Contemporary
Literary Criticism

Guide to Gale Literary Criticism Series

When you need to review criticism of literary works, these are the Gale series to use:

If the author's death date is:	You should turn to:

After Dec. 31, 1959
(or author is still living)

CONTEMPORARY LITERARY CRITICISM

for example: Jorge Luis Borges, Anthony Burgess,
William Faulkner, Mary Gordon,
Ernest Hemingway, Iris Murdoch

1900 through 1959

TWENTIETH-CENTURY LITERARY CRITICISM

for example: Willa Cather, F. Scott Fitzgerald,
Henry James, Mark Twain, Virginia Woolf

1800 through 1899

NINETEENTH-CENTURY LITERATURE CRITICISM

for example: Fedor Dostoevski, George Sand,
Gerard Manley Hopkins, Emily Dickinson

1400 through 1799

LITERATURE CRITICISM FROM 1400 TO 1800
(excluding Shakespeare)

for example: Anne Bradstreet, Pierre Corneille,
Daniel Defoe, Alexander Pope,
Jonathan Swift, Phillis Wheatley

SHAKESPEAREAN CRITICISM

Shakespeare's plays and poetry

Antiquity through 1399

CLASSICAL AND MEDIEVAL LITERATURE CRITICISM

for example: Dante, Plato, Homer, Sophocles, Vergil,
the Beowulf poet

(Volume 1 forthcoming)

Gale also publishes related criticism series:

CHILDREN'S LITERATURE REVIEW

This ongoing series covers authors of all eras. Presents criticism on authors and author/illustrators who write for the preschool through high school audience.

CONTEMPORARY ISSUES CRITICISM

This two-volume set presents criticism on contemporary authors writing on current issues. Topics covered include the social sciences, philosophy, economics, natural science, law, and related areas.

ISSN 0091-3421

Volume 37

Contemporary Literary Criticism

Excerpts from Criticism of the
Works of Today's Novelists, Poets,
Playwrights, Short Story Writers, Scriptwriters,
and Other Creative Writers

Daniel G. Marowski
EDITOR

Roger Matuz
Jane E. Neidhardt
Robyn V. Young
ASSOCIATE EDITORS

Gale Research Company
Book Tower
Detroit, Michigan 48226

STAFF

Daniel G. Marowski, *Editor*

Roger Matuz, Jane E. Neidhardt, Robyn V. Young, *Associate Editors*

Jane C. Thacker, Debra A. Wells, *Senior Assistant Editors*

Kelly King Howes, Molly L. Norris, Sean R. Pollock,
Thomas J. Votteler, Bruce Walker, *Assistant Editors*

Jean C. Stine, *Contributing Editor*
Melissa Reiff Hug, Serita Lanette Lockard, *Contributing Assistant Editors*

Lizbeth A. Purdy, *Production Supervisor*
Denise Michlewicz Broderick, *Production Coordinator*
Eric Berger, *Assistant Production Coordinator*
Kathleen M. Cook, Sheila J. Nasea, *Editorial Assistants*

Linda M. Pugliese, *Manuscript Coordinator*
Donna Craft, *Assistant Manuscript Coordinator*
Maureen A. Puhl, Rosetta Irene Simms, *Manuscript Assistants*

Victoria B. Cariappa, *Research Coordinator*
Jeannine Schiffman Davidson, *Assistant Research Coordinator*
Daniel Kurt Gilbert, Grace E. Gillis, Maureen R. Richards,
Keith E. Schooley, Filomena Sgambati, Vincenza G. Tranchida,
Valerie Webster, Mary D. Wise, *Research Assistants*

Jeanne A. Gough, *Permissions Supervisor*
Janice M. Mach, *Permissions Coordinator, Text*
Patricia A. Seefelt, *Permissions Coordinator, Illustrations*
Susan D. Battista, *Assistant Permissions Coordinator*
Margaret A. Chamberlain, Sandra C. Davis, Kathy Grell,
Mary M. Matuz, *Senior Permissions Assistants*
Colleen M. Crane, Josephine M. Keene,
Mabel E. Schoening, *Permissions Assistants*
Margaret A. Carson, H. Diane Cooper,
Dorothy J. Fowler, Anita Williams, *Permissions Clerks*

Frederick G. Ruffner, *Publisher*
Dedria Bryfonski, *Editorial Director*
Christine Nasso, *Director, Literature Division*
Laurie Lanzen Harris, *Senior Editor, Literary Criticism Series*
Dennis Poupard, *Managing Editor, Literary Criticism Series*

Copyright © 1986 by Gale Research Company

Library of Congress Catalog Card Number 76-38938
ISBN 0-8103-4411-4
ISSN 0091-3421

Computerized photocomposition by
Typographics, Incorporated
Kansas City, Missouri

Printed in the United States

Contents

Preface 7

Authors Forthcoming in *CLC* 9

Appendix 467

Cumulative Index to Authors 481

Cumulative Index to Critics 531

Vasily Aksyonov 1932- 11

Jessica Anderson 19??- 18

Russell Banks 1940- 22

Howard Barker 1946- 31

Ted Berrigan 1934-1983 42

Breyten Breytenbach 1939- 47

William F. Buckley, Jr. 1925- 53

Anita Desai 1937- 64

Stephen Dobyns 1941- 74

E. L. Doctorow 1931- 83

Allen Drury 1918- 98

Maureen Duffy 1933- 113

Thomas J. Fleming 1927- 118

Ronald J. Glasser 1940?- 130

Graham Greene 1904- 135

Donald Hall 1928- 141

Robert Hayden 1913-1980 150

Seamus Heaney 1939- 161

Ted Hughes 1930- 170

Jorge Ibargüengoitia 1928-1983 ... 182

Laura Jensen 1948- 186

Pat Jordan 1941- 193

Stephen King 1947- 197

Nella Larsen 1893-1964.......... 209

Primo Levi 1919- 220

Robert Lowell 1917-1977 231

Richard Matheson 1926- 244

Marshall McLuhan 1911-1980 251

Margaret Mead 1901-1978 268

Ved Mehta 1934- 287

John Metcalf 1938- 298

Wright Morris 1910- 309

V. S. Naipaul 1932- 318

Grace Paley 1922- 330

Pier Paolo Pasolini 1922-1975 340

Tom Paulin 1949- 352

Robert Pinget 1919- 358

Barbara Pym 1913-1980 367

Peter Shaffer 1926- 381

Gay Talese 1932- 390

Peter Taylor 1917- 406

Audrey Thomas 1935- 415

Frank Tuohy 1925- 425

William Wharton 1925- 435

Hugh Whitemore 1936- 444

Elie Wiesel 1928- 449

Nancy Willard 1936- 461

Preface

Literary criticism is, by definition, "the art of evaluating or analyzing with knowledge and propriety works of literature." The complexity and variety of the themes and forms of contemporary literature make the function of the critic especially important to today's reader. It is the critic who assists the reader in identifying significant new writers, recognizing trends in critical methods, mastering new terminology, and monitoring scholarly and popular sources of critical opinion.

Until the publication of the first volume of *Contemporary Literary Criticism (CLC)* in 1973, there existed no ongoing digest of current literary opinion. *CLC,* therefore, has fulfilled an essential need.

Scope of the Work

CLC presents significant passages from published criticism of works by today's creative writers. Each volume of *CLC* includes excerpted criticism on about 50 authors who are now living or who died after December 31, 1959. Since the series began publication, almost 1,800 authors have been included. The majority of authors covered by *CLC* are living writers who continue to publish; therefore, an author frequently appears in more than one volume. There is, of course, no duplication of reprinted criticism.

Authors are selected for inclusion for a variety of reasons, among them the publication of a critically acclaimed new work, the reception of a major literary award, or the dramatization of a literary work as a movie or television screenplay. For example, the present volume includes Ted Hughes, who was named Poet Laureate of England in 1984; Peter Shaffer, whose Tony Award-winning play *Amadeus* was adapted into an Academy Award-winning film; and E. L. Doctorow, whose novel *World's Fair* received much attention from the literary world. Perhaps most importantly, authors who appear frequently on the syllabuses of high school and college literature classes are heavily represented in *CLC;* Robert Lowell and Grace Paley are examples of writers of this stature in the present volume. Attention is also given to several other groups of writers—authors of considerable public interest—about whose work criticism is often difficult to locate. These are the contributors to the well-loved but nonscholarly genres of mystery and science fiction, as well as literary and social critics whose insights are considered valuable and informative. Foreign writers and authors who represent particular ethnic groups in the United States are also featured in each volume.

Format of the Book

Altogether there are about 750 individual excerpts in each volume—with an average of about 11 excerpts per author—taken from hundreds of literary reviews, general magazines, scholarly journals, and monographs. Contemporary criticism is loosely defined as that which is relevant to the evaluation of the author under discussion; this includes criticism written at the beginning of an author's career as well as current commentary. Emphasis has been placed on expanding the sources for criticism by including an increasing number of scholarly and specialized periodicals. Students, teachers, librarians, and researchers frequently find that the generous excerpts and supplementary material provided by the editors supply them with all the information needed to write a term paper, analyze a poem, or lead a book discussion group. However, complete bibliographical citations facilitate the location of the original source as well as provide all of the information necessary for a term paper footnote or bibliography.

A *CLC* author entry consists of the following elements:

- The **author heading** cites the author's full name, followed by birth date, and death date when applicable. The portion of the name outside the parentheses denotes the form under which the author has most commonly published. If an author has written consistently under a pseudonym, the pseudonym will be listed in the author heading and the real name given on the first line of the biographical and critical introduction. Also located at the beginning of the introduction to the author entry are any important name variations under which an author has written. Uncertainty as to a birth or death date is indicated by question marks.

- A **portrait** of the author is included when available.

- A brief **biographical and critical introduction** to the author and his or her work precedes the excerpted criticism. However, *CLC* is not intended to be a definitive biographical source. Therefore, *cross-references* have been included to direct the reader to other useful sources published by the Gale Research Company: *Contemporary Authors* now includes detailed biographical and bibliographical sketches on more than 82,000 authors; *Children's Literature Review* presents excerpted criticism on the works of authors of children's books; *Something about the Author* contains heavily illustrated biographical sketches on writers and illustrators who create books for children and young adults; *Contemporary Issues Criticism* presents excerpted commentary on the nonfiction works of authors who influence contemporary thought; *Dictionary of Literary Biography* provides original evaluations of authors important to literary history; and the new *Contemporary Authors Autobiography Series* offers autobiographical essays by prominent writers. Previous volumes of *CLC* in which the author has been featured are also listed in the introduction.

- The **excerpted criticism** represents various kinds of critical writing—a particular essay may be normative, descriptive, interpretive, textual, appreciative, comparative, or generic. It may range in form from the brief review to the scholarly monograph. Essays are selected by the editors to reflect the spectrum of opinion about a specific work or about an author's literary career in general. The excerpts are presented chronologically, adding a useful perspective to the entry. All titles by the author featured in the entry are printed in boldface type, which enables the reader to easily identify the works being discussed.

- A complete **bibliographical citation** designed to help the user find the original essay or book follows each excerpt. An asterisk (*) at the end of a citation indicates that the essay is on more than one author.

Other Features

- A list of **Authors Forthcoming in *CLC*** previews the authors to be researched for future volumes.

- An **Appendix** lists the sources from which material in the volume has been reprinted. Many other sources have also been consulted during the preparation of the volume.

- A **Cumulative Index to Authors** lists all the authors who have appeared in *Contemporary Literary Criticism, Twentieth-Century Literary Criticism, Nineteenth-Century Literature Criticism,* and *Literature Criticism from 1400 to 1800,* along with cross-references to other Gale series: *Children's Literature Review, Authors in the News, Contemporary Authors, Contemporary Authors Autobiography Series, Dictionary of Literary Biography, Something about the Author,* and *Yesterday's Authors of Books for Children.* Users will welcome this cumulated author index as a useful tool for locating an author within the various series. The index, which lists birth and death dates when available, will be particularly valuable for those authors who are identified with a certain period but whose death date causes them to be placed in another, or for those authors whose careers span two periods. For example, F. Scott Fitzgerald is found in *Twentieth-Century Literary Criticism,* yet a writer often associated with him, Ernest Hemingway, is found in *Contemporary Literary Criticism.*

- A **Cumulative Index to Critics** lists the critics and the author entries in which their essays appear.

Acknowledgments

The editors wish to thank the copyright holders of the excerpted articles included in this volume for permission to use the material and the photographers and other individuals who provided photographs for us. We are grateful to the staffs of the following libraries for making their resources available to us: Detroit Public Library and the libraries of Wayne State University, the University of Michigan, and the University of Detroit. We also wish to thank Anthony Bogucki for his assistance with copyright research.

Suggestions Are Welcome

The editors welcome the comments and suggestions of readers to expand the coverage and enhance the usefulness of the series.

Authors Forthcoming in *CLC*

Contemporary Literary Criticism, Volumes 38 and 40 will contain criticism on a number of authors not previously listed and will also feature criticism on newer works by authors included in earlier volumes. Volume 39 will be a yearbook devoted to an examination of the outstanding achievements and trends in literature during 1985.

To Be Included in Volume 38

Robert Bly (American poet and essayist)—Recognized as an important and influential contemporary poet, Bly has been praised for successfully merging the personal and the public in his work. His poems are often characterized as visionary and imagistic yet are firmly rooted in the concrete world.

Octavia E. Butler (American novelist)—Butler's "Patternist" series of science fiction novels, from *Patternmaster* to *Wild Seed*, details a future history while addressing contemporary social issues.

Guy Davenport (American short story writer, critic, and translator)—A scholar of classical literature and an experimental fiction writer, Davenport has recently published a volume of essays, *The Geography of the Imagination*, and two short story collections, *Eclogues* and *Apples and Pears*.

Michel del Castillo (Spanish-born French novelist and short story writer)—Best known for his autobiographical novel *A Child of Our Time*, del Castillo writes fiction in which the depiction of human suffering, depravity, and oppression echoes the harsh circumstances of his own background.

Mavis Gallant (Canadian novelist, short story writer, and dramatist)—Widely respected for her finely crafted fiction, Gallant centers much of her work on Canadian characters at home and abroad. Criticism will focus on her short story collection *Home Truths* and her play *What Is to Be Done?*

John Irving (American novelist)—Author of the controversial best-seller *The World According to Garp*, Irving has again inspired wide critical and popular attention with his latest novel, *The Cider House Rules*.

George S. Kaufman (American dramatist, journalist, critic, and scriptwriter)—A recipient of two Pulitzer Prizes for drama, Kaufman collaborated on such plays as *You Can't Take It With You* and *Of Thee I Sing*, which are marked by his sharp, often scathing wit.

Claude Lévi-Strauss (Belgian-born French anthropologist, essayist, and linguist)—A world-renowned figure associated with the intellectual milieu of post-World War II France, Levi-Strauss provoked widespread analysis and debate through numerous works detailing his theories of structuralism.

Jonathan Reynolds (American dramatist and scriptwriter)—Reynolds is a popular comic dramatist whose recent successful plays include *Geniuses* and *Fighting International Fat*.

Ntozake Shange (American dramatist, novelist, poet, and essayist)—Best known for her play *for colored girls who have considered suicide/when the rainbow is enuf*, Shange recently published *Betsey Brown*, a novel which explores a teenage girl's self-discovery amid the conflicts between her cultural heritage and her middle-class American surroundings.

Studs Terkel (American nonfiction writer, journalist, and dramatist)—Terkel writes social histories that emphasize the personal responses of ordinary individuals. His recent book, *"The Good War,"* examines contemporary attitudes and perceptions about World War II.

Herman Wouk (American novelist, nonfiction writer, and dramatist)—The author of such well-known works as *The Caine Mutiny* and *The Winds of War*, Wouk analyzes the experiences of Jewish-Americans through the adventures of one man in his latest novel, *Inside, Outside*.

Brian Aldiss (English novelist, short story writer, critic, and editor)—A Hugo and Nebula Award-winning science fiction author, Aldiss recently published *Helliconia Winter,* the third novel in his series about a remote planet called Helliconia.

Jorge Amado (Brazilian novelist and nonfiction writer)—Amado is recognized as one of Brazil's greatest writers, and his works have been translated into over forty languages. He is best known for his novels *Violent Land, Gabriela, Clove and Cinnamon, Dona Flor and Her Two Husbands,* and the recently translated *Pen, Sword, Camisole.*

Ann Beattie (American novelist and short story writer)—In her fiction Beattie records the disillusionment of the "Woodstock generation" as her protagonists come to terms with middle age and a suburban, middle-class lifestyle. Her latest works include *The Burning House* and *Love Always.*

Marguerite Duras (French novelist, dramatist, short story writer, and filmmaker)—Internationally recognized for her mastery of several genres, Duras is perhaps best known for her work in film and her application of cinematic techniques to the novel. Her recent prizewinning novel, *L'amant,* has furthered her reputation as an important contemporary author.

William M. Hoffman (American dramatist and editor)—Hoffman's controversial play *As Is* has been praised for his sympathetic treatment of the tragic effects of AIDS on a homosexual couple.

Garrison Keillor (American novelist and essayist)—Host of the popular radio program "A Prairie Home Companion," Keillor gained widespread recognition and praise for his bestselling novel, *Lake Wobegon Days.*

Etheridge Knight (American poet, short story writer, and editor)—Knight published his first collection of poetry, *Poems from Prison,* while serving a sentence in the Indiana State Prison. The poems in this and subsequent volumes are rooted in oral tradition and feature common, colloquial language through which Knight conveys messages of social protest.

Tim O'Brien (American novelist)—Winner of the National Book Award for his novel *Going After Cacciato,* O'Brien focuses on the theme of nuclear annihilation and social issues of the post-World War II era in his latest work, *The Nuclear Age.*

Konstantin Paustovsky (Russian fiction and nonfiction writer)—Paustovsky's six-volume autobiography, *The Story of a Life,* received considerable attention in both the Soviet Union and the West. This work chronicles his life against a historical background that includes World War I, the Bolshevik Revolution, and the Stalin purges.

Muriel Spark (Scottish-born novelist, short story writer, poet, and nonfiction writer)—Spark is best known for her witty satires which probe themes related to morality. Her recent novels include *Loitering with Intent* and *The Only Problem.*

Kurt Vonnegut, Jr. (American novelist, short story writer, and critic)—This prolific and popular author of the novel *Slaughterhouse-Five* satirizes contemporary America and Darwinism in his recent novel, *Galápagos,* which several critics consider one of his finest works.

Diane Wakoski (American poet and critic)—In her poetry Wakoski often depicts an ongoing search for fulfillment that frequently leads to loss and betrayal. Her latest books include *The Magician's Feastletters* and *The Collected Greed: Parts 1-13.*

Vasily (Pavlovich) Aksyonov

1932-

(Also transliterated as Vassily Aksenov) Russian novelist, dramatist, short story writer, scriptwriter, and author of books for children.

A popular writer in the Soviet Union for the first twenty years of his career, Aksyonov has gained increasing recognition in the United States since his emigration in 1980. His work is characterized by its surrealistic, satirical treatment of contemporary themes and reflects the historical, cultural, and ideological complexities of his homeland. He sometimes draws directly on his own experiences. Like the protagonist of what some consider his most ambitious and successful work, *Ozhog* (1980; *The Burn*), Aksyonov's childhood and adolescence were marked by the imprisonment of both of his parents during Joseph Stalin's 1937 purges. He was trained as a doctor and practiced medicine for four years before the success of his novels allowed him to become a full-time writer. Aksyonov's work flourished during the 1960s, when Soviet constraints on literature became less rigid. In the 1970s, however, his desire to expand the scope of both his subject matter and his style brought him into frequent conflict with Soviet cultural regulations. Censorship of his work, in addition to increased pressure from Soviet officials, caused him to leave his homeland. Aksyonov has since produced several new works, and his books continue to be translated into English.

Aksyonov's first two novels, *Kollegi* (1961; *Colleagues*) and *Zvezdnyi bilet* (1962; *A Ticket to the Stars*), attracted widespread attention in the Soviet Union. *A Ticket to the Stars*, which portrays rebellious Moscow teenagers on a voyage of self-discovery, is especially noted for its street slang and references to both Russian and Western popular culture. Although Soviet critics accused Aksyonov of encouraging a cynical attitude in Soviet youth, the novel was enthusiastically received by the Russian public. *Pora, moi drug, pora* (1965; *It's Time, My Friend, It's Time*), like *A Ticket to the Stars*, deals with the theme of alienation and the search for meaning, this time in the context of a love relationship. *Vsegda v prodazhe* (1965) and *Vash ubiytsa* (1977; *Your Murderer*) are avant-garde plays in which elements of popular culture and social satire are juxtaposed with such traditional forms as Russian folk humor. These and other works written before Aksyonov's departure from the Soviet Union reflect his experimental approach to style and theme. While in his early books Aksyonov wrote primarily as a spokesperson for disillusioned youth, he has developed into an innovative writer committed to fully exploring the possibilities of his craft.

Aksyonov wrote *The Burn* before he left the Soviet Union, but it was destined "for the drawer"—a term Russian writers use to describe works which would not be allowed to appear in the Soviet Union. In 1980, *The Burn* was published both in Italy and in the United States. This highly acclaimed, partly autobiographical novel was described by Anatole Shub as representing "the response of a unique writer, at the height of his powers, to a turning point.... Blending reality, memory, and fantasy in kaleidoscopic, often surrealistic fashion, it flows like a great meandering river." *The Burn* consists of three sections, each centered on the character of Tolya Von Stein-

© Jerry Bauer

bock, whose life and struggles mirror Aksyonov's in many ways. In the first section, "The Men's Club," the five protagonists—a sculptor, a writer, a surgeon, a jazz musician, and a scientist—are revealed as alternate versions of Tolya's persona. The second part, "Five in Solitary," recounts Tolya's adolescence in a gulag, where his mother was a political prisoner. The final section, "The Victim's Last Adventure," finds the five protagonists in the 1970s grappling with their knowledge of the past, the demands of the present, and the uncertainty of the future. In this novel Aksyonov employs a variety of tones to create a work in which the real and the surreal intertwine.

Ostrov Krym (1981; *The Island of Crimea*) is set on the Crimean peninsula. In this novel, Aksyonov imagines that Crimea is a society allowed to remain autonomous of the Soviet Union; its citizens enjoy an opulent, Westernized style of living. The main character, Luchnikov, weary of the society's essential shallowness, leads a movement to reunite Crimea with the Soviet Union. Critics offered various interpretations of the novel, but most agreed that it was not necessarily a rejection of Western ideals. Anthony Olcott considers it an exploration of the concept that "what freedom man possesses is a product of blind chance, threatening in its formlessness."

(See also *CLC*, Vol. 22; *Contemporary Authors*, Vols. 53-56; and *Contemporary Authors New Revision Series*, Vol. 12.)

D. MILIVOJEVIĆ

When is Aksyonov going to grow up? In the Soviet Union, he used to shock the conservative Soviet philistine public with irreverent tales of wayward Russian youth. And now with his new novel [*Ostrov Krym*] he may be trying to scandalize Western readers with lewd episodes of young girls swimming in the nude, hashish smoking, et cetera. The problem is that blasé readers in the West are less likely to be shocked than are their Russian counterparts. Moreover, social trends appear and disappear more rapidly in the West than they do in the Soviet Union. What Aksyonov is describing in *Ostrov Krym* (Crimea Island) are the mores and customs of the 1960s in the United States, transposed in location to the Crimea, with Russians being the main protagonists in the novel. (p. 137)

While the main characters and location are Russian, their behavior and actions are typically American. Unfortunately, this is the extent of the novel. There is no depth to Aksyonov's writing here. *Ostrov Krym* is, ironically, an entertaining and amusing novel to be read on a Sunday afternoon and then forgotten. (p. 138)

> *D. Milivojević, in a review of "Ostrov Krym," in* World Literature Today, *Vol. 56, No. 1, Winter, 1982, pp. 137-38.*

MARGOT K. FRANK

Aristofaniana s ljugaškami (Aristophaniana with Frogs), a collection of five plays with superb illustrations by E. Neizvestny, never officially published in the Soviet Union, shows that Aksyonov's technique and linguistic talents are particularly effective on the stage. The first play, *Vsegda v prodaže (Always for Sale),* a satirical fantasy written in 1963, actually saw performance by Moscow's Sovremennik (Contemporary) Theatre in 1965 and ran for several seasons. Its action centers on two contemporary Soviet types, a privileged journalist and a returnee from Siberia. The former indifferently misuses women, produces vapid sociopolitical jargon and ambitiously pursues his advantages, while the latter insists on honesty, decency and political as well as personal integrity. Aksyonov achieves sophistication of this stark black-white contrast by presenting the heroes as two faces of the same complex Soviet society. The second piece, a 1964 comedy formerly titled *Tvoj ubijca (Your Murderer),* now renamed *Potseluj, orkestr, ryba, kolbasa (Kiss, Orchestra, Fish, Sausage),* reflects the individual's hopeless struggle with conformist society. A reluctant conformist inadvertently creates a monstrous alter ego, which acquires a powerful independent existence. Another comedy *Cetyre temperamenta* (1967), was scheduled for presentation by the Sovremennik Theatre but in the end could not be staged. Though the play is set in the distant future, the title's four temperaments—representing choleric, melancholic, phlegmatic and sanguine citizens—echo current concerns, and in the final scene the action returns to the contemporary Soviet Union.

The 1968 title play *Aristophaniana with Frogs,* is an antique burlesque centering on the importance of poets and poetry. Greek gods pass judgment on the assembled creative community of the past, present and future, which includes Pushkin and Shakespeare. The emerging theme is that all nations and people wither without independent poetic expression. The final piece, *Caplja (Heron;* 1979), is dedicated to Aksyonov's harassed *Metropol* colleagues and partially follows the plot line of Chekhov's *Seagull.* It differs from the other plays in its realistic setting and particularly daring theme. Residents of a

Baltic resort hotel are visited by a heron from Poland, who brings feelings of a freer existence. First feared, then welcomed by the Soviet group, the heron is slain by satanic forces as a revolving stage featuring a rifle appears on the scene. Aksyonov identifies the revolving set with the Berlin wall by calling it *Mauer.* This drama, written eighteen months prior to the suppression of Polish liberalization, ends on a slightly optimistic note with the preservation of the heron's egg and a plea to bide time.

The plays face difficult translation . . . , since Aksyonov not only liberally reproduces Russian dialects and modern slang, but also incorporates neologisms and foreign words, especially Anglicisms, some of which have already become half-Russified. Only a Russian-speaking audience can appreciate the full effect of this linguistic technique. There is virtually no chance that the plays will be performed on Soviet soil in the prevailing political climate, and Russian-language stagings elsewhere are few. Like the heron's egg in the final drama, Aksyonov's creations are fated to wait. (pp. 655-56)

> *Margot K. Frank, in a review of "Aristofaniana s ljugaškami," in* World Literature Today, *Vol. 57, No. 4, Autumn, 1983, pp. 655-56.*

ANTHONY OLCOTT

[*The Island of Crimea*] is based on an irresistible "what if"; what if Crimea had been truly an island, not a peninsula, where the Whites had been able to hold out, to create their own Taiwan, snug against the belly of the bear? Part of Aksyonov's answer is an imaginative translation of Beverly Hills into Russian terms. . . . Most Westerners would kill to lead the life of Aksyonov's main character, Andrei Luchnikov, the wealthy, sexy, influential, multilingual, globe-trotting editor of the Crimea's most important newspaper; how Luchnikov's freedom of movement, of thought, and of pleasures make a Russian mouth water a Westerner can only dimly guess.

It is Luchnikov who bears Aksyonov's more serious answer to the "what if," for despite all his countless advantages, Luchnikov takes upon himself a crusade to induce his fellow Crimeans voluntarily to rejoin the Motherland, the Soviet Union. Ironically, although ideologically required to growl, the Soviets don't *want* the Crimea; they get hard currency there, the favored ones vacation there, and most of all, the Soviet leaders simply lack the heart to break another several million people to the socialist saddle.

Luchnikov, though, persists and finds a receptive audience in the West-weary Crimeans. . . . [At] the novel's conclusion, he succeeds. The Crimeans petition to become a Soviet republic; the Soviets, after months of silence, oblige, in a massive invasion which, as it were, forcibly returns Aksyonov's imagined world to our real one.

For some reason Aksyonov's publisher and early reviewers alike insist this is all good fun, a comic romp; to be sure, *The Island of Crimea* does have some good Soviet jokes, a few of Churchill's drier cracks about socialism, and many scenes of daily Soviet life, which always seem the wildest comic invention to those whom fate has spared Soviet experience. Aksyonov, though, clearly sees Luchnikov as a tragic fool, a man who confuses liberty with license, who seeks spiritual self-definition in self-debasement, a man who cannot bear the burden of his own freedom.

What elevates *The Island of Crimea* beyond anti-western jeremiad—and towards the plane of Dostoevsky's Grand Inquisitor—is that not just Luchnikov hungers and thirsts after tyranny; so too do all the other Crimeans, and so to do all the Soviets, save one, the Central Committee's expert on the island; *homo sovieticus* to the bone, he is the only one in Aksyonov's book who cherishes the freedom the island offers, however imperfectly, enough to resist its destruction.

In a sense then Aksyonov argues that there can be no "what if"; what freedom man possesses, Aksyonov gloomily implies, is a product of blind chance, threatening in its formlessness. It will disappear, *The Island of Crimea* suggests, because no man *wants* to be an island. We in the West tell ourselves easily that our fate will differ from that of the Russians, the Chinese, the Iranians; Aksyonov in this novel asks what makes us so sure. *The Island of Crimea* ought to be required reading, at least until someone among us can articulate an answer.

Anthony Olcott, "The Crimean Caper," in Book World—The Washington Post, *December 18, 1983, p. 4.*

TIMOTHY SERGAY

Although the jacket copy promises "a hilarious, ribald, lusty caper," *The Island of Crimea* is complex, long and increasingly somber. There are some good laughs—a cynical treatment of Soviet ideological blather at a Unesco conference, some foiling-the-K.G.B. high jinks following Luchnikov's disappearance from Moscow—but the novel is hardly a romp. Its ribaldry derives from the disturbing treatment of women: "Luchnikov sighed and thought to himself that he'd always preferred whores to their respectable sisters and liked Krystyna more as she was now than in her puritan guise." The female characters barely exist outside a context of promiscuity and prostitution. . . . Sometimes Aksyonov seems to be presenting his male characters' Madonna/whore mentality as an aspect of their decadence; other times he seems to share it. Either way, it is never fun.

The tone of the novel, created largely by its perception of history, is one of deepening menace: a constant assassination threat; a mortally treacherous roadway; history as "a gigantic, sleek and senseless shark," "the bitch, the Why and Wherefore"; a resignation to devouring absurdity. Luchnikov appeals repeatedly and hopelessly to God; in his final hysteria, he attributes the whole catastrophe to Hollywood. . . . (pp. 135-36)

Aksyonov's novel includes a number of themes present in the work of another expatriate Soviet author, Alexander Zinoviev [author of the political satire *The Yawning Heights*]. . . . Luchnikov's article on Stalinist dementia and the post-revolutionary triumph of mediocrity ("the gradual but eventually overwhelming takeover by incompetents and nonentities") will sound familiar to Zinoviev's readers. (p. 136)

Both authors attribute the Soviet Union's peculiar decadence to the Russian people and not to the actions of a ruling elite or to totalitarianism per se. They do so in different ways, however. Zinoviev writes literary dramatizations of sociological theory. . . . Zinoviev's concern is with the consequences of a general human nature. Aksyonov affirms the philosophically conservative idea of national character. . . . Even if the White Guard had founded a constitutional democracy on an island refuge from Bolshevism, Aksyonov suggests, the result would not be enduring open society, the Russia We Could Have Loved—at least not for long. The Sovietization of Crimea is not criminally imposed from without, against the island's Rousseauistic general will; it organizes itself from within, enthusiastically chosen by referendum in response to brilliant leadership. Welcoming banners fly on the day Soviet tanks paralyze traffic in the streets of Simferopol and the first queues form in its supermarkets.

In Aksyonov's satire, all acts of political messianism over three generations of Russians end in disaster. . . . In Aksyonov's view, scrupulously calculated and organized attempts to engineer history seem to arise periodically from the Russian culture, react with some lurking, herdish sadomasochism and end in decadence, violence and irretrievable human loss. (pp. 136-37)

Luchnikov's idea of a common fate is one of the most inventive ironies in recent Soviet émigré political satire: reunification will not restore Crimean guts and talent to all Russia; it will bring Soviet decrepitude to Crimea, at the island's own invitation. The numbing Soviet winter spills at last over sunny Yalta. The ultimate cause is apparently the Why and Wherefore, some inexorable menace inherent in Russian history.

The Island of Crimea is fairly quiet about Western history and afflictions. The portrayal of Western political and economic conditions as perfectly suitable for the development of a brutal sovietism is not meant to criticize the West but to suggest that the West will not work in the East; Western institutions simply cannot survive for long grafted onto a national character incompatible with them. But if in Aksyonov's view there is a sleek and senseless shark devouring the hopes of Russian culture, it is hard to imagine that there is not another one, perhaps of a slightly different species, devouring our own. Although less deliberately universal in scope than *The Yawning Heights*, Aksyonov's satire is no less thoughtful or impassioned. The recent English editions of both writers' works remind us that the problem of the Russian people remains the problem of civilization. (pp. 137-38)

Timothy Sergay, "The Russia that Wasn't," in The Nation, *Vol. 238, No. 4, February 4, 1984, pp. 135-38.*

ALEXANDRA HEIDI KARRIKER

[All] that the reader has come to expect from the veteran weaver of zany plots, spicy dialogue and a playful sensuousness comes to pass in Aksyonov's latest novel [*Bumazhnyĭ peĭzazh (The Paper Landscape)*]. But this is not to say that we have seen it all before. Although it shares with other recent émigré prose certain themes (the surveillance, jailing and expulsion of a Soviet citizen), stylistic techniques (stream of consciousness and shifting points of view) and a naturalistic portrayal of language (bureaucratic slang and street jargon), this novel is superior to most of the tomes which recently have inundated Western presses. The reasons are many: it is fun to read; the satire is muted; the characterization is balanced between caricature and individualization; and the elliptical sex scenes are all the more delightful for their lack of explicitness and the use of invented expressions for familiar acts or body parts.

Aksyonov, a twentieth-century master of language, has not shrugged off his nineteenth-century master's example, and all to the good. The epigraph about a drunk's meanderings, the initial discourse on the origin of the name of the main protagonist, Velosipedov, and the grotesque names in general all point to Gogol, as does the irreality of the plot. Verisimilitude is shunned for fanciful twists in the story line. . . . This spirited tale, told in the best Aksyonov tradition, proves that he is not to be relegated to that shelf which holds authors whose prime reason for being is that they are émigrés and where their works, lugubrious laments or dull diatribes, will gather dust. Aksyonov is still vibrantly entertaining.

Alexandra Heidi Karriker, in a review of "Bumazhnyĭ peĭzazh," in World Literature Today, *Vol. 58, No. 2, Spring, 1984, p. 285.*

FRANCIS KING

More than 500 pages long, *The Burn* might be described as an encyclopaedia of life in the Soviet Union during the last 50 years; but it is an encyclopaedia that has been savagely dismembered, with many of its pages lost, many mutilated and many scrawled over with irreverent graffiti, and the remainder often seeming to have been reassembled at random.

The human paper-clip that holds the remaining pages together is a young boy, Tolya Von Steinbock, whose name, at once Jewish and unproletarian, announces his exceptional and unenviable destiny. Tolya's father has already vanished in the Gulag; and in the course of the narrative his mother, with whom he has been living in exile in Siberia, is herself rearrested, leaving the boy in the charge of the religious homeopath, himself a former political prisoner, who has become her second husband. It is easy to see in Tolya's wretched childhood much of Aksyonov's own. The son of Eugenia Ginzburg, author of two remarkable books about her persecution by the authorities, he spent some time both in an orphanage for children of 'enemies of the people' and in Siberian exile with his mother. . . .

Of Tolya it may be said that the child is not merely the father of the man but the father of five men. All these five—each of whom represents not the man that Tolya becomes but the man that he has the potentiality to become—have the same patronymic, Apollinarivich; all live in Moscow and all, in their separate ways, are famous—one as a sculptor, one as a writer, one as a physicist, one as a doctor and one as a jazz musician. All are haunted by childhood memories of deprivation and persecution, all feel the need to exact expiation from one particularly brutal member of the KGB, all drink and fornicate, and all are opponents of a regime that they find at best stultifying and at worst diabolical.

The realism with which Aksyonov writes of this quintet constantly takes off into surrealism, as though a locomotive, pounding along the lines, kept transforming itself into an aeroplane. The Soviet Union is a country of almost mystical coincidences; but as in *Doctor Zhivago* the coincidences here, with the destinies of the various characters repeatedly getting snarled up with each other, burst all the fetters of conventional story-telling. Whether as former prisoners congregating in the heating system of their desolate town of exile, or as alcoholics or jazz musicians asserting their defiance of officialdom in some secret basement, Aksyonov's characters repeatedly meet under the ground. The significance of the metaphor will at once be apparent.

The picture that Aksyonov presents of people living in a state of vague fear and queasy disgust will already be familiar; but it has rarely been presented with so much savagery and bravura. In the history of Russia he sees a constant conflict between those who stretch out hands of welcome to the West and those who raise fists in resistance and even aggression. The representatives of the former are here his jazz musicians, treasuring

the records smuggled into them, and his jazz fans, aping the dress and manners of jazz fans in the States: his intellectuals, betraying each other precisely as they did in Tsarist times; and his ruling elite, hogging the consumer goods—Scotch whisky, French perfume, Italian shoes, American cigarettes—that they would deny to the proletariat. . . .

For me, this difficult but rewarding novel is most effective when, as in the passages about the misadventures of young Tolya and his mother, it indulges least in surrealistic fantasy and extravagant stylistic tricks. Others may feel differently. At all events, few more powerful indictments of the Soviet system have emerged from that unhappy country.

Francis King, "Red Jazz," in The Spectator, *Vol. 253, No. 8153, October 13, 1984, p. 29.*

RICHARD EDER

In the frivolous Western democracies, where the climate is easy, literature is almost as refined, witty and useful as a silver dish of oysters laid out on brown seaweed and garnished with cracked ice, writes Vassily Aksyonov in *The Burn*.

In the Soviet Union on the other hand, winter lasts six months. "What we like is some heavy, masochistic problem, which we can prod with a tired, exhausted, not very clean but honest finger. That is what we need, and it is not our fault."

So Aksyonov declares, with the air of a man announcing gospel and mocking it. He is speaking for the world view of Russia's intellectuals, of whom he, of course, is one. . . .

This Dostoevskian reversal of pride and self-abasement, where the former is actually the latter in disguise, and the latter the former, is the emotional heart of Aksyonov's novel. Its subject is the extraordinary 20-year passage from Stalinism through the chaotic energies of the Khrushchev thaw, and along to the gradual re-bottling of these energies during the long rule of Brezhnev. . . .

The Burn is a novel of corrosive power. Except when its highly complex style tangles on itself, it casts expansive light upon a totalitarian system loosened by hysteria and myriad small private contracts. It portrays the political old guard, brutal and naive; the slicker new class that is supplanting it; plus artists and con men who tread violently, shifting ground to survive and, sometimes, to survive with decency. (p. 3)

The novel's power is sometimes enhanced and sometimes sidetracked by its variety of tones and modes. It shifts from realism, ironic or impassioned, to a surreal displacement reminiscent of Bulgakov. There are frequent hallucinatory stretches, and characters and time-frames flow bewilderingly in and out of each other. The protagonist is five different people who are, at the same time, one person. They were all the same prison child in Siberia, and they have intermittently identical dreams and mistresses.

The book is a panorama where the hills move as well as the personages, a chessboard where the pieces won't stay still. Aksyonov is a fervent anti-totalitarian, yet, oddly enough, the Stalinist past is what comes most clearly into focus. The Siberian childhood of Tolya—precursor of the fivefold protagonist—is done with such haunting vision that it gives the reader faith, if not always success, in pursuing some of the author's more difficult stylistic advances into the present.

Siberia and Stalinism, for all their evil, remain the imaginative matrix of a whole dissident generation. Tolya, whose parents were condemned as Trotskyites, adapts with all a child's energy to a Siberian life where his mother, now widowed, is alternately in and out of jail. He is a gung-ho super-achiever in his high school, a fervent Komsomol, in love with the daughter of a prison commandant.

Only gradually does he realize that he will always be suspect by the hierarchy he is so enthusiastically trying to join. The shock opens his eyes to the endless lines of prisoners, to the plight of his mother, whose brutal re-arrest is one of the most moving sections in the book, to the torture of a friend, and to the religiosity of a Catholic deportee.

It is too much. He has a breakdown, and emerges split in five, becoming the physicist Kunitser, the physician Malkolmov, the sculptor Khvastischchev, the writer Pantelei and the jazz musician Sabler. All achieve distinction at the edges of the system while resisting it to the extent possible. But none of the five adult Tolyas is free. The absurd and painful mental stretching they are forced to perform is conveyed by the novel's swoops into surreal expressionism. (pp. 3, 13)

[Many of the events and characters] start off part-real and then, as if the pressures of the system were actually squeezing the vision, grow distorted and multicolored.

Other portions of the novel are straightforward and bitingly funny. At one point, a band of hippies invades a military drill conducted by a Stalinist major general. They distribute chocolate and flowers; eventually hippies, trainees and the major general—with a woman's girdle on his head—reel hilariously into a police station.

Aksyonov's theme is the disorder that ensued when de-Stalinization upset the existing order. Stalinist officials were alternately brutal and groveling. . . .

There is a portrait of a Stalinist secret policeman, retired on a tiny pension, who spends his time scaring other old people in the park by staring at them meaningfully. And there are merciless depictions of the Soviet mirror image of radical chic; futile conspirators; well-heeled intellectuals; wheeler-dealers who smoke Kents, drive Mercedeses, give parties animated by Scotch, sex and Pergolesi, who speak with careful scorn of the government.

The author's pyrotechnics can expand the power of the book, suggesting a desperate disorder in ways that straightforward narrative could not. At other times, the fireworks mainly smoke, getting in the reader's eyes. Under it all is Aksyonov's feeling for a kind of Russian virtue that is to be found only in Siberian exile communities—the freest towns in Russia, he writes—and among the down-and-outers in cheap Moscow bars. Gorky's lower depths have become an emblem of purity, with an errant Christian vision working among them.

Meanwhile, there is the workaday valor of Aksyonov's five Tolyas; trying to create and stay decent, stripping their mental and emotional gears in the effort. Whether in thaw or in chill, the author is saying, Soviet society allows strength only to the extremes and the hypocrites. An honorable middle ground is held at the price of madness. (p. 13)

> *Richard Eder, "A Climate Made for Manic Masochists," in* Los Angeles Times Book Review, *October 28, 1984, pp. 3, 13.*

ANATOLE SHUB

The masterwork of a sensitive writer-doctor of rare good humor and personal modesty who has few political or professional illusions, *The Burn* illuminates the daily material and spiritual experience of Russian life today as authoritatively as Gogol's *Dead Souls* etched its essential idiocy under Czar Nicholas I. That experience is so awful—so degrading, corrupting, tedious, ignoble, desperate to the point of chronic hysteria—that, with the tears of entire generations unavenged, sanity can assert itself only in the recognition of grim farce. And yet, Mr. Aksyonov realizes, Russians (and human beings generally) must go beyond such recognition and seek some saving vision of their past and future, difficult as that certainly is. With astonishing breadth and variety of form, *The Burn* simultaneously depicts both the larger Soviet reality and Mr. Aksyonov's personal quest.

It represents the response of a unique writer, at the height of his powers, to a historic turning point, and it is in large measure a dissonant requiem for the hopeful Soviet generation of the 1960's. Blending reality, memory and fantasy in kaleidoscopic, often surrealistic fashion, it flows like a great meandering river. It is in turn hilarious, tragic, evocative, mystical. Laden with allusions, symbols and witty wordplay, it invites sublime comparisons: in form with *Orlando* and *Ulysses,* in tone with the youthful art of Chagall and Shostakovich, in its substance with Andrei Biely's *Petersburg* and Mikhail Bulgakov's *The Master and Margarita.* A supremely ambitious work worthy of a great tradition, it makes Boris Pasternak's *Doctor Zhivago* seem sentimental and much of Solzhenitzyn's fiction wooden in comparison. . . .

The three books in *The Burn* unfold almost in the form of a classical sonata. The first, called, "The Men's Club," is a wild, farcical, phantasmagoric fugue on the theme of escape—mainly through alcohol and sex—from oppressive Soviet reality and memory. Each of five protagonists (a sculptor, a surgeon, a writer, a jazz saxophonist, a top-secret scientist) seeks frantically to transcend time, space and consciousness, accompanied by a madcap American professor, a hockey player, assorted whores and clowns, and, briefly, by Spiro Agnew. Each ends up in a sobering station for alcoholics. It is soon evident that all are alternate personas of the same Tolya von Steinbock, who, like Mr. Aksyonov, is a half-Jewish Russian intellectual "burned" by Stalinism.

The second book, "Five in Solitary," is a classic andante movement, more conventionally structured, often lyrical in tone. Tolya recalls his adolescence in the gulag at Magadan in 1948-49, his mother, a mysterious doctor-priest-angel and two concentration camp torturers whom we have already met (20 years later) as cloakroom attendants in Moscow's Hotel National. Once Tolya has relived these evil memories, his alter egos return, to deal with the problem of retribution—philosophically and in practice. I will not give away the plot, but it is ingenious, credible and morally satisfying.

The final book, "The Victim's Last Adventure," is a chromatic fantasy that becomes ever more exalted, imaginative and visionary, as Tolya and his surrogates lead us alternately between past and future, body and soul, earth and heaven. At issue is how an individual (and, by extension, Russia) can be free of the evil of past and present. Mr. Aksyonov's answer is in the personal-Christian tradition of Tolstoy and Pasternak, although the form this takes is Western (specifically, Roman Catholic). Mr. Aksyonov's voice remains animated, merry, playful to the end. . . .

The Burn will be read and pondered, debated and studied, for as long as literature has admirers and critics.

Anatole Shub, "The Intelligentsia in the Fires of Stalinism," in The New York Times Book Review, November 25, 1984, p. 12.

JOHN SUTHERLAND

When he still lived in the motherland, Aksyonov was a best-seller. Printed in editions of hundreds of thousands, those of his works approved by the authorities would sell out on publication day. It's hard to see him having that much success as an exile. His notion of an avant-garde, like his notion of modern (*sic*) jazz, seems stuck in the Sixties. Just as (one imagines) forward Russian youth is currently still twisting the night away, Aksyonov has written the latest Beat novel. Like Kerouac's later work, *The Burn* seems to have been written on the analogy of the saxophone improvisation, in a series of swooping solo flights. Jazz figures importantly in the novel: in the West, it is now of diminished account. For Aksyonov, hot and cool jazz retain a potent revolutionary charge. It would seem that there are clubs in Moscow, alternately just tolerated or inefficiently persecuted by the authorities, where young Muscovites make their statement by wearing jeans and coming on like fans. The Ginsberg figure in *The Burn* is the jazzman Silvester, whose great political gesture is to look like something out of last year's *Downbeat*. . . . There's a strong feel of 'reefer madness' camp about *The Burn*'s jazz scene, with the difference that Aksyonov's not laughing. *The Burn* confirms that the best destabilisation technique the Americans have had over the last thirty years of Cold War has been Willis Conover, with his Voice of America programme beaming jazz two hours a night across the Iron Curtain.

Not that Aksyonov presents his Moscow hippies as being in any sense politically vital. In one of the less ecstatic of his digressions, he analyses the essential passivity of their rebellion in the good Khrushchev years. . . . [This] is a novel enraged by the post-Khrushchev freeze, while at the same time unillusioned by the liberating capacity of the Moscow underground. And yet Aksyonov clearly feels that he must stand up and be counted among his country's long-haired, bejeaned and jazz-loving fraction. . . . (p. 20)

According to Yevtushenko, disorganisation is the Russian vice. Aksyonov goes beyond disorganisation into the narrative equivalent of drunk and disorderly. This is a novel which is high, not on experimentalism (which would exact a certain discipline), but on free-associationism. The indiscipline of *The Burn,* its rampant breaking out of bounds, insolence and improvisation, is Aksyonov's criticism of (Soviet) life. His epigraph is from Blok: 'Only a lout can scoff at Russian life.' The novel, for all its hipness, makes the same kind of loutish protest as those Americans who sewed the Stars and Stripes to the seat of their pants. (p. 21)

John Sutherland, "Red Stars," in London Review of Books, December 6 to December 19, 1984, pp. 20-1.*

JOHN UPDIKE

[*The Island of Crimea*] is a prodigious, overpopulated, futuristic fantasy based upon the premise of an island—rather than a peninsula—of Crimea that was successfully defended against the Red Armies by the Whites in 1920 and that thereafter developed, somewhat in the manner of Taiwan, into a thriving capitalist democracy. . . . At the time of our story—"late in the present decade or early in the decade to come (depending on when this book comes out)"—our hero, fabulously rich and handsome forty-six-year-old Andrei Arsenievich Luchnikov, son of Arseny Nikolaevich, one of the White Army founders, and father of Anton Andreevich, a vagabond saxophonist, has decided in his middle-generation unease to lead, from the podium of his Simferopol newspaper the *Russian Courier,* a campaign for Crimea's returning itself to the Soviet Union, democratic institutions, material prosperity, and all.

Why Luchnikov would want to do this dreadful thing, and why his movement (called the Common Fate League, or SOS) eventually captivates ninety per cent of the voting Crimeans, forms the novel's central mystery and problem. A Westerner, clearly, is reading this book from the wrong end. For all its explosive inventiveness and muffled passion, *The Island of Crimea* seems strained, stretched-out, and emotionally opaque. . . . I was most conscious in this dissident novel of allusions I was missing, from puns and pointed caricatures on up to the entire ambience, the bias of the satire. The novel, Pynchonesque in its gag names, multiplying conspiracies, and mechanical interconnections, wears an unremitting grimace; but what is being grimaced at? Crimea as an epitome of Western enterprise and decadence is plausible enough. . . . Yet satire of the West's "hysterical materialism" is not the point; the author clearly loves the idea of Crimea, "the idea of a miniature, tinselly Russia" and its "carnival of freedom." The novel's heroine, Tatyana, whose demanding roles include those of television broadcaster, Soviet sports hero's wife, Luchnikov's mistress, K.G.B. spy, and Yalta hooker, does entertain some dire thoughts about "the capitalist jungle where the very air is pornographic" and yearns to get back from Crimea to "a world where you can't get anything you need and everybody's afraid of everything, the real world." But the island of capitalist unreality, a festive blend of Southern California, Hong Kong, and Oz, inspires affection in most everybody, including Soviet officialdom. For this novel to have earned its breadth and complexity, one convinced Communist should have been represented; but all the Soviets are cheerful thugs or secret Crimeans, as baffled by Luchnikov's betrayal of his homeland as the reader is. Kuzenkov, a Kremlin higher-up, calls the Common Fate League "that sadomasochistic Idea, that snobbish guilt gone berserk!"

Some clues to "Looch"'s state of mind are offered. When visits by Crimeans to the motherland became possible, "a few of them did try to understand and immerse themselves in Soviet life, and the first was Andryushka Luchnikov." . . . He seeks out the shabby back streets that give him "a deceptive sense of the normalcy, sanity, sagacity of Russian life." . . . Hiding in the remote countryside, in the company of "foul-mouthed peasants," Luchnikov goes down on his knees in the mud and makes "a large, slow cross." Crosses multiply as the book heaves toward its apocalyptic end, and, like a refugee from farthest Dostoyevski, Luchnikov preaches to a crowd of Crimeans about his proposed "daring yet noble attempt to share the fate of two hundred and fifty million of our brethren who, through decades of gloom and untold suffering, relieved by only an occasional glimmer of hope, have carried on the unique moral and mystic mission of Mother Russia and the nations that have chosen to follow her path." This is not so much the voice of Luchnikov as a voice within him. His other voice says to Russia, "Your economy's falling apart, your politics are a pack of lies, your ideology's at a dead end." Luchnikov's contradictions and curious slippery unlikableness stem, I think, from his embodiment of ambiguity, of the ambiguous feelings of the author, who while writing this work was ever more imminently facing the prospect of exile.

"He was prepared for one vast bomb site, the smoky remains of a series of trumped-up trials and expulsions. . . Instead he found an uncanny gaiety: loft parties all over town, amateur theatricals in private flats, concerts at scientific institutes and outlying clubs . . . poetry readings by the young and struggling, meetings of the Metropol group, all-night philosophy discussions over tea, samizdat discoveries, basement exhibits. . ." Luchnikov, arriving from Crimea, is the vehicle of perception but the world perceived is Aksyonov's, down to the Metropol group—the vital, busy, "semiunderground" world of Moscow artists. "He was amazed to find so many new deviations from the ideal citizen. . . Yet here they were, living proof that life went on." This is Russia as the working writer experiences it, a mixed bag but alive and actual. Luchnikov's scheme of reintegrating Crimea with the U.S.S.R. makes sense only as a metaphor for Aksyonov's wish to remain part of a nation that is inexorably rejecting him. He will lose his language, his cultural frame of reference, and the audience that understands his frame of reference; and Russia will lose one more bright spirit. Without knowing it, Russia needs him. The dissident has not only a desire but a duty to stay. (pp. 122, 124-25)

John Updike, "Back in the U.S.S.R.," in The New Yorker, *Vol. LXI, No. 8, April 15, 1985, pp. 110-26.**

Jessica (Margaret Queale) Anderson

19??-

Australian novelist and short story writer.

Although not widely known outside of Australia, where she is a best-selling author, Anderson has won respect for the lucid narrative style of her well-crafted novels. A prevalent theme in her work is the relationship between reality and what her characters perceive to be real; tragic consequences often result from the struggle of her characters to come to terms with reality. For example, in her first novel, *An Ordinary Lunacy* (1963), a young lawyer falls in love with an accused murderess whom he defends. Although the woman is found innocent, the local gossip surrounding her arrest and allegedly promiscuous lifestyle provokes her to commit suicide. In *The Commandant* (1975), Anderson explores the psychological deterioration of a penal colony warden. Believing he can control any situation, the warden leads an expedition into the wilderness and is murdered by escaped prisoners. In her later works, *Tirra Lirra by the River* (1978) and *The Only Daughter* (1985), Anderson continues to examine the nature of personal realities. In both novels, the protagonists return from abroad to their native Australia in order to confront their pasts.

(See also *Contemporary Authors*, Vols. 9-12, rev. ed. and *Contemporary Authors New Revision Series*, Vol. 4.)

Courtesy of Australian Information Service

CHARLES POORE

In Miss Anderson's skillfully written novel [*An Ordinary Lunacy*]—a haunting tragicomedy of good and bad manners—we are reminded that society always has its barriers and frontiers. The hero of *An Ordinary Lunacy* learns that to his battering cost. His name is David Byfield. He is a steadily rising Sydney lawyer of 35, one of those perennial bachelors . . . whose matrimonial intentions, if any, are topics in the public domain. . . .

Now, as any constant novel reader will hardly be astonished to learn, David has a ruthlessly ambitious mother, Daisy—and a daisy she is, provided by Miss Anderson with all the characteristics of Freudian bloom in her toughly sunny way.

The portraiture of Daisy here occasionally threatens to run away with the book. . . .

We've learned a trifle more than we need to know about Daisy long before Miss Anderson is ready to concentrate her attention on the dramatic central plot of the novel.

And what is that? Well, David, prim and proper David, falls wildly in love with a mysterious and beautiful woman who has a murder charge—did she kill her husband?—hanging over the glorious long tresses of her head.

Tchk, tchk, tchk! Won't that infatuation imperil David's career? Of course it will. Does he care? The answer, or, at any rate, the wonderfully adroit way Miss Anderson presents the multiple choices involved in David's responses—and their effects on all and sundry—is what gives her story the useful quality of making you want to know what happened next. It's the kind of book that, when mailed out by an idealistic publisher before publication, always produces those jacketable testimonials stating just how late it kept the enthralled recipients awake. What you might call the Insomnia Factor of current literature.

And, I suspect, the Insomina Factor of *An Ordinary Lunacy* will deservedly keep many readers awake. Indeed, a decorous poll of customers should discover a fair number who appreciate its Narrative Pace and who, furthermore, will state that, governed by pleasurable antigravity elements in Miss Anderson's storytelling, they Could Not Put It Down.

> *Charles Poore, "The Insomnia Factor Helps a Tale of Strong Passions," in* The New York Times, *March 5, 1964, p. 31.*

ANTHONY WEST

[*An Ordinary Lunacy*] presents in an acute form a problem that the book reviewer has not infrequently to face—a work written on the dark side of the literary moon, in that perpetual cultural night in which it is possible to conceive and give birth to a novel in a state of complete technical and aesthetic innocence. . . .

[Since] the essential characteristic of [Miss Anderson's] storytelling method is amateurishness, it would appear that there could not be much to say for her novel as a novel. But despite these defects, there is no doubt at all that it is the product of an acute intelligence working on vital experience, or that it says something fresh about the way men behave when confronted by a certain kind of woman, or that in doing so it throws light on the quality of life as it is lived in a particular human society. (p. 86)

The phrase Miss Anderson employs for her title is from a remark by one of her characters to the effect that the physical passion that makes one person seem more desirable than another, and even a necessity, is an ordinary lunacy, a passing fever that a man should try to shake off as quickly as possible. Sex is something to be cool and amused about. That this point of view suggests Diderot brought down to the level of Bonvard and Pécuchet does not indicate any shortcoming in Miss Anderson's mental equipment; she is fully aware of the automatism and the vacuity of it. Nor is she much concerned that the shallow brand of rationalism involved is not viable. Her business with this viewpoint is to use it as a measure of the discrepancy between what the members of the society claim to be able to believe about life and about themselves and the facts of what is felt and ultimately done by them. The machine she uses as a means of liquidating the pretenses is the ambiguous sexual reputation of a woman. Her fated character is not by any means a nymphomaniac, or even promiscuous, but she creates the impression that she is. She is, instead, one of those secure, generous, and wholehearted women who gamble on their instincts and give themselves without reserve and at once to the man who arouses their passions. . . . The gift is irrevocable and absolute, but few men are men enough to be able to accept it when it is given them; the compulsions of insecurity force them to believe that a woman who gives herself immediately and unconditionally must be doing something that she has often done before and will as often do again. Miss Anderson's heroine is at last destroyed because her abundant virtue is in itself not enough to outweigh the effect on her men of their misinterpretation of it and their belief that she is to be had easily by anyone who appears to want her convincingly. So what there is in this first novel is an acutely sensed, intelligent, and discerning account of a genuinely troublesome, and most important, aspect of the psychosexual relationship between men and women written in the terms of a commonplace piece of pulp fiction. . . . It is hard to recommend, and yet even harder to dismiss, since it is a perfect act of candor and communication, in which Miss Anderson discloses to her readers the admirable sum of what she is and what she knows. (pp. 86-7)

> *Anthony West, "An Uncouth Grace," in* The New Yorker, *Vol. XL, No. 25, August 8, 1964, pp. 86-90.**

H.R.F. KEATING

[In *The Last Man's Head*] Miss Anderson has hit on an excellent situation to promote the fast growth of the personalities she has chosen. In Sydney a police detective, temporarily suspended and thus deprived of support, comes to wonder if a distant relative, a semi-unhinged joker, is not about to commit murder. The two of them, alike yet unlike, conduct a long battle of nerves, for half the book not even meeting, in a great sweep of rising tension. The story takes place in Australia, but only because Miss Anderson happens to live there. The meticulously described setting is Australian, with kookaburras complete, but it is so only because it is caught, so to speak,

accidentally in the magnifying ray Miss Anderson directs at her people.

It is the people who count and, not as quaint specimens of *homo australiensis,* but as people, with pasts going back to childhood memories, and futures, seen as the children born to them. In the course of the excellent story they are explored in depth and in width with an intensity something akin to Patricia Highsmith's. Miss Anderson, indeed, has the power to evoke so clearly and forcibly that one regrets at times that she has anxiously taken in too much. There are descriptions of gesture, stance and expression that take overlong in the telling. She has no need of these aids to vividness: hers is the true novelist's gift of bringing whatever she touches to blazing life.

> *H.R.F. Keating, "Forcing Ground," in* The Times, *London, August 22, 1970, p. 8.*

DONAT GALLAGHER

[*The Commandant*] is one of those unobtrusive books whose excellence has passed almost unnoticed. The third of Mrs Anderson's novels, it reconstructs the last months of Patrick Logan, the flogging commandant of Moreton Bay. The story opens with the arrival on the settlement of Logan's sister-in-law, Frances, who at seventeen is gauche and mildly infected with the radicalism of the imprisoned opponent of the convict system, Smith Hall. She acts as a catalyst on the Logan family, whose fortunes are precarious. . . . Frances's imprudent behaviour excites a deranged servant to touch her. By accident she sees the man after he has been flogged . . . and her utter distress enables her sister, Letty, to realize the brutality of the system her husband enforces. Letty, whom Logan loves passionately, communicates this new awareness to her husband and questions his stubbornness. Shortly afterwards Logan takes out an exploring party. Although blacks, possibly led by white escapees, harass the party, the Commandant follows straying bullocks into the bush, alone. When his body is discovered, it appears that he has been murdered by whites.

In a scene of great imaginative power, Logan's penniless widow, who must have a Colonial pension to live, influences her husband's successor to omit from the official report of Logan's death any circumstances other than those which show him to have been murdered by natives while exploring for the Crown.

No sketch of its plot can convey the subtlety of this moving novel. On one level it is a superb piece of investigative history. Was it recklessness and pride that sent Logan off on his own? Or did he willingly court his death? Mrs Anderson's explanation of Logan's motives for despair, and of his wife's seeking to distort some of the facts, is completely convincing.

But the novel will be read principally as a study of how a far from sadistic man can be tyrannical and brutal, by rule. . . . Although consistently dealing with nuances of feeling and significance, Mrs Anderson writes a lucid, decisive prose, the fruit of a sensitive but exceptionally clear mind. Her novel is not fictionalized history, but a novel of character for which historical research has provided a solid and fascinating setting.

> *Donat Gallagher, "The Enigma of Captain Logan," in* Southerly, *Vol. 38, No. 4, December, 1978, p. 477.*

CLIFFORD HANNA

Towards the end of *Tirra Lirra by the River,* Nora Porteous and a neighbour, Betty Cust, are reminiscing about Nora's dead sister, and Betty remarks: "Sometimes, when you talk about Grace, I feel I'm eavesdropping." The reader is placed in a similar position with regard to the novel for Nora's reminiscences, which occupy much of the proceedings, are very much a view from the inside. Some accommodation is made for the reader, but one senses that Nora is quite happy to be her own audience. (p. 361)

Throughout *Tirra Lirra by the River* one is reminded of a careful diarist, and in many ways this is what the novel is: a meticulous, finely written catalogue of one person's life. The novel departs from the diary format in its ordering of experience; it does not follow a chronological path, but one can imagine Nora rearranging her experiences to form a design, or a mosaic, as she had laboured over the tapestries in her youth.

Again, the diary seeks to preserve experience from time and change. Towards the end, Nora, having returned to Australia after spending a large part of her adult life in England, and after having relived her past in the house of her youth, seeks to repudiate memory, to free her mind from its past: "at present my concern is to find things". But, like the artist-figure in Tennyson's "The Lady of Shalott", the poem from which the title of the novel is taken, she has never really deserted her tower of loneliness. Tennyson's Lady could never create directly from life, but only through a mirror, and she eventually enters the outside world to die; Jessica Anderson's Lady has travelled out into the world but has carried the reflection with her. . . .

Tirra Lirra by the River is a polished piece of work that exhibits great subtlety in characterization and structure. The two stories: Nora as an old woman returning to the tower of her youth, and all it represents to her, and the idealistic young Nora departing from it, are skilfully balanced. There are no chapters as such, but seven sections, each a day in the life of the old lady, which adds weight to the idea of the diary. Each section commences with life in the present, with the old lady arriving back, meeting the neighbours, falling ill, being nursed back to health, and so on, and each fresh experience jogs her memory and propels her back into the past.

If *Tirra Lirra by the River* is a study of a mind haunted by a failed life, it is also an intimate view of life in suburban Australia between the wars. . . . [Its] view is finely drawn, the emotional landscapes meticulously rendered. Again one is reminded of the young Nora and her painstaking tapestries. (p. 362)

Tirra Lirra by the River is very much a mood piece that takes great delight in resurrecting the past, and shows great skill in evoking atmosphere. I found it a joy to read, and re-read; it pursues well-worn themes with honesty, sensitivity, and insight. (p. 363)

> *Clifford Hanna, "Camelot between the Wars," in Southerly, Vol. 40, No. 3, September, 1980, pp. 360-63.**

HARRIET WAUGH

Jessica Anderson is an Australian novelist who writes with considerable poetic intensity. In *Tirra Lirra by the River,* her talent shows in the sensibility of its elderly Australian heroine, Nora Porteous. . . . Its title is from Tennyson's poem "The Lady of Shalott." In the poem, the Lady of Shalott is cursed, so that if she looks on reality some terrible fate will befall her. She sits by her mirror and weaves pictures in cloth from the reflections of life going on in Camelot outside her window.

In Miss Anderson's novel, the girl, Nora, projects her imaginative longings onto her own Camelot, which she glimpses through the distortion of a pane of glass in the sitting-room window. . . . This vision becomes a distillation of all the possibilities of existence that she believes are waiting for her away from her mother, sister and the small town they live in. As she waits for the opportunity to leave, her frustrated creativity is expressed in making startling needlework hangings for friends. She is possessed by color and form, and knows she has genuine creative talent. But just as the Lady of Shalott is seduced by the image of Sir Lancelot to leave the loom and rush to the window . . . so does Nora leave the turret of imagination for a desert of experience, first in Sydney and later in London. . . .

These experiences, vividly recalled, are the heart of this slim novel. . . . In flashbacks the reader glimpses Nora's childhood, her first vague sexual longings that overflowed into a wider yearning for escape from the restrictions of her hometown and her marriage. . . .

There is no self-pity in Nora's story. She is a brave, interesting and resilient heroine whose strong sense of herself is never seriously under threat. She simply wishes to discover where she missed Sir Lancelot.

The Australian part of the novel works best. Miss Anderson's knowledge and feeling for the small town and Sydney give depth and conviction to the characters and the times. London seems shadowy in comparison. Nora's experiences in England are less immediate and involving, and the English characters are not so strongly delineated. The relationship between Nora and her three London friends is not very convincingly portrayed. However, the clash of Nora's youth and old age in Australia is sufficiently absorbing for this not to matter much. *Tirra Lirra by the River* is a very short and beautifully written novel.

> *Harriet Waugh, "Living without Lancelot," in* The New York Times Book Review, *February 19, 1984, p. 24.*

RONA BERG

A layer of sadness sits on [*Tirra Lirra by the River*] like a fine powder; though the plot is sentimental, its emotional grip is hard to shake off. Nora's story—the sensitive housewife oppressed by society and circumstance—is, admittedly, a tired theme, but Jessica Anderson is a graceful storyteller with the rare and quirky ability to transcend plot clichés through the emotional fidelity of her writing. A best-selling author in her native Australia, her prose is lean, intense, and clear. The perspective of an old woman, at the end of her life, with no time to change things but the will to resolve them, is cathartic: it makes a lasting impact.

> *Rona Berg, in a review of "Tirra Lirra by the River," in* The Village Voice, *Vol. XXIX, No. 21, May 22, 1984, p. 54.*

KIRKUS REVIEWS

With subtle yet firm thematic interplay, Australian novelist Anderson . . . turns the hoariest of stories—the death of a family patriarch, questions of inheritance, family ties and disgraces—into an exquisite novel of unforced volume and graceful, easy tempo. [In *The Only Daughter*] Sylvia Cornock comes home to Sydney in 1977 from her transplanted venue in Italy to attend the dying of her father Jack. . . . Jack's money, it turns out, is bequeathed to Sylvia—though not until the death of mother Molly, who'll be paid interest during her lifetime. The house will be Greta's [Jack's second wife]—if not the furniture. But the actual specifics of the bequest are no more disjointed and eccentric than the crazed patterns of loyalty and affection that ensue amid this family-under-pressure. Throughout, in fact, Anderson's great care in judging none of the characters makes them all vivid and completely believable: she sometimes writes with the acerbity of family imprisonment found in Ivy Compton-Burnett; there are also echoes of Henry Green's comic non-sequiturs of finely transcribed speech. And, aside from one small preachy sequence about expatriation, the arc of the novel is never stiff, always pliable, moving shrewdly back and forth between comic realism and social analysis. A strong, loose-jointed family novel altogether—totally convincing in its canny ear for the rhythms and tones of domestic alliance/warfare. (pp. 45-6)

A review of "The Only Daughter," in Kirkus Reviews, *Vol. LIII, No. 2, January 15, 1985, pp. 45-6.*

HILMA WOLITZER

It seems at first that [*The Only Daughter*] is more densely populated than Australia, where the action takes place. In Jessica Anderson's earlier, acclaimed novel *Tirra Lirra by the River,* a single, singular voice brilliantly narrated the story of a woman's escape from an intolerable life—instant gratification for the reader. It takes a while longer and some fierce concentration to sort out the enormous cast of this book, but it's well worth the time and effort. Through Miss Anderson's artistry, her gifts for observation, insight and humor, each character comes to life and proves essential to the complex story. . . .

The Only Daughter is filled with insidious, delicious, revealing gossip. It's through gossip that we first learn of Sylvia's arrival in Sydney and her possible intentions. And through gossip we hear of an old family scandal, involving money, of course, or "loot," as Sylvia calls it, stashed in the seats of cars. There's also violence and the threat of violence in this novel of manners. . . .

The characters in *The Only Daughter* are often startled by their own behavior, delighting or distressing one another and themselves. For the reader, there's the satisfaction of their "roundness," as defined by E. M. Forster—they're very "capable of surprising in a convincing way."

Hilma Wolitzer, "Jack Keeps Them Jumping," in The New York Times Book Review, *March 24, 1985, p. 12.*

Russell Banks

1940-

American novelist, short story writer, and editor.

In his fiction Banks often depicts ordinary people coping with difficulties in contemporary society. His settings include the Northeast and Southern regions of the United States as well as the Caribbean. Banks lived in these places, and he accurately recreates the distinct texture of each culture. Explaining his approach to fiction, Banks commented: "I don't rely on memory or observation. I rely on hallucination, what John Hawkes calls 'vision,' dream, fantasy, and system."

In his early works Banks experimented with a variety of literary forms and techniques, revealing a fondness for blending fantasy into realistically detailed stories. His first novel, *Family Life* (1975), is constructed as a fable and satirizes conventional family histories by replacing the traditional roles of father, mother, and son with a king, queen, and prince. In *Hamilton Stark* (1976) Banks concentrates on narrative technique and parodies several literary conventions in a novel about writing a novel. Stark is perceived alternately as a kind, benevolent man and as a scoundrel, yet he remains ambiguous as Banks presents the disparate viewpoints of Stark's daughter, ex-wives, and a close friend. The short story collections *Searching for Survivors* (1975) and *The New World* (1976) subtly merge the extraordinary with the ordinary. For example, in "The Conversation," included in *The New World*, Banks introduces a vision of Jesus into his portrait of an emotionally confused adolescent. A recent book, *The Relation of My Imprisonment* (1984), reflects Banks's early fictional experiments. This work, in which a prisoner publicly recants his sins against God and the religious community, is an allegorical tale modeled after a seventeenth-century literary genre popular among the Puritans.

In several of his later works Banks examines contemporary social problems. *The Book of Jamaica* (1980) centers on a white American novelist who travels to Jamaica and is appalled at the destitute circumstances of the country's native inhabitants. The novelist eventually befriends the Maroons, descendents of renegade African slaves who fight to preserve their way of life. In the interrelated stories in *Trailerpark* (1981) Banks focuses on the poor residents of a trailer-park community in New Hampshire. The inhabitants contend with alcoholism, greed, and loneliness while coping with the pressures of everyday life.

Banks interweaves American and Caribbean cultures in his highly praised novel *Continental Drift* (1985). The plot shifts between a blue-collar New Englander searching for a better life in Southern Florida and a Haitian woman who suffers endless abuse as she flees her native country for the United States. The grim paths of their lives eventually meet in the novel's tragic climax. Banks's thematic concern with displacement and flight may be interpreted as a commentary on the conditions of refugees around the world. Garrett Epps suggests that the book's title refers to Banks's vision of the state of modern humanity as "the vast, almost unprecedented human migrations of our time in which people around the globe flee

© Kelly Wise

from starvation, war, poverty, and oppression and seek a new life somewhere—anywhere—else."

(See also *Contemporary Authors*, Vols. 65-68.)

THOMAS LeCLAIR

In *Searching for Survivors* Russell Banks shares his imagination with his characters. . . . [Most] of Banks's 14 stories begin with ordinary people and work outward to fantasy or saving invention. Banks's characters want to recover or achieve some continuity with heroism, but Henry Hudson, Ché Guevara, a father enlarged by memory, and other heroes in these fictions are dead. Only the ordinary people survive, so they must create their connection. As they construct their heroes and themselves, Banks looks on, allows them their innocence and revelations, meditates the uses of illusions, measures their hazards. . . . (pp. 6-7)

Banks shuffles fact and fiction as Robert Coover did in his much-anthologized "The Babysitter," but the appeal of *Searching for Survivors* is not so much in its semi-experimental structures as in Banks's observation, language and control of tone. Because "remembering is an act of the body," he carefully attends to the physical details of his characters' fantasies as well as to the facts they try to modify. Some of the stories are journeyman stuff and several are Barthelmean oddments, but the best are as deceptive as wisdom. In them invention seems offhand and natural, artifice and circumstance one. Without being small, Banks's stories have an assurance few younger— or established—writers can match. (p. 7)

> *Thomas LeClair, in a review of "Searching for Survivors," in* The New York Times Book Review, *May 18, 1975, pp. 6-7.*

BRUCE ALLEN

[*Family Life* is a] jerky fabulistic romance set in an imaginary kingdom hedged in with heavy literary allusions, and skimming over the related sexual and other problems of "the queen, . . . the king, the youth in the slick green suit, Orgone, Dread, young Egress, and the loon." The jokes are lame indeed, the "contemporary relevance" . . . laid on with a trowel. . . . The crazy inventions resolve themselves in a climactic focus on the dead marriage of the embittered king and queen. This appallingly clumsy first novel works intermittently hard at being a sophisticated farce, but fails to conceal the sadness that lies sluggishly at its center, and appears to have been its originating force.

> *Bruce Allen, in a review of "Family Life," in* Library Journal, *Vol. 100, No. 16, September 15, 1975, p. 1650.*

G. E. MURRAY

Meet Russell Banks in the raw, in the fleshy folds of language asked to stand alone in the cold, in a striptease of imagination, in the nude places of a traditional New England consciousness.

Perhaps this is only a circular means of saying Banks' first short fiction collection [*Searching for Survivors*] excites in every way. Certainly, story after story, as his alluring veils fall, there is more and more of Banks, the writer and character, to witness.

I first met Banks in *New American Review #4* in a story called **"The Drive Home."** That was around 1968. The story has stuck with me as one of the best contemporary pieces I've read since then. In that slippery vision of windshield wipers perpetually clearing the way for destinationless travel, a twenty-five year old high school history teacher named Fletcher Bass is respectfully losing his considerable mind en route to a lifelong death in suburban Boston. On his zig-zagging jaunt "home," Bass rides a bus north to ski country with vacationing students. Faster than you can bless yourself, chanting "Peter, Paul and Mary," the wonderful kids bounce into commercial folk song, which just as quickly moves Bass to crush a few overly wholesome egos and put his foot through a guitar, to boot.

The scene is a favorite, partly because of a personal dislike for impromptu group sings, but more substantially, because it literally kicks off a theme vital to Banks' work, namely, survival by chance, nerve, and implausibility. It's good to find **"The Drive Home"** again, even discover overlooked or forgotten turns of plot. It's better to realize that Banks' first collection, unlike so many, doesn't rely on the light of one accredited jewel.

There are, for openers, three remarkable stories loosely concerned with the shadow of a revolutionary figure named Ché, who arrives little more than a rumor in places diverse as New

York's Plaza Hotel, the Outer Banks of North Carolina, and New Hampshire (Can you believe a bearded, cigar-puffing infidel in khaki togs wandering Daniel Webster's sacred hills?). (pp. 154-55)

In all of Banks' stories, there is a dancing against time, the kind of impeccable footwork required of unscarred prize fighters and storytellers to remember. With Banks, it can happen in as brief a space as the one-page tale, **"The Nap,"** or in a story which seems to precede its own first sentence and extend beyond its final punctuation, such as **"The Lie."** . . .

Surely a collection as uncommon as this almost deserves more than one title story. Almost, hell; it has *two*. The first succeeds in linking 17th-century adventurer Henry Hudson, a 1949 Hudson automobile, and an elkhound puppy named Hudson Frobisher. This story also succeeds in revealing Banks' ambitious use of metaphor. . . .

The same story provides a delightful sample of Banks' Yankee humor, exaggeration accented by an up-country affection for the security of alternatives. The scene is an unexpected meeting between Banks' narrator and a childhood friend turned stiff and superior, a would-be Boston stockbroker. The narrator reflects a droll disappointment, "No way to deny it: I truly had expected him to become a successful racing driver. Or least at least a well-known mechanic."

"Searching for Survivors (II)" takes an entirely different tack, sweeping back and forth across fierce family lines, in search of a young son lost to accident, a departed father living worlds away in a neighboring community, a brother collecting the scattered returns of his own survival. This final howl in the New Hampshire dark is as fine a piece of writing as exists in a book long on fine writing. (p. 155)

> *G. E. Murray, in a review of "Searching for Survivors," in* fiction international, *Nos. 4/5, 1975, pp. 154-55.*

TERENCE WINCH

You wouldn't like Hamilton Stark. He dumps a great variety of garbage all over his property and then shoots at it. He almost killed his father. He's a mean drunk who hates cats, dogs, and people. He is, we are told, "a self-centered, immature, violent, cruel, eccentric, and possibly insane man." And, perhaps most annoying of all, he never appears in person in this novel named after him.

Or, then again, maybe you would like him. It's quite possible he's wise and passionate and more honest than any of us. . . . He's handsome, funny, and a good dancer. He comes from an old colonial family and has a marvelous smile.

[*Hamilton Stark*] is a murder mystery / memoir / biography whose apparent purpose is to explore the ambiguous character of Hamilton Stark. The story is told by an unnamed narrator who is Stark's friend and admirer. The narrator is writing a novel about his friend Hamilton. Hamilton's daughter Rochelle, with whom the narrator is in love, is also writing a novel about her father. So this is a novel about writing a novel.

Oh no, not one of *those*, you may think. But actually Russell Banks does very well at avoiding the self-conscious and literary nature of novels about writing novels.

One reason for Banks' success is his narrator. The narrator is obsessed with Hamilton Stark, the man he calls "my hero," and with his fictionalized account of Stark's life. But like Captain Delano, the naive narrator of Melville's "Benito Cereno," Banks' narrator is sensitive and intelligent, but blind to the obvious. His faith in Hamilton is firm, his lack of self-knowledge abysmal. At one point, even the narrator himself calls into question his abilities as "a reliable witness."

The narrator frequently reflects on his "novel." Which *is* his novel? It is definitely not *Hamilton Stark*—that's Russell Banks' novel. The narrator's book (if we can pretend it exists) is the one that is really about Hamilton Stark. Banks' novel is really more about the narrator, the way *The Great Gatsby* is more about Nick Carroway than Jay Gatsby. . . . Banks suggests the possibility that Hamilton Stark is really the narrator, or a version of the narrator. The novel begins with Hamilton's suspicious disappearance and has him vanishing mysteriously at the end. And during the action of the novel, Hamilton appears only indirectly through the memories of others. Hamilton begins to seem more like a ghost of the narrator's imagination, a Doppelganger.

But ultimately these issues—Who is Hamilton Stark? Or who is the narrator? And are they the same person?—are academic. . . . The answers aren't there because the relationship between the novel's "I" and Hamilton Stark is meant to be an insoluble puzzle, just as the more conventional battle of selves in all of us remains a mystery. . . . (pp. 1, 4)

Banks will throw in almost anything, in fact, to keep you interested—the monologue of a crazed 18th-century widow; striking animal stories about drunk pigs and brutal fighting cocks; ugly barroom dramas; terrible domestic conflicts. Portraits of Hamilton Stark and the narrator emerge not out of a continuous logical narrative, but out of a collage of bits and scraps—a rambling tape-recording of one of Hamilton's five ex-wives (now overweight and old before her time), gossip, anecdote, fable, as well as the research of Hamilton's beautiful daughter. . . . Banks has skillfully used his repertoire of contemporary techniques to write a novel that is classically American—a dark, but sometimes funny, romance with echoes of Poe and Melville. (p. 4)

> Terence Winch, "The Man Who Wasn't There," in Book World—The Washington Post, *July 2, 1978,* pp. F1, F4.

ANN BIRSTEIN

[*Hamilton Stark*] is a one-man show, or, rather, a kaleidoscope with Hamilton as the brightest piece in a constantly shifting pattern. And how Mr. Banks loves to shift the pattern, using every literary device at hand, including a formal introduction to the novel, an elaborate study of the geography and history of the region, Hamilton's reminiscences, tape recordings by his wives, various addenda, philosophical digressions, footnotes, excerpts from the novel that Hamilton's *daughter* is trying to write. Sometimes all this works, and sometimes it doesn't. The use of the daughter's novel is hilarious, and so are the tapes by the wives. The little essays are often ponderous and distracting, the digressions often witty.

And is Hamilton worth all this, either philosophically or as a character? It's hard to say, because amid all the speculation one frequently forgets to wonder—a tribute to Mr. Banks. At the end his author, too, is stymied, and also bereft. Following Hamilton's EEE tracks to the top of a rise, he looks down and sees, "Nothing. *Unimaginable nothing,*" then turns around

and begins his descent. Another metaphor, but then, what's a novel without a metaphor?

> Ann Birstein, "Metaphors, Metaphors," *in* The New York Times Book Review, *July 2, 1978, p. 12.**

SYLVIA SHORRIS

[*The New World*] is divided into two sections: "Renunciation," in which [Banks's] more conventional stories appear, and "Transformation," where the writing is more experimental. **"The Conversion,"** which appears in the first section, tells of Alvin Stock, a 16-year-old New Hampshire boy, in the classic throes of tortured adolescence. . . . Alvin's most excruciating sufferings are caused by his clumsiness with girls, and during one particularly painful school dance, he sees a vision of Christ which makes him decide to be a minister. We know, however, that this will not be the final resolution for Alvin, for there are no simple resolutions, and the story is too true, too credible, to provide us with any. Banks has perfect pitch for telling of the little near-deaths we have all suffered.

Less successful but more adventurous are the stories in the second part of the book. These deal with actual people in imaginary situations: a weary, aging Simon Bolivar contemplating his life and envying a slave in **"The Rise of the Middle Class"**; Jean Hogarth, wife of the painter, William Hogarth, lying in bed one morning, unable or unwilling to move, surveying her large, healthy body and resenting its misuse by the greedy, unloving Hogarth, in **"Indisposed."**

Banks's most ambitious story is **"The New World,"** which has as its two main characters, Bernardo de Balbuena, Spanish poet and Catholic prelate, and Mosseh Alvares, a Sephardic goldsmith. Balbuena, longing for a post in Spain, Mexico, or even Lima, Peru, is sent instead to serve in Jamaica, in the 17th century a stagnating backwater. Though miserably disappointed, he gallantly writes to his friend, Lope de Vega, that we choose our own destinies. His real hopes are tied up in his epic poem, "El Bernardo," in which he creates an idealized version of himself.

Alvares is an important member of the Jewish community in Jamaica, but he, too, is an exile. Though he has a successful business and a beloved daughter, he also feels the need to create a fantasy persona, in his case, a patriarch, the hero of a story he tells his daughter one day. Both men, though alienated from their surroundings, are proud of their accomplishments under duress. But they resent that duress. They are angry at not being better situated, so they invent better situations.

Was the New World created to make the old one more endurable, just as people create fantasy lives in order to make their daily existence bearable? It's a bit farfetched, and the audacious Banks doesn't make the connection work completely. . . . But a writer willing to gamble this way deserves unlimited credit at the gaming tables. (p. 154)

> Sylvia Shorris, "Literature's Stepchild," *in* The Nation, *Vol. 228, No. 5, February 10, 1979, pp. 153-54.**

ROBERT KIELY

It is just right to call [the short fictional works collected in *The New World*] "tales." Their strongest and most common trait is a wonderful exercise of imagination. It is as though Russell Banks were a naturally gifted organist trying out the tremolos and bass tones, the foot pedals and hand stops of a new instrument.

His stories are not "fantastic tales" in the science-fiction or Gothic mode. No green people or corpses moaning in turrets. His characters and situations are familiar and ordinary to begin with, but there is nearly always a leap into the extraordinary. . . . Whatever happens, whether the reader takes it as a leap of the author's or a character's imagination, the stretching of the ordinary seems convincing and right in each case. Moral and psychological credibility are not strained.

Mr. Banks has learned the art of short fiction from great masters. Though he is never lugubrious, his unnerving habit of introducing nightmare and fairy tale into the real world resembles Poe. . . . Isaac Bashevis Singer also seems to have taught him a thing or two. Probably his least successful imitation is an elaborately labored Borges-like tale of 17th-century Jamaica. But Mr. Banks has the talent, the good sense and the daring to imitate masterful writers without fear of losing his own originality. Anyone who can turn a historical caprice—a tale told from the point of view of the wife of the 18th-century caricaturist William Hogarth—into a moody, poignant and uproarious meditation on marriage deserves watching. (p.26)

> Robert Kiely, *"Tales and Stories," in* The New York Times Book Review, *February 25, 1979, pp. 26-7.**

JEROME KLINKOWITZ

If anyone has been wondering when it would happen, here's the breakthrough novel for commercially innovative fiction in America. It could have been written by any one of a dozen deserving authors and readers should be reminded that there's lots more good stuff to be had for the digging (treasure map to come). But the truly excellent novel you can buy at your corner bookstore right now is *The Book of Jamaica* by Russell Banks.

Sunny Jamaica. . . . That's where Errol Flynn anchored his yacht in the good old days. And where the single new force in recent popular music—reggae—had its birth. But there are people dying of neglect and exploitation in Jamaica just this minute. It's not a pretty thought.

Does it bother Mick Jagger and the Studio 54 crowd? Maybe so, but who knows? It does bother Russell Banks, and his new novel is a powerful testament to human nature's alternately creative and destructive forces that seem to be both our salvation and damnation as a species on this Earth.

The story of Banks' novel is straightforward: a white American male spends some time on the island looking into the life and habits of a black religious sect, the Maroons, who are renegade descendents of slaves who'd escaped from their Spanish and British masters three centuries ago and set up their own culture in the Jamaican hills.

A sect member named Terron Musgrave introduces his narrator-friend to this group's ways and values. The narrator learns firsthand just what life in Jamaica has been for those forced to live it: a saga of exploitation at the hands of a dominant, rationalistic, colonial power, and of the creation of a uniquely imaginative way of life as a strategy to survive.

For better or for worse, Banks is a master of the techniques that make people want to read novels. As in his earlier, more experimental works, those morbidly fascinating little twists of

human existence are all here: love and sex, life and death, beauty and horror—the works.

What makes Banks so good is that he doesn't exploit his readers. . . .

The sex and violence that seem to be the necessary orchestrations of our modern American lives are perfectly justified, because—in Russell Banks' hands—they make us realize the utter danger of the places our lust and imagination take us. Did Errol Flynn, a real-life fictional character in this novel, suspect where his appetites were leading? Who knows. But no serious reader of this book can dodge that question. And that's the final profit of Banks' literary effort. . . .

[Anyone] who truly cares about the future of serious fiction in America—fiction that in turn cares about people but won't use fraudulent techniques to tell stories—will want to read *The Book of Jamaica*. And then read on.

> Jerome Klinkowitz, *"From Banks, a Novel That's the Real Thing," in* Book Week—Chicago Sun-Times, *March 9, 1980, p. 12.*

DARRYL PINCKNEY

Jamaica is the seductive setting of *The Book of Jamaica* and *The Harder They Come*—a Jamaica stricken with change, with moral contamination; suffering from an eroded sense of identity, from a complicated modernity. There is something backward in the exertions of development; Kingston is Babylon, dangerous and desperate; even the tropical heat becomes a metaphor for menacing, conspiratorial forces. Though the books share a setting, their perceptions are quite different and there are no similarities of style or tone. Russell Banks's *The Book of Jamaica* spans only a brief time and is set mostly along the northern coast of the island; Michael Thelwell's *The Harder They Come* is a chronical of generations and is set primarily in the Kingston ghetto.

Unlike Mr. Thelwell, Russell Banks is not a Jamaican, and being an outsider is the subject of his novel. His unnamed narrator develops an obsession for Jamaican culture. A 35-year-old New Hampshire college teacher, he is extravagantly sincere, alert to cultural differences, and filled with racial guilt. He travels to Jamaica first in 1975 to finish a novel and, on two subsequent visits, becomes more interested in the people than his work and is haunted by tales of Errol Flynn as a symbol of the decadent visitor. He is given to lengthy meditations on alienation and isolation and is preoccupied by the difference between his experiences and those of his new friends. (p. 15)

Well-educated and intelligent people often demonstrate a disastrous lack of imagination that affords them little gift for real experience. The narrator seems burdened by his references: "This is not a brave thing to be doing, I thought. Why, then, am I so afraid? I would have liked to have been Gauguin in Tahiti, all awash with open-eyed enthusiasm for the newly revealed alternative to bourgeois France, or Forster in India, skeptical, shrewdly compassionate, confident that what one did not know at the moment was really not worth knowing at the moment, or Dinesen in Africa, tender and secure in the tower of her absent self."

He stockpiles impressions, some of which seem inspired by marijuana. . . . He notes his "fear. . .of people whose ancestors fought generations of a just war against my ancestors. Will Americans traveling in Vietnam two hundred years from now feel as I do today?'' His task is to translate these images and educate his feelings; to re-create himself as a social being and make radical his inner life.

Much retold history of Jamaica and of slavery emerges from the narrator's curiosity. He is particularly interested in the Maroons, an autonomous people descended from the Ashanti, who successfully resisted the British. As he becomes involved with these people, his story moves from the first person to the second—''You are becoming your own stranger''—and finally to the third person, in which he becomes ''Johnny,'' the name traditionally given a trusted white. The change in point of view corresponds to ''Johnny's'' immersion in the rhythm of life around him, and illustrates a change in consciousness that will lead him to a dramatic choice. (pp. 15, 35).

> *Darryl Pinckney, "Seductive Setting," in* The New York Times Book Review, *June 1, 1980, pp. 15, 35.**

ANNA SHAPIRO

It is always a tricky thing to write about poor, uneducated people. While doing so invariably rings in a tone of high seriousness, there is always a danger of condescension. On first encountering the bad grammar and stereotypical poverty of Russell Banks's trailer-park denizens [in *Trailerpark*], one flinches. But the characters exist almost as instances or illustrations of universal truths, impossible to condescend to. One gets to know them as one gets to know people in any small community, by rumor and gossip, by laying ''one sentence beside another.'' . . .

The stories should be read slowly and reread; like the characters, they seem simple, but their simplicity is that of experience and understanding. Banks, author of the highly praised *Hamilton Stark* and *The Book of Jamaica,* writes as a professional wise man, proffering nuggets of wisdom the reader goes on pondering. What comes across as the highest moral value here is the ability to pay attention. It is a virtue Banks exemplifies. *Trailerpark* is a lucid, serious, witty frieze of a book.

> *Anna Shapiro, in a review of "Trailerpark," in* Saturday Review, *Vol. 8, No. 10, October, 1981, p. 76.*

JONATHAN YARDLEY

The dust jacket copy of *Trailerpark* begins with this curious plea: ''Read this book as you would a novel—from the beginning straight through to the end.'' Inasmuch as *Trailerpark* is elsewhere described by its publisher as ''a novel,'' it's difficult to imagine how else to read it—from the middle to the end to the beginning, perhaps? Backwards?

Never mind. The point is to read it, any old way you want. Its publisher's good-hearted protests notwithstanding, *Trailerpark* is not a novel but a collection of interrelated short stories. Each of them is uncommonly good, and the whole of *Trailerpark* is greater than the sum of its parts: it is an odd, quirky book that offers satisfactions different from those provided by the conventional, or even unconventional, novel.

Specifically, they are the satisfactions of surprising, lively writing and believably human characters, held together by no central plot line or structure; yet the book has a unifying mood and, of course, a unifying setting—the trailerpark. . . .

The occupants of the trailerpark are ''generally alone at the center of their lives.'' Among them are ''widows and widowers, divorcees and bachelors and retired Army officers, a black man in a white society, a black woman there too, a drug dealer, a solitary child of a broken home, a drunk, a homosexual in a heterosexual society—all of them, man and woman, adult and child, basically alone in the world.''

Yet it being the natural human instinct to seek community, these utterly unconnected people find themselves drawn together by the accident of living in the same place; the trailerpark, grim and dreary though it may be, is a neighborhood. And into it Banks has crowded a small but vibrant cast of characters, a human comedy in microcosm.

There are 13 stories in the book, the longest and best of these being the first and last: ''**The Guinea Pig Lady**'' and ''**The Fisherman,**'' respectively. The central character in each is a person regarded as eccentric if not downright nuts by the rest of the trailerpark, as by the community of Catamount. The treatment that each receives is uncomprehending and cruel, though each finds a way to adjust to it.

The guinea pig lady is Flora Pease, ''about forty or forty-five, kind of flat-faced and plain, a red-colored person, with short red hair and a reddish tint to her skin.'' She lives a reclusive, mysterious life in her trailer, but gradually the mystery is explained: inside she is raising guinea pigs, in great and rapidly increasing numbers, and she fears what will happen when the community discovers what she's up to. . . .

Flora's innocent decency runs up against the community's fear that the guinea pigs are dirty disease-bearers. Pressure to do something about the animals mounts to a point at which she takes peremptory action herself, then retreats from the trailerpark; her neighbors fail to tolerate or understand her, yet she emerges at the end oddly triumphant.

So does Merle Ring, the fisherman of the concluding story. He is an old and seemingly cranky fellow with a brusque manner and a penchant for homing in on the truth. During the winter he rigs up a small shack on the ice and holes up in blissful isolation, fishing through the ice. But when he wins a huge prize in the state lottery, his isolation is rudely interrupted and the greed of his fellow trailerparkers is starkly revealed.

These two stories are the framework within which the smaller parts of the book are contained—brief stories of hope and disappointment, of infidelity and murder, of betrayal and alienation. They are bleak stories set in a bleak place, yet there is a wicked comic edge to them. Banks has a terrific eye, mordant yet affectionate, for the bric-a-brac and the pathos of the American dream. . . .

The people of the trailerpark are just like people everywhere else.

Except that they live in the trailerpark. Banks catches its slightly loopy, edgy atmosphere with a nice sense of nuance and detail. His prose has a jaunty, lightly mocking quality that is entirely engaging; he's a writer who clearly enjoys what he's doing and who conveys that pleasure to his readers. *Trailerpark* is less than a novel and more than a short-story collection, and very good work all the way through.

> *Jonathan Yardley, "Life behind the Fiberglass Curtain," in* Book World—The Washington Post, *October 4, 1981, p. 3.*

DEIRDRE BAIR

[*The Relation of My Imprisonment*] is a novel, to be sure, but Russell Banks' own word, "Fiction," probably fits it best because it is also a compelling parable, allegory, exemplum and even scripture of a sort, with overtones suggesting what happens to individuals who come into conflict with their society.

The "Relation," a retelling of a personal experience, was a genre popular among 17th-century Puritans. In its usual form it was recounted by those who had been imprisoned for their deviation from rigid religious orthodoxy, and it was often a literal account of the actual details of the sinful or criminal act, told within certain literary conventions or typologies.

In general, Mr. Banks has followed both the convention and the genre. An unnamed narrator tells us that he has been imprisoned more than 12 years because his usual line of work—the building of coffins—was suddenly deemed heretical. He had been urged to turn his skills to making "high wooden cabinets with glass doors for the purpose of exhibiting fragile and expensive possessions," but at first he resisted, because his religion requires him and his brethren to devote themselves fully "to the worship and further contemplation of the power of the dead." To do so, they must lie in their coffins, for each has one and it is central to their worship. When the carpenter is imprisoned, he is temporarily deprived of his coffin and later loses it permanently to a jailer who chooses to die in his stead.

The chapters that follow form a pattern typical of the "Relation" genre; the narrator is remorseful and wants to atone after the jailer's death. He falls into lustful, orgiastic behavior. His personality becomes fragmented, so that he loses all sense of his real self. Then he has a dream—a vision—and he gains control of himself long enough to formulate a plan of action, so that he and his fellow worshippers can secure coffins for themselves. This is followed by a descent of another kind, into what the narrator calls "nostalgia," in which the carpenter fantasizes about food, money and liquor. Then he refuses to join the other inmates in their daily activity, his wife sickens and dies and he himself becomes ill. At the end, we learn that he is lying in his coffin, writing his "Relation," which he says has been "composed expressly for the use of the living," because he knows of no other way "to tender this much mercy to the dead."

All this is traditional typology, but Mr. Banks has cloaked it in a post-Modernist mantle: the form may be historical but the language is contemporary. . . . He tells us that his descriptions of events "must be taken as a type," thus insisting that we be aware of the archaic form of his narrative, all the while that he is standing apart from it, probably making sly mockery of the reader who tries to decipher it. . . .

This is a marvelously written little book, fascinatingly intricate, yet deceptively simple. Well worth reading more than once.

> *Deirdre Bair, "Parable from the Coffin," in* The New York Times Book Review, *April 1, 1984, p. 8.*

JODI DAYNARD

It is a vital sign of life when a work of fiction invites many comparisons and rests comfortably within few. Given the remarkable precedents of the author's chosen genre, that of "prison writing," *The Relation of My Imprisonment* comes as a particularly original surprise. . . .

Banks's treatment of the prison metaphor departs from its modern counterparts on several points. The most immediate is the novel's form—the "relation"—which was first used by jailed Puritan divines in the seventeenth century to relate the tests their faith had endured in prison. Each relation was read aloud to a congregation of their free brethren and framed with selected scriptures and a sermon. The relation we receive here, and which the reader may indeed find himself reading aloud at moments (so lyrical and sustained is the hero's meditation), is the testament of a coffin-maker (not a Puritan) who worships the dead. His Scripture—certain selections of which are pure gems of irony—are from a ghoulish mirror-image of the Bible. . . .

The coffin-maker is brought to trial and subsequently imprisoned after refusing to cease and desist from his perverse religion. It soon becomes apparent, however, that to incarcerate him is not a punishment but a logical extension of his belief. Imprisonment only aids and abets his coming to terms with desire, and with "the memory that begets desire," which only the living possess. To punish this fanatic with chains is to take away his last restraints. And this is where the author has made a statement that stands apart from those of his predecessors: this hero's struggle derives not from the limitations imposed upon him by society, or from the demands which civilization makes upon human instincts, but from the bitterly spare conflict of the pleasure principle versus the death wish, of human time versus the magnificent purity of infinity. . . .

[The] coffin-maker is quirky to say the least. The sanity of anyone whose antidote for anxiety is a good long rest in his coffin (portable Holy Place) is suspect. But such idiosyncracies only temporarily obscure the fact that Banks has succeeded in capturing the fundamental paradigm of human worship: the sense of infinity, the awe before something more perfect than oneself, which comes when one has surmounted the worship of desire, of human nostalgia. The longing for infinity is the product of a memory that digs back into the species' collective memory of non-being. The reader becomes aware that even the coffin-maker's worship adheres to this structure; we come to understand the attraction death holds for him, and even to anticipate with him the peaceful moments he steals, from time to time, inside his coffin.

The Relation of My Imprisonment is a strong and radical departure from Russell Banks's earlier fictions, such as *Trailerpark* and *Hamilton Stark*. Banks seems to have made a decision to address reality, human behavior, from the inside out this time, rather than, as in the past, to search external clues for signs of the life within. The faithful pre-realist style suspends us convincingly, for the most part, in an unnameable bygone time. However, it is unclear why the author allowed his narrative to retain a number of anachronisms which jar the unwilling reader from his hypnotized lull—the "newspaper" our hero sees in the prison reading room, for example, or the illnesses he describes in unmistakeably modern terms. But these are minor flaws in an otherwise solid and convincing work.

> *Jodi Daynard, in a review of "The Relation of My Imprisonment," in* Boston Review, *Vol. IX, No. 4, July-August, 1984, p. 28.*

JAMES ATLAS

From the very first sentence of *Continental Drift* Russell Banks lets it be known that he's writing a tale in which momentous things occur. The run-on prose is eager, hurried, like a breathless messenger's report. . . .

The tragedies in this novel are so awesome, so wrenching, so terrible, that it's hard to believe they're happening to ordinary people. Real-estate speculators who get in over their heads, dope dealers who get mixed up with the wrong crowd, liquor-store clerks who get held up by men willing to kill for a few dollars: these are the kinds of anonymous disasters you read about in the newspaper. In *Continental Drift* Banks has brought them to life, given them reality. His novel explores the seedy, marginal territory that has become so visible lately in American fiction—the drive-ins and shopping malls where Frederick Barthelme's characters hang out, the crummy taverns frequented by Raymond Carver's drunks, the sinister Caribbean islands where Robert Stone's nihilistic drifters end up. What distinguishes Banks from these other chroniclers of the desperate and depressed is a quality of moral outrage. By witnessing his characters' doom he rescues their lives from oblivion, invests them with significance. Every life, he reminds us, is sanctified by the same exhaustive intensity, the same will to matter.

Banks's main character, Bob Dubois, is a furnace repairman in a dilapidated New Hampshire town, one of those towns that flourished in the nineteenth century and have since fallen on hard times, hurt by the general migration from the Northeast to the Sun Belt. Bob still owes money on his car, he's got a mortgage to worry about, he has to work nights and weekends. (p. 94)

What makes Bob Dubois a great fictional character is nothing that he does; it's what he feels. Like John Updike's Rabbit Angstrom, another inarticulate, ordinary man stifled by the materiality of his needs—the money, the car, the job—and the boredom of routine, Bob has a preternatural instinct for the pathos and frailty of life. Sitting around with his girlfriend, Doris, in her apartment above Irwin's Restaurant and Lounge, he takes in her sad existence, her loneliness, the unkind things age is doing to her body. When he gets home, he's sorry for his wife, Elaine, sitting in front of the television in curlers and a flannel nightgown. He even broods over the bald spot on the back of a Sears, Roebuck salesman's head. . . . What torments Bob Dubois is our vulnerability, the fear and resentment we feel toward those we love because we know they'll die.

Lured down to Florida by the prospect of a partnership in his brother's liquor store, Bob finds himself living in a trailer, working twelve hours a day with no partnership is sight. His wife is pregnant again, and Bob is involved with the daughter of the old black man who helps out in the store. The night Elaine goes into labor, Bob is at the Hundred Lakes Motel with his new girlfriend. He tries to do the right thing, but he doesn't know how. (pp. 94, 96)

For all his weakness and simplicity of character, Bob wants to make sense of his life. He frets about his conduct and worries, within the limits of his nature and intelligence, the question of what it means to be good—unlike his brother, Eddie, who doesn't lose a lot of sleep over such matters. Crude, fast-talking, a gambler with bad instincts, Eddie is deep in a number of dubious enterprises that he just knows are going to make it big. . . .

Florida is the new frontier, "Disney World and land deals and fast-moving high-interest bank loans." Bob, though, can't make it in this brutal world. He's too cautious, too passive, too naive. Hard up for cash, sick of working in his brother's liquor store, he drifts into a more promising venture as the captain of a

fishing boat. But he's still no better off. While his partner is hauling marijuana on his sleek new yacht, Bob is knocking around on a trawler with drunken businessmen out for a good time. Drug-running isn't for him; he's too much of a "country boy at heart." Eventually he succumbs to another illicit occupation, which is supposed to be less risky: running Haitians over to the Florida beaches on his boat. "The more a man trades off his known life, the one in front of him that came to him by birth and the accidents and happenstance of youth, the more of that he trades for dreams of a new life, the less power he has"—but Bob doesn't know that. Like everyone, he imagines that his life is under his own jurisdiction, that he controls his own destiny. To say that events will prove him wrong is to put it mildly.

Entwined with Bob's story is another, the story of a young Haitian woman's struggle to reach the shores of America, which unfolds in separate chapters until the two conjoin in a shocking denouement. Banks's account of Vanise Dorsinville's life in Haiti and the humiliations she suffers at the hands of a barbarous Jamaican sea captain is uncannily vivid. He knows Haitian culture intimately—the idioms, the rituals, the desolate beauty of the poor coastal villages. His prose has a kind of hallucinatory clarity. (p. 96)

He's a novelist who clearly has been around. He's full of information about mortgages, real estate, fishing tackle, navigation, dope smuggling, boats. . . . His ability to evoke the texture of American life—of car interiors, the taste of "Dunkin' Donuts coffee in paper cups," houses with wall-to-wall carpeting and wet bars—rivals Updike's. *Continental Drift* is the most convincing portrait I know of contemporary America: its greed, its uprootedness, its indifference to the past. This is a novel about the way we live now.

Banks has been over some of this ground before in his novels and short stories, but nothing I'd read of his prepared me for this profound and gripping narrative. *Continental Drift* is a lesson in history: it shows us how ordinary, decent men can find themselves enmeshed in events of unspeakable enormity, and be destroyed by them. (pp. 96-7)

> *James Atlas, "A Great American Novel," in* The Atlantic Monthly, *Vol. 255, No. 2, February, 1985, pp. 94, 96-7.*

JEAN STROUSE

Continental Drift has only metaphorically to do with grinding tectonic plates that slowly bend subcontinents and heave mountain ranges toward the sky. The novel charts, in alternating chapters, the eventually intersecting paths of two people desperately on the move: Bob Dubois, a 30-year-old native of Catamount, N.H., who decides one cold December night in the late 1970's that he wants something better than the life he has had so far and takes off with his wife and two daughters for Florida—and Vanise Dorsinville, a Haitian woman living in a tiny cabin in the hill country near Port-de-Paix, who leaves the poverty and bitter hopelessness of her island life for the bright promise of America. Telling these powerful stories, Russell Banks has fresh things to say about a certain kind of American masculinity and some failures of the American dream. He also says problematical things about telling stories. . . .

Mr. Banks's writing . . . has a vivid, tactile quality—a neighbor of Bob's wears Scotch-plaid Bermudas with a "huge beer gut, like a weighty sack of flour, billowing out in front of him and swooping smoothly down to his pinched crotch, where enormous red legs merge like turnpike ramps.'' In scenes that might easily have become clichés, Bob seems original and full of life—yearning for his father's approval after making the all-state high school hockey team, and getting only a smile and nod, fighting with his wife in perfectly syncopated misunderstanding, deciding to kill the black kid who held up the liquor store. . . . Sometimes, though, the imagery describing Bob doesn't suit an oil-burner repairman: making love to Marguerite for the first time, he is ''gentle, but persistent, a man knocking lightly at a locked door, determined to wake his lover and not her maid.''

Near the end of his sad, downhill slide, Bob encounters the Haitian woman, Vanise. She is his emblematic opposite, heading north as he heads south, looking to the dream of America for survival itself, as Bob thrashes around after something more. . . . Early on, Vanise had lost most of her family and lived by ''letting men visit her and pay for her time and laughter and young girl's body.'' She had borne the local police chief's child and then his contempt, and she had passed, eventually, through fear to resignation and beyond, becoming a practitioner (*serviteur*) of voodoo. . . . While Bob looks for a force—luck, fate, stupidity—that will explain what happens to him, Vanise knows that she is in the hands of the gods (loas), and that if things go wrong, it is ''because the loas have not been properly fed.''

Things do go wrong. She pays a Haitian fisherman everything she has to take her, with her infant son and nephew, Claude, to Florida; he drops them off on a beach—''Biscayne Bay''—that turns out to be 600 miles from America. Praying to Christian and Haitian gods, she proceeds, with fierce will and fatalistic passivity, to make her way north. She gets raped by every man along the way, until her mind is ''an utterly silent, burned-out charnel house''; she serves the loas in fantastical ancient ceremonies; she survives—and one day Bob Dubois comes with his boat to ferry her and the boys to America. What happens next is the stuff of tragedy.

Vanise's story doesn't come as fully alive as Bob's does—it seems cloudier, more dimly perceived—in spite of the fact that Mr. Banks does more telling and less interpreting here than he does with Bob. Which brings me to the story of the story. Mr. Banks creates enormous sympathy for Bob—the way John Updike does for Rabbit Angstrom—even though both characters do some pretty terrible things. Both seem likable because they do these awful things out of a baffled, inarticulate longing to do or be or find something good. Unlike Mr. Updike, however, Mr. Banks keeps stepping in to *explain* Bob, as if talking to somebody offstage, which constantly distracts you from the illusion of fiction and draws attention to the novel's narrative voice. (p. 11)

What is the point of these intrusions, which condescend to Bob and lecture the rest of us? It is not that Mr. Banks can't create a character without such assists, since he has done that masterfully both here and in previous work. Maybe he is posing a question about storytelling itself—the process of finding narrative lines that organize, or pretend to organize, experience. Continental drift, a process invisible to the eye, moves land masses and ''explains'' puzzling geographical facts. What moves and explains men? Bob searches, in hunger and chaos and rage, for a coherence he can't find, while Vanise knows all order resides with the loas in the invisible world of magic. Maybe denying Bob the ''magic'' coherence of fiction underscores

this question precisely by undermining the story—but then, maybe not.

An ''Invocation'' at the beginning of the novel calls on one of the loas to inspire the storyteller (''bring this middle-aging, white mouth-man into speech again'') and announces: ''With a story like this, you want an accounting to occur, not a recounting, and a presentation, not a representation, which is why it's told the way it's told.'' I'm not sure that explains anything, but an ''Envoi'' picks up the sermon: ''Books get written—novels, stories and poems stuffed with particulars that try to tell us what the world is, as if our knowledge of people like Bob Dubois and Vanise and Claude Dorsinville will set people like them free. It will not. Knowledge of the facts of Bob's life changes nothing in the world. Our celebrating his life and grieving over his failure, however, will.'' They will? That argument does not work either, since we are more likely to celebrate and grieve over a character who is given real fictional life than one who is so ruthlessly explicated. (pp. 11-12)

> *Jean Strouse, ''Indifferent Luck and Hungry Gods,''*
> *in* The New York Times Book Review, *March 24,*
> *1985, pp. 11-12.*

GARRETT EPPS

Continental Drift is harrowing, bleak, often clumsy, and always compulsively readable. It reminded me of Robert Stone's *Dog Soldiers* and John Dos Passos's *U.S.A.* Like Stone, Banks has constructed a kind of super-caper novel, in which a crime and its aftermath become a metaphor for an entire moment in our national life; like Dos Passos, Banks deliberately draws on a broad canvas, attempting to dramatize social and political change in the lives of ordinary people.

The novel's title refers to the theory that all the continents were once part of a single land mass, which slowly broke up and has been drifting apart ever since. But Banks's vision is of demographic, not geological, motion—of the vast, almost unprecedented human migrations of our time in which people across the globe flee from starvation, war, poverty, and oppression and seek a new life somewhere—anywhere—else.

Although his story concerns the Caribbean boat people who are arriving in our country every day, Banks insists on a larger context, invoking images of all earth's refugees—Afghans, Somalis, Cambodians, and millions of others—as well as of the millions who help, hinder, or prey on them as they pass. (pp. 38-9)

Continental Drift is a powerful book. Its settings are convincing, particularly the section in central Florida, that fast-growth Fantasyland that has erupted out of the palmetto scrub around Walt Disney World. Bob and Elaine Dubois, a ''typical'' working-class couple who could so easily have dribbled into cliché, are subtly drawn, memorable characters; even more impressive, Banks makes Vanise and Claude Dorsinville, who begin as the kind of faceless victim-figures we are used to seeing in CARE ads, into people we not only sympathize with but toward whom we feel, by turns, admiration and exasperation. The interwoven stories never let go of the reader's emotions: I couldn't put the book down until I had finished, nor stop thinking about it after I had.

But the novel is not without its flaws. For one thing, it is unremittingly, grindingly grim, unleavened by hope, humor, or wit. For another, Banks has listened carefully to how people talk, but he hasn't always tempered his phonographic recollections with the kind of restraint fictional speech needs. The result is sometimes ridiculous. . . .

And finally, the book's insistent, unmistakably American style—long, driving sentences full of portentous clauses and incantatory refrains—sometimes bolts headlong toward self-parody. . . . (p. 39)

But the most serious criticism to which *Continental Drift* is subject is one that was also leveled at Dos Passos, and legitimately in both cases. I found myself wondering whether Banks had not diminished his characters by showing them as victims and pawns of a malign structure so much larger than they. Early in the book, Banks writes that earth's refugees are moved by "constant heroism, systematic heroism, heroism as governing principle." But on her journey across the Caribbean, Vanise waits passively for guidance from her Haitian voodoo gods—Akwe, Legba, and the fearsome god of the dead, Baron Cimitiere. These are powerful beings whose presence both character and author feel; so that the tragedy that befalls her can be seen as willed by the gods, for reasons of their own.

As for Bob Dubois, he is a victim not of spirits but of the American dream. . . . *Continental Drift* is intended as a portrait of a system destroying Dubois, who, Banks tell us, is "a decent man, but in all the important ways an ordinary man," as if his ordinariness somehow compromised his decency, or perhaps as if only an extraordinary man would have acted differently when put to the test off Boca Raton. I don't believe that; many ordinary folks—even some fishing-boat skippers I've known—wouldn't do what Dubois does; even though our system is brutal in many ways, that brutality doesn't free any of us of the burden of choice.

It's a point I would like to raise with Russell Banks, and one I hope to debate with many people who read this excellent, disturbing book. In the end, in fact, it may be the strength, not the weakness, of *Continental Drift*. Banks sends his book forth with the hope that it will "help destroy the world as it is." It may fall short of that aim, but it will leave its readers much to argue about, and that's no small accomplishment. (p. 40)

Garrett Epps, "Appointment in Florida," in The New Republic, *Vol. 192, No. 13, April 1, 1985, pp. 38-40.*

ROBERT TOWERS

Continental Drift is [Banks's] biggest and most "commercial" book, a novel that serves up melodramatic action, vividly detailed sex scenes, and lurid accounts of voodoo rituals—all accompanied by a running line of unabashed authorial comment and exhortation. Admirers of Banks's early fiction, which resisted conventional narrative, may find this objectionable, but his new book strikes me as the most interesting that he has yet produced. *Continental Drift* is an absorbing and powerful book that ambitiously attempts to "speak" to the times. (p. 36)

Following Dreiser and Dos Passos, Banks assumes in *Continental Drift* the part of a novelist-historian—in this case the historian of uprootedness and anomie in late-twentieth-century America. Consequently, his characters are presented to a considerable degree as representative types: the long-suffering wife, the big-talking, small-time operator, the various denizens of the flat, scrubby, shopping-mall landscape of central Florida and the drug-running, boating world of the Keys. Although well observed, they are not particularly interesting in themselves; they never really spring to life with Dickensian quirkiness or Dostoevskian intensity and singularity. Still, they fit into Banks's larger purposes.

The most successfully conveyed is Bob himself, the not-very-bright man of decent impulse who commits one disastrous mistake after another as he tries to cope with the exploitative and murderous aspects of life in America. Exasperating though Bob is, Banks manages to sustain our sympathy for the poor man to the end. I suspect that more than one reader—watching Bob and listening to the heartfelt banalities of his speech—will be reminded of Willy Loman (and of Biff and Hap, too) in *Death of a Salesman.*

Banks takes great risks when he intrudes and comments in the voice of the author. . . . But where he is speaking directly about his characters, particularly Bob, his voice helps to shape our responses without overwhelming them. . . . For the most part the intrusive voice provides sweep and momentum, advancing the action rather than impeding it, and this defiance of the conventions of faceless realism does much to make *Continental Drift* a vigorous and original novel. (p. 37)

Robert Towers, "Uprooted," in The New York Review of Books, *Vol. XXXII, No. 6, April 11, 1985, pp. 36-37.**

Howard Barker

1946-

English dramatist and scriptwriter.

In his plays Barker satirically explores social and political themes related to contemporary England. He often examines the economic conditions that foster immorality, for he regards capitalism as the primary reason behind political corruption, class conflict, and crime. Barker demonstrates the decadence he perceives in British society through the use of symbolic language, black humor, and violent incidents. The radical viewpoint of Barker's drama led to his early association with the English "Fringe Theater" of the late 1960s and early 1970s. Along with such Fringe playwrights as David Hare and Howard Brenton, Barker expresses extreme political and social views in unconventional dramatic forms.

In several plays Barker develops conflicts between important government officials and criminals in order to investigate the relationship between public and private morality. *Claw* (1975), for example, has as its protagonist a socially outcast young man who becomes a pimp for the Tory Home Secretary; in *Stripwell* (1975) a judge's son is involved in smuggling heroin. In both plays, the behavior of the authority figures is as unethical and immoral as that of the criminals. This ambiguity is common in Barker's work.

While Barker is concerned with conditions in contemporary England, he uses a variety of time frames in his work. In *That Good Between Us* (1977) he depicts a future British government that espouses liberal ideals yet maintains power through totalitarian means. Past and present interweave in *Fair Slaughter* (1978), in which the oppressed protagonist is seen alternately as a young soldier in the Russian Revolution and as the oldest prisoner in an English jail. Similarly, *No End of Blame* (1981) juxtaposes the life of a political cartoonist in World War I Hungary and in London during and after World War II; his freedom of expression is limited in both societies. *Victory: Choices in Revolution* (1983) is set during the English Restoration and uses the past to comment on the present. Threaded throughout these works are graphically violent and grotesque incidents, including rape, murder, and dismembered bodies, which serve as metaphors for individual and social decay.

Critical reception to Barker's plays has been mixed. Some critics contend that he is politically naive and that his work lacks unity, while others admire his skill with dramatic technique, claiming that through shock effects and coarse, highly symbolic language Barker creates powerful dramatic statements. As Steve Grant comments: "There is always something very bracing about a Barker play—even in our excess-ridden times his writing, an engaging mix of artificiality and vernacular, his imaginative plotting and spectacular gift for creating moments of literally breathtaking dramatic violence, seem to send an almost palpable thrill through an audience."

(See also *Contemporary Authors,* Vol. 102 and *Dictionary of Literary Biography,* Vol. 13.)

D.A.N. JONES

Howard Barker's first play, *Cheek* . . . , deals with the romantic frustrations of adolescence. David Caute's *The Demonstration*

. . . displays and discusses the enthusiastic idealism of libertarian students in revolt. But neither play seeks to win the nostalgic smile of compassionate middle age. We will not 'identify' with these normally disagreeable people making dangerous mistakes. Such sour, unpatronising work should be welcomed in a theatre traditionally inclined (from Anouilh to *Hair*) to get sentimental about Youth. But both these clever plays are, for different reasons, very untidy, overstuffed with matter and too many styles. . . .

[In *Cheek* a] young South Londoner, a failed Alfie, and his mother have fantasy lovers who appear on stage. . . . The boy rants, like a malcontent or Young Angry, too eloquently. He has a love-hate for his sick old father, which becomes shocking, as in Edward Bond's work: Bond-like too is the mimed motor-ride with the attempt to pick up girls.

But where did this rather timid layabout get the car and the driving lessons? When constrasting reality and fantasy, such questions of likelihood shouldn't crop up. And would such a smart and attractive mother . . . have such a vilely furnished living-room? She goes off with her son's mate . . . and the boy is left horribly nursing his father like a baby—a situation too strong for so slight a comedy.

D.A.N. Jones, "Libertarians," in The Listener, *Vol. 84, No. 2164, September 17, 1970, p. 387.**

JOHN FORD

[With] *Claw,* Howard Barker becomes a major contemporary English playwright. His previous work—notably *No-one was Saved* . . . , *Faceache* . . . and *Alpha Alpha* . . .—was clever, economical and constantly entertaining. But finally each play lacked a density at the centre. Barker seemed to be unconvinced of his own material, often sliding away from its conclusions on the skates of easy satire and fashionable cynicism. *Claw* retains all the best qualities of his tough, terse, elliptical style; but now at the centre there is a mature and unsentimental compassion.

Claw describes the life and death of one Noel Biledew. A child of the Second World War, he grows up in the rubble of South London and is shown to be as unprepossessing as his surroundings. Badsighted and pebble-lensed, he is derided as 'four-eyes' by all those who have to deal with him. His mother is unsure of his true parentage. Her husband is certainly not the father since he has lost his potency whilst in a POW camp. Old Mr Biledew never speaks to young Noel; but in his silence old Biledew is slowly developing an intellectually crippled but intuitively sound grasp of Marxism. . . .

Noel gives it a try down at the Young Communist League. There he is accepted as 'Trotsky' rather than 'four-eyes' and learns to hate the ruling class. But his new friendships also have a practical value. Abandoning theory and setting his sights clearly on the decadent lights of the enemy in Chelsea, he persuades Nora from the YCL to go with men for money. Their first practice is in a dark street, and Noel makes the mistake of soliciting a policeman. . . .

Noel finally finds his identity and becomes Claw, pimp to the aristocracy. The density and compression of Barker's writing is such that all this groundwork is achieved in less than half of the play's first act.

The second act opens with a stylistic jolt—we are in the house of the Home Secretary and his ex-chorus girl wife. But soon Claw is there, professional observer of the horrendously sophisticated thrust and parry of the pair's defunct relationship. Still a virgin in spite of his trade, he falls hopelessly for the Home Secretary's wife and is initiated in a lay-by off the A3 as she slums back to her roots. Glorious bastards, the two of them. But that is his downfall. He has become too powerful and his pimp's professional discretion has become a weapon of scandal. He must be eradicated.

The third act opens with an even more extreme stylistic jolt than the second. Two waiters serve Claw breakfast. They do not speak to him. They speak to the audience about themselves. They are both men of violence. One tells the story of the first time he planted a bomb in Northern Ireland. The second tells of his experience as an apprentice hangman before the abolition of the death penalty. Both speeches are written with an extraordinary clarity and sympathy. The men also gossip about the grubby sexual origins of pop stars, and it gradually becomes clear that they are not waiters but warders. This is a mental institution of a very special nature, and they have been selected to work there because of their particular experience. Claw appeals to his warders but gets no response. He appeals to a vision of his father. Old Biledew, now dying, condemns Claw's individualism, regrets that he did not have the vocabulary necessary to pass on his experience, and advises Claw not to despise his class but to win them. . . .

No summary, however full, can do justice to the complexity of Barker's themes. The social, psychological, sexual and political are interwoven with an unnerving dexterity—the sexual and political impotence of old Biledew, Claw's background and desire for social mobility, the psychological seeds and objective targets of violence, the difficulty of relating personal experience to a political reality when it can be of most value.

> *John Ford, in a review of "Claw," in* Plays and Players, *Vol. 22, No. 6, March, 1975, p. 35.*

J. W. LAMBERT

[One] of the more interesting of our younger generation of playwrights, Howard Barker, . . . should certainly be considered in the same league as Howard Brenton, David Hare or Trevor Griffiths. Like them he seems to find it difficult to write a play that builds, but like them he writes with a concise and penetrating wit in sharp little scenes which go some way towards disguising his play's lack of direction—particularly evident in the full-length *Claw*. . . . Mr. Barker traces the career of Noel Biledew—alias rather crudely Claw, i.e. one who claws his way up—from birth as the unwanted child of a woman of little sense whose husband is a prisoner in the second world war. . . . Claw, hated at home and despised at school for his short sight, is on his own. By way of nude pictures he is soon a quite well-set-up ponce, surviving corrupt policemen and gang warfare. It is when he tangles with the Establishment that his troubles really begin. The Tory Cabinet Minister whom he provides with tarts may seem to be easy meat, and so may his near-nymphomaniac wife, but before he knows what's happening he's discreetly shut up in an asylum. . . .

As Claw waits in the asylum for he knows not what . . . [two characters], previously appearing in several villainous roles, sit in white coats, sinister attendants. Idle conversation develops into remarkable monologues: one of them was an Irish terrorist before buying his life by taking on his present job, and recalls in numb everyday language first shooting a man, then planting a bomb; the other was the public hangman's assistant, who loved his job and his boss, and speaks a sad elegy for an abolished way of life. These speeches are at best peripheral to the play; but they are beautifully written. . . . They amply illustrate a particular quality in Mr. Barker's plays, and especially in this one: all his characters are villainous, and all are pitiful.

Somewhere beneath Mr. Barker's rather generalized satire lies an affection for people, which even when he is at his most caricatural won't let them become mere objects of his scorn.

> *J. W. Lambert, in a review of "Claw," in* Drama, *No. 116, Spring, 1975, p. 45.**

JONATHAN HAMMOND

Stripwell, revolving around a well-intentioned but morally confused judge of that name, is a comic-strip version of the crisis of liberal democracy with its so-called 'civilized values' being blown apart (literally in this case) by anarchist and other subterranean forces at work in society. Mr Justice Stripwell . . . is first seen about to pass sentence on a young hooligan . . . , who threatens him with death if he is given a prison sentence. Fearful, Stripwell goes off to lunch with his young mistress, Babs, a university-educated go-go dancer, first seen thrusting her pelvis to the strains of Stevie Wonder.

The play goes on to juxtapose Stripwell with his family, including his recalcitrant father-in-law Jarrow . . . , a Labour ex-MP of Attlee vintage, who berates the judge for his lack of any kind of commitment; his long-suffering wife Dodie . . . ; and his supercilious, conceited son, Tim . . . , just down from university and with plans to smuggle heroin in from India concealed in elephants.

Stripwell is in the habit of making surreptitious assignations with the sharp-witted Babs on the Sussex Downs, spied on by a prurient ice-cream man. . . . Eventually, he plucks up the courage to tell Dodie of his intention to leave her. . . . A hilarious scene ensues, with Dodie inviting Babs to dinner, also attended by the insolent Tim. The predictable upshot is that Babs goes off with Tim, whom she recognises as a little shit but who, in his trip to India, gives her the possibility of 'life enhancement', as she calls it. Babs tells 'Strip' (as she calls the judge) of her intention in a fraught encounter outside a Crawley strip-club; 'Strip' returns home, tail between his legs, where he vindictively shops his son to the police and meets his own violent end at the hands of the thug whom he sentenced at the play's outset.

While being consistently entertaining, watchable, as well as stylistically accomplished, the play suffers from having no consistent viewpoint of any kind. It is not really enough to condemn a bankrupt tradition of civilised non-commitment, as epitomised by the judge, without at least implying something to put in its place. Howard Barker seems to have, rightly, a pretty jaundiced view of the 'alternative' of 'experience of any kind at any price' as represented in the play by Tim and Babs; so, in an unintentionally ironic sense, the author could be said to suffer from the same basic problem as his protagonist. (p. 27)

> *Jonathan Hammond, in a review of "Stripwell," in* Plays and Players, *Vol. 23, No. 3, December, 1975, pp. 26-7.*

W STEPHEN GILBERT

Howard Barker's [*Fair Slaughter*]. . . confronts, if not rescues, the concept of revolution. The movement of the play is the life of one Gocher, first seen in Russia in 1920 'crusading against bandits'. He's due to be sent home for 'persistent use of the word capitalist' as his officer, Stavely, informs him, but before the departure he has a formative encounter with a Russian prisoner. Trying to converse, they find they have a few words in common—'proletariat' and then of course 'Lenin' and 'Trotsky'. In pantomime, the Russian tells Gocher that he was Trotsky's train driver. The Russian is killed by the White Russians and, while Stavely secretes icons as the basis of a career in art plunder, Gocher keeps the severed hand of the train driver. . . .

As war breaks out, Gocher, now a factory steward, urges his comrades to postpone subverting the bosses for the duration, out of 'loyalty to the international movement'. Taxed by his wife to choose between her and idealism, he opts for 'the real intimacy of solidarity'. As a fireman, he encounters the debauched Stavely in a conflagration and apparently brains him. . . .

The story is told by the 75-year-old Gocher to a warder, Leary, at the prison hospital. He's there because he 'brained someone with a pisspot'. 'No-one knows the sufferin' of an English idealist' Gocher tells him wryly but Leary, 'corrupted by pity', helps Gocher escape and takes him on an imagined journey to the site of the train-driver's grave. There—it's actually Dover where Lear ended his days—they encounter the gibbering, brain-damaged Stavely. Leary, by now Stalinised, wants extermination. 'There's nothing in his head' says Gocher. 'There's guilt in his head' cries Leary. '*You* told me' and he accuses Gocher of revisionism. Gocher dies after a vision of the train driver, Leary carries away the emblematic hand and Stavely dribbles over a Picasso, or a reproduction thereof.

There's something remarkably engaging and compelling about this play, much more so than in Barker's earlier work. . . . The imagery and the marshalling of forces are strikingly Bondian—knowingly, I'd guess—and as a result the figures have lost the wicked cartoon-ness of earlier plays. They take on a different dimension, having both a theatricality and a life: when Gocher remarks 'you're no jailer, Leary. You're only in the clothes', it's an appeal to a member of the same class but also an appeal beyond emblem to humanity. That, though, cannot be a distillation of the play's politics . . . can it? The trick in Bond's plays is that the analysis percolates the theatricality, that the latter is a precise manifestation of the former. *Fair Slaughter* is not as clear and eloquent. It's a nicely judged pageant history of British Communism, but I'm not sure that Barker's unprecedented engagement with his characters doesn't finally fudge his conclusion—are we to see the depth, the transformation or the hope of Communism in this rather beautiful and mystical Dover coda?

> *W Stephen Gilbert, in a review of "Fair Slaughter," in* Plays and Players, *Vol. 24, No. 11, August, 1977, p. 21.*

JEREMY TREGLOWN

There must have been people at Howard Barker's gripping but uneven new play [*That Good Between Us*] who found it an exaggeratedly pessimistic account of how things in Britain could turn out. The army, now permanently engaged in strike-breaking, has become vulnerable to communist infiltration. In his determination to eradicate left-wing influences, the Special Branch man Knatchbull edges the socialist minister inch by inch, then yard by yard into totalitarianism: she increases the number of government spies and agents provocateurs, allows imprisonment without trial and imposes censorship on the media. Of course, the play is set in the future, the publicity reassured us—it's a kind of *1984*, shall we say, or at any rate *1980*. . . . The play uses futurism as a means of releasing fact-bound imaginations so that they can look at the present in a fresh way.

Barker has collected a series of vivid and grotesque images of impoverishment, degeneracy and ruthlessness, some of them only thinly related to the main action except on a symbolic level: a bar-room stripper being insulted by a drunk homosexual; a gang-bang; a little girl in callipers discovering the mutilated corpse of a soldier on the London common where she plays; strongest of all, a half-naked man belting out 'This Could Be The Last Time' in a strangled Glaswegian falsetto as he is tipped out of a rowing boat by two Special Branch men, into a freezing dark Atlantic improvised out of black plastic rubbish bags. It's this visual resourcefulness that Barker's generation of dramatists is at last bringing into the big subsidised theatres from the fringe. . . . One is so grateful for it that it seems churlish to complain that among Barker's stage-pictures were some repetitions of other people's successes—the cabinet minister's appearances in a punt and in her garden, for example, were overshadowed by Howard Brenton's *Magnificence*—just as the often stereotyped social and political stances of the piece could have come from a number of others it has close affinities with—David Hare's *Knuckle,* or Brenton's *The Churchill Play,* or the multi-authored *Lay-By.*

But my main reservation about this powerful play—one which applies to Barker's other work too, and to Brenton's as well, for that matter—is that Barker's very visual, metaphorical imagination is let loose in a far less disciplined form in the dialogue. It's partly a matter of the law of diminishing returns, at least as far as the excretory imagery goes. Someone is accused of 'licking out the turd of treason'. . . . The Home Secretary is warned by her daughter Rhoda that a man is looking at her with 'the fixed stare of a defecating dog'. The communist Major tells his Democratic Movement that revolution will be 'a haemorrhaging of your hopes, a dysentery of your good will'. The objection to this kind of writing isn't primarily that it is schoolboyish in its obsessively narrow range of reference (though it is), but that it is falsely rhetorical and self-indulgent. So, too, are many of the less seamy speeches—Rhoda's accusation that her mother is 'A traitor and a vile deceiver of good people', for example or the Major's leaden pun about his ulcer: 'There is a terrible injustice in constitutions—not just in political ones'.

Like the social-problem novelists of the 1840s, whom both Barker and Brenton in many ways resemble, Barker over-writes for the good reason that in the end he cares less about art than about life. *That Good Between Us* follows his recent *Fair Slaughter* in incidentally attacking the way theatre can let people escape from the issues themselves, either by anaesthetising its audience or, more insidiously, by letting it feel that its imaginary participation in the suffering it sees on stage is in some quasi-religious sense a sufficient act of atonement. It's an understandable worry, but Barker can feel reassured that in his central characters at least he embodies human and political (in this case specifically Scots political) tragedy in a way that stays with us when we have left the theatre. I can't think of a play since *King Lear* which shows a man so utterly unaccommodated, in every sense, as the Glaswegian homosexual spy Billy McPhee—so inescapably degraded by the society that exploits him, and yet so capable of warmth and courage. (pp. 24-5)

> *Jeremy Treglown, in a review of "That Good Between Us," in* Plays and Players, *Vol. 24, No. 12, September, 1977, pp. 24-5.*

JOHN COLEBY

[*Fair Slaughter* and *That Good Between Us*] are never less than interesting with crisp and vigorous dialogue. *Fair Slaughter* using flashbacks and fantasy presents the dilemmas of an old style Bolshevik as the Revolution has developed from 1917 up to now, while *That Good Between Us* looks forward a few years to the situation we may find ourselves in under a Labour government forced to become repressive, even fascist, by circumstances outside its control. Fascinating characters appear and the author's insights inform his basic pessimism but the complicated structures of both plays inhibit their development into the forceful political works of the theatre one feels [Barker] was aiming to achieve. One day, he may write a major play, but neither of these is it. They leave too many openings for actors in deadly earnest to be unwittingly Coarse.

> *John Coleby, in a review of "Fair Slaughter" and "That Good Between Us," in* Drama, *No. 128, Spring, 1978, p. 81.*

PAUL ALLEN

[The character Hacker in *The Love of a Good Man*] is the gaffer of a firm which has got the contract to build the mass graveyard—garden of remembrance—at Passchendaele two years after the end of the Great War. If he does well, . . . he stands a chance of getting the plum job at Gallipoli. It is in order to do well, to finish quickly so he can get the Prince of Wales to open the place formally while he's passing, that he ends up burying . . . unnamed, undistinguished, incomplete and sickeningly brutalised bodies four to a grave.

But Hacker's ambition is not limited to monumental success as a monumental mason, and that is why he is troubled. In middle age he has conceived a taste for immortality, and the small letters on the back of the repetitive stone crosses aren't enough: he wants a son. The unseen Mrs Hacker is no sort of prospect ('like shooting into concrete') but Mrs Toynbee is. Mrs Toynbee is an upper-middle widow, beautiful but possibly mad, searching fields which are yards deep in bodies for the remains of her son. If Hacker can find the said remains he can have her. Or he could have done if the Prince of Wales hadn't come along with a better offer.

To describe Barker's sardonic epic as cynical, as some critics did, is to belittle the passion in it. The play does not simply take another axe to an already battered sacred cow; it is an angry retort to a kind of individual and corporate madness whose most disturbing factor is the ability to regenerate itself. Thus the four squaddies on graveyard duty, because there are no jobs back home in the land fit for heroes, accept the first offer which comes along. It happens to come from a Colonel recruiting for the Black and Tans in Ireland. Yes, confesses the soldier who has hitherto evinced truculently revolutionary impulses, in the meantime 'I have four children to feed'. And so it all starts again.

The play is densely plotted and gets itself bogged down in the middle act. . . . It picks up mightily, however, with the twin conclusive madnesses of a séance in which Mrs Toynbee tries to contact her dead son and gets a German instead and an opening ceremony at which neither the Prince of Wales nor a passing Bishop can find anything to say: Hacker loses Mrs Toynbee but gets Gallipoli. Only the stiff-backed equerry to the Prince, cast in the concrete of his own sense of order and discipline, knows how to behave.

The themes and the characters proliferate in the play, which is written in toughly specific language. (pp. 38-9)

> *Paul Allen, in a review of "The Love of a Good Man," in* Plays and Players, *Vol. 26, No. 6, February, 1979, pp. 38-9.*

RONALD HAYMAN

Much of Howard Barker's [early] work focuses on the tug-of-war between individual libido and social superego. *Cheek,* his first play to be produced (1970), justifies its title and sets up its tensions by taking its tone from the thrusting cockiness of the central character—outrageous by the standards of conventional behaviour, natural by the standards of a healthy boy's sexual appetite. In *Edward: the Final Days* (produced 1971), a polemic about Heath, the inventiveness is clogged up with cheap indignation, cartoonish parody, and simplistic argument.

Claw (produced 1975) is more sophisticated than any of his earlier plays in its treatment of the no-man's-land between private lust and public images. The central character is a pimp, and it was amusing to make him spectacled and virginal. The creation of Noel Biledew acted like a counterblast to the Jimmy Porter mythology: working-class boy makes middle-class girl, bold, sexy pleb versus timid, passive, effete female. Fed up with being victimized, Noel Biledew takes the name 'Claw', but fails to learn from his mother's husband, a convert to communism, that he should save his anger for his class. (p. 103)

Much of the theatrical imagery is extremely vivid, and much of the comedy is lively, especially in the second act, when the Cabinet minister's ex-chorus-girl wife mischievously seduces the unattractive Biledew. The distended third act is worst, resting—and nearly going to sleep—on the premise that the Establishment can survive only by employing ex-hangmen and ex-terrorists to staff a 'mental hospital' where they rub out social misfits who could discredit the governing elite.

Stripwell [produced 1975] is less didactic, less dependent on stereotypes, better constructed. It is also more consistently entertaining because the comedy is more organic. It is characteristic of Barker—as it was of the Marquis de Sade—to use a criminal as an incarnation of the integrity that the judge lacks. But the thug is wisely kept offstage throughout the central action, which occurs during the twelve months when he is safely in prison. If the writing is less heavy-handed than in *Claw*, it is partly because Barker is now prepared to explore his ambivalence towards the main characters, though none of them is particularly likeable. The old survivor of the first Labour government has no warmth or idealism left in him, Stripwell's wife is tiresomely fixated on her cynical son, the gogo dancer is loyal only to her own greed for experience, and we are meant to lose sympathy with Stripwell when he informs on his son, telling the police that the boy is smuggling drugs in elephants' vaginas.

Like Brenton's *The Churchill Play*, Barker's *That Good Between Us* (produced 1977) presents an alarmist picture of a future Britain in which liberal impulses go on flickering feebly in a few kindly individuals while the government gets its way by ruthlessly applying totalitarian methods, using its army like the Nazi SS and turning a blind eye when trouble-makers are 'dumped'. The female Labour Home Secretary makes gestures of holding on to the principles of democracy—'We don't want to end up like Brazil, do we?' 'Don't do violence to language or you will end up doing violence to people.' But in each of her arguments with the chief of her spy ring, she allows herself to be persuaded that the current crisis is too bad to be brought under control without a little secret killing.

Much of the writing is on the level of a script for some such television series as *The Trouble Shooters*. Unlike the notion of using elephants' vaginas for drug-smuggling, the situations in *That Good Between Us* seldom lack surface plausibility, but the pressures that the characters are putting on each other do not stand up to serious analysis, because Howard Barker has not given them any. The villain of the piece is Ronald Knatchbull, the secret service man. The scheme of the play requires him to keep eroding the vestigial decency of Mrs. Orbison, the Home Secretary. Barker is not interested in the psychological question of who or what puts pressure on Knatchbull, and he often resorts to unexplained melodramatic coincidences, as when Knatchbull turns up, with an Alsatian on a lead, at the moment that Billy McPhee is about to rape a woman whom he and two other men have dragged out of a stationary car. Anxious to prevent Knatchbull from seeming too diabolical, Barker makes him dote on his paraplegic daughter. But the

sequence in which we see them together is melodramatic. Flying a kite for her on Wimbledon Common, he trips over the dead body of a soldier, Private Hayman, a man who has been tortured and killed at Knatchbull's orders because he tried to warn the leader of a left-wing conspiracy in the army that the Special Branch was in the process of penetrating it. 'Make daddy a daisy chain,' says the nonplussed Knatchbull, trying to distract his daughter. And 'I blame the television. All this viewing. If I was a better father I'd stop it. Make you read.' But Barker is not content to let the scene rest on ironies like these. The corpse starts to talk. When Knatchbull tries to make out that he knows nothing about how the soldier died, the dead man contradicts him. When the girl asks questions which her father tries to evade, the corpse answers them: 'They tied me to a chair. Poured petrol up my nostrils. Twisted combs in my hair . . . I have never known such pain.'

The most interesting character is Godber, the quiet, unscrupulous young man who wants to win stardom as a government spy. Otherwise, he has no ambitions. 'You could put my wants into a matchbox. The rest is rat's piss so far as I'm concerned.' He tries to seduce Mrs. Orbison, and, immediately after failing, succeeds rather implausibly in seducing her radical daughter by telling her that he failed with her mother. (pp. 102-06)

One of the troubles with this kind of play is that none of its potential is ever fully developed. It was noticeable in *That Good Between Us* that the playwright tended to end each sequence just as it was becoming interesting. Godber's attempt to seduce Mrs. Orbison, for instance, ends abruptly with her saying, 'Now please go.' There is no concern with his embarrassment in getting himself out of the room, no hint of how she would behave when left alone again. Not that the play would necessarily work better if the abortive scene were developed: like melodrama and television serials, it works perfectly well, within its own terms, by jumping from one violent climax to the next. Too much energy has gone into contriving the *coups de théâtre*, not enough into organizing the relationship between them. (p. 106)

Ronald Hayman, ''The Politics of Hatred,'' in his
British Theatre Since 1955: A Reassessment, *Oxford
University Press, Oxford, 1979, pp. 80-128.*

GILLIAN GREENWOOD

[In *The Love of a Good Man,* the] combination of Barker, the fields of Passchendaele and a sharp-practising undertaker arouse expectations that hypocrisy will be exposed, that there will be a fundamental social truth for us to wrestle with. Shades of Orton. Indeed, Hacker, the undertaker, tells us early on that 'There's so much hypocrisy round here you could launch a ship on it'. Hypocrisy is exposed all over the place but one is left unsatisfied.

The play is set in 1920 amidst the debris of Passchendaele. Decaying corpses lie underfoot so Hacker and his assistant Clout have come to 'orchestrate their suffering' by carrying out a lucrative government contract to rebury them. . . .

Poor Hacker's life is further complicated by lust. He has fallen for the elegent Mrs Toynbee who, with her daughter Lalage, has come to look for the body of her son. Mrs Toynbee's presence in *The Love of a Good Man* is its major flaw. She is neither sufficiently eccentric nor grief-stricken to explain it. She is a useful butt for social comment and ribald humour and it shows. Her daughter, dragged along for the ride, is more credible. She throws herself at Soldier Riddle, an irritating, but none the less convincing bore who thinks he is much cleverer than everyone else. . . .

[*The Love of a Good Man*] is well constructed with some excellent comic dialogue and a few high moments. . . . As a comic drama it lacks substance but there are some very funny lines.

> *Gillian Greenwood, in a review of "The Love of a Good Man," in* Plays and Players, *Vol. 27, No. 5, February, 1980, p. 25.*

PATRICK BUTCHER

[Ezra Fricker, in *The Loud Boy's Life*] wants the premiership of England. In a series of carefully planned scenes of failure to achieve orgasm (social, sexual and political), Mr Barker takes us through the life of Fricker from a venal 23-year-old with a Triple First and a sense of history to a pile of ashes in the crypt of St Paul's Cathedral.

In the forbidding arena of debate on just how much Art copies Life, or vice versa Howard Barker has realised that the Real only exists to complement Art. So he regales us with a Saatchiesque woman politician . . . and a Principal who resembles less the Northern Ireland MP intended than a recent Lost Liberal Leader.

What Mr Barker has unfortunately failed to realise is that our politicians are infintely more ludicrous, amusing and pathetic than any dramatisation could ever hope to achieve. And if Art cannot be larger than Life, then it's a waste of time.

During a scene change when a voiceover begins a staccato repetition of 'Profit and Culture, Profit and Culture' I thought we were about to get a selection from Ezra Pound's Cantos. Mr Pound, like his christian namesake here was a well-known Fascist. He ended up in the nut-house. Ezra Fricker chooses a mental hospital as the location for awaiting his call to lead Parliament. From one madhouse to another, we are tempted to think. But since we're already in a theatre, that's too much like compounding a felony.

We are told during an hilarious Cabinet meeting . . . that '''Money'' doesn't want Fricker'. Since we've already attended a protracted Masonic-type gathering in the first act in which 'Money' chose him as its saviour, this, along with his paltry Cabinet rejection takes the failed orgasm into the lap of the playwright. . . .

There is an illuminating side-line in language interpretation in the use of female metaphors which highlights the general male insecurity. This is most evident during the obnoxious banquet conversation, with the pathetic parodies of women enacted by the men as party pieces. And in one telling exchange with the unlikely-named Crystal Backlawn, Fricker misinterprets her use of 'feeling'. He means 'belief'. Thus are Fricker and the Old Boys shown to be cerebral, and as such incapable of instituting any real change in the system.

The real heroes of the piece are heroines. The daughter in drag, the pregnant mum, and the wife with the gun; all of whom are prepared to make practical moves against the system. Fricker accepts its impregnability in the end. And promptly dies to prove it.

> *Patrick Butcher, in a review of "The Loud Boy's Life," in* Plays and Players, *Vol. 27, No. 6, March, 1980. p. 21.*

JOHN RUSSELL TAYLOR

[Though his] talent is as yet not entirely disciplined, Barker does have the true stuff of drama in him. His plays are things that happen on the stage, within the special circumstances of life theatre, and could not live so completely anywhere else. He does not try to tell us what we should think, or preach to us, but just tells his tale and lets us make of it what we will. This particular tale [*The Love of a Good Man*] is a somewhat cynical one of what happened—what really happened—during the creation of the giant war cemeteries with which the victors of the First World War tried to exorcise some of their war guilt and sentimentally satisfy the living by pointlessly memorialising the dead. Like all of Barker's plays that I know, this takes some sort of factual material as the basis for a myth. The period is perhaps too recent for us to be completely comfortable when a familiar character like the Prince of Wales (later Edward VIII, later still the Duke of Windsor) is brought on to be fantasised, regardless of history, in rather the way Bond does with the great Victorians in *Early Morning:* objections will keep cropping up in the order of, but George V did not die of cancer, and the Prince was never called Edward (always David) until he took that title on his accession. These remain minor objections, however. . . . [The] story, just as a story, was really gripping, even if, and partly because, we were never altogether sure exactly what it was meant to mean. (pp. 45-6)

> *John Russell Taylor, in a review of "The Love of a Good Man," in* Drama, *No. 136, April, 1980, pp. 44-6.*

ROWENA GOLDMAN

[*The Loud Boy's Life*] is vicious, decidedly unfunny even when fun is intended and, worst sin of all, at times embarrassing. The 'loud boy' of the play's title is one Ezra Fricker, a character whom Barker blatantly implies to be Enoch Powell. Mr. Barker is obviously full to the brim with indignation at what he feels to be wrong with the nation. . . .

[If] Mr. Barker intends to show what is rotten in the state of British politics he fails. What makes this failure the harder to bear is that there is brilliance in some of the writing. It is wasted, though, on a subject about which Mr. Barker seems not to know enough. He also seems to think that the free use of four-letter words is being daring when it is just being boring. Perhaps in years to come the play will be viewed as a masterpiece of contemporary political theatre, but at this stage it is simply an example of a playwright seeking to thrust his views on an audience in the same way as the politician he so clearly despises seeks to thrust his views on the man in the street.

> *Rowena Goldman, in a review of "The Loud Boy's Life," in* Drama, *No. 137, July, 1980, p. 64.*

STEVE GRANT

Barker is in many ways the Peter Pan of his generation. While other writers have toned down their early sense of moral outrage and class hatred, Barker's plays continue to carry an intense, emotional impact and a deep and often unfocused sense of political and sexual antagonism. His style is an energetic mix of comedy and declamatory phrase-making, though in *Stripwell* he demonstrated his ability to capture the more static exchanges of the middle classes. Nevertheless his sympathies seem to lie with working-class waifs like the Scot Billy McPhee in *That*

Good Between Us and Biledew, the doomed pimp in *Claw;* with old men like Gocher in *Fair Slaughter;* and, most intriguingly, with figures of moral and political ambiguity who have moved downwards or upwards in the social spectrum.

Barker's vision of contemporary society, like Brenton's in *Magnificence,* is of a huge con trick which encourages the more individualistic members of the working class to exploit each other in terms of crime and reaction: the nightmare society of spies and counter-spies that is *That Good Between Us,* the exploits of the Kray-style gangster twins in *Alpha Alpha.* Like Brenton and Edgar, Barker is an avid lampoonist and his victims have included Sir Francis Chichester, Heath, the Duke of Windsor, Enoch Powell and Lord Shinwell. In more recent works, however, he has demonstrated a more ambitious grasp of narrative, setting and characterization, while managing, through a kind of stylistic collage, to retain a good deal of the old ferocity and sexual aggression. For all his bile, he is another ambiguous writer, disgusted with the present iniquities of society and yet both respectful of old-world virtue and seemingly convinced that a great deal of humanity's problems rest in the intractable sexual warfare which permeates his plays. The undoubted confusion results in a somewhat inevitable tendency to attack the waverer and the compromiser as much and even more than the hated extremist. Labour peers who 'sold out' to the revolution abound, as do Labour police chiefs, women prime ministers and a drunken home secretary. Like Kurtz in Conrad's *Heart of Darkness,* many of Barker's establishment figures are would-be civilizers stalked by violence and madness. Cooper, the prison governor turned arsonist in *The Hang of the Gaol* is a classic example.

At his best Barker can compose immensely powerful language, particularly for those characters who burn with a sense of ignorance and helplessness. His gift for comic invention and inversion is similarly impressive. Biledew, the four-eyed diminutive pimp in *Claw* is a marvellous antithesis to Osborne's angry young man Jimmy Porter. Barker's ability to create startling *coups de théâtre* is almost unrivalled among his peers: the climax of *Stripwell* in which a young tearaway shoots the anti-hero judge after a seemingly endless moment of indecision; the seance on the field of Passchendaele in *The Love of a Good Man* and the violent conflagration between two civil servants of the opposite sex in *The Hang of the Gaol.*

Barker's main shortcomings are his inability to write parts for women that do not reverberate with what seems to be an imported sense of male sexual antagonism, and his tendency to load his more morally and politically dubious creations with a lot of leaden and barely credible self-apology and irony. So too *That Good Between Us* creates a given nightmare world of the future which, for all its power, teeters on the edge of sci-fi fantasy, while *Claw's* rivetting final act rests for its very existence on the bizarre proposition that the British Establishment keeps open extermination camps staffed by such notables as an ex-terrorist psychopath and a former hangman's assistant. It certainly seems that in Barker's plays virtue and vice stalk together. Political confusion leads to a good deal of easy moralizing but also accounts for the undoubted intensity of their vision of social and personal injustice. The comedy, though occasionally prone to the puerile, is more often deft and startling, while in a theatrical landscape often tending to sedateness and aridity, Barker can create colossal, even unforgettable confrontations out of thin air. (pp. 139-41)

> *Steve Grant, "Voicing the Protest: The New Writers," in* Dreams and Deconstructions: Alternative Theatre in Britain, *edited by Sandy Craig, Amber Lane Press, 1980, pp. 116-44.**

DIANA DEVLIN

Two volumes of Howard Barker plays [*That Good Between Us and Credentials of a Sympathiser* and *The Love of a Good Man and All Bleeding*] are . . . funny, but not fun. He writes black political farces which expose the warped ideologies and political skulduggeries of modern society to a point where ordinary human effort and good intention becomes impossible or useless. His characters are quite Dickensian—exaggerated and grotesque, yet often likeable, among them "Hacker," who features in two plays and whose main purpose in life is always to be in with the lowest tender, whether for war burials in 1920 or as caterer for a peace conference in the 1970s. The plays consist of innumerable incidents, boldly and often crudely depicted, piling up into a series of ironies and reversals that swing you from anger to laughter and to despair. My only quarrel is with the sometimes unevocative titles. *That Good Between Us* is like a spoof on John le Carré, with agents, double agents, patriots, terrorists swapping roles and chasing each other's tails and committing acts of violence under a mindless and weak-willed Home Secretary. In the same volume is *Credentials of a Sympathiser* . . . where the conduct of exploratory peace talks become an absurd tea-party of one-upmanship, as hilarious and disastrous as Ayckbourn's picnic, with a knife-twisting irony at the end. The other volume has *All Bleeding.* . . . Mainly centred on a refugee political cartoonist, it movingly exposes his defeated attempt to escape from or fight against violence and oppression from the 1930s in Hungary to modern terrorism. In the same volume is *The Love of a Good Man,* built around the War Burial Commission of 1920. The vast carnage of the first world war is to be parcelled up into a Union Jack-shaped cemetery in time for a visit by the Prince of Wales. This macabre task provides the perfect image to explore expediency, hypocrisy and the rottenness of sentimental patriotism. Barker's work demonstrates that the most "successful" sick jokes are those that succeed in making us face an unpalatable truth.

> *Diana Devlin, in a review of "That Good Between Us" and others, in* Drama, *No. 141, Autumn, 1981, pp. 51-2.*

MEL GUSSOW

Having survived world war, civil war, revolution and counter-revolution, Bela Veracek ("Vera"), the cartoonist hero of Howard Barker's acidulous new play, *No End of Blame,* arrives in England in 1936. Grateful for what he calls his "freeness," he kisses the ground. At last, he thinks, he will be able to express his savage criticism without fear of censorship.

As it turns out, England is, if anything, even less hospitable to controversy than his native Hungary or his adopted Russia. Acclaimed as a genius, Vera is treated as a token, a pawn, and, finally, as a clown who has lost his sense of humor. There is no sanctuary for the visionary, except in the madhouse, and, suggests the playwright, the only salvation is for Vera to stop flailing at injustice and to attempt to "assign the blame."

Along with David Hare and Howard Brenton, Mr. Barker is one of a young crop of virulent theatrical commentators on the collapse of English civilization, and his view is cynical in the extreme. For example, Vera receives his cruelest threat not from Stalin, but, indirectly, from Churchill.

Loosely based on the life of the celebrated cartoonist Victor Weisz ("Vicky"), *No End of Blame,* . . . is a provocative but unfulfilled play of ideas. It studies with some seriousness the use of art as an instrument of political awareness and the ineluctable fate of the dissident. Actually, Vera repeatedly poses cartooning as the antithesis to art. Cartooning, he says, can change the world; art can change only the artist. He is a quick-pen polemicist, not a man to cogitate over the future, but the annotator of the horrors of the present, someone who, in one of Mr. Barker's more apt phrases, can help people see "through the flannel."

Vera is in a rush, and so, one must conclude, is the playwright. *No End of Blame* is an outline for a play, an erratic, scattershot view of life in transit and in turmoil, and a work that too often succumbs to grandiloquence. Mr. Barker's billboard is plastered with labels about "high priests in the temple art," about trying "to catch the swinging booth of history." The loftiness of some of the dialogue seems to echo the pessimistic captions on Vera's drawings . . . , as in the underlining of an apocalyptical vision with "They grew tired of thought."

The play shows a man disillusioned and defeated by his times, and also describes the arc of those times (from 1918 to 1973). Vera could be a poet or journalist, as long as he operates in a public forum. In several respects, Mr. Barker's play reminds one somewhat of David Hare's vastly superior *Plenty,* which tells the story of the loss of ideals and the decline of England through a survivor of World War II. . . .

To borrow a sentiment from the playwright, *No End of Blame* is less art than cartoon, a broad brushstroke of a play that at crucial moments is excessive and exclamatory.

Mel Gussow, in a review of "No End of Blame," in The New York Times, December 24, 1981, p. 18.

JOHN SIMON

There is a good deal of bitter wisdom in this play [*No End of Blame*], not a little effective satire, and language that ranges from awkward to inspired. Barker's views on art, politics, society, life are never uninteresting, but the play is insufficiently fleshed out, often only a series of cartoons with gaps between and even within them. . . .

No End of Blame provides ample food for thought, and pulls off scene after dramatically effective scene. What is missing is a greater roundedness, a better sense of the interrelation of the three principal characters, and more of Veracek's private life in postwar England. And a sharper sense of detail: Hungarian intellectuals who have long lived in England might indeed have terrible accents, but they would not use *ain't* or double negatives. (p. 53)

*John Simon, "Computerized Dreams," in New York Magazine, Vol. 15, No. 2, January 11, 1982, pp. 52-3.**

EDITH OLIVER

[*No End of Blame*] tells the story, scene by scene by scene, of a Hungarian political cartoonist named Béla Veracek who eventually migrates to England. For all practical purposes, the action starts at an art class in Budapest in 1921. Veracek, whose hero is Lenin, has drawn a particularly virulent cartoon, offensive to the government in power; he is regretfully expelled by his instructor and, along with his close companion and

fellow-artist Grigor and a model (whom he eventually marries), he leaves for Moscow. But he runs into trouble there, too, with a drawing that the Writers' & Artists' Union decides undermines official policy. One of the funniest and shrewdest scenes in the play is the meeting of the union, at which the members, simulating openness of discussion but actually pouring out soft soap, persuade Veracek to tear up the drawing. He eventually gets a chance to escape from Stalin's Russia, and in 1936 he lands penniless in England, where he soon gets a job as political cartoonist on a left-wing paper. The freedom and truth he seeks (and keeps talking about) are just as elusive as ever, though—even at a wartime meeting of a left-wing faction of the R.A.F., which could be a line-for-line copy of that meeting in Moscow—and Veracek ends his days in a madhouse (along with Grigor, who followed him to England). The point of the play—that England is as restrictive and as hypocritical as anywhere else—has become a commonplace among young British writers, and Mr. Barker's version of this disaffection seems a bit too glib and easy, for overseas acceptance at least. Veracek is given to far too many long, self-serving disquisitions about the superiority—and moral superiority, that is—of cartooning to "art" (I always thought it *was* art), and while a few of the observations are acute, one soon feels that enough is enough. . . . In spite of its faults, *No End of Blame* makes an absorbing evening. (p. 85)

*Edith Oliver, "The Politics of Cartooning," in The New Yorker, Vol. LVII, No. 47, January 11, 1982, pp. 85-6.**

BENEDICT NIGHTINGALE

It is of course axiomatic that playwrights whose first names are Howard use their plays as cattle-prods, weapons with which to sting and shock the socially and politically bovine. Not that Barker's *Victory* is likely to cause as great a stir as Brenton's *Romans,* especially since it is staged at the Royal Court, where a scathing contempt for establishment authority is *de rigueur* and scabrous language, even the weird sort of four-letter baroque we get here, is perfectly acceptable. But that theatre's PR complex tells me that, when the Joint Stock Company made the curious decision to take the play to Cheltenham recently, the result was disapproval, dudgeon, and the sound of sensible shoes stomping out of the exit doors; and one can see why. Here's Charles II, the 'mad shagman', celebrating his return to the London fleshpots by compulsively humping women, the language, anyone and anything. Here's Nell Gwynne french-kissing the rotting head of Bradshaw, the regicide dug up and dismembered as part of the post-Restoration reprisals and festivities. Here's torture and sexual abuse, decadence and violence, and all else you'd expect of a Howard dealing with the corrupt aftermath of one of the few historical times of which Howards tend to approve.

It is a pustular, inventive, coarse, lurid, ebullient and really rather interesting play, covering the same period as Bond's *Restoration* but much more in the style of his *Early Morning.* The main character is Bradshaw's widow, who treks to London in search of the odds and ends of her husband that are being displayed on gates, bridges and the king's pillow. She finds them, too; but only after being reduced to beggary, raped by a randy Cavalier named Ball, briefly engaged as housekeeper by a royal trollop and, in a final climax, confronted with the sight of the raging Ball murdering the banker-husband that Charles is foisting upon her employer. This particular incident, I should explain, is by no means as random as it may sound.

Barker, like Ball, is looking for enemies and, like him, finds them in the money-men of the Bank of England. They would appear to have got rid of the fiscally importunate Charles I, brought about the Restoration when the commonwealth became unprofitable, and are now the real rulers of the land, grudgingly recognised as such by their gaudy puppet on the British throne. For Ball, for Barker, some retribution is clearly necessary.

Barker's view of history is over-simple, to say the least; but simplicity is not the impression left by the play as a whole. It is subtitled 'choices in reaction' and shows the characters making several such. Ball's death-blow is actually a desperate, doomed attempt to restore the monarchy he fought for: 'Charles Stuart, be a king!'. Charles's obsessive sex-athleticism is, at least in part, his rather pathetic way of compensating for his political impotence. Milton appears, to recommend a ceaseless series of bloody revolutions as the only means of preventing that clod, man, from institutionalising his awfulness. Mrs Bradshaw is a more interesting case, because a bad new world transforms her from a conscientious republican into a woman prepared to cheat her comrades, grovel to her enemies, exploit the already oppressed, and generally make any accommodation in order to survive and play Antigone to her husband's remains. But the most original piece of characterisation in a play that often and deliberately lurches into caricature is her companion and Bradshaw's ex-secretary: at first a flustered, bleating ninny, forever throwing up his hands in genteel anguish at the erosion of a moral and political faith he is too cowardly to stand up for himself; as it turns out, someone capable of bawling 'long live the commonwealth of equals' from somewhere inside a face sliced apart by Charles's praetorian guard.

As this suggests, Barker hasn't quite succumbed to that despair, that near-nihilism, which so often seems to afflict left-wing dramatists when they consider that past, present and future disaster-zone, England. Defiance persists. There is also the example of Bradshaw's daughter, who, while her mother is off feverishly (and, for Barker, pretty pointlessly) collecting her dead husband's offal, has been ensuring that the red meat of his ideas finds its way into print. People will presumably be able to read his views on those who exploit either the labour of others or (the play's subsidiary interest and emphasis) the relationship between the sexes. Britain may on the whole be a moral cesspit created by the hard-nosed for the hare-brained to flounder in; but there is, it seems, the odd glimmer in the murk. (pp. 26-7)

> *Benedict Nightingale, "Bad New World," in* New Statesman, *Vol. 105, No. 2715, April 1, 1983, pp. 26-7.**

DONALD CAMPBELL

Howard Barker, no less than Tom Stoppard, is a dramatist who has a deep love and respect for the music of language. Yet while Stoppard often appears to be playing a flute—or perhaps a piccolo—Barker seems happier with a trombone. *The Hang of the Gaol* [published in the volume *The Hang of the Gaol; Heaven*] resounds with imprecation, so called 'four-letter words', lavatory-wall language which is most effective in evoking the stench of a prison atmosphere. Middenhurst, the prison in question, has been destroyed by an act of arson and the play revolves around an inquiry into the incident, conducted by an irascible Scots civil servant, George Jardine, in the shell of the building. The result of this inquiry is somewhat predictable: Jardine discovers that the fire had actually been started by Cooper, the

lunatic governor of the prison, but his findings are suppressed and, despite his protestations, he himself is kicked upstairs with a knighthood. In the true traditions of the theatre, however, the weight of Barker's argument is felt not so much in the tale but rather in the manner of the telling. Apart from the language, both setting and action contribute to the general effect of excremental impurity. Anal imagery is evident throughout (on two occasions, characters actually defecate on stage) and the characters are continually seen in terms of their animal functions. On stage, this makes for a riveting presentation but, in book-form, it tends to make the gorge rise. Presumably this effect is quite deliberate, since the other play in the volume—*Heaven,* a Strindbergian fantasy for television on the theme of treason, evoking memories of the defection of Guy Burgess—reveals that Barker feels a sense of pain and revulsion at the social decay of contemporary Britain. Despite the bleakness of his vision, the bitterness of his humour, and the sense of disgust with which he seems to approach his subjects, Howard Barker's work entirely satisfies and convinces.

> *Donald Campbell, in a review of "The Hang of the Gaol; Heaven," in* British Book News, *May, 1983, p. 325.*

STEVE GRANT

Howard Barker's return to the Royal Court, with a play *Victory* set in the Restoration period, has all the makings of a Prodigal Son's reappearance in a city that has, temporarily at least, turned its back.

I remember an eminent critic of my acquaintance saying that if he ever had to review another of Barker's plays he would take up landscape gardening. . . . Two or three years ago there just seemed to be *too many* Barker plays, and familiarity, particularly when a recurring and raucously conveyed set of themes, can breed both critical and commercial contempt.

So we've all had our rest, watched our medi-dramas and spectacles, our feminist plays and performance art spectaculars. . . . Barker has returned, as brash, bold and exuberant as ever, with a piece of epic political theatre in the tradition of Brecht (though bearing little other relationship to the German Master) that is in many ways his finest work for the stage.

The English Revolution and its aftermath holds a lasting fascination for any left-wing artist or intellectual faced with the seeming stubborn intractability of the British system. . . . Barker's play makes no attempt to be 'accurate' in either fact, style or language—only Bradshaw, Milton and Charles II and his mistress, the Duchess of Devonshire, are actual historical personages, while the frame of reference is as much the conservatism of Thatcherite, post-Falklands Britain as the Monarchy of 1660. It is a play for today set in costume.

The first scene is almost the theatrical equivalent of a duelist slapping a face with his glove. Within a minute, as a group of Royalists discuss the rigours of disinterring bones and flesh for public display (one of the prerequisites for Charles' restoration, it seems) an officer called Shade (all Barker's names have a distinctly Dickensian feel about them) proceeds to use the word 'cunts' seven times in the space of half-a-minute. It is a declaration of intent and a taster for the sometimes obscenely violent sexual language which runs through the play. Barker has always been a writer obsessed with sexual gratification, with the basic bodily urges that underline and counterpoint public life and personal ambition. His heroine, the widow Bradshaw, is a woman who has lived and worked for change, but also subordinated her physical identity to a polemicist husband whose passion was 'purely nocturnal'. . . . Charles himself is a riotously unfit bawd, misunderstood (of course), by turns rakish and bored, and with the exception of a dispossessed cavalier called Ball, Bradshaw's would-be-lover and a brutally direct supporter of the monarchy, the most foul-mouthed person on stage. In Barker's plays sex, money and power are often linked together in a jerky but wild and arresting dance of death. In *Victory* that dance is carried out as a background activity, always commenting and ironically upending the main story: a 'Mother Courage' of personal reconstruction in which a widow of a puritan polemicist goes on a nightmare journey of survival, humiliation and despair in order to rescue both her husband's corpse and her own identity.

There is always something very bracing about a Barker play—even in our excess-ridden times his writing, an engaging mix of artificiality and vernacular, his imaginative plotting and spectacular gift for creating moments of literally breathtaking dramatic violence, seem to send an almost palpable thrill through an audience. The response may be hostile (I heard mutterings through the press performance) but nobody is bored. And though Barker is an undeniably OTT writer who cries out for a restraining hand, the hand of a Stoppard or even a Hare, he is a writer whose vice and virtues are impossible to separate. Thus *Victory* comes very close to being a great play. That it doesn't quite make it in the end is both saddening but, given the writer in question, also inevitable. (pp. 32-3)

Certainly one of the main faults with the play is that the second half never matches up to the first, particularly the first-half climax which is one of the greatest tours de force in the Court's recent history. Set inside the vaults of the Bank of England it begins with a riotously funny conversation between a group of bickering bankers and businessmen, arguing over the password and the calls of each other's wives, and coming clumsily to terms with the fact that paper money has replaced gold as the standard currency. . . . Moncrieff, [a] financier explains thus: 'You may remember, before the war, the King told us to pay money. Ordered us to, ye cud na argue with it. But we did na want to pay him money, so we had the war . . . Now we have a new king, an 'e still wants money from somewhere, it stands to reason. But noo, instead o' giving it to him, we lend it to him instead'. As a lecture on the rise of monetary capitalism the text is enriched by the sight of a stereotyped 'old fashioned businessman' clutching a gold bar to his bosom as means of refocusing his wealth, and a climactic sequence following the entrance of Charles and entourage in which Charles' whore is spreadeagled on a table, kissing, with great frenzy, the rotting head of the polemicist Bradshaw, a man who signed 'his dad's death warrant'. Sex, power, money, envy, lust, all coming together in a moment of pure Barker, a vivid rejigging of Webster's skull beneath the flowers, and a brilliant piece of theatre from which the play almost never recovers.

For the second half, though capable of great incidental splendours, never outstrips the first, and, indeed, falls away somewhat before the end. A scene with the blind and fugitive Milton . . . is typical: a set-piece which has the now-dishevelled and street-wise Widow slapping Milton across the face in order to free herself from the weight of received wisdom, it is more allegory than actuality. . . . While the climax to the second act in which Charles arranges a marriage between the banker Hambro and his pregnant mistress and sees the former stabbed to

death by the cavalier Ball has far too many plot strands dangling within it to be a success. Characters reappear after too long an absence. . . . The stitching is faulty and the doubts set in. So too the token optimistic finale in which Bradshaw returns home, trailing the now-crippled cavalier Ball as husband, and finds her daughter busily translating the famous 'Harmonicum Brittania' from Latin into English. A scene very reminiscent of Brenton and Bond, but no more than a sop to those of us (all of us?) who believe that life and progress must go on.

But Barker's play, for all that, is still a mighty achievement. As a writer who came to prominence in the heady, politically-optimistic Seventies, he is using the past to restore the present. In this respect the play is both a rallying call and a reminder that survival and redefinition are always uppermost in the minds of characters who have a life beyond mere utterances and ideological frameworks. It's both highly enjoyable and thought-provoking, comic and serious, and, above all, a play of great scope and ambition. Barker is back. He should be welcomed. (p. 33)

> *Steve Grant, in a review of "Victory," in* Plays and Players, *No. 356, May, 1983, pp. 32-3.*

BYRON NELSON

In the tradition of English proletarian drama . . . , Howard Barker's *Victory: Choices in Revolution* is a diatribe against the complacency and smugness of modern England. In Brechtian epic form, *Victory* presents the efforts of the widow of the regicide, John Bradshaw, to recover the mutilated body of her husband which had been exhumed and savagely abused at the Restoration of Charles II. Anachronistically the play's historical characters, such as John Milton, Mrs. Bradshaw, and Charles II, comment on the English Revolution (1640-60) in Marxist terms. By failing to root out social inequity, the Puritans are blamed for allowing the Royalists to return and lay the corrupt foundations of capitalist England. The play's clear message is a plea for Maoist continuous revolution: "Oh, all you who come after, make your revolution right!"

The heroine, called simply Bradshaw, finds the high ethical idealism of the Puritans to be hopelessly inadequate in light of the meanness of the Royalist Restoration: "We must crawl now, go down on all fours, be a dog or rabbit, no more standing up now, standing is over, standing up's for men with sin and dignity. No, got to be a dog now, and keep our teeth." Brecht's Mother Courage is the clear model for Mrs. Bradshaw; instead of waiting for the Kingdom of God she works to collect the pieces of her husband's body after its public abuse.

The quiet dignity of Bradshaw is contrasted with the near-mad prurience and scatological indecency of the court of Charles II. Obsessed with sex and pleasure, Charles plummets to the depths of human depravity, symbolically depicted by his flinging off his wig and dropping his pants: "Garments down! Out bum!" (This is *Verfremdung* at its most prosaic.) Charles' violent prurience contrasts sadly with the idealism of the defeated Puritans; the theme of the abuse of the body (politic and human) is neatly, if absurdly, united when Charles has the Countess of Devonshire reach into his pants to masturbate him while he throws skittles at the impaled head of Bradshaw. As Charles exits, one disgusted Royalist asks, "Why in Christ's name did we bring that back?"

The ill health of the nation is also depicted (improbably enough) in the vaults of the Bank of England, when Nell Gwynne innocently asks for a gold brick and, like Salome, kisses the dismembered head of the regicide. Restoration England has obviously been infected, literally and metaphorically, with the worst diseases of Europe.

At its conclusion, the play stresses the theme of national self-mutilation, as characters appear who have had their tongues or lips ripped off; yet Mrs. Bradshaw, having learned how to adapt to the new order, is pregnant and has brought home the bits of her husband for burial. However, these small triumphs scarcely earn the play its grimly mordant title, *Victory.* (pp. 555-56)

Howard Barker is best known for *Fair Slaughter,* a play about another betrayed revolution (the Russian). His *Victory* seems to have been inspired by a post-Falklands burst of nausea. . . . However, in spite of, or perhaps because of, its impassioned politics Barker's *Victory* quickly grew tiresome. Its scatological obsessiveness and its shrieking jeremiad against English complacency generate a certain energy, but the play is ultimately too strident to win converts to its political point of view. (p. 556)

> *Byron Nelson, in a review of "Victory: Choices in Revolution," in* Theatre Journal, *Vol. 35, No. 4, December, 1983, pp. 555-56.*

TONY DUNN

Howard Barker's especial strength has always been his ability to dramatise both the profound connections and the ineradicable hostilities between the various levels of a given society. This means that his historical plays have no truck with costume-drama. Period clothes, authentic language, carefully researched décor smother the contradictions of an epoch. The result is spectacle rather than drama . . . , where people may have problems but society is not fundamentally riven. The typical Barker set is some bare space—a field, a hill, a cathedral, a room—which localises the action and speech of people whose cunning, ignorance, treachery and wit are recognisably ours. What for him distinguish a period are not its characters but its issues, private and public. The rationality common to the banker Hambro and the utopian Republican Bradshaw quenches, in *Victory* (1983), the upper class sexiness of Charles II and the Cavaliers. But in *The Love of a Good Man* (1978), set on Passchendaele field in 1920, lust and desire, of and between bourgeois and worker, wolf up the cerebral social-workerism of Bridge and Lalage Toynbee. The political power of Reason is quite different in Europe 1920 as compared with England 1660. 'I use history', Barker has said, 'not for nostalgia, but to hack away at comforting images of the past in order to evoke, or unlock, feelings about the present'. . . .

Hacking is certainly central to *Pity in History,* the first of two new Barker plays for 1985. The period is again the seventeenth century, this time featuring a gang of Cromwell's Ironsides rampaging through the cathedral and crypt of the local gentry. They smash statues and pictures under the direction of Serjeant Boys and Chaplain Croop. The familiar liturgies are enthusiastically chanted. They'll win because they're stronger, and they're stronger because God's on their side. Their cook, Murgatroyd, is less ecstatic. He's dying from a stray bullet and he complains loudly and bitterly about it, until the lady of the manor, Venables, slits his throat in the crypt. (p. 9)

The second play is *The Power of the Dog* set in and around the time of Yalta (1945). . . . It is sub-titled 'Moments in History and Anti-History'. Scene 1 links the heights with the depths of the power structure. While Stalin and Churchill divide up post-war Europe, McGroot, an imported Scottish comedian, tries to entertain them. The inter-cutting between his jokes and sardonic comments and their paranoias and mistranslations accelerates as the scene proceeds. It ends with Stalin commanding that a photographer (shorter than he) be found who will fix his true image. He finally bursts into laughter at McGroot, who is puzzled and terrified.

In the last scene (10), the photographer has been found. She is Ilona, a beautiful Hungarian model, who has herself spent the war posing against the ruins of Europe and sleeping with Nazis. Between these two scenes the plot brings her, and her own photographer Victor, in contact with the Red Army which is scouring Europe of the remnants of fascism. The bulk of the play, therefore, focuses on the 'middle strata', the men and women who have to do history's dirty work. Their central concerns are politics, sex and aesthetics. Stalin's true photo parallels Matrimova's WholeFilm—'3 screens in dialectical relationship'—which parallels Sorge's cry over the body of Hannela: 'I think if you have perfect lips you are under an obligation YES, OF COURSE YOU ARE, THERE IS NO POINT LOOKING LIKE THAT IF YOU CANNOT TELL THE TRUTH'. (p. 10)

They speak no 'Russian' idiom, but Barker's familiar mix of vulgarity and formality. 'I'm fucking with Roy. Have you noticed?', inquires Tremblayev of Sorge. Ideological fixities are loosened by Ilona, the rootless, opportunist image-maker. But the attempt to create a new art and a new politics by such as Matrimova and Tremblayev is not denigrated. The play, for example, proposes, in equal measure, a satire on and an endorsement of Brecht's realism. Sorge announces: 'The proper war film is not actually about the battle, it is about the reasons for the battle. What are the reasons for the battle? Arkov?' and Arkov replies: 'It's eleven o'clock and I want to write a letter'. Yet the whole structure of *The Power of the Dog,* a series of titled episodes which parallel and cut across each other, featuring a heroine who survives through trickery, beauty and emotional coldness, is the nearest Barker has yet come to 'epic' theatre. Truth and image—now a battlefield, now a photo of a model against a battlefield, now a séance with a blonde Nazi on a battlefield—chase each other's tail throughout. But this is worlds away from the boulevard verbalising of Stoppard's *The Real Thing.* By setting his play precisely in history, the particularly bloody history of Soviet Communism's repeal of Nazi Germany, Barker gives his figures, because of all their confusion and egotism, an authentic density. *The Power of the Dog* is an intellectually rich play. It cuts more sharply from idea to idea, often within a single scene, than perhaps any previous Barker work. It therefore makes intellectual demands on actors and audience alike, and because it does so, it respects them. (pp. 10-11)

> *Tony Dunn, "The Real History of Man," in* Drama, *No. 155, 1st Quarter, 1985, pp. 9-11.*

Ted Berrigan

1934-1983

(Born Edmund Joseph Michael Berrigan, Jr.) American poet, dramatist, and critic.

Berrigan's literary career began in the 1960s when he was living in New York City, and he is sometimes linked with the so-called "New York School" of poetry, which included such poets as Frank O'Hara, Kenneth Koch, and John Ashbery. Their work is marked by emphasis on individual perception, insistence on structural freedom, and the influence of abstract-expressionist painters. A predominant feature of Berrigan's work is his unconventional manipulation of form; he rearranges the logical order of lines, creating new poems with lines from earlier works, and he experiments with the appearance of the poem on the page. Many of Berrigan's collections contain poems on which he collaborated with others. Among his best-known volumes are *The Sonnets* (1964), *Bean Spasms* (1967), *Many Happy Returns* (1969), *In the Early Morning Rain* (1970), and *Red Wagon: Poems* (1976). Poems from these and earlier, privately printed collections, as well as new poems, are included in *So Going Around Cities: New & Selected Poems, 1958-1979* (1980).

(See also *Contemporary Authors*, Vols. 61-64, Vol. 110 [obituary]; *Contemporary Authors New Revision Series*, Vol. 14; and *Dictionary of Literary Biography*, Vol. 5.)

MARVIN BELL

The Sonnets is a mimeographed workbook containing lots of talk—intense, associational, and cumulative—on being a Village poet ("Gosh, I gulp to be here in my skin!"). These sixty-six pieces seem to have been written in the hope of stumbling on one's credo in the process, for they are filled with apologies and explanations: "Everything turns into writing"; "There is no such thing as a breakdown"; "The logic of grammar is not genuine"; "I strain to gather my absurdities"; "It is a Chinese signal." And on and on. Eventually, "sonnets" consist wholly of lines from previous "sonnets".

Because I respect Mr. Berrigan's mentality and facility, I believe these poems are merely lab notes: "These sonnets are a hommage to myself / absence of passion, principles, love / The most elegant present I could get!" In **"A Final Sonnet,"** he claims to be through with "this rough magic". If that is so, I like his making these available and moving on, and I wouldn't want to be hard on such bright industry.... (pp. 371-72)

> Marvin Bell, in a review of "The Sonnets," in Poetry, *Vol. CVI, No. 5, August, 1965, pp. 371-72.*

TOM CLARK

Ron Padgett and Ted Berrigan have worked out a collaborative method that keeps things hopping. It reminds me of vaudeville partnerships, Siamese twins, Alphonse and Gaston, the Smoth-ers Brothers and "It Takes Two" by Marvin Gaye and Kim Weston.

Most of the poems and prose pieces in *Bean Spasms* are not strictly collaborations between Padgett and Berrigan. There are works composed individually by each of the authors; there are collaborations between one or the other of the authors and artists like Joe Brainard. . . .

Collaboration is the point of the book—not so much the collaboration of the authors together as the collaboration between the authors and various languages and literary forms, and other authors. What is collaborated with is the convention or model, standards in the sense a conventional model car is standard. The Italian and French languages are collaborated with, as are the sonnet form and the sestina form, the epigram, the interview, the ideogram, Richard Eberhart and Robert Frost.

Robert Frost said that rhyme is to poetry what the net is to a game of tennis, i.e., a convention producing complexity, difficulty and consequently interest. Taking this ridiculous analogy to its extreme point, we see convention as pure obstacle. *Bean Spasms* emphasizes the formality of convention to a degree of absolute tedium, which is the same as absolute hilarity. More applicable than Frost's dictum are the words of John Cage, who said "Is the door locked? No, it's open as usual." (p. 32)

Tom Clark, *"Two and Three," in* The New York Times Book Review, *March 31, 1968, pp. 32, 34.**

Hayden Carruth, *"Making It New," in* The Hudson Review, *Vol. XXI, No. 2, Summer, 1968, pp. 399-412.**

HAYDEN CARRUTH

[**The Sonnets** is an] unconventional book . . . , an experimental sequence numbered I to LXXXVIII but with a good many missing: for those who are interested, numbers 14, 20, 22, 24, 25, 28, 29, 33, 34, 35, 54, 58, 59, 60, 61, 62, 63, 69, 77, 79, 81, 86. Yes, I have, as this suggests, read these poems with care; or with as much care as I could in the time permitted a book reviewer. At first I was mystified, as I think anyone would be, coming to them unprepared. . . . Nonsensical [for example, is the fifteenth sonnet], yet it teases one with sense; and then one realizes that the lines have been rearranged. To turn it into a more or less conventional sonnet, you need only read from the two ends toward the middle, i.e. in the following sequence of lines: 1, 14, 2, 13, 3, 12, 4, 11, 5, 10, 6, 9, 7, 8. With this clue, one sees that in most of the other sonnets the lines have been displaced too, but seldom in this neat order. . . . [The eighteenth sonnet, for example,] can be put together in various ways, as a matter of fact. . . . [Yet] the original reading, the text as given by the poet, makes a kind of sense too, a felt sense which has grown perceptibly stronger from that of the fifteenth sonnet. Soon one discovers that lines and phrases are shuffled not only within poems but from poem to poem. Some—"Dear Marge, hello," for example—recur over and over. Parts of the first sonnet are picked up again toward the end of the sequence. Soon one gives up trying to rearrange the lines, which in some poems is impossible anyway, and submits to the flow of words and lines as the poet has presented them. Except for purposes of analysis, this is what we should do, of course, and it works. My own experience with the poems has produced several observations. First, my beginning dislike and distrust gave way to acceptance rather quickly, and then to enthusiasm. These poems have lyric and elegiac power, wit, complex movement, unity: they are what the poet calls them, a sonnet sequence, composed with classical intent. Secondly, though I am sure I must read the sequence several times again before I will know how all the parts function, this is nothing but what I should have to say about any long poem worth my attention. The main substance of Berrigan's sequence is clear after one reading. Thirdly, Berrigan's method is collage, like Brainard's picture or a movie by Cocteau, resembling an LSD trip, to which the poem alludes several times. But it is no random humble-jumble, of that I'm certain. These sonnets are put together, not according to a formula, since they have nothing wooden or formalistic about them, but according to a rationale of structure which is, whatever else, an elucidable rationale (though I should like to know more about those excised sonnets, what they are and why they were left out). Fourthly, this is, I believe, Berrigan's first book, at least the first I have read, and it shows some of the crudeness that characterizes most first books; I mean a tendency to be over-ambitious. Berrigan's collage is crowded, many of the parts are snippets, we must squint hard to see them. I suspect he might have given us a still stronger, more compelling sequence if he had concentrated on fewer elements and had projected them at a farther esthetic distance, thus leading us, paradoxically, not into greater simplicity but into a better integrated complexity. But this will come with experience. Meanwhile Berrigan has shown that his method is workable and that we must pay heed to what he does with it in the future. (pp. 408-10)

MICHAEL BENEDIKT

Bean Spasms is a miscellany by Ron Padgett and Ted Berrigan. What it is miscellaneous with are poems, stories, proverbs, photographs, novels, poem-puns; also interviews with famous people, made up. Not only the book, but most of the individual pieces are collaborative. One pictures its authors getting together for pleasant evenings and throwing off these pieces as a sort of by-product—about as sound a poetic esthetic as any, after all. The book's bounciness is further embellished, or established, by comic-book style drawings by Joe Brainard. . . . By not making a fuss about such things as consistency, completeness of structure (many pieces just *stop,* evidently where the writers became bored or were interrupted by events around them), or tonal range (the two hundred pages shoot at wit throughout), the collection achieves its peculiar flavor. . . . Such purely verbal experiments as [in **"The Complete Works"**] . . . , apparently the result of controlled mishearings of phrases in an English textbook, suggest of course the experiments with forced inspiration and "anti-artistic" techniques of the Surrealists. (Also suggested is the method of Eugene Ionesco's first play, *The Bald Soprano*). The Surrealists were of course also the leading twentieth-century exponents of literary collaboration. Still, we value the Surrealists for more than their pun-fun; and I would have been happier about this book had it been less obviously happy, and cultivated the Surreal sense of the higher humors, the tragi-comical character of all linguistic enterprise. (pp. 206-07)

Michael Benedikt, *"Critic of the Month, IV: The Shapes of Nature," in* Poetry, *Vol. CXIII, No. 3, December, 1968, pp. 188-215.**

STEPHEN STEPANCHEV

In a typical poem [from **Many Happy Returns**], **"Tambourine Life,"** there are random jottings that suggest the quality of Berrigan's daily life and preoccupations well enough, but they are not juxtaposed either wittily or with much metaphoric purpose: The effect is gross. The best poem in the book is **"Words for Love,"** a structured, self-analytic, and genuinely moving work.

Berrigan has also published **The Sonnets** (1964), a collection of much finer texture, with brilliant unifying recurrences of image and phrase, his most successful work to date (even though he does not say whose translation of Arthur Rimbaud's "The Drunken Boat" he uses so liberally in his "collages"). He is famous for his collaborations with Ron Padgett, **Bean Spasms** (1967), a book of poems and prose pieces in which the authors contribute alternate passages, sometimes working against each other to produce the greatest possible tension and contradiction. While this sounds intriguing, such collaborations are actually more enjoyable for the participants than the reader.

Stephen Stepanchev, *"Discovering New Poets," in* The New Leader, *Vol. LII, No. 7, April 14, 1969, pp. 28-9.**

LOUIS L. MARTZ

Berrigan's new book, **Many Happy Returns**, shows the extent to which the theory of the mobile and the uses of the daily may deteriorate in actual practice. Berrigan might be said to be demonstrating the view that William Carlos Williams expressed in *Paterson V:* "Anything is good material for poetry. Anything. I've said it time and time again." But the trouble is that Berrigan presents mainly the *material* and thus demonstrates with a flat insistence that anything, in and by itself, is not poetry. Williams says in the earlier part of that interview in *Paterson* that poetry consists of "words, rhythmically organized," and then he adds, "A poem is a complete little universe. It exists separately." In most of Berrigan's volume this rhythmical organization and poetical separation do not exist. In his search for an "open" form, Berrigan too often allows his writing to fall off into jumbles of anything, as he himself humorously admits, with a swipe at his own "mobility." . . . (p. 600)

> *Louis L. Martz, in a review of "Many Happy Returns," in* The Yale Review, *Vol. LVIII, No. 4, June, 1969, pp. 600-02.*

ALAN BROWNJOHN

[In **In The Early Morning Rain**] Berrigan exhibits a kind of experimental style which would appear to be beyond the reach of the academic ironist:

> It's 2 a.m. at Anne and Lewis's which is where
> it's at
> On St Mark's Place hash and Angel Hairs
> on our minds
> Love is in our heart's (what
> else?) dope . . .

'where it's at' is the absolute dead centre of a scene where poetry goes out to embrace random moments of turned-on consciousness, and dissolves into them. This kind of writing is difficult to criticise because it is so ungraspable, volatile and—in the end—insignificant: 'It's New Year's Eve, of 1968, & a time / for Resolution. / I don't like Engelbert Humperdinck. / I love the Incredible String Band. / The War goes on / & war is Shit.' Etc. There is a cumulative effect of verve and wild geniality, and the book is nicely presented with witty illustrations by George Schneeman. But the poetry is walking off into the margins. (p. 773)

> *Alan Brownjohn, "Absorbing Chaos," in* New Statesman, *Vol. 80, No. 2072, December 4, 1970, pp. 772-73.*

FRED MORAMARCO

Berrigan is a "New York Poet" obviously indebted to Koch, O'Hara, and Ashbery, though lacking the originality and imaginative ingenuity of any of his mentors. Occasionally his matter-of-factness is clever, more often it is simply lightweight. . . . [The poems in **In the Early Morning Rain**] are nice poems for a glum morning, when you feel like picking up on the latest gossip from the New York Poetry Scene. The illustrations by Joe Brainard, George Schneeman, and Jim Dine . . . are funny and reveal the affinities between Berrigan's poetry and the graphic arts. I don't think there's much more here to ponder. (pp. 280-81)

> *Fred Moramarco, in a review of "In the Early Morning Rain," in* Western Humanities Review, *Vol. XXV, No. 3, Summer, 1971, pp. 280-81.*

DAVID LEHMAN

The poems [in **In the Early Morning Rain**] range from the self-indulgent ("sitting now, & I'm not thinking / Nor swishing; I'm just sitting. Getting over them two / Hamburgers") to the downright insipid. Here is the complete text of **"Telegram,"** dedicated to the late Jack Kerouac:

> Bye bye Jack.
> See you soon.

Actually, Berrigan has a lot going for him, and shouldn't be wasting his time writing such moronic drivel. His first book, **The Sonnets,** was truly fine, supplying him with what he needs: a form, discipline, thinking. Otherwise his native exuberance turns into whipped cream, his wit becomes sophomoric. The narrative prose poems of **In the Early Morning Rain** show him at his best—relaxed, controlled, assured—as in the haunting **"Che Guevara's Cigars."**

In **"The Great Genius,"** another quickie poem, Berrigan writes,

> The Great Genius is
> A man who can do the
> Average thing when everybody
> Else is going crazy.

Which is almost witty, and does capture something of the crisis-conscious atmosphere currently pervading New York. But who's fooling whom? A sufficient number of us are sane enough to realize that Berrigan's genius (circa 1971) is, at best, rather average. (p. 232)

> *David Lehman, "The Whole School," in* Poetry, *Vol. CXIX, No. 4, January, 1972, pp. 224-33.**

CONNIE FLETCHER

The unevenness of [**Red Wagon**] . . . will delight some and infuriate others. The style swerves from the ingenious to the vapid, but the enduring quality in this writing is risk. **Red Wagon** holds the moments and movements Berrigan considers most dear; his best poetic antics transform the ordinary.

> *Connie Fletcher, in a review of "Red Wagon," in* Booklist, *Vol. 73, No. 12, February 15, 1977, p. 875.*

CHOICE

[Ted Berrigan and Alice Notley] (husband and wife) easily fall under the same rubric—boring. They are antique, remote; in their work there is no narrative, characterization, little imagery. What they play with mainly is polishing and repolishing language: ". . . covered thou must / dance thee here, ship / . . . lighten my eyes keep for me an apple of the eye / under the shelter of thy wings" [from Notley's *Alice Ordered Me to Be Made*] . . .; "ripped / out of her mind / a marvelous construction / thinking / no place; & you / not once properly handled / Ophelia" [from Berrigan's **Red Wagon**]. . . . Not that their language-polishing really works either: what you mainly feel confronted with is idealess, energyless blank space filled with neatly spaced words.

A review of "Red Wagon: Poems," in Choice, *Vol. 14, No. 4, June, 1977, p. 529.*

ROBERT PETERS

[The poems in *So Going Around Cities: New & Selected Poems, 1958-1979*] pick up the more self-indulgent murmurings of Frank O'Hara and circle—the cozy friendships, the contempt for the outside world, the scattered verse forms, the endless trivializing. Once in a while Berrigan nicely wrenches the old sonnet form, swings a potent image, and manages to transcend his cuteness—but not often enough.... Berrigan is nowhere as good as his mentors—O'Hara, Ashbery, Schuyler, Koch. Fashionable rather than substantial.

> *Robert Peters, in a review of "So Going Around Cities: New & Selected Poems, 1958-1979," in* Library Journal, *Vol. 105, No. 10, May 15, 1980, p. 1169.*

SARA PLATH

Readers who attempt to read [*So Going Around Cities: New & Selected Poems, 1958-1979*] ... straight through might find it unbearably monotonous, which is an indication of how little Berrigan's poetry has changed over the years. The pieces vary in density from the **"Sonnets"** to the short, spare poems that are seen in Berrigan's more recent work; but nearly all depend on a speedy, linear association of one idea to the next, rather than the controlled juxtaposition of elements. And that is exactly the virtue and challenge of what Berrigan does. As more and more new poets seem to be opting for quiet, small-voiced poems, Berrigan's sprawl and abrasiveness are refreshing.

> *Sara Plath, in a review of "So Going Around Cities: New & Selected Poems, 1958-1979," in* Booklist, *Vol. 76, No. 21, July 1, 1980, p. 1586.*

GEORGE MYERS, JR.

[*The essay from which the following excerpt is taken originally appeared in a slightly different form in* Small Press Review, *December 1980.*]

Along comes Ted Berrigan and with him a whiff of fresh air in a barnyard breeze. A lot of folks won't like Berrigan's looks: cigarette always hanging off his lower lip, a little chubby around the flanks, and *not* dressed in the latest disco outfit. Still others might gripe about the look of his poetry; it's everywhere on the page, sometimes like a giant crossword puzzle, sometimes in the form of laundry lists and highly unkempt. His twenty-year collection of new and collected poems, *So Going Around Cities,* is the best of fifteen previously published books of poetry. It's good reading, to be sure, like the epitaphs on tombstones. (pp. 106-07)

In his elegies (there are many) no antique whisperings to Ozymandias will be found, nor vapory metaphors to time gone by or gods that never existed. His odes are to Dagwood Bumstead, days he's lived and things he knows of first hand, like that old gang of his, Allen Ginsberg, Tom Veitch, John Ashbery, Peter Schjeldahl....

Berrigan seems a bit dated now, a little too drunk and carefree to really be of this world but, nevertheless, *So Going Around Cities* acts as a rousing cheer for what can become of a good

wit, wakened in his own world, not yet knuckled under by those who will have their day. (p. 107)

> *George Myers, Jr., "A Glance at Aleister Crowley, William Burroughs and Ted Berrigan," in his* An Introduction to Modern Times: Collected Essays and Reviews, *The Lunchroom Press, 1982, pp. 105-07.**

CHRIS KADISON

The publication of a Selected Poems is a benchmark in any poet's life, gathering as it does those poems seen fit to embody the career thus far. When the poet is Ted Berrigan, whose influence on the coming generation of urban poets would be hard to overstate, yet of whose twenty scattered, often mimeographed books only five appear in *Books in Print,* the occasion becomes significant to anyone with an interest in the future of the art....

The title [*So Going Around Cities*], as it should be, is instructive. "Cities"—this poetry is not so much rooted in as perfumed by a sense of place, that being invariably urban. The book's chronology follows the life's, and so we follow the poet from New York (below Fourteenth Street), remembered Tulsa, London, Chicago, Ann Arbor, Buffalo, Providence, and ever back to New York. Not descriptive in the Williams—or even O'Hara—sense, the poetry is more properly the imaginative traces of an urban *mind.* The closest Berrigan gets to nature here is looking out of an airplane at the Midwest, and some passingly mentioned, scrawny trees growing out of tenement backyards.

"Going Around"—not "walking," "riding," "through" or "in," all words imparting a sense of purpose to which true poetry is allergic. The phrase conjures up someone shuffling, wandering circle-like, pursuing hazy pleasures leisurely enough for poetry to have a chance to be heard.

And the introductory grace note "So," unsettling at first, bringing a feeling of open-endedness to both sides of the line, courting grammarians' wrath; yet how adroitly it sets up the tone of aimlessness, how lovely the stutter-step of the syllable.

In these sly pleasures outside the use of metaphor, in the seeming effortlessness of its construction, above all in its refusal to take itself too seriously, the phrase is classic Berrigan.

The work the title represents covers three decades of struggle against all that is pompous, stale, overlaid in this too-predictably somber art. If poets can be divided into those doing fine work with miniature chisels (Dickinson, Bishop, Creeley) and those painting in broad-swept strokes unafraid of the spatter so much a part of life (Whitman, Williams, O'Hara), Berrigan is firmly in the latter camp. As he once joked, this book could have been called *The Best and the Worst of Ted Berrigan.* Behind the apparent recklessness is a refusal to construct poems as airtight edifices, a deliberate turning away from the kinds of perfection at odds with experience today....

[His] fidelity to life as it is being lived (and to the mind as it skips, jumps, skids ...) extends from form to emotive content. One's chest needn't swell with passion, or (its post-Eliot counterpart still yellowing the pages of *The New Yorker,* for example) regret—before sitting down to the craft. In how many poems has death been presented as shorn of self-pity and declamation as "The heart stops briefly when someone dies, / a quick pain as you hear the news, & someone passes / from your outside life to inside. Slowly the heart adjusts / to its new weight, & slowly everything continues, sanely.'' (**"Things to Do in Providence"**)?

These points can lead to a silliness frustrating to those of us brought up on Keats' dictum "Load every vein with gold." To its credit, this book retains many of the most uncompromising forays into frivolity without which this poet could not be represented, while omitting those works (for example, **"Train Ride"**) with not much else to recommend them.

As is most urban art, this is addicted to questions of form. Probably no living American poet has done more to revitalize the sonnet. The poem with which this book begins is a fourteen line one, masterfully toned, on the death of his father. I read and enjoyed it over a dozen times before someone pointed out to me that each line has ten syllables. That is control, and one should grasp this before going on to such sprawling studies in open form as **"Tambourine Life"** (thirty-one pages), **"Bean Spasms"** (eight), and, with Anne Waldman, the virtuosic **"Memorial Day"** (twenty-eight pages).

The freedom this work imparts has for me to do with its treatment of language as something plastic, malleable, extending, as Burroughs, O'Hara and Philip Whalen have, English poesy into realms of constructivist assemblage.

This is first apparent in the early sonnets, where the same lines obsess in various poems, striking new juxtapositions and reinventing content as they do. Traceable back to Apollinaire and Rimbaud, Berrigan's abstraction approaches that in the visual arts. The poem stands not as *representation* of world or feeling, but as a feeling/world autonomous in itself—and, like cubism, this with no preferred center. . . .

In such a poetry of glittering artifice, language itself can become the chief subject, and too often, inspiration. The danger here is a kind of solipsism, of abstractions leading nowhere but themselves, poetry arising from nothing more than the poet's need to make poetry. This makes for emotionally flaccid, redundant, in a word—academic—art. Or, as Auden warned in a 1955 letter to Frank O'Hara, quoted in Perloff's *Poet Among Painters:* "I think you . . . must watch what is always the great danger in any 'surrealistic' style, namely of confusing authentic non-logical relations which arouse wonder with accidental ones which arouse mere surprise and in the end fatigue."

It is Berrigan's productivity that opens him to this charge, but I for one am grateful to see an ambitious poet err on the side of generosity. If every line is not destined to be engraved upon the lexicon, that is part of this poet's point. Still I find myself wishing for more emotional juice in much of the material here, the kind of force that issues forth from compression, and not a too easy venting of steam.

Chris Kadison, in a review of "So Going Around Cities: New & Selected Poems 1958-1979," in The American Book Review, *Vol. 5, No. 2, January-February, 1983, p. 24.**

Breyten Breytenbach

1939-

South African poet, novelist, prose writer, and short story writer.

Breytenbach is regarded by many as the foremost contemporary Afrikaans poet. In his works he alternates outrage at South Africa's governmental policies of apartheid with love for his country and its landscape. Breytenbach left his homeland at the age of twenty and eventually settled in Paris, where he married a Vietnamese woman in 1964. Considered "coloured" under South African racial laws, his wife was denied a visa until 1972, when the Breytenbachs were admitted for three months. While the visit, the subject of *A Season in Paradise* (1980), rekindled warm childhood memories, it also reinforced Breytenbach's anger at the violence and injustice of the official regime. In 1975 Breytenbach returned incognito to South Africa on a mission for a clandestine antiapartheid organization. He was subsequently arrested, tried, and sentenced to nine years imprisonment under South Africa's Terrorist Act. Breytenbach served seven of the nine years before he was released.

Breytenbach's turbulent relationship with his homeland directly informs his work. The poems in *Sinking Ship Blues* (1977), *And Death as White as Words* (1978), and *In Africa Even the Flies Are Happy: Selected Poems, 1964-1977* (1978) are unconventionally structured. Composed of sentence fragments, isolated images, and dreamlike sequences, they convey brief, intense moments rather than linear narratives. Breytenbach juxtaposes life and death, growth and destruction, and joy and sorrow, reflecting his own conflicting emotions toward South Africa. The isolation and degradation Breytenbach suffered in prison intensified his ideological opposition to the government and gave rise to two recent works: *Mouroir: Mirrornotes of a Novel* (1984) and *The True Confessions of an Albino Terrorist* (1985). The former is a collection of interrelated prose pieces that present an imagistic, surreal portrait of Breytenbach's psyche as a prisoner. The latter is an equally vivid yet more realistic examination of the South African penal system and Breytenbach's experiences as a political prisoner. His poetic background surfaces in both works, particularly in the power of his images. Nadine Gordimer commented: "If Breytenbach's imagery is to be compared with anyone's it is that of Czesław Miłosz, with whom he shares an intense response to nature and a way of interpreting politically determined events and their human consequences through the subtleties of the physical world."

(See also *CLC*, Vol. 23 and *Contemporary Authors*, Vol. 113.)

VALENTINE CUNNINGHAM

Breytenbach passed the years 1975 to 1982 in South African jails for promoting illegal trade unions in his homeland. *Mouroir*, awkward, slippery, perturbing, is his jumble of notes from that underground, a set of cryptic prison epistles with shadowy senders and shadowier recipients, a series of weird and enigmatic stories all hacked out with pain, many of them half-strangled at birth, some even still-born.

© Jerry Bauer

How to mirror systems of terror? It's one of Breytenbach's constant concerns. He solves it Borges's way in a fiction that is the mirror of enigmas—the unresolved vision through the glass, darkly. His scenes are grey deserts, empty urban labyrinths, desolate beaches. His stories come in bits, tailing off, unfinished businesses. His characters arrive abruptly. They lack explanation, and are prone to switch terrains and times and to have their names subtly doctored without notice or reason. All at sea, the reader clings to the wreckage of what's just recognisable—the multiplying prisons, camps and prisoners, the fascinated detailing of how hanged people die, the 'albocentric' obsession with the sex lives of Unwhites, and with maximum security—all the grim moves in 'South African roulette.'

It makes sense when we meet characters out of Kafka and find Hitler still stage-managing the Berlin Olympics. But otherwise the common reader's demand for clarity and conclusions is unflinchingly rebutted. There'll be no gossip, the text insists. Truth hereabouts will lie in the pell-mell jottings of inchoate distresses. The pathos, the horror, certainly get you. But, as often within the modernist compound, the formal tricksiness still seems short on total persuasion.

Valentine Cunningham, "A Season in Hell," in The Observer, *April 29, 1984, p. 23.**

JOHN WIDEMAN

Mouroir is a complex, demanding, haunting book. It is subtitled "Mirrornotes of a Novel" and like a novel, contains characters, themes and images which occur and reoccur, creating the illusion of narrative, continuity, reality unfolding. . . .

Breytenbach's work exemplifies Milan Kundera's notion of novel form, "a long piece of synthetic prose based on play with invented characters" and substance "ironic essay, novelistic narrative, autobiographical fragment, historic fact, flight of fancy." *Mouroir*'s stories are told in fits and starts; they slip in and out of focus, the prose becomes a fluid, subjective medium in which writer and reader float unbound by the constraints of traditional fiction. The reader needs to become acclimatized to the intermittent, convoluted qualities of Breytenbach's prose. The first step is surrendering *a priori* notions of what narrative should be, then allowing oneself to learn and experience what the author comprehends as "reality." *Mouroir* is difficult to read and not always under control because it makes mincemeat out of so many conventional assumptions, both philosophic and formal. Parts are as crucial as the whole. The effect is that of tapestry. The point at which the eye enters the picture space is arbitrary. You must assimilate bits and pieces before a design becomes apparent and no single, overall design necessarily enforces itself on the viewer.

Like most good innovative writing Breytenbach's *Mouroir* offers a running account of how it should be read. Hemingway's notion of a limited, fixed narrative consciousness is critiqued and mimicked in "Book, A Mirror." "The Self-Death" contains explicit instructions. "Forgive! I mean there's hardly any time left to give the information step by step a structure and a direction. As reader you will just have to read a little harder to interpret the signals." Throughout, the author lets his audience peep at the artificer. "It is thus, when you throw off the words, that you become lighter—because you obscure the matter, because the words crawl out of 'you,' devour the identity."

"Truth, after all, has more faces than a polished crystal." We are invited to confirm this perception that serves as a rationale for *Mouroir*. The author is a conjurer. He begins with nothing and then creates a richly layered, textured vision, a multifaceted reality which demands not only our cooperation, but our complicity in a daring, ingenious enterprise, an act of subversion.

Mouroir stands as a brief for the act of writing, writing as an exercise of imagination and will. Ultimately it's a treatise on power because writing in Breytenbach's view entails self-definition, a political, moral and esthetic stance towards authority. "I am the writer: I can do what I want!" A man confined in the solitary darkness of a cell faces the daily, crushing awareness of his insignificance. He can crumble before that recognition or plunge into the abyss, the void, the mirror which sits like a man's wall before his eyes. In the emptiness of the mirror a man's existence can be extinguished or celebrated. Breytenbach chooses the latter. Like Genet, like George Jackson in Soledad prison, he comes to realize "Where he doesn't look . . . remains dark" and that darkness can engulf him, destroy him unless he actively seeks and creates his reflection in the mirror.

So *Mouroir* is finally about freedom. In the funny summary "Index" which closes *Mouroir* like the rewards and punishments afterthoughts of a Victorian novel, Don Espejuelo (Sir Mirror), one of the narrator's alter egos, is revealed as the author of *"On the Noble Art of Walking in No Man's Land (translated into Afrikaans, I'm assured, as Die Oupe Lyf)."* No Man's Land can be understood as an actual country at the southern tip of Africa which racism and political repression have transformed into a nightmare landscape. No Man's Land is also the turf where Breytenbach has chosen to make his stand, the far country of imagination, dreaming, conjuring where the mind at least is free to examine its limits.

John Wideman, "In the Penal Colony," in Book World—The Washington Post, *June 24, 1984, p. 4.*

NADINE GORDIMER

Mouroir is the work of that rarity which Camus despaired of finding, an individual who has lived, as protagonist *and* victim, the central experience produced by his time and place and who possesses a creative ability equal to his experience. A poet and a painter, faced with injustice before which words and pigment seem to fail, Breytenbach put away his pen and brush and became a revolutionary. Whether he was a good one or not is something for those of us safe behind our desks to argue over. He spent seven years in a South African maximum-security prison, the ventricle-and-auricle cell of the struggle against oppression in South Africa. For a white man, to have gone through that is to have come as close as is possible to *the* experience in South Africa—that of black people.

Yet this is not a prisoner's book. It will be a crass injustice of underestimation and simplification if it is presented and received that way. In it the ordinary time-focus of a man's perceptions has been extraordinarily rearranged by a definitive experience that, the writer understands, belongs as much to the time before it happened as to the time after. Prison irradiates this book with dreadful enlightenments; the dark and hidden places of the country from which the book arises are phosphorescent with it.

Breytenbach is polylingual; he wrote his book in English and Afrikaans under a French title. Although *mouroir* is the word for "old people's home," it seems he has reinterpreted it as a dovetailing of *mourir* (to die) and *miroir* (a mirror). What Breytenbach knows, and shows by means of his recurring mirrors, eliding, reversing, breaking up events, emotions, and perceptions, is that the depth presence of prison is always there in a country where people oppress and are oppressed. A target on the stoep, set up for the innocent amusement of Afrikaner youths enjoying themselves in a seaside cottage, is not only the black man their parents and mentors are preparing them to kill but also the youths themselves, to be killed in turn. "Tuesday," an endless journey created under that title out of an actual journey and recalled throughout the book with the regularity of a calendar, is the day of release: the day on which Breytenbach himself came out of prison, and also the day of freedom, to which a name must be given if ever it is to come, to jailed and jailer, the day when, as Breytenbach expresses it *totally,* "life must be tempted back to earth." (p. 114)

Breytenbach is a writer who carries his whole life with him, all the time. His work takes on the enormous task of assuming full responsibility for what he was and is; the self cannot be disowned, either by the young Afrikaner growing up as one of the chosen *Volk,* speaking the language of the master, or by the artist fled to Paris (two generations of Afrikaner intellectuals did flee, later than but like the Hemingways and Fitzgeralds, looking hopelessly for a way out of being what they were), or by the failed revolutionary. All these personae are present in every single moment of Breytenbach's working consciousness—the consciousness of the writer, which is different from that which serves for shaving or for buying lettuce. This fusion is what makes it impossible for him to write a work that can conveniently be fitted into even the broad concept of ''story collection'' or ''novel.''

This is not to say that Breytenbach has written a book of fragments, that there is no narrative in the work. Narrative is an old railway line on which service has been discontinued. But of course service does continue; other forms of transport perform the railway's function. Inner logic (concepts, dreams, and symbols) also narrates. It has a sequence of its own, and sequence of any kind is narrative. But this sequence—unlike that of time—is highly individual, different in each subconscious and consciousness, and very, very few writers have the ability to use it as the unique shape of their work. Breytenbach is one of these, the greatly gifted. This inner logic, for which there is no recognized literary form (certainly not the long-polluted stream of consciousness, nor surreal surrender of control) is his form. (Even he cannot label it: ''Mirrornotes of a Novel''—his subtitle—will hardly do.)

With the overthrowing of time values in Breytenbach's writing comes a concomitant freeing from attachment to individual characters. If you are not going to be told what happens to them next, you don't have any obligation to identify with Minnaar or Levedi Tjeling. As Breytenbach himself airily remarks (one of his mirrors is that of ironic self-regard), these two so-called characters ''disappear from the story since they were never of any importance for its development, except perhaps as wraiths to be addressed. . . .'' At first, for reasons of habit, one misses characters, word-skeletons to be dressed up in what happens to them ''next.'' But soon an exhilarating liberty like that of a Buñuel film is granted: if someone walks into a room where the characters are being ''developed,'' why not drop them and go off with him into his life? Here is a work in which all choices (as to which way it might go) are present.

Is it, then, an alternative autobiography? (Breytenbach could have been, might be, all these people.) He writes of ''liquidating the 'I','' but also of ''an 'I,' a departure.'' He himself is the centrifuge from which all seeds are cast and sown again: the horror, the humor, the love, the knowing and unknowing, he has received from living in his world and era. Yet there is none of the self-obsession of a Henry Miller or a Céline. A world is not defined by self: he defines himself by a world—that world in which ''white is posture, a norm of civilization.'' South Africa has produced in this writer an exacerbated self-consciousness, exactly what Stalin's Russia created in Anna Akhmatova—what the English critic John Bayley has called ''the power . . . to generalize and speak for the human predicament in extremity.'' . . . Breytenbach has (has earned) this power to extrapolate suffering beyond what he has suffered himself. And as for responsibility for suffering, a one-and-a-half-page parable/parody entitled ''Know Thyself'' will leave a share of that lodged within every reader.

Writing in the English language, Breytenbach is a phenomenon of the Nabokovian rather than the Conradian order. (No space to take up what I believe is the fine difference here, except to say that Conrad is incomparably at ease in the language, whereas Nabokov's performance is *his* achievement.) A native speaker of a minor language—Afrikaans, derived mainly from Dutch—Breytenbach has a few failures in making new English words out of a collage of old ones. By contrast, his imagery is so exquisite, chilling, aphoristic, witty, that one is reminded how

that ancient and most beautiful attribute of writing has fallen into desuetude in prose. (pp. 114-15)

If Breytenbach's imagery is to be compared with anyone's it is that of Czeslaw Milosz, with whom he shares an intense response to nature and a way of interpreting politically determined events and their human consequences through the subtleties of the physical world. Once more a fusion of the creative imagination makes reality out of mere facts. For the rest, I do not think one need look for comparisons to evaluate Breytenbach's book. It is his own—perhaps the highest compliment any writer can earn.

Exactly what Breytenbach's politics are now is difficult to tell. The matter is not irrelevant; if it were, this beautiful and devastating book would be betrayed, since its chemistry is politics, that chemistry of man opposing man, of good struggling with evil, from which one sees—with a shudder—both mushroom clouds and works of art arise. (pp. 115-16)

Breytenbach's political conviction is no mythical conception of the external world; he had a conviction of the indefensible concrete cruelty and shame of white oppression of blacks, and the necessity to ally oneself with the black's struggle to free themselves. His obsession was that to make this alliance it was necessary to jump the barbed fence between artist and revolutionary, what he calls ''the contradiction between dreams and action.'' He fell—how hard and humiliatingly one gets some idea. But when he laughs at or mourns the spectacle of himself, this does not mean he disavows the truth on which the obsession was based: that South Africa is rotting in its racism, as much under a new constitution . . . as it was under the old name of apartheid.

He writes from the underground that is exile. It is impossible, for his countrymen and for all of us, to stop our ears against the excruciating penetration of what he has to say. (p. 116)

*Nadine Gordimer, ''New Notes from Underground,''
in* The Atlantic Monthly, *Vol. 254, No. 1, July, 1984,
pp. 114-16.*

NEAL ASCHERSON

Mouroir is exceedingly difficult to read. . . . [Of the nearly forty short prose works in the book, a] few, mostly those that were not written for the eye of the prison censor, are comparatively open. ''The Double Dying of an Ordinary Criminal,'' which is about a hanging (Breytenbach's prison included a much-used gallows), is both horrible and direct. But most of the rest are, at first, puzzling. Again, they require the author himself to explain what is going on. ''The texts have no symbolic intent; they only mirror and establish situations and images, situations made up of images.'' In a way, *Mouroir* is a writer's book of prose exercises, or a sculptor's yard full of seasoned blocks of old nightmare ready to be carved.

In most of these pieces, which are not quite chapters, not short stories, not what used to be described nervously as ''prose poems,'' nothing much linear or consecutive happens. Scenes emerge, detailed in the strong moonlight of Breytenbach's imagination, which then dissolve into other, disconnected scenes in a way that is literally dreamlike. (p. 23)

Occasionally, a more conventional or ''finished'' piece turns up in *Mouroir*. In ''The Temptation in Rome'' Pope Giovanni XXXV is consumed by terror that he may die before tasting pangolin's tail marinated *à l'azanienne*. The beautiful "Day of the Falling of the Stars and Searching for the Original Face" is about the seizing of a wild boy, who has been raised with a herd of deer and is now hunted by an inquisitive Academy. The Academicians trap him in a manner that suggests a recurrent theme of the book. They flash mirrors in which the wild boy for the first time perceives himself. He "advanced toward the pools of water held aloft as if by magic. He didn't realize that he was looking behind reality. He didn't know that these tongues could never be lapped up or integrated. He was not aware that he was to forgo for ever the taste of water." (pp. 23-4)

[Breytenbach's writing] is astonishingly vigorous and agile. It can also become lush, indigestible. The dazzle of broken mirror fragments is tiring to the mind; if this is indeed a writer's book of exercises, then many of them are like those acrobatic, self-congratulatory feats that violinists call "fireworks." Still, this man lived in a night that only fireworks could illuminate. By writing *Mouroir* he ensured that, while he listened in reverence to the "wind darkly blowing" through the hole broken in his *mouroir*, he did not fall through that hole and disappear into silence. (p. 24)

Neal Ascherson, *"Living in the Night,"* in The New York Review of Books, *Vol. XXXI, No. 16, October 25, 1984, pp. 23-4.*

BERNARD LEVIN

[In *The True Confessions of an Albino Terrorist* Breytenbach] includes a selection of his poems as an appendix, and as a matter of fact they are not very good; but the savage rhythms and psychedelic colours of his prose constitute poetry of a very high order indeed, making the book sing in the mind and leaving the reader with a palimpsest of horrors designed by a man consumed by twin necessities—of voiding himself of the evil he was crammed with merely by breathing the air of a South African political prison, and of making us, his readers who live in civilised safety, see and hear and smell, taste and feel, what it is like to dwell, as long as Jacob served Laban, in the tenth circle of Hell.

His technique is to alternate exact description of the details of prison life—the sadism and stupidity of the warders and interrogators, the precise nature, weight, taste and texture of the rations, the tricks used by the prisoners to outwit their jailers—with a kind of philosophic context for this photographic reality, in which he speculates, to good purpose, on the nature of evil, on the symbiotic bond that links interrogator to interrogated, torturer to tortured, even hangman to hanged man, on the trap of insanity in which the rulers of South Africa have immured themselves.

The author was not himself physically tortured, though the psychological tortures inflicted on him were such that the distinction becomes erased; the reader can be in no doubt at all that if the gas-chambers of extermination are ever set up in South Africa, there will be no lack of personnel, from the staff of Pollsmoor Prison alone, to turn the taps on, and watch, laughing, through the spyholes. . . .

He is perhaps a little too much given to assuming that every evil effect had a cause originating in a consciously evil intent; ignorance and inefficiency must have contributed much. But even as I write that lofty sentence, I recognise how easy it is

for me to do so, how hard for one who has seen, as Mr Breytenbach has, South African prison warders strip a prisoner naked, take everything out of his cell, soak floor and walls with water, and then throw through the bars an object connected to a powerful electric current. (For fun, incidentally, not to extract information.)

He pays tribute to those who still resist (unnecessarily grudging in the case of Helen Suzman), and he is devastatingly honest about the control exerted by the South African Communist Party over the African National Congress and anti-apartheid organisations abroad. . . . He sees no hope at all, not so much as the tiniest glimmer, of any reform, from within the ruling group, that will avert the inevitable catastrophe; South Africa will only change when its rulers are overthrown. He has no hope, either, that that will be soon.

Bernard Levin, *"Darkness at Noon,"* in The Observer, *October 28, 1984, p. 24.*

JOHN GROSS

Given the ordeal it chronicles *The True Confessions of an Albino Terrorist* could hardly fail to make a powerful impression, but it displays considerable artistry as well. The writing is sharp, restless, often raspingly sarcastic; a little mannered here and there, perhaps, but no matter—Mr. Breytenbach succeeds brilliantly in depicting the horror and squalor and near-madness (and sometimes the sheer madness) of the prison world into which he was thrust.

A world where cement floors have to be polished until they shine like mirrors—but he manages to convey its tedium without growing tedious himself. . . .

The jailers and security men Mr. Breytenbach describes furnish him with an unforgettable gallery of grotesques. There is the swaggering interrogator whom he nicknamed (with a nod to Ian Fleming, and to the language of Afrikaans insult) "Jiems Kont"; the fanatical Master Basie, "the big boss of the prison shrinks"; Major Schorff with his scissors and "his hogshead of angry purple blood," snipping the extra words off letters from prisoners' families that exceeded the permitted length, by however little, and flying into a rage if he thought a prisoner showed signs of behaving like a "mister," a self-respecting human being, rather than a "bandiet."

And how is the system to be brought to an end—the prison system, and the wider evil of apartheid that it exists to serve? Ultimately, Mr. Breytenbach believes, majority rule is inevitable; but if he is a long-term optimist he is a short-term pessimist, and a medium-term pessimist too. He cannot see the whites in South Africa voluntarily yielding ground, or the Western powers using their leverage to force them to; at the same time he has come to regard the African National Congress as free and democratic only "in the double-speak, Orwellian sense," and he does not think there is any chance of it transforming itself.

A bleak prospect, if he is right—though I should add that some of his political arguments strike me as rather muddled. What he does do, however, is to show us the present South African regime for what it is, and to leave us without any excuse for averting our eyes.

John Gross, in a review of "The True Confessions of an Albino Terrorist," in The New York Times, *February 5, 1985, p. 16C.*

JOSEPH LELYVELD

It has been scarcely 70 years since the dominant white group in South Africa, the Afrikaners, started to promote their crude but muscular vernacular as a modern medium suitable for all sophisticated purposes, from writing poetry to running a garrison state. Ethnic power and cultural fulfillment were seen, from the start of this campaign for linguistic self-sufficiency, as mutually reinforcing. When the time finally arrived that both seemed to have been secured, the Afrikaners were moved to a prideful gesture: as a monument to their living language, they erected a huge monolith, suggestive of a tombstone, on a mountainside in the hinterland of the Cape of Good Hope. And there, in an operatic twist, power and culture seemed to collide head on, when the pre-eminent living Afrikaans poet—some say the finest poet ever to write in the language—was charged under the Terrorism Act with plotting to blow up the Afrikaans monument.

"*That* is perhaps the one accusation to which I should privately have liked to plead guilty," Breyten Breytenbach remarks in the course of these headlong and unsparing "confessions," which document his personal misadventure in revolutionary politics and the nightmarish quality of the South African penal system. More important, . . . [*The True Confessions of an Albino Terrorist* represents] the final stage of a major cultural rupture, the poet's apostasy from the creed of Afrikaner nationalism. This did not begin in prison but, inevitably, it was completed there; and the measure of it is that, on his release at the end of 1983 after serving seven years of a nine-year sentence, he resolved to forsake Afrikaans as "the language of oppression and of humiliation" and to dictate, then rework, this book in his second language, English. (p. 1)

[The South African security police] took seven years from him, and he has now struck back with a volume that seems to have been ripped from his entrails. Mocking and sensitive, offhand and bombastic, mystical and raging—he has no time here for the classical virtues of proportion or restraint—it is a book that is almost defiantly unesthetic. Excess is only one of his responses to excess. But it is, he forces us to see, a necessary response. . . .

Taken simply as narrative, Mr. Breytenbach's "confessions" are an important contribution to a corpus of South African prison literature that has been steadily, painfully accumulating over the last quarter-century; and they are especially important since his is the first such memoir to have been written by an Afrikaner. (Albie Sachs, Ruth First and Hugh Lewin—to name three white compatriots whose prison journals preceded his—were all English-speaking leftists.) His ethnic background matters, in part, because it makes him acutely sensitive to the twisted thought patterns of his interrogators and jailers. In the poet's view, they are not other and incomprehensible, not grotesque specimens, but something even more menacing—a force for evil with which his imagination lives, unavoidably, on terms of intimacy. The result for his readers is a gallery of chilling and wholly persuasive characterizations of the genus security cop, subspecies Afrikaner. . . .

[Mr. Breytenbach] acknowledges that there are evasions and omissions in this record. Its main purpose, after all, is not documentary. The layered meanings of his title reflect his in-

tentions, which he then belittles in self-deprecatory asides. ("It will not be even a particularly searing human document," the poet-kibitzer comments at one point. "Too weak, too weak," he complains at another.) These are "confessions" in two senses, Augustinian and Orwellian—willed and forced. Examining his own soul, the poet addresses an imagined interrogator, named in a recurring play on words as "Mr. Investigator," "Mr. I," or "Mr. Eye." The imagined interrogator is apparently an alter ego, at least some of the time. "Mr. I" is also, we discover, black ("my dark mirror brother")—hence the self-designation "albino." Sometimes the poet-prisoner identifies the new "I" he is seeking with Lazarus, or the Minotaur in the maze. But he is too much of a South African to exclude the element of race; he is an albino because, he discovers, he only looks white. "I know," he exclaims with a touch of pride, "what it is like to be black in a white country."

The notion that the imagined interrogator to whom he must now confess is black points to another paradox—the possibility that white repression may serve as a prototype for the regime that will follow. It is this fear that sent Mr. Breytenbach into politics in the first place, a pursuit for which he seems to have been almost wholly lacking in vocation. At the end of his "confessions," he appends a series of self-conscious homilies or "notes" on political themes. These, along with some unsurprising, even dull, reminiscences about underworld types he encountered in prison after coming out of isolation, help to make the book overlong; and while the appendixes may be marginally useful in providing a context for foreign readers who are sure to miss various names and allusions in the main body of the text, the quality of the prose falls off sharply in them.

"To be an Afrikaner," Breyten Breytenbach declares, "is a political definition. It is a blight and a provocation to humanity." In the burned-out crucible of prison, he reinvented his identity and henceforth ceases to be an Afrikaner. The Afrikaans language monument still stands in the Cape and he is safely back in Paris. But there may have been something prophetic about the terrorism charge the security police trumped up. It is a reasonable metaphor to describe this book as an explosive device ticking away at the very foundations of the idea of a white nationalism in Africa. In that sense, and only in that sense, the poet is a "terrorist" after all. (p. 36)

Joseph Lelyveld, "Apostasy of a Prisoner-Poet," in The New York Times Book Review, *February 10, 1985, pp. 1, 36.*

ROBERT COX

It is a terrible indictment of the times we live in that so much of its great literature is prison literature. And yet it is our good fortune that men like Breyten Breytenbach can return from hell with a masterpiece.

Breytenbach, like Solzhenitsyn, survived incarceration by standing siege in the castle of his mind against evil. The comparison between the two men is inevitable, because, despite their apparent political divergence, both writers are like erupting volcanoes, their prose swirling up from the depths, majestic to behold but almost too sulphurous to breathe.

The True Confessions of an Albino Terrorist vindicates the life of the mind. Seven years as a political prisoner in South Africa—two of them in solitary confinement—produced a testament of both love and loathing for humanity. In the end it is love that overcomes loathing, as Breytenbach rises above the horrors of an underworld. (p. 5)

[Breytenbach's] literary achievement is so considerable that the political impact of *The True Confessions of an Albino Terrorist* is like the blast of a truck bomb. He holds up a mirror to the South African penal system, which in turn reflects the self-destructive madness of apartheid. Yet Breytenbach does not forget to offer ''a kind thought to some of the poor bastards who lead their twisted lives defiling mankind by extorting and oppressing and punishing and ruling in the name of 'security'.'' A remarkable man. A magnificent book. (p. 10)

> *Robert Cox, ''South Africa's Prisoner of Conscience,'' in* Book World—The Washington Post, *May 5, 1985, pp. 5, 10.*

William F(rank) Buckley, Jr.

1925-

American nonfiction writer, essayist, journalist, memoirist, novelist, and critic.

Buckley is a leading spokesperson for conservatism in the United States. He is the author of many volumes of political and social criticism; the host of "Firing Line," a syndicated television program; the founder and editor-in-chief of *The National Review;* and a columnist, lecturer, novelist, and essayist. While Buckley's outspoken, strongly conservative position on controversial issues has resulted in divided critical opinion, his engaging wit and energetic prose style are widely admired.

Buckley first received national attention with *God and Man at Yale: The Superstitions of "Academic Freedom"* (1951). Buckley challenges the "antireligious" stance of some of his professors at Yale University. He also opposes the use of certain economics textbooks which, he claims, favor "collectivism." In a review of this book, Frank D. Ashburn stated that Buckley "distorts some facts, is inaccurate often, sometimes twists conclusions, and does this while assuring the reader that he is being true to a position he repeatedly renounces." On the other hand, Max Eastman applauded *God and Man at Yale* for "its arrant intellectual courage" and called it "brilliant, sincere, well-informed, keenly reasoned, and exciting to read." The furor provoked by this book is typical of the controversy generated by Buckley's later works, including *McCarthy and His Friends* (1954), a rare defense of Senator Joseph McCarthy written in collaboration with L. Brent Bozell; *Up From Liberalism* (1959), in which Buckley advocates the abolition of liberal trends in the United States and the reinforcement of conservative values; and *Four Reforms* (1973), a short piece which proposes a repeal of the Fifth Amendment to the Constitution and argues against social welfare programs and school busing. Buckley's other nonfiction books include *The Unmaking of a Mayor* (1966), an account of his unsuccessful campaign for mayor of New York City in 1965; *Airborne* (1976) and *Atlantic High* (1982), which include anecdotes about his sailing adventures; and the journals *Cruising Speed* (1971) and *Overdrive* (1983). Buckley's representative pieces are collected in several books, including *Rumbles Right and Left* (1963) and *Right Reason* (1985).

In addition to his stature as a political and social commentator, Buckley is well regarded as a writer of spy fiction. In such novels as *Saving the Queen* (1976), *Stained Glass* (1978), and *Marco Polo, If You Can* (1981), Buckley relates the adventures of CIA agent Blackford Oakes. Buckley interweaves his fiction with historical events and figures, particularly those involved in East-West relations in postwar Europe. *See You Later, Alligator* (1985), a recent addition to the Oakes series, centers on the Cuban Missile Crisis. Critics have commented favorably on these works, praising Buckley's clear prose, fast-paced narratives, and his use of parody, caricature, and other humorous touches to offset the sometimes grim action.

(See also *CLC*, Vols. 7, 18; *Contemporary Authors*, Vols. 1-4, rev. ed.; *Contemporary Authors New Revision Series*, Vol. 1; and *Dictionary of Literary Biography Yearbook: 1980*.)

Photograph by Elizabeth Gee

McGEORGE BUNDY

The recently published book, *God and Man at Yale* . . . , written by William F. Buckley, Jr., a 1950 graduate of Yale University, is a savage attack on that institution as a hotbed of "atheism" and "collectivism." As a believer in God, a Republican, and a Yale graduate, I find that the book is dishonest in its use of facts, false in its theory, and a discredit to its author and the writer of its introduction [John Chamberlain].

Mr. Buckley's thesis rests on two propositions: first, that Yale is currently anti-Christian and anti-capitalist; and second, that Yale's alumni have a right and duty to insist that it teach "Christianity" and "individualism" as he defines them. Let us consider the method and evidence with which he tries to establish these notions.

Beginning with religion, Mr. Buckley asserts that Yale has a weak department of religion, a high degree of religious apathy in the student body, and a number of un-Christian and anti-Christian lecturers in other fields. . . .

But in fact there is no need to grant Mr. Buckley's claims. What he has done is to take the flimsiest of evidence or no evidence at all, and ignore whatever goes against his thesis. Thus on the basis of a single hearsay quotation—ripped from its context and quite unverified—he condemns as anti-religious a teacher whose profoundly religious influence I myself know from classroom experience and personal friendship. Similarly, in the teeth of the massive testimony of faculty and students alike—and quite without proof—he asserts the ineffectiveness of the saintly man who is Yale's chaplain. He makes no mention of the fact that not one of the ministers or chaplains at Yale, of any faith, agrees with his analysis; he never considers the generally agreed opinion of these and other observers that Yale is more religious than the rest of Protestant America and more religious than it was a generation ago. Most remarkable of all, Mr. Buckley, who urges a return to what he considers to be Yale's true religious tradition, at no point says one word of the fact that he himself is an ardent Roman Catholic. . . .

If possible, the economic section of Mr. Buckley's attack is still weaker. A part of this attack consists of the same sort of personal "evidence" against individuals that he uses in his religious chapter. The insidious character of this sort of innuendo and quotation from lectures lies in the fact that no outsider can readily check the context in which the statements were made. Fortunately a large part of Mr. Buckley's case rests on the theory that Yale students are enormously influenced by the views of those who write their introductory textbooks in economics, and he devotes a long section to an "analysis" of the "collectivism" of four books which have been used in recent years at Yale. (p. 50)

Mr. Buckley acknowledges that outright Marxists and Communists are exceedingly rare at Yale; he mentions none in this book. What he is attacking, and what he finds in the offending textbooks, is the more subtle menace of "collectivism," a term which remains undefined throughout his book. But let us see what he regards as evidence of this menace in the texts. First we find that these textbook writers consider nineteenth-century individualism "impractical of application" in contemporary America. . . . Then Mr. Buckley complains because a quotation he has lifted discusses the excesses of capitalism (excesses which he himself admits, at least in large part); but he omits other quotations, from the same book, in which the *over-all* success of the American economic system is bluntly and vigorously asserted.

Next we find him distressed because the texts in question argue that great inequality of wealth and income should be avoided in a healthy society. Is it ignorance or trickery that leads him to neglect the fact that this "collectivist" view dates back to Aristotle, has the support of his own Church, and is roundly endorsed by the one textbook which he praises?

He then goes on to accuse the textbook writers of "egalitarianism." An inspection of the books shows that not one of the authors supports a full leveling of incomes. . . . (pp. 50-1)

The next iniquity is that the textbooks used at Yale support a progressive income tax. This of course has been the law of the land since 1913. But Mr. Buckley feels that the writers of these books (whom he quotes indiscriminately as if they were all members of a single panel) place undue reliance on the tax, and part of his "evidence" is the fact that one of the texts wants to raise 60 per cent of federal revenue in this way; he then misquotes the recommended tax rates and fails to inform the reader, first, that on incomes between $20,000 and $100,000 the recommended rates would be a substantial reduction of those in force when the book was written (let alone now); and second, that the whole recommendation was based on the views of the Committee for Economic Development, which was led at the time by such great "collectivists" as Paul Hoffman of

the Studebaker Corporation and Beardsley Ruml of Macy's. He fails to mention that three out of four of the texts he attacks urge changes in the income tax laws to encourage venture capital.

Another claim is that these texts do not defend the institution of private property. In support of this claim Mr. Buckley enters a single quotation in which it is argued that majority opinion probably does not consider "free enterprise" to be as basic a right as the four freedoms. The quotation is evidently supposed to indicate a hostility to free enterprise, and it is therefore somewhat surprising to find that the author in question went on, in a passage ignored by Mr. Buckley, to present with evident favor three detailed and practical arguments *for* the institution of free enterprise: that it works, that it is "a central causative factor in the growth of political liberties," and that it satisfies a basic human urge. This total reversal of the author's intent is a measure of the honesty of Mr. Buckley's method, and the sample could be multiplied a dozen times.

Finally, Mr. Buckley comes to the late Lord Keynes. He argues that the texts he denounces are slavish in devotion to Keynes, whereas in fact all four contain major differences from Keynes's position—just as Keynes himself constantly revised and modified his own distinctly capitalist views. The error is unimportant except that it shows Mr. Buckley's ignorance of what he is denouncing. Moreover, the central object of his attack—the policy of fiscal adjustment to prevent a boom-and-bust cycle—is "collectivism" only if Senator Robert A. Taft is a collectivist, for it has his clearcut public endorsement. (p. 51)

In the end Mr. Buckley's indictment of Yale's economics texts turns out to be a self-indictment. This chapter shows him to be a twisted and ignorant young man whose personal views of economics would have seemed reactionary to Mark Hanna.

The worst is yet to come. Having made his "case" against Yale, Mr. Buckley has the appalling effrontery to urge that only those who will support his basic position should be alowed to teach subjects that relate to religion and economics at Yale. He goes on to argue that the alumni have a right and duty to enforce this view—unless they are themselves sympathetic to atheism and collectivism. His personal view of what a university should be is of course his own business, but in urging alumni control of Yale's educational policy he is absolutely wrong, both on the law and on the Yale tradition. His basic argument is that because the alumni pay the piper, they should call the tune. This argument has no more validity than a proposal that the religious teachings of the Roman Catholic Church should be dictated to the Pope by the Roman Catholic laymen who pay his bills. . . . Moreover, Mr. Buckley makes a fair point when he says that most alumni know too little about Yale—although he is totally wrong in his charge that this is the fault of the University authorities. (The principal evidence for this charge is that Mr. Buckley himself was once discouraged from making a speech to a large alumni audience.)

But these considerations do not add up to the conclusion that the alumni as a body have any right or duty or capacity to set the educational policies of the college. They never have and never should. (pp. 51-2)

The book winds up with a violent attack on the whole concept of academic freedom. It is in keeping with the rest of the volume that Mr. Buckley does not seem to know what academic freedom is. He leaps from one view to another, as suits his convenience, and his view of the facts depends entirely on their usefulness to his argument. . . . He totally fails to understand the vital difference between standards for hiring a professor and standards for firing him, and he has no conception whatever of the basic requirements for attracting and holding distinguished scholars. His theory seems to be that because ex-President Seymour once said he would not hire Communists, he should therefore have fired everyone who would not teach his own religious and economic views. This is one view of a free university; fortunately it is not Yale's or Mr. Seymour's.

In summary, Mr. Buckley's basic technique is that of a pretended firsthand report on the opinions and attitudes of Yale's teachers and textbooks, in which quotations and misquotations are given whatever meaning Mr. Buckley chooses to give them and not the meaning their authors intended. This method is dishonest. In addition there is a constant effort to assert that both Mr. Buckley's views and his suggestions for reform are somehow true to Yale's ancient tradition and virtues. This claim is wholly false. Mr. Buckley in fact holds views of a peculiar and extreme variety, both on economics and on the organization of a university, while his religious orientation, honorable and ancient as it is, emphatically differs from that of Yale. . . .

God and Man at Yale has the somewhat larger significance that it is clearly an attempt to start an assault on the freedom of one of America's greatest and most conservative universities. In this sense it is in some degree a sign of the times. . . . Certainly it will put the Yale authorities to an absurd amount of trouble in making answers to questions based on a set of charges that ought to be beneath contempt. (p. 52)

McGeorge Bundy, "The Attack on Yale," in The Atlantic Monthly, *Vol. 188, No. 5, November, 1951, pp. 50-2.*

MAX EASTMAN

William F. Buckley's book with the brilliant title, *God and Man at Yale,* will kick up a glorious controversy. And the controversy won't be about Yale. It will be about college education in the United States, the rights of teachers to teach what they believe, and the rights of those who employ teachers to get the kind of teaching they want. Mr. Buckley's most original and challenging idea is that essential freedom is the freedom of the customer to buy what he wants on the market. The alumni of a college who support it, and the parents who pay their children's tuition, are customers, and the commodity they are buying is education. He assumes that the customers of a college like Yale want their children taught the Christian religion and the free enterprise economy—that is the kind of education they think they are buying. And they are getting gypped, he says, on both counts.

Having just been through a Yale education, Mr. Buckley speaks with inside, or rather underside, authority on the subject, and also with great gusto. He names names and quotes quotes, and conducts himself, in general, with a disrespect for his teachers that is charming and stimulating in a high degree. . . . [Perhaps this] is the best feature of his book, certainly the most American in the old style—its arrant intellectual courage. Yale, instead of bellering, should pin a ribbon on this upstanding alumnus. His book deals a needed body-blow to the rather languidly genteel, Arrow-collarish, suavely sporty, and securely innocuous "Yale man" that inhabits the public mind.

Unfortunately, the book joins together two subjects that, in discussing education, ought to be rigidly separated, religion

and public policy—or as it reads on Buckley's banner, "God and Man." For my part, I fail to see why God can not take care of Himself at Yale, or even for that matter at Harvard. To me it is ridiculous to see little, two-legged fanatics running around the earth fighting and arguing in behalf of a Deity whom they profess to consider omnipotent. . . . Thus I think the thing to do with Mr. Buckley's chapter about God at Yale is to cross it out and forget it.

I suspect that Mr. Buckley will be crossing out that chapter himself before long. For he is very young—young enough to announce that the struggle for Christianity and individualism are, on different levels, "the same struggle"—an opinion which must have been carefully protected against reflection since nursery days. Youth, however, is not a sin, especially when evidenced by an excess rather than a paucity of logic. And that is what Mr. Buckley suffers from. . . .

His second chapter, "Individualism at Yale," is by contrast entirely mature. And it is devastating. He comes out of Yale with the conviction, and he certainly conveys it to his reader, that the politics of advancing collectivism and steadily increasing state control are being systematically inculcated in American boys who go to Yale. (p. 23)

Mr. Buckley is attacked in the current *Atlantic Monthly* by another Yale man, a very irate one, McGeorge Bundy [see excerpt above]. In his way Professor Bundy also deals a blow to the popular concept of the Yale man, for his literary manners are far from those associated with this genteel concept. It is all right to lambaste Mr. Buckley, if he makes you that mad, as "a twisted and ignorant young man." But to call him "dishonest" without detailed and cogent proof is hardly in the Yale spirit.

After reading Mr. Buckley's book and Mr. Bundy's attack on it, I remain convinced that the students of economics at Yale are being pretty well indoctrinated, by and large, with the principles of creeping socialism. Buckley's analysis of those textbooks may be somewhat impetuous—it has to be cursory—but if there is "trickery" in it, Bundy shirks what should be the easy task of proving this with texts. The cry of pain with which Buckley concludes this chapter: "Individualism is dying at Yale—and without a fight," is out of an honestly anguished heart. And it really needs no more justification than the one simple statement, which Bundy does not oppose, that in the textbooks in question "no credit is given—not even in a footnote—to the serious works of serious students who insist that abridgment of freedom is an inescapable product of government planning." (pp. 24-5)

I share the feeling of Mr. Buckley that individualism is dying, not only at Yale but all over the country, and dying at the hands of the Bigger and Bigger Government. And I want to do something about it. But I don't think the thing to do is to narrow the sphere of academic freedom. (pp. 25-6)

The question of the free-market versus the state-planned economy is under debate throughout the free world. The debate is a vital one. In the opinion of the free-market side, all our freedom—our civilization itself—is at stake. This justifies the passion, and the extremism, of Mr. Buckley's protest. For the debate is not being fairly conducted at Yale. . . .

The conclusion I draw from all this is a modest one: namely, that the debate *should be* fairly conducted. Both sides should be adequately represented. The administration should see to it that they are. And I am optimistic enough to believe that this will happen in the near future. It will happen as a direct result of Mr. Buckley's book. And that is high praise for the book, which is brilliant, sincere, well-informed, keenly reasoned, and exciting to read. (p. 26)

Max Eastman, "Buckley versus Yale," in American Mercury, *Vol. LXXIII, No. 336, December, 1951, pp. 22-6.*

SELDEN RODMAN

[*God and Man at Yale* is] an important book, perhaps the most thought-provoking that has appeared in the last decade on the subject of higher education in the United States. The advance publicity and advertising have been misleading. For its author . . . writes with a clarity, a sobriety, and an intellectual honesty that would be noteworthy if it came from a college president. That the author happens also to be a conservative, with whose specific religious and economic ideas I find myself not in sympathy, is less important than that he challenges forcefully that brand of "liberal" materialism which, by making all values "relative," honors none.

In religion Buckley is a devout Christian who believes that the "refusal to proclaim Christianity as the true religion . . . is a sample of the adulteration of religion to the point where it becomes nothing more than 'my most favorite way of living.'" In politics he is an individualist who believes that "support of the weak . . . is an automatic result of the free enterprise system" and that "abridgment of freedom is an inescapable by-product of government planning." In education he believes that it is the moral duty of a privately endowed university actively to promote through its teaching those principles of religion and political economy which the alumni (through their representatives, the Corporation and the President) profess to support. Taking Yale as a fairly typical example of the privately endowed liberal arts college, Buckley proceeds to examine its actual practice in these three categories. This is what he finds.

In the field of religion the basic courses tend to undermine rather than to fortify the average student's respect for Christianity. . . .

In the field of political economy the basic course uses four textbooks which are also used in most of the privately endowed and state universities in the nation. . . . These texts, Buckley charges, attack the free enterprise system and support, covertly or openly, state Socialism. (p. 18)

Buckley assails the "dishonesty" of the officers of the college who pronounce in their speeches and preach from the pulpit the values of Yale's Christian tradition and its championship of the free-enterprise system while conniving at contrary teachings under the shield of "academic freedom." . . . The slogan is simply used, he insists, to justify laissez faire. Thus President Seymour, himself a Christian and a believer in individualism, pronounced that academic freedom demands that the student be permitted to choose between alternatives in an atmosphere of skepticism, but did not see any inconsistency in the fact that Yale's one course in basic sociology was "taught for years by a virulently anti-religious professor" or that its only course in comparative economics is taught by a collectivist—or that Buckley was prevented from delivering a prepared address on this subject to the alumni.

But Buckley's critique goes much further than advocating merely that Yale live up to its professed ideal of presenting "both sides" fairly. . . . Buckley does not believe the student should

be shielded from different values, but he does believe the professor should speak up for what he conceives to be the truth and deflate error. To this end, scholarship and teaching, now related solely for financial convenience, should be divorced. The alumni body . . . should be consulted and polled on what really concerns it—the education of its children, the future intellectual leaders of the nation. Reform of the curriculum, he believes, would rapidly follow.

So much for Buckley's thesis. I have presented the arguments fairly because I respect the spirit and courage of their author. I applaud his assault against what he regards as the dishonesty of those who pay lip-service to one set of principles while teaching the youth, under a smokescreen of "academic freedom," other principles. (pp. 18-19)

Nevertheless (and perhaps because my philosophy took root in different soil) I see the specific issues at stake in a different frame of reference. To Buckley, the great issues today are: (1) Christianity *vs.* Agnosticism or Atheism; and (2) Individualism *vs.* Collectivism. For me, they are rather: (1) Humanism (including freedom of worship for *all* religions, and freedom of speech for non-believers) *vs.* Absolutism (whether expressed in a religion or a political creed); and (2) Individual Responsibility for the community, local, national, and world-wide, as expressed through representative government *vs.* Irresponsible Rule, whether expressed in terms of a government which permits labor to be exploited by business, or one which mobilizes labor to tyrannize through its own elite over others. I disagree also with the author's contention that "the liberal . . . is the absolute dictator in the U.S. today"—he may well be tomorrow! If he were today, MacArthur and McCarthy wouldn't be sounding off, Alger Hiss would still be running the Carnegie Foundation, and Buckley—whose economic views lie somewhere between Adam Smith and Senator Taft—would be languishing in a Federal prison. (pp. 19, 44)

Selden Rodman, in a review of "God and Man at Yale," in The Saturday Review of Literature, *Vol. XXXIV, No. 50, December 15, 1951, pp. 18-19, 44.*

FRANK D. ASHBURN

[*God and Man at Yale*] is a well-written, emotion provoking, superficially convincing tract, set down in able earnestness by a young advocate whose grip on accuracy is less firm than his grasp of assumptions. Vigorous in style, the book entices us to pardon extravagance, and could be to the casual, the uninformed, or the predisposed reader an honest, rather gallant attack on anti-Christianity and anti-capitalism at Yale, which is noted as simply *primus inter pares* in respect to its offenses. A person who can write as well as Mr. Buckley, who can arrange his arguments so persuasively, and support them so recklessly, seems certain to have a profitably polemic future.

On the day of publication the leading *Yale Daily News* editorial said: "A brilliant boy named Buckley came to Yale in 1946. He came steeped in stifling orthodoxy. He came bristling with dogmatic preconceptions. He came, a child of the Middle Ages, into a hotbed of twentieth-century intellectual ferment. . . ." And the same editorial speaks of the book as: "characterized by naivete, misinformation, quotation out of context and crassest dogmatism." . . .

Mr. Buckley distorts some facts, is inaccurate often, sometimes twists conclusions, and does all this while assuring the reader that he is being true to a position he repeatedly renounces. And to make things clear, he implies that anyone who disagrees with him should be eliminated from the Yale faculty.

Many of Mr. Buckley's charges are as unfair as they are inaccurate.... Mr. Buckley's contention comes down to his wishing all courses in religion in a university to be steeped in dogmatic theology. When Mr. Buckley came to Yale, he knew Yale's Protestant tradition. He knew its academic tradition. Yet in his book he seems to offer the alternatives that either Yale should be made intolerable for all non-Calvinists or it should be made intolerable for all who disagree with Mr. Buckley.

Mr. Buckley considers Yale anti-Christian.... Now Mr. Buckley's case could have been stronger if he had said that a considerable part of the undergraduate body, graduate students, and faculty are not greatly or at all interested in formal religion, because these groups mirror the America from which they are drawn, and that America is not predominantly religious minded, however religiously starved it may be.

Mr. Buckley believes that Yale is anti-capitalist. If one is familiar with the individuals who guide its destinies, this seems on its face improbable. If one examines the economics department Mr. Buckley's conclusions are flatly misleading....

Mr. Buckley states an ardent ambition to have the alumni more informed about Yale. In this desire the administration, the active alumni, and the faculty see eye to eye with him. He deplores the lack of alumni interest and control, while demonstrating strongly that the Yale alumni do have a large voice in university affairs. He also demonstrates their ignorance of education in general and Yale in particular. His solution apparently is to have the alumni body as a whole dictate to the administration and faculty. (p. 44)

He totally fails to distinguish between membership, with its responsibility, and administration, with its responsibility. Forty thousand individuals, many uninformed and many far away, cannot and should not administer a great institution. No more appalling fate could be reserved for a university administration and faculty than for them to abdicate their executive and pedagogical responsibilities.

Mr. Buckley is concerned about what he calls academic freedom. But his thesis, stripped to its essentials, is that the way to academic freedom is dogmatism and that the way to save capitalism is by indoctrination—a point of view shared, of course, by Marshal Stalin as a staunch supporter of what millions of people sincerely call democracy. (pp. 44-5)

If this book were anatomized, organ by organ, cell by cell, the evidence of a general metastasis would be unavoidable. There is the lesion of Mr. Buckley, then an undergraduate, not being permitted to deliver a speech very much like his book on the occasion of the dedication of a Yale war memorial.

These intramural questions would not in themselves give the book more importance than should be attached to a family quarrel. But the book does have a serious importance. *God and Man at Yale* stands as one of the most forthright, implacable, typical, and unscrupulously sincere examples of a return to authoritarianism that has appeared. Under the guise of liberty it attacks freedom; under the guise of knowledge it denies the privilege of free investigation and dissent; under the guise of defending capitalism and religion it uses the technique of Dr. Goebbels; under the guise of academic freedom it hides the somber robes of theocracy....

This book is one which has the glow and appeal of a fiery cross on a hillside at night. There will undoubtedly be robed figures who gather to it, but the hoods will not be academic. They will cover the face. (p. 45)

> *Frank D. Ashburn, in a review of "God and Man at Yale," in* The Saturday Review of Literature, *Vol. XXXIV, No. 50, December 15, 1951, pp. 44-5.*

ELMER DAVIS

In a hysterical introduction to *McCarthy and His Enemies: The Record and Its Meaning,* by William F. Buckley, Jr., and L. Brent Bozell ..., William Schlamm claims that the authors—one of them the famous expert on God and man at Yale—have "liberated a territory which for four years was terrorized by the nervous shriek." The territory is that of argument about McCarthy; the nervous shriekers who have terrorized it are the people who disagree with McCarthy—"the entrenched and the conformists, the Babbitts and the snobs—utter fools," all of them. You would think from this that nothing had ever been said on McCarthy's side of the argument—that the liberals (all of whom by definition think the same thing, so that anything any liberal says must be the opinion of them all) had had all the argument to themselves....

Their book, however, is mistitled; it deals with only some of McCarthy's enemies. Better than half of it is devoted to his original attack on the State Department and the subsequent investigation by the Tydings committee. There are a few casual references to others of his exploits, but there is nothing about those that took up most time.... (p. 63)

The book often reads like the work of a man (I have no idea which one) with reasonable ideas, who wants to be fair, revised and stiffened by somebody of a much sterner sort.... [There] is a convincing analysis of why McCarthy is wrong in holding that people who disagree with him are Communists or pro-Communists; yet only a few pages earlier the authors (or one author) were apparently very happy over "McCarthy's blows to the soft underbelly of American Liberals." ... The men he was attacking, according to Buckley and Bozell, were only "atheistic, soft-headed, anti-anti-Communist ADA Liberals."

And such men had better look out. "Some day, the patience of Americans may at last be exhausted, and we will strike out against Liberals. Not because they are treacherous like Communists; but because, with James Burnham, we will conclude that they are mistaken in their predictions, false in their analyses, wrong in their advice, and injurious to the interests of the nation."

For what it comes down to is that it doesn't much matter whether a man is a Communist or not. "We intend to eliminate traitors not so much because treason is wicked but because it gets in the way of American interests." ... There couldn't be much argument against that except the question, what is the national interest at a particular time? The authors pour scorn on the liberals who ask that; but a little earlier they had expressed more exactly what they mean—and what, if it comes to that, we all usually mean—"the national interest *as we see it.*" (pp. 65-6)

And the authors are sure that we need McCarthy and McCarthyism.... "For nearly three decades a handful of prophets—an American Resistance—tried to alert the nation to the Communist threat." It is conceivable that if they failed to alert us as much as they hoped, it was because the Fascist threat—

which this book never mentions—was more immediate and more dangerous. The defeat of that threat undoubtedly made many people realize that there was still another threat behind it, but this is concealed from the authors; they ascribe the growing realization only to the fact that "one spy scandal after another rocked the nation"—which is part of the truth but far from all. "By 1950 a genuine mobilization was under way, and Senator McCarthy—having been fairly recently mobilized himself—became one of its leaders." And now, if he should be discredited, "the mobilization will lose momentum, and perhaps grind to a dead halt." (pp. 66-7)

Communism, say the authors, has had a fair hearing in this country (as it has); we have rejected it (as we have); now we are at war with it, and there are many courses of action open to us. "McCarthyism is a weapon in the American arsenal; to the extent that out of ignorance or impetuosity or malice it urges the imposition of sanctions on persons who are not pro-Communists or security risks, we should certainly oppose it"; we should "go to the rescue of well meaning Liberals." But so long as "it fixes its goal with its present precision, it is a movement around which men of good will and stern morality can close ranks."

Which again raises the question, how precise is the present precision of McCarthyism? Some light on the authors' point of view is thrown by their final appendix on what they call "the George Marshall episode."

This was McCarthy's speech on the Senate floor, and of course under senatorial immunity, in June, 1951, accusing General Marshall of participation if not leadership in "a great conspiracy, a conspiracy of infamy so black that when it is finally exposed, its principals shall be forever deserving of the maledictions of all honest men." . . . It is true, as the authors point out, that McCarthy did not call Marshall a traitor in plain language; but "it is unreasonable to conclude that he was charging Marshall with anything less than pro-Communism," on the contention that "on those issues on which the interests of the Western powers and those of Russia conflicted, Marshall consistently sided with the policy urged by Russia." And they do not exculpate McCarthy, as they might plausibly have done, by saying that he was merely the mouthpiece for an attack written and designed by somebody else.

Nevertheless, Buckley and Bozell point out that McCarthy's conclusions were "based on a dangerous and unusual brand of reasoning" which, logically carried out, "would also brand Roosevelt and Truman as disloyal" (and, it might be remarked, President Eisenhower too). The authors, so far as can be gathered from their somewhat obscure language, do not charge any of the three Presidents with treason; and they assure us that "Marshall's loyalty is not doubted in any reasonable quarter."

Buckley and Bozell stand up for the loyalty of George Marshall. . . .

Further, for imputing treason to Marshall "McCarthy deserves to be criticized; his judgment was bad." But those who think that something else was bad and not his judgment are answered by the argument that he was quite right in "cutting Marshall down to size; he probably merits the title of America's most disastrous general."

Well, he commanded the United States Army in the biggest war we ever fought, and we won it. (pp. 67-8)

What shall we say, then, of men who call him "America's most disastrous general"? Well, it might be charitable to em-

ulate their own charity to the liberals and conclude that they are "dolts rather than traitors." (p. 68)

> Elmer Davis, "McCarthy: His Enemies and His Friends," in The Atlantic Monthly, Vol. 193, No. 5, May, 1954, pp. 63-6, 68.

MASSIMO SALVADORI

Up from Liberalism is a readable and sincere work but as a book it has many, many defects. Much of it is devoted to personalities rather than to ideas, with a good deal of rather scurrilous abuse heaped on opponents. Chapters usually begin with a comment on a book, an article, an episode; the rest consists of generalizations drawn from this single element, the author using throughout the familiar trick of identifying the particular with the universal. There is an excess of scholastic logic, as if the intellectual revolutions of the last 300 years or so—the greatest contribution of the West to man's progress—had never taken place. The reader learns what he should abandon but what is the "up" is left rather vague. Just as Marxists classify under "capitalism" the most varied systems, so Mr. Buckley under "liberalism" puts, absurdly, everything from "modern Republicanism" to integral collectivism. Strangely enough for a writer who prides himself on being a pure logician, there are quite a few contradictory statements.

With all its defects, the book is one more expression of the need deeply felt by a growing number of educated Americans to acquire a clear comprehension of the society they live in and of its ideological foundation. (p. 42)

Buckley is correct in defining as liberals those who put (besides liberty) progress, equality, reason, and the critical use of our rational powers at the center of their position. He is, of course, wrong in attributing to all American liberals an ideological materialism ill-fitting the liberals' assumption that reason (in which alone liberty is immanent) is the guide to man's action, as well as a collectivism which is the antithesis of the wider diffusion of economic power and the balance between capital and labor aimed at by New Freedom and New Deal policies.

With regard to conservatism, the author stresses "freedom, individuality, the sense of the community, the sanctity of the family, the supremacy of the conscience, the spiritual view of life." The meaning of these terms is most clearly defined through the liberal tenets Mr. Buckley criticizes: moderation, tolerance, democracy, equality, academic freedom, scientific thought, the priority of method over goals. To summarize his position he writes: "Conservatism is the tacit acknowledgment that all that is finally important in human experience is behind us."

Putting together the various points made in the book, the reader concludes that conservatism means: worship of the past, hierarchy, dogmatism, and authority—a Metternichian system in which freedom has the medieval meaning of privilege, the scourge of free societies. (pp. 42, 44)

According to Mr. Buckley, liberalism and conservatism are totally incompatible. He attributes to liberalism "the erosion of Western values"—or loss of Western influence in the world—ignoring the fact that this erosion has been the outcome of nationalism, irrationalism, monopoly capitalism, and other features of that revolt against liberalism for which conservatives feel sympathy. In a world in which most people are striving desperately—as is their right—for a better future, Buckley's conservatism has nothing to offer: his book will unfortunately be a valuable tool for Communist propagandists among Asiatic, African, and Latin American nations. (p. 44)

Massimo Salvadori, "The Future Is in the Past," in Saturday Review, Vol. XLII, No. 41, October 10, 1959, pp. 42, 44.

ELLIOTT ABRAMS

[*Four Reforms*] is Buckley's first "book" (as opposed to a collection of columns or a personal memoir) in several years.

Yet *Four Reforms* is so short that one wonders whether in writing it Buckley was not responding more to a conviction that he *ought* to write a book than to any real desire to sit down and do so. Buckley devotes only twenty-odd pages to each of his proposals, which concern welfare, aid to education, taxes, and criminal justice; this hardly provides sufficient opportunity to convert the unbelievers, and if that were Buckley's intention the book would simply be a failure. Recognizing the limitations of space, however, he has chosen a different tack. In each of four complex and highly controversial areas, he has attempted to cut through to the core of the problem with a simple, often startling, usually very conservative, proposal. . . .

Buckley's four reforms may be set forth very simply: he proposes two constitutional amendments, one to repeal the Fifth Amendment and one to forbid school busing and permit aid to parochial schools; and he proposes two statutory revisions, one to replace the progressive income tax with a flat-rate tax, and one to forbid federal welfare appropriations to the richer states. The overall program is not likely to win a very high rating from Americans for Democratic Action, but in fact, little of what Buckley has to say contains much ideological bias.

His criminal-law proposal, repeal of the Fifth Amendment, is typical. The suggestion is on its face a terrible one. Upon reading the text, however, we learn that Buckley favors neither torture nor police brutality, but is instead exercised about a number of very real problems. The first is the Supreme Court's insistence on the "exclusionary rule," the doctrine that illegally seized evidence may not be received in court. The effect of this doctrine is to frustrate, on account of police or prosecutorial misbehavior, the conviction of defendants against whom there is competent and persuasive evidence. . . . Buckley is not alone in wondering why a less costly method could not be devised to curb abuses by law-enforcement officials. Buckley is also disturbed by the endless delays which now characterize so many criminal-court calendars, and in this area too his concern is widely shared.

Buckley's objections to the present taxation and welfare systems are not fundamentally ideological either. The Internal Revenue Code is nearly incomprehensible, Buckley holds, a circumstance which encourages people to believe it is nothing but a maze of loopholes. This is on the whole an accurate charge. Buckley's reform would entail the elimination of virtually all deductions and exemptions—a system which he claims would appear more just to taxpayers than the present, irregularly progressive, one. As to welfare, dissatisfaction with the present scheme is now so widespread that there may well be no one, even among social workers, who wishes to see it continue without reform.

Buckley, then, has little difficulty demonstrating the need for change. He is less successful in proving that his proposals, if put into effect, would solve the problems to which they are addressed. (p. 74)

The reforms Buckley proposes are not novel, most having been favorites of conservatives in general and of Buckley in particular for some time now. His tax proposal, for example, may be found in identical form in Milton Friedman's *Capitalism and Freedom*, published in 1962. Now, lack of novelty is no cause for criticism, but it does lead one to wonder what the purpose of this book might be. (pp. 76-7)

If the last decade has been unkind to liberals, it can only have been demoralizing to conservatives. . . . "Conservative" intellectuals have long been wary of "conservative" politicians, fearing that their commitment was to victory and to the wealthy supporters who would arrange it or make it possible, rather than to "conservative" principles. . . .

In 1964, the massive defeat of Barry Goldwater, a man whom most conservative intellectuals considered a principled conservative in the Friedman-Buckley sense, brought to an end the dream that one of their own could be elected President. The alternative was, of course, to support a "moderate," a man who apparently shared many of their views, and could win. Nixon was the man. . . .

This dream, too, has been shattered, for the Nixon administration has compiled a record which must repel the "true" conservatives almost as much as it does liberals. The administration has not reduced the power of the state or encouraged the private ordering of our social and economic life; rather, it has simply used the power of the state to benefit a different, usually wealthier, clientele, and ultimately to preserve itself in power. . . .

Thus the dilemma is posed: if the nation is not ready to support "true" conservative principles, and if a Republican administration closely tied to big business has proved itself unpalatable, where are conservatives to turn? Buckley's answer appears to be that they must turn back to the people once again, with the same arguments and the same proposals as of old, in the hope and with the conviction that logic and good sense will in the end win out. (p. 77)

Buckley describes his reforms as "entirely procedural," and hopes they will be found to lack "ideological bias"; both comments reflect the defensiveness of a man who feels his substantive proposals and his ideological position to be a minority one.

Four Reforms seems to represent, finally, the realization that conservatives must place political education on at least as high a plane as electoral politics. The book is too brief to be meant as a theoretical contribution, or even a serious intellectual workout; it is instead meant to stir and to influence public debate. It is one of Buckley's 19th-century liberal principles that in such debate, truth must ultimately defeat error (though Buckley has lost too many battles not to understand how distant that victory may be); so, in part, he writes out of commitment to the principles of democratic politics. And to the demands of principle are added those of political expediency, for the very different sorts of defeats Goldwater and Nixon represent for "true" conservatives must show them that their views can triumph only after a great campaign of political education. Buckley writes because he loves to, but there is in this book a sense of obligation, too. (pp. 77-8)

Elliott Abrams, "Public Discourse," in Commentary, Vol. 57, No. 4, April, 1974, pp. 74, 76-8.

TERRY TEACHOUT

Mr. Buckley, needless to say, is a very funny man when it suits him, and it suits him quite often when he is writing about Mr. Oakes [the hero of his spy novels, the latest of which is *Marco Polo, If You Can*]. Indeed, his contagiously high spirits manifest themselves throughout the Blackford Oakes series in a variety of engaging ways: the sheer cheek of ventriloquizing such august personages as Dean Acheson and Dwight Eisenhower; the consummate gall implicit in the invention of, say, a KGB career man who reads *National Review* with furtive relish; and, above all, the genuine wit of Oakes himself, a delightful fellow with a decidedly impish streak. (p. 56)

It is an open secret . . . that Mr. Buckley's purpose in writing these novels is a didactic one; beneath all their disarming revelry, the adventures of Blackford Oakes are intended to explain and justify the Byzantine ways of the CIA to a wider public. In each book, the author posits an imaginary CIA operation guaranteed to set liberal teeth firmly on edge—the assassination of a bad guy in the line of duty, the assassination of a very, very good guy in order to forestall a possible strike on Western Europe by the Russians, the deliberate sabotage of the American space program so as to galvanize the general will—and then proceeds to demonstrate its historical necessity. Given such circumstances, Mr. Buckley is saying, here is the sort of thing the CIA would have done, like it or not; and, though the pill is sweetly coated with lots of good-natured sex and good-humored banter, the medicine inside is definitely for use by adults only.

In preparing these fictional briefs for the defense of his former . . . employers Mr. Buckley inevitably comes up against an ethical issue of the utmost importance to men of good will: Shall the end justify the means? "To live is to maneuver," Whittaker Chambers once said to the creator of Blackford Oakes, and that maxim could easily be taken as the unspoken moral of all four Oakes novels; but Mr. Buckley has additionally chosen to take a stronger, even more explicit stand on the eternal question of ends and means. Midway through *Saving the Queen,* the author causes his protagonist to reflect on the relevance of an old Latin tag picked up at Greyburn College: *Quod licet Jovi, non licet bovi.* "He did not fully understand it then," Mr. Buckley writes, "but did now, and though he realized it could be used in defense of indefensible propositions, nevertheless, correctly applied, it was unchallengeable: That which it is permitted for Jove to do is not necessarily permitted for a cow to do. We might in secure conscience lie and steal in order to secure the escape of human beings from misery or death; Stalin had no right to lie and steal in order to bring misery and death to others. Yet, viewed without paradigmatic moral coordinates, simpletons would say, simply: *Both sides lied and cheated*—a plague on both their houses."

Now Mr. Buckley never stoops to pretending that it is easy to lie or steal (or kill) just as long as you keep your paradigmatic moral coordinates dry. Oakes, who boggled at cold-blooded murder in *Stained Glass,* is actually driven out of the CIA by his scruples in *Who's on First.* But he knows that, in a world full of evil, those who accept the terrible responsibility of imposing the death penalty must also endlessly proclaim the innocence of the executioner or stand by as their moral authority is eroded by public cynicism; and these novels proclaim the innocence of Blackford Oakes and the rectitude of his cause with an eloquence which all their sportiveness cannot obscure. In a literary genre which has become increasingly preoccupied with the universal amorality of spies and their masters, such

an attitude has a refreshingly tonic effect. It also has an oddly familiar ring. No doubt James Bond or Willie Ashenden would have steered clear of discussing espionage in terms of its moral imperatives—but Father Brown would have been right at home talking over with Blackford Oakes the daily dilemmas of those who do wrong to do right; and it is this ethical awareness, combined with the skills of a born writer, which makes the Oakes novels the only modern thrillers that can plausibly be compared to the much-loved masterpieces of Mr. Buckley's distinguished forebear G. K. Chesterton.

In *Marco Polo, If You Can,* as it happens, the moral issues at stake are more clear-cut than usual, and emphasis is placed firmly on the machinations of Mr. Buckley's brilliant plot, with superlatively exciting results. (pp. 56, 58)

Naturally, all the patented Buckleyisms familiar to old Blackford Oakes fans are here in abundance. (Sample: "He homed in on his own, took off his sweater, sat down in the little armchair, and began to read Buckley's *Up from Liberalism.* But his mind wandered. Hardly Buckley's fault.") There's even a new character, sort of; Dean Acheson's normally showy part is trimmed to a mere walk-on this time around in order to make room for J. Edgar Hoover. Nevertheless, anyone in search of a top-notch spy thriller, political inclinations notwithstanding, need look no further than *Marco Polo, If You Can;* and anyone with lingering doubts about the wisdom of allowing Western intelligence agencies to launch covert operations ought to read it closely and think twice. (p. 58)

Terry Teachout, "The Innocence of Blackford Oakes," in National Review, *Vol. XXXIV, No. 1, January 22, 1982, pp. 56, 58.*

EVAN HUNTER

Many of the characters in William F. Buckley Jr.'s best-selling Blackford Oakes spy novels *did* at one time exist, and in *Marco Polo, If You Can* (a lovely title!) we are asked to accept not only historical actuality but the possibility that the various dialogues and schemes attributed to them are *also* real. Mr. Buckley makes it all seem possible, and moreover he seems to be having a very good time pulling the wool over our eyes. Perhaps his devil-may-care attitude accounts for why I found his new novel so enjoyable. (p. 12)

The major details in Mr. Buckley's novel concern a mole in the National Security Council during 1959 and the C.I.A.'s efforts to unmask him or her while simultaneously causing an irreparable breach between the U.S.S.R. and its then closest ally. Eventually, Blackford Oakes finds himself flying a U-2 spy plane (à la Gary Powers) along the Sino-Soviet border. But it is the adventurous Mr. Buckley himself who takes a greater risk than his hero by flying in the face of what is perhaps *the* definitive "mole" novel (John le Carré's *Tinker, Tailor, Soldier, Spy*) and managing to keep us interested and amused throughout his labyrinthine proceedings.

Mr. Buckley, with a little help from his friends, can make completely believable the subversion of an innocent Xerox machine toward devious ends, and he can write surprisingly tender love scenes, which might have been even more poignant for me had I ever fully believed that the people involved were really in the business of spying. But I'm not sure Mr. Buckley believes that, either, and being in the company of someone as charming as Blackford Oakes (and his creator) is perhaps enough to ask. (p. 17)

Evan Hunter, in a review of "Marco Polo, If You Can," in The New York Times Book Review, *January 24, 1982, pp. 12, 17.*

JOHN GREGORY DUNNE

[*Overdrive* is] the latest installment of the long-run Happy Hour that is Mr. Buckley's version of his life. As with **Cruising Speed,** his 1971 excursion along the Buckley Expressway, he sets down the events of a single week, in this instance the Monday to Monday before Thanksgiving 1981. In this eight-day period, Mr. Buckley gives speeches in Tampa, Toledo, and New York, tapes two "Firing Line" shows in Louisville, writes three newspaper columns and a piece for *TV Guide* ("Memorable Guests on 'Firing Line'"), attends *Nicholas Nickleby,* a performance of the New York City Ballet, and a concert by Rosalyn Tureck, goes sailing twice, gives a luncheon for twenty corporate executives (George Bush, the guest of honor, reneges at the last minute for reasons of state and sends in his stead UN Ambassador Jeane Kirkpatrick), has David Niven as a weekend house guest, and decides, in Louisville's Executive West Hotel, to write this book. (p. 20)

The spotlight is Mr. Buckley's alone, and he does not blink in its glare. And yet, at stage center, he is really not very giving about himself, except for that sly self-deprecation that comes so easily to the self-infatuated. In his hands, the art of being disarming is a weapon. We learn that he is ambivalent about the ballet, tries to say a rosary before he goes to sleep, has a customized 1978 Cadillac limousine lengthened two extra feet to give him additional leg room, can catnap easily in ten-minute snatches, gives forty-eight lectures a year, loves peanut butter ("I know that I shall never see / A poem lovely as Skippy's Peanut Butter"), has an unlisted telephone number, got paid ($3,000) for his *Playboy* interview, spends every February and March skiing in Switzerland. The details are often arresting, but offer no clue about the performer, only about the part he plays. (p. 28)

In the face of all this purposeful commotion, it is instructive to look for literary antecedents. If the Norman Podhoretz of *Making It* can be read as Trollope's *arriviste* Phineas Finn, with Midge Decter an unlikely Mme. Max, then with **Overdrive** we are in the country of *The Good Soldier.* It is a world of surfaces, placid and civilized. The effect is at first glinting and funny, but Mr. Buckley's vision is so hermetically focused on himself that one begins to wonder if under that coat of thin veneer there is anything but another coat of thin veneer. The spontaneous is not valued, because it opens a window of vulnerability. One remembers Mr. Buckley's celebrated television encounter with Gore Vidal, when spontaneity spurted from him like pus from a boil. "Crypto Nazi," Mr. Vidal said. "Now listen, you queer," Mr. Buckley replied. "Stop calling me a crypto Nazi or I'll sock you in your goddamn face and you'll stay plastered." This is the true territory of *The Good Soldier.*

Mr. Buckley is an anomaly in American life, a man who has been made, or who made himself, systematically déclassé. "I never knew I was an Irish Catholic until I ran for mayor of New York," he once told Martin Nolan, then a reporter for the *Boston Globe*. His father made his pile elsewhere, the initial strike in the oil business in Mexico, and having made it set about creating a style. The style was mid-Atlantic patrician, a style that his namesake son further alchemized into patrician celebrity.

Yale was the smithy where this created consciousness was forged. (It is invigorating to speculate how Mr. Buckley might have turned out had he gone to Holy Cross or Seton Hall or any of the more primitive academic *stalags* of the Irish and the Catholic.) With strenuous Christian energy, he became the quintessential BMOC, the big man on campus, skipping from success to success, from the chairmanship of the *Yale jDaily News* (via the minor scandal of a unanimous vote, having cast his own ballot for himself), to Skull and Bones, to **God and Man at Yale.** There always has been a sense of the dominant undergraduate about Mr. Buckley, a triumph of managerial style. His is a BMOC view of life; all good naturally flows to the Bones man. (p. 29)

And always he views the world with the amused condescension of the entitled. He drives to Mass with the maids, Rebeca, the "solicitous and fussy Guatemalan," and Olga, "an otherworldly and gay-spirited Ecuadorian," and on the way home discusses with them the mystery of transubstantiation. We are not told how Olga and Rebeca responded to Mr. Buckley, any more than we are told how all those "young, fresh, enthusiastic and resourceful" famous people responded to his ripostes. When it comes to the thoughts of others, Mr. Buckley exercises his *droit de seigneur;* but the *seigneur* himself seems distracted and disjointed, as he approaches his fifty-eighth birthday. The show has been on the road too long. There have been too many plane trips, too many nights spent in Executive West hotels. Mr. Buckley has spread himself so thin that he has begun to repeat himself, repeatedly. **Overdrive** is *Cruising Speed Redux* as last year's **Atlantic High** is *Airborne Redux*. In the new versions we laugh at the memory of old stories better told. The ambiance is "dictated in Switzerland, transcribed in New York." As might be expected, Mr. Buckley is unrepentant. "The unexamined life may not be worth living," he writes, "in which case I will concede that mine is not worth living." He clearly does not believe it, but his is a performance sorely in need of the very examination he refuses to give it. (pp. 29-30)

John Gregory Dunne, "Happys Days Are Here Again," in The New York Review of Books, *Vol. XXX, No. 15, October 13, 1983, pp. 20, 28-30.*

MICHAEL MALONE

[Only] an unencumbered stylist with William F. Buckley Jr.'s insouciance, intelligence and political views could have produced **The Story of Henri Tod.** Indeed, only Mr. Buckley could have written it, and that makes for a curious relation between reader and writer. . . . [Buckley himself] is now so famous a fiction in our national mythology that it is impossible to efface him when reading his fictions.

The novels, five so far, are a kind of Fourth-Reich Saga of the Cold War. Mr. Buckley slides his quite fascinatingly imagined, and appallingly conceivable, intrigues into the unknowns surrounding the secret skirmishes between *us* and *them*—the Central Intelligence Agency and Communism. "Real" people (Truman cheek by Stalin jowl) mingle with moles, gorgeous young women (many, alas, double agents) and suave young men like Blackford Oakes who are trying to make the world safe for democracy by making sure *they* don't get the hydrogen bomb (**Saving the Queen**), don't get their satellite up first (**Who's on First**), don't get along with China (**Marco Polo, If You Can**). Berlin is the geopolitical and morally symbolic center of all the books, but **Henri Tod,** like **Stained Glass** . . . deals with the crises of that city and with the gallant effort to free East Germany from Soviet control and reunify the country.

It is not coincidental that the "devilishly beautiful" spy Blackford Oakes is often found reading Mr. Buckley's books, or books by or recommended by Whittaker Chambers, or quoting letters on Berlin in National Review (also favorite reading material of Oakes's adversary in the K.G.B.); or that Oakes and his narrator so specifically and explicitly share Mr. Buckley's opinions on the dangerous drifting of our weak ship of state. Rather, it is an indication that for the author espionage novels are a kind of firing line through which he intends to convince us that Communism is Fascism, and can't be fought by warriors hamstrung by "liberal" conscience. But the author and hero share more than ideology. . . . All this notwithstanding, Blackford Oakes is no less a prepubescent fantasy of swashbuckling romance and cloak-and-dagger high jinks. Fact does not necessarily justify fiction, and Oakes is no more "realistic" than Scaramouche or Zorro or any other roguish idealist who dueled with a grin against evil. As such, his adventures make for excellent entertainment, nowhere more so than in this smoothly plotted tale of the weeks leading to the sudden rising of the Berlin Wall. . . . Some of Mr. Buckley's earlier characters do not appear in *Henri Tod*. . . . But Oakes himself, beautiful as ever, is still served to us as if he were a gourmet meal, irresistible to all. He takes his obligatory naked stroll round the room after sex while his partner wonders if he "might not have rekindled jealousy on Olympus." He still leads a charmed and charming life.

Of course, Mr. Buckley is famous for his charm also; perhaps its source lies in the audacious complacency of his extraordinary self-content. Except for an epistolary weakness for defensive justification, he would be a paradigm of Renaissance *sprezzatura*. That quality, at any rate, is what so immediately charms everyone from the Queen of England to President Kennedy when they meet Blackford Oakes. Yet, ultimately, it is not social charm but moral earnestness, increasing from novel to novel, that distinguishes Oakes from James Bond types. He is confronted with questions of choice that unsettle complacency, and time after time he (instinctively, impulsively) chooses an individual over what he himself believes to be the "good of the country."

Finally, the history evoked by Mr. Buckley makes us share those choices, and (even when we would choose differently) feel the suffering of people who have lived lives far less charmed than Oakes's. In the Oakes novels the stories of the minor characters, Russians, Hungarians, Germans, prisoners of the Cold War walls, are memorable, not the badinage. As an evangelist, Mr. Buckley should be pleased to think so. Meanwhile, I look eagerly forward to the continuing saga. Will the C.I.A. send Oakes to shoot Diem, to burglarize the Watergate or to invade Grenada?

Michael Malone, "Send in the Tanks," in The New York Times Book Review, *February 5, 1984, p. 22.*

JAMES H. ANDREWS

[With *The Story of Henri Tod*] Buckley once again has given us a rousing good yarn. He has been mindful of the novelist's obligation to serve up generous helpings of vivid description, recognizable and sympathetic characters, on-tune dialogue, and suspenseful intrigue, all spicily seasoned with Buckley's droll humor. . . .

One of the most ingenious features of Buckley's novels has been his practice of concocting fictitious but wholly plausible conversations among such notables as President Eisenhower, Nikita Khrushchev, and Dean Acheson. This time, in a masterly variation on the theme, he gives us chapters consisting solely of the stream-of-consciousness ruminations of John Kennedy. With uncanny empathy and even affection, Buckley captures the young President's intelligence, stylish phrasing, self-deprecating wit, and seriousness of purpose. The chapters are a tour de force of historical imagination and, for my money, the best in the book.

It must be said that *The Story of Henri Tod* is the most pessimistic of Buckley's novels. While the Western world suffers setbacks in some of the earlier works, the reader was left with a sense that victory still would be, or at least could be, snatched from the jaws of defeat. In this story of strategic impotence and personal betrayal, Buckley appears less sanguine about the capacity and will of the West to protect its interests and hold out hope to freedom-seeking peoples.

Learning of the President's decision not to take military action in the event the East Germans start to build the wall, Oakes recalls to a friend the foreboding of Whittaker Chambers, a convert from communism, that he had "left the winning side to join the losing side." The friend gently chides: "Despair, Blackford, is a mortal sin." There, I will continue to believe, is the authentic voice of Bill Buckley.

James H. Andrews, "Cold War Intrigue Makes for Rousing Good Spy Yarn," in The Christian Science Monitor, *February 24, 1984, p. 22.*

WILLIAM BOYD

To a degree *See You Later Alligator* is a perfectly reasonable addition to the spy-thriller genre. Aficionados may find it a little wanting in the glamour/sex stakes. Buckley is charmingly reticent about Oakes' allure and potency. . . . Also, the action creaks. . . . But this is scarcely surprising, for despite the token nods to the ingredients of the conventional spy thriller it seems to me that Buckley is interested in something altogether different. This novel—and perhaps the other five?—belong to what might be termed the didactic revisionist thriller. What Buckley relishes, and what the thriller format permits and condones, is the ability to enter the heads and dramatize the lives of real historical personages. JFK and Che get the most exhaustive treatment, but so do a host of other historical figures, major and minor. And what emerges as a lively and provocative subtext is an oblique and challenging view of the Cuban missile crisis and an intriguing interpretation of Che Guevara as dupe and to some extent scapegoat.

One wonders if Buckley, looking at the way his great rival Gore Vidal is rewriting American history through his historical novels, has decided to do the same for the 20th century through the medium of the thriller? Anyway, whatever the motives, it is the historico-political subtext that makes *See You Later Alligator* an enjoyable read and not the time-worn and predictable thriller mechanics of saving the world from destruction.

William Boyd, "Blackford Oakes Meets Che Guevara," in Book World—The Washington Post, *March 24, 1985, p. 5.*

JAY CANTOR

The plot [of *See You Later, Alligator*] is that the Russians are trying to fool the Cubans into believing that the Americans are planning to invade the island again. Fidel will then accept nuclear missiles. Bradford Oakes—Buckley's James Bond—not knowing about the missiles, is in Cuba to negotiate a hands-off-Cuba agreement while Che (for Guevara), not wanting to trade American for Soviet domination, wants a treaty with the United States rather than Soviet missiles. Will Oakes discover the missile emplacements? And will he be able to get the information back to Washington before the missiles can be armed?

This book . . . has its share of grotesque and sadistic Soviets. It, too, has playful hints of Latin sexual mysteries, daring escapes and implacable friendships. The novel is slackly written, but Buckley's prose achieves a certain energy in describing a colleague of Oakes', a former KGB agent. Repelled by Soviet sadism . . . , he has joined the winning side. Here Buckley senses a complexity in those who live beyond the law in order to serve the law—perhaps at the cost of their own damnation. This is *Realpolitik* inflected by a kind of Manichaeism. It reminds us that the word *assassin* originally named a Muslim brotherhood of gnostic politicians who would kill for the faith.

Perhaps because Che is, in his way, of this brotherhood, Buckley can, to some extent, give him his due. Guevara here is subservient to the machinations of a dictator's unpredictable, narcissistic will. He must make monstrous compromises. But Che still has a sense of what integrity means, and what cause he fights for. He provides a credible debating partner for Bradford Oakes.

Oakes himself, though, is a somewhat slight hero, unsullied by compromise because he acts so little. His main claim to the star role seems to be his good looks—the kind of beauty that can provoke exclamations even from the puritanical Guevara, who wonders how many Cuban women had sexual intercourse with American tourists, and ''. . . not by handsome athletes like you'' but with ''bloated bibulous capitalists.'' This remark would make most sense, I think, if Buckley meant to suggest a homosexual undercurrent. But the novel lacks the sensibility to deal with undercurrents. Instead, Buckley too, in the end, comes up with the unconvincing plots and words of adolescent romance, the matter of Troy without the poetry. The human dimension of politics turns out to be just another episode of *All for Love*. (pp. 3, 11)

> *Jay Cantor, ''The Soviet-Cuban-Missile-Crisis Soap Opera Twice,'' in* Los Angeles Times Book Review, *April 7, 1985, pp. 3, 11.**

Anita Desai

1937-

Indian novelist, short story writer, and author of books for children.

Desai's works have been praised by critics as important contributions to a new phase in Indian literature which centers on problems in contemporary Indian life. Desai describes her writing as an attempt to discover "the truth that is nine-tenths of the iceberg that lies submerged beneath the one-tenth visible portion we call Reality." Her fiction, therefore, is concerned primarily with exploring the emotional and spiritual states of her characters and the outside forces which influence them. Desai's sophisticated use of image and symbol supports her rich, sensuous style, and she is often acknowledged for her skillful evocation of atmosphere and place.

As Desai's characters struggle to meet the challenges of contemporary life, discordant relationships, particularly among family members, often erupt in violence. Her first novel, *Cry, the Peacock* (1963), examines a young wife's growing despair as the incompatibility of her marriage drives her to kill her husband and commit suicide. In *Voices of the City* (1965) Desai uses the city of Calcutta as a backdrop for the story of a brother and two sisters drawn into the decadence of urban life. In *Bye-Bye, Blackbird* (1971) Indian immigrants in London face the conflict between Western culture and their Eastern heritage. *Where Shall We Go This Summer?* (1975) depicts another despairing wife, and *Fire on the Mountain* (1977) examines the tense relationship between an old woman and her great granddaughter, whose erratic behavior causes destruction.

The Clear Light of Day (1980), which describes the reunion of a once affluent family, is Desai's most highly acclaimed novel. The atmosphere of the decaying family home and the hot, dusty summer adds to the spiritual malaise of two sisters as they examine their memories and come to understand the importance of the family in their lives. Desai's recent novel, *In Custody* (1984), satirically depicts a bumbling, ineffectual protagonist whose life and marriage become increasingly complicated by his relationship with an old Urdu poet. Desai has also published a collection of short stories, *Games at Twilight and Other Stories* (1978), as well as books for children and young adults.

(See also *CLC*, Vol. 19 and *Contemporary Authors*, Vols. 81-84.)

MEENAKSHI MUKHERJEE

[The essay from which this excerpt is taken was originally published in the first edition of The Twice-Born Fiction *in 1971.]*

[An] Indo-Anglian novelist whose distinctive style and intensely individual imagery deserves mention is Anita Desai. She is a comparatively young writer who has written only three novels so far, but already her style shows a strong individuality. Her language is marked by three characteristics: sensuous richness, a high-strung sensitiveness, and a love for the sound of words. In her first novel the style had a curious compatibility with her theme because the narrator of *Cry, the Peacock* is a hypersensitive young woman, tense and over-wrought. The

manner of narration reveals elements of her personality. The narrator's slow advance towards insanity is the theme of the novel, and the main pattern is the contrast between this woman's response to the world through her senses, and her husband's response through his intellect. Gautama, the husband, is cerebral by nature while Maya, the narrator, lives by her senses of touch, smell, sight and taste. . . . If the extravagance of sensuousness is somewhat oppressive . . . , it is not an inappropriate effect because this is the record of the perceptions of a woman on the brink of insanity. She is high-strung from the beginning, but before the final break-down comes, she is given some passages of startling imagery. . . . The conjecture that style in *Cry, the Peacock* is part of the device of characterization of the narrator seems plausible when we read Anita Desai's second novel, *Voices in the City*, which has some of the earlier intensity and richness, but lacks the extravagance of imagery found in the first. Also, the use of rare words is far less frequent now. In the second novel we no longer find words like 'oneirodynia', 'obmutescence', 'tenebrific', 'opsimaths', 'crepuscular', or 'sequaciousness', which were part of the general vocabulary of *Cry, the Peacock*. The second novel is not a first person narrative; it is divided into four unequal parts, telling the story of a brother, two sisters and their mother respectively, who live in separate worlds of their own but whose lives are indirectly woven together. In this case the style of narration cannot serve as a device of characterization. Only one section is an extract from a diary, hence written in the first person; the rest is in the author's own voice. If any character in the novel is akin to the neurotic narrator of the earlier novel it is Monisha, a sensitive childless young woman imprisoned in a huge oppressive joint family household. Monisha's claustrophobia and exasperation culminate in suicide, and, appropriately enough, the style and imagery in the pages from Monisha's diary come closest to the language of the heroine of *Cry, the Peacock,* another desperate woman. One complaint that the reader could have against Anita Desai is that her writing is so tense and tightly strung throughout that it leaves him breathless. But this is at the same time her strength, because it is the natural mode of expression for her uniquely personal vision. In spite of the comparative smallness of her output to date, Anita Desai is a rare example of an Indo-Anglian writer who achieves that difficult task of bending the English language to her purpose without either a self-conscious attempt of sounding Indian or seeking the anonymous elegance of public school English. (pp. 188-91)

> Meenakshi Mukherjee, "The Problem of Style," in her The Twice Born Fiction: Themes and Techniques of the Indian Novel in English, *second edition, Arnold-Heinemann Publishers, (India) Private Limited, 1974, pp. 165-97.**

DARSHAN SINGH MAINI

[Anita Desai's *Cry the Peacock* is], next to Raja Rao's book, *The Serpent and the Rope,* the most poetic and evocative Indo-Anglian novel. It has the quality of a *tour de force.* There is something in the grain of this novel which connects it with the mythopoeic and subliminal aspects of Indian life and reality. If in the end, it falls short of greatness, it's because the dramatic story is not potent and varied enough to carry the burden of sustained lyricism. In short, the paucity of events and the absence of the historical moment and sense seem to have attenuated the tale. . . . *Cry the Peacock* remains a splendid piece of writing, but not a great work of fiction. It is essentially a *nouvelle* like her latest work, *Where Shall We Go This Summer?* . . . , which is again a poetic piece homing back to that book. Clearly, Anita Desai feels that where the impulse is poetic rather than moral, social or political, it'll be dangerous to stretch the tale beyond a point. Thus, the *nouvelle* or the long short story answers best to that kind of inspiration. Henry James, Conrad and Lawrence too have written great *nouvelles* where the *single* idea or motif required an extended but intense and packed expression. The *nouvelle,* in short, has its own unique genius and character. But where it aspires to be a novel, as *Cry the Peacock* does, it's bound to encounter difficulties and doubts. The fact that Part I and Part III of the novel are a 3-page and 7-page affair respectively will show the ambiguity of the exercise. As Prologue and Epilogue, these pages may be justified, but they are too thin to carry conviction as "parts" of a novel.

Quite appropriately, however, these parts are told in the third person, and they are the authorial statements, albeit lyrical, on the chief protagonist's state of mind before and after the traumatic event towards which the story marches inexorably in Part II. And significantly, the harrowing tale of botched relationships and ominous intents is put in the mouth of Maya herself. The technique succeeds chiefly because Part III, which is a kind of requiem for the deranged heroine living in a perpetual twilight of the mind, needed to be told by someone other than

Maya. The middle story with its wave-like, sinuous movement is, thus, best rendered through her own consciousness and in her own agonised idiom. The centrality of her truth being essentially subjective, the long smothered wail of a lacerated psyche finds an apt expression.

In the opening Part, we see Maya, a childless young wife married to a reputed lawyer, nearly twice her age—a father surrogate—grieving over the death of her dog, Toto. The death motif . . . is built into the structure of the story which is an extended ode to *thanatos.* In Maya, the death-wish surfaces when in her flight from the shades, she indulges in a riot of funereal fears and musings. At the same time, she is achingly responsive to the beauty and poetry of life. The tension thus built up defines the misery of her being.

The theme of husband-wife alienation—a recurring motif in Anita Desai—is not developed in a slow, incremental manner such as we find in typical psychological novels. Through simile, metaphor and symbol, the two spouses are evoked for us as opposed archetypes. Whereas Gautama is an efficient, pragmatic, unsentimental person, a "thinking reed", in short; Maya, as her name signifies, is not only a creature of graceful illusion, but also a creature of song, dance and flower. (pp. 217-18)

Maya, for ever a prisoner of the past, lives almost perpetually in the shadow world of memories which engulf her, wave upon wave. One memory, however, a nodule of pain, has been throbbing in her consciousness, and has assumed the form of an ominous *fixation.* An albino astrologer had predicted death for one of the spouses four years after their marriage. The death of Toto has queered the pitch, and she has visions of her own dissolution and extinction.

Though Anita Desai makes little use of depth psychology as such, the interior orchestration of Maya's anguish is a tribute to her powers of poetry and penetration. The reiterative nature of the moon, drum, desert, rodent and lizard imagery (an imagery of insanity, hysteria, aridity and sliminess) in relation to Maya's premonition of death, and of the imagery of bird, tree, wind, flower and fruit in relation to her childhood felicities clearly establishes the psychological pattern. In fact, the poetry here is released as a result of the tension between these two sets of intersecting imagery.

During all this nightmare of animated and induced suffering, which shows a masochistic streak in her, she moves farther and farther away from reality. She descends into the hideous well of loneliness and unreality where the only echoes are those of the albino's dread prophecy and of the peacock's cries of death in the moment of love and orgasm. (p. 219)

As the black and sultry mood of hushed expectancy deepens, one can see the novel, like its crazed heroine, panting for a cloudburst and relief. The fury of the duststorm towards the end matches the fury of the emotional tornado whipping Maya and blowing her about. Anita Desai, like D. H. Lawrence, is exceptionally effective in portraying graphically and poetically scenes of physical and animal violence.

So Maya hurls down her husband into death in a blinding moment of unbearable agony. She has proved the albino astrologer right, and has become the instrument of her own crazy destiny! The wheel of irrationality has come full circle. (p. 220)

Cry the Peacock is a typically "feminine" novel, a novel of sensibility rather than of action. It has the quality of an orchid and of a flute about it. Its concern is almost wholly with the terrors of existence, and it achieves its effects through a series of exploding and multiplying metaphors.

In her second novel, *Voices in the City,* Anita Desai has sought to break the stranglehold of lyricism which threatened to become ingrown and autophagous in *Cry the Peacock.* Obviously, she realized the need to subordinate it to the discipline of events, and work it out rather than allow it to feed upon itself. Also, she appears to have realized the point that her first novel, despite its power and poetic appeal, was deficient in the sense of history and the sense of place. A novelist must achieve diversification of character and incident as also typicality in order to make the story a significant segment of contemporary reality. Whereas a poem could by the nature of its dialectics and mechanics turn inward and yet be viable, a novel even when doing so, has to be close to the pulse of time and to the beat of events. It does not admit of the irrationality that characterises poetry. I suppose it is the awareness of this fact which has made Anita Desai turn more outward. *Voices in the City,* then, is an effort at realizing at once the vertical and the horizontal planes of reality. That the novel somehow fails to effect such a synthesis only goes to suggest that Anita Desai has yet to strike a story that will meet the requirements of her poetic imagination. (pp. 220-21)

Anita Desai's aim [in *Voices in the City*] is to capture the polyphonic music of the metropolis, and Calcutta which forms the backdrop of the story is therefore far more realistically realized than the Delhi and Lucknow of *Cry the Peacock.* Whereas in the first novel, the cities are vague presences evoked through symbols, in the second, we are taken through the winding lanes of Calcutta and its suburbs, and feel the pulse of a city alive. Though "the monster city that lived no normal, healthy, red-blooded life but one that was subterranean, underlit, stealthy and odorous of mortality" is seldom absent from our consciousness, it's the Calcutta of the fashionable fringe and the arty set on the one hand, of the down-and-out intellectual waifs and vagrants on the other that we see here. It's not the Calcutta of a volatile and menacing proletariat, the Calcutta of barricaded streets, acid-bombs and burning buses and tram-cars. But Anita Desai does well to confine herself to the little city within city. That's why her picture is vivid, authentic and memorable as far as it goes.

At the centre of this picture is Nirode, the hero of the novel, a typical Bengali youth gone sour on his elders and betters. . . . Bitter and brutal, he is nursing an over-size grouse against the universe. His Hamletian disgust and cynicism which appear simulated and overblown do not make him the "outsider" of his fancy, despite his overt references to Camus, Baudelaire and Kafka. We find him skirting the bohemian world of booze, jazz and women because, like most of his fraternity, he is an introverted romantic and gets a "kick" out of intellectual dissipation. If he really has "dark and demoniac dreams", they do not explode into reality. He is, in fact, a type that Bengal, in particular, has been throwing up in heaps since the turn of the century. Volatile, restless, loquacious and anarchic, he can neither turn his undoubted gifts and talents to commodity and become a part of the Establishment, nor become a true revolutionary or a path-finder. He is caught in a kind of intellectual vice. His nausea indeed is nauseating. There is something hollow, something phoney about his protestations and diatribes. A rootless nihilist, he has nothing to clutch at, no religion or creed or doctrine. He is, in fact, a hang-over, twilight revolutionary who goes to seed because he has abused his intellect in the name of freedom. He cannot "connect" because he has

no shared community of values. Unlike Camus's "outsider", he makes no significant gesture to establish his credentials as one who has opted out of the "absurd" world. . . . [He] keeps one foot gingerly poised over the threshold of the Establishment, though he may never join the ranks. In Nirode, a psychic outlaw, Anita Desai has presented successfully the archetype of the Bengali rebel in search of a cause. (pp. 221-22)

Part II entitled "Monisha" is an account of the equally fractured and starved life of Nirode's married sister. To lend a tone of immediacy and anguish to the account, Anita Desai resorts to the method of the diary. It is from Monisha's long and searching and self-confronting entries in the diary that we construct the graph of her psychic life. She notices that it is the absence of "the element of love" which has made, both brother and sister "such abject rebels, such craven tragedians"! As days pass, the void in her becomes unbearable. The introduction of yet another sister, Amla, gay and provocative and destructive, hardly improves the situation. Her escapades and affairs do not quite fit into the pattern. It's as if once Nirode was emptied and done with, the novelist saw no way of carrying the story forward except through a vicarious involvement in the lives of his sisters. The two friends, Sonny and Jit Nair, as also the painter, Dharma, are necessary adjuncts to Nirode's pointless odyssey. They do not acquire enough steam to move on their own. In short, the novel gets stuck up because the hero lacking inner dynamism only repeats himself, making a parody of his essential self. There is, however, an effort in the end to salvage him. Monisha's "cloistered tragedy" culminating in suicide—a fiery ordeal described with the same intensity that characterised *Cry the Peacock*—seems to give him a momentary sense of life's "grace." . . . (pp. 222-23)

Earlier, talking to Amla, Nirode says, "All this fighting to carve out a destiny for oneself—it's nothing compared to the struggle it is to give up your destiny, to live without one—of either success or sorrow. But it's a greater victory because it brings you in the end, silence and solitude, and those are the two most powerful things of all."

But all this yearning for peace and stillness is as phoney in Nirode as his earlier "sound and fury". We are not convinced. And one wonders, if he himself is!

Voices in the City shows a different, if less intense, Anita Desai. She has obviously made a willed effort in the direction of the realistic novel. The limited success underscores a real problem for the novelist. The purely poetic novel such as *Cry the Peacock* seems to lead to a *cul-de-sac;* the realistic novel of social reality is still struggling to be born. Where will she go from here? The next novel, *Bye-Bye Black Bird* . . . gives a muted uneasy answer.

The theme of the Indian immigrant in England has so much powder for the imagination that a novelist has a tailor-made situation ready to hand. And it's a situation tractable both to comedy and tragedy at once. For in any human imbroglio involving cultural contrasts and confusion, there is, beneath the drama of irony and mirth, a nagging sense of tragedy. In electing to write on this subject, Anita Desai must have pondered the problem in some such manner. As it is, she does not have the kind of dry-eyed humour and wry compassion we associate with an R. K. Narayan. Her gift for comedy is severely limited, and it's more functional than visionary or "absurdist". Essentially, she is not a novelist of social comedy and manners, or even a novelist of ideas. As we have seen, her *forte* is the poetic novel of sensibility. But the tragic aspect which ought to have appealed to her, and which could have given the story intensity somehow remained muffled in *Bye-Bye Black Bird.* This is not to suggest, the novel set out to do one thing, and ended up with something different. Anita Desai is a careful artist in full control of her material, and as such, the novel's success is achieved within the terms of her purpose and vision. What, in fact, I have in mind is the idea of a story wherein a cultural *clash* may finally turn into a cultural *shock* with all the air of high tragedy. (pp. 223-24)

The novel opens with the arrival in England of Dev, a young Bengali student, wanting to enter the prestigious London School of Economics. He is, as we shall soon see, a paler Nirode, a sort of carry-over from Anita Desai's earlier novel. His London host, Adit Sen, with his English wife, Sarah, is set up from the start as one of the immigrant types—the Indian intellectual *manqué* who has, both by training and aptitude, imbibed the poetry of British life and settled down to an exciting discovery of his *authentic* self on these *alien* shores. Thus, the easy, natural banter which characterises the verbal skirmishes of Dev and Adit has, one feels, the quality of shadow-boxing. Dev, full of pique and prejudice, is shown reacting to the English snobbery, reserve and taciturnity in a text-book manner. He's the Bengali rebel come abroad, not to pawn away his dear Indian soul, but to keep it inviolate at all costs. Any hint of affront to one's dignity as man is to be countered with the full force of one's personality. Adit's "Englishness" is naturally a sitting target for Dev's sniping. However, his sallies are nearly always turning into squibs, for it takes Adit so little to deflect Dev's arty Anglophobia. Sarah, desperately quiet and helpless and vague will not enter the jolly fray. She knows she can be so easily misunderstood. A delicate balancing of emotion and will is needed to shore up her spiritual strength.

Though lively, the Adit-Dev thrusts and counter-thrusts have a certain air of artiness about them. It's when Dev starts "doing" his London in the company of the Sens that Anita Desai's writing assumes its natural poetic and chromatic qualities. . . . The sensuous plunge into the sights and sounds of London is clearly something that solicits her imagination in a special way. The great dowager city's civilized air, with its beautiful green parks, its rosy-cheeked and butter-fed children, its easy, unself-conscious lovers, its dreaming churches and spires, its heaving pulse and beat, is, at bottom, a spiritual experience. But, Dev's London is essentially the tourist's London, and Anita Desai cannot resist the temptation to take us along to all the familiar places of interest. It's too neat and trim and pretty to remain an enduring presence.

Meanwhile, Dev, the declared sceptic, is silently and unconsciously yielding to the spell of English life. . . . However, his passage from one state to the other has not been psychologically chartered or treated by Anita Desai. The image of Dev as "a Kafka stranger wandering through the dark labyrinth of a prison" is academic and misplaced. It's a figure of rhetoric, not of reality. Thus, his later "conversion" appears as suspect as his initial rebellion.

To give spread and density to her story, Anita Desai has brought in a few Indian and English characters other than Adit, Dev and Sarah. However, except for the spinster Emma Moffit, a decrepit, wind-blown, untidy and loosely organised landlady whose profile is "fixed" in a deliciously satirical vein, other characters such as Jasbir and Mala, Samar and Christine Langford etc. are paper-thin types; they do not acquire the pinch and bite of personality. Nor do the unspeakable Sikhs downstairs come to life. They are simply treated as a vague disturbing element, more a joke and an embarrassment than persons with their own unique problems. When a novelist is obliged to resort to static stereotypes, it's a sign, the creative imagination is not really engaged.

And when the London scenes are done, the story obligingly shifts to the fabled English countryside with its picture-postcard beauty and its idyllic charm. It appears as though the novel were proceeding according to a formula. It does seem in danger of turning into a programmatic book. But though it's the English countryside that queers the pitch and effects a spiritual crisis for Adit, we prize these pages more for their rich Keatsian descriptions than for their dramatic intent. In fact, to my mind, the change in Adit is poorly motivated, and lacks psychological veracity and depth. However, the controlled lyricism of Anita Desai, as fields and meadows, brooks and dales, bees and birds, cats and kine fill up the water-colour picture, is one of the great attractions of the book. The synaesthetic imagery of sound, colour and smell is richly evocative. (pp. 224-26)

The Hampshire home of Sarah's parents, upon which the Sens descend with their loud Indian friends is, on the whole, well done. Whilst the mother, Mrs. Roscommon-James, is a stuck-up bourgeois matron who cherishes her "precious narrowness" and her "cultivated restraint", the father, a retired physician, has lapsed in old age into a dirt farmer. It's not a place that could inspire much comfort or confidence. But Anita Desai's putative technique undermines the spirit of the crisis in Adit towards which the story is to move. To say that the brief stay in the Roscommon-James home was "marred by tactlessness, by inane misunderstandings, by loud underlining of the basic disharmony of the situation" is to substitute statement for drama. Though a few flitting moments of anxiety and the Indian *faux pas* are mildly dramatic, they do not add up to any big scene. It may not be the novelist's intention to do such a scene, but the novel seems to plead for the type of dramatic scenes we see in a poetic novelist like D. H. Lawrence.

Adit's sudden nostalgia for the Indian vastnesses and wildernesses precipitated by the visit to the Roscommon-Jameses and strengthened by the Indo-Pak War somehow is a *static* emotion. The decision to return home with Sarah who is expecting her first child is essentially Anita Desai's decision—a novelist's manipulation, in short. As for Sarah, who has few regrets leaving England, the struggle never hots up in her consciousness. Here was another opportunity missed. And when finally Adit's and Dev's roles are reversed, we are again left with a lyric statement, not a contrapuntal treatment. . . . England has said "good-bye" to one "black bird", but offered a cuckoo-nest to another. How long will the new fugitive stay? Who can tell? I wonder if Anita Desai herself can hazard a guess.

In her next book, *Where Shall We Go This Summer?* . . . , Anita Desai returns to the theme of alienation and incommunication in married life—the theme of her celebrated first novel. It appears as though she wanted to do *Cry the Peacock* over again in a more controlled and less hallucinated and exotic manner. That's perhaps why the wife's loneliness in this *nouvelle* is the loneliness of a woman, a wife and a mother—a loneliness *conditioned* by society and family. Whereas the childless Maya's *angst* is existential and metaphysical, Sita's ache is essentially domestic and temporal, though there are moments of pure terror and void even in her life, giving her state an existential dimension. The poem, by C. P. Cavafy and the verses of D. H. Lawrence used in the book apparently authenticate this aspect of the heroine's ordeal.

The *nouvelle,* divided into three almost equal parts, is once again planned as a dialectical exercise where perception (the present), memory (the past) and dream (the future) are sought to be structured in that order, and also as coextensive units of consciousness and time. But the paucity of social detail again leaves the book a flawed poem.

Part one—"monsoon '67"—which opens on a summer day in Manori, a small island off the Marve mainland, has a certain unhurried air about it at the start. But when Sita, a middle-aged woman, accompanied by two of her children, Menaka, a sharp, temperamental young girl, and Karan, a restless little boy, arrives there in a mood of desperation and doubt, the island house, deserted for over 20 years, soon becomes an apt metaphor for her condition. Unable to bear the anguish of another pregnancy, her fifth, she has bolted from Bombay in a blinding epiphany of terror, leaving Raman, her husband, in pain and despair. She had come there "in order to achieve the miracle of not giving birth". She would, she madly believes, *keep* the child *inside* her. For "wasn't this Manori, the island of miracle?" In a flashback scene, we see a desperate woman unable to control her nausea and hysteria, and panicking out of the house in a whirlwind of confused emotions. Obviously, some deep and dark upheavals are taking place in her psyche. The pent-up misery of her isolation and loneliness in the family has spilled over. A busy, indifferent husband and the grown-up children, distrustful of her melodramatic outbursts, have driven her to the edge of the precipice. As the Cavafy poem underscores her moral perplexity, she must say "No again"—"the right No", even though it "crush" her for the rest of her life! The mad idea of containing the baby in the womb for keeps is surely one of the classic cases of *regression* and retreat from reality in Freudian psychology. It's a variation on the death-wish in her—a theme explored more eloquently in *Cry the Peacock.* (pp. 226-28)

The concluding part, "monsoon '67" finds Sita still struggling to find an equation with the bored, uninvolved Menaka, and an answer to her existential dilemma. When she argues with her daughter regarding the poverty of science and statistics, and the opulence of art, possibly it's the voice of Anita Desai herself. And when one day, her husband suddenly turns up there, and she finds both children eagerly responding to his presence, she feels evermore diminished and forsaken. The "one happy moment" she can recall in a married life of protracted drift is the moment when she saw a young Muslim woman and her "aged" man in the Hanging Gardens, "a work of art", as it were. But such a weak epiphany does not connect. Nor are we prepared for the sudden glow and the decision to return to Bombay and to sanity. . . .

To sum up, Anita Desai's development as a novelist appears to be somewhat circular. She has undoubtedly brought her maverick muse under discipline, or called the muses home, so to speak. Also, during this period, she has made some authentic efforts to diversify the base of her stories. But, as I have averred earlier in this essay, she is somehow unable to invent events and episodes that may bring out the dramatic potential of her *donnees.* There are, therefore, no great scenes in her, but moments of lyric beauty and intensity. So long as her moral vision remains subservient to the poetic and metaphysical urges of her imagination, there cannot be much hope for her development. But though as a novelist, she may not, in the end, achieve a high reputation, as a prose stylist, there are few, outside of Raja Rao, to match her skill. Words appear to have a sensuous appeal for her, and she exults in the reach and power of her rhetoric. (p. 229)

Darshan Singh Maini, "The Achievement of Anita Desai," in Indo-English Literature: A Collection of Critical Essays, *edited by K. K. Sharma, Vimal Prakashan, 1977, pp. 215-30.*

PRABHU S GUPTARA

[It] is a remarkably truthful picture of Indian rural life that emerges from Anita Desai's *The Village by the Sea.* Remarkable for two reasons: first, Indian literature traditionally presents an idealized view of life; in modern times, under the influence of Western notions, it presents an inaccurately "realistic" and depressing picture. Second, Desai herself has inhabited a tortured and fantastic region of the imagination in her fiction thus far; here she emerges into the light of common day.

The story is simple enough: Hari is twelve, and his elder sister Lila, only slightly older, tries her best to cope in a house where mother is an invalid and father perpetually drunk. Hari gradually realises that the responsibility for the family is his, and he starts looking around for ways of earning money. . . .

Hari really wants to go to Bombay. Though it is only fourteen kilometres away, it seems so distant that it may as well be on the moon. The heart of the novel is Hari's journey to Bombay, how he survives and eventually thrives in it, and how he returns, changed by his experience, but knowing that he belongs in his village, and to it.

From an artistic point of view, there is a discrepancy between the articulate and knowledgeable voice of the narrator and the likely perceptions of the village protagonists. But the village is a type of India: its life is attractive, (though there are drawbacks) and this is doomed by the tides of change that are sweeping in. Yet it is these very tides that bring the possibilities of material advancement. On the whole, Desai welcomes change in *The Village by the Sea.*

This book is meant for teenagers. Anita Desai has therefore been able to smile and relax in it; and the finest fiction always transcends its intended audience. City and village, travel and social change, topography and monsoon: in Indian literature, none have ever had such fine observation or rich description lavished on them.

Prabhu S Guptara, "Indian Landscapes," in The Times Educational Supplement, *No. 3464, November 19, 1982, p. 38.*

MADHUSUDAN PRASAD

Of all the contemporary Indian-English novelists, Anita Desai . . . , avowedly "an essentially subjective writer," is indubitably the most powerful imagist. Setting great store by imagery in the novel as an art form, she regards its use as an effective technique for the articulation of her sensibility and handles it superbly. Demonstrating her fictional strategy and underscoring her essentially tragic vision of life, Desai resorts generously to imagery to vivify psychic states as well as the distinctively individual consciousness of her highly sensitive, introverted characters and the complexities of human relationships, scenes and situations, resulting in a remarkable textural density. Indisputably, her novels would have meant much less to us were it not for the transforming presence of imagery.

All six novels by Desai teem with various meaningful, functional images. On closer scrutiny, we notice that botany, zoology, meteorology, nature and color predominate as sources, and occasionally she also employs certain other stray images that, though answering immediate artistic experiences, operate on a minor level, focusing on the moods of certain characters and forming a sort of tonal chord in her novels. These minor images do not arise from what has gone before, though they do generally suggest a prefigurative pattern.

Cry, the Peacock (1963), Desai's maiden novel, abounds with momentous images, revealing her early capacity as an imagist-novelist—a remarkable quality of her craft that she has carefully maintained in all her later fiction. Exhibiting a mastery of montage technique, she dexterously deploys numerous images which, apart from creating a rich, dense texture, illuminate the protagonist Maya's obsessions and moods and develop certain secondary symbolic implications. . . .

[Zoological imagery] is quite powerful and insistent in this work, as it is in such later novels as *Where Shall We Go This Summer?* (1975) and *Fire on the Mountain* (1977). It is used as a structural device here, integral not only to the vision of the novelist but also to the theme. The first animal image deployed at the outset is that of the dead Toto, Maya's pet dog. . . . Skillfully emphasizing the death motif, Desai repeats the image of the dead Toto in different forms with a view toward objectifying Maya's psychic disorder and her ineluctable preoccupation with death, the intensity of which rises in her mind until she ultimately kills her husband.

As the tension in Maya's aberrant mind mounts, several disturbing images of slimy, crawling creatures such as rats, snakes, lizards and iguanas figure one after another. (p. 363)

In chapter 5, part 2, when Gautama wipes the face of the ailing Maya, she feels "a parasite life, creeping across" her body. She dreams of reptiles. Desai depicts Maya's final breakdown through the image of the iguana. When Maya notices the domestic cat slinking about the room, the image of the cat is replaced at once in her mind by that of an iguana, and she screams out in fright, "Iguanas! . . . Get off—I tell you, get off! Go!" . . .

Various dances have also been artistically employed in *Cry, the Peacock* . . . The cabaret dance, depicted at length in chapter 3, part 2, is not something vulgar to titillate us. As an image, it is highly significant, and it is immediately followed by the image of the bear dance that Maya recollects as a childhood experience. The cabaret dance acquires considerable significance through the juxtaposition, transforming the fantasia of Maya's subconscious mind into a contemporary reality. Besides, these images of cabaret dance and bear dance obliquely point to cruel exploitation in society. Thus both images are, in fact, victim-and-victimizer images which, though used on an experimental level here, form an important extension of Desai's prey-and-predator imagery—and it is this predation imagery that is central to her tragic vision of life and also stands out in her later novels. (p. 364)

The meteorological image of the dust storm is an important extension of the dance imagery and denotes not only the fierce storm raging in Maya's subconscious mind but also her desire for "release from bondage, release from fate, from death and dreariness and unwanted dreams." . . . Maya welcomes the storm with the pleasure of a dancer and notices in it the source of both agony and ecstasy. The most important organic image that appears repeatedly in the novel is that of the "tenebrific" albino astrologer who predicted an early death, by unnatural causes, for Maya or her husband. This image figures first in chapter 1, part 2 and later surfaces in Maya's consciousness

at certain critical moments, underscoring the death motif and developing the theme toward a climax.

In *Voices in the City* (1965) Desai extends her capacity as an imagist-novelist. This novel is strewn with meteorological images (especially those of fog, mist and air), color images (particularly the contrast between light and dark) and images of filth, ugliness, misery, poverty, decay, death and disintegration. Meteorological imagery figures in the early part of the novel, as evocations of fog, mist and air objectify the inner confusion, suffocation and frustration of the central character, Nirode. (pp. 364-65)

Color is skillfully deployed. Light and dark contrasts are used to explore the nightmare of Nirode's and Monisha's souls, suggesting their emotional "imbalance," "natural anarchism" and futile desire for solitude amid the cacophonous multitudes of Calcutta. It also reflects psychophysical parallels and brings out aspects of the illusory and paralytic existence that runs to seed. (p. 365)

Voices in the City, unlike *Cry, the Peacock,* lacks zoological imagery. However, at one point Desai does use the prey-and-predator image which she develops in novel after novel in order to crystallize her tragic vision of life. In *Voices in the City* this image occurs in the racecourse scene.

> One horse tripped on this invisible web of conflict, slid, fell and rolled. . . . [It] lay at the corner in a kicking fury. . . . Then it was hidden by a thick dark screen. . . . It was the descent of the birds who had risen, crying in triumph, from the trees, risen like a fine-woven net against the opalescent sky and, net-like, descended on the flailing horse, poured and swarmed about it, with beating wings and tearing claws, to jab and tear, jab and tear at the feast for which they had waited. . . .

Apart from this specific use of predation imagery, one also notices that Calcutta itself is, in symbolic terms, an ugly, ghastly monster in whose deadly grip three helpless victims—Nirode, Monisha and Amla—groan and gasp for life. Monisha calls Calcutta "this devil city" . . . and "the unrelenting city" . . . , while Amla is terribly repentant of having come from Bombay to this "monster city that lived no normal, healthy, red-blooded life but one that was subterranean, underlit, stealthy and odorous of mortality." . . . She complains to Nirode that "this city, this city of yours, it conspires against all who wish to enjoy it, doesn't it?" . . . This "monster city" succeeds in killing Monisha, while it leaves Nirode and Amla badly mauled. Thus the prey-and-predator imagery, studied in the light of symbolic connotation, acquires a unique dimension of effectiveness and a remarkable thematic and structural relevance. . . . Another strikingly significant image employed is that of the goddess Kali. Watching the street singer, Monisha is reminded of the Eternal Mother, the Earth Mother . . . , and in her vision the merger of the two images is expressive of the merger of the realistic with the symbolic. (The merging of the image of Nirode's mother with that of Kali at the end of the novel, however, is both unconvincing and inappropriate.) The novel also contains a few altogether different images of the river, the bird and the kite illustrating a sort of release that Nirode, Monisha and Amla all crave from the terrible oppression of the city, although these images are but loosely related to the work's central theme.

Desai has not fully exploited her capacity for image-making in *Bye-Bye, Blackbird* (1971). Nevertheless, there are certain images that do merit critical attention. In chapter 3 Desai describes the Clapham tube station. This image effectively conveys a terrible sense of claustrophobia in Dev, who, traveling by subway, feels apprehensive "of being caught, stuck in the underground by some accident, some collapse, and being slowly suffocated to a worm's death." . . . In the same chapter the inorganic image of the Battersea power station is quite significant: This "massive grey temple of power, pouring vast billows of dark smoke into an empty, breathless sky" . . . charms Dev, who notices in it "the *puja* being conducted" and hears "the clanging of great gongs and the blowing of long horns and the singing of sweet hymns." . . . Its "sacrificial bonfire" consumes his initial Anglophobia, out of whose ashes is born in him a strong Anglophilia. Thus the image of the power station has profound symbolic implications.

Desai uses quite a few images depicting, with remarkable fidelity, urban England and its bustling crowds and busy bazaars. She also paints the rural milieu quite faithfully. (pp. 365-66)

Where Shall We Go This Summer?, unlike *Bye-Bye, Blackbird,* displays Desai's superb talents for image-making. Part 1 and part 3, which deal with Sita's existentialist alienation, are strikingly replete with evocative images. Sita, a highly sensitive, emotional, middle-aged woman, already saddled with four children and now expecting her fifth, is deeply obsessed by the pervasive violence and destruction in society. Her obsession figures repeatedly through a series of caustic images embodying, in a way, the anatomy of violence and resembling droplets of acid sprinkled over our bruised consciousness. The first memorable image of violence is again of the prey-and-predator variety and occurs amid a scene in which Sita is seated on her balcony, holding a popgun and trying in vain to "keep away the crows that were attacking a wounded eagle on a neighbouring rooftop." . . . This pursuit of the prey by the predator is gruesome and ghastly even in the animal world; but it surely assumes a new dimension of horror and ugliness when transferred to the civilized world of human beings.

The other images of violence presented in the novel fall into three categories: "One small incident," "Another small incident" and "More small incidents." This technique, no doubt, suggests Desai's inadequacy of narrative resources to articulate living reality and also interferes in the esthetic pattern and structure of the novel. A few images of violence and destruction are compressed in a single passage, for example, laying stress on Sita's obsessive fear of violence and her anxiety about providing for the safety of her unborn child. (pp. 366-67)

[Part 1] contains a few color images, of which the evocations of darkness are the most significant. Highlighting the main motif of the novel, these images signify the futility of Sita's "pilgrimage" to Manori Island "for the miracle of keeping her baby unborn." . . . The island, apart from having numerous symbolic connotations, also echoes the theme of human vulnerability and the resultant conflicting demands of protection and independence. Sita looks to the island for protection, but all she gets from it is a cold welcome from islanders wary of talking to her and palms "hissing and clattering their dry leaves together harshly, like some disturbed, vigilant animals." . . . The house itself looks like "a waste of ashes."

Part 3 is remarkably free from violence and destruction. It abounds instead with the striking images of sea and sunshine, flowers and butterflies. These images reflect a sense of regen-

eration in nature and also reveal Sita's moods as well as her acute awareness of the delicate, the beautiful and the sensuous. . . . Desai also makes good use of domestic imagery in this novel, although she handles it with greater artistic skill later in *Fire on the Mountain* and *Clear Light of Day* (1980). While Sita is in Bombay, she lives in a flat on a height. Escaping city life, she later comes to Manori Island to live in the house built by her father. But to her chagrin, she discovers "a waste of ashes" and "the cold remains of the bonfire her father had lit here to a blaze." She notices dust lying "as casually as sand on a beach" and "spiderwebs" spanning "the corners of the unfurnished rooms like skeletal palm leaves." . . . Symbolically, this set of images indicates that Sita is living in an illusory world. When she realizes the futility of continuing in this illusion and comes to terms with the realities of life, she returns to the plains of Bombay. Thus Sita's living on a height, whether in Bombay or on Manori Island, reflects her conception of her self, her ego.

Of all the novels of Desai, *Fire on the Mountain* is uniquely significant, for it fully exhibits her artistically elegant patterning of numerous images rich in symbolic connotations. Adhering to the montage technique in this novel, as in *Cry, the Peacock,* she dexterously deploys several powerful botanical, zoological, atmospheric and color images that, apart from creating a remarkable textural richness and displaying her artistic ingenuity and originality, point to the symbolic centrality of the novel. The surprising thing here is that there is not much of a tale to tell; even so, the novel is spellbinding throughout. Desai amply compensates for the thin story element by skillfully drawing upon her genius for image-making and weaving a mosaic texture that charms the reader—and herein lies the uniqueness of the novel. Deprived of imagery, the work would be an ugly skeleton, chilling the reader.

The botanical image of pine trees, manifesting Nanda Kaul's desire to merge her identity with that of the trees so that she can be rid of "unwelcome intrusion and distraction," is worth consideration. Seeing a postman heading toward her, she "stepped backwards into the garden and the wind suddenly billowed up and threw the pine branches about as though to curtain her. . . . She fancied she could merge with the pine trees and be mistaken for one. To be a tree, no more and no less, was all she was prepared to undertake." . . . (p. 367)

The novel teems with numerous striking images of birds and beasts that reflect Nanda's psychic states and moods or contribute significantly to the tone of the novel. . . . (p. 368)

Desai adroitly exploits . . . zoological images for the specific purpose of characterizing Raka, who is described as "one of those dark crickets that leap up in fright but do not sing, or a mosquito, minute and fine, on thin, precarious legs." . . . Elsewhere she is "lizard-like" . . . , "an insect burrowing through the sandy loam and pine-needles of the hillsides" . . . , "a pet insect" . . . , "higher than the eagles" . . . and "an uninvited mouse or cricket." . . . These various zoological references not only define Raka's character, nature and behavior, but also externalize Nanda's deep dislike of Raka. As soon as Nanda succeeds in establishing rapport with Raka, the repulsive zoological images cease.

Although the novel is laid in the quiet seclusion of Kasauli, Desai skillfully deploys various sound images to create a tonal contrast that, apart from having a bearing on her serious vision, intensifies the mood of the novel. One significant sample is found at the beginning of chapter 7 in part 1: "Flies, too lazy for flight, were caught in . . . midday web and buzzed languorously. . . . Inside, the flies. Outside, the cicadas. Everything hummed, shrilled, buzzed and fiddled." . . . Throughout the work we hear the rustling and fluttering of leaves and twigs, flowers and wings and the characteristic chirps and cries of birds and animals. In no other novel of Desai do we notice such an admirable use of sound imagery.

Household imagery is also functional here. Unlike Sita in *Where Shall We Go This Summer?*, Nanda does not live in her house, Carignano, by choice; instead, she lives there under compulsion, since she has been deserted by her sons and daughters following the death of her husband. Carignano is situated "on the ridge" in Kasauli, and Nanda is fully satisfied with its starkness and seclusion, and with the sunshine around it. Symbolically, this quiet seclusion defines the freedom that Nanda has been able to achieve at long last in her old age. The now quiet Carignano once hummed with life before Independence; similarly, the now deserted Nanda spent a terribly busy life before the loss of her husband, ordering about "too many servants," entertaining "too many guests" and tending "so many children" and grandchildren. Thus the image of Carignano has a significant symbolic bearing on Nanda's life.

Clear Light of Day, Desai's last novel to date, is, like *Bye-Bye, Blackbird*, surprisingly deficient in the characteristic imagery which distinguishes most of her earlier novels. Desai's readers, addicted to her lyrical fervor and symbolic evocation, are bound to be rather disappointed. There are, to be sure, certain images used repeatedly in the novel: the old well, covered with green scum, at the edge of the compound in which the cow gets drowned; the bees in the Lodhi Garden which attack Bim, while Tara escapes; the white horse which Hyder Ali rides on the sand dunes by the Jumna; the father injecting Tara's ailing mother, making her feel that he is murdering her; and the nightmarish vision of Aunt Mira tearing off her clothes in an alcoholic frenzy, displaying her sad, sagging breasts and a wisp of brown pubic hair. These recurrent images possess esthetic rather than casual relevance, for the episodes used in the novel are like pieces of a thematic jigsaw puzzle which the reader has to piece together in order to obtain a clear picture of the family life in the right perspective. Here Desai has resorted but infrequently to her characteristic technique of using an image as an apparently independent artistic unit or as an objective correlative with a view toward vivifying the psychic state or emotion of a particular character. (pp. 368-69)

[It] is in the use of domestic imagery that *Clear Light of Day* excels. The feeling of stagnation and the resultant sense of boredom reigning in the ancient, unchanged house in Old Delhi to which Tara returns are evoked in the novel through the metaphor of a scummy pond. Tara feels that "part of her was sinking languidly down into the passive pleasure of having returned to the familiar—like a pebble she has been picked up and hurled back into the pond, and sunk down through the layer of green scum, through the secret cool depths to the soft rich mud at the bottom." . . . The house image is also used to objectify Tara's "dullness" and "boredom." She feels that "the fullness and the boredom of her childhood, her youth, were stored here in the room . . . as if this were the storeroom of some dull, uninviting provincial museum." . . .

In part 2 Desai limns a fine, elaborate image of the deserted house of Hyder Ali, who left the house because of the riots at the time of Indian partition and took refuge in Hyderabad. This echoes the fate of Bim, who is also deserted, by Raja and Aunt Mira: the former deliberately abandons her and goes away to Hyderabad, where he marries the daughter of Hyder Ali and settles down; the latter dies. Throughout the novel, the house is a threatening presence characterized by an explosive silence and a recurrent image of Baba grinding the old gramophone and listening to the cracked, scratchy records of the forties. It is this static image of the house that looms large in the mind of the reader, suggesting Bim's suppressed anger and bitterness.

Never otiose, Desai's imagery, which is chiefly anticipatory, prefigurative or demonstrative in nature, is always highly functional. Botanical, zoological, meteorological and color images are central to her fictional strategy and spotlight the tragic vision of life to which she, like Kamala Markandaya, is essentially committed. Her artistic image patterns, singularized by subtle interrelatedness and continuity, act on our imagination with tremendous cumulative force. Creating a mosaic of textural density in almost all her novels, Desai's imagery is wedded to rich lyricism. She is basically a powerful imagist-novelist but is also a remarkable lyrical novelist as well, and there is a subtle interaction between her imagery and lyricism. In sum, Anita Desai is the only Indian-English novelist who exploits imagery to such an extent and to such an artistic end. Certainly this is her unique achievement. (p. 369)

Madhusudan Prasad, "Imagery in the Novels of Anita Desai: A Critical Study," in World Literature Today, Vol. 58, No. 3, Summer, 1984, pp. 363-69.

SEBASTIAN FAULKS

Anita Desai's novel *In Custody* is about a man's determined defence of his own integrity and the importance of art in the face of great odds. That sounds portentous, but it is worth saying at once that this is an ambitious book, and that just because it is short and written in a way that some might call delicate (actually the prose is pretty robust) that doesn't mean it is anything less than a major attempt to tackle serious themes.

Much of it is impeccable. Deven, the hero, is a college lecturer in Mirpore, near Delhi; he is a shy man, fiercely proud of his education and devoted to literature. But he is too meek for the modern world and everyone, from his seniors at college down to the meanest beggar in Delhi, is able to manipulate him. We want Deven to succeed, to fight back, though we know that he is incapable of it. To this extent *In Custody* is a prolonged comedy of exasperation.

An old college friend, Murad, the editor of a literary magazine, bumps into Deven and offers him a chance to make his name and at the same time do great service to the dying cause of his beloved Urdu literature. He despatches Deven to interview Nur, India's greatest Urdu poet, in Delhi. This Nur is discovered living in squalor, surrounded by plagiarists, sycophants and scroungers. He has piles, no money and a drink problem. . . . The battle in Deven's heart is to retain his belief in art in such circumstances. . . .

Frequent trips to Delhi damage Deven's home and professional life. His wife Sarla thinks little of him because he has not provided her with the material things she wanted. Now his absences give her further cause for complaint. The marriage between two people of entirely different aspirations is appallingly well done; the "custody" of it drives even the mild Deven to violence. The newly fashionable occidental view that we have been too hasty in condemning arranged marriages is challenged by this story. . . .

In Custody is extraordinarily rich in incident and detail. Miss Desai is a considerable descriptive writer: small Mirpore and big Delhi are alive at once in her hands. She is very good at food, too: Nur is always ordering imaginative biryianis and fragrant rice from the bazaar. Her real skill, however, is with people. She has caught and rendered the Indian way of speaking: pedantic, highly literal, often emphasising the redundant detail, yet capable of poetry in a rhetorical way. Her characters, though all recognisable Indian types . . . , are also vividly realised.

The plot of *In Custody,* which starts at a fierce pace, stalls about half way through when Deven's visits to Nur become repetitive, and a side-plot of his dealings with the head of his Urdu department seems to deflect the narrative momentum. Throughout the book the odds are loaded so heavily against Deven that he sometimes looks like a mere embodiment of goodness in a world where every other character is there to hamper his pilgrim's progress. His unpleasantness to his wife prevents him from being too good to be true, but the novel does sometimes seem to be straining towards allegory.

This is not, I think, deliberate, but is a result of Miss Desai's wish to be clear in her fairly complicatd morality. Deven ends up bound by ties of honour, money and responsibility to the increasingly grasping poet Nur. He has exchanged the custody of his job and his marriage for this new imprisonment which he views—or rather must view—as freedom. In a sense, Deven wins the battle, because his devotion to poetry will last longer than the discomfort inflicted by the snares and tricks of those he meets. But he must be a servant, not a great man, and he must understand the almost religious paradox at the heart of his enslaved freedom. Anita Desai's handling of her theme is highly skillful, and the result, despite minor blemishes, is a considerable novel.

Sebastian Faulks, "Straining towards Allegory," in Books and Bookmen, *No. 350, November, 1984, p. 26.*

JOHN GROSS

Literature has a way of devouring those who put too much faith in it, and Deven, the ineffectual hero of Anita Desai's new novel [*In Custody*], is one of its more hapless victims. . . .

In telling Deven's story, Anita Desai avoids either farce or easy pathos; she sympathizes with his plight, and at the same time remains clear-sighted about his weaknesses. When he boasts to a colleague about knowing Nur [a famous author], he feels that the occasion calls for pomposity—''a state to which he had always secretly aspired''—and he has a temper (for ''the meek are not always mild''), which he doesn't hesitate to vent on his wife. Nur's wives are victims, too—the second of them, the poet with the painted face, a good deal more so than at first appears.

In Custody is a civilized and satisfying piece of work. As readers of Anita Desai's previous novels would expect, she writes with complete command of her material. The Indian setting, with its jumble of old and new—ancient rituals, Japanese nylon saris—is beautifully evoked, but there is no straining after local color; the descriptive detail flows naturally from the story. And running through the whole book there is a compelling sense of life's incongruities.

John Gross, in a review of "In Custody," in The New York Times, *February 22, 1985, p. 28C.*

ANTHONY THWAITE

[Anita Desai's] father was Bengali, her mother German, and her professional training and experience as a teacher have been in English. Her novels and her children's books are all written in English. . . . She was educated in Delhi, lives in Bombay, and seems most at home in a milieu that, though cosmopolitan, is essentially Indian.

That ''Indian-ness'' is acutely captured in her novels, which are full of the crosscurrents and divided loyalties of contemporary Indian life. At the same time, Desai is a writer whose double vision takes in the ''literariness'' of that life—both the Indian (particularly Urdu) tradition and the English literary tradition, which has been, sometimes uneasily, grafted on to it, ever since Macaulay's famous (or notorious) ''Minute on Education'' in the 19th century. In *Fire on the Mountain* (1977), the old university vice chancellor's widow, Nanda Kaul, unaffectedly quotes Gerard Manley Hopkins; in *Clear Light of Day* (1980), Byron, Tennyson, Swinburne, Lawrence, and Eliot are all quoted by characters who, the next moment, and equally unaffectedly, recite lines from Iqbal, the great earlier 20th-century Urdu poet. And in her latest novel, *In Custody,* the baleful figure at the very center is himself an aged Urdu poet, the fictitious Nur, who, alongside his own work, intones ''the greatest lines that were ever written by anyone''—lines from Keat's ''La Belle Dame Sans Merci.''

Anita Desai's direct use of literary references of this sort is a central part of her special gift, which is a compassionate tact in presenting people and situations poignantly, comically, and—part of both—as approximate simulacra of deflected hopes and unachieved strivings. Art is not life; some have thought art better than life; some have no time for art; but whatever the view, there is an unbridgeable gulf between the two. In Desai's fiction, it isn't so much a matter of Yeats's ''perfection of the life, or of the work'': people are almost bound to make a mess of both.

In Custody is set at a humbler level of Indian society than Desai has usually examined. Deven, the protagonist, is a low-grade lecturer in Hindi in a low-grade college in northern India. He once fancied himself as an Urdu poet, but has almost given that up. . . . [One] day he bumps into Murad, an old friend from student days who turns out to be editor of what Deven takes to be a leading Urdu literary journal. Murad . . . bamboozles him into taking on the task of interviewing possibly the greatest living Urdu poet, Nur, now old and ill and living in obscurity. The challenge is immense, but also immensely seductive. (pp. 37-8)

From then on, Deven is caught up in a hideous web of difficulties. Nur lives in Delhi, many miles from Deven's irredeemably provincial northern town of Mirpur. Just getting there is a problem. Then, when Nur is eventually tracked down, it is obvious that his great days are long over. . . .

But Nur is important to Deven, not just because of Murad's commission and the presumed ensuing glory to Deven, but because art is important. The job must be done. . . . Meanwhile, Deven's wife grumbles and rails at him whenever he comes home. She has no time for Urdu poetastering; the family needs money.

So Deven has exchanged one kind of custody for another. He slides helplessly between an arranged and loveless marriage, a dreary and ill-regarded job, and the desperations of being tied to a defunct genius, a man whose apostolic touch was meant to bring Deven good fortune. Murad won't pay him, because he hasn't produced results; Sarla, his wife, doesn't want him, because he is a hopeless breadwinner and helpmeet; Nur rejects him, because he is an irritating encumbrance in the daily battle to get satisfaction out of the short span of life that is left.

Yet Deven emerges—without anything that could be called a happy ending—as a kind of hero, a hero of art. He may be a fool, but a sort of holy fool, someone who really supposes that the gifts of the spirit are more important than the gifts of the marketplace. Reviewers of Desai's earlier novels have written of her as Chekhovian, and one can see what they mean: the sad humor of provincial lives out on the edge of something. And yet there are many differences—differences quite crucially having to do with the fact that Desai's India is a more volatile and divided place than Chekhov's pre-revolutionary Russia, in its muddled but resiliently surviving democracy, in its enormous, literate but ill-paid clerisy (college teachers like Deven, literati like Murad, as well as vast numbers of lowly civil servants), and perhaps most of all in its religious divisions, which (as religious divisions so often do) have become political divisions.

Anita Desai manages to suggest all this without making it an overt theme. Her plotting is simple, even minimal: will Deven succeed in the task that has been set him? But she is such a consummate artist that she suggests, beyond the confines of the plot and the machinations of her characters, the immensities that lie beyond them—the immensities of India. She is in no way just local, or parochial, or provincial, partly because her India, in its large-scale tangled texture, can be seen as an image—with its own local colors, smells, babble of mingling and conflicting voices—of a much larger world. It is foreign views that tend to be partial and limited. Paul Scott's India inevitably, is wholly Anglo-centric, and one in which the Indians are peripheral. Desai's [India], for all the cosmopolitan literary skill she brings to it, is an India that very few foreigners have ever penetrated: the India that is Indian. (p. 38)

Anthony Thwaite, "India Inside," in The New Republic, *Vol. 192, No. 11, March 18, 1985, pp. 37-8.*

Stephen Dobyns

1941-

American poet, novelist, and essayist.

In his poetry Dobyns combines elements of the everyday world with the surreal, offsetting his sometimes bleak or sinister vision with subtle humor. One reviewer described Dobyns's poetry as "striking and arresting, . . . tightly controlled, with precise, surreal language, undertones of deep violence, and a grim sense of humor." While in his earlier poems Dobyns maintained a tone of somewhat cynical detachment, his later work is characterized by increasing warmth and attention to human feelings.

In his first book, *Concurring Beasts* (1972), Dobyns used succinct, unemotional language to blend magic and fantasy with details and facts from the real world. Critics noted that the wit and intelligence evident in this volume are also present in *Griffon* (1976); both books drew praise for their accomplished writing and originality. In *Heat Death* (1980) one reviewer detected "moods of stark desolation offset by a crisply controlled voice" consistent with Dobyns's previous works. *The Balthus Poems* (1982) comprises poems based on paintings by the surrealist Count Balthazar Klossowski de Rola. In describing the motivation behind this volume, Dobyns said, "I tried to turn each painting into a personal metaphor to create narrative poems seemingly free from the lyrical first person voice." While *The Balthus Poems* explores the artistic process and the limits of the imagination, the poems in *Black Dog, Red Dog* (1984) are rooted in ordinary life. Gilbert Allen observes that in the later volume Dobyns "seems to be taking human emotions more seriously than in his earlier books, whose surrealistic zaniness often made the poems seem merely cerebral exercises."

In addition to his poetry, Dobyns is the author of five well-received detective novels. His first novel, *A Man of Little Evils* (1973), takes place in London and is the story of an American reporter's attempt to solve a baffling murder case. The central character of *Dancer with One Leg* (1983) is the physically and emotionally scarred Frank Lazard, a lieutenant on the Boston Fire Department's arson squad who leads the investigation of a warehouse fire. Each of Dobyns's other three novels—*Saratoga Longshot* (1976), *Saratoga Swimmer* (1980), and *Saratoga Headhunter* (1985)—involves a likable private detective named Charlie Bradshaw who is drawn, often unwillingly, into investigating various murders. Critics have noted that the attention to language Dobyns has developed as a poet enhances his fiction, and his novels are praised for their unmannered prose and inventive descriptions.

(See also *Contemporary Authors*, Vols. 45-48 and *Contemporary Authors New Revision Series*, Vol. 2.)

ROBERT D. SPECTOR

[In *Concurring Beasts*] Stephen Dobyns looks warily at the chaotic world, dislikes what he sees, and responds to its disorder in crisply controlled verse keyed to a sardonic wit one scale above cynicism. For the young poet, rejected reality frequently leads to imaginative excesses, a turn to the power of

fantasy. Dobyns maintains firm control of even the processes of imagination. For him there is "A disbelief in unicorns and concurring beasts, / he fills their places, planting his sounds, / waters them, watches them grow, their blossoms / beginning to break forth jointly."

Whether he is relating autobiographical experiences, commenting on war and politics, describing the failure in human relationships, or exploring the processes of poetry, Dobyns writes with assurance and wit. He does not overvalue his conduct and scoffs at his attempts at reformation: "Rejection's cheap when the town's shut down." Death and joviality are wryly juxtaposed, and even the horrors of political assassination are expressed through a kind of metaphysical conceit: "the room, a bullet in its chamber, / waiting to go off." Green, that symbolic color of youth and hopefulness, he observes, "becomes the color of decay." He levels idyllic pastorals by noting that at night cows go "back to the barn, banging horns, / kicking soft hooves for company" only "if the trucks don't come." For the glory of war, he offers up the prospect of body counts; to the honor of dying for one's country, he responds, "stranger, with your myth and stoney name, / what can you give me? A flag to sleep on, the quiet / of long fields, the touch of horses to close my hand."

When he says, "Sympathy has no alphabet," he ironically plays on the expression "If you want sympathy, look in the dictionary''—a detachment that, unfortunately, constitutes the major weakness in his poetry. For Dobyns's best work suffers from a lack of human warmth and feeling. Even the beautifully balanced series of poems in **"Hotel,"** poems that capture the essence of transient existence, fails to generate more than an objective view of his subject. Poems that deal with personal relations—''You sit as I do / but across the room''; ''You don't know who / I talk to, talking to you''; ''You ask for help. I can do nothing for you.''—convey clearly enough the idea of alienation, but do too little to arouse the necessary sense of anguish that their subject demands.

Nevertheless, Dobyns's accomplishment is remarkable. In his first book he has consciously created a poetic world whose values and sounds are uniquely his. Aware of the poetic influences everywhere around him, he can say: ''Now I shall begin to steal. . . . / At the rag ends of fields my words / are crouching. They know of a freight / better than the one they've been riding.'' And yet, as his introductory quotation from Nerval suggests, what he seeks is ''the power to create my own universe, to govern my dreams, instead of enduring them.'' He borrows not men's words or ways of looking at things but, rather, a kind of poetic inspiration to turn their collection of ''old coins, cat's feet'' to profit and to give value to their ''numerous glass objects / which will never be pearls.'' Far more often than not, Dobyns has succeeded.

> *Robert D. Spector, in a review of "Concurring Beasts," in* Saturday Review, *Vol. LV, No. 10, March 11, 1972, p. 80.*

THE ANTIOCH REVIEW

Precisely one-third of the poems [in *Concurring Beasts*] . . . appeared originally in *Kayak* magazine, that persistent preserve of neo-surrealism; all the poems conform almost exclusively to that poetic mode. Dobyns rarely raises his voice, mutes it with casual contractions and obsessive mid-line periods; indeed, in many of the poems no admitted ''I'' exists, so often what remains is only the eye of a distanced observer. Because of these ways, the surreal images glimmer but don't flare. The publisher's blurb speaks of Dobyns' ''control,'' of his ''elegant intellectuality,'' of his poems as ''arresting'' and of a *particular* kind. Despite what seems to be a fine and complex talent, Dobyns' poems fit the jacket copy far too well: over controlled, hyper-understated, repetitious—too often they flatten all the possible ferocity of the surreal and become simply dull.

> *A review of "Concurring Beasts," in* The Antioch Review, *Vol. 32, Nos. 1 & 2, Spring & Summer, 1972, p. 242.*

PETER COOLEY

Dobyns's poetry resembles few other current poets', though his interest in magic and his litanyesque structures might seem to relate him to many *Kayak* writers. . . . [In *Concurring Beasts*] Dobyns convinces us of his necromancer's vision by never faltering in the weaving of his spells. The tone is so perfectly controlled that we come away from each poem convinced the world must be constituted as he dreams it. . . . How could it be otherwise? we think. As in Lewis Carroll (from whom he draws an epigraph for the fifth part of his book), Dobyns always sees the fantastic as ordinary. And like Swift, he uses it in service of a satire directed against both general human foibles and the particular failings of our society. He writes by the

sentence (as Bell did by the phrase, as Levine did by the word) and has a dry wit which succeeds in winking at the surprising even within the texture of poems where the unexpected is his norm.

Especially noteworthy among *Beasts*'s poems are **"Hotel," "Continue By Waking," "Counterparts," "Contingencies," "Passing the Word"** and **"The Way of Keys."** Dobyns writes dream poetry which shows us we aren't sleeping but awake as we experience it. The objects in his poems are subject to a constant metamorphosis which is like nightmare, but in their shifting they suggest a vast potentiality to be more than themselves. As readers we participate in that potentiality and it comes to be a sort of grace.

> *Peter Cooley, in a review of "Concurring Beasts," in* The North American Review, *Vol. 258, No. 1, Spring, 1973, p. 72.*

RALPH J. MILLS, JR.

Stephen Dobyns' initial volume [*Concurring Beasts*] won the Lamont Prize for 1971, and one readily discovers the wit, intelligence, and surrealist obliquity that must have impressed the [judges], . . . for these dimensions of his work are sustained throughout. The book is so organized, at least in part, as to compose some sort of autobiographical or spiritual odyssey, with an *Entrance/Epiphany* poem to start off with and a closing section dealing with names and identities; the poems are also linked by certain recurrent details, images, and so on. In addition, there is a separate sequence, both polished and strange, called **"Hotel."** Dobyns' combination of humor and the bizarre or sinister displays itself most obviously—and to considerable effect—in his socio-political poems, where the odd, seemingly irrational constructions match with terrifying rightness the absurdity and violence of our public life, our foreign wars. . . . In the poems from the **"Hotel"** sequence we find a dreamlike atmosphere and movement that come close to the cinematic devices of Cocteau:

> She drops through a shaft of mirrors; the walls
> reflect the image of her quick descent.
> She hears nothing, is not afraid. Corridors
> open from the mirrors, long halls of ropes
> to catch a new way, leading to attics, dark
> blue rooms with flowered arches, marble floors
> so clear that each foot falls upon itself.

Stephen Dobyns' talents are unmistakable, I think, and a number of poems stand out, in spite of what appears to this reader at any rate an overall sameness which tends to blur distinctions among the various pieces, though this effect may indeed be integral to the author's intentions for giving his collection unity. Certainly, Dobyns is accomplished, and I look forward to seeing the direction his work will take. (pp. 105-06)

> *Ralph J. Mills, Jr., in a review of "Concurring Beasts," in* Poetry, *Vol. CXXII, No. 2, May, 1973, pp. 105-06.*

HENRI C. VEIT

Stephen Dobyns has written a first novel, *A Man of Little Evils* . . . , which is many steps above the usual, a subtly and imaginatively developed work, a beautifully knitted together reticulation of blurred and switching roles of pursued and pursuer. The story takes place in London and is quite simple; Jacobs, the man of many evils, is found gruesomely and efficiently murdered, and Henderson, a middle-aged and established importer of goods from Morocco, is suspect. Trevor, a hard-drinking American reporter, assigns himself to break Henderson down; they both get caught in a web of pursuit and flight that is colored by vindictiveness and by hatred of one for the other. The intimate dependence of the chased upon the chaser is pushed to the point of disintegration of personality, of fragmentation of motive. This book must not be missed.

Henri C. Veit, in a review of "A Man of Little Evils,"
in Library Journal, *Vol. 98, No. 14, August, 1973,*
p. 2341.

MARTIN LEVIN

Several people die violent deaths in this search for a missing person, but [*Saratoga Longshot*] nonetheless has a wide-eyed Charlie Brown quality about it. This is because Stephen Dobyns has given his hero, a 41-year-old cop from Saratoga, N.Y., an ingenuous nature and a kid's zest for new sights and sounds. So when Sgt. Charlie Bradshaw comes to New York City to look for the missing son of an old girlfriend, the reader is privileged to see some familiar and tawdry sights with a fresh eye.

The fact that Mr. Dobyns is a poet helps too. What develops is a suspenseful chase rich in literary texture, in which the country cop zips around lower Manhattan looking for a young punk who doesn't want to be found. The punk has a girl who should know better, some connections with cocaine dealers and involvements that suction Bradshaw right into the center of the action. Murder and mayhem in an unusually inviting climate. (pp. 32-3)

Martin Levin, in a review of "Saratoga Longshot,"
in The New York Times Book Review, *March 21,*
1976, pp. 32-3.

DONALD W. GEORGE

Griffon is a remarkably sophisticated second book, the imagery spare, the language pared. Indeed, this spareness is for me the collection's central difficulty. Most of the poems move through obscure, surreal images, which must combust spontaneously for the reader as they do for the writer if the poems are to be effective. Like . . . W. S. Merwin and Mark Strand, Dobyns seems to be trying to diminish himself, or that accumulation of memory and sensation we think of as self, as a means of appreciating—and indeed becoming—the essences of other things.

The five parts of the book record this journey. In parts one and two we find the narrator **"Putting It All Away," "Escaping Again," "Running," "Getting Through to the End,"** and **"Getting Away From It All."** The predominance of participles is particularly significant: not only are these poems about moving, they are movements in themselves. As such, whether interior or exterior journeys (and often both in one), they tend to pass by too quickly, so that the vital sense of contact with things, and of things with other things, is obscured. . . . (p. 17)

The third part introduces the character Ivan Shark, who calls himself Death, and who considerably enlivens Dobyns' poetry. **"Hunting Ivan Shark"** is a pivotal poem in the collection because it allows the narrator to strip himself ("I bait the alley with my picture, lifelike copies / of my body, clothes still

wrapped in my smell"; "I leave my footprints / for him to follow. I even leave my shadow."), and in that very act—the stripping, the writing—to confront that same antagonist, Death, who unnamed stalks the earlier poems.

In part four, following the confrontations with Ivan Shark, the narrator pauses to look at the life around him, producing two poems (**"The Television Poems"** and **"The Lives of the Chosen"**) about modern American Everymen that are sharp in all respects, and a chilling poem, **"Play In Four Acts,"** that recounts what happens to those who pause and never move again.

Thus in the last part of the book, set off with the title **"Grimoire,"** the poet moves again, but now imaginatively. Synthesizing movement and repose, he continues the extrospection begun in part four through a series of poems by as well as about our common characteristics—**"Sloth," "Gluttony," "Fear," "Doubt," "Vanity,"** etc.

Dobyns' language and imagery are consistently stimulating, if sometimes confusing, and *Griffon* is informed throughout with wit and intelligence. In his next collection I only hope he will make more presences out of his delicate sense of absences, as in these three resonant lines of **"Grief":**

> I was dancing when I
> learned of your death; may
> my feet be severed from my body.
>
>   (pp. 17-18)

Donald W. George, in a review of "Griffon," in The
Hollins Critic, *Vol. XIV, No. 2, April, 1977, pp.*
17-18.

RON SLATE

[Stephen Dobyns' first book, *Concurring Beasts,* is] filled with dislocated voices, inventive language, and odd perspectives. Since its publication, I have watched the magazines for the appearance of new poems; and on learning that Dobyns published an article on contemporary poetry in *Kayak* . . . , I immediately ordered a copy, hoping to learn more about Dobyns' motivation as a poet.

What I found was **"The Poet As Refugee,"** a stinging attack on what Dobyns calls "The Jez Plain Folks School of Poetry." . . . [In this essay Dobyns complains] about "the banality of the sensitive man," the involvement with one's own sincerity to the point of deflating language, the inability to create a distance between the experience itself and the poem as a product of experience, and therefore, the unwillingness to view poem-making as something more than bland "truth-telling."

Dobyns' antidote to this widespread complacency is more difficult to report. While he disdains poems that are written "safely from positions of content," it is also true that there are many 'plain folks' poems that deal with discontent, dissatisfaction with social order, and so forth. He suggests that the effective poet "is apparently trying to transcend his nature in order to reach some more attractive state." But how far can a poet "transcend" before constructing a poem that seems empty of personal motivation, preoccupations? All Dobyns really does, in the end, is list the poets he admires: Simic, Levine, Merwin, Strand, Justice, and others. His comments on the plain folks' "remark poems" and "what-if?" poems are important because they call attention to conventions that are overworked and overproduced, whether or not they are spawned by writers workshops, as he insists.

Dobyns' latest book *Griffon* allows us to examine his poems as a resource in this discussion. In them one finds no easy confessionalism, few gratuitous details, no descriptions of nature connected by a vague mood of introspection. Dobyns doesn't care if you think the poet is a nice guy. . . . In fact, the persona projected from these poems is that of the irascible, vociferous, if sometimes impenetrable observer. Observer of what? Human behavior, mainly. But Dobyns doesn't want to make poems that are simplistic paraphrases of "deep events," or to aim for facile conclusions. The voice he employs is "human" without being "personal"; it is not overly impressed with its own sincerity.

The title poem of the book comes first. In "**Griffon,**" it is the mythological beast that speaks, mocking, insinuating. "You think me a creature / of your dreams. You are mistaken. / You are the creatures of mine." In Grimm's fairy tale of the same name, the Griffon is a devourer of Christians, the truculent knower of all things human. To obtain answers from him, it is necessary to outwit him (via the good graces of his wife). For Dobyns, the figure might indicate the poet's attitude toward poetic insight as well as the voice he decides to employ. If the awareness of the plain folks comes too easily, without strain, then it becomes worthwhile to hide under the Griffon's bed while he talks in his sleep: you take a risk, you hear the suprahuman voice speaking of significances. And this is the voice of the poems: irritated, mistrustful, aware of frailty and folly.

Dobyns' art is the portrayal of this disgruntled mind without indulging in the excesses of pathos. He does not ask for sympathy. When not dissatisfied, the voice is one of quirky inquisitiveness. . . . Dobyns speaks *through* the various personae in this book, rather than trying to give the plain folks' impression that someone interesting is standing *beyond* the poem.

The first section of the book presents that deliberate "archetypal" voice. But in part two, another kind of poem emerges. I think Dobyns knows the dangers of always aiming for the voice of the profound "other" ("The Jez Archetypal School of Poets"?), and this section contains poems that more constantly feature the first-person, still informed by the personality of the griffon in some ways. (pp. 55-7)

Dobyns has not picked up any major new techniques in his second book. One will still sometimes find a line that contains two short, halting sentences, and poems that feature clipped diction. Moreover, he still seeks to instill the same moods in his readers. The last lines of a *Concurring Beasts* poem "**Refusing the Necessary**" are: "Without daylight, we have forgotten the sun, / accepted a darker place. Between the surface / and bottom, we may hang forever." The final lines of "**Getting Away From It All**" go: "I shall learn the songs of water / and the long green songs of trees and grass. / Closing my hands and eyes, I may learn to sleep here." A profound sense of tentativeness, a hope for a kind of ominous betterment speak out here.

Lest someone claim that Dobyns is only a poet of solipsisms (which, in large part, he is), I also insist that he offers a unique view of the world we all live in. These are the first lines of "**Moving Through Spain,**" a poem that comments on the state of the country and humanity there without falling into shallow irony, exposition, or propaganda:

> Spain is a country of small rooms. They
> lack windows. They smell of urine. Their walls
> are covered with the history of insects,
> traces of quick deaths. Between spotted laundry

> and the whistle of the swallows' wings, courtyards
> rise toward a sky of contemptuous blue.
>
> (p. 57)

Later in the book, "**The Television Poems**" show Dobyns' heavily ironic treatment of the man created by culture, going through the rounds of meaningless pleasures and chores. Dobyns risks the catalog effect here, and the poem might strike some as merely sarcastic. But there is no evidence that Dobyns excludes himself from the vision.

There are moments throughout the book where the language seems too willed, where the poet might be aware that he has a good thing going and exploits his unique stance. The "Ivan Shark" sequence does not accumulate too much for me, and are examples of the forced enigmatic statement. Still, I have a good idea of what he was trying to get across there. Basically, I'm very impressed with the work of this poet, and feel that he has not slipped from the quality of his first book. (p. 58)

Ron Slate, "Thick with Discovery," in The Chowder Review, *No. 8, 1977, pp. 55-8.*

MARY KINZIE

[In *Griffon* Stephen Dobyns'] anagogic skill far exceeds the technical display, so we must ride through an entire, splendid book on the back, it often seems, of one long declarative sentence. . . . Just as the tone is locked into an obsessive habit of declaration, many of the poems are riddles written from a uniform state of possession, an idée fixe. His idea shows itself in different forms: as the spookiness in the behavior of one's own hands; as the tendency of things to fall upward, slip aside, or plummet; and as the cloaking of the ordinary in the grotesque. (pp. 42-3)

The defiance of gravity occurs in poems like "**Our Place in Winter**" where the expectation of spring produces a constant "tilting"; in "**First Meeting with Ivan Shark**" where the "walls lean toward him; / the floor tilts and I start to fall"; in "**Getting Around Town**" where, having helped the elderly over the rail of the George Washington Bridge, he too goes "toppling into the October sky." And the most interesting recourse to this strange anti-gravity urge in Dobyns is "**The Grandfather Poem**" where the dying man, failing fast and losing his memory, "is something he is falling into." "His eyes teeter / in their sockets . . . His face slips towards the mouth." . . . The teetering and toppling of eyes and faces brings us to the obsessive use of hands, emblems of our impress on the world and often the first site of dissociation from it: "The hand on the sheet / is beginning to close. / The sheet closes up within it. / I am in a far place, / getting farther" ("**Running**"). In "**Escaping Again**" the poet leaves his body on the bed and goes to "touch all the hands in my house." It is winter and everything is dying, running down; neighbors "sit on their hands and accept stories from machines. / They can do nothing. All their clocks are dying . . . We see you at the window with your hands and negative face." The cellar thief in "**Crossroads,**" "too fat to run much", confesses, "Now the wind lives in my hands / and the crows make me thinner each day." In the last section of the book, called "**Grimoire**" (book of spells), the emblem for "**Fear**" advises, "Don't let your hand hang over the bed / in case something takes it while you sleep", while the emblem for "**Anger**" ends:

> His hands come in boxes.
> His skin is lined with knives.

His head is a mixture of phosphorous and
sulphur: strike him anywhere.

The boxed hands and inner-facing of knives in **"Anger"** re-
capitulate motifs in **"The Men With Long Faces"**:

The men with long faces have come after my knives.

. . .

Tied down in the back, my knives are forgetting.
How shall I know what is quiet without them?
How shall the darkness now keep its distance?

The feminine endings and triple rhythms create a fantastic sense
of monotony, as if we were reading Borges in a translation by
Longfellow. The question remains: why should knives keep
apart the corners of rooms, distinguish the speaker from his
pets, or sustain order by their consciousness? The symbolic
significance doesn't come clear in any one of the poems, but
I offer the following hypothesis: that the poems in *Griffon* are
all part of a long kenning designed to keep the hand away from
the knife. (While the poet waits for death, in the form of Ivan
Shark, he spends the morning cleaning knives.) Violence, and
especially that of psychological dislocation ("my clothes feel
like someone else's"), is the ruling spirit of the book. The
figures of Shark and Griffon hover about, waiting to deliver
their punch lines. . . . Laughter in the teeth of one's own grimace is one of life's great humiliations; Dobyns records it
fearfully and well. (pp. 43-5)

Mary Kinzie, "How Could Fools Get Tired!" in
Poetry, *Vol. CXXXII, No. 1, April, 1978, pp. 31-52.**

THE VIRGINIA QUARTERLY REVIEW

[*Heat Death*] continues to combine moods of stark desolation
offset by a crisply controlled voice. The subjects are dreams,
loss, cruelty, death—"the deserted beaches of the heart." With
simple, sharp strokes and a flow of grotesque images, Dobyns
shapes definitive moments or states of mind into parables that
seem already familiar. All but a few of these poems are forceful, dramatic, and convincing.

A review of "Heat Death," in The Virginia Quarterly
Review, *Vol. 56, No. 4, (Autumn, 1980), p. 146.*

J. D. McCLATCHY

A not untypical poem in [Stephen Dobyns's] first book, *Concurring Beasts* (1971), starts this way:

The three-toed Governor of Alabama eyes
the perjured hassock of our intent,
swaddled in old declarations. Mirrors
crowd his feet, gilt slippers lifted
to his nation's effort.

There is really not very much one can say about such work.
You either like it or you do not. I do not. His latest collection
[*Heat Death*] is at once more slack and more lyrical than his
earlier work. Many of the best poems in the book have the
word "Song" in their titles, and some music in their lines.
Other poems—notably **"Snow,"** the prosaic but memorable
"The Body of Romulus," and the delicate **"Getting Through
Winter"**—are fine examples of the theme-and-variations format that Dobyns is best at—the theme providing control, the
variations offering surprise. Unfortunately, these winning poems
are surrounded by—towards the end of the book, swamped

by—twaddle. Coy set-pieces abound. Whether they take to
eating Neruda or watching Peg and Bob watch TV, they are
invariably about Writing The Poem. And such writing sinks
this book, I fear, under the weight of its fatuity. (p. 236)

J. D. McClatchy, "Figures in the Landscape," in
Poetry, *Vol. CXXXVIII, No. 4, July, 1981, pp.
231-41.**

JEAN M. WHITE

[In *Saratoga Swimmer*] Stephen Dobyns offers a mystery to
savor for its lean, unmannered prose style, the backdrop of the
Saratoga racing spa, and a thoroughly likable hero without a
drop of tired cynicism.

Charlie Bradshaw is a regular, down-to-earth guy. He is middle-aged, divorced, shy with women, enjoys a beer with his
friend, Victor, an earthy, street-smart New Yorker. Charlie's
ideas about a man's loyalties and fair play, as well as his
romantic notions, come from 1940s movies. An ex-cop (*Saratoga Longshot,* 1976), Charlie now is head of security at
Lorelei Stables. When the owner is murdered while doing his
laps at the YMCA pool, Charlie reluctantly agrees to try to
find the killer despite the hostility of his former colleagues on
the police force, who would like to write off the murder as a
contract by a hit man.

The action moves swiftly with a second murder (a groom at
the stable), goon attacks on Charlie and Victor, a stable fire,
and a Hitchcock-like chase through the Saratoga Performing
Arts Center. Best of all, there is Charlie, who is an encyclo-
pedia of information about Saratoga's glory days as a racing
and gambling spa.

Where else would you learn that Arnold Rothstein, the Mr.
Big of Saratoga gamblers and the suspected mastermind of the
Black Sox baseball scandal of 1919, drank milk, collected
Whistler etchings, and employed Legs Diamond as his private
killer? Or that Rothstein, only hours before he was shot for
welching on a bet, had wagered $500,000 that Herbert Hoover
would defeat Al Smith in the upcoming presidential election?

Jean M. White, in a review of "Saratoga Swimmer,"
in Book World—The Washington Post, *December
20, 1981, p. 8.*

RICHARD JACKSON

Stephen Dobyns' *Heat Death,* the title referring to an encompassing entropy in the universe, reflects a world rapidly breaking up, a world where the relationship between discourse and
order, words and things, has already begun to disintegrate.
What he must deal with, then, as he says in a poem on the
loss of a friend's daughter, are "fragments of language, / fragments of blue sky" (**"Fragments"**). But there are no traditional
myths left, no beliefs that can shore up these fragments against
ruin. In **"How Sweet and Proper It Is,"** for example, a questor
lies down exhausted with previous questors in the tower of his
lady, his goal, and then the poem pans across the horizon to
see even more questors en route or beginning.

The solution, for Dobyns, is a surrealistic re-structuring, a
poetry populated with "refugees from / the village of the self"
which are "Turning within him moment by / moment separate
lives which / through his life he tries to / give name to or
simply discover" (**"The Photographs"**). As a result of this
internalizing, the distinctions between inner and outer, imag-

ination and reality, blur. A man sits in his house after his wife has died, hears footsteps, imagines her present, arriving, as the "room trembles with possibility. Then the fact / of her death strikes him once more and she dies" ("**Footsteps**"). In "**Getting Through Winter**" the speaker imagines a girl approaching in such terms as to suggest she is actually there, then reveals it is only a photograph he is looking at, a photograph he would place in all his windows like one of those Magritte paintings in which the canvas portrays exactly what it covers up. In "**Geese**" a man walks out into a pasture, dreams of his past, then dreaming "something touched his arm," his vision restores his lost friends. But returning home, Dobyns projects, he "keeps seeing himself pass / in cars, duck into stores, gathered with / friends around the tables of houses / he walks by at night." Now, he experiences the same touch on his arm as in the dream, and the distinction between biography and dream becomes difficult. . . . (p. 97)

> *Richard Jackson, "No Language but the Language of the Heart," in* Prairie Schooner, *Vol. 56, No. 1, Spring, 1982, pp. 91-9.**

ROBERT HASS

Stephen Dobyns writes detective novels as well as poetry. His most recent novels, *Saratoga Longshot* and *Saratoga Swimmer,* are a sort of cross between Graham Greene and Raymond Chandler set in the New York racetrack town. Dobyns also served a stretch as a reporter for *The Detroit News.* The occupations, detective, reporter, are very useful metaphors for the stance of his poetry, especially the recent *Heat Death,* which is one of the most interesting books of American poems to appear in some time. Now he is back with an odd proposal indeed. *The Balthus Poems* . . . are 32 narratives or dreamscapes based on the work of the great, strange surrealist painter, Balthus.

In his poetry Dobyns' usual physical provenance is Boston. In *The Balthus Poems* it is mostly a middle-class European turn-of-the-century drawing room, charged with peculiar innocence, a slightly voyeuristic eroticism, and an oddly becalmed inwardness which seems colored by a tinge of malice. The distortions and foreshortenings of bodies in Balthus' canvases, the fat moon-shaped faces and scarecrow postures, the way the body is posited as a strange object on the earth, belongs somehow to the glandular shock of adolescence, and many of the figures in his painting are pubescent or prepubescent children. It is this that gathers the paintings around the themes of inwardness and eroticism and death, and it is their enigma, now whimsical, now malevolent, that Dobyns is exploring.

You don't have to know the paintings to read the poems, which do not interpret them but use them as points of departure. Each poem begins by evoking a scene, sometimes a fairly strange scene. . . . Part of the pleasure of the book—its quality of being a series of puzzles and solutions to puzzles—is watching what Dobyns makes of these starting points. . . .

In detective fiction, the universe is running down. The detective hero threads his way through that urban entropy engaged in a private quest for meaning, or perhaps a private duel with meaninglessness. Dobyns, in his detective fiction, plays it straight. In these poems, in the peculiar, dreamy arrest of Balthus' interior world, he is driven to other discoveries. The detective in the poems is his own imagination. As it enters this world, it colludes with it. Detective and criminal become one, and

the criminal is the heart, or rather it is the heart as it begins to understand the body's fate.

> *Robert Hass, in a review of "The Balthus Poems," in* Book World—The Washington Post, *September 5, 1982, p. 7.*

THE NEW YORKER

Francis Lazard [in *Dancer with One Leg*] is a lieutenant in the Boston Fire Department who suffered a severe leg injury several years before we meet him, and is now attached to the Arson Squad. Lazard is a demoniac fireman, a man of absolute integrity possessed by his job. We find him here, recently separated from his wife, involved in the investigation of a fire in which two firemen were killed. The fire was unquestionably arsonous; the firemen were killed when their hose failed because of vandalistic damage to the fire hydrant; the warehouse is owned by the husband of a cousin of Lazard. We watch this obsessed man driving himself to avenge the dead firemen, to round up the vandals, to track down the arsonists, to determine the truth about his cousin-in-law, and we see him destroyed by the faults of his virtues. This is a stirring genre novel, a muscular novel of high intelligence, and a painful portrait of a tragic hero.

> *A review of "Dancer with One Leg," in* The New Yorker, *Vol. LIX, No. 16, June 6, 1983, p. 142.*

PETER STITT

The Balthus Poems, by Stephen Dobyns, is a book of subtle conceptual artistry and intellect, supremely a work of the imagination. Each of these thirty-two poems has its genesis in a painting by Balthus. . . . Insofar as the poems are narrative, describe action which progresses through time, they belong emphatically to the poet rather than to the painting or the painter. As Octavio Paz is quoted as saying in an epigraph, "In a picture things are, they do not happen." The happenings here are metaphors, personal to Stephen Dobyns and not to Balthus. Which is not to say that these poems are personal in a usual sense, that they reek of the confessional. Primarily the actions in them are imaginative or psychological: they take place within the minds of the characters described, but more importantly still in the mind of the author. The setting of these poems belongs not to the real world but to Balthus; the actions belong not to Balthus but to Dobyns. We are thus in most of them removed by at least two levels from the real world of ordinary reality.

These poems are not just "seemingly free from the lyrical first person voice"; nowhere does Dobyns, or a created speaker, speak to us using the word "I." So why is he so cagey about it in the prefatory comment? Precisely to draw our attention to the pervasiveness of the personal realm in the book—every detail, every action, every interpretation represents a choice made by Stephen Dobyns, and don't you forget it. This doesn't mean that we could study Dobyns's personality in some sly way here. It just means that this book celebrates throughout its length the power of the creative intellect, the imagination, to have things its own way. In the twenty-sixth of these thirty-two poems, we are startled not by the sudden appearance of the word "I" but of the word "you," which manages to function in much the same way. The poem, like the painting it is based on, is called "**Katia Reading**"; the second stanza begins: "All this is a painting you have seen often, and often / you have tried to determine what the girl is reading." The you is the viewer—but not just any viewer, not the reader, for as the author has also said: "My desire was to write poems that in no way would be dependent on a knowledge of the paintings or the artist." The viewer, then, is the poet, who takes this opportunity to explain the central importance of his own created world to his theory of art.

Looking more closely at the book in Katia's hands, he sees that it is "too thin for a novel; / and you have come to think it must be poetry." He then remembers "the first time / you read a poem that moved you," an experience that allowed— finally!—for a transformation of the world:

> What had your world been until then? First you
> ate something, then you bought something, then you
> went bowling; a world where men passed their lives
> peering under the hoods of cars. And like the girl
> in the painting you must have turned your head
> slightly as if from a loud noise; and you too became
> like someone who has left on a journey, someone who
> has become the answer to his own impossible riddle:
> who condemned to his room is at last free of the room.

The result of this process is the poems in this book, all of which themselves manage to break free of the "rooms" which contain them at the beginning, the paintings. (pp. 48-9)

This is, in short, a stunning book. (p. 50)

Peter Stitt, "Imagination in the Ascendant," in Po-etry, *Vol. CXLIII, No. 1, October, 1983, pp. 39-50.**

PETER STITT

The Balthus Poems is deeply concerned not with the meaning of the lives we lead but with the nature and possibilities of the process of art. Each poem illustrates the enormous power and potentiality of the unfettered imagination by telling the story that seems to be suggested by a given painting by Balthus. The poems touch upon reality only in detail and texture; everything else is made up, beginning with their genesis in Balthus' imaginary fragments. Dobyns' new book, *Black Dog, Red Dog,* by contrast, intends to achieve wisdom about the process of life, and in terms of method, the poems are far more traditional than those in *The Balthus Poems.* Here, Dobyns relies upon a narrative line so straightforward that at times we feel we are reading the naked truth.

Dobyns' goal is similar to [William] Matthews': each wants to subject the raw materials of experience to the process of thought in order to arrive at some answer, some way of living on into the future. Their methods of achieving this are quite different, however. Where Matthews brings a well-conceived and previously formulated theory to bear upon his experience, Dobyns searches through the fabric of experience itself for some little glimmer of truth, some hint of how to proceed. For example, the poem **"All That Lies Buried"** begins with the speaker walking at night amid falling snowflakes: "I catch several on my glove, / turn them over—blank on both sides. How / am I to continue with messages like these?" . . . The ideas, the subjects, are expressed through images, so that the reader can begin to feel the thought. Later the speaker remembers a bird he had watched one summer, some years ago:

> . . . Sometimes a wave
> rushed in too fast, swamping the bird which
> then shook itself and continued, and I liked that,

liked how the bird kept to the very edge.
I even thought, that's the work I want for myself;
as if that line were the division between world
and soul—the place where life itself lies hidden.
But tonight I think, isn't it living at the edge
that makes the trouble—never getting comfortable
or taking anything for granted, never trusting anything?

Undoubtedly these lines will be too direct for the taste of many readers, too literal, too sentimental. Within context, however, they work better than they do stripped naked here—and in any case, it is the general method that interests me: how wisdom emerges from the concrete, when it is needed, within the dramatic situation created by the poem's fiction.

As for the poem, it concludes with a rather different message from the one we have just seen:

> What does the water leave at the wave's edge?
> Whatever it leaves, the waves then hammer it down,
> bury it deeper and deeper under the sand, as if
> the wave's message, like the message of earth
> or snow, is simply burial—the brain's message
> to memory, the black dirt's message to a corpse.

The lines work away from the literal, the sentimental, and reach a kind of rhetorical grandeur, thanks in part to the movement of the imagery here. (pp. 861-63)

This is a book very much built upon memory; the stories it tells are recounted from many places, many times. What gives them unity is the person who speaks them, the person whose experiences they apparently are; it is his own life that he is trying to understand. These poems are almost always both entertaining and convincing; wisdom grows out of being. It would appear that Dobyns has switched mentors, to an extent, abandoning Proust (whose sensibility seems to brood over *The Balthus Poems*) in favor of Louis Simpson, master of the mundane. Dobyns' style is not nearly so plain as Simpson's, but each relies heavily on the fabric of real life for texture and story, and on the use of the telling image for meaning and resolution. (p. 863)

Peter Stitt, "Wisdom and Being in Contemporary American Poetry," in The Georgia Review, *Vol. XXXVIII, No. 4, Winter, 1984, pp. 857-68.**

GILBERT ALLEN

[In *The Balthus Poems*] Dobyns is trying to extend moments into motion, and he hopes that by doing so he will be able to deal more objectively with the concerns that lie behind both painting and lyric poetry.

It's not a bad idea. Of course, the objectivity is an illusion, regardless of the narrator's discretion, but the illusion can free the poet to explore moods and settings that he would rarely approach more directly. The accompanying danger is that this detachment will become indifference: that the poems will lack the necessity of truly outstanding work.

But if these poems are usually calm, they are rarely cold. The narrator's engagement is usually implied through his careful selection of descriptive details. And in a poem like **"Getting Up,"** Dobyns makes his analysis of the scene the poem's center. A young girl, playing in her bedroom, is about to dress for school. Once there

> she will join her friends,
> all dressed as she is,
> and together they will proceed
> through the civilized
> unwinding of their day. But now,
> naked with her cat,
> she is learning about death
> and the desire
> to kill; she is learning
> about humiliation and
> the manipulation of power. . . .

This peculiar abstraction of elegance and violence would be difficult to achieve in either a dramatic or a lyric poem. The result would seem either hysterical or condescending, rather than the filtered, steady light that we see here. . . .

Dobyns is not afraid to be clear even when he is expressing ideas, a pleasant departure from the conventions of contemporary poetry. In addition, he has the more common virtue of presenting evocative images that give his poems a painterly elegance. . . . Dobyns seems to be taking human emotions more seriously than in his earlier books, whose surrealistic zaniness often made the poems seem merely cerebral exercises. A poem such as **"Girl in White,"** on the other hand, is not flashy, but it has more substantial virtues: precise, appropriate diction and an unobtrusive style that fuses events and feelings. The poem is a fine evocation of an adolescent's sexual longing, within a world that makes its pain and beauty both more intense and more unreal.

There are fewer poems-about-poetry in this book than in Dobyns' earlier work, but the theme does surface on occasion, most interestingly in **"Katia Reading."** After the narrator describes a young girl engrossed in a book "golden with an orange spine," he broadens the context to include both himself and the reader. Dobyns' purpose, of course, is to persuade us to find in his poems the same imaginative riches that he has discovered in Balthus' work.

I would like to be more fully a believer, but Dobyns has put several obstacles in my path. First, his book is too long. Lesser poems presented as variations upon a theme often sound tired and unfocused. The endless tableau of recumbent, unclothed adolescents makes me wish that Dobyns had more respect for his reader's time. The purpose of the arts is to quell boredom, not merely to evoke or to dissect it. Too many of the Balthus poems seem like period pieces in which quaintness is equated with imaginative insight. . . . Also, the traces of coyness in lesser poems undermine the emotional intensity of the better ones. . . . Although most of the poems satisfy Pound's dictum that verse should be written at least as well as prose, there are a few lapses: a dangling participle in **"The Street,"** some needlessly repeated words and phrases, and a few cliches. (A village is "washed golden by morning light" in one poem; something is "as / inescapable as taxation or death" in another.)

But my disappointment is at least partially a measure of my delight in the book's finest poems: **"The Living Room," "Nude Resting," "The Moth," "Boy with Pigeons," "Girl in White,"** and **"Landscape at Champrovent."** *The Balthus Poems,* with some deft editorial pruning, could have been a marvelous chapbook, but it is a good read as it stands, fleshy though it may be.

Gilbert Allen, "Cool, Calm & Collected," in The American Book Review, *Vol. 6, No. 4, May-June, 1984, p. 20.*

ANDY BRUMER

The poems in Stephen Dobyns's **Black Dog, Red Dog** demand patient reading before their messages snap into focus. It seems that Mr. Dobyns, who writes mystery novels as well as poetry, will not be satisfied until he completely annihilates all vestiges of romanticism and sentimentality in his verse. But that ambition to be hard-edged proves a bit deceptive in the end.

Black Dog, Red Dog is a collection of quasi-narrative poems whose opening lines might make the best short-story writers envious: "The week the nuclear protesters stormed the gates / of the Seabrook plant was the same week you were born." Or "We had come to the English Hospital in Tangier / and my friend kept screaming none of the needles were clean." Such lines may produce a trancelike state of narrative expectancy and comfort in readers, but what follows is often as surprising and improvisational as the most abstract, nonsequential lyric poem.

One poem, **"The Gun,"** begins innocently enough with two preadolescent boys playing in a room "next to a stack of comics." Suddenly, the boy who lives in the house where they are playing is telling the other to "pull down your pants," and when he refuses, the first boy goes to a drawer and returns "holding a small gun by the barrel." Indeed, both the threatened boy and the reader are held captive by the horror of a society whose people, it sometimes seems, are possessed by the love of violence. Although the boy with the gun does little more than scare the daylights out of his friend, the mood of this opening poem sets the tone for the book, a volume in which the author restlessly struggles to free himself from a meaningless and despair-ridden existence.

So while many of the poems have the illusion of an almost documentary objectivity, they reveal instead the soulful confessions of one individual in turmoil. The violence of the world and the self is faced so squarely in this book that at times the poet has no recourse but to break into more soothing images of self-love. . . .

The significance of the black dog and the red dog is . . . revealed in the book's title poem . . . [The] protagonist is a young boy, who, after getting off his bike one evening,

> looks out toward
> red sky and darkening earth, and they seem poised
> like two animals that have always hated each other,
> each fiercely wanting to tear out the other's throat:
> black dog, red dog—now more despairing, more
>   resolved.

In dreams and mythology, the dog often symbolizes a human being's instinctual side, and the image Mr. Dobyns presents here reminds us of how ruthlessly we turn on ourselves and others when our animal natures aren't fully acknowledged and integrated. This is a harrowing book, not meant to please but to instruct.

Andy Brumer, "Experience, Instinct and Intimacy," in The New York Times Book Review, *September 23, 1984, p. 14.**

JEAN M. WHITE

In Stephen Dobyns' *Saratoga Headhunter* . . . , Charlie Bradshaw, his unassuming, good-natured private eye, makes a most welcome reappearance for his third adventure in a low-keyed, entertaining series brightened with gentle humor.

Charlie is even more woebegone than usual. He lost his steady job as a security chief for Lorelei Stables when his boss was killed in the Saratoga Springs YMCA swimming pool (*Saratoga Swimmer*). The private-eye business is not booming for him and his funny, rather seedy partner, Victor Plotz. Charlie has to get up before dawn to moonlight as a milkman for a friend, who rushed off to Santa Fe to be at the bedside of his mother, who has been dying for weeks marked with miraculous recoveries and repeated setbacks.

Then, to top it off, Charlie has to break a cozy dinner-at-home date with Doris, the waitress, when he reluctantly gives refuge to a crooked jockey-turned-informer who is fleeing the mob. And Charlie never really liked the jockey, but he always has been particularly nice to those he doesn't like because he somehow feels guilty for not liking them.

Things only get worse for Charlie. He comes home to find the headless body of the jockey slumped over his kitchen table. The townspeople and racing crowd think he sold out to the mob and turn their backs. His successful cousins—construction and hardware—are smug as they watch Charlie's muddle grow.

Then a nice old man who was a racetrack hanger-on is killed after hinting he may have some information for Charlie. So Charlie sets out to clear his own name and solve the murders (another is to come). His technique, as partner Victor observes, is to "rile up" suspects until "they come after you." *Saratoga Headhunter* ends with a mad milk-truck chase after Charlie uncovers a racing scam involving horse breeding.

Dobyns, a poet as well as novelist, writes with slyly quiet humor and tender feeling. . . .

The Dobyns mysteries are as good-natured as Charlie himself.

> *Jean M. White, "Sleuthing in Saratoga," in* Book World—The Washington Post, *May 19, 1985, p. 8.*

JIM ELLEDGE

Black Dog, Red Dog is at times nightmare-like, its narrative poems depicting a "world where everything goes wrong, / where suddenly you are making love to a corpse, / where your car plunges into a ditch." The event Dobyns records may be less traumatic—"bad mail, / bad politics, bad love"; yet, the better times also always somehow go "wrong." (p. 297)

Dobyns has trained his eye to ferret out the odd and unexpected twists life takes. **"Wedding,"** for example, never offers a view

of the nuptial rites but, instead, records his and an unidentified friend's trip to another friend's wedding, a journey that is interrupted:

> . . . I remember how you watched
> the attendants carrying the man on the stretcher
> who seemed almost delicate under his red blanket,
> although any need or fear of delicacy was past.
> I remember how you lowered your head, turning away.
> Lucky bastard, at least he's out of it, you said.
> And then the train lurched once and dragged us
>   forward.

They are "dragged . . . forward" not only to the wedding but into the future, where other tragedies await them.

At times, Dobyns is too obvious, as in **"The Earth from This Distance"** or in **"Dead Baby,"** which is, nevertheless, a chilling poem. Yet, in his best work, such obviousness reveals Dobyns's confidence, even his boldness, which permeates most of *Black Dog, Red Dog*. It may be seen in his metaphors . . . , or in his odd, yet enticing, combination of the classical with the contemporary, as in this characterization of the leader of the Arognauts: "Jason was the kind of man who if he fell from a window / would land in a passing wagon of hay; the soldier / whose breast pocket Bible stops the fatal bullet."

Dobyns's humor never elicits a belly laugh, only a grin, but serves to counteract the unwavering harshness of his vision. **"Kentucky Derby Day, Belfast, Maine,"** for example, opens humorously . . . but soon gets down to the business at hand, focusing on the losers gathered in Barbara's Lunch, "five people from the chicken plant / who . . . have been drinking beer and shots since breakfast." One is a boy whose "homemade tattoos" across "his biceps / and bare shoulders" Dobyns describes as "a poor man's / advertisement for unrequited love."

Black Dog, Red Dog is Dobyns's "dark gossip of a darker world." The secrets he discloses are his own; the hurts also. While a nostalgic impulse asserts itself in this poem or that, it affords him no respite. Instead, it serves only to underscore his pain:

> . . . in his mind is a confused memory
> of cafés and wide boulevards, of sitting
> with his friends on spring evenings, arguing
> and feeling indignant about the world
> in those days before his children were born
> when he had only his own good name to lose.

He is left, and he leaves us, with his unflinching vision, which we may not like, but whose power and honesty we cannot deny. . . . (pp. 298-99)

> *Jim Elledge, "Triumphs," in* Poetry, *Vol. CXLVI, No. 5, August, 1985, pp. 293-99.**

E(dgar) L(aurence) Doctorow

1931-

American novelist, short story writer, dramatist, essayist, and editor.

A major contemporary fiction writer, Doctorow achieved widespread recognition with the overwhelming critical and commercial success of *Ragtime* (1975), a novel which vividly recreates the turbulent years of pre-World War I America. In *Ragtime,* as in much of his fiction, Doctorow presents a multilayered narrative and historical settings and personages while exploring issues important to contemporary society. Central to Doctorow's work is his portrayal of characters who search for the material prosperity and social equality promised by the "American Dream" yet become victims of the oppressiveness of class division and capitalism. For Doctorow, history is a cyclical process in which his characters fall prey to a future over which they have no control.

Although Doctorow received little critical attention for his early novels, *Welcome to Hard Times* (1960) and *Big As Life* (1966), he was praised for his inventive approaches to the genres of the Western and science fiction as well as for his exploration of the relationship between good and evil. In *Welcome to Hard Times,* which concerns the self-destruction of a small Western town following a vicious attack by an evil outlaw, Doctorow deviates from the traditional Western novel by allowing evil to triumph. *Big As Life* is set in the near future and focuses on the reactions of New Yorkers to the possible annihilation of their city by two gigantic humanlike beings.

In his historical fiction, Doctorow examines the social realities of America's past by relying on an imaginative rendering of the times rather than strict adherence to documented fact. *The Book of Daniel* (1971), Doctorow's first major work, is a fictionalized account of the events surrounding the trial of Julius and Ethel Rosenberg, Jewish immigrants who were convicted and executed in the early 1950s for conspiracy to commit treason. The narrative focuses on the devastating impact of their deaths on their children. The novel is considered by many to be a poignant critique of the anti-Communist climate during the McCarthy era. *Ragtime* revolves around three families of different socioeconomic backgrounds and their encounters with well-known historical figures of the early twentieth century. Although some critics faulted the novel for its fanciful altering of history, many found its pseudohistorical overtones entertaining and meaningful. Critics especially admired Doctorow's prose style, which, with its strong rhythms and syncopated sentences, imitates ragtime music. Stanley Kauffmann viewed *Ragtime* as a "unique and beautiful work of art about American destiny, built of fact and logical fantasy." In *Loon Lake* (1980), Doctorow also fuses fact and fiction in his depiction of life during the Depression. Doctorow develops a cynical vision of the American Dream in this story of a man who sacrifices his moral values for wealth and social prominence. *Loon Lake* is considered Doctorow's most complex novel due to his combination of blank verse and prose and his experiments with setting, time, and multiple narrative viewpoints.

Lives of the Poets: Six Stories and a Novella (1984) consists of a series of seemingly unrelated stories connected through a

single character, a middle-aged author. Reading the work as a whole reveals this character's background and the events that have shaped his life. Critics praised Doctorow's evocation of time and space and his incisive, often ironic portrayal of Manhattan's artistic community. In *World's Fair* (1985) Doctorow recreates life in New York during the 1930s from the perspective of a young boy. Doctorow juxtaposes the hardships of the era with the youngster's vivid observations and imaginings. The novel culminates with the boy's two visits to the 1939 World's Fair in New York, which inspire him to dream about the future. Reviewers noted many autobiographical elements in *World's Fair* and suggested that this work offers a portrait of the development of Doctorow's imagination. Doctorow has also written a play, *Drinks Before Dinner* (1978). *Welcome to Hard Times, The Book of Daniel,* and *Ragtime* have been adapted for film.

(See also *CLC,* Vols. 6, 11, 15, 18; *Contemporary Authors,* Vols. 45-48; *Contemporary Authors New Revision Series,* Vol. 2; *Dictionary of Literary Biography,* Vols. 2, 28; and *Dictionary of Literary Biography Yearbook: 1980.*)

CHARLES BERRYMAN

A chorus of praise greeted the publication of E. L. Doctorow's *Ragtime* in the summer of 1975. . . . (p. 30)

The successful wave of publicity led within six months to a riptide of criticism. Early in 1976 the reviews began to turn hostile.... Seldom has a novel been so well received, then so violently attacked, and all the time so little understood. While celebrating the dynamic quality of the narrative, the reviewers did not begin to inquire about the identity of the narrator. While attacking the mixture of fiction and history, the critics failed to understand how the two fit together. (pp. 30-1)

The complexity of Doctorow's earlier novels should have alerted reviewers to the potential subtlety of *Ragtime.* Doctorow is not an artist content with offering the mere illusion of history. The story of the rise and fall of a western town is told in *Welcome to Hard Times* by a narrator who is a survivor of the history he has suffered, promoted, and perhaps invented. The story of the trial and conviction of the Rosenbergs was transformed in *The Book of Daniel* into a novel with a double narrative structure and a subtle political spectrum. Doctorow ranks high among the recent authors—Barth, Pynchon, Vonnegut—willing to experiment with the form of the novel in order to reach an artful compromise with modern history. The wide popularity of *Ragtime* does not mean that Doctorow has abandoned his experimental approach to the form of the novel or departed from the quality of his earlier work. The structure of *Ragtime* is indeed complex, and the novel's political and psychological vision is also quite intricate. But the surface of the novel is so rich with events and personalities that its dynamic life may be quickly enjoyed without pausing to analyze its remarkable structure. Thus the great popularity of the book, and the equally great incomprehension.

The first problem is to locate the narrator. Almost all of the fictional characters belong to two families: one well established in New Rochelle with a father who manufactures flags and fireworks, and a poor immigrant family with a father who makes silhouettes. Before the novel is over the families will merge and their fortunes will reverse. The narrator of the novel refers to the parents of the New Rochelle family as Father and Mother. Their only child is a little boy in a sailor suit who is seen infrequently in the book and seldom appears to be a significant character. A casual reader of the novel might not identify the little boy as the narrator, but enough is gradually revealed about his personality to allow us to see how the novel has been put together from his recollections and his research.

Doctorow does let us know just a few pages into the book that the little boy "had reached that age of knowledge and wisdom in a child when it is not expected by the adults around him and consequently goes unrecognized." Is this the "wisdom and knowledge" necessary to tell the story of his family? If the child is the narrator why does he refer to his parents as Father and Mother but always to himself in the third person as "the little boy"? A similar narrative strategy was used by Doctorow in *The Book of Daniel,* where parts of the story are told by a small boy in the first person, and parts are told by the same character in later years when he looks back upon his childhood and often refers to himself in the third person. But in *Ragtime* the mature or present narrator is never directly introduced. Instead it is necessary to infer that the little boy has the ability at a later date to look back and assemble the various pieces of his history.

Doctorow waits until chapter fifteen to reveal the qualities of the boy's mind and personality which allow him to assemble and focus the events of the novel. Only then does Doctorow explain how the boy "treasured anything discarded. He took

his education peculiarly and lived an entirely secret intellectual life." The novel is an extraordinary montage of bits and pieces discarded from the past, and it is the secret intellectual life of the little boy that saves and assembles the many images. The journal of a trip to the North Pole recorded by his father and the artistic silhouettes cut by his stepfather both eventually come into the possession of the little boy. Thus he gains the evidence necessary to tell about the journey to the Arctic with Commander Peary and to imagine the frustration of the immigrant artist cutting silhouettes on a street corner in New York.

If gathering scraps from the past is the secret activity of the little boy, what sense of order will he be able to impose upon them? "He was alert not only to discarded materials," Doctorow says of his narrator, "but to unexpected events and coincidences." Few novels since Dickens have possessed so many unexpected events and coincidences.... *Ragtime* is a comic novel, and much of the comedy depends upon the coincidences of history and fiction that come together in the mind of the narrator.

What education does the narrator have to enable him to assemble the comic patterns? "He learned nothing at school," it is reported, "so it was left to Grandfather to cultivate what might be the boy's oddity or merely his independence of spirit." Grandfather is a retired professor of classics, and he tells the boy stories from Ovid. "They were stories of people who became animals or trees or statues. They were stories of transformation." With this education it is not surprising that the little boy becomes the narrator of a novel about transformations. He will describe how his own father is transformed from a confident explorer into a frustrated and helpless man. When this parent is lost with the sinking of the *Lusitania,* the little boy will acquire a new father who has experienced an even more remarkable transformation—from an immigrant Latvian socialist to a successful Hollywood producer. While some of the historical figures in the book, J. P. Morgan and Henry Ford, discuss their belief in reincarnation, the fictional characters are shown in the stages of their metamorphoses. (pp. 31-3)

The little boy observes the changing of all things, but he is most observant when the image is his own reflection. At the end of the first chapter the boy has a chance to meet Harry Houdini. The magician unexpectedly pays a visit to the boy's family, and parks his touring car in front of their house. What does the little boy do? Characteristically he is preoccupied with "gazing at the distorted macrocephalic image of himself in the shiny brass fitting of the headlight." His world as narrator of *Ragtime* will be a series of comic mirrors.

Chapter fifteen includes a further analysis of the boy's fascination with reflected images. Doctorow moves beyond the obvious—"And then he took to studying himself in the mirror, perhaps expecting some change to take place before his eyes,"—to explore the metaphysics of mirror images: "He would gaze at himself until there were two selves facing one another, neither of which could claim to be the real one. The sensation was of being disembodied. He was no longer anything exact as a person. He had the dizzying feeling of separating from himself endlessly."... It is the narrator's experience of separation from himself that explains why he refers to himself in the third person throughout the novel. If the narrator feels the "sensation of being disembodied," it is not surprising that the reader of the novel may forget how the narrator is related to the character of the little boy. (p. 35)

The importance of mirrors in Doctorow's novel suggests how much *Ragtime* has in common with the legend of Narcissus. Does the narrator lose himself like the hero of the Greek myth in the vain pursuit of his own image? Is Doctorow's novel a reflection of Shakespeare's narcissistic Richard II who breaks the mirror in petulant despair because it shows him his own broken face? As the deposed Richard sees the glass cracked in a hundred slivers, he cannot avoid the thought of his coming destruction. "A brittle glory shineth in this face," he cries, "as brittle as the glory is the face." The narrator of *Ragtime* shows a variety of faces reflected in a decade of history, and he knows that the images will be shattered when the decade ends in war. It is not the vanity of the narcissistic quest that so much concerns Doctorow's narrator, but rather the diffraction of the image and the inevitable destruction. Mutability and death haunt the final movements of *Ragtime* on the eve of international violence. The narrator does not love what he sees in the mirror, but he is fascinated with the cycles of change. (pp. 35-6)

Does the unrecognized "knowledge and wisdom" of the little boy include a foreknowledge of the impending cycle of destruction? If the narrator is telling his story in retrospect, then of course he enjoys the omniscient perspective gained from the experience which has been sifted through recollection and supported by research. The narrator, for example, has had time to read his father's North Pole journal, and he even claims to have gained access to Houdini's private, unpublished papers. But early in the novel there is a bizarre moment when the dialogue of the little boy, not the voice of the mature narrator, reveals an accurate and unexpected knowledge of the future. At the end of the first chapter, when Houdini visits the family of the narrator, the little boy tells the magician to "Warn the Duke." The remark does not make sense to anyone present, and the boy runs away. Readers of the novel will also be puzzled because thus far in the book there has not been any mention of a duke. Only at the end of chapter thirteen will Houdini unexpectedly meet the ill-fated heir to the Austro-Hungarian throne. At that time Houdini does not remember his message for the duke. It is only at the end of the novel when Houdini is hanging upside down eleven stories over Times Square that he remembers the warning of the little boy, and realizes, now that it is too late, that perhaps he had a chance to prevent the assassination and the cycle of destruction that will follow.

Houdini's unexpected vision of the little boy at the climax of the novel is a recollection of the first and only meeting of the magician and the future narrator. How could the boy at the beginning of the book have known enough about the future to be able to advise Houdini to warn the unfortunate archduke? More than one reviewer of the novel has been disturbed by the boy's foreknowledge of the duke's fate. . . . [Yet this] criticism tends to ignore the credentials of the boy as the future narrator of the novel, and also to overlook the importance of the moment for Houdini. After the death of his mother, Houdini has followed a second career of exposing the fraud of spiritualists, soothsayers, and various charlatans with their claims of extrasensory perception and clairvoyance. But when he thinks about the warning of the little boy, Houdini decides that "it was the one genuine mystical experience of his life." His attempt to rediscover the boy, however, is frustrated. Houdini returns a week later to the home of the narrator in New Rochelle only to find that the little boy and his family have disappeared. The narrator is typically lost in the mirror of history, and Houdini is left with his inexplicable memory.

At least Houdini retains the memory of "one genuine mystical experience." The majority of the characters in the novel, whether the reflections of history or fiction, all follow adventures that are frustrating and inconclusive. The unsatisfactory nature of the heroic quest is illustrated in a variety of adventures: Commander Peary takes his expedition in search of the North Pole; J. P. Morgan attempts to contact the ancient gods of Egypt by spending a night in the Great Pyramid; Coalhouse Walker seeks justice through revolutionary violence; Houdini wishes to contact his dead mother; and Emma Goldman wants to break the tyranny of capitalism. What do all of these quests have in common? Why does Doctorow bring them all together in *Ragtime?* Doctorow's novel is a picture of Western society moving inevitably to the weapons and death of world conflict. Doctorow shows how the many adventures of human will are frustrated, and how the frustration leads to the violence of war. (pp. 36-7)

All of the quests in the novel, with the exception of the immigrant father's success in Hollywood, prove inconclusive and unsatisfactory. Commander Peary, for example, has spent most of his life planning for the moment of victory when he can be the first man to stand at the very top of the earth. But his triumph is uncertain: "No one observation satisfied him. He would walk a few steps due north and find himself going due south. On this watery planet the sliding sea refused to be fixed. He couldn't find the exact place to say this spot, here, is the North Pole.". . . The anticlimactic nature of Peary's quest is typical of what happens to the many adventurers in Doctorow's novel. Morgan expects to receive signs from Osiris in the Great Pyramid of Egypt. Instead he finds himself covered with bedbugs. Coalhouse Walker would like to have his automobile restored in a symbolic gesture of civil and racial justice. Instead he is shot by the police when he steps from the Morgan Library. Houdini intends to prove his strength against the confinement of death by escaping from a buried coffin. Instead he discovers that the weight of the earth is too much, and he must be dug from the grave by his desperate assistants.

Why do all of the adventures prove inconclusive? It is the narrator of the novel who clearly perceives the mutability of all things. Skating on the pond near his home the young boy watches "only the tracks made by the skaters, traces quickly erased of moments past, journeys taken." The novel is a vision of the many journeys and moments traced on the melting ice. It is his sense of the world in flux that informs the narrator's description of Peary's attempt to locate the North Pole—"On this watery planet the sliding sea refused to be fixed." And just as Peary "shuffled back and forth over the ice" at the inconclusive height of his quest, J. P. Morgan is described as moving blindly about in the King's Chamber of the Great Pyramid—"He paced from the west to the east, from the north to the south, though he didn't know which was which."

While the narrator of the novel recognizes that history is a comic mirror, many of the characters in the book believe in the illusions of themselves cast back by the changing times. J. P. Morgan, for example, believes that Henry Ford and himself are reincarnations of the great pharoahs who commanded the building of the pyramids. The narrator of *Ragtime* explains how Morgan is trying to escape from a world of mutability: "His desperate studies settled, inevitably, on the civilizations of ancient Egypt, wherein it was taught that the universe is changeless and that death is followed by the resumption of life." . . . But the novel at every turn reveals the vanity of Morgan's thesis. Nothing is permanent in a world that "refused to be fixed,'' and all of the adventurers are trapped by the illusions of self cast back by the turning mirror of history. The one successful character in the novel is therefore the immigrant father who can rise to power and fortune in Hollywood because he knows that history is a reel of illusions.

Even the master of illusion, Harry Houdini, also becomes its victim. All of his staged escapes are mere vaudeville tricks unless Houdini can escape from death itself. After his mother dies Houdini desperately wants to believe in the possibility of some form of supernatural life. But his visits to spiritualists and the conductors of seances all over America only convince him of their fraud and vanity. He wages a national campaign against their trickery with all of the outrage and hurt of a child who has just seen that a wizard is a humbug. Houdini may escape from jails and straitjackets and a Chinese torture machine; he may be among the first to climb into the air at the controls of his own plane; he may hang upside down eleven stories over Times Square; but the only time in his life when a true key to the future is placed in his hands Houdini does not recognize its value until it is too late. He remains just as locked in mortal time as Morgan and Peary. Only the little boy who told him years in advance to ''Warn the Duke'' will be able to separate from himself in order to put together the novel of illusions.

Houdini's attempt to break from the confinement of a buried coffin is described very early in the novel: ''He was buried alive in a grave and could not escape, and had to be rescued. Hurriedly, they dug him out. The earth is too heavy, he said gasping. His nails bled. Soil fell from his eyes. He was drained of color and couldn't stand.''. . . Some characters in the novel, nevertheless, enjoy being buried alive. The little boy and his stepsister play on the beach by covering one another with sand. ''The burial game,'' the narrator remembers, ''was their most serious pleasure.'' They lie on the beach under sculptured images of their bodies, much like the mummy of the pharaoh in his sculptured coffin, until they escape from the mound of sand and run to wash themselves in the ocean. This ritual escape from burial is sought in vain by Houdini and Morgan. Only the children of the novel, especially the narrator as the little boy, can break free from the mold of self and then baptize a new life.

All of the inconclusive quests in the novel are symptoms of the frustration and suppressed violence that will explode at the end of the book with the advent of World War I. The decade of tension prior to the war is characterized by the very title of the novel, and also by the life of the great composer Scott Joplin, who led the way in the creation of ragtime music. His words are used for the epigraph to Doctorow's novel, and his career is echoed throughout *Ragtime*. . . . [There are] many similarities between Doctorow's jazz pianist and the career of Scott Joplin. In the narrator's home in New Rochelle it is Coalhouse Walker who plays some of the famous Joplin pieces such as ''Wall Street Rag'' and ''The Maple Leaf Rag.'' After the fire station of New Rochelle is destroyed by the vengeance of Coalhouse Walker, and the newspapers of New York are competing with one another for news of the black terrorist, a picture of Scott Joplin is mistakenly printed by Hearst's *American*. Doctorow allows history and fiction to mirror one another until the reflections become interchangeable. Joplin and Walker are both reported to have come from St. Louis to New York at about the same time. Joplin's opera, *Treemonisha*, tells the story of a dark skinned infant discovered beneath a tree. The child in the opera matures through adversity to become a sym-

bol of black pride and triumph. Coalhouse Walker's son in *Ragtime* is found buried alive near the maple trees in the garden of the narrator's boyhood home. Rescued by the narrator's mother, the black child will be adopted by the narrator's family, and eventually become the minority hero of a series of films created in Hollywood by his third father. The dark child's resurrection from a shallow grave relates him symbolically to the other two children in the novel who play their burial games. The future belongs to all three children, boy and girl, black and white, who will live together in Hollywood, and serve as models for a popular film series. Their lives are thus projected by the mirrors of countless reruns into the unknown future.

Although the children in the opera and the novel live happily ever after, their fathers, with the exception of the immigrant socialist, come to violent ends. The tragic conclusion of Joplin's career is reflected in Doctorow's novel by the misfortune and death of Coalhouse Walker. More than five hundred pieces of music, including a ballet and two operas, were composed by Joplin, but his popularity rested largely upon a few pieces like ''The Maple Leaf Rag.'' He sought in vain for a producer in New York to stage *Treemonisha*. Bitterness and disappointment convinced him that racial prejudice was the cause of his rejection as a serious composer. After years of extraordinary creativity and extreme frustration, he was committed to a mental hospital. While the tension of Doctorow's novel is released in the madness of a world plunged into war, Joplin dies offstage in the mental asylum. But his counterpart in the novel, Coalhouse Walker, directs a violent challenge to the bigotry and conceit of the white community. Walker's threat to blow up the Morgan Library is the occasion for Doctorow to create the novel's most dramatic scene of revolutionary theater. Coalhouse Walker does not survive his violent protest, but the revolution will be continued; and eventually, in 1972, a successful production of *Treemonisha* will be staged in New York. *The Collected Works of Scott Joplin* were published in the same year, and thus E. L. Doctorow was prepared to write *Ragtime*.

The rhythms of violence and rebirth are syncopated in Doctorow's novel like the rich interplay of recurring themes and melodies in ragtime music. The subtlety of its narrative strategy and the complex arrangement of its mirrored images are in harmony with the words of Scott Joplin which Doctorow uses as the epigraph for his novel: ''Do not play this piece fast. It is never right to play Ragtime fast.'' (pp. 38-42)

> *Charles Berryman, '' 'Ragtime' in Retrospect,'' in* South Atlantic Quarterly, *Vol. 81, No. 1, Winter, 1982, pp. 30-42.*

DIANE JOHNSON

Like *Ragtime, Loon Lake* concerns itself with capitalism in general and with the history of union struggle in the early part of this century. Most modern writing has tended to focus on private experiences, and if an occasional didactic impulse comes on him, the writer sets up a lot of real-looking shrubs in which to hide it, in hopes that it will appear to be an aspect of the natural world. We call these realistic novels. Doctorow, impatient with ambiguity, sets up ideas like little black and white figures on top of a wedding cake, all decorated with the icing sugar of art. . . . The result is a special and characteristic concoction, not realistic and not self-consciously surreal but, rather, like an epic or a morality play, in which the poet celebrates the good, deplores the bad, and develops in a musical way the meaningful themes of his society as he sees it. (pp. 143-44)

Nature itself is an aspect of social injustice. Joe, in the last pages of the book, plunges into the icy waters of Loon Lake and comes up smiling. Nature is ice is capitalism. Loon Lake is ''a cold black lake,'' owned, loons preying on fish there, the shores haunted by the ghosts of dying Indians. It is a reflex of capitalist society and a form of selfish luxury. To the urban romantic, like Doctorow, the romantic poet of nature is a poseur. (p. 144)

But nature, which seems to an urban sensibility emblematic of spiritual desolation and selfishness, seems to the product of rural culture emblematic of goodness. Because we are not universally urban, and because the idea of nature as good (and of society as vain, bad, crowded, indifferent, etc.) is basic to a strain of Western literature since Virgil, the artist must struggle uphill in his sack. *Ragtime,* comic and working with simpler material, risked less and succeeded, but one could complain of the stately and ambitious *Loon Lake* that, by attempting to look more broadly at American history, it seems the more constrained by an ideology that explains or convokes the experience of only some Americans, without having the exemplary power of an ambiguous fictional world to expand the experience of others.

The effect of this fiction to some extent depends, then, on one's assent to the validity and explanatory power of its underlying myth of American capitalism. There are many accounts of creation. The view of American history each of us has is probably, as Frances FitzGerald has suggested, strongly conditioned by our third-grade textbooks—in some communities they're still fighting the Civil War, or celebrating the romance of religious freedom. Doctorow is particularly compelled by the stories of union brotherhood and by how poor immigrants, especially Jewish immigrants, upon arriving in America around the turn of the century, were routinely mistreated, given names they don't like, and made to live in unspeakable conditions forced on them by an exploitative ruling class. (p. 145)

Like any other idealistic and perceptive person, Doctorow has a complaint about history, that it contained brutality and villainy. The indignation that breaks through the lyricism or funny bits in all his work suggests despair about human nature itself (and why not?), but also a demand for some sort of apology, and it is here that a question arises of how the tone interferes at times with the narrative. Unless you are descended from an Ellis Island customs official or a railroad baron, you may find yourself wanting to assure the writer that all this wasn't your fault, or that history is just history, and that there is misery enough in the actual world, without its being retroactive. The twentieth-century American working class was not Earth's most pitiable group. But no doubt Doctorow pays America a kind of compliment by believing we could have been better.

He is apparently dismayed by our plurality of incongruous myths, the differences in American social conditioning which exaggerate the divisions in our national life and prevent political communion. This is the preoccupation of Penfield, in *Loon Lake,* who recalls being in Seattle during the great general strike of 1919, talking to his landlady, a woman ''proud to be free and beholden to no one.'' He is sorry that she can't understand ''the incredible tangible emotion of solidarity key word no abstract idealization but an actual feeling'' about collective effort and the labor movement and cooperation (instead of competition as exemplified by Bennett and by Joe, who gets to the Top through crime, by using the system, and by literally and figuratively screwing everybody). He's right, she can't

feel it. If we are, as in the currently fashionable view, still connected to our roots, this ''big woman large jaw blue eyes taller'' (than Penfield) was constrained by the love of solitude her ancestors felt herding their reindeer in some vast landscape. The landlady points out that the Huns had warm feelings of group solidarity. ''Nobody knows what human nature is in the raw it's never been seen on this earth,'' Warren has to admit. Defeated by the fear that even the triumph of labor would not bring utopia he goes off to Japan and studies Zen, becomes a parody of the self-involved dropout American artist. Penfield is Doctorow's wittiest invention here.

Penfield's coal-miner father had wanted him to work in the mines and to bear witness to the human suffering there. Penfield is punished for his failure of social commitment by alcoholism and violent death, twin destinies of American writers of the period. In *Loon Lake* as in *Ragtime,* punishments and rewards are appointed not by considerations of realism and not by fictional conventions of retributive justice but by Doctorow's personal scheme. In *Ragtime,* the inoffensive Father, a WASP flag manufacturer, is given sexual inadequacy, diffidence, an inability to converse, long self-exile in the frozen arctic, where parts of him become frostbitten, and finally death by drowning in an icy sea—images of ice and frigidity inundating him as they are apt to do to other non-Jewish or non-union characters. (It is notable that enthusiastic sexuality, in all the works, is a property only of those committed to the class struggle.)

Tateh is the wickedest character in *Ragtime,* risking Doctorow's vengeance by pointing ''his life along the lines of flow of American energy. Workers could strike and die but in the streets of cities an entrepreneur could cook sweet potatoes in a bucket of hot coals and sell them for a penny or two.'' But Tateh has paid his dues by being a Jewish immigrant and an artist to boot, and is rewarded by happiness, a remunerative gimmick, and the hand of Mother. Joe, in the present work, having paid his dues, is rewarded by wealth, though not, we are to assume, happiness.

It's a danger, with flat characters (in Forster's sense), that if, like broken parts of a machine, one or another doesn't work, the fiction may come to a halt. In *Ragtime,* where their flatness is part of the design, the audience knows, as at a morality play, the stereotypes: union people are good, cops are bad, WASP's are neglectful of their children, Jews are sexy, blacks are flamboyant, the rich are kinky, and so on—there's a stereotype to offend everybody, and that's the fun. (pp. 146-48)

In *Loon Lake,* the characters are rounded by the process of speaking for themselves. It's hard to be flat in the first person. None has the convincing poignancy of the brilliant characterization of Daniel in *The Book of Daniel,* but because Doctorow can only write wonderfully, even the bad Joe endears himself by his felicitous phrases, by his complexity, and by the splendid intelligence his author can't help giving him. Still, the exegetical function of the characters does somehow impede the action: the real drama lies behind the action, as in *Pilgrim's Progress*—lies in the great fable (or in this case the great program) being played on the writer's ''secret boards,'' in Emerson's phrase, to be reconstructed by the audience in part from the typology and in part from the rhetoric itself.

Philosophy is hard to illustrate, but William James devised as frontispiece to one of his father's many works on Swedenborg a picture of a man beating a dead horse. The reader may become restive, even combative, slyly imagining, under the stern gaze of the master, alternative scenarios involving cheery cops, bad union men, spontaneous, affectionate Episcopalians. Doctrine begets revisionists. The author's impatience with the moral confusion of American orthodoxy may tap a vestigial patriotic vein and release a trickle of nostalgia for our villains, tycoons like Bennett, for example, who, although wicked, were at least effective, and whom, now that we fear ourselves to be a nation of bunglers, we may remember, *pace* Doctorow, with a certain wistful admiration.

But Doctorow's faith in his version of American history, and his willingness to run the large artistic risks involved in asserting it, make him one of the bravest and most interesting of modern American novelists, flying in the face of the self-indulgent fashion for confession to write *about* something, reviving the discredited function of artist as judge, and working to find the forms for judgment. It is interesting to notice that a strong ideology often, in literature, has had the paradoxical effect of stimulating formal experiments (in Whitman and Dos Passos, for instance), but also, in this respect, one senses in *Loon Lake* Doctorow's need to interest himself.

The risk is of a retreat into manner. One can picture the rival counselors who sit on his shoulders, whispering in his ears, vying for his attention—one a kindly Marxist rabbi, the other an elegant, suavely smiling rascal, maybe somebody like Oscar Wilde. Each is nearly satisfied with *Loon Lake,* but one wishes they would go away together and leave Doctorow alone. (pp. 148-49)

> Diane Johnson, "The Righteous Artist: E. L. Doctorow," in her Terrorists and Novelists, *Alfred A. Knopf, 1982, pp. 141-49.*

FRANK W. SHELTON

Now that E. L. Doctorow has published *Loon Lake,* it is becoming increasingly clear that, taken together, his novels aim to create a panoramic view of American history from the 1880s through the 1960s. While often populating his novels with real people, Doctorow evokes American fantasies and folklore, and nowhere is that clearer than in his first novel, *Welcome to Hard Times,* his least discussed and yet arguably his best novel. (p. 7)

The book opens with that staple element of the western story, violence, here perpetrated by an imposing archetypal figure, a Bad Man who does not even have a name until later in the novel. (His name is revealed to be Turner, perhaps as an ironic reference to frontier historian Frederick Jackson Turner.) The landscape, too, is familiar: hard, rocky, barren. . . . A point implied in many westerns Doctorow makes explicit: the inextricable link between the bad men and the land. . . . Doctorow modifies the usual western formula, however. Conventionally a heroic individual appears to protect the townspeople from the bad men, but in this novel there is no hero in the usual sense. Blue, the protagonist, is unequipped to combat the Bad Man and is left with impotent rage. . . . (p. 9)

If there is no hero to look to, then people must band together for their own protection. Another change Doctorow rings on the western formula is his exclusive concern with the actual rebuilding of the town. Especially for Blue the town becomes the vanguard of civilization, the first step in the transformation of the western desert into a garden. If, as John Cawelti argues, "the Western affirms the necessity of society," Doctorow implies that society is necessary for two reasons: people come together in innate need for one another, and also, faced with an inhospitable environment, they need the protection which

numbers provide. Doctorow's concern with the social aspect of the western parallels his treatment of the workings of society in his later novels. Since society is severely criticized in them, we must also consider the nature of that civilization which the characters in *Welcome to Hard Times* struggle so tenaciously to create.

Welcome to Hard Times progresses on two planes, one concerned with the town's life and the other closely focused on the personal life of Blue. When he first comes to Hard Times, he is one of many Americans who went west to fulfill their dreams but never succeeded. . . . An orderly man, committed to the impulse of civilizing the West, he becomes town leader. Introspective and thoughtful, he seems well suited to be town mayor—at least until the Bad Man arrives. For then his inadequacies as a man of action are revealed. Like most of the other residents of the town, he is unable to face the physical threat of the Bad Man, and the memory of his cowardice fuels his commitment to help rebuild the town. He hopes that, just as the new town hides the scar of the one the Bad Man destroyed, so will it help him "bury the past." . . . In fact all his activities are aimed at compensating for past weaknesses and obliterating his memory of past failures. Personally his efforts focus on Molly, whom he feels he particularly failed when he encouraged her to go to the Bad Man. He claims Molly as his wife and takes in the orphan, Jimmy Fee, thus assuming responsibility for a family of the two survivors who were most scarred by the Bad Man. Molly is an especially interesting figure, since women play an important part in the traditional western story. Though she has been a prostitute, Blue gives her respectability by claiming she is his wife. To some extent she plays the conventional role of woman in the western—she seems weak and to need the protection of men. Yet she ultimately does not fulfill another traditional function of the woman—to represent civilization and in her presence reconcile the man to it. In at least the middle part of the novel, Blue's relationship with her is satisfactory enough to lead him to think he is burying the past. Yet even when things seem to be going well for him, Blue is sensitive enough to realize that he is interpreting events optimistically out of his immense need to do so. . . . Blue is never able to suppress for long a despair at his own weakness, and the tone of the novel alternates between hope and melancholy. These feelings coexist in him, and neither ever dominates for long.

At the same time that he is making these efforts on the personal level, Blue is also doing his utmost to attract people to help settle the new town. In the attention Doctorow pays to the business climate of the town, he shows an interest in economic factors much evident in his later novels. He suggests the continuity between the frontier entrepreneur and capitalists like Morgan and Ford in *Ragtime* and Bennett in *Loon Lake.* Certainly this goes against the grain of the traditional western, for twentieth-century capitalists, as *Ragtime* and *Loon Lake* illustrate, exploit the individual while in the West the individual is supposedly free from exploitation. Ironically the first new business concern in Hard Times is a whorehouse, a perfect example of a business which reduces people to chattel, and in fact one of the prostitutes is literally owned by the proprietor. An immigrant, and immigrants are prominent in the later novels, Zar is portrayed as the perfect merchant with his vision of the potentiality for the market economy in the West. . . . To Zar the potential of the West is not for heroic individual action, but for mercantile success. While Zar is motivated by self-interest, Blue becomes the town booster, a kind of Chamber of Commerce representative. He wants no profit for himself but has a strong commitment to the necessity of civilization.

For at least a time success appears imminent. Although winter, the time of greatest melancholy and despair, seems endless, spring does finally come, and with it a feeling of celebration. Life has begun new and fresh. In spite of his doubts, Blue sees spring as the birth of hope. . . . The coming of spring is the promise of a new life for man, the promise that past death and destruction are truly past and buried, in short the promise of the West.

And that promise seems fulfilled, both for Blue personally and for the town. Molly, Blue, and Jimmy, do appear to make a true "family," the community prospers, and in a town founded on death and destruction a wedding even takes place. Characteristically Blue explains the development of Hard Times in moral terms. . . . To him civilization is the highest good and in and of itself will defeat the threatening forces of evil.

Blue's attitude is based on a faith in the American dream, which implies that evil is outside, is other; that the individual is capable of attaining perfection; that civilization can protect the individual. Doctorow seriously calls into question the validity of that dream. Even while Blue and the others are most optimistic, a sense of fatality hangs over their lives, embodied for Blue in Molly and the scar of the old street which is never far from his thoughts. During the town's greatest success, the seeds of disintegration are present. The town's Christmas party, a time of communion and celebration, is ruined by an outbreak of the continuous argument between Zar and Isaac Maple over their business practices, and when spring comes and the miners return, the competitive and exploitative nature of the town's business climate becomes even clearer. Though Blue's well can provide water for everyone in town, Zar plans to build his own; when Blue tries to get all the businessmen to help clean the streets, only one person will cooperate. Unlike Blue, the businessmen are concerned only for themselves and have no vision of the town as a cooperative enterprise. Such short-sighted selfishness, Doctorow implies, is characteristic of American capitalism and breeds its own destruction.

On the personal level as well Blue's life disintegrates. For no matter how much Molly softens toward him, she cannot forget the Bad Man. Far from the typical domestic, civilizing woman of the western, she nurses a fanatical hatred and need for revenge. For Blue she is a constant accusation of cowardice, and her training Jimmy for the Bad Man epitomizes her rejection of Blue. As the town prospers, she withdraws into a hatred which undercuts any sense of success Blue might feel over the town's progress. On both the personal and community levels, this hopeful life falls apart practically before it begins. As Blue speculates, "Sometime between that heady evening she relented and that day we danced—there must have been a moment when we reached what perfection was left to our lives." . . . Ironically, by the time the perfection is recognized it is far in the past and cannot be recaptured. It proves as evanescent, as flimsy as the town itself.

For it becomes clear that the town was founded on an illusory dream. The anticipated expansion of the mining company never occurs, so in an economic sense the town is built on an empty hope. In fact the mining company has known for a year that it will not develop its mine further. . . . The mining company is above all else a business concern, and the people who come to Hard Times so full of hope are shown on one level to be helpless victims of economic circumstances. Realization of this

fact helps precipitate the rioting in the town, which is an unleashing of man's destructive urges.

After the rioting has begun, the Bad Man from Bodie inevitably returns to repeat his destruction. But circumstances have changed drastically since the beginning of the book, when he seemed an outside force imposing himself on Hard Times. By the end of the novel he clearly embodies forces within the residents of the town. Indeed Blue realizes, "He never left the town, it was waiting only for the proper light to see him where he's been all the time." . . . It is as if the rioting calls forth the Bad Man. The town is already on its way to disintegration, and the seeds of that disintegration can be found in the ethos of competition and exploitation of the businessmen who feel no responsibility to contribute constructively to the town. The violence of the Bad Man destroys the town because it reflects and appeals to a similar violence in the residents. On the personal level, too, Blue comes to see that Molly was never wed to him but to the Bad Man, that "She's been waiting for him, a proper faithful wife." . . . Thus evil, violence, destructiveness are not forces "other," which can be warded off by people coming together for protection; they lie within the individual and will express themselves in and through civilization.

Thus *Welcome to Hard Times* undercuts the promise of peace and opportunity which the country holds out. Filled with hope through much of its progress, the novel suggests that the hope of the West and of America is illusory. Blue laments, "Like the West, like my life: The color dazzles us, but when it's too late we see what a fraud it is, what a poor pinched-out claim." . . . In order that the reader not distance himself from the events of the novel by claiming that the story concerns only the West, Blue makes explicit the relevance of his story to all Americans. . . . The hope of Blue, of the West, of America is the hope that man can begin again, begin afresh and forget the past. But Blue comes to realize that the past is never buried; he and the other townspeople carried the Bad Man within themselves, and he had to reappear. Like *The Great Gatsby*, another exploration of the American dream, *Welcome to Hard Times* suggests that whatever dream or hope we have of beginning anew is already in the past and can never be fulfilled.

Through the character of Blue the novel is an evocation of the American need to hope. Blue regards this as his final curse, but it also leads to his heroic, if futile, killing of the Bad Man. He ultimately does face up to the Bad Man in himself and all of us and comes to acknowledge his own guilt in the drama of the town's rebirth. Even so he retains a primal innocence, an incorruptible core which exists, like Gatsby's, in his readiness for hope. As he lies dying, conscious of the futility of his life and life of the town, his final words are, "I keep thinking someone will come by sometime who will want to use the wood" . . . to rebuild the town. Just as *Ragtime* ends with the dream of an interracial society which the novel itself has shown to be far from reality, so this novel ends with a dream whose reality has been undercut by the novel itself. Yet after all man is not man, and especially not an American, if he cannot dream. (pp. 9-16)

Frank W. Shelton, "E. L. Doctorow's 'Welcome to Hard Times': The Western and the American Dream," in The Midwest Quarterly, *Vol. XXV, No. 1, Autumn, 1983, pp. 7-17.*

RICHARD TRENNER

I would like to make a few observations, fundamentally my own, about E. L. Doctorow. I need to be aggressively selective in what I say because of the sheer quantity and complexity of possibilities that haunt phrases like "a writer's development" or "a writer's relation to his culture." As such phrases apply to Doctorow, I might, for instance, consider the various narrative styles he has developed—from the (ostensibly) simple language and linear first-person story-telling of *Welcome to Hard Times* to the willfully difficult syntax, restlessly shifting point-of-view, and shuffled chronology of *Loon Lake*. Or taking up a very different sort of question—one of cultural values and the force of reputation rather than of style and language—I might speculate on Doctorow's quite rare ability to combine serious themes and big audiences. But I want instead to write about what I consider Doctorow's most important quality: his moral vision. . . . For me, at least, the essential Doctorow (if I may, for the work of analysis, posit such a quantity) is concerned with the morality of connection and disconnection—of human relatedness and unrelatedness—on various scales, from an entire society to a single family.

Doctorow is both consciously and intuitively committed to an ideal of universal justice, yet he is everywhere confronted by the failure of that ideal. It is in the tension between aspiration and disillusionment that he finds the themes of his fiction. . . . As a humanist ("All the solutions were to be found right here on earth, and the supernatural was not taken seriously," Doctorow has said of his childhood ethos), he locates the cause of failure and injustice in the social forces that ineffably combine with hearts and minds to *make* individual destinies; chief among them: politics, economics, and class hierarchies. Doctorow repeatedly presents characters struggling for fulfillment against the often destructive or repressive effects of such forces. In good fortune's arbitrary absence, the only counter-force is perception—is understanding and articulating how politics, economics, and social class deeply impinge on individual lives. And frequently, that "counter-force" can be no more than tragic knowledge or, in Doctorow's words, "the solace of shared perceptions."

How does Doctorow bear witness to the human hunger for fulfillment? The chief purely literary way, it seems to me, is through the ironic juxtaposition of contraries—contraries of a remarkable range. That range extends from (and, of course, beyond) passages that violate taboos by ironically uniting ideas or images which the prevailing social order would insist remain apart; to extended patterns of value-laden symbolism; to entire plots that yoke together mutually exclusive social classes or conflicting political philosophies. Let me give an example of each of these three strategies of ironic perception. First, consider one of Joe's raging soliloquies in *Loon Lake*. Doctorow uses a parody of a Hollywood dance sequence and alternates opposing emotions and images to represent the alienated worker's miserable relation to that ingenious instrument and metaphor of modern capitalism, the assembly line:

> Then they speed things up and I'm going too slow I drop one of the tin pots on the wrong side of the belt the guy there is throwing tires on wheel rims and giving the tubes a pump or two of air he ignores my shouts he can't take the time. And then the foreman is coming down the line to pay me a call I can't hear him but I don't have to—a red bulging neck of rage.

> And then they stop coddling us and throw the throttle to full and this is how I handle it: I am Fred Astaire in top hat and tails tossing up the screws into the holes, bouncing the frames on

the floor and catching them in my top hat of tin. I twirl the headlight kick it on the belt with a backward flip of my heel. I never stop moving and when the belt is too slow for me I jump up and stomp it along faster, my arms outstretched. Soon everyone in the plant has picked up on my routine—everyone is dancing! The foreman comes pirouetting along, putting stars next to each name on his clipboard. And descending from the steel rafter by insulated wire to dance backward on the moving parade of car bodies, Mr. Bennett himself in white tie and tails. He's singing with a smile, he's flinging money from his hands like stardust. . . .

In their direct expression of rage and exhaustion, parts of the passage are hardly ironic, of course. But generally, Doctorow's description of Joe on the assembly line—especially the bitter Fred Astaire fantasy—shows the strategy of ironic juxtaposition in the service of a radical critique brilliantly employed on a small scale.

To see the same sort of linking of contraries at work on a much broader scale, recall the symbolic force of architecture in *The Book of Daniel*. Many buildings, public and private, figure in Doctorow's tragic meditation on the fate of radicals and radicalism in post-World War II America; among them: the state psychiatric hospital to which Susan Isaacson is committed after her suicide attempt ("Designed with the idea that madness might be soothed in a setting of architectural beauty"); the pathetic business establishment of Isaacson Radio, Sales and Repair ("On the bed of the window, resting on old curled crepe paper, bleached grey, are two display radios—a table model and a console with cloth-covered doors and a combination automatic record changer. When you go inside you see that the two window display radios have nothing inside them"); the Lewins' house in Brookline, where for several years Susan and Daniel Isaacson try to live out the illusion that they are normal, middle-class children ("built for two families and designed to look as if it contained only one"); the wretched little house amid "the obscurity of Bronx architecture" in which the Isaacson family lives ("He had an odd house. It was the only house on the whole street unattached to any other"); the federal court house in Foley Square, where Paul and Rochelle Isaacson are tried and condemned ("designed to promote the illusion of solemn justice"); the prison in which the Isaacsons die ("We are clients of a new law firm, Voltani, Ampere, and Ohm. If you've seen one prison you've seen them all"); even Disneyland, where Daniel goes to confront his parents' betrayer ("What Disneyland proposes is a technique of abbreviated shorthand culture for the masses, a mindless thrill, like an electric shock, that insists at the same time on the recipient's rich psychic relation to his country's history and language and literature"). Though scarcely complete, this catalogue suggests Doctorow's method of using physical details to symbolize—generally to ironic effect—moral conditions. In *The Book of Daniel*, the narrator's parents end up in the electric chair at Sing Sing while the man who denounced them ends up in Disneyland at Christmastime. On the face of it, these are utterly different fates, but in a novel whose epigraph might well be "The failure to make connections is complicity," they are *not* so different: Doctorow locates Disneyland in "a town somewhere between Buchenwald and Belsen" and subjects it to a long and fierce mock-sociological analysis.

Finally, to illustrate what I have called Doctorow's technique of ironic juxtaposing that yokes together in entire plots mutually exclusive social classes or conflicting political philosophies, I can cite his most widely read novel, *Ragtime.* Here he places together social groups that in "real life" would almost never directly interact except in rigidly prescribed roles which acknowledge unequal power. These social groups include disfranchised blacks (represented by Coalhouse Walker and his followers); poor immigrants (like Tateh, a Latvian Jew); the white middle class (exemplified by the family from New Rochelle); radicals (like Emma Goldman); and the aristocracy of capital (the chief examples, Henry Ford and Pierpont Morgan). Only an imagination determined to forge together social contraries for moral and analytic purposes would populate one book with ironic representatives of so many different social classes. In the course of *Ragtime,* the various characters act and react in patterns that reveal the fragmenting forces of money, politics, and class—forces often inimical to individual fulfillment. But the social vision of *Ragtime* is less dark (almost genial by comparison) than the tragic meditations of its two predecessors, *Welcome to Hard Times* and *The Book of Daniel,* and Doctorow is able to give it an ending that is "happy," at least for a few of the characters. In a sunny fantasy of social justice, he closes the novel by giving Tateh, that lucky salesman of America's idealized cultural aspirations, the idea for a successful series of movies. . . .

[Tateh's idea] is a variation of Doctorow's essential moral theme of the ideal of "universal justice." To repeat the definition Doctorow once gave me of his "social ideals":

> There is a presumption of universality to the ideal of justice—social justice, economic justice. It cannot exist for a part or class of society; it must exist for all. And it's a Platonic ideal, too—that everyone ought to be able to live as he or she is endowed to live; that if a person in his genes is a poet, he be able to practice his poetry. Plato defined justice as the fulfillment of a person's truest self. That's good for starters.

(pp. 5-9)

Richard Trenner, in an introduction to E. L. Doctorow: Essays & Conversations, *edited by Richard Trenner, Ontario Review Press, 1983, pp. 1-9.*

CHRISTOPHER LEHMANN-HAUPT

To appreciate what E. L. Doctorow is up to in his sixth and latest work of fiction, *Lives of the Poets: Six Stories and a Novella,* you have to judge not the separate pieces in the book, but their relationship and the process of their unfolding.

In the first story, a thoroughly charming but somewhat conventional piece called **"The Writer in the Family,"** a youth named Jonathan, whose father has just died, is enlisted by his aunts to write letters to their aged mother, his grandmother, to create the illusion that her son isn't dead but has only moved to Arizona. Jonathan complies for a while, with spectacular success—the immigrant grandmother sees the move to fabled Arizona as a redemption of her son's failed career. But eventually Jonathan rebels, and in the act of doing so he not only achieves a deeper understanding of his father, he also takes a significant step toward becoming a true writer.

This touching, well-crafted story is followed by five more short pieces, **"The Water Works," "Willi," "The Hunter," "The Foreign Legation,"** and **"The Leather Man."** These are not as easily understood or explained. Though each is arresting in its way, as a group they are uneven in quality. **"The Water Works,"** about a drowned boy being fished out of a reservoir, has a dreamlike Gothic quality that puts one in mind of Poe. **"Willi,"** though resolved with shocking brutality when a boy reveals to his father that his mother has been making love to his tutor, starts off in a mood of Whitmanesque-hippie ecstasy that is somewhat at odds with its setting and period, which happen to be Galicia in 1910.

One isn't entirely sure what to make of these pieces. They can be read as political parables—of the system violently destroying its children in **"The Water Works"** and **"The Foreign Legation"**—the latter about a lonely suburban jogger who literally runs into a terrorist act in which a young girl is blown to pieces. They can be read for their deep psychological implications. The child betrayed by his mother in **"Willi"** becomes the man who fires a rifle-shot at a woman in **"The Hunter."** Though they read compellingly enough, there is something about them that disposes the reader to probe and speculate.

The fog disperses, however, when we come upon the book, the novella called *Lives of the Poets.* Here we encounter a writer in his 50's who has recently moved out of the Connecticut house he shares with his wife, Angel, and installed himself in a small apartment in the SoHo section of Manhattan. As he broods with wit and eloquence on the increasing absurdity of his own life and the world in general, we begin to recognize his relationship to the earlier stories in the volume.

We discover, for instance, that he is Jonathan, the writer in the earlier story, grown older and successful. We learn that the father who died young was not only a failure, but also fought violently with his wife, which suggests that the brutal ending of the story **"Willi,"** in which the father beats up the cheating wife, has deep psychological roots in the writer's childhood. As other connections reveal themselves, we begin to see that the stories constitute an autobiography of the writer's imagination. In mood and style and imagery, they are a history of the times and places in which their creator has lived.

What is the end of that history—the message in the bottle that surfaces from Jonathan's imagination? One hesitates to try conclusions because the process of revelation in *Lives of the Poets* is more vital and significant than what is revealed. But one familiar theme in Mr. Doctorow's work does emerge once again—the tendency to resolve existential dilemmas with political activism. . . .

It's true, as it has sometimes been of Mr. Doctorow's previous work, that *Lives of the Poets* comes close to reducing itself to a call for political action. But the texture and irony of the work prevail. As usual, one catches a faint whiff of the political pamphleteer in Mr. Doctorow. But, as usual too, he is fighting a losing battle with the poet who is also present.

Christopher Lehmann-Haupt, in a review of "Lives of the Poets: Six Stories and a Novella," in The New York Times, *November 6, 1984, p. C15.*

JONATHAN YARDLEY

Say one thing for E. L. Doctorow: Since the fabulously successful publication almost a decade ago of *Ragtime,* he has declined to rest on his laurels. Unlike other writers who have found profitable formulas and worked them for all they're worth, Doctorow has tried something new and venturesome each subsequent time out. He followed *Ragtime* with *Drinks Before*

Dinner, a play, and then with *Loon Lake,* a novel written in part in a form of blank verse. Now, with *Lives of the Poets,* he turns his hand to the short story; the best to be said of it is that the results are mixed but the effort, at least, is to be admired. . . .

[*Lives of the Poets*] is very well written, as all of Doctorow's work is, and the stories are not without their moments of interest. The first, **"The Writer in the Family,"** is a satisfying glimpse at the life of a man who lived "the wrong life," as seen through the eyes of a son who is trying to understand that life. In the other five stories ostensibly written by Jonathan, the narrator of the novella, there is plenty of rich prose, a preoccupation with death and loss, a sense of estrangement and incompleteness.

These, if we follow the instructions given to us by the dust jacket, we then can see as among the themes that come to the surface in the musings of Jonathan, in *Lives of the Poets.* He is a 50-year-old writer, apparently a rather successful one, who lives in suburban Connecticut with his wife and children but has just taken a small apartment in Manhattan. Supposedly it is to be a working apartment, but it also is where he proposes to entertain his lover, a woman many years his junior whom he imagines to be "my natural wife because I had never felt this with anyone, this sense of having arrived finally in my life."

Thus he finds himself inhabiting one of the "marriages of my generation," in which husband and wife are "neither married nor divorced but no longer entirely together." This has happened even though by all outward appearances his life should be happy. He is accomplished, recognized, prosperous, loved by his family: "Yet I call no one, I isolate myself, a man whose state of rest is inconsolability. I walk the streets feeling like a vagrant, I've got this stinging desolation in my eyes." He mopes around with other writers and artists, men and women whose lives are as disarranged as his if not more so, and hears tales of domestic warfare: "everything gets hung on the line as if we all live in some sort of marital tenement. Whatever happened to discretion? Where is pride? What has caused this decline in tact and duplicity?"

Not merely are marriages falling apart all around him, but so is everything else. The city is a jungle; dinner-party guests swap accounts of their most recent muggings and describe dead bodies lying unattended on sidewalks. The doorman in Jonathan's apartment building greedily eyes his new alpaca coat and hints that the gift of it could assure a degree of protection. . . .

Doctorow has pinned down just about every known nuance of life among the terminally self-indulgent, and he describes it in sharp, biting prose. He's equally good about the ominous side of Manhattan, the dirt and the noise and the everpresent threat of random violence; he is an acute social commentator, and when he puts that gift to work *Lives of the Poets* comes vigorously to life. But as an account of the writer at loose ends this novella scarcely holds a candle to Philip Roth's *The Anatomy Lesson,* a short novel that covers much the same territory in a similarly narcissistic manner but that crackles throughout with energy. *Lives of the Poets* goes only in fits and starts; it's intelligent and amusing, but essentially pointless. Can Doctorow be speaking for himself when Jonathan says, "each book has taken me further and further out so that the occasion itself is extenuated, no more than a weak distant signal from the home station, and even that may be fading"?

Jonathan Yardley, "Ruminations and Regrets," in Book World—The Washington Post, *November 11, 1984, p. 3.*

BRUCE BAWER

The dark side of the American dream is, needless to say, a familiar literary theme, and by no means an unworkable one. It served Fitzgerald well in *The Great Gatsby* and Dreiser in *An American Tragedy.* But it has yet to work for Doctorow. His approach is closer to Upton Sinclair's than to Fitzgerald's: rather than recognize that the novel's path to truth leads, of necessity, through the human soul, he peoples his novels with characters that are little more than hunks of plywood, each with its own sharply defined didactic function. There are victims of the system. . . .

Then there are the bourgeois apologists, people like Robert Lewin (who adopts Daniel and Susan in *The Book of Daniel*) and Father in *Ragtime.* They're aware of the system's injustices—against the Isaacsons and Walker, respectively—and even try to do something about them. Lewin "belongs to committees, and practices law for poor people . . . is big in the ACLU" and is "a demonstrator against Dow Chemical recruiters," and Father puts up bail for Walker. But it isn't enough for Doctorow, as he makes clear in the last sentence of the paragraph about Lewin: "When he has the time, he likes to read *The New Yorker.*" To Doctorow, it's all clear-cut: Lewin and Father, for all their humanitarianism, are part of the system. (p. 516)

That there's so little room amid all the betrayal and injustice, the madness and violence, the noble anarchy and detestable civility, for a little individual human psychology makes following the fortunes of Doctorow's characters a frustrating experience. What is it, one cannot help but wonder, that makes Coalhouse Walker so intractable? What makes him, of all the black Americans ever harassed by racists, refuse to walk away from trouble? Why does the death of Sarah transform him into a twentieth-century Nat Turner? Doctorow throws a line in somewhere about "the violence underlying all principle," and we understand we are to recognize that Walker is a man of principle, who takes the ideas he holds—ideas about justice, dignity and vengeance—as seriously as survival. Fine. But how did he get that way? Doctorow gives us no clue. To him, Walker is merely a victim of the system.

The way Doctorow sees it, we're all victims. Sometimes it seems he reserves his pity for those who make it: Mindish, the Isaacsons' supposed Communist collaborator in *The Book of Daniel,* who spends his declining years in bourgeois Santa Barbara bliss; Tateh, the destitute socialist in *Ragtime* who strikes it rich in Hollywood and gives himself a title; Joe, the working-class drifter in *Loon Lake* who is adopted by a millionaire and rises through the ranks of the Central Intelligence Agency, eventually becoming an ambassador. Happy endings? Not at all. The way Doctorow sees it, America has played its dirtiest trick on such rags-to-riches figures. By making them well-to-do, it's robbed them of the integrity and independence of mind they derived from being down and out. Success has buried them alive.

And that, believe it or not, is the general idea at work in *Lives of the Poets,* the "novella" in Doctorow's new book, *Lives of the Poets: Six Stories and a Novella.* Actually, it's not a novella at all; it's a sixty-page spiel by an unnamed speaker who, like Doctorow, is a successful 50ish liberal New York Jewish novelist. This unnamed novelist goes on about his mistress, his children, his broken marriage, his friends' marriages, his health and age, the erosion of America's moral values, the rise of ridiculous religions, the number of minorities in New York and his memories of Kenyon College (where Doctorow also went to school).

Above all, the unnamed novelist goes on about his "commitment." He's always been deeply committed, but it's not as easy as it used to be. His problem is this: he's a rich, famous writer, a friend of "Norman," a regular on the fashionable dinner-party circuit in Manhattan. He's *buried alive,* don't you see? He's oppressed by success. He's being killed with comfort. At a party at the Dakota apartment house, he watches his writer friend Leo do some serious drinking because "He's quite brilliant and has never made a dime"; but our hero knows who's *really* suffering here: "Oh Leo, I think, when you make a little money from your work you'll see what trouble is." And he's serious.

But he hasn't given up. He has abandoned his wife, kids and suburban home to live in a Greenwich Village high-rise with his young mistress. Clearly, this is meant to be taken, at least in part, as a heroic act: the man's trying to climb out of that middle-class grave, to renew his "commitment." He's like Younger Brother in *Ragtime,* who leaves his white-bread family to put on blackface and join the Coalhouse Walker gang. And— what do you know?—the man pulls it off. At the end of the story, he overcomes his stasis, his love of bourgeois comfort, and takes a family of Central American refugees into his high-rise flat. But you don't believe it for a minute. For one thing, it's out of character. For another, our unnamed novelist's act of mercy is a tired conceit that Doctorow has overused. His Ins are always harboring Outs, thereby exposing themselves to a therapeutic measure of adversity and anarchy otherwise unavailable to them. In *Welcome to Hard Times,* Blue takes in Molly and Jimmy after the devastations wreaked by the Man from Bodie leave them homeless; in *The Book of Daniel,* the Lewins take in the Isaacson children; in *Ragtime,* Mother takes in Sarah and her baby; in *Loon Lake,* the millionaire F. W. Bennett takes in Joe. Thanks to its ending, *Lives of the Poets* manages to seem both aimless and contrived, a neat trick.

The same is true of other stories in *Lives of the Poets.* Most of them are about lonely, estranged or disturbed people who are the victims of nature (symbolized variously by snow, shadows, water), history and/or America. (pp. 516-18)

In *Lives of the Poets,* there are no lives and no poets, only a handful of familiar ideas. The styles are familiar too. In some of these fictions ("Lives of the Poets," "The Writer in the Family," "The Hunter") Doctorow spells things out in that scrupulously simple *Ragtime* prose; in others ("Willi," "The Water Works," "The Foreign Legation," "The Leather Man") he tries to be artsy and mysterious in the manner of *Loon Lake.* Play it one way or the other, the song is always the same. (p. 519)

> *Bruce Bawer, "The Human Dimension," in* The Nation, *Vol. 239, No. 16, November 17, 1984, pp. 515-19.*

JAMES WOLCOTT

E. L. Doctorow has stressed in interviews that [*Lives of the Poets: Six Stories and a Novella*] is not a casual round-up. "Oddly enough, I don't think of this as a collection of stories,"

he told *Vogue.* "I think of it as a novel about a guy who has written six stories." The opening story, **"The Writer in the Family,"** is a trim reminiscence about a loyal Jewish son who writes letters to his decrepit grandmother on the noodging of his Aunt Frances. When his loyalty to his dead father triumphs over his loyalty to Aunt Frances, Doctorow's narrator becomes a Philip Roth character, smart and rebellious, capable of sabotage. The story itself is like early Philip Roth, before he began spitting fishhooks and dragon-fire, and its low-key poignance is pleasing. Unfortunately this curtain raiser is followed by a group of stories whose only character is a vague, creeping anxiety. I soon began to attach a name to this character: Nameless Dread.

Nameless Dread swims in "the yellowing rush of spumed currents" of **"The Water Works,"** where a drowned child is exhumed. Nameless Dread puts a bitch in harness in **"Willi,"** where the mating of dogs becomes a drama of brute will.... Nameless Dread drives a school bus in **"The Hunter"** and haunts the countryside in **"The Leather Man"** and stocks the shelves with ceramic erotica in **"The Foreign Legation."** In these chronicles of Nameless Dread, Doctorow sets the scene with little razor nicks of observation, his boogeyman being a beast of a thousand cuts. (pp. 31-2)

With the novella *Lives of the Poets* we abandon the world of the mod-Gothic and return to Philip Roth's Jewish-American precincts, where complaints are brewed with the morning coffee. Like Nathan Zuckerman in *The Anatomy Lesson,* Doctorow's Jonathan is a middle-aged writer in whom pain has taken up residence. (p. 32)

[Since] Jonathan is clearly an autobiographical stand-in for Doctorow (both went to Kenyon, etc.), *Lives of the Poets* is clearly a self-diagnosis meant to account for the malaise Doctorow sees around him—what he calls the "emotional exhaustion" of his circle. In other words, what ails E. L. Doctorow is what ails America. That's a pretty steep conceit, and although Doctorow loves to make lists ("fedora, homburg, Swiss Tirol, Irish tinker, deerhound, Russian lamb, baseball, tengallon, seaman watch, Greek fisher, garrison, pith or steel helmet, on me they're all dunce caps'"), he's no Walt Whitman. America isn't yodeling through his lungs. But it is making muffled distress calls. "It is not that everyone I know is fucked up, incomplete, unrealized. On the whole we are all quite game. It's life itself that seems to be wanting." So shape up, life—shape up, America. You're letting Phil and Bernie down.

Lives of the Poets is an act of vanity, but that in itself is not condemning. Imperial vanity can be a great drumming force in literature, whether it's Balzac bearing all of French society on his back, or Nabokov striding the clouds, hurling thunderbolts. The vanity of *Lives of the Poets,* however, is crabbed and pettish, like the book itself. Doctorow is crawling into his drab little box of solitude to make himself look sensitive and unbought.... Celibate in sex, celibate in fame. "A call from my mother: I saw your friend Norman's name in the newspaper, I see him all the time on television, why don't I ever see you on television? I don't know, Mom, I value my privacy. Why, she says, what are you hiding?" ... The crown of thorns to Jonathan's vanity comes when he agrees to shelter Salvadoran refugees—"definitely illegal," a lawyer assures him—and then apostrophizes, "Look, my country, what you've done to me, what I have to do to live with myself." ... Sex and politics and fame exist in *Lives of the Poets* only to certify its author's humble, monkish remove from their grubbier aspects. He marks his meek pride on his forehead with ashes. (pp. 32-3)

What's happened to E. L. Doctorow since *Ragtime*? *Loon Lake*, his 1980 novel, seemed to me an unconvincing, showy pastiche, but at least it was reaching for something—it wasn't just sitting around staring at its toenails. Perhaps it's Doctorow's thinking that needs to be straightened out. Asked in *Vogue* about the role of the writer, Doctorow replied, "I think the writer's obligation is just to tell the truth, and that's the one commitment he can't betray without destroying himself." Really? Evading the truth may be what helps free the imagination. If fiction is about telling the truth, it's also about telling beautiful lies and making what-might-have-been seem more real than what was. Doctorow told rollicking lies in *Ragtime* and gnarled, powerful lies in *The Book of Daniel*, and those are the novels which have the full breath of imagined life. *Lives of the Poets*, intent on telling the unpolished truth, is garrulous and informal and disposable—a book of blab. (p. 34)

> James Wolcott, "*Rag Time*," in The New Republic, *Vol. 191, No. 23, December 3, 1984, pp. 31-4.*

ROBERT TOWERS

[A] reader never knows what to expect in a new work by Doctorow, who has not been a writer to stay put—much less to repeat himself. One would be hard pressed to think of three major novels by the same author that differ so strikingly in subject and technique as *The Book of Daniel, Ragtime,* and *Loon Lake*. It comes, therefore, as no surprise that the six stories and the novella included in *Lives of the Poets* should be an almost defiantly mixed lot. . . .

Each of the first three stories seems to me to work effectively within its particular mode, the remaining three much less so. The disjunctive quasi surrealism of **"The Hunter"** and **"The Foreign Legation"** is simultaneously too contrived and too easy; the episodes become little more than a succession of images evoking loneliness, deprivation, boredom, and frustration—a dispiriting conglomerate—enlivened (or rather galvanized) in each case by an act of violence. **"The Leather Man"** strikes me as the only outright failure—an obscure and turbid discourse reflecting the paranoia of men who seem to be FBI agents when they are confronted with holdouts against the American Dream.

The collection's major claim to our attention is of course the novella, *Lives of the Poets,* that gives the book its title. A somber work, it assumes the form of a sourly humorous confession by a successful writer of fifty, Jonathan, who, claiming the need to isolate himself, to create a separate space for his work and his own development, has left his family home in Connecticut and moved into a studio apartment overlooking Houston Street. . . .

Jonathan is concerned over what has happened to his political convictions, presumably those of a once-committed leftist. The novella ends with his last-minute attempt to salve his humanitarian conscience—an attempt that has absurd consequences for his newly chosen way of life.

Meanwhile, there are other lives to contemplate—lives which all around him are—like the city, like the nation—beginning to unravel. Most of the couples he knows are "neither married nor divorced but no longer entirely together. There is a moving of husbands into their own digs, their own long days and nights." Angel collects stories of male perfidy, and some of these provide the most entertaining sections of the novella.

Jonathan records them with relish, with mordant wit that the narrator quickly turns against himself.

The form and tone of *Lives of the Poets,* as well as its correspondence to certain known facts of Doctorow's career, invite us to read it as a self-mocking, self-lacerating *cri de coeur* from the author of *Ragtime*. Furthermore, the jacket copy suggests that the book in its entirety may be read as a novel about the writer of the stories, which are unified and illuminated by the novella. I see no sense in either reading. Whatever the autobiographical parallels (and I am happily ignorant of their extent), the story works well enough if regarded as fiction, while the recurrence of certain images or associations from the stories hardly makes the collection a unified work. The writing itself is clumsy at times, with lots of strung-together clauses, as if Doctorow were deliberately roughing up his prose for the sake of a spurious authenticity; but there are also passages of driving power and eloquence. The evocation of the blasted city is especially effective—a city that has become the goal of wave after wave of new immigrants who seem alien and frightening to the descendants of the now "old" immigration of the Jews. While *Lives of the Poets* is hardly comparable to Doctorow's best work, it provides us with a grimacing, arresting portrait of an artist who, in midlife, finds himself consumed by that which he was nourished by. (p. 34)

> Robert Towers, "*Light and Lively*," in The New York Review of Books, *Vol. XXXI, No. 19, December 6, 1984, pp. 33-4.**

ANNE TYLER

These are the objects that Edgar Altschuler [the protagonist of *World's Fair*] buries in his time capsule: a Tom Mix decoder ring, a handwritten biography of FDR, a Hohner Marine Band harmonica, two Tootsy Toy rockets, a pair of eyeglasses and a genuine silk stocking.

Edgar is a child, of course—one of the most sympathetic and believable children to be found between the covers of a book—and his time capsule is a cardboard mailing tube lined with tinfoil. Probably it won't weather the years all that well. I can tell you a time capsule that will, though: *World's Fair,* which preserves in mint condition the sights, sounds and smells of a Bronx neighborhood in the 1930s.

Admirers of *Ragtime* and *Welcome to Hard Times* already know E. L. Doctorow's gift for depicting eras other than our own; but in *World's Fair*, he creates scenes so palpable that one suspects this novel is at least partly autobiographical. It covers Edgar's first nine years, generally from his vantage point. Two additional voices are heard at intervals—his mother's and his older brother's, each speaking in the quiet, modestly summary style of a Studs Terkel interview—but most of the book is narrated by Edgar himself, looking backward from adulthood.

Writing about a child's perceptions is risky, but we don't worry here for an instant because at the outset, the author pulls off such a coup that we know from then on we can trust him. He describes an event as seen by a baby. Edgar wakes in a wet crib, cries, is changed and taken into bed with his parents. He studies the flowers on the headboard and then the heavy window curtains, which he dislikes. "I feared suffocation," he tells us. It's that combination of past self and present self that makes this scene convincing—the past self minutely observing an "unfairly giganticized" world, the present self relaying those observations in effective adult language.

Never, though, does Edgar's grownup self presume. We never have the feeling that hindsight is falsely coloring what's described. Instead, events retain the edge of mystery lent by a child's limited comprehension. But only very slightly limited; Doctorow doesn't underestimate his young hero's capabilities.

No, what makes Edgar consistently interesting is that he's allowed a complex interior. He's not reflective beyond his years, but he *is* as reflective as we readers know children to be in real life, and he wonders silently about much that he sees going on about him, both consequential and inconsequential. . . .

The Altschulers spring to life on these pages, with all their minor triumphs and gentle pleasures and the complicated disharmonies that strain them. What's more important, a decade springs to life as well. *World's Fair* is better than a time capsule; it's an actual slice of a long-ago world, and we emerge from it as dazed as those visitors standing on the corner of the future.

> Anne Tyler, "A Child's Garden of Memories Pervades 'World's Fair'," in The Detroit News, November 10, 1985, p. 6B.

DAVID LEAVITT

[*World's Fair*] by E. L. Doctorow is a peculiar hybrid of novel and memoir. Its hero, like Mr. Doctorow, is named Edgar, and grows up in the Bronx in the 1930's; his parents, like Mr. Doctorow's parents, are named Rose and Dave; his brother, like the author's brother, Donald. The family's last name is Altschuler. One is reminded of Renata Adler's novel *Pitch Dark,* in which the heroine, Kate Ennis, must choose a name similar to, yet slightly different from, her own, and decides on Alder; in both these works, the naming strategy seems to be a kind of tipoff, a way of telling the reader that the book at hand will unapologetically combine fiction and memory.

By flaunting the artificial line dividing the true from the imagined, Mr. Doctorow not only suggests in *World's Fair* that the process of remembering is by definition a process of invention, he rejects altogether the notion that imagination and memory are ever pure of each other. His purpose in *World's Fair* seems to be to create a work that succeeds as oral history, memoir and novel all at once. Unfortunately, these disparate genres don't always make the best of bedfellows, and until its breathtaking final 100 pages, when it becomes most fully novelistic, Mr. Doctorow's new novel seems as peculiar a mix of brilliant vision and clumsy self-indulgence as the fair it so artfully describes.

World's Fair is told almost exclusively from the first-person point of view of young Edgar Altschuler, following the course of his childhood from early infancy through the age of 9, and ending with Edgar's visit to the magnificent World's Fair of 1939 in Flushing Meadow. As is appropriate to such a point of view, the large events surrounding Edgar—World War II, his father's bankruptcy, the slow burn of his parents' marriage—fall to the background and the narrative focuses on the schoolyard, park and living room which form the centers of a young boy's life. Edgar's mode is primarily recollective, and the story moves forward through time with all the fluidity of memory, stopping along the way to focus on the finely honed *tableaux vivants* of life in the Bronx during the Depression: a visit to a kosher butcher, the fall of Edgar's pensive, Yiddish-speaking grandmother into senility and rage and the delectable pleasure of buying a roasted sweet potato from a pushcart vendor on the street. Edgar is smart, adventurous, slightly vain, a passionate observer of the world around him, and in much of *World's Fair* the older Edgar describes that world in language that is both hypnotic and wonderfully precise, skillfully articulating the inarticulate passions of childhood. . . .

[Doctorow's dazzling prose] exemplifies the richness of much of this novel. There is a wonderful description . . . of the wrecked Hindenburg zeppelin ("They were not supposed ever to touch land, they were tethered to tall towers, they were sky creatures; and this one had fallen in flames to the ground''); a skilled and revealing portrait of Edgar's gentle, somewhat dopey father (his "was a peasant vision, a thing of funny papers and dialect jokes"). But what is one to make, then, of prose as artless and imprecise as [the] description of Edgar's visits to the home of his friend Meg and her mother, a "ten cents a dance" entertainer? . . .

This kind of prose, characterized by stunted or run-on sentences, narrative slackness and a blurring rather than a crystallization of detail, becomes increasingly predominant as *World's Fair* progresses, and contrasts shockingly with the hallucinatory, Whitmanesque elegance of the rest of the novel. One suspects that Mr. Doctorow is trying to recreate here the rhythms of speech, the sound of oral history, but instead has lapsed into prose that seems merely lazy.

Another problem the author comes up against—particularly in the first half of the book—is the unwavering narrowness of his recollecting protagonist's point of view. While young Edgar's perspective on the world can give rise to some magnificent descriptive passages, much of the family ritual he evokes has a kind of archetypal quality, and as a result seems disembodied. . . .

As if to compensate for sticking so closely to his child-narrator's point of view, Mr. Doctorow punctuates the novel with a kind of fractured commentary offered first by Rose and then by Donald. These interpolations suggest a larger, more adult perspective on the world Edgar describes, but unfortunately there just aren't enough of them. Rose's narration stops abruptly a quarter of the way through the novel; Donald's is limited to two short monologues. The voices in which they speak, moreover, are halting and imprecise, not the tones of people conversing or telling stories as much as the awkward, faux-sophisticated voices that people affect when talking into tape recorders. One suspects that this quality of oral history is exactly what Mr. Doctorow is trying for here—all of Rose's and Donald's remembrances are addressed to a "you" who is presumably Edgar himself—but to what end is hard to see; difficult to read and short on specific detail, these passages seem the revelations of uncomfortable people remembering under duress.

It is, in fact, only in the novel's last third, when Edgar finally goes to the fair, that Mr. Doctorow achieves the descriptive fullness and sense of narrative intention that initially seem so elusive. Edgar's meticulous accounting of the World's Fair, which he visits twice, is dizzying in its specificity, revealing the fair as a peculiar combination of noble utopian intent and vulgar sideshow. . . .

Mr. Doctorow conveys perfectly the extent to which a fair becomes a world unto itself, into which a child can become utterly absorbed. . . . It is this sense of removal from the real world—perched, in 1939, between the Depression and war—that the fair was designed to offer, and Mr. Doctorow communicates this idea by focusing on a single detail from the

World of Tomorrow—a diorama showing a utopian city of the future. . . . (p. 3)

The tragedy was, of course, that the "corner of the future" was an illusion, just as the fair was an illusion, a thing of paper and metal. Still, Mr. Doctorow insists upon the nobility of the fair's intention, just as he insists upon the nobility of his young protagonist, and of the era he lives in—an era which, for all its hopelessness, nonetheless had the imagination and faith to erect and enjoy such a monument to farsighted unreality. Such a penchant for imagination and faith in a Bronx-born child of immigrants, Mr. Doctorow suggests, is the seed of the future he will grow up to inhabit—a future that will prove to be as glamorous and unreal as the miniature World of Tomorrow at the fair, and at the same time as tragically self-deluding as the imperfect world outside the utopian enclosure at Flushing Meadow.

At the very end of *World's Fair*, Edgar, in imitation of the fair's organizers, plants his own personal time capsule in Claremont Park, then walks home practicing the "ventriloquial drone" he is trying to learn from a book called *Ventriloquism Self-Taught*. It's hard not to wonder if Mr. Doctorow means to suggest in this final image that fiction-writing itself is a kind of ventriloquism, a matter of throwing a voice out and listening for it, seeing how similar or how different it is from the voice with which one normally speaks. Biography or oral history need employ no such trickery; they can get by on the power of plain speaking.

And that, perhaps, is why *World's Fair*, as an amalgam of these genres, has a fractured and inconsistent feel to it. Its structure is that of an autobiography, beginning at the beginning and moving through the life of its protagonist with the thoroughness of a catalogue; but where a work of biography derives its imperative from the significance of the life it describes, in a novel, it is the author, not the subject, who must provide the reader with a sense of what to read for; we, as readers, expect from a novel an organizing principle more substantive than chronology, an implicit sense of direction and occasional clues, no matter how vague, that we're moving toward some revelation. And that is what seems to me to be wrong with *World's Fair*, only in its last third, where it becomes most fully novelistic, does this oddly shaped book achieve a sense of purpose and offer the rich rewards readers have come to expect from Mr. Doctorow's work. Until that point, the reader feels as if he were listening to young Edgar in the park, practicing his ventriloquial drone: a child chattering to himself, and only sometimes achieving the compelling thrown voice of true fiction. (pp. 3, 25)

> *David Leavitt, "Looking Back on the World of Tomorrow," in* The New York Times Book Review, *November 10, 1985, pp. 3, 25.*

RHODA KOENIG

I found this [*World's Fair*] . . . stodgy and trite and oppressively dull. There is no plot, merely sketches of Edgar going to the Polo Grounds with his father, going to S. Klein with his mother, playing with his dog, or wetting the bed ("Startled awake by the ammoniated mists, I am roused in one instant from glutinous sleep to grieving awareness"). Edgar experiences some sexual curiosity ("If I had the power to be invisible I would go into the girls' bathroom at P.S. 70''), but the rite of passage here is symbolic. He visits the 1939 World's Fair and, after witnessing some highly suggestive exhibits (Trylon and Per-

isphere, parachute jump, time capsule lowered into the Immortal Well), buries a time capsule of his own in Claremont Park.

Can there be a reader, from the Piedmont to Peru, who is not by now well up on lower-middle-class Jewish life in the New York of the thirties? Yet, after innumerable novels on the subject, the twenty years in which "trivia" and "nostalgia" have been growth industries, Doctorow writes as if the Grand Concourse were virgin territory, explaining social customs and radio programs in unnecessary and uninteresting detail. The peripheral characters, as well, have been heard from many times before—the loving, fretful mother; the jolly, evasive father; the bright, frustrated older brother; the atheist grandfather who (how original! how ironic!) knows the Bible better than his pious wife.

Even these limits and clichés might have been transcended if Doctorow had brought to them some vitality, some enthusiasm. But *World's Fair* seems to be broadcast to us from a great distance (or height). Although the novel is about a little boy, one is constantly aware of the much older man behind the primer prose . . . and the prose-poetry . . . , who drones on in a complacent, self-absorbed way. This book is so static, so fragmentary and dry, that, before your eyes, the letters seem to turn into lint. (pp. 96-7)

> *Rhoda Koenig, in a review of "World's Fair," in* New York *Magazine, Vol. 18, No. 46, November 25, 1985, pp. 96-7.*

EDMUND WHITE

The very modesty of E. L. Doctorow's new novel [*World's Fair*] is its most daring aspect, but it's a dare that pays off. In so many autobiographical novels the writer is tempted to gift himself with nearly perfect recall and to turn his early experiences into signs of his own later genius. Doctorow avoids these temptations and sticks close to memory, its gaps and haziness as well as its pockets of poetic lucidity. He never divines in his Jewish middle-class Bronx childhood of the 1930s the extraordinary eloquence and wisdom he was later to win for himself.

Doctorow trusts his material. He also trusts his recollections, no matter how incomplete they may be in some places. This is not a book about the deceptions of memory. In some slight instances the narrator's brother or mother, who are both given their turn to speak, may correct the facts as presented earlier, but the corrections are only a question of five dollars more or a year older. This is a novel in which the brick buildings and the summer light are as intense, as substantial and as present as in a Hopper painting.

The sentences are short, the presentation straightforward, the chronology strict. The narrator seldom indulges in psychological speculation about his past self or his parents' motives. The epic ordinariness of people's lives is the meat of this novel. That this ordinariness should apply to the story of a Jewish kid who is often ill, who fears the local hoodlums, who overhears his parents' late-night quarrels only proves how heterogeneous American life is. (p. 594)

Along the way the author examines the phenomenology of everyday life. Any book in which a young person is being inducted into the mysteries of adult life permits us to take a slow, puzzled look at conventions usually too close to be seen. With a sure touch Doctorow renders the conventions as well as the landscape against which they occur. We catch glimpses of a Woman With a Past (a childhood sweetheart's affable, pretty mother). We overhear echoes of rancor from the in-laws who think their daughter-in-law is a Spendthrift and in any event Not Good Enough (the maligned woman is the boy's mother). From the boy's point of view we learn that his happy-go-lucky father, always so jaunty and elegantly turned out, is gambling away his music store business. And we share the narrator's dismay when he discovers that his beloved older brother is flunking out of college. At the same time the decline of the family's fortunes is marked by their successively smaller, cheaper apartments.

But the problems are not overplayed. Juxtaposed against the family gloom are bright set pieces that record the weight and wonder of the visual world.... (pp. 594-95)

The characters themselves are as clear as if they had been etched out of wood with fire—that old-fashioned summer-camp technique of pyrography. Particularly memorable is the Yiddish-speaking grandma who has attacks of madness during which she thinks her daughter is poisoning her and prays that an army of Cossacks will mow her evil children down. The older brother is a mild, sensible guy, competent in the small things of life; a less observant writer would have missed him altogether. Doctorow's gift is to make his outlines firm and dark, burned into the wood to stay....

Doctorow has rooted his vision in a particular moment, place and social milieu. His attention to detail, however, never becomes just an excursion down memory lane. Mere lists of names, products and now-vanished sights can have the unwanted effect of making the past seem somehow amusing, quaint, absurd (absurd for not being up-to-date), and that approach leaves the past spayed and clawless. Doctorow finds feelings that are deep in the settings of a more innocent past. His past purrs and hisses and is capable of scratching deep enough to draw blood. (p. 595)

Edmund White, "Pyrography," in The Nation, *Vol. 241, No. 18, November 30, 1985, pp. 594-95.*

Allen (Stuart) Drury

1918-

American novelist, journalist, and editor.

A popular political novelist, Drury is best known for his first novel, *Advise and Consent* (1959), which was awarded the Pulitzer Prize in fiction. His long career as a journalist and political correspondent in Washington, D.C., provides the background for his novels of political intrigue and informs his right-wing, anti-communist stance. Drury's major concern in his fiction is the conflict between America's governing establishment and the pacifistic forces of liberalism which, in his view, serve to undermine or weaken decisive American response to the everpresent Soviet threat.

Drury's novels utilize melodramatic, fast-paced narratives and great compilations of factual detail to dramatize the intrigues and counter-intrigues, compromises, and betrayals within various governmental circles. *Advise and Consent* centers on a Senatorial battle over the confirmation of a popular liberal nominee for Secretary of State who is eventually revealed to have had communist affiliations in his youth. Drury closes the novel by stating that American democracy "represents, usually with success, a compromise between idealism and workaday realities." Subsequent novels in the *Advise and Consent* series—*A Shade of Difference* (1962), *Capable of Honor* (1966), *Preserve and Protect* (1968), *The Throne of Saturn* (1971), *Come Ninevah, Come Tyre* (1973), and *The Promise of Joy* (1976)—focus on various governmental conflicts with Third World nations, the liberal press, Washington lobbyists, and the Soviet Union.

Drury's later novels continue in the tradition of the *Advise and Consent* series but more overtly reflect his political beliefs. In *Anna Hastings: The Story of a Washington Newspaperperson* (1978) and *Mark Coffin, U.S.S.: A Novel of Capitol Hill* (1979) Drury expounds on the weaknesses and abuses of 1970s liberalism. He transfers his political interests to ancient Egypt to examine the short reign of the well-meaning but weak liberal pharaoh Akhenaten in *A God against Gods* (1976) and *Return to Thebes* (1978). In *The Hill of Summer* (1981) and *The Roads of Earth* (1984) Drury returns to the Washington political arena, centering again on a conservative government in conflict with both the liberal press and powerful Soviet forces.

Reviewers frequently challenge Drury's political views and conclusions and fault his use of heavy melodrama, unconvincing plots, and stock characters. Many readers, however, find his narratives absorbing and consider his presentation of government and politics penetrating and observant. Several of Drury's novels have been adapted for film.

(See also *Contemporary Authors*, Vols. 57-60.)

LEWIS GANNETT

[In *Advise and Consent* Allen Drury] has written the most exciting, most discriminating and most intimate novel of Washington political life yet to appear. It is also timely almost beyond belief. . . .

Photograph by Alex Gotfryd

Yet it is not a *roman à clef*. It is set in an undefined post-Eisenhower period, when the cold war with Russia is still obsessive, and the unnamed President, a former Governor of California, seems to be Republican though he is more like Roosevelt than Eisenhower. So, too, the Majority Leader in the Senate, a leading character throughout the book, is more like Lyndon Johnson than Robert Taft, but in fact he is neither.

The President has just persuaded his ineffective Secretary of State to resign and has sent to the Senate the name of a public figure who had first served the government under an administration of another party. This Robert Leffingwell appears to some Americans as a dedicated apostle of liberalism, to others . . . a smug and hypocritical "Righteous Rollo." He has enemies, and they set out to get him. . . .

What interests Mr. Drury most, and gives his story its intense drama, is not the ambivalent character of Robert Leffingwell but the interplay of force in the Senate battle over his confirmation. It is the battle in the minds of the President, the Majority Leader, the ambitious chairman of the Foreign Affairs Committee (who had hoped to be President), and his fellow committee members, and especially in the mind of the cynical and vindictive old senior Senator from South Carolina, who, though occasionally he seems cast as a villain, is yet the wittiest and most likable character in the book.

The curious fact is that Mr. Drury has managed to make almost all his characters, despite their tempestuous clashes, both credible and likable. There are no total villains in the book, though there are many fools. Motives are mixed. A fuzzy-headed, demagogic "liberal" Senator from Wyoming comes as near to being a villain as any, yet his worst fault is stupidity. Mr. Drury names and characterizes at least ninety of the hundred Senators, and his characterizations are often more pungent than gentle . . . , yet he also recognizes that in the end, influenced as their thinking may be by complex self-interests, all these officers of state will act as, on the whole, they think "right for the country." . . .

Most Americans, reading [Drury's] book, will feel that they are making discoveries, seeing things from the inside. The banter of the Senate cloakrooms, in which a Minority Leader can ask a puzzled Majority Leader what he can do to help him and mean it, is revealing and witty. As is perhaps inevitable in a Washington novel, there is a concentration on political process; and in that respect Washington, in fact as in the book, is different from the Main Streets of the nation. No woman, in the novel, seems as alive as any of a score of male characters, and that again is hardly typical of American life. . . .

Advise and Consent is a long novel, but it sustains fascination and its tension to the quirk of fate at the end. Partly this is due to Mr. Drury's own lively sense of the Experiment that is America. Here, as he says midstream, is a land that after the war succumbed to "the great Age of the Shoddy" and "the Age of the Shrug . . . when it was too hard and too bothersome to worry about tomorrow." And, as he says in his final words, this is still America, "the kindly, pleasant, greening land about to learn whether history still had a place for a nation so strangely composed of great ideals and uneasy compromises."

> Lewis Gannett, "The World of Washington, D.C., in a Dramatic, Revealing Novel," in New York Herald Tribune Book Review, August 16, 1959, p. 1.

RICHARD L. NEUBERGER

Rarely has a political tale been told with such vivid realism. In *Advise and Consent* each Senator has a name and a particular identity as a distinct personality. Here are the Senatorial primitives who thirst for other men's blood and reputations; here are the rugged symbols of quiet rectitude and patient decency; here is the stately woman Senator who has survived in a man's world. . . . Readers will seek to compare these hypothetical members of the Senate with the Senators of living reality, although Allen Drury cautions in his preface against any such undertaking. Are special human types necessarily ever repeated? . . .

Allen Drury knows Washington as Jim Bridger knew the mountain passes. He has spared no pages in giving his book color and substance in generous depth. Washington's restaurants, hotels, night spots and leading hostesses all pass in review. He protects neither the private lives of Ambassadors who poke and pry into American politics nor of the widows who set snares of sex and wealth for lonely members of the Senate. The minutiae as well as the cosmic events of government preoccupy him. (p. 1)

The story might have been more wholly credible had it ended with the Senate's roll-call vote and not in the improbable death of the Chief Executive. Far too much of a startling nature happens during the book's final sections. The reader turns to

the last page gingerly, half expecting that it may bring forth a Martian invasion of the White House lawn. . . . Nevertheless I believe that *Advise and Consent* will stand as one of the finest and most gripping political novels of our era. Many Americans will learn about their Government through its dramatic pages. I would rank it with *Revelry*, the Samuel Hopkins Adams classic about the Harding Administration, and this is high literary rating, indeed, in the field of political tales. (pp. 1, 20)

> Richard L. Neuberger, "Solons They Are, but Humans Too," in The New York Times Book Review, August 16, 1959, pp. 1, 20.

PATRICK O'DONOVAN

This single, huge and peculiar book [*Advise and Consent*] has received more praise than the *opera omnia* of most authors receive in a lifetime. Colleagues of the writer have praised its timeliness and the revelatory accuracy of its dissection of the Senate process. Literary critics have respectfully blunted their pencils before its bulk and judged it by special criteria. Particularly in Washington, people buy it and even read it and discuss it with pleasure and approval and it is quite assured of success. . . .

[In this novel], detail is heaped on detail. . . . Dialogue omits nothing. This is total recall at a typewriter. It is an attempt to present the truth by including everything. Hundreds of small conversations, dozens of biographies, innumerable incidents. There never has been such a source book in fiction. The style matches its bursting contents, rich, heavy and unselective. . . .

This is . . . a very right-wing book. The sin of the Leader of the Majority, which was to consent to blackmail of the foulest sort in order to get his measure through the Senate, is more readily forgivable than the would-be Secretary of State who is a "righteous Rollo" and had dealings with Them in the thirties. . . . The President may be great, but he interferes with the legislative process. The obstructive Southerner with his obsessive hatreds and prejudices, is, after all, a gentleman and a member of the Club's In-group. The British Ambassador is even more of a gentleman (and a peer as well) and he knows just how and when to rap out a swift and devastating rebuke to his Soviet colleague in a manner whose perfection has naturally required centuries of breeding and the habit of imperial command.

Behind and around these legitimate convictions, not often found in serious American journalism today, there is the Senate in action. In any parliamentary system that is worth its free postal arrangements the legislative body does develop a corporate personality of its own, bigger than the sum of the personalities involved and sometimes curiously at variance with the current set of members. In addition, the business of government is normally carried on and eased by innumerable private bargains and compromises which, if brought out into the clear sunlight and made to stand alone, would have a squalid and trivial air.

Yet in this senate of *Advise and Consent,* the deals seem almost to comprise the whole. The electorate is there to be wooed as a means of returning to Washington, but it plays little part in the consideration of even the Good Senators. The offices are apportioned, the Presidency passed on as cynically as a crown in a turbulent medieval court. . . .

[If] this is not a textbook on the Senate, if it is a caricature, and a sensational and dangerously distorted one, the book is something else. It is vastly entertaining. The slow interplay of archetypes is restful. The impression that you are at a keyhole looking in on the source of power is fun. It is flattering to try to fix the characters in this *Roman à clef.* Good triumphs in the good tradition. The single tragedy—and here the book almost becomes a novel—of the blackmailed Senator is genuinely moving but not too moving, because the man after all really *was* a homosexual. . . . It is a ripping tale, and thundering good yarn. It is more than that. It is a genuinely and deservedly popular book. It asks no questions. It presents no problems. It comforts and cossets. One is compelled, while foreseeing the end, to find how it works out. . . . It is the sort of book that very few can produce. It is as rare as a work of art.

It is more than a best-seller. It joins the select company of good bad books. It is almost good enough to stand with Marie Corelli and Ouida and Hall Caine. It is the equivalent of those faintly daring books that thrilled Edwardian society and sold solidly and once provided their authors with small palaces in Venice and with Rolls Royces finished in yellow basket work. Despite the acclaim and the wealth they brought their authors, such books are forgotten today. Their pleasures were too precisely attuned to the moment, their "message" too exactly directed at what was fashionably but not seriously worried over. This is a portrait of an America that never really was and which, despite the fact that the book is set in the future, has never, thank God, the slightest chance of ever being. But if you wish to know what version of the national myth is now current, then . . . *Advise and Consent* may tell you what secret image of America you now delight in but would hesitate to express too openly.

> Patrick O'Donovan, "The Current National Myth," in The New Republic, *Vol. 141, No. 11, September 14, 1959, p. 19.*

PAMELA HANSFORD JOHNSON

The mild acceptance of *Advise and Consent* by a number of reviewers in this country might almost delude me into thinking that some of my colleagues hadn't really done their homework. It is hard homework, God knows, until about page 170, when the Senatorial hearings begin: no trial scene, or its derivates, can ever flop, as every writer knows.

The story concerns the President's attempt to foist upon the Senate, as Secretary of State, a liberal called Leffingwell (Hiss model), who is not sound enough on Hard An-TI Communism. Old Seab Cooley, Senator for South Carolina (rough but good, strongly reminiscent of Joe McCarthy), gets Leffingwell smeared and traps him into lying. . . . The young chairman of the committee, Brigham Anderson, turns against Leffingwell; whereupon the President (great but bad, model FDR) has *him* smeared . . . and Anderson commits suicide. The Senate, outraged (it seems to be OK to smear bad men but not good ones) votes against Leffingwell . . . , the President dies, and somebody like Mr Truman takes over, preparing the way for the hero (model Robert A. Taft) to succeed him. Quite a yarn. And there is no doubt that when the yarn gets going, it does, despite its intolerable wafflings and repetitions, take a grip.

Now I am quite sure Mr Allen Drury is to be trusted completely on matters of Senate House procedure and Washington social life. Where everything else is concerned, I would as soon trust Billy Bunter on the *moeurs* of the modern public school. *Advise and Consent* is based, first of all, on the proposition that the West has an inherent technical military superiority over the Communist countries, a view nobody should have believed for

the last ten years; the absurd top-level and Ambassadorial charade behind the Senate House front is conducted wholly in this light. Indeed, Mr Drury's conception of the diplomatic corps makes me blink when it doesn't make me shudder. (p. 162)

Advise and Consent thoroughly depresses me. It is politically repellent and artistically null with a steady hysterical undertone. The writing is pedestrian, full of 'with a sigh', 'with a laugh', 'he chuckled', 'she blushed', 'an expessive four-letter word', and adorned by great clumsy forays into the historic present. It is morally disquieting. It doesn't condemn the McCarthy technique, except when used on characters of whom the author approves. There is not the smallest feeling for character (as apart from caricature), or for the workings of the political intellect. The political novel must be first and foremost about men, or it is nothing: Trollope, Disraeli, Hope, knew that. I cannot believe that *Advise and Consent,* which is being hugely read, and its backwoodsman principles widely assimilated, doesn't worry many of my American friends as much as it does me. (pp. 162-63)

> Pamela Hansford Johnson, "Political Soap Opera," in New Statesman, *Vol. LIX, No. 1507, January 30, 1960, pp. 162-63.*

GEOFFREY GODSELL

Allen Drury has written a second labyrinthine novel [*A Shade of Difference*] after the fashion of *Advise and Consent,* and again constructs it so cleverly that the reader always has the silken thread in his hand to find his way through it. But like so many modern buildings, it is functionally rather than aesthetically pleasing. . . .

The action takes place but six months after the Geneva conference for which President Hudson was leaving in the concluding pages of the earlier novel. At Geneva, he has called the bluff of the Soviet Union and has thus saved the world from the disaster with which it had seemed threatened. Consequently, he is now an immensely popular occupant of the White House. . . .

The reader also renews his acquaintance with many of the Congressional leaders introduced in *Advise and Consent.* . . . [Onto] center stage this time moves Senator Harold Fry, as head of the United States Delegation at the United Nations.

Indeed, as Mr. Drury indicates in his dedication, the United Nations provides the main theme for the novel, and the author clearly has as one of his purposes a plea that the newly independent countries should not strain or abuse the workings of that organization to the point of wrecking it. So determined is he to make the plea that he verges on melodrama in having Senator Fry, gravely ill, struggle to the rostrum in the General Assembly and, in a semi-deathbed scene, implore the delegates: "Let us love one another! It is all we have left." . . .

The man who sets the fuse to all the trouble in this novel is a handsome young African ruler, the M'Bulu of Mbuele—popularly known as "Terrible Terry"—who is seeking immediate independence from British rule for his country. The British have promised an orderly transfer of power within a year, but the M'Bulu has come to the United Nations to secure the General Assembly's endorsement for a British withdrawal forthwith. Of course, the Soviet bloc and most of the countries of Africa and Asia support him. But his most astute ally is the Ambassador of Panama, Felix Labaiya-Sofra.

Labaiya is married to the sister of Edward Jason, Governor of California. . . . In sponsoring and later egging on the M'Bulu, Labaiya believes that he can further two ambitions: the first, to win the Negro vote for his brother-in-law; the second, to harm the United States, whose hold on the Panama Canal he is set on loosening.

He is able to use the M'Bulu as an agent against the United States, when the young ruler is incensed by what appears to him an insufferable slighting by President Hudson. After this slighting, the Jasons fête the M'Bulu at a property they have in Charleston, and while there, he is the victim of violence resulting from school integration in South Carolina. Labaiya then introduces a motion in the United Nations censuring the United States for this incident. . . . To match this, the United States sends to the rostrum to speak against the motion a Negro member of its delegation, Congressman Cullee Hamilton, with arm in a sling after being beaten up by ruffians probably hired by a former college roommate, LeGage Shelby, who thinks the Congressman is an Uncle Tom.

The conflict between Hamilton and Shelby enables Mr. Drury to give us his version of one of the great debates within the Negro cause today—that between the moderates and the activists. But it also shows the pitfalls in this kind of novel of actuality. The author is boxed in by his need to keep close to current events. In the effort to fit recognizable characters into this framework, he comes dangerously close to stereotypes or even caricatures. Such, for example, are Mr. Drury's Negroes, in whose lives the physical side of sex is tastelessly overemphasized. The M'Bulu, too, is something of a caricature, with his polygamous family background and worship of ancestral gods to the accompaniment of thunder and lightning.

Mr. Drury is less well acquainted with United Nations procedures than with those of the Congress. A speaker before a committee, for example, does not go to a rostrum, but remains seated. And the rapporteur of a committee does not call the roll in a vote.

But for all that, one must concede Mr. Drury's skill as a writer and admire his inventiveness. What prevents *A Shade of Difference* from having lasting value is perhaps just that: it is inventive rather than creative writing.

> *Geoffrey Godsell, ''Drury: The UN Is the Sequel,''*
> *in* The Christian Science Monitor, *September 20,*
> *1962, p. 11.*

SIDNEY HYMAN

[In *A Shade of Difference*] Mr. Drury reveals himself again to be a first-class reporter, if not a first-class novelist, skilled in weaving a fascinating narrative that branches and flares on a wide canvas. Moreover, to the art he has already shown in capturing a sense of the institutional machinery of the United States Senate at work, he has now added a kindred piece of art in dealing with the institutional machinery of the United Nations General Assembly. . . .

[Two new characters] of major importance help round out Mr. Drury's cast. There is his Royal Highness, Terence Wolowo Ajkaje, better known as Terrible Terry, . . . who became the chief of his African land, M'Buele, by the route of cunning and murder. There is Representative Cullee Hamilton of California, who stands a chance of being the first Negro to be elected to the Senate. . . .

As a novelist, Mr. Drury is within his rights in inventing any character he wishes and in placing them in any kind of situation that appeals to him. But the reader is also within his own rights in wondering whether the men portrayed are really themselves—in all their tangle of emotions—or whether they are not the stereotypes of a morality play walking across the stage with identifying placards in a line of argument Mr. Drury seeks to advance.

I myself agree with much of this novel when it is read as a political essay about the wild attacks made on American purposes in the world, or when it is read as a warning to the new Afro-Asian nations about bleating a hymn of treachery while they are themselves in the teeth of a wolf. I agree with it when it is read as an essay on the travails of men of goodwill who seek a solution to incredibly complicated human problems, only to be pummeled for their efforts by forces that know only how to hate and destroy. Lastly, I agree with Mr. Drury's sharp commentary on the clichés of some American Liberals who would praise every country but their own, and who find wisdom and nobility in every body of men except the body who represent them in Washington.

Yet in Mr. Drury's own terms, it is doubtful whether the effect of this essay in the guise of a novel squares with his own thesis—dramatically expressed in the United Nations by a dying Senator Fry—that we must ''love one another.''

In the angle of vision the author brings to his portrait of most Afro-Asians there is relatively little in the way of an understanding and compassionate heart. There is very little in the way of a representation of their inner torment in their encounters with responsible power. What we have instead in this novel is a one-dimensional portrait of the new nations of Africa and Asia drawn in such a way as to make us hate them; there is no bridge of comprehensive understanding through which Mr. Drury's ''love'' can do its healing work.

> *Sidney Hyman, ''Terrible Terry at the U.N.,'' in* The
> New York Times Book Review, *September 23, 1962,*
> *p. 5.*

DONALD MALCOLM

The secret of reading the fiction of Allen Drury with pleasure and a sense of benefit is one that has been completely revealed, perhaps, only to the Pulitzer Prize Committee. The ordinary reader . . . may be puzzled to discover precisely wherein Mr. Drury's especial merit may be supposed to lie. *A Shade of Difference* . . . is not likely to resolve the perplexity. The reader will see at once that it is not the best novel of the year, but beyond that judgment he will find it difficult to proceed with assurance. One cannot speak of bad writing when there is no writing to speak of.

The chief form that non-writing takes with Mr. Drury is simple compilation. For the customary devices of narrative art, he substitutes what appear to be bills of lading. By way of evoking an atmosphere of high international glamour at the White House, he inscribes:

> The Hamiltons were among the first arrivals;
> Bob and Dolly Munson followed soon after
> with the Secretary of State and Mrs. Knox;
> other Cabinet members and their wives came
> after; the French Ambassador and Celestine Barre
> and other members of the diplomatic corps,
> with a heavy emphasis on Africa and Asia. . . .

The same method is employed to illuminate the manifold responsibilities of the President. An official has asked the Chief Executive to send along some information on "the report of the Eleven-Nation Nuclear Powers Commission," and Mr. Drury's President replies:

> "I shall. And what I recommend on the situation in Iran, and whether we should make any formal protest to India about the Prime Minister's statement, and whether it's worth trying to work things out with Indonesia, and if we should take further action on this new thing in Cuba. Also what to do about Guiana's latest, and whether or not to reply to the Soviet Union's newest charges. . . ."

Since the official to whom these remarks are addressed is the Secretary of State, who would have no use whatever for information on such matters . . . , we must conclude that the author is engaged in listing for listing's sake, a sort of book-keeperly extension of the older doctrine of *l'art pour l'art*.

It might be thought that Mr. Drury would be obliged to abandon enumeration whenever his fictional inventory mounted, by however slow degrees, to the very edge of a potentially dramatic moment, but even here, we generally find, he's got a little list. (p. 233)

The author's strong grasp of the principles of listing does not extend, unfortunately, to those literary modes that require some sense of style. From time to time in the course of the novel, Mr. Drury is mysteriously moved to try his hand at parody and burlesque, with regrettable consequences. On one such occasion, he aims a satirical kick at that easiest of all targets, the vast backside of advertising—and misses. . . . One can only stare in cold astonishment at a parody of advertising that is more repulsive in conception and more witless in execution than any advertisement it conceivably might seek to mock. On the whole, it is with a feeling of relief that one returns from such excursions to the main stream of the catalogue. . . . (p. 234)

[It] actually is possible to *compile* the bulk of a novel, but the method is not without its shortcomings. One drawback is that a story which might be told in a hundred and fifty pages or thereabouts is distended to six hundred and three. Another is that the reader, during much of the time, is mightily bored. But the most serious objection to the enumerative approach to fiction is that Mr. Drury's ideas are obscured by a superfluity of inactive words, and this is the greater pity in that his ideas appear to be highly original and even peculiar. (p. 236)

Since Mr. Drury and the great majority of his characters of all persuasions appear to believe that the end of colonialism is a good thing, on the whole, and that racial segregation is a bad thing, the political developments of the novel take place in a kind of intellectual limbo of agreement. Those who agree at all heartily, however—and this is the great curiosity of the novel—are portrayed as scoundrels and fools. The head of a Negro civil-rights organization who also serves on the United States delegation to the U.N. is shown to be working consciously against the interests of his own country. . . . The Supreme Court is represented by a Justice who calls other men "my dear boy" with emphasis and regularity and who delights in stirring up mischief on behalf of liberal causes. . . . [The] larger part of the nation's press and television, too, are shown to be entirely despicable. . . . They entertain "the automatic assumption that their own country must per se be wrong and stubborn and pigheaded and without justification, and that the enemy by the same token must have reason and justice on his side." One thinks of recent crises, and of others, not so recent, and one wonders what Mr. Drury imagines he is talking about. To be sure, it might be argued that since the novel is set in a vague near future the author intends to speak not of things as they are but of things as they might become, supposing a general disappearance of honor and sense. Yet because he mentions so many contemporary organizations by name, and pseudonymously hints at others, one wishes he had found a way to say what he means. In the absence of clarity, the reader can only surmise that Mr. Drury is possessed of a peculiar faith in a pervasive national malignity and baseness, a faith that is as uncritical, though not necessarily as endearing, as the belief of more innocent minds in Santa Claus. (pp. 236, 238, 241)

> *Donald Malcolm, "A World We Never Made," in* The New Yorker, *Vol. XXXVIII, No. 41, December 1, 1962, pp. 233-34, 236, 238, 241.*

W. G. ROGERS

A preface to this fast-stepping hard-breathing novel [*Capable of Honor*] reminds the reader that it carries on the story opened auspiciously in *Advise and Consent* and continued less excitingly in *A Shade of Difference*. Harley M. Hudson is still President. Orrin Knox is Secretary of State. Edward Jason aims at the White House. And watchdog Allen Drury is right on the job.

The chief enemy of the President and the country, too, we are told almost enough times to make us believe, is not a Communist but a columnist. Commies, in this commentator's view, have grown so big and strong we must play along with them, and in the United Nations lies the only hope of peace. . . . When rebels in Gorotoland slay Americans and destroy American property, Hudson dispatches planes and troops. The newspaper pundit, aghast, cries "War!" and comes out for Jason for President. The rest of the book tells whether Hudson runs again and how the Jason-Knox rivalry pans out.

Drury pretends the time is a decade or two hence, but that is just make-believe. Despite hints of "1984," he means 1966. There are lots more signs of today than tomorrow. A liberal-minded Senator, Rhodes scholar and Phi Bete, is easily recognizable. So is a doddering English peer. Gorotoland is a new spelling for Vietnam. And columnist Walter Dobius (christened Walter Wonderful by a vastly admiring public) is clearly Druryese for, Any Liberal Columnist. There are several live Walters. You pick one.

Drury goes whole hog. Is he afraid he has only a way-out case? Anyway, he resorts to way-out arguments. Though the President is cheered as hostilities begin, Walter Wonderful's pen is mightier than sword, gun, ship and plane together—Drury as much as swears to this. Walter's word is revered more than Holy Writ by hundreds of writers and editors, by labor, business, church, the mass of Negroes, press associations, TV networks and magazines. (pp. 54-5)

Drury finds only one reporter in the entire land who mistrusts Walter; it's a safe bet *she* would have been hood winked like the rest of us if she weren't his former wife. . . . The story ends with Storm Trooper beatings and slayings. Walter doesn't rob poorboxes or steal the widow's mite, but it's not because of any compunctions. "Capable of Honor?" Politicians, often—newsmen, almost never.

Columnist and calumny look alike to Drury. To him, or to his characters, there are only black and white, except of course Red. Perhaps a novelist cannot be condemned as novelist for the views he holds; but a reader is right to demand of him: "Show me!" This book is spectacularly short on show.

It is greatly to Drury's credit that he holds the attention of his reader, who is cannily persuaded to keep his nose to the very grindstone, evidently, on which the author ground his axe. But the story is hard for me to believe and harder still to enjoy. Fiction ought never to seem so fictional as this. (p. 55)

> *W. G. Rogers, "Walter Wonderful," in* The New York Times Book Review, *September 11, 1966, pp. 54-5.*

ROBERT B. SEMPLE, JR.

Allen Drury's highly successful fiction . . . has always, in a sense, been at war with itself. On the one hand there is Mr. Drury's capacity for telling a first-rate story that is so compelling, so authentic in detail, that the reader simply cannot let go. On the other there is his tendency to proselytize, to grind political axes openly and unashamedly.

Sadly, the second strain, his apparently irrepressible instinct to preach, has won out in his new *Capable of Honor.* Like his first two books, this one is very big, full of the kind of reportage and political expertise we might expect from a former newsman. . . . But the ax-grinding is too frequent, strident, and in the end abusive; we are inundated by cant.

The story, involving a number of characters from the earlier books, is fundamentally a sound one. Essentially, it involves the relationship of three potential Presidential candidates (the President himself, who has not yet decided whether to run; his Secretary of State; and the governor of California) to a single explosive issue of foreign policy. It also considers the relationship of all three men to a liberal columnist named Walter Dobius, reputedly the most influential pundit in the world. . . .

[Following the President's dispatch of U.S. troops to the emerging African nation of Gorotoland], everyone is out for the President and the Secretary of State. The story moves swiftly from Washington to the columnist's home in the Blue Ridge foothills to the U.N. Security Council to the climactic convention in San Francisco's Cow Palace, where the delegates render final judgment on both the foreign-policy issue and the character of the men involved.

All this is heady stuff, and nobody writing today is any better at describing a convention, building tension in the Security Council, or peering into the high councils of Government than Mr. Drury. But sooner or later—usually sooner—the author's reportorial gifts give way to long stretches of hortatory prose.

Too often the narrative halts while Mr. Drury sermonizes on the correct use of diplomacy or the evils of coexistence. Too quickly the principal characters become outlandish stereotypes. The President becomes all those dowdy Harry Trumans of the world who turn out to have more guts than anyone gave them credit for. The Secretary of State is an overblown John Foster Dulles. The governor of California is a wild cross between Jack Kennedy (he has money), Dick Nixon (he moves with the crowd), and J. W. Fulbright (he likes to negotiate). As for Walter Dobius, he is the stereotype of the knee-jerk liberal columnist.

Looking at all three novels in broad political terms, Mr. Drury has moved from the resilient anti-Establishment viewpoint of *Advise and Consent* to the impatient anticommunism of *A Shade of Difference* to a boring Old Fogeyism in *Capable of Honor.* He is clearly a conservative in domestic politics and a "hawk" in international affairs. He believes that the wise and resolute use of strength is a better deterrent to aggression than appeasement disguised as "long-range thinking."

This is a reasonable and honorable point of view. But if only Mr. Drury would shut up about it and let the point be made through character, dialog, and the spinning out of his tale.

> *Robert B. Semple, Jr., "Allen Drury's Newest Is Old Fogeyism," in* The National Observer, *September 26, 1966, p. 22.*

M. STANTON EVANS

Criticism of the Liberal press is usually dismissed, in the Liberal press, as an affront to journalistic virtue. . . .

Comes now Allen Drury—. . . whose new book [*Capable of Honor*] turns out to be a triumphantly punishing critique of the Liberal press. . . .

Drury charges, by way of openers, that the media are biased, vindictive, petty, mean-hearted, and ruinous to the national security. After establishing this, he goes on to suggest what he thinks is the matter with them.

Since he is both a journalist and a dramatic craftsman, Drury is able to present the indictment with authenticity and precision. The combination of skills makes it likely his novel will expose the workings of the Liberal press more convincingly to more people than any other such effort to date. Whether the leftward media will in consequence flog this Pulitzer Prize winner as an enemy of "the press" is an interesting question. (p. 1174)

While *Capable of Honor* is not altogether a *roman à clef*, the story line compounds many elements from contemporary politics. . . . The climactic convention battle is an obvious take-off on 1964, as TV commentators hover endlessly over Liberal aspersions, attribute dark intentions to conservatives, and cut away from conservative spokesmen for extended "analysis" by such as Dobius—all of which is a good deal closer to fact than is the journalism it satirizes. (p. 1175)

This is a well-constructed novel which, if not the equal of *Advise and Consent,* in places rises to similar heights and focuses even more intensely on the central issues of our age. As ever, Drury is most impressive when he evokes the backroom maneuvering of Washington intrigue, and he has an excellent sense for the alternating boredom, panic and exaltation of political conventions. If some of the minor characters are by necessity passion-play figurines, the major ones are well-sculpted, their resonance deepened by the Balzacian echoes from Drury's previous novels. For conservatives, the book will prove to be a long roll in the catnip; for others, good reading which should stir doubts about the frequent horror that masks itself as objective journalism. (p. 1176)

> *M. Stanton Evans, "An Enemy of the Press," in* National Review, *Vol. XVIII, No. 46, November 15, 1966, pp. 1174-76.*

GORDON MILNE

[*Advise and Consent* concentrates] upon the theme of power, a power that warps and corrodes the politicians motivated by a desire for it and taints political life with corruption. The picture of Washington given in *Advise and Consent* would certainly have struck the Founding Fathers as the epitome of a corrupt society. The Senate may show the "vitality of free men" while still not necessarily serving the true ends of popular government. . . . Because people are ultimately good, so Drury insists, the point of convergence of their self-seeking interests will ultimately be good, too. Unfortunately, the conclusion does not follow precisely from the premise, and even the premise might be regarded as suspect. Drury himself describes many, many individuals who would not be "ultimately good." When a Supreme Court justice will indulge in blackmail and when the President of the United States will "play along," the picture is black, the corruption there.

The Washington scene has a decidedly "jungl-y" air, then, in *Advise and Consent,* but it also seems, sad to say, authentically reproduced. The tan, marble-paneled fish bowl that is the Senate chamber rises before us at the beginning of the novel and remains very much in our minds throughout. In this "cave of the winds" the senators argue for their pet appropriations, debate furiously on controversial issues, and engage in various parliamentary maneuvers to secure advantage for themselves. . . . Whether in front or in back, they play a rough game, underneath the backslaps and handshakes and noble speeches. (pp. 173-74)

Of course, neither everything nor everybody is so pejoratively treated, for, as Drury reminds us toward the end of the novel, politics contains as much good as evil, the American system of government permitting "freedom" to do right as well as wrong. One does observe capable men in the Senate, one does listen to perceptive speeches on the floor (as Senator Munson's careful reminder of the legislative branch's check on the power of the executive), and one does hear intelligent and principled statements in committee hearings and caucuses. (p. 175)

Part of the book's vividness stems from its susceptibility to being read as a *roman à clef*. Certainly there is some amusement in seeing the late Senator Taft in Orrin Knox; Krishna Menon in the Indian ambassador "K.K.," a temporizing and excessively bland figure; Harry Truman in Harley Hudson; possibly Franklin Roosevelt in the President (the voice with the "happy lilt," accompanying the "toss of the head"); and surely the late Senator McCarthy in Fred Van Ackerman. But, as Irving Kristol remarks, the familiar faces are often attached to odd bodies and given unfamiliar roles, e.g., Van Ackerman as a reverse McCarthy, and the searching for identities should remain an idle, if rather captivating, game.

Although the narration retains a down-to-mud reality from beginning to end, questions arise about the author's handling of the political issue even so. Would a Supreme Court justice be so morally weak as "Tommy" Davis? Would a President . . . resort to lies, deceit, and blackmail? Could Senator Munson salve his conscience as easily as he does or be welcomed back so quickly into the fold? Would so many astute individuals continue to support Leffingwell for the secretaryship even after his uncritical penchant for peace and his fuzzy ideas about foreign policy had become well known? How plausible is the possibility that a mass movement could be started among Americans with the slogan "We would rather crawl to Moscow on our knees than perish under a bomb?" *Advise and Consent* stretches our credulity in too many instances. Drury's conclu-

sion, too, that the "good" will eventually prevail, does not, alas, seem warranted by the facts presented. It is the image of evil that lingers on.

The novel troubles one particularly, however, because it affords only qualified aesthetic satisfaction. Despite the popular acclaim and rather extensive critical approval that have been bestowed upon it, it must be considered a flawed performance. It cannot claim, for one thing, any very careful characterization, any progression beyond the one-dimensional figure. Cord Meyer rightly complains that Drury conjures up no "fully imagined and complexly motivated human beings confronting with believable anguish the hard choices that practical politics frequently present." The utterly stereotyped foreign diplomats, the English, French, and Russian ambassadors tend to prove the point, and so, too, do many of the United States officials. (pp. 175-77)

One exception to the Meyer complaint may be cited, Senator Brigham Anderson. His is a moving portrayal, with the "private fortress" as well as the public façade unveiled, and the section of the novel devoted to him is much the most impressive part of *Advise and Consent.*

The novel does possess "impressive parts," it is only fair to say, author Drury displaying a knack for spinning an engrossing narrative pattern and charging a scene with drama. The reader will not quickly forget the acerbic give-and-take of the committee hearings, the suicide sequence, the Van Ackerman censure vote. At times, to be sure, the drama verges on melodrama, the domestic poignance on sentimentality, but the reality of the Anderson marriage strain or of Senator Knox's battle with his presidential ambition cannot be denied. (pp. 177-78)

Advise and Consent, like most long novels, is simply too long, and its orderly structure cannot hide this defect. The author recounts at too great length the backgrounds of the central senators and the details of senatorial committee activity. . . . His panoramic view device is overdone also; the constant series of snippet scenes grows to resemble nothing so much as plain padding.

Drury's style causes the greatest uneasiness, veering as it does from rhapsodic overwriting to limping journalese and seldom if ever achieving a supple, natural flow. . . . [The] writing is marred by triteness of diction, too, and by some heavy-handed attempts at satire. The author, relying heavily on dialogue throughout the book, occasionally inflicts highly unrealistic conversations upon us, e.g., the exchanges between the wives of the British and French ambassadors, or the coy love passages between Mrs. Harrison and Senator Munson. (pp. 178-79)

Advise and Consent still deserves to be called a "successful illustration" of the political novel genre, however. The Washington phenomena are punctiliously ranged before us—the Senate hearing in front of the television cameras, the lavish and gossipy party, the strategy sessions of the inner circle, the incessant pursuit of senators by eager newsmen—and the role-of-the-Senate theme is thoroughly analyzed. It is disheartening, of course, to feel that Drury has demonstrated once again how in America political figures place ambition above conscience, and disheartening to realize that corruption remains the traditional thesis. Yet one is grateful that Drury has brought knowledgeability to his examination of American politics and a fair measure of competence as well. (p. 179)

Gordon Milne, "Professionals: Warren, O'Connor, and Drury," in his The American Political Novel, *University of Oklahoma Press, 1966, pp. 153-79.**

ROBERT CROMIE

It is a disappointment to report that for [*Preserve and Protect*], at least, Drury has lost the hop on his fast ball. He simply isn't the workman and storyteller he was in *Advise and Consent* or *A Shade of Difference* or *Capable of Honor*. The characters, many of whom have inhabited all four books, have lost dimension and taken on a cutout appearance, with a few notable exceptions such as the highly appealing William Abbott, Speaker of the House, who becomes President in the first few pages of the story after Air Force One crashes and kills President Harley Hudson, who has just been renominated after a convention so stormy and ugly that it recalls the Republican convention that named Goldwater. . . .

The remainder of the novel, following the crash, has a double aim: to describe the renewed fight between supporters of Orrin Knox, the Vice-Presidential nominee, and Governor Ted Jason of California, a misguided liberal millionaire, for the vacated Presidential spot. Jason, it should be added, has accepted the support of three organizations so disparate as to make his action unbelievable. One, to the far left, is headed by a psychotic United States senator. One, to the far right, is the instrument of an obvious fascist. The other is directed by a racist black leader to whom violence is the answer to everything.

It is only fair to say that Drury had the materials for an engrossing novel. From his viewpoint, I'm sure, the frequent interpolation of protests against the rising tide of violence in the country—protests which surely are justifiable and should be made—and attacks on the ''liberal'' press and ''liberal'' columnists, belong in the story. From the viewpoint of this reader, at least, they were so labored and intrusive that they did little more than slow down the action.

Certainly Drury is entitled to express his obviously sincere beliefs. But the message would have come across more clearly and forcefully if he had understated it in *Preserve and Protect* and then gone on to write a second non-fiction work, or a long essay, warning of his conviction that there is an international plot to overthrow the United States, a plot in which he feels many of its citizens are involved directly and others unwittingly; and that time grows short. . . .

Portions of the book, it must be said, move quickly and well, and occasionally there is some of the excitement which the earlier Drury novels offered to a far greater degree. But if a smooth-running story may be compared to a smooth-running motor, then *Preserve and Protect* needs its points adjusted.

> Robert Cromie, "*Pasting Up Political Cutouts*," in Book World—Chicago Tribune, *September 15, 1968, p. 6.*

M. STANTON EVANS

Drury is very much a writer with a cause, and his cause is to expose the confusions of the liberal mind in American politics. To this endeavor he brings a remarkable instinct for issues and an intimate knowledge of the political and journalistic world of Washington. These qualities have produced a series of novels that our future historian would be wise to consult if he wants to know something about the feel and shape of mid-twentieth-century politics. (p. 1225)

Preserve And Protect picks up, in chronology and theme, where Drury's last novel, *Capable of Honor,* leaves off. . . . Knox and Jason battle for their party's Presidential nomination after the incumbent chief executive is killed in a plane crash. The liberal Jason, who takes a ''dove'' stance on foreign policy, is backed by militants who try to stampede the party with violence. . . . The candidate himself seeks to reap all possible benefit from the turmoil, while ambiguously disowning it. His equivocation provides the moral center of the novel.

It would be hard to imagine a story line which more truly suggests the flavor of what has been happening in America. Drury's novelistic world is exactly like our own in that it is doubly menaced—not only by those who employ violence, but by those who explain it away or use it as a form of political blackmail. . . . It is interesting to note, indeed, that the struggle between the Jasonites and the Knoxians climaxes in a nominating session encircled by a howling mob. Considering the fact that the novel was completed four months before the Democratic convention in Chicago, this makes Drury a pretty good prophet as well as a discerning social critic.

Drury demonstrates the connection between the mentality which would speak softly to domestic anarchists and that which has led on to disaster in the cold war. The same willingness to extenuate, to meet brutality with concession and compromise, marks a certain species of the liberal mind in domestic and foreign policies alike. The people who think you can compromise with Communism abroad turn out, all too often, to be the people who would explain away terror at home. . . . No one has expressed the peculiarities of this outlook better than Drury, or shown more clearly its intolerance toward those who do not share its toleration of evil.

Along the way, Drury continues the pummeling of the liberal press which distinguished *Capable of Honor.* The celebrated ''Walter Dobius'' is once more in evidence along with other Drury-created journalists, a form of characterization in which the author excels. As a veteran Washington newsman, Drury is on familiar territory when he lampoons the one-sided coverage of the national media. The asides and the biases he attributes to the liberal reporters on the fringes of the narrative are devastating in their accuracy. (pp. 1225-26)

The weakness most frequently alleged against Drury is that his characters are one-dimensional—the good guys too insufferably good, the bad guys too impossibly bad. In many instances this is true, as it frequently is with polemical-satirical fiction. The characters in *Candide* and *Hard Times* are not particularly well-rounded, either. Drury has set out to make a philosophical point that desperately needs to be made, and he makes it well. He gives us, in sharp clear hues, an honest picture of the issues and people that are shaping our national destiny. (p. 1226)

> M. Stanton Evans, "*The Violent Explain It Away*," in National Review, *Vol. XX, No. 48, December 3, 1968, pp. 1225-26.*

W. G. ROGERS

In Allen Drury's new novel [*The Throne of Saturn: A Novel of Space and Politics*], laid about a decade in the future, the United States commits its money, scientific know-how and prestige to a manned landing on Mars. One's first reaction may be that, even if the trip lasts 18 months, it shouldn't take 18 months to read about it. It doesn't, quite, but it seems to. Despite some chilling incidents of purest melodrama, there are plodding wastes in this long book—when, instead of getting to Mars, you get nowhere.

The second reaction is more serious. Obviously, Drury believes in his story as in the Gospel. In a foreword, he thanks a score of NASA officials. However, while explicitly absolving them of responsibility for his use of materials they provided, he does credit them with underlying "facts and insights." The worrisome question is, which are "facts and insights" and which are Druryisms? How much of his weird yarn do these key officials, in a most crucial field of American endeavor, consider credible?

Do they go along with the novel's implication that the Russians plotted violence against our first Apollonians? Did they suggest to Drury that those same Russians might murder our future astronauts? Do they believe our spacecraft should be armed? Do they regard space flights as acts of war? . . . Are the jealousy, the rivalry, the despicable conniving luridly dramatized here borrowed from life? Do all astronauts and astro-scientists think no money should be spent on the poor, ill, homeless, hungry or aged—until our space program has had its slice of pie in the sky?

If a paranoid chauvinism of this intensity is rife among NASA personnel, then the whole outfit should be flushed down the drain. The novelist may stick with us, however; novelists should always be allowed to say what they think. We may thus enjoy occasional shivers, as explosions and riots blamed on sabotage cause injuries and deaths; as the President forces hapless Commander Trasker to accept two flagrant misfits in his crew of four; as a mechanical gremlin contrived by the Russians foils a launch; as justice triumphs when one American inside the capsule is shot. . . .

Drury has come a long way since *Advise and Consent*. With each of his fictions (this is the sixth) he moves further and further from story-telling, more and more into the business of laying down the law. What he gives us now, in *The Throne of Saturn*, is not a novel but a publicity release. The place for most publicity releases is the wastebasket.

W. G. Rogers, in a review of "The Throne of Saturn: A Novel of Space and Politics," in The New York Times Book Review, *February 14, 1971, p. 6.*

GEORGE E. SNOW

The Throne of Saturn is the latest in a series of books by Mr. Drury. . . . Certainly its premise is the same as the others: the struggle between the forces of a God-fearing Americanism and hordes of journalistic, acronym-inventing, intellectual, peace-at-any-price liberals. In his previous novels Mr. Drury fought this battle successfully and lucratively through the halls of Congress and the office of the presidency and in the process apparently exhausted these venerable grounds as sources for material and as platforms for his own social and political views. Thus it is only natural that he turn for further development of his theme to *the* burning issue of the current liberal-conservative face-off . . .—the incredibly expensive and controversial space program.

Quite specifically, the heroes of Drury's latest novel are NASA, the NASA technicians, and the NASA astronauts, while the villains are from the same shallow stock of characters mentioned above and consistently portrayed by Mr. Drury not only as villainous but communist-inspired and even vaguely homosexual. The reader should make no mistake about it, though this is a work of fiction and presumably created from Mr. Drury's imagination, the themes are as contemporary as today's

headlines. Their collective impact is, therefore, as insidious and divisive as any Mr. Drury has ever attempted previously.

The plot of the novel is quite simple. The action occurs in the American space program in the late 1970's where . . . the government of the United States decides to send a manned probe to Mars and thus anticipate a similar attempt by the Soviet Union. The mission is attacked from the outset by the ultra-liberal press, an immature, opportunistic United States Senator, and a labor union chief who has been an active undercover communist agent since his college days. After using every device to sabotage or prevent the flight, the group then insists that the crew be representative of all the American people and include a black man. As Mr. Drury would have it, this black American talks and acts more like Bobby Seale than an astro-scientist with a Ph.D. The author's description of him as a "race-struck, sick black child" speaks volumes about many of his own views and attitudes. Despite the sullen refusal of this stereotyped black man to join the friendly *camaraderie* of his crew-mates, the mission occurs but is finally destroyed by Soviet harassment and a western-style shoot out on the moon (during which the American black is also deliberately shot to death by one of his crew-mates because of his attempted treason). The novel ends on what Mr. Drury apparently considers an upbeat when the two survivors of this mission successfully concoct a lie about the events which had transpired, disarm criticism at home, and thereby enable yet another Mars mission to be launched.

There are any number of technical points upon which this book could be criticized: the shallow and amateurish characterization, the feeble plot, and the author's own journalistic style being just three. Yet, for all its artistic drabness, it is on the level of polemic that Mr. Drury's latest effort has to be criticized. His message is quite unmistakable and simplistic and is stressed and restressed in numerous ways throughout the novel. Mr. Drury is convinced that critics of American policies (whatever they are) are never motivated by genuine concern and genuine patriotism but rather, are "motivated by self-doubt and self-hatred which in turn is transformed to doubt and hatred for their country." If only things were that simple. For Mr. Drury and Mr. Drury's characters everything is that simple and those who continue to doubt or to express those doubts are actuated by their own ambitions, self-hatred, or are, quite simply, evil. (p. 525)

George E. Snow, in a review of "The Throne of Saturn: A Novel of Space and Politics," in Best Sellers, *Vol. 30, No. 23, March 1, 1971, pp. 525-26.*

HORACE JUDSON

Come Nineveh, Come Tyre is the fifth and penultimate novel in what the author calls the *Advise and Consent* series. Escalation has continued. Nothing less than the destruction of the American republic, and its transformation into a totalitarian dictatorship, is this book's story. It includes the assassination of a presidential candidate, the suicides of a President and a Vice President, and an incipient bloodless takeover of the U.S. by Russia. Drury's political principles have hardened into sclerotic pieties. Few would argue that the Soviet Union could never be tempted into acting out her ancient ambitions, or that U.S. military strength and civil concord are not important to keeping the peace and preserving the Constitution. But Drury finished his novel in February—and his story, that heartless bitch, has stood him up again, with the Watergate investigations and the

Agnew scandal. Characters more fascinating, events more crowded, a conspiracy against the Constitution far more plausible than anything Drury has invented. It is not Drury's country that is a helpless giant, after all. It is his novel.

> *Horace Judson, "Helpless Giant," in* Time, *Vol. 102, No. 20, November 12, 1973, p. 132.*

MARTIN LEVIN

It is too late to save Nineveh and spare Tyre. There may still be time to keep our effete civilization from becoming a terminal case. This is the nub of Allen Drury's parable in novel form [*Come Nineveh, Come Tyre*]. Its message is as clear as the graffiti on a subway car.

In his latest (and, like the others, lengthy) installment in the *Advise and Consent* series, Mr. Drury brews up a nightmare of our immediate future, when a feeble-willed Populist becomes President and falls deeper and deeper into the clutches of a pacifist cabal. With some outstanding exceptions, most of the men who surround President Jason are not bad sorts. They are merely equivocal, muddle-headed, garden-variety politicians. . . . The author drapes his novel with swags of their rhetoric, and with the bilious pontifications of "Frankly Unctuous," a nightly network sage.

Bad things begin to happen to the U.S.A. under the Jason Administration, including the Ward 7 treatment for some of the old Bosheviks who boosted the President into power. For Jason himself, a fate worse than death. And, for the country, "the endless night of the mind" envisioned by Orwell and Koestler. If you are inclined to fret over political conspiracy (who doesn't, nowadays?), this book should expand your anxieties to global size.

> *Martin Levin, in a review of "Come Nineveh, Come Tyre," in* The New York Times Book Review, *December 9, 1973, p. 47.*

EUGENE J. LINEHAN, S.J.

What happens when an author makes fiction so strange that it stretches credibility? Read this sixth, and mercifully last, novel [*The Promise of Joy*] of Allen Drury's in the series which began with *Advise and Consent* and you will find some kind of answer. It bores—precisely because so few of the characters are given any real life. The plot is so involved and so freighted with crisis and sudden tragedy that we are left not only breathless but weary of the whole thing. . . .

As one remembers, these present characters have remained somewhat constant in this long series since *Advise and Consent.* We pick up Orrin Knox of Illinois as he is nominated for and wins the Presidency. The basic platform of his party and his life is a strong stance against Communism and its imperialistic determination to conquer the world. Although the USA is within the novel involved in Panama and Gorotoland (a fictional nation in Africa), it seems clear that our author feels strongly about present promises of aid to Vietnam, Cambodia, and the rest. Are we to be peacefully passive about such interference within countries, or are we to be peacefully active to the point where we are ready, à la Kennedy and Cuba, with war against those on the side of Communism? The Soviets and Americans are set in postures which this novel explores.

The reader will decipher a thesis on the side of military strength and preparedness, of a real lack of trust in this cold war. And that's a good thesis to explore. Somehow the opposing forces are painted so naively that the novel suffers. And the excitement which is generated is incredible. . . . Within a few pages and within a short period of history so many surprises take place that one really begins to feel the grip of unreality.

And then—the newspapers and the general media coverage. There is hardly one single commentator or newspaper which does not dislike President Knox and tear at him on almost every occasion. Some of the charges made against the man seem irresponsible to a degree which allows one to wonder if the author is a disciple of Ron Zeigler and the Nixon Palace Guard who mentioned so often how badly the country was being used by the Press.

Important stuff is contained here, and as we ponder our future it is important for us to examine just where our priorities need to be. Pacifism poorly understood might be very dangerous. I do not think this novel will do much to move the debate; its promise of joy is ephemeral.

> *Eugene J. Linehan, S.J., in a review of "The Promise of Joy," in* Best Sellers, *Vol. 34, No. 24, March 15, 1975, p. 555.*

GENE LYONS

Drury's entire career as a novelist has been based upon the premise that the American political system is the only one in human history which conforms exactly to the parameters of human possibility and that everyone to the left of Roman Hruska is a traitor or a fool. No wonder he seems to be losing his grip. In six increasingly hysterical books, Drury has flogged his indefatigable politicos through enough wars, demonstrations, counter-demonstrations, riots, terrorist bombings, kidnappings and assassinations to make a year and a half in the fictive land he calls the United States look like a funhouse-mirror version of a decade and a half of the North American banana-eating republic of the same name. Not that any of these events are depicted fictionally, of course, except in Dos Passos-like headlines.

What the novels consist of are speeches, editorials, debates, crucial elections and cliff-hanging votes. Drury must have a single typewriter key that types out "The President of the United States of America," which he never fails to hit at least once every 500 words. His style is more digressive, repetitious and cliché-ridden than the early Ev Dirksen. Not a Presidential speech occurs that is not followed by at least 5 to 10 pages of fumbling parodies of the editorial responses of two newspapers, a couple of magazines and at least one TV network. The esthetic effect is rather like watching one of those speeded-up Walt Disney versions of the life and death of a yucca plant shown in super slow-motion.

If all of that seems confusing, consider the following scenario. At the end of *Preserve and Protect,* you will recall, either a Presidential nominee or his running mate had been shot to death. Since that is Drury's idea of suspense, one had to await last year's *Come Nineveh, Come Tyre* to learn that stern Orrin Knox of Illinois was dead, and that liberal Governor Edward M. Jason, . . . darling of the black-jacketed thugs of N.A.W.A.C. (National Anti-War Activities Congress), had been elected. (p. 24)

Fear not, America, for in *The Promise of Joy* N.A.W.A.C. (or is it the K.G.B.?) gets Jason instead, and the Commies get theirs. But if you think the survival of democracy is easy, may you spend eternity up to your neck in the Potomac reading the Presidential speeches of Orrin Knox by day and listening to the Presidential tapes of Richard Knix at night.

First the Russians and Chinese step up their attacks in Panama and Gorotoland, ''strategic key to the heart of Africa.'' When Knox responds firmly, The Media goes wild. . . . N.A.W.A.C. kidnaps his son and daughter-in-law, threatens to kill them if the President doesn't back off and sends Knox his son's ring finger to show they mean business. The Media, including this newspaper, The Washington Post (for chapters at a time Drury shows off his virtuoso wit by calling them the ''Pimes'' and the ''Tost''), Frankly Unctuous, the TV newsman, and all-powerful columnist, Walter Dobius, . . . all weigh in with invectives against His Presidency for fostering the climate of violence that led to the crime.

In spite of vacillation, rebellion and treason at home, Knox refuses to do the easy thing, and thank heaven for Heaven, the Lord intervenes; the Russians and Chinese attack each other with nuclear weapons, half destroying Asia, and the huddled masses of the world's editorial offices turn like fear-crazed lemmings to The President of the United States, hysterically begging the only man who has any bombs left to save the world from the consequences of forgetting that the Gospel According to H. L. Hunt is the Only Way. So ends the first half of the novel.

It is not for me to spoil the rest, but I will hint this much: by the end of the book the Chinese are swarming weaponless toward Moscow like so many army ants in a Tarzan film, and The Media, the United Nations and the pack of weak-willed hypocrites, sneering psychotics, liars, losers, time-servers and bullies that comprise the American liberal community are on the attack again, only now they want President Knox to bomb, so help me John Birch, ''The Godless Yellow Hordes of Asia.'' (pp. 24, 26)

> *Gene Lyons, ''Democracy Survives,'' in* The New York Times Book Review, *March 16, 1975, pp. 24, 26.*

JOHN SKOW

Fourteen centuries before Christ, the mystical pharaoh Akhenaten tried to sweep away the ancient pantheon of gods worshiped in Egypt. To replace the gods, he devised a kind of monotheism. Since monotheism is the modern preference, Akhenaten is now considered to have been one of civilization's heroes. But at the time his religion was very bad politics. Akhenaten failed; the ancient gods won. The surprise is not that Allen Drury, the *Advise and Consent* man, has written a book about Akhenaten [*A God Against the Gods*]—a pyramid could be made of books about him and his queen Nefertiti—but that his viewpoint is political.

It is no secret that Drury is not much of a novelist. This time he advances his narration by bringing his characters onstage alone to soliloquize about what has occurred and what bad results may be expected. Occasional modernisms . . . clink absurdly, and it is hard, when they do, to imagine the pharaoh's golden barge ghosting through chill nights on the Nile. Yet a patient reader is rewarded by some provocative notions about Akhenaten and his cousin-wife Nefertiti. . . .

Drury assumes that a power struggle seethed between the pharaohs of the 18th dynasty and the priesthood of Amen, the most powerful of the gods. Amenhotep III, an easygoing, able ad-

ministrator, failed to move firmly against the priests. When his son Amenhotep IV finally did strike at the priests, it was with a hysteria that unsettled courtiers and populace. Yet it was this man, a neurotic genius . . . , who declared the Aten, the disc of the sun, to be the one true god. Then he closed the temples of Amen, built a new capital dedicated to the Aten and took for himself the name Akhenaten, ''the son of the sun.''

The author judges these events with the professionalism of an old Washington political writer and finds that the pharaoh neglected to mend his fences. He inherited enormous popularity but wasted it in extravagance and flabby foreign policy, not to mention a gaudy love affair with his younger brother Smenkhkara. . . . By the novel's end Akhenaten has not actually reached his downfall. A sequel is promised, however, and things look dark for the son of the sun.

> *John Skow, ''Son of the Sun,'' in* Time, *Vol. 108, No. 7, August 16, 1976, p. 72.*

MICHAEL A. AHERNE

As history, Drury's first historical novel [*A God Against the Gods*] is a novel; as a novel it is even and well written, but as literature it is an allegory. . . .

Drury's Akhenaten is consumed by his passion and becomes an enigma both to his contemporaries and to the readers of his story. . . . The focus is on Akhenaten the phenomenon. The low profile with which Akhenaten the man is painted may be seen alternately as the chief strength or chief weakness of the book; by implication it must also be seen as heart and substance of the book.

Despite his strong personality and otherwise fertile brain, he never integrates his thought into a constructive policy for his nation or his people as individuals. To the contrary, his chief effect is to disorient his people, weaken his nation, change both his own love for his people and theirs for him into mutual distrust and then to fear. He does this . . . through a supreme disregard for practical administration and good planning.

The thesis is the irrelevance of great ideas, perhaps even of truth itself, to the wielding of power. What matters rather is a good show, and a simple firm hand. Drury doesn't think much of the people or of any leader who expects to do much for them. Such a leader is himself a political disease. Akhenaten, really believing in his divinity, succeeds only in exposing his humanity to the people and consequently his government to decay.

> *Michael A. Aherne, in a review of ''A God against the Gods,'' in* Best Sellers, *Vol. 36, No. 8, November, 1976, p. 245.*

JAMES R. FRAKES

[In Allen Drury's Nile from 1362-39 B.C.], all you had to do if you were worried about power bloodlines was to marry your sister or your granddaughter, pass out some grain to the peasants and then twirl the old crook and flail. The cast [of *Return to Thebes*] is familiar: stooges, plotters, double-agents, trimmers, faithful retainers, women behind the throne. . . . The events are calculatedly cleffed: assassinations, inaugural addresses, family in-fighting, church-and-state warfare, border invasions. (pp. 29, 32)

Akhenaten, 10th King and Pharaoh of the 18th Dynasty, arthritic, perhaps insane, . . . has raised all hell by appointing as Co-Regent his brother and lover, Smenkhkara. . . . The Regents are slaughtered by the book's hatchetman, Horemheb (14th and last King of the 18th), and replaced by Tutankhaten (whose tomb gets a lot of attention) and then by Aye, father of Nefertiti, who . . . forget it!

Return to Thebes (sequel to *A God Against the Gods*) is an anesthesiologist's dream—monologue after monologue all yakking about the same things, with no discernible voice-modulations, in gutta-percha phrases. Drury's aim is honorable, but to evoke in prose the savage stillness of Egyptian friezes would require the pressurized genius of Beckett or an equally rabid poet of space and spirit. The most interesting prose here is Drury's touchy "Introduction," in which he tries to disarm the Egyptologists before they attack. I am recuperating, Egypt, recuperating! (p. 32)

> *James R. Frakes, "Three Novels of Power," in* The
> New York Times Book Review, *March 20, 1977,*
> *pp. 29, 32.**

MARTIN M. BOYLAN

Many weak points mar the structure of [*Return to Thebes*]. A coherent point of view cannot be discerned because the author employs numerous characters to continue the story line. Plot development is ponderous and lacking in unity and direction. Characterization is shallow and only accentuates the paltry vocabulary, which is never eloquent and often banal. Mr. Drury should stick to the contemporary, political genre to which he is accustomed. (p. 38)

> *Martin M. Boylan, in a review of "Return to Thebes,"*
> *in* Best Sellers, *Vol. 37, No. 2, May, 1977, pp. 37-8.*

LAURENCE LEAMER

There is a touch of wit on the cover of Allen Drury's new novel. The book is called *Anna Hastings: The Story of a Washington Newspaperwoman,* but Ms. Hastings has crossed out "woman" and written "person." She has just published her own memoirs, and the novel opens with several of the reviews. . . . Each chapter begins with a snippet of the memoirs. Then Ed Macomb, Anna's former managing editor, tells his story of the same events.

What a marvelous idea! *Anna Hastings* could have been a rich satire on contemporary Washington. Anna should have been as memorable a character as Mark Twain's creation of Senator Pomeroy in *The Gilded Age.* Drury, alas, is that rarest of birds in the late 1970's: a full-feathered ideologue. He is so far to the right and so weighted down with the ballast of conservative cliché that he has managed to capsize his novel.

The narrator, needless to say, is a man of the right. He meets Anna when she is an ambitious young reporter at the beginning of World War II. . . . Anna flaunts her talent and her body. She becomes a prominent journalist. She marries Senator Gordon Hastings, a Texas millionaire. With his money she buys a newspaper, and eventually a media empire.

The Inquirer combines the trendyness of The Washington Post and the standards of objectivity of the National Enquirer with the politics of an underground newspaper. The paper publishes pictures of American atrocities in Vietnam but not those of the Vietcong. (p. 14)

Behind it all stands someone whose blood runs Kremlin pink: Talbot Farson. In the late 1960's Farson is hauled before an investigatory committee. A tape of a telephone conversation between Farson and a Russian operative is played, in which Farson promises to give the Russian the production figures on a new American bomber. But Farson is a smoothie: He talks his way out of trouble with the support of the mass media.

Anna's much-abused husband later takes on a mistress. She is not on the Government payroll. She is not a hireling of the South Koreans or the Outer Mongolians. She is simply his mistress, a crime that in Washington is taken every bit as seriously as jaywalking. Except perhaps in the White House. But this becomes the basis for the novel's other dramatic highpoint.

Anna Hastings does contain some splendid episodes as Anna steps up over the cadavers of other careers. But Mr. Drury is not about to allow a liberal like Anna that much time alone on stage. He has to haul out his ideology. A knock-'em-down conservative satire on the liberal Washington media might well have been delightful. But Drury has lost touch with the modern political world. (pp. 14, 34)

> *Laurence Leamer, "Listing to the Right," in* The
> New York Times Book Review, *August 14, 1977,*
> *pp. 14, 34.*

JOSEPH CHRISTIE, S.J.

Mr. Allen Drury's latest account of Washington cozenage [*Anna Hastings*] provides us with his usual excellent read in an atmosphere reminiscent of the Boston Pops—good technique applied to archaic themes. Indeed the ingredients are so recognizable that this reviewer is compelled by a sympathetic contagion to apply the overworked *déjà vu.* There is, as a rule, nothing wrong with a good old-fashioned receipt, but this one is bogged down in predictability. With every member of the old gang so overwhelmingly here, there is little if any place left for suspense.

It must be said of Mr. Drury that he can make the arrival in Washington of four frenetic young journalists, intent on storming its heights, look like a Homeric event, but the impression is short on durability. . . . Anna, the anti-heroine of the story, swiftly emerges as a combination of Queen Mab and *La Belle Dame Sans Merci,* ready to launch thousands of miseries calculated to keep the male element spiritually etiolated well into late middle age, while Bessie (lachrymose and fat) ekes out her years in sterile, loyal mediocrity. (pp. 164-65)

[The] story ranges through the whole tired galère from Roosevelt to Ford, bringing in again that foxy, Ervinesque old Senator from Carolina who gave Charles Laughton so much fun first time round. It is the re-emergence of this folksy antique of American political folklore that gives one pause to wonder whether Mr. Drury may have a speculative eye on Hollywood. . . .

There are some things the author of this book is uniquely qualified to say and he does so with devastating frankness. He sees much of the American Liberal Press as totally anomic—reckless in its hatred and hubris, careless to the point of treachery about the safety of the United States. His view is Actonian and thus depressing. Since none of his good guys wins though, all we have in the end is that painful fin de siècle foreboding which causes so much merriment amongst the bad guys. (p. 165)

Joseph Christie, S.J., in a review of "Anna Hastings: The Story of a Washington Newspaperperson," in Best Sellers, *Vol. 37, No. 6, September, 1977, pp. 164-65.*

MARY CLAY BERRY

The only stock Washington character who does not appear in Allen Drury's new novel about the Senate [*Mark Coffin, U.S.S.*] is the Wily Lobbyist. This must have been an oversight, for all the rest are here: the Idealistic Young Senator, newly arrived in Washington; the Stalwart Political Wife, pregnant to add visible pathos to her plight; a whole roster of senators from the Wise Old Southern Committee Chairman to the Urban Black who offers advice on how to go along and get along; the Politically Ambitious Administrative Assistant; the Protective Secretary; the Washington Hostess. In the press gallery there's the Fatherly Wire Service Reporter who has seen senators come and go, the Ambitious Investigative Reporter who is torn by a conflict between journalistic "duty" and friendship, and the Bitchy Female Journalist for whom power is an aphrodisiac.

Anyone who has watched the Senate in operation could almost put names to the faces. But only *almost,* and therein lies the flaw in this novel. Even politicians and their entourages come in shades of gray. Drury's hero, Senator Mark Coffin, is faced with a real enough dilemma—the degree to which a politician should compromise principle for political effectiveness—but, by painting everything in black and white, Drury side-steps any serious consideration of it.

Mark Coffin, U.S.S. is the story of a liberal Stanford professor's first days as the junior senator from California.... Since he led the Democratic ticket in California, helping to deliver the state for the party's presidential nominee, Senator Coffin arrives in Washington with the new president owing him a substantial political debt. Mark Coffin is also 32 and handsome, with an attractive savvy wife and two adoring small children. He is, in short, quite a politico-literary mouthful, one which taxes the digestion of any reader.

The new senator is immediately in the thick of things. He is asked to support the president's nominee for attorney general, a former district attorney from Los Angeles who has a reputation for being strong on law-and-order and rough on members of minority groups. Minutes later, Coffin is asked to back his father-in-law's bill authorizing a $10 billion increase in the Defense Department's budget. Like the white knight that he is, the new senator chooses to oppose both....

As in all fairy tales, there is a moral. Idealistic young people must continue to come to Washington to fight, however futilely, for what they believe in, if the country is to keep going....

It would be a happy, though rather boring, circumstance for all of us if Washington and the dance of legislation were as simple as Drury portrays them. What is utterly lacking in *Mark Coffin, U.S.S.* is any sense of the complexities and ambiguities of a place where there is no hard and fast truth. Because Drury's characters are caricatures, with neither the greyness that envelopes most human motivation nor a convincing depth to their sorrow and anger, the book fails to deal honestly with Senator Coffin's dilemma. Drury's readers will learn something about Senate procedure but little about the nuances which are an important part of any political process.

Mary Clay Berry, "Lying, Wheeling and Dealing," in Book World—The Washington Post, *March 18, 1979, p. E3.*

PATRICK ANDERSON

[In *The Hill of Summer,* a] new American President takes office and immediately faces the threat of war. The Soviet President is talking tough, and has ordered worldwide troop maneuvers. What is his objective? To invade Western Europe? To seize the Middle East oil fields? Because the United States has fallen behind the Soviet Union in key areas of weaponry—and thus cannot win a conventional war—the new President faces an agonizing choice: surrender or a nuclear exchange.

Fact or fiction? Many responsible people in Washington think this grim scenario is all too possible.... Unfortunately, in using this scenario—and indeed the possibility of a Soviet conquest of America—as the basis for his impassioned new novel, Allen Drury has allowed his anger to overwhelm his artistry. His novel, intended to sound the alarm, is more likely to put readers to sleep.

In his zeal to warn us of the Soviet threat, Mr. Drury has ignored plot and characterization, and has produced what is less a novel than a modern morality play, an "Everyman" in which all Good is embodied in the President of the United States and all Evil in the President of the Soviet Union. Alas, these two cosmic antagonists do not battle, they only debate, in this impossibly long-winded novel.

The United States President is a jovial but stouthearted fellow named Hamilton Delbacher.... Delbacher, unlike the former President, understands the Soviet menace, and in his first meeting with his Russian counterpart, one Yuri Serapin, he denounces the Soviet plan of world conquest and thereby sets off an international crisis.

The crisis unfolds slowly: Every hundred pages or so one side or the other will increase its defense budget or mobilize its troops. Throughout the novel Delbacher and Serapin make speeches to each other and the world. Delbacher denounces Soviet duplicity and vows to stand firm; the crafty Serapin insists that he seeks only peace. Craven American Senators and allies beg Delbacher to back down, newspaper and television editorialists accuse poor Delbacher of warmongering, while in Russia we see Serapin and his Communist cohorts swilling vodka, gobbling caviar, chortling at the pitiful, helpless Americans and toasting the American media's contribution to their cause....

After slogging through this book to find out if somehow, against all odds, President Delbacher can save America from the "Soviet conquest" promised in the novel's subtitle, we reach the final page, still awaiting Armageddon, only to learn that *The Hill of Summer* is not only a bore but a cheat. Mr. Drury does not resolve his story, he simply calls time out, and we must await a sequel to learn the fate of mankind. I for one will gladly wait forever.

Patrick Anderson, "Armageddons Avoided," in The New York Times Book Review, *March 8, 1981, p. 10.**

BURKE WILKINSON

The time is the late 1980s. The Soviets have nearly achieved their goal of world domination.... Their ongoing military maneuvers all over the world can be countered only in a very limited way by US forces, which are "outnumbered, outgunned and out-missiled."

Such is the situation, as [*The Hill of Summer*], Allen Drury's best novel since the memorable *Advise and Consent*, gets under way. We are quickly caught up in the steerageway of his narrative, soon to become undertow.

The heart of the matter is a series of confrontations between the brash new Soviet leader, Yuri Serapin, and American President Hamilton Delbacher—confrontations which take place both in private meetings and in the arena of the UN Security Council.

Logically, chillingly, the story unfolds. Because the basic themes are the "Nature of the Threat" and the survival of the Free World, the author's passionate concern for the US Senate, displayed so successfully in his earlier novel, pales a little by comparison.

In Drury's portrayal, the Soviets are convinced their ultimate goal is a moral one: USSR-induced world peace along Soviet lines, with the abrogation of the liberties free men crave. Therefore, any means, however brutal or devious, are moral too. . . .

Taking advantage of America's unbelief, Yuri Serapin, consummate actor and fanatic believer in his own star, carries the world to the brink of the abyss. . . .

Local color is at a minimum, supplied mostly by the reader himself. The Washington Monument is a "pure, pristine needle," and a Cyrus Eaton-like American industrialist has a New York apartment with "original Picassos."

Sometimes, it must be said, our credulity is strained to the limit. The Soviet defector—or is he a plant?—who plays a key role in the plot makes his getaway with only the clothes on his back, but then turns up at a secret meeting with President Delbacher in full Soviet military uniform!

Despite such lapses, the novel comes off stunningly well. The mild title is from A. E. Housman:

> On the idle hill of summer,
> Sleepy with the flow of streams,
> Far I hear the steady drummer
> Drumming like a noise in dream.

In Allen Drury's lexicon, the "hill of summer" symbolizes the American state only a few years hence, when we have grown too torpid to heed the harsh tocsin sounded by the enemy.

> *Burke Wilkinson, "Drury's Novel of Soviet Intrigue, US Apathy in the Late 1980's, Chillingly Told," in* The Christian Science Monitor, *April 22, 1981, p. 17.*

HARRY E. SEYLER

[Many of the sequels to *Advise and Consent*] have lacked the significance and immediacy of the political problem about which the actions of the characters of that first novel revolved. About this latest novel [*The Hill of Summer*], however, no one is likely to make that criticism. After a longer than customary expository beginning, Mr. Drury plunges us and his characters into an international situation in which a new President of the United States is forced by the aggressive actions of a new President of the USSR to issue an ultimatum. . . . As a political

novel the book is guaranteed to keep you reading to the end. But you will find it an unsatisfactory ending: a cliff hanger, which is designed to condition you to start salivating until you can buy the planned sequel which will be called *The Roads of Earth*.

Mr. Drury sets his novel somewhere in the late 1980's. All the dire predictions of the hawks, Russophobes, and hard liners have been justified. America has fallen hopelessly behind the USSR in tactical and strategic arms. . . . While this grim situation is, perhaps, demanded by the literary need for suspense, Mr. Drury's manner of presentation indicates that he speaks from his own conviction that such an outcome of our nation's present foreign policy is more than likely. In any case, this novel is likely to be a significant factor in strengthening the hands of those who urgently favor the resumption of an arms race by which the United States can regain a position of military supremacy over the Soviet Union.

While one is enjoying the story, one should be aware of the message. It may be that the propaganda agrees with your own views, in which case it's a bonus.

If you feel inclined to challenge or criticize aspects of the book's propaganda you will be rebuked automatically by a built-in device. You will identify yourself with one of the groups of duped or misguided Americans who have made it so difficult for President Hamilton Delbacher to unite his country against the critical danger from the Soviets. (p. 45)

> *Harry E. Seyler, in a review of "The Hill of Summer," in* Best Sellers, *Vol. 41, No. 2, May, 1981, pp. 44-5.*

EVAN HUNTER

Suppose an aging, present-day hippie, radicalized during the turbulent 1960's, decides to blow up an atomic energy plant as a protest against the society he abhors. Suppose the young daughter of a Supreme Court Justice is killed in the blast and the daughter of another Justice is rendered a vegetable for life. . . . And finally suppose the case eventually comes before the Supreme Court. Such are the suppositions Allen Drury poses in his new novel, *Decision*.

The hero is decent Taylor Barbour, the newly appointed, liberal Justice whose daughter is brain-damaged in the explosion. One of the villains is Earle Holgren, the psychopathic Harvard-graduate hippie. . . . A lesser villain is Regard (pronounced REE-gard) Stinnet, the Southern attorney general who seizes on the bombing as the launching platform for a quasi-vigilante organization called Justice NOW! Within days, it seems, Stinnet's organization attracts millions of rabid members yelling for blood.

Among the rest of the large cast of characters are Barbour's harridan wife, his newfound journalist love and the liberal female defense attorney who fears and despises Holgren but agrees with him in principle. . . . Predictably, justice in the South Carolina courts is swift and merciless. . . . Again predictably, when the case finally comes before the Supreme Court, two members of that august body must now make the most important "decision" of their lives.

That Mr. Drury is attempting a novel of ideas is beyond question. His thoughts on the spread of violence in America, however, seem as vague and unresolved as the final decision the Court hands down. Moreover, he has created such a loaded situation and peopled it with characters so obviously stamped from molds . . . that it is almost impossible to suspend disbelief or care about the outcome. One is left only with the dismaying feeling that the questions Mr. Drury raises surely deserved a more realistically probing treatment. (p. 30)

> *Evan Hunter, "Pleas and Decisions," in* The New York Times Book Review, *October 30, 1983, pp. 14, 30.**

CHARLES DeMARCO

The only positive thing about Allen Drury's latest Washington novel [*Decision*] is the discomfortingly credible situation he presents to us. Americans, already weary of rampant criminality, are pushed into openly embracing vigilantism when a maniac sabotages the opening-day ceremony of a nuclear power plant. . . .

The novel has many faults, but its most blatant rests with the characterizations. Holgren, bursting with cliches, is too simplistically crazy and evil (everyone in the novel notices his *eyes*). His female attorney is presented as a feminist who loses touch with reality by becoming infatuated with her client. Taylor Barbour, the liberal justice, is ultimately portrayed as indecisive. In general, the characters are too much of one quality, ultimately lacking any nuance or sustained believability. Their dialogue is often ponderous, the symptom of an overwritten novel.

Drury, a Washington correspondent for over 20 years, has shown an ability in the past to tell an engrossing story while ably capturing the pace and background of the nation's capital. But his latest effort is tired and overworked. And, most distressingly, it trivializes important considerations such as justice, the death penalty, and the importance of a nation's laws in fostering a humanistic society.

> *Charles DeMarco, in a review of "Decision," in* Best Sellers, *Vol. 43, No. 8, November, 1983, p. 279.*

RICHARD ELMAN

In a prefatory note to **The Roads of Earth,** Allen Drury warns of the "absolutely undeviating intention of the Soviet Union to destroy the United States and conquer the world if it possibly can." As soon as the actual novel commences, he delivers himself of a similar opinion, and then a couple of pages later on, and a couple of pages after that. By page 40 I began to get used to the sight and sound of this prophecy. . . . Mr. Drury embellishes his hortatory manner with his specific dislike for liberal politicians, humanitarians and journalists; they are all either Soviet dupes or treacherous cowards. He likes realists who will launch pre-emptive actions that will thwart Soviet intentions. In **The Roads of Earth** our Republic is hard-pressed

to withstand a series of Soviet-manufactured crises in various trouble spots around the globe. An overly ambitious Soviet chief of state grunts a lot between uttering his intentions whereas his American counterpart is genial, courtly with women, but toughminded. Needless to say, our Republic survives because this incumbent President is prepared to launch countermeasures. . . . The Russians retreat and change to a more cautious leadership which, more or less, certifies Mr. Drury's theme that using force is, at least, realistic whereas political scruples are the folly of cowards and sellouts. But, by requiring that his characters act out his political ideas—at the expense of credibility and dimension—Mr. Drury may just have created a bomb equal to anything in Soviet arsenals at present.

> *Richard Elman, in a review of "The Roads of Earth," in* The New York Times Book Review, *September 30, 1984, p. 28.*

CHRIS WALL

Roads of Earth is a soundly constructed, consistently intriguing story of a Soviet demagogue's attempts to dominate the world, and an American President's lonely crusade to stop him.

Sometime in the near future: President Hamilton Delbacher has faced down his Soviet counterpart, Yuri Serapin, under circumstances similar to the Cuban Missile Crisis. In spite of the Soviet leader's aggressive moves, he has emerged as a peacekeeper in the eyes of the world, while Delbacher is seen as a warmonger.

This misinterpretation is the fault of a self-deluded, easily manipulated media that refuses to see the truth. It's to be expected, of course, since the many media-types who pop up throughout the book are spineless, irritating wimps. . . .

With considerable skill, Drury takes us to ringing United Nations debates to the confidential chambers of the White House and Kremlin. Drury is a political scientist's Robert Ludlum; the tension derives from crisp rhetoric, bold gambles and shrewd maneuvering on both sides. The battles are fought with words, and most of the blood-spilling is done off-page. As a novel, it's skillfully written and quite engaging, even if some characters are one-dimensional.

Is it a valid warning to keep a closer eye on the Russkies? Unless you already buy that line, **Roads** is unlikely to change your mind.

Delbacher's warm, fatherly character is wholesome and appealing, and Serapin makes Stalin look like the Tooth Fairy. In short, there's nothing like a solid good vs. evil confrontation to keep you turning pages, even if the only thing you know about the Cold War is Dristan.

> *Chris Wall, "Well-Read Man for Red Menace," in* Los Angeles Times Book Review, *December 9, 1984, p. 6.*

Maureen Duffy

1933-

English novelist, dramatist, poet, short story writer, historian, translator, editor, screenwriter, and biographer.

Duffy's works record the lonely lives of society's misfits. While her protagonists come from varying educational and economic backgrounds, they invariably are outsiders in a hostile world. Exhibiting dissatisfaction with their fortunes and their unfulfilled sexual desires, Duffy's characters search for love and meaning in their lives. Duffy's writing projects a distinct sense of realism as she explores the bizarre and extreme factions of contemporary society. Although critics often fault her novels for lack of structural cohesiveness, Duffy is praised for the inventiveness and vividness of her narrative style.

Duffy's first novel, *That's How It Was* (1962), centers on the theme of social isolation. This book, a semiautobiographical account of Duffy's childhood, depicts the economic and emotional crises of alienated people. In *The Microcosm* (1966), Duffy examines the homosexual underworld of London. While *The Microcosm* deals specifically with homosexuality as a social barrier, the sexual identities of the protagonists of *Love Child* (1971) and *Londoners* (1983) are ambiguous, thus providing the plots with distinctive twists. Even when the sexual identities of her characters are clear, Duffy examines other facets of cultural alienation. Sym, in *The Paradox Players* (1967), abandons society of his own accord and lives with other dropouts in a river colony. Duffy's most extreme outcast appears in *Gor Saga* (1981). Gor, the product of a scientific experiment, is half man and half gorilla and belongs to neither world. This novel reflects Duffy's interest in animal welfare, as does *I Want to Go to Moscow* (1973), an account of an antivivisectionist group that resorts to terrorist tactics. Despite the desperate circumstances of many of Duffy's characters, they usually survive and emerge wiser as a result of their problems.

While fiction provides Duffy with her greatest audience, she also writes in several other genres. Themes prevalent in her fiction appear in both her poetry and drama. Her nonfiction works include *The Erotic World of Faery* (1972), a Freudian study of the supernatural in English literature, and the biography *The Passionate Shepherdess: Aphra Behn 1640-1689* (1977).

(See also *Contemporary Authors*, Vols. 25-28, rev. ed. and *Dictionary of Literary Biography*, Vol. 14.)

Photograph by Mark Gerson

KENNETH LAMOTT

[*The Microcosm*] is a novel about lesbians—or, more accurately, about the world in which lesbians live, the microcosm of the title. The scene is London and the principal players are the butches and femmes who frequent a bar where they meet to drink, talk, dance, break up old affairs, and begin new ones. . . .

Miss Duffy, who is clearly gifted, constructs her novel out of many discrete pieces. She is successful to a considerable degree, but I kept having the uneasy feeling that I was looking on as a prize student showed off her talents. This is largely a matter of her technique. Miss Duffy has chosen to demonstrate that, like James Joyce and goodness knows how many of his followers, she too is in command of the mock-archaic ("Great was their joy the following day when the uncle returned answer . . ."), the stream of consciousness ("he can't touch me now he can't touch me any more and you felt free for the first time . . ."), the demotic ("It's them lovely women on the telly that do it though, I mean spoil you for yourself . . ."), and so on.

I wish Miss Duffy had resisted this temptation. I would have been more moved by her book if she had depended to a greater degree on the evident authority with which she writes and on her thoroughly convincing insight into the private world of the female homosexual.

Kenneth Lamott, "Small World," in Book Week—New York Herald Tribune, *April 10, 1966, p. 14.*

ELEANOR DIENSTAG

Most homosexuals in recent literature are extraordinarily dumb. *That,* it has always seemed to me, is their real problem, not their sexual postures or partners.

This thought forcefully reasserted itself during a reading of *The Microcosm,* which features yet another "sensitive," not overly bright young protagonist named Matt—who, if you look at it one way, is like a lot of other restless heroes in contemporary fiction. Matt has a zero job pumping gasoline, daydreams incessantly, sneaks coffee breaks, gets along in bed with a wife named Rae, but often feels isolated and alone, as if there were some barrier between them. Weekends are usually spent at the Club, drinking and dancing with long-standing friends; but since Matt's old pal Carl died, they don't provide the kicks they used to. (p. 20)

Standard stuff, except for the fact that our alienated "hero" is a heroine—a butch, a "male" Lesbian. So was Carl. Rae is a female of the species. The social circle in question is the small, gossipy, competitive and slightly seamy world of London dykes.

The Microcosm is less a novel than a panoramic sweep of the Lesbian scene, much as, on the other side, John Rechy's "City of Night." Matt's story, like a theater curtain, opens and closes the action, framing it with the traditional features of the novel. Sandwiched between this emotional journey are a series of sketches of unrelated women at various stages of inversion. The point being, of course, to write not merely about *a* Lesbian, but about *the* Lesbian. This is a task that the author has mistakenly assumed could best be accomplished by stuffing us with vast amounts of what-it-is-really-like information, rather than a penetrating, subtly-drawn story of one invert's travail. (pp. 20-1)

[The characters'] portraits rely heavily on the stream-of-consciousness interior monologue. No doubt Maureen Duffy . . . hit upon this closeup technique as a means of hiding her inability to use such basic tools as dialogue and dramatic invention. She gives herself away, though, in her handling of Matt, who never has a conversation, but lectures—on morality, on religion, on the problem of leisure—while the other characters sit back in one-dimensional splendor, awaiting their own moment at the lectern. Unfortunately, it is granted.

Lesbians, one presumes, do not dwell on their condition 80 per cent of the time. Yet, in *The Microcosm,* all issues are inevitably derailed on this track, a fact which makes the novel tedious and its principal characters unbelievable. This single-mindedness might have been bearable if a spark of originality illuminated the issue. However, it takes Matt over 300 pages to discover the obvious: deviants are not like most people, and to live solely in the Lesbian world—a subculture Matt once viewed as a microcosm of the rest of society—is actually to remove oneself from life.

At one point Matt, the so-called intellectual of the novel, reflects while lighting "his" wife's cigarette: "She would never let him put it between her lips but reached out and took it from his fingers, and to him this was symbolic of their whole relationship."

It's symbolic of the level of insight and artistry of this novel, as well. (p. 21)

Eleanor Dienstag, "Members of the Club," in The New York Times Book Review, *August 11, 1968,* pp. 20-1.

THE NEW YORKER

No one character in Miss Duffy's book [*The Paradox Players*] is outstanding, although each human being and each animal is impeccably drawn and treated with thorough understanding. As a study in gray, animated and given sad meaning by the slow movement of the gray figures, gray weather, and fateful gray light, her book is a work of art. (p. 182)

A review of "The Paradox Players," in The New Yorker, *Vol. XLIV, No. 33, October 5, 1968,* pp. 181-82.

CLIVE JORDAN

In *Wounds,* Maureen Duffy . . . departs from a straightforward narrative technique. Vignettes of characters from a contemporary south London locale, and episodes in their lives, are separated by fragments of extremely intimate bedroom dialogue between two lovers no longer in their first youth. There are various mentions of wounds and operations in the novel, but what may be a more precise clue to the novel's title and structure is given in the course of the lovers' dialogue: 'The pain of love . . . is the pain of being alive. It's a perpetual wound.' Both kinds of pain are exemplified by the lives of the other characters: among them 'Kingy', the middle-aged Lesbian gardener; Alec, the sensitive West Indian adolescent, exploited by the theatrical queer, Christopher; Gliston, the veteran Labour mayor who persists in loving his unlovely borough. Amid the barren lives, there are small hopes and successes: Alec runs away to an unknown future; the public park and convenience that Gliston fights through the Council proves a haven for Wilf, the lonely old soldier, and the small black boy on his way to school to become 'same like all the rest'. Presumably the joy of the two lovers points to the private possibilities of living; and there is a further connection between the two narrative lines in that both life and love teach defiance: for Wilf, brooding on the Great War, 'we should have said no'; for the lovers, 'there's no small corner anywhere that acquiesces in darkness and destruction'. And the sections in the novel are separated by a kind of yin-yang male-female symbol repeated obsessively on the dustjacket (love as the unifier?). There is some sharply observed detail, and richly textured descriptions which occasionally overbalance into 'fine writing'. The characterisation, too, is a mixture of the imaginative and the half-achieved: 'Kingy', with her earnestness and quaintly courtly diction, is a completely individual original, but the West Indian characters seem to me courageously failed attempts to penetrate an alien experience. Despite the compensations, it must be said that such structural links as there are hardly offer themselves easily, and the extreme discontinuity of the narrative makes for difficult reading which does not always yield its own reward. (p. 22)

Clive Jordan, "Dangerous Doodles," in New Statesman, *Vol. 78, No. 1999, July 4, 1969,* pp. 21-2.*

FRANK LITTLER

[*Wounds* begins] with a fairly normal (and explicitly described) copulation, in what seems a normally situated bedroom. . . . The writhing and sweating of the anonymous sex athletes, however, are soon intercut—though not interrupted—by people from outside, a mélange of other voices, other rooms. Before these could be assigned to their owners—and not all of them at that—I found a second reading was necessary to get my bearings.

There can be no objections to a novelist who makes you work, but only in one episode could I descry a relationship between the preoccupied lovers and that hubbub outside the bedroom door. It is possible, of course, to lay too much stress on literary geometry, and *Wounds* need not be faulted for its construction. But I still don't know how the central situation relates to all these interventions. Or they to it.

However, the satellite characters interact—at least, in a fashion. Sometimes they do so with extreme mistiness, sometimes more clearly. They include an aging Lesbian, a Caribbean mother of two boys, a brace of pederasts employed in educational drama, and a mayor who obscenely defames, on the wall of a new public convenience, one of his fellow aldermen. . . .

[In one] part of the book, an oldtimer muses upon the overrated horse-and-cart days, recalling "the murderous accident—men and beasts mashed and screaming, slipping on the cobbles in the slime of dung and mud and a thin bone snapped . . ." I never witnessed such a scene myself, any more than I heard of an alderman (and I know dozens) who scratched graffiti on lavatory walls.

Might, then, Miss Duffy's talents be put to more convincing use? They might—if they have been imposed upon these bizarrely conceived scenes and characters. It seems more likely that they have burgeoned from them and are in acute need of transplanting.

> Frank Littler, *"Despite the Hubbub Outside the Bedroom Door, the Lovers Carried On,"* in The New York Times Book Review, *August 17, 1969, p. 32.*

SARA BLACKBURN

Two nameless lovers open [*Wounds*], and brief episodes about their ecstatic love-making punctuate much longer, alternating sequences about a broadly varying group of people who have in common only that they live in the same country (England) and that they've been badly hurt in ways that place absolute limits on their freedom. Some of their lives touch occasionally, and when they do, Miss Duffy is very skillful at revealing new dimensions of their characters as they appear to one another for the first time. That the reader is constantly curious about how they will perceive one another (because he knew them first) is a considerable tribute to her talent.

The characters vary in interest, and in the success with which they are presented. . . . [But] Miss Duffy's failures are always in reaching too far, never in being content with accomplishing too little. She is concerned with a world that stretches far beyond domestic drama, and is never either superficial or self-indulgent in the way she grapples with the job she's set for herself. Much of the book is even dull—perhaps because there are too many characters here, and the barrage of their sorrows sometimes gives it a somber, hopeless tone that limits rather than enhances the individual sequences. But this is a good try at a major novel by one of the most interesting young writers around today. Miss Duffy is a serious artist, and if her next novel shows even a fraction of the advance that this current one represents over her first two . . . , it will be a very good book indeed.

> Sara Blackburn, *"The World Beyond,"* in Book World—The Washington Post, *August 31, 1969, p. 8.*

JAMES R. FRAKES

Child-narrators are notoriously hazardous for an author to work with, unless the author is Twain or Salinger. Even Henry James, in writing *What Maisie Knew,* foresaw certain failure if he attempted to restrict himself to young Maisie's terminology as well as to her experience. Maureen Duffy is undaunted. Her precocious narrator [in *Love Child*], Kit, is not only a prodigy who reads Proust and Mann (Felix Krull is Kit's "protohero"), has been "more deeply influenced toward the offbeat by John Milton than by John Lennon," and is more worldly than Cary Grant; Kit is also carefully unidentified as to surname, age, or gender. The gender-game borders perilously on gimmickry: Miss Duffy plays such clever tricks with us by referring to Kit as "the child . . . it . . . a kid . . . smart guy . . . junior" and by setting up ambiguous sex-relationships that this brilliant novel threatens to devolve into an outwitting-contest. Luckily, skill spikes this threat and turns Kit's epicenism into a most effective metaphor in which Unisex represents the rarefied atmosphere of a class, a cult of "understanding" and ultra-permissiveness, a world whose emotional values have been eradicated by the intellect.

Kit's mother speaks in shaded aphorisms and walks in an aura of ultimate sophistication. Kit's economist-diplomat father flaunts his smug superiority by pretending to ignore his wife's love-affair with his latest male secretary. One of the most memorable family groups since the Hamlets of Denmark, they are "polyglot, polygamous, polymorphous, and polysyllabic." Together they compass seven dead and five living languages: "Foreign doesn't exist for us as a concept." . . .

I especially cherish the narrator's snotty remarks to the "putative reader": "You are privileged, if you ever exist, to look over my shoulder and study my recreation but you mustn't interfere with your chatter about what you like." Kit, of course, is a monster who insists on the privileges of a child. Do look over his/her shoulder.

> James R. Frakes, *"Privileged Monster,"* in Book World—The Washington Post, *April 11, 1971, p. 2.*

SUSAN HILL

[The heroine of *Love Child* is] a child of the international, intellectual jet-set. We should recognise that they have their hang-ups and strivings just as badly as lads from Nottingham. Superficially, they are different, of course: they have to come to terms with a lot of money, grand-hotel living, clever talking, parents who listen to, understand and permit all, cultural riches and the too-early acquisition of worldly wisdom.

Love Child is about these hang-ups, and it also touches on those of the hippies and draft-dodgers who frequent beaches all along the Mediterranean—some of them are fast becoming ageing juveniles, a problem in itself. But the plot tells how Kit coolly sets out to establish that her father's Greek god secretary is her mother's lover, and, having established it, to destroy him. She narrates wittily, sharply, is full of self-analysis and excuse, is hip, sophisticated, sick of being called a child, naïve, and utterly heartless. This is, I think, a heartless book. . . . But it is most admirably written. Miss Duffy has always been one of our most versatile novelists. She overloads this book with rather too much philosophical argument, and classical myth and legend, heavily charged with symbolistic meaning, weigh down the frail bark of the plot. But I found myself haunted by the book long after it was finished.

> Susan Hill, *"Heart Trouble,"* in New Statesman, *Vol. 81, No. 2093, April 30, 1971, p. 604.**

PAUL THEROUX

The title of Maureen Duffy's novel [*All Heaven in a Rage,* published in Great Britain as *I Want to Go to Moscow*] is from Blake's "Auguries of Innocence," which one of the characters conveniently quotes: "A Robin Red-breast in a cage / Puts all Heaven in a rage." But obvious dramatization of the simple truth inspires doubt, and when I finished this novel about antivivisection I began to wonder if I'd missed the point. It is about things caged and things free, and about various plots by some upper-class people who are singleminded in their desire to release animals from zoos, breeding pens and barns. It's a romp, like "The Roots of Heaven" adapted by P. G. Wodehouse, but it is a serious romp and in parts highly ingenious. (p. 16)

There is nothing very remarkable about . . . [the plot], except that Miss Duffy, who has written six other novels, brings an intelligence to bear on her theme. Here she is speculating on the possibility of man-to-animal communication (ironically, after one of the top bananas in the vegetarians has been trampled by a horse): "And if we found a species that could talk, if at least we understood what dolphins gossiped about . . . would we stop feeling that we were outside the animal kingdom, them and us, believe we were not alone with our terrible burden of intelligence that made us capable of monstrousness beyond the beasts and made us glory in our difference, would we learn in fact to love ourselves a bit?"

Most of the conspirators are too cranky to be true, and in this very literary and allusive treatment of a jokey subject the figure that stands out is that of Jarvis Chuff. There are long stretches of his prison reflections, which are excellent, his bewilderment at being free, and engaging segments of his childhood villainy. It is Chuff who is the scene-stealer, but he is sacrificed to a plot that is at best only amusing and at worst quite preposterous. Chuff is the perfect Blake figure in what is, unfortunately, a very un-Blakean book. (p. 17)

Paul Theroux, "Close Friends, Woman's Influence, Vegetarians, Femme Fatale," in The New York Times Book Review, *May 27, 1973, pp. 16-17.**

JUDY COOKE

Gor Saga is set in a not too distant future, when genetic science has advanced to a pitch of arrogance and society has polarised into warring factions, the Nons (nonachievers), the UGs (urban guerrillas) and the dominating intellectual *élite*. Since the working class are discouraged from bearing children, some substitute labour force has to be invented; hence Gor, half-ape, half-man, the creation of an evil doctor who injects a gorilla with his own semen. Gor is by no means a monster; his situation is presented with care and imagination. He is taken from his mother; then from his (human) nurse, lest she grow fond of him. His vocal chords are operated upon so that he learns to speak. He is sent from hospital to foster-parents and from foster-parents to boarding-school; all this suffering is arranged by the truly inhuman Dr Forester, whose attitude to women and children is that of an Auschwitz commandant. The novel falls uneasily between social satire and allegory. It is at its weakest when describing the home life of the Foresters, the husband a jumped-up scholarship boy whose marriage to saintly, musical Anne doesn't hold water for a moment. Whenever the focus is on Gor, the pace quickens. Maureen Duffy has always written well about lonely cities; here she evokes a derelict

Bristol, its suspension bridge in tatters and Gor loping along its streets to victory.

Judy Cooke, "Paradise," in New Statesman, *Vol. 102, No. 2644, November 20, 1981, p. 22.**

LORNA SAGE

Maureen Duffy's *Londoners* is a novel based on the curse of Babel. Her native London appears as a polyglot, infinitely subdivisible city, where people gather to trade (Asians from Africa, go-getting Eurocrats, Australians, Arabs) and where the mores of the market-place nightmarishly prevail. The market-place, moreover, is seen in its most Bohemian and down-market guise, in the form of bedsit-land in Earl's Court, where human communciation threatens to reduce itself to the wearing of an earring in the right or left ear, and where there are no homes or marriages to give the illusion of shared stabilities.

It doesn't sound, perhaps, an unfamiliar picture. But it rapidly becomes so because Ms Duffy, in calculated rebellion against received pieties, treats her frightening city as none the less survivable, and imaginable. Her narrator and spokesperson, a struggling writer called Al, who's sexually ambiguous (man or woman? straight or gay? it's more a question here of 'who's what' than 'who's who'), is out to persuade us that individual isolation is negotiable, a basis even for mutual sympathy and tolerance, that difference and division are, in short, human. Through Al, Ms Duffy connects the loneliness of writing with other kinds, and suggests that it's not by pastoral myth-making about communities, but by acceptance of our crowded solitudes, that we make a possible society.

The narrative, inevitably, is all loose ends—glimpses of brown or ivory skin, fragments of 'colourful' conversation. Ms Duffy is particularly evocative on the tragi-comedy of public transport, and on the feel of lives led on streets and in pubs (the book's opening sentence starts 'Afterwards when you get indoors'). In other ways, however, she's perhaps too deliberate, too conscious: the device of having Al translate the medieval French poet François Villon, which is meant to stress the eternity of Grub Street, and underline the polyglot theme, actually overloads a book that's anyway packed.

Lorna Sage, "How to Survive in the City," in The Observer, *October 16, 1983, p. 33.**

ANGELA McROBBIE

Londoners is a novel which explores the tensions within . . . a gay underworld characterised less by fantasy and bravado than by anonymity, fleeting pleasure, timidity, fear and the search for comfort. Often [Duffy] uses the word 'comfort' as though it were a synonym for sex. Although it's never made quite clear, Al, the narrator, struggling to make a living as a writer, is also a lesbian. This propels her, over a lifetime, into the world of predominantly male gay bars and pubs, and forces her, it seems, to take on either an asexual identity or else to spend her time with an almost exclusively male company of friends, looking on impassively as they get done up in drag or create an alternative entertainment. It's a worthy and interesting book, but depressing in the same way as *The Well of Loneliness*, Radclyffe Hall's classic lesbian novel of the 1920s. It, too, marks out the different sexual choice as a burden, a sleight of hand of nature, a force which seeks solace in an environment where pain can be transformed into neither pleasure nor anger.

Angela McRobbie, "Underworlds," in New Statesman, *Vol. 106, No. 2744, October 21, 1983, p.24.**

FRANCIS KING

The name of the central character and narrator of [*Londoners*]
is Al. Al for Alfred, for Alice or for something else? We never
learn. Like the central character and narrator of Rose Macaulay's *The Towers of Trebizond,* Al is of whatever sex that we
decide Al to be. If Al is a man, then he is a heterosexual one;
but, in that case, it is odd that he should spend so much of his
time in the company of homosexuals. If Al is a woman then
she wears trousers, constantly stands her friends and acquaintances drinks, and is attracted by other women. Whereas a
woman friend of mine is convinced that Al is a man, I am no
less convinced that Al is a woman; but that may reveal as much
about the two of us as about Al and Maureen Duffy. At all
events, in this review I shall write about Al as though he/she
is a woman. . . .

Al's life is divided between her humble, bewildered, vulnerable
neighbours and the successful, tough, affluent people among
whom she moves like an urban guerrilla foraging for a living.
The sharpness of the contrast is proof of the author's understanding of both worlds. . . .

As much at home in both these worlds as Al herself, Miss
Duffy evokes them with a combination of astringency and
affection. At one extreme, there is a telling account of how
Al gives evidence to a parliamentary committee on censorship.
At the other extreme there is a wonderful description of a drag-
act called 'The Cockettes'—'nearer to Isherwood's Berliner
ensemble than we usually come'—who march and counter-
march, union jacks at the ready, as they sing 'Land of Hope
and Glory' in a 'double parody of Mother England that drags
the emotion and lifts her skirts to show the hairy thighs in the
jutting cami-knickers.'

The book has no single narrative thread but innumerable fil-
aments, which interweave, become entangled, separate, snap

off abruptly. Al is clearly never going to see the realisation of
her dream of a film about Villon, so that when, near the close,
she is offered the job, funded by the Arts Council, of writer-
in-residence at 'Churchdown College', she is prudent to take
it. What will become of her friends and neighbours, pursuing
their untidy, often unhappy lives, we are left to guess.

The evocation of London as a city of grotesque extremes is
always moving and funny. But the strongest impression left
by the book is not of the crowds among whom Al moves but
of the solitariness of her vocation as a writer. The style is never
easy; but each paragraph churns and surges with the same
energy that keeps the city in its state of constant ferment.

Francis King, "Ambivalent," in The Spectator, *Vol.
251, No. 8103, October 29, 1983, p. 28.*

NEIL PHILIP

[Maureen Duffy] is one of those writers who seem to need to
re-learn how to write for each new novel. The result is always
interesting, and sometimes, as in her brooding and poetic *Capital,* startlingly good. King Lear and Merlin and Dick Whit-
tington and Mayhew's watercress girl add their voices to a
savage and sensuous historical pageant centred on the rise,
development and decay of London. It is a technically brilliant
piece of work, the richly textured prose modulating with precision from period to period and from character to character,
but the technique serves the novel, not vice versa. *Capital* is
a work of rare imaginative daring. It forms a loose trilogy with
two other novels about London life: *Wounds,* a fragmentary
narrative interspersing public scenes with the privacy of two
lovers, and *Londoners,* in which a writer's obsession with Villon is used to illuminate today's bedsitter urban existence. (p.
580)

*Neil Philip, "Masters (and Mistresses) of English
Prose," in* British Book News, *October, 1984, pp.
580-81.**

Thomas J(ames) Fleming

1927-

American historian, novelist, biographer, editor, and script-writer.

Fleming's numerous fiction and nonfiction works are concerned with the American Revolution and with the experiences of Irish-American immigrants. Fleming's interest in both subjects stems from his upbringing as an Irish-American Catholic. He stated: "I wanted to go back to the roots of the American character, because I felt that I had been cut off from American experience. . . . This predisposed me to write about the American Revolution. It was my attempt to acquire some American roots." At an early age, Fleming was exposed to city politics through his father, a ward leader in Jersey City, New Jersey; consequently, politics and its role in an individual's life is an important element in his writing.

While Fleming's work has a historical basis, he is praised for emphasizing the human aspects of his material. He often uses quotations from original letters, journals, and diaries to reveal the thoughts and emotions of the real people he is portraying. In such books on the American Revolution as *Now We Are Enemies: The Battle of Bunker Hill* (1960) and *Beat the Last Drum: The Siege of Yorktown* (1963), Fleming intersperses detailed descriptions of military campaigns with personal accounts by individuals who participated in the events portrayed. *For Liberty Tavern* (1976) and *Dreams of Glory* (1983) are also based on the Revolutionary War.

Although he is widely known as a historian, Fleming admits that he prefers writing novels because they give him "room to explore personal-historical experiences at a depth that you simply can't do in a history or biography because you're constricted by the evidence that you have." Several of Fleming's novels, including *All Good Men* (1961), *King of the Hill* (1966), and *Rulers of the City* (1977), deal with a political machine in a predominantly Irish city modeled after Fleming's hometown. A major theme in Fleming's fiction which does not appear in his historical works is the influence of the Roman Catholic church on his characters. *The Sandbox Tree* (1970) is a particularly strong indictment of the church's repression of individual choice. The protagonist of *The Good Shepherd* (1974) is a priest torn between his loyalty to the church and his disagreement with certain ecclesiastical policies.

In his other novels Fleming explores various aspects of modern society as well as historical subjects. A community in *A Cry of Whiteness* (1967) is divided by the racial and social strife which accompanies the busing of children for the purpose of school integration. In *Romans, Countrymen, Lovers* (1969) a successful businessman, husband, and father leaves his secure life to seek personal fulfillment and nearly destroys himself. Fleming's best-selling novel *The Officers' Wives* (1981) traces the lives of three couples after the husbands graduate from West Point in 1950. Fleming covers the years of the Korean and Vietnam wars as well as the feminist movement in America and shows how these events changed the lives of his characters and the consciousness of the country.

(See also *Contemporary Authors*, Vols. 5-8, rev. ed.; *Contemporary Authors New Revision Series*, Vol. 10; and *Something about the Author*, Vol. 8.)

Photograph by Haida Kuhn. Courtesy of Thomas Fleming

WILLARD M. WALLACE

[In *Now We Are Enemies*] Mr. Fleming examines the battle [of Bunker Hill] at all levels of activity: on the American side, from Dr. Joseph Warren, president of the Provincial Congress, to 16-year-old Corning Fairbanks, both of whom lost their lives; on the British side, from General Gage, the Governor, who watched the conflict from the North Church tower, to Evans, Howe's valet, who was shot in the arm while pouring his master a glass of wine. It is this multi-viewed method, the apt use of quotation, the piling up of incident and the terse style that give the book a vibrant immediacy and suspense. Though scholars may well challenge Mr. Fleming at points, the over-all account stands up admirably.

> Willard M. Wallace, "A Battle That Never Should Have Been," in The New York Times Book Review, September 25, 1960, p. 10.

BRUCE LANCASTER

In *Now We Are Enemies*, Thomas J. Fleming has set forth in strong, flashing colors and with a wealth of detail a full-scale narrative of the so-called "Battle of Bunker's Hill," June 17, 1775, the first to appear in a great many years. Using a vast mass of material, primary and secondary, he has constructed an account that is highly human, often moving, and admirably objective. Like a director with a revolving stage, the author skilfully maintains continuity, showing first his New England actors swinging his set to bring the British before the footlights, then switching back once more. On this shifting stage privates, sergeants, officers from ensigns to major-generals tell their particular stories of that June day, often in their own words, often in syntheses of what those words might have been, the whole blending into a swell of high, fine courage on both sides, a courage that rises above suspicion, disillusionment, stark fear, and hot slaughter.

Yet with all this action, color, drama, comedy, and tragedy the narrative drags badly at the start. For at least half a dozen chapters we are shown the protagonists in broad panorama and individual close-ups, after which the author turns to flashbacks that wander through earlier years in other countries and cities, among people and events not directly concerned with the military action under inspection. It is as though Mr. Fleming were thrusting an apprehensive toe into the water of his theme, withdrawing it hastily, hopefully testing again only to retire once more. More than 150 pages are consumed before the tempo picks up. After that, few will quarrel with the pace set. . . .

[The] strong main narrative is enlivened with carefully chosen quotes from participants. Most of these are built solidly and credibly into the story. The reconstructions may strike many as less fortunate, notably the Henry Clinton-William Howe dialogue beginning on page 10, and about all of Colonel William Prescott's speeches on Breed's Hill. And can Israel Putnam speak only in a "roar"?

There are points of fact and opinion that tend to keep eyebrows jumping. Why the House of Brunswick for the House of Hanover? It is also hard to accept the rating of first-class as applied to the Royal Marines, who at that period seem to have been in sorry shape, particularly in regard to officers. . . .

[However, the] general reader will find in this book a highly absorbing, vivid account of a Revolutionary battle whose importance to both sides, properly assayed by Mr. Fleming, far transcended its immediate results.

> *Bruce Lancaster, "Action on Breed's Hill," in Saturday Review, Vol. XLIII, No. 40, October 1, 1960, p. 23.*

FRANCIS CANAVAN

Like any other town of a respectable size, Jersey City has its quota of James Joyce types—graduates of Jesuit colleges who have lost their faith. Jake O'Connor, the central character in Thomas J. Fleming's new novel, *All Good Men* . . . , is one of these. The burden of Mr. Fleming's story is how young O'Connor, having lost all sense of meaning and purpose in life, finds his soul again in, of all places, the late Frank Hague's political machine.

Others, better qualified, may discuss the novel's literary merits. They may well conclude, too, that the book's portrayal of dubiously relevant and clearly sensational "private-life" incidents makes it unsuitable reading for the family circle. I can only say that Mr. Fleming's description of politics as practiced in Frank Hague's barony on the Hudson is thorough and accurate. To be sure, he never names the city in which his story takes place. But it is clearly, unmistakably Jersey City under the thinnest of disguises. (p. 418)

The leading politicos of the Hague era are also there, despite the conventional declaration that "all of the characters in this book are fictitious, and any resemblance to actual persons is purely coincidental." Mr. Fleming stretches coincidence pretty far.

Many of the characters are true only to type, of course. But the novel's Mayor David Shea looks, dresses, talks and acts like Mayor Frank Hague. Shea's lieutenant, Johnny Kenellen, does for him what Johnny Malone did for Hague. Matty Blair, the ward leader who organizes a revolt against Shea, in 1951, does not look like John V. Kenny. Prudence no doubt dictated lack of physical resemblance in this instance, for Mr. Kenny is still very much with us and enjoys the services of some good lawyers. But Mr. Kenny led a successful revolt against Hague, in 1949, very similar to Matty Blair's.

The political skulduggery, which Mr. Fleming describes in rich detail, is also true to life. Shea's organization does nothing in the novel which the Hague organization did not do in reality, if one can believe people who were in a position to know. Mr. Fleming's chief interest is in Jake O'Connor's dark night of the soul. But in the course of his story he writes a primer of the dark and devious ways in which the Hague machine maintained itself in power in Jersey City for 30 years.

The novelistic device by which the author does this is to have Jake's father, Ben O'Connor, fall ill on the eve of the 1951 election. Ben is Shea's leader in the 13th Ward (there were only 12 wards in Hague's Jersey City). Since Ben cannot do all of his work from a hospital bed, he is forced to ask Jake to take over some of his political chores.

Jake's first assignment requires him to drive to another part of the State, where he bribes a rural police chief to quash a charge of car stealing against the son of one of Ben's constituents. I have been told that Mayor Hague kept a fund with which to buy off State legislators who were opposing bills that Hague considered favorable to Hudson County. (pp. 418-19)

Jake also has the job of collecting the regular contributions which gamblers make to the organization in return for the privilege of operating in violation of the law. But there are no contributions from the vice racket. Dave Shea, like Frank Hague, runs a clean town.

The novel describes or alludes to a number of other political techniques, including the mass buying of votes on election day. . . .

All of the devices mentioned in the novel add up to a well-designed system for getting and keeping political power. . . .

Mr. Fleming describes the Shea organization's methods with unsparing objectivity. But he does not condemn the men who devised and used them. Quite the contrary. He feels, and makes us agree, that Ben O'Connor, master of corrupt politics, is none the less a responsible leader of his people.

Ben O'Connor, in fact, has a heart of gold. His methods are crude, sometimes ruthless, but he has the human touch. And he uses his power for his people's welfare as he understands it. Nor is this unbelievable. One can meet ward leaders in Jersey City today who, whether or not they have all of Ben O'Connor's faults, have many of his virtues. In one way or another, they are all good men. People vote for political machines quite as much out of gratitude and loyalty as out of greed and fear. (p. 419)

There remains the question of the Church. One cannot talk about Jersey City without talking about the Catholic Church; three out of four of the city's residents are at least nominally Catholic. In a curious way, despite a lot of anticlerical dialogue, the Church gets off rather easily in this novel.

Mr. Fleming presents for our admiration Msgr. Patrick O'Keefe, a tough, old-fashioned Irish pastor in whose parish Ben O'Connor spent his youth. The Monsignor understood his people. He knew, too, that a ward leader must often do things he does not like doing and which will not bear close moral scrutiny. The Monsignor was no political prude.

For our disdain we are presented with Ben O'Connor's other son, Fr. Paul O'Connor. This weak and prissy young man turns against his father and the Shea organization and openly supports Matty Blair's political revolt.

But surely this contrast of clerical types is a bit too neat. It is perfectly true that the Church has to stand above partisan political strife and that, therefore, priests should not publicly support candidates for civic office. But is there nothing more to say than that? Is our choice only between Msgr. O'Keefe and Fr. O'Connor?

Political speeches are indeed out of place in the pulpit. But sermons on such texts as "Thou shalt not steal" are quite in order, and a well-informed preacher, without naming names, can make sufficiently plain the kind of stealing he is talking about. If he wants people to respect the Church, he had better face the elementary issues of morals and politics. For when churchmen sit quietly in the midst of corruption and occasionally enjoy some tidbits from its feast, they invite—and get—contempt.

Contempt and its effect, shame, played a part in the fall of the Shea machine, as Mr. Fleming notes. The New Deal dealt a blow to the political machines everywhere in the country by furnishing as welfare services much of what the machines had conferred as favors. But even without the welfare state, the Irish politicians who dominated the great metropolitan centers would probably have found that their supporters were growing old, and their sons and daughters were growing ashamed of them and their political organization.

The descendants of the immigrants are becoming middle-class. More and more they share the middle-class political ideal. They crave, if not absolute honesty in government, at least respectability. . . .

Mr. Fleming knows all this. His novel is a drama of conflict and reconciliation between the generations. By the story's end, the older generation has learned to give way to the new, and the younger generation has learned to give the old the measure of affection and respect which is its due. Jake O'Connor is on the way to discovering the love of God through the love of his father. He is also planning to launch his own political career in a new and better style than his father ever knew.

Unfortunately, the reader is left with some doubt whether Jake's style will be new enough. The old family, ethnic and religious loyalties that, very understandably, motivated immigrant politics are simply not adequate for municipal government today. The needs of a modern city are too great and too pressing to be met by politicians whose chief merit is that they believe in "taking care" of people. The human touch is an endearing Irish trait. But the modern city needs something better than the human touch alone. (p. 420)

Francis Canavan, "The Human Touch in Politics," in America, Vol. 106, No. 12, December 23, 1961, pp. 418-20.

ROBERT HEALEY

It is somewhat unfortunate for Thomas J. Fleming that so much of his material [in *All Good Men*] has been combed through before. His shrewd, richly detailed study of the collapse of an old-fashioned Irish political machine in an Eastern city can certainly stand on its own, but its value as fresh fictional material has been diluted by other novels on the same subject. . . . The purely political scenes aside, and they are all excellent, the richest part of *All Good Men* is the developing father-son relationship, timid and begrudging at first, later budding into adult warmth and understanding.

Robert Healey, "The Many Faces of Fiction," in Books, December 24, 1961, p. 10.*

ELSWYTH THANE

Thomas Fleming has a knack for good titles. [*Beat the Last Drum: The Siege of Yorktown, 1781*], which ends with the British surrender at Yorktown, follows his *Now We Are Enemies*, which dealt with Bunker Hill, where it all began. In this second book Mr. Fleming has struck his stride in a vigorous, informal style that seldom becomes too colloquial. It makes entertaining reading, rewarding for both scholar and layman. One does not have to know—or care—very much about the end of the long war for American independence to find oneself caught up in this vivid narrative of the events, both comic and tragic, which led to that October day when the British regulars laid down their arms and gave up their colors to the victorious colonial army commanded by General Washington and his French ally, the Comte de Rochambeau. This reviewer . . . is in the unique position of reporting on a book about which there are practically no complaints. . . .

[Mr. Fleming's] ability to evoke the human being behind the record is, it would seem, one secret of making history not only intelligible but fascinating to the average reader. There were men inside the red coats—men who had foibles and high tempers and strong emotions, which they left visible in their own words written in the heat of the moment. Clinton's agonies of indecision, and Cornwallis's soldierly integrity and pride, hamstrung by his ranking officer's skill at hedging and passing the buck, emerge with contemporary force in Mr. Fleming's skilful use of quotation.

Throughout the book he has drawn freely on all the standard sources, from Washington himself to Dr. Thacher and Sergeant Lamb, plus the French accounts of Chastellux, Robin, and Rochambeau, but Mr. Fleming has added to these the obscure journals and memoirs tucked away in state historical societies' publications and privately printed material, so that his bibliography and appendix, along with an excellent index, will be of lasting value. (p. 46)

Elswyth Thane, "Bagpipes End the Sound of Battle," in Saturday Review, Vol. XLVI, No. 46, November 16, 1963, pp. 46-7.

JOSEPH G. HARRISON

For a short, concise, gripping account of the majestic achievement of the Pilgrim Fathers, [*One Small Candle: The Pilgrims'*

First Year in America] could hardly be bettered. It is written with deep reverence for what the little band of 1620 underwent in their hardship-strewn passage from the Old World to the New, and with a clear understanding of what the Pilgrim example has meant to America.

In giving his reason for writing it, Fleming says, "I grew up in an immigrant city in which there were sharp conflicts between old Americans and new Americans. I felt that my father's generation, raised in the ghetto world of Irish Catholicism, had somehow failed to grasp the deeper meaning of America, and it was this sense of loss and deprivation which has led me to spend so much of my writing career studying American origins."

What Fleming says of his father's generation, can in some measure be said of all of us. How seldom today do we take time to think back on the bitter and long-drawn struggle of the pioneers on a raw, new continent. *One Small Candle* can help recall us to a livelier memory of those days when the future of the United States was being shaped in the tiny settlement at Plymouth.

Beginning with the purchase of the Mayflower in the spring of 1620, the book closes with the Thanksgiving celebration in the fall of 1621. . . . As the tale unfolds, we feel that few adventure stories could rival this actual account of what these men, women, and children suffered for their religious, moral, and political convictions.

One cannot know the Pilgrim story too well to benefit from and enjoy reading this magnificently told tale.

> *Joseph G. Harrison, "When New England Was New,"* in The Christian Science Monitor, *December 9, 1964, p. 13.*

RODNEY F. ALLEN

In a popular narrative history [*One Small Candle: The Pilgrims' First Year in America*] Thomas J. Fleming has traced the tenacious life of the Pilgrims from their contract with the skipper of the *Mayflower* to the first Thanksgiving on the blustery shores of New England. His adroit use of quotations from original sources has permitted more than a compilation of modern scholarship, obliterating the "log cabin myths" and other folklore about the colony. The spirit of the Pilgrim enterprise has been recreated. Their fears, concerns, and aspirations are not lost in an attempt for factual completeness but are captured in the quotations and the author's flowing prose.

The closing chapters are the best in the volume. Here the separation of religious and political leadership is developed. John Carver, the first governor, is seen as indecisive, while authority gravitated to William Bradford. The Indian diplomacy of Edward Winslow and the defenses arranged by Miles Standish are outlined. And Fleming accentuates the importance of Christopher Jones, master of the *Mayflower*, in establishing the isolated enclave at Plymouth in 1620. . . .

But Fleming in his enthusiasm seems to have overstated the impact of the Pilgrims and their significance. Did later generations look back to Plymouth for "ideals and values," as he suggests, or did they absorb later legends about the settlement?

> *Rodney F. Allen, in a review of "One Small Candle: The Pilgrims' First Year in America,"* in The Social Studies, *Vol. LVI, No. 4, April, 1965, p. 156.*

R. Z. SHEPPARD

Passion, political savvy and an iron grip on the moral and philosophical complexities of government and the governed inform [*King of the Hill,* a] superheated drama of power politics in "a large American city." The author, who, we are informed, ". . . received a firsthand education in big-city politics in the Jersey City of Boss Hague," takes few pains to conceal that his inspiration was that rundown industrial city whose principal exports are a bad reputation and air pollutants.

Among his principal players are the mayor, a self-indulgent hack who took over a good thing from the "big man" and struggles ineptly to run the once well-oiled machine on old-fashioned political grease, and his assistant, a brilliant technician and renegade-Catholic nihilist whose insanely rational attempt to usurp the mayor's seat in the name of "Newpower" forcefully underscores the basic question of means and ends. There is also the reform candidate whose blend of good intentions, charm and self-doubt adds up to little more than a frail hope for the future. . . .

Bit players move briskly in and out of the wings, more important characters wrestle convincingly with their social consciences and parochial upbringings, and Mr. Fleming does some fine things with the bottomless theme of fathers and sons. My principal objection is his prose: generally overwrought, heavy-handed, relentlessly trying to pound drama out of situations that are so highly charged they should be stroked. After reading such things as "Faith looked up at the huge Irish face and suddenly saw it rotting from the inside out, like a great piece of decaying meat," and "You showed the slobs no mercy: you shredded them in the armory of your mind," it wouldn't have been too surprising if the inevitable scandal had caused the dome of city hall to erupt like a lanced boil.

> *R. Z. Sheppard, "Flourishes and Alarums,"* in Book Week—Chicago Sun-Times, *February 6, 1966, p. 14.*

MARTIN LEVIN

[*King of the Hill*] is the continuing political history of a city, not too far west of New York, that Thomas J. Fleming first described some years ago in *All Good Men*. As before, he reveals a talent for weaving large and small corruptions into a fascinating web of municipal intrigue. (p. 43)

Mr. Fleming skillfully juggles such big city by-products as scandal, graft, corruption and violence, and brings them crashing down on his civic leaders in a well-timed Götterdämmerung.

If the author's prose tends to get feverish, this is a pardonable side effect of enthusiasm, since his attitude toward his characters is sympathetic rather than clinical. He has as intense an interest in his scrofulous wedge of geography as Faulkner had in his. His characters are solidly linked together by blood, tradition and old crimes—and the rich texture of their past makes their present credible. (pp. 43-4)

> *Martin Levin, in a review of "King of the Hill,"* in The New York Times Book Review, *February 27, 1966, pp. 43-4.*

ROGER B. DOOLEY

The world [Thomas J. Fleming reveals in *King of the Hill*], with frequently startling vividness, is one of total, brutal corruption, Machiavellian double-dealing and power struggles literally to the death—to several deaths, in fact, two cold-blooded murders, another threatened and a dubious accident. Not since Harry Sylvester's 1947 *Moon Gaffney* has any novelist produced such a scathing "J'accuse" on the American Irish—and Mr. Fleming's punch is far deadlier than Mr. Sylvester's, both because this is an inside job and because he knows how to construct a tightly built plot.

Yet this very plot, so tensely effective as melodrama, may in the end keep the book from being taken as seriously as the author no doubt intended. His passionate concern for what the city has done to the Irish and vice-versa blazes forth in the ambivalent love-hatred of all the leading characters for their milieu, but within the narrow confines of the action none has the chance to grow and develop as they might have done in a more leisurely, less sensational novel. (pp. 59-60)

To me, at least, some of the minor characters come off better than the leads, perhaps because their idiosyncrasies are more sharply observed. Since Faith, Larry and Jake have all reached the same degree of disgust with their background, especially with the Church, their thoughts and conversations tend to become interchangeable, if not indistinguishable. This may be due in part to their irritating habit of continually talking to themselves by name, so that much of the book is written in a sort of second-person stream of consciousness, which at times sounds as if the author were apostrophizing them. . . .

Mr. Fleming's generally powerful prose is also flawed by a few other stylistic clichés, such as using "like" as a conjunction in the manner forever associated with Winston cigarettes and indulging in such non-transitive, Frank Merriwell verbs to convey dialogue as "He snarled," "She snapped," and "He sneered."

Come to think, he does a good deal of snarling, snapping and sneering himself, mostly in the direction of the Church. Those who cling to it are invariably dismissed as "idiots," "morons," and "rosary-rattlers," while the intelligent characters can scarely pass a Catholic institution without choking on bitter regrets for the years wasted trying to swallow all that "mush, ten centuries cold." This observation is made not on grounds of prudence but of art; it seems a violation of the writer's objectivity when his tone becomes shrill with the sound of grinding axes, especially since the Church and the clergy play no part in the action.

With all these limitations, *King of the Hill* is a compulsively readable novel, full of harsh, undeniably true observations on how our cities are run. . . . [One] hopes that a considerable public will be interested in this forceful dramatization of the seamier aspects of Irish-American politics. (p. 60)

Roger B. Dooley, in a review of "King of the Hill," in Commonweal, Vol. LXXXIV, No. 2, April 1, 1966, pp. 59-60.

ANTHONY BOUCHER

Thomas J. Fleming adapts the police procedural admirably to the purposes of the "straight" novel in *A Cry of Whiteness*, . . . which leads an insensitive career cop, temporarily assigned to a black precinct, to acts of humanity that imperil his career. This sounds, in summary, facilely moralistic; it is not at all so in Fleming's treatment, which combines living characters, powerful storytelling, a strong plot, legitimate and well-handled sex, and a subtle feeling for many levels of black-white

relationships. (One small reservation: I could wish the author had not depicted his many Roman Catholics as stupid racial bigots.) . . .

Anthony Boucher, in a review of "A Cry of Whiteness," in The New York Times Book Review, October 15, 1967, p. 57.

BERNARD F. DICK

One would like to admire [*A Cry of Whiteness*] simply because Thomas Fleming has chosen a subject which most authors would dismiss as unartistic or irrelevant: violence erupting in a Negro slum and altering the lives of all involved. At first everything augurs well. The title evokes Conrad's *Heart of Darkness*, and two lines from the novella form the epigraph. Fleming's Detective Harry Kurz was apparently suggested by Conrad's enigmatic Mr. Kurtz, and the beat to which he has been newly assigned is nicknamed, appropriately enough, "the Congo."

But soon it is all too clear that the darkness is neither ethnic nor cosmic; it is sheer murkiness that results when a novel starts as a detective story with racial overtones . . . and ends as a *Bildungsroman*. The racial issue vanishes under one of the many beds where Kurz is proving his masculinity. . . . His main problem (and the author's as well) seems to be an inability to decide whether he should be playing Studs Lonigan, Mike Hammer or James Bond. Manufactured heroes are rarely interesting, especially when their models eclipse them.

But it is in the very banality of Kurz and the other main characters that the novel takes on its fullest meaning: it is the *wrong* people who seem to get involved in race relations. . . .

A Cry of Whiteness by no means illuminates the darkness of the heart, and thus its value is more sociological than literary. But on one point Fleming is frighteningly clear: the apathetic, the ignorant, and the misguided invariably fail not only themselves but humanity.

Bernard F. Dick, in a review of "A Cry of Whiteness," in The Catholic World, Vol. 206, No. 1234, January, 1968, p. 191.

WILLIAM V. KENNEDY

[In *West Point: The Men and Times of the United States Military Academy*], Mr. Fleming quotes a member of the West Point faculty to the effect that all Army officers, graduates of the Military Academy or not, measure themselves by the standards of West Point. Essentially that is true. There has always been a danger, however, of the Academy and its graduates coming to think that West Point is the Army, and that is not true at all. Mr. Fleming acknowledges as much, but he tends to slip into this overblown concept of the role and mission of the Corps. Despite this fact, he has produced a readable account of the history of the school, one that is as comprehensive as the general reader would care to tackle. His many anecdotes are enlightening as well as entertaining. His description of the Civil War period and of the disastrous initial attempt to integrate the corps of cadets is excellent.

The early Military Academy is portrayed as a national school aimed as much, or more, at producing badly needed engineers as at producing professional soldiers. The author does his subject a service in documenting the school's outstanding success in meeting this need, and the influence of its faculty and graduates in upgrading the level of scientific education in the country as a whole.

Sylvanus Thayer, superintendent from 1817 to 1833, is depicted as the father of this contribution, as he is of the academy as a whole. (p. 422)

The author has accomplished an impressive research effort, but beyond the limits of his immediate subject the focus becomes a bit blurred. He mistakenly concludes that the Mexican War "scotched permanently any danger of antagonism" between the citizen volunteer and the West Point professional. Later references by Mr. Fleming himself make it plain that there was continuing friction throughout at least the next half-century. He has over-looked useful illustrations of latter-day pulling and hauling. (p. 423)

There are some regrettable technical flaws. Wherever Mr. Fleming can use a trite word, phrase or sentence he does so—"The primal river still flows serenely past the ancient rock." Metaphors are generally labored. One seems set up for the sole purpose of enabling Mr. Fleming to drag in his views as to the importance of Vatican II. . . . The over-all effort, however, is well worth the time of any reader who is concerned with the present and future role of the soldier in American society. (pp. 423-24)

> *William V. Kennedy, in a review of "West Point,"*
> *in* America, *Vol. 120, No. 14, April 5, 1969, pp.*
> *422-24.*

CHARLES BRACELEN FLOOD

[*West Point*] is the best book written about the United States Military Academy at West Point. It is also one of the best books ever written about any American educational institution. . . .

[Thomas J. Fleming's] feeling for both history and present-day involvement is evident in *West Point,* which emerges not as a sentimental view of The Long Gray Line, but as an exceedingly capable study by a man who is reassessing our history and institutions in terms of current international and domestic agonies. . . .

It is in describing the decades from the Civil War to the onset of World War I that the author makes his most original contribution. He points out the growing rigidity in the Academy's discipline and instruction that produced officers, and hence an Army, that was ill-prepared for the Spanish-American War and the Philippine Insurrection that sprang from it. The seldom-told tale of the first black cadets at West Point in the Reconstruction period and thereafter is set forth in all its harrowing detail.

Despite the limitations of an educational system that for some years fed upon itself, educating cadets by the book and then promptly turning them into instructors who parroted the same lessons back to a new generation of cadets, there were talented men in those times. Fleming makes the most of their stories, both as cadets and in later years. (p. 10)

Fleming closes his book with a thoughtful and deeply informed appraisal of what West Point is now. Readers will be surprised to learn that it stands fourth in the nation in terms of Rhodes Scholars produced. The author presents convincing evidence that the entering classes are the equal of any in the country. (p. 12)

> *Charles Bracelen Flood, "The Long Gray Line," in*
> The New York Times Book Review, *May 4, 1969,*
> *pp. 10, 12.*

MARSHALL SMELSER

What Fleming has done [in *The Man From Monticello: An Intimate Life of Thomas Jefferson*] is to look at life from Jefferson's point of view rather than looking from the orchestra seats at Jefferson on stage. This is not a "Life and Times," although it tells the public story too.

Where there are discrepant versions of an episode, Fleming chooses the more interesting. Where something is unknowable, he occasionally gives us plausible invention. Like Herodotus, he sometimes distinguishes his own view from tradition—as in the case of the "tradition" that Lucy Jefferson II weighed 16 pounds at birth. When the writer draws on his imagination, his fancies are always in character. . . .

Where Fleming works directly from evidence, as in deducing Martha Jefferson's boredom from her doodling on laundry lists, or in proving Jefferson's passion for independence by rhetorical analysis of the Declaration as compared with Jefferson's other state papers, he shows genuine distinction. (p. 4)

Thomas Fleming's well-constructed biography deserves attention as a highly readable story of a learned, intelligent and interesting man who never sought hero worship. (p. 5)

> *Marshall Smelser, "Thomas Jefferson from Thomas*
> *Jefferson's Point of View," in* The New York Times
> Book Review, *July 6, 1969, pp. 4-5.*

WEBSTER SCHOTT

Thomas Fleming's latest novel [*Romans, Countrymen, Lovers*] is a slice of our contemporary experience—and a swipe at making sense of it. The Romans are Roman Catholics. The countrymen are third-generation Irish and our other disenchanted compatriots. The lovers are various well-educated, middle-class businessmen and wives in differing stages of marriage, separation, and divorce. The oratorical tone of the title anticipates a command: America, Get Backbone!

Romans, Countrymen, Lovers makes all kinds of mistakes that compromise its conviction, its esthetic qualities, its capacity to expand our understanding of how and why we behave as we do. But this is a novel of serious intention, and it has moments of vigor. Fleming tries to find hope for characters who have jumped the tracks. He engages our middle-class culture at its point of maximum vulnerability—the American male attempting to lead a moral life and still make a living.

We should celebrate the author's concern: it's really unusual. Most of our literary intellectuals float or thresh outside the mainstream of bourgeois society, rejecting it out of hand. O'Hara and Auchincloss need all the help they can get. Our central culture—rife with trauma, frustration, loss—cries for intelligent exegesis. For grappling with its complexities, Fleming deserves praise.

The hero is 37-year-old Jim Kilpatrick, and the novel runs him around several circles of hell before lining him up with a sensible woman and an assistantship to a Manhattan super-executive. . . . Unsuccessful chip off a machine politician, miscast as an insurance salesman with a social conscience, an intellectual Catholic spiritually wounded by broken idealism, Jim chucks everything. He runs out on his wife and many children, sinks into alcoholism, shacks up with a wild sister-in-law in San Francisco and tests salvation via the flesh. It doesn't work. . . .

Later, Jim lucks into a job with an old college buddy in Los Angeles, succeeds as an imaginative conglomerate jack-of-all trades, and replaces his lost Catholicism with a faith in the here and now. . . .

Fleming, it seems to me, is on the side of decency, reasonableness in all respects. He depicts Jim's pal-boss as a corporation Nazi—but shows Jim finding ways to bring dignity and self-respect to swing-shift women on an assembly line. He casts Jim's wife Esther in the role of a sexual zombie. His liberated hero, however, seeks more than sexual freedom. Jim wants order, purpose, membership in the fraternity of hope. Fleming lays open the brutal competition of corporations fighting in a market economy. But he understands that institutions are extensions of human beings: he proves that humane options exist, even in corporate strategy. He suggests that power and compassion can coexist.

Why, then, does one leave **Romans, Countrymen, Lovers** more disbelieving than expanded, less confident of the novelist's insights than of his struggle to achieve them? Because Jim Kilpatrick acts but does not live; his behavior does not follow inevitably from qualities of character, but rather from his creator's programed optimism. Equally troublesome is Fleming's ambition. He wants everything. He experiments with styles (Joyce, O'Hara, even Barth) and loses control. He buries his story under a driving need to expose the failures of Catholicism, to psychoanalyze the hippie movement, to celebrate integrity in private enterprise, to dignify one man's quest for morality in sex and an open society.

His motives are beyond reproach. His motives are also beyond his capacity. It would take a Leo Tolstoy living on early retirement from General Motors, and a novel 1,000 pages long, to achieve what he has in mind.

> *Webster Schott, "How to Be Moral and Still Make a Living," in* The New York Times Book Review, *September 28, 1969, p. 55.*

ANNE FREMANTLE

[In **Romans, Countrymen, Lovers**] Thomas Fleming is bitter, not mild. He writes horridly well, making a drunk fallen-away Catholic who has left his wife and kids talk and think like it is—like it must be. His sister-in-law comes to taunt, to save, and to seduce him: "she kicked a whiskey bottle and it rolled across the fleshsmooth hotel carpet to clunk against the wall. We both watched it roll . . . Shameless, shaveless, stumbling from bottle to bottle in my greasy underwear . . . Bottle, bottle, who's got the bottle? . . ." and so on, for pages, but the cumulative effect is telling. And Mr. Fleming conveys too the exasperation of a man and of a woman by just the right touches: too drunk to drive, hero Jim winces because his wife starts up the stationwagon with a great roar, jams the accelerator, and pulls away with the usual convulsive leap. Next morning, his eight-year old Sean (with his wife's face) comes prancing into Jim's room and lets off a cap-pistol in his ear. Gradually he comes to hate all his kids, hate the weather, his job, and above all the church. . . . Jim becomes an apostle for big business, for the American way of life, lived by "men of talent and energy, the riskers and planners who produce things." He finds

Teresa, his third-time-lucky, is final surrogate for mother, church, wife and all the past besides. It is a curious credo with which to end: to believe "in another person, who understands and shares this loneliness" and in "visceral identity with Americans dead and Americans living. Losing the Catholic, losing the Irish, Jim finds the "American at last, simply, wholly, true."

> *Anne Fremantle, in a review of "Romans, Countrymen, Lovers," in* Commonweal, *Vol. XCII, No. 13, June 26, 1970, p. 324.*

PHILIP C. RULE

To be Irish, Catholic and a 21 year old senior at Mount St. Monica's in 1948 was, according to novelist Fleming [in **The Sandbox Tree**], pure hell.

Margaret Connolly, the sandbox tree, is a Galatea produced by that perverse Pygmalion, Irish-Catholic Jansenism. She is the incarnation—or at least the stereotype—of all the warped ideas on sexual morality ever promulgated by the Catholic school system.

A female Stephen Dedalus, without his incisive ability to criticize, she is caught in a tug-of-war between the young law student, Dick Thornton, a decent sort of Protestant who wants to marry her and Father Denton Malone, the sex-obsessed chaplain and dispenser of the perennial philosophy of St. Thomas at Mount St. Monica's, who in his misguided fervor wants to hurry her off to the convent as one of his spiritual prizes. . . .

More interesting, however, than Margaret and her friends— most of them in some phase of liberation from institutional Catholicism or total subservience to it—is the wild world of Irish state and local politics in which the whole story is set.

Judge James Kilpatrick, Chief Justice of the state and father of Margaret's college room-mate, Faith (an ironic name for that troubled young lady), and his neurotic, pious wife have long since gone their own ways—into separate bedrooms. . . . The sub- or, rather, parallel plot of the novel deals with the judge and his downfall.

His battles with fellow thieves and politicians frequently provide more dramatic action than does the spiritual turmoil in the souls of the younger generation. But, for anyone who has lived through the era Fleming talks about, the novel will provide a pleasure akin to that one gets in hearing fingernails scrape across the surface of a blackboard.

The book's principal weakness is that mentioned at the end by the narrator of the story: "The sententious historian is endangering the novelist."

> *Philip C. Rule, in a review of "The Sandbox Tree," in* America, *Vol. 123, No. 11, October 17, 1970, p. 296.*

PRISCILLA L. BUCKLEY

Would Protestants be interested in a novel [like **The Good Shepherd**]? . . . Probably not unless they are members of Protestants and Other Americans United for Separation of Church and State, and they will lap it up. All they have ever wanted to believe about the Church of Rome is here, the venality, the striving for power, the cynicism in high places, every sin in the book, yea even unto fornication between priest and nun. Would Catholics be interested? Very much so, but lots of them will not like it, many will loathe it, none will feel comfortable with it. Thomas Fleming wades into the middle of the galvanic struggle that has swirled in and around the Roman Catholic Church since Vatican II.... Fleming writes with assurance and strength but also with a sentimentality that leans toward maudlinism at times. (But then what are the Irish in their cups if not sentimental and maudlin?) A compelling book with a number of flaws: some characters are overdrawn, others stereotyped, the women are one dimensional. Some incidents are inherently implausible, others downright impossible. But the conflicts are real, our passions are aroused. Because of its subject matter, *Good Shepherd* is sure to be weighed for its ideological content rather than for its fictional competence. Rather a pity for a novel that probes deeply into problems that, like them or not, millions of Catholics must contend with today.

> *Priscilla L. Buckley, in a review of "The Good Shepherd," in* National Review, *Vol. XXVII, No. 7, February 28, 1971, p. 236.*

ELIZABETH NELSON

[In *The Man Who Dared the Lightning: A New Look at Benjamin Franklin*], Fleming creates a vivid, engaging portrait of his hero and views people and events from the hero's perspective.

He uses his novelist's technique ... extraordinarily well; the pace is rapid, characterization is colorful and the narrative is dramatic. Significant scenes have a theatrical flavor: Franklin's experiments with electricity (especially the opening chapter), his confrontations with members of the House of Commons and his meeting with Louis XVI at Versailles. Indeed, Fleming gives the events that lead up to the revolution and formation of the new American government an immediacy and excitement that should make the book attractive for young students of this period.

Franklin is distinguished from the man that appears in his famous *Autobiography;* this account starts "where the best known part of the autobiography ends." We do get a view of Franklin the scientist-inventor, the author of *Poor Richard's Almanack.* We are also treated to examples of Franklin's wit and ready anecdotes used to illustrate his viewpoints. This lighter side is balanced by shrewd appraisals of Franklin's actions at moments of crisis. Since Fleming's enthusiasm is infectious, we share in his satisfaction at Franklin's triumphs, especially when he wears his suit of Manchester velvet for the formal signing of the treaty of alliance with France—the same suit worn on the occasion of his humiliation before the British Lords in Council. Franklin's vulnerability is also movingly conveyed in his sorrow over his son's "defection" to the Loyalists.

While the book is a sincere portrait of Franklin and is well documented, readers of "pure" biography may well blanch at the imaginative re-creation of scenes and consciousness of characters at crucial points, or at Fleming's partiality for his subject. Secret meetings are described in detail; private reactions are directly reported rather than merely suggested. Objectivity wavers when Franklin's enemies (or even nonpartisans) are dismissed with a sharp phrase.... (pp. 323-24)

The book is not the definitive Franklin biography, but its style and treatment should make it a popular one. (p. 324)

> *Elizabeth Nelson, in a review of "The Man Who Dared the Lightning: A New Look at Benjamin Franklin," in* America, *Vol. 124, No. 12, March 27, 1971, pp. 323-24.*

GEORGE F. SCHEER

An infrequently mentioned and often misunderstood victory of the Revolution was the American repulse of a powerful British invasion of New Jersey in June of 1780....

Nearly a century ago, an eminent military historian asserted that few moments during the war "bore so directly upon the safety of the American army and the general cause" as the repulse of this offensive. But generally it has been given only passing notice by historians. [*The Forgotten Victory: The Battle for New Jersey, 1780*], Thomas Fleming's full-length account of the political machinations and battlefield actions that made up the Springfield affair, replete with colorful details and characterizations, makes both compelling reading and a convincing case for the lasting significance of the victory.

> *George F. Scheer, "Men and Battles of the Revolution," in* The New York Times Book Review, *December 16, 1973, p. 12.**

FRANCIS SWEENEY

[In *The Good Shepherd*, Thomas Fleming introduces] Matthew Mahan, archbishop of a see that sounds like Newark or Cleveland.

As an infantry chaplain Mahan had met Archbishop Roncalli, then papal Nuncio in Paris; the old diplomat and the young priest had become friends. Years later, Roncalli, now John XXIII, had picked Mahan as auxiliary bishop and unwelcome successor to Archbishop Hogan.

Mahan flies to Rome for induction into the College of Cardinals, to be an administrator dealing firmly and jovially with conservative and liberal clergy and with politicians and well-heeled benefactors. Life seems good indeed.

Yet the reader knows better. Fleming has trepanned the skull not only of Cardinal Mahan but of his secretary, Father Dennis McLaughlin, Yale Ph.D. in history and disillusioned activist, whom Mahan had chosen as secretary within a year of his leaving the Jesuits....

Mahan is troubled because he cannot agree with the teaching on birth control laid down in *Humanae Vitae* the previous year, though he does not dissent outwardly. His attitude has not been lost on the Vatican. As he kneels before Paul VI, the Pope greets him as "frater noster taciturnus"—our silent brother. So there is plenty of reason for the ulcer that flexes its talon of pain in the Cardinal's stomach....

In a climactic session with the other American bishops he defends an open-minded attitude toward optional celibacy for priests. The Vatican has asked for a united front, and he is voted down. He writes a long, candid letter to Paul VI protesting against the policies on birth control, divorce and clerical celibacy....

This is a powerful and challenging novel, which, I think, does not transcend the peril of mixing contemporary historical figures with fictional characters.

True enough, *Humanae Vitae* was a watershed of dissent in the Church, and there is widespread dissatisfaction with the

Roman Curia. But to polarize history as Fleming does is not to write a novel but a hanging sermon.

No one can quarrel with the winsome glimpses of Papa Roncalli, whom all the world loved. But to endow Paul with so many opposite qualities is unjust. On the novel's great topical issues Paul and John agree.

The characters' voices ring true, though their letters are jaunty and boring. One letter runs on for two of the book's pages describing in auctioneers' language the furniture in the Cardinal's residence. Irony is not Fleming's forte.

Readers with long memories may recall Henry Morton Robinson's *The Cardinal,* which was prime hammock reading in 1950. Fleming's is a better book, with the characters believably confronting the Church's problems and crystallizing the Church's moods.

> *Francis Sweeney, "Frater noster taciturnus—Our Silent Brother," in* The New York Times Book Review, *August 4, 1974, p. 6.*

HENRY WILKINSON BRAGDON

Seldom if ever have I reviewed a book I can more unreservedly recommend than this vivid account of the year in which the Americans decided to assume a "separate and equal station" in the family of nations. Among the virtues of *1776: Year of Illusions* are:

• It gives a broad, synoptic view of events. Fleming deals not merely with the American scene, but devotes illuminating chapters to George III and the British Parliament, to the political forces in France favoring and opposing aid to the Americans, and to the Caribbean Islands, which had an important role in promoting the American cause.

• The narrative is fast-paced and full of incident. Especially admirable are the accounts of battles, which are models of lucidity. Each one is placed in a larger context, and the most important campaigns are accompanied by useful maps.

• The principal actors come alive. Fleming's book abounds in quick, vivid, convincing sketches of military men such as Benedict Arnold, Sir William Howe, and Charles Lee, and political leaders such as George III, Edmund Burke, and John Adams.

It is Fleming's contention, which is convincing but which he perhaps belabors, that both the Americans and the British started the year 1776 handicapped by illusions that were dissipated only by bitter experience. Both sides shared the expectation that the war would be short. The British overestimated the numbers of men still loyal to the crown and so despised the rebels that they underestimated their will to fight. The Americans were rendered over-optimistic by a series of dazzling early successes....

Not the least merit of *1776: Year of Illusions* is that it shows how, amid disaster and disillusion, Washington grew in confidence, in decisiveness, and in ability to lead men.

> *Henry Wilkinson Bragdon, "1776 Comes Alive in Fast-Paced Narrative," in* The Christian Science Monitor, *November 12, 1975, p. 23.*

MARTIN LEVIN

[In *Liberty Tavern*] Thomas Fleming looks into the hearts and minds of some patriots and poltroons caught up in the Revo-

lution. The author ... seems to delight in pointing out the paradoxes that underlie politics. His protagonist is Jonathan Gifford, the tavern's owner.... Gifford is a moderate and decent man, which makes it hard for him to live with the local vigilantes who use patriotism as a screen for spite....

The other side of the coin is represented by young Anthony Skinner, the Loyalist suitor of Gifford's stepdaughter. Skinner is driven by his troubles, which include expropriation and exile, to commit atrocities on his ex-friends and neighbors.

Mr. Fleming is even-handed at pointing out the villains on both sides, investing this big historical novel with a bracing climate of political sophistication. Plus a wealth of action and intrigue that seethes around Liberty Tavern with the changing tides of the Revolution.

> *Martin Levin, in a review of "Liberty Tavern," in* The New York Times Book Review, *May 2, 1976, p. 60.*

EDMUND S. MORGAN

Thomas Fleming's *1776, Year of Illusions* gives us a narrative of only one year of the Revolution, beginning after the fighting started, with the fruitless American invasion of Canada, and closing with Washington's triumph at Trenton and Princeton. Fleming ... is concerned primarily with the war.... The Revolutionists, in Fleming's account, appear to be a minority, and 1776 was a rough year for them. Fleming blames their tribulations on their illusions, the chief of which was that independence could be won by a few bold strokes. The success of untrained militia at Bunker Hill in 1775 had filled them with confidence that they could repeat the performance at will. A few more battles like that and the British would give up. But there were no more like that, and in the face of a succession of setbacks it looked as though the Revolutionists would be the ones to give up.

Fleming writes [persuasively] ..., and the Americans he portrays are far from being one people. They are torn by conflicting loyalties and a divided leadership. Independence is a "premature child," and the congressional Declaration of it the result of clever politicking, not of popular demand. Tories seem to be everywhere, and they are not transformed into patriots until the good judgment of a Washington gradually overcomes his own and others' "Bunker Hillism" and gives his troops some victories. Only when the Revolution looks like succeeding do the people join it.

The picture may be overdrawn, but it cannot be dismissed. The author ... is a good storyteller. He does not trouble the reader with doubts or qualifications or "probablys." George III has reduced Parliament to "an obedient servant"; the tenants of Livingston Manor live "like serfs"; Howe fails to destroy Washington on Long Island because he wants to make peace. The author knows that these statements are controversial, and he does not dismiss the controversies of academic historians ..., [but] he has decided the controversies and gives his readers only the results of his decisions. It is, after all, his book. Anyone who wants another interpretation can get it elsewhere. There is much to be said for this procedure, but it may leave some readers in doubt whether a united people embraced the Revolution at the outset ... or whether they had to be dragged into it by the heels, as Fleming seems to be saying. (pp. 14-15)

Edmund S. Morgan, "The American Revolution: Was There 'A People'?" in The New York Review of Books, *Vol. XXIII, No. 12, July 15, 1976, pp. 14-18.**

J. JUSTIN GUSTAINIS

Power and conflict, it seems to me, are the essence of politics and they are basic to Fleming's novel [*Rulers of the City*]. . . . Fleming's story is set in a Midwest-American city and deals with Mayor Jake O'Connor's attempts to cope with four crises (any resemblances to the life of Richard Nixon are purely coincidental): his wealthy wife's disagreements with his social policies; his own ambition to run for the U.S. Senate; his wife's snobbish, WASPish family, who would like to see him dead, politically; and a court order to implement busing in the city's schools.

What makes this book work is not so much the above elements (which any hack writer could have dreamed up), but Fleming's ability to portray character and motivation. . . .

I will not reveal which conflicts are resolved or how; this would cheat the reader. I will mention that the busing battle is as bloody as any ever fought in South Boston, and that several characters in this novel have to make great sacrifices before order is restored. This book is tightly plotted, the characters are finely drawn, and one hell of a story is told.

With nine novels and eight solid historical works behind him, Fleming is an important American writer.

J. Justin Gustainis, in a review of "Rulers of the City," in Best Sellers, *Vol. 37, No. 6, September, 1977, p. 165.*

VALERIE HOFFMAN

[In *Rulers of the City,* the] busing issue has fractured a typical American city into warring factions and the Mayor finds himself caught between trying to keep control of the city in a controversial issue—while also trying to summon support for a bid to the Senate. . . . Although Fleming writes well, there is too little scope here to make the novel important and different. As it is, Fleming merely shows us the dilemma of a city divided into what appears to be fairly standard conceptualized points of view yet never develops it in depth so what emerges is far more artificial than what is needed to sustain a novel.

Valerie Hoffman, in a review of "Rulers of the City," in West Coast Review of Books, *Vol. 3, No. 5, September, 1977, p. 24.*

CHOICE

New Jersey is small in size but has a long and illustrious history; it is the brave author who attempts to contain its story in 200 pages. As to be expected Fleming does not entirely succeed but he has managed to produce a worthwhile popular account of the Garden State [*New Jersey: A Bicentennial History*] and presents it in a lively, readable style. There is a good balance of affection and critical comment. Some may feel that there is a disproportion of coverage of the reign of Mayor Hague in Jersey City and his ultimate domination of state politics. Residents of southern New Jersey will feel neglected because greater emphasis is given to the northern urban and industrial areas.

A review of "New Jersey: A Bicentennial History", in Choice, *Vol. 15, No. 2, April, 1978, p. 291.*

LARRY R. GERLACH

[In *New Jersey,* Thomas Fleming] has skillfully fashioned an eminently readable yet rigorously analytical historical essay about his native state that should be both entertaining and edifying to a general readership.

Conceptually, Fleming's *New Jersey* falls somewhere between a concise chronicle and an impressionistic portrait. Observing that "Divided we stand" might well serve as the state's motto . . . , he posits at the beginning that conflict—sectional, ethnic, racial, religious, social, economic, and political—has been a conspicious characteristic of life in New Jersey for more than three centuries. There follows, chronologically to 1787 and topically to the present, a discussion of the major events, trends, issues, and personalities which illustrate the theme of contentiousness.

Fleming's historical rendition is generally reliable. The inaccuracies . . . are relatively minor and do not detract from the substance of the presentation. As in all works of synthesis, the quality of the coverage of a given period or topic often reflects the nature of the extant literature. The discussion of urban-industrial New Jersey is the strongest part of the book. Here Fleming contends that Jersey was a "mirror" of the national experience: surely Paterson and Passaic are synonymous with labor violence, Standard Oil and the Camden and Amboy Railroad with corporate privilege, Woodrow Wilson and Mark Fagan with progressive reform, William Sewell and Frank Hague with "bossism." Selectivity and brevity are essential in a book of this genre, but it is regrettable that the Lenni-Lenape Indians and physiography are virtually ignored.

The development of the author's thesis is disappointing. The kinds of discord Fleming emphasizes are not peculiar to New Jersey. There is a distinctive dissonance to Jersey life, but the emphasis on political and economic matters prevents a satisfying discussion if the social and cultural bases for the state as a collection of communities without a sense of community. Nonetheless, this is a perceptive assessment of the style and spirit of Jerseyites past and present. (p. 451)

Larry R. Gerlach, in a review of "New Jersey: A Bicentennial History," in The Journal of American History, *Vol. LXV, No. 2, September, 1978, pp. 450-51.*

ROBERT H. DONAHUGH

The Stapletons are rich, powerful, and a part of American history. . . . It is decided that a family history will be written, hopefully to show the strengths and values of the good old American virtues. Jim Kilpatrick is hired as the writer; and, in the process of interviewing the family and reading documents, he learns about the weaknesses, the scandals, and the accomplishments of an extraordinary family. . . . Something for everyone [in *Promises to Keep*]: politics, incest, murder, busing, deep religious faith, miscegenation, drugs, labor disputes, genealogy, war, homosexuality, and born-again redemption. Billed as the continuation of a series, this well-written novel can be read independently. . . .

Robert H. Donahugh, in a review of "Promises to Keep," in Library Journal, *Vol. 103, No. 17, October 1, 1978, p. 2006.*

PAT GOLD

Thomas Fleming has written a dreary novel about the Stapleton family [*Promises to Keep*]. . . . Once again we have a tale of incest, corruption, greed and any other venality the author could think up. Mr. Fleming does have one saving grace—he writes historical fiction well, and in a very well written section of the book, tells an adventure tale of Theodore Roosevelt's exploration of the River of Doubt in South America. Other than that, I found *Promises to Keep* laborious reading.

> *Pat Gold, in a review of "Promises to Keep," in West Coast Review of Books, Vol. 5, No. 1, January, 1979, p. 30.*

WALTER SHAPIRO

I'll be honest. At the end of *The Officers' Wives,* by Thomas Fleming, I cried. Not the small stray tear running down the edge of your nose. No, an-honest-to-God gusher. . . .

All popular novels—and make no mistake, *The Officers' Wives* is not literature—play on basic emotions. Fleming's genius is choosing as his canvas the visceral realities of life among the officer corps in the U.S. Army as it reels from stalemate in Korea to abject defeat in Vietnam.

The subject is still too controversial, the emotions are still too raw and confused, to risk a reprise of the standard World War II combat novel. . . . Instead, Fleming wisely takes a more detached tone, building his story around three women as they grope to discharge their duties as officers' wives.

It all begins in time-honored style with three hopelessly miscast marriages as the Class of '50 graduates from West Point, or Woo Poo as it's known in Army jargon. Joanna, the brooding Catholic intellectual, marries Pete Burke, the stolid, dependable, unimaginative rock of the West Point defensive line. Amy, the ambitious socialite from Vassar, devotes her life to transforming George Rosser from an amiable cipher to a general. Honor, the beautiful, but vapid, southern belle mistakenly believes that brilliant, cynical Adam Thayer can become her Ashley Wilkes.

Aware that much of America has lost its instinctive sympathy for the Army officer corps, Fleming builds on many of our preconceptions about military life.

The Officers' Wives is not, however, a diatribe against the Army. Fleming carefully develops a tone of realistic ambivalence, one that balances honor and bravery against brutality and careerism. (p. 4)

Strangely enough, given the richness of the material, *The Officers' Wives* is sometimes slow going. Fleming follows the mechanical pattern of devoting alternate chapters to each of the three women, even though the cold-blooded Amy and the passive Honor are far too one-dimensional to sustain your interest.

Moreover, the writing, generally pedestrian, suffers Fleming's occasional aspirations to art. You wince at overwritten passages like, "Invariably, Pete's negative feelings crept into their bedroom, the place where almost all disguises fail and so many compromises collapse."

Much of the padding in this 645-page novel comes from Fleming's rather obvious attempts to create a documentary feel. There is the obligatory "Where were you when Kennedy was shot?" scene. Amy flies to Saigon for a clandestine weekend

with Adam just in time for the 1968 Tet offensive. In the early 1950s, Joanna reads the short stories in *Cosmopolitan* and finds them better than expected, especially one "by a writer named Kurt Vonnegut."

But these are quibbles. In the end, what produced my tears was Col. Pete Burke's sense of duty and personal honor. Fleeing from a failed marriage, he fights on in Vietnam, long after the war becomes hopeless, long after the smart officers like George Rosser have requested reassignment to Germany. Reading *The Officers' Wives* is an emotionally wrenching experience. Not because it is a great novel, but because it allows a spark of patriotism to emerge from the carnage in Vietnam. (pp. 4, 12)

> *Walter Shapiro, "Keeping the Home Fires Burning," in Book World—The Washington Post, March 29, 1981, pp. 4, 12.*

JANE LARKIN CRAIN

[*The Officers' Wives*], which spans the political and cultural history of America from the days of the Korean War to the aftermath of the Vietnam era, opens with the weddings of three graduating West Point cadets and their college sweethearts on a sunny day in June 1950.

In this sprawling tale of military life, the overlapping destinies of these six characters unfold. . . .

Orchestrating these histories, Mr. Fleming is attentive to both the dynamics of his characters' private lives and to the wider worlds in which they develop. He dissects the workings of class and careerism, brings in an array of fully realized supporting characters and captures vividly the ambiance of locales from Japan through Saigon to Washington, D.C.

Thomas Fleming, who can be ranked with Herman Wouk and James Jones, has written a satisfying novel that illuminates matters as diverse as the changing status of women, the ordeals and consolations of marriage, the permutations of religion—or any form of idealism—that arise in a rapidly changing culture and the bitter fallout from America's involvement in Vietnam. He probes the heart of the American experience over the last 30 years with subtlety and intelligence. He mourns the loss of a sometimes arrogant but undeniably heady American innocence, speculates on the promise of what endures and closes on a note of cautious affirmation.

> *Jane Larkin Crain, in a review of "The Officers' Wives," in The New York Times Book Review, April 12, 1981, p. 14.*

PUBLISHERS WEEKLY

Set in 1780, this well-crafted if somewhat protracted spy story [*Dreams of Glory*] opens as the burly British are about to seize Charleston. The bad guy here is Major Beckford, a homosexual who does everything he can to ensure British domination of the virgin America. The good guy is no less than the cherubic Calem Chandler, a humanitarian, abolitionist chaplain who embodies the sincere if naïve democratic spirit of the late-18th century. In between lies (literally) Flora Kuyper, a bitter spy-whore with a penchant for laudanum elixirs employed by the British to "entertain" Washington's guileless troops. What Flora's paymaster Beckford doesn't take into account, however, is Flora's obsession with her proud and brutal slave and lover, Caesar. When Caesar is murdered, Flora vows to avenge his death, and she spends the story seducing both British and

American soldiers in search of his killer. Fleming has used personal diaries, journals, letters, and memoirs to pull together this saga, which is sure to engage those who liked his *The Officers' Wives.*

> *A review of "Dreams of Glory," in* Publishers Weekly, *Vol. 223, No. 13, April 1, 1983, p. 57.*

LORALEE MacPIKE

[*Dreams of Glory*] is taken from actual diaries, journals, letters, and papers of the Stapleton family, one of whose members was a Congressman during the war. Fleming's historical background is accurate and evocative. The main focus of the intrigue is a British plot to capture George Washington just at the height of American disenchantment with a painful, bloody, and apparently ill-omened rebellion against the superior powers and the supercilious self-assurance of the British. . . . The attempted British abduction of Washington becomes a focal point for eddying loyalties and for an examination of beliefs about human nature, about honor, about love. The richness of incident and character which makes the book seem so true to our ideals of Revolutionary America, however, also makes it very difficult to keep the characters straight and to follow the overly complex action. (pp. 53-4)

> *Loralee MacPike, in a review of "Dreams of Glory," in* West Coast Review of Books, *Vol. 9, No. 5, September-October, 1983, pp. 53-4.*

PUBLISHERS WEEKLY

Widely admired for his histories, his biographies and his ability to blend history into convincing fiction, Fleming [in *The Spoils of War*] offers a historical novel as accomplished and compelling as his bestselling *Officers' Wives,* and richer in scope. The period covered is post-Civil War America, the focus of attention the impact of the war on the lives and consciousness of Northerners. . . . The story dramatically encompasses White House politicking, Wall Street power plays, trade union violence, nascent U.S. imperialism, spurred by the likes of William Randolph Hearst and Theodore Roosevelt, and the Spanish-American war. It does so, moreover, entirely through the loves and ambitions of some remarkably real-seeming people.

> *A review of "The Spoils of War," in* Publishers Weekly, *Vol. 227, No. 2, January 11, 1985, p. 67.*

KATHY PIEHL

Yellow journalism, the woman suffrage movement, labor strikes, and Wall Street panics fill the pages [of *The Spoils of War*]. Often these events (and the historical figures involved) swamp the personal relationships of the major characters and lessen our interest in them as individuals. Readers who like romance served with heavy doses of social and political history might enjoy this novel and its textbook lessons. (pp. 179-80)

> *Kathy Piehl, in a review of "The Spoils of War," in* Library Journal, *Vol. 110, No. 3, February 15, 1985, pp. 179-80.*

Ronald J. Glasser

1940?-

American nonfiction writer and novelist.

Glasser's works are based on his experiences as a doctor. In the late 1960s he was an officer in the Army Medical Corps stationed at the United States Evacuation Hospital at Camp Zama, Japan. Since his discharge in 1970 Glasser has practiced pediatric medicine in Minnesota. His best-known book, *365 Days* (1971), is a collection of sketches about the wounded American soldiers he met during the Vietnam war. Critics praise this work for its understated yet moving prose style and its brutally accurate description of the war. *Ward 402* (1973) centers on a young girl dying of leukemia and concerns the battle between her parents and doctors over her medical treatment. Glasser addresses the controversial issue of prolonging life by artificial methods and analyzes the effects of such circumstances on those involved. His next two books, *The Body Is the Hero* (1976) and *The Greatest Battle* (1976), are also nonfiction works. The first is a history of immunology beginning with the experiments of French scientist Louis Pasteur; the second is an exposition of Glasser's theories about the causes of cancer and the impediments to finding a cure. In his first novel, *Another War, Another Peace* (1985), Glasser again dramatizes the physical and emotional hardships of American soldiers serving in Vietnam. The narrative focuses on the relationship between a young Army doctor and an enlisted soldier and their reactions to the war and the Vietnamese people.

Time Magazine

THOMAS LASK

The last chapter of [*365 Days*], published separately as **"The Burn Ward,"** is already justly famous. The rest of the book deserves to be. It will be, too. Its quiet eloquence, its factual precision, its emotional restraint braided into the horror and pain of the subject matter make it a book of great emotional impact. The writings in this series of sketches of the war in Vietnam are virtually flawless. There isn't a false note, a soft center in any of them. Dr. Glasser's fluency comes not from any literary manipulations but from his commitment to what he is saying. . . . [He] never preaches. But that does not mean that he has no point of view. It's in what he is telling us.

The sketches, all true, incidentally, though they often have the shaping grace of fiction, are focused on the war in Indochina. But the theme is not that war. The war is the cause and excuse for the book, but the theme is the waste of war, the destruction of our American young. . . .

The book has the structure of a fugue and its two subjects are counterpointed as tightly as in a work of Bach. One is the enormous organization, effort and technical proficiency that go into saving a soldier's life. If the wounded get to Japan, the percentage of those saved is startlingly high: 98 per cent. The other is the equally great organization, effort and technical proficiency that go into making our soldiers killers. The sophistication of the weaponry, the daring with which they are used and the bravery of the Americans who use them are engrossingly described. On the one hand we have the sweeps, the patrols, the never-ending booby traps, the explosive fire-

fights, the supporting gunships, the artillery barrages—all in unbearable heat and jungle. On the other hand we have the selflessness of the medics, of the copter pilots who go in to take the men out, and the procedures that start as soon as the men are taken out. The killing and healing are joined by some logic somewhere, I know, but in more than one place in the book, they simply sound insane. . . .

Hovering over these chapters is the aimlessness of it all, of chance happenings and lack of design. Dr. Glasser cites few people with a strong commitment to the war. There is loyalty to the unit or to the group but not to ideology. But the soldiers are not neutral in their feelings for the Vietcong. They hate them, as they do most of the Vietnamese they encounter.

What we call atrocities are related in every chapter. They are born of frustration, of fear, of seeing comrades killed in beastly ways. And so, in animal-like reaction, the troopers strike back. After one bloody and merciless encounter, the helicopter pilots gathered the bodies of the enemy dead and dumped them in the path of the retreating Vietcong. On the other hand the decimation of the people of South Vietnam is one of the open sores of this brutal conflict.

He wrote the book, the author says, to fill in the record. He wanted to restore something to the kids that was free of doctrine and polemics. And he has done so. It's a book as nearly objective as one can be in a cause that has so divided the country.

Thomas Lask, "Vietnam: Children's Crusade," in The New York Times, *September 11, 1971, p. 25.*

MURRAY POLNER

Written in New Journalese, [*365 Days*] has a major shortcoming: its failure to reproduce authentic dialogue. The author never set foot in Vietnam yet he purports to relate, for example, the specific conversation between soldiers as they debate whether to kill an officer they hate. That flaw, however, is offset by the scenes in Army hospitals in Japan, where Glasser served as a major in the Medical Corps.

He has set out to relate simply and starkly what it meant to be a wounded and sometimes dying eighteen-, nineteen-, and twenty-year-old combat trooper. Except for the published reminiscences of the brave and loyal young men who have actually served in combat, not many better books on the horrors of war and its effect on individuals have yet appeared. (pp. 46-7)

In the final and best-written chapter, Glasser tells of David, a nineteen-year-old in a "burn ward." His body is charred, his temperature often hovers close to 106 degrees, and his days are marked by the only treatment available—the whirlpool which painfully tears off his dead skin so that new skin may perhaps grow. In the end, David, near death, pleads with his doctor (who accompanied his own brother's body back to the States): "I don't want to go home alone."

There are other memorable portraits. "Joan" is not a M*A*S*H nurse but a real woman. Overworked, filled with pity, but trying desperately to remain detached in order to survive emotionally, she permits herself an affair while on leave in Hong Kong, and is nearly killed in a rocket attack when she returns to Vietnam. A white infantryman awakens in a Zama, Japan, recovery room without his leg, and screams obscenities in his anguish. Black soldiers pass through the wards, and Glasser wonders about their special kind of meaningless sacrifice. . . .

Bitter, confused, feeling betrayed, longing to be home and whole again, the victims of this war are a special class—several million young men largely from the lower-middle and working classes who, lacking any alternatives, are compelled to serve. You have to "see the patients," writes Glasser, "broken and shattered at eighteen and nineteen. . . ." Kids. Fifty thousand of them now dead, and God knows how many crippled for life. *365 Days* is a graphic reminder of what this war is all about. (p. 47)

Murray Polner, in a review of "365 Days," in Saturday Review, *Vol. LIV, No. 37, September 11, 1971, pp. 46-7.*

PETER S. PRESCOTT

Glasser rarely succumbs to . . . emotion [in *365 Days*]. His is a peculiar book: the most convincing, most moving account I have yet read about what it is like to be an American soldier in Vietnam—and yet, it *is* peculiar. It is a collection of stories: true stories, Glasser tells us, and I don't doubt it, but Glasser has nonetheless made these true stories read as if they were fiction. They are told with the fiction writer's eye for organization, detail, impact and compression. All right. And it is all right, too, that he was in Japan and did not personally

observe many of these incidents, but has recreated what others have told him. . . .

The book is dedicated "to the memory of Stephen Crane" and you could drop a couple of Crane's war stories—"The Upturned Face," for instance—into this book and not even notice a ripple, so carefully does Glasser adhere to Crane's approach to war reporting. Still, these stories *are* romantic. Glasser wanted to "give something to these kids" and what he gives them is the dignity of battle, which, in this war, is debatable. . . .

I admire the details: about the way the Tet offensive began, with the killing of cooks and perimeter guards; about the varieties of booby traps; about the way Americans shoot a Vietnamese girl and then strip her, cutting off her nose and ears for the edification of the villagers. I admire particularly the pilot who says, "the gooks use greenish-blue tracers. I swear to God they're lovely coming up at you." I admire all this and everything else Glasser does in this fascinating book, but I am disturbed by it, too, not because of what it tells us about ourselves, which we are now coming to understand, but because it is, perhaps in spite of Glasser's intention, an invitation to a kind of military romanticism. For all the horror there is the subtle suggestion that because war can be exciting, heroes are heroes, even if what they do is unjust and appalling. (p. 102)

Peter S. Prescott, "The 'Dignity' of Battle," in Newsweek, *Vol. LXXVIII, No. 11, September 13, 1971, pp. 101-02.*

LOUIS SIMPSON

365 Days is dedicated to the memory of Stephen Crane, but the writing is closer to Hemingway, the laconic style of most Americans who write about war or, for that matter, personal relations. Americans are determinedly laconic, as though any extravagance in expressing feeling would loosen their grip on sanity. . . . A little of Stephen Crane's poetry would come as a relief. But, of course, the author does not aim to relieve. He wants to excoriate the reader and, like Wilfred Owen, make him feel the pity of war. Books such as this may indeed move us to pity, but their authors are mistaken if they think that this will change anything. Pity has never put a stop to war. A particular war, however, can be stopped by showing that it is absurd and taking political measures to stop it.

Glasser's concluding sketch, the portrait of a young man who is dying from burns, expresses all his pity. Just when the young man is beginning to want very much to live he feels himself beginning to die. He begins with hope, moves to sullen anger, and ends by pleading with the doctor to go with his coffin back to the States. Glasser speaks of the courage of the patients: I am glad that he speaks of it, for though the war has been abominable, and the United States will never again be a country that one can love with a whole heart, some of these young men have shown a great deal of courage. Not the least of the disasters of war is that it requires most of the human virtues. But, in this war, to what purpose? These Americans have been no less misguided than the British when they fought the Boers. They have been sustained only by pride in their companies, and when the war is over they will have nothing to show for it but their wounds. (pp. 735-36)

Louis Simpson, "Nothing to Show but Their Wounds," in The Listener, *Vol. 87, No. 2253, June 1, 1972, pp. 735-36.*

PETER S. PRESCOTT

[*Ward 402*] is like an otter: as Falstaff said of Mistress Quickly, it is neither fish nor flesh, and a man knows not where to have it. The publisher calls it alternatively Dr. Glasser's "new volume" and a "dramatic narrative," which means he will not say whether it is fact or fiction. Glasser clearly intends to claim the license of both modes. "Everything actually happened," he writes, but "the events did not all occur in the same sequence, or in the same hospital, or to the same people; some I witnessed, others I heard of."

It is an extraordinary disclaimer. For fiction it is superfluous; we expect novelists to rearrange reality. For nonfiction it won't do; we expect the writer, even within the amorphous confines of the "nonfiction novel," to assume responsibility for the integrity of the events he reports—which is to say that he may select, condense and emphasize at will, but he may not redistribute, without regard to time and space, facts and rumors of which he is aware; he may not in short create collages.

Despite its sins, *Ward 402* is good red herring. It *is* a "dramatic narrative"—intern stories, of which we have recently had many, usually are. The narrator of this one (Dr. Glasser, I presume?) is serving time on a children's ward in a huge, distinguished, anonymous research hospital. The schedule is grueling and interns, dulled by fatigue, become sloppy, even callous. The children are terribly ill: some are wasted by diarrhea or diabetes, others lack kidneys or the clotting factor that stops bleeding. For sheer melodramatic effect nothing beats a medical emergency—knives and needles, pumps and fumbling fingers plunged into bodies turning black and purple, lungs filling with water—"This is what it's all about," the intern thinks. With children it is worse; we rarely imagine children in desperate pain. We know intellectually that a certain number of children must die—it is the only way to run a universe—but why not snuff them out at birth? Why wait for them to develop as individuals and then torture them? Glasser does not explore the question, that is not a doctor's business, but he exploits the poignancy of the situation.

To this age-old drama he adds a new one, the drama of technology. . . .

Still this is a book specifically about human concern. It is a book with a thesis. Doctors, Glasser says, are so trained to believe in the miracle of medicine that they act as if they were gods interpreting disease to man; they no longer talk to patients and their relatives as if they were human beings with human anxieties and needs. To illustrate his point, Glasser presents to his intern an 11-year-old girl dying of leukemia. The girl's father claims some knowledge of hospital procedures and insists that his daughter only be made comfortable until she dies. The intern rebels, of course: the child must be put on a protocol of drugs designed to obtain a remission that may, just possibly, last long enough for a cure to develop. To keep the child alive becomes a grisly business. . . . The intern pulls the plug on the child's life-sustaining machine when he has learned his lesson in humanity.

Except—except that the issues are never joined. The angry father is not simply a man who needs to be understood; he needs to be arrested. Pulling the plug on a terminal patient may be commendable, but it prompts more complex ethical reactions than a simple awareness of maturity and competence. Nor does Glasser really explore the questions attending the use of a protocol of drugs designed to serve better the needs of leukemia researchers than the child whose life depends upon it.

Two years ago in a book called *365 Days*, Glasser gave us a sequence of stories about American soldiers in combat in Vietnam. It worked better than this one does. Glasser knew no more about combat in Vietnam than he could deduce from service in a hospital in Japan. Yet his stories, equally as invented, equally as true as this one, worked in part because so little that seemed authentic had been written about soldiers in that war, in part because Glasser refrained from moralizing, and in part because combat stories are as old as story-telling itself. Here we have one story, and it is certainly readable. But it fails as fiction because its author is unequal to the moral situations he creates and because his characters have been plucked from the common reservoir of stereotypes maintained by novelists of tertiary talent. It fails as nonfiction because the author refuses to vouch for the accuracy of its design, the relatedness of the events he puts before us.

Peter S. Prescott, "Doctors as Gods," in The New Republic, *Vol. 169, Nos. 7 & 8, August 18 & 25, 1973, p. 23.*

TOM BUCKLEY

[In *Ward 402* an] 11-year-old girl, . . . suffering from advanced leukemia, . . . is brought by her parents to a great teaching and research hospital, not for treatment but to die as quickly and painlessly as possible. . . .

[Her father] knows that the disease is invariably fatal, a bit of information that came as a surprise to me, and that remissions, when they occur, are apt to be brief and are gained at the price of considerable pain. To spare his daughter this, he has permitted her to waste away at home in the months since the original diagnosis.

His timing has been so good that she is practically dead when she is brought to the hospital . . ., when, in what seems a plot convenience, only the gallant pediatrics resident and the bumptious interne, who tells the story, are on duty. They begin a heroic effort to save the child's life, thereby angering not only her father but also the head of their department, who in the interests of a vast research project he heads has established rigid guidelines for the treatment of the disease.

Within a month, the child is dead, having suffered a horrifying series of complications, described in gruesome detail. The interne, who betrays his inexperience by involving himself emotionally with the child, wonders, "Had we performed a miracle or taken part in a disaster?"

These conflicts provide the basis for an examination of several social and ethical problems of medicine: Whether a terminally ill patient should be kept alive by heroic measures, whether doctors are treating the disease and ignoring the patient and his or her family, to what extent the requirements of research can coexist with those of treatment, and to what extent the medical profession has failed to police itself.

Dr. Glasser, who was widely praised for his previous work, *365 Days*, . . . has taken a different, and it seems to me, much less successful approach in *Ward 402*.

He has . . . attempted a work of fiction. As such, it does not meet even the debased standard of that craft's flourishing medical subdivision. . . .

[As] the author seems to be arguing for greater communication between physicians and laymen, he clouds his writing by unexplained technicalities and jargon.

Next to the girl's father, who should have been persuaded to enter the hospital's psychiatric division for an extended stay or, failing that, should have been prosecuted for child abuse, the narrator, at least for me, emerges as the most disagreeable character in the book. His ego spreads through its pages like a leaking bedpan. . . .

Indeed, the only time *Ward 402* rises above its emergency-room sensationalism and becomes quietly persuasive is when the proverbially remote and autocratic chief of the department is speaking:

"'What we would like to do,'" he tells the girl's father, "'if you agree, is to use a special protocol of medications for your daughter, where dosages and time of treatment have already been established.'". . .

"'But in the end, she'll die anyway, Right?'

"'Yes, she will die anyway.'"

> Tom Buckley, "The Pathology of Pain," in The New York Times, *September 8, 1973, p. 29.*

HARRY SCHWARTZ

Dr. Ronald J. Glasser's two previous books, *365 Days* and *Ward 402,* quickly and deservedly established him as one of the leading contemporary physician-writers. His ability to move his readers emotionally while accurately describing the front lines, where doctors and very sick people come together, won him a large audience. But [*The Body Is the Hero*] is a rather different kind of book.

The Body Is the Hero is essentially a history of immunology. . . . In his polished prose Dr. Glasser tells also the grim story of what happens when the immune system goes berserk and seeks to destroy the body of which it is part, or when, as in transplant rejection, it frustrates the most ingenious efforts of modern medicine to cure kidney or heart disease.

If any college is thinking of giving a course on Biology for Poets—in which general concepts and leading ideas are all, and grimy details are of no interest—this would be an ideal textbook. But readers for whom prose poems are not enough, who want to understand the intricacies of the immunological system and would find a diagram or two of great help, will most likely be confused and annoyed by this book.

> Harry Schwartz, in a review of "The Body Is the Hero," in Saturday Review, *Vol. 3, No. 15, May 1, 1976, p. 36.*

JUNE GOODFIELD

[Most] of the cancers of Western society, some 75-80 per cent it is estimated, appear to be self-inflicted and . . . we could eliminate them if we chose. . . .

This is the theme of *The Greatest Battle,* the fourth book to flow from the fluent pen of Ronald Glasser. . . . Almost the most forceful sentence in the book is the very first, in the preface, when he reveals that "During the Christmas holidays last year, of the twenty-three children admitted to the largest pediatric ward of the University of Minnesota Hospitals in a single day, eighteen had cancer." It is a shocking statistic; one which, as a society, we are still far too complacent about, and as the author goes on to insist, it is not as if we were ignorant of this situation. We know the facts and we know the remedies, but the mixture of vested interests, fatalism and indifference will no doubt ensure that this situation improves slowly, if at all.

Glasser takes us easily through the basic facts of cancer, in fine detail but with the ease of explanation that we have come to expect of him. So we come quickly to see how and why the chemicals that are poisoning our atmosphere are equally playing havoc with our bodies. (p. K3)

Chapter after chapter the evidence relentlessly piles up from nicotine, to thalidomide to Red Dye 2. There are plenty of horror stories and sometimes he is kinder than he should be. One chapter tells how in Chicago 70,000 children were affected by twin errors of "medical judgment" and "medical prudence." After World War II, X-rays became a routine treatment and irradiation of infants and children was standard procedure. It was observed that children when young were susceptible to colds and upper respiratory infections but gradually grew out of them—any grandmother could tell you that. But this coincided—it was also observed—with the shrinking of the thymus gland. These two facts are in fact related, for when an infant has its full complement of immune protective bodies the gland shrinks away, its job done. But when it was realized that X-rays could shrink the thymus artificially someone made the erroneous deduction that this would reduce the incidence of colds and at the touch of a button there was a cure for demanding parents and fussy babies. Without any proof of efficacy whatever, high energy beams were directed into babies' chests, not only onto the thymus but tonsils and adenoids. So these children were deprived of a gland vital for their proper immune function, and so have grown up with a variety of immune deficient diseases. But worse, the X-rays later generated cancer in other places, like the thyroid gland.

Some 15 to 20 years later, as they always do in cancer, the chickens came home to roost. In 1970 a definitive paper appeared which showed that 15 per cent of all adults who had developed thyroid cancers between 1946 and 1968 had been given X-ray treatment to the chest in their earlier years. What was really ominous was the malignant state of these tumors. Glasser calls this story a "medical error," surely an understatement in view of the fact that the damaging effects of radiation had been known for years before!

The publishers claim that this book may well have the stunning impact of Rachel Carson's *Silent Spring.* I wish this were true but I doubt it. For one thing Rachel Carson had the advantage that she was telling us something not only shocking but new. Glasser is telling us something shocking, but we have known about this for some time. Next, Carson has a wonderfully evocative and forceful way with words, and fluent writer though Glasser may be, he is no match for her as a stylist. Even more important, he evades an issue that Rachel Carson did not evade. To be fair to Glasser it is an issue that almost everyone is evading, so far as environmental cancers are concerned. For it is no longer a medical problem, so much as an ethical and political one, in which personal and governmental ethics are involved.

What is needed is not more exposure but practical action even if vested interests are involved, the kind of practical action that Rachel Carson initiated and inspired. If Glasser from his popular position could mobilize people and politicians and industry too—or if he could mobilize Ralph Nader—then maybe some impact could be made. (pp. K3, K5)

June Goodfield, in a review of "The Greatest Battle," in Book World—The Washington Post, *January 9, 1977, pp. K3, K5.*

PUBLISHERS WEEKLY

From the acclaimed author of **365 Days** comes [**Another War, Another Peace**] a poignant story of one man's passage from ignorance to cynicism in the Vietnam War. David, a self-assured doctor, has opted for a year of duty in Vietnam instead of two more in the U.S. Assigned to a remote base, he is given the nebulous duty of traveling to the surrounding villages every day to dole out free vitamins and pills to the natives. His driver, an enlisted man named Tom, is the antithesis to David's scholarly naiveté. Tom is young but tuned into the toughest intricacies of the war. As the two men make their rounds to the villages on the distant outskirts of the base, they begin to learn that the terror of the war is closer to them than they ever imagined. Just as they have broken down the barrier between officer and soldier and effected a closer relationship, they meet disaster head on. . . . David is soon overwhelmed by the devastating horror of the Tet offensive, and the book ends with the ring of real experience. Sharply focused and painfully truthful, the novel is a chapter of the war that illuminates the entire saga.

A review of "Another War, Another Peace," in Publishers Weekly, *Vol. 227, No. 7, February 15, 1985, p. 89.*

JOE KLEIN

[**365 Days**] was remarkable for its clarity, compassion and intelligence, and it is rightfully considered one of the early classics of Vietnam literature. The same compassion and intelligence are present in **Another War, Another Peace,** but the story is too contrived and preachy to be entirely convincing. Dr. Glasser is at his best when David and Corporal Griffen are out in the countryside treating the Vietnamese, who "seemed to have no weight to them, no substance; they were like creatures from a lighter planet." His ability to explain medical procedures is evident here, but he also creates a living, breathing, recognizable and quirky character in Griffen. The other characters—doctors, back at the base—tend to be cardboard blowhards who say things about the war, pro and con, that have already been said far too many times. Even David, apparently Dr. Glasser's alter ego, is too naïve at the novel's beginning and too knowing at the end to be very affecting.

Still, Dr. Glasser has a wonderful eye for detail. His descriptions of heat, pain and the confusion of an ambush—the staples of any war novel—are often perceptive.

Joe Klein, "Soldiers and Doctors," in The New York Times Book Review, *April 21, 1985, p. 26.*

TIMOTHY S. DYSON

[**Another War, Another Peace**] presents many of the elements necessary for quality fiction. It utilizes terse, authentic dialogue. The geography is alive with detail. The central figure, David, is able to gain our interest and evoke our sympathy. The plot follows maturation's ancient path: innocence / disillusionment / realization. Terror, fear, absolute emptiness—all these powerful emotions are skillfully etched into the reader's unconsciousness. Then, what's missing? Power: True intensity is lacking. Not due to a narrative flaw but to a lens that has already flooded our senses with the very images Glasser presents. We've already seen emaciated, displaced Vietnamese villagers. We've already seen blood-spattered troops get med evac'd out of an LZ. We've heard too many experts talk about a lack of strategy and combat fatigue. Mr. Glasser's trying to surf in a tidal wave.

Luckily, he's a pretty good surfer! He is able to dissect the war into a few key instants of real raw energy. . . . We witness the utter futility of war when a trooper, surrounded by skilled surgeons and modern equipment, dies on the operating table. We hear the eerie quiet that engulfs a man who knows "it ended before either of us got here."

The only problem I encountered with this book was one of staging. . . . We go out on endless and uneventful med cap patrols. We view the nuts and bolts of daily Army medical life. We meet supporting cast members who do not have much input. This effort to portray the war's aura saps some of the strength out of the book's impact. Only in the last third of the novel do we get the moments of real energy.

It is to Glasser's credit that this book gives us a unique glimpse into the most watched war in history. He is a skilled author. His ability to give us true insight into the Vietnam conflict is testimony to his skill. (pp. 125-26)

Timothy S. Dyson, in a review of "Another War, Another Peace," in Best Sellers, *Vol. 45, No. 4, July, 1985, pp. 125-26.*

Graham (Henry) Greene

1904-

English novelist, short story writer, dramatist, travel writer, memoirist, author of books for children, journalist, critic, essayist, scriptwriter, and editor.

A widely acclaimed and popular author throughout his long career, Greene is best known for his novels, most of which pursue his obsession with the darker side of human nature within the contexts of spy thrillers or adventure stories. These novels are considered suspenseful and entertaining, and they quickly move the reader into the physical and moral conflicts of the stories. Greene is described by many critics as a Catholic writer: the human struggle between faith and doubt and the despair and alienation of modern humanity are constant themes in his work. Despite such religious elements, Greene contends that he is an intellectual nonconformist, and he rejects systematic adherence to formal precepts of religion.

World travel has been an integral part of Greene's life. His impressions and experiences during these trips are recorded in his nonfiction and contribute to the authenticity of detail and setting in his novels. His journey to Mexico in 1938, for example, is documented in *The Lawless Roads: A Mexican Journey* (1939) and provides the setting of his best-known novel, *The Power and the Glory* (1940). His trips to Africa resulted in the travelogues *Journey without Maps* (1936) and *In Search of a Character: Two African Journals* (1961) and the novels *The Heart of the Matter* (1948) and *A Burnt-Out Case* (1961). *Getting to Know the General: The Story of an Involvement* (1984) is set in Panama and chronicles Greene's association with the late General Omar Torrijos Herrera. This memoir extends beyond a portrait of the leader to a commentary on the turbulent political conditions in Central America.

Greene's early novels are dominated by religious themes and are considered his finest work. *Brighton Rock* (1938), *The Power and the Glory,* and *The Heart of the Matter,* which received the James Tait Black Memorial Prize, explore the gray moral area between right and wrong and examine the relationship between sin and redemption. *The Power and the Glory* is representative of Greene's treatment of character and theme. In this novel, thematic concerns are worked out more through characterization than through plot. In his story of the persecution of a priest by a police lieutenant, Greene pits political and secular conventions against spiritual and religious beliefs. The priest, like the police lieutenant, is a complex character capable of both good and evil acts. For Greene, the sinner is often a saint, while the idealist is dangerous.

In addition to his Catholic novels, Greene has written comedies and spy fiction, which he catalogues as "entertainments." *Our Man in Havana* (1958) is set in Cuba months before Fidel Castro's revolution. The novel satirizes the British Secret Service working in Cuba and the corruption of the pre-revolutionary regime. *Travels with My Aunt* (1969) details the madcap adventures of an eccentric older woman introducing her conventional nephew to the wild and carefree side of life. *The Human Factor* (1978) concerns a British double agent who attempts to aid black South Africans by leaking information

Photograph by Figaro/Gamma-Liaison

to the Soviet Union. This novel displays the complexity of character that marks all of Greene's work.

The publication of *The Tenth Man* (1985) constituted a significant literary event. Originally written as a screenplay in 1944, the manuscript was shelved and forgotten until its discovery in 1983. Like many of Greene's Catholic novels, *The Tenth Man* examines the protagonist's conscience after a single act of cowardice and exemplifies the moral dilemmas inherent in Greene's best works. In praise of the novel, John Carey stated that "the 40-year eclipse of *The Tenth Man* is just a by-product of the dark processes that have generated some of the most compelling fiction of our age."

(See also *CLC*, Vols. 1, 3, 6, 9, 14, 18, 27; *Contemporary Authors*, Vols. 13-16, rev. ed.; *Something about the Author*, Vol. 20; and *Dictionary of Literary Biography*, Vols. 13, 15.)

JOHN SPURLING

[Jorge Luis Borges, Anthony Powell, Vladimir Nabokov, Samuel Beckett, and Graham Greene] are all writers born around the turn of the century, all romantics with sheltered childhoods who have had to face up to the twentieth-century failure of the Victorian world-order and the questioning of its values in both public and private terms. Borges and Powell, by their different techniques for neutralizing themselves, have evolved into classicists; Nabokov, driven out of his own country by the revolution, turned Russia into a fairy-tale landscape for ever out of reach and therefore for ever potent as a romantic standard by which to judge his characters' and the world's inadequacy; Beckett, like Greene a rebel against the world that sheltered him and a voluntary exile, retreated into the cave of himself. Only Greene has tried to retain the romantic forms of the old world—including the romantic protagonist and the romantic self within the protagonist—and to use them as the direct expression of a reality which conflicts with the original content of the forms. If it is a bold solution, it is also rather naïve. If it makes things easy for the conservative reader and plays a part in Greene's enormous popularity, it raises increasing problems of credibility as the novels get older and are more objectively analysed.

Romanticism and reality will seem to square with one another only as long as the particular brand of romanticism is shared by the author and his or her public. Once that becomes suspect, or even ludicrous, the work loses its current value and drops away into the past, to be remembered, if at all, only as a forerunner, a historical phenomenon, a book for children or the basis for adaptations to another medium. Some of the work of Buchan, Hope and Haggard, for example—Greene's second-division masters—will survive in this way, in spite of the now embarrassingly 'period' attitudes it enshrines. Clearly Greene's rather too schematic reaction against those attitudes—his substitution in the make-up of his protagonists of weakness, corruption, disloyalty and uncertainty for the strength, integrity, loyalty and self-confidence that characterize Buchan's and Haggard's imperialist heroes—will date in its turn, though for the present it is still sufficiently widely shared by readers and imitated by younger writers to appear normal and therefore realistic. The question is how much will remain when the attitudes have lost their savour. Three things, I suggest, which are perhaps only three aspects of the same thing, guarantee Greene's staying-power.

The first is that behind the attitudes—the authorial *pensées,* the preaching of Javitt and others, the forced similes—Greene does explore real pain and unhappiness and not always solely in his protagonists. The pain is felt through his protagonists, but it is often drawn off the subsidiary characters, the protagonists acting as a kind of central conduit for whatever *Angst* or suffering is around, much in the way that a priest does or is supposed to do. In this sense, one can say that Greene's fiction has a genuine religious dimension, not to be confused with that melodramatic backdrop of good and evil which he used as a way of raising the stakes and laying on the colours.

I am not certain whether Greene himself is fully conscious of this active core in his work—if he were, I suspect he would have formulated it more obviously into a *pensée* or a sermon—but it accounts not only for the powerful effect some of his books have had on those in need of spiritual comfort but also for the ordinary reader's feeling that, for all the mud that can be thrown at the rhetorical style, the over-controlled plots, the morality-play characters and the artificial theology, these are not negligible fictions. Why does the whisky priest in *The Power and the Glory* turn back into danger and sacrifice his life in order to hear a criminal's confession, why is it so appalling that Scobie can't make his confession, why does Fowler in *The Quiet American* wish that there was someone to whom he could say he was sorry for causing Pyle's death? These are not just Catholic quibbles. Even the irreligious Brown wonders

whether the happiest moment he and his mistress ever knew was not the time when they trusted each other with mutual self-revelations instead of caresses.

The act of confession, in itself and regardless of its ritual orthodoxy—the sharing of one's pain with someone else—is a movement towards 'the city called Peace of Mind', just as the schoolboy Greene was pulled back from despair by his visit to the psychoanalyst. Yet Scobie and Castle can approach that city only by complete withdrawal into themselves. The tension set up between these two incompatible kinds of happiness— or at least temporary alleviations of unhappiness—is at the heart of *The Heart of the Matter,* as of all Greene's best work. Indeed, it is there in most of his work in some form; only that in the novels which are most likely to outlast the decay of their overt attitudes—*The Heart of the Matter, The Power and the Glory, The Quiet American, The Comedians*—it is tauter and more deeply lodged in the story.

The second thing that makes Greene more than a temporary phenomenon is, paradoxically, what is most contemporary about him: his settings and situations. In spite of its distortions, Greeneland is real. No European writer since Conrad has put the hot, poor and foully governed places of the earth on paper as vividly as Greene. This is not to say that he has described them as they are, from the point of view of God or even of their inhabitants, but as they appeared and smelt and felt and tasted to the European visitor in the middle decades of the twentieth century. Nor are these simply heightened descriptions—or a good travel writer or journalist might have done them as well—but, like Conrad's, they are moral landscapes, characterizations of what is there and of whom it is experienced by. In other words, they contain to a remarkable degree the history and politics of both parties to the encounter. The political part of Greene's plots is fairly standard and even banal— inevitably so, since tyrants, spies, corruption and oppression are hardly newer than human society—but, just as the spiritual element is to be found not in his well-publicized Catholic backdrop but buried deep in his protagonists, so the true political element is intrinsic to his settings and forms a kind of parallel to the spiritual element, for it too involves the tension between apartness and collusion.

The European is safe and in control of himself so long as he keeps the place at arm's length, but the place offers him—and surely it's the reason he came there—loss of control, a temporary unburdening, the opportunity to give and receive. Scobie gives way and then regains control, Querry holds on to himself and then gives way, Brown's is a long process of slipping into collusion with the place, Fowler thrashes to and fro. And of course the fact that, since the days of Conrad, the Europeans have resigned their empires to the United States makes collusion easier for Greene's characters than it was for Conrad's, whose apartness was supported and indeed demanded by a whole society and its patriarchal ethos. From Scobie, who still inhabits a largely Conradian tropic, to Brown and Plarr in their especially squalid pockets of the new American hegemony, Greeneland documents and mythologizes this transitional phase of history, providing the equivalent to Dickens's early industrial London, say, or Chekhov's pre-revolutionary Russia. In so far as the subsidiary characters in Greene's novels have an existence independent of the protagonists, it is as emanations of their political landscapes. To read Greene's novels is to be haunted ever afterwards by places and times with human features or humans who are half made up of places and times. The dentist and the half-caste in *The Power and the*

Glory are the ghosts of pre-war Mexico; the two young guards in the roadside watchtower in *The Quiet American* are Vietnam in the last days of the French; Rycker and Deo Gratias in *A Burnt-Out Case* are the Congo when it was still Belgian, and so on.

The third thing takes us back to the *pensée*. . . . In a generation or two, if it doesn't already, this kind of detachable sentiment, which can be put into the mouth of any protagonist, will sound as quaint as some of Richard Hannay's sentiments. But in that the protagonists' self-examinations, however slickly expressed, reflect those of a man who could never forgive or forget the process of growing up, they will continue to have meaning: not just for students of the particular author Graham Greene, but for any reader trapped in that narrow but sometimes lifelong defile leading from dependence and immaturity to responsibility for one's own actions and the happiness of others. It is one of the central themes of literature, especially of English literature, and although it may have been handled with broader sympathy and deeper understanding by the greatest writers—including Greene's own first-division masters, James and Conrad—it has never been done with more intimate passion than by Greene. (pp. 71-5)

> *John Spurling, in his* Graham Greene, *Methuen, 1983, 80 p.*

PATRICK MARNHAM

In the winter of 1976, Graham Greene, who was living in Antibes, received a mystifying telegram from Panama which was signed by a stranger. It stated that General Omar Torrijos Herrera, the head of state, had invited him to Panama and that an air ticket was at his disposal. Mr. Greene recognised the outlines of an adventure. He flew to Panama but, when he arrived, there was no sign of the man who had signed the telegram. There was a car to meet him, however, and on the following day he was taken to see the General. Their first conversation seems to have been mutually baffling. The General, who spoke no English, wanted to know why Mr. Greene had spent so much of his life in the Caribbean. Greene, who speaks little Spanish, communicated with the aid of an interpreter, a sergeant in the General's bodyguard known as 'Chuchu'. This sergeant spoke English, French, Italian and German, and had once been a professor of Marxist philosophy; he first introduced himself to Mr. Greene in the guise of a chauffeur. Chuchu and Greene became close friends, and it is Sergeant Chuchu who is the real hero of [*Getting to Know the General*].

Over the next five years, until General Torrijos died in a plane crash, Greene revisited Panama again and again, always at the General's rather baffling invitation (it is never suggested, for instance, that General Torrijos had read any of the author's books.) But Greene came to love this leader, who was unorthodox enough to suggest once that he send a hit-man to Antibes to sort out the local gangsters. At first, Mr. Greene travelled to Panama with the intention of writing a novel based on his experiences, but that project never took off. 'I was trying mistakenly to use real characters', he explains, 'the General, Chuchu . . . They had emerged from life and not from the unconscious and for that reason they stood motionless like statues in my mind—they couldn't develop, they were incapable of the unexpected word or action—they were real people and they could have no life independent of me in the imagination.'

Deprived of a novel, he has written instead this loosely structured account of some fairly disorganised journeys. In the company of Chuchu, life took on an increasingly picaresque guise. Much time was spent in search of the perfect rum punch, or in pursuit of some girl who had caught the eye of either the General or Chuchu. (p. 25)

Greene describes Torrijos as a democrat who wanted a country which was socialist but not Marxist, and who dreamt of a Central America which would be independent but no threat to the United States. He says that Torrijos signed a treaty which gave Panama less than he wanted, because he knew how close to violence his people were, and he wanted to save them from it. If the US Senate had refused to ratify the treaty, Torrijos would have been left 'with the simple solution of violence which had often been in his mind, with desire and apprehension balanced as in a sexual encounter'.

But *Getting to Know the General* is not simply about Panama, it is about Central America, and that means it is about El Salvador and Nicaragua. In view of Greene's approval for Torrijos's social democratic ideas, the author's almost unqualified enthusiasm for the Sandinista regime in Nicaragua is surprising. The chief plank in Greene's current politics seems to be his opposition to the military, economic and cultural domination of the United States, but that—as he has himself pointed out so frequently—does not mean that its opposite, in this case authoritarian Communism, must be supported. Yet it is towards that sort of Communism that such influential members of the Sandinista junta as Comandante Tomas Borge are drawn. Mr Greene is well aware of the self-conscious posturing of some of the priests who defy Rome in order to support the junta. But he also ascribes the opposition of the Archbishop of Managua to 'wounded vanity' in losing his weekly television spot. This is an inadequate explanation, as is confirmed by the recent decision of the senior archbishops in Costa Rica, Honduras, Guatemala and El Salvador to sign a statement saying that the Catholic church in Nicaragua is being persecuted. Greene, however, at this stage in his long quarrel with Catholic orthodoxy, is apparently happy to see the conservative side of his church suffer a little persecution, and is equally happy that men such as Tomas Borge should overrule the Archbishop of Managua in deciding which Mass should be televised in Nicaragua. He sees no danger of an atheist triumph over Christianity here. As he says in this book, 'If one takes a side, one takes a side, come what may'. Until perhaps one changes the side one takes, as a re-reading of *The Lawless Roads* might suggest.

Somewhere Mr Greene has written that a writer should be careful of where he travels in peacetime, since he may be sent back there in time of war. Perhaps a novelist should also be careful of the situations in which he places his characters; for it was surely more than coincidence that the author of *The Honorary Consul* should have been chosen as an intermediary in a real kidnapping case. In 1980, Mr Greene, by then thoroughly involved in Latin American politics, was approached by the South African foreign service to assist in the release of the South African ambassador to El Salvador who had been kidnapped by the guerrillas. Despite his determined efforts, he failed to persuade the guerrilla leader, Salvador Cayetano, to have mercy on his hostage. The ambassador eventually died in captivity. The man responsible for his death was undoubtedly Cayetano. That, too, is surprising in a writer who had depicted the plight of the political hostage with such memorably imaginative understanding. And perhaps that, too,—that narrowing of sympathy—is part of the price of 'taking sides'. (pp. 25-6)

Getting to Know the General is an absorbing account of an unexpected adventure; the story of one more stroke of luck or genius which has characterised a life punctuated by the apt choice of people and regions about to become topical. It is an essential addition to the fragmented autobiography of *A Sort of Life* and *Ways of Escape*. It is also a moving record of the 'dead man whom I loved', Omar Torrijos, who may or may not have been assassinated in 1981. As for what on earth Mr Greene was doing out there, my own theory is that it was not Torrijos who devised it all but Chuchu—Chuchu, who did read English and who was familiar with the work of this gringo author. But if Mr Greene had originally received a summons to Panama from a 'Sergeant Chuchu', would he have gone? That first telegram must have been one of the Sergeant's more ingenious jokes; and *Getting to Know the General* is a record of its many delightful consequences. (p. 26)

Patrick Marnham, ''Sergeant Chuchu's Guest,'' in The Spectator, *Vol. 253, No. 8151, September 29, 1984, pp. 25-6.*

JOHN SPURLING

Getting to Know the General is subtitled 'The Story of an Involvement', but the trouble is that . . . [it] lacks a plot. There is the signing of the Canal Treaty in Washington, which Greene attended as a Panamanian delegate; there is the civil war in Nicaragua bubbling off-stage . . . ; there is a solid and humorously conceived second character, in the shape of Torrijos' most faithful aide, known as Chuchu, a poet and ex-professor of Marxist philosophy; and there are a few shadowy figures such as ex-president Arias, 'Senor V.' and the President's Chief of Staff, Colonel Flores, who look ready to play the parts of Black Michael and Rupert of Hentzau. But nothing really happens on stage and we end up with a rather scrappy travelogue, intermittently enlivened with episodes of discomfort and misunderstanding which miss becoming farce because they too, like the incipient adventure story, lack a plot. . . .

Such desultory experiences, of course, are the stuff of life and, used as telling details, of lifelikeness in a novel, but they are of little use to a romancer of Greene's type unless he can thread them on to a strong story-line. He tried and failed to do so in an abortive novel called *On the Way Back,* then settled for this memoir when he heard the news of Torrijos' sudden death.

Greene is justly famed for his atmospheric settings, but he has never been a very careful observer of human behaviour. The minor characters in his novels are rapid, serviceable sketches, contributions both to the atmosphere and to the swiftly running plot; his major ones are usually self-projections. Very little of Torrijos emerges beyond his boyish charm and enthusiasm and Greene's great admiration for him; indeed one hardly learns more about him from the book than is already conveyed by Bernard Diederich's photo on the dustjacket of old-timer Greene and young cowpuncher Torrijos (actually in his forties) smiling shyly at each other across a table under a palm tree. (p. 32)

John Spurling, ''Panamania,'' in New Statesman, *Vol. 108, No. 2794, October 5, 1984, pp. 31-2.*

CHRISTOPHER DICKEY

In Vietnam the Pentagon counted bodies as a measure of victory. In El Salvador in 1980 and 1981 the State Department began counting them as a measure of defeat. . . . But columns of numbers do nothing to make sense of a world where the bullet-shattered bodies of peasants and students become as common on some roads as the corpses of hapless animals. To decipher such madness you search for consolation in the voices of experience and art; you read, for instance, Gabriel García Márquez. . . .

And you read Graham Greene. It is Greene who knows about the protocol of suffering, the elite's traditional notion that the physical side of political persecution is reserved for the poor; in his words, for "the torturable class." It is Greene who evokes countries where cruelty sweeps over the land like a searchlight. It is Greene who explores the oppression and ecstasy of Catholicism; Greene whose "whisky priests" turn up in garrison towns along the front lines of war, full of faith and Scotch on the edge of death.

Greene's *The Quiet American,* published in 1955 about Vietnam, is especially good to read in Central America. It deals with Washington's persistent notion that a political center, a Third Force, can be found—or manufactured out of whole cloth—in the midst of a war and in the face of much-needed revolution. It is about the arrogance of American moral and political certainty and the danger of American innocence. . . .

Now Greene, 80 years old, has written [*Getting to Know the General*], his own new book about Central America. It is not a novel but a memoir, a "tribute to a man whom . . . I had grown to love." Greene calls it "the story of an involvement" with the late General Omar Torrijos, the hard-drinking, hard-bargaining dictator of Panama. But it is also a quiet essay on the intrigue, the emotions, and the personal dangers of leading revolutions in America's backyard. (p. 26)

A dangerous enemy, Torrijos was, for Greene, a wonderful friend. But love and friendship foster loyalties and responsibilities so intense they can be self-destructive. That was the great theme of *The Human Factor,* one of Greene's best recent books and it is the great flaw, I think, in this one. Greene is vulnerable to "the Friends of my Friend, Omar Torrijos, in Nicaragua, El Salvador, and Panama," to whom he dedicates this book. Torrijos understood these people in ways that Greene either does not or will not admit to, and Greene's tone in dealing with such characters as Carpio or Borge is tentative and uncertain. You sense his puzzlement at the way some of them have behaved since Torrijos's death, and he finds himself making repeated excuses for them. . . .

Of the Central Americans Greene encounters outside of Panama, in fact, only Edén Pastora's is a really credible portrait. Pastora was virtually a disciple of Torrijos and, indeed, when Pastora made his decision to leave Nicaragua in 1981, he went to Panama to consult with the General. He was there when the General died. But Greene does not appear to have known Pastora well. He is not a friend of his. Paradoxically, Greene's picture of him is much the better for that. (p. 28)

[The book's] emotions, the economy of style, and, I would say, the politics are exactly right. One wishes that Greene were writing a novel about Pastora, or indeed about Torrijos the romantic revolutionary, "bored and haunted by his public image," or about Chuchu Martinez. . . . Greene, too, wished he could find the novel hidden in this material. He gives us its title, tells us its outline, even quotes a sharp little passage from it. But the characters, he tells us, never quite took on their own life in fiction and he could not find his way clear to write it. So we are left with *Getting To Know The General,* and it seems to be here by default. This is a disappointment; it is not Greene at his best and he seems to know it. But it is Greene, nonetheless, and as election-oriented discussions of Central America steadily slide away from the reality of experience there toward the comfortable abstractions of statistics and centers-between-the-extremes and Third Forces created mainly for American consumption, it is good to hear Greene's voice again. (p. 29)

Christopher Dickey, "J'Adore," in The New Republic, *Vol. 191, No. 16, October 15, 1984, pp. 26-9.*

CHRISTOPHER LEHMANN-HAUPT

[*The Tenth Man* is a] very readable novella indeed. Jean-Louis Chavel, a wealthy Parisian lawyer, is among 30 prisoners being held in a Gestapo prison in occupied France. Their German captors announce that three of them must be executed; it doesn't matter who. The prisoners draw lots. Chavel is one of the losers. In a panic, he offers to give his fortune to anyone who will take his place. Another prisoner named Janvier Mangeot steps forward, ready to die for his family's security. The trade is made.

After the war, Chavel, conscience-stricken, poor and unable to find work, shows up at his family's old provincial estate, now occupied by Janvier Mangeot's mother and sister. Introducing himself as Jean-Louis Charlot, a prison-mate of Janvier and a witness to the death-exchange, he is hired as a handyman with the special task of looking out for the hated Jean-Louis Chavel. Soon, Charlot has fallen in love with the sister. Then, one night, a man appears at the door announcing himself as Jean-Louis Chavel.

On its face *The Tenth Man* is about the problem of atoning for an act of instinctive cowardice, a not unfamiliar theme in English literature, especially given its prominence in Joseph Conrad's "Lord Jim." Yet Mr. Greene does not really explore the problem. There is no discussion of the meaning or cause of Chavel's instinctive act. There are no characters who might act out subtle variations of Chavel's behavior. His path to his ultimate destiny is an avenue without side streets or detours, along which he gallops like a beast with blinders on.

Moreover, the surreal atmosphere of the prose, combined with its highly contrived plotting, serves to lend *The Tenth Man* a dreamlike quality. It is as if the ending inspired the story rather than the other way around, as if the narrator had fantasized the action just so as to arrive at the self-annihilating conclusion. Once again, as so often happens with a Graham Greene story. It is not so much the narrative that arrests us as the nature of the emotions that inspired such a narrative.

Christopher Lehmann-Haupt, in a review of "The Tenth Man," in The New York Times, *March 4, 1985, p. C17.*

JOHN CAREY

Greene wrote *The Tenth Man* in 1944, under contract to MGM, and it has gathered dust in their archives ever since. . . . It is very short, and a masterpiece—tapped out in the lean, sharp-eyed prose that film-work taught Greene to perfect. The idea for the story first came to him, he tells us, in 1937, and its burden of social guilt marks it as a Thirties text, despite its wartime setting.

Socially, it offers compensation to the small-shopkeeping class for Greene's earlier abuse. In *Stamboul Train* (1932) the good communist Dr. Czinner explains that the truly despicable bourgeois is not the professional gentleman, who may well be wise, just and brave, but the small shopkeeper, as represented by Mr. and Mrs. Peters, who are vulgar, poorly-spoken, and on a Cook's Tour. This version of communism fitted in neatly with the disdain for "trade", and respect for the professions, traditional in such locales as Berkhamsted School. But among Chavel's fellow prisoners in *The Tenth Man,* whose courage shames him, small shopkeepers are prominent—a greengrocer, a tobacconist, and Mangeot who is a shopkeeper's son. True, these are French shopkeepers, which for a romantic like Greene carries a glamour unattainable in English commercial circles. But the social message is markedly less complacent than in *Stamboul Train,* for all that.

Not that, in the end, [*The Tenth Man*] is a political novel. Religion enters, and usurps it, in the last few pages. Madame Mangeot falls ill, and a priest is fetched to administer the sacrament. He is a humdrum priest, in galoshes, but from the moment he arrives with his little case, everything changes. God has come in.

To the Protestant mind there is something undignified about a deity you can carry around like a tin of biscuits. But for Greene it has clear advantages. The one aspect of religion he has never been wholly convinced of is, he admits, the existence of God. In this position, a church which offers unquestionable dogma is naturally helpful. Besides, the palpable, dramatic God of Catholicism is better value in a thriller, because He raises the stakes. Chavel realises, at the end, that he confronts, in Carosse, not a fat actor but Satan.

Perhaps this gives us a clue to the nature of Greene's need for God, which seems rather unusual. One result of his childhood indoctrination during the Great War is that he finds life significant only when it is dangerous. Safe suburban normality disgusts him. He has always been drawn to troublespots—Malaya, Indo-China, Vietnam. Central America. God appeals, because He brings risk into every moment of life, balancing man between the colossal extremes of heaven and damnation. Like Russian Roulette. He can make even Berkhamsted Common exciting.

Greene says he had entirely forgotten about *The Tenth Man* till MGM came across the typescript. Even entitling a later book *The Third Man* did not remind him. In another writer that might seem careless. But for Greene forgetting is as important as memory. Forgetting consigns the stuff of life to the creative depths of the subconscious, which he has always trusted. Several of his stories have been written straight out of dreams. So the 40-year eclipse of *The Tenth Man* is just a by-product of the dark processes that have generated some of the most compelling fiction of our age.

John Carey, "Living Made Dangerous," in The Sunday Times, *London, March 10, 1985, p. 45.*

DAVID PROFUMO

The psychological realism of [*The Tenth Man*] is considerable, despite the many coincidences. A characteristic Greene figure, the lawyer is victim of a crucial moment of failure, and his cowardice infects him with shame. Betrayal of his birthright echoes the crime of the collaborators at large, and his constant fear of discovery provides a genuine *frisson*. His personal history wears the aura of a dark fairy tale, a dream in which he is transformed into someone else and revisits the scene of his childhood like a stranger, exploring areas of the house previously forbidden him, where the carpet stops. . . .

Falling as it does in the fertile period of Greene's 'Catholic' novels—midway between *The Power and the Glory* (1940) and *The Heart of the Matter* (1948)—its spiritual concerns are of a piece with them, especially in the tension between evil and the greyer shades of morality. The novel also offers insights regarding his work for the cinema, and there are two film-sketches appended, one of which *(Nobody to Blame)* is a prototype of *Our Man in Havana*. Like virtually all his stories, there is an inherent cinematic potential here, particularly in his focus on suggestive details—an inexpertly shaved moustache, a stopped watch—and on symbolic effects: 'The light moved steadily away from the cell; it rolled up like a carpet from one end to the other. The dusk eliminated Janvier while the clerk sitting by Voisin could still find light enough to write by.'

The Tenth Man would still make a powerful film, though a movie of that very name was reviewed by Greene himself in 1936, a year before he recorded the first idea for his novel. The melodrama and narrative wrinkles don't matter much, in the end, as the story has that essential ingredient of excitement. The only incredible thing about this reverberant fable is that the author could ever have forgotten having written it.

> David Profumo, "Imposters on the Run," in The Spectator, Vol. 254, No. 8176, March 23, 1985, p. 25.

ELIOT FREMONT-SMITH

[*The Tenth Man*] is a vintage Greene thriller (what he usually dubbed an "entertainment"), mordantly eerie and quite enjoyable. Greene himself, in a perplexed and slightly indignant introduction, finds the novel "very readable—indeed I prefer it in many ways to *The Third Man*." He was in fact working on *The Third Man* in 1948—and already, he admits, all memory of anything called *The Tenth Man* had slipped away.

This is weird. Greene's reputation as a novelist, both serious and sleuthing, was well established by 1944. The acclaimed *Brighton Rock* (1938) had been followed by *The Confidential Agent, The Power and the Glory,* and most recently *The Ministry of Fear,* which was published in 1943 while Greene was still working for the Foreign Office. The following year he quit that position and, to make ends meet (for acclaim was hardly bankable in those days—*Brighton Rock* sold 8000 copies and *The Power and the Glory* had a wartime print of only 3500), sold himself to M-G-M.

How he must have hated those two years, to have suffered such amnesia; the unrevised canon continues with *Nineteen Stories* (1947), *The Heart of the Matter* (1948), and then *The Third Man* (1950). Or perhaps he didn't consider *The Tenth Man* really his. Certainly M-G-M didn't—either then or nearly 40 years later when it dug the manuscript out of its vault and startled hawking it to publishers. . . .

A friend of mine, full of literary suspicion, thinks it will all turn out to be a ruse, a clever sales gimmick to hype a brand new Graham Greene novel that might otherwise receive only ho-hum notice. M-G-M is going along with it, he hisses, to hype the inevitable movie. I don't believe it—though if *The New Yorker* can be sold to a chain, I suppose anything is possible. . . .

The Tenth Man is eerie and detached, and also relentless in suspense. There are neat, concise observations along the way, about class distinction and the dislocation of time: "When a war ends one forgets how much older oneself and the world have become; it needs something like a piece of furniture or a woman's hat to waken the sense of time." All of Greene's themes are here—the atmosphere of oppression, the corruption of authority, the pessimism not quite balanced by the presence of grace, manifesting itself in moral paradox—but one eats them on the fly, as it were. This is a brief, fast story, and so resolutely unpretentious that when the most common food-for-thought is offered—"People are quite aware of the sorrow there always is in lust, but they are not so aware of the lust there is in sorrow"—it goes down like caviar.

The book's ending is unhappy, but there's a pleasing twist or two. It's not the deepest stuff, but as entertainment it has a cutting edge. In short, *The Tenth Man* is a professional job, and I don't care when it was written, though it's always fun to speculate, as Greene, I think, knows.

> Eliot Fremont-Smith, "Another Greene World," in The Village Voice, Vol. XXX, No. 13, March 26, 1985, p. 39.

ELIZABETH CHRISTMAN

Though short and somewhat undeveloped, [*The Tenth Man* is] pure Greene. The protagonist is a hallmark Greene type, a middle-aged man weighed down with guilt and failure. (pp. 316-17)

The plot has fascinating turns and complications, managed with Greene's economical deftness. It is a plotty story, of course: it was written for a movie. There are some fortuitous coincidences. (p. 317)

Character portrayal is sketchy. Greene gives no satisfactory analysis of why the middle-aged, childless widower wants so passionately to live. Still more shadowy is young Janvier's motive for giving up his life to enrich his mother and sister, who are not desperately poor. There are a couple of throwaway hints. Janvier coughs a lot; perhaps he knows he's going to die soon anyway. He and his sister are twins, with an exceptional bond between them; perhaps giving his life for her is almost like saving a part of himself. Greene might have fleshed out these hints if he had had novel publication rather than a movie in view.

Once past the spare beginning, Greene unfolds more spaciously the consciousness of a man running or hiding from a disgraceful moral failure. No writer is better than Greene at dramatizing moral failure or at tracing its effects down the years on a man's life. (pp. 317-18)

Charlot is like Scobie in *The Heart of the Matter* who has betrayed both his wife and his mistress; like the whisky priest in *The Power and the Glory* who has had an illegitimate child; like Rowe in *The Ministry of Fear* who has killed his wife in pity for her sufferings. Like these other protagonists, Charlot finds a way to atone for the evil he committed—a drastic atonement, but then it was a drastic act, buying a man's life.

The Tenth Man is not a Graham Greene masterpiece, but it is a welcome addition to the canon. (p. 318)

> Elizabeth Christman, "Something to Be Ashamed Of," in Commonweal, Vol. CXII, No. 10, May 17, 1985, pp. 316-18.

Donald (Andrew) Hall (Jr.)

1928-

American poet, essayist, autobiographer, editor, dramatist, critic, and author of books for children.

A respected writer, educator, and editor, Hall is best known for his poetry. He contends that "the poem is a vehicle for self-discovery," and his work reflects this inward focus. Hall is eager nevertheless to share his poems and participates frequently and enthusiastically in public readings. He writes with particular attention to sound, valuing a poem's aural quality as much as, if not more than, its appearance on the page. Critics have linked Hall with such poets as Robert Bly, James Wright, and James Dickey, who favor simple, direct language combined with surrealistic imagery. Hall has identified as crucial to his conception of poetry a force he calls "the vatic voice," which provides the inspiration for his poems. The vatic voice exists in everyone, says Hall, but the careful attention poets pay to it allows them to produce their work.

Hall garnered critical acclaim with his first major work, *Exiles and Marriages* (1955). At this early stage of his career, Hall wrote in a tightly structured style which featured a formal application of rhyme and meter. By the late 1950s, his approach had changed significantly, as he explained: "My early poetry concentrated on form entirely. I was concerned that poetry should be only technique, and perfectly finite. . . . By 1954 I had begun to distrust the vanity of technique, and I began to learn that what I called technique covered small ground. Working with syllabics and free verse . . . , I tried to extend my range, and to make poems which were more expressive and imaginative." The poems in *A Roof of Tiger Lilies* (1966) and *The Alligator Bride: Poems New and Selected* (1969) exemplify this looser yet more complex and self-examining style. Critics noted in these works and in *The Town of Hill* (1975) ambiguous images and phrases that, while expressed in direct, unadorned language, are not always easily grasped.

In 1975 Hall left his professorship at the University of Michigan to devote his time to writing at his family's farm in New Hampshire. The poetry in *Kicking the Leaves* (1978) reflects his feelings on returning to a place rich with memories and links with his past. Many of the poems explore and celebrate the continuity between generations, as Hall reminisces about the past and anticipates the future. Similarly reflective is *String Too Short to Be Saved: Childhood Reminiscences* (1961; revised, 1979), a collection of prose narratives inspired by Hall's childhood summers spent with his grandparents on the same New Hampshire farm where he now lives.

In addition to his poetry, Hall has written many prose works. In *Marianne Moore: The Cage and the Animal* (1970) he analyzes Moore's poetry, and *As the Eye Moves: A Sculpture by Henry Moore* (1973) is an appreciation of the work of this renowned sculptor. In *Remembering Poets: Reminiscences and Opinions* (1978) he recounts his conversations with and impressions of T. S. Eliot, Ezra Pound, Dylan Thomas, and Robert Frost. Hall has also authored several books on the craft of writing, including *Writing Well* (1973), *To Keep Moving* (1980), and *The Weather for Poetry* (1982). *Goatfoot, Milktongue,*

Photograph by Michele McDonald. Courtesy of Donald Hall

Twinbird (1978) collects interviews, articles, and short pieces on poetry and other poets.

Hall has said that had he not become a poet he would have liked to be a great athlete, and his canon includes two volumes on sports: *Dock Ellis in the Country of Baseball* (1976) and *Fathers Playing Catch with Sons: Essays on Sport (Mostly Baseball)* (1984). One of Hall's books for children, *Ox-Cart Man* (1979), won a Caldecott Medal. He is also the author of a play, *An Evening's Frost* (1966), based on the work of Robert Frost.

Critical response to Hall's work has generally been favorable. His carefully crafted poetry and thoughtful prose are widely praised for their clarity and integrity. Robert Bly observed that Hall "is not prolific, he does not have an immense number of good poems, but when a poem is good, it is solid all the way through, and absolutely genuine."

(See also *CLC*, Vols. 1, 13; *Contemporary Authors*, Vols. 5-8, rev. ed.; *Contemporary Authors New Revision Series*, Vol. 2; *Something about the Author*, Vol. 23; and *Dictionary of Literary Biography*, Vol. 5.)

GERALD BURNS

Donald Hall's book of new and selected [*The Alligator Bride*] is valuable firstly because you get the poems he reads so well—

"Self-portrait as a Bear," "The Poem," "Woolworth's," "Crew-cuts," "Lovers in Middle Age," and "Gold." . . . *The Alligator Bride* is a document, not a book; it opens with a sonnet, moves on to a sestina than which only Zukofsky's "Mantis" is more readable, fools around for a while and stops dead. Like many post-Auden forties Americans, he begins to question the value of a lifetime of well-made poems. So he stops writing and retools, and comes back more daring but still Donald Hall. It's this part the histories will get wrong. **"The Foundations of American Industry"** isn't *that* far from **"Old Houses."** He doesn't chuck the armory of writing tricks he learned in the days you learned writing tricks—the first and last poems in the book depend on the last-line vista. There's less Hall as politely interested describer, more getting *inside* the thing. But the Vegetal Blessing—"where a quarrel / of vines crawls into the spilled body of a plane," the end of **"Digging,"** the rowboat in **"The Farm," "The Stump"**—the detached comment of falling rain or falling snow—are habits he never breaks. In the archetypal Hall poem, a state of affairs is remolded (or quick-frozen) by the mere assertion of lyricity; it's not that there are poppies in the toilet bowl and vines in the computer but that there *are*, don't you see. Hall's abiding approach ignores the shift in form, and it seems to me that the surreal works best in what he's done as part of those lyrical assertions. That's why I don't love **"The Long River"** and **"The Alligator Bride"** more. However important they are for the history of his writing, more people could have written them. I'd swap them both for **"The Lone Ranger."** What Hall teaches me always is that importance has nothing to do with value. (p. 214)

> *Gerald Burns, "Why Johnny Can't Write," in* Southwest Review, *Vol. LV, No. 2, Spring, 1970, pp. 211-15.**

THE VIRGINIA QUARTERLY REVIEW

In his introduction to the anthology "Contemporary American Poetry" (1962) Hall, pointing to certain poems by Bly and Simpson among others, notes a kind of imagination new to American poetry; "This imagination is irrational, yet the poem is usually quiet and the language simple; there is no straining after apocalypse. There is an inwardness to these images, a profound subjectivity. . . . To read a poem of this sort, you must not try to translate the images into abstractions. . . . You must try to be open to them, to let them take you over and speak in their own language of feeling." These same characteristics manifest themselves with increasing frequency in Hall's own poetry written during and since that time, a development which may be easily observed in [*The Alligator Bride*]. . . . It is interesting to note on the book jacket what Hall says of his title poem: "The story is one that, if you leave yourself open to the language of dreams, is available to everyone. . . . You may not translate anything in the poem, you have to *float* on it." Again, the insistence on the reader's leaving himself open—to the language of dreams, to the language of feeling—and not attempting to *translate* the images. Fine, in theory. But the problem is that often in Hall's later work the experience of the poem is *not* available to the reader, however earnest Hall is in his attempt to share the vision. Sometimes the images simply do not provide a surface on which one can "float." One wonders if there is not too much of the "inwardness" Hall spoke of earlier. This is not to fault Hall's general approach, for the kind of poetic experience he suggests is wonderfully afforded in Wilbur's recent "Walking to Sleep,"

for example. Nor are these negative points intended to deny Hall's successes. The collection allows a fresh look at his early work, which has been out of print, and offers new poems that indicate a continually deepening poetic awareness. (pp. xliv, xlvi)

> *A review of "The Alligator Bride," in* The Virginia Quarterly Review, *Vol. 46, No. 2 (Spring, 1970), pp. xliv, xlvi.*

HAYDEN CARRUTH

Although Donald Hall's [*The Alligator Bride: Poems Selected and New*] offers work both recent and early (the latter somewhat revised) and although it clearly shows his poetic manner shifting to accommodate, or at least to accompany, the changing styles of 20 years, certain features are consistent from beginning to end; consistent and curiously old-fashioned. We are reminded of the period when Hall began to write, the late forties and early fifties.

The past, Hall says, is better than the present. Grandfathers are superior to fathers, middle-aged lovers make better love than young lovers. The values of early generations of New Hampshire farmers were more humane and reasonable than the values of their descendants. In his own life the poet's progress toward middle age, or even old age, brings him nearer to freedom, discovery, and a wise appreciation of pleasure.

Yet because this progress ends in death, and because past values are irretrievably past, Hall's attitude is touched with inevitable irony. His celebration of pleasure is imbued with a sense of loss. He is, in short, hung up on the conventional dilemma of metaphysical poets, which he meets by conventional means: his poems are elegiac in tone, and civil, subdued and orderly in manner. The alternative, he would say, is insanity.

There is obvious truth in this, and obvious importance too. . . . But this is not the truth that most Americans want to hear today. Nor is Hall's poetic decorum, with its roots in literary tradition, what attracts their notice. . . .

A second point concerns Hall's attitude toward natural objects. For him they are things to be manipulated in the poet's favor, "objective correlatives." A stone, tree, bird or animal is significant only as it transmits meanings from outside itself, meanings which are verbally imposed. This is the attitude of Yeats, Eliot, and many great poets of 40 years ago. Call it Neo-Symbolism or Post-Symbolism if you will; it is still Symbolism, and its roots are deep in the Transcendental past.

To the great majority of American poets today, however, working under the influence of Pound, Williams, Zukofsky and the Black Mountain school, this view is not only wrong but evil. The objects of our world have their own meanings, natural meanings, which poets have no right to manipulate. Instead the poet's work is to represent the objects in their pristine selfhood, not as symbols of his feeling but as counterparts, or simple presences. . . .

The point here is that, next to the clear-cut poems of the objectivists, Hall's symbolic poems, even his leanest and sharpest, are likely to seem murky and portentous by comparison.

Yet sometimes it is easier to judge a poet who is out of fashion than one who is in. If a poem projects through its facade of quaintness, so to speak, and genuinely touches us, then probably it is a success. How great a success doesn't matter; we call it, loosely but reasonably, a good poem. Hall's most famous poem, his early **"Elegy for Wesley Wells,"** in which the poet grieves for the death of a New Hampshire farmer and the values he represents, is not a good poem. . . .

But a few of Hall's poems from the middle and later parts of his book do break through: **"The Snow," "The Stump," "The Long River," "Swan,"** perhaps three or four others. These, more cleanly written and less derivative than the early poems, have attracted strong advocates and many readers, and doubtless have earned a place, in the New England tradition.

> *Hayden Carruth, "A Celebration of Pleasure Imbued with a Sense of Loss," in* The New York Times Book Review, *September 13, 1970, p. 38.*

THE NEW YORKER

[*Dock Ellis in the Country of Baseball* is a] lively, original book about the former Pirate pitcher (now a Yankee) who almost from the moment he came up to the majors has been one of baseball's most controversial figures. In his major-league career, Dock Ellis has, among other things, hurled a no-hitter while suffering from a hangover, intentionally hit three batters in a row and accused professional baseball of being racist and reactionary. . . . [Donald Hall] is a friend of Ellis's, and he describes him with candor and affection, showing Ellis to be cool, proud, articulate, sensitive, occasionally haughty, and often troubled. (At several points, Ellis talks movingly of being tired and depressed—of days when he wants nothing to do with baseball.) The book touches all the bases of the standard baseball bio—the childhood pranks, the teen-age brush with the law, the rescue by a kindly ex-ballplayer, the difficult years in the minors—but it does so in prose that is brisk and energetic. Some of the best passages are those in which Hall describes the eccentric little duchy that he imagines to be the Country of Baseball—a pastoral place, inhabited largely by boys and young men, where time passes differently and ghostly figures from the past sometimes take an occasional lap around the outfield. (pp. 171-72)

> *A review of "Dock Ellis in the Country of Baseball," in* The New Yorker, *Vol. LII, No. 34, October 11, 1976, pp. 171-72.*

SAMUEL R. CROWL

The outfields are snowy, dark, and deep now in the country of baseball, and for those of us longing to be back in the stands, Don Hall's [*Dock Ellis in the Country of Baseball*] is the ideal winter solace. We like to make metaphor with the ease and grace and geometry of baseball's poetry in motion, so it is ironically appropriate that poet Hall meets his match in pitcher Ellis. After Hall's brief but glorious introduction to baseball's geography, Ellis takes over and dominates every turn in our tour. Hall pitches his inquires into the tangled web of Ellis's life, and Dock responds with prose poems of startling depth. We see that Ellis's bad-nigger reputation is precisely dependent upon his insistence on spinning metaphors at literal-minded teammates, managers, and sportswriters. As with Ali, the sports section can't contain him. Ellis has much to teach us all about the liabilities of language, especially if our infield or E.R.A. is slipping. One of the rare delights for me in watching the bond develop between Hall and Ellis, is being witness to the marvelous meals they share at Pigall's (for the uninitiated, one of two great French Restaurants in Cincinnati). I can see Don Whittle beaming graciously in the background as Hall and Ellis

throw delicious soft curves to one another, in and around every course. This is a book for the connoisseur.

> *Samuel R. Crowl, in a review of "Dock Ellis: In the Country of Baseball," in* The Ohio Review, *Vol. XVIII, No. 1, Winter, 1977, p. 115.*

DONALD DAVIE

Hall knows as much about poetry as anyone in America; instead of staying with that relatively austere and respectable concern, [in *Remembering Poets: Reminiscences and Opinions*] he has chosen—with a humility and generosity that are characteristic—to navigate in the murkier waters of the poetry scene, that is to say, of the poet's relation with his public. And so he has written a book about what it means to be a poet in the English-speaking world in the 20th century.

His account is not speculative, but grounded in particular episodes and occasions recalled and recreated with the richness and nuance of the great storyteller or—that rarer creature—the great biographer. [Dylan Thomas, Robert Frost, T. S. Eliot, and Ezra Pound] come before us as individual, fallible human beings trying to cope with the conditions of 20th-century living while yet not betraying their poetic calling. The difficulty of that—in the long run the impossibility of it—could have provided Hall with many an easy irony; instead, what he makes it yield is sorrow and sometimes anger.

There are some places—notably in the poignant pages devoted to a self-accusing Ezra Pound known through several days in Rome in the early 1960's—where the book provides information that will have to be taken account of by responsible scholars. . . . But these are incidental bonuses. The central achievement is in humanizing the poetic endeavor, by bringing it down once again to the fact of an isolated individual trying to speak to, and be heard by, his concerned contemporaries.

I suspect that Donald Hall has written a modern classic. Certainly his unassuming memoir of these four poets can most valuably, for the common reader, bypass and cut through many shelves' worth of learned commentaries and exegeses. He proffers from time to time, notably on Eliot, his own ultimately Freudian explanation of why, alike in the life and in the writings, a poet's career took the shape it did. I am not persuaded—because I'm not persuaded by the Freudian schema that in its outlines Hall takes to be axiomatic. But that, too, is beside the point: The diagnoses are tentative, the evidence is presented with a fullness and a fairness that permit and even invite quite different explanations. And no one can afford to disagree with Hall's central and passionate contention—that great poetry is a record of sanity maintained and achieved, not of sickness pushed to the hysterical and suicidal limit. If there is a sickness in the life of each of these poets—and we must surely agree with Hall that there is—in three of the cases (Thomas is the exception) the lives and the poetry show us the sickness not indulged and exacerbated, but heroically if partially surmounted by, and in the interest of, the art. (pp. 15, 33)

> *Donald Davie, "Frost, Eliot, Thomas, Pound," in* The New York Times Book Review, *February 19, 1978, pp. 15, 33.*

MARJORIE PERLOFF

By definition, the literary memoir presupposes an intimate connection between a writer's life and his work: a look, a gesture, a particular conversation, an observed eccentricity, a remembered incident—all these provide potential insights into the work itself. It is all the more curious that Donald Hall, who modestly refers to his memoirs of Dylan Thomas, Robert Frost, T. S. Eliot, and Ezra Pound [*Remembering Poets: Reminiscences and Opinions*] as "literary gossip," repeatedly denies that such a connection exists and urges us to "split poem from poet." . . .

But why then write literary gossip? What good does it do us to know that Pound didn't know his way around Rome or that Thomas bullied his wife or that Frost worried about what suit to wear to a reading? Hall's "gossip" is, moreover, fairly thin because . . . Donald Hall, by his own admission, barely knew the four poets who are his subject. His role was, from the beginning, that of middleman: it was Hall who arranged the poetry readings, who brought the car around, who made introductions, who interviewed Eliot and Pound for the *Paris Review*. Frost and Eliot expressed a polite if rather perfunctory interest in Hall's own poems; Thomas and Pound had never read them.

If Hall's book is short on anecdote, it is long on general reflections as to the "meaning" of poet's lives; not for nothing is his book subtitled *Reminiscences and Opinions*. His central thesis is that "The poet who survives is the poet to celebrate." "In our culture," he notes, "an artist's self-destructiveness is counted admirable, praiseworthy, a guarantee of sincerity. There seems to be an assumption . . . that it is natural to want to destroy yourself; that health is bourgeois or conventional." Hall deplores this cult of the suicidal artist. "Thomas," he declares, "was a minor poet, rather than a major one, because he was a drunk," whereas Eliot, Pound, and Frost survived heroically and therefore became great poets.

Hall is quite right, I think, to debunk the myth of art as self-destruction, a myth propagated by such studies as A. Alvarez's *The Savage God* (1972) and reinforced by the actual suicides of Sylvia Plath, Anne Sexton, and John Berryman. But I am not sure that Hall's own view of poetic "survival" is finally more satisfactory than the one he opposes.

Dylan Thomas, who Hall first heard read at Harvard in 1950, is seen as "a small unsmiling figure, huge belly, pudgy face, nose like the bulb on a Klaxon horn, chinless, red-faced, pop-eyed, curly-haired, with an expression at once frightened and insolent. Out of this silly body rolled a voice like Jehovah's, or Ocean's, or Firmament's." . . . The portrait of Thomas that emerges from the memoir is that of a bullying, cowardly, sometimes charming, but wholly irresponsible genius who committed "public suicide" by drinking himself to death. But why was he a drunk? Because, Hall posits, he chose "suffering . . . as punishment for the sin of writing poems." Brought up by his mother "in a Welsh church of Devil and sin," he must have felt that "When he became a poet he joined the Devil's party."

This version of the poet's dilemma is, to say the least, questionable. Baudelaire, who believed fervently in Satan, took all sorts of drugs and yet wrote some of the greatest poems of the 19th century; Joyce, brought up on fire-and-brimstone sermons of the sort described in the *Portrait of the Artist,* drank a great deal but became, in Hall's terms, a heroic survivor; Lawrence, whose early religious training surely resembled that of Thomas, happened to have none of Thomas's vices. The point is, I think, that great artists somehow marshal their forces and preserve themselves from the total self-destruction of a Dylan Thomas

because they know that there is work to be done. Quite possibly, Thomas became a drunk just because he knew in his heart of hearts that he was a minor poet, rather than the other way around. (p. 30)

Hall's speculations about Frost do not take us much further. Frost is presented neither as the Good Gray Bard of New England nor as the monster Lawrence Thompson made of him in his recent biography, but as a vain, peculiarly petty man who could also be very endearing. Hall skillfully describes Frost's astonishing need for approval, his longing, even at the height of his fame, for total devotion from the crowd. Frost was competitive and aggressive, never letting anyone, not even Donald Hall the prep school boy, win a round. Here is Hall's explanation:

> . . . he was a guilty man, and guilty over the wrongs he felt he had done to people he loved. . . . Therefore, perhaps he courted love, *any* love, even the kind he took from his Stanford audience, to assuage his conviction that he was *bad*. The need for love and applause was a need for forgiveness.

This may well be the case, but it doesn't really tell us much about Frost's peculiar genius. (pp. 30-1)

Hall's memoir of Eliot is scanty for Eliot was a very private person and in his few meetings with Hall, he revealed singularly little. Hall has, however, a "psychological notion" about Eliot, a notion admittedly based only on second-hand knowledge of the poet. He argues that Eliot's "bad marriage" to Vivien Haigh-Wood "was crucial to Eliot's poetry," that she was "blessing and curse, Muse and death's head." Eliot married a "death-muse" because his mother was a poet, and "To marry the Mother is at the same time wholly forbidden and wholly desirable." So he posits, "Eliot married Vivien in order to be impotent, to suffer, and to write poems."

Against this Freudian banality, I would set Lyndall Gordon's well-informed and careful account of Eliot's disastrous marriage in *Eliot's Early Years.* . . . The evidence about Eliot's personal life is, as everyone knows, not yet in, but we do know, from Vivien's diaries and Eliot's letters, that the poet was evidently a virgin when he married at the age of 26, that he was genuinely smitten by Vivien's charm, that the revelation of his subsequent impotence was a deep shock both to himself and to his wife, and that far from being the catalyst that plunged him into the writing of poetry, this terrible marriage almost prevented Eliot from writing at all. "Prufrock," surely one of Eliot's greatest poems, was written before he met Vivien: *The Waste Land* was written during his recovery from mental breakdown at Lausanne, away from his wife; *Four Quartets* was composed after he and Vivien had formally separated. . . . Hall's assumption that artists must "pay a price"—whether that price is a hopeless marriage (Eliot) or alcoholism (Thomas) or the suicide of one's children (Frost)—ignores two very simple facts: (1) even non-artists tend to pay "a price" for whatever it is they achieve in their lives; and (2) generalizations about "the sufferings of the artist" are always dangerous, for artists are, finally, as different from one another as they are from the rest of us.

The same Romantic assumptions govern the Pound memoir. Hall met Pound when he was sent down to Rome in 1960 to interview him for the *Paris Review:* he was apprehensive about meeting the "difficult" Ezra Pound but found to his surprise that Pound was lonely, sweet, shy, generous . . . , and totally unpredictable. Gay and talkative one minute, he lapsed the next into stony silence or collapsed on his sofa-bed as if he had just suffered a stroke. Such sudden "attacks" as well as the fabled silence of Pound's last years lead Hall to conclude:

> The hell in Ezra Pound's chest had to do with Mary, with Dorothy, with Olga, and with others. . . . At the end of the lives of our great poets, the domestic life is a desert of anguish— perhaps on account of choices made for the sake of the self and its passion and its poetry, choices which in the retrospect of old age appear destructive and cruel. . . . [Pound] returned to his personal Inferno, a hell constructed by the arrogance and madness of his middle age.

This is a dramatic cautionary tale but the facts don't support it. Hugh Kenner remarked in a recent interview that although the European physicians who treated Pound could not agree on a diagnosis, there is no doubt that Pound's health collapsed in 1959-1960, just at about the time when Hall conducted the interview. (p. 31)

The 74-year-old poet was, in other words, a very sick man. His "personal Inferno," as Hall melodramatically calls it, is at least as attributable to physical as to psychological causes. Nor should we make too much of Pound's "cruelty" to Dorothy Pound and Olga Rudge, both of whom were quite willing to do anything for him. . . . One could turn the tables on Hall and ask how many men, whether poets or not, have had a wife and mistress as devoted as Dorothy and Olga, or a daughter as loving as Mary de Rachelwitz?

If Hall's theorizing repeatedly flounders, as I think it does, it is perhaps because his set of memoirs is only ostensibly about Thomas, Frost, Eliot, and Pound. Hall's real subject is himself, as his conclusion **"Gladness and Madness"** reveals. "Artists of vast ambition seldom die happy," Hall announced, leaving us to wonder who it is that does die happy. "Most people," he continues, "avoid (the poet's) despair at the end of life by following simple maxims: don't be ambitious; take it easy; be a *good* father, mother, citizen. . . ." But the poet can't take this way out. "You will never be any good as a poet unless you arrange your life and your values in the hope of writing great poems—always knowing . . . that you may well have 'messed up your life' for nothing."

Here Hall gives himself away. Throughout the book, he has been assuming, rather naively, that poets "arrange their lives and values in the hope of writing great poems," evidently because this is what he himself did. An extraordinarily precocious boy, Hall "decided to become a poet" at 14. By the time he was 16, he had already published poems in Little Magazines; later he was an editor of the Harvard *Advocate* and won an important fellowship to Oxford. He became a well-known anthologist, editor, interviewer, and critic—a genuine man of letters. But I think it is not unfair to say that, despite all his "arranging," Hall has not lived up to his early poetic promise.

Perhaps this doesn't matter. Hall himself insists: "This book records a portion of my education. Whether my own poems look worthy in retrospect is irrelevant: I grew up as a poet, for better or worse, among other poets." But Hall's evaluations of his poetic fathers suggest that the status of his own poems is not, after all, irrelevant. He longs to convince us that the aspiring poet cannot help but "mess up a part of his own life or the lives of others"—"for the selfish sake" of his art. He

believes, in short, that the aspiration toward greatness—his own aspiration—is in itself admirable; the sufferings it may cause others or himself are justified so long as he endures, survives, dares to continue.

Such Romantic glorification of the poet's enterprise (as distinct from the production of good poems) is perhaps just as misguided as the cult of self-destruction. *Remembering Poets* is an oddly dispiriting book for it demonstrates, quite unwittingly, that becoming a poet is one thing, and wanting and *planning* to become one, quite another. As for "literary gossip," one wishes that Donald Hall had chosen to give us some juicy tales about the poets of his own time and place. (pp. 31-2)

> *Marjorie Perloff, in a review of "Remembering Poets: Reminiscences and Opinions," in* The New Republic, *Vol. 178, No. 18, May 6, 1978, pp. 30-2.*

JUDITH GLEASON

"The oral tradition!" exclaims Donald Hall on the dust jacket of *Ox-Cart Man,* a story handed down from an old man to a boy, old man to a boy, old man to the present author's cousin. This is the New England heritage . . . , and there is nothing metaphoric about it, nothing heroic. Metonymic from start to finish, it isn't really a story either (no baited-breathed "and then? and then?") but rather the genesis and flat unfolding of a series of modest transactions made by an industrious, thrifty householder at the Portsmouth (Maine) market once upon an October. Each item that he sells stands for a time of year and a spell of work: a bag of wool sheared from sheep in April, a box of maple sugar left over from the March tapping. Waste not, want not. It is the prudent metonymy of proverbial wisdom, a road leading to and fro, to market and home again with implements and utensils for next year's increased comforts and more efficient production. No fanciful, phantom Moebius strip, the road to market is common sense, but alas in this case marred by a scene of hypocritical tenderness when the householder, having sold his faithful ox, kisses him good-bye on the nose. Life was simpler then. Then always is. "As if human beings could be perennial plants," says Donald Hall in the publicity release. But they aren't. And neither are oxen. Burdensome heritage. (pp. 73-4)

> *Judith Gleason, "That Lingering Child of Air," in* Parnassus: Poetry in Review, *Vol. 8, No. 2, Spring-Summer-Fall-Winter, 1980, pp. 63-82.**

BRENT SPENCER

"Poems are never *about* anything," Donald Hall says in **Goatfoot, Milktongue, Twinbird.** "The sensual body of the poem is pleasure—the sounds of it, the weight of it." And this is the note Hall strikes throughout this collection of interviews, essays, and notes on poetry. . . . Hall believes that we are drawn to poetry by the set of pre-verbal pleasures the title of his book identifies. It is a strange book, rich in insights about poetry, literary gossip, and reminiscence. Strange because there's a looseness to the organization that makes the work seem more like a transcription of intelligent talk than a volume of literary criticism. And this is refreshing.

He speaks of the poem as a "sensual body" reaching us through our mouths, "which are warm in the love of vowels held together." This is Milktongue—the mouth-pleasure poetry satisfies. The poem also reaches us through our leg muscles, which dance to the rhythm and syntax of the line. This is

Goatfoot. And Twinbird is the pleasure in resolution that can come through rhyme and meter and in other ways. These Hall identifies as the psychic origins of poetry.

Some of what Hall says has been said before. Wordsworth, for example, says similar things about poetry in the *Preface*. But Hall's emphasis on the sensual body of the poem is fresh. We're far from Eliot's classicism here, but we're also at least a neighborhood away from Williams's imagism. And I suppose, too, we're somewhere down the street from the Eastern, mystical element in contemporary poetry. "A poem is one man's inside talking to another man's inside," Hall paraphrases Wordsworth. "Inwardness" is the condition poetry urges in us. In a book like *The Town of Hill,* Hall himself attempts to achieve this through a juxtaposition of the fantastic and the realistic. In the more recent poems of *Kicking the Leaves* he tries to achieve it through memory.

Hall sees the poet as both *poiein* and *vates,* maker and mystic, whose control of the vision and song is only marginal. As Hall puts it, "The Priestess does not know what she says, but she knows that she says it in dactylic hexameter." And what Goatfoot, Milktongue, and Twinbird do is lull us into accepting the poem on its own terms without intellectualizing it and without civilizing it into something else. Accepting this means never being bothered by the but-what-does-it-mean question readers sometimes cry out in exasperation. It means only the shape of the sounds sitting on the tongue, the rhythmic throb of the body, and the awareness of the almost magical correspondences among sounds and things.

If there is a problem with the book, it is in the sometimes contrived sound of the questions put to Hall in the interviews. In each case, though, it is merely the voice of an admirer asking questions calculated to elicit answers already known and appreciated. The answers and observations give the book a gnomic character. (pp. 30-1)

Hall is a generous, clear headed reader of poetry with as much concern for the audience of poetry as for the "sensual rune" that is the poem. For a poet who has been acquainted with some of the major poets of this century . . . , he is never coy or superior about what he knows, and he knows a great deal. The book is pretty clear proof of that.

Although shaping the language is Hall's major concern in poetry (he has said, "If I can get a string of four diphthongs in a row, it drives me wild"), the imagery of the dream-vision is what dominates *The Town of Hill.* The speaker in these poems sounds like a man who has just been awakened from a nightmare, and his faintly quizzical voice seems to come to us from the darkness where he tries to piece together his half-real, half-unreal imaginings—about a town so small that a fern's breath can blow it away; a convocation of dead presidents, each affecting postures of vanity or self-pity; articles of clothing lost but living lives of their own. Sometimes his dream-visons are threatening, as in **"Sudden Things,"** where he must protect a houseful of children and old people from escaped wild animals. A strange, evocative poem, it is not the best in the collection but is important for its careful development of the dream imagery and narration. Here all things are out of control, and no matter what he does, he can't stop them; the only way old dangers are done away with is when new, greater dangers take their places, and whatever he fears might happen does happen. . . . (p. 31)

The poetry in this small book deals with much more than the delicious confusion of dream and reality. Hall is a sort of poet-cartographer—the best kind of poet to be—who explores and charts the rapidly shifting borders between dream and reality, the conscious and unconscious, the solemn and absurd. He does this by skillfully juxtaposing image with image, thought with thought. (pp. 31-2)

[In some] poems visions that seem disquieting at first turn out to be inviting, and he embraces them as he does in **"White Apples."** . . . There is unfathomable depth to a line like "white apples and the taste of stone" that verifies the belief that poetry does much more than what plain one-step-in-front-of-the-other prose can do. It is a line so unparaphrasable and indefinable, yet so appropriate, that we are caught off guard by it, lured into new ranges of feeling—and it is brought off with a sureness and economy that make it seem all the more magical. This is what Hall means in *Goatfoot, Milktongue, Twinbird* by the nonrational element in poetry.

Other poems, like **"To a Waterfowl,"** **"The Space Spiders,"** and **"Poem With One Fact,"** also take the reader by surprise, but by the direction of the narrative rather than by surprising but appropriate imagery. They are change-up pitches disguised as poems, seeming at first to be only incredibly funny show-pieces by which Hall displays his capacious wit, but near the end they change in tone and intention, they subvert our expectations, and they face the reader squarely if not quite fully seriously. **"To a Waterfowl,"** Hall's mock send-up of poetry readings, ends in unexpected tongue-in-cheek condemnation of the reader who laughs at the expense of Hall's amiable but dotty patrons of poetry. No one—least of all the poet in the poem—winds up with any shred of dignity left. . . . The effects of these poems do not depend on the surprise ending. Instead, the endings send new pulses of meaning throughout the rest of the poem. The endings themselves are less important than how they make the reader react to the whole.

Unearthly stillness is the mood of the title poem, where the effect is achieved, again, by juxtaposition—the mixture of pastoral innocence with something vaguely but persistently threatening. (pp. 32-3)

String Too Short to be Saved is a book with a magic title. The publisher calls it "recollections" and "memoirs." Hall has called it a collection of stories. In them he tells of boyhood summers on his grandfather's New England farm. The stories are true in the only real sense—to life if not to history. (p. 34)

We hear a rich chorus of voices in this book: the hired man arguing with his employer, Hall's grandfather, about haying: "Yew jist sind up all yew kin sind up and I kin take ceer of what yew kin sind up"; old voices singing "There's a Long, Long Trail A-Winding"; the grandfather asking himself a question he knows the answer to already ("Lawyer Green. Now how does that begin?"), or remembering another story ("One day—I was away somewhere—your grandmother was alone and a gypsy woman come to the door.").

The stories show both of the main characteristics of Hall's poetry—the attention to language and to detail. And they show a real storyteller at work, something we get a taste of in *Kicking the Leaves.* Each book throws light on the other, both coming as they do from the same source.

Going back to his past was undoubtedly good for Hall, and seems to have opened the way for the expression of deeper feelings. Some of the early poems—I'm thinking of poems like those in *The Yellow Room*—are self-conscious in their use of language and image. This is true also of some of the poems in *The Town of Hill,* where the fantastic sometimes seems like a convenient barrier that keeps him from confronting what really matters in his life. *String Too Short to be Saved* was originally published in 1960, but a look at *Kicking the Leaves* shows that the past is still with him constantly and that he is working out ways to integrate past, self, and poetry.

The poems in *Kicking the Leaves* are mostly poems of memory, yet not mere reminiscence. The effort in these poems is to look for that part of the past that lives on into the present. They are, for the most part, poems about the gifts the past brings to us, the gifts of the dead. . . . These are poems, in the end, about dying. The poet looks to his past because he feels himself slowly becoming a part of that past, "taking a place in the story of leaves."

Hall writes about himself and death, his own and others', with no trace of sentimentality. He does not get misty-eyed about the past, though he regrets what is lost. . . . In *Goatfoot, Milktongue, Twinbird* Hall says, "For some poets place is golden and the golden place like the golden age is usually unattainable—either because it is in the historical past or because it is in the biographical past of the poet, or both." Hall is the kind of poet he describes, and the place that is golden for him, that he has really only fully discovered in the most recent poetry, is the hilly ground and wild growth of the New Hampshire farm where he spent his summers. But . . . he never drags the past kicking and screaming into the present. He has reverence, not an obsession, for the past.

The basic quality of Hall's poetry in [*Kicking the Leaves*] is the sense of discovery, of the journey over a rugged terrain to an almost inaccessible spot where he finds something of great value. It cannot be brought back to civilization except in song. It may be that the terrain is physical, as it so often is in *String*— the discovery of the valley full of fallen rock maples, the discovery of the old locomotive in the woods. Or the journey may be inward, a dream journey, as it is in some of the poems in *The Town of Hill.* Lyric poetry, according to Hall, urges the condition of inwardness, which is achieved in the new poems through memory, the hard road the spirit travels. (pp. 34-6)

The pleasure that comes from the sound of the poem *is* the poem, and Hall is the king of the vowel. . . . Part of what makes Hall so good is that he knows the language inside out. And, reading his poetry, we realize that he is a poet who knows that poetry is alive in the mouth and in the sounds it makes in the air, not lying on the narrow bed of the page.

Everywhere in these poems are doomed civilizations; the remains of a roast pig are "like the map of a defeated country," his father's old, ivy-covered dairy is "like a Mayan temple, / like a pyramid grown over with jungle vines," small stones are locked together in a wall "like the arched / ramparts at Mycenae." And it's true—reading Hall's poetry is like visiting an ancient country where everything you see, everything you touch, is centuries old, filled with history.

The major question these poems seem to raise is whether a concern for the past is regressive. For Wordsworth, memory is redemptive. And there is a sense that Hall is doing something similar to what Wordsworth is doing in the *Prelude* and elsewhere. For both, things are charged with meaning; everything in nature is infused with its own history and the history of the race. Hall makes us feel the significance of the cycle of life and death—for a field of clover and timothy growing and being cut down generation after generation; for leaves dying and falling to be replaced by others that die and fall; for generations

of old men reciting poems and stories while they milk their cows, living and dying on the only land they know, defining their own existence somewhere between the endless cycle of the field's growth and the "mountains that do not change." Part of him wants to be the boy again, to return "to the countryside / where I lay as a boy / in the valley of noon heat," but part of him also knows he must find his own place in the cycle, that he must build the "house of dying." . . . (pp. 36-7)

One characteristic of Hall's best poetry—whether the earlier, more surreal work or the more recent narrative work with its longer, more relaxed line—is an ability to bring out deep-rooted fears by the balance and interplay of his imagery. The result is often an eerie calm that overlies the poems. This is true of an older poem like **"The Alligator Bride."** It's true also of a more recent poem I've mentioned, **"White Apples."** And it's true of the newer poems, though there the images don't jar against each other as they do in the earlier poems. They are all part of a whole, part of life on a New Hampshire farm. The eeriness comes from the clarity of the observation and thought they set in motion in the mind. . . . In the new poems Hall is looking more closely than ever at what he fears and what he knows he must accept, what is behind the screen door of the house in **"The Town of Hill,"** the trip "to the village of nightfall."

In the country of Donald Hall, there is a town so small the breath of a fern could knock it over. There the lion is loose in the garden, zebras, rattlesnakes, wildebeests, and cougars, and woodchucks on the lawns and in the tennis courts. There is a funeral procession for the dead brain cells. There is a dead pilot still strapped into the cockpit of his crashed plane in the jungle, the vines reaching through the broken windows. Other citizens in the country of Donald Hall are Dock Ellis and Henry Moore. In this country cheeses grow old and settled in their ways. There are horses named "Lady Ghost" and "Mackerel" and other names in the pasture of dead horses. The Alligator Bride poses in white lace on the bare wood floor. The country of Donald Hall is cold nights in New Hampshire and cold nights in Ann Arbor. It is poetry readings at Oxford and haying under the eye of Mt. Kearsarge. In the country of Donald Hall, the land and the past are alive and come down the mountainside to you, asking for water with their hats in their hands. Sit down with them. Give them water. (pp. 37-8)

> *Brent Spencer, "The Country of Donald Hall: A Review Essay," in* Poet and Critic, *Vol. 12, No. 3, 1980, pp. 30-8.*

BARRY WALLENSTEIN

In 1975, approaching fifty, Donald Hall quit his teaching post at the University of Michigan in Ann Arbor and moved to the farm in New Hampshire that had been in his family since his great-great grandfather. He had spent his childhood summers there and it remained a fixed place of security and wonder no matter how far he roamed. There are two recent books celebrating life at the ancestral farm, with photos of it adorning both covers. *Kicking the Leaves,* a book of poems, appeared in 1978. The book being reviewed here, *String Too Short to be Saved,* is a series of prose recollections that first appeared in 1961. It was reissued in 1979, with the addition of a most interesting epilogue.

String, despite the publisher's blurb, is not a collection of short stories. The separate yet interconnected reminiscences and narratives do not contain the tensions or resolutions associated with the short story. Instead, these are eleven extended episodes primarily about the poet's grandfather, and life on the farm as experienced by the boy and distilled through the many stories the old folks tell. The dominant mood is nostalgic and the method straightforward, marred only occasionally by the inflated "poetic" voice. . . . Yet overall the book's style is reflective, clear and easygoing. The book is full of country gossip—nothing sensational and no attempt to jazz it up.

The many close-up scenes, descriptions of nature and life on the farm, make no pretense about being objective. The poet's selectivity and evaluative memory of family and place give the book its flavor and its frequent mood of elegy and longing. . . .

Early in the book, Hall says that the "idea of their (the old folks') mortality was never far from the surface of my day," and this idea tinges every story or reminiscence that follows. Thus the book's real interest does not lie in the reminiscences themselves or in the description of nature . . . but in the love Hall feels for his family, his forebearers. He communicates their life with detail and ethical insight. About his grandfather he makes this careful distinction: "He always seemed adequate to his own poverty and bad luck, and he never denied a fact in his life. A time I remember really seeing him in depression was over someone else."

The nostalgia over times gone by and loved ones gone under is partly comprised of a living conservatism hinted at in the book's wonderfully ironic epigraph. It is an anecdote that tells of a man who is cleaning out the attic of a New England home and finds a box "full of tiny pieces of string. On the lid of the box there was an inscription in an old hand: 'String too short to be saved.'" Everything is saved on the farm. Hall would prefer the word preserved. . . .

In the last chapter, **"Out of the Garden,"** Hall makes a concrete association hinted at in a few places throughout the book: "My poems were keens over the dead, glorifying him (grandfather) as the saint of a destroyed civilization". . . . By the time he wrote the epilogue in 1975 he recognized that he had "made that familiar confusion of personal loss with social decay."

The final lines from the title poem of *Kicking the Leaves* extoll the lighter theme presented by the new epilogue:

> Now I leap and fall, exultant, recovering
> from death, on account of death, in accord
>   with the dead
> the smell and taste of leaves again,
> and the pleasure, the only long pleasure,
>   of taking a place
> in the story of leaves.

Ultimately the prose book expresses a moral imperative that goes beyond mere nostalgia and personal need. The author realizes the insight that "to be without history is like being forgotten." The book remembers and indeed memorializes an era in history as well as the family of a precocious boy who started reading and writing poems at a very young age. Fans of Donald Hall's poetry will gain from this book, especially if it is read in conjunction with *Kicking the Leaves.*

> *Barry Wallenstein, in a review of "String Too Short to Be Saved," in* The American Book Review, *Vol. 3, No. 3, March-April, 1981, p. 3.*

THE VIRGINIA QUARTERLY REVIEW

[The essays in *To Keep Moving: Essays 1959-1969*] not only chronicle many of the trends, concepts, crises, and surprises

of American poetry of a decade ago, but they also obliquely highlight the intellectual development of one of our foremost poets, Donald Hall. Poet, editor, educator, and literary historian, Hall has already shown us how well he can write about matters literary with his recent, marvelous book, *Remembering Poets.* This volume, an eclectic hodgepodge of essays on various subjects ranging from the uses of free verse to Wordsworth . . . to the value of reading, includes some pieces too brief or glib to be of anything more than documentary interest, but the longer essays, especially **"Poems Without Legs"** and **"Whitman: The Invisible World,"** are always engaging. In all of these selections it is obvious that Hall is enjoying himself, that he is someone who loves to discourse, and that he is willing to discourse on any subject. And that is the mark of a natural-born essayist. (pp. 128-29)

> *A review of "To Keep Moving: Essays 1959-1969," in* The Virginia Quarterly Review, *Vol. 57, No. 4 (Autumn, 1981), pp. 128-29.*

PUBLISHERS WEEKLY

Sports writing is a favored avocation of noted poet Donald Hall; it allows him to step out of himself and relax. And as a sports writer, Hall ranks with the greats. Baseball is the focal point of his attention; he observes that this is the sport accounting for the most memorable prose. Yet Hall's baseball writing is different from that of many other sports writers: there is a quiet depth and emphasis on the continuity, the tradition passed on from fathers to sons, that is not found in the works of Bernard Malamud or Roger Angell. Football is also chronicled [in *Fathers Playing Catch with Sons: Essays on Sport (Mostly Baseball)*], from the innocent losses at the author's own Hamden High to the lost innocence of the neo-professional world of big-time college football. Basketball and even ping-pong also come under Hall's scrutiny (the latter only because of his ability to twist his body underneath the cellar beams and around the furnace, winning matches against those who fancied a poet could have no athletic prowess at all). This is a wonderful collection of essays (and two poems) that no lover of sports and fine writing should miss.

> *A review of "Fathers Playing Catch with Sons: Essays on Sport (Mostly Baseball)," in* Publishers Weekly, *Vol. 226, No. 24, December 14, 1984, p. 49.*

THOMAS POWERS

There are some pretty wild spots in the hills of Vermont and New Hampshire. Just about all of them were farms once upon a time, but they've grown back to forest now, and you might see a deer, or a fox if you're lucky, or even one of those strange solitaries who dress and speak (a word or two at a time) like men but choose to live apart from men. The poet Donald Hall, whose *Ox-Cart Man* won the Caldecott Medal in 1980, has written a new book [*The Man Who Lived Alone*] that tells the story of such a man with amazing economy.

He has no name. He lives on the side of Ragged Mountain in a one-room camp cluttered with stuff—old nails he's collected and straightened, wasps' nests hanging on railroad spikes, stacks of yellowing newspapers, Bell jars filled with a season's produce from his garden and orchard. He's as native to the area as an old bear and just as shy of men.

He can do things—build a shotgun from scratch, for example. Think about that for a minute. Not much money passes through his hands. He works on the town roads for a couple of weeks each year to make the money to pay his taxes. Sometimes he does carpentry or shingles a roof for a neighbor. He has only one friend, or at least Mr. Hall only mentions one—Nan, two years younger, apparently a first cousin once removed. They lived together as children for a while, and he built his camp up the mountain from her family farm—what people of this sort call the home place. Most of what he does he does for her and her children and her grandchildren and finally her great-grandchildren.

We meet him when he is 6 years old. We leave him 70 years later, with his gray beard long enough to cover the darns on his shirt. Not much happens in between. "One year he stopped reading because he couldn't hold the newspaper far enough away. A couple of years later he found an old pair of glasses that somebody had dropped on the road and he went back to reading the Bible every day."

This is a love story, although the word "love" is not mentioned. The man who lives alone in fact lives as close to Nan, the object of his love, as the laws of consanguinity and the accidents of his life have allowed him to get. His extra love—of which, Mr. Hall makes it clear, there is a great deal—is given to places and two fellow solitaries, a mule and an owl.

Some years ago Mr. Hall wrote a wonderful book called *String Too Short to Be Saved,* about the New Hampshire farm on which he spent summers as a child. I remember a character in it a lot like the man who lived alone. On the evidence, Mr. Hall is still thinking about this real person and what his life meant. . . . *The Man Who Lived Alone* is a children's book only in the sense that it's the size and shape of a children's book and includes beautiful illustrations . . . , as children's books are supposed to. I think children will like it. I know I did.

Thomas Powers, in a review of "The Man Who Lived Alone," in The New York Times Book Review, *January 13, 1985, p. 26.*

BERT ATKINSON

Always leave it to the poetic mind to make us aware of the boundaries of our sensibility. Donald Hall, a distinguished poet and critic, does just this in *Fathers Playing Catch With Sons.* His essays vary in tone and mood, but all are concerned with the metaphors that sport provides through tradition and seasonal ritual. . . . The title essay is a warm, humorous account of his brief stay at the Pittsburgh Pirates' spring training camp in the early 1970's. On a freelance assignment, he was an observer and out-of-shape participant. It also reveals a part of Mr. Hall's adolescence that is preserved and refracted through an adult mind. His love for the sport gives him relaxation from his craft and a place where "the child [in him] can walk." The most notable essay is a reprint of the first chapter of Mr. Hall's book *Dock Ellis in the Country of Baseball* that can stand alone as a profile of the former Pirates pitcher. It lends substance to what otherwise would be a tenuous collection. Another essay, **"Proseball: Sports, Stories, and Style,"** is an appreciation of baseball writing in which Mr. Hall evaluates some of the best writers of the genre. In **"Baseball and the Meaning of Life,"** he becomes philosophical to show how baseball bridges the generations. Yet all the time, he reminds us that while baseball is a diversion for the fans, it is a serious business for the players and the owners. Mr. Hall's performance here assures us that, in his prose about sport as well as in his poetry, metaphor remains alive and well.

Bert Atkinson, in a review of "Fathers Playing Catch with Sons: Essays on Sport (Mostly Baseball)," in The New York Times Book Review, *February 10, 1985, p. 25.*

Robert (Earl) Hayden

1913-1980

(Born Asa Sheffey) American poet, essayist, editor, and dramatist.

Hayden is a major black American poet whose literary achievements are widely recognized. His poetry is elegant and dignified and exhibits a strong sense of form. Though not strictly adhering to traditional structures, his poems are tightly controlled and somewhat detached in tone. During the 1960s Hayden came into conflict with the proponents of the "Black Arts" movement, who accused him of denying his Afro-American heritage and adopting writing standards prescribed and practiced by the white literary establishment. Hayden maintained that black poets should be judged by the same criteria as other writers, and he warned against "ghettoizing" black writers, thereby separating them from the rest of the literary world and limiting their audience. Hayden was a follower of the Bahá'í religion, and his faith has had a significant impact on his work. The Bahá'í tenets include a belief in the essential oneness of all people and in the importance of the artist's work as a means of praising God and serving humankind. Hayden devoted a large portion of his work to exploring black concerns and celebrating black history and culture.

Born and raised in a Detroit ghetto neighborhood called "Paradise Valley," Hayden attended Detroit City College (now Wayne State University) and the University of Michigan, where he studied with W. H. Auden. As a student Hayden read and admired the poets of the Harlem Renaissance, especially Countee Cullen, Langston Hughes, and Orrick Johns, as well as such other renowned poets of the period as Carl Sandburg and Edna St. Vincent Millay. Hayden's early work shows the influence of these writers and is considered somewhat imitative, but in his later works his style became more clearly his own. The concerns central to all of Hayden's work are evident in *Heart-Shape in the Dust* (1940), *The Lion and the Archer* (1948), and *Figures of Time* (1955). Some of his most famous poems are included in these books: "Middle Passage," a narrative which describes the passage of a slave ship carrying blacks from Africa to America; "Runagate Runagate," about the underground railroad; and "Frederick Douglass," an unrhymed sonnet commemorating the great black leader.

Hayden did not gain widespread recognition until the mid-1960s. In 1966 *A Ballad of Remembrance* (1962) won the grand prize for poetry at the first World Festival of Negro Arts in Dakar, Senegal. With *A Ballad of Remembrance* and the books that followed—*Selected Poems* (1966), *Words in the Mourning Time* (1970), *The Night-Blooming Cereus* (1972), and *Angle of Ascent: New and Selected Poems* (1975)—Hayden broadened his range of topics and altered the tone of his poetry. While still focusing much of his attention on black experience, Hayden began to write poems about travel, art, family, the Bahá'í religion, and other subjects. John S. Wright noted that this later poetry is "less embossed, less erudite, more serene even when dealing with the violence and chaos of the time, unguardedly conversational, and measurably freer." In 1976 Hayden was appointed poetry consultant to the Library of Congress. This honor was significant both because Hayden

was the first black writer to hold the position and because it confirmed his stature in American literature.

In *American Journal* (1978) Hayden continued to explore and celebrate the history and achievements of black Americans. This volume includes poems on such important black pioneers as Phillis Wheatley, Paul Lawrence Dunbar, and Matthew Hensen, the explorer who traveled to the North Pole with Admiral Robert Peary. "Elegies for Paradise Valley" evokes the sights and sounds of Hayden's Detroit childhood. "American Journal" is a long narrative chronicling the impressions of an observer from another planet who visits the United States. Robert G. O'Meally called *American Journal* "a book of unforgettable images of America and her people, a prayerful report from one of our most hauntingly accurate, and yet hopeful, recorders." Hayden's posthumous publications include *Collected Prose* (1984) and *Collected Poems* (1985).

(See also *CLC*, Vols. 5, 9, 14; *Contemporary Authors*, Vols. 69-72, Vols. 97-100 [obituary]; *Something about the Author*, Vols. 19, 26; and *Dictionary of Literary Biography*, Vol. 5.)

ROBERT HAYDEN [INTERVIEW WITH JOHN O'BRIEN]

[*This interview was originally published in* Interviews with Black Writers, *written by John O'Brien, in 1973.*]

[O'Brien:] *Are you sometimes struck by the mystery of your art?*

[Hayden:] I've always felt that poetry and the poetic process are pretty mysterious. What is it that makes one a poet? What are you doing when you write a poem? What is poetry? The feeling of mystery is no doubt intensified because you can't deliberately set out to be a poet. You can't become one by taking courses in creative writing. You are born with the gift, with a feeling for language and a certain manner of responding to life. You respond in a particular way to yourself, to the basic questions that concern all human beings—the nature of the universe, love, death, God, and so forth. And that way of responding, of coming to grips with life, determines the kind of poetry you write. Once you discover you're a poet—and you have to find out for yourself—you can study the art, learn the craft, and try to become a worthy servitor. But you can't *will* to be a poet. This is an age of overanalysis as well as overkill, and we've analyzed poetry and the poetic process to a point where analysis has become tiresome, not to say dangerous for the poet. And for all our investigations, mysteries remain. And I hope they always will.

Do you see a progression in your work? Do you realize that you are writing poetry today that you could never have succeeded with ten years ago?

I've been very much aware of that. Yes. I think I'm now writing poems I couldn't have written ten or fifteen years ago. But I should add that some of my best-known poems were written back then. But there've been changes in outlook and technique since, and so I'm able to accomplish, when I'm lucky, what I once found too difficult to bring off successfully. I didn't know enough. Still, there are elements, characteristics in my work now, that seem always to have been present. Certain subjects, themes, persist, and—perhaps—will continue to give my work direction. My interest in history, especially Afro-American history, has been a major influence on my poetry. And I have a strong sense of the past in general, that recurs in much of my work. I don't have any nostalgia for the past, but a feeling for its relationship to the present as well as to the future. And I like to write about people. I'm more interested in people than in things or in abstractions, philosophical (so-called) ideas. In heroic and "baroque" people especially; in outsiders, pariahs, losers. And places, localities, landscapes have always been a favorite source for me. I once thought of using *People and Places* as the title for one of my books. Despite changes in outlook and technique over the years, the qualities I was striving for as a younger poet are the same ones I'm striving for today, basically. I've always wanted my poems to have something of a dramatic quality. I've always thought that a poem should have tension—dramatic and structural. And I've always been concerned with tone, with sound in relation to sense or meaning. I sometimes feel that I write by the word, not by the line. I'm perhaps oversensitive to the weight and color of words. I hear my words and lines as I write them, and if they don't sound right to me, then I know I'll have to go on revising until they do. I revise endlessly, I might add.

Did you ever fear that you might stop developing as a poet, that perhaps in another year or two years you would have exhausted yourself?

Oh, yes. A year or so ago—before I'd completed *The Night Blooming Cereus*—I was afraid I'd never be able to write a new poem again. . . . I went stale, felt I was repeating myself, had nothing more to say. I've been through all this before,

many times in fact. *Cereus* . . . was a breakthrough for me, and no doubt that's why it's my favorite book up to now. Writing it released me, also confirmed ideas and feelings I'd had before, but distrusted. I began to move in a new direction and to consolidate my gains, such as they were.

When you first started writing, were there poets that you tried to imitate and hoped you would be as good as, some day?

When I was in college I loved Countee Cullen, Jean Toomer, Elinor Wylie, Edna St. Vincent Millay, Sara Teasdale, Langston Hughes, Carl Sandburg, Hart Crane. I read all the poetry I could get hold of, and I read without discrimination. Cullen became a favorite. I felt an affinity and wanted to write in his style. . . . All through my undergraduate years I was pretty imitative. As I discovered poets new to me, I studied their work and tried to write as they did. . . . I reached the point, inevitably, where I didn't want to be influenced by anyone else. I tried to find my own voice, my own way of seeing. I studied with W. H. Auden in graduate school, a strategic experience in my life. I think he showed me my strength and weaknesses as poet in ways no one else before had done. (pp. 116-18)

I know that your religion has greatly affected your poetry. Have your religious views changed since writing "**Electrical Storm,**" *where you recorded a near encounter with death? There seems to be a skepticism in that poem, absent in your most recent volume of poetry,* **Words in the Mourning Time.**

No, not actually. I'm only suggesting the skepticism I might have felt earlier in my life. This wasn't a factor at the time I wrote the poem. I've always been a believer of sorts, despite periods of doubt and questioning. I've always had God-consciousness, as I call it, if not religion.

Do you think that there is a religious dimension to the work of the poet? Is there a special role that he must play in a century like ours?

Being a poet is role enough, and special enough. What else can I say? I object to strict definitions of what a poet is or should be, because they usually are thought up by people with an axe to grind—by those who care less about poetry than they do about some cause. We're living in a time when individuality is threatened by a kind of mechanizing anonymity. And by regimentation. In order to be free, you must submit to tyranny, to ideological slavery, in the name of freedom. And, obviously, this is the enemy of the artist; it stultifies anything creative. Which brings me to my own view of the role of the poet, the artist. I am convinced that if poets have any calling, function, *raison d'être* beyond the attempt to produce viable poems—and that in itself is more than enough—it is to affirm the humane, the universal, the potentially divine in the human creature. And I'm sure the artist does this best by being true to his or her own vision and to the demands of the art. This is my view; it's the conviction out of which I write. I do not set it up as an imperative for others. Poetry, all art, it seems to me is ultimately religious in the broadest sense of the term. It grows out of, reflects, illuminates our inmost selves, and so on. It doesn't have to be sectarian or denominational. There's a tendency today—more than a tendency, it's almost a conspiracy—to delimit poets, to restrict them to the political and the socially or racially conscious. To me, this indicates gross ignorance of the poet's true function as well as of the function and value of poetry as an art. With a few notable exceptions, poets have generally been on the side of justice and humanity. I can't imagine any poet worth his salt today not being aware of social evils, human needs. But I feel I have the right to deal with these matters in my own way, in terms of my own understanding of what a poet is. I resist whatever would force me into a role as politician, sociologist, or yea-sayer to current ideologies. I know who I am, and pretty much what I want to say.

There's an impersonal tone in almost all of your poetry. You're removed from what you write about, even when a poem is obviously about something that has happened to you.

Yes, I suppose it's true I have a certain detachment. I'm unwilling, even unable, to reveal myself as directly in my poems as some other poets do. Frequently, I'm writing about myself but speaking through a mask, a persona. There are troublesome things I would like to exteriorize by writing about them directly. One method for getting rid of your inner demons sometimes is to be able to call their names. I've managed to do so occasionally, but not very often. I could never write the confessional poems that Anne Sexton, Robert Lowell, John Berryman have become identified with. And perhaps I don't honestly wish to. Reticence has its aesthetic values too, you know. Still, I greatly admire the way Michael S. Harper, for example, makes poems out of personal experiences that must have been devastating for him. He's a marvelously gifted poet. I agree that poets like Harper and Lowell do us a service. They reveal aspects of their lives that tell us something about our own. One of the functions of poetry anyway. I think I tend to enter so completely into my own experiences most of the time that I have no creative energy left afterward. (pp. 119-21)

Do you think of yourself as belonging to any school of poetry? Do you place yourself in a romantic tradition as well as a symbolist?

I don't know what to say to that. I suppose I think of myself as a symbolist of a kind, and symbolism is a form of romanticism by definition. I've often considered myself a realist who distrusts so-called reality. Perhaps it all comes down to my being a "romantic realist." How would I know? Leave classification to the academicians. I do know that I'm always trying in my fumbling way to get at the truth, the reality, behind appearances, and from this has come one of my favorite themes. I want to know what things are, how they work, what a given process is, and so on. When I was writing **"Zeus over Redeye,"** for instance, I studied the booklets I picked up at the Redstone Arsenal so I'd learn the correct terminology, get the facts about rocket missiles. I scarcely used any of this information, but it gave me a background against which my poem could move. (p. 121)

Except when you are dealing with an obvious historical situation, you depend upon the present tense in your poems.

I've made a superficial—very superficial—analysis of the recurrence of the present tense in my poems, and I think I may be using it to achieve dramatic immediacy and because in a sense there is no past, only the present. The past is also the present. The experiences I've had in the past are now a part of my mind, my subconscious, and they are there forever. They have determined the present for me; they exist in it.

*There appears to be a progression in your long poem **"Words in the Mourning Time."** The first few sections catalogue the madness of our age, particularly that of the 1960s. Yet love enters in the last section and restores what appeared to be a hopeless condition. I'm not sure how you move from the vision*

of the evils to one of love. Were you suggesting that love comes after the violence and killing, or perhaps because of them?

The final poem is the culmination, the climax of the sequence. For me, it contains the answers to the questions the preceding poems have stated or implied. If I seem to come to any conclusion about injustice, suffering, violence at all, it's in the lines about man being "permitted to be man." And it's in the last poem, written originally for a Bahá'í occasion. Bahá'u'lláh urged the absolute, inescapable necessity for human unity, the recognition of the fundamental oneness of mankind. He also prophesied that we'd go through sheer hell before we achieved anything like world unity—partly owing to our inability to love. And speaking of love, I try to make the point, in the elegy for Martin Luther King in the section we're discussing, that love is not easy. It's not a matter of sloppy sentimentality. It demands everything of you. I think it's much, much easier to hate than to love. (pp. 123-24)

In **"Monet's 'Waterlilies'"** *you refer to "the world each of us has lost." Is it a world of innocence, of childhood?*

I'm absolutely cold to the voguish and overused theme of "lost innocence." Maybe I'm just too pseudo-Freudian. I might have been thinking about childhood, though surely not about innocence. But no, I can't honestly say I was even thinking about childhood. I grant the poem could be so interpreted without doing too much violence to its meaning. Certainly, children, as we all know, live in a fantasy world, in a realm of the imagination that's forever lost to them when they grow up. But each of us has known a happier time, whether as children or as adults. Each of us has lost something that once gave the world a dimension it will never have again for us, except in memory. A botched answer, to be sure, but the best I can offer at the moment.

Is it through art that one is able to recapture it or at least become highly conscious of it?

Sometimes. That particular Monet helps me to recapture something—to remember something. I would say that one of the valuable functions of all the arts is to make us aware, to illuminate human experience, to make us more conscious, more alive. That's why they give us pleasure, even when their subjects or themes are "unpleasant." (pp. 127-28)

Robert Hayden and John O'Brien, "A 'Romantic Realist', " in Collected Prose *by Robert Hayden, edited by Frederick Glaysher, The University of Michigan Press, 1984, pp. 115-28.*

MICHAEL S. HARPER

[Robert Hayden] was a man of considered reserve, with an unsuppressible elegance, his bowties, watch-chain and old man's comforts giving him the glow of a courtly preacher who was summoned to give the word, and well he did, recalling his early childhood testifying days in Detroit's "Paradise Valley", scenes captured by the images of a sanctified Second Baptist Church Service in his **"Witch Doctor"** poem, which conjured up the *high-falutin'* church talk of a would-be saviour in the tradition of a Daddy Grace. Hayden spent his early days in the 'save your sight' school program, sometimes playing the violin, and picking up the lore of his adopted parents, the Haydens; and when he was to 'finish' Detroit City College (later Wayne State University) as a Spanish major, and do research on the WPA's Federal Writers Project gathering the folkstuff of his people, he spoke of the neighbors who slipped him book money, small coins and, on rare occasions, a dollar bill, to help him get through school—they made him proud as he made them sing in poetry. Hayden has been called a stellar poet of remembrance with a symbolist bent for mysticism and for the cryptic phrasings of the bizarre and the occult, but most folks saw him as a consummate storyteller who had the pace, coloration and detailed finish of a romantic, with an iconoclastic air. His poetic heroes, Dunbar and Keats, pushed him toward *The Tempest* and the ancestors: Pa Hayden for one, whom Hayden memorialized in the sonnet, **"Those Winter Sundays"**:

> Speaking indifferently to him,
> who had driven out the cold
> and polished my good shoes as well.
> What did I know, what did I know
> of love's austere and lonely offices?

Hayden said, in an interview, that he wrote **"Frederick Douglass,"** his great accentual sonnet of religious American possibility, for the future, when 'man was permitted to be man.' He dreamed of freedom and literacy, a perennial dream of humane transformation. There is no lost Eden in Hayden's *oeuvre;* he was a most elegant prognosticator of the future— a Baha'i for almost forty years—and a craftsman par excellence. His knowledge of poetic traditions led him beyond many of the experiments steeped in a conscious modernism; his **"Middle Passage,"** a poem in eight voices which borrowed from ships' logs and court testimony, slave and master, was written, in part, to answer Eliot's *The Waste Land* with the addition of a broad and pungent social reality—'Voyage through death / to life upon these shores'. His recalling the schizoid past's brutalities was always shaped to light the future. He was a poet of the discovery of self as art, not a proponent of the confessional mode, but a poet of design who saw patterns of consciousness in the foibles and fascinations of the most public and private surfaces. These surfaces that Hayden polished always opened through a trapdoor to a 'striptease of reality'— no "deep image" for him but the deep pit, lest the poet— "squalored in that pit"—forget his wings. His last poems display utter candor and embossed technique, with no self-consciousness; the poems **"A Letter From Phillis Wheatley"** ... and **"Paul Laurence Dunbar"** ... are talismans of his inheritance, and his possibility. The unknown visitor from elsewhere in his title poem, *American Journal,* is more than any observer ("must be more careful item learn to use 'okay' / their pass word 'okay'") and less than any spokesman for the country, though his voice suggests the inner reexamination of that *quiddity* hidden in the word made flesh, those sacred documents that brought form and geography together.... (pp. 231-33)

Hayden's ballads reveal a story told, offhandedly, of a storytelling people, for he was a national poet in the voicings he could capture in a phrase; he could also recall Wallace Stevens and take us into that hidden arena of transcendence.... (p. 233)

Hayden has been working as a liberator in the only world he knew, ours. That spiritual realm he refers to in his poems is glow and afterglow of rockets and science fiction. The poem he was working on, and to which he hoped to return, at the end, was for Josephine Baker; his notes and drafts might tell us one day whether he made that deadline. As a figure who, increasingly, will earn his rightful place in our hearts, in our minds and libraries and anthologies, his epitaph ought be the poems he gave us.... (pp. 233-34)

Michael S. Harper, "Remembering Robert E. Hayden," in The Carleton Miscellany, *Vol. XVIII, No. 3, Winter, 1980, pp. 231-34.*

GARY ZEBRUN

The great poets of the 20th century *have* achieved angles of ascent, transcendences of beauty, even though modern pressures of cruelty and destructiveness have made these ascents seem more precarious and uncertain than ever before. Eliot's measured dance in his "Four Quartets," his great ascent, is forever shadowed by the first horror of "The Wasteland." William Carlos Williams, as his contemporary Wallace Stevens noted in the preface to the 1934 edition of Williams's *Collected Poems,* insisted that "life would be untolerable except for the fact that one has, from the top, such an exceptional view of the public dump ..." All the wonder and solace that Yeat's poems can provide have their genesis in what he called in his famous closure to "The Circus Animal's Desertion," *the foul rag and bone shop of the heart*. It is out of Robert Hayden's own version of these dark and dingy places, completely grounded in the history of America and his own lifetime, in **"Hiroshima Watts My Lai,"** that his wellspring of plangency—and transcendence—takes place.

The voice of the speaker in Hayden's best work twists and squirms its way out of anguish in order to tell, or sing, stories of American history—in particular the courageous and plaintive record of Afro-American history—and to chart the thoughts and feelings of the poet's own private space. Both histories— the personal and historical ones—are transfigured into Hayden's poems, which are striking examples of what Emerson said a poem must be: "spheres and cubes, to be seen and smelled and handled." What one sees, smells, and touches in his poetry is the human imagination *searching* for something else besides the muck of history or of one's own foul rag and bone shop.... (p. 22)

The speaker in the 3rd section of the poem, **"Stars,"** describes another seeker, *Sojourner Truth,* who "comes walking barefoot / out of slavery / ancestress / childless mother / following the stars / her mind a star." One of the primary human truths, Hayden believes, is freedom, the first principle on which America was founded and from which it has repeatedly strayed. It is personified here as a childless mother, the ironic and complex figure of the first freed black American desiring to give birth to free sons and daughters. But this figure remains sheer desire, starlight; she is a paradoxically painful and encouraging reminder that freedom (especially in this crazy winding down of the 20th century) remains, for many Americans, an unfulfilled desire. There is a rift between what is and what one desires, and these barren facts of life and brilliant dreams of the imagination become a compelling and *challenging* tension in much of Hayden's poetry.

Throughout his work this urge to find relief from the horror and constriction of ordinary life remains simply the wish for transcendence, a kind of prayer, expressed, for example, in the 5th section of the remarkable series, **"Beginnings,"** the first poem in the collection *Angle of Ascent:*

> Floyd Collins oh
> I guess he's a goner,
> Pa Hayden sighed,
> the Extra trembling
> in his hands.

Poor game loner
trapped in the rock
of Crystal Cave, as
once in Kentucky coal-
mine dark (I taste the
darkness yet)
my greenhorn dream of
life. Alive down there
in his grave. Open
for him, Blue Door.

In this poignant lyric about the trapped miner, Floyd Collins, Hayden portrays how inextricably tangled are our human dreams and the hard, like Kentucky coal, realities of our lives. Here is the greenhorn dream of life (reminiscent of both the speaker's childhood and our first innocence, our lost Eden), and the Blue Door (the hoped-for opening in the earth and way out for the trapped miner). These rich, appealing images of beauty and solace, however, are checked by the first appearance of the father, trembling with fear and grief from the bleak news of Collins's disaster and by the coal mine darkness itself, so powerful that the speaker can taste it, in which the splendor of crystal and innocence and relief is trapped. The lyric form itself becomes in Hayden's difficult style a troubled, almost imprisoned voice of the heart. Beginning here with the wholly plain lines "Floyd Collins oh / I guess he's a goner, Pa Hayden signed, the Extra trembling / suddenly in his hands," the poem suddenly shifts to the trapped, worried voice of sorrow, trapped in the rock / of Crystal Cave, as / once in Kentucky coal-mine dark . . . ," until it makes its transcendence, or noble wish for it, which is perhaps the only solace left for late 20th century poets: "Open / for him, Blue Door." . . . It is in poems, like this one, so finely crafted, that Hayden earns a place in literary history as one of the few contemporary poets of major distinction—a knowledgeable, competent, and inspired craftsman—who illustrates what may be in store for our poetry descending from Dickinson, Whitman, Frost, and Williams.

Somehow a striking sense of beauty, precarious as it is amidst material ugliness and threatening social and political actions, does emerge in these poems. In **"The Night Blooming Cereus"** the speaker describes a night vigil during which he waited, hoping to see the heavy bud break into flower. "We waited," he says, "aware / of rigorous design." And the design that Hayden witnesses is as bewildering and contradictory as the design that Robert Frost describes in his famous poem called "Design." As in Frost's poem where assorted characters of death and blight meet, the dimple fat spider devouring the dead moth, against the background of the beautiful white heal-all, Hayden's night blooming cereus, a promise of so much beauty, both repells and fascinates the speaker. So, although he imagined it "packed / tight with its miracle . . . ," it seems, as it struggles to bloom, like an "eyeless bird head, / beak that would gape / with grotesque life-squak." Notice how tight, how compressed the language of these lines themselves are, not only representing the closed bud of the flower, but the *enclosed* place of consciousness, both of which contain so much beautiful possibility struggling to break out. When the cereus flower blossoms, it appears as a symbol of the hard earned and short-lived beauty, older than man himself; as the cry of doom that is existential in its source. . . . (pp. 23-4)

"Elegies for Paradise Valley," one of Hayden's recent poems included in the volume, *American Journal,* is a collection of ballad-like poems about Hayden's dead kin and acquaintances from his childhood: Madam Artelia, Auntie Belle, Miss Alice,

Jim—the Watusi prince, and especially Uncle Crip. The Paradise Valley of the title is a city slum in which one of the many voices of the poem remembers a junkie who died in maggots there and recalls the hatred for his kind he saw glistening like tears in the policemen's eyes. The title is no mere display of cleverness, or bitterness, but a roadsign for the reader that is packed with irony and poignant half-truths. City slum that Paradise Valley is, it goes beyond its surface decay, for it contains the sacred or nearly sacred characters that the poet brings powerfully before us. . . . **"Elegies for Paradise Valley"** is one of Hayden's finest poems, it provides a rich example of the numerous tonal variations present in his work, including humor, anger, uncertainty, and love. His characters seem at once real and mythic. His ability to shift into voices quickly and effortlessly might remind a reader of some of the dramatic scenes in *Moby Dick,* in which Melville has created a flurry of believable voices: Ishmael, Queequeg, Pip, Starbuck, and Ahab, all about to speak on the deck of the Pequod.

Robert Hayden, supremely concerned with craft, insists on exploring the fictions and truths of the heart that only a poet fastened to experience can convey. In particular, he studies the noble and tragic history of Afro-Americans as he charts the contradictory feelings of a *thinking* man, black or white. There is throughout his poetry a recurring elegiac tone. It is this plaintive note, this wellspring of plangency, that gives Hayden's poetry a signature of its own and that places him as an important link in an American tradition of soul-searching. This tradition received its first brilliance with Hawthorne and Melville, with Whitman and Dickinson, was extended to Frost and Crane, and during our time has passed to Lowell and Hayden. They have sought the spiritual in the land and in the heart, they have insisted on keeping up the highest order of technical brilliance (the craft of writing), and they have not balked at the difficulty and darkness which threaten their searches.

In his poetry, Robert Hayden is ceaselessly trying to achieve his angle of ascent, his transcendence, which must not be an escape from the horror of history or from the loneliness of individual mortality, but an ascent that somehow transforms the horror and creates a blessed permanence. This task, as he indicates in the swirling contradictions of his verse, might well be a folly. Nonetheless, it is *his* necessary folly and the single glorious folly that the human race in its vast imagination holds dear. . . . (pp. 25-6)

> *Gary Zebrun, "In the Darkness a Wellspring of Plangency: The Poetry of Robert Hayden," in* Obsidian: Black Literature in Review, *Vol. 8, No. 1, Spring, 1981, pp. 22-6.*

JOHN S. WRIGHT

In one of the quieter moments in the expanded edition of his last book, *American Journal,* Robert Hayden offers a rare, unmediated comment on the trajectory of his life: "When my fourth decade came, / I learned my name was not my name. / I felt deserted, mocked . . . And the name on the book was dead, / like the life my mother fled, / like the life I might have known." Other names, unwanted names—"Four Eyes. And worse"—kept Hayden inside and isolated as a boy, plying his abysmally poor eyesight with books. So "Old Four Eyes fled / to safety in the danger zones / Tom Swift and Kubla Khan traversed." That world of the artist's imagination seems to be a place of refuge but is in fact a danger zone, Hayden later concluded, because art is both cruel and mysterious. (pp. 904-05)

The mystery of his own art he was most sanguine about, saw himself, in fact—in that veiled, allusive way he usually treated the details of his own biography—as a "mystery boy" looking for kin. If Robert Earl Hayden had been a confessional poet, he would probably have made more capital out of a life rich with the dramatic tension he wanted his poems to have. He would have worked more pointedly the flamboyant ironies of a World War I era boyhood in the "Paradise Valley" section of Black Detroit. He would have exposed and explored how his work's almost ritual preoccupation with identity, with names, and with ambiguous realities reflected the bruising fact that "Robert Hayden" was his adoptive, not his legal name and that discovering what that "real" name was served as part of his initiation into fuller manhood. If the confessional mode had better fit him, he would have chronicled also the "burdens of consciousness" that his dual commitment to human freedom and artistic integrity made him bear; he would have logged the jagged confrontation with the Black Arts writers which ultimately turned his long tenure at Fisk University into a trial of words and which made him for a moment seem a naysayer to blackness and so become one of a younger generation's many scapegoat kings.

But Hayden was not a confessional poet like so many of his contemporaries because, as he acknowledged, he entered his own experiences so completely that he had no creative energy left afterward. He could admire the way that Anne Sexton, Robert Lowell, John Berryman, and Michael Harper made poems out of devastating personal experiences; but he countered, in his own defense, that "reticence has *its* aesthetic values *too.*" And so, with words at least, he wore the mask, and won in wearing it the detached control and objectivity without which poetic marvels like his most widely acclaimed poem, **"Middle Passage,"** would not have been possible. From the apprentice work of his earliest book, *Heart Shape in the Dust* (1940), to the closing lines of *American Journal*, he pushed toward the mastery of materials, outlook, and technique that would enable him to strike through the masks reality wore. And so he made himself, like the Malcolm X of his honorific poem **"El-Hajj Malik El-Shabazz,"** one of Ahab's Native Sons, though rejecting Ahab.

The continuities in the progressive unmaskings, which Robert Hayden described as his "slim offerings over four decades," are striking. His absorption with the past, especially the black past, provided one axis of subject and theme for him—an absorption that brooked no lost Edens, no nostalgia, but which transformed archetype and artifact into a poetry of revelation. At the same time, he was drawn more to the dramas of human personality than to things or abstractions or philosophical ideas. In *American Journal*, as in all his books, the places, landscapes, and localities he re-creates so minutely live primarily through his heroic and what he called "baroque" people—more often than not outsiders, pariahs, even losers. As he revealed in an interview with John O'Brien [see excerpt above], Hayden thought of himself as a "symbolist of a kind," as a "realist who distrusts so-called reality," as a "romantic realist." And he couched his symbolist explorations of human suffering and transcendence in a world-view permeated by an omnipresent, though never obtrusive, "God-consciousness." Poetry, indeed all art, he felt, was "ultimately religious in the broadest sense of the term"; if poets have any calling beyond fulfilling the demands of their craft, he insisted, "it is to affirm the humane, the universal, the potentially divine in the human creature." (pp. 905-06)

Far from embodying any naïve optimism or sentimental religiosity, Hayden's vision of the human predicament and of human possibility presents love as characteristically an *agon*, presents God and nature as beneficences shrouding caprice or indifference, presents our slow progress toward the godlike in man as a scourging, scarifying journey through maze and madness. That "voyage through death to life upon these shores" (which his **"Middle Passage"** chronicles, for example) discovers its metaphors for sin, sickness, and salvation in the historic matrix of the Atlantic slave trade and racial slavery. But the death wish, the masks, the phantasms that lure the crew and cargo of the slave ship *Amistad* figure no less potently in the timeless and seemingly antithetical "easeful azure" world of disquieting natural beauty to which the awestruck persona of Hayden's **"The Diver"** descends.

But lest we overstress the dark side of Hayden's poetic world, I should add that nothing in his work is *less* ambiguous, nothing *more* affirming of human hopes for illumination, perfection, and freedom than his gallery of portraits sketching the possibilities for heroic action in the face of even the most murderous and dispiriting forces. The flight *to* and fight *for* freedom dramatized in **"Runagate, Runagate,"** the rectifying resurrecting images in his **"Ballad of Nat Turner,"** the transcendent fortitude captured in his dedicatory sonnet **"Frederick Douglass,"** the unbowed tradition of communal artistry celebrated in **"Homage to the Empress of the Blues"**—combine to create a lineage of heroic *presences* painted in rich hues and delivered from oppression and obscurity, presences to which all of us, at the level of will and aspiration, are kin.

As in the collections containing these earlier poems, in *American Journal* Hayden's portraits of the famous and the faceless alternate. The opening poem, **"A Letter from Phillis Wheatley,"** is suffused with all the ironist's recognition of incongruities and his controlled acceptance of them: the Sable Muse holds tears and outrage in check with exquisite syntax and diction and with the somber humor that, in Idyllic England, notes the Serpent's hiss on the flickering tongues of the "foppish would-be wits" who dub her the "Cannibal Mockingbird," humor that dispels unseemly gloom with the amusement won from a soot-faced English chimney sweep's query, "Does you, M'Lady, sweep chimneys too?" Hayden's rendering of John Brown, originally commissioned to accompany a portfolio of paintings by Jacob Lawrence, reveals a man not cruel, not mad, but unsparing, a life with the "symmetry of a cross," driven by the "Fury of truth, its enigmas, its blinding illuminations." These familiar lives Hayden counter-weights with those of the anonymous Rag Man who faces the wind and the winter streets with scarecrow patches "and wordless disdain as though wrapped in fur," rejecting the world and its fleeting pity; or **"The Tattooed Man,"** a "grotesque outsider" whose body is a bizarre, sideshow mosaic that feeds his pride and repels the love he wants but "cannot (will not?)" cleanse his flesh to win. His is the heroism of the stoic ("all art is pain / suffered and outlived") and of the realist ("It is too late / for any change / but death. / I am I").

The poetic inspiration behind Hayden's images of the heroic came early in his career and stayed late. The apprentice poems of *Heart-Shape in the Dust* were largely imitative of the themes and conventions of the New Negro Renaissance, and reflected a young poet still in search of his voice. These first poems nonetheless made the rich storehouse of legend and lore (acquired by Hayden as a folklore researcher for the Federal Writer's Project in the late thirties) into an enduring framework for later achievements. In this first book, his long mass chant **"These Are My People,"** his portrait of gallows-bound slave rebel Gabriel Prosser, the blues-toned resilience he pictures in the "po' colored boy" of **"Bachanale"**—all offered shadings of the ordinary extraordinary heroic spirit that Hayden would continue to sing long after the formulaic stridency and vaguely socialistic ideology in which these poems were couched had disappeared from his poetic scheme.

During these formative years, Hayden absorbed and reconciled a variety of poetic influences—Dunbar, Cullen, Langston Hughes, Millay, Sandburg, Hart Crane, Stephen Vincent Benét, Eliot, and Yeats. In his second book, *The Lion and the Archer* (written with Myron O'Higgins and published in 1948), and in *Figures of Time* (1955) Hayden showed the impress of what he later called "a strategic experience" in his life: as a graduate student at the University of Michigan he had studied with W. H. Auden, and Auden had shown him his strengths and weaknesses as a poet in ways no one else had done. *The Lion and the Archer* and *Figures of Time* presented Hayden *as stylist* moving toward the baroque, the surreal, and away from what he rejected as "chauvinistic and doctrinaire." The dated dialect and colloquialism of his earliest work gave way now to dense, sculpted language which glittered and whirled like a prism. And though his folk themes and heroic motifs acquired a new kind of grandeur, his audience—his black readers in particular—were not uniformly pleased with the changes. *Heart-Shape in the Dust* had been praised in *Opportunity* magazine as "a true marriage of form and content, a happy fusion of mastery of technique with the rough and raw material of life." And Robert Hayden had been pictured to be a worthy challenger to Langston Hughes and Sterling Brown as an interpreter of Afro-American experience.

But as the scathingly sarcastic review in *Crisis* magazine of *The Lion and the Archer* showed, Hayden's movement toward a more complex and consciously modernist poetry exacted the high price of what would be a recurrent accusation: that he had abandoned his people and his political commitments for a poetry of arcane, overwrought diction and professional pretension.

There is little doubt that Hayden's development as a poet has placed increasing demands on his readers; and Hayden himself—unceasingly self-critical—has acknowledged that he was inclined to be "perhaps oversensitive to the weight and color of words." But the poetic language and form he experimented with during that crucial phase of his career was no mere library poet's fixation on the ornamental and esoteric, nor any reclusive linguistic introversion. Hayden was seeking ways, on his own terms, to make the techniques of innovations of the New Poetry movement of the twenties and thirties his own, to bring *all* the resources of the English language—classical and vernacular, popular and academic—to bear on the illumination of Afro-American experience. He had "always wanted to be a Negro poet . . . the same way Yeats is an Irish poet." So he had always resisted the private temptation and the public call to restrict himself to the treatment of exclusively black experience. Yet he felt it was no paradox that he consistently found his most intensely universal symbols for human striving and strife in the materials of Afro-American life.

So with the appearance in 1962 of his fourth book, *A Ballad of Remembrance,* it was a Robert Hayden "meditative, ironic, and richly human"—qualities he ascribes to Mark Van Doren in that volume's title poem—who, full-voiced and with consummate control, created from "the rocking loom of history"

and the scenes of modern American life the sweeping mosaic of word, color, image, syntax, music, and portraiture that won him the grand prize for poetry at the first World Festival of Negro Arts at Dakar, Senegal, in 1966. With this book the recognition of Hayden's achievements on the terms he sought it—as a poet and not as "a species of race-relations man"—was assured. . . . (pp. 906-09)

[The poetry Robert Hayden wrote in the last decade of his life] was less embossed, less erudite, more serene even when dealing with the violence and chaos of the times, unguardedly conversational, and measurably freer—freed now, as one perceptive reviewer realized, through an imagination given wings by wisdom, style, and the science of language.

That hard-won freedom permitted Hayden in *American Journal* to return with greater imaginative detachment and detail than before to the scenes of the childhood where, by his own acknowledgment, "cruel and dreadful things happened and I was exposed to all kinds of . . . really soul-shattering experiences in the home and all around me." And indeed, the book's emotional center lies in the *Elegies for Paradise Valley* stirred by the poet-persona's memory of a seance his mother arranged with a counterfeit gypsy to contact the spirit of a murdered uncle. Returning with Uncle Crip from now vanished rooms and dead streets to flood the poet's mind are the names and faces that make Paradise Valley a human kaleidoscope. And here in kaleidoscopic whirl, carefully wrought but unobtrusive, are all of Hayden's trademarks as a poet: the sensuous delight with aural texture and rhythm; the fluid syntactic and semantic shifts between the spare and the ornamental, the colloquial and the esoteric; the line lengths expanded and contracted for sinuous and staccato effects; the haiku-like concentration of image. Limned with panoramic sweep and surreal juxtapositions amidst a progression of subtly shifting stanzaic forms, human character here takes on the intense coloration of the exotic, the idiosyncratic, the alien, yet is shaded as almost always in Hayden's work by the common bonds of dying, of loving, and of evil. Hayden's persona, whose first remembrance is of a junkie dying in maggots below his bedroom window, closes the eight-part reverie with a recollection of his own guilty boyhood impulses and his ruefully imagining himself "the devil's own rag babydoll."

By contrast, the poems in the book's fourth section—on a loose spectrum of personal, religious, social, and political themes—are less intensely dramatic and ironic; and those that treat expressly elements of Hayden's Bahai faith veer unperturbingly but less arrestingly toward the sectarian and declamatory. **"Double Feature"** playfully affirms the momentary relief cinematic fantasy offered to childhood comrades besieged by the miasmic ills of urban poverty. **"Killing the Calves"** links by cautious simile the squander abundance breeds with the murderous horror of My Lai. In **"The Year of the Child,"** Hayden orchestrates a rite of passage for his newborn grandson, bestowing names as protective talismans "in a world that is / no place for a child." And in **"The Islands"** the collision the narrator feels between the tropics' lush "chromatic torpor" and the islanders' oppression-bred scorn, hostility, and raucous anger develops in lyric counterpoint first to the momentary fusion of his voice with their patois (a recurrent Hayden technique) and, then, to his release from history's endless, enervating evils in the fleeting, transcendental beauty of a "morning like a god in peacock-flower mantle dancing."

In the fifth and final section of *American Journal*, three poems complete the volume's progression from symbolic refractions of the racial past to transracial evocations of the space-age present and future. "The Snow Lamp," an excerpt from a work in progress whose opening suggests the spirit and mode of an Eskimo song-poem, revolves around the black codiscoverer of the North Pole, Matthew Henson, whose exploits with Peary's 1909 expedition were apotheosized in folk tales by Greenland Eskimos, the Inuit. The shifts in narrative voice from Inuit chanter to detached observer to the collective mind of the imperiled expedition achieves dramatically Hayden's characteristic illumination of a discrete experience or subject through probings from multiple viewpoints within a poem or a thematic group of poems. The "lunar wastes" of wind and snow that Miypaluk (Henson) traverses are transposed in "Astronauts" into the moonscape of shadow and glare where the space age's "heroic antiheroes, / smaller than myth and / poignantly human" voice a "Wow" and "Oh, boy" entirely inadequate to the "Absolute Otherwhere" their machines have transported them to. Finally, in the title poem of *American Journal,* the perspective moves dialectically to that of a baffled Alien contemplating and "curiously drawn" to an "america as much a problem in metaphysics as / it is a nation earthly entity an iota in our / galaxy an organism that changes even as i experience it." In this closing poem the turmoil, ambivalent feelings, and divided loyalties that characterized Hayden's personal past; his preoccupation with extremes and variegations and "paradox on paradox" and the riddle of identity—all commingle in a last wearing of the mask, his closing meditation on his native land. Even in this most alien guise, detachment from the American conundrum for Robert Hayden remains only a tenuous device of art, his Alien's bafflement and the veiled preachments of the Counselors light years away too transparent a contrivance to hide the galling human mystery whose "essence quiddity," for all the opulence of his imagination, all the power and precision of his craft, the artist/Alien at the end "cannot penetrate or name." Michael Harper . . . described Robert Hayden in a recent tribute [see excerpt above] as "a man of considered reserve, with an unsuppressible elegance, his bow-ties, watch-chain and old man's comforts giving him the glow of a courtly preacher summoned to give the word, and well he did." That word, at the end, was a question for the Furies that drove this "mystery boy," who had looked so reverently, so transfiguringly, for kin and who made his fluent prayers for illumination and perfection seem so well answered. (pp. 909-11)

> *John S. Wright, "Homage to a Mystery Boy," in* The Georgia Review, *Vol. XXXVI, No. 4, Winter, 1982, pp. 904-11.*

VILMA RASKIN POTTER

He is dead and the honors are no longer important: not the Library of Congress, not Dakar, not the academic encomiums from Fisk to Michigan, the prizes, the fellowships. What is important is what has always been—the poems gathered into a single collection called *Angle of Ascent.* The gift of Robert Hayden's poetry is his coherent vision of the black experience in this country as a continuing journey both communal and private. This journey begins in the involuntary suffering of the middle passage and continues across land and into consciousness. His poems are full of travelers whose imagination transforms the journey. In the striking sonnet, "Frederick Douglass," Hayden names the journey "this freedom, this liberty, this beautiful / and terrible thing, needful to man as air." He celebrates Douglass' dream that makes "lives grown out of

his life." These lives become the various dreamers of Hayden's canon. From his earliest published volume, *A Ballad of Remembrance,* to the last, *American Journal,* a traveler's perspective of our American experience is his most striking theme.

The black epic journey, a "voyage through death" is the subject of his complex, brilliant early poem, "Middle Passage." An anonymous narrator controls the tone of the poem from horror to celebration. The narrator is concealed as a witness, yet his is the ironic intelligence that judges, condemns, celebrates. He hears and reports the testimonies of those oceanic voyagers who are the poem's European voices. The epic black journey is recounted in a collage of white voices: hypocrites hymning in New England of Jesus walking upon the waters, scoundrel shipowners, deck officers, maritime lawyers, sick seamen. Into this sequence is threaded Shakespeare's song of Ariel in a fine double irony. It parodies the European civilization's great poet while it extends Shakespeare's text to emphasize the profound rage of the enslaved.

> Deep in the festering hold thy father lies,
> of his bones New England pews are made,
> those are altar lights that were his eyes.
>
>   (p. 51)

Here Ariel and, as an echoing voice, the narrator speak as the victims. In a vivid conclusion, all that suffering and hatred is transformed by "the timeless will." Now the white speaker is urbane, Spanish; the scene is the Connecticut courtroom, 1841; it is the trial of the *Amistad* resisters and particularly of Cinquez, the leader. At the end of the poem, Cinquez becomes the "deathless primaveral image" whose life "transfigures many lives." Thus the voyage through death of "Middle Passage" becomes a voyage into life, an affirmation of will, struggle, resistance.

Hayden created a group of poems which resonate with continuity of the theme of the Middle Passage and the unfulfilled but "deep immortal wish" of Ariel's song. One of these, "Runagate Runagate," is designed like "Middle Passage": a multitude of voices testify; some are famous, some anonymous. The oceanic voyage is now an overland journey of the underground railroad whose wheels and people hum together the poem's refrain, "'Mean mean mean to be free." In "The Dream (1863)," Hayden combines a formal narrator's voice with the nineteenth century folk voice of a young black soldier writing home to an old woman, Sinda. . . . For the letter writer, the change from slave into soldier completes the meaning of the journey into a free life. It is not so for Sinda, the dreamer with an African name: her imagination demands more than northern buckras in warrior postures. Hayden sets Sinda into a landscape of birdsong and blooming tree—but her dream is unfulfilled. These overland journey poems Hayden wrote acknowledge the incompleteness of the dream; they become, therefore, a poetry of dreamers, of scouts, of seekers.

Some of Robert Hayden's dreamers are historic figures. The star poems of *Angle of Ascent* celebrate Sojourner Truth; Nat Turner and Frederick Douglass are in *A Ballad of Remembrance;* in the newest group are Phillis Wheatley and Matthew Henson. But many dreamers are plain folks. Mattie Lee scurries joyfully aboard a U.F.O. wearing "the dress the lady she cooked / for gave her." Sometimes the anonymous dreamer seems to be Hayden himself—alert, ironic, peering into the heart of things. In "Tour 5" and "Locus," the Middle Passage continues in an ordinary trip south. It becomes the historical American journey, "the route / of highway men and phantoms, / of slaves and armies.'' The poet interlocks the dreamers (Indians, Blacks, Spanish, southern whites) in brutal historic ceremonies which produce our ''adored and unforgiven past.'' (pp. 52-3)

The last Hayden work is called *American Journal.* At this writing only portions have been published, yet it is evident that the Black-American passage, the transfiguring immortal wish continued to be Hayden's theme. In **''A Letter from Phillis Wheatley''** the woman compares the middle passage with her own safe experience. Her imagination, like Hayden's, is free; her expressive voice is ironic and sedate. She recognizes the serpent in the English Eden. She marvels at God, not at the English.

Hayden chooses Matthew Henson, polar explorer, for **''The Snow Lamp,''** a poem in three voices: an Eskimo, an invisible poet-narrator, and Henson. The narrator speaks of the stuff of adventure: expansive wastes, pain, desolation, the dire dark. The Eskimos celebrate Henson-Miypaluk, skilled with sledges, dogs, the hunt, women—skilled with life. But only the voyager himself may say why he goes. Only Henson knows why for twenty years, he followed the meridians to their end. Hayden does not choose Henson's ultimate 1906 journey; his great journeyer illustrates the continuity of a dream, and, therefore, is taken at a point of incompleteness. Henson crosses ''through darkness dire / as though God slept / in clutch of nightmare.'' And at the last, it is the voice of the traveler we hear in his note for a remote cairn: ''We are verminous. We stink like the Innuits. We fight the wish to die.''

The title poem of *American Journal* is a journal entry of a traveler from some Galactic Elsewhere who has reached out towards ''life upon these shores.'' He reports ironically upon the strange Americans:

> . . . this baffling
> multi people   extremes and variegation their
> noise restlessness their almost frightening
> energy

He reports it all: the noisy buckras Sinda saw, the **''Tour 5''** paradoxes and vanities, the tensions between myth and experience. At last he points to a unifying, pervasive passion for life. This *élan vital* brought together in Hayden's imagination the middle passage and the whole unfinished American journey. Courage, say the poems of Robert Hayden, courage! We are all travelers to life upon these shores. (pp. 54-5)

Vilma Raskin Potter, ''A Remembrance for Robert Hayden: 1913-1980,'' in MELUS, *Vol. 8, No. 1, Spring, 1982, pp. 51-5.*

THE VIRGINIA QUARTERLY REVIEW

This volume of poems [*American Journal*], assembled just before his death, is vintage Hayden, even if for the most part it is Hayden in a minor key. The verse is as lean, meticulous, and resonant as ever, but some of its colors are faded and its sounds quieted. There is nothing here comparable to the sensual intensity of such earlier poems as the **''Fantasia for Tiger Flowers,'' ''The Diver,'' ''Witch Doctor,''** or **''Middle Passage.''** The tone of the collection might be described rather as wise and serene in its recognition of pain and complexity, even though Hayden has not compromised his long preoccupation with bigotry, hatred, and violence. What is best here, in fact, is what Hayden has always done best, however it may be muted. On the one hand, there is the meditation on history

made personal and immediate, as in the epistolary impersonation of Phyllis Wheatley and the sequence for John Brown. On the other hand, there are the personal poems of memory that become the definition of a community. The most ambitious section of the book is the eight-poem sequence about ghetto life, **''Elegies for Paradise Valley.''** Both kinds of poem demonstrate anew what a compassionate poet Hayden was, and how much he found his distinctive voice by assuming in defense of history the voices of the lost, defeated, or forgotten.

A review of ''American Journal,'' in The Virginia Quarterly Review, *Vol. 58, No. 4 (Autumn, 1982), p. 134.*

G. E. MURRAY

Ironically, as the last original work we shall have from Hayden, *American Journal* represents an array of new beginnings for this important yet long overlooked poet. It shows Hayden to be moving in a great many positive directions. The book's opening selection, for instance, **''A Letter from Phillis Wheatley,''** audaciously recreates the voice of the black colonial poet, circa 1773. . . . From these mellow and subservient tones, Hayden turns to a vastly more radical historical perspective, that of abolitionist John Brown. . . . The entire five-part sequence **''John Brown''** is impressive for its tight metrical control, visual impact and the ''haunting stark / torchlight images,'' as well as for its pursuit of ''Fury of truth: fury / of righteousness.'' These are and have always been concerns for Hayden, in spite of his wide range of poetic forms, lyric measures and voices. But occasionally, ''righteousness'' overwhelms the art, as with **''Homage to Paul Robeson.''** . . . This seems as dull— and, one supposes, as necessary—as dishwater. While this ''homage'' to the black singer and social reformer might well be better suited to prose, Hayden remains true to his medium, which more often than not proves an acceptable vehicle for his thoughts and desires, even when a particular poem falls short of its artistic mark.

Hayden's poetry has an indelible honesty and directness. He stares at the world and his life intently. He is honestly sentimental. His carefully pitched voice operates as a well-conditioned boxer, throwing a burst of glancing jabs as set-up, then delivering other blows at considerable length and effect. The result is a fine coordination between eye and ear, and a sense of completeness to this final book, albeit one of fragments and new vistas. Indeed, as one rereads and interrelates Hayden's work, something remarkable begins to occur. The world Hayden observes comes into clearer focus by virtue of his ways of looking at it, what he manages to cope with and capture. The poems do not consist of extraordinary high points; instead each poem becomes part of a more intricate music. Each poem proceeds by small increments and builds into larger, more deliberate structures which peak unobtrusively. Only after the plain and forceful voice stops, the poem ends, and we are drifting back from it, do we have the opportunity to regard the echoes and reverberations for all they are worth.

The best example of this is **''Elegies for Paradise Valley,''** a series of eight diverse and far reaching poems set in Hayden's boyhood Detroit. The sequence opens abruptly and convincingly. . . . Soon after, Hayden alters and expands his expression to summon all the personal troubles of the times he has recollected. . . . It is apparent what purpose is served by this litany of appelations as Hayden focuses on the secrets of growing up rough and, sometimes, ready. Hayden proves to be a poet willing to return or go out to whatever can tell him what he is. And this is no common trait among our many poets. Hayden's poems yield pleasure and wisdom. They are the learned, meditative, witty and melancholy leavings of a craftsman who won't constrain his art or his life for the sake of any accommodation, literary or otherwise.

Two of this book's most exceptional poems are memorable for their curious circumstances and renderings. First is the tantalizing **"The Snow Lamp,"** a poem described as "in progress" and now, with Hayden's passing, one that will remain fragmentary. The poem's subject is Peary's 1909 expedition to the North Pole. Its main character is Matthew Henson, a black man in Peary's group, who became a legend among the Greenland Eskimos. . . . Composed with an ear for the sound and spirit of an Eskimo song-poem, this foreshortened work exhibits fascinating possibilities, especially as Hayden begins to explore the nature of demon in both Eskimo and expeditionist souls.

Finally, the title poem purports to be the chronicle of an alien from another galaxy here to observe our American strangeness: The concept is well-executed, and appropriate, for Hayden, as a black man who lived in the United States all his life, knew how it felt to be a socially risky outsider looking in. The poet's feelings are understandably mixed. . . .

> confess i am curiously drawn   unmentionable   to
> the americans   doubt i could exist among them for
> long however   psychic demands far too severe
> much violence   much that repels   i am attracted
> none the less   their variousness their ingenuity
> their élan vital   and that some thing   essence
> quiddity   i cannot penetrate or name
>
> (pp. 651-54)

Hayden *did* penetrate and name his essences—his indefatigable quest for learning and analysis, his ethnic virtues—in order to produce a testimony to faith even in the face of social and cultural ignorance. Dedication to the life of his art enabled Hayden to understand that "we are for an instant held shining / like memories in the mind of God." (p. 654)

> *G. E. Murray, "Struck by Lightning: Four Distinct Modern Voices," in* Michigan Quarterly Review, *Vol. XXII, No. 4, Fall, 1983, pp. 643-54.**

R. G. O'MEALLY

[Robert Hayden's *Collected Prose* is an] extraordinarily important collection of prose works by a major American poet. Most of the pieces were first published obscurely, some are first published here. All present well-crafted and telling parts of Hayden's story and artistic philosophy. A chapter from an unfinished autobiography, a speech as dialogue between poet and his disquieting inquisitor, a play, essays, prefaces, and interviews make up this carefully edited volume and form a picture of a complex, dedicated man who believed very fervently that making poems was a prayerful activity, one to which he gave every ounce of his strength. He wrote about this painful, sacred process of creating art; and he wrote about heroes, friends, family, and history—especially Afro-American history. What makes his work live is not just his choice of subject but his stylistic experimentations with "forms and techniques I have not used before—to arrive at something really my own, something patterned, wild, and free." Some of the prose here not only sheds light on the poetry but itself attains this "pat-

terned, wild, free" standard of eloquence. Hayden fought off ideologues and racists, white and black, who wanted his work (or that of "the" black community) defined too narrowly. The record of his side of that emotional fight (which, sadly, limited his production of poems) is recorded in these pages.

> *R. G. O'Meally, in a review of "Collected Prose," in* Choice, *Vol. 22, No. 4, December, 1984, p. 556.*

JOSEPH A. LIPARI

Neglected for much of his life, Hayden in the last 15 years has been generally recognized as an important black writer. A formal poet, Hayden . . . combined an intimate knowledge of evil with an acute appreciation of the sublime. . . . Struggling to escape early influences, he wrote most powerfully about the things he knew best, from black people and their history to garden flowers: "That belling of / tropic perfume—that / signalling / not meant for us." This collection of his later work [*Collected Poems*] evidences the variety and abiding strength of the work and the dignity of the poet.

> *Joseph A. Lipari, in a review of "Collected Poems," in* Library Journal, *Vol. 110, No. 10, June 1, 1985, p. 130.*

JIM ELLEDGE

Despite its title, Hayden's most recent is not a *Collected Poems* in the usual sense. His first three books, which are chock-full of exciting poems, are not represented. Instead, it begins, oddly, at midcareer, with Hayden's 1962 volume *A Ballad of Remembrance* . . . and concludes with two selections from the previously unpublished *The Snow Lamp.* Yet, the work from the six volumes that are included is representative and in no way slight. Marked by wisdom, without being stodgy, Hayden's poetry is a blend of unrivaled craftsmanship with a sharp, unrestrained vision. His subjects encompass the whole of human experience, from the extremely personal but never obscure (**"Approximations"**) to the historical but never pedantic (**"Belsen, Day of Liberation"**). His technique is similarly varied. Hayden is as adept with haiku, imitations of Eskimo song-poems, or sonnets as he is with free verse.

> *Jim Elledge, in a review of "Collected Poems," in* Booklist, *Vol. 81, No. 21, July, 1985, p. 1504.*

EDWARD HIRSCH

In **"American Journal,"** the last poem in [*Collected Poems*] Robert Hayden—who once said that "nothing human is foreign to me"—wryly assumes the voice of an extraterrestrial observer reporting on a "baffling / multi people," a country of charming and enlightened savages, "brash newcomers lately sprung up in our galaxy." The engaged yet alienated observer was a fitting persona for a man who always identified with the figure of the outsider and who often referred to himself as an "alien at home." . . .

[It is] revealing that Hayden's alien stand-in observes and contemplates not the entire earth but only the portion of it called America, a place which is, as he says, "as much a problem in metaphysics as / it is a nation." For Hayden, America represented "a kind of microcosm," a heterogeneous new world working out an emblematic destiny. He was repelled by our "strangering" racial distinctions but intensely attracted to our ideal of freedom and, like his alien ethnographer, he spent much of his intellectual energy trying to penetrate and name some American "essence" or "quiddity." However internationalist he was in outlook, his life's work makes clear that he was an American poet, deeply engaged by the topography of American myth in his efforts to illuminate the American black experience. He read American history as a long, tortuous struggle in psychic evolution, an exercise in humanity. An alien at home, he nonetheless contended with America as the place where "we must go on struggling to be human." His *Collected Poems* should become one of our exemplary poetic texts. . . .

Hayden's *Collected Poems* brings together work from nine books written over more than forty years. His first volume, *Heart-Shape in the Dust,* published in 1940, and his two pamphlets, *The Lion and the Archer* (1948) and *Figure of Time: Poems* (1955), are poorly represented here because he came to feel they poorly represented him. He considered his early poems "'prentice pieces" and only a limited number survived for publication in his first mature volumes, *A Ballad of Remembrance* (1962) and *Selected Poems* (1966). Hayden's early work dutifully followed the themes and forms of the Harlem Renaissance and relied heavily on his experience as a folklore researcher for the Detroit branch of the Federal Writers' Project in the late 1930s. As his work progressed, he began to shed his first poetic models: Edna St. Vincent Millay, Carl Sandburg, Langston Hughes, and, most important, Countee Cullen. Slowly he developed a consciously modernist style, a type of tersely written symbolic lyric, often with an Afro-American inflection, that was all his own.

By the time of *A Ballad of Remembrance,* which starts off the *Collected Poems,* Hayden had already developed his characteristic style: "meditative, ironic, richly human," as he wrote of Mark Van Doren. He was a "romantic realist," a formal lyricist with a feeling for the baroque, a symbolist poet who distrusted external reality but nonetheless felt compelled to grapple with history. Like his mentor Auden, with whom he studied, Hayden's work is a little anthology of poetic forms, though in general he favored two types over others: the spare, well-chiseled, "objective" lyric and the long, fragmentary, collage-like history poem. Hayden was never prolific and his *Collected Poems* is not a long book—in addition to *A Ballad of Remembrance,* it consists of *Words in the Mourning Time, The Night-Blooming Cereus, Angle of Ascent* and *American Journal.* And yet it has a profound and passionate scope. Every one of its poems is meticulously crafted. (p. 685)

Freedom is the great subject of Hayden's work, his poetic touchstone. He considered the need for freedom a constant beyond history—"the deep immortal human wish,/ the timeless will," as he said in **"Middle Passage"**—but understood that the struggle for freedom takes place inside history. In a number of long poems dealing with nineteenth-century America (which he once planned as a unified series to be called *The Black Spear)* Hayden rediscovered and celebrated a group of individual heroes, primarily blacks, who ferociously opposed slavery: Sojourner Truth, who "comes walking barefoot / out of slavery"; Cinquez, who led the successful slave rebellion on the *Amistad*; Harriet Tubman, who escaped from slavery and then became one of the most spectacular agents of the underground railroad, continually making the hard journey from "Can't to Can";

Nat Turner; John Brown; and, of course, Frederick Douglass. Hayden's characteristic method in these poems is the collage, a form which works by the ironic juxtaposition of different voices. In **"Middle Passage,"** for example, he mixes his own descriptive commentary with the voices of slave traders, hymn singers and even the dead. So, too, he splices together and adapts descriptions from journal entries, ships' logs, depositions and the eyewitness accounts of traders. These formal innovations give his history poems an uncanny ethnographic basis, a profound sense of the human suffering caused by slavery.

Like Harriet Tubman, all Hayden's heroes "Mean mean mean to be free," and lead others to freedom. Their legacy is the lives their lives insure: the nameless slaves escaping to freedom in **"Runagate Runagate,"** the "many lives" transfigured in **"Middle Passage."** This idea is resoundingly expressed in Hayden's sonnet to Frederick Douglass . . . . Hayden's fine rhetorical poem, reminiscent of Hopkins's sonnet "That Nature Is a Heraclitean Fire," asserts that what matters is not freedom for the self alone but the communal realization of the dream. In this sense he is a utopian poet.

Hayden's historical and public poems are counterbalanced by personal lyrics like **"Homage to the Empress of the Blues"** **"Mourning Poem for the Queen of Sunday,"** **"'Summertime and the Living . . . ,'"** **"The Rabbi"** and, my personal favorites, **"The Whipping"** and **"Those Winter Sundays."** Written at various times during his life, these poems rely on childhood experiences in a Detroit slum ironically known as Paradise Valley. Hayden refused to sentimentalize his past—as a child growing up his primary desire was to escape the world that surrounded him, and he also determined to remember it accurately. He was born Asa Sheffey but raised as Robert Hayden (a duality that haunted him) and he knew both his natural and foster parents. He was bound to his childhood as the foster son of poor working-class people and remained committed to what he liked to call "folk" people: poor, uneducated, dignified, all those who quietly fulfilled "love's austere and lonely offices."

There is a certain detachment even in Hayden's most personal lyrics, a slight distancing of what he calls "the long warfare with self / with God." He once said that "Reticence has its esthetic values, too," and his typical method was to exteriorize and objectify the past by speaking about it in the third person, or by using the disguise of a persona. In a sense he was like the diver in the opening lyric of the *Collected Poems*: a man who needed to keep control as he moved down into the oceanic depths, who longed to fling aside his mask and be done forever with the "vain complexity" of the self but continually managed to pull himself away from the silenced wreck and re-commence "the measured rise." There is a muted but powerful longing for transcendence in Hayden's work, and the diver is close kin to the figure of the old man with bloodstained wings in **"For a Young Artist,"** who begins sprawled out in a pigsty but ends by somehow managing to fly again, "the angle of ascent/ achieved." Both the diver and the old man are figures of the triumphant artist. (pp. 685-86)

Edward Hirsch, "Mean to Be Free," in The Nation, *Vol. 241, No. 21, December 21, 1985, pp. 685-86.*

Seamus (Justin) Heaney

1939-

Irish poet, critic, essayist, translator, and editor.

Heaney's poetry reveals his skill with language and his command of form and technique. In his poems, Heaney balances personal, topical, and universal themes. He approaches his themes from a modest perspective, creating depth of meaning and insight while remaining accessible to a wide audience. Heaney's attempts to develop poetic language in which meaning and sound are intimately related result in concentrated, sensually evocative poems characterized by assonant phrasing, richly descriptive adjectives, and witty metaphors. Critics note that Heaney is concerned with many of contemporary Northern Ireland's social and cultural divisions. For example, Irish and Gaelic colloquialisms are often intermingled with more direct and straightforward English words for a language that is both resonant and controlled. Viewing the art of poetry as a craft, Heaney stresses the importance of technique as a means to channel creative energies toward sophisticated metaphysical probings. He explores a wide range of subjects in his poems, including such topics as nature, love, the relationship between contemporary issues and historical patterns, and legend and myth. Although critics debate Robert Lowell's assessment of him as "the greatest Irish poet since Yeats," they agree that Heaney is a poet of consistent achievement.

Heaney's childhood in a rural area near Ulster, Northern Ireland, informs much of his poetry, including his first volume, *Death of a Naturalist* (1966), for which he won immediate popular and critical success. In most of these poems, Heaney describes a young man's responses to beautiful and threatening aspects of nature. In "Digging," the poem which opens this volume, he evokes the rural landscape where he was raised and comments on the care and skill with which his father and ancestors farmed the land. Heaney announces that as a poet he will metaphorically "dig" with his pen. In many of the poems in his next volume, *Door into the Dark* (1969), he probes beneath the surface of things to search for hidden meaning. Along with pastoral poems, Heaney focuses on rural laborers and the craftsmanship they display in their work.

Heaney left Northern Ireland when the "troubles" resumed in 1969. After teaching in the United States, he settled with his family in the Republic of Ireland. The poems in *Wintering Out* (1972) reveal a gradual shift from personal to public themes. Heaney begins to address the social unrest in Northern Ireland by taking the stance of commentator rather than participant. After having read P. V. Glob's *The Bog People,* an account of the discovery of well-preserved, centuries-old bodies found in Danish bogs, Heaney wrote a series of poems about Irish bogs. Some of the bodies found in Danish bogs are believed to have been victims of primitive sacrificial rituals, and in *Wintering Out* Heaney projects a historical pattern of violence that unites the ancient victims with those who have died in contemporary troubles. In *North* (1975), which some consider his finest collection, Heaney continues to use history and myth to pattern the universality of violence. The poems in this volume reflect his attempt to tighten his lyrics with more concrete language and images.

Photograph by Caroline Forbes, reproduced by permission of Faber and Faber Ltd

The poems in *Field Work* (1979) concern a wide range of subjects. Critics praised several love poems dealing with marriage, particularly "The Harvest Bow," which Harold Bloom called "a perfect lyric." In the ten-poem sequence "The Glanmore Sonnets," Heaney describes a lush landscape and muses on such universal themes as love and mortality, ultimately finding order, meaning, and renewal in art. Other books of significance by Heaney include *Preoccupations: Selected Prose 1968-1978* (1980) and *Sweeney Astray* (1984). The former, which includes prose pieces on the origins and development of his poetry as well as essays on other poets, lends insight into Heaney's poetics. *Sweeney Astray,* a story-poem based on the ancient Irish tale *Buile Suibhne,* relates the adventures of Suibhne, or Sweeney, as he is transformed from a warrior-king into a bird because of a curse. The narrative follows Sweeney's exile from humanity and his wanderings and hardships as a bird, mixing prose descriptions of events with lyrical renderings of Sweeney's ravings as he responds to the harshness and beauty of nature.

Heaney's next volume of poetry, *Station Island* (1984), is made up of three sections. The opening part consists of lyrical poems about events in everyday life. The title sequence, which comprises the second section, is based on a three-day pilgrimage undertaken by Irish Catholics to Station Island, where they seek spiritual renewal. While on Station Island, Heaney ruminates on personal and historical events and encounters the souls of dead acquaintances and Irish literary figures who inspire him to reflect upon his life and art. In the third section, "Sweeney Redivivus," Heaney takes on the persona of Sweeney, attempting to recreate Sweeney's highly sensitized vision of life. Although critics debated the success of the three individual sections, most agreed that *Station Island* is an accomplished work that displays the range of Heaney's talents.

(See also *CLC*, Vols. 5, 7, 14, 25; *Contemporary Authors*, Vols. 85-88; and *Dictionary of Literary Biography*, Vol. 40.)

IRVIN EHRENPREIS

Only the most gifted poets can start from their peculiar origin in a language, a landscape, a nation, and from these enclosures rise to impersonal authority. Seamus Heaney has this kind of power, and it appears constantly in his *Poems 1965-1975*. One may enter his poetry by a number of paths, but each joins up with others. Nationality becomes landscape; landscape becomes language; language becomes genius.

For a poet, language is first; and in considering this, I may clarify my meaning. Speech is never simple, in Heaney's conception. He grew up as an Irish Catholic boy in a land governed by Protestants whose tradition is British. He grew up on a farm in his country's northern, industrial region. As a person, therefore, he springs from the old divisions of his nation.

At the same time, the theme that dominates Heaney's work is self-definition, the most natural subject of the modern lyric; and language, from which it starts, shares the old polarities. For Heaney, it is the Irish speech of his family and district, overlaid by the British and urban culture which he acquired as a student.

The outcome is not merely a matter of vocabularies and accents. Even the smallest constituents bifurcate. In the poet's ear, vowels are soft and Irish; consonants are hard and English. Heaney once said he associated his personal pieties with vowels and his literary awareness with consonants. So also the vocabularies and etymologies (sometimes fanciful) have their ground. For softness and hardness belong to the landscape of the poet's childhood, to its bogs and farms, its rivers and mountains. Consequently, we hear lines from poems translating sound into terrain and nationality. . . .

Instead of being hemmed in by the old divisions, Heaney lets them enrich his expression. Fundamental to his process of self-definition is a refusal to abandon any part of his heritage. The name of the family farm, Mossbawn, divides itself between the soft Irish bog of "moss" and a word meaning the fortified farm, or "bawn," of a British settler. The Heaneys' farm actually lay between a "bog" of yielding peat and the cultivated "demesne" of Moyola Park—belonging to a peer who had served as head of the British establishment. It was bordered as well by townlands with malleable Gaelic names, Anahorish and Broagh. But it looked out on Grove Hill and Back Park, firm with the definitive consonants of a ruler's voice. What the poet means to accomplish is a union of the two traditions [as stated in "A New Song"]:

> But now our river tongues must rise
> From licking deep in native haunts
> To flood, with vowelling embrace,
> Demesnes staked out in consonants.

Heaney incorporates these subtle attitudes into a coherent literary self. He feels eager, as he says of some English poets, to defend a linguistic integrity, to preserve the connection of his own speech with "the descending storeys of the literary and historical past." Historically, therefore, he can identify himself with the English tradition and oppose it in turn to the Latin of the conquerors of Britain.

In "Freedman," for example, he begins with Latinate diction and ends with short English words as he traces his evolution from a shy Northern Irish student of the master culture ("subjugated yearly under arches") into a poet acknowledged by readers in New York and Melbourne ("poetry wiped my brow and sped me").

The same poem illustrates the characteristic, pervasive gravity of the poet's wit. He describes himself going through the streets of Belfast on Ash Wednesday with a touch of ashes on his forehead, and links the mark to the humble, earthbound status of the native Roman Catholic Irish before their Protestant governors. . . .

The habit of digging into the history of the words he uses comes from the same impulse as a wish to tie the images of the poems to a racial past. In his writing as in his character, the poet tries to root the present age in the oldest, elemental patterns of his poeple, and then to relate the people to the countryside that fostered them, ultimately reminding us of the situation of all humanity in nature. Love for a woman must be like love for a region; and the features of the homeland call up the countryside the poet knows best. In "Polder" (from the recent book *Field Work*) Heaney speaks of embracing after a quarrel as a reclaiming of territory from the sea.

Quite deliberately, the poet tries to describe elements of landscape in human terms and people he loves as reminding him of animals. The humor and wit convey affection, but they also suggest a wish to be at home in the world, to surmount the barriers between man and beast. If a stream turns into a woman ("Undine") and a woman into an otter ("Otter"), Heaney implies that his own devotion to the countryside links up with his attachment to people. . . .

The yearning toward a racial past takes powerful forms. It is characteristic of Heaney that when he wished to find symbols adequate to the ordeal of his countrymen, he should have turned to an ancient mystery which reaches toward the hidden aspects of human nature. This is the problem of the so-called "bog people," or bodies found in Danish bogs, where they were placed from the time of the early Iron Age. Heaney accepts the view that at least some are the remains of a fertility ritual. But he uses them in his poems to suggest that modern terrorism, rather than meaning a breaking with the past, belongs to an archetypal pattern. In a forceful passage, he indicates the strain on his character as he contemplates the national agony; for he too feels the yearning to be not a recorder or singer but a heroic actor in the terrible drama. . . .

The poet's triumph is to bring the ingredients of history and biography under the control of his music. Technique, says Heaney, "entails the water-marking of your essential patterns of perception, voice and thought into the touch and texture of your lines."

Here again he accepts traditions that join England to Ireland; for his verse reminds us of the short lines (often octosyllabic), the couplets and quatrains of Swift, who liked to mix coarseness with idealism, humor with anger, observation with fantasy, and honesty with love. Heaney's expressive rhythms support his pleasure in re-echoing syllables and modulating vowels through a series of lines to evoke continuities and resolutions. He has learned from Yeats without being suffocated by him. (p. 45)

Irvin Ehrenpreis, "Digging In," in The New York Review of Books, *Vol. XXVIII, No. 15, October 8, 1981, pp. 45-7.**

DENIS DONOGHUE

Sweeney Astray is a version—for the moment call it that, rather than a translation—of *Buile Suibhne* (Sweeney's Frenzy), an Irish poem written sometime between the years 1200 and 1500, in the period between the late Middle-Irish and early Modern-Irish. The poem recites the adventures of Suibhne Geilt, son of Colman Cuar, and king—or at least lord—of Dal Araidhe, the northern half of County Antrim. His adventures began when he drove out of his lands one Ronan Finn, a priest, who was marking out a place for his church. Ronan cursed Suibhne and called upon God to afflict him with many evils. At the Battle of Magh Rath—the present Moira—Suibhne went mad, driven wild by the horrors of the battle. By Ronan's curse he was changed into a bird, and forced to live a miserable life in exile from his home, his wife, and every domestic satisfaction. In the end, he is restored to himself and reconciled to Christianity through the ministry of the priest Moling. Killed by the throw of a spear, as Ronan ordained, he receives a Christian burial.

It is clear that the lore from which the poem arose is as early as the ninth or tenth century. There are three independent manuscripts. The most important one was probably written between 1671 and 1674; another probably in 1721-1722; and the third, the earliest but not the best, in 1629. J. G. O'Keeffe, who edited and translated the poem for the Irish Texts Society in 1913, settled upon the 1671-74 one for his copy-text. It is a mixture of narrative passages in prose and lyrical sections in verse: the verse is mostly Suibhne's lament for his lost greatness, or his rueful sense of the life available to him as a bird. One lyric section of extraordinary power invokes the order of nature which has replaced, for Suibhne, the order of society and fellowship.

Much of the sentiment of the poem arises from the conflict between pagan and Christian values in early Ireland, a theme dear to many writers including Yeats, Austin Clarke, and Frank O'Connor. Heaney makes much of Sweeney's—we can call him that now—association with the north of Ireland, the west of Scotland, and in the end the south of Ireland. Tact prevents him from making anything of the association between Sweeney and himself, two poets driven to fury if not to madness by the horrors of war in the north of Ireland. Heaney emphasizes rather the significance of Sweeney as an artist, at odds with a society to the pitch of frenzy. . . .

Buile Suibhne is a difficult poem. It is my impression that Heaney found it, line by line, hard to deal with. Many of his prose passages are far prosier than the Irish. How do you translate into English a work in prose and verse which developed in some rambling fashion over several centuries of Irish expression, oral and written? Heaney has chosen to stick to the common style of his own lyric poems for his copy-text, but to include archaic words from time to time. The problem is that some crucial words in the English lack the force of the Irish. "Astray" doesn't, even in the north of Ireland, have the force of *"ar buile,"* which means frenzied. In the north, I

remember, we said that someone was "astray in the head," meaning daft or simpleminded: not the same ailment. I don't know what American readers will make of such words as "rath" and "erenach," though recourse to the O.E.D. will discover "cantreds" and "scuts." Those who know John Crowe Ransom's poems will have no problem with Heaney's "thole." . . . But I'm not persuaded by Heaney's version of *"roclodhadh a chedfadha."* O'Keeffe gives "his senses were overcome," which is sound enough, but Heaney gives "his senses were mesmerized," which is too modern. (p. 28)

Heaney comes into his own eloquence when the Irish poem sets him free in ways we have known since *North* and his earlier books. When Sweeney comes back to rebuke his faithless wife Eorann, she sweet-talks, saying that she'd like to be like him, a bird, and fly away with him. I wish, she says, that we were together, and that feathers would grow on our bodies— *"co ttigeadh clumh ar ar ttaobh"*—"in light and darkness I would wander with you every day and night." Heaney's version warms it more:

> I wish we could fly away together,
> be rolling stones, birds of a feather;
> I'd swoop to pleasure you in flight
> and huddle close on the roost at night.

It's beautiful; though it's hard to think of rolling stones now without striking against the other Rolling Stones.

I'm sure we haven't heard the last of Heaney's Sweeney. Indeed, I gather that Heaney has been writing new poems in some relation to Sweeney. No wonder: if Yeats had Crazy Jane, Heaney is entitled to his Mad Sweeney. In a country as mad as Ireland, there is no lack of theme. (pp. 28-9)

Denis Donoghue, "A Mad Muse," in The New Republic, *Vol. 190, No. 3615, April 30, 1984, pp. 27-9.*

BRENDAN KENNELLY

One of the crucial signs of a genuine imagination is its ability to give new life to old myths, stories and legends. By the criterion, *Sweeney Astray,* a complete translation of the medieval Irish work *Buile Suibhne,* shows that Seamus Heaney's imagination is continuing to deepen in intensity and range.

Sweeney is cursed by a Christian cleric named Ronan whom he has insulted and humiliated. As a result, he becomes a mad outcast, a paranoid fugitive from life, a shifty victim of panic who lives on watercress and water and is driven to the tops of trees, from which vantage point he gazes down, terrified yet furiously articulate. From the heights of his mad agony, Sweeney makes sad, beautiful, thrilling poems. He is the voice of darkness and nightmare but also, in his naked and ravaged loneliness, the celebrant of the natural beauty of Ireland. This paranoid is a superb poet, and it takes a superb poet to capture, in translation from the Irish, the full range of pain and beauty in Sweeney's poetry. Seamus Heaney has produced an exhilarating version of this most unusual story poem.

And it *is* a story poem. Many poets, impatient with the sometimes irritating machinery of narrative, would have cut the story and gone for the climactic lyrical moments. In his introduction Mr. Heaney admits he found himself faced with this temptation: "My first impulse had been to forage for the best lyric moments and to present them as poetic orphans, out of the context of the story. These points of poetic intensity, rather than the overall organization, establish the work's highest artistic level and offer the strongest invitations to the translator of verse. Yet I gradually felt I had to earn the right to do the high points by undertaking the whole thing: what I was dealing with, after all, is a major work in the canon of medieval literature.''

That passage perfectly illustrates Mr. Heaney's patient sense of responsibility toward and respect for the original work. In the art of translation, this sense is vitally connected with the quality of the ultimate product—in this case, with a new, exciting creation that seems to grow into an original work. Some prose passages and even some of the poems are relatively flat, deliberately so. The original is also prose and poetry, but it is only as one reads and rereads Mr. Heaney's version that one realizes that the counterpointing of prose with poetry intensifies the climactic lyric moments. To my mind, this is true of Irish literary works as far apart in time as the Old Irish epic dominated by the hero Cuchulain, *Tain Bo Cuailgne,* and Joyce's *Ulysses.* Both have heavy, tedious moments, but also an ecstatic, soaring quality. We appreciate the moments of flight all the more deeply because we have been earthbound for a while.

Something similar happens in *Sweeney Astray.* A number of the prose passages have clarity and solid force; but they remain prose. These slow moments stress the poem's intensity. . . .

This balancing of slowness with speed, casualness with concentration, is not merely a linguistic technique or structural device; it reflects the very core of the poem. Sweeney is mad, in this world. His inspired frenzies occur on a familiar stage. To the other characters on that commonplace stage, he is a driven figure raving gibberish. Sweeney in his turn sees them as if he were a mad Adam driven alone through a lunatic Eden. The language of the poem reflects this gulf—between the ''civilized'' and the outcast, the accepted and the accursed, agonized aimlessness and calm resoluteness, the man of pain and the men of purpose. Mr. Heaney, in his magical way, balances all these matters with a strong sense of drama and unfailing control.

I mentioned Sweeney as the man of pain apart from the men of purpose. *Sweeney Astray,* I believe, will come to be seen as a compelling poem of human pain—the vague yet vivid pain of the waking imagination, an almost unutterable loneliness. ''I am the bare figure of pain,'' Sweeney cries. . . .

If the poem were kept at . . . [an intense] pitch from beginning to end, it would become almost unendurable. Flann O'Brien, who used the figure of Sweeney in his comic novel *At Swim-Two-Birds,* realized this, and so his Sweeney makes us laugh aloud even as we are touched with pity. This dual response enriches the novel and the reader's experience. Mr. Heaney has little or none of O'Brien's intellectual iciness. Nor does he have O'Brien's brilliant cruelty or devastating sense of comedy, though there are a few quietly comic moments in *Sweeney Astray.* What Mr. Heaney offers as an alternative to Sweeney's pain is Mr. Heaney's own lyric gift, his inimitable music. If there is anything in this work that balances the poetry of pain, it is the poetry of praise. And what is praised most beautifully and convincingly is the landscape of Ireland, its fields, meadows, hills, rivers, mountains, glens, the sea's eternal caress and threat. . . .

In one of his poems, called **"The Harvest Bow,"** Mr. Heaney says, ''The end of art is peace.'' At the end of this work, Sweeney finds his own kind of peace. But what one remembers most about *Sweeney Astray* is the delicate, dramatic balance between pain and praise. The poem is a balanced statement about a tragically unbalanced mind. One feels that this balance, urbanely sustained, is the product of a long, imaginative bond between Mr. Heaney and Sweeney.

> Brendan Kennelly, ''Soaring from the Treetops,'' in The New York Times Book Review, *May 27, 1984, p. 14.*

PAUL MULDOON

The title-sequence of Seamus Heaney's sixth collection [*Station Island*] finds him on Station Island, Lough Derg, more commonly known as St Patrick's Purgatory. It's the setting for a pilgrimage undertaken by thousands of Irish men and women each year. For three days they fast and pray, deprive themselves of sleep, and walk barefoot round the station 'beds'—circles of rough stones said to be the remains of monastic huts. A place, then, strongly associated in the Irish mind with self-denial, contemplation, spiritual renewal; a place, too, that has attracted writers like Sean O'Faolain, Denis Devlin, William Carleton and Patrick Kavanagh; a place where the individual might decently ruminate on his relationship with society.

This setting affords Seamus Heaney a remarkable opportunity, of which he takes remarkable advantage, to ruminate, not only on his very special relationship with a society which has taken him to its heart, but on religion, sex and the dead. The sequence takes the form of a series of meetings with 'familiar ghosts'. There's Simon Sweeney, 'an old Sabbath-breaker' who urges him to 'Stay clear of all processions!' Heaney is nonetheless drawn into the trail of pilgrims for the island. On the way he meets the shade of Carleton. . . . Later on, on Station Island itself, Kavanagh addresses him. . . .

If these meetings with writers seem a touch self-regarding (the 'self' being that of the 45-year-old, smiling public man who virtually admonishes Carleton for not recognising him—'then with a look that said, *who is this cub anyhow,'* and 'whoever you are, wherever you come out of'), Heaney is by and large attractively open, self-doubting, sometimes self-critical, as when his cousin Colum McCartney rebukes him:

> The Protestant who shot me through the head
> I accuse directly, but indirectly, you
> who now atone perhaps upon this bed
> for the way you whitewashed ugliness and drew
> the lovely blinds of the *Purgatorio*
> and saccharined my death with morning dew.

Section VII of **"Station Island"** is indeed a great deal less saccharined in its portrayal of a sectarian murder than **"The Strand at Lough Beg"** (*Field Work*). . . . Throughout this sequence Seamus Heaney is resolutely questing and questioning, constantly refining and redefining. He is, for example, now more likely to question the received opinions and stock responses of Irish Catholicism and Irish Nationalism, though the drift of the most intensely lyrical passage of **"Station Island"** would seem to suggest that the fatalism of both have marked him indelibly. . . .

The **"Station Island"** sequence forms the middle section of this book, though it is not as important to the overall effect as the blurb-writer would have us believe. Heaney's strength resides still in the short lyric, of which a group of 25 makes up the first part, and, I believe, the core, of the collection. Here Heaney has managed to give a further resonance to his precise descriptions of 'small' fixtures of the physical world. . . .

The best poems in the first section of *Station Island* seem to me to be small masterpieces: "**A Hazel Stick for Catherine Ann**", "**Changes**", "**Sloe Gin**'" and, above all, "**Widgeon**". . . . In the third section of the book, however, Heaney rather 'expectedly' throws his voice through the figure of Sweeney, the Ulster king who's cursed by Saint Ronan and is transformed into a bird-man. In a note to *Station Island* Heaney writes: 'A version of the Irish tale is available in my *Sweeney Astray*, but I trust these glosses can survive without the support system of the original story.' I feel he's mistaken in that. With the exceptions of "**Holly**" and "**An Artist**", these 20 pieces need all the support they can get. They are either unintelligible . . . or all too intelligible. . . . (p. 20)

Not even the weak third section of *Station Island* can take away from the fact that this is a resourceful and reliable collection, his best since *Wintering Out*. In the unlikely event of a truly uninvited shade being summoned up in some reworking of the "**Station Island**" sequence, I suspect that its advice to Seamus Heaney would be along the following lines. 1. That he should, indeed, take the advice he gave himself as long ago as 1975— 'Keep your eye clear as the bleb of an icicle'—but take it quietly rather than rehearse it again and again. 2. General Absolution is too much for even a Catholic confessional poet to hope for. 3. That he should resist more firmly the idea that he must be the best Irish poet since Yeats, which arose from rather casual remarks by the power-crazed Robert Lowell and the craze-powered Clive James, who seemed to have forgotten both MacNeice and Kavanagh. In the meantime, Heaney is a very good poet indeed—which is enough to be going on with.

[*Sweeney Astray*] Heaney's version of the Middle Irish Romance *Buile Suibhne* ("The Frenzy of Sweeney") is a masterful act of repossession. Though he's much indebted to J. G. O'Keefe's edition, published in 1913 by the Irish Texts Society, Heaney brings great exuberance and tenderness to the story of the king of Dal-Arie. . . . For years Sweeney will hop, skip and jump over the length and breadth of Ireland, and indeed Britain (where he spends a year with another madman, Alan), until his death at the hands of a swineherd. Sweeney's hardships already have some popular literary currency, in the work of Flann O'Brien . . . and W. D. Snodgrass . . . ; but Heaney's version, at once scholarly and readable, is unputdownable, a ripping yarn. Section 40 of *Sweeney Astray*, acknowledged by O'Keefe to be 'the most interesting poem of the story', is lovingly presented by Heaney as Sweeney's praise of the trees of Ireland.

The problems raised by *Sweeney Astray* are common to any process of translation from one language to another: in this case, from one world-picture to another. It is impossible to take into account the insatiable and deep-rooted Gaelic interest in the lore of place-names, which is not always so riveting in English. Nor can the complexities of the many verse-forms used in *Buile Suibhne*, with their stress on assonance and alliteration and internal rhymes, be conveyed in English: Heaney's version does at least convey something of the rhyme-scheme. . . . Seamus Heaney's retelling of Sweeney's story must rank with Thomas Kinsella's *The Tain* as the most significant recent contribution to the body of Gaelic literature available in English. (pp. 20-1)

> Paul Muldoon, "*Sweeney Peregraine*," *in* London Review of Books, *November 1 to November 14, 1984, pp. 20-1.**

ELIZABETH JENNINGS

Even the vigour of language, the mastery of subtle cadence and the easy engagement with his own and history's past which were often evident in Seamus Heaney's first four books of poems—*Death of a Naturalist, Wintering Out, Door into the Dark,* and *North*—did not prophesy accurately the range of subject and form which were to be found in *Field Work*. Nor did that volume prepare us for the further depth and development of this richly satisfying substantial new volume, *Station Island*.

Heaney's first three books were often concerned with his eventful, pastoral childhood, his marriage and with the tragic public events of Ireland. His fourth book *North*, was very specifically devoted to the closeness of the poet's sympathies with all that hurts and happens in Northern Ireland.

Field Work was a true advance, a book full of surprises both in themes and forms. Heaney ventured warily into the sonnet-form and here made use of a technique which has become more and more evident in his work. This is a habit of deviating from a strict form or rhyme-scheme when obeying the rules would make a given poem appear too easily achieved. This is clearly deliberate, and, usually, if we find any departure from a normal procedure, this is the reason.

Above all, Heaney is a natural poet, a man who writes only when he must. He has called verse-making 'A love-affair between the gift and craft', and he has also spoken quite unselfconsciously of "**The Muse**". He is an extremely Irish poet most especially in language, but he is not a poet in the Yeatsian mould; not for him high-mannered seriousness or intentional rhetoric. He is serious, of course, but it is the gravity which grows in his roots, not one which is obtrusive in the finished artefact. Heaney twice refers to Joyce in *Station Island*. Unlike Joyce, though, his language and purposes are clear with the shining of a pool; he is always an accessible poet.

There is much that is new in *Station Island,* notably the title piece, a sequence in 12 parts. A group of lyrical poems precedes this long one, and another meditative section follows it. Heaney loves the objects of the past. Examples of this delight are to be found here in "**Sandstone Keepsake**" and in the group of six short poems called "**Shelf Life.**" . . .

Throughout *Station Island,* we find a poet in complete command of language, image and form. Heaney possesses a rich vocabulary and, everywhere, his love of the concrete, his quick eye and ear, his compassion for and love of simple things and daily activities are evident. His "**Shelf Life**" shows us an artist delighting in his surroundings, loving the sea and the country-side, recording, like the good Nature poet he can often be, an awareness of the past in the ever-moving present.

The third poem in this brief sequence is entitled "**Old Pewter**" and it is a fine example of the way Heaney can draw an abstract idea out of tangible mementos. . . .

Never before has Heaney shown so confidently his close engagement with the poet's private events. In *Field Work,* he wrote love poems and elegies. In the first section of this new book, he writes with deep pleasure of married love and of his children. . . .

He also demonstrates his pleasure and pride in his family in "**A Kite for Michael and Christopher**". . . . (p. 30)

In "**The Railway Children**", he writes a poem about his own childhood. It has that authentic ring of true poetry which defies literary criticism and can only be called pure magic. This poet is an adept at spell-binding and offers it most joyfully in this poem. . . . All we can do with a spell such as this is smile and nod our heads.

Heaney displays immense virtuosity in this volume. He uses many verse-forms: a very individual form of *terza-rima,* blank verse, stanzas of short lines. And his themes range from evocations of his own past to the profound study of his purposes as a poet.

The title poem, **"Station Island",** is located in the place of that name in Ireland which, for over a thousand years, has been a place of pilgrimage. In the best sense, this is a dark poem often relieved by flashes of light, the true light of dawn, the occupation of the sun, the luminous but fitful brilliance of a world preoccupied by death and the caprices of time. Heaney calls it 'a sequence of dream encounters with familiar ghosts. . . .' Yet there is no absorbed introversion here, no neurotic self-searching. Heaney is felt as a presence who is above all engrossed in the figures of old friends who appear in his mind's eye but who also have a place in this holy locale. Here the poet rediscovers his own Roman Catholicism, but this religion is more of a symbol to him than a creed pondered on dialectically.

In **"Station Island",** Heaney is chided for his mis-directions, his wasting of time and language. There is considerable self-awareness in this remarkable and ambitious sequence. (pp. 30-1)

This is a rich and noble sequence and the whole of this volume illuminates our own dark searchings. Yet Heaney never reaches pat conclusions; he is always exploring the furthest possibilities of language. His stylistic gusto is controlled by a refusal to be satisfied with facile answers. He is a poet who belongs to that great, masculine tradition which we find so resonantly in Yeats and Louis MacNeice. (p. 31)

> *Elizabeth Jennings, "The Spell-Binder," in* The Spectator, *Vol. 253, No. 8159, November 24, 1984, pp. 30-1.*

DERWENT MAY

Unease and uncertainty are the hallmarks of Seamus Heaney's new poems [in *Station Island*]. And he knows it. One poem describes a woman 'aiming' an iron at the linen on an ironing-board:

> To work, her dumb lunge says,
> is to move a certain mass
>
> through a certain distance,
> is to pull your weight and feel
> exact and equal to it.
> Feel dragged upon. And buoyant.

The word 'certain' there is more than just an algebraic 'x'— the word brims with the idea of confidence and rightness. And Heaney is certainly offering us an image here of the making of a good poem and what we can find in it.

These fine lines show up, however, both by what they say and how they say it, the prevailing uncertainty in many of the other poems in *Station Island.* The subject-matter of this new collection is explicitly doubt, hesitation, guilt. The long central sequence which gives its name to the book describes a return, in imagination, to an island on Lough Derg where Roman Catholics go on penitential pilgrimages. Here Heaney meets many unsettling ghosts from his past, all making him uneasy

about his religion, his sex-life, his poetry and his politics. Perfectly good subjects: the trouble is that in reading about them one too often feels the iron swerving out of control, even dropping to the floor. The 'exact and equal' feeling, the buoyancy, are missing.

One emotion that seems especially overworked here is guilt. It is not in the least surprising that Heaney, like many Northern Ireland Catholics, has disturbing, confused feelings about his relationship with the Republican movement. In his last book, *Field Work,* he had a poem about the murder of his young second cousin; here, he has that cousin revile him for the way in which, in that poem, Heaney

> whitewashed ugliness and drew
> the lovely blinds of the *Purgatorio*
> and saccharined my death with morning dew.

Brilliant lines, again! Yet the poem as a whole leaves one thinking that Heaney is just brooding here on a private problem, rather fruitlessly as far as we are concerned, rather self-importantly as far as he thrusts it on us in this unresolved state. Perhaps it is helpful to him to write it; but he has not given us an 'exact and equal' poem. . . .

Another aspect of this emotional unease, more conspicuous in this book than hitherto, is a kind of coyness about various sexual experiences, dropping big hints, then quickly shutting up, as in a poem about a visit to Hardy's birthplace, where the visiting couple went into a damp-floored wood

> where we made an episode
> of ourselves, unforgettable,
> unmentionable.

This is all we are told—and that is far too much. Again, the evocation of people and objects from his childhood often seems over-intense and sentimental. A girl is evoked, the first, it seems, to have given him any sexual pleasure; but the swirl of images proves, after the flutter of sound has passed, to be patronising and even conventional. . . .

Verbally, the unease in these poems comes out either in a rather Lowell-like attempt to catch the immediacy of a feeling in a flying detritus of words, or, more deliberately, in a loading of every rift, as it were, with uranium, in the hope of explosions going off in all directions. Yet, in Heaney's abundant invention of images, such weaknesses still sit very close to his superlative gifts—as can be seen by comparing two lines in the very first poem in *Station Island.* This describes, first, the poet running behind his wife along an Underground tunnel to get to the Albert Hall on their honeymoon, the new wife's buttons springing off her new coat in the rush; then, apparently on a later occasion, the poet in angry mood walking in front of his wife, metaphorically picking up the buttons, refusing to look back but still hoping she is behind him. It's a fine conception, even if the rifts of such a short poem are positively overloaded with allusions to Daphne and Apollo, Orpheus and Eurydice and Hansel and Gretel. One line goes: 'Honeymooning, moon-lighting, late for the Proms'. It nicely catches a mood of glamour and fun inextricably intertwined, the first 'moon' picked out and doubled by the second, then the 'light' slipping through its alliteration into 'late'. Yet, in meaning, the line doesn't stand up. 'Moonlighting' cannot escape its primary sense of 'having two jobs'; and there seems no way in which that can apply to the couple on this rather formal honeymoon. So the pleasing initial effect of the line is undermined, and one ends up dissatisfied by it. (p. 53)

Heaney shows himself a venerator, but an independent-minded one, in his other new book, a translation mainly in verse of a medieval Irish poem, *Buile Suibhne,* or, as he puts it, **Sweeney Astray.** . . . King Sweeney assaulted St Ronan and was turned into a bird living in the treetops. There he sang his mad, sad songs, an archetype of the exile who turns to poetry, and Heaney has translated them with an excellent blend of melancholy, tale-tellerish surprises and Lucky-Jim humour. . . .

The confidence and ease of this translation, combined with the words of the last ghost on Station Island, the ghost of James Joyce, make me think that Heaney will recover all his buoyancy. Joyce says to him:

> Let go, let fly, forget.
> You've listened long enough. Now strike your
> > note.

Heaney will be aiming the iron again. (p. 54)

Derwent May, "Seamus Heaney's New Poems," in The Listener, *Vol. 112, No. 2889, December 20 & 27, 1984, pp. 53-4.*

ROBERT PINSKY

With characteristic wit and penetration, Heaney has given [**Station Island**] and its central sequence, a title of many senses. A station is a place where one must stand, or habitually stands, and because "station" is a military, social, and religious term—denoting steps in a pilgrimage as well as the stations of the cross—the idea of a station recalls the whole web of inherited communal ties and responsibilities. In seeming opposition, 'island" suggests isolation; but the terms reverse in relation to Heaney's country, Ireland, which is an island, and an island whose artists have sometimes stationed themselves somewhat apart from those inherited ties.

It is also characteristic of Heaney's shrewd attention to the world around him that he took the term from experience, personal and communal. Station Island is an island on Lough Derg, in County Donegal, also called St. Patrick's Purgatory, where pilgrims still go for a three-day exercise that includes "stations" re-creating Patrick's vigil and fasting on the site. The poem is bold enough to be consciously Dantesque in elements like its encounters with figures from the poet's life, and tactful and wise enough that the project does not seem overweening or vainglorious.

One striking thing about the sequence is how immensely powerful the narrative is: so artful and so at home with the verse, that the best sections deserve comparison with Frost's narrative poems. Even more than the previous books, this one establishes that along with his wonderful gifts of eye and ear, Heaney has the gift of the storyteller. The power to tell a story compactly, in a way that suggests that it could be told with such force only in verse, appears with particular clarity in the poem's seventh section, where the poet encounters the victim of a political killing, an admired schoolmate and football teammate ("the one stylist on the team"). . . . [This] section is a poem you might want to read aloud to friends, and the more of it you hear or read, the more impressive it is. . . . [The] way the full and partial rhymes shape the march of syntax without hobbling it, echoing the great model's *terza rima* just enough; the way the language is colloquial without windiness or strain; the rapid, natural transitions from the poet's voice to the interlocutor's, and from description to narrative; small telling contrasts between heightening ("knocking, knocking") and

lowering ("I had the sense"), so that the elements of the divine and of human comedy become credible.

Just the same, at some point Heaney decided not to write an epic, decided that this work was not going to be as large as that. The sections and their actions stand out in stronger relief than the actions of the whole, which is the poet's gathering of himself for new pastures. He chooses to pay homage to the past, rather than to re-create it as an epitome or global whole. This measured loyalty, a kind of quit-fee to the past, is the sequence's theme and its limiting boundary.

In the first section, he meets a kind of village bad-man who cuts wood on Sunday, "with a bow-saw, held / stiffly up like a lyre." "Stay clear of all processions," this figure advises. In subsequent poems, the interlocutors are various of the empowered dead: historical figures, like the 19th-century Protestant convert and author William Carleton, or James Joyce, who has the last word.

Before that last word, the poet pays debts and respects, some of them to fosterers and alter-selves: to a parish priest who died young on a mission to Africa, a teacher, a childhood sweetheart, a fanatic young political thug dead in prison, a murdered cousin the poet has written about, who questions whether that writing—an earlier, memorable poem in **Field Work**—was true enough. . . . This atonement is more like a discharged responsibility than a life's project: an island of devotion rather than an extended path of pilgrimage. . . . The last of such payments, in the penultimate poem, is given to a fondly remembered priest who once said "Read poems as prayers . . . and for your penance / translate me something by Juan de la Cruz." The translation is elegantly grave and straightforward, and precedes the final encounter with Joyce.

As if echoing the profane woodcutter of the first section, the severe word-crafter, with his voice "eddying with the vowels of all rivers," counsels against all processions in his own way. He greets the poet on the tarmac of the parking lot, not on the island itself, and urges work-lust, independence, freedom from the dead fires of the past, and uncumbered adventure into "the dark of the whole sea." In the poem's last line, isolated and single after the processional of tercets, "the downpour loosed its screens round his straight walk."

Those concluding two words, with their implication of a strict course, exactly defined (though into a shrouded and storm-swept terrain), indicate in a way that the sequence is less a summing-up than a tentative pointing forward. The sequence is an inspiring, masterful work that successfully evokes its great predecessors partly by declining their epic terms. In any case, the book as a whole is a rich and commanding work, one more indication that Seamus Heaney is a leading figure in a generation of poets that may be making already, and partly unnoticed, a new, various and powerful poetry in English. (pp. 38-9)

Robert Pinsky, "Poet and Pilgrim," in The New Republic, *Vol. 192, No. 3657, February 18, 1985, pp. 37-9.*

NICHOLAS CHRISTOPHER

From the first poem in Seamus Heaney's remarkable new collection [**Station Island**], it is clear we are in the hands of a master. He makes it all seem too easy. One of the infernal shades in the title poem advises the poet after his descent to hell "that the main thing is to write / for the joy of it." He surely does.

The ear will pick up more than the eye in these poems, whether urban, rural or otherworldly. We find ingenious rhymes and off-rhymes ("solder" and "alder," "option" and "iron"), metrical versatility and a subtle sense of play. There is seldom any fat or flatness in Mr. Heaney's rhythms. When he packs a punch, he does it with music and music's echoes. In the shorter, meditative lyrics in the first and third sections of the book (the latter narrated by Sweeney, the legendary exiled king of Ulster whose medieval story Mr. Heaney translated last year), he works his stanzas with wonderful confidence. His lines are rarely overloaded. Rather, it is the triplets and quatrains he frequently employs that make the poems move. One is reminded of Wilfred Owen and W. H. Auden, John Clare and Thomas Hardy, poets who worked confidently with the stanza form, achieving delicate strokes with a broad medium and often on a very large canvas.

As in Hardy's work (Hardy is celebrated affectionately in the poem called **"The Birthplace"**), there is a generosity of spirit, an abundant, assured energy in Mr. Heaney's poems. His is a world of powerful ebbs and flows beneath deceptive surfaces. We find a deep, magical apprehension of the physical world that recalls Yeats's observation on Celtic tradition: "Once every people in the world believed that trees were divine . . . and that deer, ravens and foxes, and wolves and bears, and clouds and pools, almost all the things under the sun and moon, and the sun and moon, were not less divine and changeable." . . .

There are no folksy, down-home or miniaturist tendencies in his presentation of natural subjects. His voice is complex and his eye keen, but as with any inspired poet, he is after transformations, not reproductions. Nature is neither antagonist nor sounding board but a component of the human imagination. Life changes before our eyes if we are willing to see, to discard our comfortable blindfolds, to change ourselves. . . .

It is no coincidence that the long poem **"Station Island"** recalls Dante's purgatory and Odysseus' visit to Tiresias in the underworld. But the ghosts here are modern Irish ghosts—terrorists and their victims, a young priest, an old man. In his notes, Mr. Heaney informs us that the poem is a series of "dream sequences set on Station Island on Lough Derg in Co. Donegal." Also called St. Patrick's Purgatory, the island has been the site of pilgrimages for over 1,000 years. Its "stations" are what Mr. Heaney calls units of the pilgrim's penitential exercises during a three-day vigil. . . . We know from the outset that it is an ancient route (with modern pitfalls) the poet follows here, down and down, deep into himself on a footpath trod by many ghosts, good and evil, and finally into the bowels of Ireland itself. It is not a journey for weak hearts.

We come upon a ghost in the seventh section, a young shopkeeper roused from his bed by strangers and shot:

> His brow
> was blown open above the eye and blood
> had dried on his neck and cheek.

After describing his killers to the poet and being informed that they were jailed, he stands silent, "forgetful of everything," and the poet breaks his cadence, pulling us far back, as if inverting a telescope:

> Through life and death he had hardly aged.
> There always was an athlete's cleanliness
> • shining off him and except for the ravaged

> forehead and the blood, he was still that same
> rangy midfielder in a blue jersey
> and starched pants, the one stylist on the team,

> the perfect, clean, unthinkable victim.

That last line lies buried like a shard at the poem's center and works its way to the surface throughout the narrative.

"Station Island" is a brilliant, spiraling poem that carries us to hell, in and out of the fire and back to the rainy jetty where the shade of Joyce, a tall, straight, "fish-cold" man who "seemed blind"—Tiresias and Virgil in one—guides us again into the world of the living with a bit of acid advice: . . .

> ". . . Let go, let fly, forget.
> You've listened long enough. Now strike your note."

Some of Seamus Heaney's finest work—his best since *North* (1975)—is in this collection. *Station Island* is that rarity, a book of poems to be read through rather than dipped into. There is bone and sinew and song here, and an urgency that grabs you by the sleeve—sometimes by the throat—and makes your blood race. Read it aloud.

> *Nicholas Christopher, "A Pilgrim in County Donegal," in* The New York Times Book Review, *March 10, 1985, p. 9.*

RICHARD ELLMANN

After the heavily accented melodies of Yeats, and that poet's elegiac celebrations of imaginative glories, Seamus Heaney addresses his readers in a quite different key. He does not overwhelm his subjects; rather he allows them a certain freedom from him, and his sharp conjunctions with them leave their authority and his undiminished. There are none of Yeats's Olympians about; the figures who appear in Heaney's verse have quite human dimensions. Nature for him does not mean the lakes, woods, and swans visible from the big house. Instead, a farmer's son, Heaney sees it as the "dark-clumped grass where cows or horses dunged, / the cluck when pith-lined chestnut-shells split open" (the latter a line that Hopkins would have welcomed). These and much else are things to remember "when you have grown away and stand at last / at the very centre of the empty city." . . .

Auden complained that Yeats was willing to sacrifice sense to sound. Heaney escapes such an imputation: his sounds are contained, clipped, unlingering, "definite / as a steel nib's downstroke, quick and clean." Even his lyrical passages are tightly reined. . . . Rhymes, when he uses them, are resolutely unemphatic, more obvious effects being shunned. He is fond of assonance, which, as Austin Clarke said, "takes the clapper from the bell of rhyme." Irish poetry since Yeats has been at pains to purge itself of the grand manner, and Heaney austerely excludes it except on state occasions. He likes tough words that sound like dialect, though they are respectably lexical, such as flenge or loaning or slub silk or scutch or Joyce's tundish. Occasional Irish words such as "aisling" (vision) make their appearance. (There were more in [the books that preceded *Station Island*]). Compared with Yeats, this contemporary poetry marks its difference by subdued rhythms, less clamant philosophy, less prophetic utterance. "Glimmerings are what the soul's composed of," Heaney declares.

Although unpretentiousness is characteristic of Heaney's verse, the term is not adequate to describe his assured reticences, his unearthing of apt and unexpected images, his proneness to see the visible world as a substance compounded from materials no longer visible but still suspended in it. Behind facts lie myths, not airy ones but myths so durable they seem facts too. . . .

Heaney has always been fond of myth, of what in **"Gifts of Rain"** in an earlier book he called self-mockingly "my need for antediluvian love." He feels inside him "a whole late-flooding thaw of ancestors," including the Tolland man and the Graballe man. Not anthropological ancestors only. A little room is found for godlike presences, of Diana or Venus, of the Irish Niamh and the fertility sprite, the brazen sheelagh na gig. A cornfield becomes the cornfield of Boaz where Ruth labored. Ghosts belong to the congeries of backgrounding selves, and so he praises Hardy, whose grave he visits in one poem [in *Station Island*], for "the unperturbable ghost life he carried." Looking at a pump in **"Changes,"** Heaney hears its prehistory, "the bite of the spade that sank it," and all that has happened to it since.

At moments this sense of objects as being like people dragging their histories with them moves toward allegory, as in **"A Kite for Michael and Christopher,"** where the soaring kite reminds the poet humorously of the soul, and the sudden feeling of the kite's weight makes him feel "the strumming, rooted, long-tailed pull of grief." He reminds his beloved that their bodies are temples of the Holy Ghost in order to compare the feeling of her underbreast to that of a ciborium in the palm, as if Christianity existed to supply him with erotic imagery. He hunts for precedents for his own feelings, and lights on Milosz's sense of being caught between participating actively in history and contemplating a motionless point, and on Chekhov's recognition of slavery on Sakhalin even as he tries to waken the free man in himself.

[*Station Island*] has three sections. The lyrics in the first exhibit Heaney's ability to blend recollection with immediate feeling. Wry, spare, compressed, subtle, strange, they have a furtive intensity and excitement. "Poems that explode in silence, / without forcing, without violence," are what he aims at here. He gives only fleeting glimpses of himself, often mocking, as when, in **"Sandstone Keepsake,"** he is "a silhouette not worth bothering about, / out for the evening in scarf and waders," and "from my free state of image and allusion" looks across at watchtowers in Northern Ireland.

The situation in Ulster plays a large part in these poems. Though Heaney apologizes in one for "my timid circumspect involvement," and in another explains, "I have no mettle for the angry role," he cannot for long, as an Ulsterman, take his eyes off the victims on both sides. Yet he acknowledges, as Yeats did, a certain bewilderment, and in one poem, **"Away from It All,"** presents that with indirection, using a lobster "fortified and bewildered" as it reaches the boiling pot. In a no-win situation, the poet's duty is to register compassion, not partisanship.

In the other two sections of his book Heaney offers, as he has not before, two series of connected poems. One of them is based upon *Sweeney Astray,* his translation published last year of the *Buile Suibhne.* (p. 19)

The act of translation suggested a kinship of souls as well as of sounds between Heaney and Sweeney, and he exploits this in his new book. The series of poems with the general title **"Sweeney Redivivus"** offers glosses on the original, somewhere between the point of view of the legendary king and that of the contemporary poet. Heaney has a lyric earlier in the book which he calls **"Making Strange,"** and the effect of these new poems is to take the poet out of the sphere of being in which he usually locates himself so firmly. . . . He has to unlearn and learn again from this new perspective of Sweeney among the starlings. He can even reconsider Ronan's exiling curse and wonder whether it was not rather that he himself chose to desert the ground and groundlings, so "pious and exacting and demeaned." . . . The Sweeney persona enables Heaney to overcome the earth's gravity, to reconsider all things from the vantage point of weightlessness. The solid Heaney world melts a little. At the same time, though no longer "mired in attachment," Sweeney never really leaves the earth behind, and subjects it to sharp and undetached scrutiny, relieved by playfulness.

These poems have their curious effect of stepping backward and forward at once as tanks and steering wheels appear before the twice-born Sweeney's eyes. Good as they are, they are surpassed by the other section, **"Station Island,"** which gives its name to the book. The connected lyrics here represent Heaney's most ambitious work. Station Island, sometimes known as St. Patrick's Purgatory, is an island in Lough Derg, County Donegal, to which for hundreds of years people have made pilgrimages. Among these were two writers, William Carleton and Patrick Kavanagh. . . . Both these predecessors appear to Heaney in the course of the poem, for at Lough Derg, as Yeats says in "The Pilgrim," "All know that all the dead in the world about that place are stuck."

Heaney, no longer a believer, has had the happy thought of making the pilgrimage an all souls' night, with frequent use of Dantean terza rima. The poet encounters a series of familiar ghosts, a woodcutter he has known, an old master from his Anahorish School, a priest friend who died of fever in a mission compound, an athletic schoolfellow killed by the IRA and a second cousin killed by a Protestant, an archaeologist, his mother, a first girlfriend. They tell their stories to this Irish Dante, and tell them well, and implicate him in their replies. But the main burden is carried by Carleton at the beginning, and by Joyce, no Lough Derg pilgrim, at the end. . . . Joyce completes Heaney's pilgrimage by rejecting it: "Your obligation / is not discharged by any common rite," he tells him. When Heaney raises the question of the Irish using the English language, Joyce is impatient:

> "The English language
>   belongs to us. . . ."

(pp. 19-20)

In Heaney's poem, Joyce confines himself to the question of the artist's career. There is much to be said for this unportentous vision. It seems fitting that Heaney should find his model not in Yeats, constantly trying to break through the façade of what is, but in Joyce, who "found the living world enough" if sufficiently epiphanized. Joyce's message is a reaffirmation, with the authority of an immortal, of what Heaney has meant in speaking of himself as "an inner émigré" and claiming "a migrant solitude."

Many of these poems have a tough rind as though the author knew that for his purposes deferred comprehension was better than instant. Obliquity suits him. Heaney's talent, a prodigious one, is exfoliating and augmenting here. (p. 20)

Richard Ellmann, "Heaney Agonistes," in The New York Review of Books, *Vol. XXXII, No. 4, March 14, 1985, pp. 19-20.*

Ted Hughes

1930-

(Born Edward James Hughes) English poet, dramatist, script-writer, short story writer, author of books for children, editor, critic, essayist, and translator.

Named Poet Laureate of England in 1984, Hughes is a versatile poet who is perhaps best known for creating powerful poems that feature bold metaphors and resonant language, imagery, and speech rhythms. He often describes natural phenomena and animals through evocative language, and he also comments on the human condition through the use of myth and symbol. Hughes contends that Western civilization has over-valued intellectual faculties, dividing humans from both their instinctual urges and from nature. He suggests that the poet can be a reunifying source by employing such creative energies as imagination and emotion, as well as rationalization, to probe the mysteries of nature and life. In Hughes's poetry, according to Seamus Heaney, "racial memory, animal instinct and poetic imagination all flow into one another with an exact sensuousness."

Hughes began writing during the 1950s when English poetry was being influenced by a group of writers collectively labeled The Movement. Unlike such Movement poets as Philip Larkin, Kingsley Amis, and D. J. Enright, who wrote about urban life with ironic detachment, emotional constraint, and urbane wit, Hughes's early poetry is emotionally intense and features elaborate imagery and natural settings. His first book, *The Hawk in the Rain* (1957), made an immediate impact on critics, poets, and readers. The poems in this volume display charged, assonant language which critics likened to that of Gerard Manley Hopkins. Many of these poems are voiced from the perspectives of animals, describing their sensations and actions as they participate in natural cycles. These verses introduce Hughes's extensive examination of the overly rational actions of humans as compared to the instinctual actions of animals. Critics were particularly impressed with the sensual language of "The Thought-Fox," one of Hughes's most anthologized poems. *Lupercal* (1960), Hughes's second volume, confirmed his reputation as an important and inventive young poet. Although many of the poems are more subdued, contemplative, and conversational than his earlier verse, others focus on brutality in nature and celebrate the untamed natural world. Several poems in *The Hawk in the Rain* and *Lupercal* offer social criticism or focus on the indignities of war.

Wodwo (1967), Hughes's next major book, contains poems, short stories, and a script for a radio play. The title sequence of poems concerns a fantastic creature who originally appeared in the medieval poem *Sir Gawain and the Green Knight*. Early in *Wodwo*, the creature asks, "What am I?" and undertakes a quest for identity by exploring its surroundings. These poems reveal Hughes's increasing interest in and use of myth. Hughes's next major book, *Crow* (1970), is considered his most startling achievement. The poems follow the adventures of Crow from the genesis of life to nuclear apocalypse. Crow experiences individual and universal tragedies and assesses both human pretension and life itself with coldly sardonic observations. Many of the poems, or "Crow songs," are intended to shock the reader through black humor, violence, and sexual im-

agery. Although several critics contend that the violence is often gratuitous and ultimately nihilistic, others agree that the work has powerful implications deriving from the depth of symbolic meaning developed in the poems. They note that the ravenous crow is an appropriate commentator on the grim realities of life: crows are carrion eaters and are symbols of ill-omen in many cultures, and the grating voice of the crow appropriately reflects the tone and content of the poems. Crow suffers the malevolence of nature and humans but reveals a determination to survive and endure.

In several volumes and pamphlets following *Crow*, Hughes continues to develop a mythic interpretation of life. *Gaudete* (1977), a long narrative poem, presents a tragicomic portrait of a clergyman who is spirited away and replaced by a sexually voracious substitute. During the course of this poem, Hughes explores some of the dualistic traits associated with males and females, humanity and nature, and Christian and pagan myths. *Cave Birds: An Alchemical Cave Drama* (1977) concerns a being that has denied its natural instincts in favor of a wholly rationalistic view of life. The individual poems in this volume follow the being as it experiences "ego death" and is symbolically reborn. Critics debated the effectiveness of Hughes's symbolic presentations in these works.

The poems in *Remains of Elmet* (1979), *Moortown*, (1979), and *River* (1984) offer vivid descriptions of animal life and nature and generally project a more positive view of humanity than Hughes's previous works. *Remains of Elmet* traces the history of the Elmet region of England as it developed from an ancient kingdom to a modern industrial area. Critics were especially impressed with Hughes's recreation of the region's haunting landscape. *Moortown* is composed of four sequences of poems. The "Moortown" sequence, which was singled out for acclaim by critics, recounts in diary form Hughes's experiences as a dairy farmer deeply engaged in the birth and death cycles of animals. This sequence also includes several elegies to Jack Orchard, Hughes's farming partner. The poems in *River* follow a series of rivers through the course of a year, describing their sundry landscapes and animal life. These volumes reveal what many agree to be Hughes's finest qualities as a poet: his ability to evoke the natural world in rich, sensuous detail and his unsentimental yet respectful view of life. According to Keith Sagar, Hughes's work as a whole represents an attempt to recover "the lost sense of the sacredness of nature."

Although Hughes has distinguished himself primarily as a poet, he is also respected for his many other literary endeavors. In particular, critics praise his careful editing of the posthumously published work of his late wife, the poet and novelist Sylvia Plath. Hughes's insightful social and literary criticism and his poems and books about poetry for children have also been commended.

(See also *CLC*, Vols. 2, 4, 9, 14; *Children's Literature Review*, Vol. 3; *Contemporary Authors*, Vols. 1-4, rev. ed.; *Contemporary Authors New Revision Series*, Vol. 1; *Something about the Author*, Vol. 27; and *Dictionary of Literary Biography*, Vol. 40.)

P. R. KING

Hughes has so far published eight major collections (as well as several limited editions published by small presses) in just over two decades. He has also written poetry and prose for children, plays for radio and stage, short stories, and some very fine critical essays. In *Poetry in the Making* (1967) he has also published one of the most exciting and useful accounts of poetry for younger readers. This is a very full range of work and represents a great variety of forms and intentions. Within the eight major volumes of poetry there is also a great variety of subject and treatment. This is a fact sometimes overlooked by readers unduly influenced by the label of 'animal poet' or 'nature poet' that was attached to Hughes in the early sixties. Too great an attention to this early aspect of his poetry has led to misunderstanding and even dislike of Hughes's later work.

In *The Hawk in the Rain* and *Lupercal* it is certainly the poems about animals and nature that make the greatest impact. His creation of hawks, jaguars, pikes and thrushes are vivid, vibrantly energetic exercises in taking the reader into the very feelings and actions of the animals, and these poems must rank as the best of their kind since *Birds, Beasts and Flowers* by D. H. Lawrence (with whom Hughes shares some preoccupations). But Hughes's total output encompasses far more subjects than animals and far more moods, feelings and ideas than are contained in these intense, strenuously active descriptions. He is also capable of writing with tenderness, or with quiet, lyrical grace, or with a sense of play and humour. However, it is true that the dominating impression that his poems leave with a reader is a sense of the vigour and frequently violent energies of both the non-human world and the inner world of man's own emotions.

In fact it is not his especial concern for animals that seems to have drawn Hughes to write about them so frequently in his poetry. It is rather that he sees in them the most clear manifestation of a life-force that is distinctly non-human or, rather, is non-rational in its source of power. Hughes observes in modern man a reluctance to acknowledge the deepest, instinctual sources of energy in his own being, an energy that is related to the 'elemental power circuit' of the universe and to which animals are closer than man. Hughes's concern, therefore, has always been wider than the simplistic labelling of him as 'animal poet' implies. It is true that he began in the first two books by exploring the primal energies of the animal and natural world that stressed the absolute otherness of that world. Since then he has moved on to express a sense of sterility and nihilism in modern man's response to life, a response which he connects with the dominance of man's rational, objective intellect at the expense of the life of the emotions and imagination. In *Crow* he created a mythical story to express this nihilistic universe and to show that beneath the feelings of complete despair there was still an active voice of unyielding energy and survival—the voice of the Crow. In *Gaudete*, he has gone on to explore in symbolic terms the divided nature of modern man's soul and the need to reconcile the inner and outer lives of man if his sense of pain and evil is not to become self-destructive. (pp. 109-10)

[It] is possible to perceive a developing task in his work. Briefly, that task is to explore and express what he has called 'the war between vitality and death'. It is a war he sees most clearly waged in the natural world where no consciousness of self intervenes to manipulate an animal's response to his condition. Man, as a result of the power of his consciousness (his intellect and imagination), is able to stand back from the situation that confronts him and not just respond instinctually. His capacity to do so is both a strength and a weakness. Hughes seems to be suggesting that in modern man it has become a serious weakness because he has allowed too large a gap to develop between his consciousness and his instinctual reaction to his condition. He has cultivated his rational, cognitive powers too exclusively, neglecting his inner world of feelings, imagination and instinct, and has therefore divided his own nature, cutting himself off from the natural energies of the universe. In **"Myth and Education,"** a key essay for an understanding of his attitudes, he writes of the way in which modern man has narrowed his vision until he is looking only at the outer world. He regards this as a consequence of the rise of the scientific ideal of objective intelligence but sees our too exclusive concern with such intelligence as producing a rigid and suicidal stupidity.... [The] inner world of our bodies, of our 'archaic energies of instinct and feeling', is rapidly being lost to us. The traditional means of embracing and humanizing these energies was religion. Without religion these powers have become dehumanized and our inner life 'a place of demons'. Cut off from those powers, 'All we register is the vast absence, the emptiness, the sterility, the meaninglessness, the loneliness.' Having depicted this situation, Hughes has gone on to seek a means of reconciliation with those inner powers. The traditional means of such a reconciliation has been the use of the imagination, which has been called 'creative' and 'divine' because it has the power to help us negotiate between the inner and outer worlds. The traditional language of this negotiation has been religion, myth and symbol. In his later poetry, Hughes seems to be making increasing use of myth and symbol to explore man's divided nature and to express some kind of resolution. This is not to suggest that he is moving towards some religious stance (in the Christian sense). It appears he looks back beyond Christian sources towards myths which have their beginnings in the experience of seasonal and natural cycles, and which express an almost fatalistic acceptance of suffering while celebrating the sheer power and energy of the life process itself. The tool to re-create an understanding of these sources is the imagination and the artist is its guardian. The artist and his work are thus the key to the resolution of these conflicts. . . . (pp. 110-11)

If this is the task that Hughes has undertaken, it is a difficult one for an artist living in a civilization that prefers to think no longer in terms of myth—that appears, indeed, even to pride itself on its demythologizing fervour. The immensity of the task and the belief in the artist as a last guardian of essential truths can lead to a poetry with an aim that may sometimes elude its grasp, and may, in fact, lead to the inconsistencies of voice and tone that some critics point to in the poetry. Hughes himself has spoken of writing from 'three separate characteristic states of mind, which are fairly different', and these states of mind may reflect different possibilities of expression as well as different experiences. The voice of nihilism in many *Crow* poems, the voice of confused search in *Wodwo* and the voice of divided man in *Gaudete* are only some of the voices of a poet who seeks to express our modern sense of ourselves as varied and contradictory. (p. 112)

> *P. R. King, "Elemental Energy: 'The Poetry of Ted Hughes'," in his* Nine Contemporary Poets: A Critical Introduction, *Methuen, 1979, pp. 107-51.*

BLAKE MORRISON

Ted Hughes's last collection, *Remains of Elmet,* did much to check the view that from *Crow* onwards his work has been deteriorating. It wasn't just that his description seemed more under control. . . . There was also Hughes's powerful feeling for the Calder Valley: the charting of its decline and the affection shown towards inhabitants like the **"Crown Point Pensioners"** were something quite new and unexpected in a poet who'd never previously shown much empathy for humans or their history. This healthy development is in some measure consolidated in *Moortown:* his poems about a farm-labourer, an auctioneer, a tramp have a surprising warmth. There is also, though, the half-baked existentialism and numskull historicising of **"A Motorbike"**. . . . (pp. 22-3)

There are similar worries with **"Foxhunt"**; the creature which trotted so delicately into Hughes's imagination in **"The Thought-Fox"** is here ruthlessly hunted down, deprived of its freedom not so much by hounds as by the author himself, whose anti-hunt propagandising hasn't, in any case, Wilde's flair for epigram: 'A machine with only two products: / Dog-shit and dead foxes' does not have the ring of 'the unspeakable in full pursuit of the uneatable'.

And yet the title sequence which opens *Moortown* is on the whole Hughes back to his best. Quickly written and hardly revised, the sequence is a kind of dairy-diary, a journal of everyday life and livestock. Though there are moments of pleasure and relief, life on the Hughes farm is predominantly struggle: the animals won't co-operate; the tractor can only be started after a titanic fight with 'shackle-pins bedded in cast-iron cowshit'; and activities like shearing and dehorning are much messier than city-folk might suppose. . . . It's in the poems about birth (and there's an extraordinary rate of lambing and calving on this farm) that Hughes is at his best: the delicacy of the new-born brings out his own delicacy. Some editing might

have helped: after the first half-dozen similes for afterbirth—jelly, jetsam, plastic apron, tent-rope, tattered banner, flag . . .—Hughes understandably enough runs out of new ones. But what's impressive about these poems is that they touch on fundamental issues of birth, life, work, death, without ever losing sight of a familiar, knowable world: the description of a mother and her calf lying 'face to face like two mortally wounded duellists' has its metaphysical implications, but there's an immediate physicality too.

Sadly, this lesson is not learnt throughout the rest of *Moortown,* where Hughes breaks open the myth-kitty, brings out a predictable cast of Prometheus, Adam, etc. There's an arbitrariness about it all nicely summed up in a poem entitled **"Life is trying to be life"** which begins 'Death is also trying to be life'. In these wham-bam dealings with polarities and paradox everything can equally well be its opposite—the grave wants to be a cradle, the cradle wants to be a grave, and I want to read something else. (p. 23)

> *Blake Morrison, "Yous & Is & Doths & Thees," in* New Statesman, *Vol. 99, No. 2546, January 4, 1980, pp. 22-3.**

BEN HOWARD

Hughes's powers are peculiar. They spring in part from his rhetoric—graceful, aggressive, or studiously ugly, according to his will—and from a talent for tapping buried psychic energies. But their central origin, one suspects, lies in his gift for making poems into battlegrounds, where warring ideas and currents of feeling can have it out. Tensions crackle—and ironies abound. Though an ally of the id, of impulse and spontaneity, he has crafted some of the tightest, strictest poems of his generation. Though an enemy of rationalism, he has achieved startling successes through such rationalistic means as pattern, rhyme, and meter. He has deplored the "virus of abstraction" in Western thought, and has argued that puritanical repression breeds violence and destruction. And yet in his own work he has often resorted to abstraction, and has often seemed the celebrant, if not the proponent, of violence and destruction. Opposed to the "subtly apotheosized misogyny of Reformed Christianity," he has ironically become, in a part of the feminist mind, an arch villain of male oppression. In the matter of style, he has praised the unadorned directness of such poets as Keith Douglas, while veering in his own work from polished elegance to hyperbolic special effects. At his best, he has seemed an inspired musician; at his worst, a dubious shaman. And now he has taken a fresh and unexpected turn. By the standards of *Crow* and *Gaudete*, his newest poems [in *Cave Birds, Remains of Elmet,* and *Moortown*] seem plain, reflective, and curiously anecdotal. In his own way and to his own ends, he is finding a place for himself in the English meditative tradition. Crow has been spotted near Tintern Abbey. (pp. 253-54)

Hughes's native Yorkshire, the rock cliffs and the moors, excites [his] imagination with its "strange strength." As Hughes puts it, the landscape re-ignites "the ancient instincts and feelings in which most of our body lives," the "prehistoric feelings" deadened by civilization. Landscape affected Hughes at an early age. He grew up in a valley, confined by a wall of rock whose "evil eye" looked down upon his birth. . . . Hughes's only escape was to the moors, a desolate but exhilarating atmosphere, where the light was at once both "gloomily purplish and incredibly clear . . . as if objects there had less protection than elsewhere." And so a polarity developed between the "gloom, oppression, constriction, and deathliness" of the rock, and the "clarity, excitement, (and) exposure" of the moors. (p. 255)

The rock and the moors have their counterparts in Hughes's moral vision, where the rock becomes the force of puritanical rationalism, and the moors become a metaphor for the inner life. More precisely, the rock becomes an emblem of the civilized order—its rationality, morality, and repression of instinct—while the moors become a theater for the exploration of the inner life, the world of "final reality." The opposition is fundamental to Hughes's thought. It undergirds a vision in which hawks, crows, and falcons are the heroes, and the enemies are puritanical rationalism and the "ferocious virus of abstraction." In Hughes's words: "The inner world, separated from the outer world, is a place of demons." And it is puritanical rationalism which divides mind from body, the life of thought from the life of instinct, the outward world from the inner. Relegated to the confines of the id, man's "baser nature" grows "cannibal murderous with deprivation," and the conscious mind is cut off from dimensions of experience which once made "life worth living," the "lost awareness and powers and allegiances of our biological and spiritual being. (pp. 255-56)

Hughes's image of the psyche is part of a larger vision of Western history and "the soul-state of our civilization." Grounded in the theories of Robert Graves, Hughes's world view centers on the figure of the White Goddess, the creative-destructive deity ousted by Jehovah. When the exiled goddess returns, it is no longer as a principle of fertility but as a perversely destructive force, a serpent in Paradise, wreaking havoc upon the repressive, civilized order. The conflict of pagan goddess and Christian oppressor animates several poems in *Wodwo* . . . (esp. **"Karma," "Logos,"** and **"Gog II and III"**). It underlies Hughes's interpretation of English history, in which the medieval, pre-Christian goddess of natural law is drawn into court by the Puritan Jehovah. More recently, it appears in Hughes's essay on the environmental crisis (**"The Environmental Revolution"**), which bemoans the "fanatic rejection of Nature" and declares that "the story of the mind exiled from Nature is the story of Western Man." (p. 256)

Cave Birds (1978) is a fresh assault. Produced in collaboration with Leonard Baskin, it is a series of short poems juxtaposed with grotesque, cartoonlike drawings of rapacious feathered creatures. (p. 257)

What has revealed itself in *Cave Birds* is an "alchemical cave drama," in which an Everyman, identified with platonism and with Logos divorced from the body, is accused of an unnamed crime and brought to trial. Spectral birds invade him: the "summoner," "the interrogator," "the judge," "the executioner," the "gatekeeper." Swallowed by a raven, he undergoes several ordeals. In the end he marries an earthly woman and is reborn as a falcon.

Hughes has summarized the story and its significance. The protagonist, who has denied his dark, instinctual side,

> is confronted in court with his victim. It is his own demon whom he now sees for the first time. The hero realizes he is out of his depth. He protests as an honorable platonist, thereby re-enacting his crime in front of his judges. He still cannot understand his guilt. He cannot understand the sequence of cause and effect.

From this description, one might have expected a narrative poem, or perhaps a dramatic dialogue. Instead, Hughes has preferred a sequence of monologues interspersed with surrealistic anecdotes. . . . Its strategies are not so much dramatic as rhetorical, and its strengths lie mainly in single lines and short passages (e.g., "You shall see / How tenderly she has wiped her child's face clean / Of the bitumen of blood and the smoke of tears"), where the force and variety of the rhythms make up for a lack of genuine drama. (pp. 257-58)

[**"The Owl Flower"**] is the penultimate poem of the sequence. The hero has just been married. He is about to be reborn as a falcon. . . . This scene ought to have been climactic. We are witnessing a momentous upheaval in which the hero's puritanical will, his rational denial of his demon, has at last been overcome. He has been forced to accept his instinctual self. The hero's trauma ought to have been affecting—and even cathartic.

What makes it merely embarrassing is Hughes's choice of tactics, which distance the reader and undermine the dramatic illusion. Instead of dramatizing an anguished transformation, Hughes's comic-strip diction ("big terror descends"), his profusion of Gothic images and metaphors (the spinning coffin, the cauldron of tongues, the "mummy grain"), and his near-hysterical tone evoke the image of a frenzied stage manager fumbling with ropes and pulleys and recorded screams. Even the explosive verbs ("scalds," "spins," "bursts") have soggy fuses.

Elsewhere Hughes is less theatrical and more convincing. . . . One can respect Hughes's boldness and his effort to symbolize his deepest convictions, but there's not much to be said for his devices or for the creaking artifact they have produced.

Remains of Elmet (1979), another collaboration, is more personal and far more restrained. At points it is very moving. This time Hughes has collaborated with Fay Godwin, who has taken a group of photographs of the Calder valley. Situated west of Halifax, this region was (in Hughes's description) "the last ditch of Elmet, the last British Celtic kingdom to fall to the Angles." The poems are Hughes's response to the photos.

Hughes's collaborations are instructive. They help define a many-sided poet. If Baskin brings out the caricaturist in Hughes, Godwin draws out the contemplative: the meditative realist rooted in locale. (pp. 257-60)

The title poem epitomizes the series. Personal and impersonal history merge in a single statement. . . . (p. 260)

Not all of the poems are so austere. Hughes's subjects range from rhododendrons, curlews, and dry walls to the parsonage at Haworth and the legend of a milkmaid killed by foxes. Haunted by the ghost of Emily Bronte and dogged by the pathetic fallacy, Hughes often seems unable to leave well enough alone. A delicate, empathic poem about curlews ends with the lines

> Drinking the nameless and naked
> Through trembling bills

undoing all that has come before. An unfortunate tree is subjected to "unending interrogation by wind" and "tortured by huge scaldings of light"; and when it tries to "confess" it cannot "bleed a word." Another kind of excess occurs in an otherwise powerful study of the skeleton of a sheep, whose bones have "tumbled apart, forgetting each other." . . . It's disheartening to see one of Hughes's more expressive mannerisms—the ending of a line with an adverb ("anyway," "ironically")—hardening into a habit. Elsewhere (as in "digesting utterly") this idiosyncrasy produces an effect of colloquial vigor, but here it produces only awkwardness. Hughes's language is more complicated than his subject. The object of contemplation has yet to achieve parity with the poet's response.

Moortown (1979) brings Hughes closer to such a balance. . . . Up until recently, his own work has been weighted heavily in favor of the subjective. "[The] real problem," he suggests, "comes from the fact that outer world and inner world are interdependent at every moment. We are simply the locus of their collision." Such collisions have been frequent in Hughes's art, but until recently it is the inner world which has collected damages.

That is why *Moortown* represents a turning point, if not a landmark, in Hughes's development. The book includes three ambitious sequences, two of which (**"Prometheus on his Crag"** and **"Adam and the Sacred Nine"**) are aggressive, rhetorical treatments of mythical subjects. The real interest of the book, however, lies in the title sequence: a group of thirty-four poems which document Hughes's experience as a farmer in Devon. At their strongest these pieces have the qualities Hughes has admired in Keith Douglas: the "freshness and trenchancy of a jotting," and "the obsession to get the facts down clear and straight, with no concessions to so-called poetry."

The facts are often gruesome. One episode [**"February 17th"**] begins in stillbirth—and ends in decapitation. . . . The language is heightened not by analogical leaps or telescoping contexts but by its energetic rhythms and intense concentration. In the narrative that follows, the speaker beheads the lamb in order to free it. The poem ends with the extrication:

> Then like
> Pulling myself to the ceiling with one finger
> Hooked in a loop, timing my effort
> To her birth-push groans, I pulled against
> The corpse that would not come. Till it came.
> And after it the long, sudden, yolk-yellow
> Parcel of life
> In a smoking slither of oils and soups and syrups—
> And the body lay born, beside the hacked-off head.

Though rich in tropes—the soups and syrups, the parcel, the pull to the ceiling—this passage is notable for its plainness and its fidelity to the facts of the outer world. The tropes penetrate the outer world. They also objectify the poet's response, though here that purpose seems secondary.

And throughout the sequence, whether his subject is cows or sheep, a difficult birth or a gory dehorning, Hughes subordinates "so-called poetry" to an accurate rendering. Even his figures serve mainly to illuminate his subjects, as when he writes of a fox who "runs still fresh, with all his chances before him." The figure serves not so much to display the poet's invention or chronicle his emotions, as to evoke the fox's desperation.

The obvious danger is that the "outer world" will subsume the inner, and that the writing will become pedestrian. A few poems (**"Tractor"** in particular) fall into that trap, but on the whole Hughes maintains an even balance. In one unusual instance [**"Orf,"** the] poem divides itself equally between objective fact and subjective response. (pp. 261-64)

Hughes has always had access to mysteries. In the past, however, he has attended mainly to the inner life, and his poems have been distinguished by their bold associative leaps, their openness to inner terror. He has been terror's ambassador, bringing the ravages of madness into the light. He has trafficked in the supernatural and has dwelt imaginatively among otherworldly birds. In his new work he has not lost his gift for wonder—or his taste for gore—but he has turned his attention back to the earth, and has addressed the brutality of ordinary life. Intuition—and perhaps his own best instincts—have returned him to the things of this world. (p. 265)

Ben Howard, "*Terror's Ambassador*," in Parnassus: Poetry in Review, *Vol. 8, No. 2, Spring-Summer-Fall-Winter, 1980, pp. 252-65.*

CAROL BERE

At fifty, Ted Hughes is no longer the wunderkind of British poetry, the angry young man squaring off against the patricians of the literary establishment. But whether personal tragedy or the natural attritions of time have—or could—pacify him is another issue. He has been likened to Lear stalking the heath, his blistering rage challenging the quixotic elements. And everything about Hughes gives shape to this image: the towering physical presence; the resonant voice, a seeming fount of power only marginally contained; the out-sized linguistic gifts—at times, stamped with unmistakable authority; at other times, a turbulent avalanche of overwrought images.

It is not surprising, then, that critics rarely harbor neutral feelings toward Hughes's poetry. He has been dismissed as a connoisseur of the habits of animals, his disgust with humanity barely disguised; labeled a "voyeur of violence," attacked for his generous choreographing of gore; and virtually written off as a cult poet, the private preserve of those specialized in arcane areas of mythology and Jungian psychology. Still others consider him to be the best poet writing today—admired for the originality and command of his approach; the scope and complexity of his mythic enterprise; and the apparent ease and freshness with which he can vitalize a landscape, free of any mitigating sentimentality.

And the poetry provides sufficient corroborating evidence for all of these claims. For what we are faced with in Hughes is a poet whose very strengths generate their own built-in possibilities for excess. It is precisely the wide range of his risk-taking—his constant assault on what Geoffrey Hill calls the "recalcitrance of language"—that makes works such as the highly original *Crow* and even such unwieldy endeavors as *Gaudete* both provocative as well as problematic. Hughes's despair with the ability of language to convey varied states of feeling is self-evident and, at times, the poetry may founder on the "titanic extravagance" of his verbal gymnastics. Still, to read the compelling title sequence of the recently published *Moortown* is to be reminded once again of his remarkable ability to suggest the interrelationships between all areas of life—the beauty and the tragedy inherent in the simple fact of existence. When Hughes writes like this, I wonder if anyone could have said things better.

Since the publication of *Wodwo* in 1967, Hughes's poetry seems to have developed along two relatively distinct lines, although obviously both are the product of the same complex poetic vision, the "same knot of obsessions" as Hughes would say. These lines express Hughes the mythmaker embarked on what has been referred to as a large-scale spiritual quest and the

English nature poet who is very much of his time and his place. . . . [The] working out of his mythological undertaking begins in some of the poems in *Wodwo* such as "Logos" and moves through *Crow, Gaudete, Cave Birds* and, perhaps, more glancingly, "Prometheus on His Crag" [a sequence of poems reprinted with some variations in *Moortown*]. The nature and animal poems, clearly inscribed with Hughes's preoccupations and often charged with a volatile restlessness, emerge in the early volumes, *The Hawk in the Rain, Lupercal* and *Wodwo* as well as in the later more fully-developed sequences: the magnificent *Season Songs* (ostensibly written for children but should be required reading for all adults); *Remains of Elmet* and, now, the "Moortown" sequence. (pp. 427-28)

There is a new compelling generosity to Hughes's writing in the "Moortown" sequence, thirty-four poems that center on his farming experiences in Devon. Hughes has always had an enviable ability to dramatize nature, to isolate the vital spirit of life frequently submerged in the routine cares of everyday existence. But often there was a discordant note—a deliberate camouflaging of feeling. In the "Moortown" poems, though, there is an intense feeling of personal involvement and Hughes's descriptive powers are at their best in poems that open out to comment on the movements of natural process, the life and death cycles of the universe. (p. 428)

[The] feeling of familiarity, of belonging, informs much of Hughes's most powerful nature poetry. It is not a vision of nature as a healing, restorative power in the Wordsworthian sense; rather, it is a feeling of at-oneness, of a developing sense of the equal susceptibility of both man and nature to the seemingly unknowable movements of the higher forces of the universe. The stark opening poem, "Rain," dramatizes the painful vulnerability of the almost defenseless farmland and its inhabitants, perpetual victims of the tireless assaults of wind and rain. . . . Or, consider "March Morning Unlike Others" with its sympathetic portrait of the earth, fragile in its recuperation from the grim ravages of winter. . . .

And the bludgeoning strokes that characterize some of Hughes's animal poems are gone as he describes the difficult process of "Dehorning," the painful death-in-life struggle of the lamb in "February 17th," or the child's sighting of the dead lamb in "Ravens." (p. 429)

Certainly, as I have already intimated, the most striking quality of "Moortown" is the personal strain, Hughes's own sense of the passing of time. The recent *Remains of Elmet,* set in his native Yorkshire, recalls a steady catalogue of deterioration—of the erosion of the land and the inevitable loss of personal relationships. Here, again, the sense of the relentless encroachments of time with its attendant personal losses is urgent. In "Coming Down Through Somerset," for instance, Hughes's response as he spies a dead badger on the road is uncharacteristically plaintive. . . .

Perhaps the most stirring evocation of loss can be found in the beautifully crafted final cluster of poems that form the elegy to Jack Orchard, Hughes's father-in-law and farming partner. Written with a quiet simplicity and candor, the poems are ways of remembering—ways of being in touch with a man whose seeming indestructibility was leveled ironically by the single-minded incursions of cigarettes. (p. 430)

To move from Hughes's affecting elegy to "Prometheus on His Crag" (the sequence immediately following "Moortown") requires an emotional shift in gears that seems far too abrupt. Perhaps one should only read the volume at designated inter-

vals. For "Prometheus" is a complex, demanding—sometimes problematic—work that also asks some knowledge of Hughes's treatment of myth. The obvious question of exotic specialization surfaces again and the only defense can be that, despite some vagaries of structure, "Prometheus" is rewarding. (p. 431)

[Many] of the concerns of Hughes's poetry over the years can be found in his treatment of the Prometheus myth: the threatening bird of prey, similar to Crow, who must be confronted; the concentration on the female principle; the notion that the birth of the son threatens the position of the father. And the idea of the divided self, or mind at war with nature can be found in Hughes's early animal poems as well as in the later more fully-articulated sequences. Hughes's Prometheus is not particularly introspective. He has none of the fury or hate of Aeschylus' Prometheus who rages at his fate. Nor does he have the majestic sweep of Shelley's Prometheus. Rather, he assesses his condition squarely with neither rancor nor recrimination; he raises the eternal Promethean questions about the relative nature of power and wisdom, or good and evil in the universe; and with neither assurances nor clear-cut resolutions, he makes the necessary leap of faith, toward reintegration, toward a positive transcendence of the self.

Although connected thematically, the lyrics appear to be spare, self-enclosed units which are occasionally undermined by jarring syntactical constructions—the blending of the abstract and the concrete that has become something of a trademark of the later poetry. Interior monologues of Prometheus interweave in a somewhat arbitrary fashion with more explanatory lyrics that comment on or describe the evolving movements of the myth. Hughes has described the sequence as a "limbo . . . a numb poem about numbness." It is this, but it is also inexact to rest with this definition. For Prometheus also intimates possibilities of reintegration, of rebirth into a higher form. The final poem, for instance, with its beautiful combination of visual and aural effects movingly dramatizes Prometheus' transfiguration—his rebirth and the consequent renewal of all nature. Most striking, perhaps, is the powerful contrast between the marvelous vision of a world sprung alive by the rebirth of Prometheus (in language reminiscent of *Crow*) and the muted, mystical vision of the final stanzas. (pp. 432-33)

There is no reason to assume that Hughes's direction will change measurably in the future: the mythological quest seems to be in full progress while the nature poems continue to appear in scattered periodicals. His reach is wide, his production formidable. Perhaps what Hughes has written of the poet Laura Riding's efforts to forge a distinct poetic voice can best be said of him, "her poems embody both a search and a discovery of how precisely the job can be done." (p. 434)

Carol Bere, " 'How Precisely the Job Can Be Done' :
Ted Hughes's 'Moortown'," in The Literary Review,
Vol. 24, No. 3, Spring, 1981, pp. 427-34.

TERRY GIFFORD AND NEIL ROBERTS

The spirit of celebration, humility and respect that underlies [the poems about farming in *Moortown*] derives in part from their personal significance. In 1978 these poems were published in limited edition as *Moortown Elegies,* and in a strong sense all the poems derive elegiac qualities from the writer's engagement with the life and death of one man, Jack Orchard, with whom [Hughes] farmed at Moortown Farm. . . . The vivid immediacy yet universal vision of these poems recalls *Season Songs,* but in these poems the observer is also participant,

which involves responsibility. This is the price of man's finding his place in the natural world and the consequence of his specifically human contribution. In a dramatically developed, poignant poem, **"Ravens"**, the writer explains to a three-year-old child that a lamb 'died being born. We should have been here, to help it.' In the final sentence of the poem Hughes reflects that this lamb was 'lucky' in making its 'first day of death' into a momentarily paradisal world. The emphasis on 'this one' paradoxically reminds the reader of other lambs born in other conditions, such as those described in **"February 17th"**. . . .
In this poem there is no division between man and animal, which was such a dominant theme in Hughes's early poems, and which often tended to be expressed to man's discredit. In this poem those divisions are resolved in practical action of such urgency and intensity that they are not an issue. Indeed the poem's rhythm of the repeated word 'push' builds towards a harnessing of the natural force of the birth push. The archetypal undercurrents of all this are rightly undeveloped, but undoubtedly contribute to the poem's depth of effect. Similarly the symbolic meeting-point of birth and death is hinted at only in an entirely literal description of the cut-off head of the lamb 'sitting in the mud / With all earth for a body'. Characteristically the language here presents not an imagined vision, as if from *Gaudete,* but a symbolic moment as it arises in everyday practical life.

Part of our response to the poem is the belief that the writer has had this experience, and in reading it we inwardly measure ourselves against the actions the poem describes. An important part of its effect is the reader's respect for the man who has undergone this trial. The writer's feelings, however, are never expressed; the poem is entirely focused on responses to necessity. These actions represent, in fact, not unusual qualities of character, but the necessities of a particular way of life, and our admiration of the poet's capacity to act leads to our admiration of the uniquely human engagement in the creative-destructive processes of nature that farmers undertake in their daily work.

In the final six poems that engagement is celebrated by specific reference to the life and death of Jack Orchard. Here is a human life that had the toughness, sureness, vitality and wholeness that Hughes had previously observed only in animals. **"A monument"** evokes all those qualities in a poem which recalls the stubborn man erecting a fence in December rain in a thorny copse, 'using your life up'. The final phrase catches the tone of pathos and celebration that makes each of these six poems so moving. A simple description of Jack Orchard shearing a sheep also breaks new ground for Hughes. **"A memory"** is a quite unironical description of a man 'mastering' an animal. In **"The Bull Moses"**, for example, Hughes's treatment of the bull's subjection focuses entirely on the mystery of the animal's own inner being. The role of man was small in that poem because the bull had consented to the imposition of the human ego—that inexplicable consent was the poem's theme. In **"A memory"** there is no ego imposition, but an engagement that is unconcerned about the self, even at a physical level: 'Heedless of your own surfaces'. In this unromanticized heroic poem a cigarette is

> Preserving its pride of ash
> Through all your suddenly savage, suddenly gentle
> Masterings of the animal.

Here is a master-craftsman who is in total command of his own nature. He is not, like the men in **"Thrushes"** for example, a victim of his potentialities, but his emotional character is ex-

pressed in the practical skill of his craft. This is an individual human image of the wholeness of self and relatedness with material reality which is felt towards in the symbolic images of *Crow, Gaudete* and *Cave Birds.*

These fine poems represent better than anything else what is obviously different in *Moortown* from what has gone before. It has been a long discipline of imaginative objectivity that has brought Hughes to the point where positive connections between man and nature can be expressed, and in directly personal terms. For us this sense of connection has always been one of the main criteria by which Hughes's work should be judged. Hughes's poetry has not been striving towards mystical transcendence or for some supposedly invulnerable stance. In it he is seeking a position of practical engagement with the world that is utterly honest stripped of self-deceptions, humble and respectful but at home in the only world, that is our life and our death. Certainly such a search is not without its dangers, but what is remarkable in the development of the poetry of Ted Hughes is not only the small proportion of failures but the consistency of focus that runs through the varied forms of the successes. No doubt he will continue to surprise us, but we look forward to the developing presence in his work of the unimaginably hard-earned sense of the fitness, dignity and responsibility of being human expressed in **"The day he died."** . . .

> From now on the land
> Will have to manage without him.
> But it hesitates, in this slow realisation of light,
> Childlike, too naked, in a frail sun,
> With roots cut
> And a great blank in its memory.

(pp. 249-53)

Terry Gifford and Neil Roberts, in their Ted Hughes: A Critical Study, *Faber and Faber, 1981, 288 p.*

SANDRA McPHERSON

At stake is pleasure. At issue, how we like to be shocked and like to be delighted. We are going to study a poet who has power to shock and delight for part of a book and we will try to understand why pleasure waxes and wanes in two different kinds of poetry he likes to write.

The first sixty-four pages of *Moortown* contain high-horse-power rural documentaries, and I frankly love them. They are rich in sensuous detail and livewire diction. Who could predict that page after page of calves and lambs being born would fascinate? We might not predict this because we don't have first-hand experience with such birthings. But with Hughes's comprehensive descriptions, each difficult birth is individualized. There are recoveries, there are deaths, there is animal grief with the full impact of human grief, and there are other poems that unsentimentally describe happiness and exhilaration. It's *Genesis 1* in loving detail. And it's an active poetry, describing loading bales before an approaching storm, starting a recalcitrant tractor, stringing fences. . . . That is only half the sentence. Hughes is better than Adam because he doesn't stop at names. He writes as an expert on what activities he sees. . . .

Hughes's animal poems are homages, poems of praise, affectionate descriptions. In fact, as we will see later in the book, if his attitude toward his subject is not one of amazement and respect, if his motivation (if we can guess it) is not one of curiosity, his poems tend to sound harsh; the abrasive is Hughes's weakest mode. But there is no weakness in the long section called **"Moortown."** The more he details, the stronger his poems become. These animal subjects are important to him and he tends to their every need. And with charm: he chooses a black and white cow to stand under the rainbow end; he gravitates toward the dumb calf as if following the Biblical injunction, "Bring me your poor, your weak"; he notes one cow has "White eyelashes / To fringe her beauty." If you liked *All Creatures Large and Small* on public television, you will like being told "We force-feed her with medical powder mix. / We brim her with pints of glucose water" because there is drama in these lifesavings. . . .

But the book contains many pages of another kind of poem that might be introduced by this story: I once met a man, an expert in his field, who claimed that putting city kids in a room painted like the seashore, with sea-sounds piped in and beach-balls in good supply, would be just as beneficial to them as bussing them to the beach for the day. The difference between those two degrees of reality is, however, apparent to most people. When Hughes leaves for the country and helps a half-born calf in delivery and gets his boots muddy, he gives us rich energized poetry. But few are likely to write anything but a satirical poem at the indoor beach. Similarly, when Hughes writes of mythical animals and heavenly landscapes, the writing is most of the time unpalatable, unattractive, even slightly ridiculous. Some of these poems in the sections **"Prometheus on His Crag," "Earth-Numb,"** and even **"Adam and the Sacred Nine"** glower at us. Hughes wants to cover the side of life expressed by his summation that "the laws of space and matter are bitter." In Hughes the results are often cartoon-ish. . . . (p. 18)

The Prometheus poems are cartoons compared to the documentary animal poems. The animal poems seemed complete; in the Prometheus poems something starts to be missing. Why? For one thing, in myth, first-hand observation cannot be one of the techniques. . . . The cosmic landscape is not the most fertile for Hughes's imagination. . . . Even the visual form of the mythical poems changes: spareness, frequent one-line stan-zas take the place of the hefty form of the bucolic poems. Is schematic the word for such writing as this: "Death also is trying to be life. / Death is in the sperm like the ancient mariner / With his horrible tale. Death mews in the blankets—is it a kitten? / It plays with dolls but cannot get interested." This is a blueprint compared to the deathscenes of the lambs. The structural inventiveness of the "Moortown" poems has been replaced in the mythic poems by formulaic passages. . . . (pp. 18-19)

Hughes's imaginary world has little in it to like. When he describes the effect of the *Grosse Fuge* the reader wants to cry, "Enough make-believe! Enough!" . . . Give us back the cows that stand, at twilight, "waiting, like nails in a tin roof," the cows that, "Battling the hay bales from me . . . / Jostle and crush, like hulls blown from their moorings / And piling at the jetty." (pp. 19-20)

Hughes has to write out of love to make the most of his gifts. His poems which try so hard to shock give us a shock as dry and pleasureless as electric shock treatment; but his poems which grow from close contact with their subject have the real healing effect and are as healthy a poetry as is being written today. (p. 22)

Sandra McPherson, "Ted Hughes's 'Moortown', Real and Imagined," in The American Poetry Review, *Vol. 11, No. 1, January-February, 1982, pp. 18-22.*

ALAN WILLIAMSON

It was Matthew Arnold, writing of Keats, who invented the phrase "natural magic," to describe the pleasure poetry gives us simply by a vivid recapturing of sensation, apart from any moral or intellectual vision it contains. The early work of Ted Hughes, whose *New Selected Poems* has recently been pub-lished, is perhaps the preeminent poetry of natural magic in our time. . . .

Natural magic is still there in Hughes' recent work, though more sporadically. Like a number of poets on our side of the Atlantic, Hughes has gotten looser in weave as he has gotten older; a cult of spontaneity leads him to let in easy words—"splendor," "infinite," "savage," "sweet"—which his early poems would have avoided. But the sheer energy of observation and empathy remains. In **"An October Salmon,"** Hughes tries to enter the mind of the fish that has returned to its upstream pool, and has nothing to do but wait for death. Its tattered flesh, once a "sea-going Aurora Borealis of . . . April power," is now "[Death's] clownish regimentals, her badges and dec-orations." The imagery of clothing suggests an overriding met-aphor: the salmon, in its selfless obedience to instinct, is bru-tally "stitched" or "richly embroidered" into the continuum of nature. . . .

One feels that these are the themes that have always drawn forth Hughes' most powerful writing about nature: what it is like to live meshed with one's environment, without fore-thought or afterthought; what it is like not to care that one kills; what it is like not to care that one dies.

Does Hughes' poetry have a moral vision? Or is it simply, amorally envious of the unconsciousness of nature? Thinking about this, my mind goes back to an early poem about the debate in Parliament over the abolition of the cat-o-nine-tails:

> "To discontinue it were as much
>   As ship not powder and cannonballs
>   But brandy and women." (Laughter.)
> Hearing which
>   A witty profound Irishman calls
>   For a "cat" into the House, and sits to watch
>   The gentry fingering its stained tails.
>
> Whereupon. . .
>   quietly, unopposed,
>   The motion was passed.

The optimistic reading of this would be that we are cruel through habit and ignorance; the pessimistic reading, that we are ig-norant in order to indulge our cruelty, but that shame saves us from ourselves. Taken either way, the passage is the work of a serious moral thinker, though one deeply interested in vio-lence and sadism.

This level of intelligence is hard to find in the nihilistic cult of mere survival, the schoolboy blasphemies, of *Crow*. Indeed, rereading Hughes' theological poems, one is mainly struck by their obsessively painful sexual imagery—especially the image of the female devouring the male. Poems explicitly about sex-ual combat, on the other hand, retain considerable moral in-telligence—probing the hidden aggression in romantic com-munion (**"Lovesong"**), the aggression of grief and guilt (**"The Contender," "Prospero and Sycorax"**). Pondering these things, one cannot help remembering that Hughes has had to lead a tragic erotic life in public, and not (like Lowell or Berryman) by his own choice, or in the role of hero. The few sections

Hughes has preserved here from the notorious *Gaudete* tell the story of a man who, paralyzed by his relation to a dead woman (''what I did only shifted the dust about''), now slowly begins to return to life. From a human point of view, that is very much the spectacle which the second half of *New Selected Poems* presents: under the grim mask of the illusionless survivor, occasional glimpses of the moral man struggling to go on.

Alan Williamson, ''Ted Hughes: Poet in a Land-scape,'' in Book World—The Washington Post, *July 18, 1982, p. 10.*

NEIL PHILIP

Ted Hughes's *New Selected Poems* leaves one in no doubt that he is a major poet: one whose voice and vision are unique, and potent. In this selection, made by the poet himself from a large body of work, there are inevitably poems which seem weak, or slack, or posturing; there are certainly some which are brutal, recalling all the arguments over the years about the Hughes's attitude to violence: whether his fascistic hawk, whose 'manners are tearing off heads', is being explored or glorified. Violence *is* important to Hughes: but, it seems to me, as a concentration or explosion of energy rather than for any superficial bootboy glamour. And those poems which summon doubts are far outweighted by those which are assured, persuasive, richly rewarding, stubborn and bare as rock though they are. There is a tenderness, too, in a poem such as **''Bride and Groom Lie Hidden for Three Days''**, which will surprise those who think of Hughes as a harsh, ungiving poet. Much of Hughes's later work is organized in sequences—*Crow, Cave Birds, Gaudete*—which in turn break down into smaller sequences and coalesce into larger ones. It is difficult to select from these without causing the reader some difficulty, and readers unfamiliar with them will probably be more immediately moved by the early poems such as the magnificent, perfectly balanced **''The Thought-Fox''**, by the rugged landscape poems from *Remains of Elmet,* and by the extracts from the 'verse farming diary' *Moortown.* These last show Hughes exercizing his considerable descriptive gifts to the full, particularly in an extraordinary and powerful series of poems about sheep and lambs. . . . He is a religious poet in everything he writes: the anti-bible of *Crow,* the parables of God's unconscious; the beautiful hymns which conclude *Gaudete,* many of which appear here; the enigmatic **''Adam and the Sacred Nine''**; even, or especially, the animal poems. A weak poem, **''Earth-Numb''**, gives a significant account of his creative process: 'Something terrified and terrifying / Gleam surges to and fro through me'. That something terrified and terrifying has been the subject of Hughes's concentrated attention throughout his career. His intensity can lead him to over-simplify; it can lead to glibness, as in the word-play in **''Earth-Numb''** on 'hunted' and 'haunted', or at the end of **''Heptonstall''** on 'tries' and 'tires'. But it has also led him to seek out fundamental truths about man's relationship to the natural world and to God, in a language with the strength, suppleness and economy of dialect and a style so stripped and incisive it compels us to share his perceptions. (pp. 507-08)

Neil Philip, in a review of ''Selected Poems 1957-1981,'' in British Book News, *August, 1982, pp. 507-08.*

DICK DAVIS

Ted Hughes is a very popular poet, and *River,* which contains a sequence of his poems accompanied by Peter Keen's pho-

tographs, clearly sets out to be a popular book—it looks more at home on the coffee-table than in the library or on the schoolmaster's desk. If this gives poetry and fine photography a wider audience then that is all to the good, but I think two distinct kinds of popularity have been confused here and the end result is something of a squeamish compromise.

Hughes's reputation rests on his very individual vision of the natural world. . . . He is popular for this very reason—he brings back to our suburban, centrally-heated and, above all, *safe* lives reports from an authentic frontier of reality and the imagination. His poems speak to us of a world that is constantly true in a way that we know our temporary comforts cannot be. He is anything but a pretty poet. But this is a relentlessly pretty book. . . .

The photographs confirm this notion: they are very fine, with a limpid transparency and grace, they accurately catch elusive qualities of clear light (particularly dawn light); those that approach abstract patterns, for example of snow or lichen or water-ripples, are especially beautiful. But opposite one such moment of still contemplation (a few trees' reflections in slightly shifting water) we have Hughes's description of a cormorant and 'the dinosaur massacre-machine' that constitutes its brain. The two images do not complement each other so much as get in each other's way, and Hughes's vision (not to speak of Keen's) seems too exclusive to brook contradiction. Further, a Hughes poem holds its reader almost by an act of hypnosis; his celebrated empathy with the creatures of his poems is achieved by a staring concentration on their presence and uniqueness, the reader feels he shares this concentration, he is drawn in and momentarily possessed by the reality Hughes evokes. A contradictory image on the opposite page can only be a distraction, no matter how fine it is.

Frequently there *is* some correlation between the poems and the photographs that are placed together, but it is usually an arbitrary similarity of subject-matter rather than any deeper convergence of mood or understanding. . . .

A particular story of struggle and survival runs through the book—that of the salmon. Its course is charted from conception to death, but it is the old salmon, veteran of voyages and the buffetings of its arduous life, that most impressively engages Hughes's imagination. It is perhaps going too far to see the fish as chiefly a self-image—they are undoubtedly and very physically salmon before they are anything else—but in the same way that his fox evoked the young poet exploring experience and transmuting it by his gaze, so these stubborn survivors do convey something of the way in which Hughes has doggedly and single-mindedly pursued his idiosyncratic and difficult vision. Not that the book is wholly elegiac—it contains a marvellously celebratory poem on the 'marriage' of snow and the river, and, beginning with a description of death it ends with the hatching of salmon eggs, as if by leaving life's cycle at its most optimistic moment it offered a defiant reversal of the direction of individual existence—but in general it is the poems concerned with age and endurance that are the most convincing.

Dick Davis, ''Country Codes,'' in The Listener, *Vol. 111, No. 2840, January 12, 1984, p.23.*

JOHN MOLE

Ted Hughes has never really been away from the river. It's his bloodstream. Dark brown god, soft sweet runner, muscle and fluency, primeval depths and surface dazzle, it has served him as a living metaphor—a tributary for patient contemplation, and a headlong rush inviting total immersion. . . .

When, as he often does, he speaks of fishing—most recently on a taped reading [*Ted Hughes and Paul Muldoon*]—his observations are those of a poet defining his art: "The sort of fishing where the angler sits beside the water and waits is just as curious as the sort where he wades up or down the river sometimes up to his chest in the water. I've enjoyed both." Of course, anyone who knows Hughes' work will smile at the word *curious* on which the observation turns. It couldn't be less innocent, just as it is impossible to imagine Hughes sitting anywhere without already being up to his chest (at least) in an ether of primal energies.

He has always been the most possessed of observers. Even his patience is impetuous, tense and populated with the poetry it is about to become. So fierce, in fact, is the sense of *presence* in his often overwhelming poems that any attempt to disengage their author from these energies—and to sort out the genuine from the manufactured—feels like an intrusion for which a price will have to be paid. Where criticism is concerned, it sometimes seems as if Hughes has become invulnerably identified with the sensational drama of his method, and one is not a little reminded of that *Punch* cartoon in which a timid visitor stands at the doorway to William Blake's workroom and calls out, through a teeming cloud of phenomena, "Mr. Blake, may I speak with you *alone*?"

For the time being, though, it must be enough to say that his latest collection, *River*—a bursting package of all that is best and most suspect in Hughes—is a lavish production. Its 43 poems, accompanied by Peter Keen's cold-crystal photographs, celebrate a year in the life of the river, watched at all times of the day and night, and the life and death of everything that surrounds and is contained in it. "*Only birth matters* / Say the river's whorls"—and the tone is sustained at a high pitch of amazed and grateful witness where death takes equal shares in the glamour, where for **"An October Salmon"** "this was inscribed in his egg. / This chamber of horrors is also home." For Hughes, life and death are always seeking a communion, or synthesis. They chase each others' tails while the river, in certain moods, "Acts fishless . . . / Fully occupies with its calisthenics / Its twistings and self-wrestlings", and in others is the "primitive, radical / Engine of earth's renewal" or renewing *itself* with a sort of charmed viscosity. . . . (p. 46)

The poems ingest images plundered from every level of experience. In **"A Rival"**, for example, a cormorant's "fossil eye-chip" unites prehistory with advanced technology, and then, having briefly undergone a Hammer Horror transformation into "An abortion-doctor / Black bag packed with vital organs / Dripping unspeakably", the bird is off "over the sea's iron curtain" with a cleverly timed frisson of contemporary politics left troubling the waters. This is brilliant, but one can't help glimpsing an element of opportunist contrivance in Hughes' exhaustive pursuit of analogies. The bird is swallowed up by the invention it has given rise to, and no amount of beautiful sound—"Sanctus Sanctur / Swathes the blessed issue"—or vigorous stretches of language can give it the simple life it *also* deserves.

To suggest that Hughes often goes too far is, no doubt, an ungrateful, short-sighted response to his work. Every page of *River* is as full of sustained and challenging complexities as it is of random phrase-making. Nevertheless, too unquestioning

an involvement in a process where he seems to be appropriating the universe is in danger of repressing real doubts as to whether he is sometimes not also floundering in a vacuum of brilliance. A considerable degree of uncertainty cannot detract from his stature, though, and as a witness to poetry's sheer power of affirmation he has few equals. . . . (pp. 46-7)

John Mole, "The Reflecting Glass," in Encounter, *Vol. LXII, No. 3, March, 1984, pp. 46-52.*

J. D. McCLATCHY

When **"The Thought-Fox"** first fluttered the henhouse of English poetry in 1957, Hughes seemed a force of nature. When I think back now on poems like **"Pike"** and **"Thrushes,"** on **"Thistles"** and **"Gnat-Psalm,"** I remember a pulsing, nearly ritualistic intelligence, a descriptive and rhythmical precision. But from *Crow* on, the lines seemed to come unstitched, the mythic gestures sounded hollow. *Gaudete*'s novelistic imbroglio (a cross between *The Bacchae* and *Cold Comfort Farm*) and *Moortown*'s farming diary were both shambling affairs. Perhaps because of Hughes's work during this period in the theater, one felt his lines were no longer written but delivered, and played to the balcony; because of his writing for children, it seemed he dealt in the most obvious ways with Fantasy and Significance, and the results were banal.

But whatever the poet's misjudgments have been, it would be an error on any reader's part to underestimate Hughes's capacity to change. In a way he has always been a restless poet, experimenting now with voices, now with subjects, his head cocked for a new access to imaginative strength, whether ecstatic or elemental. *River* marks such a change in his career. If it seems a leap forward it has been accomplished by retracing his steps, and so perhaps it should be called not a change but a recovery. It is a welcome and an exciting one.

The poems stand up very well indeed, one by one. Yet the book is really an elaborate sequence. The title tells all. Though many rivers are invoked, and some named (the Dee, the Sligachan, the Gulkana), the sequence starts with the idea of river—first seen, as in the mind's eye, from a great height. . . . In closer focus, we see the seasons the river reflects, the small lives that live on it (oak and catkin, cormorant, the blood-mote mosquito, the old anglers), the trout and salmon that move mysteriously beneath it, a world before man that includes him: "I share it a little," the poet says. (pp. 39-40)

His underwater creatures are primitive but not grotesque: sleek muscle, "bowed and fervent, / But their hearts are water." There is something inherently touching about descriptions of this threatened and vanishing life, as well as a fascinating vocabulary. And Hughes's refracted perspective allows him the transparency of natural calm and meditative depth; it dispels the violence, even as it magnifies the power and fragility. In a **"River Barrow"** the poet watches, his senses indistinguishable from the scene. . . . The whole book is similarly unhurried but taut. There is a dark wit (as in **"Ophelia"**) or a delicate wit (as in **"Japanese River Tales"**), a masterful ease that neither avoids nor belabors its effects. (p. 40)

Of course Hughes is up to something more than evocative writing. . . . There is everywhere in this book an Ovidian resonance: "So the river is a god / Knee-deep among reeds, watching men, / Or hung by the heels down the door of a dam." And if *River* is, finally, a fable, I would dip back to another sequence of poems about a river for the key. At the end of his 1820 sonnet-series *The River Duddon*, Wordsworth sounds the organ note. . . . Hughes is up to no less. The last half-dozen poems in *River* rise to Wordsworth's point in identifying the river with art itself. Still, Hughes gives it a personal inflection. It is hard not to detect a wry self-portrait in **"October Salmon."** . . . And then, in **"Fairy Flood,"** to witness the relation of poet to muse. . . . The Form remains, says Wordsworth—the river, the idea of the river, the enabling "power" that is the source of both river and poem. This new volume by Ted Hughes is the evidence of that power and an eloquent tribute to it. . . . (pp. 40, 42)

> *J. D. McClatchy, "The Return of Ted Hughes," in The New Republic, Vol. 191, No. 3633, September 3, 1984, pp. 39-40, 42.*

HELEN VENDLER

The new Poet Laureate of England, Ted Hughes, now in his mid-fifties, has written a water book, *River* . . . , to match his 1979 earth book, *Moortown*. In *Moortown*, Hughes' animal surrogates were chiefly sheep and lambs; in *River*, they are fish, eels, and insects. Hughes notices in nature what suits his purpose: if he wants to wince at man's naïveté, he writes about the innocent lamb ignorant of its fate; if he wants to write about disability, he describes a dying insect. In **"A March Calf"**, for example (from the 1954 volume *Season-Songs*), Hughes is the knowing speaker observing the lamb for the slaughter. . . . In **"A Cranefly in September"** (from the same book), Hughes is the "giant" who watches the crippled cranefly "with her cumbering limbs and cumbered brain." . . . Poems like these imply, as Hughes wishes to imply, that we, too, are only animals in the universe, and live and die as helplessly and as unavoidably as any other animal form. But the poems shade rather too easily into a form of sadism. Hughes no doubt means to include himself in the human family of deceived lambs; but the writer of the poem is undeceived, and the irony is tinged with the relish of superior power, if only the superior power of knowledge. The giant who watches the cranefly takes the diagnostic tone of a doctor watching a terminal case: he "knows she cannot be helped in any way." It is not Hughes' frustration at his own helplessness that the poem illuminates but, rather, the triumph of his biological knowledge. . . . (p. 66)

For a long time, Hughes has represented himself as the man who has seen into the bottomless pit of aggression, death, murder, holocaust, catastrophe. There, in the pit, he has faced not only the physical evils of mutilation and extinction but also the moral squalor attending on the brute survival instinct, the impulse to prey on others out of self-interest. His earlier surrogate forms, the hawk and the crow—in *Lupercal* (1960) and *Crow* (1971)—are his vehicles for facing base instinct. Crow, for instance, watches a suicide; when it is over "And the body lay on the gravel / Of the abandoned world . . . / Crow had to start searching for something to eat." . . . These are the poems of a man convinced that social hypocrisy has prevented such unlovely truths from appearing in poetry except in an "ethical" poetry condemning them. Hughes is determined to unveil these instincts, to show himself and others, through such animal surrogates, in the most predatory and self-serving light. Needless to say, there is a self-sadism here, which, when Hughes splits himself in two—the watcher and the watched—turns into what appears to be sadism toward the foolish lamb and the stumbling cranefly.

In fact, Hughes' gaze has been so relentlessly selective as he looks at the world that all the arguments made against any "naturalistic" writer apply to him. If a hundred lambs are adequately born and one is not, Hughes' poem will savagely concern itself with the exception. His anger against a world containing stillbirths may be his conscious motive for writing; but what reader will not see in **"February 17th"** (from *Moortown*) Hughes' powerful imaginative appetite for naming and ornamenting disaster? . . . To the argument "But that was exactly how it was" one can only put the counterargument: This is a poet who wants to write words like "blood ball swollen" and "sliced . . . throat strings" and "hacked-off head." Poems are, at one level, experiments in getting certain sounds and phrases and grammatical forms down on paper; and Hughes likes violent phrases, thick sounds, explosive verbs.

Hughes grew up, as every commentator on him remarks, with a sense of violence and death. This is attributed by Hughes himself, and by his critics, following him, to his having internalized his father's experiences of the First World War. As the poems **"Out"** and **"TV Off"** tell us, the elder Hughes was wounded and left piled with the dead for two days; later, though outwardly healed, he never recovered from that memory of lying "Golden-haired, while his friend beside him / Attending a small hole in his brow / Ripened black." It may be true, as Hughes says, that "the shrapnel that shattered my father's paybook / Gripped me," and that Hughes' writing replays a child's monstrously enlarged imaginings of trench warfare, mutilation, and death. But something more has been added. Hughes mixes sexual intercourse into the brew of war and death, and his blighted imagination, though it occasionally mentions joy, tends to speak even of that with the exhaustion of one who knows all the moves in the erotic battle and finds a perverse fascination in the stylizations of victimage. In [*River*], a damselfly who kills her mate during intercourse serves Hughes as a sexual symbol. . . . Less violent matings interest Hughes proportionately less; he insists on demystifying "love" into its most aesthetically lethal biological instance. It cannot be aesthetic for Hughes, one suspects, without its fatality.

Hughes has by now found many ways to embody his wounded sense of the world; catastrophe (the stillborn lamb), predatory acts (by the hawk, by butchers), sexual victimage (the damselfly), suicide (Ophelia), and, in this book, hunting and fishing. He tears off the bandages to expose the "red unmanageable life," the raw flesh of existence. And he must find not only adequate emblems but adequate formal means. For him, this has meant putting the world into parables, which have an air of reducing things to their most basic terms. . . . The irreducible child in Hughes, for whom reality is always large and looming, relishes parables as he relishes cartoon images.

In the new volume, cartoon appears in **"Night Arrival at Seatrout"** as a fantasy by a grimmer Disney. It is an autumn night, and Hughes fishes amid menacingly eroticized rural scenes. . . . The seatrout leaps, snarls, and shivers; lobworms couple; earth sings under her breath. . . . Though this would like to appear pagan, it is in fact neo-pagan and symbolist, a "hard," revisionist view of Keats' apparently softer autumn. Hughes' neo-paganism was learned at Lawrence's knee, and his parables are Lawrentian, too. So are his repetitions (a formal means revived by Lawrence and frequent in Hughes). . . . "Dark," "darker," "darkened," "darkness," "dark," "blood-dark," "dark"— all these variants occur in eight lines, as though, in Lawrentian intensification, one could mesmerize oneself farther into sensation by reiteration of a single hypnotic word. The hope of simplification through intensity explains as well Hughes' continued attachment to fixed, repeated sentence forms, as though a furrow once plowed could only be cut deeper and deeper.

On the other hand, against these simplifications of form and language, which play, we might say, the role of fate in Hughes' universe (incorporating the immutable, the geometric, the rigid, the reduced, and the physical laws regulating space and time), there appear a number of variable forms, playing, we could say, the role of free will. It was in Hopkins that Hughes first found a model for this variable side of his otherwise obsessive nature—a side both visual and kinetic, and more animal than human. The intellectual side of Hughes is entirely aligned with fate; only his physical, sensual being escapes into freedom. In a remarkable poem on growing old, **"October Salmon,"** Hughes sketches brilliantly the moment of male adolescence. . . . This pure kinetic energy is often coarsened and brutalized by Hughes, when it is too theatrically tethered to his Celtic, even Scandinavian, gloom, or when it is too orgasmically "spasming" (his coinage) on the page, or when it is too imitatively re-creating Hopkins' larks and kestrels. But at its best, reined in, it gives Hughes' poems their tensile strength. Hughes has found it difficult in the past to moderate his touch. When he presses just hard enough, not too hard; he raises the English pastoral (Hopkins through Hardy through Lawrence) to a sharper and bleaker pitch. In **"The Vintage of River Is Unending,"** Keatsian autumn—the ripeness, the grapevines, the sweetness, the gathered grain and swelling fruit, the weighted boughs, the river, the cider press—finds itself concentrated as in a burning glass in Hughes' praise of the river of being. . . . (pp. 66-8)

If this vocabulary of praise seems startling coming from the Hughes of wounds and blood, talon and fang, it is no less startling that Hughes' frequent abandon, in *River,* of the iron maiden of his habitual sentence structure. *River* is altogether a more flexible book, it seems to me, than its predecessors. Hughes is still recognizably himself in the thrust and momentum of his lines, in his choice of the animal world as human mirror, and in his interest in determined biological patterns. But he has readjusted his focus. As Crow, he was predatory and avian; as lamb, he was victim and mammal; now he goes lower on the evolutionary scale, and becomes eel, fish, insect. The cooling of the blood into a subaqueous current tempers Hughes' lines. They are still headstrong, still governed more by a linear sexual drive of instinctual will, more by the rhythms of biological birth and decay. Hughes seems to have decided, somewhat in the manner of Whitman, that if there ever was any death it led forth life. In the baldest statement of the book, Hughes hails, in italics, the river's perpetual "toilings of plasm" as the salmon spawn:

Only birth matters
Say the river's whorls.

Hughes' new vitalism participates in the same mystic obscurantism that animated his earlier convictions about rapacity and death. But because it exchanges the drilled bullet-gaze of Crow for a more sensuous, free-ranging, and associative registering of the natural scene, the vitalism seems more comprehensive and more adequate to natural existence, and even to human existence. (p. 68)

In the new book, Hughes tries to feel life through "the dance-orgy of being reborn," chiefly in the life cycle of the salmon. He writes of eggs and sperm, of salmon spawning, of insect copulation, of "exhumations and delirious advents." He rises to a rhapsody:

And this is the
liturgy
Of the earth's tidings—harrowing,
crowned—a travail
Of raptures and rendings.

Around that climax are arranged, in this new volume, the tatters of man's mortal dress as it is about to be cast aside—leper-cloths, a frayed scarf, a mask, a shroud, the "crude paints and drapes" of death. Man becomes "death's puppet," and "the masks and regalia drift empty."

In the perfection of the river, all evil, says Hughes, is suspended. The river is the "primitive, radical / Engine of earth's renewal," washing everything to the pure ablution of the sea, "back to the sea's big re-think." In his early combination, in *Crow,* of powerful drama and fine-grained observation, Hughes had praised the power of human consciousness to rise above mortality. . . . But, on the evidence of his lifework, Hughes makes poems less to praise consciousness or to construct something beautiful than to reverse an evil spell. In **"Stealing Trout on a May Morning"** (from *Wodwo,* 1967), Hughes wrote down the deepest truth about his own poetic. As he stands deep in a river fishing, a flood of panic seizes him, "tearing the spirits from my mind's edge and from under." He is magically rescued from terror by the leap of a trout, which gets "a long look" at him. At that moment, the charm is wound up:

So much for the
horror:
It has changed places.

Hughes' evil spirits have been cast out into the Gadarene swine of objectified nature.

Hughes has gone about the world finding vessels in nature for his private horrors; once the poison is emptied into the natural vessel and the poem has fixed it there, the horror has changed places—of course, only for a moment. For the spell to work, the poem has to be adequate to its object, one presumes; but, even so, the aesthetic end is subordinated to the therapeutic one. These priorities need to be reversed if the poems are to bear the strain well and long.

And it does seem as though a certain flagging in the horror had enabled Hughes to detach from his compulsive spell-casting and to look, at least sometimes, on his natural images with more reverie than exorcism. The most beautiful poem in *River,* to my mind, is **"October Salmon,"** Hughes' long self-elegy, masked as an elegy for a dying salmon. . . . **"October Salmon,"** was first published two years ago, in Hughes' *New Selected Poems,* but the tonality it embodies recurs throughout *River,* struggling for its poise against Hughes' equally recurrent, and more typical, violence and victimization. Hughes' remarkable adjectival gift and his propulsive rhythms may find a balance in epic poise. If they do, and if the obsessive rituals of the poetry are harmonized with aesthetic as well as therapeutic ends, Hughes may become an ampler poet of consciousness. Even if they do not, his glare into the machinery of evolutionary law results in a strong contemporary individual scanning of the rites of human life. (pp. 68, 70)

Helen Vendler, "Raptures and Rendings," in The New Yorker, *Vol. LX, No. 48, December 31, 1984, pp. 66-8, 70.*

Jorge Ibargüengoitia

1928-1983

Mexican novelist and dramatist.

An author of humorous satire, Ibargüengoitia objectively probed Mexico's political and social realities and suggested that unprincipled individuals were a product of corrupt Mexican values. The first of his novels to be translated into English, *Las muertas* (1977; *The Dead Girls*), is a fictional rendering of an actual event that concerns a white slavery and prostitution network run by two Mexican sisters. Ibargüengoitia's documentary-style narrative utilizes the viewpoints of authorities, victims, and victimizers to show how a sensational and tragic scandal was overlooked as a commonplace occurrence in Mexico. *Dos crímenes* (1979; *Two Crimes*) centers on a political radical whose shallow revolutionary principles are undermined by greed when he becomes involved in a family's competition for a dying uncle's inheritance. This novel relies on the more traditional elements of suspense and humor; according to John Sutherland, *Two Crimes* "is less starkly objective than *The Dead Girls* and seems more affectionately tolerant of Mexican corruption." Ibargüengoitia's play *El atentado*, written in 1962 but banned in Mexico until 1975, is a sardonic treatment of José de León Toral's assassination of President-elect Alvaro Obregón in 1928. Sam L. Slick considers this work "significant in Mexican letters, for it honestly and courageously scrutinizes the marrow of national consciousness." Ibargüengoitia died in a 1983 Madrid airplane disaster.

(See also *Contemporary Authors*, Vol. 113 [obituary].)

© Jerry Bauer

SAM L. SLICK

The annals of twentieth-century crime contain few cases more outrageous and perverse than that of the Poquianchi sisters in Mexico. Encompassing an incredible number and variety of criminal and immoral acts, the Poquianchis' story stunned the world. . . .

Las muertas is rigorously based upon the infamous Poquianchis and their network of white slavery. The novel skillfully recreates the complicated developments of the case from the early 1950s to the sisters' arrest in 1964. Thinly disguising the characters and locales of the real incident, Ibargüengoitia avoids sensationalism and softens the sordid and grotesque with touches of humor. His treatment of the villains and victims serves to add a human dimension to an otherwise pathetic cast of assassins and child prostitutes. Although the novel will shock some, Ibargüengoitia's fictionalized version is less shocking than the unvarnished truth.

Aside from being spectacularly interesting, *Las muertas* is also one of the best-written Mexican novels of recent vintage. Noteworthy is the manipulation of narrative perspective which controls the story's unfolding by means of restrictive viewpoints. . . . This does not prevent Ibargüengoitia, however, from intervening actively in the narration to guide the reader through a maze of criminal insanity. . . . Ibargüengoitia's pseudo-objective approach to his fiction, which is in turn based on fact, will intrigue readers. Utilizing the disparate views of

victims, perpetrators and prosecutors, the author weaves a brilliant tale which seems to humorously mimic the macabre but ever-popular *notas rojas* of the Mexican press. . . .

Las muertas is a superb novel and a highlight in Mexican narrative.

Sam L. Slick, in a review of "Las muertas," in World Literature Today, *Vol. 53, No. 1, Winter, 1979, p. 79.*

SAM L. SLICK

[Originally written in 1962, *El atentado*] was not performed in Mexico . . . until 1975, having been successfully banned by authorities for some thirteen years. The play's explosive political content undoubtedly accounts for its long-delayed publication. Classifying the work as a "documental farce," Ibargüengoitia insists that any similarity between his play and actual Mexican history is "not by accident, but because of a national disgrace."

El atentado is a thinly disguised account of José Toral's assassination of President-Elect Obregón in 1928. Although the characters' names are fictitious, those familiar with Mexican history will have no trouble identifying the historical counterparts. . . . In three fast-moving acts Ibargüengoitia reconstructs the folly and corruption surrounding the whole sordid affair. The author forgoes virtually all character development to suggest a mechanistic, almost matter-of-fact unfolding of events. . . .

El atentado, aside from being a highly controversial play, is significant in Mexican letters, for it honestly and courageously scrutinizes the marrow of national consciousness.

> *Sam L. Slick, in a review of "El atentado," in* World Literature Today, *Vol. 53, No. 3, Summer, 1979, p. 481.*

DAVID WILLIAM FOSTER

Although he has not received quite the national and foreign acclaim of writers like Gustavo Sainz or José Agustín, Ibargüengoitia is one of the best Mexican writers of the last two decades. . . . His great gift is to write deceptively simple novels that are nevertheless carefully plotted and pregnant with social meaning; elements of urbane humor and treacherous irony serve to enhance his eminently "readerly" prose. . . .

Like his previous novel *Las muertas* . . . , *Dos crímenes* is a crime novel in which the elements of mystery, villainy and plot resolution explicate a complex social structure wherein the crime itself is less perfidious than the society that makes it a logical consequence of human behavior within the confines of that structure. The same society makes the crime necessary, condones it and covers up for it—all in the name of business as usual.

While that schema is a classic variant of the crime novel, Ibargüengoitia provides it with a fresh twist by showing how the chain of violent events is unleashed through a series of lies told by the protagonist to protect himself from a lie created by the police in order to protect itself from . . . and so on. Escaping from a false accusation as a terrorist, the protagonist seeks refuge in the home of his wealthy uncle in a small town, only to alter unwittingly but violently the machinations of a plot by relatives to obtain an inheritance from the old man. The town, its values and power structure are a microcosm of Mexico, and the homology between the protagonist's alleged terrorist activities and the societal structures the town represents is unmistakable.

> *David William Foster, in a review of "Dos crímenes," in* World Literature Today, *Vol. 55, No. 1, Winter, 1981, p. 69.*

LONNIE WEATHERBY

[*The Dead Girls*] is about small-town political corruption, deception, and intimidation—a microcosmic representation of the Mexican body politic. The two Baladro sisters operate a bawdy-house. Through a series of unfortunate yet comedic circumstances they become responsible for the death and clandestine burial of several employees. . . . The author's writing vascillates between black comedy and farce. However, style and form are mere flash; the book lacks the fire of imagination and scope that could have rendered it more than just another novel with a familiar theme and exhausted message.

> *Lonnie Weatherby, in a review of "The Dead Girls," in* Library Journal, *Vol. 108, No. 3, February 1, 1983, p. 221.*

JOHN MELLORS

According to the author's note [in *The Dead Girls*], 'Some of the events described herein are real. All the characters are imaginary'. The book examines and reconstructs the events leading to the discovery of the bodies of six prostitutes in a small Mexican town. . . . [It] is the novelist's skill, not the researcher's industry, that gives *The Dead Girls* its laconic force. The book is episodic, and there are many ups and downs, with a few flat stretches, as the reader rides the buses between the three brothels that had housed the dead girls.

Ibargüengoitia gives his story a spicily pungent flavour by including a number of vividly-told anecdotes about strange happenings in unfamiliar places. One such is the account of the annual fair at Ocampo. . . . At this fair in 1950 a fourteen-year-old girl was sold into prostitution. At twenty-seven she developed paralysis during an abortion. The other whores tried to cure her by applying hot irons to a wet blanket placed over her paralysed side. The sick woman's skin stuck to the blanket and came off with it. She died. (pp. 135-36)

> *John Mellors, "Bad Dads," in* London Magazine, *n.s. Vol. 23, Nos. 1 & 2, April & May, 1983, pp. 133-36.**

JOHN WALSH

Ibargüengoitia adds to the canon of Latin American exotica with this insidiously absorbing study of death and corruption among the shanty towns of the Mexican interior.

Apparently based on fact, [*The Dead Girls*] concerns the discovery of the bodies of six prostitutes. . . . There is no question of 'whodunnit'—the book takes the form of a carefully unemotional marshalling of information in the manner of police reportage—but the plot's momentum is supplied by the more basic form of 'what-on-earth-will-happen?'. . . .

Serafina and Arcángela are businesswomen from first to last, who become proprietresses of a brace of brothels, premises both licensed and popular. They enlist the services of waifs and strays and teenagers who think they are going off to become servants, all in the interests of profits and enterprise. They are entirely un-villainous. They seem destined to flourish. . . . [But from] motives of political expediency, the Governor outlaws prostitution, as a sop to local businessmen who are reluctant to cough up his increases in the rates. The sisters, together with their complement of 26 employees, have to move on. But the local judiciary rules against them and, rapidly acquiring refugee status, they move illegally into the closed-down Casino, behind sealed doors. . . .

From being a tale of love and successful entrepreneurship, *The Dead Girls* shifts into a claustrophobic study of what amounts to a closed community, a passionate sorority turned in upon itself. We are offered, at arm's length, a series of how they all got there, how they feel towards each other, and how the community comes to disintegrate through a series of bizarre accidents.

It's not a terribly appealing novel (character is defined mostly by action or the most basic motivation) but it has a tautness and a clinical fascination that stays in the mind.

> *John Walsh, in a review of "The Dead Girls," in* Books and Bookmen, *No. 335, August, 1983, p. 37.*

JOHN SUTHERLAND

The Dead Girls was hailed as a work of literary subtlety, which none the less contrived to generate the traditional visceral appeal of the thriller. The story was one of mass murder in a small-town Mexican brothel. Assembling a sequence of first-hand accounts, the narrative artfully uncovered behind the newspaper version a farcically accidental chain of violence. What seemed sensational turns out to be banal. The ironic-documentary technique of *The Dead Girls* (which has the enigmatic epigraph 'Some of the events described herein are real') has roots in literary history which go back as far as Wilkie Collins and even Defoe, the supranational father of crime fiction. But Ibargüengoitia's barbs are local, contemporary and political. *The Dead Girls* sets up a sharply comic juxtaposition of the business infrastructure of prostitution with Mexico's formal charades of law enforcement, public morality and government bureaucracy.

Two Crimes is a better novel. In manner, it is less starkly objective than *The Dead Girls* and seems more affectionately tolerant of Mexican corruption. Most of the narrative is in the form of an autobiographical retrospect by the hero, Marcos González, also known as 'El Negro'. Marcos is a political radical in the evening, a minor civil servant by day. He is forced into hiding, after giving refuge to a terrorist. This first crime is not exactly an act of commitment; Marcos is simply too embarrassed to tell the man to go away. He flees Mexico City, a step ahead of the police, and makes for Muérdago, where a rich uncle lives. . . . Marcos is gradually sucked into his family's furious competition for the old man's fortune when he dies. Comic and melodramatic complications ensue. Inheritance hunting, seduction, adultery and finally murder for gain (the second crime) take over as the main preoccupations of Marcos's existence.

Insidiously, he is transformed into a petty bourgeois. He is no longer a revolutionary on the run, but a nephew on the make. The regression, of which the ingenuous hero is unaware, is beautifully handled, with the remote, understated finesse that seems Ibargüengoitia's narrative stock-in-trade. And again, the novel makes sly points about Mexico's extraordinary confusion of revolutionary idealism and low capitalist greed. . . .

The Dead Girls was all unfolding, making its effects by the simple accretion of facts and different perspectives on facts. *Two Crimes* employs the more traditional fictive techniques of suspense and surprise. (Not to give away the novel's twists, El Negro survives not only police persecution but three attempts on his life by jealous relatives and ends up a happily married restaurateur.) As a coda, the narrative switches briefly to the report of a bystander to the main events; but this detached winding-up does not sever the friendly relationship which has formed between the reader and the hero.

John Sutherland, "On the Run," in The Listener, *Vol. 112, No. 2870, August 9, 1984, p. 26.*

MICHELE SLUNG

Two Crimes is a beautifully imagined and structured tale. There's an air of mischief about it, but that doesn't mean that it's not serious—and the fact that it is, *au fond*, serious doesn't detract from its charm. The exotic setting, a small Mexican town rather off the beaten track, is immensely appealing and yet just the slightest bit disorienting at the same time. Stepping back for a moment from the mosquitoes and the eucalyptus, the tortillas

and the mariachis, one quickly sees, though, that the situation is a familiar one: a rich man, plus greedy relatives, equals murder.

But, restored to this firmer ground, still the reader is kept pleasantly off balance. Where's it all taking us—the clues dropped both carefully and unobtrusively, the touchy, shifting alliances, the maneuverings of Marcos, our young hero, whose cleverness can't combat fate? And there are mysteries within the mystery. If, indeed, we know what the first crime is likely to be, the substance of the second one—remember, the book is called *Two Crimes*—remains a puzzle until the story concludes. But it just may be, too, that there are more crimes than the title indicates—three, four, even more. For all the transported trappings of the classic British mystery, Ibarguengoitia resembles Friedrich Durrenmatt, not Agatha Christie, and the ambiguities of culpability are abundant.

From Asa Zatz's translation, which appears to serve the author very, very well, one finds Ibarguengoitia to be a writer with a genius for tightly vivid descriptions, short word paintings that immediately hit the senses, as flavor on the tongue. . . .

The town itself appears like this—"The sound of sparrows squabbling shrilly could be heard nearby. The Lenten cobalt sky hung over Muerdago. Visible on our left were the pink steeples of the church, two-story houses, and the laurel trees in the town square. The rest of the visual field encompassed the flat city of rooftops, relieved at intervals by a tower, a dome, and a solitary ash tree, and cultivated parcels stretched out all the way to the background of the mountains in the distance." Doesn't this convey not only the landscape, so clearly evoked, but also a place where the surface tranquility is soon to be shattered?

Marcos has come to Muerdago to lay low for a while, having dispatched his girlfriend to another spot. He's concocted a not implausible explanation for his arrival, having to do with a mining investment he wants his uncle Ramon to make, and Ramon, grateful to be distracted from the hovering, covetous clan around him, decides to go along with it. . . . However, Marcos, for all that he's gotten pretty good at thinking on his feet, is quickly in over his head, both because he seduces two of his cousins (a mother and her daughter) simultaneously and because he's unable to gauge the depths of the passions in the family circle he's returned to. With his own concerns (are the cops on his trail?) to worry about, he fails to notice that he's a match to a waiting powder keg. Naturally, once he gets the picture, it's too late.

In the novel's second half, Don Pepe [a pharmacist who is Uncle Ramon's best friend] turns detective, and what has been, up until this point, blackly comedic, now seems mostly black. Ibarguengoitia . . . lets no one off the hook, even though he seems to have some affection for even the rogues and deadbeats among his characters. *Two Crimes* is in no way a kindly book; still, it gives off a curious air of benevolence against the violence, as if, perhaps, in this small domestic drama, the author's canvas is actually larger. A politically committed writer, Ibarguengoitia would not waste such a situation: one can love one's country and deplore the ways in which it destroys itself.

Michele Slung, "Mystery and Murder, Mexican Style," in Book World—The Washington Post, *September 16, 1984, p. 7.*

JULES KOSLOW

In [*Two Crimes*], the late Jorge Ibargüengoitia misses by a wide margin one of his apparent objectives—to create a fast-paced suspense thriller loaded with shady types from south of the border and suffused with Mexican color. The protagonist, Marcos Gonzáles, is a crafty antihero with a larcenous heart. He has an amorphous connection with a group of sketchily drawn terrorists and gets involved with an assortment of undistinguished and indistinguishable male relatives itching to get their filthy hands on an ailing rich uncle's pesos. In an attempt to capture the attention of readers with an eye for eroticism, the author also introduces a couple of well-endowed female relatives who just can't resist the mawkish sexual come-ons of Marcos Gonzáles who, it seems, is in a continual state of sexual excitation. The purposeless comings and goings of a host of relatives blur whatever suspense is aroused by the old-hat plot teasers: Who is going to get dear old uncle's dough and will someone finally succeed in killing him in order to get it? The lack of suspense and excitement is somewhat compensated for by Ibargüengoitia's crisp writing, which often impresses, frequently titillates and sometimes amuses. . . . His not unsubstantial literary abilities are often in evidence, especially when he manages to turn a neat phrase, describe an oddball character or illuminate with clarity and wry humor an everyday happening. But these very decent literary achievements do not compensate for the novel's defects of plot, character and suspense.

> *Jules Koslow, in a review of "Two Crimes," in* The New York Times Book Review, *September 23, 1984, p. 28.*

ELIZABETH HANLY

At first, *Two Crimes* seems a simple invitation to fun and frolic, but Jorge Ibargüengoitia is sly. It slowly dawns on you that he's probing the dark side of experience, caressing it until secrets are delivered up. The novel begins with a dinner party, the fifth anniversary of the Chamuca's "giving herself" to Marcos, our hero. . . . Word comes that the authorities are on their way—something about the burning of El Globo department store. Already the police have everyone else from the party in custody. Marcos isn't a fool; he understands that innocence is no protection.

The hungover couple fling themselves into hurried leave-taking, and plan to meet again shortly on an obscure beach. Marcos, meanwhile, travels to the equally obscure town of Muérdago and tries to con his pesoed uncle into a phoney investment that will yield enough for several months of seaside bliss. But uncle is surrounded by cousins who wait with varying degrees of patience for him to die. Each attempts to protect the family interests from this intruder. There's Amalia: blond hair, black eyebrows, feathered spike mules. . . . Amalia's brothers are Mexico's answer to the Three Stooges; when not plotting anti-Marcos activities, they romp over the countryside with a mariachi band. And then there's the Gringo, Amalia's husband Jim, a marksman who pulls up his socks a lot, while insisting that Marcos join him early in the a.m. to hunt plump little birds.

Impervious to the scams around him sits the master manipulator—half-paralyzed, one-eyed Uncle Ramón. The old man is genuinely fond of Marcos and vice versa. Even as they ply each other with fake wills and money schemes, both are beaming. (p. 4)

No trace here of Fuentes's ancient gods and ancient memories. Nor does the land carve away at its people as in the tales of Juan Rulfo. Ibargüengoitia's is a secular world, focused on power, pressure, and the ins and outs of emotion. He sets up a morality tale, aware that his characters are beguiling enough to wreak havoc with such frameworks. *Two Crimes* is an endless cycle of value judgment interruptus.

Poor Marcos—the police, led by invincible Pancho, never stop looking for him. . . . Finally Ramón dies, not from natural causes. Cross-cutting curls the two plots into a tidy gallows knot enveloping Marcos, in custody for two crimes he didn't commit. Yet even when the hairpin turns have nowhere else to go, they don't let up. The last one, appropriately stunning, illustrates just how close to the edge the novel has always hovered. In the midst of this murder and mayhem, who finally pocketed Ramón's millions? Justice, my love, even your scent is gone. (p. 5)

> *Elizabeth Hanly, in a review of "Two Crimes," in* VLS, *No. 31, December, 1984, pp. 4-5.*

Laura (Linnea) Jensen

1948-

American poet.

Jensen's poems are often centered on ordinary events and objects, yet she evokes a sense of mystery through complex imagery and unusual syntax. She has identified authors of children's literature, particularly Laura Ingalls Wilder, as influences on her work. Tess Gallagher describes Jensen's poems as "full of riddles, music, childhood memories, and the ritual comforts that words can give." Jensen's first major book, *Bad Boats* (1977), reveals her penchant for quirky, apparently unconnected images and phrases. While response to her work was generally favorable, critics pondered the effectiveness of the expressionistic quality of her verse. *Memory* (1981) was also well received. In his review of this volume, J. D. McClatchy observed that while *Bad Boats* seemed to him "flat and confused," Jensen "knows now what she wants, and goes after it with ingenuity and poise."

(See also *Contemporary Authors*, Vol. 103.)

FLOYD SKLOOT

[*Bad Boats*] is a book of staunch isolation, of night and absence, of "a landscape where we take in turn / what is bleak and empty."

A typical Jensen mood, as in **"Here in the Night."** is agitated separation:

> There is a dog barking here in the night,
> here in my happiness where my neighbor
> forgets all about me. The other has run
> all his bath water, all the pressure that sang
> in the pipes. I am waiting for my bouillon,
> and while I drink it I will be happier still.

The mood does not necessarily make for agitated language. Quite the opposite is generally true and the effect of this surface calm is to enhance the sense of smouldering terror, deep upset. There is an uneasy, uncertain truce. . . . (pp. 88-9)

Consistent with mood, a typical Jensen tone, as in **"Winter Evening Poem,"** is controlled distress, a kind of assured gloom. . . . I do not find the perception all that unique. What makes Jensen particularly impressive, and her work compelling, is the constant effort to control the way her perceptions threaten to eliminate her sense of self. (p. 89)

The dangers inherent in writing from a posture like Jensen's are numerous. One can, and Jensen occasionally does, become too facile in presenting the perceived emptiness and absurdity ("I watch whim, with narrow eyes, / fly into darkness like an arrow"), the futility of human endeavor ("Bored is the farmer, / and drawn in the jaw / while children have dynasties crashing.") or the difficulty of happiness. . . . Such facility, if overindulged, will produce exercises rather than poems.

But Jensen's strategies in *Bad Boats* suggest awareness of the limits of perspective from which she can say: "I am a soul without a body" or "I am nothing / like a sailboat just touching water / carrying a wake behind, I turn / like air on air." She

is open and direct, then assumes various shapes and voices (seller of Ajax samples, Indian, a "large animal / no one can name"), first or third person, speculates, states, speaks to mules, turns directly to the reader, tinkers with situations, watches the pressure under which she puts her languages. After a poem like **"Amigo Acres,"** in which Jensen assembles but does not resolve a multitude of concrete images . . . , she places **"Water Widow,"** which is among the most lyrical and hazy poems in the book. . . . The variety and pace are carefully calculated, I think, and serve to keep this poet of sadnesses . . . interesting and effective: "The reason for sadness is less clear / when nothing has been said."

As the book progresses, Jensen's symbols accumulate and begin to intensify the impact of individual poems. Of particular interest are birds, especially owls. . . . The owl "wakes in sunset / and his lenses do not change," a quality Jensen admires, at least in part because "Everything happens after dark; / night blooms; the owls do not turn away." Her symbols—birds, winter, windows, night, snow—are most traditional, but her use of them is toward a skewed romanticism in which nonpresence or negation seem to be desired as ends in themselves. . . . Watchfulness becomes a means of survival in poem after poem rather than as a means toward comprehension, and being watched can be a major threat. . . . (pp. 89-90)

The enemy is what holds one in place against one's will ("They are bad boats and they hate their anchors"). But in a story, one can choose confinement and be pleased. . . . Though Jensen may say, "I betray my sister when I see her," she chooses to stay and continue seeing: "One no more takes flight / than one must take one's flight / as an example." Poets are seen as "peculiar foreigners" by the very subject matter they observe and attract.

At her zaniest, Jensen can turn the fear of being watched into a delightfully comic flight. **"After I Have Voted"** is worth quoting . . . :

> I move the curtain back,
> and something has gone wrong.
> I am in a smoky place,
>
> an Algerian cafe.
> They turn the spotlight toward me;
> the band begins to play.
>
> The audience stares back at me.
> They polish off their glasses.
> They ask the waiter, "Who is she?" . . .

[This poem] is Jensen at her most disarming. Beneath the loony flow of events is a familiar pattern of negative attention: a situation turning against her, betrayal by putting her on display, the private activity (secret balloting: a cherished personal right) going public. There is deep pain when the individual is constrained (as with the bad boats), when one is not left alone to sort things out, cast one's vote, devise one's private truths. (pp. 90-1)

In her weakest work, Jensen lapses into comfortable stylistic habits: At least a dozen poems place far too much weight upon the use of questions. . . .

These mannerisms, though, are not inconsistent with Jensen's way of understanding what she sees. *Bad Boats* is a strong book, rich and pleasing despite its occasional flaws or poems that simply don't work too well. . . . (p. 91)

> Floyd Skloot, *"Something Better than Ourselves,"* in The Chowder Review, *Nos. 10 & 11, 1976, pp. 88-92.*

FANNY HOWE

The strange title poem for [*Bad Boats*] is, on the surface, about boats that float loose, overturn, are generally "ready to be bad," anything to avoid settling, being anchored. As the title poem it sums up the dark and drifting nature of the poems throughout the book.

Jensen constructs a thicket of images, both austere and glittering and often does not attempt interpretation. The words are there, as emotional as music, and just as abstract. This evasion of stated meaning is "badness." . . .

The value, or beauty, of such lines depends on a suspension of thought. It is all expressionistic. And frequently Jensen rings true. The poems are not remotely radical in form but use traditional line endings and depend, too heavily I think, on repetition for impact.

[A] terse formality, especially when repeated, produces some tension between the drifting quality of the images and the poet's self-conscious construction of a poem. But the technique is an old one now, and vaguely sentimental. Luckily it doesn't ruin the whole effect of the book, which contains many serious and vivid poems. The "badder" they are, the better they are.

> Fanny Howe, *"Prose Poems and Poetry Poems,"* in The New York Times Book Review, *November 13, 1977, p. 82.*

TESS GALLAGHER

In a beautiful preface to his poems, the Irish poet Sean O'Riordain, who died in March of 1977, describes the child-mind as it relates to poetry, perception, and being in a way that enlivens an old idea: it is when we give ourselves over to the child-mind that we are most able to enter the appearances of the natural world. (p. 118)

[Wonder, a word O'Riordain uses in his preface,] applies to Jensen's work both in the sense of her ability to evoke amazement in the seemingly ordinary and also as wonder*ing*, questioning of what others take for granted. Jensen literally puts us under appearances in **"Cloud Parade,"** a poem which appears in both *Anxiety and Ashes* and *Bad Boats*. Its carnival atmosphere compels us to stand at attention, re-seeing the earthly parades of our childhoods, those flat-on-the-back afternoons of fashioning animals and objects from the clouds, "attics and beds, men with moustaches / heels over heads." Then the magician's exclamatory "Scarves! Echoes! Pavilions!" and we are in a world in which even the smoke from the fireplace is "beautifully made, / in deference to the cloud parade." The world is infused with cloudness; our walking-around earthly pursuits are no longer the main event.

Jensen's strong attachment to the work of various childrens' writers has perhaps helped sustain a simplicity of statement, a lightly moralistic tone, and a sense of being which repopulates the world by giving animals and objects back their power to act on us and to be dignified and humiliated by our own actions.

Primary among these childrens' writers has been Laura Ingalls Wilder. Her books about pioneer life, moving by covered wagon from Wisconsin, where she was born in 1867, to Kansas, Minnesota, and the Dakota Territory, have been an inspiration to Jensen. (pp. 118-19)

Wilder's stories are full of real hardships on the way to rescues. . . . [In *The Long Winter*], for instance, Laura and Carrie stumble through a blizzard to the warmth of their home.

> Laura sat stiffly down. She felt numb and stupid. She rubbed her eyes and saw a pink smear on her hand. Her eyelids were bleeding where the snow had scratched them. The sides of the coal heater glowed red-hot and she could feel the heat on her skin, but she was cold inside. The heat from the fire couldn't reach that cold.

This internal cold that cannot be reached by the heat of the fire gives some sense, I think, of the emotional center out of which many of the poems in *Anxiety and Ashes* were written. The activity of writing these poems might be compared to the way one must keep blowing on the hands in freezing weather while heading toward a hope of warmth. The revivals are momentary and need to be renewed since the cold is steady, the breath partial. Beside Wilder's bleeding eyelids, Jensen's motions are more subtle, as when she "forgets geriatrics" or notes in **"In the Hospital"** that the cups are "made in Occupied Japan."

It's hard for me to read this last phrase without irony since Jensen was herself at that time (Spring 1974) in the occupied Japan of the hospital in which that poem was written. She must have sensed during this time that the poems were a foil to that occupation, a way of preserving choice. (p. 120)

The captive life of the patient resembles that of the child. There are the pill givings, the feedings, the blood takings, the various impersonal invasions of the body. **"In the Hospital"** keeps insisting on memory. . . . Although not made specific in the poem, it is the memory of her grandmother's death which comes back to Jensen in her own hospitalization. Remembering that loss becomes a way of telling what endures, of accompanying the self with familiar presences during a confinement. (pp. 120-21)

Forgetfulness is the pain, the fear through which Jensen discovers extremes of tenderness and performs unexpected transformations. The weather itself [in **"In the Hospital"**] seems a message, the falling snow making visible the breaths of the absent grandmother. The snow, which reminds her of flowers, also reminds her that unseen beauties co-exist with harshnesses *when we remember they do.* Memory then becomes a way of restoring, of returning the love of the grandmother to the self in an alien situation, the "answer to the answer to a prayer."

It *is* brutal that our lives come down to us "like a cord of firewood / burning," that is, already aflame with those inherited predispositions over which we fear limited control and the prospect of ashes. But phoenix-like in Jensen these ashes "sprout." (p. 121)

The final vision of **"Anxiety and Ashes"** is a mocking one in which "The match laughs / at the joke of the body, / nudges the wick, / and laughs." This laughter occurs also at the end of **"In the Hospital"** but with some resolution and less taunting:

> Didn't I always understand
> the snow and the laughter, the bay leaves
> of the cupboards resting in the snow.

The speaker up until now has been looking out a window toward a spectre, "the bent man and his / frosty plumes of breath." Then a potentially violent thing happens. The interior of the house, the cupboards with their store of bay leaves, are dumped into the snow, but in such a disarming way that it seems the cupboards are being received by the snow. The verb "resting" engineers a final vulnerability, the opening of the heart which the poem has been moving toward. Although the laughter here belongs to the speaker's helplessness during the occupation, it is also joyous and reflexive as the speaker's own triumph in delivering the contents of the cupboards into the snow. This is an act of truce. . . . (pp. 121-22)

Breath is a hinge, spilling us beyond our wills, back into the larger air. Memory, closely allied to breath, returns us to that larger consciousness in which we are an extension of those who preceded us, making us "followers of air" and, by sound association, flowers of air. (p. 122)

[**"In the Hospital"** is] perhaps the most complex, successful, and autobiographical of Jensen's poems in these books and allows us our closest view of the speaker. **"In the Hospital"** is an arrival poem because it confronts anxieties by transforming elements of fear, snow, loss of breath, loss of memory, loss of self into beauty. "Beauty is made by fear," Jensen says in a later poem **"Writing Your Love Down"** in *Bad Boats.* As in this line, an aphoristic brand of wisdom begins to take

charge in the more recent poems. Often the concrete partakes of the abstract and vice versa. That is, actual elements are carried into the unseen and conversely, the unseen moves into the elemental: breath into frosty plumes into snow, snow into flowers, snow into tears, into white cinders and in the reverse: lives into cordwood, *forgetfulness* like a message on one of the *cups, love* in the oval *lips* of *cups,* the *glass* the thin walls of the missing grandmother's *clothes,* all manifestations of one another. Unseen and seen, appearance and disappearance revive each other. So in **"Baskets"** we find the bird's color entering the basket woven near a river. The bird will fly away at the end of the poem in the speaker's own statement that she cannot fly.

Jensen often does various turns on the word "nothing" and the attempt, invariably, is to subdue the vacancy of that word. Just as often, she uses a negative to insert a positive. In **"Animal,"** a poem which proceeds as a riddle, she reassures us that "nothing *is* too thin to endure the danger". . . "even the snake / bakes on his own rock." The last verse of the poem identifies that keeper who is "cousin to the crow's collection" as comfort itself.

> I am that other animal,
> comfort. Everything,
> even the winds that threaten,
> come to me.

Comfort has become the controlling element by the end of the poem so it is a generosity when comfort receives the menacing winds, here become animal and needful. (pp. 122-23)

Even though personification and anthropomorphism have been poorly esteemed as poetic currency of late, Jensen manages to make it work most of the time. (p. 123)

Jensen's lyric jumps in the poems enlarge spatial and rhythmic possibilities although they also cause some confusion which unbalances the reader from time to time. Madeline DeFrees suggested that the mind in these poems is a solitary one, one used to allowing itself to range and is therefore not always aware of its own jumps or, in company, when it has moved too quickly or forgotten to bridge a thought. Jensen accomplishes these leaps often with statement as in "The swallow would like to help us all." Suddenly it seems as if the swallow *has* volunteered by the sheer impact of this saying. We even want to trust the swallow because, unlike us, he "has never mistaken a path for a river." The sheer excitement of the way a swallow moves might be an apt metaphor for the exuberance of Jensen's own jerks, sudden flights, and nervy flittering. We're taken inside the emotional world of the swallow when she tells us "excitement makes him sad," for it seems "that he has a troubled memory; / that he is too happy about flight." In these sudden shifts there is a constant "troubling" of the memory by the very structure of the poem. As with the swallow, if the memory is troubled, flight becomes disjunctive, too happy, that kind of glad-sadness akin to hysteria. This "too happy flight" carries an implicit criticism. Perhaps it's a part of the modern condition: the way we convince ourselves into false happiness in order to keep the motion up. Consequently we're thrown more and more outside memory and meaning. Jensen's efforts toward coherence in this "too happy flight" might be seen as a series of landings which release into the next consideration.

The use of the collective "we" serves as a gathering force in many of the poems and this gives a foothold where the movement is sudden. "We" remember "ghosting it / with headlights, water witching anywhere, / anywhere, and with a turkey wishbone.'' Here again this emblem of childhood becomes an implement of hope. In our desperation to find the wished for water we are handed a miniature witching stick in the turkey wishbone and made to see ourselves in that remembered state of faith when well water *could* be anywhere, when breaking the wishbone *could* affect one's future because it was believed. As readers we feel over-sized and our childhood means of sustaining hopefulness becomes lilliputian. (pp. 124-25)

The apples of the last stanza [of **''Well Water''**] involve a rather private reference to a poem of mine called ''Apples From the Ground'' in which I steal some apples from a landlady's backyard. The ''you'' then points to the dedication but also to the speaker who is in a self-accusatory mood.

> What you took in apples I took in handfuls
> from a watering can,
> the well water meant for the flowers.
> The smell of the gravel is as it should be.
> The rain is ahead of me already on the path.

That the water should be set aside, *meant* for the flowers, is a state of concern for other-than-self that I'm thankful to be returned to. We live in such a state of arrogance with the natural world that we tend to appropriate it; how right it is to remember that the water does not belong to us, that we are borrowers and takers. Luckily, the rain, like language, replenishes, is always ahead of us on the path, beyond our needs, our de-servings and usuries. So the poem ends with nature balancing out the speaker's appropriation of the water. The well will fill again, which signals a restoration that the natural world takes upon itself.

The image of the well reappears in Jensen so often that it would seem to be a key to the emotional anxieties of the poems. Again we are like Alice in that we might suddenly fall down one of these wells. As in the line from **''Tantrum,''** ''The body takes the throat / like an enemy tower,'' we are always on the verge of this take-over, this lapse in our own control in which we hear ourselves speaking from far off ''as hail rattles on a board fence, / as the telephone wires / take the snow to be a mountain.'' (p. 125)

[Jensen] sometimes leaves out entirely the event which occa-sioned the poem. . . . In **''Household,''** a farmer's wife sends a packet of needles with her daughter who is going to the city. It's possibly unclear that the speaker is the farmer's wife. Because the needles take on a personality and are ''stubborn,'' the method is somewhat surreal: ''a fingertip is sleeping in a thimble; there is ''a haystack of needles,'' / ''needles spending their lives now / forgotten from raincoats in a rush.'' This poem comments under its surface on the making of poems: ''It is not easy to sew with an ignorant needle.'' Needle here could read ''word.'' The poem proceeds to use words as if they don't know what they mean. It sews with an ignorant needle and the result is one of the most purely musical passages in the book, echoing childrens' riddles:

> Once building a needle, once building a weed
> was a young time, once, that leaves itself be
> a wheedling eye, a thread of light
> between ins and the reputable grasses,
> their brass teasing eyes to believe.

> If there were no trouble, borrowing,
> the troubles would be in the rivers

> and the rivers would be rivers
> that the troubled find.

Here the language doubles back on itself, carrying us blindly into the next stitch but arriving miraculously at a feeling of wisdom beyond reason and sense, a finding, but no ordinary prosaic finding. The assonance and repetition are the inner coherence that bind the seam. (pp. 125-26)

Bad Boats carries over many of the poems I've already spoken of, but the new poems, as the title indicates, add a scolding, ironically moralistic tone, as though a mother had appeared on the scene. The loneliness of the poems is less self-inflicted and seen to be the general condition, as in **''Here in the Night''** where the speaker says:

> When I feel bad I wonder why they do not come
> to help me, why they let me go on this way,
> but who are they? And what are they, but alone?

A dog barking anonymously in the first line becomes personal in the last line, barking ''as if it were caring for me.'' The speaker has the sense of other activities going on in adjacent apartments and this causes a dollhouse effect so that we as readers view the aloneness and togetherness of the ''they'' at once, as though the front of the house were torn away.

I remember a conversation with an East Coast editor friend to whom I had shown this poem. He objected to ''but who are they? And what are they, but alone'' as sentimental. This word has come up again in relation to Jensen's reliance on repetition noted in a rather hastily taken view of the book in *The New York Times Book Review* [see excerpt above by Fanny Howe]. I want to suggest, perhaps dangerously, that this designation signals a very real difference in East and West Coast sensi-bilities as regards what is tolerable or ''enough'' in what a poem volunteers emotionally. . . . What in the East would be excess is in the West a sign of full spiritedness, willingness, and to admit the essential vulnerability of one's humanity is not an embarrassment or redundant, but rather the impulse to invite, to share.

I don't mean to insist on polarities which depend on such generalizations that the truth is blotted out by the exceptions one begins to advance. Nonetheless, I would protect the way Jensen's poems at such points speak directly out of the gen-erosity in that sensibility one seems to find especially now in the West, one which still allows candor without cynicism. (p. 127)

If anything, I'd like to see the fullness in Jensen's poems enlarged upon. In the less successful poems one has the feeling of a scaffolding along which images collide and intersect pre-cariously, and mystery sometimes withholds essential connec-tions. Restraint is a large part of our excitement about what is given in the poems, but the nature of that restraint is still developing, and it appears to be getting more clear-headed in poems such as **''Praise,''** **''Patience Is A Leveling Thing,''** and **''As The Window Darkens.''**

Jensen's poems continually invite the reader back. She manages a high degree of complexity and seems to break many of what have been thought to be the ''rules.'' The passive verbs and simple syntax are deceptive. They cause an evasiveness (''Hap-piness is a thread to find'' . . . ''Happiness is one lucky clo-ver'') that eludes even as it defines. Jensen's use of repetition— ''This is the time for it / this is the best time for it''—gives an eerie sense of the inevitable in such poems as **''The Red Dog''** and **''House Is An Enigma.''** She is so animated by the presences of her poems that they seem almost to write themselves out of the surety of her consciousness. Their unpredictable movement is what delights. . . . [Most] of Jensen's subjects are everyday, familiar happenings made consequential by a rare intimacy and mystery. They are full of riddles, music, childhood memories, and the ritual comforts that words can give. . . . (p. 128)

> *Tess Gallagher, "Scarves! Echoes! Pavilions!" in* Parnassus: Poetry in Review, *Vol. 6, No. 1, Fall-Winter, 1977, pp. 118-28.*

WILLIAM LOGAN

[*Bad Boats* offers] the freshest use of surrealism since W. S. Merwin and Charles Simic. All the anger in [Jensen's] poetry is projected onto the landscape, so we have the rare difficulty and pleasure of reading poetry that represents tumultuous internal states without cataloguing the tedious days of the author. Behind every sharp vision lurks a reproach. . . .

She lives in a dangerous world where "Salt falls from the sky into my clothes." In the disturbed backwaters of the unconscious, the most benign view can take on threatening postures. . . . Jensen writes as if there were nothing that could not be altered by her seeing it, and her language often has the surprising exactness of Wallace Stevens. The *mise-en-scenes* she favors are the country and the sea. . . .

Like some complex tragedy, her visions are both terrifying and funny; they create a poetry of elegance and fear. The risks Jensen takes—odd juxtapositions and tortuous transitions—cause their share of failures, but experience may later manage what her invention now unleashes. *Bad Boats* is a remarkable opening effort.

> *William Logan, in a review of "Bad Boats," in* Book World—The Washington Post, *March 12, 1978, p. E5.*

THE VIRGINIA QUARTERLY REVIEW

[Laura Jensen's poems] have a subdued, personal voice masking a quiet intensity. In [*Bad Boats*], the best pieces are poignant, dramatic, depicting the faces of the artist in short, straightforward syntax and complex, intricately connected thoughts. Dense, surreal images form delicate constructs tenuously related or not quite holding together. Often lyrical and moving, some are too unfocused and obscure, so precarious is this type of deep imagist poetry—language almost effacing itself, attempting to metamorphose completely into image. What holds our attention and admiration is the compelling mixture of the exotic and familiar and the strange provocative dream-logic of image and observation.

> *A review of "Bad Boats," in* The Virginia Quarterly Review, *Vol. 54, No. 2 (Spring, 1978), pp. 56-7.*

ROBERT McDOWELL

Laura Jensen has written a book, *Bad Boats,* that is sure to receive a lot of attention. Unfortunately, much of it will be for the wrong reasons. She is a versatile young poet whose work is always lively, whose skillful observations never overrate her own importance. In her world the poet is just another element, not a loud ringmaster in a sequined tux. She avoids, or has already outgrown, the guise most often befitting a young poet,

that of the creature of limited experience looking at herself. Even in the few poems in which her presence is a tangible part, it is transformed into a universal being. (p. 379)

I have said that this book will often be praised for the wrong reasons. Many, especially the ardent proponents of the young, will want to call it an exceptional book, implying that the poet can expect to be lured to Hollywood or the Himalayas to prepare for the arrival of her legion of imitators. *Bad Boats* is not an exceptional book; it is one in which the poems race from one beautiful moment to another, but the course between is full of potholes. The problem is fairly common, especially among Jensen's less-talented peers. It is the result of a lack of patience and, again, common sense. Many poets are too readily seduced by the sensational, by the startling image designed to jar the habitually lethargic reader. The pressure to produce such an image, often at the expense of making sense in the poem, is constantly applied by teachers, friends, and publishers (this is where current writing schools are bad, if they are bad at all). The consequent failure to achieve the perfect sense of the poem is an unconscious one on the part of the poet, but it is a failure nonetheless. Any sensitive reader cannot help but be aware of it. Instead of being seduced by the sensational, he feels as if he has merely bumped heads with the mediocre. Jensen's title poem provides a timely example. . . . Every line is good, but the lines don't really work together. The reason is that the poet's attitude toward her subject has not been clarified. *Why are the boats bad?* They are bad because of their initiative *and* because they lack it. They are bad because they would "demolish the swagger and the sway," then because "they cannot wind their own rope." In a short poem you can't have it both ways. The poet must take a side. As it stands, **"Bad Boats"** is a not very satisfactory poem that exists too much for the sake of its wonderful last line; and a poem that lives for its last line quickly assumes the posture of a stale joke with an all-too-predictable punch line. This should not happen to a poem in which, as I have said, all the lines are excellent and the basic idea is intriguing.

This problem is found in too much poetry to be ignored, but it is easily corrected with a little more thought, a little more work. If I use Jensen as an example, it is because she is so much better than the common violator. The poem is more important than the individual image, and there are times when this poet remembers and shows us what she can do. **"House Is an Enigma," "The Cloud Parade," "Dreaming of Horses,"** and **"An Age"** are fine poems displaying a tough sensibility, a hyper-active intelligence, and thorough "working out" of the subject matter. At her best Jensen is better than almost any of the young poets writing today. *Bad Boats* is one uneven book that is worth the reader's time. It is full of bad writing—of a high caliber—, but it is also full of moments that make me feel as if I have made an important discovery. (pp. 380-81)

> *Robert McDowell, in a review of "Bad Boats," in* The Hudson Review, *Vol. XXXI, No. 2, Summer, 1978, pp. 379-81.*

VERNON SHETLEY

Laura Jensen belongs to the "expressionist" school, the majority party among young American poets. I borrow this apt label from Donald Hall, who feared that this expressionist tendency would become a new orthodoxy; his fears have been confirmed. So many of her contemporaries have adopted this style, as the rich and idle adopt fashionable maladies, that it takes some time to realize how genuine and necessary Jensen's voice is. The form of her perceptions and feelings calls forth the method of her poems; this first volume [**Bad Boats**] has an undiluted vigor rare anymore even among the originators of this mode.

Mark Strand suggests that this expressionist school is a new "international style," a kind of imagination shared worldwide. Indeed, at its most mechanical, the expressionist poem reads as if versified from a prose translation of an unknown original. But in America the sources of this mode, or at least of its operating principles, may yet be found not in the cosmopolitan analogues sought by Strand but within the American tradition. It is a less than universally acknowledged fact that the standards of Imagism remain the standards by which most American poems get written. Imagism eschewed discursiveness and abstraction, juxtaposed images directly, and even more than making it new, tried to keep it moving. In its orthodox form, the expressionist poem features an impersonal narrator delivering a series of images without comment or connection, much as Swift's philosophers conversed wordlessly with objects drawn from large sacks. Jensen's faults are the faults of the Imagist attitude. When she fails, she does so because she adopts this grab-bag approach; the poems choke in a flood of images without context, as if berserk mills were turning out parts faster than human hands could assemble them.

When Jensen succeeds, however, she is working on another level altogether. The impersonality of her voice results not from a mass-produced diction but from a real innocence of perception. . . . (pp. 230-31)

Jensen is not among those that affect a primitive clarity and purity; the emotions in her poems are mixed, unstable, and ambiguous, as the primal emotions are. The best poems in this volume combine disparate material, disjunctions in syntax, continual twists in diction, to build single, complex moments of feeling. They cohere around circular structures or patterns of recurrence, moving with an oblique but rigorous poetic logic that is the greatest satisfaction of this fine first volume.

> *Vernon Shetley, "A Babel of Tongues," in* Poetry, *Vol. CXXXIV, No. 4, July, 1979, pp. 226-33.**

ROBERT HUDZIK

Jensen's poems illuminate a shadowy, ghost-like realm delicately formed in opposition to the willful, hurtful, everyday world. As in **Bad Boats** . . . Jensen [in **Memory**] makes unexpected connections, transforming ordinary things into magical spirit-objects. . . . Her verse tends to be tenuous and abstract, like memory itself, linked to reality through a series of startling, evocative images. . . . A fine, emotionally involving collection from an expressive, intuitive poet who, at her best, returns to us like a kite and "tells / what it is like in the altitude."

> *Robert Hudzik, in a review of "Memory," in* Library Journal, *Vol. 107, No. 13, July, 1982, p. 1329.*

MARY KINZIE

[In **Memory,** Laura Jensen applies] some of the same methods as Louise Glück: the forcible paring of settings to their lunar minimum; manipulation of an often helplessly buffeted speaker among frozen particulars; the mingling of present with past; permeable temporality; the openness of one element (air, water,

flesh) to another; and both Glück and Jensen are wont to dwell on states of psychological paralysis. But whereas Glück is brisk, even business-like in approaching her material head on, Laura Jensen leaves the impression of having accidentally stumbled upon her fearful and nauseated images of the self:

> Out on the beach the mussels caught
> at it, what you overturned;
> the crabs scattered, running
> with one glance
> at some horrible maturity.

These lines [from "**Tapwater**"] affect by their power of suggestion, directed at the unnamable—a method that lies at the core of all gothic romance. But Jensen also permits the amusing crabs to act their part, all running sideways as if "with one glance" back at what scattered them, the girl on the beach. With the phrase "some horrible maturity," the poet betrays her great weakness for the exaggerated, slightly off-center puff. She writes elsewhere of "unrelenting wings," "tactile evening," "virtuous coracle," and "expedient humanity." The off-centeredness is made more troublesome by a second mannerism, the coy surreal, which in the work of many who have been encouraged to pursue the quirky in their sensibilities produces mere varieties of makeshift. Finally, of course, a cultivated eccentricity is simply another convention, but in extreme or youthful cases one that deprives itself of the order a convention can and should provide.

The stanza from "**Tapwater**" above, despite its small charm, has no stamina for carrying through the suggestion that horror at the thing (a dead animal?) turned over on the beach is actually horror of one's own crime—a deed to which the mind pivots and clings like a mussel, fastening itself, sucking. Rather, the associations into which Jensen allows the poem to drift do nothing to support or sustain one another. Suddenly, a bird appears in the speaker's hands that was not there until the crabs scattered; the speaker prays to it, mentions "the others," alludes to oncoming death—all eerie little turns entirely wanting in aesthetic or narrative significance.

At the same time, I don't believe that Jensen is trying for a purely verbal accidence of emblem groups. The most successful poems in **Memory** (hardly for Jensen a cerebral title) are those in which the perceiving mind pivots feelingly upon an object. One example is "**Kite**," about the arrangement by age-groups of the aisles in a dime store; another is "**Kitchen**," in which each ingredient in the larder is interpreted ("Onions are the same tunes / to their centers," "Milk is a satisfied whisper"); these are mild, coherent, unobjectionable poems. Jensen is also fond of debris, and does not shrink from surface listing. . . . But like the prose into which this kind of thing necessarily drifts, her poems of greater ambitions, especially political ones, are diffused into aimless spurts of descriptive energy; from the fifty lines of "**Tenor**," the portrait of an anti-war mother, the following is the only one where something true has been precisely centered in the watching mind: the sky is said to be "deepened by a jet, tiny and high." In the end, one is frustrated by the narrowness of the range of those poems of Laura Jensen to which genuine response is possible.

> *Mary Kinzie, "Haunting," in* The American Poetry Review, *Vol. 11, No. 5, September-October, 1982, pp. 37-46.**

THE VIRGINIA QUARTERLY REVIEW

The clarity and consistency of the poems in [**Memory**] . . . is impressive. There is a sure sense of craft and grace in the best poems which enrich the distinct vision they present. These are acts of definition; of the self, the world, and the imaginative universe, achieved through a sharp focus on the details and objects that make up our experience. At times the poems seem reserved or willed, but the best poems confront this world with a dreamlike sense of focus and texture, attempting to assimilate the inevitable pain and relief of our lives.

A review of "Memory," in The Virginia Quarterly Review, *Vol. 59, No. 1 (Winter, 1983), p. 26.*

J. D. McCLATCHY

Everywhere there are birds in [*Memory*]: finches, starlings, gulls, crows, penguins, sparrows, eggs. Some are observed, some remembered, some figurative, but all have the emblematic force of the falcon in the title-poem: "The falcon knows the falconer / with both its eyes. Like memory, it / returned when it was unexpected. / Like memory it is a weight on the arm, / missed sorely when it is missing." That falcon is Jensen's nightingale or skylark, the High Romantic symbol for the natural life of art beyond human powers. She writes in her new book, then, about what is missing, what she unexpectedly finds when tolled back to her sole self. Of one of her birds she asks "that you teach me the boundary / between shell-charity and flight." *Memory* seeks to walk that boundary. Jensen's first book, *Bad Boats* (1977), seemed to me flat and confused. *Memory* is neither. Jensen knows now what she wants, and goes after it with ingenuity and poise. Several voices sound throughout: one is an eerily slow stutter, dealing the facts of a fantasy; another is incantatory, set to evoke a poem's subject, though sometimes it never comes (this is the school of Inspired Babble); another is the vulnerable, knowing child's voice—and in these poems Jensen puts me in mind of *"Der Erlkönig."* The control in other poems—like the brilliant **"To a Stranger (at the End of a Caboose),"** or **"Poem,"** or **"West Window"**—points not only to this poet's tightrope balance, but also to what these poems balance themselves above: a treacherous empty space in her life. When, in **"West Window,"** wondering at being a woman "who is no more than tenant, daughter, / follower, fan, vine, parade, and borrower," and having catalogued her small possessions, she asks herself

> It is all here in a cluttered cache,
> my luck, my dreams, and privacy. How well
> I have seen the temporal fact of it all, but
> less every moment do I want to leave it all,
> or carry it with me. I ask, not where can I go,
>
> but how can I go, as the shawl and the shelf
> grow dearer and I more within, more within?

it could well be a hospital room she is describing. In **"The Creature from the Black Lagoon"** and **"'Wind Saves Woman in Leap from Building',"** there is the same struggle, unsettling but never sensational; the reader never has the sense that either the poet's experience or his own feelings are being exploited. Jensen knows what it is "to walk / in the brief sweet world of the saved," and what it is not to. Many fine poems in *Memory* (let me also single out **"Somali Legend," "Hot Spell,"** and **"The Woman"**) record that troubled knowing.

J. D. McClatchy, in a review of "Memory," in Poetry, *Vol. CXLIII, No. 3, December, 1983, pp. 169-70.*

Pat(rick M.) Jordan

1941-

American nonfiction writer, journalist, memoirist, critic, and novelist.

Jordan is best known for his books about sports in the United States. He is particularly noted for capturing the personal interaction among athletes, a skill informed by his three years as a minor league pitcher in the Milwaukee Braves organization. In his first nonfiction book, *Black Coach* (1971), Jordan examines the effects of racial attitudes on a predominantly white high school football team after their white coach is replaced by a black man. *Chase the Game* (1979) chronicles the lives of three inner-city high school basketball players and their foundering hopes for professional careers. In *A False Spring* (1975), Jordan recalls his unsuccessful attempt to enter major league baseball. Among Jordan's other works are *Suitors of Spring* (1973) and *After the Sundown* (1979), which present biographical profiles of notable athletes. *The Cheat* (1984), Jordan's first novel, concerns a journalist's attempts to cope with various professional and personal problems.

(See also *Contemporary Authors*, Vols. 33-36, rev. ed.)

Photograph by Al Szabo. Courtesy of Pat Jordan

JONATHAN YARDLEY

A subject of the sort that sportswriting usually shies away from is central to Pat Jordan's *Black Coach:* the role of high-school football in desegregation. The book, which is very well-written, is about a black man named Jerome Evans, who was named head coach when the white and black schools of Burlington, NC, were merged. . . . Jordan is much less concerned with what happened on the field (the team, in fact, did very well) than with the impact of Evans on the town and that of the town on Evans. It is not a roaring success story . . . , but there is great bitterness and, in the end, a sense as powerful as ever of the distance between black and white.

That is the real reason why Jordan's book is good: it recognizes that sport is a part of life, not an unimportant one, and that life is more complex than sports-page headlines. The story is often not who won, or how, but in what way the game, the players and the audience reflect the society of which they are a part. The best baseball fiction—novels by Ring Lardner, Mark Harris, Bernard Malamud and Robert Coover—has recognized that. So does the best sports journalism: it avoids mythmaking, places sport in perspective, and acknowledges that the English language is a delicate instrument to be handled with respect—that the old clichés and the old reportorial forms ought to be abandoned. The good young sportswriters—Jordan, Merchant, Axthelm, Lipsyte, Deford, Angell—are working to those purposes. The trouble is, there are so damnably few of them, and even fewer places in the profession where their efforts are appreciated and encouraged. (p. 23)

> Jonathan Yardley, "*Babe Ruth Still in His Heaven,*" in The New Republic, *Vol. 165, No. 25, December 18, 1971, pp. 21-3.**

DESMOND MATTHEWS, S.J.

Black Coach is mainly the story of Burlington, North Carolina, and its people and the conflict which arose when Cicero Abraham Frye, the white football coach of the town's predominantly-white Walter Williams High School, was replaced by Jerome Evans, a black.

Would the players and assistant coaches take orders from this man, or would Frye manage to destroy Evans before the school year even began? Would the first warm night of the football season bring the townsfolk out to cheer or riot? Would success spoil Jerome Evans?

These and allied questions make up the thesis of this thoroughly boresome book. If you are interested in the lucubrations of a bevy of black cheerleaders, the mouthings of a man like Frye and of his pathetic "red-neck" friends and acquaintances, then read this book. And do so if you are interested in the somewhat dubious philosophy of Jerome Evans who apparently is so self-conscious that, to quote his own words, "everybody is looking at me." . . .

I honestly don't think that any high school football coach, be he white or black, is of sufficient interest to the general public to write even a colorless book about him. And that indeed is what Pat Jordan has set out to do. The account is banal, the book is banal. It occurs to me that it may have been intended for teenagers, and not for adults at all. If so, it is boring to teenagers, several of whom I let read it, lest I was being too critical of it.

Desmond Matthews, S.J., in a review of "Black Coach," in Best Sellers, *Vol. 31, No. 19, January 1, 1972, p. 444.*

KIRKUS REVIEWS

Talk of spring training is in the air and it's enough to gladden the winterized heart of even the most coldblooded among us. And by the time [*The Suitors of Spring*] is in the stores and libraries, the national pastime will be preparing for Opening Day—for some of us an event better than Christmas and the Fourth of July put together. Grandstand cognoscenti are urged to get into shape by reading Pat Jordan's small but warming collection of baseball profiles—they gleam like flashing spikes and are as colorful as today's harlequin uniforms.... Jordan talks about and with some very recognizable names—the Mets' top-property Tom Seaver, happy-go-lucky Sudden Sam McDowell, former Boston Braves great and now much traveled pitching coach Johnny Sain, the zany Bo Belinski who rode to fame and glory on the first no-hitter in California history, and a wonderfully long piece which traces the rise of young Bruce Kison from the minors to Pirate hero of the 1971 play-offs and World Series. And some very unknown names—aging Woody Huyke who catches for the Waterbury (Conn.) Pirates and who knows that at 33 he'll never make it to the big time but who remains cheerful even when he pops up.... This might not be in the same league as last year's *Boys of Summer*, but it will do quite nicely as a warm-up exercise.

A review of "The Suitors of Spring," in Kirkus Reviews, *Vol. XLI, No. 3, February 1, 1973, p. 166.*

JAMES A. PHILLIPS

Virtually every day a new sports book comes out, usually one written by a star capitalizing on his notoriety, ephemeral as it may be.... For the greater part, however, sports books are detailed histories of technique, frustrations, and eventual success glamorized and glorified by the pen of a professional writer. Not so with *A False Spring.* Pat Jordan got a $45,000 total bonus, but he never pitched a game in Milwaukee County Stadium and never again spoke to Warren Spahn.... The money was half what he wanted, especially in view of the fact that he had pitched four consecutive no-hitters as a Little Leaguer. But as any eighteen-year-old star rationalizes, this is merely the start of a fantastic career, so a smaller bonus isn't such a big deal.

Poor Pat, however, was destined to such nothing baseball towns as McCook, Davenport, Eau Claire, and Palatka. All the work (and deception) he ... had gone through for years came to naught with Pat's unconditional release from the Braves after three sometimes promising but consistently unproductive years in the minors....

What is engaging about this story of sports failure is the concomitant story of personal growth. Pat was youth growing into manhood, much the way that youth always grows into manhood: slowly, naively, trustingly, humorously, and often painfully. From insecure to aloof, from hero-worshiper to self-designated star, from virgin to customer, and, most importantly, from observer to interpreter, he grew and learned. And

he has used the thirteen years since the end of his career to reminisce and look back warmly on all those who were so much a part of him and his. In no other sports book have I read such incisive, albeit subjective, descriptions of people from a person's past.... Thinking about what might have been seems to have sharpened the eye and pen of Pat Jordan. He strikingly remembers everyone: the "bird dogs" who first scouted him, his first manager, first woman, first prostitute, first helpful coach, people who gave him a space in their home and an opportunity to be part of their lives....

What *Catcher in the Rye* did for prep school dropouts, *A False Spring* might well do for pro sports dropouts.

James A. Phillips, in a review of "A False Spring," in Best Sellers, *Vol. 35, No. 2, May, 1975, p. 35.*

PETER ANDREWS

Broken Patterns is a book about challenges and the athletes who rise to meet them in women's sports, sometimes at a fearful cost. Pat Jordan, a former professional athlete himself and a first-rate writer, presents us with a series of deftly etched portraits of women sports figures and the price they paid for "breaking the pattern" of traditional society to dedicate themselves to sport. These are not the money superstars like Chris Evert, but women like Lillian Ellison, now in her 40's and still working as a professional wrestler under the name of "The Fabulous Moolah." A fascinating gallery of dedicated, driven people.

Peter Andrews, in a review of "Broken Patterns," in The New York Times Book Review, *May 29, 1977, p. 18.*

CAROL KEON

The basic premise [of *Broken Patterns*] led me to believe that this would be a hard-hitting work by a feminist about feminists, but—alas(!)—Pat Jordan is a male—a fact which comes through all too loud and clear. Although he is sensitive to the struggles, as well as to the uniqueness of these women, he fails to present a clear picture of just what patterns are broken: stereotyped roles of women or of athletes?

Some characters in this work make a feminist's hair stand on end: "The only thing we have going for us when we play sports is that we can compete more gracefully than men, although not as well. Once we destroy the illusion of femininity we're defeating the whole purpose of women's sports." Sez who?! The conversations with the younger women are more reassuring. Perhaps they have indeed broken some patterns, as the title promises. Survival in a hostile world or the furious struggle to protest one's femininity are no longer motivating forces.... The most refreshing treatment, however, is that of a Women's field hockey team, for whom playing well appears to be their only goal. Blood-thirsty competition, individual stardom, and fanatical "beating-the-guys-really-turns-me-on" attitudes are graciously absent.

Curiously, Mr. Jordan is at his best when he writes neither about women nor about sports, but rather when he describes his milieu. In the Willye B. White chapter he captures masterfully the bigotry and despair of the deep South from which she escaped via sports. The seedy squalor and smalltown mediocrity of the audience at the Fabulous Moolah's wrestling match make an indelible impression. Jordan's description of

El Paso reveals the eye of a painter and the soul of a poet. He should develop this talent further and leave women's things to women!

> *Carol Keon, in a review of "Broken Patterns," in* Best Sellers, *Vol. 37, No. 3, June, 1977, p. 85.*

VICTOR KANTOR BURG

Chase the Game is about sports insofar as sports are about individuals, families and neighborhoods: about private wishes and the public arenas in which these hopes take their form and are played out. Primarily, but not exclusively, a story of three young lives, this book is a narrative of loss and combat and play.

Frank Oleynick, Barry McLeod and Walter Luckett grew up and were famous as basketball players in the slums of Bridgeport, Connecticut.... All of them had special promise and an unusual blend of black and white influences on their lives and on the style of their games.... None lived up to the promise that each had demonstrated as a youth. And talent, and what becomes of it, Pat Jordan's abiding concern and passion, underlies this story....

One of Jordan's finest talents—fully displayed here—is his depiction of the look and feel of intersections: streetcorners, rivalries, relatives, the visible forms of anger and friendships and games. The scenes in this book of street life and family life in the multi-faceted ghetto and the way that heterogeneity is expressed on a basketball court, the intersecting of generations and nationalities; the interactions form the substance of *Chase the Game.* Olyenick, McLeod and Luckett were friends, neighbors, cousins and combatants; the complexity and liveliness of their relationships are surely and powerfully presented. This is a book for young readers as well as adults, but only those young readers—and only those adults—who are prepared for a grown-up view of the sports world....

No present-day American writer of whom I know has any better ability to portray a full spectrum of ages, sexes, classes, environments and races. It is a pleasure to have a new book of his to read; the cumulative effect of all his books is beginning to be considerable.

> *Victor Kantor Burg, "How They Played the Game," in* The Christian Science Monitor, *May 10, 1979, p. 19.*

JOSEPH P. LOVERING

[*Chase the Game*] is readable mainly because [Jordan] dramatizes the young men's lives through their talk and their interactions. Both the talk (loaded with vulgarities and obscenities) and their associations with one another exhibit clearly the aimlessness of this existence. Obviously Jordan knows the game of basketball, and knows these young men very well too. The book does well, I think, in bringing a focus upon the exploitation of athletic ability, by communities, by colleges and by professional organizations. Yet in Jordan's book I do not think the focus is quite clear enough on the root causes. For one who sees this problem so clearly in its dimensions, the author seems to me to be too content merely to lay down a concrete depiction of it in these pages.

> *Joseph P. Lovering, in a review of "Chase the Game," in* Best Sellers, *Vol. 39, No. 4, July, 1979, pp. 129-30.*

PUBLISHERS WEEKLY

In the American jockocracy, second in interest only to the practicing athlete is the former player, whose days of glory—or dreams of glory—are gone. [In *After the Sundown*] Jordan, himself a former pitcher ..., looks at a group of ex-athletes to determine what they have become.... The individual stories combine to make a book of interest to any sports buff.

> *A review of "After the Sundown," in* Publishers Weekly, *Vol. 216, No. 9, August 27, 1979, p. 380.*

BOOKLIST

[*After the Sundown* contains a] curious mixture of eight thought-provoking journalistic profiles, written between 1972 and 1977, that tend to focus on athletes past their prime whose chief self-image is still wrapped up in who they were—or might have been. One of the pieces is autobiographical, as was Jordan's *False Spring* ..., and is no kinder than those on Jim Bouton, Art Heyman, Bo Belinsky, Philip Hill, and Richard Connors—all of whom exhibit ambivalence about themselves, at best.

> *A review of "After the Sundown," in* Booklist, *Vol. 76, No. 9, January 1, 1980, p. 648.*

PUBLISHERS WEEKLY

Jordan's first novel [*The Cheat*] has the requisite elements of formula fiction: it features a handsome protagonist who has a wife and a mistress and enough lurid sexual encounters to make the book a snap to read. What's missing here is a veracity in the writing and the characters. Much of the dialogue is stilted ... and the repartee is so macho, cool and hip that one winces at the clinkers. Bobby Giacquinto is [a journalist and] a "stud." He loves his wife, but she won't let him make love to her, so he becomes involved with Sheila—slightly older, a loner, and uncompromising.... When he is assigned to chronicle the career of a once-famous baseball pitcher who ended up a destitute, forgotten alcoholic, he stumbles upon another story involving a second pitcher, a holier-than-thou evangelical crusader who has an unsavory connection with the dead former star. Suddenly Bobby is at a crossroads where he must decide between his marriage and his mistress, and, morally, at the point of choice between being a lifelong cheat at his profession or opting for a courageous resolution. Unfortunately, Jordan's skills are not up to the telling of this tale.

> *A review of "The Cheat," in* Publishers Weekly, *Vol. 226, No. 5, August 3, 1984, p. 54.*

ROBERT W. CREAMER

Mr. Jordan is ... a first-rate observer and not a bad writer.... *A False Spring,* about his own unsuccessful experience as a bonus-baby pitcher in the minor leagues, was a blunt and sometimes unpleasant work. But it holds up on rereading and remains one of the most revealing books ever written about baseball. Even better was his *Chase the Game,* an extraordinary account of the intertwined lives of three basketball-playing kids from a Connecticut ghetto, two white, one black, who go on to college and the pros before tumbling, almost inevitably, back toward the ghetto.

Mr. Jordan is entranced by failure, his own in baseball, for example, and those of his young basketball players as they encounter the realities of life in the National Basketball Association. Perhaps he sees elements of classical tragedy in this, with flaws of character rather than external forces ultimately bringing down the hero. In any case, he pursues the same theme fictionally in *The Cheat*.

Bobby Giacquinto, the hero of this novel, is a big, good-looking Connecticut Italian in his 40's. Like Mr. Jordan, he was a terrific pitcher when he was a schoolboy and for the past 15 or 20 years has been a successful professional writer. A few years ago, Mr. Jordan was sued after writing an eye-opening magazine story about a prominent straight-arrow athlete; Giacquinto also writes a revealing magazine story about a prominent straight-arrow athlete and is sued.

How much further the parallels between the author and the fictional Giacquinto extend I don't know, but serious writers often twist autobiographical material to suit their fictional needs, and Mr. Jordan is very serious about his writing. . . .

Mr. Jordan's depiction of Giacquinto's frustration and ambivalence is admirably done, and his sensitive and refreshing descriptions of some aspects of the middle-aged affair are awfully good. For instance, the scene in which Giacquinto and Sheila first venture into love-making after she undergoes a mastectomy is particularly well done. Unfortunately, the demands of the plot—the story Giacquinto pursues and writes, the magazine's distortion of it, the subsequent lawsuit—and the two-dimensional caricatures of such key figures as the self-righteous athlete the hero is writing about and the magazine's glib lawyer damage the book badly. So do some of the sexual passages, which read more like adolescent daydreams than serious fiction. Nor is painstaking devotion to careful writing consistently evident—there are enough "furrowed brows" in this book to grow all the corn in Iowa.

Thus for all Pat Jordan's skill and hard work, the book is a failure. Reading it is like watching a pitcher throw five or six strong innings before being bombed out in the seventh. He's good enough to be heard from again.

> Robert W. Creamer, "Love After 40," in The New York Times Book Review, *October 28, 1984, p. 20.*

ELIZABETH MILLKEN

[*The Cheat*] is a good story, but unfortunately it is not the one Mr. Jordan wants to tell us. He is too much concerned with Bobby Gianquinto's messy life. Bobby writes fluff for magazines and commits adultery compulsively. He is a cheat. We are given lists of his women that rival Leporello's catalogue of Don Giovanni's exploits, with anatomical descriptions that are much more intimate and not nearly as entertaining. Then Bobby falls in love with Sheila. She inspires him to write and write well. She redeems him. The reader is not so uplifted. We are treated to the same heavyhanded and dehumanizing sexual details in this relationship that we saw in Bobby's other affairs. He even makes love to the poor woman on the floor of his office just as he did with all those other broads. Tacky. It seems Pat Jordan missed the mark here and this novel should have concentrated on the subject he has written so well about before, the baseball player.

> Elizabeth Millken, in a review of "The Cheat," in Best Sellers, *Vol. 44, No. 9, December, 1984, p. 327.*

Stephen (Edwin) King

1947-

(Has also written under pseudonyms of Richard Bachman and John Swithen) American novelist, short story writer, scriptwriter, nonfiction writer, and autobiographer.

King is a prolific and popular author of horror fiction. In his works, King blends elements of the traditional gothic tale with those of the modern psychological thriller, detective, and science fiction genres. His fiction features colloquial language, clinical attention to physical detail and emotional states, and realistic contemporary settings that help make supernatural elements convincing. King's wide popularity attests to his talent for creating stories in which he emphasizes the inability to rationalize certain facets of evil in seemingly commonplace situations.

King's interest in the demonic and the paranormal is evidenced in his protagonists, whose experiences and thoughts often reveal psychological complexities or abnormalities. His first novel, *Carrie* (1974), concerns a socially outcast high school girl whose emotional insecurities lead her to take violent revenge on her taunting classmates by means of telekinetic powers. In *The Shining* (1977) malevolent spirits in a remote resort hotel gradually manipulate a caretaker to attempt to murder his wife and child. Similarly, a haunted car in *Christine* (1983) gains control of an angry and alienated teenage boy. Other works in which such elements recur include *The Dead Zone* (1979) and *Firestarter* (1980).

Some of King's novels are variations of classic stories of fantasy and horror. For example, *'Salem's Lot* (1972) is a contemporary version of Bram Stoker's *Dracula* set in a New England town. King's apocalyptic epic *The Stand* (1978) is close in structure to J.R.R. Tolkien's *The Lord of the Rings* in its tale of a deadly virus and the battle between the surviving forces of good and evil. *Pet Sematary* (1983), which is a variation on W. W. Jacobs's short story "The Monkey's Paw," tells of a physician who discovers a supernatural Indian burial ground in which the dead return to life. *The Talisman* (1984), written in collaboration with horror writer Peter Straub, also recalls *The Lord of the Rings* in its creation of a fantasy world in which a boy searches for a cure for his mother's cancer.

King has admitted writing five novels as Richard Bachman to avoid publishing too many works under his own name. These novels seldom contain elements of the macabre or occult, focusing instead upon such themes as human cruelty, alienation, and morality. In *Rage* (1971), a psychopath shoots a teacher and holds the students hostage, singling out one pupil for physical and mental torture. *The Long Walk* (1979) and *The Running Man* (1982) focus on near-future societies in which people compete to the death in ritualistic games. *Roadwork* (1981) explores a man's reaction as he watches his family, work, and home destroyed by corporate and governmental forces beyond his control. *Thinner* (1984) concerns the fate of an obese man who begins to lose weight following a gypsy's curse.

King's short story collections *Night Shift* (1977) and *Skeleton Crew* (1985) comprise detective, science fiction, and horror tales. *Stephen King's Danse Macabre* (1981) includes autobio-

© Jerry Bauer

graphical essays and a critical history of the horror genre in films, television, and literature. *Different Seasons* (1982) consists of four novellas which, like the Bachman novels, focus upon terrors of daily life. King has also written scripts for the films *Creepshow* (1982), in collaboration with director George Romero, and *Cat's Eye* (1985), which present comic-book style vignettes of horror.

(See also *CLC*, Vols. 12, 26; *Contemporary Authors*, Vols. 61-64; *Contemporary Authors New Revision Series*, Vol. 1; *Something about the Author*, Vol. 9; and *Dictionary of Literary Biography Yearbook: 1980*.)

WALTER KENDRICK

[Money] and fame are as nothing compared to the eminence asserted by *Stephen King's Danse Macabre*. For the first time King isn't telling us a story, he's talking about himself—his opinions, his ideas, how he got to be so eminent. . . . We can even pay $65 if we want to, for an autographed limited edition of King's ego-trip. Now that's eminence.

The ostensible subject of *Danse Macabre* isn't really Stephen King; it's the genre of horror fiction as manifested during the last 50 years in magazines, books, movies, and on TV. . . . [But] there's nothing here to interest an aficionado, and a newcomer to horror (if anyone older than six could be so innocent) will get no worthwhile guidance either from King or from the dozens of pointless illustrations that pad out his already over-stuffed pages. The only interesting thing in *Danse Macabre* is Stephen King, and the only interesting thing about him is the phenomenon of his success. How on earth can such an aggressively vapid nincompoop have risen so high so fast?

Danse Macabre makes it seem inevitable. As King tells it, the horror tradition leads directly to him, its culmination. In fact, though, since horror fiction doesn't really develop but scours the same ground again and again, the genre is a vast junkyard, heaped with the leavings of other writers, through which Stephen King singlemindedly sifts, scavenging.

Until now it's been easy to dismiss him. Reviewers have been doing it every time he comes out with a new book, and most of them will probably do it to this one, too. If you value wit, intelligence, or insight, even if you're willing to settle for the slightest hint of good writing, all King's books are dismissible, and *Danse Macabre* is the worst of the bunch. It's hard to tell which is worse—the utter vacuity of the ideas or the foolish flatulence of their expression. Lest you think I'm a snob ("I'm no snob," says King in a footnote, "and if you are, that's your problem"), let me give you some samples of the wit and wisdom of Stephen King.

On international affairs: "that old poop the Ayatullah (sic) Khomeini." On television: "the bottomless pit of shit." . . .

But I'm not being fair. It's a strange thing to say about a professional writer, but it's unfair to quote Stephen King. His words are the worst thing about him. The man can't write. Sound asleep I can turn out a better sentence than he could on the brightest day he ever had. King and I are about the same age (going on 34). I'm smarter than he is, better looking, too, I think. So why am I cranking out this review for peanuts while he rakes in millions? Because he's a genius. God damn it.

I've had this problem with Stephen King ever since, a few years ago, a friend of mine forced a paperback of *'Salem's Lot* on me and said, "Read this. You'll love it." . . . I read *'Salem's Lot*—furiously, monomaniacally. . . . I was enthralled. I finished the whole thing in four hours.

I hated myself in the morning; I felt glutted and dirty, as if I'd just swallowed a gallon of Cool-Whip. King's prose has a lot in common with this synthetic goo that can never go stale because it was never fresh: it's a featureless flood of cliches, uniformly tasteless and absolutely unthreatening, never asking you to feel or think anything that isn't totally familiar. And though his books are always monstrously too long, somehow this is soothing, too, because you can slither through whole pages in a second, confident that the general drift suffices; the words don't matter.

Later I read *The Shining* (I bought it myself). It confirmed my first judgment: Stephen King works by shotgun-overkill. *The Shining* trots out every imaginable haunted-house cliche at least three times, with no effect to make them add up to a total or converge on any goal. . . . [Yet the novel is effective] because each of King's prepackaged shocks works at its moment and can be forgotten as his endless prose gushes past.

I suppose this sounds patronizing, but I'm tremendously envious of what King does, and I have to do something to appease my meaner emotions. There's unmistakable genius in Stephen King, and though it's genius of a trivial kind . . . , still it's inimitable. . . . King . . . [writes] with such fierce conviction,

such blind and brutal power, that no matter how hard you fight—and needless to say, I fought—he's irresistible.

Everybody knows (even King admits it) that though horror fiction seems to aim at making your flesh creep, it's the most reassuring of genres, since all the ghoulies and ghosties it conjures up get comfortably dispersed at daybreak, and since it scrupulously avoids all the real horrors of life. . . . Horror fiction is invincibly complacent. Its final message always is: You already know all you need to know, and everything you know is true.

King is aware of this much, and it's not surprising that he should be. What is surprising, though, is that in his real life, at least as *Danse Macabre* portrays it, the same rule prevails. Nothing more complacent than the life King describes, nothing more satisfied with things as they are, always were, and always must be, could be imagined by even the most fiendish of horror writers. . . . [He] leads the perfect prefab American life, a nonstop margarine commercial.

In order to succeed in horror fiction, you seem to need the ability to ignore real life altogether, to dispose for good of the irksome myth that a writer must write from experience, even if that experience be only the rollercoaster ride of his own heart. King's life contains no pinnacles, no abysses; it sets him free to forage in the junkyard of his genre, where nothing need be done but what's been done before, where the writer's raw material isn't raw at all—it's predigested. . . .

Vapid, formless, unoriginal, questioning nothing and adding nothing to our knowledge, Stephen King deserves his eminence. Lord knows, I can't match it; I never seriously thought I could, but *Danse Macabre* has convinced me. At this point I could launch into a melancholy attack on the moral bankruptcy of a culture that rewards the masturbatory escapism of a Stephen King while relegating to obscurity much better writers (me, for example) who refuse to pander to its senile desires. But that would be a cliche, too. If King is a symptom of our culture, so am I—only he has genius, and all I have is misgivings.

> Walter Kendrick, "Stephen King Gets Eminent," in The Village Voice, Vol. XXVI, No. 18, April 29-May 5, 1981, p. 45.

MICHELE SLUNG

Danse Macabre, a one-man flea market of opinions and ideas, will certainly be a treat for those avid readers of horror, fantasy and science fiction who like nothing better than to sit around, after a George Romero double-feature followed by a late-night rerun of "The Twilight Zone," and recall the great days of E. C. Comics. However, for those who have little interest in accompanying Mr. King on a highly discursive ramble through byways lined with other people's monsters and mad scientists, this book may prove both boring and baffling, a trick instead of a treat. . . .

Excess is Mr. King's stock-in-trade, and he has used his prodigious energies over the years to soak up vast quantities of material about weird literature and film. In a spirit of the utmost good humor and generosity, he now spews out all the thoughts he's been storing up, sharing his crotchets and promoting his pets. Mr. King, who possesses an enviable superabundance of imagination, suffers from a less enviable logorrhea. Along with hundreds of names, relevant and irrelevant, . . . we are exposed to thousands of Kingian pronouncements; there is nothing that doesn't elicit an opinion from him—or a definitive statement.

As he admits, he cannot resist "following any trace of interesting scent." He digresses with glee, never reins in his garrulity and always says what he is thinking—a veritable fetishist of his own synaptic responses. It's one thing to learn what were the books and movies of Mr. King's youth, another to be told what year he was toilet-trained (1950). But perhaps one ought to overlook this self-indulgence, a flaw by almost any standards, since the flood of his prose is swept along by so much warm affection for a sort of writing that, outside a narrow circle, is often underappreciated. . . .

Mr. King approaches the various notions he explores as if he were handling a midway bumper car: He drives up to a concept and bangs it from all directions, particularly those beliefs that he holds most fervently: "Story *must* be paramount over all other considerations in fiction" and "The horror story is in many ways an optimistic, upbeat experience."

Danse Macabre ranges widely over the past 30 years, even pausing to touch on what Mr. King considers the "*bedrock of horror fiction . . . you gotta scare the audience.*" A clearly stated dictum, which only Mr. King would deem it necessary to elaborate on immediately: "Sooner or later you gotta put on the gruesome mask and go booga-booga."

Mr. King's class-clown mannerisms—his fascination with nose picking and clogged pores, his fondness for words such as puke, yuch and dreck—are partly a defense mechanism, I believe. He has serious thoughts and ambitions and wants to be taken seriously; at the same time, he's a little bit jumpy about it.

I grew up at exactly the same time as Mr. King, and our touchstones for that period are identical. . . . Like Mr. King, I remember worrying about the three lives of Herbert Philbrick, the challenge posed by Sputnik I, and "the spectre of juvenile delinquency."

There's a lot of sociology interwoven among the trivia about comic books like Tales From the Crypt and movies like *The Thing,* not the least of which is what it was like to grow up in the 1950's and come of age in the 60's.

Anyone susceptible to the lure of good or bad "fright artistry" will acknowledge all the contradictions inherent in explications of it. We hear from Mr. King that the horror genre "deliberately appeals to all that is worst in us," yet is also nutritive, "salt for the mind." It can "be reactionary, anarchistic, and revolutionary all at the same time." Moreover, Mr. King proposes "that only people who have worked in the field for some time truly understand how fragile this stuff really is, and what an amazing commitment it imposes on the reader or viewer or intellect and maturity." Kids, on the other hand, get it right off the bat, lifting "the weight of unbelief with ease." (pp. 15, 27)

Not all moviegoers or readers enjoy being scared, and some believe "that an interest in horror is unhealthy and aberrant," a tenet Mr. King struggles mightily to refute. He succeeds, although by the end of *Danse Macabre* he's reeling groggily from the effort. But then, despite my reservations about his stylistic predilections and my cavils about his tastelessness, I was on his side from the very start.

Many of us are drawn to the horror story, as Pandora to the box or Jonathan Harker to the forbidden rooms in Castle Dracula, though we are protected by the safety net of fictional distance. Mr. King simply wants to remind us of what Joseph Conrad once wrote in *Lord Jim:* "As long as there is any life before one, a jolly good fright now and then is a salutary discipline." (p. 27)

Michele Slung, "Scare Tactics," in The New York Times Book Review, *May 10, 1981, pp. 15, 27.*

BRIAN MORTON

It has never been clear quite how we should take Stephen King. His hugely successful novels—*Carrie, The Shining, Salem's Lot* and now *Firestarter*—each combine a curiously dogmatic documentary realism with a pretentious and "literary" portrayal of abnormal psychology, while at the same time a wry dismissiveness undermines the horror, suggesting that King may indeed be putting us on. Like film-maker John Carpenter, King is a deft manipulator of his audience; his books tease and taunt our innate fears, never confirming their reality, never denying their existence.

Stephen King's Danse Macabre . . . is the horror writer's homage to his genre. Part autobiography, part analysis, the book connects King's own practice to the horror novels and films of the past 30 years. What links all of these, or King's selection from them, is a cathartic relief, close to laughter, as we face down our fears; this is true even at the extremes of H. P. Lovecraft, Carpenter's *Halloween,* Hooper's *Texas Chainsaw Massacre,* where laughter is, quite consciously, part of the horror. In the era of Treblinka, Manson's "Helter Skelter", the "White Night" at Jonestown, horror and sf movies build psychic bulwarks which compress and contain the whole process of alienation, always ending with the comforting news that "The present danger . . . is over." . . .

The unease King generates in *Danse Macabre* stems from a simple stylistic idiosyncrasy. He writes about "disestablishment and disintegration", "the set of reality", our "phobic pressure points" but instantly highlights the pomposity of much of this with [slang] expressions. . . . There is little consistency of argument or tone. Lee Oswald becomes "a nurd with a fourteen dollar mail-order gun"; Albert Camus and pop star Billy Joel are flung together; both it seems, write (or sing) about Strangers.

King's embarrassment at the whole venture is instructive. As a working practitioner, and a phenomenally successful one, he is clearly ill at ease with the intellectual formulations which attach themselves to his chosen genre. Horror, almost uniquely, links the graduate seminar with the best-seller lists; Erich Segal's *Love Story* fits no academic curriculum, *Carrie* does and has. King's belief that horror is central to our collective awareness, that it "dances" evilly through our lives, is best served when he avoids an acquired jargon. His gobbets of psychoanalysis and cultural sociology are spread only unevenly on his autobiographical base. It is never clear how well King understands his borrowed methodologies. . . . His awareness of its artistic potential is constantly underlined by its irruption into everyday life: JFK's assassination; rock'n roll destruction; Vietnam; most poignantly, an October afternoon in 1957 when a matinee of *Earth vs. the Flying Saucers,* attended by the ten year old King is interrupted to announce the Cold War shock of Sputnik I. . . .

The culture-shocked ten year old is still in there. So too in his books, the confusions of intent and register suggest much about our age and the writer's ambivalent role; what a dream to be paid for disgust and horror, and what an anxiety. Perhaps, as he constantly suggests, Stephen King is quintessentially the child of our times.

Brian Morton, *"Carrie on Screaming,"* in The Times Educational Supplement, *No. 3399, August 21, 1981, p. 18.*

DOUGLAS E. WINTER

Stephen King's novel of journey, *The Stand* (1978) . . . , signaled a definite turning point in his fiction. Prior to this work, his novels and short stories were structured, for the most part, within the boundaries of the traditions of horror. *The Stand* would be the first of several highly successful novels that transcended specific literary formulas. . . .

Like Tolkien's famous *The Lord of The Rings*, *The Stand* takes the form of a noble quest and employs a host of characters, some heroic, some darker and indeed monstrous. . . . *The Stand* creates a modern myth, portraying the timeless struggle between good and evil in terms and geography distinctly American yet subtly alien: evil haunts not dark, clammy caverns or mist-laden mountains, but the cornfields of Nebraska, the backroads of Montana, and the oil refineries of Indiana. Its seat of power is not Mordor but Las Vegas. Evil does not strike with sorcerous spells . . . , but with .45 caliber pistols, radio-controlled explosives, Phantom jets, and nuclear warheads. . . . (p. 55)

In the brief introductory note to his American epic poem *Paterson;* William Carlos Williams described the essential quality of the modern epic: ''A taking up of slack; a dispersal and a metamorphosis.'' So too are these essential qualities of *The Stand*. The novel's first third is a creation myth involving the ''taking up of slack'': the birth of a new world through the destruction of our modern world. The motive force is a ''superflu'' that escapes from a secret military installation. Called ''Captain Trips'' . . . , the superflu is 99.4% pure, not unlike Ivory Soap, and its infection is always fatal. Only six-tenths of one percent of the population, who are inexplicably immune to the superflu, survive its cleansing onslaught. (p. 56)

Much of the power of King's epic draws upon the juxtaposition of the world that was with the post-apocalypse wasteland. The Gothic tradition has always played a major, but unspoken role in apocalyptic fiction, and *The Stand*, much like Mary Shelley's *The Last Man* (1826) and Shirley Jackson's *The Sundial* (1958), brings that tradition to the foreground. In particular, apocalyptic fiction implicitly invokes the ''dual life'' or ''dual landscape'' theme present in most Gothic fiction and, indeed, used as a touchstone for much criticism of all nineteenth-century literature. . . . This portrayal of duality attempts to burrow beneath surface illusions to reach the inevitably dark reality below. Thus, in Bram Stoker's *Dracula* (1897), the king vampire's castle is schizoid: its upper levels include a Victorian library and well-furnished apartments, while underneath lie labyrinthine vaults; likewise, Dr. Seward's mansion encloses an insane asylum. Similar landscapes are presented in *The Stand*—for example, the Disease Center in Vermont is a bright, sterile environment that exudes order and authority but is transmuted to a maze-like chaos, filled with death and dread.

This duality of life and landscape is the central metaphor of *The Stand*. Superimposing the illusions of our modern world upon the ravished landscape of catastrophe, King explores the strange mixture of myth and reality that comprises our perception of America. . . . (pp. 56-7)

This dual landscape, psychic and geographic, provides the setting for the remainder of the novel, which takes the form of the quest so common in epic literature. The ''dispersal'' and ''metamorphosis'' quickly focus on the traditional epic struggle of man against monster: Odysseus confronting Scylla and Polyphemus, Beowulf squaring off with the Dragon. By the Fourth of July, less than three weeks after the epidemic begins, only the immune remain, and a new America rises purposefully from the human rubble. The survivors are visited with strange and often highly personalized dreams involving two recurring images: a dark, faceless man offering enticement and threat, and an ancient black woman who exudes peace and sanctuary. These images form the parameters of a choice between good and evil in which each individual's intrinsic predisposition plays an important role, and that choice divides the survivors into opposing camps: the evil forces at Las Vegas, the forces of good at Boulder, Colorado. (pp. 57-8)

The protagonist of *The Stand* is Stu Redman, the factory worker from Arnette, Texas, his soft-spoken, stoic reliability evoking Gary Cooper, Clint Eastwood, and other archetypal American heroes. He is the character to whom we are first introduced, and he is one of the few lead characters to survive the novel; as his last name suggests, he is the new native American. Yet despite his traditional heroic and American qualities, his role is one of continuum—he does not change through the course of the novel. The critical character is burnt-out rock musician Larry Underwood, whose internal strife places him on the knife-edge between good and evil, hinted at by his name. As his mother ironically realizes before dying of the superflu that Underwood may have communicated to her: ''(T)here was good in Larry, great good. It was there, but this late on it would take a catastrophe to bring it out.'' . . . Underwood is particularly interesting because he lacks traditional heroic qualities; he is self-destructive and avoids taking personal responsibility.

The entwined fates of Redman and Underwood culminate in the novel's final third, when ''the stand''—the confrontation between good and evil—occurs. . . . When Redman, Underwood, and two others go to take ''the stand,'' Redman's leg is broken *en route;* he must be left alone in the desert while the others proceed to Las Vegas. His ''stand'' takes place in isolation, as if it were a reaffirmation of his individualism. Underwood, the rock performer, must take the center stage, this time to die before the masses. (pp. 58-9)

The focal point of the wrong—west—side of the Rocky Mountains is Randall Flagg, the Dark Man, the ''Walkin Dude.'' His earliest memory is of attending school with Charles Starkweather, but he also recalls meeting Lee Harvey Oswald in 1962, riding with the Ku Klux Klan, cop-killing with black men in New York City, and whispering plans to Donald DeFreeze about Patty Hearst. (p. 59)

Yet Randall Flagg is neither Satan nor his demonic spawn. He is an atavistic embodiment of evil, the ''last magician of rational thought.'' . . . Flagg is the epitome of the Gothic villain: his appearance is indistinct, malleable, a collection of masks. . . . Like many Gothic villains, Flagg is curiously inept, helplessly watching his well-laid plans go awry at every turn. He is a rhetorician of self, seemingly obsessed with convincing himself and others of his importance and destiny. And as the novel's climax discloses, Flagg, like Tolkien's Sauron, is a straw man who literally collapses when confronted. (pp. 59-60)

Although the most mystical of King's novels, *The Stand* is also his most explicitly didactic work. The paradoxes of myth and reality that seemingly riddle the fabric of American society are the Gordian Knot, split and unwinding in the ruins. This sociopolitical subtext poses difficult questions about order and authority. Humans need companionship, but companionship produces society, which in turn seemingly requires order. To have order, someone must have authority—and someone must be subject to that authority. Order and authority benefit us by providing a stable society and technological change. However, they also mean oppression, the atomic bomb and the spectre of Captain Trips. . . . (p. 61)

> *Douglas E. Winter, in his* Stephen King, *Starmont House, 1982, 128 p.*

STEVE GALLAGHER

For a while now, I've been trying to come to terms with something I cannot easily understand. As I've gradually been sliding into fandom over the last couple of years, I've also been falling out of love with SF. . . . I'd like to talk about a minor SF work that made a brief appearance on the bookstands and then faded away without leaving much of a trace. It was called *The Long Walk* by one Richard Bachman; I think I saw a single medium-temperature review of the book in a British fanzine.

Rumor reached me a couple of weeks before it appeared that *The Long Walk* was, in fact, a pseudonymous effort from Stephen King, and so I went looking. King is one of those writers whose works I tend to devour. . . . He's what I'd call an invisible stylist; subtle without being obviously clever, stylish without being showy, providing dazzle without obvious razzle . . . I hate him. . . .

Not everybody agrees with me about King; the commonest criticism I've heard is that his books are out of balance, his attention to character exceeding his attention to plot. All I can say is, I've never found it to be so. . . . Faith was restored by my discovery of the *Gunslinger* series . . . , a thundering dud. I fell on it with relief. . . .

[*The Long Walk*] had an indifferent cover with one of those "in the great tradition of . . ." copy lines that serve more as a warning-off than as encouragement; in this case, the "great tradition" was that of *Rollerball*. The similarities are so superficial that they're barely worth talking about; near-future society, public catharsis achieved through a nationally-hyped contest involving genuine suffering and death. However, whilst the *Rollerball* movie turned out to be little more than Conan on rollerskates, *The Long Walk* avoided showy action and heroics; here the story is of a group of ordinary teenagers, all volunteers, walking until they drop. Those who drop and don't get up are shot where they lie; at the end, the single survivor is declared the winner and allowed to name his own reward.

And that's really all the plot there is. Internal evidence for the book being one of King's is high and for me, convincing. . . . The no-frills, sharply evocative style is immediately recognizable, and there are at least two images that reappear, word-for-word, elsewhere in King books. . . .

The Long Walk is by no means a poor work, so I think we have to look elsewhere for an explanation of the pseudonym. Maybe it covers a collaboration, but I don't believe this. More likely, is the idea that it's a response to genre pressures. (p. 35)

The Long Walk isn't the best SF I've ever read, but it's better than most. What really elevates it for me is the craft-quality that is brought to bear on a simple subject, a few dozen kids shuffling down a road and gradually reducing in numbers. . . . [There] isn't a slack passage in any of the 250 pages. Imagine the toughness of it as a writing exercise; you're not even allowed to vary the ages of your characters to provide differentiation. That the characters stand clearly and separately in the reader's mind without needing any of the old pulp "tags" is a clear indication that what we have here is no simple hackery, but the real stuff, clearly previsualized and sincerely executed. (p. 36)

> *Steve Gallagher, "Standing by Jericho," in* Science Fiction Review, *Vol. 12, No. 1, February, 1983, pp. 35-6.*

DIANE C. DONOVAN

[In Bachman's *The Running Man*] America in the year 2025 is a nation of abject poverty which exists alongside a wealthy community. The tie that binds these two opposing poles is the FreeVee, which produces TV game shows in which the stakes are not money but life and death. Ben Richards, a poor man with a sick child and a foul mouth, sets out to beat the odds, entering the game show where the nation is his hideout and the cash stakes rest upon his ability to survive in a world of hunters eager to see him die. The fast-moving plot with a variety of complex twists and turns will maintain the interest of SF readers. . . . [An] intriguing, unusual plot with moral undertones, provides a combination of action and unexpected developments which older readers used to complex plots will welcome for leisure reading material.

> *Diane C. Donovan, in a review of "Running Man,"* in Voice of Youth Advocates, *Vol. 6, No. 1, April, 1983, p. 44.*

JAMES EGAN

Stephen King uses several genres of popular literature in his work, two of the most important of which are the Gothic and detective modes. That these modes are related, that they share several characteristics, has not gone unnoticed. Many Gothicists have also written detective novels. . . . Though the literary relationship between the genres is familiar, Stephen King's use of them is distinctive and striking. He sets the two in opposition and their opposed relationship helps to define his literary aesthetic. The rational, empirical, deductive procedures of detection are mocked by the Dark Forces which hold sway in his fiction.

Throughout his work King shows an awareness, by means of allusions to and citations of other modern Gothicists, that he writes in a Gothic mode. . . . King refers to Bram Stoker, Algernon Blackwood and H. P. Lovecraft. It is these Gothicists . . . , to whom King is primarily indebted. Of course, many gothic props, devices and character types permeate his fiction. . . . Vampires are central to *'Salem's Lot,* while assorted demonic characters parade through *The Stand.* John Rainbird in *Firestarter,* Randy Flagg in *The Stand* and Gregg Stillson in *The Dead Zone* are all Gothic villains, reincarnations of an old stock-character type. . . . Many of King's settings (the Overlook Hotel in *The Shining* and the Marsten House in *'Salem's Lot,* to cite but two) are manifestly Gothic as well.

Perhaps most important, the aesthetic texture of his fiction is Gothic. King writes what David Punter calls "paranoiac fiction," a mode which Punter identifies closely with Gothicism. In King's world little can be trusted, for that world lacks security and stability. Punter also demonstrates that Gothicism is heavily involved with taboos—culturally, morally or psychologically forbidden areas. King has, in *Danse Macabre,* acknowledged his fascination with taboos. . . . The Gothic novel, as Elizabeth MacAndrew points out, puts "the ordinary world in touch with the mysterious." . . . [Horror] is—ubiquitous, conspiratorial, enduring. . . . The evil and dread [King] deals with are, moreover, both immanent and transcendent, located in the dark corners of the psyche as well as in the dark corners of the universe. Yet for King the mysterious is not unequivocally evil—a complex moral ambiguity surrounds the actions of such characters as Carrie White, John Smith and Charlie McGee. . . . [The] author "endorses neither a rational nor a supernatural explanation" of character or event. King, like other Gothicists, typically refuses to allow the reader "an end of it": the supernatural phenomena he evokes remain "at large, both in the story and in the reader's mind." . . . In short, King's stock-in-trade is metaphysical mysteries which resist explanation.

However, King is also very familiar with detective fiction and continues to write in the genre. His first professional sale, in fact, was a mystery-detective story—**"The Glass Floor."** . . . That King has been noticed by the detective-writing establishment is evidenced by John D. MacDonald's introduction to *Night Shift,* King's collection of short stories. . . . Moreover, murder, police procedures and other matters, both criminal and non-criminal, requiring investigation and detection in the narrow and broad senses of those terms, are fundamental features of his fiction. (pp. 131-34)

When one examines how King treats detection in his work, it is apparent that his Gothic and detective modes are antithetical. King pits police procedures and rational investigations of all sorts against the transcendent mysteries of his Gothic universe. A sizeable portion of *The Dead Zone's* plot is devoted to the mystery of the Castle Rock killer; that portion may be described as a police-procedural. The investigation flounders, however, because of one of detective fiction's commonest cliches—faulty procedures and sub-par investigators. None of the investigators is able to accept the simple premise that the murderer could be one of them: a small-town boy, a cop. In this overlooking of the obvious one hears a distant echo of Poe's "The Purloined Letter." Sheriff George Bannerman's tactics and the standard operating procedures of the FBI produce either irrelevant data or no leads at all. Although Bannerman has clues that point to Frank Dodd, a Castle Rock cop toward whom Bannerman has a fatherly disposition, the sheriff has lost his objectivity and impartiality in dealing with Dodd. This failing is one reason why the investigation is dead-ended. . . . Frank Dodd is not a supernatural antagonist, but simply one who makes no mistakes and who has remarkable good luck. As a result, standard procedures can't catch him.

Enter John Smith, psychic. At "wit's end," Bannerman calls Smith and presents him with the accumulated clues. Very quickly, Smith's ESP alerts him to the identity of the killer. . . . Ironically, it is Smith's psychic power and his "methods" which alarm Bannerman, who distrusts and resents Smith at first. But the story's point is clear—the crime can be solved only by a method which transcends the pat rationalities of police procedures.

Having disposed of Frank Dodd, Smith turns to a more complex and ambiguous matter, the apprehension of a dangerous political criminal, Gregg Stillson. The FBI cannot prove that Stillson is guilty of anything, much less the political "crimes" Smith's psychic vision tells him Stillson will commit in the future. Crimes which haven't happened can't be crimes. There is no way to investigate the future; to understate the issue, the future is not tangible and empirical. . . . In the final third of the novel, Smith becomes a full-fledged psychic detective, using second-sight and following parapsychological clues: *The Dead Zone's* conclusion is thus the culmination of a lengthy tracking and chase scenario. . . . Smith has apparently done a "good" deed, but troubling questions remain. Has Smith not engaged in a criminal act by attempting to assassinate Stillson? Who is to say that Smith's psychic intuition about Stillson's capability for starting a nuclear war was correct? Weren't Stillson's rights violated? Wasn't he presumed to be guilty and pursued by a psychic vigilante instead of being proven guilty? Don't Smith's actions have disturbing implications for the normal, rational procedures of law enforcement? To these questions *The Dead Zone* offers no answers. (pp. 135-37)

The White Commission Report and several other "studies" cited in [*Carrie*] are equivalent to a scientific and psychological investigation of Carrie's case. Data of all sorts has been collected, including eyewitness testimony about Carrie's death and the Chamberlain holocaust itself. Unquestionably, the Commission is in possession of many reliable facts and much empirical information, from which they draw some accurate conclusions about telekinesis and Carrie White. Under the circumstances, they reconstruct what could easily be considered a "logico-temporal" sequence of events.

However, the fact remains that the White case simply overwhelms the procedures of detection and scientific inquiry for a variety of reasons and in a variety of ways. . . . The Commission cannot even detect the extent of Carrie's guilt because, ironically, there is so little *empirical* proof that Carrie actually caused the damage. There were "witnesses" to Carrie's destructive intentions; however, the witnesses "heard" only psychic messages from Carrie. . . . The criminal investigation fails in Carrie's case because there is so little conventional, empirical evidence that she was guilty of any criminal acts.

The investigation of Carrie's psyche is equally inconclusive. . . . Was Carrie in full control of her telekinetic ability? At one point Carrie herself recognizes that it has grown alarmingly fast. . . . There is also considerable confusion in Carrie's mind over her own identity. She wonders whether her power is divine or demonic. . . . Carrie clearly had religious fantasies of vengeance, perceiving herself on several occasions as an avenging angel of the Lord. Was Carrie suffering from the same religious mania which affected her mother? The Commission pays little heed to the possibility of transcendent moral realities, whether divine or demonic, in Carrie's life. The cause-and-effect conclusions psychologists draw negate the occult or preternatural aspects of her experience. As a result of that negation, the conclusions they draw are largely invalid. (pp. 140-42)

Scientific detection, then, has concerned itself with irrelevant trivia and has drawn many faulty or misleading rational conclusions. . . . By disregarding the complexities of Carrie's telekinesis and confusing the issue of her motives and behavior, the Commission fails to reach the metaphysical plane on which much of Carrie's story took place. The White Commission neglects to report on the Gothic universe.

A mystery is likewise central to King's plot in *The Shining*. This time Jack Torrance is the investigator. Unlike his counterparts in the stories referred to earlier, Torrance is neither a police detective, a scientist, nor a psychologist. He is an amateur, a literary-historical detective who wants to research the history of the Overlook hotel and write a book about his findings. Jack's search begins when he finds a "scrapbook" about the Overlook in the hotel's basement. He pores through the scrapbook, spending increasing amounts of time in the cellar, and then consults newspaper records to fill in blanks in the Overlook's history. However, as Torrance follows the clues, he rather than the mystery becomes unraveled. The investigation releases Jack's inner demons (guilt, suicidal tendencies, insecurity, paranoia) and exposes him to the Overlook's transcendent evil.

Virtually as soon as Jack opens the scrapbook, an eerie haze settles over him and his family. . . . Torrance's mind turns to suicides, strange deaths, the ghosts of the Overlook. Soon he becomes obsessed by the scrapbook and is driven to discover whose it was and how it wound up in the cellar. Self-destructive impulses surface as Jack calls Stuart Ullman and harangues the outraged hotel manager about the Overlook's sordid past. . . . The book is a catalyst and a lure—the more Jack probes into the clues the worse both he and the mystery become. In the cellar, mulling over the book and other documents from the Overlook's past, he has a grotesque dream of his family-abusing father, a dream which foreshadows his own fate. While Jack broods in the cellar, his world begins to crumble. . . . Not until he has degenerated into a demonic lackey of the hotel, who plans to kill his family to please his "employer," does Torrance learn the deepest secrets of the scrapbook. His detective work ends when he is told that the supernatural "manager" of the Overlook left the scrapbook for him to find. . . . At this point only a few traces of the human remain in the detective. To the bitter end, the Overlook has teased his curiosity about itself, his desire to solve its riddles. (pp. 142-43)

The patterns which characterize King's use of detective and Gothic motifs are clear. Detectives of every sort are present in his novels: local police, state and federal investigators, physical scientists, psychologists, literary and historical sleuths, amateurs and professionals. . . . They earnestly apply logic, sift through factual data and employ the latest scientific aids available—all in an attempt to establish a plausible "logico-temporal" order of events. . . . King's sleuths have wandered into uncharted territory, the Gothic universe, where standard operating procedures are inoperative or counterproductive. King's Gothic universe is sentient and it characteristically reacts with anger to those who pry into its secrets. (p. 144)

> *James Egan, "Antidetection Gothic and Detective Conventions in the Fiction of Stephen King," in* Clues: A Journal of Detection, *Vol. 5, No. 1, Summer, 1983, pp. 131-46.*

ANNIE GOTTLIEB

Besides being a literate and sometimes lyrical prose stylist, Mr. King is one or our pre-eminent novelists of parenthood and its piercing vulnerabilities, a distinction he reclaims for himself in *Pet Sematary*. His portrayal of contemporary life, especially in small town New England—a setting he returns to again in this new book—is sensuous and accurate to the detail. He has been criticized for throwing in too many brand names, but that's time-capsule realism. The macabre irony of paying for a child's coffin with a MasterCard—a detail from *Pet Sematary*—is specific to our age.

Even as a horror writer, Mr. King delivers more than just a masterful handling of the conventions. . . . [It] is in the spaces of unease among . . . familiar gargoyles that Mr. King really shows his art. He is obviously an intelligent, sensitive and voluptously terrified man who writes horror stories as a way of worrying about life and death. . . . King's most original and chilling inventions are innocuous objects or animals that the anxious imagination animates with a subtle, horrid menace. In *Firestarter*, it was a faintly sexual garbage disposal unit. In *The Shining*, it was a live fire hose. And in *Pet Sematary*, it's a white cat named Church (short for Winston Churchill) who is . . . well, not quite a cat anymore.

To begin at the beginning, there is something very wrong in Ludlow, Maine. . . . Whatever it is, it is there in Ludlow, waiting in the Pet Sematary that the kids keep up in the woods and in the old Micmac Indian burying ground beyond it.

Into this disturbed field wanders (or is lured?) Louis Creed, a physician in his 30's, with his wife, 5-year-old daughter and infant son. Creed is in the venerable tradition of the rational man . . . , whom the dark powers love to get hold of and rend. His rationality is his flaw. He lacks sufficient kinship with darkness to evade it. . . .

As a doctor, Louis Creed thinks he accepts death. But it's an unexamining, shallow-rooted acceptance. What he can't bear is his wife's and daughter's fear of death, a fear precipitated by a visit to the Pet Sematary. Actually Rachel and Ellie are both far more resilient than he is, and they eventually come to terms with death in their emotional way. . . . When Church is killed by a truck . . . it seems both compassionate and logical that the kind old man across the road should take Creed into the woods and show him the town's dark secret—how to "fix" Church, but good. But not so good. [When the cat returns to life following its burial], Creed has made a Faustian bargain. He has sold his soul for the power to give life—after a fashion. . . . Now there is no going back.

Like most of Mr. King's novels, *Pet Sematary* loses credibility toward the end, as it gains in gore. Loss of control of, and perhaps interest in, his material after the midpoint is a recurrent flaw (disastrous in *The Stand* and *The Shining*) that Mr. King has moderated but not entirely overcome. Nor is *Pet Sematary* his best book as a piece of writing. (To me, that honor goes to *Cujo*—also, interestingly, the King novel in which the supernatural element is most muted and metaphorical.) It is, however, his grimmest. Through its pages runs a taint of primal malevolence so strong that on each of the three nights it took me to read it, both my companion and I had nightmares. Reader, beware. This is a book for those who like to take their scare straight—with a chaser of despair.

> *Annie Gottlieb, "Something Lurks in Ludlow," in* The New York Times Book Review, *November 6, 1983, p. 15.*

DOUGLAS E. WINTER

In early 1979, King was serving as writer-in-residence at the University of Maine. His rented house bordered a major truck route—a road that seemed to consume stray dogs and cats. Despite precautions, one day a passing truck claimed his daughter's cat, and King was faced with the disconcerting tasks of explaining to his daughter what had happened and then burying the cat.

It was on the third day after the burial, he reports rather ominously, that the idea for [*Pet Sematary*] came to him.

What would happen if a young family were to lose their daughter's cat to a passing truck, and the father, rather than tell his daughter, were to bury the cat on a remote plot of land—something like a pet cemetery. And what would happen if the cat were to return the next day, alive but fundamentally different—fundamentally *wrong*. And then, if a member of that family were to fall victim to another passing truck. . . . The book would be a conscious retelling of W. W. Jacobs' "The Monkey's Paw," that enduring short story about parents who literally wish their son back from the dead. (pp. 1, 11)

Precisely because of King's closeness to its subject matter, *Pet Sematary* is one of the most vivid, powerful and disturbing tales he has written. His hallmarks—effortless, colloquial prose and an unerring instinct for the visceral—are in evidence throughout, but this novel succeeds because of King's ability to produce characters so familiar that they may as well have lived next door for years.

Louis Creed, a young physician, has moved his family from Chicago to Maine, where he will manage a university infirmary. Creed is apparently the most hard-headed of rationalists: "He had pronounced two dozen people dead in his career and had never once felt the passage of a soul." His wife, Rachel, on the other hand, shrinks with preternatural fear from the very thought of death. . . . When an elderly Downeaster, Jud Crandall, takes the Creeds to visit the "Pet Sematary" in the woods behind their rented house, their 6-year-old daughter, Ellie, immediately fears for the life of her cat, wryly nicknamed Church. . . .

Ellie's cat indeed dies, and Crandall initiates Creed into the secret that lies beyond the Pet Sematary—an ancient burial ground long-abandoned by Indians. Creed buries the cat there, and it returns—awkward, loathsome to touch, stinking of sour earth, but *alive*—setting the stage for a haunting moral dilemma: whether, regardless of the cost, death should be cheated. When . . . [Creed's infant son] is killed, Louis Creed's mourning is not that of a sentimental Pieta, but the driven ambition of a Faust. Should he take the body beyond the Pet Sematary? "You do it because it gets hold of you," Crandall warns. "You do it because that burial place is a secret place, and you want to share the secret . . . You make up reasons . . . they seem like good reasons . . . but mostly you do it because you want to."

"Death is a mystery, and burial is a secret," King tells us here, and in those few words pinpoints the key to his popularity and the abiding lure of the uncanny for writers and readers alike. . . . But as *Pet Sematary* makes clear, the horror story—at its most penetrating, important moments, those of the immaculate clarity of insight which we call art—is not about make-believe at all. It is a literature at whose heart lies our single certainty: that, in Hamlet's words, "all that live must die." And the horror story, like a ride on a good roller coaster, serves as a full-dress rehearsal for death. In the darkness, the night, the eternal negation of the grave, we gain access to truths about life that we might not otherwise find. . . .

Pet Sematary delivers, not simply for those who love a tale well told, but for those who like to think about what they read. Despite some faults—King moves his actors on and off stage

with undue convenience and occasionally lapses into the overwriting that has marred his lengthier novels—this book offers the rare exhilaration of being scared within the safe limits of art, and the opportunity to exercise our need, as rational beings, to grapple with the fact of our mortality. (p. 11)

> *Douglas E. Winter, in a review of "Pet Sematary,"* in Book World—The Washington Post, *November 13, 1983, pp. 1, 11.*

MICHAEL E. STAMM

For several years there have been rumors that Stephen King had written a novel even he felt might be too horrifying ever to publish. *Pet Sematary* (a child's spelling) . . . is that novel. . . . [It] is a harrowing story, plumbing depths of blackness King has never reached—nor, I think, wanted to reach—before. The novel returns to the Maine of '*Salem's Lot* (1975) and *The Dead Zone* (1979), country that King knows and loves, and depicts it in prose that is almost poetry. But it is a darker poetry this time; the landscape is peopled with ancient shadows drifting more and more thickly around the lives of the storied inhabitants, and the reader senses the coming of a night [without] end.

Pet Sematary is—as always with King—a powerful story, but it is not *quite* the book it could have been. The characters are fractionally less complete than usual; they are sometimes seen in glimpses, their individual natures occasionally obscured by plot exigencies—seldom a King weakness. The tale is quite grim, and seems somehow unfinished; the last chapter seems almost to have been thrown together for an ending which is (and I use no hyperbole whatsoever) relentlessly horrifying, but somehow inappropriate—as well as less complex and frightening than it might have been, ghastly though it is. It is as if King wanted to get *out* of the story's awful darkness and was less careful than usual about how he did so. . . .

Pet Sematary is nevertheless a great read, and King treats its horrors for the most part seriously and with ruthless honesty as well as compassion and insight, and craft which shades often into real art. A disturbing book, it is probably not the place for readers new to King to start; it will be snapped up by King fans—though it may tell them things about life, and death, that they would rather not know. (p. 36)

> *Michael E. Stamm, in a review of "Pet Sematary,"* in Science Fiction & Fantasy Book Review, *No. 20, December, 1983, pp. 35-36.*

JOSEPH F. PATROUCH, JR.

Stephen King is surely a fantasist, the kind who makes us face, in a variety of disguises, what each of us sees as the ultimate irrationality of the universe: our own personal deaths. (p. 9)

[Some] of King's stuff is clearly and indisputably science fiction. The short story, "**I Am the Doorway**," for example, is about an astronaut returned from orbiting Venus and the curious disease he brings back with him. And *The Stand:* a mutated virus escapes the lab and kills 99.9 percent of the people on earth, and the survivors must band together to survive, a staple in science fiction at least since Mary Shelley's *The Last Man*.

A second point: when I started reading through King's books this summer. . . . I began with *Carrie*. I didn't understand then (and I don't understand now) how anyone can read *Carrie* as anything other than science fiction. *Carrie* is not possessed; she is simply a young girl afflicted with secret hidden powers of the human mind, secret hidden powers that she is too young and immature and confused to control. Her secret hidden power is telekinesis, a wild talent we have all read about many times over the years. Actually, *Carrie* is a science fiction novel . . . , the type in which scientifically implausible things like faster-than-light drives and parallel worlds and time travel have been accepted into the science fiction canon because of the work of a whole tradition of writers since H. G. Wells.

A third point: King clearly likes children afflicted with secret hidden powers of the human mind. Beside Carrie, we have Danny Torrance in *The Shining,* Leo Rockway in *The Stand,* and of course the pyrokinetic Charlie McGee in *Firestarter.* Science fiction characters all, and King has read his science fiction and knows these characters. . . . So it seems to me that we shouldn't forget that Stephen King, whatever else he may be, is also a science fiction writer.

One final "it seems to me" before I quit. Science fiction writers are constantly talking about "breaking out of category" to the big audience and therefore the big money. *Stranger in a Strange Land* and *Dune* were two of the first books to show that scientific novels could do this. One of the more fascinating things about what King has done is that he has found a new way to break out of category. He located and exploited an area where science fiction and occult/psychic/horror novels might be said to overlap. I really wonder how *Carrie* escaped being published as another 2500-copy "Doubleday SF line" novel. . . . Pulling off this marketing coup may just be the most fantastic thing Stephen King has yet done. (pp. 9-10)

> *Joseph F. Patrouch, Jr., "Stephen King in Context,"* in Patterns of the Fantastic, *edited by Donald M. Hassler, Starmont House, 1983, pp. 5-10.*

MICHAEL E. STAMM

[*Cycle of the Werewolf*] is really a short novella, told in 12 chapters, one for each month of a year in Tarker's Mills, Maine. As always in King's work, the milieu is beautifully done; the strokes of characterization are broad but very sure, the people convincing, and the sense of place is wonderfully realized.

As a werewolf story . . . it isn't unusually impressive; though it is strongly hinted fairly early, the identity of the werewolf is not revealed until late in the story, and so not much is done with the nature of the werewolf itself. Always seen from *outside,* the monster might almost be considered a metaphor for the monstrous, irrational darkness that sometimes erupts into the light of 'normal' life; the story has some of the same feeling as *'Salem's Lot,* which is no small praise.

> *Michael E. Stamm, "Not for the Average King Fan,"* in Fantasy Review, *Vol. 7, No. 2, March, 1984, p. 32.*

KEN TUCKER

[Two] chums-in-horror [King and Straub] have yoked their word processors together to attempt the creation of the ultimate boy's book [*The Talisman*]. . . . Their plucky little hero, 12-year-old Jack Sawyer, has a Hollywood has-been hag for a mother; she is dying of cancer. Her husband long dead . . . , she and Jack leave Hollywood for a little hotel in New Hampshire, where Lily Sawyer assumes she'll die in peace.

Fat chance: Jack, noble and ordinary, clenches his prepubescent fists and determines to save his mom. He meets up with a wise old black man—the same stereotype we've met in King's *The Shining;* let's face it, it's Scatman Crothers—who shows him how to enter (or "flip," in the pervasive jargon of the book) into an alternate world: the Territories, a parallel universe peopled with "twinners"—medieval folks who bear a rough correspondence to their Earth equivalents. This is a literary device as awkward as it is to explain, and all it accomplishes in the novel is to enable Jack to flip into the Territories and arrive dressed in the proper period clothing, so he doesn't alarm the peasants.

What *The Talisman* amounts to is Straub and King's variation of *The Lord of the Rings,* with the mythos of the story lowered to the everyday language King deploys so well. All the clichés of the fantasy novel are here: a mythic quest, strange creatures that help or hurt, a callow youth who grows to manhood over the course of the book. But Straub and King add something: the kid's name is Jack Sawyer; the first section of the book is called "Jack Lights Out." Are you—duh—beginning to get it? . . . S&K seemed to think that writing a book that crosses Twain with Tolkien would be really keen.

Well, about half of it is. The first half, when we can still enjoy the screechy rants of Jack's mother, and before our hero gets stuck in the Territories slaying slobbering werewolves and pondering the meaning of being a man for hundreds of pages at a time. The exceptionally kind, humorous yet wholly unsentimental empathy Stephen King has shown for children in every book he's written is evident here in the early scenes of Jack's utter desolation upon realizing that he's in for a long, long adventure—one that may result in his mother's death. It is, of course, impossible to ascribe anything to one particular writer in a collaboration. . . . Nonetheless, Jack Sawyer's breezy conversational style and the casual way the supernatural scares the shit out of the kid in the opening chapters of *The Talisman* is far more reminiscent of King in *Pet Sematary* than Straub in name-your-choice. To put it another way: the first half of *The Talisman* is concerned with scariness-through-simple-story-telling, King's trademark; the second half is obsessed with literature-through-delirium, Straub's favorite affectation. . . .

It's also interesting that *The Talisman* isn't particularly scary; doesn't really try to be. There is a lot of graphic violence, but it is overwhelmed by all of the sappily good friends Jack makes in the course of his journeys. *The Talisman* reads like a detailed draft for a big-budget family fantasy film. . . .

> *Ken Tucker, "Boo! Ha-ha, You Sap!"* in The Village Voice, *Vol. XXIX, No. 43, October 23, 1984, p. 53.**

ANNA SHAPIRO

[*The Talisman*] is *The Wizard of Oz* written as a boy's adventure, with spacey adumbrations on the theme of good and evil and their symmetry in the universe. Jack Sawyer is the boy, his scarecrow is an old black man named Speedy Parker, his cowardly lion is a cheerful werewolf and the Tin Woodman is his human but ultra-rational cousin Richard. The yellow brick road may be U.S. 40, while Oz is a quaint country known as the Territories. . . . The talisman, the object of his quest, is the Wizard. Unlike the Wizard, the little crystal ball is not a fraud but "the axle of all possible worlds" with which Jack's mother, a former Sandra Dee-type actress known as the "Queen of the B's," and her "twinner," the Queen of the Territories, will be able to rise from their deathbeds. . . . There are quantities of blood and of worms crawling out of things, and of each character's verbal tag tacked to every utterance—"Yeah bob," "Right here and now," "God pound his nails," "Can you gimme hallelujah,"—until you could hum them in your sleep. Tricky typography stands in for description until it seems the purpose was to circumvent language rather than use it, and the black and white fairy-tale logic goes a metaphysical gray toward the end. *The Talisman* is absorbing but not, oddly enough, fun to read.

> *Anna Shapiro, in a review of ''The Talisman,'' in* The New York Times Book Review, *November 4, 1984, p. 24.*

JANICE EIDUS

[In Richard Bachman's *Thinner,* the] overweight and affluent Billy Halleck, a successful lawyer, lives comfortably in Fairview, Conn., where (like all his neighbors) he worships money, sex and food. Clearly, though, something terrible is destined to befall Billy. We know this because *Thinner* is really by Stephen King, the reigning king of literary terror. . . . And, indeed, terror does arrive when a band of gypsies comes to town and Billy, not paying attention to his driving, runs over and kills a gypsy woman. The gypsies retaliate by placing an amusingly ironic curse on the portly Billy. He will grow so thin . . . that he will die. The novel's suspense supposedly lies in whether—and how—he can convince the stubborn gypsies to remove the curse. But *Thinner* is so burdened with cardboard characters, seemingly endless descriptions of Billy's weight loss and painful jokes ("A conductor's voice shouted in his mind, *Next stop Anorexia Nervosa! All out for Anorexia Nervosa!''*) that the terror and suspense never fully materialize. Instead, it becomes far more suspenseful trying to guess whether Mr. King/Bachman will ever tire of using the brand names he incessantly tosses about. We learn far more about Lacoste shirts, Rolex watches, Bausch & Lomb soft contact lenses and Jordache jeans than the people wearing them. Finally, though, even that bit of suspense fades . . . , and *Thinner,* for all its padding, can be seen for what it is—a pretty thin book.

> *Janice Eidus, in a review of ''Thinner,'' in* The New York Times Book Review, *April 14, 1985, p. 27.*

DAVID ANSEN

The Stephen King triptych movie, *Cat's Eye,* . . . [succeeds] at whipping up some droll shivers. The drollery, however, may be more essential here than the shudders: the tone is closer to the comic horror of *Christine* than to the jump-out-of-your-seat moments in *Carrie.* Satirical sadism informs the first episode . . . [about] a heavy smoker who puts himself in the hands of an outrageous outfit called Quitters, Inc., run by a jovial maniac . . . who has devised some brutally effective methods for keeping a guy off the evil weed. . . .

The second tale revolves around the twin addictions of gambling and power. An odious Atlantic City high roller . . . makes a deal with an aging tennis pro . . . who wants to run off with his wife. If the tennis pro can walk around the five-inch ledge of his high-rise apartment, he can have the wife and loot for life. Lewis Teague, the director, does cliff-hanger suspense very well, but can't conceal the lack of novelty in King's script.

The final episode involves a terrific alley cat [and] a little girl . . . who wants a pet and a nasty gremlin that lives inside her

bedroom wall. This creature . . . manages to be equally hilarious and horrific as it climbs onto [the little girl's] bed, holds her nose and attempts to steal her breath away. A far more accomplished anthology than *Creepshow, Cat's Eye* assumes an honorable but not exalted position in the multimedia King empire. But expect as many giggles as goose bumps: this is a movie which features cameos by Christine the car, Cujo the dog and a hardback copy of *Pet Sematary.*

> *David Ansen, ''Catcalls and Wolf Whistles,'' in* Newsweek, *Vol. CV, No. 18, May 6, 1985, p. 73.**

PETER NICHOLLS

Skeleton Crew makes it obvious that King is not worried now, if he ever was, about his pulp-magazine past. There are stories here from 1968 onwards. . . . These days he can afford to be amused by his own juvenilia . . . and rightly so. The early stories are pretty good, but the real winners are recent.

There are two poems (better than some of you might have expected) and 20 stories. Four stories are classics. The other 16 are, without exception, highly readable; eight definitely above average and none of them contemptible. Other critics might call the score a little differently, but overall there can be no argument: the big guy from Bangor, Maine, has made another touchdown. (p. 1)

King is, of course, well known as an excellent contriver of laid-back New England dialect . . . , and also of a generalized downmarket prose, either straight-from-the-shoulder or filtered-through-the-beercan. But it would be a mistake for King to become over-confident about his mastery of the common touch. In his afterword he tells an anecdote about the difficulty he had in selling a story (**''Mrs. Todd's Shortcut''**) to women's magazines. It seems that two of them turned it down ''because of that line about how a woman will pee down her own leg if she doesn't squat.'' Well, Steve, I don't want to be difficult, but the same line made me wince too, and it didn't do a bit of good to the story; it makes a likeable narrator seem momentarily insensitive, even vulgar. I suspect that a lot of us plain folks who admire King's work do so in spite of, and not because of, this sort of thing. . . .

But one's adverse judgments are really quite mild. Several of the stories, as with too many genre short stories, are of the kind which one describes to friends in sentences that begin ''Did you ever read the story about . . . ?'' . . . [**''Survivor Type''**] is well told, but once you have heard someone say, ''Did you ever read the story about the man on the desert island who got so hungry he ate himself?,'' there is not a lot of point in reading the actual story. As gross-outs go, I preferred the scene in **''The Raft''** where a teen-age couple, menaced by a floating and carnivorous blob, make desperate love. . . .

The short story is not, on the face of it, a form to which King's undoubted talents are suited. Polished gemstones of precision are not his line, and mandarins and collectors of lapidary delights should seek their pleasures elsewhere. One joins King for more leisurely, outdoor pursuits: a ramble through the graveyard perhaps, with the chill of fall in the air.

Even in the short story, however, King's refusal to be hurried can pay dividends, especially in **''Mrs. Todd's Shortcut,''** a vibrant, memorable tale about a young woman obsessed with the possibility of finding ever shorter automobile routes between her home village and Bangor, 79 miles as the crow flies. As the shortcuts become more elaborate, the back roads wilder and the distance shorter, it is no longer certain through what dimension these tracks are cutting, but some nasty little animals get caught up in the radiator grille. Part of the story's strength lies in the ironical, moving contrast between the relaxed telling of the tale and the mad hurry it encapsulates.

The other three classics vary in tone. **"The Monkey,"** perhaps, cuts closest to the white dead bone in its tale of a children's toy which laughs and bangs its cymbals when death is due. Here King's well known sore spot (highly visible in *Pet Sematary*), which has to do with parental love and fear and mortal threats to children, is hectically picked at yet again. On a much more expansive and amusing note, **"The Mist"** (almost a short novel) is by far the best supermarket-menaced-by-horrible-monsters story ever likely to be written, and some of the nastiest monsters are human. . . .

Finally, something out of the way for King: a piece of true-blue surrealism, beautifully judged and paced, **"Big Wheels: A Tale of the Laundry Game (Milkman⁄2)"**. The horror in this one bubbles up through the beercans that are central to its imagery, and the reader discovers more about the soft white underbelly of blue-collar life than he could conceivably want to know.

Skeleton Crew is probably better than the first collection, *Night Shift*, and as good in its very different way as the second, *Different Seasons*. King does not have too much to worry about, though he has one failing, perhaps because he likes to be liked. In a few too many stories (including the last, **"The Reach"**) he sacrifices the hard edge of his vision for something that can only be called cute. (p. 7)

> *Peter Nicholls, "Beach Blanket Books: 'Skeleton Crew',"* in Book World—The Washington Post, *June 16, 1985, pp. 1, 13.*

CHUCK MOSS

Skeleton Crew is a veritable cornucopia of the nasty, the horrible, the cruel, or the just plain unearthly. "Here's a chance to really grab people by the gag reflex and throttle them," King once said of one of these stories, a macabre little tale of self-cannibalism called **"Survivor Type,"** at a time when no editor would publish it. . . .

Along with **"Survivor,"** which reaches for your gorge as advertised, this compendium includes **"The Raft,"** a ditty of some sweet college students and a waterborne Thing that will make you swear off skinny dipping forever. It also includes **"Nona,"** whose moral appears to advise against picking up hitchhikers; **"Here There be Tygers,"** which suggests that the next time your kids report monsters in the bathroom, you'd better believe them. . . .

It also includes several examples of King as science fictioneer. **"Beachworld,"** for one, is competent sci-fi—and of course, even in the far future, the bottom line is horror.

What's the deal here? Is King genuinely obsessed with the macabre, or is he just writing what sells? A little of both, probably. . . .

Now, there's nothing wrong with this. Heck, we all love to be scared. Who doesn't like reading a story that ruins your day, makes you afraid to sleep, and leaves an ugly image that haunts you for weeks? So why, after staggering from King's spook house, does a body feel, well, just a little used?

Perhaps because there's a calculating undertone to this project: King knows just what reflexes to grab and how to grab them. Rather than poking around in the id, he sticks his finger down your throat—and there's a big difference. Read *Skeleton Crew*, by all means, if you're devoted to King or to horror as a genre. But don't be surprised if you find it 1980s state of the art: effective, cold, technically perfect—and ultimately banal.

> *Chuck Moss, "Multiple Shivers from a Champion of the Game,"* in The Detroit News, *June 16, 1985, p. 2K.*

MICHAEL R. COLLINGS

King has not divorced [his novels written under the pseudonym of Richard Bachman] from his others; they explore many of the same themes from different perspectives. In style, theme, structure, and characterization, they are identifiably Stephen King.

Stylistically, the five novels [*Rage, The Long Walk, Roadwork, The Running Man,* and *Thinner*] reflect King's techniques, although to differing degrees. There is the same emphasis on realism of presentation through the constant, almost insistent use of brand names to establish the validity of the world King has chosen to explore. His prose is crisp, clear, often blunt—long a trademark in King's fiction. The language is likewise blunt, often crude, but rarely gratuitously so. King does not hesitate to use non-standard diction, but usually reserves it for specific purposes in characterization. The Bachman novels are, if anything, freer in their use of objectionable language than the novels published under King's name.

Similarly, King treats sexuality with greater openness here than in many of his other novels. Characters discuss sexuality and sex acts with less reserve; narrators present the acts in more graphic detail. . . . *Rage* and *The Long Walk* concentrate openly and frankly on developing adolescent sexuality, as did *Carrie*, with the consequence that much of the text is devoted to discussions, comparisons, and denials of characters' sexual identities. *Roadwork* traces a disintegrating marriage through separation, isolation, and infidelity into madness and death; in this sense, it closely parallels *The Shining*, with the systematic destruction of relationships between Jack, Wendy, and Danny Torrance. (pp. 15-16)

As in many of King's novels and short stories, however, sexuality is ambiguous. Necessary for survival, it is also destructive, particularly for adolescents not yet mature enough to cope with their own struggles and the struggles of others. Charlie Decker (*Rage*) and Ray Garraty (*The Long Walk*) each find individual outlets for their fears and frustrations, one through external violence, the other through punishing his body literally to the point of death. . . . The characters actions and the reactions of adults surrounding them are frequently referred to in sexual terms. . . . In sexual terms, no one is secure. (p. 16)

Sexuality transcends merely the individual, however. The Bachman novels also reflect another insistent motif in King's fiction, the disintegration or fragmentation of the family. . . . Ultimately, fathers become threats: Carl Decker describes graphically what he would do to anyone sleeping with his wife, unaware that young Charlie is listening and remembering crawling into his mother's bed after Carl left for work. Throughout *Rage*, Charlie refers to the Cherokee nose-job, an image that epitomizes his hatred of his father. His mother is not much better, however, with her insular attitudes. (pp. 16-17)

Fragmentation leads, in turn, to isolation. The central characters in each of the Bachman novels is increasingly isolated. They lose family, friends, life itself. Charlie Decker makes his own isolation, locking himself away from parents, teachers, friends, and forcing the students he imprisons in the classroom to undergo a similar isolation. (p. 17)

Isolation in turn suggests helplessness, a final motif that unifies the Bachman novels and makes them an inherent part of King's imagined universe. In spite of everything—pain, suffering, death—no one can finally do anything. Characters become enmeshed by social pressure, politics, the external environment; they can no longer control themselves, their actions, or the action of others. (pp. 17-18)

In addition, there are a number of minor elements that clearly connect the Bachman novels with King's larger body of works. Cancer as threat underlies much of his fiction. . . . Cancer strikes without warning, an unseen time-bomb "no larger than a good sized walnut" [in *Roadwork*]. . . .

Thus far, I have said little that could not apply to virtually any of King's fictions. The Bachman novels stand alone, however, in that they develop these images, define these themes, detail these motifs without concentrating on horror. Except for ***Thinner,*** each seems more science fictional or mainstream than we have come to expect in King. The novels contain images of horror, of course. . . . [The] descriptions assert an image of horror, but do not attempt to create the visceral response associated with horror. (p. 18)

This final characteristic is what fully differentiates the earlier Bachman novels from King's other works. They are insistently non-horrific; what horror they evoke is of a radically different order than vampires or ghosts or malevolent, sentient Plymouth Furies can create. More like ***Cujo*** than ***The Shining,*** they assert the actuality of horror within the commonplace. (pp. 18-19)

Michael R. Collings, in his Stephen King as Richard Bachman, *Starmont House, Inc., 1985, 168 p.*

Nella Larsen

1893-1964

American novelist and short story writer.

Larsen is often associated with the Harlem Renaissance, an era of extraordinary achievement in black American art and literature during the 1920s and 1930s. Drawing much of her material from her friendships with Harlem's literary and social elite, Larsen examines the psychological consequences faced by middle-class black women searching for spiritual fulfillment and material prosperity in a male-dominated, race-conscious society.

Larsen's first and best-known novel, *Quicksand* (1928), is a semiautobiographical account of a woman whose racial and sexual confusion contributes to her unfulfilled quest for identity. Like Larsen, the protagonist, Helga Crane, is an educated and cultured young woman of mixed black and Danish ancestry. Helga's refusal to come to terms with her sexuality and her inability to find happiness in either black or white society leads her into a degrading marriage to a semiliterate rural preacher. Larsen was praised for her use of such metaphors as suffocation and drowning to depict Helga's psyche. Arthur P. Davis contends that Helga is "the most intriguing and complex character in Renaissance fiction."

In *Passing* (1929), her only other novel, Larsen relates the tragic story of a light-complexioned black woman who chooses to "pass" as white for economic security and social status. Unlike most novels that discuss the subject of "passing" in broad sociological terms, Larsen develops the theme on an individual psychological level. Although it was less successful than *Quicksand*, Robert Bone considered the novel "the best treatment of the subject in Negro fiction."

Courtesy of Moorland-Springarn Research Center

THE NEW YORK TIMES BOOK REVIEW

Quicksand is not part of the tradition which began long ago when Mrs. Stowe pictured for us Simon Legree beating Uncle Tom, nor is it very much in the tradition which began recently when Van Vechten pictured for us the bright lights and social subtleties of Harlem. Miss Larsen cannot help being aware that the negro problem is a real one, cannot help being aware that negro exhibitionism, in the manner of *Nigger Heaven,* is a vivid and interesting spectacle; but she is most of all aware that a novelist's business is primarily with individuals and not with classes, and she confines herself to the life of Helga Crane.

Helga Crane is the daughter of a negro father and a Scandinavian mother. Her father disappears and her mother remarries, this time a white man. Her mother dies and her mother's people do not like her. An uncle, however, educates her and she becomes a teacher in an efficient negro school. Her life there, her complacent, respectable fiancé, her standardized work, her conventional friends, become unbearable. Robert Anderson, the Principal, tries to restrain her from going away by holding out to her the ideal of service, but in the end he antagonizes her and she runs off.

After suffering in Chicago from poverty and loneliness, Helga lands a good job in New York and becomes part of upper

Harlem life. She re-encounters Anderson, whom she really loves. . . . Nothing comes of their new meeting except that Anderson begins going with Anne, Helga's best friend. Helga comes into some money and goes to Copenhagen to visit an aunt. In Copenhagen she enjoys a curious social success, and even wins a proposal of marriage from a talented painter. But now, with Anderson subconsciously in her mind, she longs for America. She returns to attend Anne and Anderson's wedding.

When it is too late, Helga understands her feeling for Anderson. Depressed, she is exalted by a negro revival and marries an eloquent but ignorant preacher. They go down South and Helga bears him children. She sinks into a slough of disillusionment and indifference. She tries to fight her way back to her own world, but she is too weak and circumstances are too strong.

Miss Larsen offers here no tragedy of ignorance, or of lack of opportunities, or of unfair discrimination, or even of unfitness. The essential tragedy has little to do with Helga's being a negro—no more, at least, than if she were Asiatic or Jewish. Helga has her chances, the reasonable, average number of chances which come to most human beings. In Harlem and Copenhagen she could have made a place for herself. She could have married the man she loved, but her own nature was against her. (pp. 16-17)

This is an articulate, sympathetic first novel, which tells its story and projects its heroine in a lucid, unexaggerated manner.

In places, perhaps, it is a little lacking in fire, in vitality one finds it more convincing than moving. But it has a dignity which few first novels have, and a wider outlook upon life than most negro ones. (p. 17)

> "A Mulatto Girl," in The New York Times Book Review, *April 8, 1928, pp. 16-17.*

ROARK BRADFORD

Here again is the old theme of mixed blood, Negro and Scandinavian, this time, with the North, South, Chicago, Harlem and even Denmark for the backgrounds. The result is interesting.

Sharper pens than Miss Larsen's have dipped into this muddy brown ink and have come out blunted or inarticulate. Duller pens too have tried it and have written verbosely. . . .

The real charm of [*Quicksand*] lies in Miss Larsen's delicate achievement in maintaining for a long time an indefinable, wistful feeling—that feeling of longing and at the same time a conscious realization of the impossibility of obtaining—that is contained in the idea of Helga Crane. (Helga is an idea more than she is a human being; drawing character does not seem to be one of Miss Larsen's major accomplishments.)

Whether it is possible to hold that feeling throughout the entire length of the book is a matter for speculation. It runs beautifully and artistically through the maze of realities and artificialities: the prim correctness of the school at Naxos; the mad rush of Chicago; the intellectual absurdities of Harlem; the cold gentleness of Copenhagen. Now it is languidly encased in the comforts of civilized culture, now it trembles uncertainly to the straining rumble of old Africa. But always it is there—a wistful note of longing, of anxiety, of futile searching, of an unconscious desire to balance black and white blood into something that is more tangible than a thing that merely is neither black nor white, of a nervous, fretful search for that will o' the wisp called happiness.

It leads directly to a splendid emotional climax. The brief scene is at a party in Harlem. Helga is alone for a moment with the man who first understood that strange emotions swelled within her bosom. . . . Her nerves are tuned to a high pitch; her soul is stirred; savagery tears at her heart; the black blood chokes the white, and Africa rumbles through her veins. And the man—suddenly the veneers of civilization crackle about him and—well, the reader is as tense as the two actors in the drama.

But alas! Without knowing just where it comes from, the reader suddenly catches a faint odor of talcum powder. And from that point on the book—in this reviewer's opinion—suffers from odors. Burnt cork, mostly.

In spite of its failure to hold up to the end. [*Quicksand*] is good. No doubt it will be widely read and discussed. The reader, to get the maximum enjoyment, should begin with a mind as free as possible of racial prejudices and preconceived notions and conclusions. Miss Larsen seems to know much about the problems that confront the upper stratum of Negroes, and, happily, she does not get oratorical about what she knows. She is quite sensitive to Negro life, but she isn't hysterical about it. There is a saneness about her writing that, in these hysterical literary times, more than compensates for her faults.

> Roark Bradford, "Mixed Blood," in New York Herald Tribune Books, *May 13, 1928, p. 22.*

THE SATURDAY REVIEW OF LITERATURE

Put together to a large extent from autobiographical materials, Miss Larsen's story of the life and struggles of a mulatto woman, the daughter of a negro man and a Scandinavian woman, is no more than mildly interesting. [*Quicksand*] has a distinctly cosmopolitan touch, as its principal character moves from Tuskegee, called Naxos in the book, to the upper circles of Copenhagen society, from Copenhagen to New York, and from New York back to a little Alabama town as the wife of a typical negro minister of the revivalistic type.

Miss Larsen is herself the daughter of a negro by a Danish woman, and most of the important incidents of the book follow her own life closely. . . . [However], it is in her one direct departure from her own life story as the framework of her book that she becomes wholly unconvincing. She would have us believe that her young and attractive mulatto woman, after life has failed to please her, could fall in love with and marry a man far beneath her in every respect and be willing to bear his children—one a year—and to endure the unutterable stupidity of an Alabama village.

A great love even between two people so different as her Helga Crane and the Reverend Mr. Pleasant Green might account for such strange behavior, but there is nothing to indicate that any such feeling exists.

The silly assertion on the jacket of the book that "it is almost the only Negro novel of recent years which is wholly free from the curse of propaganda" indicates, it appears to this reviewer, that the jacketeer has not read much of the new fiction dealing with the negro. Most of it is altogether free from propaganda, freer indeed, than Miss Larsen's book.

> A review of "Quicksand," in The Saturday Review of Literature, *Vol. IV, No. 43, May 19, 1928, p. 896.*

W.E.B. Du BOIS

I think that Mrs. Imes, writing under the pen name of Nella Larsen, has done a fine, thoughtful and courageous piece of work in . . . [*Quicksand*]. It is, on the whole, the best piece of fiction that Negro America has produced since the heyday of Chesnutt, and stands easily with Jessie Fauset's *There is Confusion,* in its subtle comprehension of the curious cross currents that swirl about the black American. . . .

Nella Larsen . . . has seized an interesting character and fitted her into a close yet delicately woven plot. There is no "happy ending" and yet the theme is not defeatist like the work of Peterkin and Green. Helga Crane sinks at last still master of her whimsical, unsatisfied soul. In the end she will be beaten down even to death but she never will utterly surrender to hypocrisy and convention. Helga is typical of the new, honest, young fighting Negro woman—the one on whom "race" sits negligibly and Life is always first and its wandering path is but darkened, not obliterated by the shadow of the Veil. White folks will not like this book. It is not near nasty enough for New York columnists. It is too sincere for the South and middle West. Therefore, buy it and make Mrs. Imes write many more novels.

> W.E.B. Du Bois, in a review of "Quicksand," in The Crisis, *Vol. 35, No. 6, June, 1928, p. 202.*

EDA LOU WALTON

To tell the story of a cultivated and sensitive woman's defeat through her own sex-desire is a difficult task. When the woman is a mulatto and beset by hereditary, social and racial forces over which she has little control and into which she cannot fit, her character is so complex that any analysis of it takes a mature imagination. This, I believe, [is why] Miss Larsen is too young to have the book, *Quicksand,* as a first novel. The attempt is to present Helga Crane not as a young colored woman, but as a young woman with problems unique to her temperament, and her background one largely of her own choice. Supposedly, save for a deep-rooted weakness, she has the vitality to manipulate the machinery of her days. But of this we are never quite convinced. As portrayed, the character is not quite of one pattern. Now it is Helga, the aesthete, the impulsively intelligent girl whom we feel; now it is Helga, the mulatto, suffering from an inferiority complex about her mixed ancestry, her lack of social status. Since she is supposedly complex, her character should be turned to us as a jewel of many facets. Instead we get it as a piece of bright red glass or as smoke-colored.

Besides the difficulty of incomplete characterization there is the fault of fine-writing in the worst sense of that word. The opening paragraph is a good example of that elaborateness of uninteresting detail into which Miss Larsen plunges in order to assure us that her Helga is cultured and modern. (p. 212)

Miss Larsen writes a little too carefully of the objective evidences of culture and too carelessly of the refinement within the woman herself. We are told again and again that Helga is restless, unhappy, passionate, but we don't believe it until, arbitrarily, Miss Larsen introduces proofs of action.

Quicksand is, for all this comment, a good tale, and a good first novel. Miss Larsen's prettiness of style may, with more writing, become power. She will undoubtedly learn a more effectual working out of laws of cause and event within characters. She has already the ability to interest us in her people and their problems.

But she has not in this first book anything of the usual richness and fullness of character presentation, or the zestful interest in life in Harlem that other novelists of Negro life have given us. (p. 213)

> *Eda Lou Walton, in a review of "Quicksand," in*
> Opportunity, *Vol. VI, No. 7, July, 1928, pp. 212-13.*

MARGARET CHENEY DAWSON

Among white people there seem to be two common attitudes toward Negroes, one that they are a different order of beings with utterly foreign feelings and thoughts, the other that they are, in a sad, luscious way, entirely romantic. Nothing startles the white man so surely as the discovery of a simple, dignified routine in the life of educated Negroes.... This technique has been used in Negro fiction before, but not, I think, in the unselfconscious, taken-for-granted way in which Miss Larsen uses it in *Passing.* Indeed, she seems so unaware of its effectiveness that she throws all the emphasis of her story onto those spectacular phases of the race problem which are more commonly supposed to be interesting. Nevertheless, it remains one of the most arresting things in her book.

Passing refers to the quiet slipping across the color line practiced by so many fair-skinned Negroes, and the story concerns particularly the fate of Clare Kendry, white-faced, golden-haired beauty, whose passage was completely successful until a yearning for her own kind led her to take fatal risks. Opposed to this precarious, rootless existence and passionately anxious for a recognized stability, stands Irene Redfield, Clare's old schoolmate. Between these two the race issues develop, then become tangled and obscure. At first, Irene protects Clare out of race loyalty; later because she fears that detection and divorce from the ignorant Mr. Kendry (a white man) would leave Clare free to finish the seduction of her own husband, Brian. Throughout she holds a curious attitude toward Clare—another interesting aspect to the white reader—a mixture of contempt and admiration, envy and disgust. In the end, when Kendry discovers Clare at a Harlem party, Irene's emotions merge into sheer hatred.... They called Clare's fall from the window "death by misadventure." But Irene herself was not quite sure.

Any novel that deals with a public problem can be judged either for the sharpness of its point in controversy or for distinction of style. As a piece of writing. *Passing* can only be called adequate. Perhaps the romanticism that associates the Negro with powerful rhythms and broad good humor is false as far as this newer generation is concerned. It is doubtless well that we be pricked to consciousness of growing sobriety and responsibility among them. But the flat, unimpassioned sentences are a disappointment to an expectancy of beauty. However, that strange excitement arising from the mere mention of race, as from the word sex, holds one's interest to the end.

> *Margaret Cheney Dawson, "The Color Line," in*
> New York Herald Tribune Books, *April 28, 1929,*
> *p. 6.*

THE NEW YORK TIMES BOOK REVIEW

Nella Larsen is among the better negro novelists. She writes a good, firm, tangible prose, and her dialogue is convincing except when she is trying to give you an idea of how intellectual people talk at a party. While she is neither as rhythmical nor as pungent as Claude McKay, and nowhere near as much a creature of the five senses, she still manages to capture color, scent and atmosphere in her simple, direct sentences. She is not especially concerned with presenting her milieu; apparently she is willing to take for granted that her reader knows that negroes live in Harlem and Chicago. Unlike other negro novelists, and white novelists who write about negroes, she does not give her following a bath in primitive emotionalism. She is not seeking the key to the soul of her race in the saxophone to the exclusion of all else.

What she is after in *Passing* is the presentation of two psychological conflicts. Both are set forth from one point of view: that of Irene Redfield, a negro woman who, although she has a skin light enough to "pass" for Caucasian, prefers to maintain her racial integrity. The first conflict concerns the attitude of Irene Redfield toward another woman of some negro blood, a quite lovely girl who is "passing" for white. The second problem of *Passing* is the lovely girl's unquenchable desire for negro company, even when it is liable to endanger the life with a white man that she has built up for herself....

Miss Larsen is quite adroit at tracing the involved processes of a mind that is divided against itself, that fights between the dictates of reason and desire. She follows the windings of Irene Redfield's thought without chasing the fleeting shades of cerebral processes into blind alleys; hence she is not a good stream-of-consciousness writer, but rather a good recorder of essentials.

There are two criticisms to be made of *Passing*. The most serious fault with the book is its sudden and utterly unconvincing close, a close that solves most of the problems that Miss Larsen has posed for herself by simply sweeping them out of existence through the engineered death of Clare Kendry, the girl who is passing. The second fault may not be a fault at all; it may merely reveal a blind spot in the reviewer. But fault or not, Clare Kendry seems a little too beautiful to be true; she seems to be Miss Larsen's apotheosis of half-caste loveliness. . . . But perhaps she is not as lovely as all that; perhaps she just seems that way to Irene, through whose eyes she comes to the reader.

But in spite of the suspiciously "made" ending, and in spite of Clare's posed beauty, *Passing* is on the whole an effective and convincing attempt to portray certain aspects of a vexatious problem. The fact that it is by a girl who is partly of negro blood adds to the effectiveness. . . .

"Beyond the Color Line," in The New York Times Book Review, *April 28, 1929, p. 14.*

W. B. SEABROOK

Negro writers seldom possess a sense of form comparable to that of Miss Nella Larsen. Her new novel, *Passing,* is classically pure in outline, single in theme and in impression, and for these reasons—if for no others—powerful in its catastrophe. The whole tragedy is prepared and consummated in less than fifty thousand words, without the clutter of incident and talk which impede the progress of most novels, and without a single descent, so far as this reviewer could perceive, into sentimentality. The sharpness and definition of the author's mind (even when her characters are awash in indecision) are qualities for which any novel reader should be grateful. . . .

As a matter of technique, Miss Larsen should either have told us the story of Clare Kendry directly, without the device of an intervening personality, or else have made the device-character interesting enough to mean something to us. As it is, we are impatient with Irene Redfield's tortures because they cut off our view of Clare.

It is in the creation of that character, not always perfectly realized but always strongly felt, that Miss Larsen's best achievement lies. Form alone could not do this. (p. 1017)

In describing the gradual surrender of Clare to the fascination of the Negro, her final return and death, Miss Larsen has made an unusually powerful appeal to the sensibilities and imaginations of her readers.

In some other respects the author has not been so successful. Although the writing is of good quality in general, it does occasionally lapse into the sort of jargon we call "literary." There is no reason, for example, for Miss Larsen to say "the rich amber fluid" when she means tea. . . . These occasional elaborations are disconcerting in a work which otherwise seems so clear and chaste. Similarly, one wonders whether the author does not slightly exaggerate the wit and elegance of the salons of Harlem. Such wit and tone as Miss Larsen describes ("brilliant, crystal-clear and sparkling," with "nonsensical shining things" being thrown into "the pool of talk") have not been common this side the water, or indeed anywhere else since the eighteenth Century. And when examples of this esprit are given

("you're as sober as a judge," is the first of them) one wonders what Madame du Deffand would have had to say about them.

These occasional evidences of self-consciousness are undoubtedly due to the fact that Miss Larsen, like most other Negro writers, is aware of a mixed audience; a large proportion of her readers must be white people, which is to say, either uncomprehending or hostile. But there is a great deal less of this self-consciousness in Miss Larsen than in most writers of her race. She has produced a work so fine, sensitive, and distinguished that it rises above race categories and becomes that rare object, a good novel. (pp. 1017-18)

W. B. Seabrook, "Touch of the Tar-brush," in The Saturday Review of Literature, *Vol. V, No. 43, May 18, 1929, pp. 1017-18.*

ESTHER HYMAN

Miss Nella Larsen has felt the innate drama of her protagonists [in *Passing*] but her well-planned story, written with a quiet and careful artistry, has not completely fulfilled the promise inherent in her theme. Her three central characters are well realized. . . . But there is not sufficient depth to the background against which these are painted. Even in these days of tolerance and broad-mindedness towards artistic forms, a mere forty thousand words are not sufficient to develop a theme of importance against a firm and satisfying background.

The device of taking for granted the reader's interest in and knowledge of life among Harlem's cultured upper class would be successful in a short story and is not without effectiveness here. But the dramatic climax lacks conviction, not so much because of its inherent improbability as because of the insufficiency of the preparation—it needs a very decided push, such as could scarcely escape the attention of a crowd of people with gaze concentrated upon the victim, to send a woman hurtling through a window. Against a more richly-painted background these creations of Miss Larsen would have stood out as memorable figures. (p. 428)

Esther Hyman, in a review of "Passing," in The Bookman, *New York, Vol. LXIX, No. 4, June, 1929, pp. 427-28.*

MARY FLEMING LABAREE

I like *Passing* for its calm clear handling of a theme which lends itself to murky melodrama. But this quality of calmness and clearness does not and has not entailed the blinking of a single element in the stupid Nordic complex and its unlovely sequelae. The tragedy is told with an economy of words, but its full import is unmistakable. A throb of *the urge to speak out* runs through it.

Also . . . we have a competent piece of story-telling: both plot and people move logically to their appointed end. Yet somehow, it fails to be a great story, and with the given ingredients, it might have been great and greatly moving. I wish with all my heart that instead of bringing forth another novel next year, Mrs. Imes would, after a decade of brooding, give the world its needed epic of racial interaction between thinking members of the American social order belonging to both African and European stocks.

Mary Fleming Labaree, in a review of "Passing," in Opportunity, *Vol. VII, No. 8, August, 1929, p. 255.*

ROBERT BONE

Drawing upon much the same material as Jessie Fauset, Nella Larsen was more successful in infusing it with dramatic form. Even her less important novel, *Passing* (1929), is probably the best treatment of the subject in Negro fiction.... Unfortunately, a false and shoddy denouement prevents the novel from rising above mediocrity. *Quicksand* (1928), on the other hand, is tightly written; its subtleties become fully apparent only after a second reading. The narrative structure of the novel is derived from a central, unifying metaphor; its characterization is psychologically sound; and its main dramatic tension is developed unobtrusively but with great power. (p. 102)

The key to the narrative structure of *Quicksand* is contained in a passage toward the end of the novel in which Helga Crane rebels against her lot as a brood mare: "For she had to admit it wasn't new, this feeling of dissatisfaction, of asphyxiation. Something like it she had experienced before. In Naxos. In New York. In Copenhagen. This differed only in degree." Helga's quest for happiness has led her, floundering, through a succession of minor bogs, until she is finally engulfed by a quagmire of her own making. The basic metaphor of the novel, contained in its title, is supported throughout by concrete images of suffocation, asphyxiation, and claustrophobia. Associated always with Helga's restlessness and dissatisfaction, these symbols of a loathsome, hostile environment are at bottom projections of Negro self-hatred.... (p. 103)

On one level, *Quicksand* is an authentic case study which yields readily to psychoanalytic interpretation. Each of the major episodes in Helga's life is a recapitulation of the same psychological pattern: temporary enthusiasm; boredom, followed by disgust; and finally a stifling sense of entrapment. Then escape into a new situation, until escape is no longer possible. Race is functional in this pattern, for it has to do with Helga's initial rejection and therefore with her neurotic withdrawal pattern. Her tendency to withdraw from any situation which threatens to become permanent indicates that she is basically incapable of love or happiness. No matter how often she alters her situation, she carries her problems with her.

Deserted by her colored father and rejected by her white stepfather, Helga's quest may be viewed as the search for a father's love. The qualities of balance and security which she finds so appealing in Danish society; her attraction for Dr. Anderson, an older married man; her desire for "nice things" as a substitute for the security of parental love; and her belated return to religion can all be understood in these terms. Her degrading marriage to a jackleg preacher who "fathers" her in a helpless moment plainly has its basis in the Oedipal triangle. Her unconscious need to be debased is in reality the need to replace her mother by marrying a "no-account" colored man not unlike her gambler father. Such an interpretation can never be a substitute for aesthetic criticism, but it is useful as verification of Larsen's psychological depth and skillful characterization.

The dramatic tension of the novel can be stated in terms of a conflict between Helga's sexuality and her love for "nice things." Her desire for material comfort is static; it is the value premise on which the novel is based.... Helga's sexuality, on the other hand, is dynamic; its strength increases until she is overwhelmed and deprived of the accouterments of gracious living forever.

At Naxos, during the period of her frigid romance with James Vayle, Helga's inner conflict is as yet only dimly perceived.... After a visit to a Harlem cabaret, she discovers "a

shameful certainty that not only had she been in the jungle, but that she had enjoyed it." In Copenhagen, when Axel Olsen paints a sensual portrait of Helga, she denies the likeness, only to be told: "You have the warm, impulsive nature of the women of Africa, but the soul of a prostitute."

Olsen's insight is fully justified by Helga's subsequent behavior. Disappointed by her chosen lover, she sells herself in marriage to the Reverend Green. The meaning of the marriage, as far as Helga is concerned, is plain enough.... Lest the thematic significance of Helga's sexuality be lost upon the reader, Larsen poses the alternatives once more at the end of the novel: "It was so easy and so pleasant to think about freedom and cities, about clothes and books, about the sweet, mingled smell of Houbigant and cigarettes in softly lighted rooms filled with inconsequential chatter and laughter and sophisticated timeless music. It was so hard to think out a feasible way of retrieving all these agreeable, desired things. Later. When she got up. By and by." ... (pp. 104-05)

At this point the tone of the novel, which arises from the author's attitude toward her material, becomes decisive. Helga's tragedy, in Larsen's eyes, is that she allows herself to be declassed by her own sexuality. The tone of reproach is unmistakable. It is this underlying moralism which differentiates *Quicksand* from the novels of the Harlem School. It is manifested not in Helga's behavior, which is "naturalistic" and well motivated, even inevitable, but in the symbols of luxury which are counterposed to the bog, in the author's prudish attitude toward sex, and in her simple equation of "nice things" with the pursuit of beauty.

A comparison of Larsen's best novel with the best work of Claude McKay may help to sharpen the contrast. Objectively, Helga Crane's fate is not much different from that of Bita in *Banana Bottom*. Bita, too, having been educated for something "higher," returns to a folk existence in the end. That one author interprets this event as a tragedy and the other as a natural expression of cultural dualism is a measure of their respective attitudes toward bourgeois society. Two normative judgments are involved: an evaluation of "nice things" and an evaluation of the folk culture. Nella Larsen sees beauty only in "gracious living," and to her the folk culture is a threatening swamp. Yet within the limits of her values she has organized one aspect of Negro life into a complex aesthetic design. (pp. 105-06)

Robert Bone, "The Rear Guard," in his The Negro Novel in America, *revised edition, Yale University Press, 1965, pp. 95-108.*

HIROKO SATO

Quicksand is a very cleverly wrought novel. If you compare it with Jessie Fauset's novels, it will become evident what a gifted writer Nella Larsen is. She knows the craft of fiction: how to write effectively and economically, how to keep artistic unity, and how to maintain the proper point of view. Her interest lies mainly on the psychological and not on the social side of the matter. The title, *Quicksand,* signifies the heroine Helga Crane's sexual desire, which was hidden beneath her beautiful and intelligent surface and came up at an unexpected moment and trapped her. (pp. 83-4)

This book is an interesting and curious one. The heroine is always looking for a place where she could find peace of mind. It seems to me as if she is a forerunner of Joe Christmas of

William Faulkner's *Light in August*. As a child of a white mother and black father, Helga could not identify herself with either race. Nella Larsen uses materialism and sensuousness to express these two worlds. In Helga these two tendencies exist together.... It is impossible to satisfy these two sides at the same time. White people were deprived of vitality and haunted with the anxiety for existence, while "everything had been taken from those dark ones, liberty, respect, even the labor of their hands." It seems to me that Nella Larsen, using a very particular situation of mixed blood, expresses a tragic situation which faces us, our loss of our identity in this dehumanized and materialistic society and our need for materialistic comfort.

Mr. Robert Bone thinks that Nella Larsen gives a moral judgment on Helga [see excerpt above].... (p. 87)

He is wrong. There is no moral judgment at the end of the book. Certainly toward the end Helga longed for the niceties of the world.... This is what her white blood desires. To the end, Nella Larsen watches Helga with her cool naturalist's eyes. She never says which side—white or black—is better. There is compassion for the heroine, but no moral judgment on her. (pp. 87-8)

Nella Larsen is not concerned with race problems in the ordinary sense, nor does she glorify blackness. She does not use the race for protest or propaganda. In that sense she is, as Mr. Robert Bone says, a rearguard of the Harlem Renaissance. Yet in her technique and treatment of her subject she is with the most advanced of the time. She is a very sophisticated writer and she is able to present her subject with wide perspective: a personal problem can be expanded to a race problem, then to a universal one. She is the first one among the black writers who has attained this artistic accomplishment. Though she has written only one good book, she can be regarded as one of the best black writers up to now. (p. 89)

> *Hiroko Sato, "Under the Harlem Shadow: A Study of Jessie Fauset and Nella Larsen," in* The Harlem Renaissance Remembered, *edited by Arna Bontemps, Dodd, Mead & Company, 1972, pp. 63-89.**

ARTHUR P. DAVIS

Nella Larsen is usually grouped with Jessie Fauset because both play up the same kind of folk, the Negro middle class; both treat passing as a major phenomenon in upper-stratum Negro life; and both practically ignore the presence of the "other" blacks. There is, however, a difference in the treatment of these themes. Nella Larsen is far more intense and bitter than Fauset in her attitude toward an America which forces upon Negroes the agony and frustrations they must endure simply because of the accident of color. And yet this bitterness is seldom overt in her writings. She expresses it, as a good artist expresses it, through the realistic and believable experiences and attitudes of her creations. (p. 94)

[*Quicksand*] is a fascinating case study of an unhappy and unfortunate woman. It is important to emphasize Helga's individuality because there is a temptation to blame everything that happens to her on racial grounds.... Although Helga's mixed ancestry and the race situation in America naturally influence her, Miss Larsen seems to be saying that they are not the sole causes of Helga's tragedy. She is the victim of her own inability to make the right decisions, a hang-up which the author suggests *may* come from frustrated love, or from

brooding over a father who deserted his family, or from strong unsatisfied sexual urges, or from all of these causes as well as the racial situation. Helga is a superb creation. With the probable exception of Kabnis in Toomer's *Cane,* she is the most intriguing and complex character in Renaissance fiction.

The quicksand motif is used very skillfully in this work. The quicksand, of course, is Helga's own vacillating inner self, which the author renders with appropriate images of suffocation, sinking, drowning, and enclosure. The author is skillful in other respects. Although her dialogue in *Quicksand* is inclined to be too scanty, even inadequate on occasion, she nevertheless is an excellent narrator. More like a drama than a novel, *Quicksand* moves from crisis to crisis, giving small details only when absolutely necessary. Unlike other Harlem novelists, Miss Larsen never deserts the delineation of her major character in order to bring in sensational matter. Her picture of a Negro college in the South is skeletal (compare Ellison in *Invisible Man* on the same subject); her cabaret scenes compared with those of McKay are mild; her Harlem street scenes lack the fullness and preciseness of those of Fisher; and her Southern small town scene has no lynching, no confrontation between white and black. Her main objective was the analysis of the neurotic Helga Crane, and she allowed nothing to take the reader's attention away from this goal.

Passing, though not as good a novel as *Quicksand,* is a moving story of a "tragic mulatto" who crossed the line and then tried to return. The present-day reader may wonder at this morbid concern of new Negro novelists with the passing theme; and ask why. The answer, of course, is not simple, and it may not be understood at all by young blacks, particularly those who believe in black nationalism. But there are reasons which seemed valid at the time. First of all, there was economic motivation. When almost every job of any consequence in the white world, including those of street-car conductors and street cleaners, were closed to the Negro, it was only natural for those who could pass to take advantage of their color. There was also the matter of simple convenience like a meal in a decent restaurant or a room in a modern hotel when one shopped downtown or took a trip to another city. There was always present the pleasure of fooling "Cap'n Charlie" (the white man) who, having set up the foolish caste laws, was then unable to tell who was or who was not a Negro. And there was on occasion a deeper compulsion on the part of a few Negroes to pass—a certain "call of kind" which transcended the routine motivations for crossing the line. Most passers tended to return to the race. This last kind returned only when forced to by discovery. Whatever the present-day reader may think of passing, the New Negro novelist was aware of its dramatic possibilities in fiction, and most of them treated the theme in their novels. (pp. 96-7)

Clare, like Helga in *Quicksand,* is a complex creation; unlike Helga, however, she is hard, amoral, and utterly selfish in her search for happiness or, at least, contentment. She does not hesitate to take (or try to take) whatever she desires, including her friend's husband. She seems to have one overriding urge: to return to the Negro world which she left. In her case, however, the return trip ends in tragedy. Clare Kendry belongs with that group of "tragic mulattos" gracing the works of George Washington Cable, Dion Boucicault, and other earlier writers, but she emerges as an individual, not as a stereotype. One tends to pity, in spite of her ruthlessness, this poor, mixed-up child of a bad background, married ironically to a "nigger-hating" white husband. One finds in her a tragic symbol of the whole irrational concern in America over color and race.

It is unfortunate that Nella Larsen limited herself to two novels. She was a sensitive writer, with great skill in narration. It is reasonable to assume, given her intelligence, that she would have improved her fiction techniques if she had written more. As it is, she produced in *Quicksand,* one of the better novels of the Harlem Renaissance. (pp. 97-8)

Arthur P. Davis, "First Fruits," in his From the Dark Tower: Afro-American Writers, 1900 to 1960, *Howard University Press, 1974, pp. 61-136.**

ADDISON GAYLE, JR.

Quicksand is a novel almost modern in its plot and conflicts. More so than [George Schuyler's] *Black No More,* it seeks to broach the wider question of identity, not the loss of it, but the search for it, and to suggest that this search in a world, race mad, must produce serious psychological problems of the spirit and soul. Helga cannot accept the definition of herself as Black in the terminology of whites or affluent Blacks; therefore, she is forced into a self-destructive encounter with her own fantasies, forced to discover the realities of the world of poverty and desperation. Unlike the black middle class she cannot accept the argument that pigmentation of skin does not indicate a difference in cultural and historical values, cannot believe that the true images of black people do not reside in the "primitive" aspects of lower-class black life.

Thus her romanticism of the "poor suffering Black," in the final analysis, causes her undoing. For her identity cannot be discovered here, any more than it can in the life-style of the middle class or of whites, and the major flaw in the character of Helga is that she knew nothing of her true history and roots. She is incapable, therefore, of maintaining her balance in a world in which conflicting forces demand that she surrender her individuality. Her real conflict is not due to skin color, but to the inability to find self-validation in a world in which all choices are equally reprehensible. That this is the dilemma of Helga Crane does not suggest that it is the dilemma of the author, also.

For though better executed, technically, than *Black No More,* and presenting dimensions of the problem of identity which did not occur to Schuyler, Miss Larsen's novel by implication, at least, suggests, in the fate of the heroine, that the black middle-class values, no matter how imitative, are far superior to those of the white world or to that world of the black poor fantasized in the dreams of Helga Crane. Those who survive the novel, the Anne Greys, the Andersons, and the Vayles, imitative white men and women, though they may be, are conscious of an identity, no matter how flawed, which moves them outside that depicted in the writings of either Van Vechten or Jean Toomer. Theirs is a passive acceptance of the superiority of white images over black, and the ability to accept these minimize psychological difficulties of the kind encountered by Helga Crane.

Thus the middle-class-black reader of the twenties had little difficulty in choosing the fate of Anne Grey, hypocritical and pretentious, over that of Helga Crane, doomed to the quicksand of poverty and want. Anne is, after all, made in the image of James Weldon Johnson's protagonist [in *The Autobiography of an Ex-Coloured Man*]; she is cognizant of the fine distinctions between the black middle class and the black poor as is George Schuyler; unlike her friend, therefore, she engages upon no quest to establish her identity, stays clear of the life-style so akin to that of those suggested in the fiction of Jean Toomer.

The tragedy of Helga Crane and Nella Larsen, as well, however, is that neither knew of the values of courage and endurance depicted in the life-style of Toomer's men and women, and therefore looked upon black life as lived by the poor through the distorted lenses of white sociologists. In their flight from themselves, Blacks have all too often accepted the same images of each other as have whites.

Nella Larsen's second novel, *Passing* (1929), differs fundamentally from the first. In terms of character development, organization, and fidelity to language, the second, divided into three sections—"Encounter," "Re-encounter," and "Finale"—is superior to the first. Though this structure makes for a more well-knit novel, none of her characters possess the stature of a Helga Crane, and Miss Larsen loses both focus and emotional intensity in her attempt to balance Irene Redfield and Clare Kendry against one another. . . . The experiences of both are juxtaposed in the novel, with the result that Clare's act of passing receives more extensive treatment than Irene's adoption of white-middle-class values. (pp. 111-12)

The dramatic intensity of *Passing* is derived from Miss Larsen's contrast between Irene and Clare. . . . Passing, as dramatized through the experiences of Clare, entails secrecy, deception, loss of identity, and eventually tragedy. It means to be separated from a life-style, which, for Clare, as for Helga, offers up romantic images of sensation and atavism, to lose something, in the James Weldon Johnson sense, of one's own soul. Even Clare's act of passing is suspect, based more upon expediency and hope of escaping poverty than upon commitment to a belief in the superiority of Euro-American values. . . . (p. 113)

Irene's life, by comparison, is superior to that of her friend. Though she has more than a casual interest in "passing," having done so in a small way, in department stores, etc., and, to the reader, seeming at times to resent the color of her husband (tea-colored) and of her son (dark), her interest is merely that of a curious woman, one interested in knowing the ". . . hazardous business of passing, this breaking away from all that was familiar and friendly to take one's chances in another environment. . . ." Possessing the symbolism of the white world, Irene has little reason to completely adopt its images. The wife of a doctor, she has servants, security, and near dictatorial powers over her family. As a black woman, she has more prestige, let alone power, than would be accorded her were she white under similar circumstances. It is this knowledge that induces the paranoia concerning Clare and Brian. For without Brian, the symbols Irene has acquired disappear. Prestige and standing in the black community amount to nothing in the absence of her doctor husband; her plan to send her children to Europe to study, where they will learn nothing of either sex or race, impossible of bearing fruition were Brian to desert her. Her standing in the white community as a representative of "respectable Blacks" and her role as missionary to the black poor must be forfeited with the loss of her husband. In light of her possessions, it takes no great leap of the imagination to believe that Clare Kendry met her death at the hands of Irene Redfield.

Aspects of Miss Larsen's personal life bear heavily upon both of her novels. Like Helga Crane, she was the product of a mixed marriage, and like both Irene Redfield and Clare Kendry, her own marriage was beset by turmoil. Her conflict between possible marriage to a white man and attempting to make a go of her marriage, all combine to present her as one beset by the problem of psychic dualism—the major theme in *Quick-*

sand and *Passing*—and accounts for her ambivalence concerning the meaning of blackness. Here she is both analogous to, and different from, Schuyler and Johnson. In the final analysis, her characters, Helga, Anne, Irene, and Clare, must either find their identities in the world of the black middle class, or face disaster. Not as partial to this class as either Johnson, Schuyler, or Jessie Fauset, and privy to its hypocrisies and pretensions, nevertheless, she believes that it is far superior to the lower class, and in some instances, for those like Irene Redfield, offers opportunities that the white world does not. Yet, both novels evidence the fact that she was not altogether happy with this special class, that she was capable of understanding, though not forgiving, their shortcomings. They wished, after all, to be both American and Negro, and yet Negro with limitations, defining the term in ways that moved them outside the sphere of less fortunate Blacks.

Like Miss Larsen herself, and Helga Crane, more specifically, theirs is a romanticism based upon repression or ignorance of the true facts concerning the black poor and their life-style. For Helga, nuances of the problem, occasioned by confusion of images, appear; for the black poor are both symbols of atavism and of the Christ figure, the poor suffering wards of American society. . . . (pp. 113-14)

Read Miss Larsen's novels and discover the disaster which awaits those who search for identity through fantasy—either by passing into the white world or affectuating too close an association with the poor of the black world. In the final analysis it is better to be Irene Redfield than either Helga Crane or Clare Kendry, though happiness is not, and cannot be, the key to the character of either. For the question is not one of happiness for Miss Larsen, but one of survival. Those characters in her novels, beset by problems of identity, are doomed to destruction; only those who accept the fact that identity is a prerogative of a special class of people are capable of surviving. Theirs is not so much the finding of an identity, but the creation of one out of material bequeathed by both the white and the black worlds. (pp. 114-15)

> *Addison Gayle, Jr., ''The Confusion of Identity,'' in his* The Way of the New World: The Black Novel in America, *Anchor Press, 1975, pp. 97-128.**

CLAUDIA TATE

Nella Larsen's *Passing* (1929) has been frequently described as a novel depicting the tragic plight of the mulatto. . . . Though *Passing* does indeed relate the tragic fate of a mulatto who passes for white, it also centers on jealousy, psychological ambiguity and intrigue. By focusing on the latter elements, *Passing* is transformed from an anachronistic, melodramatic novel into a skillfully executed and enduring work of art. (p. 142)

Ostensibly, *Passing* conforms to the stereotype of the tragic mulatto. However, many factors make such an interpretation inadequate. The conventional tragic mulatto is a character who ''passes'' and reveals pangs of anguish resulting from forsaking his or her Black identity. Clare reveals no such feelings; in fact, her psychology is inscrutable. Moreover, Clare does not seem to be seeking out Blacks in order to regain a sense of racial pride and solidarity. She is merely looking for excitement, and Irene's active social life provides her with precisely that. An equally important reason for expanding the racial interpretation is that alone it tends to inhibit the appreciation of Larsen's craft. Larsen gave great care to portraying the characters; therefore, the manner of their portrayal must be

important and ultimately indispensable to interpreting *Passing*'s meaning. Thus, the ''tragic mulatto'' interpretation not only is unsuited to the book's factual content, but also disregards the intricately woven narrative.

An understanding of *Passing* must be deduced not merely from its surface content but also from its vivid imagery, subtle metaphors, and carefully balanced psychological ambiguity. For example, although the story has a realistic setting, it is not concerned with the ordinary course of human experience. The story develops from a highly artificial imitation of social relationships which reflect Irene's spiritual adventures. These characteristics are more compatible with the romance than with the tragedy. (pp. 142-43)

The work's central conflict develops from Irene's jealousy of Clare and not from racial issues which are at best peripheral to the story. The only time Irene is aware that race even remotely impinges on her world occurs when the impending exposure of Clare's racial identity threatens to hasten the disruption of Irene's domestic security. Race, therefore, is not the novel's foremost concern, but is merely a mechanism for setting the story in motion, sustaining the suspense, and bringing about the external circumstances for the story's conclusion. The real impetus for the story is Irene's emotional turbulence, which is entirely responsible for the course that the story takes and ultimately accountable for the narrative ambiguity. The problem of interpreting *Passing* can, therefore, be simplified by defining Irene's role in the story and determining the extent to which she is reliable as the sole reporter and interpreter of events. We must determine whether she accurately portrays Clare, or whether her portrait is subject to, and in fact affected by, her own growing jealousy and insecurity. In this regard, it is essential to ascertain precisely who is the tragic heroine— Irene who is on the verge of total mental disintegration or Clare whose desire for excitement brings about her sudden death. (p. 143)

Long before we encounter Clare Kendry, Larsen creates a dense psychological atmosphere for her eventual appearance. In the very first paragraph of the narrative, Larsen describes Clare's letter from Irene's point of view. . . . Larsen uses ambiguous and emotional terminology to refer to Clare's letter: ''alien,'' ''mysterious,'' ''slightly furtive,'' ''sly,'' ''furtive,'' ''peculiar,'' ''extraordinary.'' Repeated references to the letter's beguiling unobtrusiveness and its enthralling evasiveness heighten the mystery which enshrouds both the almost illegible handwriting and its author. The letter itself is animated with feline cunning—''a thin sly thing.'' From one perspective the letter is insubstantial; from another, it possesses ''extraordinary size.'' The letter rejects every effort of precise description. Provocative, bewitching, vividly conspicuous and yet elusive, the letter resembles the extraordinary physical appearance of Clare Kendry as she is later described, sitting in Irene's parlor. . . . (pp. 143-44)

In the next paragraph of the introductory section there are numerous references made to danger which incite a sense of impending disaster. The suspense is associated first with the letter and then with Clare. The letter is, to use T. S. Eliot's term, ''an objective correlative,'' in that it objectifies abstract aspects of Clare's character, and its very presence reflects her daring defiance of unwritten codes of social propriety. Like Clare herself, the letter excites ''a little feeling of apprehension,'' . . . which grows in intensity to ''a dim premonition of impending disaster,'' . . . and foreshadows the story's tragic ending.

The letter, therefore, is a vivid though subtle narrative device. It foreshadows Clare's actual arrival and characterizes her extraordinary beauty. It also suggests abstract elements of Clare's enigmatic character which evolve into a comprehensive, though ambiguous portrait. Furthermore, it generates the psychological atmosphere which cloaks Clare's character, rendering her indiscernible and mysterious.

Irene is literally obsessed with Clare's beauty, a beauty of such magnitude that she seems alien, impervious, indeed inscrutable.... On one occasion we are told that "Irene turned an oblique look on Clare and encountered her peculiar eyes fixed on her with an expression so dark and deep and unfathomable that she had for a short moment the sensation of gazing into the eyes of some creature utterly strange and apart.".... On another occasion, Irene puzzles "over that look on Clare's incredibly beautiful face.... It was unfathomable, utterly beyond any experience or comprehension of hers." ... Irene repeatedly describes Clare in hyperbole—"too vague," "too remote," "so dark and deep and unfathomable," "utterly strange," "incredibly beautiful," "utterly beyond any experience...." These hyperbolic expressions are ambiguous. They create the impression that Clare is definitely, though indescribably, different from and superior to Irene and other ordinary people. (p. 144)

Irene is characterized as keenly intelligent, articulate and clever. In this regard, the social gatherings seem to be more occasions for her to display a gift for witty conversation than actual events. Whether in the midst of a social gathering or alone, Irene often falls prey to self-dramatization, which is half egoism and half ironic undercutting for the evolving story.... Hence, her personal feelings are confined to an outer shell of superficial awareness. Although she is further portrayed as possessing an acute awareness of discernment, she tends to direct this ability entirely toward others and employ hyperbole rather than exact language for its expression. Her perceptions, therefore, initially seem generally accurate enough, until she becomes obsessed with jealousy.

As the story unfolds, Irene becomes more and more impulsive, nervous and insecure, indeed irrational. She tends to jump to conclusions which discredit her credibility as a reliable source of information. For example, on several occasions Irene assumes that Clare questions her racial loyalty.... On another occasion, she assumes that Clare is involved with the man who escorted her to the Drayton Hotel dining room.... And eventually, she concludes that Clare and Brian are having an affair.... Each of her assumptions may indeed be correct, but we observe no tangible evidence of their support; consequently, we cannot know with any certainty whether or not Irene's suspicions are true.

Although we only know the external details of Clare's life, we observe the fatal essence of Irene's psychology. We have also noted that thematic information is seldom communicated directly, but implied through dramatic scenes. Hence, Irene's character, like Clare's, achieves cohesion from the suggestive language Irene employs (especially when describing Clare), the psychological atmosphere permeating her encounters with Clare, and the subtle nuances in characterization. The realistic impact of incidents in and of themselves neither fully characterizes Irene nor conveys the novel's meaning. Meaning in *Passing,* therefore, must be pieced together like a complicated puzzle from allusion and suggestions. Irene gives form to Clare, but we are left with the task of fashioning Irene from her reflections of Clare's extraordinary beauty.

The ambiguous ending of *Passing* is another piece of the puzzle. The circumstances surrounding Clare's death support several interpretations. The most obvious interpretation is that Irene in a moment of temporary insanity pushed Clare out of the window. This interpretation has received widest acceptance, although the manner in which Larsen dramatizes Irene's alleged complicity receives no serious attention at all. Critics take her involvement in Clare's death for granted as merely a detail of the plot. A close examination of the events surrounding Clare's death, however, reveals that the evidence against her, no matter how convincing, is purely circumstantial. No one actually observes Irene push Clare, and Irene never admits whether she is guilty, not even to herself.... [At the] moment Clare falls through the open window, ... Irene responds by saying that "she wasn't sorry. (That she) was amazed, incredulous almost." ... Larsen provides no clarification for Irene's remark or its emotional underpinning. We do not know whether she is simply glad that Clare is permanently out of her life by means of a quirk of fate, whether she does not regret killing her, or whether she has suffered momentary amnesia and therefore does not know her role in Clare's death. In fact, Larsen seems to have deliberately avoided narrative clarity by weaving ambiguity into Irene's every thought and expression. For example, shortly after Clare's fall, Irene wonders what the other people at the party may be thinking about the circumstances surrounding Clare's death. Her speculations further cloud the narrative with other possible explanations for Clare's death.... A literal interpretation of this passage suggests that Clare may have accidentally fallen through the open window, or that she may have committed suicide. The passage can also be interpreted to mean that Irene hopes that the guests willl mistakenly assume her innocence in their effort to arrive at a more agreeable explanation than murder. Of course, the passage may merely reflect Irene's genuine attempt to deduce what the others would necessarily conclude in light of her innocence. A few moments later, Irene fiercely mutters to herself that "it was an accident, a terrible accident." ... This expression may be merely her futile effort at denying involvement in murder. Or, it may be her insistence that she is indeed innocent, through she suspects that no one will believe her. Or, she could be uncertain of her involvement and struggling to convince herself that she is innocent. In all cases we must be mindful that there is still no tangible proof to support one interpretation over another. Although we may be inclined to accept the conventional interpretation, we must remember that all evidence is circumstantial, and we cannot determine Irene's guilt beyond a reasonable doubt.

In reference to other explanations for Clare's death ..., we note that the possibility of accidental death is the least satisfying interpretation. Consequently, we disregard it, despite its being a plausible assumption as well as the conclusion which the authorities reach.

The last alternative—suicide—tends to be inadvertently neglected altogether, inasmuch as Clare's motives are not discernible. Nothing is left behind, neither note nor explaining discourse, to reveal her motives. However, this interpretation does deserve consideration, since it enhances the ambiguous conclusion and draws heavily on Larsen's narrative techniques of allusion and suggestion.

Early in the text we are given the circumstances surrounding the death of Clare's father. When his body was brought before her, she stood and stared silently for some time. Then after a brief emotional outburst, (s)he glanced quickly about the bare room, taking everyone in, even the two policemen, in a sharp look of flashing scorn. And, in the next instance, she . . . turned and vanished through the door (never to return)." . . . the last scene in the story bears a striking resemblance to this, and the motives for Clare's behavior in the early scene suggest a possible motive for her suicide. "Clare stood at the window, as composed as if everyone were not staring at her in curiosity and wonder. . . . One moment Clare had been there . . . the next she was gone." . . . In both instances Clare surveys the fragments of her life, and in both she vanishes, leaving behind a painful situation which she cannot alter. In the latter, she is utterly alone, and suicide is the ultimate escape from the humiliation that awaits her. *Passing*'s conclusion defies simple solution. . . . What I am certain of, though, is that *Passing* is not the conventional tragic mulatto story at all. It is an intriguing romance in which Irene Redfield is the unreliable center of consciousness, and she and not Clare Kendry is the heroine.

Larsen's focus on a mulatto character, the plagiarism scandal surrounding her short story, **"Sanctuary,"** published in 1939, and aspects of her personal life probably account for the sparsity of serious, critical attention given to her work. Critics, of course, hastily comment on Larsen's skill as they either celebrate other Harlem Renaissance writers or look ahead to the socially conscious writers of the '30s. Few address the psychological dimension of Larsen's work. They see instead a writer who chose to escape the American racial climate in order to depict trite melodramas about egocentric black women passing for white. This critical viewpoint has obscured Larsen's talent and relegated *Passing* to the status of a minor novel of the Harlem Renaissance. But Larsen's craft deserves more attention than this position attracts. *Passing* demands that we recognize its rightful place among important works of literary subtlety and psychological ambiguity. (pp. 144-46)

> *Claudia Tate, "Nella Larsen's 'Passing': A Problem of Interpretation," in* Black American Literature Forum, *Vol. 14, No. 4, Winter, 1980, pp. 142-46.*

MARY HELEN WASHINGTON

[*Quicksand* and *Passing* examine the problems of] the marginal black woman of the middle class, who was both unwilling to conform to a circumscribed existence in the black world and unable to move freely in the white world. We may perhaps think this is a strange dilemma for a black woman to experience or certainly an atypical one, for most black women then, as now, were struggling against much more naked and brutal realities and would be contemptuous of so esoteric a problem as feeling uncomfortable among black people. Is there anything relevant in the lives of women who arrogantly expected to live in Harlem in the middle-class enclave of Sugar Hill, to summer at resorts like Idlewild in Michigan, to join exclusive black clubs and sororities? Weren't the interests that preoccupied Larsen in her work just the spoiled tantrums of "little yellow dream children" grown up? (pp. 44, 47)

Her preoccupation with the theme of marginality was the first venture into an ocean that blacks would navigate in somewhat larger numbers as the Afro-American experience is modified for some of us by greater access to education, economic resources, and social mobility. One subtle effect of this change has been the loosening of the more obvious ties of commonality between the privileged few and the majority of the black community—ties that may have had a clearer purpose when racial barriers were more stark. (p. 47)

There are a few clues about why Nella Larsen fell silent as a literary voice. In 1930 she was accused of plagiarizing a story that was published in *Forum* magazine. Though she was supported by her editor, who had seen several drafts of the story, she was nonetheless devastated by the criticism. Then in 1933 she was divorced from her husband. . . . The divorce was crudely sensationalized by one widely read black newspaper. (p. 48)

These two events of public shame, plus a fragile and vulnerable personality, a sense of oddness that made her seem strange even to her friends, and a deep-seated ambivalence about her racial status combined to reinforce her sense of herself as the Outsider and may finally have pushed her into a life of obscurity.

Always there is the ambivalence: in her personal correspondence Larsen is detached and aloof speaking about "the Negroes" as though she were observing a comic opera, and yet there is the unmistakable race pride as she observes the style and coping power of poor blacks in the South. She once wrote in a letter to Carl Van Vechten, a white novelist and critic of the Harlem Renaissance period, that she found poor Southern blacks quaint and amusing. . . . Then she hastens to add that the poor whites by comparison are tragic and depressing.

What happens to a writer who is legally black but internally identifies with both blacks and whites, who is supposed to be content as a member of the black elite, but feels suffocated by its narrowness, who is emotionally rooted in the black experience and yet wants to live in the whole world not confined to a few square blacks and the mentality that make up Sugar Hill?

Her two novels give no indication that Nella Larsen ever solved this problem of duality. All of Larsen's women characters choose self-destruction and yet her novels sensitively explored the consciousness of the marginal black woman. Larsen's characters—Helga Crane, Irene Redfield, and Clare Kendry—are black women out of step with their time, as middle-class black women in the 1920s. Like strange projectiles, or plants trying to sustain themselves without roots or nourishment, they are detached and isolated from the black community. Helga Crane feels claustrophobic in the black Southern college and in black Harlem where she is forced to observe taboos and conventions that constrict her spirit. The proscription against wearing bright colors (because bright colors supposedly emphasize a dark-skinned woman's blackness) amuses her, for example, but she sees it as one of the innumerable internal controls people already under severe restraints must submit to. Even more intolerable for Helga is the absolute law against any kind of interracial mixing, which Helga's Harlem friends consider an act of disloyalty to the race. One woman in *Quicksand* is ostracized because she is seen dancing publicly with white men. Helga is never able to completely deny her blackness, so she lives with resentment and rancor, having to "ghettoize" her own life.

In Larsen's second novel, *Passing,* one can see most clearly how she failed to resolve the dilemma of the marginal woman. The central character, Clare Kendry, is married to a white man and has been passing for white all of her married life. Passionate and daring, the mysterious Clare lives in both the black and white worlds, feeling no permanent allegiance to either nor any of the classic anguish of the tragic mulatto. This golden and graceful woman is simply determined to escape the poverty of her childhood and to have whatever she wants in life regardless of the price or the danger.

Passing becomes, in Larsen's terms, a metaphor for the risk-taking experience, the life lived without the supports other black women clung to in order to survive in a white-dominated, male-dominated society. One clear indication of Clare's striving for autonomy is that she is never called by her married name, Mrs. Bellew. She is only and always Clare Kendry, a woman of such passion and vitality that she mocks the shallowness of her childhood friend, the pretentious and proper Irene Redfield.

Why does Clare pass for white? Because it enables her to marry a man of means. Because she, like most other black women of the 1920s, if she achieved middle-class status, did it by virtue of a man's presence in her life, by virtue of his status—a grandfather who owned an undertaking business, a father who became a doctor, a husband elected to public office.

Larsen's failure in dealing with this problem of marginality is implicit in the very choice of "passing" as a symbol or metaphor of deliverance for her women. It is an obscene form of salvation. The woman who passes is required to deny everything about her past—her girlhood, her family, places with memories, folk customs, folk rhymes, her language, the entire long line of people who have gone before her. She lives in terror of discovery—what if she has a child with a dark complexion, what if she runs into an old school friend, how does she listen placidly to racial slurs? And more, where does the woman who passes find the equanimity to live by the privileged status that is based on the oppression of her own people?

Larsen's heroines are all finally destroyed somewhere down the paths they choose. Helga Crane loses herself in a loveless marriage to an old black preacher by whom she has five children in as many years. She finally retreats into illness and silence, eventually admitting to herself a suppressed hatred for her husband. *Passing*'s Irene Redfield suspects an affair between her friend Clare (recently surfaced from the white world) and her black physician husband. This threatens her material and psychological security. In the novel's melodramatic ending, she pushes Clare off the balcony of a seventeenth-floor apartment and sinks into unconsciousness when she is questioned about Clare's death.

And Nella Larsen, who created Helga and Irene, chose oblivion for herself. (pp. 48, 50)

But unlike the women in her novels, Larsen did not die from her marginality. . . . She lived through the conflicts of the mar-

ginal woman and felt them passionately. Why didn't she leave us the greater legacy of the mature model, the perceptions of a woman who confronts the pain, alienation, isolation, and grapples with these conundrums until new insight has been forged from the struggle? Why didn't she continue to write after 1929?

If there are any answers to these questions, we have to look again in the two novels to find them. Both novels end with images of numbness, suffocation, blunted perceptions, loss of consciousness, invisibility. It is a world even more restricted than that in Ralph Ellison's *The Invisible Man*, another novel about marginality and the Afro-American experience. The "invisible man" at least has the choice of a range of work options, mobility, and political activism. Who can imagine a black woman character replicating the intense activities of a black man who—in literature and life—is at least sometimes physically free to hop a freight North or to highball it down the track from coast to coast as a Pullman porter, to organize and lead political movements without apology, to wield the tools of an occupation other than personal sevice and earn a living by sheer physical skill? And the characters in the literature of white women move through a variety of places and experiences with relative ease when compared to black women. They can be artists in Europe or illustrators in New York or farmers in Iowa or retirees in Florida without suffering the permanent absence of community. In their insistence that black women are estranged from the right to aspire and achieve in the wide world of thought and action, *Quicksand* and *Passing* are brilliant witnesses to the position of a colored woman in a white, male world.

She did not solve her own problems, but Larsen made us understand as no one did before her that the image of the middle-class black woman as a coldly self-centered snob, chattering irrelevantly at bridge club and sorority meetings, was as much a mask as the grin on the face of Stepin Fetchit. The women in her novels, like Larsen, are driven to emotional and psychological extremes in their attempts to handle ambivalence, marginality, racism, and sexism. She has shown us that behind the carefully manicured exterior, behind the appearance of security is a woman who hears the beating of her wings against a walled prison. (p. 50)

Mary Helen Washington, "Nella Larsen: Mystery Woman of the Harlem Renaissance," in Ms., *Vol. IX, No. 6, December, 1980, pp. 44, 47-8, 50.*

Primo Levi

1919-

(Has also written under pseudonym of Damianos Malabaila) Italian memoirist, short story writer, novelist, poet, and scriptwriter.

An Italian Jew and a survivor of the Nazi concentration camp at Auschwitz, Levi is best known for his Holocaust memoirs *Se questo è un uomo* (1947; *If This Is a Man*) and *La tregua* (1958; *The Reawakening*). According to H. Stuart Hughes, what distinguishes the former book from more sensational accounts of Nazi horror is "its tone of moderation, of equanimity, punctuated by an occasional note of quiet humor." A similarly temperate tone characterizes Levi's other work, which is noted for its sympathetic insight into human nature and its essentially optimistic outlook. Levi's recently translated novel *Se non ora, quando?* (1975; *If Not Now, When?*) has also received considerable attention.

In 1943 Levi was arrested for anti-Fascist Resistance activities and deported to Auschwitz. Following the camp's liberation by Russian troops in 1945, a series of Soviet bureaucratic delays forced Levi and his fellow prisoners to undergo a long railway detour through Eastern Europe before returning home. Upon his return to Italy, Levi wrote *If This Is a Man*, based on his experiences as an inmate at Auschwitz. Conceived as "a serene study of certain aspects of the human soul," the book was commended for its sensitive treatment of the ruthless politics that dictated camp survival and its compassionate portrayal of both victims and victimizers. Refusing to "nourish hatred," according to Levi, for either his oppressors or the German people in general, he sought instead to extract positive value from the experience and to increase his understanding of the ordeal. In *The Reawakening* Levi relates his return home through Eastern Europe and the liberated prisoners' sense of joy and celebration. Described by Charlotte Saikowski as an account of "the journey back to sanity and identity," the memoirs are above all a lyrical affirmation of life. Levi's insistent faith in humanity is again expressed in *Shema* (1976), a collection of poems also based on his Holocaust experiences.

Before World War II Levi received formal training as a chemist, and he returned to this profession after the war. His knowledge of chemistry and his "absolute need to write" about his wartime experiences have informed much of his fiction. For Levi, as H. Stuart Hughes notes, "the chemist incarnated the eternal struggle to pry open the secrets of the universe." Levi's early short story collections *Storie naturali* (1966) and *Vizio di forma* (1971), written pseudonymously, describe his postwar experiences as technical director of a paint company in a blend of fantasy, science fiction, and personal reminiscences. Though neither book has been translated into English, Levi's next collection, *Il sistema periodico* (1975; *The Periodic Table*), gained him international notice. In this work Levi bases each story on a different chemical element, with each element evoking for him a memory of a person or past event. Levi's humor balances his serious reflections throughout the book. Noting the "relentlessly inquisitive" intelligence of the book, Alvin H. Rosenfeld praised Levi's ability "to forge an unusual synthesis of scientific learning and poetic sensibility." Levi's short

© Jerry Bauer

story collection *Lilít e altri racconti* (1981) also blends reminiscence and personal reflection.

Levi's first novel to be translated, *Se non ora, quando?* (1975; *If Not Now, When?*), examines the notion that Jews passively surrendered to the Nazis because of religious injunctions. Based loosely on historical fact, the book relates the odyssey of an Eastern European Jewish partisan unit that actively resists Nazi oppression. The novel celebrates the positive emergence of a collective Jewish consciousness.

(See also *Contemporary Authors*, Vols. 13-16, rev. ed. and *Contemporary Authors New Revision Series*, Vol. 12.)

ALFRED WERNER

The place is Auschwitz, but the narrative would fit any one of the scores of *Konzentrationslager* the Nazis established in their vast, hellish empire. . . . What raises [Levi's] memoirs [*If This Is a Man;* later republished as *Survival in Auschwitz: The Nazi Assault on Humanity*] high above other descriptions of man-made horror is the author's humanity, the deep interest he took in fellow-prisoners, his penetration of the gruesome sociological structure and, finally, his talent for terse statement.

Levi is a forty-year-old Italian chemist. In December, 1943, he was captured by Fascist militia and turned over to the SS, to be shipped from his native land to the death factory in Upper Silesia. . . .

''Man's capacity to dig himself in, to secrete a shell, to build around himself a tenuous barrier of defense, even in apparently desperate circumstances, is astonishing and merits a serious study.'' These are the observations of one who, having been assigned to the ''Buena Project,'' lived to see the end of tyranny, while the majority of his fellow-prisoners went ''up the chimney.''

We know by now all that is worth knowing about the mad laws and logic that characterized a German concentration camp, about the terror by which the SS subjugated and demoralized the gray mass of helpless prisoners. But we can never hear enough about those who managed to resist corruption and to retard their moral disintegration, in the realization that their personalities were in far greater danger than their lives. . . .

What Levi calls ''the divine spark'' was extinguished soon in the multitudes, doomed to a quick death from exhaustion. He is forced to admit, unhappily, ''Survival without renunciation of any part of one's own moral world . . . was conceded only to very few superior individuals, made of the stuff of martyrs and saints.''

Levi himself seems to belong to the latter category, if only because even Auschwitz could not kill his confidence in man's moral nature. . . . Levi refused to draw the conclusion that man was ''fundamentally brutal, egotistic, and stupid in his conduct'' when removed from civilized restraints. Though Germans, and especially German prisoners assigned to police their Jewish fellow-inmates, were responsible for his daily torture, he would not indulge in generalizations.

Liberation came precisely a year after Levi's arrival at Auschwitz. . . . Levi went home and wrote his book, which was published in 1947. After the lapse of a dozen years, it is still overwhelmingly fresh and powerful in English translation, a useful reminder of events we must never forget.

> Alfred Werner, ''Amid Suffering, the Divine Spark,'' in Saturday Review, Vol. XLIII, No. 1, January 2, 1960, p. 23.

DAVID CAUTE

If This is a Man is in a class of its own, and its . . . pages comprise a stark prose-poem on the deepest sufferings of man. . . . Levi was a quiet, frail chemist, an Italian Jew whose existence was shattered one day in 1944 when he and his kind were bundled like cattle on to a German train. . . . Levi, a civilian, a member of an oppressed race, fragile and naive, was to experience the depths of human degradation. His story is told without melodrama, without self-pity, but with a muted passion and intensity, an occasional cry of anguish, which makes it one of the most remarkable documents I have read.

In Auschwitz the layers of civilisation were quickly peeled. The battle was not bilateral, for the oppressed themselves had to prey on their weaker comrades if they were to win favour and survive. The majority, it seems, soon lost the will to live. Chronic malnutrition, brute force, indescribable filth, the constant threat of the gas chambers and, above all, the complete severance of contact with the outside world . . .—it was a sub-human existence in which only the super-human could survive.

In a POW camp there may be Red Cross parcels and mail from home. In Auschwitz there was neither. To find a friend was indeed a feat, but to steal his last square inch of bread was not immoral, only the recognition of the ultimate jungle law, the survival of the fittest. Each man was driven in on the wasted bag of skin and bones which was himself. . . .

Although Signor Levi reveals himself a born writer, even a great artist, he has written nothing since this book was first published in Italy in 1947. Perhaps he wrote only to banish a dark nightmare from his soul: perhaps there is nothing else to say.

> David Caute, ''Man a Prisoner,'' in New Statesman, Vol. LIX, No. 1514, March 19, 1960, p. 410.*

WERNER J. CAHNMAN

[*If This Is a Man* is] documentary evidence of the first order of the inhumanity of man to man in our time. Here is literally a report from hell: the detached, scientific, unearthly story of a man who descended to the nether world at Auschwitz and returned to the land of the living. (p. 638)

What this report offers in words of pitiless clarity is insight into the workings of human nature in society, which no contrived experiment will ever reveal. To conduct it on human beings would be a crime, and to conduct it on animals would miss the point, namely, whether the object observed is indeed ''a man.'' If society and the ethical code it implies are suddenly taken away from us, we are human no more. . . . [It is insufficient] to say that punishment is visited here on virtue and reward on sin, because the very concepts ''virtue'' and ''sin'' have disappeared. . . . While hope is conducive to survival in one set of circumstances, it leads one into a trap on another occasion seemingly similar to the first. . . . The prisoner who carved on the bottom of his bowl the words, ''Don't try to understand,'' was wise.

The knowledge that human nature can be effectively dehumanized by depriving it of the braces of societal norms and by exposing it instead to non-norms, rigidly enforced, is thoroughly discomforting, but it is counterpoised by the example of those few who retain their human quality by keeping alive the memory that such a thing ever existed. This is a most important truth in social psychology: as long as we remember, we cannot be entirely swayed by the emotions and deprivations of the moment. As long as we remember, we can plan. (pp. 638-39)

Perhaps we have here before us a perfect theoretical model for the anomie of our time. The bewildered youth of the postwar generations revolts not so much against conflicting norms as against normlessness. Their grip on what is essentially human is loosened, and in desperation they become wall scribblers, vandals, and killers. The very permissiveness of our society, then, produces the destructive urge which ends in totalitarianism. To say the least, this is a lead which is worth following up.

At any rate, this book and whatever lesson it contains should be presented as serious reading matter. . . . Primo Levi's slim report, to be sure, is only one of many, but it seems to come nearest to suggesting the kind of theory of the dehumanizing process which we need if we are to know what to guard against. (p. 639)

Werner J. Cahnman, in a review of "If This Is a Man," in American Journal of Sociology, *Vol. LXV, No. 6, May, 1960, pp. 638-39.*

CHARLOTTE SAIKOWSKI

[For Levi], as for many others, liberation brought to an end the physical horrors and outrages of the Lager. But the journey back to sanity and identity—the return home—still lay ahead.

The Reawakening [published in Great Britain as *The Truce*] is a moving account of that journey—a senseless, tragic, sometimes humorous odyssey through Eastern Europe.

At the Polish city of Katowice 800 Italians are loaded into a convoy of trucks. They set out eastward, hopefully for Odessa where a ship will take them home. But at the Ukrainian town of Zhmerinka the convoy inexplicably turns northward, with 800 Romanians added to the hapless group.

There was no logic, no reason, for this tortuous trek—just the inanity of war. . . .

The story of these wandering exiles is one of nights on wooden planks, of ice-cold dawns, of vagabonding, haggling for food, searching for human contacts. It is a tale of hunger, disillusion, uncertainty, boredom, inertia.

Yet it is not depressing. Mr. Levi writes with astonishing lack of bitterness or hatred. He tells of these "wanderings on the margins of civilization" without rancor—indeed, with compassion and humor.

The author seems far less concerned with his own plight than with the experiences of those around him. He himself never emerges clearly as a personality; but through his sensitive, deftly drawn portraits one is introduced to a wonderful array of characters—fellow exiles, camp commandants, Soviet officers. . . .

Whether Mr. Levi is describing the joy which greeted the end of the war, the spectacle of demobilized Red Army soldiers streaming back to their homes, the delicious comfort of a bowl of hot soup, the comic operation of procuring a chicken in a Byelorussian village, or his "rediscovery" of the wonders of nature, his graphic prose sings with vitality. . . .

[Levi's] chronicle stands as a tribute to the patience and endurance of the human spirit.

Charlotte Saikowski, "Detour to Freedom," in The Christian Science Monitor, *May 27, 1965, p. 9.*

VIRGILIA PETERSON

The Reawakening begins in January, 1945, when the human wreckage left behind by the retreating Nazis to die was liberated by the Russians. What happened to Mr. Levi and his fellow-survivors between then and the day, some 10 months later, when he was finally repatriated makes the burden of the book.

Perhaps because Mr. Levi cleansed himself of the worst of his horror in an earlier book called *If This Is a Man,* perhaps because the 20 years since his experience have shifted his perspective, but also and in large part because he seems to be by nature a philosopher, he achieves in this book a remarkable objectivity, often managing to be funny at his own expense, yet never for a moment tempering the Goyaesque gruesomeness intrinsic to the tale.

The book opens as the emaciated, half-frozen Mr. Levi . . . and another inmate of the camp have just tipped the body of a fellow-prisoner off a stretcher into the snow on the edge of the overflowing, putrescent common grave. Looking up they see on the far side of the barbed wire, staring at them in silence, four mounted Russian soldiers. No word of greeting is exchanged. . . .

The war, of course, was not over when Auschwitz was liberated. West of that monument of infamy, the Russians were still engaged in mortal combat with the Nazis. It stands to reason, therefore, that they did not know what to do with the uprooted scarecrows from all over Europe who now fell into their charge. But what they actually did do . . . exceeds the boundaries of reason itself.

Herded into freight cars, the liberated were transported east through Poland, then north into Russia, where they spent the whole summer in a village on the steppes near Minsk, after which they rode the rails for 35 consecutive days. . . . The author has made a map of all the places they passed through, but no map could show the shuntings and sidings, the delays, the perils, and the absurdities of this incredibly senseless journey.

The journey gives the book its pace and sense of destiny, but what rivets the reader's eye are the scenes Mr. Levi reenacts with a novelist's art, the desperate black-market shenanigans in Cracow streets, the uproarious celebration the Russians staged for the deportees on the day of victory, . . . the pathetic ingenuity with which the involuntary travelers turned their leaking, rattling, odoriferous freight cars into homes.

Most of all it is the people in these pages who burn their way into the reader's mind: the 3-year-old, nameless, speechless Auschwitz-born child with its blazing eyes; the jaunty Greek who bought and sold everything including women; . . . and the clumsy but for the most part well-meaning Russians—people sprung up from the lower depths of our times, people whom the author presents with a Gogol's sense of humanity and absence of moral judgment. This story of the way back from death to life, recounted by Mr. Levi with pity for others and none for himself, gives an unforgettable picture of the struggle of the holocaust's survivors to survive their own survival.

Virgilia Peterson, "Road Back from Death," in The New York Times Book Review, *November 7, 1965, p. 85.*

PAUL BAILEY

[The two books *If This is a Man* and *The Truce*] should be read as one. Although a crude over-simplification, it is nevertheless essentially true that *If This is a Man* is about the descent into, and *The Truce* about the flight away from, hell. The statement is crude because the first book, despite its appalling subject, is not dispiriting. Levi does not flinch from setting down the unbelievable details of that cruelty born of the 'mystique of barrenness', but then neither does he paint them in lurid colours to press his point home. The facts are surely enough. What finally emerges, paradoxically, from the book is a sense of Man's worth, of dignity fought for and maintained against all the odds. . . .

If This is a Man and its sequel are books about a man among men: there are no saints and no heroes in the accepted sense. Indeed, what Levi says of his friend Leonardo in *The Truce* could with equal justice apply to himself:

Besides good fortune, he also possessed another virtue essential for those places: an unlimited capacity for endurance, a silent courage, not innate, not religious, not transcendent, but deliberate and willed hour by hour, a virile patience, which sustained him miraculously to the very edge of collapse.

And Levi did have good fortune, though the phrase is an obscenity when one thinks of the horrors that he and Leonardo and the other survivors were forced to combat. But he was not 'selected' and by some miracle he was ill with scarlet fever when the Germans fled from Auschwitz in January 1945, taking all the healthy prisoners with them. The healthy, who numbered almost 20,000, vanished on the march. . . . The work by this time was the work of healing, of finding and sharing food with the helpless, not the humiliating drudgery imposed upon them by the SS. . . . It is on this note of hope that *If This is a Man* ends: with the [prisoners], tired and hungry, creeping out of the shadows and slowly becoming men again.

Still, the book is not all blackness, though the tone of the narrative is elegiac and those millions of accusing ghosts haunt its every sentence. Levi does not omit from his story the faint glimmers of light that came on rare occasions to shine briefly out of the evil murk. (p. 245)

But *The Truce* is almost all light. It tells of Levi's journey home to his native Turin and the quiet, hesitant note of hope and renewal that ends the first book is transformed into something like a trumpet blast in its pages. The reader's eyes open with Levi's as he becomes aware of the abundant life about him. Like the great novels he devoured as a youth . . . , it is a celebration of other men's uniqueness. In Auschwitz he had learned a new morality, one that had made him more tolerant of the failings of others, and he draws a clear line in *The Truce* between the good thieves and the bad, the genuinely strong man and the vicious bully. There are unforgettable portraits of the people he met or who shared his journey with him: Cesare, from the Roman slums, making fish fatter with the aid of a syringe and selling them to gullible Russian peasants; . . . the ministering angel, Dr Gottlieb; the stately Moor of Verona, warding off friendship with obscenities. But the self-styled Colonel Rovi is perhaps the most incredible character of them all—an official interpreter at Katowice camp who cannot speak a word of German or Russian, dressed in a uniform composed of Soviet boots, a Polish railwayman's cap and a jacket and a pair of trousers from an unknown source.

In conclusion, I should like to stress how easy it would have been for Levi to have simply let everything pour out of him. He chose to build instead: out of the mud, the blows dealt without anger, out of that unique humiliation he has constructed two incomparable works of art, written in a careful, weighted and serenely beautiful prose. . . . In Italy they are rightly regarded as classics, but not—as yet—of the safe kind. I hope they will one day be so regarded here. . . . I hope they find their way into the hands of the practitioners of the new sentimentality—those who try to persuade us, with increasing shrillness, that Man is vile; the artists who use the terrible fact of the camps for emotional and aesthetic effect, and the critics who compare their grimmer brand of kitsch to *King Lear* and the paintings of Goya's last years. Levi, who has confronted the experience, could not be persuaded that our short time on earth is just a matter of waste disposal. He has heard songs other than those of the crow. (pp. 245-46)

Paul Bailey, "Saving the Scaffolding," in New Statesman, *Vol. 82, No. 2109, August 20, 1971, pp. 245-46.*

MIRNA RISK

Reviewers who had thought that the research chemist Primo Levi had exhausted his talent as a writer after *Se questo è un uomo* . . . [and *La tregua*] and who reacted fairly coldly to his subsequent collections of science fiction short stories had to change their minds after reading *Il sistema periodico*. The title of this collection of twenty-one stories, which refers to Mendeleev's table of elements, suggests a thematic unity: every story is titled after the element closest to its theme. The first one, **"Argon,"** compares this so-called inert gas to Levi's own Jewish ancestors. . . . The other stories are moments of Levi's experiences as a student, as a prisoner in Auschwitz, as a writer and most of all as a chemist. . . . **"Chromium,"** possibly the best piece, describes Levi's return to chemical research after the concentration camp and his need to communicate what he had experienced, so as to rediscover humanity in himself. His passion for solving chemical problems and his frantic writing worked simultaneously to help him reenter life with enthusiasm. . . .

But the book is something more than just an autobiography; it mirrors continuously the historical events of the author's generation—Fascism, the Resistance, the postwar years, people who died, people who kept on working. And another thread runs through the stories, as can best be seen in the last of them, **"Carbon."** The chemical history of an atom of carbon is followed through the centuries, till it eventually enters Levi's own brain, gives Levi's hand a certain impulse and leads it to impress the final full stop of the book on paper. There is no divorce between matter . . . and spirit; only through mutual interaction does man develop.

The language is clear, lucid, always extremely concrete; it adds to the fascination of the book because of its very concreteness and nonliterariness.

Mirna Risk, in a review of "Il sistema periodico," in World Literature Today, *Vol. 51, No. 1, Winter, 1977, p. 75.*

ANNE STEVENSON

[Poetry] of social concern stands or falls according to the passionate, rhetorical engagement of the poet. That this engagement must not be egotistical, but tragic, personal and musical, is made evident by such writers as Primo Levi. . . . Levi, in his collected poems [*Shema*], writes out of an experience of suffering which he not only observed but knew. . . . Levi has written two volumes of autobiography, but his poetry is devoid of self-concern. It concentrates on the horror of all human suffering, calling on his readers to consider what has been. Unfortunately, Levi's English translators, Ruth Feldman and Brian Swann, have not printed the originals of his poems. Except for one, **"Shema"** which is included in the Italian, Levi's poems in this edition have lost their music. (p. 492)

Anne Stevenson, "Plumed Hat, Bare Head," in The Listener, *Vol. 97, No. 2504, April 14, 1977, pp. 491-92.*

ALVIN H. ROSENFELD

[*If This Is a Man*], a portrait of the human being *in extremis*—of man ''on the bottom''—is pervaded by the manifold ironies of the literature of absurdity, a literature that renders the utter senselessness of happenings. Grounded in a humane intelligence and persistently curious and observant, it is turned toward whatever remains of the human face after it has been pummeled and befouled by the crime of the camps, barbarized almost beyond recognition but, in rare instances here and there, still retaining a countenance of fraternal decency and brightness.

Levi's story spans the period . . . of the author's incarceration in Auschwitz, a year that seemed ''a journey toward nothingness.'' . . . A man of intellect and civilized manner, who thought in Cartesian categories and once believed that he inhabited a sensible world, Levi found himself suddenly in a place so radically deformed as to disarm thought itself. There is water at the camp, but men and women dying of thirst are forbidden to drink it. Their bunks are made and stand before them, but the dead-weary inmates are not permitted to occupy them. . . . As the blows begin and herds of people are marched off to their deaths, a band plays *Rosamunda*. A brightly illuminated sign across the door reads ''Arbeit Macht Frei'' [''Work Makes Freedom''], but the workers are clearly slaves and most of what they do is senseless, unproductive labor. (p. 56)

For a man trained in thought and guided by its habits, . . . [the intellectual loss] was a drastic one, but it proved to be only one of many deprivations. Stripped of his clothing, his shoes, his hair, even his name, the inmate of Auschwitz soon became, as Levi learned, ''a hollow man, reduced to suffering and needs, forgetful of dignity and restraint.'' . . . Even language, perhaps the final protest against full expropriation, was disarmed and emptied of its normal capacities to function, for in the ''perpetual Babel'' of the camps ''no one listens to you.'' . . . Dispossession, in sum, was all but total.

The literary form that Levi's memoir takes to convey this radical reduction of the human is an intricate and especially interesting one, for the author has written a kind of reverse *Erziehungsroman*, a narrative of *mis*education or an unlearning and relearning of human possibilities. A rationalist inhabiting a place governed by absolute irrationality, Levi sees life devolving to its most elementary forms, all of them to be mastered in order to withstand the camp's clearly perceived plan: ''to annihilate us first as men in order to kill us more slowly afterwards.'' . . . As a matter of basic self-defense, then, the inmates, removed as they are from the social patterns of the civilized order, travel a route that takes them from an accomplished adulthood back to the earliest of childhood beginnings, learning all over again how to eat, how to wash, how to relieve themselves, how to stand, how to dress, how to stay warm, how to sleep, even newly how to talk the special language of the camp. Those who failed at their lessons almost certainly would perish. (pp. 56-7)

[The language] is naturalistic, yet Levi does not place his final perceptions in a merely Darwinian notion of human survival. Given the social structure of the camp, according to which ''the privileged oppress the unprivileged,'' he understood early that survival depended on ''the struggle of each one against all.'' . . . At the same time, he learned . . . other lessons that were likewise basic yet transcended the brute nature of the war of the fit against the less fit. . . . [They] illustrate the necessities of moral survival, even though they might involve nothing more than a washing of one's hands or the simplest gestures of

kindness. . . . [Lessons such as these] strengthened the will to resist deprivation and avoid succumbing to the degradation that precedes and announces death. (p. 57)

> *Alvin H. Rosenfeld, ''Holocaust and History,'' in his* A Double Dying: Reflections on Holocaust Literature, *Indiana University Press, 1980, pp. 37-61.**

RUFUS S. CRANE

The stories [in *Lilít e altri racconti*] are very readable and will appeal to almost all readers. The **''Passato prossimo''** stories, apparently based on the writer's experiences in a German concentration camp, will be of interest to readers who have some knowledge of the situation in Germany and Italy in World War II. The stories in the other two categories [**''Futoro anteriore''** and **''Presente indicativo''**] treat a variety of subjects: astrology, tourism, fantasy, a Roman soldier on duty at Hadrian's Wall in Britain, and more wartime stories. The title of the volume comes from the story of a girl in a concentration camp in Germany who is a constant source of trouble. As long as God continues to sin with Lilith—who, according to rabbinical writings, was supposed to be the first wife of Adam—there will always be grief, sorrow and bloodshed on earth. All the tales without exception could bear retelling, but one story alone will illustrate the high quality of the writing and the ability of the author to portray intense emotion and human feelings. . . . The story in question is **''Il ritorno di Lorenzo.''**

Lorenzo is dead now, and there is no longer any reason to hold back the telling of his remarkable story. He was a bricklayer, a civilian, who was working in France at the time that country fell to the Germans in 1940. He was sent to Auschwitz and put to work in the same concentration camp as the narrator. Unlike the narrator, who was a Jew and an inmate of the camp, Lorenzo was neither a prisoner nor an internee and for that reason received better rations. Throughout the long period they were there Lorenzo, at great risk, managed to share his rations with the narrator. In January 1944, when the Russians were about to reach the camp, the Germans disbanded the Italian group and told them to take off. Lorenzo started out for Italy on foot and eventually reached his home. . . . Lorenzo looked up the narrator's family and told his mother that her son was certainly dead since all Jews at Auschwitz had been sent to the gas chambers. Five months later, however, the narrator arrived home. He went to see Lorenzo, who was drinking heavily and caring less and less about life. The narrator tried in vain to help his friend and benefactor but did finally manage to get him into a hospital. Lorenzo soon escaped because they would not give him any wine. He was found outside, dying, and was taken back to the hospital, where he died in solitude and loneliness.

We learn that Lorenzo helped many prisoners at the camp, Italian and non-Italian. He was a benefactor for the inmates, to whom he gave hope and dignity as well as his rations. The depiction of this Christlike figure, even down to the death/crucifixion by alcohol, is drawn to just the right degree. There is no sentimentality or strained description, no overreaching the mark. The author writes evenly and effectively. . . . Primo Levi is indeed an excellent writer. (pp. 83-4)

> *Rufus S. Crane, in a review of ''Lilít e altri racconti,'' in* World Literature Today, *Vol. 57, No. 1, Winter, 1983, pp. 83-4.*

ROSARIO FERRERI

[Levi] constructs his latest novel, *Se non ora, quando?*, on the plausible historical odyssey of a group of Jews from Eastern Europe during World War II.

As in his first novels, Levi's characters define their individuality in terms of their ability to resist annihilation; but in *Se non ora, quando?* the protagonists learn to identify with a Jewish partisan unit and acquire a new sense of dignity unknown to their forebears. Initially the characters are shadows living in the memories of their devastated homes and families, but the need to take a stand and gather energy pushes them to search their memories for traditional values. . . . Behind the actual fight and the surrounding circumstances is the epic story of the emergence of Jewish consciousness and a feeling of dignity; on another level it is the drama of modern man's quest for self-identity.

Basing his descriptions on historical fact, Levi tells the story of the little-known partisan groups which grew up around the Russian front on both sides of the Nazi lines. The itinerary of adventures takes the protagonists from the steppes of Russia to Italy. . . . As a document, the book is invaluable and extremely interesting. Indeed, previous books by Levi have been well received internationally because their documentary content presented such essential human experience and their subject (the concentration camps) was portrayed in an arresting way with the obvious attempt to universalize one group's experience. The characters generally did not, however, exist independently of the facts and ideas expressed. In this latest book, on the contrary, the individual characters and the various resistance groups leave their definite imprint. Sketched with subtle humor, *Se non ora, quando?* is Levi's first novel fully deserving of the definition. (pp. 265-66)

> *Rosario Ferreri, in a review of "Se non ora, quando?"* in World Literature Today, *Vol. 57, No. 2, Spring, 1983, pp. 265-66.*

H. STUART HUGHES

[*Se questo è un uomo*], Primo Levi's account of his ten-month stay in the place that has become the supreme symbol of Nazi frightfulness, occupies a special niche in concentration-camp literature. (p. 77)

What made his book distinctive? Above all, its tone—its tone of moderation, of equanimity, punctuated by an occasional note of quiet humor. By his own account, Levi had resolved to lift to a level of universality the unspeakable experiences he had been through—to compose "a serene study of certain aspects of the human soul." Rather than pouring out his indignation in a white-hot torrent, as so many others did, he fashioned his book in two stages: first he wrote his chapters "not in logical succession but in order of urgency"; only later, and with a calmer mind, did he fuse them together in accordance with a literary "plan."

Much of what he wrote was familiar when it appeared; much has become still more familiar since. In particular, Levi took care to detail the special circumstances that had enabled him to survive. In common with others who lived to tell the tale, he freely recognized a series of fortunate accidents: his stay in Auschwitz proved short, less than a year; . . . his competence as a chemist eventually entitled him to sheltered work in the neighboring Buna factory. . . . With the approach of the Red Army, the SS guards evacuated the bulk of the prisoners west—

a gruesome winter trek, in which nearly all perished. Levi was one of several hundred too sick to tramp through the snow, who were left behind to await the Russians.

This final ten-day phase of survival, unguarded and abandoned to the bitter January cold, was the only one that Levi narrated in full grisly detail. And for a reason both moral and aesthetic: this was when the Nazis triumphed in defeat, when they broke the spirit even of those who had held out until then, when their former captives sank to less than men. As prisoner after prisoner froze or starved, the remaining human norms collapsed. "It is no longer man who, having lost all restraint, shares his bed with a corpse. Whoever waits for his neighbor to die in order to take his piece of bread is, albeit guiltless, further from the model of thinking man than the most . . . vicious sadist."

Kameraden, ich bin der Letzte! ["Comrades, I am the last!"] Such had been the desperate cry of a rebellious prisoner at the moment of his hanging. . . .

The word "last" he never fully explained. But the implication seemed clear: the prisoner put to death had belonged to a secret ring of resisters and saboteurs that had linked camp to camp; presumably the others had been caught and slaughtered one by one; he, the victim, was the only man of courage left. Evidently the spectators thought so too: no "murmur . . . of assent" to his words rose from their ranks; they shuffled off in silence, overwhelmed by a sense of shame.

In the carefully articulated structure of Levi's book this figured as the collective emotional climax. But it was an earlier episode, narrated in a handful of short, packed sentences, that gave the clue to Levi's personal universe of emotion and value, that unleashed his own cry of anguish. The moment was again one of unbearable tension: the periodic "selection" of the prisoners listed for death. Among those spared was an old Jew called Kuhn. That night oblivious to the fate of his fellows, oblivious to the "abomination" which had just occurred, the wretch prayed aloud to his God, in the hearing of all, giving thanks for his deliverance. "If I were God," was Levi's grim comment, "I would spit out Kuhn's prayer upon the ground."

Why the sudden breakthrough of passionate revulsion? Why did Levi turn on one of his coreligionists his strongest words of scorn? Perhaps the clue may be found in his repeated statement that he could "nourish" no hatred for the German people. He hated no people as such. If he and his fellow Italian Jews clung together, if they shared their sorrows and their tormented dreams of home, it was not through antipathy toward the others—it was because they were so helpless and so few. They did not form a great mass like the Jews from the East. They were not tough and resilient and adept at the arts of barter and theft like the Greek Jews of Salonica. . . . They were gentle, educated, and defenseless. "All lawyers, all with degrees," their numbers soon fell from more than a hundred to forty, since they were no good at manual labor, since it was easy to steal their food, since they were slapped from morning till night. (pp. 78-80)

For such as these, the act of giving thanks for a special favor bestowed from on high smacked of a notion of Judaism that they had abandoned generations ago. The "ecumenical humanism" which had taken its place admitted of no limitations on a universal claim to sympathy. Thus, when on his return home Primo Levi was seized by an irresistible compulsion to reckon up what he had been through, it had nothing to do with paying off old scores; it meant to deepen one's understanding of an evil so vast and irreparable that it had permeated the lives of one and all. *Der Mann hat keine Ahnung,* the man has no glimpse of the truth, he wrote, relapsing into the German of the concentration camp, when, twenty-two years after the war's end, his former superior in the Buna chemical laboratory, who by an odd chance had become his business correspondent, suggested a friendly reunion. What shocked Levi was not so much the memory of the unfeeling way this man had treated him nearly a quarter-century before; it was the German's total incomprehension of the evil which he and his countrymen had either done or countenanced; it was the implicit request for "absolution"—coupled with the insufferable suggestion that Levi had transcended his own Judaism by following the Christian injunction to love one's enemies! (p. 80)

As Levi's first book had told of his descent into the inferno, so his second [*La tregua*] recorded his struggle up again to the land of the living, his effort to purge himself of the "poison of Auschwitz" that tormented his dreams. . . . [Levi] had the happy sensibility of an amateur anthropologist: he knew the trick of turning boredom into education. (pp. 81-2)

Levi's undimmed curiosity served him well in the process of recovering his sense of himself as a human being. And the fellow human beings he encountered along his way—a mixed bag of hardy survivors—provided one after another the subjects he needed for a magnificent series of vignettes to document what he had learned and was still learning about mankind's infinite, its universal capacity to rebound from disaster. (p. 82)

It was toward [the Russians] that Levi's steady, gravely ironic gaze was directed most intensely; it was from them that he learned the most about the common humanity he was striving to understand. He knew only a few words of their language; in Auschwitz his scientist's fluent knowledge of German had given him access to the mentality of his captors and a command of the lingua franca of their victims; on his journey home he was reduced to observation from the outside. But what he discovered rang true: he caught the maddening contrast between natural warmheartedness and official insensitivity that has baffled successive waves of subsequent visitors. . . . [The] demobilized men of the Red Army, whom he watched day after day along an endless road, trudged home—"often barefoot, . . . some singing lustily, others gray-faced and exhausted— they scarcely seemed conquerors. Yet behind them (and him), he noted, lay "the inscrutable Soviet bureaucracy, an obscure and gigantic power, . . . suspicious, negligent, stupid, contradictory and . . . as blind as the forces of nature." This dread force had rounded up the collaborationist Ukrainian women who Levi also saw coming home, crammed into "roofless cattle trucks," joyless and hopeless, humiliated and shamed. Levi "watched their passage, with compassion and sadness," as " a new testimony to . . . the pestilence which had prostrated" his continent.

So he refrained from judgment on his Russian hosts. He took advantage, rather, of his enforced sojourn among them, to learn what they could teach, by action and gesture, of the colossal evil they had at once suffered, inflicted, and survived. On balance, their resilience and their vitality gave him greater reason for hope than for dismay. (pp. 82-3)

"The awesome privilege of our generation and of my people": so Primo Levi summed up what the vicissitudes of his wartime existence had taught him. Twelve years later he was prepared to add that his "baggage of dreadful memories" had become a "treasure." The affirmative tone is startling. (p. 84)

H. Stuart Hughes, "Two Captives Called Levi," in his Prisoners of Hope: The Silver Age of the Italian Jews, 1924-1974, *Cambridge, Mass.: Harvard University Press, 1983, pp. 55-85.**

BETTY FALKENBERG

In his novel *Elective Affinities*, Goethe drew on chemistry— the way, for example, alkalines and acids interact—to drive home the inexorable nature of the attractions between his characters. In *The Periodic Table,* Primo Levi turns chemistry's Periodic Law into a system for weighing and elucidating certain chosen elements of his own past.

One is struck in both cases by the unlikely aptness of the chemical metaphor: its ability to render precise images and at the same time to yield endlessly rich associative material from the unconscious and from myth. As did Goethe some 200 years earlier, Levi really lives in the scientific and literary realms, so there is never a sense of straining. Indeed, his deep human commitments and profound sense of calling give this professional chemist's vocabulary a totally new dimension and urgency. . . .

This third work—originally published in Italy in 1975—is again a memoir. But by its very design and concept it is also a highly conscious artifice that clearly jumps the genre. Each chapter focuses on a person, an experience or some facet of the author's past that evokes or corresponds in "weight" to a chemical element. . . .

Just as the chemical metaphor throws light on the human element, the language—like "all languages on the frontier and in transition"—reveals wonderful truths about its users. Contrasts between its rugged Piedmontese texture and its solemn Hebrew inlay thus cause Levi to ponder another more general conflict: between the divine vocation of the Jews scattered among the Gentiles and the daily misery of their existence, mitigated by laughter born of the tension. . . .

"Iron," a truly compelling chapter, deals with a youthful friendship. "Sandro climbed the rocks more by instinct than technique, trusting to the strength of his hands and saluting, ironically, in the projecting rock to which he clung, the silicon, calcium and magnesium he had learned to recognize in the course on mineralogy.". . . Never in quest of memorable feats, what was important to him was "to know his limitations, to test and improve himself." But none of this helped. "Sandro was Sandro Delmastro, the first man to be killed fighting in the Resistance with the Action Party's Piedmontese Military Command. . . . He lived completely in his deeds, and when they were over nothing of him remains—nothing but words, precisely."

The implicit irony in that statement is typical of Levi's mental bent. Opposites inhere, if not in things themselves, then in our perception of them. With matter as with man, with words as with actions, we are ever in an adversary relationship. Our function is to take the blows and to hand them out. The nobility of man lies in making himself "the conqueror of matter" because "understanding matter is necessary to understand the universe and ourselves." But matter . . . is no less difficult to comprehend than any human adversary. (p. 16)

Levi raises his attitude of neither condoning nor altogether condemning to a moral precept. In a world where grand principles, grand rhetoric and grand schemes have created so much havoc, it is the human scale that is to be honored. Appropriate to the measure of man, then, is the Periodic Table, a precise if modest poetry that can be used to ward off the stench of Fascist "Truths," the misty mystique of dogma.

"Vanadium" gives this theme its most eloquent treatment. The chapter again addresses the Auschwitz years, but through a new and startling confrontation. . . .

While employed in a varnish factory in the '60s, Levi is obliged to ask a German supplier to investigate some faulty shipments. His supplier's name is Müller; the name of the suspect substance is naphenate. In a letter, however, Müller spells it "naptenate." Now memory's curious wheels begin to turn. At the lab in Auschwitz where Levi was put to work there was also a Müller who said "naptylamin," instead of "napthylamin." Levi writes a personal letter to Müller. A correspondence ensues, and as Müller's persona is revealed a whole typology of German postwar mentality emerges. The deplorable events of Auschwitz are attributed vaguely to Man. . . . [Müller] claims to have had no knowledge "of any proviso that seemed aimed at the killing of the Jews"—even though on clear days the flames of the crematorium were visible from his factory.

Müller has read Levi's book on Auschwitz. He sees in it "an overcoming of Judaism, a fulfillment of the Christian precept to love one's enemies, and a testimony of faith in Man. . . ." He winds up the letter with an urgent request for a meeting, preferably on the French Riviera. "Eight days later I received from Mrs. Müller the announcement of the unexpected death of Doktor Lothar Müller in his sixtieth year of life."

A more flamboyant writer would have ended on that dramatic note. Instead, the final chapter ["**Carbon**"] follows the course of a single atom of carbon that lies buried in limestone, until with a blow of the pickax it is freed, "plunged into the world of things that change." Ultimately it enters the author's body, where it partakes of his decision on the place for the last period.

The impishness of the conclusion is of course calculated—but calculated to restore. And "restorative" is perhaps the word that best describes this beautiful gem of a book. It is no accident that the chosen element, carbon, is an "impurity." Impure for Levi is synonymous with life-giving, with Jewishness, with all that was despised by Fascist and Nazi ideologues. Yes, his final injunction is: Immerse yourself in such impurity. (p. 17)

Betty Falkenberg, "Organic Chemistry," in The New Leader, *Vol. LXVII, No. 21, November 26, 1984, pp. 16-17.*

ALVIN H. ROSENFELD

The 21 pieces in *The Periodic Table,* each named after an element, are . . . at one and the same time rigorous "confrontations with Mother-Matter" and vividly drawn portraits of human types—analytical "tales of militant chemistry" and imaginative probings of personal, social and political experience. It is rare to find such diverse aims in combination, and rarer still to find them so successfully integrated in a contemporary work of literature. Yet that is what we have in this beautifully crafted book, the most recent and in many ways the most original of Mr. Levi's three volumes of autobiographical reflection. . . .

The book's first piece, **"Argon,"** . . . is a homage to the author's Jewish ancestors, themselves a breed apart. Intent on retrieving his innumerable aunts and uncles from a legendary past, Mr. Levi at the same time rescues for posterity snatches of their lost language, a local version of Judeo-Italian that combined Hebrew roots with Piedmontese endings and inflections. . . . The revivification of this jargon (which Mr. Levi elsewhere refers to as a kind of "Mediterranean Yiddish") and of some of the people who once spoke it is a sizable accomplishment and, in its linguistic precision and playful wit, sets the tone and direction for the pieces that follow. . . .

To Mr. Levi there are no such things as emotionally neutral elements, just as there are no emotionally neutral men and women. Thus, whether a given story's focus is on friendship, mountain-climbing, early encounters with love or the troubled status of being a Jew in Mussolini's Italy, the author is able to strike a fitting correlation with one of the elements. Mercury, "always restless," is "a fixed and volatile spirit." Zinc, by contrast, is "a boring metal," "not an element which says much to the imagination" (it requires the presence of impurities to react, and in Fascist Italy, as Mr. Levi's imagination seizes upon the analogy, the Jew was to be the impurity—in his case, almost proudly so). There are elements, such as iron and copper, that are "easy and direct, incapable of concealment"; others, such as bismuth and cadmium, that are "deceptive and elusive." The point of these figurations is to revive "the millennial dialogue between the elements and man" and to show that in none of its aspects is nature impermeable to intelligence.

The intelligence made manifest throughout this book is a relentlessly inquisitive one, dedicated to understanding the most subtle dimensions of matter and of man. At once analytic and novelistic, it is the intelligence of a writer who has been able to forge an unusual synthesis of scientific learning and poetic sensibility, of rational procedures and moral perceptions. Its aim, therefore, is both to comprehend and to create, and thereby to keep from being victimized by all outward assaults, spiritual as well as material. . . .

[For] all of its musings upon the enigmas of matter, *The Periodic Table* is best read as a historically situated book and will mean most to those readers who are alert to the mind's engagements with moral as well as physical truths. Thus **"Iron,"** dedicated to Sandro Delmastro, a fellow chemistry student (and the first Resistance fighter to be killed in the Piedmont), is primarily about the nobility of friendship, as **"Phosphorus"** is more a tale of sexual attraction than it is an anatomy of life in the laboratory. Both pieces, set in the 1940's, have far more to do with the vagaries of human relationships under the Italian racial laws than with the laws of chemistry.

The real attraction of *The Periodic Table,* therefore, lies in the author's ability to probe human events with as much discriminating power as he probes nature and in his refusal to surrender the sovereignty of independent inquiry to either stolid matter or a stupid and savage politics. If one sees the book in this way, it is not difficult to understand how chemistry became for Mr. Levi as much a "political school" as a trade. . . .

The Periodic Table is not an angry or a brooding book. On the contrary, it is a work of healing, of tranquil, even buoyant imagination. The meditative power of *Survival in Auschwitz* and *The Reawakening* is fully evident but is joined by a newly acquired power of joyful invention.

Alvin H. Rosenfeld, "Elements of a Life," in The New York Times Book Review, *December 23, 1984, p. 9.*

PAUL WEST

Levi published *The Periodic Table* 10 years ago: an extraordinary, nimble, fluent book from an extraordinary life, part autobiography, part fiction, but essentially something like a memoir of elemental matter. . . . Here are the rites of passage— young man hunting a career in science, falling in love, winning the highest academic honors, doing vital and also trivial experiments, mountaineering, getting sucked into the rapids of power politics—intimately related to the ineluctable matrix of all life. . . .

Levi's main aim is to get across what almost any sentient mind ought to find in its context, savoring the intricate and invisible and quirky material relationships that surround us. Like Dreiser, he sees the human as a chemism, but goes far beyond, humanizing his chosen chemicals into performers in an erudite drama whose rules framed themselves in the first few seconds of the Big Bang. It is an amazing, delightful conception, linking Levi to such writers as Sir Thomas Browne and Francis Ponge; he doesn't stick as closely to the periodic table as I'd hoped (he ignores atomic weight, as well as 82 of the elements), doesn't always give the titular element full play in the chapter named for it, and doesn't seem to want to exploit the table as a structure-conferring device.

Yet such carping is the measure of the man's originality. This is one of the most intelligent books to come along in years, not only because it reveals a fine mind having sport with things it knows backwards, but also because, with articulate and near-mystical infatuation, it exposes the riddles of material being.

> Paul West, *"Formulas for Literary Alchemy,"* in Book World—The Washington Post, *December 30, 1984, p. 7.*

PUBLISHERS WEEKLY

[In *If Not Now, When?*] the [holocaust] experience is not recalled but deeply imagined, with humor, respect, dignity— with what Irving Howe in a warmhearted introduction astutely calls Levi's "moral poise." Here the Jew is portrayed not as victim but as active agent affirming his humanity against impossible odds. Unfolding in the war years 1943-1945, the action is set in Eastern Europe, where a band of Jewish partisans— some of them onetime Soviet soldiers, some escapees from the Nazi charnel-houses—are locked in rear-guard, tangential, guerrilla warfare against the enemy, actions strategically insignificant and inherently futile. Save for one thing: that far more than actions on the grand scale—those that win wars and define history—these obscure, courageous deeds will breathe life into the virtually extinguished human spirit. That we do now know Levi's work better is something of a scandal.

> A review of *"If Not Now, When?"* in Publishers Weekly, *Vol. 227, No. 8, February 22, 1985, p. 151.*

IRVING HOWE

[After World War II], back in Italy, [Levi] heard from a friend reports about a Yiddish-speaking partisan unit that had survived the fighting in Eastern Europe and somehow had ended up in Milan. This story, together with the stories he had heard in Auschwitz, seems to have lodged itself deeply in his mind, though it was not until many year later . . . that he would come back to the Yiddish partisans. In 1982 he published a novel based on their experiences, with the title *If Not Now, When?*

A great success in Italy, *If Not Now, When?* should be read first of all as a tribute to those East European Jews who tried to offer some resistance to the Nazis. It is a gesture of solidarity and, in a quiet way, identification. The immediate occasion for this novel, Levi has written, was a noisy controversy—and probably a fruitless one too—that has been raging for several decades about the behavior of the Jews during the Holocaust:

> Did [the Jews] really allow themselves to be led to the slaughter without resistance? . . . In my opinion, this discussion is unhistorical and polluted by prejudices. As a former partisan and deportee, I know very well that there are some political and psychological conditions in which resistance is possible, and others in which it is not. (p. 14)

[After the war], Levi began to make notes, and then a coherent account from his notes, about the Auschwitz experience. He knew, or in the course of writing learned, that with materials so dreadful in nature, so without historical precedent and therefore so resistant to conceptual grasp, the writer needs most of all to keep a strict discipline of exactitude in recall and description. . . . How difficult and at times impossible this discipline can be, anyone who has read Holocaust memoirs and fictions can testify. It requires an emotional restraint and a steadiness of creative purpose that can seem almost indecent to demand from survivors. Yet if such memoirs are to constitute more than a howl of rage or pain, there is no other way to write them.

Speaking about Levi's first book, the recollection of Auschwitz entitled *If This Is a Man* (1947), H. Stuart Hughes finds its point of distinction in Levi's "equanimity, punctuated by an occasional note of quiet humor" [see excerpt above]. That is right, but I would also speak about a quality in Levi's work that might be called moral poise. I mean by this an act of complete reckoning with the past, insofar as there can be a complete reckoning with such a past. (pp. 14-15)

Close to the finely woven surface of *If This Is a Man* there hover all the terrible questions that the Holocaust has forced upon us, questions about the nature of man and the absence of God, or, if you prefer, the failure of man and the search for God. But Levi is sufficiently shrewd a writer to avoid a head-on collision with his theme—even when writing about the Holocaust, a writer needs a little shrewdness. Perhaps later; perhaps future generations will be able to "make sense" of it all, but not now. (p. 15)

Toward those . . . with whom he shared suffering and death, Levi is invariably generous. He writes not so much to record the horrors, though there is no shortage of them in *If This Is a Man,* but to salvage memories of human beings refusing, if only through helpless symbolic gestures, to cease being human. There is a stirring passage in *If This Is a Man:* Levi recalls a day when he and a few other prisoners were put to work scraping an underground gasoline tank. They worked in almost total darkness, and the work was very hard. Then, from some inner fold of memory, Levi began telling the young French prisoners about Dante's great poem, reciting the lines,

> Think of your breed; for brutish
>   ignorance
> Your mettle was not made; you were
>   made men,
> To follow after knowledge and
>   excellence.

Coming "like the blast of a trumpet, like the voice of God," these lines flood the hearts of the prisoners, so that "for a moment I forget who I am and where I am" and the wretched might suppose they are still human beings. . . .

If one can detect traces of a "Jewish" spirit or tone in Levi's first book, then. . . . [*The Reawakening*] seems rather more "Italian." Something of what we like to suppose as essentially Italian—a gaiety of voice, a fine, free pleasure in the things of this world—breaks through in *The Reawakening,* even as its figures still bear the stigmata of the camps. The book . . . moves with a strong, even lyrical, narrative force. It is filled with vibrant sketches of former prisoners and stray soldiers, mostly young, who marvel at their own survival. In their rags and in the midst of their hunger, they are overwhelmed with a guilty joy at being free to savor the commonplace sensations of existence. The book itself also radiates that guilty joy, as its narrator yields to the pleasure of being able to smile at misadventures that still carry pain but, in representing a return to the realm of the human, can be endured, even accepted.

Wandering across Poland and Russia, Levi and his companions enact a curious version of picaresque adventure. Outwardly, along the skin of narrative, *The Reawakening* appears to follow the traditional pattern of picaresque: a series of more or less comic episodes loosely strung together with a central narrator-observer who does not so much act on his own as "receive" the actions of others. But in basic spirit the book is anti-picaresque. Between the external form of the narrative and its inner vibrations of memory there is a strong nervous tension—like that between the first hesitant taste of freedom and the overpowering image of the camps. To sustain this tension throughout the narrative is a remarkable feat of literary craft.

Levi has a special gift for the vignette, and in this book it reaches an easy fruition. He moves from figure to figure, each of whom enacts a sort of ritual return to life by yielding to the delights of free sensation, even the sensation of that bewilderment and pain that is one's own, not imposed. (p. 16)

Soon after *The Reawakening* appeared in English translation, a British critic, John Gross, wrote some thoughtful comments upon reading it:

> We are all predisposed to praise books by concentration camp survivors; and indeed no record of that most terrible of experiences can be without value. Under the circumstances, it usually seems tactless to raise questions of literary merit. . . . Yet the sad fact is that the quality of the writing *does* count, however harrowing the subject, and that much of [Holocaust] literature . . . is effective only at the level of poignant documentary. To have been a witness, and a survivor, and a born writer was a rare combination.

Now, on the face of it, Gross is surely right: "the quality of the writing *does* count." Yet even while nodding agreement, we are likely to notice within ourselves a decided inner resistance. Before so intolerable a subject, may not the whole apparatus of literary criticism, with all its nice discriminations and categories, seem incongruous, even trivial? (pp. 16-17)

I am inclined to think that there is no easy answer, perhaps no answer at all, to this problem. The more sensitive writers on Holocaust themes have apparently felt that their subject cannot be met full-face or head-on. . . . If approached at all, the Holocaust must be taken on a tangent, with extreme wariness, through oblique symbols, strategies of indirection, and circuitous narratives. Yet the irony is this: no sooner do we speak about ways of approaching this subject than we return to a fundamental concern of literary criticism, thereby perhaps acknowledging that John Gross was right, after all, in what he wrote about Levi's work. . . .

If Not Now, When? is a curious work of fiction. Levi stakes everything on his capacity to imagine experiences that by their very nature must be alien to him. And it is *because* these experiences—the ordeals of the East European Jews—are not known to him firsthand that he chooses to take the risk of rendering them. Since he has had "to reconstruct an era, a scenario, and a language [Yiddish]" which he "knew only spottily" the result cannot quite have the sensuous immediacy and abundance of many episodes in *The Reawakening.*

Yet it's in *If Not Now, When?* that certain of Levi's strongest literary gifts are allowed full play. All along he had shown a large and "natural" gift for narrative movement, although his early books, by their very nature, could not bring that gift to full development. But *If Not Now, When?* speeds along with an accumulating energy, even suspense, its treatment of the struggle undertaken by the powerless Jewish partisans resembling somewhat an adventure story. True, a strange kind of adventure, with pitifully few possibilities for external action. It's rather an adventure in which a few desperate acts and small deeds must be taken as tokens of a large spiritual intention. What these partisans do has little military significance, it is closer to gesture than achievement; but through their raids and escapades they are trying to establish that a pacific people can muster the use of arms without, perhaps, abandoning its deep repugnance at having to take up arms. . . .

Quite the strongest part of the novel is, I think, the one in which the two stragglers, Mendel and Leonid, stumble upon the "republic of the marshes," an encampment of Jews who have fled the Nazi terror of the cities and are now huddling together in a precarious community. Levi's evocation of life in this little oasis is simply brilliant, starting with his physical description of the place and proceeding to sharply etched portrayals of the figures who have here found a moment or two of rest. This little settlement comes to seem emblematic of the Jewish situation during these years—a moment of breath before asphyxiation, a wish to hold together even though everyone knows this to be impossible. It is like the soul's last cry for air and sun.

Later, the novel changes course, and Levi presents an often fierce and exciting story of partisan activities: their relations with Russian and Polish guerrilla fighters, their occasional encounters with the Germans, and their inner crises and transformations. Reading this portion of Levi's book, I found myself responding to it less as a depiction of events supposedly happening than as an effort by this writer . . . to thrust himself into the situation of the East European Jews, indeed, to become one with them. It's as if the novel here turned into a kind of exemplary fable, a story mediated through the desires of a writer who has yielded himself utterly to unseen brothers and sisters in martyrdom.

And I felt about Primo Levi: he is a friend, this writer who creates for us a miniature universe of moral striving and reflectiveness, filtered through ordeals of memory, reinforced by resources of imagination. I kept hearing the voice of a man struggling to retrieve the sense of what it means in the twentieth century to be, or become, a *Mensch*. (p. 17)

Irving Howe, "How to Write about the Holocaust," in The New York Review of Books, *Vol. XXXII, No. 5, March 28, 1985, pp. 14-17.*

BERNARD KNOX

Guerilla warfare against the German forces of occupation in France, Italy and Yugoslavia is a familiar theme for the Western reader, documented by personal memoirs and recreated in impressive novels and films. . . . Primo Levi's novel [*If Not Now, When?*] introduces an aspect of that huge and ferocious war which is entirely unfamiliar—Jewish partisans. It is the story of the suffering, struggles and exploits of a small band of Jewish irregulars who fight their way westward, all the way to Italy, the staging area for Palestine. (p. 3)

The book is fiction but it is firmly based on reality—the stories of Jewish refugees arriving at an assistance center in Milan at the end of the war. "Some bands similar to the one I have aimed to portray," Levi writes in an Author's Note, "really did arrive in Italy; men and women whom years of suffering had hardened but not humiliated, survivors of a civilization . . . that Nazism had destroyed to its roots. Exhausted, these survivors were still aware of their dignity." . . . [Levi] has also studied the documents, in English, Italian, Yiddish and German, which deal with Jewish resistance movements in the east. But there is nothing bookish about his narrative; Levi is one of modern Italy's most skillful and original writers. His characters are vibrantly alive; their voices resound with the unmistakable vigor and humor of East European Yiddish as we know it from such writers as Isaac Bashevis Singer; by some miracle of transformation Levi's Italian simulation of a language he himself knows "only marginally" has emerged as salty, vigorous English in William Weaver's fine translation.

This tale of resistance and escape, varying in tone from epic to picaresque, presents a realistic picture of partisan life, of a world in which the obsessive fear of encirclement, the fatigue and privation of the hunted, find their only compensation in the proud conviction that it is better to go to your death fighting than like sheep to the slaughter. (p. 14)

Bernard Knox, "Primo Levi's Prelude to an Exodus," in Book World—The Washington Post, *May 19, 1985, pp. 3, 14.*

Robert (Traill Spence) Lowell (Jr.)

1917-1977

American poet, dramatist, editor, translator, critic, and novelist.

Widely considered the most influential American poet of the mid-twentieth century, Lowell is acclaimed for his revolutionary contributions to the confessional movement and for his mastery of the techniques of modernism. The strength of tradition predominant in his work—both the English and European literary traditions and the social traditions of his Puritan heritage—distinguishes his poetry from the work of other confessionalists. Likewise, his candor and the intensity of his dark vision set him apart from the formalists with whom his life and art were intimately connected.

Lowell's private life was marked by profound emotional and spiritual turmoil. Nicknamed "Cal" in his school days after the infamous Roman ruler Caligula because of his manic behavior, Lowell later suffered bouts of madness that frequently resulted in hospitalization. His emotional instability, precarious family relations, and the increasing disorder of modern society contributed to his inner turbulence. Lowell reacted strongly to the rapidly changing social and political climate of his time; his refusal to serve in World War II resulted in a one-year sentence in a federal penitentiary, of which he served about six months, and his objection to the Vietnam War led him to publicly decline an invitation to the White House Festival of the Arts in 1965. The intensity of Lowell's private life and his response to the world around him form the thematic core of his art.

Lowell was born into an established New England family whose ancestors include the literary figures Amy Lowell and James Russell Lowell. His social position, formal education, and early interest in poetry brought him into contact with nearly every significant American poet of his time. At St. Mark's School in Massachusetts, where he was a student from 1930 to 1935, he began writing poetry under the guidance of academic poet Richard Eberhart. From 1935 to 1937 Lowell studied at Harvard University. There he first encountered the poetry of William Carlos Williams, which perhaps most significantly influenced Lowell's break in the 1950s from the formal style of his early works to the openness of form and content of his confessional poems. Lowell was nevertheless unhappy at Harvard, and in the summer of 1937 he accompanied novelist Ford Madox Ford on a journey to the home of poet and critic Allen Tate. Lowell spent the summer with Tate and his wife, the novelist Caroline Gordon, and became involved with the circle of artists known as the Southern Fugitives. Basically formalist in their aesthetics, the group aimed to create a literature utilizing the best qualities of modern and traditional art. Lowell immersed himself fully in the activities of the Fugitives, and their influence in varying degrees can be seen throughout his career. At the end of the summer Lowell enrolled at Kenyon College in Ohio, where he studied with poet Randall Jarrell and Fugitive poet and critic John Crowe Ransom, and graduated *summa cum laude* in 1940 with a degree in classics. He also took graduate courses at Louisiana State University from 1940 to 1941 under the guidance of the leading New Critics Robert Penn Warren and Cleanth Brooks.

Lowell's first book, *Land of Unlikeness* (1944), with its metrical intricacy, formal approach, and critical introduction by Allen Tate, clearly reflects the influence of the Southern literati. At the center of the book is Lowell's response to the turbulent political events of World War II and his conversion to Roman Catholicism in reaction to the Protestantism of his heritage. Highly mannered yet almost violent in their rebelliousness, the poems contain much religious symbolism. Despite the unpolished nature of the collection, it earned Lowell moderate acclaim and introduced him as an important new voice in modern poetry. His next collection, *Lord Weary's Castle* (1946), was awarded the Pulitzer Prize in poetry and firmly established Lowell's presence in American literature. In "The Kingdom of Necessity," one of the most influential early reviews of Lowell's work, Randall Jarrell observed that the oppositional pull between "that cake of custom in which all of us lie embedded" and "everything that is free or open, that grows or is willing to change" can be seen at the heart of Lowell's work. "The Quaker Graveyard in Nantucket," the book's most acclaimed poem and one of Lowell's most famous works, exemplifies these dual forces. Revolving around the death of Warren Winslow, Lowell's cousin who died while serving in the Navy, the poem displays Lowell's characteristic historical awareness as well as his acute sensitivity to the chaos and failures of the modern world. *The Mills of the Kavanaughs*

(1951) is largely considered an ambitious although unsuccessful attempt to explore new poetic techniques. Written in the form of dramatic monologues, the poems in this collection are marked by highly rhetorical, symbolic language, resulting in a work that is regarded by most critics as convoluted and burdensome.

Lowell's next collection of verse, *Life Studies* (1959), was described by Steven Gould Axelrod as a work of "brilliantly original art." This volume signals a breakthrough in both content and style and is regarded by many critics as Lowell's greatest achievement. Abandoning the formal concerns of his first three collections, Lowell turned to free verse and created the poetic voice of intense personal concern that characterizes the best confessional poetry. In this work he incorporated the aesthetic of common speech introduced to him by William Carlos Williams and the clear, sharp imagism of Elizabeth Bishop. Lowell's profound emotional energy, the depth of his self-scrutiny, and his synthesis of private and public concerns marks this as one of the most influential volumes of postwar poetry. In *For the Union Dead* (1964) Lowell continued in the confessional vein but placed increasing emphasis on the interplay of past and present and the social and political. Whereas *Life Studies* revolves primarily around Lowell's emotionally charged family history, *For the Union Dead* confronts more specifically the spiritual hollowness of the technologically advanced modern society and its alienating effect on the individual.

Throughout the remainder of his life Lowell continued to write and revise extensively, drawing on his strong sense of personal history and literary tradition as well as the problems in his private life and the world around him. His output during these years was considerable. The first half of *Near the Ocean* (1967) contains Lowell's free translations of the work of Horace, Juvenal, Dante, and others in the manner of his earlier work, *Imitations* (1961). The second half consists of poems written in couplets, reminiscent of the formal style of his earliest volumes. *Notebook 1967-1968* (1969; revised, 1970), a combination of formal and informal concerns, was revised and expanded in 1973 into three separate volumes of unrhymed sonnets: *For Lizzie and Harriet, The Dolphin,* and *History*. Lowell's last collection, *Day by Day* (1977), which, according to Helen Vendler, is characterized by its "disarming openness," led to comparisons with *Life Studies*. Both works are noted for their piercing autobiographical frankness and openness of poetic form. Expressing tenderness as well as anguish, this collection shows Lowell reviewing his life and confronting his death with a quietness of tone not evident in his earlier works.

Never fully satisfied with his own art, Lowell continually revised his work, and many poems appear in significantly different forms in various collections. In addition to his poetry and translations, or "imitations," Lowell wrote several plays, most notably *The Old Glory* (1964), a series of three short works—*Benito Cereno, Endecott and the Red Cross* and *My Kinsman, Major Molineux*—in which he explores the American past through adaptations of stories by Herman Melville and Nathaniel Hawthorne.

Despite the diverse changes in form that characterize his art, Lowell's drive to express his personal torment and the struggles of the nation provides a connective thread, resulting in a unified and distinguished body of work. Lowell's fusion of the formal concerns of modernism and the personal concerns of confessionalism, his vision of the inextricability of the public and private selves, and the superior talent with which he crafted

his work have established him as a central figure of postwar American poetry.

(See also *CLC*, Vols. 1, 2, 3, 4, 5, 8, 9, 11, 15; *Contemporary Authors*, Vols. 9-12, rev. ed., Vols. 73-76 [obituary]; and *Dictionary of Literary Biography*, Vol. 5.)

HELEN VENDLER

[The essay from which this excerpt is taken was written in 1978.]

Lowell began as a writer of an obscure and oblique poetry, which struggled violently with murky feeling, invented baffling displaced sufferings like those in *The Mills of the Kavanaughs*, resisted interpretation, and discovered original resources in traditional forms. This poetry, in spite of its difficulty, attracted wide attention and praise, so much so that its very strength was the greatest obstacle to Lowell's poetic progress. *Life Studies* disappointed readers attached to Lowell's earlier "Catholic" manner, and the lean and loose-jointed poems which are now his most famous work had to wait some time for popular acceptance. Just as *Life Studies* entered the anthologies, Lowell returned to a species of formality, writing innumerable sonnets (collected in *Notebook* and subsequent volumes), compressing life with what seemed extraordinary cruelty and candor into a Procrustean and unyielding shape. These poems have not yet been assimilated—except in a voyeuristic way—into the American literary consciousness. "It takes ten years," Lowell said dryly of popular acquiescence.

Now he has ended, in *Day by Day*, as a writer of disarming openness, exposing shame and uncertainty, offering almost no purchase to interpretation, and in his journal-keeping, abandoning conventional structure, whether rhetorical or logical. The poems drift from one focus to another; they avoid the histrionic; they sigh more often than they expostulate. They acknowledge exhaustion; they expect death. Admirers of the sacerdotal and autocratic earlier manner are offended by this diminished diarist, this suddenly quiescent volcano. But Lowell knew better than anyone else what he had given up: "Those blessèd structures, plot and rhyme— / why are they no help to me now," he begins his closing poem, "**Epilogue.**" He had been willing to abandon plot and rhyme in writing poems about things recalled—in order to make that recall casual and natural. But now, in his last poem, he wanted "to make something imagined, not recalled," and wished to return to plot and rhyme. But the habit of the volume held, and the last testament is unrhymed and unplotted, as unstructured apparently as its companions. Despairingly, Lowell contrasts himself with the "true" artists, the painter, feeling himself to be like Hawthorne's Coverdale, only an American daguerrotypist:

> Sometimes everything I write
> with the threadbare art of my eye
> seems a snapshot,
> lurid, rapid, garish, grouped,
> heightened from life,
> yet paralyzed by fact.

Lowell here anticipates all that could be said, and has been said, in criticism of his last book: that his art does not go clothed in the gorgeous tapestry of his earlier work, but is threadbare; that he is making capital of the lurid and garish episodes of his life—adolescent cruelty, family scandal, madness, three marriages; that his poems are rapid sketches rather than finished portraits; that he is hampered by his allegiance to fact without even the compensating virtue of absolute truthfulness, since all is heightened by compression and focus. After this devastating self-criticism, the only self-defense can be the anti-bourgeois question "Yet why not say what happened?" (pp. 157-59)

Abandoning the showy "objective correlatives" for his life which fill the earlier poetry, Lowell prays in his last poem for the "grace of accuracy," which he found in the Dutch realists, from Van Eyck to Vermeer. There is in this volume a painstaking description of Van Eyck's Arnolfini marriage portrait. The couple are not beautiful: the husband stands "long-faced and dwindling," the wife is pregnant; the husband "lifts a hand, / thin and white as his face / held up like a candle to bless her . . . / they are rivals in homeliness and love." In the background of the portrait, Lowell sees all the furniture of their common life: "The picture is too much like their life— / a crisscross, too many petty facts"; a candelabrum, peaches, the husband's wooden shoes "thrown on the floor by her smaller ones," the bed, "the restless marital canopy." This "petty" domestic inclusiveness is what Lowell now proposes to write about in place of his former metaphysical blazes, even in place of his former carefully casual "life studies." We know at least, then, that the aesthetic of the last work was not an unconscious or an unconsidered one. Whether it is, as some would say, a rationalization after the fact, justifying, *faute de mieux,* an exhausted invention, only history can tell; some will see in these pieces a shrewdness of choice and an epigrammatic wit that suggest consummate art. (pp. 159-60)

How, then, are we to read these late poems? Not, certainly, for the blessèd structures of plot and rhyme; not for the hard-driving compression of the late sonnets; not for the transforming and idealizing power of lyric; not for the diamond certainties of metaphysical verse; not for the retrospective and elegiac stationing of figures as in *Life Studies;* not for the visionary furies of youth. One afternoon in spring, I walked with Lowell through Harvard Yard. "Did you see that Christopher Ricks had written a piece [see *CLC,* Vol. 9] about me?" he said. "No, what did he say?" I asked. "He said I'm violent," said Lowell with a mixture of humor and irony. "And Ehrenpreis says you're comic" [see *CLC,* Vol. 8], I said. "Why don't they ever say what I'd like them to say?" he protested. "What's that?" I asked. "That I'm heartbreaking," he said, meaning it.

And so he is. If this book is read, as it should be, as a journal, written "day by day," as a fragment of an autobiography (Lowell called his poems "my verse autobiography,") it is heartbreaking. It records his late, perhaps unwise, third marriage; the birth of a son; the very worst memories suppressed from *Life Studies,* memories of having been an unwanted child and a tormented adolescent; exile in Britain and Ireland; the death of friends; clinical depression and hospitalization, lovemaking and impotence; distress over age; fear of death. Against all this is set the power of writing—"universal consolatory / description without significance, / transcribed verbatim by my eye."

Readers who demand something more than the eye's verbatim transcript, who do not ask whether in fact there is anything more, may not find these poems heartbreaking. But the Wordsworth who said that the meanest flower that blows could give thoughts that do often lie too deep for tears would, I think, understand the tears underlying these "petty facts" of one man's existence. (pp. 160-61)

And yet, for all their air of verbatim description, these poems, like all poems, are invented things. They are invented even in

little. Lowell once handed me a draft of a new poem, called **"Bright Day in Boston."** It begins, "Joy of standing up my dentist, / X-ray plates like a broken Acropolis . . . / Joy to idle through Boston." I was struck by the *panache* of standing up one's dentist, and said so; "Well, as a matter of fact," said Lowell sheepishly, "I actually *did* go to the dentist first, and *then* went for the walk." But in the poem, "the unpolluted joy / And criminal leisure of a boy"—to quote earlier verses—became fact, where in life they had been only wish. The life of desire is as evident in these poems as the life of fact. Medical prescriptions are both named and rejected: "What is won by surviving, / if two glasses of red wine are poison?" The Paterian interval becomes ever smaller: "We only live between / before we are and what we were." Lowell looks in terror to "the hungry future, / the time when any illness is chronic, / and the years of discretion are spent on complaint— / . . . until the wristwatch is taken from the wrist." These deathly truths, unrelieved by any prospect of afterlife or immortality, are, I think, what dismay many readers. How squalid and trivialized a view of death, they may feel—chronic illness, complaint, and that last hospital gesture, the wristwatch taken from the wrist. But over against that end, Lowell sets a flickering terrestrial Eden: "We took our paradise here—how else love?" That "A man love[s] a woman more than women" remained for him an insoluble and imprisoning mystery: "A man without a wife / is like a turtle without a shell." "Nature," says Lowell who is part of nature, "is sundrunk with sex," but he would "seek leave unimpassioned by [his] body." That leave was not granted him: he stayed with women till the end of the party, "a half-filled glass in each hand— / . . . swayed / by the hard infatuate wind of love."

In this last accuracy the poet cannot even see himself as unique, unusual, set apart. There is the humility of the generic about this volume, in spite of its pride in its poetic work. As far as he can see, Lowell tells us, each generation leads the same life, the life of its time. No one in the present is wiser or more foolish than those in the past or the future. No fresh perfection treads on our heels; nor do we represent any decay of nature. This attitude distresses those who come to poetry for hope, transcendence, the inspiriting word. (pp. 162-63)

In a class lecture on Arnold, Lowell once said that "Dover Beach" had been criticized, "in the old days of the New Critics," for not continuing the sea imagery in the last stanza; "But I think by then," Lowell went on, "you've had quite enough of it." His sense of the fluidity of life's events and of human response pressed him into some of the same discontinuity of imagery, and drew the disapproval of purists in structure. Lowell believed—I am quoting another class—that the poem "is an event, not the record of an event"; "the lyric claims to produce an event; it is this for which it strives and which it sometimes brings off." Like an event, the lyric can be abrupt, odd-shaped, irregularly featured, and inconclusive. The important thing is the presence of "exciting or strenuous writing"—what one finds in Henry James, he said, on every page, good or bad. Power and wistfulness stood, for Lowell, in inverse relation: he praised the "tender" poems at the end of *Leaves of Grass* while remarking nonetheless how different in tone Whitman's later poetry, written when he was ill, was from the poetry of his "great healthy days." We might say the same of Lowell's last collection. The impetuousness of the "manic statement" is gone: mania is now viewed with apprehension and horror: "I grow too merry, / when I stand in my nakedness to dress." Even poetry itself can seem to want conviction: it becomes merely a compulsive "processing of words," a ''dull instinctive glow,'' refueling itself from ''bits of paper brought to feed it,'' which it blackens. (pp. 163-64)

Lowell once quoted Eliot on Coleridge: ''By the time he wrote the *Biographia Literaria* he was a ruin, but being a ruin is a sort of occupation.'' (T. S. Eliot actually wrote in *The Use of Poetry and the Use of Criticism*: ''Sometimes, however, to be 'a ruined man' is itself a vocation.'') The remark reveals a good deal about Eliot, but Lowell's citation is interesting in itself: it conveys the conviction of the artist-survivor that there is always something to be made of life, even of its orts and offal, its tired ends, its disappointments and disgusts, its ironies. The sense of the end of life must find some expression, even if in what Stevens called ''long and sluggish lines.'' Without endorsing an imitative form, we can yet find in Lowell's casualness, his waywardness, his gnomic summaries, his fragmentary reflections, authentic representations of a sixty-year-old memory.

Not every poem, I suppose, succeeds in giving ''each figure in the photograph / his living name.'' But the poet who had decided that ''we are poor passing facts,'' felt obliged to a poetry of deprivation and of transient actuality, lit up by moments of unearthly pained happiness. . . . The poetry of ''poor passing facts'' entails the sacrifice in large part of two aspects of Lowell's poetry that had brought him many admirers: his large reference to European literature, through his allusions and translations (which he called ''Imitations''); and his political protest. In that earlier grandeur of literary scope, as well as by the moral grandeur of defiance and protest, Lowell seemed to claim a vision and power for poetry that many readers were happy to see affirmed. Others were more pleased by the development, beginning in *For the Union Dead* and culminating in Lowell's final volume, of a humbler style, that of a man, in Rolando Anzilotti's fine description, ''who confronts directly and with courage his own failures, his faults and despairings, without seeking comfort, without indicating solutions to cling to. Feeling is revealed with the subtlest delicacy and candor, in its essential being.'' ''The eye of Lowell for the particular which becomes universal,'' Anzilotti continues, ''is precise and perfect; . . . we are far away from the oratory, from the bursting out of emotion in tumultuous rhythms, that appeared in **'The Quaker Graveyard.'**'' This line of writing, as Anzilotti points out, remained in equilibrium with the national and moral concerns evident in *Near the Ocean* and *Notebook;* not until this final volume did the precise eye and the quotidian feeling become the dominant forces in Lowell's aesthetic. The allusions in this last collection come from an occasional backward glance to favorite passages—a line of Dante, a line of Horace—but the poetic mind turns less and less to past literature, more and more to the immediacy of present event. There is only one poem in the volume that springs from a political impetus; **''Fetus,''** prompted by the trial, in Boston, of a doctor accused of making no effort to keep an aborted fetus alive. And even the poem quickly leaves its occasion behind and engages in a general meditation on death, that ''black arrow'' arriving like a calling-card ''on the silver tray.'' It is perhaps significant that this poem is the least successful, to my mind, in the group, in part because Lowell no longer has the moral sureness to condemn or approve the abortion. He sees only the grotesquerie of the medical procedure, of the trial court, and of the biological shape of ''the fetus, the homunculus, / already at four months one pound, / with shifty thumb in mouth— / . . . Our little model. . . .'' . . . Social forms disappear in this last phase of Lowell's writing, and public moral witness disappears with them. The solitary human

being, his life extending only as far as the domestic circle, becomes the topic of attention. . . . The personal is seen as the locus of truth, insight, and real action.

And when Lowell writes about the personal, he spares himself nothing, not the patronizing doctor in the asylum addressing Caroline, ''A model guest . . . we would welcome / Robert back to Northampton any time''; not the susurrus of public or private comment about madness having attacked him even in this third, scandalous marriage:

> If he has gone mad with her,
> the poor man can't have been very happy,
> seeing too much and feeling it
> with one skin-layer missing;

not a murderously detached self-portrait among the other mad:

> I am a thorazined fixture
> in the immovable square-cushioned chairs
> we preoccupy for seconds like migrant birds.
>
> (pp. 164-67)

The grand drama of the manic has ended, and it is the depressive side of illness, without the illusions of mania, which gives its tone to these latter poems. As the horizon narrows, the smallest sensations of living—waking up alive, seeing the spring—suffice. ''I thank God,'' says Lowell, ''for being alive— / a way of writing I once thought heartless.'' Heartless because selfish, solipsistic—or so he thought when he was young, and had heart for all the world, or so it seemed. Recognizing the fury of political statement as a displacement of fury against parents, he can no longer permit its unmediated and thoughtless energy. In the poem to his mother, he admits, ''It has taken me the time since you died / to discover you are as human as I am . . . / if I am.'' (p. 168)

Nothing remains for Lowell, then, after he has jettisoned formal religious belief, social protest, a twenty-year marriage, even residence in America, except memory and the present moment. (p. 169)

In writing this last volume, Lowell pleased himself, listening with some inner ear to the inner life of the poem, deciding with mysterious certainty when it was finished, when it had found its equilibrium. I think that the instinctive principles on which he worked will become clearer with time. One writes poetry, he said, by instinct and by ear, and his own instincts and ear were pressing toward a poetry ever more unconventional, ever less ''literary.'' He admired the way Coleridge, in his ballads, could be ''showily simple and get away with it.'' He sought that ostentatious simplicity himself. He added that though Coleridge's verse epistle to Sara Hutchinson—the first version of the Dejection Ode—was embarrassing, yet it was ''a long apologetic masterpiece—something is lost by making it an ode.'' What is lost is the spontaneity, the heartbreak, the domestic anguish—all that appears in Lowell's journal written day by day. No doubt it could all have been transformed into odes; that was his old manner. But the something that was lost in such a case now seemed to him more precious than the something that is found. His last book, however casual it may seem, is not a collection of unconsidered trifles. (pp. 169-70)

''Not to console or sanctify,'' says Stevens, speaking of the aim of modern poetry, ''but plainly to propound.'' The plain propounding . . . , if too severe, for some tastes, is to others profoundly assuaging. We are lucky in America in our poetry of old age: Whitman's, Stevens', and now Lowell's. Such poetry never can speak to the young and form their sensibilities as can the poetry of passion and hope and revolutionary ardor; but it sums up another phase of life, no less valuable, no less moving, no less true. (p. 171)

Helen Vendler, ''Robert Lowell's Last Days and Last Poems,'' in Robert Lowell: A Tribute, *edited by Rolando Anzilotti, Nistri-Lischi Editori, 1979, pp. 156-71.*

STEVEN GOULD AXELROD

''Risk was his métier,'' Lowell said of Ulysses, a symbol of himself. Throughout his career, Lowell demonstrated an astonishing willingness and ability to make his writing new. ''My books have changed,'' he once explained. ''It doesn't really matter whether one style is better than the last. When it no longer serves, you must adventure.'' Despite this characteristic modesty, he was an ambitious poet, and like other American poets before him—Whitman, Pound, Williams, Eliot—he spoke with different voices. Each of his books embodies his struggle to find a way to say the thing he had then to say. None succeeds completely. The books, and the individual poems, are imperfect because not fully distinct from the indeterminacy of the life that produced them. Lowell's ''failure,'' if we want to call it that, is an inextricable feature of his ambition, is indeed part of what his poems are about: his attempt to create a language in which he could more fully realize his being.

He thus stands firmly within the main line of American poetry. Roy Harvey Pearce has observed that ''American poems record the discovery, rediscovery, and again and again the rediscovery of the Fall into Existence—American Existence.'' Lowell's poetry microcosmically recapitulates that repeated rediscovery. Lowell once commented that American literature looks like ''a bravado of perpetual revolution,'' and so indeed does his own poetic career.... Yet for all its dynamism, his poetic oeuvre is unified. At its center is Lowell himself, discovering, altering, creating the conditions of his own existence.

Although the style of Lowell's art changed radically over the years, its essentially experiential character remained constant. ''The thread that strings it together,'' he remarked, ''is my autobiography''; ''what made the earlier poems valuable seems to be some recording of experience and that seems to be what makes the later ones.'' ''Experience'' does not mean only what ''happened'' to Lowell, for that formulation would place too much emphasis on an active but unilateral environment, and would reduce the experiencer's mind to the passive role of a transmitting lens. The mind itself is active, trembling to ''caress the light.''.... ''Experience'' more truly means the sum of the relations and interactions between psyche and environment. It grows from the Cartesian dualism of inner and outer, but through its interpenetrating energies abolishes the dualism. Just as experience mediates between self and world, partaking of both, so Lowell's poems mediate between himself and his world, and between his personal history and that of his readers. His poems are structures of experience. They both record his life and assume a life of their own; and as they transform the poet's life into the autonomous life of art, they reenter his life by clarifying and completing it. (pp. 3-5)

In choosing poems from his early, privately printed book *Land of Unlikeness* to reprint two years later in his first commercial book *Lord Weary's Castle,* Lowell chose the poems that he felt were ''more experienced,'' ''more concrete.'' A decade later, in *Life Studies,* he rejected the impersonal and metrically regular mode of *Lord Weary's Castle* entirely because he found he

''couldn't get [his] experience into tight metrical forms.'' In changing his style and subject matter, he turned away from the canons of Modernist formalism, precisely because Modernist esthetics, from Hulme, Eliot, and Pound on, tended to view the poem as a world of its own, lacking reference to the poet and culture that produced it. Lowell came to see that—at least for himself and perhaps for others—the relationship of art to human experience was too elemental for an ''Impersonal theory of poetry,'' as Eliot called his own early theory, to do anything but block up the springs of inspiration. Lowell explained to Frederick Seidel in 1960 that ''writing seems divorced from culture somehow. It's become too much something specialized that can't handle much experience. It's become a craft, purely a craft, and there must be some breakthrough back into life.'' *Life Studies,* a book about ''direct experience and not symbols,'' was just such a breakthrough. All of Lowell's subsequent work centered around his quest for the craft and inspiration to bring even more experience into his art, and his related quest to account for the place art makes in experience. (pp. 5-6)

Lowell did not write poems in hopes of achieving immortal fame, ''grass on the minor slopes of Parnassus.''.... His ''open book,'' he suggests in *History,* amounts to no more than an ''open coffin,'' doomed like his corporeal self to perish in time, though more slowly. Poetry had an entirely different value for Lowell, an existential value: it proved its maker was ''alive.''.... Thus he viewed himself as engaged in the quintessential labor of the American poet. For the difference between American and other writers, he once argued, is that in America ''the artist's existence becomes his art. He is reborn in it, and he hardly exists without it.''

Believing that ''the artist's existence becomes his art,'' Lowell made himself into the classic figure of the American poet, a Whitman for our time, though a more tragic one, as befits our time. Like Whitman's, his conception of poetry closely resembles that of Ralph Waldo Emerson. (pp. 6-7)

Although Lowell's metaphysics differed from Emerson's, he wrote out of a neo-Emersonian conviction that poetry is ''neither transport nor a technique'' but rather a verbal manifesting of experience that itself takes its place within experience. Robert Lowell, like Emerson, lived in his art, at the place where deed meets word, or in his own terms, where ''what really happened'' connects with the ''good line.''

Lowell's esthetic places his art at the center of American literary tradition. In his seminal essay on this topic, ''The Cult of Experience in American Writing,'' Philip Rahv termed the affirmation of individual experience the ''basic theme and unifying principle'' of American writing. Rooted in Puritan antinomianism, fostered by Jeffersonian democratic idealism, and formulated most eloquently by Emerson, this theme preoccupies the American literary mind. Whether the protagonist is Hester Prynne or Isabel Archer breaking out of conventionality through intense personal suffering; Huck Finn or Jake Barnes trusting his own senses in opposition to society's conventional unwisdom and a friend's illusory book learning; Ishmael going to sea, Thoreau going to Walden, or Ike McCaslin going to the woods . . .—the principle is always the same, the growth of consciousness and the deepened sense of personal identity resulting from immersion in firsthand experience. (pp. 8-9)

Thus, in the radically experiential and existential qualities of his poetry, Lowell continues the central quest of the American imagination. But his accomplishment is even more significant than that. He has made himself an Emersonian "reconciler" for our time. For despite the wholeness advocated by Emerson and exemplified in good measure by Whitman, experience in American literature has tended to fragment itself. Early in this century Van Wyck Brooks lambasted American culture for failing to achieve an organic conception of life. Rather, Brooks argued, American literature drifts chaotically between two extremes—the extremes, simply put, of understanding experience intellectually and understanding it through the emotions. Brooks applied to these extremes his celebrated labels "highbrow" and "lowbrow," and termed the failure of our writers to synthesize the two "a deadlock in the American mind." This kind of dualism may have originated, as Edwin Fussell has suggested, in America's divided loyalties between Old World and Western Frontier; or it may have originated in class difference. Whatever its source, some version of the highbrow-lowbrow dualism has been discerned by most students of American literature. Philip Rahv, for example, argued that American literature composes itself into a debate between "palefaces" and "redskins." The "palefaces" (Henry James, T. S. Eliot, and Allen Tate would belong to this party) produce a patrician art which is intellectual, symbolic, cosmopolitan, disciplined, cultured. The "redskins" (Walt Whitman and William Carlos Williams would tend to belong here) produce a plebeian art which is emotional, naturalistic, nativist, energetic, in some sense *un*cultured. . . . This dualism appears within Lowell's poetic career as well, as he felt himself caught between two competing kinds of poetry whose extreme forms he called (echoing Lévi-Strauss) "cooked" and "raw." The two strongest individual influences on his artistic development were first the "paleface" Tate, and then the "redskin" Williams. But like the very greatest of American poets, Lowell tried to diminish this split, to repair the "broken circuit" of American culture. His goal was not the middlebrow's bland insensitivity to *any* kind of experience, but rather the unified central vision of what Emerson termed "the complete man" among partial men.

To borrow one of his own metaphors, Lowell's poetry "clutches only life," for it is based on his belief that "art and the life blood of experience can't live without each other." . . . [His] major poetic changes . . . grew out of his deepening sense of the relationship between art and experience. In his youthful period, under the direct tutelage of Allen Tate and the pervasive influence of T. S. Eliot, Lowell fit his personal experience into impersonal mythic patterns. He conceived of his life as being in service to the poetic idea, as needing to be depersonalized and transformed into art. He constructed verbal icons out of his experience, the most ambitious and powerful of these being **"The Quaker Graveyard in Nantucket."** In his second, "revolutionary" phase, he learned, under the approving eye of William Carlos Williams, to bring his undisguised personal experience to the forefront of his poetry. Exercising a brilliantly original art, he produced an album of "photographs" of experience, his Confessional masterpiece *Life Studies.* In the third, long period of his maturity, Lowell continued to explore the domain along the boundary where life meets art. He now conceived of experience as being more inward than in his *Life Studies* stage: not isolable events from the past but a fusion of immediate impressions with consciousness itself. Experience in this sense, as T. S. Eliot wrote long ago, is indefinable except that it is "more real than anything else." In the great poems of this period—**"For the Union Dead,"** the **"Near the Ocean"** sequence, and *The Dolphin*—Lowell revealed the truth of a human heart and mind, his own. (pp. 9-12)

Lowell's poems plunge into, and thereby affirm for himself and for us all, the infinite possibilities for human life in the actual world. They embody a complex process of clarifying and thus culminating his experience; and then, since poems are themselves real, they take their rightful place within experience, leaving author and reader alike altered. Lowell once said of Thoreau that the most wonderful and necessary thing about his life was the courageous hand that wrote it down. The words apply equally to himself. (p. 12)

Steven Gould Axelrod, in his Robert Lowell: Life and Art, *Princeton University Press, 1978, 286 p.*

ROBERT B. SHAW

Coming to terms with Robert Lowell's last books is no simple matter. To begin with, the sheer amount of work in the three volumes is intimidating. There are 368 poems in *History* (1973); although the great majority of these appeared in one or both of the earlier versions of the sequence Lowell at first called *Notebook,* they are in many cases significantly revised, and some eighty new poems have been added. *The Dolphin* (1973) contains 104 separate poems or sections. *Day by Day,* published shortly before the poet's death in 1977, contains sixty-three poems and three "translations." The proportions of any one of these books seem bold if set beside any of Lowell's earlier collections: *Life Studies,* his most famous book, has only twenty-three poems and derives much of its bulk from its thirty-five-page chunk of autobiographical prose. How well did the poet's late-attained fluency serve him? Do his last works exhibit an expansion of scope or a weakening of critical instinct?

In dealing with such questions one is bound to reflect on Lowell's formal strategies. *History,* like the two versions of *Notebook* which preceded it, is a collection of unrhymed sonnets. The same is true of *The Dolphin.* For some six years Lowell subjected himself to the confines of iambic pentameter and of units of fourteen lines. *Day by Day* is different: free verse, often freer than any Lowell had previously written. Again, questions arise. For example: Can we fairly consider these pieces as individual poems, or must they be treated as components of the sequences in which they have been painstakingly arranged? And more basically: How effectively do Lowell's chosen forms convey the taxing, at times excruciating, burden of experience he took it upon himself to express?

No one has been more aware of such questions than Lowell was himself, as instanced by his tireless rewriting of his lines, and yet more tireless reworking of his themes. In his final years it often seemed that he was determined to prove that genius is an infinite capacity for taking pains. . . . *History* is a massive record of this scrupulosity. Anyone who compares it with the two previous versions of *Notebook* is likely to emerge at once dizzied from the demands of collation and respectful of Lowell's tireless willingness to improve his work. In numerous instances he has tightened his argument, removed inconsequence, intensified his imagery and clarified his references. What one is bound to find most striking, however, is the radical reordering of contents which, with the addition of the new poems, gives the book as a whole a weight and definitive structure that its preceding versions did not have.

The earlier formats of the work had suggested that it was to be seen as a kind of diary in verse, covering "a summer, an autumn, a winter, a spring, another summer," the years in question being 1967-68. There was an awkwardness about this; Lowell was constantly drawn to escape the frame of his own

self-imposed structure, shifting his attention fitfully from present to past, from personal concerns to historical vignettes.
Handcuffed to the calendar, the poet was hindered in giving
an artistic design to the work; it proved impossible under this
system to achieve narrative tension, to build toward a climax.
In arranging **History** Lowell had the courage to sever the intuitive, often ineluctable web of connections which had tugged
him backward and forward in time. To our relief and his, he
has opted for linearity. After a few introductory pieces which
establish the poet's point of view, the subjects hew to a traditional chronology: from Adam and Eve through the Old Testament to the Greeks and Romans, to the Middle Ages and
beyond—until, after the first hundred pages, we arrive at the
poet's personal reminiscences. In the second half of the book
the course of his own life is pursued, decade by decade, up
through his meditations on the time in which he is writing, the
later 1960s. If we have lost certain arresting juxtapositions
under this scheme, we have gained an impressive sense of
momentum.

The plan of **History** runs the risk of exciting shallow derision:
here is a poet who sees himself as the high point toward which
Western civilization has been striving for centuries. But an
unprejudiced reading will discover a great deal beyond comfortable egotism in Lowell's procedure. His aim here appears
to be to relate his personal experience to that of humanity at
large, to view his situation as an artist in the twentieth century
with the deeper understanding which a sense of the past affords.
The two halves of this book are meant to illumine one another:
to cite the pun which is surely latent in the title, "history"
and "his story" are virtually the same story in the end. The
relation of the two is like that of macrocosm to microcosm.

Of course Lowell *as* a historian fails to observe contemporary
practice. He offers anecdotes, not statistics, concentrates not
on social forces operating over long periods but on individuals
in moments of crisis. There is something engagingly Victorian
about his narrative flair, his appetite for colorful characters
and illustrative incidents. One is reminded of Carlyle's assertion, "The history of the world is but the biography of great
men." It is indeed the great men on whom Lowell focuses,
but he sees them in the light of an even more familiar Victorian
dictum, Lord Acton's "Power tends to corrupt, absolute power
corrupts absolutely." (pp. 515-17)

Both directly and implicitly, the book calls the power of state
into question by contrasting it with the fructifying power of
imagination. (p. 517)

In the two **Notebook** versions, Lowell's own confrontations
with the state in the 1960s were central. One couldn't read
them without thinking of the Lowell whom Norman Mailer
brilliantly mythologized in *The Armies of the Night*. In **History**
the poet's political involvements—his opposition to the Vietnam war, his support of Eugene McCarthy—are subordinated
to the more encompassing theme of political and imaginative
power confronting one another since statecraft began. The positive images that linger in the mind after reading this work are
not self-important ones of the poet on the steps of the Capitol,
but those relating to his poetic apprenticeship in which he
generously evokes his mentors, whether known personally or
in books. Lowell is particularly adept at combining appreciation
with shrewd analysis in such tributes. Often he hits the target
with a single characterizing phrase, as when he speaks of the
"harsh luminosity" of Randall Jarrell. Of the new poems, two
seem helpful in obliquely defining certain of Lowell's own
aims and preoccupations. One is on Thoreau [entitled **"Tho-**

reau Z"]. . . . The other, called **"The Poet,"** is on Thomas
Hardy. . . . (pp. 518-19)

In each of these pieces the poet's affinity to his subject comes
through without having to be stated. The qualities he praises
are those he seeks to emulate. Like Thoreau, Lowell was a
New Englander at odds with his region, and more generally
with the American imperialism which he saw as Puritan self-
righteousness writ large. Like Thoreau he had a gift for fierce
denunciation, which flared forth early in such a poem as **"Children of Light"** and was to be rekindled in later pieces prompted
by public occasions: **"For the Union Dead," "Waking Early
Sunday Morning,"** and many others. A final parallel to Thoreau can be seen in Lowell's conscientious practice of civil
disobedience, for which he spent more time in jail than Thoreau
did. If reading the Thoreau poem reminds us of Lowell's civic
concerns, reading the Hardy poem reminds us just as vividly
of the more intimately personal side of his work. Hardy's
baffled estrangement from his wife, and his reawakened love
for her following her death make him a model for poets treating
themes of disillusionment and troubled domesticity. I think
that Lowell, when dealing with three complexly troubled marriages, aimed for something like the "acrid sweetness" of tone
in Hardy's great series of elegies, "Poems of 1912-13."

One can read these portraits of artists as contributing to Lowell's portrait of himself, as I have been doing. Or one may
prefer to appreciate the grace and economy with which they
have been made. The easy familiarity of the style coexists with
a vigilant control of detail. . . . **History** offers more in the way
of stylistic interest than might at first appear. Its grand proportions may distract us at first from focussing on fine details,
but the details are there and are well worth attending to. I
suspect it will come to rank high among Lowell's works not
only for the audacity of its design but also for the solid and
subtle craftsmanship that shaped its many facets.

I wish I could feel equal enthusiasm for **The Dolphin**. Although
I find more to admire in each re-reading of **History,** this continuation of Lowell's chronicle leaves me cold. The material
is relentlessly domestic: we are told of the breakup of Lowell's
marriage to Elizabeth Hardwick and the beginning of a new
life in England with Caroline Blackwood, who bore his son
and eventually became his third wife. I suppose the model for
this is something like *Modern Love*, but **The Dolphin** lacks the
firm contours and the steady tone of high Victorian melancholy
that make Meredith's poem such a memorable combination of
narrative and lyric modes. . . . I believe the most successful
parts of **History** are those in which Lowell stands at a contemplative distance from his subject—as in his profiles of writers,
his views of his own past, or his speculations touching the
aims of art. Much of **The Dolphin** suffers from the lack of such
a distance. Without an adequate interval for meditation, Lowell
is no better than the rest of us in giving clarity to the flux of
experience, the never slackening passage of moment on moment. (pp. 519-21)

Of course, Lowell recognized the risk of documentary tedium
he was running. He has made a valiant attempt to enhance the
significance of his story by recurring at key junctures to the
symbol of the dolphin. The dolphin is the poet's savior, keeping
him afloat in life's tempestuous seas, as in the Greek myth the
poet Arion was rescued from drowning by a dolphin. It is his
muse, his inspiration, searching out the matter of poetry. . . .
The figure of the dolphin has its ominous aspect, suggesting
at times not so much a benign muse as a seductive siren or
mermaid, luring the poet out beyond his depth. Finally (and

here is where the reader may have trouble evaluating the symbol) the dolphin is at some points quite starkly equated with Caroline Blackwood. . . . The reader is discomfited in following the flickering back and forth between the mythic and the literal aspects of the figure. Like Graves's White Goddess and the real Laura Riding, Lowell's dolphin and the real Caroline Blackwood don't quite fuse to an adequate symbolic presence. . . . There are some passages of lyric beauty, as in the first and last poems of the book . . . , but the effect of these is oddly foreign to Lowell's genius. At his best, in other works if not here, Lowell succeeds in bringing the factual and the visionary together, while these lines achieve their music by leaving the factual behind. One hears a voice of handsome resonance, but it seems not quite Lowell's own.

After *The Dolphin,* an adventurous experiment gone wrong, Lowell recovered his authentic voice in *Day by Day.* I mean ''his authentic voice'' more or less literally. Anyone who spent time with Lowell in his last years—even only occasionally, as I did—will feel that these poems come closer than any of his others to approximating his manner in conversation. He came to see the move to free verse, which facilitated a speaking tone of voice, as a liberation from ''the sonnet's cramping and military beat.'' As with any effect of ease in poetry, this one entailed strenuous labor. . . . His efforts succeeded in bringing to the page the verve and unpredictability of his talk—typically magnanimous but with moments of cheerful malice, hovering in clouds of generality only to plummet hawklike upon some targeted particular. The greater range of tone here allows for moments of humor, albeit of a mordant sort. One sees this particularly in the monologues Lowell creates for aged VIPs. (pp. 521-23)

Mortality haunts the poet as much as it does any of his imagined personae. . . . Given that he is so often conscious of fragility, it is remarkable that in this book Lowell mustered the energy to subject his life, past and present, to one of his most searching inquisitions. His renewed attention to subjects he had treated in past books surprisingly avoids repetitiveness. What Lowell offers are tellingly augmented views of material used before, or the same material seen from arrestingly different angles. As he grew older, he looked back on events and people in his past with wider sympathy and awakened understanding. He was unwilling to let bygone days be fossilized either in his thought or his writing. (pp. 523-24)

When he comes to deal with his present experience in *Day by Day,* Lowell shows the same flexibility of approach that he adopts toward his past. A number of poems dealing with one of his periodic breakdowns can be usefully compared with those on the same theme in *Life Studies.* Again, the new poems are less schematic and stylized. A cocoon of protective numbness surrounds Lowell's earlier accounts of derangement. There is less of that here; poems like ''Visitors,'' ''Three Freuds,'' ''Home'' and ''Shifting Colors'' are startlingly immediate in describing a bout of madness and its exhausted aftermath.

While it would be easy to continue itemizing fine poems and passages in *Day by Day,* the book as a whole is difficult to assess. A considerable part of its power . . . comes of its conscious use of retrospection, recapitulation. Perhaps it is a flaw in a book of poems that it should not yield its full effect without reference to the poet's earlier writing. But isn't self-reference, continuity of intention, a characteristic of the greater poets? One wouldn't begin reading Yeats with *Last Poems and Plays* or Eliot with *Four Quartets.* Lowell seems to have arranged the book so that the notion of returning would linger in the

reader's mind from the start; he placed first the long poem ''Ulysses and Circe'' which ends with the return of Ulysses to Ithaca, and followed this with ''Homecoming,'' an account of his own return to a summer resort of his youth. Both poems contemplate the tenacity with which the aging consciousness seeks to salvage what it can from the past. The Ulysses poem is by any reasonable measure one of Lowell's finest. (pp. 525-26)

Ironically, it was in the midst of his own return, to America, to Elizabeth Hardwick, that Robert Lowell died, shortly after the publication of *Day by Day.* It would not be my wish here, in viewing a lifework of this magnitude, to rank certain portions of it ahead of others. Whatever judgments later critics will arrive at, I believe that Lowell is one of those poets whose every phase of development may be studied with respect and frequent pleasure. His last poems worthily close the circle he set out to trace almost forty years before. (p. 526)

> *Robert B. Shaw, ''Lowell in the Seventies,'' in* Contemporary Literature, *Vol. 23, No. 4, Fall, 1982, pp. 515-27.*

MARK RUDMAN

Part of the tragedy of Lowell's death at sixty is that he was on his way to becoming a great poet of old age: mellow, reflective, funny, and always—could he be else?—intense. The poems in *Day by Day* are mainly meditations on past actions. Although there are a few grim harbingers of death, the book is about living out the afterlife in this life. (p. 175)

All his life Lowell was trying to become comfortable with imperfection and in *Day by Day* he does. The book was an open door for him and it contains the most flexible verse he ever wrote. The fourteen-line girdle is gone. While retaining always the integrity of the line, he seemed to let his thoughts drift where they would, sometimes dredging, sometimes drifting, but following his Muse. Many of the poems directly confront the question of his art—but he gives himself the freedom here that he sought in *Life Studies* and then backed away from in successive books. Some of the key poems are ''Ulysses and Circe,'' ''Last Walk,'' ''Since 1939,'' ''Art of the Possible,'' ''In the Ward,'' ''Death of a Critic,'' ''Domesday Book,'' ''The Spell,'' ''The Withdrawal,'' ''Wellesley Free,'' ''Grass Fires,'' ''Turtle,'' ''Visitors,'' ''Shifting Colors,'' and ''Unwanted.''

As with *Life Studies* and *History,* the first poem in *Day by Day,* ''Ulysses and Circe,'' contains a line that could define Lowell's stance in the book: ''Risk was his métier.'' . . . Gifted with an associative mind, he had previously shackled himself with fixed subject matter and forms. The formal devices used in these late poems are exaggerated versions of his earlier style. He uses more syntactical ambiguity in these poems; more unfinished thoughts, unusual line breaks, and enforced pauses between statements. . . . [The] real risk, as Lowell perceived it, was to distinguish, for the poem, memory from imagination, fact from truth. Blake, for one, made a clear distinction between the two. Did Lowell? Lowell worried that he had become too reliant on ''the threadbare art of [his] eye,'' and paralyzed by the facts he recorded. . . . (pp. 177-78)

And yet the ''facts'' in these final poems are never recorded—they are blessedly smudged by imagination. That's the sign of a powerful imagination—the ability to transform memory in the process of recollection—to give it form: to sing. In ''**The**

Withdrawal," . . . when Lowell looks back, he sees "a collapsing / accordion of my receding houses," a whole life—

> and myself receding
> to a boy of twenty-five or thirty,
> too shopworn for less, too impressionable for more—
> blackmaned, illmade
> in a washed blue workshirt and coalblack trousers

Lowell continues to hit the nerve of what we can never know about ourselves: the selves he remembers are always imagined, decisively seen, perceived, rendered, but not fixed or unidimensional. The movement forward in time and the movement backward are one and the same. The body moves forward in space, the imagination backward in time, and, in the gap between the remembered scene and the feeling, Lowell leaves white space replete with significance and without pretension. . . . The cost of Lowell's self-estrangement is that the body and mind have never been one, but is there anyone who does not suffer from this malady? Only one who, like the narrator of Beckett's *How It Is,* can exist wholly in the present tense, like the ocean, someone who just *is;* to be in that condition of being one must put aside all worldliness, all remorse.

In *Day by Day* Lowell begins to make use of depression and aging much in the same way Beckett made use of impotence and despair. Beckett's cosmic anguish is more interesting than Lowell's personal depression and yet Lowell appeals to our common humanity. He engages us with his unanswered, unanswerable questions—alternating currents of pain and doubt. (pp. 179-80)

Despite his immersion in the quotidian, in this book Lowell is not writing for himself as in a journal, jotting down whatever comes into his head and then sifting through it for good lines. He simultaneously addresses others and himself, his inner self, his deep invisible "I." His candor is endearing, but lends no real transparency. Many of the poems remain opaque and mysterious, prismatic, riddled with possibilities of meaning which he doesn't attempt to clarify.

Even at the end of the book Lowell still fears that he hasn't submitted the data to the transforming power of the imagination, and to this fear there is no absolute or final answer. He worries that his work is too close to life and, consequently, not art: "everything I write / . . . seems a snapshot, / . . . paralyzed by fact." But what Lowell calls memory could be called imagination.

> Yet why not say what happened?

The criticism that he levels against himself in **"Epilogue"** pertains more to his past than his present work, faults he had overcome after the relentlessly willed decade of fourteen-liners and the "relevant" poetry of the late sixties. I think that Lowell was in a transitional phase, in the process of becoming a meditative poet, unfamiliar with his own emerging self and poetic voice, unable to evaluate its quality, and that he had already achieved "the grace of accuracy" he aspired to when he seized Vermeer's eternal moment in these lines, as "the sun's *illumination*"—not the sun—is "stealing like the tide across a map / to his girl solid with yearning." Lowell died after having once again opened up some new terrain for poetry and the poetic imagination to explore. (pp. 188-89)

> *Mark Rudman, in his* Robert Lowell: An Introduction
> to the Poetry, *Columbia University Press, 1983, 205 p.*

VEREEN M. BELL

Robert Lowell's poetry is identifiable by nothing so much as its chronic and eventually systematic pessimism. One is hard pressed to come forward with even remotely sanguine or assuaging poems from Lowell's canon, and the few that we might call forth seem in the end to be momentary aberrations in an otherwise desolate philosophical context. Whatever spirit of affirmation that we think we perceive in Lowell's work we must always suspect ourselves of projecting upon it, being less willing than Lowell himself to yield to the implications of a nihilism of such an absolutized form—being, as it were, more Nietzschean than Lowell was able to be. What encourages us to find such pictures in the clouds is the element in his work that I consider to be fully as significant as its chronic pessimism (by which I contradict myself slightly); this feature is Lowell's conditioned and wholly understandable reluctance to accept the consequences of his own vision—a kind of scruple that causes him to consider again and again what life might be if it were not in fact what it is. (p. 1)

In his preface to **Land of Unlikeness,** Allen Tate represented Lowell as one of the few poets of his generation who retained "at least a memory of the spiritual dignity of man." For Tate a concept such as "spiritual dignity" necessarily implied a teleology, Christian or otherwise, without which auxiliary and dependent concepts such as dignity and heroism become increasingly subjective, debatable, and ambiguous. Once the teleology unravels, the personal idealism that it sustained begins to seem merely conditioned and vestigial, and this process results in the kind of demoralized ambivalence that is the salient characteristic of Lowell's work. Nietzsche regarded all teleologies and metaphysical systems as expressions of nihilism in disguise, since they were indications that "man [had] lost faith in his own value," and he exhorted his audience to transform the nihilism of despair—which occurs when religious and philosophical systems fail to support belief and identity—into a nihilism of affirmation. In his early poems Lowell was working his way through the crises of nihilism that Nietzsche describes, but he was never able to break through fully to the other Nietzschean side, to give credence to the exaltation of subjectivity or to the desirability of the human reappropriation of the world. The secular Augustinian scruple prevails in his thought as well.

As he moves painfully along the metaphysical spectrum implied in my title ["Nihilist as Hero"]—which, of course, is really his—Lowell in the poems becomes increasingly problematic to himself, as an artist and as a human being, and this effect is evident in his work as markedly in its technique as in its content. Form and value in Lowell's work do not so much collaborate and cohere as test and challenge each other, continually. Frank Kermode might say of Lowell's career, as he has said of Sartre's *La Nausée,* that it represents a "crisis in the relation between fiction and reality, the tension of dissonance between paradigmatic form and contingent reality." Lowell's nihilism is complicated by the unregulated intervention of internally surviving paradigms. Hayden Carruth addresses precisely this issue in his tribute to Lowell just after Lowell's death [see *CLC,* Vol. 9]. Carruth calls attention to the number of poets of Lowell's generation who died early, as if broken finally by an indefinable anxiety and guilt.

> They had inherited from their elders—Eliot,
> Pound, Stevens, Williams, Auden, even Frost—
> an enormous metaphysical awareness, an enormous apparatus for moral, psychological, and
> aesthetic inquiry, without anything to use it on.

They were in a vacancy ("the unredeemable world"). They had neither faith nor doubt, neither art for its own sake nor the natural environment. Everything had been used up . . . [Finally] they came to understand, one way or another, that their sin was their own existence.

If the first negational stage of nihilism is a necessary transition, as Nietzsche argued, to the affirmational—"the sign of a crucial and most essential growth, of the transition to new conditions of existence"—it stands to reason that this first dangerous phase might also never be wholly transcended. Lowell was somehow perpetually in transition, between the negation of old values and the affirmation of new ones, and he makes Nietzsche by comparison seem ingenuously romantic. (pp. 1-3)

One thing above all a poet must take care not to do is lose morale, since poetry is, if nothing else, morale apotheosized. Yet very few of the traditional consolations of the poet seem to have had any therapeutic relevance for Lowell at any point in his life. The facsimile of Christian theism that motivates his early work is, in its way, more terrifying an implication than the glum agnosticism of the later, and is not at all orthodox. Eastern religions seem not to have interested him at any stage. Romantic supernaturalism, like Roethke's or Dickey's, is virtually absent from his work. He could neither sentimentalize his own childhood nor, therefore, childhood in general or the myth of innocence. His view of history was antimelioristic. Sexual love was, in the poems at any rate, at least as problematic as redemptive. Most of the friends he writes about, by the time they get written about, are either dying or dead. Any infatuation with the Nietzschean will to power he might have cherished in his younger days seems to have dissipated altogether by the time of *Notebook* and *History,* where historical and mythological *übermenschen* are systematically debunked and vulgarized. Over the long haul his compulsive sincerity produces in him an ambiguous attitude even toward art. Lowell was a studious and learned man. Mythology, literature, music, painting constituted for him an alternative universe, one that was not irrational and that therefore absorbed him powerfully. On the other hand, his own style grew increasingly less "literary," and thus indirectly he expressed a distrust of literature's ability to affirm anything usefully meaningful or truthful about human life. In *Notebook* the allure of posterity is mocked repeatedly. So all that is left finally, when this is summed up, is an art which, as Sartre said, reclaims "the world by revealing it as it is but as if it had its source in human liberty," and not only does this minimal, stubbornly human thing but calls attention at every stage to the fact that that is what it is doing.

In the memorable last sentence of the **"Afterthought"** appended to *Notebook* Lowell said: "In truth I seem to have felt mostly the joys of living; in remembering, in recording, thanks to the gift of the Muse [an ironic shading here], it is the pain." This statement calls attention to the fact that, naive views of confessional poetry notwithstanding, the Robert Lowell in life and the Robert Lowell in the poems were substantively different people, the Lowell in life—in and often out of health—having been a considerably more vivid and robust figure than his readers, extrapolating, might be expected to conjure. The divergence is not easy to account for, but it suggests that Lowell the poet was a watchful, Kierkegaardian critic of Lowell the man, analytical and unappeasable. (pp. 5-6)

A related point that needs to be raised here is that Lowell's identity, at least his poetic one, was uniquely and inextricably entwined with the history of his own time, and with human history generally. (p. 6)

When he writes about Colonel Shaw's unwavering integrity and sense of purpose and of the disintegration of Boston into "civic sandpiles," it is he himself who is Colonel Shaw's foil, pining for "the dark downward and vegetating kingdom" of the old South Boston Aquarium and taking some comfort from the next-best thing, his television set, crouching before it to watch the "drained faces of Negro schoolchildren rise like balloons" on the screen. **"For the Union Dead"** is in fact a model of the way in which history and the poet's life interact in Lowell's poems. The poet in that poem is more like Boston than he is like Colonel Shaw, an aspect of the process that he deplores; and the tone of the poem, consistent with the behavior of the poet in the poem, is not that of moral outrage but that of an observer who seems to be content to be different to the extent that he observes. This effect is very carefully managed, and it produces something near to the reverse of the covert sanctimoniousness that compromises most such cultural criticism. It also deepens the sense of hopelessness by which we and the poet participate in the dehumanizing process. (p. 7)

The effect of the pressure of history is to narrow the gap for Lowell between art and life and therefore to foreclose any chance of redemption through mere sensibility. Jarrell wrote about this long ago: Lowell, he said, "seems to be condemned both to read history and to repeat it" [see *CLC,* Vol. 1]. One cannot achieve human authenticity finally without being historical; but to achieve authenticity at the expense of repeating the history of this particular century, and of having it internalized, virtually ensures an unwinnable contest with moral despair and self-contempt.

Describing what he calls Lowell's "poetry of experience," Steven Gould Axelrod says that "Lowell did not write poems in hopes of achieving immortal fame, 'grass on the minor slopes of Parnassus' . . . His 'open book,' he suggests in *History,* amounts to no more than an 'open coffin,' doomed like his corporeal self to perish in time, though more slowly. Poetry had an entirely different value for Lowell, an existential value: it proved its maker was 'alive'" [see excerpt above]. Axelrod quotes Lowell as saying that in America "the artist's existence becomes his art. He is reborn in it, and he hardly exists without it." Lowell's comment comes in an interview with A. Alvarez in which the main subject becomes America's famous cultural schizophrenia. On the one hand it is a country whose "democracy was based, theoretically, on certain abstract principles that were lacking in Europe" (Alvarez), founded "on a constitution" rather than "on a history and a culture." "We were founded," Lowell says, "on a Declaration, on the Constitution, on Principles, and we've always had the ideal of 'saving the world.'" On the other hand it is a country whose "moral sense" seems thwarted by its own "general rootlessness and mobility," because of which "nothing seems to last, neither objects, nor relationships, nor even the landscape" (Alvarez). For Lowell this abstracted quality of American life is epitomized by the city of New York.

> You can't touch a stone in London that doesn't point backwards into history; while even for an American city, New York seems to have no past. And yet it's the only city that sort of provides an intellectual, human continuum to live in . . . [If] you removed it, you'd be cutting out the heart of American culture. Yet it is a heart with no past. The New York of fifty years

ago is utterly gone and there are no landmarks; the record of the city doesn't point back into the past. It has that sheer presence which, I think, is not the image of mobility you talk about.

Alvarez: This kind of driving force, moving into the future all the time, without a past at all, as though the wake were closing up behind it . . .

Lowell: And it has a great sheer feeling of utter freedom. And then when one thinks back a little bit, it seems all confused and naked.

It is in this context that Lowell offers his observation about the American artist's existence becoming his art. The language in places is curiously Nietzschean. The remarks describe a country that is simultaneously idealistic and nihilistic and a poet, living in history, who is all too aware of how deeply identified he and his native country are.

Axelrod does not comment upon the odd circumstance that what "proves its maker is alive" (a honeycomb, in the first instance) is also described as an "open coffin." Lowell's commentators tend to want to make the poems seem more conventionally affirmative than they truly are. The irony in this case is very dark and represents Lowell at a low point in existential morale, where being alive is next to being dead, and where the poem alone is the sign that the poet has kept going nevertheless. It is thus also a sign—as silence would not be—that the poet, with every possible reason to do so clearly before him, has not been willing to give up on experience or on his wavering commitment to extort from experience some unmediated value that remains for him imaginable but stubbornly undisclosed. (pp. 7-9)

> *Vereen M. Bell, in his* Robert Lowell: Nihilist as Hero, *Harvard University Press, 1983, 251 p.*

JAMES E. B. BRESLIN

In February 1977, announcing a joint reading that the two men were to give at St. Mark's-in-the-Bowery, the New York *Times* described Allen Ginsberg and Robert Lowell as "opposite ends of the poetic spectrum." While "Howl" and *Life Studies* are certainly the crucial texts in any account of the transformation of American poetry in the late 1950s, it is easy to see what the *Times* had in mind, even in 1977 when the cleavage between the two men was not as sharp as it was, say, in 1957. Ginsberg, the son of Jewish immigrant parents from Newark, began his career as the poetic prophet of the bristling, zany defiance of the beat generation, while Lowell, whose ancestry extended back by way of Amy Lowell and James Russell Lowell to colonial New England, started out with the active support of those fastidious literary authorities—Eliot, Ransom, Tate—that the antics of the beats were most designed to antagonize. Ginsberg—the rhapsodic hip visionary; Lowell—the ironic and reserved aristocrat. Both poets, it is true, were eventually drawn toward confessional writing: but if Ginsberg at least begins his revelations by immersing himself in immediate feeling and thought, Lowell always preserves some personal distance and artistic control. Hence, Ginsberg gives us his prophetic *howl,* while Lowell provides life *studies.* (p. 110)

Both Ginsberg and Lowell began as religious sensibilities writing in traditional verse forms, though there was every difference between Lowell's devotional Catholicism and Ginsberg's

ecstatic mysticism. . . . [Both poets] shared a sense of attenuation and crisis in American poetry, and they sought to renovate their art by going outside literature to a referential language and an open poetics. With weak actual fathers, both poets were especially eager to find literary mentors and in [William Carlos Williams] they discovered a benign paternal figure who provided poetic models for the alternatives they were seeking. . . . Like Ginsberg, Lowell did not derive image, phrase or rhythm from Williams: to be like Williams you had to write unlike Williams. Moreover, the older poet was no Virgil who guided his poetic successor through eternal realms; Williams, instead, presided over Lowell's "breakthrough back into life." From *Land of Unlikeness* (1944) to *Life Studies* (1959) Lowell's career marks a slow, painful, and sometimes frightening journey toward something that originally repelled him—physical actuality; *Life Studies* itself enacts such a journey.

Nevertheless, in spite of some common poetic targets and a common poetic source in Williams, the differences between Lowell and Ginsberg remain basic; and they are differences not just of poetic style but of ultimate assumption. "Howl" describes, in its crackling, rhapsodic language, a tormented passage through a sordid urban world, an ordeal that issues in revelation of the absolute: "Pater Omnipotens Aeterna Deus"; **"Life Studies"** reviews familial past with an outward air of casual detachment—tightening at moments into stern and terrifying insights—in order to renounce absolutes and, in **"Skunk Hour,"** to accept the imperfections of a secular world. The autobiographical realism of *Life Studies* implicitly rebukes Ginsberg's visionary idealism.

"We [Americans] have some impatience with prosaic, everyday things of life—I think those hurt us," Lowell told an interviewer. He admires a writer like Frost for his "directness and realism," his "abundance and geniality": "the virtue of a photograph but all the finish of art." Ginsberg, on the other hand, might stand as exemplary for all that Lowell finds suspect and dangerous in American poetry and culture. Our culture, formed on abstract principles rather than a long tradition, is idealistic, and this is precisely what makes it dangerous, for "violence and idealism have some occult connection." Hemingway claimed that all American literature began with *Huckleberry Finn;* Lowell claimed that "American literature and culture begin with *Paradise Lost.*"

> I always think there are two great symbolic figures that stand behind American ambition and culture. One is Milton's Lucifer and the other is Captain Ahab: these two sublime ambitions that are doomed and ready, for their idealism, to face any amount of violence.

Lucifer and Ahab: radical individualists whose passionate ambitions made them heroic and whose fanatical idealism made them doomed and demonic. According to Lowell, American writers, similarly impatient with limits and tortured by otherness, imperiously avoid the prosaic and "leap for the sublime." Poetry is then imagined to be something far grander than a mere craft; it becomes the means to transcendence and self-apotheosis. . . . Like Ahab's, the American poet's furious quest for heroic independence becomes emotionally exhausting and self-destructive. Dissociated from historical, social, and physical realities, which hurt by confronting them with limitations, our poets fall into what Lowell calls "the monotony of the sublime."

As literary history, Lowell's account is provocatively inadequate; he may be able to explain many of the features of ''Howl,'' but not its humor; and he cannot explain even the existence of books like *The Beautiful Changes* and *A Change of World*. Lowell can account for Crane but not Williams, much of Whitman but very little of Frost. Lowell's theory is most valuable when understood as a projection onto the American past of his own struggles as a beginning poet. (pp. 111-13)

Ginsberg's notebooks of the late forties and early fifties open a kind of boundless space for the writer—allowing for self-analysis and self-expression, transcription of dreams and fantasies as well as actual persons, places, and events, experiments in spontaneous writing. Lowell's notebooks from the mid- and late forties . . . are, in contrast, strikingly nonintrospective and narrowly literary. Into them, in a small, tense, crabbed script, Lowell copied poems he admired and worked on his own poetry. Rather than providing a chance to release the flow of creative energy, these notebooks record Lowell's scrupulous efforts to wrench turbulent feelings into compressed language and form—a stumbling, laborious, deliberate, and back-breaking struggle for perfection of style. It is an elevated, a grand style—a gnarled sublimity toward which Lowell does not so much leap as he carefully climbs, as if up a slippery, rocky mountain where any error would be disastrous.

Each of the poems in *Lord Weary's Castle,* for instance, evolved gradually through numerous changes of word, image, rhythm, idea, and the writing of many of the poems was carried on at the same time. Lowell's deliberation, at once cautious and ambitious, sometimes results in an overworked verbal surface that stifles emotional impact. But Lowell's disciplined procedures also created the intricate force of particular poems and the elaborate unity of the book as a whole. Indeed, Lowell's critics have, if anything, underestimated the degree to which verbal cross references, the pairing of poems, and the unfolding drama of a spiritual quest pull these poems together into a single work. As a whole, *Lord Weary's Castle* records a quest through the confusion and violence of the years just before and just after the end of World War II—a quest for personal sanctity. But if the young Lowell yearns, angrily, for the stasis of a disembodied perfection, his strongest poems are made dynamic by their tracing of the movements of the poet's consciousness as he desperately searches for spiritual illumination. (pp. 113-14)

In *Lord Weary's Castle,* the poet yearns for some principle of absolute order that will resolve conflicts within the poet and violence in the world; the poems, often packed almost to the breaking point with division and disorder, dramatize the *search* for resolution, something that . . . is more often anticipated than actually achieved. (p. 117)

Strenuous, compressed, and oracular, the language of *Lord Weary's Castle* seems inspired by such poets as Hopkins, Thomas, and Crane. ''Like Thomas, Crane is subjective, mystical, obscure and Elizabethan,'' an admiring Lowell wrote in 1947; and as late as 1961 Lowell ranked Crane as ''the great poet'' of the generation before his own, because ''all the chaos of his life missed getting sidetracked the way the other poets' did.'' Yet from the beginning Lowell was equally ''preoccupied with technique, fascinated by the past, and tempted by other languages.'' If he wanted his poems to be ''loaded and rich,'' he also wanted (unlike Crane) to build them on a foundation that was ''perfectly logical.'' His characterization of Hopkins in a 1945 essay reveals the young Lowell's personal and literary ideal: an ''inebriating exuberance'' ''balanced''

by a ''strict fastidiousness.'' The appeal of such fastidiousness explains Lowell's enthusiasm when he first met Allen Tate: ''I became converted to formalism and changed my style from brilliant free verse, all in two months.'' Crane might be the greater poet but Tate ''was somehow more of a model and he had a lot of wildness and a lot of construction.'' Combining wildness and construction, loaded language and formal severity, the young Lowell aimed at becoming the total poet, the culmination of the modern movement.

But in his own more impatient and imperious way Lowell participated in the postwar domestication of modernism. Unlike Wilbur and Rich, Lowell saw that traditional poetic forms could not simply be inherited, that in the modern era such forms require justification *in the work.* ''Shelley can just rattle off terza rima by the page, and it's very smooth, doesn't seem an obstruction to him,'' Lowell observed; but when ''someone does that today and in modern style it looks as though he's wrestling with every line and may be pushed into confusion, as though he's having a real struggle with form and content.'' Of course, this is just how it should look if such forms are to seem authentic. In other words, Lowell energizes—and validates—his external forms by making the poem record the resistance to such forms posed by contemporary chaos and confusion. Yet it remains the case that in both religious and poetic ways *Lord Weary's Castle* contains disruptive energies by submission to a preexisting order—precisely the kind of order modernism had tried to abolish.

Lowell's Puritan severity, his ''symbolic armour'' and his gnarled Miltonic splendor make a peculiar combination, but all three manifest a desire for what he later called ''the attenuate ideal.'' Reservations about this poetic project began to trouble Lowell in the late forties. (pp. 118-19)

Fears that his own writing had become overly rhetorical, narrowly literary, and more than a little secondhand prompted Lowell to explore character and plot in the dramatic monologues of *The Mills of the Kavanaughs* (1951). But Lowell's move toward narrative only made clearer the limits of his ''intemperate, apocalyptic'' style. . . . (p. 120)

The interval of eight years between *The Mills of the Kavanaughs* (1951) and *Life Studies* (1959) felt like ''a slack of eternity'' until his autobiographical poems came as a ''windfall'' in two ''spurts'' of writing in 1957 and 1958. The interval was a time of personal anguish and literary frustration for Lowell; but it was also a time of gathering of forces in Lowell's struggle to renounce a tense, ungainly symbolic mode and descend to the actual, the riches of days. Like Pound before him, Lowell sought restoration for a decadent poetry in ''the prose tradition''; but unlike Pound, he was not looking for *le mot juste* of Stendhal or Flaubert. Rather, he was after a realistic fullness of representation that he found in writers like Chekov and Tolstoy. (pp. 120-21)

Life Studies ultimately renounces tight, external forms and preestablished symbolism; it discards rhetorical sublimity and religious myth in a quest to enter a demystified present. Lowell touches what had hurt him most, the prosaic and everyday, and he finds that his fiery creative self can survive within the quotidian. In literary terms, the achievement of *Life Studies* is twofold. Lowell creates what he calls ''the confession given rather directly with hidden artifice''; at the same time he makes the book as a whole a self-conscious meditation on the problem of a confessional language. . . . Throughout *Life Studies* Lowell remains aware of the tension between the flux of temporal experience and the stasis of literary form; he constantly calls attention to the dangers of turning "life" experiences into poetic "studies.". . . [The] four parts of *Life Studies* are stages in the process of finding a language of process . . . , [finding] a way of writing that would preserve, rather than annihilate, his life. (p. 124)

The notion that confessional poetry is solipsistic is so ingrained that the phrase "confessional solipsism" is like the phrase "communist aggression": you never see the first word without the second. Yet *Life Studies* shows Lowell's journey "beyond the Alps" into the rich riverbottom of otherness; in **"Skunk Hour"** his mountain-climbing imagination at last comes to earth. . . . *Life Studies* records the formation of an ego which can manage experience without being impositional, and this project entails a more complicated model of psychic life than does "Howl," with its polarizing of repressive and visionary consciousness. In Lowell's book physical objects—say, the items in **"Father's Bedroom"**—possess a matter-of-fact literalness, but they also acquire metaphoric depth from their context in a particular poem, in the whole book. This combination of literal surface with metaphoric substructure allows Lowell to compose his experience into literary shapes that do not *seem* impositional: "the confession given rather directly with hidden artifice." This technique, by no means novel in twentieth-century poetry, helps explain why *Life Studies,* though an insurgent work, did not provoke the kind of literary scandal that "Howl" did.

Unlike both Olson and Ginsberg, Lowell can, then, allow and even strive for an aspect of the self that remains outside of immediate experience or feeling. Lowell's ironic detachment, however, points up the limits and occasional weaknesses of *Life Studies.* If the book proceeds by moving closer to the emotions that are "breaking up" the poet's composure, even the **"Life Studies"** poems remain at some distance from their emotional sources. A line like "Grandpa! Have me, hold me, cherish me!" . . . is unusual for its emotional directness, and Lowell lacks the compelling emotional drive of a Ginsberg or a Plath. The "Olympian poise" of the boy in **"My Last Afternoon"** is father to the adult poet, for whom it also functions as a defense against terror. Lowell's early poems had often seemed as if they were about to explode under the weight of their own intensity; in *Life Studies,* especially in poems like

"Terminal Days at Beverly Farms," "Father's Bedroom," "For Sale," "Sailing Home from Rapallo," "During Fever," the writing can become emotionally slack and all-too-deftly literary under the direction of Lowell's coolly understated irony.

A poet like Plath illustrates the dangers of a confessional poetry at the other end of the spectrum. Feelings from the past are reawakened in all their raw violence, but they then turn against her and sweep her along in a "suicidal / drive." Lowell's defenses, necessary for survival, are part of an effort to gain perspective on the personal past. Not wanting to be swallowed up by it, he does not fantasize about abolishing it either. The existence of such a perspective, however, raises a crucial question: upon what ground does Lowell base his implicit claim to be able to detach himself from himself and to break from the fixations of his past? The answer is that in *Life Studies* Lowell has silently assumed psychoanalysis as the frame through which he studies his past life. . . . I do not mean to imply that *Life Studies* should be read as a cryptic text in which primal scenes, family romances, and juicy Freudian symbols have been tucked away. Critics have already examined *Life Studies* from a psychoanalytic point of view, and while no Freudian critic has ever concluded that a writer he decided to explore turned out to be lacking in latent content, I don't disagree with the conclusions these critics have reached. I want, rather, to emphasize that psychoanalysis provided Lowell with a way of thinking about his life. . . . This point of view affected Lowell's choice of parental figures as subjects of the poems, his emphasis on loss, and the need to work through loss, his picture of his relation with his wife as repetition of his relation with his mother; even more important, the self-revising movements of the **"Life Studies"** poems create mixed, ambivalent images of parental authorities, as opposed to the static simplifications of [the prose pieces included in *Life Studies*]. Like a patient in treatment, the poet proceeds from idealizations (both positive and negative) to ambivalent perceptions—again, a step Ginsberg cannot yet take in "Howl." The psychoanalytic notion of ambivalence thus performs a crucial *literary* function in **"Life Studies."** (pp. 140-42)

James E. B. Breslin, "Robert Lowell," in his From Modern to Contemporary: American Poetry, 1945-1965, *The University of Chicago Press, 1984, pp. 110-42.*

Richard (Burton) Matheson

1926-

American novelist, short story writer, and scriptwriter.

Matheson blends elements of fantasy, horror, and science fiction in stories about ordinary people suddenly caught in extraordinary circumstances. His stories examine the psychological impact of the unexpected upon an individual rather than presenting a larger social or historical perspective. Throughout his fiction Matheson centers on paranoia and persecution; other concerns in his work include the occult, time travel, life after death, and the scientific rationale for supernatural phenomena. Matheson's protagonists are usually alienated middle-class males who experience several emotional changes throughout the course of their adventures. The helplessness and isolation of his characters is reinforced by Matheson's spare prose style and his use of black humor.

Matheson's best-known works of fiction are the novels *I Am Legend* (1954) and *The Shrinking Man* (1956). Both of these works contain elements of science fiction in what are essentially nightmare tales. *I Am Legend* concerns the last human being on an earth inhabited by vampires; *The Shrinking Man* is about a man who fights for survival while gradually shrinking to nothingness. In two other novels Matheson creates a mood of romantic fantasy. *Bid Time Return* (1975) and *What Dreams May Come* (1978) treat time travel and life after death, respectively, in the context of uniting the protagonist with a loved one. Matheson has also written several thrillers and *The Beardless Warriors* (1960), a novel set during World War II.

Matheson is also well known for his screenplays for television and film. He contributed to such television series as "The Twilight Zone," "Star Trek," and "Alfred Hitchcock Presents," and several films, including *The Incredible Shrinking Man, The Young Warriors, The Omega Man,* and *Somewhere in Time,* were adapted from his novels. Among Matheson's most widely acclaimed teleplays is "Duel" (1971), which was adapted from one of his short stories. "Duel" is a tense story of a solitary traveler pursued by a huge transport truck whose driver is never seen. Another of Matheson's successful scripts for television is "The Morning After," a stark portrayal of the problems of alcoholism.

(See also *Contemporary Authors,* Vols. 97-100 and *Dictionary of Literary Biography,* Vols. 8, 44.)

DANIEL TALBOT

"A teen-ager don't bring anything to war but himself," says tough (but really soft-hearted) Sergeant Cooley in Mr. Matheson's first novel [*The Beardless Warriors*], which is about a squad of eighteen-year-old recruits and their assault on a German town in December, 1944. The quote is effective if somewhat superficial. . . . (p. 22)

The plot and situations in Mr. Matheson's book are [not original] . . . ; you've seen it all before in a hundred Hollywood war pictures—but at least the story is well told, unpretentious, and continually absorbing. Hackermeyer has had a loveless childhood, is insecure, morose, even morbid in his thoughts;

he has a death-wish, and no feeling for other people; but, slowly, as he is whisked through the hell of war, he learns understanding, compassion, love. He even finds a "father" in Sarge Cooley, who guides him in the path of manhood. Mr. Matheson writes his story simply and solidly, the dialogue is exact, the characters believable and pitiable, the circumstances chilling and horrible.

Especially effective are Mr. Matheson's descriptions of combat—vivid, terse, and realistic. The growing change in Hackermeyer is predictable yet strangely moving, and though many of the novel's incidents are by now war-genre clichés, the author seems aware of them, usually placing in Hackermeyer's mind the thought that what he's doing reminds him of some old "B" movie—a pretty clever way of anticipating criticism. Stylistically, the author occasionally overworks his metaphors, and certainly overuses self-invented, hyphenated adjectives . . . , but on the whole his book shows a narrative excellence and descriptive talent that is quite commendable. (pp. 22-3)

The Beardless Warriors is clean, readable, and honest. I don't think . . . [it] is a particularly important book or a very memorable one either; maybe if the theme ("Perhaps love is the answer") were farther removed from the Paddy Chayefsky-type penny-analyst naturalism the novel's over-all impression would be deeper. As it stands, the characters are likable, the battle scenes are clearly, graphically detailed, the dialogue is truthful; *The Beardless Warriors* would—with a different, snappier title—make a very good movie. (p. 23)

Daniel Talbot, "Understudies to Violence," in Saturday Review, Vol. XLIII, No. 34, August 20, 1960, pp. 22-3.*

WILLIAM WISE

In December, 1944, the tide of battle in Western Europe changed briefly and for the last time. . . . It was during these weeks that American infantry troops suffered their heaviest casualties since the D-Day landings. Replacements were rushed to the front, many of them 18-year-olds with only a minimum of basic training and no combat experience. One of these 18-year-olds, Everett Hackermeyer, is the principal character in Richard Matheson's fast-paced and gripping war novel, *The Beardless Warriors.*

Ten days of combat are seen through Hackermeyer's eyes, beginning with his assignment to a decimated rifle squad on Dec. 8. They are ten grim and terrible days of bloodshed and carnage. By the time they are over and the town of Saarbach has been taken, Hackermeyer has been transformed from a green recruit into a veteran, and the reader has experienced the sounds, sights and smells of war in many of their most intimate and appalling forms. If some of the author's descriptions of death and destruction are too strong for the squeamish, he can hardly be held to account. He has not invented infantry warfare—he has merely written about it in a plain, honest and compelling way. . . .

[Mr. Matheson] has been less successful in his attempt to tell the personal story of Hackermeyer, a lonely adolescent who finds a measure of self-respect through the understanding and kindliness of an older man, Sergeant Cooley, his squad leader. In action, both the sergeant and Hackermeyer are credible figures. Between skirmishes, at moments when they must divulge their innermost feelings, they tend to become awkward and momentarily unbelievable—two mouthpieces of the author expressing his views in words that could hardly be their own.

Happily, these moments are few and brief. For most of its length, *The Beardless Warriors* proceeds to paint an individual and memorable picture of battle. It does so with almost none of the interminable flashbacks, the grandiose philosophizing or the bogus love stories that have marred many over-long and highly praised war novels of the past decade.

William Wise, "Soldier's Testing," in The New York Times Book Review, August 28, 1960, p. 27.

TALIAFERRO BOATWRIGHT

"Teen-agers make good soldiers because they are unthinking machines . . . smoothly operating machines. . . . Then, too, there is the high order of the teen-ager's reflexes. . . . At the same time, they're highly idealistic about concepts which an older man would question. Like *Mom . . . America . . . Democracy . . . Liberty.* . . . They can be fired into a rage by them . . . of course the thing is, if you kill off all the teen-agers, who's going to be left to reach maturity?"

Thus Guthrie, one of the eighteen-year-old warriors in Richard Matheson's hyperthyroid new war novel [*The Beardless Warriors*] to his peers. His position is essentially that of the novel as a whole, although the novel as a whole is more ambitious in theme, more extensive in permutating the varieties of teen-age experience and more searching in its analysis of what makes a youth a soldier.

Actually, the burden of the book is how those who are "left" reach maturity, the slow, groping, agonizing process by which a youth becomes a man. In *The Beardless Warriors* this process is compressed into a time span of two weeks of combat. As relative time goes, this, of course, can be a lifetime, and is almost that for Everett Hackermeyer, the stolid, humorless, shy, uncommunicative private who is the book's central character.

The plot revolves around the son-father relationship that develops between the orphaned Hackermeyer and his squad leader, Sergeant Cooley. . . . Cooley in battle is everywhere. He is the fount of knowledge, the protector, the exhorter, the punisher—in short, the father image. Hackermeyer turns out to be a natural soldier. . . .

The battle is a tough assault on a German town called Saarbach, the time is December, 1944. The characters are all members of one infantry squad (or their replacements). The fighting is vicious.

For this reader it is made too much of a hell. Too many varieties of combat challenge and individual response are packed into a short space of time for anything like a true picture, no matter how realistic the details. Similarly, Cooley is more symbol than flesh and blood. Hackermeyer, Guthrie and the rest of the "beardless warriors," however, are extremely well done. Their fears and anxieties, their gropings toward manhood and their behavior under fire make this a good novel in spite of its sensationalism.

Taliaferro Boatwright, "A Novel of Teen-Age Soldiers in Battle," in New York Herald Tribune Book Review, September 4, 1960, p. 4.

PUBLISHERS WEEKLY

[*Shock III* consists of thirteen] short stories in the fantasy-science fiction field. In **"Girl of My Dreams"** a woman can dream of future accidents and her evil husband uses the information she supplies to extort money from people for telling them the time and place of their impending trouble. **"Tis the Season to Be Jolly"** is a dialect story about a hillbilly family falling apart—literally. There are also a space-ship story, a time-machine story, a haunted house story and others populated by supernatural creatures. The author has some clever ideas but too often he tries to stretch material for a short-short to a longer length and pads with arch dialog. A grab-bag collection.

A review of "Shock III," in Publishers Weekly, Vol. 189, No. 6, February 7, 1966, p. 92.

DAMON KNIGHT

The hypothetical reader who, looking up from one of the books dealt with in this chapter, should remark, "This isn't half bad," would be wrong. These books are half bad. They are the work of an infuriating small group of highly talented writers, who operate "by the seat of their pants," in the innocent conviction that their every word is golden.

A totally bad book is a kind of joy in itself, like a completely ugly dog; but these in-betweens, in which the author seems on alternate pages a genius and an idiot, are almost unbearable.

Take, for instance, a good, hard look at *I Am Legend*, by Richard Matheson. This story of the last live man, in a world where everyone else has become a vampire, has frequent moments of raw power: it's a theme perfectly adapted to Matheson's undisciplined, oh-my-God style, and he has developed it, in many places, with great ingenuity and skill. The book is full of good ideas, every other one of which is immediately dropped and kicked out of sight. The characters are child's drawings, as blank-eyed and expressionless as the author himself in his back-cover photograph. The plot limps. All the same, the story could have been an admirable minor work in the tradition of *Dracula,* if only the author, or somebody, had not insisted on encumbering it with the year's most childish set of "scientific" rationalizations. For instance: vampirism is caused by a bacillus. Matheson's hero evolves this notion, apparently by opening a physiology text at random and stabbing with the thumb, and tests it by examining a specimen of vampire's blood under the microscope. He "proves" it by finding one—count it—one bacillus in the specimen. Previously, we are told, the world's medical experts had failed to isolate the cause of the epidemic. Probably they were harder to satisfy.

On this slender foundation the hero erects a theory which has half the ten-dollar words of immunology in it, but does not make a nickel's worth of sense. Vampires can't be killed by bullets, for instance, because the bacillus causes the secretion of a—hold your hat—*powerful body glue* that seals up the bullet holes. (The bacillus also "provides energy," by the way, and makes the dog teeth grow.) Antibiotics won't work because—hold it again—the victims' bodies can't fight germs and make antibodies at the same time. It can't be done, believe him. It's a trap.

About a third of the book is taken up with this nonsense, which has been stuffed in with no gentle hand. The early part of it reads exactly as if Matheson had sat down with a first draft and an editor's letter beside him, copied off the questions (How does the hero, who knows no anatomy, always manage to hit the heart with his oaken stake? Why don't the vampires burn his house down if they want to get him out so badly?) and answered them with the first thing that came into his head. . . . (pp. 63-4)

• • • • •

Richard Matheson is a prim young man whose considerable talent is usually submerged in an indiscriminate creative gush. Like most of his literary generation, he has no sense of plot; in each story he puts together a situation, carries it around in circles until he gets tired, then introduces some small variation and hopefully carries it around some more, like a man bemused in a revolving door. His stories sometimes reach their goal by this process, but only, as a rule, when there is no other possible direction for the story to take; more often they wind up nowhere, and Matheson has to patch on irrelevant endings to get rid of them. Of the stories collected in *The Shores of Space,* **"Blood Son," "Trespass"** and **"The Curious Child"** are botches of this kind. Other, slighter stories such as **"The Funeral," "Clothes Make the Man"** and **"The Doll That Does Everything"** are almost as weak, but are saved by Matheson's impudence.

Except for whimsy, Matheson's dramas are all domestic, not to say banal, and their hero is almost always Matheson himself. He has a profound interest in the trivia of his daily life and in his own uninspired conversation, which he reproduces without irony. At its best, by sheer honesty and intensity of emotion,

this kind of thing turns into art, as in **"The Test,"** Matheson's harrowing story of an old man losing his grip on life. **"Steel,"** although it is built on a creaking sports-pulp plot and an even creakier set of robots, achieves tragic stature.

At its worst, Matheson's bare natural style, with its corner-drugstore vocabulary and inflections, is thin and dull. Apparently realizing this, he makes frequent efforts to jazz it up; I would lay odds that he owns and uses a thesaurus. He cultivates George Meredith's "he said" avoidances: "the little man asided," "Marian sotto voiced," "he dulceted." He has a sure touch for the gaudy solecism ("other right concaved his stomach"; "The count bicarbonated"), for the unnecessary word ("unwanted garbage"), and for unconscious anatomical humor. . . . (pp. 239-40)

As for the science in his stories, the less said about it by Matheson the better. When he sticks to one implicit assumption (euthanasia in **"The Test,"** or the one survivor of atomic war in **"Pattern For Survival"**), his work is often compact and witty. The Earth is apparently about to be destroyed by collision with a flaming comet in **"The Last Day,"** but Matheson never says so, he merely shows you the red horror in the sky, and with hardly any effort you can forget the Victorian nonsense and concentrate on the astonishingly effective prig's-eye view of humanity under sentence of death.

When, on the other hand, he feels obliged to expound the science background of a story, the results are pitiful. ("'That clinches it!' he said. 'Mars has two-fifths the gravity of Earth. They'd need a double heart to drive their blood or whatever it is they have in their veins.'")

Like many another talented writer, Matheson got into this field more or less by accident, found that it paid, and never bothered to learn its basic techniques. It's hard to know whether to be more grateful to him for minor masterpieces like **"The Test"** and **"The Last Day,"** or more annoyed by the piles of trash he has left for us to wade in. . . . (p. 240)

• • • • •

[*The Shrinking Man*] is the story of one Scott Carey, a young man who suddenly begins shrinking exactly one-seventh of an inch every day. The story proper begins when he is five-sevenths of an inch tall and has been marooned in his own cellar forty-four days, with five more to go before he becomes zero inches tall and whiffs out like a candle flame.

Previous stages in his descent are told as interruptions: the focus is on Carey's last five days, his loneliness and hardships, his struggles to get food, and his occasional encounters with a grudge-bearing black widow spider. (p. 279)

The cellar episodes vary from unintentional comedy like this ("'Son of a bitch!' he yelled, and he kicked the cracker to bits. . .") through long stretches of boredom, to occasional incongruous bits of truth, as when Carey is shocked and stunned by the impacts of gigantic water drops. The most striking lapse in logic, for readers who have seen this subject handled before in science fiction, is Matheson's neglect of the square-cube law.

Other things being equal, a small object has proportionately less volume (and therefore less mass) than a large one. If our measuring sticks were to shrink at the same time, there would be no difference, but they don't: atoms and molecules provide an absolute standard of size, and in practice, so do the minimal sizes of living cells, and the fineness of muscle fiber. So a flea can perform gymnastic feats on spindling legs, while an elephant lumbers clumsily on massive ones. It follows that a man Carey's size could jump like a grasshopper, and could lift objects many times his own weight. But Carey pants and struggles to carry a pin, and toils up a wicker chair as if it were Everest. When, near the end of the book, he finally realizes he can fall long distances without being hurt, and does so, the event is totally incredible because nothing else in the book prepares you for it: earlier, when Carey tries a much shorter fall, Matheson would have you believe the shock is agonizing.

A few drops of genuine feeling are distilled from this brew, as when, on his last night, Carey faces extinction without hope or fear: but the following scene, when he wakes up still alive and still shrinking, is perfectly ludicrous—evidently the author has some vague idea that minus numbers and microscopic sizes are the same thing.

Like . . . *I Am Legend,* this one is a drama of alienation. In the former book, everybody but the hero was a vampire; in this one, everybody else is a giant. *The Shrinking Man* is at one point strikingly reminiscent of *Alice in Wonderland:* when Carey is the wrong size to climb the cellar steps, the door is open; when he's the right size, the door is shut.

In the before-cellar episodes, Matheson, using quantity of emotion as a substitute for quality, runs through a kind of bathroom-sink collection of vulgarities which, if written and published about a real person, would be called yellow journalism. The story line is purposeless and repetitive; about seven tenths of it is padding, but every now and then Matheson succeeds in registering the eerie scenic effects for which he is noted. In one short passage, when the forty-two-inch hero hitches a ride from an aging, drunken homosexual, Matheson's prose and his characters come brilliantly to life, as if the author wanted to prove that he really *can* write, when not churning out this sludge.

The rest of the book, like much of Matheson's work, is a dismal interior monologue, endlessly reflecting the author's own stream of consciousness at its most petty and banal. (pp. 280-81)

> *Damon Knight, in his* In Search of Wonder: Essays on Modern Science Fiction, *revised edition, Advent: Publishers, 1967, 306 p.*

BENJAMIN PAUL JOHN PRZEKOP

To begin with a massive understatement, let us say that [*Hell House*] is not your run-of-the-mill "ghost story" about a "haunted" house. Yes, the house does have a record which plays by itself, a door which locks by itself, and the traditional rocking chair which rocks by itself. But it also contains the spirit (the psychic force, if you will) of an incredibly fiendish man (its former owner and leader of the debauched inhabitants that once lived there, Emeric Belasco), who can cause tables, chairs and knives to fly at people, who can instill lesbian and exhibitionist urgings in a formerly sedate matron, who can seduce a deeply religious medium, and who can summon, generally speaking, innumerable mental and physical phenomena to aid in his complete destruction of anyone who dares threaten his reign of horror in *Hell House.* Richard Matheson's novel about a possessed house and its would-be conquerors is an artfully written piece of fiction, containing just enough gore, perversity, and terror to delight the most demanding and most seasoned of "horror story" readers, while maintaining more than enough credibility-potential to avoid offending or disappointing the more serious student of well written novels. . . .

Matheson's book moves with unhurried, unfaltering steps towards its logical, and deadly conclusion. His depth of detail on psychic phenomena more than suspends any disbelief we might entertain. It is a shocking book, totally absorbing in its progression, brutally compelling in its conclusion; a book well worth one long, scary night's reading, if just for the "Hell" of it.

> *Benjamin Paul John Przekop, in a review of "Hell House," in* Best Sellers, *Vol. 31, No. 10, August 15, 1971, p. 220.*

NEWGATE CALLENDAR

In most Gothic novels . . . the story ends with a rational explanation of whatever spooks, poltergeists and other phenomena were used. Somebody has been trying to drive the heiress mad, nine cases out of ten. But in Richard Matheson's *Hell House,* the haunted house is really, demonstrably haunted. There is a vicious ghost, or series of specters, on hand.

In to exorcise them come a medium, a parapsychologist-physicist, and an ex-medium who has lost his powers, or so he thinks. They enter a very evil house, one that not even Mrs. Radcliffe could have imagined. In this house are materialization, possession, Satanism, the works. . . . Belasco House is a terror.

Matheson's book is a fine horror story, all the more in that he seems to take for granted that spirits can walk the earth. Few of the dated trappings of the genre are used. There is a final confrontation between the forces of evil and a lone antagonist that even has certain elements of humor. A walloping good book of its kind.

> *Newgate Callendar, in a review of "Hell House," in* The New York Times Book Review, *August 29, 1971, p. 27.*

MARTIN LEVIN

If past and present exist simultaneously, as J. W. Dunne and others have speculated, might it not be possible to sneak back and forth in time? [In *Bid Time Return,* this] well-worn springboard is a limber jumping-off place into a day in the year 1896, where a 36-year-old writer named Richard Collier feels very much at home. Here, at the Coronado Hotel, a Pacific pleasure dome in the grand style, Collier picks up a *déjà vu* romance with an actress of the nineties. Elise McKenna is an ingenue in the Maud Adams mold, and Collier is dead sure that their paths have crossed before. How else to explain his name on an old hotel register dated November 20, 1896? The writer, who has bad troubles in the present days, buys himself a Gay Nineties suit of clothes at a costumer's, and before you can say J. B. Priestley, he is holding hands with his beloved. Whether it be teleportation or delirium, Richard Matheson fashions his hero's wanderings into a fine, atmospheric trip.

> *Martin Levin, in a review of "Bid Time Return," in* The New York Times Book Review, *March 30, 1975, p. 21.*

THE CRITIC

And you thought there was no life after Warren Beatty? Nonsense. Author Matheson bases [*What Dreams May Come*] on the studies by Elizabeth Kübler-Ross and Raymond Moody regarding the human experience of death and the after-life and it's quite a trip what with the astral shells, etheric doubles, concentric spheres of existence and all sorts of auras to pass through on the way to wonderful ''Summerland'' where a glorified ''all mental'' body disports itself free of all earthly encumbrances. Actually, Matheson does a pretty fair job of pulling readers along his celestial science-fiction orbit but if you're not a dog-lover you may want to bail out when long-dead old rover shows up to greet his newly arrived master.

> *A review of ''What Dreams May Come,'' in* The Critic, *Vol. 37, No. 8, October, 1978, p. 7.*

TED KRULIK

Among the many movies that enticed audiences [during the 1950s and 1960s] with visions of giant insects and mutated beings were two that avoided the cliché of the [bug-eyed monster]: *The Last Man on Earth* (1964) and *The Incredible Shrinking Man* (1957). Both of these movies had their genesis in books written by a single author in the 1950s, Richard Matheson. The Vincent Price film *The Last Man on Earth,* later remade with Charlton Heston as *The Omega Man,* was originally entitled *I Am Legend* (1954); *The Incredible Shrinking Man,* prior to its movie release, was simply called *The Shrinking Man* (1956).

Both novels describe the terrible consequences of man-made forces. Instead of the threat of the usual giant insect or mutant, unnatural forces, related to the release of nuclear energy, affect ordinary people and change their environments in drastic ways. These two novels offer a fresh slant to the Things-Better-Left-Untouched motif so often used in science fiction since the dropping of the Hiroshima bomb.

At their core, *I Am Legend* and *The Shrinking Man* take us into the thoughts and feelings of ordinary men struggling to survive in highly unusual circumstances. In *I Am Legend,* Matheson has reworked the last man on earth theme; his protagonist, Robert Neville, is the last living man plagued by an army of the living dead—vampires. Scott Carey, in *The Shrinking Man,* is separated from society by his decreasing size, until he must survive alone in an alien world created by the increasing immensity of the basement in which he is trapped.

Trivial domestic details and descriptions of everyday objects present a clear contrast with the strangeness of the situations in which Neville and Carey find themselves. In *The Shrinking Man,* the increasing size of familiar objects creates a sinister realm that Scott Carey must cope with. Because of his altered sense of scale, an ordinary oil burner becomes a huge thundering tower. The wall beside it appears as an enormous cliff, the strewn sand on the floor is seen as a vast desert, and a common spider seems to be a frightful creature as tall as he is.

Part of the horror that the reader feels about Carey's predicament is in the fact that he no longer has control over the paraphernalia that people take for granted. The familiar has become a terrible, unknown frontier; at the same time, there is a fascination about the threats that might lurk in such a minuscule world.

In *I Am Legend,* an attention to domestic details forms an ironic comparison with Robert Neville's situation. Contrasted with the daily routines of making a life for himself are Neville's supernatural preparations. While he carefully washes his hands and makes sandwiches and coffee for a seemingly pleasant little trek, he also sharpens stakes and carries them in a bag like a latter-day Van Helsing, to be used in the well-known way against vampires.

An integral part of the dream of being the last person on earth is the freedom to roam anywhere one wants, to enjoy all the fruits of civilization left to him. Significantly, such a fantasy has the bonus of freedom from the responsibilities we all face in tending to a job, a home, automobile, family, and the other activities that whirl around our lives. In the world of Robert Neville, we see this fantasy come to life. All the fruits of modern technology lie before him, for his use alone. He has no responsibilities to any other people. His only responsibility is to himself, to maintain a comfortable existence, and to assure his own survival.

Matheson reveals a belief that living in an unknown frontier can be beneficial to man. Natural self-reliance in facing a wilderness is missing from our machine-age existence. As horrible as Scott Carey's life in *The Shrinking Man* has become in his cellar world, he philosophically reflects on his condition. . . . Thus we see a common bond between Matheson's protagonists. Carey and Neville are representative of the frontier spirit, seeking survival in the face of cruel hardships.

The lengthy, mundane descriptions of Neville's daily life in *I Am Legend* might seem tiresome to the reader, but they vividly illustrate what we would have to go through if we had to rebuild civilization around our needs. . . . But Matheson doesn't leave it at that; he instills a nightmare aspect into this fantasy of our childhood—other beings out there, trying to get at and kill the protagonist. With its step-by-step description of Neville's actions, *I Am Legend* breathes realism into everyman's nightmare of being chased and almost caught by creatures from beyond the grave. As night falls, Neville must hit and shove and scratch his way back into his house when he realizes he had been outside too long. Using all his strength, he closes the front door on the arm of one vampire, crushing it until it is broken and useless. Then Neville pushes the limb back out and locks the door.

The reader feels a catharsis with Neville's success at warding off the vampires' attacks. In a violent world, Neville has the strength to meet violence with violence. With his stoic, self-reliant way of life and his dynamic physical struggle against the vampires, he is a hero we can admire.

For Scott Carey, however, an important part of his problem is concerned with failing strength and failing masculinity as he shrinks. He simply can't punch his way out of his predicament the way Robert Neville could. He is fighting his own feelings of weakness and loss in addition to any real enemy. This loss of strength is in part the reason why he becomes trapped in the cellar in the first place; he fights a losing battle with a creature that, under normal conditions, he would have nothing to fear from. A bird twice his size forces Carey against the cellar window when he inadvertently finds himself locked out of his house. Using snow from the ground, Carey tries to chase off the attacking bird, but to little avail. He doesn't have the strength or forcefulness that Neville has. As a result, Carey is beaten back and falls into the cellar, from which he finds no escape. In counterpoint to the fantastic situation, a tiny man fending off an ordinary bird, is the realism of the scene, expressed through selected details of the exterior of the house, the cellar window, and the snow. (pp.1-4)

Although author Damon Knight seemed to frown on Matheson's homespun technique when he wrote: "He has a profound interest in the trivia of his daily life"[see excerpt above], it is Matheson's ability to capture a sense of realism in a few lines of scenery which allows the reader to take the imaginative leap necessary. The author's detailed method makes plausible the nightmare thoughts that many people share, at least as children. The process of seeking some credible scientific excuse for the mythologies and superstitions of the human imagination is an important part of Matheson's writings. (pp. 4-5)

In *I Am Legend,* the reader learns with Neville that the vampire state develops from a germ like any other disease. With his discovery of the *bacillus vampiris* on a microscope, Neville wipes away all the superstitious fears of centuries. Although Matheson's pseudoscientific explanations may not stand up to informed scrutiny, it is remarkable how much his bacillus can explain. (p. 5)

Matheson uses similar medical terminology to describe the reasons for Scott Carey's condition in *The Shrinking Man.* The immediate biological cause of his shrinking is an irreversible and persistent loss of specific bodily elements, such as nitrogen, creatinine, phosphorus, and calcium; these elements are associated with development of tissue and muscle, and bone. Matheson is attempting to deal with one of the basic considerations of the SF genre, "the what if—" question. What if a person could shrink? How might it happen? What experiences might he have? By using medical jargon that sounds half-reasonable to answer some of these questions, the author shows a high regard for the science behind the unknown.

Damon Knight points out a serious problem in the construction of *The Shrinking Man.* Matheson's story is inconsistent in its showing of Carey's weaknesses and physical incapabilities. Knight's argument is that Carey should not have been shown struggling hard to lift large objects and scale mountainous terrains if, at the end of the novel, he discovers that a fall of hundreds of feet leaves him unhurt. An explanation comes to mind, but it is not based on any scientific rationale. It was important for dramatic effect, for keeping in character with the failing strength of Scott Carey, that he struggle for each small gain in his basement world. Matheson's motivation for showing Carey surviving a fall that should have killed him had nothing to do with scientific accuracy or relative stresses in differing molecular densities. Carey's survival from that great fall illustrated that he was no longer part of the human race in any physical sense. His physical being had finally taken on all the attributes of an insect, not just in size. His world had become an alien realm beyond our experience. (pp. 5-6)

Matheson's use of science is a means to an end; it brings realism to the predicament of his characters. That realism helps the reader to identify with Neville and Carey. To Matheson, scientific advance can be a dangerous thing to the individual. His people have simple, domestic worries and share genuine feelings with us; science is a disruptive force that is capable of ripping such a person from all that he knows. (p. 7)

Robert Neville shares the gain of a new insight almost directly with the reader. He changes our view of the sinister presence of the dead-returned-to-life through his discovery of a scientific reason for vampirism. The vampire is no longer a creature of mystery and mystical powers; here is a science that explains the reason for a vampire's existence and all the myths surrounding our understanding of them. The reader finds a new way of looking at all superstitious fears, not only of the vampire. By making a vampire a known quantity, with a scientific basis, Robert Neville gives us a reason to reflect that the unknown need not be fearful.

Neville's realization at the end of the novel that he is the one who is different from the others gives the reader a new slant on the makings of civilization. The reader, like Neville, always had assumed that a truly civilized society sought to better itself, removing the undesirable elements and improving on the better qualities of people and the community. In essence, society encourages health, strength, and achievement, while hoping to eliminate disease, poverty, and criminality. When we learn that a new civilization is in the developing stages, one that is infected with the sickness that caused the world-wide death and creation of vampires, a new civilization that is seeking to destroy all the remnants of past human society, our assumptions are shaken. (pp. 7-8)

In a jarring moment, Scott Carey in *The Shrinking Man,* trapped in his basement, is thrust into a radically distorted perspective of his former world. As he walks toward his shelter under the water heater, a thunderous noise disrupts the cellar world. A huge, other-worldly figure looms over him, shaking his minuscule world with shoes several times his own height. Some new understandings strike Carey simultaneously: the new shock that the cellar realm he accepted can be disturbed by the life "out there;" the vision of a person the size he once was; and the realization that this monstrosity with elephantine dimensions was once his wife, Louise.

When Carey wonders afterward why he didn't try to call to her, he realizes that he no longer has any relationship to his wife, or to the world he once knew. The reader understands that there is no way for Carey to go back, that he does not belong in that world. In an almost literal way, Scott Carey is a fish abruptly taken out of his fishbowl. While he is still able to view his old way of life, he becomes aware that he must forge a new one.

In his first weeks of shrinking, Carey confronted a basic truth about human nature. . . . So much of our relationships with other people depend on our physical presence, on what we are, measured in feet and inches, in comparison with others around us. (pp. 8-9)

"Why not go out?" It is a question that occurs for both Carey and Neville. For Carey, soon to disappear from the world of humanity, letting the spider catch him was all that was needed. "It would be a hideous death, but it would be quick; despair would be ended." Robert Neville need only heed the call of the vampires for all his problems to be resolved. "Why go through all this complexity when a flung-open door and a few steps would end it all?" However, Matheson's characters belong to a literary tradition in which the hero must grapple with all obstacles and attempt to endure. Locked helplessly in his home each night, Neville's expression of contempt is typical of the hero: "I'll kill every mother's son of you before I'll give in!"

When the infected people came with guns to break in to Neville's house, he put up a valiant effort to defend his home and himself. Having been forewarned of their coming, his defense seemed as heroic as the men at the battle of the Alamo, who knew death would come at the end. Seriously wounded and taken prisoner, Neville's reasons for not leaving when he had the chance appear flimsy, but are the stuff that makes ordinary men attempt extraordinary actions in the face of the greatest dangers: "I was too used to the . . . the house. It was a habit, just . . . just like the habit of living. I got . . . used to it." Weak from his wounds, Neville refused to accept the reality of his death. . . . Only when Neville saw the fear on the faces of the infected people, and understood what that fear meant, did he relinquish his hold on life.

Although Scott Carey had more readily accepted the coming of death, he expressed doubts about how that death would take shape. . . . Throughout the novel, Carey was assailed by doubts about his reason for struggling so hard to survive. Many times the means to end his life were put in his path: jumping off a table top to his death, falling down a bottomless hole he found in the cellar floor, or letting hunger and thirst take their final toll on him. Why go on if he faced nonexistence in a few more days?

The affirmation of a will to live continuously overcame Carey's thoughts of death. It seemed that there might be a purpose to his surviving as far as he had. (pp. 10-11)

His resolution to climb the "cliff" was made with this reaffirming of purpose to his life. Carey intended not only to reach the bread he needed for nourishment, but to fulfill his need to kill the spider and have sole domain of his universe. . . . (p. 11)

Matheson's final point in both novels is bonded by a common theme. In their variant ways, Scott Carey and Robert Neville are able to continue after the end of their existence. The events in *I Am Legend* lead to two important revelations of Neville's. First, he realizes he should have foreseen the development of a race of beings who could be infected by the bacteria but who would not become vampires. He sums up his realization in three words: "Bacteria can mutate."

Neville's second discovery embodies the author's prime motive behind the story's title and presents the ultimate purpose of Neville's life. . . . As the last of the human race, Neville realizes, as we do, that a new future race of beings could view us as infamous and the stuff of mystical fears. His death not only has meaning, but the future race will remember him until the end of its time.

The concluding revelation in *The Shrinking Man* closely parallels that of *I Am Legend* in its intention to shock the reader as the protagonist is shocked (or surprised). It also reveals the purpose of Carey's existence, his uniqueness as a thinking creature who is smaller than a mote of dust. (p. 12)

Unlike the ironic but sad end of Robert Neville, Scott Carey's life holds the promise of continued existence in undreamed-of worlds. On the morning after his shrinking was supposed to take him from the face of the earth, he awoke. "He looked up again at the jagged blue dome. It stretched away for hundreds of yards. It was the bit of sponge he'd worn." His surprise and understanding of the "blue dome" mirrors our own. His revelation, like Neville's, comes after life as we know it has no further meaning.

Throwing aside the artificial measurements of mathematics, Carey understood that nature has no such limitations. "To nature there was no zero. Existence went on in endless cycles. It seemed so simple now. He would never disappear, because there was no point of nonexistence in the universe." With new energy and new joy, Scott Carey ran to face the infinite worlds awaiting him. The last words of the movie version encompassed the full meaning of Carey's story. Amid church music and the ringing of bells, Carey's own voice jubilantly told us: "I still exist!"

The popular appeal of these two novels rests on two qualities of any good work of literature: the universality of their themes, and the strong delineation of the characters and their conflicts. *I Am Legend* and *The Shrinking Man* express the universality of such themes as fear of darkness and the nightmare creatures we all fear it may contain; prejudice against anyone who is different from us, and the converse fear that we may be seen as different from others; and a real concern about changes within ourselves because of the world we have made. The novels are vividly personal because of the myriad particulars of Neville's and Carey's lives that Matheson takes the time to describe. We recognize those particulars because they are so much a part of our own lives. Like them, we all must confront our fears and weaknesses; we must endure beyond our mistakes, our embarrassments, and our personal humiliations. Matheson's characters are multifaceted and given to human frailty. They are like us in their drives and desires and they resemble us in our failures and need for the company of others.

The two novels discussed here are good examples of the genre of science fiction in that they describe ordinary human beings in unusual circumstances, and use the language of science as explanation. But they are more than that. They are worthwhile depictions of human endurance and human cares in a world gone haywire, one that looks very much like ours. (pp. 13-14)

Ted Krulik, "Reaching for Immortality: Two Novels of Richard Matheson," in Critical Encounters II: Writers and Themes in Science Fiction, *edited by Tom Staicar, Frederick Ungar Publishing Co., 1982, pp. 1-14.*

(Herbert) Marshall McLuhan

1911-1980

Canadian nonfiction writer, critic, poet, and editor.

McLuhan gained notoriety during the 1960s for his controversial theories on communications and for the experimental literary forms in which he presented his concepts. "McLuhanism" is a term critics apply to his theories and to the aphorisms and puns he commonly used to stimulate reader curiosity and to draw attention to his ideas. The most famous McLuhanism—"the medium is the message"—is a pivotal concept in his beliefs. McLuhan emphasized that human societies are shaped by the nature of their communications mediums; thus, the mediums through which society communicates more greatly affect society than the content of the messages being relayed. He argued further that recently developed electronic mediums—particularly television, which has become the dominant form of communication in the twentieth century—are significantly altering contemporary lifestyles and initiating a new stage in human development. These theories are elaborated in his two most important works, *The Gutenberg Galaxy: The Making of Typographic Man* (1962) and *Understanding Media: The Extensions of Man* (1964). The former book presents a historical foundation for McLuhan's claims, while the latter, which became a bestseller and provoked widespread public and critical debate, examines the implications of new electronic technologies.

While he was a student and later a professor of English literature, McLuhan became intensely interested in communications and popular culture. After publishing several essays of literary criticism, McLuhan composed his first book dealing with communications mediums, *The Mechanical Bride: Folklore of Industrial Man* (1951). This book contains illustrated ads that appeared in American magazines and sardonic commentary by McLuhan on the techniques of advertising. In the mid-1950s McLuhan directed a seminar on culture and communications at the University of Toronto; he was also a founder and editor, along with anthropologist Edmund Carpenter, of *Explorations,* a journal which provided a forum for studies in communications. The book *Explorations in Communications* (1960), edited by McLuhan and Carpenter, collects essays which originally appeared in their journal. During the late 1950s McLuhan directed a project on media that was cosponsored by the United States Office of Education and the National Association of Educational Broadcasters, and in 1963 he was named head of the Center for Culture and Technology at the University of Toronto.

In *The Gutenberg Galaxy,* which won the Governor General's Award for critical prose, McLuhan claims that four major stages in human development are directly related to significant changes in the means of human communication. During the first stage, preliterate humans communicated primarily by oral means and used a balance of the five senses to make meaning of the world. McLuhan contends that preliterate societies were necessarily collective in structure and encouraged active participation of tribal members due to their reliance on oral communication. With the creation of the alphabet, a new stage of life evolved in which humans began to rely on non-

Photograph by Karsh of Ottawa

oral forms of communication. The invention of the printing press in the fifteenth century effected a third stage in which humans began to rely primarily on the sense of vision, since printed matter had become the dominant form of mass communication. "Typographic man" began to make meaning of life in much the same way that books convey messages—by emphasizing sequential and linear thought patterns and arguments relying on logic and rationalism. McLuhan claims that books fragmented society by promoting individualistic pursuit of knowledge. The new electronic mediums are creating a fourth stage, according to McLuhan, changing human communication from the "visual-conceptual" mode of books to the "audile-tactile" mode of mediums like television. Whereas print media tend to fragment society, the new electronics technology, particularly the mass availability of television, will effect a web of interdependence that can unite humanity in a "global village."

In *Understanding Media* McLuhan concentrates on the new electronics technologies and examines their effect on contemporary life. This book made McLuhan an international celebrity; he was a popular lecturer who frequently spoke on college campuses and in corporate meeting rooms. Critics acknowledged the important implications of his theories and the fact that he was exploring aspects of popular culture that had been neglected by social scientists. Despite McLuhan's popularity, critical response to *The Gutenberg Galaxy* and *Understanding Media* was largely negative. Many critics cited McLuhan's montage-like presentation of ideas as a major obstacle in conveying his ideas. McLuhan attempted to duplicate in typographic form the ways in which electronic mediums convey messages, relying on repetition, generalizations, puns, and a rapid delivery. Many critics claimed that his arguments were undeveloped, illogical, and obscure. McLuhan countered this by saying that his ideas were meant to be "probes" rather than logically argued theses and that he was primarily interested in stimulating discussion of the new electronic technologies as a means toward understanding and controlling them. In retrospect, most critics view him as an important figure for having drawn attention to the relationship between communication and culture in the contemporary world. Hugh Kenner, a companion of McLuhan's during their college days and a lifelong friend, blamed critics for misconstruing McLuhan's intentions by concentrating on his style rather than the validity of his ideas. Kenner, who disagreed with many of McLuhan's theories, stated that McLuhan "was taken at his (printed) word, just as if in his outrageous one-liners he hadn't intended audience participation, or hadn't counted on his audience to fill out and correct all those comic-book formulations."

McLuhan contributed to his notoriety during the 1960s by being widely accessible and by presenting his ideas in a variety of mediums. According to James P. Carey, McLuhan became "a prophet, a phenomenon, a happening, a social movement." *The Medium Is the Massage* is the title of a book, a record album, and a television special, all of which appeared in 1967. On the television program, which aired on the National Broadcasting Company, McLuhan explained that this title "is intended to draw attention to the fact that a medium is not something neutral—it does something to people. It takes hold of them. It rubs them off, it massages them, it bumps them around." In the book McLuhan explained the importance of examining communications mediums: "All media work us over completely. They are so pervasive in their personal, political, esthetic, psychological, moral, ethical, and social consequences that they leave no part of us untouched, unaffected, unadulterated."

Although McLuhan is best remembered for his communications theories, he wrote several other works. *Counterblast* (1954; revised, 1967) is a collection of his poetry. *The Interior Landscape* (1969) is a collection of the literary criticism he wrote between 1943 and 1962. McLuhan also edited and wrote the introduction for a volume of poems by Alfred, Lord Tennyson, *Selected Poems* (1956). His other works on communications and popular culture include *War and Peace in the Global Village: An Inventory of Some of the Current Spastic Situations That Could Be Eliminated by More Feedforward* (1968), on which he collaborated with Quentin Fiore; *Culture Is Our Business* (1970); *Take Today: The Executive as Drop-Out* (1972); and, in collaboration with his son, Eric, and Kathy Hutchon, he published *The City as Classroom: Understanding Language and Media* (1977) and *Media, Messages, and Language: The World as Your Classroom* (1980).

(See also *Contemporary Authors*, Vols. 9-12, rev. ed., Vol. 102 [obituary] and *Contemporary Authors New Revision Series*, Vol. 12.)

In this volume commentary on Marshall McLuhan will focus on his first four books: *The Mechanical Bride, The Gutenberg Galaxy, Understanding Media,* and *The Media Is the Massage.*

DAVID L. COHN

[*The Mechanical Bride: Folklore of Industrial Man*, according to McLuhan,] "makes a few attempts to attack the very considerable currents and pressures set up around us today by the mechanical agencies of the press, radio, movies, and advertising." The use of large reproductions of advertisements illuminates the text and often powerfully reinforces it.

Herbert McLuhan is, happily, an indignant man. He is angry at many things. They range from what he calls "The Ballet Luce"—the magazines Time, Life, Fortune—to the Great Books program of the University of Chicago to Emily Post and co-education in our schools. Other blasts are leveled at the professional mortician, Charles McCarthy, Thornton Wilder, life insurance salesmen, the New Look in masculine apparel, Momism, hosiery ads, the comic-strip and Reader's Digest.

Righteous anger has its uses, but it is here often abused to the detriment of the author's thesis that we are wallowing in vulgarity and shabbiness of values. A passionate no-sayer, he is sometimes carried away by his anger. Not content, for example, with celebrating a man of whom he approves—Al Capp and his Li'l Abner—he sets Capp a little above Mark Twain and then applies the club to some of Capp's contemporaries. . . .

One can often share the author's indignation while believing that with some display of humor on his part he might have made his book more corrosively cleansing. As it is he is nearly always as solemn as Nazi propagandists who told Germans that we were a decadent people because we had tree-sitters, marathon dances and jazz bands. . . .

It is no derogation of McLuhan's book to say that some of it is repetitive and covers familiar ground. The Bible, by a process that would have horrified economical Greek writers, frequently achieves emphasis by repetition; nor can one strike out too often against the shabbiness of many of our values. Yet the idiocies of advertising, television, radio and the movies might yield the more to a less strident treatment than the author has given them. If he had toned down his words now and then, and had permitted himself a little humor—"amusement" to which he is given is not the same thing—his would have been a better book for a wider audience. Too often, however, his own voice is lost amid his voice shouting to be heard.

> David L. Cohn, "A Touch of Humor Wouldn't Hurt,"
> in The New York Times Book Review, *October 21,
> 1951, p. 26.*

THE NEW REPUBLIC

[In *The Mechanical Bride*] Mr. McLuhan has assembled and commented on 59 examples, with illustrations, of attempts to get inside the "collective public mind" through advertisements, newspaper headlines, comic strips, etiquette books, science fiction and the like, to play for profit or other advantage on human fears and longings, to "manipulate, exploit and control." . . . The study of these specimens is important, Mr. McLuhan suggests, to help us find out why and how we are bamboozled, how we may guide our world "in more reasonable courses." The idea of the book is excellent, its purpose admirable; unfortunately the effectiveness of the work is all but destroyed by an inflated and professorial style and by the author's predilection for positively blood-curdling puns.

A review of "The Mechanical Bride: Folklore of Industrial Man," in The New Republic, *Vol. 125, No. 22, November 26, 1951, p. 21.*

JOHN SIMON

[*The essay from which this excerpt is taken originally appeared in* The New Republic, *October 8, 1962.*]

If there is anything that characterizes this rather characterless age in which we live, it is its inability to make choices. In politics, it seems impossible to choose between disarmament and an arms race, and perfectly well-meaning people find themselves embracing both. (p. 272)

As might be expected, the apologists of the choiceless society were hardly likely to keep us waiting for their appearance. As might further be expected, the gigantic task of defending the choice of choicelessness was not going to be undertaken by any casual casuist, but would require the emergence of men with considerable resourcefulness, erudition, and authority. Such a one is Professor McLuhan . . . [in] *The Gutenberg Galaxy,* a study of the starring role typography played in the shaping of human thought and life. The thesis of the book is that man was once tribal and fully developed in all his senses, *i.e.,* in the jargon of the trade, "audile-tactile"; "Touch," McLuhan suggests, "is not so much a separate sense as the very interplay of the senses." But the invention of the phonetic alphabet and, particularly, of printing, stressed man's visual-conceptual orientation and development, until everything from his politics to his art, from his science to his commerce, became lineal, sequential, organized according to a perspective and logic that were merely the hypertrophy and hegemony of the visual or conceptual. But the coming of the telegraph, films, radio, television and other mass media, which demand the use of various senses and which reduce the world to a tribal village, creates a new revolution comparable to the typographic one but in the inverse direction. McLuhan claims that if we can understand the nature of this revolution, we can avoid being its victims. Perhaps, then, it would be more accurate to describe him, not as the apologist, but as the dupe of the new technologies.

As McLuhan summarizes his book, the typographic world "is the method of the fixed or specialist point of view that insists on repetition as the criterion of truth and practicality. Today our science and method strive not toward a point of view but to discover how not to have a point of view, the method not of closure and perspective but of the open 'field' and suspended judgment. Such is now the only viable method under electronic conditions of simultaneous information movement and total human interdependence." It follows that McLuhan's hero and model should be Harold Innis who, he alleges, "was the first person to hit upon the *process* of change as implicit in the *forms* of media technology. The present book," McLuhan continues, "is a footnote of explanation to his work." (pp. 273-74)

Let us consider, for the sake of our survival as readers and writers in the global village of the structuralist age, how Mr. McLuhan's book without a point of view is put together. It is, as he says himself, a footnote, but a footnote made up of footnotes. I would guess that it is about three quarters quotations, with the remaining quarter chiefly a connecting text introducing and commenting on the quotations, but also slipping in some assertions startling in their boldness and, occasionally, their irreconcilability. To turn his book "audile-tactile," he divides it into short, overlapping chapters which tend to have as little beginning and end as possible, and which may consist, for example, of quotations from Dom Jean Leclercq's *The Love of Learning and the Desire of God,* W. W. Rostow's *The Stages of Economic Growth,* Frazer's *The Golden Bough,* and the Opies' *Lore and Language of Schoolchildren* cheek by jowl. Such chapters are introduced by superscriptions in twenty-point bold face italics. . . . To make the book more of a "field," page numbers appear only on the rectos, so that one must frequently swivel one's head (a tactile phenomenon) to find out on what page one is. The book, moreover, is full of the new words of the electronic tribe: analogate, auditorially, haptic, specialisms, decentralism, etc.; as well as phrases like "civil defence against media fall-out," "Greek celature as a take-off strip for medieval manuscript culture," or "the Montaigne kodak trick of snapshotting moments," and other such felicities, meant, perhaps, to activate our olfactory sense as well.

Underneath it all, McLuhan plays the history-of-ideas game, and plays it, I am afraid, none too well. Though he avers that what is bad is not print culture but only its effect on those who do not comprehend its bias, distinctions certainly become blurred when McLuhan blames "the Gutenberg galaxy" for everything from the "compartmentalizing of human potential" to the French Revolution, and speaks of "the natural victims of print" and "people reduced to things" by it. Furthermore, McLuhan does not have the encyclopedic learning with which to back up his generalizations: often we feel that a single book on a large topic holds him in thrall, and a vast historical question is supposed to be resolved by a single contemporary quotation. With medieval deference to authority, McLuhan keeps making his obeisance to this or that "major work" or "grand study"—favorite critical terms of his. One's confidence is further shaken by references to the Bavarian composer, Carl Orff as a Viennese musician, or to Umberto Boccioni, whose painting was far more important, as just a sculptor. It is, then, typical for McLuhan to make a contestable generalization about Spanish culture on the basis of two books (one a collection of essays by various hands), quotations from which are used, to say the least, deviously; thus Casalduero's statement that Don Quixote and Sancho "are of the same nature with a difference in proportion" is supposed to demonstrate that print in Spain was "effecting a new ratio in the senses."

Indeed, this is McLuhan's worst failing: the wholesale reinterpretation of texts to prove his preconceived argument. He offers lengthy misreadings of *King Lear, The Dunciad,* and *Finnegan's Wake,* among others. . . . (pp. 274-75)

Even more remarkable are Mr. McLuhan's contradictions, as when Euclidean geometry is still so "tactile-muscular" that later scholars criticized it for its pusillanimity, but Euclidean space is "linear, flat, straight, uniform" and a product of that literacy which, in turn, produced print culture. (p. 276)

McLuhan's conclusion is that visual orientation resulted in the fiasco of "mechanical matching, not imaginative making . . . in the arts and sciences, in politics and education until our own time." But when it comes to suggestions for dealing with the present cultural crisis which, true apologist or dupe that he is, . . . he offers no more help than he did in his previous book,

The Mechanical Bride. . . . Like Poe's sailor, we are supposed to study the maelstrom, and so discover the way out. But that is a faulty analogy. Beyond Poe's maelstrom was safety; beyond the trends that engulf our world there is no terra firma, no other world. And it is not typography or the sequential view that does us in, but any multiplication and vulgarization of ideas: the fact that the masses demand mass-production—in a way which Ruskin and Morris could not foresee, and which McLuhan's "field" view avoiding choice cannot concede— spells the end of culture, typographical or otherwise. I do not know just what about television, for example, Professor McLuhan would have us understand. How the tube works? The shoddiness of sponsors, agencies, and programs? The cloddishness of the public which dooms attempts at improvement? How would that help us to anything but choiceless acquiescence? It seems preferable to hold on to the pitifully individualistic, non-audile-tactile values of print culture: for the betterment of life, it is not death that needs understanding, but life. (pp. 276-77)

> John Simon, *"Pilgrim of the Audile-Tactile," in his* Acid Test, *Stein and Day Publishers, 1963, pp. 272-77.*

FRANK KERMODE

[The theme of *The Gutenberg Galaxy*] is the overdevelopment, since Gutenberg, of the visual function, both in language and in other fields, with consequent disturbances in the whole organism. Typographical man is individualist and has a fixed point of view; he also has an idea of time and space which is arbitrary, though it seems to him instinctive; it is based on the invention, early in the typographical era, of perspective. Type carried on the work of the phonetic alphabet, which, with its de-tribalising power, had created open societies and Euclidean geometry. Our sense of causation is shaped by our visual apprehension of spatio-temporal relations. (pp. 76-7)

Since no aspect of modern life is unaffected by the rise and fall of visual technology, McLuhan has to work in very diverse fields. He does this by making a florilegium of extracts from specialists in anthropology, physics, spelling reform, art, liturgiology, theology, and most other subjects. His authorities stretch from Opie to Giedion, Heisenberg to Chaytor, Ong (a specially heavy debt, this) to Panofsky. Some of the authorities are unknown to me even by name, and I daresay specialists might find the book partial in its treatment of their interest, as I myself found it very odd on Shakespeare. But these bundles of miscellaneous learning add a lot to the interest of the book, and they are brought to bear on the central theme. McLuhan is enormously well-read, and one learns a lot from him. Yet he reminds me a little of the Ice Age hunters who come into the argument at one point, and are said to have discovered in the natural contours of the rock the image of the animal they sought. "A few lines, a little carving, or some colour, are enough to bring the animal into view." Thus, perhaps, does McLuhan do his reading. (p. 77)

[It] seems undeniable that the printing press changed our notions of time. . . . It also altered our concept of space and of antiquity. (Curiously, McLuhan has nothing to say about the anthropological retribalisation of Greece that has taken place in this century.) That print also brought on the Reformation, as McLuhan argues, seems much more dubious, though of course that event has been related to the development of *homo economicus,* and he wasn't possible (according to this thesis) without the individualising, quantifying agency of print. It seems

possible on the Gutenberg thesis to trace most of the disagreeable elements of life in this epoch to movable type; and what can't be so explained can be attributed to its forerunners. Thus McLuhan says that print destroyed monodic song and substituted polyphony; and if you argue that pre-typographical popes sometimes had to act in order to save the words of the mass from melismatic encroachment, the answer would probably be that, with literate-manuscript men, the coming event cast its shadow before. I suppose there could be a very considerable list of objections to specific elements in the book, where the author's eye for "contour" leads him into positions of this kind.

It is now time to enter more general objections. The antithesis between oral and visual cultures seems to be too strongly asserted. Searching for evidence that the "ratio of the senses" was once less distorted by the supremacy of the visual, we cannot in the nature of the case get much farther back than the beginning of written records; you can argue that the damage was done by then, but this weakens the case for its having been caused largely by printing. For the senses always seem to have been thought of as existing in a hierarchy, usually with sight at the head of it. For Plato as for Shakespeare, sight was the "most pure spirit of sense": for Plato, as for typographic man, touch was the lowest of the senses. If we have reversed the position and put "tactility" at the top, we are returning—if anywhere—to pre-literacy, to the primitive. Everybody from Socrates on—perhaps from Cadmus on—is what McLuhan calls a "literacy victim." It's no use blaming it on Gutenberg that all our knowledge is translation into visually-dominated stereotypes, those bad substitutes for some tense, explosive ideogram.

Furthermore, there is an aspect of post-Gutenberg man almost too obvious to mention, but one has to, since the author also finds it so. This is the strong anti-typographical counter-current in our culture. Antiquity viewed in perspective may be an achievement of typographic man; but so is the creation of a civilisation heavily dependent upon, and imitative of, that remote world. The typographic men of the 16th and 17th centuries revered the oral rhetoric and the recited epic of Rome; the 18th century made a hero of the bard Homer. Typographic man invented counterpoint and bar-measures; but he also fought counterpoint, imitated ancient monody, and made possible modern opera. The poets have gone on insisting that theirs is an oral art. . . . We typographic men have certainly paid our respects to oral culture.

McLuhan might well answer that this merely shows how men of high sensibility react naturally against the typographical attempt to reduce their sensoria, and hanker after the original state of nature, oral, tactile, simultaneous. But Tharmas fell; or, to use a Blake reference employed by McLuhan, God was unable to keep us "from single vision and Newton's sleep." (pp. 77, 80-1)

Mr. McLuhan never uses the expression "dissociation of sensibility," but he is always talking about it and in a very literal way; no one else has ever made out so encyclopaedic a case for this ubiquitous and central modern notion. He quotes with approval a description of "the print-made split between head and heart" as "the trauma which affects Europe from Machiavelli to the present" and thinks the Unconscious is a sort of slag-heap where we dump the débris left by the wasteful processes of a distorted sensory equipment. Our materialist technologies have destroyed "Imagination, the Divine Body." What used to be the "ordinary transactions between the self and the world'' have now to be simulated in Symbolist poetry and called illogical. McLuhan shows signs of resistance to enslavement by the dissociation myth; he says much modern primitivism is fraudulent or ignorant, and is anxious to preserve whatever is good in the Gutenberg technology so that it may be of benefit in the different future. But I don't think this is sufficient to disarm one's critique of satisfaction. Why give this splendid new dress to our old friend dissociation? The whole doctrine is itself a nostalgic reaction against typographic culture.

There is, naturally, a case for understanding better the success of the doctrine. What matters is not whether the dissociation happened, but that we feel happier to suppose it did, and work on the historical contours like the Ice Age hunters, or the millennialists; it is one of those schemes described by Mircea Eliade as ways of evading the terrors of actual history. We ought to ask ourselves why at a moment like the present (after the relevant historiographical debate has been on for years) we find such obvious comfort in historical or pseudo-historical explanations.

Mr. McLuhan's book is a work of historical explanation, and its merits as well as its defects are related to this. He tries to say everything relevant about a changing culture by free borrowing from many authorities, whose material is organised around a central myth. This is the method of the *specula*, or of the old hexemeral commentaries, which organised an encyclopaedia into a commentary on the Six Days of Creation. All knowledge was therefore related and manageable; and the Fall explained why things had so evidently gone awry. This was the Genesis Galaxy. Mr. McLuhan substitutes the printing-press for Genesis, and the dissociation of sensibility for the Fall. In so doing he offers a fresh and coherent account of the state of the modern mind in terms of a congenial myth. In a truly literate society his book would start a long debate. (pp. 81-2)

> *Frank Kermode, "Between Two Galaxies," in* Encounter, *Vol. XX, No. 2, February, 1963, pp. 76-7, 80-2.*

DWIGHT MacDONALD

[*Understanding Media: The Extensions of Man*] is one of those ambitious, far-ranging idea-books that is almost certain to be a *succes d'estime* and may well edge its way onto the bestseller lists. It has all the essentials: a big, new theory about an important aspect of modern life—in this case what is called Mass Media, or Communications—that is massively buttressed by data and adorned with a special terminology. . . .

Mr. McLuhan's book outdoes its predecessors in the scope and novelty of its theory, the variety of its data (he has looted all culture, from cave paintings to Mad magazine, for fragments to shore up against the ruin of his System) and the *panache* of its terminology. My only fear is he may have overestimated the absorptive capacities of our intelligentsia and have given them a richer feast of Big, New ideas than even their ostrich stomachs can digest. (p. 1)

Compared to Mr. McLuhan, Spengler is cautious and Toynbee positively pedantic. His thesis is that mankind has gone through three cultural stages: a Golden Age of illiterate tribalism that was oral, homogeneous, collective, non-rational and undifferentiated; a Silver Age (the terms are Ovid's, not his) that set in after the invention of the alphabet during which the spoken

word began to be superseded by the written word, a decay into literacy that was facilitated by the fact that alphabetic writing is easier to learn and use than Egyptian hieroglyphs or Chinese ideograms, whose desuetude he deplores; and the present Iron Age that was inaugurated by movable-type printing, an even more unfortunate invention, and that is visual, fragmented, individualistic, rational and specialized. McLuhan's *The Gutenberg Galaxy* . . . is really Vol. 1 of the present work, describing the socio-cultural changes, mostly bad, brought about by the post-Gutenberg multiplication of printed matter, with its attendant stimulation of literacy. A gloomy work.

Understanding Media is more cheerful. It is about a fourth Age into which for over a century we have been moving more and more rapidly, with nobody realizing it except Mr. McLuhan: the Electronic Age of telegraph, telephone, photograph, phonograph, radio, movie, television and automation. This is a return to the Golden Age but on a higher level, as in the Hegelian synthesis of thesis and antithesis; or a spiral staircase. These new media are, in his view, making written language obsolete, or, in his (written) language, the Electronic Age ''now brings oral and tribal ear-culture to the literate West (whose) electric technology now begins to translate the visual or eye man back into the tribal and oral pattern with its seamless web of kinship and interdependence.''

This preference for speech over writing, for the primitive over the civilized—to be fair, McLuhan's Noble Savage is a more advanced model than Rousseau's, one equipped with computers and other electronic devices that make writing, indeed even speech, unnecessary for communication—this is grounded on a reversal of the traditional hierarchy of the senses. Sight, Hearing, Touch was Plato's ranking, and I imagine even in the Electronic Age few would choose blindness over deafness or touch over either of the other two. But McLuhan's 75 per cent of new material includes a rearrangement to Touch, Hearing, Sight, which fits his tropism toward the primitive. He seems to have overlooked the even more primitive Taste and Smell, which is a pity, since a historical-cultural view based on them would have yielded at least 90 per cent new material.

If I have inadvertently suggested that *Understanding Media* is pure nonsense, let me correct that impression. It is impure nonsense, nonsense adulterated by sense. Mr. McLuhan is an ingenious, imaginative and (above all) fertile thinker. He has accumulated a great deal of fresh and interesting information (and a great deal of dull or dubious information). There is even much to be said for his basic thesis, if one doesn't push it too far (he does). . . . It is when he develops his ideas, or rather when he fails to, that I become antipathetic.

One defect of *Understanding Media* is that the parts are greater than the whole. A single page is impressive, two are ''stimulating,'' five raise serious doubts, ten confirm them, and long before the hardy reader has staggered to page 359 the accumulation of contradictions, non-sequiturs, facts that are distorted and facts that are not facts, exaggerations, and chronic rhetorical vagueness has numbed him to the insights. . . . (pp. 1, 14)

If he had written, instead of a long book, a long article for some scholarly journal, setting forth his ideas clearly—and once—Mr. McLuhan might have produced an important little work. . . . At the worst, it would have been Provocative, Stimulating, maybe even Seminal. And Readable. But of course he wrote the book because he couldn't write the article. Like those tribesmen of the Golden Age, his mind-set doesn't make for either precision or brevity. . . .

Alas. A writer who believes that truth can be expressed only by a mosaic, a montage, a *Gestalt* in which the parts are apprehended simultaneously rather than successively, is forced by the logic of the typographical medium into "a fixed point of view" and into much too definite conclusions. And if he rejects that logic, as McLuhan tries to, the alternative is even worse: a book that lacks the virtues of its medium, being vague, repetitious, formless and, after a while, boring. (p. 14)

Dwight MacDonald, "Running It Up the Totem Pole," in Book Week—The Sunday Herald Tribune, *June 7, 1964, pp. 1, 14-15.*

DEBORAH A. HOLMES AND GEORGE ZABRISKIE

[*The Gutenberg Galaxy*] presented the thesis that the invention of the alphabet, and later the printing press, progressively transformed an oral, tactile, tribal culture into a specialized, fragmented society characterized by visual perception, the use of logical, sequential organization and a fixed point of view. Earlier, McLuhan . . . had written *The Mechanical Bride,* an elaborate spoof on the stereotyped excesses of a society dominated by mechanical technology. In *Understanding Media,* which carries history up to President Kennedy's assassination, he returns to the final theme in *The Gutenberg Galaxy:* electronic technology will take us back to oral, tactile tribalism.

The Gutenberg Galaxy, published in 1962, contained the promise of *Understanding Media* in its final section. With only two years between books, it seems that McLuhan was pressed to finish this new one and many of its disappointments . . . must be charged to haste. . . . Yet the book represents fresh and constructive thinking—insights, to use the author's own vocabulary—on the nature of media and their psychic and social consequences. In the wake of considerable controversy over his ideas, it is time to take a close look at what McLuhan is up to in *Understanding Media.*

McLuhan's concept of media includes not only the technology of communications but *any* socially affective technology. He treats media as extensions of the human personality, an approach adapted from the psychology of William MacDougall, who considered personality extension to begin with such simple things as the use of hand tools. McLuhan carries this MacDougallian theory into all things, with an inclusive view of media and the broadest possible interpretation of their effects. . . . Furthermore, to McLuhan, media as extensions of personality have particular analogies to parts of the human body: electric technology is an extension of the central nervous system.

From his view of media as extensions of personality, McLuhan proceeds to his second thesis: the medium is the message. He explains: ". . . the 'message' of any medium or technology is the change of scale or pace or pattern that it introduces into human affairs." In other words, the social effects resulting from the action of any medium of communication, and from its interaction with other media, transcend the cognitive content of the medium. Media of pure technology, such as artificial illumination, of course have a content *only* in terms of the message, i.e., the social implications.

The content of one medium is always another. The content of writing is speech; the content of speech is thought. Speech "is

an actual process of thought, which is in itself nonverbal." He continues:

> An abstract painting represents direct manifestations of creative thought processes as they might appear in computer designs. What we are considering here, however, are the psychic and social consequences of the designs or patterns as they amplify or accelerate existing processes.

This paragraph defines McLuhan's fundamental interests and the basis of his dynamics. One need add only his particular definition of hot and cold media:

> A hot media is one that extends one single sense in "high definition." High definition is the state of being well filled with data. A photograph is, visually, "high definition." A cartoon is "low definition" simply because very little visual information is provided. . . . Hot media are, therefore, low in participation, and cool media are high in participation or completion by the audience.

This polarity of "hot" and "cold," which pervades the book, is McLuhan's chief methodological error. It has the superficial appearance of crispness, but lends itself to fuzziness and meaningless categorizations which have little to do with McLuhan's central ideas. Polarities can be useful intellectual tools, but they tend to inhibit the description of dynamic processes, which seems to be the function of *Understanding Media.*

Radio and television are McLuhan's main interests. Radio is a hot medium (little audience participation) while TV is cool (great audience participation). He tends to disregard the highly auditory construction of much American programming, in which the visual image actually plays a subsidiary role. His theoretical TV audience gives constant and undivided attention to the shadow land of the screen, watching programs in which the visual constructs are all-meaningful. Actually, it is possible to experience many TV programs without looking at the picture. Here again, McLuhan's hodge-podge methodology betrays him.

Television, he affirms, is "tactile" and "tribal." Tactile, because it lacks definition; tribal, because it is "preliterate." . . . The ill-defined TV image . . . charms the nonliterate because he is forced to participate in fulfilling its creation. In McLuhan's view, the intellectual tends to reject the specific experience and its quality, while the young and non-intellectual, and those of subliminal literacy, identify with the experience without understanding it. He lists the social and psychological changes: the dead-pan expressions of the young, the virtual abolishment of adolescence in the traditional sense, a move toward involvement and participation in *depth*—or "getting with it."

His terminology of "tactile" and "tribal," when applied to the electronic age, is used to indicate change from the visual and specialized values of the Gutenberg era. But it is used as if it might imply progression. This leads to the paradoxical proposition that as we progress (change) we regress (revert to earlier behavior).

When he discusses media, McLuhan seems unaware that he is describing the witchcraft of our time. Media, in effect, are the irrational elements which motivate part of our irrational behavior. Unfortunately, McLuhan identifies with the irrationality of the media he describes, with a result analogous to

Montague Summer's literal belief in magic. The believer, as analyst, is undone by his belief. This acceptance of processes as descriptive models may account in large part for McLuhan's methodological floundering. (pp. 194-95)

The method of presentation in *Understanding Media* is essentially that of the *Gutenberg Galaxy*. A sequence of insights, as verbal *Gestalten* intended to correspond to the field approach of behavior, are configured into the grand *Gestalt* of a book. . . . This method was used more successfully in the *Galaxy* than in *Understanding Media,* which is primarily concerned with the present, rather than history. *Understanding Media* is too diverse, its content and arguments too sweeping, to stay within the orientation and limits of his mosaic framework. Methodologically, McLuhan seems to be striving for some kind of modular concept: a set of interchangeable, reusable intellectual building blocks which can be used over and over again in a variety of ways and still present bright new faces. . . .

As one reads the book, one wonders whether McLuhan is presenting illuminations or attempting the preliminary model of a system. . . . [He] might have gained something by treating his material as a continuum rather than in episodic disconnection. Except through artifice, life doesn't really live that way.

For any consideration of "the psychic and social consequences" of media, some psychological orientation is necessary. McLuhan's might be described as broadly eclectic, leaving some questions about its structure and organization. One is never quite certain whether the element of consistency is merely lurking or really lacking in the "mosaic image." His indebtedness to MacDougall has already been mentioned. Not only in the formal organization of the book, but in the text itself, through his insistence on "insight" and his elaboration of field theory, *Gestalt* psychology is given a good run for its money. Consciously, for reasons often obscure, he tends to reject Freudian and post-Freudian psychoanalytic theory except for a brief quotation from C. G. Jung, even though it would serve to bolster his projections more adequately than his numerous literary quotations. He is aware that somehow we have become "conscious of our unconscious," but he fails to apply that awareness where it might lead to a better understanding. . . .

McLuhan rejects value judgments and the idea of "content" in the usual sense. "It is wise to withhold all value judgments when studying these media matters, since their effects are not capable of being isolated." For better or worse, the man deserves to be taken at his word. Unfortunately, it is possible to find statements which seem to be implied value judgments . . . and it is equally possible to misconstrue some of his neutral statements as judgments of "content." McLuhan demands that others be more careful in the role of reader than he was in the role of writer. . . .

Nowhere does the haste with which this book was written betray the inclusive view of media more than in the chapters on "Number" and "Clocks." In the "Number" chapter his insights appear and disappear. . . . In this chapter and elsewhere, he sees the use of the binary number system by computers and other data-processing apparatus as a return to tribal counting methods. This mystical view ought to have been tempered by the realization that the modern use of the binary system derived from the inherent limitation of electrical switches to the two basic positions: *on* and *off*. (p. 195)

Like the chapter on "Number," the chapter called "Clocks: the Scent of Time" is little more than diffuse speculation. The

time concepts enforced by the era of data processing and information handling systems necessary for space technology are strangely absent from his discussion, except that "the electronic age . . . found that instant speeds abolish time and space and return man to an integral in primitive awareness." . . .

Neither *The Gutenberg Galaxy* nor *Understanding Media* is a literary book either in the canonical, scriptural way of the New Criticism, or in the offhand way of those volumes in which English professors give a bookish view of books and the world. Yet reviewers have tended to treat McLuhan as if he were writing literary books instead of descriptions of social and technical dynamics. Unfortunately, McLuhan himself drags in enough odd bits of literary misinterpretation to make a respectable article for the established journals of that business. As soon as one makes the noises of a literary critic or an English professor, the woods become full of literary critics and English professors who can make the same kind of noise, and louder. It is not easy for anyone else to believe that Andrew Marvell anticipated Einstein in precisely the way McLuhan would have him. At another point, misquotation and misunderstanding of Yeats join hands. To believe that *Among School Children* is concerned with movies is as difficult as it is to find the line "a spume upon a ghostly paradigm of things" in the poem. . . .

McLuhan's interpretations of Shakespeare and Donne are not less or more ridiculous than other perceptions embodied in much literary criticism, but in the light of McLuhan's own approach, they serve only to fog his intended meanings. This literary appeal to authority (his own) to bolster his arguments is methodologically weak and accomplishes little more than space filling. We have stressed methodology throughout this discussion because it is McLuhan's fundamental weakness— not merely the fact that some of his separate insights are erroneous or far-fetched.

A further flaw springs from his facile acceptance of a probable good possibly inherent in electronic technology. He is, of course, sound in saying that if we do not understand the nature and effects of the new media we shall lose by default that much control over our environment. Yet his own approach suggests no realistic methods of control and his general air of hopefulness has no sounder basis than a total pessimism might.

While McLuhan relates TV to every cultural phenomenon of our time from seamless stockings to paperback books, he fails, except for passing mention of the Kennedy assassination, to relate it for better or worse to the perverse violence of our time. . . . To what extent television, with its underlying emotional mode of terror, is related to this phenomenon is a question McLuhan neither raises nor attempts to answer. Tracing back, through McLuhan's own statements, "the medium is the message." And, following his nesting-box concept of media, in which one medium always contains another, we get back to human thought itself. The medium may, in the case of gratuitous violence, reflect the world—but circularly, it may also be implicated in its creation. The dynamics of this area of behavior certainly deserve more consideration than the cool medium and hot issue of the small car or the qualities of a successful TV master of ceremonies.

McLuhan gives a clue when he says: "Everybody experiences far more than he understands. Yet it is experience, rather than understanding, that influences behavior, especially in collective matters of media and technology where the individual is almost inevitably unaware of their effect upon him." His statement hangs in mid-thought, leaving the reader to relate it to something. Here again is the failure, not of concept but of construct, which flaws the whole work. What might have been one of the most important books of its decade has been so poorly put together that its most realistic claim remains that of being a series of highly stimulating speculations. In reading it, one learns as much about McLuhan as about media. (p. 196)

Deborah A. Holmes and George Zabriskie, "The Cybernetic Caveman," in The Nation, *Vol. 199, No. 9, October 5, 1964, pp. 194-96.*

CHRISTOPHER RICKS

Understanding Media cuts off its extension of man to spite its face. How can Mr McLuhan possibly use the medium of the *book* (typographic, linear, fragmented) in order to speak in this way about the electronically instantaneous? On his own terms, a book cannot but enforce the typographical attitudes which he insists are cramping Western man. If his arguments are true, how silly to annul them by using a medium which has no option but to annul them.

He wriggles in this unmentioned predicament, and does his best to escape by abandoning all the sequential virtues of a book. He says the same thing on every page, and repeats whole chunks when he feels like it—which is perhaps one kind of instantaneity. He praises the Eastern ('oral') mode of thought. . . . But if this 'oral' tradition could be incorporated in a book, his arguments would all collapse. The attempt may be pluckily preposterous, but the outcome is not just 'seeming' redundancy. The moral position, too, is shaky, and not even the quotation from Pope Pius XII about media quite manages to shore it up. Mr McLuhan may insist that he is 'withholding all value judgments when studying these media matters,' but in fact his terms are about as neutral as a bigot. (p. 925)

Very well—people were wrong to ignore the nature of a medium. But that doesn't beautify the airy hauteur to which the arguments rise whenever they confront facts, earthy political facts. Possibly radio does inevitably inflame, and TV does cool, but the authorial tone is too epigrammatically Olympian. 'Had TV occurred on a large scale during Hitler's reign he would have vanished quickly. Had TV come first there would have been no Hitler at all.' Vanished? Like a Walt Disney ogre? So confident a magic wand does not like the fact that there are facts. Can we be quite so sure that Nazi TV would have had no choice but to intervene so coolingly and so effectively? Is 'content' (even anti-semitic content) really a matter of total indifference in comparison with 'the medium proper'? Mr McLuhan may perhaps be right, but Hitler seems to me a subject where too serene a confidence in one's own theories can easily look unfeeling. After all, there are those of us who would have traded all of Pope Pius's words about mass media for just a word or two about the massacre of the Jews.

Mr McLuhan's confidence, quite without irony, sees the computer as a type of the Holy Ghost: 'The computer, in short, promises by technology a Pentecostal condition of universal understanding and unity.' So much for greed, crowding, hunger, and all the hard facts which make universal understanding and unity a matter of intractable things as well as of language and media. When Mr McLuhan invokes his Pentecost, there is no doubt about the mighty rushing wind, but where are the tongues of fire?

It seems that we have been fools, but now at last we will be put right about it all, though our patient teacher can't quite prevent his eyelid from drooping disdainfully. 'It is not the increase of numbers in the world that creates our concern with population,' rather it is 'our electric involvement in one another's lives'. Our 'concern' may well have been pricked by the media, but it is not entirely evolved from them, since there remains the glumly objective fact of the increasing population, a fact which to any man who wants to live as something more than 'a student of media' is in itself a cause of concern. Could it be that Mr McLuhan averts his eyes from the fact because the Catholic Church wishes it weren't a fact? When the facts would be embarrassing, Mr McLuhan passes by on the other side. It seems that 'literate man' is a warped creature, 'quite inclined to see others who cannot conform as somewhat pathetic.' And then, without a pause: 'Especially the child, the cripple, the woman, and the coloured person appear in a world of visual and typographic technology as victims of injustice.' But in this world, the world of facts as well as of media, coloured people do not merely *appear* (thanks to tricksy typography) to be victims of injustice, they *are* such. Not every single individual, of course, but quite enough for Mr McLuhan's enlightened detachment to get tarnished. He long-sufferingly tut-tuts—how naive of people to be upset by circumstances, instead of realising that it is all just the built-in preconceptions of media.

Media, apparently, and not moral convictions, get things done: 'the real integrator or leveller of white and Negro in the South was the private car and the truck, not the expression of moral points of view.' Notice 'was', as if it were all a thing of the past, so that now the historian can bask in equanimity. Notice, too, that it isn't said that the truck was in the end the most effective or most important integrator or leveller—no, it was 'the real' one, which leaves 'moral points of view' (a prettily placid piece of phrasing) as merely unreal. . . . Since everybody else will talk about nothing but 'content', he will talk about nothing but media—nice, neutral, omnipotent media.

There is a similar stoniness when he discusses 'labour-saving' devices, toasters or washing-machines or vacuum cleaners: 'Instead of saving work, these devices permit everybody to do his own work. What the 19th century had delegated to servants and housemaids we now do for ourselves.' Oh no we don't. When we switch on the automatic washing machine, Mr McLuhan and I are not in any meaningful sense doing the same *work* as servants used to do. There is something unimaginative about a deftness that is so very interested in 'devices' and so little interested in how 19th-century servants really did work. 'Today, in the electronic age, the richest man is reduced to having much the same entertainment, and even the same food and vehicles as the ordinary man.' Try telling that to the many ordinary men who live in 'the other America', let alone three-quarters of the globe. Mr McLuhan may claim the license of a prophet, but even a prophet will be the more humane if he does not state as today's fact what may perhaps one day come to pass.

Such indifference to fact is not always politically disagreeable, but it is always absurd. (pp. 925-26)

The style is a viscous fog, through which loom stumbling metaphors. And Mr McLuhan's subject, after all, is the imagination and the emotions. Nothing could be less imaginative than all this talk of 'a complex and depth-structured person', especially as the depth resembles a sump: 'people begin to sense a draining-away of life values.' What we need is 'the mosaic of the press' which 'manages to effect a complex many-levelled function of group-awareness.' Fortunately 'the tactile mesh of the TV mosaic has begun to permeate the American sensorium'—hence the 'complex togetherness of the corporate posture'. What makes it all so grisly is that this unfelt, unfeeling and nerveless style is forever insisting on how media grip, how they touch, how they create. (p. 926)

Christopher Ricks, "Electronic Man," in New Statesman, *Vol. LXVIII, No. 1761, December 11, 1964, pp. 925-26.*

NEIL COMPTON

The typical reader of *Commentary* is living in a numbed and somnambulistic trance, self-hypnotized by his visual, linear bias. As for the magazine itself, it is an extremely hot medium . . . perversely devoting most of its space to matters which are peripheral to the real problems of modern culture. The ads are the best part of the journal.

These conclusions are forced upon anyone who accepts the main argument of *Understanding Media.* They are not the eccentric maunderings of a madman. On the contrary, Marshall McLuhan is one of the most brilliant sociocultural theorists writing today. I have been shamelessly pilfering his work for years, and others have been doing it too. . . . For all that, McLuhan is a somewhat lonely figure with many admirers but few disciples. His cocksure wisecracking manner, his extravagant generalizations, and his maddeningly repetitive style tend to repel fastidious readers. Even a strong sympathizer is likely to find irritation and illumination fairly evenly blended in his books. . . .

He began as a relatively conventional observer of the mass media. *The Mechanical Bride* is a brilliant application of the techniques of iconography and literary criticism to such hitherto neglected phenomena as advertisements, comic strips, and newspapers. Though McLuhan now apparently repudiates its essentially hostile and derisive tone, many will feel that this devastatingly witty and high-spirited work is his finest achievement. Between *The Mechanical Bride* and his next book, McLuhan edited *Explorations,* an extraordinary periodical devoted to the study and criticism of all types of communication. In its pages one can trace McLuhan's gradual shift from ironic contemplation to total immersion in the destructive element of modern media. The Old and New Testaments of the faith that followed this baptism are *The Gutenberg Galaxy* (1962) and its successor *Understanding Media.* (p. 79)

[In *The Gutenberg Galaxy* and *Understanding Media*] McLuhan faced an insoluble problem of method. How is it possible to diagnose and attack the distortions caused by phonetic literacy while using the very medium one is deploring? He has tried to resolve the dilemma by arranging his books in a "mosaic" of separate chapters which can be read in any order (thus making necessary a good deal of repetition). Since he regards the idea of cause and effect as an illusory linear abstraction, McLuhan tries to avoid making use of it, preferring to suggest the kind of configuration implied by the word "galaxy." Unfortunately, the English language does not lend itself very well to this kind of non-syntactical juxtaposition, so he is forced to fall back on such vague rhetorical flourishes as "That is why . . ." or "In the same way. . . ." His favorite mode of discourse is the enthymeme (or incomplete syllogism) which bookmen of detached private character like myself may be forgiven for thinking a vice rather than a revolutionary method of apprehending the universe. Nevertheless, *The Gutenberg Galaxy* is a most exciting book, full of brilliant insights (if one may risk

a visual metaphor) and valuable information about communication habits past and present. McLuhan is immensely well-read for a man with a grudge against print, and he quotes liberally from some fascinating and out-of-the-way writers and scholars.

If the earlier book concentrated on the past and its consequences for the present, *Understanding Media* is mainly devoted to the contemporary revolution in communications and its consequences for the future. It ought to be the fulfillment of the author's career as a cultural prophet. Unfortunately, though there is more than enough to reward persevering readers . . . , the book lacks the concentration and coherence of its predecessor. (p. 80)

The crisis of our time is that our visual and fragmented culture is inadequate to the electronic technology with which we have to cope. McLuhan reserves his most mordant wit to jeer at literary intellectuals whom he thinks more remote from understanding the world in which they live than the teen-age fans of any disc-jockey. And so long as the educated remain obstinately wedded to the irrelevant values of print-culture, the danger increases that man will slip back into that "Africa of the mind" from which the alphabet liberated our remote ancestors.

McLuhan confuses his thesis by an abortive—and at times even ludicrous—attempt to categorize media as "hot" and "cool." A hot medium extends one single sense in "high definition" (i.e., well filled with data). Cool media are low in definition and therefore require participation or completion by the audience. . . .

The coolest of all is television. McLuhan is so anxious to distinguish TV from old-fashioned hot media that he tries to deny that it is visual: because the TV screen shows "light through" rather than "light on," and the image is a low-definition shifting mosaic mesh, it has a haptic or tactile quality—in contrast to cinema which is highly visual and therefore hot. Eccentric judgments of this kind seem to arise from McLuhan's apparent compulsion to relate every phenomenon of modern life to his theories. Almost casually he "explains" why Kennedy beat Nixon (what would he have said if a few thousand votes had shifted the election the other way?), why mesh nylons are more sensuous than sheer (are they?), why baseball is declining (is it?), why the guards let Jack Ruby kill Lee Oswald, and why B. O. is unforgivable in literate societies. His critics understandably make fun of this intellectual megalomania.

But no review of *Understanding Media* should close on such a note. In this apocalyptic age, a pusillanimous correctness may be far more foolish than the wildest of insufficiently supported generalizations. While most scholars bury their heads in the private little sand plots they have marked out as their "field," McLuhan obstinately takes all knowledge for his province. Like the great writers that he admires—Rabelais, Cervantes, Pope, Joyce—he strives to be a man of "integral awareness." I expect to be equally inspired and infuriated by his next book. (p. 81)

Neil Compton, "The Cool Revolution," in Commentary, *Vol. 39, No. 1, January, 1965, pp. 79-81.*

HAROLD ROSENBERG

We all know that radio, the movies, the press do things to us. For McLuhan they also *are* us: "They that make them," he quotes the Psalms, "shall be like unto them." So *Understanding Media* is nothing less than a book about humanity as it has been shaped by the means used in this and earlier ages to deliver information.

McLuhan's account of the effects of the media upon the human psyche lies between fact and metaphor. The instrumentalities through which words, images, and other human signals reach us transform our bodies as well as our minds. Our eyes are bulged out by vacuum tubes, our ears elongated by transistors, our skin ballooned by polyesters. . . . In his first book, *The Mechanical Bride,* . . . unmistakably inspired by Duchamp's erotic apparatuses, McLuhan dealt with the pop creations of advertising and other word-and-picture promotions as ingredients of a magic potion, "composed of sex and technology," that was populating America with creatures half woman, half machine. "Noticed any very spare parts lately?" he inquired in a subhead of his title chapter. The legs, bust, hips of the modern girl have been dissociated from the human person as "power points," McLuhan claimed, reminding the reader that "the Hiroshima bomb was named 'Gilda' in honor of Rita Hayworth." Man, to McLuhan, often appears to be a device employed by the communications mechanisms in *their* self-development. "Any invention or technology," he writes in *Understanding Media,* "is an extension or self-amputation of our physical bodies, and such extension also demands new ratios or new equilibriums among the other organs and extensions of the body. There is, for example, no way of refusing to comply with the new ratios or sense 'closure' evoked by the TV image."

In McLuhan's *The Gutenberg Galaxy,* the analysis of how the human organism has been remodelled by a single communications medium is turned into a full-scale interpretation of Western history. (p. 129)

Understanding Media is McLuhan's goodbye to Gutenberg and to Renaissance, "typographic" man; that is, to the self-centered individual. As such, it takes its place in that wide channel of cultural criticism of the twentieth century that includes writers like T. S. Eliot, Oswald Spengler, D. H. Lawrence, F. R. Leavis, David Riesman, Hannah Arendt. *Understanding Media,* McLuhan's most neatly ordered and most comprehensive book, is an examination of how the eye-extended, print-reading individualist of the past five centuries is in our time undergoing metamorphosis under the bombardment of all his senses by new electronic media, the first of which was the telegraph. (pp. 129-30)

Of all crisis philosophers, McLuhan is by far the coolest. Though his notion of the "externalization" or "numbness" induced in the consumer of today's popular culture accords with Eliot's "hollow men," Reisman's "other-directedness," and Arendt's "banality," he is utterly unsympathetic to any concept of "decline." The collective trance of his contemporaries is to his mind a transitional phenomenon—one that recurs in all great historic shifts from one dominant medium to another. Current unfeeling and anxiety parallel states prevalent in the early Renaissance, when the printed document was replacing the hand-written script. Regarding us all in this light, McLuhan is immune to despair; in his terms, the theory that the modern world is a cultural wasteland is meaningless. What, he might ask, makes the inwardness of yesterday preferable to the shallowness of tomorrow, if both are by-products of more or less effective devices for conveying information? As the phonetic alphabet carried man from tribalism to individuality and freedom, the new electric media are taking him beyond "frag-

mented, literate, and visual individualism." If man today is part machine, this is not an effect of the Industrial Revolution. Technologies have been a component of human living for three thousand years, and our loftiest feelings have derived from that segment of us that is least ourselves: "By continuously embracing technologies, we relate ourselves to them as servo-mechanisms. That is why we must, to use them at all, serve these objects, these extensions of ourselves, as gods or minor religions. An Indian is the servo-mechanism of his canoe, as the cowboy of his horse or the executive of his clock." In line with Toynbee (the idea of the Eskimo as a merman, the cowboy as a centaur, is his), McLuhan has superseded Marx's "fetishism of commodities" with a fetishism of the medium to explain the forms of belief by which men have been governed in various epochs. Societies in which the sacred played a greater role than it does in ours were simply those ruled by media of communication more primitive than the visual. "To call the oral man 'religious,'" McLuhan observed in *The Gutenberg Galaxy,* "is, of course, as fanciful and arbitrary as calling blondes bestial."

McLuhan, then, is a modernist to the hilt; his own "sacred" touchstones are Cézanne and abstract art, the new physics, *Finnegans Wake.* His is the kind of mind that fills with horror the would-be conservator of values (a Leavis, a Yeats, a Lukács). He is not tempted in the slightest to dig in at some bygone historical moment. Accepting novelty as inevitable, he is not only a modernist but a futurist. In his latest mood, he regards most of what is going on today as highly desirable, all of it as meaningful. His position is to be inside change; he is given over to metamorphosis on principle. The present world-wide clash between the new and the old arouses him to enthusiasm, since "the meeting of two media is a moment of truth and revelation from which new form is born." It is this appreciation of innovating forms that distinguishes McLuhan from other writers on popular culture. Instead of discovering menace in the chatter of the disc jockey and the inanities of the commercial, or relief in New Wave films or in Shakespeare and ballet on TV, McLuhan probes beyond the content of the media to the impact of each medium itself as an art form. What takes place at any moment in the rectangle of the comic strip or on the screen of the TV set may not be worth serious reflection. But as you look, or look and listen, in the particular way demanded by the comic strip or the television image, something is slowly happening to one or more of your senses, and through that to your whole pattern of perception—never mind what gets into your mind. Hence the first axiom of *Understanding Media* is "The medium is the message." Radio tells us about bargains in second-hand cars, the great books, the weather, but the ultimate effect of radio is that, day after day, it is displacing reading and reintroducing on a new, technological level the oral communication of preliterate societies—or, as McLuhan calls it, "the tribal drum." The effect of a tale differs depending on whether we read it, hear it, or see it on the stage. McLuhan therefore ridicules the reformist idea that changes in programming could alter the cultural mix now produced by the popular arts. (pp. 130-32)

A remarkable wealth of observation issues from the play of McLuhan's sensibility upon each of today's vehicles of human intercourse, from roads and money to games and the computer. After *Understanding Media,* it should no longer be acceptable to speak of "mass culture" as a single lump. Each pop form, this work demonstrates, has its peculiar aesthetic features: the comics, a crude woodcut style; TV, a blurred "iconic" image shaped by the eye of the viewer out of millions of dots (in contrast to the shiny completed image of movie film). A further aesthetic complexity of the popular media pointed out by McLuhan lies in their division into "hot" and "cool." The hot medium, like radio and newspapers, is aggressive and communicates much information, while the cool, like TV and the Twist (also open-mesh stockings and dark glasses), is reticent and tends to draw its audience into participation. The varieties of aesthetic influences by which modern man is showered ought to dissolve the belief, prevalent among intellectuals, that today's man in the street, in contrast to the peasant or the bushman, has been cut down to a bundle of simple reflexes. (p. 132)

In sum, McLuhan has built a philosophy of history on art criticism, which he has directed not at styles in literature, painting, or architecture but at the lowly stuff of everyday life. In doing this, he has also sought to recast the meaning of art and literature since the Renaissance by finding in Shakespeare, Pope, or Blake "galaxies" of meaning related to the aesthetics and metaphysics of print. He has experimented with form in his own writings; that is, he has tried to function as an artist. *The Mechanical Bride* was a kind of early pop art, with a layout like a museum catalogue and with headlines, clips of advertising art, comic-strip boxes. *The Gutenberg Galaxy* and *Understanding Media* regard the human habitation as an enormous art pile, a throbbing assemblage of things that communicate, and they try to make it comprehensible by means of a mosaic of exhibits and comments that the author's "circulating point of view" has assembled from widely separated fields; McLuhan is attempting to imitate in his writing the form of the TV image, which he describes as "mosaic." The effort to develop an open, expressive social-science investigation in place of the customary learned research report may in time produce important results; McLuhan's version of this new form has the virtue of allowing the author to pick up bits of observation (e.g., that girls in dark glasses are engaged in "cool" communication) that are usually excluded, and it also enables him to bring into focus a remarkable spread of information (e.g., the measurement of time by smell among the ancient Chinese and among modern brain-surgery patients). McLuhan's concern for style tempts him into discharges of epigrams, wisecracks, and puns. These have abated in *Understanding Media,* but the titles are still haunted by gags ("Money: The Poor Man's Credit Card," "The Photograph: The Brothel-Without Walls"). Some of this wit is low-grade ("Movies: The Reel World") even if we consider bad puns to be in keeping with the pop spirit. However, formulas like "If it works it's obsolete," to suggest the rate of change in media, and "Today, even natural resources have an informational aspect," more than balance the account.

McLuhan, then, is a kind of artist, and his quick leaps from datum to axiom ("Take off the dateline, and one day's paper is the same as the next") are often aesthetically pleasurable. In his communications-constructed world, the artist is the master figure—in fact, the only personage whom he differentiates from the media-absorbing mass. The artist, McLuhan believes, anticipates the changes in man that will be wrought by a new medium and through his work adjusts the collective psyche to it. Thus the artist provides an antidote to the numbness induced by changeover. Painting has long since gone beyond being a merely visual medium; praising someone for having a "good eye," as if a modern painting were an object to be taken in by a single sense, is tantamount to praising him for being out of date. A Kandinsky or a Mondrian is actually apprehended through a "resonating interplay" of the whole keyboard of sense and consciousness; no wonder that eye-trained people

continue to ask, "What does it mean?" One of McLuhan's most valuable contributions is to help dissolve the craft-oriented concept that modern art works still belong in the realm of things contemplated instead of being forces active in "the unified field of electric all-at-onceness" of tomorrow's world community.

Unfortunately, despite his insights into form, McLuhan's organization of his own ideas is far from first-rate. As a composition, *Understanding Media* is often out of control; "circular" perspective becomes synonymous with going round in circles. Endlessly repetitious, the book, for all its rain of bright intuitions, creates a total effect of monotony. This repetitiousness probably reflects McLuhan's uneasiness about his ability to make himself clear. For there are in his thesis inherent ambiguities. Given the advanced nature of the electric media, the implication is that older forms, like the book and the stage, are obsolete and that film and comic strip are the art forms of the future. In clinging to a sense extension (the eye) that has been surpassed, the novelist is a reactionary—except for the beatnik who gives readings in coffeehouses. Even being an individual is retrogressive, so turn the dial and slip into the new global kraal. Much as McLuhan lauds the artist, he has pitted the pop media against him, in disregard of the fact that the masterpieces of this century have been paintings, poems, plays, not movies or TV shows. The point is that while McLuhan is an aesthete, he is also an ideologue—one ready to spin out his metaphor of the "extensions" until its web covers the universe; if clothes are media, and trees and policemen are, too—if, in short, all of creation "speaks" to us—McLuhan is discussing as media what used to be called "Nature," and his notion of the "sensuously orchestrated" man of the future is a version of the pantheistic hero. He is a belated Whitman singing the body electric with Thomas Edison as accompanist. Yet to expect Adam to step out of the TV screen is utopianism of the wildest sort. For McLuhan, beliefs, moral qualities, social action, even material progress play a secondary role (if that) in determining the human condition. The drama of history is a crude pageant whose inner meaning is man's metamorphosis through the media. As a philosophy of cultural development, *Understanding Media* is on a par with theories that trace the invention of the submarine to conflicts in the libido or the decline of the handicrafts to the legalization of interest on loans. (pp. 133-35)

McLuhan has taken with deadly literalness his metaphors of the media as extensions of the body and of a nervous system outside ourselves. . . . His susceptibility to figures of speech leads him to describe possibilities of technological innovation as if they were already achieved facts. In his world, money and work are things of the past; we live on credit cards and "learn a living" as managers of computers, and the struggle, backwash, surprise of real events are somnambulistically brushed away. The chilly silence of science fiction reigns over a broad band of McLuhan's temperament.

These deficiencies might be decisive were there to arise a McLuhan "school" of cultural interpretation through media analysis. If one judges McLuhan as an individual writer, however, what remain paramount are his global standpoint and his zest for the new. As an artist working in a mixed medium of direct experience and historical analogy, he has given a needed twist to the great debate on what is happening to man in this age of technological speedup. Other observers have been content to repeat criticisms of industrial society that were formulated a century ago, as if civilization had been steadily emptied out since the advent of the power loom. As against the image of our time as a faded photograph of a richly pigmented past, McLuhan, for all his abstractness, has found positive, humanistic meaning and the color of life in supermarkets, stratospheric flight, the lights blinking on broadcasting towers. In respect to the maladies of de-individuation, he has dared to seek the cure in the disease, and his vision of going forward into primitive wholeness is a good enough reply to those who would go back to it. *Understanding Media* is a concrete testimonial (illuminating, as modern art illuminates, through dissociation and regrouping) to the belief that man is certain to find his footing in the new world he is in the process of creating. (pp. 135-36)

> Harold Rosenberg, "Philosophy in a Pop Key," in
> The New Yorker, *Vol. XLI, No. 2, February 27,*
> *1965, pp. 129-36.*

ARTHUR M. SCHLESINGER, JR.

Devotees of the prophet will not find much that is new in his latest communique: but, to do Professor McLuhan justice, *The Medium Is the Massage* is intended not to offer new illuminations but to sum up the present status of the revelation. As for the unanointed, they will find here the McLuhan argument in its simplest form, stripped of the historical and sociological patter which filled *The Gutenberg Galaxy* and *Understanding Media.* (p. 1)

What then is McLuhanism? It is a chaotic combination of bland assertion, astute guesswork, fake analogy, dazzling insight, hopeless nonsense, shockmanship, showmanship, wisecracks, and oracular mystification, all mingling cockily and indiscriminately in an endless and random monologue. It also, in my judgment, contains a deeply serious argument. After close study one comes away with the feeling that here is an intelligent man who, for reasons of his own, prefers to masquerade as a charlatan.

His contention is that the emergence of electronic technology is confronting modern man with a crisis of consciousness. Societies, he suggests, have always been "shaped more by the nature of the media by which men communicate than by the content of the communication." Hence the medium is not only the message but, in a typical feeble McLuhan joke, the massage. . . . Where Marx located the motive force of history in changes in the means of production, McLuhan locates it in changes in the means of communication. (pp. 1-2)

[Every] new technology creates a new environment and today "the instantaneous world of electric informational media," McLuhan argues, is beginning once again to alter the presuppositions of life. Where the print culture gave experience a frame and viewed it in sequence and from a distance, electronic communication is simultaneous and collective: it "involves all of us, all at once." All this means a tremendous strain on inherited modes of perception. . . .

As the electronic revolution gathers momentum, McLuhan warns, it will overturn all traditional patterns of thought and behavior. This situation accounts, for example, for the peculiar urgency of the current generational conflict. One generation has mistrusted another since Adam; but the gap between generations has rarely been so intensely perceived as today. The first generation to be reared in an electronic culture, McLuhan notes, instinctively understands the new environment, shucks off the rational-visual past, lives "mythically and in depth." Young

people do not look for detached patterns—for ways of relating themselves to the world, *a la* nineteenth century": they demand instead a *"participation mystique."* It is this situation, too, according to McLuhan, which has created the contemporary assault on privacy and the "very serious dilemma between our claim to privacy and the community's need to know." Indeed, we are reaching the point, he concludes somewhat obscurely, where "remedial control, born out of knowledge of media and their total effects on all of us, must be exerted."

But how to precipitate our official culture, so hopelessly enslaved by the Gutenberg galaxy, into an awareness of the new environment? Humor, in McLuhan's view provides "our most appealing anti-environmental tool." I am sure he is right and only wish that his own jokes were better. He plainly sees himself as a card, but his experiments in wit end up as wheezes and sub-Joycean plays on words: not only the medium as massage but a pleased description of his new book, for example, as "a collide-oscope of interlaced situations." His better weapon is simply his vivid, and generally exaggerated, account of the way in which electric technology is reshaping "patterns of social interdependence and every aspect of our personal life."

One may read McLuhanism as perspective or as prophecy. The perspective enables him to say many things—some subtle and impressive, as on privacy or on the generational conflict, some forced and dubious, as on TV commercials—about our contemporary culture. The prophecy is less lucid and, I think, entraps him in inherent contradictions.

He thus suggests that the electronic world will replace Gutenbergian analysis and specialization by a new environment of all-at-once organic communion. He apparently means two very different things by this: one is the ability of the computer to handle a mass of variables in a single motion; the other is, so to speak, the ability of the young to study while the radio is on. The first is technical, functional, and precise: the second is subjective and intuitive. Yet he seems to confuse them—or at least to fuse them into a single order of perception. "The future of language," he has even said in one of his more rhapsodic moments, "will not be as a system of classified data or meanings. . . . The future of language presents the possibility of a world without words, a wordless, intuitive world, like a technological extension of the action of consciousness."

This vision of a wordless utopia is not highly convincing. For what he has elsewhere called the "mosaic pattern of simultaneous projection" cannot, I think, solve other than technical problems. I doubt that the best computer will ever make decisive political or moral judgments; or that the wholly cybernated society will ever divest itself of the need for exact statement and sequential logic; or that the great issues of politics or ethics will be solved by the impressionism of the subliminal drama. For the medium is only part of the massage; the message is the massage too. While electric circuitry will unquestionably affect—and may in time revolutionize—our modes of perception and communication, it cannot abolish the need for consecutive reason and systematic analysis without, in the end, sapping its own foundations.

But I am sure it is wrong to read McLuhanism as prophecy. One suspects, indeed, that he is indulging his version of the future primarily for the shock of the thought and the pleasure of the scandal. Underneath the hyperbole and the vaudeville there remains a significant and fertile truth. If one cannot explain history entirely as a result of alterations in the means of communication, any more than one can explain it entirely as a result of alterations in the means of production, we never-theless stand in debt to McLuhan for a marvelously stimulating insight into the dynamics of change—and for the gaiety and aplomb with which he conducts his campaign to heighten our awareness of the processes taking place in the depths below consciousness. (p. 2)

Arthur M. Schlesinger, Jr., "The Plugged-In Generation," in Book Week—World Journal Tribune, *March 19, 1967, pp. 1-2.*

TOM NAIRN

A cult, or intellectual fashion, is the contagious diffusion of ideas felt to be significant. By this process new notions and attitudes emerge a-critically, as intuitions, changing our ap-prehension of things almost before we are fully aware of their meaning. The importance of McLuhanism in this sense can be measured by the range of its diffusion: it affects not only in-tellectuals, students, theorists of media and communication, but also business men and the users of the mass media, poli-ticians and advertising men. What matters initially is to un-derstand *why* this happens, and this is probably the most fruitful approach to McLuhan's writings. There is little point in sneer-ing at the PR slickness of the cult, or the vested interests that have made McLuhan No 1 speaker in the US after-dinner cir-cuit: such success is only possible because of the genuine wide appeal of his ideas. There is little point, either, in an academic textual approach to books which notoriously are composed in deliberate defiance of scholarly values, by an author who thinks that jokes and puns are a better form of communication than long-faced 'serious' analysis. For those worried by the diffi-culty of McLuhan, incidentally, the latest book *The Medium is the Massage* is the best introduction to him, although it lacks the intellectual fascination of the others. The title, of course, is a characteristic joke-pun rendering of his equally character-istic aphorism 'The Medium is the Message'—his way of say-ing that the form, or structure, of a given system of commu-nication affects society more deeply than what it transmits.

The ideas which filter out through McLuhan's gnomic prose are not in fact excessively difficult, and they appeal as apparent explanations of a great variety of contemporary experience. There may be less than meets the eye in McLuhan but one must look first at what he seems to be saying, the source of his influence and his status as a modern myth-figure. . . .

At the moment, what is going on is 'the recreation of the world in the image of a global village', through the 'electronic in-terdependence' of modern means of communication. In McLuhan's eyes, this revolution we are living through is the ultimate phase of a long historical process. (p. 362)

The print era was analysis, fragmentation, repetition, the vic-tory of a certain sort of rationality. But this era is already over, although we are unwilling (or unable) to grasp the fact. It has been ended by an even more drastic upheaval: the 'implosion' of instantaneous electric communication has thrown back to-gether what Gutenberg sundered, and brought about a new multisensible world of wholeness and all-at-onceness. Such is the 'message' of the new 'medium', which has so far reached its most advanced form in television. Intellect is no longer isolated in a corner, or on a professorial rostrum; it can be literally everywhere at once, in the 'cosmic membrane that has been snapped round the globe by the electric dilation of our various senses'. The different aspects of this process are most

interestingly discussed in *Understanding Media,* and re-em-phasised in *The Medium is the Massage:*

> We now live in a *global* village . . . a simul-taneous happening. We are back again in acous-tic space. We have begun again to structure the primordial feeling, the tribal emotions from which a few centuries of literacy divorced us.

The book, the neatly printed page, are the originally 'square' things. They made a world of literalness, while the new media have made a world of *myth*. In the square world, meaning was 'content' that could be manifested in different 'forms'; in the myth world this visual metaphor becomes useless.

McLuhan's ideas are themselves mythical, a part of the world he depicts. This is at once the source of his appeal, and of the disquieting unreality of that appeal. Reading him is rather like undergoing an hallucination. . . . However—to quote the slo-gan printed on the cover of *The Medium*—the point is also to help us 'contemplate what is happening', to explain and un-derstand, and act meaningfully within, the myths woven about us by the new environment. This implies stepping outside the dimension of myth, it implies the critical detachment which McLuhan mythicises as outmoded, at the same time as he struggles to achieve it. The content of McLuhan's myth is a delirious, one-sided emphasis upon the importance of media and communication in society; the form appropriate to the delirium is precisely the bizarre, disjointed non-argument at first glance so disturbing. (pp. 362-63)

To anyone who can extricate himself from the McLuhanite trance for a few moments, it is reasonably clear that the . . . *actual* use made of media like television, in our society and others, far from uniting humanity against these facts, reinforces our acceptance of them. When he produced his dazzling study of American advertising *The Mechanical Bride* (1951), this aspect of the problem was at least present to him. In the preface, he explains how he wants to analyse 'visual symbols that have been employed in an effort to paralyse the mind', and so create 'a citadel of inclusive awareness amid the dim dreams of col-lective consciousness'. From *The Gutenberg Galaxy* (1962) onwards, he seems to have felt that this was a rear-guard at-titude, that no walls could stand against the dreams. The ad-vantage of his new position was the extreme vividness with which he conjures up the facts he is interested in—rather than 'drawing our attention' to them, he puts them in our presence. But he achieves this at the cost of merging into the dim dreams himself.

His position is that the form, the overall structure of the dream is more important than what is dreamt. The former knits the world together, restores a unity between thought and feeling, and offers a means of escape from the estrangement of his-tory—it prefigures the 'psychedelic' transformation of the en-vironment by mind, and this is freedom according to Marx's vision of the world, as well as McLuhan's. . . .

McLuhan is a monomaniac who happens to be hooked on something extremely important. We ought to be grateful. But the colossal evasiveness, the slipshod reasoning and weak-kneed glibness accompanying the mania make him dangerous going. He has rapidly acquired the reputation of being a prophet, or a charlatan, or both. In fact, he is neither. Capable of the most brilliant and stimulating insight into relationships other historians and social theorists have ignored, he systematically fails to develop this insight critically. Consequently, his view of the connection between media and society is an unbelievable shambles: his dream-logic turns necessary conditions into suf-ficient conditions, half-truths into sure things, the possible into a *fait accompli*. His chaos is like that of Jean-Luc Godard: good ideas, lost in a pyrotechnics which is ultimately banal—the 'message' of *The Medium is the Massage,* all in big letters on a black ground, is 'There is absolutely no inevitability as long as there is a willingness to contemplate what is happen-ing.' Because he is so unwilling to contemplate the contradic-tions actually existing in our media-world, he can all too easily become an apologist of that existence. That is, of the present use being made of media in our sort of society, the dream-nightmare we grope our way through daily.

Yet, while he so often appears to be arguing that whatever is, is right—producing a sort of new Idealism to suit the conditions of advanced capitalist society, in fact—other images counter this meaning. A favourite one, to which he returns again in *The Medium,* is that of the sailor who is sucked down into a whirlpool in Edgar Allan Poe's story *The Descent into the Maelstrom.* He escaped by studying what was happening to him, the action of the vortex. McLuhan identifies this with our predicament, 'our electrically-configured whirl'. His writing is so like the vortex itself, that its effect must be the opposite most of the time. But if one can avoid plunging headlong into what he says and use him critically, then he is the best guide to our maelstrom. (p. 363)

Tom Nairn, "Into McLuhan's Maelstrom," in New Statesman, Vol. 74, No. 1906, September 22, 1967, pp. 362-63.

ARNOLD ROCKMAN

The McLuhan movement offers the sociologically-oriented ob-server an opportunity to watch an intellectual fashion in the process of formation. Whether the new fashion will become a new style of thinking is debatable, though to my mind Mc-Luhanism has the feel of a long-term movement which might represent a major shift in our way of looking at the world. . . .

McLuhanism is primarily a cultural fashion. Yet it might turn out to be a long-term revolution, since it bears many of the earmarks of other revolutionary beginnings in the social, po-litical and religious realms. Moreover, it conforms in a most satisfying manner to the archetypal myth of the hero. In this myth, the charismatic leader living in a province remote from the heart of empire attracts to his side a small band of disciples whose prime role is to spread the word of the master even though they suffer ridicule in their own country. Meanwhile, those who guide the destinies of empire are gripped by a feeling of *malaise* and disquiet that all in the empire is not as it should be. They search for wonders, signs, oracles. They hear of the new master with a new word to preach. They invite him to the capital and shower him with honour and glory. Only then do the master's compatriots in the remote province recognize their native son. (p. 29)

The successful revolutionary leader offers a new world-view which he and his disciples claim will replace the old, "con-ventional wisdom" about how the world is supposed to work. . . . McLuhan tells us that "the medium is the message," that "the electric media" are "retribalising" the human race into one "global village," and that the whole of technology consists of "extensions of man." These are all powerful slogans and phrases designed to reshape our ways of thinking and feeling about the world and our place within it.

Behind the slogans and the phrases a complex network of ideas constitutes a framework for replacing an old ideology with a new one. The new ideas are rarely presented or received as a set of logical propositions, for once a set of ideas is logically justified it has lost some of its fresh-minted quality. Logical justification must come after the creative discovery. . . .

Today, McLuhan's notion that the forms and styles of "me-dia"—the alphabet, print, radio, television, painting, the urban environment, the computer, and anything else he chooses to regard as a "medium"—are more profound in their psychic and social consequences than the content of the medium strikes many people as not only illogical but also absurd.

The slogans and arguments of a prophet must appear to his contemporaries the height of absurdity and extremism. In order to gain a hearing for the new truth, the prophet exaggerates the force and application of his concepts until they seem capable of re-ordering the experience of his listeners and giving it new meaning and justification. His followers are usually those who feel out of step with the main drift of their society, who, as one critic has put it, "experience a real or apparent loss of wealth, power or prestige." (p. 30)

Few North American academics before McLuhan and his circle had paid equal and serious attention to the forms and styles of cities, literature, psycho-analysis, and mass media. For the first time, a fully enfranchised academic in a fully reputable dis-cipline was advocating the study of popular culture without apology, prior judgment or condemnation. Those who helped to make and distribute the artifacts of that popular culture were no longer required to feel, as Lewis Coser has put it, "sys-tematic alienation and frustration." They could stand a little taller when they met their university colleagues instead of adopting their usual apologetic and humble stance. It is not surprising that McLuhan and his ideas should become world-famous in a relatively short time. . . .

McLuhan's rise to fame as charismatic leader from obscure beginnings has not entailed very much of either struggle or martyrdom. At the most, his more conventional colleagues who are repelled by his slogans and poetic analogies make weak jokes about the medium and the message, but they have not subjected him to the hostile indifference or withering scorn with which Freud was first greeted.

Why should McLuhan be treated differently? First, he has paid attention to those phenomena whose makers and distributors have easy access to the publicity mill. These second-class cit-izens of the republic of letters outside the academy are flattered by his attention. They pay in kind, a hundred-fold. Second, most other intellectual leaders have not had waiting for them a worldwide network of communications media to spread their gospel "at electric speeds," in McLuhan's Whitmanesque phrase. (p. 32)

Unlike most other literary intellectuals who sometimes pay attention to business, McLuhan does not despise it, disparage it or knock it to the ground, neither does he advocate any politically radical action against the business élite. His attitude to business is similar to his attitude to formal education: its leaders cannot be blamed for their ineptitude since they do not understand what they are doing. They "are hypnotised by the amputation and extension of their own beings in a new technical form." Unlike the usual posture of intellectuals in the secular, radical tradition who thunder against the makers of popular culture, McLuhan, perhaps because of his Catholic convic-tions, is more charitable and not so quick to judge.

It is this attitude of tolerant charity combined with a hard-headed yet poetic intellect which distinguishes McLuhan from so many other critics of contemporary culture. Without any such intention, he provides the partisans of consensus politics with a non-partisan, non-political ideology with which anyone, Left or Right, may agree. He strips away from Marxism its intimate link between class consciousness and the relation of men to the means of production. He leaves only the relation of persons to their technology. From Freud he strips away the super-ego and its role in social control as a censor of socially undesirable wishes and activities, and leaves only the relation between the body and its senses and the ''patterns of information'' perceived and ''processed'' by that body.

Many commentators have criticised this excessively simplistic notion of the link between the human person and the characteristic style of a society's technology in any given period. No doubt these criticisms are justified. But McLuhan's work, unlike the comparable attempts of a Toynbee or a Spengler to explain everything, is not presented as finished thesis but as running commentary on his own thought processes, as one side of a great conversation in which anyone may take part. ''I'm perfectly prepared to scrap any statement I ever made about any subject,'' he told Gerald Stearn, ''once I find that it isn't getting me into the problem.''

Revelations like this one help to make him popular among non-enfranchised intellectuals and among the general public. They also make him unpopular with his academic *confrères*. In conventional scholarship there is an accepted style of presentation which may be studied in any journal devoted to the ideas and research of any academic discipline. In that style, articles are written as if even tentative findings are part of an objective body of authoritative knowledge completely detached from the person who did the research and wrote the article. This feeling of authority and pseudo-objectivity is conveyed through avoidance of the first person, through exaggerated use of the passive voice and through over-indulgence in modifiers and verbs which transmit feelings of hesitancy and lack of personal commitment. (p. 35)

If the more conventional scholars feel a sense of outrage, they have only themselves to blame. Few of them have genuinely tried to bridge the ever-increasing gap between specialist discourse appropriate to the practice of a priestly craft and a widely understood public language.

Sociologists seem to be especially hurt by the fact that McLuhan has galloped all over ''their'' territory and found it wanting. They have answered his incursions by silence. One may immerse oneself in the scholarly sociological journals published during the last few years and emerge almost completely unaware that a man named McLuhan has been indulging in a fascinating exercise in intuitive sociology. Among the orthodox academic psychologists, one will find the same indifference, even though one might have thought that McLuhan's speculations on the relation between technology and psyche would excite some comment and, at the very least, one or two experiments.

Yet, despite the neglect of orthodox scholars in the social sciences and by the brand-name literary journals, perhaps even *because* of this indifference, McLuhan is seen as intellectual hero by almost any intellectual or artist who feels not quite respectable when judged by the standards of the academic church. McLuhan is the legitimator of profane objects, activities, attitudes, and thoughts. . . .

Lewis Feuer has remarked that the founders of the Royal Society were impelled by a ''hedonist-libertarian'' ethic which ''restored science together with the life of the senses.'' In a similar manner, McLuhan seems to have found a way to restore social enquiry not only with the life of the senses but also with the life of the morally-committed intellect. (p. 36)

> *Arnold Rockman, ''McLuhanism: 'The Natural History of an Intellectual Fashion','' in* Encounter, *Vol. XXXI, No. 5, November, 1968, pp. 28-36.*

HUGH KENNER

Marshall McLuhan noticed long ago that the ''content'' of a medium is always a previous medium. He also remarked that we don't see a medium itself, save as packaging for its content. That helps ease new media into acceptability. Genteel folk once learned to tolerate movies by thinking of them as packaged plays or packaged books. Likewise, we sidle up to the computer, saying over and over that it's nothing but an electrified filing system. ''Word processing'' is another incantation. Souls are safe in proximity to *words*. (p. 71)

No reader of newsmagazines will fail to remember how Bill Gates (Harvard dropout) founded Microsoft, how Steven Jobs (Reed dropout) and Stephen Wozniak (Berkeley dropout) founded Apple. No, the filing-system model lacks explanatory power. Passion for filing systems, even electrified ones, does not bring about such a transformation of hierarchies. Yes, something has altered. Marshall McLuhan again:

> The drop-out situation in our schools at present has only begun to develop. The young student today grows up in an electrically configured world . . . not of wheels but of circuits, not of fragments but of integral patterns. . . . At school, however, he encounters a situation organized by means of classified information. The subjects are unrelated. They are visually conceived in terms of a blueprint. The student can find no possible means of involvement for himself, nor can he discover how the educational scene relates to the ''mythical'' world of electronically processed data and experience that he takes for granted.

In 1964 that seemed one of McLuhan's wilder remarks. No longer. Today we find it pertinent that even when computers were far from ubiquitous he was observing the medium instead of its content, ''files.'' He was foreseeing, moreover, a dramatic *effect* of the medium. And instances of his prescience multiply. Once brushed off by the *New Yorker* as a ''pop philosopher,'' the author of **Understanding Media** is starting to look like a prophet.

That is all the more remarkable since ''the oracle of the electric age'' (a phrase coined by *Life*) wouldn't drive a car, never turned on a radio, barely glanced at television, and checked out movies by popping in on them for twenty minutes. Apart from the Olivier *Henry V*, at which he'd been trapped on a social occasion, I don't know of a movie he saw from beginning to end. ''Marshall McLuhan Reads Books,'' said a bumper sticker, graffito of the scandalous truth. He did indeed read books, and, other than talk and scribble, he did little else.

Such disdain for inconvenient fact could erode your confidence. . . . His world was full of people who didn't know their business, such as nearly all of his fellow English professors.

But though he was often wrong himself, as when he discerned "the abrupt decline of baseball," he never had the patience to sit through a ball game.

In those days he countered niggling by sheer assertion. It was after my time that he discovered a generic answer. People who raised objections were detailists, specialists, locked into local patterns: instances of what had happened to the Western psyche after Gutenberg gave his *coup de grâce* to the old oral culture by persuading everybody that one thing must follow another the way each printed word follows, on its line, the word that precedes it. Nigglers were confined to "the neutral visual world of lineal organization," and the specialist was one who "never makes small mistakes while moving toward the grand fallacy."

I have sometimes wondered if Marshall didn't evolve his whole theory of media as a way to explain why there seemed to be people who tried to interrupt his monologues. What cataclysm of history had spawned *them?* Why, literacy, with its first-things-first-let's-keep-it-all-straight syndrome. Were they not the very people who kept wincing at somebody's grammar? The word "grammar" itself derives from the Greek word for a written mark. That would have been enough to get him started. Much as Saul found a kingdom while out hunting for his father's asses, Marshall McLuhan found his skeleton key to the social psyche. Thereafter he kept it hanging on a hook labeled "Media," and never bothered to explain what Media were.

Media included not only magazines and television but also roads, wheels, railways, electricity, numbers, clocks, money—they all did things we had once tried to do with our senses and our bodies; that was why he called them "extensions of man." Adjusting to any new medium, since it strained what had been a bodily and sensual relationship (his word was "ratio"), meant anguish and anxiety. So "the mediaeval world grew up without uniform roads or cities or bureaucracies, and it fought the wheel, as later city forms fought the railways; and as we, today, fight the automobile."

Media came in two flavors, "hot" and "cool." The hot ones saturate you with information; paradoxically, you are then passive, uninvolved, as when you half listen to the radio. The cool ones draw back and leave you filling in. TV, with its inferior picture detail, is cool; hence its viewer's rapt involvement.

Though his pronouncements on the electronic age and its global village made him briefly famous, what he really knew was literacy, and what he developed most fully was his insight into its consequences. What literacy achieves is the "hot" storage and retrieval of *words only,* as though their choice and sequence constituted the whole of human communication. But in the heat of conversation, relatively little is communicated by words. Silences, intonations, advances and withdrawals, smiles, and the whole repertory of body language—these in their elaborate dance enact most of what is happening.

Screen them out, leave only the silent words on a page, and your first requirement is *more* words. The dialogue Henry James's people exchange is wordier by a factor of at least three than any speech human ears have ever heard. James was making up for the absence from printed pages of what normal grammar and diction do little to convey, the ballet of interaction. (He brought written prose to its extreme of articulation just before radio took over).

The next thing you need is a fairly strict one-two-three order, because written words exist only in space, and can presuppose only the words that came before them. Things on a line of print cannot overlap. This is the "linearity" on which McLuhan harped. Talkers allude to what they've not said, or have said on another occasion, or they will say later, or needn't say save by gesture or dawdle or pause; but once discourse is controlled by writing, as even the spoken discourse of literates tends to be, its syntax (think of James again) grows fairly elaborate, out of need for strict systems of subordination among items that can be produced only one after another. Examine the sentence you've just read.

Finally, literates come to believe that controlled linearity is order, all else disorder: that the cosmos itself is structured like a Jamesian utterance, with primary, secondary, tertiary clauses. If any sentence of **Understanding Media** might have turned up without irrelevance anywhere in any chapter, that was because McLuhan thought that prose should work like the mind, not the other way round. Whatever he was thinking of grew in iconic power the more rapidly he could relate it to a dozen other things, if possible in the same breath. So he got called "the professor of communications who can't communicate," an academic Harpo unable to stick to a point. His point was that there is never a "point." Points are Euclidean junctures in such sentences as come to life only in diagrams.

There are aspects of his plight Beckett might have invented. What language may *say* in a literate society McLuhan deemed of little importance compared with what literacy had done to the literate. I once heard him deny that anything Plato wrote could match in importance the fact that in a given classroom all copies of *The Republic* have the same word at the same place on the same numbered page. Hence "The Medium Is the Message," his most quoted and most suicidal oversimplification. For it was precisely *what* he said that he wanted understood; moreover, what he said *in writing*. Using writing to expound the effects of writing was like explaining water to a school of fish. Fish understand nothing of water, but they judge you by the way you move your flippers. He got snubbed by print-swimmers who deemed measured prose a measure of character.

So obsessed was his readership by "content" that detractor and disciple alike tended to think he was talking about the effect of the medium on the message it carries: TV is highly visual, for instance, hence its fondness for crowds and confrontations. But that barely concerned him. (He said TV was "tactile.") What obsessed him is clearer after twenty years: the effect of the mere *availability* of new media on people's sense of who and what they are. (pp. 71-3)

McLuhan deemed it of far more moment that life in a print-oriented culture restructures the soul of even a total illiterate. Not only does he know that other people know things he doesn't, but he also picks up ambient assumptions about first-things-first. In not being felt at all, the latter effect reaches deeper than any felt deprivation.

Likewise, said McLuhan, all of us have been reconstituted by TV, whether we choose to watch the tube or not: "The utmost purity of mind is no defense against bacteria." . . . [It is] not because of someone's adroitness at packaging that Ronald Reagan sits in the Oval Office but Richard Nixon in itchy exile, Jimmy Carter in limbo. Articulate *opinion* of Nixon and of Carter got formed in print, still our only medium of articulate opinion. And yet, it was the omnipresence of television that determined what kind of opinions the older medium, print, could form and seem credible.

This means that in the television age even non-watchers gravitate toward ''cool'' personalities. Nixon was too jowly and affirmative to pass muster, Carter too morally opinionated. . . . The prevalent perception of ''wake-me-when-it's-over'' Reagan is that he falls asleep: a caricature that affirms his ultimate ''cool.'' When you have to tell the President what's happening, that is your ultimate participation. . . .

Yes, we're governed by carcicatures, because we perceive by them. There's no better instance than the regnant caricature of McLuhan, shared by print-folk who thought they were attending to his text and bypassing the electronic media, the wrong thing to do. For he was presupposing TV's cool collaboration, not print's hot ''specialist,'' ''fragmented'' reading. Like another guide to the future, Bucky Fuller, McLuhan was discarded as unintelligible. Willy-nilly, trapped in hot print in an age of cool TV, he was taken at his (printed) word, just as if in his outrageous one-liners he hadn't intended audience participation, or hadn't counted on his audience to fill out and correct all those comic-book formulations. The apostle of ''cool'' came on ''hot,'' a blunderbuss Nixon of the Media Era, and coolness made a joke of him and discarded him. (p. 73)

Hugh Kenner, ''McLuhan Redux: Further Thoughts on the Medium as Message,'' in Harper's, *Vol. 269, No. 1614, November, 1984, pp. 71-3.*

Margaret Mead

1901-1978

American anthropologist, essayist, nonfiction writer, and autobiographer.

Mead is credited with making anthropology accessible to the general public. By incorporating psychology, sociology, and economics into her studies of primitive societies and applying her results to contemporary Western civilization, Mead expanded the scope of this relatively new discipline. Her ability to communicate her findings to nonprofessionals in a clear and stimulating prose style resulted in widespread public interest in anthropology and helped establish Mead as a prominent figure in American culture. A large part of her field work was conducted among South Pacific societies. She reported her findings in such works as *Coming of Age in Samoa: A Psychological Study of Primitive Youth for Western Civilization* (1928), *Growing Up in New Guinea: A Comparative Study of Primitive Education* (1930), and *Sex and Temperament in Three Primitive Societies* (1935). Her interests included such diverse topics as adolescent sexuality, health and nutrition, the role of women in society, the role of society in shaping the individual, and the importance of international communication for future world survival. Many of her personal observations on these subjects appeared as essays in *Redbook* magazine. Mead was a renowned lecturer, a member of numerous academies and associations, the recipient of many honors and awards, and a prolific writer who published over twenty-five popular and scientific works.

Mead began her professional field work in 1925, studying adolescent girls on the Samoan islands as a fellow for the National Research Council. Her study resulted in *Coming of Age in Samoa,* her most famous and controversial work. This account of idyllic cultural harmony stimulated public and professional interest in anthropology; it also exemplifies Mead's scientific approach, which has often been questioned by professionals. A formidable challenge was recently issued by Derek Freeman, one of Mead's most adamant detractors, who claims in his study *Margaret Mead and Samoa: The Making and Unmaking of an Anthropological Myth* (1983) that Mead's conclusions are unfounded and in part a result of personal biases. He further asserts that her emphasis on cultural over biological determinism is misleading and draws into question the "nature versus nurture" controversy in anthropology.

In addition to the extensive field notes based on her studies in the South Pacific, Mead published numerous works that concentrate on contemporary Western concerns. *Male and Female: A Study of the Sexes in a Changing World* (1949) applies results from her observations of sex roles in seven primitive cultures to modern American society; *Continuities in Cultural Evolution* (1964) explores the process of social evolution; *A Way of Seeing* (1970) and *Aspects of the Present* (1980) collect Mead's essays written with Rhoda Metraux for *Redbook* magazine in which they take an anthropological approach to contemporary American issues; and *Culture and Commitment: A Study of the Generation Gap* (1970) addresses the transferral of information from one generation to the next. As with much of her writing, the effects of a rapidly changing society are central to these works. Likewise, *Twentieth Century Faith:*

Photograph by Layle Silbert; © 1985

Hope and Survival (1972) and *World Enough: Rethinking the Future* (1975) explore the future in terms of global communication, universal human interdependency, and the interplay of science, technology, and religion.

Mead has been charged with subjectivity and a lack of professionalism for incorporating speculation and intuition into her work. However, Ward Goodenough reflects much critical opinion by claiming that Mead "raised important questions about things both scientists and the lay public were taking for granted about human behavior.... That her own empirical research in connection with these questions was of questionable quality and that at times she overstated her case are minor matters compared with the role she played in raising these questions and stimulating others to examine them."

(See also *Contemporary Issues Criticism*, Vol. 1; *Contemporary Authors*, Vols. 1-4, rev. ed., Vols. 81-84 [obituary]; *Contemporary Authors New Revision Series*, Vol. 4; and *Something about the Author*, Vol. 20.)

GEORGE A. DORSEY

[As] Professor Boas points out in his Foreword to Dr. Mead's extraordinarily illuminating and valuable book [*Coming of Age in Samoa*], anthropologists have long suspected that "much of what we ascribe to human nature is no more than a reaction to the restraints put upon us by our civilization.'' Dr. Mead's painstaking investigations confirm the suspicion. Our sex misbehaviors and insanities are merely by-products of our civilization. In this respect, and to that extent, it is our civilization that is unnatural; not Samoan culture.

The subtitle of Dr. Mead's book is: ''A Psychological Study of Primitive Youth for Western Civilization.'' She is more than a psychologist (and a competent one at that); she is primarily an anthropologist. . . . She not only learned the Samoan language but lived Samoan fashion in villages still fairly unspoiled by the progress of civilization. This combination of training and intimate contact with native life enabled Dr. Mead to do an extraordinarily brilliant and, so far as I am aware, unique piece of work. . . .

I have characterized *Coming of Age in Samoa* as an extraordinarily illuminating book. So it is. But the light it throws is on love's coming of age in Vienna and all points west in civilization. Therein lies the importance of this contribution to knowledge. For, after all, what is of primary concern to us is not whether Samoans are as beset with sex problems and sex psychoses as we are, but whether our sex psychoses are inherent in human nature and hence inevitable, or are excrescences, cultural phenomena, social diseases that flourish in our civilization.

> George A. Dorsey, ''Natural or Savage?'' in New York Herald Tribune Books, *September 2, 1928, p. 4.*

THE NEW YORK TIMES BOOK REVIEW

Are the difficulties of the transition from childhood to adult life due to adolescence itself, and therefore universal and unavoidable, . . . or are they the result of the impact between developing youth and a civilization which at once restrains and complicates?

Anthropology has been asking this question for a long time. Now, in an extraordinary fashion, an anthropologist has answered it.

With the National Research Council's fellowship in Biological Science, Miss Mead went to Samoa to study the development of youth under what may paradoxically be called a highly developed primitive life. It was a life highly developed because it presented a distinct pattern of civilization which for long ages ''other members of the human race had found satisfactory and gracious''; it was primitive because it not only lacked the appurtenances of modern progress, but subsisted with very simple standards and needs; in every way it presented a vast contrast to all of Western civilization. In this pattern of life Miss Mead fitted herself, studying the language, living as the people lived, making them her friends; she was with them for nine months. . . . Her findings [presented in *Coming of Age in Samoa*] confirm the suspicion of the scientist that in the ''coming of age'' of human life, ''much of what we ascribe to human nature is no more than a reaction to the restraints put upon us by our civilization,'' and offer invaluable material against which to study better the conditions and problems of our own youth.

As Miss Mead's careful scientific work deserves the most earnest tribute, so her method of presenting its results calls for the highest praise. Her book, broad in its canvas and keen in its detail, is sympathetic throughout, warmly human yet never sentimental, frank with the clean, clear frankness of the sci-entist, unbiased in its judgment, richly readable in its style. It is a remarkable contribution to our knowledge of humanity.

> ''The Adolescent,'' in The New York Times Book Review, *November 4, 1928, p. 19.*

RUTH BENEDICT

Our most careful psychological studies and tests suffer a common limitation; they are pot-bound within the restrictions of our western civilization. Their roots are tightly circumscribed by the definitely fixed limitation of our tradition. We pile statistics upon statistics, and the logical doubt is still left that we may be studying, not ability, but ability to succeed in New York; not adolescence, but adolescence in America. . . .

In the matter of the psychological test we are becoming continually more canny, but we have not scrutinized in the same way our popular theories of adolescence. The studies that have been made have been all in the setting of the twentieth-century western world. Are the facts they so abundantly report due to the fixed characteristics of the life cycle, or to similar circumstances working over and over again to create like situations?

This is the problem Dr. Mead answers from the evidence of Samoa [in *Coming of Age in Samoa*]. . . . And the upshot of the matter is that it is precisely at adolescence that the Samoan girl is at peace with the universe.

It is not any one simple variation of our own schemes that has brought about this different result. As Dr. Mead shows, some of the forces that have been at work, like the low evaluation of personality differences, are distasteful to us; and the most fundamental one of all, the simplicity of the choices open to the Polynesian girl, we could recapture only at the price of civilization itself. But the placing of the girl in the economic scheme, the systematic lowering of the effect of decisions, the handling of sex, are all full of that illumination that comes of envisaging very different possible ways of handling invariable problems. . . .

As Professor Boas says in his Foreword, most ethnological descriptions of primitive peoples give us almost no picture of the individual's problems and solutions in his own culture, and it is because in this book the representation has been reversed that we find answers to questions most ethnologists leave unanswered. Dr. Mead has sketched the suave and gracious background of Polynesian culture as it was interpreted in Samoa, but she has sketched it as it affects the life of the growing girl. It is culture not as a strange static scene, catalogued for reference, but existence as the individual lives it out and modifies it by his own life history, and readers who have rejected many accounts of primitive peoples may find this one to their liking.

Certainly those who are interested in the way in which the social environment can select and underscore now one, now another, of human potentialities, will find here much illustrative material intelligently presented. Is it possible, we ask ourselves, that a people can exist all of whose virtues are the social graces, who have in themselves so little violence, are so little concerned with mystery, with supernatural forces? For the Samoans live in the well charted seas of social amenities, and they take no notice of the regions that lie outside.

Not only is *Coming of Age in Samoa* challenging to the educator and to the parent of growing children, but the anthropological student of psychological problems among primitive peoples should not miss the program of research in the appendix with its due weight given to differences in culture, and the student of sex problems will find here an example of consistent cultural behavior in a society that develops no neuroses in its members. It is a book for which we have been waiting.

Ruth Benedict, "The Younger Generation with a Difference," in The New Republic, *Vol. LVII, No. 730, November 28, 1928, p. 50.*

ROBERT H. LOWIE

In her Samoan field-work [which informs her *Coming of Age in Samoa*] Dr. Mead deliberately set herself a task distinct from the traditional ethnographer's. Ignoring the conventional descriptive pattern, she concentrated on the individual's reactions to his social setting—specifically, the adolescent girl's adjustment. . . . The author further departs from ordinary practice in pointing a moral. One of her principal theses is that the sexually uninhibited Samoan adolescent is thereby freed from the stress and strain characteristic of *our* adolescents, hence these disturbances are not rooted in original nature, but in the repressive agencies of our society. Therefore—but I am afraid Dr. Mead has not been quite ingenuous in her applied anthropology and fortunately readers of this journal are not concerned with pedagogical sermonizing.

However, there is one basic point that concerns us. Miss Mead's graphic picture of Polynesian free love is convincing. It falls in line with the reports of earlier travellers; it is supported by Dr. Handy's evidence from the Marquesas; and from another Oceanian area we have Dr. Malinowski's Trobriand observations. Nevertheless, this is not the whole story. The author knows it . . . and even enlarges on it—in an appendix. There we read as follows . . . :

> But it is only fair to point out that Samoan culture, before white influence, was less flexible and dealt less kindly with the individual aberrant. Aboriginal Samoa was harder on the girl sex delinquent than is present-day Samoa. And the reader must not mistake the conditions which have been described for the aboriginal ones, nor for typical primitive ones. Present-day Samoan civilization is simply the result of the fortuitous and on the whole fortunate impetus of a complex, intrusive culture upon a simpler and most hospitable indigenous one. . . .
>
> (p. 532)

How are the two pictures to be reconciled? On the one hand, we are shown licensed freedom precluding mental derangements; on the other, we see all girls of rank originally subjected to the defloration rite and the *taupo* liable to the death penalty for unchastity. If it is only modern Samoa that connives at free love, it may still remain true that adolescence is not necessarily a quasi-pathological condition; but the *social* applications become banal. . . . [It] is one thing to have a community treat the individual's sex life as an individual matter when the society is in a normal state; quite another, to find it unconcerned with his amours when abnormal contacts destroy old standards and fail to impose substitutes. The reformer must face the question whether any *normal* society can and will practice that lofty detachment found in Samoa nowadays.

But Dr. Mead's pedagogical theses, whether sound or not, should not obscure her solid contributions to ethnographic fact and method. Her picture of child life is among the most vivid

I know. . . . Along with other records from the same general area Dr. Mead's account . . . throws doubt on a proposition I have hitherto vigorously maintained, viz., the universality of the individual family. The question involved is not at all that of consanguinity, but of a differential bond between a restricted group—mother, child, mother's spouse—as against the rest of the universe. In Polynesia this bond does seem to be exceptionally loose and to be superseded by more widely diffused ties.

On some points made by Dr. Mead I must frankly avow skepticism. It is hard to believe that all but the youngest boys and girls should fail to use ordinary kinship terms correctly . . . ; or, in an absolute way, that Samoan children do not learn to work through learning to play. . . . It is hard to understand how certain conclusions could have been arrived at. Says Dr. Mead:

> The Samoan girl never tastes the rewards of romantic love as we know it. . . . . .

Query: What, never? And: Who are "we"? Unless the Samoans are different from other Polynesians, they indulged in the luxury of romantic love precisely like other folk, to wit, in their fiction. Only after the most thoroughgoing search in Samoan folk-literature had yielded no trace of the sentiment, should I feel disposed to accept a negative result. Finally, perhaps from a Plains Indian bias, I am not convinced by Dr. Mead's picture of the "low level of appreciation of personality differences." . . . With due regard to the insolence of seniority and of caste, I suspect that here, too, the normal aspect of ancient Samoan life has been blurred by the blighting contact with European civilization. "The new influences have drawn the teeth of the old culture." . . . When tattooing declines, the differences in fortitude on the victims', or in skill on the artists', part would naturally fade away; and so with other aspects of aboriginal life. Plains Indians no longer go on the warpath; but the record of their mad competitive strivings has remained, and modern equivalents, though diluted, are not lacking. Would a similar, i.e., historical, approach to Samoa yield comparable results? I deny nothing; I am asking for information.

These reservations should not be taken to obscure the value of Dr. Mead's achievement. Dealing with problems incomparably subtler than those which usually engage the ethnographer's attention, she has not merely added much in the way of illuminating information but also illustrated a new method of study that is bound to find followers and to yield an even richer harvest. (pp. 533-34)

Robert H. Lowie, in a review of "Coming of Age in Samoa: A Psychological Study of Primitive Youth for Western Civilization," in American Anthropologist, *n.s., Vol. 31, No. 3, July-August, 1929, pp. 532-34.*

ISIDOR SCHNEIDER

Growing Up in New Guinea is an even more interesting book than Miss Mead's widely and deservedly praised *Coming of Age in Samoa*. It is worked out in the same way. A generalized biography (which, however, takes on personality with each case mentioned) of the native child from birth to entrance into adult society, is followed by a comparison with our own society, in relevant particulars.

The researches for this book were carried on not in New Guinea proper but on Manus Island in the Admiralty Group, an archipelago to the northeast of New Guinea. (p. 329)

If the book had appeared as a modern *Gulliver's Travels,* the description of Manus society would have sounded like a bitter satire on American life.

Trade obsesses this people. Every social occasion, from birth to marriage, is made an opportunity for investment through gift exchanges. Respect for property is the first and one of the only two social obligations taught to children. Property even acts as a determinant of personality, the man of property being aggressive and overbearing, while the poor man is humble and shamefaced. . . . The lagoon rings not with music and dancing, as one would suppose in a tropical society, but with the squabbling voices of debtors and creditors. Like other traders, they are a people without art. Their houses are furnished with the fine carved work of their neighbors, which, however, they do not learn to prize above trade value. . . .

As if to finish off the satire, the Manus are the Puritans of Oceania. Adultery is uncommon; prudery is joined with respect for property as the only social instruction given to children. Frigidity among women is taken for granted and the sexual relation is a secret act comparable in offensiveness to evacuation.

This is adult life among the Manus. The life of the children is completely apart. They lead spoiled, selfish existences. They can make any demand upon their parents and they give nothing in return, run no errands, perform no household tasks. . . . The attitude of the children is one of contempt for adult life. . . .

The opportunities presented by such a society for analogies with our own are well used by Miss Mead. It was a task which she had good excuses for evading, but she regarded it as a responsibility of the anthropologist. She undertakes it with intelligence and courage and without prophetic self-consciousness. (p. 330)

> *Isidor Schneider, "Manus and Americans," in* The New Republic, *Vol. LXIV, No. 831, November 5, 1930, pp. 329-30.*

THE NEW YORK TIMES BOOK REVIEW

[Again Margaret Mead] has written an excellent book about primitive life [*Growing Up in New Guinea*]. . . . Miss Mead has the rare faculty of combining scientific observation with happiness of literary expression. In the hands of a person less gifted this material would have been interesting to the student of human behavior but dull to the ordinary reader. Under this author's pen, the pages produce a rare clarity of portraiture of humans and habits. One is also grateful to Miss Mead for the directness and lack of convention with which she writes. . . .

Miss Mead, in the second half of her book, throws an illuminating and rather disconcerting light on the similarity of Manus civilization and our own. The respect for the Manus man of property who owns dogs' teeth, beads, pigs and oil is no less than the respect American civilization has for wealth and the outward signs thereof. A native culture the Manus have not, and neither, according to Miss Mead, have we. Our greatest crime, in the light of Manus observation as well as in American, lies in the education, or, rather, lack of education of our young. This is an era of experimentation in American schools, most of the experiments being directed toward greater freedom and less discipline for the growing child. Miss Mead asks the question, and it is one educators might well ponder upon, Where is the adult American, the product of these schools,

to learn the discipline and adjustment that the life will demand of him?

> To treat our children as the Manus do, permit them to grow up as the lords of an empty creation, despising the adults who slave for them so devotedly, and then apply the whip of shame to make them fall in line with the course of life which they have never been taught to see as noble or dignified—this is giving a stone to throw to those who have a right to good bread.

Provocation to thought is in this paragraph, as the author intended there should be. There is much more in this book that will serve as a prod to thinking.

> *"Primitive Life in New Guinea," in* The New York Times Book Review, *November 16, 1930, p. 22.*

RUTH BENEDICT

[*Sex and Temperament in Three Primitive Societies*] is about the old question of the differences between men and women, but it is as fresh and unhackneyed as an exploration in Mars. [Dr. Mead] has looked at men and women on the other side of the globe, and she has described the kind of men and the kind of women who make up three hitherto unknown tribes of New Guinea. Just as in *Coming of Age in Samoa* she showed how even so natural a crisis as adolescence can be met and passed in a given society without storm and stress and in *Growing Up in New Guinea* how another culture readily moulds its children to its requirements, so in this still richer volume she has described tribes each of which has a different version of the female role in life, and each of which regularly produces women shaped to its pattern.

In our own civilization it is a fundamental tenet that certain temperaments are womanly and certain temperaments are manly. The characteristics do not always fit, and then we regard a woman as masculine and a man as feminine, and devote elaborate psychological analysis to these aberrations. The first two tribes Dr. Mead studied in New Guinea do not have to meet any such difficulties: they expect men and women to be moved by the same emotions and to value the same rewards. Men are not the aggressive sex and women the fostering and maternal. Rather, in the Arapesh tribe, men and women are equally expected to be mild and fostering; in the Mundugumor tribe both sexes are equally expected to be violent and aggressive. In neither case do the natives have any idea that these two kinds of character have anything to do with sex. . . .

The third tribe, the Tchambuli, like western civilization, thoroughly recognizes the gulf fixed between male character and female character, but they have reversed our formulation. Tchambuli men are playboys, living on sufferance of their women. Women are the secure, co-operative group whose role it is to manage the economic life and make the wheels of life go round. Men are the artists, the hangers-on, waiting timidly until the women court them, and secure only in the kindly unobsessive tolerance and appreciation of their womenfolk. The description of Tchambuli is less detailed than the other descriptions, but Tchambuli seems to be the closest approach to female dominance that has yet been described for any society. Curiously enough, it occurs in a patrilineal tribe.

Dr. Mead's conclusion is that no matter how important a role sex differences may play in a society that has defined certain kinds of behavior in this fashion, they are clearly not a matter of inalienable human nature. A society may require one special kind of response to life and require it of both sexes, or it may recognize two kinds and allot one to either sex. But how and to what degree do societies succeed in accomplishing this? In her answers to these questions Dr. Mead has made her greatest contributions to ethnological study. She describes the nursing habits, the conflicts of babyhood, the situations that are formative in the young child, and she shows the manner in which the unbelievably malleable infant child is inducted into the role it will play as an adult. It is a story for every one who is interested in child training.

Similarly she asks how many and what kind of persons receive only partially the stamp of their society. She discusses the deviants in each society, and the nature and degree of their conflicts. . . . Maladjustment in each society is a function of the cultural ideal, and no anthropologist has investigated so carefully the nature of the conflicts and the kinds of personality that in each society predispose an individual to maladjustment. Dr. Mead has developed an intensive technique for the study of children and of deviants in field work among primitive peoples, and its importance is abundantly demonstrated in this volume.

> *Ruth Benedict, "A Man Isn't a Man for a' That—in New Guinea," in* New York Herald Tribune Books, *June 2, 1935, p. 5.*

MALCOLM COWLEY

[In *Sex and Temperament in Three Primitive Societies*, Miss Margaret Mead] drew a general lesson from her observation of . . . three savage tribes. The lesson was that most of the so-called masculine and feminine traits are social rather than biological, acquired rather than instinctive. . . .

In the argument leading to this radical conclusion there are some links of which the weakness is obvious even to a non-anthropologist and non-sojourner among the Papuan aborigines. Thus, on the basis of Miss Mead's own records, it is not true that "neither the Arapesh nor the Mundugumor have made any attitude specific for one sex." The attitude of restlessness, of continually seeking new distractions, is a trait of the Arapesh men; their wives call them "Walk-Abouts" or "Never-Sit-Downs." Among the Mundugumor, the attitude of reckless self-exposure in warfare is specifically male. Among all three tribes, even the women-ruled Tchambuli, it is taken for granted that the men will have a monopoly of hunting, trading, fighting, painting and wood-carving, whereas the women will stay at home and preserve the continuity of tribal life. If all the researches of all the anthropologists were added together, it might be shown that a few male and female characteristics have prevailed everywhere. After all, the men are stronger than the women and are unhampered by pregnancy. The matriarch has to be gentler and more conniving than the patriarch. Even the Tchambuli women are careful not to rule their husbands too openly, for, as the men say, "We might become so ashamed that we would beat them."

Yet it seems to me that Miss Mead is essentially right in her principal conclusions about sex and temperament and the lack of a real connection between them. She is right in saying that most of the traits connected with social classes are also non-hereditary, are roles invented as if by a dramatist and imposed as if by a dictator. There is no more biological basis for class distinctions than there is for the belief of the Mundugumor that only a child born with the umbilical cord wrapped round its

neck can become an artist. And Miss Mead is justified in her emphasis on the infinite adaptability of human nature. This, indeed, is the lesson pointed by the studies of almost all the modern anthropologists. After scattering over the world for thirty years, they are now carrying home the results of their studies. They have to report that nothing is humanly impossible, that there is certainly no inferno in which man has not managed somehow to live and probably no Utopia toward which he might not rise.

> *Malcolm Cowley, "News from New Guinea," in* The New Republic, *Vol. LXXXIII, No. 1070, June 5, 1935, p. 107.*

HORTENSE POWDERMAKER

[In *Sex and Temperament in Three Primitive Societies*] Dr. Mead has undertaken "to discover to what degree temperamental differences between the sexes were innate and to what degree they were culturally determined, and furthermore to inquire minutely into the educational mechanisms connected with these differences." . . . [The] part of the study dealing with the influences which mold the personality in childhood is of much significance and value to those interested in trying to understand how an individual takes on his cultural rôle, and is a subject much neglected by students of primitive societies.

The reader of any book about an unknown people is forced to picture the society according to the author's interpretation. Observers might differ in their interpretation of the same society. For instance, in discussing the consummation of marriage among the Arapesh, the author writes that it is done "without haste, without a due date to harry them with its inevitableness." The assumption is that the setting of a date for a marriage ceremony is a harrowing experience for a normal person. This is open to question. If there is a justifiable doubt in the interpretation of rather well-known phenomena of our society, there is still more leeway for differing in the interpretation of little-known societies. (pp. 221-22)

The author concludes from her observations that the personalities (or temperaments) of the two sexes can be and are socially produced, and that behavior cannot be regarded as sex-linked. The obvious physiological differences between the sexes and the psychiatric implications of these on personality are not discussed, and in the introduction, Dr. Mead says that she will not discuss any universal or fundamental sex differences. To omit a study of these in a study of sex and temperament seems to run counter to what modern psychiatric theory teaches about their significance, and is similar to the case of an economist making a study of our economic system and deciding to leave currency and material goods completely out of consideration. . . .

In the final chapter the author makes a plea that our culture should allow all types of personalities to function and be considered of equal social value. One does not question the desirability of such tolerance, but one may question its feasibility. The book is devoted to showing that all personality types arise purely out of culture. At the same time we are urged to achieve a completely unselective society. Could such a society exist? If so, how would personality types arise? (p. 222)

> *Hortense Powdermaker, in a review of "Sex and Temperament in Three Primitive Societies," in* The Annals of the American Academy of Political and Social Science, *Vol. 181, September, 1935, pp. 221-22.*

DAVID RIESMAN

Margaret Mead begins *Male and Female*—after a brilliant introductory discussion of the meaning of scientific questions and anthropological methods of posing and answering them—with a description of how the different ways of handling boy babies and girl babies in seven South Sea cultures help to determine sex roles and sex expectations in the children. Her field work, in its subtlety, is far removed from the "diaperology" about which her school of anthropology is often kidded by people unsympathetic with the beginning steps of a science. For she sees that what matters is not so much what is done to the child in strict terms of a formula for feeding or toilet training as how the formula is mediated to the child of each sex through the parent of one sex—and how this in turn reflects the parent's and creates the next generation's whole style of life, particularly its acceptance or rejection of or its anxiety about its sex role.

Moreover, Dr. Mead further complicates her account by suggesting that differences in temperament—that is, in body type or constitution—may cut across differences in stylization of sex roles; so that a boy whose temperament is similar to that of boys in some other class or culture and atypical in his own may be stamped as "feminine," and seek either to become more of a "man" by dissociating himself from his body and the native gifts that go with his body-type, or move altogether in the opposite direction toward homosexuality or transvestitism. . . .

Underneath, however, the variations and restructurings of sex roles accomplished by culture and temperament, Dr. Mead sees certain biological clues as tending to produce different outlooks in men and women. It is characteristic, she suggests, for women to *be* women simply by growth through the definite stages of menarche, loss of virginity, motherhood, and menopause: a girl has merely to await these stages in her body's cycle for them to come about. As against this, men have no such time-bound indices of being; for them the problem is one of *becoming* male by constant reassertions of potency, of achievement. . . . However, in modern monogamous societies, where women outnumber men and the birth rate has fallen, the situation is somewhat different, for many women must learn how to be women without being wives and mothers.

The material from the South Seas is used to prove with concrete illustrations the point made by John Stuart Mill in *The Subjection of Women*: that if one sex defines too narrowly the role of the other, it also cramps its own role. This holds for the roles assumed in sexual intercourse, in the family, and in occupations. (p. 376)

Dr. Mead finds her cross-cultural material useful in getting away from the continuing battle in the United States between those surviving feminists who are concerned with proving that women have qualities virtually identical with men and those whom, to coin a word, one might term "feminine-ists," soured of feminism and concerned with proving that women are basically dependent creatures who, as in romances of the ante bellum South, were happier before "emancipation." By pointing to the mild Arapesh—or the violent Mundugumor—Dr. Mead has good case studies of the monotony of an "equality" between the sexes based on likeness rather than the cultivation of difference. On the other hand, by pointing to the Iatmul, she can show the strain put on men—and, derivatively, on their wives—by a culture that exaggerates the differences by keeping women at home and assigning to men the performance of bombastic ceremonial. (pp. 376-77)

When Dr. Mead brings . . . notions and comparisons to the study of contemporary American patterns of sex roles and sex training, she does so not to suggest that solutions to American problems can be found by adopting the sex stylizations in vogue among the Arapesh, or even among the sex-happy Samoans. She uses the knowledge of other cultures as a tool of insight into her own, not as a prescription. (p. 377)

Margaret Mead sees the sexes in contemporary America caught in vicious circles of mutual emulation, manipulation, and fear. She also observes that the ideal that each conjugal family should have a separate home of its own condemns many women who attain it to being more isolated than they would like, while the families who must live with relatives or in crowded quarters feel somehow wrong or wronged. This physical freezing of living arrangements into a single ideal—in which unimaginative city planning and the housing industry, or lack of an industry, co-operate—both symbolizes and reinforces the freezing of ideals of sex role and family life by which Americans try to cope with their fluid social system.

Though Dr. Mead has her own ideals—she has gone beyond the cultural relativism so necessary to the development of anthropology—she is terribly aware of the dangers of idealism for Americans, who are apt to bridge the gap between ideals and current practice either by cynical kicking of the ideal or ruthless kicking of the practice. And this danger is especially great in the field of sex roles, where Americans have often abused the findings of psychological and sociological studies—not to speak of the myths of love presented in novels in which no one ever has a cold, a contraceptive, or complications—to make impossible demands on themselves and on others, without regard to individual constitution or, often, to the mood of the moment. Yet Dr. Mead believes that Americans are still sufficiently experimental to be capable of building new patterns of male and female roles that exploit the wisdoms of the body and the wisdoms of all relevant cultural experience.

Any book that attempts so much runs into difficulties. As Dr. Mead is aware, her readers will find it hard to keep straight the threads of seven South Sea cultures, or the seven times seven threads in the American pattern, even though this is limited to the middle class in the East and Midwest. In my opinion there is not sufficient accent on a limited number of themes, but instead a too-great receptivity to concepts from the whole panorama of the human sciences. But perhaps that is the male in me speaking, wanting to order the data around while Dr. Mead is still listening to them. Dr. Mead herself does the very useful thing, in an appendix, of saying where and from whom she learned what; so that the reader can appraise her perspective. Not for anything would she so standardize vantage points that one could not tell whether a book, or a review, was written by a man or a woman. (pp. 377-78)

David Riesman, "Of Men and Women," in The Nation, *Vol. 169, No. 16, October 15, 1949, pp. 376-78.*

C. E. M. JOAD

[Miss Mead's] descriptions of the more intimate details of primitive life are remarkable no less for their detachment than for their delicacy. In the second half of [*Male and Female*] she applies the same technique to a study of the habits of her American compatriots.

This book has been extensively reviewed and highly praised; its author has been called "a great teacher," and the word "genius" has been used. It is relevant in the light of these encomiums to make one important criticism. The book is badly written, the style is obscure and it is unnecessarily overlaid with technical jargon. Miss Mead, in fact, has not mastered the art of saying what she means clearly, simply and shortly. As a result it is often extremely difficult to tell what her sentences mean. . . .

So much having been said by way of disparagement, it would be ungracious not to come out handsomely with the avowal that the book represents a great achievement; indeed, for originality of material, freshness of treatment and wisdom of conclusion, there has been nothing like it in the anthropological field since the days of Rivers and Malinowski.

Its interest for the general reader is as various as it is intense. (p. 221)

The lessons to be drawn from this important book are, I think, two. First, that if you trace the way in which children grow to be men and women—if you note what they are taught, and particularly what they are taught about their bodies and the mysteries of birth, of marriage and of death, consider the behaviour which at different periods of their lives is expected of them and the ideals of maleness and femaleness which are put before them—you cannot but conclude that our civilisation lays the worst possible foundation for happy, easy sexual relations in maturity. Secondly, that over the last fifty years standards of behaviour, and more particularly of sexual behaviour, have changed so rapidly and so radically that it is harder than it has ever been for young people to adjust themselves. How, indeed, can people be expected to adjust themselves to an environment which is always changing? (pp. 221-22)

> *C. E. M. Joad, "Courtship and Mating," in* The New Statesman & Nation, *Vol. XXXIX, No. 990, February 25, 1950, pp. 221-22.*

SOL TAX

Human evolution, we may say, begins with the development of tools, languages, traditions and values which change and pass from one generation to the next outside the continuing genetic system. Eventually, most of the behavior of our peculiar genus and species is "cultural," and man self-consciously separates himself from the rest of nature; we seem no longer subject to laws of evolution. Only as the very success of our peculiar genus threatens us with the fate of many others before it—extinction—do we come back to the naturalistic view, and ask whether this species cannot use its extraordinary knowledge to change the direction of its evolution.

Margaret Mead may be the first with sufficient experience both to understand the complexity of the problem and not be dismayed. The path to the future which she indicates we may take begins with solid footprints of verified knowledge of human behavior. In [*Continuities in Cultural Evolution*] she provides a good and very interesting sample of our knowledge of this sort, much greater in quantity than many suppose, most of it quite recent and much of it still unpublished. (p. 3)

If one includes the voluminous footnotes, this may indeed be the richest book we have about how the sciences themselves, or at least the human sciences, actually operate. The blurb on the jacket may understate the book's merits when it says it is a "significant contribution to the contemporary dialogue on the nature of human participation in the evolutionary process and the place of the individual in history." It is not impossible

that this book in time will be seen to have integrated and refocused large parts of the human (or behavioral or social) sciences. It is an extraordinary contribution to the study of how information is exchanged among human individuals and groups, an important integration of ideas and knowledge about education, cultural diffusion, continuity, and change. At least half of the book is explicitly about that basic human process—learning—which Miss Mead has studied from her first field work with children in Samoa and New Guinea and includes findings reported at the most recent conferences on cybernetics. Here is available a distillation of much significant, new, analytical-experimental knowledge of psychology tested against a broad comparative experience of the real world.

Professional anthropologists have long appreciated Miss Mead's technical competence but wondered at her popular writing, lecturing and conferencing. In her new book she frankly and explicitly spurns a great deal of the theoretical literature "in which a small group of human scientists, writing primarily for one another, cite a minimum of evidence but present a maximum of contradictory arguments *ad argumentum.*"

She is equally frank in preferring to document her own conclusions with her own field data and with ideas expressed in her presence, usually at conferences. She tends to go to the human laboratory rather than to the theoretical contributions of others. The result is good because she is a good judge of relevance and worth, and because she travels to some of the most interesting places and talks with some of the most extraordinary people in the world. (pp. 3, 20)

> *Sol Tax, "The Great among Others," in* The New York Times Book Review, *August 9, 1964, pp. 3, 20.*

BETTY J. MEGGERS

In recent years, principally through the efforts of Leslie A. White and Julian H. Steward, cultural evolution has achieved general acceptance as the theory that best accounts for differences exhibited between extinct and functioning cultures through time and space. This approach can be likened to reconstruction of biological evolutionary pathways by comparison of structures of extinct and living animals. As was the case in biology, the fact of evolution has been accepted in anthropology in advance of the ability to explain the underlying mechanism by which it takes place. Biologists have recently made considerable progress in laying bare the genetic basis for variability in plants and animals, and the manner in which this variability is acted upon by natural selection resulting in evolutionary modification and speciation. Much less attention has been paid to the underlying mechanics of cultural evolution, and [*Continuities in Cultural Evolution*] is significant as an attempt to deal in popular terms with this important subject. . . .

Taking her cue from the fact that cultural behavior is learned behavior, Mead notes that the unique fact about man is his ability to transmit knowledge, whereas in many other animals "ability to learn has far outrun their ability to transmit what they have learned." . . . Further, "we may hypothesize that the ability to learn is older . . . than is the ability to teach," and it must be recognized that "there are many kinds of learning, each of which is itself dependent on styles of teaching." . . . Cultures differ in the amount and type of behavior that is recognized as learnable as opposed to "natural," and these differences can have important consequences for diffusion: "As long as the house form, the method of fighting, the dances, or the ceremonies of the next tribe are thought of as part of their physical being, no diffusion will occur. . . . The next step, in which People A borrows some item of behavior from People B, requires the implicit recognition that this behavior has been learned by those who display it now and so can be learned by others.'' . . . (p. 1397)

The final four chapters, in which [Mead's] propositions about culture and its evolution are applied to the present world situation, are disappointing. Having devoted the bulk of the text to showing how cultural barriers inhibit acceptance of new ideas, she recommends selecting primitive and isolated groups in remote parts of the globe for ''live storage'' of the choice elements of modern western culture in case of atomic holocaust. In the face of her observation that man seems unable to confront a new reality that eliminates traditional separation between ''us'' and ''them,'' she outlines an international floating conference group that will meditate upon and propose solutions for social and cultural problems. That more realistic measures cannot be proposed is in itself testimony to the limitations of our knowledge.

While it is possible to dispute certain of Mead's views and proposals, this book should be welcomed if only because of the attempt it makes to join together two points of view traditionally in opposition. Our literature abounds with more or less heated discussions about ''organic vs. superorganic'' or ''psychological vs. cultural'' explanations of human behavior. Although Mead has been a leader in many fields of psychological investigation, she demonstrates a thorough comprehension of the cultural evolutionary point of view as well. Recognizing that for certain purposes it is fruitful to consider culture independent of human beings, or human beings independent of culture, she feels that since man's uniqueness consists in his inability to survive except in a man-made environment, attention should be directed to the manner in which he has acted on and reacted to this artificial setting. Her belief that investigations in this area will produce results relevant to solution of problems of how and why cultures have changed or failed to change in different times and places seems justifiable. We know enough about cultural pressures behind psychological attitudes to recognize that they must be fantastically complicated and that they must operate in unsuspected ways. Although we may catch a glimpse of their operation, as Mead has done, our perceptions are as limited as those of microbiology before the invention of the electron microscope and the centrifuge. It is to be hoped that her book will stimulate attention to this neglected field of investigation. (pp. 1398-99)

> *Betty J. Meggers, in a review of ''Continuities in Cultural Evolution,'' in* American Anthropologist, *Vol. 66, No. 6, December, 1964, pp. 1397-99.*

JOHN LEONARD

Raymond Aron, in his most recent book *The Elusive Revolution,* observes: ''A professor would have to be very ignorant indeed to be more ignorant than his students, particularly in their first years at university.'' Margaret Mead, in this slim volume of shining intelligence [*Culture and Commitment: A Study of the Generation Gap*], sees the situation from a less comfortable point of view. The young, she says, know something the rest of us refuse to admit. They know that ''there are no adults anywhere in the world from whom they can learn what the next steps should be.'' What the next steps should be . . . a deceptively simple and ultimately horrifying formu-

lation to describe that most notorious of holes, the Generation Gap.

For the dissident young, writes Dr. Mead, ''the past . . . is a colossal, unintelligible failure and the future may hold nothing but the destruction of the planet.'' One needn't subscribe wholly to such an apocalyptic vision, it being the nature of young men to build Taj Mahals of anguish around an inadequate sex-life. . . .

But something is going on . . . that can't be sloughed off as glandular irregularities. . . . Dr. Mead suggests that the something is a new world culture, which she calls ''prefigurative,'' . . . based upon a profound revision of authority roles, the nature of dependency and the ''location of the future.''

Her concepts are perfectly straightforward. In a ''postfigurative'' culture—primitive societies, small religious and ideological enclaves—children learn primarily from their forebears. . . . In a timeless culture, the oldest among us is the inevitable model; the youngest, the child, is so much Silly-Putty on which a role is pressed.

In a ''cofigurative'' culture—such ''great civilizations'' as our own, incorporating change—both children and adults learn from their peers, playmates, fraternity brothers, colleagues. The grandfather, hopelessly anachronistic, has been wheeled off to the nearest Gerontion Garden for figs and Estrogen. . . .

''Prefigurative'' culture is what is happening to us. The young, in their apprehension of ''the still unknown future,'' assume new authority; teach us by asking questions we were too busy to worry about; require of us a nurture, an environment, that instead of pressing forms upon the child invites his limitless inquiry. Accustomed as we are to being thumped on the head with slogans—''the collapse of the family, the decay of capitalism, the triumph of a soul-less technology''—we may resist Dr. Mead's quiet and common-sensical notion that the pace of change has so accelerated that traditional forms of culturally incorporating it are insufficient. We resist at our peril. . . .

It is impossible to do justice to [Dr. Mead's] weaving of fine details into this convincing tapestry . . . but one must suggest the wisdom, the pithy distillations, of this book. We require, says Dr. Mead, a biological and ecological model of our world which repudiates ''the old calculus of gain and loss,'' which substitutes a model of ''negative entropy,'' the mutuality of gain by interreaction in a single environment.

She is optimistic, and so embarrasses old gloom-mongers like me. . . . One must pray that her postfigurations will prevail.

> *John Leonard, ''Dr. Mead vs. the Gloom-Mongers,'' in* The New York Times, *January 8, 1970, p. 39.*

EDGAR Z. FRIEDENBERG

Culture and Commitment presents the texts of a series of lectures delivered at the American Museum of Natural History in March, 1969, in celebration of its centennial. Miss Mead has herself been for more than 40 years professionally concerned with the processes—crucial to anthropology—by which culture is transmitted from one generation to another; her classic *Coming of Age in Samoa* was published in 1928. This little book, however, adds very little to the literature on intergenerational conflict which, though recently marked by several works of real distinction like Theodore Roszak's *The Making of a Counter Culture,* . . . seems already too voluminous.

Miss Mead's intention is to state, in a form acceptable to a popular audience, a general theory by which current conflict between the generations can be explained. The very fact that such conflict is now world-wide relieves her of the necessity . . . of considering specifically American aspects of the conflict; while the fact that she speaks as an anthropologist permits her to couch her argument solely in terms of conflicting patterns of culture without looking behind those patterns to examine the social and economic processes that generate them. Since Canadian, French and Japanese youth are as disaffected as our own, she can eliminate the Vietnam war and the draft as fundamental sources of conflict; while the fact that such hostilities occur in Communist countries as well as capitalist is taken to eliminate the whole question of capitalism or imperialism, with its specific forms of alienation. She searches, instead, for factors common to relations between the generations throughout the world.

At this level of generality, Miss Mead comes up with a threefold classification of relations between the generations, according to the prevalent rate of social change. When the rate is slow, so that children grow up secure in the knowledge that, for good or ill, their lives will be similar to those of their parents, the parents serve as models and authorities. . . . (pp. 1, 25)

When the rate of social or technological change becomes so rapid that parents no longer lead the kinds of lives their children may expect to lead, they can no longer serve as models and much of their authority is lost. . . . Authority then shifts to the peers who become the source of norms. But the parents retain, at least, the power to abdicate and thereby facilitate and share in—indeed insist on—their children's success. . . .

When change becomes yet more rapid, however, the parents can neither prepare their children for emancipation nor accept it. Communication between the generations can continue only if its direction is reversed; i.e., the parents must consent to learn from the children who, like the children of pioneers, are at home in the world their parents find hostile and need to control. . . .

Miss Mead, on the record, practices her own doctrine—a charming, if archaic custom. She is, I believe, the only public figure to advocate to a Congressional committee that marijuana be simply legalized and the harassment of the young to this extent thereby reduced. But Miss Mead's heuristic approach to generational conflict does not involve her in a discussion of the "politics of pot," or the politics of anything else. Her "postfigurative," "cofigurative" and "prefigurative" cultures . . . say nothing at all about the moral or political content of intergenerational conflict. The result is wholly noncontroversial and makes no specific demands; in structure, *Culture and Commitment* resembles *A Christmas Carol*, with Margaret Mead suggesting that Scrooge be benign, but offering no explanation of or response to the despair of the young that the world has become as loveless, commercial and tawdry as Christmas itself. (p. 25)

> *Edgar Z. Friedenberg, in a review of "Culture and Commitment: A Study of the Generation Gap," in The New York Times Book Review, March 8, 1970, pp. 1, 25-6.*

KENNETH E. BOULDING

[*Culture and Commitment: A Study of the Generation Gap*] originated in the Man and Nature Lectures which Margaret Mead delivered at the American Museum of Natural History in March, 1969. The appendix on the film, slides, and music used in the lectures makes one realize how much must have been lost in translating this event to print. Those who attended the lectures must have had a rare privilege. Nevertheless, a good deal remains even in cold print and the book is a testament (one hopes not the last one) to the life of one of the most energetic and remarkable women of our time. In it indeed Dr. Mead sums up what she has learned from the past and what she hopes for the future.

The book centers around three additions to the English language, and very useful words they are—post-figurative, co-figurative, and pre-figurative, which are descriptive of different modes of transmission of culture in different types of society. Post-figurative societies are those in which the culture is transmitted, with very limited opportunities for change, from each generation to the next. (p. 339)

The modern world, however, has produced what Dr. Mead calls co-figurative cultures, in which the younger generation especially draws its culture not so much from its elders as from its peers. . . . In co-figurative cultures . . . the impact of change is so great that the world the elders grew up in has passed away, either because of rapid internal change, or because of impact from the outside. (p. 340)

Then in the modern world Dr. Mead detects what we call the pre-figurative culture, in which the rate of change is so great that only the younger generation understands what is going on at all and the older generation has to learn from them. It is in cultures of this kind that the generation gap is most evident because the children have not the slightest intention of growing up to be like their elders and the elders in no sense form a model to the children. In these societies, furthermore, there develops a great variety of cultures, so that the individual growing up has a certain choice as to what he shall be. Identity and commitment are no longer determined for him, but represent an act of choice.

One sees the beginning of this phenomenon in what I have elsewhere called religions of convincement, as opposed to religions of confirmation, for religions of convincement almost force the child to be pre-figurative and to select an identity and a commitment. The problem becomes more acute as the number of possible cultures proliferates. On the question of how these choices of identity and commitment to culture are made, Dr. Mead is for the most part silent. The romantic illusion that each person has only one true self that must be fulfilled is clearly nonsense in the modern world. Still, it is by no means easy to see how the commitment to an identity, which must be a commitment to the imitation of a model, either of a personal hero or an abstract ideal of life, is actually performed. The anomic cultures that we see all around us reflect the difficulty of making satisfactory commitments to an identity. While this book raises a question of the utmost importance, therefore, it does not provide us with much of an answer.

As one would expect in a book that originated in a series of lectures, the text is full of tantalizing asides and *obiter dicta* which one would like to see spelled out further. . . . The most tantalizing question of all . . . is whether the co-figurative and pre-figurative cultures are merely transitional stages towards an eventual post-figurative culture which will include all that has gone before. Only post-figurative cultures are stable, that much is clear, and the enormous dynamic of change in which we find ourselves today clearly cannot go on forever. At some time within the next hundred years we must begin to make preparations for what I have called the re-entry and landing on spaceship earth. As we approach towards a much more stable, though one hopes high-level, developed society, the post-figurative culture will presumably take over again, although its mode of transmission may be very different. Any fundamental breakdown of the cultural transmission process would lead to disaster. One hopes Margaret Mead will take up these questions in a later volume. (pp. 340-41)

> *Kenneth E. Boulding, "Tantalizing Questions," in* The Virginia Quarterly Review, *Vol. 46, No. 2 (Spring, 1970), pp. 339-41.*

BENJAMIN DeMOTT

How goes it with culture critics? Is a consensus in the works? Will these new American sages ever agree about what's right and wrong with the times? . . .

Culture critics are given to highly idiosyncratic literary tones, methods, and self-images. Neutralize all divisive factors save this latter one—spiky individuality—and the prospect of culture-crit concord would still seem remote.

For a glimpse of the quality of the individualities in question, consider the case of Margaret Mead, whose observations about American life appear regularly in *Redbook,* a mass-circulation women's magazine. *A Way of Seeing* is a compilation of the best of her columns, with Rhoda Metraux credited as co-author. The tone is teacherly, unflappable, optimistic. . . . [Dr. Mead's] method is to begin by stating a traditional or popular understanding of one or another custom or convention, and thereafter to cast that understanding in doubt by summarizing statistical and other evidence suggesting its breakdown. The gap disclosed between myth and fact is represented as a social problem, whereupon a solution is tentatively advanced. (p. 23)

[Part] of Dr. Mead's individuality derives from the firmness of her belief in the pliancy of men and institutions, and from her occasionally beamish enthusiasm for radical social innovations. Other sources of individuality are the author's conviction of personal incorruptibility and the intensity of her self-regard. The latter qualities appear most vividly in an account of a revisit, with a TV camera crew, to Peri village, scene of Dr. Mead's memorable *Growing Up in New Guinea.* She describes, with perky satisfaction, episodes of showbiz ghoulishness and exploitation—director and crew hanging about impatiently for good footage of a real-life death scene, turning hot lights on a wretched woman in childbirth—and immediately thereafter she praises her own and her camera crew's "integrity, empathy and insight." But that one or two features of this critic's makeup aren't charming only intensifies her distinctiveness. Dr. Mead clearly is one of a kind—nobody easily tamed or caged in consensus. (pp. 23-4)

> *Benjamin DeMott, "New Longings Abroad in the Land," in* Saturday Review, *Vol. LIII, No. 27, July 4, 1970, pp. 23-6.**

NOBUO SHIMAHARA

Perhaps the timely publication of *Culture and Commitment* was anticipated by sensitive students of contemporary culture who have given attention to Mead's frequent commentaries on American youth. But even for her, this was a bold attempt because she had to reduce her enormous miscellaneous obser-

vations on cultural process and generation change to a little over a hundred pages. . . . For without adequate regard for the variations and complexity of the issue discussed, Mead makes sweeping generalizations which are poorly substantiated. In this sense, it would not be unfair to say that her book was written for a journalistic purpose. Furthermore, impressed by the role of technology as an overwhelming force for cultural transformation, Mead tends to overstate the impact of technology upon the fabrics of values and characterological structure. She argues that technology has cut off "irreversibly" the young from the elders and the past, resulting in accelerating generational discontinuities with respect to values, attitudes, and behavior patterns. Her profile of the generation gap is more impressionistic than descriptive, it has more appeal to laymen than to cautious empiricists.

In essence, Mead's book is intended to clarify the direction of the generational change in American and other technologically developed cultures. The overall aim is brilliantly achieved, and indeed, she offers a number of valuable insights. (pp. 159-60)

Having occurred within a very short period of one generation, [the technological developments of the last two and a half decades] . . . shatter the sense of direction and certainty on the part of the adults to whom the past can no longer serve as the guide. There is also no guide for the youth. This predicament calls for the emergence of the prefigurative culture where a sincere dialogue between the elder and younger generations must be established.

Mead romanticizes youth not in a Rousseauistic sense, but because of her impression that they are capable of purer imagination, wider vision, and more passion than the elders. They, says she, "know better" our crises and imperative needs for the commitment to harmony and peace. The adults who still have little faith in the young must realize that the future depends upon the communication between the two generations and the establishment of a vocabulary which will facilitate their communication.

Mead criticizes justifiably the older generation for its stubbornness and insensitivity to change. The adults, she insists, must learn a new model for themselves so that they can learn from youth. Youth's participation in the power structure where the adults regulate their lives is urgent if the generation gap is to be solved.

Culture and Commitment will widely generate reflection and discussion on the part of students and their teachers, and hopefully children and their parents. (p. 161)

> *Nobuo Shimahara, in a review of "Culture and Commitment: A Study of the Generation Gap," in* Teachers College Record, *Vol. 72, No. 1, September, 1970, pp. 159-61.*

RICHARD J. MARGOLIS

[*A Rap on Race*] does not explain how it happened, but the impresario who brought Margaret Mead and James Baldwin together was plainly a minor genius—the kind of brassy broker who in another time might have introduced Florence Nightingale to Franz Kafka. . . . Consider Baldwin: the passionate exile, the middle-aged Cassandra, brooding prophet of the fire next time. And Mead: the cool anthropologist, rational grandmother, symbol of common sense to millions of Americans.

An odd couple. Yet for two days last August, as a tape recorder eavesdropped, these two improbable communicants waged a remarkable Socratic marathon. Mead played a rather sharp-tongued Socrates to Baldwin's suffering Phaedo. . . .

[Baldwin] predicts that "the Western world will either live by what it professes to believe in or it will cease to exist." . . . He writes off white Americans who "go along singing like Doris Day in the sun and the rain," and never hear their black compatriots weeping. "I no longer care," he protests, "whether white people hear me or not."

At first Mead gentles him. Politely she translates his black chauvinism into excusable village parochialism. . . .

Later she begins to lose patience. "You treat the country as if it had one problem," she complains. "It has a lot more than one problem."

"Yes," replies Baldwin, "but that one problem . . . has obsessed me all my life."

It is a weakness she apparently cannot condone. One should see through a glass clearly, eclectically. Over the years she has gathered a quiverful of facts, astonishing arrows with which she now tries to puncture Baldwin's ballooning bitterness. She is mistress of the academic put-down. . . .

She is willing to grant him his peculiar racial pain—"I have never suffered as you have," she tells him—but she would rather rap on the whole human race. . . .

At times it all seems too much for Baldwin. "I'm a poet," he reiterates. "I never learned anything through my mind. I learned whatever I've learned from my heart and my guts." And so they struggle to find each other, the sensitive poet and the sensible humanist, each feeling the weight of the brother they have in common.

Baldwin tries to come of age in Mead's milieu, and as the marathon draws to a close, one suspects that his instincts are at least equal to her intellect.

> *Richard J. Margolis, "Useful Talk by an Odd Couple," in* Life *Magazine, Vol. 70, No. 21, June 4, 1971, p. 22.*

RICHARD ELMAN

No fuss. No bother. Eliminate dirty smudges on the fingertips, broken nails, and messy erasure marks. You don't need to revise, rethink, or rewrite. You don't even need to write. . . . Sealed inside your own angry mortal human vacuum, to be just as fatuous as Margaret Mead and James Baldwin about the crisis of our time—particularly race—all you have to do is talk and not listen, always avoid expressing your feelings openly, refer constantly to other times and other cultures with historical and/or pseudohistorical truths, interrupt whenever possible, call yourself a prophet or a poet, insist that you are being emotionally sincere and/or objectively rational, and record it all on tape, to be transcribed later as a book. . . .

Announce that "love is the only wisdom." Assert such "in the name of your ancestors." Denounce any and all assertions of "racial guilt." Speak out fearlessly against the plight of Chicanos, Filipinos, Sephardic Jews of Israel. Presto! You're off the hook. You've got a book. You haven't had to say anything at all, and it will probably sell fairly well. This is called instantaneous wisdom, although some may call it *A Rap on Race.*

Basically, it will be the same old bilge you've heard from the fellow on the next stool to you in the saloon. . . .

Caution: You must either be a world-famous white liberal anthropologist, or a brilliant black writer, or else there isn't much of an audience for this sort of thing except among your friends, or in taverns and bars where people generally call it baloney. But wisdom and baloney are as blither is to blather; here and there ideas are speckled like pieces of fat in a slab of Hebrew National, though most of it is pretty bland, chewy stuff. We're all capable of it, but only some of us ever bother to publish it. (p. 5)

[Eventually, Mead and Baldwin grew] so angry and muddled that [Baldwin] was being accused of mouthing anti-Semitic nonsense and, as a final quid pro quo, he lumped her among his potential enemies and victimizers. Rather smugly, the anthropologist had said she could not possibly be a racist because of her impeccable upbringing and because she had once or twice coddled babies in Africa, Samoa, West Irian. Baldwin countered by asking how could he be an anti-Semite since one of his best friends was Jewish. . . .

Margaret Mead and James Baldwin both agreed that touch is a necessity in human communications, but there is no record from this transcript that they ever did. Nor do we get any idea of what their feelings toward each other really were from tone of voice, or facial expression, or what they did with their hands and feet. On television, maybe Professor Mead can explain, from a social scientist's perspective, what she meant by her remark that "When the Irish get angry they're in love," and, of course, provide the necessary data; and I would also like to see Baldwin live up to his compassionate boast that he can "dance and sing as well as the Yemenites do. And pay the same price for it."

In the meantime, though, this sort of thing, if obviously impassioned, well-intentioned, and not always wrong-headed, is still not much more than a cut above the sort of thing that most blacks and whites are saying to each other now that we're all supposedly getting together. (p. 14)

Better luck next time, Professor Mead and Mr. Baldwin. For the rest of us, I think we better start talking to each other and stop listening to wise men and women among us except when they deign to write down what they have to say in novels and plays and poems and essays and, yes, then revise, if necessary. (p. 16)

> *Richard Elman, "About the Black Accused and the White Accusers: 'A Rap on Race'," in* The New York Times Book Review, *June 27, 1971, p. 5.*

WILFRID C. BAILEY

Together, Mead and Metraux, examine a wide variety of topics related to modern society [in *A Way of Seeing*]. These include cities, role of children, police, Christmas, New Year, the two-party system, women in politics, Mrs. Roosevelt, student power, race, parenthood, marriage and divorce, population control, education, nudists, sex education, aggression, and Gypsies. The individual essays represent the authors' personal responses to events at different moments in time. As such, they reflect the changing scene at home and abroad. (p. 822)

A Way of Seeing is neither a book on anthropology nor a book for anthropologists. In fact, some of the essays show little relationship to anthropology and could have been written by most anyone. Margaret Mead claims that as an anthropologist she has developed a special way of seeing our country and its problems. She makes a great point of the fact that she and Rhoda Metraux grew up a decade apart and that, in turn, their children were born a decade apart. However, this seems to have no relationship to the essays, except insofar as they represent a combination of views. (p. 823)

> *Wilfred C. Bailey, in a review of "A Way of Seeing," in* American Anthropologist, *Vol. 73, No. 4, August, 1971, pp. 822-23.*

DAVID DONALD

[*A Rap on Race*] is not a book that contributes much to our understanding of race, or to racial understanding. Very early in the dialogue it becomes evident that neither Baldwin nor Mead represents any considerable intellectual constituency. The novelist, who has for years spent most of his time in France, is out of touch with young American blacks; as a forty-six-year-old, he admits that American Negroes of the 1970's "could no longer turn to my generation for anything at all." Though he understands, and in an abstract way sympathizes with, the strivings of young Negroes for separatism and black power, he has no part in their movement. "The trouble is," he confesses, "that I'm really neither black nor white." Neither is Miss Mead, who was brought up in a comfortable Northern community free from prejudice and who has spent much of her distinguished career living among primitive peoples of a different race. She knows, one suspects, more about growing up in Samoa than in the suburbs.

Much of their conversation resembles an old-fashioned revival meeting, where one speaker after another mouths truths and truisms, to a chant of "Amen" from his listeners. Both Mead and Baldwin agree, and echo each other, that race is the most pressing issue of our time; that American society is in a bad way; that racial prejudice is deplorable; that the black power movement is inevitable and probably beneficial. On only one topic is there real disagreement. Baldwin insists that all white Americans are guilty of the atrocities committed against black people throughout our past. . . . Sharply Mead dissents: "I will *not* accept any guilt for what anybody else did. I *will* accept guilt for what I did myself. . . . I absolutely refuse racial *guilt*."

Precisely what American whites, past or present, are supposed to be guilty of neither speaker explains. Both Baldwin and Mead conclude that the problems of the present are rooted in the past, and both make much of what they call "the historical point of view." It is not, however, evident from these dialogues that either knows much about American history, and they show no acquaintance with the voluminous and controversial literature dealing with the history of the American Negro and the institution of slavery.

Though *A Rap on Race* says little that is significant or new about its topic, this is nevertheless a fascinating book, because it offers self-drawn character portraits of two exceptionally interesting people. High-strung and voluble, Baldwin dominates the early stages of the conversation. In a tone verging on hysteria, he pictures the United States as a jungle where black men are ruthlessly hunted and killed. (pp. 619-21)

Low-keyed and understated at the outset, Mead asserts herself gradually by making minor corrections on Baldwin's incidental points. . . . When Baldwin claims that the Nazis exterminated Jews in the name of Christianity, she observes that he is employing neither good theology nor good history but is just making "an anti-establishment remark." "Yeah, all right," concedes Baldwin. "I'll accept that, because I'm not equipped to argue it."

Miss Mead is clearly superbly equipped to argue anything, and from this point her primacy in the dialogue is obvious. While Baldwin reverts to childish tricks of making faces at her remarks or of trying to fluster her by calling her "Meg," she implacably exposes his extravagances. No, she corrects him, mass production is not an unmitigated evil, apartment buildings are not all horrors, Americans are not universally apathetic. (p. 621)

A Rap on Race certainly does not take anybody far in exploring the most serious issue of our times. But it does serve as a superb demonstration of how effectively a skilled teacher can tie an unwary but loquacious pupil into knots. And perhaps it may also serve to remind a gifted novelist that he should return to his field of fiction. (p. 622)

> *David Donald, "A Fascinating Book," in* The Virginia Quarterly Review, *Vol. 47, No. 4 (Autumn, 1971), pp. 619-22.*

JANE HOWARD

More than an account of her professional beginnings, [*Blackberry Winter: My Earlier Years*]—presumably the first half of Dr. Mead's autobiography—is a hymn to her own family in particular and the idea of families in general. Although none of her own three marriages endured, she takes enormous pleasure in having finally become a mother herself, at age 38. . . .

What one misses most in this lucid, witty record hearteningly free of jargon, is more candor about the author's three husbands. Not much passion informs her accounts of how Luther Cressman, Reo Fortune and Gregory Bateson entered her life and left it, all apparently before she was 40. Was there no rancor, no unpleasantness, when these unions were put asunder? Was everybody really all that grownup and civilized? Didn't Luther mind being replaced by Reo, and did Reo bow out so peaceably for Gregory? Was she perhaps even a little bit to blame herself?

We are offered few marital vignettes of the sort that lend charm to Dr. Mead's sketches of her forebears: we only know that Reo, whom it made nervous to watch her houseclean, once refused to fetch a thermometer when her temperature was 105° and that Gregory, since their divorce, has misspent his energy on "records that are not in themselves priceless or timelessly valuable."

Not to carp, though. Perhaps no man is a permanent match for the likes of Dr. Mead, and, if not, so what? *Blackberry Winter,* an agreeable rummaging through a crowded but tidy attic, makes some instructive points. It argues eloquently for the continuity of generations, and the gift of complete and sustained attention between parents and children. "Watching a parent grow," she observes, "is one of the most reassuring experiences anyone can have, a privilege that comes only to those whose parents live beyond their children's early adulthood." She commends, too, the trying task of "sweeping one's mind clear of every presupposition." Valid aims, these, and worthy of reflection.

> *Jane Howard, "There's No One Like Margaret," in* The New York Times Book Review, *November 12, 1972, p. 49.*

ANN BELFORD ULANOV

[In *Twentieth Century Faith: Hope and Survival*] Mead expresses her confident faith in 20th-Century man. She speaks to the reader much as a beloved grandmother—a figure highly honored in Mead's thought—might share a vision of life's meaning and its future possibilities with the younger generation. Technology, she asserts, has no hope of altogether successful application to the [world's] problems. . . . But faith in this century—faith in God and confidence in ourselves—can have no future, she says, without the practical knowledge and implementation that science provides. Out of a vision of the interpenetration of science and religion, Mead envisions imaginative and practical approaches to such problems and concerns as birth control, the human need for ritual, . . . and a theology of some cultural depth. What we need to build, she argues, is a human culture in which all can share, through universal symbol systems, in everything from spatial measurements and road signs to scientific formulas. This book should be of special interest to theologians, natural scientists, and social scientists.

> *Ann Belford Ulanov, in a review of "Twentieth Century Faith: Hope and Survival," in* Library Journal, *Vol. 97, No. 21, December 1, 1972, p. 3922.*

WILL DAVISON

Margaret Mead, America's anthropologist laureate, is both child to the 20th century and parent. She has devoted her threescore years and ten to the "proper study of mankind," and is preeminently qualified to address herself to man's faith, hope and survival. This she does, in [*Twentieth Century Faith: Hope and Survival*] . . . , 16 collected pieces, written between 1953 and 1971, which comprise the 25th volume of the Religious Perspectives series.

Several broad themes stand out—science and technology, religion and spirituality, culture and civilization—but, typically, all are important to the author only as they relate to man past, present and future.

The greatest, and most interesting, part of the book deals with culture, which is, of course, the author's forte. **"Cultural Man"** (1966) is a brilliant essay on the meaning of anthropology and how it can be used to enhance and reinforce Christianity. And with what knowledge and delight she writes not only about children but also about the aged! . . .

[In] abundance are the now familiar earmarks of Margaret Mead's work: disinterested observation; wisdom and understanding; hopeful anticipation; liberal open-endedness. The book is an interesting journey through the evolution of her thought over the last two decades.

> *Will Davison, in a review of "Twentieth Century Faith: Hope and Survival," in* The New York Times Book Review, *January 7, 1973, p. 37.*

GEORGE W. STOCKING, JR.

[It] struck me while reading *Blackberry Winter* that surely one of the great moments in the history of anthropology must have occurred early in 1933 on the Sepik in Northeast New Guinea, when Margaret Mead, her second husband Reo Fortune, and her later-to-be third husband Gregory Bateson, with whom she was then falling in love, sat around "cooped up together" in a "tiny eight-foot-by-eight-foot mosquito room," . . . thrashing out their ideas on the interrelated variation of sex roles,

inborn temperaments, and human cultures. Three important figures in the history of anthropology, tangled in a complex maze of interpersonal relations, themselves representative of three different English-speaking cultures (American, New Zealand, and British), who had collectively worked in no less than eight non-Western cultures—bringing all this to bear on a question of fundamental anthropological and continuing general intellectual interest. (pp. 95-6)

In their cell on the Sepik, the three of them arrayed the New Guinea cultures they had studied in a "fourfold system" based on "culturally defined temperamental expectations for men and women in each one." . . . There was one empty slot in the scheme, which Mead hypothesized (and later confirmed by fieldwork carried on with Bateson) might be filled by Bali. In all of this, the three were conscious that their own temperaments could also be arrayed schematically, with Bateson and Mead together at one pole in strong contrast to Fortune. So far as one can judge from Mead's account, however, it does not seem to have occurred to them that here, too, there might be a missing (female) type. Nor do they seem to have explored the implications of all this for the fieldwork on which their typologizing was based.

Mead does recognize that the pattern a particular fieldworker discovers "is one of many that might be worked out through different approaches to the same human situation," . . . and that the differences they had found between cultures might have "nearly as much to do with us, as individuals, as it had to do with the nature of the cultures we studied." . . . But in general, her discussion of fieldwork method tends to emphasize the scientific character of it all—or rather, her attempt to introduce rigorous and systematic methods *into* ethnographic work. And although she confides that she found Arapesh culture "thin" . . . and Mundugamor "loathsome" . . . , there is no serious doubt that she had penetrated to the essential character of their cultural handling of sexual and temperamental differences.

Let us assume that she did, for there is no doubt that she was an extraordinary fieldworker. All the more interesting, then, is her account of the experiences that formed the pattern of her own personality. That it should be less than totally revealing is hardly surprising. Autobiography is after all a privileged form of communication. . . . Perhaps the most that one can ask is that the general "truth" of a person's life be somehow accessible in the particular body of concrete detail selected from all its moments. It seemed to me that Mead accomplished this brilliantly in her portrait of Ruth Benedict (*An Anthropologist at Work*). And although *Blackberry Winter* is at points rather elliptical . . . for a book which Mead apparently worked on over a fairly long period, it does in fact reveal to us, directly or indirectly, a great deal about the culture and personality of Margaret Mead. (p. 96)

> *George W. Stocking, Jr., "Growing Up to New Guinea," in* Isis, *Vol. 65, No. 226, March, 1974, pp. 95-7.*

ROBERT H. DONAHUGH

In a felicitous blending of words and photographs [*World Enough: Rethinking the Future*], Mead and [Ken] Heyman seek to make comprehensible to today's reader the social and technological interdependence of the world's people. Citing the end of World War II as the time when all the wrong directions were explored, Mead traces the thrust of technology and its imposition on areas and people not prepared for or even needing it. . . . The scope of the book is breathtaking, but the clarity and sanity of Mead's prose carries the reader along. . . . [This] work should stimulate much thought and conversation.

> *Robert H. Donahugh, in a review of "World Enough: Rethinking the Future," in* Library Journal, *Vol. 101, No. 5, March 1, 1976, p. 701.*

RODERICK NORDELL

For half a century since the celebrated ***Coming of Age in Samoa,*** Dr. Mead has been adding to her knowledge of little-known cultures and the hardly less confounding patterns of the well-known civilization nearer home. In the new ***World Enough: Rethinking the Future*** . . . she draws on it all to combine the broad and sometimes controversial generalizations to which she has earned a right—and the sudden close-in detail of which her memory must be full.

In partnership with Ken Heyman's skilled photographs from many countries, Dr. Mead's words not only declare a needed change in 20th-century thinking, they exemplify it. This fresh attitude to mind breaks away from the narrow, horizon-bound residue of days before communications made the world a global village. It connects what individuals do anywhere to the potential effects felt everywhere in an age when, for example, babies in remote deserts have become dependent on the quality control of powdered milk produced thousands of miles away. . . .

What the Mead-Heyman book tries to do—and to a considerable extent does—is to provide an experience of the world that makes one feel the relationships of each to all. The question is whether humanity will move fast enough to achieve a world view balancing technology, nature, and mankind—which this book is not alone in advocating.

A reader's admiration is qualified by Dr. Mead's failure to display a political awareness as strong as her other kinds. She says that it is good for the world to believe that the Chinese have "found a better solution than we have" to the problem of relating the "millions who must be fed" to a "meaningful way of life." But references to rigorous planning are the nearest she comes to hinting at the communist repression that makes the political price of the Chinese solution too high for emulation. . . .

[Dr. Mead also responds] to the changes of the past quarter century, the technology that has both brought benefits and interfered with the natural processes of life. She sees that the resulting dilemmas cannot be solved either by getting rid of technology or by simply throwing more technology at them.

So she rejects the now familiar concept of Planet Earth as a spaceship, insofar as it suggests people are simply "human components" on a vehicle that can be preserved through proper engineering. She does see help in the human inventions from writing to television that permit for the first time every kind of human experience to be shared. . . .

For all the problems Dr. Mead sees, she believes that "it is open to us" to correct the damage done to the earth and its inhabitants.

> *Roderick Nordell, "Coming of Age on Planet Earth," in* The Christian Science Monitor, *March 19, 1976, p. 14.*

ROSALIE H. WAX

Most of the letters in [***Letters from the Field***] were written, not to a particular individual, but to a varied, known, and loved group of people. And such is their straightforward style and eloquence that a reader, in some magical fashion, finds herself or himself taking, not the role of a student or critic, but the role of a friend or sympathetic colleague. To read letters from a friend in the field when that friend is Margaret Mead is a unique experience.

There are field letters from Samoa, Manus, the Omaha Reservation, New Guinea, Bali, and Iatmul, from a second visit to Manus, and from many subsequent, shorter trips. The time span extends from 1925 to 1975, and each of the major field expeditions is prefaced by an introduction explaining the relevant personal, academic, and scientific circumstances. As a bonus, the volume opens with the most illuminating and helpful short statement about the importance of fieldwork that I have ever read.

Mead's vivid and uninhibited descriptions of what she sees and what she does are, in turn, moving, amusing, horrifying, and awe inspiring. . . . (pp. 90-1)

With the present-day emphasis on women's studies and women's liberation, it is well that we are reminded that Mead initiated the comparative study of women (and children) in other cultures more than 50 years ago, and that she has probably done more research on women and contributed more factual and insightful information about them than any other anthropologist—and, perhaps, any other human being. And, given her independence and originality, it is not surprising to learn that, on occasion, female critics have accused her of antifeminism, whereas male critics have accused her of rampant feminism. (p. 92)

It is greatly to Mead's credit that . . . she spoke for sanity, tolerance, a respect for all peoples, and a concern for the human and scientific values of fieldwork. This volume of letters helps us to appreciate her abilities and her moral courage. (p. 98)

> *Rosalie H. Wax, "Notes from a Pioneer," in* Natural History, *Vol. LXXXVII, No. 2, February, 1978, pp. 90-4, 98.*

JAMES SLOAN ALLEN

If letters should informally disclose their author's life and thought, Margaret Mead's [***Letters from the Field 1925-1975***] . . . should be prized. For they do this and more: They chart the growth of anthropology, the shifting relationships between undeveloped and advanced societies, and the waning of tribal life. . . . [A] spirit of novelty and keen responsiveness to cultural detail never leaves Mead's letters; nor does the transparent, descriptive prose that lets the reader see what Mead sees; nor does her affection for the tribal cultures.

But Margaret Mead does change, along with the cultures she studies. Like anthropology itself, her observations grow more comprehensive and analytic as she learns to look beyond the sights and sounds of rituals, manners, and emotional incidents to the social structures and psychological patterns they signify; and she smiles at the naïveté of her early work. Then, with new methods of study and with the passing of years, the letters reflect the gradual transformation of primitive societies as they come under Western influence: Custom and superstition yield to education, rationality, and worldly worry. And, as she steeps herself in the evidence and meaning of these changes, Mead assumes the character we all know: less the scientist than the sage—alive with ideas, facts, and feelings about how to remedy the modern world's discontents.

> *James Sloan Allen, in a review of "Letters from the Field 1925-1975," in* Saturday Review, *Vol. 5, No. 9, February 4, 1978, p. 38.*

KIRKUS REVIEWS

People apparently asked Margaret Mead *everything*—and she took the opportunity, in the columns from *Redbook* (1963-79) reprinted [in *Margaret Mead: Some Personal Views*], to tell them what she thought they should know. . . . In freeing children of both sexes from constraints, she observed, "we may be destroying the set of motives that have made men the great achievers and innovators of civilization." Women, on the other hand, should not be accepted for combat service because, hang on, they're "too fierce": whereas boys grow up learning the rituals of fighting, women fight only to defend their homes and their young. Her views were not culture-bound, however. In 1963 she took an advanced position on abortion (though she has second thoughts by '71), drug addiction, and homosexuality. . . . Nor did she hesitate to deliver herself of opinions on off-track betting, international spying, the authorship of Shakespeare's plays—or how come she thought she was "an authority on everything"? Of all that's in this grab-bag, though, Mead is most impressive on matters of moral consequence—like the Andean plane crash in which, she explains, the survivors' faith turned cannibalism into ritual. Like its predecessor volume *A Way of Seeing* (1970), spot-nourishment for the Mead following.

> *A review of "Margaret Mead: Some Personal Views," in* Kirkus Reviews, *Vol. XLVII, No. 13, July 1, 1979, p. 782.*

DORIS GRUMBACH

[*Aspects of the Present*, a] selection of a decade's worth (1969-1979) of Margaret Mead's Redbook essays, demonstrates the variety and depth of her interests: She cared passionately about the shape and direction of American culture (in the same way that she had cared in her anthropological studies about the cultures of the South Seas), about peace, the problems and rights of women, the survival of the American family, the health and education of children, about clean air, about the values of the American past and its rituals of celebration—Christmas, Halloween, the Bicentennial and other events.

But the most interesting of these thoughtful pieces (on which she collaborated with anthropologist and friend Rhoda Metraux) are the most radical ones. In 1927 she wrote: "The time has come, I think, when we must recognize bisexuality as a normal form of human behavior." At 74 her acute and sympathetic "way of seeing" (to use the title of her earlier collection of essays) made it possible for her to acknowledge "our human capacity to love members of both sexes." Her views on crime and punishment are equally "mind-expanding" (her term for changing traditional attitudes toward taboos and cultural beliefs). She writes: "We make our own criminals"—and later: "We have concentrated too much on criminals . . . instead of asking what needs they serve and what general attitudes in our society—or in the whole of modern society—are reflected in their actions." . . .

In *Blackberry Winter,* Margaret Mead's autobiography, she said: "I speak out of the experience of my own lifetime of seeing past and future as aspects of the present." This is exactly what she accomplished in her journalism: a rich and humane vision of the freedom possible in our lives.

> *Doris Grumbach, in a review of "Aspects of the Present," in* The New York Times Book Review, *July 27, 1980, p. 13.*

ALAN J. DeYOUNG

As every person reading this review would probably agree, Margaret Mead was surely one of the most cogent and respected cultural anthropologists to appear before the American public in this century. . . . One of the major problems when an important scholar goes public, however, is that the context of his work may become lost or blurred by both the community of scholars from whence the work originated, and by the larger public to whom most of the messages are addressed. While Margaret Mead was leagues ahead of most scholars who chose to educate non-specialists in the findings of their specialization, [*Margaret Mead: Some Personal Views*] does not accomplish this mission as much of her other work does. As the title suggests, the content of this book concerns primarily personal opinions. To be sure, much of what constitutes Dr. Mead's personal views can usually be traced to insight developed in her scholarly work. Unfortunately, the linkages between Dr. Mead's opinion and its basis in her cross-cultural studies are usually unclear in the series of brief positions developed in this book. . . .

[The] text is organized into eleven chapters which *Redbook* editors, and ostensibly Dr. Mead, found of special interest to its readers. These chapters include the titles: "Men and Women, Children, Parenthood, The Human Condition, Personal Choices," etc. As such titles suggest, the book is full of short cross-cultural vignettes and personal opinions which suggest Dr. Mead's insight, wit, and candor. Yet, for a scholarly audience, this series of vignettes and opinions beg many of the questions which many of us would like to be pursued. For example, one of the questions asked of Dr. Mead to which she responds in this collection concerns her opinion of the status of only children in modern American society. She responds by saying that only children may actually be happier and perhaps greater achievers as adults than children in larger families. While such an assessment seems quite plausible and even consistent with some research in social psychology, the context for Dr. Mead's response in the article seems to come as much from a description of her own daughter's feelings on this issue as it does from cross-cultural experience of the work of social scientists in other fields. One is left at the end of this one page response to the question with the impression that cultural anthropology can answer such a complex question in two paragraphs, rather than suggest a host of possibilities which is more the emphasis among contemporary anthropologists.

In addition to answering some very difficult questions a bit too superficially for many of us, there are also quite a few pages in this text devoted to questions which only readers of *Redbook* would find of great interest.

Whether or not Dr. Mead favored fluoridation of public water supplies, how much homework she thought was enough for high school students, or her opinion of international espionage certainly may interest a popular audience.

[It] is doubtful that those interested in a serious introduction to Dr. Mead's scholarly work would benefit by a discussion of such topics.

All in all, **Margaret Mead: Some Personal Views** is an interesting and entertaining piece. It clearly demonstrates those qualities of candor, humor and outspokenness which were trademarks of one of the greatest social scientific personalities to emerge in the United States. As a serious piece of work for consideration by a scholarly community, however, this book has important weaknesses. Read it to whet your appetite for Dr. Mead's more serious efforts, or read it to get a cross-cultural perspective to topics dealt with by Ann Landers. Don't read this piece to see the current status of cultural anthropology. . . .

> *Alan J. DeYoung, in a review of "Margaret Mead: Some Personal Views," in* Educational Studies, *Vol. 11, No. 3, Fall, 1980, pp. 270-71.*

ROBERT KANIGEL

[In 1928 *Coming of Age in Samoa* appeared]; critics of the day realized it was something more than just another dry anthropological treatise. "Warmly human, yet never sentimental, frank with the clean, clear frankness of the scientist," wrote one [see excerpt above from *The New York Times Book Review*, November 4, 1928]. For another, it was "an extraordinarily brilliant and, so far as I am aware, unique piece of work" [see excerpt above by George A. Dorsey].

What Mead was doing, she explained in a preface, was a kind of experiment, using the natural laboratory furnished by a primitive island culture: Were the *Sturm und Drang* of the teenage years, their nervousness and rebellion, inevitable? "Were these difficulties due to being adolescent," Mead wondered, "or to being adolescent in America?" And any society where familiar teen-age pathology was absent, she pointed out, would show nurture was responsible, not nature—culture, not genes.

But for 12 chapters, as Mead immerses her readers in the life of the island, this overarching question recedes to the background: We rise to the sound of cocks crowing, and to "the insistent roar of the reef." We watch boys going off to fish in their dugout canoes, girls looking after the smaller children, or weaving their mats. We encounter the odd, floating, ever-permeable Samoan household where, faced with even a breath of discontent, one just moves out of one thatched hut and into another nearby. We're treated to a chapter on the role of dance, the one area of island life where excellence is rewarded, not discouraged in the name of getting along. Finally, after dark, it's "under the palm trees," the indigenous euphemism for clandestine lovers not so clandestinely coupling.

We read a broad survey of this irresistibly charming culture. But it is a "survey"; it is anthropology, science, and occasionally does read like a journal article. . . . Such detached academic language is not typical; yet there's just enough of it to suggest that Mead didn't completely bridge the gap to "popular" writing.

Then comes Chapter 13. Abruptly, what had been merely interesting begins to glow, as if the author had been holding back, husbanding energy, like a baseball pitcher lazily warming up before the first high, hard one. . . .

[She] returns, almost triumphantly, and with liberated energies, to her original question . . . : Is the pathology of adolescence inevitable, or just an artifact of Western civilization? Well, she replies, if her carefree, well-adjusted Samoan girls are any measure, it's certainly *not* inevitable. . . .

Samoa is a more forgiving society than ours, Mead notes—a place where a "low-grade moron would not be hopelessly handicapped," and where those afflicted with "slight nervous instability" can get along just fine.

Suddenly, it's *Western* society that swings under her magnifying lens—nervous, chaotic, furiously paced. The 60 years since her work first appeared have left us even more nervous, and the lessons to be drawn from the gentle Samoans that much more telling.

> *Robert Kanigel, "ReReading," in* Los Angeles Times Book Review, *June 20, 1982, p. 2.*

ELIOT MARSHALL

Derek Freeman, an anthropologist at the University of Australia, set off some academic fireworks in February with a devastating critique of Margaret Mead's research on Samoa. . . .

The explosion burst on the front page of the *New York Times* in the form of a description of Freeman's book, due to be published by Harvard University Press in the spring. The book, it said, challenged the accuracy of Mead's work and could "intensify the often bitterly contested nature versus nurture controversy."

Freeman sharply criticizes the founders of American cultural anthropology—Franz Boas, Ruth Benedict, and Mead—and gives support to the opposing "biological" view which holds that hereditary factors are at least as important as culture in shaping human behavior. . . .

Thus Freeman has earned his instant notoriety on two counts: for debunking a prominent figure and rekindling the sociobiology furor. (p. 1042)

What is the quality of Freeman's evidence against Mead? "Massive," says Ernst Mayr, professor of zoology at Harvard and a distinguished analyst of Darwinian theory. He read Freeman's manuscript and urged Harvard to publish it. Princeton and Yale were also after the book. Perhaps one of the most critical reviewers is Bradd Shore, an anthropologist at Emory who last year published the results of his own fieldwork in Samoa. He says, "Freeman has a justly deserved reputation for being a meticulous scholar. I'm sure there aren't any mistakes in the facts." John Whiting, a distinguished Harvard anthropologist, says, "Freeman did a good job, but he clearly had the ax out for Margaret."

The only adamant skeptic is [anthropologist Lowell Holmes], who says, "Freeman includes all of my criticisms of Mead, but doesn't mention that I think her basic thesis is right: Samoa is an easier-going culture than ours." Holmes' case is particularly interesting because he was the first to make a thorough restudy of Mead's work, spending several years in Samoa. (pp. 1042-43)

The core of Freeman's argument is that Mead was ill prepared to do fieldwork when she decided to go to Samoa at the age of 23. She had just changed disciplines, leaving psychology to study under Franz Boas, Columbia's eminent professor of anthropology. Because she was inexperienced and ill trained, Freeman writes, what she saw in Samoa was not the real society that existed there, but a fictional one, elements of which were fixed in her imagination before she left New York.

As a consequence, Freeman believes, American anthropology has inherited a mistaken view of Samoa and, with it, the bias of Mead and her teachers—that human behavior can be analyzed sensibly without reference to human biology.

The most important bias Mead brought with her to Samoa, in Freeman's view, was her wish to find a "negative instance" that would disprove the concept that human nature follows universal patterns. This would bolster the antibiological outlook of her professor, Franz Boas, a life-long opponent of the eugenics movement. . . .

In the early 1920's, Freeman writes, Boas gave his students a new idea: someone should study adolescence to see whether any cultures produced behavior very different from the Western norm, which was a pattern of rebellion and turmoil. The research would involve sifting the biological from the cultural influences, a complex undertaking.

This was the task that Mead accepted, "an impossibly difficult problem to foist upon a graduate student as sparsely experienced" as she, Freeman writes. He points out that she was not fluent in Samoan; she spent only 9 months in the country; she lived with an American family the whole time; and village life was badly disrupted by a hurricane while she was there.

Freeman concludes that Mead, overwhelmed, opted for the simple way out and provided Boas with the observations that she thought would best fit his thesis. She reported that Samoan adolescence was very different from ours—sexually lax, unconstrained, and "the age of greatest ease." Mead found not only that adolescence was carefree, but that the entire Samoan ethos was casual. . . .

Freeman rebuts this portrait of Samoa with historical data and recent observations of his own in nine categories. It is enough to consider two: aggression and sexual mores. Mead wrote that the Samoans are "one of the most amiable, least contentious and most peaceful peoples in the world." She also claimed that they "never hate enough to want to kill anybody." Freeman cites accounts given by visitors to Samoa begining in 1787 and running through the police records of 1966. There were consistent reports of fights, affrays between villages, and murders. He calculates that the per capita rate of assault in Western Samoa during the mid-1960's was five times higher than that of the United States.

Mead's description of Samoan sexual customs was perhaps the most celebrated part of her book, certainly one that helped sales. The Samoans, she wrote, have the "sunniest and easiest attitudes towards sex," tolerating a period of free lovemaking among adolescents before marriage. "Marriages make no violent claim for fidelity," she wrote, and "jealousy, as a widespread social phenomenon, is very rare." Freeman says that on this, the most critical subject in her study, Mead got the picture exactly reversed. According to him, Samoa "is a society predicated on rank, in which female virgins are both highly valued and eagerly sought after." (p. 1043)

[Freeman] also describes the cult of virginity—the taupou system—as "central to the sexual mores of the Samoans" and "one of the principal characteristics of the cultures of Western as against Eastern Polynesia." This was the traditional practice of selecting girls to serve as taupou, or official virgins, an emblem of pride for the village they lived in. Taupou were married with great ceremony, but before consummation, they

were made to undergo a public trial of their virginity. (The trial disappeared as Christianity advanced in Samoa.) A taupou took great risks if she compromised her status, for angry villagers and relatives in some cases were said to have beaten taupou to death upon failure to pass the test of virginity.

Mead's explanation for these stories was that the taupou took on the "onus of virginity" for the whole adolescent female population, leaving the throng to be promiscuous. Freeman says just the opposite, that although taupou were of noble rank, every family aspired to follow the noble ideal.

Mead also wrote that a taupou could avoid embarrassment in her premarriage test simply by asking the officiating chief not to embarrass her. But then, the accounts of taupou being beaten seemed incongruous. Mead explained that this probably happened only when they failed to provide a little chicken blood for the ceremony or failed to warn the officials beforehand of their compromised status. . . .

This interpretation, Freeman writes, is a "travesty," and he calls the stories of adolescent promiscuity "fible-fables." He believes Mead was simply "duped" by the adolescents she interviewed. Embarrassed by her questions about sex, they may have decided to tell her entertaining stories. . . .

The cult of virginity made sexual relations difficult, not simple, Freeman concludes, and he closes his case with some data on rape. Many observers over the years have commented on the number of rapes in Samoa. Freeman cites this historical record and his own calculation that the incidence of forcible rape in Samoa in 1966 was twice that of the United States and 20 times that of England.

Even more common in Samoa is an unusual form of surreptitious rape, known as moetotolo or "sleep crawling," in which young men try to destroy the virginity of sleeping girls. If this is included, the incidence of rape, according to Freeman, rises to "one of the highest to be found anywhere in the world." This hardly bears out Mead's statement in 1938 that "the idea of forcible rape or of any sexual act to which both participants do not give themselves freely is completely foreign to the Samoan mind."

Despite its thoroughness, Freeman's book is unbalanced in a way. At the age of 66 and at the apex of his career, he is attacking the first work of a graduate student in anthropology, a pioneering study written almost 60 years ago. Why did Freeman wait until now to make this case? Freeman explains that he, Holmes, and others did point out some of Mead's errors in the 1950's and 1960's. She responded with a monograph in 1969 that partly defended *Coming of Age in Samoa* and partly conceded its shortcomings. . . .

Holmes, who broke off correspondence with Freeman in 1967 because of the offensive way he was investigating Mead's personal life in Samoa, still defends Mead's interpretation. While Samoans are sometimes violent, Holmes says, "I never heard of any rape. I never saw a fistfight in 4 years living there. Moetotolo never occurred in any village I was in, as far as I heard." Holmes cites an article he published in 1978 summarizing years of psychometric testing on the Samoans. "Again and again, on all different varieties of tests, the people come out as gentle, cooperative, low-key, and submissive." He is puzzled by the attention Freeman is getting. "There must be a hate-Mead club in America." . . .

Of course, Freeman is aiming to do more than simply refute Mead's portrait of Samoa. Throughout the text, he hints at ways in which Samoan behavior might be taken to illustrate biological mechanisms at work. In his final chapter, he makes a plea for "giving full cognizance to biology, as well as to culture" in order to prevent anthropology from becoming "isolated in a conceptual cul de sac." He believes that "anthropology in America is a schizophrenic system: you have cultural anthropologists and physical anthropologists, and they have nothing to do with one another." What is needed, he says, is more attention to human biology, cooperation between the disciplines, and far more sophisticated methods for analyzing the data. (pp. 1043-44)

> *Eliot Marshall, "A Controversy on Samoa Comes of Age," in* Science, *Vol. 219, No. 4588, March 4, 1983, pp. 1042-45.*

WARD GOODENOUGH

In the article "A controversy on Samoa comes of age" [see excerpt above]. . . , Eliot Marshall reviews questions that have been raised by the advance publicity given to Derek Freeman's book [*Margaret Mead and Samoa*], in which Freeman severely criticizes the work of Margaret Mead in Samoa and, I gather, what he considers to be the theoretical stance of cultural anthropology in the United States. Marshall suggests that cultural anthropology in America now faces the necessity of having to confront its current standards and practices relating to ethnographic research and also its theoretical emphasis on the cultural determination of human behavior.

The impression is conveyed that standards of ethnography have not changed since the 1920's and that Margaret Mead's work is typical of how ethnographic research is conducted. Neither impression could be farther from the truth. In more than 40 years as a student and teacher of cultural anthropology, I cannot recall Mead's *Coming of Age in Samoa* or *Social Organization of Manua* ever being cited as models of how ethnographic research ought to be done. (p. 906)

Whatever may be the popular repercussions of Derek Freeman's book, . . . Margaret Mead does not and never has exemplified for anthropologists the highest standards of ethnographic field research. Neither do the views she has expressed in regard to the role of culture versus biology in human behavior accurately reflect where anthropology stands today. Her contributions to science lie elsewhere. She raised important questions about things both scientists and the lay public were taking for granted about human behavior, namely, our own customary views regarding differences in the behavior of immigrants of different ethnic background, regarding the inherent nature of men and women, and regarding the behavior of adolescents. She raised these questions at a time when experiments in conditioning behavior by psychologists and the findings of clinical psychology and psychoanalysis were demonstrating a great deal about the degree to which behavior, even genetically programmed behavior, is affected by or is a product of experience. It was a time when it was appropriate to call attention to the enormous role of custom and tradition in structuring experience. That her own empirical research in connection with these questions was of questionable quality and that at times she overstated her case are minor matters compared with the role she played in raising these questions and stimulating others to examine them. Some of the great figures in the history of science have been, themselves, poor field or laboratory researchers but have inspired the kinds of questions that have helped to move the research enterprise along.

Margaret Mead also had the capacity to stimulate the lay public to look at things differently and to accept the idea that common assumptions about human nature needed to be questioned. It is for this reason, not their scientific accuracy, that her books have been widely used in introductory social science courses. They turned students on.

The lay public is now learning what professional anthropologists have long known about the quality of her early ethnographic fieldwork, done in her youth. It is inevitably an occasion for public excitement because, through the inspiring role she played, Margaret Mead had become a national institution by the end of her career. But there is no need, therefore, for scientists to conclude that there is a crisis in anthropology. The crisis is in the public's view of a public idol. (pp. 906, 908)

> *Ward Goodenough, "Margaret Mead and Cultural Anthropology," in* Science, *Vol. 220, No. 4600, May 27, 1983, pp. 906, 908.**

TODD G. BUCHHOLZ

Derek Freeman's refutation of one of the heroes of American academia [*Margaret Mead and Samoa: The Making and UnMaking of an Anthropological Myth*] has incited responses from many angry social scientists. The ensuing controversy has raised questions not just about the stature of Margaret Mead but about the mission of anthropology and the present-day implications of the debate over "nature versus nurture," or biology versus culture, that dominated anthropology during the first half of this century.

Freeman, professor of anthropology emeritus at the Australian National University, begins by telling the story of a bright young Margaret Mead who traveled to primitive Samoa in 1925 to discern whether Samoans were significantly similar or dissimilar in disposition to Western, "civilized" peoples. A student of Franz Boas, professor at Columbia University and leader of the school of cultural determinism, Miss Mead was in fact searching for proof of so great a variety in human life as to make untenable the notion of a universal human nature. She was looking, writes Freeman, for a single "negative instance"—for

> in anthropology you only have to show once that it is possible for a culture to make, say, a period of life easy, where it is hard everywhere else, to have made your point.

Miss Mead's specific goal was to expose a negative instance in adolescent life. (p. 78)

Freeman, who spent time in Western Samoa as a graduate student in the 1940's and again years later, proceeds to erase her negative instance from the anthropological ledger. The contrast between Mead's and Freeman's findings is startling. . . .

In two hundred pages Freeman grabs, tears, and shreds Margaret Mead's research to pieces. To be sure, he is not the first to dispute her findings. Many Samoans, in fact, have called Miss Mead a liar. Freeman brands this "an interpretation that I have no hesitation in dismissing." Instead, he terms her illprepared, her research casual. For example, she apparently had not read previous reports on Samoa, although "the institutions and traditions . . . had . . . been very extensively documented long before Mead first set foot on Ta'u in 1925." Moreover, she spent only nine months, did not live with a Samoan family, and did not speak the native language. Since she was working with what she termed "primitive groups," she assumed their ways of life "were simple enough to be grasped quickly." Her conclusions about Samoan sex were based largely on conversations with a small sample of girls. Freeman, who speaks the language fluently, surmises that the girls may have teased Miss Mead with stories of easy and expert intercourse.

Freeman's critique of Margaret Mead's methods is solid, and one is tempted to regard it as closing the case for cultural determinism. But his own techniques are not quite exemplary, either. Rather than focusing solely on the particular group of Samoans (on the island of Ta'u) who provided Mead's negative instance, Freeman assumes that all Samoan tribes are alike . . . and then he compounds the error by ignoring time differences in gathering data (he finds "no reason to suppose that Samoan society and behavior changed in any fundamental way during the fourteen years between 1926, the year of the completion of Mead's inquiries, and 1940, when I began my own observations of Samoan behavior. . . .") As several critics have pointed out, British Western Samoa, where Freeman went as a student, is two hundred miles away from Ta'u, and there are significant historical and political differences between them.

Still, even if one eliminates all of the data adduced from other Samoan islands, Freeman does provide enough testimony to argue convincingly the case against pure cultural determinism: coming of age in Samoa is not that different from coming of age in, say, San Francisco. The idea of a universal human nature is rescued from Margaret Mead's "negative instance." (p. 79)

Todd G. Buchholz, "Cultural Determinism," in Commentary, *Vol. 77, No. 1, January, 1984, pp. 78-80.*

Ved (Parkash) Mehta

1934-

Indian-born American autobiographer, nonfiction writer, essayist, novelist, and scriptwriter.

Mehta is best known for his autobiographical works, most of which were originally published in *The New Yorker*, where he has been a staff writer since the early 1960s. Blind since the age of three, Mehta has written extensively about his childhood in India and his years at the Arkansas State School for the Blind, where his father sent him when he was fifteen. Mehta writes with warmth, humor, and insight of the people and places he has known. He is also widely respected for his works on social, political, and intellectual figures and trends. Reviewers admire Mehta's success in overcoming the obstacles of blindness and praise his accomplished prose style.

Mehta gained recognition with the publication of his first book, *Face to Face* (1957), an account of his childhood in India and his experiences at the Arkansas school. Critics were impressed by his considerable literary talents and by his refusal to let his blindness hinder him. In *Walking the Indian Streets* (1960), Mehta recounts his return to India after college and his travels there with a friend. Mehta's next autobiographical work, *Daddyji* (1972), focuses on his father's life and ends with the author's departure at the age of five for a school for the blind in Bombay. Mehta's mother is the central character of *Mamaji* (1979). In *Vedi* (1982) Mehta describes his life at the Bombay school. His most recent autobiographical volume, *The Ledge between the Streams* (1984), chronicles Mehta's life between his return home from a short stay at the Bombay school and his departure for America at age fifteen.

Mehta's books on intellectual and political topics are also acclaimed. *Fly and the Fly-Bottle: Encounters with British Intellectuals* (1963) records Mehta's conversations with leading British historians and philosophers. In *The New Theologian* (1966) Mehta explores contemporary movements in theology through interviews with eminent figures in the field. *Portrait of India* (1970), the first of four books on the changing social and political situation in India, presents a disturbing picture of conditions in that country. *Mahatma Gandhi and his Apostles* (1977) is considered an important work in the vast amount of literature on Gandhi. In this book Mehta attempts to portray Gandhi as a fallible, somewhat eccentric human being and assesses his impact on India. *The New India* (1978) centers on the first term of Indira Gandhi's leadership and her defeat in 1977, which Mehta saw as a victory for the common people of India. In *A Family Affair: India under Three Prime Ministers* (1982) Mehta discusses India's political climate under Morarji Desai, Charan Singh, and Indira Gandhi.

Mehta has also written a novel, *Delinquent Chacha* (1967), about an eccentric elderly Indian, and a filmscript, *Chachaji, My Poor Relation*, based on this novel. *The Photographs of Chachaji* (1980) recounts the filming of this story for British television.

(See also *Contemporary Authors*, Vols. 1-4, rev. ed. and *Contemporary Authors New Revision Series*, Vol. 2.)

© Jerry Bauer

GERALD W. JOHNSON

Ved Mehta is only twenty-three years old and totally blind, but he has already accomplished something in the world. Although a native of Gujrat, in India, and a Hindu, he has given to an American educational institution an honorable eminence it had never achieved before. This is the Arkansas State School for the Blind, which took Mehta in when all other American institutions had refused him, and liberated him from the prison of blindness so successfully that he was able to go on to Pomona College in California, where he graduated as a Phi Beta Kappa and won a scholarship at Balliol College of Oxford University where he is now.

It is extraordinary when a man at twenty-three has the material for an autobiography that deserves the serious attention of the intelligent, and still more extraordinary when a man so young can present his material in an arresting fashion. But [as he shows in *Face to Face*] Mr. Mehta has both material and ability, which means that the Arkansas school has the distinction of having released a powerful mind that under other circumstances probably would never have developed more than a small fraction of its strength.

A little over half of the book is devoted to a blind boy's life in modern India. Ved Mehta's father was a physician who had taken his medical training in England and returned to become an official of the Public Health Service. It was therefore an upper-class household, though not of the princely group, nor of the wealthy commercial group. At the age of three the boy contracted meningitis which destroyed his vision, but left him physically sound otherwise. The affliction came so early that he has no memory of sight, which he considers is an advantage, rather than the reverse, because he is free from the regretful memories that haunt those who once could see.

Blind or not, he has drawn a picture of Indian family life that is vivid in the extreme. His father's official duties included constant tours of inspection on which he sometimes took Ved along; and through touch, taste, hearing and smell the boy acquired an experience of Indian life far beyond the narrow circle of the family. . . .

When the boy was between fourteen and fifteen the doctor was stationed at Lahore, a city that at the time of partition went to Pakistan; the Mehtas, being Hindus, lost everything and became refugees. The story of the riots and subsequent life among the displaced persons is matter-of-fact and all the more moving on that account.

The American section follows and is difficult to describe. No other foreigner has written about the United States in quite this style. There is neither eulogy nor denunciation in it. The Arkansas school was poorly equipped and under-staffed. Life there was far from luxurious and instruction was not always of the best. Fanaticism, racial and religious, intruded once or twice. All this Mehta noted and set down precisely. He closes that episode without any extravagance of any kind. But one thing they did have—excellent instructors to teach the blind how to move about confidently. So there he was liberated, physically and mentally, and there is no doubt that he knows it.

He writes of Pomona College and the rest of his American experience coolly, exactly, never hesitating to mention what he did not like, yet in it all is the tension of strong emotion. It is a young man writing about his home. He wastes no time in effusive thanks because he assumes that anybody must know that he is grateful. This reticence is a higher compliment to the country than any other he could pay.

He goes back to India, after a couple of years at Oxford, not knowing what he will do. He has been warned that he will be a maladjusted person, doomed to suffer bitter disappointment, neither an oriental nor an occidental. That is not news to him. He has already suffered many disappointments and his affliction has always made him maladjusted; but he seems to have realized that the maladjusted person who does not become embittered and inert is a powerhouse. He effects changes, he gets things done. His book leaves you guessing, but its fine quality is that you are guessing with a high heart.

> *Gerald W. Johnson, "From India Came a Sightless Man with a Clear Vision," in* New York Herald Tribune Book Review, *August 18, 1957, p. 6.*

HERBERT L. MATTHEWS

Ved Mehta plays an extraordinary trick on his prospective readers and on anyone who does not know about him or has not read his previous book, *Face to Face.* Mr. Mehta, a Punjabi Hindu, now 25 years old, has been completely blind since the age of 3. He has written [*Walking the Indian Streets*] about his return to India after ten years' absence as if he had normal vision.

His publishers carefully play the game, saying nothing on the jacket blurb to indicate that the author is blind. Even in the half-dozen quotations from reviews of Ved Mehta's first book, *Face to Face,* they allow no word to appear that would show the book was a moving, sensitive, perceptive account of a blind Hindu boy's childhood in India and schooling in the United States. The normally tragic fact of blindness and the remarkable way in which Ved overcame it to make a fruitful, tender and gay life for himself is what gave *Face to Face* its quality and its soul.

Now Ved Mehta has written a book about his experiences in Delhi, Calcutta and Katmandu in Nepal as if he were just another bright, gay, frivolous youth going back to his family and his struggling nation and to come away after a year, chastened and thoughtful, with a faith in India's future that seems more than anything to have been given to him by some hours spent with that most wonderful of Indians, Jawaharlal Nehru.

Mr. Mehta is doing in this book what he does in life. He asks no quarter and he lives, in so far as it is humanly possible, as if he could see. Knowing he is blind, we can only regard this work as an astonishing tour de force. Read as a continuation of the autobiographical *Face to Face,* it is fascinating to see Ved Mehta's reactions on being confronted with the new India he left as a schoolboy of 15.

As a book of, by and about Ved Mehta it holds continual interest. As a book about contemporary India one must sorrowfully record that it tells little that is new, important or significant. How could it be otherwise? Mr. Mehta has learned to minimize his handicap amazingly, but it naturally remains a severe handicap. The author has tried to do the impossible.

Anyone reading the book simply as an account of India today by a young Hindu in possession of all his faculties will get an entertaining and touching work with flashes of deep insight. It is deliberately keyed to an almost frivolous and cynical gaiety, with the serious and genuine emotions the author experiences hidden under a veneer of indirection, understatement and mockery. . . .

Ved Mehta handicaps himself doubly in *Walking the Indian Streets.* He cannot help his blindness and has, indeed, turned it by a miracle of will power and courage into something resembling an asset, but he could not hope to write a book about India as if he were not blind.

He has done so, and it would be unfair to say that, even taken at its face value, this book is a failure. Mr. Mehta had his family roots in India and spent his childhood there. He speaks some of the languages and applies a brilliant, thoughtful mind to what he hears and learns. "A bummy month" . . . is spent with his friend, Dom Moraes, son of the famous Bombay editor and author, Frank Moraes. They "see" Delhi and Calcutta like college tourists on a binge and hence they do not really see these extraordinary cities. Ved touches the heart of India in talks with the old family tailor and, most of all, with Premier Nehru.

So it is a book about India, but it is better to read it as a book about Ved Mehta.

> *Herbert L. Matthews, "A Native's Homecoming," in* The New York Times Book Review, *August 21, 1960, p. 14.*

MARCUS CUNLIFFE

What we hear about [in *Fly and the Fly-Bottle: Encounters with British Intellectuals*] are the views, habits and personalities of two groups of British intellectuals—philosophers and historians. They turn out to be mostly Oxford people, though the author looks in at Cambridge to see the historians Herbert Butterfield and E. H. Carr, finds much material in London (the headquarters of Arnold Toynbee), and even goes to Utrecht to seek out the Dutch scholar, Pieter Geyl. In general, and perhaps rightly, Oxford is the focus of Mr. Mehta's interviews. . . .

Mr. Mehta is a deft interviewer. He tells us what the people he meets look like, how their voices sound, what they eat and drink, what books they have on their shelves. He uses his dialogues to present, with wit, economy and an air of authenticity, several complicated concepts and controversies. Thus we are given a lucid digest of Oxford's linguistic approaches to philosophy, and of other approaches such as those of A. J. Ayer and Stuart Hampshire. . . .

Certain doubts persist, at any rate in my mind. Mr. Mehta's method is highly effective, and the interview is becoming almost a characteristic art form of our time. But in its very nature it raises difficulties. Is it always accurate? How prominent a part ought the interviewer to play?

Mr. Mehta supplements his records of conversations with quotations from printed work, and he is certainly far less unjust (or malicious) about the scholars he meets than some of them are about one another. Even so, I am bothered by the kind of off-the-cuff anthology that emerges. More important, it would be a pity if this book unwittingly conveyed the impression that intellectuals as a whole are odious and futile, or that British intellectuals exhibit unpleasant forms.

Mr. Mehta has not said this and clearly does not mean to say it. But he expresses some dismay at the constricted nature of the zones of controversy, the intermixture of personal antipathies, and the circularity of some of the arguments. The intellectual activity is always on the edge of silliness because it must always push ideas to their limits. To define, to refine, to generalize is to risk sounding fussy, eccentric, ingrown; and linguistic philosophy is among the most vulnerable of such types of inquiry.

So, too, for the unhistorical, are disputes about history. What does it *matter* whether the Tudor gentry were on the way up or on the way down? But what are the consequences of not caring? Only a hair, Omar Khayyam speculates, "perhaps divides the False and True." The intellectual must always seek that hair and having found it proceed to split it. His pursuits, as Mr. Mehta on the whole brilliantly suggests, are pursuits in more than one sense: he chases that which is bound to elude him.

> Marcus Cunliffe, "Inquisitory Interviews," in The New York Times Book Review, *August 18, 1963, p. 12.*

DAVID CAUTE

When the earliest of the separate chapters which comprise Mr. Mehta's new book [*Fly and the Fly-Bottle*] originally appeared in the *New Yorker,* the despair which at first typified the reaction of his victims soon gave way to collective common-room outrage, and belated appeals for fair play to menacing talk of libel. But neither Mr. Mehta nor the spirit of inquiry

is easily deterred. Having, more in sorrow than in anger, dispatched Oxford philosophers, he returned to the scene of the crime and proceeded to wreak havoc among the more distinguished protagonists of recent historical controversies. Discarding his rapier for a bludgeon, he resorted now to overt mayhem, cracking down on renowned skulls as a prelude to the cannibalistic munching of jagged bone and raw flesh.

From what particular standpoint the author delivers his judgments (often implicit, but usually lethal) remains a matter for not very profitable conjecture. If he harbours a distinct credo of his own, beyond the conventional wisdom of that elastic organ the *New Yorker,* then we, his readers, have not been asked to shoulder its burden. Himself a Balliol man, he is evidently familiar enough with the English academic ethos to understand it, while being sufficiently detached both in spirit and in situation (he now lives in New York) to dissect impartially its more fanciful excursions into the realm of the absurd. And if the first person singular of Mr. Mehta's second autobiographical book, *Walking the Indian Streets,* has imperceptibly shed some of its commitment to Balliol, the mysteries of Blackwell's and the charm of the men's garment vendors of the Turl, then it would be churlish to complain; a fixed point of reference is, after all, the mark of a pedant, and the streets of Oxford no less than those of Delhi demand a certain detachment of the disinterested observer. Alienation grows poorly out of the soil of unequivocal admiration. . . .

Mr. Mehta has interviewed a considerable number of eminent philosophers and historians, and if it has proved beyond his range (and whose range is it not beyond?) to read all their works, he has at least fashioned a series of workable syntheses out of second-hand opinions and casual gossip. But if we are dull enough to regard truth as the objective narration of events in a logically related context, if our wish to understand can compete with our pleasure at being entertained, then I fear that Mr. Mehta can only provide us with a transparent, if intelligent, example of literary post-impressionism. (p. 424)

[It] would be useful to know under what guise the interrogator presented himself on each separate occasion. But Mr. Mehta does not tell us. Balliol man though he may be, he is ambiguous about the nature of his sources. Yet he is a phenomenally quick and acute observer, marvellously adept at grasping and conveying the essence of a personality as it might appear in the first twenty minutes of a direct confrontation. As for those heroes who are now dead (Wittgenstein, Namier, Tawney), one can only admire his subtle use of varied reminiscences, his ability to suggest the shape and weight of the gravestone supporting the multi-coloured wreaths. (pp. 424-25)

Mr. Mehta's philosophers emerge (and rightly so) with distinctly more credit than his historians. The amateur (a term which embraces both Mr. Mehta and myself) is inclined, when allowing himself the luxury of a broad survey, to regard philosophy as a residual subject whose major revolutions take the form of capitulations, whose permanent advances are effected only when one of the sciences can justly claim as its own a province of knowledge previously regarded as a field for pure speculation. Consequently, if the kingdom of philosophy must constantly accommodate itself to diminishing frontiers, one is apt to sympathise with the philosophers who confine their attentions to the meaning of words and the meaning of meaning, to the bastions, in short, which show the greatest promise of impregnability. And yet the distressing incompetence of our practising historians in their efforts to travel happily from the particular to the general, from the cause of one thoroughly

examined event to the question of the laws of historical causation, reveals how disastrous this withdrawal of our philosophy
into its inner shell has been. The streams of narrow specialis-
ation flow ever wider apart. . . .

Also, one must agree with [Mr. Mehta] that the historians have
hashed up their chances. Few first-year undergraduates would
allow themselves to father some of the tendentious trivia we
have had to suffer over the last few years. (p. 425)

If this is true, it must be acknowledged that Mr. Mehta himself
has not shrunk from adding another straw to the haystack of
legend and libel which by now buries the real issues at stake.
Brilliant in his handling of men, he is less at ease with their
ideas.

All in all, however, *Fly and the Fly-bottle* is a small bomb.
While some of the anger it will invoke may be justified, some
will surely spring from a sinking sense of chilled recognition.
Often Mr. Mehta has caught dons with their trousers down, or
persuaded them to undress, while seeming to admire the em-
broidery on their invisible gowns. Talented, perceptive and
fertile of imagination as he is, he has on this occasion too often
forgotten that subjective truth and its objective first cousin do
not always marry well. And if his true province lies with the
former, he may yet, as a short-story writer and novelist with
a remarkable command of language and the insights of an artist,
travel rapidly from the realm of necessity to the realm of freedom. (p. 426)

> *David Caute, "High Table and Low," in* The Spec-
> tator, *Vol. 211, No. 7058, October 4, 1963, pp.
> 424-26.*

ANTHONY KENNY

Four years ago Ved Mehta published *Fly and the Flybottle,*
account of contemporary philosophers and historians. Philosophers of my acquaintance thought the book not quite accurate
about philosophy, but very entertaining about the historians.
Historians cautioned me about the historical parts, but were
glad to see the philosophers exposed for what they were.

In his latest book [*The New Theologian*] . . . , Ved Mehta has
not taken the precaution of splitting the opposition. This time
he deals entirely with theologians, taking as his starting point
the Bishop of Woolwich's book *Honest to God.* He describes
the controversy over that book, reproducing in some detail the
arguments of MacIntyre and Jenkins designed to convict the
Bishop of atheism. The main part of *The New Theologian* is
based on three sets of interviews with theologians in the United
States, in England, and Germany. . . .

The virtues and vices of the book will be familiar to readers
of Ved Mehta's earlier work. Brisk summaries of the theologians' doctrines alternate with vivid descriptions of their hab-
itats. The records of the interviews are enlivened by the author's
unique talent for reproducing idiosyncrasies of speech rhythm.
But the reader is encouraged to feel that he has learnt more
than he really has about what these men stand for. He is tempted
to feel that he need not take the Archbishop of Canterbury
seriously because he comes out with quintuples of 'yes'es, and
to feel that he has Bultmann and Barth placed when he learns
that one wore grey pinstripe and the other liked snails.

The interview treatment seems to me fairest when dealing with
those writers whose reputation is based mainly on popular
pamphlets or television interviews; it seems extremely unfair

to serious scholars like Barth and Bultmann. In this book perhaps the fairest and fullest account is contained in the biography
of Bonhoeffer; the method is seen at its worst in the treatment
of Reinhold Niebuhr. We are given an account of a brief conversation in which Niebuhr criticised Tillich for other-world-
liness. But most of what is said about Niebuhr consists of
trivial details. . . .

> *Anthony Kenny, "Instant Theology," in* New States-
> man, *Vol. 73, No. 1876, February 24, 1967, p. 264.**

JOHN WAIN

[The central character of *Delinquent Chacha*] is a feeble-minded
posturer, devious without having the strength of character to
be definitely criminal, rather like an Indian version of Isherwood's Mr. Norris. "*Chacha*," we learn on the first page, is
Hindustani for "uncle," and the book is narrated by the nephew
who watches in horrified fascination as Delinquent Chacha acts
out the farcically tragic pattern of his delusions. To him, the
British Raj was India's golden hour; since 1945 everything has
declined; bereft of British example, the Indians are a mere
rabble, etc., etc. The nephew goes to England to attend Oxford
University; Delinquent Chacha manages to follow him there.
This should be the opening of an amusing story, but opportunity
after opportunity is missed, till the reader is driven to conclude
that Mr. Mehta, a lively enough writer in other forms, has no
flair for the novel. He has created an interesting comic character, but seems unable to set him in motion in a story. The
book opens in India, but immediately leaves it, so that we get
no impression of Indian life, and we certainly get no impression
of England; in spite of the years he spent there, Mr. Mehta
has no ear for the way English people talk. . . .

Delinquent Chacha, with his worship of everything English
and his romantic obsession with "Ox-Ford," is absurd, but he
is absurd in a vacuum; there is no firm position, either Eastern
or Western, against which his flutterings are silhouetted. The
nephew, who might at least have had the attitudes of a Westernized Indian, is given no character at all and remains a mere
hole in the story. Like *A Passage to India,* the book pivots on
a long trial scene, but in Mr. Mehta's hands the scene, for lack
of wit and observation, has no reality and fails to rise to that
authentic nightmare quality which all good trial scenes have.
The story folds in on itself and collapses into boredom; a pity,
because the opening fifty pages are not without fresh and amusing passages.

> *John Wain, "The Way of Some Flesh," in* The New
> York Review of Books, *Vol. VIII, No. 12, June 29,
> 1967, p. 28.**

BERNARD D. NOSSITER

At a durbar in Gangtok, where the former Hope Cooke is first
lady, a Sikkimese politician whispered to Ved Mehta: "You've
lived in America. We have an American Gyalmo. My question
is this: If there is a war between Sikkim and India, will America
fight on Sikkim's side? I would like your opinion."

Innocent and aggressive, ingenuous and faintly sinister, the
query epitomizes the subcontinent that Mehta has rediscovered
[in *Portrait of India*]. It is a riot of contradiction, a mixture of
ascetic withdrawal and irritated sensibility, pathetic, proud and
frequently absurd. The unreal remark is precisely the sort of
illuminating quote that Mehta, with his sensitive ear, repeatedly
catches.

He has escaped the trauma of many of the brightest Western-educated Indians, paralyzed by an unresolved struggle between the values and manners of their birthplace and those of the newer world in which they live and work. Mehta, however, responds to this dilemma, even in its slightest form. His sympathy reflects a rare synthesis, an attitude that draws strength from both his heritage and the insights of his adopted culture. . . .

In the best *New Yorker* tradition, he adopts a neutral stance. His *Portrait,* really an impressionist arrangement of brush strokes, loosely strings together the disparate accounts he wrote for the magazine. It is as deliberately formless and themeless as the complex subcontinent.

Mehta, however, deftly permits an implicit theme to emerge, that whatever one says of India its opposite is equally true. He reports on the deeply religious impulse animating the great crowd of pilgrims at the Khumba mela in Allahabad and finds himself immersed in the sacred confluence of the Ganges and the Jumna; he also tells of the shocking cruelty that drowned hundreds in the crush there twelve years earlier. He discovers a few genuine saints. However, they are more likely to look like Jayaprakash Narayan, who abandoned politics to help landless laborers, than the self-advertised brand, like the giggling Maharishi. . . .

Nowhere does Mehta hint at his own burden, total blindness since childhood. Somehow, he has converted this into a writer's asset, an ear that misses little of consequence and an emotional imagination that brings him close to a patronizing district commissioner in Nagaland, inhibited coeds at a "modern" university, the crass movie stars of Bombay.

Mehta suggests that, like Narayan, he is troubled by Indians' lack of "community sense," a social discipline that is a prerequisite for development. But more often than not, he expresses an unobtrusive pride in his country's struggle to escape from misery, a sentiment that sometimes leads to dubious judgments. . . .

Urbane and urban, Mehta has little to say about the villages where four of five Indians live. He traveled to Bihar and Orissa during the great drought, but there is no report of what he found. These are minor signs of commission and omission; however. Far more important is what he has accomplished, a brilliant collection of sketches that make accessible a remarkably impenetrable world. And all of this is rendered in an effortless prose that marks a skilled and painstaking craftsman.

> Bernard D. Nossiter, *"Whatever Can Be Said of India, the Opposite Also Is True," in* Book World— Chicago Tribune, *May 10, 1970, p. 6.*

MERVYN JONES

A recurrent Indian phenomenon is a storm of indignation over a book—not because it is 'obscene', as in this country, but because it is 'an insult to India'. The main flashpoints in recent years have been V. S. Naipaul's *An Area of Darkness* and Ronald Segal's *The Crisis of India*. . . . What the Indians are really saying is that it's high time for someone to write a sympathetic book about their country. By this I don't mean, and nor do they, a laudatory book; I mean a book whose author tries to feel as Indians feel about their manifold problems.

There may not be a storm about [Mr Mehta's *Portrait of India*]. His view of India is by and large depressing, and he scratches

at the sensitive spots like Kashmir and Nagaland, but it would be unjust to call him hostile. Anyway, his book is far too boring to generate excitement. No Indian and no friend of India, however, could plod through these 520 pages without disappointment. . . . Mr Mehta is a writer and scholar of some renown: he has his roots in India, though he has lived in the West since the age of 15; he spent 'many months' in the country gathering material for his book, he was able to meet anyone from the Prime Minister downward, and one can gauge the advantages extended to him from the fact that he was allowed to visit the normally closed areas on the Chinese frontier. The book does indeed contain a great deal of information. . . . But a portrait is precisely what it is not. Reaching the end, one has a curious sense of emptiness. India must be somewhere, but it isn't here.

One fairly important defect is that the book is significantly out of date. Mr Mehta was in India in 1966, and tells us in detail about events which preceded his visit and which he has to recount from old press-cuttings, such as the Kashmir riots of 1964—events which, as in this case, had no lasting consequences. There is even a chapter about the old Nizam of Hyderabad, which any journalist would have tossed into the wastebasket when the Nizam died. We are told about the monsoon failure and food shortage which dominated the scene in 1966, but nothing about the green revolution and the bumper crops which in more recent years have transformed the overall food situation (if not the condition of the poor). Facts and figures are based on 1963 or 1964 statistics, described as 'the latest available'. . . . I fail to see why Mr Mehta, whose note of acknowledgements is dated October 1969, couldn't have used 1968 statistics. One might not complain about this if Mr Mehta were not so keen on seeking an effect of breathless immediacy; he is fond of the word 'today', often uses the historic present, and several times prints his rough notes as if he had no time to turn them into connected prose. A dated quality in the impressions and even the facts might be compensated by a reflective note in discussion, but this we never get.

I have to say, moreover, that I do not trust Mr Mehta's visual descriptions. There is nothing to be ashamed of in being blind, and Mr Mehta would not be the first blind writer to achieve a remarkable power of perception. But phrases like 'an elfin face', 'unevenly dyed hair', and 'a sly smile' are descriptive in a way that can only be derived from sight. Necessarily, they are personal; a smile that looks sly to me may look shy or intelligent to you. One must deduce that someone smiled, and some third person (unidentified) told Mr Mehta that the smile was sly. No writer has the right to offer the reader observations which appear to be his own, and are not.

So much for method. As for the content, the immense vacancy in the book is that it tells us nothing about the India where 80 per cent of the people live—rural India. As we are led from Delhi to Bombay to Calcutta to Madras, we must ask how anyone could spend many months in the country without placing the emphasis where it so manifestly belongs. (pp. 380, 382)

The distortion in the book, therefore, is the same as in the impressions of the average visitor, who sees India at its two extremes. The visitor naturally meets well-to-do Indians who speak English, and who (depending on his contacts) may include politicians, businessmen, officials, artists and intellectuals. The visitor also sees beggars, destitutes, and people who sleep in the streets, who strike him with a sense of shock and confirm what he has heard about 'starving India'. Perhaps he goes to the Home for the Dying in Calcutta, which is now well established in the semi-journalistic circuit and predictably gets a chapter in *Portrait of India*. The truth is that India is an extremely complex society. Many people (roughly a third of the total) live in abject misery and hunger, but many more are grappling with varying success with a range of social, economic and cultural problems. Most of the latter, as well as most of the former, are in the villages. The corpse by the roadside is a part of India, but the village hospital and the peasant co-operative are a part of India too. This is what I mean by sympathy—an understanding of effort and contest in Indian life, not merely of difficulty and despair. Without this, there can be no portrait. (p. 382)

> *Mervyn Jones, "Empty Canvas," in* New Statesman, *Vol. 80, No. 2062, September 25, 1970, pp. 380, 382.*

PAUL SCOTT

Ved Mehta closes [*Daddyji*] at the moment when he himself was thrust crying through a window of the Frontier Mail on the railway station at Lahore. That was in 1939. He was not quite five. He was dressed in a yellow suit and was on his way to an American mission school for the blind in Bombay.... In this scene we get a glimpse of the writer-in-embryo, of the young Mehta already lighting his dark landscape of memory and desire with recollections and impressions, with details built up from chance remarks, and transforming it through a mysterious alchemy of his own into a vivid picture of astonishing depth.

Since the publication of his first experiment in autobiography, *Face to Face,* he has avoided making any reference to his physical disability and has not seemed to welcome conjecture about the methods he uses to achieve his extraordinary visual effects, which even from a sighted man would be outstanding. But in *Daddyji,* which glows with the light and colours of India, the blindness is once again admitted....

[Here] is Mehta senior, affectionately but objectively observed and celebrated in a short book which, beautifully balanced and judged, tells us far more about the individual experience and ambitions of middle-class Indians than many a studious work several times its length. Mehta senior, who read medicine in Lahore, London, the United States and, of all places, Sardinia, and gave up the chance to practise in England (which he adored) for the very Hindu reason that other members of the family had to have their chance of a western education, was the main span in the bridge which his father Lalaji ... threw across the notorious gulf separating east and west, thereby linking the Punjabi village where the Mehtas originated with the island of Manhattan where Lalaji's grandson has been a respected contributor to the *New Yorker* this past 12 years.

Conceived as a series of cameos of village and urban family life from the end of the last century to the end of the first 40 years of this, *Daddyji,* intimate, personal, is as well a history of modern India in the making. This is a country where the cow lies down quite happily with the computer, and in his especially tender and dispassionate way, Mr Mehta tells us why.

> *Paul Scott, "Lighting the Dark Landscape of Memory," in* The Times, London, October 19, 1972, p. 10.

LEONARD A. GORDON

Having experienced the scenes of India's partition (movingly chronicled in *Face to Face*) and Gandhi's call for nonviolence at a time of communal war, Mehta has recently visited close disciples of Gandhi including some who are attempting to carry on the Mahatma's work a generation after his assassination. The first and third parts of [*Mahatma Gandhi and His Apostles*] consist almost entirely of quotations from interviews with these disciples. From these quotations a vivid picture of Gandhi is created, and that is about all one can say for this book. The middle part is a pedestrian summary of chapters from Gandhi's autobiography interlaced with a few quotations from standard biographies of Gandhi by B. R. Nanda and Louis Fischer, as well as from the more interpretive works of Erik H. Erikson and N. K. Bose.

Mehta mocks the gargantuan efforts of those who are now compiling Gandhi's collected writings and the work of his last secretary and official biographer, Pyarelal. These official memorialists do approach Gandhi with reverence, but they also perform the valuable function of preserving and editing material. They should not be lightly dismissed by so slight a scholar as Mehta, who seems not to have consulted even a fraction of the relevant documents. His disregard for historical sources other than a few interviews and secondary books leads to numerous errors about the history of the period from 1920 to 1947. Mehta does not know the objectives and organization of the Non-co-operation movement of 1921-22, the political role of Gandhi in the 1930s, nor the split in the Marxist camp during World War II. (p. 26)

The small contribution of this book is in the quotations from the disciples. From these the flesh-and-blood Gandhi, particularly the personal man, steps forth. We hear anew of Gandhi's experiments with food, sexual discipline and basic hygiene. The late C. Rajagopalachari, one of the most intelligent Gandhians and a leader in his own right, told Mehta that Gandhi was one of the hungriest and most highly sexed men he had known. This simple but accurate statement helps to untangle the Mahatma's rationalizations for his rigid dietary rules and his endless arrangements for sexual temptations to prove his purity.

Mehta has spent so much time with the private Gandhi, fascinated like his subject with food, sex and hygiene, that we learn almost nothing about the man's great appeal and political skills. Since Mehta is concerned with the impact and memory of Gandhi, he might have investigated the varied responses to the Mahatma among different groups and regions in Indian society. (pp. 26-7)

> *Leonard A. Gordon, "The Marginal View," in* The Nation, *Vol. 225, No. 1, July 2, 1977, pp. 26-8.**

JOHN GRIGG

[In *Mahatma Gandhi and His Apostles,* Ved Mehta] has written about the officially acclaimed father of the Indian nation, and the result is an outstanding book, which rescues Gandhi from the dead hand of the hagiographers, without offering him as a human sacrifice to trendy cynics and debunkers.

Interview is one of Mr Mehta's favourite techniques, and he uses it extensively in this book. The first chapter consists of a long and meticulous description of Gandhi's daily routine at his Sevagram *ashram,* near Wardha, based upon the recollections of an unnamed female apostle who travelled with the author through the villages of central India. This brings Gandhi to life in all his sublimity and crankiness.

Next, by a fine stroke of art, Mr Mehta introduces us to the contemporary Gandhi cult and to some of its high priests. We visit the Gandhi Cremation Ground, the Gandhi Exhibition, the Gandhi National Memorial Museum, the Gandhi Peace Foundation and the offices of the Collected Works of Mahatma Gandhi (which occupy about 30 rooms of a large government building). We meet Gandhi's chief secretary, Pyarelal, who is writing his master's life at stupendous length and can hardly hope to complete it. How strange, Mr Mehta reflects, that one 'who lived in such starkly simple circumstances should be so encumbered after death'.

The opening section of the book ends with chapters entitled 'Family' and 'Benefactors'. In the latter, there is a fascinating interview with the octogenarian, G. D. Birla, who was one of Gandhi's chief financial backers, and in whose garden he was assassinated. . . .

In the middle section we are given a brief but lucid account of Gandhi's career. Mr Mehta is no Pyarelal; he tells the story in little more than 100 pages. But though the narrative moves swiftly, it omits nothing essential, and is throughout aglow with illuminating detail. . . .

The last section of Mr Mehta's book contains a number of interviews with surviving Gandhians, including the eccentric Madeleine Slade who, it appears, was fixated on Beethoven before turning to Gandhi 50 years ago, and has now turned back again to Beethoven. Among political Gandhians, Mr Mehta unfortunately chose to interview Gulzarilal Nanda, who is no longer active, rather than Morarji Desai—thus missing a notable scoop.

Perhaps because he is blind, the author goes out of his way, as in previous books, to convey the visual effect of every person and every scene. Some may feel that he slightly overdoes this, but the descriptions are often revealing and, at times, very funny. (p. 220)

> *John Grigg, "Across the Black Waters," in* The Listener, *Vol. 98, No. 2522, August 18, 1977, pp. 220-21.*

PAM JABLONS

The most striking feature of [*The New India*] is that much of what is admirable about it—its cogent homogenization of facts—is also what renders it ultimately unsatisfying. Ved Mehta depends excessively on letters written by other (often anonymous) Indians, newspaper stories filed by New York *Times* and Washington *Post* correspondents, and magazine articles from the *Economist, Surge International* and *Seminar*. Upon finishing *The New India,* one is left with the feeling that its intelligent and rather dispassionate author has chosen to compile rather than analyze; indeed, there are so many lengthy quotations it is sometimes hard to tell where the quotations stop and the author begins.

Mehta believes that these sources accurately portray the mood of the nation from June 26, 1975 to March 21, 1977, the period immediately preceding and including the Emergency rule. He further suggests that the experiences of those two years—in a country where 5,000-year-old traditions coexist with modern technology—are representative of the "new" India. But in the aftermath of Indira Gandhi's defeat at the polls by octogenarian

Morarji R. Desai (covered all too briefly in the last chapter), it seems implausible that the already concluded era should be regarded as "new."

Even if this book is seen as an historical overview rather than an original contribution—there are less than a dozen sentences worth underlining to the student of Indian culture and history—it fails for the very reasons Mehta so often criticizes other journalists. To begin with, it is superficial (Mrs. Gandhi is compared to Mussolini, Hitler, Stalin, and Nixon; her regime is "Orwellian"; "no poor country," we are told, "can be an ideal democracy"). Secondly, it is self-defeating ("There has been," Mehta writes in the concluding paragraph, "such an onrush of material and testimony—most of it formless and contradictory—about things that happened during the Emergency that it will be years before anyone can hope to sift through it"). Finally, and inexcusably, it is bland. (p. 22)

The pivotal figure of these difficult times is Indira Nehru Gandhi, who metamorphosed from the Prime Minister of the world's largest democracy—"the land of every seventh person in the world," as Mehta nicely puts it—into a despotic Kashmiri queen. . . . Accordingly, in the fifth of the book's 11 chapters she is profiled—all too faintly, alas. Her childhood, her relationship with her parents, her education, and her marriage are summarized in one paragraph of crisp prose. . . .

[Mehta is] not without his prejudices, which would be more palatable were they less insidiously couched. For example, early in the book . . . he writes: "He (Nehru) did not appoint his daughter, for instance, to any high government post or encourage her to acquire any personal power." Fair enough, yet four chapters later he writes: "For most of the time that Nehru was Prime Minister, Indira lived with her widowed father, serving not only as his official hostess but his confidante; she was his sole heir. In 1959, mainly because of her family's position in recent Indian history, she was given a major commission: she was made the president of the Congress Party."

The author should have added that at the time her father was Prime Minister, and played a significant role in assigning the post of party president. True, there are substantial differences in character between father and daughter, but there are similarities to be found as well if one is willing to penetrate the Nehru mystique.

Moreover, judging from my own observations, Mehta misinterprets some of the events he describes. Writing of the Emergency, he claims that "The mass support for the opposition parties, so much in evidence during the protest demonstrations and processions, simply melted away—a confirmation of the fact that the conflict between Congress and those parties was in essence just a quarrel among middle class politicians." Coming as it does after pages of discussion of Mrs. Gandhi's "terror tactics," this is curiously insensitive to the role that fear played in those days—a fear aggravated by tales of retaliation against recalcitrants that pervaded the country. (p. 23)

This is the crux of the issue and, quite possibly, of Mrs. Gandhi's electoral defeat. That the poverty-stricken, superstitious, illiterate, and oppressed villager believed he had a right to redress, and mustered the courage to vote against the 'cow and the calf' despite prevailing rumors that the elections were monitored and Janata supporters would be punished, is more than "the most hopeful sign of democracy in a poor country." It is glorious.

Mehta quotes John Kenneth Galbraith describing India as "a functional anarchy," and adds: "If that is what it is, it is certainly an anarchy that functioned best after the establishment of the British raj, in 1858. . . . The 'Indianization' of India that has been going on since independence is becoming a kind of regression to the days before the raj." But the period of British colonialism and the thinking that accompanied it have expired, as has Indira Gandhi's regime. It is time for a revised portrait of the country—one more genuinely new than *The New India*. (pp. 23-4)

Pam Jablons, "Trapped in the Past," in The New Leader, *Vol. LXI, No. 8, April 10, 1978, pp. 22-4.*

CLARK BLAISE

The third volume of Ved Mehta's familial biography [*Mamaji*] opens irresistibly: In Lahore over a century ago, an accursed couple (10 of their infants have died) seek guidance from a holy woman. She tells them where to find a half-buried statue of the goddess Durga. Worship it for six months, and they will be delivered of a son. That prophesied son—Ved Mehta's maternal grandfather, "Babuji"—led the family out of squalor and superstition, gained wealth and a title, fathered 15 children and died a centenarian in 1973. *Mamaji* closes in the year 1938 with the author, only 3 and already blind from the effects of meningitis, being taken by his mother (Babuji's daughter, Mamaji) on furtive missions to seers and healers. Despite being a doctor's wife and a lawyer's daughter, she remained convinced, at least in an active part of her, that blindness was a spell to be lifted by prayer and flagellation. But we are now in the modern world, "Daddyji's" world of Western medicine. Even though one seer is able to describe the occasion of Ved Mehta's initial infection with eerie precision, her prescribed cure—Durga worship—this time proves ineffective.

Within that wavering symmetry falls the unshapely tale of Mamaji—good wife, fierce mother, neglected daughter. Unlike the earlier volumes in this de facto trilogy—*Face to Face* in 1958 and *Daddyji* in 1972—*Mamaji* is less a study of a remarkable individual than a sober and unsentimental account of the fracturing of an intact but ignorant world.

The three volumes (more are promised) now survey more than a century in the daily lives of two reasonably typical (which is to say, utterly extraordinary) Punjabi families. They might also be said to embrace the world: from Daddyji's ancestral village . . . to the alleys of Mamaji's Lahore, the Indian student hostels of London, the butchery of Partition, and finally America, where the author won a series of scholarships and eventually settled, a staff writer with The New Yorker. The personal narratives are compelling; the larger design is inescapable.

In the foreward to *Face to Face* Ved Mehta at 22 wrote: "No one man's experience or reflections were sufficient to justify or inspire a book. But India, where I had been born and brought up, was." While that stern dismissal of individual inspiration is a bit strident, it does suggest the scale of the author's ambition. Blindness is a metaphor, not a subject; an urgent geometry of continual self-placement. But the larger coordinates are not delivered by touch and hearing; they derive from *place:* history, society and family.

Daddyji, I should acknowledge, remains for me the most satisfying of the three Mehta family memoirs, an absorbing personal narrative and a suggestive allegory of colonialism. *Mamaji* is longer and more diffuse, dominated not by a single character but by larger social forces. Attitude replaces psychology. In the West, we conveniently label that attitude "submissiveness" and tend to inflate or demean it, depending on our politics. *Mamaji* at its best goes a long way toward describing the concomitant of wifely submissiveness, and that is inexplicable fear. Mamaji yields to terrors that lack specific or psychological origins; she turns from unfamiliar expectations with a potentially violent apostasy. This is a way of saying, perhaps, that the book is indeed faithful to the condition of women of Mamaji's generation; we can glimpse, but never fully appreciate, the cultural barriers she cannot transcend. (pp. 7, 51)

Mamaji was married in the traditional manner (and by a bit of permissible fraud) to a worldly young doctor just back from England who expected the proverbial perfect bride: educated, English-speaking and a nightingale. . . . What Daddyji got was a Punjabi-speaking, musically untrained teen-ager, who'd been removed from school at the first hint of menstruation. In the beginning she begs her husband not to beat her or turn her out (not that he would); in later life she will violate his orders and take her blind son on repeated visits to religious quacks, following piously their injunctions to leave meat at crossroads, donate gold in the shape of eyeballs, flog the boy and treat his eyes with caustic solutions of antimony. Her life, full and rich by any standard, is scarred by many such instances of terror and ignorance. Ved Mehta does not solicit an easy compassion. The tone remains detached.

If the center is slightly undefined, the periphery offers compensation. Babuji's diaries anchor the book in the density of Indian family life: birth, marriage, death and education (always education; the family owes everything to the sacrifices made in its name, and exam results are entered as faithfully as the other three vital statistics). Daddyji's rampant social life—bridge and tennis—is here rendered through Mamaji's uncomprehending eyes. What might appear as a mild flirtation remains inconclusive; a different corruption is thus revealed. . . .

Family is the tidiest metaphor for the vastness of India. To understand its compelling and often terrible hold is to possess a special understanding of the culture. Ved Mehta patiently delivers that understanding and courageously presents it without intepretation, limiting even its expected "warmth" in the service of a sharper clarity. (p. 51)

Clark Blaise, "Family Memoir," in The New York Times Book Review, *October 21, 1979, pp. 7, 51.*

GEOFFREY MOORHOUSE

Ved Mehta had been enlisted by an American television outfit to script a film about India and Chachaji became its focal point—a sad, quaint relic from the fringes of Mehta's own family, who also symbolised the Indian capacity for survival against powerful odds. The film won a prize and Mehta [in *The Photographs of Chachaji*] tells the story of how it was made. He does this deftly, waspishly and, for all his own Americanisation after 30 years out of India, with a deep instinct for what is pertinent in that wonderful but confusing subcontinent.

I do wish, though, that he wouldn't insist on piling up crude visual images . . . which would be irritating from anyone's pen: from a blind writer it's bizarre.

Mehta's own irritation is reserved for the television people and I'm with him there. "I could warm up to the idea of an expose of Morarji Desai,'' says one early on, and from start to finish the prize-winning producer is portrayed as brash, insensitive and vaccilating in about equal parts.

There's a cruel but (alas) hilarious description of a bewildered Chachaji trying to catch a bus while staying in shot, which is merely another dogged episode in a lifetime as everybody's pawn. And a lovely moment when he is transported from Delhi back to his old village where he discovers, delightedly, that he can recall prayers his old guru has forgotten. Mehta is at his best in recording the beholden, plaintive, submissive moods of the old man, and his astonishment when at last he saw the finished film. "It seemed as if I was having a holy audience with myself in Heaven."

> Geoffrey Moorhouse, *"A Holy Audience," in* Manchester Guardian Weekly, *June 14, 1981, p. 22.**

JANET MALCOLM

Every good autobiography raises the question of whose story to credit—that of the intelligent, critically observing, narrating adult or that of the uncomprehending, dumbly accepting, experiencing child. In *Vedi*, Ved Mehta's extraordinary memoir of the four years he spent as a young child in an appalling place in Bombay called the Dadar School for the blind, the tension between the two "I's" is particularly pronounced. The adult "I" is outraged by what his father did to him when he abruptly removed him—a blind child not yet five—from his affectionate and comfortable middle-class home in the Punjab and sent him a thousand miles away to an orphanage for destitute blind children located in a mosquito-ridden industrial slum, where he was to contract typhoid within three months (and suffer repeated bouts of it), and where he lived for four years under the harshest of physical conditions and received the most pitifully rudimentary of educations. But the child "I" is unconcerned about the things that pain and appall the grown-up "I." He is a high-spirited, strong-willed, eager little boy, so intent on exercising his child's prerogative of enjoyment that he seems almost unaware of the cruelty and difficulty of his predicament. . . . Thus, in *Vedi*, paradoxically, it is the knowledgeable narrator who suffers over the monstrous events of the story, while the ignorant child at their center accepts them with composure, and even, amazingly, a kind of gaiety.

In *Vedi*, for the first time in his mature writing, Mehta writes from the perspective of total blindness. The book is entirely without visual descriptions. We follow the blind child into the orphanage, and, like him, we never learn what the place or any of the people in it looked like. We hear, we feel, but we see nothing. We are dislocated and disoriented. As the child misses the familiar persons and things of home, so the reader misses the customary visual clues of literature. One feels a kind of sensory deprivation throughout the book—almost a lack of enjoyment—even as one experiences the excitement that an original work engenders. Not the least of *Vedi*'s originality is this very stylistic denial, which amounts to an approximation of the experience of blindness. As we grope though the early sections of the book, trying to get our bearings in its alien literary environment, we are like tourists in a foreign country who have to struggle with themselves not to commit the absurdity of rejecting the very foreignness they have traveled to experience. The country of the blind is exotic indeed, and Mehta takes us to places in its bleak, impassable terrain that no one from the sighted world has previously penetrated. . . .

The principal of the school, Mr. Ras Mohun, though sighted, was somehow exempted from the resentment and fear that the blind children extended to the sighted world, perhaps because of his benignity and genuine interest in the blind. He was a man in his early thirties, a Bengali Christian convert, who had worked with missionaries among the blind and the deaf and had studied at the Perkins Institution for the Blind in America. His wife, who "was the same height he was," was a little less kind, though hardly a villainess. The villains of the book are poverty, disease, and blindness. Vedi arrived at the school a healthy, sturdy little boy, with fat cheeks that the other children kept pulling at in wonder. . . .

In a few months time, Vedi became as sickly and fever-ridden as the rest, and when he went home for Christmas vacation, his parents removed him from the school. Unaccountably, they sent him back a year later, and once again he fell into a brutal physical decline. When he came home for his second Christmas vacation, his clothes hung from him and his head was so severely infested with ringworm that his father, a doctor, decided to risk baldness, and even brain damage, by having him undergo X-ray treatments, then the only remedy for the condition. . . .

In his books about his parents, *Daddyji* (1972) and *Mamaji* (1979), which form a trilogy with *Vedi*, Mehta draws a sharp contrast between his rational, decisive, tough-minded, Western-educated, physician father and his superstitious, backward, uneducated, childish, tender-hearted mother. Typically, when her son went blind, the mother refused to accept the fact and dragged him around to faith healers and quacks, in the confident belief that the blindness was a temporary punishment for some transgression in this or a previous life. And typically, the father clutched at the idea of "progressive, Western methods of educating the blind" as the answer to his son's tragic predicament (for which, as Mehta unhappily suggests in *Daddyji*, recounting the events that led up to the loss of his eyesight, he may have been responsible).

But, paradoxically, it was the emotional, irrational, childish, fanciful, "Indian" parts of Ved Mehta's nature that were his strongest defense against the harsh actuality of Dadar. The Western values and qualities that his father represented, and that he mistakenly believed the school to embody—realism, pragmatism, stoicism, common sense—had little survival value in the extreme situation that the five-year-old blind child was placed. (p. 3)

Because of his family's superior status—and, more to the point, the money that his father sent every month—Vedi received special treatment at the school. He ate his meals with the Ras Mohuns instead of with the other children, and was exempted from chair-caning instruction. But Mrs. Ras Mohun found it inconvenient to honor the agreement that he also sleep in the principal's quarters, and so he was put into the boys' dormitory, though he was given a special bed, with a mattress and mosquito netting; the other boys slept on bare wood slats, unprotected from mosquitos. The move to the dormitory was a fortunate one: it brought the child into the life of the school, its real life of mischief, gossip, fighting, ghost-story telling, sex play (called "boy mischief"), cruelty, savagery, camaraderie. . . .

There is a scene toward the end of the book that freezes the blood. It takes place at Dadar in the boys' dormitory, and it concerns Jaisingh, a boy who is blind, deaf, dumb, and retarded—a large, helpless, miserable, barely human creature, whom Mr. Ras Mohun calls "the Dadar School's Helen Keller," and whom the other children dislike. . . . Jaisingh is given to crying at night, making eerie moaning and wailing sounds, and when this happens, the Sighted Master, who is in charge of the boys' dormitory, subdues him by beating him with a shoe. The Sighted Master is a sinister, shadowy figure without name or any other characteristics besides his brutality and lowness. One night, both Jaisingh and another pathetic child named Ramesh begin howling together, awakening everyone in the dormitory. Vedi hears the Sighted Master get up, and as he passes his bed he hears him mutter, "I will finish Ras Mohun's Helen Keller." Vedi hears the Sighted Master walk toward the howling boys, and hears him remove a plank from one of their beds. As Vedi and the other boys listen in terror, first Ramesh's howling and then Jaisingh's abruptly stop. The next day, both Ramesh and Jaisingh are gone. They are never seen again at Dadar. Whether the Sighted Master actually killed the two boys—as the other boys speculate—is unclear. What really happened is never known.

What really happened? This is the question that impels every autobiographer, and that gives autobiography its special epistemological interest. In Mehta's taut, strong, ironic memoir, he restively ponders the question of what his experience at the Dadar School had been, worrying it and turning it this way and that and finally letting it lie there in all its unanswerability—like the question of what happened to Ramesh and Jaisingh, like the question, perhaps, of what happened to all of us in our childhoods. . . . Neither of the two "I's" through which the story of a childhood is told is trustworthy: the testimony of the child, who was there, is lacking in understanding; the testimony of the adult, who is ominiscient, is lacking in authenticity. At best, an uneasy truce between the child (memory) and the man (understanding) is achieved. In an epilogue, Mehta states the problem of the two "I's" with almost shocking explicitness. As an adult, he returns to the school. . . . (p. 4)

He learns that many of his classmates had died of consumption at an early age. He reports a depressing meeting with Deoji, his best friend at the school, who "confirmed this fact and that fact, but what he really succeeded in confirming was the divide between us—both before, during, and after our first meeting, when I was a child, and before, during, and after our last meeting, when I was a man." His final encounter is with Rajas, a girl at the school, now a destitute woman living in a squalid tenement in Dadar. He does not remember her at all. He presses her for details about himself at the school. To the narrator's disappointment—and to the reader's elation—she has only one thing to say about him: "I remember that you were a very jolly child." (p. 6)

Janet Malcolm, "School of the Blind," in The New York Review of Books, *Vol. XXIX, No. 15, October 7, 1982, pp. 3-4, 6.*

ROBERT L. HARDGRAVE, JR.

Drawn from Ved Mehta's continuing portrait of India in *The New Yorker* magazine, *A Family Affair* is an account of Indian politics under three prime ministers: Morarji Desai, Charan Singh, and Indira Gandhi. Covering the period from 1977 through 1980, the greater portion of the book is devoted to the Janata government and its cast of characters. The title is taken from Mehta's theme: "A study of Indian politics has to be a study of the shifting power and influence of its ruling families and their close and distant relatives, for although India is the world's largest parliamentary democracy, . . . it is also a traditional feudal society, organized around the principles of caste and family." . . .

Despite Mehta's serious purpose, he rarely cuts below the surface of personality or politics. Much of the book is a chronicle of rumors and allegations emanating from New Delhi, a report of the fads, idiosyncrasies, and machinations of the "celibate Janata leaders." This is not without interest, but it provides little real understanding of the political and social forces shaping Indian political life. (p. 191)

In contrast to the vanity and ineptitude of the Janata leaders, Indira Gandhi emerges as the master politician. She stages an impressive comeback; "derails" Morarji Desai, Jagjivan Ram, and Charan Singh; and she regains power, with Sanjay, her younger son, as heir apparent. Sanjay's death in June 1980 provides the centerpiece for Mehta's reflections on dynastic democracy in India. The book should have ended here, for the final chapter, "Nepotism and Discord," is a patchwork of news items and afterthoughts. Mehta, a writer of remarkable perception, should have given us a better book. (pp. 191-92)

Robert L. Hardgrave, Jr., in a review of "A Family Affair: India Under Three Prime Ministers," in The Journal of Asian Studies, *Vol. XLIII, No. 1, November, 1983, pp. 191-92.*

AINSLIE EMBREE

Central to most good autobiographies is the process of arranging and selecting memories of the past, of remembering events and emotions that served as the foundation on which a life was built. What makes *The Ledge Between the Streams* . . . a remarkable, perhaps even a unique, book is that it is not so much about remembering as forgetting. Again and again in this account of his Indian childhood, which is the fourth in a series of autobiographical works, Ved Mehta returns to the theme that what he wanted to forget, and to make others forget, was that he was blind. An astonishing achievement of the book is that the reader forgets it too and remembers it only with the realization that the ordinary events of a young boy's life are being carried out, not just in darkness, but in a self-created world of visual imagination.

One example of this is the little boy's participation in that most Indian of pastimes, battles with kites flown from rooftops. The strings are covered with powdered glass, and the object is to fly your kite in such a fashion that you cut another's string, so that you can then add his fallen kite to your store. Jumping from roof to roof and handling the sharp string is a dangerous and exciting business for anyone, but especially for a boy who did all this "by sensing the currents of air and by listening to the patter of feet on a roof, to the scrapes of shoes along a wall."

On another occasion, during a holiday in the mountains, the headstrong boy forced the men who rent ponies along the mountain trails to let him ride one despite their sensible objections. He recalls that as he galloped along, "I forgot all about my blindness." Even more splendidly difficult was learning to ride a bicycle despite bruises, cuts and the screams of his distracted mother. Then one day he took his bike out on the highway and, by listening to their talk and laughter, followed his sisters through traffic to their school. "Three smart sisters and their little brother" was the phrase he kept repeating to himself, trying to forget the qualification that kept rising to the surface, "blind brother."

All this is narrated without a hint of either self-pity or boasting; nor is there the least suggestion that we are being provided with an improving lesson on the values of grit and determination. What we are given, through the easy elegance of Mr. Mehta's literary craft, is a narrative that moves in at least three constantly shifting and intersecting worlds.

There is, first of all, the one of the little boy, who by a kind of sleight of hand manages to do impossible things and to make them appear commonplace. This world is encapsulated in that of the Mehta family, which the author has examined in his other autobiographical works, and it is hard to separate his extraordinary achievements from the nature of Indian family life and the kind of support he received from his family, especially his father. Many authors have tried to convey the complexities and strengths of the Indian family system through both novels and memoirs, but few have succeeded as well as Mr. Mehta, despite the fact that the members of his family, with their education, prosperity and access to Western society, were in no sense typical.

The Ledge Between the Streams could have been a novel, but through the realities of an unusual little boy and his family, Mr. Mehta re-creates one of the dramatic moments of modern history, the partition in 1947 of the Indian subcontinent into the nation-states of India and Pakistan. This is the third world that intersects in Ved Mehta's book with the smaller ones of himself as a little boy and of his family. The political and social causes of the partition of India and the agonies and miseries that accompanied it have been explored in hundreds of books, but I do not know of any other account that conveys so vividly, and yet without histrionics, the meaning of the events of the summer of 1947. . . .

[The] great world of nations being born touched the world of the little blind boy. Through dogged persistence, his father persuaded Lady Mountbatten to get him admitted, against all the rules, into a school for soldiers who had been blinded in war. This was a step toward fulfilling the dream of Ved and his father of his going to America, where he could get the kind of education not then available to the blind in India. The book ends with his acceptance by the Arkansas School for the Blind. When Prime Minister Nehru asked, ''Why Arkansas?'' the boy answered in deep embarrassment, ''That's the only place that would have me.'' There is no looking forward in the book, no assurance of a satisfactory outcome of the flight from India, except, perhaps, in the dark farewell of the old uncle who says to the boy, ''People who go to America nowadays never come back.''

Ainslie Embree, ''Leaping Without Looking,'' in The New York Times Book Review, *May 6, 1984, p. 14.*

John Metcalf

1938-

English-born Canadian short story writer, editor, novelist, essayist, and critic.

Metcalf is known in Canada for his elegant short fiction and his caustic satires of Canadian academic life. Critics frequently compare his compressed, concise prose style to poetry, and Metcalf himself believes "that stories should be approached not as things to be understood but rather as things to be lived through and experienced." Barry Cameron contends that "for Metcalf, the short story is an approximation of poetry in that it offers to the reader . . . a brief but intense emotional insight."

Through his work as editor of the *Best Canadian Stories* series and as a compiler of several other short story anthologies, Metcalf has gained respect for his promotion of the contemporary Canadian short story. His own short fiction is often considered his most successful work. In the stories collected in his first book, *The Lady Who Sold Furniture* (1970), Metcalf contrasts perceptions of childhood innocence with the resentments of adulthood. The stories in Metcalf's second collection, *The Teeth of My Father* (1975), explore adolescent consciousness and introduce new concerns to Metcalf's fiction, notably the conflict between the artist and society and between the artist's public and private lives. The story "The Years in Exile" deals with its author-persona's realization that his childhood, while extremely remote, is more interesting and real to him than his present experiences. *Girl in Gingham* (1978), in addition to the title novella, contains the novella *Private Parts*. Both of these works also focus on the relationship between art and life. *Girl in Gingham* concerns a divorced man's invention of his ideal woman from the bare details provided by a computer dating service and the subsequent discrepancies between his fantasies and reality. *Private Parts* is a story of a man who realizes he cannot recover the passion he experienced as a boy rebelling against his mother's repressive attitudes.

Metcalf's most vitriolic fiction is based on his personal experiences as an educator in Canada. These works usually have as protagonists British teachers or professors of literature transplanted from London to Canada. These characters, like Metcalf himself, are often dissatisfied with the poor quality of education and literary criticism in their adopted country. Metcalf's comic novella *Going Down Slow* (1972), an attack on Montreal's education system, depicts an idealistic teacher who is castigated for his rebellious but concerned attitude, while his colleague is rewarded for his conformity and opportunism. Metcalf's novel *General Ludd* (1980) is described by Keith Garebian as "a satire on a writer's solitary, somewhat crazy battle against the forces of cultural destruction." This work focuses on a professor whose personal commitment to literature tempts him to destroy a communication arts complex that he feels has subverted the true value of language. Metcalf sums up the rhetorical concerns of these works in a more direct manner in *Kicking Against the Pricks* (1982), a collection of essays, personal reminiscences, and an interview.

(See also *Contemporary Authors*, Vol. 113.)

Photograph by Sam Tata

ROBERT WEAVER

The echoes that one hears in *Going Down Slow* began in England a few years after the end of the Second World War, and the noises were made by a group of writers who were called Angry Young Men (by now, apparently, most of them would be called Embattled Old Tories). These writers represented the provincial, redbrick university graduates trying to muscle in on the Oxford- and Cambridge-educated Establishment in London.

In *Going Down Slow* we have an English immigrant teacher thumbing his nose at the stuffy educational establishment in Montreal. . . . What we get . . . is an immigrant's-eye view of Montreal, and the portait isn't a flattering one. I don't doubt that a similarly unflattering novel could be written about Toronto or Vancouver or Edmonton from the immigrant's point of view, and indeed Wyndham Lewis did it for Toronto thirty years ago. (pp. 50-1)

It isn't entirely fair to compare *Going Down Slow* with the early novels by Kingsley Amis, John Wain and John Braine. It's more sophisticated and more contemporary than their books were, even when they seemed to be bringing something modern into postwar English fiction. *Going Down Slow* is really quite a nasty, sour novel—deliberately so—and its effect on us ought to be therapeutic. What somehow limits my admiration for it is that John Metcalf's short stories proposed that he was capable of a book of fiction with a greater emotional range. (p. 51)

Robert Weaver, "Outsider's Views of Africa and Montreal," in Saturday Night, *Vol. 87, No. 11, November, 1972, pp. 50-1.**

PATRICIA MORLEY

Metcalf's first novel [*Going Down Slow*] is a free-swinging and very funny attack on the Establishment. The target is The System, not simply the Montreal high school system but the whole North American credo: athletics and sports cars are important but art isn't; conformity and hypocrisy will be rewarded; and what matters can be put on a Kardex file. The treatment is comic but the humour is black, and at times as bitter as the bile that teacher David Appleby retches up at the novel's end.

Appleby (advance oneself *by* giving an *apple* to the teacher?) is a young Englishman just over from Britain, a newcomer to the teaching game. A latter-day Quixote, he thinks he can vanquish prejudice, prudery and pettiness singlehanded. He does get in quite a few blows and succeeds in making his antagonist look thoroughly ridiculous. It's a Pyrrhic victory, for The System defeats him in the end.

Metcalf is already known for his short fiction. *The Lady Who Sold Furniture,* a collection of short stories, was published in 1970, and his fiction has appeared in periodicals and anthologies. Several of these short pieces have classroom settings and themes which anticipate this novel. They depict a system that tends to brutalize teacher and student alike, a system penalizing the imaginative and forcing the independent spirit to conform. In *Going Down Slow,* David's fellow teacher Jim is willing to play by the rules of those in power. Jim goes in for guidance, administration, and higher degrees. He ends with a fat OISE grant and a white Galaxy 500 with red upholstery. David, a born loser, gets to retain his hated job, at the cost of betraying his girl and sacrificing both his freedom and his self-respect. In capitulating to The System, it's downhill all the way. . . .

Genuine satire has a moral base, and Metcalf is a moralist, an idealist-*cum*-cynic, although that seems like a strange combination. (p. 102)

Although a summary of the novel's concerns suggests something out of *This Magazine is About Schools,* this is fiction not journalism, and rather brilliant fiction at that. Teacher David tells [his student and lover] Susan that a writer depends upon literary tradition. Writer Metcalf has obviously taken his own advice. Many of his comic techniques are straight out of Firbank and Waugh. (p. 103)

The element of fantasy found in many of Metcalf's stories is negligible in this novel, but mordant humour is a common denominator. The novel is told in the third person, but centred in David's iconoclastic point of view and his wry sense of humour. David has his own standard of values . . . and they are not those of The System. The story takes on something of the bouncy, irrepressible manner of its leading character.

In the first half of the novel, David's sense of superiority to the Montreal Yahoos may begin to irritate you. But as the trap closes around him . . . , as his friend Garry betrays him and Jim takes off in his Galaxy 500, you're likely to agree with

Metcalf: vomiting is the suitable response to the obscenities of The System. (p. 104)

Patricia Morley, "Poisoned by the System," in Canadian Literature, *No. 58, Autumn, 1973, pp. 102-04.*

ANTHONY BRENNAN

One is not surprised to learn that a couple of John Metcalf's avowedly autobiographical characters [in *The Teeth of My Father*] were eager collectors of butterflies in their past. The patience to wait, to stalk and then to pounce, the ability to skewer the victim and devote careful attention to his variegated hues are all key elements of Metcalf's story telling style. There are not many writers in Canada who have real venom. There is Richler, of course, but few others who can like Metcalf, make you laugh out loud at the accuracy of their barbs.

In **"Beryl"**, for example, he presents the stumbling comic opera of an inexperienced, romantic university student and a blunt, practical factory girl. He reels off a string of incongruous and unpromising settings for the progress of the romance, culminating in the ultimate seduction on an orange living room carpet while three vicars natter away on TV about miracles, and a bed-ridden grandmother hammers on the bedroom floor aloft for a cup of tea. It is that kind of juxtaposition—the pursuit of heroism and romance in ludicrous conditions that is Metcalf's strong suit. He is here in territory heavily clumped over by Amis but he does not share the nasty glee which makes Amis at times seem like a drearily superior adolescent.

In **"Gentle as Flowers Make the Stones"** we are treated to the mock-heroics of survival against the philistines by a poet who combines the acerbity of Amis and the cunning of Donleavy's Sebastian Dangerfield. Metcalf pursues a delicate balance in writing the story. He counterpoises against the poet's steady, restless search for an artistically satisfying adaptation of a Martial epigram, the detritus of a day of mundane events in the writer's attempt to stay afloat and feed himself. (p. 123)

Four of the eight stories in this collection have that 'don't let the bastards get you down' embattled quality that was the essence of Metcalf's novel *Going Down Slow.* The danger of this mercilessly precise tone is that the stories draw us in successfully only when the main character seems to be fired with some of Metcalf's own splenetic bile. He writes best about those bitter ex-patriate English intellectuals maddened by the feeling that they have come down in the world, savagely certain that their newly adopted country does not come up to their high standards. . . . **"The Practice of the Craft,"** the slightest story in the collection, fails for me because Metcalf gives Neil Peters none of that inner flame flickering to stay alive against all the odds with which he usually energizes his main characters. The actor on tour in New Brunswick worries about his wife's infidelities at home in Toronto, acts in a play about a wife's infidelities, reads himself to sleep in a lonely hotel room with a biography of Neville Chamberlain—it all seems a little too glib and predictable. The detail though accurate is wearily contrived. I cannot care much about Neil Peters because the writer doesn't seem to care much about him. It is the only story in the collection which has the air of being cranked out a little mechanically. It is not the slightness of the story which is disappointing. **"A Thing They Wear"** about the initiation of two boys into the mystery of the menstrual pad is even slighter and yet is brilliantly brought off with just the right emphasis, shading and detail.

Like Alice Monro and Hugh Hood, with whom Metcalf can be grouped as an outstanding practitioner of short fiction, the skill which forces itself on your attention is the way he produces the right tonality out of a mosaic of detail. . . . He knows his characters and situations with certainty. He does not hint and nudge. He delights you with pinpoint accuracy, the exactly right quality of a word as it locks into place—you know that it has been searched for carefully, that Metcalf was not satisfied until he got it right. **"The Years in Exile"** about an aging writer living in Canada but drifting back constantly to memories of his boyhood in England is a *tour de force* of accumulated detail. Metcalf's credo as a writer is what the story itself celebrates—particular life. (pp. 123-24)

Metcalf is very good at catching what he himself calls "reverberations" and tonalities—the delicate shifts in human relationships. In the title story he sews together fragments of autobiographical fiction with tatters of memory about his eccentric father. The events described are not dramatic turning points but rather random selections from the flow of life which give us, nevertheless, an intimate sense of character and place out of all proportion to the brief space they take up. There is here a kind of Carlos Williams' concentration on the ordinary to make it yield up secrets.

In **"The Strange Aberration of Mr. Smythe"** the chaotic concert of a German Boys Brass Band in the Edinburgh Pleasure Gardens whereby a drunken MC ex-R.A.F. type gradually grows more and more insulting until he is leading the audience in a chorus of 'Hitler had only got one ball' to the band's rendition of Colonel Bogey we have the funniest piece of sustained humour in recent Canadian fiction. (p. 124)

I do not always have the same feeling about the rightness of the total structure of the stories. In **"The Years in Exile"** the juxtaposition of past and present, the luminous childhood memories of England and the flat routine of old age in Canada seems a little flimsy, arbitrary and undeveloped. In **"The Practice of the Craft"** the weaving of time sequences does not have quite that sense of inevitability that the detailed observation within the stories so often has.

The blurb on the book's jacket tells us that "As always, Metcalf is poised, urbane, affectionate, amused." Three of the tags one cannot quarrel with, but affection is only spasmodically present. There is a warm sympathy in the memories of childhood and of his father but not notably elsewhere. Hopefully he will develop this side of his talent and avoid the kind of wallowing disgruntlement Amis has fallen into. At the moment, however, the territory still most easily within his grasp is that inhabited by what Mencken termed the 'boobery'. In **"The Flowers that Bloom in Spring"** we have the embattled schoolteacher being overwhelmed as he stems the tide of miseducation by trying to get his students to focus on the object, the particular detail, the real world. Even though we have come across it before in *Going Down Slow* it is a fitting close to this book. David fights gamely to clear away all the crud that the ignorant smear over the beauty and ugliness of the quotidian world. (p. 125)

The teeth of the title are the ill-fitting choppers Metcalf's father endlessly remakes with a do-it-yourself kit. He realizes years later that his father would have been broken hearted had he ever produced an undeniably perfect pair. One has the same feeling about Metcalf's response to the imperfect world. He keeps his teeth sharp because he enjoys the task of chewing it out. Since there is little chance of the world achieving perfec-

tion immediately we can look forward to many years of Metcalf's brilliant observations of particular life. If you like a wide range of humour, devastatingly accurate character portrayal, consistently high quality, and a delightfully skilled handling of language you should buy Metcalf's collection of stories right away. (pp. 125-26)

> *Anthony Brennan, in a review of "The Teeth of My Father," in* The Fiddlehead, *No. 105, Spring, 1975, pp. 123-26.*

BARRY CAMERON

The Teeth of My Father reveals powerfully and unequivocally where John Metcalf's real strengths as a writer lie and what his sense of the short story is: for Metcalf, the short story is an approximation of poetry in that it offers to the reader, through the subtlety and complexity of its linguistic and imagistic patterns, a brief but intense emotional insight. (p. 36)

The positive features of . . . earlier stories are again evident. . . : Metcalf's talent for capturing the mood and idiom of childhood, his strict control of point of view in which that which is perceived becomes the reactions or responses of the perceiver, the tightness of narrative structure, the suggestiveness of concrete details, the economy of diction, and his skillful juxtaposition of the romantic or pastoral with the reality of social existence.

Marking a thematic and stylistic departure for Metcalf, . . . [five of the stories] are thematically interrelated and form a self-contained sequence. All five stories are concerned in different ways with different aspects of the same dilemma: the relationship between the artist and society or the relationship between the artist's execution or performance of his craft and his own personal life. The movement from the first to the fifth story reveals a progressive internalization of the problem. For example, the first story, **"The Strange Aberration of Mr. Ken Smythe,"** although in some ways a comic—bitterly comic—story, metaphorically dramatizes the artist's essentially vulnerable position vis-a-vis a hostile and unappreciative audience. The fifth story, **"The Years in Exile,"** through a first-person *persona* who is a novelist, explores the built-in tension of an artist's life in terms of a split within the artist's own mind in that the *persona's* memories of his childhood in England—because he has "fictionalized" the past—are more real to him than his present moment in Canada as a famous novelist.

Both of these stories exemplify Metcalf's use of thematically suggestive details and his tendency to use the paragraph as a rhetorical device to emphasize the importance of an image by the implied status provided in the isolating, separating, effect of the paragraphing. (pp. 36-7)

"The Practice of the Craft" deals blatantly with the tension between the performance of the artist's craft and his own personal life. It is the story of a professional actor who is playing the lead role in a West End farce about a man whose younger wife is unfaithful to him and who is suffering the same fate in his own personal life as the character he portrays in the play. The rhetorical thrust of the story suggests that in order to practice the craft, it might be necessary for the artist to sacrifice the reality of his own life for the craft itself. The agony of this dilemma is emphasized by the ironic parallel between the actor's own situation and the plot of the play: every night, in a small provincial theatre, he acts out a farce of the tragedy of his own life, and he will continue, must continue, to perform this ritualistic masochism because he is a "professional" actor. His pain is the price he must pay for what he is. Such a story might evoke a stereotyped sentimentality, but Metcalf nicely obviates the possibility by allowing the actor, in four one-sentence paragraphs that dramatize the dilemma through antithetical juxtaposition, to accept his pain and to mock it simultaneously. . . .

"Gentle as Flowers Make the Stones" concerns a poet who lives purely and simply for the art that he practices. Despite the exigencies of his life—his need for money, food, shelter, even human companionship—he must practice his craft. Throughout the story, he is composing a poem in his mind, and the completion of the poem, which is the climax of the story, occurs during a moment of sexual climax with a woman who is emotionally desperate for him. But while the entire sexual encounter is taking place, all that is going on in his mind is the completion of the poem that he has been working on all day: to be an artist, on one level, is to be cut off from all genuine human contact.

Perhaps Metcalf's best story, the title piece, "The Teeth of My Father," is at once a moving elegy for Metcalf's father and a summing-up of his rhetorical concerns as a writer. Like the other stories in the sequence, it deals with the relationship between the artist's execution of his craft and his own personal life, but it does so more subtly by exploring the reality of fiction as opposed to the factual reality of life. Early in the story, which incorporates whole stories or parts of others that Metcalf has previously written, the speaking "I" utters a remark that is both an admonition to and a directive for the reader: "I have decided to tell the truth." . . . The story appears to be—indeed, admits to be through the speaking voice of the "I"—"the truth," but a truth that is a supreme piece of fiction. "The Teeth of My Father" is about the craft of fiction itself—about the artist's act of shaping or manipulating experience to give it a greater reality—and there are occasions in the story when Metcalf deliberately shatters the art illusion (the narrator's comments on the incorporated story "Biscuits," for instance) to draw attention to the art itself and to his performance as fiction writer. Like all Metcalf's stories in this collection, "The Teeth of My Father" demonstrates the brilliantly austere craftsmanship of John Metcalf as a short story writer. These stories are, quite simply, the works of an artist. (p. 37)

> Barry Cameron, "In Praise of the Craft," in The
> Canadian Forum, Vol. LV, No. 653, August, 1975,
> pp. 36-7.

JOHN MUGGERIDGE

In these alienated times what a novelist needs is not roots, but withered roots. John Metcalf . . . unearths his particular set in *Private Parts,* the first of [*Girl in Gingham*'s] two novellas and a mawkishly sentimental account of growing up sexually repressed among North of England Methodists during the 1940s. . . .

Bound with *Private Parts* comes *Girl in Gingham,* a sprightly well-crafted piece refreshingly free of sentimentality and sexology. . . . *Girl in Gingham* discusses a real issue: the connection between technology and happiness. All of us half believe in its existence. Whatever our education we turn the pages of a sales catalogue expectantly. In Metcalf's story Peter Thornton, a divorced fine-arts expert, is persuaded by his friends to try a computer dating service. They have a good laugh over filling out the questionnaire, but when the calls start coming

in, Thornton returns them. . . . The climax in *Girl in Gingham* is reached when the connoisseur comes face to face with the last of his computerized lovers. This is by far the best part of either novella. The scene in the Port and Starboard Restaurant where Thornton, amid the liturgical comings and goings of waiters, finds out that he has met his soul mate, is handled with taut precision. Metcalf even manages to inject it with that rarest of all ingredients in modern fiction, effective melodrama.

The book's main flaw is Metcalf's alienation from the New World. He complains, for instance, about the barbaric spelling of Canadian Tire. Readers who don't know rugger songs are simply lacking in culture, Metcalf's roots, however authentically withered, are on the wrong side of the Atlantic.

> John Muggeridge, "Sex and the Dating Service," in
> Maclean's Magazine, Vol. 91, No. 12, June 12, 1978,
> p. 73.

JOHN MILLS

John Metcalf's narrator in *Private Parts,* one of the two novellas in this new book [*Girl in Gingham*], looks back on an experience, primal in its way, involving a village idiot who worked on his uncle's farm in the north of England during the war. (p. 175)

[*Private Parts*] deals at one level with childhood sexuality—with the routine business of masturbation, of fumblings with the other sex, of the bright fantasies of adolescence, of finally losing one's virginity. As such it invites comparison with *Portnoy's Complaint,* but it is better than Roth's slick, chic, opportunistic, and shallow book by a long way; and its comedy is in part created by a spare, understated, classical style beyond Roth. . . . In our century subject matter like this has only just been released for imaginative literature from the clutches of psychologists and pox doctors in whose hands, so to speak, it resided from the death of Havelock Ellis to the advent of Lenny Bruce. Thus it is still fresh enough to be entertaining in its own right, and most of us can, from a plain description of someone else's experience, enjoy the frisson of recognizing our own. But the novella doesn't stop there. The narrator's father is a self-effacing Methodist minister whose eccentricity is only revealed to the son much later in life and after the former's death. Parental authority goes by default to a fanatical, perhaps diabolical, mother. It is she who teaches the narrator that life is joyless or, if it is not, that it then should be and that flesh is sinful. Her Manichaeanism extends beyond this simple body-spirit dichotomy to include, in its polarities, regions of the body. Thus, when she bathes her son she leaves his genitals out but hands him a sponge and orders him to "wash yourself" thereby setting up in the boy's mind a moral inferiority residing in the private parts of the title. There is no forgiveness in the narrator for this kind of thing. . . . As he grows past puberty, however, he engages this woman in battle. He disobeys her; he introduces taboo subjects, like the derivation of the word "bugger," at dinner table. When he takes her on, he is conscious that he is also doing battle with the entire puritan, life-denying, ethical tradition which he inherits and which he also associates with dark north-of-England towns and bleak moorlands. . . . In one of the story's most brilliant and harrowing scenes, his mother discovers a copy of a nudist magazine from which he is in the habit of culling masturbation images and makes him kneel with her in prayer, dragging him to the floor, wallowing in a sadistic orgy of religiosity sexual in its intensity until he is reduced to a "shuddering, tear-wracked hysteria." . . . (pp. 175-76)

How, in conventional morality, ought this boy to be punished? He is clearly not, in accordance with Baden-Powell's *Scouting for Boys,* one of those "decent clean-living chaps who will have nothing to do with this beastliness." Will he go blind? Catch tuberculosis? Rachitis? ("Will I be OK if I just do it in strong sunlight?") The modern, liberated adult, of course, rightly laughs at such myths. He will tend to replace them with canting nonsense of his own. He might say that the child stands in danger of preferring fantasy to reality. (So what?) Or he might say, as Norman Mailer says somewhere, that he will pay for masturbation by sluggishness of sexual response in later life. By and large, however, it is *all right* to masturbate. But what about hating his Mum? About not forgiving her? Will he not pay for *that?* The liberal permitter might argue that the boy will eventually grow to tolerate his mother, to love her even, as he begins to understand her and to recognize the nature of her problems. On the other hand, of course, why should he learn to love that which is hateful, to tolerate the intolerable? . . . What, then, given this background, happens to him in later life?

It is here that Metcalf's narrative darkens. In the final section of the book the narrator, whose name, we discover, is written up in his university catalogue as T. D. Moore . . . is observed washing dishes after a party. It is early morning and he can't sleep. A hangover partly explains his gloom. On the other hand, there is much to be gloomy about: he teaches at a university, some would say a form of purgatory in itself, to support his art. His art consists of writing "finely tuned" stories in a minor key about "loneliness and self-discovery." A partitioned-off section of the basement between furnace and washing machine serves him as a study. So much for the life that "would be lived in the sun." The "laughter," the "beautiful women, warm flesh" all have been reduced to this stale domesticity, his sex-life withered to a Saturday morning fumble while the children are pre-occupied with a television programme. His wife, in any case, is not as attractive to him as she used to be.

At first sight it looks as though Metcalf is punishing Moore for his sexual fantasies and hatred of his mother by plunging him into boredom and alienation. In fact, however, Moore knows exactly what has happened to him:

> It's as if I exhausted all my passion by the age
> of sixteen: nothing since has compared with the
> drama of that battle of wills, a titanic struggle
> fought against the backdrop of Hell.

It is against this backdrop that his sense of being was at its most intense. The backdrop is removed. He wins his various battles. But without the melodrama of conflict his sense of being begins to wane. Boredom and alienation are the penalties for "winning through" to a lack of belief. He is also aware that to his children he is almost a Bronze-Age figure who pre-existed TV and the Age of Permission. Is he depriving his children of this strong experience of selfhood by refusing to provide them with a melodramatic household like the one provided for him by his mother? What alternative is there to living blandly and producing bland and spineless children whose demands are no sooner stated than they are met? (pp. 176-77)

Metcalf ends *Private Parts* by having Moore finding a second-hand store in an "unfamiliar" part of Montreal. On some obscure impulse he walks in and buys a sextant. . . . I suppose

one could argue that Metcalf is using this sextant as a rebus—a punning device. On the other hand, an allegorist might say that the point of a sextant is that one focusses part of it on the sun, an image of transcendence, and another on the horizon, an image of the earth, the material. A Jungian would probably want to know what seas the narrator hopes to navigate towards the goal of totality. But the true meaning of this sextant is Metcalf's secret and I hope he keeps it to himself. All I know is that it ends perfectly, one of the most profound and delightful works of fiction I have read in a long time.

The subject matter of *Girl in Gingham* is more secular than that of *Private Parts* and thus its power and interest are consequently diminished. It is a third-person narrative concerning a divorcee who—lonely, bored, and depressed—finds himself acquiescing in a friend's hoax whereby his name is placed on a computer dating list. The computer presents him with a list of women some of whom he is able to disqualify by phone, another he actually encounters in the highly neurotic flesh. These episodes are hilarious. It is one of Metcalf's great strengths as a writer that he is able to reinforce the comedy with which he treats his material with the fundamental seriousness of the protagonists' situations. In *Girl in Gingham* the hero, between his attempts at romance, tries to live his day-to-day life but cannot adjust to the absence of his wife. In desperation he phones the last number on his list and subsequently meets his ideal—the girl of the title. But Metcalf does not allow him to enjoy her, and, in fact, the narrative takes a strange, even grotesque, twist which does not seem to me to be anything other than gratuitous. It is as though Metcalf *really,* in this story, wants to punish his protagonist but for reasons he doesn't make clear to the reader. Or perhaps he wishes to create a romantic mood in his reader then castigate him for it. (pp. 177-78)

> *John Mills, in a review of "Girl in Gingham," in*
> The Fiddlehead, *No. 118, Summer, 1978, pp. 174-78.*

ROBERT A. LECKER

Both stories [in *Girl in Gingham*] are marked by Metcalf's deft handling of narrative voices which are linked to subtly cohering formal structures. . . .

In *Private Parts* we encounter a narrator who is conscious—all too conscious—of the aesthetic implications of the autobiographical fragments he presents. "I find I can't distinguish between real and imagined events," he says. Life, as he sees it, is "mainly lies." To put it another way, life in *Private Parts* is always seen in terms of art, and thus it comes as no surprise to learn that the narrator is himself a writer dedicated to mythologizing the "sequence of anecdote and reflection" which constitute the private parts of memory. (p. 27)

The most obvious feature of *Private Parts* is the "frenzied," "feverish" obsession with the meaning and mechanics of Sex ("Such words as 'desire' or 'lust' are pallid counters for the raw actuality"). Although virtually every page is studded with alternately grotesque and amusing pictures of masturbation, perversion, and mini-catalogues of genitalia, each of these descriptions serves more importantly to reveal the narrator's anxious, insecure mind. By the end of the story we realize that the "private parts" referred to are not only sexual but spiritual, social, and aesthetic: fragments are drawn together to create a unified character who lives "alone in silence" and apart from love.

Girl in Gingham is about Peter Thornton and the identity crisis he experiences after his marriage collapses. By using a third person point of view which allows him to digress upon the social and psychological conditions accounting for Peter's present state of mind, Metcalf is able to comment on a hypocritical, technology-governed world which mechanizes love and transforms feeling into a stilted, role-played response. Set in contrast to a real but thwarted internal desire for family, friendship, and community is an external, computerized lifestyle which promises romance at the flick of a switch. Peter submits to completing a questionnaire from a CompuDate service. . . . The ironies of the story develop (hilariously and pathetically) as a succession of ''ideal'' mates are revealed in all their neurotic and self-deluding glory. . . . [Each] of the potential ''Computer Compatibles'' is aligned with symbols and gestures that enrich our understanding of the multi-levelled nature of Peter's quest. Like the narrator of *Private Parts* Peter is forced to make fiction of reality in order to find rituals of stability in the midst of chaos. He not only mythologizes the past but dramatizes the future, perceiving each woman he is about to meet as the heroine in a great fantasy of love. The perfect ''girl in gingham'' never appears, but Peter persists in calling the last name on his list because the ''final chapter'' which would provide ''a fitting conclusion to this dismal adventure'' had to be lived out. It is only through his meeting with Anna that the romantic fantasies that have haunted Peter are violently cast aside in a series of carefully structured scenes which lead up to a brutally realistic conclusion. As a mark of Metcalf's skill, we see that the larger thematic conflicts between dream and reality, art and life are reflected and respected in the most minute details and objects: toothpicks, drinking glasses, an unopened box—all function toward illuminating the general design.

Near the end of *Private Parts* the narrator tells us that (much like Metcalf's own writing) his work has been described as '''sensitive' and 'finely-tuned explorations of loneliness and self-discovery.''' That comment could well be applied here, but there is also technical competence—style and form working together to produce entertainment *and* significance. (p. 28)

Robert A. Lecker, ''Private Art,'' in The Canadian Forum, *Vol. LVIII, No. 684, September, 1978, pp. 27-8.*

MICHAEL SMITH

Ned Lud (with one d) was an English lunatic who in a fit of rage smashed up a Leicestershire weaver's mill and thereby inspired the destructive Luddite movement of the early 1800s to adopt his name. His spiritual descendant in John Metcalf's novel [*General Ludd*] is James Wells, poet, winner of the Governor General's Award, whose alcoholic frenzy is directed not at industrial mechanization but the production of kitsch. As writer in residence at St. Xavier's University his target is the new Communication Arts Complex where, to his horror, students learn about ''listening skills'' and ''the societal uses of advertising.'' He blames television in particular for the illiteracy, cultural poverty, debasement of feeling, and distortion of reality that surround him every day.

Wells's reaction to this pervasive mediocrity . . . alternates between sour disbelief and drunken sprees, which twice land him in hospital. A prisoner of society, he searches for escape in grotty night spots and a rural winter retreat, but without success. . . . [It's] no surprise when he finally unleashes his fury on one of his adult students, Itzic Zemermann, a pathetic, crippled Jew who has survived the Nazi concentration camps only to become a persistent writer of atrocious, pseudo-pastoral verse. Of course, the confrontation ends in disaster.

We know it *has* to end in disaster, because Zemermann is so heaped with the trappings of a victim. For while Metcalf's previous fiction has been marked by finesse, he writes here with the deftness of an anvil. . . . His characters seldom have any more dimension than the stick-figures that Wells habitually doodles, and tend to find themselves introduced, then thoughtlessly forgotten. Perhaps because Wells leads a portable, self-contained existence as a poet, Metcalf neglects to give even him more than the sketchiest of pasts. It's one of the novel's mysteries that Wells should be so infatuated with his rather ordinary girlfriend, Kathy Neilson, and that she should see anything appealing in him—yet their relationship is central to Wells's eventual downfall.

It's easy to agree with Metcalf's attack on the mass media, whose simplifications, jargon, and clichés seem to have corrupted every level of society, but as a novel *General Ludd* is overly obsessed with his message. As a result, the chapters mostly comprise a collection of comic set-pieces—a faculty reception, a poetry reading, and so forth—to which Wells, as the first-person narrator, applies his caustic, single-minded commentary. Stripped of these cameo performances, the book is no more complicated than an extended short story. The climactic scene where Wells plots to destroy the Communication Arts Complex is telegraphed from the moment he sets foot in the place, not to mention the obvious historical hint in the title.

Michael Smith, ''Kitsch 22: A Pass Option in Mediocrity,'' in Books in Canada, *Vol. 9, No. 7, August-September, 1980, p. 9.*

BARBARA CAMPBELL

John Metcalf's latest novel, *General Ludd,* will fan the flames of many a jaded academic, with its scathing attack on Canada's literary society. . . .

Sparing nobody, from a crippled aspiring poet, Itzic Zemermann, to a muddled university dean, Metcalf's humour is at times superb. However, it is coloured by ferocious cynicicm, suggesting a distorted vision that almost destroys credibility. This is unfortunate, since the central figure, Jim Wells, who is obsessed with restoring a respect for literature, clarifies some serious problems in Canadian publishing.

Through describing Wells' stint as writer-in-residence at Montreal's fictional St. Xavier University, Metcalf reduces eccentric professors, disrespectful students, and the bureaucratic system to absurdity. As Wells becomes deeply depressed, his drinking increases. His verbal diatribes, liberally peppered with eloquent poetry as well as base profanity, are frequently more tedious than entertaining. Paradoxically, his struggle for higher ideals only drags him deeper into depravity, and mental illness. . . .

The novel ends with a reference to the approaching spring. However, this essentially static plot, with disjointed episodes, shallow characters, and Wells' poorly developed relationship to Kathy Neilson, belies such positive growth. Like the original General Lud, who led a violent movement to gain rights for textile workers, Wells' struggles and Metcalf's novel create a great fuss, that leads nowhere.

*Barbara Campbell, in a review of "General Ludd,"
in* Quill and Quire, *Vol. 46, No. 10, October, 1980,
p. 35.*

CARY FAGAN

During the course of [*General Ludd,* protagonist Jim Wells] is
poet-in-residence at St. Xavier's, a second-rate university in
Montreal, where he falls in love with a faculty member, Kathy
Neilson, goes on several self-destructive binges, tries to destroy
the university's sophisticated Communication Arts Complex,
and ends up in a mental institution.

Sounds like an exciting and moving plot. It isn't, primarily
because Metcalf is so interested in scoring satiric points and
staging comic set-pieces, that he doesn't take the time to develop real characters with emotions we can understand. Although Wells narrates the novel, we never get to know him
well enough to believe he is the genius/madman that Metcalf
assumes he is. . . . And yet Metcalf expects us to react emotionally to the rare moments of human feeling he does provide—Wells and Kathy falling in love, Wells discovering that
the *Collected Poems* of his late friend and idol, John Caverly,
has been remaindered. These moments come too quickly after
the satire, and the shift from cardboard characters to real people
is bewildering.

As for the satire, *General Ludd* has made me realize how
difficult it is to criticize in a novel and still hold the reader's
interest. Even when I agreed with Wells's anger, I found his
ranting tedious and unoriginal. Metcalf starts off right by making his attacks humorous. . . . But Metcalf quickly loses his
touch. Near the end, he has his mouthpiece Wells list his
complaints as if he were reciting a laundry list. . . . Another
fault in Metcalf's criticism is its superficiality. He points to
the symptoms alright . . . , but he doesn't try to discover *why*
we have them, or who is trying to turn our country into a vast
Eaton Centre. The intimation Metcalf gives is that we *deserve*
it. Whenever he mentions us, the ordinary people (that is, not
true poets) it is with hatred and disgust. (p. 39)

But perhaps Metcalf's criticism is most ineffective because it
is so heartless. Why should we hate TV and fast food and
shopping malls? Because they alienate us from things of real
value, and especially from each other. Wells feels so superior
and is so self-obsessed that he is incapable of loving, something
that Metcalf cannot see. Wells says he loves Kathy, but we
never see it, or feel it. There is a general lack of caring among
the characters in the book, and Metcalf himself does not try
to understand any character who is not a persona of himself;
so he relies on stereotypes, of gays, Indians, Portuguese, Russians, and especially, Jews.

Itzic Zemermann, for example, is a character central to the
novel. At first he is introduced purely for comic effect, comic
because: 1. he is Jewish; 2. he has a funny accent; 3. he is
extremely pushy; 4. he is a cripple; 5. he is a survivor of the
Holocaust; 6. he writes bad poetry. Metcalf gets all the laughs
out of a wheel-chair that he can. . . . And yet, some interesting
and important themes could be raised through Itzic; the amoral
cruelty of a fate that strikes a man with both a concentration
camp and then polio, the pathetic truth that tragedy does not
always give rise to great art.

But Metcalf does not pursue these ideas. Instead, he uses Itzic
as the central metaphor for all that Wells sees as wrong in our
society. . . . There are many ways Metcalf could have attacked

the misuse of language in this country, but to do it by ridiculing
a handicapped Jewish survivor who uses English as a second
language is, to be kind, a bad choice. And the scene where
Wells becomes so *earnest* in sermonizing to Itzic on the real
value of poetry that Itzic has a heart attack and dies, is inex-
cusable.

In *General Ludd* there are a few moments of real human emotion and good satiric humour, but they are overwhelmed by
Metcalf's disturbing fundamental beliefs and values. The writer
thinks he is holding a mirror up to our faces to show us who
we really are. He ought to turn the mirror around and take a
hard look at himself. (pp. 39-40)

Cary Fagan, "Misguided Accuser," in The Canadian Forum, *Vol. LX, No. 705, December, 1980-
January, 1981, pp. 39-40.*

GEOFF HANCOCK [INTERVIEW WITH JOHN METCALF]

HANCOCK: *Is it safe to say that you're very pessimistic about
the educational system in Canada? Your narrator in* **General
Ludd** . . .

METCALF: The narrator in *Ludd* is apoplectic on the subject.
And so am I. Who isn't pessimistic, other than "educators"?
The quality of education has declined everywhere over the last
50 years as the number to be educated has risen. (pp. 99-100)

In **Going Down Slow** *and* **General Ludd** *you manage to criticize
both the high schools and the universities, at least in Quebec.*

Not a difficult feat. Yes, they've formed subject matter simply
because I've spent a lot of my professional life as a teacher. . . .
But the educational systems haven't really been subject matter
for me. More backgrounds. *Going Down Slow* is less about
school systems than about a love affair which ends in betrayal
through compromise. Though I suppose it's the system which
forces the compromise.

*In fact, in your dramatic scheme, the system becomes the an-
tagonist?*

Yes, that's probably true not only with the educational world
but with the world in general. And particularly with the world
as I experience it in North America. I'm violently in conflict
with the dominant nature of North American society and this
affords me at varying times great distress and great amusement.

This is what you want to write about in your work?

No, it isn't what I *want* to write about. It's what I've been
almost *driven* to write about. One writes about where one lives.
I happen to live in Canada. I *have* been writing about Canada
from the viewpoint of being an immigrant to this country and
I get considerable mileage out of the comic and serious contrasts between Canada and Europe. But it's all emotionally
complicated. (pp. 100-01)

*What did you learn from Evelyn Waugh? Did you learn form,
did you learn structure? Did you learn the difference between
the novel, the novella, the story?*

No, No, nothing like that. I heard a voice and I saw a tremendous craftsman manipulating words in a delicious order.
I was offered an example of something damn close to perfection. I suppose I learned a great deal about timing and pacing,
about precision and crispness. (p. 103)

He's so difficult to talk about. In . . . [a] *Paris Review* interview
he was asked what he felt about criticism and he said,

"Naturally I abhor the Cambridge movement of criticism" (by which he meant F. R. Leavis and the Scrutineers) "with its horror of elegance and its members mutually encouraging uncouth writing."

Now I'd like to expand on that because I consider my own work to be fairly elegant and it's something I've suffered for at the hands of readers and critics. Critics in Canada don't have a horror of elegance. They don't even know it's there. . . .

You can't *explain* elegance. It's pointless to try. (p. 104)

You're something like your character Jim Wells in that you're also inside and outside the system at the same time. In **General Ludd,** *Wells as a writer is inside the system yet harshly critical of it.*

Personally, I'm very much outside the system. I cannot conceive of anything more horrible than being inside. I make raids into enemy territory every now and then when funds are running low. But I don't really think that the people who employ me pretend that I'm massively *with* them.

Does that also apply to where you stand in Canadian Literature? Waugh's comment about Leavis and the Cambridge school of criticism might also apply to critics in Canada. CanLitCrit tends to deal with the ideas *of a fiction and not usually with the technical accomplishment.*

Well. Let's take that in two parts. I don't think I stand *anywhere* in the CanLit Scheme. . . . My work suffers from a paucity of Indians and Myth. I have very few readers and the critics are still largely baying at the thematic moon. (pp. 104-05)

Now as to the critics and their horror of elegance and their mutually encouraging uncouth writing. Says it all, doesn't it? All the criticism we've had in the last ten years has been intellectually embarrassing. Patricia Morely, John Moss, Clara Thomas—I'd rather read Eddie A. Guest *and* fail my Wasserman Test. Our newspaper reviews are not unusually illiterate. (p. 105)

In your own work, you comment quite strongly on various aspects of Canadian writing. Do you see yourself as a satirist or moralist?

Certainly there's a satirical bent, even perhaps a moralistic bent in my writing. And I mean moralistic in a bad sense. An element of preaching, I'm afraid—I certainly wouldn't deny that.

I was going to say that **General Ludd** *is like a one-man demolition derby.* **Private Parts: A Memoir** *is almost an allegory with the River Eden, the fall from grace, sermonettes . . .*

What a revolting word! But, yes. I don't think **Parts** is moralistic at all. But I wouldn't defend **Ludd** against that charge. **Ludd**'s very much a public book. This comes back to what we were talking about before. Canada drives me into opposition—loving opposition, of course. And opposition does tend to encourage sermonizing and castigation and fulminating like one of the gloomier prophets. . . .

If one cares about what Canada could become, it's difficult to restrain criticism of what it *is*. Which is a mess. And it's a mess for interlocking reasons. Take our cities as an example. For the most part, they're visual slums. This isn't simply because we have bad architects. It's because those with money have bad taste. They have bad taste, in part, because of our educational system and its dominant values—which reflects our political system. There are many people staggeringly wealthy

in Canada but the rich middle class wields no artistic influence as it does in other countries. (p. 111)

The whole ethos of Canada is one of Take. We've not yet grown to a point where people think of ways to give. It's a place from which people extract—as though it were a vast mine—and all they leave behind is ugly tailings. This attitude seems to permeate every aspect of Canadian life. Big Bucks. Top Dollar. How is it possible *not* to hate that?

Do you see your fiction, then, as an instrument by which this may be changed?

No, I'm not *that* bloody daft. Fiction doesn't work that way. But something I say might touch a heart here or there . . . I suppose that behind a lot of my fiction there hovers a ghost of somewhere else—Europe, England—where there's a different kind of attitude towards the country, where there's been a much longer tradition of passionate caring for place.

This is very apparent if you place **Girl in Gingham** *and* **Private Parts** *side by side.*

Yes. The idea of the divorced person is particularly significant to me for reasons which extend beyond the purely personal. I somehow see divorce as being metaphorical in many ways for life in Canada. Everybody knows what we're divorced *from*—from the land itself, from anything resembling a cohesive society, from a past, from our countries of origin. . . . The events in *Girl in Gingham*—CompuMate and all the wounded people—suggest, I hope, more than the literal.

I have a pessimistic view of what we've wrought in Canada, a view not far removed from Levine's conclusion to *Canada Made Me*. That doesn't mean that I have contempt for all the individual lives in Canada but the totality of those lives has not created a society yet. We traded one form of wilderness for another—bush for shopping centres.

It sounds arrogant, I suppose, but I want to add my 5-cents worth in my special field to try and raise the standards of one part of our life here. The standards are so very obvious and cast a strong and *uncomfortable* light. We're so frightened of the idea of excellence—and with damn good reason.

You certainly apply those standards to your work, your stories, the rhythms of the sentences, the words, the relationship of one word to another, even the punctuation has a considerable sense of grace and style.

I hope so. I repeat myself but stories are verbal structures. Everyone is so busy grubbing about to find an unfindable "what" that they pay no attention to the "how"—and it's the "how" that *is* the "what". I'm using these terms because I'm referring to John Ciardi's little book *How Does a Poem Mean?* Every English teacher in the country ought to have a copy. We don't read *King Lear* for its silly, pantomime story. We read it because it's written in words that have been forged into compelling order.

In fact, that's something that you often do in your own work. You use words almost for their own sake. Your stories are just filled with very unusual words, odd words, strange-sounding words, words that send us off to the dictionary.

I certainly hope I *don't* use words for their own sake. I only use words that seem to me entirely appropriate within the context and that produce the rhetorical effect I wish to achieve. I certainly don't put words into my stories which *I* have to find in dictionaries. (pp. 112-13)

You also use pieces of words and once carefully examined the code letters in a telegram. Letters themselves have a specific weight.

Well the examination of a telegram's code letters was to indicate something of the emotional context of the person doing the examining but, yes, I have a deep and probably neurotic interest in what you might call the *calligraphic* look of words on a page. It's part of writing well. All writers do it to some extent.

In fact, the text and typeface of your pages look almost like John Cage compositions. You've got the bold type, the italic type, upper case, lower case, the sentence fragments, and all kinds of voices and textures moving in and out; there's a counterpoint, almost like music to the ear and certainly to the eye.

Yes, that's deliberate. For example, over the past few years I've been working out a system of double and single quotation marks to indicate differing levels of voice. And my use of paragraphing is to get different weights and emphases—rather than for syntactical purposes. I write and re-write endlessly to get the exact look and feel of what it is I'm saying. (pp. 113-14)

*Did it take you a while to find your narrative voices? In **General Ludd** the narrative voice is entirely different from that of any of your other work. There's more of a barb in it, more of a sharp tone.*

Well, you're making the assumption that that's my tone or my voice. It's the voice of the narrator. The voice of the narrator in **Private Parts** is very different. The voice of the narrator in **"The Years in Exile"** very different again.

Is voice important to you in your fiction?

I think it's the centre of all fiction. . . .

Do you follow the traditional shape of the story, the so-called dramatic triangle? With a climax and a denouement, strong narrative hook, or do you like the Clark Blaise, Mavis Gallant kind of story that turns around, goes back inside itself? Or do you just follow your intuition and find the shape of the story as you discover it? (p. 116)

A lot of my early stories were very traditional in form—epiphany stories. The only way I wasn't traditional, perhaps, was that I always worked with great intensity, very close-up. And then I wrote some stories which were less traditional in form and the last story I wrote was even modish—or appeared to be.

Most critics seem to have me pegged as a very traditional writer. I'm not sure why. Stories like **"The Teeth of My Father"** and **"The Eastmill Reception Centre"** aren't Katherine Mansfield exactly. But I don't follow any school or manner. To use your word, I just *discover* the right shape.

I write each page 20 times over and it's in that rewriting that I eventually find the shape it has to be. I start with a sentence which I might elaborate and expand for half a page. That elaboration throws off an image, say, which I recognize as being what I wanted from the start. So I scrap the half page and start again from that image and then go on to a second sentence. In that second sentence, the same thing might happen again. It's a process of chipping away endless layers of language.

Of course, I know what the story's "about" before I start. That's more or less irrelevant. What the story's really about is the operation of language.

And how language reveals scenes, images . . .

Exactly. I think some people consider my stories rather pedestrian—full of *detailed*, factual *things*. But those people haven't read closely enough—haven't given their whole attention to those things—because it's out of giving yourself totally to the evoked *thing* that meanings and significances arise. Some of my stories, though concrete, are very mysterious. **"Keys and Watercress"** is a good example. (p. 118)

Where do stories start for you? With scenes, an image, a character, an object, with an emotional gathering in your heart?

They certainly never start with an idea. There's nothing I want to say to anybody. I want to make people *feel*. I want them to live inside the experience of the story and by doing that, by responding to the story's texture and rhetoric, they'll find that meanings *grow out of* the seemingly meaningless.

Stories can start for me with a sound or a scene or a detail which is dreamlike or surrealistic in its intensity. This detail, say, might be remembered from the distant past or it might be something I saw yesterday which jumped at me. (p. 119)

Where do your characters come from? How do you bring your characters to move through the story?

I don't know where characters come from. I'd say they usually come somehow from voices. Whenever I read detective stories or thrillers—those kinds of books which tell you for half a page what someone looks like—I always skip that description because I can never really visualize the person. On the other hand, the character's only got to speak two or three sentences and I get a fairly immediate mental picture of what they look like. Dialogue works so quickly to invent character. And the voice, the vocabulary, the rhythms, the sentence patterns—everything they say *implies* their past history, social status, education, etc. etc. So I work back from the voice to be able to see them clearly. The voices will tell you everything if you'll only listen.

Do you think in sequences of stories, interlocked stories?

I'm pleased you asked that. There seems to be a vogue in Canada for sequences of stories and I think I know exactly why. It's because it turns the story collection into something that's just a touch closer to a novel. (pp. 119-20)

Different rhetorics, amazingly different and various worlds, different voices—that's the joy of a story collection. I just can't see why one would wish to restrict oneself to eight stories about the same character or eight stories about alienation in Hamilton, Ont. (p. 120)

Surely the only way of judging a collection of stories is by asking if each story, individually, succeeds in creating a real world, if each one, individually, is an entrancing performance. And if it does and if it is, in God's name, what more could you ask for?

So, in fact, that's what connects all your works?

There might well be more. I'm not a critic. But for me, the one demand is that the work be done well. This desire for an expressed "philosophy" seems to me basically philistine. Or French. (pp. 120-21)

Do you feel more comfortable with short stories than novels?

Yes, definitely. I like the novella form, too. I've said this often before—that the story form is close to poetry. With a novel, you can chuck in bits and pieces of anything that appeals to you. You can expand scenes outrageously if you like them or truncate them if they're boring you and nobody really seems to notice. With a story, you've got to get it dead right. A beat or two off and it's ruined. I just cannot control language and shape over 300 pages the way I can over 20.

How do you feel about your last novel, **General Ludd?**

Mixed feelings. It's most probably a failure as a cohesive work of art. I was insufficiently distanced. Yet, on the other hand, I think it contains chunks which are funnier than anything that's ever been written in Canada. Which isn't a particularly arrogant or immodest comment when you consider the competition. I think the book's probably worth preserving for the nightclub scene, the chapter with Julia Hetherington, the Russian writers—and a few other odds and sods. But Flaubert it ain't.

You often use women characters to bring out the softer aspects of the male characters. And in fact Jim and Kathy's relationship in **General Ludd** *is one of your most successful.*

Well, that doesn't say much for earlier relationships. It's probably a suicidal thing to do in our literary climate but I want to be honest about the book. I don't need critics to tell me the book's flaws. I've got a more lively awareness about my own work than they have. And I judge my work by comparing it with the best, with the *great* comic writers—Naipaul, Waugh, Waterhouse, etc.

It's a troubled book. I was setting out to write comedy, dark comedy admittedly, but somehow got overmastered by rage so that there's a blurring between Jim Wells as character and me as writer. And this pulls the book out of sharp focus. I wish it were a better book. But the next one will be because I learned a lot from writing **Ludd**.

But you were talking about Kathy. I was unhappy about her all the way through the writing. She isn't realized well. I feel she's very much a lay figure, as it were. The problem for me was that the book was Jim's voice. Kathy was more or less a plot device, a balancing force of reason, a counterweight. But I didn't *care* about her. She wasn't real to me. She wasn't *alive* in the way that Julia Hetherington's alive. I loved that Julia chapter—all those deranged kids—and the way it turns emotional direction at the end becoming quietly sad. *Beautiful* writing. (pp. 121-22)

But I don't mind that the book's less than perfect because in doing it I learned a great deal about my weaknesses and strengths. It crystalized for me some important ideas or feelings about character.

Can you expand on that?

Sure. I realized through writing **Ludd** that what really *delights* me is caricature and cartoon. And I'm thinking now of ways of applying caricature to the story form. I think the thing that saves **Ludd,** for me, is the series of portraits. . . . All these gave me delight. Other parts of the book were willed. (pp. 122-23)

One last question: Where are you taking your fiction now? Or where is your fiction taking you?

As I was saying a minute ago, I'm brooding about caricature and all the implications of that. It suggests extensive formal changes. I suspect I'm working up to something *broadly* comic. But it will most likely be stories or novellas. . . .

I'm exploring, as I've always been exploring so far as I can see, ways of playing with language, with rhetoric, to make my worlds, in the plural, real and compelling. (p. 123)

Geoff Hancock and John Metcalf, in an interview in The Canadian Fiction Magazine, *No. 39, 1981, pp. 97-123.*

MORRIS WOLFE

[In *Kicking Against the Pricks*] Metcalf lashes out—satirically, we're told—at the Canadian literary community, whose greatest sin, it seems, is that it hasn't given one John Metcalf the respect and attention he deserves. Everywhere Metcalf turns he runs into pricks. . . . I think Metcalf even suspects *me* of being a prick. (p. 31)

Morris Wolfe, "Sticks and Stones: From the Perplexities of Modern-Day Etiquette to Yet One More Shameful Episode in Canadian History," in Books in Canada, *Vol. 11, No. 9, November, 1982, pp. 30-1.**

ROBIN SKELTON

John Metcalf is so good a writer that any book in which he discusses his own beliefs and working methods cannot fail to be of more than usual interest, even this one [*Kicking Against the Pricks*] where only three of the nine parts command re-reading. These three are the opening interview of Metcalf by Geoff Hancock [see excerpt above], which is conversational, candid, shrewd and frequently funny; the essay on his childhood and early reading, which is revelatory: and his study entitled **"Punctuation as Score",** which should be placed on the short list of essential reading for writers and studied with care.

In the first two of these, the mixture of gossip, critical assertions, verbal squibs, self-analyses and satirical reflections is effective because the tone is that of friendly, if acidulous, conversation. In the essay on punctuation, which, unhappily, is quoted extensively in the preceding interview, the tone is consistently serious, the writing precise and lucid. In the other essays, however, the wholly justified jeremiads on the paucity of readers for Canadian books, the ludicrous incompetence of reviewers, the appalling state of our educational system and the dangerous absurdity of what J. B. Priestly called our Ad-mass Civilization, are marred by comments and asides whose frivolity entertains even while it undermines one's faith in the reliability of the author's judgement. His verdicts on the work of other writers are made casually, summarily, as if no appeal were possible, and yet his contention that Irving Layton is one of our best poets and W. P. Kinsella one of our worst writers is, at the very least, disputable. . . .

Indeed, Metcalf exposes his tastes more efficiently than he explains his judgments. And his tastes lead him to praise a small number of writers who appear to be close friends. . . . Others, who may or may not be as interesting, are consigned to outer darkness. . . .

Almost none, save the dead, escape whipping. In the anecdotal essays on the Montreal Story Tellers group and on being a writer-in-residence, authors are largely portrayed as eccentric, hard-drinking, arrogant, irresponsible and lazy; many readers might well ask why such people should be taken seriously. The answer is, of course, that many writers delight in self-mockery and distrust pretension, and that good literature is only rarely written by the humourless and sober. . . .

Metcalf is certainly inconsistent. He maintains that the content of a novel is unimportant and that ''what *is* important is how the work is performed'' and then castigates writers for their subject matter. He praises elegance and cocks snooks. He states that ''a mass readership and a literary writer are incompatible'' and considers P. G. Wodehouse a master. Had H. L. Mencken not already used the title this book could well have been called ''Selected Prejudices''.

Metcalf clearly sees himself as a member of an aristocracy, as did Waugh, and like Waugh he seeks to relieve our sacred cows of their distressing inflation by summary puncture. Like Waugh, he sees himself also as out of step with the times, and it is this that enables him to follow passionate prophecies of disaster with derisive and capering comedy.

Robin Skelton, ''John Metcalf Goads the Literary Establishment,'' in Quill and Quire, *Vol. 48, No. 11, November, 1982, p. 23.*

Wright (Marion) Morris

1910-

American novelist, short story writer, essayist, critic, memoirist, and photographer.

A prolific writer who has published works in a variety of genres, Morris is best known for his novels, in which he focuses on such themes as the quest for identity, relationships between males and females, the effects of the past on people's lives, the relativity of knowledge, and the values associated with material success. He explores these themes while experimenting with various narrative techniques and deemphasizing plot and action. Morris's works feature distinctly American settings and characters whose personalities are revealed by how they define and pursue "the American Dream." Most of his works are set in the Midwestern Plains area; he recreates Midwestern idioms and catalogues recognizable objects while evoking subtle meaning and pathos in the lives of ordinary people. David Madden says: "Bringing into focus a representative part of America, [Morris] has sought the meaning of legends, myths and realities of America as they survive and prevail in the minds of common men; the uncommon exists for the edification of the common."

Morris's novels have consistently garnered critical respect. His first novel, *My Uncle Dudley* (1942), relates the adventures of middle-aged Dudley and his young nephew, the Kid, as they cross America by automobile. This work introduces several thematic elements which recur in Morris's fiction, including the journey-quest motif and the significance of clichés in American life. An example of the way in which Morris uses clichés and audacious characters in his work occurs when the title character of *My Uncle Dudley* spits in the eye of a corrupt policeman. Two of Morris's best-known works are *The Field of Vision* (1956), which won the National Book Award, and *Ceremony in Lone Tree* (1960). These works have several characters in common and offer different perspectives of past events to reveal their lasting significance on the lives of the characters. Two other important novels, *Fire Sermon* (1971) and *A Life* (1973), involve characters similar to Uncle Dudley and the Kid. In *Fire Sermon*, Kermit, an orphaned boy, journeys with his Uncle Floyd and undergoes a symbolic passage into maturity. In *A Life*, Uncle Floyd comes to terms with his past and the prospect of mortality. *Plain's Song: For Female Voices* (1980), another acclaimed work, represents Morris's most extensive exploration of female characters. Morris received the American Book Award for this novel.

Other works by Morris include his photo-texts, *The Inhabitants* (1946), *God's Country and My People* (1968), and *Wright Morris: Photographs and Words* (1983). These books combine photographs of recognizable artifacts of the Midwest with prose passages that correspond to the pictures. In his works of literary criticism, *The Territory Ahead* (1958) and *Earthly Delights, Unearthly Adornments: American Writers as Image Makers* (1978), Morris discusses a number of American writers, focusing on their use of personal experience as material for their fiction. *A Bill of Rites, A Bill of Wrongs, A Bill of Goods*

Courtesy of Josephine Morris

(1968) offers Morris's views on contemporary American culture.

Morris has also published several volumes of memoirs. *Will's Boy: A Memoir* (1981) covers the first twenty years of Morris's life and includes excerpts from his novels to show how he reworked actual experiences into his fiction. *Solo: An American Dreamer in Europe, 1933-34* (1983) recounts Morris's somewhat disillusioning experiences during his travels in Europe as a young man. *A Cloak of Light: Writing My Life* (1984) is a more conventional autobiographical account of his early struggles to become a writer and his personal life up to 1960.

While Morris is esteemed by critics as an important contemporary American writer, he has never enjoyed a wide readership. John Aldridge descibed him as "the least well-known, and most widely unappreciated important writer alive in this country." The deemphasis of plot and action in his works and his experimentation with the conventions of the novel have been cited as possible reasons for his lack of popular success. Nevertheless, critics praise his ability to use ordinary language and experience to create meaningful stories, as well as his skillful use of a variety of literary techniques.

(See also *CLC*, Vols. 1, 3, 7, 18; *Contemporary Authors*, Vols. 9-12, rev. ed.; *Dictionary of Literary Biography*, Vol. 2; and *Dictionary of Literary Biography Yearbook: 1981*.)

GRANVILLE HICKS

Those of us who strongly admire the work of Wright Morris— a not altogether inconsiderable number of not altogether inconsiderable people—are always wondering why everybody doesn't see his writings as we see them, as one of the most imposing edifices on the contemporary literary horizon. We, who look forward to each book of his as it is announced, and talk about it with excitement when it appears, cannot understand why so many pulses remain calm. Morris has been read, has been praised, has been honored. When anyone sets out to list the best living novelists, his name is usually mentioned. But not always, not automatically, as it ought to be. There is a new aristocracy of men and women of letters—admired by the discriminating and read by the many and therefore, in this affluent age, freed from economic pressures and limitations. That Morris is not yet among them indicates that both he and the reading public are getting less than they deserve. (p. ix)

[Prior to the collection titled *Wright Morris: A Reader,* he wrote] nineteen books: three excursions with camera and typewriter, two collections of essays, fourteen novels. What the French would call *un oeuvre.* We have here the results of more than twenty-five years of disciplined productivity, to be read and enjoyed and meditated upon. As the books appeared, critics were sometimes puzzled because each was different from what had gone before it. This variety is one of his great qualities, and yet I can say, as one who has read them all, that all his books hang together. (pp. ix-x)

There are no villains in Morris's work. Unlike certain of his contemporaries, he finds it no easier to believe in absolute evil than in absolute good, and he has little use for the doctrine of original sin, even as a metaphor. His people are always mixtures of traits that may seem either good or bad according to the circumstances in which one encounters them.... Morris finds people frequently pathetic, often terribly exasperating, and endlessly fascinating.

There are no villains and no heroes of the romantic sort, but Morris does have heroes of his own variety. That is, there are characters who are set apart from the mass of men by virtue of special qualities. We find examples in his first novel, *My Uncle Dudley,* and in his most recent, *In Orbit.* The distinguishing characteristic of a Morris hero is audacity; he is a man who refuses to accept the limitations by which other men are held prisoner. Dudley is no model citizen; on the contrary, he is, when occasion requires, an unscrupulous con man. But he has a boldness that attracts other men to him, and he gets his little bunch of misfit refugees two-thirds of the way across the continent. As Morris sees it, audacity reveals itself in appropriate gestures, and the book ends with a foolish but magnificent gesture on Dudley's part.

In [*In Orbit*], Jubal Gainer, a high school dropout, in the course of a day engages in a fist fight, steals a motorcycle, is accused of rape (of which he is at least guilty in intention), beats one man, and stabs another. Although Jubal is unaware of it, each violent act he performs is a symbolic gesture. He is a kind of natural force, like the tornado that simultaneously visits the town. Some of the more thoughtful of the townspeople who are involved in Jubal's escapades feel the significance of his deeds. One is Hodler, editor of the local newspaper.... [When] Jubal has vanished, Hodler listens to the unhelpful replies that bystanders give to the sheriff. "Did they all dream of being a man on the loose? Envied by inhibited, red-blooded men, pursued by comical galoots like the Sheriff. He went that-a-way.

With the thoughts, fantasies, and envious good wishes of them all.''

In *The Huge Season* we have an apparently more conventional hero, Charles Lawrence, who tries to make the audacious gesture a way of life. He makes such an impression on his associates that, more than twenty years after his death, his example is the central fact in their lives.

One of the most interesting specimens is Gordon Boyd, the ''successful failure'' of *The Field of Vision* and *Ceremony in Lone Tree.* The former occupies a key position in the Morris canon, for it examines several recurrent themes: the relativity of all knowledge, nostalgia and the general problem of the past, the possibilities of human transformation, and the role of heroism. As a boy and young man, Boyd made a series of gestures that evoked the astonished admiration of his companion, Walter McKee: he tried to walk on the water, made off with the pocket of a famous baseball player, and kissed McKee's girl, Lois Scanlon. Although he has never forgotten that there was something special about Boyd, McKee knows that, by conventional standards, he has been a success and Boyd a failure. (pp. xii-xv)

At the end of *The Field of Vision* Boyd seems to have won a victory of sorts, but in *Ceremony in Lone Tree* the situation is not so clear.... We ... learn that Lois engaged herself to McKee so soon after Boyd kissed her because she was afraid of being roused as Boyd had roused her. Although she has managed to seem as much ''on the ice side'' as her husband, her passions have been inhibited but not destroyed. McKee remains as stolid as ever, but, though he is willing to bear witness to Boyd's past heroism, he does not want him in his present. Boyd, ''a completely self-unmade man,'' has at last come to terms with his past; what he will do with the present is another matter.

If certain of Morris's characters are audaciously active, others are disturbingly passive, none more so than Will Brady in *The Works of Love.* (p. xv)

Brady is a man alone, not always in the flesh but always in the spirit. He establishes a profitable egg business, but money gives him little pleasure. He builds expensive houses, but doesn't know how to live in them. There are women in his life, but they do not stay there long. He has a son, or a boy who passes as his son, and loves him dearly but cannot come close to him. ''Why are you so different?'' the boy asks him, and he can't answer. In time his life dwindles away until his only human contacts are with his landlady, waitresses in the cheap restaurants in which he eats, and other casual acquaintances who will listen to the tales he makes up about his son. (p. xvi)

It is a moving book and nowhere more moving than in the pathos of the ending. Brady periodically writes a postcard to his son, but then he doesn't mail it, because he wants to wait until he has moved into less disreputable quarters. Such a card is found on his body when it is drawn out of a stinking Chicago canal.... (pp. xvi-xvii)

If some of Morris's men are passive, several of his women are active enough to take your breath away. The earliest appearance of the species was in a short story called ''The Ram in the Thicket,'' published in *Harper's Bazaar* in 1948. In 1951 the story grew into a short novel, *Man and Boy.* The first part covers the same ground as the story: the rising of Mr. Ormsby, the emergence of Mrs. Ormsby, and their preparations for a trip to Brooklyn, where she is to christen a ship named after their son, Virgil Ormsby, killed at Guadalcanal. In the second part, devoted to the trip, Mrs. Ormsby talks with a young soldier, Private Lipido, and the boy's questions and comments illuminate the relationship of the Ormsbys one to another and the relationship of each to the son. In the end, after winning a skirmish with the Navy, Mrs. Ormsby grandly performs her duty.

In the short story Mrs. Ormsby is a disagreeable character, not only domineering but self-indulgent, not merely bossing Ormsby but enslaving him. This effect is somewhat softened in the novel, and as the story proceeds we are forced to recognize her virtues, as is Private Lipido, at first a scoffer. It is a funny book, with page after page of amusing dialogue, but the intent, of course, is serious. (p. xvii)

Mrs. Porter in *The Deep Sleep* is in essentials like Mrs. Ormsby, though superficially different. Mrs. Porter is married to a judge, and they have an ample house on the Main Line. The story occupies something less than twenty-four hours the day after Judge Porter's death. The Porters' daughter—their only living child, for a son died in the war—has come home with her husband, Paul Webb, an artist. The judge's mother, in her ninety-ninth year, is still an occupant of the house. The only other important character—and he is very important as a key to all the others—is Parsons, the Porters' handyman and the judge's confidant. The daughter, Katherine, realizes that neither she nor her father has been able to live in the house: "They had worked out a way of doing their living somewhere else." Parsons, who tells Webb that Mrs. Porter is a woman of principle and has no human failings, is aware of and sympathetic to the judge's occasional exasperation and frequent escapes. To Webb his mother-in-law is a holy terror and cause for wonder, but, as Private Lipido in *Man and Boy* ended by cheering for Mrs. Ormsby, so Webb pays a final tribute to Mrs. Porter. (p. xviii)

When, in *The Field of Vision*, Gordon Boyd encounters McKee in Mexico City and asks him how he is, he is told, "Mrs. McKee and me couldn't be happier." The appalling thing is that, most of the time, McKee believes it. And it seems altogether probable that Mr. Ormsby and Judge Porter would make the same affirmation. Since, as we have seen, Lois Scanlon married McKee because she did not want passion in her life, it scarcely seems fair that she should blame him for being dull and matter-of-fact, but she does, and she punishes him. Her revenge is less unconscious than Mrs. Ormsby's and Mrs. Porter's, for she has some idea what it is she has missed.

There are women in Morris's work who are not at all like Lois McKee. The first example, perhaps, is Lou Baker in *The Huge Season*—"Montana born *aus* Bryn Mawr chick," who has "the ring of gold in an age of brass"—but the best specimen is the girl in *Love Among the Cannibals* who is known as "the Greek." The narrator of the story is Earl Horter, who writes words for the popular songs for which Irvin K. Macgregor, Mac, provides the music. Horter has to work hard to get the phony touch that he knows is essential to success in the business; to Mac it comes natural.

In Hollywood to work on a movie, they spend most of the time on the beach, and it is there that Mac meets Billie Harcum, a would-be singer from the South. Horter sees Eva Baum at a party, and immediately falls for her. In the place that probably has the highest concentration of phonies in the world, she is perfectly genuine. Instead of running away from passion, as Mrs. Ormsby, Mrs. Porter, and Mrs. McKee do, she welcomes

it. Unlike Billie Harcum, who has a price and collects it, the Greek gives herself freely. (p. xix)

Since he created the Greek, Morris has portrayed a number of young women who might be regarded as daughters of Eva. In *Ceremony in Lone Tree* Etoile Momeyer, niece of Lois Scanlon McKee, has her aunt's beauty and none of her inhibitions: she wants her cousin Calvin and gets him. The girl Boyd picks up and calls Daughter is a more sophisticated example of the species. Seventeen-year-old Cynthia in *What a Way to Go* represents a variety of goddesses to a variety of men, but she chooses middle-aged Professor Soby as the man most likely to help her discover what she really is. The most appealing of the seekers for the new freedom is Chickpea in *One Day*. Almost as young and just as eager for life as Cynthia and Etoile, she is exposed to more kinds of experience than they are, for she belongs to the generation that has ideas about changing the world. (p. xx)

In *The Territory Ahead* Morris has written: "The history of fiction, its pursuit of that chimera we describe as reality, is a series of imaginative triumphs made possible through technique." None of his contemporaries has a more brilliant record of technical experimentation than Morris. His innovations are not showy, nor does he waste much time talking about them. He is not interested in experiment for its own sake; he is simply trying to find the right way of getting at reality. Technique is not only a way of expression but also a means of discovery.

Morris's first novel, *My Uncle Dudley,* is a straightforward first-person narrative, the narrator being a participant in the action but not the central figure. Even here, however, the telling of the story from the Kid's point of view shows a good deal of technical sophistication. The second novel, *The Man Who Was There,* attempts a more difficult problem, for the man of the title isn't there; he is missing in action in the Pacific. Agee Ward is given to us by the reports of certain individuals who were influenced by him and through descriptions of a series of photographs of him and of artifacts associated with him. The persons who bear witness are humble souls, but they make it clear that Agee Ward was there and therefore, in a significant way, still is.

With *Man and Boy* Morris introduced two narrative methods that he has used, with variations, a number of times. In the first place, the action is concentrated into a short space of time, a matter of hours. This is also true of *The Deep Sleep, The Field of Vision, Ceremony in Lone Tree, One Day,* and *In Orbit.* In the second place, the story is told from several specified points of view, each chapter bearing the name of the person through whose eyes we are looking. The general method is used in *The Deep Sleep, The Field of Vision, Ceremony in Lone Tree,* and *One Day.*

The Field of Vision is the most tightly woven of all Morris's novels. The action takes place in the two hours or so occupied by a bullfight. During most of this time the seven characters are sitting together on the shady side of the ring, and the sections are presented from the points of view of five of the seven. Each of the five is living in his own world, and no two, as Morris specifies, see the same bullfight. Indeed, there are two persons—Paula Kahler and Scanlon—who don't see the bullfight at all. The reader not only has to try to make out what is going on in the present; he has to reconstruct the strange relationship of Boyd and the McKees, the mysterious past of Dr. Lehmann and Paula, and the mythic past of Scanlon.

Brilliant as the construction of *The Field of Vision* is, *The Huge Season* is an even better example of Morris's skill in the solution of problems of form. Morris set out to contrast a group of persons as they were in the late Twenties and as they were in the early Fifties and also to contrast the two periods. The problem, of course, was time, and, although Morris could probably have solved it by the use of flashbacks, at which he is adept, he found a better way, a way calculated to give life to both parts of the story and emphasis to the contrast. There are two narratives in alternating chapters, one with "The Captivity" as its running title and the other with "Peter Foley." The former, written in the first person, is Foley's account of what happened to him and his friends in college. The latter tells in the third person about Foley's experiences on May 5, 1952, when he is moved to seek out some of these former comrades. Each story is wonderfully dramatic, and they perfectly balance and support one another.

After succeeding so well with the tight construction of these two novels, Morris deliberately relaxed his hold in order to get a different sort of effect. Like *My Uncle Dudley, Love Among the Cannibals* is told in the first person, and its movement is largely shaped by external events. *Ceremony in Lone Tree,* though it follows the same pattern as *The Field of Vision,* to which it is a sequel, is not so tautly held and has an air, deceptive of course, of improvisation. *What a Way to Go* is pleasantly playful in both content and form. *Cause for Wonder,* returning to the problem of past and present, resembles *The Huge Season* in form. *One Day* is given a firm structure by the limited period of time imposed on the action, but it is one of the most varied of Morris's novels and the longest. *In Orbit,* on the other hand, is the shortest, but in its free-swinging way it covers a lot of ground. To analyze it is to recognize that under the appearance of artlessness lies an art that has matured through a quarter of a century. (pp. xxiv-xxvi)

From the beginning [Morris] has written in the vernacular; seldom does one find in his novels a word that cannot be heard in the day-to-day speech of moderately well-educated Americans. The rhythms of his prose, moreover, are basically the rhythms of ordinary talk. (p. xxvi)

This flexible, conversational, amusing, unpretentious style, which is in fact extremely artful, can serve many purposes. (p. xxvii)

Like many of his fellow-countrymen, especially those on the farms and in the small towns, Morris is likely to use a deadpan irony when he is the most serious. In *The Works of Love,* for instance, we read such passages as this: "It might be going too far to say that Will Brady lived in this house, as he spent his time elsewhere and usually had other things on his mind. But he came back there every night, went away from there every morning, and something like that, if you keep at it, gets to mean something." Always he relies on indirection: "When a man has lost something he would like to get back, say a wife, a boy, or an old set of habits, he can walk around the streets of the city looking for it. Or he can stand on a corner, nearly anywhere, and let it look for him." Many of his characters coin epigrams: Warren Howe, in *Cause for Wonder,* remarks, "My uncle, Fremont Osborn, came too late for God and too early for the Farm Security Administration."

Clichés are an essential part of Morris's style. Whereas most writers think about clichés, only in the hope of avoiding them, he uses them for his own purposes. Horter and Mac in *Love Among the Cannibals* specialize in clichés, Mac by nature,

Horter by intent. "Every cliché in the world," Horter reflects, "once had its moment of truth. At some point, if you traced it back, it expressed the inexpressible." In time, of course, the cliché becomes a poor substitute for thought and feeling and imagination. Morris, by twisting a cliché so that you have to look at it, shocks you out of your insensitivity. *God's Country and My People* he has named his latest book: "The men called it God's country—but the women asked, who else wants it?" "The plow that broke the plains lies buried in the yard," he observes, "and it is clear that the plains won the return engagement." Of his Uncle Harry he writes: "He was strong as a horse, stubborn as a mule, slow as molasses, smart as a whip, but what there was that was human in his nature was slow to emerge." (pp. xxviii-xxix)

Morris's figures of speech, which are numerous, are usually derived from familiar artifacts or commonplace experience, from the stuff of ordinary life. In *The Field of Vision* . . . the bullring reminds Gordon Boyd of a hub cap. In *Cause for Wonder* Warren Howe sees M. Dulac in bed as "a small fox waiting for the appearance of Little Red Riding Hood." In *The Huge Season* the watch that had belonged to Foley's father serves to indicate Foley's relationship to the past and hints at the differences between the generations: "Time, for my father, seemed to be contained in the watch. It did not skip a beat, fly away, or merely vanish, as it does for me. So long as he remembered to wind the watch Time would not run out." (p. xxx)

Some people are puzzled or distracted or even offended by Morris's style. It seems to many of us, however, that he has forged an almost perfect instrument for the expression of his understanding of life and feeling about it. That it is so close to the vernacular is one source of its vitality; it echoes the voices of living people. Like most speech, it calls for response. Although it flows so unpretentiously, it constantly challenges the reader to take his part in the activity of a creative imagination. That is one reason why Morris so often interrupts himself with a paradox, an apparent non sequitur, or a wisecrack; he demands a more than perfunctory participation. Although he is not a difficult writer in the *avant-garde* sense of the adjective, there is always much more in his books than immediately meets the eye or the ear.

Being an intelligent and responsive human being, Morris is a man of ideas. Ideas are important to him; he respects his own and pays courteous attention to others'. His ideas, it ought to be unnecessary to say, are never present in the fiction as ideas; they are implicit, never explicit. But Morris has published two books that are expository by intent: one a discussion of, for the most part, literary matters, the other a critique of contemporary culture.

In *The Territory Ahead* he talks about certain American writers, past and present: Thoreau, Whitman, Melville, Mark Twain, Henry James, Hemingway, Wolfe, Fitzgerald, Faulkner. A careful reader and uncommonly well informed, he talks impressively about all these men. At the moment, however, we are concerned with his general ideas, two in particular. First he emphasizes the danger of the artist's relying on raw material, and cites Thomas Wolfe as the horrible example. (pp. xxxi-xxxii)

His second thesis is that nostalgia has been the curse of American literature, and he illustrates this theory by examining the successes and failures of the writers mentioned above. What seems to be more important than the general idea itself is the light it sheds on Morris's work. At the start and for a long time thereafter he was concerned with his own past and the conditions that shaped it. All of the plains books, including **The Inhabitants** and **The Home Place,** grew out of this concern, and it has served him well; he has not repudiated his earlier books, nor is there any reason why he should. In time, however, he was troubled by his enslavement to the past, and **The Territory Ahead** expresses his rebellion. The characters in his following novel, **Love Among the Cannibals,** live wholly in the present, and the same thing is true of **What a Way to Go** and **In Orbit. Cause for Wonder** is a new and in large measure successful attempt to make imaginative use of the past in the present. From this point of view, the text of **God's Country and My People** is important. The pictures, taken more than twenty years ago, were part of Morris's attempt to get at the past by means of a camera. But the text is proof that at last he has exorcised nostalgia.

A Bill of Rites, A Bill of Wrongs, A Bill of Goods is a book about the crazy world we live in. Reading it, one alternates between laughter and outrage. Ours is a shoddy culture, Morris says, built on greed, ruthlessness, and hypocrisy. The evidence is everywhere and he produces enough of it to give us all the jitters.

Many American writers have done their best work when they were comparatively young and thereafter have declined. Henry James is the conspicuous exception—a man who not only went on writing through decade after decade but also went on growing as a writer. As Morris approaches his sixtieth birthday, he is still going strong, full of energy, full of plans, and, to play Morris's game with clichés, full of promise. (pp. xxxii-xxxiii)

> *Granville Hicks, in an introduction to* Wright Morris: A Reader, *by Wright Morris, Harper & Row, Publishers, 1970, pp. ix-xxxiii.*

JIM MILLER

Wright Morris is . . . an archeologist of the everyday, an author who records with melancholy detachment the mute artifacts, small talk and gestures used to bridge painful gaps between husband and wife, father and son, past and present. For nearly 40 years, in 30 books of hardscrabble fiction, essays and photography, he has chronicled his passion for the prosaic, in part by treating the men and women of middle America as if they were icons of a lost civilization. Often admired, his books are too rarely read. . . . Now his unusual odyssey has reached a climax of sorts with the publication of **Will's Boy,** a memoir as somber and moving and finely etched as anything Morris has ever written.

He was born in 1910 in Central City, Neb. His mother died six days later. His father, Will Morris, was jovial but remote. . . . Drifting from town to town along the rim of the Platte River, his father floundered in the egg business and cavorted with loose women while he was left to fend for himself: "I was half an orphan." In 1925 father and son moved East.

In Chicago, Morris wooed his first girl and "learned the art of fiction," telling her tales of his "life and great times." A few years later, on a visit to his mother's people in Idaho, he met his past firsthand: "Seated around the table to which four leaves had been added were the parts of my life that had proved to be missing. My impression of them all—the old man already dozing, the sisters with their open, affectionate faces, the warmth I felt to be accepted as one of their number—restored to my

mind an image of the good life that I had once glimpsed and put behind me."

He found another part of himself—and a fresh respect for the quixotic pioneer—when he spent the winter in Texas with his uncle, a man foolishly determined to farm the arid panhandle. He helped him plow the parched soil and watched clouds on the horizon rain someplace else. . . . (p. 77)

Will's Boy, like Morris's other books, is written in a pensive vernacular of stark purity and droll wit, and it flows with a compelling sense of integrity. By interpolating italicized passages from **The Works of Love** and several other novels, Morris implies that his life, at least as he now imagines it, contains the essence of his fiction: the lonely sweep of the plains, the flinty, inhibited characters, the "impression of time as a liquid in which all things [are] suspended." Although the story ends when he enters college, long before he becomes a novelist, it also evokes the consuming nature of his need to write: "I am a camera," he remarks at the outset—"but who it is that clicks the shutter I do not know."

The quest for identity torments his most sympathetic characters. In **Plains Song,** the fiercely independent Sharon Rose, a symbol of feminist revolt, runs away from the farm and the aunt who raised her. Like Morris himself, she can leave her past behind—but she can't get over it. After one unsettling visit home, "Sharon felt herself in limbo, neither coming nor going, seized with a longing that had no object." She only finds a measure of peace years later, at the aunt's funeral: "Whatever life held in the future for her, it would prove to reside in this rimless past, approaching and then fading like the gong of a crossing bell." By lingering over such ceremonies—his work abounds with funerals and family reunions—Morris makes us uncomfortably aware of how we each must define ourselves, often against our will, in terms of a shared past—particularly before death.

Some of his most striking inventions are characters gone blind or crazy and slowly dying: Tom Scanlon in the remarkable **Ceremony in Lone Tree,** . . . Uncle Floyd in **Fire Sermon,** . . . Cora, the aunt in **Plains Song.** Set in their ways, their minds clouded by pressing memories, they dwell amid old impressions that diminish until the mysterious primordial core of a personality is laid bare. In **Plains Song,** the aged Cora's being congeals around a scar on one hand, left years before when her newlywed husband assailed her chastity: "In the dawn light she found that she had bitten through the flesh of her hand, exposing the bone."

Such memories may bring order to a life but they afford no solace. In **Will's Boy,** as in his best novels, Morris offers a bleak view of the human condition—one reason he hasn't found a large audience. Reading him also requires patience: his slow pace and plain speech invite a wistful kind of meditation. Then, there is the sort of objection that H. L. Mencken raised against Willa Cather: "I don't care how well she writes, I don't give a damn what happens in Nebraska." But when his measured cadences quicken and crack, when he lets one of his taciturn characters vent feeling or run wild or drift into space, then this plain world can suddenly seem fearful and wondrous and altogether gripping—a grave allegory of the strange spirit we Americans call our own.

Like them or not, Morris's rigid plainsmen, with their harebrained schemes and haunted children, form a vivid part of our national heritage. (pp. 77-8)

Jim Miller, "Plain Talk from the Plains," in News-week, *Vol. XCVIII, No. 2, July 13, 1981, pp. 77-8.*

BRUCE MANUEL

[*Will's Boy: A Memoir*] is a shimmering, impressionistic memoir, conjured up by fondling "pebbles . . . in the mind's secret pockets." The prose is unsmudged, crystalline. It recaptures the innocence, resilience, nonchalance, and dawning awareness of Morris's bittersweet boyhood during the second and third decades of this century.

Though autobiographical, the account is enriched by the skill and imagination of this gifted writer of fiction.

Morris's youth and adolescence were as bleak, yet as open and breezy, as the plains of Nebraska, where he was born. As a boy in Omaha, he went to school when he chose to, plucked chickens and candied eggs for his father, and ate in cafeterias that doled out meal tickets in exchange for eggs. On Saturdays he might play Ping-Pong or baseball or marbles. . . .

As a teen-ager in Chicago he filled orders on roller skates in the stockroom at Montgomery Ward, led Bible discussions on Sundays at the YMCA, and supervised rowdy young men in the "Y" lobby, where his unbeaten streak of Ping-Pong conquests inspired awe. . . .

Also included in these recollections are an adventurous motor trip to California with his father . . . ; Morris's return to Chicago and enrollment in City College; his brief stint at an evangelical college near San Francisco; his short-lived job driving a tractor on an uncle's ranch in Texas; and finally his entry into the college of his dreams in Pomona, Calif.

Yet *Will's Boy* strikes me as being not about these events so much as the changing perceptions that carry us inexorably to adulthood. Near the beginning, Morris observes, "I am a camera, but who it is that clicks the shutter I do not know." Near the end, as the snapshots began to fit together into a mosaic, he remarks, "I was no longer a boy. What I was was not clear."

Will's Boy captures some of the enchanting certainties and mysteries of childhood. Frequently it freezes the frame to offer a clear look at the imperceptible process of growing up. And it gives a refreshing glimpse of a younger America—not so darkened by disillusionment and cynicism. . . .

Bruce Manuel, "Shimmering Memoir of a Midwestern Boyhood," in The Christian Science Monitor, *July 29, 1981, p. 17.*

NOEL PERRIN

Until he was 8, Wright Morris [as depicted in *Will's Boy: A Memoir*] lived a more or less ordinary life. It's true that he had no mother—she died when he was six days old—and no brothers or sisters. But he had a father, a telegraph agent for the Union Pacific railroad. He had a house to live in and a housekeeper to look after him. He even went to school.

In 1918 all that changed. One night his father came back from Omaha with a new car. . . . In the new car was a new wife, a pretty girl named Gertrude, much nearer the little boy's age than the father's. At that moment domesticity ceased, and the life of a picaro began. Within a year the three of them had moved from Central City to Schuyler to Kearney to Omaha. (p. 12)

After she left, the father divided his time between candling eggs in his dingy Omaha office and looking for a third wife. The boy, now 10 years old, started a small business delivering notes for a fee of 25 cents. Wright Morris doesn't *say* that these notes were mostly to do with assignations (he likes being cryptic), but he implies it. . . .

[For] several years the father more or less drifted away, while the boy lived with a family named Mulligan and went to school. Then, when he was almost 14, his father repossessed him. A Mrs. Van Meer had come into the father's life, and she looked like good pickings. The two Morrises moved into her house. The first night there, Mrs. Van Meer's almost-grown daughter Claudine came into the boy's basement room for a bedtime visit. Soon her mother shouted down the stairs. "She thinks we're down here doing something dirty," Claudine told him. "You want to?"

Wright Morris's whole childhood was like this. After the Van Meers came a brief spell in a reformatory, and then when he was 15 a series of adventures. . . . As the book ends, Morris is 20 and about to start serious education.

A story like this could be told as a series of burlesque adventures, Auntie Mame style. How wacky we all were! How eccentric! What a scream!

That is not Wright Morris's way at all. He is very much alive to the comic possibilities in his father's life and his own childhood—but like a good Westerner, he prefers to tell the story with a straight face.

He is even more aware of the serious possibilities of life, and especially of childhood. What really interests him is the growth of awareness. The book begins in a kind of imagism—the random impressions of a small boy in Central City—and gradually becomes clear and narrative and orderly as the boy grows up. The dawn of consciousness to 10 A.M., so to speak. Despite the very different kind of childhood described, the book has much in common with Henry James's *Notes of a Son and Brother* and much with Wordsworth's *Prelude*.

My one serious complaint is that the book is too short. Because of the imagism and because of Mr. Morris's fondness for quoting passages from his own novels . . . , the narrative takes a while to come to full power. Much too soon after it does, the story is over; I could wish this book twice its length. But even as it is, *Will's Boy* immediately takes its place as one of Wright Morris's half-dozen best books. (p. 13)

Noel Perrin, "Young Picaro," in The New York Times Book Review, *August 16, 1981, pp. 12-13.*

CHRISTOPHER LEHMANN-HAUPT

[*Solo: An American Dreamer in Europe, 1933-34* is] a charming account of a year spent in Europe 50 years ago by the prolific novelist and author of an earlier autobiographical memoir, *Will's Boy*. . . .

Mr. Morris admits that a violent storm he experienced while crossing the Atlantic in a freighter was not as vivid to him as a storm he had read about in Conrad. And there are few places in Europe he will approach without a literary scene in mind, most of them from the pages of Thomas Mann.

But whatever his nature when he set forth. Europe did not live up to his image of it. He went first with his high hopes to Paris, but after two days of drizzle, the city of lights "looked to me like one big dirty puddle.'' Symbolically enough—though Mr. Morris is too plain-spoken to underline the point—he bought two apples from a peddler, ''about the size of golf balls,'' and found them full of worms. . . .

Yet the loss of illusion in *Solo* is in no way depressing. Indeed one has to stop reading and think about the text in order to imagine the young traveler's disenchantment. This is because he seems to welcome with good-humored equanimity whatever befalls him in Europe. He visits an Austrian Schloss and gets caught for the winter in a scene painted by Bruegel, a ''world out of time'' so marvelously eccentric that no single detail, such as the presence of a tomahawk-wielding cigar-store Indian in one of the castle's halls, can begin to capture the flavor.

In Grosseto, Italy, he and a friend are woken up and placed under arrest for no discernible reason by an entire troop of nervous young soldiers wearing plumes in their helmets and swords on their belts. In Paris, he gets caught trying to shoplift Céline's *Journey to the End of Night,* but a police inspector is so delighted with his prisoner's interest in literature that he immediately paroles him.

All of these experiences, and others, seem to bounce off the narrator without leaving cuts or bruises. Occasionally, there are feelings of elation, despair or anger. Even more occasionally, there are references to the author's dawning awareness that he is gathering material for future fictions. But mostly he is a camera—a dilapidated Kodak Brownie—snapping away.

Why do we read with such relish if the author doesn't grow or even react to his experiences all that dramatically? As much because of the details as anything. A washer attached to a pipe-stem, ''green as the bit in the mouth of a horse,'' that enables a train conductor to talk without removing his pipe from his mouth, the bright red earmuffs worn by the chauffeur of the Austrian castle's master, an acquaintance's suit worn so thin at the knees that his underwear shows through when he is seated—such details, recalled from half a century ago, are set down as in an intricate still life composed with deadpan humor. The more you look the more you see, and the more you see the more you delight.

If the Europe he visited took him pleasantly outside the flux of time, then Mr. Morris has returned the favor. To our pleasure.

> *Christopher Lehmann-Haupt, in a review of ''Solo: An American Dreamer in Europe, 1933-34,'' in* The New York Times, *May 31, 1983, p. C13.*

JAMES ATLAS

Wright Morris's *Solo* is one of the few memoirs I've read that admits it's possible to go abroad and have a crummy time. His plain-spoken but vivid account of a year he spent in Europe after college is embarrassingly truthful. . . . There may be those fortunate enough to have lucked into the bawdy, rollicking Paris of Henry Miller, but for this reviewer, anyway, Mr. Morris's doleful experience is more like it.

Like every literary sojourner, he embarked with ''extravagant expectations.'' He had read Oswald Spengler, had even written to the author to clear up a point in *The Decline of the West.* But his knowledge of Europe seems to have been rudimentary, even by the standard of Twain's gawking innocents abroad. . . . When a Viennese medical student aboard the freighter bearing him to Europe insisted Vienna was more interesting than Paris,

young Morris followed him there and eventually ended up in a castle on the Danube that could have been the one Kafka's K tried unavailingly to enter. Snow drifted through the open windows and had to be carted off; chamber pots made the air unbreathable; servants slept behind the stove; the lady of the house, Madame Deleglise, lay in bed all day reading French novels and showed up for dinner ''dressed like one of the Three Musketeers or Cyrano de Bergerac.'' No wonder Mr. Morris calls it a winter ''spent out of this world.''

What comes through in his account, apart from the mad comedy of it, is the author's utter passivity. He submits to lugging Madame Deleglise's odorous dog out to the woods in a basket; drags wood and water up the snowy slopes; keeps a vigil in the barn all night to make sure a sow doesn't crush her litter of newborn piglets while they're suckling—only to have one served up for dinner. No sooner does he embark on a bicycle tour of Italy than the hapless tourist lands in prison. (It turns out that Mussolini had passed through town while Mr. Morris was obliviously snapping photographs.)

Mr. Morris regards these travails with equanimity. His authorial voice is tolerant, unflappable, bemused. But he was clearly taking it all in. Half a century later, he can recall every detail of that year, every bizarre character encountered in the course of his pilgrimage. . . . (pp. 7, 24)

It's when he pauses to draw conclusions that Mr. Morris goes awry. ''I was full of the mystery of the time that had passed,'' he muses upon returning home, ''the *Wanderjahr* that was already far behind me, like a clock that had just started.'' Why do memoirists go in for these post-game wrap-ups? There is so much observed detail in *Solo,* so many memorable characters and episodes, that Mr. Morris needn't have said anything about what it all means. Do we really need to know that in Venice his ''jumbled impressions mingled the sordid, the earthly, and the unearthly, in a way that exceeded my understanding''? Or that when he witnessed a loutish servant pursuing a kitchen maid with ''a butchered pig's tail sticking out of his fly like a corkscrew penis,'' he felt ''something had ripped the veil to the past, just as I was passing, and I had seen through it''?

There is something schoolmarmish about Mr. Morris's attitude toward his experience. The determination to become a writer is hardly a shameful theme in a memoir, but Mr. Morris can't seem to refer to his ambition without becoming that Midwestern hayseed depicted in so many of his novels, chewing on a piece of straw and shuffling his feet. A novel by Henri de Montherlant inspires him to meditate on how the art of the novel ''combined what was new with what was old.'' A storm at sea prompts him to brood on how much less profound he is than Conrad. Caught shoplifting a novel by Céline, he gets involved in a literary discussion with the detective, who asks him if he plans to be a writer: ''Oh fateful question! Did I?''

These feeble meditations bring us no closer to Mr. Morris, who remains a shadowy figure throughout. He refers on occasion to the girl he left back home but never gives us any sense of who she was or what became of their relationship; and his accounts of various narrowly averted seductions are scarcely comprehensible if one hasn't read the first volume of Mr. Morris's autobiography, *Will's Boy,* a poignant account of his desolate childhood in the company of a widowed father whose tireless philandering ''deepened what was prudish'' in Mr. Morris's character, ''a vein that ran deep.'' This diffidence inhibits his narrative, giving it a certain annoying mystery. What was he looking for in Europe? Why did he give in so readily to others' wishes? Why was he afraid of girls? We'll never know.

"Raw material, an excess of both material and comparatively raw experience, has been the dominant factor in my own role as a novelist," Mr. Morris declared in *Earthly Delights, Unearthly Adornments.* But it's what the novelist does with his material, not simply what happened, that matters. Mr. Morris has returned obsessively in his work to the same traumatic incidents—the death of his mother, the failure of his father's chicken farm, his lonely adolescence in Chicago—but somehow he's never quite gotten at why they hold such power over him.

For all its reticence, *Solo* is a departure of sorts; Paris seems to have finally liberated Mr. Morris's imagination. His description of what it's like to wander aimlessly through the Tuileries; to hang out at the American Club on the Boulevard Raspail; to take up with the weird assortment of students, tourists and would-be artists who populate the cafes is the best I've read since Frank Conroy's *Stop-Time.* (pp. 24-5)

> James Atlas, "Going Abroad and Having a Bad Time," in The New York Times Book Review, June 5, 1983, pp. 7, 24-5.

KIRKUS REVIEWS

Following *Will's Boy* and *Solo,* this new volume of Morris' autobiography [*A Clock of Light: Writing My Life*] begins with the writer now poised on the brink of his career: college in California; marriage to a nameless coed (referred to only as "my wife"); WPA-level poverty; a move eastward to Cape Cod; and then the first photo-texts (*The Inhabitants, The Home Place*) that launched his professional-writing life. From the subsequent decades, Morris gives the greatest emphasis to his peripatetic, solitary wanderlusts—especially car-trips to Mexico, a locale that fills him with affection, then fascination and doubt. . . . And the domestic details of his later life do eventually emerge, somewhat obliquely: his odd, if not quite loveless, marriage; hints of infidelity on both sides (with vaguely lesbian innuendos); a final break at age 50; and a new beginning with a young art-dealer named Jo. But the emotional substance of Morris' later life . . . seems to be largely obscured in this memoir: the specter of what is left unsaid dominates the book—like a horizon that the writer keeps always behind him, out of sight. Morris portrays himself as a plugger, a "glowworm," the wearer of a "cloak of light." With literary people, he is amiable but inconstant, a man who makes alliances uneasily and rarely, an essential loner. And Morris' style here—contrapuntal, unrhapsodic, sometimes even tight-lipped—adds to this sense of dislocation, of half-darkened views. Again, as in his previous autobiographical writings, Morris' feel for the conjunction of a specific time-and-place is on ample display—with personal, impressionistic illumination of the settings in his fiction (excerpts of which are interspersed throughout). But, far less vivid than *Will's Boy,* this curious sequel is more an imagistic collage than a directly involving memoir—frequently haunting in its spooky reticence, yet finally unsatisfying. (pp. 1091-92)

> A review of "A Clock of Light: Writing My Life," in Kirkus Reviews, Vol. LII, No. 22, November 15, 1984, pp. 1091-92.

JONATHAN YARDLEY

[*A Cloak of Light: Writing My Life*] is the concluding volume of Wright Morris' autobiographical trilogy, and a considerable

departure from its predecessors. *Will's Boy* and *Solo,* which tell the story of the author's first two decades, are slender, elegiac books in which specific autobiographical detail is of less moment than Morris' attempt to mythologize his own life, to locate himself within the larger American experience; it is a bold effort, and a successful one. *A Cloak of Light,* by contrast, is autobiography of a more conventional sort. It supplies, in ample detail, the customary accounts of career, travel and notable friendships; all of this is interesting to anyone who has read the first two books or who is familiar with Morris' substantial body of other work, but after *Will's Boy* and *Solo* it comes as rather a letdown.

A Cloak of Light picks up where *Solo* left off, with the author back from a memorable stay in Europe and enrolled at Pomona College, in California, in the mid-'30s. He describes himself here, much as he did at the end of the previous book, as "one of those fools who persists in his folly, never mind what"; his folly is his self-preoccupation and his obsessive desire to explore and understand his past by writing about it, as the book's subtitle emphasizes. Not merely that, but he soon discovered himself to be "a writer addicted to compactness, and economy of statement," who began to develop a style that was distinctly his own. . . .

It was a style that, however original and appealing, was not calculated to win the hearts of editors or publishers. Morris was a long time getting published, and when he did it was to the general indifference of the reading public; for years he underwent the familiar experience of good reviews and poor sales, with the result that he moved around from publisher to publisher as one after another came to judge him a poor risk. He made himself an even less promising commercial prospect by working on books, beautiful but expensive to produce, that combined text and photographs, at which he also excelled, but which raised the question: "Was he a writer who liked to take photographs, or a photographer who liked to do a little writing? In either case, it played hell with the publisher's intent to establish a new author." (p. 3)

In all these years Morris was hooked on writing, and his entire life centered upon it. He married at a relatively early age, but was often separated from his wife for long periods as the two pursued their separate interests, and in 1961 they divorced; for some reason he never names her, referring to her throughout as "my wife," a practice that is both puzzling and irritating. Though his writing is quintessentially American in tone and subject matter, he spent a good deal of time out of the country, especially in Mexico, travels through which occupy substantial parts of the book. As he became more widely known he started to make the literary rounds, to lecture and teach, and to establish friendships with authors and publishers; he writes most winningly about Loren Eiseley and Saul Bellow, he adds still more to the legend of Maxwell Perkins, and he tells an amusing tale on Dorothy Canfield Fisher.

There is enough of this in *A Cloak of Light* to satisfy the reader's appetite for anecdote and gossip, but Morris does not really seem to have his heart in it; his writing often loses its edge in these passages, which suggests nothing so much as that he is going through the motions. Where the book comes to life is in those sections that explore Morris' past, his character and his literary impulses. He is a reflective, introspective writer who returns over and again to ideas and thoughts, viewing them from different angles and in the light of new experience: his "fascination with structures and artifacts," his sense of himself as a "missing person," his interest in "the maintenance of connections'' between past and present, his love of the American vernacular, his ''ongoing preoccupation with fact and fiction, with what is real-seeming in the world I perceive around me, and the fiction we produce to mirror that world.''

What becomes clear from all of this rumination is that Morris is one of those rare people who quite simply was born to write. He had no choice. This provides the answer to the question he posed to himself at a point when he had at last begun to acquire a reputation: . . .

> [''What] I was doing came naturally. To cease
> to do it seemed an unnatural, destructive act.
> In May of 1958 I saw that I was one of those
> determined to persist in his folly.''

To call it folly is, of course, Morris' self-mocking conceit; the self-evident truth is that his is a passionate, unwavering commitment that he has pursued for half a century with the utmost seriousness. He has gotten neither the fame nor the wealth that his accomplishments should have earned for him, but in the middle of his eighth decade he seems unfazed by this. The work matters more than the recognition for it; Morris seems confident in the knowledge, as certainly he should be, that his work is good. (p. 13)

> *Jonathan Yardley, ''The Achievement of Wright Morris,'' in* Book World—The Washington Post, *February 3, 1985, pp. 3, 13.*

EDWARD ABBEY

In this droll, delightful and richly quotable book [*A Cloak of Light*] Mr. Morris recounts his own pilgrimage along the open yellow road of American optimism. Rather than describe in detail his career as a writer he concentrates on the essential self-shaping of his life, with quotations from his many novels and essays serving as commentary on the personal history. Through writing he strives to make sense of his own life and of American lives in general, and to save and recapture what might otherwise be forgotten. . . . (pp. 9-10)

Memory and imagination ally themselves against entropy, against the landfill of history. A work of art may be, after all, the best reply anyone can make to the immense brutality of the power institutions—government, science, industry, religion, war—that tyrannize our lives. Whether or not this has been his primary purpose, Mr. Morris's 19 novels and many other books serve to vindicate the integrity of the individual in an age of mass production and mass destruction. . . .

So far Mr. Morris has not achieved (he's only 74) the kind of fame and wealth that have been the fortune or maybe misfortune of a dozen or so living American novelists. None of his books ever sold very well, he tells us, and as a result he has enjoyed the acquaintance of many different publishers. . . . However, Mr. Morris does not bellyache about the odd whims of the literary marketplace but simply goes on writing the kind of books he writes—concentrated, humane, intense, precise as micrometrics in style and thought. . . .

The publisher says *A Cloak of Light* is the concluding volume of this autobiography. Not so, I hope, for this book brings us only to 1960 and Wright Morris's 50th year. I for one hope to read the rest of the story, in the author's own words, straight through to the denouement—whatever the deadline may be. The writer, says Mr. Morris, is ''born to soar, sustained by nothing more than his cloak of light.'' Keep on soaring, Wright Morris.

> *Edward Abbey, ''Reruns of a Happy Life,'' in* The New York Times Book Review, *February 17, 1985, pp. 9-10.*

BRUCE ALLEN

Morris's style [in *A Cloak of Light*] is wonderfully pictorial, characterized by odd juxtapositions of words and images. He doesn't sound quite like anyone else, as he recounts misadventures (being ''picked up as a vagrant, and charged with being a possible spy'' in South Carolina), or as he offers deadpan descriptions of the wonders he's seen. Morris sees the humor, even the absurdity, in his own personality, ambitions, and actions; his good nature and energy come through strongly in these pages, as does his photographer's habit of viewing things from an unconventional angle, trying out grouping and framing tactics as he looks at them.

We see how ideas and images rolled around in his mind (often for years), changing shape, waning and waxing in intensity, ending up transformed in his fiction. Morris explains, perhaps better than any other writer has, how the traveler's lust for new places and sensations ''provokes and sustains imagemaking, the supreme form of daydreaming.'' He wrestles with the idea of art as self-fulfillment (against ''real losses'' it opposes ''imaginary gains'') and examines via metaphor—the title image of ''a cloak of light''—what it is that seems to make the writer different, and distant, from other people; that protective, sustaining nimbus which surrounds him, enfolding him in his own sensitivity, fragility, and (Morris freely admits it) egotism. The resulting self-portrait makes this one of Wright Morris's most accessible and attractive books.

> *Bruce Allen, ''The Memoirs of Wright Morris: Views from an Unconventional Angle,'' in* The Christian Science Monitor, *February 28, 1985, p. 20.*

V(idiadhar) S(urajprasad) Naipaul

1932-

Trinidadian-born English novelist, essayist, and short story writer.

Naipaul is among the world's most highly regarded contemporary writers. His work centers on the Third World, including countries in Africa, Asia, South America, and the Caribbean. Born in Trinidad to Indian parents, Naipaul left the island at eighteen to attend school in England, where he has lived ever since. He has spent much of his life traveling, and his work usually expresses the viewpoint of a stateless wanderer who observes his surroundings from a peripheral position. Naipaul cites Joseph Conrad as a major influence, and critics have noted that the dark, brooding atmosphere, tropical settings, and alienated perspective in Naipaul's prose resemble similar qualities in Conrad's work. Although his detached stance and bleak, skeptical outlook have made Naipaul's work controversial, his lucid style, skillful use of dialect, and observant eye are highly praised.

In his first four novels—*The Mystic Masseur* (1957), *The Suffrage of Elvira* (1958), *Miguel Street* (1959), and *A House for Mr. Biswas* (1961)—Naipaul drew on his Trinidadian background for subject matter. The most highly acclaimed of these early works, *A House for Mr. Biswas*, is based on facts from Naipaul's life. Like Mr. Biswas, Naipaul's father was a Trinidadian journalist of Hindu extraction who frequently clashed with his wife's large, powerful Brahmin family and with the Indian community in Trinidad yet managed to instill his abilities and journalistic aptitude in his son. The novel was praised for its humorous tone, vivid characterizations, and underlying pathos. Naipaul's early novels were republished in 1984.

The social awareness evident in Naipaul's early work has become more prominent as his career has developed. *The Middle Passage: Impressions of Five Societies—British, French and Dutch in the West Indies and South America* (1962) is written in the form of a travelogue, or a record of impressions by an outsider, and is the first of Naipaul's nonfiction books to examine the societies of developing countries. *An Area of Darkness* (1964) describes Naipaul's travels to India. His harsh portrayal of this country caused some critics to accuse him of arriving in India with a rigid bias in favor of Western tradition and ideology. *India: A Wounded Civilization* (1977) generated similar criticism.

A negative appraisal of life in the Third World is also apparent in Naipaul's later novels and short stories. The short novel and stories which comprise the Booker McConnell Prize-winning *In a Free State* (1971) involve characters whose alienation stems from a loss of cultural identity. *Guerrillas* (1975) takes place on a Caribbean island recently liberated from colonial rule where the involvement of an American couple with a native rebel leader ends in tragedy. In *A Bend in the River* (1979), an Indian merchant tries unsuccessfully to establish himself in a newly independent African country. Each of these novels contains elements of sexual and political violence within an atmosphere of impending chaos, causing some reviewers to conclude that Naipaul views Third World societies as es-

© Lütfi Özkök

sentially hopeless. However, most critics agree that his fiction displays narrative skill and command of language.

The controversy surrounding Naipaul's work intensified with the publication of *Among the Believers: An Islamic Journey* (1982), in which he examines the Islamic revival in Iran, Pakistan, Malaysia, and Indonesia. Naipaul presents a scathing picture of the civil and social disorder in these countries and attributes it to the dominance of Islamic fanaticism. The accusation most often leveled at Naipaul was that he had merely confirmed preconceived notions about his subject rather than attempting a deeper analysis of the Islamic religion and its impact. Edward Said observed that "Naipaul carries with him a half-stated but finally unexamined reverence for the colonial order," and other reviewers affirmed this complaint, citing Naipaul's distaste for everything non-Western as a major weakness in his work. Yet several critics defended *Among the Believers*, praising Naipaul's style as skillful and sensitive. In a review of the book, D. J. Enright characterized Naipaul as "a fair-minded observer and brave explorer, and, in the mode of the best old-fashioned travel writers, a good, quick describer of nature and of men."

Finding the Centre: Two Narratives (1984) created much less controversy. In the first section, "Prologue to an Autobiography," Naipaul recounts the story of his own beginnings as a writer. This narrative was particularly noted for Naipaul's poignant depiction of his father's life and influence. The second section, "The Crocodiles of Yamoussoukro," concerns a visit Naipaul made to the Ivory Coast, an economically and politically stable African republic. Reviewers detected a warmer, more accepting tone in this piece than in Naipaul's previous examinations of the Third World.

(See also *CLC*, Vols. 4, 7, 9, 13, 18; *Contemporary Authors*, Vols. 1-4, rev. ed.; and *Contemporary Authors New Revision Series*, Vol. 1.)

JAMES CAMERON

The affinity of uppercrust Islam with the old Brits of the brave Imperial days was understandable if not especially lovable; both sides were hierarchical, didactic and somewhat boring. It was also discriminatory; officials and the Army always got on with Muslims in a way they never did with Hindus or pagans or Christians or intellectuals. This broadly might have been said about all the Empire in the East.

It is therefore immensely interesting to have [in *Among the Believers*] the Islamic scene examined in the context of today by another sort of outsider. V. S. Naipaul is neither a European nor a Muslim. As a novelist, essayist and historian he has now become a respected and established part of the contemporary Anglo-Saxon literary scene, but he is, in fact, a Hindu, though as he will insist neither devout nor conformist. In fact he was grown up before he ever saw India, and wrote a pretty scathing book about it, *An Area of Darkness,* which gave great offence to the Indian *literati,* who are not used to being critically examined by, as it were, their own kith and kin. V. S. Naipaul, who was born in Trinidad, could not have cared less.

The Muslim world which reads *Among the Believers* will not exactly take him to their hearts either. V. S. Naipaul has a tremendously keen eye for flaws. In no way does he offer judgment theologically, and in no way is he a cynic. He is immensely generous and understanding, even to a way of life that he clearly feels to be the essence of intolerance. But he is a truly admirable reporter, which means he will delight reporters and exasperate zealots, which is as it should be.

Among the Believers is just what the title says: an account of a philosophical journey in a spirit of genuine yet neutral enquiry through four major Muslim societies—Iran, Pakistan, Malaysia and Indonesia. In each the basics of Islam differ sharply with dogmatic variations on the common theme, each with one or another kind of turmoil, each with Islam's introspective torment at trying to drive a contemporary world into the enlightenment of backwardness. (p. 21)

V. S. Naipaul presents everything through the minds and eyes of the young zealots (or sometimes cynics) who were his interpreters and guides. He was very smart or lucky with them; they varied from fanatics to communists, from mullahs to wits, from the dead-pan to the elusive. . . .

Mr Naipaul's background equips him well for this study, at once intricate and simple. He was without religious faith himself. But 'Muslims were part of the small Indian community of Trinidad into which I was born; it could be said that I had known Muslims all my life. I knew little of their religion. My own background was Hindu, and I grew up with the knowledge that Muslims, though ancestrally of India and therefore like ourselves in many ways, were different. . . . The difference was more a matter of group feeling, and mysterious: the ani-

mosities our Hindu and Muslim grandfathers had brought from India had softened into a kind of folk-wisdom about the unreliability and treachery of the other side.'

That folk-wisdom did not accompany him on his journey through Islamic lands. The Muslims he met he usually liked and respected; his observations are gentle and generous, kind and bitter and above all honest. Mr Naipaul has a perceptive eye for social detail; if nothing else *Among the Believers* is a first-class piece of travel reportage.

From Iran, which has replaced a tyranny with a sort of limbo, he moves on to Pakistan, where Islamic ideals long since foundered in a State created uniquely for Muslims. From its very beginning the institution of Pakistan was never seen as a political achievement but as a victory for the Faith, complete in itself. Its curse was to be ruled by a succession of crazed idealists and self-seeking soldiers . . . and, of course, to have no oil.

Iran was different; Iran was 'the confusion of a people of high mediaeval culture awakening to oil and money, a sense of power and violation and a knowledge of a great new encircling civilisation. That civilisation couldn't be mastered. It was to be rejected, and at the same time it was to be depended on.'

The progression to Malaysia and Indonesia was less traumatic. They are more tranquil places, or at least project themselves as such; even the last generation's ugly Indonesian conflicts were less religious than civil. Nevertheless the reflection returns constantly to Naipaul, as it does to everyone who travels through this strange dream: what does Islam do about poverty?

Why, answers the good and believing Muslim: it teaches you to endure it.

The conclusion, if there is one, is that the religious ideal of Islam is *organically* related to the social order which is created. The rejection of the one will necessarily involve the rejection of the other. God is almighty, and Allah is His prophet. Take it or leave it, my children; that is how it is.

From one who has travelled through these regions, there is one more thing to say about V. S. Naipaul's book: one wishes one had written it. (p. 22)

> *James Cameron, "Trans-Arabia," in* The Spectator, *Vol. 247, No. 7995, October 3, 1981, pp. 21-2.*

EDWARD SAID

Naipaul the writer now flows directly into Naipaul the social phenomenon, the celebrated sensibility on tour, abhorring the post-colonial world for its lies, its mediocrity, cruelty, violence, and maudlin self-indulgence. Naipaul, demystifier of the West crying over the spilt milk of colonialism. The writer of travel journalism—unencumbered with much knowledge or information, and not much interested in imparting any—is a stiff, mostly silent presence in [*Among the Believers: An Islamic Journey*], which is the record of a visit in 1979-80 to Iran, Pakistan, Malaysia, Indonesia. What he sees he sees because it happens before him and, more important, because it confirms what, except for an occasionally eye-catching detail, he already knows. He does not learn: *they* prove. Prove what? That the 'retreat' to Islam is 'stupefaction'. In Malaysia Naipaul is asked: 'What is the purpose of your writing? Is it to tell people what it's all about?' He replies: 'Yes, I would say comprehension.' 'Is it not for money?' 'Yes. But the nature of the work is important.'

Thus Naipaul travels and writes about it because it is important, not because he likes doing it. There is very little pleasure and only a bit more affection recorded in this book. Its funny moments are at the expense of Muslims, wogs after all, who cannot spell, be coherent, sound right to a wordly-wise, somewhat jaded judge from the West. Every time they show their Islamic weaknesses, Naipaul the phenomenon appears promptly. A Muslim lapse occurs, some puerile resentment is expressed, and then, *ex cathedra,* we are given a passage like this:

> Khomeini required only faith. But he also knew the value of Iran's oil to countries that lived by machines, and he could send the Phantoms and the tanks against the Kurds. Interpreter of the faithful, he expressed all the confusion of his people and made it appear like glory, like the familiar faith: the confusion of a people of high medieval culture awakening to oil and money, a sense of power and violation and a knowledge of a great new encircling civilization. It was to be rejected: at the same time it was to be depended on.

Remember that last sentence and a half, for it is Naipaul's thesis as well as the platform from which he addresses the world: the West is the world of knowledge, criticism, technical know-how and functioning institutions, Islam its fearfully enraged and retarded dependant, awakening to a new barely controllable power. The West provides Islam with good things from the outside, for 'the life that had come to Islam had not come from within'. Thus the entire existence of 800,000,000 people is summed up in a phrase, and dismissed. . . .

After such knowledge what forgiveness? Very little obviously. The Islamic characters encountered by Naipaul, those half-educated schoolteachers, journalists, sometime revolutionaries, bureaucrats and religious fanatics, they exude little charm, arouse scant interest or compassion. One, yes, one person only, an Indonesian poet, suggests some nobility and intelligence. Carefully set and dramatised, Naipaul's descriptions, however, invariably tend to slide away from the specific into the realm of the general. Each chapter ends with some bit of sententiousness, but just before the end there comes a dutiful squeezing out of Meaning, as if the author could no longer let his characters exist without some appended commentary that aligns things clearly under the Islam/West polarity. (p. 21)

It is not just that Naipaul carries with him a kind of half-stated but finally unexamined reverence for the colonial order. That attitude has it that the old days were better, when Europe ruled the coloureds and allowed them few silly pretensions about purity, independence, and new ways. It is a view declared openly by many people. Naipaul is one of them, except that he is better able than most to express the view perhaps. He is a kind of belated Kipling just the same. What is worse, I think, is that this East/West dichotomy covers up a deep emptiness in Naipaul the writer, for which Naipaul the social phenomenon is making others pay, even as a whole train of his present admirers applauds his candour, his telling-it-like-it-is about that Third World which he comprehends 'better' than anyone else.

One can trace the emptiness back a few years. Consider, for instance, **"One Out of Many"**, a deft story published in *In a Free State* (1971). At the very end of the tale Santosh, the Bombayan immigrant to Washington, watches the city burn. It is 1968: blacks run amuck and, to Santosh's surprise, one of them scrawls *Soul Brother* on the pavement outside his

house. 'Brother to what or to whom?' Santosh muses. 'I was once part of the flow, never thinking of myself as a presence. Then I looked in the mirror and decided to be free. All that my freedom has brought me is the knowledge that I have a face and have a body, that I must feed this body and clothe this body for a certain number of years. Then it will be over.' Disavowal of that admittedly excited community of Sixties revolutionaries is where it begins. Seeing oneself free of illusion is a gain in awareness, but it also means emptying out one's historical identity. The next step is to proceed through life with a minumum number of attachments: do not overload the mind. Keep it away from history and causes; feel and wait. Record what you see accordingly, and cultivate moral passions.

The trouble here is that a mind-free body gave birth to a super-ego of astonishingly assertive attitudes. Unrestrained by genuine learning or self-education this persona—Naipaul the ex-novelist—tours the vulnerable parts of his natal provenance, the colonial world he has been telling us about via his acquired British identity. But the places he visits are carefully chosen, they are absolutely safe, places no one in the liberal culture that has made him its darling will speak up for. Everyone knows Islam is a 'place' you must criticise. *Time* did it, *Newsweek* did it, the *Guardian* and the *New York Times* did it. Naipaul wouldn't make a trip to Israel, for example, which is not to say that he wouldn't find rabbinical laws governing daily behaviour any less repressive than Khomeini's. No: *his* audience knows Israel is OK, 'Islam' not. And one more thing. If it is criticism that the West stands for, good—we want Naipaul to criticise those mad mullahs, vacant Islamic students, cliché-ridden revolutionaries. But does he write *for* and *to* them? Does he live among them, risk their direct retaliation, write in their presence so to speak, and does he like Socrates live through the consequences of his criticism? Not at all. No dialogue. He snipes at them from the *Atlantic Monthly* where none of them can ever get back at him.

What is the result? Never mind the ridiculous misinformation . . . and the potted history inserted here and there. The characters barely come alive. The descriptions are lackadaisical, painfully slow, repetitious. The landscapes are half-hearted at best. How can one learn about 'Islam' from him? Without the languages, he talks to the odd characters who happen by. He makes them directly representative of 'Islam', covering his ignorance with no appreciable respect for history. (pp. 21-2)

Little of what took place in 1979 is mentioned here. Naipaul's method is to attack Islamic politics without taking account of what its main currents and events are. In Pakistan Zia's much-resented, much-resisted (US assisted) assault on Pakistani civil society is nearly invisible to Naipaul. Indonesian history is the Japanese occupation, the killing of 'the communists' in 1965, and the present. The massacres of East Timor are effaced. Iran is portrayed as a country in the grip of hysteria; you would not know from Naipaul that a tremendous post-revolutionary battle, occurring while he was there, continues to go on. All this to promote an attitude of distant concern and moral superiority in the reader.

Despite its veneer of personal impressionism then, this is a political book in intention. On one level Naipaul is the late 20th-century heir of Henry MacKenzie who in *The Man of Feeling* (1771) averred that 'every noble feeling rises within me! every beat of my heart awakens a virtue—but it will make you hate the world! No . . . I can hate nothing; but as to the world—I pity the men of it.' That these men happen to be brown or black is no inconvenience on another level. They are to be castigated for not being Europeans, and this is a political pastime useless to them, eminently useful for anyone plotting to use Rapid Deployment Forces against 'Islam'. But then Naipaul isn't a politician: he's just a Writer. (p. 22)

Edward Said, *"Expectations of Inferiority," in* New Statesman, *Vol. 102, No. 2639, October 16, 1981, pp. 21-2.*

FOUAD AJAMI

In 16 works of fiction and nonfiction written over a period of some 20 years, V. S. Naipaul has been taking his readers to remote, inaccessible places in the third world. *Among the Believers,* his new book, is the chronicle of a seven-month journey he made in 1979 and 1980 to Iran, Pakistan, Malaysia and Indonesia in search of Islam. It displays all of Naipaul's major themes, his great talent as a writer and his increasing limitation of vision.

We can see in this book, perhaps more than in Naipaul's previous writings, the dilemma of a gifted author led by his obsessive feelings regarding the people he is writing about to a difficult intellectual and moral bind. He expressed this dilemma in **"Conrad's Darkness,"** the concluding essay in his last book, *The Return of Eva Perón:*

"It came to me that the great novelists wrote about highly organized societies. I had no such society; I couldn't share the assumptions of the writers; I didn't see my world reflected in theirs. My colonial world was more mixed and secondhand, and more restricted. The time came when I began to ponder the mystery—Conradian word—of my own background: that island in the mouth of a great South American river, the Orinoco, one of the Conradian dark places of the earth. . . ."

No romantic illusions brought to those dark places—"half-made societies that seemed doomed to remain half-made"—could satisfy Mr. Naipaul, for he knew from experience the bleak landscape and petty ways of "the bush"—his favorite metaphor for the third world. . . .

But he has repeatedly traveled back into the bush from London, his adopted home, and the restrictions of the third world have continued to torment and limit him. He feels that those dark places cannot sustain vision or produce great art, yet they remain the major subject of his work. Naipaul's concern with his fellow colonials has taken him from the West Indies, the setting of most of his books, to India (*An Area of Darkness, India: A Wounded Civilization*), Africa (*A Bend in the River*), Argentina (*The Return of Eva Perón*), and now Iran, Pakistan, Malaysia and Indonesia. He doesn't, however, go to those places to "meditate" on them—a Conradian term—but increasingly to express his bewilderment and "rage"—a Naipaulian word—at what he finds there.

In his brief foreword to *The Return of Eva Perón,* he spoke of the "obsessional nature" of the essays in the book and admitted that his "themes repeat." Those themes have by now become Naipaul trademarks: third-world revolutionaries who rant about cultural "authenticity" but who at bottom are really "hustlers," their heritage a "bogus past," their causes nothing but "jargon" and "borrowed ideas" and "sentimental hoax," their Western admirers either media people looking for "jesters" or "revolutionaries who visit centers of revolution with return air tickets." He has written again and again about the "frenzy" that drives third-world people to undo their world and brings them face to face with their own limits and mediocrity.

In regard to his subject matter, Naipaul has been in his own words "at once too close and too far." The consoling detachment enjoyed by someone less threatened by what he writes about, like Conrad, has been denied Naipaul. On the other hand, he cannot achieve real proximity to the places he depicts. There is, increasingly, in his work more of the "political panic" he says in the Conrad essay he carried with him from Trinidad to London. His travels have become not journeys to other places but journeys into himself—bleak re-enactments of the fear of the bush he experienced in childhood. He has become more and more predictable, too, with serious cost to his great gift as a writer. The books set in the West Indies have always demonstrated a masterly grasp of the material, and his work about India has at least been inspired by his ancestry, but in *Among the Believers* Naipaul is on considerably less familiar ground, and because the book seems to have no central theme, readers must depend on the testimony of the witnesses Naipaul picks to interview. (p. 7)

Ever the gifted novelist, Naipaul tells the story best when he lets some of his characters open up and reveal themselves. In Iran, for example, the tension in the twin revolutions against the Shah—that of Khomeini and the mullahs and that of Abolhassan Bani-Sadr and the secular nationalists—is illuminated through Behzad, a young leftist from a provincial town who is a science student in Teheran. In spite of the mullahs, Behzad says, he initially wanted to claim the revolution as his own. He wanted to believe that the mullahs could be pacified and handled, and that he and his fellows would inherit the new world. But the two revolutions went their separate ways, and young people like Behzad discovered that one form of tyranny can be replaced by another. "For the third time in this century the people of Iran have been broken," he says.

Malaysia comes together in Shafi, a 32-year-old Malay in Kuala Lumpur. At one time a building contractor in a village to the north, he now works for ABIM, a major Moslem youth movement. In Pakistan there is Ahmed, a high civil servant, a man of Sind, a devout Muslim with a feel for history. For Ahmed, as for so many others in Pakistan, the dream of a Moslem state has gone bad. But faith, somehow, survives. "If the state failed, it wasn't because the dream was flawed, or the faith flawed; it could only be because men had failed the faith." In Indonesia, Muhammad Imaddudin Abdul Rahim represents the new Islam. Imaddudin (an Arab name meaning "pillar of the faith") would like Islam to cleanse the country, so he offers it in the form of "mental training courses" to members of Indonesia's young middle class.

All four of them, like so many others they stand for, bring to their religion and tradition modern demands and anxieties. This creates pressures, for today's needs are great. The outside world at once tempts and threatens Moslems. Many of them enter that world, but they can enter it only partly. When they fail to deal with it, they retreat into their shell. When they surrender to it, guilt seizes them. (p. 30)

This theme comes close to being Naipaul's central theme, and in dealing with it he lets his personal feelings get in the way of his presentation. He chides Moslems for being "made" by the Western world they reject. Instead of trying to understand these people, Naipaul is ready to judge them. In his desire to discover their hidden vulnerabilities and point out their contradictions, their need for outside goods and outside approval, he tends to miss the drama and the real meaning of their situation. He forgets that it is part of the painful process of history that people are always made by the world they reject and that the rage at it they express is in large measure rage at themselves.

In addition to this limitation of vision, one gets the distinct feeling of superficiality in this book. Of the holy city of Qom, Naipaul writes: "Qom's life remained hidden." It is probably fair to say that much of the territory he covered remained hidden to him. The places he went to confused and eluded him, denied him entry. He was in a hurry; he wanted to see "Islam in action." But the people he wanted to comprehend were ambiguous and guarded, and under no obligation to reveal themselves to a traveler. Inside the large international hotels, visitors came to talk with him, but his questions frequently seem rigged and their answers canned. He wanted them to explain to him the secrets of their motivations, the cause of their rage. Over and over again he asked them for blueprints—how would they build an economy? keep a state together?—and repeatedly they had no blueprints to come up with, but only the confusions of their certainties, their reliance on metaphysics, the belief that all the answers could be found in sacred texts.

"We read," Naipaul says in his Conrad essay, "to find out what we already know." Most Naipaul readers will take to this book an image of Islam as a world of anarchy and rage, partly because of recent developments in the Middle East—so dramatically revealed in the assassination of President Anwar el-Sadat of Egypt—but partly also because that is the image of the third world that they have been taking away from Mr. Naipaul's work for some time now. (pp. 30, 32)

Naipaul's third-world interpretations have acquired the prestige they have in the West because he is so gifted a writer and also because he has often presented a believable image of places most writers before him were able to see only through the mists of illusion. Timing, too, had something to do with his success; he made his appearance at a point when there was great disillusionment in the West with the affairs of the third world. So many revolutions had failed; so much jargon had been discredited; so much of the modern veneer on third-world countries had cracked. Eventually, no one who really wanted to come to terms with the third world felt he could dismiss Naipaul or slight his work. But he has continued to depict the same thing over and over: a world where the oppressed often turn out to be as vicious as their oppressors; where the promises of redemption lead into blind alleys of fear and terror.

Some third-word critics have blamed Naipaul for not being a real crusader or revolutionary himself, but it is, as he would say, not the task of writers to remake societies. Where I do fault Naipaul, however, is on the depth of his material, and for me *Among the Believers* is his thinnest and least impressive book. What he has said of Conrad must surely apply to himself as well: "Conrad's experience was too scattered; he knew many societies by their externals, but he knew none in depth."

It has been a Naipaulian assumption that only men who live in remote, dark places are "denied a clear vision of the world." This is the major theme of much of his work. And many men who have left the third world to settle in other places have a tendency to think this way as well. . . . Their intellectual vocations often allow them to look at their own countries and similar ones with a critical eye, and to feel that they have a right to judge and interpret the places they have broken with. But these same men usually approach the civilization of the West with awe and leave it unexamined.

Were Naipaul to want really to come to terms with his own past, and to determine whether any men have a clear vision of the world, he would have to set his work (as he once had to set his imagination in order to appreciate Conrad) somewhere far away from the third world, somewhere in the West perhaps. . . .

More and more the women and men in [Naipaul's] fiction and political essays appear to be unsupported by anything of value, diminished and disfigured, vain, insincere, crazed, dishonest. Surely, as Conrad would tell us, this is too simple a view of things. . . . Were Naipaul to meditate on places less haunted for him by old ghosts, he might come to realize some of the truths that Conrad learned; that darkness is not only there but here as well; that all men and societies are haunted by their own demons; that all of us are denied a clear vision of the world. (p. 32)

Fouad Ajami, "In Search of Islam," in The New York Times Book Review, *October 25, 1981, pp.* 7, 30, 32.

JULIO MARZAN

Each chapter [of *Among the Believers*], each country, makes it clear that Naipaul, apparently obsessed by the third world, traveled to confirm about Islam the third world flaws he knew he would find: institutionalized hypocrisy, blind idealism, and the failure to match lofty ideology with performance. *Among the Believers* starts out being a treatise on these themes but evolves into something else: as in a picaresque novel, Naipaul's dialogues with his diverse people-metaphors teach us more about him. *Among the Believers* isn't about the visited countries, but about Naipaul among the believers over whom, in a civilized manner, his personality looms as the hero embodying a presumed, schematically articulated Westernism. *Among the Believers* is a nonfiction companion to *A Bend in the River*, many of whose themes are repeated here.

Like Salim, the anagrammatic hero in that novel, Naipaul diminishes Islam and by implication dismisses all religion. This message is also conveyed by the title, *Among the Believers*, which in fact prominently misrepresents this book. Deep down Naipaul must know that, like Islam, his clean, efficient "universal civilization" is a visible structure built on the same sort of bottomless metaphysical foundation. Islam, however crude it may be, fills that black hole with Allah and the Koran, which are subsequently exploited for political ends. On the other hand, what Western wars and conquests—especially the Cold War—have not pretended to be holy? Belief isn't in question in this book, only non-Western and specifically Islamic beliefs, whose worst features are set in relief against selected aspects of the West. For all his years in the civilized world, Naipaul has yet to direct one of his uncompromising essays at the West. In the absence of such an essay, his otherwise engrossing thoughts on the Third World serve as so much literate Westernist agit-prop, which the flattered and applauding First World will eventually find disappointingly, if exquisitely, shallow. Naipaul's West—because unexamined—remains uncontaminated by flaws of the human condition and its history. His is a vague and idealized West whose inventions and conveniences are observed from a poetic distance.

Criticizing the West would debilitate Naipaul's literary persona, which now stands strong and impervious: disagreeing with him submits you to a rigged scheme in which he transforms compassion into a form of weakness or collusion with the hypocrisy he loathes. And this gimmick disturbs because Naipaul asks hard questions of the third world that it is asking of itself—like questioning the value of ideology in the face of poverty. Underlying Naipaul's writing there is also a positivist vision of an inexorable advance throughout history of a "universal civilization," before whose patent superiority the past should peaceably surrender. He forgets that when the West had set out to share this civilization, its inability to resist enslaving or exploiting those it *believed* racially inferior was part of the reason why the colonized often chose to remain backward, free at least of self-doubt. Blondes, to this day, will invariably have more fun.

Hence, despite its merits (the vivid sense of being there, in the desert, in the bazaar), *Among the Believers* lacks a humanizing sense of the parallel Western beliefs that, say, cause the English to despise the influx, from the Caribbean, from Asia, of imperialism's debris. Like the Argentines criticized in *The Return of Eva Peron,* boastful of being neither "niggered up" nor half-Indian, Naipaul invokes a distance of Culture between himself and the world of low-grade, dark-skinned men, and that distance, turbulent with his ruthlessness, overpowers the effect of his incisive prose.

> Julio Marzan, "Romance of the Golden West," in The Village Voice, *Vol. XXVI, No. 45, November 4-10, 1981, p. 43.*

MARVIN MUDRICK

V. S. Naipaul (who *comes from* there and even *looks like* them) has been saying it for a quarter of a century now, it's what you always knew about the Third World but didn't dare tell anybody except your favorite bartender: East is East but West is Best. Till now, in default of a larger audience, Naipaul has been saying it to the readers of highbrow writing, those fit but few who hold their annual convention in the nearest telephone booth. Yet ripeness is all. Now, having made the timeliest possible in-depth and low-profile tour of the latest Third-World powder-kegs and tinderboxes and sleeping giants, he returns brimming with the latest evidence for his same old news behind the news [*Among the Believers*] only, now at last he gets to say it in thunder for Dick Cavett and the Book-of-the-Month Club: Damn the wogs: Kipling was right all the time. Naipaul complains that the weekly newsmagazines encourage Islamic barbarism (the noisiest barbarism of the moment) by their toothless and respectful coverage of it, that they "[were] helping to make the history they recorded. Islam was pure and perfect; the secular, dying West was to be rejected; that was the message." The Muslims are coming! (p. 130)

Naipaul isn't an opportunist, though the opportunity having come he takes it with a vengeance because it's vengeance that he has in mind: against the lesser breeds, against his own past, his life as a third-generation East Indian in the black-and-brown West Indies, where—trying to emulate (to ape) the lordly Europeans who have already quit and gone back to civilization— the blacks and East Indians seem to him sick jokes, seem in his raging phrase "like monkeys pleading for evolution" (in *The Middle Passage,* published twenty years ago, which is his horrified account of his visit home from grateful permanent exile in England; and he doesn't feel a bit better twenty years after). The catchword in *Among the Believers* is "rage." According to Naipaul the dynamo that charges up these believers isn't so much belief as rage; and Naipaul is their brother and, more than he knows, their advocate, because though he himself isn't a believer—quite the contrary—he too is charged up with rage: that they should *presume!* and furthermore he takes their

rage far more seriously than any Westerner except a *Time* or *Newsweek* reporter would. (pp. 130-31)

For somebody as usually desperate as Naipaul is about everything he comes from and broods over, bitching and moaning, wringing his hands, in as theatrical a fix as the people he writes about with their "frenzies and frustrations," he's most of the time a surprisingly expert, resilient, expansive writer (and very well read in "litritcher and poultry," as they are called by the down-home caricatures in his most nearly genial book of fiction, *Miguel Street*). If only he weren't so single-mindedly committed to his conclusions, so incapable of thinking about them, so exasperated and revived by all the irrefutable evidence he compulsively collects. A believer he's been interviewing asks him, "what is the purpose of your writing? Is it to tell people what it's all about?" and Naipaul answers, "Yes. I would say comprehension"—a sound answer, but one that doesn't predict or justify the current of foregone conclusions that oppressively steers the reader through Naipaul's books. In fact Naipaul already *knows* "what it's all about"—You see? you see? it's as bad as I told you!—and he doesn't try to comprehend, he doesn't reflect on his material, he's content to react to it with rage and shame. His most admired book— it has been compared, but not by me, to Dickens—is *A House for Mr Biswas,* his novel about an East Indian family in Trinidad: while reading it the reader never doubts the locale, the circumstances, the people; but if there's a more relentlessly depressing novel around I haven't read it. . . . Indeed it's so uniformly depressing that Naipaul himself can't believe it is, but later in the novel keeps imagining he has sweetened the earlier part with happy scenes and amiable characters and relationships that just aren't there. . . . The trouble is that Naipaul has a taste for horrors only, minor or major, the grandest of which is the slow-motion destruction of the Shorthills estate by the family as by a pillaging army on holiday; and finally the book isn't—though in excerpts it may seem so—funny because horrible beyond verisimilitude or acceptability, it's just horrible as a betrayal of family secrets, a proxy confession of impotence, a protracted cry of rage and shame against the lesser breeds who can't build a house or cultivate a field or develop or even convincingly adopt or imitate a civilization. (pp. 132-34)

Naipaul is so much of a one-idea writer (How do these barbarians have the *nerve* to set themselves up against the West?) that sooner or later the idea begins to seem too big for thinking about and too small for a book:

> How could he read, how could he judge, how could he venture into the critical disciplines of another civilization, when so much of his own history had been distorted for him, and declared closed to inquiry? (According to Islam, "history must serve theology.") And how strange, in the usurped Freemasons' Hall of Rawalpindi, to talk of the English political novel and the distortions of colonialism, when in that city in a few weeks, in the name of an Islam that was not be be questioned, the whipping vans were to go out, official photographs were to be issued of public floggings, and one of the country's best journalists was to be arrested and photographs were to show him in chains.

This paragraph occurs on page 210, almost exactly halfway through *Among the Believers,* but it would be quite as appropriate, with a few modifications of detail, on almost any other page; and many or most of Naipaul's interjections, expostulations, ruminative asides, paroxysms of testiness provoked by brutal, ignorant, and "parasitic" Islam are quite as versatile and interchangeable. Maybe he ought to have looked at his idea in a different way, maybe he ought to have written a different book, maybe he ought to have observed less and thought more. Aside from his shrewd interviewing and reporting and the force of his obsession, the book he sat down and wrote is monotonously alarmist, it's as questionable as the hot-from-the-presses "news items" which according to Naipaul these nuts share with one another while they plot the takeover and regeneration of the decadent West: e.g. that Scandinavia ("always liberal and wise") has already "fallen" to Islam and "France was half Muslim; in England hundreds were converting every day." *Among the Believers* isn't a world-drama the portentous ending of which hasn't yet been written, it's *Grand Guignol* with Dracula makeup and howls from the wind-machines in the wings as Islamic fanaticism threatens the very foundations of civilization: The sky is falling! the sky is falling! "Nineteen seventy-three was the year of the oil-price rise, the year when money for Arab oil seemed to come like a reward for the Arab faith." But if the oil money was God-given, God was in one of those tricky and double-talking moods the West has become accustomed to, He was showing these belated nations that money isn't everything—as Naipaul points out in the smartest paragraph in his book:

> The pleasures of money in Malaysia were simple. Money magnified the limitations of places like Malaysia, small, uneducated, and coming late to everything. Money—from oil, rubber, tin, palm oil—changed old ways. But money only turned people into buyers of imported goods, fixed the country in a dependent relationship with the developed world, kept all men colonials.
>
> (pp. 136-37)

These are the facts. Money doesn't produce goods, it can only buy them; the West may be the great Satan, but if you want goods and more than parochial political power there's no substitute for Western technology and mass-education (even when they speak Japanese; so thousands of Japanese children learn violin by the mass-teaching Suzuki method in order when grown up to play Viennese music in American and European symphony orchestras). Besides, as Naipaul never comes close to acknowledging, if the U.S. and the Soviet Union go to war over Persian Gulf oil, it won't have anything to do with Islam, any more than the Vietnam War had to do with Buddhism. Naipaul lets himself get so caught up in Third-World rhetoric that he sometimes ignores the likelier inferences and writes as if he half-believes this chickenhouse hubbub about the revolutionary power of Islam: Does he expect the Bedouins led by Rudolph Valentino to come sweeping like the simoom out of the desert descending on Bloomingdale's with fire and sword and no-limit Visa cards?

An idea that Naipaul touches on only in passing (though with graphic illustrations that should have alerted him to its significance) might have been a luckier one to take up: that it isn't just Western technology that makes the difference, it's a difference between peoples that nobody likes to mention in these days of cultural anthropology when we (in the West!) are taught to believe that a culture which practices human sacrifice isn't worse (or better) than one which doesn't, that a culture with a long history of energy and work and achievement isn't any better (though perhaps it's worse) than one in which the masses

have been shitting all over the landscape from time immemorial. In Malaysia, for example, where the Chinese constitute less than half the population they do almost all the work and business (and are arbitrarily excluded from political power because otherwise they would have everything). Or in Indonesia: "Resentment of Chinese; of foreigners; of people with skills Indonesians didn't have"; and "the gentle Masood . . . had said, '*Millions* will have to die'" (many of these "gentle" Muslims are just aching to incite and command indispensable and gigantic massacres; "the idea of human quality," as Naipaul notes, "occurs only in certain societies"). . . . Why can the Chinese (and Japanese) do what the Malaysians and Indonesians can't? Nineteenth-century travelers in Russia, as well as indignant nineteenth-century Russians, have written that, approaching a village in the outback, one could immediately identify it as either native Russian (ramshackle, sluggish, foul) or an immigrant German settlement (clean, orderly, well-constructed, cheerful). The will to work and learn is important, nor is it necessarily restricted to masters and conquerors (the Chinese continued to have it during their centuries of subservience to outsiders; the Jews have always had it); cultures differ in their recognition or encouragement of it, and these differences have the most extensive consequences over millennia of history. It's an idea that Eric Hoffer has been usefully reflecting on for decades, and it's a better idea than Naipaul's. (pp. 137-38)

Marvin Mudrick, "The Muslims Are Coming! The Muslims Are Coming!" in The Hudson Review, *Vol. XXXV, No. 1, Spring, 1982, pp. 130-38.*

MICHIKO KAKUTANI

Filled with a Dickensian gallery of antic characters and animated by a mordant black humor that recalls Evelyn Waugh, the first three novels by V. S. Naipaul [*The Mystic Masseur, The Suffrage of Elvira,* and *Miguel Street,* collected in *Three Novels,*] bear little surface resemblance to his more recent fiction. It was his fourth novel, *A House for Mr Biswas,* that established his reputation, and in a sense, these earlier stories are still the immature fruit of his apprenticeship. They are less dense, less allusive than the later novels, and in place of the brooding vision of the third world embodied in such books as *Guerrillas* and *A Bend in the River,* there is a humorous appreciation for the vitality of the populous Caribbean world.

Still, Mr. Naipaul once remarked, "all my work is really one; I'm really writing one big book," and despite their comic touches, these novels give us intimations of the direction he would move in—a fact that makes their reissue of unusual interest to followers of his work. The Trinidad depicted here, after all, belongs to the author's world of "half-made societies," places, as he once wrote, where "the West is packing its boxes, waiting for the helicopters," and it suffers from the same lack of coherence and civilizing values that Mr. Naipaul misses in India (*A Wounded Civilization*), Africa (*A Bend in the River*) and South America (*The Return of Eva Perón*). The difference in portrayal is largely one of tone: satire and irony have not yet hardened into cynicism and despair.

An outsider by circumstance as well as temperament—he grew up in Trinidad, the grandson of a Brahman who had emigrated from Uttar Pradesh, India—Mr. Naipaul was eager to leave his homeland and make a career for himself in England, and the characters in these early novels share a similar desire to escape. Their own country, as they see it, is ignorant, superstitious and dumb. "He borrow money to buy one of them dentist machine thing and he start pulling out people teeth, just like that," observes one cynic in *The Mystic Masseur.* "The boy killing people left and right, and still people going. Trinidad people is like that." . . .

If he is skeptical about the old, backward ways of the Caribbean, however, Mr. Naipaul is equally contemptuous of those former colonials who—not unlike an earlier version of himself—are so eager to become imitation English gentlemen. It is a theme developed at length in such later works as *The Mimic Men,* and already, in these novels, much of the humor comes from the islanders' hapless efforts to import an alien culture and adopt the ways of the West.

Parablelike in form, *The Mystic Masseur,* for instance, shows the making of a "mimic man." In the course of turning a career as a faith healer into political success, the hero, Ganesh, buys a complete set of Everyman's Library, perfects "his prose to a Victorian weightiness" and installs, in his house, a musical toilet-paper rack that plays "Yankee Doodle Dandy." He attends legislative-council meetings with other representatives who affect jodphurs and monocles, and by the end of the book has become a British representative at Lake Success. Of course, by then, he is no longer good old "Pundit Ganesh"—he has changed his name to G. Ramsay Muir.

In *Miguel Street*—less a story than a portrait of a town, laid out in a series of quick character sketches—a brothel owner known as Bogart adopts the hard-boiled manner of his namesake; and in *Elvira,* a village politician uses every bit of American electioneering jargon he can think of to further his campaign: "Win With Harbans" and "You Can't Live Without the Heart. You Can't Live Without Harbans."

The most sophisticated of these early novels, *Elvira,* is the story of a village election, and it is also a satiric examination of the consequences of political change. Mr. Naipaul has never bought that popular romantic vision that has a brave new world rising from the dust of the empire, and the slapstick goings-on in Elvira betray a deep skepticism of progress. . . .

In the end, Harbans's efforts almost come to naught when a stray dog triggers the voters' superstitions, nearly setting off a panic. As one character remarks: "Everybody just washing their foot and jumping in this democracy business. But I promising you, for all the sweet it begin sweet, it going to end damn sour." It is an observation, we now know, that will come to dark and violent fruition in Mr. Naipaul's later work.

Michiko Kakutani, in a review of "Three Novels,"
in The New York Times, *January 17, 1983, p. C20.*

D.A.N. JONES

Vidiadhar Naipaul won a scholarship to Oxford in 1950 and is now Trinidad's most famous writer of English. It was colonial Trinidad, he records, that helped him become a writer, by sending him to England: but it was self-governing Trinidad that sent him on 'a colonial tour in 1960—and by this accident I became a traveller.' Much of his fiction and travel-writing reflects a strong interest in the question of where he—and people in like case, colonials or ex-colonials—fit in. Do they belong to the community or are they always on the periphery? If they are 'outsiders', where is the inside, the centre?

In his novel of 1967, *The Mimic Men,* an ambitious West Indian observes that the Carribbean islands offer a bad start for a man

who wants to make his mark in the great world. They are populated by 'mimic men', he says: they are part of 'the suburbs of the world'. He quotes an old Greek proverb, to the effect that no man can be great unless he comes from a great city.

Naipaul has travelled adventurously around the suburbs of the world, those Third World territories that used to be outposts of empire. He has inspected the successor states and reported his findings with a severity that seems designed to challenge the paternalist sentimentality that comes so easily to those of us who think of ourselves as descendants of the white imperialists. But now, in *Finding the Centre,* he reports on a recent visit to the Ivory Coast with a sort of wondering enjoyment and approval. The old words of magic are not too strong: he has been fascinated, enchanted, 'glamoured' (a favourite Naipaul word) by West Africa.

The Ivorian narrative is entitled **"The Crocodiles of Yamoussoukro"**, this being the ancestral village of that powerful prince, President Houphouet-Boigny, who has been trying, for many years, to turn Yamoussoukro into a great and famous city, under the tutelary protection of sacred crocodiles. The reader is as surprised as Naipaul himself that the author should feel almost at home in this exotic community, as he instructs himself in Ivorian mysteries, seeing the new nation (*Ex Africa semper aliquid novi*) as an ancient heartland, a centre, not merely as one of the suburbs of the world.

The other narrative in *Finding the Centre* is called **"Prologue to an Autobiography"** and blends an account of Naipaul's beginnings as a writer with his middle-aged discoveries about the old subject-matter of his youth, Trinidad and his father. It is a sort of *recherche du temps perdu:* sometimes he is peeling off the onion-skin from his early fiction, as if progressing toward the heart of the subject-matter, and sometimes he is adding new outer layers, memories of memories.

A House for Mr Biswas, probably his most popular novel, was the story of a man like his father, a Trinidad newspaperman, an adventurous spirit pushing out against the bars of convention: he had felt oppressed by the orthodoxies of Trinidad, the general will of his people, especially the rigorously conservative Hinduism of his wife's extended family, a formidable tribe. Naipaul's fourth novel, first published in 1961, *A House for Mr Biswas* is now reissued with a new introduction by the author, written in a spirit of serenity, glee and candour that harmonises well with the mood of the two narratives in *Finding the Centre.* . . . Trinidad has become more real to the world because of *A House for Mr Biswas.* Naipaul suggests in his new introduction that the reality of the book derives from . . . memories of memories: it begins with 'events twice removed, in an antique "pastoral" time, and almost in a land of the imagination'. He was a town boy with little knowledge of 'the Trinidad Indian village way of life', so he made it up from childhood memories of his father's conversation and from the short stories, his father's own way of looking back on the past.

Mr Biswas is comical in his role as the dissident in-law: he snipes cockily at the caste-consciousness of his wife's family, mocking their choice of a Roman Catholic school for their children. . . . Mr Biswas himself flirts with a set of 'protestant' or reforming Hindus, the Aryans, he dabbles in Christianity, he causes irritation with his non-Indian books and the vulgar Fleet Street style of his newspaper work. Naipaul's father was like that, but for him the family situation wasn't comical. *Finding the Centre* reveals the severity of the pressure he suffered.

In 1970 an American writer in Russia, after reading Naipaul's fiction, sent the author a newspaper cutting about his father, published in 1933. The headline was: 'Writer Kowtows to Kali to Escape Black Magic Death.' The story began: 'Threatened with death by the Hindu goddess Kali, Seepersad Naipaul, native writer, today offered a goat as sacrifice to appease the anger of the goddess. . . .' This story surprised Naipaul: it had not been in his father's cuttings-book. He thought it might have been a journalistic joke, cooked up by his father and his genial editor, an 'Amazing Scenes' addict. But he learned that it represented a genuine public humiliation for his father—who, he now remembered, detested the Kali cult and had complained that his mother-in-law was a votaress of that order. Naipaul discovered that his father's newspaper work had been accept-able to the family when he could act as their herald, reporting political meetings which took place in the main family house, but not when he 'got people into the paper whether they wanted it or not'. There was trouble over his reports of an election and a riot in which members of the family were involved. Matters came to a head when the reporter was encouraging Indians to get their cattle vaccinated, scientifically, although they preferred to perform religious sacrifices to Kali, the black mother-goddess. The reforming journalist was told that unless he himself performed this rite, in public, he would surely die.

So, he surrendered. . . . Then he tried to write about his humiliation in jaunty, Fleet Street style, on the front page of the Sunday paper. '*Mr Naipaul Greets You!—No Poison Last Night.* Good morning, everybody! As you behold, Kali has not got me yet . . .' Soon he was quite ill.

His son pieced the story together from the newspaper library, some forty years later, and asked his mother: 'What form did my father's madness take?' She replied: 'He looked in the mirror one day and couldn't see himself. And he began to scream.' This is not comedy, but tragedy. The very word is Greek for 'the song of the goat', presumably derived from the idea of the goat as totem or sacrifice. The younger Naipaul seems not dispirited by the tale but more inclined to admire his father for his spirit, his sense of vocation, against such odds: the man has become heroic. The little communities of Trinidad begin to seem like Greek cities where serious things happen: not suburban, not off-the-map.

This is the main story, told with craft discursiveness, in **"Pro-logue to an Autobiography"**. It is echoed poetically in the second part of *Finding the Centre*, when Naipaul reports on the ceremony of feeding the crocodiles at Yamoussoukro: there is a tall, thin man in a skullcap and a flowered gown who throws live chickens to crocodiles in the newly created lake, using a long, thin knife to kill any chicken that escapes the jaws. The lake is near to the fine new golf-course and near to the long walls of Houphouet-Boigny's Presidential palace: these walls surround his ancestral house, where the ceremonies are less public than the feeding of the crocodiles, a spectacle open to visitors and convenient for motorists.

Naipaul asked several Ivorians about the ritual significance of the President's crocodiles. The only straightforward explana-tion came from Mr Bony, a former Minister of Education. Mr Bony said that the crocodile was the totemic animal of the President's family, just as the panther was for Mr Bony's fam-ily. There were two worlds, said Mr Bony, the world of work-aday reality and the world of the spirit. . . . They seek each other out—rather as power and authority seek each other, in Roger Scruton's formulation, to create our own political es-tablishment. . . .

A new cult among the Ivorians is called the Celestial Christians: they come from Ghana and have only been in the Ivory Coast for three years, so they are anxious to make their mark. Naipaul followed up one of their success stories: they had driven out an evil spirit which had persistently started magical fires in a harmless schoolmaster's house, and they complacently ex-pressed their regret that the schoolmaster had wasted so much money on fetishes and Muslim *marabout* magic. A letter to the newspaper, offering 'A Scientific Explanation', was dis-regarded.

Mr Biswas, that fictional amalgam of Naipaul and his father, might have expressed scorn and distaste for all this magic—as for Naipaul's stories about the severed human heads still needed for the funeral rites of Ivorian princes. But Naipaul tells his tales with more satisfaction than scepticism. The magic-haunted regime of Houphouet-Boigny is, after all, more stable, prosperous and popular than other West African governments, so often overturned by sergeants and flight-lieutenants with progressive, Biswas-like ideas. What Naipaul wants to know is whether the 'modern' world of motorways, hotels and golf-courses can be quite real to the Ivorians. He is taken with Mr Bony's talk of two worlds, one spiritual, one workaday, and associates it with his idea that West Africans have a world of the day and a world of the night: in the latter, weak women become powerful sorcerers and beggars become princes. (p. 15)

Hearing of this night life in the Ivory Coast, Naipaul was reminded of the beliefs and customs of black slaves in old Trinidad. 'A king of the night, a slave by day, would be taken about by his fellows in a litter. To the outsider, to the slave-owner, the African night world might appear a *mimic* world, a child's world, a carnival. But to the African it was the true world: it turned white men to phantoms and plantation life to an illusion.' Who are 'the mimic men' now?

It was with a different sort of Caribbean-inspired notion that he came to the Ivory Coast. He had been attracted by the idea of France in Africa—'a private fantasy, based on my own love of the French language, a special schoolboy love, given me at Queen's Royal College in colonial Trinidad by teachers, many of them black or partly black, who were themselves in love with the French language and an idea (hinted at, never stated) of an accepting, assimilating France'. For all their faults as colonisers, the French have often been said to be more skilled in assimilating their subjects than the standoffish British. But the Ivorians whom Naipaul met seemed to regard the French rather as useful tools, for the daytime superstructure, than as a civilisation to supersede their own. One of them found the French too placid, unstimulating, compared with the British.

The Ivorians he talked with most were not unlike Mr Biswas in the way they threw out general statements and epigrams—often 'modern' and Western in tone—without attempting a consistent philosophy. Djedje, the young man who attempted to guide Naipaul among the magicians, told him: 'Without civilisation, everyone would be a sorcerer.' What did he mean by civilisation? Some equivalent of an established church, per-haps, to keep the spiritual world under control. Djedje told Naipaul that sorcerers might hide their secrets from him if they discovered that he was a Hindu, since Hindus had a great reputation as magicians: however, Naipaul was the same colour as a European. This surprised Naipaul, who thinks himself quite a different colour, and he decided that Djedje was 'ra-cially, an innocent'.

His relations with black people here are different from the world of Mr Biswas in Trinidad. Mr Biswas liked to read in *Huck-*

leberry Finn about 'nigger Jim who had seen ghosts and told stories' but he was not at ease when his editor sent him out to interview 'deserving destitutes'—which might mean that he would be accosted by 'burly negroes, pictures of health and strength', demanding money: 'Indian, give me a shilling!' Among the Ivorians there was a different sort of 'racial awareness'. Those with general ideas about Africa and the African race had got them from another continent: 'a man like Djedje still knew only about the gods and the tribes.' What Naipaul seems to have found among the Ivorians is an intriguing, encouraging reflection of the ex-colonial, ancient-and-modern dilemma faced both by his real-life father and by Mr Biswas: the Ivorians had their own equivalent of the choice between vaccinating cattle or sacrificing to Kali, and they had the confidence to reconcile the two. (pp. 15-16)

D.A.N. Jones, "The Enchantment of Vidia Naipaul," in London Review of Books, *May 3 to May 16, 1984, pp. 15-16.*

FERDINAND MOUNT

V. S. Naipaul's work is . . . remarkable in several ways; that he has written first and last, for nearly 30 years, about unsettled individuals and unsettled societies—which, after all, comprise a large proportion of the world's population—without at any point deviating into the sentimental or the didactic, and without falling for any of the comfortable cure-alls that will soothe or explain away the realities: not religion, or socialism, or capitalist development, or indeed political enthusiasm of any sort. He never fails to take careful aim. His scorn withers its victims without parching the surrounding landscape; his pity for the helpless and the bewildered does not drench the continent; and his capacity for farce is reined in, sometimes too much so for the reader who is constantly hoping for every page to be as funny as the funniest pages of *A House for Mr Biswas*. There is a continuing fineness of discrimination at work, an unwavering seriousness of purpose; temptations to take the easy scores are always resisted. This all makes him sound dry and getting drier; yet there is a glorious free swing about his most recent novel, *A Bend in the River*—a triumphant proof that he has not lost the art of letting go.

Finding the Centre is a relaxation of another sort. In these two 'personal narratives', Naipaul deviates from his usual retiring, almost mannered impersonality to offer what he calls a **"Prologue to an Autobiography"**; this is followed by a piece—**"The Crocodiles of Yamoussoukro"**—which shows the writer 'going about one side of his business' in a manner which has become familiar to us; here Naipaul is in the Ivory Coast, but the technique is the same as that which he has practised in India, the West Indies, the Middle East, the Congo and elsewhere:

> To arrive at a place without knowing anyone there, and sometimes without an introduction; to learn how to move among strangers for the short time one could afford to be among them; to hold oneself in constant readiness for adventure or revelation; to allow oneself to be carried along, up to a point, by accidents; and consciously to follow up other impulses—that could be as creative and imaginative a procedure as the writing that came after.

Naipaul finds this kind of travel-work glamorous. He also finds it demanding and exhausting (to the rooted homebody, it sounds a bit bleak too). (p. 21)

A Map of the World, a recent play by David Hare, . . . [concerns] an author who is unmistakably modelled on Naipaul—witty, fastidious, uncompromising. The character is not treated wholly unfairly . . . and is given the best lines, certainly better than those given to the other rather disillusioned characters who are milling around the milieu of the same Third World conference. Still, the impression is left that a writer, or indeed any person who does not associate himself wholeheartedly with the struggles of the Third World is a dubious character or, at the very least, poses a moral question.

This familiar misunderstanding about literature is widely shared by politicians and public persons of all sorts. The fallacy is that political commitment indicates warmth and humanity, while detachment is the sign of a cold fish and a dead soul. Yet what could be colder and deader than to shovel so many ill-assorted and ill-used beings into some huge makeshift bin of ideology or nationality? By paying attention to them as individuals the author gives proper value to the diversity and poignancy of their experience; to say that he immortalises their plight is not to say that he is indifferent to it. (pp. 21-2)

[In **"The Crocodiles of Yamoussoukro"**] I think Naipaul strains for effect a little. . . . The idea of spiritual completeness is not confined to Africa. Country people almost everywhere have, or used to have, much the same feelings of amused superiority as they contemplated the frantic scurryings of townees with their childish fads.

The sight of a stain on the wall of a modern flat in Abidjan where the tropical rain has penetrated reminds the narrator of something an expatriate has said to him earlier: 'Africa seeps through'. But in that sense, England seeps through too. So do most places. In **"The Crocodiles of Yamoussoukro"** we have in fact been quietly, unconsciously carried over the border which divides reporting from creating, the setting down of experience from the working up of material, journalism from art.

Yet the working up of mumbo-jumbo (in the strict sense of that term) is essential to Mr Naipaul's narrative; for the mumbo-jumbo is the background to the people he is really dealing with—the expatriates, the marginal, the displaced, the half-Europeans; this mixture of excitement and fear is what lures them to the edge of the jungle and keeps them there. It is their story which is to be told.

And story-telling is the driving force of Naipaul's work: 'any attempt at narrative can give value to an experience which might otherwise evaporate away.' It is precisely the inconsequential which most needs consequences; the story which has no point or twist which most needs a beginning, middle and an end. The narrative impetus dignifies, sharpens, intensifies effects, whether of pathos or humour. Narrative and simplicity. How beautifully and clearly Naipaul starts his autobiographical fragment by telling the story of how he wrote *Miguel Street*, a collection of Trinidad tales which has the carefree fluency of so many of his first books: he was sitting in a gloomy little office in the BBC; he describes the room and he sets down the first sentence he tapped out on the old typewriter and the magical feeling of having written it: *Every morning when he got up Hat would sit on the banister of his back verandah and shout across, 'What happening there, Bogart?'*

I read *Miguel Street* years ago; that first sentence brings it all back in a rush, and to recall the rush of pleasure is to present as moral a justification as any, if justification were needed, which it isn't. (pp. 22-3)

Ferdinand Mount, "No Home for Mr Biswas," in *The Spectator, Vol. 252, No. 8130, May 5, 1984, pp. 21-3.*

EDWARD HOAGLAND

[V. S. Naipaul's] novels picture a kind of limitless postcolonial space and liberty—a delirium of liberty—but madness or star-vation awaits any poor soul who suffers a misstep. Hindu in his origins, Trinidadian by birth . . . and a grateful resident of England for the past 34 years, he writes with an exile's jitters and takes a mordant view of most national truisms. Home, wherever home is, is likely to be a patchwork of religious and racial sects, hostile or incommunicado toward each other. But of course to set out from home is still more precarious. (p. 1)

Life in Britain has . . . made him intensely fastidious and gin-gerly on his returns to what is called the third world; in fact he usually goes loaded for bear. But when he leaves the first-class, high-rise hotels where he carefully situates himself, he remains as openhearted as any writer to the actual sight of poverty, of stunted hopes and blighted opportunities. And fame as a novelist has not spoiled Mr. Naipaul as a travel writer, which is uncommon enough to be phenomenal. He doesn't wander through exotic hamlets distracting himself with re-sentment that nobody has heard of him. Part of his fidelity may be due to his regarding the trips themselves as little novels, each with a set of characters, risks and dilemmas, which he follows out to see how they're resolved, and part to his ex-pressed kinship with Joseph Conrad, the meat of his career lying in these "meditations" in tropical climates.

He combines a British-style matter-of-fact professionalism—a book every year or two, 18 at present count—with the des-perately serious ambition of so many New World novelists, who seem prepared to stake their very lives on conveying one grand vision. He writes, as he says in the extraordinary au-tobiographical fragment [in *Finding the Center*], from a central "hysteria" or fear, which is that of personal extinction, a fear kept at bay only by writing, the vocation bequeathed to him (along with the fear) by his father, who after a frail but prom-ising apprenticeship was indeed destroyed. . . .

Finding the Center contains . . . [the] vivid **"Prologue to an Autobiography"** and another long essay, **"The Crocodiles of Yamoussoukro,"** about a visit Mr. Naipaul paid to the Ivory Coast at the end of 1982, and the balanced view of Africa he sought there. He had just turned 50 and perhaps it marks a sea change in him that he was in search of a balanced view. Over the years he could virtually be counted upon, when on a trip to the third world, to smash it and bash it. With Zaire and Argentina, in *The Return of Eva Peron* (1980), one might not argue with the fear and despair the destinations he had chosen aroused in him; but *India: a Wounded Civilization* (1977) is far less convincingly acerbic, polemical and dour, and is written as though by an author who doesn't know that all civilizations are wounded. *Among the Believers* (1982) is a vitriolic tour of several Moslem countries which, in my opinion, evinces an inherent antipathy to the religion of Islam so naked and severe that a book taking a comparable view of Christianity or Judaism would have been hard put to find a publisher in the United States.

Of Great Britain, his residence for so long, he has written relatively little—presumably that will some day follow this "Prologue"—but expatriate though he is, in both fiction and nonfiction, he has seldom failed to give vent to his exasperation at British or other Western expatriates whom he has encoun-tered abroad. That they should have voluntarily left the very place he struggled to find a refuge in seems to have been a sore point with him. So have his numerous bouts with African or Asian intellectuals who have not followed his path to Oxford and permanent European exile. A man much touched by pov-erty and abandonment, but a man of many irritations, he has seemed intolerant of educated men who were still comfortable where they were born, unless they were Europeans.

His novels include marvelous evocations of Trinidad, as well as one masterpiece, *A Bend in the River,* set in deepest Africa, and I wouldn't quibble with his means of arriving at a mas-terpiece, but his previous journalism has contained so many rancorous interviews that I have been impatient to see him acknowledge some personal element of painful history to ac-count for such cantankerousness when traveling out of England. *Finding the Center* does not spell out a connection between his childhood wounds and his snappish bent, but the evidence of pain, upheaval, demoralization and terror is in the memoir, alongside his customary surges of affection, intuition and com-passion and his quite peerless gift for being utterly specific about each person he brings to mind.

After finishing the "Prologue," he went off at once to the Ivory Coast, which he chose because it was in West Africa, where he had never been, was French-influenced, not English, and was a success story. Not Guinea or Uganda, but "African success, France in Africa—those were the glamorous ideas that took me out." And **"The Crocodiles of Yamoussoukro"** is replete with a wise good humor appropriate to somebody who has just found himself to be half a century old. . . .

[No] artist of Mr. Naipaul's stature is likely to travel anywhere without finding whatever he has already set his sights on. Not the high new office buildings, the vast golf course and miles of cropland around Yamoussoukro, the President's birthplace, which is being built up into an Ivorian Brasília; but the croc-odiles. It is impossible for a distant reader to know how much significance these reptiles' existence really has for anybody, apart from Mr. Naipaul. Conceivably he *is* portraying the heart of the country by concentrating on the crocodiles. His intuitions tell him so, and he impressively summons, from a couple of university people, testimonials to the round-the-clock bustle of Africa's traditional spirits, who busily surpass during the night every feat of a Western technology that is activated only during the day. Yet he may also be distorting somewhat in the way a writer would who visited the United States and focused heav-ily on the peculiar ritual of future captains of industry tearing down the goal posts after a Yale-Princeton game.

Otherwise, Mr. Naipaul's chief prism during this quick trip was the observations of other foreigners, black as well as white. He can command such resonance and intensity that he was able to work in what seems to be a scattery and accidental manner and yet come back with a lovely and profound vignette, full of honest changes of judgment about particular people, gen-erally on the side of appreciating them better. . . . (p. 44)

Reconciliation is one of the themes in each of the essays. However, Mr. Naipaul's contempt for Islam remains. "In a commercial street . . . one African, white-capped and in a Mus-lim gown, was doing his midday prayer, kneeling and bending forward in a private stupor.'' Moslem—but never Christian or Jewish—prayer is by its nature a ''stupor.'' This sort of slur, together with his previously dependable flaying of the third world nations he visited, has made him popular with sectors of the American intellectual community who do not ordinarily pay much attention to contemporary novelists, and he has developed here the odd celebrity of an Erskine Caldwell in Russia: brilliant local portraiture being touted for purposes of disparagement as an accurate picture of a whole continent that readers, it can be assumed, will never visit.

But Mr. Naipaul is a wild card. His politics are more complicated than they may seem; or part of his politics may have been simply rage. *A Bend in the River, In a Free State, A House for Mr. Biswas, The Return of Eva Peron, Finding the Center—* these are books written from a more varied intelligence than any other writer can now reliably muster. Mr. Naipaul has quoted Conrad: ''To awaken the sense of true wonder. That is perhaps a fair definition of the novelist's purpose in all ages.'' And if he can continue to free himself from his strange mesh of antipathies—becoming as free of them as Conrad—he might indeed become a kind of double for his literary hero for our own *fin de siècle.* (p. 45)

> *Edward Hoagland, ''Staking His Life on One Grand Vision,'' in* The New York Times Book Review, *September 16, 1984, pp. 1, 44-5.*

MAGGIE LEWIS

V. S. Naipaul's pair of narratives in *Finding the Center* seem unrelated at first. One is autobiographical; the other is a reflection on superstition in the Ivory Coast. As you read, though, they turn out to be circling the same themes in startlingly different ways.

Naipaul tells his **''Prologue to an Autobiography''** almost shyly. He starts with the moment he wrote the first sentence of the first book he got published, a book about a man who lived with Naipaul's family in Trinidad. He brings out one loop of revelation after another, but cautiously, never telling all at once. We see his impoverished life as a young colonial and Oxford graduate in London. He works through concentric rings of memory, historical fact, and disclosures by family members. The story takes us to Venezuela 27 years later to visit the subject of that first sentence, back to his childhood in Trinidad, and further back to his grandparents' emigration from India.

This is mainly a heartbreaking portrait of his father, a reporter who covered the Indian community for the Trinidad Guardian. It is also a portrait of himself as a son. He writes about his father's downfall with such tenderness that you can imagine him as a small boy. (p. 19)

[The] image of the young Naipaul, writing that first published sentence in a state of desperate ambition, suddenly makes sense. You feel you have ''found the center'' with him.

Which makes **''The Crocodiles of Yamoussoukro''** all the more chilling.

Here, Naipaul investigates the crocodiles that the President of the Ivory Coast keeps at his tribal village, Yamoussoukro,

which has been made a monument of modernity as a testament to Ivory Coast's development. Daily, they are thrown a live chicken to eat in front of an audience. Naipaul talks to people about other strange happenings and then puts the events side by side to see if they shed light on one another.

But his questions keep leading to the ''world of night, the world of darkness,'' as one African calls it, the world of animistic belief and supposed supernatural powers. Many of the people he talks to are foreigners who have chosen to live here and who love it, like the woman from Martinique who says that ''life is so big'' with the addition of this ''other world.''

Yet poking through the satisfaction and ''wholeness'' these people say they feel are the grisly little details he keeps wondering about. In the Ivory Coast, the servants of a chief are still buried with him, Naipaul is told. If they run away at his death, children are sacrificed instead. Someone tells him that, when the newspaper reports a child's disappearance, that child has been sacrificed. The newspaper describes a house that mysteriously keeps catching on fire, and attributes this phenomenon to evil spirits. . . .

Naipaul's shyness has become stealth. He tells you about human sacrifice calmly, in the middle of charming descriptions of the expatriates and Ivorian intellectuals and admiring comments on Ivorian development. It is as if you had found these things out by mistake. You don't even know whether to believe him, since he has said this is not a journalistic investigation. You feel alone in an alien world.

Naipaul has succeeded in passing along his terror of superstitious thinking to the reader. At the end of the book, I yearned for the beginning with something like homesickness. The African life, with its integrated belief system in which ''the world of darkness'' is an accepted part of the terrain of thought, contrasts with Naipaul's edgy, alienated sense of the tight horizons of his childhood. But I turned back and reread **''Prologue to an Autobiography''** because I couldn't leave the book that way. In this book, the *search* for the center *is* the center, and Naipaul makes the reader search, too.

In **''The Crocodiles of Yamoussoukro''** he pretends to withhold judgment, like a polite visitor, but in putting the two views of sacrifice together he really makes a severe judgment indeed. His aloof style in the second narrative is confusing. He seems to be writing about Westerners and Western-educated Ivorians' enchantment with ''the world of darkness.'' But *Finding the Center* could be read as a condemnation of Africans for being backward, written by someone who spoke more often with Westerners living in Africa than with natives. He reports that he looked away when the chicken was eaten by the crocodile— a perfectly sensible response. But why search for the meaning of something you aren't willing to look at?

What does come through clearly is that his search of newspapers, relatives' memories, and his own feelings in **''Prologue to an Autobiography''** is crucial. This is a chilling book that should be read 1½ times. (p. 20)

> *Maggie Lewis, ''The Dark Night of Superstition: Two Tales,'' in* The Christian Science Monitor, *October 31, 1984, pp. 19-20.*

Grace Paley

1922-

American short story writer and essayist.

Paley's inventive style and the political and social causes advocated in her work have generated significant critical attention despite her small literary output. Her stories are often fragmented and open-ended, and she frequently ignores conventional development of plot and characterization. Paley's fiction gains vitality and originality through economical language, precise imagery, experimentation with form, and recreation of urban American idioms, particularly Yiddish-American dialect. She usually centers on female characters who attempt to hold their families together or who persevere on their own following failed love relationships. These women, like Paley, are frequently politically oriented; for the sake of their children and the world, they demonstrate for safe parks, march in antiwar protests, and oppose the use of nuclear arms and energy. However, most critics contend that her style is as important as her subjects. According to Jonathan Baumbach, Paley's ability to deal with "the most risky and important themes in a style in which words count for much, sometimes almost for all," allows her to combine "what has been called the 'tradition of new fiction' in America with the abiding concerns of the old."

Paley has published three collections of short stories: *The Little Disturbances of Man* (1959), *Enormous Changes at the Last Minute* (1974), and *Later the Same Day* (1985). In the first collection she establishes her characteristic narrative tone, which alternates between humor and sadness, and develops the lower-class New York milieu in which almost all of her stories are set. The highly regarded story "An Interest in Life" displays Paley's concern with ordinary people caught in unexceptional circumstances that nonetheless hold important meaning in their lives. On the surface, this story relates a husband's desertion of his wife and four children, yet it distills into a study of a woman's will to survive what a character calls "the little disturbances of man."

The experimental nature of the stories in *Enormous Changes at the Last Minute* provoked a wide range of critical response. Several critics considered this volume a major work, while others noted an uneven quality and obtrusive political themes in some of the stories. Marianne DeKoven pointed out that "Paley's concern is not mimesis or verisimilitude, but rather the problem of creating a literary form which does not strike one as artificial; which is adequate to the complexity of what we know." In a widely discussed story in this collection, "A Conversation with My Father," Faith, a fiction writer, argues with her father about the merits of her unconventional storytelling methods. The father wants her to write stories in the manner of Guy de Maupassant and Anton Chekhov. In the end, observed DeKoven, "emerges the statement, crucial to Paley's work, that traditional themes can no longer be treated *truthfully* by formally traditional fiction: formal inventiveness and structural open-endedness not only make fiction interesting, they make it 'true to life.'"

In *Later the Same Day* Paley continues to explore the themes of her first two collections. Several of the stories revolve around

© Nancy Crampton

characters from her earlier work who are older but still outspoken. Faith, whom many critics regard as Paley's alter ego, appears in several stories as a wisecracking yet sensitive observer of contemporary life. Critical response to this collection was generally positive, and several critics asserted that Paley is among the most important and innovative of contemporary American short story writers. Robert Harris stated: "Miss Paley has achieved a reputation as a writers' writer, as one of the best short story writers we have, because of her uncanny ability to juxtapose life's serious and comic sides in stories whose essential truths are set forth with freshness and lucidity."

(See also *CLC*, Vols. 4, 6; *Contemporary Authors*, Vols. 25-28, rev. ed.; *Contemporary Authors New Revision Series*, Vol. 13; and *Dictionary of Literary Biography*, Vol. 28.)

PATRICIA MacMANUS

The glad tidings from this reviewer's corner are of the appearance of a newcomer possessed of an all-too-infrequent literary virtue—the comic vision. Grace Paley is the writer, and heretofore, apparently, her light has been confined to some of the smaller quarterlies. Now, however, *The Little Disturbances of Man* brings together ten of her short stories, and a welcome event it is. While they may not, to be sure, fully satisfy confirmed plot-watchers, they are by no means simply "mood" stories—rather, they are marked throughout by a well-defined and artfully guileless form of narrative progression. But the heart of the matter in these tales is their serio-comic stance: character revealed through the wry devices that man contrives, consciously and unconsciously, to shore up his uncertain existence and, sometimes, to salvage laughter from lamentation. (p. 28)

The people in these tales exist on the far periphery of the Important world; and the themes are as the title states: the little disturbances of man—"little" vis-à-vis cosmic catastrophes, but major to the personal business of daily living. A middle-aging, sanguine-spirited "bachelor girl" recollects an amorous past on the eve of her marriage to a long-ago beau; a determined teen-ager cons a bemused young soldier into a thoroughly entangling alliance; a husband-abandoned wife and mother wait out the idolized prodigal's return, imperturbably confident; a pixilated youth who lives in a philodendron-decorated automobile and functions as a kind of curb-service problem consultant; a girl's long, frustrated need for love is examined from her own viewpoint—and from the viewpoint of the man she wants. These are a few of the characters who move through the oblique human comedy of Mrs. Paley's stories. Small-time people, in terms of the world worldly, they none the less reflect the perdurable instinct of most people everywhere to improvise ways and means of accepting the indifferent universe. (pp. 28-9)

Patricia MacManus, "Laughter from Tears," in The New York Times Book Review, *April 19, 1959, pp. 28-9.*

THOMAS LASK

[Miss Paley] is everything the people quoted on the dust jacket [of *The Little Disturbances of Man*] say she is: A writer of "wild imagination," whose "toughness and bumpiness arise out of . . . the daring and heart of a genuine writer of prose"; her writing "takes off into a realm that borders on the surreal"; her work is "sexy, crazy, funny"; she "has a girl's charm and a woman's strength"; she is "a natural." Miss Paley comes endorsed by Philip Roth, Donald Barthelme, Harvey Swados, Jerome Charyn, Herbert Gold, Susan Sontag—a list that establishes a good line of credit.

Miss Paley is a natural all right. No die will ever be made from her style. Every imitation will have to be built up each time from the first sketches.

She doesn't merely use words. She kites them, skitters them, schoons them along the frozen surface of our minds. There is something elfin about her but nothing frail or dainty. Her imagination is inverted, but look at the world through her lenses and you will discover a hive of dislocated men and women, driven by their appetites, by lofty but not always adequate codes of behavior and morality. Circumstances knock their plans into the ashcan, but they bounce back as if they had a hot line to the Almighty. She has a wonderful faculty of making everything in her stories seem new and unused.

Thomas Lask, "Three but Not of a Kind," in The New York Times, *March 23, 1968, p. 29.*

GRANVILLE HICKS

The case of Grace Paley is unique. She published a first book of short stories, *The Little Disturbances of Man,* in 1959. It caused no great stir, but it so impressed a certain number of people that its reputation has steadily grown. Out of print for some time, it has now been reissued. . . .

The book's contents are described as "eleven stories of men and women at love." This is not exactly a novel subject, but Miss Paley has brought to it depth of feeling, fresh powers of observation, and a personal, vigorous style. Look at the first paragraph of the first story, **"Goodbye and Good Luck"**:

> I was popular in certain circles, says Aunt Rosie. I wasn't no thinner then, only more stationary in the flesh. In time to come, Lillie, don't be surprised—change is a fact of God. From this no one is excused. Only a person like your mama stands on one foot, she don't notice how big her behind is getting and sings in the canary's ear for thirty years. Who's listening? Papa's in the shop. You and Seymour thinking about yourself. So she waits in a spotless kitchen for a kind word and thinks—poor Rosie. . . .

Rosie goes on to make it clear to her niece that she is not to be pitied. When she was a girl, she fell in love with a popular actor in the Yiddish theater, and became his mistress. He was a charmer, a matinee idol: "On the opening night, in the middle of the first scene, one missus—a widow or maybe her husband worked too long hours—began to clap and sing out, 'Oi, oi, Vlashkin.'" The affair followed a strange course over many years, and now, as she wants the niece to understand, it has reached a strange but to her satisfying climax.

It is Miss Paley's masterly use of the vernacular that makes us feel Rosie's vitality. In this, as in several other stories, the language is that of persons who have been influenced by Yiddish, and Miss Paley knows how to get the most out of the colorful idioms of that speech; but the voice is always unmistakably her own—alive, eager, fearless, a little tough, a little tender.

There are extraordinary characters: Josephine, the thirteen-year-old who goes after and nearly gets her man; Shirley Abramovitch, who plays the leading part in the public school Christmas play because she has the loudest voice; Eddie Teitelbaum, an inventive boy whose ingeniousness gets him into serious trouble. Most of the stories are told in the first person, and in most of these the narrator is a woman. One or two of the characters are grotesques, and their stories could be described as far-out, but Miss Paley's great gift is for making something remarkable out of the commonplace. (p. 29)

Granville Hicks, "Some Stopped Short and Sold," in Saturday Review, *Vol. LI, No. 17, April 27, 1968, pp. 29-30.**

MARIANNE DeKOVEN

In contemporary fiction, the impulse to recreate form is at loggerheads with the impulse to tell about everyday life. Grace Paley is a rare contemporary who feels both impulses, and in her work they cohere. It would be easy to read her stories without recognizing that they give two very different kinds of pleasure—the intellectual, aesthetic pleasure of inventive language and form, and the emotional, moral pleasure of deftly handled, poignant theme—without realizing that one was having the best of two historically sundered fictional modes.

Though Paley has published only two collections of stories, *The Little Disturbances of Man* and *Enormous Changes at the Last Minute,* she is nonetheless an important writer—important in the significance of the fictional possibilities she realizes rather than in the uniform merit of her published work. She is not always at her best. But when she is, Paley reconciles the demands of avant-garde or postmodern form for structural openness and the primacy of the surface with the seemingly incompatible demands of traditional realist material for orchestrated meaning and cathartic emotion.

"A Conversation With My Father," in *Enormous Changes,* makes of this seeming incompatibility an argument between father and daughter, from which emerges the statement, crucial to Paley's work, that traditional themes can no longer be treated *truthfully* by formally traditional fiction: formal inventiveness and structural open-endedness not only make fiction interesting, they make it "true-to-life." Paley's concern is not mimesis or verisimilitude, but rather the problem of creating a literary form which does not strike one as artificial; which is adequate to the complexity of what we know. Her narrator in **"A Conversation With My Father"** calls traditional plot "the absolute line between two points which I've always despised. Not for literary reasons, but because it takes away all hope. Everyone, real or invented, deserves the open destiny of life." Her father, arguing that plot is the truth of tragedy, wants her to write like Chekhov or Maupassant: "Tragedy! Plain tragedy! Historical tragedy! No hope. The end." Paley's narrator-surrogate, arguing for open-ended hope and change, clearly bests her father in the conversation. But in the story, Paley gives him the last word: the setting is his hospital room, and he speaks from what we may assume is his deathbed. His lecture on writing is "last-minute advice," and the closing speech, from father's pain to daughter's guilt, is his: "'How long will it be?' he asked. 'Tragedy! You too. When will you look it in the face?'"

The assertion of hope through change and open-endedness is therefore neither easy nor unambiguous. As the literary father sees, an inevitable component of optimistic belief in saving the situation through "enormous changes at the last minute" is evasion of genuine and unavoidable horror, the father's tragedy. As Faith herself says in **"Living"** (*Enormous Changes*), "You have to be cockeyed to love, and blind in order to look out the window at your own ice-cold street."

Paley herself, though endorsing in the structure of her fiction the narrator's point of view, is increasingly ambivalent about traditional storytelling. (pp. 217-18)

Though linear storytelling is attractive to Paley's moral-political sensibility, and she feels guilty that she doesn't write that way, the marrow of her fictions remains "enormous changes at the last minute." (p. 218)

Paley places the tragic material which interests and moves her within an antitragic structure of sudden, abrupt transformations, "enormous changes," but the tragic material is nonetheless left intact. There is none of the hollow laughter, the mocking, alienated distance from pathos that is characteristic of serious modern fiction. But transformation undercuts tragic inevitability—fictional structure becomes tragedy's antidote rather than either its vehicle or its negation—and, equally important, as we will see, transformation undercuts the sentimentality that so easily trivializes pathos.

The people Paley's narrator in **"A Conversation With My Father"** would accuse of having merely "literary reasons" for rejecting traditional plot might explain the "enormous change" as an interesting substitute for outworn, tedious literary convention (linear plots are stale and boring), infusing new life into fiction. But Paley's structures are more than that. They are rooted not only in an assertion of open-endedness and possibility, and in a nonlinear vision of life's events, but also, ultimately, in a profound commitment to freedom as a primary value (nonlinearity is not as alien to Paley's politics as it might appear). For many postmodernists, that freedom is problematic; tangled with fear of chaos on one hand and of authority on the other. . . . But the freedom implied for Paley by "enormous changes," the freedom from inevitability or plot, is synonymous with hope; hence her larger assertion that open-endedness in fiction is the locus of "the open destiny of life," to which everyone is *"entitled"*—a strongly political statement. . . . Tentatively and comically, Paley offers fiction's "enormous changes" as a warbling counternote to the tragic gong, even in twentieth century political life, that notoriously unredeemed domain.

The tragic subject matter of Paley's work reaches the reader emotionally as pathos, a tricky entity because it so easily becomes sentimental. However, pathos remains pathos in Paley's work: she jerks no tears but neither does she freeze them. Instead, she distracts the reader from pathos at dangerous moments, when sentimentality threatens, by calling attention to her wildly inventive, comic language and imagery. In those moments when her language takes on the burden of simultaneously communicating and distracting from pathos, Paley creates a unique and fascinating literary object.

In **"Faith in the Afternoon"** (*Enormous Changes*), Faith, recently abandoned by her husband, is visiting her parents in their old people's home, "The Children of Judea." Faith's mother belongs to the "Grandmothers' Wool Socks Association," governed by the formidable Mrs. Hegel-Shtein, who rolls noiselessly in and out of everyone's privacy "on oiled wheelchair wheels." Mrs. Hegel-Shtein is an ineluctable and pitiless purveyor of sad stories. She forces Faith's mother, who wants to spare her daughter more unhappiness, to discuss the tragic fates of various of Faith's childhood friends, beginning with Tess Slovinsky, whose first child was a "real monster," and:

> "[The second] was born full of allergies. It had rashes from orange juice. It choked from milk. Its eyes swoll up from going to the country. All right. Then her husband, Arnold Lever, a very pleasant boy, got a cancer. They chopped off a finger. It got worse. They chopped off a hand. It didn't help. Faithy, that was the end of a lovely boy. That's the letter I got this morning just before you came."
>
> Mrs. Darwin stopped. Then she looked up at Mrs. Hegel-Shtein and Faith. "He was an only son," she said. Mrs. Hegel-Shtein gasped. "You said an only son!"

Mrs. Hegel-Shtein is vulnerable to Arnold Lever's gruesome fate through her love of her own "only son," Archie. Faith's mother tells Arnold Lever's story from the great distance of the comic grotesque. He does not represent the kind of pathos Paley is interested in: his is sensational horror, not the unostentatious, commonplace pain of everyday life. Because she feels deeply Mrs. Hegel-Shtein's commonplace pain, Paley reaches a moment of potential sentimentality, her cue for magnificent writing: ''On deep tracks, the tears rolled down her old cheeks. But she had smiled so peculiarly for seventy-seven years that they suddenly swerved wildly toward her ears and hung like glass from each lobe.'' The image of Mrs. Hegel-Shtein's tears swerving along deep tracks, formed by seventy-seven years of peculiar smiling, to hang from her ear lobes like crystals, is so striking that it appropriates most of our attention as we read, preventing us from noticing particularly the pathos which we nonetheless feel. The fate of Mrs. Hegel-Shtein's tears is exactly the fate of our own. They fall, but they are ''wildly'' diverted along literally comic tracks to become something other than tears, something not at all commonplace; in fact, something transcendent: they crystallize into literary epiphany.

Pathos is neither transformed nor displaced by language: it remains intact, registered at a more or less subliminal level. But it combines with the startling, comic-bizarre language and imagery to make a profound literary moment which we experience simultaneously as a unity beyond both pathos and language, and also as a concatenation of the two separate elements, each maintaining its integrity.

For Paley, ''life'' need not be rescued from sordid insignificance by ''literature.'' She does not translate or transform one into the other, but rather allows them to coexist in her work, partly separate, partly clashing, partly fused. We do not look *through* her images to find the meanings behind them; instead, the arresting, startling language and imagery comprise one element of the fiction, the feelings and meanings they communicate another. We receive them with different kinds of attention.... (pp. 219-21)

But just as often as they function separately in Paley's work, prose surface and story come together in the peculiar way of Mrs. Hegel-Shtein's tears, in those moments when language must suddenly distract the reader from pathos, misleading us about the primary emotion of the fictional material. Again, in the best of those moments, surface and feeling register on the one hand separately, as strangely irreconcilable, and on the other harmoniously, as an irreducible literary epiphany. (p. 222)

At the heart of Paley's engagement with everyday life is her deep empathy with her characters. Even the deserters and betrayers she allows their ''reasons,'' as she might say, and the rest she actively likes—a stance even more unusual in serious postmodern fiction than her assertions of hope in the face of our despair. It is not surprising that this uncommon empathy, which is really the condition of adherence to subjects of everyday life, is the province of a woman. Empathy and compassion are legacies of sexism that women do well to assert as privileged values rather than reject as stigmata of oppression. Uncomfortable as it makes her to write in such a predominantly male tradition, as a woman in the avant-garde, Paley is in an especially propitious position to unite interesting forms with important themes. She uses innovative form much as she uses innovative activism, to make new the endlessly dreary and shameful moral-political world we inhabit. (pp. 222-23)

Marianne DeKoven, ''Mrs. Hegel-Shtein's Tears,'' in Partisan Review, *Vol. XLVIII, No. 2, 1981, pp. 217-23.*

MICHIKO KAKUTANI

In one of the stories in Grace Paley's new collection [*Later the Same Day*], a story titled **''The Expensive Moment,''** a Chinese woman, who is visiting America, turns to her New York host and says: ''Now I would like to see how you live. I have been to meetings, one after another and day after day. But what is a person's home like? How do you live?'' That, of course, is exactly what Grace Paley tries to do in these sad, funny, elliptical stories—show how people live day to day in New York City, show how the public events of history (mainly the noisy disruptions of the 1980's) conjoin with our private lives, and how we continue to seek, even after disappointment and loss, some approximation of our youthful dreams.

Although the neighborhood of the Village is the same and some of the characters, too, are acquaintances from earlier Paley stories—most notably Faith, the author's feisty yet simpatico alter ego—the people in this collection are older than before, more given to remembering love and ambition than experiencing it anew. Most of them, as the narrator of **''Love''** observes, have settled into a ''homey life in middle age with two sets of bedroom slippers'' and are trying to cope with the fact that their families and their sense of attachment have slowly dwindled: their parents are dead now or confined to homes for the aged, their children grown and departed for lives of their own, or impolitely reticent—forgetting to call home on the holidays or simply reluctant to articulate their secrets.

Responsibility—to one's family, one's friends and to social ideals—remains the dominant concern of Mrs. Paley's characters....

Mrs. Paley at times resorts to blunt, unnecessary explication.... And at other times, Mrs. Paley tries so hard to stress the universality of her characters' dilemmas that she unwittingly reduces them to abstract wraiths. Her writerly gifts are for naturalism, not for surrealism or the symbolic, and such tales as **''At That Time, or the History of a Joke,'' ''In the Garden,''** and **''This is a Story about My Friend George, the Toy Inventor''** become little more than nervous, haphazard sketches about ill-defined people—they neither move in the quick, surprising circle of a good parable nor loft the mundane up into the heights of sunny metaphor.

Mrs. Paley is clearly at her best when she is writing, in a straightforward manner, about people she knows well—lapsed intellectuals and committed liberals, who spend their free time passing out antiwar leaflets, going to China, attending ''cultural events'' and arguing the fine points of Marxist and feminist doctrine....

Well-versed in the pompous rhetoric of the ideological and adept at dramatizing themselves as good Samaritans, these characters could easily become obnoxious—and they frequently are—but Mrs. Paley is not merely interested in satirizing their pretensions. She is also interested in investigating the ways in which they use their high-minded concerns about the state of the world at large as a distraction from more private troubles. It is easier, for most of them, to babble on about patriarchy in China or ''the bravery of that private inclusive intentional community'' than to face up to a friend's slow death from cancer, a husband's infidelity or a daughter's maturation into fatness and despair.

Indeed, the lives of Mrs. Paley's characters are riddled with illnesses, failures of love and busted promises. More often than not, their well-laid plans for themselves and their families are out of sync with some larger pattern of fate, and through no fault of their own they fall apart, fall down, fall victim to ''God's chemical mistakes and society's slimy lies.'' A woman goes to visit her aged parents at a sanitarium and hears her father announce that he wants to get a divorce. A couple's two young daughters are kidnapped, never to be returned. A man watches his pretty daughter, Cissy, tumble into madness and incoherence, and ends up using the money he'd saved for his retirement to pay for a hospital that cannot repair her mind.

What's left for these people to do is to talk, for in talking, in making up stories—or lies—about their problems, there is at least the hope of understanding what has happened to them and why. Frequently, they don't do such a good job of listening to one another—Mrs. Paley's characters are constantly interrupting others, changing the subject or making abortive jokes—but in the end, maybe, that doesn't really matter. For them, as for Mrs. Paley, the process of telling stories is itself a redemptive and necessary act.

> Michiko Kakutani, in a review of "Later the Same Day," in The New York Times, April 10, 1985, p. C20.

ROBERT R. HARRIS

Ask writers of varying dispositions and sensibilities, and Grace Paley's name is almost certain to be mentioned in any list of admired colleagues. During the last 25 years she has published just three slim volumes of short stories—*The Little Disturbances of Man* (1959), *Enormous Changes at the Last Minute* (1974) and now *Later the Same Day* [1985]. The three books contain 45 stories, and not all are first-rate. Yet Miss Paley has achieved a reputation as a writers' writer, as one of the best short-story writers we have, because of her uncanny ability to juxtapose life's serious and comic sides in stories whose essential truths are set forth with freshness and lucidity. Her best stories have staying power, and a few can justifiably be called brilliant.

Miss Paley's work has an honesty and guilelessness about it, qualities made all the more luminous by an artfully intricate prose style full of surprises. Her (mostly) plotless narratives seem straightforward until a turn of phrase catches you off guard and, quietly but purposefully, breaks your heart. Irony is crucial in her stories, though she does not use it to sentimentalize or mock her characters but to delineate the offbeat ways in which they muddle through their lives, facing up to hurt without forfeiting their humanity.

The people Miss Paley writes about are likely to be, as she said in *Enormous Changes,* "revisionist Communist revisionist Trotskyite and revisionist Zionist registered Democrats," New York Jews who still find that "new little waves of anti-Semitism lap the beaches of their accomplishment." They are also New York's blacks, Italians, Puerto Ricans and Irish. Her female characters tend to be "somewhat combative pacifists" (as Miss Paley has described herself) from Greenwich Village, who counseled draft resisters during the Vietnam War and who are worried about nuclear power and chemical pollution. These women raise their children alone, live with divorced men, have love affairs. They are, Miss Paley writes in *Later the Same Day,* "the soft-speaking tough souls of anarchy" who are apt to consider "the mistake of the World Trade Center, Westway, the decay of the South Bronx, the rage in Williamsburg" their "private" troubles.

Some 30 years ago, Miss Paley was one of the first writers to portray accurately the hard, at times desperate, lives of divorced mothers. Hers is a feminism that while hardly strident is still intense. In *Little Disturbances,* men are likely to "ded-

icate with seeming good will thirty days and nights, sleeping and waking, of truth and deceit to the achievement of a moment's pleasure." And they often act badly. As one woman puts it in *Later the Same Day:* "They pay me with a couple of hours of their valuable time. They tell me their troubles and why they're divorced and separated, and they let me make dinner once in a while." The women take it all in stride, still connect with men even if in a desultory way. . . .

But Miss Paley allows her male characters to explain why they might be thought of as less than perfect. "I was once a pure-thinking English major," a hardworking businessman says in *Later the Same Day,* "but alas, I was forced by bad management, the thoughtless begetting of children, and the vengeance of alimony into low practicality."

The finest stories in Miss Paley's first two collections are those about Faith and her sons, Richard and Anthony (Tonto). Faith figures in nine of the 17 stories in *Later the Same Day;* three tell of events witnessed by her during a single day. And once again, Miss Paley is at her best in the Faith stories. . . .

"**Friends**"—in which Faith and two friends visit the gravely ill Selena—brings Faith's life story up to the present. She is now 48. Her mother is dead. Richard and Tonto . . . have grown up. Richard has turned to radical politics. He is a member of something called the League for Revolutionary Youth and is apt to call collect from Paris. Tonto, 18, "believes that the human race, its brains and good looks, will end in his time." Selena's daughter, Abby, "one of that beloved generation of our children murdered by cars, lost to war, to drugs, to madness," was found dead long ago in a distant city. Reminiscing, Selena tells Faith, "You know the night Abby died, when the police called me and told me? That was my first night's sleep in two years. I *knew* where she was."

The concern of parents for the vulnerability of their children is pervasive in Miss Paley's stories, and the deft handling of this what's-to-become-of-them theme gives her writing extraordinary power. In "**Anxiety**," Faith watches some children riding on their fathers' shoulders after school and worries "how to make sure that they gallop safely home through the airy scary dreams of scientists and the bulky dreams of automakers." In "**Ruthy and Edie**," Ruth's granddaughter, Letty, who is just learning to talk, complains that Ruth is squeezing her too hard, but Ruth senses that "she'd better hold her even closer, because, though no one else seemed to notice—Letty, rosy, and soft-cheeked as ever, was falling, already falling, falling out of her brand-new hammock of world-inventing words onto the hard floor of man-made time." . . .

The half-dozen very short stories (two to five pages long) Miss Paley has included in *Later the Same Day* don't work. They seem pat, offering quick bits of insight in clever contexts not developed enough to allow Miss Paley's artistry to shine through. No matter, in light of the accomplishment of the longer stories. . . .

Ever since *Little Disturbances* appeared in 1959, rumors have circulated that Miss Paley was writing a novel. When *Enormous Changes* was published 15 years later, she seemed to defend herself when she said she wrote short stories because "art is too long and life is too short." A decade later, she has given us another collection of remarkable stories. It's been worth the wait, for Miss Paley is one of the few who write about people who actually believe in things passionately (for example, feminism, helping the poor, civil rights) and say so. She demonstrates how history and politics can move and change—and victimize—people, and makes us care about her characters even if we disagree with them. This is fiction of consequence.

Robert R. Harris, "Pacifists with Their Dukes Up," in The New York Times Book Review, *April 14, 1985, p. 7.*

ANNE TYLER

American short-story writers are a tough breed in any event—standing firm in a country where the average reader prefers a novel—but Grace Paley must be one of the toughest. Not only does she continue to produce stories, and usually very brief ones; she continues to speak in a voice so absolutely her own that a single line, one suspects, could be identified as hers among a hundred other lines. She is resolute, stalwart, vigorous. She is urban to an unusual degree, cataloging both the horrors and the surprising pockets of green in her native New York City. And she is unique, or very nearly unique, in her ability to fit large-scale political concerns both seamlessly and effectively onto very small canvases.

The stories collected in *The Little Disturbances of Man* . . . and *Enormous Changes at the Last Minute* . . . brought to our attention a particular kind of heroine: the gritty, embattled urban mother. Sometimes on welfare, sometimes not, generally between husbands, fiercely protective of her children but often a little sloppy with her housekeeping, this woman had different names but always the same amused, ironic voice—a sort of "Oh, well" tone, accompanied by a shrug of the shoulders. In the case of Faith, the most endearing of these women, the shrug was meant solely for her own messy life, never for the messy state of the world, which she was constantly hoping (and picketing, and petitioning) to alter.

Faith is the character who emerges most clearly from this new collection [*Later the Same Day*] and she's the one who gives special meaning to the title. It is, indeed, later the same day: the woman we observed rearing her two little boys alone and dealing with the middle age of her parents is now middle-aged herself. Now she is coping with her parents' old age and with the eventual death of her mother. She is facing the fact that even though romantic love continues to interest her, it will have to be weighted with a history of past loves. And when she worries about her sons, it is because they are beyond her reach, out in that very world she's been trying to change all these years. . . .

Faith has hung on to her political fervor, as have the other characters in this collection. In **"Anxiety"** a woman leans out her apartment window to harangue a young father. "Son," she says, "I must tell you that mad men intend to destroy this beautifully made planet. That the murder of our children by these men has got to become a terror and a sorrow to you, and starting now, it had better interfere with any daily pleasure." In the old days, she reflects, these windows were full of various women issuing their orders and instructions. It's a thought that calls up an instant image of the Paley heroine: arms akimbo, jaw set pugnaciously, but her head now grayer and body thicker.

When characters meet on these pages, it's at the National Meeting of Town Meetings or the League for Revolutionary Youth. When they travel, it's to observe socialist societies. When they start a conversation with an attractive man, their subject is the ecological damage in Vietnam. Yet they avoid self-righteousness; they're not offensive. The reason, I believe, is that Grace Paley never loses sight of the personal. She is in touch with those individual lives affected by the larger issues; she can tally the cost of what she calls the "expensive moment," the private sacrifice that historical considerations may demand. (p. 38)

There is humor, too; that always helps—a kind of running thread of humor underlying nearly every passage. And there's an earthy, angular style of speech. If I had to summarize this book's best feature, though, I would quote a single sentence. It's a line referring to Faith and her friends, but it describes Grace Paley's stories equally well: "They were all, even Edie, ideologically, spiritually, and on puritanical principle against despair." (p. 39)

Anne Tyler, "Mothers in the City," in The New Republic, *Vol. 192, No. 7, April 29, 1985, pp. 38-9.*

ALIX KATES SHULMAN

In *Later the Same Day* . . . Grace Paley plunges us back into the lives of a group of Greenwich Village characters (in both senses) who entered literature in her 1959 collection, *The Little Disturbances Of Man*. Here they all are: Faith, the protagonist or narrator of many of the stories; her neighbors; the local shopkeepers; Faith's pals from the antiwar movement, playground, and PTA; their children, lovers, ex-lovers, husbands, ex-husbands (who sometimes switch roles within the group), aging parents, and even a reappearing grandparent (whom the reader recognizes by the frozen herring he carries in his pocket). The settings too are familiar. By now some of the characters, most of them good leftists, have visited the People's Republic of China (the focus of two stories in this collection), and sometimes they go back to Brooklyn to relive the past or visit the Children of Judea Home for the Golden Ages, Coney Island Branch; but despite what Faith calls "my wide geographical love of mankind," we seldom see them north of 14th Street. There are newcomers to the scene—friends of the original crew, visitors from China, a younger playground crowd, shtetl ancestors—but they enter the book as naturally as new people enter our lives: they're political comrades, neighbors, relatives, friends of friends. All are rendered with that wildly comic Paley charm, her generous politics, her perfect ear-hand coordination. Again she tells her sad/funny stories and wry parables, in a wisecracking, ironic New York voice that sounds like no other—except, amazingly, Isaac Babel.

Going from *Little Disturbances* to *Later the Same Day* we hardly notice that time has passed. True, the kids we saw in the playground in earlier stories may have grown up, some swallowed by "history" (living underground, dead of an overdose, mad, gone to California, or off "in different boroughs trying to find the right tune for their lives"); the married couples memorialized by having sandwiches named after them at the Art Foods Deli may have gotten divorced; and some of the sandbox mothers of 20 years before are turning 50 or starting to die. But Paley can do for time what astro physicists do for space: whether stretching or shrinking it, they deepen the mystery with every advance in describing it. As her narrator comments, "the brain at work pays no attention to time and speedily connects and chooses." Knowing this, Paley blithely sprinkles her stories with lines like, "Hello, my life, I said. We had once been married for twenty-seven years, so I felt justified" or, "What did you do today with your year off?" In a Paley story connections are forged—between generations, eras, cultures, continents—to show how different worlds are essentially the same; thus Later the Same Day might be 40 years later—

as in the story **"Ruthy and Edie,"** which begins when Ruthy and Edie are children, then halfway through rushes ahead to Ruthy's 50th birthday party—or it might be a century earlier, when Faith's ancestors (activists like Faith and her friends) opposed the tyranny of the Tsar. With its vision of universal reconciliation, Paley's sensibility simply cannot be restricted by the ordinary boundaries of space or time.

Paley has sometimes been criticized for allowing her passionate commitment to politics to "interfere" with her art, but the two feed each other, are in fact one. Paley is as political as García Marquez or Camus. In story after story she demonstrates the inseparability of "private" and "public" passions—especially the passion to save the children, which she implicitly equates with saving the world. In Paley's universe children ("babies, those round, staring, day-in-day-out companions of her youth"), the ever-precarious next generation, are the raison d'être of political action. When Faith asks herself, recalling the PTA struggles of a bygone time, "Now what did we learn that year?" her answer is "The following: Though the world cannot be changed by talking to one child at a time, it may at least be known."

These lines are from **"Friends,"** one of my favorite stories in the new collection. In it, as elsewhere in Paley's work, the urgency of '60s radicalism is expressed through the intimacies formed by parents around their children. . . .

If the bond of love between parent and child is the motive force of politics and the affective center of Paley's art, then the worst thing that can happen is the severing of that bond. The event that haunts most of Paley's stories is the loss or disappearance of a child, occasionally of a parent. Even if they don't die, they leave. . . .

The ever-present threat to the children is a metaphor for the danger hanging over the world. The image of the Biblical Abraham, Sarah, and their nearly sacrificed Isaac that recurs in several stories is an image of the madness men are capable of. (For Paley, it is mostly men who threaten the world. In an early story, **"The Long-Distance Runner,"** Faith says of men, "First they make something, then they murder it. Then they write a book about how interesting it is.") Fathers are always running off: "I think I have a boy who's nine," muses one. **"The Story Healer,"** in which a middle-aged Faith contemplates having another child, ends with Faith meditating on "that Isaac, Sarah's boy—before he was old enough to be taken out by his father to get his throat cut, he must have just lain around smiling and making up diphthongs and listening, and the women sang songs to him and wrapped him up in such pretty rugs." But such innocence is always precarious. (p. 9)

Paley's stories are metaphysically open-ended, preserving the hope that Later the Same Day anything may happen—even, as her second collection proclaims in its equally inspired title, Enormous Changes at the Last Minute. Not through miracles or deus ex machinas—for as Faith says, "miracles don't happen and if they do they're absolutely explainable"—but because of the boundless range of life's possibilities. The optimistic affirmation that marks every Paley story, no matter how sad the subject or grim the event, is rooted in her faith in these unpredictable outcomes. She keeps enlarging her view of every calamity, even war, sickness, betrayal, death, until it can support a hopeful—or at least undespairing—interpretation. ("This is probably a comedy, this crummy afternoon.") Speaking of mortality, Faith remarks: "Luckily, I learned recently how to get out of that deep well of melancholy. Anyone can do it."

You grab at roots of the littlest future, sometimes just stubs of conversation. Though some believe you miss a great deal of depth by not sinking down down down."

Notice the final sentence here, acknowledging the other side—a frequent Paley touch. It's a mark of Paley's extraordinary empathy and compassion that her affirmations are usually balanced with an undertone of doubt, humility, or fear. Ever fairminded, she gives equal time to the dour, sour, or just negative view—without, however, permitting the hopeless to triumph. . . . (pp. 9-10)

The pessimistic vision, though seldom voiced by the protagonist or first-person narrator, nevertheless is usually done justice by Faith's beloveds: her father, son, husband, or friend. In the complex story **"Dreamer in a Dead Language"** (about, among other things, the restless desire to move on that most Paley men exhibit), Faith's father complains to her about her mother, his optimistic lifetime mate, "She doesn't see the Bissel twins, eighty-four years old, tragic, childish, stinking from urine. She sees wonderful! A whole lifetime together, brothers! She doesn't see, ach! Faithy, she plain doesn't see!"—and so enables *us* to see. . . .

This scrupulous allowance for the negative, this concession to the other side, is a large part of Paley's affirmative wisdom, her version of Gramsci's famous revolutionary formula—pessimism of intellect, optimism of will. . . .

"Listening" is a companion piece to the charming opening story, **"Love"**; together they enclose the collection like parentheses. Both stories are about the relation of art to life, of language to love, memory, and forgiveness. Here Paley is at her most playful, allowing her characters to send each other secret messages by inventing stories of their own or invoking other Paley characters from other stories. In **"Love,"** which opens with a poem, Faith creates fictions from reality while Jack creates reality from fiction. He taunts Faith with stories of his old girlfriends, including one Dotty Wasserman, a character in *Little Disturbances*. Faith asks, "What do you mean, Dotty Wasserman? She's a character in a book. She's not even a person"—then goes on to tell a story about a lover of her own, referred to in the opening poem. When Jack asks, "How come I don't know the guy?" Faith further mixes up life and art by retorting, "Ugh, the stupidity of the beloved. It's you, I said."

To each of them, the lover created by the imagination is at least as real as the model. In Paley's work, art—story-telling—creates consciousness, and thereby reality. Art makes the private public, the forgotten remembered, the silent heard. There are hints of these purposes throughout the book. In **"Friends,"** Faith claims the right to name her friends so that "those names can take thickness and strength and fall back into the world with their weight." The subject of each generation's language, proclaims the narrator of **"The Story Healer,"** is "how to save the world—and quickly." In **"The Expensive Moment"** (a story in which Chinese and American artists—"cultural workers"—meet), the purpose of mysterious red and green acrylic circles painted like signatures at the scene of a prison break is explained: "They were political prisoners. Someone has to not forget them." But in **"Love"** and **"Listening,"** the relation of art to life is addressed explicitly. As Faith walks through the neighborhood imagining the past toward the end of **"Love,"** she muses: "How interesting the way [the brain] glides to solid invented figures from true remembered wraiths. By God, I thought, the lover is real. The heart of the lover continues, it has been propagandized from birth.''

So in **"Listening,"** Faith accepts responsibility for the stories she has told and those she has neglected, what has been ''propagandized'' and what has not. In this final story of the collection, responsible, fair-minded Paley generously gives the last word not to Faith but to one of Faith's critics. Cassie makes her first appearance in the book on its penultimate page to accuse Faith of writing about all their friends except her: "Listen, Faith, why don't you tell my story? You've told everybody's story but mine.... Where is *my* life? It's been women and men, fucking, fucking. Goddamnit, where the hell is my woman and woman, woman-loving life in all this? . . .

''Cassie, I finally said, I don't understand it either; it's true, though, I know what you mean.... How can you forgive me?''

''Forgive you? She laughed.... You are my friend, I know that, Faith, but I promise you, I won't forgive you, she said. From now on, I'll watch you like a hawk. I do not forgive you.''

Not only are these the last words of the story; they stand as the last words of the book. Perhaps they contain a promise for the next one. (p. 10)

Alix Kates Shulman, ''The Children's Hour,'' in VLS, No. 36, June, 1985, pp. 9-10.

CAROL IANNONE

Grace Paley believes that art has a practical function—to make ''justice in the world.'' And for that reason, she adds, ''it almost always has to be on the side of the underdog.'' Like certain other writers who started out in the 50's, Mrs. Paley is concerned with ''little people,'' mostly women, individuals with small-scale lives and low horizons, people harried or baffled by the disorderly rush of existence.

Mrs. Paley is a writer with a large reputation built on a small output. Considered by many to be a master of the short-story form, she has to her credit just three slim volumes after nearly three decades of writing. By way of explanation, she claims that ''art is too long and life is too short.'' In her case ''life'' has included raising two children and now also embraces teaching, but mainly it involves politics. Indeed, Mrs. Paley's fight against injustice is not confined to her art. A long-time activist, she has for decades been a member of the War Resisters' League and has campaigned for draft resistance, prison reform, environmentalism, feminism, and the nuclear freeze; she has been distributing leaflets, signing statements, organizing protests, marching and/or sitting down for various causes since she opposed civil-defense drills as a PTA mother in Greenwich Village in the 50's. (p. 54)

Whatever the final assessment of Grace Paley's art, her first collection [*The Little Disturbances of Man*] did reveal a degree of talent and ingenuity. Her style can be fresh and explosive. She works by sound, allowing one idiosyncratic voice, complete with New York or Yiddish intonation, to shape content and perception through a kind of wryly comical perspective. Sometimes the technique fails—the perspective (as in **"The Floating Truth," "A Woman Young and Old," "The Pale Pink Roast"**) being so limited or fragmented as to prevent a proper understanding of scope or significance. But other stories touch and move and prod and tickle the reader into the character's world. **"Goodbye and Good Luck," "The Loudest Voice,"** and **"The Contest"** are examples—all, not coincidentally, on Jewish themes; later attempts at other voices (black, Irish, etc.) were less successful.

By the time she was writing the stories that were to become her second collection, however, the Vietnam war had intervened and Mrs. Paley's radical sympathies were given new opportunities to flourish. *Enormous Changes at the Last Minute* accordingly reflects this deeper political involvement. Some stories openly celebrate activism. In addition, the little people are now identical with ''the oppressed''—the poor, the young, runaways, welfare mothers, single mothers, pregnant teenagers, drug addicts, criminals. In general, the collection is less attractive than the first. Some of the stories still have a modicum of recognizable shape (**"Faith in the Afternoon"**) but a good number are just skimpy throwaways, poorly thought out and obscure little fragments (**"Debts," "The Gloomy Tune," "Living," "Wants," "Politics," "Come On, Ye Sons of Art"**), suggesting that the author had other things on her mind. (pp. 54-5)

For the most part, Mrs. Paley's brand of activism has aroused as much admiration as her fiction. ''A Woman of Principle'' went the headline of a *Newsweek* box accompanying the review of her most recent collection [*Later the Same Day*]. ''These Four Women Could Save Your Life'' was the title of a piece on her and three other anti-nuclear activists; an adjoining photo of Mrs. Paley had her looking like a visionary, eyes flashing into the distance. Interviewers are agreeably impressed with her sweetly untidy appearance, and see a connection between her warm womanliness and her politics: ''It's this pleasure in caring for others,'' one has suggested, ''that makes her activism seem so undogmatic and natural, a lyrical extension of the kind of work women have always done.'' Critics marvel at the six or so days she has spent in jail and at the risks she has taken in signing documents that might have brought federal prosecution.

Critics also find interesting links between her art and her politics. ''Start by trying to save a few lives on paper, and you might end an activist like Paley, protesting the waste of lives in the Vietnam war,'' goes one clever analysis. (p. 57)

Mrs. Paley herself proudly allows that her writing has grown more political over the years, that her characters are now seen to be living and talking their activism: ''how to save the world— and quickly.'' And she has always readily admitted that her political commitments have affected the quantity of her output (''I'm easily distractable''). But the influence her politics has had on her work goes beyond relative superficialities like these right to the very substance and form of her imagination (as the Marxists might have told us), and shows how a writer of some ability can founder on the shoals of ideology.

In one of Mrs. Paley's stories, the heroine, a writer, has a conversation with her father about the nature of her craft. The father pleads with her to write a straightforward story in the manner of Chekhov, with recognizable characters, with beginning, middle, and end, the whole informed by a tragic sense of life. But the heroine, who is clearly Mrs. Paley herself, defends her quirky, elliptical, inconclusive, plotless style as proffering more hope. ''Everyone, real or imagined, deserves the open destiny of life,'' she declares. Her idea seems to be that the Chekhovian style forecloses life's possibilities, while writing like her own, full of whimsical condensations and lacunae, keeps them alive. This is probably the way she means her art to make ''justice in the world,'' as she has put it—to preserve by the imaginative act the open destiny that life itself denies.

But in fact there is something in the working of Mrs. Paley's imagination which does less to free than to confine. The notion of the open destiny even becomes itself a kind of tyranny, precluding choice, achievement, change, or progress. An example is the view of Jewish history that Mrs. Paley filters through Faith, a recurrent character often taken as her alterego. To Faith's mind, Jews are meant to represent some quintessential idealism for the rest of the human race—the newspaper in the Children of Judea home to which Faith's parents retire is entitled *A Bessere Zeit*, a better time; Jews are supposed to float free of the quotidian (upside down, perhaps, like the figures in the paintings of Marc Chagall). But the Jews of today, and especially in Israel, have defaulted on their charge, and so must be dismissed. . . . To continue to fire Mrs. Paley's imagination, it seems, it is necessary not only to have been an underdog but to remain one.

Something similar happens in her view of women. Jews having passed the cup of pure innocence, women now fill in as conscience of the race in Mrs. Paley's work. She condemns the "masculinist enterprise of war," and the evils of the "man-owned state"—the Vietnamese orphan airlift, for example, is something only men could have thought of, she wrote in *Ms.* (When an experienced airlift worker wrote in answer that the operation had on the whole most certainly been executed by women, Mrs. Paley's reply simply failed to acknowledge this point.) Her male characters tend to be self-absorbed, befuddled, childish. In **"The Long-Distance Runner"** (from *Enormous Changes at the Last Minute*), Faith says of men: "First they make something, then they murder it. Then they write a book about how interesting it is." Mrs. Paley does allow men a necessary place in her world (mostly for having sex and making babies), but the really important connections are among women and children.

Yet Mrs. Paley's conception of women seems to demand that they be (like the wandering Jews) at least somewhat unattached—single women bearing children, abandoned wives, welfare mothers, many "unmarried on principle."

Faith almost always has a man around, but it's not always the same man. Other heroines lack men; some have men but no husbands, or at least no husbands of their own, and even in longstanding relationships the characters are casually unfaithful. It is as if, in Mrs. Paley's imagination, secure marriage collapses the "open destiny" and somehow supports patriarchy, injustice, war, and nuclear arms. What marriages do appear in her fiction tend to be traps for husband or wife.

Unfortunately, the alternatives to marriage are also traps. Mrs. Paley's characters may display movement, but their lives lack any distinct sense of development. In **"An Interest in Life,"** for example (from her first collection), a sexy young mother of four is flatly abandoned by her sexy young husband. She struggles in her tough, street-wise way with the single-mother welfare life and shortly takes up with a former suitor, now a not terribly contented family man. But she suspects that her husband will return one day, and at the story's end she imagines what his homecoming will be like—a triumphant replay of their previous ardors, which got her into trouble in the first place. Similarly, Faith, from story to story, gets older and her children grow up, and like her friends she travels "around half of most of the nearly socialist world," but she never really seems to change.

Even the *idea* of enormous changes at the last minute, the "anything can happen" feeling that Mrs. Paley's admirers profess to find in her stories, turns out to be not really about change in the sense of progress or development or insight but about change as the pull of chance, time, age, impulse, lust, desire, fear, passion, and assorted other random pressures. Sometimes the enormous changes are fantastical. . . . Sometimes the stories involve experiences that are too large for the people undergoing them, and too large for the author as well. In **"The Expensive Moment"** and **"Ruthy and Edie,"** radical mothers wonder about their children, though without any insight. In **"A Little Girl,"** an unhappy runaway is brutally raped by a degenerate and then dies gruesomely by being thrown or throwing herself out the window. Mrs. Paley uses a first-person narrator, a friend of the rapist, to tell this story, but neither she nor the narrator is able to make any sense of it, and **"A Little Girl"** remains simply a sensationalistic horror story.

Truth to tell, Mrs. Paley exhibits a grim determinism about life that is the opposite of hope. Occasionally she even acknowledges this tendency, while managing to make it seem like an asset. Counsels Faith: "It's very important to emphasize what is good or beautiful so as not to have a gloomy face when you meet some youngster who has begun to guess" the bitter truth about life. A dialogue between Faith and her son Tonto (short for Anthony) also illustrates this tendency. They are discussing Abby—the daughter of Faith's friend Selena—one of "that beloved generation" of the 60's, in this case wrecked by drugs. Tonto wants to know why Faith and Selena "never realized about Abby," presumably meaning why they never saw her problems until it was too late. Faith offers what amounts to an excuse: "Listen, Tonto. Basically, Abby was O.K. She was. You don't know what their times can do to a person." (pp. 57-8)

Here we have an inadvertent literary insight into Mrs. Paley's own temperamental incapacity to assign responsibility to individuals, which is something deadly in a writer of fiction. Perhaps it is because Marxist regimes view people not as responsible, accountable individuals but as variables, human "units" in some larger system, that Mrs. Paley feels such kinship with them. But no artist can really afford to see people this way, through the wrong end of the telescope. What "their times can do to a person" is simply an alibi, a way out of the task of understanding character.

Of course Mrs. Paley has her *ideological* sense of the importance of human individuality, but she cannot make this come alive in her work. In **"Samuel,"** a young boy, probably Hispanic, is fooling around with some friends while riding between two subway cars. A sudden stop is induced when the emergency cord is pulled by an older man, and Samuel falls to his death on the tracks. Samuel's mother becomes inconsolable. Even after the birth of another child, "she immediately saw that this baby wasn't Samuel . . . never again will a boy exactly like Samuel be known." The message is clear, but Samuel was not actually ever known to us in the first place, because Mrs. Paley did not have the patience to fill him out.

Similarly, in **"Faith in the Afternoon,"** we hear the story of a woman afflicted, Job-like, with one awful punishment after another. The story seems intended to stimulate an awareness of the terrible vulnerability of the human condition, but the woman's sorrow is never realized, we just hear about it. In the very same story, Mrs. Paley does achieve a moment of genuine pathos, between Faith and her father, but she turns from it abruptly (as her father turns from Faith), ending the story.

Thus the most enormous change at the last minute is Mrs. Paley's way of copping out on her material, leaving the reader hanging with curious contrasts, baffling leaps, deep-sounding but puzzling last lines—all the truth falling through those empty holes.

Paradoxically, this self-appointed champion of little people manages to make their lives even littler than they supposedly are. It is not life that is so limited, it is Mrs. Paley's imagination, an imagination formed and finally trapped by ideology and therefore entirely unable to make much of the world as it is, let alone suggest a means of transcending it. (p. 58)

Carol Iannone, "A Dissent on Grace Paley," in Commentary, Vol. 80, No. 2, August, 1985, pp. 54-8.

ROBERT TOWERS

The title, *Later the Same Day,* is apt, for a number of the characters from the earlier collections now reappear, suitably aged. Preeminent among these is Faith, the narrator of some of the stories—a wry and somewhat combative woman with old left sympathies and "a yellow dog contract with Bohemia." She has two lively sons, Richard and Tonto, a succession of mates (Ricardo, Clifford, Philip, Jack), and a cluster of women friends (Ruth, Ann, Susan), who mostly have children and no husbands and who consider themselves socialists of one stripe or another. Faith also has a pair of elderly parents, now living in a Jewish old people's home in Coney Island. The passage of time has not been kind. (p. 27)

In **"Dreamer in a Dead Language,"** Faith visits her parents at the Children of Judea home and is exposed to a cruel irony: her intelligent, lively, restless old father complains about the disappearance of brains (the brains of the other residents) all around him, only to reveal that his own mind is slipping: he would like to leave the home and divorce his wife of many years but can't because, he says, they were never married in the first place. Faith's panicky response to all this is to shock the old man with an account of her own love life and then to flee. In a typical ending, in which the tragic is halfway converted into the absurd, the stricken Faith takes her two boys to Brighton Beach and encourages them to bury her up to the armpits in the sand, leaving her arms free, as she instructs the elder, "so I can give you a good whack every now and then when you're too fresh."

["**Dreamer in a Dead Language,**" "**Friends,**"] and one other, "**Somewhere Else,**" which juxtaposes an incident on a tour of China with an incident in the South Bronx, are not only characteristic but first-rate, worthy of the company of the previous collections. But *Later the Same Day* as a whole shows, I am afraid, a considerable dropping off in both inspiration and achievement. While she is wonderfully skilled in suggesting not only the locutions but the rhythms of Jewish-American speech of the immigrant generation, Grace Paley is far less convincing when she adopts the tongue of a middle-aged black woman who has seen lots of troubles (in "**Lavinia: An Old Story**") and tries to force it into the quirky Paley mode ("I said: Mama, I see you just defile by leaning on every will and whim of Pa's"). This story, like several others ("**A Man Told Me the Story of His Life,**" "**Zagrowsky Tells**"), seems to have been written from an enlightened point of view rather than from the inspired waywardness of the author's imagination. Still others strike me as slight or diffuse or, in the case of "**Listening,**" as so self-consciously cute in both language and sentiments as to seem almost a parody of the Paley mannerisms. But even when she is not in top form, Grace Paley is apparently incapable of writing a story that does not, through some flash of insight or turn of phrase, provide its moment of distilled pleasure. (pp. 27-8)

Robert Towers, "Moveable Types," in The New York Review of Books, Vol. XXXII, No. 13, August 15, 1985, pp. 26-9.

Pier Paolo Pasolini

1922-1975

Italian poet, novelist, essayist, filmmaker, critic, editor, and short story writer.

Although recognized outside his country primarily as a filmmaker, Pasolini is well known in Italy for the outspoken views on Marxism and religion he presents in his poetry, novels, and essays. During the course of his versatile and controversial career, his observations on Catholicism, communism, and the existing social order alternately pleased and angered conservatives and leftists alike. Central to Pasolini's life and works is his despair over Italy's impoverished conditions and his anger over the indifference of the materialistic bourgeoisie.

Born and educated in Bologna, Pasolini was the son of a career army officer. His father's long absence as a prisoner of war in Kenya and his brother's execution as a partisan by the Fascists forced political awareness upon Pasolini at an early age. His childhood and early adult experiences in the poverty-stricken village of Casarsa, located in the province of Friuli, inspired his lifelong identification with the poor. Following a brief period with the Italian army just before the Italian surrender to the Allied forces in 1943, Pasolini returned to Casarsa, where he was strongly influenced by the ideas of Karl Marx and Antonio Gramsci, the leading theoretician of Italian communism. In 1950 Pasolini moved to Rome and became immersed in the slum life of that city.

Pasolini has been called one of the most notable poets to have emerged during post-World War II Italy. He wrote his earliest poetry in the northern Italian peasantry's native Friulian language in the hope of creating a literature accessible to the poor. Pasolini rejected the official Italian language because he believed that it had been created by and for the bourgeoisie. These early poems appear in his first booklet of verse, *Poesie a Casarsa* (1942), and in an expanded and revised version, *La meglio gioventu* (1954). Pasolini's poetry centers on his renunciation of Catholicism and his endorsement of Marxist beliefs. Other early poems, along with some experiments in the tradition of religious poetry, are collected in his second volume, *L'usignolo della Chiesa Cattolica* (1958). The poetry of *Le ceneri di Gramsci* (1957; *The Ashes of Gramsci*) and *La religione del mio tempo* (1961; *The Religion of My Time*) reflects, among other beliefs, Gramsci's idea of a "popular national literature." Pasolini's later poetry, *Poesia in forma di rosa* (1964) and *Poesie* (1970; *Poems*), is more autobiographical and confessional, yet the political concerns central to the majority of his works are still evident.

Pasolini's experiences in the Roman slums and his impressions of urban poverty inspired two novels: *Ragazzi di vita* (1955; *The Ragazzi*) and *Una vita violenta* (1959; *A Violent Life*). These highly controversial novels were largely responsible for Pasolini's notoriety. *The Ragazzi* centers on a group of youths whose poverty has led them to a life of violence, crime, and indiscriminate sex. Rejecting the official language of the bourgeoisie, Pasolini liberally utilizes Roman dialect and slang. Though free of authorial intrusion, the work is considered an indirect attack on the Italian establishment; its depiction of Italian young people was particularly shocking. Harshly re-

© Lütfi Özkök

alistic in its explicit language and political implications, *The Ragazzi* angered many factions of the community and resulted in Pasolini's prosecution for obscenity, for which he was acquitted. *A Violent Life* is the second book of his unfinished trilogy on street life. Similar in theme and milieu to *The Ragazzi*, *A Violent Life* was praised abroad for its realism and the characterization of its protagonist.

Nearly all of Pasolini's nonfiction works reflect his continued interest in the ideas of Marx and Gramsci. His essays on political and literary subjects are collected in *La confusione degli stili* (1957), *Passione e ideologia* (1960), and *Empirismo eretico* (1972).

During the last fifteen years of his life, Pasolini made films in which he sought to combine his socialist sensibilities with a profound, nondenominational spirituality. His films were often anti-Catholic in their implications and controversial due to their explicit sexual subject matter. Among his best-known films are *Accattone* (1961), *Il vangelo secondo Matteo* (1964; *The Gospel According to Saint Matthew*), *Teorema* (1968; *Theorem*), and *Salò o le 120 giornate di Sodoma* (1975; *Salò: 120 Days of Sodom*).

Pasolini was murdered in 1975. His death is considered an ironic end to a life spent absorbed in and concerned with the violent nature of contemporary society. As Robert Wells notes,

"Pasolini's death was clearly not an unhappy freak but a horribly apt consequence, foretold in detail by himself, of the act of absolute opposition which his life and work together represent." Two previously unpublished autobiographical novels, *Amado mio* and *Atti impuri,* were published under the title *Amado mio* in 1983. These works explore Pasolini's homosexuality and his emotional torment over what he saw as the disintegration of Italian society.

(See also *CLC,* Vol. 20 and *Contemporary Authors,* Vols. 93-96, Vols. 61-64 [obituary].)

ROBERT CRICHTON

[Because of a need for self-deception on the part of the Italian peasantry], the first condition imposed on Italian writers is that they make life bearable and acceptable. To his credit, Pasolini chose not to do this. He wrote, instead, [*The Ragazzi,* about] . . . the street urchins of Rome, specifically the ones who came to age in the disjointed and disillusioning years after the war, the way they were. . . .

So the roof fell in. Pasolini had broken the code. In fairness to critics the use of the title word was partly to blame. *Ragazzi* actually means "kids," and the term thus implies that the book is a picture of all Italian youth. Pasolini is actually writing about a sub-breed—the deserted, desperate, homeless waifs of Italy known as *scugnizzi.* The word derives from the verb *scugnare,* which means "to gyrate, to spin around like a top," which is marvelously descriptive. (p. 4)

This is not a novel, but a loosely connected series of sketches, verbal pictures, unresolved short stories and fragments of life, sometimes revolving around a boy named Riccetto, sometimes around his friends and sometimes around no one in particular. There is no effort to transfigure experience or to make any of it meaningful, even that which is meaningless. The result is an imbalanced mass of behavioristic description, whose intent is not to re-create a human being or a life, but to expose a condition of life.

This in itself needn't have been fatal if the approach had been different. Pasolini seems to be saying that one can't question, one can't reflect, probe, comment; one can only record. While reading his book, I had the distinct image of the author trailing his subject through the weeds of the vacant lots where most of the scenes take place—hand-held camera whirring quietly, recording, recording, but always only the surface of things, life as seen through a strip of film darkly. It came as no surprise to learn that the publisher compares his work with the neo-realist films ("Shoeshine," "The Bicycle Thief") that came out of Italy just after the war, or that Pasolini has spent the major part of his energies in film making during the last ten years.

Pasolini's book, "the noncommitted" novel, represents a kind of writing that continues to have an effect on American writers and intellectuals, is generally considered "serious" (it rarely contains any humor) and is rewarded with a highly inflated respect. Because the author is really a camera, because the writing is really notes for a future producer, the prose often lacks energy, becomes secondary. To cover this lapse of literary imagination, however, writers have discovered the winning effect of what used to be thought of as "existential" prose. More recently, it has come to be known as a sort of "white style," where everything is impersonal, dry, devoid of emo-

tion, not abstract in the way of Kafka, but transparent in the way of film.

There is always the sensation of a lens between the matter and the beholder. The effect, worked at, is one of flatness. The tone is down, everything down, always down, very fashionably down—and that is ultimately the word for the style, fashionable. (pp. 4, 44)

There is almost a perverse misplacement of emphasis in this fashionable writing. In *The Ragazzi,* pages are devoted to stealing six or eight cauliflowers and a paragraph or two to burning a boy at the stake.

There are a few writers who use these techniques in a legitimate way. I think of Cesare Pavese and Tomasso Landolfi, both simple and quiet, almost as if in protest to their loquacious countrymen. For some reason their writing is genuine, there is the hint of genius operating and the simplicity of the prose strikes one as stemming from compressed intelligence.

But for the others—and for this novel—there is a sensation of the writing being fashioned because the style is fashionable, that it is an artifice, not an art, a stylization and not a style. (p. 44)

Robert Crichton, "Ragazzi Will Be Ragazzi, and Sometimes They'll Be Scugnizzi," in The New York Times Book Review, *November 10, 1968, pp. 4, 44.*

OLGA RAGUSA

[*The essay from which this excerpt is taken was written in 1969.*]

[In a review of Carlo Emilio Gadda's novel *Quer pasticciaccio brutto de via Merculana*], Pasolini presents Gadda as simultaneously accepting and rejecting the social reality of Italy as created by the middle classes in the wake of the *Risorgimento.* The resultant ambivalence caused that feeling of despondent anguish and that "tragically mixed and obsessive style" which are the marks of Gadda's helpless and ever renewed fury at finding institutions which are potentially good turned into organizations which are actually bad. "Gadda belongs to an historical time," Pasolini concludes, "when it was impossible to see the world—this magma of disorder, corruption, hypocrisy, stupidity, and injustice—in a perspective of hope."

The full significance of this statement becomes apparent when we examine Pasolini's two novels, [*Ragazzi di vita* and *Una vita violenta*]. . . . In both Pasolini would like to see the world "in a perspective of hope" but both of them fall short of being true documents, the first of the "magma of disorder . . . and injustice" which must be destroyed, the second of the awakening of the social consciousness through which this destruction will be effected.

Ragazzi di vita is a novel because it deals with a group of fictional characters, the course of whose life we follow during a determined period of time. But it could just as easily be conceived of as a series of vignettes or episodes only loosely related to one another, whose main function is the representation of a milieu rather than the construction and revelation of a character. *Ragazzi di vita* came out at the height of the neorealistic vogue and was read at first as a document of the desperate conditions of the Roman subproletariat in the disconsolate slums springing up with unbelievable rapidity on the outskirts of the city.

The documentary aspect of the book appeared to be underlined by the glossary of dialect terms and underworld jargon which Pasolini provides at the end. To some readers the list seems incomplete and insufficient, although it is true, as Pasolini claims in his covering note, that comprehension of the story or of any one episode of it is not really impeded by the inability to translate into standard Italian every one of the rude, vulgar, obscene expressions which occur in the speech of its protagonists. Pasolini feels that no reader coming upon these words for the first time could fail to grasp their meaning through intuition of the context in which they are used. And indeed the dialogue which makes up so much of the book is little more than a string of curses, cries, expletives, urgings, exclamations—the typical "conversational" exchanges which occur when people do not *speak* to one another but simply, almost by the accident of propinquity, share common experiences.

Dialogue in novels has often been used to discuss important philosophical problems or to introduce the author's personal convictions. Nothing could be further from Pasolini's practice. His message is never entrusted to the words of his characters. Rather it is implicit in his representation of selected conditions, or, in some rare cases, in his own narrated third-person comment on what he is telling. (pp. 256-57)

The time span covered by **Ragazzi di vita** goes from the liberation of Rome in 1944 to the early Fifties. Riccetto, who might be considered the principal character if for no other reason than that he is most frequently on stage, lives through the years of his adolescence: he is eleven and receiving his first communion when the story begins, eighteen and having served a three-year term in jail when it ends. In noting with precision the exact limits of the historical situation which serves as background, Pasolini is fulfilling one of the desiderata of the esthetics of neorealism, which calls for the concrete rooting of fiction in a definite and verifiable reality. But **Ragazzi di vita** is in no sense an historical novel. It has nothing of Pratolini's *Metello* (1956) where historical events are made part of the plot. Nor do historical events shape its story as they do, in however muted a manner, in Verga's *I Malavoglia,* for instance. **Ragazzi di vita** gives back the "color" of a time only in an episodic, allusive manner. Thus we have in the early pages of the book the description of the pilfering of food and other necessities characteristic of day-to-day existence in occupied Rome. There is reference to the emergency housing of the homeless and the destitute—as a matter of fact, Riccetto's mother is killed in the collapse of an old school building which had been turned to this use. And there is the endless stream of "things," objects of all sorts from sewer lids to automobile tires to articles of furniture. . . . We have, in other words, the landscape made familiar by films such as *Bicycle Thief* (1948), but without the underlying ethic of that film which dealt with man's effort to make good, to find his place in society through his work. (p. 258)

The truth of the matter is that Riccetto and his friends are outsiders, typical juvenile delinquents unable and unwilling to make the compromises necessary to find their way into a social order, and that it is therefore difficult to consider their stories as representative of a socio-historical condition. Though **Ragazzi di vita** can be read as a Marxist indictment of the capitalist society which makes lives such as it describes possible, it is in no way an example of socialist realism, for it sets up no exemplary hero who through his awareness of the dynamics of social change can become the potential founder of a new order. **Ragazzi di vita** is the representation of a nether world

no less absolute than that of *Quer pasticciaccio*. No broad and happy road leads out of this world, toward that triumph of reason which Marxist writers, mindful of their Enlightenment origins, like to prognosticate.

But if the vision of the road leading to the transformed society is missing in **Ragazzi di vita,** it is not because Pasolini, as we have seen in his review of *Quer pasticciaccio,* does not consciously believe in its existence. It is simply that he has lost sight of it while telling his story, while exploring with loving attention the teeming life of the Roman underworld. For that underworld has a vitality for him, a gay insouciance, a forceful optimistic *élan, a joie de vivre,* that obscures its horror. (p. 259)

The first reviewers of **Ragazzi di vita** singled out its social nihilism and its literary estheticism for special criticism. Pasolini's insistence on a monotonous and unrepresentative segment of the Roman subproletariat seemed to them a deformation and a stylization of reality which went counter to the fundamental documentary intention of neorealism. Moreover, an episode such as the one in which the thoughts of a couple of mongrel dogs during a fight are recorded as though spoken in the same dialect used by the human protagonists of the book was cited as a clamorous instance of that flight from naturalistic objectivity to decadent self-indulgence which was also underlined by the picaresque aspects of the novel.

In an essay on Italian dialect poetry which he had written some years earlier, Pasolini had already implicitly defended his narrative approach in **Ragazzi di vita.** In speaking of the Roman poet, Gioacchino Belli, the nineteenth century interpreter of the feelings and opinions of the city's unruly populace, he emphasized, as many other observers had done, the uniqueness of the Roman citizenry, those descendants of the *plebs* of antiquity, who in the midst of splendid testimonials of their past have always lived and continue to live outside of history, that is, outside the awareness and the dynamics of change. To the ideal of progress conceived in terms of social betterment, these people substitute the excitement of life lived exclusively for the moment, the happy-go-lucky acceptance of whatever opportunities, however slight and brief, chance offers them. To represent this "aristocratic Roman proletariat"—the expression is Pasolini's—in their saga of roguish adventure is thus, Pasolini claimed, to reflect the "real" Rome, the Rome that rebels against the political and economic structures of bourgeois society *not* by taking a conscious position against them but by simply ignoring them. And to use the Roman dialect to record the inner content of the fictional lives of these people (dialect is used only in the dialogue parts of the book and in some rare cases of stream of consciousness) is to apply the general rule later formulated by Pasolini in his answer to a questionnaire on the novel sponsored by the periodical *Nuovi argomenti:* "If the character and milieu chosen by the novelist are proletariat, let him use dialect in part or wholly; if they are middle-class, let him use the *koiné.* In this way he cannot go wrong." By *koiné* Pasolini means the uniform, nondialect Italian usage of the petite bourgeoisie as formed by the unification of Italy. . . . **Ragazzi di vita,** it should be remembered, was written and is set in the period immediately preceding the new levelling and cohesive forces of Italy's "economic miracle," which were to do so much to destroy the nation's compartmentalized subcultures and to turn large segments of its proletariat into a middle class—without, however, the contributions of Marxism.

Pasolini's second novel, **Una vita violenta** is in part an answer to the more justified objections raised against **Ragazzi di vita.**

Pasolini, a convinced and avowed Marxist, was especially sensitive to the critics who took him to task for ideological inadequacy, for having escaped into the private world of a kind of eternal adolescence and primitiveness instead of attempting to represent the awakening social consciousness of the masses on their way to claim their place in the sun. Thus Tommaso Puzzilli, the protagonist of *Una vita violenta,* is seen as more fully rounded than Riccetto and is made to undergo a political education which changes his initial heedless spontaneity into a sense of responsibility toward others. Whether the book for all its orthodox intentions is as successful as its predecessor is questionable. My own feeling is that the first part of *Una vita violenta* is more effective than the second and that the episodes most strongly reminiscent of *Ragazzi di vita* are what saves it from being a completely pedestrian and unimaginative illustration of a thesis. (pp. 260-62)

[There are certain] episodes in the first part of the book which mark a departure from *Ragazzi di vita:* Tommasino's participation in a "rumble" staged by a group of Fascist sympathizers, and the revolt of the women of Pietralata against the police, who are rounding up their suspect husbands and sons. But the most striking innovation has to do with technique. It is in a flashback at the beginning of Part Two that we are told of the Puzzillis' coming to Rome as refugees during the war, of how they were forced to leave the country, where their land and animals and the father's job as caretaker in the public schools had permitted them to live quite comfortably, much better than they now live in Rome. Still, in the long run they turn out to be more fortunate than many of their new neighbors, for they are assigned an apartment in the complex of public housing being built in the no-man's-land of Pietralata. It is to this apartment that Tommaso returns after his stint in jail for having stabbed a heckler during a street fight, and it is at this point that the thrust of the narrative changes.

Tommaso appears to have left his adolescence behind him. He finds work and becomes a respectable member of society.... At the beginning of this turning point, however, Pasolini introduces the theme of death. First there is the brief report of the sudden death of Tommasino's two baby brothers, an episode which makes a strong appeal for sympathy from the reader by bringing into view the injustices and deprivations which reduce human life to the level of animal, or even insect, life. Then there are the first symptoms of Tommasino's tuberculosis, which eventually leads him to a long stay in a city hospital. There he meets and learns to admire and respect a group of Communists who are organizing and supporting the hospital attendants in a strike. Tommasino joins the party upon his release. But the story is now rapidly approaching the end. Tommasino dies in a new tubercular attack, brought on by his trying to save a prostitute during a flood.

As can be seen, Pasolini's intention in *Una vita violenta* was to write a novel which would follow the classical pattern by being the complete and exemplary story of a central character. In this respect *Una vita violenta* is not different from the social novels of the nineteenth century, from Zola, for instance. But while Pasolini is excellent at catching the "feeling" of the life of his protagonists, he is less successful with the concreteness of historical background. He leaves the reader with strong sense impressions: unpleasant odors, rough and dirty textures, deformed limbs, blemished skins, rotting clothing, mud, heaps of garbage. But there is little or nothing in the book which will help a future reader to reconstruct the complexity of an epoch. Pasolini's talent is lyrical and sentimental, not narrative and

historical. That is why the episode of the "talking" dogs, tucked away in the flow of euphoric slang, is the real clue to the quality of his art. (pp. 263-64)

> *Olga Ragusa, "Gadda, Pasolini, and Experimentalism: Form or Ideology?" in* From "Verismo" to Experimentalism: Essays on the Modern Italian Novel, *edited by Sergio Pacifici, Indiana University Press, 1970, pp. 239-69.**

T. O'NEILL

With few exceptions, the novels published [in Italy in the 'fifties] were of a uniformly mediocre level of content and form. Novelists seemed much more concerned not with *what* they had to say but with *how* they were to say it. Once more, it seemed, the *questione della lingua* was raising its ugly head.

In this situation the figure of Pier Paolo Pasolini is important not only because of the contribution he was to make to the linguistic controversies of the 'fifties, but also because in the essentially eclectic nature of it there can be seen mirrored the various influences that were at work in those years.

If in future years the novels of Pasolini will be only of marginal interest to the literary historian, they will undoubtedly be of prime interest to the historical philologist as documentary evidence of a renewed interest in the linguistic problem which characterized the 'fifties in Italy. It is, therefore, of value that the attitude to the *questione della lingua* in Pasolini be documented. (p. 63)

[From] the early poetry in dialect, *Poesie a Casarsa* of 1942, through the two important *saggi, La poesia dialettale del Novecento* of 1952 and *La poesia populare italiana* of 1955, to the 'Roman' novels, *Ragazzi di vita* of 1955 and *Una vita violenta* of 1959, ... the linguistic theory evolved by Pasolini over the years is put into practice.

In the poetry, dialect has a twofold function: that of a private, unchanging language through which is expressed the private, unchanging world of the poet, ... but also that of a *reaction* against Fascist culture and conformity in order to participate of true reality.... (pp. 63-4)

[In the 'Roman' novels, dialect] is used to provide an alternative to the existing language, an escape from a civilization in a state of linguistic crisis, which, given the link in Pasolini between language and society, indicates a crisis *tout court.*

However, contrary to what some critics think, in the novels, dialect is not, as it had been prevalently in the poetry, a means of escape from society but rather an alternative to a language in crisis, a basis on which can be constructed a *new* language commensurate with a new social reality. (p. 64)

[According to Pasolini], over the centuries Italian has not been the language of the whole Italian people, but only of a restricted, educated minority, a literary élite which, more often than not, has coincided with the ruling class in society.

Just as the main social aim of the élite was to maintain the purity of the class, so, linguistically, its main aim was to maintain the purity of the language. The result of this was that the pure literary language established by Petrarch was preserved intact across the centuries. Thanks to the purists, it was not allowed to develop and to draw energy and vitality from its development, but was maintained in its state of original purity as a language of the class in power, spoken only by them and not by the majority of Italians. As a result of this, the literature of that society tended to have the limitations of it and its official expression: it was non-popular, written by and for an élite, and therefore tended to be rhetorical and divorced from reality.

This linguistic-literary situation held true until such times as the politico-social situation in Italy underwent a radical change. This came about with Unification, which, although not radically modifying the hierarchy of Italian society, did nevertheless tend to shift the emphasis from the hitherto restricted élites of government to the larger, emergent liberal middle-class on whom the hopes of Italy were now centred. They, however, did not come up to the hopes that had been placed in them, tended to be conservative and, in effect, ended up as the breeding ground of Fascism. The conservative nature of the language was maintained and, if anything, accentuated during the *ventennio nero*. With the Resistance there came the recognition of the moral and social emptiness of Fascism and a reaction against it at all levels, including the linguistic one. Following on from this, there was a shift away from interest in the 'pure' tradition of Italian literature—Dante of the *pietrose,* Petrarch, Leopardi—to the 'realist' one—Dante of the *Commedia,* Boccaccio, Manzoni, Verga—a line which, although fairly continuous and which had included several major authors, had tended nevertheless to be considered inferior to the 'pure' tradition.

There also resulted from this an upsurge of interest in popular literature and a renewed attention to works in dialect under the influence of Pavese's recommendation that a return be made to dialect in order to deny it, to raise it up to the level of *lingua.* (pp. 65-6)

The change of emphasis in Pasolini's attitude to dialect, seen now as the basis for a new Italian language, is the clear result of the various influences on him between 1942 and the mid-'fifties—influences ranging from the purely philological and literary to the more openly ideological.

Among the wide-ranging philological influences, the most notable and the most constant has been Contini. . . .

Pasolini had evidently been attracted by the interest of Contini in Petrarch and the results of that interest in the field of stylistic criticism.

The interest of Contini in Petrarch went back to at least the early 'forties, when he produced his *Saggio d'un commento alle correzioni del Petrarca volgare.* Here, there was already to be found *in nuce* one of his main ideas, namely that of the numerous Petrarchan revisions being an attempt to produce a purified and, in its way, eternal, atemporal language, by removing from it those impurities—generally realistic details—which stopped him achieving this end. (p. 66)

It is not surprising . . . that in the critical writings of Pasolini the *questione della lingua* be seen not only from a philological point of view, but also from a socio-political one; that the 'folgorante schema' of Contini be interpreted in the light of the theories of Pasolini's other master, Gramsci, as they are expounded in *Letteratura e vita nazionale.* (p. 68)

[The] 'concezione nuova' of Gramsci was to widen the horizons of Italian national life to include all classes of society. In order that this be put into effect, it would be necessary for the Italian intellectual to break free from the reactionary conservatism which had come with the *Controriforma,* for only when this had been done would he be able to contribute to the foundation of a truly national culture. According to Gramsci, it is precisely the inexistence of this national-popular culture which is at the root of the *questione della lingua,* and this for two reasons: the non-popularity of Italian literature and the lack of a true Italian Romanticism—Romanticism in the sense of a living bond of unity between intellectual and people. Both of these causes he traces to an absence of unity in the cultural life of the nation.

It is this deep schism in the cultural life of the nation that Pasolini takes up from Gramsci: Italian literature is not popular, but is the preserve of an élite, and the reason for this can be found in the social history of the country. . . . (pp. 68-9)

[In *La confusione degli stili* of 1957], Pasolini, in the guise of a writer looking for a new language in which to express the new reality of post-war Italy, reviews the state of Italian since Unification. The new language for which he is searching cannot be that instituted at Unification since it, too, was merely a restricted language like the *italiano colto* it had replaced, alive only in its dialects. It has, instead, to come from a renewal of political and social life; it has, in a word, to have an ideological premise. (p. 69)

Pasolini, following on from Gramsci and seeing not only in post-Unification literature but also in post-Resistance literature the continuance of *italiano colto,* turned away to that Italian 'vivo solo linguisticamente nei suoi dialetti' which would constitute the basis of the renewed language.

However, since Pasolini is not simply a theoretical philologist with strong ideological tendencies but also a creative writer, it is natural that he be influenced by those writers in whose works he sees his theories put into practice. These are mainly four: Pascoli, Moravia and Gadda, and Belli.

Although the influence of Pascoli is extremely limited, since his linguistic innovations were not based, as in Manzoni and Verga, on ideological premises, his 'storia psicologico-linguistica' . . . attracts Pasolini because in the 'appassionata velleitarietà di ricercatore' of Pascoli, in his 'sperimentalismo,' especially the infusion into the literary language of live elements from other sources, especially from the dialects, he, Pasolini, finds mirrored his own intentions in that same direction. What is more, his own linguistic innovations, unlike Pascoli's, will be more valid and enduring because based on the firm conviction that desire to change the language of a given society is basically at one with a desire to modify that society itself. It is this same firm conviction that he finds in both Moravia and Gadda, and it is for this reason that he is attracted to them.

Apart from the ideological intent in Moravia's novels, what especially attracts Pasolini to him is that he sees illustrated there, albeit in a completely different milieu, his own theory of linguistic mimesis. In an article in *L'illustrazione italiana* he pointed out that Moravia performed 'sostanzialmente la mia stessa operazione'; that he, too, regressed 'dentro l'anima d'un parlante, a un livello culturale inferiore al suo, e ne prende le abitudini, il carattere, la psicologia, la lingua.' The truth of this statement, that the basic texture of Moravia's novels is built essentially around a linguistic mimesis in which every single word spoken and thought by the character is faithfully recorded on the written page, can be verified on any page of his novels.

This interest in Moravia's technique of linguistic mimesis already to be seen in the novels with a middle-class setting was increased when the focus of Moravia moved in the direction chosen by Pasolini himself, namely, towards the people. (pp. 70-1)

Gadda, too, like Moravia, is fundamentally a moralist, intent on depicting in its true reality, in its essential corruptness and absurdity, Italian bourgeois society; but, unlike the Roman writer who tends to be clinical and impersonal in his approach, the Lombard writer portrays society not with detachment, but with irony and sarcasm. . . .

It is Gadda's use of language that especially attracts Pasolini, and in this he singles out as its most predominant feature its baroque element: what he called in a review of the author's *Novelle del Ducato in fiamme* in 1954 'un barocco realistico.' This 'barocco realistico' he links up with the plurilinguistic tradition indicated by Contini. . . . (p. 72)

However, the society depicted by both Moravia and Gadda is that of the Italian bourgeoisie, and the language used to depict it is the language of that class, namely the *koinè*, product of Unification. Moreover, the society depicted is a society in crisis and, consequently, the language used to depict it is also a language in crisis. It is this close link between subject-matter and language—language as a mirror of society—that particularly attracts Pasolini to both Gadda and Moravia, but it is also this same link that of necessity limits his interest, because he is not intent on depicting a society in crisis—that is already presupposed—but rather on depicting a *new* class, the *sottoproletariato*, which through participation in history will be able to replace the now moribund bourgeoisie, and, what is more, he is intent on representing it in its own language, . . . which, given its vitality—a vitality reflecting that of the society from which it derives—will replace the *italiano colto*, which will die along with the society of which it is a product. This intention on the part of Pasolini of depicting a newly emerging class about to take the place of the bourgeoisie now in its twilight years, and of depicting it with its own language, draws him much closer to the Roman poet, Belli, than to either Moravia or Gadda.

From a reading of the pages devoted to Belli and the 'plebe romana' in the section *Roma e Milano* of **La poesia dialettale del Novecento** it is quite evident how similar is the world of Pasolini to that of Belli and how similar is the language used by them both.

There is no fundamental difference between the lives of the *ragazzi di vita* in the *borgate* of Rome described by Pasolini and those of the *plebe* of Belli in the popular, wretched districts of Rome during the pontificate of Gregory XVI.

Both live out an existence that is ahistorical and unconscious. The *sottoproletariato* unaware of the socio-political importance of the masses in post-war Italy because unaware of the rôle it has to play in history, repeats in a contemporary setting the situation of the Bellian *plebe* in the nineteenth century, it too unaware of the social, popular turmoil going on around it in those years of Risorgimento ideals. This lack of awareness of one's existence in history—of a social conscience—is perpetuated through an unwillingness on the part of society to educate these masses, to ameliorate their situation—in the works of Pasolini, unwillingness on the part of the bourgeoisie, jealous of its privileges and determined to keep them intact; in the sonnets of Belli, unwillingness on the part of the Papacy, it too like Pasolini's bourgeoisie, jealous of its privileges and its unique situation and, it too, determined to keep them intact.

As a consequence of this, both the Pasolinian *sottoproletariato* and the Bellian *plebe* live out their existence in a 'society' that is immutable, unchanging, with no hope of betterment, condemned to an existence of misery and squalor, both economic and moral as a result of social injustice.

Like Pasolini, Belli also believed that the poor alone were capable of possessing the complete truth of life because their humanity had not been destroyed or falsified through wealth or power, which tended to make men insincere and ridiculous. As a result of this situation, both the *sottoproletariato* and the *plebe* have managed to preserve that naturalness and spontaneity that would have been lost through social conformity, that 'énergie,' as Stendhal called it. . . . (pp. 72-4)

It is precisely this 'énergie,' this natural spontaneity, that is the predominant characteristic of both the *plebe* and the *sottoproletariato*, and it is the depiction of such that both Pasolini and Belli aim at.

This realistic depiction of the Roman populace *in toto* at which Belli aimed . . . is evidently the aspect of Belli that most attracts [Pasolini], because he undoubtedly sees in it his own 'mimesi ambientale' and in Belli as in Pasolini the success of this hinges largely on the language used. The most important feature of this is not so much the choice of dialect—a reaction against a prevalently Humanistic literary tradition—as the mimetic qualities of the one chosen, namely, Romanesco. In his sonnets, Belli invariably has recourse to the spoken language, the most notable feature of which is this mimetic quality. The word in Belli is always associated with the gesture, so much so that he could justifiably refer to the speech of his characters as being *manesco*, especially when they were expressing violent sentiments.

Pasolini, too, has tried to adopt this . . . in his 'Roman' novels, although here, as distinct from Belli, he has to describe physically what in fact ought to come across in the dialogue, but which in his novels fails to do so because of the inherent poverty of its content.

In addition to the *manesco*, mimetic quality of the dialect, there is also to be considered its vulgarity. Belli is constantly and uncompromisingly indecent. The crudity of both Belli and Pasolini can be defended as being inherent in the nature of Romanesco and also, on occasions, as being artistically justifiable. What it is difficult to justify in the case of Pasolini is an *indiscriminate* crudity.

Finally, there is to be considered the social awareness of both authors. The socialist-humanitarian sympathies of Pasolini are also found in Belli, who in a prevalently Arcadian period was steeped in the leading writers and thinkers of Europe. (pp. 74-5)

This is not to say that Pasolini is a twentieth-century Belli, repeating in a modern context what Belli did in the nineteenth century, without there being any great difference between them. Belli has created a *complete* world and not—as has Pasolini—only a specific part of one. . . . The *sottoproletariato* of Pasolini . . . forms the basis of a [class] pyramid, but—unlike in Belli—it is generally unaware of the existence of the other strata and, except on a few rare occasions, does not give itself to judging them, because it is incapable of doing so. As a consequence of this awareness, Belli is a dramatic poet, because there is in him and in his society a conflict and an awareness of it. On the other hand, Pasolini is not a dramatic writer, because this consciousness of a conflict does not exist. Although the choice of setting implies on his part a criticism of the social structure and also, indirectly, of the Papacy that should allow such a situation to exist, the other sections of society, especially the Church, do not enter upon the scene, as in Belli, to create this conflict.

These are the main sources of Pasolini's theory on language, but what of the theory itself? Theory is concerned with what *ought* to be, not with what *is,* and if the linguistic theory of Pasolini tells us what *ought* to constitute a language which, in keeping with his ideals, will be at once both popular and national, it fails to take account of what *is,* in practice, modern Italian, both spoken and written. Pasolini's theory of language does not only not tie in with current linguistic trends in Italy, but actually goes completely against them. (pp. 75-6)

Why is it . . . that Pasolini should be so consistently off the mark in this particular field? The main reason is not hard to find, and, as is only to be expected, it is socio-political. Pasolini is almost perpetually blinded to the true state of language in Italy because he is so taken up, not so much with the linguistic state of Italy, as with the anti-bourgeois polemic that runs throughout his work.

In addition to this, however, Pasolini is off the mark because he tends to consider the *questione della lingua* almost exclusively at an *oral* level. He almost always sees language in its practical, day-to-day usage without considering it also as a means of communication on a literary level; a means by which man, through his creative faculties, can give expression to what is deepest and noblest in him. (p. 77)

It is when Pasolini's ideas on dialect are seen in the broader concept of the theory and aims of literature that their limitations are seen to the fullest, and it is because they refuse to see the *questione della lingua* divorced from the problems of literature in general that so many of Italy's leading writers—sympathetic to Pasolini in other respects—find themselves against him on this point. These writers, briefly, consider art not only as a *representation* of reality—i.e. the Pasolinian thesis of 'mimesi ambientale'—but also—and especially—as an *interpretation* of reality. They give special emphasis to the fact that literature is one of the highest expressions of man's intellect, and as such requires a language capable of expressing it adequately. They rightly point out that dialect with its restrictions would not produce a national-popular literature, but would rather tend to produce the very results its advocates were hoping to avoid— namely, a restriction of its popularity to those who were capable of understanding the dialect used. In short, an indiscriminate use of dialect would not open up the field of literature to an even greater reading public, but, if anything, would merely transfer it from an aristocratic élite to—in the case of Pasolini— a subproletarian élite, but an élite nevertheless.

A much greater awareness of the truth of Italy's linguistic situation on the part of Pasolini is to be seen in the poems in *Poesia in forma di rosa,* written between 1961 and 1964. In this strongly autobiographical collection, there is a repudiation on his part of the Marxist, populist doctrines that permeated the poems, novels and critical essays of the 'fifties, in favour of a new political stance called 'opposizione pura,' i.e. a new social *engagement* with no narrow party bias. As a consequence of this, there is also a modification of his linguistic theories so closely bound up as they were with his political ones. The 'Roman' novels of Pasolini, however, even if they are, as he himself now admits, the result of 'l'errore nella questione linguistica,' will remain, nevertheless, as valuable documents of

an interesting, even if eclectic, and, as it resulted, transitory resurgence of the *vexata quaestio.* (pp. 77-8)

> T. O'Neill, ''Il Filologo Come Politico: Linguistic Theory and Its Sources in Pier Paolo Pasolini,'' in Italian Studies, *Vol. XXV, 1970, pp. 63-78.*

JOHN GATT-RUTTER

Whatever one feels about the quality of individual poems of Pasolini's, there is no doubt, first, that he made extended discourse once again possible in Italian poetry and, second, that he did so by involving poetry, desperately, with the real world, the 'external' world, and its problems—something which a whole generation of 'committed' and 'neo-realist' poets failed to bring off. The Italian panoramas that fill much of Pasolini's poetry, with their too exquisite descriptive colour and pervasive, ambiguous sexuality, do not succeed as epic, but they form sweeping limbs of an unquenchable spate of discourse, rich in different levels of terminology and linguistic and metaphorical resourcefulness to the point of facility. Plethora, perhaps; Pasolini's intellectual strength is not proportionate to his verbosity or emotionalism, granted. Yet his 'sofferto esibizionismo', truthful if only in the uncomfortable awareness of its own falsity, is one of the few convincingly authentic things to have broken through the impeccable form and the monstrous egotism of recent and not so recent Italian poetry. Pasolini's pretexts and his self-indulgence are so transparent as not to matter. He goes on and on, book after book, laying bare his obscure political conscience—for such is the gist of nearly all his poetry, apart from some finely rhetorical polemical or satirical invective, literary controversy and projects for future poems, narratives, plays or films.

Pasolini's poetry, then, is an emotional and ideological sorting-yard. It remains to a more resolute mind to turn the instrument he has created to more solid purpose. From the later 1960s, Pasolini also used poetry for the dramatic monologues inserted in the experimental novel *Teorema* (1968) or as the medium for his plays: nor is the dramatic 'voice' always a mere disguise for Pasolini's own. But if in these later works Pasolini adopts his new-found poetic discourse for the dramatic monologues of the tortured bourgeois soul, his Roman prose narratives of the 1950s offend literary propriety in the opposite sense, by resorting to crude dialect.

Ragazzi di vita (1955) consists of loosely linked stories about the juvenile delinquent fringe of the shanties and slums on the outskirts of Rome. The stories collected in *Alí dagli occhi azzurri* (1965) were written in the same years as *Ragazzi,* or a little later, and extend the panorama of that same subproletarian world of pimps and prostitutes, thieves and scroungers. Pasolini amply characterises this world in the long poem **"La ricchezza"** (in *La religione del nostro tempo,* 1961) as well as in his **"Appunti per un poema popolare"** in *Alí.* . . . Ferretti castigates this area of Pasolini's writing for its 'estetismo del lercio' ('aestheticism of the sordid') and hastens over it with evident embarrassment, as a self-indulgence unworthy of a Marxist. Non-Marxist critics have tended to show equal distaste but usually pass it off as an aesthetically motivated rejection of a merely documentary realism, a realism relying on the direct transcription of raw dialect and yet not exempt from *estetismi* and sentimental and moralistic intrusions by the author. (pp. 43-4)

[What few critics can stomach is that] one senses that Pasolini's real solidarity is with . . . [the] teeming 'low life', the non-working world, as against the despised working world. It is his outdated Romantic primitivism—which Pasolini readily and half-penitently confesses—that cannot be tolerated by Order.

Pasolini counted some of the pieces of *Alì* among the best he had done—**"La notte brava"**, **"Accattone"**, **"Mamma Roma"**, **"La ricotta"**. . . . *Una vita violenta* (1959) is an edifying but unsuccessful attempt to transcend this immemorial 'low life': Pasolini tries to make a novel, complete with central character, Tommaso Puzzilli, who progresses 'positively' from total unawareness to Fascist thuggery and then to Communism and the—to Pasolini—*petit bourgeois* dream of marriage, home and respectability. **"Accattone"** and **"Mamma Roma"** (which Pasolini filmed in uncompromising dialect) show 'society' as a world out of reach of the respective protagonists, who are pulled back irresistibly into their gutter. The ever-present risk of death, or the near-death of prison, lends a baroque drama to their lives. Mamma Roma's despairing tirade on the inescapable heredity of her kind ends with the unanswerable and all too answerable: 'E allora, de chi è la colpa? La responsabbilità?' ('Well then, whose fault is it? Who's responsible?'), to which the author's literary response is the image of the dirty scrap of paper carried along the road and left there by the sea wind (*Alì dagli occhi azzurri* . . .). The pathos of this contrasts with the pathos, in **"Accattone"**, of the virginal Stella finally consenting to whore for the upkeep of her abominable lover—and finding herself, in the event, unable to go through with it. Then **"La notte brava"** renders the dizzy wheeling of fortune with a fantastic, deadly gaiety unknown to the complacent Boccaccio, while social fatality is most inexorably worked out in **"Mignotta"**.

The charge of irresponsible, self-indulgent irrationalism forms the refrain of criticism of Pasolini. But what he presents, in various guises, is *pre-rational:* that is, a reality that Reason has failed to deal with or has simply ignored. To go on ignoring it—that is indeed irrational. The pre-rational in Pasolini's Roman works is the gaiety, viciousness and pointlessness of the life of those who lack an 'honest' livelihood or refuse to be serfs to those who 'perché ciànno un po' de grana in saccoccia se credono chissà che sono!' (*Alì* . . . : 'just because they've got some money in their pockets take themselves for God knows who!'). In *Teorema* (1968) and the verse-plays, the pre-rational wreaks its vengeance on the bourgeois world that has reduced everything to a semblance of rationality. In the guise of the male genitalia, the pre-rational destroys that flimsy conventional world: the stranger in *Teorema* (also a film) who ravishes maidservant, son, daughter, mother and father; in *Affabulazione* . . . , the father's curiosity and loving envy of his son's sexuality, most explicitly enacted, ending with son stabbing father with a knife—given by the father—that represents that sexuality. In each work, *la ragione* is Pasolini's target, in opposition to his notion of *religione contadina* in *Teorema* and sexuality as *mistero* in *Affabulazione*. Ideologically, Pasolini makes the banal error of confusing the false rationality of the bourgeois-communist world diarchy with 'Reason' as such. . . . Artistically, his high bourgeois tragedy is transparently contrived and pretentious. He flounders, and his vaunted *canone sospesa* ('open canon') is no excuse. Yet the potency of his writing and of his imagination—both in overall design and in the details—survives the frequently frightful lapses and ramblings of his verse.

Pasolini's main interest was to turn to the *cinema di poesia*. On the whole, his literary work produced foundations rather than edifices. It remains to be seen whether some other writer will build further on those foundations. (pp. 45-6)

John Gatt-Rutter, "Pier Paolo Pasolini: After Eros," in his Writers and Politics in Modern Italy, *Holmes & Meier Publishers, Inc., 1978, pp. 41-6.*

WALLACE P. SILLANPOA

The closing section of *L'usignolo della Chiesa Cattolica* (1958), containing verse composed between 1943 and 1949, carries the subtitle, *La scoperta di Marx.* War and the Italian Partisan response had transformed Pasolini, leading him to the conviction that life demands "qualcos'altro che amore / per il proprio destino." For the young Pasolini, that "something other" prompted a probe into an alternative world view, grounded in reason, synthesized in Marx, and calling for a commitment to popular political struggle. Within a short period of time, this newly explored world view began to intrude upon the sentimental universe of the poet's earlier verse, linguistically and thematically circumscribed by his maternal Friuli.

Pasolini's idiolect thus evolved into the idiom of a wider historical and class perspective, but without ever causing the poet to dismiss his previous experience. Pasolini's topocentric perspective widened, that is, and allowed the peasant world of Friuli, a world of primitive innocence and religious fatality, to assume even greater mythic proportions in the course of this investigation of a Marxist rationalism. During these years, first as a witness to Partisan struggles, and then as a sympathizer to the uprisings of Friulan day laborers, Pasolini participated in the local politics of the Italian Communist Party. But also in these years, he helped found, together with other young Friulans, the *Academiuta de lengua furlana,* a small circle dedicated to the philological study and social diffusion of Friulan language and culture. Thus Pasolini's early formation joined a sentimental attachment to the linguistic and cultural environment of his adolescence to an examination of Marxist rationalism and political ideology. (pp. 120-21)

[In] 1948 Pasolini was forced to abandon his region and his people under personal and political circumstances that left deep scars. Amid the disinherited of Rome's shantytowns (*borgate*), he felt painfully torn from the world of his youth. That emotional and ethical energy previously nourished through his contact with Friuli was thus diverted to these emarginated urban poor who, lured by the promises of postwar industrial reconstruction, were leaving behind their Southern agrarian communities to find themselves amid the wretched conditions of those inhabiting the periphery of many large Italian cities. The poet's myth of an a-temporal and a-rational Friuli was hence transferred to the neoprimitive and socially incohesive topography of Rome's dispossessed. . . . *Ragazzi di vita,* Pasolini's celebrated novel begun in 1950 and published in 1955, emerged from this newly uncovered social and linguistic reality.

At the same time, some of the verse Pasolini composed while in Rome marked the survival of his passionate attachment to the *locus amoenus* of his youth. . . . Once removed from his native setting and confronted with the back-street humanity of Rome's periphery, however, Pasolini found it difficult to reconcile the poetic concepts of his earlier work to the expressive demands of his present writings. While Friuli quite often appeared in his verse as a natural utopia, by contrast, the Roman *borgate* of his novels *Ragazzi di vita* and *Una vita violenta* (1959) seem an inferno of degradation and disassociation. In his esthetic treatment of the socially downtrodden, Pasolini nonetheless tempered this hellish world with residues of primitive purity and adolescent innocence present beneath the coarse language and brutal(ized) faces of its inhabitants. In the end, death triumphs over the instinctual guile and bruised grace of these *ragazzi di vita,* as the novelist underscores the social and political pathos of this cast-off race and class. But, as just stated, Pasolini never dismissed the primordial virtues of a simpler world, and so it is in Rome during the early 1950's that he came to believe his primitive innocents the victims of a Neocapitalism that he claimed would eventually destroy the very humanity of these people as it swept away time-honored linguistic and social patterns.

In truth, that afore-mentioned rupture in Pasolini's poetry had already manifested itself to some extent at the time of his "discovery of Marx." One such example can be found in **"Testament Coran,"** a part of the verse in dialect written between 1947 and 1952. Here Pasolini depicts a young peasant in Friuli who joins the Partisans and is then captured and hung by the Nazis. While dying, the boy-soldier commits his image to the conscience of the rich, as he sadly salutes the courage, pain, and innocence of the poor.

Similarly, the underlying evangelism of **Poesie a Casarsa** (1941-1943) gradually replaced a traditional peasant demand for an avenging afterlife with a here-and-now vindication. In one poem, now part of **La meglio gioventù** containing all of Pasolini's verse in dialect, the peasants' figure of Christ crucified, index of a future retribution, takes on the workclothes and identity of a laborer who promises more than an atonement to come. (pp. 121-23)

[The] passage of Pasolini's rhapsodized race from a natural-religious state to an historical-political one was greatly influenced by the catalytic intrusion of external events. The esthetic and sensual aura of a poeticized Friuli gave way to the cruel incandescence of the War and Resistance and stirred the poet's ethical consciousness. The Resistance, above all, deeply affected Pasolini (as it did an entire generation), modifying his poetic sensibility. (p. 123)

[Throughout] the 1950's, the example of the Sardinian revolutionary [Antonio Gramsci] played an important role in defining Pasolini's pronounced conflict between the pull of a visceral and esthetic passion and a call to rational, ideological exactitude. It was precisely this conflict that became the ferment of much of Pasolini's later works.

Although the volume's title poem was actually composed in 1954, **Le ceneri di Gramsci** was published in 1957. These poems, written in Italian (and not in dialect) occupy a special place in postwar Italian literature, for they signal a significant departure from pre- (and post-) war Hermeticism.

Contesting the Hermetics' mystique of the word, Pasolini models his verse on a rejuvenation of certain traditional stylistic modes (*e.g.,* adjectivization; the *terzina,* reminiscent of post-Dantean didactic and satirical verse; the *poemetto,* evoking the Romantic-patriotic poetry of the *Risorgimento*), motivated by the desire for a return to a 'civil' poetry that might effectively challenge the Hermetic postulates of absolute self-expression and pure lyricism. At the same time, Pasolini's 'civil' poetry shares little with various strains of postwar prose *à thèse,* nor does it confuse reportage with poetic expression. Instead, his verse proceeds from a conflict experienced between public commitment and poetic predilection—instinct and reason. Within a context based on seemingly irreconcilable antitheses, Gramsci represents a world of reason and ideological precision both guiding and goading the poet. This world clashes with Pasolini's visceral-irrational feelings that ultimately precede his ide-

ology. Thus, **Le ceneri di Gramsci** records a struggle between reason (Gramsci) and passion (Pasolini).

A note to the text establishes Rome as the location of that collection's title poem: specifically, the Testaccio (working-class) quarter; the English cemetery; Gramsci's grave. It is an "autunnale/maggio" in the mid-1950's, a decade once anticipated with hope by the Resistance.... The poet, "capitato/ per caso" into Rome's cemetery for non-Catholics, finds there a "mortale/pace" that shuts out the industrious clatter of the nearby proletarian neighborhood, providing a proper situation for his colloquy with Gramsci. This setting lends an immediate air of elegy that reduces all color and contour to an achromatic grey in a meeting of the living dead. (pp. 124-25)

From the beginning, then, the poem's metaphoric progression rests on a series of contrasts. The juxtaposition of the cemetery's quiet to the frenzy of the surrounding neighborhood is the first in succeeding analogical contrasts that culminate in the poet's self-reflexion and refraction in his hero—who is simultaneously his antagonist. Attraction and repulsion result from Pasolini's thirst for vitalistic passion and Gramsci's somber reminder of the need for rational articulation.... (p. 125)

Elegy renders Pasolini's evocation of Gramsci the commemoration of a lost ideal, for Gramsci, as person and precept, undergoes a figurative transformation. The force of **"Le ceneri di Gramsci"** is discharged through an extension of personal conflict ... to a general, and generational, crisis.... In bemoaning the loss of the hopes and ideals of the Resistance, Pasolini indirectly censures the *pis-aller* of the 1950's, while implying that the 'committed' poet and critic of his times must paradoxically operate within and without conventional political structures. Gramsci, meanwhile, must necessarily remain a luminary ..., iconically remote and ideally distant from the poet's inner torment.... Thus Pasolini's Gramsci lives only insofar as he is 'ashes'; insofar as his presence is experienced emblematically and at a defining distance. Without this figure, Pasolini's visceral passion would have no ballast. Gramsci is thus made to assume the role of an ideological counterpoise.... (p. 126)

Wallace P. Sillanpoa, "Pasolini's Gramsci," in MLN, *Vol. 96, No. 1, January, 1981, pp. 120-37.*

ALEXANDER STILLE

Influenced by Rimbaud and the decadent poets, [young Pasolini] saw the Friulian dialect as a "language of pure poetry"; because of its unfamiliarity to most Italians, it would "prolong the lag between sound and meaning." Some critics believe that Pasolini's early lyrics, published in 1942, are his highest poetic achievement.

Poems omits this early verse. While the Friulian dialect would arguably lose too much in translation to make inclusion worthwhile, one misses a selection from his second book, *The Nightingale of the Catholic Church,* which was written in standard Italian. Instead, *Poems* concentrates on the mature "public verse" that Pasolini wrote after moving to Rome in 1949. This is a curious mixture of political and personal confession, of ideological speechifying shot through with flashes of brilliance, with, every now and then, moments of equilibrium when political and personal passions coincide with great force....

At his best, Pasolini created an outrageous synthesis of Christian imagery, Marxism and private despair. The suffering of Italy was transformed into his own personal Calvary....

Pasolini did not live up to his potential as a poet, and clearly he knew it. . . . But his early lyric inspiration never entirely left his poetry and redeems even his harsher polemics. (p. 87)

Alexander Stille, "Poet, Martyr, Myth," in The Nation, Vol. 235, No. 3, July 24-31, 1982, pp. 86-8.

PIA FRIEDRICH

[In] *Teorema,* the fundamental motifs of Pasolini's intellectual itinerary come together: his religious and social entreaties, the "disillusionment with history," the critique of the bourgeois condition as painful self-criticism and confession, and the myth of a primitive innocence existing prior to the bourgeoisie, which "has exchanged the soul for the conscience."

This chapter refers to the written work, and the author explains its genesis on the cover-leaf: "In truth, *Teorema* was born as a piece in verse, about three years ago; then it was transmuted into a film and, simultaneously, into the story the film was taken from and which the film corrected. . . ." Despite the close connection between the two versions, the book does not constitute the scenario of the film, but it clarifies the film's parable. The text cannot be precisely placed within any one literary genre. It is a series of prose statements, bare and intimately lyrical, characterized by a pace that is at once dreamy and precise, alternating with long poetic and sometimes heavily didactic insertions. (pp. 89-90)

[In] *Teorema* for the first time the author describes the bourgeoisie from the inside, and his "autobiographical hatred" leads him to express himself in a judgmental manner. The anti-bourgeois polemic in this book thus assumes that trace of conventionality that one might expect, but remains sufficiently problematical to give rise to a number of interpretations, ranging from the social to the religious, moral, ideological, and even psychoanalytical.

It is neither *Teorema*'s narrative "medium" . . . nor the novelty of its situation, nor its psychoanalytical background that makes the book unique among Pasolini's works. It is of central importance rather as a summation of motifs. . . . [The] text of *Teorema* elaborates and synthesizes Pasolini's entire thematics of the 1960s. In the works of that decade one may in fact glimpse an unsuppressible aspiration, becoming ever more taut and strained, toward an Absolute that is as essential as it is unknowable. In this sense *Teorema* is of primary importance: Its philosophical connotation is that of an uncompromising idealism. The dominating force is the anxiety of "intuition," if we wish to use Bergson's definition; or of "transcendental apperception" in a Kantian sense; or of Schopenhauer's "Will." The process of approach is so irrational (as suits the poet?) that the whole itinerary of the romantic experience can be helpful in analyzing this extemporaneous product of anguished spiritualism. (pp. 91-2)

Pasolini's spirit is by nature Christian; that is to say, he must bring to account the experience and conditioning of Catholicism, if not simply the archetype of Mediator-Savior-Demiurge present in all religions, positive and otherwise: At this point the figure of the mysterious Guest [who, in the story, visits a typical bourgeois family, one by one physically possesses them, then abruptly leaves] and the chance of redemption he offers to the bourgeois family enter in. The idea that, in general terms, the road to the Divine passes through a sexual dimension is anything but new to one who is familiar with the psychology of religion and the history of rituals.

The palingenetic and cathartic element of sexuality in *Teorema* has the same significance as cannibalism (Pasolini seems to be gradually rediscovering the entire repertory of ritual) will have in *Porcile,* where the main character, captured and condemned by a scandalized society, proclaims the famous line: "I have eaten my father and my mother and I tremble with joy!" That is, awareness is achieved by the overcoming of the existential condition of carnal filiation (in psychoanalytic terms, the overcoming of the birth trauma of separation).

In Hebrew terminology specifically, "knowledge" connoting physical union symbolizes the achievement of global contact with reality. Pasolini's quotation of a passage from the book of Jeremiah in the "Enclosures" to *Teorema* facilitates our reading of the symbols: "O Lord, thou hast deceived me; and I was deceived; thou art stronger than I, and hast prevailed (also in a physical sense): I am in derision daily, every one mocketh me" (Jeremiah 20:7).

Many of the attributes of the arcane figure of the Guest are derived from the religious inventory: the Revealer, Innocence, the Destroyer, the Adorable One. Others . . . denote heavily physical characteristics. On the whole, the identity of the mysterious Visitor seems to be without precise philosophical implications: All the elements of the parable, not to mention the basic allegorical sense, make him rather the "mediator" of an authenticity that is primitive and instinctual spontaneity of being. The Guest is the hypothetical means to a life marked by absolute fidelity to one's own nature, prior to any moralistic social conditioning. The miracle consists in his offer to the bourgeois of a chance to recover this state of primitive innocence and human dignity. At the disappearance of the Guest, everyone finds himself alone with the privilege of a truth too pitiless and radical to be lived, except by the maid Emilia. She belongs to this rural subproletariat world which, like the Friuli of his childhood and adolescence, is assumed by the poet to be the mythic receptacle of sacredness. Emilia returns to this world and its religious peace, and her miracles are the proof of her identification with the arcane forces of nature.

The bourgeois father, Paolo, is spared at least in part from the total devastation that sweeps away the other members of the family. He is the "mature adult male," the one who does not "lose or betray God," the most spiritual member of the family. In him we recognize the close presence of the author. The only one of the family not to have yielded to instinct without thinking, he is also the one who comes the closest to salvation. He gives the factory away to his workers and, in the large, crowded station of Milan, strips off all his clothing. The renunciation of material possessions, motivated not by love but by a sense of guilt, cannot guarantee his salvation. Salvation for him appears when, finally naked on the sand of a desert both eternal and new, he utters the "cry" of one who, at the limit of annihilation, finally "knows." . . . (pp. 92-4)

The meaning of this unseemly bestial "cry," which shook the spectators of the film and was interpreted in the most imaginative ways, could express the newly acquired awareness that—in order to "know" and "exist"—the stripping away of clothing and factories is not enough. One must be naked not in symbol, but in reality.

Thus the bourgeois father has managed to bring his "knowledge" to fruition and to touch redemption, while the others, son, daughter, and wife, "betray" and remain hopelessly cast out.

It is at this point that the interpretive resources of psychoanalysis (taken on by Pasolini as a new dimension of knowledge, although at a rather elementary level) become indispensable. Characteristic of all the Visitor's couplings with the various members of the bourgeois family is the prefiguration of incest. Within psychoanalysis, incest is a typical ingredient of salvation, an obligatory element of the process of overcoming the Oedipal complex by going backwards, "killing the primordial father again" and recovering the purity and freedom of Being.

The father and mother recognize their son in the Guest; the son and daughter see him as brother and father. Through incest, therefore, every member of the family receives the revelation of his own most intimate nature. However, at the Guest's departure each one falls back into the lack of authenticity of his or her previous experience, and the new emptiness is only the clearer and more distressing.

The poetic passages which, like a series of explanatory monologues, make up the Appendix of the first part of the book, become extremely important for the interpretation of this particular level of the narrative. Here the autobiographical element emerges with cruel evidence. In the case of [the son] Pietro we learn that his contact with the Visitor has revealed to the boy his "diversity." The acceptance of this truth, which is the transfiguration of "diversity" as awareness of the separation as an individual, is shadowed by fear and the inability to live it to the full. . . . (pp. 94-5)

The truth is too harsh and radical for Pietro, like [his younger sister] Odetta or [his mother] Lucia, to resolve to live by it completely. The young man leaves his home and family circle and falls into a sudden, rabid devotion to an abstractly mechanical form of art. His awareness of the mystifying randomness of his performance almost obviously brings us back to the heart of anti-avant-garde polemic, without excluding, once again, a deep autobiographical matrix. . . . (p. 96)

[Odetta] expresses her refusal to live in her choice of an obstinate madness. Her doggedly clenched fist, which will not open, is another evident Freudian symbol.

Lucia, the mother, will seek the "truth" revealed to her by the Guest in the experience of empty, degrading sexual dissipation. . . . She too, finally, evades the necessary choice in the easy consolation of a little country church, filled with all the cherished sentimental attributes of traditional religion.

The deliberateness of *Teorema*'s narrative structure is reaffirmed on this level in Emilia's "corollaries." There should remain no doubt that the sub-proletariat constitutes Pasolini's ideological and sentimental weakness. Since Emilia, by virtue of being a member of the subproletariat, is outside history, she has no need of the regenerative "trauma." By a real intervention of a deus ex machina, she need not travel the hazardous road of self-recognition: She is already an immediate candidate for salvation, even sainthood, just by having encountered the Lord's Anointed, who frees her from her historical condition of slavery.

In the formal construction of the text, the conclusion of Emilia's story, in its successive phases, acts as a counterpoint to the conclusion of the other stories: The maid seated motionless on the beach, intimately involved in the process of her gradual illumination, surrounded at first by the timid curiosity of the peasants and then protected by their acceptance, is contrasted with Odetta, motionless in the bed of a luxury hospital, with her fist rigidly closed and her family around her, dully recognizing themselves in the opaque madness of the girl. The miracles finally wrought by Emilia are followed by the demonstration of Pietro's creative impotence; Lucia's sterile attempt to find refuge in the melancholy little church of the "ancient terrible religion" is followed by the confirmation of Emilia's "sainthood," her levitation, her reabsorption into the mystery of the cosmic forces.

The "corollaries" of the father, however, are placed within the structure of the text in such a way that they evidently complement Emilia's, as we have already observed. The quintessential bourgeois, who reads Tolstoy and lives his contradictions to the full, breaking with his own world and refusing authority and possessions, is the incarnation of the only alternative to salvation. Salvation eludes him because he is bourgeois: This constitutes the flagrant over-simplification upon which the allegory of *Teorema* hinges, and the self-destructive inconsistency of the author. (pp. 96-7)

Teorema is a work in which analysis, description, and motivation dissolve in the face of the absolute relevance of facts. The text is predominantly visual; the characters are identified through the schematic precision of the "data" and the "corollaries," which assume the function that subjective focusing has in cinematographic technique. The exclusion of psychological inquiry points up the emblematic quality of the protagonists, and the verification of their basic experience is, from this point of view, evidential: The "love" of the five for the Guest is without any psychological connotation; every episode starts out *in medias res* when the respective protagonists are already hopelessly enamored of the visitor, and ends with their coupling. The Guest gives himself in carnal union with an impartial, understanding serenity that reaffirms the emblematic intention of the whole.

The aspect of the language of *Teorema* which Pasolini defined as "dreamy and ephemeral" shows that "recourse to oneirism" of the Freudian type which Michel David has found in the verses of *Poesia in forma di rosa*. In *Teorema* this recourse is developed to the point of becoming a fundamental stylistic preoccupation, sometimes mechanically exhibited. The behavior of the five characters is registered through episodic nuclei unconnected by a temporal link, so that the order or presentation could be changed without changing the narrative results. The key events that presuppose even a vague "before" and "after" are the appearance of the Guest and his departure. Around these "occurrences" other "occurrences" take place, as in a dream, outside any concept of past and future, in a continuous present revealed mainly through verbal syntax, sometimes rather laboriously. We do not find in *Teorema* (or in *Poesia in forma di rosa*) psychological and poetic time substituted for the normal coordinates of succession, following the procedure of the revolution in perceptions inaugurated by the works of Marcel Proust. . . . Here as in a dream, the relation between cause and effect is expressed in occurrences, and these very occurrences, according to one of the many didactic statements in the text, "happen at the same time in the same place." (pp. 99-100)

In constant and consistent relation to the suffering and the ideological choice of the poet, *Teorema* fits into the same literary myth, as abstract as it is individual, with [Pasolini's] other works, but with differing expressive choices. The eternal ingredients of sexual mysticism, purifying and purified narcissism, natural religiosity filtered from time to time through popular Christian forms, or stretched to recover an absolute and ideal essentiality, are still present and pressing. Despite reservations of a general and ideological nature and those due to the heaviness of abused psychological and religious symbols, *Teorema* merits a positive judgment. (p. 100)

> *Pia Friedrich, in her* Pier Paolo Pasolini, *Twayne Publishers, 1982, 151 p.*

JON COOK

Lutheran Letters brings together some of the last pieces that Pasolini wrote before his murder by a male prostitute in 1975. They present a fascinating and disturbing convergence of obsession and reason. Pasolini's obsession is sexual, homoerotic, and its subject is his relation with the street boys of Rome and Naples. . . . Reason and obsession combine to make a repeated statement about the character of contemporary Italian society, which, according to Pasolini, has been overtaken by something close to a catastrophe, the catastrophe of consumer capitalism. This new power manifests itself in various ways: 'enormous quantities, superfluous goods, a hedonistic function'. Its offer of abundance is deceitful, however, because, in reality, it destroys life, whether that life is embodied in the natural environment, in the physical appearance of Pasolini's beloved young men or in an active popular culture. In particular, the destruction of this last is felt as the most painful loss, the one to which the others can be connected. . . .

What has been lost is precisely something *different* from this bourgeois culture of consumption, and what this means for Pasolini is a loss not so much in what can be explicitly stated as a value but in a capacity for self-definition and the regulation of a meaning which is not simply in the interests of the powers-that-be. Bound by the compulsion to consume, the subordinate classes are neither respected nor feared by their rulers but managed in an irresponsible and destructive way. (p. 23)

Evidently a gloomy picture, and there are various means of distancing or denying it close at hand. Pasolini's argument can be understood as a peculiarly exacerbated version of the embourgeoisement thesis—the argument that as workers become more affluent they lose their radicalism—and this has been around long enough for us all to forget it. Or *Lutheran Letters* can be read as little more than the rationalisation of Pasolini's disturbed sexuality: the well-to-do intellectual who once found sexual pleasure with working-class youth now finds himself rejected or humiliated and then projects his own loss as the loss of his national culture. Or a more insidious and chauvinistic response takes over. At his own repeated insistence, Pasolini writes about the specificity of Italian life and culture and we all know that, whatever their strong points, the Italians couldn't run a play-group let alone a national government if they tried. After all, what do we hear in Pasolini's book but the written equivalent of voices typically raised in an endless and hysterical public debate which will never get anywhere because it's in the interests of its participants that it should never end.

I doubt that any of these responses can be sustained. Whatever the differences in the tone of public debate, Pasolini's Italy of 1975 anticipates Thatcher's Britain: an irresponsible government swayed by the interests of the multi-nationals and finance capital, a denial of the future, a lack of compassion, the destruction of the environment. . . . As for Pasolini's homoerotic passion, *Lutheran Letters* does not suggest a rationalisation so much as a risk undertaken, a willingness to use the delicate register of desire as a way of comprehending a language of bodies and objects which cannot be arrived at by other, more conventionally rational means. When this connects with Pasolini's strenuous immersion in an Italian tradition of reflection on the nature of good government, the legacy of Machiavelli and Gramsci, the effect is a rare kind of moral grandeur. (pp. 23-4)

> *Jon Cook, ''Reason and Obsession,'' in* New Statesman, *Vol. 107, No. 2759, February 3, 1984, pp. 23-4.*

Tom Paulin

1949-

English-born Irish poet and critic.

In his poetry Paulin often ruminates on liberty and justice. He is interested in the various ways these concepts are interpreted and practiced by individuals, societies, and governments, particularly those of Northern Ireland, where he makes his home. In several poems Paulin examines his themes from a historical or political perspective. He frequently describes the Irish landscape, finding in it appropriate images and metaphors to extend the implications of his social themes. These concerns are apparent in the collection *A State of Justice* (1977) and have been developed further in subsequent works. In *The Strange Museum* (1980) and *Liberty Tree* (1983), Paulin also concentrates on such personal themes as love and hope and examines the ways in which history and art shape the human perception of reality. Critics praise his subtle, unrhetorical approach, his effective use of understated language, and his craftsmanship, all of which contribute to poems that are typically low-key yet poignant.

Ireland and the English Crisis (1984) is a collection of Paulin's social and literary criticism. In these pieces Paulin focuses on such topics as contemporary Irish politics, the study of literature, and the various ways that writers respond to political issues.

(See also *Dictionary of Literary Biography*, Vol. 40.)

Photograph by Mark Gerson

ANNE STEVENSON

The uses of adversity have rarely been sweet in recent years, but in Northern Ireland they have produced some remarkable poetry. Tom Paulin's first collection, *A State of Justice*, contains a number of technically accomplished, highly serious poems. Though by no means all the poems are about 'the troubles', Ulster is there in the background, resonating with didactic seriousness throughout. Paulin, however, is no propagandist, not even for peace. Instead, he is a muller-over of the predicament, preoccupied with the abstract idea of justice and the restrictions a 'just state', in an ironic sense, sets on individual freedom. Much of the book constitutes a criticism of any state's answer to violently conflicting human needs. . . . The question Paulin asks in one way or another throughout this book is whether it is possible to achieve a humane peace in a country like Ulster without the imposition of force by the state. His answer is mostly a grim 'no', but still he keeps the question open, worrying it with images of the natural landscape around Belfast which at least provides an alternative idea. . . .

The laconic tone Paulin has adopted—his style falls somewhere between that of Larkin and of Douglas Dunn—usually suits his theme. There are times, though, when he pares his poems down to the point of obscurity. Some of his dramatic monologues need more explanation. Who would guess from the nine lines of **"Newness"** that it is about an old Antrim wife remembering her wedding day? And what is the situation between mother and son in **"In Antrim"**? On the other hand, two dramatic poems, **"Provincial Narratives"** and **"A Traveller"** are masterpieces of understatement. Paulin is especially sen-

sitive to the nuances of class distinction. His best poems suggest that the differences between the rich and the poor in Ireland can be taken as an allegory of the relationship between England and Ireland itself.

The command of subtlety and allusion Paulin has achieved in *A State of Justice* is certainly admirable, and perhaps a stoic, unrhetorical approach to the tragedy of Ireland is the right one for the temperament of a British audience. (p. 491)

> Anne Stevenson, "Plumed Hat, Bare Head," *in* The Listener, *Vol. 97, No. 2504, April 14, 1977, pp. 491-92.**

P. R. KING

[Paulin] has emerged as one of the most interesting of an important group of Ulster poets whose work has been published against the background of political violence in Northern Ireland. Paulin's poetry frequently deals with aspects of his Irish background or uses Ulster for its setting, but the themes of the poems have a more universal significance than this localized subject matter might suggest. This significance is seen particularly in the themes of justice and responsibility which dominate the finest poems in his first collection, *A State of Justice* (1977). (p. 228)

The poems in *A State of Justice* are composed of scenes, situations, events and narratives taken from memories of childhood, from aspects of life in Ulster and from stories the poet has gathered from the lives of his family and friends. They frequently begin as descriptions of people and places, or as narratives, and develop into an exploration of personal and social states of being, often ending in an image that expresses that state with almost symbolic force. The predominant idiom is colloquial and the style, although capable of expressing an idea with force, is usually deliberately low-keyed. But the calm surface tone of this unforced style moves on a groundswell of unease and unresolved tensions. These tensions centre on the idea of justice. The state of justice is both personal and political, and many of the poems examine the pull between natural justice and institutionalized justice: between justice as a human desire for equity and the politicizing of that desire with its consequent danger of interpreting justice as retribution. The individual is caught between his need for a fair order and the danger that the state will exploit this in a partial and dogmatic justice. It is a tension which takes on an urgency and importance in the work of a writer conscious of the political unrest in Ulster. (pp. 228-29)

> *P. R. King, "Three New Poets: Douglas Dunn, Tom Paulin, Paul Mills," in his* Nine Contemporary Poets: A Critical Introduction, *Methuen, 1979, pp. 220-43.**

ANDREW MOTION

Like most good poets, Tom Paulin is obsessed. In his first collection, *A State of Justice,* he pursued the issues raised by his title with relentless fascination, and in his second, *The Strange Museum,* he is even more determined. Not that his interests are quite the same as they were. He is still concerned with justice and necessary organisation, but his two overriding preoccupations—in abstract as well as specific terms—have become love and history. On page after page he uses the ideas of 'grace' and 'great gentleness' associated with the former, and the fierce impersonality suggested by the latter, to frame an argument that he knows cannot be easily solved. His purpose isn't to isolate one from the other, since love might then decline into vacuous civility, and history connote what he calls 'The forced jubilance of a crowd / That is desolate and obedient'. Instead, he tries to keep them in watchful alliance, and to position himself as a sentry on their frontier—minimising the potential defects of both sides, and arranging for their several virtues to combine.

Introducing this kind of border imagery isn't simply an accident of style. Paulin's poems encourage its use by employing it themselves to fulfil a number of related functions. One, predictably, is to describe Irish politics; another is to summarise international social distinctions . . . ; and a third is to summon up enriching echoes of the poet to whom he owes most: Auden. Just as Auden's early poems inhabit a world of spies and boundaries, so Paulin's convey a series of vulnerable divided states where 'private faces' seek and cannot find a role in 'public places'. . . .

Auden's influence on Paulin hasn't simply been a matter of directing his attention to ways in which the machinery of state threatens individuality. It has also helped to shape the nature and scope of his imaginative response. The effect is less evident in language and rhythm than in narrative strategies (Paulin normally confines himself—sometimes rather too rigorously— to what he has dubbed 'terse fricative cadences'). Nearly all his most interesting poems adapt technique associated with short stories, and the control of their glancingly-reported incidents owes a good deal to Auden's practice in poems like 'Gare du Midi'. The result is not that an awareness of their poetic ancestry detracts from their original merits, but that they realise in literary terms what they seek in political ones: a sensitive and compassionate sense of history.

The complexity of this achievement is intensified, and its significance increased, by virtue of the fact that Paulin's poems combine their discussion of historical processes with an examination of their own narrative authenticity. . . . ["**The Other Voice**"] mingles an account of history with a meditation on art, to illuminate the pressures and deceptions of both. . . . The ideas contained in this poem—implicitly as well as explicitly— are evident throughout *The Strange Museum.* Again and again it tackles the vulnerability of idealism, the resilience of hope, and the danger to human nature of purely functional pragmatism. It's not often that contemporary British poets treat these things at all—let alone with such serious good sense. The scale of its ambitions, and the intelligence with which they are fulfilled, make it a continuously exciting book.

> *Andrew Motion, "On the Frontier," in* New Statesman, *Vol. 99, No. 2559, April 4, 1980, p. 517.**

DICK DAVIS

Tom Paulin's poetry is good of its dour kind. In the first eight pages [of *The Strange Museum*] we have 'a dead light', 'a brute and sallow light', 'sour light' and 'the light is dull'. The prevailing tone is one of accidie in which a 'grey tenderness' is the most one can hope for. Many poems (among them "**The Harbour in the Evening**", for me the best in the collection) are concerned with waiting for an undefined release. A hint of salvation comes in the frequent references to art which Mr Paulin's conscience sees chiefly as a fascinating danger—he continually admonishes himself to have none of its blandishments. The book is well written (though the mentors Heaney and Lowell are ubiquitous) with a kind of deliberate drabness. I would give in to those blandishments, Mr Paulin.

> *Dick Davis, "Temporary Wealth," in* The Listener, *Vol. 103, No. 2664, June 5, 1980, p. 729.**

NEIL CORCORAN

In his second book, *The Strange Museum,* Tom Paulin finds a sustaining abstract metaphor for the condition, or plight, of the contemporary Irish writer caught, in the very language he uses, in a web of crossed loyalties, afflicted with the responsibility of extreme self-consciousness about his own inheritance and 'tradition'. Paulin imagines himself, in an image that carries obvious Marxian reverberations, held static in the 'long lulled pause / Before history happens, / when the spirit hungers for form.' In a poem called "**A Partial State,**" Ireland before the present troubles is defined as 'Stillness, without history'. And Trotsky, a central presence in the book, is seen at the Finland station 'Plunging from stillness into history' and is imagined uttering a self-definition in the long, mysterious, effortlessly inventive poem, "**The Other Voice**". . . . Mandelstam in the same poem is an intricately opposed figure who leaves a buttery in the Kremlin 'Because I could never stay / In the same room as Trotsky' and celebrates his own hermetic withdrawal. . . . [Oppositions] and confrontations, which are the oppositions and confrontations of his own present history before they are anything else, are probed with a fine analytical passion in Paulin's work. Now fully absorbing, and making manifest, the lessons Auden has to give him, Paulin seems capable of being articulate in poetry not only about his 'history' or, indeed, about what he understands of historical process itself, but about how history may be said to happen in poems. The dour, fricative, tight-lipped cadences of these poems insist on the most problematic confrontation of all, the confrontation between the lyric impulse and the responsible, and responsive, primacy of political analysis. . . . In poems such as ["**What is Fixed to Happen**"], Paulin seems—as he has Trotsky say of Byron—'Forced by more than himself'. His meditation on specific re-imagined moments of his history, and his attempt to find a context for them elsewhere in history, his forcing them into the re-presentation of allegory, as in the poem "**The Strange Museum**" itself, seems as responsible and moving an act as the very different strategy Seamus Heaney developed in *North*. But Paulin's essential quality is a kind of Marvellian compaction of an insistent personal cadence with a generous, clear-eyed, unsentimental public responsibility which measures and weighs the difficulties a poem has in assuming a position, and goes ahead. . . . (p. 55)

> *Neil Corcoran, "Stillness into History," in* PN Review, *Vol. 7, No. 4, 1980, pp. 55-6.**

DONALD CAMPBELL

Sometimes poetry needs to be obscure. The poet, faced with the near-impossible task of expressing the inexpressible, cannot always be expected to pull it off with a diverting clarity. Tom Paulin is a youngish Irish poet—[*Liberty Tree*] is his third collection—who is much concerned with the complex considerations of the Irish identity. In dealing with those, Paulin employs a great deal of poetic cunning—using analogue, riddle and, often enough, some esoteric nouns, adjectives and verbs—to gain a deeper perspective on the perplexities of modern Ireland. In "**Manichean Geography**", for instance, the description of a remote outpost of the British Empire is full of images which relate back to Northern Ireland, while in "**What Kind of Formation Are B Specials?**" an attempt is made to empathize with the predicament of the Poles. By considering his Irishness from a variety of fresh and unexpected angles, Paulin is not so much drawing parallels as identifying correspondences, seeking to use one situation to reach some kind of understanding of the other. Nor are such correspondences limited by time and place: . . . in "**S/He**" one of Chekhov's *Three Sisters* suddenly pops up in Londonderry. This kind of technique has almost endless possibilities, making for an absorbing, demanding poetry, never completely accessible, often infuriatingly difficult, but always more than worthy of attention. Paulin's superb technical control, his distinctive tone of voice and his slightly off-beat sense of humour are all qualities which support the genuine tension of his verse and make *Liberty Tree* an immensely satisfying collection. (pp. 640-41)

> *Donald Campbell, in a review of "Liberty Tree," in* British Book News, *October, 1983, pp. 640-41.*

DEREK MAHON

Paulin is a frankly political poet, intellectually in a line of descent from those Belfast radicals who attached themselves to Wolfe Tone and the ideals of the French Revolution. He dreams (don't we all?) of a 'sweet, equal republic' whose roots, for him, lie in the dark soil of Protestant Ulster, for which he

entertains a not unfamiliar love-hate. . . . His love is reserved for a might-have-been and a not-yet, his enmity (which is graphic and exhilarating) for treasonable clerks like the pseudo-poet 'Rupert Brookeborough'. He prefers (don't we all?) figures like Chénier and Mandelstam who died significant deaths in the open air.

Liberty Tree is full of exciting phrases, lines, even whole poems; but I am bothered by Paulin's tendency to make notes, his impatience to get an idea into verse and get on to the next one, so that the implications of an image or a scenario are not worked through. . . .

The most striking feature of this collection . . . is a deliberate roughening of texture. Although he still dreams 'of grace and reason', more in tune with his present mood is the

> gritty
> sort of prod baroque
> I must return to
> like my own boke.

Except for Simmons, his predecessors have tended to put 'poetry' first. What Paulin puts first is the engaged imagination—a commitment, a devotion even, to the harsh realities of oil-drum and tumbril; and the cacophonous new music of his verse mimics those realities in a way not heard before. His poetic voice affects the spine like crushed glass under a kitchen door. (p. 27)

> *Derek Mahon, "Quaat?" in* New Statesman, *Vol. 106, No. 2747, November 11, 1983, pp. 27-8.**

JOHN MOLE

The ghosts that haunt Tom Paulin's poetry are ancestral—at various removes—and his response to them holds a middle ground between recognition and detachment. On a recent tape-recorded reading [*Seamus Heaney and Tom Paulin*] he speaks of his admiration for the novels of Joseph Conrad—particularly *Under Western Eyes*—and his own preoccupation with a map of Ulster in which history and fiction dissolve into each other would seem to owe not a little to Conrad's method of narration at a distance; a technique of creating perspective and clearing spaces within which character, event and ideologies can jostle and cohere into analysis. One can almost hear the knowingly bewildered tones of the Professor of Languages speaking in "**Martello**": "Can you *describe* history I'd like to know? / Isn't it a fiction that pretends to be fact . . . ?", and the reply is fact that presents itself with all the selective, atmospheric detail of fiction:

> And the answer that snaps back at me
> is a winter's afternoon in Dungannon,
> the gothic barracks where the policemen
> were signing out their weapons in a stained register,
> a thick turbid light and that brisk smell of fear
> as I described the accident and felt guilty—
> guilty for no reason, or cause, I could think of.

The guilt, perhaps, is occasioned by the artistry at work on the material, the very effectiveness of the perception becoming (like a prize-winning newsreel shot) reprehensibly vivid, "snapping" back in two senses of the word. But, then, the observer is also Paulin's *creation,* and what may at first seem like confession becomes—in the context of the various voices of *Liberty Tree*—part of his analysis of guilt.

The juxtaposition of dialects, slogans, locations at the same time exact in their topography and symbolic in their resonance (''the dead centre of a faith'', ''the territory of the Law'', etc.) set up a scenario in which the poet is manipulator, investigator, and just one more character picking his way across an echoing minefield of private and public concerns. This is much more the case in this new book than in Paulin's previous collections where the poems often stood more confidently on their own, and the result involves a degree of confused obscurity; but taken overall as a montage of cross-cutting full of brilliant flashes and linking commentary done in different voices, it demands thoughtful reading.

John Mole, in a review of ''Liberty Tree,'' in Encounter, *Vol. LXII, No. 3, March, 1984, p. 49.*

DICK DAVIS

Amy Clampitt has a linguistic tic that is in keeping with her preoccupations—she loves French that has been domesticated into English—déshabillé, protégé, ombré, repoussé, velouté, longueur, grisaille, fouettés and the like. Tom Paulin has a similar tic, but his is for using dour, obscure adjectives that end in 'y'—choggy, humpty, schisty, clabbery, claggy, gourly, screggy, glooby, biffy and so on (after a while this begins to read as self-parody). And the mean-spiritedness of such language is typical of his concerns. . . . His poems [in *Liberty Tree*] are about lack—of joy, nationhood, purpose, freedom, light—and their emotional atmosphere is one of fear, boredom, hatred, self-disgust. The language seems pitched as a relentless attack on complacency, and if the reader takes the book seriously the aggression and disgust are finally wearying, we feel bullied by it. Even so, Paulin's vision of how things are comes across with a stark and undeniable intensity. A few comic poems about the pretensions of empire would provide some relief ('a brave wee hymn to the sten-gun') were it not clear that these too come out of hatred rather than anything else; it makes you feel like asking him Allen Ginsberg's (probably apocryphal) question to David Cecil, 'Say man what do you *love?*' An alarming development is that many of the poems are extremely cryptic; I hope Paulin is not catching the irritating 'now you see me now you don't' disease of too much recent poetry.

Dick Davis, ''Screggy and Co.,'' in The Listener, *Vol. 112, No. 2867, July 19, 1984, p. 25.**

DENIS DONOGHUE

Tom Paulin's way with poetry is to seek an equilibrium between the immediacy of experience and patterns suggested by natural life, the seasons, the ebb and flow of things. His favourite season is in-the-beginning: some of the most stirring passages in *Liberty Tree* imagine an aboriginal landscape and the freedom of starting out. . . . In **''The Book of Juniper''** Paulin imagines a social and political narrative corresponding to the plentitude of the tree: the juniper, the rudimentary dictionaries say, is an evergreen coniferous shrub or tree with hard blue berries, yielding an oil used in medicine as stimulant and diuretic. Add to that a discrimination of juniper-kinds, including the savin or *Juniperius sabina,* the *genièvre,* and the family of gymnosperm, not to speak of the Grimms' tale of ''The Juniper Tree'' and Eliot's allusion to it in ''Ash Wednesday''. What more would an analogist want, touching upon earthly presence, racial memories and desires? Paulin doesn't resort to all the poetries already adhering to the juniper tree, but only to as many as he

needs to incite his desire for a new beginning under the best auspices. The political use he makes of the emblem is to dream

> of the sweet
> equal republic
> where the juniper
> talks to the oak,
> the thistle,
> the bandaged elm,
> and the jolly jolly chestnut.

Charming, no doubt, but a long shot of dreaming at a time when RUC men in Belfast are killing people with plastic bullets and the IRA are practising their craft with bullet and bomb.

Paulin's response to these immediacies is erratic. Sometimes his poems take a superior attitude to their themes. In **''Desertmartin''** he sets his lithe intelligence against the 'parched certainties' he ascribes to the Protestant villagers. . . . (pp. 22-3)

Some of Paulin's poems of Northern Ireland are clear enough, though their politics seem to me naive. But some are bound to be opaque to readers who have not had the privilege of living in the North. I lived there for nearly all my youth, but some of Paulin's dialect-poems are dark to me. In **''A New Look at the Language Question''** (1983) he made a fair case for Irish dialect as a poetic language, by analogy with the 'hoard of relished words' by which members of a family express their kinship. I have no quarrel with the sentiment. But I don't see that anything would be lost by adding a few notes to such a book as *Liberty Tree*. Paulin's readers are expected to know that 'the Big Man' is Ian Paisley, and to know or guess the parts played in the history of the North by 'Munro, Hope, Porter and McCracken'. Maybe they know that 'sheugh' means ditch. . . . But readers can't be expected to know that 'prod' means Protestant or that 'the Cruiser' is Conor Cruise O'Brien. Gourly is gurly or rough, a corrie is a mountain-hollow, a spooly is (I presume) a linen-worker.

Some other words require guesswork or a fairly big dictionary. . . . I'm all for notes.

The equilibrium Paulin looks for would justify his sense of local immediacy by implying that it is sanctioned by the larger certainties of natural and planetary life. If he's right in the large sequences, he's probably sound on the small ones. A poet sensitive to the 'meek astringency' of juniper-oil is likely to be reliable when astringencies stop being meek and take to the gun. The rhetoric is astute, but not finally convincing. . . .

Paulin has learnt, probably from Seamus Heaney, how to put his sense of immediate provocation under the protection of natural and epic grandeurs. I'm surprised that the rhetorical procedure—which is just as questionable as Yeats's—hasn't been much reflected on. People plagued with immediacy are grateful for the release offered in a time-comprehending pastoral, but the release is specious, no historian really sees a pure narrative before him. (p. 23)

Denis Donoghue, ''Making Sense,'' in London Review of Books, *October 4 to October 17, 1984, pp. 22-3.**

MARY HOLLAND

In the introduction to his timely, angry book [*Ireland and the English Crisis*], Tom Paulin compares what he perceives to be a crisis in English literature with 'the desperate wrecked state of Northern Ireland.' Both are symptoms of a malaise, cultural as well as political, which has now reached crisis point in Britain. . . .

The task that Paulin has taken on himself in many of these essays, as in his poetry, is that of Stephen Dedalus, 'to forge the uncreated conscience of my race.' He is primarily concerned with Northern Ireland's Protestants. His own attitudes were shaped originally by growing up in an Ulster Protestant community and he is consumed with the desperate plight of a people who often seem, even to themselves, to belong neither to Britain nor to Ireland.

Until about 1980 Paulin shared their assumption that Northern Ireland was and should continue to be part of the United Kingdom. His understanding of just how passionately that view is held is demonstrated here in essays on Carson, Louis MacNeice and, most notably, in a brilliant analysis of the Rev Ian Paisley, which draws together the theological and political roots of this complex cleric and explains his continuing appeal to the Protestant working class.

The troubles in the North brought Paulin to re-reading Irish history. This in turn gave him a different political perspective on Irish writers, particularly James Joyce, whose work is a recurring theme in this book. Now he cherishes hopes of a future in which Protestants and Catholics may share a nonsectarian republic. Until that Utopian dream is realised he works for a 'fifth province' of the mind, a cultural sanctuary in which Irish artists must try to lay together foundations for a new political reality. . . .

He goes on to describe how difficult it is to resist the seduction of a large British audience which can lead, in effect, to the artist being colonised. Some Irish writers have been able to resist such cultural domination. Paulin cites Wilde and Joyce, both of whom paid a heavy price in humiliation and exile when they were alive.

The situation of the exiled writer crops up again and again, as does the problem of audience. In a sympathetic essay on Solzhenitsyn, for example, Paulin argues that he has always written for a Russian audience and has nothing but contempt for Western values. This has not saved him from being appropriated by Western critics who find his writings comfortable. Paulin describes Solzhenitsyn's relations with the other Russian writers thus: 'Here as so often in Russian writing we seem to be eavesdropping on an intense family quarrel. Culturally that enormous country seems to be passionately provincial—everyone knows each other and there is much malicious gossip, sudden tenderness and equally sudden rage.'

Not very different from the quarrels on the current state of English in our academic institutions, at least as Paulin describes them. In his essay **'English Now'** he puts himself curiously on the side of those like Christopher Ricks 'who believe that it is a teacher's job to uphold the canon of English literature.' He sees those who would favour broadening the syllabus to include, for example, TV soap operas, as barbarians at the gates. While one has sympathy with this view it is a pity that this essay relies less on the rigorous arguments which characterise most of Paulin's book. Instead he is often abusive in a way which he does not substantiate in the text. Critics with whom he disagrees are described as 'infinitely tedious,' 'stupidly philistine' and 'alas, fatally dull.'

Contrast this with his riveting study of another academic subject, **"A New Look at the Language Question,"** in which he traces the way that English itself has been politically institu-

tionalised and the limitations this places on writers who are not English but write in that tongue.

Once again one is drawn back to Ireland and to the two figures who dominate this book, Joyce and Paisley. Unlikely companions for his hoped-for 'fifth province'? Maybe, but Tom Paulin clearly thinks they would get along rather well.

> *Mary Holland, "Fifth Province," in* The Observer, *January 20, 1985, p. 46.*

JOHN HORGAN

Paulin's voice—in poetry as in criticism—is informed, independent, argumentative. Coming from the Northern Protestant and Unionist tradition (although born in England), he believed firmly until 1980 that the union with Britain was essential, but has travelled quite a distance since then. Conor Cruise O'Brien, meanwhile, has been voyaging in the opposite direction, setting out as a dutiful supporter of the Anti-Partition League and ending up as undoubtedly the Northern Unionists' favourite Southern politician. Reading Paulin's withering essay on O'Brien [in *Ireland and the English Crisis*] is like watching, in helpless fascination, a head-on collision between two powerful locomotives, each fuelled by its own distinct, and potent, renegade angst. One of Paulin's most surprising discoveries is that 'the writing of Irish history . . . is now, and will be for the foreseeable future, inescapably *political*.' It is difficult to imagine that the writing of history ever has been—or will be—anything else: but to make matters worse, there is the absence in Ireland of any agreed history at all. The class analysis which Paulin would prefer to the tribal versions of Irish history, and of which he sees the embryonic beginnings in some of the public statements by UDA leaders, is a dodgy bet. This may be one more initiative which will have to bow to the tribal realities: many a Northern Ireland Labour Party election meeting in Belfast, even in the hungry Thirties, was dramatically and effectively disrupted by the heckle from the back of the crowd: 'Whaur's yer flag?' There is probably some truth in Paulin's assertion that militant Protestantism has more than a little in common with militant Republicanism—the fact that each has adopted 'socialism' as a tag-word shows a shared populism, at least. But part of the reason for the Northern gridlock is that each section of the community is internally split. No political leader on either side, therefore, can attempt to deliver political support for any solution—or even amelioration—of the present impasse without exposing himself to the accusation of weakness, of selling the pass. Protestant disillusion with Britain may yet prove to be the lubricant of a political solution, but the line between wishful thinking and hard analysis, even in Paulin's lucid and persuasive prose, is sometimes a bit difficult to draw. Even if one hesitates before some of his arguments, however, his account of the Irishness—in a politically specific and uncompromising sense—of writers as disparate as MacNeice, Wilde, Joyce and Trevor is a sinewy corrective to the Paddywhackery and pious exegesis that sometimes passes for criticism on the summer school circuits. (p. 11)

> *John Horgan, "Local Heroes," in* London Review of Books, *February 7, 1985, pp. 11-12.**

JENNIFER FITZGERALD

The unifying spirit behind this collection of essays and reviews [*Ireland and the English Crisis*] is summed up in the title: Shifting the cultural perspective, Tom Paulin no longer sees "the Irish question" or "the Irish crisis" as a long-running subplot in the drama of British history; instead he identifies a crisis of confidence, in particular in English literary criticism, which may be resolved or at least illuminated from the more clearly defined vantage point of Irish stability. This is, of course, only one (perhaps overemphasized) reading of the multi-layered ironies built into the title, but the question of culture—where do we stand? to whom do we speak?—informs each of these rather eclectic reviews with the impetus of personal political commitment. Paulin is particularly effective in revealing the distortions imposed by the assumptions of the English cultural norm, so that his shift in perspective provides a new and often invigorating light to literary reviewing.

"Culture" is a loaded word, which Paulin treats with less respect than is wise. His sensitivity to cultural imperialism evaporates in the heat of the specific "English crisis" of contemporary literary criticism, as evidenced in the Introduction and the essay **"English Now."** As "the pursuit of perfection," "culture" is dangerously severed from its roots in experience and becomes an autonomous absolute which encourages authoritarianism: Students reared on television should be *made* to learn prosody and grammar and to appreciate classical texts. Enter the poet rather than the Irishman, vigorously defending the independence of the author and his or her own creation from the external forces of the Marxist and the structuralist: *Viva* the individual genius. Instead of evolving a positive *Defence of Poesy,* however, Paulin responds negatively, selecting critical extremes as clay pigeons in this shooting-down exercise. "Cultural studies" which legitimate the analysis of *Coronation Street* or *Crossroads* are scathingly dismissed, with the implication that "culture" is the preserve of the highbrow (a writer is described as "highly cultured," apparently because he "sprinkles his text with impressive bits of Greek, Latin, Italian and German").

This ideological confusion may result from Paulin's internal dialectic—whether to pledge allegiance to life or to art—which emerges subterraneously from the reviews. He emphasizes D. H. Lawrence's deliberate artistry in an attempt to counterbalance the critical effusions of "life" as aesthetic norm, but the reader senses his reluctance to embrace the other extreme. He assesses Derek Mahon as "an intransigent aesthete who rejects life almost completely and considers only the flotsam and jetsam along its fringes" with as much unease as approval. He is obviously feeling for the middle ground. . . . Yet when it comes to history and politics, Paulin abandons the middle ground with a move distinctly to the left, finding himself on the other side of the fence from the autonomous poet. As a participant in history he declares his interest, uncovering the bias which constitutes the so-called disinterestedness of others. He demolishes Conor Cruise O'Brien's vaunted nonpartisanship by unveiling his silent support of the status quo, which only appears sensible and apolitical because its ideology is accepted as norm. Applying *Antigone* as a matrix to the Northern Ireland troubles, O'Brien seriously distorts the text, and misreads the tragedy altogether in the exercise of Benthamite moral bookkeeping: The contrast with Paulin's own translation of the play *The Riot Act* could hardly be starker.

Paradoxically, then, despite his avowed anti-deconstructionism, the strength of Paulin's arguments stems from his acceptance of the inevitability of interest, the necessity of establishing the perspective dictated by one's position in society: "the critic must come out in the open and say '*credo*.'" Detached judgment is only an intellectual con-trick which the committed individual—and by virtue of being human we are *all* commit-

ted—eschews. It is unfortunate that having established the impossibility of sophisticated objectivity, Paulin's yearning after a truth as absolute as possible tempts him from the path of reality into the cave of Platonic ideals. . . .

While the chimera of a New Ireland is Paulin's political pipedream, the inconsistencies in his shift in position can be traced to his ambivalent identities. Socially and politically, he accepts responsibility for his Irishness; he is thus intrinsically sensitive to the morse code of cultural diversity (challengingly examined in . . . **"A New Look at the Language Question,"** reprinted here). Accepting a national destiny ought not, however, to entail exclusiveness, antagonism, violence; as he tries to transcend political chauvinism in his pluralist vision, so he also gives wings to art, attempting to exceed the boundaries of experience through autonomous value. The point at which social and economic constraints are relaxed into a purer form of "culture" is not identified, and I suspect he will never be able to put his finger on it. "Culture" is not begotten by hope on idea; it is the ensemble of what already exists, the hidden rules by which people live and interpret their lives. Irish culture of the here and now is tragically different from the Platonic entity that Paulin imagines. It is not a question, as posed in his diatribe on deconstructionism and the Centre for Contemporary Culture at Birmingham, of preferring *Crossroads* to *Middlemarch* but of recognizing that *Middlemarch* may have little to say to the characters of *Crossroads* (and vice versa). The ideal reader of English literature, the ideal Irish identity cannot be forged by imposing the rules of prosody or civility, but by discovering how and why we are cast as personages in our own drama. Cultural studies, including both the English canon and contemporary art forms such as film, provide the key which may eventually unlock the door of conditioning and allow the actors to control their own creation.

Many of the reviews in this collection are very brief. The justification for publishing them lies in Paulin's obsession with cultural definition which overrides the ad hoc nature of such writing. This preoccupation illuminates the most appropriate criticism (on Wilde and Joyce, for example) but can also blinker his reading. The contradictions it engenders may be symptomatic of its as-yet half-baked form. One receives the strong impression that in bringing together his writing of the last few years, Paulin is reviewing himself, beginning the process of sifting and self-arguing which will eventually lead to an acutely original thesis. The material of the later study, as it appears in this eclectic and random form, does not carry enough weight as criticism *per se.* The two longer essays, **"English Now"** and **"A New Look at the Language Question,"** make their own points validly enough, but they could go much further if their tantalizingly diverse perspectives were integrated and consolidated. Paulin's ideas are burgeoning, but they have as yet to be subject to the discipline of comprehensive digestion. This is not to underestimate the fine intelligence that begets them, but this book is a halfway stage, a no-man's land bristling with potent contradictions. . . . Premature publication may not enhance the quality of this particular volume, but the polemic it has stimulated should cross-fertilize some of this powerful material. The potential for a whole new cultural critique for Ireland lies within Paulin's reach if he would only reconcile his own contradictions and take a long, hard look at the realities of Irish experience, North and South.

Jennifer Fitzgerald,"A New Cultural Critique for Ireland," in *Irish Literary Supplement, Vol. 4, No. 1, Spring, 1985, p. 21.*

Robert Pinget

1919-

Swiss-born French novelist, dramatist, short story writer, scriptwriter, journalist, and translator.

Pinget is a practitioner of the *nouveau roman* or antinovel, a fictional mode developed in the 1950s by writers rebelling against the conventions of the traditional novel. Composed primarily by French authors, including Alain Robbe-Grillet, Claude Simon, and Nathalie Sarraute, antinovels are objective fictional pieces which present reality without authorial interpretation. Pinget's work reflects the style of the antinovel in its fragmented prose and absence of plot, narrative, and chronological development. He establishes within each work a distinct narrative tone, which grows increasingly confused as it futilely attempts to find meaning in a meaningless world.

Pinget's first fictional work, *Entre Fantoine et Agapa* (1951; *Between Fantoine and Agapa*), is composed of surreal and fantastic stories set in an imaginary province bordered by the communities of Fantoine and Agapa. This region resurfaces regularly in Pinget's fiction; its exact and copiously detailed description provides the only stable point of reference Pinget offers his readers. Pinget next wrote several moderately successful absurdist novels before he achieved widespread acclaim with *L'inquisitoire* (1961; *The Inquisitory*). Considered by many his finest work, the novel centers on the interrogation of an old man by the police. The man apparently witnessed a crime, yet the nature of the crime remains ambiguous, as do the characters involved. The testimony shifts from incident to incident, becoming increasingly vague and finally inconclusive. Pinget demonstrates how memory distorts the past and suggests that the nature of reality is ultimately elusive.

Pinget's novels written after *The Inquisitory* reveal a trend away from the fantastic, playful quality of his early work toward an increasing concern with perversion, violence, and death. Sinister crimes provide the crux of these novels: *Le libera* (1968; *The Libera Me Domine*) investigates the ten-year-old murder of a young boy, and *Passacaille* (1969; *Passacaglia*) begins with a bleeding corpse lying on a dungheap. In these novels, rumor and speculation eventually obscure reality until nothing is certain or verifiable. The little boy could have been strangled or drowned, or he might never have existed. Similarly, the bloodied corpse is perceived alternately as the town simpleton, the postman, and as a lifelike scarecrow. With *L'apocryphe* (1981) Pinget moved even further from any semblance of storyline, shifting narrative focus between a possible death, an inventory of furniture, and descriptions of seasonal change. In this work plot is again deemphasized as Pinget concentrates on language, recreating the spoken word and revealing how hearsay and gossip alter the truth.

Pinget has also written a number of plays, some of which he adapted from his novels. *Lettre morte* (1960; *Dead Letter*) is based on *Le fiston* (1959; *No Answer* or *Monsieur Levert*), in which an old man writes a long letter to his prodigal son. *Ici au ailleurs* (1962; *Clope*) is derived from *Clope au dossier* (1961; *Clope's File*), which contrasts spiritual aspirations with secular activities. Pinget's plays are strongly influenced by the work of Samuel Beckett. Both dramatists employ a minimum of

props and sets, and their plays focus on the isolation and alienation of individuals attempting to make sense of an absurd world.

While Pinget has not received the recognition that Robbe-Grillet and Beckett have earned, critics generally praise his stylistic innovations and note his contribution to the French literary tradition. Robert Henkels comments: "The wit, the flashes of recognition, the essential consistency (despite all the whimsical aberrations) of his wanderings in language all serve to make him a serious and meaningful innovator in the world of fiction in our fluid, indeed antirational, late twentieth century."

(See also *CLC*, Vols. 7, 13 and *Contemporary Authors*, Vols. 85-88.)

JOHN STURROCK

[Pinget] represents what you might call the bucolic element in the anti-novel. His stories are all of them set in his own weirdly eventful corner of the French countryside, in a landscape of the mind to be found "Between Fantoine and Agapa," as the title of his earliest, ground-breaking collection of stories had it. (p. 11)

There could be no finer introduction to the mind-boggling uncertainties of life in that blighted arcadia between Fantoine and Agapa than *The Libera Me Domine*. . . . The uncertainties come about because his narrators are men obsessed, with a fearsome urge to reconstruct the past; the one thing they have no time or mind for is the immediate present. The past, however, won't play the game, it won't be reconstructed; there are plenty of bits of it lying to hand, picturesque shreds of local legend, but they don't fit together. Instead of one past in this novel there are many, all contradictory of one another. What happens on one page is likely to cancel out what happened on the page before. Events quickly change their nature, people equally quickly change theirs, and the result is a hilarious inability to come to any fixed conclusions at all. Like each of Mr. Pinget's novels, *The Libera Me Domine* is the record of someone failing lamentably to construct a single coherent story, but that record is so rivetingly, so eloquently told, that this failure has to go down as a thumping success.

It seems that a small boy was once murdered in the village. Little Louis Ducroux was found strangled in the woods one hot July day. Or did he have his throat cut by a sex maniac? Or did he drown accidentally in the lake? But then, wasn't it actually one of the other Ducroux children who died, and wasn't he knocked down by a lorry in the village street? No, surely that wasn't a child but one of the grown-ups, Mlle. Lorpailleur the prissy schoolteacher, who was knocked off her bike. Etc. The novel is like some demented coroner's inquest, where the identity of the victim changes with each new question, until it is doubtful whether there was a victim at all.

It is the events themselves that are dead: All the many engaging scenes that are first dreamed up, then redreamed and then erased in *The Libera Me Domine* are said to have taken place a statutory 10 years ago, apart from one or two especially signal episodes of local history that can be dated, equally arbitrarily, to 1873. Which is to say that the facts are happily beyond recall, and we are adrift on an ocean of rumor. Nothing that gets said commands any lasting credence at all.

Yet if this is high farce, it is farce with a black lining to it. The unknown killer of little Louis has never been caught, he is still ''on the run,'' as the novel regularly reminds us. Nor will he be caught, because Mr. Pinget's killer is the killer who will sooner or later get every man, woman and child of us: death itself, the ultimate conclusion that haunts this desperately inconclusive novel, as it haunts all of Mr. Pinget's work.

In *The Libera Me Domine*, death migrates with dreadful ease from character to character, changing its form as it goes. And it turns up just as grotesquely in the shorter, more somber novel, *Passacaglia*, in which a troublesome, inexplicable corpse turns up lying—where else?—on a dunghill. Unless, that is, it's an overly naturalistic scarecrow removed from the farmer's field, or the postman in an alcoholic trance, or the village idiot having an attack. Whatever the perfectly unattainable facts of the case may be, the imagination, which is the hero of any Pinget novel, lurches helplessly off into morbid speculation.

Simpletons, inebriates and crackpots frequent the scene so as to show how futile the storyteller's ambitions are, for these wandering, vacuous minds are typical of his sources of information as he strives to make himself the archivist of an unreliable community—the ''deficiency'' of his sources is one of many recurring complaints voiced by the narrator of *Passacaglia*. But he keeps at it nonetheless, working at what he poignantly calls his ''laborious accumulation of straws in the wind.'' He has to keep at it: He is nothing more than a voice trying to make up a story, and to stop—to fall silent—is also a death. Mortality can only be kept at bay for as long as the voice continues.

Mr. Pinget's are spoken novels, written in order to be heard. His chief interest in writing them, he has said, is to impersonate a particular ''tone'' of voice and to sustain this over many pages. In a book such as *The Libera Me Domine,* the voice is beautifully consistent and rhythmic, and its monologue is irresistible. Mr. Pinget composes his books with the rigor and artful variations of a piece of music. . . . His language is much more artful, more richly inventive than any genuine spoken language: it is the printed word's tribute to the power of the spoken word. (pp. 11, 55)

John Sturrock, ''Pessimistic Diversions,'' in The New York Times Book Review, *April 29, 1979, pp. 11, 55.*

JOHN UPDIKE

[The essay from which this excerpt is taken originally appeared in a slightly different form in The New Yorker, *September 17, 1979.]*

It is with some embarrassment that a reviewer recommends to readers a writer whom he scarcely understands, whose works are more than a little exasperating, and who furthermore writes with a high degree of colloquiality in a foreign language. Yet Robert Pinget, as glimpsed through translation and through the cloudy layers of his own obfuscations, does seem one of the more noble presences in world literature, a continuingly vital practitioner of what, a weary long quarter-century ago, was christened *le nouveau roman.* . . .

Pinget's first book, *Between Fantoine and Agapa,* was published in 1950, and ever since he has explored a fictional terrain of which the local city is Agapa and the rather interchangeable villages are Fantoine and Sirancy. (p. 417)

His most successful and best known work is *The Inquisitory* (1962); it won the Prix des Critiques, became a best-seller in France, and still does seem his masterpiece. Its question-and-answer form, though extended beyond all plausibility, yet served to mold and control the contrary pulls toward anarchy in Pinget's work—one his utter trust in the vagaries of monologue, and the other his inexhaustible circumstantial interest in the doings, geography, and personalities of his fictional countryside. This second quality distinguishes him from Beckett and gives him a distant cousinage with Balzac and Faulkner. If we can imagine a Faulkner who began with the combative intellectual playfulness of Queneau or Jarry, or a *Sound and the Fury* that concludes with everyone dissolved in Benjy's idiocy, we start to taste Pinget. . . .

Pinget's plots deliberately defy summary. His novels are mystery novels that end with the mysteries compounded. *The Libera Me Domine* (an awkward collection of words based upon the French title, *Le Libera*—referring to the phrase in the Latin funeral Mass corresponding to the Biblical ''Deliver me, O Lord'') opens with talk, in an unspecified voice, about the violent death, ten years earlier, of four-year-old Louis Ducreux. (p. 419)

At the novel's end, we do not know who killed the Ducreux boy . . .; but we do feel we have lived in a provincial French village and experienced its tedium and its entertainments (lunch at the manor house, a dance concert at a local *pension*) at a bone-deep level no logic-bound tale could have reached. For in fact human events, whether they be Kennedy's assassination or Watergate or how we spent the day before yesterday, have a permanently unsettled shape once past the instant in which they occur, and Pinget's reverberations of hearsay are less anti-realistic than they appear. He could not be so surreal were he not so inventive, and so genially at home in the popular mind. Fantoine is always there for him, as Frenchman's Bend was for Faulkner and Macondo is for Gabriel García Márquez. In this village where everything is dubious, we never doubt the existence of the village.

Passacaglia (a type of Italian or Spanish tune, originally played on the guitar while the musician was passing though the streets) is a much shorter work than *The Libera Me Domine,* and its French publication came a year later, in 1969. Again, there has been a mysterious violent death—this time, a body found on a dunghill. (p. 421)

A man, called "the master," sits in a cold room of a shut-up country house ("the garden was dead, the courtyard grassy") looking at an old book, making notes in the margin; he has just torn the hands off the clock in the room. The body on the dunghill at first appears to be his ("the man sitting at this table a few hours earlier, found dead on the dunghill"), but then it becomes that of an idiot the master adopted in the past who has mutilated himself with a chain saw (or fallen off a ladder or swallowed a sponge). (pp. 421-22)

"Turn, return, revert." "In the margin beside an empty phrase." "His life having emigrated elsewhere." These are some of the phrases that recur, making the music of the passacaglia. Some program notes, by scholars of Pinget, are appended, and among them Dr. Stephen Bann links the phrases "Something broken in the mechanism" and "Death at the slightest deficiency in thought" with Descartes's *"Cogito, ergo sum":* the master is about to stop thinking, the universe is winding down, the hands are off the clock. Were it not so deeply embedded in the palpable atmosphere of an afflicted house and the surrounding damp, chill fields, such a significance would seem merely schematic and cerebral. But Pinget's work always outraces what might be said about it. His notion of haunting, of being haunted, for instance, is neither fashionable nor prescribed—Robbe-Grillet's manifestos called for universal demystification—yet it permeates Pinget's microcosm as strongly as the smell of earth.

An end game of a refreshed sort is being played here; though modern art has exhausted art's possibilities, the world goes on, idiotically. Unable to write stories, Pinget can still write about the popular will to make a story: "This is where people's imaginations take over and make them start questioning everything again." A kind of cave art, like Dubuffet's rough-textured daubs, arises from the voices of hearsay and gossip amid the final dilapidation of the mansions of nineteenth-century narrative. One test of an artistic method is how much of the seemingly arbitrary it can absorb and re-present as intrinsic; on this score Pinget is infinitely absorptive but unevenly successful in creating an illusion of coherence. *Passacaglia,* in part because it is shorter, is a more intense, somber, and moving work than *The Libera Me Domine. The Libera* ends with a funeral; *Passacaglia* weaves death itself into an arrested moment in a cold room of a shut-up house.

Such a description may not prepare a reader for the genuine difficulty and truculence of Pinget's fiction. Even a short book

of his feels long, and though he has outgrown the Beckettian vaudeville of early novels like *Baga,* the willful confusion of his anti-plots, the repetitions of their circular unwinding, and the author's refusal to take a clarifying position above the voices he records all make for a rocky read. Yet a certain incidental delight lives in many a well-struck phrase, and a real psychology and topology and sociology press toward us through the words. Unlike Beckett, he has not turned his back on the seethe of circumstance, or, like the mature Joyce, taken refuge in nostalgic reconstruction. For all his flouting of conventional expectations and all the sly comedy of his rambling village talebearers, Pinget strikes one as free of any basically distorting mannerism or aesthetic pose. His recourse remains to the real, without irony. In a France of smiling mandarins and chilly chic, he manifests the two essential passions of a maker: a love of his material and a belief in his method. (pp. 422-23)

John Updike, "Robert Pinget," in his Hugging the Shore: Essays and Criticism, *1983. Reprint by Vintage Books, 1984, pp. 417-23.*

ROBERT M. HENKELS, JR.

Marshall Mcluhan has endorsed a notion that the magazine *House Beautiful* has (and had) been preaching for years—that a man sees his house as an extension of himself. Henry James' artists inhabit a world of philosophically finite, prescribed phenomena. They gaze out at a single garden from the house of fiction they inhabit together. Their observations of activity in the garden may differ, but only because the windows are of different sizes and the angle of observation varies. In the Jamesian scheme of things, novelists may react to reality in many ways, but their broad experience of life is shared. Some writers are more perceptive than others and see the garden in greater detail and with greater precision than others. But to look out and see a unicorn munching on a rose, like the man in James Thurber's fable, would clearly have put the Victorian novelist beyond the pale as credible spectator of the real world.

In *The Inquisitory,* Pinget, like Henry James, uses a dwelling as a metaphor for the act of perception. Before erecting the Château de Broy, however, Pinget had gleefully torn up the Victorian novel's floor of reasoned discourse, dismantled its gables of authorial omniscience, and smashed its gingerbread trim of plot. The Château de Broy's corridors afford the reader glimpses into closed-off chambers of perception: the walls twist and curve, masking hidden stairways; the floors and ceiling give way, embracing the everyday and the imaginary. Thus learning is presented as a cyclical, ever-new, and ongoing activity.

The experience that James would communicate must pass through the same filtering agents that Pinget struggles to remove. Sense impressions go first through the censor of the conscious mind and then flow out through a screen of conventionalized forms as a "work of art." For Pinget, there are as many gardens as there are spectators, and so his work strives to interpose a minimum number of walls between reader and writer. Working at the outer limits of rationality, Pinget refuses to speak through a closed window. He tries rather to break through, to make the lines of words on the page as permeable as the castle walls, so that the reader will not simply understand his vision but will participate in its articulation.

Pinget's vision is not the only vision, of course, and his particular narrative approach does not invalidate the more traditional attitude toward the relationship of author and reader. But he is a remarkably honest, unflinching explorer of his own skeptical view of life, which he conveys through written commentary as fragmented and inconsecutive as his own version of life's non sequiturs. The wit, the flashes of recognition, the essential consistency (despite all the whimsical aberrations) of his wanderings in language all serve to make him a serious and meaningful innovator in the world of fiction in our fluid, indeed antirational, late twentieth century.

Pinget's fiction mirrors change and flux—change from the surrealist tales to the satiric *"récits"* and the fuguelike recent works, flux in the return of familiar voices. (pp. 219-20)

The technique of shifting from realistic description to poetic experimentation makes the relationship between Pinget and his reader uncommonly subtle and complex. Like a skilled wrestler, Pinget turns to his own purpose the thrust of his reader's conditioned responses to the novel. He entices him into his world with the hint of a conventional story. Then he shifts with the rapidity of a well-executed switching maneuver, and the reader finds himself upside down. What is more, through the patterned response of his expectations, the reader has participated in the process in spite of himself. Stephen Bann, when writing of Pinget's work, dusted off the learned word "anagogical," which a dictionary defines as "having a spiritual meaning or sense referring to heavenly life, relating to or arising from the striving of inner psychic forces toward progressive or lofty ideals, relating to the psychotherapeutic interpretation of dreams and with emphasis on anagogic striving." In Pinget's case, all three meanings apply. (p. 221)

Unfortunately for Pinget, too many of his readers have failed to understand the purpose behind his elaborate parodies, and too many reviewers have missed the point of his having satirized their stereotyped, rigid manner of thinking, reading, and searching. Until now, the author's joke has backfired to such an extent that some critics have praised his chronicle for the wrong reasons. A discouraging number of readers have blandly accepted Pinget's chronicle at face value. Reviewers have praised the "neorealistic" portrayal of provincial life in **The Inquisitory** and the photographic accuracy of detail in the description of the boarding house in **Someone.** Such critics have complained about the "contradictions," which they cannot understand since they refuse to accept, or are unable to recognize or understand, Pinget's objectives—which is to say, the works themselves. (pp. 221-22)

Pinget's fiction has often been neglected, despite Robbe-Grillet's and Beckett's praise, because it seems to hesitate between accepting and rejecting traditional conventions. But **The Libera Me Domine, Recurring Melody, Fable,** and **That Voice** give ample proof that, after having carefully cleared the ground, Pinget has found a new and innovative idiom. His work is only now beginning to find its public. One may hope that his continuing quest will attract the attention it deserves. (p. 222)

Paradoxically, the very ambivalence that has kept Pinget's work from reaching a wide audience constitutes one of his chronicle's most rewarding features. Pinget's novels *must* interest the adventurous general reader, the critic, and the literary historian precisely because he uses the "well-made" novel as a point of departure toward something new. The most dynamic and interesting currents of contemporary French fiction run through Pinget's turbulent prose. His work incorporates and juxtaposes the rejection of a well-established tradition of expression and the groping search for a new mode of communication. And it

does so with both arresting urgency and keen wit. French writers tend to work very tightly within their own literary heritage. Turning his back on the past is therefore an anguishing decision for a French writer, and this bold act of renunciation gives Pinget's novels an atmosphere of tension. On the more individual level, French novelists often circle in on their target in concentric circles like an onion. They zero in on the secret garden of their own reality or their own expressivity with dread and anticipation. Anticipation of the flowers they may find. Dread that the garden door will open onto nothing. The anguish of Pinget's latest works indicates clearly that Pinget has thrown himself into the game, unreservedly, risking all.

But Pinget's quest is unlikely to end in failure, for it shows how the novel flows on, renewing itself by challenging limits. Pinget's mock epic, with each component a fleeting moment in a broader, shifting perception, gives tonic proof that the novel remains vital. For life entails change, and only that which is alive can die. (pp. 222-23)

> *Robert M. Henkels, Jr., in his* Robert Pinget: The Novel as Quest, *The University of Alabama Press, 1979, 277 p.*

NEAL OXENHANDLER

Hearing Pinget's voice in 1980 the effect of surprise diminishes. It is a quiet voice, scanning precise effects. As for radical ambiguity, Pinget's master trope, it is what we are living by these days. Since the death of God and the novel there has been nothing besides doubt. Doubt as to who we are, doubt as to the noumenal—does this typewriter exist? Doubt as to who killed cock robin. Maybe it was Robert Pinget or even a case of suicide.

In Pinget's **Libera** there may have been three murders: a little boy lost in the forest, another run down at an intersection, a man named Serinet killed by his brother-in-law. With Pinget violence becomes the ultimate fact of life. . . .

Around the murders one voice (or several, the critics disagree on this) weaves a litany of suspicion, complaint, accusation. Everything it describes changes in the process, like the famous gas molecules of Heisenberg's experiment.

The fascination exerted by [**The Libera Me Domine** and **Passacaglia**] is not in the domain of the referential—what happened, who did what to whom—but rather in the kind of reading they impose on us. The subtlest form of violence is that which the novelist does to his reader.

The case can be made for post-modern fiction as parody. That is, it depends for its cogency on a set of conditioned reflexes, formed by reading the traditional novel. So for instance we begin automatically to register the characters of **Libera.** Verveine, the druggist, is a compulsive note-taker and is keeping a diary of the crimes. Mlle Lorpailleur, the school teacher, is a sadistic gossip who writes up the crimes in the town newspaper. . . .

Such notations are suspect. As the characters begin to multiply (as many as in one of Pynchon's huge novels), their actions fuse. The same action may be borrowed by another character, or two or three. We are never sure of the identity of the little boy with the red wooly who wanders off into the forest. Or who was crushed at the intersection. It could have been Frédéric or Jean-Claude. Or perhaps a girl named Lorette. . . .

Voice is the thread the reader holds onto as he navigates Pinget's labyrinth. (p. 19)

It is never quite the same voice from novel to novel. Yet there are recurrences. A quality of fake resignation, hiding anger at a failed life. A perverse interest in excrement and death. A limping yet indomitable rhythm. Above all, an obsession with details and the need to get it right, to report things exactly as they occurred. Which is the most difficult task of all. Not only because memory fails, because people lie, because the senses betray. But rather because the very existence of things is at stake. I come back to the noumenal—this typewriter. Does it exist? (pp. 19-20)

In *Passacaglia* . . . , somebody is ruminating about the death of a man not quite right in the head. What was his relationship to the owner of the estate? He too is found dead, slouched over his desk, his notebook fallen to the floor.

X number of bodies is found on the dungheap, genitals slashed with a pruning fork. Other victims include the postman and a passing tourist. Everybody is suspect. Pinget has called this novel an attempt ''to exorcise death by magical operations with words.'' To it he has given the name of a formalized dance— the passacaglia. How can we tell the dancers from the dance? Who killed them? Is the passacaglia not only the dance of death but the doctor's rumination on his friend, the Master? Or does the Master himself speak, through his notebooks?

We have no right to ask these questions. If we choose to play the game of post-modern reading, we cede all rights to the novelist. He is our Master, our lover and executioner. Each time we catch ourselves expecting a plot or character to ''jell'' we mutter a hasty *mea culpa.*

Yet if these novels do in fact depend on reading reflexes generated by the tradition, if they are essentially parodistic or ironic (depending for effect on a subliminal echo in the reader's mind), then reading them is always a doubled act.

As Pinget's long rumination called a novel chatters through the passive mind, we supply a thematic obbligato, correcting each scene, each event, each phrase with the echo of what it might have been in a traditional novel. If we stop doing this, as post-modernist novelists demand, we lose the intertextual dimension of the work. In a sense we lose it altogether. A word that does not reverberate is a dead word.

Yet however we thematize it, the text is *there*. It does not solicit us as does the realist text. It stands aloof. Unfolding, formal as a dance, it traces an arabesque on the grey skies of those countrysides Pinget calls Fantoine, Agapa, Sirancy-la-Louve.

The names of the innumerable characters interlock in an undecipherable code. Assonancy, rhyme, interior duplication are phantom solutions. So Lorpailleur, Lattirail, Loiseleur. Ducreux, Cruze, Crottar, Crottet, Descreux. They *almost* describe a meaning (attirail = pomp, show; crotte = turd, one thinks of Beckett's Turdybaba); yet that is not quite the point.

About the turds. They recur frequently, most explicitly at Mlle de Bonne-Mesure's tea-party where the guests see the cat shit in the window-box. Or was it in the rhododendrons? Pastoralist though he may be, Pinget equates excrement with Nature. Like Nature it is everywhere.

We come closer to the point in the title *Libera Me Domine* (only the first word used as title of the French text). The phrase is from the litany for the dead: ''Free me, Lord, from eternal

death.'' Perhaps after all that is why Pinget writes. Or why anybody writes. To trick the dark angel. To send a syllable echoing through time. To *speak* before uttering that final quack.

Pinget was one of the first to work toward a new problematics of reading, his novels among the first to challenge the aesthetics of the realist novel. They are muted, low-key works. There is not the humour of Beckett nor the geometric hard edges of Robbe-Grillet. But if you enter them, they do finally compose a world. In the way that Balzac composes a world with his *Scenes of Country Life*. Bernanos used to say that the country priest heard things in the confessional that would render his sophisticated urban colleagues mute with horror. Such are the deeds that occur in Pinget's quiet countryside. You sit there, like the priest in the confessional, straining to hear. The penitent mumbles or speaks in a rush. At the end, you are not sure what you heard. But you think: after this knowledge what forgiveness?. . .

Pinget fills an essential niche in the evolution of French fiction. His schizoid lucidity, the last step in the history of French Cartesianism, is an important lesson in the pathology of reason. Like so many other post-modern novelists he points towards a possibility of transcendence. A Liberation that lies beyond obsession and reason both. Perhaps only encountered when we turn the last page and the novelist's voice is stilled. (p. 20)

Neal Oxenhandler, in a review of ''The Libera Me Domine'' and ''Passacaglia,'' in The American Book Review, *Vol. II, No. 4, May-June, 1980, pp. 19-20.*

ROBERT HENKELS

Nowhere is the search for constancy and transcendence in a world of unremitting change expressed more poignantly and hilariously than in Pinget's nineteen novels, in which that quest works itself out through the act the author knows best, that of writing. Ostensibly, his latest novel [*L'apocryphe*] is about many disparate things: the comings and goings of a mysterious shepherd, the murder of an old man, visits to an insane asylum, the revision of a manuscript, inventories of furniture, descriptions of landscapes, reminiscences of Virgil's *Georgics*, a compendium of botanical maxims, the passage of the seasons— the whole interlarded with phrases in Latin and autocritical comments on the text. But what interests Pinget far more than these anecdotal shards is what he calls ''la façon de dire,'' the fugal interplay of tone of voice, shifting connotation, and movement from one level of language to another; and he signals to the reader the way in which the book is intended to be read by its title, ''apocryphal—of doubtful authorship or authenticity, false, spurious.'' Structurally and stylistically Pinget underscores the aleatory nature of his prose. The novel is divided into two parts, the second a reprise of the first with extensive variations. (pp. 926-27)

Part I contains eighty fragments and Part II sixty-three. Within individual fragments incomplete sentences occur frequently. Speakers and subjects change unpredictably. The sentence subjects tend to be veiled and unspecific (''quelqu'un,'' ''d'autres,'' ''on''). The verbs slide over into the speculative realm of the conditional. As a result, images take on multiple values or are taken through variations, as in a Bach fugue. The novel opens with the image of a shepherd, which recurs with variations throughout the book. Is this a description of a figure on a Greek vase, a farmer from Pinget's beloved Touraine, a bow in the direction of Virgil's yeoman farmer, an idealized image of the novelist, or an allusion to Christ, the Good Shepherd? The title suggests that it signifies all these possibilities at once and no single one exclusively. In the alternation between affirmation and uncertainty the fragments resonate from one to the other, like voices in an echo chamber, in pleasing and intricate patterns. But just as this novel is far more than the sum of its anecdotal parts, so also does it transcend its architectonic "tour de force." As the novel progresses, elegiac childhood memories and lyrical evocations of the ballet of the seasons occur with increasing frequency.

Without minimizing the tedium and frustration of the search for meaning, . . . Pinget's prose suggests an imminent transcendence that would give the text and the life that formed it value and meaning. In the religious context the Apocrapha are those books of the Bible that many feel to be divinely inspired yet are not recognized as part of the holy canon. The poetic passages in this book and the simple but moving suggestion of hope make its title doubly appropriate. . . . (p. 927)

> *Robert Henkels, in a review of "L'apocryphe," in*
> The French Review, *Vol. 55, No. 6, May, 1982, pp. 926-27.*

ANNA OTTEN

On a superficial level [*L'apocryphe*] is a detective story about a possible murder, suicide or case of insanity. There is a suspicion of what may have happened but no proof, and it is impossible to unravel testimony around what is a dead center, a hole, in the fabric of the text. . . . [An] old man has died and left his heirs a great many notes—obviously in preparation for a book. There are remembrances, ruminations, questions, commentaries, varying accounts of people and places, and aphorisms. Since several persons have added their own comments and annotations to these already contradictory notes, the uncertainty that prevails prompts suspicions of all kinds.

On another level the book is about writing itself. Pinget stresses capturing reality in language and finding the right "tone." He frequently refers to impressions from his reading—Virgil's bucolics, for instance. From them he retains the image of a shepherd, seen variously through field glasses, on an ancient cup, as an illustration in a book, on a tapestry—the image appears several times in the text. It clearly plays an important role, perhaps to show the difficulty of capturing an image or "reality"—whose very existence is questioned—in black letters on the white page. Pinget also uses intertextuality, weaving into the novel a few strands of his previous works. . . .

L'apocryphe offers a wealth of impressions, as the text moves rapidly and images and places alternate; the focus glides from bright to dark, from despair to joy, from agreeable humor to biting satire. Like a composer, Pinget plays variations on his themes, always returning to the beginning but never to the same theme. Some questions remain: When is the shepherd Virgil's pastor, and when is he instead the "Good Shepherd"? What is a beautiful book? Most of the questions cannot be answered, but *L'apocryphe* seems to come as close as possible to the idea of a beautiful book.

> *Anna Otten, in a review of "L'apocryphe," in* World Literature Today, *Vol. 56, No. 1, Winter, 1982, p. 69.*

RONALD De FEO

Of the leading practitioners of the *nouveau roman*, Robert Pinget has always been the least representative. Over the years,

he has emerged as a very individual voice, a writer who has expanded and refined new techniques and who continues to experiment and grow. Although Pinget's work is as intellectually vigorous and demanding as that of his colleagues, it possesses an earthiness, intimacy and urgency that theirs often lacks. Set mostly in an imaginary domain comprised of the small city of Agapa and the provincial towns of Fantoine and Sirancy, Pinget's novels are as rooted to the earth as Faulkner's, while in their concerns and manner they are close to the work of Pinget's friend Samuel Beckett. Like Beckett, Pinget is intent upon rendering a questioning, solitary voice, one that is often vague, confused and even a bit mad, lost in a labyrinth of its own words. Pinget's narratives, like Beckett's, are free-associative and self-perpetuating, but whereas Beckett's narrators seem to be forever searching for a clarification of themselves and their positions, Pinget's repeatedly, hopelessly, try to arrive at some truths about past events, to retrieve those events from the obscurities of the past and to fix them once and for all.

Pinget studied law before becoming a professional writer, so it is not surprising that the central event in many of his novels is a crime of some sort and that the narrator often comes across as an investigator, though of a very cosmic variety. Violent deaths or, more accurately, possibly violent deaths—for doubt haunts these narratives—are explored in *Clope au dossier, The Inquisitory, The Libera Me Domine, Passacaglia* and the latest novel to appear in English, *That Voice.*

Like the brief and haunting *Fable* . . . *That Voice* is composed of fragments; but in this book the fragmentation and jumbled chronology are so extreme that at first the reader feels lost. As he reads on, however, the pieces, the snatches of narrative voice, begin to fall into place. What emerges is not a story in any traditional sense, but rather a pattern of obsessional concerns and questions generated by Alexandre Mortin, a wealthy old man in a provincial town who has spent much of his time taking notes on trivial daily events and attempting to reconstruct his past. Using Mortin's absurd struggle as a foundation, Pinget ingeniously creates parallel difficulties: the narrative voice struggles to control the disorderly text and the reader must work to fit together recurrent phrases and images.

Matters are further complicated by Mortin's nephew Théodore, who, after the old man dies, pores over his chaotic papers. These contain, in addition to confused metaphysical speculations, supposedly startling revelations about certain townspeople. Théodore is determined to put them in order, "until the day when he realizes that he himself has become this juggler at the end of his tether, and that the story of this contorted, concocted, controversial manuscript is now well and truly his own, Mortin reincarnated in his nephew." What Pinget has fashioned is not merely a strange, fractured text about an old man, his papers and their effect, but an elaborate and brilliant meditation on memory and the attempt to establish a reality before it vanishes into nothingness, and on writing itself. (pp. 20-1)

With each new book Pinget refines his style further, and as a result his narratives have become increasingly abstract and difficult. *The Inquisitory* (1962), which is filled with typically precise *nouveau roman* descriptions of interiors, is almost traditional compared with *That Voice,* where we are not even certain who is speaking or if there is a central voice. At times we think we are hearing Mortin, at others his nephew, at still others an omniscient narrator who conveys snippets of town gossip and describes a host of contradictory events. The narrator gives several accounts of Mortin's death—from both natural and unnatural causes. But Pinget assures us in his brief preface that the voice is "the same from beginning to end, despite the diversity of tones"—which makes *That Voice* a particularly complex, dream-infused monologue. The reader may well hesitate to tackle such a seemingly vague and self-destructive narrative, which repeatedly undercuts all expectations. But if he accepts the challenge, he will find himself working with a remarkably suggestive text, whose unanswered questions point to larger questions that elude us all.

Published simultaneously with *That Voice* is Pinget's first book, *Between Fantoine and Agapa,* which appeared in French in 1951. Composed of brief surrealist sketches in which language is teased and poked fun at, and in which words and objects are removed from their usual contexts, the book recalls the playful verbal experiments of Raymond Roussel, Raymond Queneau, Henri Michaux and André Breton. It also reminds us that Pinget's early work was rather clownish. Still, we find in *Between Fantoine and Agapa* many concerns that are treated in a more somber and intricate manner in his later books. The presentation of fragmentary thoughts and actions in **"Monsieur Maurice"** suggests Pinget's mature style. The artist in **"The Swan Café"** who suspects the cashier of wrongdoing anticipates the questioning narrators of the novels to come. In **"The Pumpkins,"** Pinget might be describing his obsessed narrators or addressing critics of his future work when he notes that "man is really the most pumpkin-headed. He can't write 'in the beginning' without being obsessed by 'at the end.'" (p. 21)

Some may dismiss Pinget as too obscure, but his difficulties bring rewards that are not to be had from more accessible and commonplace fiction. As the Pinget narrator struggles futilely to arrive at a truth, he reminds us of nothing less than the fleeting nature of reality and existence. (p. 22)

Ronald De Feo, "Lost Voices, Imaginary Cities,"
in The Nation, *Vol. 237, No. 1, July 2, 1983, pp.*
20-2.

JOHN UPDIKE

What can one say of Pinget . . . except that he conveys, amid much willful murk, an impression of integrity, intelligence, and power? He is a dark author, placidly settled amid his favorite village odors of damp stone and rotting wood (anyone who has stepped into an old French farmhouse will recognize the aroma), and mysteriously content to churn and rechurn the chronic garbled rumors of perversion and homicide that make up his plots, if he can be said to have plots. This reviewer naïvely hoped that a consecutive reading of a work Pinget produced in 1951 [*Between Fantoine and Agapa*] and one published in 1980 [*That Voice*] would clarify what the author had been "up to;" and indeed certain differences in texture and machination are apparent. But it cannot be said that Pinget began as anything but oddly, opaquely himself; his surrealism has been constant, though its field of operation has become more rural and, as it were, medieval and hellish.

One might suppose *Between Fantoine and Agapa* to have a certain geographical focus and to lay claim to the imaginary territory of provincial France where the later fictions—preëminently *The Inquisitory* (1962), still Pinget's most impressive and cogent work—more or less take place. Alas, one is fooled again, for the little book is a collection of disconnected pranks, or prose poems, which take place not so much between Fantoine and Agapa as between Pinget's ears. . . . But for . . . two

tales, there is no mention of Fantoine or Agapa, and the subject matter gravitates toward the mythic and the facetiously geographic—episodes take place in Manhattan, Menseck, the Forest of Grance, and Florence, and characters include Don Quixote, a parrot called Methuselah, Aeschylus and his maidservant Aglaia, and the Persian king Artaxerxes. . . .

Pinget . . . shows something of the antic sunniness of Raymond Queneau and of Beckett's clownish desolation. His playful dabbling with history and myth suggests a host of experimental modernists, from Borges to Barth, from the *Fabrications* of the late Michael Ayrton to the *Eclogues* of our contemporary Guy Davenport. Literary experiment and surrealism have certain natural channels into which to run, it would appear, not so unlike the well-worn grooves of realism; nonsense, being an inversion of sense, is condemned to share a certain structure with it, and its finitude of forms. Pinget, even in this early, rather frolicsome and eclectic work, does look forward to what is to become his mature tone. The last and longest piece in *Between Fantoine and Agapa* is titled **"Journal,"** and, though concerned with such absurdities as snowstorms of fingernail clippings and dwarfs sold at auction to be used as candelabra by religious communities, it foreshadows the sinister cruelty and gloom of the later work. (p. 96)

That Voice concerns—Well, what *does* it concern? The phrase *"manque un raccord"* ("a missing link") is used seventeen times in the French text, the translator claims on the jacket's back flap, and a phrase rendered as "impossible anamnesis" ("anamnesis" = "recalling to mind") returns a number of times also, as do "invincible fatigue," "traces of effacement," "psspss," "take a hair of the night that bit you," and "an invisible manitou." The author, in a special preface to the American edition, assures us that "the structure of the novel is precise, although not immediately apparent. The different themes are intermingled. One cuts into another point-blank, then the other resumes and cuts into the first, and so on until the end." The two themes named are "the theme of the cemetery" and "that of the gossip at the grocery.". . .

Pinget locates us in the gently moldering, nowhere solid hell (a word that originally denoted not so much punishment as a simple bleak survival in a vague netherworld) of communal remembering, of mutual awareness, never exact, never erased. "Something else is being prepared beyond people's consciousness, it had to be reshaped first, we have been at pains to do so." And we, it must be admitted, have been at pains to read the result. Could the impression Pinget creates be conveyed less exasperatingly, less numbingly? Perhaps not, since its theme, to a degree, is the exasperation and numbingness of our human, social, forgetful, banal existence. (p. 97)

[This] reviewer would be doing less than his duty if he did not admit that he found *That Voice,* as an experience of readerly immersion in a fabricated world, less compelling and more mannered than, say, Pinget's *Libera Me Domine,* which it resembles in ambition and milieu. The sinister, shifting rumors of dark deeds done amid rural stagnation had a force there that here seems lost amid the pleasures of a self-professedly intricate counterpoint. A perfected artistic method can serve, unfortunately, to insulate the artist, to dull his recourse to the actual. *Between Fantoine and Agapa,* for all its buffoonery, was a venture into the unknown; *That Voice* is a demonstration of a master's method, in a territory thoroughly subdued. (p. 99)

John Updike, "Between Pinget's Ears," in The New
Yorker, *Vol. LIX, No. 21, July 11, 1983, pp. 96-9.*

ROBERT COOVER

What happens between Fantoine and Agapa [in the title story of the collection ***Between Fantoine and Agapa***] is that a family of campers, stopping for a picnic lunch, is frightened by an incomprehensible sign that reads, "Alopecia-impetrating prohibited." An innkeeper whom they ask about the sign is no help, being too preoccupied with a grandmother who has mistaken her jam pot for a chamber pot. A dictionary suggests that what is prohibited is obtaining a patchy baldness from competent authority. What can that mean? Well, that night in Agapa, the campers' son wakes up and vomits jam, frightening his mother, whose hair stands on end—"but not for long, because half an hour later she was bald as a coot."

Language has invaded reality, remaking it; a strange sign has invoked a plot. The familiar cause-and-effect world was displaced by a seemingly nonsensical one the moment they turned off the main highway toward Agapa, but now what is holding this tale together? Not much, except the voice of the narrator and his quest for meaning, but it is a quest now completely undermind by incongruity, irresolvable mystery and at the end a kind of comic terror. That is—"in embryo," as the author himself says in the preface—the essence of the art of Robert Pinget. For what has really happened between Fantoine and Agapa is that one of our major contemporary artists has discovered (if not yet explored) his territory. . . .

Mr. Pinget belongs to that French literary movement known somewhat by default as "the new novel," a group of writers united by contempt for the conventional bourgeois novel and its implicit ideology (especially the notions of causality, normative human nature, coherent chronology and the "well-ordered universe") and by their enthusiasm for innovation and iconoclasm. Their common influences include Kafka, Joyce, Beckett (who is often counted in their number), Jean-Paul Sartre, the phenomenologists and the earlier Expressionists and Surrealists.

Mr. Pinget is perhaps the most consistent (some might say narrow), least aggressive but most enigmatic and playful member of the group, which has a tendency to veer toward a kind of dour intellectual self-absorption. He does not share the zest for theory and manifesto that characterizes so many of the others—Alain Robbe-Grillet, for example, or Nathalie Sarraute or Michel Butor—but is rather, one might say, the movement's poet.

What convictions he does have about literature he prefers to bury deep in the structure of his texts, allowing them to emerge out of their own insistence upon the truth. In the story called **"Ubiquity,"** for example, he offers what at first seems to be a lesson on how to write an opening sentence if the writer wants to suggest that two events occurred at the same time. But what actually happens in the story is that the whole idea of synchronicity—indeed, any kind of coherent chronology—is reduced to absurd comedy in which the narrator meets his wife six months after he marries her, people visit and kiss themselves or wait for themselves in the rain in three different places at once and everybody ends up in the same bed, which is in Bucharest and probably Manhattan and Paris as well, if anywhere at all.

This power of the text over its author, together with its corollary, the instability of all narrative statements, is at the center of Mr. Pinget's art. In these early stories, he still seems manipulative, an author playfully demonstrating his ideas about writing with witty contrivances. Later, in his novels, as these notions take on greater depth and mystery, he will surrender to them, letting the text tell him what happens next. (p. 15)

For Mr. Pinget . . . writing a novel is a kind of chase. Once the prey has been released, it must be recaptured. "One thing alone interests me in the novel," he has said, "to capture *the tone of a voice.*" He repeats that in the preface to ***That Voice,*** a work first published in Paris in 1980. The narrator sets out—in this case, on a nighttime exploration of the village cemetery—hoping for the best. . . . Stories proliferate and intertangle. Characters do too. Perhaps they are all one story, one character, theme and variations. Inquisitors enter the text to try to find out. They become trapped there and turn into characters with stories of their own. They engage in disputations. Relevant books and papers on the matter appear, get quoted, disappear. Characters erase one another from the text. "In short," as he concludes, "it's all as clear as mud."

Yet clarity—at least in terms of traditional narrative—is not Mr. Pinget's goal in ***That Voice*** or any of his other works. Reality is his goal, and clarity is not one of its attributes, nor is logic—"I don't give a damn for logic!" he has been heard to exclaim. (Not surprisingly, we find constant uneasy shifts of verb tense and frequent use of the conditional.) Paradox is an attribute, ambiguity is, as is insubstantiality, even that of the questing self. And if the narrator lacks substance, so must all narrative statements. The central story in ***That Voice*** is one of theft and murder—or was it suicide and failure? Who can say when the names in the story have been plucked from tombstones and the plots from the gossip of cafes and markets and point of view is a dead convention from discredited mythologies? "'The old rumors being mixed up with the new ones,' poor Alexandre repeated, 'that's why my head feels like a factory.' And he went back up to his room and made notes, voices from all around, from before, from last night, from afterwards, I am their spokesman here."

The original quest, which may actually have been for a kind of substance, an effort to locate the self in something like life, ends here in these voices, or rather, because they merge finally into one communal voice, in ***That Voice.*** And that voice, once captured, is its own reward, for the author discovers near the end, "all of a sudden, like a dew, the love of what has been said."

The result is both truthful and beautiful . . . , though this does not seem to be Mr. Pinget's conscious intention. "I am now convinced," he says in **"Journal,"** the most fecund and inventive of the pieces in ***Between Fantoine and Agapa,*** "that in a work of art we do not try to conjure up beauty or truth. We only have recourse to them—as to a subterfuge—in order to be able to go on breathing." (pp. 15, 21)

> *Robert Coover, "When Language Invades Reality,"* in The New York Times Book Review, *September 25, 1983, pp. 15, 21.*

ROBERT M. HENKELS

Fantoine—the realistic representation of the trivial goings on in a small French country town, its gossip, its intimations of scandal, its fears and its underlying despair.

Agapa—the domain of the extraordinary, home of a transcendent love of humanity and language; the source of liberating laughter where one senses, from time to time, the tantalizing hope of salvation.

Whether considered in terms of his treatment of language, literary conventions, or narrative structure, Robert Pinget's fiction oscillates between the poles suggested by the two sleepy hamlets that dot the landscape of his imaginary province. Pinget delights in making the strange familiar and the familiar strange. Or rather, through an evolving mastery of increasingly complex devices, Pinget combines each way of seeing as the two eyes combine to make one vision. (p. 361)

Pinget's most recent novels, including *That Voice,* bring techniques of repetition and alternation to bear on words, phrases, and themes. Any sense of plot or linear progression of the story line has been reduced almost to the zero point—either through the truncation of the narrative into shorter and shorter fragments or through the accumulation of details. The reader receives too little information (or too much) to ground the story in a continuum of cause and effect. Thus, in *That Voice,* as in *Between Fantoine and Agapa,* language serves as the book's subject and object. Here, however, the author highlights the denotative and connotative power of words by repeating them in subtly varying combinations.

The closest exercise from everyday life to the process to which Pinget subjects words and themes in *That Voice* is the attempt to locate a misplaced object through a painstaking reconstruction of the recent past. One begins with recollections firmly established in certainty and works back onto increasingly hypothetical ground. Failure to find the answer to the problem brings the seeker back again and again to the starting point until the quest itself is cast in doubt and the process of seeking overshadows the object of the search.

Pinget called attention to this comparison when he described *That Voice* as "a triple amnesis." ("Amnesis" means literally "the recalling to memory of things past," and, in psychoanalytical terms, "a patient's rememberance of the early stages of his illness." The latter meaning is most significant, since Pinget describes his own writing as a compulsion of sickness.) In the novel *That Voice* the narrator recalls the elements of his story; Pinget relates the work to the images, themes, and forms of this continuing chronicle; and the reader struggles to recall what has gone before and to relate it to the words before his eyes. Formally, the text recomposes itself in reascending order.

That Voice unfolds through the contrapuntal recurrence of three themes: a mysterious stranger writing on a slate in a cemetery; events surrounding Pinget's alter-ego writer-figure, Mortin; and village gossip about these and other matters. As in baroque music, leitmotifs and variations (here read "themes and words") return in different keys or contexts, and in different orders, here in reverse. . . . To the reader caught up in complex and contradictory variations at the informational level, this structure seems anything but obvious. To perceive its outline one must step back from the level of words as communication to the level of words as expression or as music, much as one must do when viewing an impressionist painting. Close attention to the text's spacing on the page helps bring the recurring structure into clearer perspective. The serial blocks of the novel's first half are set off by double spacing between paragraphs. The recapitulating quest for what has been lost in the beginning of the second part of the book runs together without typographical points of reference. The text rambles on, doubling back onto itself, growing by accretion until it abrubtly ends. (pp. 361-62)

Whatever form his fiction takes, Pinget's quest strives for a reconciliation of the wonderful and the ordinary, of the immanent and the transcendent. Something precious has been lost in Pinget's world somewhere between Fantoine and Agapa. Perhaps it is the magic of this inexplicable equilibrium. (p. 362)

Robert M. Henkels, in a review of "Between Fantoine and Agapa" and "That Voice," in The Southern Humanities Review, *Vol. XVIII, No. 4, Fall, 1984, pp. 361-362.*

Barbara Pym

1913-1980

English novelist, nonfiction writer, and editor.

Pym's novels are wry comedies of manners frequently compared to the work of Jane Austen for their quiet, temperate tone and subtle psychological insights. Described by Barbara Everett as "romantic anti-romances," the novels focus on solitary women and the conflict between their romantic notions of love and the mundane reality of their lives. Although Pym wrote six moderately successful novels between 1950 and 1961, her career lapsed for sixteen years due to her publisher's opinion that her novels were no longer contemporary in subject or commercially viable. Doubting both the quality of her work and her own critical abilities, Pym continued to write but published very little. In a 1977 *Times Literary Supplement* poll, poet Philip Larkin and biographer Lord David Cecil both designated her as one of the most underrated writers of the century. This prompted critical reappraisal and resulted in a great increase in the popularity of her works. Prior to her death Pym published three additional novels which were favorably received. All of her early fiction has been reissued, some available for the first time in the United States, and several posthumous volumes have recently been published.

Pym sets most of her fiction in the British drawing room; her characters include an assortment of spinsters, clergymen, and anthropologists. By continually emphasizing mundane, commonplace details over action, Pym reveals both the psychological subtleties of her characters and the trivial nature of their lives. Her characteristic themes—the disparity between the sexes, rejection, disappointment, and the quiet acceptance of an obscure existence—are introduced in her first novel, *Some Tame Gazelle* (1950). The book focuses on two spinsterly sisters living in a small English village, one of whom falls in love with a clergyman but discovers that her own romantic naiveté has led her to feelings he does not share. Filled with touches of humor, the novel characteristically avoids both bitterness and profundity through the sympathetic treatment of the characters' shortcomings and their ineffectual lives. Pym's depiction of men as insensitive and oblivious comes to the fore in *Excellent Women* (1952), which revolves around a lonely woman whose societal value lies in her role as peacemaker for a variety of anthropologists and their friends and spouses. Pym's subsequent novels also focus on unrequited love and the relationship of the individual to society. The protagonists of *Jane and Prudence* (1953), *Less Than Angels* (1955), *A Glass of Blessings* (1958), and *No Fond Return of Love* (1961) wrestle with frustration, loneliness, and disillusionment, yet in an unobsessed manner, often finding consolation in their solitude.

Pym's works published following her long literary exile—*Quartet in Autumn* (1977), *The Sweet Dove Died* (1978), and *A Few Green Leaves* (1980)—although perhaps more subtly refined, reflect the same concerns and approach of her earlier works. This is also true of the posthumously published novels *An Unsuitable Attachment* (1982) and *Crampton Hodnet* (1985), both of which were written early in her career. An additional posthumous publication, *A Very Private Eye: An Autobiography in Diaries and Letters* (1984), reveals insights into Pym's life

and fiction and displays the same skillful evocation of details and gentle humor found in her novels.

(See also *CLC*, Vols. 13, 19; *Contemporary Authors*, Vols. 13-16, Vols. 97-100 [obituary]; *Contemporary Authors New Revision Series*, Vol. 13; *Contemporary Authors Permanent Series*, Vol. 1; and *Dictionary of Literary Biography*, Vol. 14.)

WILLIAM BRADLEY HOOPER

Considering the growing readership [in the United States for Pym's novels, the reissue of *Less Than Angels*] will be warmly received. Not Pym's best, the novel is certainly not plain, either. With typically shrewd satire, an intricate plot, and characters so apparently ordinary that their very ordinariness is attractive, Pym depicts the amorous adventures of a circle of acquaintances—anthropologists, for the most part—that includes spinsters, private eccentrics, and young men and women in need of pairing up. *Less Than Angels* is in no way dated; its continued freshness is to be marveled at.

William Bradley Hooper, in a review of "Less Than Angels," in Booklist, *Vol. 77, No. 9, January 1, 1981, p. 615.*

JOHN McALEER

Although the novel of manners by definition strives to defend the existing social order, the best specimens have, with therapeutic intent, a strong satiric thrust. On that account the death of Barbara Pym, in January 1980, is a serious loss to the genre.... Her satire, laced with vitriol, is reminiscent of Waugh's. Her canvas, however, is small. Anglican spinsters preside at its center. They are not Miss Marples, but wistful, unfulfilled women, the odd bits left in the tiderack by the retreating ocean of empire.

Even so, *Less Than Angels* is rollicking fun. Catherine Oliphant is at the center of a community of anthropologists, and mistress to one of them, Tom Mallow, though merely his moment's fancy. Others in the group are Father Gemini, a Catholic priest, the Lydgates, brother and sister, and Deirdre Swan, who will oust Catherine from her place. These are wonderfully literate people who chat about Tennyson and Arnold and the classics....

With the aid of a French anthropologist who examines the manners of the English village—he has the same interest he would show in cataloguing the traits of the aborigines of the Australian Outback—we come to realize that Pym actually is examining her elite grouping of British anthropologists as though they were, indeed, exotic specimens of an all but extinct society. It's really deliciously funny when Father Gemini, in the company of the sinister Father Serpentelli, decamps at the end with the funds meant to support the research of the others, and all are left, high and dry, presumably to wither away and vanish from view even as they continue to brood, in lofty detachment over the social structure and land-tenure practices of societies scarcely less bizarre than their own. Miss Pym disposes nicely indeed.

> *John McAleer, in a review of "Less Than Angels,"*
> in Best Sellers, *Vol. 40, No. 12, March, 1981, p. 428.*

DAVID KUBAL

[Barbara Pym's] is a world of repression, which both pains the self and permits it to survive, relatively secure from the forces that would absorb it. The focus is on the female whose ability to persist is even more heroic than the male's, because she is denied his opportunity for variety and liberty, limited though those advantages are. Having learned from birth to suffer the curtailment of pleasure, Miss Pym's women, moreover, have grown in courage and self-sufficiency superior to men. The bitter irony is that the female still must wait on the male's call. But even if she is never beckoned, she retains the resources to remain alone, distinct, and individual. The professional middle class men of her novels have no such strength; alone they turn foolish and disoriented, needing a woman, if only to make the tea and type their research papers. Nonetheless, for Miss Pym, despite the fact that the woman must assume an ostensibly subservient position in any coupling, she is better off with a man, since she can find at least some pleasure, and hence some dignity, in the relationship. Besides, with the right kind of man, one who is willing to settle in, she is safer than when she is alone. In Miss Pym's world as in Freud's, it is the case, as Imlac told Rasselas, that "Human life is everywhere a state in which much is to be endured, and little to be enjoyed." (p. 462)

Yet there is something to be enjoyed, as we see in her recently re-issued novel [*Less Than Angels*], first published in 1955.... *Less Than Angels* is particularly welcome, since it may be her best. It is a more richly humorous and generous book than the ones she wrote immediately before her death. It also offers the prospect of a number of compensating pleasures, some moderate, others rather exotic, designed to allay the discontents of a highly civilized life.

Near the beginning of the novel two silly graduate students in anthropology "stopped outside a cinema and were gazing at a poster which showed a young woman . . . reclining seductively in a transparent negligée across what seemed to be Niagara Falls. 'I have that seminar paper to prepare,' said Mark reluctantly. 'Yes, of course,' said Digby meekly." Their muted sexual ache for Marilyn Monroe, their begrudging resignation, and their recourse to work suggest the central, although unstated, drama of the novel. It is the sad condition of middling Englishmen, unwilling heirs of Victorian morality and decorum, in the 1950s. The situation of women is, of course, more frustrating. These young anthropologists, like their grandfathers, have the prospect of field work in Africa to look forward to. Catherine Oliphant, the heroine, who thinks of herself as Jane Eyre, has only the vague possibility of some Rochester to pursue. That she finds him, decked out in an African fertility mask in a suburban garden, is her good fortune, a reward earned for her steadfastness. Observed from an adjoining house by a widow and a spinster, with whom she has been staying since the death of Tom Mallow, her apparently platonic lover, a young anthropologist who was accidentally killed in an African political riot, Catherine joins Alaric Lydgate in a fertility ritual. Rhoda Wellcome, the spinster, reports: "'They're going right to the bottom of the garden. Now he seems to be cutting something and Catherine is helping him—what *can* they be doing? Why, now she's standing up and her arms are full of rhubarb! What a strange girl she is. . . . What odd turns life does take!'" Still, it is Alaric who is the more fortunate, because "Like so many men, he needed a woman stronger than himself, for behind the harsh cragginess of the Easter Island façade cowered the small boy, uncertain of himself."

If this last notion is condescending and snobbish, it is also somehow a necessary protection for women to adopt against the power of the male in such a society. If Catherine Oliphant, an orphan, yearns for a husband and a family, as well as for suburbia, she also realizes the dangers to her self in those mergers. If secure pleasure, therefore, is a necessity, so is independence. To be avoided, on the one hand, is the loss of the self in sexuality and institutions; to be feared, on the other, is the diminishment entailed in repression and disconnectedness. Striking a balance between the needs of pleasure and of autonomy constitutes the spiritual adventure of the modern self. That Barbara Pym can imagine the achievement of such an effort, done with grace and humor, is itself a rare accomplishment in contemporary literature. It also should alert the reader to the fact that her comic novels of manners are informed by a subtle intelligence that is serious, germane, and, more than anything else, healthy. (pp. 462-63)

> *David Kubal, in a review of "Less Than Angels,"*
> in The Hudson Review, *Vol. XXXIV, No. 3, Autumn, 1981, pp. 462-63.*

DENISE P. DONAVIN

The late Barbara Pym has left another beguiling novel [*Jane and Prudence*] to enchant U.S. readers. It concerns an unusual

British spinster, Prudence Bates, who is a worldly, attractive Londoner engrossed in "the rapture and misery and boredom of her love for Arthur Grampian," then for Fabian Driver, then Geoffrey Manifold.... [Prudence's friend] Jane is a remarkable clergyman's wife—remarkable for her cheery countenance as she ponders poetry instead of parish matters and unsuccessfully copes with household obligations. Jane is busy throughout the novel fretting over Prudence's love life and seeking an appropriate husband for her from the supply of bachelors in the country village her husband has been assigned to. Pym's appealing characters carry this modest plot beautifully, with charm and wit.

> *Denise P. Donavin, in a review of "Jane and Prudence," in* Booklist, *Vol. 78, No. 3, October 1, 1981, p. 179.*

JAMES CAMPBELL

There is much in *An Unsuitable Attachment* that is good. Barbara Pym's gently satirical touch is sure of itself for the first 50 or so pages, in which the main characters are introduced.... In this area, Barbara Pym is an expert. The genius of her characterisation is in the way that her creations are immediately recognisable as types....

[The danger of establishing characters as types], of course, is that they occasionally topple over the verge of their personalities and become caricatures. With as good a writer as Barbara Pym, this doesn't happen often; but a case in point is the shrill Lady Selvedge, who is not quite convincing as the great celebrity at the parish fête.

Having introduced her characters, Barbara Pym seems not to have known quite what to do with them. There are too many characters of approximately equal 'weight' in the novel, and the particular 'attachment' of the title is not developed sufficiently beyond the others.... [In addition] there are too many scenes which appear to have no justification other than that of adding length. In true comic tradition, the novel concludes with the pairing off of the main couple and hints at the prospects for others; however, being set in a world where the 'dear and familiar' tradition (symbolised by the church) is being overthrown by unthinking iconoclasts such as Penelope, and thinking ones such as the anthropologist Stonebird, the attachments in this comedy are ironic.

Barbara Pym is the most *English* of modern novelists: little happens that one would be unlikely to see from the kitchen window; her narrative winds through nervous dinner parties and chance encounters on the street; situations abound in which manners and 'the right way of putting things' are to the fore. She satirises this affliction with just the right amount of subversive edge, but in the end one feels that she would not really like things to be other than they are. There are many pages in this novel which show a fine writer in control of her material, and her followers will want to read it. Finally, though, I am not all that surprised that her publishers rejected it....

> *James Campbell, "Kitchen Window," in* New Statesman, *Vol. 103, No. 2657, February 19, 1982, p. 25.**

PENELOPE LIVELY

[In *An Unsuitable Attachment*] John Challow, the male half of the unsuitable attachment, is perhaps not fully rounded as a character, but the vaguely unspecified unsuitability of the match seems to me just one of those indeterminate unsettling situations that are a Pym characteristic. Her narrative line has often been slight—though none the less oddly gripping—and for the rest, ... we are back on the old territory. It is a wonderful book: hilarious, unexpected, touching and occasionally faintly disturbing. Anyone who has enjoyed Barbara Pym—plus any misguided soul who so far has not—is going to want to read it.... The cast is, in a sense, familiar: two sisters, one married to a clergyman, assorted neighbours including an anthropologist. So is the plot, heralded on the first page as we meet the sisters, twenty-five-year-old Penelope and Sophia, the vicar's wife, displaying furtive interest in the newly arrived bachelor down the road. We have men and we have women, the wed and the unwed, and the conflict is on. All Barbara Pym's novels are about the war of genders (not the sex war, which is something rather different) first and foremost, long before they are (as most critics have claimed) about social nuances.... What all the novels do is to present a situation in which bachelors and spinsters and husbands and wives are locked in subtle combat, pursue or are pursued, prey on one another. I am always surprised that the feminists have never claimed Barbara Pym (though I suspect she would have indignantly rejected any such affiliation); of all women novelists no one has dealt so effectively with male aspirations. Pym men are frequently vain, complacent, self-absorbed and parasitical. One thinks, with what infinite pleasure, of Archdeacon Hoccleve in *Some Tame Gazelle*. And when they are in pursuit of an available unmarried woman it is with one thing in mind, and one thing only: getting their thesis typed, or their shirts washed, their supper cooked, their sheets turned sides to middle.

The men usually win, technically. They evade marriage, or marry the other woman, they secure the required services. But the women are the moral victors; they provide a rich and biting commentary. They endure and observe and walk off with all the best lines; their beady eyes are turned on the unsuspecting male, noting that his shoes are not quite right, or his manners wanting.... (pp. 76-7)

The delicacies [of *An Unsuitable Attachment*] lie, as usual, in how the tale is told. Barbara Pym's prose has always had a deceptive simplicity; she is telling a story, first and foremost, and the reader is lulled by the steady onward march of the narrative into an unsuspecting calm. Only on the next page does the delayed-action effect of a phrase or remark hit you with its full impact.... Again and again, comfortable and unsuspecting as a Pym hero (inappropriate word) one reads a page, turns over, only to be brought up short by the realisation of what has just been said, the appreciation of some barbed comment, the implication of a remark.... [There] is a phrase that I shall cherish for a long time: "a mild social occasion." We know exactly what is meant by that....

Most of the social occasions in *An Unsuitable Attachment* are mild: little dinners, a church bazaar, an anthropological garden party. But the human undercurrents are not. And, funny and deft as it is, this novel is not without those darker reflections that herald the bleaker vision of *Quartet in Autumn*, which I suppose must be thought of as the best of the lot.... Behind the wit and fun lie the sombre ghosts that are Barbara Pym's theme: loneliness, rejection, solitary courage. (p. 78)

> *Penelope Lively, in a review of "An Unsuitable Attachment," in* Encounter, *Vol. LVIII, No. 4, April, 1982, p. 76-8.*

MARILYN BUTLER

[The] principal characters [of *An Unsuitable Attachment*], all offspring of deceased Anglican clergymen, might be the equivalents of Jane [Austen] herself. Like any Austen novel, *An Unsuitable Attachment* makes a cluster of courtships an occasion to uncover the lives of genteel and near-genteel friends and neighbours.

As matchmaker in chief, the part of a Mrs. Bennet or an Emma, Sophia Ainger the vicar's wife does her best to manoeuvre Rupert Stonebird into the arms of sister Penelope. . . . Stonebird proves as impervious as his name, or rather begins to develop instead a low-key passion for Ianthe Broome, while Penny fails to get her man through too much stage-management and too much trying, rather in the style of Harriet Smith or Mary Bennet.

Sometimes the debt to Austen is verbal and explicit: 'The day comes in the life of every single man living alone when he must give a dinner party.' Minor characters are almost recognisable, Sister Dew, good-hearted parish helper, is the equivalent of Mrs Jennings or Miss Bates. The mean Lady (Muriel) Selvedge, who comes to open the Church bazaar and lunches en route near Victoria for 3s 9d, might be based on the entrepreneurial Lady Denham in *Sanditon*. Ianthe's aunt, Bertha, married to the rector of a fashionable Mayfair parish, blends the hypochondria of *Sanditon's* Diana Parker with the injudicious high living of Dr Grant in *Mansfield Park*. . . .

The mystery then is why Miss Pym is not really like Miss Austen at all, why Austen readers could find her thoroughly disturbing.

Jane Austen and her contemporaries had a frank curiosity about one another's personalities and lives which often at the time came under fire as vulgar prying. . . . The same curiosity about people and their relationships, possessions and environment is an academic subject now, called social anthropology.

For the older reader and indeed the older critic, time has stood still as far as the literature of character is concerned. The 19th-century novel, according to this unreconstructed view, gives us something closer to life than any other art form; realism gives us reality and naturalism nature. It is precisely this kind of reader and this kind of critic who most firmly believes in Barbara Pym as a latterday Jane Austen, a novelist in the great 19th-century tradition involved in the transparent reproduction of familiar localised life. Which is odd, because Barbara Pym, far from being an old-style characteriser, seems bent on a reappraisal of technique that ends by making the familiar very strange.

In some Pym novels—*Excellent Women,* for example, and now *An Unsuitable Attachment*—the Anglican parish is invaded by a professional anthropologist: here it is the eligible bachelor himself, Rupert Stonebird. . . . Barbara Pym's men, whether anthropologists, vicars or vets, don't relate well to others and don't notice detail; their professional status earns them cachet in the world of her novels, but their skills remain theoretical, and comically outstripped by the amateurish curiosity of women. Still, it seems significant that while Jane Austen led the life of a vicar's daughter, Barbara Pym worked as Assistant Editor of the anthropological journal *Africa*. . . .

In developing her novelist's craft in the 1950s, and in working for *Africa*, Barbara Pym was exposed to prevailing ideas of what social anthropology was about. Of these, perhaps the dominant fashion, and certainly the one that seems most clearly reflected in her novels, is functionalism. In an attempt to order the social sciences on similar lines to the physical sciences, the functionalist compared individual human beings to cells or molecules, and saw them interconnected by their social relations to the organic whole which is society at large; social life was the interaction of individuals and of the organised groups to which they belonged. . . . There can't be much doubt that in her first and by general consent better group of novels, Barbara Pym makes use of this hypothesis concerning man in his social relations. *An Unsuitable Attachment,* seventh and last of the early series, actually looks like a deliberate attempt at a functionalist novel, even if the experiment is leavened with irony.

In acknowledgement that 'character' is no longer what it was, the heroine Ianthe Broome is presented in a format that is virtually computer-ready, or at least ready for entering on one of the card-indexes which Ianthe spends her working life compiling. She is catalogued at every appearance by her suitable clothing . . . , her abstemious but carefully orthodox taste in food and drink, her irreproachably tasteful vocabulary and piety to the memory of her mother, the canon's widow. The people in the novel react to Ianthe wholly in terms of these outward and visible indices. Rupert Stonebird wants to marry her, rather than Penny, because her outfit is always an ensemble . . . , while rival Penny wears a lopsided beehive hairdo, a borrowed dress that comes apart at the seams and footwear at odds with the dress. Another of Ianthe's unlucky suitors, the librarian Mervyn Cantrell, wants to marry her because her house contains a Pembroke table. (p. 16)

This is all rather like Elizabeth Bennet's joke when she is asked how she began to love Mr Darcy: 'I believe I must date it from my first seeing his beautiful grounds at Pemberley.' But in Jane Austen's moral world, a heroine would not in all earnestness attempt a kind of auctioneer's valuation of a marital partner, as the sum of all his worldly goods. Barbara Pym's heroine assesses her suitors by such signs, and they her. Characters are identified in the first instance by the jobs they do, though women—acknowledged subordinates—are also defined by the support they give voluntarily to the parish, by running tea parties, opening bazaars and visiting the sick. All the leading women are named somewhere in terms of their relationship to socially more significant men—Canon's daughter, vet's sister, vicar's wife, vicar's wife's sister. . . .

Most thoughts and actions are determined by social pressures: Pym people lead anything but a rich inner life. . . .

If characters are strangely and bleakly transformed in the Pym world, so, too, are institutions. . . . Barbara Pym's subject is the Church of England at parish level. . . . At a very superficial reading, she could just be made into a proselytiser for the Anglican way. St. Basil's is led from its Victorian vicarage by Mark, who is glad to have a working parish rather than the more fashionable St Ermin's, after which his wife Sophia hankers. Mark has chosen an appropriate patron saint, it would seem, since the original St Basil, an early Christian father, was a famous preacher, a believer in a community life of shared work, an advocate of taking religion into the city rather than privately out into desert places. So the original function of the Church as an institution is cunningly brought into play, but it is very clear that Barbara Pym sees few signs of its purposeful operation at the present time. . . .

Barbara Pym's portrait of the Anglican way in London NW cannot in the end seem anything but critical. Mark and Sophia are, for example, commented on, even parodied, by their next-door neighbours, the veterinary surgeon Edwin Pettigrew and his sister Daisy. Where Mark and especially Sophia, childless, lavish too much kindness on their cat Faustina, the Pettigrews outdo them by running an entire cattery in their basement. . . .

Mark and Edwin are . . . comically alike as priests of their respective orders. Their professional lives take them almost wholly among women, with whom neither is naturally equipped to deal. Edwin is 'an expert at calming and reassuring the agitated and often hysterical women who brought their animals to see him', but he could not focus on his own wife, and she has long since left him. Mark struggles to pay enough attention to Sophia. When the parish group sets out for Rome, Mark and Edwin, its only two men . . . , behave very similarly. Mark abstractedly studies the confessionals in St Peter's, Edwin the distended tail glands of an Aberdeen terrier spotted in the Via Botteghe Oscure. In the amphitheatre at Ostia Antica, both are briefly called upon to show their professional paces, which they do with characteristic ineffectuality. . . .

In Italy the peculiarities of the parish of St Basil are even accentuated. Daisy Pettigrew behaves more battily than at home, pursuing the lean ubiquitous Roman cats with tins of catfood, while Sophia pines obsessively for Faustina. Pym uses Italy in a schematic way reminiscent of Forster, though not, alas, Forster at his most engaging: some of her characters find love there, but on the whole the unfamiliar taste of libido is not so much releasing as guilty and unpleasant. Otherwise what they meet is a grotesque version of what they knew before. . . . The Italian for Holy Spirit (subject of the best-known work of the real St Basil) flashes out over Rome in neon lights, but only as the name of a bank. Ianthe muses that one takes comfort from chance signs, including those which mean to say something else. This may express a sincere, rare perception by Barbara Pym herself about the private aspect of religion, but the subject of her novel is its institutional working, and here the sense of comic futility is unmistakable.

In his brief introduction, Philip Larkin recounts how this seventh Pym novel was rejected in 1963 by the publisher of the first six . . . because the publisher's readers just did not like it. Perhaps they disliked the boldness with which the anthropological Miss Pym has imposed her meaning externally: where there's enough extraneous commentary to be noticed, there's usually too much to be assimilated, and that's probably the case with *An Unsuitable Attachment*. Perhaps they noticed how often Pym's ingenious sociology leads her into impasses in psychology. Philip Larkin complains that there is not enough of Ianthe falling in love, and in fact there is never enough of characters' feelings for one another. . . . There isn't enough evidence, and indeed one powerful current of feeling which in real life would be strong in such a world, that between the novel's many women, finds no direct expression at all. Instead, keeping up with Jane Austen traps Barbara Pym into a conventional plot, a network of courtship rituals which by 1960 belong almost wholly to literature and not to real life. Whatever *Pride and Prejudice* may pretend, marriage does not mean as much to a woman now as it is made to mean for Penny, nor her own work as little.

Jane Austen's novels are liked by a very wide range of readers, which surely includes most mature literate men. . . . Is Barbara Pym, too, a novelist for older men? Certainly they have so far been more gallant and vociferous than women in championing her, Lord David Cecil, John Bayley and Philip Larkin have paid her tribute as a superb observer of comic detail, and as

the delineator of a world, the Anglican parish, which has a Betjemanesque charm. . . . Philip Larkin in the present introduction gives more attention to the woman than to the artist, and sketches a portrait which might be that of Ianthe Broome when he describes the 'unassuming modesty' with which Pym received her eventual success, and the 'innocent irony' characteristic of her letters.

In an age of feminist consciousness, this is not much of a bid for the woman reader's vote. And in fact every woman reader of Barbara Pym that I know has found her charm resistible. Perhaps it is because her heroines so emphatically fall short of heroic stature. . . . Yet she surely should not be read thus unironically, as though she invited us to sympathise with her characters, instead of inducing us to see them, as she does, from a lair in the long grass.

Philip Larkin writes of the 'undiminished high spirits' of the early Pym novels, this one included, but he is surely mistaken: again, the meekness of her art seems singularly deceptive. It was a coup to borrow the insights of functionalism, out of the stable that was to give us structuralism, and, without the faintest surface hint of the *nouveau roman,* nevertheless challenge the comfortable clichés through which the naturalistic novelist underwrites a certain view of reality. She lived to see her reputation made by admirers who on the whole emphasised her continuity with tradition. Of this fame, Philip Larkin says briefly that 'the irony of the situation was not lost on her.' Maybe not, but it's growing only slowly on everyone else. (p. 17)

> *Marilyn Butler, "Keeping Up with Jane Austen," in*
> London Review of Books, *May 6 to May 19, 1982,*
> *pp. 16-17.*

EDITH MILTON

Both Barbara Pym and Bernice Rubens belong to that honorable sorority of English novelists whose writing seems to compel from critics, almost in reflex response, murmurs about Jane Austen. This is no doubt because these novelists are women, because they both have a crisp style, a mocking eye and a sharp focus upon the intimate details of social behavior. Above all it is because they are expected to know their place and not to slip from the exquisite quarters allotted to their talents into anything vast, like history and metaphysics, or anything chaotic, like fantasy and unbridled passion.

But the modest scale of *An Unsuitable Attachment,* like that of most of Barbara Pym's fiction, is entirely deceptive. She has a genius for slanting her view of the restricted lives of her characters so that they shine, still, with reflections of an ancient greatness that the world they live in no longer affords. The bygone mysteries of the Church of England and the lost snobberies of empire return as ghostly and gently comic echoes of themselves in the habits and pretensions of Barbara Pym's people, who, like the good antiques that furnish their rented bed-sitters and the good manners that decorate their lives, are no longer quite appropriate to the present day. Their lives commemorate the death of a civilization. . . .

[Among] other things [*An Unsuitable Attachment*] is a celebration of unsuitability. A titled lady of impeccable ancestry, for instance, steals her neighbor's pudding at lunch; the parish expedition to Rome no sooner sets foot in the Holy City than it rushes to find an English tea shop; and a clergyman collides with a determined parishioner as they both race to demonstrate the principles of brotherhood by sitting next to a black man.

The novel's list of the unsuitable is splendid and endless. In their confusion about who they are and how they should behave, the characters eye each other, hoping to find out what someone else thinks of them so they will know what to think of themselves. This does not help enormously, since what other people think is usually based much less on their insight than on their insecurities. Ianthe Broome, particularly, is perceived by the other characters in the way least useful to her: as the inheritor of all the graces of a time gone by, a creature who owes it to everyone's high opinion of her to keep herself as inviolate as a rare antique. Her choice between her own instincts and everyone else's advice is the central tension of the novel, which begins, "They are all watching me, thought Rupert Stonebird," and which describes social intercourse as an interchange of constant, mutual misperception. . . .

[That the manuscript met with] rejection seems quite incredible, and even without the distressing hiatus in Barbara Pym's writing to which it led, it would be unforgivable. *An Unsuitable Attachment* is a paragon of a novel, certainly one of her best, witty, elegant, suggesting beyond its miniature exactness the vast panorama of a vanished civilization. (p. 11)

> Edith Milton, "Worlds in Miniature," *in* The New York Times Book Review, *June 20, 1982, pp. 11, 25.*

ANATOLE BROYARD

[Perhaps Pym's] most brilliant achievement was the portrait of what might be called The Woman Who Overflows Her Situation. This woman, this archetype, this unsung heroine of the ordinary life, is always reaching for a further reference, always trying, in E. M. Forster's sense, to connect the low and the high, the near and the far, the everyday and the eternal.

Jane, of *Jane and Prudence,* is perhaps the best example of The Woman Who Overflows Her Situation. Tall, thin, so badly dressed as to be satirical, Jane is the wife of a vicar in a village near London. Since her husband presides over heaven and hell, limbo is Jane's dominion. It is her job to see to all the things that are too petty, too vague or ill defined, too *human,* for him to deal with. But while a vicar's wife is supposed to be a halo, a rather dim halo, around his head, Jane is more like a searchlight.

The author of a book of essays on minor 17th-century English poets, Jane is always ready with a confounding quotation, one that inadvertently exposes all the awkward implications of what had seemed to be an innocent condition. . . .

When Mrs. Doggett, a large, elderly woman who is a power in the parish, mentions that she's going to her dressmaker for a fitting, Jane says, "How grand that sounds, having clothes specially fitted so that they are exactly your shape and nobody else's." The remark is uncomfortable because it comes too close to Mrs. Doggett's shape. It is too vivid, too particular, too enthusiastic. We are reminded that, in the church, enthusiasm once meant heresy.

A vicar's wife should be hearty but not enthusiastic, responsive but not rhapsodic. Jane is always saying the kind of thing that most of us repress as being too romantic or poetic or farfetched. But Jane sees it as her duty in life, her sacred calling, to fetch from afar. . . .

After giving a dinner party, Jane asks her friend Prudence how she thought the evening went. "Very well," Prudence answers.

"It was a lovely chicken." "A lovely chicken!" Jane repeats with a wild laugh, as she sees all her efforts, all her talents, all the loveliness of the world stuffed into a chicken. . . .

"How convenient women were," a male character observes in another of Miss Pym's novels—"the way they were always 'just going' to make coffee or tea or perhaps had just roasted a joint in the oven or made a cheese soufflé." Jane, though, is inconvenient: She is always just going to quote a difficult or disturbing poem or burst the confines of an orderly situation. If she were not married, she would be a "distressed gentlewoman," another of Miss Pym's favorite types. In England in the 1950's, a subdued and wistful distress was seen as the natural condition of any gentlewoman, as she lived on her "small independence," her modest portion of freedom.

To call Jane a fine example of Miss Pym's irony is not enough, because every serious writer, good or bad, is ironical these days. What is so pleasing about Miss Pym's irony is the fact that, like Mrs. Doggett's clothes, it is specially fitted; it is exactly Jane's shape and nobody else's. It is cozy as opposed to cosmic irony, warm, not cold, sweet rather than bitter. It is not a grandiose defeat but an incorrigible enthusiasm running through life like a dog chasing a bird.

> Anatole Broyard, "Overflowing Her Situation," *in* The New York Times Book Review, *August 15, 1982, p. 27.*

BARBARA BROTHERS

In her novels, which sparkle with compassion, humour, and the wit of understatement, Pym contrasts her characters and their lives with those which have been presented in literature to mock the idealised view of the romantic paradigm and to emphasise that her tales present the truth of the matter. Though the men in her novels are not cast as heroes nor the women as goddesses of love and inspiration, the fantasy shapes the expectations of the characters. In Pym's novels women continue to be the 'second sex' more because of fantasy than because of political or social factors. Men, behind the mask of responsibility for society, make it little less than a 'holy privilege' for a woman to enter into their service. But that service lacks the rewards of love and meaning that adolescent romantic fantasies project for it. The life of a wife, Pym suggests, is little different from the life of the spinsters of the church who 'dote' upon the clergy. Love is not a flame, let alone a constant one. Men are more interested in their comfort and self-importance than in causes. And women, though not by nature self-effacing and good creatures, frequently pretend to be. Pym perceives that little has changed in the contemporary world: women are still psychic victims of what might be considered a self-serving, male-created myth that a woman fulfils herself only through love. . . . Women are neither more nor less heroic, original, petty or self-serving than are men. She attacks the myth because it has prevented both men and women from seeing and accepting themselves as they are.

Like Woolf and other feminists, Pym chides novelists for not telling the truth about women's lives. The sins of novelists in the world according to Pym are both sins of omission and sins of commission. In *Quartet in Autumn,* Letty no longer reads novels for there are none which reflect 'her own sort of life . . . [as] an unmarried, unattached, ageing woman'. . . . By not dramatising the life of the unmarried woman or that of the woman who is neither in love nor the object of some man's love, novelists, Pym suggests, have contributed to society's perception that such women have no lives of their own. What is more, the 'unattached' woman herself has been made to feel that she is a spectator of rather than an actor on the world's stage. (pp. 62-3)

The consensus among Pym's characters is that such women, if they are to become participants in the drama of life, must find a way to serve others. . . .

Pym maintains that while the silences of fiction have made it seem that the unmarried woman is a voyeur of life, the portrayal of women in fiction, on the other hand, has helped to create the image of woman as one who loves and serves. In *Jane and Prudence,* Jane Cleveland finds a model for her role as a clergyman's wife in the novels of Yonge, Trollope, and the other Victorians. But she is disillusioned with herself when she fails to be the 'gallant, cheerful' . . . wife who manages the household on 'far too little money', gets along well with the parishioners, and rears a large family. Jane is ineffectual in running the house and in helping with church activities, and she doesn't 'feel so very much of a mother' . . . since she has only one child. Her greatest gift is recalling quotations or analogies from literature which somehow always miss the mark. (p. 64)

Pym makes the point in *Less Than Angels* that the education of women and women's liberation have done little to alter the expectation that women are to serve a man whose mission is thought to be to civilise the world. The 'changed position of the sexes', which we have heard so much about, means only that 'now . . . women . . . [are] more likely to go off to Africa to shoot lions as a cure for unrequited love than in the old days, when this had been a man's privilege'. . . . Little, if anything, has happened to make 'the relations between men and women any more satisfactory', . . . for their characters and their roles are still stereotyped. Though, as one young anthropologist observes, two people may live together in 1950 without being married, the parts they are expected to play and do play are still unchanged. (p. 65)

Pym seems to feel that at least a part of the reason why education has not made a difference is that a woman's education is anachronistic, as Kate Millett has pointed out in *Sexual Politics*. . . . Females are educated in the humanities and the social sciences; they are taught the ideals of Renaissance humanism but not the facts of the hard sciences. . . . What it leads to for more than one woman in Pym's novels is landing a husband because she has the 'learning' to do an index for his book! Though a man is writing the book and a woman indexing it, Pym leaves no doubt that his mind is no more original than hers. (pp. 65-6)

Pym depicts in detail what it means to be a man's muse or his 'looking-glass'. Her wives, spinsters, and young and middle-aged hopefuls spend their days washing surplices, arranging church jumble sales, darning socks, cooking boiled chicken with white sauce, typing manuscripts, compiling indexes and preparing tea for the clergymen, anthropologists, and historians, the men who do the 'real' work in the world. Women do those things that a man does not want to do, for everyone knows 'men did not usually do things unless they liked doing them'. . . .

Though their lives as helpmates are unromantic, women cling to the notion that men and their world are as noble as they have been portrayed. When Dr Grampian says to Prudence [in *Jane and Prudence*] that 'things have been rather trying lately', she wonders what things. 'Men did not have quite the same trials as women—it would be the larger things that worried

him, his health, his work . . .'. . . . She does not perceive that which the reader perceives: as a single working women she has precisely the same problems that Arthur has.

In Pym's novels, so powerful is the mythic weight of man's responsibilities that her women fail to perceive not only that their jobs are often no different from a man's but also that a woman's needs are no different or less substantial. Jane Cleveland reflects with amusement on the woman in the café who insists on a 'man's needs' when she serves Jane one egg and her husband, Nicholas, two, and wonders why a man is thought to need more meat and eggs than does a woman. Her husband, however, finds nothing unusual about the portions. . . . Women, after all, must be satisfied with less in return for being one of those things a man needs, even if only for such 'arduous or thankless' tasks as compiling an index. It is enough for them to be 'allowed to love' a man, as one of Pym's women puts it in *No Fond Return of Love*. . . . (pp. 66-7)

To emphasise that romance in fiction and romance in life are never quite the same, Pym has Catherine Oliphant, a short story writer in *Less Than Angels,* question a scene she has just written. A lover in a novel may quote lines from Tennyson . . . , but it is unlikely that a lover who exists outside the pages of fiction would. . . . Catherine must decide that it is time fiction reflected more accurately life as women experience it, for we learn in *A Glass of Blessings* that she has rewritten the story. The 'women under the drier at the hairdresser's', . . . whom Catherine imagines reading the story, learn instead of 'a young man and girl holding hands in a Greek restaurant, watched by the man's former mistress'.

Pym's women who look for romance and excitement do not find it. Jane Cleveland acquiesces to the realities of life as a clergyman's wife. She dresses in frumpy clothes and listens to gossip, hoping to find in others' lives the passion her own lacks. But, of course, she never does. (p. 69)

As if to emphasise that she is chronicling rather than creating the lives of women and the men the women meet, know, and in some instances even love, Pym has characters in later novels meet or discuss characters from earlier novels. We learn in *A Glass of Blessings,* for instance, of Prudence having yet another 'unsatisfactory love affair' with Edward Lyall, the MP she meets on a train at the close of *Jane and Prudence*. . . . What we learn of characters' later actions is predictable, for life in a Pym novel is not made up of crisis and denouements. As one character of Pym's remarks, 'There was something almost frightening and at the same time comforting about the sameness of it all'. . . . Love, won or lost, effects no metamorphosis of character.

Pym's novels dramatise the point E. M. Forster makes in *Aspects of the Novel:* 'love is neither so intense nor such an ever-present interest as novelists have led us to believe'. People, unlike characters, are not nearly so 'sensitive' to love. None of the four central characters in *Quartet in Autumn* are in love, nor do they want to be. They find it difficult even to remember those 'loves' they have known—mother, father, wife. Letty does not even understand romantic love. . . . She has had beaus, but she has never experienced the desire to make her life a part of theirs, or theirs a part of hers. (pp. 69-71)

[As] Pym emphasises, women have had their image of being a female shaped by poets, novelists, and writers of popular drama, musicals, and pulp fiction. Imaginative creations have also shaped their expectations of men, love, and life. As subscribers to Boots Book-lover's Library or its lists, holders of degrees in humanities from Oxford, and viewers of television dramas and advertisements, they have had life presented to them as a love story and man and his work depicted as hardly less important than that of divine messengers. While Pym gently mocks women's naïvety and their romantic susceptibilities, she incisively exposes male pretentiousness, men's pompous acceptance of their own importance, and their vain belief in the myth they have created. (p. 71)

Pym's novels, then, call the whole myth into question. In them she turns the myth back into fiction. She constantly reminds her readers that neither characters, nor love, nor destiny is as grand as it has been portrayed. (pp. 72-3)

Pym rejects as romantic the fictional and historical idea that life is lived in pursuit of noble ends. The sermons her clergymen preach are dull, the scholarship of her anthropologists and literary historians picayune, and the work of her government officials insignificantly routine. Tom Mallow in *Less Than Angels* dies 'accidentally shot in a political riot, in which he had become involved more out of curiosity than passionate conviction'. . . . And, though John Akenside is an important enough figure to have someone edit his letters, he 'had a finger in nearly every European political pie at the time of his death, . . . one had never been sure what it was he actually did'. . . .

Pym mocks the pretentiousness of tragedy but proclaims the dignity of the quotidian. That those who have been ignored by fiction and by history, those who have neither jobs of importance nor loved ones who depend upon them, who are elevated by neither cause nor passions, are worthy of being attended to is the posture which informs Pym's fictional world. (p. 77)

Though her portrayal of life focuses on its mundaneness and on her characters' self-deceptions and self-pretensions, Pym's is not the pen of a satirist. She depicts her characters' psychic landscapes with the compassionate understanding of a humanist and celebrates their successes in being individuals despite the pressures of an impersonal society which would make them into nothing more than spinsters, clergymen, or clergymen's wives. . . . Because her characters do not conform to the model by which our society and fictions confer value upon men and women, Pym raises the question of what it means to be human, and, in particular, what it means to be among those fiction has ignored. (p. 79)

> *Barbara Brothers, "Women Victimised by Fiction: Living and Loving in the Novels of Barbara Pym," in* Twentieth-Century Women Novelists, *edited by Thomas F. Staley, Barnes & Noble Books, 1982, pp. 61-80.*

ANNE TYLER

Barbara Pym's plots, like Jane Austen's, often seem drawn from the daydreams of a refreshingly sensible and not obviously beautiful woman. In these daydreams the woman who finally bags her man is also, by coincidence, refreshingly sensible and not obviously beautiful. There's an important distinction, though. With Jane Austen the man was well worth the trouble. With Barbara Pym half the point is the absurdity of any woman's making so much fuss over someone as vain and pretentious as, say, Aylwin Forbes, the so-called hero of *No Fond Return of Love.*

Aylwin, the editor of a literary journal, is the kind of man who lists his hobbies as "conversation and wine." Unpacking his bags in a new room, he must find space for his yeast tablets,

his stomach powder and the framed photograph of his wife, who left him because of his infidelities. Do his weaknesses give pause to Miss Dulcie Mainwaring, our sensible and not obviously beautiful heroine? Not for an instant, though she's far too perceptive to miss noticing them.

Dulcie, an indexer-proofreader who meets Aylwin at a learned conference, has no more than a nodding acquaintance with him when she begins tracking down clues to his life like an only slightly less exuberant Nancy Drew. It seldom occurs to her that there's anything strange about a grown woman's lurking around a man's mother-in-law's house, or skulking in his brother's church, or journeying all the way to Taviscombe to spy on his mother's hotel. In fact, what makes this book so funny is her absolute unselfconsciousness. (pp. 1, 22)

As in all of Barbara Pym's novels, character is everything. Each figure is swiftly, brilliantly defined, from Dulcie herself, who firmly believes that "Life's problems are often eased by hot milky drinks," to Aylwin, who goes off on a trip with a Henry James novel and comes back talking like Henry James, to Dulcie's not so dear friend, Viola, who is given to statements like "It was kind of you to bring the tea, even though it was Indian." The closest attention is paid to even the most insignificant passer-by briefly glimpsed in a restaurant. Mild-mannered though Dulcie Mainwaring may be, she's also devilishly sharp of eye, and people observed from her point of view are not allowed to get away with much.

Chronologically, *No Fond Return of Love* falls somewhere in the middle of Barbara Pym's published works. It's more certain of its themes than the earlier books: There are several explicit statements about the importance of the trivial in the scheme of things and about the relative goodness of unassuming, ordinary people. . . .

Even more than in her other books, there are allusions to the characters' awareness of themselves as inhabitants of a novel—a tantalizing device that tends to lead readers to search for clues where perhaps none exist. Viola is "a disappointment . . . like a character in a book who had failed to come alive"; and when Dulcie finally gives Aylwin what for, she reflects that if this had been romantic fiction, "he would have been struck by how handsome she looked when she was angry, the sea breeze having whipped some colour into her normally pale cheeks."

In a stodgy Taviscombe dining room, a novelist appears—"a woman of about forty, ordinary-looking and unaccompanied . . . nobody took much notice of her." Is the novelist Barbara Pym? Has she, in her unobtrusive, quirky way, dropped in on her own story? If so, what fools those other guests are not to notice her! She is the rarest of treasures; she reminds us of the heartbreaking silliness of daily life. (p. 22)

> *Anne Tyler, in a review of "No Fond Return of Love," in* The New York Times Book Review, *February 13, 1983, pp. 1, 22.*

ISA KAPP

In the canny, delectable novels of the British writer Barbara Pym, we can count on finding sanctuary from the enormous liberties and vast territory that have been gained by modern fiction. Miss Pym's unworldly cast—absentminded vicars beaming kindly over their spectacles, stilted anthropologists back from Africa with charts and kinship diagrams, accommodating clergymen's daughters snug in their modest legacies of Hepplewhite chairs and Victorian ornaments—preordains an absence of garish crime, sexual revelation, or hearts of darkness.

The setting, comfortably confining, is usually the parish church. "I sometimes thought how strange it was that I should have managed to make a life for myself in London so very much like the life I had lived in a country rectory when my parents were alive. But then so many parts of London have a peculiarly village or parochial atmosphere that perhaps it is only a question of choosing one's parish and fitting in to it," muses Mildred Lathbury, the narrator of Miss Pym's second and most benign novel, *Excellent Women*, preparing us for a tale of personal rather than cosmic crisis. In Mildred's style, serene and accepting, an elusive Pym seasoning—a compound of marinating self-deprecation and salty accuracy—is usually present to counteract her mild manners. Nevertheless, her genteel hesitations, her persistent decorum make it obvious that the novelist sees no excuse for turning the chaos within us into anarchy without. Unlike the star fiction writers of the last few decades, Barbara Pym is not much attracted to chaos, whether linguistic or emotional, and nurtures instead an implausible fascination for everything that is orderly and habitual. (p. 234)

[Although] the precision of Miss Pym's observation of speech, manner, and mentality is awesome, the radius of her novels is startlingly narrow. There is more *not* happening in them than happening. The best-willed matchmaking goes awry, and a good many of the characters of both genders manage to avoid getting married or even falling authentically in love. . . . For Barbara Pym, love is a vagrant impulse, evanescent and untrustworthy, quite unlike the desire for security and routine, for tea, and for a pleasant room. (p. 239)

Logically enough, children rarely poke their disrupting heads into the proceedings. . . . Other oppressions that Miss Pym does not inflict upon her readers include argumentation, violence, intellectuality, politics, or even overly long, intense conversations. And despite the cozy familiarity with every aspect of the lives of the clergy, even a powerful emotional entanglement with either the theology or the spirituality of religion is noticeably absent.

To a considerable extent this deliberate avoidance of "action" is the result of Barbara Pym's unbudgeable honesty. (pp. 239-40)

Although Miss Pym does write mainly about male and female spinsters, about men and women who are timid, reserved, and unenterprising, who huddle into the church for safety and companionship, it would be a great mistake to confuse her restrictedness with triviality. She means us to sense that many of the predicaments and habits she describes are to be found everywhere: women without occupation, happenstance marriage, foolishly envisioned romance, and—always a major Pym theme—the need to adapt to one's limitations. These subjects are as alive among Scandinavian teak and glassy condominiums as they were among Victorian bric-a-brac.

Calm as the narrator's voice may be, a Pym novel is never lacking in suspense. Much more than a comedy of manners, it is a drama of disposition, willpower, and ethics, a closer relation of E. M. Forster and Henry James than of those busier and giddier novelists with whom this writer is usually linked: Angela Thirkell, Anthony Powell, and Iris Murdoch. Miss Pym does not sermonize us in quite the self-satisfied way that Jane Austen did. She does have a rather exacting glossary of vices and virtues, but it must be admitted that the vices are mild ones like vanity, irritability, indifference, and condescension,

and her reproaches are equally mild. Partly this is just plain subtlety, a fictional trait going rapidly into disrepute.

One of the great joys of reading Barbara Pym is that she laces her prosaic situations irrepressibly with stanzas of wonderful poetry. Like the novels, the poems confirm her conviction that the lives we live can be frugal, circumscribed, sometimes ego dampening—but not without their pleasures—and that there is more to be salvaged in any predicament than we suspect. One of the very few writers who makes virtue seem genuinely appealing, she is able to persuade us that neatness, thrift, secondhand clothes, and meager meals are no obstacle to happiness, and that doing what we ought is itself a pleasure of high quality. (p. 240)

There is no doubt that Barbara Pym is an extraordinarily forebearing and compassionate writer, but it is the layer beneath those warm qualities, a layer of sheer spinal firmness and imperturbable detachment that puts her into the rank of first-rate novelists. That detachment is what we meet in every successful comic with a straight face, and along with it goes a many-layered intelligence: the ability to see several things at the same time, not only the poignancy, the pity of it all (*that* most of us can see), but the risible oddness of our behavior and the miraculous resilience of our nature. (p. 242)

> *Isa Kapp, "Out of the Swim with Barbara Pym," in* The American Scholar, *Vol. 52, No. 2, Spring, 1983, pp. 237-42.*

MICHAEL GORRA

"If only one could clear out one's mind and heart as ruthlessly as one did one's wardrobe," Belinda Bede muses toward the end of *Some Tame Gazelle*. But, of course, one can't, and her words sum up her situation. . . . Miss Pym doesn't treat Belinda's thought as a summation; it's just a single sentence dropped into the middle of a conversation with her sister, Harriet, about whether or not to get rid of an old green dress. All the big moments in this novel are like that—quiet, offhand realizations presented without a trace of bravado, as if they were accidents. They astonish only when one steps away from them and sees how deftly they are woven into and illuminate the uneventful surface of the narrative. A big scene, confrontation, consummation of any kind—all are unthinkable. Yet Miss Pym's restraint isn't an evasion but precisely the point.

Belinda and Harriet live on a comfortable unearned income in an unnamed English village. . . . [Harriet] is silly and giddy and extremely happy; when she receives a proposal from a visiting librarian, she turns it down because she knows that marriage would interfere with her love of coddling curates. Belinda is sharper, more censorious and less happy. She has quotations for all occasions, but most of her "scraps of culture" aren't very good ones: early 19th-century verse by Thomas Haynes Bayly, for example, from whom the novel's epigraph comes: "Some tame gazelle, or some gentle dove: / Something to love, oh, something to love." (p. 12)

As with most of the men in Miss Pym's novels, it's hard to see the point of [Henry, the target of Belinda's affection]. . . . But that's just what Miss Pym intends. Belinda's affection has no logical cause; her love for this pompous and feckless clergyman is her limitation, her self-definition and her blind spot. She knows his faults but wills herself into ignorance and believes that her love lends her a dignity that her sister lacks. But Belinda fools nobody except herself, and even Harriet, whose behavior is more transparent, thinks her sister sentimental.

Harriet has a permanent suitor, an Italian count resident in their village whose proposals she always graciously refuses. Belinda tells him that he "'mustn't lose hope. . . . I know she is fond of you and even if she will not love you, always remember'—her eyes lighted on the works of Alfred, Lord Tennyson—'that it is better to have loved and lost than never to have loved at all. I always think those lines are such a great comfort; so many of us have loved and lost.' She frowned: nobody wanted to be one of many, and she did not like this picture of herself, only one of a great crowd of dreary women. Perhaps Tennyson was rather hackneyed after all."

The passage is characteristic of Miss Pym's compressed and seemingly casual way of letting her characters unwittingly reveal themselves, and its delicacy warrants the frequently made comparison to Jane Austen. Belinda dodges the implications of her words; she shifts the blame to Tennyson and refuses to see herself as she sees another character, as "one of the many thousand respectable middle-aged spinsters, the backbones or busybodies of countless parishes." . . .

Miss Pym's world is one of chaos barely reduced to order; her work is not as complacent as the surfaces of the scenes she describes. The quiet motion of the novel brings Belinda to the point of self-recognition. Finally she is aware that others regard her life as "pathetic" and that she really has no answer for them. But that acceptance only leads her to a self-knowledge so ingrained that it allows her to lose the pain of self-awareness. . . .

In places Miss Pym directs the reader's response to her characters too firmly, noting, for example, that Belinda spoke "loyally" or "irrelevantly." But nothing else suggests the typical rough edges of a first novel. *Some Tame Gazelle* is a completely controlled and realized consideration of the themes to which this unusually consistent writer returned in her nine succeeding novels, even when, as in *Less Than Angels* or *Quartet in Autumn,* she moved her setting from a country parish to a more anonymous London. This novel has all the quiet skill, the tough, reasonable wit and, above all, the calm integrity of Barbara Pym's best work. (p. 18)

> *Michael Gorra, "Restraint Is the Point," in* The New York Times Book Review, *July 31, 1983, pp. 12, 18.*

FRANCES TALIAFERRO

Quite early in *Some Tame Gazelle,* Belinda Bede quietly reflects on her life: "There was something frightening and at the same time comforting about the sameness of it all." Barbara Pym's admirers will sigh with pleasure, reassured that we can still breathe the pure serene of that sameness, still make the acquaintance of those menopausal virgins, those comely curates, those clerics and ladies in a mild and civilized dither. . . . The date [of the novel's original publication]—1950—is of little importance. Pym's characters move in a parish frieze as timeless as the procession on the Grecian Urn, but Keats's pastoral was a cold one, and with few exceptions the world of Barbara Pym is clement and comfortable. (p. 74)

The comforts of ritual are part of the pleasure of reading and rereading Barbara Pym. Characters behave exactly as they are expected to: Count Bianco can last only a few months without proposing to Harriet; the Archdeacon can be counted on to lace

his sermons with quotations from *Urn Burial* and Young's *Night Thoughts;* in a burst of enthusiasm Harriet will begin to knit a pullover for the current curate, and Belinda will more soberly finish it. The conversation at a dinner party will predictably include such subjects as the picturesque costume of the ancient Etruscans, and someone will always make one of those well-meant, inept comments that Barbara Pym records with such relish. (In this case, the Bishop of Mbawawa remarks of the soup, "It reminds me of our native fermented porridge.")

As if to acknowledge her interest in such rituals, Barbara Pym includes anthropologists in several of her later novels, but her true kinship (as has often been pointed out) is with her predecessors among the novelists of manners. *Some Tame Gazelle* often echoes Jane Austen, particularly in the characterization of the sisters and in the ironic symmetries of its gentle plot. Barbara Pym has Trollope's gift for distinguishing and choreographing a large cast of characters; with Angela Thirkell, the other Barsetshire novelist, she shares a sense of humor that alternates between donnish wordplay and a giddy appreciation of the ridiculous.

Barbara Pym is, however, very much herself. One reads her not only for civility and order—one can find them in the opening chapters of most country-house murder mysteries—but also for the delicacy with which she perceives small climatic variations in the temperate zone of the emotions. Many readers will feel that *Some Tame Gazelle* lacks the depth of Barbara Pym's reflective last novel, *A Few Green Leaves.* I think this early book succeeds at something more difficult: it is that literary miracle, an entertaining novel whose two central characters are intelligent, contented, and good. (p. 75)

> *Frances Taliaferro, in a review of "Some Tame Gazelle," in* Harper's, *Vol. 267, No. 1599, August, 1983, pp. 74-5.*

CHRISTINE B. VOGEL

The last of Barbara Pym's novels to be made available in the United States, *Some Tame Gazelle,* written in 1950, was actually the first published in England. In it the author of *Excellent Women* and *No Fond Return of Love* introduces readers to what has become known as the "World of Pym"—English country villages with their population of middle-aged spinsters, clergymen and a gaggle of assorted village eccentrics and visitors.

Harriet and Belinda Bede, the heroines of *Some Tame Gazelle* are two of Pym's many "excellent women." They are middle-aged, unmarried, religious (Church of England, naturally) and endlessly willing to give of themselves to those around them. . . .

Surrounding these two wonderfully realized ladies is a cast of equally memorable supporting characters. (p. 1)

Nothing much actually happens in *Some Tame Gazelle,* for Pym is a minimalist when it comes to storyline. What does occur is the ordinary goings-on of country life. The archdeacon's garden party, his sermon on Judgment Day and an evensong and a slide presentation by a visiting bishop are probably the novel's highlights. Yet from such simple stuff Pym has fashioned a precise portrait of human experience, using delicate irony, penetrating insight, and genuinely delightful humor.

Much as Jane Austen's miniaturized world of the provincial gentry of Regency England is well suited to her examination of social mores and pretensions, so the circumscribed existence of Pym's characters serves as a perfect backdrop for her finely targeted psychological portraits.... Pym's people are those one might see every day yet never notice because they are so commonplace and unexciting, concerned more with boiled chicken and knitted vests than with dioxin spills and thermonuclear war.

But Pym gives them importance. She shows us their thinking, details their small comforts, exposes their essential solitude, all without sentimentality. She demonstrates, particularly in the case of Belinda Bede, that the state of being alone can be a vocation more worthy of praise than pity.

In addition, throughout *Some Tame Gazelle,* Pym shows a particular gift for illustrating, totally without cruelty, the ways in which the faintest glimmer of romance can turn her sensible spinsters and aging gentlemen into absolute twits.

I've no doubt that those who have savored Barbara Pym's later novels will find much to please them here. And those, making a first acquaintance with her, will surely be delighted, moved and impelled to seek out other works by a novelist who was once—but is certainly no longer—obscure. (p. 14)

> *Christine B. Vogel, "A Sip of Pym's Number One,"*
> in Book World—The Washington Post, *August 21,*
> *1983, pp. 1, 14.*

PETER KEMP

Disappointment is a theme that never let Barbara Pym down.... [Her novels'] titles—*Less Than Angels, No Fond Return of Love, The Sweet Dove Died*—often wryly acknowledge life's fallings-short. Their narratives—resembling some mix of *Cranford* and *Crockford* in their singular congregations of spinsters and ministers—quizzically chronicle the rueful, resilient strategies by which genteel celibates try to fend off feelings of loneliness and unfulfilment.

A Very Private Eye—'a kind of autobiography composed of extracts from Barbara Pym's letters and journals from 1932 to 1979, and following her from student at an Oxford college to spinster in an Oxfordshire cottage—brings out the closeness of these fictional concerns to her life. One of 'the unwanted lovers of this world', like so many of her protagonists, she eventually found herself settling, with self-amused chagrin, into an existence offering 'no intense joy but small compensations, spinsterish delights'. When *A Very Private Eye* opens, though, this seems a remote prospect. The Barbara Pym who bounds into view as an undergraduate is an unexpectedly extrovert figure....

Milton's presence on the scene is just one of many indications of Barbara Pym's passionate attachment to English poetry. The first undergraduate she fell for aroused her interest by reciting 'To His Coy Mistress'. More usually, though, it's poetry's power to console, not stimulate, that attracts her. Depressions brought on by the foundering of love affairs are eased by disconsolate leafings through *The Oxford Book of Victorian Verse* in search of 'appropriate lines' to chime in with her jangled feelings. Initially, this gingerly application of the purple patch to the emotional wound can seem somewhat theatrical. But, in later life, apt allusions are handled with a plucky irony worthy of the most mettlesome moments in her fiction. Learning that she has a cancer of the breast, she jokes, '"Oh little lump"'—almost a subject for a metaphysical poem'.

The Barbara Pym audible in such utterances seems so distinct from the gushing girl of the first entries as to be almost another person. And as if aware that her Oxford persona didn't represent her true self, she gave her a different name—'Sandra', an alter ego personifying the dashing figure she wanted to cut. Sandra, however, wasn't fated to last long, being dispatched by a traumatic affair with an older student. Jilted by him, Barbara Pym dropped with startling abruptness from Sandra's kittenishness into premature middle age. At 25, in letters quivering with pained and painful sprightliness, she is regularly referring to herself as 'a spinster lady who has been crossed in love', 'this old brown spinster', 'this poor old spinster'. Consolidating this, all her subsequent involvements with men turned out to be letdowns. Gradually, she opted for 'a quieter, narrower kind of life ... Bounded by English Literature and the Anglican Church and small pleasures.' From the heart of it, she wrote her books.

A sense of having missed out was their source as well as subject. This made the halting of her fictional career in 1963 doubly hurtful. (p. 23)

The three rather autobiographical novels published after her long silence demonstrate [her refusal to abandon writing or ignore her situation's reality].... *The Sweet Dove Died*—'a chunk of my life'—is, for all the suaveness of its comedy, resolutely unsparing about emotional humiliations and makeshifts. *Quartet in Autumn*—a novel about obsolescence, written as she approached retirement, and containing an ultimate in Barbara Pym's studies of want: a character who wastes away through malnourishment—brings a brisk matter-of-factness to its surveys of slow decline. Her last book, *A Few Green Leaves,* constitutes an outstanding feat of undauntedness. Aware—as *A Very Private Eye* makes clear—that she was dying when she wrote it, she fills it with equally contemplated intimations of mortality.... Ripely, [*A Few Green Leaves*] represents a culmination of that quiet, cheery stoicism she so rewardingly portrays and disappointedly practised. (p. 24)

> *Peter Kemp, "'One of the Unwanted Lovers of This*
> *World'," in* The Listener, *Vol. 112, No. 2869, Au-*
> *gust 2, 1984, pp. 23-4.*

GAIL POOL

A Very Private Eye is, as the editors intended, "another book by Barbara Pym": a collection of her diaries, working notebooks and letters to close friends.... Despite the book's subtitle ["An Autobiography in Diaries and Letters"], it isn't an autobiography—there are far too many gaps—but that doesn't necessarily diminish it. In the externals, Pym's life doesn't seem to have been especially eventful. Of most interest is Pym's unusual sensibility, which created the peculiar world of her fiction and which we can follow through this selective record.

A Very Private Eye reveals that when Pym was quite young she had already mapped out the terrain she and her fictional characters would inhabit. It is striking that early on she assumed the role of spinster, a role which her fiction explored in depth.... Even in her first novel, *Some Tame Gazelle,* begun when she was only 21 and based largely on people she knew at Oxford, Pym figures as a spinster of 50, living with her sister, participating in village affairs and still nurturing a flame for her first love (Henry), now the archdeacon and married to someone else.

Of course, at this early stage, Pym's spinster persona is partly humorous. *Some Tame Gazelle* and her letters to Henry and [his wife] Elsie are meant to be satirical, and her Oxford diaries show Pym is aware of the social comedy she creates in seeking Henry out, arranging to be at certain places at certain times so she will "happen" to meet him, much as her heroines will do in the novels. But the spinster image is not treated with such humor in the war journals, as Pym, 30 and involved in a series of messy attachments, finds the role becoming reality. (pp. 88-9)

Why Pym, a dynamic and apparently popular young woman, should have assumed the role of spinster so early is somewhat puzzling. But, in a sense, the role provided her with her life's work. She explored the position and the point of view of the single woman, and even when she allowed her heroines to marry, she lavished most of her attention on their unmarried state.

After the war, Pym's diaries become working notebooks filled with tiny details and bits of observation, as one would expect from a novelist whose work was characterized by—and criticized for—its emphasis on trivia.

"What is wrong with being obsessed with trivia?" Pym wrote in 1970. "Some have criticised *The Sweet Dove* for this. What are the minds of my critics filled with? What *nobler* and more worthwhile things?" At the simplest level Pym felt, as she wrote in 1943, that "it adds to the pleasure of life to notice things," but her "obsession" went much deeper and was intrinsic to her world view. Ordinary people living ordinary lives—her main fictional interest—*were* obsessed with trivia, Pym believed.... Life, in both its pleasant and its unpleasant aspects, is largely a matter of detail for Pym's characters. Her heroines aren't entirely satisfied with living at this level, but they come to terms with it.

This was much the case with Pym herself, who delighted in ordinary life ... but wasn't satisfied without the "extraordinary," which for her meant writing....

Pym's journals of the 1960s and 1970s show her coming to terms with ordinariness, settling into village life with her divorced sister, Hilary, much as she had prophesied in *Some Tame Gazelle*. They also show her coming to terms with failing health: breast cancer in 1971, a mild stroke in 1974. And they show her taking literary success, when it finally came, in her stride, moving on, making notes for a new novel, not dwelling on regrets. (p. 89)

A Very Private Eye is a moving account. As in the novels, much of the emotion is off the page, and its impact may hit us only upon reflection.... As the editors intended, the autobiography illuminates the fiction. It does so almost too well, forcing us to see the limitations of all happy endings. (p. 90)

Gail Pool, "Excellent Women," in The Nation, *Vol. 239, No. 3, August 4-11, 1984, pp. 88-90.*

ROSEMARY DINNAGE

In 1966 Barbara Pym records in her diary that she is reading an account of someone that "made me laugh—people lying ill in the Dorchester and dying in Claridges." "My own story," she goes on, "judiciously edited from these notebooks would be subtler and more amusing." This reinforces the feeling given by the diaries [of *A Very Private Eye*] that, frank and entertaining as they are, they conceal as well as reveal. For

what *is* Barbara Pym's own story? Why did she choose the words "subtle" and "amusing" for it, and do they quite fit the life history as told in diaries and letters here? The "story" ostensibly is the quiet progress of an unmarried lady novelist who produced ten books, very gently satiric ones. (p. 15)

It seems that in life and in fiction Barbara Pym could not envisage the plot of woman gratified or triumphant. Even "splendid," which might mean something quite different, to her means being stoical in dreary circumstances. Perhaps she needed to write so much that love affairs were deliberately chosen for their fruitlessness; a friend, she reports, "thinks perhaps this is the kind of love I've always wanted because absolutely *nothing* can be done about it." ...

The diaries show little sign of introspection and psychological complication. When they are not concerned with the various men preoccupying her they act as a kind of ragbag for the odd and Pym-like observation. Lunch hours, for instance, she makes rather a specialty of: overheard conversations in the Kardomah café in Kingsway, rambles around City churchyards where shabby dignified women drink coffee from plastic cups. She keeps modestly up with the times: John Lennon, so "like a very plain middle-aged Victorian female novelist." ...

Interspersed among the later diaries are her letters to the poet Philip Larkin, first an epistolary admirer and then, after a nervous meeting, a friend. Larkin, something of a male, poetic Pym (or alternatively she was something of a female, prose Larkin) was an ideal correspondent and the letters seem to hover on the verge of laughter....

Few diaries give us the whole person and the whole life; most diarists make it a receptacle for a particular kind of diary-fodder, and this is true here. We have to glimpse the life sometimes across gaps and between lines. For one thing, in spite of the numberless references to things ecclesiastical, we do not know anything about Barbara Pym's faith—whether it was fiery or *terre-á-terre*, whether it had remained solid since childhood or had fluctuated. Clearly it was central to her life....

So can her book lead us to understand how it was that she saw her story as "subtle" and "amusing"? It might have had the makings of being tragic, but avoided that. Perhaps it was amusing because, at the least, she never ceased to be an entertainer; and subtle, because she was a subtle person. "Comic and sad and indefinite" sums it up best, as it does all our lives:

> "I'm so glad you write *happy* endings," said Mabel. "After all, life isn't really so unpleasant as some writers make out, is it?" she added hopefully.
>
> "No, perhaps not. It's comic and sad and indefinite—dull, sometimes, but seldom really tragic or deliriously happy, except when one's very young."

(p. 16)

Rosemary Dinnage, "Comic, Sad, Indefinite," in The New York Review of Books, *Vol. XXXI, No. 13, August 16, 1984, pp. 15-16.*

PUBLISHERS WEEKLY

Cause for rejoicing—a fine new Pym novel! A very early work written just as World War II began in 1939, *Crampton Hodnet* is a romantic comedy about unsuitable attachments set in a quintessentially Pym world of spinsters, clergy and academics in North Oxford in the 1930s. The plot is more slight than those spun by the mature Pym, but charmed by the sharp characterizations and the brilliant dialogue, readers will overlook its flaws. Pym enunciates here a theme that she probes more searchingly in her later books—the difficulties of reconciling romantic fantasy with the reality of life. . . . [The novel] adds to our knowledge of Pym as a writer and as a person. But these are secondary virtues: this very funny novel can stand on its own as entertaining fare.

> *A review of "Crampton Hodnet," in* Publishers Weekly, *Vol. 227, No. 16, April 19, 1985, p. 69.*

ALICE DIGILIO

Crampton Hodnet is a novel held together not so much by its plot or characters as by its tone—a tone which, in its self-deprecatory wryness is instantly recognizable as Barbara Pym's.

Pym wrote most of the novel in 1939, set it aside during the war, and then grew disenchanted and turned to other more promising work, like her masterful *Some Tame Gazelle*. Ultimately, she felt, *Crampton Hodnet* had become dated and unpublishable. Today, we can see how wrong she was, for *Crampton Hodnet* is not only publishable, it is timeless. The story is set in Oxford during the '30s—most particularly that uppercrust enclave on the university's outskirts called North Oxford. Like many such neighborhoods North Oxford never changes very much. Barbara Pym satirizes its quirks and self-importance with gentle glee.

The cast of characters will be familiar to Pymites: two spinsters, in this case an older Miss Doggett and her thirty-ish companion Miss Morrow; the obligatory young curate, Mr. Latimer, a lodger in Miss Doggett's house; Francis Cleveland, a middle-aged don, his frumpy but likable wife Margaret and their beautiful daughter Anthea; plus a succession of undergraduates, college masters, clergymen and dons.

If *Crampton Hodnet* has a problem, it is that Pym seems never to have made up her mind whose consciousness would anchor the novel. She bounces us from Miss Morrow's to Francis Cleveland's, to Mr. Latimer's point of view, to name only a few, in dizzying succession. They all have their contributions to make to her finely drawn portrait of their small world, but Pym might have been wiser to let Miss Morrow, whose sensibility and wit seems so nearly her own, lead us through the novel's episodes.

> *Alice Digilio, "Teatime at Oxford," in* Book World— The Washington Post, *June 9, 1985, p. 9.*

PAUL BAILEY

This determinedly jolly little novel [*Crampton Hodnet*] was written in 1939 and 1940. . . .

For such an early work, the writing and plotting are extraordinarily assured. The narrative breezes along in the merriest possible way. Almost everything is played for laughs in this one of all Barbara Pym's books that can be accurately described as a performance. Miss Doggett, the nosy old spinster, and her paid companion, Jessie Marrow, are much more obviously comic in *Crampton Hodnet* than they are in the later *Jane and Prudence,* where the comedy is tempered by irony. Miss Morrow is by far the most interesting and sympathetic of the North Oxford performers if only because the head on her shoulders

seems to be functioning intelligently. Her thoughts give *Crampton Hodnet* what depth it has, which isn't much.

Yet the book is funny, at times almost a hoot—to use the appropriate period word. It's like a parody of the later fiction, a cheerful send-up of that same material she turned to melancholic purpose. Romantic attachments in *Crampton Hodnet* are especially ludicrous, none more so than that between dark-eyed Barbara Bird and her handsome, middle-aged tutor Francis Cleveland.

A certain cynicism lies buried beneath the jauntiness. . . . Love, it is implied, is a tiresome inconvenience, a waste of time and energy, particularly when the object of a girl's high-minded affections is such an ineffectual drip.

Francis is not isolated in his drippiness. *Crampton Hodnet* could be read as a feminist tract in cosy disguise, given the chronic inadequacies of its male characters. The sharp Miss Morrow rejects Mr Latimer's proposal of marriage with a justified sense of rightness: she knows a curate on the look-out for a drudge when she sees one. Mr Killigrew, wearing crêpe-soled shoes that guarantee that he won't be heard when he creeps up on people, is a nasty neuter gathering gossip for the ancient mother who rules over him. Simon Beddoes is a philanderer whose small talk sounds mechanical, and Michael and Gabriel, the homosexuals who do *entrechats* in the park, are the true ancestors of Sandy and Julian, of beloved memory from 'Round the Horne' and 'Beyond Our Ken.' The male, in North Oxford in 1935, was decidedly the weaker of the species.

Barbara Pym, so cruelly neglected for most of her writing life, is now being over-praised. It is common practice to compare her with Jane Austen, whose art transcends the charming, the pleasingly ironic. The depth of understanding of the human heart displayed in 'Persuasion' was beyond Miss Pym's engaging powers, as it is beyond those of the majority of novelists. It's as well to remember that, in our anxiety to do this talented author belated justice.

> *Paul Bailey, "Period Hoot," in* The Observer, *June 30, 1985, p. 23.*

PICO IYER

Pym's patient, diffident women—blue of stocking, not of blood—treat life as if it were a book they were not writing, but reading. So too, Pym is determined to have almost no designs upon the reader, no great expectations, no intricate patterns except in her plot. Her charm lies in her innocence of literary fashion, her willingness to sew together a series of shrewd observations into nothing more, nor less, than a solid, old-fashioned entertainment.

From the deflationary title of *No Fond Return of Love* to its benevolent conclusion, Pym restricts herself to the narrow imaginative limits occupied by her unprepossessing heroine. Like the rest of Pym's fiction, this novel resembles nothing so much as a cramped, somewhat lonely little bed-sitter complete with floral wallpaper, well-made bed and pot of strong tea. Psychically, the weather forecast always calls for mild drizzle; the menu generally offers up macaroni cheese, tomato soup and boiled potatoes, with Nescafe for pudding; the dramatis personae include nobody except timid scholars, spinsterish researchers and bachelor clergymen. And all the excellent women are, of course, themselves vicars—unrewarded consolers and confession-takers who choose to live vicariously.

Pym catches the tiny tremors and shy sorrows of these women manqués with such glancing precision, balancing amusement and sympathy so evenly (and instinctively) that every incident becomes, as the heroine regards a friend, "at once comic and pathetic." Her eye infallibly alights upon all the humble objects that are, as she puts it, "mean" unless or until they are transfigured by sentiment. Above all, she expertly calibrates the gradations of embarrassment, regret and disappointment. "Life," she ventures, "is often cruel in small ways." The sentences that stick here, and the sentences that sting, are always spoken softly: "It is sad, she thought, how women longed to be needed and useful and how seldom most of them really were," or "Perhaps it is sadder to have loved somebody 'unworthy' and the end of it is the death of such a very little thing, like a child's coffin."

The transforming grace of Pym's measured compassion is that she brings to her sheltered characters the same strict wistfulness they bring to the world, yet treats their lackluster good nature no more kindly than does the world. Many of her heroines are as polite, well-meaning and earnest as Paddington Bear; their element is innocence, and their natural environment a schoolgirl's world of crushes and mild-mannered schemes, lessons and secret treats. They are still guileless enough to regard a librarian as glamorous, compare an old professor to Rupert Brooke, listen with beating hearts to a lecture on "the terrors and triumphs of setting out a bibliography correctly." And in the end, their deepest sorrow is that they are unable to abandon this sweet naivete, yet much too sensible to allow themselves the luxury of foolishness or hope. The absence of glitter from their lives is only made the sorrier by the absence of illusions; the inalienable sadness of Pym's forgotten characters lies less in the drabness of their lives than in their steady and unsentimental acknowledgement of that drabness. (pp. 289-90)

Pym's women are, in addition, much too practical to linger on their disappointments: they recognize that these must be borne bravely, and alone. And their sadness is tenacious because it involves no bitterness and no prospect of epiphany. Their lives, the heroine thinks, have "the inevitability of Greek drama."

But in reality, of course, her life proves to be all inevitability and no drama, all sorrow and no sweep. It is not a dark star that hangs over such destinies, just a very dim one. (p. 290)

Though Pym's devices are certainly [careful] . . . , they refuse to draw attention to themselves. Pym is content to allow features to remain features without becoming themes. Thus the names in her novel are by no means carelessly chosen, but nor are they transparent: the still pretty, but entirely unromantic heroine is called "Dulcie" (though she does in a moment of panic seize upon the alias of Miss Lamb).

When the brave, goodhearted, lonely heroine is seen through the eyes of her sweet eighteen year-old niece—as a bland, joyless dullard—we do not see so much as feel her hurt. And though Christianity is a constant presence in Pym's novels, their mater-of-fact moral is that the meek, however blessed, will not inherit the earth.

Pym takes trouble all the while to observe the rules of storytelling. She organizes her fiction with brisk aplomb and drives her story forward at a smart, spritely pace. Every strand of plot is assiduously tied together with an economy and a reliance on coincidence that makes her universe a small world as well as a world of small horizons. Although she indulges herself cautiously by obliquely defending her art ("People blame one for dwelling on trivialities . . . but life is made up of them," muses Dulcie, while a housekeeper assures her elsewhere, "Oh, I know it's a trivial detail, but these are the things that make up life, aren't they."), she makes few claims for it. Notably conscientious toward her reader, she tells her story and, when it is finished, stops. She does what she can do, and nothing more.

This can, on occasion, make her universe almost suffocatingly cosy. . . . It also means that one of her books is almost indistinguishable from another and that her entire oeuvre can be—as a Pym character might put it—quite pleasant, but a little tiresome. (pp. 290-91)

Pico Iyer, "Tricks of Self-Consciousness," in Partisan Review, *Vol. LII, No. 3, 1985, pp. 286-91.**

Peter (Levin) Shaffer

1926-

(Has also collaborated with Anthony Shaffer under joint pseudonym of Peter Antony) English dramatist, scriptwriter, novelist, and critic.

Shaffer is best known for his popular dramas *Equus* (1973) and *Amadeus* (1979). He has earned a reputation for consistent craftsmanship through his work in several theatrical genres, including domestic tragedy, farce, short and extended revue, and psychological and historical drama. Shaffer's plays, which often involve such themes as love, death, and salvation, explore the moral values of his characters. He is by his own admission "fascinated by the endless ambiguity of the human situation, of the conflict between two different kinds of right."

Shaffer has never been linked to a particular dramatic movement, and he has demonstrated his versatility with each new play. His first play, *Five Finger Exercise* (1958), is a domestic drama in which a German tutor in a middle-class English home is mistakenly accused of seducing his employer's wife. The play ends on an ambiguous note as the tutor attempts suicide and the family is forced to reexamine their definitions of loyalty and trust. This work won the New York Drama Critics Circle Award for Best Foreign Play in 1960. Shaffer's next production, the double bill of *The Private Ear* and *The Public Eye* (1962), achieved commercial success despite a general reluctance on the part of English playgoers to attend one-act plays. The first play concerns a shy clerk's realization that a girl for whom he cares falls short of his fantasies; the second is about a detective who attempts to convince a client that suspicions regarding his wife's fidelity are unfounded and may be rooted in a subconscious desire to control her. The farcical structure of a later one-act play, *Black Comedy* (1965), revolves around a device Shaffer borrowed from Japanese Kabuki theater. As the characters are seen stumbling around a well-lighted stage in imaginary darkness, their identities and actions become hilariously confused.

Shaffer's most successful dramas are based in myth and explore the psychological motivations of his characters. His innovative use of masks, music, and dance illuminate thematic concerns, and his conflicts are developed through characters who function as dramatic foils. *The Royal Hunt of the Sun* (1964) reenacts the sixteenth-century conquest of Atahualpa's Inca empire by Spanish conquistador Francisco Pizarro. The play focuses on the debased qualities of both characters and the relationship that evolves between them. The psychological drama *Equus*, for which Shaffer received the Antoinette Perry (Tony) Award and the New York Drama Critics Circle Award in 1975, explores the spiritually-based motivations of a stable boy who is institutionalized after blinding six horses that he believes are deities. The boy's disillusioned psychiatrist faces his own personal conflict when he questions whether the boy's "treatment" will strip him of a rare and precious spiritual passion, thus relegating him to a mundane, normative existence. Shaffer's exploration of the human psyche culminates in *Amadeus,* a drama of jealousy and revenge which he describes as "a fantasia on events in Mozart's life." In this play, a successful court composer of moderate ability contemplates

© Jerry Bauer

with bitter irony why his pious devotion to God has been ignored, while the vulgar, self-centered Mozart is blessed with genius. Realizing that God chose to reward him by allowing him to recognize the power of Mozart's music, the composer takes his ultimate revenge on God and humankind by poisoning his rival. *Amadeus* won a Tony Award in 1981.

Shaffer has also contributed to screenplay adaptations of *Equus* and *Amadeus*. While the film *Equus* was faulted by critics for its simplistic symbolism, the film *Amadeus* earned international praise. A collaboration between Shaffer, director Milos Forman, and producer Saul Zaentz, *Amadeus* won an Academy Award for Best Picture, and Shaffer received an Academy Award for Best Screenplay Adaptation.

(See also *CLC*, Vols. 5, 14, 18; *Contemporary Authors*, Vols. 25-28, rev. ed.; and *Dictionary of Literary Biography*, Vol. 13.)

In this volume commentary on Peter Shaffer is focused on the film adaptation of his drama *Amadeus*.

DAVID DENBY

I sat through *Amadeus,* Milos Forman and Peter Shaffer's [film] adaptation of Shaffer's popular play, with painfully divided feelings. Some of this exuberant, large-scale movie is charming and inventive, and some of it is pitifully trashy.... Shaffer and Mozart—what a combination! Peter Shaffer is an author of overemphatic middlebrow problem plays, Mozart the supreme instance of the unknowability of genius.

Mozart's ease is baffling, insolent, finally heartrending. He never overwhelms your senses; most of his music isn't even *loud.* Yet an unexpected modulation, a woodwind commenting quietly above the melodic line, a blending of two voices, and suddenly you are cast into a state of almost unbearable melancholy. He can be subtle—no wonder most of his contemporaries were indifferent to him. In Prague, Mozart was a genuine popular success, but in Vienna, where he lived most of the last ten years of his life, he was merely one of many composers turning out music for court, concerts, opera houses, and private homes; he was fashionable for a while and then forgotten.

It is Shaffer's conceit that only one of Mozart's Viennese contemporaries, the immensely successful court composer Antonio Salieri, actually "heard" Mozart—that Salieri alone had a modern conception of Mozart's qualities. Decades after Mozart's death, it was rumored that Salieri had accused himself of poisoning the young composer. From this sensational and probably fictional instance of neurotic self-loathing, Shaffer has woven a gaudy tale. The entire movie is told from the point of view of the old man. In the play, Salieri spoke directly to the audience; in the movie, he speaks to a priest eager to hear his confession. In his youth, he says, his envy of Mozart turned into a quarrel with God. He, Salieri, asked nothing more than to serve God with music, yet God chose to make him a mediocrity and to speak instead ... through the work of an eccentric, bumbling, and loutish *boy.* Salieri vows to destroy Mozart in order to revenge himself on God.

The movie shows Mozart's years in Vienna through the prism of Salieri's envy.... [The] material has been conceived as a comedy of humiliation, with the inept Mozart invariably making a fool of himself in front of the powerful men who might help him if he would only act properly subservient....

The portrait is only a partial truth: Mozart may have been inept, but he did grow up around aristocrats, and some of their manners must have rubbed off on him.... [In the film, Mozart] is just a nice American kid running around in a wig.... [He] doesn't convey the sense of depths hidden away, and maybe Forman didn't want him to....

[However, Salieri] uses his big nose, thick eyebrows, and dark beard for their full weight of misery. When Salieri hears Mozart's music, [he] appears to be entering paradise and hell at the same time—he looks ecstatic yet stricken. The most entertaining and emotionally satisfying scenes in *Amadeus* begin with Salieri's responses to Mozart's work. Shaffer and Forman give us a kind of high-powered music-appreciation lesson, in which Salieri, masochistically proud of his powers of discrimination, celebrates the beauties of the adagio movement of the Serenade in B-flat for Thirteen Winds....

For anyone who's ever cared for Mozart, this sort of thing is irresistible—perhaps the juiciest dramatization in movie history of the emotional power of classical music. We get to hear the music with "modern" ears...; at the same time, we watch the period productions, which are buoyant and funny. (p. 93)

Salieri's narration allows Forman to jump in and out of scenes quickly.... It's Shaffer's dramaturgy that wears us down. Shaffer, who has a fondness for heavyweight ironies and dialectical oppositions, keeps pounding away at Salieri's envy and his complaint against God—scene after scene of this ranting stuff. The quarrel with God is a familiar, hammy property of the "serious" Broadway/West End theater, and it doesn't mean much to an audience eager to understand the source of supreme talent and murderous envy.

Does Shaffer spend so much time with Salieri because Mozart eludes his understanding, too? His Salieri talks of Mozart as if he were a later version of Jesus—literally the incarnation of God's voice—and the movie supports this grandiose, melodramatic, and creepy idea. Jesus returns, carrying the Word, and again he's betrayed. But in an odd way, this view of Mozart does more to belittle than glorify him, for if Mozart speaks with the voice of God, he is no longer the author of his own talent, and his painful education at his father's hands and endless hard work mean nothing. Shaffer keeps insisting that Mozart destroys the peace of self-confident mediocrities, but actually the notion of the composer as God's dummy—a sort of divine Charlie McCarthy—is consoling to mediocrities.

The last third of *Amadeus* is a lurid disaster. Giddy from his own conceit of a betrayed Jesus-Mozart, Shaffer wildly misrepresents Mozart's relations to his wife and father and goes way past Salieri's self-accusation of murder by poison. This Salieri murders Mozart by sadistically driving him crazy.... (p. 94)

What Shaffer and the other melodramatists of Mozart's early death cannot admit is that Mozart, tired of failing in Vienna, largely withdrew in his final years; he no longer *cared* that much.... Like millions of other young people in the eighteenth century, he just *died.* This is unbearably tragic, but it's useless to imply, as this movie does, that his society was unworthy of him and that *we* would have had the taste and courage to appreciate his genius. Actually, the society that turned away from Mozart was probably the only one that could have produced him. If he had been lucky enough to live another twenty years, his audience would have caught up to him.... In his early death, there is cause for grief, but not for all this tearful breast-beating. (pp. 94-5)

David Denby, "Mozartomania," in New York Magazine, *Vol. 17, No. 38, September 24, 1984, pp. 93-6.**

PETER SHAFFER

The cinema is a worrying medium for the stage playwright to work in. Its unverbal essence offers difficulties to anyone living largely by the spoken word. Increasingly, as American films grow ever more popular around the world, it is apparent that the most successful are being spoken in Screenspeak, a kind of cinematic esperanto equally comprehensible in Bogota and Bulawayo. For example, dialogue in heavy-action pictures, horrific or intergalactic, now consists almost entirely of the alternation of two single words—a cry and a whisper—needing translation nowhere on the planet: *'Lessgidowdaheer!'* and *'Omygaad!'* Mastery of this new tongue is not easy for older writers.

Equally dismaying has to be the endemic restlessness of filmgoers. In his mind's ear as he writes for the live theatre, the dramatist can presume the attentiveness of his audience: its mutual agreement to listen, and to remain in one place while the performance is going on. No such agreement exists among movie audiences. Indeed the very word 'movie' nowadays can as accurately describe the viewers of films as films themselves. I never really understood the meaning of the phrase 'upward mobility' until I had experienced a Manhattan cinema on a recent Saturday night. (pp. 50-1, 56)

[But] for the enthusiasm of Milos Forman I doubt if there would be a film of *Amadeus* at all. He met me in London after the very first preview of the play . . . and declared without hesitation that what I had actually written was a natural film, and that if I were ever willing to let him do so, he would direct it. In this assertion he persisted for two years.

Persistence was coupled with perceptiveness. When finally I cautiously agreed to explore the possibility of working with him, he sensed quite plainly my . . . dissatisfaction with all previous films of my own plays in particular. When I asked him what he would do with my piece, he told me what he would *not* do: turn it into a stagey hybrid, neither play nor picture. He also pointed out that the film of a play is really a new work, another fulfillment of the same impulse which had created the original. . . . During this process a fair amount of demolition work would go on, some of it perhaps painful to the author. In the case of *Amadeus,* its operatic stylization would probably have to go, and its language would have to be made less formal, though not, of course, more juvenile.

Actually, my own personal taste in cinema inclines very much to the operatic and stylized—the opening sequence of *The Magnificent Ambersons,* for example, or the iconographic groupings in the First Part of *Ivan the Terrible*—but I also sensed, as we talked, how this vigorous man's brand of naturalism, infused with his huge humor and his obvious passion for my material, might make an enthralling new thing out of it. The possibility of working with him was suddenly very tempting. . . .

From the start we agreed upon one thing: we were not making an objective Life of Wolfgang Mozart. This cannot be stressed too strongly. Obviously *Amadeus* on stage was never intended to be a documentary biography of the composer, and the film is even less of one. Certainly we have incorporated many real elements, new as well as true. . . . But we are also blatantly claiming the grand license of the storyteller to embellish his tale with fictional ornament and, above all, to supply it with a climax whose sole justification need be that it enthralls his audience and emblazons his theme. I believe that we have created just such a climax for the film of *Amadeus.*

To me there is something pure about Salieri's pursuit of an eternal Absolute through music, just as there is something irredeemably impure about his simultaneous pursuit of eternal fame. The yoking of these two clearly opposed drives led us finally to devise a climax totally different from that of the play: a night-long encounter between the physically dying Mozart and the spiritually ravenous Salieri, motivated entirely by the latter's crazed lust to snatch a piece of divinity for himself. Such a scene never took place in fact. However, our concern at this point was not with facts but with the undeniable laws of drama. (p. 56)

Some people may find this new climax hard to accept. Others may rejoice in it as a horribly logical end to the legend. To me it seems the most appropriate finish to our black fantasia. Even on stage I had to create a final confrontation quite outside historical record. I had to recognize and honor the change of atmosphere from clear Enlightenment to murky Gothic which

inevitably occurred once the figure of the Masked Messenger was introduced. In the film this recognition is more carefully prepared for. Indeed the motif of masked people goes all through the picture—paralleling to some extent Mozart's own preoccupation with them. After all, the three great Da Ponte operas are all concerned with the dramatic effects of wearing disguise.

What pleased me best about this resolution is that we were able to construct a scene which is highly effective in cinematic terms, yet wholly concerned with the least visual of all possible subjects: *music itself.* I do not believe that a stage version of this scene would have been half as effective. (pp. 56-7)

[Our] joint movie is definitely the first and last of the metamorphoses of *Amadeus.* Unlike *Equus* it will not also become a ballet; unlike *The Royal Hunt of the Sun* it will not become an opera. Above all, and no matter how fortunate our effort may prove in its reception, it will spawn no sequels. There will be no television series of half-hour dramas in which Salieri plots a different method of murdering Mozart each week, only to be frustrated by the wily little genius in the twenty-ninth minute. Even Milos Forman will agree that there can be a limit to adaptation. (p. 57)

> *Peter Shaffer, "Mostly Mozart: Making the Screen Speak," in* Film Comment, *Vol. 20, No. 5, September-October, 1984, pp. 50-1, 56-7.*

JASCHA KESSLER

[*Amadeus*] offers us a heavy dose of pseudoprofundities, in a formulation composed of nothing but worn-out truisms. Never mind that the sets and costuming are accurately researched and opulent, and that all the character-actors mug their cameos with stock Eighteenth Century stage-mannerisms . . . movies have specialized in this flummery from the beginning. Never mind that the dialogue is what you would hear from the mouths of 12-year old Americans today, and in no way represents the speech and behavior of Austrian aristocrats and artists of the 1770's. The mass audience of the movies would like to think itself on an equal footing with the elites of the past, and in fact in fantasy it is, because the camera lets us stand in the same room with the royalty itself. . . .

However, above all the other inauthenticities of Shaffer's *Amadeus,* there are two that made this movie simply unbearable to me, though doubtless they will account for its box-office success, and . . . even help to put Mozart recordings into homes that seldom trouble with classical, that is, "Highbrow" music the way that Bo Derek's use of Ravel's "Bolero" got that piece into bedrooms and aerobics classes everywhere. The first absurdity is Shaffer's intensive attack on the Genteel. In that vulgar tradition of supposed refinement, artistic geniuses such as Mozart are angelic human beings too, as if their beautiful creations must have come from equally beautiful lives and minds. This smarmy prejudice may have come into full flower in the Nineteenth century along with the snobbery of the nouveau riche and plumbing. . . . But in fact the Genteel tradition has been dead for most of this century, and Shaffer's depiction of Mozart as an earthy fellow, and not a bloodless, porcelain figurine, is meant to shock us as though we were still under Queen Victoria's censorship. . . . It throws everything off kilter: we are not in the 1880's. The great fraudulence of *Amadeus,* however, lies in its principle theme. . . . [Salieri's] narration of Mozart's career, foreshortened to look as if it all took place in Vienna, is meant to tell us that [he] made his pact with the Devil in order to vent his rage at the God he still worships, the God who flummoxed him by creating that . . . immoral, adolescent scamp. And the point of it all is simply that this successful failure, this ambitious, obsessed Salieri cannot avoid doing God's work. Ever since Milton's *Paradise Lost,* this has been a famous "theological" chestnut. Shaffer uses this cliche most vulgarly, even making Salieri drag the *Requiem Mass* from the lips of a dying Mozart during a long night in which Salieri takes it down from dictation all the while surprised at the orchestration, and marvelling at the "divine" logic of the music, as though God himself were dictating it to him through the medium of a poisoned carcass called Amadeus. (Shaffer calls him Amadeus, by the way; Salieri calls him Mozart. How heavyhanded can you get?) It's as corny a dramatic irony as has been perpetrated in a long time, and I found this maudlin piety disgusting in the extreme. . . . If it had even remotely happened this way in historical fact, one might have had to put up with it; but this is merely a dramatic fiction. Is it Shaffer putting us on? He was after all quite serious in another piece of kitsch, the movie called *Equus.* As drama, [*Amadeus*] is not only a hackneyed, but a repulsive . . . inauthentic, way of popularizing the sublime . . . as though such a thing were possible. I think everyone who had anything to do with making [*Amadeus*], an example of cultural pretentiousness at its intellectual best today, ought to be ashamed.

> Jascha Kessler, "*Peter Shaffer: 'Amadeus',*" in a radio broadcast on KUSC-FM—Los Angeles, CA, October 12, 1984.

RICHARD A. BLAKE

For Peter Shaffer, playwright and screenwriter, the human condition is one of helpless madness. [In *Amadeus*] God descends incarnate to redeem His people and is devoured by them. . . .

Amadeus is a revenge play. Antonio Salieri . . . is the court composer to the Holy Roman Emperor Joseph II. He is dedicated to his monarch and to his God, who he prayerfully thanks for each painfully completed score. . . . When young Mozart . . . bursts on the Vienna court like the Beatles on Liverpool, Salieri is stunned. Through this foul-mouthed, bottom-pinching boor, Salieri hears "the voice of God," music more wondrous than he had ever imagined. It is unfair. Salieri, having strained his resources to achieve mediocrity, determines to destroy his young rival. . . .

How is it possible, Salieri muses, for Mozart, so crude and manifestly unworthy, to be gifted with genius? "We are all equal in the eyes of God," the priest tells him, but Salieri and everyone else know that is a lie. God anoints geniuses and trifles with the mediocre. Salieri recalls the moment when, tormented with his own limitations and the genius of Mozart, he burns his crucifix as an act of defiance against an unjust God.

By his dramatic gesture of blasphemy, Salieri moves the story into the realm of theology. He has identified Mozart's music as the voice of God. By his determination to destroy Mozart, he claims the power to frustrate the Incarnation. Here is the paradox. As a skilled student of music, he alone in all of Vienna seems to be able to appreciate the theophany that has come in the person of the crude, but gifted, adolescent from Salzburg. He alone knows that through Mozart, God has visited his people, and the thought that God has chosen such a vulgar prophet drives him to the edge of insanity.

Salieri challenges God's wisdom. By his rectitude, cold rationality and reliance on human effort, he tries to replace the God of frivolity, caprice and mystery. . . . Salieri in the closing moments glides among the mad as their patron saint. Mankind, left to its own devices and raving in its own mediocrity and rationality, holds no future. Salieri and the asylum he represents have banished hope.

Amadeus is more than two and a half hours long, but it ended all too quickly. One yearns for it to go on and on. Peter Shaffer adapted his play to the screen and Milos Forman . . . was able to fuse the psychological intent of the play with philosophical and theological questions and, importantly, with the glorious music of Wolfgang Amadeus Mozart. . . .

This was the most powerful film I have seen in a long time. Why? The characters, the Prague settings and the celestial music of Mozart, of course. But here sits Salieri, the reviewer and critic, recognizing excellence but incapable of producing it. Here rests the plight of the human condition, that furious tension between what might be and what really is. For believers, there remains the question: Why is the Incarnation so capricious? Why does the spark of divinity glow in such unlikely crevices: dissolute artists, unbearable saints?. . . Salieri could not answer those questions, and they drove him to murder and insanity. Neither could Shaffer, and they drove him to drama.

> Richard A. Blake, "God's Grandeur," in America, Vol. 151, No. 10, October 13, 1984, p. 210.

JOHN SIMON

Total eclipse . . . overtakes what is now billed grandiosely as *Peter Shaffer's Amadeus,* as if anyone else would be rash enough to claim it. Bad as the play was . . . , Shaffer's screenplay, written under the supervision of and directed by Miloš Forman, is immeasurably worse. This preposterous story contrives that Salieri—outraged that, despite a vow of chastity and service to God, he is gifted with only a middling talent . . .—vows hatred for God and destruction to Mozart. Since, despite the baseless legend about the lesser man's poisoning his great rival, the facts cannot be easily squared with anything more than Salieri's animosity toward Mozart, it is Shaffer who is the real poisoner of the well of truth with a tale whose implausibility is matched only by its vulgarity. One does, however, discern yet another chapter in Shaffer's continuous lament over his own mediocrity and inability to break with convention—themes that cropped up in *The Royal Hunt of the Sun* and *Equus* as well.

For the movie version of *Amadeus,* additional characters had to be dragged in—the allegedly despotic Leopold Mozart; the insufferable mother-in-law, Frau Weber; the spying maid, Lorl; and Schikaneder with his chicanery—while existing ones had to be beefed up. As a result, the new characters remain rushed and superficial, whereas Constanze becomes the stereotypical loving but nagging wife, a cliché from which the play's foreshortening dubiously saved her. The new scenes are often crass scatology, as when Mozart sticks out his behind at Archbishop Colloredo. . . . The play's crude Freudianizing, whereby the Commendatore is really Mozart's dead father, has been retained and grossly hammered in. . . . And it has been expanded, by having Frau Weber's stridulous yammerings at her son-in-law turn into the coloratura aria of the Queen of the Night! (pp. 56-7)

Particularly cheap is the conceit—new in the movie version—that the moribund Mozart dictated the *Requiem* to Salieri, who wrote it down in a prolonged ecstasy of love-hate. . . . Salieri turns into an orgasmic Molly Bloom even as Mozart turns into an idiot requiring the Latin text to be translated for him by Salieri so that the great unwashed in the movie audience should be able to follow—which they won't anyway.

Most appalling is the ending, with Salieri dying illogically in a lunatic asylum. Here madmen more horrific than in *Marat/Sade* are hideously chained or caged along the walls of a corridor down which Salieri is being wheeled. "Mediocrities everywhere, I absolve you," he mutters. At least in the play this referred to the audience; in the movie, even that simplistic irony becomes an abject copout. . . . Boo and *O, Weh!* (p. 57)

                                    *John Simon, "Bizet's Carmen, Shaffer's Amadeus,"
                                    in* National Review, *Vol. XXXVI, No. 20, October
                                    19, 1984, pp. 55-7.**

STANLEY KAUFFMANN

Lucky are those who see the film of **Amadeus** without having seen the play. Peter Shaffer's original was markedly different in the London and New York productions that I saw, but both of them used theatrical conceits as if they were virtuosity, when in fact they were padding for a thin body. . . . Shorn of this spurious decor, the film fares somewhat better.

Shaffer's screenplay . . . is a more straightforward narrative; it goes on too long and it heaves toward a dreadfully contrived climax, but in the main it's a visually lively piece that tells a story about Mozart and Salieri. Not *the* story: those familiar with Mozart's life may die the death of a thousand cuts unless they agree from the start to a romance. Still, that romance is presented here with much less of Shaffer's undergraduate playwriting cleverness, less tinselly rhetoric, and a lot of nice things to look at. With, of course, a great many bits of Mozart's music—bits only, yet ravishing, more than in the play and played more sonorously. . . .

The story takes off from the myth that Salieri, the Viennese court *Kapellmeister* more successful than Mozart yet jealous of him, poisoned the younger man. . . . Shaffer's notion is neither to prove nor disprove the poisoning but to assume that Salieri believes himself responsible for the death, principally because he is so jealous of Mozart. Thirty-four years later, plagued by his obsession, Salieri attempts suicide, and soon afterward dies. In the play the old man recounts the story to us, with flashbacks, as he tries to redeem himself with future generations. This abominable idea is shucked in the film: Salieri recounts the story, with flashbacks, to a priest who visits him in the hospital after the suicide attempt. The wiping off of greasepaint metaphysics—by making the narrative a straight confession—helps immensely.

It would take too much time to dwell on all the liberties with fact. Just a few samples: Where is Aloysia, Mozart's sister-in-law, so important in his life? . . . [Why] would Mozart on his deathbed dictate some of his Requiem Mass to Salieri? First, what remains of the score is in Mozart's firm hand; second, the one composer at the deathbed was, apparently, Süssmayr. But let's generously allow factual license to Shaffer as we do to Schiller for *Mary Stuart* and Brecht for *Galileo*, and see what we get in return for our generosity. (p. 30)

The fundamental question in the film, as in the play, is the justice of God. Was it just of God to make the scatological, arrogant Mozart a supreme genius, thinks Salieri, while his own decent behavior and hard work are rewarded only with serviceable talent? The justice of God is an old question in drama but, more often than not, is taken as unfathomable in mortal life, to be explained hereafter. . . . The muzziness of Shaffer's exploration is exposed by one question: Would Salieri have been any less jealous of Mozart's genius if the other man had been conventionally well spoken and modest? The implication is that Salieri is more incensed by bad manners than jealous of genius.

The very close of the film, however, has a power that the play lacked. In the play, the last lines were addressed by Salieri to the audience: "Mediocrities everywhere—now and to come—I absolve you all! Amen!" He raised his arms, and we heard a beautiful bit of Mozart. It seemed both presumptuous and self-exculpatory for Shaffer. In the film we, the future, are left out of it. Salieri is being wheeled down the corridors of the hospital through a crowd of lunatics chained to the walls, and it's to these lunatics that he speaks those lines. This gives irony, not impertinence, to his act of absolution. And the final sound is not Mozart's music but Mozart's high-pitched, irritating giggle. That's good. (pp. 31-2)

                                    Stanley Kauffmann, "Divertimento," in The New
                                    Republic, *Vol. 191, No. 3640, October 22, 1984,
                                    pp. 30-2.*

PAULINE KAEL

[*The essay from which this excerpt is taken was originally published in* The New Yorker, *October 29, 1984.*]

The story of a genius who isn't appreciated and dies in poverty has the same basic appeal whether its subject is Stephen Foster or Wolfgang Amadeus Mozart. That's not the kind of story the director Miloš Forman and the writer Peter Shaffer set out to tell in **Amadeus,** but it's essentially what they wound up with, and that appeal is probably what saves the movie from being a disaster. *Amadeus* has a very complicated surface—there's a steady stream of rhetoric about high-flown things. But after a while the rhetoric cancels itself out, and what we see is the unworldly Mozart . . . caught in a web of intrigue by his enemy, the unctuous Hapsburg court composer Salieri . . . , and worked to death, in 1791, at the age of thirty-five. (p. 249)

Peter Shaffer can give clichés a glitter, and the polarities that are his specialty may sound convincingly clever at the beginning of his plays, but when he starts to add elements the polarities are contradicted, and the conflicts become highly abstruse and drift off into the murk. (p. 250)

At first, it's quite funny when the slimy-smooth Salieri complains that his exertions—his always doing the proper thing, studying, going to church—haven't been rewarded. He's the least humble of Christians—he seems to expect God to give him exact value for every prayer he has ever delivered. (He's like a kid saying to Mommy, "I was always a good boy and ate my spinach and did my homework, but you love my brother more than you love me—and he uses dirty words and chases girls.") Salieri thinks that because he suffers so much he should be a genius.

The movie, though, by showing you Mozart as a rubber-faced grinning buffoon with a randy turn of mind, as if that were all there was to him, begins to lend credence to Salieri's mad notion that Mozart doesn't have to do a thing—that his music is a no-strings-attached, pure gift from God. The tone of many of the incidents and details is quite opaque. Are Mozart's bushy white wigs (and the sometimes faintly pinkish ones) a shaky attempt at historical fidelity, or is it Shaffer's or Forman's thought that the young audience will identify with Mozart if he's made to look like Harpo Marx as a rock star? (The effect was also used in the stage version.) Many of the scenes appear to support Salieri in his belief that Mozart's prankish obscenities and his boastfulness are proof that he's unworthy of his artistic gift. Ribald cloacal jokes were an accepted part of ordinary people's conversation in the Vienna of the day, but in the movie Mozart is the only person who seems to enjoy talking dirty. And the movie doesn't make it apparent that his scatological games and his carousing were quick vacations from his work. . . . (p. 251)

There's nothing but confusion at the heart of the movie: it's a semi-realistic musical biography of Mozart built on a madman's justification for envy. . . . The corniness in *Amadeus* is that the view of artistic accomplishment which Salieri spouts—that if art comes without plodding it must be a gift from above—is at least half shared by the writer and the director. They don't appear to register that the whole notion of dictation from God is an insult to Mozart. (pp. 251-52)

[The] use of Mozart's music to illustrate snippets of his life and to provide the film with comic (and gothic) punctuation is offensive. . . . Each time you hear the music, it invalidates the movie's bumpkin Mozart, with his hideous, high-pitched whinny-giggle. And if you've read Mozart's letters you know this twerp couldn't have written them. But Forman's crudeness is a form of showmanship—not one I respect but one I'm forced to acknowledge. He trudges through the movie as if every step were a major contribution to art, and he keeps the audience hooked the same way people were hooked by Hollywood's big, obvious, biographical epics. . . .

There are some real aberrations in this movie, such as a shot of Salieri in a cuckoo's nest where the passageways are lined with bare-chested loonies chained to the walls. . . . There's also a long deathbed sequence—the muzziest part of the movie—with Mozart, who looks as if he'd been painted light green, innocently and pathetically dictating his "Requiem" to Salieri, who's plotting to steal the music. And it's definitely one plot too many. The episode totally fuddles the fratricidal issues; Salieri seems about to echo the boy's cry to his God in *Equus*—"Make us one person." (p. 252)

> *Pauline Kael, "Mozart and Bizet," in her* State of the Art, *E. P. Dutton, 1985, pp. 249-57.**

RICHARD COMBS

The antagonists of Shaffer's plays often seem not just pairs or *doppelgängers* but twins; both their interconnectedness and their rage to differentiate themselves have a biological necessity. One might see it reflected in such incidental details as the 'doubled' chorus of *Amadeus,* the two *venticelli* (gossip-mongers) who attend Salieri, or in Shaffer's own twin-hood with the Shaffer of *Sleuth,* Anthony. . . . It's a powerful, protean theme, bursting out of the historical circumstances of Inca conquest or the musical scandals of eighteenth-century Vienna. Which is one reason why the form of his plays may be so mutable, so open to adaptation, since the passions and *angst* of 'collaboration' are so much part of their essential subject. *Amadeus* the movie, then, is both something of an anomaly, and rather hard to discuss. Its physical detail, the elaborate

period recreation and the visualisation of Mozartian opera, give the subject a solidity and finality. . . . But there is nothing in the treatment of the theme—the eternal tug of war between Salieri and Mozart over the arbitrary dispensation of divine (fatherly?) gifts—that suggests it is doing anything but passing through on its way to other metamorphoses, other collaborations.

The most significant change, in fact, between the published play and Shaffer's screenplay underlines this—a new deathbed scene for Mozart in which Salieri literally collaborates with the expiring composer, hurriedly taking down dictation for the "Requiem Mass". In the end, he comes to share in some small way in the divine gifts he had believed by rights to be his. . . . So in some small way also Salieri is elevated by this final collaboration, is perhaps even elevated by the sheer God-defying scale of his scheme to hound Mozart to his death and then claim the "Requiem Mass" . . . as his own music to be played at Mozart's funeral, usurping "God's creature" while commemorating him. . . .

On the other hand, more is made in the play than in the film of Mozart's (historical) accusation that he had been poisoned by Salieri. To the Salieri of the play, this was a lie in which he allowed Mozart to believe because it represented a truth (he had spiritually poisoned him) and because Salieri hoped thereby to achieve an ignominy which would allow him to atone for what he had done. God's revenge was that nobody believed the lie, and Salieri was sentenced "to endure thirty-two years of being distinguished . . . I survived to see myself become extinct". These differences don't affect the fate of either man, but they are permutations on character and motive, on Mozart and Salieri's relationship to each other and to God, which make the creative possibilities within their rivalry more important than an acceptable delineation of that rivalry. Shaffer's obsessions have absorbed the Salieri-Mozart story (rather than vice versa), and it seems he could go on spinning out variations on their secret, baleful relationship to fill any number of TV half-hour dramas.

The film, finally, is left to fill out one of these variations in a way that is helpful but not exactly essential. . . . Mozart's father Leopold is . . . more of a solid presence, to give psychological credence to the way Salieri will torture Mozart through his sense of guilt after the old man's death. Unfortunately, this kind of 'psychological' support doesn't add much to the cosmic family games that Shaffer is playing. Similarly, Mozart's one or two defiant speeches about creating his operas out of the stuff of real life (and his own life) instead of unchanging conventions about gods and goddesses are supported by more detailed scenes of his devising *The Magic Flute* for a popular audience. But the play is only tangentially about a revolution in the concept of the artist, or the artist as revolutionary, or the emergence of the Romantic spirit, and this material seems a curious interruption. Much of what the film does, in fact, looks like mere theatrical over-elaboration of what was theatrically more quixotic in the original. At the same time, it is hard to identify any interpretative element that is not strictly part of Shaffer's protean treatment of his theme. The auteurist finger of suspicion, however, might point at . . . Forman for the unfortunate decision to 'place' Salieri's confession in the context of a madhouse. (p. 15)

> *Richard Combs, in a review of "Amadeus," in* Monthly Film Bulletin, *Vol. 52, No. 612, January, 1985, pp. 14-15.*

DAVID THOMSON

Mozart is to Salieri as Randall McMurphy, the hero of Forman's *One Flew Over the Cuckoo's Nest*, is to Nurse Ratched: He has more fun. But creative enthusiasm is no more reliable than long hair, or fucking, to out-think tyranny. Something in the appetizing rush of *Amadeus* nagged at me. Was it all fringe benefits, like . . . the crisp-edged, cut-out isolation of the Dolby sound? The period was fulsome but as easily lifted off as a hat. And did the head come off with the hat? If this was art, it stayed at the level of gastronomy, flattering appetite and taste, indulging cruelty and complacency, and ignoring its crush on property. And now that worry has spread so that not all the Mozart Köchel counted could ease it. There's something wrong, and it's not disguised by polish and reticence. For how can you listen to that music and settle for Peter Shaffer's mannered agony over its giddy composer and his wicked mastermind agent?

Of course, Mozart can look after himself. He no more needs a hit play or a school-bus movie than Dickens or Tolstoy need "Masterpiece Theatre." In fact, Mozart is an innocent thug to the movie's enterprise: Time and again, as music takes over from all else, the wretchedly cute story insists on coming back and reducing this work and that opera to mood music for Wolfie's unhappy life and Salieri's delicious dilemma. (At least Salieri listens to the music. The movie Mozart is so much more inclined to live out his scapegrace life, dithering over wigs, but knowing every note. Anything, as long as he doesn't have to think.)

I walked out of a public screening . . . behind two ladies telling themselves that to enjoy the movie you really needed a great knowledge of Mozart's music. But isn't the movie aimed at a passing familiarity with a few motifs and the overall gloss that Mozart was an unruly, impolite genius who may safely be kept up on the shelf, where he can do no harm? It may even enhance this reverent voodoo about genius that, allegedly, some other lesser composer willed his death. Artists, after all, lead such wild lives, and genius means never having to be bored. The two ladies set me thinking that what I had missed on seeing *Amadeus* again was a running commentary from those scabrous housewives on "Monty Python's Flying Circus" to lacerate its classic piety: "Oh, look dear, he's doing *Il Seraglio* now. Isn't he lovely?" In our stupefied and bereft cultural awareness, Mozart is a more winning martyr than Christ. If only God could talk back to Salieri—then they could share their pique, like a couple of queens trashing their reckless best boy.

There's another Mozart who could be served by the film, because we might then recognize a man interested in more than partying and music. And maybe the two ladies have a point here in wanting knowledge—except that if you once began to follow the intricate drama of *The Marriage of Figaro* you'd walk out when the movie abandons it and head for the nearest opera house. Mozart the dramatist never deserved the brazen gimmickry of Peter Shaffer, nor shared his dislike of people. The variety of his music is not just technical; it mirrors the depths and differences of human nature. The music is always thinking. This Mozart is one of the greatest influences on *La Regle du Jeu* and *The Golden Coach*. His preoccupation with the human heart and the flux of misunderstanding make the Shaffer-Forman irony feel like a slick patter.

If ever *Amadeus* could let us see what any of the operas are about—or why the music seems "beautiful"—it would have to dispense with the idiot's delight that has the composer as a farting, giggling buffoon out of *Animal House*. The historic

Mozart may have offended and baffled his contemporaries; but it is more important to realize how and why his music had those effects, and can have them still. In both cases, it is because he showed us ourselves. He was not a music-maker without mind or character, a note-smith who tricked up tunes as chronically as he played with billiard balls and ran words backward. He was a composer always responding to life. The worst crime against history in the play and the film is not in painting Mozart as a brat or Salieri as the lizard of murderous envy; it is in presenting Mozart as unaware of what is going on, while Salieri is a sleek Iago. And it is sheer hypocrisy to try to pretend that this wizard Salieri is a mediocrity.

Salieri has no mercy on his wretchedness, his sin, his mediocrity—but he's loving it all, especially the sound of his unending, eloquent disdain. It's the only heartfelt thing in the play or the film, granted that the music is a given, a sound cue that allows Salieri the masochist to suffer and sing. He is a remarkable character: implausible in so many ways, impossible even, but a music that teaches us to hear. Now that he is on film, he may be seen as the most striking and ambivalent new character since Norman Bates in *Psycho*—another step in the movies' walking out with glib scoundrels. (pp. 70-1)

In the play, Salieri is master of the show. The stage is his *Huis Clos,* and the lights are his torture tools; he can go from age to youth by putting on a powdered wig; he can call his memories into being, or freeze them long enough for a sardonic aside. He is undying Death, taunting the audience for being "Ghosts of the Future." No wonder Forman recognized a movie when he saw the play: Salieri has life trapped on a Moviola. . . .

Salieri is a storyteller like Clifton Webb's Waldo Lydecker in *Laura*. His real text is, "See what a clever devil I have been." The contrite pose of confession is exposed by his and his makers' indifference to God. This is not "forgive me" but "remember me"; the shame is all pride. He has not a jot of reverence for anything outside his own head. Mozart's music is less what the kid has composed than the miracle Salieri has heard. He is the perfect critic, the only one who knows how good it is, alone with the art. Wolfgang is conventionally brash, but he is not as conscious of his music as is Salieri. How could he be? He lacks the necessary refinement, or the itch for ownership.

Because Mozart is so slaphappy, there is a kind of mistake involved in his being the composer of such music. But Salieri can set the error right by dint of control, eloquence, and appreciation. He is the dank tunnel of history, a cultural bowel, a born director who must shit on the world. And he is a talker. Not as much in the film as on the stage, but still wooed by the mortified sound of his own voice, and by the stink of his ordure. He is a cobra who can imitate the wail of the pipe and writhe to it at the same time. He wears dark colors not out of self-denial; he is in mourning for the voided Enlightenment. . . .

Still, it is hard to get worked up about losses for Salieri. He is as loathsome as he must be a treasure for actors. Has anyone ever been less than riveting in the part? The man is all poseur and no character, pretending to faith so that he may put his crucifix in the fire. . . . If you can stand a minute of his floating disdain, it could go on forever. Talk is his music, and he knows he has no equal. It is like listening to the hilarious accounts by some old theatrical queen of all his disasters and humiliations. The longer he goes on about his own bitter pills, the more celebrated he becomes. Salieri is a kind of Rasputin:

Poison doesn't work on him; his metabolism converts it to candy.

And yet. For the film, someone has had second thoughts. Shaffer wrote the screenplay, just as he made extensive revisions when his play moved from London to America. Perhaps the movie's ending is his fresh thought, or maybe one should trust the taskmaster Forman. . . . (p. 72)

Is there a hint there of one composer putting another through hoops, bringing him to heel by virtue of superior understanding? If so, the movie is rebuke enough to Forman. Who can believe that the skilled Shaffer wanted Leopold Mozart to figure so large and useless in the action, or condoned the several scenes that show and romanticize a Life of Mozart, even to deathbed imagery taken from *The Death of Chatterton*? No, I think this is a version that Forman has cajoled into being, and which Shaffer transcribed. There's no reason to blame him or sympathize with Shaffer; the play was remorselessly whimsical and unappetizing. But it was, at least, a whole, a repressed threnody to an impossible love affair between a lapsed but prancing cardinal and an ignoble savage.

The play could as easily turn on painting or gardening as music; it might be better still if Mozart and Salieri were rival pastry cooks. But something in Forman must have been disturbed by the nastiness, or by its hideous frankness. Perhaps he guessed the large audience would want someone more worthy of being liked. . . . And so there is a scene of reconciliation in this *Amadeus*, the best thing in the movie and its one fluttering attempt to escape Schaffer's cage. (pp. 72-3)

The reconciliation is a screenwriter's joy pulled down from an earlier era of Hollywood's Great Composers. For what happens here is that Mozart is too enfeebled by illness actually to write down the ending of his *Requiem Mass*. In history, that unfinished work (K. 626) was completed by Franz Sussmayr. But in the film, the secretly gratified and overtly solicitous Salieri discovers Mozart's helplessness. . . . And so he offers help, without spite or trick, in his one moment of humility and human sympathy. . . .

It was Salieri who saw that all Mozart's scores had the quality of fair copies, the inspiration landing on the page like a cat. And then Salieri must suffer the returned Constanze's hostility and see his best work shut up in a cabinet, one with a glass front. The scene lets us learn something about music—it amounts to an analysis of part of the *Requiem*—and it sees the odious smile of masquerade and superciliousness fall away from Salieri. A true friendship is reached. It is very moving, and the best moment [Salieri] has because it is the quietest and the most self-effacing. He suddenly becomes a plain man.

The scene, in fact, is profound enough to explode everything that has gone before it. It spells out the first worry I had: that no one really appreciative of Mozart could wish him harm. This has to be a matter of opinion, and of our response to the material. There are few cases in history to support one side or another; and although the film says nothing about this, biographers are sure that the old rumors about a plot and Salieri's part in it were false. I do not mean to belittle the human capacity for envy, malice, or evil. But neither do I want to enshrine it. The best measure I can offer of Mozart's genius—a subject so obvious but mysterious that it might henceforth be left out of movies, along with such passions as sexual intercourse, dying, and the sun—is that Salieri's envy is so real and active because he does *not* understand the music. He *is* the film, a fine gesture of despair. (p. 73)

Salieri reminds me of Hollywood people. He's a deal-maker, a cynic, a gossip, a connoisseur, a manipulator advertising his love of the instant "sizzle" in the medium. He has made personal arts out of sarcasm and loathing, and he serves them up like nouvelle cuisine. He passes for the intelligent man of feeling; he is called a class act, and he is a lean aerobics sensualist and a killer at pun charades. There isn't a tune he can't whistle backward, or one he could write that wouldn't play as well in reverse. And he is drowning out genius, substance, his very medium with works he despises. One day a Mozart may kill him. We will all of us have to watch out. Genius is a dangerous thing, always wanting us to think and feel instead of gorge ourselves. (p. 75)

David Thomson, "Salieri, Psycho," in Film Comment, *Vol. 21, No. 1, January-February, 1985, pp. 70-5.**

C. J. GIANAKARIS

Shaffer's most striking and effective technique [in *Amadeus*] was to steep the film in great quantities of Mozart's own music on screen and in the background, via the sound track. Shaffer has called the movie "a fantasia on events in Mozart's life," and as such it represents his further evolved speculations on the deeper meanings of great art and music in the lives of flawed human beings. Mozart's life, based wholly on music, deserves the radical employment of music in the film as correlative. (pp. 89-91)

Why did Shaffer believe that he could discipline music, an abstract art form, to serve him as both theme and technical tool in the movie *Amadeus?* Audiences should be aware that music has always held a unique position in Shaffer's own life and career. At one time a music critic, Shaffer has embedded music in each of his previous dramas for the stage as important thematic metaphors. His concentration on Mozart is a natural extension of his lifelong pursuit of the transcendent values he knew existed in musical art. . . . To manifest man's craving for some ultimate ideal in his life, Shaffer originally fashioned a Salieri who alone would recognize the divinity in the music pouring from Mozart's pen. Shaffer expands on this point, when writing: "What I wanted to emerge clearly from the play is the obsession of a man, Salieri . . . with finding an absolute in music."

Shaffer refused to call the movie just an adaptation; he considered it rather "a parallel work" to the original play. His design relied on the fact that films are amenable to the inclusion of much music, compared to the stage. Through music, Shaffer hoped to help movie audiences understand what it was in Mozart's music that became Salieri's ideal as well as his torment. To that end, Shaffer wrote into his film script detailed instructions for vast quantities of Mozart selections on the sound track. Mozart's career "arena" was the musical performance of his works; accordingly, Shaffer built into the action numerous recital, concert, and operatic episodes connoting Mozart's artistic life and the general musical world of Vienna in his day. (pp. 91-2)

With so much of Mozart's music playing on the sound track, and with samples of Salieri's music, as well, Shaffer intended that audiences should actually hear a contrast between Mozart's voice and the conventional musical sounds of the era. Audiences should also comprehend, as a result, the allusions in the script to "too many notes"—the accusation aimed at Mozart's music by taste setters in the court of Emperor Joseph II—and to "tonic and dominant"—Mozart's description of the boring Italian musical style of the time. Thus, people attending the movie could draw their own conclusions concerning the musical tastes of Mozart's day which reflected disapproval of his daring, threatening tonalities and musical forms.

Shaffer's concept for an enveloping musical backdrop won Forman's acceptance on a purely separate basis. Forman envisioned a Mozart figure portrayed as more sympathetic in the film than he was shown in the theatre. Forman also wanted Mozart positioned more prominently in the action. . . . Mozart's own compositions, played throughout the film, help to keep attention on him at all times, while also providing a shocking contrast between the "voice of God" and the "obscene child"—both of course being the single person Mozart. (p. 92)

A simple gathering together of the chief musical pieces heard in the movie fails utterly to convey the many techniques used and effects gained thereby. Scenes featuring a musical performance in the plot—usually a concert or opera—are designed to fit the action with blueprint accuracy. Even when a complete act or movement is not shown, the section used is surgically inserted to allow the music to breathe and bloom, without bringing the plot action to a halt. One cannot fail to perceive that Mozart's music, as such, is given highest priority in the film. Scenes were deliberately planned to fit the compositions, not the other way around. . . . As a result, perhaps not since *The Red Shoes* from the late 1940s has music played such an organic part in the shape and soul of a motion picture. (p. 93)

[In] scenes not picturing musical performances, the background score is taken entirely from Mozart. Even then, the excerpts are not cut or arranged, but left in Mozart's notations and orchestrations. One result is a welcome crispness. At the same time that the music enriches the visual moment, it reinforces our awareness of Mozart's unsurpassed genius at composition. The film breathes Mozart's music, creating an effect of its omnipresence to underscore Salieri's paranoia concerning the threat of his younger colleague's work.

A striking and original effect is gained by the use of music to segue from one episode to another, emphasizing causal and associative relationships in the process. This brilliant *coup de cinéma* in Shaffer's script always evokes great positive responses from audiences seeing the movie. (p. 94)

A final specimen revealing the musical dimensions of the *Amadeus* picture comprises the entire late section. . . . In an amazing episode that is just barely credible, the exhausted and dying Mozart lies propped up in his bed, dictating to Salieri the remainder of the partly done *Requiem Mass*. . . . As soon as the notations are imprinted on paper, the sounded music of what had just been dictated is heard over the sound track. By such fits and starts, verbal dictation is conveyed to paper, the written version in turn transformed into the powerful music of the *Requiem* which we then hear.

Simultaneously, brief visual shots interjected into the dictation pattern show Mozart's wife, Constanza, boarding a coach to begin an overnight journey back home to be with her husband. The total effect is of contrapuntal visual shots and musical phrases. The music comes from Mozart's glorious *Requiem*, and it floods the movie theatre to accompany the visual portraits of worried wife, frenetic rival Salieri copying furiously, and fading Mozart. The fusion of visual pictures with enveloping music creates a powerful movie effect not soon forgotten. . . .

Has Shaffer's huge dosage of music led to a successful rendering of *Amadeus?* Box-office success is one matter, of course, and artistic success possibly another. . . . [Aesthetically] we can say that the movie does achieve much of Shaffer's initial intention. The enormous investment of energy and money to create this film in parallel forms to a musical composition pays off handsomely. (p. 95)

If one has reservations about the lavishly filmed *Amadeus,* they probably grow out of problems introduced because of cinematic objectives. Despite filling the scenes realistically with figures only alluded to in the play . . . Forman's more literal medium ends up actually simplifying the story's conflict. The price for breadth and scope is focus and complexity of thought. When rehabilitating the character of Mozart, even modestly compared to the stage version, the movie leaves him more an annoying, whinnying prodigal than a tragic figure whose own actions betray his career time after time.

Concomitantly, as the center of the movie shifts away from Salieri and his spiritual conundrum concerning art and godhead, the story line is simplified yet further. For the movie, the main plot action becomes a straight-line tale of HOW DID SALIERI RUIN MOZART? The "intrigue" quotient is diminished when motives are set forth in such bold outline. As another result, the film too often takes on an episodic rhythm. The episodic shape, in turn, leads to a longer movie than perhaps needed. (pp. 95-6)

The movie of *Amadeus,* then, has permitted playwright Peter Shaffer an opportunity to develop even further than in the play his conjectures on music and art, and their possible relationship to the divine. (p. 96)

                    C. J. Gianakaris, "Drama into Film: The Shaffer Situation," in Modern Drama, *Vol. XXVIII, No. 1, March, 1985, pp. 83-98.*

Gay Talese

1932-

(Born Gaetano Talese) American nonfiction writer, essayist, journalist, critic, and editor.

Talese is best known as one the first practitioners of New Journalism, a type of expository writing that blends reporting with such fictional techniques as extended dialogue, shifting points of view, and detailed scene-setting. Among the topics Talese has examined are organized crime, the power structure behind *The New York Times*, and the sexual revolution in America. He is highly regarded for his exhaustive research on these subjects; the investigations of some of his topics have taken him years to complete. Talese's popularity has been enhanced in part by the provocative issues he examines in his work.

Talese spent twelve years at *The New York Times*, working his way from copy-boy to reporter. He achieved local acclaim for his human interest articles about New York street life and people with unusual occupations. These stories inform the content of his early books, *New York: A Serendipiter's Journey* (1961) and *The Bridge* (1964). The first work relates Talese's impressions of Manhattan, while the second is a brief documentary about the men who built the Verrazano-Narrows Bridge, which links Brooklyn and Staten Island. In 1961 Talese began writing free-lance articles for *Esquire* magazine, developing a style of reporting that closely follows the tenets of New Journalism. His profiles of such diverse people as Broadway producer Joshua Logan and boxer Floyd Patterson earned him national recognition. Talese published these and other celebrity profiles written for *Esquire* in *The Overreachers* (1965) and *Fame and Obscurity* (1970).

In 1965 Talese left *The New York Times* to pursue his literary interests. His first major work, *The Kingdom and the Power* (1969), studies the internal power structure of the paper and its influential stature in the United States. Talese traces the history of the newspaper from the late 1890s, when it was purchased by Adolph Ochs, to the present under the leadership of Arthur Ochs Sulzberger, Ochs's grandson. In addition to anecdotes about his former coworkers, Talese also describes the rivalries between the various editors and executives of the paper. In his review of the book, Ben H. Bagdikian found these power struggles informative, for "the outcome of the *Times*'s conflicts will . . . [influence] public policy in the United States."

With the cooperation of Bill Bonanno, the son of New York Mafia leader Joe Bonanno, Talese spent six years researching his next major book, *Honor Thy Father* (1971). In a 1973 interview, Talese described this work as a book about failure, "how the second generation failed to match the sum of the strengths of the older generation." By focusing the narrative on the lives of Bill Bonanno, his wife, and his children, Talese depicts an intimate and poignant picture of life in the Mafia. He also provides a history of the organized crime group, from its origins in Sicily to its influence in America. *Honor Thy Father* was praised for its unique portrait of the Mafia and for its absence of sensationalism and stereotype in describing the people involved.

© 1986 Nancy Crampton

After nine well-publicized years of research, Talese published his most ambitious book, *Thy Neighbor's Wife*, in 1980. Primarily a historical overview of sexual behavior and attitudes in the United States, this controversial work also contains portraits of prominent publishers of erotica, including Hugh Hefner, the founder of *Playboy* magazine, as well as sketches of several middle-class married couples who engage in such unconventional practices as mate-swapping. The more sensational aspects of *Thy Neighbor's Wife*, particularly Talese's own experiences working in a Manhattan massage parlor and his participatory visits to sex communes in California, received the most attention. Several critics faulted the book for ignoring homosexuality, feminism, and the effects of sexual permissiveness on America's youth. However, Talese was praised for his analyses of several literary obscenity trials which are now considered legal precedents and for his investigation of censorship in the United States.

(See also *Contemporary Issues Criticism*, Vol. 1; *Contemporary Authors*, Vols. 1-4, rev. ed.; and *Contemporary Authors New Revision Series*, Vol. 9.)

LEO LERMAN

Mr. Talese's Manhattan notebook [*New York: A Serendipiter's Journey*] is composed of glimpses and statistics. Not only does he tell about mediums and other occultists but of a man who earns his living by impersonating George Washington, and of another "who as a child wanted to grow up and become a mosaic ***." The latter is tattooed with 244 pictures; his name, Joe Dracula. . . .

Then there are the policewomen, "masquerading as naïve and lovesick doxies," who are out to get the goods on the city's gypsy fortunetellers.

Despite patches of over-exuberance such as are inevitable when writing love letters, *New York: A Serendipiter's Journey* will be valuable both to readers who do not know the city at all and to those who know it intimately. . . .

[Most] of all, however it is about New Jersey-born Gay Talese's love affair with our town. He is mad about her, but I do not think he wants to make an honest woman of her. The theme of his book, he tells us, is "New York is not a summer festival." That may be, but Mr. Talese's book is most certainly a year-round New York celebration.

> *Leo Lerman, "Tattoos and Wicked Gypsies," in* The New York Times Book Review, *July 23, 1961, p. 16.*

HERBERT MITGANG

It is about 35 years since Hart Crane's *The Bridge* aimed to represent the Brooklyn Bridge as the main symbol of modern America's aspiration and achievement. No such claim is made for Gay Talese's *The Bridge,* a factual account of the building of the Verrazano-Narrows Bridge linking Brooklyn to Staten Island. The titles are the same but not the times. . . .

In one chapter, the author tells us about the mixed-blood Mohawk Indians who rent rooms in the North Gowanus section of Brooklyn and drive 400 miles on weekends to visit their families on the Caughnawaga reservation near Montreal. They are the sons of the iron workers who built the Empire State Building and George Washington Bridge. The reader is taken for a ride from an Indian bar on Nevins Street to the reservation in Canada and then back in time for Monday morning's bridge work.

The statistics are here too, and some do-it-yourself directions for bridge builders, based on the lessons learned in this century about suspension bridges. . . .

The reporting, photographs and drawings work together handsomely and make *The Bridge* a vibrant document.

> *Herbert Mitgang, "Stitchers of Steel," in* The New York Times Book Review, *January 17, 1965, p. 51.*

PETE HAMILL

The Overreachers is a collection of magazine articles held together by what strikes me as a forced theme. It is supposed to be about men who "take that extra step," who "make the same mistakes, the same stupid, reckless, dramatic, wonderful mistakes." Some of the subjects actually qualify: Floyd Patterson, Frank Costello, Josh Logan, Peter O'Toole. Unfortunately, the Paris Review crowd, the editors of Vogue, and woolheads like Romy Schneider and Christina Paolozzi do not. And there is a closing section about the change of seasons in New York that doesn't fit at all.

This is probably not Talese's fault. Editors want something to hang books on, and this was as good as any. But taken one at a time, the pieces are examples of how really good the magazine article can be. Talese is interested in character, and the things men do, and his pieces are not clotted with facts. . . . The new journalists have learned their lessons well, have learned as much about their craft from Chekhov or Dostoevsky or Flaubert or Turgenev as they have from city editors. Talese's pieces on Peter O'Toole and Floyd Patterson can stand on their own as writing, with no apologies for anything. The others are all stylishly, gracefully written and are weaker only because their subject matter is less interesting. (pp. 17-18)

> *Pete Hamill, "Limelight Gone Sour," in* Book Week—The Sunday Herald Tribune, *June 13, 1965, pp. 17-18.**

BEN H. BAGDIKIAN

Books about newspapers fall into familiar categories, ranging from memoirs of people-meet-such-interesting-newspapermen to treatises on the anatomy and physiology of communications organisms. [*The Kingdom and the Power,* Talese's history of The New York Times] is a different kind of book. It is done in the novelistic style of Truman Capote, William Manchester and Theodore White, moving real contemporary men through real contemporary events. . . .

But this is not just another book about organization men scheming to reach the top. Men lust for power in newspapers as they do elsewhere, but with a difference. An organization like The Times has unique stakes compared with General Motors or Proctor & Gamble. The outcome of the Times's conflicts will not influence the design of radiator grilles or detergent containers but of public policy in the United States. Every public and private leader in Washington and New York, and every newspaper editor reads a paper like The Times before he starts his day, and adjusts to the version of reality created on Page One by the men who struggle in this book. During the period Talese describes these men and their views were the subject of intense, almost obsessive concern by the most powerful policy-makers in the country.

So the hero (heroine? villain? victim?) of the book is The Times itself, . . . that envelops the men who struggle to control it and in the end influences their lives more than they influence it.

It is a fascinating book, compelling for those addicted to newspapers, and to anyone else who lets himself get caught up in the interplay of the characters, whether or not he recognizes the bylines. The author had wide access to his sources, though his book will be a bitter pill for some who granted it. . . .

His writing is lively, aided by an eye for irreverent detail that reminds you constantly that this is not an official biography. Frederick Birchall, a former acting managing editor, is introduced in one scene, "one day while driving his car with one hand on the steering wheel and the other on the Baroness's leg."

Talese flicks the scalpel with joy. . . .

The book is rich in intimate detail, personal insights and characterization. While The Times turns its face to the world with a stiff upper lip and all the news that's fit to print, in this book the men of The Times emerge not as godlike models of intrepid journalism but as unique individuals who, in addition to other human traits, have trouble with their ambitions, alcohol, wives and analysts.

But this is the book's weakness. It implies value in professional newspapermen on the basis of personal idiosyncrasy. Individual tastes are important, but so is man's perception of reality, of issues, and of public events, which, after all, are the substance of his trade. It is interesting to learn the kind of woman and clothing that turns on a particular editor, but there is more to judgments of journalists than bedmates or haberdashers.

Inevitably, much has to be taken on faith, like the author's descriptions of men's inner thoughts annd motives. And there are times when this faith is shaken by unfairness, including that toward the late publisher, Orvil Dryfoos, and toward James Reston. Talese depicts Dryfoos as a rather precious agent of the Establishment, criticizing him and Reston because they ordered the story of the Government's preparations for the Bay of Pigs "toned down, moved to a less prominent place on the page, its headline minimized, and any reference to the imminence of the invasion eliminated" (which I agree was a bad decision).

While Talese uses this incident as a key to Dryfoos's character, he does not credit the same character for making courageous anti-Establishment decisions that offended important people at The Times . . . and offended powerful people in government. . . . (p. 8)

Talese is least convincing in areas he does not know well—Washington and foreign affairs—not a small failing in a book about The Times. His final description of New York's attempt to dominate their Washington bureau, despite its being an arcane matter for the outside world, is, in Talese's hands, a genuinely moving drama. . . .

Despite its flaws, the book creates moving scenes and personalities. Seldom has anyone been so successful in making a newspaper come alive as a human institution. It is a story that many ambitious newspapers would wish their best writers to produce—about someone else. (p. 30)

> Ben H. Bagdikian, "The Hero (Villain? Victim?) Is 'The New York Times'," in The New York Times Book Review, *June 8, 1969, pp. 8, 30.*

A. J. LANGGUTH

[*The Kingdom and the Power*] is fascinating, laden as it is, behind a genial facade, with adroit and ill-natured tattle. Talese is a romantic who can find glamour in that drab factory on 43rd Street and excitement in dissecting its cautious managers. His long gallery of portraits begins with Adolph Ochs, the publisher who built [*The New York Times*] into a world institution, and concludes with his grandson, the current publisher, Arthur Ochs "Punch" Sulzberger. Around them, maneuvering for position in serpentine ways, twist the dozens of editors and executives who must put out the newspaper each day. (p. 29)

To judge from Talese, the editors are not so much interested in publishing a paper as securing a higher spot on the masthead. Harrison Salisbury's trip to Hanoi was interesting, Talese would grant that, but he manages to convey that its real importance was in forestalling attempts to dislodge Salisbury from his post as assistant managing editor.

The same technique that makes the book so readable adds to Talese's problems in capturing the essence of his characters. Taking material from extensive interviews, Talese has fash-

ioned a narrative that tells, in Talese's words, what each editor thought and felt at his moment of bureaucratic crisis. Since Talese seldom quotes them directly, the reader hears mostly a smooth omniscient voice that sees all, tells all, but misses in its crystalline high style any distinctive rough edges. (p. 31)

> A. J. Langguth, "Tales of the Times," in The New Republic, *Vol. 160, No. 26, June 28, 1969, pp. 29-33.*

C. H. SIMONDS

You can see them Sunday mornings on the Upper East Side, in the Village, in Brooklyn Heights, chicly dressed but sleepy-eyed, hastening to the newsstand where waits, in towering piles, the Sunday *New York Times*. Home it goes, a five-pound slab of newsprint that by dusk has dissolved into a wall-to-wall strew in the livingroom, leaked into the bathroom, gotten mixed in with the rumpled bedclothes, leaving its readers glassy of eye, sour of stomach, hung over, listless with an almost post-coital *tristesse*. The day is gone. They might have fixed the faucet, played some tennis, flown a kite with the children; instead they have read the Sunday *Times*.

They seem to have derived little pleasure from the act. It is a duty—a religious duty, Gay Talese would jump to say: The daily *Times* is prayers, the Sunday edition is Mass (sheer mass). Talese is fond of metaphor-stretching—beginning with the title, [*The Kingdom and the Power*] his book is peppered with facile religious allusions. . . . In fact, reverence is the only word for what the *Times* evokes. Put the *Times* reader at a houseparty weekend in thither Vermont, or transfer him to the Omaha branch, and he will fret. He misses those eight drab columns with their constipated headlines, the magisterially self-assured editorials, the agate listings of arriving and departing ships, visible satellites, out-of-town buyers, debutantes, English football results. "You don't have to read it all," the paper's promotion department assures us, "but it's nice to know it's all there." How nice? Is the absent reader fretful in part because amid his loss he feels a teensy bit relieved? (p. 810)

It is as an institution that Talese examines the *Times*, but he stops regrettably short. He has written, he tells us, "a human story of an institution in transition . . . a factual story of several generations of *Times*men and the interplay within (among?) those generations, the internal scenes and confrontations and adjustments that are part of the vitality and growth of any enduring institution." Fine as far as it goes, but there is too little consideration of the sources, extent and effects of the *Times'* considerable power; too many scenes and confrontations, too much novelistic scene-setting and picture-painting. . . .

[A] chronicle of executive maneuvering might be interesting; in Talese's hands it is tiresome for two reasons. First, there is the *Times'* pace: There are no lightning coups at the *Times*, everything moves with the speed of erosion; it may take a decade to ease a man upstairs, or downstairs, or over to an obscure desk behind a post. Second, there is Talese's pace; more precisely, his inability to follow the main line of the story and dovetail in the background, asides and subplots so that they support instead of obscure. . . . We have peeked into dozens of offices, and we have skipped around in time, too, for well over a century, since the first Ochs landed on American soil. . . . [Then] we move on through the rest of the book, still hopscotching in time and space, through more offices, past more editors, reporters, wives, children, ancestors. Quite plainly, Talese is under the influence of Truman Capote's "nonfiction novel'' and the highly personal reportage of Norman Mailer; quite sadly, he is not up to their level. The stream of consciousness is muddied. The juxtaposition of events does little to enlighten, much to confuse. (p. 811)

C. H. Simonds, ''Printed to Fit,'' in National Review, *Vol. XXI, No. 31, August 12, 1969, pp. 810-12.*

JOSEPH EPSTEIN

The Kingdom and the Power is about an attempt to change the *Times*—specifically, about an attempt on the part of certain of the New York editors to divest the paper's Washington bureau of its long-held independent status as the most powerful of the *Times*'s many dukedoms. Great institutions, however, are changed only by stealth or revolution. In this instance, the method was stealth; the effort, abortive; the reverberations within the *Times,* cataclysmic; the net effect, some shifting of personnel and responsibilities, some changes in title—and business pretty much as usual. But on the single piece of intrigue which is the occasion for this book, Talese has hung an extremely readable history of the *Times,* an account of its mechanics and machinations, and a virtual glory-hole of gossip about its owners, editors, and reporters. (p. 96)

[In the] long, involuted account of the struggles of these men for power, what is dismaying is how little those struggles have to do with any serious intellectual issues or questions of journalistic quality. What is at stake above all else is power, simple and naked. Strange things happen to a man when he becomes an editor of the *Times*. In agreeing to accept an editorship a man has also to agree in his own mind to swap the satisfactions of the by-line and the freedom of the reporter's life for the anonymous power of the executive. In so doing a man gives up his trade while retaining his ambition; where that ambition formerly might have driven him toward excellence in his craft, it now drives him toward power in his job, which at the *Times* means greater and greater control over larger and larger segments of the paper. This, of course, was what the effort of the New York editors to curtail the independence of the *Times*'s Washington bureau was really all about. Such issues as existed, if not invented in the first place, quickly receded to the background, and in the final analysis the outcome was decided on the basis of one man's having more clout with the publisher than another. (pp. 96, 98)

Already in Talese's last pages one can hear the rumblings of the next round of the struggle for power at the *Times*. Let us hope that whoever writes the story of this one has the energy and thoroughness of Gay Talese and, in addition, a quality the subject really deserves—more of the eye and touch of Evelyn Waugh. (p. 98)

Joseph Epstein, ''Paper Politics,'' in Commentary, *Vol. 48, No. 3, September, 1969, pp. 95-6, 98.*

STUART W. LITTLE

One can hang around the backstage of Broadway theaters watching rehearsals endlessly without observing anything of real dramatic interest among the principals involved. But Gay Talese is the most patient, observing, and penetrating of reporters. When he is on the scene, sooner or later, the director and the star will erupt in a titanic quarrel as Joshua Logan and Claudia McNeil do in **"The Soft Psyche of Joshua Logan."** In *Fame and Obscurity,* a collection of portraits by Gay Talese

. . ., mostly from *Esquire,* the dramatic moment usually comes. . . .

In this superb collection, Talese follows Frank Sinatra cutting a record, the beaten Floyd Patterson dealing uncertainly with some boys who have been teasing his daughter in school, Frank Costello, Joe Louis, and Alden Whitman dealing with the ultimate deadline as the chief obituary writer of *The New York Times*. Employing some trick of mental acrobatics, Talese somehow gets inside the life of his subjects, writing from within the shell of their existence. In his long piece on the building of the Verrazano-Narrows Bridge, standing out more vividly than the tall towers of the world's largest suspension span, are the swarm of people who built it or were affected by its building—the boomers, the dispossessed residents of Bay Ridge, the daredevil Indian rivet gangs driving Cadillacs up to Canada on Friday nights to visit their wives.

Talese finds meaning in the lives of the obscure, meaninglessness in fame. His sure handling of color and feeling and happening in every story is one of the most interesting feats in today's journalism.

Stuart W. Little, ''The Omnipresent Reporter,'' in Saturday Review, *Vol. LIII, No. 28, July 11, 1970, p. 53.*

COLIN MacINNES

[*Honor Thy Father* could have been a] splendid opportunity . . . for an ''inside story'' of a bizarre and significant sector of the American scene; yet I am sorry to say Mr. Talese fails to seize it. . . .

[What we have] is a lengthy recapitulation of American gangster history that is by now quite generally known. There are also enormous chunks describing the day-to-day life of Bill Bonanno which, apart from his being who he is, are of no particular interest. The portrait of a minor mobster in decline has a certain melancholy fascination, though what is said in pages would often be better put in paragraphs. The whole tone of the book is rather sentimental, and curiously snobbish: one is reminded, at times, as the author evokes his alarming and deplorable characters, of the voice of a gossip columnist.

Most disconcerting of all is Mr. Talese's attitude in describing these events and personalities. Bill, he implies, is a nice guy and a victim of circumstance, and at no point does the author assess him and his world from any clear standard of personal opinion. I am not, of course, saying it is a writer's business to ''judge'' any other human creature, but it certainly is to measure him by some identifiable code of human conduct. . . .

Perhaps the most interesting sections of *Honor Thy Father* are not those where Mr. Talese is rather cosily describing Bill and his devoted family, but where he tries to assess the financial structure of organized crime in the United States. He is also excellent on the historical origins of the Mafia, and does well to remind us that it was originally a secret society founded to defend Sicilian rights against their oppressors. The sections on the recent emergence of major black gangsters have an unfortunate relevance here, since this is also in part a consequence of the oppression of a minority group by the majority.

If I have been damning with faint praise, I would conclude by saying I do think the book will interest many readers. Perhaps the public as a whole is not so different from artists in its preoccupation with crime and criminals. The themes of so much fiction, films and television are proof of this; and Mr. Talese's book at least has the advantage of dealing with real, and not invented, personalities and social problems. (p. 18)

Colin MacInnes, "Does the ----- Really Exist?" in The New York Times Book Review, October 31, 1971, pp. 2, 18.

PETE HAMILL

[In *Honor Thy Father*] Talese has constructed one of those sturdy Victorian novels that take us beyond the curtains to look at human lives; that the story he tells is about actual people makes the feat somewhat more compelling, but that is not crucial. After the principals are all gone, the book will remain, a family saga as important as any we've seen in this country. It is a book about fathers and sons, about trust and betrayal, about the old style and the new; it is, of course, a tragedy, because the genre of the family saga, real or imagined, always seems to turn out that way. But the book is also a stunning comment on America and the failure of its romantic promise.

Pete Hamill, "Bonanno and Son," in Book World— The Washington Post, November 7, 1971, pp. 4, 8, 10.

RICHARD J. CATTANI

[*Honor Thy Father*] is as much a domestic study which fits into the new white-ethnic genre as it is reportage on the world of crime. Talese shows how the Sicilian underworld—which took a monopolistic hold on American crime after prohibition—has been disintegrating along with the ethnic awareness and early immigrant conditions of the Sicilian-Americans themselves. . . .

Some critics have complained that Talese's book, which he thinks of as journalism, is too novelistic. And at moments the drama does catch Talese running too hard.

Others have said he has gotten too close to his subject, abandoning moral perspective.

Yet Talese has managed a unique feat in befriending the Bonanno family, poring over family photo albums with them, observing the worn places in the rugs of their private past. . . . He gives an intimate portrait of the Bonanno family—the dapper, magnetic father, the confounded and grasping son, and Rosalie the young wife—trying to adjust to the overbearing disrupter of their circle which, in the end, is of course not simply the father, but the family tradition of crime itself.

Richard J. Cattani, "FBI at the Keyhole, Strangers on the Sofa," in The Christian Science Monitor, December 9, 1971, p. 15.

RONALD DWORKIN

Why does America love the Mafia?

For the same reasons, it seems, as it loved the cowboys. The heroes of the Westerns were exotic, because they came from what was meant to be a different though ancestral country. They were familiar nevertheless, because they were made to talk and think in ways drawn from the romantic culture of those who went to the movies—until the cowboys went to the movies themselves and allowed nature to copy art. Now [in *Honour Thy Father*] Bill Bonanno and his sidekicks ride the range of

those dreary Brooklyn streets in plain black Fords, putting in at neon spaghetti-houses instead of saloons, drinking Chianti instead of red-eye, and calling each other by titles they might have learned from books about Al Capone.

The appeal of the cowboys was nostalgic, because their country was disappearing while it was celebrated. The nostalgia is more complicated in the case of the Mafia. What is disappearing is not the Prairie but that other American frontier, the ethnic society of racial neighbourhoods, corrupted foreign tongues and mysterious foreign skills and specialities, like the Jew's craft in retail trade and the Italian's cruelty and love of vengeance. Prohibition fell upon this America, and it was a great mother of racial legends. The economy demanded gangs—they were the most efficient way of providing booze while protecting hypocrisy—and since everything else was ethnic, so were the gangs. . . . That society is breaking down, not because the melting-pot has worked, but because the post-industrial society has made all the ethnic groups want the same kinds of job and home and life. The Mafioso is an anachronism, like Quixote and the Marlboro man, a hold-over from a time treasured mostly because it is gone. The theme of the Mafia stories is that he will not disappear—at least, not yet. (pp. 232, 234)

The Mafia of the stories serves the role of a myth that denies change, but it serves another purpose as well. . . . The Mafioso kills in a way that satisfies . . . [Americans'] taste for violence without fear: his murders are neither indiscriminate nor pointless nor political, and they threaten no one who does not live by choice in that world. There is nothing more frightening in the murder of Anastasia in a barber's shop, or Crazy Joe Gallo in an Italian clam-bar, than in the shooting of a claim-jumper drawing to a straight in the Dodge City Saloon. On the contrary. The violence of the Mafia is violence that supports rather than threatens things as they are. Bill Bonanno told Gay Talese, with extraordinary insight, that crime that panders to vice, like prostitution and the numbers racket, is constructive because it allows the straight society its moralism on the cheap.

Even the Mafia style must be a comfort to Middle America. Talese's book was read by the Bonannos, whose help was necessary, and it reads like a house biography. . . . The Mafiosi are family men: they fear God, take care of the garden and play with the children whenever they can. Bill Bonanno takes a mistress, but this is part of his flirtation with an alien world and the divided family closes ranks in support of his wife. The same morality discriminates between good and bad crime . . . and the Bonannos, as they tell it, draw the line at drugs. . . .

The criminal law, which still confuses crime with morals, contrives to put a lot of money into gambling, sex and drugs, and this money will pay for a good deal of both organisation and competition. There is little doubt that Italo-Americans continue to have a corner in this work, but the gang killings may have no more to do with the noble code of the Godfather than the sordid murders in the Klondike really had to do with the code of the West. (p. 234)

Ronald Dworkin, in a review of "Honour Thy Father," in The Listener, Vol. 88, No. 2265, August 24, 1972, pp. 232, 234.

PAUL ROBINSON

"She was completely nude." So begins [*Thy Neighbor's Wife*, an] examination of sex in America by Gay Talese. . . .

The opening sentence suggests that Talese has left himself fully vulnerable to attack. Its banality and clumsy redundancy ("nude," after all, implies "completely") are worthy of a bad pornographic novel. The effect, however, is not entirely unintentional, and *Thy Neighbor's Wife* is a better book than its inauspicious beginning would lead one to expect. For all its minor annoyances and substantial heft, it makes interesting, informative, and sometimes even titillating reading.

I should note immediately that its subject is much narrower than the advance publicity has suggested. Talese himself calls it "a book about sex in America," and he describes its theme as "the redefinition of morality." But in reality, he treats only limited aspects of American sexual life. The book has essentially two subjects: first, the proliferation of sexually explicit literature during the last three decades, and second, the emergence in the same period of a new pattern of extramarital sexuality, especially among middle-class men.... Left virtually untouched ... are premarital sex, homosexuality, geriatric and infantile sexual behavior, and the characteristic sexual experiences of poor, nonmetropolitan, and black Americans. Moreover, the subject is explored largely from a male perspective, and few women, I imagine, will recognize themselves in these pages. None of my criticisms is intended to be disqualifying, since the matters Talese does address are large and complex. But readers anticipating something more inclusive should be warned.

The book's strengths and limitations derive from a single intellectual predilection: like any good reporter, Talese conceives of the recent history of sexual customs as a "story," or, as he puts it himself, as "one of the most important stories of his lifetime." Stories display certain characteristics: they have shape and drama, they are dominated by personalities, and, at their best, they express a point of view. The most successful parts of Talese's book are precisely those that lend themselves to "storial" treatment. Thus, for example, his account of the rise and fall (and ultimate consolidation) of Hugh Hefner's Playboy empire is told with enviable skill. The characters spring immediately to life, the identification of Hefner's private fantasies and public accomplishments is ingeniously demonstrated, and even the physical details of the publisher's houses, airplane, and daily routine are tellingly rendered.

Nearly as good is the account of the various legal imbroglios, most of them ending before the Supreme Court, that have punctuated the emergence of sexually explicit literature in the past quarter century. Here, too, Talese has a story to tell: colorful personalities, dramatic confrontations, and the satisfying sense of resolution that a court ruling lends to violent antagonisms. (p. 105)

Talese's second theme—the new style of infidelity—gives him more trouble. Unlike the vicissitudes of the Playboy empire or the history of censorship, it is not a story. It can't be adequately encompassed through an account of individual characters; it lacks clear dramatic contours; and it raises moral questions that only the most poised and rigorous intelligence can negotiate successfully. The subject best lends itself to two possible approaches: the sociological, such as Alfred Kinsey pursued in his monumental studies of 1948 and 1953; or the novelistic, such as one finds in, say, John Updike's *Couples*. Talese's procedure falls, none too happily, between these stools.

He begins by accepting the sociologist's rigorous empirical premises: "The names of the people in this book are real, and the scenes and events described on the following pages actually

happened." Everything about the book argues that Talese, save for isolated rhetorical extravagances and an occasional lapse into self-deception, has been faithful to his word. Nevertheless, he isn't willing to express his findings in the highly abstract statistical form that a commitment to historical realism usually implies. Rather, he wants to convey something of the concrete feeling and nuance of changing sexual mores—in other words, he wants to convey just those things that are inaccessible to the sociologist because they don't allow of systematic treatment.

He attempts to escape this predicament by way of autobiography and what might be called projected autobiography. To his credit, Talese has the frankness to acknowledge this tactic and even to introduce it explicitly into his text. He ends with an explanation (in the third person) of how he came to write the book, which leaves no doubt that the new style of infidelity he describes is in large measure his own infidelity....

Talese is too intelligent to generalize blithely from his limited data. For the most part, he is satisfied merely to intimate that his own experience and that of the Sandstone habitués prefigure America's sexual future. His procedure is self-consciously impressionistic, and he seldom makes bolder claims for his findings than would a good novelist. Still, one does not come away from this book, as one did from the Kinsey volumes, with the confident sense of having found out how things really are.

Judged, then, as a work of gentle introspection and astute but essentially casual social observation, *Thy Neighbor's Wife* must be counted a success. Within its own self-imposed limits, it has only two important shortcomings. First, it is infected by a subtle overinflation, In order to heighten the sense of drama, the characters are lent a weightiness that they can't always bear. Each dalliance, it seems, must have existential resonances and reflect profound psychological shifts. People aren't simply horny, they are dissatisfied with their lives. They don't just want to get laid, they are seeking escape from bourgeois conformity. Talese's refusal to let his characters be the prosaic and insipid figures that they sometimes must have been soon grows tiresome.

A more serious fault is the author's moral diffidence. He is not certain in his own mind exactly how he feels about the sexual changes he describes. On the one hand, he appreciates the case for liberation. Indeed, he has benefited from it in his own life. But he is sensitive enough to recognize that something valuable has been endangered in the process.... One might argue that he has the courage to expose his own moral confusion. Yet it seems fair to expect those who make a public matter of their sexuality to demonstrate a firmer grasp of the issues than the rest of us bemused creatures. (p. 106)

Paul Robinson, "The Talese Report," in Psychology Today, *Vol. 13, No. 11, April, 1980, pp. 105-06.*

ROBERT SHERRILL

Thy Neighbor's Wife [is] an imperfect inventory of contemporary sexual activities and hang-ups. [Talese's] emphasis is on sex as a business. (p. 1)

At best it is little more than expansion of what any semiconscious newspaper reader already knows: that the establishment is a pretty clumsy monitor of morality, that there is a great deal of money to be made by those persons clever and daring enough to circumvent the establishment's strictures, and that society's sex taboos are falling like an aged lothario's ardor.

Although Talese is practical enough to admit that money is the chief motivation of the sex industry, he also seems to be arguing that virtually all purveyors of erotica are created by childhood oppression.

Hugh Hefner, it seems, founded *Playboy* in reaction to his parents, those ''relics of the Victorian era.'' This appraisal becomes a bit strained, however, when we learn a few pages later that mama contributed $1,000—one of the biggest donations Hefner got—to publishing the first issue and daddy later became the magazine's accountant. (pp. 1-2)

Talese's case histories of publishers would make Miss Lonelyhearts turn purple. He describes Larry Flynt, founder of *Hustler,* as ''an eighth-grade dropout, a dirt-poor Kentucky sharecropper's son.'' *Screw*'s Alvin Goldstein, child of a stuttering mother and a father who kept hardcore pics in the bureau drawer, was, according to Talese, a masochistic drifter until he found his place in smut. The psyche of William Hamling, once California's most successful porn publisher, was shaped, the book says, by the ''sex-denouncing nuns and priests'' of his Chicago childhood. Marvin Miller, another rich pornographer, grew up on welfare and was first arrested at the age of 6. . . .

Next to Hefner, the featured player on Talese's psychoanalyst's couch is John Williamson, the brooding offspring of a crippled, part-time bootlegger. Williamson founded Sandstone Retreat, a 15-acre Los Angeles hideaway. Some of his early followers in a group-marriage experiment were people who had grown up in households where sex was equated with, or practiced as, various kinds of abuse and perversion. Later Sandstone expanded into a sex club open to anyone who could pay the dues or had enough prestige to give the joint some class. . . .

A visitor to Sandstone's basement, Talese says, would have seen in the semidarkness a churning sea of bodies and would have heard ''sighs, cries of ecstasy . . . the slap and suction of copulating flesh.'' Makes your hair stand on end, doesn't it? No? . . .

[The] most irritating aspect of *Thy Neighbor's Wife,* aside from the bad psychiatry, is the bad writing. Talese smothers you in clichés and soap-opera language. . . . Sometimes his lushness is hilarious, as when he calls a transcontinental trollop ''a beautiful vagrant bird in tireless flight.''

For a book that pretends to be a broad survey, there are some strange omissions. Where's Bob Guccione of *Penthouse,* who pushed the pink much farther into mass circulation than Hefner ever dared to do? And why is there not one mention of the whorehouse industry? Has it disappeared?

Still, there are pluses. Talese does an excellent job reviewing the court battles between bluenoses and freethinkers over the past century or so. . . .

It's just too bad that Talese has to be so heavy-handed. In trying to get a good grip on sex he squeezes it to death. In trying to make kinky sex seem ordinary he only succeeds in making ordinary sex seem kinky. *Thy Neighbor's Wife* offers sex without elegance or mystery and—most dread defect of all—without even a touch of humor. Can this really be American sex? Say it ain't so, Henry Miller. (p. 2)

> *Robert Sherrill, ''Selling Sex in America,'' in* Book World—The Washington Post, *April 27, 1980, pp. 1-2.*

ELIOT FREMONT-SMITH

Talese, a pioneer of personally involved and novelistically structured journalism, is not an *analytical* writer. He is a seemingly inexhaustable interviewer of others and himself, a listener and recorder and arranger, but not a complicated questioner. The assumption that he is, and that [*Thy Neighbor's Wife*] more than scratches the surface (or underside) of ''the social and sexual trends of the entire nation,'' has led and will continue to lead to much critical effluvia. . . .

Thus I myself leapt to denigrate Talese's vaunted research with the discovery, on page 47, of a reference to a ''1913 Jaguar'' (there is no such make for that year; details upon request). And thus there is going to be a lot of *tsk-tsk*ing over the virtual absence from the book of the effects of feminism and homosexual consciousness.

The fault—and it is first of all the book's—is that it pretends to be more encompassing and coherent than it is. In fact, its substantive materials are quite modest. (p. 40)

Talese has very little to say, of broad and substantive interest, about the whyfores and whithers of changing American sexual mores. What he does do is weave together a bunch of stories that would have remained isolated but for his own *physical* enterprise of traveling around the country and then organizing a narrative suspense. The main stories have to do with male masturbation, an experiment with wife-swapping and the establishment of a sexual retreat (Sandstone), and the development of erotic commerce (principally, massage parlors and masturbation magazines)—all related from a straight, middle-class, male point of view. There is also some history—the Oneida community of the 19th century (much more puritan, I think, than Talese suggests), the Comstock laws, and the major court battles that have, over the last 20 years, radically altered legal conceptions and restrictions of obscenity.

There is no question that the country has undergone an enormous shift of attitude about sexual behavior, but Talese's concentration is on specific tales, mostly fringe, and on spinning connections between them, both as writer and researcher/experiencer, that seem to widen their scope and significance and reveal new fact—that monogamy, for instance, is on the way out and that that's a good thing.

In fact, the wife-swapping story—and it is fascinating—is ultimately a story of failure, and very sad. . . .

At the end, Talese seems to glimpse the difficulty, the void at the center of the book. Try as he does, he cannot really pull it together in the big and meaningful way intended; the incidents are one place, their true effects somewhere else. . . .

I don't know about thee, but this seems to me an achievement of sorts—circa many years ago, but touching all the same. It shouldn't destroy marriage, or drive critics crazy. (p. 41)

> *Eliot Fremont-Smith, ''Thy Neighbor's Old Lady,'' in* The Village Voice, *Vol. XXV, No. 17, April 28, 1980, pp. 39-41.*

BENJAMIN DeMOTT

[*Thy Neighbor's Wife* undeniably establishes] Talese's standing as that most familiar, if not most universally admired, American character, The Unblinking Eyewitness. Few writers have lived so long, traveled so far, on the frontiers of the sexual revolution. In this not invariably sunny quarter Talese is the man, to paraphrase Whitman. Whether in suffering or in ecstasy, he saw. He has been there.

It's true, of course, that much of his book's substance derives from digging in periodical and newspaper files and in libraries, rather than from on-the-spot sightings along group-sex sectionals and in massage-parlor cubicles. As a serious chronicler of "the redefinition of morality" in America . . . , the author of *Thy Neighbor's Wife* felt himself obliged, in the name of comprehensiveness, to treat many matters more abstract than the actualities of coupling. He devotes chapters to the landmark court cases—literary . . . and nonliterary—that were the vehicle of judicial advance from punitive positions about explicitness to the permissive doctrine of "redeeming social value," and later to amendments stressing the right of individual communities to specify their own standards of obscenity. . . . There is, in addition, a discussion of the financing of the "revolution of the senses"—problems of capital formation in the men's magazine industry, stages in the development (from Russ Meyer onward) of "the multimillion dollar 'skin flick' market," the building of the *Playboy* empire. . . . (p. 98)

And, in order to measure more precisely the modern "departure from conventionality," Talese functions, intermittently, as historian. He provides a catalogue of recent events and inventions contributing to the shaping of new attitudes—the Pill, legalized abortion, sex therapy clinics, Esalen, the Berkeley Free Speech Movement, frontal nudity on the legitimate stage (*Hair*) and in art films (Antonioni's *Blow-up*), others. He undertakes to describe levels of sexual repressiveness in the past through a survey of nineteenth-century opinion regarding masturbation. And he focuses briefly on various theoretical and practical initiatives encouraging free and communal love—the fifteenth-century Adamites, Brook Farm, John Humphrey Noyes's Oneida community (the latter is seen, I believe unjustifiably, as a precursor of the Sandstone Retreat).

As might be guessed from the author's enthusiastic talk of a "quiet rebellion" against "an inhibiting force," the perspective throughout most of *Thy Neighbor's Wife* is resolutely positive: You and I have come a long way, babe. . . . Yesterday rich aesthetes alone were permitted to appreciate artistic representations of human nudity; today these treasures are democratically available in centerfolds. Yesterday possessiveness and exploitativeness were norms beyond challenge in marriage; today, owing to the idealism of the founders of Sandstone, among others, these norms have been called into question. Yesterday the arena of sex was joyless and solemn; today there's room for hilarity and glee. . . . We've leaped forward, in short—in Talese's view—from shame to happy expressiveness, from unacknowledged burning to relaxed acceptance of our pleasures, from superstition to light. Therefore—inevitably—a book about sex in America must take the form of a paean to Progress.

It's a mindless form, in my opinion, far out of touch for much of its length with the best current thinking about the behavior and attitudes it presumes to describe. I know of few historians, anthropologists, or semiologists nowadays who don't consider it a mistake to seal off change in sexual attitudes and behavior from the broader structures of life, as though such change occurred in some inviolable theater of ideas, Benightedness and Enlightenment wrestling each other, one on one, for domination of the human future. . . . [No] writer of consequence in the field shares Gay Talese's vacuous faith in the autonomy of the so-called sexual revolution.

The reason this vacuity isn't fatal to *Thy Neighbor's Wife* is partly that Talese is journalistically adept at ferreting out undernoticed intricacies of overpublicized events—sexual curiosities past and present, revelatory details of the personal life of celebrities, numberless other items of "feature interest." (pp. 98-9)

In the end, though, it's merely the author's alertness to piquant sidebar material that distracts attention from his weak intellectual scaffolding. The case is that, lodged in the middle of his book, as utterly unpredictable and unassimilable as a sermon on *radix malorum est cupiditas* would seem if encountered midway through, say, *How You Can Become Financially Independent by Investing in Real Estate,* is a narrative of liberation that's extraordinary in its crude emotional power, and that burned off, for me, swiftly and irresistibly, much of the jungle of progress-prattle surrounding it.

The story in outline is simple. John Bullaro, a young insurance salesman, *un homme moyen sensuel,* married, occasionally unfaithful to his wife, is drawn into an affair with an exceptionally independent married woman, Barbara Williamson. (These are real names, the author says; this is real life.) Barbara assures John Bullaro that her husband John Williamson has no objection to her infidelity—welcomes it, in truth, because he does not believe in marital possessiveness. John Bullaro is unaware that this strikingly unconcerned cuckold is a mechanical engineer turned sensual engineer who, self-schooled in the theories of Wilhelm Reich and the elitist visions of Ayn Rand, and afflicted with on-the-job ennui, is planning the experimental center that one day will be world-renowned as Sandstone. Disbelieving Barbara Williamson's asseverations, John Bullaro is filled with fear when her husband arranges to lunch with him—but the man not only confirms what his wife has said, he invites John Bullaro to drop by his house to meet a group of similarly liberated folk. Skeptical, wary of entrapment, John Bullaro pays the visit, becomes acquainted with the sexual experimenters for whom John Williamson is guru, and, enticed by a glimpse of forbidden delights, commences a new life. He initiates his wife, Judith, into the mysteries of mate-swapping and group sex, over her protest, and gradually the couple's commitment to Williamson the guru strengthens. They contribute labor and other resources to the refurbishing of the buildings that are to be reborn as Sandstone—Williamson's embryonic Celestial City. Judith Bullaro falls in love with the guru. The Bullaro center—family life, children—does not hold. John Bullaro dwindles into jealousy, and, under the tutelage of the guru, attempts to purify himself through acts of ritual isolation and exposure in the California desert—separation from the human community. But in the sequel he loses wife, children, family, job, and home. . . .

Nightmares, in sum, garish and sensational—as many as a half-dozen—are distributed throughout the Bullaro-Williamson chapters of the book. Soap, catchpenny lubriciousness, and side-show chills jostle each other in these scenes. Repeatedly as one reads one finds oneself wanting to hoot at the extravaganza, the spectacle of lordly, half-educated Faustians, self-styled Ayn Randian Leaders, imagining themselves as instructors to nature, exhorting their presumed inferiors to break every chain of attachment to the past, to common humanity, ordinary trust, ordinary shame. What have we here but a hideously farcical reduction of the decent aspirations of democratic individualism? What response to such madness could be appropriate except a chortle?

But loss is not mocked—not substantial human loss, not when accompanied by deep and intense awareness that it is self-caused, and that alternatives existed. Two hundred pages before the end of *Thy Neighbor's Wife* we see John Bullaro contemplating the wreckage of his days, recalling in despair the "first sexual encounter with Barbara at the insurance convention in Palm Springs, the emergence of John Williamson as a problem solver, the nude evenings in the Williamsons' house on Mullholland Drive . . ." That teasing time, rich in intimations of holiday release, seemed "so exhilarating and liberating"—and now Bullaro understands it as nothing other than "a preamble to destruction and chaos." Whatever love and order had been the stability of his life he had "sacrificed to the whim of experimentation and change." (p. 100)

I can imagine a reader of taste and good sense refusing sympathy to this victim, stiffening against the current of sentimentality. But the refusal is difficult; I was moved.

The author himself seems not to have been. The entire hundred-page Bullaro *exemplum* seems indeed to have had minuscule impact, psychological or otherwise, upon him. After dutifully running it through, he returns to the upbeat chronicle of Reason Triumphant, as though no real interruption had taken place. . . .

Thy Neighbor's Wife says a good deal, I'd argue, about the impacted condition of moral discourse in the late twentieth century. A fair conclusion is that we can bear reminders of the profound historical admonitions against covetousness and betrayal only if they're spotted into alien surroundings, allowed to peep out through the scrim as though by accident, claiming no more than an impatient and reluctant attention. Cameo appearances. Yet I remain impressed that Gay Talese, eyewitness, represented so fully the pathetic anguish of his experimenting couple. Despite chic obtuseness and intellectual naiveté, he possesses, as a good reporter, the ability to recognize (if not to understand) a whole story when it's proffered. Beyond this he has an honorable sense of obligation: whole stories, assimilable or no, deserve to be passed along in their fullness. Thanks to these gifts, nourished in this instance by a purely professional code (what besides purely professional codes survives?), the paean to Progress in *Thy Neighbor's Wife* may self-destruct. (p. 101)

> Benjamin DeMott, ''A Sexual Pilgrim's Progress,'' in The Atlantic Monthly, *Vol. 245, No. 5, May, 1980, pp. 98-101.*

JOHN LEONARD

Thy Neighbor's Wife is a pile of anecdotes, stapled together at random, of recipes instead of people, of ingredients and tics of personality and vehement longings: new uses for old organs! The enigmatic anus! More than 20 years ago, sizing up his competition in *Advertisements for Myself,* Norman Mailer decided that J. D. Salinger was "no more than the greatest mind ever to stay in prep school." In *Thy Neighbor's Wife,* nobody seems ever to have graduated from junior high—certainly not Talese. (p. 56)

Writing a book about sex in America, Talese almost totally ignores feminism. Gay liberation doesn't interest him. Children, conveniently, do not exist; if they did exist, they would make group sex—Tinkertoys! Erector Sets!—an unseemly hassle. Freud is trivialized. Marx isn't even mentioned. Can you imagine what Marx would have said after one long look at the

romper room in which we live? I can: He would have reminded us that the "fetishism of commodities" includes the vibrator.

For Talese, the sexual revolution seems to mean that more people are getting more of it and not feeling quite so bad afterward. Off, then, to California, where we remove our disposable clothes and go to water bed and discuss "primary" versus "secondary relationships."

Really, Talese should have had a long talk with the autumnal Freud about greed and bad faith. Is sublimation really necessary? If I defer my gratification, will you defer yours? Would Freud, smoking his sad cigar, be interested to hear that Hefner began as a cartoonist, doing obscene parodies of the Dagwood-and-Blondie comic strip? That Arthur Bremer, wearing a vest and a tie, failed to achieve orgasm in a massage parlor only a month before he shot and paralyzed Governor George Wallace?

What has possessed Talese, whom I have met and who has never before been dull? The reporter in him founders. He starts to tell us about obscenity prosecutions in this country, on which Irving Wallace was more informative in his novel *The Seven Minutes;* he digresses to discuss sex clubs, about which Jerzy Kosinski was more entertaining in his novel *Passion Play;* then we find him in the middle of a casual précis of D. H. Lawrence, about whom one would do better to consult Norman Mailer in *The Prisoner of Sex;* but he has already moved on to Wilhelm Reich, about whom Paul Robinson had much more to say in *The Freudian Left;* however, now he is explaining Ayn Rand, who needs no explanation for anyone who read the review of *Atlas Shrugged* by Whittaker Chambers—the famous ex-Communist who translated *Bambi*—in the pages of *National Review,* a magazine without pubic hair. . . . And so on.

Nor, in his books on *The New York Times* and the Mafia, was Talese so slapdash. Because Hefner's magazine has a lead time of months instead of weeks, I am reading *Thy Neighbor's Wife* in 1979 in manuscript, and possibly the publisher will clean it up some, but don't bet on it. The San Francisco earthquake happened in 1906, not, as Talese has it, in 1904. The Free Speech Movement in Berkeley was launched in 1963, not in 1965. And while he may have wound up as a Los Angeles Ram, the Bernie Casey who cohabited with Max Lerner and Alex Comfort and Daniel Ellsberg at Sandstone in the nude spent most of his professional football career with the San Francisco 49ers. (pp. 57-8)

I quibble because I get the feeling that there is something disheartened and desperate about Talese's slapdash, as if he wanted to escape in a hurry from his own book, as if the subject had begun to mystify and alarm him, as if he were afraid he could not come back normal, after all those years in massage parlors and *New York* magazine and *Esquire.* Out in the world, we seethe. Is the act itself, no holds barred, merely reactional and hygienic, a kind of horizontal jog? Or does it partake of something deeper, down in the dreams? He is sometimes the little boy outside the window of the toy-sex shop, about to slaver; at other times he seems to fear that it won't work, we'll be punished, members of the John Birch Society ought not to behave this way, hedonism lacks sincerity, the compass has gone crazy.

Who knows? I certainly don't, but I didn't write a book on what I didn't know. . . .

Closing *Thy Neighbor's Wife,* looking around at romper room, I wonder whether in the postindustrial whatever-it-is, we insist on service stations for a baffled eros. Cars need filling stations; maybe the rest of us need emptying, on odd and even days. How sad. The critic Irving Howe has written of our new "psychology of unobstructed need." Sexuality is proposed as "the ground of being, and vital sexuality the assurance of a moral life." But what if "the needs and impulses of human beings clash . . . if the transfer of energies from sexuality to sociality" doesn't go smoothly? . . .

These are questions Talese didn't ask himself, as if his revolution were all Woodstock and no Altamont, all Bunnies and no Mansons. Is anybody happier? Missing from *Thy Neighbor's Wife* are history and stamina and celebration and mystery, along with birth, blood, death and beauty, not to mention earth, fire, water, work, politics and everything else that isn't our urgent plumbing, that refuses to swim in our libidinal pool—everything that used to distinguish us from paramecia. Who wants to be a god in such a universe? (p. 58)

> *John Leonard, in a review of "Thy Neighbor's Wife,"*
> *in* Playboy®, *Vol. 27, No. 5, May, 1980, pp. 56-8.*

BARBARA GRIZZUTI HARRISON

"The only sin passion can commit is to be joyless." Somebody wonderful said that in a novel; and it is a fitting epigraph for [*Thy Neighbor's Wife*]—which is about as exciting as Bowling for Dollars, only much much much longer. . . .

Not only is *Thy Neighbor's Wife* boring, it is grim. Poor Gay Talese has managed to produce a book that is as pious and self-righteous as those little religious tracts distributed by sad gray men who invite us to go to hell for thinking nasty thoughts. Actually, those tracts—written, as they are, with a certain verve and a rather charming disregard for syntax—are far more titillating than Talese's pompous tome about (I guess) the sexual revolution. *Thy Neighbor's Wife* is also written without regard to syntax, but it has as little charm as a manual on plumbing, which it in many ways resembles. (p. 33)

I don't want to give you the impression that *Thy Neighbor's Wife* is totally without redeeming social value. It's good for a chuckle now and then. As when Talese tells us that in the course of his arduous research—nine years' worth—he spoke to some "admittedly monogamous couples." Now there's a fetching phrase. Gone are the days when monogamy was the love that dared not speak its name; if married couples are now so brave as to "admit" to monogamy, what horrible crimes will be broadcast next? I'm also taken with Talese's notion that masseuses are "the Florence Nightingales of masturbation." He does have a way with words. As when he tells us that a nude model, "aware only of her body as an inspired instrument . . . felt internalized as she danced." The trouble is, I'm not sure what the words mean. Have you felt internalized lately? (p. 34)

Talese makes me laugh. I can't help it; he ought to make me angry, but he makes me laugh.

He doesn't make me laugh when he tries to pass himself off as a populist—as opposed to those "elitists" among us who find pornography distasteful. . . . Convince me—Talese can't—that Goya's maja and a picture of a woman being fed through a meat-grinder appeal to the same instincts and impulses. Nowhere does Talese even attempt to define the difference be-

tween erotica and pornography. I would have found that interesting.

Never does he tell us where the kids of all these sexual libertines are, or what they think of their parents' carryings on. I would have found that interesting. I find it ludicrous—and if Mr. Talese believes his own words he's even dopier than I think he is—that the men at Sandstone were there to bridge the generation gap. . . . (pp. 34-5)

One might also laugh at Talese's rabid anti-Catholicism (it can't have escaped your notice that all his books have biblical titles), were it not so pitiable; one might also say pathological. Irish Catholic mothers, who are invariably married to drunken fathers, and "latent homosexual" priests are the villains in this book (though "dour Jewish women" come in for their share of blame). His hatred of the Church is so intense that it causes Talese to desert, momentarily, his fierce advocacy of the First Amendment. . . .

Talese parrots Reich: he mistakenly holds that "religious tradition" regards sex as "evil," and that religious leaders "deny the body." But it is not the Church that denies the body—hence the promise of an earthly resurrection; it is the pornographers who deny the body by objectifying it—hence "Hefner would not print any advertising that focused on male problems or worries, such as baldness, physical frailty, or obesity." Talese is wildly out of control, he can't help himself. He even places pimps in "Lenten-purple" automobiles. (p. 35)

The Church (which Talese, in his monomania, confuses with the Puritans) may indeed have contributed to an atmosphere of sexual repression—look what it led to: Talese. But by Talese's own admission, only six Catholics have served on the Supreme Court during its nearly 200-year history. This is a fact not to be disregarded when one is talking about obscenity trials. Talese does talk about obscenity trials, and this is potentially fascinating material. But precisely because of his myopic secularism, he does not place obscenity trials in any social context—which is what I would call more than a slight flaw in a book that is touted as a social history. It is enough for him to cast the Church as villain; cultural and secular forces at work are blithely disregarded, as are the opinions of women. There has been a melt-down at the core of this book; it is hollow.

Talese's bigotry is bound to offend me because I am Catholic. But one does not have to be Catholic to be offended by Talese's hatred for the penis. He may not know he hates the penis, but he does. . . . If ever a man were more to be pitied than scorned it is Gay Talese.

Who has the effrontery to suggest that only "man-hating" feminists are offended by whips and chains and manacles and kiddie porn? . . . A *good* feminist is someone like Betty Dodson, who is "cunt positive," and who invites men to "consciousness-raising sessions." . . . A *good* feminist believes that "marriage is a form of prostitution. . . . Saving sex for my lover was my gift to him in exchange for economic security." . . . (pp. 35-6)

While Talese consorts with these "cunt positive" women—who seem to me more than a little cuckoo—he wonders fleetingly why few women are "aroused by the sight of an erect penis *unless* they are warmly disposed to the man who (is) attached to it." Well, if he's writing a book about the sexual revolution, he ought to do more than wonder fleetingly. It has not escaped my notice that many, if not most, men differ from many, if not most, women in their approach to sex. Never—in 548 pages—does Talese seriously explore the reasons for this contrast between the sexes.

Or the love that exists between men and women. (p. 36)

Barbara Grizzuti Harrison, in a review of "Thy Neighbor's Wife," in The New Republic, *Vol. 182, No. 18, May 3, 1980, pp. 33-6.*

ROBERT COLES

Gay Talese, the well-known journalist who has a knack for taking on projects others would believe to be awesomely difficult, if not impossible (the workings of the Mafia, for example) now offers [in *Thy Neighbor's Wife*] a report (the result of no less than nine years of work) on just how far some of us have willingly, gladly strayed not only from 19th-century morality, but from the kind that most of the 20th century has taken for granted. His method of inquiry is that of "participant-observation"; as a matter of fact, I doubt any so-called "field worker" can claim to have surpassed Mr. Talese with regard to personal involvement. He talked with men and women who have embraced uninhibited or unconventional sexuality, but he also became a distinct part of a world he was trying to comprehend. That is, he not only worked in Manhattan's massage parlors, he became a beneficiary of their favors. . . .

Yet this long narrative will probably disappoint those with prurient interests. It is not an exhibitionist's confession; it is not a journalist's contribution to pornography. Mr. Talese will be made a good deal richer than he already is by this book, but one suspects a substantial number of his readers will find him surprisingly restrained. He has a serious interest in watching his fellow human beings, in listening to them, and in presenting honestly what he has seen and heard. He writes clean, unpretentious prose. He has a gift, through a phrase here, a sentence there, of making important narrative and historical connections. We are given, really, a number of well-told stories, their social message cumulative: A drastically transformed American sexuality has emerged during this past couple of decades. . . .

There are some first-rate sections in *Thy Neighbor's Wife* on that matter: the social history of pornography, the legal history of book and magazine banning; there is also a very valuable political and cultural history of some of America's sexual utopian communities, going back to the 19th century. Those who have associated the town of Oneida, N.Y. with the manufacture of silverware will be interested to learn that such an industry was but one of many set in prosperous motion by a group of people converted to "Perfectionism"—a communitarian, polygamous group anxious to show the world that both property and love can be shared quite generously among a particular group of human beings. And those who want an account of the Supreme Court's complex encounters with X-rated films and certain boldly, explicitly sexual magazines will be grateful for the careful discussion that subject receives.

But informative as such chapters are, they turn out to be enlightening digressions. The heart of Mr. Talese's book is the life stories he presents—factual accounts of men and women not provided disguises. . . .

The tone of the book varies—a reflection, surely, of the author's complicated, if not ambiguous responses to what he witnessed and sometimes took part in (now gingerly, one surmises, now with few if any reservations). Mr. Talese is at his best when he is away from the high-pitched cosmopolitanism of California—in the Midwest or the rural South. . . .

But no matter the geography, Mr. Talese pays attention to more than sex; we get, repeatedly, the textures of a given social scene. He can be a controlled but touching writer, anxious to convey the melancholy, the hurts of a particular life, yet able to stop short of sentiment. I had not expected to feel anything but repulsion for some of the people described in this book; yet, as is often the case when a good writer looks beneath the surfaces of life, even the kind that seems cheap or tawdry or twisted or just plain foolish, strangely compelling proofs are discovered—reminders that here, too, is a moment of important human truth. (p. 3)

What Mr. Talese claims is that the "polymorphous perverse" of Freud has now become enough a part of our everyday social life to merit a study that took a long time to do and to write up. His evidence—the range of his informants, the geographic and cultural spread of his investigation—seems to bear him out. Whether he is describing a rising tide or one now already at ebb (as with some descriptions of "youth" and their "behavior" made in the recent past) is hard to know. But one thing comes across loud and clear: The people who embraced sexuality for various reasons—be they mainly personal, or for commercial profit—are still, like the rest of us, slouching toward Jerusalem; that is, are as mean and self-centered and vain and ungenerous and nasty, from time to time, as the rest of us "unliberated" ones. And Mr. Talese notably skirts an extremely important subject: what happened to the children whose parents got caught up in the "growth centers" and "people changes" and "love nets" this book describes? We hear little about those boys and girls; they seem set aside, forgotten, handed over (we are several times told) to a succession of baby sitters—as if love for a "neighbor's wife" matters more by far than the welfare of mere children.

What kind of ethical responsibilities are at work in such lives? One wonders, too, about the moral sensibility presumably at work in this book. The author is quick to scorn our hypocrisies and self-serving pieties. He mocks some of our Supreme Court Justices. He confesses his various lusts. He mentions his wife and children—the troubling effect his work had on them. But exactly what does he think of Hugh Hefner, of the life he lives—all those oiled and powdered women, an endless succession bought by a demanding millionaire in the service of his sexual megalomania? Does Gay Talese want such a fate for any woman—for his daughters? And what about the women who give all those Manhattan massages—why the reluctance to look at their lives, to comment on their situation? Has this shrewd journalist, this accomplished storyteller not once been inspired by the above-mentioned to a cautionary tale he can share with us—maybe even to shed his "cool" with an outburst of disgust? Who ought to get "love" (if that is the right word here) from whom—and at what cost of human dignity? What happens to a culture, a civilization, when sexual fantasies become for increasing numbers a reigning preoccupation—one vast Id, with the Ego and Super-Ego mere straws in the brisk wind of a given social history?

I don't think those are the questions of a few sexual puritans, or for that matter, a few narrow-minded, influential burghers, anxious to stifle the physical aspirations of others. Ordinary men and women all over the world wonder about such matters;

do so not necessarily because they are "inhibited," because they have yet to become "liberated," but out of their humanity. As philosophers once knew to put it—and would that they did so more often these days: what is the meaning of life, and how ought one to live it? (p. 39)

Robert Coles, "Transforming American Sexuality," in The New York Times Book Review, *May 4, 1980, pp. 3, 38-9.*

VIRGINIA JOHNSON-MASTERS

[*Thy Neighbor's Wife*] is a scholarly accumulation of information, laced with enough erotic content to entertain most anyone.

It will be regrettable if *Thy Neighbor's Wife* is regarded primarily as a biography of Hugh Hefner, even though Hef's life, times, and the saga of *Playboy* magazine comprise a major segment of the book and provide it with an important part of its structural design. But Talese's tome is much more than one person's biography. It is a meticulously researched context of people, events, and circumstances through which a reader can follow the breakdown of the repressive sexual myths that have dominated our society until quite recently. It is also possible, in this vast amount of material, to perceive the resulting social struggle to establish a sexual value system that serves more of the people more of the time, while they try to cope simultaneously with their "sex is pleasure and pleasure is sin" lessons of childhood. (p. 199)

The focus of *Thy Neighbor's Wife* is always sexual, but the content informs at least as much as it titillates. Paradoxically, it reads as easily as a children's book while presenting some very sophisticated material. For those who don't shy from the opening erotica of Chapter One, interest should be easy to establish and maintain. This is a lengthy book, however, where those with a fascination for explicit information about the lives and sexual behavior of others must wade through many layers of factual material that they may find boring.

It might be suggested that those who are less intellectually inclined read until they become restless with a segment they consider pedantic, mark it for later, and move forward along the story line. It would be unfortunate, though, if the reader who skips in this fashion should fail to return another time to the portions previously avoided. Dry though they may seem, much of their content is landmark information about things that are continuing to influence and control our sexual destinies.

Small wonder Gay Talese took eight years to research and write this book. Although his initial announcement of a planned review of "sex in America" seemed rather grandiose, he seems to have reasonably accomplished his goal. He has produced an internal as well as external picture of sexual practices in our society: How people feel and what they expect, as well as how they really act, in situations where sex is a crucial factor. (pp. 199-200)

On a personal note, I was immensely relieved to find that Gay Talese the writer did not disguise himself as Gay Talese the sociologist/psychologist, in the fashion of many published journalists today. His work is obviously *his* work, *his* perspective, and not material claimed from the work of scientists in professional journals. There is maturity and skill in the way Talese depicts the individual uniqueness of erotic stimulation, not

clinically but graphically revealed in descriptions of people's sexual feelings and behavior. He obviously understands, at least as a writer, the nature of erotic response and sources of sexual stimulation better than most people, not simply in terms of technique but in terms of the mind, emotions, and expectations. . . .

I cannot state that I know all times, places, and events presented in this book are absolutely accurate. My impression is, though, that the degree of accuracy of historical information is high. I will offer the opinion, however, that *Thy Neighbor's Wife* provides something rather difficult to come by in these days of sex-related media bombardment: a definitive overview of the sexual attitudes, behavior, and expectations prevalent in society during the past and present centuries, together with what surely is the most comprehensive guide to contemporary sources of sexual influence, with one notable exception.

Mr. Talese chose to omit any real mention of the contributions towards "redefining sexual mores" made by members of the scientific community. It is curious that he offers only a minimal reference to Dr. Kinsey, and a few sentences about Masters and Johnson. This omission calls for some scrutiny of Talese's bias in viewing the totality of America's sexual scene. Perhaps the author felt it of too little importance to let his book show that it is the scientific and health-care communities that are primarily responsible for dignifying the sexual condition in contemporary society and that, more than any other group, they have fostered social acceptance of sexuality as a vital, crucial dimension of personality. (p. 200)

Virginia Johnson-Masters, "'Scholarly and Erotic . . .'," in Vogue, *Vol. 170, No. 6, June, 1980, pp. 199-200.*

RICHARD WOODS, O.P.

Like *Playboy,* which Talese as a journalist may properly admire, *Thy Neighbor's Wife,* for all its fascination with female genitalia, is by a male, about males, for males. Heterosexual to a Kinseyan fault, moreover, Talese smoothly passes over issues of gay liberation and that of other oppressed sexual minorities even more completely than he did that of women. Yet it *is* important that in the contemporary revolution of sexual consciousness and behavior, at least in the affluent portions of the globe, liberation is not confined to white, married, upper-middle-class, heterosexual urban males whose foibles and fantasies have too long dominated the media.

Still, one can't entirely suppress the feeling that there is something important, even valuable about discovering the pathetic misadventures of now notorious pornographers and libertines— both the peddlers of smut and their antagonists, such as the puritannical Comstock. Talese studies, considers, reports, but does not slaver over the sometimes sordid, more often embarrassing scenes of their youth and young adulthood. He is a camera, not unrelated to Isherwood's hero, charting photographically and often with gritty realism the path of sexual wreckage littering some of the cultural and personal expressways of the late 20th century. He seems unwilling or perhaps unable to assume a definite moral or ethical stance in regard to his material, however, despite his announced agenda.

Although *Thy Neighbor's Wife* may lack some essential ingredients of great literature—imagination, charm, wit and insight—it is not devoid of compassion in its candid view of celluloid and tabloid sexuality. It is a studiously tedious path this Vergil leads us along into the dessicated gulleys of a cultural and spiritual wasteland. But not into hell, which after all has a tragic aspect that bespeaks the greatness of the stakes in life's gamble. No Francesca da Rimini suffers eternally here in the company of her forbidden lover. The tourist in Talese's inferno is met largely by boring and insipid customers bent on satisfying their genital itches in an incessant masturbatory roulette. *Thy Neighbor's Wife* is an epitaph on the gravestone of passion. For too often Talese reminds us, sometimes almost eloquently, in matters and manners sexual, it is a small, small world after all. (p. 4)

> *Richard Woods, O.P., in a review of "Thy Neighbor's Wife," in* The Critic, *Vol. 38, No. 22, June 11, 1980, pp. 2-4.*

THE ECONOMIST

Thy Neighbor's Wife is not an inclusive study of sex in America, nor is it the definitive work on "the redefinition of morality". There are scholarly historical passages on pornography cases and on utopian American communities. But there are no homosexuals, no happy monogamous couples, no sensitive portrayals of women. The only contemporary issues that get systematic treatment are pornography, middle-class infidelity and masculine lust and longing. (p. 107)

Mr Talese does not seem certain how he feels about the sexual changes he describes. Nor does he have a firmer grasp than the rest of mankind on the complex issues he explores. The conflicting enticements of monogamy and variety leave him in a moral fog along with his characters, mostly middle-class men escaping from a repressed background like himself.

In fact, the author and his protagonists are locked in a time warp. They are still fighting against the repression of the 1950s while the rest of the United States is now grappling with the confusions of the 1980s. Towards the end of the book Mr Talese writes that "the initiators were almost always men, the inhibitors almost always women". This sums up his views about men and women: the men are supposed to try, the women are supposed to resist.

This was the basic social pattern of male-female relationships before the so-called sexual revolution, and the breaking down of this dynamic is what the revolution was all about. But Mr Talese and his ilk appear to define the new sexual freedom as a licence to do whatever turns them on and to perpetuate the double standard.

As a result, they are stuck in the traditional male mould no matter how many new experiences they undergo or fantasies they fulfill. They remain eternal adolescents, defying mother, longing for a sexually assertive woman and terrified if they meet her.

The most provocative issues raised by this book do not concern bedroom behaviour but pornography and literature. Where does social observation end and bad taste start? Was it worth countless miles and dollars for the author accurately to inform us exactly how Mr Hefner and his ex-wife Mildred petted during their courtship? Is more learned by participating in painstakingly detailed bedroom scenes of living people than by peering into those of fictional characters? Does the non-fiction novel, as this book has been described, turn its audience into Peeping Toms?

Although these issues are an integral part of his assignment, Mr Talese does not directly address them in his book. As a result, his book remains a piece of reportage, trying to tell a story perhaps too changeable, too unwieldy and far too personal for anyone to depict properly—or even improperly. (pp. 107-08)

> *"Peeping Toms," in* The Economist, *Vol. 275, No. 7139, June 28, 1980, pp. 106-08.*

GILLIAN WILCE

Thy Neighbour's Wife doesn't raise questions, except by default. I shouldn't imagine it raises much else either. It didn't give me so much as a frisson of fellow-feeling. A compelling communication of sensual pleasure, a re-presentation of people *enjoying* themselves, might have provided more of a rationale for the book. As might the offering of premises for argument about sexual mores in the West today. The vaunted objectivity proves merely dull and frustrating. There's no passion here—mental, ethical, sexual or even anthropological. And there's no sense of humour or proportion either. Mr Talese solemnly claims to be dealing with one of the greatest issues of his time. But you begin to have doubts about his discernment of issues when he equates the sexual jealousy of one John Bullaro with the deaths of Robert Kennedy and Martin Luther King. Of course sexual jealousy is painful, very, but it's hardly in the same league as assassinations and riots. And if there is a connection, a reason why we should see them all as part of the same 'turmoil', Mr Talese omits to tell us.

Moreover, there isn't even the echo of a giggle in his voice when he reveals that 'in his more visionary moments, sitting in his round bed in his private aeroplane . . . Hugh Hefner saw himself as the embodiment of the masculine dream'. The relentless length at which he describes Hefner's life and furniture suggests it's all too probable that Gay Talese shares this 'vision'. It's all the fault of the penis, you see, that 'most honest organ', 'endlessly searching, sensing, expanding, probing, penetrating, throbbing, wilting and wanting more'. The penis (and you may have missed this bit in biology class) is 'rooted in man's soul'; it certainly seems to have tipped Mr Talese off balance.

As you might infer from his organic orientation, Mr Talese is not so hot on the sexual nature of women. He doesn't understand them; he says so. He occasionally comments favourably on some woman's 'masculine' ability to take her sexual pleasure as she pleases and without fuss. He makes a gesture towards feminism in his chapter on Betty Dodson and her paintings. But he doesn't even try to consider sexual roles off the couch, or homosexuality, or sex education, or the possible limits of freedom. No reason he should, of course, except that his subtitle—'sex in the world today'—sort of suggested that he just might.

What Mr Talese mostly writes about is sex as a commodity. . . . He talks at one point about the fast-food business of sex. His visit to Europe—made in the interests of research but productive of exactly one paragraph—served only to confirm his view that 'women sold sexual pleasure; men bought it', everywhere. And, even if he is sometimes, in some places, partly right, he does not seem to have noticed what it is that he has said, let alone wondered whether it matters and why it should be so.

This is a smooth-surfaced, silicone book, manufactured for a market. But it is a disappointing buy, over-packaged, over-sold and unsatisfying. (pp. 17-18)

Gillian Wilce, ''Market Values,'' in New Statesman,
Vol. 100, No. 2577, August 8, 1980, pp. 17-18.

BARBARA LOUNSBERRY

The work of Gay Talese offers a vivid, though rarely recognized, illustration of personal mythos and the new journalism.... If any writer should be free of projecting his own mythos on his material, Talese, with his tireless legwork, should be the one. And yet, an analysis of Talese's writings to date reveals a persistent personal mythos: Talese's intense preoccupation with the relationship between fathers and sons and with the continuation of the paternal legacy. Whether writing about bridge builders, gangsters, movie stars, or *The New York Times,* Talese tends to define the essence of these disparate entities in terms of the key parent-child relationship. In these works he expands the specific dilemma of how to honor one's real-life father in a changing age to the more universal question of how to honor the national spirit, the American dream of our forefathers, in a similarly changing and diminished era. Thus the individual ''psychodramas'' of Talese's subjects become the national psychodramas of us all.

The article **''The Soft Psyche of Joshua Logan''** [collected in *Fame and Obscurity*] offers a clear and simple illustration of Talese's mythos. The ''news peg,'' or journalistic excuse, for this piece was the 1963 opening of Joshua Logan's new play, *Tiger Tiger Burning Bright,* and Logan's attempt to make a Broadway comeback after such past glories as *South Pacific.* Talese is quick to note the similarity of the play's plot to Logan's own parental conflict: *Tiger Tiger Burning Bright* is about ''a mother who dominates her children in a dream world she has created in Louisiana—a play that gradually, as rehearsals progressed, churned up more and more memories for Logan, haunting memories of his days in Mansfield, Louisiana.'' ... In his author's note to *Fame and Obscurity,* Talese wrote that one of his ambitions is to remain with his subjects long enough ''to see their lives change in some way.'' Most of his writings gradually mount to some dramatic crisis which is revelatory of the son's success or failure in living up to his father's (or mother's) spiritual tradition or expectations. In a conversation in **''The Soft Psyche,''** Logan shares the personal psychodrama behind his present theatrical effort. (pp. 518-19)

Talese ends this article with the fate of Logan's venture. *Tiger Tiger Burning Bright* opens to praise, but Logan, ill, is unable to attend opening night....

[In *The Bridge*], a more extended work, Talese is able to move beyond the simple individual parental obsession of a famous figure like Logan to suggest the broader, indeed national, implications of the theme. Bridge builders, indeed, *literally* ''span'' the nation and regard themselves, Talese tells us, as ''the last of America's unhenpecked heroes.'' ... Across the ten chapters which make up this work, Talese stresses family relationships again and again, particularly emphasizing the difficulties sons experience in trying to escape the dangerous family tradition of bridge building.... (p. 520)

Chapter 6 of *The Bridge* is entitled ''Death on a bridge,'' and here we see Gerard McKee, a handsome, popular youth from a ''boomer'' [bridge building] family, fall to his death from the Verrazano span. Gerard has two brothers who are also boomers, and his father—''a man whom Gerard strongly resembled—had been hit by a collapsing crane a few years before, had had his leg permanently twisted, had a steel plate inserted in his head, and was disabled for life.'' ... Of all the

mourners at Gerard's funeral, James McKee suffers the most: '''After what I've been through,' he said, shaking his head, tears in his eyes, 'I should know enough to keep my kids off the bridge.''' ... But McKee doesn't, and *The Bridge* ends with another son's death on the next bridge in Portugal. Talese's title explicitly links his vision of the nation with Hart Crane's in his famous poem of the same name. Both works proffer the bridge as a symbol of hope for a permanent spanning to some vast national ideal, and yet both show the negations that in the present somehow keep us from achieving the affirmations of Whitman's American prophecy. Failure, death, or, at best, a short-lived success like Joshua Logan's are the fates of the sons of bridge builders. (p. 521)

The legacy of another kind of national monument, *The New York Times,* becomes a similar haunting burden for each generation of ''sons'' in **The Kingdom and the Power**.... Those who read **The Kingdom and the Power** carefully will find more than just the ''human history of an institution in transition'' which Talese claims; they will find a powerful arraignment of that institution, many of its top executives, and the U.S. Establishment as well. Talese creates this indictment through subtle equating and interweaving of three father figures. He begins by establishing the central subject of his book as the transmission of the *Times* tradition from Adolph Ochs to each generation of his successors. The *Times* tradition is also projected (through religious rhetoric) as being a veritable patriarchal religion to Ochs and his fellow *Times*men. Finally, Talese equates the *Times*'s tradition/religion with the secular vision of the U.S. Establishment. To the extent that Talese also continuously undercuts this Establishment, particularly for its indifference to the lower classes, his book indicts *The Times* as an example of the American Dream gone wrong, of American idealism gone elitist. (pp. 521-22)

[From] his first chapter on Talese carefully presents his ultimate conflict (between New York and Washington and between different styles of *Times* leadership) through the figures of managing editor Clifton Daniel and former Washington Bureau Chief James Reston. **The Kingdom and the Power** begins with Daniel and ends with Reston. In between, the two men—of similar backgrounds but antithetical styles—engage in a struggle for control of the future of *The Times,* and in the end Adolph Ochs's grandson must decide between them. His crisis and his decision, then, will reveal his faithfulness to his patriarchal heritage and the future direction of the *''Times*ian'' liturgy.

The Daniel/Reston conflict is posed, however, in a most sophisticated manner. Although Talese sees in Daniel and Reston distinctly different aspects of the *Times*'s corporate personality and uses them in this symbolic way, in no sense does he present the two in any simple or diametric opposition. They are both, after all, faithful sons of *The Times.* My feeling is that Talese chooses to begin his story of *The New York Times* with Clifton Daniel because Daniel epitomized to him the ''public image'' of *The Times*—the image which Talese wishes to debunk. (p. 524)

Clifton Daniel ... represents *The Times* as a whole—its public façade and its private struggle with tradition.... Yet Daniel also represents a slightly new style for *The Times* with his interests in the women's and society pages, the columns on culture and the arts. James Reston, however, represents ... a more fundamental element in the newspaper. With the grand-patriarch now thirty years gone, Reston is the living *Times* executive who, in Talese's eyes, most embodies the past, the *Times* ''tradition,'' and particularly the distinctive Ochsian philosophy of religious idealism and business pragmatism. Talese, indeed, goes to great length to link Reston with the holy *Times* triumvirate of tradition, religion, and the U.S. power Establishment. Unlike Daniel (but like Adolph Ochs), Reston is a legacy builder. He becomes, Talese tells us, "the *paterfamilias*" of his Washington bureau . . . , establishing a line of succession passing from himself to Tom Wicker and Max Frankel, and standing up and protecting his "sons" from New York attack. (p. 525)

The crisis to the fourth successor, Adolph Ochs's grandson Punch Sulzberger, came over the appointment by Daniel of James Greenfield to replace Tom Wicker as Washington bureau chief in 1968, and over Reston's subsequent opposition. This is the final moment of conflict toward which the entire volume builds. Talese increases the suspensefulness of this climactic moment by describing Punch Sulzberger in ambiguous terms. To Talese, he is one of the "older young men . . . caught between the prismatic vision of the generation above and the one below."' . . . Sulzberger is thus, like so many sons in Talese's work, a son caught between the past and the future. We are also told that he has been a failure to his father in the past and that even his office suite as publisher on the fourteenth floor of the *Times* building revealed his uncertain and ambiguous posture. (pp. 525-26)

Thus Punch Sulzberger, the latest son, has failed his father in the distant past, and, by folding *The Times's* overseas edition, has shown himself not sentimentally bound to his father's vision in the recent past. Will he choose the past (Reston) over the present (Daniel) at this moment? This passage by Talese perhaps most clearly reveals Punch Sulzberger's (and the United States's) dilemma: "Sulzberger now more than ever wanted to experiment with modern systems and to learn more about them; his newspaper could not merely follow the formulas of his father or grandfather. *The Times* would have to preserve what was inviolable in its tradition, yet adjust to the changing trends and new tools."' . . . (p. 526)

"Preserve what was inviolable in its tradition." That is the key phrase, for what is inviolable in Adolph Ochs's *Times* tradition is its place as righteous spokesman for the U.S. Establishment. And so when the chips are down (unlike Bill Bonanno in *Honor Thy Father* who proves a failure to his father's image), Punch Sulzberger proves himself a faithful son and grandson, a faithful heir and preserver of the Ochsian theocracy; he chooses, of course, Washington and Reston over New York and Daniel.

In Talese's language (as well as in my own) there is something distressingly sinister about this gesture of "honoring thy father." Punch Sulzberger's decision to preserve and elevate the past, the "tradition" as embodied in James Reston, is distressing to the degree that Talese has also suggested the elitism, and thus limitation, of that tradition. Here we have the anti-Establishment, anti-*Times* motif which Talese weaves all through his volume. In Talese's view, the American society is divided into the "haves" and "have-nots," and the elitist circles of the rich and powerful hardly even recognize, much less support, the have-nots. Indeed, at repeated points in the volume Talese ironically juxtaposes the nearsighted elitist world of the Establishment with the real problems and suffering of the poor. . . . (p. 526-27)

James Reston is particularly characterized by Talese as associated with Establishment elitism. And this is the man and the spirit triumphing at the end of *The Kingdom and the Power.* Reston sees the future dominated by a "new class of public

servant," which is nothing less than an Establishment clique "operating within the 'triangle' of the university-foundation life, the communications media, and the government."' . . . His method of reporting what the young people of the nation are thinking and saying is to print the remarks of college valedictorians—the elite of the youth—in *The Times.* Surely this limited elitist view is criticized by Talese in *The Kingdom and the Power,* and surely, to this degree, James Reston is the villain of the work. (p. 527)

Talese has created a most subtle, artful work of journalistic history in the way he undercuts *The Times* at the same time he is carefully presenting its story. *The Times* may be *the* U.S. newspaper, but to the extent (as Talese repeatedly suggests) that it was from its beginning and continues to be an organ firmly linked to the elitist U.S. power establishment, its history and tradition represent a limitation and even a falsification of the original vision of our forefathers. And to the extent (as Talese's rhetoric also implies) that its history is a microcosm of United States history, its falsification of the original Jeffersonian dream of equality and justice, under the pressures of money and power, illustrates the fate of the nation in the late twentieth century.

Iphigene Sulzberger's comment that Talese "didn't know what he was talking about" raises some important questions regarding personal mythos and the new journalism. To what extent does Talese's mythos—his preoccupation with the generational legacy throughout all his writing—offer valid and meaningful insights into the history of *The New York Times?* Is the mythos more revelatory of Talese (and his own personal and literary obsessions) than of *The Times?*

These are important questions for both writers and readers, for here is a case where evidently nothing has actually been "invented," yet the personal mythos is everywhere apparent. Writers of hybrid factual/fictional forms need to become more conscious of their own personal mythoi, of the subjects to which they are repeatedly drawn, of the facets of a subject upon which they repeatedly focus. Such consciousness might enable them to control more rigorously their subjectivity, their tendency to see in the subject an enactment of their own mythos. Talese, for example, should ask: "Is the parent/child relationship the significant conflict in this history, or are there other facets more 'true' that my personal mythos is obscuring?" At the least, such consciousness could aid new journalists to rein in their subjectivity rather than let it roam, as at present, unchecked. (p. 528)

Thus both writers and readers of the new journalism, the docudrama, and other hybrid forms of fact and fiction would do well to remind themselves repeatedly of the inescapable subjectivity of the genre. Readers should tell themselves that they are reading, not *the* truth about *The New York Times,* American bridge builders, or Joshua Logan, but *a* truth, one vision. They need to be alert as they read for signs of the author's personal mythos and to recognize that there are ways to test the validity of such subjective visions. The validity of Talese's equation of *The Times's* "tradition" with the power Establishment can be judged, for example, by asking how often *The Times* took stands opposed to the Establishment, as in the Pentagon papers case. Such questions would lead the reader to other *Times* histories and away from the tyranny of the single source. Ultimately they could lead readers to a richer appreciation of both the subject and the writer's mythos.

Finally, readers must recognize that new journalists frequently employ nonfictional subjects (historical events and personages) merely as springboards for larger subjects which engage them. One might argue, for example, . . . that Gay Talese's *real* subject is the repeated failure of the United States to live up to the spiritual ideals of its forefathers. Thus readers of the new journalism must assess the validity of two literary projects rather than one, recognizing that most frequently, as is true with Gay Talese, it is the larger truth which is compelling, while the literal truth of the events or personages can be viewed with a more cynical eye. (p. 529)

Barbara Lounsberry, ''Personal Mythos and the New Journalism: Gay Talese's Fathers and Sons,'' in The Georgia Review, *Vol. XXXVII, No. 3, Fall, 1983, pp. 517-29.*

Peter (Hillsman) Taylor
1917-

American short story writer, dramatist, and novelist.

Taylor is considered one of the most accomplished short story writers in contemporary American literature. In his stories he focuses on urban, upper middle-class Southern family life and explores such regional concerns as the collapse of traditional values and the consequences of the shift from agrarian to urban society. While his fiction is firmly rooted in the concerns of a specific locale, Taylor is praised for achieving universal relevance in his works. Taylor sees himself "writing about people under certain circumstances, but always concerned with the individual experience and the unique experience of [each] story." His stories are tightly structured, and his precise characterization and subtle denouements have led critics to compare his works with those of Henry James and Anton Chekhov.

Taylor's first collection, *A Long Fourth and Other Stories* (1948), was well received. With this book, Taylor established the themes and milieu which he has continued to explore throughout his career. The title story, regarded as one of Taylor's best, expresses several of the author's predominant themes. The narrative centers on a prosperous Nashville woman and her attempts to prepare a memorable weekend for her son, who will visit her from New York before joining the army. Several circumstances undermine her plans and reveal the lack of tradition and order in her seemingly well-mannered life. The story comments on the changing values of society and dramatizes the suffering of people unable to reconcile themselves to social change.

Taylor's mastery of the short story form was secured with the publications of *The Widows of Thornton* (1954), *Happy Families Are All Alike: A Collection of Stories* (1959), and *Miss Lenora When Last Seen and Fifteen Other Stories* (1963). The second collection contains the story "Venus, Cupid, Folly, and Time," which won the O. Henry Award. The stories in these collections display Taylor's characteristically gentle tone as he chronicles conflicts beneath life's surface through the subtle revelations of his characters.

The short stories selected for *The Old Forest and Other Stories* (1985) span Taylor's entire career. The title story is considered one of his finest depictions of the effects of social pressure on individual behavior. Jonathan Yardley stated that *The Old Forest and Other Stories* provides "a generous, incomparably rewarding introduction to the work of an American writer who, more than any other, has achieved utter mastery in short fiction."

(See also *CLC*, Vols. 1, 4, 18; *Contemporary Authors*, Vols. 13-16, rev. ed.; *Contemporary Authors New Revision Series*, Vol. 9; and *Dictionary of Literary Biography Yearbook: 1981*.)

© Thomas Victor 1986

KENNETH CLAY CATHEY

Peter Taylor is at once among the most promising of our newer writers, and the most limited. His productions to date reveal a sensitive perception, a keen observation, and a remarkable ability to control his materials; yet the range of subjects upon which he has chosen to draw is surely one of the narrowest in present day literature. However, this range is an important and hitherto neglected one. As Robert Penn Warren has said, "Peter Taylor's stories, are officially about the contemporary, urban, middle-class world of the upper South, and he is the only writer who has taken this as his province." Mr. Warren's list of qualifying adjectives might be made still more explicit by saying that Taylor writes about people in Nashville, Memphis, Chattanooga, St. Louis, and the hypothetical little town of Thornton, Tennessee. Moreover, these people always belong to old, traditional families, the land-owners-moved-to-the-city. There is a further circumscription within this scope in that he has written only one story in which a real effort is made to characterize an adult male. Taylor seems to have intentionally restrained himself to showing the impact of his world upon women and children, especially women.

Nevertheless, the narrow limits of his range are completely overshadowed by the success of his efforts within them. The very restriction perhaps contributes to the fact that his tone of lively interest coupled with personal detachment never once falters. Taylor knows his fictional world intimately, but he himself is not part of it; he can depict its victories (such as they are) and its tragedies minutely, but he never becomes personally entangled in them. Almost, his tone reaches the Classical serenity. (pp. 9-10)

When he first began writing, his chief interest was, by his own admission, not so much in subject matter as in the search for what he called "the pure story." By this term he seems to have meant that he was seeking for a narrative situation which could be presented in a straightforward manner, without flashbacks or digressions, and with little or no exposition. The "pure story" would be one possessing a high degree of artistic immediacy; it would, in Henry James's words, present a direct impression of life. It can be speculated that the effort to obtain this immediacy first led Taylor into choosing as subject matter the world he knew best, the "middle-class South," and into concentrating on the elements of that world which would have the strongest direct appeal to the rank and file of readers, family affairs. By selecting such subject matter, and it is to be remarked that not a single piece of Taylor's work fails to consider the chief character or characters in relation to their family life, he assured himself that he would be dealing with a basic situation which required little exposition. Accordingly, his earlier stories, such as **"Skyline"** (1939) and **"Like the Sad Heart of Ruth"** (1941), show a tightness of structure and an avoidance of digressions which actually seem to threaten the artistic value of the work by hampering the clear expression of the meaning. In **"The Fancy Woman,"** (1940), for instance, the action begins (in the very first paragraph) on an evening, extends through all of the next day and ends on the second morning. In this space the characters indulge in no memories of what has preceded and make only occasional references to anything outside the immediate scene. Unfortunately this structure, constantly stressing the forward motion, leaves the author little or no time to make really clear just what the conflict in the story consists of, so that it seems closer to a sketch than a short story.... [The] structure of Taylor's early stories is so tight, the progression so chronologically straightforward, that the struggles of his characters lack the vitality and intensification which alone can lead them to a true moral revelation within the circumscribed limits of the story. Taylor, in his search for the "pure" form, seems to have forgotten that no one stretch of time is more interesting than another except as it condenses, concentrates or intensifies the meaning of previous stretches. (pp. 10-11)

"A Long Fourth" (1946) finds him trying for the first time to depict a truly dramatic conflict rather than a merely dramatized scene in which some traces of struggle are evident. The story runs to about twice the length ... of his previous efforts and reveals a structure which is far different from the tight narratives of his earlier pieces. It opens with something of a leisurely pace in that the stream of consciousness of the central character is often used to supply exposition by means of flashbacks. In addition, **"A Long Fourth"** is the first of Taylor's stories to incorporate exposition stemming directly from the omniscient narrator. This variation of structure is important because it allows Taylor more opportunity to create the exact atmosphere of contemporary middle-class family relations in all their subtlety: doubly important when we realize that the family atmosphere is the real antagonistic force in all Taylor's works. **"A Long Fourth"** marks the first occasion on which he allowed himself enough structural freedom to include incidents that serve to illuminate the more recondite aspects of the setting. The events of this story seem at first reading to be a somewhat confused mass of happenings—some minor, some striking— which occur during a long, Fourth-of-July weekend while a middle-aged woman entertains various people and parties before her son goes off to the war. When new characters are introduced, Taylor shows no reluctance to stop his narrative long enough to sketch in the exact relation each bears to the central family group, especially to the mother. The story is impressive even at an initial reading for its vivid characterization and accurate rendering of the scene. Taylor's unusual power of observation transforms, as it were, the familiar, ordinary setting and turns it into something a bit magical, something easily remembered despite the dangers of banality from the subject. It is possibly one of his finest attributes that he can thus create an artistic world which is consistent within itself and yet bears so many points of resemblance to the real world that all of us know. The story is also outstanding in that it introduces an element which is of considerable importance in most of his work—the question of race relations and the status of Negroes in the modern South. The delicacy with which Taylor handles this theme is seen in the fact that it never once obtrudes itself so strongly into the central action that the piece becomes one of the "problem" stories of which we have had too many in recent fiction. As pointed out, Taylor's artistic world is consistent within itself: the presence of the Negro servants and their influence on some of the family activities is recognized, but the center of attention properly remains with the woman whose spiritual development is the real subject.

The chief fault of **"A Long Fourth"** is much the same as the difficulty which dogged him from the very beginning; he does not make clear just what is the influence of the conflict upon the central character. She clearly undergoes some moral revelation, for the author plainly states that she felt the final incident was "a larger and more general inquiry into her character than ... ever ... before." Unfortunately, the reader is not sure as to the specific nature of this inquiry, although we can speculate that it concerns her revaluation of the loyalties by which she has lived and which gave her existence meaning. The reader feels that the author knew clearly what he wanted to say but left part of it unsaid on the assumption that a "good" story should leave something to the reader's own power of interpretation. True, a good story is suggestively "incomplete," but the reader feels cheated when there is a distinct impression that the things left unsaid are consciously withheld by the author rather than stemming from a subject which is too universal to be totally comprehended by any single mind. Nevertheless, **"A Long Fourth"** marked an important stage of Taylor's development; in it he finally found his true subject, on which he could speak with authority, to be a depiction of the dissolving of traditional conceptions about family relationships: conceptions which included much that was useful, more that was hampering to modern life; much that was repulsive, more that was attractive to the sentiments of every one of us. In short, the story marks the clarification of Taylor's own view of life.

It is probable that at this time Taylor himself felt his chief weakness to be a vagueness in clearly outlining dramatic conflicts, for his next story, **"Allegiance"** (1947), is clearly constructed in such a way as to place the conflict at the center of attention. It does not plunge pell-mell into the action; rather it proceeds leisurely for a time, allowing the author space to present adequate exposition. The story opens with the entrance of a Nashville boy, in England with the American army, into the London parlor of an aunt who long ago shocked the entire family by completely severing all ties of kinship and going off to live a life of her own in a foreign country. Much use is made of the stream of consciousness technique in this opening section so as to allow the narrator (the boy) to indulge in flashbacks which set the scene by condensing the entire life history of the woman, who is the chief center of interest. He remembers her "romantic" quality and the aura of glamor which her independence lent her in the eyes of those who knew her as children. However, the dramatic structure of the story is shown by the fact that on the very first page the narrator reveals that this woman had in the past done some "grievous wrong" to his mother and that the family had been nursed on hatred of her (the aunt). This revelation immediately rouses a keen interest in the reader, an interest which is not disappointed, for the conflict is sharply illumined when the aunt soon afterwards makes the statement that the boy was always the member of his family most like herself, and he begins worrying over whether or not he is about to "betray someone or something." Having thus put into motion what seems to be the central action of the story, Taylor then wisely alternates between dialogue and reflections by the narrator in order to further characterize the aunt and introduce details about the boy's past, both of which help bring the story to an effective climax. The aunt alludes to the narrow provincialism of her Nashville family life, against which she had rebelled, and the reader expects the resolution of the conflict to make some more or less universal comment on family relationships that are too restrictive. Unfortunately, the story begins to fail at this point.

By attempting to concentrate the meaning of a woman's lifetime into a single dramatic moment, Taylor comes upon a methodological procedure which seems peculiarly fitted to the illumination of his chosen subject matter, the obligations and advantages of family bonds in a world of dissolving loyalties. However, he does not yet seem to be able fully to control this method, for he seriously neglects an adequate elaboration of the conflict itself after he has set the scene. Apparently what happened was that he became involved in the latter part of the story in an effort to show that "each moment and indeed everything in the lie and body of the world must have in itself a latent magic which might be exploited." Although this is a very interesting idea (and one which recurs at other places in Taylor's work), the author fails to find objective correlatives for it in the action of the story, the last half of which is taken up with very subtle and introspective conjectures on the narrator's part as to whether or not the old lady's youthful rebellion was caused by a realization that the actual, the present moment, is more important than altruism or personal honor. The reader can only regret that this striking theme is expressed mostly by direct statement instead of being embodied artistically so as to show *why* the old lady came to such a conclusion. The dramatic possibilities latent in the situation could probably have been extended to an objective solution of the problem.

This lack of objectification is one of the chief faults of Taylor's earlier work and one which it is hard to see how he avoids even now since he practically never deals with violent action of any sort, preferring to draw his events from the quieter, everyday side of family affairs. Conversations, reunions, visits, minor domestic crises—these are the external substance of Taylor's stories. Therefore, "**Allegiance**" ends with several questions unanswered in the reader's mind; yet the skill with which the complication was built up and the vivid selection of details to suggest the atmosphere of an expatriate Southern lady's parlor in London (without allowing this atmosphere to dominate the drama, however) show that Taylor is beginning to achieve sufficient mastery of his structural techniques to allow him to center the reader's interest on what the story says about life rather than what it says about the author's private ideas (his point of departure), which is the mark of an artist as differentiated from a technician.

In the work that followed "**Allegiance**" Taylor showed evidences of intentional experiments with structure by venturing

into the realm of another genre; in 1949 he published his . . . play, *The Death of a Kinsman.* The fact that he turned his attention to this form shortly after the appearance of "**Allegiance**" seems to indicate that he wanted to try something which he could perform with total freedom from all elements extraneous to the drama. The play is obviously experimental. It is incapable of holding an audience's attention throughout an actual stage performance since the entire first half accomplishes nothing but exposition, but it does succeed in making the essential conflict and its results very clear by the end. Like his stories, it deals with the effect of a close-knit family atmosphere on the central character—this time a maiden aunt who justifies her position of economic gratuitant by assiduously relieving the wife and mother of the burden of caring for the five children. The author makes it clear that both women realize they are playing "rôles" which descend from the traditional Southern composition of large families, the aunt's role having been actually obviated by modern economic changes which have made it possible for her to maintain a separate living if she so desired. For the first time, Taylor finds an adequate objectification of the antagonistic forces by introducing a housekeeper whose age, sex, and lack of immediate family make her a counterbalance to the maiden aunt. (pp. 11-15)

The basic success of Taylor's dramatic experiment in *The Death of a Kinsman* would seem to indicate that he had finally perfected the essential elements of his structural technique, even though he still showed some clumsiness in handling exposition. It is a feature of first importance, though, that he realized both here and in "**Allegiance**" that whatever exposition is necessary to the full delineation of the dramatic conflict should not be sacrificed to an effort to "present a direct impression of life." Taylor was apparently ready at this time to enter upon a period of real artistic accomplishment in the highest sense of the word, combining a steady view of life with technical excellence. Instead he embarked upon another structural experiment which led to his greatest failure.

In 1950 he published his only long piece to date, *A Woman of Means,* which he always refers to as a novelette rather than a novel. It is hard to ascertain exactly why this work is so much less impressive than his better short stories. Perhaps it is because he reverted to a subject and method which he had used in some of his earliest efforts. Instead of dealing with a family in all its relations and connections with the social background, he concentrated on showing the development of a thirteen year old boy under the tutelage of a step-mother. To do this he adopted the first person singular point of view, which he handles less well than the omniscient viewpoint for which he shows a decided preference in the total body of his work. The structure of *A Woman of Means* shows serious faults. In reality it seems to be two short stories poorly woven together, for the reader's attention is sharply split between interest in the fortunes of the youthful narrator, who in the process of the story first comes to an awareness of his existence as an individual personality, and interest in the character of the step-mother, who suffers a nervous breakdown, possibly because of the boy's newly-declared independence. Unfortunately, the two storylines are not synthesized well enough for the reader to perceive any direct connection. (pp. 15-16)

Perhaps the main trouble lay in the fact that Taylor was so accustomed to writing short stories that he really did not perceive the differences of structure demanded by the longer form, this difference being essentially (as Mark Schorer says) the depiction of a moral *evolution* instead of the moral *revelation* which is central to the short story. Taylor distinctly arranges the incidents in such a manner as to lead up to the two separate revelations that come to the two chief characters, but he does not embody the changes in enough objective incidents to show how the revelations affected the lives of the characters after they occurred. He comes closer to showing an evolution for the boy than for the step-mother; yet the woman's story occupies the position of greatest interest, the end of the book. As stated, these faults may be the result of Taylor's not perceiving the true nature of novel (or novelette) structure; but it is more probable that they result from the effort to depict the psychology of an adolescent boy, which by its nature cannot help but seem rather too thin a subject to support a sustained effort now that the initial surge of interest in Freudian conceptions has died down.

From 1949 till 1951 Taylor was engaged in writing a series of nine stories for *The New Yorker,* among which are his finest efforts to date, especially **"Porte-Cochere," "Uncles," "What You Hear from 'Em," "Two Ladies in Retirement,"** and **"Bad Dreams."** For the most part, they deal with various aspects of the feminine view of Southern life and with the status of present day Negroes. This latter theme becomes increasingly important until it occupies the entire scene in Taylor's most recently published story, **"Bad Dreams."**. . . **"Bad Dreams"** and **"Two Ladies in Retirement,"** his most dramatically effective pieces, reveal central facets of Taylor's mature thought. Both are much like **"A Long Fourth"** in that a rather leisurely, expository opening emphasizes the fact that the atmosphere will be very important in the working out of the theme. However, in **"Bad Dreams"** a better job is done of dispersing the necessary exposition throughout the body of the action than in **"Two Ladies in Retirement."** Taylor shows unmistakeable signs of having profited by the dramatic experiment of his play, for in both stories he outlines the conflict distinctly, embodies it in a sufficient number of incidents, and devotes enough space to the denouement to make clear to the reader the essential nature of the moral revelation that takes place. (pp. 16-17)

The most outstanding feature of Taylor's writing to date is that he has shown an almost uninterrupted improvement in both technique and content. Significantly, his very last story to appear [thus far, **"Bad Dreams,"**] is certainly his best from the standpoint of form, and probably from the standpoint of the ideas it expresses as well. His later efforts, impressive as artistic achievements in themselves, are even more impressive as portents of his future productions, coming as they do at a time when the authors of fiction (as Malcolm Cowley has pointed out) have realized the limitations of the older types of writing and are crying out for some new direction. Perhaps Peter Taylor can offer part of that direction by continuing to make valid statements about the external world we live in. (p. 18)

> *Kenneth Clay Cathey, "Peter Taylor: An Evaluation," in* The Western Review, *Vol. 18, No. 1, Autumn, 1953, pp. 9-19.*

THOMAS DANIEL YOUNG

[Much] of Taylor's fiction is concerned with the changes that have occurred in the quality of life available in a society that is rapidly shifting from agrarian to urban in orientation. . . . Taylor's stories are set in the places in which he lived and

knew well—Trenton, Nashville, St. Louis, and Memphis. . . . A careful, cautious writer, over the past thirty years he has published six collections of short stories, a novel, and three dramas.

The protagonist of the Taylor story is usually a resident of a middle-sized city of the upper South, although he is more often than not one or two generations removed from a small Southern town, usually the fictitious Thornton, Tennessee. These quiet tales of domestic life almost always reveal—just beneath the level of the slightly perturbed world of families, businesses, servants, and matter-of-factness on which the principal action occurs—a sense of deep tragedy, disorder, and often impending doom. Many of these tales are leisurely told by a narrator who is urbane, witty, sophisticated, nostalgic—very much like Taylor himself—a gentleman who is confiding in a lady or another gentleman, someone who shares the creature comforts of those who belong to the financially secure, and often wealthy, world of the upper-middle class: doctors, lawyers, businessman, judges, college presidents, and even governors. Theirs is a society securely rooted in tradition and history, but the courteous, patient confidante in his matter-of-fact, understated manner often reveals to his listeners an unsuspected characteristic of this placid, most natural of all possible worlds. What he presents is something that is always significant, usually much broader in application than the precisely delineated world in which it occurs, and nearly always unsettling and disturbing—sometimes so shocking and horrible that the narrator's auditor is filled with disgust or terror. Stories such as **"Venus, Cupid, Folly, and Time"** describe spiritual incest and suggest the possibility of physical incest as well. **"A Spinster's Tale,"** narrated by a young girl, reveals the distorted, grotesque horrors of a warped, neurotic imagination. **"The Fancy Woman"** presents a sordid, illicit affair between a hard drinking, good-time girl and a brutish, egocentric, pleasure-seeking but unfeeling member of the so-called respectable wealthy class. Although no reference is made specifically by either of the principal characters in the story, the Negro maid in **"Cookie"** exposes the emptiness, the meaninglessness of the marriage between a successful, middle-aged doctor and his wife. After the maid has revealed that it is a well-known fact around town that the doctor is meeting "the ladies" at the home of a friend of his, and after he has left for another assignation, the wife first thinks she will fire Cookie because she cannot have "a servant of mine talking to my husband like that." After thinking the matter over—although she will never admit what the reader surely knows—she tells her husband, "I'll speak to her tonight. It'll never happen again." She is caught in a loveless union from which she can never escape and can only think, pathetically, perhaps it will not be true; or in some way the pain will be easier to bear, if she does not admit the glaringly evident truth, even to herself.

The world of Peter Taylor's stories includes the inevitable nostalgia and feeling of separation that accompanies one's leaving his hometown, the nagging ever-present realization that one can never recapture the feelings, the aspirations, and the experiences of his youth. The constant awareness of his own mortality, of his movement from innocence through experience to death, is like a cancer forever growing larger within him. (The best of these stories is **"At the Drug Store."**) That world includes, too, an ambiguous view of the family: not only a unifying, civilizing institution but one that is simultaneously stultifying, imprisoning, and destructive of one's individual development. (**"In the Miro District,"** one of his most recent stories, delineates poignantly and compellingly the unhappy results of a family's accepting the stereotype that a grand-father and his grandson should be buddies. The individual personalities and differences will not permit this kind of relationship between persons of different generations.) Taylor's segment of the world that he knows so well embraces, too, a disintegrating tradition, the deterioration of family, the tensions of love—of family, of home, of parents, of childhood sweethearts—and the loneliness that always follows the realization that one is cut off from tradition and family; that in the modern materialistic world, with its hurry, efficiency, and constant anxieties, free, open honest communication is virtually impossible. This is the world which, Robert Penn Warren says, Taylor "has made his own forever." As one critic has pointed out, "Peter Taylor is our southern Chekov, as Faulkner was our Dostoevsky"; the violence forever lying just beneath the seemingly peaceful exterior is always boiling and threatening to explode.

Taylor's well-crafted stories of the gentlefolk of the upper South are not propaganda pieces. He is attempting, as good artists always are, to reconstitute reality, not to make some comment about a particular social order. His stories, as Robert K. Morris . . . has observed, reveal to us a "particular kind of sensibility: a sensibility encased in memories that have saddened or weakened it without having totally destroyed or done violence to it." Few authors in modern southern literature equal Taylor in his ability to ferret out the secret motives that move his people to act precisely as they do. . . . (pp. 92-6)

Although for almost thirty years Taylor's stories have retained their sure and certain grasp of the unique quality of Tennessee mores and manners, his attitude toward this territory, which he has staked out as his exclusive property, has not changed a great deal. This amazingly consistent view of reality is dramatically revealed, most readers believe, in one of his early stories, the title story in his first collection.

The focus of this early narrative, **"A Long Fourth,"** is upon Harriet Wilson, a Nashville housewife approaching middle-age, who is preparing for a visit home from her son, a journalist living in New York. He is coming for a long weekend before being inducted into the army during World War II. Harriet has induced all members of her family and household staff—her husband, her two daughters, her cook, Mattie, and Mattie's nephew, B. T., a general handyman around the place—to assist her in making this visit one that Son will long remember. She has planned a party, a family friend is to entertain them with a dinner party, and there are scheduled periods for family togetherness.

Despite her attention to every possible detail, all does not work out as expected, and a consideration of all of these insignificant details that will not fit into her preconceived mold reveals how chaotic and traditionless her seemingly placid and ordered life really is. (p. 96)

Allen Tate develops a disturbing picture of a society that has lost its traditions, as the one depicted in Peter Taylor's stories is in the process of doing. A social order without manners, religions, morals, or codes, Tate writes, always ends in chaotic or violent action. Taylor writes of social order in transition, as **"A Long Fourth"** and many of his other stories reveal, of a people moving from a closely knit, ordered community to an urbanized society, a people who are slowly losing their traditional values. Seldom does Taylor suggest that organized

religion affects the behavior of his characters. Although there is the semblance of a social order composed of polite, well-mannered, civilized, compassionate people, there are too many loveless marriages, too much sham and hypocrisy, too many empty and meaningless gestures for us to put much faith in the stability of the materially acquisitive, thing-oriented society to which Taylor's characters belong. (pp. 98-9)

Thomas Daniel Young, "The Contemporary Scene," in his Tennessee Writers, *The University of Tennessee Press, Knoxville, 1981, pp. 77-111.**

JONATHAN YARDLEY

[*The Old Forest and Other Stories*] contains one novella, one short play and a dozen stories. The 14 pieces were originally published over four decades, from 1941 to the present, and they display Taylor in his full range of themes, settings and moods. This is to say that they provide a generous, incomparably rewarding introduction to the work of the American writer who, more than any other, has achieved utter mastery in short fiction. By comparison with *The Old Forest and Other Stories,* almost everything else published by American writers in recent years seems small, cramped, brittle, inconsequential; among American writers now living, only Eudora Welty has accomplished a body of fiction so rich, durable and accessible as Taylor's.

The pity (not to mention the oddity) of it is that he has done this almost entirely unnoticed by the larger world of serious readers, who simply have no idea what a treat they have missed. . . . In some measure, perhaps, this can be explained by his refusal to follow literary fashion; nowhere in his work is to be found the language of the gutter, his treatment of sexual business is subtle and reticent, his references to academic life are more often mocking than reverential, and he has not once in all these years corrupted a piece of fiction in order to advance his political opinions.

Rather, in all these years Taylor has quietly—though not, I believe, without deep frustration at the neglect to which he is subjected—gone about the business of transforming the small world he knows best into a place that has the look of a universe. This world is centered about the two Tennessee cities of Memphis and Nashville, with occasional forays to St. Louis and beyond. Its principal residents are white people of the middle and upper-middle classes, though this being the South there are also many black people who, in the self-centered and wildly mistaken view of the whites are "completely irresponsible and totally dependent upon us." This world's central preoccupation, as stated by the narrator of the title [story] of the collection, is with "the binding and molding effect upon people of the circumstances in which they are born."

Perhaps more than any other it is this theme that gives Taylor's fiction its universality; no matter what world a person may be born into, his stories say, that is the world that shapes him, and this we all have in common. Read superficially, Taylor seems to be a chronicler and defender of the old Southern order, a society that suppresses women and oppresses blacks. Yet as the stories in *The Old Forest* make abundantly clear, from the outset his strongest sympathies have been with the powerless, and his abiding interest has been in discovering what strategies they devise for acquiring such power as may be available to them. He depicts the world as it exists rather than the world as we wish it might be, so some of the social settings and personal relationships in these stories may seem unfortunate to today's enlightened reader; but the truth is that his portrait of the white middle-class South, though drawn with sympathy and affection, is as withering as any we have. . . .

"**The Old Forest**" is the best of the stories in this collection, and the most characteristic in that it so comprehensively summarizes Taylor's work: not merely his settings and themes, but the marvelous subtlety and ingenuity of his leisurely, humorous storytelling method. But it is the best of an exemplary group. Mention certainly must be made of "**The Gift of the Prodigal**" and "**A Friend and Protector**," both of which examine the vicarious life; of "**Promise of Rain**" and "**The Little Cousins**," stories about children and their parents; of "**A Long Fourth**" and "**Two Ladies in Retirement**," which have much to do with matters of race; and of the short play, *The Death of a Kinsman*, which in its exploration of "family happiness" and "how well we know our roles and how clearly defined are our spheres of authority" is another paradigmatic example of Taylor's art.

Gathered together as they now are, all of these tales serve admirably as a supplement to Taylor's *Collected Stories*. . . . Like that earlier volume, *The Old Forest* is both a thorough sample of Taylor's work in all its diversity and consistency, and clear evidence of his steady maturation over these four decades. Unlike most American authors, he is a better writer at 65 than he was at 45. . . . It is significant that the two finest stories here, "**The Old Forest**" and "**The Gift of the Prodigal**," are also the two most recent; midway through his seventh decade, Taylor is still expanding his world and his understanding of it.

Taylor has been compared, by Randall Jarrell and others, to Anton Chekhov; certainly both are virtuosos of the short story and of human psychology. But in the literature of his own country, Taylor can be compared to no one except himself; he is, as every word in this book testifies, an American master.

> *Jonathan Yardley, "Peter Taylor: The Quiet Virtuoso," in* Book World—The Washington Post, *January 27, 1985, p. 3.*

RICHARD EDER

Peter Taylor, a master of the American short story, is only partly thought of today as a Southern writer. His "collected stories," brought out several years ago, ranges more widely. Now, with *The Old Forest,* comes a thematic re-winnowing. The 14 stories center about the loss of patrician assurance— the English call it "bottom"—associated with what, up to the 1950s, was still known as the Southern Way of Life.

The loss has been compared to the decline of the Russian landed classes in the 19th Century, and Taylor's portrayal of it has been compared to Chekhov. Taylor explores the subtleties of class entropy with precision and gentleness. But, the effect is not really Chekhovian; it is something coarser. The difference lies not so much in the art as in the material.

Chekhov plays and stories show us free spirits in cages. Taylor's Tennesseans are simply caged spirits. They may be aware of their decline and announce it with a disenchanted, if woolly, courage, but what they announce is hollowness more than frailty. The feverish sensibility, the flare of swallows at sunset are not

there. These are broody hens whose eggs are being taken from them at supper time, one by one.

Written over the past 40 years, the stories mostly take place among families who have moved to Memphis or Nashville or St. Louis but whose roots lie in prosperous farm estates. The families are still prosperous, though there have been reverses.

Their memories and assumptions, in any case, are of prosperity tinged by the shadows of a Depression past and an economic re-ordering to come. And if the economic underpinnings are beginning to teeter, the social verities are clearly under siege. Most of these stories tell of the shock.

Sometimes shock is coupled with a step or two toward wider understanding. In "**The Gift of the Prodigal**," a wealthy widower, accustomed to bailing out Ricky, his wastrel son, and considering it a cross to bear, suddenly realizes there is more pleasure than martyrdom in it. "I am listening gratefully to all he will tell me about himself, about any life that is not my own," the old man reflects as Ricky begins his latest plea for help. . . .

Usually the understanding is less clear. Taylor is writing about a silted-up society; his narrators, imbued with its assumptions, only see vaguely what lies outside. . . .

Often, there is no understanding at all, only pain. Nowhere is the blindness and the pain greater than in the relation of these white families to their black servants. . . .

The families retain the feudal expectation that they will provide the protection and their Negroes will provide the devotion and the work. In story after story, both the protection and the devotion are riddled and collapse. In one of the best stories, "**A Long Fourth**," a gently reared woman is undermined into panic and hysteria by her suppressed realization that the barriers between her and her two black servants are no longer dependable.

The woman protagonist is both silly and vindictive; yet Taylor has made her bafflement not only real and moving, but a symbol of a more general upheaval and disarray. She comes to us directly, through her own feelings; in other stories, Taylor uses a distant narrator, perhaps an uncle or a brother.

The distanced narrators can be a burden. They are priggish, endlessly garrulous about old passions and quarrels, and their insight is a tiny chink in their obliviousness. Taylor makes his points with them. What he fails to do in a number of the stories—"**The Old Forest**" itself, among others—is to validate them. They are so opaque and tedious that by the time they laboriously achieve their moment of truth, we are in danger of no longer caring.

In "**Bad Dreams**," the narrator is virtually suppressed, and it may be the best story in the collection. It stands out, in any case, for telling of change from the point of view of the blacks. A married couple, servants to a white family, are suddenly told to share their quarters with an old black man from the country. He is dirty and peculiar; he threatens the precarious status and hopes achieved by the man and woman who have cut themselves off from their own country roots. Yet he is the only one who can soothe their baby when the infant wakes in hysterics from a bad dream.

Taylor's point about the unsoundness of Southern gentility in changing times is made here in reverse, and most movingly. Bert and Emmeline, for all their pretentions, are authentic struggling spirits. We care more about them than we do about the privileged dispossessed in most of the other tales, whose nostalgia is for power and comfort, and never for anything much more magical.

> *Richard Eder, in a review of "The Old Forest and Other Stories," in* Los Angeles Times Book Review, *February 3, 1985, p. 1.*

ROBERT TOWERS

The Old Forest and Other Stories, is welcome as a reminder of just how good Peter Taylor can be. Though the amount of new work is not extensive . . . , the long title story reveals Mr. Taylor at the very apex of his powers and several other recent pieces succeed handsomely in his familiar vein.

The title story, typically, deals with a minor crisis affecting affluent families in one of the larger cities of the middle South; in this case the city is Memphis (in other Taylor stories it is frequently Nashville and occasionally St. Louis) and the families belong to the upper reaches of its society. The men are cotton brokers, lawyers and newspaper publishers with access, when they need it, to the mayor. The women, involved in the social rituals of their caste (debuts, formal engagements, splendid weddings with their attendant parties, membership in the Memphis Country Club), wield their own kind of power. All know well how to join ranks when a crisis occurs. Characteristically, Mr. Taylor's approach to this material is retrospective, that of an older man looking back upon—and trying to make sense of—something that happened four decades before. (p. 1)

But the main interest of **"The Old Forest"** lies not so much in the action itself or its denouement as in the novelistic density of observation, analysis and reflection in which they are embedded. The fact that Peter Taylor's best stories are like miniature novels has been noted before. His narrative method is to hover over the action, to digress from it, to explore byways and relationships, to speculate on alternative possibilities—in short, to defy the conventions of brevity and concentration that we usually associate with the genre. What results is often a thickly populated microcosm of an entire society, with its assumptions, virtues, loyalties and snobberies revealed. The retrospective approach lends itself to such an effect. . . .

I found myself equally absorbed in **"The Gift of the Prodigal"** and **"A Friend and Protector,"** both of which embody one of Mr. Taylor's favorite themes—that of vicarious living. In the first, a rich, ailing old widower is repeatedly forced to bail his black-sheep son, Ricky, out of scrapes and costly scandals. . . . What is revealed is that the father, despite his complaints about Ricky, feeds avidly upon his son's misadventures, that in the gloom and pain of his own decline he can't wait for the details, however disreputable, of any life that is not his own.

In **"A Friend and Protector,"** there is an analogous relationship between Jesse, a "bad" Negro (Mr. Taylor avoids the term "black," which would be anarchronistic applied to the time he is writing about) and the respectable, affectionate white family that employs him and protects him from the consequences of his often violent antisocial behavior. At the disastrous climax the adolescent narrator realizes that "purplish-black, kinky-headed" Jesse, now in ruin, has been encouraged to act out the self-destructive impulses that his employers cannot permit themselves to indulge, however dissatisfied they are "with the pale *un*ruin of their own lives."

Such vicariousness is fundamental to Mr. Taylor's art. He almost never renders anguish firsthand or from the inside. We see it through the eyes of others—often a child or teen-ager—or hear about it as something that happened long ago. While he is eminently Southern in his concentration on family relationships that include not only parents and children but also a large cast of grandparents, spinster aunts, widowed uncles and country cousins and extend to the surrounding and sustaining servants, Mr. Taylor avoids the melodrama and extreme situations that we associate with writers like Faulkner or Flannery O'Connor. His fiction could hardly be less gothic or rhetorical. Death takes place offstage; where sex is concerned, bedroom doors are kept firmly closed. He is very much an artist of the "normal," who finds sufficient drama in the crises and perturbations that affect even the best-regulated families. Not all of Mr. Taylor's stories work; sometimes his failure to endow his situations with adequate energy and tension can result in the tedious analysis of the humdrum.

While *The Old Forest* contains several pieces from previous collections that do not seem worth resurrection (the weakest being a stylistic experiment, **"Allegiance,"** that reads like a parody of Henry James), we can be grateful for the inclusion of two fine early stories—**"Porte Cochere"** and **"The Scoutmaster."** . . .

Whatever it lacks in volume, Peter Taylor's voice—measured, civilized and oddly affecting—continues to make itself heard through the contemporary uproar. Those attuned to his special note prize it highly. It would be almost true to say that no one else writes that way anymore. (p. 26)

> *Robert Towers, "A Master of the Miniature Novel," in* The New York Times Book Review, *February 17, 1985, pp. 1, 26.*

WALTER CLEMONS

Like Poe's purloined letter, Peter Taylor is hidden in plain sight. He is . . . one of the best American storytellers now or ever, and yet it's not hard to find literate friends who don't know his name. . . . I'll try not to be a scold about Taylor's lack of fame. Don't read either [*Collected Stories* or *The Old Forest and Other Stories*] because you ought to; try Taylor because he's irresistibly beguiling.

"There," a characteristic Taylor story with a characteristically unassertive title that gathers meaning as you read it, has a narrator with "a mixture of masculine frankness and almost feminine gossipiness." Taylor, a Southerner, is an expert gossip. Like a great actor whom you don't catch "acting," he's a great writer you seldom catch "writing." He simply buttonholes you and starts telling you things. When he's done, he's anatomized a society. His stories have the resonance of novels.

"The Old Forest" is one of his finest. A Memphis gentleman reminisces about the week before his wedding in 1937 when he was in a car wreck with a girl of lower social status, a pal with whom he wasn't having an affair. She jumped out of the car and went into hiding, and his marriage couldn't take place until it was settled that no harm had come to her. One of Taylor's memorable earlier stories, **"Miss Leonora When Last Seen,"** turned on a similar disappearance; here, the vanishing of the girl from the car becomes a mystery that exposes the strata of polite society in entirely unexpected ways. We expect the familiar distinction between "nice" girls and "bad" ones.

Both categories are dissolved. The resolution Taylor quietly provides is original. . . .

Taylor may have been underestimated not only as a result of his devotion to the short story—never a road to fame—but also because he's failed to deliver the expected Gothic vision of life in the South. In **"Venus, Cupid, Folly and Time"** he set up a situation with which Tennessee Williams could have had a field day and then calmly undermined every hope of revelation of incest and depravity by simply telling how a practical joke went wrong and distanced a brother and sister from each other for the rest of their lives. This is an indelible story. So are—in the *Collected Stories*—**"Heads of Houses," "What You Hear from 'Em?"** and—in the new collection—**"The Gift of the Prodigal"** and **"Porte Cochere."** It's a shame Taylor isn't as famous as he deserves to be. Maybe that will now be corrected.

Walter Clemons, "Southern Comfort," in News-week, *Vol. CV, No. 10, March 11, 1985, p. 74.*

OLIVER CONANT

A distinctive literary voice is a rare achievement, rarer still when it possesses the affability of the one that speaks to us in [*The Old Forest and Other Stories*]. Informal, almost chatty, yet always cultivated, it invites us into these tales . . . with a graciousness that reflects the author's Southern roots. And we soon come to feel we are his guests, installed on some rustic porch or verandah, listening in the course of a long hot afternoon to his ever-flowing stream of anecdotes and recollections.

For all of its spontaneity, though, Taylor's artistry is highly conscious, schooled in the prose masters of the past century. At times it is exhibited in cadences and complications reminiscent of Henry James, at other times in a certain urgent, surprising lyricism that is clearly his own. He is superb at evoking a sense of place (the grand columned ante-bellum mansions, the neat rows of cotton brokers' offices with their steep wooden stairs, high ceilings and windows over the Mississippi), at accurately recording varieties of black and white speech, and at building situations full of tension and conflict.

True, too many of the stories end inconclusively, a weakness that can get to be no less irritatingly predictable than a series of pat resolutions. Occasionally the prose is awkward, as in the following example of one character's thought about another: "The degree of her long anxiety for the special accidental qualities which would make up the naturalness of our meeting is patent in the pleasure she takes from its realization."

But despite such sporadic false notes Taylor manages to re-create the manners, morals and servants of the Southern upper-middle class in cities like Memphis and Atlanta during the decade separating the Great Depression and World War II. (p. 18)

Some of Taylor's concerns, of course, are universal: first love, the trials of fatherhood, loneliness, old age. Among the themes arising directly out of his regional subject matter perhaps the most salient involve the complex set of deferences, allegiances and obligations that both linked and distinguished old money, country club types from less exalted whites, and the similarly complicated, more intimate, but sometimes horribly destructive relationships between blacks and the white families they served. In all the stories social relations have a palpable presence, a power to bind and mold. If you lived here you knew your place

exactly, and everybody else's as well, whether you happened to be a debutante, a field hand, a landowner, or a businessman.

Thanks to this extreme specificity, *The Old Forest* seems virtually free of the communal anomie so common in contemporary fiction, and of the concomitant alienation and weightlessness. On the contrary, society is too much with Taylor's people; its manifest, manifold oppressions and outbursts of astonishing cruelty help us avoid the silly mistake of assuming that the minute gradations of individual pain delineated in the typical *New Yorker* story, or even the grandiose despair of such writers as Norman Mailer, exhaust the evils of American existence.

The title story is a rich blend of class tensions and conflicted passions. Nat, a cotton broker's son engaged to marry the tall, splendid debutante Caroline Braxley, also enjoys the friendship of the more winsome Lee Ann Deehart. She is a short, hazel-eyed beauty from what a Proust-reading member of Nat's circle refers to as "the Memphis demimonde"—which turns out, unglamorously, to consist of the relatively independent daughters of respectable but generally unprosperous tradesmen. . . .

It is a measure of Taylor's power of sympathy that even if we reject the antique social and sexual mores that shape events in **"The Old Forest,"** we are made to understand why Caroline Braxley could feel Nat's entanglement might expose her to scandal.

Indeed, because Taylor is a conservative writer he is concerned about increasing our respect for the old: the "primeval" forest of the title, the old houses, the old codes of decorum in Southern speech and manners. In the book this respect coexists uneasily with Taylor's clear-eyed assessment of the rigidities of the past. . . .

Of the entries that dramatize racial divisions, **"Friend and Protector"** is the most moving. It presents a perverse symbiosis: The more prosperous and socially connected cotton broker Andrew Nelson becomes, the more his black servant Jesse Munroe gets into trouble with the law. Actually, Jesse's wildness is encouraged by Nelson, who takes pleasure in it partly as an expression of his own repressed instincts, partly as a means of flaunting his power and influence over the authorities every time Jesse gets into a scrape and needs rescuing. The outcome is tragic: Jesse's violence finally lands him in a lunatic asylum, safe at last from his "friend and protector."

It is plain to the reader—and, I think, to Taylor—that the cotton broker's self-serving posture implies a denial of his servant's moral responsibility—one of the meanings of racism. We are not encouraged to condemn Nelson in an easy or absolute manner, however. Jesse, ironically, considers himself his employer's "friend and protector." . . .

It is therefore not really apparent exactly how Taylor would have us respond to Nelson's racism, or to the racism that pervaded his milieu. The author does seem to resist the idea that the kinds of relationships he delineates were expressions of systematic oppression. Only two of his characters (in **"A Long Fourth"**) clearly condemn this aspect of Southern society: the son of a Memphis physician and his female companion, the Left-wing editor of a "birth-control magazine." Both are intellectuals who have made the momentous move to New York, and neither is drawn very sympathetically. The woman talks in abstractions, declaring herself in favor of "Equality: economic and social"; the son's rejection of Southern racism is accompanied by a blurted announcement that he feels "no real tie" to his old Tennessee home. I have the impression that this confession of rootlessness renders the son's opposition to "the system" either irrelevant or suspect for Taylor, since his art depends on social connectedness.

On the other hand, diffused in these stories is a dark message strikingly at odds with their lively and charming narration: that human relationships can be fixed, inescapable and destructive. Taylor, who like his long-time friend Robert Penn Warren loves all that is good and true in the old ways of the world he depicts, nowhere idealizes the pre-civil rights South. But his book gives no hint of the profound transformation that would soon be effected precisely by abstract ideas of equality and justice. (p. 19)

Oliver Conant, "Tales from the Verandah," in The New Leader, *Vol. LXVIII, No. 4, March 25, 1985, pp. 18-19.*

Audrey (Grace) Thomas

1935-

American-born Canadian novelist, short story writer, and scriptwriter.

Thomas is one of Canada's most respected fiction writers. She is primarily concerned with exploring "the terrible gap between men and women," and her novels and short stories focus on problems in relationships, including those between parents and children. Critics have noted the similarities between Thomas's life and the lives of her characters; the autobiographical nature of her writing is one of its most distinctive features. Thomas's style makes clear her interest in and skillful use of language and various stylistic devices. She experiments with shifts in narrative perspective, puns, paradoxes, and literary allusions. As a result, her work requires the active participation of the reader. In keeping with her fascination with words, many of Thomas's protagonists are writers who struggle with the difficulties of their craft. Thomas is praised for her tightly controlled yet flexible prose and for her compassionate representation of contemporary life.

Thomas's first novel, *Mrs. Blood* (1970), is also the first of three novels to chronicle various stages in the life of Isobel Cleary, who, like Thomas, is an American-born woman transplanted to Canada. In *Mrs. Blood,* Isobel experiences a miscarriage while living in Africa with her husband and two children. *Songs My Mother Taught Me* (1973) tells the story of Isobel's unhappy childhood. In *Blown Figures* (1975), Isobel returns to Africa to try to discover what became of her child's body. All three novels exemplify the concerns of Thomas's work in their exploration of the traumas involved in male-female relationships, in parenthood, and in self-awareness. Another of Thomas's major themes—the conflicts a writer faces when attempting to integrate his or her personal and creative lives—is explored in the novellas which make up *Munchmeyer and Prospero on the Island* (1972). Like the three novels centered on Mrs. Blood, these novellas are interconnected. *Munchmeyer* concerns a writer who leaves his wife and family to live out his rather vague creative impulses. In *Prospero on the Island,* a woman is writing the novel about Munchmeyer while living with her children in a cabin on an island.

A similar situation is presented in *Latakia* (1979). This novel focuses on two lovers, each of whom are writers, and follows them to various cities around the world as they struggle with their relationship and with the problems of writing. The woman is in the process of writing an autobiographical novel, echoing the novel-within-a-novel mode of *Munchmeyer and Prospero on the Island.* The protagonist of *Intertidal Life* (1984), Alice Hoyle, is also working on a book. Like Thomas, Alice is the mother of three daughters and lives on a Canadian Gulf island. The novel follows her relationships with her children, her mostly absent husband, and her friends and neighbors while she tries to finish her own novel. Critics praised this work for its dynamic portrayal of a creative, loving woman who attempts to adapt to the circumstances of her life.

Thomas's short stories reinforce and often duplicate the themes, characters, and situations in her novels. The stories in *Ten Green Bottles* (1967) and *Ladies & Escorts* (1977) reflect Thom-

as's interest in modern relationships and the failure of men and women to interact harmoniously. *Real Mothers* (1982) includes several stories centered on the links between parents and children, particularly in regard to divorce and the breakup and redefinition of families. Thomas was lauded for her effective descriptions of the pain and tenuousness of these circumstances as well as the joy and satisfaction that sometimes make them more bearable.

(See also *CLC,* Vols. 7, 13 and *Contemporary Authors,* Vols. 21-24, rev. ed.)

MARY McALPINE

[Audrey Thomas is] the possessor of a strange talent. *Munchmeyer and Prospero On the Island,* two novellas in one small volume, make a haunting and fascinating book written in an oddly erratic style. The style in *Munchmeyer* suits the theme, which is a man's desire to escape from living and its bondage. Both novellas are set on the coast of [British Columbia], where wild beauty intensifies either happiness or unhappiness; where Canada's suicide statistics are highest.

The first short novel, *Munchmeyer,* is told by Munchmeyer himself, a growing-older student-teacher with four children and a harmless wife who clicks him to craziness with her knitting needles. (She makes sweaters for the children and for him: "Martha, forgive me, I left one in the movies the other night . . . I cannot wear your mark upon my back.") He decides he must escape. He must write. He must be free—of what? "Martha. Or life? But isn't that what I'm opting for?" He brutalizes his loving bewildered Martha and forces her to leave him, and enters his own hallucinatory hell of threatening homosexuals, empty department stores with moving escalators, the Miracle Girl and her sea-washed coffin, his desperate loneliness. Yet always he stays on the rim of reality. . . .

Presumably—because with Mrs. Thomas' tales you can't be sure where imaginary and "real" happenings stop and start—Munchmeyer takes a suite of rooms. "Here, looking out of his window and onto this determined street, he would write as he had never been able to write before, above that life, but not completely removed from it." The room has a yellow bed, which appeals to him and he thinks of his Martha-like landlady saying, "Now, I know he'll need a yellow bed.—"

> 'And did it ever occur to you once that whole day that you'd sleep with me?'

> 'Never,' he said honestly. 'I saw you as the drab Mrs. Lodestone and was grateful to you because of the yellow bed.'

> Not knowing Thomas (her artist-husband) had painted it.

Here is where Mrs. Thomas is irritatingly brilliant. She grabs you and takes you down into that in-between world of truth and deception with her jerky juxtapositions, her sometimes staccato writing; and, although her characters are shadowy, they involve and often hurt you. I wish, however, that Munchmeyer had been less shadowy and a bigger figure, a better writer. He is too thin; he tempts contempt. . . .

On her Gulf island where Miranda Archer is writing her story of Munchmeyer—we're in the second novella, *Prospero On the Island*—sex and love are welcomed and fulfilling. So is living. She loves her cabin, which she's rented for a year to write the book, the beach, her weekend husband Fred, the solitude of island life, her children, and the view from her window. . . . (p. 44)

She sees "like a diver in a diving bell." *Munchmeyer* is the more successful short novel. In it Audrey Thomas can withdraw and let her escape-fancy follow her shadowy man through his hellish shadowy underworld. But this will not work with *Prospero On the Island* because here, I think, she is attempting whole life and reality—at least the happiness of living (although for that of course you need the escape of imagination). But she will not become involved; she stays in her diving bell.

Miranda's life is quite simple: picnics with her two-year-old Toad, writing with pleasure, love-making with Fred by firelight—the richness of life in interrupted solitude. She meets and perhaps falls in love with a painter, whom she names Prospero. She knows Sweeney, his friend with smelly socks, and husbandless Frankie with her many children, her laughter and efficiency. But they are flimsy people; even Miranda herself is a shadow. "Ah Prospero, my dear, I am not what you think I am." But she doesn't anywhere suggest what he or she thinks or is.

Perhaps this passage exemplifies Audrey Thomas' failure in the last novella:

'Sometimes, driving home on Sunday nights . . . I don't seem to be getting anywhere; I'm sure I've passed that clump of trees before—those rocks, that shadow. And sometimes I don't care, am quite content to drive like this . . . until I die. No desire to find out what's at the end of the road, no fear either. Just a kind of sleepy stillness and the peace. I remember lying in the warm sea off the coast of Africa, eyes closed, face lifted to the sky. The same feeling of being gently *taken* somewhere. The feeling Munchmeyer sees on the face of the Miracle Girl.

'Then human voices wake us and we drown.'

I wish they had wakened Audrey Thomas; she might, or might not, have drowned. (p. 45)

Mary McAlpine, " 'I Cannot Wear Your Mark Upon My Back'," in Saturday Night, *Vol. 87, No. 7, July, 1972, pp. 44-5.*

GEORGE WOODCOCK

Ladies and Escorts is a collection of stories which includes West Africa . . . and British Columbia among its settings, adds Mexico and a couple of more dubious locales, and presents the puzzling but always intriguing variety of tones that comes when one collects stories written at various times and in various moods, and published in different kinds of magazines whose only thing in common was a liking for Audrey Thomas's work and perhaps for its aura of personality.

Indeed, it may be this palpable personal aura that most clearly links the stories and at the same time explains their appeal. Audrey Thomas is no Flaubertain objectivist, no adherent of the theory that the writer must immolate herself in the task of creating a work that will be self-consistent and self-sustaining. One is always aware of the sensibility at work in her writing, of the autobiographical—almost the confessional—urge as a carefully hidden yet ever present element. The things these stories describe (the curious intrusion into West African family life narrated in **"Joseph and his Brother,"** the ambiguous and inconsequential encounter between a pregnant white woman and an Indian youth described in **"Kill Day on the Government Wharf,"** the bizarre pretences that surround the breakup of a woman writer's marriage in **"Initram"**) may have happened to Audrey Thomas (either as participant or witness), but that is not the important thing. The important thing is that they *could have* happened, they are options, and what is ultimately interesting is not the boundaries of the action but what lies beyond, what is implied in the wry twist of recognition in which each story turns upon its necessary illusions. It is indeed in the tenuousness of her conclusions, the flimsiness of her boundaries, that Audrey Thomas's largeness of vision lies. But that would not make her the excellent fiction writer she is, if the willingness to live beyond definition and finality in terms of experience and feeling were not accompanied by an exactness of expression in prose that is the result of years of dedicated practice. (pp. 99-100)

George Woodcock, "Oberon's Court," in Wascana Review, *Vol. 11, No. 2, Fall, 1976, pp. 98-102.**

MARGARET ATWOOD

[*The essay from which this excerpt is taken was originally published in* The Globe and Mail, *April 16, 1977.*]

More than most writers, [Audrey Thomas] is constantly weaving and re-weaving, cross-referencing, overlapping, even repeating her materials. Both [*Ten Green Bottles* and *Ladies & Escorts*] are collections of short stories; but, though Thomas' novels threaten to fragment, to splinter into their component images, the experience of reading these books together is much like reading a novel. The stories reinforce and echo each other. . . . (p. 268)

Thomas once said that she writes about "the terrible gap between men and women," and the phrasing is an indication of her even-handed approach. For though her women are usually bewildered, afraid of not being loved, unable to cope and dependent on men though resentful of them, her men are far from being the potent, capable figures these women suppose them to be. When she writes from the point of view of a male character, we are likely to discover a man who feels smothered by such clinging vines, or who feels literally crushed—as in **"Aquarius"**—by a woman's flaunted sexuality. Men, in their turn, visualize their women as all-powerful goddesses who mock and diminish them. Neither side is able to imagine its own power, only that of the other. It is typical of a Thomas heroine that she should long for a simple domestic life, with husband and children, something pastoral, with a wood stove and home-spun yarn, only to find she is hopeless at lighting fires and afraid of everything outside the door, and that her husband is up to something with the next-door neighbour, while she herself is attracted by the young Indian fisherman down at the fishing dock.

The distance between men and women is only one of the "terrible gaps" Thomas writes about. Her characters often exist in a state of prolonged culture shock. Men against women, reality against arcadia, Europe against America, and, even more starkly, the white West against some country further south, Africa or Mexico—these are the collisions whose psychic contusions she traces. When Thomas' heroines aren't locking themselves in alien bathrooms for fear of snakes, they sometimes have a somnambulistic courage. The white woman dreamwalking through a foreign culture, aware of its dangers but not of what they are, unable to understand her surroundings but sure some important truth is hidden there, is a recurrent figure in the Thomas landscape. Isobel of the accomplished novel *Blown Figures* appears again in *Ladies & Escorts,* but the prize sleepwalker here is the hippychild Caroline of **"Rapunsel,"** wandering alone through Africa doing a little vibe-collecting and sketching and keeping a journal in one of Thomas' favourite languages, mirror-writing. Africa finally manifests itself to her not as the friendly nuns and colourful market figures, but as a man she may or may not have dreamed, whose face she never sees. "Why did you come here?" he asks, before threatening to rape or kill her. . . . Her heroines are terrified of Africa because it is terrifying, and because—like sexual love—they can neither understand nor control it. Part of the darkness is in them, but, if we are to believe Thomas' work at all, part of it is really there, just as in her Mexican stories the grotesque lives of her characters find their counterparts in the actual images supplied to them by Mexico itself. Thomas didn't need to invent **"The More Little Mummy in the World,"** a mummified baby on public display which gives her a fitting reflection of her heroine's abortion. (This, by the way, is yet another appearance of the lost unborn child, a central image in Thomas' work from the beginning.)

Thomas is a writers' writer, which shouldn't prevent her from being a readers' writer as well. She has enormous verbal skills: a passion for words—words as games, words as magic or refrain, words as puzzle or multi-leveled pun—a wonderful ear for dialogue and dialect, a flexible style. Her fascination with language for its own sake accounts for much of the sheer panache of her writing, though it occasionally leads her into less successful excesses. . . . She is at her best when her stylistic gifts and her obsession with language are reflected by her material. Her finest stories not only demonstrate language, they are about language: the impossibility, and the necessity, of using it for true communication.

Her best stories, too, are about the difficulty of doing whatever it is that she does as a writer. She is not at heart a "storyteller," that is, a constructor of plots which will carry in themselves the weight of her meaning. In fact, she is at her least convincing with her most "finished" plots. Instead she is a fictionalizer. "Writers are terrible liars," she begins one story. She then confesses that the story before it was an inflated distortion of an actual event, and proceeds to tell another story which we are tempted to believe is more "true," until we come to the end and discover the author and the principle character giggling over what names they will have in the story and even what name the story will have. The story, even if "true," is revealed as an artefact. This device—the story told, re-told in a different way, exposed, told again—occurs throughout Thomas' writing. Take the curious case of the African cook-steward. This man appears in two of Thomas' novels, *Mrs. Blood* and *Blown Figures*. In these his name is Joseph, and it is Joseph also in one story from *Ten Green Bottles*. In another story a figure clearly based on the same man is called Samuel. He is back again in *Ladies & Escorts,* but this time we are given an entirely different version of where he came from and what happened to him. Is the author just "using material" in one story but telling the truth in the other? We will never know.

Thomas' work is not like a mystery story, where a series of hidden clues add up finally to the one, the inevitable truth. Rather it is—as a whole, and also in its parts—more like a folk-tale collected in several variant forms. No one story is the true story, but the sum of the stories is. A reader will either love this approach for its richness and its surreal echo effects or be very frustrated by it. Those who insist on the cut and dried should probably avoid Thomas.

It's amazing that Audrey Thomas has managed to write as much as she has in the last ten years: three novels, two novellas, and two books of stories. Despite her output and its ambition, range and quality, she has not yet received the kind of recognition such a body of work merits, perhaps because she is that cultural hybrid, an early-transplanted American. Of course her work has flaws; everyone's does. She can be sentimental, repetitious, and sometimes merely gossipy. But page for page, she is one of [Canada's] best writers. (pp. 268-71)

Margaret Atwood, "Audrey Thomas: 'Ten Green Bottles', 'Ladies & Escorts'," *in her* Second Words: Selected Critical Prose, *Toronto: House of Anansi Press, 1982, pp. 268-71.*

I. M. OWEN

The American-born Canadian writer Audrey Thomas has written [*Latakia,*] a novel about an American-born Canadian writer named Rachel who is writing an autobiographical novel. The danger of getting trapped in an infinite regression . . . is avoided by giving the novel—Audrey Thomas's, not Rachel's—the form of a monologue in which Rachel imagines herself talking to her recent lover, a younger writer named Michael who has now returned to his wife, about their life together. The narrative keeps shifting in time and place, at random and without warning; sometimes the scene is in Crete where Rachel is now living, sometimes in Vancouver where the affair started, sometimes on a freighter in the Atlantic or the Mediterranean, sometimes in New York, Montreal, Las Palmas, Rome, Latakia, or Athens. That's the way our private thoughts work, of course. But when we want to interest someone else in our experiences we generally try to arrange the events in a logical sequence. And one of the objects of a novel is to interest someone else in a story.

When Margaret Laurence plays about with the time-sequence in *The Diviners* there's a point to it, but *The Diviners* is a large and complex story. *Latakia* isn't. Rachel meets Michael and falls in love with him. He leaves his wife Hester to live with her. They travel together; he keeps in touch with Hester; they try a *ménage à trois* that fails; he ends up back with Hester. These three are the only characters; there are other figures, but they are not much more than stage props. Most of them are Greeks; Rachel can speak some Greek . . . but not enough to enable her to see more than the surfaces of the people's lives. Hers is a tourist's-eye view: she can speak of ''a Greek, nurtured on centuries of worship of physical perfection, especially in the male,'' as if there had been no intervening centuries of well-wrapped Eastern Orthodoxy and Islamic domination between Praxiteles and the present.

But then Rachel and Michael don't do much thinking, except about themselves. ''I thought you were the biggest egotist I had ever met,'' she says; ''you thought the same of me.'' They were both right. The reader wonders what the novels of such people would be like, and Rachel supplies the answer: ''I *can* write about other people, I just don't choose to.'' She implies that Michael wouldn't be able to if he chose. . . .

Rachel is obsessively in love with this repellent person—so obsessively that doubts don't seem to enter her mind even when early in their liaison he calls her seven-year-old daughter ''you little fucking bitch.'' As for Michael, his obsession is with the satisfaction of having two women in love with him. (Hester is mostly off stage, and there's little to explain what's going on in *her* mind.)

Occasionally Rachel tries to derive from her abject condition a significant feminist statement:

> I had never loved anyone, physically, the way that I loved you. When you touched me, my flesh smoked. That was the great power you had over me. For the first time in my life, I really understood the politics of male chauvinism, the conscious (or often unconscious) use of the power bestowed by genitals and the System.

That's simply silly. Rachel has had to wait until the age of 38 to experience a feeling that's familiar, surely, to most males. So if it has to do with the politics of sexual chauvinism, women must have been in charge of the world all along, after all.

Each episode, it should be said, is shrewdly observed and written with style and wit. Audrey Thomas is a very good writer. I just wish she had emulated Mavis Gallant, who sometimes writes a novel and then pares it down until it emerges as a short story. *Latakia* could have made a striking short story. By stretching it out over 176 pages and then shuffling the pages into a random order, the author hasn't done her small subject a bit of good.

I. M. Owen, ''Three on a See-Saw,'' in Books in Canada, *Vol. 8, No. 10, December, 1979, p. 11.*

RUSSELL M. BROWN

The publisher calls *Latakia* a novel on the front cover; on the back it is referred to as a travelogue. Really it is neither, but rather . . . the raw material from which novels get made. This book is closer to confessional prose than to fiction—it is at once autobiographical fragment and a strongly-felt meditation on a failed love affair. Perhaps *Latakia* is best described as rumination: a thorough, thoughtful chewing over of only partially digested experience. What the book gives us, after all, is not so much a record of events as one of the patterns which the mind makes as it circles around troubling moments in its past, assessing and reassessing them. Since the account does not move in an ordered or chronological fashion, its present comes to be juxtaposed with the past in a way that makes disappointing outcomes stand uncomfortably close to promising beginnings: reality repeatedly mocks expectation. . . .

The reader's experience of *Latakia* is not a simple one. . . . Thomas gives us only Rachel's version of things. Frank and sometimes fiercely self-revealing though it is, we find ourselves unable to forget how one-sided it must be. If we remain sympathetic despite this, it is because we come to believe that we would have felt the same and been equally unable to see any point of view but our own. This is the only way a work so personal can succeed: by abolishing distances and making us participants. Still, we frequently find ourselves struggling *for* some distance from this text—longing for a more removed point from which to contemplate the many unsignalled ironies, sort out the unreflected-upon compulsions of these people, and think about their unexamined motives.

Thomas does not give us the room for such detached reflection, nor does she want to. Throughout this has been a work of vindication rather than of explanation: the writer bringing her craft to her defense. Rachel's last words call our attention to this, (if it was not already evident.) As an author she no longer values life as it has been lived, but as it can be recast into art—an art where hers will always be the final word. ''And remember,'' she tells us in closing, ''the best revenge is writing well.''

Russell M. Brown, ''Life After Man,'' in The Canadian Forum, *Vol. LX, No. 700, June-July, 1980, p. 38.*

BARBARA NOVAK

Real Mothers is a particularly unified collection. Although the narration shifts in tone from story to story, stylistically it remains consistent, a single voice struggling from parenthesis to parenthesis toward the intuitive goal that the mother, sleeping under the moon with her daughter in **''Natural History,''** achieves for a fleeting instant: ''wholeness, harmony, radiance: all of it making a wonderful kind of sense.'' . . .

[*Real Mothers* includes] stories in which a woman's sense of responsibility toward her child is in conflict with her sense of responsibility toward her mate. Thomas examines this problem in two stories, one comic and one tragic. In **"Real Mothers"** the idea is distilled into a conflict between the need to nurture and the need to be nurtured. The latter wins out ("Sometimes, I think that you're the mother and I'm the teenager, Marie-Anne!") as the mother relinquishes control over herself and her two daughters to the demands of a selfish, brutal lover. First excluded, then emotionally and physically neglected, her children leave her to live with their father, much to her anguish. In **"Harry and Violet"** a woman is caught in the middle, trying to satisfy the needs of daughter and lover. . . . A balance is struck, but it is quickly upset with a comically inevitable twist at the end. (p. 19)

Thomas's women grapple with . . . [an] insidious fear, most evocatively presented in **"Natural History."** The *leitmotiv* in this story is the moon: "And the moon up there, female, shining always by reflected light, dependent on the sun, yet so much brighter, seemingly, against the darkness of the sky; so much more mysterious, changing her shape, controlling the waters, gathering it all in her net." The moon, inspiring a host of old wives' tales, is to be feared. The mother in this story prays for her daughter (named after the sunflower) to be "strong, yet loving." At the end of the story she shields her from the moonlight.

Thomas's women are afraid, not of men, but of themselves, of their own strengths and needs. They are afraid of their strength, because loneliness may well be the price they have to pay for it. And they are afraid of admitting their need of men, of allowing themselves to become dependent, for then they risk being mere reflections, like the moon, or like the "wasted light" reflected from the eyes of animals at night. But even the cat in **"Natural History"** doesn't like to sleep alone: "The cat was old, but very independent, except for wanting to sleep inside at night."

The images in **"Natural History"** reverberate throughout the entire collection. In a story called **"Out in the Midday Sun"** a woman conceals a letter from her husband, knowing that when she shows it to him he will leave her. The letter is not from a lover, but from a publisher accepting a manuscript she wrote secretly. She knows that her success will upset the balance of power with her writer-husband, will equalize it, and destroy the relationship. **"In the Bleak Mid-Winter"** is about a *ménage à trois* involving two women: one dependent, one independent. Their lover caters to the woman who needs him the most.

Thomas's stories are created with such a complete mastery of form that to discuss them in linear terms is to do them an injustice. One story begins with a quote from a guidebook in the Jeu de Paume, the Impressionist gallery in Paris: "A picture must be built up by means of rhythm, calculation and selection." This approach applies equally well to all the stories in Thomas's collection. (pp. 19-20)

Thomas demands much more of her readers than most writers, but the rewards are much greater, too. (p. 20)

> Barbara Novak, "Lunar Distractions," in Books in Canada, Vol. 11, No. 2, February, 1982, pp. 18-20.*

ELEANOR WACHTEL

"Where are all the strong men now that there are all these strong women?" asks a character in Audrey Thomas's newest

and most accomplished collection of stories, *Real Mothers*. The collection takes up a subject—the failure of modern relationships—that has perhaps even supplanted love and romance as a preoccupation of our time. Thomas tackles it with an honesty and immediacy at once powerful and familiar.

Her characters, however great their need for independence, don't want to be alone. They require the physical and emotional presence of another person, a body in their bed, even if it's simply "the reassuring back of the puzzle who was her husband." Connection fails because ties between individuals are unequal. Increasingly, as women seize power, or come to assume it subtly from vain, weak men, relationships dissolve, or last only as long as the women maintain the charade of male dominance. "It's easier without a man . . . but is it better?"

In **"Out in the Midday Sun,"** a professor seduces and runs off with his brilliant female students as a way of suppressing them. If, like the amaryllis, they somehow find new soil in which to flower again, this self-fulfilment is a betrayal, an infidelity that terminates the relationship. The professor is exposed and undone; he must seek a fresh admirer to con.

While women grope for a balance between independence and involvement, men have different expectations, preferring unqualified devotion. Like petty godlings, they are content with the form, insensitive to nuance. In **"Galatea,"** the wife realizes that her marriage depends on her accepting the role of dabbler; she, however, chooses to stay and manipulate her (professor) husband rather than take herself seriously and thus become so threatening he'd be forced to leave.

If men live in self-delusion, they are spared the pain of self-knowledge. Only Thomas's women bleed. Men are more vulnerable now, she seems to be saying, but also more callous. In one of the book's slighter stories, **"In the Bleak Mid-Winter,"** Johanna, one of two women in a *ménage à trois*, rebels against the self-centered male corner of the triangle. In taking up with a workman in the Greek hotel where the three are staying, she undermines her lover's pretensions. Then she silences his impotent anger with the reassurance: "It's all right, Patrick. I told them that you were my brother." Appearances are intact.

"Crossing the Rubicon" is a stylistically brilliant story in which the multiple narrative threads enable Thomas to underline women's ambivalence. A writer, to avoid having to work on a difficult story, is helping her daughter make Valentine treats. By thinking about "the woman in my story," she is able to give her a sense of determination and assurance that the author herself lacked. In the story within a story, the character parts from an encounter with an old lover, who has chosen to remain with his wife. The writer has the character end the encounter in style: "And she doesn't look back. In my story, that is. She doesn't look back in my story."

Thomas often introduces into the mix of these relationships the significant but frequently unacknowledged presence of a child. "Separated children" are the by-products of broken marriages; they form the apex of contemporary triangles—a woman, her lover, and her child. If the 1960s signified sexual awakening, and the 1970s was a period of sexual politics, then the 1980s just might be dominated by the politics of the family, with Audrey Thomas one of its most astute commentators. In her analysis, for a couple not to have children is a symptom of an inadequate relationship. Yet it later appears that the only prospering relationship is the one between parent and child, as portrayed in the most tender of these stories, **"Natural History."**

This relationship too can founder. In the title story, Marie-Anne, a middle child, comforts her mother when her father forsakes them for a young student of his. . . . The closeness she enjoys with her mother is shattered by her mother's new lover, a nasty young man who resents his paramour's children. When the mother is unable to face the inexorable choice between lover and children, Marie-Anne must do it for her.

The impulse behind these stories is the same one which informed Thomas's first published prose, **"If One Green Bottle . . ."** . . .—a need to organize pain. Thomas doesn't shrink from depicting the dark side of life, yet her writing is infused with a zest for living—a sensuous appreciation of colours and tastes, curiosity, and a pleasure in simple, old-fashioned activities, like making cookies or walking on the beach. There's a recognition of the richness of small joys that cooler chroniclers of modern affairs, like Ann Beattie and Mavis Gallant, eschew. (pp. 51-2)

Real Mothers is Thomas at her most relaxed—but it is a carefully crafted casualness. Some of the earlier work seems, by comparison, skilful but slightly contrived, with a certain self-conscious quality of "good writing" enhanced by a show of erudition. *Real Mothers* gives us Audrey Thomas leaning over the kitchen table: a raconteur who seems to ramble until the strands suddenly draw together like a net. Elliptical, personal imagery has been replaced by anecdote, while the ear for dialogue, the fascination with language, foreign words and their origins, remain unchanged. (p. 52)

> *Eleanor Wachtel, "Contemporary Triangles," in* Saturday Night, *Vol. 97, No. 4, April, 1982, pp. 51-2.*

BARBARA GODARD

Any doubt as to whether Thomas is one of our major writers should be dispelled in this new collection of short stories [*Real Mothers*]. . . .

Thomas plays on the duplicity, the multiplicity of language, its paradoxes and overlaps opening up the space of the book, demanding an active participation on the part of the reader. The story is not in the words but in the space between them and around them. In contextualizing her narratives, Thomas makes her language performative. This strategy is announced in the epigraph to **"Galatea":** "A picture must be built up by means of rhythm, calculation and selection." Thomas' stories evolve through such modulation, plane grafted onto plane, perspective piled onto perspective. Much of the rich complexity as well as the surprise develops from the sudden shifts between perspectives—between the child's story and the mother's in **"Real Mothers,"** between the husband's story of his life and the wife's in **"Galatea."** . . . And Thomas' stories oscillate between these modes—between the timeless, fantastic world of the tale and a pattern of infinite regression, Godel's theorem. In **"Crossing the Rubicon,"** there are many levels of narrative: the story the narrator is trying to write in a self-reflexive narrative, enfolded within the story of her own life evoked through childhood memories, and counterpointed against those of her daughter's life and the present interaction with the daughter as they bake cupcakes. Both of the first stories focus on the break up of a love affair, that of the story trying to write itself being projected into the future tense, contrasting with the weight of trivia from her "rag bag mind." In the story being composed, the woman doesn't look back when she says good-bye to her lover. However, the story we actually read is about Lot's wife and the function of memory.

Characteristically, clashes between perspectives are signalled by disjunctions in language. In Montreal, where the affair ends, the sign "Arretez" is ignored by the woman, who runs into the road. Other abrupt switches into a foreign language underline the difficulties of comprehension between individuals. "PAIN DORE. 'Golden pain' is the first thing that comes to her; then 'golden bread'. She stops to look it up. 'Canada: Pain doré. France: pain perdu. French Toast'." Even within the French language there is no agreement; golden break wars with lost bread. The implication is that any relationships constructed on the basis of linguistic communication are bound to falter; this is so because so much noise or static is registered between sender and receiver. (p. 110)

This technique is a familiar one from Thomas' other books. One of her most common metaphors for the problematic nature of language is travelling in foreign countries, adrift on the cross-cultural confusions and the multiple meanings of words. As the stories intercut, the enfolding of story within story underlines these inadequacies of language. . . . [Expanding] on Henry James' principle of reflectors but accentuating the breaks, Thomas illustrates a facet of perception only recently being taken into account by feminist sociologists. What is clear is that there is *no single* story of family life or marriage; there are as many stories as there are individuals involved. Each character brings his or her story with him or her. Emphasis consequently is not on description but on the act of telling, characters becoming grammatical beings embedding their stories in the narrative as it grows through accumulation in the manner of *The Arabian Nights.* To speak is to live; such is the magical power of the narrative act, a power which Thomas foregrounds in **"Out in the Midday Sun"** where the man writes "swiftly and easily," "automatically," with a black pen "magic, like the broom of the sorcerer's apprentice." But as this allusion makes clear, while Thomas believes in the power of language—a life giving, fantastic power—this makes her all the more aware of the lie that is narrative. In this clash of perspectives is located Thomas' analysis and judgement of truth and lies, memory, private and public story telling—all potentially fallible. (p.111)

Another of Thomas' images foregrounds the clash that lies between stories, between perspectives—that of the stereopticon which the narrator remembers playing with as a child, taking two photographs at different angles which take on depth at "the right distance from everything." Memory becomes an important distancing element and the characteristic Thomas narrator mulls over the past in an effort to attain the "illusion of solidity." Everything, however, is open to new interpretation as another viewpoint is injected.

In two stories Thomas highlights this process as she rewrites well known stories and inverts them. In **"Galatea"** the wife claims she has fallen in love with the river and asks her writer-husband—a devourer of dictionaries and encyclopedias—where there are any myths about this. Inverting the story of the classic Galatea, he replies that it is usually the River God who pursues the nymph. His ignorance here is a key element in underlining the untold story. It is his wife who is the artist in the family; she is the one who has moulded his stories, eavesdropped on conversations for him, developed the settings in which to locate his characters. The collaboration is conveyed through another allusion, inverted and changed in a new context. The word "incarnadine," so famous to readers of *MacBeth*, is translated here from being a reference to the blood, death and madness created by an ambitious woman, to having association with the Incarnation, the Word made flesh (the couple's "literary" offspring). In his deployment of the word, we become aware that the husband has absorbed her painterly eye. Context and word play off ironically against each other; such is this structure of loss.

A similar story unfolds in **"Out in the Midday Sun"** which despite its reference to Noel Coward is a pastiche, a rewriting from an inverted female perspective of Hemingway's "The Snows of Kilimanjaro." The name of the mountain tells it all—the violence of an American bitch undoing a man. Here a series of allusions to Hemingway . . . sets the scene for the revelation that the woman is going to make to her husband. She has been his brilliant student whom he has married. Although she loves him, she has lived in this house under false pretences. Not content to be there when he has wanted her (did he marry her to shut her up, she wonders), she has been writing in secret and the book is about to be published. Her husband has had two wives before her, she interjects into her thoughts in the midst of a conversation about Hemingway's many wives, and, by implication, he is chasing the same fear of creative impotency as the American writer. As the story unfolds in Thomas' hands from the female perspective, the woman is not the destructive force. Rather the problem lies within the male who cannot bear to have his dominancy challenged by the black pen of the apprentice sorcerer.

The play on edges occurs not just between one art form and another—between the narratives of one sex and another—but also between art and life. This is made clear in **"Déjeuner sur l'herbe."** In the famous impressionist painting alluded to here, there is a sharp incongruity between nude figures and pastoral landscape. In the story, platonic friends visit Paris. Their lack of involvement with each other—their twin beds—reflect their tourist disinterestedness and their non-involvement in the human suffering they witness about them. On their last day, they look for a place to picnic, deciding to eat in a cemetery, thereby flaunting their detachment. As the woman is posing with a wreath of artificial poppies for yet another tourist photo, a woman comes along emptyhanded, having abandoned the kitten she had earlier been carrying. The photo is interrupted; the woman reacts by looking for the kitten while the man says there is nothing they can do. At this point she "snaps" and calls out tauntingly to him to end the artifice of their lives, inviting a realignment of foreground and background, a breaking of the pictorial codes by which they have been living. She throws back at him the slogans they have been seeing on walls: "Don't touch! . . . Don't get involved." Aestheticism divorced from human emotions and from human relationships is destructive, Thomas implies. But within the story there is no solution offered. In the final line, the man throws back another question: "'And what if you do?' (. . .) 'What then?'"

What then indeed? As I have been suggesting, the collisions of perspective in Thomas' work are conveyed through a series of images of perception and through linguistic devices which open up the gap between language and feeling. These include the lost child—word not incarnate—the foreign word—slippery indeterminate in translation—the ironic or inverted allusion—working explicitly on convention to explode meaning. Working to effect a similar disjunction and interrogation of the hermeneutic process are cliché, ambiguity, and definition. Cliché, like allusion, points to the fact that the impact of Thomas' fiction rests on its deployment of conventions and "realistic"

expectations which are then frustrated by the next section or sentence or word. Her syntax is like Camus' *écriture blanche* which Sartre described: "there is a small death between each sentence"—indeed, between each word as "real mothers" demonstrates. Here the word "real" is an equivocal word situated at the point where two sequences of semantic or formal associations intersect. The one set of associations comes from the sign's immediate context, its syntactical position, and relates to the issue of being a *true* mother—loyal, self-sacrificing, carrying out the tasks to assure her children's well-being (all that goes with the cliché "motherhood"). The other set of associations comes from a wider context, from another text within the text which develops from the mother's quest for authenticity. Her first steps toward a life of her own where she is involved with school work and a lover to the exclusion of her children's demands raises the question: "How can one be real and be a mother?" The children's understanding of the word clashes with the mother's understanding of the word. Increasingly they are involved in a classic triangle—children and lover in a tug-of-war for mother. Within the story the differing concepts of reality are reflected in the mother's changing language as she moves to a new sense of self. "Coping" is "one of her mother's new words," as is "separated." The latter word opens a wider gap, for as the daughter Anne-Marie reflects, no one ever heard of "separated" children (though the word more appropriately describes her psychological state than it does her mother's). In **"Crossing the Rubicon,"** the clichés of married and family relationships (those "real mothers") are underlined in the clichéd phrases of the candied hearts being put on the birthday cupcakes—phrases like "Be My Sugar Daddy" or "You're a Slick Chick."

Ambiguity—present, in fact, in most stories—is highlighted in **"Ted's Wife."** This occurs even in the opening description of this woman where Phyllis (known for her "mots justes") describes her as "the alternate selection." The story is immediately focussed into a broader context—ultimately into the story *not* told—in an attempt to elucidate an answer to the implied question: "alternate to whom?" In most stories, the narrators or characters resort to dictionaries in an attempt to stop the drift of words, seeking out the precise meaning of a term. . . . But the greatest onslaught on received meanings or the conventions of speech is revealed in the child's answer to her father in **"Natural History."** "And what are strangers?" asked her father gently. The child's reply was very serious: "Strangers are usually men." Social context, questions of dominance or difference, leave their mark on language. It is as much a well of private experiences as it is a vehicle for public communication. One function is continuously intersecting with another. That Thomas thinks of language as a paradigm is clear in **"Timbuktu"** where in referring to the West African custom of respecting women and not harassing them because they have power and status she uses the term "lingua franca." Here the paradigmatic level intrudes ungrammatically into the level of syntax.

If, as I have been suggesting, Thomas specializes in this ungrammaticality and creates structures of loss, she does offer her readers presents in compensation. There are, for instance, the joys accompanying the rediscovery of an obsolete word, a dinosaur eliminated by cultural evolutions. . . . Thomas' polishing of such lost linguistic jewels opens the texts up beyond the mimetic level to involve the reader's life story as well as those of the characters.

Again, her use of allusion invokes the same mechanisms of recall and textual explosion, though operative not in the gap between text and life, but in that between one text and another. Intertextuality, as in the direct quotation of an interchange from Durrell's *Balthazar* in **"Harry & Violet,"** as well as calling forth memories of reading the Alexandria quartet, foregrounds Thomas' narrative model. For Durrell's intersecting, conflicting personal visions of a chain of actions—written to illustrate, as the epigraph informs us, that $E = MC^2$—are reflected in the spatial and temporal relativity in Thomas' work which makes *story,* the narrative unfolding of an action, the only reality.

If I have focussed on the semiotic delights of Thomas' texts, it is not to deny there are any mimetic ones. On the contrary, the carefully selected and polished language is the foundation on which is built an examination of the present realities of women's lives as they struggle for a sense of selfhood (**"Timbuktu"**), wrestle with conflicting demands of children and husband/lovers (**"Harry & Violet"**), or deal with the complex web of miscomprehensions which are the conventions of relationships between members of the opposite sex (**"In the Bleak Mid Winter"**). In all these situations, conflicting emotional demands or role expectations are threatening to split women apart. These are the very areas where the struggle of contemporary women to redefine conventions is at its sharpest, because conventions here coincide with our deepest emotional bonds. The dangers of not being involved leads one into the grammar of family life which in **"Real Mothers"** seems to deny authenticity to women. Only in the intersecting paradoxes of Thomas' narratives can these conflicting demands be reconciled. Fiction becomes a strategy for reinforcing wholeness and integration in a world that threatens to come apart. But it is a trick, this "illusion of depth and solidity," a trick of the distance and the multiple frames. Nonetheless, the illusion of careful surfaces that Thomas has created ensures that there is an appeal to the heart in these stories, just as the self-reflexive nature of the narratives offers the mind the consolation of form. (pp. 111-14)

*Barbara Godard, in a review of "Real Mothers,"
in* The Fiddlehead, *No. 135, January, 1983, pp. 110-14.*

URJO KAREDA

Audrey Thomas's writing has been with us for almost two decades, and her output has been substantial.... Her stories have appeared in national publications and have won competitions and awards, but somehow she has never achieved her rightful place in the hierarchy of Canada's best writers. Her writing tends to be racier, ruder, more raw than that of her contemporaries in the Ontario-centred, female-dominated literary establishment. Thomas puts bluntness before elegance, and her prose is a kind of burr on the silky eloquence that characterizes the writing of Margaret Atwood and Alice Munro, or the mythic cadences of Margaret Laurence's work. Her mercilessly satiric instincts expose the intellectual and emotional confusions of her characters....

Whether *Intertidal Life* becomes her breakthrough book remains to be seen. It is not without flaws, but it is an ambitious, complex work, profoundly feminist in its arguments and sensibilities. It is a candid exploration of the sadomasochistic substructure of male-female relationships. It is as clear-headed about emotional needs, sexual hunger, and the territorial imperative of an intelligent temperament as it is about the ache of betrayal, the humiliation of desire, and the infinite emptiness

of loss. And because Thomas's own personality seems so shrewd, honest, and resiliently affirmative, the novel manages to seem celebratory about the vital but doomed struggle of men and women to understand one another.

The central character, Alice, is, like Thomas, a writer with three daughters, living on an island very like the author's own Galiano. A present course of action—preparing food, coping with the daughters, trying to find time to write—reverberates with fragments from the past. Her stormy love for and marriage to Peter, a painter, has ended messily: he has deserted Alice and their daughters, yet keeps circling around, as if for refuelling stops between relationships with several women, most of whom share the ironic distinction of having first been Alice's confidantes.

Thomas elaborates upon themes and techniques from her earlier work, but also pursues patterns within a wider world of literature, most obviously the novels of Virginia Woolf. Alice seems a very distant, sexy Canadian cousin of Woolf's Mrs. Ramsay in *To the Lighthouse,* balancing a journey toward self-understanding with children, random visitors, and what's-for-dinner. (A lighthouse figures iconographically in *Intertidal Life* as well.)

The author's most arresting achievement is the translation of Alice's consciousness—her nerve-end tensions, her encyclopedic distractions, her comic missiles, her self-pity as well as her self-loathing—into a prose that never becomes whiny or enervated. The structure—as in Woolf—is subtle and allusive, a weave of memories, sensations, associations, and reassessments.... Thomas's collage technique, in which the most intimate erotic detail can be followed by a pedantic tiptoe through a dictionary, is touched, even transformed, by intelligence, and an omnivorous curiosity. Her inquiry is into what remains after everything else is cut away.

There is a dark subplot—which Thomas insists, rather arbitrarily, on keeping mysterious—about a serious illness that threatens Alice even as she is rallying her psychic resources. As in Atwood's *Bodily Harm*—whose metaphor of breast cancer Thomas may be echoing here—images of mutilation abound.... (p. 50)

The characters who enter Alice's circle of sympathy are generously handled. Thomas's child characters remain among the most credible in Canadian fiction, and the island's gentle and unfocused eccentrics who wander through the novel retain, against the author's almost irrepressible satiric instinct, their integrity. In an odd way, Thomas is less fair to Alice's ex-husband Peter than Alice is herself. For all the forgiveness and understanding that Alice seems determined to shove in his direction, he remains distinctly weightless, a man in hiding, caught at best only in half-glimpses. This has the effect of making Alice her own antagonist—there is no opposition similarly strong and muscular—but she has enough contradictory impulses and warring confusions to sustain both roles. Transcendence becomes a vision of passivity: "And what do I want? In which direction, now, do I want to move? Or could I please for the next little while just be a stone, washed by the sea, warmed by the sun, unmoving?" ...

Intertidal Life doesn't rank with Audrey Thomas's finest writing, but its desire to reach us, to tell so much, to keep questioning, are the strengths of an exceptional, expressive will. (p. 51)

Urjo Kareda, "Sense and Sensibility," in Saturday Night, *Vol. 100, No. 1, January, 1985, pp. 50-1.*

WAYNE GRADY

There are textual reverberations, what Baudelaire might have called correspondences, among Audrey Thomas's four novels. She often plunders her own earlier work in order to supply images and details for the new. Thus an episode from the 1970 novel *Mrs. Blood* turns up again, altered and inflated, as **"Degrees,"** a short story published two years ago in *Saturday Night*. The epilogue to Part I of *Mrs. Blood*—the passage in *Alice's Adventures in Wonderland* in which the Cheshire Cat observes that Alice must be mad, otherwise she wouldn't be in Wonderland—is echoed now in *Intertidal Life,* where it is given emphasis by the fact that the main character is named Alice.... Both Isobel in *Blown Figures* (1975) and Alice in *Intertidal Life* recall fathers who used to sing:

> Oh, the only girl I ever loved
> had a face like a horse and Bug-gy.

And both Alice and Rachel (in *Latakia,* 1979) are writers who are trying to come to terms in their books with the fact that they have been rejected by men who have loved them.

The form of *Intertidal Life* is itself a borrowing from two earlier books. The present work is part novel, written in the third person, and part commonplace book, written in the first person; and the book alternates between "she" and "I" in much the same way that *Mrs. Blood* alternated between passages by Mrs. Blood and Mrs. Thing. There is also the echo of Thomas's 1972 book, *Munchmeyer and Prospero on the Island,* in which the second novella is a diary kept by Miranda, who is writing the first novella.

Alice's commonplace book is meant, we learn early on, as a place where Alice "would finally bring all the words and definitions and phrases I have copied out for years on scraps of paper. But I need it now for something else. I need it to stay sane." At one point, when Alice is buying jigsaw puzzles for her daughters, she imagines herself as one of the boxes: "Alice Hoyle: 1,000 Interlocking Pieces." The commonplace book is Alice's attempt to put all those interlocking pieces together.

The threat to her sanity is the desertion by her husband Peter, one of those vaguely depressing trendies who after 14 years of marriage has decided that a trial separation, during which he could learn not to be "uptight" (this is in 1979) and "locked into the Protestant work ethic," would be worth the physical and financial suffering it inflicts on his wife and three daughters. (p. 32)

Section I of the novel is a long wail, a prolonged venting of Alice's grief, which takes the simultaneous forms of despair and anger: "How dare he walk away," she rages in the commonplace book. "'I'll call you during the week.' I vowed I wouldn't talk to him but of course I did. And cried. 'Hello, old friend,' he said in his soft, *caring* voice. But I'm not stupid, I could hear the 'end' in 'Friend'...."

Alice shares her island with a group of superannuated hippies who have taken over a clutter of abandoned cabins in Coon Bay. At first she feels no great antipathy toward them—two of them have become her friends, and her husband has, in a sense, gone over to them—but her real friends are two women, Stella and Trudl, and it is this triad or sisterhood that is the real focus of the novel.

Stella's husband has died, and Trudl has left hers, and so the three women share at least one common bond. (Alice and Stella also share Peter, but Alice doesn't discover that until later.) The hippies, Alice realizes, are "takers," uninterested in any-

thing outside their own self-absorption.... Alice's new orientation is with the women, the "givers"; and by the end of Section I she has accepted the fact that her husband has gone over to the "takers."

In Section II, Alice's acceptance assuages her grief: "When I'm not full of rage I'm sad," she notes in her commonplace book, and the dominant note of this section is sadness, with occasional dips into resignation tempered by anguished cries of rebellion. She is moon-driven, up and down with the tides.

Water imagery is an important element throughout the book: in Section I Alice is "struggling in the icy waters of Peter's rejection"; now she can almost joke about it ("Your honour, we drifted apart"). The book's title identifies the metaphor—"intertidal life" is a biological reference to the myriad crusty creatures that live in trapped puddles of water when the tide has receded.... Alice and her children observe the pile worms and limpets, the starfish, mussels, and hermit crabs, and admire their ability to survive. "We could all learn a lesson from limpets," Alice writes. "They really know how to hang on."

By the end of the book, though, Alice is off limpets, just as she has gone off hippies. Intertidal creatures "just go about eating each other." She has come to see all life as intertidal, a lunatic frenzy of directionless activity between the overwhelming oceans of birth and death, and we are reminded of the world of difference that exists between Miranda's association with water and Ophelia's....

The plunge into early maritime exploration has given Alice (and us) a hint at the true nature of her own plight. "Women have been shanghaied," she tells Stella, "and now we are waking up and rubbing our eyes and murmuring, 'Where are we?'" Women's response, she says, is to incite "some kind of mutiny," but not one intended to regain freedom. "We don't want to be let out at the nearest port or unceremoniously tossed overboard ... what we really want is to be officers and captains ourselves."

This is all fairly orthodox feminism, and there is not much that is mutinous in *Intertidal Life.* Peter is such a wimpy piece of asparagus that his passage from Alice's life ought to have been an occasion for joy rather than the 280 pages of *angst* it engenders. The commonplace-book motif gives the action of the novel, such as it is, a certain distance, a lack of immediacy: events and even emotions are reported rather than experienced, and the difference between high and low tide never seems to be more than a few inches.

But the positive side of distance—control—is also here. Thomas is a superbly controlled writer, and her prose is tight and unflawed. As the exploration of the emotional state of a woman approaching middle age who has suddenly to come to terms with a New World (not necessarily a real one), *Intertidal Life* has a warm, quiet intensity. It is a novel about freedom—some of Thomas's characters are born free, some achieve freedom, and some, like Alice, have had freedom thrust upon them—and a surfeit of freedom may be said to be the most toxic carcinogen of the 20th century. *Intertidal Life* is undoubtedly Thomas's best novel to date. (p. 33)

Wayne Grady, "Littoral Truths," in Books in Canada, *Vol. 14, No. 4, May, 1985, pp. 32-3.*

ALBERTO MANGUEL

The life in question [in *Intertidal Life*] belongs to Alice, a happily married writer, with three daughters, a house on one of Vancouver's islands, and a husband who has just told her he's in love with another woman. As the title suggests, Alice is caught between tides: marriage and separation, present and past, acquiring knowledge and losing herself in despair. Like her looking-glass namesake, Alice finds that her world is somehow wrong—its geography has shifted. The rules by which she lived, the certainty she felt, no longer seem true.... Two women follow Alice's itinerary: "I" and "she." "I" is Alice herself, mirrored in her writer's notebooks; "she" is the other Alice, a character seen from a distance by an anonymous narrator. It's curious that the intimate Alice, the "I," is the least revealing. "I" discloses her thoughts as they drift by; "she" describes Alice's actions. And it is through what Alice does, rather than what she thinks, that her voyage is mapped.

Virginia Woolf, in *A Room of One's Own,* accused Kipling of writing "only with the male side of his brain." The reverse charge cannot be leveled against Audrey Thomas. Her men, as much as her women, grow and tremble and change: Alice's husband of 14 years, Peter; Harold, the deaf neighbor with whose girlfriend Peter becomes involved; the hippie Raven, a leftover from the '60s, self-centered and conceited. All three defy conventional labels—even Peter, the villain, whose tactlessness is revealed when he offers Alice a copy of Rilke's *Letters to a Young Poet,* thereby (he feels) displaying true interest in her writing.

Much has been made of the symbolic importance of female characters in Canadian literature, both in the works of women writers . . . and their male counterparts. . . . In *Survival,* a now classic "thematic guide to Canadian literature," Margaret Atwood posits the Rapunzel fairy-tale as the pattern for all "realistic" novels about "normal" women: there's the imprisoned Rapunzel, her guardian parents or husband, the tower of society in which she's kept, and her lover-liberator. As Atwood points out, Rapunzel and her tower are one and the same. This is certainly true of Alice and her island society: they suffer the same betrayals, yearn for the same self-knowledge. Atwood also remarks that Canadian literature yields "a bumper crop of sinister Hecate-Crones," but "Why are there no Molly Blooms?" Alice is Molly Bloom on the verge of self-discovery.

The character, reaching the shores of her own self, harks back to the archetypical image of woman as land. In *Intertidal Life,* Audrey Thomas explores not only Alice's identity but that of her country, Western Canada, for which a history must be invented, myths dug up, features painfully reconstructed. The epigraphs that open each section of *Intertidal Life,* taken from *A Spanish Voyage to Vancouver,* make the association clear: "Part of the following day," reads the first quote, "was employed in arranging and setting in order our records of observations, charts and calculations . . . in order that they might be in good order and not convey a confused idea of the information gained." The tides which Alice sees are also those of her physical world, the world which 18th century explorers gave to the European writers as a symbol of unlimited freedom. It constitutes the backdrop (and sometimes the foreground) of Alice's inner voyage. . . . The landscape lends its reality to the characters. . . .

[*Intertidal Life*] appears as the culmination of the search for a character that was never quite defined before. Perhaps in the much-neglected *Blown Figures* or in *Songs My Mother Taught Me,* there are sketchier versions of Alice circling the primary question: Who am I? In *Intertidal Life* the question is answered. Explorer and explored become one at last.

Alberto Manguel, "Stranded," in The Village Voice,
Vol. XXX, No. 32, August 6, 1985, p. 50.

Frank Tuohy

1925-

(Born John Francis Tuohy) English novelist, short story writer, biographer, scriptwriter, and travel writer.

Tuohy's novels and stories are set in countries where he has lived and taught, including England, Brazil, Poland, and Japan. He focuses on the influence of social customs and physical settings on his characters, some of whom are expatriates who feel culturally displaced, while others are natives who feel alienated in their own societies. Although some critics consider the view of life projected in his fiction to be somber and pessimistic, Tuohy is respected for his witty and insightful observations of anxieties that arise from social conflicts. According to Dennis Drabelle, "Tuohy reminds us that our terrible aloneness is, paradoxically, something we all have in common."

Tuohy's first two novels, *The Animal Game* (1957) and *The Warm Nights of January* (1960), are set in Brazil, where he lived for six years. He won praise for his strong technical skills and particularly for his detached yet evocative narrative style. *The Animal Game* centers on an English expatriate who observes people suffering various hardships as they seek happiness and companionship. In *The Warm Nights of January*, a French female artist falls in love with a Brazilian man, but their cultural biases eventually undermine their relationship. Tuohy's third novel, *The Ice Saints* (1964), is set in Poland, where the bleak urban landscape reflects and contributes to the despondency of the characters. This novel centers on a Polish husband, his English wife, and their young son. The wife's sister visits the couple in Poland and informs them that their son has been willed an inheritance. Misunderstandings arise as the sister attempts to convince the boy to return with her to England. Generally considered Tuohy's finest novel, *The Ice Saints* was awarded the James Tait Black Memorial Prize.

Tuohy's admirers claim that the straightforward presentation of events and subtle evocation of pathos in his short stories resemble the artistry of Anton Chekhov. The stories in his first collection, *The Admiral and the Nuns, with Other Stories* (1962), are set in Brazil, Poland, and England, and focus on characters who are forced to acknowledge uneasy truths about themselves or their loved ones. In *Fingers in the Door and Other Stories* (1970) Tuohy concentrates on English settings and characters who suffer emotional hardships due to class distinctions. In several pieces in *Live Bait and Other Stories* (1978) Tuohy probes the influence of cultural values on individuals in Poland and Japan. *The Collected Stories of Frank Tuohy* was published in 1984. Tuohy's other publications include a travelogue, *Portugal* (1968), and the literary biography *Yeats* (1976).

(See also *Contemporary Authors*, Vols. 5-8, rev. ed.; *Contemporary Authors New Revision Series*, Vol. 3; and *Dictionary of Literary Biography*, Vol. 14.)

BEN RAY REDMAN

[*The Animal Game* is] one of the most entertaining books that have come my way in a long time, a comedy of manners in which tragic and ridiculous fibres are interwoven.

Photograph by Mark Gerson

Mr. Tuohy refuses to name the country and city of his novel, but there is no doubt that the country is Brazil and the city São Paulo. At the center of the action is Celina Fonseca, beautiful and amorous, daughter of an ancient Portuguese family, helplessly infatuated with Gregory Cowan, a disreputable English film director of undisclosed origins, who treats Celina like a common prostitute. In the wings, observing the play, stands Robin Morris, well-bred employee of a British oil company, through whose eyes we see much of the comedy.

But, although they have leading parts, Celina and Cowan and Morris are not the best realized characters. Mr. Tuohy scores with his minor characters, the best of them being Betty, Celina's stepmother from Philadelphia, who spends much of her life in an amiable alcoholic haze.

This novel revolves on its axis instead of progressing, and the author's control of form does not match his wit. But his wit is so pervasive, the serious intentions underlying it so evident, his powers of observation so keen, and the quality of his writing so excellent, that it would seem almost churlish to ask for anything more.

Ben Ray Redman, in a review of "The Animal Game," in The Saturday Review, *New York, Vol. XL, No. 39, September 28, 1957, p. 35.*

FLORENCE HAXTON BULLOCK

With the words "Far away, on the precarious underside of the world," the young English novelist Frank Tuohy begins his impressive *The Animal Game,* set in an unnamed South American country. That same flavor of wonder tinged with horror carries on throughout his story of a group of Anglo-Americans and Europeans brought into accidental, dramatic relationship because they are temporary exiles from their homes while they carry on their business and other assignments in an alien culture. . . .

The unusual quality of Mr. Tuohy's novel lies in his capacity for close observation of human emotions, regardless of moral or other implications, and his artful precision in capturing them in words. Violence and futility become meaningful and to a degree beautiful in his hands. He is in the best sense of the word, unconventional. . . .

Much in little is the salient characteristic of *The Animal Game*—offering by suggestion a distant view of much while presenting, oh so casually, the immediate little. Mr. Tuohy in his first novel smoothly channels into literature his rare, and intense, perceptive powers.

> *Florence Haxton Bullock, "Well-Told Tale of Exiles," in* New York Herald Tribune Book Review, *September 29, 1957, p. 7.*

RICHARD HORCHLER

A sad young man, but stiff-lipped, Frank Tuohy offers [in *The Animal Game*] yet another version of "The Waste Land." His rendering is unusual chiefly in that he sees the nightmare which is life most hideously epitomized in present-day Brazil.

The central character of *The Animal Game* is an Englishman who has come to South America in the employ of a British oil company. He is cautious, ineffectual, slightly ludicrous. In every way, from his flannel suit and suede shoes to his timid desire "not to get involved," he is out of place in a land of burning sun, endemic folly—and the "animal game." This last is the state lottery, in which certain numbers are designated by the names of animals, and it symbolizes the recklessness and irrationality which mark the way of life in this milieu. . . .

Tempted many times, the Englishman does not succumb; he never buys a ticket.

He observes the game, however, at closer range than he would like, as he is drawn into the lives of some of the desperate participants. Many of them are ridiculous, but all are lost souls—betrayed women, defeated men, drunkards, homosexuals, political fanatics, foreigners pathetically "keeping up standards" in the land of exile. All the lives move relentlessly toward calamity—violent death, madness, or an equally destructive ennui. . . .

A Brazilian hell has some special characteristics—climate and topography, obviously, Latin-American political instability, religion and religiosity, Latin notions on the position of women. There is also, it seems, a ruinous conviction of national futility and absurdity. The natives speak of South America as "a tragedy really, or perhaps a farce." Essentially, however, its horrors—of triviality, loveless eroticism, meaninglessness—are those seen elsewhere many years ago by Eliot, Waugh, Huxley, the earlier trackers in the deserts of our times.

Unfortunately, Mr. Tuohy's cosmic madhouse, too sad to be funny and too mean to be tragic, is in the end only depressing. A moralist without a moral, Mr. Tuohy does not judge, does not interpret, does not respond emotionally to the world he describes. The detachment of his tone is violated—occasionally, and very slightly—only by hints of weariness and distaste.

Mr. Tuohy's writing is unobtrusively excellent, his control of his material remarkably firm, his imagination both strong and subtle. For all its limits, *The Animal Game* is a notable first novel, and if its author were willing "to get involved," as his hero is not, he might someday write a truly important book.

> *Richard Horchler, "Lament of the Exiles," in* The New York Times Book Review, *October 13, 1957, p. 48.*

MAURICE RICHARDSON

Mr Tuohy's first collection of short stories makes an impression, borne out by his novels, of one of those slowly but surely and satisfactorily developing talents. Poles, mainly in Brazil, are the principal subjects of *The Admiral and the Nuns, with Other Stories.* The title story is focused on the very sad young wife, native of South Kensington, of one particularly difficult and drunken specimen. Mr Tuohy is particularly deft at trapping that strange, oblique, off-beat quality which you find in even the least interesting Pole. He finds it in present-day Poland which is the setting for one story, an encounter with a disgruntled student. He notices, too, the peculiar penchant of Poles abroad for certain types of crime and racket. His last and longest story about a wistful young refugee engaged in a hopeless piece of ineffectual drug-smuggling in Brazil is neat and vivid and unsensational. (p. 649)

> *Maurice Richardson, "Damned Up North," in* New Statesman, *Vol. LXIII, No. 1625, May 4, 1962, pp. 649-50.**

MICHELE MURRAY

There is hardly a page of Frank Tuohy's collection of stories [*The Admiral and the Nuns*] that does not bear the mark of an intelligent observer, a skilled writer. Yet the presence of these qualities only serves to point up that they alone are not enough to make a book memorable. Unfortunately, Mr. Tuohy does not provide very much more, so that his stories, pleasant and enjoyable to read, slip almost immediately out of mind.

At first, there is the pleasure of reading fiction set in unaccustomed places and dealing with an unusually wide variety of characters. Of the dozen stories, five are set in Brazil and four in Poland, with the remaining three taking place in England. But Mr. Tuohy's attitude is unfailingly that of the emotional tourist, so that our final pleasure remains our first one: the novelty of exotic material.

In story after story, at the moment of expected emotional pressure, he dissipates the climax, so that the work rather than seeming incomplete while plumbing the depths in the best Chekhovian manner, *is* incomplete, an exercise in cliff-hanging. The stories display the posture of a casual visitor, arriving on a luxury cruise, who stops over in one city or another for a few days. Just when he is becoming a bit more closely acquainted with the place, getting drawn into its alien pattern, the boat whistle calls him back and, untouched, he resumes shipboard life and watches the city fade from sight, feeling at most mild twinges of nostalgia.

[**"The Admiral and the Nuns"**] which promises to be an interesting exploration of a young Englishwoman, who is the daughter of an admiral, the product of a convent school, who is married to a rough Polish workman and completely lost in a Brazilian community hacked out of the bush, simply evaporates. . . . (pp. 626-27)

The best story in the book, which is pendant to the title piece, is also long and also set in Brazil. **"A Survivor in Salvador"** tells of a hallucinated few days in the life of an elderly Polish nobleman who has come to the end of the line in the old Brazilian city of Salvador, where he is supposed to deliver a package of cocaine, earning a small fee in return. Reaching the contact only seconds before the police, he flees with the package but with no money and no knowledge of the language. How he survives, not only materially, but also in his estimate of himself as a man, makes a thoroughly satisfying story. Three or four more like it would have given body and particularity to what is now only another commonplace collection. (p. 627)

> *Michele Murray, "An Exotic Tour," in* Commonweal, *Vol. LXXVII, No. 24, March 8, 1963, pp. 626-27.*

HOKE NORRIS

Frank Tuohy is a British writer of cosmopolitan interests and scope. His manner is somewhat like that of Chekhov—quiet, deceptively matter-of-fact, without compromise or illusion or any desire to prettify the ugly—yet he finds beauty where others might find only moral or physical squalor. Thus equipped, he explores in the twelve stories comprising **The Admiral and the Nuns** . . . the truths of struggle, of degradation, of compensation and redemption—among London artists, in the Poland of tyranny and agony, in the decadence of tropical Latin America.

In the South America of the title story . . . we meet a "hopelessly, slothfully inadequate" woman, who is in grave difficulty because "her upbringing had provided her with too many retreats into the cosiness of class and religion." In South America, too, we perceive in the angers and the apoplexy of the old hands, with their contemptuous approach to the "natives," the tattered banners of British colonialism. (p. 45)

In Poland we witness the chilling consequences of an infernal State mechanism—a man turned into a spy for the regime that had persecuted him. But in Poland we may also laugh (however briefly) over the plight of a music critic denied a passport because he was reported to have been "in contact with Western diplomats": he had arranged the mating of his dog with that of an ambassador.

These are but a few examples of the sensitive stories that make **The Admiral and the Nuns** a splendid achievement. It is a book that deserves a wider audience than it probably will have. (pp. 45-6)

> *Hoke Norris, in a review of "The Admiral and the Nuns," in* Saturday Review, *Vol. XLVI, No. 12, March 23, 1963, pp. 45-6.*

FRANCIS HOPE

[**The Ice Saints**], set in Poland, is both good and plain. It is free enough from current orthodoxy to portray some Poles as conformist bores—notably Witek Rudowski, English teacher at Biala Gora University, an unimaginative scholar and an inglorious party member. His wife is English, and an English aunt leaves their son Tadeusz a legacy, which wife and sister-in-law plan to use to smuggle Tadeusz out into the free air of Knightsbridge. The plot miscarries, disastrously, in a skilfully mounted crescendo of suspicion, stupidity, bad luck, national and ideological incomprehension; everyone is sadder, and a few wiser, at the end. Mr Tuohy's Poland is a cold, harsh country, described in unemphatic, economical language: detached but not aggressively knowing, he covers an astonishing area in 213 pages. The grimness never becomes peevish: his Polish characters are worn out by overwork and mutual distrust, his English ones varyingly stupid fish out of water. . . . But some passages are also comic, almost light-hearted in a traditionally Polish 'desperate' way; and the pleasure of his technical mastery never flags. (p. 60)

> *Francis Hope, "Poland Plain," in* New Statesman, *Vol. LXVIII, No. 1739, July 10, 1964, pp. 60-1.**

PETER DEANE

For the first hour [**The Ice Saints**] was one of the most depressing novels I have read, if only because of the persistently bleak picture it draws of post-war Poland. . . .

Returning later, I realized that while I was getting an extensive sight-seeing trip, I wasn't getting much of a novel. In fact, Mr. Tuohy seems interested in his story only in so far as it serves as a vehicle for his grim tour. Consequently, when Rose Nicholson comes to Poland to tell her sister and her Party-loyal brother-in-law, Witek, that their young son has come into an inheritance back in England, she is less a harbinger of dangerously mixed blessings than an inquisitive tourist whom the author uses to give us his impressions of the landscape.

It is of only minor importance that Rose is so distressed and appalled by what Mr. Tuohy sees that she conspires with her sister to get the boy out of the country, and unwittingly brings ruin to the family. Mr. Tuohy is primarily concerned with getting Rose distressed and appalled. To accomplish this end, she sees as many gloomy and impoverished sights and meets as many oppressed and cynical Poles as her visa permits.

With Poland happening in the foreground, the novel meantime seems more and more contrived to fit Rose's itinerary. Major relationships are only briefly sketched. Motivations are made up on the spot, and the author continually has to step forward to explain what he hasn't shown dramatically.

By the time Rose has an affair (which we barely glimpse) with a Pole (a spy) who reveals the inheritance to the Party, thereby bringing disaster and a rapid ending, the reader may begin to question the author's trustworthiness, both as a novelist and as a guide. I don't mean to imply that the picture he presents of Poland is untrue or necessarily one-sided, but rather that its credibility is jeopardized by the sparseness of the novel proper.

Because he has used the trappings of fiction to pass along information and his own opinions, and because he treats his characters mainly as spokesmen, Mr. Tuohy, while never quite sounding propagandistic, often risks discouraging the reader's confidence.

> *Peter Deane, "From Pole to Pole," in* Book Week— The Sunday Herald Tribune, *September 20, 1964, p. 28.*

AILEEN PIPPETT

In [*The Ice Saints*] an English legacy is willed to a Polish boy.... Rose Nicholson, posing as a tourist, visits her elder sister who is married to a Polish professor to discuss in privacy the best way of insuring that 14-year-old Tadeusz really benefits under the will....

Her sister, unhappily married, tired of hard work and poverty, is ready to cooperate, but the professor is alarmed.... The boy himself is a fervent patriot who comes to regard his pretty young aunt as a temptress trying to seduce him from devotion to his native land.

Frank Tuohy, an English novelist who has lived in Poland, deals with the problem in human and practical terms. Rose finds her harrassed sister almost a stranger in whose cramped quarters a visitor is unwelcome, so she takes every opportunity to travel around. In this way, many aspects of life behind the Iron Curtain in 1960 are revealed. The picture is painted in shades of gray, for everywhere Rose goes she is frustrated by failure to make any real contact with people for whom conformity and duplicity are the rule....

There is no argument, for acceptance of conditions as they are is essential to survival, ambition is forbidden, hope is a daydream and enthusiasm is reserved for parades.

The benumbing effects of this prevailing atmosphere of resignation could have spread to the story, turning a novel into a tract, had not the author avoided this trap by the suppleness of his writing and the diversity of scenes described. Rose is nearly corrupted by a sense of guilt at being better off and knowing her way of escape is open, but her natural resilience enables her not to succumb to apathy....

She leaves Poland by plane, seeing below her "a whole landscape waiting for explanation." Yet it is a landscape with figures, and they are alive although temporarily frozen in the pious attitudes of a religion in which they no longer believe. Frank Tuohy succeeds in suffusing this desolating picture with a kind of luminosity springing from clear-headed, warm-hearted attempts to understand. His book is a remarkable achievement, a tribute to his skill as an artist and his honesty as a thinker.

> Aileen Pippett, "Where Hope Is a Dream," in The New York Times Book Review, September 20, 1964, p. 4.

FRANK McGUINNESS

[Frank Tuohy is] an author whose later work abundantly fulfils the promise shown in his first book. Indeed, not to cast him in too flattering a light, both *The Warm Nights of January* and his latest novel *The Ice Saints*—the one an enormously sensitive and complex study of a fading French artist's affair with a Brazilian negro, the other a refreshingly unblinkered survey of contemporary Poland—reveal Tuohy as a highly intelligent and gifted writer whose present claim to a place in the front rank of current British novelists is surely beyond dispute. And yet, when all this has been said, one is forced to admit that the spectacular success enjoyed by numerous other writers over this same period has constantly evaded him.... The sad truth is that present tastes are overwhelmingly geared to the vulgar, the superficially tough and the flamboyant whereas Tuohy can only provide the subtle, the searchingly sympathetic and the reflective.... Tuohy gives us creatures of flesh and blood—individual, involved and erratic—when most of us are looking

for cardboard puppets which will mouth the same empty slogans that invite our vigorous applause and strike the old familiar attitudes with which we can so easily and flatteringly identify ourselves.... Here is a novelist with an astonishing flair for vivid and warm characterization which—even more remarkably—asks precious little from either the heroic or the sensational. Bella, the central figure of *The Warm Nights of January*, is a superb creation who, if lacking the immediate bawling impact of the Joe Lamptons and Arthur Machins who stud so much current literature, is, in the final analysis, infinitely more convincing, varied and alive. In her, Tuohy has achieved that rare phenomenon—a woman who is good without being either prissy or dull. It is the *totality* of her as a person that is so consummately contrived. Tuohy recognises that if her goodness embraces tolerance, charity and undemanding love, it can also emerge as weakness, stupidity and self-indulgence.

In all his books, Tuohy reveals a strong preoccupation with the plight of the exile. This, I imagine, is important to him because it allows him to catch his characters in the raw, when they are at their most exposed and vulnerable, unable to conceal their emotions behind the habits and customs of their own society. In *The Animal Game*—a first novel which, it should be said, is more notable for its mature achievements than its promise—the character thus stranded is a young Englishman who becomes helplessly embroiled in a riot of Latin passion before he learns that one can only help those one loves and to whom, therefore, one is hopelessly partisan. Here again, no less than in his later books, Tuohy exhibits his tremendous range of sympathy and understanding in the treatment of his characters, most particularly, perhaps, in the relationship of Mrs Newton and her husband. She is a woman almost totally lacking in charm or grace whose surliness eventually drives her husband away from her. There is, in all conscience, little to recommend her either before or after the estrangement and yet Tuohy slowly rouses sympathy for her and the realization that misery is no less painful or distressing because it is brought on by one's own obtuseness and cruelty.

The Ice Saints, the most recent of Tuohy's novels, is set in modern Poland, a fact which I confess would ordinarily have set my teeth on edge in anticipation of another glowing account of the people's paradise.... Fortunately, Tuohy's vision is unclouded by prejudice and his examination of the promised land is detached, cool and penetrating. (pp. 94-5)

> Frank McGuinness, in a review of "The Animal Game," "The Warm Nights of January," and "The Ice Saints," in London Magazine, n.s. Vol. 4, No. 9, December, 1964, pp. 93-6.

MARY BORG

Frank Tuohy's collection of short stories, *Fingers in the Door*, has the control, incision and intelligence one has come to expect of this immaculate writer. The stories deal in the small, apparently insignificant moments which reveal the clues to lives. His sphere is mostly that faded, repressed, genteel, suburban world behind privet hedges or monkey puzzle trees, where people's participation in the lives of others is more unappreciated than marginal. Each story glances at the effect of apparently trivial moments....

Frank Tuohy is superb at the exact pinpointing of unacknowledged social awkwardness, of the effect of one life on another, when people are unaware of the roles they are playing. He uses the short story to display the full tragedies of selfishness, the deliberate or unknowing blindness to the needs of others which make for either social unease or real disaster. The stories are beautifully written, the middle-class evasion of expressive dialogue exactly caught. It is a very accomplished collection, though I personally should like another novel as good as *The Ice Saints* rather than more snippets, however well contrived.

Mary Borg, "Family Troubles," in New Statesman, *Vol. 79, No. 2044, May 15, 1970, p. 699.**

KINGSLEY SHORTER

"We classify in order to deal with one another, and then we die." Thus Frank Tuohy, in a characteristically bleak short story from his new collection, *Fingers in the Door.* . . . The English, of course, are particularly expert at the deadly art of social classification, and Tuohy—in this book as elsewhere—shows himself a taxonomist second to none. The title story is set in the "home counties," that bastion of the English petite bourgeoisie; the eponymous fingers belong to an upwardly mobile real-estate man who has the social ineptitude to get them mangled in a train door. Although he is in dreadful pain, his ex-typist wife, hagridden with snobbery, is concerned only that he should not make a scene in front of the other first-class passengers, while their vapid teen-age daughter accuses him of ruining her day. . . .

In a manner strongly reminiscent of Angus Wilson, the human impoverishment of Tuohy's characters is underscored by the manicured graciousness of the English countryside. The public-school boy locked in the incommunicable anguish of puberty, the real-estate man with his crushed fingers, the retired soldier facing social and sexual obsolescence, all are mocked by the "gleaming landscape" that holds them in bourgeois parenthesis.

If Tuohy confined himself to the evocation of milieu and the pinpointing of social types, he would perhaps be no more than a very clever genre artist, specializing in, say, English Uptight. The pain in many of his stories pertains more to embarrassment, which passes, than to true psychic injury, which does not. But Tuohy knows that class, like race or creed, is only one of the grosser and more visible ways we "classify in order to deal with one another," he recognizes that classification is a never-ending process pursued at every level of consciousness down to the very minutiae of existence. In the best of these stories Tuohy uses the magnifying glass of art to show the process operating at the wincing interface between life and life, where solitude seeks redress. And here, in the mute agony of his characters, he reveals the *reductio ad absurdum* of the class system: the dreadful discovery that one is all alone, the solitary member of a class of one.

Perhaps, as Tuohy muses at one point, "the idea of God is the only escape from the categories and the classifications." But the middle-class English who inhabit these pages have no idea of God to speak of, nor do they have rituals that might deliver them from the solitary confinement of private experience and restore to them a sense of human community. (p. 15)

Like the shock of icy water, Tuohy's work takes one's breath away. Yet one has doubts. Nobody *has* to see the world in terms of such unrelieved gloom; in the end it is hard not to feel that Tuohy has an ax to grind. Sometimes the cards are too visibly stacked against the characters for their suffering to be edifying. Pain must be manifestly inescapable; if it is circumstantial, if it derives only from a situation the author has

patently contrived, it loses its authenticity. Take a story like **"The Trap."** A charmless Polish girl, betrayed by "the competing puritanisms of Church and State," pursues her English teacher to London, there to receive the inevitable rebuff. After a disastrous evening he finally manages to put her on the tube train. "The doors slid shut. There was a minute before the train started and he watched her standing there. She did not look at him any more, but was making small half-blind movements, like an animal searching incredulously round the walls of its trap."

It is an excruciating tale, but the effect is to shock rather than to move, and there is a gratuitous brutality in the manner as well as the matter that I find repellent. Tuohy is not altogether innocent of a certain vivisectionist relish. One is reminded of the paintings of Francis Bacon: flayed torsos on butcher's hooks, humanity as raw meat. . . .

Is there not a powerful undercurrent of misogyny in these stories? Tuohy tends to write about helpless, retiring men and self-sufficient, even aggressive women. Women are seen as a sexual threat, an embarrassing nuisance, a dykish joke, or at best an alien form of life to be dealt with at a respectful distance. . . .

Interestingly, in several of these stories the only relief from the prevailing gloom is a nostalgia for male-bonding activities—notably soldiering—contrasted with the present misery of dependence on family or female relatives. . . .

These stories are the work of a master craftsman; I couldn't put the book down. Yet I feel a little ashamed of enjoying them as much as I did. Perhaps this has something to do with what one might call the pornography of social unease. Such people as Tuohy creates do exist, after all, but one should not be too fascinated by their misfortunes. In the end I was glad to close the book. (p. 16)

Kingsley Shorter, "Humanity as Raw Meat," in The New Leader, *Vol. LIII, No. 19, October 5, 1970, pp. 15-16.*

ROBERT MOSS

Tuohy's twelve stories [in *Fingers in the Door*], set mostly in England, cover the period from 1940 to the present. They embrace a wide variety of human pain, ignoring the barriers of class, age, and background. . . . [Most] of Tuohy's sufferers are isolated, condemned to a cold, cheerless world where help and sympathy are seldom obtained.

Even those who are most convinced that English fiction is dead will find things to admire in Tuohy's work. His style is sure-footed and supple; each shading and nuance falls perfectly into place. (p. 45)

Tuohy is also a discerning social commentator, and no grain in the British caste system is too fine to escape his eye. In **"A Palladian Bridge,"** for example, the hero, Page-Barlow, is asked about his double name by a farm girl who works at his school. He reflects: "He knew it had been something to do with money, in the past, but at the back of his mind his mother loomed up, telling you you did not discuss money with servants." Indeed, if Tuohy has an outstanding gift it is the ability to interlace his stories with well-observed details. The tranquil beauty of English gardens, the miniature class warfare of nannies in the park, the shabbiness and disorientation of post-war London, chalk streams in the countryside, queues in the city—

Tuohy captures them all with marvelously accurate rhythms and colors.

Tuohy's sense of style and his talents as a social observer are prominent assets. Unfortunately, there is another side to the ledger. The author's command of mood and his handling of character and situation are frequently faulty. The glazed, mannered surfaces of **"Thunderbolt,"** a study of false gentility and youthful passion, are almost as baroque—and boring—as *Last Year at Marienbad,* which they resemble. **"A Life Memberhip,"** dealing with an injured worker fleeced by his social betters, mistakes predictability for inevitability; it telegraphs every punch and labors every irony. It is illustrative of Tuohy's central fault: a literary technique that is inadequate to his gloomy vision of life. Too often, he locks his characters into impossibly grim situations. . . . Tuohy's pessimism is too insistent; it is tortured out of characters and circumstances where it does not rightfully belong.

Perhaps the most unflattering thing one can say about a writer's work is that it reminds one of better work elsewhere. Tuohy's story **"A License,"** about the painful collisions of a sensitive adolescent with thick-skinned adults, brings to mind the infinitely subtler treatment of this situation in Elizabeth Bowen's *The Death of the Heart.* Similarly, Tuohy's obsession with disillusionment, where a particular event is seen as a procession of small, grimy ironies, sends one back to George Orwell's *Keep the Aspidistra Flying* rather than on to more Tuohy.

Fingers in the Door is a work of competence and occasional excellence, but no more. If, in the gallery of English short-story writers, Tuohy ranks somewhat above H. E. Bates and V. S. Pritchett, he is still significantly below Katherine Mansfield and Graham Greene. (pp. 45-6)

> *Robert Moss, in a review of "Fingers in the Door and Other Stories," in* Saturday Review, *Vol. LIII, No. 45, November 7, 1970, pp. 45-6.*

JOHN MOLE

Any biographer of Yeats must be aware of the odds against his subject attracting immediate sympathy. . . . [There] are many for whom Yeats remains a resonant poseur, and a cultural authoritarian with a propensity for calling the police.

This last habit is one to which Frank Tuohy's admirable new biography [*Yeats*] draws attention; and it is characteristic of his approach that he does it with a humour which quietly insists on Yeats's humanity, his bewilderment in the face of events that an impractical vision often set in motion. What emerges is the portrait of a man who was not silly like us, but uniquely silly. Tuohy is almost relentless in his inclusion of cartoons by Beerbohm and comments by observers or intimates. . . .

None of this is to suggest that Tuohy confirms the popular prejudice against Yeats. Rather, he accepts it as inevitable, making the most of everything which seems most extraordinary, as an enticement to further understanding. A short biography can only hope to present the course of the poet's life in such a way as will send readers to, or back to, the poems to discover how the 'base metal of his ideas'—and idiosyncrasies—'are transformed by the nature of his personal vision'. Enough of the poems are quoted to point the direction, and, though there is little attempt at critical assessment, the crucial importance of several, particularly 'The Second Coming', is made clear by a few deft observations.

> *John Mole, "Ballyphallus," in* The Listener, *Vol. 96, No. 2481, October 28, 1976, p. 544.*

DENIS DONOGHUE

Frank Tuohy's *Yeats* is a straightforward biography, sensible, well-written, and beautifully illustrated: the photographs are superb. The background, Ireland in the nineteenth century, is well sketched, with judicious paragraphs on Daniel O'Connell, Thomas Davis, Mangan, the Famine years, the rise and fall of Parnell. Mr. Tuohy is satisfied that Yeats's life is most accurately seen through his friendships. "And say my glory was I had such friends," Yeats writes in "The Municipal Gallery Revisited," somewhat coyly. Mr. Tuohy takes Yeats at his word, the account he gives of John Butler Yeats, George Russell, Mohini Chatterji, Dowden, John O'Leary, Hyde, Rolleston, Morris, Madame Blavatsky, Wilde, Florence Farr, Maud Gonne, Lady Gregory, and all the other immortals is in keeping with Yeats's own version in the *Memoirs* and *Autobiographies.* Mr. Tuohy does not insist upon his own reading of these people. In general, he takes Yeats's word for most things: the accepted Yeats mythology is not strained to accommodate any other interpretations.

There is one exception to this rule: Yeats's occult interests. On one page Mr. Tuohy writes two skeptical passages as dry as anything I have seen in Yeatsian commentary. On Yeats's part in the Order of the Golden Dawn, he asks: "No fewer than fourteen medical men had joined the Golden Dawn by 1900; which has lasted better, their medical knowledge or their mystical speculation?" And a few lines earlier: "Yeats's world, it might be said, comprised everything that is not the case." Yvor Winters said nothing more astringent than that about Yeats. But I am not convinced that astringency is required: it is a bit late to be scandalized by theosophy and magic. Besides, Yeats's attitude to such mysteries was a mixture of credulity and skepticism: just when you think he is ready to believe any kind of nonsense, he draws back into a common sense as dry as anyone else's. I still think that the matter can be explained by Yeats's desire to fill his mind with congenial images. The element he most admired in esoteric procedures was their air of ritual, pattern, form, and symmetry. Mr. Tuohy is somewhat harsh when these topics arise; but generally he is good-humored, lively, and informative. The book does not pretend to be the first or the last word on Yeats's life: it is an interim work. (p. 4)

> *Denis Donoghue, "The Hard Case of Yeats," in* The New York Review of Books, *Vol. XXIV, No. 9, May 26, 1977, pp. 3-4, 6, 8.**

WILLIAM BOYD

Many of the stories in Frank Tuohy's latest collection [*Live Bait and Other Stories*] have a foreign context—and are all the better for it. This represents a partial return to the worlds of his first exceptional volume *The Admiral and the Nuns* (1962) and, I'd like to think, a move away from the less remarkable *Fingers in the Door* (1970), which dwelt a little too lengthily on the foibles of the gin-and-tonic belt. Not that Tuohy's observations aren't generally valuable; but when the scene shifts abroad the grim predictability that dulls most English short stories recedes and his own subtle talent emerges. . . .

[There] is an almost palpable widening of horizons and effect in Tuohy's foreign stories. For example, the callous randiness of a retired professor groping a former student in **"A Summer Pilgrim"**; or the candid lust of a rebarbative businessman searching downtown Tokyo for his Japanese mistress in **"Nocturne with Neon Lights."**

In comparison, the local offerings—**"The White Stick," "Love to Patsy"** and **"A Ghost Garden"**—with their familiar middle-class intellectual background, appear whimsical and affected. It is essentially the feeling of over-worked parochialism that is responsible for the ordinariness of the long title story, a rather ponderously symbolic tale of a lonely and unpopular boy and his attempts during a summer holiday to catch a huge pike in the lake of a nearby manor house. It is not merely a question of more exotic scenery adding extra spice; Tuohy's strength lies in the way he captures the unusual mood and viewpoint of the expatriate, the exile and the temporary alien. The barriers of language and culture give rise to a slightly baffled and tentative querying of reality; perspectives shift and blur, appearances bemuse and all our certainties suddenly lack foundation. (p. 554)

> William Boyd, "Aliens," in New Statesman, Vol. 96, No. 2484, October 27, 1978, pp. 554-55.*

JOHN MELLORS

Reading Frank Tuohy's novels and short stories is like being taken on a package holiday abroad in the company of a witty, cynical guide, a guide who knows the expatriate communities as well as the indigenous peoples, who has observed natives and foreigners interacting and, however well-intentioned and tolerant in the beginning, sliding inevitably into misunderstanding and mistrust. (p. 59)

Tuohy's view of life was already fully formed in his first novel, *The Animal Game* (1957). Indeed, in that book he is more bitter, more dogmatic about the impossibility of successful close relationships between people of different race, than in anything he has written since. As an Englishman abroad, 'you were set apart, without even an attitude to fall back on. This was the constant and unadmitted condition of those who live habitually abroad—you ended up in a complete moral vacuum'. Tuohy appears to believe that the nearer you try to get to someone with an entirely different cultural background, the worse will be your failure and the more damage you will do. (pp. 59-60)

In *The Animal Game* the native-foreigner misunderstandings seem only to highlight Tuohy's pessimism about the whole human condition. We are all foreign bodies to one another. Life is a lottery (the 'game' of the title), and lucky the man who draws the role of spectator rather than that of participant. There is a telling scene in this novel in which Celina, an educated woman from an old local family (the country is unspecified but it is obviously Brazil), drives out of the city into the hills. She sees some Japanese children walking along the road. When she calls to them they stare blankly. 'They live here, she thought, where I have lived all my life, and I know nothing about them, nothing whatever. This idea gave her a feeling of complete alienation, of belonging to a world so broken up that no relationships existed at all, each person wading ahead alone through the mess until death'. It is a bleak prospect, and all that Tuohy can advise us to do is to accept our lot and alleviate it by enjoying whatever simple pleasures we can obtain. (p. 60)

In *The Warm Nights of January* (1960), Tuohy is rather more relaxed. Bella, a French expatriate in Rio, lives with a young black Brazilian, Hadriano. There is plenty of scope for misunderstanding here, especially when Bella wants something more than sexual satisfaction from her bedfellow. . . . Bella suffers occasionally from what one might call 'alien's ennui': 'like all exiles, she experienced sudden yawning voids, where in her own country some habit of life or small social obligation would have ordered fulfilment'. However, at the end of the novel Tuohy relents, and we leave Bella with the prospect of contentment now that she has settled for the pleasures of Hadriano's physical presence, the proximity of the sea and the freshness of the food in the street-market: 'anything was possible on this tolerant shore, in this nonchalant atmosphere that made even the guilt of the past fade to a companionable shadow. She was grateful for the limitations of her life'. That seems to be Tuohy's recipe. Limit your expectations. Be thankful for small mercies.

Once you have adapted yourself to a pessimistic view of life, staying on the edge of commitment and involvement, observing from the sidelines the antics of those who are caught in the toils of love, politics or religion, you will survive and might even extract a little quiet enjoyment from the passing show. In *The Ice Saints* (1964) people suffer because they have not learnt that lesson. They try to bridge the gaps between the Slav and Anglo-Saxon cultures, between communism and liberalism, and between adulthood and adolescence. They meddle. They pry. They want to help. They think they should live up to Forster's motto, 'only connect'. Tuohy is no Forsterian. Stay aloof would be his advice. When you come to gaps, don't try to fill them in or build across them. His attitude is summed up at the end of this book when Rose, the visitor from England, is leaving Poland and her sister's family which she has tried so clumsily and unsuccessfully to help. Rose is in a train on an 'abysmally sad' rainy day:—'Today was one of the chill weeping days in the early part of May, the days of the Ice Saints, St. Pancras, St. Servace and St. Boniface, whose arrival affords a reminder that all is by no means well with the year. If you had confidence in the Spring, your trust was misplaced: it will let you down. And if you are a pessimist you can give the satisfied snort of those whose worst fears are justified, and continue toting the burden of existence a little further on'. The mood, like the weather, is chillier in Poland than it was in Brazil in the warm January nights. But although Tuohy's worst fears for his characters are usually justified, he never gives a 'satisfied snort'. He does not despise his earnest, well-meaning busybodies. He sympathizes even where he cannot condone. (pp. 61-2)

In his most recently published short stories, *Live Bait,* Tuohy portrays the Japanese, those 'connoisseurs of tedium', as skilfully as he has painted Brazilians and Poles. In the Japanese character, he points out, there is 'an intense fury of the will which hides behind all the decorum and docility'. Rather than play the part of a homosexual in a play, a student has the fury of will to kill himself—and his classmates are too polite to explain to their teacher the reason for his absence. Of course, the English expatriates come in for some stick, too. When one of them loses his temper and shouts and waves his arms, the reaction of the Japanese present is to turn their backs on him, leaving him in a 'solipsist's nightmare, in which everything exists except yourself'.

It is, indeed, one of Tuohy's specialities to bring out the oddness of the English character by contrasting it with the quirks in the make-up of people of other nationalities. In **'Evening in Connecticut'**, Michael, an English guest at a dinner in the home of a distinguished American academic, is aware of himself being unforthcoming in a very British way. He makes the effort 'to forget the wry, slightly emetic essence of his Britishness, like an overdose of angostura in a glass of gin', but he finds it painfully hard to respond to someone who gives him the impression of being 'on heat for interesting conversation'. At the end of the evening he has to confess to his host that he has upset some of the other guests: 'Cultural differences. One doesn't always interpret the signals correctly'.

There are many delights in reading Tuohy. He is a fastidious writer, not a finnicky, self-conscious stylist, but a careful craftsman who orders the right words in the right places. Sometimes he lets his characters handle words with the same care. In a story in **Fingers in the Door,** a schoolboy thinks that his father would call one of the school maids 'a whore'—and then the boy revises his thought, 'No, ''tart'' was the correct word: it had the sticky sourness of old men's desires'. Tuohy's witticisms are thoughtful, not just plays upon words: the sort that you can savour again and again, coming back to them as to a favourite passage in a poem.... Tuohy's characters can be both sexy and violent, but when he portrays them as such Tuohy keeps his style restrained and, so to speak, well-mannered. He can be delicately erotic and suggestive:—'Her bare brown arms were raised and he noticed the patches of mouse-fur under her arms. He decided that she kept them because somebody had asked her to'. The comment following the observation conjures up the whole affaire. Above all, of course, Tuohy is the reporter and analyst of 'cultural differences'. Michael in Connecticut didn't always interpret the signals correctly, but Tuohy is the interpreter who never misses a nuance. (pp. 62-3)

John Mellors, ''Foreign Bodies: The Fiction of Frank Tuohy,'' in London Magazine, *n.s. Vol. 18, No. 11, February, 1979, pp. 59-63.*

FRANCIS LEVY

Almost all the stories constituting [*Live Bait and Other Stories*] deal with characters who find themselves thrust into a foreign culture or milieu. In one a Japanese student journeys to the West to visit a poet who had been her professor many years before.... The title work concerns a humbly born English boy who lives in the shadow of a magnificent estate where he likes to fish. He is allowed into the upper class world through a casual friendship. The story recounts his rude awakening to the cruelty of class distinction.

Tuohy ... has a fine eye for social mores. What's more, apart from the depiction of individual conflict, his evocations of life in varying countries can be just as illuminating. (p. 1)

However, cross-cultural observation is really only a surface for Tuohy. In the course of these stories he uses it to dramatize the difficulty of communicating through words. Coming from different backgrounds each of his characters places a stress on language that emphasizes its weakness. Yet learning another tongue or even sharing one from the start is no guarantee of understanding. (pp. 1, 4)

But this linguistic problem also has another side. The most complex stories in this collection go beyond the simple ironies of misinterpretation. Tuohy seems to have been influenced by that tradition of writers—E. M. Forster is the most famous—who have used ethnic contrasts to reflect on the mysteries of

communication. For this reason, however much cultural differences symbolize human isolation, they can also set the stage for forms of understanding that transcend the limits of language alone. In the story about Polish university life, **''The Candidate,''** which is one of the most fully drawn in the collection, the dénouement is brought about by an indirect set of circumstances. At the beginning of the tale, party regulars are trying to influence the admission process. But the unconscious crisscrossing of values between the younger generation of Poles who care more about camaraderie than social position, and a liberal-minded Western professor who is loath to go along with favoritism, effect a set of reversals by which just choices are inadvertently made.

At times Tuohy's stories suffer from overschematization.... But for the most part these stories exhibit a kind of lyrical compression that's at the heart of the form. Tuohy's strength lies in using simple situations that create a deep sense of character. In reading his best stories one only regrets that the author didn't linger long enough to develop the sense of a fuller world. (p. 4)

Francis Levy, ''Charting the Limits of Communication,'' in Book World—The Washington Post, *February 11, 1979, pp. 1, 4.*

PETER KEMP

A connoisseur of consternation, Frank Tuohy fills his short stories with blushings and blenchings, dried mouths and sweating palms. Shaming encounters, often involving hot-faced adolescents, are a speciality. His plots elbow shrinking figures into sticky situations. Like some nervous tic, the word ''embarrassed'' pulses through his prose. Triggering off the appalled hilarity that is his forte, social life becomes a minefield of gaffes and gaucheness. Everywhere, treacherous tripwires bring down high-minded efforts to cross class or national barriers.

Proximity, in [the pieces in *The Collected Stories of Frank Tuohy*], generates discomfiture: an English lecturer and a priggish Polish girl he's reluctantly accompanied to the cinema, cringe side by side during the sex sequences of an arty film; an effete young man and a nursing sister he's invited out as a thank-you present sit, rigid with awkwardness, through a lewdly ''progressive'' play. In two stories—reinforcing the idea of propinquity as ordeal—a pair of characters perched at a restaurant table strain not to graze each others' knees....

Physical closeness, in Tuohy's world, stresses real isolation—something his shrewder characters realise. Several times, bridges appear in his fiction—but only to throw into relief unspannable gulfs....

Seeing the world as a vast mosaic of tiny territories between which there's scant contact, Tuohy excels at vivid encapsulatings of place or social niche. His stories set in England focus on enclaves of jealously-preserved gentility, with particular attention given to private schools, establishments—presented as more concerned with class than classes—that feature as training-camps for the socially-dominant. Not that even the staid snobs and county brutes who loom so large in the path of Tuohy's wobbly social climbers are without their own embarrassments—usually caused by strayings from the sexual strait and narrow by some black sheep of the family....

Grotesque partnerships are standard in this fiction. A mismatched marriage receives scrutiny in the opening story. Recurrently, after this, Tuohy closes in on estranged mates and strained relations. Failed friendships—often the casualties of some bungled bid at international liaison—are everywhere: especially in those stories placed in Poland. There, clammy with a sense of guilt, repression and inadequacy, well-meaning English visitors are shown incurring mortifying rebuffs or provoking increased constraint through blundering attempts to achieve rapport. Poland gives a grim twist to another Tuohy preoccupation, too; what in his English stories is the social unease of being stared at heightens into the political nightmare of being under surveillance.

It's Japan, though, that seems most congenial to Tuohy's purposes—a country where embarrassment is an ever-present and even lethal threat. One story mentions a Japanese bride who committed suicide after breaking wind at her wedding ceremony. In another, a Tokyo student—distraught at having to kiss another man on stage during a production of Miller's *A View from the Bridge*—kills himself. Culture clashes aren't usually as fatal as this in Tuohy's work, but they're ubiquitous, with verbal stumbling-blocks especially likely to cause upsets. Putting up Babel-like barriers in the cosmopolitan stories, language also serves as a means of segregation in the English ones, with their close attention to idioms and accents that indicates origins.

Always precisely registered—from the shibboleths of the shires to give-away vulgarisms—speech in Tuohy's fiction seems primarily a device by which members of social groups signal their presence to each other and repel outsiders: almost a biological mechanism for proclaiming status and standing ground. Linked to this is Tuohy's fondness for likening his characters to creatures—everything from birds to boars. Surfacing with particular ferocity in the final story, **"Live Bait"**, this technique breaks humanity down into hordes of different species, each programmed to some distinctive pattern of behaviour, circling each other warily, aggressively or forlornly. It's a savage vision. But—when combined, as it is in Tuohy's tragi-comedies of errors, with crisp near-epigrammatic prose and aghast wit—it makes for exhilarating fiction.

> *Peter Kemp, "Tuohy and Embarrassment," in* The Times, *London, December 23, 1984, p. 42.*

PETER S. PRESCOTT

Why Frank Tuohy's work isn't better known in this country I can't guess. Tuohy must be counted—with V. S. Pritchett and William Trevor—as one of the best living English practitioners of the short story. There's more than a superficial resemblance among these three writers' works: none has any use for experimentation with form or language; each writes deeply traditional stories about human vulnerability, psychological exploitation and the festering injuries imposed by class or cultural distinctions. Loneliness figures largely in their work, as it does in most short stories, but Tuohy tends to push loneliness a step further: to desperation. His characters ("the former Countess Milewska") are often superannuated, out of place. Their very survival seems to be in question.

Witty though many of Tuohy's stories are, they're extremely pessimistic; some seem positively misanthropic. Most of Tuohy's characters are in some way abused, and all suffer. The pain they endure may be gratuitous, or deserved; it may be self-inflicted, or brought on by the brutality of others, or endemic in the human condition. But it is real pain and it is not going to go away. Whether he's writing a brief anecdote about

a girl betrayed by her date in a pub, or a leisurely narrative about a pubescent boy's awakening to a fallen adult world in which sex and class are used as weapons, Tuohy never suggests that life will improve. The best his people can hope for is a temporary truce, a postponement of misery sure to come, or a quick flick of stylish revenge. . . .

Pain, desperation, deceit, betrayal, a priggish attitudinizing that replaces genuine emotion: these elements flourish in most of the 36 stories in [*The Collected Stories of Frank Tuohy*], but nowhere more clearly than in **"The Admiral and the Nuns."** An Englishwoman bred among the London gentry finds herself in an obscure Brazilian city, married to a Polish technician of peasant instincts. Both attempt to impress themselves upon the narrator, an English visitor. The woman is trivial and insensitive; she ignores her reduced condition by dwelling on her past. The Pole is a brute. At a dance, he gets drunk and makes a pass at an underage girl. For this, he's humiliated by some pretentious English expatriates—and for a moment we're tempted to sympathize with his dizzy wife. But only for a moment. Tuohy is adept with the whiplash effect: Ah! You thought that about my character? Now try this. The former gentlewoman proves impervious to shame: "She was one of those people whom experience leaves untouched." . . .

In **"The Admiral and the Nuns," "Two Private Lives"** and other stories, [Tuohy] captures the tensions of a small foreign community: all the debilitating strictures of one national culture rawly exposed to another. Here, as in most of his stories, his people exploit each other. Sometimes the survival of one seems to depend on another's help. . . .

Tuohy works several variations on his theme of one person's fearful need for another. It's a useful device for an author who writes so often about deception and betrayal. In one story, an Englishman in Tokyo plunges into the maze of unnamed streets in an attempt to find his Japanese mistress, who has given him a false address. In another, a seedy Polish prince, cast loose in a Brazilian city with a packet of cocaine he can't sell, turns for support to an underage prostitute. . . . When the girl seems to leave him, we can feel the city close indifferently about this penniless rogue, and sense his anguished recognition that he has no resources left. . . .

Unexpectedly, Tuohy gives us a lovely low-key ghost story and a few outright comedies. Comedy has always been one of the principal vehicles for conveying a bleak view of mankind. Tuohy's very good at it, but he employs it only rarely. More often, he relies on wit, a different thing entirely.

> *Peter S. Prescott, "The Whiplash Effect," in* Newsweek, *Vol. CV, No. 5, February 4, 1985, p. 78.*

DENNIS DRABELLE

Frank Tuohy is one of those literary conservationists who would no more waste a word than leave the tap running while they go answer the phone. The rigor of his prose can make quite short stories—36 of them in [*The Collected Stories*] . . .—seem full-bodied and not completely fathomed.

Tuohy's minimalist approach contrasts sharply with the effusiveness of, say, William Faulkner, who augmented his sentences with qualifications, embellishments, and sonorities, all designed to depict the towering passions of larger-than-life characters. Tuohy's characters are modeled more closely to life's actual scale, and his style keeps pace with the cadence of ordinary speech. He achieves forcefulness by the exactness of his observations, especially when he scrutinizes small matters that might elude other writers's notice. . . .

Some of his best stories capitalize on his familiarity with transcultural predicaments. . . .

The multiplicity of stories, settings, and nationalities reaches its apex in **"The Potlatch of Esmeralda,"** in which a black Brazilian woman and a white Spanish man befriend each other in Paris. At times such intricate combinations can be so dazzling as to obscure Tuohy's artistic aims.

Often, though, the easiest way of ascertaining what an artist is up to is by examining his failures. There are few of them in this omnibus volume. . . . But one, called **"Windows,"** is instructive. To my mind it falls short because it reveals the author red-handedly forging a connection—between two separate sightings, an ocean and several years apart, of naked women in windows. At any rate, the closing lines are telling, if tendentious: "Whatever your experiences are, it is you who choose them to make the pattern. The girls at the windows belonged to him because he was alive. The two separate visions he had been given reminded him that he was unique, and that, because we are unique, we are alone."

The same themes are sounded more subtly and effectively in several other stories. Connections are made, uniquenesses rendered. Few of us go around talking about those evanescent moments that preoccupy our idling minds: the naked women fleetingly seen or, in another story, the "tear bubbles" that "trickle slowly across" a child's eyeballs while he lies on the ground, gazing at the sky. . . . By retrieving such discardable moments, by chronicling the vagaries of personal down-time, Tuohy reminds us that our terrible aloneness is, paradoxically, something we all have in common.

Dennis Drabelle, "A Wide World of Stories," in Book World—The Washington Post, *February 17, 1985, p. 9.*

William Wharton

1925-

(Pseudonym of unidentified author) American novelist.

Wharton is best known for his acclaimed first novel, *Birdy* (1979). An idiosyncratic fantasy about a young man's obsessive desire to become a bird, *Birdy* has been widely praised for Wharton's successful rendering of a difficult plot. The story revolves around Birdy and his friend Al, who shared a childhood interest in birds. As the two boys matured, they drifted apart; Al developed new interests, while Birdy sank deeper into his obsession with birds. Reunited in a World War II army hospital, Al helps the doctors understand Birdy, who has escaped reality by regressing fully into his fantasy world. The narrative alternates between present and past and between the points of view of Al and Birdy. While critics mentioned various flaws, *Birdy* was almost unanimously hailed as a powerful and moving novel; Robert Towers claimed that "*Birdy* contains many passages of almost incandescent beauty, passages where exact observation, combined with an exalted state of feeling, find expression on what might be called a visionary level," and Robert R. Harris declared that *Birdy* "is so accomplished in style, so assured of its grip on the reader, that one can easily doubt whether it really is a *first* novel." *Birdy* won the American Book Award for best first novel in 1980.

Wharton's subsequent novels have not received the acclaim of *Birdy. Dad* (1981) revolves around John Tremont, a middle-aged man who attempts to nurse his dying father and relate to his teenage son, Billy. As with *Birdy,* the story is revealed through flashbacks; the narrative shifts between the voices of John and Billy and the fantasies of John's father, who slips into a dream world he has invented as a means of coping with his shrewish, demanding wife. *Dad* has been praised for its examination of the relationship between father and son; however, it has been faulted for sentimentality and an insensitive portrait of the mother. *A Midnight Clear* (1982) tells the story of a group of young intellectuals assigned to combat duty during World War II. Wharton again uses both past and present perspectives and contrasts grim reality with escapes into fantasy. Sherwood Williams contends that the "matter-of-fact narration and offhand conversational style turn a quirky fantasy into a drama of convincing reality," but many reviewers claim the narrative and characterizations in *A Midnight Clear* are less successful than in Wharton's preceding works. Likewise, *Scumbler* (1984), which develops the character of an American painter living in Paris, is generally considered less polished and compelling than his earlier novels. Wharton himself is a painter who has lived in France for most of the past twenty-five years; although he chooses to conceal his identity to maintain his "personal privacy," the autobiographical nature of *Scumbler* and his other novels has been cited.

(See also *CLC,* Vol. 18; *Contemporary Authors,* Vols. 93-96; and *Dictionary of Literary Biography Yearbook: 1980.*)

JACK BEATTY

You feel like a bum for not being moved by a novel like *Dad.* It's an exploitation machine about a middle-aged son nursing his sick and dying parents. Since most of us either have faced or will soon face this, we're suckers for a novel that, on the one hand, teases our fears and guilts yet, on the other, renders even the bedpan scenes bearable by making the son loving, competent, and inexhaustible—just the way we would want to be in his shoes.

How can an author miss with material like this? Buoyed by the son's sterling example, we should finish *Dad* with our fears purged and our hopes renewed, ready to face the second worst thing in life. But we don't—or I didn't, and my advice to you is *caveat emptor*—because William Wharton is so busy establishing the son's ability to handle the situation that its full awfulness never registers with us. It doesn't seem to get him down, so why should it bother us? The emphasis is on coping, not on anguish, either his or his parents'. Scenes that should be rending emerge as flat behavioral descriptions. Perhaps we're supposed to understand that the son's flat voice is his way of distancing himself, but since it's a first-person narrative we get the story only through him, and if he's distanced, so are we. Wharton may have gone behaviorist to avoid sentimentality, but why work against your material like that? We're ready to weep when we open a novel with a title like *Dad,* so why not push us beyond sentimentality into something deeper and more complicated?

Dad is framed by two telegrams of equally dreadful import. The first informs Jack Tremont, a 52-year-old American expatriate artist in France, that his mother has had a serious heart attack. . . . The second telegram, which reaches him in Philadelphia months later, informs him that his father has died. Between the telegrams lie 350 pages of medical and psychiatric reportage relieved only by displays of Jack's moral athleticism. . . .

The cause of Dad's death is not exactly clear but the text suggests it's Mom, who is depicted as a fanged harridan, a real life-hater. Here Wharton is following the profitable lead of Judith Guest, who gave us the loving father/killer-mother duo as *Ordinary People.* Add Mrs. Kramer of *Kramer vs. Kramer* to this list of hard mamas, and you have the makings of a ponderous generalization about the state of our culture. . . . (p. 38)

Dad is bound to be praised as "daring" or—God help us—"experimental" because it features three narrative voices. The largest part of the book belongs to Jack. . . . Jack is joined at Dad's by the second narrator, his son, Billy, a 19-year-old dropout from the University of Santa Cruz. . . . The sole poetic note in the novel and, in fact, the only writing of any rhetorical appeal belongs to the third voice, Dad's. . . . Dad has dreamed up a whole world for himself over the years, a place to hide when Mom is too much with him.

It's at least a poignant idea—that a factory worker who was brought up on a farm would long to have a farm of his own. However, when Dad goes on to describe this dream farm, locate it in Cape May, New Jersey, number its chickens and hogs and fenceposts, and tell us how far it is from Philadelphia, poignancy rapidly fades. Did Wharton think this ludicrously explicit fantasy could be moving? Perhaps not, since it is the clinical aspect of Dad's secret life that seems to interest him. Thus he has Jack take Dad to the main modern enemy of poetic suggestion, a psychiatrist: Dad is a "successful schizophrenic." You could look it up in R. D. Laing.

Late in the novel, Jack asks himself, "What is it that keeps fathers and sons so far apart?" Since he gave Jack that line, Wharton must think that what he is showing here is the distance between his fathers and sons. But he must have lost control of his material, because nature rarely has witnessed less ambivalence between fathers and sons. Next to these guys, the cuddly father and son from *Ordinary People* look like fugitives from the *Brothers Karamazov*. Jack bears no discernible scars from the struggle to get free of his father: his love for Dad is full and unclouded. Dad himself begins lovable and grows more so, until he becomes quite insufferable. Jack is lovable too; and you can bet Billy loves him. So for all *Dad*'s naturalistic detail, its inventory of excretions and eructations, it is a romance, what Ann Douglas has called a "male weepie." . . . To get the shadow of our fathers off our lives and yet still love them—that is the conflict faced by most men and women. But you'd never know it from *Dad*. Its predecessor, the much praised *Birdy*, was called "magical," and that helpless adjective will doubtless be pasted on *Dad*. There is magic in it, all right, but it is not in Dad's Cape May fantasy world. It's in Wharton's Edenic pictures of fathers and sons.

He makes the men dears but gives Mom lines like: "If that wop (her son-in-law) thinks he can keep me from eating with my own daughter and my grandchildren, then he has another thing coming. I'll tell you that!" Meanwhile, Dad is coming on like Erich Segal. . . . He's such a swell guy. Why, though, is Mom a stinker? (pp. 38-9)

[Wharton's text shows a] proximate cause: it's a response to the way the men in her life have treated her, which is like a troublesome pet. Jack, for example, is a regular ringmaster, forever congratulating himself on his skill in handling Mom. . . . When Mom starts to lose faith in Dad's recovery, Jack gets her where she bleeds, in her Catholic conscience, by telling her that despair is the worst sin of all. That shuts the old girl up pronto!

After seeing Jack snap the whip we can easily imagine that Dad has been bouncing his own carom shots off Mom for 50 years. His technique at least is subtle. For instance: Dad has long wanted a couch at the Salvation Army store, but has been afraid of what Mom would say if it should suddenly show up in her living room. So he takes Mom to the store and baits a trap for her with a show of gallantry: "Johnny, we're probably wearing mother out with all this coming and going; let's sit down on this nice-looking couch here and take a little rest." He pretends it's Mom who discovers the couch and by this strategem foxes her into buying it. Yuk. Yuk.

This is odious. Is Wharton unaware of what he's showing us? He gives every sign of being in the dark. . . . [Wharton] seems not to have read his own novel. And who can blame him? *Dad* is for people who hate Mom. (p. 39)

> *Jack Beatty, "Put the Blame on Mame," in* The New Republic, *Vol. 184, No. 20, May 16, 1981, pp. 38-9.*

BENJAMIN DeMOTT

One of the best-selling half-truths of our literary times—basic to the work of Kurt Vonnegut, Ken Kesey, J. D. Salinger and many of their superiors and inferiors—is that only madmen are wise. And one of the more ingenious fictional treatments of that idea in the 1970's was William Wharton's *Birdy*. . . .

The novel was widely praised for some closely observed chapters, printed in italics, dramatizing the hero's success at persuading pigeons and canaries to regard him as one of themselves. I, too, liked parts of those chapters, but I found the work as a whole badly formula-ridden. The celebrations of the joys of looniness seemed stale. . . . And the bad-mouthing of mental consciousness seemed downright sophomoric. . . . The overall effect was that of pop D. H. Lawrence—cliché dressing up in bird feathers in hope of passing itself off as Soaring Thought.

The pseudonymous author of *Birdy* shifts focus a little in *Dad*. The book's two narrators are John Tremont, a 52-year-old American artist residing in France who's called back to California to care for his ailing parents, and Billy Tremont, his son, a University of California (Santa Cruz) dropout who's planning on supporting himself as a day laborer abroad while finishing a first book. The narrative frame is a transcontinental automobile ride—the first leg of the pair's journey back to Europe—taken at the conclusion of John Tremont's struggle to straighten out his elders' mental and physical lives.

Flashbacks show us the complications of that struggle (they're traceable to the uncaringness of the American medical establishment and to the meanness and self-absorption of Tremont's hatefully ignorant mother). The foreground of the tale is the drama of father and son attempting to fathom each other's nature, tastes and prospects during conversations (or inward ruminations) about speed limits, rock stars and ambition. (One notices occasional echoes here and elsewhere in the book of Robert Pirsig's "Zen and the Art of Motorcycle Maintenance.") There's also a series of italicized interpolations putting us in touch with the dream world of John Tremont's aged father, who has been driven crazy by his wife's unrelenting carping and prudery.

The most likable aspect of *Dad* is Tremont's performance as nurse and nurturer of his father and son. His attempt to rescue the old man first from senility, then from a coma, is humiliating, exhausting and arrestingly described. His attempt to explain his objections to the youth culture and its idols to his son is admirably forthright about the values underlying the critique.

I'm sorry to say, though, that *Dad* nevertheless struck me as even more formula-ridden than its predecessor. One reason for this is the density of stereotypes in this book—lovable Pops, hateful Moms, innocent kids. Another, more important reason is the peculiarly megalomanic thrust of the book's sentimentality. Where *Birdy* embraced a comparatively up-to-date softheadedness, namely anti-rationalism, *Dad* embraces all kinds. On the one hand it offers reverent portraits of motorcycles and motorcycle repairmen, contrasts between cold ugly WASPS and sexy beautiful blacks (and between kind happy hippies and murderous money-grubbing physicians), sermons against competition and psychology and sociology, panegyrics on Art. And, on the other hand, it slips down Memory Lane to produce a golden-hearted prostitute (or rather madam), an overnight moral conversion (a racist awakens suddenly to the sweet spirit of universal love), . . . and other old-timey hankie dampeners.

Here and there in *Dad* the old and new interpenetrate, as when the elderly youth-culture critic drops his Lewis Stone/Judge Hardy manners and reveals himself to be a person who loves good grass and pops a wicked pill. There's a sense, indeed, in which **Dad** qualifies as a sort of handbook on the modern politics of treacle—a manual of instruction on how to be, simultaneously, pro tearjerking and pro mind blowing. . . .

I believe there's room just now for a lively work of fiction dramatizing the continuing possibility that parents and children can care deeply for each other. And the nurturing sections I've mentioned hinted for a time that **Dad** had a chance of becoming that work. But this hope faded fast. Well before the middle **Dad** was distinctly recognizable as, at its mushy core, only another Father's Day promotion.

> *Benjamin DeMott, "Fathers and Sons," in* The New York Times Book Review, *May 24, 1981, p. 8.*

PAUL GRAY

Dad portrays both the loss and the continuity in [the] irrevocable process of change. Author William Wharton creates a middle-aged hero who must simultaneously witness the rapid decline of his father and the growing independence of his own son. . . . But **Dad** is more than a chronicle of pain and dissolution. It shows how stories that began with love can end that way too. . . .

The presence of [Dad's] obsessive, comforting [farm] vision links **Dad** to **Birdy** (1979), Wharton's acclaimed first novel about an adolescent boy who wants to become a canary and fly. But **Dad** is a rather more tenuous success than its predecessor. For one thing, it dissipates some of its power in prolixity. When Dad goes through his brief recovery, Tremont notes, within a few pages, "he's like a seventeen-year-old . . . he could have some feelings of being physically thirteen or fourteen years old. . . ." These sound like random thoughts, not the shaped statements of a narrator on top of his material. Tremont's treatment of his mother also provokes uneasiness. He seems blind to his bias against her, even though his own words reveal how eager he is to free his father by reining her in.

Ultimately, the effectiveness of **Dad** lies beyond logic. The novel has the feel of an intense autobiography, not recollected in tranquillity but dashed off from life, with all its uncertainties, mixed motives and false starts preserved intact. Wharton, himself an artist and an American expatriate in France, has photographed this story instead of painting it. But, like the best snapshots, **Dad** is touching, commemorative and candid.

> *Paul Gray, "A Time to Live and to Die," in* Time, *Vol. 117, No. 22, June 1, 1981, p. 77.*

ROGER SALE

While reading William Wharton's wonderful novel, **Dad,** I could not help imagining, as many will, the circumstances of its composition. It has the tone of intense personal quest that leads the reader to such speculations. . . .

Wharton seems to intend to be no more efficient than life is, because he knows better than to try to control as a novelist more than he can record as a son. So he records it, and the result is an experiment in discovering, one that refuses to impose a form. Not an academic effort which tries to show what style, form, or point of view can do, but something richer: to find out what happened, who these people are.

Patterns do begin to emerge, some early on that are tough to spot then since the narrative twists and turns so suddenly, now hopeful, now depressing. Mom has, among other childhood

troubles, seen two sisters die of tuberculosis in the bed the three slept in as children. She has had two nervous breakdowns by the time she meets her husband when she is seventeen. So she has grown to feel that only the narrow way, the controlled way, the hysterically clean way, can fend off disaster. Brewer's yeast and boiled vegetable juices for the kids. A short leash for the husband. Schedules and prejudices for everything. Her daughter protects herself by becoming an ironist and flees by marrying "a wop." Her son protects himself by becoming a painter, and flees, to "live with foreigners." In a sense, the novel is about what happens to Dad as a result. . . .

Wharton insists on the plain style; he allows himself only exclamation marks and an occasional loftiness, but no higher than that Mom is "a diesel engine inside a canoe." He allows himself to invent some passages of Dad's alternative world, and to do some scenes between Johnny and his son told from the son's point of view; these are strained, overdone. The rest is written, and the result is the sense that nothing is as wonderful, as awful, as wearying, as mysterious, as growing old. It may even be that Wharton is such a fine novelist because he is a very good son. Stranger things have happened.

Still, as one rereads the book, something seems askew. The book should have been called *Mom and Dad,* but it couldn't have been because Wharton in this book has been unable to forgive Mom. Dedicate a book to naked search, yes, but then the writer is not free to choose the materials. What emerges here is a blockage of feeling. Mom is no villain, and Wharton and Johnny always can "understand" Mom, but her pain and travail are too often and too finally allowed to be the cause of everyone else's. Dad is described in soft light, Mom in harsh florescent, and if Wharton can "see" this, he cannot control it, account for it, and so, in a book where the other women are wonderfully described, one wants only to record the fact of the bias, and to say that here such a failure matters. But not enough to keep **Dad** from being a fine novel I hope will be read.

> *Roger Sale, "Life with Father," in* The New York Review of Books, *Vol. XXVIII, No. 13, August 13, 1981, p. 44.*

MELVIN MADDOCKS

Fathers have seldom been safe with writers as sons. Kafka, Joyce, D. H. Lawrence—could three writers of the same generation have been less alike? Yet they are one man in their singular grievance against father. From the time fiction became self-scrutinizing—that is, "modern"—father has played an important and generally sinister role in explaining writing sons to themselves. (pp. 107-08)

[Now there] is a new intimacy to the old adversaries. Father and son are no longer seen as separate fates, moving in opposite directions, polarizing. A poem by Anthony Hecht pictures Aeneas carrying his aging father on his shoulders. This literal intertwining of lives—this alternation of roles: burden and carrier—seems to be what American writing about fathers and sons has lately come to. (p. 109)

Dad, the new novel by William Wharton, is perhaps the most explicit statement yet of the American writing son's premise: that he must not only understand and forgive father; he must also love him in order to be saved himself. Wharton has one other novel behind him, **Birdy** . . . , in which the protagonist with a kind of lyrical madness tries to turn himself into a bird.

A reader of *Dad* is tempted to say that Wharton is now telling the story of a man trying to turn himself into an angel: the perfect son—surely even more of a miracle. (p. 110)

Wharton is not a graceful writer. The prose (including the dialogue) lies flat and bleak—a 1980s version of Theodore Dreiser. But the style—or lack of it—suits the subject. Like Dreiser, Wharton cuts to the plain graceless heart of the matter; and like Dreiser he is sufficiently powerful and unrelenting to compel us to see how much literary gloss goes into our usual novelist's notion of "reality." Because he lacks the guile or skill to vary his pace Wharton makes his reader experience almost at firsthand the low-grade time that constitutes much of life. Ordinary American existence is laid out here in its full monotony: the hours spent before the television set; the miles one drives (and drives again) when one resides at a number like 10432 on—small irony—Colby Lane....

At the center of this uneventfulness quietly sits the very embodiment of ordinariness—Dad. Dad is a farm boy from Wisconsin who moved to Philadelphia in his teens when the farm got sold. First he became a carpenter. Then he went into a General Electric plant, and twenty-five years passed like one of those dreams-with-no-plot that torment a dreamer in slow motion. After Philadelphia came thirty years around Los Angeles, as he worked at a Douglas factory....

Older than his years, sick, disastrously combining a banal mind with early senility, a man incapable of showing any real affection, Dad is the least charming of human beings. "You're old when most people would rather have you dead," Wharton writes, and Dad seems to qualify. (p. 111)

As a nurturing son, Jack has been as ordinary as Dad.... From the beginning he is homesick for his wife and eight-year-old son in Paris, and for his work. Yet he stays on for almost six months in all, popping Valium and sleeping pills, exacerbating his high blood pressure and losing twenty pounds. He is determined to bring back Dad from the land of the dead, as if his own life depends on it. He plays Dad's beloved Bing Crosby records. He plants him in his rocker in front of his favorite soap operas. He pats him on the head.

Nothing brings back the departed intelligence—no trick, no familiar ritual, no new sign of caring. The face has been wiped clean of "a whole layer of civilization." When left to himself, the old man ends up on all fours, crawling back to infancy and then beyond to a prehuman state. Eyes as vacant as two pieces of glass, Dad defecates in his bed or wherever he happens to be....

At last the deck is stacked as no writing son has stacked the deck before. Filling Jack Tremont's nostrils with stench, dumping this imbecilic bag of bones smeared with excrement on his shoulders, Wharton asks in effect: *Now can a son love a father?*

Then suddenly, as if he cannot stand the brutal question he has asked himself and his reader, Wharton turns deus ex machina. Dad magically pulls himself together, and the novel falls apart. It becomes, in fact, a different novel with different characters bearing the same name, as though Wharton had written a Version I and Version II. After Dad's body comes to match the low state of his brain . . . , the old man springs back to complete health—a most impressive, if inexplicable, case of mens sana in corpore sano. Only this is another Dad. An interesting Dad. A lovable Dad. (p. 112)

In a scene that must be regarded as a climax Dad smokes pot among the last of the hippies. "These natural children-people

can be a reminder of how humans are meant to be," Wharton in II solemnly observes. Can this actually be what he intends his novel to say? Seldom does a book so good become so bad.

There have been flaws from the beginning, particularly Mom—a glib and heartless caricature. Mom is a nonstop complainer, a bullying genius at emotional blackmail; a typed composite of the worst moms from Philip Wylie to Philip Roth. But now it is no longer just a question of wrong touches: *Dad* simply slips out of control....

Have we gone through honest agony to arrive at such commonplace announcements as "A good part of the world's troubles are built around death fears"? The worst sin possible to a novelist the Wharton of Version II commits: He provides a logical explanation for suffering. Dad is officially diagnosed as a schizophrenic....

It is almost a relief when this second Dad turns catatonic again. One longs for resurrection, but with a single important proviso: When the stone is rolled away, the right body must come forth.

To speculate on why Wharton revises his own story would be to fall into the trap of literary psychoanalysis oneself. But it may be worth noticing again that when writing sons set out to make fathers lovable, they tend to make them carefree clowns or irresponsible rascals—that is to say, not fathers at all. And so to Wharton's terrible question—Can a son love a father when he is sick, stinking, idiotic, and full of death?—must be added a second question: Can a son love a father when he is potent, in his prime, and exercising authority? Those lovable fathers have a way of becoming twice as immature as their sons. Is the strategy of making father a cute child and loving him the only alternative to making him odious and killing him? (p. 113)

In his innocence, in his anxiety, Wharton cannot take no for the answer to any of his questions.... Version II is a desperate attempt—wrong as art, right as aspiration—to *prove* that more is possible between fathers and sons. We cannot live with its stipulation of success. It is Version I—the struggle and the failure—that convinces us.

The test of a powerful novel, as distinguished from a good novel, is that it puts the reader into solitary confinement with its author's obsession. *Dad* passes the test. It is by his own almost fanatical refusal to hate or quit that Wharton persuades us, as a more sophisticated writer might not, that love in its usual "Yes, but . . . " form is as possible between fathers and sons as elsewhere; and that such love is redeeming, if not quite the pure salvation Wharton dreams of. This may seem to be a modest breakthrough into the self-evident, but the father-and-son novel has been a genre self-satisfied for too long with facile hates and facile loves, time-lagging behind novelists' perceptions on other subjects. After *Dad* the stock attitudes ought not to be quite so easy to fall into again. (p. 114)

> *Melvin Maddocks, "Living Fathers and Literary Sons," in* The Sewanee Review, *Vol. XC, No. 1, Winter, 1982, pp. 107-14.*

THOMAS R. EDWARDS

December 1944, the Ardennes Forest: An under-strength American Intelligence and Reconnaissance squad unenthusiastically mans a quiet observation post in a remote, deserted chateau. From the standpoint of military history, with the Battle of the Bulge impending, this is a bad situation. It is, however, a good situation for a war novel. In *A Midnight Clear,* William Wharton . . . gives us both a gripping tale of military action and a perhaps less successful account of the human stakes in war.

The I and R squad in question consists of two soldiers in their 20's and also four teen-agers drawn (to their dismay) from the Army Specialized Training Program in American colleges to help fill up the depleted ranks of combat troops late in the war. Known somewhat derisively in the regiment as The Whiz Kids, they are very bright, very young, very green about war and other things. They soldier by the book, carefully and rather well, but it seems that for them war is a kind of game, to be played seriously but not closely pertinent to anything outside its own structures and rules.

A part of the game is to feel their involuntary association as a family relationship. The older men serve as the parents—"Father" Mundy, the dropout Catholic seminarian, and "Mother" Wilkins, with his obsession for neatness. The smart, affectionately impudent children are Miller, the mechanical genius and poet; Shutzer, the organizer who wants to go into advertising; Gordon, the health nut and would-be-doctor; and (as the story's narrator) Sergeant Knott, whose talent is for drawing but who finds himself in unwelcome command. . . . Together they agree to resist the Army and its style by eschewing obscene language.

At the chateau, they attend to their duty. . . . But the duties of family domesticity engage them more fully as they tend the fire, make decent hot meals, find real mattresses to sleep on and, above all, keep themselves amused. . . . But the main diversion is games: chess, homemade crosswords, a fiercely competitive form of (cardless) duplicate bridge. They become aware of a squad of Germans in the area who also seem oddly unwarlike, making snowmen, engaging the Americans in snowball fights, setting up a Christmas tree and throwing a Yule party at which carols are sung and gifts exchanged.

This book is not a fantasy but a realistic novel, and in fact these Germans are looking for a safe way to surrender. But their behavior, in the season of peace and good will, suggests that something can resist war's mindless brutality, which is opposed (though not always defeated, as the book's violent ending seems to say) by the ability of soldiers to disbelieve in war.

The Whiz Kids, and evidently their German counterparts too, *feel* no allegiance to national or ideological causes, to the structures of command that mean to control their service or even to the personal roles war asks them to play. They do of course play them, knowing the penalties for not doing so, but inside they remain civilians, truly devoted only to the civil values of love, self-respect, intellectual freedom, physical subsistence and sheer pleasure. What preserves them is the private hope that they are not what they seem, as Knott reflects when they find themselves in a mirrored bedroom at the chateau:

"I stop in front of one mirror, straighten, try to recognize myself; who is this, who am I?" . . . (p. 13)

It's the amused self-disbelief recorded in so many wartime photos of troops momentarily at ease.

Mr. Wharton conveys this disbelief thoroughly and lovingly, but it is not a new or strong enough idea to create the moral resonance he evidently wants for his war story. Two related problems of execution seem to muffle such resonance needlessly. There is a curious trickiness of narrative perspective in

Knott's occasional admission that he's not "telling a story" as it occurs but "writing a book" many years later. . . . Similarly, the present existence of some of his comrades is alluded to before we learn what happened to them all in the Ardennes. But the fact of survival is all we are given, with virtually nothing to indicate what Knott has turned out to be like in middle age. The narrative presence is that of the bright, flippant, frightened 19-year-old he was during the war scenes, with little that suggests the present contemplating the past in a stable ironic way.

Also, Knott's narrative, especially in its earlier parts, is almost embarrassingly cute. Although some of the worst moments have to do with his tediously recurrent intestinal troubles, . . . puerile humor is general throughout the squad until the action gets serious. Presumably Mr. Wharton means to show young minds wondering what tone to take toward their experience, but the wit is too forced to be affecting or even funny.

A Midnight Clear seems in a number of ways unsure about the effects it wants. The soldiers never quite jell as characters; though each is assigned particular interests and "family" roles, I had trouble remembering which was which. The "family" and the "games," interesting in themselves, seem diagrammatic and overdetermined. Though I respect Mr. Wharton's determination to keep things literal and realistic, it seems to me that his material would have benefited from a little more messiness of theme, a little more mystery or fantasy or symbolic intimation, the sort of thing someone like William Golding or John Fowles or (closer to home) Thomas Berger might have done with it. I may just be missing the point, but for me *A Midnight Clear,* absorbing as it is at the level of action and event, doesn't achieve a convincing deeper coherence. (pp. 13, 45)

Thomas R. Edwards, "Young at War," in The New York Times Book Review, *September 12, 1982, pp. 13, 45.*

PETER S. PRESCOTT

A writer whose first novel is fulsomely praised must pay forever after an excruciating tax: with each new book his readers will demand a repeat performance. I think it's fine that with his third novel [*A Midnight Clear*] the pseudonymous William Wharton hasn't attempted anything as mesmerizing as *Birdy,* his first—he means to write a different kind of story. As before, he deals with young men, contrasting the unpleasant world of reality with one more attractive, in which normal laws of behavior appear to be suspended, but there the resemblance ends. This time, Wharton has written a war story—not an exercise in realism, but not quite a fable either; what happens in it seems to point nowhere beyond itself. . . .

The narrator, Will Knott (nicknamed "Won't"), is 19. Recently promoted to sergeant, he leads a diminished squad of six young men with IQ's so high they've been assigned to a special corps. . . .

In the stillness before the final German push, Will is ordered to lead his squad on an extended patrol to a deserted chateau, there to huddle against the bitter cold [and] stand guard. . . . As snow descends, the Germans make their presence known . . . by delivering a Christmas tree, complete with candles, carols and presents. "It's crazy!" Will says, understating the case. "This whole war's gone off track somehow!"

Indeed it has. Are the Germans proffering some kind of Trojan horse? Will's crowd is smart enough to be more skeptical than they are—after all, war teaches skepticism, and whatever the Germans are up to, this procedure cannot bode well for our side. Wharton means to show us that this elite squad, just because it is so bright, will outsmart itself—and yet I think he may have outsmarted himself as well. He doesn't strike the right distance between realism and fantasy; the plot, if you examine it (and I advise you not to), will seem just improbable. Among other venial sins, Wharton interrupts his narrative to tell us what the survivors of this incident are doing now. Who cares? Minor quibbles, these, and I certainly don't mean to carp. I had a good time with this story: its suspense and pace, and its likable young men unhappily disguised as warriors, easily overcome its awkwardnesses.

> Peter S. Prescott, "A Fantasy of Men at War," in *Newsweek*, Vol. C, No. 11, September 13, 1982, p. 77.

ARNOLD KLEIN

[*A Midnight Clear*] is a first-person story entirely in the present tense, and about five times as long as it should be. Indeed, it ought to be retitled *A Midnight Dreary*. . . .

The double dose of immediacy resulting from present tense and first person brings every action of this small story into a positively exhausting sharp focus. . . . (p. 249)

Will Knott is supposed to be an intelligent young man, but . . . Wharton has not succeeded in giving him a very intelligent narrative voice. In fact, his characterizations are merely epithets. . . . Such stereotyping is standard war-story procedure, but in a novel attacking soldierly values one expects something less musty. Musty, too, is Wharton's tacit assumption of complicity from his readers. He writes about World War II with the deep disgust of the post-World War I era; today, pre-World War III, we tend to think of those conflicts as quite different from one another. Nonetheless, it would be easier to agree with the author that war is senseless if Will Knott were not such a drone. . . .

And another thing. Doesn't it seem to you that you've heard this tale of ill-fated surrender before? Somewhere . . . a movie, maybe . . . isn't it all . . . familiar? Perhaps Wharton padded out his novel because, reduced to basics, it would have made a somewhat conventional short story. And yet *A Midnight Clear*, despite its length, has remained a short story; . . . it lacks the dimensions and complexity of a novel. (p. 250)

> Arnold Klein, "Video 2, Fiction 0," in *The Nation*, Vol. 235, No. 8, September 18, 1982, pp. 248-50.*

SHERWOOD WILLIAMS

The soldiers in William Wharton's new novel [*A Midnight Clear*] are so wholesome they almost seem more like characters from "Leave It to Beaver" than GIs serving on the German front in December 1944. . . .

The reader's sense of isolation from the real world is heightened by the novel's unusual setting, which seems drawn in equal parts from the Brothers Grimm and grim reality. Staked out in an abandoned château in the middle of the snow-dusted Ardennes Forest, the men are detached from all sense of time and only sporadically in touch with either side of the fighting. . . .

If this fairy-tale scenario seems slightly unreal in a World War II novel, the incongruity is purely intentional. Wharton reveals the ugliness of war far better by reminding us of the joy of life than by pedantically documenting the brutality of battle.

Like the title character of Wharton's acclaimed first novel, *Birdy,* Sergeant Knott reacts to the confining pressure of combat by searching for uplifting mental escapes. "I'm having my usual trouble," he remarks at one point, "noticing how beautiful the world is just when there's a chance I might be leaving it."

Such cynical wisecracks serve to turn potentially maudlin situations like the men's Christmas celebration into events of beguiling intensity. Knott's matter-of-fact narration and offhand conversational style turn a quirky fantasy into a drama of convincing reality. As the fairy-tale falls apart and the novel is pulled toward its explosive conclusion, we come to realize that we have been emotionally blitzed by a novelist of remarkable power.

> Sherwood Williams, "WWII Saga of Remarkable Power," in *The Christian Science Monitor*, November 5, 1982, p. B5.

ROBERT TOWERS

A Midnight Clear has a stirring story to tell, a war story that follows a classical line of action. . . . A handful of very young American soldiers is sent on a reconnaissance mission in unfamiliar territory, where they make contact with an enemy who seems eager to make friendly contact with them. . . . But a terrible blunder occurs, and war, with all its brutality, stamps out the small fire of common humanity that has barely begun to shed its light in the thickening gloom. (p. 38)

The action of *A Midnight Clear* is well sustained, providing abundant opportunities for suspense, alarm, sentiment, comedy, terror, and grief. The catastrophe is properly appalling (though one anticipates its coming and has already guessed the identity of the blunderer). The details of the deserted château which the squad uses as an outpost, of the dense woods and snow, of the myriad discomforts (cold, wetness, diarrhea, etc.) of soldiering—all of these are made graphic enough. Still, the novel does not work. There are several reasons for this failure, the most damaging having to do with Wharton's use of a first-person narrator. . . .

[Apart from] clichés, technical lapses damage the narrator's credibility. Is Won't's narration that of a youngster from whom a considerable degree of callowness might be expected or that of a man in his late fifties, looking back? We are invited to assume the former, but what then are we to do with the sudden leaps from the novel's "present" (1944) to our own inflation-ridden present (1982)—with, for instance, Won't's comment that "Forty dollars was a lot of money in those days"? At another point he interrupts the flow of the novel's events (Won't is in his tent, about to go to sleep) to introduce expository material by saying, "There is a typical military briefing coming up soon but I think I should give our real briefing here while I'm supposed to be drifting off to sleep." In a different kind of novel such violations of the imagined present could be made integral to the mode of narration, but *A Midnight Clear* has not been set up that way; except for these and a few other such breaks, the narrative movement is linear and rendered entirely in the callow, corny language of the nineteen-year-old Won't. Consequently, the inconsistencies seem merely crude.

The recorded dialogue of the Whiz Kids is wholly lacking in the intellectual playfulness and range of reference that we might expect from such high scorers; worse, it is afflicted with the banality of Won't's language and his laborious strainings for humor.... The clichés extend to their characterizations as well, especially to that of Shutzer, the squad's "professional Jew," who is given to such outbursts as "Those filthy, Nazi, Kraut-headed, super-Aryan, motherfucking bastards.... We should shove them in their gas ovens and wipe them all out...." (Never mind that "motherfucking" was a term still confined to the black ghettos in 1944 and that a GI was not likely to have heard of the gas ovens at that date.)

Nowhere in *A Midnight Clear* do I find the visionary power or the passages of incandescent description that made the author's first novel, *Birdy,* so striking; nor do I find anything comparable to the painfully felt, honestly rendered account of family life that more than compensated for the rather amateurish construction of his second novel, *Dad.* Were it not for these accomplishments, a reader might be inclined, on the basis of this most recent production, to dismiss the pseudonymous William Wharton as a well-intentioned hack. (p. 39)

> Robert Towers, "American Graffiti," in The New York Review of Books, *Vol. XXIX, No. 20, December 16, 1982, pp. 38-40.* *

TOM O'BRIEN

[William Wharton] is one of the finest writers in English today. His previous works, *Birdy* and *Dad,* drew on experiences of family life and war to create rich, powerful, and vivid treatments of a prevalent modern theme, the close proximity of certain types of madness and imaginative moral vision. *A Midnight Clear,* however, is somber, almost monotonous.... At its best, *A Midnight Clear* is a moving allegory about the difficulties of making peace, not war.

Unfortunately, it takes some time to get *A Midnight Clear* moving, and it remains potent only as an allegory because Wharton leaves his most effective weapon behind, his gift for describing inspired insanity in his two previous novels. (pp. 155-56)

The narrative voices in both [*Birdy* and *Dad*], moreover, are dominated by an urgent, pained need to communicate. Reading Wharton is like being buttonholed by a modern version of the Ancient Mariner reciting a story of Dostoevsky translated into English by Lenny Bruce. There are times when one has to put down his books not because they are boring, or, on the other hand, too thrilling, but simply because of the need to break from a draining but powerful conversation with a friend in an emotional crisis. *Dad* and *Birdy* are grueling both in what they give and what they take, full of frank talk and genuinely tough confrontations; their tone is vulgar, earthy, earnest, immediate. The language is quick, notational, dominated by the present tense even when recollecting, and peppered by sharp wit and home truths.... [With] small brushstrokes and the accumulative Niagara-like force of his prose, Wharton domesticates madness and insinuates how all strong feeling—in all of us—borders an abyss.

This is no more true than in the last one hundred pages of *Birdy,* when the hero's friend tries to help him recover in a mental hospital after World War II.... It is a loony, magnificent novel, not only in its treatment of a brotherly kind of friendship, but also in its contrast between Birdy's harmless

pastoral among the parakeets and the larger madness of modern weapons.

A Midnight Clear brings together these concerns with war and family life, but without Wharton's usual interest in madness. The army squad is a microcosm, both of family and social types.... (p. 156)

But Wharton's "family" in *A Midnight Clear* is made of wit, not substance. We never get to care for the individual fates of the soldiers or feel for them as we do for the characters in *Dad* and *Birdy.* A war book, ironically, replaces bang with whimper. In part, the problem is structural: Wharton spends too much time describing the family and self-indulgently delineating its superiority to the army before the real story truly begins. The only time these opening sections come alive involves remembrances of training camp before the squad got to the cold plains of northern France. If Wharton wanted us to catch boredom as the essence of military life, he has succeeded, and in so doing committed the imitative fallacy. Were it not for faith engendered by *Dad* and *Birdy,* I would not have continued.

Most importantly, the narrative voice of *A Midnight Clear* is cool and detached. "Won't" recalls the events from calm retrospect, many years after the fateful Christmas. In *Birdy* and *Dad,* the narrators recollect past events too, but in the middle of a present crisis—a crisis usually generated by some form of both sublime and pitiable dementia that adds an especially poignant and simultaneously terrifying aspect to the climax. In *A Midnight Clear,* Wharton pursues his sense of extraordinary human riches destroyed by the madness of the so-called normal world, but without a crisis and a genuine Quixote at the center, he never soars. *Birdy* and *Dad* catch something essential about life: the pain we suppress for the sake of social sanity, but must acknowledge in some form lest we scream. *Birdy* and *Dad* are cathartic wrestlings with that pain, and finally function like exorcisms. *A Midnight Clear* is like taps.

My advice: buy the earlier books and read them instead. (pp. 156-57)

> Tom O'Brien, "Potent Only as Allegory," in Commonweal, *Vol. CX, No. 5, March 11, 1983, pp. 155-57.*

PUBLISHERS WEEKLY

William Wharton is the pseudonym of an expatriate American painter who lives in Paris, as does the protagonist-narrator of his new book [*Scumbler*]. The title comes from a painting term (to modify the effect of a painting with an overlay of opaque color); the narrator calls himself "Scum" or "the Scumbler"; like much else in this disappointing novel, it is a heavy-handed device.... Among the improbable events the Scumbler recounts here is the purchase of 42 of his paintings by a wealthy American couple, an event that temporarily astonishes the Scumbler and his family with fiscal solvency. The lazily organized narrative is composed of many such vignettes, all celebrating the Scumbler's artistic processes and illuminating his midlife crisis. Many passages, especially the ones in which Scum delivers panegyrics to an artist's creativity, are platitudinous, pretentious and boring. Sad to say, this is a tedious, inconsequential novel, not even convincing as fantasy, a medium in which Wharton has previously *(Birdy, Dad)* excelled.

> A review of "Scumbler," in Publishers Weekly, *Vol. 225, No. 12, March 23, 1984, p. 67.*

TOM LeCLAIR

Scumbler is Mr. Wharton's fourth novel in five years. While all may not have been written during that span, he should heed the advice Kafka posted on his wall: "Wait." **Birdy, Dad** and **A Midnight Clear** had powerful subjects—madness, senility, war—and emotional effects. Though admittedly autobiographical, these novels were distanced from the author's present circumstances. In *Scumbler,* Mr. Wharton works closer to home. He too is an American painter who has spent much of the last two decades with his family in Paris. This life, no matter how originally Mr. Wharton may be living it, is by now a literary situation, as familiar as adolescence in an unpleasant school or age in a baseball novel, a convention requiring literary sophistication and subtlety—a waiting art—to make it carry weight or comedy. Mr. Wharton knows the tradition and competition . . . , yet *Scumbler* seems hurried into existence, reported rather than composed, talked, not typed. . . .

In Mr. Wharton's prose, numbing spreads everywhere, vitiating a possibly sympathetic character, his observations, other people, even fun. Scumbler is a justifiably angry alien. Imprisoned as a conscientious objector in World War II, he was split from his first family and then denied a passport to leave the United States. But his attacks on America . . . come in clichés heard nightly on American television, a railing unimproved by his suffering or residence in France, which is described in postcard jottings. As for his happy second family, we hear only scolding from his wife and nothing from his kids.

Mr. Wharton can do quick comic turns, his hero's stumbling into and tip-toeing out of scrapes, magnifying danger and exaggerating his mother wit. The plot enlarges this pattern. Scumbler decides in winter that he's in a late-life crisis, travels to Spain, where he passes tests mostly of his own making, and returns renewed in spring, ready to resist the temptation of sudden money. Unfortunately, his inescapable "nit-picking desire to tell all" spoils effects large and small, clogging up comedy with diary detail and trite moralizing. . . . His little comments on art, time and life are usually simply embarrassing. . . .

First-person narrators are not, I know, their makers. J. P. Donleavy's roguish Ginger Man, John Hawke's Papa Cue Ball (in "Second Skin") and Joyce Cary's artist, Gulley Jimson (in "The Horse's Mouth")—comic characters of whom Scumbler seems a composite—have their stylistic limitations too, but they're not banal. Triviality, to be rewarding, must be shared or symbolic, representative of some social stupidity, an instructive dumbness. *Scumbler* is only Scumbler—scrambler, bumbler, mumbler, an artistic failure.

Tom LeClair, *"Painting Himself into a Corner,"* in The New York Times Book Review, *June 3, 1984, p. 40.*

VALERIE MINER

Scumbler is a marvelously vital novel about the power of imagination to create and to re-create life. The fey narrator names himself after "scum of the earth" because of his affection for the people he paints on the streets of Paris. . . . Presented as 23 self-portraits, the first-person, present-tense story elicits intimate connnection between writer and reader. . . .

Like his pseudonymous author, Scumbler is an American-sometime-expatriate who sometimes supports his family by painting. . . . Scumbler also is seemingly ageless, juxtaposing "weird" adolescent diction with wise-old-man maxims. His emotional power is tested in openness, tenderness and stability. However, he does emerge as endearingly fallible in his self-obsessions and in his sometimes irresponsible impetuosity. . . .

Perhaps the most satisfying canvases are those where he steps into the pleasure of his work. The sustaining spirit is a joyful tranquillity, at once the source of his art, an inspiration to do his work and a wholly separate momentum which carries him through the rest of his life. . . .

Given Scumbler's seductive intimacy, it's hard to keep a distance on his book. In many senses, it feels like an autobiography. Sometimes the aphorisms seem flip or facile. Is that part of his nature or a failure in the writing? Sometimes he does things that seem stupid or self-indulgent. Is one being critical of the character, the narrator or the author? Is the reader uncomfortable with Scumbler's uninhibited abandon or simply jealous of it? . . .

Valerie Miner, *"Seductive Intimacy of an Alter Ego,"* in Los Angeles Times Book Review, *June 10, 1984, p. 4.*

CHRISTOPHER PORTERFIELD

"Always distrust professed honesty," says Scumbler. . . . "It's the ultimate con job." This seems an odd assertion from a character whose narrative is one long profession of emotional candor, sensitivity, creativity and individuality. William Wharton's novel [*Scumbler*] is no con job, however, but something perhaps harder to take: a credo of total, devout and sometimes excruciating sincerity. (p. 86)

Old Scum might seem more engaging and colorful if he were not so familiar: another in a long line of romantics who disdain the bourgeois "scramble for outside things like money or status," a lesser descendant of that definitive rogue-genius Gulley Jimson, hero of Joyce Cary's *The Horse's Mouth.* For a man who claims that most of his life has been "a flight from boredom," Scum has an amazing tolerance for bull-session profundities. . . .

The pseudonymous William Wharton . . . is himself an American painter who lived many years in Paris, so it is no surprise that his street scenes and descriptions of the painterly process are vividly authentic. His chapter on Scum's attempt to paint a self-portrait that would transport him out of the temporal dimension makes a stirring set piece. But his identification with his character is so complete that the novel seems to be spun from their shared fantasy fulfillment. . . .

"I think I hurt people by living," Scum maintains. "My maniacal insistence on living my own life is in itself a terrible violation of everybody else." The reader sees little of such conflict. Insofar as the other characters have any life outside of Scum's ruminations, they are as simple and warm-hearted an assortment of waifs and eccentrics as can be found anywhere this side of William Saroyan. Indeed, like Saroyan's, Wharton's writing has often seemed like a race between originality and sentimentality. In *Scumbler,* the sentimentality is way out in front. (p. 87)

Christopher Porterfield, *"Too True,"* in Time, *Vol. 123, No. 24, June 11, 1984, pp. 86-7.*

JOSE YGLESIAS

"Look around, how do you like it here, inside my head? A bit messy, isn't it?" [The protagonist of *Scumbler*] asks this question two-thirds of the way into the novel, and you might forbearingly agree—so many are the pleasures in it, so grand the reservoir of admiration for [Wharton's] three previous novels—but you had better watch out. Wharton may be having you on, like Dostoyevsky in *The Possessed* apologizing for not being a better storyteller.

Even so, Wharton never lies to you; he is always direct and plain-spoken and unambiguous, like a man who keeps his eyes on yours as he tells you his story. If he doesn't put on the dog, as he might say, neither does he eschew the skills and ploys that the most elliptical of modernist writers have developed. In the above quotation there are strains of James Joyce and Gertrude Stein, but totally transmuted. He doesn't lean on precedent: he'd be writing this way no matter what—because he's a regular Joe and that's the way a regular Joe talks. Never for a moment do you feel that some literary notion has been imposed on his (or our) natural sensibilities.

Take the title, *Scumbler*. It seems the perfect epithet for an unsuccessful painter living in Paris with his wife and kids, engaged in more activities and possessed by more obsessions than a man in late middle age can handle. If the book were not prefaced by the dictionary definition of scumbling . . . I should have thought of it, at least on a first impression, as a modern picaresque novel about a man in midlife crisis, and not missed either its fun or humanity. Yet how much richer to see, at the same time, that his overlapping adventures amount to a multifaceted cubist self-portrait.

But enough fanciness; it would anger Wharton. Here then, under another name, is the middle-aged hero of *Dad* (and very likely the young man of *Birdy* and the sergeant of *A Midnight Clear*) at home in Paris pursuing his busy, settled life. . . . (p. 250)

Every one of [his adventures is] . . . a marvel of interest for the reader (Wharton, after all, kept one enthralled for pages on end in *Birdy* with the courtship of a pair of canaries) but not for Scumbler. He knows he's an old man now and for him to question the life and art that he has chosen, or to contemplate its coming to a disillusioned end, is unbearable.

Suddenly he is forced to make his old choices over again: he receives an offer for a nice California nest that would solve all his financial problems. He decides, in accordance with his ideals, that he must turn it down. The decision gets him back to work, to his old life, but when he tells his wife after the fact, she protests, "You never think of anybody but yourself. You treat everybody and everything as if we're all part of one big painting, a painting of *your* life, a self-portrait, a *selfish* portrait, and we're all only background."

It is her first deeply felt complaint about their life together, and it shows him that his obsessions, his life's choices, his freedom, have impinged on others, cost them dearly. He has turned out to be the kind of man he wished not to be: an egotist. . . .

He comes out of it all in a typical Scumbler way and he takes us with him, for he does not live for art alone, he is no Gulley Jimson. And we go along willingly. Even so, this funny-looking old man . . . comes dangerously close to being, as Chesterton said about Dickens's characters, the sort of person we run to in fiction but run from in life.

On the dust jacket of each new book the pseudonymous William Wharton tells us another fact about his life. This time he says that he is a painter who also writes. I don't believe that for a minute; it must be the other way around. (p. 251)

Jose Yglesias, "Rescue Operations," in The Nation, *Vol. 239, No. 8, September 22, 1984, pp. 250-51.*

JOHN BATESON

Scumbler is better than a lot of novels being published today, in large part because Wharton writes well about a subject that is close to him. Scumbler is a 60-year-old flower child, an American painter of free spirit living in Paris. . . . Since Wharton himself is a painter . . . , it's not surprising that his character is deftly drawn and his story engrossing. Indeed, if that were all he aimed for, his book would be a success. The problem is, Wharton has pretensions of more.

"Scumbler," he says in the jacket copy, "investigates at a profound level one man's efforts to take on the big issues: death, meaning, time, dreams. . . . Reading this book can be a creative experience."

Inasmuch as reading itself is a creative experience (the reader imagines scenes and people, tries to understand thoughts, feel emotions, follow the action in his mind and, with the best of books, comes away a different person), Wharton is correct. However, *Scumbler* is not profound and the so-called "big issues" are given the most cursory review. Wharton does offer a few thoughts about art and the creative process that may improve readers' appreciation the next time they visit an art gallery . . . , but most readers will be unaffected.

Most readers will—or should—be offended by the lines of poetry that litter almost every page (in capital letters, no less. According to a printer's note, Wharton wanted the whole book set in caps. Mercifully, it wasn't). The poetry is simplistic to the point of being juvenile and bears little relation to what precedes or follows. It disrupts an otherwise fluid narrative and heightens the basic flaw: *Scumbler* begs to be taken more seriously than it deserves.

The book lacks depth. This is ironic since "scumbling" is an artistic term that relates to layering, but it is not a crime for a novel. It's just not the stuff of literary heaven.

"This book may easily be read merely as 'The Confessions of a Paris Street Painter,'" says Wharton, "however, it's more than that."

Sorry, Bill, it's not. But as "The Confessions of a Paris Street Painter," it's okay.

John Bateson, "Minor Portrait of the Artist," in San Francisco Review of Books, *September-October, 1984, p. 8.*

Hugh Whitemore

1936-

English dramatist and scriptwriter.

Whitemore is best known for his plays *Stevie* **(1977) and** *Pack of Lies* **(1983).** *Stevie* **is a stage biography of poet and fiction writer Stevie Smith that incorporates samples of her witty writings into the dialogue and extended monologues of the title character. Set in the suburban apartment where she lived a mundane life with her aunt, the play is highlighted by Smith's observations on life, which are often playfully humorous yet hint at her underlying despair.** *Pack of Lies* **is based on an actual case of espionage that occurred in a London suburb in the early 1960s. Whitemore deemphasizes suspenseful plot action to focus on the Jacksons, whose best friends and neighbors, the Krogers, are alleged by government agents to be spies. After the Jacksons allow the agents to use their home for purposes of surveillance, they begin to feel repugnance for their duplicity towards their friends. Whitemore probes the theme of betrayal as it relates to friendship and patriotic duty.**

Whitemore has written film adaptations for *Stevie* **and Rebecca West's novel** *The Return of the Soldier.* **He has also written several television plays and the script for the mini-series about Alger Hiss,** *Concealed Enemies.*

ANTHONY CURTIS

The eccentricity of the English, or rather of one gifted and highly individual English lady, is celebrated in Hugh Whitemore's *Stevie.* . . . I remember meeting Stevie Smith, whose life-story this is . . . , but I do not recall anything much she said. This is not surprising because it emerges from this play that she saved up her best remarks for her verse which shows great simplicity combined with great feeling for people whose lives are precariously balanced on the edge of despair. . . .

It is hard to explain why the piece is so moving. . . . [Perhaps] is lies in the fascination of seeing a woman of exceptional gifts encased in a mask of ordinariness. She conformed cheerfully; she had a dullish city job which she quite enjoyed, led a dull suburban life which she loved, and yet she flourished as an artist. . . . The whole show well deserved its unexpected West End success.

Anthony Curtis, in a review of "Stevie," in Drama, *No. 125, Summer, 1977, p. 57.*

EDITH OLIVER

[*Stevie*] is largely, though not entirely, a skillful arrangement, by Hugh Whitemore, of Miss Smith's own words, taken from short stories and recollections, and above all from the deadly light verse of her despairing temperament. The poems, in their deceptive simplicity, arise from the script as effortlessly as they appear to have arisen in her. All the action takes place in the living room of 1 Avondale Road, Palmers Green, a suburb of London where the spinster poet lived with her aunt. . . . Sitting over the teacups with her aunt, she begins to tell the audience about herself and her life, breaking into imitations of schoolmistresses and neighbors and of colleagues at the pub-

lishing house where she works as a secretary. She plays some scenes with her aunt and with [a] man, who acts the parts of an unsuccessful suitor in her youth and of a somewhat put-upon, though devoted, escort in her sixties—until her death, in 1971, at sixty-eight. The scene with the suitor, by the way, in which she breaks off an engagement, is the only one that seems false and sounds off-key; I doubt that many of those words are Miss Smith's. The best words are the poems, of course, but there are also good ones in her conversations (many of them with the audience) and in the stories she tells about herself as we trace her steps from childhood on. (pp. 78, 80)

[*Stevie*] presents and then shatters the stereotype of the English spinster. For all her unsuitable clothes (too young or too frisky or just plain god-awful), her acid comments, the sprightliness that masks her desperation and her obsession with death, the cigarettes she continually lights, the nips at the bottle, Stevie Smith . . . is a humorous, shrewd, complex woman, like no one else on earth. Her understanding of herself is deep and complete, and she is capable of every emotion—most notably defiance. (p. 80)

Edith Oliver, "Miss Smith and Miss Maxwell," in The New Yorker, *Vol. LV, No. 2, February 26, 1979, pp. 78, 80.*

JOHN SIMON

Stevie Smith was the most curious of poets: in form, somewhere between D. H. Lawrence and nursery rhymes; in content, between Hilaire Belloc and Paul Eluard. A Blakean innocence coexists in her work with surreal arcana, while her prosody shuttles between doggerel and sophisticated *vers libre.* With that strange poetry . . . went an equally strange life, consisting of office work, passionate party going, and near recluseveness in London's remote Palmers Green. There, with her aggressive book clusters confronting the shabby gentility of her maiden aunt's furnishings, she lived in tender mutual care and irony with her childhood protectress—her "Lion Aunt," as she called her.

Hugh Whitemore's stage biography *Stevie,* is less a play than a collage of true anecdotes, poems, and a little journalistic narration held together by a minimum of invented dialogue. Whitemore . . . has proceeded here with good sense and finesse, allowing Stevie to effervesce almost uninterruptedly and bringing in the aunt only when necessary to complete the picture of a mildly unusual sort of domesticity. The third character, Man, is a composite of various friends, suitors, and interviewers; he is used very sparingly—often merely as a laconic, self-effacing narrator. Out of these three . . . there emerges an image of understated but intense humanity, of a prosaic life made poetic by Stevie's fiercely personal, slightly daffy, yet ultimately vatic view of existence, worthy of a latter-day, megalopolitan Emily Dickinson.

The drama and comedy here are, naturally, on a small scale, but not brittle or "literary." "I bought this hat at a jumble sale for only five shillings," Stevie remarks. "Tremendous bargain but perhaps a bit of a mistake.'' Or: ''Some people think that because I never married, I don't know anything about emotion. They're wrong; I loved my aunt.'' Such lines are exhilaratingly absurd or smilingly melancholy in context; there is enough unassuming laughter and loveliness in *Stevie* to provide a steady flow of pleasure, whether it is, strictly speaking, a play or not.

John Simon, ''Stevie's Little Wonders,'' in New York Magazine, *Vol. 12, No. 11, March 12, 1979, pp. 74-5.**

IRVING WARDLE

Bob and Barbara [in *Pack of Lies*] are a nondescript middle-aged couple, live in Ruislip with hardly a care in the world when—out of the blue—they are visited by a gentleman from Whitehall who informs them that their neighbours may be harbouring a Russian spy, and that he requires their front bedroom as a surveillance post.

Bob overrides Barbara's objections and agrees; and, sure enough, the wanted man is observed leaving the house of their two best friends, Peter and Helen. In due course, the authorities move in and mop up the nest of traitors. The whole operation goes like clockwork except that, unfortunately, Barbara then dies of a heart-attack.

There are hardly any other events, much less any melodrama, and we never get to see the wanted man. Though perhaps this is unnecessary, as he is named as Gordon Lonsdale; and . . . Hugh Whitemore's play is based on the memory of the Ruislip survivors.

In the circumstances, it would be impertinent for any playwright to exploit such material as an imaginative launching pad. Why, then, present it as a play at all?

The answer, conclusively justified in *Pack of Lies,* is that the very banality of the story gives it a moral force beyond the scope of the most sensational plot.

As we first see them, the Ruislip couple exemplify British private life. . . . Their daily round of housework, and parenthood may look deadly dull, but they are both decent, affectionate people, who happen never to have been required to make a serious choice.

When the moment does arrive, the element of choice is taken out of their hands. Stewart, the Whitehall man . . . simply refers apologetically to the Official Secrets Act and moves his girl agents into the house: just as he periodically waves his pipe in the air and asks: ''You don't mind if I . . . ?'' He is going to have his smoke whatever they say.

The effect on the couple of the scheme is catastrophic and extremely painful to watch. . . .

Mr. Whitemore's main achevement is to show Barbara simultaneously disintegrating and acquiring articulacy. He does this partly through displaced climaxes. Barbara remains stoically tight-lipped with Stewart and secretive with Helen.

But when her daughter is discovered to have taken a forbidden motor-bike ride, [Barbara] explodes in a terrifying paroxysm of wrath, hurling her satchel at her head and screaming: ''I'll never trust you again''. It is also she who speaks the play's epitaph on what Stewart and his kind have done to families such as hers. ''Why should he bother about us? We're the kind of people who stand in queues and don't answer back'' . . . .

[There is] awkwardness [in] the solo narrative scenes. But this is a small imperfection in a play whose tone and values are otherwise so exactly judged.

Irving Wardle, ''Torment of Spies Best Friends,'' in The Times, *London, October 27, 1983, p. 13.*

RICHARD ZOGLIN

On a chill December night in 1948, Whittaker Chambers led two investigators from the House Committee on Un-American Activities into a pumpkin patch on his Maryland farm. From inside a hollowed-out pumpkin he produced several rolls of microfilm: copies of secret Government documents that, he claimed, had been passed to him in the 1930s by a State Department official named Alger Hiss, when both men were members of a Soviet espionage ring.

A few days later, HUAC members, spurred on by first-term California Congressman Richard Nixon, called Eastman Kodak to check on the film's emulsion numbers. They got bad news: the film could not have been manufactured before 1945, which meant that Chambers must be lying. Furious, Nixon phoned Chambers to demand an explanation. But minutes later, Kodak called back to apologize for its mistake: the film could indeed have been made in 1938. . . .

Such were the bizarre twists and turns of the notorious Hiss-Chambers case. In the decades since the case dominated the headlines, the facts have all but disappeared under the symbolic baggage piled on them. . . .

To its great credit, *Concealed Enemies,* a four-hour, three-part docudrama in PBS's *American Playhouse* series, clears away much of that baggage and concentrates instead on one of the most fascinating political mystery stories of the century. The drama, with a script by British Playwright Hugh Whitemore, begins on Aug. 3, 1948, the day that Chambers electrified a HUAC hearing by naming Hiss as a Communist. Chambers by then had been out of the Communist Party for ten years, and was working as a senior editor for *Time.* The climax is set in a courtroom almost 18 months later, when Hiss—who denied all charges and has continued to do so to this day—was convicted at a second trial for perjury. (His first trial ended in a hung jury.) The intervening events make compelling drama: the discovery of the ''pumpkin papers''; the search for the Hisses' old Woodstock typewriter, allegedly used to retype the secret documents; the investigation into a homosexual phase in Chambers' past; the charges and denials, the courtroom theatrics and, as ever, the uncertainties. . . .

The show's most serious flaw is the congenital problem of many docudramas dealing with controversial events: a dogged inscrutability. Remaining neutral on the issue of Hiss's guilt, the show presents a mass of incidents—some important, some irrelevant, some canceling others out—that are engrossing from moment to moment. But the end result is a sort of dramatic entropy that can be frustrating.

Richard Zoglin, ''A Bizarre Political Mystery,'' in Time, *Vol. 123, No. 19, May 7, 1984, p. 108.*

RALPH DE TOLEDANO

[*Concealed Enemies* is a] TV script that repeatedly confuses dramatization with fictionalization. Written by Hugh Whitemore, an accomplished TV and stage playwright, *Concealed Enemies* plunges into fiction in its opening sequences by falsifying the genesis of Whittaker Chambers's appearance before the House Committee on Un-American Activities (HCUA). When Chambers took the stand on August 3, 1948, neither Representative Richard Nixon nor the HCUA had the vaguest idea of what his testimony would be, and the naming of Hiss as a Communist conspirator in the State Department rocked the committee as much as it did the nation.

Chambers, in fact, had been subpoenaed almost as an afterthought to corroborate the testimony of spy-courier Elizabeth Bentley on Communist infiltration of the Federal Government. The TV script, however, has a Catholic priest, given name identification only, pouring the poison of what he had presumably been told by Chambers into Nixon's ear before the most sensationally accurate of the HCUA's hearings had begun. (p. 56)

In like manner, there are fictional conversations between John Foster Dulles and his brother Allen that impute corrupt political motives to their very marginal role in the case. Nowhere are we told that Hiss left the State Department after he had been self-trapped in some substantial lies to Secretary of State James F. Byrnes about his Communist complicity. *Concealed Enemies* also stands mute on the prejudicial conduct of the first trial judge and his refusal to dismiss the foreman of the jury despite solid information that he had declared, even before the unfolding of the evidence, that Alger Hiss would not be convicted as long as he sat on the jury. Interestingly, the gross impropriety of allowing a Hiss partisan to remain on the jury was part of the first version of the TV script but somehow disappeared from the PBS production.

All of this is peripheral. Where *Concealed Enemies* strikes its strongest blow for Alger Hiss is in those sequences dealing with the Hiss Woodstock on which the incriminating State Department documents that Hiss delivered to Chambers for transmission to the Soviet Union were typed. The typewriter was the "immutable witness" in the case—and defense and prosecution witnesses agreed during the two trails that the State Department documents had been copied on the same machine as correspondence written by Priscilla Hiss at the time. There was never, during the trail or since then, the slightest doubt that Priscilla Hiss's letters and the State Department copies had emerged from the same typewriter.

But *Concealed Enemies* would have none of this, so a fictional conversation between FBI Director J. Edgar Hoover and two of his colleagues—a conversation in which Hoover orders them to suppress evidence concerning the Woodstock—pops up in the script, playing the serial-numbers game that Hiss and his lawyers attempted in their unsuccessful efforts before the courts to win a new trial on the basis of the mythical "forgery by typewriter." Hiss's first move to flank the damning testimony of the "immutable witness" was to tell the grand jury which indicted him that Chambers had crept into the Hiss home undetected in the dead of night to type the hundreds of pages of documents and then to disappear by dawn's early light.

Yet for all of these transgressions, this pandering to Hiss and his benighted supporters, *Concealed Enemies* has its virtues. The Whittaker Chambers I knew never comes through, but at least he is shown as a man of principle and compassion, not the plotter and conniver so dear to the polemicists of the liberal press. Being a PBS production it could not say forthrightly that Hiss was guilty of treason, which both Whitemore and Elstein made it clear to me that they believed, but at least it suggested that Chambers might have been telling the truth. It missed the root meanings of the case—the meanings that were so eloquently expressed in the Chambers autobiography, *Witness*—reducing it all to cops-and-robbers melodrama. But it did adumbrate a little of the nature of the accusing protagonist. For this, from a script approved by Alger Hiss and bearing the dubious imprimatur of PBS, we may be thankful. (pp. 56-7)

Ralph de Toledano, in a review of "Concealed Enemies," in National Review, *Vol. XXXVI, No. 11, June 15, 1984, pp. 56-7.*

LEO SAUVAGE

In a season that is on the way to leaving its mark as one of the least creative in New York theater history, Hugh Whitemore's *Pack of Lies* . . . is a welcome interruption. Although theme and development are badly shaken toward the end by two unnecessary—and therefore particularly irritating—digressions into hackneyed magazine realism, the British import retains a substantial amount of truth.

It concerns the Jacksons and the Krogers, neighbors in the middle-class London suburb of Ruislip. On our side of the stage we have Bob and Barbara Jackson . . . with their daughter Julie. . . . Peter and Helen Kroger . . . , a Canadian couple, moved in about five years ago across the street. . . . The two families have become best friends. . . . The Krogers—most often Helen—drop in frequently at the Jacksons, who are seldom invited to reverse the situation. Because Peter works at home and visitors may disturb him, the Jacksons find nothing odd about this. At least not until the day a certain Mr. Stewart . . . makes his appearance and Barbara starts thinking about coincidences.

Mr. Stewart looks as though he worked for British Intelligence, and he does. . . . Stewart asks for permission to station a female agent at the window of Julie's room. . . . The Jacksons don't like the idea of having a stranger in their house all day, even a woman. Yet they are good citizens, Bob is a kind of civil servant, and Stewart says it is important. . . .

Pack of Lies should not be viewed as simply a spy story, however. Its strength derives from probing friendship and friendship betrayed. Barbara Jackson will be increasingly upset not by hearsay or neighborly domestic quarrels or the perfidious insinuations of an Iago named Stewart, but by the dawning of an unbelievable, morally repugnant truth and her own response to it. Since no suspense is involved, it may be revealed that the Krogers turn out to be Soviet spies and, incidentally, are Americans rather than Canadians. They have told a great many lies about themselves. Does this mean their friendship is made of lies too?

Barbara cannot bear the very idea that Helen's seemingly openhearted relations with her and displays of fondness for Julie could be insincere. . . . She feels betrayed and at the same time sees herself as a betrayer.

Indeed, in her eyes the real liar of *Pack of Lies* is Barbara Jackson. Having agreed to pretend nothing has changed, she is distressed to the point of physical illness by each little step forward in the investigation. She wonders whether Helen is hiding as much as she herself is at this point. After all, the Krogers' lies did not necessarily cancel the possibility of genuine affection. Nor had they exploited their British friends in Ruislip for their spying purposes. . . .

[Stewart] too, though, leaves open the possibility that the Krogers might not have been feigning their love for Barbara, Julie and Bob. That merely further agitates Barbara. She doesn't like people spying for the Russians, of course, but it isn't hatred of these unmasked enemies that is breaking her heart. (p. 18)

About two thirds of *Pack of Lies* is an impressive drama using the Jacksons' discovery that the Krogers are enemy spies as background for the classical problems of friendship. I have rarely witnessed such a deep silence for so long in a theater: Nobody coughed, nobody shifted in his seat, dropped anything, unwrapped a candy. . . .

Where Whitemore went wrong, breaking the tension and spoiling the impact, was in suddenly deciding to switch the focus to the motivations of his spies in two superficial monologues. These lower the play to the level of cheap clichés. . . .

What a pity Whitemore made the shift. As the play goes on it dissolves into undramatic bits of what the *Playbill* tells us are true events of 1960-61. The playwright, we are further told, planned a so-called docudrama, something he is clearly not very good at. Implausibilities that might be ignored in a psychological context are weaknesses in a spy story. . . .

In addition, it stretches the imagination to have a British couple sufficiently impressed with the country's security service to let agents stay for weeks in the family castle. That would be unlikely if there were a good reason for the continued surveillance, and there isn't. One of the two security people sees the man she is looking for enter the Krogers' home the very first weekend. . . . We are left to guess what agents Thelma . . . and Sally . . . are watching for over the following weeks. . . . (p. 19)

Leo Sauvage, "Pick of the Pack," in The New Leader, *Vol. LXVIII, No. 1, January 14-28, 1985, pp. 18-19.**

CLIVE BARNES

Hugh Whitemore's absolutely engrossing play [*Pack of Lies*] is based on a true spy story that rocked Britain in 1960. . . .

Whitemore unfolds his play with the matter-of-fact lack of ceremony of a documentary—which, in unimportant part, it is. But he permits his central characters explanatory monologues during the action, which adds a depth of reality to the play's naturalism.

It helps show the characters and illustrates Whitemore's theme of very ordinary people placed under extraordinary and unforeseen stress. A stress impossible to rationalize in terms of duty or patriotism. And a stress so historically irrelevant that virtually no one reading the newspaper story of the spy-bust would give it even a casual first thought, let alone a second one.

Whitemore has a neat hand with unvarnished dialogue that has the voiceprints of actuality to it. . . .

It is amazing how well *Pack of Lies* holds the interest, even though you know the outcome, there is no mystery, and scarcely any suspense.

But it has ordinary people going about their extraordinary business caught perfectly in the focus of a play's prism. And that, and that alone, is much more than enough for an evening of dynamic theater.

Clive Barnes, "'Pack of Lies' Revives Broadway," in New York Post, *February 12, 1985. Reprinted in* New York Theatre Critics' Reviews, *Vol. XXXXVI, No. 2, Week of February 4, 1985, p. 380.*

FRANK RICH

[*Pack of Lies*] tells a cold war spy story about KGB agents and purloined NATO secrets, but its author won't settle for entertaining the audience with anything as trivial as a suspense yarn. This is a play about the morality of lying, not the theatrics of espionage, and, in Mr. Whitemore's view, lying is a virulent disease that saps patriots and traitors alike of their humanity.

The playwright, who has the aspirations but not the skills of a Graham Greene or John LeCarré, may be too high-minded for his own good. *Pack of Lies* . . . comes across as a terribly polite English attempt at a Lillian Hellman melodrama; it's too flimsy and low-keyed to support its weighty polemical message and yet too pretentious to cover its ideological bets with cheap cloak-and-dagger thrills. . . .

[There] are dull stretches to go along with the script's gaping substantive loopholes. In Act 1, the author takes far too long to establish both his story and the humdrum domestic atmosphere: The play only perks up when the actors periodically double as narrators to provide the plot and character exposition that is lacking in the innocuous scenes proper. Mr. Whitemore further uses these monologues to elevate the play's flat language—often by tossing in fruitily portentous descriptions of the weather in which, for dramatic purposes, a rainstorm can be likened to "the end of the world."

Mr. Whitemore—who wrote *Concealed Enemies,* last year's television mini-series about Alger Hiss—also cuts important dramatic corners. No matter how many times we're told that the Jacksons and Krogers are close friends, that friendship is never credibly conveyed on stage: There's so little intimacy between the couples to start with that we're not as jolted as we should be when that intimacy proves a sham.

Nor is there any reason . . . for Mr. Whitemore's failure to take us into the Krogers' living room. We're easily as curious about their private conflicts as we are about the Jacksons': Surely they have paid their own price for betraying friends and country. But the spies' behavior is explained (and, by default, condoned) only by a single, last-minute biographical paragraph invoking such inevitable buzz words as "the Depression" and "the Rosenbergs."

By caricaturing history so glibly, Mr. Whitemore completely abdicates his intellectual authority to argue or substantiate his case that, as Barbara eventually puts it, informing on spies is "the same rotten game" as spying itself. Like so many other docudramas, *Pack of Lies* is a pack of simple, appealing half-truths—elevated by honest, high-powered actors to the persuasiveness of fact.

Frank Rich, "'Pack of Lies' at the Royale," in The New York Times, *February 12, 1985, p. C13.*

PAUL BERMAN

The line that naturally comes to mind in [connection with *Pack of Lies*] . . . is E. M. Forster's "If I had to choose between betraying my country and betraying my friend, I hope I should have the guts to betray my country." That line has a nice ring. It cuts through a lot of pious cant about service to country.

But as a general proposition on betrayal, it is, to anyone not an aristocrat or a Mafioso, unacceptable. . . . The rest of us think there's more to like than the well-being of one's little social group. Our loyalties are broader, and since loyalties sometimes conflict, we know that in certain extreme circumstances personal betrayals are unavoidable.

The point has often been made on stage. The doctrine of moral relativity—the idea that moral commitments are never absolute (except rhetorically) but always depend in the last analysis on circumstances—was for many years a favorite theatrical theme, especially among left-wing playwrights. Bertolt Brecht used it in *The Measures Taken,* where he showed that the earnest young comrade must be cruelly betrayed in the higher interest of the Chinese Revolution. Clifford Odets did something similar in *Till the Day I Die,* where the fine young husband must be falsely denounced and driven to his death in the interest of the anti-Nazi resistance. Likewise Lillian Hellman in *Watch on the Rhine.* These plays are, it's true, faintly malodorous in retrospect. . . . One might even describe the plays I've cited as morality tales for a movement devoted to amorality. But that's a historical note. Brushing history aside, considering merely what the plays show on stage, the argument they make is unimpeachable.

What, then, are the circumstances that can justify personal betrayal? Brecht, Odets and Hellman supply an adequate answer. Betrayal requires two conditions to be justified. The first touches the outside world. There must be an extreme social crisis. . . . The second condition touches the betrayer's inner thoughts. His eyes must be open: blind stabs can never be justified morally, even if for some reason they accomplish a useful task. A justified betrayer must recognize the enormity of the social crisis; his political understanding must be large. And he must recognize the enormity of his betrayal; his moral understanding must be equally large. He must recognize that he himself, having violated simple laws of decency, will never be the same. . . . He must accept this consciously. He must, in short, be a great person, equal to the tragedies that history imposes. If he is anything less than great, if in any way his understanding and motives prove less than exemplary, then his act will be repulsive, and nothing but repulsive. (pp. 343-44)

The Jacksons in *Pack of Lies* are hardly great, and Whitemore didn't mean to make them so. He meant to show that they were victims of police manipulation or perhaps that fate is unkind. The smooth-talking police official manages to get them to avoid questioning what they are doing for weeks on end. The political issues—whether danger comes more from Scotland Yard or from Soviet spies, the duty of standing by the state versus the duty of not standing by the state—are never discussed, or only perfunctorily so. . . . Gradually Mrs. Jackson does grasp the repugnant aspect of betraying her friends and begins to feel sick about it. Chitchat between her and Mrs. Kroger becomes uncomfortable, then unbearable. But the die is cast. What you are meant to feel by the end of the play, I think, is empathy for Mrs. Jackson, who has been so cruelly used by Scotland Yard, and indignation that the police would do such things—even if such things were unavoidable.

But what kind of person could respond this way? My indignation was at the Jacksons. They don't have to submit. They could throw the police out and inform their friends; or they could think the cold war through and embrace patriotic duty with a full sense of the accompanying tragedy. They could act; but they don't act, they temporize; and since temporizing means mindless betrayal of friends through obedience to the state, they emerge as repulsive from the start, far more repulsive than Whitemore seems to know. He seems to think the situation is ambiguous—when it's merely complicated. As for shifting blame to the police, this strikes me as a kind of cowardice. Police are always heartless. That doesn't excuse anyone.

Whitemore does no better with the Krogers. These people live a life of betrayal. They betray Britain to the Soviet Union, and in a fashion they betray the Jacksons, as Mrs. Jackson observes, since the Jacksons would never have struck up a neighborly intimacy if they'd known about the radio transmitter in the basement and what was happening to British submarine secrets there. What, then, are the moral parameters from the Krogers' point of view? Surely these people claim a justification. Their motive might be deep sympathy with the victims of economic exploitation, which might impel them to serve the Soviet Union, thinking that Soviet communism represents justice. The motive might be fear of the K.G.B. Having worked for the K.G.B. before, in America, they might now find a K.G.B. gun to their heads and have to dance as they are told. The play in fact cites both motives. But it never evokes the appropriate feelings. You don't tremble with fear for the Krogers, nor do you tremble with solidarity for the Soviet Union. You merely watch these motives get pushed around like pieces on a chessboard. The whole point about complicated questions of loyalty and betrayal is that one must understand through the heart. But the heart in *Pack of Lies* isn't big enough to take in the Krogers. So the Krogers, too, emerge as cheap people, engaged in large betrayals without adequate justification and without sufficient understanding from the playwright.

What is it about these espionage cases of a generation ago that brings out the smallness in people, the shying away from truth? The early cold war period was a small, cursed era. *Pack of Lies* was written with decent intentions but manages only to be faithful to that small, cursed quality. The Kroger case was a footnote to the Rosenberg case, and the Kroger play turns out to be almost a footnote to the Rosenberg debate—almost as mean, almost as nasty. (p. 344)

[A] play that could explain why people like the Krogers might have wanted to support the Soviets, and how they might have got involved in espionage, and been caught, and ruined their lives serving a Soviet tyranny that was nothing like the vision of social justice they started out to serve, how the betrayers were betrayed, and how not only they but the people around them were destroyed in the aftermath of those benighted decisions and events—*that* would be a play. Audiences would flock to a work like that. The balconies would fill with people weeping their eyes out and thinking hard thoughts—not softheaded easy ones—about morality and treachery. (pp. 344-45)

Paul Berman, in a review of "Pack of Lies," in The Nation, *Vol. 240, No. 11, March 23, 1985, pp. 343-45.*

Elie(zer) Wiesel

1928-

Rumanian-born American novelist, memoirist, journalist, short story writer, essayist, and dramatist.

Among the most important authors of Holocaust literature, Wiesel is also considered an eloquent spokesman for contemporary Judaism. Through his fiction, prose poems, essays, and dramas, he has attempted to reconcile the evil of Nazi Germany and the apparent indifference of God, thereby reaffirming his life and faith. His novels, written chiefly in French in a highly lyrical, impressionistic prose style, frequently juxtapose past and present to examine the effects of the Nazi horror on the Jew. Although Wiesel's stories and essays focus upon seemingly exclusive Judaic concerns and issues, many critics contend that their relevance lies in his ability to speak all persecuted people and, by extension, for humanity itself. Daniel Stern stated, "not since Albert Camus has there been such an eloquent spokesman for man."

Wiesel was fifteen years old when he and his family were sent to the Auschwitz concentration camp. He was almost seventeen when he exited the Buchenwald camp; his parents and younger sister did not survive. For ten years Wiesel vowed silence, finding the experience incomprehensible and language insufficient to convey its brutal significance. Wiesel lived in France after the war, studying at the Sorbonne and working as a journalist for several French newspapers. In 1954, inspired by French novelist François Mauriac, Wiesel determined to confront his past, to "bear witness" for the Holocaust's silenced dead, and to post his experience as a warning to all future generations. His memoir-novel *Un di velt hot geshvign* (1956) became, in its shorter French form, *La nuit* (1958; *Night*). The book is a powerful account of Wiesel's death-camp experiences and of his destroyed faith in God. Wiesel's ensuing novels explore fate and the effect of the Holocaust upon present experience. Their characters, like Wiesel himself, seek to cull some meaning from a senseless, absurd past and to regain their faith in God and humanity. *L'aube* (1961; *Dawn*) concerns a young Jewish terrorist who executes a British soldier during the struggle for Jewish independence in Palestine but discovers that he has forsaken his innocence and religious ideals forever. In the strongly autobiographical *Le jour* (1961; *The Accident),* an Israeli foreign correspondent who is nearly killed by a taxi gradually realizes that his subconscious guilt over surviving other victims of the Holocaust has led him to seek his own death.

Wiesel's later novels elaborate on his themes of self-discovery, moral choice, and the idea of an absurd and unjust God. In *La ville de la chance* (1962; *The Town Beyond the Wall*), a confused Jewish Holocaust survivor penetrates the Hungarian Iron Curtain to confront an indifferent ex-Nazi guard from his past before deciding that revenge and madness are merely escapes from moral responsibility. In *Les portes de la forêt* (1964; *The Gates of the Forest),* a Jewish refugee similarly rediscovers his faith amidst quiet episodes in America and violent partisan struggles in his native Hungary. *Le testament d'un poéte Juif assassiné* (1981; *The Testament*) concerns a Russo-Jewish writer who realizes, as he is about to die in the Stalinist purge of 1952, that he has misplaced his faith in God by blindly

© Jerry Bauer

supporting the Soviet cause. Wiesel's recent novel *Le cinquieme fils* (1984; *The Fifth Son*) is about a young American who travels to Europe to kill a sadistic ex-Nazi officer whom his father mistakenly believed he had executed following the war. The young man finds himself unable to kill his father's persecutor, however, when he is confronted with the man's incomprehension and lack of an explanation for his deeds. Wiesel's mythopoeic dramas *Zalmen; ou la folie de Dieu* (1966; *Zalmen, or the Madness of God*) and *Le proces de Shamgorod* (1979; *The Trial of God*) address the notion of a cruel and unjust God and weigh human responsibility for God's judgments.

In the mid-1960s Wiesel extended his commitment to speak for victims of the Holocaust by focusing on contemporary Jewish victims of oppression in his nonfiction. *Le Juifs du silence* (1966; *The Jews of Silence*) is both an eyewitness report of Jewish persecution in the Soviet Union and a plea for global Jewish solidarity. Wiesel further examines the political and moral effects of world apathy upon today's oppressed people in stories and autobiographical fragments collected in *Le chant des morts* (1966; *Legends of Our Time*) and *Entre deux soleils* (1970; *One Generation After*). Although Wiesel states in the former book that "Nothing has been learned, Auschwitz has not even served as a warning," he also emphasizes the need for the modern Jew to "impose a meaning on what perhaps has none and draw ecstasy from nameless, faceless pain.'' This idea is again explored in *Un Juif aujourd'hui* (1976; *A Jew Today*), a collection of autobiographical sketches, essays, and dialogues in which Wiesel expresses shame for the past and a cautious hope for the future. To be a Jew today, Wiesel insists, implies a sense of historical consciousness and a need to keep ''singing . . . louder and louder.'' Wiesel has addressed similarly affirmative aspects of Judaism through his humanistic examinations of Jewish biblical figures and legends. Beginning with *Célébration hassidique: Portraits et légendes* (1972; *Souls on Fire*), Wiesel expounds on his belief that Hasidism's modern relevance lies in its example of how to live joyfully in an incomprehensible and absurd universe. Ensuing collections of Wiesel's biblical portraits, based on lectures delivered at various international universities, include *Four Hasidic Masters and Their Struggle Against Melancholy* (1978), *Five Biblical Figures* (1981), and *Somewhere a Master* (1982).

Wiesel's work often generates disagreement among critics. While some reviewers consider his plots and characters mere vehicles for rhetorical concerns and question whether his fiction is art or polemic, others praise his sensitive insight into human behavior, his moral candor, and his ability to objectively examine the Holocaust and its effect upon modern Jewish thought. Despite the range of critical opinion, Wiesel's fiction is widely regarded as among the most passionate and powerful of all Holocaust writing.

(See also *CLC*, Vols. 3, 5, 11; *Contemporary Issues Criticism*, Vol. 1; *Contemporary Authors*, Vols. 5-8, rev. ed.; and *Contemporary Authors New Revision Series*, Vol. 8.)

LAWRENCE L. LANGER

Although Elie Wiesel has announced many times in recent years that he is finished with the Holocaust as a subject for public discourse, it is clear from his latest book, *A Jew Today,* that the Holocaust has not yet finished with him. Almost from his first volume to his last, his writing has been an act of homage, a ritual of remembrance in response to a dreadful challenge ''to unite the language of man with the silence of the dead.''. . .

The essays, diary excerpts, dialogues, letters and legends in *A Jew Today*—following the pattern of the earlier *One Generation After*—are loosely linked excursions into memory and the contemporary scene. The past of Auschwitz casts its shadow over discussions of starvation in Biafra, apartheid in South Africa, and Israel's defensive wars. Is the world's indifference *then* a reminder or precedent for the world's behavior *now?* Is Wiesel foolish to take so seriously Solzhenitsyn's bizarre conclusion in the Gulag volumes that Hitler was more moderate than Stalin, the NKVD crueler than the Gestapo, the Nazi murder of six million Jews less significant than Stalin's massacre of 20 million of his own people? Is he correct in supposing that the crank efforts to discredit the Holocaust (by arguing that it never happened) represent a prelude to attacks on remembrance itself?

Certainly his alarm is genuine, though here and there it may be misplaced. How many human beings will ever believe—Wiesel says many already do—that ''the death factories never existed. . .?'' How persuasive is his argument that the ''professor or shopkeeper who disregarded facts and warnings and clung to illusion, refusing to admit that people could so succumb to degradation'' were really engaged in a form of resistance? If the state of Israel had disregarded similar ''facts and warnings'' in recent decades, it would have sealed its doom.

Refusal to see reality and life through the enemy's eyes may seem a victory in retrospect, but amidst present dangers would it not make potential victims more vulnerable once again?

If Elie Wiesel returns compulsively to the ruins of the Holocaust world, it is not because he has nothing new to say. His grandfather Dodye Feig, the French Catholic novelist Francois Mauriac . . . , his birthplace Sighet—we have met them all before, in talks, fugitive essays, earlier writings. Somehow the mind is not disturbed by a sense of *deja vu*, but rather startled by Wiesel's need to keep alive a part of himself that will always be a stranger to the world he inhabits now. . . . Although he knows that only madness lies at the end of the journey leading him once more back to Sighet, he still returns, accompanied by his wife and a television crew, to film the pilgrimage. What it does for him is a mystery; what it does for us is to verify, lest we forget, that once there was a Jewish past that is no more, and that there are moments when futile gestures to recapture it are as necessary and meaningful as sensible efforts to create the future.

In *A Jew Today,* Wiesel maintains a fragile balance between the two worlds: pride in the Jewish future—pride . . . in the human future, for which Jewish destiny in the 20th century is a paradigm—and despair at the Jewish past (which of course is also our human past). He dramatizes the dilemma of fashioning a possible future out of an impossible past. . . .

In three brief dialogues called ''**A Father and His Son**,'' ''**A Mother and Her Daughter**,'' and ''**A Man and His Little Sister**,'' . . . we get a glimpse of the painful truth that survival may not be the supreme blessing after all, and that those who were left ''behind'' still possess the power to summon the survivor back into the realm of night. The dialogues typify language's attempt to solace memory, arrest extinction, preserve in a frozen moment of literary time images of a ruined past. We are silent partners at this verbal ritual to rescue from oblivion the uncompleted lives of a mother, father, and sister who did not survive but left a heritage of unforgettable anguish for the son and brother who did.

Although if we were to select a single word to describe the tone that pervades many of the essays in *A Jew Today* we would have to choose ''melancholy,'' Wiesel still manages to face the human condition with the resilience of hope. Despair would be a profanation of the dead. Despite a past that evokes remorse and a future that invites anguish, says Wiesel, Jews must continue to sing. To celebrate the endurance of the Jew, to chronicle his sadness, to awaken once more memories of the Holocaust that mocked the one and fertilized the other unto eternity—these are some of the mingled motives that animate the spirit of Wiesel's volume and endow it with life.

> Lawrence L. Langer, *''The Inescapable Anguish,''* in Book World—The Washington Post, *October 29, 1978, p. 3E.*

ALEXANDRA JOHNSON

In his newest book [*A Jew Today*], a compendium of essays, dialogues and portraits, Wiesel confirms his unusual place as our most eloquent if prolific writer on silence. This paradox is history's, not his. Its roots lie coiled in the ashes of the holocaust through which Wiesel survived as an adolescent. As an adult it burdened him with the survivor's dilemma. Should one speak, recount, warn? Can one? And if so, how?

Intrinsic to every one of his books is this moral issue. To bear witness is both imperative and impossible. "Should one shout, or whisper?" How can one relate what transformed a young Hungarian boy for whom "all things seemed simple and miraculous" to a countryless adult. . . ?

For Wiesel such questions . . . cut so deeply that he vowed silence over them. For 10 years. To render explanation, however inchoate, was impossible. Language was simply inadequate. Metaphor profaned the dead and blasphemed the living. The holocaust, unlike words, was not an approximation. Silence, then, became the survivor's dark eloquence.

One of the most powerful essays in this collection describes how his own silence was shattered. In 1954, Wiesel . . . interviewed the august French writer François Mauriac. Unexpectedly pitted in heated discussion over the holocaust, Mauriac chided him, "You are wrong not to speak." One year later, Wiesel sent him the completed manuscript of his first novel, *Night*. A lexicon for the living had been invented.

"An Interview Unlike Any Other" is just that. In six pages it evokes a scene of almost Biblical magnitude. With chilling clarity Wiesel underlines the abyss that separates, perhaps irrevocably, the survivor's experience from the rest of humanity's. Yet what surfaces here is the fierce concern, the common humanity that unites and ultimately transcends the distance that yawns between the old Catholic and the young Jew.

Such an essay is emblematic of Wiesel's ability to summon the universal point out of the deeply partisan problem. In this current collection he broadens his subject matter even further. Cutting across cultural lines, he investigates racism in South Africa, famine in Biafra, terrorism in the Middle East, and fiction in the Soviet Union.

The core of his collection, though, is a philosophical meditation on Jewish identity. For him, to be a Jew is, foremost, to be possessed of a historical consciousness. . . . To understand the past is to safeguard the present. . . .

Moreover, to be Jewish "means asserting spirituality in a world that denies spirituality; it means singing ... louder and louder." For Wiesel's Jew "his mission was never to make the world Jewish but, rather, to make it more human." . . .

Writing is Wiesel's means of affirming life even if it means recounting all that conspires against it. Aware of his duty to testify accurately, he developed a style that adheres rigorously to its message. For the survivor, style *is* substance. . . .

Wiesel's most ardent theme [is] the culpability of the passive. To witness is to participate; to participate is to condone. If incuriosity was for Swift society's worst vice, then for Wiesel it's indifference. The latter, he notes, is love's opposite, not hate. Thus, if survivors "had the strength to write those words, we must have the strength to read them."

Indeed, to understand Jewish history is to begin to see its parallels in today's world. . . . Today's lesson is still that of Cain and Abel: to kill another is to kill part of oneself. To persecute one segment of society is to undermine it altogether.

A Jew Today is an excellent introduction to Wiesel's life and work. For those intimate with his writing, it represents a rich reworking of themes, a rich testimony of conscience. Throughout the moral exposition and historical reflection, one can quite literally hear a human voice. It is the voice that throughout all Wiesel's work continues the questions and deepens the answers.

Alexandra Johnson, "Holocaust: The Silence Screams," in The Christian Science Monitor, *November 22, 1978, p. 21.*

MAYO MOHS

Just about everyone is stung in [*A Jew Today*]. American Jews for not shouting loud enough when they knew what was happening in Hitler's concentration camps; European Christians for standing idly by or keeping silent against the encircling terror. Even God is indicted. The tone echoes an ancient Jewish tradition, epitomized in the fiercely mystical Hasidic teachers whose stories Wiesel tells so well, men taking issue with the Master when the universe is out of joint. . . .

In his books and in the essays, letters and diary excerpts that make up this new volume, the Holocaust haunts every word. Wiesel's special accomplishment is that he has assigned himself the excruciating role of witness to the century's great crime without losing his hold on sanity and compassion.

The author is at his best in a section titled "Legends of Today." The parables are brief, ironic and heartbreaking. Here is one prisoner refusing the demand of a German officer to revile Jehovah. . . . There are other more pitiful tales: the family that can hide only one child safely, and must choose which one. Or a girl in a schoolroom, asking if there is no excuse, no mitigating evidence, for the Jewish Kapos in the camps: "Is there nothing, nothing at all to be said on behalf of my father?"

The diary excerpts reveal the breadth of Wiesel's concern. He mourns the death of Biafra and the extermination of an Indian tribe in Paraguay, confessing that his own indifference has made him an accomplice. He recognizes South Africa's enduring loyalty to Israel, but scorns apartheid and sides with the rebels of Soweto. In a selection of letters, though, he is less successful. One, to a young Palestinian Arab, expresses empathy, but then proceeds to lecture the young Arab on Jewish suffering and Arab terror, never mentioning the sometimes disproportionate Israeli reprisals.

Wiesel's hottest outrage is reserved for the so-called scholarship of revisionists who call the Holocaust a myth, or in the words of Northwestern Professor Arthur Butz, "the hoax of the century." Replies Wiesel: "Where has a people disappeared? Where are they hiding?" In fury, he asks why academics have not boycotted Butz and why students have not walked out on his classes.

In fact, there seems little danger that such revisionists will be taken seriously. . . . While Elie Wiesel lives and writes, there will be no rest for the wicked, the uncaring or anyone else.

Mayo Mohs, "Jeremiah II," in Time, *Vol. 112, No. 26, December 25, 1978, p. 81.*

JACK RIEMER

It must have been such a remarkable scene when these lectures [collected in *Four Hasidic Masters and Their Struggle Against Melancholy*] were given at Notre Dame. On the platform Elie Wiesel, scion of Viznitz, who but for the Holocaust would have probably lived out his years in the village of Sighet. And in the audience priests and nuns who had probably never heard of Naftali of Ropshitz or Pinchas of Koretz or any of these figures that Wiesel brings to life in these lectures. (p. 316)

What exactly are these lectures? They are not formal factual discourses, although they are obviously the product of much learning and of first-hand acquaintance with the primary sources. They are essentially the retelling of a saga and the recreation of a special moment in Jewish history, a moment in which a corps of charismatic people rose to heights of friendship and concern for each other, for their disciples, and for the world that is rare.

"Friendship" and "concern" are the key motifs of this book. For Wiesel, Hasidism is not a theology or a philosophy. It is not an abstract system of ideas or a conception of the Deity. It is a friendship and a concern for people and for God. Hasidism is the opposite of solitude. It is a sense of being bound up together with all other human beings in their joy and in their distress and of being bound up with God in his joy and in his distress.

At the heart of Hasidism was this kinship, this relationship between Rebbe and disciple, a relationship in which each affected the other. The Rebbe gave hope and spirit and meaning out of his heart to his people, but there were more of them than there were of him, and they wore away at his spirit as much as or more than he uplifted theirs. And so these men who could move others to joy were themselves stricken with melancholy. (pp. 316-17)

The story with which this book begins sets the tone for all that follows. A disciple once came to Pinchas of Koretz and begged for help. The disciple confessed that his world was filled with turmoil and sadness, that all words seemed empty, all men seemed bestial, all life seemed dull. He pleaded with the Rebbe to tell him what to do.

"Go and study," said the Rebbe. "It is the only remedy I know. Torah contains all the answers. Torah *is* the answer."

"Woe unto me," said the disciple, "I *can't* study. So shaky are my foundations, so all-pervasive are my doubts that my mind finds no anchor. I open the Talmud and contemplate it but aimlessly. I remain riveted to the same page, to the same problem. What must I do, Rebbe, what must I do?"

When a Jew can provide no answer, he at least has a tale to share. And so Rebbe Pinhas of Koretz invited the student to come closer, and then said with a smile: "Know, my young friend, that what is happening to you also happened to me. When I was your age I stumbled over the same obstacles. I, too, was filled with doubts and questions. I wallowed in doubt, I was locked in despair. I tried study, prayer, meditation—in vain. I tried penitence, solitude, silence—in vain. Then one day I learned that Rebbe Israel Baal Shem Tov would be coming to our town. Curiosity led me to the place where he was receiving his followers. When I entered he was just finishing his prayers. He turned around and saw me, and I was convinced that he was seeing me, me and no one else—but so was everyone else in the room. The intensity of his gaze overwhelmed me, and I felt less alone. And strangely, I was able to go home, to open the Talmud, and to plunge into my studies once more. You see," said Rebbe Pinhas of Koretz, "the questions remained questions, but I was able to go on . . ."

And then Wiesel explains the tale in words that are a succinct summary of what Hasidism is all about: "What did Pinhas of Koretz try to teach his young visitor? One: not to give up; even if some questions are without answers, to go on asking them just the same. Two: one must not think that one is alone and that one's inner tragedy is exclusively one's own, others have

gone through the same sorrow and endured the same anguish. Three: one must know where to look and to whom. Four: God is everywhere, even in pain, even in the search for faith. Five: a good story in Hasidism is not about miracles, but about friendship and hope—the greatest miracles of all."

I like that last sentence for its gentle irony and its truth. It seems to be a put-down of miracles which so many think is what Hasidism was all about. But then it turns out to be an affirmation of friendship and hope, which are the real core of Hasidism, and which are also miracles, perhaps the greatest miracles of all. (p. 317)

[As] Elie Wiesel demonstrated at Notre Dame, and as is becoming more and more clear to . . . a society such as ours that is so fragmented, that needs so much to create a sense of community, . . . to a society that is able to set foot on the moon but does not know how to lift a head up from the ground, to such a society the story of Hasidism and its efforts to give man dignity and joy and purpose on this planet speaks with power and with relevance. (p. 318)

Jack Riemer, "Miracle of Friendship & Hope," in Commonweal, Vol. CVI, No. 10, May 25, 1979, pp. 316-18.

LOTHAR KAHN

Wiesel's one previous attempt at theatre, *Zalmen ou la folie de Dieu,* was marred by excessive verbosity and lack of dramatic intensity. These flaws, while still faintly discernible, are no longer disturbing in this newest work [*Le procès de Shamgorod*]. . . . As in nearly all of his books since *Night,* which dwelled on the horrors themselves, Wiesel continues the survivor's dialogue with God. To be more precise, the survivor of Shamgorod insists on a *trial* of God.

In this play, set in an East European town on 25 February 1649—the eve of the festival of Purim—three Purim "players" arrive at the inn of Shamgorod, expecting to perform the traditional Purim play for the Jews of the town. Alas, they have all been slaughtered in a recent pogrom—all, that is, but the innkeeper and his daughter, who has lost her sanity. . . . [Into] the inn steps the village priest, now to proselytize, now to warn that the innkeeper and his guests must flee. But the innkeeper will not be dissuaded from conducting the trial [of God]. All roles for the trial are filled but that of "defender of God." An outsider appears and volunteers for the part. Only near the end is his identity revealed—the defender turns out to be Satan.

This is an intellectually stimulating, provocative play, daring in its conception, imaginative in its execution. It is also a moving play. This historical distancing of the Holocaust and resulting trial of God may be the most impressive effort by Wiesel since *The Gates of the Forest.*

Lothar Kahn, in a review of "Le procès de Shamgorod," in World Literature Today, Vol. 53, No. 3, Summer, 1979, p. 553.

HARRY JAMES CARGAS

Terrifying. That's the only way to describe the new play [*The Trial of God*] by Elie Wiesel. The effect of this drama is to shame us all. If now, after all that we know about the Holocaust, we can still be fooled by Satan regarding that tragic event, how would we have behaved in the midst of the Nazi era?

The plot is set in 1649: a Jewish innkeeper and three wandering Jewish minstrels decide to put God on trial because of the massacre of their people in a pogrom. The time is the feast of Purim, and an air of unreality pervades. Songs are sung, masks are worn—but an atmosphere of doom touches all.

The trial cannot proceed, however, until a defense attorney is found. It will not be easy to defend an apparently indifferent, perhaps even hostile Creator. Eventually, a stranger named Sam eagerly accepts the role. Sam is skillful and manipulative. He blames humans for the crime and finds God blameless. He suggests that the dead might be grateful for a quick release from this terrible earth.... Sam insists that faith must be boundless; the task of humans is to glorify, not judge, God.

Only in the end do we learn for certain that Sam is Satan; we remember that it is Purim, Sam has worn a mask and we have been deceived—too easily.... [We] are easily victimized by Wiesel, and this powerful drama ought to teach us something valuable about ourselves. (p. 803)

> *Harry James Cargas, "Wiesel's Genius," in* The Christian Century, *Vol. XCVI, No. 26, August 15-22, 1979, pp. 803-04.*

D. M. THOMAS

In this austere, uncomfortable novel [*The Testament*], Elie Wiesel relates a 20th-century Jewish odyssey. Born in Russia before the Revolution, Paltiel Kossover becomes a poet and a Communist. To the grief of his Orthodox Jewish parents, he travels to Western Europe to serve his new faith. He is in Germany at the sickening moment when it becomes clear that its people are turning to fascism and anti-Semitism; he escapes to the turbulent political debates of Paris. He has a brief, moving interlude in Palestine, carrying out a secret mission. Wherever he goes he takes his phylacteries and his Jewish learning, like a burdensome suitcase that just *might* be useful. He experiences the brotherhood, misery and disillusionment of the Spanish Civil War; then returns to France.

When Nazism threatens that country, he makes his way uncertainly back to the Soviet Union. He welcomes the outbreak of war against Hitler joyfully.... After the victory, Kossover becomes a card-carrying member of the party, his poetry is published, his reputation flourishes, he marries and has a son. In 1952 he is arrested, in Stalin's sudden turning against the Jews. Like the real-life Jewish poets, he is shot—in the town of his birth. His odyssey is over.

Unlike Odysseus, but like the real Jewish poets, and millions of humbler Jews in our time, he is expunged from the record. Even his death is wiped out. Or so it seems. But there is a testament, and a witness. Kossover's interrogator, despairing of extracting evidence from him by torture, encourages him to write his autobiography. No poet could resist such a clever ploy. Kossover, recanting his apostasy, denounces the false religion of communism, and places himself firmly back in the Judaic fold. It is all, of course, excellent evidence against him. The poet's uncomfortable truths will never see the light of day; they will die with him. Except that the hidden stenographer becomes moved by the prisoner's words, and resolves to keep them alive. Years later he passes the testament on to Kossover's son, Grisha. Grisha, who is a mute, has arrived in the new state of Israel. In fragments interwoven with the testament itself, we see him beginning his new life and learning to know his father.

For us—reading over his shoulder, as it were—the testament of the fictional poet is clearly intended by the author to carry a representative authority. Kossover's is the voice of traditional religion, but he has also been a convert to secular religion. He is a poet, too: the voice of truth and humanity. Unfortunately, for most of the novel he does not write like a poet. The pressure of crowding in too many journeys causes the author to crowd *out* the rich complications of life and relationships; for much of the way the testament is a rather lifeless chronicle. Kossover's "burning, incandescent verses" turn out to be mediocre. The prose style strains pretentiously for effect at the most intense points....

Yet in the end, with moving unexpectedness, the dry bones live. The quickening occurs with the onset of the Second World War; and the surge of intensity in the writing may be not unconnected with the fact that Wiesel was himself a victim of the Nazis, in the concentration camps. Be that as it may, his hero and narrator suddenly begins to testify with the bleak and searing eloquence that his calling, and his situation, would seem likely to evoke. For the first time, his prison cell becomes real, instead of a fictional device for the narrative. There are wonderful, painful accounts of his attempt to save the life of a dying German soldier; of coming to the house of his parents and discovering that they have been taken off in the cattle trucks. Now, there is no straining for effect, but absolutely the right words for ultimate horror: "Between the world and myself, between my life and myself, there was this dark mass of infinite, unspeakable, tumultuous sadness; it encompassed the first man killing the last." Poems about his father do, at last, burn. The novel reaches a climax of tragic power, as the stenographer-witness describes the pre-dawn execution. In more than one sense, the author has wrested life out of death.

It is a very masculine book. The women with whom Kossover has brief, joyless affairs, and the woman he marries, are little more than shadows. The theme of father and son dominates. The absence of the feminine, together with the—more understandable—absence of lyricism and humor, makes for an uncompromisingly severe novel. There is, too, the suggestion of a "Keep Out" sign for non-Jewish readers. "Funny," observes Kossover, "everything seems to bring me back to Jewish memory." This is so apparent that it risks diminishing his universal humanity; yet there are no signs that Wiesel takes account of this.

If he intends his poet to be the Good Man, sincere even when he was misguided—and I believe he does—then it is strange that he has him *joining* the Communist Party of the Soviet Union in 1946, the year of renewed hardline persecution of writers.... *The Testament* has both the strengths and limitations of having been written from inside the Jewish consciousness. The strengths, however, are stronger than the limitations. When the author's voice, through his hero's, finally bursts into flame, lit by the ashes of the dead, it speaks with authority.

> *D. M. Thomas, "Caught in the Web of History," in* Book World—The Washington Post, *April 12, 1981, p. 1.*

JEFFREY BURKE

[Wiesel's] sixth novel, *The Oath* (1976), described a pogrom in an East European village, where the tenuous coexistence of Christian and Jew was not unlike that of Communist and Jew under Stalin.

The Testament expands on a brief episode in *The Oath,* whose narrator, Azriel, a survivor of a pogrom, is recruited by a Jewish agent of the Comintern to promulgate the Communist ideal among Talmudic students. Shortly after a fierce rabbi reprimands him for forgetting that "a Jew's place is among Jews," Azriel hears that the agent has been recalled to Moscow and executed during the first purges. Doubly chastened, he abandons the revolution.

The hero of *The Testament* is a minor poet named Paltiel Kossover, a fictional victim of Stalin's purge of Russian-Jewish writers and artists on August 12, 1952. While in prison awaiting execution, Kossover writes a memoir, a "testament" of his activities for the revolution. . . . Having grown up amid religious persecution, Kossover is eager to believe the Communist propagandizing of a fellow Talmudic student whose Russia, transformed by revolution, is now "the one country where Jews feel at home and live in security." The irony of that statement comes both from Kossover himself, who is writing with hindsight in prison, and from Mr. Wiesel, who is orchestrating a dialectic between Judaism and Communism from which no synthesis will ever issue.

As he embarks on a grand tour that will take him into influential Communist-Jewish circles over the next three decades, Kossover promises his father that he "will remain a Jew" and "put on (his) phylacteries every morning." In the heady political fervor of Berlin, Paris and Barcelona, he finds his religious faith yielding more and more to the revolution.

But his religious conscience is intermittently revived by a "professor-adventurer-mystic" named David Aboulesia, who drifts into the narrative to deliver, as Kossover at one point describes them, "speeches on the apocalyptic outcome of history." Kossover's tour ends after service in the Red Army during World War II. He settles in Moscow, marries a staunch Communist and works energetically for the Party: "I found in the Communist Revolution an ideal that suited me. I was doing useful work and I was doing it as a Jew." There again is Mr. Wiesel's dialectic. Kossover is enough of a Communist to call Moscow home and enough of a Jew to be caught in Stalin's purge. Unlike Azriel, he learns his lesson too late. He writes from prison: "Truth, for a Jew, is to dwell among his brothers."

From Azriel's 10-page brush with Communism in *The Oath* to the more than 200 pages of revolutionary "testament" in this book, Mr. Wiesel has not substantially improved on his lesson, although he has woven it into a larger swatch of history. Neither the character nor the chronicle matters so much as the lesson the author derives from joining the two. And *The Testament* as a whole works not as a novel but as a contrived illustration of themes the author has treated somewhat less schematically in other books.

Alternating with sections from Kossover's narrative are episodes in the life of his son, who was an infant at the time of his father's arrest and comes to know him first through his collection of poems, *I Saw My Father in a Dream,* and eventually through the testament. Grisha Kossover grows up in Russia as one of the Jews of silence, with the additional stigma of having a "criminal" father. The boy has developed a strong attachment to his father through the book of poems, and he finds his mother's affair with a neighbor a painful betrayal. To make matters worse, the lover persistently interrogates the boy about his feelings for his father, until Grisha, in a fit of rage, bites off his own tongue.

Silence, in all of Mr. Wiesel's novels, is the legacy of the dead, whether from pogrom, holocaust or purge. . . . Grisha Kossover's muteness dramatizes the difficulty of speaking for the dead.

It is not necessary to know the author's other novels to recognize the importance of this theme. He alludes to it frequently in *The Testament.* Characters, events, at times it seems even history itself, all exist merely to make a point. Having made it, time and again, Mr. Wiesel leaves the reader little else to take from his novel.

Moreover, Mr. Wiesel must be held responsible—along with his wife, who translated the novel—for writing that slips into triteness or purple prose or redundancy. While in "the primitive jungle where anything goes," Paltiel Kossover is said to have discovered that "Inge was teaching me something else too, something better. Lucky for me." One might excuse this as Paltiel's own way of talking about sex . . . ; but it is hard to excuse "the die was cast with irrevocable certainty." (pp. 15, 35)

No one can or would deny the seriousness and necessity of Elie Wiesel's role as witness. Santayana's famous warning about those who cannot remember the past being condemned to repeat it underlies the author's work. It is natural that such a mission would remain uppermost in the writer's mind, but that the requirements of art should proportionately diminish in significance is not an acceptable corollary. *The Testament* is the most extreme example of Mr. Wiesel's tendency, evident in other novels, to sacrifice the demands of craft to those of conscience. (p. 35)

> *Jeffrey Burke, "Jews under Stalin," in* The New York Times Book Review, *April 12, 1981, pp. 15, 35.*

SHIMON WINCELBERG

Like nearly all of Wiesel's stories and novels of the past two decades, except on a more ambitious scale, *The Testament* chronicles a European Jew who tries, as a Jew, to survive in the toxic environments of the 20th century. And it does so from the vantage point of Jewish mysticism as homely and unstudied as brushing one's teeth. The characters live in a world where those in literal search of the Messiah are ordinary fellow-travelers one may encounter on a train to Paris. . . . The supernatural becomes comprehensible and necessary to us—if only we too could learn to view it through the eyes of the poet, the eccentric or the child.

Similarly, Wiesel's courage in being at times overtly sentimental reminds us that there *is* much in life to be sentimental about, that occasionally we need to let ourselves simply *feel,* without irony, without cynicism, without objectivity. Irony is what he reserves for almost casual asides: "In war, all people become Jews without realizing it." . . .

Kossover is one of the relatively minor victims of the mad and dying Stalin, who in a single day in 1952 destroyed nearly all of the Soviet Union's great Yiddish writers. "I have written this novel to restore their deaths to them and to imagine what their lives might have been," Wiesel tells us. In the process we also learn why he himself will not let go of our buttonhole. (p. 17)

Wiesel's artless art, the sheer authority of his own personality in a modest role early on, compel one to believe [*The Testa-*

ment] absolutely. While some of his previous tales may at times have lacked narrative momentum, the wonder of his company, whether as a minor protagonist or a witness or a detached narrator, has always been to make us see and feel the preciousness of life with a child's matter-of-fact anticipation of something miraculous that could happen at any moment.

There is a prologue about Kossover's mute son, whose first night in Jerusalem impels him only to sit down and write. Is he too a poet? "No, not like his father. In place of his father."

That seems to me to capture Elie Wiesel's own propulsive force. He seeks to use his talent and indeed his life to fill in for all those of our century who have been prematurely silenced. An impossible task, of course, an act of hubris, an invitation to mockery. And yet, more often than not he successfully restores a faint echo of millions of lost voices without ever exploiting either them or us. Thanks to artists like Elie Wiesel, "the dead are not mute." (p. 18)

> *Shimon Wincelberg, "Echoes of the Silenced," in*
> The New Leader, *Vol. LXIV, No. 12, June 15, 1981,*
> *pp. 17-18.*

ROBERT McAFEE BROWN

[Wiesel] was working on [*The Testament*] back in 1967 when the Six Day War disrupted his writing schedule and his life, and *A Beggar in Jerusalem* was his response to those events. There have been many intervening volumes, but *The Testament,* now published after fifteen years, may well turn out to be Wiesel's greatest work to date. (p. 226)

The Testament represents a watershed in Wiesel's writings. It is painted with a wide brush on a vast canvas. The holocaust is there—it will always be in Wiesel's writings—but so are many other things. The action covers over half a century of European history. The protagonist, Paltiel Kossover, a Russian Jew, endures a pogrom in his youth, migrates to Germany after embracing communism, flees to Paris after Hitler comes to power, works for the party in France, fights in the Spanish Civil War, is with the Russian troops in World War II, and then makes it in post-war Russian literary society as a poet. Ah, for once a Jewish success story? Not so. For Paltiel is a victim of the Stalinist purge of Jews, and the book is his "testament" before the court that will eventually be the instrument of his execution on orders from above.

It is the story of hundreds of Jewish artists in Russia since World War II. Indeed, the status of Jews in Russia has been an increasing concern of Wiesel's from *The Jews of Silence* (1966) through *Zalmen, or The Madness of God* (1974) to *The Trial of God* (1979). But it is not just the story of a ruthless state destroying a sensitive person; it is also the story of a sensitive person struggling between the claims of his Jewish faith and the idealism of his embrace of communism, attempting to put the two of them together.... As [Kossover] tells his tale, he comes to the ironic realization, "I lived a Communist and I die a Jew." ... An outer story of activity, fighting, hating and loving, is also an inner story of unbearable tensions, ideological and theological conflicts, hopes and disappointments. We are told of Paltiel's "testament" that "every word contains a hidden meaning." ... And that is true for the reader of the book that surrounds his "testament" as well. We have to deal with the observation that for a Jew to live in a Christian world is to know the meaning of fear; we have to confront what it meant, after the war, to visit Majdanek; we

have to struggle with the image of God as a "grave-digger," not, perhaps, the one who kills, but the one who is reduced to the task of rounding up and disposing of the corpses. (pp. 226-27)

So on one level it is a terrible picture that emerges, actions full of devastating consequences. And yet ... there is something else. The important thing for Wiesel is always that the story be told. He truly believes that words have power (else why would he write under such moral compulsion?). The tale must be kept alive. When it is told, it can produce change. So tyrants must always suppress the tale. The Stalinist court thought it had done so with Paltiel Kossover. The purgers would themselves be purged. Paltiel's testimony would never be read. His story would never be told. But it was. An invisible man, the court stenographer, outwitted the cunning of all the secret police. An invisible man made Paltiel visible. And he tells the story to ... a mute, Kossover's son. And Grisha Kossover, though mute, will speak. The story will live. It will be told. And it will change those who hear it.

That is our final assurance against the holocaust revisionists. They want to kill the story. They want to substitute another story, a false one, just like the Stalinist courts. But they will not succeed. That is the message of hope that informs *The Testament:* they will not succeed. A curious irony—Wiesel, who of all people would have reason to despair, becomes the one of all people most able to instill hope. (p. 227)

> *Robert McAfee Brown, "Keeping the Story Alive," in* Theology Today, *Vol. XXXVIII, No. 2, July, 1981, pp. 224-27.**

CHOICE

[In *Five Biblical Portraits,* Wiesel] confronts the biblical text as a modern: he addresses questions to the text, answers back, accepts certain lines of thought and rejects others, turns the themes around and around, and reads the texts from a cultural and sometimes very personal standpoint. Wiesel brings his own modern sensibilities to the subject; both his sense and use of narrative concision and the wealth of rabbinic commentaries that reflect earlier struggles with Saul, Jonah, Jeremiah, Elijah, and Joshua—the five personalities dealt with here.... Wiesel makes the powerful biblical individuals he treats accessible and, by rereading and meditating on them, shows how the Bible and traditional religious literature can be made personal for modern man. Only rarely does Wiesel focus on issues of the "survivor"—and, at those points, he introduces very private twists to the text. At the same time, through modulated allusions, links to contemporary political issues and events are made.

> *A review of "Five Biblical Portraits," in* Choice, *Vol. 20, No. 1, September, 1982, p. 110.*

LOTHAR KAHN

[*Contre la mélancolie: Célébration hassidique II* is a collection of] portraits of the Hasidic holy men who insisted on celebrating God and life no matter what miseries they were forced to suffer. "Man owes it to himself to refuse despair," is the saying attributed to one of Wiesel's masters. Another speaks of the need to pull joy from a seemingly endless, nameless sea of sorrow....

Wiesel assigns to each of his rabbis a *qualité maîtresse*. Thus he speaks of Rabbi Pinhas and Hasidic wisdom, of Aharon and Hasidic fervor, of Wolfe and humility, of Moshe-Leib and compassion, of Baroukh and Hasidic wrath. Within the basic unity of attitude toward life, there existed among the Hasidic leaders a large variety of personalities, philosophies, degrees of piety, originality. Wiesel characterizes their individuality and outlook through legends about them, through maxims and sayings attributed to them and through brief biographical sketches. It is easy to forget that these Hasidic rabbis, rulers over their disciples and adherents, were not European monarchs or saints or Popes, but that their domain only extended over small villages—though their fame extended far beyond them. But in Jewish history, and especially in Hasidic history, these masters were titans of the spirit and valiant fighters for the celebration of life.

To his studies, based on Yiddish and Hebrew sources, Wiesel brings the art of the novelist, his unique style that operates somehow more effectively here than in other facets of his work. The book is infinitely rich in its countless bits of wisdom, in its insights into a movement that seemed a dynamic and revolutionary force in Judaism, and in its insights into men who refused to accept melancholy, whatever life's vagaries.

> *Lothar Kahn, in a review of "Contre la mélancolie: Célébration hassidique II," in* World Literature Today, *Vol. 56, No. 4, Autumn, 1982, p. 747.*

FREDERICK A. HOMANN, S.J.

[In *Somewhere a Master: Further Hasidic Portraits and Legends*] we have Hasidic story, tales of men seeking God in faith and pain. Hasidim are "fervent ones," Hasidism a Jewish tradition with roots in the Psalms and Talmud. Israel Baal Shem Tov (1700-1760) rekindled this movement of inwardness and faith in the hamlets and ghettos of Eastern Europe, in Poland, Galicia, and the Ukraine. A long line of intense rebbes (spiritual guides) soon expanded his work.... Wiesel has more tales: strikingly diverse leaders come out of the shadows for us, pique our interest, and retreat quickly into silence. The angry Barukh of Medzibozh with his passionate love for the people, the humorous but deeply fearful Naphtali of Ropshitz, the enigmatic "Seer of Lublin," Jacob Isaac Horowitz, each mirrors the pain and hope of a poor, persecuted community at times divided in itself. Some, Mitnagdim (adversaries), opposed to the "new" sect as revolutionary, knew they must try not to fear men, but only God. Deep religious passions were there. Both sides fought out of conviction, out of deep commitment and desire to profess the validity of their ideas and beliefs.

The masters with all their power and flaws fire Wiesel's imagination. He knows their tales are to be told, not studied, lived, not analyzed. A Hasidic story is more about Hasidim than about their colorful, idiosyncratic guides. It's also as much about those who tell it as about those who lived it in painful loneliness. Their hold on Wiesel has never been stronger, their questions of faith and commitment are his. Few of his readers will escape their tug.

> *Frederick A. Homann, S.J., in a review of "Somewhere a Master: Further Hasidic Portraits and Legends," in* Best Sellers, *Vol. 42, No. 9, December, 1982, p. 361.*

TED L. ESTESS

In *Somewhere a Master*—four chapters of which originally appeared in *Four Hasidic Masters* (1978)—[Wiesel] continues his retrieval of Hasidic legends begun in *Souls on Fire* (1972). It is a distant kingdom, this kingdom of Hasidism, altogether antithetical and vulnerable to the kingdom of death he encountered at Auschwitz. Arising in the 18th century, Hasidism swept through Eastern Europe and restored hope to thousands of disheartened Jews. The accent of the movement was on passion, love and trust; its enemies were despair, resignation and indifference; its fruits were simplicity, laughter, community and the presence of God.

As in *Souls on Fire*, Wiesel focuses on the various Rebbes in *Somewhere a Master*, looking always for each one's dream and legend, the secret of his power. The secret of Rebbe Pinhas, we learn, was wisdom and an obsession with friendship; of Rebbe Wolfe, humility and a willingness to "suffer rather than cause suffering"; of Rebbe Aharon, "hitlahavut—fervor, enthusiasm." Wiesel finds anger in Rebbe Barukh, compassion in Rebbe Moshe-Leib, laughter in Rebbe Naphtali....

Wiesel's portraits are engaging and disturbing. With them, he seeks to evoke the Rebbes' secret powers, for himself and for his readers. "A man can do without many things," he has said, "but not without a teacher." *Somewhere*, he almost desperately seems to be saying, there *must* be a teacher, who can stir the memory and charge the imagination for the living of a human life in our time.

There is, however, a somber tone throughout these powerfully rendered sketches. Each of Wiesel's beloved Masters was divided within, for each suffered the steady encroachment of melancholy. It is as though each knew in advance what Wiesel knows in retrospect: the terrible vulnerability of love in a world of hate and indifference. (p. 397)

> *Ted L. Estess, in a review of "Somewhere a Master: Further Hasidic Portraits and Legends," in* America, *Vol. 147, No. 20, December 18, 1982, pp. 396-97.*

MARK J. MIRSKY

Elie Wiesel's *Somewhere a Master* so puzzled me that I went back to read his earlier *Souls on Fire*, to which the book jacket claims the present volume is a "sequel."... Unhappily I must report that this second collection is inferior to that first presentation in *Souls on Fire* of the lives and sayings of the Hasidic masters. Perhaps the problem is that having written once about this world, merely changing the cast of characters and introducing new rabbis and their courts does not jog Wiesel's narrative talents. Instead of his sure sense of timing, the careful cutting of history, anecdote and personal observation which gives the first book its fire, we have a dispersed voice, which occasionally hectors the Hasidic tales, reducing some to the level of elementary school moral lectures.

Somewhere a Master has its wonderful moments—my favorite is the reply of the sainted, humble Reb Itzikl to another Master. "The Kotzker asked him why he had hired a cynic as his private secretary. 'I'll tell you,' said Reb Itzikl. 'All private secretaries become cynical—so why wait?'" Yet my impression is that this "sequel" was a hasty job. Elie Wiesel's remarks about the religious Jews who opposed Hasidism, the Mitnagdiim, are shallow clichés. His denigration of the Gaon of Vilna, acknowledged by most modern scholars to be one of the unique figures in the evolution of modern Jewish thought, is ill-informed. . . . Again and again in *Somewhere a Master* one meets anecdotes from the earlier book. Having given a generalized but enthusiastic portrait of the major Hasidic figures in *Souls on Fire*, the far more difficult task of dealing with minor figures fell to the lot of this book. But since the less intriguing *rebbes* had already swum in and out of the ken of the greater, more than accretion of anecdote was called upon to give the sequel a guiding idea or organizing principle. Since Elie Wiesel seems to have no notion of recent scholarship about Eastern Europe, its Hasidic courts, he has nothing new to report either.

The most interesting possibility of *Somewhere a Master* lurks in the book's failure. For even Wiesel admits that his enthusiasm for his heroes, the wonder-working, Zen-speaking *rebbes*, falls short at times. Many of them end their lives in despair, horror, delirium. . . .

Wiesel's own book testifies against its heroes, making plain the egotism of men who dreamed themselves at the center of the Universe like the Seer of Lublin—who jumped from his roof, to provoke the Messiah—jarring the reader and forcing one to read between the lines of anecdotes. For a while Wiesel reads with us, but inevitably he breaks off to resume his job of assembling yet another popular volume on the saints of this mass movement.

Hasidism still agitates many Jews, educated and uneducated, today, to joy. Yet somewhere in the 19th century, it lost a revolutionary élan which it has yet to recover. One wants Wiesel to return to the far more difficult unsentimental task of understanding what went awry with the charisma which awoke not only the poor, but the middle class, to the creation of a society of celebrants in which the boundary between future joy and present fears would be annulled.

> *Mark J. Mirsky, "Fast Year at Marienbad," in* Book World—The Washington Post, *January 16, 1983, p. 11.**

WILLIAM A. HARTFELDER, JR.

Based on lectures delivered at Boston University and the 92 Street "Y" in New York, [the biographies in *Five Biblical Portraits*] are more a collection of sermons than lectures. The author's lyrical prose, his use of the medium of biography, and his drawing upon Rabbinic Midrash and Talmudic Aggadah to fill in the "gaps" of the biblical text combine to lead the reader on a superbly crafted homiletical journey.

The author highlights the paradoxical and painfully human side of his biblical subjects. We feel the chiaroscuro agony of Jeremiah who knows that "only if he tells the truth about what may and will happen is there a chance for it not to happen; only if he tells the truth can it prove to be false." We share in the loneliness of Saul who, misunderstood himself, could never understand others. He was incapable of going beyond his solitude even at the moment of death. It was fitting that Saul killed Saul for suicide means "a wish to be at once executioner and victim, mortal creature, and Angel of Death."

The author is not content, however, simply to bring his biblical portraitures to life only within their own periods. He also probes their relevance for contemporary human existence. He shows us how the fiery Elijah belongs not only to all the tribes, but to all of us. Elijah embodies humankind's "eternal need for poetry and [its] eternal quest for justice."

Readers of Hebrew may raise an occasional eyebrow at the author's renditions of the biblical text. Similarly, those unfamiliar with the rabbinic sages may not fully appreciate their profoundly reverent yet sometimes fanciful comments. But do not most effective sermons contain an admixture of profundity and fancy? Every reader will be intellectually stimulated and spiritually enriched by these biblical portraits executed by a consummate artist. (p. 72)

> *William A. Hartfelder, Jr., in a review of "Five Biblical Portraits," in* Theology Today, *Vol. XL, No. 1, April, 1983, pp. 71-2.*

JACK RIEMER

The chapters in [*Somewhere a Master*] are not essays, not formal biographies. . . . One who wishes to learn all of the factual details of these masters' lives is advised to go elsewhere. One who wishes to know their innermost being should come here.

Each chapter is a kind of a confrontation. It is as if the author has summoned up the master from the grave in order to ask him a question, *the* question: *what can your life teach me about my life,* what wisdom do you have that can help me here and now? (p. 502)

This is not a work of objective history, that records dates and facts and figures. It is a spiritual search, almost a detective story, an effort to catch the echo of the soul beneath the words, beneath the stories. Each of these masters lived at many levels. Each one revealed a little and hid a lot. And so one must listen carefully to the tales and one must read between the lines of the writings in order to find the real master. One must hear what is said, and one must also listen for what is left out. (pp. 502-03)

Who is a real master? Often the one who denies that he is. And who possesses the profoundest truths? Often the one who seems the most simple.

They were an extraordinary collection of spirits, these Hasidic masters of the last two centuries. They were people who inspired others and yet suffered loneliness themselves. They were people who led groups and yet hungered for privacy, people who sustained others and yet lived with heartache themselves.

And for Wiesel, and hopefully for his readers too, the tense of the verb in that last paragraph is not quite right. We should say not that "they were" but "they are," for their tales are still being told, and as long as they are these masters still live, these messages still reverberate. (p. 503)

> *Jack Riemer, "Confrontation with the Masters," in* Commonweal, *Vol. CX, No. 16, September 23, 1983, pp. 502-03.*

RONALD D. PASQUARIELLO, F.M.S.

It is because they are the product of Elie Wiesel's practiced pen that these tiny tales and fragments of tales [collected in *The Golem*] do not drift off into a sea of irrelevance. The book nowhere has the power of his excellent fiction, nor of his *Souls on Fire*, the first volume of his series of portraits of the Hasidic Masters. There, and in subsequent similar volumes, one could sense him wrestling with each Rabbi on every page for the Rabbi's truth. Here too Wiesel's struggle with the meaning of Jewish faith after Auschwitz and Buchenwald is clearly evident. These tales of the Golem jar the faith of the believing reader, opening him up to the work of grace.

The Golem is a shadowy figure, for good reason. The book is about God, and God's concern for his people. With tales and legends and myths, it is usually necessary to read between the lines, to reach for the Story behind the story, the Word behind the words. Not here. The Golem exists only to save his people, the Jews of sixteenth century Prague in this case, from the heinous, antisemitic acts of the gentile population. Mute, made of clay, and given life through the faith of Rabbi Yehuda Loew, the Golem goes about Prague in secret, uncovering the trumped up charges of the gentiles against individual members of the local community. Eventually, at the behest of the Rabbi, the Golem leaves. The narrator asks for his return, knowing the Golem's work is not done.

> *Ronald D. Pasquariello, F.M.S., in a review of "The Golem," in* Best Sellers, *Vol. 43, No. 11, February, 1984, p. 429.*

D. M. THOMAS

"A novel about Auschwitz is either not a novel or it is not about Auschwitz," Elie Wiesel observed in a recent interview.... Art implies coherence, form, vitality and beauty; and therefore the Holocaust rejects art, even if art finds itself increasingly drawn to the Holocaust. If art and the Holocaust are incompatible, what possible excuse can be found for the novel which, not aiming to be art, uses the Holocaust in order to entertain? (p. 1)

If Wiesel—who endured it, who is wise, and a marvelous writer—finds the Holocaust beyond understanding and beyond narration, that is good enough for me. I accept his view. There is, of course, a paradox: one cannot write about that genocide, and yet one must, because it is a central event of our century. For a Jew, there are no other events. Elie Wiesel's way of coping with the impossible dilemma is ... "not to replace silence with words, but to add silence to the words, to surround words with silence." (pp. 1, 4)

[*The Fifth Son*] is a very silent novel, a narrative almost without events. Its narrator is a young man growing up in Brooklyn, in the radical, frenetic atmosphere of the late '60s. He has a politically-conscious girlfriend, and tries acid, but essentially he lives in the almost wordless home of his parents. His mother has gone out of her mind, and is simply lost—away somewhere; his father, Reuven, writes his secret letters to his son Ariel, pores over ancient Jewish books in the library where he works, and once every month discusses passionately with a friend the ethics of killing. Reuven cannot tell his living son about the past. But gradually it is revealed: the small-town ghetto in which Reuven was head of the Jewish councillors, responsible to a cultivated Nazi sadist, the "Angel"; the beautiful, angelic son whom that Angel tortured to death; Reuven's revenge, after the war, when they found the Angel, tried him, and executed him with a grenade.

But was he, in fact, dead? The young Jewish American, understanding at last his father's torments, his mother's madness, carries out some investigations and finds that the Angel survived the grenade attack and is now a successful businessman. Resolving to take his own revenge, the young man travels to Germany and at last confronts the Angel in his office. In fictional, novelistic terms, the encounter is anti-climactic; the Jew can do no more than tell the Angel who he is, and thereby confront him with the past. Faced with Death itself, in the form of an uninteresting German businessman, the spirit of vengeance just goes away....

Clearly, in this scene, can be heard the silence surrounding the words. Useless to ask the Angel to explain how he could have enjoyed torturing and killing Jews, including the child Ariel. His life is spared, not from any ethical consideration, but from a sudden feeling of emptiness, the void. People move from life to death in the book, but we do not see them die. Even the death of Ariel, of such importance to the story that one would expect the novelist to steel himself to describe it, takes place off-stage, so to speak. It is a cruel death; that is all we hear of it.

The author's reticence, reminiscent of Greek tragedy, is wonderfully effective and moving. We are reading a superb novel which doesn't want to be a novel; which brilliantly uses novelistic techniques (such as the mysterious, gradually unveiled letters to Ariel) while shuffling them off with distaste; an art which does not want to be art. Even the name Reuven Tamiroff strikes an unreal, faintly absurd note, for *The Fifth Son* is not about fictional individuals but about the Jewish race. Ariel is, by contrast, the perfect and apocalyptic name; so is Angel. When the Angel orders the Jews he is about to kill to bow down and worship him, as if he were God, we are harrowed to the core by the thought that he *is* God. For He allowed it to happen, and Wiesel says he does not understand His silence either.

The book's triumph is that it implicitly recognizes the impossibility of dealing with the Holocaust in art, and thereby begins to find a language with which to confront the task. No word is thrown away, and the construction is masterly....

The term "novel" ... becomes increasingly inadequate as a description of a certain kind of literature, written out of a conviction that the reality of our epoch overwhelms fiction; a form of writing which still needs the conventions of plot and characterization, but as symbols of history. *The Fifth Son* is of that kind, along with the works of Pasternak and Solzhenitsyn.... Poem would be, I think, a more truthful description. I suggest that if we substituted poem for novel in the opening quotation of this review, Elie Wiesel's statement would no longer be valid. Poems can be written about the Holocaust—and *The Fifth Son* grandly proves it. They can, and must, be written by Jews and Gentiles alike; for we are all, in our time, children of the Holocaust. (p. 4)

> *D. M. Thomas, "Between Words and Silence," in* Book World—The Washington Post, *March 17, 1985, pp. 1, 4.*

RICHARD F. SHEPARD

There are two main currents running through [*The Fifth Son*] by one who has come to be a most-heard voice of the Holocaust, a voice that is humanistic and universal even as it is Jewish-minded and special. There is the story of the Brooklyn-born young man of the 1980's, whose father, onetime head of the Jewish Council in a German-run ghetto in Poland, shrouds his life in silence and whose mother has gone mad and lives on in an institution.

There is also the searching, philosophical question of revenge. Is it ever justified? When may one kill an oppressor, and what are the reasons that permit it? These matters constitute the comment that ties the generations together, that are the axis on which the story revolves. . . .

Mr. Wiesel is essentially a poet, or at least as much of a poet that any fine writer who deals with such mighty themes must be. . . . It is, in the Wiesel style, writing that is not intent on name-brand detail, in the fashion of the documentary novelist, but writing that seeks to capture in one passage after another the sensitivities and the moods that are the realities of our lives. The realities he writes about are rooted in the Nazi past but extend to New York, to Israel, to drugs, to the entire world.

"Most people think that shadows follow, precede or surround beings or objects. The truth is that they also surround words, ideas, desires, deeds, impulses and memories," a character, a man who deals in shadows, says. And it is shadows that Mr. Wiesel is himself dealing with here, the shadows cast by an unhappy past and that threaten to darken, by our own thoughts, our very future. A shadow is not a shadow, he is saying: it is as real as the flesh that shapes it.

How well he represents the feeling of children born to Holocaust survivors, only those children themselves can say: and, as with anything in life, one suspects there are as many re-actions as there are people. But the author does make all of us "children" of that generation, all of us who were not there, in the sense that he outlines for us the burdens of guilt, of revenge, of despair, and passes on to us his own ideas on how he balances those burdens while leaving us to decide how to deal with them in our own minds.

> Richard F. Shepard, "After the Horror," in The New York Times, *March 21, 1985, p. C29.*

FREDERIC MORTON

A survivor of Auschwitz and Buchenwald, Mr. Wiesel writes eloquently in Yiddish, French and English. His nonfiction books have proved him almost the equal of Martin Buber in person-alizing the remoter reaches of Jewish lore. *Souls on Fire* ren-dered the Hasidic masters with an intensity that, bypassing the cheaply nostalgic, engaged the religious roots of nostalgia. In *Messengers of God,* he gave Old Testament heroes modern faces without corrupting their timelessness. A Deuteronomic fervor has charged his essays and speeches on the Jewish tragedy. . . .

[*The Fifth Son*] once more shows [Wiesel] to be a first-rate rhetorician. In other words, he wields a gift dangerous to the creative writer. Rhetoric can be dangerous but not necessarily fatal, as shown by his play *The Trial of God,* which tackles the most bedeviling of theological problems—theodicy, or the justification of the divine in the presence of evil. Here Mr. Wiesel had the rather marvelous nerve to cast Satan as the defense counsel of the Lord of Hosts. He got away with it—succeeded brilliantly—because his cunning rhetoric distilled the moral paradoxes involved. Of course, *The Trial of God* may be as difficult to stage as, say, the Book of Job. I've only read it, and it's the sort of reading that sticks.

Can I say the same of *The Fifth Son*? Like other of his novels, its ambition is absolute. It strives to give ultimate horror its ultimate expression. In view of Mr. Wiesel's history and ethical energy, that ambition is understandable, but in *The Fifth Son* it remains once more unrealized.

At first the story invites and intrigues, employing a narrative line more original than in any of his novels I know. The narrator is the stepchild of a Holocaust survivor, and thus he makes a

perfect metaphor for the consequences of survivorship. . . . In *The Fifth Son,* the experience of surviving the Holocaust falls like a curtain between father and son. The book's action con-cerns the son's vain attempts to break through his father's unmerciful emotional veil. At last the son resolves to force his father to open up, to become a real father. He decides to carry out a task the older man left uncompleted. During the war, Reuven, the father, tried but could not kill the SS officer who murdered his son. The stepson discovers the SS officer's new identity in West Germany and sets out to execute him. . . .

This is an excellent dramatic premise, with undertones that need voicing in the Holocaust aftermath. But they are never really heard, because the drama doesn't breathe. Instead of describing the texture of the father's absence, the story offers only a void. The son is less a person than an intermittently interesting philosophical construct. The scene shifts from Brooklyn to Germany, but we get little sense of Brooklyn and none of the countryside around Frankfurt. Gloom grays every syllable, but it is not a cumulative, magic gloom. Yet all along we feel each scene's latent power. We feel that Mr. Wiesel is capable of transforming his story into revelation. Why doesn't he?

A clue might lie in a passage in which the narrator meditates on an incipient love affair. "To forget," he muses, "there is nothing like the awakening of the senses." Sensuousness would make the son forget his mission, forget the murderous burden of the Holocaust. But that sentence also seems to hint at Mr. Wiesel's possibly self-imposed limitations as a novelist. It's as if Auschwitz had forever tainted his senses, and they were therefore not to be trusted as instruments of the imagination. Is that why Mr. Wiesel lapses into abstractions at critical points in the novel? Is that why he avoids the light-dark, sweet-sour shadings of the concrete details that allow us to cope with the bafflements of life and death? He is already one of our most accomplished orators about a great darkness in our time. He could be—should be—its definitive dramatist.

> Frederic Morton, "Execution as an Act of Inti-macy," in The New York Times Book Review, *March 24, 1985, p. 8.*

D. KEITH MANO

[The theme of *The Fifth Son*] is: "Children of survivors are almost as traumatized as the survivors themselves." Fair enough, and Wiesel has a decent style: honest, lucid, if over-abstract, *French* you might say. . . . But the whole disinvolves: imagery is either missing or tentative, except as it will approach [the Nazi sadist] Lander. Without the Holocaust background to sup-ply dread resonance, these would be people of just moderate interest. You compensate for them, as, in friendship, you would compensate for someone with a serial number tattooed on his or her arm. *The Fifth Son* reads more like Biblical commentary than fiction.

Structure, too, has been misconceived. Wiesel withholds data as one would in a suspense-novel format. What secret is father stashing away from Ariel II? What drove mother mad? . . . You learn in time—and it isn't so surprising after all—that a younger son, Ariel, was tortured to death by Lander. This new, dead Ariel sucks spirit and identity from Ariel II: personae commingle. Guilt, of course, cross-fertilizes. . . . Has Ariel II been swindled of love by memory? Poignant dilemma, but, with so much information held back, the dead Ariel becomes just a daubed, sudden, insubstantial wraith. His murder doesn't support enough weight (amid all those other murders), even though he is rather hastily spoken of as the "future of Davarowsk." Wiesel can't manage point of view well enough. He doesn't have the flexible ventriloquy of William Styron, say. Plot will out too slowly and, with it, also too slowly, a reader's emotional allegiance.

Yet this is the Holocaust and still provoking. Both father and son will make incompetent, near-frivolous attempts to execute Lander—even though revenge is clearly forbidden by Jewish law. . . . Davarowsk Jews call him Angel or simply Death. One owning so much fatal power must come out of revelation, not the bourgeoisie. That would be exquisite terror: to suppose an ordinary man capable of such imposing evil. Worse, how can punishment, even capital, accommodate this crime? It would create a humiliating equation: Lander = 20,000 Jews. Ariel, head to head, can only inquire in awe, "How could you inflict such suffering without its leaving a mark on your face?" Lander is, in some real sense, beyond retribution, under special immunity. Such questions get asked of the Maker, not of middle-aging German men.

Ariel II, after this confrontation, will resolve that Lander "no longer held any real interest for me." Catharsis of a correct, if somewhat disquieting, kind. . . . We must never forget Auschwitz or Dachau. But it is about time we stopped celebrating—for our obsessive attention has done just that, celebrate—the murderers and their impenetrable sensibility. They are an enigma: one that will enfeeble us with puzzlement. They steal focus from their victims and numb compassion in curiosity. (pp. 57-9)

D. Keith Mano, "An Omen or Three," in National Review, *Vol. XXXVII, No. 13, July 12, 1985, pp. 57-9.*

Nancy Willard

1936-

American poet, novelist, short story writer, essayist, critic, and author of books for children.

Willard blends fantasy and reality to create works in which the ordinary becomes extraordinary. Her work is marked by a powerful imagination and sense of wonder at common, everyday occurrences. Noting her "precise statement of vision," Jascha Kessler finds in Willard's work the voice "of an imagination that is not trendy in its subjects, nor cliché-ridden in its observation, which is always clear and simple."

Willard's work embraces a wide range of genres. Perhaps best known for her fiction for children, she has also written numerous adult works, including poetry, fiction, and criticism. Willard first established her literary reputation as a poet in the collections *In His Country* (1966), *Skin of Grace* (1967), and *A New Herball: Poems* (1968). In many of these poems she examines a single, commonplace object in great detail, thereby creating a fresh image untainted by traditional perceptions. Her imaginative approach also characterizes the poems in *Nineteen Masks for the Naked Poet: Poems* (1971), *The Carpenter and the Sun: Poems* (1974), and *Household Tales of Moon and Water* (1982). In a review of *Household Tales of Moon and Water*, Bruce Bennett cites Willard's ability to illuminate the mystery of common objects, commenting: "Snow, soap bubbles, cocoons, an icicle: everything is revealed in wonder, as if newly created." Willard's approach to poetry is also evident in her critical study *Testimony of the Invisible Man: William Carlos Williams, Francis Ponge, Rainer Maria Rilke, Pablo Neruda* (1968), which connects the four poets in terms of their attention to the concrete aspects of daily life.

Like her poetry, Willard's fiction is mystical and displays a sense of enchantment. The stories in *Childhood of the Magician* (1973), which are linked by a young, female protagonist, portray the poignance and pathos of the transition from childhood to adulthood. *Angel in the Parlor: 5 Stories and 8 Essays* (1983) further reveals her talents as a storyteller. Willard's first novel, *Things Invisible to See* (1984), is a fanciful exploration of the conflicts between life and death and good and evil. This work centers in a pair of twins who grow up in a small town where animals talk and spirits return from the dead. As several critics note, however, the fantasy does not intrude on the story's credibility. Michiko Kakutani comments: "[The] strange and unexpected are not irrational events in need of explanation; they are simply divine manifestations of love and faith."

(See also *CLC*, Vol. 7; *Children's Literature Review*, Vol. 5; *Contemporary Authors*, Vols. 89-92; *Contemporary Authors New Revision Series*, Vol. 10; *Something about the Author*, Vols. 30, 37; and *Dictionary of Literary Biography*, Vol. 5.)

DENISE LEVERTOV

[*The preface from which this excerpt is taken was written in 1968.*]

There was a time—years ago—when I felt puzzled by what then seemed contradictory in all that the . . . two great poets [Rilke and Williams] seemed to represent. It is easy to find

© Eric Lindbloom

superficial polarities: to see Rilke as aristocratic, mystical, and concerned with "high language," Williams as democratic, pragmatic, and devoted to contemporary idiom, for instance. I did not try to worry the matter through to a conclusion. It seemed enough to care so much about them both and to know the ferment of them both working in my life. Now [in *Testimony of the Invisible Man: William Carlos Williams, Francis Ponge, Rainer Maria Rilke, Pablo Neruda*] Nancy Willard, without troubling her head about polarities, calmly . . . places both upon a common ground, that same ground of open, devoted, curious, loving attention to *things* where Ponge so emphatically stands also. It is always a betrayal to effect reconciliations merely by ignoring distinctions; but to point out what *is* shared by two such different poets is not a betrayal but an act not unrelated to what Rilke said love was, "a mutual bordering and guarding of two solitudes."

Ponge is a poet I came to much later than to Rilke and Williams and whose work I don't pretend to yet know well, but who began to become important for me from the moment I first read the lines about an oyster that are cited in Chapter III of this book. The icy spring water of Ponge's phenomenological clarity—I am thinking here of Gaston Bachelard's use of the term—is both familiar and enticing to one who has taken "No ideas but in things" seriously, not mistaking it for "No ideas," but understanding that it means the poet can discover the universal only in the local—in the concrete particulars both of the material world and of language itself. (pp. x-xi)

Though I have thought I detected in some Neruda poems a rhetoric I distrusted, that is, an overextension of feeling and language, one has only to read some of the poems quoted in Chapter IV—for example, the ''Oda al Elefante''—to note that here too, song arises from precise and open vision.

It is a virtue of these essays that parallels are not forced. Nancy Willard does not try to squeeze all four poets into one small esthetic rowboat. But I think she does a service in juxtaposing for us what is genuinely related in their concern and thus making understandable how it happens that they can live side by side as powerful forces, yet not in conflict, in the minds of other writers. If I find myself wishing she had focused not only on the correspondences in their basic attitudes but on their very different senses of form and rhythm, I qualify that wish by the recognition that this book, by its very nature—as a first map of an intuited territory, a place in imagination where Nancy Willard wants, as I do, to find her own bearings and live—is a beginning, not an end. (p. xi)

> *Denise Levertov, in a preface to* Testimony of the Invisible Man: William Carlos Williams, Francis Ponge, Rainer Maria Rilke, Pablo Neruda *by Nancy Willard, University of Missouri Press, 1970, pp. ix-xi.**

MORDECAI MARCUS

[In *Testimony of the Invisible Man*] Miss Willard approaches four modern poets . . . to show how they strive to efface the barriers between the self and the things of this world, to achieve a communion that becomes all that matters. Her tone is reverential, and her general assumption seems to be that the goals of these poets are the highest a poet can aspire to—an approach perhaps reminiscent of T. S. Eliot's early essays but more puzzling than Eliot's because we are told very little about the kinds of approaches and inadequacies which are left behind by her admired poets.

In her introduction Miss Willard lets the poets speak mostly for themselves, and though there and in later chapters she makes brief mention of their continuities with Imagists and Symbolists, she makes no use of extensive scholarship on this subject. Miss Willard cites commonplaces of poetic theory as if they were both novel and special to her poets. (p. 88)

Miss Willard praises Neruda thus: ''Such a poem is a gift, the signature of his love.'' But the preceding lines quoted from Neruda are pure statement, and one wonders why Miss Willard's phrase would not apply to poems by Keats or Hopkins or Elizabeth Bishop. This is not to deny the efficacy of such a phrase as the measure of a deeply treasured response, but Miss Willard writes *as if* this kind of response were more appropriate for the poets she celebrates than for other great poets.

Miss Willard thinks that Williams's poems rarely reveal a personality, which she takes to be a measure of their successful incorporation of the world, and she thinks that Williams almost always presents ideas without statements and through images. These views are mistaken. Miss Willard accurately observes that Williams sensitizes fictive personae, as in ''The Widow's Lament in Springtime,'' but how can she miss the passionately inquisitive, ingenuously surprised, delighted, and angered man who strides through the world of Williams's poems? Williams's early poems use a variety of indirect techniques to incorporate

ideas and feelings, and only a few of these approach statement. But in such great middle and late poems as ''The Semblables,'' ''Burning the Christmas Greens,'' and most strikingly in ''The Descent,'' Williams uses an abundance of statement and abstract metaphor. I cannot as easily follow her arguments about the foreign-language poets, but I strongly suspect similar inaccuracy there.

Miss Willard's reverence and tenderness for her material is quite moving and sometimes connected to excellent observations (usually undeveloped), and since her vantage point seems largely that of the practicing and questing poet, perhaps one should not ask for in-depth scholarship from her. But she lists an applicable bibliography and she makes intellectual statements which ask to be taken seriously. I cannot tell why her homework is so inadequate to her tasks. (pp. 88-9)

> *Mordecai Marcus, ''On Greatness,'' in* Prairie Schooner, *Vol. XLV, No. 1, Spring, 1971, pp. 88-9.*

FRANCINE DANIS

''Her poems don't draw blood or blow your head off,'' admits Stanley Poss in *Western Humanities Review* [see *CLC*, Vol. 7]. True. Nancy Willard's poems are not violent or militant, not startling at all—unless one is startled at encountering joy in the work of a female poet of the 1970's. Willard's poetry, bright, graceful, and often playful, radiates womanly fullness, contentment, and reverence. In mood and language, her five slender volumes of poetry—*In His Country, Skin of Grace, Nineteen Masks for the Naked Poet, A New Herball,* and *Carpenter of the Sun*—might be called, collectively, a contemporary woman's psalter, and though the world of these domestic psalms is relatively small in terms of geography and experience, it is a realm transformed by humor and tenderness, conveyed through skillfully crafted language—a clean, subtle use of imagery, sound effects and figurative language.

The impulse behind the transformation of the ordinary can be seen in Willard's own critical writings. In a book-length critical study, *Testimony of the Invisible Man,* she deals with the work of four writers (William Carlos Williams, Francis Ponge, Rainer Maria Rilke, and Pablo Neruda) whom she categorizes as *Ding*-poets. Her description of a *Ding*-poet as the true artist also gives us a clue as to her own artistic theory:

> The artist is one who has freed himself from the molds that language and a life of action try to force on human vision, and therefore we say he sees things as they are. The *Ding*-poet does not make up a new world; he shows you the old one. . . .

Or, again:

> The new poetry will be as impure as our bodies, soiled by sweat and usage and traffic with the things of this world. If you can keep this joyful contact with things, you are already a poet . . . , for being a poet means living so selflessly that nothing is alien to your singing. . . .
>
> (pp. 126-27)

[Consider] some of the means by which Willard achieves the control, grace, and precision which rescue her poems of praise and affection from the pitfalls of sentimentality. . . . [In *Testimony of the Invisible Man*] Willard constantly speaks of abandoning fixed views of objects in order to enter into those objects and discover anew their true qualities. Willard draws on one of Neruda's images to make this notion concrete, saying that "the poet who takes his residence on earth seriously is like the deep-sea diver: he practices his birth again and again.". . .

A primary way in which the artist "practices his birth again and again" has to do with the way he looks at things. John Cage once said it well: "I am trying to check my habits of seeing, to counter them for the sake of greater freshness. I am trying to be unfamiliar with what I'm doing." Many of Willard's uses of figurative language seem to flow out of that kind of creative unfamiliarity and to aim at creating the same outlook in us. . . . Willard also employs similes with great precision, suggesting with a single detail a whole scene, mood, or insight. Speaking for instance of an assault trial, the persona of **"Clearing the Air"** recollects that the defendant "sat in a box, docile as old shoes.". . . In a lighter mood, **"First Lesson"** opens by musing on a box of eggs, "the lid raised to show / a jury noncommittal / as the bald heads of / a dozen uncles.". . . (pp. 129-30)

Willard's use of figurative language is often enhanced by her control over sound effects. Short *a's* and quick *c's* and *r's,* for instance, contribute to the rhythm and diction of the lines "rapid as argument, / acrobatic as a conversation / of mutes"—lines that move as agilely as the hand-motions they describe. (p. 130)

Willard's poetry frequently exhibits a delight in profusions of color, texture, or taste. Yet even the most strongly sensory poems move through description to insight. Willard could say of herself what she writes of Neruda in *Testimony:* "Seeing a thing well is not enough: he wants you to love it.". . . True, **"Patisserie"** makes its point directly: "The sweet flesh you love does not satisfy, / Nothing grows old and nothing endures.". . . Yet even there, the moral is softened by being expressed as an admonition of the bespectacled shop-owner, and also by forming a refrain which in its recurrence suggests the cloying quality of "the sweet flesh" itself. (p. 131)

[Such poems as **"Crewel," "Skin of Grace,"** and **"Tapestry Makers"**] suggest that Willard's poetry not only celebrates the wholeness of what exists but also affirms the possibility of wholeness in what is not yet healed. Her use of craft to reveal content reflects the timeless belief that art can, indeed must, be part of that healing process. "You are healed," she declares, "When you know to praise.". . . If, through reading Willard's poetry of praise, her domestic psalms, we feel that "grace" has become more fleshly while green peppers, wooden blocks, and crewel-work have become less mundane, then the poet has realized her own definition: "art is not a selection from the world but a transformation of it into something that praises existence.". . . (pp. 133-34)

Francine Danis, "Nancy Willard's Domestic Psalms," in Modern Poetry Studies, *Vol. IX, No. 2, Autumn, 1978, pp. 126-34.*

ROBERT PACK

True storytelling begins with the sense of wonder. Why does the universe exist rather than nothing? Why did he meet her by the willow tree that windy day? What happened next? Did they get married? Did he die? In this remarkable collection of stories and essays [*Angel in the Parlor*], Nancy Willard wonders her stories into form and wonders about the art of wondering. In effect, her essays are stories about stories, how they have their roots both in experience and in invention. If her childhood

seems to have been magical, it is because she has not lost her sense of enchantment in its recounting. (p. xi)

The universe that Willard's imagination inhabits is enchanted because everything in it has its story, everything is touched with the animation of her own delight in the thoughtful act of looking. In this book the reader can witness the products of Willard's imagination in their completed form and at the same time glimpse the resources of her particular experiences that she has shaped into stories. And therein lies her dominant theme—how people either fail or succeed in inventing the lives that finally they must call their own. Their fictions of themselves must bear the weight of what they feel. . . . The story that Willard creates is a fabric of the fictions each character creates for himself or herself, and this composite fiction is the "lie" that enables the reader to see into the representative truth of her characters. (p. xii)

Willard is right in assuming that the fictions we invent, the life of the imagination, are an essential part of the reality of human life. And so the supernatural in her work, the aura of enchantment that often surrounds her objects and people, must be seen as what the mind adds to the perceived world of events and images. A dreamlike or impressionistic sense of things gives expression to the feelings that inevitably are associated with what we call the actual. Even the most recalcitrant realist must acknowledge the existence of human fantasy, of wishing and making believe. It is as if we live in two worlds at once, and these worlds of the literal and the imagined are always merging or clashing, each contending for our allegiance.

In the world of the actual the universal law is that everything is causally connected, and therefore description is essentially linear. Explanation or interpretation must show how things connect in sequence, motivation causing action, one action leading to the next. But in the world of imagination such necessity may be suspended briefly to allow an imaginative premise to take the place of a cause. In Willard's hands, the real and the imagined are joined and enhance one another. (pp. xii-xiii)

[Her] narration possesses the freedom to reject explanation for presentation, to apprehend an image or an action in the intensity of the moment in which it is witnessed. For example, in a poem inspired by a literal reading of a newspaper headline on a sports page, **"Buffalo Climbs Out of Cellar,"** Willard restores the life of the buffalo by making him a four-legged buffalo again. She gives us his predicament and his story. We know how he must feel, and so we care. But as artist she does not tell us, nor does she have to, how he got there in the first place, for that would be another story. (pp. xiii-xiv)

Robert Pack, in an introduction to Angel in the Parlor: 5 Stories and 8 Essays *by Nancy Willard, Harcourt Brace Jovanovich, Publishers, 1983, pp. xi-xiv.*

BRUCE BENNETT

"Night Light," the first poem in [*Household Tales of Moon and Water*] . . . , concludes: "It is time to turn on the moon. / It is time to live by a different light." The "moon" is china, made in Japan and cost ten dollars; the "different light" is imagination, which plays upon and illuminates common objects until each shines forth in its essential mystery. Snow, soap bubbles, cocoons, an icicle: everything is revealed in wonder, as if newly created. The poet has ushered us into a realm where sacramental and magical are coterminous, where healing and miracle are easily achieved, provided we are patient. . . .

Blake is invoked in the book's second poem, **"Vision and Late Supper,"** and his presence can be felt throughout; clearly, for Willard too, "everything that lives is Holy."

Willard's preferred methods of discourse are proverb . . . and paradox. . . . As her title suggests, she is pre-eminently a story-teller, whether her tales take the form of parables, like the memorable **"Out of War,"** or playfully render characters and scenes, as in the fourteen-poem closing sequence, **"My Life on the Road with Bread and Water."** Action in her poems often involves an unfolding, or a peeling and paring away. We participate, for instance, in the triumphal emergence of the calla lily, "pushed out of the earth / like a note in a bottle." Slicing into a pepper, in **"How to Stuff a Pepper,"** we find we have entered "a moon, spilled like a melon, / a fever of pearls / a conversation of glaciers." Her metaphors also unfold, or richly succeed themselves: the interior of the pepper "is a temple built to the worship / of morning light."

Birth and death, the subject of many of these poems, are, for Willard, inextricable. In **"The Child. The Ring. The Road."** the speaker addresses a dying child: "Good-bye, I say, when we touch the door / which winks to receive you / into its corridors, green, so green; / you have glided into a stem." The door image recurs in **"Arbor,"** where, for a woman "at the end of her life," it leads to "another country." . . . In Nancy Willard's world, grace is pervasive, and spirit, like the humble Indian pipe, is "everywhere present, / everywhere unseen." (p. 314)

> Bruce Bennett, *"Poems Magical, Poems Mordant,"* in The Nation, *Vol. 236, No. 10, March 12, 1983, pp. 314-15.*

THE VIRGINIA QUARTERLY REVIEW

Half whimsical, half sinister, [the poems in *Household Tales of Moon and Water*] have the simplicity and magic of children's folktales: water, fire, mud, bread, and many other natural objects become personalities with special powers and wisdom. . . . Willard's wide-ranging imagination infuses the ordinary with mystery and surprise. This gets a bit strained at times . . . , yet overall it is a pleasing and striking collection, admirable for the way it focuses steadily on the domestic world and raises the most commonplace events to a larger, almost mythic significance.

> A review of *"Household Tales of Moon and Water,"* in The Virginia Quarterly Review, *Vol. 59, No. 2 (Spring, 1983), p. 62.*

PUBLISHERS WEEKLY

Willard's gifts are evident . . . [in the] eight engaging essays and five stories [collected in *Angel in the Parlor*], tales in which she navigates skillfully between earthy reality and heights of fantasy, never creating a doubt to stir disbelief. One finds it reasonable, for instance, that in **"The Doctrine of the Leather-Stocking Jesus,"** a little girl changes her younger brother into a donkey. When she can't turn him back into himself, God appears in answer to her prayer and solves the problem in a stunning lesson about the immutability of things. The witty, revealing essays give the reader graphic examples of how Wil-

lard, in [Robert Pack's] phrase, "wonders her stories into form and wonders about the art of wondering" [see excerpt above].

> A review of *"Angel in the Parlor,"* in Publishers Weekly, *Vol. 224, No. 11, September 9, 1983, p. 57.*

RHODA YERBURGH

Willard's stories and essays [in *Angel in the Parlor: 5 Stories and 8 Essays*] display and then explain the art of storytelling. . . . Willard's world is saturated with Christian dogma, humor, fantasy, compassion, and the strain that comes from lying accurately in the service of a deeper truth. The essays explain the steps in the writing process; dream, memory, magic, craft. Sprightly conversations between the writer and her muse show us how she "wakes the water" in the well of her abundant imagination. Either the stories or the essays would have made a satisfactory volume; together they exceed the sum of their parts.

> Rhoda Yerburgh, in a review of *"Angel in the Parlor: 5 Stories and 8 Essays,"* in Library Journal, *Vol. 108, No. 17, October 1, 1983, p. 1879.*

JASCHA KESSLER

The "water" poems [in *Household Tales of Bread and Water*] are a set of 15 short poems, in a pseudo-folktale style, and the sequence is called **"My Life on the Road with Bread and Water."** The epigraph is taken from an African folktale, and reads, "There was once a woman who loved a river. " The Water of the sequence is the name of the man (or river) she loved; the bread is what she bakes, Willard being . . . an intensely, domestic, householding poet, but someong who . . . holds her house with tender whimsy. . . . [Her] attention is given mostly to her little boy, seen as a fetus once nearly lost, and as a curious, very little child. . . .

Some of her best poems are written for her little son, and in the poem titled, **"For You, Who Didn't Know,"** we can see how she combines an anecdote about the delivery of her first baby with reflective, and charming whimsy, a whimsy that usually attempts to offer something gnomically wise, though it is wisdom that charms and does not carry us down with the strain of forced profundity. In other words, she has that trick she must have garnered from Emily Dickinson, a model for the indirectly metaphysical and the softly-speaking female voice, if there ever was one. . . .

Willard's way with words and language is not novel, or original, but her voice is recognizably her own, because it is the voice of poetic craft and precise statement of a vision that is securely set in her own path, of an imagination that is not trendy in its subjects, nor cliché-ridden in its observation, and which is always clear and simple.

> Jascha Kessler, *"Nancy Willard: 'Household Tales of Moon and Water',"* in a radio broadcast on KUSC-FM—Los Angeles, CA, September 19, 1984.

MICHIKO KAKUTANI

Things Invisible to See is a novel about baseball in the way that *The Natural* by Bernard Malamud is a baseball story, a coming-of-age novel, in the way that William Wharton's *Birdy* is a story about adolescence: [*Things Invisible to See*] moves freely between the mundane and the metaphysical, the present and the remembered past, transiting the gap between the real and the fantastic the way the finest children's books do—nimbly and without the slightest trace of self-consciousness or guile.

In Nancy Willard's fictional world, the strange and the unexpected are not irrational events in need of explanation; they are simply divine manifestations of love and faith. So adept is the author at melding the ordinary with the magical that we do not even question the novel's surreal, penultimate scene, in which an exhibition baseball game becomes a celestial contest, waged—as in Ingmar Bergman's "Seventh Seal"—with that nastiest of opponents, Death. . . . [Miss Willard] writes of small-town life during World War II with a genuine nostalgia—neither sentimental nor contrived—for the innocence Americans once possessed; and she makes a teen-age love story—about a pair of brothers and the two girls they fancy—reverberate, gently, with larger, darker questions about the human condition.

Miss Willard creates pictures of daily life so precisely observed that they leave after-images in the reader's mind. . . . [The] scenes of ordinary life dissolve with celluloid ease into more extraordinary ones: animals carry on strange conversations with their owners, ghosts walk the night, and dead sports heroes come back to assert their prowess.

What keeps a reader from completely falling under Miss Willard's spell has to do not with a paucity of language or imagining, but from a surfeit. When she attempts to address philosophical issues, her prose tends to become willfully poetic . . . , and at other times, metaphors proliferate with such vigor that the reader feels lost in a jungle of pretty images and allusions. Phrases like "the pale green Monopoly board of his future" are simply more distracting than they are evocative.

The overall narrative, too, is crammed with subsidiary characters—who seem to have been included simply because they possess a picturesque eccentricity or two. And certain scenes read more like dazzling set-pieces than necessary parts of the story. Such flaws, however, are redeemed by the sheer power of Miss Willard's talent. In the end, the novel probably most resembles an old-fashioned crazy quilt—eclectic and a little over-embroidered, but all in all a charming work of improvisation, held together by the radiance of its creator's sensibility.

> *Michiko Kakutani, "The Real and Fantastic," in* The New York Times, *January 12, 1985, p. 13.*

RICHARD EDER

In the interest of letting their readers know what to expect of the books they buy, publishers might consider branching out from blurbs and flap summaries. For example, they could print on the jacket the names of any animals to be encountered.

There is a cat in Nancy Willard's romantic fantasy, and it is called Cinnamon Monkeyshines. That tells you something. If the name strikes you as warm and inveigling, *Things Invisible to See* is likely to inveigle you. If not, possibly not.

My own feeling about animals is that generally they would be better off with numbers. I realize that puts me at a captious extreme from the Cinnamon Monkeyshines camp. Perhaps the fair thing is to stand a little apart from judgment and take a presentational approach, the kind sometimes used with the newborn: "My, that *is* a baby."

My, this *is* a romantic fantasy. . . .

Willard has written poems, short stories and a number of children's books. *Things Invisible* is told something like a children's book for grown-ups. The characters divide into quite marvelous and quite awful. The whimsies are cut to large and extra-large sizes.

Some of them are funny and crisp. Two sisters are so close and prickly that one of them can smell the scorch of the other's ironing when they are talking by phone. They share responsibility for an amiable old father and an impossible old mother, swapping them regularly and keeping track of mother days and father days in an account book. . . .

On the other hand, the magic interventions are put to a lot of work to advance such a sweet and small plot. Willard's supernatural is as cozy as a long Sunday afternoon with the heat turned up. There is some highly adorned language. Willard uses such phrases as "God, who watches and winds the footage of humanity. . . ."

She is an exuberant and fanciful writer, but she over-arranges her tale. If *Things Invisible to See* were a refrigerator, it would be ornamented with kittens and quotations from William Blake.

> *Richard Eder, in a review of "Things Invisible to See," in* Los Angeles Times Book Review, *January 20, 1985, p. 1.*

SUSAN FROMBERG SCHAEFFER

[*Things Invisible to See*] has the quality of a fairy tale, its landscape both phantasmagoric and real, as if one were seeing reality filtered through someone else's dream. It is deceptively simple, a paradigm of life as a Manichaean conflict between good and evil, a parable in which Thanatos is in constant contention with Eros, a modern morality play in which God is firmly in place and the Devil no less so. It is a tribute to Nancy Willard's talent that these themes unfold almost beyond the border of the reader's awareness. And it is a mark of her ability that the novel never crosses from sentiment into sentimentality. *Things Invisible to See* is an altogether marvelous book—a modern-day "Everyman." (p. 12)

Nancy Willard has written a lovely, moving parable of life as a playing field on which the desire to live must continually contend with the forces opposing it. It is a courageous book—courageous because Miss Willard has dispensed with almost all the devices an author ordinarily uses for self-protection. There is no authorial detachment here, no distancing irony, no refusal to take full responsibility for her frankly religious view of the world.

She creates a world in which there is a constant interplay between the living and the dead, between things visible and invisible. . . . All the truly good characters constantly die and are resurrected, coming back with mysterious powers that allow them to heal or to see into the future. Nothing is ever new but everything is always changing. . . .

"In Paradise, on the banks of the River of Time," Miss Willard writes in her opening sentence, "the Lord of the Universe is playing ball with his archangels. . . . What a show!" And with each toss of the ball, disasters and deaths occur as well as miracles and births. Only God "brings things to pass and gives them their true colors." *Things Invisible to See* is a visionary rendering of how God makes amends, reweaves patterns and sets things to rights. Miss Willard transforms reality into something endlessly magical, and she does all this without apologizing for what she believes in. (p. 13)

Susan Fromberg Schaeffer, "Playing Ball with Death," in The New York Times Book Review, *February 3, 1985, pp. 12-13.*

JEREMIAH TAX

[Two years ago] a remarkable first novel by Percival Everett called *Suder* told the hilarious and touching story of a fictional third baseman for the Seattle Mariners in a syncopated, highly improvisational style that read like jazz. If you missed it, look for it. Now comes another first novel, ***Things Invisible to See*** . . . , a kind of fairy tale for adults that seems to fly off into space, propelled by the author's imagination, like a baseball off a Louisville Slugger. As Everett did with *Suder,* Willard provides a strong, compelling narrative to carry the reader along on her flights of imagery and analogy. (p. 6)

Willard leaves no doubt about what kind of a tale this is. . . . [In] the second [paragraph of the book], the highly fluid plot begins to flow from its source: "In the damp night of the womb, when millions of chromosomes are gearing up for the game of life, the soul of Willie says to the soul of (twin brother) Ben,

'Listen, you can be first-born and get out of this cave first if you'll give me everything else. Brains, charm, and good looks.'" (pp. 6-7)

The scene is Ann Arbor, Michigan in the years just before and after the start of World War II. Willard, who grew up in Ann Arbor, teaches English at Vassar. She has written three books of short stories and eight books of poetry. It is often tempting to say that the eye and empathy of the poet are at work in her descriptions of small-city life, though poets are not our only reliable observers. But Willard's language is indeed poetic, and there is never a false or discordant note as she works out the destinies of the twins following the bargain in the womb.

Her story's climax is a baseball game. . . .

Who wins the game and why—if either side does—and what it all means are among the questions that Willard leaves to each of us. Readers of the manuscript have concluded happily that the result is a triumph of "life" over "death." My view is that the author has deliberately presented us with a standoff, a tie. You may have other ideas. (p. 7)

Jeremiah Tax, "A GI Makes a Bet with Death and a Fantastic Baseball Game Ensues," in Sports Illustrated, *Vol. 62, No. 9, March 4, 1985, pp. 6-7.*

Appendix

The following is a listing of all sources used in Volume 37 of *Contemporary Literary Criticism*. Included in this list are all copyright and reprint rights and acknowledgments for those essays for which permission was obtained. Every effort has been made to trace copyright, but if omissions have been made, please let us know.

THE EXCERPTS IN CLC, VOLUME 37, WERE REPRINTED FROM THE FOLLOWING PERIODICALS:

America, v. 147, December 18, 1982 for a review of "Somewhere a Master: Further Hasidic Portraits and Legends" by Ted L. Estess; v. 151, October 13, 1984 for "God's Grandeur" by Richard A. Blake. © 1982, 1984. All rights reserved. Both reprinted with permission of the respective authors./ v. 106, December 23, 1961; v. 120, April 5, 1969; v. 123, October 17, 1970; v. 124, March 27, 1971. © 1961, 1969, 1970, 1971. All rights reserved. All reprinted with permission of America Press, Inc., 106 West 56th Street, New York, NY 10019.

American Anthropologist, n.s. v. 31, July-August, 1929./ v. 66, December, 1964 for a review of "Continuities in Cultural Evolution" by Betty J. Meggers; v. 73, August, 1971 for a review of "A Way of Seeing" by Wilfred C. Bailey. Copyright 1964, 1971 by the American Anthropological Association. Both reproduced by permission of the American Anthropological Association and the respective authors.

The American Book Review, v. II, May-June, 1980; v. 3, March-April, 1981; v. 5, January-February, 1983; v. 6, May-June, 1984. © 1980, 1981, 1983, 1984 by *The American Book Review*. All reprinted by permission.

American Journal of Sociology, v. LXV, May, 1960. © 1960 by The University of Chicago. Reprinted by permission of The University of Chicago Press.

American Mercury, v. LXXIII, December, 1951.

The American Poetry Review, v. 11, January-February, 1982 for "Ted Hughes's 'Moortown', Real and Imagined" by Sandra McPherson; v. 11, September-October, 1982 for "Haunting" by Mary Kinzie. Copyright © 1982 by World Poetry, Inc. Both reprinted by permission of the respective authors.

The American Scholar, v. 52, Spring, 1983 for "Out of the Swim with Barbara Pym" by Isa Kapp. Copyright © 1983 by the author. Reprinted by permission of the publishers.

The Annals of the American Academy of Political and Social Science, v. 181, September, 1935 for a review of "Sex and Temperament in Three Primitive Societies" by Hortense Powdermaker. © 1935, renewed 1962, by The American Academy of Political and Social Science. Reprinted by permission of the publisher and the Literary Estate of Hortense Powdermaker.

The Antioch Review, v. 32, Spring & Summer, 1972. Copyright © 1972 by the Antioch Review Inc. Reprinted by permission of the Editors.

The Atlantic Monthly, v. 254, July, 1984 for "New Notes from Underground" by Nadine Gordimer. Copyright © 1984 by the author. Reprinted by permission of Russell & Volkening, Inc. as agents for the author./ v. 245, May, 1980 for "A Sexual Pilgrim's Progress" by Benjamin DeMott; v. 255, February, 1985 for "A Great American Novel" by James Atlas. Copyright 1980, 1985 by The Atlantic Monthly Company, Boston, MA. Both reprinted by permission of the respective authors./ v. 188, November, 1951 for "The Attack on Yale" by

The Midwest Quarterly, v. XXV, Autumn, 1983. Copyright, 1983, by *The Midwest Quarterly,* Pittsburg State University. Reprinted by permission.

MLN, v. 96, January, 1981. © copyright 1981 by The Johns Hopkins University Press. All rights reserved. Reprinted by permission.

Modern Drama, v. XXVIII, March, 1985. Copyright *Modern Drama,* University of Toronto. Reprinted by permission.

Modern Poetry Studies, v. IX, Autumn, 1978. Copyright 1978, by Media Study, Inc. Reprinted by permission.

Monthly Film Bulletin, v. 52, January, 1985. Copyright © The British Film Institute, 1985. Reprinted by permission.

Ms., v. IX, December, 1980 for ''Nella Larsen: Mystery Woman of the Harlem Renaissance'' by Mary Helen Washington. © 1980 Ms. Magazine Corp. Reprinted by permission of the author.

The Nation, v. 169, October 15, 1949./ v. 199, October 5, 1964; v. 225, July 2, 1977; v. 228, February 10, 1979; v. 235, July 24-31, 1982; v. 235, September 18, 1982; v. 236, March 12, 1983; v. 237, July 2, 1983; v. 238, February 4, 1984; v. 239, August 4-11, 1984; v. 239, September 22, 1984; v. 239, November 17, 1984; v. 240, March 23, 1985; v. 241, November 30, 1985; v. 241, December 21, 1985. Copyright 1964, 1977, 1979, 1982, 1983, 1984, 1985 *The Nation* magazine, The Nation Associates, Inc. All reprinted by permission.

The National Observer, September 26, 1966. © Dow Jones & Company, Inc. 1966. All rights reserved. Reprinted by permission of *The National Observer.*

National Review, v. XVIII, November 15, 1966; v. XX, December 3, 1968; v. XXI, August 12, 1969; v. XXVII, February 28, 1971; v. XXXIV, January 22, 1982; v. XXXVI, June 15, 1984; v. XXXVI, October 19, 1984; v. XXXVII, July 12, 1985. © by National Review, Inc., 150 East 35th Street, New York, NY 10016; 1966, 1968, 1969, 1971, 1982, 1984, 1985. All reprinted with permission.

Natural History, v. LXXXVII, February, 1978. Copyright the American Museum of Natural History, 1978. Reprinted with permission from *Natural History.*

The New Leader, v. LII, April 14, 1969; v. LIII, October 5, 1970; v. LXI, April 10, 1978; v. LXIV, June 15, 1981; v. LXVII, November 26, 1984; v. LXVIII, January 14-28, 1985; v. LXVIII, March 25, 1985. © 1969, 1970, 1978, 1981, 1984, 1985 by The American Labor Conference on International Affairs, Inc. All reprinted by permission.

The New Republic, v. LVII, November 28, 1928; v. LXIV, November 5, 1930; v. LXXXIII, June 5, 1935; v. 125, November 26, 1951./ v. 191, October 22, 1984 for ''Divertimento'' by Stanley Kauffmann. Copyright © 1984 by Stanley Kauffmann. Reprinted by permission of Brandt & Brandt Literary Agents, Inc./ v. 141, September 14, 1959; v. 160, June 28, 1969; v. 165, December 18, 1971; v. 169, August 18 & 25, 1973; v. 178, May 6, 1978; v. 182, May 3, 1980; v. 184, May 16, 1981; v. 190, April 30, 1984; v. 191, September 3, 1984; v. 191, October 15, 1984; v. 191, December 3, 1984; v. 192, February 18, 1985; v. 192, March 18, 1985; v. 192, April 1, 1985; v. 192, April 29, 1985. © 1959, 1969, 1971, 1973, 1978, 1980, 1981, 1984, 1985 The New Republic, Inc. All reprinted by permission of *The New Republic.*

New Statesman, v. LIX, January 30, 1960; v. LIX, March 19, 1960; v. LXIII, May 4, 1962; v. LXVIII, July 10, 1964; v. LXVIII, December 11, 1964; v. 73, February 24, 1967; v. 74, September 22, 1967; v. 78, July 4, 1969; v. 79, May 15, 1970; v. 80, September 25, 1970; v. 80, December 4, 1970; v. 81, April 30, 1971; v. 82, August 20, 1971; v. 96, October 27, 1978; v. 99, January 4, 1980; v. 99, April 4, 1980; v. 100, August 8, 1980; v. 102, October 16, 1981; v. 102, November 20, 1981; v. 103, February 19, 1982; v. 105, April 1, 1983; v. 106, October 21, 1983; v. 106, November 11, 1983; v. 107, February 3, 1984; v. 108, October 5, 1984. © 1960, 1962, 1964, 1967, 1969, 1970, 1971, 1978, 1980, 1981, 1982, 1983, 1984 The Statesman & Nation Publishing Co. Ltd. All reprinted by permission.

The New Statesman & Nation, v. XXXIX, February 25, 1950.

New York Magazine, v. 12, March 12, 1979; v. 15, January 11, 1982; v. 17, September 24, 1984; v. 18, November 25, 1985. Copyright © 1979, 1982, 1984, 1985 by News America Publishing, Inc. All reprinted with the permission of *New York* Magazine.

New York Herald Tribune Book Review, August 18, 1957; September 29, 1957; August 16, 1959; September 4, 1960. © 1957, 1959, 1960 I.H.T. Corporation. All reprinted by permission.

New York Herald Tribune Books, May 13, 1928; September 2, 1928; April 28, 1929; June 2, 1935. © 1928, 1929, 1935 I.H.T. Corporation. All reprinted by permission.

New York Post, February 12, 1985. © 1985, News Group Publications, Inc. Reprinted from the *New York Post* by permission.

The New York Review of Books, v. XXIX, October 7, 1982 for ''School of the Blind'' by Janet Malcolm; v. XXX, October 13, 1983 for ''Happy Days Are Here Again'' by John Gregory Dunne; v. XXXII, March 14, 1985 for ''Heaney Agonistes'' by Richard Ellmann; v. XXXII, March 28, 1985 for ''How to Write about the Holocaust'' by Irving Howe. Copyright © 1982, 1983, 1985 Nyrev, Inc. All reprinted by permission of the respective authors./ v. VIII, June 29, 1967; v. XXIII, July 15, 1976; v. XXIV, May 26, 1977; v. XXVIII, August 13, 1981; v. XXVIII, October 8, 1981; v. XXIX, December 16, 1982; v. XXXI, August 16, 1984; v. XXXI, October 25, 1984; v. XXXI,

D. McClatchy; v. CXLIII, October, 1983 for "Imagination in the Ascendant" by Peter Stitt; v. CXLIII, December, 1983 for a review of "Memory" by J. D. McClatchy; v. CXLVI, August, 1985 for "Triumphs" by Jime Elledge. © 1965, 1972, 1973, 1978, 1979, 1981, 1983, 1985 by The Modern Poetry Association. All reprinted by permission of the Editor of *Poetry* and the respective authors.

Prairie Schooner, v. XLV, Spring, 1971; v. 56, Spring, 1982. © 1971, 1982 by University of Nebraska Press. Both reprinted from *Prairie Schooner* by permission of University of Nebraska Press.

Psychology Today, v. 13, April, 1980. Copyright © 1980 (American Psychological Association). Reprinted with permission from *Psychology Today* magazine.

Publishers Weekly, v. 189, February 7, 1966; v. 216, August 27, 1979; v. 223, April 1, 1983; v. 224, September 9, 1983; March 23, 1984; v. 226, August 3, 1984; v. 226, December 14, 1984; v. 227, January 11, 1985; v. 227, February 15, 1985; v. 227, February 22, 1985; v. 227, April 19, 1985. Copyright © 1966, 1979, 1983, 1984, 1985 by Xerox Corporation. All reprinted from *Publishers Weekly,* published by R. R. Bowker Company, a Xerox company, by permission.

Quill and Quire, v. 48, November, 1982 for "John Metcalf Goads the Literary Establishment" by Robin Skelton. Reprinted by permission of *Quill and Quire* and the author./ v. 46, October, 1980. Reprinted with permission of *Quill and Quire.*

San Francisco Review of Books, September-October, 1984. Copyright © by the *San Francisco Review of Books* 1984. Reprinted by permission.

Saturday Night, v. 87, November, 1972 for "Outsider's Views of Africa and Montreal" by Robert Weaver; v. 97, April, 1982 for "Contemporary Triangles" by Eleanor Wachtel; v. 100, January, 1985 for "Sense and Sensibility" by Urjo Kareda. Copyright © 1972, 1982, 1985 by *Saturday Night.* All reprinted by permission of the respective authors./ v. 87, July, 1972. Copyright © 1972 by *Saturday Night.* Reprinted by permission.

Saturday Review, v. XLII, October 10, 1959; v. XLIII, January 2, 1960; v. XLIII, August 20, 1960; v. XLIII, October 1, 1960; v. XLVI, March 23, 1963; v. XLVI, November 16, 1963; v. LI, April 27, 1968; v. LIII, July 4, 1970; v. LIII, July 11, 1970; v. LIII, November 7, 1970; v. LIV, September 11, 1971; v. LV, March 11, 1972; v. 3, May 1, 1976; v. 5, February 4, 1978; v. 8, October, 1981. © 1959, 1960, 1963, 1968, 1970, 1971, 1972, 1976, 1978, 1981 *Saturday Review* magazine. All reprinted by permission.

The Saturday Review, New York, v. XL, September 28, 1957. © 1957 *Saturday Review* magazine. Reprinted by permission.

The Saturday Review of Literature, v. IV, May 19, 1928; v. V, May 18, 1929; v. XXXIV, December 15, 1951.

Science, v. 219, March 4, 1983; v. 220, May 27, 1983. Copyright 1983 by the AAAS. Both reprinted by permission of the publisher.

Science Fiction & Fantasy Book Review, n. 20, December, 1983. Copyright © 1983 by Science Fiction Research Association. Reprinted by permission.

Science Fiction Review, v. 12, February, 1983 for "Standing by Jericho" by Steve Gallagher. Copyright © 1983 by the author. Reprinted by permission of the author.

The Sewanee Review, v. XC, Winter, 1982. © 1982 by The University of the South. Reprinted by permission of the editor of the *Sewanee Review.*

The Social Studies, v. LVI, April, 1965. Copyright © 1965 Helen Dwight Reid Educational Foundation. Reprinted with permission of the Helen Dwight Reid Educational Foundation, published by Heldref Publications, 4000 Ablemarle Street, N.W., Washington, DC 20016.

South Atlantic Quarterly, v. 81, Winter, 1982. Copyright © 1982 by Duke University Press, Durham, N.C. Reprinted by permission of the Publisher.

Southerly, v. 38, December, 1978 for "The Enigma of Captain Logan" by Donat Gallagher; v. 40, September, 1980 for "Camelot between the Wars" by Clifford Hanna. Both reprinted by permission of the publisher and the respective authors.

The Southern Humanities Review, v. XVIII, Fall, 1984. Copyright 1984 by Auburn University. Reprinted by permission.

Southwest Review, v. LV, Spring, 1970. © 1970 by Southern Methodist University. Reprinted by permission.

The Spectator, v. 211, October 4, 1963; v. 247, October 3, 1981; v. 251, October 29, 1983; v. 252, May 5, 1984; v. 253, September 29, 1984; v. 253, October 13, 1984; v. 253, November 24, 1984; v. 254, March 23, 1985. © 1963, 1981, 1983, 1984, 1985 by *The Spectator.* All reprinted by permission of *The Spectator.*

Sports Illustrated, v. 62, March 4, 1985. © 1985 Time Inc. Reprinted courtesy of *Sports Illustrated.*

THE EXCERPTS IN CLC, VOLUME 37, WERE REPRINTED FROM THE FOLLOWING BOOKS:

Atwood, Margaret. From *Second Words: Selected Critical Prose*. Toronto: House of Anansi Press, 1982. Copyright © 1982, O. W. Toad Limited. All rights reserved. Reprinted by permission.

Axelrod, Steven Gould. From *Robert Lowell: Life and Art*. Princeton University Press, 1978. Copyright © 1978 by Princeton University Press. All rights reserved. Excerpts reprinted with permission of Princeton University Press.

Bell, Vereen M. From *Robert Lowell: Nihilist as Hero*. Harvard University Press, 1983. Copyright © 1983 by the President and Fellows of Harvard College. All rights reserved. Excerpted by permission.

Bone, Robert. From *The Negro Novel in America*. Revised edition. Yale University Press, 1965. © 1958 by Yale University Press, Inc. Revised edition © 1965 by Yale University. All rights reserved. Reprinted by permission of the author.

Breslin, James E.B. From *From Modern to Contemporary: American Poetry, 1945-1965*. University of Chicago Press, 1984. © 1983, 1984 by The University of Chicago. All rights reserved. Reprinted by permission of The University of Chicago Press and the author.

Brothers, Barabara. From "Women Victimised by Fiction: Living and Loving in the Novels of Barbara Pym," in *Twentieth-Century Women Novelists*. Edited by Thomas F. Staley. Barnes & Nobles, 1982. © Thomas F. Staley 1982. All rights reserved. By permission of Barnes & Noble Books, a Division of Littlefield, Adams & Co., Inc.

Collings, Michael R. From *Stephen King as Richard Bachman*. Starmont House, 1985. Published and copyright © 1985 by Starmont House, Inc. All rights reserved. Reprinted by permission.

Davis, Arthur P. From *From the Dark Tower: Afro-American Writers, 1900 to 1960*. Howard University Press, 1974. Copyright © 1974 by Arthur P. Davis. All rights reserved. Reprinted by permission of Howard University Press.

Friedrich, Pia. From *Pier Paolo Pasolini*. Twayne, 1982. Copyright 1982 by Twayne Publishers. Reprinted with the permission of Twayne Publishers, a division of G. K. Hall & Co., Boston.

Gatt-Rutter, John. From *Writers and Politics in Modern Italy*. Holmes & Meier, 1978. Copyright © 1978 John Gatt-Rutter. All rights reserved. Reprinted by permission of Holmes & Meier Publishers, Inc., IUB Building, 30 Irving Place, New York, NY 10003.

Gayle, Addison, Jr. From *The Way of the New World: The Black Novel in America*. Anchor Press, 1975. Copyright © 1975 by Addison Gayle, Jr. All rights reserved. Reprinted by permission of Doubleday & Company, Inc.

Gifford, Terry and Neil Roberts. From *Ted Hughes: A Critical Study*. Faber and Faber, 1981. © 1981 by Terry Gifford and Neil Roberts. All rights reserved. Reprinted by permission of Faber and Faber Ltd.

Grant, Steve. From "Voicing the Protest: The New Writers," in *Dreams and Deconstructions: Alternative Theatre in Britain*. Edited by Sandy Craig. Amber Lane Press, 1980. Copyright © Amber Lane Press Limited, 1980. All rights reserved. Reprinted by permission.

Hayden, Robert and John O'Brien. From "Robert Hayden," in *Interviews with Black Writers*. By John O'Brien. Liveright, 1973. Copyright © 1973 by Liveright Publishing Corporation. Reprinted by permission of Liveright Publishing Corporation.

Hayman, Ronald. From *British Theatre Since 1955: A Reassessment*. Oxford University Press, Oxford, 1979. © Oxford University Press 1979. All rights reserved. Reprinted by permission of A. D. Peters & Co. Ltd.

Henkels, Robert M., Jr. From *Robert Pinget: The Novel as Quest*. University of Alabama Press, 1979. Copyright © 1979 by The University of Alabama Press. All rights reserved. Reprinted by permission.

Hicks, Granville. From an introduction to *Wright Morris: A Reader*. By Wright Morris. Harper & Row, 1970. Introduction copyright © 1970 by Harper & Row, Publishers, Inc. All rights reserved. Reprinted by permission of Harper & Row, Publishers, Inc.

Hughes, H. Stuart. From *Prisoners of Hope: The Silver Age of the Italian Jews, 1924-1974*. Cambridge, Mass.: Harvard University Press, 1983. Copyright © 1983 by the President and Fellows of Harvard College. All rights reserved. Excerpted by permission.

Cumulative Index to Authors

This index lists all author entries in the Gale Literary Criticism Series and includes cross-references to other Gale sources. References in the index are identified as follows:

AITN: *Authors in the News*, Volumes 1-2
CAAS: *Contemporary Authors Autobiography Series*, Volumes 1-2
CA: *Contemporary Authors* (original series), Volumes 1-116
CANR: *Contemporary Authors New Revision Series*, Volumes 1-16
CAP: *Contemporary Authors Permanent Series*, Volumes 1-2
CA-R: *Contemporary Authors* (revised editions), Volumes 1-44
CLC: *Contemporary Literary Criticism*, Volumes 1-37
CLR: *Children's Literature Review*, Volumes 1-9
DLB: *Dictionary of Literary Biography*, Volumes 1-45
DLB-DS: *Dictionary of Literary Biography Documentary Series*, Volumes 1-4
DLB-Y: *Dictionary of Literary Biography Yearbook*, Volumes 1980-1984
LC: *Literature Criticism from 1400 to 1800*, Volumes 1-3
NCLC: *Nineteenth-Century Literature Criticism*, Volumes 1-11
SAAS: *Something about the Author Autobiography Series*, Volume 1
SATA: *Something about the Author*, Volumes 1-42
TCLC: *Twentieth-Century Literary Criticism*, Volumes 1-19
YABC: *Yesterday's Authors of Books for Children*, Volumes 1-2

A. E. 1867-1935 . . . . TCLC **3, 10**
See also Russell, George William
See also DLB 19

Abbey, Edward 1927- . . . . CLC **36**
See also CANR 2
See also CA 45-48

Abé, Kōbō 1924- . . . . CLC **8, 22**
See also CA 65-68

Abell, Kjeld 1901-1961 . . . . CLC **15**
See also obituary CA 111

Abish, Walter 1931- . . . . CLC **22**
See also CA 101

Abrahams, Peter (Henry) 1919- . . . . . CLC **4**
See also CA 57-60

Abrams, M(eyer) H(oward)
1912- . . . . CLC **24**
See also CANR 13
See also CA 57-60

Abse, Dannie 1923- . . . . CLC **7, 29**
See also CAAS 1
See also CANR 4
See also CA 53-56
See also DLB 27

Achebe, Chinua
1930- . . . . CLC **1, 3, 5, 7, 11, 26**
See also CANR 6
See also CA 1-4R
See also SATA 38, 40

Ackroyd, Peter 1917- . . . . CLC **34**
See also CA 25-28R

Acorn, Milton 1923- . . . . CLC **15**
See also CA 103
See also AITN 2

Adamov, Arthur 1908-1970 . . . . . CLC **4, 25**
See also CAP 2
See also CA 17-18
See also obituary CA 25-28R

Adams, Alice (Boyd) 1926- . . . . . . CLC **6, 13**
See also CA 81-84

Adams, Douglas (Noel) 1952- . . . . CLC **27**
See also CA 106
See also DLB-Y 83

Adams, Henry (Brooks)
1838-1918 . . . . TCLC **4**
See also CA 104
See also DLB 12

Adams, Richard (George)
1920- . . . . CLC **4, 5, 18**
See also CANR 3
See also CA 49-52
See also SATA 7
See also AITN 1, 2

Adamson, Joy(-Friederike Victoria)
1910-1980 . . . . CLC **17**
See also CA 69-72
See also obituary CA 93-96
See also SATA 11
See also obituary SATA 22

Addams, Charles (Samuel)
1912- . . . . CLC **30**
See also CANR 12
See also CA 61-64

Adler, C(arole) S(chwerdtfeger)
1932- . . . . CLC **35**
See also CA 89-92
See also SATA 26

Adler, Renata 1938- . . . . CLC **8, 31**
See also CANR 5
See also CA 49-52

Ady, Endre 1877-1919 . . . . TCLC **11**
See also CA 107

Agee, James 1909-1955 . . . . TCLC **1, 19**
See also CA 108
See also DLB 2, 26
See also AITN 1

Agnon, S(hmuel) Y(osef Halevi)
1888-1970 . . . . CLC **4, 8, 14**
See also CAP 2
See also CA 17-18
See also obituary CA 25-28R

Ai 1947- . . . . CLC **4, 14**
See also CA 85-88

Aiken, Conrad (Potter)
1889-1973 . . . . CLC **1, 3, 5, 10**
See also CANR 4
See also CA 5-8R
See also obituary CA 45-48
See also SATA 3, 30
See also DLB 9, 45

Aiken, Joan (Delano) 1924- . . . . CLC **35**
See also CLR 1
See also CANR 4
See also CA 9-12R
See also SAAS 1
See also SATA 2, 30

Ajar, Emile 1914-1980
See Gary, Romain

CONTEMPORARY LITERARY CRITICISM, Vol. 37

Akhmatova, Anna
1888-1966............... CLC 11, 25
See also CAP 1
See also CA 19-20
See also obituary CA 25-28R

Aksakov, Sergei Timofeyvich
1791-1859.................. NCLC 2

Aksenov, Vassily (Pavlovich) 1932-
See Aksyonov, Vasily (Pavlovich)

Aksyonov, Vasily (Pavlovich)
1932-.................... CLC 22, 37
See also CANR 12
See also CA 53-56

Akutagawa Ryūnosuke
1892-1927................. TCLC 16

Alain-Fournier 1886-1914 .... TCLC 6
See also Fournier, Henri Alban

Alarcón, Pedro Antonio de
1833-1891.................. NCLC 1

Albee, Edward (Franklin III)
1928-..... CLC 1, 2, 3, 5, 9, 11, 13, 25
See also CANR 8
See also CA 5-8R
See also DLB 7
See also AITN 1

Alberti, Rafael 1902-.............. CLC 7
See also CA 85-88

Alcott, Amos Bronson
1799-1888.................. NCLC 1
See also DLB 1

Alcott, Louisa May 1832-1888..... NCLC 6
See also CLR 1
See also YABC 1
See also DLB 1, 42

Aldiss, Brian (Wilson) 1925- .... CLC 5, 14
See also CAAS 2
See also CANR 5
See also CA 5-8R
See also SATA 34
See also DLB 14

Aleichem, Sholom 1859-1916...... TCLC 1
See also Rabinovitch, Sholem

Aleixandre, Vicente
1898-1984................ CLC 9, 36
See also CA 85-88
See also obituary CA 114

Alepoudelis, Odysseus 1911-
See Elytis, Odysseus

Alexander, Lloyd (Chudley)
1924-........................CLC 35
See also CLR 1, 5
See also CANR 1
See also CA 1-4R
See also SATA 3

Alger, Horatio, Jr. 1832-1899..... NCLC 8
See also SATA 16
See also DLB 42

Algren, Nelson
1909-1981.............. CLC 4, 10, 33
See also CA 13-16R
See also obituary CA 103
See also DLB 9
See also DLB-Y 81, 82

Allen, Heywood 1935-
See Allen, Woody
See also CA 33-36R

Allen, Roland 1939-
See Ayckbourn, Alan

Allen, Woody 1935-..............CLC 16
See also Allen, Heywood
See also DLB 44

Allingham, Margery (Louise)
1904-1966...................CLC 19
See also CANR 4
See also CA 5-8R
See also obituary CA 25-28R

Allston, Washington
1779-1843.................. NCLC 2
See also DLB 1

Almedingen, E. M. 1898-1971......CLC 12
See also Almedingen, Martha Edith von
See also SATA 3

Almedingen, Martha Edith von 1898-1971
See Almedingen, E. M.
See also CANR 1
See also CA 1-4R

Alonso, Dámaso 1898-.............CLC 14
See also CA 110

Alta 1942-........................CLC 19
See also CA 57-60

Alter, Robert 1935-...............CLC 34
See also CANR 1
See also CA 49-52

Alther, Lisa 1944- ....CLC 7
See also CANR 12
See also CA 65-68

Altman, Robert 1925-.............CLC 16
See also CA 73-76

Alvarez, A(lfred) 1929-......... CLC 5, 13
See also CANR 3
See also CA 1-4R
See also DLB 14, 40

Amado, Jorge 1912- ....CLC 13
See also CA 77-80

Ambler, Eric 1909- .... CLC 4, 6, 9
See also CANR 7
See also CA 9-12R

Amichai, Yehuda 1924- .... CLC 9, 22
See also CA 85-88

Amiel, Henri Frédéric
1821-1881.................. NCLC 4

Amis, Kingsley (William)
1922-............CLC 1, 2, 3, 5, 8, 13
See also CANR 8
See also CA 9-12R
See also DLB 15, 27
See also AITN 2

Amis, Martin 1949-.............. CLC 4, 9
See also CANR 8
See also CA 65-68
See also DLB 14

Ammons, A(rchie) R(andolph)
1926-............ CLC 2, 3, 5, 8, 9, 25
See also CANR 6
See also CA 9-12R
See also DLB 5
See also AITN 1

Anand, Mulk Raj 1905-..........CLC 23
See also CA 65-68

Anaya, Rudolfo A(lfonso)
1937-.......................CLC 23
See also CANR 1
See also CA 45-48

Andersen, Hans Christian
1805-1875.................. NCLC 7
See also CLR 6
See also YABC 1

Anderson, Jessica (Margaret Queale)
19??-.......................CLC 37
See also CANR 4
See also CA 9-12R

Anderson, Jon (Victor) 1940- ......CLC 9
See also CA 25-28R

Anderson, Lindsay 1923- ....CLC 20

Anderson, Maxwell 1888-1959 .... TCLC 2
See also CA 105
See also DLB 7

Anderson, Poul (William)
1926-.......................CLC 15
See also CAAS 2
See also CANR 2, 15
See also CA 1-4R
See also SATA 39
See also DLB 8

Anderson, Robert (Woodruff)
1917-.......................CLC 23
See also CA 21-24R
See also DLB 7
See also AITN 1

Anderson, Roberta Joan 1943-
See Mitchell, Joni

Anderson, Sherwood
1876-1941............... TCLC 1, 10
See also CA 104
See also DLB 4, 9
See also DLB-DS 1

Andrade, Carlos Drummond de
1902-.......................CLC 18

Andrews, Cicily Fairfield 1892-1983
See West, Rebecca

Andreyev, Leonid (Nikolaevich)
1871-1919.................. TCLC 3
See also CA 104

Andrézel, Pierre 1885-1962
See Dinesen, Isak
See also Blixen, Karen (Christentze
Dinesen)

Andrić, Ivo 1892-1975 ....CLC 8
See also CA 81-84
See also obituary CA 57-60

Angelique, Pierre 1897-1962
See Bataille, Georges

Angell, Roger 1920-......... ....CLC 26
See also CANR 13
See also CA 57-60

Angelou, Maya 1928- .... CLC 12, 35
See also CA 65-68
See also DLB 38

Annensky, Innokenty
1856-1909................. TCLC 14
See also CA 110

Anouilh, Jean (Marie Lucien Pierre)
1910-..................CLC 1, 3, 8, 13
See also CA 17-20R

Anthony, Florence 1947-
See Ai

Anthony (Jacob), Piers 1934-......CLC 35
See also Jacob, Piers A(nthony)
D(illingham)
See also DLB 8

Antoninus, Brother 1912-
See Everson, William (Oliver)

Antonioni, Michelangelo 1912- .....CLC 20
See also CA 73-76

Antschel, Paul 1920-1970
See Celan, Paul
See also CA 85-88

Apollinaire, Guillaume
1880-1918................TCLC 3, 8
See also Kostrowitzki, Wilhelm Apollinaris de

Appelfeld, Aharon 1932- ....CLC 23
See also CA 112

Apple, Max (Isaac) 1941-.......CLC 9, 33
See also CA 81-84

Aquin, Hubert 1929-1977.........CLC 15
See also CA 105

Aragon, Louis 1897-1982.......CLC 3, 22
See also CA 69-72
See also obituary CA 108

Arbuthnot, John 1667-1735.........LC 1

Archer, Jeffrey (Howard)
1940-.......................CLC 28
See also CA 77-80

Archer, Jules 1915-...............CLC 12
See also CANR 6
See also CA 9-12R
See also SATA 4

Arden, John 1930-.........CLC 6, 13, 15
See also CA 13-16R
See also DLB 13

Arguedas, José María
1911-1969................CLC 10, 18
See also CA 89-92

Armah, Ayi Kwei 1939-........CLC 5, 33
See also CA 61-64

Armatrading, Joan 1950-..........CLC 17
See also CA 114

Arnim, Achim von 1781-1831.....NCLC 5

Arnold, Matthew 1822-1888......NCLC 6
See also DLB 32

Arnow, Harriette (Louisa Simpson)
1908-....................CLC 2, 7, 18
See also CANR 14
See also CA 9-12R
See also DLB 6
See also SATA 42

Arp, Jean 1887-1966...............CLC 5
See also CA 81-84
See also obituary CA 25-28R

Argueta, Manlio 1936- ....CLC 31

Arquette, Lois S(teinmetz)
See Duncan (Steinmetz Arquette), Lois
See also SATA 1

Arrabal, Fernando 1932-.....CLC 2, 9, 18
See also CANR 15
See also CA 9-12R

Arrick, Fran.....................CLC 30

Artaud, Antonin 1896-1948.......TCLC 3
See also CA 104

Arthur, Ruth M(abel)
1905-1979....................CLC 12
See also CANR 4
See also CA 9-12R
See also obituary CA 85-88
See also SATA 7
See also obituary SATA 26

Arundel, Honor (Morfydd)
1919-1973....................CLC 17
See also CAP 2
See also CA 21-22
See also obituary CA 41-44R
See also SATA 4
See also obituary SATA 24

Asch, Sholem 1880-1957.........TCLC 3
See also CA 105

Ashbery, John (Lawrence)
1927-..... CLC 2, 3, 4, 6, 9, 13, 15, 25
See also CANR 9
See also CA 5-8R
See also DLB 5
See also DLB-Y 81

Ashton-Warner, Sylvia (Constance)
1908-1984....................CLC 19
See also CA 69-72
See also obituary CA 112

Asimov, Isaac
1920-............. CLC 1, 3, 9, 19, 26
See also CANR 2
See also CA 1-4R
See also SATA 1, 26
See also DLB 8

Aston, James 1906-1964
See White, T(erence) H(anbury)

Asturias, Miguel Ángel
1899-1974...............CLC 3, 8, 13
See also CAP 2
See also CA 25-28
See also obituary CA 49-52

Atheling, William, Jr. 1921-1975
See Blish, James (Benjamin)

Atherton, Gertrude (Franklin Horn)
1857-1948...................TCLC 2
See also CA 104
See also DLB 9

Atwood, Margaret (Eleanor)
1939-........CLC 2, 3, 4, 8, 13, 15, 25
See also CANR 3
See also CA 49-52

Auchincloss, Louis (Stanton)
1917-.................CLC 4, 6, 9, 18
See also CANR 6
See also CA 1-4R
See also DLB 2
See also DLB-Y 80

Auden, W(ystan) H(ugh)
1907-1973....... CLC 1, 2, 3, 4, 6, 9, 11, 14
See also CANR 5
See also CA 9-12R
See also obituary CA 45-48
See also DLB 10, 20

Auel, Jean M(arie) 1936- ....CLC 31
See also CA 103

Austen, Jane 1775-1817.........NCLC 1

Avison, Margaret 1918- ....CLC 2, 4
See also CA 17-20R

Ayckbourn, Alan
1939-.................CLC 5, 8, 18, 33
See also CA 21-24R
See also DLB 13

Aymé, Marcel (Andre)
1902-1967....................CLC 11
See also CA 89-92

Ayrton, Michael 1921-1975.........CLC 7
See also CANR 9
See also CA 5-8R
See also obituary CA 61-64

Azorín 1874-1967.................CLC 11
See also Martínez Ruiz, José

Azuela, Mariano 1873-1952...... TCLC 3
See also CA 104

"Bab" 1836-1911
See Gilbert, (Sir) W(illiam) S(chwenck)

Babel, Isaak (Emmanuilovich)
1894-1941...............TCLC 2, 13
See also CA 104

Babits, Mihály 1883-1941....... TCLC 14
See also CA 114

Bacchelli, Riccardo 1891-..........CLC 19
See also CA 29-32R

Bach, Richard (David) 1936-.......CLC 14
See also CA 9-12R
See also SATA 13
See also AITN 1

Bachman, Richard 1947-
See King, Stephen (Edwin)

Bagehot, Walter 1826-1877...... NCLC 10

Bagnold, Enid 1889-1981..........CLC 25
See also CANR 5
See also CA 5-8R
See also obituary CA 103
See also SATA 1, 25
See also DLB 13

Bagryana, Elisaveta 1893- ....CLC 10

Baillie, Joanna 1762-1851........ NCLC 2

Bainbridge, Beryl
1933-.......CLC 4, 5, 8, 10, 14, 18, 22
See also CA 21-24R
See also DLB 14

Baker, Elliott 1922-................CLC 8
See also CANR 2
See also CA 45-48

Baker, Russell (Wayne) 1925-......CLC 31
See also CANR 11
See also CA 57-60

Bakshi, Ralph 1938-..............CLC 26
See also CA 112

Baldwin, James (Arthur)
1924-......CLC 1, 2, 3, 4, 5, 8, 13, 15, 17
See also CANR 3
See also CA 1-4R
See also SATA 9
See also DLB 2, 7, 33

Ballard, J(ames) G(raham)
1930-...............CLC 3, 6, 14, 36
See also CANR 15
See also CA 5-8R
See also DLB 14

Balmont, Konstantin Dmitriyevich
1867-1943.................TCLC 11
See also CA 109

Balzac, Honoré de 1799-1850..... NCLC 5

Bambara, Toni Cade 1939- ....CLC 19
See also CA 29-32R
See also DLB 38

Banks, Iain 1954-.................CLC 34

Banks, Lynne Reid 1929-..........CLC 23
See also Reid Banks, Lynne

Author Index

Banks, Russell 1940-.............CLC 37
See also CA 65-68

Banville, Théodore (Faullain) de
1832-1891..................NCLC 9

Baraka, Amiri
1934-.......CLC 1, 2, 3, 5, 10, 14, 33
See also Baraka, Imamu Amiri
See also Jones, (Everett) LeRoi
See also DLB 5, 7, 16, 38

Baraka, Imamu Amiri
1934-........CLC 1, 2, 3, 5, 10, 14, 33
See also Baraka, Amiri
See also Jones, (Everett) LeRoi
See also DLB 5, 7, 16, 38

Barbey d'Aurevilly, Jules Amédée
1808-1889..................NCLC 1

Barbusse, Henri 1873-1935 .... TCLC 5
See also CA 105

Barea, Arturo 1897-1957 .... TCLC 14
See also CA 111

Barfoot, Joan 1946-.............CLC 18
See also CA 105

Baring, Maurice 1874-1945 .... TCLC 8
See also CA 105
See also DLB 34

Barker, George (Granville)
1913-.......................CLC 8
See also CANR 7
See also CA 9-12R
See also DLB 20

Barker, Howard 1946- ....CLC 37
See also CA 102
See also DLB 13

Barker, Pat 19??-.................CLC 32

Barnes, Djuna
1892-1982........ CLC 3, 4, 8, 11, 29
See also CANR 16
See also CA 9-12R
See also obituary CA 107
See also DLB 4, 9, 45

Barnes, Peter 1931-................CLC 5
See also CA 65-68
See also DLB 13

Baroja (y Nessi), Pío
1872-1956..................TCLC 8
See also CA 104

Barondess, Sue K(aufman) 1926-1977
See Kaufman, Sue
See also CANR 1
See also CA 1-4R
See also obituary CA 69-72

Barrett, (Roger) Syd 1946-
See Pink Floyd

Barrett, William (Christopher)
1913-........................CLC 27
See also CANR 11
See also CA 13-16R

Barrie, (Sir) J(ames) M(atthew)
1860-1937..................TCLC 2
See also CA 104
See also YABC 1
See also DLB 10

Barrol, Grady 1953-
See Bograd, Larry

Barry, Philip (James Quinn)
1896-1949................. TCLC 11
See also CA 109
See also DLB 7

Barth, John (Simmons)
1930-......CLC 1, 2, 3, 5, 7, 9, 10, 14,
                                    27
See also CANR 5
See also CA 1-4R
See also DLB 2
See also AITN 1, 2

Barthelme, Donald
1931-...... CLC 1, 2, 3, 5, 6, 8, 13, 23
See also CA 21-24R
See also SATA 7
See also DLB 2
See also DLB-Y 80

Barthelme, Frederick 1943-........CLC 36
See also CA 114

Barthes, Roland 1915-1980 ....CLC 24
See also obituary CA 97-100

Bassani, Giorgio 1916- ....CLC 9
See also CA 65-68

Bataille, Georges 1897-1962.......CLC 29
See also CA 101
See also obituary CA 89-92

Baudelaire, Charles
1821-1867..................NCLC 6

Baum, L(yman) Frank
1856-1919.................. TCLC 7
See also CA 108
See also SATA 18
See also DLB 22

Baumbach, Jonathan 1933- ..... CLC 6, 23
See also CANR 12
See also CA 13-16R
See also DLB-Y 80

Baxter, James K(eir)
1926-1972...................CLC 14
See also CA 77-80

Bayer, Sylvia 1909-1981
See Glassco, John

Beagle, Peter S(oyer) 1939- ....CLC 7
See also CANR 4
See also CA 9-12R
See also DLB-Y 80

Beard, Charles A(ustin)
1874-1948.................. TCLC 15
See also CA 115
See also SATA 18
See also DLB 17

Beardsley, Aubrey 1872-1898 ..... NCLC 6

Beattie, Ann 1947-..........CLC 8, 13, 18
See also CA 81-84
See also DLB-Y 82

Beauvoir, Simone de
1908-........... CLC 1, 2, 4, 8, 14, 31
See also CA 9-12R

Becker, Jurek 1937- .... CLC 7, 19
See also CA 85-88

Becker, Walter 1950-
See Becker, Walter and Fagen, Donald

Becker, Walter 1950- and
Fagen, Donald 1948- ....CLC 26

Beckett, Samuel (Barclay)
1906-......CLC 1, 2, 3, 4, 6, 9, 10, 11,
                                14, 18, 29
See also CA 5-8R
See also DLB 13, 15

Beckman, Gunnel 1910-...........CLC 26
See also CANR 15
See also CA 33-36R
See also SATA 6

Becque, Henri 1837-1899........ NCLC 3

Beddoes, Thomas Lovell
1803-1849.................. NCLC 3

Beecher, John 1904-1980...........CLC 6
See also CANR 8
See also CA 5-8R
See also obituary CA 105
See also AITN 1

Beerbohm, (Sir Henry) Max(imilian)
1872-1956.................. TCLC 1
See also CA 104
See also DLB 34

Behan, Brendan
1923-1964...........CLC 1, 8, 11, 15
See also CA 73-76
See also DLB 13

Behn, Aphra 1640?-1689 ....LC 1
See also DLB 39

Belasco, David 1853-1931........ TCLC 3
See also CA 104
See also DLB 7

Belcheva, Elisaveta 1893-
See Bagryana, Elisaveta

Belinski, Vissarion Grigoryevich
1811-1848.................. NCLC 5

Belitt, Ben 1911- ....CLC 22
See also CANR 7
See also CA 13-16R
See also DLB 5

Bell, Acton 1820-1849
See Brontë, Anne

Bell, Currer 1816-1855
See Brontë, Charlotte

Bell, Marvin 1937-............ CLC 8, 31
See also CA 21-24R
See also DLB 5

Bellamy, Edward 1850-1898 ...... NCLC 4
See also DLB 12

**Belloc, (Joseph) Hilaire (Pierre Sébastien
René Swanton)**
1870-1953................ TCLC 7, 18
See also CA 106
See also YABC 1
See also DLB 19

Bellow, Saul
1915-.....CLC 1, 2, 3, 6, 8, 10, 13, 15,
                            25, 33, 34
See also CA 5-8R
See also DLB 2, 28
See also DLB-Y 82
See also DLB-DS 3
See also AITN 2

Belser, Reimond Karel Maria de 1929-
See Ruyslinck, Ward

Bely, Andrey 1880-1934......... TCLC 7
See also CA 104

Benary-Isbert, Margot
    1889-1979....................CLC 12
  See also CANR 4
  See also CA 5-8R
  See also obituary CA 89-92
  See also SATA 2
  See also obituary SATA 21

Benavente (y Martinez), Jacinto
    1866-1954.................... TCLC 3
  See also CA 106

Benchley, Peter (Bradford)
    1940-..................... CLC 4, 8
  See also CANR 12
  See also CA 17-20R
  See also SATA 3
  See also AITN 2

Benchley, Robert 1889-1945 ...... TCLC 1
  See also CA 105
  See also DLB 11

Benedikt, Michael 1935-........ CLC 4, 14
  See also CANR 7
  See also CA 13-16R
  See also DLB 5

Benet, Juan 1927- ....CLC 28

Benét, Stephen Vincent
    1898-1943................... TCLC 7
  See also CA 104
  See also YABC 1
  See also DLB 4

Benn, Gottfried 1886-1956....... TCLC 3
  See also CA 106

Bennett, (Enoch) Arnold
    1867-1931.................. TCLC 5
  See also CA 106
  See also DLB 10, 34

Bennett, George Harold 1930-
  See Bennett, Hal
  See also CA 97-100

Bennett, Hal 1930-................CLC 5
  See also Bennett, George Harold
  See also DLB 33

Bennett, Jay 1912-.................CLC 35
  See also CANR 11
  See also CA 69-72
  See also SATA 27

Bennett, Louise (Simone)
    1919-......................CLC 28
  See also Bennett-Coverly, Louise Simone

Bennett-Coverly, Louise Simone 1919-
  See Bennett, Louise (Simone)
  See also CA 97-100

Benson, Jackson J. 1930-..........CLC 34
  See also CA 25-28R

Benson, Sally 1900-1972...........CLC 17
  See also CAP 1
  See also CA 19-20
  See also obituary CA 37-40R
  See also SATA 1, 35
  See also obituary SATA 27

Benson, Stella 1892-1933 .... TCLC 17
  See also DLB 36

Bentley, E(dmund) C(lerihew)
    1875-1956................. TCLC 12
  See also CA 108

Bentley, Eric (Russell) 1916- ....CLC 24
  See also CANR 6
  See also CA 5-8R

Berger, John (Peter) 1926-...... CLC 2, 19
  See also CA 81-84
  See also DLB 14

Berger, Melvin (H.) 1927-.........CLC 12
  See also CANR 4
  See also CA 5-8R
  See also SATA 5

Berger, Thomas (Louis)
    1924-.......... CLC 3, 5, 8, 11, 18
  See also CANR 5
  See also CA 1-4R
  See also DLB 2
  See also DLB-Y 80

Bergman, (Ernst) Ingmar
    1918-.......................CLC 16
  See also CA 81-84

Bergstein, Eleanor 1938- ....CLC 4
  See also CANR 5
  See also CA 53-56

Bernanos, (Paul Louis) Georges
    1888-1948................... TCLC 3
  See also CA 104

Bernhard, Thomas 1931- .... CLC 3, 32
  See also CA 85-88

Berrigan, Daniel J. 1921-...........CLC 4
  See also CAAS 1
  See also CANR 11
  See also CA 33-36R
  See also DLB 5

Berrigan, Edmund Joseph Michael, Jr.
    1934-1983
  See Berrigan, Ted
  See also CANR 14
  See also CA 61-64
  See also obituary CA 110

Berrigan, Ted 1934-1983 ....CLC 37
  See also Berrigan, Edmund Joseph
    Michael, Jr.
  See also DLB 5

Berry, Chuck 1926-...............CLC 17

Berry, Wendell (Erdman)
    1934-.................CLC 4, 6, 8, 27
  See also CA 73-76
  See also DLB 5, 6
  See also AITN 1

Berryman, John
    1914-1972..... CLC 1, 2, 3, 4, 6, 8, 10,
                      13, 25
  See also CAP 1
  See also CA 15-16
  See also obituary CA 33-36R

Bertolucci, Bernardo 1940- ....CLC 16
  See also CA 106

Besant, Annie (Wood)
    1847-1933................... TCLC 9
  See also CA 105

Bessie, Alvah 1904-1985...........CLC 23
  See also CANR 2
  See also CA 5-8R
  See also obituary CA 116
  See also DLB 26

Beti, Mongo 1932-................CLC 27

Betjeman, John
    1906-1984...........CLC 2, 6, 10, 34
  See also CA 9-12R
  See also obituary CA 112
  See also DLB 20
  See also DLB-Y 84

Betti, Ugo 1892-1953............. TCLC 5
  See also CA 104

Betts, Doris (Waugh)
    1932-...............CLC 3, 6, 28
  See also CANR 9
  See also CA 13-16R
  See also DLB-Y 82

Bidart, Frank 19??-...............CLC 33

Bienek, Horst 1930-........... CLC 7, 11
  See also CA 73-76

Bierce, Ambrose (Gwinett)
    1842-1914?............... TCLC 1, 7
  See also CA 104
  See also DLB 11, 12, 23

Binyon, T(imothy) J(ohn)
    1936-......................CLC 34
  See also CA 111

Bioy Casares, Adolfo
    1914-.................. CLC 4, 8, 13
  See also CA 29-32R

Bird, Robert Montgomery
    1806-1854.................. NCLC 1

Birdwell, Cleo 1936-
  See DeLillo, Don

Birney (Alfred) Earle
    1904-...................CLC 1, 4, 6, 11
  See also CANR 5
  See also CA 1-4R

Bishop, Elizabeth
    1911-1979...... CLC 1, 4, 9, 13, 15, 32
  See also CA 5-8R
  See also obituary CA 89-92
  See also obituary SATA 24
  See also DLB 5

Bishop, John 1935- ....CLC 10
  See also CA 105

Bissett, Bill 1939-.................CLC 18
  See also CANR 15
  See also CA 69-72

Biyidi, Alexandre 1932-
  See Beti, Mongo
  See also CA 114

Bjørnson, Bjørnstjerne (Martinius)
    1832-1910.................. TCLC 7
  See also CA 104

Blackburn, Paul 1926-1971 ....CLC 9
  See also CA 81-84
  See also obituary CA 33-36R
  See also DLB 16
  See also DLB-Y 81

Blackmur, R(ichard) P(almer)
    1904-1965................ CLC 2, 24
  See also CAP 1
  See also CA 11-12
  See also obituary CA 25-28R

Blackwood, Algernon (Henry)
    1869-1951.................. TCLC 5
  See also CA 105

Blackwood, Caroline 1931- ...... CLC 6, 9
  See also CA 85-88
  See also DLB 14

Blair, Eric Arthur 1903-1950
  See Orwell, George
  See also CA 104
  See also SATA 29

Blais, Marie-Claire
1939-............ CLC 2, 4, 6, 13, 22
See also CA 21-24R

Blaise, Clark 1940-.............. CLC 29
See also CANR 5
See also CA 53-56R
See also AITN 2

Blake, Nicholas 1904-1972
See Day Lewis, C(ecil)

Blasco Ibáñez, Vicente
1867-1928................. TCLC 12
See also CA 110

Blatty, William Peter 1928-......... CLC 2
See also CANR 9
See also CA 5-8R

Blish, James (Benjamin)
1921-1975................... CLC 14
See also CANR 3
See also CA 1-4R
See also obituary CA 57-60
See also DLB 8

Blixen, Karen (Christentze Dinesen)
1885-1962
See Dinesen, Isak
See also CAP 2
See also CA 25-28

Bloch, Robert (Albert) 1917-....... CLC 33
See also CANR 5
See also CA 5-8R
See also DLB 44
See also SATA 12

Blok, Aleksandr (Aleksandrovich)
1880-1921................. TCLC 5
See also CA 104

Bloom, Harold 1930-.............. CLC 24
See also CA 13-16R

Blume, Judy (Sussman Kitchens)
1938-.................. CLC 12, 30
See also CLR 2
See also CANR 13
See also CA 29-32R
See also SATA 2, 31

Blunden, Edmund (Charles)
1896-1974.................... CLC 2
See also CAP 2
See also CA 17-18
See also obituary CA 45-48
See also DLB 20

Bly, Robert 1926- ..... CLC 1, 2, 5, 10, 15
See also CA 5-8R
See also DLB 5

Bochco, Steven 1944?-
See Bochco, Steven and Kozoll, Michael

Bochco, Steven 1944?- and
Kozoll, Michael 1940?- .... CLC 35

Bødker, Cecil 1927-.............. CLC 21
See also CANR 13
See also CA 73-76
See also SATA 14

Boell, Heinrich (Theodor) 1917-1985
See Böll, Heinrich
See also CA 21-24R
See also obituary CA 116

Bogan, Louise 1897-1970.......... CLC 4
See also CA 73-76
See also obituary CA 25-28R
See also DLB 45

Bogarde, Dirk 1921-.............. CLC 19
See also Van Den Bogarde, Derek (Jules
Gaspard Ulric) Niven
See also DLB 14

Bograd, Larry 1953-.............. CLC 35
See also CA 93-96
See also SATA 33

Böhl de Faber, Cecilia 1796-1877
See Caballero, Fernán

Boileau-Despréaux, Nicolas
1636-1711.................... LC 3

Böll, Heinrich (Theodor)
1917-1985..... CLC 2, 3, 6, 9, 11, 15,
27
See also Boell, Heinrich (Theodor)

Bolt, Robert (Oxton) 1924- .... CLC 14
See also CA 17-20R
See also DLB 13

Bond, Edward 1934-...... CLC 4, 6, 13, 23
See also CA 25-28R
See also DLB 13

Bonham, Frank 1914-.............. CLC 12
See also CANR 4
See also CA 9-12R
See also SATA 1

Bonnefoy, Yves 1923-.......... CLC 9, 15
See also CA 85-88

Bontemps, Arna (Wendell)
1902-1973................. CLC 1, 18
See also CLR 6
See also CANR 4
See also CA 1-4R
See also obituary CA 41-44R
See also SATA 2
See also obituary SATA 24

Booth, Martin 1944-.............. CLC 13
See also CAAS 2
See also CA 93-96

Booth, Philip 1925-.............. CLC 23
See also CANR 5
See also CA 5-8R
See also DLB-Y 82

Booth, Wayne C(layson) 1921- ..... CLC 24
See also CANR 3
See also CA 1-4R

Borchert, Wolfgang 1921-1947 .... TCLC 5
See also CA 104

Borges, Jorge Luis
1899-.......CLC 1, 2, 3, 4, 6, 8, 9, 10,
13, 19
See also CA 21-24R

Borowski, Tadeusz 1922-1951 ..... TCLC 9
See also CA 106

Borrow, George (Henry)
1803-1881................. NCLC 9
See also DLB 21

Bosschère, Jean de
1878-1953................. TCLC 19

Bourget, Paul (Charles Joseph)
1852-1935................. TCLC 12
See also CA 107

Bourjaily, Vance (Nye) 1922-........ CLC 8
See also CAAS 1
See also CANR 2
See also CA 1-4R
See also DLB 2

Bourne, Randolph S(illiman)
1886-1918................. TCLC 16

Bowen, Elizabeth (Dorothea Cole)
1899-1973...... CLC 1, 3, 6, 11, 15, 22
See also CAP 2
See also CA 17-18
See also obituary CA 41-44R
See also DLB 15

Bowering, George 1935-.......... CLC 15
See also CANR 10
See also CA 21-24R

Bowering, Marilyn R(uthe)
1949-...................... CLC 32
See also CA 101

Bowers, Edgar 1924-.............. CLC 9
See also CA 5-8R
See also DLB 5

Bowie, David 1947-.............. CLC 17
See also Jones, David Robert

Bowles, Jane (Sydney)
1917-1973.................... CLC 3
See also CAP 2
See also CA 19-20
See also obituary CA 41-44R

Bowles, Paul (Frederick)
1910-................ CLC 1, 2, 19
See also CAAS 1
See also CANR 1
See also CA 1-4R
See also DLB 5, 6

Box, Edgar 1925-
See Vidal, Gore

Boyd, William 1952-.............. CLC 28
See also CA 114

Boyle, Kay 1903-.......... CLC 1, 5, 19
See also CAAS 1
See also CA 13-16R
See also DLB 4, 9

Boyle, Patrick .... CLC 19

Boyle, T. Coraghessan 1948-....... CLC 36

Brackenridge, Hugh Henry
1748-1816................. NCLC 7
See also DLB 11, 37

Bradbury, Edward P. 1939-
See Moorcock, Michael

Bradbury, Malcolm (Stanley)
1932-...................... CLC 32
See also CANR 1
See also CA 1-4R
See also DLB 14

Bradbury, Ray (Douglas)
1920-............... CLC 1, 3, 10, 15
See also CANR 2
See also CA 1-4R
See also SATA 11
See also DLB 2, 8
See also AITN 1, 2

Bradley, David (Henry), Jr.
1950-...................... CLC 23
See also CA 104
See also DLB 33

Bradley, Marion Zimmer
1930-...................... CLC 30
See also CANR 7
See also CA 57-60
See also DLB 8

Bragg, Melvyn 1939-..............CLC 10
See also CANR 10
See also CA 57-60
See also DLB 14

Braine, John (Gerard) 1922-..... CLC 1, 3
See also CANR 1
See also CA 1-4R
See also DLB 15

Brammer, Billy Lee 1930?-1978
See Brammer, William

Brammer, William 1930?-1978.....CLC 31
See also obituary CA 77-80

Brancati, Vitaliano
1907-1954................. TCLC 12
See also CA 109

Brancato, Robin F(idler) 1936-.....CLC 35
See also CANR 11
See also CA 69-72
See also SATA 23

Brand, Millen 1906-1980 ....CLC 7
See also CA 21-24R
See also obituary CA 97-100

Brandes, Georg (Morris Cohen)
1842-1927................. TCLC 10
See also CA 105

Branley, Franklyn M(ansfield)
1915-........................CLC 21
See also CANR 14
See also CA 33-36R
See also SATA 4

Brathwaite, Edward 1930-........CLC 11
See also CANR 11
See also CA 25-28R

Brautigan, Richard
1935-1984....... CLC 1, 3, 5, 9, 12, 34
See also CA 53-56
See also obituary CA 113
See also DLB 2, 5
See also DLB-Y 80, 84

Brecht, (Eugen) Bertolt (Friedrich)
1898-1956..............TCLC 1, 6, 13
See also CA 104

Bremer, Fredrika 1801-1865..... NCLC 11

Brennan, Christopher John
1870-1932................. TCLC 17

Brennan, Maeve 1917- ....CLC 5
See also CA 81-84

Brentano, Clemens (Maria)
1778-1842................. NCLC 1

Brenton, Howard 1942- ....CLC 31
See also CA 69-72
See also DLB 13

Breslin, James (E.) 1930-
See Breslin, Jimmy
See also CA 73-76

Breslin, Jimmy 1930- ....CLC 4
See also Breslin, James (E.)
See also AITN 1

Bresson, Robert 1907-.............CLC 16
See also CA 110

Breton, André 1896-1966..... CLC 2, 9, 15
See also CAP 2
See also CA 19-20
See also obituary CA 25-28R

Breytenbach, Breyten
1939-.................... CLC 23, 37
See also CA 113

Bridgers, Sue Ellen 1942-..........CLC 26
See also CANR 11
See also CA 65-68
See also SAAS 1
See also SATA 22

Bridges, Robert 1844-1930....... TCLC 1
See also CA 104
See also DLB 19

Bridie, James 1888-1951 .... TCLC 3
See also Mavor, Osborne Henry
See also DLB 10

Brin, David 1950- ....CLC 34
See also CA 102

Brink, André (Philippus)
1935-................... CLC 18, 36
See also CA 104

Brinsmead, H(esba) F(ay)
1922-........................CLC 21
See also CANR 10
See also CA 21-24R
See also SATA 18

Brittain, Vera (Mary)
1893?-1970...................CLC 23
See also CAP 1
See also CA 15-16
See also obituary CA 25-28R

Brodsky, Iosif Alexandrovich 1940-
See Brodsky, Joseph
See also CA 41-44R
See also AITN 1

Brodsky, Joseph
1940-................CLC 4, 6, 13, 36
See also Brodsky, Iosif Alexandrovich

Brodsky, Michael (Mark)
1948-........................CLC 19
See also CA 102

Bromell, Henry 1947-..............CLC 5
See also CANR 9
See also CA 53-56

Bromfield, Louis (Brucker)
1896-1956................. TCLC 11
See also CA 107
See also DLB 4, 9

Broner, E(sther) M(asserman)
1930-........................CLC 19
See also CANR 8
See also CA 17-20R
See also DLB 28

Bronk, William 1918-.............CLC 10
See also CA 89-92

Brontë, Anne 1820-1849......... NCLC 4
See also DLB 21

Brontë, Charlotte
1816-1855................NCLC 3, 8
See also DLB 21
See also DLB 39

Brooke, Henry 1703?-1783 .... LC 1
See also DLB 39

Brooke, Rupert (Chawner)
1887-1915................ TCLC 2, 7
See also CA 104
See also DLB 19

Brookner, Anita 1938- .... CLC 32, 34
See also CA 114

Brooks, Cleanth 1906- ....CLC 24
See also CA 17-20R

Brooks, Gwendolyn
1917-.............. CLC 1, 2, 4, 5, 15
See also CANR 1
See also CA 1-4R
See also SATA 6
See also DLB 5
See also AITN 1

Brooks, Mel 1926-.................CLC 12
See also Kaminsky, Melvin
See also CA 65-68
See also DLB 26

Brooks, Peter 1938-................CLC 34
See also CANR 1
See also CA 45-48

Brooks, Van Wyck 1886-1963......CLC 29
See also CANR 6
See also CA 1-4R
See also DLB 45

Brophy, Brigid (Antonia)
1929-................... CLC 6, 11, 29
See also CA 5-8R
See also DLB 14

Brosman, Catharine Savage
1934-........................CLC 9
See also CA 61-64

Broughton, T(homas) Alan
1936-........................CLC 19
See also CANR 2
See also CA 45-48

Broumas, Olga 1949- ....CLC 10
See also CA 85-88

Brown, Claude 1937- ....CLC 30
See also CA 73-76

Brown, Dee (Alexander) 1908- .....CLC 18
See also CANR 11
See also CA 13-16R
See also SATA 5
See also DLB-Y 80

Brown, George Mackay 1921-.......CLC 5
See also CANR 12
See also CA 21-24R
See also SATA 35
See also DLB 14, 27

Brown, Rita Mae 1944- ....CLC 18
See also CANR 2, 11
See also CA 45-48

Brown, Rosellen 1939- ....CLC 32
See also CANR 14
See also CA 77-80

Brown, Sterling A(llen)
1901-.................... CLC 1, 23
See also CA 85-88

Brown, William Wells
1816?-1884................. NCLC 2
See also DLB 3

Browne, Jackson 1950-............CLC 21

Browning, Elizabeth Barrett
1806-1861................... NCLC 1
See also DLB 32

Browning, Tod 1882-1962 ....CLC 16

Bruccoli, Matthew J(oseph)
1931-........................CLC 34
See also CANR 7
See also CA 9-12R

Author Index

Bruce, Lenny 1925-1966..........CLC 21
See also Schneider, Leonard Alfred

Brunner, John (Kilian Houston)
1934-..................... CLC 8, 10
See also CANR 2
See also CA 1-4R

Bryan, C(ourtlandt) D(ixon) B(arnes)
1936-.......................CLC 29
See also CANR 13
See also CA 73-76

Bryant, William Cullen
1794-1878.................. NCLC 6
See also DLB 3, 43

Bryusov, Valery (Yakovlevich)
1873-1924.................. TCLC 10
See also CA 107

Buchheim, Lothar-Günther
1918-........................CLC 6
See also CA 85-88

Buchwald, Art(hur) 1925- ....CLC 33
See also CA 5-8R
See also SATA 10
See also AITN 1

Buck, Pearl S(ydenstricker)
1892-1973.............. CLC 7, 11, 18
See also CANR 1
See also CA 1-4R
See also obituary CA 41-44R
See also SATA 1, 25
See also DLB 9
See also AITN 1

Buckler, Ernest 1908-1984.........CLC 13
See also CAP 1
See also CA 11-12
See also obituary CA 114

Buckley, William F(rank), Jr.
1925-.................. CLC 7, 18, 37
See also CANR 1
See also CA 1-4R
See also DLB-Y 80
See also AITN 1

Buechner, (Carl) Frederick
1926-.................CLC 2, 4, 6, 9
See also CANR 11
See also CA 13-16R
See also DLB-Y 80

Buell, John (Edward) 1927-........CLC 10
See also CA 1-4R

Buero Vallejo, Antonio 1916- ......CLC 15
See also CA 106

Bukowski, Charles 1920- ...... CLC 2, 5, 9
See also CA 17-20R
See also DLB 5

Bulgakov, Mikhail (Afanas'evich)
1891-1940..............TCLC 2, 16
See also CA 105

Bullins, Ed 1935-............ CLC 1, 5, 7
See also CA 49-52
See also DLB 7, 38

**Bulwer-Lytton, (Lord) Edward (George Earle
Lytton)** 1803-1873 .... NCLC 1
See also Lytton, Edward Bulwer
See also DLB 21

Bunin, Ivan (Alexeyevich)
1870-1953.................. TCLC 6
See also CA 104

Bunting, Basil 1900-1985..........CLC 10
See also CANR 7
See also CA 53-56
See also obituary CA 115
See also DLB 20

Buñuel, Luis 1900-1983 ....CLC 16
See also CA 101
See also obituary CA 110

Burgess, Anthony
1917-.....CLC 1, 2, 4, 5, 8, 10, 13, 15,
22
See also Wilson, John (Anthony) Burgess
See also DLB 14
See also DLB-Y 84
See also AITN 1

Burke, Kenneth (Duva)
1897-.................... CLC 2, 24
See also CA 5-8R
See also DLB 45

Burns, Robert 1759-1796........... LC 3

Burns, Tex 1908?-
See L'Amour, Louis (Dearborn)

Burnshaw, Stanley 1906- .... CLC 3, 13
See also CA 9-12R

Burr, Anne 1937-.................CLC 6
See also CA 25-28R

Burroughs, Edgar Rice
1875-1950.................. TCLC 2
See also CA 104
See also DLB 8
See also SATA 41

Burroughs, William S(eward)
1914-............. CLC 1, 2, 5, 15, 22
See also CA 9-12R
See also DLB 2, 8, 16
See also DLB-Y 81
See also AITN 2

Busch, Frederick 1941-...... CLC 7, 10, 18
See also CAAS 1
See also CA 33-36R
See also DLB 6

Bush, Ronald 19??-...............CLC 34

Butler, Samuel 1835-1902 .... TCLC 1
See also CA 104
See also DLB 18

Butor, Michel (Marie François)
1926-............. CLC 1, 3, 8, 11, 15
See also CA 9-12R

Buzzati, Dino 1906-1972..........CLC 36
See also obituary CA 33-36R

Byars, Betsy 1928-...............CLC 35
See also CLR 1
See also CA 33-36R
See also SAAS 1
See also SATA 4

Byatt, A(ntonia) S(usan Drabble)
1936-.......................CLC 19
See also CANR 13
See also CA 13-16R
See also DLB 14

Byrne, David 1953?-..............CLC 26

Byrne, John Keyes 1926-
See Leonard, Hugh
See also CA 102

Byron, George Gordon (Noel), Lord Byron
1788-1824.................. NCLC 2

Caballero, Fernán 1796-1877 .... NCLC 10

Cabell, James Branch
1879-1958.................. TCLC 6
See also CA 105
See also DLB 9

Cable, George Washington
1844-1925.................. TCLC 4
See also CA 104
See also DLB 12

Cabrera Infante, G(uillermo)
1929-.................... CLC 5, 25
See also CA 85-88

Cain, G. 1929-
See Cabrera Infante, G(uillermo)

Cain, James M(allahan)
1892-1977.............. CLC 3, 11, 28
See also CANR 8
See also CA 17-20R
See also obituary CA 73-76
See also AITN 1

Caldwell, Erskine 1903- ...... CLC 1, 8, 14
See also CAAS 1
See also CANR 2
See also CA 1-4R
See also DLB 9
See also AITN 1

Caldwell, (Janet Miriam) Taylor (Holland)
1900-1985................. CLC 2, 28
See also CANR 5
See also CA 5-8R
See also obituary CA 116

Calisher, Hortense 1911- ...... CLC 2, 4, 8
See also CANR 1
See also CA 1-4R
See also DLB 2

Callaghan, Morley (Edward)
1903-.................... CLC 3, 14
See also CA 9-12R

Calvino, Italo
1923-1985........ CLC 5, 8, 11, 22, 33
See also CA 85-88
See also obituary CA 116

Campbell, John W(ood), Jr.
1910-1971....................CLC 32
See also CAP 2
See also CA 21-22
See also obituary CA 29-32R
See also DLB 8

Campbell, (Ignatius) Roy (Dunnachie)
1901-1957.................. TCLC 5
See also CA 104
See also DLB 20

Campbell, (William) Wilfred
1861-1918.................. TCLC 9
See also CA 106

Camus, Albert
1913-1960...... CLC 1, 2, 4, 9, 11, 14,
32
See also CA 89-92

Canby, Vincent 1924-.............CLC 13
See also CA 81-84

Canetti, Elias 1905-......... CLC 3, 14, 25
See also CA 21-24R

Cape, Judith 1916-
See Page, P(atricia) K(athleen)

Čapek, Karel 1890-1938.........TCLC 6
See also CA 104

Capote, Truman
1924-1984...... CLC 1, 3, 8, 13, 19, 34
See also CA 5-8R
See also obituary CA 113
See also DLB 2
See also DLB-Y 80, 84

Capra, Frank 1897-..............CLC 16
See also CA 61-64

Caputo, Philip 1941-..............CLC 32
See also CA 73-76

Cardenal, Ernesto 1925-...........CLC 31
See also CANR 2
See also CA 49-52

Carey, Ernestine Gilbreth 1908-
See Gilbreth, Frank B(unker), Jr. and
    Carey, Ernestine Gilbreth
See also CA 5-8R
See also SATA 2

Carleton, William 1794-1869...... NCLC 3

Carlisle, Henry (Coffin) 1926-......CLC 33
See also CANR 15
See also CA 13-16R

Carman, (William) Bliss
1861-1929................... TCLC 7
See also CA 104

Carpentier (y Valmont), Alejo
1904-1980................ CLC 8, 11
See also CANR 11
See also CA 65-68
See also obituary CA 97-100

Carr, John Dickson 1906-1977 ......CLC 3
See also CANR 3
See also CA 49-52
See also obituary CA 69-72

Carr, Virginia Spencer 1929- ......CLC 34
See also CA 61-64

Carrier, Roch 1937- ....CLC 13

Carroll, Jim 1951-................CLC 35
See also CA 45-48

Carroll, Lewis 1832-1898........ NCLC 2
See also Dodgson, Charles Lutwidge
See also CLR 2
See also DLB 18

Carroll, Paul Vincent
1900-1968...................CLC 10
See also CA 9-12R
See also obituary CA 25-28R
See also DLB 10

Carruth, Hayden
1921-................CLC 4, 7, 10, 18
See also CANR 4
See also CA 9-12R
See also DLB 5

Carter, Angela 1940-..............CLC 5
See also CANR 12
See also CA 53-56
See also DLB 14

Carver, Raymond 1938-....... CLC 22, 36
See also CA 33-36R
See also DLB-Y 84

Cary, (Arthur) Joyce
1888-1957................... TCLC 1
See also CA 104
See also DLB 15

Casares, Adolfo Bioy 1914-
See Bioy Casares, Adolfo

Casey, John 1880-1964
See O'Casey, Sean

Casey, Michael 1947- ....CLC 2
See also CA 65-68
See also DLB 5

Casey, Warren 1935-
See Jacobs, Jim and Casey, Warren
See also CA 101

Cassavetes, John 1929-...........CLC 20
See also CA 85-88

Cassill, R(onald) V(erlin)
1919-.................... CLC 4, 23
See also CAAS 1
See also CANR 7
See also CA 9-12R
See also DLB 6

Cassity, (Allen) Turner 1929- ......CLC 6
See also CANR 11
See also CA 17-20R

Castaneda, Carlos 1935?-..........CLC 12
See also CA 25-28R

Castro, Rosalía de 1837-1885 ..... NCLC 3

Cather, Willa (Sibert)
1873-1947................ TCLC 1, 11
See also CA 104
See also SATA 30
See also DLB 9
See also DLB-DS 1

Catton, (Charles) Bruce
1899-1978...................CLC 35
See also CANR 7
See also CA 5-8R
See also obituary CA 81-84
See also SATA 2
See also obituary SATA 24
See also DLB 17
See also AITN 1

Caunitz, William 1935-...........CLC 34

Causley, Charles (Stanley)
1917-........................CLC 7
See also CANR 5
See also CA 9-12R
See also SATA 3
See also DLB 27

Caute, (John) David 1936-........CLC 29
See also CANR 1
See also CA 1-4R
See also DLB 14

Cavafy, C(onstantine) P(eter)
1863-1933................ TCLC 2, 7
See also CA 104

Cavanna, Betty 1909- ....CLC 12
See also CANR 6
See also CA 9-12R
See also SATA 1, 30

Cayrol, Jean 1911- ....CLC 11
See also CA 89-92

Cela, Camilo José 1916-........ CLC 4, 13
See also CA 21-24R

Celan, Paul 1920-1970 .... CLC 10, 19
See also Antschel, Paul

Céline, Louis-Ferdinand
1894-1961........CLC 1, 3, 4, 7, 9, 15
See also Destouches, Louis Ferdinand

Cendrars, Blaise 1887-1961 ....CLC 18
See also Sauser-Hall, Frédéric

Césaire, Aimé (Fernand)
1913-.................... CLC 19, 32
See also CA 65-68

Chabrol, Claude 1930-............CLC 16
See also CA 110

Challans, Mary 1905-1983
See Renault, Mary
See also CA 81-84
See also obituary CA 111
See also SATA 23
See also obituary SATA 36

Chambers, Aidan 1934-...........CLC 35
See also CANR 12
See also CA 25-28R
See also SATA 1

Chambers, James 1948-
See Cliff, Jimmy

Chandler, Raymond
1888-1959................. TCLC 1, 7
See also CA 104

Chaplin, Charles (Spencer)
1889-1977...................CLC 16
See also CA 81-84
See also obituary CA 73-76
See also DLB 44

Chapman, Graham 1941?-
See Monty Python
See also CA 116

Chapman, John Jay
1862-1933................. TCLC 7
See also CA 104

Char, René (Emile)
1907-................. CLC 9, 11, 14
See also CA 13-16R

Charyn, Jerome 1937- .... CLC 5, 8, 18
See also CAAS 1
See also CANR 7
See also CA 5-8R
See also DLB-Y 83

Chase, Mary Ellen 1887-1973.......CLC 2
See also CAP 1
See also CA 15-16
See also obituary CA 41-44R
See also SATA 10

Chateaubriand, François René de
1768-1848.................. NCLC 3

Chatterji, Saratchandra
1876-1938.................. TCLC 13
See also CA 109

Chatterton, Thomas 1752-1770....... LC 3

Chatwin, (Charles) Bruce
1940-........................CLC 28
See also CA 85-88

Chayefsky, Paddy 1923-1981.......CLC 23
See also CA 9-12R
See also obituary CA 104
See also DLB 7, 44
See also DLB-Y 81

Chayefsky, Sidney 1923-1981
See Chayefsky, Paddy

Cheever, John
1912-1982...... CLC 3, 7, 8, 11, 15, 25
See also CANR 5
See also CA 5-8R
See also obituary CA 106
See also DLB 2
See also DLB-Y 80, 82

Cheever, Susan 1943- ....CLC 18
  See also CA 103
  See also DLB-Y 82

Chekhov, Anton (Pavlovich)
  1860-1904................TCLC 3, 10
  See also CA 104

Chernyshevsky, Nikolay Gavrilovich
  1828-1889...................NCLC 1

Cherry, Caroline Janice 1942-
  See Cherryh, C. J.

Cherryh, C. J. 1942-.............CLC 35
  See also DLB-Y 80

Chesnutt, Charles Waddell
  1858-1932...................TCLC 5
  See also CA 106
  See also DLB 12

Chesterton, G(ilbert) K(eith)
  1874-1936................TCLC 1, 6
  See also CA 104
  See also SATA 27
  See also DLB 10, 19, 34

Ch'ien Chung-shu 1910-..........CLC 22

Child, Lydia Maria 1802-1880 .... NCLC 6
  See also DLB 1

Child, Philip 1898-1978 ....CLC 19
  See also CAP 1
  See also CA 13-14

Childress, Alice 1920-......... CLC 12, 15
  See also CANR 3
  See also CA 45-48
  See also SATA 7
  See also DLB 7, 38

Chislett, (Margaret) Anne
  1943?-......................CLC 34

Chitty, (Sir) Thomas Willes 1926-
  See Hinde, Thomas
  See also CA 5-8R

Chomette, René 1898-1981
  See Clair, René
  See also obituary CA 103

Chopin, Kate (O'Flaherty)
  1851-1904................TCLC 5, 14
  See also CA 104
  See also DLB 12

Christie, Agatha (Mary Clarissa)
  1890-1976...........CLC 1, 6, 8, 12
  See also CANR 10
  See also CA 17-20R
  See also obituary CA 61-64
  See also SATA 36
  See also DLB 13
  See also AITN 1, 2

Christie, (Ann) Philippa 1920-
  See Pearce, (Ann) Philippa
  See also CANR 4

Chulkov, Mikhail Dmitrievich
  1743-1792....................LC 2

Churchill, Caryl 1938- ....CLC 31
  See also CA 102
  See also DLB 13

Churchill, Charles 1731?-1764 .... LC 3

Ciardi, John (Anthony) 1916-......CLC 10
  See also CAAS 2
  See also CANR 5
  See also CA 5-8R
  See also SATA 1
  See also DLB 5

Cimino, Michael 1943?- ....CLC 16
  See also CA 105

Clair, René 1898-1981 ....CLC 20
  See also Chomette, René

Clampitt, Amy 19??-..............CLC 32
  See also CA 110

Clare, John 1793-1864 .... NCLC 9

Clark, (Robert) Brian 1932- ......CLC 29
  See also CA 41-44R

Clark, Eleanor 1913-........... CLC 5, 19
  See also CA 9-12R
  See also DLB 6

Clark, Mavis Thorpe 1912?- ....CLC 12
  See also CANR 8
  See also CA 57-60
  See also SATA 8

Clark, Walter Van Tilburg
  1909-1971.................CLC 28
  See also CA 9-12R
  See also obituary CA 33-36R
  See also SATA 8
  See also DLB 9

Clarke, Arthur C(harles)
  1917-............ CLC 1, 4, 13, 18, 35
  See also CANR 2
  See also CA 1-4R
  See also SATA 13

Clarke, Austin 1896-1974........ CLC 6, 9
  See also CAP 2
  See also CA 29-32
  See also obituary CA 49-52
  See also DLB 10, 20

Clarke, Austin C(hesterfield)
  1934-......................CLC 8
  See also CA 25-28R

Clarke, Shirley 1925- ....CLC 16

Clash, The.......................CLC 30

Claudel, Paul (Louis Charles Marie)
  1868-1955...............TCLC 2, 10
  See also CA 104

Clavell, James (duMaresq)
  1924-................ CLC 6, 25
  See also CA 25-28R

Cleaver, (Leroy) Eldridge
  1935-.....................CLC 30
  See also CANR 16
  See also CA 21-24R

Cleese, John 1939-
  See Monty Python
  See also CA 112, 116

Cleland, John 1709-1789 .... LC 2
  See also DLB 39

Clemens, Samuel Langhorne 1835-1910
  See Twain, Mark
  See also CA 104
  See also YABC 2
  See also DLB 11, 12, 23

Cliff, Jimmy 1948-................CLC 21

Clifton, Lucille 1936- ....CLC 19
  See also CLR 5
  See also CANR 2
  See also CA 49-52
  See also SATA 20
  See also DLB 5, 41

Clutha, Janet Paterson Frame 1924-
  See Frame (Clutha), Janet (Paterson)
  See also CANR 2
  See also CA 1-4R

Coburn, D(onald) L(ee) 1938-......CLC 10
  See also CA 89-92

Cocteau, Jean (Maurice Eugene Clement)
  1889-1963............CLC 1, 8, 15, 16
  See also CAP 2
  See also CA 25-28

Coetzee, J(ohn) M. 1940-...... CLC 23, 33
  See also CA 77-80

Cohen, Arthur A(llen) 1928- .... CLC 7, 31
  See also CANR 1
  See also CA 1-4R
  See also DLB 28

Cohen, Leonard (Norman)
  1934-.......................CLC 3
  See also CANR 14
  See also CA 21-24R

Cohen, Matt 1942-................CLC 19
  See also CA 61-64

Colegate, Isabel 1931-.............CLC 36
  See also CANR 8
  See also CA 17-20R
  See also DLB 14

Coleridge, Samuel Taylor
  1772-1834................. NCLC 9

Colette (Sidonie-Gabrielle)
  1873-1954............TCLC 1, 5, 16
  See also CA 104

Collier, Christopher 1930-
  See Collier, Christopher and Collier, James
    L(incoln)
  See also CANR 13
  See also CA 33-36R
  See also SATA 16

Collier, Christopher 1930- and
  Collier, James L(incoln)
  1928-......................CLC 30

Collier, James L(incoln) 1928-
  See Collier, Christopher and Collier, James
    L(incoln)
  See also CLR 3
  See also CANR 4
  See also CA 9-12R
  See also SATA 8

Collier, James L(incoln) 1928- and
  Collier, Christopher 1930-
  See Collier, Christopher and Collier, James
    L(incoln)

Collins, Hunt 1926-
  See Hunter, Evan

Collins, (William) Wilkie
  1824-1889.................. NCLC 1
  See also DLB 18

Colman, George 1909-1981
  See Glassco, John

Colum, Padraic 1881-1972.........CLC 28
  See also CA 73-76
  See also obituary CA 33-36R
  See also SATA 15
  See also DLB 19

Colvin, James 1939-
  See Moorcock, Michael

Colwin, Laurie 1945- . . . . **CLC 5, 13, 23**
See also CA 89-92
See also DLB-Y 80

Comfort, Alex(ander) 1920- . . . .**CLC 7**
See also CANR 1
See also CA 1-4R

Compton-Burnett, Ivy
1892-1969 . . . . **CLC 1, 3, 10, 15, 34**
See also CANR 4
See also CA 1-4R
See also obituary CA 25-28R
See also DLB 36

Comstock, Anthony
1844-1915 . . . . **TCLC 13**
See also CA 110

Condon, Richard (Thomas)
1915- . . . .**CLC 4, 6, 8, 10**
See also CAAS 1
See also CANR 2
See also CA 1-4R

Connell, Evan S(helby), Jr.
1924- . . . . **CLC 4, 6**
See also CAAS 2
See also CANR 2
See also CA 1-4R
See also DLB 2
See also DLB-Y 81

Connelly, Marc(us Cook)
1890-1980 . . . .**CLC 7**
See also CA 85-88
See also obituary CA 102
See also obituary SATA 25
See also DLB 7
See also DLB-Y 80

Conrad, Joseph
1857-1924 . . . .**TCLC 1, 6, 13**
See also CA 104
See also SATA 27
See also DLB 10, 34

Conroy, Pat 1945- . . . .**CLC 30**
See also CA 85-88
See also DLB 6
See also AITN 1

Constant (de Rebecque), (Henri) Benjamin
1767-1830 . . . . **NCLC 6**

Cook, Robin 1940- . . . .**CLC 14**
See also CA 108, 111

Cooke, John Esten 1830-1886 . . . . . **NCLC 5**
See also DLB 3

Cooper, James Fenimore
1789-1851 . . . . **NCLC 1**
See also SATA 19
See also DLB 3

Coover, Robert (Lowell)
1932- . . . .**CLC 3, 7, 15, 32**
See also CANR 3
See also CA 45-48
See also DLB 2
See also DLB-Y 81

Copeland, Stewart (Armstrong) 1952-
See The Police

Coppard, A(lfred) E(dgar)
1878-1957 . . . . **TCLC 5**
See also CA 114
See also YABC 1

Coppola, Francis Ford 1939- . . . .**CLC 16**
See also CA 77-80
See also DLB 44

Corcoran, Barbara 1911- . . . .**CLC 17**
See also CAAS 2
See also CANR 11
See also CA 21-24R
See also SATA 3

Corman, Cid 1924- . . . .**CLC 9**
See also Corman, Sidney
See also CAAS 2
See also DLB 5

Corman, Sidney 1924-
See Corman, Cid
See also CA 85-88

Cormier, Robert (Edmund)
1925- . . . . **CLC 12, 30**
See also CANR 5
See also CA 1-4R
See also SATA 10

Corn, Alfred (Dewitt III)
1943- . . . .**CLC 33**
See also CA 104
See also DLB-Y 80

Cornwell, David (John Moore) 1931-
See le Carré, John
See also CANR 13
See also CA 5-8R

Corso, (Nunzio) Gregory
1930- . . . . **CLC 1, 11**
See also CA 5-8R
See also DLB 5, 16

Cortázar, Julio
1914-1984 . . . . . **CLC 2, 3, 5, 10, 13, 15,
33, 34**
See also CANR 12
See also CA 21-24R

Corvo, Baron 1860-1913
See Rolfe, Frederick (William Serafino
Austin Lewis Mary)

Ćosić, Dobrica 1921- . . . .**CLC 14**

Costain, Thomas B(ertram)
1885-1965 . . . .**CLC 30**
See also CA 5-8R
See also obituary CA 25-28R
See also DLB 9

Costello, Elvis 1955- . . . .**CLC 21**

Couperus, Louis (Marie Anne)
1863-1923 . . . . **TCLC 15**
See also CA 115

Cousteau, Jacques-Yves 1910- . . . . . .**CLC 30**
See also CANR 15
See also CA 65-68
See also SATA 38

Coward, Nöel (Pierce)
1899-1973 . . . . **CLC 1, 9, 29**
See also CAP 2
See also CA 17-18
See also obituary CA 41-44R
See also DLB 10
See also AITN 1

Cowper, William 1731-1800 . . . . . . **NCLC 8**

Cox, William Trevor 1928-
See Trevor, William
See also CANR 4
See also CA 9-12R

Cozzens, James Gould
1903-1978 . . . .**CLC 1, 4, 11**
See also CA 9-12R
See also obituary CA 81-84
See also DLB 9
See also DLB-Y 84
See also DLB-DS 2

Crane, (Harold) Hart
1899-1932 . . . .**TCLC 2, 5**
See also CA 104
See also DLB 4

Crane, R(onald) S(almon)
1886-1967 . . . .**CLC 27**
See also CA 85-88

Crane, Stephen
1871-1900 . . . .**TCLC 11, 17**
See also CA 109
See also DLB 12
See also YABC 2

Craven, Margaret 1901-1980 . . . . . .**CLC 17**
See also CA 103

Crawford, F(rancis) Marion
1854-1909 . . . . **TCLC 10**
See also CA 107

Crayencour, Marguerite de 1913-
See Yourcenar, Marguerite

Creasey, John 1908-1973 . . . .**CLC 11**
See also CANR 8
See also CA 5-8R
See also obituary CA 41-44R

Crébillon, Claude Prosper Jolyot de (fils)
1707-1777 . . . .**LC 1**

Creeley, Robert (White)
1926- . . . .**CLC 1, 2, 4, 8, 11, 15, 36**
See also CA 1-4R
See also DLB 5, 16

Crews, Harry 1935- . . . . **CLC 6, 23**
See also CA 25-28R
See also DLB 6
See also AITN 1

Crichton, (John) Michael
1942- . . . . **CLC 2, 6**
See also CANR 13
See also CA 25-28R
See also SATA 9
See also DLB-Y 81
See also AITN 2

Crispin, Edmund 1921-1978 . . . .**CLC 22**
See also Montgomery, Robert Bruce

Cristofer, Michael 1946- . . . .**CLC 28**
See also CA 110
See also DLB 7

Crockett, David (Davy)
1786-1836 . . . . **NCLC 8**
See also DLB 3, 11

Croker, John Wilson
1780-1857 . . . . **NCLC 10**

Cronin, A(rchibald) J(oseph)
1896-1981 . . . .**CLC 32**
See also CANR 5
See also CA 1-4R
See also obituary CA 102
See also obituary SATA 25

Cross, Amanda 1926-
See Heilbrun, Carolyn G(old)

Crothers, Rachel 1878-1953 . . . . . . **TCLC 19**
See also CA 113
See also DLB 7

Crowley, Aleister 1875-1947 ...... **TCLC 7**
See also CA 104

Crumb, Robert 1943- ....**CLC 17**
See also CA 106

Cryer, Gretchen 1936?- ....**CLC 21**
See also CA 114

Csáth, Géza 1887-1919......... **TCLC 13**
See also CA 111

Cudlip, David 1933- ....**CLC 34**

Cullen, Countee 1903-1946 ...... **TCLC 4**
See also CA 108
See also SATA 18
See also DLB 4

Cummings, E(dward) E(stlin)
1894-1962........ **CLC 1, 3, 8, 12, 15**
See also CA 73-76
See also DLB 4

Cunningham, J(ames) V(incent)
1911-1985................ **CLC 3, 31**
See also CANR 1
See also CA 1-4R
See also obituary CA 115
See also DLB 5

Cunningham, Julia (Woolfolk)
1916-.......................**CLC 12**
See also CANR 4
See also CA 9-12R
See also SATA 1, 26

Cunningham, Michael 1952- ....**CLC 34**

Dąbrowska, Maria (Szumska)
1889-1965....................**CLC 15**
See also CA 106

Dabydeen, David 1956?-..........**CLC 34**

Dagerman, Stig (Halvard)
1923-1954................. **TCLC 17**

Dahl, Roald 1916- ....**CLC 1, 6, 18**
See also CLR 1, 7
See also CANR 6
See also CA 1-4R
See also SATA 1, 26

Dahlberg, Edward
1900-1977............. **CLC 1, 7, 14**
See also CA 9-12R
See also obituary CA 69-72

Daly, Maureen 1921-.............**CLC 17**
See also McGivern, Maureen Daly
See also SAAS 1
See also SATA 2

Däniken, Erich von 1935-
See Von Däniken, Erich

Dannay, Frederic 1905-1982
See Queen, Ellery
See also CANR 1
See also CA 1-4R
See also obituary CA 107

D'Annunzio, Gabriele
1863-1938.................. **TCLC 6**
See also CA 104

Danziger, Paula 1944-.............**CLC 21**
See also CA 112, 115
See also SATA 30, 36

Darío, Rubén 1867-1916......... **TCLC 4**
See also Sarmiento, Felix Ruben Garcia
See also CA 104

Darley, George 1795-1846 .... **NCLC 2**

Daryush, Elizabeth
1887-1977................ **CLC 6, 19**
See also CANR 3
See also CA 49-52
See also DLB 20

Daudet, (Louis Marie) Alphonse
1840-1897.................. **NCLC 1**

Daumal, René 1908-1944 .... **TCLC 14**
See also CA 114

Davenport, Guy (Mattison), Jr.
1927-.................... **CLC 6, 14**
See also CA 33-36R

Davidson, Donald (Grady)
1893-1968........... **CLC 2, 13, 19**
See also CANR 4
See also CA 5-8R
See also obituary CA 25-28R
See also DLB 45

Davidson, Sara 1943- ....**CLC 9**
See also CA 81-84

Davie, Donald (Alfred)
1922-...............**CLC 5, 8, 10, 31**
See also CANR 1
See also CA 1-4R
See also DLB 27

Davies, Ray(mond Douglas)
1944-.......................**CLC 21**
See also CA 116

Davies, Rhys 1903-1978 ....**CLC 23**
See also CANR 4
See also CA 9-12R
See also obituary CA 81-84

Davies, (William) Robertson
1913-................**CLC 2, 7, 13, 25**
See also CA 33-36R

Davies, W(illiam) H(enry)
1871-1940................. **TCLC 5**
See also CA 104
See also DLB 19

Davis, Rebecca (Blaine) Harding
1831-1910.................. **TCLC 6**
See also CA 104

Davison, Frank Dalby
1893-1970...................**CLC 15**
See also obituary CA 116

Davison, Peter 1928-..............**CLC 28**
See also CANR 3
See also CA 9-12R
See also DLB 5

Davys, Mary 1674-1732 .... **LC 1**
See also DLB 39

Dawson, Fielding 1930-.............**CLC 6**
See also CA 85-88

Day, Thomas 1748-1789 .... **LC 1**
See also YABC 1
See also DLB 39

Day Lewis, C(ecil)
1904-1972.............. **CLC 1, 6, 10**
See also CAP 1
See also CA 15-16
See also obituary CA 33-36R
See also DLB 15, 20

Dazai Osamu 1909-1948......... **TCLC 11**
See also Tsushima Shūji

Defoe, Daniel 1660?-1731............ **LC 1**
See also SATA 22
See also DLB 39

De Hartog, Jan 1914- ....**CLC 19**
See also CANR 1
See also CA 1-4R

Deighton, Len 1929- .... **CLC 4, 7, 22**
See also CA 9-12R

De la Mare, Walter (John)
1873-1956.................. **TCLC 4**
See also CA 110
See also SATA 16
See also DLB 19

Delaney, Shelagh 1939-............**CLC 29**
See also CA 17-20R
See also DLB 13

Delany, Samuel R(ay, Jr.)
1942-.................... **CLC 8, 14**
See also CA 81-84
See also DLB 8, 33

De la Roche, Mazo 1885-1961......**CLC 14**
See also CA 85-88

Delbanco, Nicholas (Franklin)
1942-.................... **CLC 6, 13**
See also CAAS 2
See also CA 17-20R
See also DLB 6

Delibes (Setien), Miguel
1920-.................... **CLC 8, 18**
See also CANR 1
See also CA 45-48

DeLillo, Don 1936- ......**CLC 8, 10, 13, 27**
See also CA 81-84
See also DLB 6

De Lisser, H(erbert) G(eorge)
1878-1944.................. **TCLC 12**
See also CA 109

Deloria, Vine (Victor), Jr.
1933-......................**CLC 21**
See also CANR 5
See also CA 53-56
See also SATA 21

Del Vecchio, John M(ichael)
1947-......................**CLC 29**
See also CA 110

Dennis, Nigel (Forbes) 1912-........**CLC 8**
See also CA 25-28R
See also DLB 13, 15

De Palma, Brian 1940-............**CLC 20**
See also CA 109

De Quincey, Thomas
1785-1859.................. **NCLC 4**

Deren, Eleanora 1908-1961
See Deren, Maya
See also obituary CA 111

Deren, Maya 1908-1961 ....**CLC 16**
See also Deren, Eleanora

Derleth, August William
1909-1971....................**CLC 31**
See also CANR 4
See also CA 1-4R
See also obituary CA 29-32R
See also SATA 5
See also DLB 9

Derrida, Jacques 1930-............**CLC 24**

Desai, Anita 1937-............. **CLC 19, 37**
See also CA 81-84

De Saint-Luc, Jean 1909-1981
See Glassco, John

De Sica, Vittorio 1902-1974 . . . . CLC **20**

Destouches, Louis Ferdinand 1894-1961
    See Céline, Louis-Ferdinand
    See also CA 85-88

Deutsch, Babette 1895-1982 . . . . CLC **18**
    See also CANR 4
    See also CA 1-4R
    See also obituary CA 108
    See also DLB 45
    See also SATA 1
    See also obituary SATA 33

De Vries, Peter
    1910- . . . . CLC **1, 2, 3, 7, 10, 28**
    See also CA 17-20R
    See also DLB 6
    See also DLB-Y 82

Dexter, Pete 1943- . . . . CLC **34**

Diamond, Neil (Leslie) 1941- . . . . CLC **30**
    See also CA 108

Dick, Philip K(indred)
    1928-1982 . . . . CLC **10, 30**
    See also CANR 2, 16
    See also CA 49-52
    See also obituary CA 106
    See also DLB 8

Dickens, Charles 1812-1870 . . . . . NCLC **3, 8**
    See also SATA 15
    See also DLB 21

Dickey, James (Lafayette)
    1923- . . . . CLC **1, 2, 4, 7, 10, 15**
    See also CANR 10
    See also CA 9-12R
    See also DLB 5
    See also DLB-Y 82
    See also AITN 1, 2

Dickey, William 1928- . . . . CLC **3, 28**
    See also CA 9-12R
    See also DLB 5

Dickinson, Peter (Malcolm de Brissac)
    1927- . . . . CLC **12, 35**
    See also CA 41-44R
    See also SATA 5

Didion, Joan 1934- . . . . CLC **1, 3, 8, 14, 32**
    See also CANR 14
    See also CA 5-8R
    See also DLB 2
    See also DLB-Y 81
    See also AITN 1

Dillard, Annie 1945- . . . . CLC **9**
    See also CANR 3
    See also CA 49-52
    See also SATA 10
    See also DLB-Y 80

Dillard, R(ichard) H(enry) W(ilde)
    1937- . . . . CLC **5**
    See also CANR 10
    See also CA 21-24R
    See also DLB 5

Dillon, Eilis 1920- . . . . CLC **17**
    See also CANR 4
    See also CA 9-12R
    See also SATA 2

Dinesen, Isak 1885-1962 . . . . . . CLC **10, 29**
    See also Blixen, Karen (Christentze
    Dinesen)

Disch, Thomas M(ichael)
    1940- . . . . CLC **7, 36**
    See also CA 21-24R
    See also DLB 8

Disraeli, Benjamin 1804-1881 . . . . . NCLC **2**
    See also DLB 21

Dixon, Paige 1911-
    See Corcoran, Barbara

Döblin, Alfred 1878-1957 . . . . TCLC **13**
    See also Doeblin, Alfred

Dobrolyubov, Nikolai Alexandrovich
    1836-1861 . . . . NCLC **5**

Dobyns, Stephen 1941- . . . . CLC **37**
    See also CANR 2
    See also CA 45-48

Doctorow, E(dgar) L(aurence)
    1931- . . . . CLC **6, 11, 15, 18, 37**
    See also CANR 2
    See also CA 45-48
    See also DLB 2, 28
    See also DLB-Y 80
    See also AITN 2

Dodgson, Charles Lutwidge 1832-1898
    See Carroll, Lewis
    See also YABC 2

Doeblin, Alfred 1878-1957
    See also CA 110

Doerr, Harriet 1914?- . . . . CLC **34**

Donleavy, J(ames) P(atrick)
    1926- . . . . CLC **1, 4, 6, 10**
    See also CA 9-12R
    See also DLB 6
    See also AITN 2

Donnell, David 1939?- . . . . CLC **34**

Donoso, José 1924- . . . . CLC **4, 8, 11, 32**
    See also CA 81-84

Donovan, John 1928- . . . . CLC **35**
    See also CLR 3
    See also CA 97-100
    See also SATA 29

Doolittle, Hilda 1886-1961
    See H(ilda) D(oolittle)
    See also CA 97-100
    See also DLB 4, 45

Dorn, Ed(ward Merton)
    1929- . . . . CLC **10, 18**
    See also CA 93-96
    See also DLB 5

Dos Passos, John (Roderigo)
    1896-1970 . . . . . CLC **1, 4, 8, 11, 15, 25,
                                                        34**
    See also CANR 3
    See also CA 1-4R
    See also obituary CA 29-32R
    See also DLB 4, 9
    See also DLB-DS 1

Dostoevski, Fedor Mikhailovich
    1821-1881 . . . . NCLC **2, 7**

Douglass, Frederick
    1817-1895 . . . . NCLC **7**
    See also SATA 29
    See also DLB 1, 43

Dourado, (Waldomiro Freitas) Autran
    1926- . . . . CLC **23**
    See also CA 25-28R

Dowson, Ernest (Christopher)
    1867-1900 . . . . TCLC **4**
    See also CA 105
    See also DLB 19

Doyle, (Sir) Arthur Conan
    1859-1930 . . . . TCLC **7**
    See also CA 104
    See also SATA 24
    See also DLB 18

Dr. A 1933-
    See Silverstein, Alvin and Virginia
    B(arbara Opshelor) Silverstein

Drabble, Margaret
    1939- . . . . CLC **2, 3, 5, 8, 10, 22**
    See also CA 13-16R
    See also DLB 14

Dreiser, Theodore (Herman Albert)
    1871-1945 . . . . TCLC **10, 18**
    See also CA 106
    See also DLB 9, 12
    See also DLB-DS 1

Drexler, Rosalyn 1926- . . . . CLC **2, 6**
    See also CA 81-84

Dreyer, Carl Theodor
    1889-1968 . . . . CLC **16**
    See also obituary CA 116

Droste-Hülshoff, Annette Freiin von
    1797-1848 . . . . NCLC **3**

Drummond de Andrade, Carlos 1902-
    See Andrade, Carlos Drummond de

Drury, Allen (Stuart) 1918- . . . . CLC **37**
    See also CA 57-60

Dryden, John 1631-1700 . . . . LC **3**

Duberman, Martin 1930- . . . . CLC **8**
    See also CANR 2
    See also CA 1-4R

Dubie, Norman (Evans, Jr.)
    1945- . . . . CLC **36**
    See also CANR 12
    See also CA 69-72

Du Bois, W(illiam) E(dward) B(urghardt)
    1868-1963 . . . . CLC **1, 2, 13**
    See also CA 85-88
    See also SATA 42

Dubus, Andre 1936- . . . . CLC **13, 36**
    See also CA 21-24R

Duclos, Charles Pinot 1704-1772 . . . . . LC **1**

Dudek, Louis 1918- . . . . CLC **11, 19**
    See also CANR 1
    See also CA 45-48

Dudevant, Amandine Aurore Lucile Dupin
    1804-1876
    See Sand, George

Duerrenmatt, Friedrich 1921-
    See also CA 17-20R

Duffy, Maureen 1933- . . . . CLC **37**
    See also CA 25-28R
    See also DLB 14

Dugan, Alan 1923- . . . . CLC **2, 6**
    See also CA 81-84
    See also DLB 5

Duhamel, Georges 1884-1966 . . . . CLC **8**
    See also CA 81-84
    See also obituary CA 25-28R

Dujardin, Édouard (Émile Louis)
1861-1949.................. TCLC **13**
See also CA 109

Duke, Raoul 1939-
See Thompson, Hunter S(tockton)

Dumas, Alexandre (*père*)
1802-1870.................. NCLC **11**
See also SATA 18

Dumas, Alexandre (*fils*)
1824-1895.................. NCLC **9**

Dumas, Henry (L.) 1934-1968...... CLC **6**
See also CA 85-88
See also DLB 41

Du Maurier, Daphne 1907- ..... CLC **6, 11**
See also CANR 6
See also CA 5-8R
See also SATA 27

Dunbar, Paul Laurence
1872-1906............... TCLC **2, 12**
See also CA 104
See also SATA 34

Duncan (Steinmetz Arquette), Lois
1934-........................CLC **26**
See also Arquette, Lois S(teinmetz)
See also CANR 2
See also CA 1-4R
See also SATA 1, 36

Duncan, Robert
1919-.............. CLC **1, 2, 4, 7, 15**
See also CA 9-12R
See also DLB 5, 16, 37

Dunlap, William 1766-1839....... NCLC **2**
See also DLB 30, 37

Dunn, Douglas (Eaglesham)
1942-........................CLC **6**
See also CANR 2
See also CA 45-48
See also DLB 40

Dunn, Stephen 1939-.............CLC **36**
See also CANR 12
See also CA 33-36R

Dunne, John Gregory 1932-........CLC **28**
See also CANR 14
See also CA 25-28R
See also DLB-Y 80

Dunsany, Lord (Edward John Moreton Drax
Plunkett) 1878-1957......... TCLC **2**
See also CA 104
See also DLB 10

Durang, Christopher (Ferdinand)
1949-........................CLC **27**
See also CA 105

Duras, Marguerite
1914-........... CLC **3, 6, 11, 20, 34**
See also CA 25-28R

Durrell, Lawrence (George)
1912-........... CLC **1, 4, 6, 8, 13, 27**
See also CA 9-12R
See also DLB 15, 27

Dürrenmatt, Friedrich
1921-............. CLC **1, 4, 8, 11, 15**
See also Duerrenmatt, Friedrich

Dylan, Bob 1941-..........CLC **3, 4, 6, 12**
See also CA 41-44R
See also DLB 16

East, Michael 1916-
See West, Morris L.

Eastlake, William (Derry) 1917-.....CLC **8**
See also CAAS 1
See also CANR 5
See also CA 5-8R
See also DLB 6

Eberhart, Richard 1904- .... CLC **3, 11, 19**
See also CANR 2
See also CA 1-4R

Echegaray (y Eizaguirre), José (María
Waldo) 1832-1916........... TCLC **4**
See also CA 104

Eckert, Allan W. 1931-.............CLC **17**
See also CANR 14
See also CA 13-16R
See also SATA 27, 29

Eco, Umberto 1932- ....CLC **28**
See also CANR 12
See also CA 77-80

Eddison, E(ric) R(ucker)
1882-1945.................. TCLC **15**
See also CA 109

Edel, (Joseph) Leon 1907- ..... CLC **29, 34**
See also CANR 1
See also CA 1-4R

Eden, Emily 1797-1869......... NCLC **10**

Edgeworth, Maria 1767-1849 ..... NCLC **1**
See also SATA 21

Edmonds, Helen (Woods) 1904-1968
See Kavan, Anna
See also CA 5-8R
See also obituary CA 25-28R

Edmonds, Walter D(umaux)
1903-........................CLC **35**
See also CANR 2
See also CA 5-8R
See also SATA 1, 27
See also DLB 9

Edson, Russell 1905-.............CLC **13**
See also CA 33-36R

Edwards, G(erald) B(asil)
1899-1976.......................CLC **25**
See also obituary CA 110

Ehle, John (Marsden, Jr.)
1925-........................CLC **27**
See also CA 9-12R

Ehrenbourg, Ilya (Grigoryevich) 1891-1967
See Ehrenburg, Ilya (Grigoryevich)

Ehrenburg, Ilya (Grigoryevich)
1891-1967............... CLC **18, 34**
See also CA 102
See also obituary CA 25-28R

Eich, Guenter 1907-1971
See also CA 111
See also obituary CA 93-96

Eich, Günter 1907-1971..........CLC **15**
See also Eich, Guenter

Eichendorff, Joseph Freiherr von
1788-1857.................. NCLC **8**

Eigner, Larry 1927- ....CLC **9**
See also Eigner, Laurence (Joel)
See also DLB 5

Eigner, Laurence (Joel) 1927-
See Eigner, Larry
See also CANR 6
See also CA 9-12R

Eiseley, Loren (Corey)
1907-1977....................CLC **7**
See also CANR 6
See also CA 1-4R
See also obituary CA 73-76

Ekeloef, Gunnar (Bengt) 1907-1968
See Ekelöf, Gunnar (Bengt)
See also obituary CA 25-28R

Ekelöf, Gunnar (Bengt)
1907-1968....................CLC **27**
See also Ekeloef, Gunnar (Bengt)

Ekwensi, Cyprian (Odiatu Duaka)
1921-........................CLC **4**
See also CA 29-32R

Eliade, Mircea 1907-..............CLC **19**
See also CA 65-68

Eliot, George 1819-1880......... NCLC **4**
See also DLB 21, 35

Eliot, T(homas) S(tearns)
1888-1965....... CLC **1, 2, 3, 6, 9, 10,**
13, 15, 24, 34
See also CA 5-8R
See also obituary CA 25-28R
See also DLB 7, 10, 45

Elkin, Stanley L(awrence)
1930-............. CLC **4, 6, 9, 14, 27**
See also CANR 8
See also CA 9-12R
See also DLB 2, 28
See also DLB-Y 80

Elledge, Scott 19??-...............CLC **34**

Elliott, George P(aul)
1918-1980....................CLC **2**
See also CANR 2
See also CA 1-4R
See also obituary CA 97-100

Ellis, A. E. ....CLC **7**

Ellis, (Henry) Havelock
1859-1939.................. TCLC **14**
See also CA 109

Ellison, Harlan 1934- .... CLC **1, 13**
See also CANR 5
See also CA 5-8R
See also DLB 8

Ellison, Ralph (Waldo)
1914-................... CLC **1, 3, 11**
See also CA 9-12R
See also DLB 2

Elman, Richard 1934-.............CLC **19**
See also CA 17-20R

Éluard, Paul 1895-1952 .... TCLC **7**
See also Grindel, Eugene

Elvin, Anne Katharine Stevenson 1933-
See Stevenson, Anne (Katharine)
See also CA 17-20R

Elytis, Odysseus 1911- ....CLC **15**
See also CA 102

Emecheta, (Florence Onye) Buchi
1944-........................CLC **14**
See also CA 81-84

Emerson, Ralph Waldo
1803-1882.................. NCLC **1**
See also DLB 1

Empson, William
      1906-1984....... CLC 3, 8, 19, 33, 34
      See also CA 17-20R
      See also obituary CA 112
      See also DLB 20

Enchi, Fumiko 1905-..............CLC 31

Ende, Michael 1930-..............CLC 31
      See also SATA 42

Endo, Shusaku 1923-....... CLC 7, 14, 19
      See also CA 29-32R

Engel, Marian 1933-1985.........CLC 36
      See also CANR 12
      See also CA 25-28R

Enright, D(ennis) J(oseph)
      1920-.................. CLC 4, 8, 31
      See also CANR 1
      See also CA 1-4R
      See also SATA 25
      See also DLB 27

Ephron, Nora 1941-......... CLC 17, 31
      See also CANR 12
      See also CA 65-68
      See also AITN 2

Epstein, Daniel Mark 1948-........CLC 7
      See also CANR 2
      See also CA 49-52

Epstein, Jacob 1956-..............CLC 19
      See also CA 114

Epstein, Leslie 1938-..............CLC 27
      See also CA 73-76

Erdman, Paul E(mil) 1932-........CLC 25
      See also CANR 13
      See also CA 61-64
      See also AITN 1

Erenburg, Ilya (Grigoryevich) 1891-1967
      See Ehrenburg, Ilya (Grigoryevich)

Eseki, Bruno 1919-
      See Mphahlele, Ezekiel

Esenin, Sergei (Aleksandrovich)
      1895-1925.................. TCLC 4
      See also CA 104

Eshleman, Clayton 1935-..........CLC 7
      See also CA 33-36R
      See also DLB 5

Espriu, Salvador 1913-1985........CLC 9
      See also obituary CA 115

Evans, Marian 1819-1880
      See Eliot, George

Evans, Mary Ann 1819-1880
      See Eliot, George

Evarts, Esther 1900-1972
      See Benson, Sally

Everson, R(onald) G(ilmour)
      1903-......................CLC 27
      See also CA 17-20R

Everson, William (Oliver)
      1912-................. CLC 1, 5, 14
      See also CA 9-12R
      See also DLB 5, 16

Evtushenko, Evgenii (Aleksandrovich) 1933-
      See Yevtushenko, Yevgeny

Ewart, Gavin (Buchanan)
      1916-......................CLC 13
      See also CA 89-92
      See also DLB 40

Ewers, Hanns Heinz
      1871-1943.................. TCLC 12
      See also CA 109

Ewing, Frederick R. 1918-
      See Sturgeon, Theodore (Hamilton)

Exley, Frederick (Earl)
      1929-.................... CLC 6, 11
      See also CA 81-84
      See also DLB-Y 81
      See also AITN 2

Ezekiel, Tish O'Dowd 1943-.......CLC 34

Fagen, Donald 1948-
      See Becker, Walter and Fagen, Donald

Fagen, Donald 1948- and
      Becker, Walter 1950-
      See Becker, Walter and Fagen, Donald

Fair, Ronald L. 1932-..............CLC 18
      See also CA 69-72
      See also DLB 33

Fairbairns, Zoë (Ann) 1948-.......CLC 32
      See also CA 103

Fairfield, Cicily Isabel 1892-1983
      See West, Rebecca

Fallaci, Oriana 1930-..............CLC 11
      See also CANR 15
      See also CA 77-80

Fargue, Léon-Paul 1876-1947.... TCLC 11
      See also CA 109

Farigoule, Louis 1885-1972
      See Romains, Jules

Fariña, Richard 1937?-1966........CLC 9
      See also CA 81-84
      See also obituary CA 25-28R

Farley, Walter 1915-..............CLC 17
      See also CANR 8
      See also CA 17-20R
      See also SATA 2
      See also DLB 22

Farmer, Philip José 1918-...... CLC 1, 19
      See also CANR 4
      See also CA 1-4R
      See also DLB 8

Farrell, J(ames) G(ordon)
      1935-1979....................CLC 6
      See also CA 73-76
      See also obituary CA 89-92
      See also DLB 14

Farrell, James T(homas)
      1904-1979.............CLC 1, 4, 8, 11
      See also CANR 9
      See also CA 5-8R
      See also obituary CA 89-92
      See also DLB 4, 9
      See also DLB-DS 2

Farrell, M. J. 1904-
      See Keane, Molly

Fassbinder, Rainer Werner
      1946-1982....................CLC 20
      See also CA 93-96
      See also obituary CA 106

Fast, Howard (Melvin) 1914-.......CLC 23
      See also CANR 1
      See also CA 1-4R
      See also SATA 7
      See also DLB 9

Faulkner, William (Cuthbert)
      1897-1962...... CLC 1, 3, 6, 8, 9, 11,
                                    14, 18, 28
      See also CA 81-84
      See also DLB 9, 11, 44
      See also DLB-DS 2
      See also AITN 1

Fauset, Jessie Redmon
      1884?-1961....................CLC 19
      See also CA 109

Faust, Irvin 1924-..................CLC 8
      See also CA 33-36R
      See also DLB 2, 28
      See also DLB-Y 80

Federman, Raymond 1928-........CLC 6
      See also CANR 10
      See also CA 17-20R
      See also DLB-Y 80

Feiffer, Jules 1929-............. CLC 2, 8
      See also CA 17-20R
      See also SATA 8
      See also DLB 7, 44

Feinstein, Elaine 1930-...........CLC 36
      See also CA 69-72
      See also CAAS 1
      See also DLB 14, 40

Feldman, Irving (Mordecai)
      1928-........................CLC 7
      See also CANR 1
      See also CA 1-4R

Fellini, Federico 1920-...........CLC 16
      See also CA 65-68

Felsen, Gregor 1916-
      See Felsen, Henry Gregor

Felsen, Henry Gregor 1916-........CLC 17
      See also CANR 1
      See also CA 1-4R
      See also SATA 1

Fenton, James (Martin) 1949-......CLC 32
      See also CA 102
      See also DLB 40

Ferber, Edna 1887-1968..........CLC 18
      See also CA 5-8R
      See also obituary CA 25-28R
      See also SATA 7
      See also DLB 9, 28
      See also AITN 1

Ferlinghetti, Lawrence (Monsanto)
      1919?-...........CLC 2, 6, 10, 27
      See also CANR 3
      See also CA 5-8R
      See also DLB 5, 16

Ferrier, Susan (Edmonstone)
      1782-1854.................. NCLC 8

Feuchtwanger, Lion
      1884-1958.................. TCLC 3
      See also CA 104

Fiedler, Leslie A(aron)
      1917-................. CLC 4, 13, 24
      See also CANR 7
      See also CA 9-12R
      See also DLB 28

Field, Eugene 1850-1895......... NCLC 3
      See also SATA 16
      See also DLB 21, 23, 42

Fielding, Henry 1707-1754..........LC 1
      See also DLB 39

       CONTEMPORARY LITERARY CRITICISM, Vol. 37

Fielding, Sarah 1710-1768 . . . . LC 1
See also DLB 39

Fierstein, Harvey 1954- . . . . .CLC 33

Figes, Eva 1932- . . . . .CLC 31
See also CANR 4
See also CA 53-56
See also DLB 14

Finch, Robert (Duer Claydon)
1900- . . . . .CLC 18
See also CANR 9
See also CA 57-60

Findley, Timothy 1930- . . . . .CLC 27
See also CANR 12
See also CA 25-28R

Fink, Janis 1951-
See Ian, Janis

Firbank, (Arthur Annesley) Ronald
1886-1926. . . . . TCLC 1
See also CA 104
See also DLB 36

Firbank, Louis 1944-
See Reed, Lou

Fisher, Roy 1930- . . . . .CLC 25
See also CANR 16
See also CA 81-84
See also DLB 40

Fisher, Rudolph 1897-1934 . . . . . . TCLC 11
See also CA 107

Fisher, Vardis (Alvero)
1895-1968. . . . . .CLC 7
See also CA 5-8R
See also obituary CA 25-28R
See also DLB 9

FitzGerald, Edward
1809-1883. . . . . NCLC 9
See also DLB 32

Fitzgerald, F(rancis) Scott (Key)
1896-1940. . . . . .TCLC 1, 6, 14
See also CA 110
See also DLB 4, 9
See also DLB-Y 81
See also DLB-DS 1
See also AITN 1

Fitzgerald, Penelope 1916- . . . . .CLC 19
See also CA 85-88
See also DLB 14

FitzGerald, Robert D(avid)
1902- . . . . .CLC 19
See also CA 17-20R

Flanagan, Thomas (James Bonner)
1923- . . . . .CLC 25
See also CA 108
See also DLB-Y 80

Flaubert, Gustave
1821-1880. . . . . NCLC 2, 10

Fleming, Ian (Lancaster)
1908-1964. . . . . CLC 3, 30
See also CA 5-8R
See also SATA 9

Fleming, Thomas J(ames)
1927- . . . . .CLC 37
See also CANR 10
See also CA 5-8R
See also SATA 8

Fo, Dario 1929- . . . . .CLC 32
See also CA 116

Follett, Ken(neth Martin)
1949- . . . . .CLC 18
See also CANR 13
See also CA 81-84
See also DLB-Y 81

Forbes, Esther 1891-1967. . . . . .CLC 12
See also CAP 1
See also CA 13-14
See also obituary CA 25-28R
See also DLB 22
See also SATA 2

Forché, Carolyn 1950- . . . . .CLC 25
See also CA 109
See also DLB 5

Ford, Ford Madox
1873-1939. . . . . .TCLC 1, 15
See also CA 104
See also DLB 34

Ford, John 1895-1973. . . . . .CLC 16
See also obituary CA 45-48

Forester, C(ecil) S(cott)
1899-1966. . . . . .CLC 35
See also CA 73-76
See also obituary CA 25-28R
See also SATA 13

Forman, James D(ouglas)
1932- . . . . .CLC 21
See also CANR 4
See also CA 9-12R
See also SATA 8, 21

Forrest, Leon 1937- . . . . .CLC 4
See also CA 89-92
See also DLB 33

Forster, E(dward) M(organ)
1879-1970. . . . . . CLC 1, 2, 3, 4, 9, 10,
13, 15, 22
See also CAP 1
See also CA 13-14
See also obituary CA 25-28R
See also DLB 34

Forster, John 1812-1876. . . . . NCLC 11

Forsyth, Frederick 1938- . . . . CLC 2, 5, 36
See also CA 85-88

Forten (Grimk), Charlotte L(ottie)
1837-1914. . . . . TCLC 16

Foscolo, Ugo 1778-1827 . . . . NCLC 8

Fosse, Bob 1925- . . . . .CLC 20
See also Fosse, Robert Louis

Fosse, Robert Louis 1925-
See Bob Fosse
See also CA 110

Foucault, Michel
1926-1984. . . . . CLC 31, 34
See also CA 105
See also obituary CA 113

**Fouqué, Friedrich (Heinrich Karl) de La
Motte** 1777-1843. . . . . NCLC 2

Fournier, Henri Alban 1886-1914
See Alain-Fournier
See also CA 104

Fournier, Pierre 1916- . . . . .CLC 11
See also CANR 16
See also CA 89-92

Fowles, John (Robert)
1926- . . . . . .CLC 1, 2, 3, 4, 6, 9, 10, 15,
33
See also CA 5-8R
See also DLB 14
See also SATA 22

Fox, Paula 1923- . . . . CLC 2, 8
See also CLR 1
See also CA 73-76
See also SATA 17

Fox, William Price (Jr.) 1926- . . . . . .CLC 22
See also CANR 11
See also CA 17-20R
See also DLB 2
See also DLB-Y 81

Frame (Clutha), Janet (Paterson)
1924- . . . . .CLC 2, 3, 6, 22
See also Clutha, Janet Paterson Frame

France, Anatole 1844-1924 . . . . TCLC 9
See also Thibault, Jacques Anatole
Francois

Francis, Dick 1920- . . . . CLC 2, 22
See also CANR 9
See also CA 5-8R

Francis, Robert (Churchill)
1901- . . . . .CLC 15
See also CANR 1
See also CA 1-4R

Frank, Anne 1929-1945 . . . . TCLC 17
See also CA 113
See also SATA 42

Franklin, (Stella Maria Sarah) Miles
1879-1954. . . . . TCLC 7
See also CA 104

Fraser, Antonia (Pakenham)
1932- . . . . .CLC 32
See also CA 85-88
See also SATA 32

Fraser, George MacDonald
1925- . . . . .CLC 7
See also CANR 2
See also CA 45-48

Frayn, Michael 1933- . . . . CLC 3, 7, 31
See also CA 5-8R
See also DLB 13, 14

Frederic, Harold 1856-1898. . . . . . NCLC 10
See also DLB 12, 23

Fredro, Aleksander 1793-1876 . . . . NCLC 8

Freeman, Douglas Southall
1886-1953. . . . . TCLC 11
See also CA 109
See also DLB 17

Freeman, Mary (Eleanor) Wilkins
1852-1930. . . . . TCLC 9
See also CA 106
See also DLB 12

French, Marilyn 1929- . . . . CLC 10, 18
See also CANR 3
See also CA 69-72

Freneau, Philip Morin
1752-1832. . . . . NCLC 1
See also DLB 37, 43

Friedman, B(ernard) H(arper)
1926- . . . . .CLC 7
See also CANR 3
See also CA 1-4R

Friedman, Bruce Jay 1930-...... CLC 3, 5
See also CA 9-12R
See also DLB 2, 28

Friel, Brian 1929-................CLC 5
See also CA 21-24R
See also DLB 13

Friis-Baastad, Babbis (Ellinor)
1921-1970...................CLC 12
See also CA 17-20R
See also SATA 7

Frisch, Max (Rudolf)
1911-......... CLC 3, 9, 14, 18, 32
See also CA 85-88

Fromentin, Eugène (Samuel Auguste)
1820-1876................. NCLC 10

Frost, Robert (Lee)
1874-1963...... CLC 1, 3, 4, 9, 10, 13,
15, 26, 34
See also CA 89-92
See also SATA 14

Fry, Christopher 1907-...... CLC 2, 10, 14
See also CANR 9
See also CA 17-20R
See also DLB 13

Frye, (Herman) Northrop
1912-........................CLC 24
See also CANR 8
See also CA 5-8R

Fuchs, Daniel 1909-........... CLC 8, 22
See also CA 81-84
See also DLB 9, 26, 28

Fuchs, Daniel 1934-..............CLC 34
See also CANR 14
See also CA 37-40R

Fuentes, Carlos
1928-........... CLC 3, 8, 10, 13, 22
See also CANR 10
See also CA 69-72
See also AITN 2

Fugard, Athol 1932-......CLC 5, 9, 14, 25
See also CA 85-88

Fuller, Charles (H., Jr.) 1939-.....CLC 25
See also CA 108, 112
See also DLB 38

Fuller, (Sarah) Margaret
1810-1850.................. NCLC 5
See also Ossoli, Sarah Margaret (Fuller
marchesa d')
See also DLB 1

Fuller, Roy (Broadbent)
1912-..................... CLC 4, 28
See also CA 5-8R
See also DLB 15, 20

Futrelle, Jacques 1875-1912...... TCLC 19
See also CA 113

Gadda, Carlo Emilio
1893-1973...................CLC 11
See also CA 89-92

Gaddis, William
1922-........... CLC 1, 3, 6, 8, 10, 19
See also CA 17-20R
See also DLB 2

Gaines, Ernest J. 1933- ..... CLC 3, 11, 18
See also CANR 6
See also CA 9-12R
See also DLB 2, 33
See also DLB-Y 80
See also AITN 1

Gale, Zona 1874-1938............ TCLC 7
See also CA 105
See also DLB 9

Gallagher, Tess 1943-..............CLC 18
See also CA 106

Gallant, Mavis 1922-.......... CLC 7, 18
See also CA 69-72

Gallant, Roy A(rthur) 1924- ....CLC 17
See also CANR 4
See also CA 5-8R
See also SATA 4

Gallico, Paul (William)
1897-1976...................CLC 2
See also CA 5-8R
See also obituary CA 69-72
See also SATA 13
See also DLB 9
See also AITN 1

Galsworthy, John 1867-1933...... TCLC 1
See also CA 104
See also DLB 10, 34

Galt, John 1779-1839............ NCLC 1

Gann, Ernest K(ellogg) 1910- ......CLC 23
See also CANR 1
See also CA 1-4R
See also AITN 1

García Lorca, Federico
1899-1936................TCLC 1, 7
See also CA 104

García Márquez, Gabriel
1928-.......... CLC 2, 3, 8, 10, 15, 27
See also CANR 10
See also CA 33-36R

Gardner, John (Champlin, Jr.)
1933-1982...... CLC 2, 3, 5, 7, 8, 10,
18, 28, 34
See also CA 65-68
See also obituary CA 107
See also obituary SATA 31, 40
See also DLB 2
See also DLB-Y 82
See also AITN 1

Gardner, John (Edmund)
1926-........................CLC 30
See also CANR 15
See also CA 103
See also AITN 1

Garfield, Leon 1921-..............CLC 12
See also CA 17-20R
See also SATA 1, 32

Garland, (Hannibal) Hamlin
1860-1940................... TCLC 3
See also CA 104
See also DLB 12

Garneau, Hector (de) Saint Denys
1912-1943................. TCLC 13
See also CA 111

Garner, Alan 1935-..............CLC 17
See also CANR 15
See also CA 73-76
See also SATA 18

Garner, Hugh 1913-1979..........CLC 13
See also CA 69-72

Garnett, David 1892-1981 ....CLC 3
See also CA 5-8R
See also obituary CA 103
See also DLB 34

Garrett, George (Palmer)
1929-..................... CLC 3, 11
See also CANR 1
See also CA 1-4R
See also DLB 2, 5
See also DLB-Y 83

Garrigue, Jean 1914-1972 .... CLC 2, 8
See also CA 5-8R
See also obituary CA 37-40R

Gary, Romain 1914-1980..........CLC 25
See also Kacew, Romain

Gascar, Pierre 1916-
See Fournier, Pierre

Gaskell, Elizabeth Cleghorn
1810-1865................... NCLC 5
See also DLB 21

Gass, William H(oward)
1924-............. CLC 1, 2, 8, 11, 15
See also CA 17-20R
See also DLB 2

Gautier, Théophile 1811-1872..... NCLC 1

Gaye, Marvin (Pentz)
1939-1984...................CLC 26
See also obituary CA 112

Gee, Maurice (Gough) 1931-.......CLC 29
See also CA 97-100

Gelbart, Larry (Simon) 1923-......CLC 21
See also CA 73-76

Gelber, Jack 1932- .... CLC 1, 6, 14
See also CANR 2
See also CA 1-4R
See also DLB 7

Gellhorn, Martha (Ellis) 1908- .....CLC 14
See also CA 77-80
See also DLB-Y 82

Genet, Jean 1910- ..... CLC 1, 2, 5, 10, 14
See also CA 13-16R

Gent, Peter 1942-..................CLC 29
See also CA 89-92
See also DLB-Y 82
See also AITN 1

George, Jean Craighead 1919- .....CLC 35
See also CLR 1
See also CA 5-8R
See also SATA 2

George, Stefan (Anton)
1868-1933................ TCLC 2, 14
See also CA 104

Gerhardi, William (Alexander) 1895-1977
See Gerhardie, William (Alexander)

Gerhardie, William (Alexander)
1895-1977....................CLC 5
See also CA 25-28R
See also obituary CA 73-76
See also DLB 36

Gertler, T(rudy) 1946?- ....CLC 34
See also CA 116

Gessner, Friedrike Victoria 1910-1980
See Adamson, Joy(-Friederike Victoria)

Ghelderode, Michel de
1898-1962................ CLC 6, 11
See also CA 85-88

Ghiselin, Brewster 1903- ....CLC 23
See also CANR 13
See also CA 13-16R

Giacosa, Giuseppe 1847-1906 ..... TCLC 7
See also CA 104

Gibbon, Lewis Grassic
1901-1935................... TCLC 4
See also Mitchell, James Leslie

Gibran, (Gibran) Kahlil
1883-1931................ TCLC 1, 9
See also CA 104

Gibson, William 1914- ....CLC 23
See also CANR 9
See also CA 9-12R
See also DLB 7

Gide, André (Paul Guillaume)
1869-1951............... TCLC 5, 12
See also CA 104

Gifford, Barry (Colby) 1946-.......CLC 34
See also CANR 9
See also CA 65-68

Gilbert, (Sir) W(illiam) S(chwenck)
1836-1911.................. TCLC 3
See also CA 104
See also SATA 36

Gilbreth, Ernestine 1908-
See Carey, Ernestine Gilbreth

Gilbreth, Frank B(unker), Jr. 1911-
See Gilbreth, Frank B(unker), Jr. and
Carey, Ernestine Gilbreth
See also CA 9-12R
See also SATA 2

Gilbreth, Frank B(unker), Jr. 1911- and
Carey, Ernestine Gilbreth
1908-.......................CLC 17

Gilchrist, Ellen 1939- ....CLC 34
See also CA 113, 116

Gilliam, Terry (Vance) 1940-
See Monty Python
See also CA 108, 113

Gilliatt, Penelope (Ann Douglass)
1932-................. CLC 2, 10, 13
See also CA 13-16R
See also DLB 14
See also AITN 2

Gilman, Charlotte (Anna) Perkins (Stetson)
1860-1935.................. TCLC 9
See also CA 106

Gilmour, David 1944-
See Pink Floyd

Gilroy, Frank D(aniel) 1925-........CLC 2
See also CA 81-84
See also DLB 7

Ginsberg, Allen
1926-........CLC 1, 2, 3, 4, 6, 13, 36
See also CANR 2
See also CA 1-4R
See also DLB 5, 16
See also AITN 1

Ginzburg, Natalia 1916-........ CLC 5, 11
See also CA 85-88

Giono, Jean 1895-1970........ CLC 4, 11
See also CANR 2
See also CA 45-48
See also obituary CA 29-32R

Giovanni, Nikki 1943-........ CLC 2, 4, 19
See also CLR 6
See also CA 29-32R
See also SATA 24
See also DLB 5
See also AITN 1

Giovene, Andrea 1904-............CLC 7
See also CA 85-88

Gippius, Zinaida (Nikolayevna) 1869-1945
See also Hippius, Zinaida
See also CA 106

Giraudoux, (Hippolyte) Jean
1882-1944................. TCLC 2, 7
See also CA 104

Gironella, José María 1917-.......CLC 11
See also CA 101

Gissing, George (Robert)
1857-1903.................. TCLC 3
See also CA 105
See also DLB 18

Glanville, Brian (Lester) 1931- ......CLC 6
See also CANR 3
See also CA 5-8R
See also DLB 15
See also SATA 42

Glasgow, Ellen (Anderson Gholson)
1873?-1945................ TCLC 2, 7
See also CA 104
See also DLB 9, 12

Glassco, John 1909-1981 ....CLC 9
See also CANR 15
See also CA 13-16R
See also obituary CA 102

Glasser, Ronald J. 1940?- ....CLC 37

Glissant, Edouard 1928-...........CLC 10

Glück, Louise 1943- .... CLC 7, 22
See also CA 33-36R
See also DLB 5

Godard, Jean-Luc 1930-...........CLC 20
See also CA 93-96

Godwin, Gail 1937-.......CLC 5, 8, 22, 31
See also CANR 15
See also CA 29-32R
See also DLB 6

Goethe, Johann Wolfgang von
1749-1832................... NCLC 4

Gogarty, Oliver St. John
1878-1957................. TCLC 15
See also CA 109
See also DLB 15, 19

Gogol, Nikolai (Vasilyevich)
1809-1852.................. NCLC 5

Gökçeli, Yasar Kemal 1923-
See Kemal, Yashar

Gold, Herbert 1924- .... CLC 4, 7, 14
See also CA 9-12R
See also DLB 2
See also DLB-Y 81

Goldbarth, Albert 1948-............CLC 5
See also CANR 6
See also CA 53-56

Goldberg, Anatol 19??-............CLC 34

Golding, William (Gerald)
1911-........CLC 1, 2, 3, 8, 10, 17, 27
See also CANR 13
See also CA 5-8R
See also DLB 15

Goldman, Emma 1869-1940 ..... TCLC 13
See also CA 110

Goldman, William (W.) 1931-.......CLC 1
See also CA 9-12R
See also DLB 44

Goldmann, Lucien 1913-1970 ......CLC 24
See also CAP 2
See also CA 25-28

Goldsberry, Steven 1949-.........CLC 34

Goldsmith, Oliver 1728?-1774....... LC 2
See also SATA 26
See also DLB 39

Gombrowicz, Witold
1904-1969............... CLC 4, 7, 11
See also CAP 2
See also CA 19-20
See also obituary CA 25-28R

Gómez de la Serna, Ramón
1888-1963....................CLC 9
See also obituary CA 116

Goncharov, Ivan Alexandrovich
1812-1891................... NCLC 1

Goncourt, Edmond (Louis Antoine Huot) de
1822-1896
See Goncourt, Edmond (Louis Antoine
Huot) de and Goncourt, Jules (Alfred
Huot) de

Goncourt, Edmond (Louis Antoine Huot) de
1822-1896 and Goncourt, Jules (Alfred
Huot) de 1830-1870 .... NCLC 7

Goncourt, Jules (Alfred Huot) de 1830-1870
See Goncourt, Edmond (Louis Antoine
Huot) de and Goncourt, Jules (Alfred
Huot) de

Goncourt, Jules (Alfred Huot) de 1830-1870
and Goncourt, Edmond (Louis Antoine
Huot) de 1822-1896
See Goncourt, Edmond (Louis Antoine
Huot) de and Goncourt, Jules (Alfred
Huot) de

Goodman, Paul
1911-1972..............CLC 1, 2, 4, 7
See also CAP 2
See also CA 19-20
See also obituary CA 37-40R

Gordimer, Nadine
1923-.......... CLC 3, 5, 7, 10, 18, 33
See also CANR 3
See also CA 5-8R

Gordon, Caroline
1895-1981.............. CLC 6, 13, 29
See also CAP 1
See also CA 11-12
See also obituary CA 103
See also DLB 4, 9
See also DLB-Y 81

Gordon, Mary (Catherine)
1949-.................... CLC 13, 22
See also CA 102
See also DLB 6
See also DLB-Y 81

Gordon, Sol 1923-.................CLC 26
See also CANR 4
See also CA 53-56
See also SATA 11

Gordone, Charles 1925- .... CLC 1, 4
See also CA 93-96
See also DLB 7

Gorenko, Anna Andreyevna 1889?-1966
See Akhmatova, Anna

Gorky, Maxim 1868-1936 .... TCLC 8
See also Peshkov, Alexei Maximovich

Author Index

Goryan, Sirak 1908-1981
  See Saroyan, William

Gotlieb, Phyllis (Fay Bloom)
  1926-.........................CLC 18
  See also CANR 7
  See also CA 13-16R

Gould, Lois 1938?-........... CLC 4, 10
  See also CA 77-80

Gourmont, Rémy de
  1858-1915.................TCLC 17
  See also CA 109

Goyen, (Charles) William
  1915-1983..............CLC 5, 8, 14
  See also CANR 6
  See also CA 5-8R
  See also obituary CA 110
  See also DLB 2
  See also DLB-Y 83
  See also AITN 2

Goytisolo, Juan 1931-....... CLC 5, 10, 23
  See also CA 85-88

Grabbe, Christian Dietrich
  1801-1836................... NCLC 2

Gracq, Julien 1910-..............CLC 11

Grade, Chaim 1910-1982.........CLC 10
  See also CA 93-96
  See also obituary CA 107

Graham, R(obert) B(ontine) Cunninghame
  1852-1936.................TCLC 19

Graham, W(illiam) S(ydney)
  1918-.........................CLC 29
  See also CA 73-76
  See also DLB 20

Graham, Winston (Mawdsley)
  1910-.........................CLC 23
  See also CANR 2
  See also CA 49-52

Granville-Barker, Harley
  1877-1946.................TCLC 2
  See also CA 104

Grass, Günter (Wilhelm)
  1927-.......CLC 1, 2, 4, 6, 11, 15, 22,
                                        32
  See also CA 13-16R

Grau, Shirley Ann 1929- .... CLC 4, 9
  See also CA 89-92
  See also DLB 2
  See also AITN 2

Graves, Robert 1895- ......CLC 1, 2, 6, 11
  See also CANR 5
  See also CA 5-8R
  See also DLB 20

Gray, Amlin 1946-................CLC 29

Gray, Francine du Plessix
  1930-   ....CLC 22
  See also CAAS 2
  See also CANR 11
  See also CA 61-64

Gray, John (Henry)
  1866-1934................ TCLC 19

Gray, Simon (James Holliday)
  1936-.................CLC 9, 14, 36
  See also CA 21-24R
  See also DLB 13
  See also AITN 1

Greeley, Andrew M(oran)
  1928-.......................CLC 28
  See also CANR 7
  See also CA 5-8R

Green, Hannah 1932-........ CLC 3, 7, 30
  See also Greenberg, Joanne
  See also CA 73-76

Green, Henry 1905-1974 .... CLC 2, 13
  See also Yorke, Henry Vincent
  See also DLB 15

Green, Julien (Hartridge)
  1900-.................... CLC 3, 11
  See also CA 21-24R
  See also DLB 4

Greenberg, Ivan 1908-1973
  See Rahv, Philip
  See also CA 85-88

Greenberg, Joanne (Goldenberg)
  1932-.................. CLC 3, 7, 30
  See also Green, Hannah
  See also CANR 14
  See also CA 5-8R
  See also SATA 25

Greene, Bette 1934-..............CLC 30
  See also CLR 2
  See also CANR 4
  See also CA 53-56
  See also SATA 8

Greene, Gael........................CLC 8
  See also CANR 10
  See also CA 13-16R

Greene, Graham
  1904-.......CLC 1, 3, 6, 9, 14, 18, 27,
                                        37
  See also CA 13-16R
  See also SATA 20
  See also DLB 13, 15
  See also AITN 2

Gregor, Arthur 1923-..............CLC 9
  See also CANR 11
  See also CA 25-28R
  See also SATA 36

Gregory, Lady (Isabella Augusta Persse)
  1852-1932.................. TCLC 1
  See also CA 104
  See also DLB 10

Grendon, Stephen 1909-1971
  See Derleth, August (William)

Greve, Felix Paul Berthold Friedrich
  1879-1948
  See Grove, Frederick Philip
  See also CA 104

Grey, (Pearl) Zane
  1872?-1939................ TCLC 6
  See also CA 104
  See also DLB 9

Grieg, (Johan) Nordahl (Brun)
  1902-1943................. TCLC 10
  See also CA 107

Grieve, C(hristopher) M(urray) 1892-1978
  See MacDiarmid, Hugh
  See also CA 5-8R
  See also obituary CA 85-88

Griffin, Gerald 1803-1840 .... NCLC 7

Griffiths, Trevor 1935-............CLC 13
  See also CA 97-100
  See also DLB 13

Grigson, Geoffrey (Edward Harvey)
  1905-........................CLC 7
  See also CA 25-28R
  See also DLB 27

Grillparzer, Franz 1791-1872 ..... NCLC 1

Grimm, Jakob (Ludwig) Karl 1785-1863
  See Grimm, Jakob (Ludwig) Karl and
  Grimm, Wilhelm Karl

Grimm, Jakob (Ludwig) Karl 1785-1863
  and **Grimm, Wilhelm Karl**
  1786-1859.................. NCLC 3
  See also SATA 22

Grimm, Wilhelm Karl 1786-1859
  See Grimm, Jakob (Ludwig) Karl and
  Grimm, Wilhelm Karl

Grimm, Wilhelm Karl 1786-1859 and
  Grimm, Jakob (Ludwig) Karl
  1785-1863
  See Grimm, Jakob (Ludwig) Karl and
  Grimm, Wilhelm Karl

Grindel, Eugene 1895-1952
  See also CA 104

Grove, Frederick Philip
  1879-1948................. TCLC 4
  See also Greve, Felix Paul Berthold
  Friedrich

Grumbach, Doris (Isaac)
  1918-................... CLC 13, 22
  See also CAAS 2
  See also CANR 9
  See also CA 5-8R

Grundtvig, Nicolai Frederik Severin
  1783-1872.................. NCLC 1

Guare, John 1938-..........CLC 8, 14, 29
  See also CA 73-76
  See also DLB 7

Gudjonsson, Halldór Kiljan 1902-
  See Laxness, Halldór (Kiljan)
  See also CA 103

Guest, Barbara 1920-.............CLC 34
  See also CANR 11
  See also CA 25-28R
  See also DLB 5

Guest, Judith (Ann) 1936-...... CLC 8, 30
  See also CANR 15
  See also CA 77-80

Guild, Nicholas M. 1944-..........CLC 33
  See also CA 93-96

Guillén, Jorge 1893-1984 ....CLC 11
  See also CA 89-92
  See also obituary CA 112

Guillevic, (Eugène) 1907-.........CLC 33
  See also CA 93-96

Gunn, Bill 1934- ....CLC 5
  See also Gunn, William Harrison
  See also DLB 38

Gunn, Thom(son William)
  1929-...............CLC 3, 6, 18, 32
  See also CANR 9
  See also CA 17-20R
  See also DLB 27

Gunn, William Harrison 1934-
  See Gunn, Bill
  See also CANR 12
  See also CA 13-16R
  See also AITN 1

Gurney, A(lbert) R(amsdell), Jr.
　1930-.........................CLC 32
　See also CA 77-80

Gustafson, Ralph (Barker)
　1909-.........................CLC 36
　See also CANR 8
　See also CA 21-24R

Guthrie, A(lfred) B(ertram), Jr.
　1901-.........................CLC 23
　See also CA 57-60
　See also DLB 6

Guthrie, Woodrow Wilson 1912-1967
　See Guthrie, Woody
　See also CA 113
　See also obituary CA 93-96

Guthrie, Woody 1912-1967 ....CLC 35
　See also Guthrie, Woodrow Wilson

Guy, Rosa (Cuthbert) 1928-........CLC 26
　See also CANR 14
　See also CA 17-20R
　See also SATA 14
　See also DLB 33

Haavikko, Paavo (Juhani)
　1931-.................... CLC 18, 34
　See also CA 106

Hacker, Marilyn 1942- .... CLC 5, 9, 23
　See also CA 77-80

Haggard, (Sir) H(enry) Rider
　1856-1925.................. TCLC 11
　See also CA 108
　See also SATA 16

Haig-Brown, Roderick L(angmere)
　1908-1976....................CLC 21
　See also CANR 4
　See also CA 5-8R
　See also obituary CA 69-72
　See also SATA 12

Hailey, Arthur 1920-..............CLC 5
　See also CANR 2
　See also CA 1-4R
　See also DLB-Y 82
　See also AITN 2

Haley, Alex (Palmer) 1921- ..... CLC 8, 12
　See also CA 77-80
　See also DLB 38

Hall, Donald (Andrew, Jr.)
　1928-.................. CLC 1, 13, 37
　See also CANR 2
　See also CA 5-8R
　See also SATA 23
　See also DLB 5

Hall, (Marguerite) Radclyffe
　1886-1943.................. TCLC 12
　See also CA 110

Halpern, Daniel 1945-..............CLC 14
　See also CA 33-36R

Hamburger, Michael (Peter Leopold)
　1924-.................... CLC 5, 14
　See also CANR 2
　See also CA 5-8R
　See also DLB 27

Hamill, Pete 1935-.................CLC 10
　See also CA 25-28R

Hamilton, Edmond 1904-1977.......CLC 1
　See also CANR 3
　See also CA 1-4R
　See also DLB 8

Hamilton, Gail 1911-
　See Corcoran, Barbara

Hamilton, Mollie 1909?-
　See Kaye, M(ary) M(argaret)

Hamilton, Virginia (Edith)
　1936-.......................CLC 26
　See also CLR 1
　See also CA 25-28R
　See also SATA 4
　See also DLB 33

Hammett, (Samuel) Dashiell
　1894-1961............CLC 3, 5, 10, 19
　See also CA 81-84
　See also AITN 1

Hammon, Jupiter
　1711?-1800?.................. NCLC 5
　See also DLB 31

Hamner, Earl (Henry), Jr.
　1923-.......................CLC 12
　See also CA 73-76
　See also DLB 6
　See also AITN 2

Hampton, Christopher (James)
　1946-........................CLC 4
　See also CA 25-28R
　See also DLB 13

Hamsun, Knut 1859-1952 ..... TCLC 2, 14
　See also Pedersen, Knut

Handke, Peter 1942-......CLC 5, 8, 10, 15
　See also CA 77-80

Hanley, James 1901-.......CLC 3, 5, 8, 13
　See also CA 73-76

Hannah, Barry 1942- ....CLC 23
　See also CA 108, 110
　See also DLB 6

Hansberry, Lorraine
　1930-1965....................CLC 17
　See also CA 109
　See also obituary CA 25-28R
　See also DLB 7, 38
　See also AITN 2

Hanson, Kenneth O(stlin)
　1922-.......................CLC 13
　See also CANR 7
　See also CA 53-56

Hardwick, Elizabeth 1916-.........CLC 13
　See also CANR 3
　See also CA 5-8R
　See also DLB 6

Hardy, Thomas
　1840-1928.............TCLC 4, 10, 18
　See also CA 104
　See also SATA 25
　See also DLB 18, 19

Hare, David 1947-.................CLC 29
　See also CA 97-100
　See also DLB 13

Harlan, Louis R(udolph) 1922-.....CLC 34
　See also CA 21-24R

Harper, Frances Ellen Watkins
　1825-1911.................. TCLC 14
　See also CA 111

Harper, Michael S(teven)
　1938-.................... CLC 7, 22
　See also CA 33-36R
　See also DLB 41

Harris, Christie (Lucy Irwin)
　1907-.......................CLC 12
　See also CANR 6
　See also CA 5-8R
　See also SATA 6

Harris, Joel Chandler
　1848-1908.................. TCLC 2
　See also CA 104
　See also YABC 1
　See also DLB 11, 23, 42

**Harris, John (Wyndham Parkes Lucas)
　Beynon** 1903-1969
　See Wyndham, John
　See also CA 102
　See also obituary CA 89-92

Harris, MacDonald 1921-...........CLC 9
　See also Heiney, Donald (William)

Harris, Mark 1922-...............CLC 19
　See also CANR 2
　See also CA 5-8R
　See also DLB 2
　See also DLB-Y 80

Harris, (Theodore) Wilson
　1921-.......................CLC 25
　See also CANR 11
　See also CA 65-68

Harrison, James (Thomas) 1937-
　See Harrison, Jim
　See also CANR 8
　See also CA 13-16R

Harrison, Jim 1937- .... CLC 6, 14, 33
　See also Harrison, James (Thomas)
　See also DLB-Y 82

Harriss, Will(ard Irvin) 1922-......CLC 34
　See also CA 111

Harte, (Francis) Bret(t)
　1836?-1902.................. TCLC 1
　See also CA 104
　See also SATA 26
　See also DLB 12

Hartley, L(eslie) P(oles)
　1895-1972.................. CLC 2, 22
　See also CA 45-48
　See also obituary CA 37-40R
　See also DLB 15

Hartman, Geoffrey H. 1929-.......CLC 27

Haruf, Kent 19??-.................CLC 34

Harwood, Ronald 1934-...........CLC 32
　See also CANR 4
　See also CA 1-4R
　See also DLB 13

Hašek, Jaroslav (Matej Frantisek)
　1883-1923.................. TCLC 4
　See also CA 104

Hass, Robert 1941- ....CLC 18
　See also CA 111

Hauptmann, Gerhart (Johann Robert)
　1862-1946.................. TCLC 4
　See also CA 104

Havel, Václav 1936-...............CLC 25
　See also CA 104

Haviaras, Stratis 1935-............CLC 33
　See also CA 105

Hawkes, John (Clendennin Burne, Jr.)
  1925-......CLC 1, 2, 3, 4, 7, 9, 14, 15,
                                            27
  See also CANR 2
  See also CA 1-4R
  See also DLB 2, 7
  See also DLB-Y 80

Hawthorne, Nathaniel
  1804-1864...............NCLC 2, 10
  See also YABC 2
  See also DLB 1

Hayden, Robert (Earl)
  1913-1980..........CLC 5, 9, 14, 37
  See also CA 69-72
  See also obituary CA 97-100
  See also SATA 19
  See also obituary SATA 26
  See also DLB 5

Haywood, Eliza (Fowler)
  1693?-1756....................LC 1
  See also DLB 39

Hazzard, Shirley 1931-...........CLC 18
  See also CANR 4
  See also CA 9-12R
  See also DLB-Y 82

H(ilda) D(oolittle)
  1886-1961....... CLC 3, 8, 14, 31, 34
  See also Doolittle, Hilda

Head, Bessie 1937-...............CLC 25
  See also CA 29-32R

Headon, (Nicky) Topper 1956?-
  See The Clash

Heaney, Seamus (Justin)
  1939-........... CLC 5, 7, 14, 25, 37
  See also CA 85-88
  See also DLB 40

Hearn, (Patricio) Lafcadio (Tessima Carlos)
  1850-1904...................TCLC 9
  See also CA 105
  See also DLB 12

Heat Moon, William Least
  1939-......................CLC 29

Hébert, Anne 1916-......... CLC 4, 13, 29
  See also CA 85-88

Hecht, Anthony (Evan)
  1923-................. CLC 8, 13, 19
  See also CANR 6
  See also CA 9-12R
  See also DLB 5

Hecht, Ben 1894-1964.............CLC 8
  See also CA 85-88
  See also DLB 7, 9, 25, 26, 28

Heidegger, Martin 1889-1976......CLC 24
  See also CA 81-84
  See also obituary CA 65-68

Heidenstam, (Karl Gustaf) Verner von
  1859-1940...................TCLC 5
  See also CA 104

Heifner, Jack 1946-...............CLC 11
  See also CA 105

Heilbrun, Carolyn G(old)
  1926-......................CLC 25
  See also CANR 1
  See also CA 45-48

Heine, Harry 1797-1856
  See Heine, Heinrich

Heine, Heinrich 1797-1856........NCLC 4

Heiney, Donald (William) 1921-
  See Harris, MacDonald
  See also CANR 3
  See also CA 1-4R

Heinlein, Robert A(nson)
  1907-............ CLC 1, 3, 8, 14, 26
  See also CANR 1
  See also CA 1-4R
  See also SATA 9
  See also DLB 8

Heller, Joseph
  1923-.......... CLC 1, 3, 5, 8, 11, 36
  See also CANR 8
  See also CA 5-8R
  See also DLB 2, 28
  See also DLB-Y 80
  See also AITN 1

Hellman, Lillian (Florence)
  1905?-1984..... CLC 2, 4, 8, 14, 18, 34
  See also CA 13-16R
  See also obituary CA 112
  See also DLB 7
  See also DLB-Y 84
  See also AITN 1, 2

Helprin, Mark 1947-.....CLC 7, 10, 22, 32
  See also CA 81-84

Hemingway, Ernest (Miller)
  1899-1961...... CLC 1, 3, 6, 8, 10, 13,
                                19, 30, 34
  See also CA 77-80
  See also DLB 4, 9
  See also DLB-Y 81
  See also DLB-DS 1
  See also AITN 2

Henley, Beth 1952-...............CLC 23
  See also Henley, Elizabeth Becker

Henley, Elizabeth Becker 1952-
  See Henley, Beth
  See also CA 107

Henley, William Ernest
  1849-1903...................TCLC 8
  See also CA 105
  See also DLB 19

Hennissart, Martha
  See Lathen, Emma
  See also CA 85-88

Henry, O. 1862-1910 .... TCLC 1, 19
  See also Porter, William Sydney

Hentoff, Nat(han Irving) 1925-.....CLC 26
  See also CLR 1
  See also CANR 5
  See also CA 1-4R
  See also SATA 27, 42

Heppenstall, (John) Rayner
  1911-1981...................CLC 10
  See also CA 1-4R
  See also obituary CA 103

Herbert, Frank (Patrick)
  1920-................. CLC 12, 23, 35
  See also CANR 5
  See also CA 53-56
  See also SATA 9, 37
  See also DLB 8

Herbert, Zbigniew 1924- ....CLC 9
  See also CA 89-92

Herbst, Josephine 1897-1969.......CLC 34
  See also CA 5-8R
  See also obituary CA 25-28R
  See also DLB 9

Herder, Johann Gottfried von
  1744-1803.................. NCLC 8

Hergesheimer, Joseph
  1880-1954................. TCLC 11
  See also CA 109
  See also DLB 9

Herlagñez, Pablo de 1844-1896
  See Verlaine, Paul (Marie)

Herlihy, James Leo 1927-...........CLC 6
  See also CANR 2
  See also CA 1-4R

Herriot, James 1916-..............CLC 12
  See also Wight, James Alfred

Hersey, John (Richard)
  1914-.............CLC 1, 2, 7, 9
  See also CA 17-20R
  See also SATA 25
  See also DLB 6

Herzen, Aleksandr Ivanovich
  1812-1870................. NCLC 10

Herzog, Werner 1942- ....CLC 16
  See also CA 89-92

Hesse, Hermann
  1877-1962...... CLC 1, 2, 3, 6, 11, 17,
                                       25
  See also CAP 2
  See also CA 17-18

Heyen, William 1940-......... CLC 13, 18
  See also CA 33-36R
  See also DLB 5

Heyerdahl, Thor 1914-............CLC 26
  See also CANR 5
  See also CA 5-8R
  See also SATA 2

Heym, Georg (Theodor Franz Arthur)
  1887-1912.................. TCLC 9
  See also CA 106

Heyse, Paul (Johann Ludwig von)
  1830-1914.................. TCLC 8
  See also CA 104

Hibbert, Eleanor (Burford)
  1906-......................CLC 7
  See also CANR 9
  See also CA 17-20R
  See also SATA 2

Higgins, George V(incent)
  1939-................CLC 4, 7, 10, 18
  See also CA 77-80
  See also DLB 2
  See also DLB-Y 81

Highsmith, (Mary) Patricia
  1921-.................. CLC 2, 4, 14
  See also CANR 1
  See also CA 1-4R

Highwater, Jamake 1942-..........CLC 12
  See also CANR 10
  See also CA 65-68
  See also SATA 30, 32

Hill, Geoffrey 1932-.........CLC 5, 8, 18
  See also CA 81-84
  See also DLB 40

Hill, George Roy 1922-............CLC 26
  See also CA 110

Author Index

Hill, Susan B. 1942- . . . . .CLC 4
See also CA 33-36R
See also DLB 14

Hilliard, Noel (Harvey) 1929- . . . . . .CLC 15
See also CANR 7
See also CA 9-12R

Himes, Chester (Bomar)
1909-1984. . . . . .CLC 2, 4, 7, 18
See also CA 25-28R
See also obituary CA 114
See also DLB 2

Hinde, Thomas 1926- . . . . CLC 6, 11
See also Chitty, (Sir) Thomas Willes

Hine, (William) Daryl 1936- . . . . . . .CLC 15
See also CANR 1
See also CA 1-4R

Hinton, S(usan) E(loise) 1950- . . . . . .CLC 30
See also CLR 3
See also CA 81-84
See also SATA 19

Hippius (Merezhkovsky), Zinaida
(**Nikolayevna**) 1869-1945 . . . . . TCLC 9
See also Gippius, Zinaida (Nikolayevna)

Hiraoka, Kimitake 1925-1970
See Mishima, Yukio
See also CA 97-100
See also obituary CA 29-32R

Hirsch, Edward 1950-. . . . . .CLC 31
See also CA 104

Hitchcock, (Sir) Alfred (Joseph)
1899-1980. . . . . .CLC 16
See also obituary CA 97-100
See also SATA 27
See also obituary SATA 24

Hoagland, Edward 1932- . . . . .CLC 28
See also CANR 2
See also CA 1-4R
See also DLB 6

Hoban, Russell C(onwell)
1925- . . . . CLC 7, 25
See also CLR 3
See also CA 5-8R
See also SATA 1, 40

Hobson, Laura Z(ametkin)
1900- . . . . CLC 7, 25
See also CA 17-20R
See also DLB 28

Hochhuth, Rolf 1931- . . . . CLC 4, 11, 18
See also CA 5-8R

Hochman, Sandra 1936-. . . . . CLC 3, 8
See also CA 5-8R
See also DLB 5

Hochwälder, Fritz 1911-. . . . . .CLC 36
See also CA 29-32R

Hocking, Mary (Eunice) 1921- . . . . .CLC 13
See also CA 101

Hodgins, Jack 1938- . . . . .CLC 23
See also CA 93-96

Hodgson, William Hope
1877-1918. . . . . TCLC 13
See also CA 111

Hoffman, Daniel (Gerard)
1923-. . . . . CLC 6, 13, 23
See also CANR 4
See also CA 1-4R
See also DLB 5

Hoffman, Stanley 1944- . . . . .CLC 5
See also CA 77-80

Hoffmann, Ernst Theodor Amadeus
1776-1822. . . . . NCLC 2
See also SATA 27

**Hofmannsthal, Hugo (Laurenz August
Hofmann Edler) von**
1874-1929. . . . . TCLC 11
See also CA 106

Hogg, James 1770-1835 . . . . NCLC 4

Holden, Ursula 1921- . . . . .CLC 18
See also CA 101

Holland, Isabelle 1920-. . . . . .CLC 21
See also CANR 10
See also CA 21-24R
See also SATA 8

Holland, Marcus 1900-1985
See Caldwell, (Janet Miriam) Taylor
(Holland)

Hollander, John 1929- . . . . .CLC 2, 5, 8, 14
See also CANR 1
See also CA 1-4R
See also SATA 13
See also DLB 5

Hollis, Jim 1916-
See Summers, Hollis (Spurgeon, Jr.)

Holt, Victoria 1906-
See Hibbert, Eleanor (Burford)

Holub, Miroslav 1923- . . . . .CLC 4
See also CANR 10
See also CA 21-24R

Honig, Edwin 1919-. . . . . .CLC 33
See also CANR 4
See also CA 5-8R
See also DLB 5

Hood, Hugh (John Blagdon)
1928-. . . . . CLC 15, 28
See also CANR 1
See also CA 49-52

Hope, A(lec) D(erwent) 1907- . . . . . . .CLC 3
See also CA 21-24R

Hopkins, John (Richard) 1931-. . . . . .CLC 4
See also CA 85-88

Horgan, Paul 1903-. . . . . .CLC 9
See also CANR 9
See also CA 13-16R
See also SATA 13

Horwitz, Julius 1920- . . . . .CLC 14
See also CANR 12
See also CA 9-12R

Hougan, Carolyn 19??-. . . . . .CLC 34

Household, Geoffrey (Edward West)
1900-. . . . . .CLC 11
See also CA 77-80
See also SATA 14

Housman, A(lfred) E(dward)
1859-1936. . . . . TCLC 1, 10
See also CA 104
See also DLB 19

Housman, Laurence
1865-1959. . . . . TCLC 7
See also CA 106
See also SATA 25
See also DLB 10

Howard, Elizabeth Jane
1923-. . . . . CLC 7, 29
See also CANR 8
See also CA 5-8R

Howard, Maureen 1930-. . . . . . . CLC 5, 14
See also CA 53-56
See also DLB-Y 83

Howard, Richard 1929- . . . . CLC 7, 10
See also CA 85-88
See also DLB 5
See also AITN 1

Howard, Robert E(rvin)
1906-1936. . . . . TCLC 8
See also CA 105

Howells, William Dean
1837-1920. . . . . TCLC 7, 17
See also CA 104
See also DLB 12

Howes, Barbara 1914- . . . . .CLC 15
See also CA 9-12R
See also SATA 5

Hrabal, Bohumil 1914-. . . . . .CLC 13
See also CA 106

Huch, Ricarda (Octavia)
1864-1947. . . . . TCLC 13
See also CA 111

Hueffer, Ford Madox 1873-1939
See Ford, Ford Madox

Hughes, Edward James 1930-
See Hughes, Ted

Hughes, (James) Langston
1902-1967. . . . . . . CLC 1, 5, 10, 15, 35
See also CANR 1
See also CA 1-4R
See also obituary CA 25-28R
See also SATA 4, 33
See also DLB 4, 7

Hughes, Richard (Arthur Warren)
1900-1976. . . . . CLC 1, 11
See also CANR 4
See also CA 5-8R
See also obituary CA 65-68
See also SATA 8
See also obituary SATA 25
See also DLB 15

Hughes, Ted 1930-. . . . . CLC 2, 4, 9, 14, 37
See also CLR 3
See also CANR 1
See also CA 1-4R
See also SATA 27
See also DLB 40

Hugo, Richard F(ranklin)
1923-1982. . . . . .CLC 6, 18, 32
See also CANR 3
See also CA 49-52
See also obituary CA 108
See also DLB 5

Hugo, Victor Marie
1802-1885. . . . . NCLC 3, 10

Humphreys, Josephine 1945-. . . . . . .CLC 34

Hunt, E(verette) Howard (Jr.)
1918-. . . . . .CLC 3
See also CANR 2
See also CA 45-48
See also AITN 1

Hunt, (James Henry) Leigh
1784-1859. . . . . NCLC 1

Hunter, Evan 1926-........CLC 1, 11, 31
See also CANR 5
See also CA 5-8R
See also SATA 25
See also DLB-Y 82

Hunter, Kristin (Eggleston)
1931-........................CLC 35
See also CLR 3
See also CANR 13
See also CA 13-16R
See also SATA 12
See also DLB 33
See also AITN 1

Hunter, Mollie (Maureen McIlwraith)
1922-........................CLC 21
See also McIlwraith, Maureen Mollie
Hunter

Hurston, Zora Neale
1901?-1960..............CLC 7, 30
See also CA 85-88

Huston, John (Marcellus)
1906-........................CLC 20
See also CA 73-76
See also DLB 26

Huxley, Aldous (Leonard)
1894-1963...... CLC 1, 3, 4, 5, 8, 11,
18, 35
See also CA 85-88
See also DLB 36

Huysmans, Charles Marie Georges
1848-1907
See also Huysmans, Joris-Karl
See also CA 104

Huysmans, Joris-Karl
1848-1907..................TCLC 7
See also Huysmans, Charles Marie Georges

Hyde, Margaret O(ldroyd)
1917-........................CLC 21
See also CANR 1
See also CA 1-4R
See also SATA 1, 42

Ian, Janis 1951-..................CLC 21
See also CA 105

Ibargüengoitia, Jorge
1928-1983..................CLC 37
See also obituary CA 113

Ibsen, Henrik (Johan)
1828-1906.............TCLC 2, 8, 16
See also CA 104

Ibuse, Masuji 1898-..............CLC 22

Ichikawa, Kon 1915-..............CLC 20

Idle, Eric 1943-
See Monty Python
See also CA 116

Ignatow, David 1914-........CLC 4, 7, 14
See also CA 9-12R
See also DLB 5

Immermann, Karl (Lebrecht)
1796-1840..................NCLC 4

Inge, William (Motter)
1913-1973...........CLC 1, 8, 19
See also CA 9-12R
See also DLB 7

Innaurato, Albert 1948-..........CLC 21
See also CA 115

Innes, Michael 1906-
See Stewart, J(ohn) I(nnes) M(ackintosh)

Ionesco, Eugène
1912-..........CLC 1, 4, 6, 9, 11, 15
See also CA 9-12R
See also SATA 7

Irving, John (Winslow)
1942-................CLC 13, 23
See also CA 25-28R
See also DLB 6
See also DLB-Y 82

Irving, Washington 1783-1859 .... NCLC 2
See also YABC 2
See also DLB 3, 11, 30

Isaacs, Susan 1943-..............CLC 32
See also CA 89-92

Isherwood, Christopher (William Bradshaw)
1904-................CLC 1, 9, 11, 14
See also CA 13-16R
See also DLB 15

Ishiguro, Kazuo 1954?-...........CLC 27

Ishikawa Takuboku
1885-1912................TCLC 15

Ivask, Ivar (Vidrik) 1927- ....CLC 14
See also CA 37-40R

Jackson, Jesse 1908-1983.........CLC 12
See also CA 25-28R
See also obituary CA 109
See also SATA 2, 29

Jackson, Laura (Riding) 1901-
See Riding, Laura
See also CA 65-68

Jackson, Shirley 1919-1965 ....CLC 11
See also CANR 4
See also CA 1-4R
See also obituary CA 25-28R
See also SATA 2
See also DLB 6

Jacob, (Cyprien) Max
1876-1944..................TCLC 6
See also CA 104

Jacob, Piers A(nthony) D(illingham) 1934-
See Anthony (Jacob), Piers
See also CA 21-24R

Jacobs, Jim 1942-
See Jacobs, Jim and Casey, Warren
See also CA 97-100

Jacobs, Jim 1942- and
Casey, Warren 1935-........CLC 12

Jacobson, Dan 1929-.......... CLC 4, 14
See also CANR 2
See also CA 1-4R
See also DLB 14

Jagger, Mick 1944-
See Jagger, Mick and Richard, Keith

Jagger, Mick 1944- and
Richard, Keith 1943-........CLC 17

Jakes, John (William) 1932- ....CLC 29
See also CANR 10
See also CA 57-60
See also DLB-Y 83

James, C(yril) L(ionel) R(obert)
1901-.......................CLC 33

James, Daniel 1911-
See Santiago, Danny

James, Henry (Jr.)
1843-1916...............TCLC 2, 11
See also CA 104
See also DLB 12

James, M(ontague) R(hodes)
1862-1936...................TCLC 6
See also CA 104

James, P(hyllis) D(orothy)
1920-........................CLC 18
See also CA 21-24R

James, William 1842-1910...... TCLC 15
See also CA 109

Jandl, Ernst 1925-...............CLC 34

Jarrell, Randall
1914-1965.........CLC 1, 2, 6, 9, 13
See also CLR 6
See also CANR 6
See also CA 5-8R
See also obituary CA 25-28R
See also SATA 7

Jarry, Alfred 1873-1907......TCLC 2, 14
See also CA 104

Jean Paul 1763-1825.............NCLC 7

Jeffers, (John) Robinson
1887-1962...........CLC 2, 3, 11, 15
See also CA 85-88
See also DLB 45

Jefferson, Thomas 1743-1826 .... NCLC 11
See also DLB 31

Jellicoe, (Patricia) Ann 1927-.......CLC 27
See also CA 85-88
See also DLB 13

Jennings, Elizabeth (Joan)
1926-.....................CLC 5, 14
See also CANR 8
See also CA 61-64
See also DLB 27

Jennings, Waylon 1937-...........CLC 21

Jensen, Laura (Linnea) 1948- ......CLC 37
See also CA 103

Jerrold, Douglas 1803-1857.......NCLC 2

Jewett, Sarah Orne 1849-1909 .... TCLC 1
See also CA 108
See also SATA 15
See also DLB 12

Jhabvala, Ruth Prawer
1927-...................CLC 4, 8, 29
See also CANR 2
See also CA 1-4R

Jiles, Paulette 1943-...............CLC 13
See also CA 101

Jiménez (Mantecón), Juan Ramón
1881-1958...................TCLC 4
See also CA 104

Joel, Billy 1949-.................CLC 26
See also Joel, William Martin

Joel, William Martin 1949-
See Joel, Billy
See also CA 108

Johnson, B(ryan) S(tanley William)
1933-1973..................CLC 6, 9
See also CANR 9
See also CA 9-12R
See also obituary CA 53-56
See also DLB 14, 40

Johnson, Charles 1948-.............CLC 7
See also CA 116
See also DLB 33

Johnson, Diane 1934- .... CLC **5, 13**
See also CA 41-44R
See also DLB-Y 80

Johnson, Eyvind (Olof Verner)
1900-1976................... CLC **14**
See also CA 73-76
See also obituary CA 69-72

Johnson, James Weldon
1871-1938................ TCLC **3, 19**
See also Johnson, James William
See also CA 104

Johnson, James William 1871-1938
See Johnson, James Weldon
See also SATA 31

Johnson, Lionel Pigot
1867-1902.................. TCLC **19**
See also DLB 19

Johnson, Marguerita 1928-
See Angelou, Maya

Johnson, Pamela Hansford
1912-1981................ CLC **1, 7, 27**
See also CANR 2
See also CA 1-4R
See also obituary CA 104
See also DLB 15

Johnson, Uwe
1934-1984............. CLC **5, 10, 15**
See also CANR 1
See also CA 1-4R
See also obituary CA 112

Johnston, Jennifer 1930- .... CLC **7**
See also CA 85-88
See also DLB 14

Jones, D(ouglas) G(ordon)
1929-...................... CLC **10**
See also CANR 13
See also CA 29-32R
See also CA 113

Jones, David
1895-1974............. CLC **2, 4, 7, 13**
See also CA 9-12R
See also obituary CA 53-56
See also DLB 20

Jones, David Robert 1947-
See Bowie, David
See also CA 103

Jones, Diana Wynne 1934-......... CLC **26**
See also CANR 4
See also CA 49-52
See also SATA 9

Jones, Gayl 1949- .... CLC **6, 9**
See also CA 77-80
See also DLB 33

Jones, James 1921-1977 ...... CLC **1, 3, 10**
See also CANR 6
See also CA 1-4R
See also obituary CA 69-72
See also DLB 2
See also AITN 1, 2

Jones, (Everett) LeRoi
1934-........CLC **1, 2, 3, 5, 10, 14, 33**
See also Baraka, Amiri
See also Baraka, Imamu Amiri
See also CA 21-24R

Jones, Madison (Percy, Jr.)
1925-........................ CLC **4**
See also CANR 7
See also CA 13-16R

Jones, Mervyn 1922-..............CLC **10**
See also CANR 1
See also CA 45-48

Jones, Mick 1956?-
See The Clash

Jones, Nettie 19??-................ CLC **34**

Jones, Preston 1936-1979.......... CLC **10**
See also CA 73-76
See also obituary CA 89-92
See also DLB 7

Jones, Robert F(rancis) 1934- .... CLC **7**
See also CANR 2
See also CA 49-52

Jones, Terry 1942?-
See Monty Python
See also CA 112, 116

Jong, Erica 1942-.......... CLC **4, 6, 8, 18**
See also CA 73-76
See also DLB 2, 5, 28
See also AITN 1

Jordan, June 1936- .... CLC **5, 11, 23**
See also CA 33-36R
See also SATA 4
See also DLB 38

Jordan, Pat(rick M.) 1941- ....CLC **37**
See also CA 33-36R

Josipovici, G(abriel) 1940-.......... CLC **6**
See also CA 37-40R
See also DLB 14

Joubert, Joseph 1754-1824........ NCLC **9**

Joyce, James (Augustine Aloysius)
1882-1941.............. TCLC **3, 8, 16**
See also CA 104
See also DLB 10, 19, 36

Just, Ward S(wift) 1935- .... CLC **4, 27**
See also CA 25-28R

Justice, Donald (Rodney)
1925-..................... CLC **6, 19**
See also CA 5-8R
See also DLB-Y 33

Kacew, Romain 1914-1980
See Gary, Romain
See also CA 108
See also obituary CA 102

Kacewgary, Romain 1914-1980
See Gary, Romain

Kafka, Franz
1883-1924.............. TCLC **2, 6, 13**
See also CA 105

Kahn, Roger 1927- ....CLC **30**
See also CA 25-28R

Kaiser, (Friedrich Karl) Georg
1878-1945.................. TCLC **9**
See also CA 106

Kallman, Chester (Simon)
1921-1975................... CLC **2**
See also CANR 3
See also CA 45-48
See also obituary CA 53-56

Kaminsky, Melvin 1926-
See Brooks, Mel
See also CANR 16

Kane, Paul 1941-
See Simon, Paul

Kanin, Garson 1912-.............. CLC **22**
See also CANR 7
See also CA 5-8R
See also DLB 7
See also AITN 1

Kaniuk, Yoram 1930-............. CLC **19**

Kantor, MacKinlay 1904-1977 ......CLC **7**
See also CA 61-64
See also obituary CA 73-76
See also DLB 9

Karamzin, Nikolai Mikhailovich
1766-1826.................. NCLC **3**

Karapánou, Margaríta 1946-.......CLC **13**
See also CA 101

Karl, Frederick R(obert) 1927-.....CLC **34**
See also CANR 3
See also CA 5-8R

Kassef, Romain 1914-1980
See Gary, Romain

Kaufman, Sue 1926-1977........ CLC **3, 8**
See also Barondess, Sue K(aufman)

Kavan, Anna 1904-1968........ CLC **5, 13**
See also Edmonds, Helen (Woods)
See also CANR 6

Kavanagh, Patrick (Joseph Gregory)
1905-1967................... CLC **22**
See also CA 25-28R
See also DLB 15, 20

Kawabata, Yasunari
1899-1972............CLC **2, 5, 9, 18**
See also CA 93-96
See also obituary CA 33-36R

Kaye, M(ary) M(argaret)
1909?-.................... CLC **28**
See also CA 89-92

Kaye, Mollie 1909?-
See Kaye, M(ary) M(argaret)

Kazan, Elia 1909- .... CLC **6, 16**
See also CA 21-24R

Kazantzakis, Nikos
1885?-1957................ TCLC **2, 5**
See also CA 105

Kazin, Alfred 1915-............... CLC **34**
See also CANR 1
See also CA 1-4R

Keane, Mary Nesta (Skrine) 1904-
See Keane, Molly
See also CA 108, 114

Keane, Molly 1904-............... CLC **31**
See also Keane, Mary Nesta (Skrine)

Keates, Jonathan 19??-............CLC **34**

Keaton, Buster 1895-1966 ....CLC **20**

Keaton, Joseph Francis 1895-1966
See Keaton, Buster

Keats, John 1795-1821 .... NCLC **8**

Keene, Donald 1922-............. CLC **34**
See also CANR 5
See also CA 1-4R

Keller, Gottfried 1819-1890....... NCLC **2**

Kelley, William Melvin 1937- ......CLC **22**
See also CA 77-80
See also DLB 33

Kellogg, Marjorie 1922-........... CLC **2**
See also CA 81-84

Author Index

Kemal, Yashar 1922- .... CLC 14, 29
See also CA 89-92

Kemelman, Harry 1908-........... CLC 2
See also CANR 6
See also CA 9-12R
See also DLB 28
See also AITN 1

Keneally, Thomas (Michael)
1935-........ CLC 5, 8, 10, 14, 19, 27
See also CANR 10
See also CA 85-88

Kennedy, John Pendleton
1795-1870................... NCLC 2
See also DLB 3

Kennedy, Joseph Charles 1929-
See Kennedy, X. J.
See also CANR 4
See also CA 1-4R
See also SATA 14

Kennedy, William 1928-..... CLC 6, 28, 34
See also CANR 14
See also CA 85-88

Kennedy, X. J. 1929- .... CLC 8
See also Kennedy, Joseph Charles
See also DLB 5

Kerouac, Jack
1922-1969...... CLC 1, 2, 3, 5, 14, 29
See also Kerouac, Jean-Louis Lebrid de
See also DLB 2, 16
See also DLB-DS 3

Kerouac, Jean-Louis Lebrid de 1922-1969
See Kerouac, Jack
See also CA 5-8R
See also obituary CA 25-28R
See also AITN 1

Kerr, Jean 1923-................. CLC 22
See also CANR 7
See also CA 5-8R

Kerr, M. E 1927-............ CLC 12, 35
See also Meaker, Marijane
See also SAAS 1

Kerrigan, (Thomas) Anthony
1918-...................... CLC 4, 6
See also CANR 4
See also CA 49-52

Kesey, Ken (Elton)
1935-.................. CLC 1, 3, 6, 11
See also CA 1-4R
See also DLB 2, 16

Kessler, Jascha (Frederick)
1929-......................... CLC 4
See also CANR 8
See also CA 17-20R

Kettelkamp, Larry 1933-......... CLC 12
See also CANR 16
See also CA 29-32R
See also SATA 2

Kherdian, David 1931-......... CLC 6, 9
See also CAAS 2
See also CA 21-24R
See also SATA 16

Khodasevich, Vladislav (Felitsianovich)
1886-1939.................. TCLC 15
See also CA 115

Kielland, Alexander (Lange)
1849-1906................. TCLC 5
See also CA 104

Kiely, Benedict 1919- .... CLC 23
See also CANR 2
See also CA 1-4R
See also DLB 15

Kienzle, William X(avier)
1928-........................ CLC 25
See also CAAS 1
See also CANR 9
See also CA 93-96

Killens, John Oliver 1916-........ CLC 10
See also CAAS 2
See also CA 77-80
See also DLB 33

King, Francis (Henry) 1923-........ CLC 8
See also CANR 1
See also CA 1-4R
See also DLB 15

King, Stephen (Edwin)
1947-................. CLC 12, 26, 37
See also CANR 1
See also CA 61-64
See also SATA 9
See also DLB-Y 80

Kingman, (Mary) Lee 1919- .... CLC 17
See also Natti, (Mary) Lee
See also CA 5-8R
See also SATA 1

Kingston, Maxine Hong
1940-................... CLC 12, 19
See also CANR 13
See also CA 69-72
See also DLB-Y 80

Kinnell, Galway
1927-.......... CLC 1, 2, 3, 5, 13, 29
See also CANR 10
See also CA 9-12R
See also DLB 5

Kinsella, Thomas 1928- .... CLC 4, 19
See also CA 17-20R
See also DLB 27

Kinsella, W(illiam) P(atrick)
1935-....................... CLC 27
See also CA 97-100

Kipling, (Joseph) Rudyard
1865-1936............... TCLC 8, 17
See also CA 105
See also YABC 2
See also DLB 19, 34

Kirkup, James 1927-.............. CLC 1
See also CANR 2
See also CA 1-4R
See also SATA 12
See also DLB 27

Kirkwood, James 1930- .... CLC 9
See also CANR 6
See also CA 1-4R
See also AITN 2

Kizer, Carolyn (Ashley) 1925-...... CLC 15
See also CA 65-68
See also DLB 5

Klausner, Amos 1939-
See Oz, Amos

Klein, A(braham) M(oses)
1909-1972.................. CLC 19
See also CA 101
See also obituary CA 37-40R

Klein, Norma 1938-.............. CLC 30
See also CLR 2
See also CANR 15
See also CA 41-44R
See also SAAS 1
See also SATA 7

Klein, T.E.D. 19??-.............. CLC 34

Kleist, Heinrich von
1777-1811................. NCLC 2

Klimentev, Andrei Platonovich 1899-1951
See Platonov, Andrei (Platonovich)
See also CA 108

Klinger, Friedrich Maximilian von
1752-1831.................. NCLC 1

Klopstock, Friedrich Gottlieb
1724-1803.................. NCLC 11

Knebel, Fletcher 1911-........... CLC 14
See also CANR 1
See also CA 1-4R
See also SATA 36
See also AITN 1

Knowles, John 1926-......CLC 1, 4, 10, 26
See also CA 17-20R
See also SATA 8
See also DLB 6

Koch, Kenneth 1925- .... CLC 5, 8
See also CANR 6
See also CA 1-4R
See also DLB 5

Koestler, Arthur
1905-1983....... CLC 1, 3, 6, 8, 15, 33
See also CANR 1
See also CA 1-4R
See also obituary CA 109
See also DLB-Y 83

Kohout, Pavel 1928-............. CLC 13
See also CANR 3
See also CA 45-48

Konrád, György 1933- .... CLC 4, 10
See also CA 85-88

Konwicki, Tadeusz 1926-....... CLC 8, 28
See also CA 101

Kopit, Arthur (Lee)
1937-................. CLC 1, 18, 33
See also CA 81-84
See also DLB 7
See also AITN 1

Kops, Bernard 1926-.............. CLC 4
See also CA 5-8R
See also DLB 13

Kornbluth, C(yril) M.
1923-1958.................. TCLC 8
See also CA 105
See also DLB 8

Kosinski, Jerzy (Nikodem)
1933-.......... CLC 1, 2, 3, 6, 10, 15
See also CANR 9
See also CA 17-20R
See also DLB 2
See also DLB-Y 82

Kostelanetz, Richard (Cory)
1940-....................... CLC 28
See also CA 13-16R

Kostrowitzki, Wilhelm Apollinaris de
1880-1918
See Apollinaire, Guillaume
See also CA 104

Kotlowitz, Robert 1924- . . . . .CLC 4
See also CA 33-36R

Kotzwinkle, William
1938- . . . . .CLC 5, 14, 35
See also CLR 6
See also CANR 3
See also CA 45-48
See also SATA 24

Kozol, Jonathan 1936- . . . . .CLC 17
See also CANR 16
See also CA 61-64

Kozoll, Michael 1940?-
See Bochco, Steven and Kozoll, Michael

Kramer, Kathryn 19??- . . . . .CLC 34

Krasicki, Ignacy 1735-1801 . . . . NCLC 8

Krasiński, Zygmunt
1812-1859. . . . . NCLC 4

Kraus, Karl 1874-1936. . . . . TCLC 5
See also CA 104

Kristofferson, Kris 1936- . . . . .CLC 26
See also CA 104

Krleža, Miroslav 1893-1981. . . . . . . .CLC 8
See also CA 97-100
See also obituary CA 105

Kroetsch, Robert 1927- . . . . CLC 5, 23
See also CANR 8
See also CA 17-20R

Krotkov, Yuri 1917- . . . . .CLC 19
See also CA 102

Krumgold, Joseph (Quincy)
1908-1980. . . . . .CLC 12
See also CANR 7
See also CA 9-12R
See also obituary CA 101
See also SATA 1
See also obituary SATA 23

Krutch, Joseph Wood
1893-1970. . . . . .CLC 24
See also CANR 4
See also CA 1-4R
See also obituary CA 25-28R

Krylov, Ivan Andreevich
1768?-1844. . . . . NCLC 1

Kubrick, Stanley 1928- . . . . .CLC 16
See also CA 81-84
See also DLB 26

Kumin, Maxine (Winokur)
1925- . . . . CLC 5, 13, 28
See also CANR 1
See also CA 1-4R
See also SATA 12
See also DLB 5
See also AITN 2

Kundera, Milan
1929- . . . . .CLC 4, 9, 19, 32
See also CA 85-88

Kunitz, Stanley J(asspon)
1905- . . . . .CLC 6, 11, 14
See also CA 41-44R

Kunze, Reiner 1933- . . . . .CLC 10
See also CA 93-96

Kuprin, Aleksandr (Ivanovich)
1870-1938. . . . . TCLC 5
See also CA 104

Kurosawa, Akira 1910- . . . . .CLC 16
See also CA 101

Kuttner, Henry 1915-1958. . . . . . . TCLC 10
See also CA 107
See also DLB 8

Kuzma, Greg 1944- . . . . .CLC 7
See also CA 33-36R

Labrunie, Gérard 1808-1855
See Nerval, Gérard de

**Laclos, Pierre Ambroise François Choderlos
de** 1741-1803 . . . . NCLC 4

**La Fayette, Marie (Madelaine Pioche de la
Vergne, Comtesse) de**
1634-1693. . . . . LC 2

Laforgue, Jules 1860-1887 . . . . NCLC 5

Lagerkvist, Pär (Fabian)
1891-1974. . . . . .CLC 7, 10, 13
See also CA 85-88
See also obituary CA 49-52

Lagerlöf, Selma (Ottiliana Lovisa)
1858-1940. . . . . TCLC 4
See also CLR 7
See also CA 108
See also SATA 15

La Guma, (Justin) Alex(ander)
1925- . . . . .CLC 19
See also CA 49-52

Lamartine, Alphonse (Marie Louis Prat) de
1790-1869. . . . . NCLC 11

Lamb, Charles 1775-1834 . . . . NCLC 10
See also SATA 17

Lamming, George (William)
1927- . . . . CLC 2, 4
See also CA 85-88

LaMoore, Louis Dearborn 1908?-
See L'Amour, Louis (Dearborn)

L'Amour, Louis (Dearborn)
1908- .CLC 25
See also CANR 3
See also CA 1-4R
See also DLB-Y 80
See also AITN 2

**Lampedusa, (Prince) Giuseppe (Maria
Fabrizio) Tomasi di**
1896-1957. . . . . TCLC 13
See also CA 111

Lancaster, Bruce 1896-1963 . . . . . . .CLC 36
See also CAP-1
See also CA 9-12R
See also SATA 9

Landis, John (David) 1950- . . . . .CLC 26
See also CA 112

Landolfi, Tommaso 1908- . . . . .CLC 11

Landwirth, Heinz 1927-
See Lind, Jakov
See also CANR 7

Lane, Patrick 1939- . . . . .CLC 25
See also CA 97-100

Lang, Andrew 1844-1912. . . . . TCLC 16
See also CA 114
See also SATA 16

Lang, Fritz 1890-1976 . . . . .CLC 20
See also CA 77-80
See also obituary CA 69-72

Langer, Elinor 1939- . . . . .CLC 34

Lanier, Sidney 1842-1881. . . . . NCLC 6
See also SATA 18

Larbaud, Valéry 1881-1957. . . . . . . TCLC 9
See also CA 106

Lardner, Ring(gold Wilmer)
1885-1933. . . . . .TCLC 2, 14
See also CA 104
See also DLB 11, 25

Larkin, Philip (Arthur)
1922- . . . . .CLC 3, 5, 8, 9, 13, 18, 33
See also CA 5-8R
See also DLB 27

Larsen, Nella 1893-1964. . . . . .CLC 37

Larson, Charles R(aymond)
1938- .CLC 31
See also CANR 4
See also CA 53-56

Latham, Jean Lee 1902- . . . . .CLC 12
See also CANR 7
See also CA 5-8R
See also SATA 2
See also AITN 1

Lathen, Emma . . . . .CLC 2
See also Hennissart, Martha
See also Latsis, Mary J(ane)

Latsis, Mary J(ane)
See Lathen, Emma
See also CA 85-88

Lattimore, Richmond (Alexander)
1906-1984. . . . . .CLC 3
See also CANR 1
See also CA 1-4R
See also obituary CA 112

Laurence, (Jean) Margaret (Wemyss)
1926- . . . . .CLC 3, 6, 13
See also CA 5-8R

Lavin, Mary 1912- . . . . CLC 4, 18
See also CA 9-12R
See also DLB 15

Lawrence, D(avid) H(erbert)
1885-1930. . . . . .TCLC 2, 9, 16
See also CA 104
See also DLB 10, 19, 36

Lawrence, T(homas) E(dward)
1888-1935. . . . . TCLC 18
See also CA 115

Laxness, Halldór (Kiljan)
1902- . . . . .CLC 25
See also Gudjonsson, Halldór Kiljan

Laye, Camara 1928-1980 . . . . .CLC 4
See also CA 85-88
See also obituary CA 97-100

Layton, Irving (Peter) 1912- . . . . CLC 2, 15
See also CANR 2
See also CA 1-4R

Lazarus, Emma 1849-1887 . . . . NCLC 8

Leacock, Stephen (Butler)
1869-1944. . . . . TCLC 2
See also CA 104

Lear, Edward 1812-1888 . . . . NCLC 3
See also CLR 1
See also SATA 18
See also DLB 32

Lear, Norman (Milton) 1922- . . . . . .CLC 12
See also CA 73-76

Leavis, F(rank) R(aymond)
1895-1978. . . . . .CLC 24
See also CA 21-24R
See also obituary CA 77-80

Leavitt, David 1961?- ....CLC 34
See also CA 116

Lebowitz, Fran(ces Ann)
1951?-....................CLC 11, 36
See also CANR 14
See also CA 81-84

Le Carré, John
1931-.............CLC 3, 5, 9, 15, 28
See also Cornwell, David (John Moore)

Le Clézio, J(ean) M(arie) G(ustave)
1940-.........................CLC 31
See also CA 116

Leduc, Violette 1907-1972 ....CLC 22
See also CAP 1
See also CA 13-14
See also obituary CA 33-36R

Lee, Andrea 1953-................CLC 36

Lee, Don L. 1942-.................CLC 2
See also Madhubuti, Haki R.
See also CA 73-76

Lee, (Nelle) Harper 1926-..........CLC 12
See also CA 13-16R
See also SATA 11
See also DLB 6

Lee, Lawrence 1903-..............CLC 34
See also CA 25-28R

Lee, Manfred B(ennington) 1905-1971
See Queen, Ellery
See also CANR 2
See also CA 1-4R
See also obituary CA 29-32R

Lee, Stan 1922- ....CLC 17
See also CA 108, 111

Lee, Vernon 1856-1935...........TCLC 5
See also Paget, Violet

Leet, Judith 1935-................CLC 11

Le Fanu, Joseph Sheridan
1814-1873..................NCLC 9
See also DLB 21

Leffland, Ella 1931-..............CLC 19
See also CA 29-32R
See also DLB-Y 84

Léger, (Marie-Rene) Alexis Saint-Léger
1887-1975
See Perse, St.-John
See also CA 13-16R
See also obituary CA 61-64

Le Guin, Ursula K(roeber)
1929-.................CLC 8, 13, 22
See also CLR 3
See also CANR 9
See also CA 21-24R
See also SATA 4
See also DLB 8
See also AITN 1

Lehmann, Rosamond (Nina)
1901-.........................CLC 5
See also CANR 8
See also CA 77-80
See also DLB 15

Leiber, Fritz (Reuter, Jr.)
1910-.........................CLC 25
See also CANR 2
See also CA 45-48
See also DLB 8

Leithauser, Brad 1953-............CLC 27
See also CA 107

Lelchuk, Alan 1938-................CLC 5
See also CANR 1
See also CA 45-48

Lem, Stanislaw 1921-..........CLC 8, 15
See also CAAS 1
See also CA 105

L'Engle, Madeleine 1918-.........CLC 12
See also CLR 1
See also CANR 3
See also CA 1-4R
See also SATA 1, 27
See also AITN 2

Lennon, John (Ono)
1940-1980....................CLC 35
See also Lennon, John (Ono) and
McCartney, Paul
See also CA 102

Lennon, John (Ono) 1940-1980 and
McCartney, Paul 1942- ....CLC 12

Lennon, John Winston 1940-1980
See Lennon, John (Ono)

Lentricchia, Frank (Jr.) 1940-......CLC 34
See also CA 25-28R

Lenz, Siegfried 1926- ....CLC 27
See also CA 89-92

Leonard, Elmore 1925-........ CLC 28, 34
See also CANR 12
See also CA 81-84
See also AITN 1

Leonard, Hugh 1926- ....CLC 19
See also Byrne, John Keyes
See also DLB 13

Lerman, Eleanor 1952-.............CLC 9
See also CA 85-88

Lermontov, Mikhail Yuryevich
1814-1841...................NCLC 5

Lesage, Alain-René 1668-1747.......LC 2

Lessing, Doris (May)
1919-........CLC 1, 2, 3, 6, 10, 15, 22
See also CA 9-12R
See also DLB 15

Lester, Richard 1932-.............CLC 20

Leverson, Ada 1865-1936........ TCLC 18

Levertov, Denise
1923-.........CLC 1, 2, 3, 5, 8, 15, 28
See also CANR 3
See also CA 1-4R
See also DLB 5

Levi, Primo 1919- ....CLC 37
See also CANR 12
See also CA 13-16R

Levin, Ira 1929-................ CLC 3, 6
See also CA 21-24R

Levin, Meyer 1905-1981............CLC 7
See also CANR 15
See also CA 9-12R
See also obituary CA 104
See also SATA 21
See also obituary SATA 27
See also DLB 9, 28
See also DLB-Y 81
See also AITN 1

Levine, Philip
1928-...........CLC 2, 4, 5, 9, 14, 33
See also CANR 9
See also CA 9-12R
See also DLB 5

Levitin, Sonia 1934- ....CLC 17
See also CA 29-32R
See also SATA 4

Lewis, Alun 1915-1944...........TCLC 3
See also CA 104
See also DLB 20

Lewis, C(ecil) Day 1904-1972
See Day Lewis, C(ecil)

Lewis, C(live) S(taples)
1898-1963........ CLC 1, 3, 6, 14, 27
See also CLR 3
See also CA 81-84
See also SATA 13
See also DLB 15

Lewis, (Harry) Sinclair
1885-1951............... TCLC 4, 13
See also CA 104
See also DLB 9
See also DLB-DS 1

Lewis, Matthew Gregory
1775-1818..................NCLC 11
See also DLB 39

Lewis, (Percy) Wyndham
1882?-1957...............TCLC 2, 9
See also CA 104
See also DLB 15

Lewisohn, Ludwig 1883-1955 .... TCLC 19
See also CA 107
See also DLB 4, 9, 28

Lezama Lima, José
1910-1976................ CLC 4, 10
See also CA 77-80

Li Fei-kan 1904-
See Pa Chin
See also CA 105

Lie, Jonas (Lauritz Idemil)
1833-1908...................TCLC 5

Lieber, Joel 1936-1971 ....CLC 6
See also CA 73-76
See also obituary CA 29-32R

Lieber, Stanley Martin 1922-
See Lee, Stan

Lieberman, Laurence (James)
1935-.................... CLC 4, 36
See also CANR 8
See also CA 17-20R

Lightfoot, Gordon (Meredith)
1938-.......................CLC 26
See also CA 109

Liliencron, Detlev von
1844-1909................. TCLC 18

Lima, José Lezama 1910-1976
See Lezama Lima, José

Lind, Jakov 1927-.........CLC 1, 2, 4, 27
See also Landwirth, Heinz
See also CA 9-12R

Lindsay, David 1876-1945 .... TCLC 15
See also CA 113

Lindsay, (Nicholas) Vachel
1879-1931..................TCLC 17
See also CA 114
See also SATA 40

Lipsyte, Robert (Michael)
1938-.......................CLC 21
See also CANR 8
See also CA 17-20R
See also SATA 5

Author Index

Liu E 1857-1909 . . . . TCLC 15
See also CA 115

Lively, Penelope 1933- . . . . CLC 32
See also CLR 7
See also CA 41-44R
See also SATA 7
See also DLB 14

Livesay, Dorothy 1909- . . . . CLC 4, 15
See also CA 25-28R
See also AITN 2

Llewellyn, Richard 1906-1983 . . . . . . CLC 7
See also Llewellyn Lloyd, Richard (Dafydd
Vyvyan)
See also DLB 15

Llewellyn Lloyd, Richard (Dafydd Vyvyan)
1906-1983
See Llewellyn, Richard
See also CANR 7
See also CA 53-56
See also obituary CA 111
See also SATA 11

Llosa, Mario Vargas 1936-
See Vargas Llosa, Mario

Lloyd, Richard Llewellyn 1906-
See Llewellyn, Richard

Lockhart, John Gibson
1794-1854 . . . . NCLC 6

Lodge, David (John) 1935- . . . . CLC 36
See also CA 17-20R
See also DLB 14

Logan, John 1923- . . . . CLC 5
See also CA 77-80
See also DLB 5

Lombino, S. A. 1926-
See Hunter, Evan

London, Jack 1876-1916 . . . . . . TCLC 9, 15
See also London, John Griffith
See also SATA 18
See also DLB 8, 12
See also AITN 2

London, John Griffith 1876-1916
See London, Jack
See also CA 110

Long, Emmett 1925-
See Leonard, Elmore

Longfellow, Henry Wadsworth
1807-1882 . . . . NCLC 2
See also SATA 19
See also DLB 1

Longley, Michael 1939- . . . . CLC 29
See also CA 102
See also DLB 40

Lopate, Phillip 1943- . . . . CLC 29
See also CA 97-100
See also DLB-Y 80

López y Fuentes, Gregorio
1897-1966 . . . . CLC 32

Lord, Bette Bao 1938- . . . . CLC 23
See also CA 107

Lorde, Audre (Geraldine)
1934- . . . . CLC 18
See also CANR 16
See also CA 25-28R
See also DLB 41

Loti, Pierre 1850-1923 . . . . TCLC 11
See also Viaud, (Louis Marie) Julien

Lovecraft, H(oward) P(hillips)
1890-1937 . . . . TCLC 4
See also CA 104

Lowell, Amy 1874-1925 . . . . TCLC 1, 8
See also CA 104

Lowell, James Russell
1819-1891 . . . . NCLC 2
See also DLB 1, 11

Lowell, Robert (Traill Spence, Jr.)
1917-1977 . . . . . CLC 1, 2, 3, 4, 5, 8, 9,
11, 15, 37
See also CA 9-12R
See also obituary CA 73-76
See also DLB 5

Lowndes, Marie (Adelaide Belloc)
1868-1947 . . . . TCLC 12
See also CA 107

Lowry, (Clarence) Malcolm
1909-1957 . . . . TCLC 6
See also CA 105
See also DLB 15

Loy, Mina 1882-1966 . . . . CLC 28
See also CA 113
See also DLB 4

Lucas, George 1944- . . . . CLC 16
See also CA 77-80

Lucas, Victoria 1932-1963
See Plath, Sylvia

Ludlum, Robert 1927- . . . . CLC 22
See also CA 33-36R
See also DLB-Y 82

Ludwig, Otto 1813-1865 . . . . NCLC 4

Lugones, Leopoldo
1874-1938 . . . . TCLC 15
See also CA 116

Lu Hsün 1881-1936 . . . . TCLC 3

Lukács, Georg 1885-1971 . . . . CLC 24
See also Lukács, György

Lukács, György 1885-1971
See Lukács, Georg
See also CA 101
See also obituary CA 29-32R

Lurie, Alison 1926- . . . . CLC 4, 5, 18
See also CANR 2
See also CA 1-4R
See also DLB 2

Luzi, Mario 1914- . . . . CLC 13
See also CANR 9
See also CA 61-64

Lytle, Andrew (Nelson) 1902- . . . . . . CLC 22
See also CA 9-12R
See also DLB 6

Lytton, Edward Bulwer 1803-1873
See Bulwer-Lytton, (Lord) Edward (George
Earle Lytton)
See also SATA 23

Maas, Peter 1929- . . . . CLC 29
See also CA 93-96

Macaulay, (Dame Emile) Rose
1881-1958 . . . . TCLC 7
See also CA 104
See also DLB 36

MacBeth, George (Mann)
1932- . . . . CLC 2, 5, 9
See also CA 25-28R
See also SATA 4
See also DLB 40

MacCaig, Norman (Alexander)
1910- . . . . CLC 36
See also CANR 3
See also CA 9-12R
See also DLB 27

MacDiarmid, Hugh
1892-1978 . . . . CLC 2, 4, 11, 19
See also Grieve, C(hristopher) M(urray)
See also DLB 20

Macdonald, Cynthia 1928- . . . . . CLC 13, 19
See also CANR 4
See also CA 49-52

MacDonald, George
1824-1905 . . . . TCLC 9
See also CA 106
See also SATA 33
See also DLB 18

MacDonald, John D(ann)
1916- . . . . CLC 3, 27
See also CANR 1
See also CA 1-4R
See also DLB 8

Macdonald, (John) Ross
1915-1983 . . . . CLC 1, 2, 3, 14, 34
See also Millar, Kenneth

MacEwen, Gwendolyn 1941- . . . . CLC 13
See also CANR 7
See also CA 9-12R

Machado (y Ruiz), Antonio
1875-1939 . . . . TCLC 3
See also CA 104

Machado de Assis, (Joaquim Maria)
1839-1908 . . . . TCLC 10
See also CA 107

Machen, Arthur (Llewellyn Jones)
1863-1947 . . . . TCLC 4
See also CA 104
See also DLB 36

MacInnes, Colin 1914-1976 . . . . . CLC 4, 23
See also CA 69-72
See also obituary CA 65-68
See also DLB 14

MacInnes, Helen 1907- . . . . CLC 27
See also CANR 1
See also CA 1-4R
See also SATA 22

Macintosh, Elizabeth 1897-1952
See Tey, Josephine
See also CA 110

Mackenzie, (Edward Montague) Compton
1883-1972 . . . . CLC 18
See also CAP 2
See also CA 21-22
See also obituary CA 37-40R
See also DLB 34

Mac Laverty, Bernard 1942- . . . . CLC 31
See also CA 116

MacLean, Alistair (Stuart)
1922- . . . . CLC 3, 13
See also CA 57-60
See also SATA 23

MacLeish, Archibald
1892-1982 . . . . CLC 3, 8, 14
See also CA 9-12R
See also obituary CA 106
See also DLB 4, 7, 45
See also DLB-Y 82

MacLennan, (John) Hugh
1907- .... CLC 2, 14
See also CA 5-8R

MacNeice, (Frederick) Louis
1907-1963.............. CLC 1, 4, 10
See also CA 85-88
See also DLB 10, 20

Macpherson, (Jean) Jay 1931- ...... CLC 14
See also CA 5-8R

Macumber, Mari 1896-1966
See Sandoz, Mari (Susette)

Madden, (Jerry) David
1933- .... CLC 5, 15
See also CANR 4
See also CA 1-4R
See also DLB 6

Madhubuti, Haki R. 1942- .... CLC 6
See also Lee, Don L.
See also DLB 5, 41

Maeterlinck, Maurice
1862-1949.................. TCLC 3
See also CA 104

Maginn, William 1794-1842...... NCLC 8

Mahapatra, Jayanta 1928- .... CLC 33
See also CANR 15
See also CA 73-76

Mahon, Derek 1941- .... CLC 27
See also CA 113
See also DLB 40

Mailer, Norman
1923- ...... CLC 1, 2, 3, 4, 5, 8, 11, 14,
                                                28
See also CA 9-12R
See also DLB 2, 16, 28
See also DLB-Y 80, 83
See also DLB-DS 3
See also AITN 2

Mais, Roger 1905-1955 .... TCLC 8
See also CA 105

Major, Clarence 1936- .... CLC 3, 19
See also CA 21-24R
See also DLB 33

Major, Kevin 1949- .... CLC 26
See also CA 97-100
See also SATA 32

Malamud, Bernard
1914- ...... CLC 1, 2, 3, 5, 8, 9, 11, 18,
                                               27
See also CA 5-8R
See also DLB 2, 28
See also DLB-Y 80

Mallarmé, Stéphane
1842-1898.................. NCLC 4

Mallet-Joris, Françoise 1930- ...... CLC 11
See also CA 65-68

Maloff, Saul 1922- .... CLC 5
See also CA 33-36R

Malouf, David 1934- .... CLC 28

Malraux, (Georges-) André
1901-1976........ CLC 1, 4, 9, 13, 15
See also CAP 2
See also CA 21-24R
See also obituary CA 69-72

Malzberg, Barry N. 1939- .... CLC 7
See also CANR 16
See also CA 61-64
See also DLB 8

Mamet, David 1947- .... CLC 9, 15, 34
See also CANR 15
See also CA 81-84
See also DLB 7

Mamoulian, Rouben 1898- .... CLC 16
See also CA 25-28R

Mandelstam, Osip (Emilievich)
1891?-1938?.............. TCLC 2, 6
See also CA 104

Manley, (Mary) Delariviere
1672?-1724.................... LC 1
See also DLB 39

Mann, (Luiz) Heinrich
1871-1950.................. TCLC 9
See also CA 106

Mann, Thomas
1875-1955............. TCLC 2, 8, 14
See also CA 104

Manning, Olivia 1915-1980 ..... CLC 5, 19
See also CA 5-8R
See also obituary CA 101

Mano, D. Keith 1942- .... CLC 2, 10
See also CA 25-28R
See also DLB 6

Mansfield, Katherine
1888-1923................ TCLC 2, 8
See also CA 104

Marcel, Gabriel (Honore)
1889-1973.................... CLC 15
See also CA 102
See also obituary CA 45-48

Marchbanks, Samuel 1913-
See Davies, (William) Robertson

Marinetti, F(ilippo) T(ommaso)
1876-1944................ TCLC 10
See also CA 107

Markandaya, Kamala (Purnalya)
1924- .... CLC 8
See also Taylor, Kamala (Purnalya)

Markfield, Wallace (Arthur)
1926- .... CLC 8
See also CA 69-72
See also DLB 2, 28

Markham, Robert 1922-
See Amis, Kingsley (William)

Marks, J. 1942-
See Highwater, Jamake

Marley, Bob 1945-1981 .... CLC 17
See also Marley, Robert Nesta

Marley, Robert Nesta 1945-1981
See Marley, Bob
See also CA 107
See also obituary CA 103

Marmontel, Jean-François
1723-1799.................... LC 2

Marquand, John P(hillips)
1893-1960................ CLC 2, 10
See also CA 85-88
See also DLB 9

Márquez, Gabriel García 1928-
See García Márquez, Gabriel

Marquis, Don(ald Robert Perry)
1878-1937.................. TCLC 7
See also CA 104
See also DLB 11, 25

Marryat, Frederick 1792-1848 .... NCLC 3
See also DLB 21

Marsh, (Edith) Ngaio
1899-1982.................... CLC 7
See also CANR 6
See also CA 9-12R

Marshall, Garry 1935?- .... CLC 17
See also CA 111

Marshall, Paule 1929- .... CLC 27
See also CA 77-80
See also DLB 33

Marsten, Richard 1926-
See Hunter, Evan

Martin, Steve 1945?- .... CLC 30
See also CA 97-100

Martínez Ruiz, José 1874-1967
See Azorín
See also CA 93-96

Martínez Sierra, Gregorio 1881-1947
See Martínez Sierra, Gregorio and Martínez
Sierra, María (de la O'LeJárraga)
See also CA 104, 115

Martínez Sierra, Gregorio 1881-1947 and
**Martínez Sierra, María (de la
O'LeJárraga)** 1880?-1974 .... TCLC 6

Martínez Sierra, María (de la O'LeJárraga)
1880?-1974
See Martínez Sierra, Gregorio and Martínez
Sierra, María (de la O'LeJárraga)
See also obituary CA 115

Martínez Sierra, María (de la O'LeJárraga)
1880?-1974 and **Martínez Sierra,
Gregorio** 1881-1947
See Martínez Sierra, Gregorio and Martínez
Sierra, María (de la O'LeJárraga)

Martinson, Harry (Edmund)
1904-1978.................... CLC 14
See also CA 77-80

Masaoka Shiki 1867-1902....... TCLC 18

Masefield, John (Edward)
1878-1967.................... CLC 11
See also CAP 2
See also CA 19-20
See also obituary CA 25-28R
See also SATA 19
See also DLB 10, 19

Mason, Bobbie Ann 1940- .... CLC 28
See also CANR 11
See also CA 53-56

Mason, Nick 1945-
See Pink Floyd

Mason, Tally 1909-1971
See Derleth, August (William)

Masters, Edgar Lee
1868?-1950.................. TCLC 2
See also CA 104

Mastrosimone, William 19??- ......CLC 36

Matheson, Richard (Burton)
1926- .... CLC 37
See also CA 97-100
See also DLB 8, 44

Mathews, Harry 1930- .... CLC 6
See also CA 21-24R

Matthias, John (Edward) 1941- ...... CLC 9
See also CA 33-36R

Matthiessen, Peter
  1927-..................CLC 5, 7, 11, 32
  See also CA 9-12R
  See also SATA 27
  See also DLB 6

Maturin, Charles Robert
  1780?-1824..................NCLC 6

Matute, Ana María 1925-.........CLC 11
  See also CA 89-92

Maugham, W(illiam) Somerset
  1874-1965.............CLC 1, 11, 15
  See also CA 5-8R
  See also obituary CA 25-28R
  See also DLB 10, 36

Maupassant, (Henri René Albert) Guy de
  1850-1893..................NCLC 1

Mauriac, Claude 1914-.............CLC 9
  See also CA 89-92

Mauriac, François (Charles)
  1885-1970..................CLC 4, 9
  See also CAP 2
  See also CA 25-28

Mavor, Osborne Henry 1888-1951
  See Bridie, James
  See also CA 104

Maxwell, William (Keepers, Jr.)
  1908-..................CLC 19
  See also CA 93-96
  See also DLB-Y 80

May, Elaine 1932-..................CLC 16
  See also DLB 44

Mayakovsky, Vladimir (Vladimirovich)
  1893-1930..................TCLC 4, 18
  See also CA 104

Maynard, Joyce 1953-.............CLC 23
  See also CA 111

Mayne, William (James Carter)
  1928-..................CLC 12
  See also CA 9-12R
  See also SATA 6

Mayo, Jim 1908?-
  See L'Amour, Louis (Dearborn)

Maysles, Albert 1926-
  See Maysles, Albert and Maysles, David
  See also CA 29-32R

Maysles, Albert 1926- and **Maysles, David**
  1932-..................CLC 16

Maysles, David 1932-
  See Maysles, Albert and Maysles, David

Mazer, Norma Fox 1931-.........CLC 26
  See also CANR 12
  See also CA 69-72
  See also SAAS 1
  See also SATA 24

McBain, Ed 1926-
  See Hunter, Evan

McCaffrey, Anne 1926- ....CLC 17
  See also CANR 15
  See also CA 25-28R
  See also SATA 8
  See also DLB 8
  See also AITN 2

McCarthy, Cormac 1933-..........CLC 4
  See also CANR 10
  See also CA 13-16R
  See also DLB 6

McCarthy, Mary (Therese)
  1912-.............CLC 1, 3, 5, 14, 24
  See also CANR 16
  See also CA 5-8R
  See also DLB 2
  See also DLB-Y 81

McCartney, (James) Paul
  1942-..................CLC 35
  See also Lennon, John (Ono) and
    McCartney, Paul

McClure, Michael 1932-........ CLC 6, 10
  See also CA 21-24R
  See also DLB 16

McCourt, James 1941-.............CLC 5
  See also CA 57-60

McCrae, John 1872-1918........ TCLC 12
  See also CA 109

McCullers, (Lula) Carson
  1917-1967...........CLC 1, 4, 10, 12
  See also CA 5-8R
  See also obituary CA 25-28R
  See also SATA 27
  See also DLB 2, 7

McCullough, Colleen 1938?-.......CLC 27
  See also CA 81-84

McElroy, Joseph 1930-.............CLC 5
  See also CA 17-20R

McEwan, Ian 1948-..................CLC 13
  See also CA 61-64
  See also DLB 14

McGahern, John 1935-......... CLC 5, 9
  See also CA 17-20R
  See also DLB 14

McGinley, Phyllis 1905-1978.......CLC 14
  See also CA 9-12R
  See also obituary CA 77-80
  See also SATA 2
  See also obituary SATA 24
  See also DLB 11

McGinniss, Joe 1942-.............CLC 32
  See also CA 25-28R
  See also AITN 2

McGivern, Maureen Daly 1921-
  See Daly, Maureen
  See also CA 9-12R

McGrath, Thomas 1916-..........CLC 28
  See also CANR 6
  See also CA 9-12R
  See also SATA 41

McGuane, Thomas (Francis III)
  1939-..................CLC 3, 7, 18
  See also CANR 5
  See also CA 49-52
  See also DLB 2
  See also DLB-Y 80
  See also AITN 2

McHale, Tom 1941-1982........ CLC 3, 5
  See also CA 77-80
  See also obituary CA 106
  See also AITN 1

McIlwraith, Maureen Mollie Hunter 1922-
  See Hunter, Mollie
  See also CA 29-32R
  See also SATA 2

McInerney, Jay 1955-.............CLC 34
  See also CA 116

McIntyre, Vonda N(eel) 1948-......CLC 18
  See also CA 81-84

McKay, Claude 1890-1948....... TCLC 7
  See also CA 104
  See also DLB 4, 45

McKuen, Rod 1933-............ CLC 1, 3
  See also CA 41-44R
  See also AITN 1

McLuhan, (Herbert) Marshall
  1911-1980..................CLC 37
  See also CANR 12
  See also CA 9-12R
  See also obituary CA 102

McManus, Declan Patrick 1955-
  See Costello, Elvis

McMurtry, Larry (Jeff)
  1936-............. CLC 2, 3, 7, 11, 27
  See also CA 5-8R
  See also DLB 2
  See also DLB-Y 80
  See also AITN 2

McNally, Terrence 1939- .... CLC 4, 7
  See also CANR 2
  See also CA 45-48
  See also DLB 7

McPhee, John 1931-.............CLC 36
  See also CA 65-68

McPherson, James Alan 1943- .....CLC 19
  See also CA 25-28R
  See also DLB 38

McPherson, William 1939-.........CLC 34
  See also CA 57-60

McSweeney, Kerry 19??- ....CLC 34

Mead, Margaret 1901-1978 ....CLC 37
  See also CANR 4
  See also CA 1-4R
  See also obituary CA 81-84
  See also SATA 20
  See also AITN 1

Meaker, M. J. 1927-
  See Kerr, M. E.
  See Meaker, Marijane

Meaker, Marijane 1927-
  See Kerr, M. E.
  See also CA 107
  See also SATA 20

Medoff, Mark (Howard)
  1940-..................... CLC 6, 23
  See also CANR 5
  See also CA 53-56
  See also DLB 7
  See also AITN 1

Megged, Aharon 1920-.............CLC 9
  See also CANR 1
  See also CA 49-52

Mehta, Ved (Parkash) 1934- ....CLC 37
  See also CANR 2
  See also CA 1-4R

Mellor, John 1953?-
  See The Clash

Meltzer, Milton 1915-.............CLC 26
  See also CA 13-16R
  See also SAAS 1
  See also SATA 1

Melville, Herman 1819-1891 ......NCLC 3
  See also DLB 3

Mencken, H(enry) L(ouis)
    1880-1956.................. **TCLC 13**
    See also CA 105
    See also DLB 11, 29

Mercer, David 1928-1980.......... **CLC 5**
    See also CA 9-12R
    See also obituary CA 102
    See also DLB 13

Meredith, George 1828-1909..... **TCLC 17**
    See also DLB 18, 35

Meredith, William (Morris)
    1919-.................. **CLC 4, 13, 22**
    See also CANR 6
    See also CA 9-12R
    See also DLB 5

Mérimée, Prosper 1803-1870...... **NCLC 6**

Merrill, James (Ingram)
    1926-........ **CLC 2, 3, 6, 8, 13, 18, 34**
    See also CANR 10
    See also CA 13-16R
    See also DLB 5

Merton, Thomas (James)
    1915-1968.......... **CLC 1, 3, 11, 34**
    See also CA 5-8R
    See also obituary CA 25-28R
    See also DLB-Y 81

Merwin, W(illiam) S(tanley)
    1927-........ **CLC 1, 2, 3, 5, 8, 13, 18**
    See also CANR 15
    See also CA 13-16R
    See also DLB 5

Metcalf, John 1938-.............. **CLC 37**
    See also CA 113

Mew, Charlotte (Mary)
    1870-1928.................. **TCLC 8**
    See also CA 105
    See also DLB 19

Mewshaw, Michael 1943-.......... **CLC 9**
    See also CANR 7
    See also CA 53-56
    See also DLB-Y 80

Meynell, Alice (Christiana Gertrude
    Thompson) 1847-1922........ **TCLC 6**
    See also CA 104
    See also DLB 19

Michaels, Leonard 1933-....... **CLC 6, 25**
    See also CA 61-64

Michaux, Henri 1899-1984...... **CLC 8, 19**
    See also CA 85-88
    See also obituary CA 114

Michener, James A(lbert)
    1907-.............. **CLC 1, 5, 11, 29**
    See also CA 5-8R
    See also DLB 6
    See also AITN 1

Mickiewicz, Adam 1798-1855..... **NCLC 3**

Middleton, Christopher 1926-...... **CLC 13**
    See also CA 13-16R
    See also DLB 40

Middleton, Stanley 1919-.......... **CLC 7**
    See also CA 25-28R
    See also DLB 14

Miguéis, José Rodrigues 1901-..... **CLC 10**

Miles, Josephine
    1911-1985.......... **CLC 1, 2, 14, 34**
    See also CANR 2
    See also CA 1-4R
    See also obituary CA 116

Mill, John Stuart 1806-1873..... **NCLC 11**

Millar, Kenneth
    1915-1983........ **CLC 1, 2, 3, 14, 34**
    See Macdonald, Ross
    See also CANR 16
    See also CA 9-12R
    See also obituary CA 110
    See also DLB 2
    See also DLB-Y 83

Millay, Edna St. Vincent
    1892-1950.................. **TCLC 4**
    See also CA 104
    See also DLB 45

Miller, Arthur
    1915-.......... **CLC 1, 2, 6, 10, 15, 26**
    See also CANR 2
    See also CA 1-4R
    See also DLB 7
    See also AITN 1

Miller, Henry (Valentine)
    1891-1980.......... **CLC 1, 2, 4, 9, 14**
    See also CA 9-12R
    See also obituary CA 97-100
    See also DLB 4, 9
    See also DLB-Y 80

Miller, Jason 1939?-.............. **CLC 2**
    See also CA 73-76
    See also DLB 7
    See also AITN 1

Miller, Walter M(ichael), Jr.
    1923-.................. **CLC 4, 30**
    See also CA 85-88
    See also DLB 8

Millhauser, Steven 1943-.......... **CLC 21**
    See also CA 108, 110, 111
    See also DLB 2

Milne, A(lan) A(lexander)
    1882-1956.................. **TCLC 6**
    See also CLR 1
    See also CA 104
    See also YABC 1
    See also DLB 10

Miłosz, Czesław
    1911-............ **CLC 5, 11, 22, 31**
    See also CA 81-84

Miró (Ferrer), Gabriel (Francisco Víctor)
    1879-1930.................. **TCLC 5**
    See also CA 104

Mishima, Yukio
    1925-1970.......... **CLC 2, 4, 6, 9, 27**
    See also Hiraoka, Kimitake

Mistral, Gabriela 1889-1957...... **TCLC 2**
    See also CA 104

Mitchell, James Leslie 1901-1935
    See Gibbon, Lewis Grassic
    See also CA 104
    See also DLB 15

Mitchell, Joni 1943-.............. **CLC 12**
    See also CA 112

Mitchell (Marsh), Margaret (Munnerlyn)
    1900-1949.................. **TCLC 11**
    See also CA 109
    See also DLB 9

Mitchell, W(illiam) O(rmond)
    1914-...................... **CLC 25**
    See also CANR 15
    See also CA 77-80

Mitford, Mary Russell
    1787-1855.................. **NCLC 4**

Modiano, Patrick (Jean) 1945-..... **CLC 18**
    See also CA 85-88

Mohr, Nicholasa 1935-........... **CLC 12**
    See also CANR 1
    See also CA 49-52
    See also SATA 8

Mojtabai, A(nn) G(race)
    1938-.............. **CLC 5, 9, 15, 29**
    See also CA 85-88

Momaday, N(avarre) Scott
    1934-.................. **CLC 2, 19**
    See also CANR 14
    See also CA 25-28R
    See also SATA 30

Monroe, Harriet 1860-1936...... **TCLC 12**
    See also CA 109

Montagu, Elizabeth 1720-1800.... **NCLC 7**

Montague, John (Patrick)
    1929-...................... **CLC 13**
    See also CANR 9
    See also CA 9-12R
    See also DLB 40

Montale, Eugenio
    1896-1981.............. **CLC 7, 9, 18**
    See also CA 17-20R
    See also obituary CA 104

Montgomery, Marion (H., Jr.)
    1925-...................... **CLC 7**
    See also CANR 3
    See also CA 1-4R
    See also DLB 6
    See also AITN 1

Montgomery, Robert Bruce 1921-1978
    See Crispin, Edmund
    See also CA 104

Montherlant, Henri (Milon) de
    1896-1972.................. **CLC 8, 19**
    See also CA 85-88
    See also obituary CA 37-40R

Monty Python.................... **CLC 21**
    See also Cleese, John

Mooney, Ted 1951-.............. **CLC 25**

Moorcock, Michael (John)
    1939-.................... **CLC 5, 27**
    See also CANR 2
    See also CA 45-48
    See also DLB 14

Moore, Brian
    1921-.......... **CLC 1, 3, 5, 7, 8, 19, 32**
    See also CANR 1
    See also CA 1-4R

Moore, George (Augustus)
    1852-1933............... **TCLC 7**
    See also CA 104
    See also DLB 10, 18

Moore, Marianne (Craig)
    1887-1972...... **CLC 1, 2, 4, 8, 10, 13,**
                                              19
    See also CANR 3
    See also CA 1-4R
    See also obituary CA 33-36R
    See also DLB 45
    See also SATA 20

Moore, Thomas 1779-1852........ **NCLC 6**

Author Index

Morante, Elsa 1918- .... CLC 8
See also CA 85-88

Moravia, Alberto
1907- .... CLC 2, 7, 11, 18, 27
See also Pincherle, Alberto

Moréas, Jean 1856-1910 .... TCLC 18

Morgan, Berry 1919- .... CLC 6
See also CA 49-52
See also DLB 6

Morgan, Edwin (George)
1920- .... CLC 31
See also CANR 3
See also CA 7-8R
See also DLB 27

Morgan, Frederick 1922- .... CLC 23
See also CA 17-20R

Morgan, Robin 1941- .... CLC 2
See also CA 69-72

Morgenstern, Christian (Otto Josef Wolfgang)
1871-1914................... TCLC 8
See also CA 105

Mori Ōgai 1862-1922 .... TCLC 14
See also Mori Rintaro

Mori Rintaro 1862-1922
See Mori Ōgai
See also CA 110

Mörike, Eduard (Friedrich)
1804-1875 .... NCLC 10

Moritz, Karl Philipp 1756-1793 ...... LC 2

Morris, Julian 1916-
See West, Morris L.

Morris, Steveland Judkins 1950-
See Wonder, Stevie
See also CA 111

Morris, William 1834-1896 .... NCLC 4
See also DLB 18, 35

Morris, Wright
1910- .... CLC 1, 3, 7, 18, 37
See also CA 9-12R
See also DLB 2
See also DLB-Y 81

Morrison, James Douglas 1943-1971
See Morrison, Jim
See also CA 73-76

Morrison, Jim 1943-1971 .... CLC 17
See also Morrison, James Douglas

Morrison, Toni 1931- .... CLC 4, 10, 22
See also CA 29-32R
See also DLB 6, 33
See also DLB-Y 81

Morrison, Van 1945- .... CLC 21
See also CA 116

Mortimer, John (Clifford)
1923- .... CLC 28
See also CA 13-16R
See also DLB 13

Mortimer, Penelope (Ruth)
1918- .... CLC 5
See also CA 57-60

Moss, Howard 1922- .... CLC 7, 14
See also CANR 1
See also CA 1-4R
See also DLB 5

Motley, Willard (Francis)
1912-1965 .... CLC 18
See also obituary CA 106

Mott, Michael (Charles Alston)
1930- .... CLC 15, 34
See also CANR 7
See also CA 5-8R

Mowat, Farley (McGill) 1921- ...... CLC 26
See also CANR 4
See also CA 1-4R
See also SATA 3

Mphahlele, Es'kia 1919-
See Mphahlele, Ezekiel

Mphahlele, Ezekiel 1919- .... CLC 25
See also CA 81-84

Mrożek, Sławomir 1930- .... CLC 3, 13
See also CA 13-16R

Mueller, Lisel 1924- .... CLC 13
See also CA 93-96

Muir, Edwin 1887-1959 .... TCLC 2
See also CA 104
See also DLB 20

Mujica Láinez, Manuel
1910-1984.................... CLC 31
See also CA 81-84
See also obituary CA 112

Muldoon, Paul 1951- .... CLC 32
See also CA 113
See also DLB 40

Mull, Martin 1943- .... CLC 17
See also CA 105

Munro, Alice 1931- .... CLC 6, 10, 19
See also CA 33-36R
See also SATA 29
See also AITN 2

Munro, H(ector) H(ugh) 1870-1916
See Saki
See also CA 104
See also DLB 34

Murdoch, (Jean) Iris
1919- ...... CLC 1, 2, 3, 4, 6, 8, 11, 15,
22, 31
See also CANR 8
See also CA 13-16R
See also DLB 14

Murphy, Sylvia 19??- .... CLC 34

Murry, John Middleton
1889-1957................. TCLC 16

Musgrave, Susan 1951- .... CLC 13
See also CA 69-72

Musil, Robert (Edler von)
1880-1942.................. TCLC 12
See also CA 109

Musset, (Louis Charles) Alfred de
1810-1857................... NCLC 7

Myers, Walter Dean 1937- .... CLC 35
See also CLR 4
See also CA 33-36R
See also SATA 27, 41
See also DLB 33

Nabokov, Vladimir (Vladimirovich)
1899-1977....... CLC 1, 2, 3, 6, 8, 11,
15, 23
See also CA 5-8R
See also obituary CA 69-72
See also DLB 2
See also DLB-Y 80
See also DLB-DS 3

Nagy, László 1925-1978 .... CLC 7
See also obituary CA 112

Naipaul, Shiva 1945-1985......... CLC 32
See also CA 110, 112
See also obituary CA 116

Naipaul, V(idiadhar) S(urajprasad)
1932- .... CLC 4, 7, 9, 13, 18, 37
See also CANR 1
See also CA 1-4R

Nakos, Ioulia 1899?-
See Nakos, Lilika

Nakos, Lilika 1899?- .... CLC 29

Nakou, Lilika 1899?-
See Nakos, Lilika

Narayan, R(asipuram) K(rishnaswami)
1906- .... CLC 7, 28
See also CA 81-84

Nash, (Frediric) Ogden
1902-1971.................... CLC 23
See also CAP 1
See also CA 13-14
See also obituary CA 29-32R
See also SATA 2
See also DLB 11

Nathan, George Jean
1882-1958................. TCLC 18
See also CA 114

Natsume, Kinnosuke 1867-1916
See Natsume, Sōseki
See also CA 104

Natsume, Sōseki
1867-1916................ TCLC 2, 10
See also Natsume, Kinnosuke

Natti, (Mary) Lee 1919-
See Kingman, (Mary) Lee
See also CANR 2

Naylor, Gloria 1950- .... CLC 28
See also CA 107

Neihardt, John G(neisenau)
1881-1973.................... CLC 32
See also CAP 1
See also CA 13-14
See also DLB 9

Nekrasov, Nikolai Alekseevich
1821-1878.................. NCLC 11

Nelligan, Émile 1879-1941 .... TCLC 14
See also CA 114

Nelson, Willie 1933- .... CLC 17
See also CA 107

Nemerov, Howard
1920- .... CLC 2, 6, 9, 36
See also CANR 1
See also CA 1-4R
See also DLB 5, 6
See also DLB-Y 83

Neruda, Pablo
1904-1973........ CLC 1, 2, 5, 7, 9, 28
See also CAP 2
See also CA 19-20
See also obituary CA 45-48

Nerval, Gérard de 1808-1855 ..... NCLC 1

Nervo, (José) Amado (Ruiz de)
1870-1919.................. TCLC 11
See also CA 109

Neufeld, John (Arthur) 1938- ...... CLC 17
See also CANR 11
See also CA 25-28R
See also SATA 6

Neville, Emily Cheney 1919- ....CLC 12
See also CANR 3
See also CA 5-8R
See also SATA 1

Newbound, Bernard Slade 1930-
See Slade, Bernard
See also CA 81-84

Newby, P(ercy) H(oward)
1918- .... CLC 2, 13
See also CA 5-8R
See also DLB 15

Newlove, Donald 1928- ....CLC 6
See also CA 29-32R

Newlove, John (Herbert) 1938- .....CLC 14
See also CANR 9
See also CA 21-24R

Newman, Charles 1938- .... CLC 2, 8
See also CA 21-24R

Newman, Edwin (Harold)
1919- ....CLC 14
See also CANR 5
See also CA 69-72
See also AITN 1

Newton, Suzanne 1936-............CLC 35
See also CANR 14
See also CA 41-44R
See also SATA 5

Ngugi, James (Thiong'o)
1938-................CLC 3, 7, 13, 36
See also Ngugi wa Thiong'o
See also Wa Thiong'o, Ngugi
See also CA 81-84

Ngugi wa Thiong'o
1938-................CLC 3, 7, 13, 36
See also Ngugi, James (Thiong'o)
See also Wa Thiong'o, Ngugi

Nichol, B(arne) P(hillip) 1944-......CLC 18
See also CA 53-56

Nichols, Peter 1927- .... CLC 5, 36
See also CA 104
See also DLB 13

Niedecker, Lorine 1903-1970.......CLC 10
See also CAP 2
See also CA 25-28

Nietzsche, Friedrich (Wilhelm)
1844-1900............... TCLC 10, 18
See also CA 107

Nightingale, Anne Redmon 1943-
See Redmon (Nightingale), Anne
See also CA 103

Nin, Anaïs
1903-1977........ CLC 1, 4, 8, 11, 14
See also CA 13-16R
See also obituary CA 69-72
See also DLB 2, 4
See also AITN 2

Nissenson, Hugh 1933- .... CLC 4, 9
See also CA 17-20R
See also DLB 28

Niven, Larry 1938- ....CLC 8
See also Niven, Laurence Van Cott
See also DLB 8

Niven, Laurence Van Cott 1938-
See Niven, Larry
See also CANR 14
See also CA 21-24R

Nixon, Agnes Eckhardt 1927- ......CLC 21
See also CA 110

Norman, Marsha 1947-............CLC 28
See also CA 105
See also DLB-Y 84

Norris, Leslie 1921-................CLC 14
See also CANR 14
See also CAP 1
See also CA 11-12
See also DLB 27

North, Andrew 1912-
See Norton, Andre

North, Christopher 1785-1854
See Wilson, John

Norton, Alice Mary 1912-
See Norton, Andre
See also CANR 2
See also CA 1-4R
See also SATA 1

Norton, Andre 1912-.............CLC 12
See also Norton, Mary Alice
See also DLB 8

Norway, Nevil Shute 1899-1960
See Shute (Norway), Nevil
See also CA 102
See also obituary CA 93-96

Nossack, Hans Erich 1901-1978 .....CLC 6
See also CA 93-96
See also obituary CA 85-88

Nova, Craig 1945-............. CLC 7, 31
See also CANR 2
See also CA 45-48

Nowlan, Alden (Albert) 1933-......CLC 15
See also CANR 5
See also CA 9-12R

Noyes, Alfred 1880-1958 .... TCLC 7
See also CA 104
See also DLB 20

Nunn, Kem 19??-.................CLC 34

Nye, Robert 1939-................CLC 13
See also CA 33-36R
See also SATA 6
See also DLB 14

Nyro, Laura 1947-................CLC 17

Oates, Joyce Carol
1938-.....CLC 1, 2, 3, 6, 9, 11, 15, 19, 33
See also CA 5-8R
See also DLB 2, 5
See also DLB-Y 81
See also AITN 1

O'Brien, Darcy 1939-.............CLC 11
See also CANR 8
See also CA 21-24R

O'Brien, Edna
1932-............ CLC 3, 5, 8, 13, 36
See also CANR 6
See also CA 1-4R
See also DLB 14

O'Brien, Flann
1911-1966......... CLC 1, 4, 5, 7, 10
See also O Nuallain, Brian

O'Brien, Richard 19??-............CLC 17

O'Brien, Tim 1946-............ CLC 7, 19
See also CA 85-88
See also DLB-Y 80

O'Casey, Sean
1880-1964........ CLC 1, 5, 9, 11, 15
See also CA 89-92
See also DLB 10

Ochs, Phil 1940-1976 ....CLC 17
See also obituary CA 65-68

O'Connor, Edwin (Greene)
1918-1968....................CLC 14
See also CA 93-96
See also obituary CA 25-28R

O'Connor, (Mary) Flannery
1925-1964...... CLC 1, 2, 3, 6, 10, 13, 15, 21
See also CANR 3
See also CA 1-4R
See also DLB 2
See also DLB-Y 80

O'Connor, Frank
1903-1966................ CLC 14, 23
See also O'Donovan, Michael (John)

O'Dell, Scott 1903- ....CLC 30
See also CLR 1
See also CANR 12
See also CA 61-64
See also SATA 12

Odets, Clifford 1906-1963 ...... CLC 2, 28
See also CA 85-88
See also DLB 7, 26

O'Donovan, Michael (John) 1903-1966
See O'Connor, Frank
See also CA 93-96

Ōe, Kenzaburō 1935- .... CLC 10, 36
See also CA 97-100

O'Faolain, Julia 1932- .... CLC 6, 19
See also CAAS 2
See also CANR 12
See also CA 81-84
See also DLB 14

O'Faoláin, Seán
1900-.................CLC 1, 7, 14, 32
See also CANR 12
See also CA 61-64
See also DLB 15

O'Flaherty, Liam
1896-1984................. CLC 5, 34
See also CA 101
See also obituary CA 113
See also DLB 36
See also DLB-Y 84

O'Grady, Standish (James)
1846-1928.................. TCLC 5
See also CA 104

O'Hara, Frank
1926-1966............... CLC 2, 5, 13
See also CA 9-12R
See also obituary CA 25-28R
See also DLB 5, 16

O'Hara, John (Henry)
1905-1970...... CLC 1, 2, 3, 6, 11
See also CA 5-8R
See also obituary CA 25-28R
See also DLB 9
See also DLB-DS 2

Okigbo, Christopher (Ifenayichukwu)
1932-1967....................CLC 25
See also CA 77-80

Olds, Sharon 1942- ....CLC 32
See also CA 101

Olesha, Yuri (Karlovich)
   1899-1960....................CLC 8
  See also CA 85-88

Oliphant, Margaret (Oliphant Wilson)
   1828-1897..................NCLC 11
  See also DLB 18

Oliver, Mary 1935-........... CLC 19, 34
  See also CANR 9
  See also CA 21-24R
  See also DLB 5

Olivier, (Baron) Laurence (Kerr)
   1907-......................CLC 20
  See also CA 111

Olsen, Tillie 1913-............. CLC 4, 13
  See also CANR 1
  See also CA 1-4R
  See also DLB 28
  See also DLB-Y 80

Olson, Charles (John)
   1910-1970...... CLC 1, 2, 5, 6, 9, 11,
                            29
  See also CAP 1
  See also CA 15-16
  See also obituary CA 25-28R
  See also DLB 5, 16

Olson, Theodore 1937-
  See Olson, Toby

Olson, Toby 1937-................CLC 28
  See also CANR 9
  See also CA 65-68

Ondaatje, (Philip) Michael
   1943-................ CLC 14, 29
  See also CA 77-80

Oneal, Elizabeth 1934-
  See Oneal, Zibby
  See also CA 106
  See also SATA 30

Oneal, Zibby 1934-...............CLC 30
  See also Oneal, Elizabeth

O'Neill, Eugene (Gladstone)
   1888-1953................ TCLC 1, 6
  See also CA 110
  See also AITN 1
  See also DLB 7

Onetti, Juan Carlos 1909- ...... CLC 7, 10
  See also CA 85-88

O'Nolan, Brian 1911-1966
  See O'Brien, Flann

O Nuallain, Brian 1911-1966
  See O'Brien, Flann
  See also CAP 2
  See also CA 21-22
  See also obituary CA 25-28R

Oppen, George
   1908-1984..............CLC 7, 13, 34
  See also CANR 8
  See also CA 13-16R
  See also obituary CA 113
  See also DLB 5

Orlovitz, Gil 1918-1973 ....CLC 22
  See also CA 77-80
  See also obituary CA 45-48
  See also DLB 2, 5

Ortega y Gasset, José
   1883-1955..................TCLC 9
  See also CA 106

Orton, Joe 1933?-1967 .... CLC 4, 13
  See also Orton, John Kingsley
  See also DLB 13

Orton, John Kingsley 1933?-1967
  See Orton, Joe
  See also CA 85-88

Orwell, George
   1903-1950.............TCLC 2, 6, 15
  See also Blair, Eric Arthur
  See also DLB 15

Osborne, John (James)
   1929-.................CLC 1, 2, 5, 11
  See also CA 13-16R
  See also DLB 13

Osceola 1885-1962
  See Dinesen, Isak
  See also Blixen, Karen (Christentze
   Dinesen)

Oshima, Nagisa 1932-.............CLC 20
  See also CA 116

Ossoli, Sarah Margaret (Fuller marchesa d')
   1810-1850
  See Fuller, (Sarah) Margaret
  See also SATA 25

Otero, Blas de 1916-.............CLC 11
  See also CA 89-92

Owen, Wilfred (Edward Salter)
   1893-1918.................. TCLC 5
  See also CA 104
  See also DLB 20

Owens, Rochelle 1936- ....CLC 8
  See also CAAS 2
  See also CA 17-20R

Owl, Sebastian 1939-
  See Thompson, Hunter S(tockton)

Oz, Amos 1939-...... CLC 5, 8, 11, 27, 33
  See also CA 53-56

Ozick, Cynthia 1928- .... CLC 3, 7, 28
  See also CA 17-20R
  See also DLB 28
  See also DLB-Y 82

Ozu, Yasujiro 1903-1963 ....CLC 16
  See also CA 112

Pa Chin 1904-....................CLC 18
  See also Li Fei-kan

Pack, Robert 1929- ....CLC 13
  See also CANR 3
  See also CA 1-4R
  See also DLB 5

Padgett, Lewis 1915-1958
  See Kuttner, Henry

Page, Jimmy 1944-
  See Page, Jimmy and Plant, Robert

Page, Jimmy 1944- and
   Plant, Robert 1948- ....CLC 12

Page, P(atricia) K(athleen)
   1916-..................... CLC 7, 18
  See also CANR 4
  See also CA 53-56

Paget, Violet 1856-1935
  See Lee, Vernon
  See also CA 104

Palamas, Kostes 1859-1943 .... TCLC 5
  See also CA 105

Palazzeschi, Aldo 1885-1974 ....CLC 11
  See also CA 89-92
  See also obituary CA 53-56

Paley, Grace 1922- .... CLC 4, 6, 37
  See also CANR 13
  See also CA 25-28R
  See also DLB 28
  See also AITN 1

Palin, Michael 1943-
  See Monty Python
  See also CA 107

Pancake, Breece Dexter 1952-1979
  See Pancake, Breece D'J

Pancake, Breece D'J
   1952-1979...................CLC 29
  See also obituary CA 109

Parker, Dorothy (Rothschild)
   1893-1967...................CLC 15
  See also CAP 2
  See also CA 19-20
  See also obituary CA 25-28R
  See also DLB 11, 45

Parker, Robert B(rown) 1932-......CLC 27
  See also CANR 1
  See also CA 49-52

Parks, Gordon (Alexander Buchanan)
   1912-..................... CLC 1, 16
  See also CA 41-44R
  See also SATA 8
  See also DLB 33
  See also AITN 2

Parnell, Thomas 1679-1718 .... LC 3

Parra, Nicanor 1914- ....CLC 2
  See also CA 85-88

Pasolini, Pier Paolo
   1922-1975................ CLC 20, 37
  See also CA 93-96
  See also obituary CA 61-64

Pastan, Linda (Olenik) 1932-.......CLC 27
  See also CA 61-64
  See also DLB 5

Pasternak, Boris
   1890-1960.............. CLC 7, 10, 18
  See also obituary CA 116

Patchen, Kenneth
   1911-1972.............. CLC 1, 2, 18
  See also CANR 3
  See also CA 1-4R
  See also obituary CA 33-36R
  See also DLB 16

Pater, Walter (Horatio)
   1839-1894.................. NCLC 7

Paterson, Katherine (Womeldorf)
   1932-..................... CLC 12, 30
  See also CLR 7
  See also CA 21-24R
  See also SATA 13

Patmore, Coventry Kersey Dighton
   1823-1896.................. NCLC 9
  See also DLB 35

Paton, Alan (Stewart)
   1903-................. CLC 4, 10, 25
  See also CAP 1
  See also CA 15-16
  See also SATA 11

Paulding, James Kirke
   1778-1860.................. NCLC 2
  See also DLB 3

Paulin, Tom 1949-...............CLC 37
See also DLB 40

Pavese, Cesare 1908-1950 .... TCLC 3
See also CA 104

Payne, Alan 1932-
See Jakes, John (William)

Paz, Octavio 1914-..... CLC 3, 4, 6, 10, 19
See also CA 73-76

Peake, Mervyn 1911-1968 ....CLC 7
See also CANR 3
See also CA 5-8R
See also obituary CA 25-28R
See also SATA 23
See also DLB 15

Pearce, (Ann) Philippa 1920-.......CLC 21
See also Christie, (Ann) Philippa
See also CA 5-8R
See also SATA 1

Pearl, Eric 1934-
See Elman, Richard

Peck, John 1941-...................CLC 3
See also CANR 3
See also CA 49-52

Peck, Richard 1934- ....CLC 21
See also CA 85-88
See also SATA 18

Peck, Robert Newton 1928-........CLC 17
See also CA 81-84
See also SAAS 1
See also SATA 21

Peckinpah, (David) Sam(uel)
1925-1984....................CLC 20
See also CA 109
See also obituary CA 114

Pedersen, Knut 1859-1952
See Hamsun, Knut
See also CA 104

Péguy, Charles (Pierre)
1873-1914.......... TCLC 10
See also CA 107

Percy, Walker
1916-.......... CLC 2, 3, 6, 8, 14, 18
See also CANR 1
See also CA 1-4R
See also DLB 2
See also DLB-Y 80

Pereda, José María de
1833-1906................. TCLC 16

Perelman, S(idney) J(oseph)
1904-1979........ CLC 3, 5, 9, 15, 23
See also CA 73-76
See also obituary CA 89-92
See also DLB 11, 44
See also AITN 1, 2

Peretz, Isaac Leib
1852?-1915................. TCLC 16
See also CA 109

Perrault, Charles 1628-1703 .... LC 2
See also SATA 25

Perse, St.-John 1887-1975 ...... CLC 4, 11
See also Léger, (Marie-Rene) Alexis Saint-
Léger

Pesetsky, Bette 1932-.............CLC 28

Peshkov, Alexei Maximovich 1868-1936
See Gorky, Maxim
See also CA 105

Peterkin, Julia (Mood)
1880-1961....................CLC 31
See also CA 102
See also DLB 9

Peters, Robert L(ouis) 1924-........CLC 7
See also CA 13-16R

Petrakis, Harry Mark 1923- ....CLC 3
See also CANR 4
See also CA 9-12R

Petry, Ann (Lane) 1912-...... CLC 1, 7, 18
See also CANR 4
See also CA 5-8R
See also SATA 5

Phillips, Jayne Anne 1952-..... CLC 15, 33
See also CA 101
See also DLB-Y 80

Phillips, Robert (Schaeffer)
1938-.......................CLC 28
See also CANR 8
See also CA 17-20R

Piccolo, Lucio 1901-1969 ....CLC 13
See also CA 97-100

Piercy, Marge
1936-.......... CLC 3, 6, 14, 18, 27
See also CAAS 1
See also CA 21-24R

Pincherle, Alberto 1907-
See Moravia, Alberto
See also CA 25-28R

Piñero, Miguel (Gomez) 1947?-......CLC 4
See also CA 61-64

Pinget, Robert 1919-........ CLC 7, 13, 37
See also CA 85-88

Pink Floyd.......................CLC 35

Pinkwater, D(aniel) M(anus)
1941-.......................CLC 35
See also Pinkwater, Manus
See also CLR 4
See also CANR 12
See also CA 29-32R

Pinkwater, Manus 1941-
See Pinkwater, D(aniel) M(anus)
See also SATA 8

Pinsky, Robert 1940-.......... CLC 9, 19
See also CA 29-32R
See also DLB-Y 82

Pinter, Harold
1930-........CLC 1, 3, 6, 9, 11, 15, 27
See also CA 5-8R
See also DLB 13

Pirandello, Luigi 1867-1936...... TCLC 4
See also CA 104

Pirsig, Robert M(aynard)
1928-...................... CLC 4, 6
See also CA 53-56
See also SATA 39

Plaidy, Jean 1906-
See Hibbert, Eleanor (Burford)

Plant, Robert 1948-
See Page, Jimmy and Plant, Robert

Plante, David 1940-........... CLC 7, 23
See also CANR 12
See also CA 37-40R
See also DLB-Y 83

Plath, Sylvia
1932-1963...... CLC 1, 2, 3, 5, 9, 11,
14, 17
See also CAP 2
See also CA 19-20
See also DLB 5, 6

Platonov, Andrei (Platonovich)
1899-1951................. TCLC 14
See also Klimentov, Andrei Platonovich

Platt, Kin 1911-..................CLC 26
See also CANR 11
See also CA 17-20R
See also SATA 21

Plimpton, George (Ames)
1927-.......................CLC 36
See also CA 21-24R
See also SATA 10
See also AITN 1

Plomer, William (Charles Franklin)
1903-1973................. CLC 4, 8
See also CAP 2
See also CA 21-22
See also SATA 24
See also DLB 20

Plumly, Stanley (Ross) 1939-.......CLC 33
See also CA 108, 110
See also DLB 5

Poe, Edgar Allan 1809-1849 ...... NCLC 1
See also SATA 23
See also DLB 3

Pohl, Frederik 1919-..............CLC 18
See also CAAS 1
See also CANR 11
See also CA 61-64
See also SATA 24
See also DLB 8

Poirier, Louis 1910-
See Gracq, Julien

Poitier, Sidney 1924?-.............CLC 26

Polanski, Roman 1933-............CLC 16
See also CA 77-80

Police, The.......................CLC 26

Pollitt, Katha 1949-...............CLC 28

Pomerance, Bernard 1940-.........CLC 13
See also CA 101

Ponge, Francis (Jean Gaston Alfred)
1899-.................... CLC 6, 18
See also CA 85-88

Poole, Josephine 1933- ....CLC 17
See also CANR 10
See also CA 21-24R
See also SATA 5

Pope, Alexander 1688-1744 ....LC 3

Popa, Vasko 1922-................CLC 19
See also CA 112

Porter, Katherine Anne
1890-1980..... CLC 1, 3, 7, 10, 13, 15,
27
See also CANR 1
See also CA 1-4R
See also obituary CA 101
See also obituary SATA 23, 39
See also DLB 4, 9
See also DLB-Y 80
See also AITN 2

Author Index

Porter, Peter (Neville Frederick)
1929-...................CLC 5, 13, 33
See also CA 85-88
See also DLB 40

Porter, William Sydney 1862-1910
See Henry, O.
See also CA 104
See also YABC 2
See also DLB 12

Potok, Chaim 1929-......CLC 2, 7, 14, 26
See also CA 17-20R
See also SATA 33
See also DLB 28
See also AITN 1, 2

Pound, Ezra (Loomis)
1885-1972..... CLC 1, 2, 3, 4, 5, 7, 10,
13, 18, 34
See also CA 5-8R
See also obituary CA 37-40R
See also DLB 4, 45

Powell, Anthony (Dymoke)
1905-..........CLC 1, 3, 7, 9, 10, 31
See also CANR 1
See also CA 1-4R
See also DLB 15

Powell, Padgett 1952-.............CLC 34

Powers, J(ames) F(arl)
1917-....................CLC 1, 4, 8
See also CANR 2
See also CA 1-4R

Pownall, David 1938- ....CLC 10
See also CA 89-92
See also DLB 14

Powys, John Cowper
1872-1963...............CLC 7, 9, 15
See also CA 85-88
See also DLB 15

Powys, T(heodore) F(rancis)
1875-1953...................TCLC 9
See also CA 106
See also DLB 36

Pratt, E(dwin) J(ohn)
1883-1964....................CLC 19
See also obituary CA 93-96

Preussler, Otfried 1923-...........CLC 17
See also CA 77-80
See also SATA 24

Prévert, Jacques (Henri Marie)
1900-1977....................CLC 15
See also CA 77-80
See also obituary CA 69-72
See also obituary SATA 30

Prévost, Abbé (Antoine Francois)
1697-1763.....................LC 1

Price, (Edward) Reynolds
1933-....................CLC 3, 6, 13
See also CANR 1
See also CA 1-4R
See also DLB 2

Price, Richard 1949-..........CLC 6, 12
See also CANR 3
See also CA 49-52
See also DLB-Y 81

Priestley, J(ohn) B(oynton)
1894-1984.............CLC 2, 5, 9, 34
See also CA 9-12R
See also obituary CA 113
See also DLB 10, 34
See also DLB-Y 84

Prince (Rogers Nelson) 1958?-......CLC 35

Prince, F(rank) T(empleton)
1912-.......................CLC 22
See also CA 101
See also DLB 20

Pritchard, William H(arrison)
1932-.......................CLC 34
See also CA 65-68

Pritchett, V(ictor) S(awdon)
1900-..................CLC 5, 13, 15
See also CA 61-64
See also DLB 15

Procaccino, Michael 1946-
See Cristofer, Michael

Prokosch, Frederic 1908-...........CLC 4
See also CA 73-76

Proust, Marcel 1871-1922 ..... TCLC 7, 13
See also CA 104

Pryor, Richard 1940- ....CLC 26

P'u Sung-ling 1640-1715.............LC 3

Puig, Manuel 1932-.......CLC 3, 5, 10, 28
See also CANR 2
See also CA 45-48

Purdy, A(lfred) W(ellington)
1918-....................CLC 3, 6, 14
See also CA 81-84

Purdy, James (Amos)
1923-.............CLC 2, 4, 10, 28
See also CAAS 1
See also CA 33-36R
See also DLB 2

Pushkin, Alexander (Sergeyevich)
1799-1837...................NCLC 3

Puzo, Mario 1920-.........CLC 1, 2, 6, 36
See also CANR 4
See also CA 65-68
See also DLB 6

Pym, Barbara (Mary Crampton)
1913-1980............. CLC 13, 19, 37
See also CANR 13
See also CAP 1
See also CA 13-14
See also obituary CA 97-100
See also DLB 14

Pynchon, Thomas (Ruggles, Jr.)
1937-........CLC 2, 3, 6, 9, 11, 18, 33
See also CA 17-20R
See also DLB 2

Quasimodo, Salvatore
1901-1968....................CLC 10
See also CAP 1
See also CA 15-16
See also obituary CA 25-28R

Queen, Ellery 1905-1982 .... CLC 3, 11
See also Dannay, Frederic
See also Lee, Manfred B(ennington)

Queneau, Raymond
1903-1976..............CLC 2, 5, 10
See also CA 77-80
See also obituary CA 69-72

Quin, Ann (Marie) 1936-1973.......CLC 6
See also CA 9-12R
See also obituary CA 45-48
See also DLB 14

Quinn, Simon 1942-
See Smith, Martin Cruz

Quoirez, Françoise 1935-
See Sagan, Françoise
See also CANR 6
See also CA 49-52

Rabe, David (William)
1940-...................CLC 4, 8, 33
See also CA 85-88
See also DLB 7

Rabinovitch, Sholem 1859-1916
See Aleichem, Sholom
See also CA 104

Radcliffe, Ann (Ward)
1764-1823...................NCLC 6
See also DLB 39

Radnóti, Miklós 1909-1944 ...... TCLC 16

Rado, James 1939-
See Ragni, Gerome and
Rado, James
See also CA 105

Radomski, James 1932-
See Rado, James

Radvanyi, Netty Reiling 1900-1983
See Seghers, Anna
See also CA 85-88
See also obituary CA 110

Raeburn, John 1941-..............CLC 34
See also CA 57-60

Ragni, Gerome 1942-
See Ragni, Gerome and Rado, James
See also CA 105

Ragni, Gerome 1942- and
Rado, James 1939-...........CLC 17

Rahv, Philip 1908-1973 ....CLC 24
See also Greenberg, Ivan

Raine, Craig 1944- ....CLC 32
See also CA 108
See also DLB 40

Raine, Kathleen (Jessie) 1908-.......CLC 7
See also CA 85-88
See also DLB 20

Rand, Ayn 1905-1982.......... CLC 3, 30
See also CA 13-16R
See also obituary CA 105

Randall, Dudley (Felker) 1914-......CLC 1
See also CA 25-28R
See also DLB 41

Ransom, John Crowe
1888-1974........ CLC 2, 4, 5, 11, 24
See also CANR 6
See also CA 5-8R
See also obituary CA 49-52
See also DLB 45

Rao, Raja 1909-...................CLC 25
See also CA 73-76

Raphael, Frederic (Michael)
1931-.................... CLC 2, 14
See also CANR 1
See also CA 1-4R
See also DLB 14

Rattigan, Terence (Mervyn)
1911-1977....................CLC 7
See also CA 85-88
See also obituary CA 73-76
See also DLB 13

Raven, Simon (Arthur Noel)
1927-.......................CLC 14
See also CA 81-84

Rawlings, Marjorie Kinnan
    1896-1953.................. TCLC **4**
    See also CA 104
    See also YABC 1
    See also DLB 9, 22

Ray, Satyajit 1921-.............. CLC **16**

Read, Herbert (Edward)
    1893-1968.................... CLC **4**
    See also CA 85-88
    See also obituary CA 25-28R
    See also DLB 20

Read, Piers Paul 1941-...... CLC **4, 10, 25**
    See also CA 21-24R
    See also SATA 21
    See also DLB 14

Reade, Charles 1814-1884 .... NCLC **2**
    See also DLB 21

Reade, Hamish 1936-
    See Gray, Simon (James Holliday)

Reaney, James 1926-.............. CLC **13**
    See also CA 41-44R

Rechy, John (Francisco)
    1934-.............. CLC **1, 7, 14, 18**
    See also CANR 6
    See also CA 5-8R
    See also DLB-Y 82

Redgrove, Peter (William)
    1932-........................ CLC **6**
    See also CANR 3
    See also CA 1-4R
    See also DLB 40

Redmon (Nightingale), Anne
    1943-........................ CLC **22**
    See also Nightingale, Anne Redmon

Reed, Ishmael
    1938-.......... CLC **2, 3, 5, 6, 13, 32**
    See also CA 21-24R
    See also DLB 2, 5, 33

Reed, John (Silas) 1887-1920...... TCLC **9**
    See also CA 106

Reed, Lou 1944-.................. CLC **21**

Reid, Christopher 1949-........... CLC **33**
    See also DLB 40

Reid Banks, Lynne 1929-
    See Banks, Lynne Reid
    See also CANR 6
    See also CA 1-4R
    See also SATA 22

Reiner, Max 1900-
    See Caldwell, (Janet Miriam) Taylor
        (Holland)

Remark, Erich Paul 1898-1970
    See Remarque, Erich Maria

Remarque, Erich Maria
    1898-1970................... CLC **21**
    See also CA 77-80
    See also obituary CA 29-32R

Renard, Jules 1864-1910 .... TCLC **17**

Renault, Mary
    1905-1983.............. CLC **3, 11, 17**
    See also Challans, Mary
    See also DLB-Y 83

Rendell, Ruth 1930- .... CLC **28**
    See also CA 109

Renoir, Jean 1894-1979 .... CLC **20**
    See also obituary CA 85-88

Resnais, Alain 1922-.............. CLC **16**

Rexroth, Kenneth
    1905-1982........ CLC **1, 2, 6, 11, 22**
    See also CA 5-8R
    See also obituary CA 107
    See also DLB 16
    See also DLB-Y 82

Reyes y Basoalto, Ricardo Eliecer Neftali
    1904-1973
    See Neruda, Pablo

Reymont, Wladyslaw Stanislaw
    1867-1925................... TCLC **5**
    See also CA 104

Reynolds, Jonathan 1942?- .... CLC **6**
    See also CA 65-68

Reznikoff, Charles 1894-1976 .... CLC **9**
    See also CAP 2
    See also CA 33-36
    See also obituary CA 61-64
    See also DLB 28, 45

Rezzori, Gregor von 1914-........ CLC **25**

Rhys, Jean
    1894-1979........ CLC **2, 4, 6, 14, 19**
    See also CA 25-28R
    See also obituary CA 85-88
    See also DLB 36

Ribeiro, Darcy 1922-.............. CLC **34**
    See also CA 33-36R

Ribeiro, João Ubaldo (Osorio Pimentel)
    1941-........................ CLC **10**
    See also CA 81-84

Ribman, Ronald (Burt) 1932-....... CLC **7**
    See also CA 21-24R

Rice, Elmer 1892-1967 .... CLC **7**
    See also CAP 2
    See also CA 21-22
    See also obituary CA 25-28R
    See also DLB 4, 7

Rice, Tim 1944-
    See Rice, Tim and Webber, Andrew Lloyd
    See also CA 103

Rice, Tim 1944- and
    Webber, Andrew Lloyd
    1948-........................ CLC **21**

Rich, Adrienne (Cecile)
    1929-.......... CLC **3, 6, 7, 11, 18, 36**
    See also CA 9-12R
    See also DLB 5

Richard, Keith 1943-
    See Jagger, Mick and Richard, Keith

Richards, I(vor) A(rmstrong)
    1893-1979............... CLC **14, 24**
    See also CA 41-44R
    See also obituary CA 89-92
    See also DLB 27

Richards, Keith 1943-
    See Richard, Keith
    See also CA 107

Richardson, Dorothy (Miller)
    1873-1957................... TCLC **3**
    See also CA 104
    See also DLB 36

Richardson, Ethel 1870-1946
    See Richardson, Henry Handel
    See also CA 105

Richardson, Henry Handel
    1870-1946.................. TCLC **4**
    See also Richardson, Ethel

Richardson, Samuel 1689-1761....... LC **1**
    See also DLB 39

Richler, Mordecai
    1931-............. CLC **3, 5, 9, 13, 18**
    See also CA 65-68
    See also SATA 27
    See also AITN 1

Richter, Conrad (Michael)
    1890-1968................... CLC **30**
    See also CA 5-8R
    See also obituary CA 25-28R
    See also SATA 3
    See also DLB 9

Richter, Johann Paul Friedrich 1763-1825
    See Jean Paul

Riding, Laura 1901-............. CLC **3, 7**
    See also Jackson, Laura (Riding)

Riefenstahl, Berta Helene Amalia 1902-
    See Riefenstahl, Leni
    See also CA 108

Riefenstahl, Leni 1902-............ CLC **16**
    See also Riefenstahl, Berta Helene Amalia

Rilke, Rainer Maria
    1875-1926.............. TCLC **1, 6, 19**
    See also CA 104

Rimbaud, (Jean Nicolas) Arthur
    1854-1891................... NCLC **4**

Ritsos, Yannis 1909- .... CLC **6, 13, 31**
    See also CA 77-80

Rivers, Conrad Kent 1933-1968 ..... CLC **1**
    See also CA 85-88
    See also DLB 41

Robbe-Grillet, Alain
    1922-.........CLC **1, 2, 4, 6, 8, 10, 14**
    See also CA 9-12R

Robbins, Harold 1916-.............. CLC **5**
    See also CA 73-76

Robbins, Thomas Eugene 1936-
    See Robbins, Tom
    See also CA 81-84

Robbins, Tom 1936- .... CLC **9, 32**
    See also Robbins, Thomas Eugene
    See also DLB-Y 80

Robbins, Trina 1938- .... CLC **21**

Roberts, (Sir) Charles G(eorge) D(ouglas)
    1860-1943................... TCLC **8**
    See also CA 105
    See also SATA 29

Roberts, Kate 1891-1985 .... CLC **15**
    See also CA 107
    See also obituary CA 116

Roberts, Keith (John Kingston)
    1935-........................ CLC **14**
    See also CA 25-28R

Robinson, Edwin Arlington
    1869-1935................... TCLC **5**
    See also CA 104

Robinson, Jill 1936-.............. CLC **10**
    See also CA 102

Robinson, Kim Stanley 19??-....... CLC **34**

Robinson, Marilynne 1944- .... CLC **25**
    See also CA 116

Robinson, Smokey 1940- ....CLC 21

Robinson, William 1940-
See Robinson, Smokey
See also CA 116

Roddenberry, Gene 1921- ....CLC 17

Rodgers, Mary 1931- ....CLC 12
See also CANR 8
See also CA 49-52
See also SATA 8

Rodgers, W(illiam) R(obert)
1909-1969...................CLC 7
See also CA 85-88
See also DLB 20

Rodriguez, Claudio 1934-.........CLC 10

Roethke, Theodore (Huebner)
1908-1963........ CLC 1, 3, 8, 11, 19
See also CA 81-84
See also DLB 5

Rogers, Sam 1943-
See Shepard, Sam

Rogers, Will(iam Penn Adair)
1879-1935................... TCLC 8
See also CA 105
See also DLB 11

Rogin, Gilbert 1929-..............CLC 18
See also CANR 15
See also CA 65-68

Rohmer, Eric 1920-...............CLC 16
See also Scherer, Jean-Marie Maurice

Roiphe, Anne (Richardson)
1935-..................... CLC 3, 9
See also CA 89-92
See also DLB-Y 80

**Rolfe, Frederick (William Serafino Austin
Lewis Mary)** 1860-1913..... TCLC 12
See also CA 107
See also DLB 34

Rölvaag, O(le) E(dvart)
1876-1931................ TCLC 17
See also DLB 9

Romains, Jules 1885-1972 ....CLC 7
See also CA 85-88

Romero, José Rubén
1890-1952................. TCLC 14
See also CA 114

Rooke, Leon 1934-............ CLC 25, 34
See also CA 25-28R

Rosa, João Guimarães
1908-1967...................CLC 23
See also obituary CA 89-92

Rosenberg, Isaac 1890-1918...... TCLC 12
See also CA 107
See also DLB 20

Rosenblatt, Joe 1933- ....CLC 15
See also Rosenblatt, Joseph
See also AITN 2

Rosenblatt, Joseph 1933-
See Rosenblatt, Joe
See also CA 89-92

Rosenthal, M(acha) L(ouis)
1917-.......................CLC 28
See also CANR 4
See also CA 1-4R
See also DLB 5

Ross, (James) Sinclair 1908- ....CLC 13
See also CA 73-76

Rossetti, Christina Georgina
1830-1894................... NCLC 2
See also SATA 20
See also DLB 35

Rossetti, Dante Gabriel
1828-1882................... NCLC 4
See also DLB 35

Rossetti, Gabriel Charles Dante 1828-1882
See Rossetti, Dante Gabriel

Rossner, Judith (Perelman)
1935-................... CLC 6, 9, 29
See also CA 17-20R
See also DLB 6
See also AITN 2

Rostand, Edmond (Eugène Alexis)
1868-1918................... TCLC 6
See also CA 104

Roth, Henry 1906-...........CLC 2, 6, 11
See also CAP 1
See also CA 11-12
See also DLB 28

Roth, Philip (Milton)
1933-......CLC 1, 2, 3, 4, 6, 9, 15, 22,
                                        31
See also CANR 1
See also CA 1-4R
See also DLB 2, 28
See also DLB-Y 82

Rothenberg, Jerome 1931-..........CLC 6
See also CANR 1
See also CA 45-48
See also DLB 5

Roumain, Jacques 1907-1944 .... TCLC 19

Rourke, Constance (Mayfield)
1885-1941................. TCLC 12
See also CA 107
See also YABC 1

Rovit, Earl (Herbert) 1927-.........CLC 7
See also CA 5-8R

Rowson, Susanna Haswell
1762-1824................... NCLC 5
See also DLB 37

Roy, Gabrielle 1909-1983...... CLC 10, 14
See also CANR 5
See also CA 53-56
See also obituary CA 110

Różewicz, Tadeusz 1921- .... CLC 9, 23
See also CA 108

Ruark, Gibbons 1941-..............CLC 3
See also CANR 14
See also CA 33-36R

Rubens, Bernice 192?- .... CLC 19, 31
See also CA 25-28R
See also DLB 14

Rudkin, (James) David 1936- ......CLC 14
See also CA 89-92
See also DLB 13

Rudnik, Raphael 1933-.............CLC 7
See also CA 29-32R

Ruiz, José Martínez 1874-1967
See Azorín

Rukeyser, Muriel
1913-1980..........CLC 6, 10, 15, 27
See also CA 5-8R
See also obituary CA 93-96
See also obituary SATA 22

Rule, Jane (Vance) 1931-..........CLC 27
See also CANR 12
See also CA 25-28R

Rulfo, Juan 1918- ....CLC 8
See also CA 85-88

Runyon, (Alfred) Damon
1880-1946................. TCLC 10
See also CA 107
See also DLB 11

Rushdie, (Ahmed) Salman
1947-..................... CLC 23, 31
See also CA 108, 111

Rushforth, Peter (Scott) 1945-......CLC 19
See also CA 101

Russ, Joanna 1937-...............CLC 15
See also CANR 11
See also CA 25-28R
See also DLB 8

Russell, George William 1867-1935
See A. E.
See also CA 104

Russell, (Henry) Ken(neth Alfred)
1927-.......................CLC 16
See also CA 105

Ruyslinck, Ward 1929-............CLC 14

Ryan, Cornelius (John)
1920-1974...................CLC 7
See also CA 69-72
See also obituary CA 53-56

Rybakov, Anatoli 1911?- ....CLC 23

Ryga, George 1932-...............CLC 14
See also CA 101

Sabato, Ernesto 1911-......... CLC 10, 23
See also CA 97-100

Sachs, Marilyn (Stickle) 1927-......CLC 35
See also CLR 2
See also CANR 13
See also CA 17-20R
See also SATA 3

Sachs, Nelly 1891-1970...........CLC 14
See also CAP 2
See also CA 17-18
See also obituary CA 25-28R

Sackler, Howard (Oliver)
1929-1982...................CLC 14
See also CA 61-64
See also obituary CA 108
See also DLB 7

Sade, Donatien Alphonse François, Comte de
1740-1814................... NCLC 3

Sadoff, Ira 1945- ....CLC 9
See also CANR 5
See also CA 53-56

Safire, William 1929-..............CLC 10
See also CA 17-20R

Sagan, Carl (Edward) 1934- ....CLC 30
See also CANR 11
See also CA 25-28R

Sagan, Françoise
1935-............. CLC 3, 6, 9, 17, 36
See also Quoirez, Françoise

Sainte-Beuve, Charles Augustin
1804-1869................... NCLC 5

Sainte-Marie, Beverly 1941-
See Sainte-Marie, Buffy
See also CA 107

Sainte-Marie, Buffy 1941- ....CLC 17
  See also Sainte-Marie, Beverly

Saint-Exupéry, Antoine (Jean Baptiste Marie
    Roger) de 1900-1944 .... TCLC 2
  See also CA 108
  See also SATA 20

Saki 1870-1916................. TCLC 3
  See also Munro, H(ector) H(ugh)

Salama, Hannu 1936- ....CLC 18

Salamanca, J(ack) R(ichard)
    1922-.................... CLC 4, 15
  See also CA 25-28R

Salinas, Pedro 1891-1951....... TCLC 17

Salinger, J(erome) D(avid)
    1919-.................CLC 1, 3, 8, 12
  See also CA 5-8R
  See also DLB 2

Salter, James 1925-................CLC 7
  See also CA 73-76

Saltus, Edgar (Evertson)
    1855-1921.................. TCLC 8
  See also CA 105

Samarakis, Antonis 1919-...........CLC 5
  See also CA 25-28R

Sánchez, Luis Rafael 1936- ....CLC 23

Sanchez, Sonia 1934-...............CLC 5
  See also CA 33-36R
  See also SATA 22
  See also DLB 41

Sand, George 1804-1876.......... NCLC 2

Sandburg, Carl (August)
    1878-1967....... CLC 1, 4, 10, 15, 35
  See also CA 5-8R
  See also obituary CA 25-28R
  See also SATA 8
  See also DLB 17

Sandburg, Charles August 1878-1967
  See Sandburg, Carl (August)

Sandoz, Mari (Susette)
    1896-1966....................CLC 28
  See also CA 1-4R
  See also obituary CA 25-28R
  See also SATA 5
  See also DLB 9

Saner, Reg(inald Anthony)
    1931-........................CLC 9
  See also CA 65-68

Sansom, William 1912-1976...... CLC 2, 6
  See also CA 5-8R
  See also obituary CA 65-68

Santiago, Danny 1911- ....CLC 33

Santmyer, Helen Hoover 1895-.....CLC 33
  See also CANR 15
  See also CA 1-4R
  See also DLB-Y 84

Santos, Bienvenido N(uqui)
    1911-........................CLC 22
  See also CA 101

Sarduy, Severo 1937- ....CLC 6
  See also CA 89-92

Sargeson, Frank 1903-1982........CLC 31
  See also CA 25-28R
  See also CA 106

Sarmiento, Felix Ruben Garcia 1867-1916
  See also CA 104

Saroyan, William
    1908-1981....... CLC 1, 8, 10, 29, 34
  See also CA 5-8R
  See also obituary CA 103
  See also SATA 23
  See also obituary SATA 24
  See also DLB 7, 9
  See also DLB-Y 81

Sarraute, Nathalie
    1902-...........CLC 1, 2, 4, 8, 10, 31
  See also CA 9-12R

Sarton, (Eleanor) May
    1912-...................... CLC 4, 14
  See also CANR 1
  See also CA 1-4R
  See also SATA 36
  See also DLB-Y 81

Sartre, Jean-Paul
    1905-1980...... CLC 1, 4, 7, 9, 13, 18,
                           24
  See also CA 9-12R
  See also obituary CA 97-100

Sassoon, Siegfried (Lorraine)
    1886-1967....................CLC 36
  See also CA 104
  See also Obituary CA 25-28R
  See also DLB 20

Saura, Carlos 1932-...............CLC 20
  See also CA 114

Sauser-Hall, Frédéric-Louis 1887-1961
  See Cendrars, Blaise
  See also CA 102
  See also obituary CA 93-96

Sayers, Dorothy L(eigh)
    1893-1957............... TCLC 2, 15
  See also CA 104
  See also DLB 10, 36

Sayles, John (Thomas)
    1950-................ CLC 7, 10, 14
  See also CA 57-60
  See also DLB 44

Scammell, Michael 19??- ....CLC 34

Schaeffer, Susan Fromberg
    1941-................ CLC 6, 11, 22
  See also CA 49-52
  See also SATA 22
  See also DLB 28

Schell, Jonathan 1943- ....CLC 35
  See also CANR 12
  See also CA 73-76

Scherer, Jean-Marie Maurice 1920-
  See Rohmer, Eric
  See also CA 110

Schevill, James (Erwin) 1920- ....CLC 7
  See also CA 5-8R

Schisgal, Murray (Joseph)
    1926-........................CLC 6
  See also CA 21-24R

Schlee, Ann 1934- ....CLC 35
  See also CA 101
  See also SATA 36

Schmitz, Ettore 1861-1928
  See Svevo, Italo
  See also CA 104

Schneider, Leonard Alfred 1925-1966
  See Bruce, Lenny
  See also CA 89-92

Schnitzler, Arthur 1862-1931 ..... TCLC 4
  See also CA 104

Schorer, Mark 1908-1977 ....CLC 9
  See also CANR 7
  See also CA 5-8R
  See also obituary CA 73-76

Schrader, Paul (Joseph) 1946-.....CLC 26
  See also CA 37-40R
  See also DLB 44

Schreiner (Cronwright), Olive (Emilie
    Albertina) 1855-1920 .... TCLC 9
  See also CA 105
  See also DLB 18

Schulberg, Budd (Wilson) 1914- .....CLC 7
  See also CA 25-28R
  See also DLB 6, 26, 28
  See also DLB-Y 81

Schulz, Bruno 1892-1942 .... TCLC 5
  See also CA 115

Schulz, Charles M(onroe)
    1922-........................CLC 12
  See also CANR 6
  See also CA 9-12R
  See also SATA 10

Schuyler, James (Marcus)
    1923-...................... CLC 5, 23
  See also CA 101
  See also DLB 5

Schwartz, Delmore
    1913-1966.............. CLC 2, 4, 10
  See also CAP 2
  See also CA 17-18
  See also obituary CA 25-28R
  See also DLB 28

Schwartz, Lynne Sharon 1939-.....CLC 31
  See also CA 103

Schwarz-Bart, André 1928-...... CLC 2, 4
  See also CA 89-92

Schwarz-Bart, Simone 1938-........CLC 7
  See also CA 97-100

Sciascia, Leonardo 1921- .... CLC 8, 9
  See also CA 85-88

Scoppettone, Sandra 1936-.........CLC 26
  See also CA 5-8R
  See also SATA 9

Scorsese, Martin 1942-............CLC 20
  See also CA 110, 114

Scotland, Jay 1932-
  See Jakes, John (William)

Scott, Duncan Campbell
    1862-1947.................. TCLC 6
  See also CA 104

Scott, F(rancis) R(eginald)
    1899-1985....................CLC 22
  See also CA 101
  See also obituary CA 114

Scott, Paul (Mark) 1920-1978.......CLC 9
  See also CA 81-84
  See also obituary CA 77-80
  See also DLB 14

Scudéry, Madeleine de 1607-1701..... LC 2

Seare, Nicholas 1925-
  See Trevanian
  See also Whitaker, Rodney

Sebestyen, Igen 1924-
  See Sebestyen, Ouida

Sebestyen, Ouida 1924-............CLC 30
See also CA 107
See also SATA 39

Seelye, John 1931-................CLC 7
See also CA 97-100

Seferiades, Giorgos Stylianou 1900-1971
See Seferis, George
See also CANR 5
See also CA 5-8R
See also obituary CA 33-36R

Seferis, George 1900-1971 ...... CLC 5, 11
See also Seferiades, Giorgos Stylianou

Segal, Erich (Wolf) 1937-....... CLC 3, 10
See also CA 25-28R

Seger, Bob 1945- ....CLC 35

Seger, Robert Clark 1945-
See Seger, Bob

Seghers, Anna 1900-..............CLC 7
See Radvanyi, Netty

Seidel, Frederick (Lewis) 1936-.....CLC 18
See also CANR 8
See also CA 13-16R
See also DLB-Y 84

Seifert, Jaroslav 1901- ....CLC 34

Selby, Hubert, Jr.
1928-.................CLC 1, 2, 4, 8
See also CA 13-16R
See also DLB 2

Sender, Ramón (José)
1902-1982...................CLC 8
See also CANR 8
See also CA 5-8R
See also obituary CA 105

Serling, (Edward) Rod(man) 1924-1975
See also CA 65-68
See also obituary CA 57-60
See also DLB 26
See also AITN 1

Serpières 1907-
See Guillevic, (Eugène)

Service, Robert W(illiam)
1874-1958................. TCLC 15
See also CA 115
See also SATA 20

Seton, Cynthia Propper
1926-1982...................CLC 27
See also CANR-7
See also CA 5-8R
See also obituary CA 108

Settle, Mary Lee 1918-............CLC 19
See also CAAS 1
See also CA 89-92
See also DLB 6

Sexton, Anne (Harvey)
1928-1974...... CLC 2, 4, 6, 8, 10, 15
See also CANR 3
See also CA 1-4R
See also obituary CA 53-56
See also SATA 10
See also DLB 5

Shaara, Michael (Joseph)
1929-......................CLC 15
See also CA 102
See also DLB-Y 83
See also AITN 1

Shaffer, Anthony 1926-............CLC 19
See also CA 110
See also CA 116
See also DLB 13

Shaffer, Peter (Levin)
1926-..............CLC 5, 14, 18, 37
See also CA 25-28R
See also DLB 13

Shalamov, Varlam (Tikhonovich)
1907?-1982...................CLC 18
See also obituary CA 105

Shamlu, Ahmad 1925- ....CLC 10

Shange, Ntozake 1948-......... CLC 8, 25
See also CA 85-88
See also DLB 38

Shapiro, Karl (Jay) 1913-..... CLC 4, 8, 15
See also CANR 1
See also CA 1-4R

Sharpe, Tom 1928- ....CLC 36
See also CA 114
See also DLB 14

Shaw, (George) Bernard
1856-1950................. TCLC 3, 9
See also CA 104, 109
See also DLB 10

Shaw, Irwin 1913-1984...... CLC 7, 23, 34
See also CA 13-16R
See also obituary CA 112
See also DLB 6
See also DLB-Y 84
See also AITN 1

Shaw, Robert 1927-1978 ....CLC 5
See also CANR 4
See also CA 1-4R
See also obituary CA 81-84
See also DLB 13, 14
See also AITN 1

Sheed, Wilfrid (John Joseph)
1930-.................. CLC 2, 4, 10
See also CA 65-68
See also DLB 6

Sheffey, Asa 1913-1980
See Hayden, Robert (Earl)

Shepard, Jim 19??- ....CLC 36

Shepard, Lucius 19??-.............CLC 34

Shepard, Sam 1943- ......CLC 4, 6, 17, 34
See also CA 69-72
See also DLB 7

Sherburne, Zoa (Morin) 1912- .....CLC 30
See also CANR 3
See also CA 1-4R
See also SATA 3

Sheridan, Richard Brinsley
1751-1816.................. NCLC 5

Sherman, Martin ....CLC 19
See also CA 116

Sherwin, Judith Johnson
1936-.................. CLC 7, 15
See also CA 25-28R

Sherwood, Robert E(mmet)
1896-1955................. TCLC 3
See also CA 104
See also DLB 7, 26

Shiel, M(atthew) P(hipps)
1865-1947.................. TCLC 8
See also CA 106

Shiga Naoya 1883-1971............CLC 33
See also CA 101
See also obituary CA 33-36R

Shimazaki, Haruki 1872-1943
See Shimazaki, Tōson
See also CA 105

Shimazaki, Tōson 1872-1943 ...... TCLC 5
See also Shimazaki, Haruki

Sholokhov, Mikhail (Aleksandrovich)
1905-1984................. CLC 7, 15
See also CA 101
See also obituary CA 112
See also SATA 36

Shreve, Susan Richards 1939-......CLC 23
See also CANR 5
See also CA 49-52
See also SATA 41

Shulman, Alix Kates 1932-...... CLC 2, 10
See also CA 29-32R
See also SATA 7

Shuster, Joe 1914-
See Siegel, Jerome and Shuster, Joe

Shute (Norway), Nevil
1899-1960...................CLC 30
See also Norway, Nevil Shute

Shuttle, Penelope (Diane) 1947-......CLC 7
See also CA 93-96
See also DLB 14, 40

Siegel, Jerome 1914-
See Siegel, Jerome and Shuster, Joe
See also CA 116

Siegel, Jerome 1914- and
Shuster, Joe 1914- ....CLC 21

Sienkiewicz, Henryk (Adam Aleksander Pius)
1846-1916.................. TCLC 3
See also CA 104

Sigal, Clancy 1926- ....CLC 7
See also CA 1-4R

Silkin, Jon 1930- .... CLC 2, 6
See also CA 5-8R
See also DLB 27

Silko, Leslie Marmon 1948-........CLC 23
See also CA 115

Sillanpää, Franz Eemil
1888-1964...................CLC 19
See also obituary CA 93-96

Sillitoe, Alan 1928- .... CLC 1, 3, 6, 10, 19
See also CAAS 2
See also CANR 8
See also CA 9-12R
See also DLB 14
See also AITN 1

Silone, Ignazio 1900-1978..........CLC 4
See also CAP 2
See also CA 25-28
See also obituary CA 81-84

Silver, Joan Micklin 1935-.........CLC 20
See also CA 114

Silverberg, Robert 1935- ....CLC 7
See also CANR 1
See also CA 1-4R
See also SATA 13
See also DLB 8

Silverstein, Alvin 1933-
See Silverstein, Alvin
  and Silverstein, Virginia B(arbara
  Opshelor)
See also CANR 2
See also CA 49-52
See also SATA 8

Silverstein, Alvin 1933- and **Silverstein,**
  Virginia B(arbara Opshelor)
1937-......................CLC 17

Silverstein, Virginia B(arbara Opshelor)
1937-
See Silverstein, Alvin and Silverstein,
  Virginia B(arbara Opshelor)
See also CANR 2
See also CA 49-52
See also SATA 8

Simak, Clifford D(onald) 1904-......CLC 1
See also CANR 1
See also CA 1-4R
See also DLB 8

Simenon, Georges (Jacques Christian)
1903-..............CLC 1, 2, 3, 8, 18
See also CA 85-88

Simenon, Paul 1956?-
See The Clash

Simic, Charles 1938-.........CLC 6, 9, 22
See also CA 29-32R

Simms, William Gilmore
1806-1870...................NCLC 3
See also DLB 3, 30

Simon, Carly 1945-...............CLC 26
See also CA 105

Simon, Claude 1913-.........CLC 4, 9, 15
See also CA 89-92

Simon, (Marvin) Neil
1927-.................CLC 6, 11, 31
See also CA 21-24R
See also DLB 7
See also AITN 1

Simon, Paul 1941-................CLC 17
See also CA 116

Simonon, Paul 1956?-
See The Clash

Simpson, Louis (Aston Marantz)
1923-................CLC 4, 7, 9, 32
See also CANR 1
See also CA 1-4R
See also DLB 5

Simpson, N(orman) F(rederick)
1919-.....................CLC 29
See also CA 11-14R
See also DLB 13

Sinclair, Andrew (Annandale)
1935-....................CLC 2, 14
See also CANR 14
See also CA 9-12R
See also DLB 14

Sinclair, Mary Amelia St. Clair 1865?-1946
See Sinclair, May
See also CA 104

Sinclair, May 1865?-1946......TCLC 3, 11
See also Sinclair, Mary Amelia St. Clair
See also DLB 36

Sinclair, Upton (Beall)
1878-1968.............CLC 1, 11, 15
See also CANR 7
See also CA 5-8R
See also obituary 25-28R
See also SATA 9
See also DLB 9

Singer, Isaac Bashevis
1904-........CLC 1, 3, 6, 9, 11, 15, 23
See also CLR 1
See also CANR 1
See also CA 1-4R
See also SATA 3, 27
See also DLB 6, 28
See also AITN 1, 2

Singh, Khushwant 1915-..........CLC 11
See also CANR 6
See also CA 9-12R

Sinyavsky, Andrei (Donatevich)
1925-........................CLC 8
See also CA 85-88

Sissman, L(ouis) E(dward)
1928-1976................CLC 9, 18
See also CA 21-24R
See also obituary CA 65-68
See also DLB 5

Sisson, C(harles) H(ubert) 1914-.....CLC 8
See also CANR 3
See also CA 1-4R
See also DLB 27

Sitwell, (Dame) Edith
1887-1964.................CLC 2, 9
See also CA 9-12R
See also DLB 20

Sjoewall, Maj 1935-
See Wahlöö, Per
See also CA 65-68

Sjöwall, Maj 1935-
See Wahlöö, Per

Skelton, Robin 1925-..............CLC 13
See also CA 5-8R
See also AITN 2
See also DLB 27

Skolimowski, Jerzy 1938-..........CLC 20

Skolimowski, Yurek 1938-
See Skolimowski, Jerzy

Skrine, Mary Nesta 1904-
See Keane, Molly

Škvorecký, Josef (Vaclav)
1924-.......................CLC 15
See also CAAS 1
See also CANR 10
See also CA 61-64

Slade, Bernard 1930- ....CLC 11
See also Newbound, Bernard Slade

Slaughter, Frank G(ill) 1908- ......CLC 29
See also CANR 5
See also CA 5-8R
See also AITN 2

Slavitt, David (R.) 1935-........ CLC 5, 14
See also CA 21-24R
See also DLB 5, 6

Slesinger, Tess 1905-1945....... TCLC 10
See also CA 107

Slessor, Kenneth 1901-1971........CLC 14
See also CA 102
See also obituary CA 89-92

Smart, Christopher 1722-1771 ...... LC 3

Smith, A(rthur) J(ames) M(arshall)
1902-1980...................CLC 15
See also CANR 4
See also CA 1-4R
See also obituary CA 102

Smith, Betty (Wehner)
1896-1972...................CLC 19
See also CA 5-8R
See also obituary CA 33-36R
See also SATA 6
See also DLB-Y 82

Smith, Cecil Lewis Troughton 1899-1966
See Forester, C(ecil) S(cott)

Smith, Dave 1942-................CLC 22
See also Smith, David (Jeddie)
See also DLB 5

Smith, David (Jeddie) 1942-
See Smith, Dave
See also CANR 1
See also CA 49-52

Smith, Florence Margaret 1902-1971
See Smith, Stevie
See also CAP 2
See also CA 17-18
See also obituary CA 29-32R

Smith, Lee 1944- ....CLC 25
See also CA 114
See also DLB-Y 83

Smith, Martin Cruz 1942-.........CLC 25
See also CANR 6
See also CA 85-88

Smith, Martin William 1942-
See Smith, Martin Cruz

Smith, Patti 1946- ....CLC 12
See also CA 93-96

Smith, Sara Mahala Redway 1900-1972
See Benson, Sally

Smith, Stevie 1902-1971......CLC 3, 8, 25
See also Smith, Florence Margaret
See also DLB 20

Smith, Wilbur (Addison) 1933-.....CLC 33
See also CANR 7
See also CA 13-16R

Smith, William Jay 1918-...........CLC 6
See also CA 5-8R
See also SATA 2
See also DLB 5

Smollett, Tobias (George)
1721-1771.....................LC 2
See also DLB 39

Snodgrass, W(illiam) D(e Witt)
1926-...............CLC 2, 6, 10, 18
See also CANR 6
See also CA 1-4R
See also DLB 5

Snow, C(harles) P(ercy)
1905-1980....... CLC 1, 4, 6, 9, 13, 19
See also CA 5-8R
See also obituary CA 101
See also DLB 15

Snyder, Gary 1930-..... CLC 1, 2, 5, 9, 32
See also CA 17-20R
See also DLB 5, 16

Snyder, Zilpha Keatley 1927- ......CLC 17
See also CA 9-12R
See also SATA 1, 28

Sokolov, Raymond 1941- . . . . .CLC 7
See also CA 85-88

Sologub, Fyodor 1863-1927 . . . . TCLC 9
See also Teternikov, Fyodor Kuzmich

Solwoska, Mara 1929-
See French, Marilyn

Solzhenitsyn, Aleksandr I(sayevich)
1918- . . . . .CLC 1, 2, 4, 7, 9, 10, 18, 26, 34
See also CA 69-72
See also AITN 1

Sommer, Scott 1951- . . . . .CLC 25
See also CA 106

Sondheim, Stephen (Joshua)
1930- . . . . .CLC 33
See also CA 103

Sontag, Susan
1933- . . . . CLC 1, 2, 10, 13, 31
See also CA 17-20R
See also DLB 2

Sorrentino, Gilbert
1929- . . . . .CLC 3, 7, 14, 22
See also CANR 14
See also CA 77-80
See also DLB 5
See also DLB-Y 80

Soto, Gary 1952- . . . . .CLC 32

Souster, (Holmes) Raymond
1921- . . . . CLC 5, 14
See also CANR 13
See also CA 13-16R

Southern, Terry 1926- . . . . .CLC 7
See also CANR 1
See also CA 1-4R
See also DLB 2

Southey, Robert 1774-1843 . . . . NCLC 8

Soyinka, Akin-wande Oluwole 1934-
See Soyinka, Wole

Soyinka, Wole 1934- . . . . . .CLC 3, 5, 14, 36
See also CA 13-16R

Spacks, Barry 1931- . . . . .CLC 14
See also CA 29-32R

Spark, Muriel (Sarah)
1918- . . . . CLC 2, 3, 5, 8, 13, 18
See also CANR 12
See also CA 5-8R
See also DLB 15

Spencer, Elizabeth 1921- . . . . .CLC 22
See also CA 13-16R
See also SATA 14
See also DLB 6

Spencer, Scott 1945- . . . . .CLC 30
See also CA 113

Spender, Stephen (Harold)
1909- . . . . .CLC 1, 2, 5, 10
See also CA 9-12R
See also DLB 20

Spicer, Jack 1925-1965 . . . . CLC 8, 18
See also CA 85-88
See also DLB 5, 16

Spielberg, Peter 1929- . . . . .CLC 6
See also CANR 4
See also CA 5-8R
See also DLB-Y 81

Spielberg, Steven 1947- . . . . .CLC 20
See also CA 77-80
See also SATA 32

Spillane, Frank Morrison 1918-
See Spillane, Mickey
See also CA 25-28R

Spillane, Mickey 1918- . . . . CLC 3, 13
See also Spillane, Frank Morrison

Spitteler, Carl (Friedrich Georg)
1845-1924 . . . . TCLC 12
See also CA 109

Spivack, Kathleen (Romola Drucker)
1938- . . . . .CLC 6
See also CA 49-52

Springsteen, Bruce 1949- . . . . .CLC 17
See also CA 111

Spurling, Hilary 1940- . . . . .CLC 34
See also CA 104

Staël-Holstein, Anne Louise Germaine Necker, Baronne de
1766-1817 . . . . NCLC 3

Stafford, Jean 1915-1979 . . . . . CLC 4, 7, 19
See also CANR 3
See also CA 1-4R
See also obituary CA 85-88
See also obituary SATA 22
See also DLB 2

Stafford, William (Edgar)
1914- . . . . CLC 4, 7, 29
See also CANR 5
See also CA 5-8R
See also DLB 5

Stanton, Maura 1946- . . . . .CLC 9
See also CANR 15
See also CA 89-92

Stark, Richard 1933-
See Westlake, Donald E(dwin)

Stead, Christina (Ellen)
1902-1983 . . . . .CLC 2, 5, 8, 32
See also CA 13-16R
See also obituary CA 109

Stegner, Wallace (Earle) 1909- . . . . . .CLC 9
See also CANR 1
See also CA 1-4R
See also DLB 9
See also AITN 1

Stein, Gertrude 1874-1946 . . . . . . TCLC 1, 6
See also CA 104
See also DLB 4

Steinbeck, John (Ernst)
1902-1968 . . . . . . CLC 1, 5, 9, 13, 21, 34
See also CANR 1
See also CA 1-4R
See also obituary CA 25-28R
See also SATA 9
See also DLB 7, 9
See also DLB-DS 2

Steiner, George 1929- . . . . .CLC 24
See also CA 73-76

Steiner, Rudolf(us Josephus Laurentius)
1861-1925 . . . . TCLC 13
See also CA 107

Stephens, James 1882?-1950 . . . . . . TCLC 4
See also CA 104
See also DLB 19

Steptoe, Lydia 1892-1982
See Barnes, Djuna

Stern, Richard G(ustave) 1928- . . . . . .CLC 4
See also CANR 1
See also CA 1-4R

Sternberg, Jonas 1894-1969
See Sternberg, Josef von

Sternberg, Josef von
1894-1969 . . . . .CLC 20
See also CA 81-84

Sterne, Laurence 1713-1768 . . . . LC 2
See also DLB 39

Sternheim, (William Adolf) Carl
1878-1942 . . . . TCLC 8
See also CA 105

Stevens, Mark 19??- . . . . .CLC 34

Stevens, Wallace
1879-1955 . . . . TCLC 3, 12
See also CA 104

Stevenson, Anne (Katharine)
1933- . . . . CLC 7, 33
See also Elvin, Anne Katharine Stevenson
See also CANR 9
See also DLB 40

Stevenson, Robert Louis
1850-1894 . . . . NCLC 5
See also YABC 2
See also DLB 18

Stewart, J(ohn) I(nnes) M(ackintosh)
1906- . . . . CLC 7, 14, 32
See also CA 85-88

Stewart, Mary (Florence Elinor)
1916- . . . . CLC 7, 35
See also CANR 1
See also CA 1-4R
See also SATA 12

Stewart, Will 1908-
See Williamson, Jack

Sting 1951-
See The Police

Stitt, Milan 1941- . . . . .CLC 29
See also CA 69-72

Stoker, Bram (Abraham)
1847-1912 . . . . TCLC 8
See also CA 105
See also SATA 29
See also DLB 36

Stolz, Mary (Slattery) 1920- . . . . .CLC 12
See also CANR 13
See also CA 5-8R
See also SATA 10
See also AITN 1

Stone, Irving 1903- . . . . .CLC 7
See also CANR 1
See also CA 1-4R
See also SATA 3
See also AITN 1

Stone, Robert (Anthony)
1937?- . . . . CLC 5, 23
See also CA 85-88

Stoppard, Tom
1937- . . . . . CLC 1, 3, 4, 5, 8, 15, 29, 34
See also CA 81-84
See also DLB 13

Storey, David (Malcolm)
1933- . . . . .CLC 2, 4, 5, 8
See also CA 81-84
See also DLB 13, 14

Storm, Hyemeyohsts 1935- . . . . .CLC **3**
   See also CA 81-84

Storm, (Hans) Theodor (Woldsen)
   1817-1888 . . . . NCLC **1**

Storni, Alfonsina 1892-1938 . . . . . . TCLC **5**
   See also CA 104

Stout, Rex (Todhunter)
   1886-1975 . . . . .CLC **3**
   See also CA 61-64
   See also AITN 2

Stow, (Julian) Randolph 1935- . . . . .CLC **23**
   See also CA 13-16R

Stowe, Harriet (Elizabeth) Beecher
   1811-1896 . . . . NCLC **3**
   See also YABC 1
   See also DLB 1, 12, 42

Strachey, (Giles) Lytton
   1880-1932 . . . . TCLC **12**
   See also CA 110

Strand, Mark 1934- . . . . CLC **6, 18**
   See also CA 21-24R
   See also DLB 5
   See also SATA 41

Straub, Peter (Francis) 1943- . . . . . .CLC **28**
   See also CA 85-88
   See also DLB-Y 84

Strauss, Botho 1944- . . . . .CLC **22**

Straussler, Tomas 1937-
   See Stoppard, Tom

Streatfeild, Noel 1897- . . . . .CLC **21**
   See also CA 81-84
   See also SATA 20

Stribling, T(homas) S(igismund)
   1881-1965 . . . . .CLC **23**
   See also obituary CA 107
   See also DLB 9

Strindberg, (Johan) August
   1849-1912 . . . . TCLC **1, 8**
   See also CA 104

Strugatskii, Arkadii (Natanovich) 1925-
   See Strugatskii, Arkadii (Natanovich) and
      Strugatskii, Boris (Natanovich)
   See also CA 106

Strugatskii, Arkadii (Natanovich) 1925-
   and **Strugatskii, Boris**
   (Natanovich) 1933- . . . . .CLC **27**

Strugatskii, Boris (Natanovich) 1933-
   See Strugatskii, Arkadii (Natanovich) and
      Strugatskii, Boris (Natanovich)
   See also CA 106

Strugatskii, Boris (Natanovich) 1933- and
   Strugatskii, Arkadii (Natanovich) 1925-
   See Strugatskii, Arkadii (Natanovich) and
      Strugatskii, Boris (Natanovich)

Strummer, Joe 1953?-
   See The Clash

Stuart, (Hilton) Jesse
   1906-1984 . . . . CLC **1, 8, 11, 14, 34**
   See also CA 5-8R
   See also obituary CA 112
   See also SATA 2
   See also obituary SATA 36
   See also DLB 9
   See also DLB-Y 84

Sturgeon, Theodore (Hamilton)
   1918-1985 . . . . .CLC **22**
   See also CA 81-84
   See also obituary CA 116
   See also DLB 8

Styron, William
   1925- . . . . CLC **1, 3, 5, 11, 15**
   See also CANR 6
   See also CA 5-8R
   See also DLB 2
   See also DLB-Y 80

Sudermann, Hermann
   1857-1928 . . . . TCLC **15**
   See also CA 107

Sue, Eugène 1804-1857 . . . . NCLC **1**

Sukenick, Ronald 1932- . . . . . . .CLC **3, 4, 6**
   See also CA 25-28R
   See also DLB-Y 81

Suknaski, Andrew 1942- . . . . .CLC **19**
   See also CA 101

Summers, Andrew James 1942-
   See The Police

Summers, Andy 1942-
   See The Police

Summers, Hollis (Spurgeon, Jr.)
   1916- . . . . .CLC **10**
   See also CANR 3
   See also CA 5-8R
   See also DLB 6

Summers, (Alphonsus Joseph-Mary Augustus)
   Montague 1880-1948 . . . . TCLC **16**

Sumner, Gordon Matthew 1951-
   See The Police

Susann, Jacqueline 1921-1974 . . . . . . .CLC **3**
   See also CA 65-68
   See also obituary CA 53-56
   See also AITN 1

Sutcliff, Rosemary 1920- . . . . .CLC **26**
   See also CLR 1
   See also CA 5-8R
   See also SATA 6

Sutro, Alfred 1863-1933 . . . . TCLC **6**
   See also CA 105
   See also DLB 10

Sutton, Henry 1935-
   See Slavitt, David (R.)

Svevo, Italo 1861-1928 . . . . TCLC **2**
   See also Schmitz, Ettore

Swados, Elizabeth 1951- . . . . .CLC **12**
   See also CA 97-100

Swados, Harvey 1920-1972 . . . . .CLC **5**
   See also CANR 6
   See also CA 5-8R
   See also obituary CA 37-40R
   See also DLB 2

Swarthout, Glendon (Fred)
   1918- . . . . .CLC **35**
   See also CANR 1
   See also CA 1-4R
   See also SATA 26

Swenson, May 1919- . . . . CLC **4, 14**
   See also CA 5-8R
   See also SATA 15
   See also DLB 5

Swift, Jonathan 1667-1745 . . . . LC **1**
   See also SATA 19
   See also DLB 39

Swinburne, Algernon Charles
   1837-1909 . . . . TCLC **8**
   See also CA 105
   See also DLB 35

Swinfen, Ann 19??- . . . . .CLC **34**

Swinnerton, Frank (Arthur)
   1884-1982 . . . . .CLC **31**
   See also obituary CA 108
   See also DLB 34

Symons, Arthur (William)
   1865-1945 . . . . TCLC **11**
   See also CA 107
   See also DLB 19

Symons, Julian (Gustave)
   1912- . . . . CLC **2, 14, 32**
   See also CANR 3
   See also CA 49-52

Synge, (Edmund) John Millington
   1871-1909 . . . . TCLC **6**
   See also CA 104
   See also DLB 10, 19

Syruc, J. 1911-
   See Miłosz, Czesław

Tabori, George 1914- . . . . .CLC **19**
   See also CANR 4
   See also CA 49-52

Tagore, (Sir) Rabindranath
   1861-1941 . . . . TCLC **3**
   See also Thakura, Ravindranatha

Talese, Gaetano 1932-
   See Talese, Gay

Talese, Gay 1932- . . . . .CLC **37**
   See also CANR 9
   See also CA 1-4R
   See also AITN 1

Tamayo y Baus, Manuel
   1829-1898 . . . . NCLC **1**

Tanizaki, Jun'ichirō
   1886-1965 . . . . CLC **8, 14, 28**
   See also CA 93-96
   See also obituary CA 25-28R

Tarkington, (Newton) Booth
   1869-1946 . . . . TCLC **9**
   See also CA 110
   See also SATA 17
   See also DLB 9

Tate, (John Orley) Allen
   1899-1979 . . . . . . CLC **2, 4, 6, 9, 11, 14,
                                       24**
   See also CA 5-8R
   See also obituary CA 85-88
   See also DLB 4, 45

Tate, James 1943- . . . . CLC **2, 6, 25**
   See also CA 21-24R
   See also DLB 5

Tavel, Ronald 1940- . . . . .CLC **6**
   See also CA 21-24R

Taylor, C(ecil) P(hillip)
   1929-1981 . . . . .CLC **27**
   See also CA 25-28R
   See also obituary CA 105

Taylor, Eleanor Ross 1920- . . . . .CLC **5**
   See also CA 81-84

Taylor, Elizabeth
   1912-1975 . . . . CLC **2, 4, 29**
   See also CANR 9
   See also CA 13-16R
   See also SATA 13

Taylor, Kamala (Purnaiya) 1924-
   See Markandaya, Kamala (Purnaiya)
   See also CA 77-80

Taylor, Mildred D(elois) 19??-......CLC 21
   See also CA 85-88
   See also SATA 15

Taylor, Peter (Hillsman)
   1917-................CLC 1, 4, 18, 37
   See also CANR 9
   See also CA 13-16R
   See also DLB-Y 81

Taylor, Robert Lewis 1912-........CLC 14
   See also CANR 3
   See also CA 1-4R
   See also SATA 10

Teasdale, Sara 1884-1933........ TCLC 4
   See also CA 104
   See also DLB 45
   See also SATA 32

Tegnér, Esaias 1782-1846........ NCLC 2

Teilhard de Chardin, (Marie Joseph) Pierre
   1881-1955.................. TCLC 9
   See also CA 105

Tennant, Emma 1937- ....CLC 13
   See also CANR 10
   See also CA 65-68
   See also DLB 14

Teran, Lisa St. Aubin de 19??-.....CLC 36

Terry, Megan 1932- ....CLC 19
   See also CA 77-80
   See also DLB 7

Tertz, Abram 1925-
   See Sinyavsky, Andrei (Donatevich)

Teternikov, Fyodor Kuzmich 1863-1927
   See Sologub, Fyodor
   See also CA 104

Tey, Josephine 1897-1952 .... TCLC 14
   See also Mackintosh, Elizabeth

Thackeray, William Makepeace
   1811-1863.................. NCLC 5
   See also SATA 23
   See also DLB 21

Thakura, Ravindranatha 1861-1941
   See Tagore, (Sir) Rabindranath
   See also CA 104

Thelwell, Michael (Miles)
   1939-.......................CLC 22
   See also CA 101

Theroux, Alexander (Louis)
   1939-.................... CLC 2, 25
   See also CA 85-88

Theroux, Paul
   1941-............ CLC 5, 8, 11, 15, 28
   See also CA 33-36R
   See also DLB 2

Thibault, Jacques Anatole Francois
   1844-1924
   See France, Anatole
   See also CA 106

Thiele, Colin (Milton) 1920-........CLC 17
   See also CANR 12
   See also CA 29-32R
   See also SATA 14

Thomas, Audrey (Grace)
   1935-.................. CLC 7, 13, 37
   See also CA 21-24R
   See also AITN 2

Thomas, D(onald) M(ichael)
   1935-................. CLC 13, 22, 31
   See also CA 61-64
   See also DLB 40

Thomas, Dylan (Marlais)
   1914-1953................. TCLC 1, 8
   See also CA 104
   See also DLB 13, 20

Thomas, Edward (Philip)
   1878-1917................. TCLC 10
   See also CA 106
   See also DLB 19

Thomas, John Peter 1928-
   See Thomas, Piri

Thomas, Joyce Carol 1938-........CLC 35
   See also CA 113, 116
   See also SATA 40
   See also DLB 33

Thomas, Lewis 1913- ....CLC 35
   See also CA 85-88

Thomas, Piri 1928- ....CLC 17
   See also CA 73-76

Thomas, R(onald) S(tuart)
   1913-.................... CLC 6, 13
   See also CA 89-92
   See also DLB 27

Thompson, Francis (Joseph)
   1859-1907................. TCLC 4
   See also CA 104
   See also DLB 19

Thompson, Hunter S(tockton)
   1939-.................. CLC 9, 17
   See also CA 17-20R

Thoreau, Henry David
   1817-1862................. NCLC 7
   See also DLB 1

Thurber, James (Grover)
   1894-1961............. CLC 5, 11, 25
   See also CA 73-76
   See also SATA 13
   See also DLB 4, 11, 22

Thurman, Wallace 1902-1934 ..... TCLC 6
   See also CA 104

Tieck, (Johann) Ludwig
   1773-1853................. NCLC 5

Tillinghast, Richard 1940-.........CLC 29
   See also CA 29-32R

Tindall, Gillian 1938- ....CLC 7
   See also CANR 11
   See also CA 21-24R

Tocqueville, Alexis de
   1805-1859................. NCLC 7

Tolkien, J(ohn) R(onald) R(euel)
   1892-1973......... CLC 1, 2, 3, 8, 12
   See also CAP 2
   See also CA 17-18
   See also obituary CA 45-48
   See also SATA 2, 32
   See also obituary SATA 24
   See also DLB 15
   See also AITN 1

Toller, Ernst 1893-1939 .... TCLC 10
   See also CA 107

Tolson, Melvin B(eaunorus)
   1900?-1966.................CLC 36
   See also Obituary CA 89-92

Tolstoy, (Count) Alexey Nikolayevich
   1883-1945.................. TCLC 18
   See also CA 107

Tolstoy, (Count) Leo (Lev Nikolaevich)
   1828-1910............TCLC 4, 11, 17
   See also CA 104
   See also SATA 26

Tomlin, Lily 1939-................CLC 17

Tomlin, Mary Jean 1939-
   See Tomlin, Lily

Tomlinson, (Alfred) Charles
   1927-..................CLC 2, 4, 6, 13
   See also CA 5-8R
   See also DLB 40

Toole, John Kennedy
   1937-1969....................CLC 19
   See also CA 104
   See also DLB-Y 81

Toomer, Jean
   1894-1967............CLC 1, 4, 13, 22
   See also CA 85-88
   See also DLB 45

Torrey, E. Fuller 19??-............CLC 34

Tournier, Michel 1924-...... CLC 6, 23, 36
   See also CANR 3
   See also CA 49-52
   See also SATA 23

Townshend, Peter (Dennis Blandford)
   1945-.......................CLC 17
   See also CA 107

Trakl, Georg 1887-1914 .... TCLC 5
   See also CA 104

Traven, B. 1890-1969.......... CLC 8, 11
   See also CAP 2
   See also CA 19-20
   See also obituary CA 25-28R
   See also DLB 9

Tremblay, Michel 1942-..........CLC 29

Trevanian 1925-..................CLC 29
   See also Whitaker, Rodney
   See also CA 108

Trevor, William
   1928-................CLC 7, 9, 14, 25
   See also Cox, William Trevor
   See also DLB 14

Trilling, Lionel
   1905-1975............. CLC 9, 11, 24
   See also CANR 10
   See also CA 9-12R
   See also obituary CA 61-64
   See also DLB 28

Trogdon, William 1939-
   See Heat Moon, William Least
   See also CA 115

Trollope, Anthony 1815-1882 ..... NCLC 6
   See also SATA 22
   See also DLB 21

Troyat, Henri 1911- ....CLC 23
   See also CANR 2
   See also CA 45-48

Trudeau, G(arretson) B(eekman) 1948-
   See Trudeau, Garry
   See also CA 81-84
   See also SATA 35

Trudeau, Garry 1948-.............CLC 12
   See also Trudeau, G(arretson) B(eekman)
   See also AITN 2

Truffaut, François 1932-1984 ......CLC **20**
  See also CA 81-84
  See also obituary CA 113

Trumbo, Dalton 1905-1976 ....CLC **19**
  See also CANR 10
  See also CA 21-24R
  See also obituary CA 69-72
  See also DLB 26

Tryon, Thomas 1926- .... CLC **3, 11**
  See also CA 29-32R
  See also AITN 1

Ts'ao Hsüeh-ch'in 1715?-1763........ LC **1**

Tsushima Shūji 1909-1948
  See Dazai Osamu
  See also CA 107

Tsvetaeva (Efron), Marina (Ivanovna)
  1892-1941.................. TCLC **7**
  See also CA 104

Tunis, John R(oberts)
  1889-1975.................CLC **12**
  See also CA 61-64
  See also SATA 30, 37
  See also DLB 22

Tuohy, Frank 1925- ....CLC **37**
  See also DLB 14

Tuohy, John Francis 1925-
  See Tuohy, Frank
  See also CANR 3
  See also CA 5-8R

Turco, Lewis (Putnam) 1934- ......CLC **11**
  See also CA 13-16R
  See also DLB-Y 84

Tutuola, Amos 1920-........ CLC **5, 14, 29**
  See also CA 9-12R

Twain, Mark
  1835-1910............TCLC **6, 12, 19**
  See also Clemens, Samuel Langhorne
  See also DLB 11

Tyler, Anne 1941- ....CLC **7, 11, 18, 28**
  See also CANR 11
  See also CA 9-12R
  See also SATA 7
  See also DLB 6
  See also DLB-Y 82

Tyler, Royall 1757-1826.......... NCLC **3**
  See also DLB 37

Tynan (Hinkson), Katharine
  1861-1931.................. TCLC **3**
  See also CA 104

Unamuno (y Jugo), Miguel de
  1864-1936................ TCLC **2, 9**
  See also CA 104

Underwood, Miles 1909-1981
  See Glassco, John

Undset, Sigrid 1882-1949........ TCLC **3**
  See also CA 104

Ungaretti, Giuseppe
  1888-1970............. CLC **7, 11, 15**
  See also CAP 2
  See also CA 19-20
  See also obituary CA 25-28R

Unger, Douglas 1952- ....CLC **34**

Unger, Eva 1932-
  See Figes, Eva

Updike, John (Hoyer)
  1932-......CLC **1, 2, 3, 5, 7, 9, 13, 15,**
                        23, 34
  See also CANR 4
  See also CA 1-4R
  See also DLB 2, 5
  See also DLB-Y 80, 82
  See also DLB-DS 3

Uris, Leon (Marcus) 1924-...... CLC **7, 32**
  See also CANR 1
  See also CA 1-4R
  See also AITN 1, 2

Ustinov, Peter (Alexander)
  1921-.........................CLC **1**
  See also CA 13-16R
  See also DLB 13
  See also AITN 1

Vaculík, Ludvík 1926- ....CLC **7**
  See also CA 53-56

Valenzuela, Luisa 1938-.........CLC **31**
  See also CA 101

Valera (y Acalá-Galiano), Juan
  1824-1905.................. TCLC **10**
  See also CA 106

Valéry, Paul (Ambroise Toussaint Jules)
  1871-1945................ TCLC **4, 15**
  See also CA 104

Valle-Inclán (y Montenegro), Ramón (María)
  del 1866-1936 .... TCLC **5**
  See also CA 106

Vallejo, César (Abraham)
  1892-1938 .... TCLC **3**
  See also CA 105

Van Ash, Cay 1918- ....CLC **34**

Vance, Jack 1916?-...............CLC **35**
  See also DLB 8

Vance, John Holbrook 1916?-
  See Vance, Jack
  See also CA 29-32R

Van Den Bogarde, Derek (Jules Gaspard
  Ulric) Niven 1921-
  See Bogarde, Dirk
  See also CA 77-80

Van der Post, Laurens (Jan)
  1906-.......................CLC **5**
  See also CA 5-8R

Van Doren, Carl (Clinton)
  1885-1950................. TCLC **18**
  See also CA 111

Van Doren, Mark
  1894-1972................ CLC **6, 10**
  See also CANR 3
  See also CA 1-4R
  See also obituary CA 37-40R
  See also DLB 45

Van Druten, John (William)
  1901-1957.................. TCLC **2**
  See also CA 104
  See also DLB 10

Van Duyn, Mona 1921- .... CLC **3, 7**
  See also CANR 7
  See also CA 9-12R
  See also DLB 5

Van Itallie, Jean-Claude 1936- ......CLC **3**
  See also CAAS 2
  See also CANR 1
  See also CA 45-48
  See also DLB 7

Van Peebles, Melvin 1932-...... CLC **2, 20**
  See also CA 85-88

Van Vechten, Carl 1880-1964......CLC **33**
  See also obituary CA 89-92
  See also DLB 4, 9

Van Vogt, A(lfred) E(lton)
  1912-.........................CLC **1**
  See also CA 21-24R
  See also SATA 14
  See also DLB 8

Varda, Agnès 1928-...............CLC **16**
  See also CA 116

Vargas Llosa, (Jorge) Mario (Pedro)
  1936-.......CLC **3, 6, 9, 10, 15, 31**
  See also CA 73-76

Vassilikos, Vassilis 1933- .... CLC **4, 8**
  See also CA 81-84

Verga, Giovanni 1840-1922....... TCLC **3**
  See also CA 104

Verhaeren, Émile (Adolphe Gustave)
  1855-1916................. TCLC **12**
  See also CA 109

Verlaine, Paul (Marie)
  1844-1896.................. NCLC **2**

Verne, Jules (Gabriel)
  1828-1905.................. TCLC **6**
  See also CA 110
  See also SATA 21

Very, Jones 1813-1880........... NCLC **9**
  See also DLB 1

Vian, Boris 1920-1959 .... TCLC **9**
  See also CA 106

Viaud, (Louis Marie) Julien 1850-1923
  See Loti, Pierre
  See also CA 107

Vicker, Angus 1916-
  See Felsen, Henry Gregor

Vidal, Eugene Luther, Jr. 1925-
  See Vidal, Gore

Vidal, Gore
  1925-........CLC **2, 4, 6, 8, 10, 22, 33**
  See also CANR 13
  See also CA 5-8R
  See also DLB 6
  See also AITN 1

Viereck, Peter (Robert Edwin)
  1916-.........................CLC **4**
  See also CANR 1
  See also CA 1-4R
  See also DLB 5

Vigny, Alfred (Victor) de
  1797-1863.................. NCLC **7**

Villiers de l'Isle Adam, Jean Marie Mathias
  Philippe Auguste, Comte de,
  1838-1889.................. NCLC **3**

Vinge, Joan (Carol) D(ennison)
  1948-.........................CLC **30**
  See also CA 93-96
  See also SATA 36

Visconti, Luchino 1906-1976.......CLC **16**
  See also CA 81-84
  See also obituary CA 65-68

Vittorini, Elio 1908-1966 ..... CLC **6, 9, 14**
  See also obituary CA 25-28R

Vliet, R(ussell) G. 1929-...........CLC **22**
  See also CA 37-40R

Author Index

Voigt, Cynthia 1942-..............CLC 30
  See also CA 106
  See also SATA 33

Voinovich, Vladimir (Nikolaevich)
  1932-......................CLC 10
  See also CA 81-84

Von Daeniken, Erich 1935-
  See Von Däniken, Erich
  See also CA 37-40R
  See also AITN 1

Von Däniken, Erich 1935-.........CLC 30
  See also Von Daeniken, Erich

Vonnegut, Kurt, Jr.
  1922-...... CLC 1, 2, 3, 4, 5, 8, 12, 22
  See also CANR 1
  See also CA 1-4R
  See also DLB 2, 8
  See also DLB-Y 80
  See also DLB-DS 3
  See also AITN 1

Vorster, Gordon 1924-...........CLC 34

Voznesensky, Andrei 1933-..... CLC 1, 15
  See also CA 89-92

Waddington, Miriam 1917-........CLC 28
  See also CANR 12
  See also CA 21-24R

Wagman, Fredrica 1937-..........CLC 7
  See also CA 97-100

Wagner, Richard 1813-1883 ...... NCLC 9

Wagoner, David (Russell)
  1926-................. CLC 3, 5, 15
  See also CANR 2
  See also CA 1-4R
  See also SATA 14
  See also DLB 5

Wahlöö, Per 1926-1975 ....CLC 7
  See also CA 61-64

Wahlöö, Peter 1926-1975
  See Wahlöö, Per

Wain, John (Barrington)
  1925-.................. CLC 2, 11, 15
  See also CA 5-8R
  See also DLB 15, 27

Wajda, Andrzej 1926-.............CLC 16
  See also CA 102

Wakefield, Dan 1932-.............CLC 7
  See also CA 21-24R

Wakoski, Diane
  1937-.............. CLC 2, 4, 7, 9, 11
  See also CAAS 1
  See also CANR 9
  See also CA 13-16R
  See also DLB 5

Walcott, Derek (Alton)
  1930-............. CLC 2, 4, 9, 14, 25
  See also CA 89-92
  See also DLB-Y 81

Waldman, Anne 1945- ....CLC 7
  See also CA 37-40R
  See also DLB 16

Waldo, Edward Hamilton 1918-
  See Sturgeon, Theodore (Hamilton)

Walker, Alice
  1944-............ CLC 5, 6, 9, 19, 27
  See also CANR 9
  See also CA 37-40R
  See also SATA 31
  See also DLB 6, 33

Walker, David Harry 1911-........CLC 14
  See also CANR 1
  See also CA 1-4R
  See also SATA 8

Walker, Edward Joseph 1934-
  See Walker, Ted
  See also CA 21-24R

Walker, Joseph A. 1935- ....CLC 19
  See also CA 89-92
  See also DLB 38

Walker, Margaret (Abigail)
  1915-.................... CLC 1, 6
  See also CA 73-76

Walker, Ted 1934-................CLC 13
  See also Walker, Edward Joseph
  See also DLB 40

Wallace, Irving 1916- .... CLC 7, 13
  See also CAAS 1
  See also CANR 1
  See also CA 1-4R
  See also AITN 1

Wallant, Edward Lewis
  1926-1962................. CLC 5, 10
  See also CA 1-4R
  See also DLB 2, 28

Walpole, Horace 1717-1797.......... LC 2
  See also DLB 39

Walpole, (Sir) Hugh (Seymour)
  1884-1941................... TCLC 5
  See also CA 104
  See also DLB 34

Walser, Martin 1927-.............CLC 27
  See also CANR 8
  See also CA 57-60

Walser, Robert 1878-1956 ...... TCLC 18

Walsh, Gillian Paton 1939-
  See Walsh, Jill Paton
  See also CA 37-40R
  See also SATA 4

Walsh, Jill Paton 1939-...........CLC 35
  See also CLR 2

Wambaugh, Joseph (Aloysius, Jr.)
  1937-.................... CLC 3, 18
  See also CA 33-36R
  See also DLB 6
  See also DLB-Y 83
  See also AITN 1

Ward, Douglas Turner 1930-.......CLC 19
  See also CA 81-84
  See also DLB 7, 38

Warhol, Andy 1928-..............CLC 20
  See also CA 89-92

Warner, Francis (Robert le Plastrier)
  1937-......................CLC 14
  See also CANR 11
  See also CA 53-56

Warner, Sylvia Townsend
  1893-1978................. CLC 7, 19
  See also CANR 16
  See also CA 61-64
  See also obituary CA 77-80
  See also DLB 34

Warren, Robert Penn
  1905-........CLC 1, 4, 6, 8, 10, 13, 18
  See also CANR 10
  See also CA 13-16R
  See also DLB 2
  See also DLB-Y 80
  See also AITN 1

Washington, Booker T(aliaferro)
  1856-1915.......... TCLC 10, CLC 34
  See also CA 114
  See also SATA 28

Wassermann, Jakob
  1873-1934................... TCLC 6
  See also CA 104

Wasserstein, Wendy 1950-........CLC 32

Waters, Roger 1944-
  See Pink Floyd

Wa Thiong'o, Ngugi
  1938-................CLC 3, 7, 13, 36
  See also Ngugi, James (Thiong'o)
  See also Ngugi wa Thiong'o

Waugh, Auberon (Alexander)
  1939-......................CLC 7
  See also CANR 6
  See also CA 45-48
  See also DLB 14

Waugh, Evelyn (Arthur St. John)
  1903-1966...... CLC 1, 3, 8, 13, 19, 27
  See also CA 85-88
  See also obituary CA 25-28R
  See also DLB 15

Waugh, Harriet 1944-..............CLC 6
  See also CA 85-88

Webb, Charles (Richard) 1939-......CLC 7
  See also CA 25-28R

Webb, James H(enry), Jr.
  1946-......................CLC 22
  See also CA 81-84

Webb, Phyllis 1927- ....CLC 18
  See also CA 104

Webber, Andrew Lloyd 1948-
  See Rice, Tim and Webber, Andrew Lloyd

Weber, Lenora Mattingly
  1895-1971....................CLC 12
  See also CAP 1
  See also CA 19-20
  See also obituary CA 29-32R
  See also SATA 2
  See also obituary SATA 26

Wedekind, (Benjamin) Frank(lin)
  1864-1918................... TCLC 7
  See also CA 104

Weidman, Jerome 1913-............CLC 7
  See also CANR 1
  See also CA 1-4R
  See also DLB 28
  See also AITN 2

Weinstein, Nathan Wallenstein 1903?-1940
  See West, Nathanael
  See also CA 104

Weir, Peter 1944- ....CLC 20
  See also CA 113

Weiss, Peter (Ulrich)
  1916-1982................. CLC 3, 15
  See also CANR 3
  See also CA 45-48
  See also obituary CA 106

Weiss, Theodore (Russell)
  1916-................... CLC 3, 8, 14
  See also CAAS 2
  See also CA 9-12R
  See also DLB 5

Welch, James 1940-............. CLC 6, 14
  See also CA 85-88

Weldon, Fay
1933-............ CLC 6, 9, 11, 19, 36
See also CANR 16
See also CA 21-24R
See also DLB 14

Wellek, René 1903-............... CLC 28
See also CANR 8
See also CA 5-8R

Weller, Michael 1942-............ CLC 10
See also CA 85-88

Weller, Paul 1958-................ CLC 26

Welles, (George) Orson
1915-1985.................. CLC 20
See also CA 93-96

Wells, H(erbert) G(eorge)
1866-1946............. TCLC 6, 12, 19
See also CA 110
See also SATA 20
See also DLB 34

Wells, Rosemary................... CLC 12
See also CA 85-88
See also SAAS 1
See also SATA 18

Welty, Eudora (Alice)
1909-.......... CLC 1, 2, 5, 14, 22, 33
See also CA 9-12R
See also DLB 2

Werfel, Franz (V.) 1890-1945 ..... TCLC 8
See also CA 104

Wergeland, Henrik Arnold
1808-1845.................. NCLC 5

Wersba, Barbara 1932- .... CLC 30
See also CLR 3
See also CA 29-32R
See also SATA 1

Wertmüller, Lina 1928- .... CLC 16
See also CA 97-100

Wescott, Glenway 1901-........... CLC 13
See also CA 13-16R
See also DLB 4, 9

Wesker, Arnold 1932-........... CLC 3, 5
See also CANR 1
See also CA 1-4R
See also DLB 13

Wesley, Richard (Errol) 1945-....... CLC 7
See also CA 57-60
See also DLB 38

West, Jessamyn 1907-1984...... CLC 7, 17
See also CA 9-12R
See also obituary SATA 37
See also DLB 6
See also DLB-Y 84

West, Morris L(anglo)
1916-.................... CLC 6, 33
See also CA 5-8R

West, Nathanael
1903?-1940............... TCLC 1, 14
See Weinstein, Nathan Wallenstein
See also DLB 4, 9, 28

West, Paul 1930-.............. CLC 7, 14
See also CA 13-16R
See also DLB 14

West, Rebecca 1892-1983..... CLC 7, 9, 31
See also CA 5-8R
See also obituary CA 109
See also DLB 36
See also DLB-Y 83

Westall, Robert (Atkinson)
1929-........................CLC 17
See also CA 69-72
See also SATA 23

Westlake, Donald E(dwin)
1933-.................... CLC 7, 33
See also CANR 16
See also CA 17-20R

Whalen, Philip 1923-........... CLC 6, 29
See also CANR 5
See also CA 9-12R
See also DLB 16

Wharton, Edith (Newbold Jones)
1862-1937................. TCLC 3, 9
See also CA 104
See also DLB 4, 9, 12

Wharton, William 1925-....... CLC 18, 37
See also CA 93-96
See also DLB-Y 80

Wheatley (Peters), Phillis
1753?-1784.................... LC 3
See also DLB 31

Wheelock, John Hall
1886-1978................... CLC 14
See also CANR 14
See also CA 13-16R
See also obituary CA 77-80
See also DLB 45

Whelan, John 1900-
See O'Faoláin, Seán

Whitaker, Rodney 1925-
See Trevanian
See also CA 29-32R

White, E(lwyn) B(rooks)
1899-1985............... CLC 10, 34
See also CLR 1
See also CANR 16
See also CA 13-16R
See also obituary CA 116
See also SATA 2, 29
See also DLB 11, 22
See also AITN 2

White, Edmund III 1940-..........CLC 27
See also CANR 3
See also CA 45-48

White, Patrick (Victor Martindale)
1912-........... CLC 3, 4, 5, 7, 9, 18
See also CA 81-84

White, T(erence) H(anbury)
1906-1964................... CLC 30
See also CA 73-76
See also SATA 12

White, Walter (Francis)
1893-1955................ TCLC 15
See also CA 115

Whitehead, E(dward) A(nthony)
1933-........................CLC 5
See also CA 65-68

Whitman, Walt 1819-1892........ NCLC 4
See also SATA 20
See also DLB 3

Whitemore, Hugh 1936-..........CLC 37

Whittemore, (Edward) Reed (Jr.)
1919-........................CLC 4
See also CANR 4
See also CA 9-12R
See also DLB 5

Whittier, John Greenleaf
1807-1892.................. NCLC 8
See also DLB 1

Wicker, Thomas Grey 1926-
See Wicker, Tom
See also CA 65-68

Wicker, Tom 1926-................CLC 7
See also Wicker, Thomas Grey

Wideman, John Edgar
1941-................ CLC 5, 34, 36
See also CANR 14
See also CA 85-88
See also DLB 33

Wiebe, Rudy (H.) 1934-..... CLC 6, 11, 14
See also CA 37-40R

Wieners, John 1934-................CLC 7
See also CA 13-16R
See also DLB 16

Wiesel, Elie(zer)
1928-................CLC 3, 5, 11, 37
See also CANR 8
See also CA 5-8R
See also AITN 1

Wight, James Alfred 1916-
See Herriot, James
See also CA 77-80

Wilbur, Richard (Purdy)
1921-..................CLC 3, 6, 9, 14
See also CANR 2
See also CA 1-4R
See also SATA 9
See also DLB 5

Wild, Peter 1940-..................CLC 14
See also CA 37-40R
See also DLB 5

Wilde, Oscar (Fingal O'Flahertie Wills)
1854-1900................ TCLC 1, 8
See also CA 104
See also SATA 24
See also DLB 10, 19, 34

Wilder, Billy 1906- ....CLC 20
See also Wilder, Samuel
See also DLB 26

Wilder, Samuel 1906-
See Wilder, Billy
See also CA 89-92

Wilder, Thornton (Niven)
1897-1975...... CLC 1, 5, 6, 10, 15, 35
See also CA 13-16R
See also obituary CA 61-64
See also DLB 4, 7, 9
See also AITN 2

Wilhelm, Kate 1928-...............CLC 7
See also CA 37-40R
See also DLB 8

Willard, Nancy 1936- .... CLC 7, 37
See also CLR 5
See also CANR 10
See also CA 89-92
See also SATA 30, 37
See also DLB 5

Williams, C(harles) K(enneth)
1936-........................CLC 33
See also CA 37-40R
See also DLB 5

Williams, Charles (Walter Stansby)
1886-1945................ TCLC 1, 11
See also CA 104

Williams, (George) Emlyn
    1905-.........................CLC 15
    See also CA 104
    See also DLB 10

Williams, John A(lfred)
    1925-..................... CLC 5, 13
    See also CANR 6
    See also CA 53-56
    See also DLB 2, 33

Williams, Jonathan (Chamberlain)
    1929-.........................CLC 13
    See also CANR 8
    See also CA 9-12R
    See also DLB 5

Williams, Joy 1944-...............CLC 31
    See also CA 41-44R

Williams, Paulette 1948-
    See Shange, Ntozake

Williams, Tennessee
    1911-1983....... CLC 1, 2, 5, 7, 8, 11,
                                15, 19, 30
    See also CA 5-8R
    See also obituary CA 108
    See also DLB 7
    See also DLB-Y 83
    See also DLB-DS 4
    See also AITN 1, 2

Williams, Thomas (Alonzo)
    1926-.........................CLC 14
    See also CANR 2
    See also CA 1-4R

Williams, Thomas Lanier 1911-1983
    See Williams, Tennessee

Williams, William Carlos
    1883-1963....... CLC 1, 2, 5, 9, 13, 22
    See also CA 89-92
    See also DLB 4, 16

Williamson, Jack 1908-............CLC 29
    See also Williamson, John Stewart
    See also DLB 8

Williamson, John Stewart 1908-
    See Williamson, Jack
    See also CA 17-20R

Willingham, Calder (Baynard, Jr.)
    1922-.........................CLC 5
    See also CANR 3
    See also CA 5-8R
    See also DLB 2, 44

Wilson, A(ndrew) N(orman)
    1950-.........................CLC 33
    See also CA 112
    See also DLB 14

Wilson, Andrew 1948-
    See Wilson, Snoo

Wilson, Angus (Frank Johnstone)
    1913-......... CLC 2, 3, 5, 25, 34
    See also CA 5-8R
    See also DLB 15

Wilson, Brian 1942-...............CLC 12

Wilson, Colin 1931-.............CLC 3, 14
    See also CANR 1
    See also CA 1-4R
    See also DLB 14

Wilson, Edmund
    1895-1972......... CLC 1, 2, 3, 8, 24
    See also CANR 1
    See also CA 1-4R
    See also obituary CA 37-40R

Wilson, Ethel Davis (Bryant)
    1888-1980....................CLC 13
    See also CA 102

Wilson, John 1785-1854......... NCLC 5

Wilson, John (Anthony) Burgess 1917-
    See Burgess, Anthony
    See also CANR 2
    See also CA 1-4R

Wilson, Lanford 1937-...... CLC 7, 14, 36
    See also CA 17-20R
    See also DLB 7

Wilson, Robert (M.) 1944-....... CLC 7, 9
    See also CANR 2
    See also CA 49-52

Wilson, Sloan 1920-...............CLC 32
    See also CANR 1
    See also CA 1-4R

Wilson, Snoo 1948-...............CLC 33
    See also CA 69-72

**Winchilsea, Anne (Kingsmill) Finch, Countess
    of** 1661-1720 .... LC 3

Winters, (Arthur) Yvor
    1900-1968.............. CLC 4, 8, 32
    See also CAP 1
    See also CA 11-12
    See also obituary CA 25-28R

Wiseman, Frederick 1930-.........CLC 20

Witkiewicz, Stanislaw Ignacy
    1885-1939................... TCLC 8
    See also CA 105

Wittig, Monique 1935?-...........CLC 22
    See also CA 116

Wittlin, Joseph 1896-1976........CLC 25
    See also Wittlin, Józef

Wittlin, Józef 1896-1976
    See Wittlin, Joseph
    See also CANR 3
    See also CA 49-52
    See also obituary CA 65-68

Wodehouse, P(elham) G(renville)
    1881-1975......... CLC 1, 2, 5, 10, 22
    See also CANR 3
    See also CA 45-48
    See also obituary CA 57-60
    See also SATA 22
    See also DLB 34
    See also AITN 2

Woiwode, Larry (Alfred)
    1941-..................... CLC 6, 10
    See also CANR 16
    See also CA 73-76
    See also DLB 6

Wojciechowska, Maia (Teresa)
    1927-.........................CLC 26
    See also CLR 1
    See also CANR 4
    See also CA 9-12R
    See also SAAS 1
    See also SATA 1, 28

Wolf, Christa 1929-........... CLC 14, 29
    See also CA 85-88

Wolfe, Gene (Rodman) 1931-......CLC 25
    See also CANR 6
    See also CA 57-60
    See also DLB 8

Wolfe, Thomas (Clayton)
    1900-1938............... TCLC 4, 13
    See also CA 104
    See also DLB 9
    See also DLB-DS 2

Wolfe, Thomas Kennerly, Jr. 1931-
    See Wolfe, Tom
    See also CANR 9
    See also CA 13-16R

Wolfe, Tom 1931-..... CLC 1, 2, 9, 15, 35
    See also Wolfe, Thomas Kennerly, Jr.
    See also AITN 2

Wolitzer, Hilma 1930-.............CLC 17
    See also CA 65-68
    See also SATA 31

Wonder, Stevie 1950- ....CLC 12
    See also Morris, Steveland Judkins

Wong, Jade Snow 1922-...........CLC 17
    See also CA 109

Woodcott, Keith 1934-
    See Brunner, John (Kilian Houston)

Woolf, (Adeline) Virginia
    1882-1941................. TCLC 1, 5
    See also CA 104
    See also DLB 36

Woollcott, Alexander (Humphreys)
    1887-1943................... TCLC 5
    See also CA 105
    See also DLB 29

Wouk, Herman 1915-........... CLC 1, 9
    See also CANR 6
    See also CA 5-8R
    See also DLB-Y 82

Wright, Charles 1935- ...... CLC 6, 13, 28
    See also CA 29-32R
    See also DLB-Y 82

Wright, James (Arlington)
    1927-1980...........CLC 3, 5, 10, 28
    See also CANR 4
    See also CA 49-52
    See also obituary CA 97-100
    See also DLB 5
    See also AITN 2

Wright, Judith 1915-.............CLC 11
    See also CA 13-16R
    See also SATA 14

Wright, Richard (Nathaniel)
    1908-1960....... CLC 1, 3, 4, 9, 14, 21
    See also CA 108
    See also DLB-DS 2

Wright, Richard B(ruce) 1937-......CLC 6
    See also CA 85-88

Wright, Rick 1945-
    See Pink Floyd

Wright, Stephen 1946- ....CLC 33

Wu Ching-tzu 1701-1754 .... LC 2

Wurlitzer, Rudolph
    1938?-.................. CLC 2, 4, 15
    See also CA 85-88

Wylie (Benét), Elinor (Morton Hoyt)
    1885-1928................... TCLC 8
    See also CA 105
    See also DLB 9, 45

Wyndham, John 1903-1969........CLC 19
    See also Harris, John (Wyndham Parkes
    Lucas) Beynon

Wyss, Johann David
1743-1818 . . . . NCLC 10
See also SATA 27, 29

Yanovsky, Vassily S(emenovich)
1906- . . . . CLC 2, 18
See also CA 97-100

Yates, Richard 1926- . . . . CLC 7, 8, 23
See also CANR 10
See also CA 5-8R
See also DLB 2
See also DLB-Y 81

Yeats, William Butler
1865-1939 . . . . .TCLC 1, 11, 18
See also CANR 10
See also CA 104
See also DLB 10, 19

Yehoshua, Abraham B.
1936- . . . . CLC 13, 31
See also CA 33-36R

Yep, Laurence (Michael) 1948- . . . . .CLC 35
See also CLR 3
See also CANR 1
See also CA 49-52
See also SATA 7

Yerby, Frank G(arvin)
1916- . . . . CLC 1, 7, 22
See also CANR 16
See also CA 9-12R

Yevtushenko, Yevgeny (Aleksandrovich)
1933- . . . . .CLC 1, 3, 13, 26
See also CA 81-84

Yglesias, Helen 1915- . . . . CLC 7, 22
See also CANR 15
See also CA 37-40R

Yorke, Henry Vincent 1905-1974
See Green, Henry
See also CA 85-88
See also obituary CA 49-52

Young, Al 1939- . . . . .CLC 19
See also CA 29-32R
See also DLB 33

Young, Andrew 1885-1971 . . . . .CLC 5
See also CANR 7
See also CA 5-8R

Young, Edward 1683-1765 . . . . LC 3

Young, Neil 1945- . . . . .CLC 17
See also CA 110

Yourcenar, Marguerite 1913- . . . . . .CLC 19
See also CA 69-72

Yurick, Sol 1925- . . . . .CLC 6
See also CA 13-16R

Zamyatin, Yevgeny Ivanovich
1884-1937 . . . . TCLC 8
See also CA 105

Zangwill, Israel 1864-1926 . . . . TCLC 16
See also CA 109
See also DLB 10

Zappa, Francis Vincent, Jr. 1940-
See Zappa, Frank
See also CA 108

Zappa, Frank 1940- . . . . .CLC 17
See also Zappa, Francis Vincent, Jr.

Zaturenska, Marya
1902-1982 . . . . CLC 6, 11
See also CA 13-16R
See also obituary CA 105

Zelazny, Roger 1937- . . . . .CLC 21
See also CA 21-24R
See also SATA 39
See also DLB 8

Zhdanov, Andrei A(lexandrovich)
1896-1948 . . . . TCLC 18

Zimmerman, Robert 1941-
See Dylan, Bob

Zindel, Paul 1936- . . . . CLC 6, 26
See also CLR 3
See also CA 73-76
See also SATA 16
See also DLB 7

Zinoviev, Alexander 1922- . . . . .CLC 19
See also CA 116

Zola, Émile 1840-1902 . . . . TCLC 1, 6
See also CA 104

Zorrilla y Moral, José
1817-1893 . . . . NCLC 6

Zoshchenko, Mikhail (Mikhailovich)
1895-1958 . . . . TCLC 15
See also CA 115

Zuckmayer, Carl 1896-1977 . . . . . . .CLC 18
See also CA 69-72

Zukofsky, Louis
1904-1978 . . . . CLC 1, 2, 4, 7, 11, 18
See also CA 9-12R
See also obituary CA 77-80
See also DLB 5

Zweig, Paul 1935-1984 . . . . .CLC 34
See also CA 85-88
See also obituary CA 113

Zweig, Stefan 1881-1942 . . . . TCLC 17
See also CA 112

Author Index

Cumulative Index to Critics

Aalfs, Janet
Jane Rule 27:422

Aaron, Daniel
Claude Brown 30:38
Thornton Wilder 15:575

Aaron, Jonathan
Tadeusz Różewicz 23:363

Aaron, Jules
Michael Cristofer 28:96
Jack Heifner 11:264

Abbey, Edward
Wright Morris 37:317
Robert M. Pirsig 6:421

Abbott, James H.
Juan Benet 28:21

Abbott, John Lawrence
Isaac Bashevis Singer 9:487
Sylvia Townsend Warner 7:512

Abbott, Shirley
Eudora Welty 33:425

Abeel, Erica
Pamela Hansford Johnson 7:185

Abel, Elizabeth
Jean Rhys 14:448

Abel, Lionel
Samuel Beckett 2:45
Jack Gelber 6:196
Jean Genet 2:157
Yoram Kaniuk 19:238

Abernethy, Peter L.
Thomas Pynchon 3:410

Abicht, Ludo
Jan de Hartog 19:133

Ableman, Paul
Brian Aldiss 14:14
Beryl Bainbridge 22:45
Jurek Becker 19:36
William Boyd 28:39
William S. Burroughs 22:85
J. M. Coetzee 23:125
Len Deighton 22:116
Elaine Feinstein 36:171
William Golding 17:179
Mary Gordon 13:250
Mervyn Jones 10:295
David Lodge 36:273
Michael Moorcock 27:351
Piers Paul Read 25:377
Mary Renault 17:402
Anatoli Rybakov 23:373
Andrew Sinclair 14:489
Scott Sommer 25:424
D. M. Thomas 22:419
Gore Vidal 22:438
A. N. Wilson 33:451

Abley, Mark
Margaret Atwood 25:65
Clark Blaise 29:76
J. M. Coetzee 33:109
Harry Crews 23:136
John le Carré 28:226
William Mitchell 25:327
Brian Moore 32:312
Michael Ondaatje 29:341, 342
Agnès Varda 16:560
Miriam Waddington 28:440

Abraham, Willie E.
William Melvin Kelley 22:249

Abrahams, Cecil A.
Bessie Head 25:236

Abrahams, William
Elizabeth Bowen 6:95
Hortense Calisher 2:97
Herbert Gold 4:193
A. N. Wilson 33:451
Joyce Carol Oates 2:315
Harold Pinter 9:418
V. S. Pritchett 5:352

Abrahamson, Dick
Fran Arrick 30:19
Sue Ellen Bridgers 26:92
Jean Craighead George 35:179
John Knowles 26:265
Norma Fox Mazer 26:294

Abrams, Elliott
William F. Buckley, Jr. 37:59

Abrams, M. H.
M. H. Abrams 24:18
Northrop Frye 24:209

Abramson, Doris E.
Alice Childress 12:105

Abramson, Jane
Peter Dickinson 12:172
Christie Harris 12:268
S. E. Hinton 30:205
Rosemary Wells 12:638

Achebe, Chinua
Ayi Kwei Armah 33:28
Amos Tutuola 29:435

Acheson, Dean
Art Buchwald 33:92

Acheson, James
William Golding 17:177

Acken, Edgar L.
Ernest K. Gann 23:163

Acker, Robert
Ernst Jandl 34:198

Ackerman, Diane
John Berryman 25:97
Arthur C. Clarke 35:119

Ackroyd, Peter
Brian Aldiss 5:16
Martin Amis 4:19
Miguel Ángel Asturias 8:27
Louis Auchincloss 6:15
W. H. Auden 9:56
Beryl Bainbridge 8:36
James Baldwin 5:43
John Barth 5:51
Donald Barthelme 3:44
Samuel Beckett 4:52
John Berryman 3:72
Richard Brautigan 5:72
Charles Bukowski 5:80
Anthony Burgess 5:87
William S. Burroughs 5:92
Italo Calvino 5:100; 8:132
Richard Condon 6:115
Roald Dahl 6:122
Ed Dorn 10:155
Margaret Drabble 8:183
Douglas Dunn 6:148
Eva Figes 31:163, 165
Bruce Jay Friedman 5:127
John Gardner 7:116
Günter Grass 4:207
MacDonald Harris 9:261
Joseph Heller 5:179
Mark Helprin 10:261
Russell C. Hoban 7:160
Elizabeth Jane Howard 7:164
B. S. Johnson 6:264
Pamela Hansford Johnson 7:184

G. Josipovici **6**:270
Thomas Keneally **10**:298
Jack Kerouac **5**:215
Francis King **8**:321
Jerzy Kosinski **10**:308
Doris Lessing **6**:300
Alison Lurie **4**:305
Thomas McGuane **7**:212
Stanley Middleton **7**:220
Michael Moorcock **5**:294;
   27:350
Penelope Mortimer **5**:298
Iris Murdoch **4**:368
Vladimir Nabokov **6**:358
V. S. Naipaul **7**:252
Joyce Carol Oates **6**:368
Tillie Olsen **13**:432
Grace Paley **6**:393
Frederik Pohl **18**:411
Davi Pownall **10**:418, 419
J. B. Priestley **9**:441
V. S. Pritchett **5**:352
Thomas Pynchon **3**:419
Frederic Raphael **14**:437
Simon Raven **14**:442
Peter Redgrove **6**:446
Keith Roberts **14**:463
Judith Rossner **9**:458
May Sarton **4**:472
Tom Sharpe **36**:400
David Slavitt **5**:392
Wole Soyinka **5**:398
David Storey **4**:529
Peter Straub **28**:409
Glendon Swarthout **35**:403
Frank Swinnerton **31**:428
Paul Theroux **5**:428
Thomas Tryon **11**:548
John Updike **7**:488; **9**:540
Gore Vidal **8**:525
Harriet Waugh **6**:559
Jerome Weidman **7**:518
Arnold Wesker **5**:483
Patrick White **4**:587
Roger Zelazny **21**:469

Acton, Gary
D. M. Pinkwater **35**:320

Acton, Harold
Anthony Powell **31**:318

Aczel, Tamas
Heinrich Böll **27**:63

Adachi, Ken
David Donnell **34**:157, 159

Adam, G. F.
Rhys Davies **23**:143

Adamic, Louis
Woody Guthrie **35**:182

Adamowski, T. H.
Simone de Beauvoir **4**:47

Adams, Agatha Boyd
Paul Green **25**:197

Adams, Alice
Lisa Alther **7**:14
C.D.B. Bryan **29**:106
Joyce Carol Oates **33**:291
Cynthia Propper Seton **27**:429
Joy Williams **31**:463

Adams, Franklin P.
James M. Cain **28**:43

Adams, George R.
Lorraine Hansberry **17**:190
Ann Petry **18**:403

Adams, J. Donald
Erich Maria Remarque **21**:327

Adams, Jacqueline
Al Young **19**:479

Adams, James Truslow
Esther Forbes **12**:206

Adams, John
Roy A. Gallant **17**:131

Adams, John J.
Jack Vance **35**:421, 422

Adams, Laura
Norman Mailer **11**:340

Adams, Leonie
John Crowe Ransom **4**:428

Adams, M. Ian
Juan Carlos Onetti **10**:376

Adams, Percy
James Dickey **7**:81

Adams, Phoebe-Lou
Chinua Achebe **26**:11, 13
Richard Adams **18**:2
Joy Adamson **17**:3
Nelson Algren **33**:17
Beryl Bainbridge **5**:40
Ann Beattie **18**:38
David Bradley, Jr. **23**:81
André Brink **18**:68
Robert Cormier **12**:133
Margaret Craven **17**:80
Roald Dahl **18**:109
Peter Davison **28**:100
José Donoso **32**:154
G. B. Edwards **25**:151
John Ehle **27**:105
John Fowles **15**:234
Dick Francis **22**:150
Günter Grass **22**:196
Dashiell Hammett **5**:161
James Herriot **12**:282
George V. Higgins **18**:234
Jamake Highwater **12**:285
Bohumil Hrabal **13**:290
Langston Hughes **35**:219
P. D. James **18**:275
David Jones **7**:189
Garson Kanin **22**:232
Jerzy Kosinski **6**:285
William Kotzwinkle **14**:311
Halldór Laxness **25**:292, 300
Harper Lee **12**:341
Yukio Mishima **9**:385
N. Scott Momaday **19**:317
Berry Morgan **6**:340
Joyce Carol Oates **6**:374
Tillie Olsen **13**:433
Sylvia Plath **17**:352
Reynolds Price **6**:426
Jean Rhys **19**:394
Darcy Ribeiro **34**:102
João Ubaldo Ribeiro **10**:436
Philip Roth **15**:452

Françoise Sagan **17**:419
Khushwant Singh **11**:504
Jean Stafford **19**:431
Christina Stead **8**:500
Douglas Unger **34**:116
R. G. Vliet **22**:441
Joseph Wambaugh **18**:532

Adams, Richard
Robert Newton Peck **17**:338

Adams, Robert M.
Peter Brooks **34**:521
Adolfo Bioy Casares **13**:87
R. V. Cassill **23**:105
John Cheever **25**:121
Eleanor Clark **19**:105
Edward Dahlberg **7**:63
William Empson **34**:337
Max Frisch **32**:194
Peter Matthiessen **11**:361
Mary McCarthy **14**:362
Alberto Moravia **18**:348
Robert M. Pirsig **4**:404
Severo Sarduy **6**:485
Mary Lee Settle **19**:409
Edmund Wilson **24**:469

Adams, Robert Martin
John Barth **10**:24
Samuel Beckett **14**:74
Jorge Luis Borges **10**:66
Richard Brautigan **12**:61
Anthony Burgess **10**:90
Lawrence Durrell **13**:185
T. S. Eliot **10**:171
William Faulkner **11**:201
Carlo Emilio Gadda **11**:215
William H. Gass **2**:154
José Lezama Lima **10**:321
Vladimir Nabokov **11**:393
Flann O'Brien **10**:363
Thomas Pynchon **11**:453
Alain Robbe-Grillet **10**:437
J.R.R. Tolkien **12**:586
Angus Wilson **2**:472

Adams, Robin
Frank Herbert **12**:279
Roger Zelazny **21**:470

Adams, Robin G.
Joan D. Vinge **30**:409

Adams, S. J.
Ezra Pound **13**:453

Adams, Stephen D.
James Purdy **28**:380

Adams, Timothy Dow
Leon Rooke **25**:394

Adcock, Fleur
John Berryman **13**:83
Maurice Gee **29**:178, 179
Robert Lowell **11**:331
David Malouf **28**:268
Peter Porter **13**:453

Adelman, Clifford
John Berryman **3**:71

Adelman, George
Frank B. Gilbreth, Jr. and
   Ernestine Gilbreth Carey
   17:156

Adereth, M.
Louis Aragon **22**:36

Adkins, Laurence
Eilís Dillon **17**:96
Farley Mowat **26**:336

Adler, Anne G.
John Jakes **29**:250

Adler, Bill
Marvin Gaye **26**:132

Adler, Dick
Ross Macdonald **1**:185

Adler, Jerry
Leon Uris **32**:437

Adler, Joyce
Wilson Harris **25**:207

Adler, Renata
Mel Brooks **12**:75
Francis Ford Coppola **16**:232
Joan Micklin Silver **20**:346

Adler, Thomas P.
Edward Albee **11**:13
Harold Pinter **15**:424
Sam Shepard **17**:446
Stephen Sondheim **30**:389

Aers, Lesley
Philippa Pearce **21**:284

Aeschliman, M. D.
William Mastrosimone **36**:291
Tom Stoppard **34**:282

Agar, John
Jonathan Baumbach **6**:32
Laurie Colwin **5**:107
Joy Williams **31**:462

Agee, James
Frank Capra **16**:156
Charles Chaplin **16**:193
Maya Deren **16**:251
Carl Theodor Dreyer **16**:256
Alfred Hitchcock **16**:339, 342
John Huston **20**:158, 160
Buster Keaton **20**:188
Laurence Olivier **20**:234
Billy Wilder **20**:456

Agee, Joel
Aharon Appelfeld **23**:38
Günter Grass **32**:202

Agena, Kathleen
Charles Wright **13**:613

Aggeler, Geoffrey
Anthony Burgess **2**:86; **5**:85;
   13:123; **22**:69

Aghazarian, Nancy
Milton Meltzer **26**:304

Agius, Ambrose, O.S.B.
Edward Dahlberg **7**:64

Ahearn, Kerry
Wallace Stegner **9**:509

Aherne, Michael A.
Allen Drury **37**:108

Ahokas, Jaakko A.
Paavo Haavikko **18**:206; **34**:169
Frans Eemil Sillanpää **19**:418

Ahrold, Robbin
Kurt Vonnegut, Jr. **3**:501

Aidoo, Christina Ama Ata
Ayi Kwei Armah **33**:24

Aiken, Conrad
William Faulkner **8**:206
St.-John Perse **11**:433
I. A. Richards **24**:370
Carl Sandburg **35**:345
Karl Shapiro **15**:475

Aiken, David
Flannery O'Connor **10**:365

Aiken, William
David Kherdian **6**:281

Aithal, Rashmi
Raja Rao **25**:373

Aithal, S. Krishnamoorthy
Raja Rao **25**:373

Aitken, Will
Carlos Saura **20**:319

Ajami, Fouad
V. S. Naipaul **37**:321

Aklujkar, Ashok
R. K. Narayan **28**:301

Alazraki, Jaime
Jorge Luis Borges **19**:45
Pablo Neruda **2**:309; **7**:261

Albers, Randall
Ai **14**:8

Albert, Walter
Blaise Cendrars **18**:90

Albertson, Chris
Laura Nyro **17**:313
Stevie Wonder **12**:662

Aldan, Daisy
Maya Angelou **35**:32
Phyllis Gotlieb **18**:193
Howard Nemerov **36**:306
Joyce Carol Oates **33**:294

Alden, John R.
Bruce Lancaster **36**:245

Alderson, Brian W.
Aidan Chambers **35**:98
Leon Garfield **12**:226
Jean Craighead George **35**:177
William Mayne **12**:395, 401

Alderson, S. William
Andre Norton **12**:464, 466, 470

Alderson, Sue Ann
Muriel Rukeyser **10**:442

Alderson, Valerie
E. M. Almedingen **12**:6
Noel Streatfeild **21**:412

Aldiss, Brian
J. G. Ballard **3**:33
Frank Herbert **12**:272
Jack Williamson **29**:450

Aldiss, Brian W.
Isaac Asimov **26**:38
Philip K. Dick **30**:116
Robert A. Heinlein **26**:162
Jack Williamson **29**:456

Aldrich, Nelson
Piri Thomas **17**:497

Aldridge, John W.
Nelson Algren **33**:17
James Baldwin **4**:42
Donald Barthelme **2**:39
Saul Bellow **2**:49, 50
Louis-Ferdinand Céline **7**:47
John Cheever **3**:105
John Dos Passos **4**:131
James T. Farrell **4**:157
William Faulkner **3**:150
William Gaddis **3**:177; **6**:193
Joseph Heller **5**:177; **36**:224
Ernest Hemingway **3**:231, 233
James Jones **3**:261
Frederick Karl **34**:552
Jerzy Kosinski **2**:231
Richard Kostelanetz **28**:216
Alison Lurie **5**:260
Norman Mailer **1**:193; **2**:258
Mary McCarthy **3**:327, 328
Wright Morris **3**:342; **18**:352
John O'Hara **2**:323
Katherine Anne Porter **3**:392
Philip Roth **4**:459
Alan Sillitoe **3**:447
William Styron **3**:472
John Updike **2**:439
Gore Vidal **22**:431
Robert Penn Warren **1**:356
Eudora Welty **2**:461
Colin Wilson **3**:536
Edmund Wilson **2**:474
P. G. Wodehouse **2**:478

Aldridge, Judith
Ruth M. Arthur **12**:27
Honor Arundel **17**:14, 15, 18

Alegria, Fernando
Jorge Luis Borges **2**:71
Pablo Neruda **28**:309

Alessandri, Tom
Czesław Miłosz **31**:263
Jim Shepard **36**:407

Aletti, Vince
Marvin Gaye **26**:130, 131, 132
Laura Nyro **17**:312
Prince **35**:325
Smokey Robinson **21**:342, 345
Stevie Wonder **12**:656, 660

Alexander, Alex E.
Stephen King **26**:234

Alexander, Edward
Cynthia Ozick **28**:348
Isaac Bashevis Singer **11**:503

Alexander, Jean
Richard Peck **21**:296

Alexander, John R.
Robinson Jeffers **2**:215

Alexander, Michael
Donald Davie **5**:113
Ezra Pound **7**:336

Alexander, William
Carl Sandburg **4**:463

Alexandrova, Vera
Mikhail Sholokhov **7**:420

Alfonso, Barry
Van Morrison **21**:239

Alford, Steven E.
Doris Betts **28**:34

Algren, Nelson
Clancy Sigal **7**:424

Ali, Ahmed
Raja Rao **25**:366

Ali, Tariq
Jules Archer **12**:19

Alig, Tracy
John Gregory Dunne **28**:121

Alkalimat, Abd-Al Hakimu Ibn
C.L.R. James **33**:219

Allaby, Michael
Jacques-Yves Cousteau **30**:107

Allen, Blaine
Monty Python **21**:223

Allen, Bob
Waylon Jennings **21**:206
Willie Nelson **17**:305

Allen, Bruce
Richard Adams **5**:6
Russell Banks **37**:23
David Bradley, Jr. **23**:81
Raymond Carver **36**:103
J. M. Coetzee **33**:108
Julio Cortázar **5**:110
Stanley Elkin **6**:168
John Gardner **8**:236; **28**:162
Mary Gordon **13**:250
Thomas Keneally **5**:212
Kenneth Koch **5**:219
Peter Matthiessen **7**:211
Wright Morris **18**:354; **37**:317
Iris Murdoch **6**:347
Joyce Carol Oates **6**:369
Kenzaburō Ōe **36**:346
Seán O'Faoláin **32**:343
Manuel Puig **5**:355
John Sayles **10**:460
Isaac Bashevis Singer **6**:509
Paul West **7**:524
Patrick White **5**:485
A. N. Wilson **33**:457

Allen, Bruce D.
Jane Rule **27**:417

Allen, Carol J.
Susan Fromberg Schaeffer
11:491

Allen, Constance
Robin F. Brancato **35**:70

Allen, Dexter
Mary Lee Settle **19**:408

Allen, Dick
Margaret Atwood **2**:20
Wendell Berry **6**:61
Hayden Carruth **7**:40
Paul Goodman **2**:169
Thom Gunn **6**:221
Richard F. Hugo **6**:245
Philip Levine **2**:244
Jayanta Mahapatra **33**:277
Lisel Mueller **13**:400

George Oppen **7**:281
Judith Johnson Sherwin **7**:414

Allen, Don
François Truffaut **20**:397

Allen, Frank
Jayanta Mahapatra **33**:279

Allen, Gay Wilson
Carl Sandburg **10**:447

Allen, Gilbert
Stephen Dobyns **37**:80

Allen, Henry
Robert M. Pirsig **4**:403

Allen, James Sloan
Margaret Mead **37**:281

Allen, John A.
Eudora Welty **14**:564

Allen, John Alexander
Daniel Hoffman **13**:288

Allen, L. David
Arthur C. Clarke **18**:106

Allen, Louis
Shusaku Endo **14**:161
Shiga Naoya **33**:373

Allen, Merritt P.
Walter Farley **17**:116
Andre Norton **12**:455

Allen, Michael
Richard F. Hugo **32**:239

Allen, Michael S.
Richard F. Hugo **32**:247

Allen, Patricia H.
Zilpha Keatley Snyder **17**:469

Allen, Paul
Alan Ayckbourn **33**:45, 46
Howard Barker **37**:34
C. S. Forester **35**:159

Allen, Ralph G.
Eric Bentley **24**:51

Allen, Rodney F.
Thomas J. Fleming **37**:121

Allen, Steve
S. J. Perelman **23**:335

Allen, Tom
Ralph Bakshi **26**:73
Vittorio De Sica **20**:97
Rainer Werner Fassbinder
20:115
Kon Ichikawa **20**:186
Yasujiro Ozu **16**:450
Pier Paolo Pasolini **20**:270
Sidney Poitier **26**:361
Carlos Saura **20**:321
Jerzy Skolimowski **20**:354

Allen, Tom, S. C.
Mel Brooks **12**:81

Allen, Walter
A. Alvarez **5**:17
Kingsley Amis **1**:5
Riccardo Bacchelli **19**:31
Saul Bellow **1**:30
Elizabeth Bowen **1**:40

Paul Bowles **1**:41
Truman Capote **1**:55
Ivy Compton-Burnett **1**:61
James Gould Cozzens **1**:66
Edward Dahlberg **1**:71
John Dos Passos **1**:79; **8**:181
Margaret Drabble **22**:120
Lawrence Durrell **1**:85
James T. Farrell **1**:98; **8**:205
William Faulkner **1**:101
E. M. Forster **1**:104
John Fowles **4**:170
William Golding **1**:120
Nadine Gordimer **33**:179
Henry Green **2**:178
Graham Greene **1**:132
L. P. Hartley **2**:181; **22**:211
Ernest Hemingway **1**:142
Richard Hughes **1**:149
Aldous Huxley **1**:150
Christopher Isherwood **1**:155
Pamela Hansford Johnson
    1:160; **27**:217
Doris Lessing **1**:173
Richard Llewellyn **7**:206
Bernard Malamud **1**:197
Olivia Manning **19**:300
John P. Marquand **2**:271
Carson McCullers **1**:208
Henry Miller **1**:221
Wright Morris **1**:231
John Mortimer **28**:282
Iris Murdoch **1**:234
P. H. Newby **2**:310
Flannery O'Connor **1**:255
John O'Hara **1**:260
William Plomer **4**:406
Anthony Powell **1**:277
Henry Roth **2**:377; **11**:487
J. D. Salinger **1**:298
William Sansom **2**:383
C. P. Snow **1**:316
John Steinbeck **1**:325
William Styron **1**:330
Frank Swinnerton **31**:426
Allen Tate **2**:427
Gore Vidal **22**:434
Robert Penn Warren **1**:355
Evelyn Waugh **1**:358
Glenway Wescott **13**:592
Rebecca West **7**:525
Angus Wilson **2**:471

Allen, Ward
Donald Davidson **2**:112

Allen, Woody
S. J. Perelman **15**:419

Alley, Phillip W.
Franklyn M. Branley **21**:18

Allott, Miriam
Graham Greene **18**:193

Allsop, Kenneth
J. P. Donleavy **6**:139
Eva Figes **31**:161
Thomas Hinde **6**:238

Alm, Richard S.
Betty Cavanna **12**:99
Maureen Daly **17**:89
Mary Stolz **12**:548

Alma, Roger
Philippa Pearce **21**:291

Almansi, Guido
Alan Ayckbourn **18**:27
Italo Calvino **22**:90
Mario Luzi **13**:354

Almon, Bert
Gary Snyder **32**:394

Alonso, J. M.
Rafael Alberti **7**:11
Jorge Luis Borges **9**:117

Alpern, Joyce
Christopher Collier and James
    L. Collier **30**:71

Alpert, Hollis
Vincent Canby **13**:131
Howard Fast **23**:156
C. S. Forester **35**:169
Daniel Fuchs **8**:220
William Kotzwinkle **14**:311
Olivia Manning **19**:300
Ernesto Sabato **23**:375
Budd Schulberg **7**:402
Melvin Van Peebles **20**:410

Alstrum, James J.
Ernesto Cardenal **31**:74

Altbach, Philip G.
Jonathan Kozol **17**:252

Alter, Robert
S. Y. Agnon **4**:11
Yehuda Amichai **9**:23
John Barth **9**:71
Donald Barthelme **8**:49
Saul Bellow **3**:48, 49; **33**:69
Heinrich Böll **27**:68
Jorge Luis Borges **2**:76; **6**:94
R. V. Cassill **23**:104
Leslie Epstein **27**:130
Leslie A. Fiedler **13**:212
John Hollander **8**:298
Jerzy Kosinski **2**:232
Doris Lessing **22**:285
Norman Mailer **3**:312; **11**:342
Bernard Malamud **3**:30, 321;
    27:299, 305
Claude Mauriac **9**:366
Elsa Morante **8**:402
Alberto Moravia **18**:346
Vladimir Nabokov **2**:302; **8**:414
Hugh Nissenson **4**:380
Flann O'Brien **7**:269
Amos Oz **33**:299
Manuel Puig **10**:420
Thomas Pynchon **9**:443
Raymond Queneau **10**:429
Philip Rahv **24**:353
Alain Robbe-Grillet **6**:468
Earl Rovit **7**:383
André Schwarz-Bart **4**:480
Isaac Bashevis Singer **11**:501;
    15:507
J.I.M. Stewart **7**:465
William Styron **15**:527
John Updike **2**:444
Kurt Vonnegut, Jr. **8**:531
Elie Wiesel **3**:526
Abraham B. Yehoshua **13**:618;
    31:467

Alterman, Loraine
Ray Davies **21**:96
Jesse Jackson **12**:291
Gordon Lightfoot **26**:279
Carly Simon **26**:408
Andrew Lloyd Webber and Tim
    Rice **21**:428

Altieri, Charles
Robert Creeley **2**:107
Robert Duncan **15**:191
Denise Levertov **28**:238
Robert Lowell **15**:345
Charles Olson **29**:332
Gary Snyder **32**:390

Altman, Billy
Elvis Costello **21**:75
Ray Davies **21**:102
Peter Townshend **17**:537, 539
Brian Wilson **12**:652

Alvarez, A.
Aharon Appelfeld **23**:38
John Berryman **2**:58; **3**:65
Albert Camus **4**:89
William Empson **19**:154
Eva Figes **31**:168
E. M. Forster **1**:109
Carlos Fuentes **22**:165
Dashiell Hammett **3**:218
Seamus Heaney **25**:247
Zbigniew Herbert **9**:271
Russell C. Hoban **25**:266
Miroslav Holub **4**:233
Edwin Honig **33**:210
Dan Jacobson **14**:289
Philip Larkin **3**:275
Robert Lowell **3**:300
Hugh MacDiarmid **4**:309
Norman Mailer **3**:312
Cynthia Ozick **28**:351
David Plante **23**:346
Sylvia Plath **2**:335; **3**:388
Jean Rhys **4**:445
Jean-Paul Sartre **4**:475
Edith Sitwell **9**:493
Aleksandr I. Solzhenitsyn **7**:436
Robert Stone **23**:428
Patrick White **3**:521
Elie Wiesel **3**:527
Yvor Winters **4**:589

Alvia, Sister
Robert Newton Peck **17**:339

Aly, Lucile F.
John G. Neihardt **32**:336

Amacher, Richard E.
Edward Albee **1**:5

Amado, Jorge
João Ubaldo Ribeiro **10**:436
João Guimarães Rosa **23**:348

Amanuddin, Syed
James Welch **14**:559

Amberg, George
Jean Cocteau **16**:229

Ambrose, Stephen E.
Cornelius Ryan **7**:385

Ambrosetti, Ronald
Eric Ambler **9**:20

Ames, Alfred C.
Joy Adamson **17**:5

Ames, Carol
John Berryman **25**:96

Ames, Evelyn
J. B. Priestley **5**:351

Ames, Katrine
Gordon Parks **16**:460

Amiel, Barbara
Margaret Atwood **15**:37
Jack Hodgins **23**:228
Chaim Potok **14**:429
A. W. Purdy **14**:435
Jane Rule **27**:422

Amis, Kingsley
Ray Bradbury **10**:68
Arthur C. Clarke **13**:155
Ivy Compton-Burnett **1**:60
Ilya Ehrenburg **18**:132
Leslie A. Fiedler **4**:159
Ian Fleming **30**:137, 139
Christopher Isherwood **14**:278
Philip Roth **1**:293
Elizabeth Taylor **29**:408
Arnold Wesker **3**:517

Amis, Martin
J. G. Ballard **6**:27
Saul Bellow **33**:70
Malcolm Bradbury **32**:56
Peter De Vries **7**:77
Bruce Jay Friedman **5**:127
Ernest J. Gaines **3**:179
John Hawkes **7**:141
Philip Larkin **13**:337
Iris Murdoch **4**:367
Vladimir Nabokov **8**:412
Shiva Naipaul **32**:325
Roman Polanski **16**:472
Philip Roth **6**:475
John Updike **34**:293
Fay Weldon **11**:565
Angus Wilson **34**:582

Ammons, A. R.
Mark Strand **18**:514

Amory, Cleveland
Art Buchwald **33**:94
Rod McKuen **1**:210
Rod Serling **30**:357

Amprimoz, Alexandre
Joe Rosenblatt **15**:448

Amy, Jenny L.
Robert Newton Peck **17**:343

Anders, Jaroslaw
Tadeusz Konwicki **28**:209

Andersen, Richard
Robert Coover **32**:124

Anderson, A. J.
Charles Addams **30**:16
Jeffrey Archer **28**:11
Russell Baker **31**:32
Art Buchwald **33**:93

Anderson, David
Albert Camus **4**:89, 90
William Golding **3**:197, 198
Jean-Paul Sartre **4**:477

Anderson, David C.
L. E. Sissman **9**:491

Anderson, Elliott
Vladimir Nabokov **3**:354

Anderson, George
Piri Thomas **17**:499

Anderson, H. T.
Herbert Gold **14**:208
Erich Segal **10**:467

Anderson, Isaac
Agatha Christie **12**:114
August Derleth **31**:127, 128
Joseph Krumgold **12**:316

Anderson, Jack
Philip Levine **4**:286
George MacBeth **2**:252

Anderson, James Douglas
Louis R. Harlan **34**:190

Anderson, Jervis
James Baldwin **8**:41
Michael Thelwell **22**:415

Anderson, Joseph L.
Akira Kurosawa **16**:396

Anderson, Lindsay
Luis Buñuel **16**:129
Vittorio De Sica **20**:84
John Ford **16**:305, 306
Elia Kazan **16**:362
Fritz Lang **20**:205
Yasujiro Ozu **16**:447

Anderson, Michael
Edward Bond **6**:85
Tennessee Williams **11**:577

Anderson, Patrick
David Cudlip **34**:39
Allen Drury **37**:110
Ward Just **4**:266

Anderson, Poul
Poul Anderson **15**:14
Fritz Leiber **25**:303
Erich von Däniken **30**:423

Anderson, Quentin
Leon Edel **29**:171
Vladimir Nabokov **3**:351

Anderson, Reed
Juan Goytisolo **10**:244; **23**:184

Anderson, Robert W.
Helen MacInnes **27**:279

Anderson, Sherwood
Carl Sandburg **35**:342

Anderson, William
Stephen Sondheim **30**:397

André, Michael
Robert Creeley **2**:107

Andrejevic, Helen B.
Walter Dean Myers **35**:296

Andrews, James H.
William F. Buckley, Jr. **37**:62

Andrews, Nigel
John Cassavetes **20**:47
Sam Peckinpah **20**:277
Jerzy Skolimowski **20**:350

Andrews, Peter
Philip Caputo **32**:105
Michael Crichton **6**:119
Peter De Vries **28**:108
Ken Follett **18**:157
Arthur Hailey **5**:157
Richard F. Hugo **32**:249
Pat Jordon **37**:194
Peter Maas **29**:305
D. M. Pinkwater **35**:319
Martin Cruz Smith **25**:413
Irving Stone **7**:471

Andrews, Sheryl B.
Barbara Corcoran **17**:70
James D. Forman **21**:119
Virginia Hamilton **26**:149
S. E. Hinton **30**:204
Isabelle Holland **21**:148
Mollie Hunter **21**:158
Andre Norton **12**:460
Barbara Wersba **30**:430

Angell, Roger
Brian De Palma **20**:80
Bob Fosse **20**:126
Steve Martin **30**:249
Gene Roddenberry **17**:413
Paul Schrader **26**:395
Lina Wertmüller **16**:600

Angier, Carole
Stevie Smith **25**:421

Angle, Paul M.
Milton Meltzer **26**:299

Angogo, R.
Chinua Achebe **11**:2

Annan, Gabriele
Aharon Appelfeld **23**:37
Simone de Beauvoir **4**:47
Heinrich Böll **9**:111
Laurie Colwin **23**:129
I. Compton-Burnett **34**:500
Anita Desai **19**:133
Iris Murdoch **11**:388
Jean Rhys **19**:391
Hilary Spurling **34**:500
Sylvia Townsend Warner **19**:459

Annan, Noel
E. M. Forster **4**:166

Anozie, Sunday O.
Christopher Okigbo **25**:350

Anselm, Felix
Hermann Hesse **17**:194

Ansen, David
Lillian Hellman **34**:349
George Roy Hill **26**:208
Stephen King **26**:243; **37**:206
Sidney Poitier **26**:362
Prince **35**:328

Ansorge, Peter
Howard Brenton **31**:59
Trevor Griffiths **13**:256
David Hare **29**:213
Sam Shepard **6**:495
Snoo Wilson **33**:460

Anthony, Robert J.
Isaac Asimov **26**:38

Appel, Alfred, Jr.
Fritz Lang **20**:211
Vladimir Nabokov **1**:240; **2**:300

Appel, Benjamin
Nelson Algren **33**:11
Glendon Swarthout **35**:399

Apple, Max
T. Coraghessan Boyle **36**:56
John Gardner **10**:222

Appleyard, Bryan
Alan Ayckbourn **33**:46
Samuel Beckett **29**:64

Aptheker, Herbert
W.E.B. Du Bois **13**:180

Araújo, Virginia de
Carlos Drummond de Andrade **18**:4

Arbuthnot, May Hill
Frank Bonham **12**:53
Franklyn M. Branley **21**:18
Betsy Byars **35**:73
Julia W. Cunningham **12**:164
Maureen Daly **17**:91
Jesse Jackson **12**:290
Joseph Krumgold **12**:320, 321
Madeleine L'Engle **12**:350
Emily Cheney Neville **12**:452
Alvin Silverstein and Virginia B. Silverstein **17**:455
Mary Stolz **12**:553
Noel Streatfeild **21**:412
Rosemary Sutcliff **26**:436
Jade Snow Wong **17**:566

Archer, Eileen A.
Diana Wynne Jones **26**:228

Archer, Eugene
Ingmar Bergman **16**:46
Bernardo Bertolucci **16**:83
Federico Fellini **16**:271
John Huston **20**:164, 165
Sam Peckinpah **20**:272

Archer, Marguerite
Jean Anouilh **13**:18

Archer, Mildred
John Donovan **35**:142

Arendt, Hannah
W. H. Auden **6**:21

Argus
Josef von Sternberg **20**:370

Arias, Ron
Rudolfo A. Anaya **23**:25

Aristarco, Guido
Satyajit Ray **16**:474

Arkhurst, Joyce E.
Mildred D. Taylor **21**:419

Arland, Marcel
Françoise Sagan **17**:416

Arlen, M. J.
Art Buchwald **33**:90

Arlen, Michael J.
Alex Haley **12**:254

Armes, Roy
Michelangelo Antonioni **20**:38
Robert Bresson **16**:114
Claude Chabrol **16**:170
Jean Cocteau **16**:228
Federico Fellini **16**:284
Pier Paolo Pasolini **20**:265
Alain Resnais **16**:505
Alain Robbe-Grillet **4**:449
Agnès Varda **16**:556

Armour, Robert A.
Fritz Lang **20**:214

Armour-Hileman, Vicki
Gary Soto **32**:403

Armstrong, Judith
Philippa Pearce **21**:292

Armstrong, Louise
John Donovan **35**:142

Armstrong, Marion
Fletcher Knebel **14**:308

Armstrong, William A.
Sean O'Casey **1**:252; **9**:407

Arnason, David
Amos Tutuola **14**:540

Arnett, Janet
Roderick L. Haig-Brown **21**:146

Arnez, Nancy L.
Alex Haley **12**:250

Arnheim, Rudolf
Maya Deren **16**:253

Arnold, A. James
Aimé Césaire **19**:99

Arnold, Armin
Friedrich Dürrenmatt **15**:193

Arnold, Gary
Woody, Allen **16**:4

Arnold, Marilyn
John Gardner **18**:177

Arnolt, Vicki
Hermann Hesse **17**:215

Arnson, Curtis
A. B. Yehoshua **31**:470

Aronowitz, Alfred G.
John Lennon and Paul McCartney **12**:364
Peter Townshend **17**:526

Aronson, James
Donald Barthelme **1**:18
Saul Bellow **1**:33
James Dickey **1**:73
John Fowles **1**:109
John Knowles **1**:169
John Updike **1**:345
Eudora Welty **1**:363

Aros, Andrew
Christopher Fry **14**:189

Arpin, Gary Q.
John Berryman **10**:48
Edwin Honig **33**:215

Arrowsmith, William
Dino Buzzati **36**:88

Arthos, John
E. E. Cummings **12**:146

Arthur, George
Monty Python **21**:226

Arthur, George W.
Judy Blume **12**:47
Robert Crumb **17**:85

Artinian, Robert W.
Jean-Paul Sartre **24**:411

Arvedson, Peter
Roy A. Gallant **17**:131

Arvin, Newton
Leon Edel **29**:168

Asahina, Robert
Woody Allen **16**:12
Mel Brooks **12**:80
Caryl Churchill **31**:86
Brian De Palma **20**:82
Athol Fugard **25**:175
Jean-Luc Godard **20**:153
Werner Herzog **16**:334
George Roy Hill **26**:208
Steve Martin **30**:249
Pier Paolo Pasolini **20**:270
Eric Rohmer **16**:538
Sam Shepard **34**:270
Joan Micklin Silver **20**:346
Steven Spielberg **20**:366
Lanford Wilson **36**:463

Ascher, Carol
Simone de Beauvoir **31**:39, 42

Ascherson, Neal
Beryl Bainbridge **14**:38
Breyten Breytenbach **37**:49
André Brink **36**:72
Leslie Epstein **27**:129
Rolf Hochhuth **18**:256
György Konrád **10**:304
Tadeusz Konwicki **8**:327
Milan Kundera **4**:278
Tadeusz Rózewicz **9**:465
Yevgeny Yevtushenko **1**:382

Aschkenasy, Nehama
Amos Oz **27**:361

Asein, Samuel Omo
Alex La Guma **19**:276
Ezekiel Mphahlele **25**:342
Derek Walcott **25**:451

Ashbery, John
A. R. Ammons **2**:13
Elizabeth Bishop **9**:89
Philip Booth **23**:75
James Schuyler **23**:390

Ashburn, Frank D.
William F. Buckley, Jr. **37**:56

Ashcroft, W. D.
Janet Frame **22**:146

Ashley, L. F.
Rosemary Sutcliff **26**:433

Ashlin, John
William Mayne **12**:390

Ashton, Dore
Octavio Paz **10**:392

Ashton, Thomas L.
C. P. Snow **4**:504

Asimov, Isaac
Arthur C. Clarke **35**:117
Roy A. Gallant **17**:127, 128
Carl Sagan **30**:338

Asinof, Eliot
Pete Hamill **10**:251

Asnani, Shyam M.
Mulk Raj Anand **23**:21

Aspel, Alexander
Ivar Ivask **14**:286

Aspler, Tony
William F. Buckley, Jr. **7**:36
William Gaddis **8**:226
Josef Škvorecký **15**:510

Astor, Judy
Italo Calvino **33**:99

Astrachan, Anthony
Joseph Brodsky **36**:77
Agnes Eckhardt Nixon **21**:246
Vladimir Voinovich **10**:509

Atchity, Kenneth
Jorge Luis Borges **2**:71
Virginia Spencer Carr **34**:423
John Dos Passos **34**:423
Leon Edel **29**:174
James Jones **3**:261
Stephen King **26**:241
Robert Penn Warren **4**:581

Athanason, Arthur N.
Pavel Kohout **13**:326

Atheling, William, Jr.
Isaac Asimov **3**:17
Arthur C. Clarke **1**:58
Harlan Ellison **1**:93
Robert A. Heinlein **1**:139;
    3:227

Atherton, J. S.
Anaïs Nin **11**:398

Atherton, Stan
Margaret Laurence **6**:290

Athos, John
L. P. Hartley **22**:214

Atkins, Anselm
Robert Bolt **14**:90

Atkins, John
L. P. Hartley **2**:182

Atkinson, Bert
Donald Hall **37**:149

Atkinson, Brooks
Robert Anderson **23**:30
Enid Bagnold **25**:76
Sally Benson **17**:49
Paddy Chayefsky **23**:112
William Gibson **23**:174, 175
Paul Green **25**:195
Lorraine Hansberry **17**:182
Fritz Hochwälder **36**:232
Garson Kanin **22**:230
Jean Kerr **22**:254, 255

Arthur Miller **26:315
Elmer Rice **7**:361
Irwin Shaw **23**:397
Stephen Sondheim **30**:376, 377

Atkinson, Joan L.
Sue Ellen Bridgers **26**:92

Atkinson, Michael
Robert Bly **10**:58

Atlas, Jacoba
Mel Brooks **12**:78
Joni Mitchell **12**:436

Atlas, James
Russell Banks **37**:27
Samuel Beckett **6**:37
Frank Bidart **33**:76
Marie-Claire Blais **6**:82
C.D.B. Bryan **29**:105
Raymond Carver **22**:102
J. V. Cunningham **3**:122
Peter Davison **28**:102
Alan Dugan **6**:144
Leon Edel **34**:535
John Gardner **34**:548
Paul Goodman **4**:198
Graham Greene **27**:172
Mark Harris **19**:206
John Irving **23**:248
Randall Jarrell **6**:261
Galway Kinnell **5**:217
Thomas McGrath **28**:277
W. S. Merwin **5**:287
Wright Morris **37**:315
John O'Hara **6**:386
Kenneth Rexroth **6**:451
Laura Riding **7**:375
Delmore Schwartz **4**:478
L. E. Sissman **9**:490
Christina Stead **32**:411
James Tate **2**:431
Richard Tillinghast **29**:414
John Updike **34**:294
C. K. Williams **33**:444
Angus Wilson **34**:583
Richard Yates **23**:482

Attanasio, Paul
C.L.R. James **33**:123

Attebery, Brian
Lloyd Alexander **35**:26
James Thurber **25**:437

Atwell, Lee
Michelangelo Antonioni **20**:39
George Roy Hill **26**:199

Atwood, Margaret
Frederick Barthelme **36**:50
Ann Beattie **18**:38
Marie-Claire Blais **6**:80
E. L. Doctorow **18**:126
Janet Frame **22**:148
Susan B. Hill **4**:227
Erica Jong **6**:267
A. G. Mojtabai **5**:293
Tillie Olsen **13**:432
Marge Piercy **14**:420; **27**:381
Sylvia Plath **11**:451
A. W. Purdy **14**:430
James Reaney **13**:472
Adrienne Rich **3**:429; **11**:478;
    36:365

Cynthia Propper Seton **27:425
Audrey Thomas **7**:472; **37**:417

Aubert, Rosemary
Patrick Lane **25**:288

Auchincloss, Eve
Vera Brittain **23**:93
Brigid Brophy **29**:93
Bruce Chatwin **28**:71
Mavis Gallant **18**:171
R. K. Narayan **7**:257
Gilbert Rogin **18**:457

Auchincloss, Louis
Katherine Anne Porter **7**:316

Aucouturier, Michel
Aleksandr I. Solzhenitsyn **7**:432

Auden, W. H.
Joseph Brodsky **4**:77
Cleanth Brooks **24**:101
Kenneth Burke **24**:121
William Dickey **28**:116
Loren Eiseley **7**:90
Daniel Hoffman **23**:237
Christopher Isherwood **14**:281
Chester Kallman **2**:221
C. S. Lewis **27**:261
Adrienne Rich **36**:364
J.R.R. Tolkien **1**:336; **12**:564
Andrei Voznesensky **1**:349
James Wright **28**:461

Auriol, Jean-George
René Clair **20**:57

Auster, Paul
John Ashbery **6**:14
John Hollander **8**:300
Laura Riding **7**:375
Giuseppe Ungaretti **7**:484

Austin, Allan E.
Elizabeth Bowen **22**:61
Roy Fuller **28**:155

Austin, Anthony
Ilya Ehrenburg **34**:434
Anatol Goldberg **34**:434

Auty, Martyn
John Landis **26**:273

Avant, John Alfred
Eleanor Bergstein **4**:55
Rosellen Brown **32**:63
Gail Godwin **5**:142
Gayl Jones **6**:266
José Lezama Lima **4**:291
Carson McCullers **12**:427
Joyce Carol Oates **6**:371, 373
Tillie Olsen **4**:386
Patrick White **5**:486

Averill, Deborah
Frank O'Connor **14**:395

Avery, Evelyn Gross
Richard Wright **14**:597

Axel-Lute, Melanie
Will Harriss **34**:193

Axelrod, George
Gore Vidal **4**:556

Axelrod, Rise B.
Anne Sexton **15**:471

Axelrod, Steven
Robert Lowell 2:249

Axelrod, Steven Gould
Saul Bellow 6:60
Allen Ginsberg 36:192
Robert Lowell 37:235

Axhelm, Peter M.
Saul Bellow 13:66
Allen Ginsberg 36:192
William Golding 10:232

Axthelm, Pete
Peter Gent 29:180
Robert Lipsyte 21:210
Gilbert Rogin 18:457

Ayd, Joseph D., S.J.
Louis Auchincloss 18:26

Ayer, A. J.
Albert Camus 9:152

Ayers, William R.
Lewis Thomas 35:414

Ayling, Ronald
Sean O'Casey 11:409; 15:405

Ayo, Nicholas
Edward Lewis Wallant 10:515

Ayre, John
Austin C. Clarke 8:143
Mavis Gallant 7:110
V. S. Naipaul 13:407
Mordecai Richler 5:378

Baar, Ron
Ezra Pound 1:276

Babbitt, Natalie
Joan Aiken 35:19
Paula Danziger 21:85
Lois Duncan 26:106
William Mayne 12:395
Katherine Paterson 12:403, 486
Robert Westall 17:559

Babby, Ellen R.
Michel Tremblay 29:427

Babenko, Vickie A.
Yevgeny Yevtushenko 13:620

Bach, Alice
Norma Klein 30:238
Sandra Scoppettone 26:400
Jill Paton Walsh 35:432

Bachem, Michael
Christa Wolf 29:464

Bachman, Charles R.
Sam Shepard 17:442

Bachmann, Gideon
Shirley Clarke 16:215
Federico Fellini 16:283
Jean Renoir 20:290
Luchino Visconti 16:572

Backscheider, Nick
John Updike 5:452

Backscheider, Paula
John Updike 5:452

Bacon, Leonard
Eric Bentley 24:43

Bacon, Martha
John Donovan 35:140
Walter Farley 17:118

Bacon, Terry R.
Robert Creeley 11:137

Bader, Julia
Vladimir Nabokov 23:303

Baer, Barbara L.
Harriette Arnow 7:16
Christina Stead 5:403

Bagchee, Syhamal
John Fowles 33:166

Bagdikian, Ben H.
Gay Talese 37:391

Bagnall, Norma
Robert Cormier 30:84
M. E. Kerr 35:248
Norma Klein 30:241

Bagshaw, Marguerite
Farley Mowat 26:337

Bailey, Anthony
James Baldwin 17:38
A. J. Cronin 32:138
John Gregory Dunne 28:124
David Plante 23:342

Bailey, Bruce
George Ryga 14:474

Bailey, Hilary
Maya Angelou 35:33

Bailey, James
Andrei Voznesensky 15:553

Bailey, Jennifer
Norman Mailer 28:255

Bailey, Nancy I.
Roch Carrier 13:142

Bailey, O. L.
Eric Ambler 6:2
Robert Bloch 33:84
Dick Francis 2:142
George V. Higgins 4:223
Maj Sjöwall 7:501
Mickey Spillane 3:469
Per Wahlöö 7:501

Bailey, Paul
Maya Angelou 35:33
James Baldwin 15:43
Elizabeth Bishop 32:44
Isak Dinesen 29:164
Gabriel García Márquez 3:180
Nadine Gordimer 10:239
Kazuo Ishiguro 27:202
P. D. James 18:274
Yasunari Kawabata 2:223
Louis L'Amour 25:278
Primo Levi 37:222
Brian Moore 3:341
Alberto Moravia 11:384
James Purdy 2:351
Barbara Pym 37:379
Philip Roth 3:437
Muriel Spark 5:400
David Storey 2:426
Elizabeth Taylor 29:410
Paul Theroux 11:531

Gore Vidal 6:550
Tennessee Williams 7:544

Bailey, Peter
Nikki Giovanni 2:165
Melvin Van Peebles 2:447

Bailey, Wilfrid C.
Margaret Mead 37:278

Bair, Deirdre
Russell Banks 37:27
Simone de Beauvoir 31:42
Samuel Beckett 6:43

Baird, James
Djuna Barnes 8:49

Baird, Jock
Paul McCartney 35:293

Baker, A. T.
A. R. Ammons 5:30

Baker, Betty
Scott O'Dell 30:269

Baker, Carlos
Truman Capote 19:79
Ernest Hemingway 6:234;
30:180
Elizabeth Spencer 22:401
John Steinbeck 21:366
Jessamyn West 17:546

Baker, Charles A.
Robert Altman 16:25

Baker, David
Marvin Bell 31:51

Baker, Donald W.
Edward Dahlberg 7:63

Baker, Houston A., Jr.
James Baldwin 1:16
Arna Bontemps 1:37
Gwendolyn Brooks 15:92
Sterling A. Brown 1:47
W.E.B. Du Bois 1:80
Ralph Ellison 1:95; 3:145
Leon Forrest 4:163
Langston Hughes 1:149
LeRoi Jones 1:163
Ann Petry 1:266
Ishmael Reed 2:369; 6:449
Jean Toomer 1:341
Richard Wright 1:380

Baker, Howard
Caroline Gordon 6:206
Katherine Anne Porter 1:273

Baker, James R.
William Golding 3:200; 17:169,
175

Baker, John Ross
Wayne C. Booth 24:94

Baker, Kenneth
Walter Abish 22:18
Leon Rooke 25:391

Baker, Nina Brown
Madeleine L'Engle 12:344

Baker, Peter
Lindsay Anderson 20:12
Vittorio De Sica 20:89

Baker, Rob
Albert Innaurato 21:196

Baker, Roger
Poul Anderson 15:11
Beryl Bainbridge 4:39
James Blish 14:83
John Buell 10:81
Paula Fox 8:217
Janet Frame 3:164
John Hawkes 1:139
Jerzy Kosinski 1:172
Alistair MacLean 13:359
Larry McMurtry 3:333
Harold Robbins 5:378
Herman Wouk 9:580
Rudolph Wurlitzer 2:483
Helen Yglesias 7:558
Roger Zelazny 21:466

Baker, Ruth
Frank B. Gilbreth, Jr. and
Ernestine Gilbreth Carey
17:152

Baker, Sheridan
Alan Paton 25:358

Baker, William
William Carlos Williams
13:606

Baker, William E.
Jacques Prévert 15:437

Bakerman, Jane S.
Toni Morrison 22:318
Ruth Rendell 28:385
May Sarton 14:481

Bakker, J.
William Gaddis 19:189

Bakshy, Alexander
Frank Capra 16:153
Charles Chaplin 16:188
René Clair 20:57, 58
Rouben Mamoulian 16:418,
419

Balakian, Anna
Louis Aragon 22:42
André Breton 9:132; 15:90
René Char 9:164
Monique Wittig 22:472

Balakian, Nona
Taylor Caldwell 28:58

Baldanza, Frank
Alberto Moravia 2:293
Iris Murdoch 1:235
James Purdy 2:350; 4:424;
10:421

Baldauf, Gretchen S.
C. S. Adler 35:15
Larry Bograd 35:63

Baldeshwiler, Eileen
Flannery O'Connor 1:255

Balducci, Carolyn
M. E. Kerr 12:297
Norma Klein 30:237

Baldwin, James
Alex Haley 8:259
Langston Hughes 35:216
Norman Mailer 8:364
Richard Wright 21:438

Bales, Kent
Richard Brautigan **5**:71

Ballard, J. G.
Philip K. Dick **10**:138
Harlan Ellison **13**:203
Frederik Pohl **18**:410
Robert Silverberg **7**:425

Ballet, Arthur H.
Thornton Wilder **35**:439

Balliett, Whitney
James Baldwin **17**:44
Ann Beattie **18**:40
R. V. Cassill **23**:103
Richard Condon **4**:105
C.L.R. James **33**:224
Pamela Hansford Johnson **27**:218
William Melvin Kelley **22**:247
Walter M. Miller, Jr. **30**:255
Clancy Sigal **7**:424

Ballif, Gene
Jorge Luis Borges **6**:87
Vladimir Nabokov **6**:351
Sylvia Plath **11**:449
Alain Robbe-Grillet **6**:464
Nathalie Sarraute **8**:469

Ballstadt, Carl
Earle Birney **6**:78

Balm, Trixie A.
David Bowie **17**:63

Baltensperger, Peter
Robertson Davies **25**:129

Bambara, Toni Cade
Gwendolyn Brooks **2**:81
June Jordan **23**:256
Ntozake Shange **25**:396

Bamborough, J. B.
F. R. Leavis **24**:300

Banas, Mary
T.E.D. Klein **34**:71

Band, Arnold J.
S. Y. Agnon **14**:2

Bander, Edward J.
Jules Archer **12**:16

Bandler, Michael J.
Roger Kahn **30**:233
Chaim Potok **14**:430; **26**:369
Elie Wiesel **11**:570

Banfield, Beryle
Rosa Guy **26**:143

Bangs, Lester
Chuck Berry **17**:51
David Bowie **17**:63
David Byrne **26**:97
Jimmy Cliff **21**:64
Mick Jagger and Keith Richard **17**:225, 226, 236
John Lennon **35**:266
John Lennon and Paul McCartney **12**:381
Bob Marley **17**:270, 271
Paul McCartney **35**:283
Joni Mitchell **12**:437
Jim Morrison **17**:289, 290, 292

Van Morrison **21**:234, 238
Jimmy Page and Robert Plant **12**:474, 476
Lou Reed **21**:306, 310, 317
Bob Seger **35**:381, 382
Bruce Springsteen **17**:481
Lily Tomlin **17**:523
Peter Townshend **17**:536
Frank Zappa **17**:586, 587, 591

Banks, Joyce
Ruth M. Arthur **12**:28

Banks, R. Jeff
Mickey Spillane **13**:527

Banks, Russell
William McPherson **34**:85
Joyce Carol Oates **19**:355

Bann, Stephen
Lawrence Durrell **27**:99
Elaine Feinstein **36**:172
Ernst Jandl **34**:195
William Kotzwinkle **35**:257
Seán O'Faoláin **32**:341
J.I.M. Stewart **32**:422

Bannerman, David
Allan W. Eckert **17**:104

Bannikov, Nikolai
Anna Akhmatova **25**:29

Banning, Charles Leslie
William Gaddis **10**:210

Barber, Michael
Simon Raven **14**:443
Gore Vidal **4**:557

Barber, Raymond W.
Jean Lee Latham **12**:324

Barbera, Jack Vincent
John Berryman **8**:88

Barbour, Douglas
Marilyn R. Bowering **32**:47
Matt Cohen **19**:111
Louis Dudek **11**:160
Ursula K. Le Guin **22**:265
Gwendolyn MacEwan **13**:358
B. P. Nichol **18**:368
Michael Ondaatje **14**:407
Joe Rosenblatt **15**:446
Rudy Wiebe **6**:566
Gene Wolfe **25**:472
Roger Zelazny **21**:466

Barbour, Joan
Anne McCaffrey **17**:282

Barclay, Pat
Robertson Davies **7**:72
Farley Mowat **26**:344

Bardeche, Maurice
René Clair **20**:61

Bargad, Warren
Yehuda Amichai **22**:29
Amos Oz **8**:436
Abraham B. Yehoshua **13**:617

Bargainnier, Earl F.
Agatha Christie **12**:126
Peter Dickinson **35**:132

Barge, Laura
Samuel Beckett **10**:34; **11**:39

Bargen, Doris G.
Stanley Elkin **27**:122

Barghoorn, Frederick C.
Aleksandr I. Solzhenitsyn **4**:508

Barish, Jonas A.
Jean-Paul Sartre **24**:408

Barker, A. L.
Edna O'Brien **5**:311

Barker, Felix
Alan Ayckbourn **33**:48

Barker, Frank Granville
Margaret Drabble **10**:163
J. B. Priestly **9**:442

Barker, George
Brian Aldiss **5**:14

Barker, Shirley
Bruce Lancaster **36**:244

Barkham, John
A. J. Cronin **32**:137, 138
Nadine Gordimer **33**:176
Alan Paton **25**:359

Barksdale, Richard K.
Gwendolyn Brooks **5**:75
Langston Hughes **15**:294

Barnard, Caroline King
Sylvia Plath **17**:361

Barnden, Louise
Eva Figes **31**:166

Barnes, Anne
Laurie Colwin **23**:128

Barnes, Bart
J. B. Priestley **34**:362
Irwin Shaw **34**:368

Barnes, Clive
Enid Bagnold **25**:78
John Bishop **10**:54
Alice Childress **12**:104, 105
Caryl Churchill **31**:85, 89
Michael Cristofer **28**:96
Gretchen Cryer **21**:77, 78, 80
Lawrence Ferlinghetti **2**:134
Harvey Fierstein **33**:154
Athol Fugard **25**:176
Larry Gelbart **21**:126, 127
Jack Gelber **14**:193
Simon Gray **9**:240
John Guare **29**:203, 207
Lorraine Hansberry **17**:191
David Hare **29**:211
Jack Heifner **11**:264
Arthur Kopit **1**:170; **33**:252
David Mamet **34**:219
Mark Medoff **23**:292
Peter Nichols **36**:326, 330
Monty Python **21**:226
John Mortimer **28**:286
Richard O'Brien **17**:322
David Rabe **33**:345
Gerome Ragni and James Rado **17**:378, 380, 383, 386, 387
Anthony Shaffer **19**:413
Sam Shepard **17**:436, 437, 438, 441; **34**:267
Neil Simon **31**:394, 399, 400
Stephen Sondheim **30**:380, 388

Tom Stoppard **1**:328; **34**:274
Elizabeth Swados **12**:556
Lily Tomlin **17**:517
Andrew Lloyd Webber and Tim Rice **21**:425, 427, 430, 432
Michael Weller **10**:525
Hugh Whitemore **37**:447
Lanford Wilson **7**:547; **36**:459, 464

Barnes, Harper
James Tate **2**:431

Barnes, Hazel F.
Simone de Beauvoir **31**:44

Barnes, Howard
Irwin Shaw **23**:396
Tennessee Williams **30**:454

Barnes, John A.
John Gardner **30**:157

Barnes, Julian
Richard Brautigan **5**:72; **9**:124
Vincent Canby **13**:131
Agatha Christie **12**:120
James Clavell **6**:114
Len Deighton **7**:76
B. S. Johnson **6**:264
Pamela Hansford Johnson **7**:184
G. Josipovici **6**:270
Richard Llewellyn **7**:207
Alistair MacLean **13**:359
Vladimir Nabokov **6**:359
Joyce Carol Oates **9**:402
Chaim Potok **26**:373
Richard Price **12**:490

Barnes, Ken
Bob Seger **35**:380

Barnes, Peter
John Huston **20**:162

Barnes, Regina
James T. Farrell **4**:158
Geoffrey Household **11**:277

Barnett, Abraham
John Ehle **27**:102

Barnett, Ursula A.
J. M. Coetzee **23**:121
Ezekiel Mphahlele **25**:336

Barnouw, Dagmar
Elias Canetti **14**:120
Doris Lessing **6**:295

Barnstone, William
Jorge Luis Borges **6**:93

Barnstone, Willis
Jorge Luis Borges **9**:120

Baro, Gene
Dannie Abse **29**:12
Brigid Brophy **29**:91
R. V. Cassill **23**:103
Carolyn Kizer **15**:308
Henri de Montherlant **19**:324
Auberon Waugh **7**:512

Barolini, Helen
Lucio Piccolo **13**:441

Baron, Alexander
Bernard Malamud **2**:268

Barr, Alan P.
Akira Kurosawa **16**:405

Barr, Donald
Robert Bloch **33**:83
Mary Renault **17**:392
George Tabori **19**:435
T. H. White **30**:444

Barrenechea, Ana María
Jorge Luis Borges **1**:38

Barrett, Gerald
Jerzy Kosinski **10**:305

Barrett, Nina
T. Coraghessan Boyle **36**:62

Barrett, William
Nelson Algren **33**:12
Samuel Beckett **2**:48
Albert Camus **2**:99
Arthur C. Clarke **4**:105; **35**:116
William Faulkner **3**:154
Leslie A. Fiedler **24**:188
Romain Gary **25**:186
William Golding **17**:168
Martin Heidegger **24**:271
Ernest Hemingway **3**:238
Hermann Hesse **2**:191
Fletcher Knebel **14**:308
Halldór Laxness **25**:292
Yukio Mishima **27**:336
Philip Rahv **24**:358
Alain Robbe-Grillet **2**:377
Françoise Sagan **17**:423
Leon Uris **7**:491
Yvor Winters **32**:460

Barrow, Craig Wallace
Madeleine L'Engle **12**:351
Paul Muldoon **32**:318

Barrow, Geoffrey R.
Blas de Otero **11**:425

Barry, Elaine
Robert Frost **26**:125

Barry, Iris
Charles Addams **30**:12
Fritz Lang **20**:200, 201
T. H. White **30**:439

Barry, John Brooks
T. S. Eliot **6**:165

Barry, Kevin
John Berryman **6**:65

Barsam, Richard Meran
Leni Riefenstahl **16**:522

Barson, Anthony
Chaim Potok **26**:371

Bartelme, Elizabeth
Alice Walker **27**:454

Barth, J. Robert
Tom Stoppard **34**:274

Barthel, Joan
Joe McGinnis **32**:305

Barthelme, Donald
Werner Herzog **16**:334

Barthes, Roland
Georges Bataille **29**:39
Michel Foucault **31**:171
Raymond Queneau **5**:357

Bartholomay, Julia A.
Howard Nemerov **6**:360

Bartholomew, David
Larry McMurtry **11**:371
Lina Wertmüller **16**:597

Bartkowech, R.
Alain Robbe-Grillet **14**:462

Bartlett, Lee
Lawrence Ferlinghetti **27**:137

Bartley, E. F.
Jacques-Yves Cousteau **30**:105

Bartley, Edward
Donald E. Westlake **33**:438

Barton, Mrs. G. V.
H. F. Brinsmead **21**:28

Barzun, Jaques
Lionel Trilling **11**:539

Baskett, Sam S.
Ronald Bush **34**:530
T. S. Eliot **34**:530

Baskin, Barbara H.
Betsy Byars **35**:72
Virginia Hamilton **26**:156
Zoa Sherburne **30**:363
Barbara Wersba **30**:432

Baskin, John
Helen Hooven Santmyer **33**:360

Basler, Roy P.
Melvin B. Tolson **36**:428

Bass, Judy
Barbara Guest **34**:447
H. D. **34**:447

Bassan, Maurice
Flannery O'Connor **21**:261

Basso, Hamilton
Paul Green **25**:195
Halldór Laxness **25**:291
Andrew Lytle **22**:292

Bassoff, Bruce
William H. Gass **8**:244

Batchelor, John Calvin
Ann Beattie **18**:39
Thomas M. Disch **36**:125
William Golding **17**:179
Mark Helprin **10**:262
Frank Herbert **35**:207
Steven Millhauser **21**:220
Joyce Carol Oates **19**:355
Walker Percy **18**:400
David Plante **23**:344
Peter Rushforth **19**:407

Batchelor, R.
André Malraux **9**:353

Bates, Ernest Sutherland
T. S. Stribling **23**:445
Rebecca West **31**:453

Bates, Evaline
Ezra Pound **3**:397

Bates, Gladys Graham
Sally Benson **17**:48
Laura Z. Hobson **25**:268

Bates, Graham
Pär Lagerkvist **7**:198

Bates, Lewis
E. M. Almedingen **12**:2

Bates, Marston
Peter Matthiessen **32**:286

Bates, Ralph
Edwin Honig **33**:208

Bateson, F. W.
W. H. Auden **6**:24
John Gardner **2**:151

Bateson, John
William Wharton **37**:443

Bati, Anwer
Ken Russell **16**:551

Battcock, Gregory
Andy Warhol **20**:415

Bauer, Arnold
Carl Zuckmayer **18**:555

Bauer, William
John Buell **10**:82

Baugh, Edward
Derek Walcott **25**:450

Bauke, J. P.
Jakov Lind **4**:292

Bauke, Joseph P.
Heinrich Böll **27**:60

Baum, Alwin L.
Alain Robbe-Grillet **14**:458

Baum, Betty
Robert Westall **17**:556

Baumann, Michael L.
B. Traven **8**:520; **11**:535, 537

Baumbach, Elinor
Sylvia Ashton-Warner **19**:22

Baumbach, Jonathan
Robert Bresson **16**:117
Truman Capote **8**:132
R. V. Cassill **23**:106
Ralph Ellison **1**:95
John Hawkes **4**:212
Stanley Kubrick **16**:377
Norman Mailer **4**:318
Bernard Malamud **1**:197, 199
Mary McCarthy **5**:275
Wright Morris **1**:232
Flannery O'Connor **1**:256
Grace Paley **6**:393
J. D. Salinger **1**:299
Scott Sommer **25**:424
William Styron **1**:330
Peter Taylor **1**:333
Michel Tournier **36**:435
Edward Lewis Wallant **10**:511
Robert Penn Warren **1**:355

Baumgarten, Murray
Jorge Luis Borges **19**:52

Baumgold, Julie
Truman Capote **34**:325

Bauska, Barry
Dick Francis **22**:151

Bawer, Bruce
Robert Creeley **36**:121
E. L. Doctorow **37**:92
Gary Snyder **32**:400
C. K. Williams **33**:448

Baxter, Charles
J. R. Salamanca **15**:464

Baxter, John
John Ford **16**:312
Josef von Sternberg **20**:375

Baxter, Ralph C.
Allan W. Eckert **17**:104

Bayles, Martha
Anita Brookner **34**:141

Bayley, John
Anna Akhmatova **11**:9
W. H. Auden **2**:27, 28
Joseph Brodsky **36**:79
Anthony Burgess **4**:85
D. J. Enright **8**:203
E. M. Forster **22**:136
M. M. Kaye **28**:197
Philip Larkin **33**:267
Robert Lowell **4**:296
Czesław Miłosz **31**:260
Amos Oz **11**:428
Vasko Popa **19**:375
Anthony Powell **10**:417
Christopher Reid **33**:349
Varlam Shalamov **18**:479
Stevie Smith **25**:420
Aleksandr I. Solzhenitsyn
  4:511; **7**:444; **10**:479; **18**:499
T. H. White **30**:444
Alexander Zinoviev **19**:486

Baylis, Jamie
Edmund White III **27**:481

Bazarov, Konstantin
Ivo Andrić **8**:20
Heinrich Böll **3**:76
James A. Michener **1**:214
Aleksandr I. Solzhenitsyn
  2:411; **10**:483

Bazelon, David T.
Dashiell Hammett **19**:193

Bazin, André
Robert Bresson **16**:111
Luis Buñuel **16**:131
Charles Chaplin **16**:200
Orson Welles **20**:435

Bazzdlo, Gretchen
Lee Kingman **17**:246

Beach, Glyger G.
Ouida Sebestyen **30**:348

Beach, Joseph Warren
John Dos Passos **25**:137
Carl Van Vechten **33**:388

Beacham, Richard
Howard Brenton **31**:67

Beacham, Walton
Erskine Caldwell **8**:124
Paul West **14**:568

Beagle, Peter S.
J.R.R. Tolkien **12**:567

Critic Index

Bean, Robin
  Bob Fosse **20**:121
  Pier Paolo Pasolini **20**:258, 259
  Carlos Saura **20**:313

Beards, Virginia K.
  Margaret Drabble **3**:128

Beardsley, Doug
  Ralph Gustafson **36**:218

Beardsley, Monroe C.
  Wayne C. Booth **24**:99

Beatie, Bruce A.
  J.R.R. Tolkien **3**:477

Beattie, Munro
  Daryl Hine **15**:282
  Irving Layton **15**:323
  Dorothy Livesay **15**:341
  A.J.M. Smith **15**:516

Beatty, Jack
  Ann Beattie **18**:39
  Isabel Colegate **36**:112
  George V. Higgins **18**:235
  Ward S. Just **27**:230
  Bernard Mac Laverty **31**:256
  William Maxwell **19**:308
  Alice Munro **19**:346
  Shiva Naipaul **32**:326
  V. S. Naipaul **18**:362
  R. K. Narayan **28**:301
  Alexander Theroux **25**:432
  Paul Theroux **15**:534; **28**:427
  William Trevor **25**:443
  William Wharton **37**:435

Beatty, Jerome, Jr.
  Larry Kettelkamp **12**:305

Beatty, Patricia V.
  John Fowles **33**:169

Beatty, Richmond C.
  Donald Davidson **13**:166

Beauchamp, Gorman
  E. M. Forster **10**:183

Beauchamp, William
  Elizabeth Taylor **4**:541

Beaufort, John
  Amlin Gray **29**:201
  Sam Shepard **34**:268
  Martin Sherman **19**:416
  Stephen Sondheim **30**:394
  Tom Stoppard **34**:277
  Elizabeth Swados **12**:560
  Tennessee Williams **19**:473
  Lanford Wilson **36**:465

Beaujour, Michel
  Georges Bataille **29**:45

Beauman, Sally
  Julia O'Faolain **19**:359
  Leon Rooke **25**:390
  Monique Wittig **22**:473

Beaupre, Lee
  Ralph Bakshi **26**:67

Beauvoir, Simone de
  Violette Leduc **22**:260
  Henri de Montherlant **19**:322

Beaver, Harold
  William S. Burroughs **15**:112
  Daniel Fuchs **22**:161
  Allen Ginsburg **13**:241
  Joyce Carol Oates **11**:404
  Flannery O'Connor **21**:278
  Sharon Olds **32**:346

Bechtel, Louise S.
  Margot Benary-Isbert **12**:31, 32
  Franklyn M. Branley **21**:16
  Walter Farley **17**:117
  Henry Gregor Felsen **17**:121,
    122
  Margaret O. Hyde **21**:171
  Carl Sandburg **35**:354
  Zoa Sherburne **30**:360
  Mary Stolz **12**:546
  Noel Streatfeild **21**:399, 400,
    401
  Rosemary Sutcliff **26**:425, 426
  John R. Tunis **12**:596
  Lenora Mattingly Weber **12**:632

Beck, Alfred D.
  Franklyn M. Branley **21**:16
  Margaret O. Hyde **21**:172

Beck, Marilyn
  Rod McKuen **1**:210

Beck, Richard
  Frans Eemil Sillanpää **19**:417

Beck, Warren
  William Faulkner **11**:197;
    14:171

Becker, Alida
  Penelope Lively **32**:277

Becker, Brenda L.
  Mary Gordon **22**:187

Becker, George J.
  John Dos Passos **15**:183
  Upton Sinclair **15**:500
  T. S. Stribling **23**:446

Becker, Lucille Frackman
  Louis Aragon **3**:14
  Michel Butor **11**:80
  Henri de Montherlant **19**:325
  Georges Simenon **2**:398, 399;
    8:488; **18**:481

Becker, May Lamberton
  Betty Cavanna **12**:97, 98
  Maureen Daly **17**:88
  Walter Farley **17**:115
  Henry Gregor Felsen **17**:119
  Esther Forbes **12**:207
  Jesse Jackson **12**:289
  Noel Streatfeild **21**:397, 398,
    399
  John R. Tunis **12**:594, 595
  Leonora Mattingly Weber
    12:631, 632

Becker, Stephen
  Jerome Siegel and Joe Shuster
    21:355

Beckett, Samuel
  Václav Havel **25**:230
  Sean O'Casey **11**:405

Beckham, Barry
  Piri Thomas **17**:499

Beckman, Susan
  Jack Hodgins **23**:234

Beddow, Reid
  Iris Murdoch **22**:328

Bedell, Thomas
  John Gardner **30**:155

Bedford, William
  Robert Lowell **15**:342
  Eugenio Montale **18**:342

Bedient, Calvin
  A. R. Ammons **8**:13
  John Ashbery **15**:29
  W. H. Auden **2**:27
  Samuel Beckett **1**:24
  Marvin Bell **31**:50
  Leonard Cohen **3**:110
  Edward Dahlberg **7**:67
  Donald Davie **10**:120
  Richard Eberhart **11**:178
  T. S. Eliot **13**:196
  Louise Glück **7**:119
  John Hawkes **4**:215
  Seamus Heaney **25**:242
  Anthony Hecht **19**:209
  Joseph Heller **5**:178
  Geoffrey Hill **5**:184
  Daniel Hoffman **6**:243
  Ted Hughes **2**:202; **4**:235
  David Ignatow **7**:182
  Donald Justice **19**:236
  Thomas Kinsella **4**:271; **19**:256
  Philip Larkin **5**:228
  Robert Lowell **3**:303
  George MacBeth **5**:264
  James Merrill **8**:381
  Joyce Carol Oates **2**:314; **3**:362
  Octavio Paz **4**:398
  Sylvia Plath **14**:426
  Jon Silkin **6**:498
  Dave Smith **22**:386
  Stevie Smith **25**:416
  Mark Strand **18**:520
  James Tate **25**:429
  R. S. Thomas **6**:532
  Charles Tomlinson **4**:545, 547
  Mona Van Duy **7**:499
  Robert Penn Warren **10**:523;
    18:534, 538
  John Hall Wheelock **14**:571
  Richard Wilbur **9**:568
  James Wright **5**:520

Bednarczyk, Tony
  Edmund Crispin **22**:111
  William X. Kienzle **25**:274

Bedrosian, Margaret
  William Saroyan **29**:361

Beer, John
  E. M. Forster **22**:131

Beer, Patricia
  W. H. Auden **6**:19
  Beryl Bainbridge **18**:33
  Christopher Fry **14**:188
  Seamus Heaney **14**:241
  Eleanor Hibbert **7**:156
  Lisel Mueller **13**:400
  Alice Munro **10**:357
  Peter Redgrove **6**:447

Beerman, Hans
  Hermann Hesse **17**:199

Beesley, Paddy
  Horst Bienek **11**:48

Begley, John
  Oriana Fallaci **11**:191

Begley, John J., S.J.
  Erich von Däniken **30**:426

Begnal, Michael
  Vladimir Nabokov **23**:309

Behar, Jack
  T. S. Eliot **13**:198
  Rod Serling **30**:355

Behrendt, Stephen
  Richard Tillinghast **29**:417

Beichman, Arnold
  Art Buchwald **33**:94
  Arthur Koestler **1**:170
  Anthony Powell **3**:400

Beidler, Peter G.
  Leslie Marmon Silko **23**:407

Beidler, Philip D.
  David Rabe **33**:343

Beja, Morris
  Lawrence Durrell **4**:145
  William Faulkner **3**:153
  Nathalie Sarraute **4**:466

Belben, Rosalind
  David Plante **23**:347

Belgion, Montgomery
  André Malraux **4**:334
  I. A. Richards **24**:373

Belitt, Ben
  Jorge Luis Borges **2**:75
  Robert Lowell **4**:297
  Pablo Neruda **1**:247
  Ayn Rand **30**:292

Belkind, Allen
  Amos Oz **27**:361
  Ishmael Reed **13**:480
  Kurt Vonnegut, Jr. **22**:447

Bell, Anthea
  Katherine Paterson **30**:285
  Otfried Preussler **17**:377

Bell, Bernard
  William Styron **3**:473

Bell, Bernard W.
  Jean Toomer **4**:550; **22**:427

Bell, David
  Joyce Carol Oates **19**:356

Bell, De Witt
  William Dickey **28**:118

Bell, Frederick J.
  Ernest K. Gann **23**:162

Bell, Gene H.
  Jorge Luis Borges **9**:118
  Alejo Carpentier **8**:135
  Vladimir Nabokov **6**:360

Bell, Ian F. A.
  Ezra Pound **10**:404

Bell, Lisle
Charles Addams **30**:12, 13
Frank B. Gilbreth, Jr. and
Ernestine Gilbreth Carey
17:152
Ogden Nash **23**:316
Frank G. Slaughter **29**:374

Bell, Madison
William Caunitz **34**:35
Lisa St. Aubin de Teran **36**:421

Bell, Marvin
Ted Berrigan **37**:42
F. R. Scott **22**:375
Dave Smith **22**:387
Miriam Waddington **28**:437

Bell, Millicent
Margaret Atwood **2**:19
Lynne Reid Banks **23**:40
Peter De Vries **2**:113
Janet Frame **22**:144
Eugenio Montale **7**:231
John O'Hara **2**:325
Anne Tyler **28**:430

Bell, Pearl K.
Martin Amis **4**:20
John Ashbery **6**:12
Beryl Bainbridge **4**:39
James Baldwin **4**:40; **15**:42
William Barrett **27**:24
Ann Beattie **18**:40
Saul Bellow **8**:70
Marie-Claire Blais **6**:81
Louise Bogan **4**:69
William F. Buckley, Jr. **7**:35
Anthony Burgess **22**:77
John Cheever **15**:130
Eleanor Clark **5**:106
Arthur A. Cohen **7**:51
Len Deighton **7**:76
William Faulkner **6**:177
Paula Fox **2**:140
Nadine Gordimer **5**:146
Juan Goytisolo **5**:149
Günter Grass **4**:206
Graham Greene **3**:214
Joseph Heller **5**:180; **36**:226
Mark Helprin **22**:222
Josephine Herbst **34**:454
George V. Higgins **7**:157
Maureen Howard **5**:189
John Irving **13**:293
Ruth Prawer Jhabvala **8**:311
Charles Johnson **7**:183
Diane Johnson **5**:199
Uwe Johnson **10**:284
James Jones **10**:291
Milan Kundera **4**:277; **19**:270
Elinor Langer **34**:454
Philip Larkin **13**:337
John le Carré **5**:232
Alison Lurie **4**:307
Bernard Malamud **18**:321
Peter Matthiessen **5**:275
Mary McCarthy **14**:360
John McGahern **5**:281
James A. Michener **29**:313
Steven Millhauser **21**:217
A. G. Mojtabai **9**:385
Toni Morrison **22**:323
V. S. Naipaul **7**:254
Amos Oz **5**:335

Cynthia Ozick **7**:288
Walker Percy **8**:438
Marge Piercy **18**:409
Anthony Powell **3**:403
J. F. Powers **8**:447
Mario Puzo **36**:359
Ishmael Reed **6**:448
Adrienne Rich **6**:459
Jill Robinson **10**:439
Philip Roth **15**:455
J. R. Salamanca **15**:463
Susan Fromberg Schaeffer
22:367
Anne Sexton **6**:494
Alix Kates Shulman **10**:475
Stephen Spender **5**:402
D. M. Thomas **22**:421
Mario Vargas Llosa **6**:546
Patrick White **3**:523
Edmund Wilson **24**:483

Bell, Robert
Honor Arundel **17**:12
H. F. Brinsmead **21**:27
Robert Cormier **12**:137
Eilís Dillon **17**:95, 96
Mollie Hunter **21**:163
Madeleine L'Engle **12**:350
William Mayne **12**:390, 399
Robert Westall **17**:555, 557

Bell, Vereen M.
E. M. Forster **1**:107
Ted Hughes **9**:281
Richard F. Hugo **18**:260
Robert Lowell **37**:239

Bellamy, Joe David
Donald Barthelme **13**:60
Sam Shepard **4**:490
Kurt Vonnegut, Jr. **4**:564
Tom Wolfe **35**:462

Bellman, Samuel Irving
Saul Bellow **8**:81
Jorge Luis Borges **6**:91
Jerome Charyn **5**:103
Leonard Cohen **3**:109
Stanley Elkin **6**:169
William Faulkner **3**:152
Leslie A. Fiedler **4**:160, 161
Bruce Jay Friedman **3**:165
William H. Gass **15**:258
Ernest Hemingway **3**:234
Yoram Kaniuk **19**:239
Jack Kerouac **3**:263, 264
Meyer Levin **7**:205
Bernard Malamud **1**:197; **3**:320,
325
Saul Maloff **5**:271
Wallace Markfield **8**:380
James A. Michener **5**:288
Harry Mark Petrakis **3**:382
Philip Roth **3**:435
John Updike **3**:487
Elie Wiesel **5**:490

Belloc, Hilaire
P. G. Wodehouse **22**:479

Bellow, Saul
Camilo José Cela **13**:144
Ilya Ehrenburg **18**:131

Bellows, Silence Buck
Frank B. Gilbreth, Jr. and
Ernestine Gilbreth Carey
17:155
Zilpha Keatley Snyder **17**:471

Bell-Villada, Gene H.
Gabriel García Márquez **15**:254
Mario Vargas Llosa **31**:442

Beloff, Max
Paul Scott **9**:477

Beloof, Robert
Stanley J. Kunitz **6**:285
Marianne Moore **4**:360

Belton, John
Claude Chabrol **16**:177

Bemrose, John
Scott Elledge **34**:430
Frank Herbert **35**:206
Leon Rooke **34**:251
D. M. Thomas **31**:434
E. B. White **34**:430

Benchley, Nathaniel
Art Buchwald **33**:92
Robert Newton Peck **17**:337

Bendau, Clifford P.
Colin Wilson **14**:585

Bender, Marylin
Alix Kates Shulman **2**:395

Bender, Rose S.
Babbis Friis-Baastad **12**:214

Bender, William
Neil Diamond **30**:110
Andrew Lloyd Webber and Tim
Rice **21**:423

Bendiner, Elmer
Piri Thomas **17**:498

Bendow, Burton
Grace Paley **4**:393

Benedict, Joan
Arthur C. Clarke **35**:123

Benedict, Ruth
Margaret Mead **37**:269, 271

Benedikt, Michael
Ted Berrigan **37**:43
David Ignatow **14**:276
Galway Kinnell **2**:230
Charles Simic **22**:379
Richard Wilbur **3**:532

Benestad, Janet P.
M. E. Kerr **12**:300

Benet, Rosemary
Enid Bagnold **25**:74

Benét, Stephen Vincent
Walter D. Edmonds **35**:147,
150
Bruce Lancaster **36**:241, 242
Carl Sandburg **35**:347, 348

Benét, William Rose
Alvah Bessie **23**:60
Sterling A. Brown **23**:95
Agatha Christie **12**:111
August Derleth **31**:136
Robert Francis **15**:235

Ogden Nash **23**:316
John G. Neihardt **32**:331
Carl Sandburg **35**:347

Benford, Gregory
Arthur C. Clarke **35**:128

Benham, G. F.
Friedrich Dürrenmatt **11**:174

Benjamin, Cynthia
Madeleine L'Engle **12**:351

Benjamin, David A.
John D. MacDonald **27**:274

Benn, M. B.
Michael Hamburger **14**:234

Bennett, Bruce
Brad Leithauser **27**:240
Mary Oliver **34**:247
Katha Pollitt **28**:367
Richard Tillinghast **29**:416
Nancy Willard **37**:463

Bennett, C. S.
Rosemary Sutcliff **26**:427

Bennett, Joseph
Philip Booth **23**:75
Anthony Hecht **8**:266

Bennett, Michael Alan
Walter M. Miller, Jr. **30**:258

Bennett, Spencer C.
John Lennon and Paul
McCartney **12**:365

Bennett, Steven D.
William Kotzwinkle **35**:258

Bennett, Virginia
Truman Capote **19**:80

Bennett, Wendell C.
Thor Heyerdahl **26**:190

Benoff, Symme J.
C. S. Adler **35**:11

Bensen, D. R.
Glendon Swarthout **35**:399

Bensheimer, Virginia
Mary Oliver **34**:247

Benson, C. David
Anthony Powell **31**:314
P. G. Wodehouse **22**:484

Benson, Gerard
Leon Garfield **12**:229

Benson, Jackson J.
Ernest Hemingway **6**:232
John Steinbeck **9**:517

Benson, Mary
Athol Fugard **14**:189

Benson, Sheila
Jerzy Skolimowski **20**:355

Benson, Thomas W.
Wayne C. Booth **24**:89

Benstock, Bernard
William Gaddis **3**:177
Flann O'Brien **7**:270
Sean O'Casey **5**:317

Critic Index

Benston, Alice N.
W. S. Merwin 2:276

Bentkowski, Tom
John Lennon 35:275

Bentley, Allen
Morris L. West 6:564

Bentley, Eric
Robert Anderson 23:29
Sally Benson 17:50
Truman Capote 19:81
Charles Chaplin 16:205
I. A. Richards 24:388
Robert Penn Warren 8:536
Orson Welles 20:434
Tennessee Williams 30:461
Herman Wouk 9:579

Bentley, Joseph
Aldous Huxley 1:152

Bentley, Phyllis
Pearl S. Buck 11:69
Noel Streatfeild 21:394

Benton, Michael
Alan Garner 17:146

Bere, Carol
Ted Hughes 37:174

Berenda, Carlton W.
Nevil Shute 30:372

Berendt, John
Phil Ochs 17:333

Berendzen, Richard
Carl Sagan 30:332, 336

Berets, Ralph
Saul Bellow 15:47
John Fowles 3:163

Berg, Beatrice
Agnes Eckhardt Nixon 21:243

Berg, Rona
Jessica Anderson 37:20

Berg, Stephen
Guillevic 33:191

Berge, Jody
Betsy Byars 35:73

Berger, Arthur Asa
Robert Crumb 17:85
Stan Lee 17:257
Monty Python 21:228
Charles M. Schulz 12:529
Jerome Siegel and Joe Shuster
21:360

Berger, Charles
Olga Broumas 10:77
James Merrill 18:331
Frederick Seidel 18:474

Berger, Harold L.
Frank Herbert 12:278
Walter M. Miller, Jr. 30:261

Berger, John
Lindsay Anderson 20:11

Berger, Joseph
Liam O'Flaherty 34:355

Berger, Matt
Roger Zelazny 21:474

Berger, Peter L.
Andrew M. Greeley 28:171
Shiva Naipaul 32:326

Bergin, Thomas G.
Aldo Palazzeschi 11:432
Lucio Piccolo 13:440
Salvatore Quasimodo 10:429
João Guimarães Rosa 23:349

Bergman, Andrew
Frank Capra 16:159
Isaac Bashevis Singer 11:499

Bergman, Andrew C. J.
Peter Benchley 4:53
Guy Davenport, Jr. 6:124

Bergmann, Linda Shell
Ishmael Reed 13:479
Ronald Sukenick 4:531

Bergonzi, Bernard
Kingsley Amis 2:6, 9
W. H. Auden 6:22
Amiri Baraka 33:52
John Barth 3:39
Heinrich Böll 27:60
Paul Bowles 2:79
Anthony Burgess 2:85
R. V. Cassill 23:106
David Caute 29:108, 121
Donald Davie 10:123
Nigel Dennis 8:173
Ilya Ehrenburg 18:135
Richard Fariña 9:195
Ian Fleming 30:131
John Fowles 2:138
Paula Fox 2:139
Geoffrey H. Hartman 27:189
Aldous Huxley 35:244
B. S. Johnson 6:262
Doris Lessing 3:283
William Maxwell 19:307
Iris Murdoch 2:297
Flann O'Brien 4:383
Anthony Powell 3:400
Thomas Pynchon 3:408
Alain Robbe-Grillet 4:447
Siegfried Sassoon 36:392
Andrew Sinclair 2:401
C. P. Snow 4:501; 13:508
Evelyn Waugh 1:357; 3:510
Angus Wilson 2:473; 25:461

Berke, Roberta
John Ashbery 25:55
Allen Ginsberg 36:187
Charles Olson 29:335
Katha Pollitt 28:366
Craig Raine 32:353

Berkley, Miriam
Cynthia Voight 30:420

Berkman, Leonard
Tennessee Williams 30:468

Berkman, Sylvia
Peter Matthiessen 32:285

Berkowitz, Gerald M.
Neil Simon 31:396
Tom Stoppard 29:397

Berkson, Bill
Frank O'Hara 2:320
Jerome Rothenberg 6:477

Berkvist, Margaret
Babbis Friis-Baastad 12:213

Berkvist, Robert
Isaac Asimov 26:36
Allan W. Eckert 17:105
Earl Hamner, Jr. 12:258
Robert A. Heinlein 26:161
S. E. Hinton 30:205
Farley Mowat 26:337
Andre Norton 12:456, 457
Kin Platt 26:348, 352
Mary Rodgers 12:493

Berlin, Isaiah
Aldous Huxley 3:254

Berlin, Normand
Roman Polanski 16:469
Tennessee Williams 30:473

Berman, Bruce
Rainer Werner Fassbinder
20:105

Berman, Jeffrey
E. M. Forster 22:129

Berman, Michael
Milan Kundera 19:267

Berman, Neil
Robert Coover 15:143

Berman, Paul
C.L.R. James 33:221
Peter Nichols 36:334
Isaac Bashevis Singer 11:501
Gary Snyder 32:400
Michel Tournier 36:439
Hugh Whitemore 37:447

Berman, Ronald
William F. Buckley, Jr. 18:81
Ronald Bush 34:532
T. S. Eliot 34:532

Berman, Susan K.
Fredrica Wagman 7:500

Bermel, Albert
Ed Bullins 1:47
Jean Genet 10:227
Christopher Hampton 4:211
Megan Terry 19:439

Bermel, Joyce
Hilma Wolitzer 17:562

Bernays, Anne
Alice Adams 6:1
Stratis Haviaras 33:203
Adrienne Rich 11:474

Berner, Robert L.
André Brink 18:68; 36:69
Bessie Head 25:233
Alan Paton 10:388

Berner, Steve
Louis L'Amour 25:281

**Bernetta (Quinn), Sister Mary,
O.S.F.**
Allen Tate 4:539
See also Quinn, Sister Mary
Bernetta, O.S.F.

Bernhardt, William
François Truffaut 20:380

Bernikow, Louise
A. S. Byatt 19:77
Muriel Rukeyser 6:479

Berns, Walter
Daniel J. Berrigan 4:57

Bernstein, Burton
George P. Elliott 2:131

Bernstein, Jeremy
Lewis Thomas 35:413

Bernstein, Paul
James Clavell 25:127

Bernstein, Richard
Marguerite Duras 34:162

Bernstein, Samuel J.
Robert Anderson 23:33

Bernstein, Theodore M.
Isaac Asimov 26:36

Berrigan, Daniel, S.J.
Horst Bienek 7:28
Denise Levertov 28:243
Thomas Merton 11:373

Berry, Faith
Amiri Baraka 33:54

Berry, Jason
Steven Goldsberry 34:55

Berry, Mabel
Maureen Daly 17:91

Berry, Margaret
Mulk Raj Anand 23:12

Berry, Mary Clay
Allen Drury 37:110

Berry, Patricia
Walter Dean Myers 35:298

Berry, Wendell
Hayden Carruth 4:94

Berryman, Charles
E. L. Doctorow 37:83
Joseph Heller 36:227
Gore Vidal 22:435

Berryman, John
Saul Bellow 10:37
T. S. Eliot 13:197
Ernest Hemingway 10:270
Randall Jarrell 13:299
Ezra Pound 13:460

Bersani, Leo
Julio Cortázar 2:104
Jean Genet 2:158
J.M.G. Le Clézio 31:243
Norman Mailer 8:364
Henri de Montherlant 19:328
Alain Robbe-Grillet 1:288
Robert Wilson 7:551

Berthel, John H.
Nevil Shute 30:367

Berthoff, Warner
Alex Haley 12:245
Norman Mailer 3:313
Iris Murdoch 3:345
Vladimir Nabokov 3:352
Muriel Spark 3:464

Edmund Wilson **2**:475; **3**:538

Bespaloff, Rachel
Albert Camus **9**:139

Bessai, Diane
Austin C. Clarke **8**:142

Besser, Gretchen R.
Julien Green **3**:205

Besser, Gretchen Raus
Nathalie Sarraute **31**:380, 381, 382

Bessie, Alvah
Norman Mailer **3**:319

Best, Alan
Fritz Hochwälder **36**:237

Bester, Alfred
Isaac Asimov **3**:16
Robert A. Heinlein **3**:227

Bester, John
Masuji Ibuse **22**:225, 226
Kenzaburō Ōe **10**:372

Beston, John B.
Patrick White **18**:544

Bethell, Nicholas
Aleksandr I. Solzhenitsyn **7**:441

Betsky, Celia B.
A. Alvarez **5**:19
Max Apple **9**:32
Harriette Arnow **7**:15
Don DeLillo **10**:135
Margaret Drabble **2**:119
John Hawkes **4**:217
Doris Lessing **10**:315
Iris Murdoch **4**:370
Tim O'Brien **19**:358
Marge Piercy **14**:419

Bettelheim, Bruno
Lina Wertmüller **16**:599

Bettersworth, John K.
Milton Meltzer **26**:300

Betts, Whitney
Winston Graham **23**:192

Bevan, A. R.
Mordecai Richler **5**:377

Bevan, David G.
Pier Paolo Pasolini **20**:268

Bevan, Jack
Arthur Gregor **9**:253

Bevington, Helen
Peter Davison **28**:101
Louis Simpson **4**:500

Bewick, E. N.
H. F. Brinsmead **21**:28

Bewick, Elizabeth
Josephine Poole **17**:371

Bewley, Marius
A. R. Ammons **2**:11
John Berryman **2**:56
Kenneth Burke **24**:124
C. Day Lewis **6**:128
Thomas Kinsella **4**:270
Hugh MacDiarmid **2**:253

Sylvia Plath **2**:335
Herbert Read **4**:440
Charles Tomlinson **2**:436

Bezanker, Abraham
Saul Bellow **1**:32
Isaac Bashevis Singer **3**:454

Bianco, David
James Purdy **10**:426

Biasin, Gian-Paolo
Dino Buzzati **36**:86
Umberto Eco **28**:131
Carlo Emilio Gadda **11**:211
Leonardo Sciascia **8**:473

Bibby, Geoffrey
Thor Heyerdahl **26**:192

Bick, Janice
Christie Harris **12**:269

Bickerton, Dorothy
Melvin Berger **12**:41

Bickman, Martin
Alfred Kazin **34**:555

Bidart, Frank
Robert Lowell **9**:336

Bien, Peter
Yannis Ritsos **6**:462

Bienstock, Beverly Gray
John Barth **3**:41

Bier, Jesse
James Thurber **5**:434

Bierhaus, E. G., Jr.
John Osborne **11**:423

Bierman, James
Snoo Wilson **33**:463

Bigger, Charles P.
Walker Percy **8**:440

Bigsby, C.W.E.
Edward Albee **9**:6, 9; **13**:4
James Baldwin **13**:51; **17**:33
Imamu Amiri Baraka **14**:43; **33**:58
Lorraine Hansberry **17**:185
Arthur Miller **10**:342; **26**:321
Willard Motley **18**:357

Bilan, R. P.
Margaret Atwood **25**:62
F. R. Leavis **24**:310
Rudy Wiebe **14**:574

Bilik, Dorothy Seidman
Bernard Malamud **27**:296

Bill, Rise
Richard Peck **21**:301

Billings, Robert
Marilyn R. Bowering **32**:47

Billington, Michael
Howard Brenton **31**:56
David Mamet **34**:218
Snoo Wilson **33**:459

Billington, Rachel
Malcolm Bradbury **32**:58

Billman, Carol W.
Arthur Kopit **18**:290
Laurence Yep **35**:474

Binder, Lucia
Cecil Bødker **21**:12

Binding, Paul
Jurek Becker **19**:36
Rolf Hochhuth **18**:256
Brian Moore **19**:334

Binham, Philip
Paavo Haavikko **18**:207, 208;
34:172, 174, 177
Hannu Salama **18**:460

Binns, Ronald
Samuel Beckett **29**:55
John Fowles **4**:171

Binyon, T. J.
Eric Ambler **9**:21
William Boyd **28**:40
Matthew Bruccoli **34**:416
Peter Dickinson **12**:175, 176
Paul E. Erdman **25**:154
Ross Macdonald **34**:416
Ruth Rendell **28**:384

Birbalsingh, F. M.
Mordecai Richler **13**:485

Birch, Ian
David Byrne **26**:95

Birchall, Jonathan
Elizabeth Jane Howard **29**:246

Bird, Caroline
Milton Meltzer **26**:299

Bird, Christopher
Colin Wilson **14**:584

Birkerts, Sven
Blaise Cendrars **18**:97
Max Frisch **32**:193
Brad Leithauser **27**:241
Michel Tournier **36**:441

Birmingham, Mary Louise
Jesse Jackson **12**:289

Birnbaum, Henry
Gil Orlovitz **22**:332

Birnbaum, Larry
Frank Zappa **17**:595

Birnbaum, Milton
Aldous Huxley **3**:255; **4**:239

Birnbaum, Phyllis
Shiga Naoya **33**:365

Birney, Earle
A.J.M. Smith **15**:513

Birney, Hoffman
Bruce Lancaster **36**:243

Birrell, Francis
René Clair **20**:59
Rouben Mamoulian **16**:420

Birstein, Ann
Russell Banks **37**:24
Iris Murdoch **4**:370
David Plante **23**:343
Sylvia Plath **17**:352

Bishop, Christopher
Buster Keaton **20**:189

Bishop, Claire Huchet
Joseph Krumgold **12**:316
Noel Streatfeild **21**:401

Bishop, Elizabeth
Flannery O'Connor **15**:408

Bishop, Ferman
Allen Tate **2**:428

Bishop, John Peale
E. E. Cummings **12**:142

Bishop, Lloyd
Henri Michaux **8**:390

Bishop, Michael
Arthur C. Clarke **35**:125
Guillevic **33**:192, 193, 194
Stephen King **26**:238
Ursula K. Le Guin **22**:275
Fritz Leiber **25**:307

Bishop, Morris
Ogden Nash **23**:323

Bishop, Tom
Jean Cocteau **8**:145
Julio Cortázar **2**:103
Raymond Queneau **5**:359
Claude Simon **9**:482

Biskind, Peter
Elia Kazan **16**:371
Sam Peckinpah **20**:278
Lina Wertmüller **16**:588

Bissell, Claude T.
Hugh Garner **13**:234

Bissett, Donald J.
Walter Dean Myers **35**:296
Colin Thiele **17**:493

Bjorkland, Beth
Ernst Jandl **34**:200

Bjornson, Richard
Charles R. Larson **31**:240

Black, Campbell
Mary Renault **17**:400
Isaac Bashevis Singer **6**:507

Black, Cyril E.
André Malraux **1**:203

Black, Susan M.
Art Buchwald **33**:89
Pamela Hansford Johnson **27**:219
Elizabeth Spencer **22**:400

Black, W. E.
John G. Neihardt **32**:332

Blackburn, Sara
Lynne Reid Banks **23**:41
Marie-Claire Blais **22**:58
C.D.B. Bryan **29**:102
R. V. Cassill **4**:95
Don DeLillo **27**:77
Peter Dickinson **12**:169
Rosalyn Drexler **2**:120
Maureen Duffy **37**:115
Jim Harrison **6**:225
Maxine Hong Kingston **12**:313
Alan Lelchuk **5**:244

David Madden 5:266
Michael McClure 6:316
Toni Morrison 4:365
Marge Piercy 3:384
Alix Kates Shulman 2:395
Elizabeth Spencer 22:402
Gillian Tindall 7:473
Anne Tyler 28:431
David Wagoner 5:474
Fay Weldon 6:562

Blackburn, Thomas
Sylvia Plath 17:344

Blackburn, Tom
Kingsley Amis 2:6

Blackford, Staige D.
M. M. Kaye 28:201

Blackman, Ruth
Sylvia Ashton-Warner 19:20

Blackman, Ruth Chapin
Ayn Rand 30:294

Blackmon, W. D.
Antonia Fraser 32:185

Blackmur, R(ichard) P.
Cleanth Brooks 24:102
E. E. Cummings 8:154; 12:140
T. S. Eliot 24:159
Archibald MacLeish 14:336
Marianne Moore 13:393
John Crowe Ransom 5:363
I. A. Richards 24:389
Allen Tate 4:536
Lionel Trilling 24:450
Yvor Winters 32:456

Blackwood, Caroline
Ingmar Bergman 16:49

Blades, Joe
Bob Fosse 20:123

Blaha, Franz G.
J. P. Donleavy 4:125

Blair, Karin
Gene Roddenberry 17:408, 411

Blair, Walter
Ogden Nash 23:320

Blais, Marie-Claire
Elizabeth Bishop 13:88

Blaise, Clark
Ved Mehta 37:294
Salman Rushdie 23:365

Blake, George
John Cowper Powys 9:439

Blake, Nicholas
Margery Allingham 19:12
Agatha Christie 12:113

Blake, Patricia
Josephine Herbst 34:453
Elinor Langer 34:453
Cynthia Ozick 28:355
Aleksandr I. Solzhenitsyn
  1:319; 7:439
Andrei Voznesensky 1:349

Blake, Percival
Leonardo Sciascia 8:474

Blake, Richard A.
Norman Lear 12:331
George Lucas 16:411
Monty Python 21:224
Peter Shaffer 37:384
Morris L. West 33:433

Blakeston, Oswell
Michael Ayrton 7:19
Peter Dickinson 35:131
Gabriel García Márquez 3:180
Paul Theroux 15:535
Trevanian 29:430
P. G. Wodehouse 2:480

Blamires, David
David Jones 2:216, 217; 4:260;
  13:308

Bland, Peter
Norman MacCaig 36:283
Louis Simpson 32:378
Derek Walcott 25:457

Blanford, S. L.
Honor Arundel 17:13

Blaser, Robin
Jack Spicer 18:506

Blasi, Alberto
José Donoso 32:161

Blasing, Mutlu Konuk
Elizabeth Bishop 32:44

Blassingame, Wyatt
Harriette Arnow 7:15

Blaydes, Sophia B.
Simon Gray 9:242

Blazek, Douglas
Robert Creeley 2:107
W. S. Merwin 5:286
Diane Wakoski 4:573

Bleikasten, André
Flannery O'Connor 10:366

Bleiler, E. F.
Isaac Asimov 26:58

Blewitt, Charles G.
Fumiko Enchi 31:140
John Gardner 30:154

Blicksilver, Edith
Leslie Marmon Silko 23:409

Blindheim, Joan Tindale
John Arden 13:26

Blish, James
Poul Anderson 15:11
John Brunner 10:77
Theodore Sturgeon 22:411
Roger Zelazny 21:465

Blishen, Edward
Alan Garner 17:150
William Golding 27:159
William Mayne 12:391, 394
Amos Tutuola 29:441

Bliss, Corinne Demas
Stratis Haviaras 33:205

Bliss, Michael
Hugh Hood 28:195

Bliss, Shepherd
Frederick Wiseman 20:477

Bliven, Naomi
Marie-Claire Blais 22:58
Brigid Brophy 29:93
Louis-Ferdinand Céline 4:103
Agatha Christie 12:125
Isak Dinesen 29:163
Andrea Giovene 7:117
Andrew M. Greeley 28:170
Eugène Ionesco 6:257
Anthony Powell 7:343
Emlyn Williams 15:578
Monique Wittig 22:471

Bloch, Adèle
Michel Butor 8:120
Pär Lagerkvist 7:200

Blodgett, E. D.
D. G. Jones 10:285
Sylvia Plath 3:388

Blodgett, Harriet
Colin MacInnes 23:285
V. S. Naipaul 4:375

Blomster, W. V.
Christa Wolf 14:594

Blomster, Wes
Günter Grass 32:201
Siegfried Lenz 27:256

Błonski, Jan
Czesław Miłosz 11:377

Blonston, Gary
Tom Robbins 32:374

Bloom, Harold
A. R. Ammons 5:25; 8:14; 9:26
John Ashbery 4:23; 9:41; 13:30;
  15:26, 33
W. H. Auden 6:16
Saul Bellow 6:50
Frank Bidart 33:77
Jorge Luis Borges 6:87
Alfred Corn 33:114
James Dickey 10:141
Northrop Frye 24:226
Allen Ginsberg 6:199
Seamus Heaney 25:246
Anthony Hecht 13:269
Daryl Hine 15:282
John Hollander 8:301, 302;
  14:264
Galway Kinnell 29:284
Philip Levine 9:332
Robert Lowell 8:355
Archibald MacLeish 8:363
Norman Mailer 28:260
James Merrill 8:388
Howard Moss 7:249; 14:375
Howard Nemerov 36:300
Robert Pack 13:439
W. D. Snodgrass 10:478
Mark Strand 18:517
Robert Penn Warren 8:539;
  18:535
Charles Wright 13:614
A. B. Yehoshua 31:474

Bloom, J. Don
Alvin Silverstein and Virginia
  B. Silverstein 17:454

Bloom, Janet
Linda Pastan 27:368

Bloom, Robert
W. H. Auden 1:10; 11:13

Blotner, Joseph L.
Cleanth Brooks 24:116
J. D. Salinger 1:295

Blount, Roy, Jr.
Steve Martin 30:248

Blow, Simon
Julia O'Faolain 19:360
Sylvia Plath 11:451
Anthony Powell 31:317
Isaac Bashevis Singer 6:510
Scott Spencer 30:408
A. N. Wilson 33:452

Blue, Adrianne
Simone de Beauvoir 31:44
Buchi Emecheta 14:160
Henri Troyat 23:461
John Edgar Wideman 34:300

Bluefarb, Sam
Leslie A. Fiedler 13:213
Bernard Malamud 1:196; 9:350
Chaim Potok 26:370
John Steinbeck 5:407
Richard Wright 3:546

Bluestein, Gene
Bob Dylan 12:189
Richard Fariña 9:195

Bluestone, George
Nelson Algren 10:5

Blum, David
Peter Handke 15:268

Blum, Morgan
Peter Taylor 18:522

Blumberg, Myrna
Ronald Harwood 32:225

Blumenberg, Richard M.
Alain Resnais 16:510

Blumenfeld, Yorick
John Berger 19:37
Yevgeny Yevtushenko 1:382

Blundell, Janet Boyarin
Maya Angelou 12:14; 35:31, 32

Bly, Robert
A. R. Ammons 5:28
Carlos Castaneda 12:94
Gunnar Ekelöf 27:111, 115
David Ignatow 14:274
Robert Lowell 4:297
Pablo Neruda 28:306, 315
Francis Ponge 18:419

Blythe, Ronald
Roy Fuller 28:158
William Golding 17:178
Ronald Harwood 32:224
Erica Jong 6:267
Alice Munro 6:341
Joyce Carol Oates 6:368
Jean Rhys 19:391
Wilbur Smith 33:375
David Storey 8:506
A. N. Wilson 33:458

Boak, Denis
André Malraux **4**:330

Boardman, Gwenn R.
Yasunari Kawabata **2**:222
Yukio Mishima **2**:286

Boas, Franz
Zora Neale Hurston **30**:209

Boatwright, James
Harry Crews **23**:132
John Ehle **27**:104
Paul Horgan **9**:278
David Leavitt **34**:79
James McCourt **5**:278
Gore Vidal **6**:549
Robert Penn Warren **1**:356

Boatwright, John
Walker Percy **8**:438

Boatwright, Taliaferro
Ernest K. Gann **23**:165
Richard Matheson **37**:245
Emily Cheney Neville **12**:450

Bobbie, Walter
Stephen King **12**:309

Bobbitt, Joan
James Dickey **15**:173
William Price Fox **22**:140

Bochner, Jay
Blaise Cendrars **18**:93

Bochtler, Stan
Cecil Bødker **21**:12

Bock, Philip K.
John G. Neihardt **32**:335

Bocock, Maclin
Donald Barthelme **23**:44

Bodart, Joni
John Gardner **30**:154
Frank Herbert **12**:272
Rosemary Wells **12**:638

Bode, Carl
Katherine Anne Porter **7**:318

Bodo, Maureen
Gore Vidal **10**:504

Boe, Eugene
Christina Stead **2**:421

Boek, Jean K.
Vine Deloria, Jr. **21**:113

Boeth, Richard
Len Deighton **22**:114
John O'Hara **2**:324

Bogan, Louise
W. H. Auden **1**:9
Richard Eberhart **19**:140
Barbara Howes **15**:289
Patrick Kavanagh **22**:235
Marianne Moore **13**:396; **19**:338
W. R. Rodgers **7**:377
Muriel Rukeyser **15**:456
Frederick Seidel **18**:474

Bogart, Gary
Sol Gordon **26**:137
Kristin Hunter **35**:228
Robert Newton Peck **17**:340

Bogdanovich, Peter
Alfred Hitchcock **16**:343

Bogen, Don
Frank Bidart **33**:80
Richard F. Hugo **32**:251

Bogstad, Janice M.
Barbara Wersba **30**:433

Bohn, Chris
Bob Marley **17**:272

Bohner, Charles H.
Robert Penn Warren **1**:354

Bok, Sissela
Vladimir Nabokov **1**:245

Boland, John
Brian Aldiss **5**:15
John Dickson Carr **3**:101
Richard Condon **4**:106
Harry Kemelman **2**:225
Michael Moorcock **5**:293

Bold, Alan
Robert Graves **1**:130

Boles, Paul Darcy
Truman Capote **19**:81

Bolger, Eugenie
Hortense Calisher **8**:125
José Donoso **4**:130

Bollard, Margaret Lloyd
William Carlos Williams **9**:571

Bolling, Doug
John Barth **27**:30

Bolling, Douglass
E. M. Forster **9**:206
Doris Lessing **3**:290
Clarence Major **19**:296
Rudolph Wurlitzer **4**:598;
  15:588
Al Young **19**:478

Bolotin, Susan
Eva Figes **31**:167
Jay McInerney **34**:81
Gloria Naylor **28**:304

Bolton, Richard R.
Herman Wouk **9**:580

Bond, Kirk
Carl Theodor Dreyer **16**:260

Bondy, François
Günter Grass **2**:173

Bone, Robert
William Melvin Kelley **22**:247
Nella Larsen **37**:213
Paule Marshall **27**:309
Melvin B. Tolson **36**:430
Jean Toomer **22**:425

Bone, Robert A.
James Baldwin **1**:15; **17**:29
Amiri Baraka **33**:53
Arna Bontemps **1**:37
W.E.B. Du Bois **1**:80
Ralph Ellison **1**:95; **3**:142
Jessie Redmon Fauset **19**:170
Langston Hughes **1**:147
Zora Neale Hurston **7**:171
Willard Motley **18**:357

Ann Petry **1**:266
Jean Toomer **1**:341
Richard Wright **1**:378
Frank G. Yerby **1**:381

Bongiorno, Robert
Carlo Emilio Gadda **11**:209

Boni, John
Kurt Vonnegut, Jr. **5**:465

Boniol, John Dawson, Jr.
Melvin Berger **12**:40, 41

Bonner, Joey
Bette Bao Lord **23**:279

Bonney, Mary Anne
Erich von Däniken **30**:427
Jonathan Keates **34**:201
Ann Schlee **35**:374

Bontemps, Arna
Langston Hughes **35**:215
Zora Neale Hurston **30**:213
Ann Petry **18**:403
Jean Toomer **13**:551

Booker, Christopher
Andrea Lee **36**:254
Tom Wolfe **35**:457

Booth, James A.
Ayi Kwei Armah **33**:30
Carl Sagan **30**:338

Booth, Martin
Thomas M. Disch **36**:126
Ted Hughes **14**:272
John Matthias **9**:361
Christopher Reid **33**:351
Gilbert Sorrentino **14**:500
Yevgeny Yevtushenko **26**:469

Booth, Philip
Hayden Carruth **18**:87
William Dickey **28**:117
Richard Eberhart **11**:176;
  19:140
Randall Jarrell **1**:159
Maxine Kumin **13**:327
Mary Oliver **19**:361
Louis Simpson **7**:426

Booth, Rosemary
Marilynne Robinson **25**:388

Booth, Wayne C.
M. H. Abrams **24**:13
Kenneth Burke **24**:133
Susan Fromberg Schaeffer
  22:367
Hunter S. Thompson **17**:507

Borden, Diane M.
Ingmar Bergman **16**:78

Bordewich, Fergus M.
Agnes Eckhardt Nixon **21**:246

Bordwell, David
Charles Chaplin **16**:199
François Truffaut **20**:389
Orson Welles **20**:445

Borg, Mary
Eva Figes **31**:163
Bessie Head **25**:232
Elizabeth Jane Howard **29**:245
Françoise Sagan **17**:426
Frank Tuohy **37**:428

Borges, Jorge Luis
Adolfo Bioy Casares **4**:63
Orson Welles **20**:453

Boring, Phyllis Zatlin
Miguel Delibes **18**:117

Borinsky, Alicia
Manuel Puig **5**:355

Borkat, Robert F. Sarfatt
Robert Frost **9**:222

Borland, Hal
John Ehle **27**:103
Farley Mowat **26**:333, 335

Boroff, David
R. V. Cassill **23**:104, 105
William Melvin Kelley **22**:247

Boroff, David A.
John A. Williams **13**:598

Borroff, Marie
John Hollander **2**:197
Denise Levertov **2**:243
William Meredith **4**:348
James Merrill **2**:274

Borrus, Bruce J.
Saul Bellow **15**:57

Bosley, Keith
Eugenio Montale **7**:229

Bosmajian, Hamida
Louis-Ferdinand Céline **3**:103

Bosse, Malcolm
Walter Dean Myers **35**:297

Boston, Howard
Eilís Dillon **17**:93, 94
Jean Lee Latham **12**:323
Farley Mowat **26**:333

Bosworth, David
Robert Stone **23**:430
Kurt Vonnegut, Jr. **12**:629

Bosworth, Patricia
Nora Ephron **31**:159

Botsford, Judith
Franklyn M. Branley **21**:19

Boucher, Anthony
Margery Allingham **19**:13
Robert Bloch **33**:83
Taylor Caldwell **28**:65
Agatha Christie **12**:115, 116,
  117
John Creasey **11**:134
Edmund Crispin **22**:109, 110
C. Day Lewis **6**:128
August Derleth **31**:137, 138
Jan de Hartog **19**:131
Evan Hunter **31**:219, 220
Len Deighton **22**:113, 114
Eilís Dillon **17**:95
Howard Fast **23**:158
Timothy Findley **27**:140
Thomas J. Fleming **37**:122
Dick Francis **22**:150
John Gardner **30**:151, 152
Winston Graham **23**:193, 194
Patricia Highsmith **2**:193
P. D. James **18**:272
M. M. Kaye **28**:198

Harry Kemelman 2:225
Colin MacInnes 23:282
Mary Lee Settle 19:409
Anthony Shaffer 19:413
Mary Stewart 7:467; 35:388,
  389, 390, 391
Julian Symons 2:426; 14:523

Boucher, Norman
Thomas Merton 34:467
Michael Mott 34:467

Bouise, Oscar A.
Allan W. Eckert 17:103
Eleanor Hibbert 7:155
Per Wahlöö 7:501

Boulby, Mark
Hermann Hesse 11:272; 17:207

Boulding, Kenneth E.
Margaret Mead 37:276

Boulton, James T.
Harold Pinter 6:406

Boumelha, Penny
Howard Nemerov 36:309

Bouraoui, H. A.
Nathalie Sarraute 2:385

Bourdillon, Jennifer
Otfried Preussler 17:374

Bourjaily, Vance
Kay Boyle 19:66
David Bradley, Jr. 23:80
Roald Dahl 18:109
Jim Harrison 14:235
Philip Roth 9:460
Helen Hoover Santmyer 33:358
John Sayles 14:483
George Tabori 19:436

Bourne, Mike
Jimmy Page and Robert Plant
  12:476
Pink Floyd 35:305
Frank Zappa 17:588

Bourne, Randolph
Carl Van Vechten 33:385

Bourneuf, Roland
Hubert Aquin 15:17

Bousoño, Carlos
Vicente Aleixandre 36:30

Boutelle, Ann E.
Hugh MacDiarmid 2:253

Boutrous, Lawrence K.
John Hawkes 3:223

Bova, Ben
James A. Michener 29:314

Bova, Benjamin W.
Franklyn M. Branley 21:17

Bowden, J. H.
Peter De Vries 28:112

Bowden, Laurie
Zibby Oneal 30:280

Bowe, Clotilde Soave
Natalia Ginzburg 11:228

Bowen, Barbara C.
P. G. Wodehouse 10:538

Bowen, Elizabeth
Henri de Montherlant 19:322

Bowen, John
Arthur Kopit 1:171
Randolph Stow 23:433

Bowen, Robert O.
Andrew Lytle 22:293
Flannery O'Connor 21:259

Bowen, Roger
Philip Larkin 18:297

Bowen, Zack
Padraic Colum 28:90

Bowering, George
Milton Acorn 15:9
Margaret Atwood 2:19
Margaret Avison 2:29
Earle Birney 4:64
D. G. Jones 10:288
Margaret Laurence 3:278
Denise Levertov 15:336
Gwendolyn MacEwan 13:357
John Newlove 14:377
A. W. Purdy 6:428
Mordecai Richler 5:374
Audrey Thomas 7:472; 13:538

Bowering, Marilyn
Patrick Lane 25:285

Bowering, Peter
Aldous Huxley 4:237

Bowers, A. Joan
Gore Vidal 8:526

Bowers, Marvin
L. E. Sissman 9:491

Bowie, Malcolm
Yves Bonnefoy 9:114

Bowles, Gloria
Diane Wakoski 7:505

Bowles, Jerry G.
Craig Nova 7:267

Bowra, C. M.
Rafael Alberti 7:7

Boxer, David
Raymond Carver 22:98

Boyce, Burke
Esther Forbes 12:205

Boyd, Alex
Walter Dean Myers 35:298

Boyd, Ann S.
Ian Fleming 30:145

Boyd, Blanche M.
Renata Adler 8:5

Boyd, Celia
Honor Arundel 17:16

Boyd, Ernest
Padraic Colum 28:86, 87

Boyd, John D.
Theodore Roethke 11:483

Boyd, Malcolm
Andrew Lloyd Webber and Tim
  Rice 21:425

Boyd, Robert
James Purdy 2:350

Boyd, William
J. G. Ballard 36:47
William F. Buckley, Jr. 37:62
Margaret Drabble 22:126
Gabriel García Márquez 15:252
Penelope Gilliatt 13:238
William Golding 27:162
Steven Millhauser 21:221
John Mortimer 28:288
Irwin Shaw 23:399
Frank Tuohy 37:430
Kurt Vonnegut, Jr. 22:451
Gordon Vorster 34:122
Stephen Wright 33:468

Boyer, Robert H.
Roger Zelazny 21:473

Boyers, Robert
Saul Bellow 3:57
Ingmar Bergman 16:79
Alan Dugan 6:143
Louise Glück 22:173
Witold Gombrowicz 7:125;
  11:241
Robinson Jeffers 2:214; 3:258
Arthur Koestler 6:281
Robert Lowell 8:349; 9:336
Sylvia Plath 11:447
Adrienne Rich 7:364
Theodore Roethke 8:457
W. D. Snodgrass 2:406
Gary Snyder 2:406
Richard Wilbur 6:569

Boylan, Martin M.
Allen Drury 37:109

Boyle, Kay
James Baldwin 1:15
Tom Wicker 7:534

Boyle, Ted E.
Kingsley Amis 2:6
Brendan Behan 1:26

Boylston, Helen Dore
Betty Cavanna 12:97
Henry Gregor Felsen 17:120
Lee Kingman 17:243

Boynton, H. W.
Frank Swinnerton 31:421

Bozek, Phillip
Hugh MacDiarmid 19:285

Bracher, Frederick
John Cheever 15:127
James Gould Cozzens 11:127

Bracken, Paul
Jonathan Schell 35:369

Brackman, Jacob
Renata Adler 31:11
Robert Crumb 17:84
Melvin Van Peebles 20:411

Bradbrook, M. C.
T. S. Eliot 1:91; 2:130
William Empson 33:137

Bradbury, John M.
Allen Tate 24:446

Bradbury, Malcolm
J. G. Ballard 14:40
Saul Bellow 33:65
Malcolm Bradbury 32:55
A. S. Byatt 19:75
Ivy Compton-Burnett 10:109
John Dos Passos 8:181
D. J. Enright 31:147
E. M. Forster 4:167; 10:180
John Fowles 3:162; 4:172
William Gaddis 8:227
Joseph Heller 36:226
Thomas Hinde 6:240
Aldous Huxley 4:244
Alfred Kazin 34:555
Michael Mott 15:379
Iris Murdoch 4:367; 11:388
John O'Hara 11:413
Ezra Pound 34:508
Piers Paul Read 25:378
Frank Sargeson 31:365
C. P. Snow 4:505
Gilbert Sorrentino 14:501
Muriel Spark 2:418
E. Fuller Torrey 34:508
Lionel Trilling 9:531
Gore Vidal 33:411
Evelyn Waugh 8:543
Angus Wilson 5:513

Bradbury, Maureen
Phyllis Gotlieb 18:193

Bradbury, Ray
Ray Bradbury 15:86

Bradford, Melvin E.
Donald Davidson 2:111, 112;
  13:167
William Faulkner 1:102; 3:155;
  18:149
Walker Percy 3:381
Allen Tate 2:429

Bradford, Richard
A. B. Guthrie, Jr. 23:199
M. E. Kerr 12:300
James Kirkwood 9:319
Scott O'Dell 30:270

Bradford, Roark
Nella Larsen 37:210

Bradford, Tom
Ray Bradbury 10:69

Bradley, Jerry
Gary Soto 32:401

Bradley, Marion Zimmer
Thomas M. Disch 36:128

Bradley, Sculley
Robert Frost 3:169

Bradlow, Paul
Frederick Wiseman 20:469

Brady, Ann P.
T. S. Eliot 15:213

Brady, Charles A.
David Kherdian 6:281
C. S. Lewis 14:322

Brady, Owen
Richard Wright 21:460

Brady, Patrick
Albert Camus **9**:147

Brady, Veronica
Thomas Keneally **19**:245

Braestrup, Peter
James H. Webb, Jr. **22**:454

Bragdon, Henry Wilkinson
Thomas J. Fleming **37**:126

Bragg, Melvyn
Kingsley Amis **13**:14
Saul Bellow **25**:84
William F. Buckley, Jr. **18**:82
E. M. Forster **2**:136
John le Carré **28**:227
Tom Sharpe **36**:401

Bragg, Pamela
Frank Bonham **12**:52

Bragin, John
Jean-Luc Godard **20**:133
Jean Renoir **20**:297

Braginsky, Dorothea D.
Judith Guest **30**:173

Braine, John
Richard Llewellyn **7**:207
Fay Weldon **9**:559

Braithwaite, E. R.
J. G. Ballard **36**:38

Braithwaite, William Stanley
T. S. Stribling **23**:439

Bramwell, Gloria
Richard Wright **21**:439

Branden, Nathaniel
Ayn Rand **30**:296

Brander, Laurence
E. M. Forster **15**:224
Aldous Huxley **18**:269

Brandriff, Welles T.
William Styron **11**:514

Brandt, G. W.
John Arden **13**:23

Brasillach, Robert
René Clair **20**:61

Brater, Enoch
Samuel Beckett **6**:42; **9**:81;
   14:78; **18**:51; **29**:63
Harold Pinter **27**:389
Tom Stoppard **29**:398

Braudy, Leo
John Berger **2**:54
Thomas Berger **3**:63
Bernardo Bertolucci **16**:90
Richard Condon **4**:107
Alfred Hitchcock **16**:347
Norman Mailer **1**:193; **8**:368
Jean Renoir **20**:301
Susan Sontag **31**:415

Braudy, Susan
Nora Ephron **17**:112

Braun, Devra
Lillian Hellman **18**:225

Braun, Eric
John Landis **26**:273
Elaine May **16**:433

Braun, Julie
Philip Roth **4**:453

Braver-Mann, Barnet G.
Charles Chaplin **16**:188

Braybrooke, Neville
Graham Greene **1**:130
François Mauriac **4**:337

Brazier, Chris
David Byrne **26**:94
The Clash **30**:44
Mick Jagger and Keith Richard
   17:239
Bruce Springsteen **17**:482
Paul Weller **26**:443

Brée, Germaine
Louis Aragon **3**:12
Marcel Aymé **11**:21
Samuel Beckett **10**:27
Stanley Burnshaw **13**:128
Albert Camus **1**:54; **11**:93
Louis-Ferdinand Céline **1**:57
Jean Cocteau **1**:59
Georges Duhamel **8**:186
Jean Giono **4**:183
Julien Green **3**:203
André Malraux **1**:202
François Mauriac **4**:337
Raymond Queneau **2**:359
Jules Romains **7**:381
Jean-Paul Sartre **1**:306; **7**:397

Breen, Jon L.
Robert Lipsyte **21**:210

Bregman, Alice Miller
Milton Meltzer **26**:301

Breit, Harvey
James Baldwin **2**:31

Breitrose, Henry
Shirley Clarke **16**:215

Brench, A. C.
Mongo Beti **27**:41

Brendon, Piers
Donald Barthelme **5**:53
Rosalyn Drexler **2**:119
Daphne du Maurier **6**:146
Tom Sharpe **36**:398
Wilbur Smith **33**:376
Robert Penn Warren **4**:582
Morris L. West **33**:432

Brennan, Anthony
W. P. Kinsella **27**:235
John Metcalf **37**:299
Jane Rule **27**:420

Brennan, Anthony S.
Samuel Beckett **14**:80
Clark Blaise **29**:72

Brereton, Geoffrey
Lucien Goldmann **24**:239

Breschard, Jack
Billy Joel **26**:213

Breskin, David
Sterling A. Brown **23**:100

Breslin, James E.
T. S. Eliot **6**:166

Breslin, James E. B.
Robert Lowell **37**:241

Breslin, Jimmy
Gore Vidal **8**:525

Breslin, John B.
Charles Addams **30**:16
Gail Godwin **31**:196
Andrew M. Greeley **28**:177
C. S. Lewis **6**:308
Phyllis McGinley **14**:368
Tom McHale **5**:281
Wilfrid Sheed **10**:474
Susan Sontag **13**:516

Breslin, Patrick
Miguel Ángel Asturias **8**:25
Romain Gary **25**:189
Paul Theroux **15**:534

Breslin, Paul
Philip Booth **23**:77
Michael S. Harper **22**:209
Geoffrey Hill **18**:239
Daniel Hoffman **23**:242
William Meredith **22**:303
Charles Olson **29**:334
James Schuyler **23**:391

Bresnick, Paul
James Purdy **10**:425

Breton, André
Luis Buñuel **16**:152

Brew, Claude C.
Tommaso Landolfi **11**:321

Brewer, Joan Scherer
Sol Gordon **26**:138

Brewster, Ben
Yasujiro Ozu **16**:455

Brewster, Dorothy
Doris Lessing **1**:173

Brickell, Herschel
Harriette Arnow **7**:15
Julia Peterkin **31**:303

Bricker, Karin K.
Mavis Thorpe Clark **12**:131

Brickner, Richard P.
Anthony Burgess **2**:86
Jerome Charyn **8**:136
Frederick Exley **11**:186
Frederick Forsyth **2**:137
Herbert Gold **7**:120
Evan Hunter **31**:222
William Kotzwinkle **14**:309
Phillip Lopate **29**:300
Cormac McCarthy **4**:341
Vladimir Nabokov **3**:355
Harry Mark Petrakis **3**:383
Muriel Spark **3**:465
Richard B. Wright **6**:581

Bridges, Les
Mickey Spillane **3**:469

Bridges, Linda
Donald Barthelme **5**:55
Alistair MacLean **13**:359
Georges Simenon **8**:487

Brien, Alan
Kingsley Amis **2**:6
Alan Ayckbourn **8**:34
Trevor Griffiths **13**:255
Ann Jellicoe **27**:205
John Osborne **5**:333
Harold Pinter **6**:418
N. F. Simpson **29**:365, 366
Wole Soyinka **14**:505
Tennessee Williams **8**:547

Brien, Dolores Elise
Robert Duncan **15**:188

Brigg, Peter
Arthur C. Clarke **13**:148
Frank Herbert **35**:204

Briggs, Julia
Leon Garfield **12**:234
Diana Wynne Jones **26**:227
Philippa Pearce **21**:290

Briggs, Kenneth A.
Thomas Merton **34**:463
Michael Mott **34**:463

Brignano, Russell Carl
Richard Wright **4**:594

Brink, Andre
James A. Michener **29**:312

Brink, André P.
Breyten Breytenbach **23**:83, 84

Brinkmeyer, Robert H., Jr.
Caroline Gordon **29**:189

Brinnin, John Malcolm
John Ashbery **6**:12
Ben Belitt **22**:49
Allen Ginsberg **6**:201
Galway Kinnell **1**:168
William Meredith **13**:372
Sylvia Plath **1**:269
Muriel Rukeyser **27**:404
William Jay Smith **6**:512

Brinsmead, H. F.
H. F. Brinsmead **21**:28

Brinson, Peter
Jean Renoir **20**:289

Bristol, Horace
Pearl S. Buck **7**:33

Britt, Gwenneth
Vittorio De Sica **20**:94

Brittain, Victoria
Ngugi wa Thiong'o **36**:319

Britten, Florence Haxton
Carl Van Vechten **33**:394

Brivic, Sheldon
Richard Wright **9**:585

Brizzi, Mary T.
C. J. Cherryh **35**:109

Brock, H. I.
Zora Neale Hurston **30**:209

Brockway, James
Beryl Bainbridge **10**:16
Angela Carter **5**:102
J. P. Donleavy **4**:126
Mavis Gallant **7**:111
Penelope Gilliatt **10**:230

Critic Index

Julien Green **3**:205
Susan B. Hill **4**:228
Ursula Holden **18**:257
Frederic Raphael **14**:438
Piers Paul Read **10**:435
Muriel Spark **5**:399; **8**:495
Frank Swinnerton **31**:428
Emma Tennant **13**:537

Broderick, Dorothy M.
Fran Arrick **30**:18
H. F. Brinsmead **21**:27
Lois Duncan **26**:101
James D. Forman **21**:119
Nat Hentoff **26**:185
Jesse Jackson **12**:655
Stephen King **26**:239

Brodin, Dorothy
Marcel Aymé **11**:22

Brodrick, Jeffrey
John Gregory Dunne **28**:127

Brodsky, Arnold
Stevie Wonder **12**:655

Brodsky, Joseph
Anna Akhmatova **25**:26
Czesław Miłosz **11**:376
Eugenio Montale **9**:388

Brody, Patricia Ann
Joan Armatrading **17**:9

Brogan, D. W.
Bruce Catton **35**:88

Brogan, Hugh
Peter Ackroyd **34**:389
T. S. Eliot **34**:389
Mervyn Peake **7**:301

Bromberg, Pam
Lillian Hellman **18**:229

Brombert, Victor
Robert Alter **34**:517
Peter Brooks **34**:520
St.-John Perse **4**:398
Nathalie Sarraute **31**:378
Michel Tournier **36**:439

Bromell, Nicholas
Derek Walcott **25**:456

Bromfield, Louis
Conrad Richter **30**:310, 312

Bromwich, David
Conrad Aiken **5**:10
A. R. Ammons **9**:2
John Ashbery **15**:34
Ben Belitt **22**:54
Elizabeth Bishop **32**:37
Hayden Carruth **10**:100
Leslie Epstein **27**:127
Robert Frost **9**:266
John Hawkes **4**:216
John Hollander **5**:187
Richard Howard **7**:167
Thomas Kinsella **19**:253
Doris Lessing **3**:288
Jay Macpherson **14**:346
Penelope Mortimer **5**:299
Michael Mott **15**:380
Iris Murdoch **3**:348; **6**:347
Howard Nemerov **9**:394

Robert Pinsky **9**:416
Stanley Plumly **33**:315
Eric Rohmer **16**:532
Anne Sexton **10**:467
Charles Simic **9**:479
Stevie Smith **8**:492
Muriel Spark **3**:465
Paul Theroux **5**:427
Robert Penn Warren **13**:572
Elie Wiesel **3**:528
Joy Williams **31**:462
Charles Wright **13**:615

Broner, E. M.
Maxine Hong Kingston **19**:250

Bronowski, J.
Kathleen Raine **7**:352

Bronson, A. A.
Joe Rosenblatt **15**:448

Bronstein, Lynne
Trina Robbins **21**:338

Brook, Stephen
Howard Brenton **31**:69
David Mamet **34**:218
Anthony Powell **31**:321

Brooke, Jocelyn
Elizabeth Bowen **1**:39

Brooke, Nicholas
Anne Stevenson **7**:462

Brooke-Rose, Christine
Ezra Pound **7**:328

Brookner, Anita
Ursula Holden **18**:259
Colleen McCullough **27**:320
Fay Weldon **19**:469

Brooks, Anne
Maureen Daly **17**:87
Mary Stolz **12**:548

Brooks, Cleanth
William Empson **19**:152
William Faulkner **18**:148;
  28:144
Ernest Hemingway **30**:179
Randall Jarrell **1**:159
Marianne Moore **10**:347
Walker Percy **6**:399
I. A. Richards **24**:396
Allen Tate **4**:539; **11**:522
Eudora Welty **33**:415
Yvor Winters **32**:458

Brooks, Ellen W.
Doris Lessing **3**:284

Brooks, Gwendolyn
Kristin Hunter **35**:225
Melvin B. Tolson **36**:426

Brooks, Jeremy
A. J. Cronin **32**:140
Michael Frayn **31**:188

Brooks, John
Ernest K. Gann **23**:163

Brooks, Peter
Louis Aragon **22**:39
Roland Barthes **24**:28
J.M.G. Le Clézio **31**:246
Violette Leduc **22**:262
Alain Robbe-Grillet **1**:287

Brooks, Rick
Andre Norton **12**:467

Brooks, Robert M.
Andrew M. Greeley **28**:169

Brooks, Taye
Cecil Bødker **21**:12

Brooks, Thomas R.
Muriel Spark **18**:506

Brooks, Valerie
Beryl Bainbridge **22**:47

Brooks, Van Wyck
Upton Sinclair **15**:497

Broome, Peter
Robert Pinget **7**:306

Brophy, Brigid
Kingsley Amis **2**:5
Simone de Beauvoir **2**:42
Hortense Calisher **2**:95
Ivy Compton-Burnett **3**:111
William Faulkner **1**:102
Ernest K. Gann **23**:167
Jean Genet **2**:157
Joanne Greenberg **30**:162
Ronald Harwood **32**:223
Shirley Hazzard **18**:213
Patricia Highsmith **2**:192
W. Somerset Maugham **1**:204
Henry Miller **2**:281
Françoise Sagan **3**:443; **6**:482
Georges Simenon **2**:397
Elizabeth Taylor **2**:432
Evelyn Waugh **3**:509

Brophy, James D.
W. H. Auden **11**:15

Brose, Margaret
Giuseppe Ungaretti **11**:558;
  15:538

Brosman, Catharine Savage
Simone de Beauvoir **31**:39
Jean-Paul Sartre **13**:503

Brosnahan, John
Robert Coover **32**:127
Michael Cunningham **34**:40
John Jakes **29**:250
Stephen King **26**:236
David Leavitt **34**:78
Larry McMurtry **27**:333
Wilbur Smith **33**:377
Gordon Vorster **34**:122

Brothers, Barbara
Elizabeth Bowen **15**:79
Barbara Pym **37**:372

Brotherston, Gordon
Ernesto Cardenal **31**:71

Brotman, Sonia
Margaret O. Hyde **21**:176, 177

Broughton, Glenda
Hilma Wolitzer **17**:563

Broughton, Panthea Reid
William Faulkner **6**:175
Carson McCullers **4**:345

Broun, Heywood Hale
Roger Kahn **30**:231

Brousse, Charles
William Mastrosimone **36**:291

Brown, Alan
Marie-Claire Blais **22**:59
Ernest Hemingway **19**:217

Brown, Ashley
Caroline Gordon **6**:204, 206;
  13:241
Allen Tate **2**:428

Brown, Calvin S.
Conrad Aiken **3**:4
William Faulkner **18**:149;
  28:142

Brown, Chip
Joe McGinniss **32**:303

Brown, Clarence
Jorge Luis Borges **19**:48
Joseph Brodsky **36**:77
Czeslaw Milosz **5**:292
Vladimir Nabokov **1**:242

Brown, Constance A.
Laurence Olivier **20**:239

Brown, Cynthia
Barbara Corcoran **17**:75

Brown, Dee
Vine Deloria, Jr. **21**:112

Brown, Deming
Alexander Zinoviev **19**:487

Brown, E. K.
Louis Dudek **19**:136
E. J. Pratt **19**:382

Brown, Edward Hickman
Nadine Gordimer **33**:180
Doris Lessing **22**:279

Brown, Edward J.
Ilya Ehrenburg **18**:136

Brown, F. J.
Arthur Koestler **3**:271
Alberto Moravia **2**:293
Mario Puzo **1**:282
Muriel Spark **2**:417

Brown, Frederick
Louis Aragon **3**:13
Jean Cocteau **1**:60

Brown, Geoff
Woody Allen **16**:8
Walter Becker and Donald
  Fagen **26**:79
Jackson Browne **21**:35
Dario Fo **32**:172
Marvin Gaye **26**:132
Satyajit Ray **16**:495
Smokey Robinson **21**:345, 350
Joan Micklin Silver **20**:342
Peter Weir **20**:425
Brian Wilson **12**:648

Brown, Georgia A.
Lynne Sharon Schwartz **31**:388

Brown, Harry
Hollis Summers **10**:494

Brown, Ivor
J. B. Priestley **2**:346

Brown, J. R.
Michael Frayn **31**:192

Brown, Jennifer
Richard Peck **21**:300

Brown, John L.
Helen MacInnes **27**:281
Marguerite Yourcenar **19**:484

Brown, John Mason
Charles Addams **30**:13
Eric Bentley **24**:46
Paul Green **25**:193
Laura Z. Hobson **25**:270
Thornton Wilder **35**:436, 437
Tennessee Williams **30**:457

Brown, John Russell
John Arden **6**:8
John Osborne **5**:332
Harold Pinter **6**:408, 413
Arnold Wesker **5**:482

Brown, Kenneth R.
Sam Peckinpah **20**:275

Brown, Linda
Alan Ayckbourn **33**:43

Brown, Lloyd W.
Imamu Amiri Baraka **3**:35;
33:56
Wilson Harris **25**:212
Langston Hughes **10**:281
Paule Marshall **27**:313

Brown, Margaret Warren
Jean Lee Latham **12**:323

Brown, Merle E.
Kenneth Burke **2**:88
Geoffrey Hill **18**:236
Philip Larkin **18**:295

Brown, Pam
Billy Joel **26**:215

Brown, Ralph Adams
Henry Gregor Felsen **17**:121
Andre Norton **12**:455
John R. Tunis **12**:595

Brown, Richard
Douglas Adams **27**:14
John Kennedy Toole **19**:443

Brown, Robert
Stanley Elkin **14**:157

Brown, Robert McAfee
Elie Wiesel **5**:493; **37**:455

Brown, Rosellen
Margaret Atwood **8**:28; **15**:39
Marilyn French **18**:158
Toni Morrison **22**:321
Tim O'Brien **7**:272
May Sarton **4**:471
Judith Johnson Sherwin **7**:414
Diane Wakoski **4**:572

Brown, Royal S.
Brian De Palma **20**:78

Brown, Russell M.
Clark Blaise **29**:69, 73
Robert Kroetsch **5**:221
Leon Rooke **25**:392
Audrey Thomas **37**:418

Brown, Ruth Leslie
John Gardner **2**:151
Gilbert Rogin **18**:457

Brown, Slater
Jerome Siegel and Joe Shuster
21:353

Brown, Spencer
Edward Hoagland **28**:185
John McPhee **36**:297

Brown, Stephen P.
David Brin **34**:135
Kim Stanley Robinson **34**:105
Lucius Shepard **34**:108

Brown, Sterling
Zora Neale Hurston **30**:211

Brown, Steve
Arthur C. Clarke **18**:107

Brown, T.
Louis MacNeice **10**:323

Brown, Terence
Kingsley Amis **2**:6
Seamus Heaney **25**:240
Michael Longley **29**:293
Derek Mahon **27**:288

Brown, William P.
John Brunner **10**:78

Browne, Joseph
Larry McMurtry **27**:334

Browne, Ray B.
Irving Wallace **13**:569

Browne, Robert M.
J. D. Salinger **12**:511

Browning, Dominique
Susan Cheever **18**:101

Browning, John
Snoo Wilson **33**:466

Browning, Preston M., Jr.
Flannery O'Connor **3**:367;
21:275

Brownjohn, Alan
Dannie Abse **7**:1; **29**:16
Ted Berrigan **37**:44
Elizabeth Daryush **19**:120
Donald Davie **5**:115
C. Day Lewis **6**:128
D. J. Enright **31**:149, 153
Elaine Feinstein **36**:168
Roy Fisher **25**:157, 159
Roy Fuller **28**:157, 158
W. S. Graham **29**:197
Geoffrey Grigson **7**:136
Thom Gunn **18**:199
Seamus Heaney **7**:148
Hermann Hesse **17**:215
Geoffrey Hill **18**:239
Elizabeth Jennings **14**:292
Thomas Kinsella **4**:270
Philip Larkin **5**:226
Penelope Lively **32**:275
Michael Longley **29**:291
George MacBeth **9**:340
Norman MacCaig **36**:283, 284
Derek Mahon **27**:287
Edwin Morgan **31**:273

Leslie Norris **14**:388
Linda Pastan **27**:370
Kenneth Patchen **18**:393
Peter Porter **33**:326
Anthony Powell **7**:341
Craig Raine **32**:349
Christopher Reid **33**:349
Marilynne Robinson **25**:388
Alan Sillitoe **19**:420
Louis Simpson **7**:428
D. M. Thomas **13**:541
Ted Walker **13**:567
Yevgeny Yevtushenko **26**:467

Brownjohn, Elizabeth
Philip Larkin **5**:227

Broyard, Anatole
Walter Abish **22**:17
William Barrett **27**:19
Frederick Barthelme **36**:53
Saul Bellow **2**:52; **33**:67;
34:545
Claude Brown **30**:39
Rosellen Brown **32**:63, 64
William F. Buckley, Jr. **18**:83
Frederick Busch **18**:84
Italo Calvino **33**:99
Elias Canetti **25**:113
Raymond Carver **36**:100
John Cheever **25**:119
Arthur A. Cohen **31**:94
Laurie Colwin **23**:129
Pat Conroy **30**:76
Len Deighton **22**:119
John M. Del Vecchio **29**:151
Peter Dickinson **12**:176; **35**:137
José Donoso **8**:179
Lawrence Durrell **27**:97
Nora Ephron **17**:111
Jules Feiffer **8**:217
Elaine Feinstein **36**:169
Ken Follett **18**:156
Daniel Fuchs **34**:545
John Gardner **28**:164
John Gardner **30**:158
Penelope Gilliatt **10**:229
Herbert Gold **14**:208
Günter Grass **2**:172
Lillian Hellman **18**:227
Mark Helprin **22**:221; **32**:230
Richard F. Hugo **32**:241
Garson Kanin **22**:232
Yoram Kaniuk **19**:239
Donald Keene **34**:566
Benedict Kiely **23**:266
Jerzy Kosinski **10**:307
Helen MacInnes **27**:283
Bernard Mac Laverty **31**:256
Bernard Malamud **2**:266
Bobbie Ann Mason **28**:272
James A. Michener **29**:316
A. G. Mojtabai **15**:378
Wright Morris **18**:353
Edna O'Brien **13**:415
Michael Ondaatje **14**:410
Cynthia Ozick **28**:351
Robert B. Parker **27**:367
Marge Piercy **14**:420
Anthony Powell **31**:317
V. S. Pritchett **15**:442
Barbara Pym **37**:372
Anne Redmon **22**:342
Jean Rhys **19**:393

Marilynne Robinson **25**:387
Philip Roth **3**:436; **22**:356
Françoise Sagan **9**:468; **17**:427;
36:380
Nathalie Sarraute **8**:473
Mark Schorer **9**:473
Lynne Sharon Schwartz **31**:390
Georges Simenon **8**:488
J.I.M. Stewart **32**:421, 422
Peter Taylor **18**:527
Lisa St. Aubin de Teran **36**:422
Trevanian **29**:429, 430
William Trevor **25**:445
Anne Tyler **11**:553
John Updike **2**:440; **9**:539;
15:545
Eudora Welty **33**:423
Joy Williams **31**:463
Hilma Wolitzer **17**:563

Bruccoli, Matthew J.
James Gould Cozzens **11**:131
John O'Hara **3**:370

Bruce-Novoa
Gary Soto **32**:404

Bruchac, Joseph
Chinua Achebe **26**:21

Bruckner, D.J.R.
Thomas Merton **34**:465
Michael Mott **34**:465

Brudnoy, David
James Baldwin **2**:33
Robin Cook **14**:131
Bob Fosse **20**:123

Bruell, Edwin
Harper Lee **12**:342

Brukenfeld, Dick
Joyce Carol Oates **3**:364

Brumberg, Abraham
Aleksandr I. Solzhenitsyn
4:514; **18**:498

Brumer, Andy
Stephen Dobyns **37**:81
Mary Oliver **34**:246

Brummell, O. B.
Bob Dylan **12**:183

Brunette, Peter
Archibald MacLeish **14**:338

Bruning, Peter
Ward Ruyslinck **14**:472

Brushwood, John S.
Gregorio López y Fuentes
32:280

Brustein, Robert
Edward Albee **3**:6, 7; **25**:37
Jean Anouilh **1**:6
Enid Bagnold **25**:77
James Baldwin **4**:40; **17**:28
Brendan Behan **1**:26
Robert Bolt **14**:88
Christopher Durang **27**:89, 91
Federico Fellini **16**:278
Dario Fo **32**:176
Michael Frayn **31**:193
Athol Fugard **25**:178
Jack Gelber **1**:114

Jean Genet **1**:115
William Gibson **23**:175
John Guare **29**:208
A. R. Gurney, Jr. **32**:219
John Hare **29**:219
Ronald Harwood **32**:227
Joseph Heller **3**:228
Lillian Hellman **34**:350
Rolf Hochhuth **4**:230
William Inge **1**:153
Eugène Ionesco **1**:154
Arthur Kopit **18**:287; **33**:252
Stanley Kubrick **16**:378
David Mamet **34**:223
William Mastrosimone **36**:290
Mark Medoff **23**:294
Arthur Miller **6**:330
John Osborne **5**:332
Harold Pinter **1**:266; **3**:385,
    386; **15**:426; **27**:392
David Rabe **33**:346
Gerome Ragni and James Rado
    17:379
Ronald Ribman **7**:357
Jean-Paul Sartre **4**:476
Murray Schisgal **6**:489
Peter Shaffer **5**:386
Sam Shepard **17**:442; **34**:269
Martin Sherman **19**:416
Stephen Sondheim **30**:403
Tom Stoppard **3**:470; **15**:524;
    29:406
Ronald Tavel **6**:529
C. P. Taylor **27**:447
Jean-Claude Van Itallie **3**:492
Gore Vidal **4**:552, 553
Peter Weiss **3**:514
Arnold Wesker **5**:482
Tennessee Williams **19**:470
Lanford Wilson **36**:465

Brutus, Dennis
Alan Paton **25**:361

Bruun, Geoffrey
Thomas B. Costain **30**:95, 96,
    98, 99
Marguerite Yourcenar **19**:480

Bryan, C.D.B.
Jonathan Baumbach **23**:54
Julio Cortázar **2**:103
Norma Klein **30**:236
Craig Nova **7**:267
Tom Wolfe **35**:452

Bryant, J. A., Jr.
Allen Tate **14**:530
Eudora Welty **1**:361; **5**:480

Bryant, Jerry H.
James Baldwin **8**:41
John Barth **2**:36
Saul Bellow **2**:52
William S. Burroughs **2**:91
Ronald L. Fair **18**:140
Ernest J. Gaines **18**:165
Nikki Giovanni **19**:191
Joseph Heller **3**:228
James Jones **3**:261
Norman Mailer **2**:260
Bernard Malamud **2**:266
Carson McCullers **4**:344
Toni Morrison **4**:366
Flannery O'Connor **2**:317

Walker Percy **2**:333
Thomas Pynchon **2**:353
Ayn Rand **3**:423
Ishmael Reed **32**:362
John Updike **2**:441
Kurt Vonnegut, Jr. **2**:452
John A. Williams **5**:497

Bryant, Nelson
Jacques-Yves Cousteau **30**:105
James Herriot **12**:282

Bryant, Rene Kuhn
Thomas Berger **8**:83
Heinrich Böll **6**:84
John Fowles **6**:187
Paula Fox **8**:219
John Hersey **7**:154
Doris Lessing **10**:316
James A. Michener **5**:291

Bryden, Ronald
Peter Barnes **5**:49
David Hare **29**:212
Doris Lessing **6**:299
Shiva Naipaul **32**:324
Peter Nichols **5**:306
Françoise Sagan **17**:421
David Storey **4**:529
Peter Straub **28**:408
Paul West **7**:525

Buache, Freddy
Luis Buñuel **16**:138

Bucco, Martin
René Wellek **28**:452

Buchanan, Cynthia
Norman Mailer **2**:263

Buchen, Irving H.
Carson McCullers **10**:334

Buchholz, Todd G.
Margaret Mead **37**:285

Buchsbaum, Betty
David Kherdian **6**:280

Buck, Philo M., Jr.
Jules Romains **7**:378

Buck, Richard M.
Andre Norton **12**:457

Buckle, Richard
John Betjeman **2**:60

Buckler, Ernest
Hugh Hood **15**:283
Frank Swinnerton **31**:427

Buckler, Robert
Elia Kazan **6**:274
Thomas Williams **14**:582

Buckley, James J., Jr.
Pat Conroy **30**:77

Buckley, John
Jim Harrison **33**:196

Buckley, Kathryn
Joan Barfoot **18**:36

Buckley, Leonard
Ronald Harwood **32**:224

Buckley, P. L.
Helen MacInnes **27**:282

Buckley, Peter
Lily Tomlin **17**:522
Andy Warhol **20**:420

Buckley, Priscilla L.
Eric Ambler **6**:4
Thomas J. Fleming **37**:124

Buckley, Reid
William McPherson **34**:88

Buckley, Tom
Steven Bochco and Michael
    Kozoll **35**:48
Michael Cimino **16**:212
Ronald J. Glasser **37**:132
Irving Wallace **13**:570

Buckley, Vincent
T. S. Eliot **3**:138

Buckley, Virginia
Katherine Paterson **12**:487

Buckley, William F., Jr.
William F. Buckley, Jr. **7**:35
Len Deighton **22**:118
Lillian Hellman **14**:257
John le Carré **28**:226
Monty Python **21**:229
Gerome Ragni and James Rado
    17:381
Aleksandr I. Solzhenitsyn **4**:511
Hunter S. Thompson **17**:513
Garry Trudeau **12**:590
Tom Wolfe **2**:481

Buckman, Peter
Elaine Feinstein **36**:168
Tom Sharpe **36**:400

Buckmaster, Henrietta
Kristin Hunter **35**:223
Maxine Hong Kingston **19**:250
Paule Marshall **27**:310
Barbara Pym **19**:387

Bucknall, Barbara J.
Ursula K. LeGuin **13**:349

Budgen, Suzanne
Jean Renoir **20**:299

Budrys, Algis
Piers Anthony **35**:35
Isaac Asimov **26**:52
Robert Bloch **33**:84
John W. Campbell, Jr. **32**:78,
    80
C. J. Cherryh **35**:102, 103,
    104, 108
Arthur C. Clarke **35**:124
Robert A. Heinlein **26**:174
Fritz Leiber **25**:307
Frederik Pohl **18**:412
Keith Roberts **14**:464
Kim Stanley Robinson **34**:106
Lucius Shepard **34**:109
Arkadii Strugatskii and Boris
    Strugatskii **27**:435
Jack Williamson **29**:457
Gene Wolfe **25**:473, 475
Roger Zelazny **21**:479

Buechner, Frederick
Annie Dillard **9**:178

Buell, Ellen Lewis
Lloyd Alexander **35**:22
E. M. Almedingen **12**:3
Isaac Asimov **26**:35
Margot Benary-Isbert **12**:31
Dino Buzzati **36**:83
Betty Cavanna **12**:97, 98
Maureen Daly **17**:90
Walter Farley **17**:115
Henry Gregor Felsen **17**:120,
    122
Esther Forbes **12**:207
Roderick L. Haig-Brown
    21:134
Lee Kingman **17**:243
Joseph Krumgold **12**:317
Jean Lee Latham **12**:32
Madeleine L'Engle **12**:345
William Mayne **12**:389
Andre Norton **12**:456
Scott O'Dell **30**:267
Otfried Preussler **17**:374
Carl Sandburg **35**:354
Mary Stolz **12**:545, 546, 547,
    548, 549, 550, 551, 552
Noel Streatfeild **21**:396, 397,
    398, 399
John R. Tunis **12**:593, 594,
    595, 596
Jill Paton Walsh **35**:430
Lenora Mattingly Weber **12**:631
Maia Wojciechowska **26**:451

Buell, Frederick
A. R. Ammons **8**:17

Bueno, J.R.T., Jr.
Roderick L. Haig-Brown
    21:136

Buffalohead, W. Roger
Vine Deloria, Jr. **21**:110

Buffington, Robert
Wayne C. Booth **24**:92
Cleanth Brooks **24**:111
Frederick Busch **18**:85
Donald Davidson **2**:112
John Crowe Ransom **4**:430,
    437

Bufithis, Philip H.
Norman Mailer **11**:342

Bufkin, E. C.
Iris Murdoch **2**:297
P. H. Newby **2**:310

Buford, Bill
Gabriel García Márquez **27**:151

Buhle, Paul and Fiehrer, Thomas
Ernesto Cardenal **31**:79

Buitenhuis, Peter
Harry Mathews **6**:314
William Trevor **7**:475
Richard Yates **23**:479

Bukoski, Anthony
W. P. Kinsella **27**:237

Bullins, Ed
Alice Childress **12**:106

Bullock, Florence Haxton
John Ehle **27**:102
Laura Z. Hobson **25**:268
Elizabeth Jane Howard **29**:242
Frank Tuohy **37**:426
T. H. White **30**:440

Bulman, Learned T.
Henry Gregor Felsen **17**:122
Margaret O. Hyde **21**:171
Jean Lee Latham **12**:323, 325
Andre Norton **12**:456

Bumpus, Jerry
Mario Vargas Llosa **15**:552

Bumsted, J. M.
Bruce Catton **35**:95

Bundy, McGeorge
William F. Buckley, Jr. **37**:53

Bunnell, Sterling
Michael McClure **6**:321

Bunster, Elizabeth
Sylvia Murphy **34**:91

Bunting, Basil
Hugh MacDiarmid **4**:313

Bunting, Charles T.
Elizabeth Spencer **22**:403

Bunting, Josiah, III
James H. Webb, Jr. **22**:453

Burbank, Rex
Thornton Wilder **1**:364

Burch, Noel
Alain Resnais **16**:496

Burg, Victor
Richard Elman **19**:150

Burg, Victor Kantor
Pat Jordan **37**:195

Burger, Marjorie
Walter Farley **17**:116, 117

Burger, Nash K.
Walter D. Edmonds **35**:153
Elizabeth Spencer **22**:400

Burger, Otis Kidwell
Lynne Reid Banks **23**:40

Burgess, Anthony
Kingsley Amis **1**:6; **2**:8
James Baldwin **1**:16
Samuel Beckett **1**:23; **3**:44
Saul Bellow **1**:31
Elizabeth Bowen **1**:40; **3**:82
Brigid Brophy **6**:99; **29**:94, 95
William S. Burroughs **1**:48
Italo Calvino **22**:92
Albert Camus **1**:54
Louis-Ferdinand Céline **7**:46
Agatha Christie **1**:58
J. M. Coetzee **23**:126
Ivy Compton-Burnett **1**:62
Don DeLillo **13**:178
Peter De Vries **28**:109
E. L. Doctorow **18**:125
Lawrence Durrell **1**:87
T. S. Eliot **3**:139
E. M. Forster **1**:107
Carlos Fuentes **13**:231

Gabriel García Márquez **27**:156
Jean Genet **1**:115
Penelope Gilliatt **2**:160
William Golding **1**:121
Günter Grass **1**:125; **11**:251
Henry Green **2**:178
Graham Greene **3**:207
Joseph Heller **1**:140
Ernest Hemingway **1**:143;
  3:234
Aldous Huxley **1**:151
Christopher Isherwood **1**:156
Pamela Hansford Johnson **1**:160
Erica Jong **18**:278
Alfred Kazin **34**:562
Arthur Koestler **1**:169; **3**:270
John le Carré **9**:326
Colin MacInnes **4**:314
Norman Mailer **1**:190; **28**:262
Bernard Malamud **1**:199; **3**:322
Olivia Manning **19**:301
Mary McCarthy **1**:206; **24**:345
Henry Miller **1**:224
Manuel Mujica Láinez **31**:285
Iris Murdoch **1**:235
Vladimir Nabokov **1**:244; **3**:352
Flann O'Brien **1**:252
Lucio Piccolo **13**:440
Reynolds Price **13**:464
J. B. Priestley **2**:347
Alain Robbe-Grillet **1**:288
J. D. Salinger **1**:299
William Sansom **2**:383
Alan Sillitoe **1**:307
C. P. Snow **1**:317
Muriel Spark **2**:416
Paul Theroux **11**:528
D. M. Thomas **31**:431
John Wain **2**:458
Evelyn Waugh **1**:359; **3**:510
Angus Wilson **2**:472
Edmund Wilson **3**:538

Burgess, Charles E.
William Inge **8**:308

Burgess, Jackson
Robert Altman **16**:22
Stanley Kubrick **16**:380

Burgess, John
Satyajit Ray **16**:476

Burgin, Richard
Isaac Bashevis Singer **23**:420

Burhans, Clinton S., Jr.
Joseph Heller **3**:230
Ernest Hemingway **8**:283;
  30:188
Kurt Vonnegut, Jr. **8**:530

Burian, Jarka M.
Václav Havel **25**:223

Burk, Anne M.
Fumiko Enchi **31**:140
William Kotzwinkle **35**:254

Burke, Frank
Federico Fellini **16**:298

Burke, Jeffrey
Carolyn G. Heilbrun **25**:256
Thomas Keneally **19**:248
Ted Mooney **25**:330
Alberto Moravia **18**:349
Jayne Anne Phillips **15**:420

Richard Price **12**:492
Lewis Thomas **35**:410
Elie Wiesel **37**:453

Burke, Kathleen
René Wellek **28**:454

Burke, Kenneth
Wayne C. Booth **24**:90
William Empson **33**:146
Clifford Odets **28**:325
John Crowe Ransom **24**:363
Theodore Roethke **11**:479
James Thurber **25**:435
Glenway Wescott **13**:590

Burke, Susan E.
Cynthia Propper Seton **27**:424

Burke, William M.
John A. Williams **5**:497

Burkholder, Robert E.
Pat Conroy **30**:78

Burkman, Katherine H.
Harold Pinter **27**:384

Burkom, Selma R.
Doris Lessing **1**:174

Burnett, Constance Buil
Frank B. Gilbreth, Jr. and
  Ernestine Gilbreth Carey
  17:153

Burnett, Michael
James Thurber **5**:440

Burnett, W. R.
Mari Sandoz **28**:403

Burnham, David
Clifford Odets **28**:329
Emlyn Williams **15**:577

Burns, Alan
Michael Moorcock **27**:348
Ann Quin **6**:442
C. P. Snow **1**:317

Burns, Gerald
W. H. Auden **4**:33
John Berryman **6**:62, 63
Austin Clarke **9**:169
Donald Hall **37**:141
Seamus Heaney **7**:147
Donald Justice **19**:236
Robert Lowell **5**:256
Frank O'Hara **5**:324
Charles Olson **5**:328
Ezra Pound **5**:348
Gary Snyder **5**:393
William Stafford **4**:520
Diane Wakoski **11**:564

Burns, J.
Noel Hilliard **15**:280

Burns, James
Maurice Gee **29**:177

Burns, John F.
James A. Michener **29**:313

Burns, Landon C., Jr.
Mary Renault **17**:395

Burns, Martin
Kurt Vonnegut, Jr. **12**:608

Burns, Mary M.
Lloyd Alexander **35**:28
Cecil Bødker **21**:14
Alice Childress **12**:107
Barbara Corcoran **17**:77
Peter Dickinson **12**:171; **35**:136
Lois Duncan **26**:102
Jean Craighead George **35**:178
Bette Greene **30**:171
Jamake Highwater **12**:287
Isabelle Holland **21**:154
Mollie Hunter **21**:164
Diana Wynne Jones **26**:230
M. E. Kerr **12**:297, 298
Lee Kingman **17**:247
Jean Lee Latham **12**:325
Norma Fox Mazer **26**:290
Anne McCaffrey **17**:282
Nicholasa Mohr **12**:445
Andre Norton **12**:471
Scott O'Dell **30**:274
Robert Newton Peck **17**:340,
  342
Carl Sandburg **35**:357
Ann Schlee **35**:372
Ouida Sebestyen **30**:350
Noel Streatfeild **21**:410
Maia Wojciechowska **26**:457
Laurence Yep **35**:470

Burns, Robert
A. J. Cronin **32**:140

Burns, Stuart L.
Ernest Hemingway **30**:197
Jean Stafford **4**:517

Burns, Wayne
Alex Comfort **7**:52,53

Burnshaw, Stanley
James Dickey **10**:141

Burroughs, Franklin G.
William Faulkner **3**:157

Burrow, J. W.
Aldous Huxley **3**:254
J.R.R. Tolkien **3**:482

Burroway, Janet
James Leo Herlihy **6**:235
Mary Hocking **13**:284
Masuji Ibuse **22**:227
Paule Marshall **27**:310

Burstein, Janet Handler
Isak Dinesen **29**:160

Burt, Struthers
Kay Boyle **19**:62

Burton, Dwight L.
Betty Cavanna **12**:99
Maureen Daly **17**:88

Burton, Thomas
Alfred Hitchcock **16**:338

Busch, Frederick
J. G. Farrell **6**:173
John Hawkes **7**:140
William Kotzwinkle **35**:256
Alice Munro **10**:356
Jim Shepard **36**:406
Paul Theroux **28**:426
Paul West **7**:523

Critic Index

Bush, Kent
Thor Heyerdahl **26**:190

Bush, Roland E.
Ishmael Reed **3**:424

Busi, Frederick
Alain Resnais **16**:513

Butcher, Patrick
Howard Barker **37**:36

Butkiss, John F.
Lee Kingman **17**:246

Butler, Christopher
I. A. Richards **24**:401

Butler, Colin
Hermann Hesse **17**:214

Butler, Florence W.
Henry Gregor Felsen **17**:120

Butler, G. P.
Siegfried Lenz **27**:251
Martin Walser **27**:466

Butler, Geoff
Rolf Hochhuth **18**:256

Butler, Marilyn
Brigid Brophy **29**:98
Barbara Pym **37**:370

Butler, Michael
Heinrich Böll **11**:58
Ernst Jandl **34**:197

Butler, Rupert
Laurence Olivier **20**:239

Butler, William Vivian
John Creasey **11**:135

Butscher, Edward
John Berryman **3**:67
Shusaku Endo **14**:162
John Gardner **3**:185
Jerzy Kosinski **6**:282
Richard Kostelanetz **28**:218
John Sayles **14**:483
Philip Whalen **29**:445
James Wright **5**:519
Rudolph Wurlitzer **4**:598

Butt, John
Carlos Fuentes **10**:208

Buttel, Robert
Seamus Heaney **25**:241

Butterick, George
Ed Dorn **18**:129

Butterick, George F.
Charles Olson **29**:327

Butwin, Joseph
Richard Brautigan **12**:62

Byars, Betsy
Jean Craighead George **35**:180
Kin Platt **26**:350

Byatt, A. S.
Malcolm Bradbury **32**:51
Penelope Fitzgerald **19**:174
Antonia Fraser **32**:179
Diane Johnson **13**:305
Pamela Hansford Johnson
　27:221

Amos Oz **11**:429
V. S. Pritchett **15**:440
C. P. Snow **13**:514

Byer, Kathryn Stripling
Carolyn Kizer **15**:309

Byers, Margaret
Elizabeth Jennings **5**:197

Byers, Nancy
Jean Lee Latham **12**:324

Byrd, James W.
Willard Motley **18**:357

Byrd, Max
Jorge Luis Borges **6**:93
Peter DeVries **10**:136

Byrd, Scott
John Barth **1**:17

Byrns, Ruth
August Derleth **31**:131

Byrom, Thomas
Frank O'Hara **13**:423

Byron, Stuart
Woody Allen **16**:12
John Lennon **35**:265

Cabrera, Vicente
Juan Benet **28**:23

Cadogan, Mary
Joan Aiken **35**:17
Antonia Fraser **32**:185
William Mayne **12**:404
Noel Streatfeild **21**:143

Cahill, Daniel J.
E. L. Doctorow **18**:121
Jerzy Kosinski **2**:232

Cahn, Victor L.
Tom Stoppard **29**:397

Cahnman, Werner J.
Primo Levi **37**:221

Caidin, Martin
Ernest K. Gann **23**:166

Cain, James M.
James M. Cain **28**:45

Cain, Joan
Camilo José Cela **13**:147

Cain, William E.
Wayne C. Booth **24**:97

Cairns, Scott C.
Michael S. Harper **22**:209

Calas, Nicholas
André Breton **9**:125

Calder, Angus
T. S. Eliot **2**:128
Alex La Guma **19**:273
Ngugi wa Thiong'o **36**:310

Calder, Robert L.
W. Somerset Maugham **15**:369

Caldicott, Leonie
Michael Frayn **31**:191

Caldwell, James R.
Muriel Rukeyser **27**:407

Caldwell, Joan
Margaret Laurence **13**:344
Audrey Thomas **7**:472

Caldwell, Mark
Thom Gunn **32**:214
Lewis Thomas **35**:415

Caldwell, Stephen
D. Keith Mano **2**:270

Caless, Bryn
Joan Aiken **35**:20
Penelope Lively **32**:275
J.I.M. Stewart **32**:421

Calisher, Hortense
Yukio Mishima **2**:289
Vladimir Nabokov **1**:246
Raja Rao **25**:365
Christina Stead **5**:403

Callaghan, Linda Ward
Gene Roddenberry **17**:414

Callahan, John
Michael S. Harper **7**:138

Callahan, John F.
Alice Walker **5**:476

Callahan, Patrick
Wendell Berry **27**:33

Callahan, Patrick J.
C. S. Lewis **3**:297
George MacBeth **2**:251
Alan Sillitoe **1**:308
Stephen Spender **2**:420

Callan, Edward
W. H. Auden **1**:9, 11; **14**:30
Alan Paton **4**:395; **25**:363

Callan, Richard J.
José Donoso **11**:147
Octavio Paz **19**:364

Callanan, Deirdre G.
Mary Oliver **34**:249

Callenbach, Ernest
Ingmar Bergman **16**:60
Charles Chaplin **16**:198
Shirley Clarke **16**:218
John Ford **16**:309
Alfred Hitchcock **16**:342, 344
Elia Kazan **16**:367
Satyajit Ray **16**:482
Andy Warhol **20**:418
Orson Welles **20**:438

Callendar, Newgate
Eric Ambler **4**:18
Isaac Asimov **9**:49
T. J. Binyon **34**:34
William Peter Blatty **2**:64
Robert Bloch **33**:83, 84
William F. Buckley, Jr. **18**:81, 83
Robert Cormier **12**:136
John Creasey **11**:135
Edmund Crispin **22**:111
Rhys Davies **23**:147
Peter Dickinson **12**:170, 171, 177; **35**:131, 132, 136
Paul E. Erdman **25**:153, 154
Howard Fast **23**:160, 161
Dick Francis **22**:152

John Gardner **30**:154, 155
Nicholas M. Guild **33**:186, 187
Ronald Harwood **32**:226
Carolyn G. Heilbrun **25**:252, 254
Richard F. Hugo **32**:242
Evan Hunter **11**:279, 280
P. D. James **18**:272
James Jones **3**:262
Harry Kemelman **2**:225
William X. Kienzle **25**:275, 276
Emma Lathen **2**:236
Elmore Leonard **28**:233
Robert Ludlum **22**:289
Ross Macdonald **14**:336
Helen MacInnes **27**:284
Richard Matheson **37**:247
Robert B. Parker **27**:363, 364
Ellery Queen **11**:458
Ruth Rendell **28**:383, 384, 385, 386, 387
Georges Simenon **2**:399
Martin Cruz Smith **25**:412
Wilbur Smith **33**:375, 376, 377
Mickey Spillane **3**:469
J.I.M. Stewart **14**:512; **32**:420, 421
Julian Symons **32**:425
Trevanian **29**:429
Vassilis Vassilikos **8**:524
Gore Vidal **22**:434
Donald E. Westlake **7**:528, 529; **33**:436, 437, 438

Callery, Sean
Mario Puzo **36**:358

Callow, Philip
Andrew Sinclair **2**:400

Calta, Louis
N. F. Simpson **29**:367

Caltabiano, Frank P.
Edward Albee **25**:39

Calverton, V. F.
Langston Hughes **35**:213

Cambon, Glauco
Michael Hamburger **14**:234
Robert Lowell **8**:348
Eugenio Montale **7**:224
Giuseppe Ungaretti **7**:482; **11**:555; **15**:536
Elio Vittorini **14**:543

Cameron, Ann
Tom Robbins **9**:454

Cameron, Barry
John Metcalf **37**:300
A. W. Purdy **14**:432

Cameron, Ben
Edward Albee **25**:38
Howard Brenton **31**:66

Cameron, Eleanor
Lloyd Alexander **35**:25
Julia W. Cunningham **12**:164
Leon Garfield **12**:226
Alan Garner **17**:138
Nat Hentoff **26**:184
Mollie Hunter **21**:159, 160
Joseph Krumgold **12**:320

William Mayne **12**:393
Emily Cheney Neville **12**:452
Philippa Pearce **21**:283
Rosemary Sutcliff **26**:434

Cameron, Elspeth
Margaret Atwood **13**:4
Timothy Findley **27**:145

Cameron, Ian
Michelangelo Antonioni **20**:20
Nagisa Oshima **20**:247

Cameron, J. M.
David Caute **29**:110

Cameron, J. R.
T. H. White **30**:447

Cameron, James
V. S. Naipaul **37**:319

Cameron, Julia
Judith Rossner **6**:469

Camp, Raymond R.
Roderick L. Haig-Brown
21:135

Camp, Richard
Leon Garfield **12**:221

Campbell, Alex
Ian Fleming **30**:142

Campbell, Barbara
Henry Gregor Felsen **17**:124
John Metcalf **37**:303

Campbell, Colin
Muriel Rukeyser **27**:408

Campbell, Donald
Howard Barker **37**:39
Caryl Churchill **31**:83
Norman MacCaig **36**:287
Tom Paulin **37**:354

Campbell, Gregg M.
Bob Dylan **6**:157

Campbell, James
William S. Burroughs **22**:84
Frederick Forsyth **36**:176
Kazuo Ishiguro **27**:202
Bernard Mac Laverty **31**:254
Vladimir Nabokov **23**:314
Ngugi wa Thiong'o **36**:318
Barbara Pym **37**:369

Campbell, Josie P.
E. L. Doctorow **18**:123

Campbell, Mary Jo
Isaac Asimov **26**:51
Arthur C. Clarke **35**:126

Campbell, Patricia
Kin Platt **26**:353

Campbell, Patty
Fran Arrick **30**:17
Sol Gordon **26**:138, 139
Norma Klein **30**:241
Stan Lee **17**:262
Norma Fox Mazer **26**:292
D. M. Pinkwater **35**:318
Kin Platt **26**:353, 355
Sandra Scoppettone **26**:402

Campbell, Peter
Frank Sargeson **31**:371

Camper, Carol
H. D. **31**:212

Canary, Robert H.
Robert Graves **11**:256

Canavan, Francis
Thomas J. Fleming **37**:119

Canby, Henry Seidel
Pearl S. Buck **18**:75

Canby, Peter
Randolph Stow **23**:438

Canby, Vincent
Lindsay Anderson **20**:16
Ralph Bakshi **26**:66, 68, 72, 76
Shirley Clarke **16**:218
Brian De Palma **20**:72, 74, 75, 79, 80
Vittorio De Sica **20**:95, 97
Marguerite Duras **20**:99
Rainer Werner Fassbinder **20**:113, 120
Federico Fellini **16**:290
Bob Fosse **20**:123
George Roy Hill **26**:205, 207
Alfred Hitchcock **16**:359
John Landis **26**:273
Nagisa Oshima **20**:249
Piers Paolo Pasolini **20**:262, 265
Sam Peckinpah **20**:276
Sidney Poitier **26**:357, 359
Richard Pryor **26**:380
Carlos Saura **20**:316
Paul Schrader **26**:391, 394
Martin Scorsese **20**:323, 330
Jerzy Skolimowski **20**:348
François Truffaut **20**:393
Peter Weir **20**:428

Canham, Erwin D.
Russell Baker **31**:27
T. H. White **30**:447

Canham, Patience M.
John Donovan **35**:140

Candlin, Enid Saunders
Bette Bao Lord **23**:280

Cannella, Anthony R.
Richard Condon **10**:111

Cannon, JoAnn
Italo Calvino **11**:92

Cannon, Margaret
Frederick Forsyth **36**:176

Cansler, Ronald Lee
Robert A. Heinlein **3**:227

Cantarella, Helene
Jules Archer **12**:15
Dino Buzzati **36**:87

Cantor, Jay
William F. Buckley, Jr. **37**:63

Cantor, Peter
Frederic Raphael **2**:367

Cantwell, Mary
Alan Sillitoe **19**:421
Julian Symons **32**:428
Fay Weldon **36**:445

Cantwell, Robert
Erskine Caldwell **14**:94
Upton Sinclair **15**:498

Capers, Charlotte
Mary Lee Settle **19**:409

Capey, A. C.
William Golding **17**:177

Capitanchik, Maurice
E. M. Forster **2**:135
Yukio Mishima **6**:338
Michael Moorcock **27**:348

Caplan, Brina
John Gardner **18**:176
Lillian Hellman **18**:226
Larry McMurtry **27**:331
Joy Williams **31**:465

Caplan, Lincoln
Frederick Buechner **6**:103

Caplan, Pat
Colleen McCullough **27**:319

Caplan, Ralph
Kingsley Amis **1**:6

Capouya, Emile
Amiri Baraka **33**:52
Albert Camus **2**:98
Camilo José Cela **13**:145
Robert Coover **7**:57
Howard Fast **23**:158
Paul Goodman **7**:129
James Leo Herlihy **6**:234
Ignazio Silone **4**:493
Aleksandr I. Solzhenitsyn **1**:320
Robert Stone **23**:425
Dalton Trumbo **19**:445

Capp, Al
Charles Chaplin **16**:194
Mary McCarthy **5**:276

Capps, Benjamin
Christie Harris **12**:262

Caprio, Betsy
Gene Roddenberry **17**:411

Caputi, Jane E.
Steven Spielberg **20**:363

Caputo, Philip
Thomas McGuane **18**:322

Caputo-Mayr, Maria Luise
Peter Handke **8**:261

Caram, Richard
Anne Stevenson **7**:463

Card, Orson Scott
Roger Zelazny **21**:472

Cardinal, Roger
André Breton **15**:86

Cardullo, Robert J.
Robert Altman **16**:37

Carduner, Art
Ingmar Bergman **16**:69

Carens, James F.
Evelyn Waugh **27**:472

Carew, Jan
John Irving **13**:292
George Lamming **2**:235

Carey, John
Richard Bach **14**:35
Lawrence Durrell **4**:147
Richard Eberhart **3**:135
William Empson **8**:201
D. J. Enright **4**:155
Graham Greene **37**:139
Doris Lessing **6**:292
Norman MacCaig **36**:283
John Updike **7**:489

Carey, Julian C.
Langston Hughes **10**:278

Cargas, H. J.
Jacques-Yves Cousteau **30**:105

Cargas, Harry James
Elie Wiesel **37**:452

Cargill, Oscar
Pearl S. Buck **7**:32

Cargin, Peter
Michael Cimino **16**:208

Carhart, Tom
Stephen Wright **33**:467

Carleton, Joyce
Patrick Modiano **18**:338

Carleton, Phillips D.
Halldór Laxness **25**:290
Frans Eemil Sillanpää **19**:417

Carlile, Henry
Stanley Plumly **33**:313

Carls, Alice-Catherine
Tadeusz Różewicz **23**:363

Carlsen, G. Robert
Frank Herbert **12**:273

Carlson, Dale
M. E. Kerr **12**:296
Rosemary Wells **12**:638

Carlson, Michael
James Fenton **32**:166

Carmer, Carl
A. B. Guthrie, Jr. **23**:197
Zora Neale Hurston **30**:212
Bruce Lancaster **36**:244

Carmody, Rev. Francis R., S.J.
Roy A. Gallant **17**:129

Carne, Rosalind
Caryl Churchill **31**:90

Carne-Ross, D. S.
John Gardner **3**:185
Eugenio Montale **7**:222

Carollo, Monica
Margaret O. Hyde **21**:177

Caron, Paul A.
M. E. Kerr **35**:249

Carpenter, Bogdana
Zbigniew Herbert **9**:274

Critic Index

Carpenter, Frederic I.
  William Everson **14**:163
  Robinson Jeffers **2**:212; **11**:311;
    15:300
  Carson McCullers **12**:417
  Conrad Richter **30**:313
  Jessamyn West **17**:547

Carpenter, John R.
  Zbigniew Herbert **9**:274
  Greg Kuzma **7**:196
  John Logan **5**:255
  James Schevill **7**:401
  Gary Snyder **2**:407
  Diane Wakoski **2**:459
  Peter Wild **14**:581
  Charles Wright **6**:580

Carpenter, Richard C.
  Kay Boyle **19**:63, 64

Carpio, Rustica C.
  Bienvenido N. Santos **22**:363

Carpio, Virginia
  Andre Norton **12**:464

Carr, Archie
  Peter Matthiessen **32**:285

Carr, John
  George Garrett **3**:190

Carr, Patrick
  Peter Townshend **17**:540
  Neil Young **17**:580

Carr, Roy
  John Lennon and Paul
    McCartney **12**:379

Carr, Terry
  Kim Stanley Robinson **34**:107
  Lucius Shepard **34**:108

Carroll, David
  Chinua Achebe **1**:1
  Jean Cayrol **11**:107

Carroll, Paul
  John Ashbery **2**:16
  Robert Creeley **2**:106
  James Dickey **2**:116
  Allen Ginsberg **2**:163
  Frank O'Hara **2**:321
  W. D. Snodgrass **2**:405
  Philip Whalen **6**:565

Carruth, Hayden
  Ai **14**:9
  A. R. Ammons **9**:30
  W. H. Auden **1**:11
  Ted Berrigan **37**:43
  John Berryman **2**:56
  Earle Birney **6**:75
  Robert Bly **15**:68
  Edward Brathwaite **11**:67
  Charles Bukowski **5**:80
  Cid Corman **9**:170
  Robert Creeley **8**:153
  J. V. Cunningham **3**:121
  Babette Deutsch **18**:119
  Annie Dillard **9**:177
  Robert Duncan **2**:122
  Loren Eiseley **7**:91
  Clayton Eshleman **7**:97, 98
  Robert Frost **10**:198
  Tess Gallagher **18**:169

  Jean Garrigue **8**:239
  Arthur Gregor **9**:251
  H. D. **8**:256
  Marilyn Hacker **9**:257
  Donald Hall **37**:142
  Jim Harrison **14**:235
  William Heyen **18**:230
  John Hollander **8**:301
  Edwin Honig **33**:215
  Richard Howard **7**:166
  David Ignatow **7**:174, 175,
    177; **14**:275
  June Jordan **11**:312
  Denise Levertov **8**:346
  Philip Levine **2**:244
  Phillip Lopate **29**:299
  Audre Lorde **18**:309
  Robert Lowell **4**:299; **9**:338
  Archibald MacLeish **14**:337
  W. S. Merwin **8**:390
  Josephine Miles **2**:278
  Frederick Morgan **23**:297
  Howard Nemerov **2**:306
  Charles Olson **9**:412
  Robert Pinsky **9**:417
  J. F. Powers **1**:280
  Kenneth Rexroth **2**:370
  Reg Saner **9**:468
  Anne Sexton **2**:390; **4**:484
  Judith Johnson Sherwin **15**:480
  Leslie Marmon Silko **23**:406
  W. D. Snodgrass **18**:492
  Gilbert Sorrentino **7**:448
  Raymond Souster **14**:502
  R. G. Vliet **22**:443
  David Wagoner **15**:559
  Diane Wakoski **2**:459; **4**:574
  Theodore Weiss **8**:545
  Louis Zukofsky **2**:487

Carson, Dale
  Gunnel Beckman **26**:87

Carson, Katharine W.
  Claude Simon **9**:485

Carson, Neil
  Arthur Miller **26**:327
  George Ryga **14**:472, 473

Carson, Rachel L.
  Jacques-Yves Cousteau **30**:101

Carson, Tom
  The Clash **30**:44, 50
  Steve Martin **30**:247
  Paul McCartney **35**:287
  Van Morrison **21**:239
  The Police **26**:363
  Richard Pryor **26**:378
  Lou Reed **21**:315
  Paul Simon **17**:467
  Paul Weller **26**:446
  Brian Wilson **12**:653
  Neil Young **17**:582
  Frank Zappa **17**:594

Cart, Michael
  Virginia Hamilton **26**:148
  S. E. Hinton **30**:204

Carter, Albert Howard, III
  Italo Calvino **8**:126
  Thomas McGuane **7**:213

Carter, Angela
  John Hawkes **27**:197
  Thomas Keneally **5**:210
  Christina Stead **32**:414

Carter, Anne
  Eilís Dillon **17**:100
  Josephine Poole **17**:373

Carter, Betty
  Robert Cormier **30**:85
  Jean Craighead George **35**:179

Carter, Boyd
  Gregorio López y Fuentes
    32:280

Carter, Lin
  J.R.R. Tolkien **1**:339

Carter, Mary
  Maxine Kumin **28**:221

Carter, Paul
  Eugenio Montale **9**:387

Carter, Robert A.
  Arthur Gregor **9**:253

Carter, Steven R.
  Isaac Asimov **19**:28
  Julian Symons **14**:523

Carver, Ann Cathey
  Lucille Clifton **19**:109

Cary, Joseph
  Dino Buzzati **36**:94
  Eugenio Montale **7**:223; **9**:386
  Giuseppe Ungaretti **7**:482
  Louis Zukofsky **18**:558

Casari, Laura E.
  Adrienne Rich **11**:479

Case, Brian
  Steven Bochco and Michael
    Kozoll **35**:53

Casebeer, Edwin F.
  Hermann Hesse **3**:245

Caserio, Robert L.
  Gilbert Sorrentino **7**:449

Casey, Carol K.
  Eleanor Hibbert **7**:156

Casey, Daniel J.
  Benedict Kiely **23**:260

Casey, Ellen Miller
  Maya Angelou **35**:31

Casey, Jane Barnes
  Peter Taylor **18**:527

Casey, John
  T. Alan Broughton **19**:73
  John D. MacDonald **27**:275
  Breece D'J Pancake **29**:346

Casey, John D.
  Jim Harrison **33**:197

Cashin, Edward J.
  Walker Percy **14**:411

Caspary, Sister Anita Marie
  François Mauriac **4**:337, 338

Casper, Leonard
  Flannery O'Connor **6**:375
  Bienvenido N. Santos **22**:361,
    362, 365

Cassada, Jackie
  Piers Anthony **35**:40, 41
  Jeffrey Archer **28**:14

Cassal, Gould
  Irwin Shaw **23**:395

Cassidy, John
  Dannie Abse **29**:21

Cassidy, T. E.
  Jessamyn West **17**:545

Cassill, R. V.
  Mavis Gallant **7**:110
  Joanne Greenberg **30**:161
  Thomas Hinde **6**:241
  William Kotzwinkle **35**:254
  James Alan McPherson **19**:309
  Tom Robbins **32**:367
  Irwin Shaw **7**:413
  Wilfrid Sheed **2**:393
  Christina Stead **2**:422
  Thomas Williams **14**:581

Cassirer, Thomas
  Mongo Beti **27**:43

Casson, Lionel
  Mary Renault **17**:399

Castor, Gladys Crofoot
  Betty Cavanna **12**:98

Catalano, Frank
  David Brin **34**:134

Catania, Susan
  Alvin Silverstein and Virginia
    B. Silverstein **17**:452

Catanoy, Nicholas
  Mircea Eliade **19**:147, 148

Cate, Curtis
  Romain Gary **25**:185

Cathey, Kenneth Clay
  Peter Taylor **37**:406

Catinella, Joseph
  Christopher Isherwood **1**:157
  Joel Lieber **6**:311
  Bernard Malamud **1**:201

Catling, Patrick Skene
  William Trevor **25**:447

Cattani, Richard J.
  Gay Talese **37**:394

Causey, James Y.
  Camilo José Cela **4**:95

Caute, David
  Breyten Breytenbach **23**:86
  Jean Genet **5**:137
  Lucien Goldmann **24**:236, 242
  Primo Levi **37**:221
  Ved Mehta **37**:289
  Lionel Trilling **9**:531

Cavan, Romilly
  Derek Walcott **4**:574

Caviglia, John
  José Donoso **11**:149

Cavitch, David
William Stafford **4**:521

Cawelti, John G.
Dashiell Hammett **19**:195
Mario Puzo **6**:430
Mickey Spillane **3**:468

Cawley, Joseph A., S.J.
Isabelle Holland **21**:150

Caws, Mary Ann
André Breton **2**:81; **9**:125
Yves Bonnefoy **9**:113
Blaise Cendrars **18**:92

Caws, Peter
Michel Foucault **31**:177

Caylor, Lawrence M.
Marion Zimmer Bradley **30**:31

Caywood, Carolyn
Joyce Carol Thomas **35**:406
Joan D. Vinge **30**:415

Cecchetti, Giovanni
Eugenio Montale **7**:221

Cecil, David
Aldous Huxley **3**:252

Cederstrom, Lorelei
Doris Lessing **22**:281

Ceplair, Larry
Alvah Bessie **23**:61

Cerf, Bennett
John O'Hara **2**:324

Cerf, Cristopher
Peter De Vries **28**:105

Cevasco, G. A.
Pearl S. Buck **18**:77

Chabot, C. Barry
Frederick Exley **11**:187

Chabrol, Claude
Alfred Hitchcock **16**:357

Chace, William M.
Ezra Pound **4**:415

Chadwick, Joseph
Julio Cortázar **33**:123

Chaillet, Ned
Athol Fugard **9**:232
Hugh Leonard **19**:281

Chamberlain, Ethel L.
E. M. Almedingen **12**:8

Chamberlain, John
James Gould Cozzens **11**:131
Aldous Huxley **35**:232
Mary McCarthy **3**:326
Ayn Rand **30**:293
Conrad Richter **30**:329
Carl Van Vechten **33**:395
Sloan Wilson **32**:449

Chamberlain, John R.
Julia Peterkin **31**:303, 304

Chamberlin, J. E.
Margaret Atwood **8**:28
George MacBeth **5**:265
W. S. Merwin **3**:338
Charles Tomlinson **4**:547;
6:535, 536
David Wagoner **5**:475

Chambers, A.
S. E. Hinton **30**:204

Chambers, Aidan
Alan Garner **17**:145, 147
William Mayne **12**:404
Philippa Pearce **21**:293
Robert Westall **17**:555

Chambers, Colin
Howard Brenton **31**:63
Peter Shaffer **18**:477

Chambers, D. D.
Alan Paton **25**:359

Chambers, D.D.C.
Matt Cohen **19**:111

Chambers, Robert D.
Ernest Buckler **13**:120
Sinclair Ross **13**:492

Chambers, Ross
Samuel Beckett **9**:77

Chametzky, Jules
Edward Dahlberg **14**:134
Isaac Bashevis Singer **1**:313

Champagne, Roland A.
Roland Barthes **24**:32
Marguerite Duras **11**:167
Romain Gary **25**:188

Champlin, Charles
Julio Cortázar **33**:135
Don DeLillo **27**:84
John Hawkes **27**:196
Manuel Puig **28**:373
Evelyn Waugh **27**:476

Chanady, Amaryll B.
Julio Cortázar **34**:331

Chandler, D. G.
Len Deighton **22**:117

Chang, Charity
Barbara Corcoran **17**:74

Changas, Estelle
Elia Kazan **16**:368

Chankin, Donald O.
B. Traven **8**:517

Chapin, Katherine Garrison
Allen Tate **4**:536

Chapin, Nancy
Jean Craighead George **35**:179

Chaplin, William H.
John Logan **5**:253

Chapman, Abraham
Kristin Hunter **35**:225

Chapman, John
Stephen Sondheim **30**:376, 378

Chapman, Raymond
Graham Greene **1**:133

Chapman, Robert
Anthony Burgess **4**:83
Ivy Compton-Burnett **3**:112

Chappell, Fred
George Garrett **3**:191
Richard Yates **7**:554

Chappetta, Robert
Bernardo Bertolucci **16**:88
Roman Polanski **16**:466

Charles, Faustin
David Dabydeen **34**:148

Charnes, Ruth
M. E. Kerr **12**:303

Charques, R. D.
Ian Fleming **30**:130
Nevil Shute **30**:368

Charters, Ann
Charles Olson **5**:326

Charters, Samuel
Robert Creeley **4**:117
Robert Duncan **4**:142
Larry Eigner **9**:180
William Everson **5**:121
Lawrence Ferlinghetti **6**:182
Allen Ginsberg **4**:181
Charles Olson **5**:329
Gary Snyder **5**:393
Jack Spicer **8**:497

Charyn, Jerome
Kōbō Abé **8**:1
Martin Amis **9**:26
J. G. Ballard **36**:41
David Bradley, Jr. **23**:79
T. Alan Broughton **19**:72
R.H.W. Dillard **5**:116
Elizabeth Jane Howard **7**:165
Margaríta Karapánou **13**:314
William Kotzwinkle **14**:311
Richard Price **12**:492
James Purdy **10**:424; **28**:381
Ishmael Reed **32**:356
Leon Rooke **34**:254
Judith Rossner **9**:457
Luis Rafael Sánchez **23**:383
Mario Vargas Llosa **31**:443
Joseph Wambaugh **18**:533
Jerome Weidman **7**:518
Donald E. Westlake **33**:438
Kate Wilhelm **7**:538

Chase, Edward T.
Nat Hentoff **26**:181

Chase, Gilbert
Louis Aragon **22**:35

Chase, Ilka
Art Buchwald **33**:87

Chase, K.
Josephine Miles **34**:244

Chase, Mary Ellen
Nadine Gordimer **33**:179

Chase, Richard
Saul Bellow **1**:27
Philip Rahv **24**:351

Chasin, Helen
Laurie Colwin **23**:128
Alan Dugan **6**:144
May Sarton **4**:472

Chaskel, Walter B.
Robert Lipsyte **21**:208

Chassler, Philip I.
Meyer Levin **7**:205

Chatfield, Hale
Gil Orlovitz **22**:334

Chatfield, Jack
William F. Buckley, Jr. **18**:83

Chatham, Margaret L.
Isaac Asimov **26**:50
Roy A. Gallant **17**:133

Chatterton, Wayne
Nelson Algren **33**:15

Chaudhuri, Una
Salman Rushdie **31**:357

Chazen, Leonard
Anthony Powell **3**:402

Cheatwood, Kiarri T-H
Ayi Kwei Armah **5**:32

Cheever, John
Saul Bellow **10**:43

Cheever, Susan
Susan Isaacs **32**:254

Chelton, Mary K.
Jay Bennett **35**:46
Anne McCaffrey **17**:281

Chemasi, Antonio
Christopher Durang **27**:88

Cheney, Brainard
Donald Davidson **2**:112
Flannery O'Connor **1**:254;
21:261
Julia Peterkin **31**:307

Chernaik, Judith
Beryl Bainbridge **14**:39
Amos Oz **27**:360

Cherry, Kelly
John Betjeman **10**:53

Cherry, Kenneth
Vladimir Nabokov **8**:413

Cheshire, Ardner R., Jr.
William Styron **11**:518

Chesnick, Eugene
John Cheever **7**:48
Nadine Gordimer **7**:133
Michael Mewshaw **9**:376

Chester, Alfred
Terry Southern **7**:454

Chettle, Judith
Nadine Gordimer **33**:181
Judith Guest **30**:176

Cheuse, Alan
Alejo Carpentier **11**:100
Carlos Fuentes **13**:231
John Gardner **5**:132
Nicholas M. Guild **33**:189
Stephen King **26**:241
Jerzy Kosinski **15**:317
Elmore Leonard **28**:237; **34**:215
André Schwarz-Bart **4**:480
B. Traven **11**:534
John Edgar Wideman **34**:298

Chevigny, Bell Gale
Toni Cade Bambara **19**:32
Julio Cortázar **15**:148
Paule Marshall **27**:311
Tillie Olsen **4**:387

Chew, Shirley
Wilson Harris **25**:211

Chiari, Joseph
Jean Anouilh **8**:23
Jean Cocteau **8**:144

Chiaromonte, Nicola
Eric Bentley **24**:45

Child, Ruth C.
T. S. Eliot **24**:169

Childress, Alice
Joyce Carol Thomas **35**:405

Childs, E. Ira
Peter Townshend **17**:534

Chinn, Nick
Trina Robbins **21**:338

Chitre, Dilip
Jayanta Mahapatra **33**:277

Chomsky, Noam
Saul Bellow **8**:81

Christ, Carol P.
Doris Lessing **22**:283
Ntozake Shange **25**:401

Christ, Ronald
Chinua Achebe **26**:13
Jorge Luis Borges **2**:70, 73;
  4:75
José Donoso **8**:178
Gabriel García Márquez **3**:179
Leonard Michaels **25**:315
Pablo Neruda **5**:301; **7**:260
Octavio Paz **3**:375; **4**:397;
  6:398
Manuel Puig **5**:354; **28**:370
Luis Rafael Sánchez **23**:384
Mario Vargas Llosa **9**:542

Christensen, Paul
Ed Dorn **18**:128
Charles Olson **29**:331

Christgau, Georgia
Joan Armatrading **17**:8
Bob Marley **17**:273
Prince **35**:323

Christgau, Robert
Chuck Berry **17**:54
Richard Brautigan **9**:124
Jimmy Cliff **21**:62
Mick Jagger and Keith Richard
  17:225, 237
C.L.R. James **33**:225
John Lennon **35**:273
John Lennon and Paul
  McCartney **12**:358
Carly Simon **26**:407
Patti Smith **12**:539
Peter Townshend **17**:525
Stevie Wonder **12**:658, 659

Christiansen, Robert
Jackson J. Benson **34**:413

Christiansen, Rupert
John Steinbeck **34**:413

Christie, Ian Leslie
Ken Russell **16**:541

Christie, Joseph, S.J.
Allen Drury **37**:109

Christison, Kathleen
Amos Oz **33**:304

Christman, Elizabeth
Graham Greene **37**:140

Christon, Lawrence
Monty Python **21**:229

Christopher, Nicholas
Seamus Heaney **37**:167

Chrzanowski, Joseph
Jorge Luis Borges **19**:49
Carlos Fuentes **22**:167

Chubb, Thomas Caldecot
Thomas B. Costain **30**:97
C. S. Forester **35**:171
Zora Neale Hurston **30**:209

Chupack, Henry
James Purdy **28**:379

Church, D. M.
Arthur Adamov **25**:16
Albert Camus **32**:94

Church, Richard
Robert Frost **26**:113
Erich Maria Remarque **21**:324

Churchill, David
Peter Dickinson **12**:175
Mollie Hunter **21**:161

Churchill, R. C.
John Cowper Powys **15**:433
P. G. Wodehouse **10**:537

Churchill, Winston
Charles Chaplin **16**:189

Ciardi, John
Robert Frost **13**:223
Stanley Kunitz **14**:312
Melvin B. Tolson **36**:425
Richard Wilbur **14**:576
William Carlos Williams
  13:602

Cifelli, Edward
John Ciardi **10**:106

Cioffi, Frank
Gilbert Sorrentino **22**:397

Ciplijauskaité, Biruté
Gabriel García Márquez **3**:182

Cismaru, Alfred
Simone de Beauvoir **2**:43
Albert Camus **11**:95
Aimé Césaire **19**:96
Marguerite Duras **6**:149; **11**:164
Eugène Ionesco **9**:289
Robert Pinget **13**:442

Cixous, Helen
Severo Sarduy **6**:485

Claire, Thomas
Albert Camus **9**:150

Claire, William F.
Stanley Kunitz **11**:319
Sylvia Plath **17**:347
Allen Tate **9**:521
Mark Van Doren **6**:541

Clancy, Cathy
Piri Thomas **17**:502

Clancy, James H.
Albert Camus **32**:91

Clancy, Joseph
A. J. Cronin **32**:139

Clancy, Thomas H.
Andrew M. Greeley **28**:170

Clancy, William P.
Carson McCullers **12**:413
Brian Moore **7**:235

Clapp, Susannah
Caroline Blackwood **9**:101
Elaine Feinstein **36**:170
Penelope Fitzgerald **19**:172
Antonia Fraser **32**:184
Maurice Gee **29**:177
Ursula Holden **18**:257
Margaríta Karapánou **13**:315
Seán O'Faoláin **7**:274
George MacBeth **9**:340
David Plante **7**:308
Barbara Pym **19**:386
Cynthia Propper Seton **27**:427,
  428
Frank G. Slaughter **29**:378
A. N. Wilson **33**:450
Hilma Wolitzer **17**:562

Clare, Anthony
Susan Sontag **13**:518

Clarens, Carlos
Eric Rohmer **16**:530, 531

Clareson, Thomas D.
James Blish **14**:83
Arthur C. Clarke **35**:120
Thomas M. Disch **36**:124
Aldous Huxley **35**:237
Gene Wolfe **25**:475, 477

Clark, Barrett H.
Paul Green **25**:192

Clark, Edwin
Carl Van Vechten **33**:390, 393

Clark, Eleanor
A. J. Cronin **32**:133

Clark, G. J.
T. J. Binyon **34**:33

Clark, Gerry
Bernice Rubens **19**:405

Clark, Jeff
William Kotzwinkle **35**:255

Clark, J. Michael
Jean Toomer **22**:426

Clark, John R.
Doris Betts **6**:69
Alan Sillitoe **1**:308

Clark, Katerina
Vasily Aksenov **22**:28

Clark, Tom
Ted Berrigan **37**:42
Philip Whalen **29**:447

Clark, Walter Van Tilburg
A. B. Guthrie, Jr. **23**:198

Clarke, Edward J.
Walter D. Edmonds **35**:148

Clarke, Gerald
Edward Albee **25**:37
Larry Gelbart **21**:126
Gore Vidal **2**:449
P. G. Wodehouse **2**:480

Clarke, Henry Leland
Melvin Berger **12**:38

Clarke, Jane H.
Jesse Jackson **12**:289

Clarke, Kenneth
Jesse Stuart **14**:516

Clarke, Loretta
Paul Zindel **6**:587

Clarke, Pauline
Rosemary Sutcliff **26**:437

Clarkson, Paul R.
Robert Kroetsch **23**:269

Clarkson, William
Donald Davie **31**:112

Claudel, Alice Moser
David Kherdian **9**:317

Clausen, Christopher
T. S. Eliot **10**:171

Clay, Carolyn
Mario Vargas Llosa **31**:446

Clay, George R.
Conrad Richter **30**:317

Clayton, John
Richard Brautigan **12**:63

Clayton, John Jacob
Saul Bellow **6**:50

Clements, Bruce
Robert Cormier **12**:137
Richard Peck **21**:297

Clements, Robert J.
Pablo Neruda **2**:308
Irving Stone **7**:469
Vassilis Vassilikos **4**:551

Clemons, Walter
Lisa Alther **7**:12
Max Apple **33**:20
James Baldwin **5**:43
Saul Bellow **6**:55
Peter Benchley **8**:82
Jackson J. Benson **34**:409
Anita Brookner **34**:140
G. Cabrera Infante **5**:96
E. L. Doctorow **6**:133
Nora Ephron **17**:113
J. G. Farrell **6**:173
Joseph Heller **5**:176, 182
George V. Higgins **7**:158
Maureen Howard **5**:189
Erica Jong **4**:263
Milan Kundera **4**:276
Doris Lessing **6**:302
Alison Lurie **4**:305
Ross Macdonald **1**:185
James McCourt **5**:278
Carson McCullers **1**:210
Vladimir Nabokov **6**:354
Donald Newlove **6**:364
Joyce Carol Oates **2**:316; **3**:363
Flannery O'Connor **2**:317

Grace Paley **4**:391
Robert M. Pirsig **4**:403
Manuel Puig **5**:354
Adrienne Rich **6**:458
Isaac Bashevis Singer **3**:456
Martin Cruz Smith **25**:412
Raymond Sokolov **7**:430
John Steinbeck **34**:409
Peter Taylor **37**:412
Gore Vidal **33**:411
Tom Wicker **7**:534
Richard B. Wright **6**:582

Clerc, Charles
Thomas Pynchon **33**:335

Clery, Val
Brian Moore **32**:307

Clever, Glenn
E. J. Pratt **19**:383

Clifford, Gay
Staley Middleton **7**:221
Bernice Rubens **19**:403

Clifford, Paula M.
Claude Simon **9**:485

Clifford, William
Walter Farley **17**:116

Cline, Edward
John Gardner **30**:156

Cline, Ruth
C. S. Adler **35**:14

Clinton, Craig
John Arden **15**:24

Clinton, Dana G.
Sue Ellen Bridgers **26**:91
Ouida Sebestyen **30**:346

Clinton, Farley
William Safire **10**:447

Cloonan, William
André Malraux **13**:368
Tom Robbins **32**:365

Close, Peter
Jack Vance **35**:423

Cloudsley, Donald H.
Glendon Swarthout **35**:401

Cloutier, Pierre
Hugh Hood **15**:285

Clouzot, Claire
John Cassavetes **20**:45
Andy Warhol **20**:419

Clucas, Humphrey
Philip Larkin **5**:227

Clum, John M.
Paddy Chayefsky **23**:115
Peter Shaffer **14**:487

Clurman, Harold
Edward Albee **2**:2; **5**:14; **25**:37
Robert Anderson **23**:28
Jean Anouilh **3**:12
Fernando Arrabal **2**:15; **9**:41
Alan Ayckbourn **5**:37; **8**:35;
18:30
Samuel Beckett **2**:47; **6**:33
Howard Brenton **31**:57

Lenny Bruce **21**:52
Ed Bullins **1**:47; **5**:83
Albert Camus **32**:84
Alice Childress **12**:106
D. L. Coburn **10**:108
Padraic Colum **28**:88
E. E. Cummings **8**:160
Christopher Durang **27**:89
Brian Friel **5**:129
Jean Genet **2**:158
William Gibson **23**:174
Trevor Griffiths **13**:256
John Guare **14**:220
Bill Gunn **5**:153
Christopher Hampton **4**:211,
212
Lorraine Hansberry **17**:190
Lillian Hellman **18**:226
Rolf Hochhuth **4**:230
Fritz Hochwälder **36**:233
William Inge **8**:308
Eugène Ionesco **4**:250
Ann Jellicoe **27**:209
Preston Jones **10**:296
Jean Kerr **22**:254
Arthur Kopit **18**:287, 291
David Mamet **15**:355, 356
Terrence McNally **4**:347;
7:217, 218
Mark Medoff **6**:322
Arthur Miller **1**:218; **6**:335
Jason Miller **2**:284
Yukio Mishima **27**:337
Sławomir Mrozek **13**:399
Peter Nichols **36**:326
Clifford Odets **2**:320; **28**:330,
334
John Osborne **5**:330
Miguel Piñero **4**:402
Harold Pinter **6**:405, 410, 415,
419; **15**:426
David Rabe **4**:426; **8**:450, 451
Terence Rattigan **7**:355
Eric Rohmer **16**:537
Tadeusz Różewicz **23**:361
Anthony Shaffer **19**:413
Peter Shaffer **5**:388
Sam Shepard **6**:496, 497;
17:437, 442
Neil Simon **11**:496
Bernard Slade **11**:508
John Steinbeck **5**:408
Tom Stoppard **1**:327; **4**:526;
5:411; **8**:501; **15**:521
David Storey **5**:417; **8**:505
Elizabeth Swados **12**:557
George Tabori **19**:437
Megan Terry **19**:438
Gore Vidal **2**:450
Joseph A. Walker **19**:454, 455
Richard Wesley **7**:519
Morris L. West **33**:428
Thornton Wilder **6**:573; **35**:445
Tennesse Williams **2**:465;
5:500, 504; **7**:545; **30**:459,
470
Lanford Wilson **7**:549; **14**:592

Clute, John
Douglas Adams **27**:13
Isaac Asimov **26**:58
Samuel R. Delany **14**:147

Fritz Leiber **25**:308
Gene Wolfe **25**:478

Cluysenaar, Anne
Edwin Morgan **31**:273
László Nagy **7**:251
Jon Silkin **6**:498

Coady, Matthew
Monty Python **21**:223

Coale, Samuel
Donald Barthelme **23**:49
John Cheever **25**:118
Jerzy Kosinski **3**:273; **6**:284
Alain Robbe-Grillet **6**:468

Coates, John
Patrick White **18**:545

Coates, Ken
Aleksandr I. Solzhenitsyn
18:500

Cobb, Carl W.
Vicente Aleixandre **36**:23

Cobb, Jane
Taylor Caldwell **28**:61
Betty Cavanna **12**:97
Henry Gregor Felsen **17**:120
Frank B. Gilbreth, Jr. and
Ernestine Gilbreth Carey
17:154, 155
Lee Kingman **17**:243
James Schuyler **23**:387
Zoa Sherburne **30**:361
Mary Stolz **12**:547

Cobb, Richard
René Clair **20**:68

Cockburn, Alexander
P. G. Wodehouse **22**:480

Cocks, Geoffrey
Thomas Pynchon **18**:437

Cocks, Jay
Mel Brooks **12**:77
Michael Cimino **16**:208
Neil Diamond **30**:113
Werner Herzog **16**:326
Richard Lester **20**:231
Gordon Parks **16**:460
Pink Floyd **35**:310
Harold Pinter **3**:388
Prince **35**:329
Lou Reed **21**:316
Bruce Springsteen **17**:480
François Truffaut **20**:383
Frank Zappa **17**:587

Cocks, John C., Jr.
Federico Fellini **16**:274

Cockshott, Gerald
John Ford **16**:307

Coe, Richard L.
Lily Tomlin **17**:521

Coe, Richard N.
Jean Genet **1**:117
Eugène Ionesco **6**:251

Coelho, Joaquim-Francisco
Carlos Drummond de Andrade
18:4

Coffey, Barbara
François Truffaut **20**:393

Coffey, Warren
Flannery O'Connor **21**:262
Kurt Vonnegut, Jr. **3**:494

Cogell, Elizabeth Cummins
Ursula K. LeGuin **13**:348

Coggeshall, Rosanne
Lee Smith **25**:408, 409

Cogley, John
Dan Wakefield **7**:502

Cogswell, Fred
Earle Birney **1**:34
Phyllis Gotlieb **18**:191
Ralph Gustafson **36**:217
Joe Rosenblatt **15**:446

Cohan, Steven
Iris Murdoch **31**:286

Cohan, Tony
William Caunitz **34**:36

Cohen, Arthur A.
Joseph Brodsky **4**:77
Cynthia Ozick **3**:372
Marguerite Yourcenar **19**:483

Cohen, Dean
J. P. Donleavy **1**:76

Cohen, Debra Rae
Anne McCaffrey **17**:283
The Police **26**:365
Carly Simon **26**:413

Cohen, Edwin
Woody Guthrie **35**:194

Cohen, F.
Romain Gary **25**:189

Cohen, George
Robin Cook **14**:131
Nicholas M. Guild **33**:188

Cohen, Gerda
Eva Figes **31**:166

Cohen, Henry
Aimé Césaire **19**:96
Anne Hébert **29**:233

Cohen, J. M.
Yevgeny Yevtushenko **13**:619

Cohen, Joseph
Cynthia Ozick **28**:356
Siegfried Sassoon **36**:388
A. B. Yehoshua **31**:475

Cohen, Keith
Julio Cortázar **33**:132

Cohen, Larry
Jules Feiffer **2**:133

Cohen, Mitchell
David Byrne **26**:98
John Lennon **35**:274
Paul McCartney **35**:292
Prince **35**:326
Smokey Robinson **21**:351
Brian Wilson **12**:652
Neil Young **17**:578

Critic Index

Cohen, Mitchell S.
Elaine May **16**:433

Cohen, Nathan
Mordecai Richler **5**:371

Cohen, Phyllis
Kin Platt **26**:349
Zoa Sherburne **30**:362

Cohen, Richard
Joseph Heller **36**:229

Cohen, Robert
Farley Mowat **26**:336

Cohen, Ron
Amlin Gray **29**:201

Cohen, Sarah Blacher
Cynthia Ozick **28**:347

Cohen, Stephen F.
Aleksandr I. Solzhenitsyn
18:497

Cohn, David L.
Marshall McLuhan **37**:252

Cohn, Dorrit
Alain Robbe-Grillet **1**:289

Cohn, Ellen
Lily Tomlin **17**:517

Cohn, Jeanette
Hilma Wolitzer **17**:564

Cohn, Nik
Mick Jagger and Keith Richard
17:234
Paul Simon **17**:465
Bruce Springsteen **17**:480

Cohn, Ruby
Edward Albee **1**:4; **2**:4
Fernando Arrabal **18**:20
James Baldwin **2**:32
Imamu Amiri Baraka **2**:35
Djuna Barnes **4**:43
John Dos Passos **4**:133
Lawrence Ferlinghetti **2**:134
John Hawkes **4**:215
Robinson Jeffers **11**:310
Kenneth Koch **5**:219
Robert Lowell **11**:324
Arthur Miller **2**:279
Harold Pinter **6**:405
Kenneth Rexroth **11**:472
Thornton Wilder **15**:569
Tennessee Williams **2**:465

Cohn-Sfetcu, Ofelia
Hubert Aquin **15**:15

Coker, Elizabeth Boatwright
Julia Peterkin **31**:307

Colby, Elbridge
James D. Forman **21**:119

Colby, Harriet
Enid Bagnold **25**:72

Colby, Rob
Olga Broumas **10**:76

Colby, Thomas E.
Hermann Hesse **17**:206

Colcord, Lincoln
C. S. Forester **35**:164, 168

Coldwell, Joan
Marie-Claire Blais **13**:96

Cole, Barry
J.M.G. Le Clézio **31**:245
Ann Quin **6**:442

Cole, Diane
Pat Barker **32**:13
Harriet Doerr **34**:152

Cole, John N.
Edward Abbey **36**:20

Cole, Laurence
Jean Rhys **2**:372

Cole, Margaret
Eva Figes **31**:164

Cole, Sheila R.
Julia W. Cunningham **12**:166

Cole, Terry M.
Sonia Levitin **17**:263

Cole, William
Charles Causley **7**:42
Alex Comfort **7**:54
Richard Condon **10**:111
Louis Simpson **7**:429
R. S. Thomas **6**:531

Coleby, John
Howard Barker **37**:34
E. L. Doctorow **15**:180
Robert Nye **13**:413
David Rudkin **14**:471
Wole Soyinka **36**:411
George Tabori **19**:438
Francis Warner **14**:553

Colegate, Isabel
Susan B. Hill **4**:227
Joyce Carol Oates **6**:369

Coleman, Alexander
Alejo Carpentier **11**:99
José Donoso **11**:145; **32**:152
Pablo Neruda **2**:309
Nicanor Parra **2**:331
João Guimarães Rosa **23**:350, 352
Marguerite Yourcenar **19**:484

Coleman, Sister Anne Gertrude
Paul Vincent Carroll **10**:95

Coleman, Arthur Prudden
Joseph Wittlin **25**:466

Coleman, John
Chinua Achebe **26**:12
Robert Altman **16**:44
Mel Brooks **12**:79
Isabel Colegate **36**:108
Marguerite Duras **20**:102
George Roy Hill **26**:201
Kon Ichikawa **20**:180
Garson Kanin **22**:231
Elia Kazan **16**:367
Jack Kerouac **2**:227
Pier Paolo Pasolini **20**:266
Pink Floyd **35**:313
Sidney Poitier **26**:361
Simon Raven **14**:439
Satyajit Ray **16**:487
Bernice Rubens **31**:350
Jerzy Skolimowski **20**:354

Leon Uris **7**:490
Orson Welles **20**:452

Coleman, Jonathan
Evan Hunter **31**:227

Coleman, Ray
Joan Armatrading **17**:8
Neil Diamond **30**:113
Billy Joel **26**:215
John Lennon **35**:265
Bob Marley **17**:268, 269

Coleman, Robert
Stephen Sondheim **30**:376

Coleman, Sidney
Roger Zelazny **21**:467

Coles, Don
Clark Blaise **29**:71
Graham Greene **27**:174

Coles, Robert
Eldridge Cleaver **30**:57
Shirley Ann Grau **4**:208
Nat Hentoff **26**:182
Kenneth Koch **8**:324
Jonathan Kozol **17**:249
Cormac McCarthy **4**:343
John McPhee **36**:297
Milton Meltzer **26**:298
Thomas Merton **34**:464
Michael Mott **34**:464
Tillie Olsen **13**:432
Walker Percy **14**:415
Ezra Pound **34**:505
Muriel Rukeyser **10**:442
William Stafford **7**:461
William Styron **1**:331
Gay Talese **37**:400
E. Fuller Torrey **34**:505
C. K. Williams **33**:446
Frederick Wiseman **20**:467
James Wright **3**:544

Coles, W. E., Jr.
Ann Swinfen **34**:577

Colimore, Vincent J.
John Gardner **30**:153

Colley, Iain
John Dos Passos **25**:140

Collier, Carmen P.
Pearl S. Buck **7**:32

Collier, Christopher
Esther Forbes **12**:212

Collier, Eugenia
James Baldwin **2**:33
Melvin Van Peebles **2**:447

Collier, Michael
Delmore Schwartz **10**:463

Collier, Peter
Earl Rovit **7**:383

Collings, Michael R.
Piers Anthony **35**:37
Dino Buzzati **36**:92, 94
Stephen King **37**:207

Collings, Rex
Wole Soyinka **5**:397

Collins, Anne
André Brink **36**:65
James Clavell **25**:126
Stephen King **12**:311
Manuel Mujica Láinez **31**:283
Joyce Carol Oates **33**:295

Collins, Bill
Jack Vance **35**:427

Collins, Bob
Gene Wolfe **25**:478

Collins, Glen
Fran Lebowitz **36**:248

Collins, Harold R.
Amos Tutuola **5**:443

Collins, J. A.
Christopher Fry **14**:185

Collins, Michael
Dannie Abse **29**:20
Tom Wolfe **15**:584

Collins, Michael J.
Donald Davie **31**:118

Collins, Ralph L.
Elmer Rice **7**:360

Collins, Robert G.
George Lucas **16**:412

Colmer, John
Shirley Hazzard **18**:215

Colombo, John Robert
B. P. Nichol **18**:366

Colum, Mary M.
Vera Brittain **23**:89

Colum, Padraic
Patrick Kavanagh **22**:234
Rosemary Sutcliff **26**:433

Columba, Sister Mary, P.B.V.M.
Rosemary Wells **12**:638

Combs, Richard
Woody Allen **16**:4
Robert Altman **16**:24
John Cassavetes **20**:48, 53
Claude Chabrol **16**:182
Brian De Palma **20**:76
Rainer Werner Fassbinder
20:107, 117, 120
Werner Herzog **16**:322, 323, 333
Elaine May **16**:431
Gordon Parks **16**:459
Sidney Poitier **26**:361, 362
Paul Schrader **26**:388, 396, 399
Martin Scorsese **20**:330, 331, 332
Peter Shaffer **37**:386
Jerzy Skolimowski **20**:353
François Truffaut **20**:393
Peter Weir **20**:425, 427
Orson Welles **20**:453

Commager, Henry Steele
Bruce Catton **35**:83, 85, 86
Esther Forbes **12**:209
MacKinlay Kantor **7**:194
Carl Sandburg **35**:348, 352

Compton, D. G.
Samuel Beckett 3:47
Frederick Buechner 2:84
John Gardner 2:151
Bernard Kops 4:274
Vladimir Nabokov 6:352
Frederic Prokosch 4:422

Compton, Neil
Marshall McLuhan 37:259
Tom Wolfe 35:453

Compton-Burnett, Ivy
Ivy Compton-Burnett 15:139

Conant, Oliver
Renata Adler 31:15
Saul Bellow 33:69
Edna O'Brien 36:338
Peter Taylor 37:413

Conarroe, Joel
John Berryman 8:91; 13:76
Malcolm Bradbury 32:57
Alfred Corn 33:121
Leon Edel 34:536
Stanley Elkin 27:124
Richard Howard 7:167
Brad Leithauser 27:240
Philip Levine 33:275
Howard Nemerov 2:307
Anne Sexton 2:391
W. D. Snodgrass 2:405

Conaty, Barbara
Carolyn Hougan 34:60

Condini, N. E.
Denise Levertov 28:241

Condini, Nereo
Eugenio Montale 7:230
Octavio Paz 19:368
David Plante 23:345
Isaac Bashevis Singer 6:511
Tom Wolfe 9:579

Condon, Richard
John le Carré 15:324

Conley, Timothy K.
William Faulkner 9:200

Conlogue, Ray
Anne Chislett 34:144

Conn, Stewart
Elaine Feinstein 36:169
Anne Stevenson 7:463

Connell, Evan
Carlos Fuentes 22:170
Trevanian 29:431

Connell, Evan S., Jr.
Simone de Beauvoir 2:43
James Dickey 2:116
Gilbert Rogin 18:459
Wilfrid Sheed 2:392

Connelly, Christopher
Jim Carroll 35:81
Paul McCartney 35:293

Connelly, Kenneth
John Berryman 1:34

Connelly, Robert
Luchino Visconti 16:565

Conner, John W.
E. M. Almedingen 12:5
Honor Arundel 17:15, 16
Jay Bennett 35:42
Judy Blume 12:44
Frank Bonham 12:53
James D. Forman 21:118
Nikki Giovanni 4:189
Jesse Jackson 12:290
Madeleine L'Engle 12:348,
349, 350
Robert Lipsyte 21:209
John Neufeld 17:309
Zoa Sherburne 30:363
Glendon Swarthout 35:402
Lenora Mattingly Weber 12:635
Barbara Wersba 30:430
Maia Wojciechowska 26:455,
456

Connole, John M.
Thor Heyerdahl 26:191
Margaret O. Hyde 21:172

Connolly, Cyril
Ernest Hemingway 6:225
Louis MacNeice 4:315
Ezra Pound 4:408, 414

Connolly, Francis X.
C. S. Forester 35:168
T. H. White 30:441

Connor, Anne
Norma Klein 30:244

Conover, Roger
Paul Muldoon 32:316

Conover, Roger L.
Mina Loy 28:250

Conquest, Robert
Roy Fuller 28:149
Norman MacCaig 36:280
Ezra Pound 7:334
Aleksandr I. Solzhenitsyn
2:413; 4:513

Conrad, George
Helen MacInnes 27:280

Conrad, Peter
Beryl Bainbridge 22:46
F. R. Leavis 24:307
David Lodge 36:272

Conrad, Randall
Luis Buñuel 16:145

Conrad, Robert C.
Heinrich Böll 27:65

Conradi, Peter J.
John Fowles 33:174
Harold Pinter 27:391

Conron, Brandon
Alice Munro 19:343

Conroy, Jack
Charles Bukowski 2:84

Consiglio, Alberto
Rouben Mamoulian 16:421

Contoski, Victor
Robert Duncan 2:123
David Ignatow 7:175
David Kherdian 6:281
W. S. Merwin 18:334
Czesław Miłosz 11:376
Marge Piercy 6:403; 18:405;
27:374
Charles Simic 9:480

Conway, John D.
Paul Vincent Carroll 10:98

Coogan, Daniel
Antonia Fraser 32:184

Coogan, Tim Pat
Brian Moore 19:332

Cook, Albert
Djuna Barnes 4:43
André Malraux 4:327

Cook, Bruce
Kingsley Amis 8:11
James Baldwin 3:32; 17:39
Heinrich Böll 6:84
William S. Burroughs 1:49
Evan S. Connell, Jr. 4:109
Gregory Corso 1:64
Robert Duncan 1:83
John Gregory Dunne 28:122
Allen Ginsberg 1:118; 36:194
Lillian Hellman 8:281
John Jakes 29:248
Marjorie Kellogg 2:224
Thomas Keneally 5:211
Jack Kerouac 1:166
Jerzy Kosinski 1:171
Ross Macdonald 2:256
Norman Mailer 1:193
Brian Moore 7:235
Charles Olson 1:263
Ezra Pound 1:276
Ayn Rand 30:299
Budd Schulberg 7:403
Irwin Shaw 7:413
Georges Simenon 2:399
Gary Snyder 1:318
Glendon Swarthout 35:401
Dalton Trumbo 19:446, 448
Arnold Wesker 5:484
William Carlos Williams 1:372

Cook, Carole
Robert Coover 32:122
Janet Frame 22:149
V. S. Pritchett 15:443
Lynne Sharon Schwartz 31:391
Eudora Welty 14:565

Cook, David
Roald Dahl 18:108
Camara Laye 4:283
Ngugi wa Thiong'o 36:321

Cook, Fred J.
Peter Maas 29:303

Cook, John
Robert Kroetsch 23:274
Patrick Lane 25:286

Cook, Jon
William Empson 34:539
Pier Paolo Pasolini 37:351

Cook, Martha E.
Donald Davidson 19:128

Cook, Reginald L.
Robert Frost 1:111

Cook, Richard M.
Carson McCullers 12:429
Edmund Wilson 24:486

Cook, Roderick
Harry Mathews 6:314
John McPhee 36:293
Berry Morgan 6:340
Paul Theroux 28:422

Cook, Stanley
William Golding 17:173
Mollie Hunter 21:168

Cooke, Alistair
C. S. Lewis 27:260

Cooke, Judy
Maureen Duffy 37:116
H. D. 31:207
Peter Rushforth 19:406
John Updike 23:477

Cooke, Michael
Eldridge Cleaver 30:58

Cooke, Michael G.
Ronald L. Fair 18:141
Alex Haley 12:246, 252
Gayl Jones 9:308
Margaríta Karapánou 13:314
George Lamming 4:279
Michael Mott 15:381
Joyce Carol Oates 9:403
Jean Rhys 4:445
William Styron 1:331
John Updike 2:443
Alice Walker 9:558
Robert Penn Warren 4:581

Cookson, William
David Jones 4:260
Hugh MacDiarmid 4:310

Cooley, Peter
Stephen Dobyns 37:75
Daniel Halpern 14:231
Daniel Hoffman 13:286
Ted Hughes 2:201
David Ignatow 14:275
Stanley Plumly 33:313
Gary Soto 32:402
Peter Wild 14:581

Coolidge, Elizabeth S.
Jill Paton Walsh 35:431

Coolidge, Olivia
Christopher Collier and James
L. Collier 30:71

Coombs, Orde
James Baldwin 8:40

Coon, Caroline
Joan Armatrading 17:8

Cooney, Thomas E.
Sloan Wilson 32:447

Critic Index

Cooper, Arthur
Richard Adams **5**:5
Ralph Bakshi **26**:70
Richard Condon **6**:115
Michael Crichton **2**:109
J. P. Donleavy **6**:142
Frederick Forsyth **36**:174
Ward S. Just **4**:266; **27**:228
John le Carré **3**:281
James A. Michener **5**:290
Wright Morris **7**:245
Gordon Parks **16**:459
Ishmael Reed **6**:450
Philip Roth **2**:378
Irwin Shaw **7**:414
David Storey **5**:417
Gore Vidal **6**:549
Fay Weldon **6**:563

Cooper, Carolyn
Louise Bennett **28**:30

Cooper, Ilene
C. S. Adler **35**:12, 13, 15
Norma Fox Mazer **26**:294

Cooper, Jane
Muriel Rukeyser **15**:456

Cooper, Keith B.
Milton Meltzer **26**:306

Cooper, Nina
Gabriel Marcel **15**:362

Cooper, Philip
Robert Lowell **4**:300

Cooper, Susan
John Donovan **35**:142
Mollie Hunter **21**:160
Mildred D. Taylor **21**:419
Colin Thiele **17**:494, 495

Cooper, William
C. P. Snow **19**:427

Cooperman, Stanley
Langston Hughes **35**:215
Evan Hunter **31**:218
W. S. Merwin **1**:212
Philip Roth **3**:438
Marguerite Yourcenar **19**:481

Coover, Robert
Julio Cortázar **34**:333
José Donoso **4**:127
Carlos Fuentes **8**:224
Gabriel García Márquez **15**:253
Robert Pinget **37**:365
Manuel Puig **28**:371
Ernesto Sabato **23**:381

Cope, Myron
George Plimpton **36**:352

Copland, R. A.
Noel Hilliard **15**:279

Copland, Ray
Frank Sargeson **31**:368, 370

Coppage, Noel
David Bowie **17**:66
Jackson Browne **21**:42
Neil Diamond **30**:114
Janis Ian **21**:184
Mick Jagger and Keith Richard **17**:233

Waylon Jennings **21**:202, 203, 204, 205
Kris Kristofferson **26**:266, 270
John Lennon **35**:263, 268
Gordon Lightfoot **26**:279, 280, 281, 282, 283
Paul McCartney **35**:282
Joni Mitchell **12**:439
Willie Nelson **17**:304
Laura Nyro **17**:314
Phil Ochs **17**:334
Buffy Sainte-Marie **17**:431
Bob Seger **35**:378, 379
Carly Simon **26**:407
Neil Young **17**:583

Corbin, Louise
Jean Renoir **20**:293

Corcoran, Neil
Tom Paulin **37**:353

Cordell, Richard A.
Taylor Caldwell **28**:56, 59
August Derleth **31**:136

Cordesse, Gérard
William S. Burroughs **15**:110

Core, George
Virginia Spencer Carr **34**:421
John Dos Passos **34**:421
Scott Elledge **34**:428
Andrew Lytle **22**:293
Edna O'Brien **8**:429
Seán O'Faoláin **7**:273
John Crowe Ransom **2**:364; **5**:366
Jean Rhys **14**:447
William Styron **1**:331
Allen Tate **4**:537
William Trevor **9**:529
E. B. White **34**:428

Coren, Alan
James Thurber **25**:440

Corey, David
Wilbur Smith **33**:377

Corey, Stephen
William Stafford **29**:386

Corke, Hilary
Isaac Asimov **26**:37
John Cheever **3**:106
A. N. Wilson **33**:452

Corliss, Richard
Renata Adler **31**:13
Alan Ayckbourn **33**:50
Ingmar Bergman **16**:58
Steven Bochco and Michael Kozoll **35**:49
Larry Gelbart **21**:128
Amlin Gray **29**:200
Stephen King **26**:243
Richard Lester **20**:224
David Mamet **34**:222
Garry Marshall **17**:277
Tom Stoppard **34**:273, 280

Corman, Cid
Kon Ichikawa **20**:179
George Oppen **13**:433
Philip Whalen **29**:447

Corn, Alfred
Elizabeth Bowen **15**:78
Robert Frost **34**:474
John Hollander **8**:302
Czesław Miłosz **22**:310
Eugenio Montale **18**:339
Frederick Morgan **23**:299
Boris Pasternak **7**:300
William H. Pritchard **34**:474
Reg Saner **9**:469
James Schuyler **23**:390
L. E. Sissman **18**:489

Cornell, George W.
Andrew M. Greeley **28**:174

Cornish, Sam
Douglas Unger **34**:117

Cornwell, Ethel F.
Samuel Beckett **3**:45
Nathalie Sarraute **8**:471

Corodimas, Peter
Ira Levin **6**:305
Françoise Sagan **17**:425
Glendon Swarthout **35**:401

Corr, Patricia
Evelyn Waugh **1**:356

Corradi, Juan E.
Joan Didion **32**:145

Corrigan, Mary Ann
Tennessee Williams **11**:571, 575

Corrigan, Matthew
Charles Olson **5**:328

Corrigan, Maureen
T. Gertler **34**:52
Frank Lentricchia **34**:571

Corrigan, Robert W.
Edward Albee **5**:11
John Arden **6**:9
Saul Bellow **6**:51
Robert Bolt **14**:89
Friedrich Dürrenmatt **8**:196
Michel de Ghelderode **6**:197
Arthur Miller **1**:218
John Osborne **5**:332
Harold Pinter **6**:417
Thornton Wilder **5**:494

Corrigan, Sylvia Robinson
Sylvia Plath **17**:350

Corrington, John William
James Dickey **1**:73
Marion Montgomery **7**:233

Cort, David
Jules Archer **12**:16

Cort, John C.
Helen MacInnes **27**:279

Cortázar, Julio
Jorge Luis Borges **8**:102
Luisa Valenzuela **31**:437

Cortínez, Carlos
Octavio Paz **10**:393

Corwin, Phillip
Kay Boyle **5**:67
Siegfried Lenz **27**:249

Cosgrave, Mary Silva
Maya Angelou **12**:13; **35**:32
Robert Lipsyte **21**:208
Paul Zindel **26**:472

Cosgrave, Patrick
Kingsley Amis **3**:8
J. V. Cunningham **31**:102
Robert Lowell **4**:300
Ruth Rendell **28**:384, 386
Georges Simenon **3**:452
Julian Symons **14**:523

Cosman, Max
Sylvia Ashton-Warner **19**:21

Costa, Jean-Charles
Pink Floyd **35**:306

Costello, Bonnie
Elizabeth Bishop **32**:29
Philip Levine **33**:275
Howard Nemerov **36**:307

Cott, Jonathan
Bob Dylan **6**:156
Mick Jagger and Keith Richard **17**:234
John Lennon **35**:261
John Lennon and Paul McCartney **12**:356
Jim Morrison **17**:287
Van Morrison **21**:236
Patti Smith **12**:542
Andrew Lloyd Webber and Tim Rice **21**:423

Cotter, James Finn
Robert Bly **10**:62
Philip Booth **23**:76
Peter Davison **28**:104
William Everson **14**:167
Nikki Giovanni **19**:192
Thom Gunn **18**:204
Daniel Hoffman **23**:243
Denise Levertov **28**:243
Laurence Lieberman **36**:262
Jayanta Mahapatra **33**:280
Josephine Miles **34**:245
Frederick Morgan **23**:298, 300
Howard Nemerov **36**:309
Robert Phillips **28**:364
Robert Pinsky **19**:371
May Sarton **14**:482
Barry Spacks **14**:511
James Tate **25**:429
Richard Tillinghast **29**:416
Mark Van Doren **6**:542
David Wagoner **15**:559
John Hall Wheelock **14**:571

Cottrell, Robert D.
Simone de Beauvoir **8**:58

Coughlan, Margaret N.
E. M. Almedingen **12**:4

Coult, Tony
Edward Bond **23**:65

Cournos, John
R. V. Cassill **23**:102
Carl Sandburg **35**:354

Courtivron, Isabelle de
Violette Leduc **22**:263

Couto, Maria
Salman Rushdie **23**:367

Covatta, Anthony
Elio Vittorini **6**:551

Coveney, Michael
Athol Fugard **5**:130
Sam Shepard **6**:496
Snoo Wilson **33**:462

Cowan, Doris
Marian Engel **36**:164

Cowan, Louise
Caroline Gordon **13**:243
John Crowe Ransom **5**:363
Allen Tate **2**:431
Robert Penn Warren **6**:555

Cowan, Michael
Norman Mailer **8**:371

Cowan, Paul
Edmund White III **27**:480

Cowan, Robert
Billy Joel **26**:214

Cowasjee, Saros
Mulk Raj Anand **23**:19

Cowen, Robert C.
Jacques-Yves Cousteau **30**:102
Margaret O. Hyde **21**:174

Cowie, Peter
Michelangelo Antonioni **20**:24
Ingmar Bergman **16**:50, 65
Nagisa Oshima **20**:249, 256
Satyajit Ray **16**:480
Jean Renoir **20**:294, 296
Eric Rohmer **16**:531
Jerzy Skolimowski **20**:353
Orson Welles **20**:451

Cowley, Malcolm
Conrad Aiken **10**:3
Louis Aragon **22**:34, 35
Cleanth Brooks **24**:116
Pearl S. Buck **7**:31; **11**:71
Erskine Caldwell **14**:93
E. E. Cummings **3**:118
John Dos Passos **4**:135
Howard Fast **23**:154
William Faulkner **8**:210; **28**:142
Robert Frost **4**:173
Ernest Hemingway **13**:270;
19:212
Arthur Koestler **33**:229
Doris Lessing **6**:303
Margaret Mead **37**:272
John O'Hara **2**:325
Ezra Pound **4**:407
Upton Sinclair **15**:500
Allen Tate **24**:439
James Thurber **5**:430

Cowley, Robert
Woody Guthrie **35**:185

Cox, C. B.
James Baldwin **17**:27
William Golding **17**:163
David Lodge **36**:267
Norman MacCaig **36**:283

Cox, David
Wilfrid Sheed **4**:489

Cox, James M.
Robert Frost **26**:118

Cox, Kenneth
Hugh MacDiarmid **4**:311
Ezra Pound **4**:413
C. H. Sisson **8**:490
Louis Zukofsky **7**:562; **11**:582

Cox, Martha Heasley
Nelson Algren **33**:15

Cox, Robert
Breyten Breytenbach **37**:51

Cox, Shelley
Tish O'Dowd Ezekiel **34**:46

Cox, Terrance
W. P. Kinsella **27**:238

Coxe, Louis
David Jones **2**:217
Mary McCarthy **24**:344
Anne Sexton **2**:391

Coxe, Louis O.
Sloan Wilson **32**:445

Coy, Jane
Norma Fox Mazer **26**:291

Coyle, Cathy S.
Paula Danziger **21**:83
Diana Wynne Jones **26**:224

Coyle, William
Frank Herbert **35**:201

Coyne, John R., Jr.
David Caute **29**:116
Frederick Forsyth **5**:125
Dick Francis **2**:142
E. Howard Hunt **3**:251
Ward Just **4**:266
Robert Lipsyte **21**:211
Donald E. Westlake **7**:528
Tom Wolfe **2**:481

Coyne, Patricia S.
Kingsley Amis **3**:10
Erica Jong **4**:265
Joyce Carol Oates **9**:402
Wilfrid Sheed **2**:395
Elizabeth Spencer **22**:402
Morris L. West **6**:564

Crabtree, Paul
Louis Auchincloss **18**:27

Crace, Jim
William Least Heat Moon
29:225

Cracroft, Richard H.
A. B. Guthrie, Jr. **23**:199

Craft, Robert
Aldous Huxley **5**:193

Craft, Wallace
Eugenio Montale **7**:230

Crago, Hugh
Andre Norton **12**:460
J.R.R. Tolkien **12**:573

Craib, Roderick
Bernard Malamud **3**:322

Craig, Barbara J.
Sandra Scoppettone **26**:405

Craig, D. A.
Thomas Bernhard **32**:17

Craig, David
Piers Paul Read **25**:375
Frank Sargeson **31**:365

Craig, George
Samuel Beckett **29**:62
Michel Butor **15**:115

Craig, Patricia
Joan Aiken **35**:17, 20
Beryl Bainbridge **18**:33
Joan Barfoot **18**:36
Elizabeth Bowen **22**:67
Rosellen Brown **32**:68
Antonia Fraser **32**:185
Carolyn G. Heilbrun **25**:257
Penelope Lively **32**:274
Bernard Mac Laverty **31**:252
William Mayne **12**:404
Joyce Carol Oates **33**:295
Edna O'Brien **8**:429
Frank O'Connor **23**:330
Julia O'Faolain **19**:360
Katherine Paterson **12**:485
Frederic Raphael **14**:438
Noel Streatfeild **21**:413
Fay Weldon **19**:468
A. N. Wilson **33**:451

Craig, Randall
Jean Genet **2**:160
Bernard Pomerance **13**:444
Robert Shaw **5**:390
Sam Shepard **4**:489
E. A. Whitehead **5**:489
Snoo Wilson **33**:461

Crain, Jane Larkin
Alice Adams **13**:1
Caroline Blackwood **9**:101
André Brink **18**:66
E. M. Broner **19**:72
Rosellen Brown **32**:63
William F. Buckley, Jr. **18**:81
Sara Davidson **9**:175
Lawrence Durrell **6**:153
Leslie Epstein **27**:129
Thomas J. Fleming **37**:128
Bruce Jay Friedman **5**:126
John Gardner **5**:134
Gail Godwin **8**:248
Shirley Ann Grau **9**:240
Milan Kundera **4**:276
Alan Lelchuk **5**:244
Doris Lessing **6**:299
Grace Paley **4**:394
Walker Percy **6**:401
Kathleen Raine **7**:353
C. P. Snow **6**:518
Muriel Spark **5**:398
Mario Vargas Llosa **6**:545
Gore Vidal **4**:555
David Wagoner **5**:474
Frederick Wiseman **20**:474
Sol Yurick **6**:583

Crane, Hugh M.
Andrew M. Greeley **28**:175

Crane, John K.
T. H. White **30**:448

Crane, Lucille
Winston Graham **23**:194

Crane, Peggy
Joy Adamson **17**:6
Jean Rhys **14**:446
Wilbur Smith **33**:376

Crane, R. S.
Cleanth Brooks **24**:104

Crane, Rufus S.
Primo Levi **37**:224

Cranford, Beaufort
John McPhee **36**:299

Crankshaw, Edward
Yuri Krotkov **19**:264
Aleksandr I. Solzhenitsyn **1**:319

Cranston, Maurice
Michel Foucault **31**:178

Cranston, Mechthild
René Char **14**:126

Craven, Avery
Bruce Catton **35**:87

Crawford, John W.
Julia Peterkin **31**:302

Crawford, Pamela
Andy Warhol **20**:418

Creagh, Patrick
Giuseppe Ungaretti **7**:484

Creamer, Robert W.
Peter Gent **29**:182
Pat Jordan **37**:195

Creekmore, Hubert
Langston Hughes **35**:214

Creeley, Robert
Robert Duncan **4**:141
William Everson **5**:121
Robert Graves **6**:210
Charles Olson **5**:326; **29**:326
Ezra Pound **3**:395
William Stafford **4**:519
William Carlos Williams **5**:507
Louis Zukofsky **4**:599; **18**:559

Creighton, Joanne V.
Joyce Carol Oates **19**:348

Creighton, Luella
Dalton Trumbo **19**:444

Crenshaw, Brad
Frank Bidart **33**:78

Crew, Gary
Wilson Harris **25**:217

Crews, Frederick
Geoffrey H. Hartman **27**:187

Crews, Frederick C.
E. M. Forster **13**:219
Shirley Ann Grau **4**:207
Philip Roth **2**:379

Crews, Harry
Elliott Baker **8**:39
Pat Conroy **30**:80

Crichfield, Grant
E. M. Forster **22**:135
Barry Hannah **23**:210

Critic Index

Crichton, Michael
Frederick Forsyth **2**:136
Kurt Vonnegut, Jr. **3**:495

Crichton, Robert
Pier Paolo Pasolini **37**:341

Crick, Bernard
Arthur Koestler **33**:243

Crick, Francis
Michael McClure **6**:319

Crick, Joyce
Michael Hamburger **5**:159
Botho Strauss **22**:408
Christa Wolf **29**:464

Crider, Bill
Robert Cormier **30**:82
Stephen King **12**:310

Crinklaw, Don
John Gardner **3**:186
David Lodge **36**:268

Crinkley, Richmond
Edward Albee **2**:3

Crisler, Ben
Art Buchwald **33**:88, 89

Crisp, Quentin
Graham Greene **18**:198
Molly Keane **31**:234
Stevie Smith **25**:422

Crist, Judith
Lindsay Anderson **20**:17
Mel Brooks **12**:81
John Cassavetes **20**:52
Julia W. Cunningham **12**:163
George Roy Hill **26**:196
Harry Kemelman **2**:225
Jean Kerr **22**:256
Richard Lester **20**:231
Laurence Olivier **20**:241
Nagisa Oshima **20**:249
Sidney Poitier **26**:358
Satyajit Ray **16**:488
Alain Resnais **16**:514
Ken Russell **16**:547

Croce, A.
John Gregory Dunne **28**:121

Croce, Arlene
Ingmar Bergman **16**:47
Shirley Clarke **16**:217
Vittorio De Sica **20**:88
Jean-Luc Godard **20**:128
John Huston **20**:163
Stanley Kubrick **16**:377
Satyajit Ray **16**:475
Stephen Sondheim **30**:382
François Truffaut **20**:381

Croft, Julian
Robert D. FitzGerald **19**:182

Croft, L. B.
Yevgeny Yevtushenko **13**:620

Cromelin, Richard
Walter Becker and Donald
Fagen **26**:79
David Bowie **17**:58

Cromie, Robert
Allen Drury **37**:105

Crompton, D. W.
William Golding **17**:171

Croome, Lesley
Diana Wynne Jones **26**:225

Crosby, John
Donald E. Westlake **33**:437

Crosland, Margaret
Isabel Colegate **36**:113

Cross, Michael S.
Frank Herbert **12**:279

Cross, Nigel
I. Compton-Burnett **34**:496
Hilary Spurling **34**:496

Cross, Richard K.
Richard Eberhart **19**:143

Crossman, R.H.S.
Arthur Koestler **33**:234

Crossmann, Richard
David Caute **29**:117

Crouch, Marcus
Ruth M. Arthur **12**:28
Margot Benary-Isbert **12**:34
Cecil Bødker **21**:13
Larry Bograd **35**:64
H. F. Brinsmead **21**:32
Peter Dickinson **12**:175
Leon Garfield **12**:228
Alan Garner **17**:144
Diana Wynne Jones **26**:229,
230, 231, 232
Andre Norton **12**:464
Katherine Paterson **30**:285
Philippa Pearce **21**:289
Noel Streatfeild **21**:403
Rosemary Sutcliff **26**:432, 438,
440

Crouch, Stanley
James Baldwin **17**:42
Marvin Gaye **26**:134
Ishmael Reed **13**:480; **32**:359

Crouse, Timothy
Carly Simon **26**:406

Crow, John
Harlan Ellison **13**:203

Crowder, Richard H.
Carl Sandburg **1**:300; **15**:467

Crowe, Linda
Honor Arundel **17**:13

Crowl, Samuel R.
Donald Hall **37**:143

Crowne, Thomas
David Donnell **34**:155

Crowson, Lydia
Jean Cocteau **8**:148

Crowther, Bosley
Jean Cocteau **16**:222, 223, 227
Carl Theodor Dreyer **16**:256
Federico Fellini **16**:270
John Ford **16**:305, 309
John Huston **20**:157, 158, 159,
161
Kon Ichikawa **20**:178
Elia Kazan **16**:360, 363

Norman Lear **12**:326
Laurence Olivier **20**:234
Alain Resnais **16**:498
Carlos Saura **20**:314
Nevil Shute **30**:367
Josef von Sternberg **20**:375
Agnès Varda **16**:554
Andrzej Wajda **16**:577
Jessamyn West **17**:548
Billy Wilder **20**:455, 457, 462

Crozier, Andrew
Ed Dorn **18**:128

Cruickshank, John
Patrick Lane **25**:289

Crump, G. B.
Tom Stoppard **15**:519

Crunk
See also Robert Bly
James Wright **28**:462

Crunk
See also James Wright
Gary Snyder **32**:386

Cruse, Harold
Eldridge Cleaver **30**:63

Cruse, Harold W.
W.E.B. Du Bois **2**:120

Cruttwell, Patrick
Sylvia Ashton-Warner **19**:23
Adolfo Bioy Casares **4**:63
Jerzy Kosinski **3**:274
Iris Murdoch **2**:296
I. A. Richards **24**:392
Patrick White **7**:529

Cryer, Dan
Michael Ende **31**:143

Cuddon, J. A.
Peter De Vries **2**:114
James Purdy **4**:423
Frederic Raphael **2**:367
Ann Schlee **35**:372
Claude Simon **4**:497

Culbertson, Diana
Alberto Moravia **7**:243

Cullen, Elinor S.
Ruth M. Arthur **12**:26

Cullen, John B.
Len Deighton **22**:114

Culler, Jonathan
Harold Bloom **24**:75
Wayne C. Booth **24**:96
Geoffrey H. Hartman **27**:184
Walker Percy **8**:439
George Steiner **24**:433

Culligan, Glendy
Rosa Guy **26**:140

Cully, Kevin
Manlio Argueta **31**:21

Culpan, Norman
Mollie Hunter **21**:167
Andre Norton **12**:470, 471
Roger Zelazny **21**:464, 465,
472

Cumare, Rosa
Flann O'Brien **5**:317

Cumming, George M. A., Jr.
Piers Anthony **35**:38

Cumming, Joseph B., Jr.
Richard O'Brien **17**:325

Cummings, Peter
Northrop Frye **24**:225

Cunliffe, Marcus
Alfred Kazin **34**:556
Ved Mehta **37**:289
Irving Stone **7**:469

Cunliffe, W. Gordon
Heinrich Böll **11**:57
Günter Grass **1**:126
Uwe Johnson **10**:283

Cunningham, John
Isabelle Holland **21**:150

Cunningham, Laura
Richard Price **6**:427

Cunningham, Valentine
Jeffrey Archer **28**:12
Louis Auchincloss **6**:15
Djuna Barnes **29**:32
John Barth **5**:51
Donald Barthelme **3**:43
Samuel Beckett **29**:67
Richard Brautigan **12**:70
Breyten Breytenbach **37**:47
Pearl S. Buck **18**:80
Alejo Carpentier **8**:134
Margaret Craven **17**:79
Donald Davie **31**:120
Len Deighton **4**:119
Don DeLillo **13**:179
Ilya Ehrenburg **18**:137
Buchi Emecheta **14**:159
Shusaku Endo **7**:96; **14**:161
Eva Figes **31**:164
Penelope Fitzgerald **19**:172
Frederick Forsyth **5**:125
Mervyn Jones **10**:295
Anna Kavan **5**:206
William Kennedy **28**:204
William Kotzwinkle **5**:220
Mary Lavin **4**:282
J.M.G. Le Clézio **31**:248
Colin MacInnes **4**:314
Bernard Mac Laverty **31**:255
Stanley Middleton **7**:220
Yukio Mishima **4**:358
Vladimir Nabokov **3**:355
Hans Erich Nossack **6**:364
David Plante **7**:307
Bernice Rubens **19**:404
Salman Rushdie **23**:366
Ward Ruyslinck **14**:471
Françoise Sagan **9**:468
William Sansom **6**:484
Randolph Stow **23**:437
Emma Tennant **13**:536
Lisa St. Aubin de Teran **36**:422
Paul Theroux **8**:513
Gillian Tindall **7**:474
Ludvík Vaculík **7**:495
Kurt Vonnegut, Jr. **22**:450
Harriet Waugh **6**:559
Arnold Wesker **5**:483

Patrick White **4**:587

Cuppy, Will
Agatha Christie **12**:112, 113
August Derleth **31**:127

Curley, Thomas
Laura Z. Hobson **25**:272

Curley, Thomas F.
Pamela Hansford Johnson
27:218

Curran, Charles
Vera Brittain **23**:93

Curran, Mary Doyle
Nadine Gordimer **33**:180

Curran, Ronald
Joyce Carol Oates **33**:293

Curran, Thomas M.
Shusaku Endo **19**:161

Current-Garcia, Eugene
George Seferis **11**:494

Currie, William
Kōbō Abé **8**:2

Curry, Andrew
Robert Phillips **28**:361

Curtin, Edward J., Jr.
Manlio Argueta **31**:20

Curtis, Anthony
Alan Ayckbourn **18**:30; **33**:41
Caryl Churchill **31**:84
David Hare **29**:213
Ronald Harwood **32**:227
W. Somerset Maugham **15**:365
J. B. Priestley **5**:351
Hugh Whitemore **37**:444

Curtis, C. Michael
Sara Davidson **9**:175
Annie Dillard **9**:179
George Plimpton **36**:354

Curtis, Charlotte
Bette Bao Lord **23**:279

Curtis, Jerry L.
Jean Genet **10**:224

Curtis, Penelope
Katherine Paterson **12**:485

Curtis, Simon
Donald Davie **5**:113
Seamus Heaney **7**:151

Curtius, E. R.
William Goyen **14**:209

Cuscuna, Michael
Jim Morrison **17**:289

Cuseo, Allan
Michael Cunningham **34**:42
Sam Shepard **34**:270

Cushing, Edward
Aldous Huxley **35**:233

Cushman, Jerome
Jascha Kessler **4**:270

Cushman, Kathleen
Kurt Vonnegut, Jr. **12**:610

Cushman, Keith
Roger Angell **26**:28
Marilyn French **18**:157
Mark Schorer **9**:474

Cushman, Robert
Edward Bond **23**:71

Cusimano, Jim
Lou Reed **21**:309

Cutler, Bruce
Louis Simpson **7**:428

Cutter, William
S. Y. Agnon **4**:15

Cutts, John
Frank Capra **16**:157
Carl Theodor Dreyer **16**:258
Lorraine Hansberry **17**:184

Cyclops
Larry Gelbart **21**:126, 127
Garry Marshall **17**:275

Czajkowska, Magdalena
Tadeusz Rózewicz **9**:463

Czarnecki, Mark
Anne Chislett **34**:144
W. P. Kinsella **27**:238
Lewis Thomas **35**:414
Michel Tremblay **29**:419

Dabney, Lewis H.
William Faulkner **6**:174

Dabney, Lewis M.
Edmund Wilson **24**:482

Dabydeen, David
David Dabydeen **34**:147

Dacey, Philip
Arthur Gregor **9**:255

Daemmrich, Horst S.
Eugène Ionesco **11**:289

Dahlie, Hallvard
Hugh Hood **28**:192
Brian Moore **1**:225; **7**:237
Alice Munro **10**:357

Daiches, David
W. H. Auden **1**:8
Saul Bellow **3**:55
Elizabeth Bowen **1**:39
Anthony Burgess **22**:71
Arthur A. Cohen **31**:92
Ivy Compton-Burnett **1**:60
Elizabeth Daryush **19**:119
C. Day Lewis **1**:72
T. S. Eliot **1**:89
William Empson **3**:147
Christopher Fry **2**:143
Robert Graves **1**:126
Henry Green **2**:178
H. D. **31**:202
Aldous Huxley **1**:149
Hugh MacDiarmid **2**:252
Louis MacNeice **1**:186
Bernard Malamud **3**:323
I. A. Richards **24**:384
Henry Roth **6**:473
Edith Sitwell **2**:403
Stephen Spender **1**:322
Evelyn Waugh **1**:356

René Wellek **28**:443

Daiker, Donald A.
Hugh Nissenson **4**:381

Dale, Peter
John Berryman **2**:58
Basil Bunting **10**:84
Stanley Burnshaw **13**:128,129

Daley, Robert
Mark Harris **19**:200
John R. Tunis **12**:597

Dalgliesh, Alice
Margaret O. Hyde **21**:173
Madeleine L'Engle **12**:346, 347

Dallas, Karl
Jimmy Cliff **21**:63
Janis Ian **21**:185
Joni Mitchell **12**:435
Jim Morrison **17**:287
Phil Ochs **17**:330
Frank Zappa **17**:593

Dalton, David
Mick Jagger and Keith Richard
17:239
Jim Morrison **17**:292
Lou Reed **21**:314
Smokey Robinson **21**:347
Paul Simon **17**:466

Dalton, Elizabeth
E. M. Broner **19**:71
Vladimir Nabokov **1**:245
John Updike **1**:344

Dalton, Margaret
Yevgeny Yevtushenko **26**:461

Daltry, Patience M.
Mary Stewart **35**:391

Daltry, Patrice M.
Lee Kingman **17**:245

Daly, Jay
Roger Zelazny **21**:470

Daly, Maureen
Mary Stolz **12**:551

Daly, Mike
Ray Davies **21**:90

Dame, Enid
Chaim Potok **7**:322

D'Amico, Masolino
Umberto Eco **28**:130

Dana, Robert
Yukio Mishima **2**:286

Dangerfield, George
Taylor Caldwell **28**:55
Rayner Heppenstall **10**:272
Compton Mackenzie **18**:313
Carson McCullers **12**:410
Nevil Shute **30**:367
Noel Streatfeild **21**:397
Frank Swinnerton **31**:424, 425
Carl Van Vechten **33**:394

Daniel, Glyn
Thor Heyerdahl **26**:191

Daniel, Helen
David Malouf **28**:265

Daniel, John
Ann Quin **6**:441
Isaac Bashevis Singer **6**:507

Daniel, Lorne
Andrew Suknaski **19**:432

Daniel, Mary L.
João Guimarães Rosa **23**:354

Daniel, Robert
Yvor Winters **32**:458

Daniel, Robert D.
Walker Percy **14**:414

Daniel, Robert W.
W. D. Snodgrass **10**:478

Daniels, Jonathan
T. S. Stribling **23**:440

Daniels, Les
Trina Robbins **21**:338
Jerome Siegel and Joe Shuster
21:359

Daniels, Robert V.
Larry Woiwode **10**:540

Danielson, J. David
Simone Schwarz-Bart **7**:404

Danis, Francine
Nancy Willard **37**:462

Danischewsky, Nina
Ruth M. Arthur **12**:26
Peter Dickinson **12**:167

Danner, G. Richard
Eugène Ionesco **15**:298

D'Arazien, Steven
Hunter S. Thompson **9**:528

D'Arcy, David
Shiva Naipaul **32**:328

Dardess, George
Jack Kerouac **5**:213

Dareff, Hal
Jonathan Schell **35**:362

Darling, Cary
Prince **35**:325

Darling, Frances C.
Henry Gregor Felsen **17**:120

Darlington, W. A.
Shelagh Delaney **29**:143

Darnton, John
Shiva Naipaul **32**:325

Darrach, Brad
George V. Higgins **4**:224
Joyce Carol Oates **2**:313
Ezra Pound **7**:336
Irving Stone **7**:471

Darragh, Tim
Kem Nunn **34**:94

Dasenbrock, Reed Way
Ngugi wa Thiong'o **36**:324

Das Gupta, Chidananda
Satyajit Ray **16**:481

Dasgupta, Gautam
John Guare **29**:204
Albert Innaurato **21**:191
Arthur Kopit **33**:248

Datchery, Dick
Agatha Christie **12**:120
Trevanian **29**:430

Dathorne, O. R.
Mongo Beti **27**:45
Christopher Okigbo **25**:347

Dauenhauer, Richard
Paavo Haavikko **18**:206; **34**:170

Dault, Gary Michael
Joe Rosenblatt **15**:447, 448

Dauster, Frank
Gabriel García Márquez **3**:182

Davenport, Basil
Daphne du Maurier **11**:162
Carson McCullers **12**:409
Frank Swinnerton **31**:424

Davenport, G.
J.R.R. Tolkien **3**:482

Davenport, Gary
Seán O'Faoláin **14**:406

Davenport, Gary T.
E. M. Almedingen **12**:4
Matt Cohen **19**:113
Timothy Findley **27**:142
Frank O'Connor **23**:326
Seán O'Faoláin **7**:275

Davenport, Guy
E. M. Almedingen **12**:4
Ayi Kwei Armah **33**:24
Michael Ayrton **7**:17
Beryl Bainbridge **8**:36
Thomas Berger **8**:82
Wendell Berry **8**:85
Richard Brautigan **12**:58
Frederick Buechner **2**:82
Paul Celan **10**:101
Louis-Ferdinand Céline **3**:104
John Cheever **25**:116
Evan S. Connell, Jr. **4**:110
Harry Crews **23**:132
Joan Didion **1**:75
J. P. Donleavy **4**:124
G. B. Edwards **25**:151
Günter Grass **22**:197
Donald Hall **13**:260
Miroslav Holub **4**:233
Benedict Kiely **23**:267
Frederick Morgan **23**:296
Michael Mott **15**:379
Charles Olson **6**:388; **9**:412
Nicanor Parra **2**:331
Chaim Potok **2**:338
James Purdy **2**:350
Gilbert Sorrentino **22**:394
J.I.M. Stewart **7**:466
Harriet Waugh **6**:560
Eudora Welty **14**:564
Richard Wilbur **6**:569
Louis Zukofsky **2**:487; **4**:599;
   7:560

Davey, Frank
Margaret Atwood **25**:68
Bill Bissett **18**:58
E. J. Pratt **19**:380
Joe Rosenblatt **15**:446

Daviau, Donald G.
Ernst Jandl **34**:196

David, Jack
B. P. Nichol **18**:369

Davidon, Ann Morrissett
Simone de Beauvoir **8**:57
Grace Paley **4**:391
Gore Vidal **4**:557

Davidson, Andrea
Larry Bograd **35**:63

Davidson, Edward
Carl Van Vechten **33**:390

Davidson, Michael
Jack Spicer **18**:509

Davidson, Peter
Sylvia Plath **17**:346

Davidson, Richard B.
Christie Harris **12**:266

Davie, Donald
A. R. Ammons **5**:30
John Berryman **8**:87
Austin Clarke **6**:112
Elizabeth Daryush **19**:120
T. S. Eliot **15**:210
Thom Gunn **18**:202; **32**:212
Donald Hall **37**:143
Michael Hamburger **5**:159
Anthony Hecht **8**:267
John Hollander **8**:299
Galway Kinnell **5**:217
Norman MacCaig **36**:288
John Peck **3**:377
Peter Porter **33**:317
Ezra Pound **13**:456
F. T. Prince **22**:339
Siegfried Sassoon **36**:391
Andrew Sinclair **14**:488
Paul Theroux **11**:529
J.R.R. Tolkien **12**:572

Davie, Michael
Michael Scammell **34**:491
Aleksandr Solzhenitsyn **34**:491

Davies, Brenda
René Clair **20**:65
Jean Renoir **20**:296

Davies, Brian
Robert Bresson **16**:103
Claude Chabrol **16**:168

Davies, Norman
Czesław Miłosz **31**:269

Davies, R. R.
Joanne Greenberg **7**:135
Diane Johnson **5**:198
William Sansom **6**:482

Davies, Ray
Ray Davies **21**:88

Davies, Robertson
Marie-Claire Blais **22**:57
John Fowles **33**:171
William Golding **27**:160
John Irving **23**:248
Iris Murdoch **31**:292

Davies, Russell
Richard Condon **8**:150
Donald Davie **31**:111
Joan Didion **8**:177
Elaine Feinstein **36**:168, 169
Michael Hamburger **14**:234
Thomas Hinde **11**:273
Francis King **8**:321
Fran Lebowitz **36**:249
Norman MacCaig **36**:286
S. J. Perelman **15**:418
Harold Pinter **27**:386
Kate Roberts **15**:445
Josef Škvorecký **15**:511
C. P. Snow **19**:429
William Trevor **9**:528
John Updike **23**:477

Davis, Arthur P.
Arna Bontemps **18**:64
Langston Hughes **35**:219
Nella Larsen **37**:214
Ann Petry **18**:404

Davis, Bolton
Breece D'J Pancake **29**:350

Davis, Charles E.
Eudora Welty **33**:417

Davis, Charles T.
Robert Hayden **5**:68

Davis, Cheri Colby
W. S. Merwin **13**:383; **18**:332

Davis, Christopher
Diana Wynne Jones **26**:225

Davis, Deborah
Julio Cortázar **5**:109

Davis, Dick
Ted Hughes **37**:178
Norman MacCaig **36**:288
Edwin Morgan **31**:276
Tom Paulin **37**:353, 355
Peter Porter **33**:325
Craig Raine **32**:353
Anne Stevenson **33**:381
D. M. Thomas **31**:430

Davis, Elmer
William F. Buckley, Jr. **37**:57

Davis, Elrick B.
A. B. Guthrie, Jr. **23**:197

Davis, Fath
Toni Morrison **4**:366

Davis, George
Claude Brown **30**:40
George Lamming **2**:235
Clarence Major **3**:320

Davis, Gladys
Vera Brittain **23**:90

Davis, Hassoldt
Nevil Shute **30**:365

Davis, Hope Hale
John Cheever **8**:140
Oriana Fallaci **11**:190
Sloan Wilson **32**:448

Davis, Jack L.
Charles R. Larson **31**:239

Davis, James
Gretchen Cryer **21**:78

Davis, Jorja
Sandra Scoppettone **26**:405

Davis, Jorja Perkins
Sol Gordon **26**:139

Davis, L. J.
Richard Brautigan **12**:71
Anthony Burgess **22**:71
Richard Condon **4**:106
Robert Cormier **30**:82
Peter De Vries **7**:78
John Gregory Dunne **28**:121
Stanley Elkin **4**:153
Leon Forrest **4**:163
Lois Gould **4**:200
Hannah Green **3**:202
A. B. Guthrie, Jr. **23**:200
John Hersey **2**:188
Stanley Hoffman **5**:184
James Jones **10**:291
Ward S. Just **27**:226, 227
William Kennedy **6**:274
Richard Kostelanetz **28**:213
Ira Levin **6**:307
Colin MacInnes **23**:284
Larry McMurtry **27**:326
John O'Hara **2**:324
J. F. Powers **8**:448
Philip Roth **2**:379
Françoise Sagan **6**:481
Tom Sharpe **36**:404
Ronald Sukenick **4**:531
Paul Theroux **28**:424
J.R.R. Tolkien **8**:516
Vassilis Vassilikos **8**:524
Richard B. Wright **6**:582

Davis, Lavinia
Margot Benary-Isbert **12**:31
Maureen Daly **17**:90

Davis, Lavinia R.
Rosemary Sutcliff **26**:425, 426

Davis, M. E.
José María Arguedas **10**:10

Davis, Mary Gould
Betty Cavanna **12**:98
Esther Forbes **12**:207
John R. Tunis **12**:595, 596

Davis, Michael
Pink Floyd **35**:308

Davis, Ossie
Lorraine Hansberry **17**:184

Davis, Paxton
Eric Ambler **9**:18
George Garrett **3**:189
S. E. Hinton **30**:205
Paul Zindel **26**:480

Davis, Richard
Woody Allen **16**:2
Claude Chabrol **16**:169
Larry Gelbart **21**:126
Ken Russell **16**:541

Davis, Richard A.
Sam Shepard **17**:439

Davis, Rick
Richard Brautigan **9**:125
Richard Condon **10**:111

Davis, Robert Gorham
Saul Bellow **2**:49
Paul Bowles **19**:57
John Dos Passos **1**:78
A. B. Guthrie, Jr. **23**:197
Josephine Herbst **34**:451
Elinor Langer **34**:451
Halldór Laxness **25**:291
Irwin Shaw **23**:396
William Styron **3**:472

Davis, Robert Murray
Anthony Powell **31**:316
John Steinbeck **21**:387
Evelyn Waugh **1**:359

Davis, Stephen
Jimmy Cliff **21**:63, 64
Bob Marley **17**:267
Jimmy Page and Robert Plant **12**:480
Lou Reed **21**:307
Carly Simon **26**:407
Brian Wilson **12**:645

Davis, Thulani
Joyce Carol Thomas **35**:407

Davis, Thurston
John le Carré **28**:229

Davis, William V.
Robert Bly **15**:63, 67

Davison, Peter
Robert Creeley **8**:151
Robert Frost **4**:175
Tess Gallagher **18**:169
Doris Grumbach **13**:257
Robert Hass **18**:209
John Hollander **8**:298
Galway Kinnell **2**:229
Denise Levertov **8**:345
Sylvia Plath **2**:337
Anne Sexton **8**:482
William Stafford **7**:460

Davison, Will
Margaret Mead **37**:280

Davy, Charles
René Clair **20**:61
Rouben Mamoulian **16**:422

Davy, John
Arthur Koestler **1**:169

Dawidoff, Robert
Joyce Carol Oates **33**:293

Dawson, Dorotha
Walter Farley **17**:115
Noel Streatfeild **21**:399

Dawson, Helen
David Storey **4**:529

Dawson, Jan
Robert Altman **16**:20, 21
Rainer Werner Fassbinder **20**:116, 118
Werner Herzog **16**:328
Roman Polanski **16**:470
Jerzy Skolimowski **20**:349
François Truffaut **20**:392
Andrzej Wajda **16**:583

Dawson, Margaret Cheney
Nella Larsen **37**:211
Noel Streatfeild **21**:395

Dawson, Rosemary
Betty Smith **19**:422

Day, A. Grove
James A. Michener **1**:214

Day, Doris M.
Peter Shaffer **14**:487

Day, Douglas
Robert Graves **1**:127

Day, James M.
Paul Horgan **9**:278

Daymond, Douglas M.
Mazo de la Roche **14**:150

Daynard, Jodi
Russell Banks **37**:27
Sylvia Murphy **34**:92

De Aguilar, Helene J. F.
Vicente Aleixandre **36**:28

Deal, Borden
Doris Betts **28**:33

Deal, Paula Nespecca
C. J. Cherryh **35**:114

Dean, Joan F.
Peter Shaffer **18**:475

Dean, Joan Fitzpatrick
Tom Stoppard **29**:401

Dean, Leigh
Robert Cormier **30**:87
Lois Duncan **26**:108

DeAndrea, Francis T.
Nicholas M. Guild **33**:188

Deane, Peter
Frank Tuohy **37**:427

Deane, Seamus
Seamus Heaney **7**:150
Thomas Kinsella **19**:253
Derek Mahon **27**:289

Deas, Malcolm
Bruce Chatwin **28**:70

Debicki, Andrew P.
Dámaso Alonso **14**:15
Claudio Rodríguez **10**:439

De Bolt, Joe
John Brunner **8**:110

Debrix, Jean R.
Jean Cocteau **16**:223

DeBuys, William
Paul Horgan **9**:279

Decancq, Roland
Lawrence Durrell **8**:191

De Charmant, Elizabeth
Giorgio Bassani **9**:74

Deck, John
Harry Crews **6**:17
Henry Dumas **6**:145
J. G. Farrell **6**:173
Michael Moorcock **5**:294
John Seelye **7**:406

de Costa, René
Pablo Neruda **28**:311

Decter, Naomi [later Naomi Munson]
Judy Blume **30**:20

Dector, Midge
Leon Uris **7**:491

DeCurtis, Anthony
Leonard Michaels **25**:316

Dee, Jonathan
Raymond Carver **36**:107

Deedy, John
J. P. Donleavy **4**:123
Nora Ephron **17**:114
Upton Sinclair **11**:498

Deemer, Charles
Renata Adler **8**:7
James Baldwin **17**:38
John Cheever **3**:108
Peter Handke **5**:165
Bernard Malamud **3**:324

Deen, Rosemary F.
Randall Jarrell **6**:259
Galway Kinnell **3**:268

Deer, Harriet
Stanley Kubrick **16**:387

Deer, Irving
Stanley Kubrick **16**:387

DeFalco, Joseph
Ernest Hemingway **30**:185

De Feo, Ronald
Martin Amis **4**:21
Beryl Bainbridge **8**:37
Thomas Bernhard **3**:65
William S. Burroughs **2**:93
Dino Buzzati **36**:94
José Donoso **4**:128
Frederick Exley **11**:187
Eva Figes **31**:169
William Gaddis **6**:195
Gabriel García Márquez **2**:149; **10**:216
John Gardner **5**:131, 134
Graham Greene **6**:219
John Hawkes **1**:138
Richard Hughes **11**:278
Dan Jacobson **4**:255
Jerzy Kosinski **1**:172
Iris Murdoch **6**:345
Howard Nemerov **6**:360
Robert Pinget **37**:363
Sylvia Plath **1**:270
Anthony Powell **3**:404
Manuel Puig **28**:369
James Salter **7**:388

Gilbert Sorrentino **3**:461
William Trevor **7**:477
John Updike **5**:460
Mario Vargas Llosa **31**:445
Angus Wilson **5**:514

Deford, Frank
Martin Scorsese **20**:334

Degenfelder, E. Pauline
Larry McMurtry **7**:213

Degnan, James P.
Kingsley Amis **2**:10
Roald Dahl **1**:71
John Knowles **26**:258
J.M.G. Le Clézio **31**:247
Wilfrid Sheed **2**:394

Degnan, James P., Jr.
Betty Smith **19**:424

de Horá, Seán
William Kennedy **34**:210

Deitz, Paula
Frederick Busch **18**:84

De Jonge, Alex
Dick Francis **22**:151
Robert A. Heinlein **26**:165
Frank Herbert **23**:219
Frederik Pohl **18**:413
Aleksandr I. Solzhenitsyn **9**:506
D. M. Thomas **22**:417
Roger Zelazny **21**:471, 472

Dekker, George
Donald Davie **8**:166

Dekle, Bernard
Saul Bellow **1**:32
E. E. Cummings **1**:69
John Dos Passos **1**:80
William Faulkner **1**:102
Robert Frost **1**:111
Langston Hughes **1**:148
John P. Marquand **2**:271
Arthur Miller **1**:219
John O'Hara **1**:262
J. D. Salinger **1**:300
Upton Sinclair **1**:310
Thornton Wilder **1**:366
Tennessee Williams **1**:369
William Carlos Williams **1**:371

DeKoven, Marianne
Grace Paley **37**:331

De la Fuentes, Patricia
Gary Soto **32**:405

Delahanty, Thornton
Rouben Mamoulian **16**:419

Delamater, Jerome H.
Jean-Luc Godard **20**:145

Delaney, Marshall
See Fulford, Robert

Delany, Paul
A. Alvarez **5**:19
Margaret Atwood **4**:24
John Berger **19**:39
Vera Brittain **23**:93
Anthony Powell **31**:322

Delap, Richard
Fritz Leiber **25**:306

Critic Index

De la Roche, Catherine
Jean Renoir 20:288

De la Torre Bueno, J. R., Jr.
Roderick L. Haig-Brown
21:134, 135, 137

Delattre, Genevieve
Françoise Mallet-Joris 11:355

De Laurentis, Teresa
Italo Calvino 8:127

De Laurot, Edouard L.
Paddy Chayefsky 23:111
Federico Fellini 16:270

Delbanco, Nicholas
Max Apple 33:18
Frederick Busch 10:93
Graham Greene 9:251
Doris Grumbach 13:257

Deligiorgis, Stavros
David Kherdian 9:318

Delius, Anthony
Breyten Breytenbach 23:86
Alan Paton 25:361

Della Fazia, Alba
Jean Anouilh 1:7

Dellar, Fred
Smokey Robinson 21:345

Dellett, Wendy
Ann Schlee 35:373

Delong-Tonelli, Beverly J.
Fernando Arrabal 9:36

Del Rey, Lester
Marion Zimmer Bradley 30:26,
27
John W. Campbell, Jr. 32:77
C. J. Cherryh 35:103, 104, 105
Frederik Pohl 18:412
Jack Williamson 29:461
Roger Zelazny 21:471

De Luca, Geraldine
Aidan Chambers 35:99
Robert Cormier 30:83
Mollie Hunter 21:168
J. D. Salinger 12:517
Sandra Scoppettone 26:403

De Man, Paul
Harold Bloom 24:72
Georg Lukács 24:323

DeMara, Nicholas A.
Italo Calvino 11:87

DeMarco, Charles
Allen Drury 37:112

Demarest, Michael
Michael Crichton 6:119

DeMaria, Robert
Diane Wakoski 2:459

De Mauny, Erik
Ilya Ehrenburg 34:435
Anatol Goldberg 34:435

Dembo, L. S.
Donald Davie 31:110
Charles Olson 2:327
George Oppen 7:283
Robert Phillips 28:362
Louis Zukofsky 2:488

DeMeritt, William
Bernard Mac Laverty 31:252

Demetz, Peter
Lucien Goldmann 24:241
Rolf Hochhuth 18:250
Georg Lukács 24:328

De Mille, Richard
Carlos Castaneda 12:95

Demorest, Stephen
David Byrne 26:95
Lou Reed 21:313
Neil Young 17:579

Demos, E. Virginia
Larry Kettelkamp 12:307

Demos, John
Gunnar Ekelöf 27:113

DeMott, Benjamin
Margaret Atwood 2:20
James Baldwin 2:32
John Barth 14:58
Jorge Luis Borges 2:70
Lenny Bruce 21:49
Anthony Burgess 13:126
Vincent Canby 13:132
Truman Capote 19:84
Eleanor Clark 19:107
Robert Coover 15:142
E. L. Doctorow 18:124
T. S. Eliot 2:127
John Fowles 33:171
John Gardner 28:165
Barry Hannah 23:210
Joseph Heller 36:223
Mark Helprin 32:230
Nat Hentoff 26:183
Russell C. Hoban 7:162; 25:266
John Irving 23:250
Doris Lessing 2:240
Norman Mailer 28:258
Mary McCarthy 14:357
Margaret Mead 37:277
Henry Miller 2:283
A. G. Mojtabai 29:318
Philip Roth 9:462
Josef Škvorecký 15:512
William Styron 15:526
Gay Talese 37:396
Alexander Theroux 25:433
Paul Theroux 28:425
William Trevor 14:537
Anne Tyler 28:432
John Updike 5:459
Kurt Vonnegut, Jr. 2:453
John Wain 15:562
Derek Walcott 14:550
William Wharton 37:436
Patrick White 18:547
Maia Wojciechowska 26:456

DeMott, Robert
Mary Oliver 19:362
Judith Johnson Sherwin 15:480

Dempsey, David
Patrick Boyle 19:67
James M. Cain 28:48
R. V. Cassill 23:103
Janet Frame 22:143
Ernest K. Gann 23:162
Martha Gellhorn 14:195

Willard Motley 18:357
Nevil Shute 30:370
Terry Southern 7:454
Glendon Swarthout 35:400
Leon Uris 32:431

Dempsey, Michael
Robert Altman 16:20
Lindsay Anderson 20:14
Francis Ford Coppola 16:248
John Huston 20:171
Richard Lester 20:226
George Lucas 16:408
Ken Russell 16:546
Paul Schrader 26:387

Demuth, Philip
Jerome Siegel and Joe Shuster
21:363

Denby, David
Woody Allen 16:2
John Cassavetes 20:55
Francis Ford Coppola 16:237,
241, 245
Brian De Palma 20:81
Bob Fosse 20:126
Werner Herzog 16:334
John Landis 26:272, 274
Richard Lester 20:232
Richard Pryor 26:380
Paul Schrader 26:392, 396, 398
Martin Scorsese 20:325
Peter Shaffer 37:382
Joan Micklin Silver 20:345
Steven Spielberg 20:366, 367
Andy Warhol 20:419

Deneau, Daniel P.
Hermann Hesse 3:249
Jakov Lind 1:178
Amos Oz 27:360
Alain Robbe-Grillet 4:449

Denham, Paul
Louis Dudek 11:159

Denham, Robert D.
Northrop Frye 24:227

Denisoff, R. Serge
Woody Guthrie 35:193

Denison, Paul
Ward S. Just 27:227

Denne, Constance Ayers
Joyce Carol Oates 6:372

Denney, Reuel
Conrad Aiken 1:3

Dennis, Sr. M., R.S.M.
E. M. Almedingen 12:1

Dennis, Nigel
Louis-Ferdinand Céline 1:57
William Golding 17:167
Günter Grass 11:253
Robert Pinget 7:305
E. B. White 10:531

Dennis, Patrick
Françoise Sagan 17:422

Dennison, George
Claude Brown 30:37
Paul Goodman 4:197

Denuel, Eleanor P.
Laura Z. Hobson 25:273

DeRamus, Betty
Joyce Carol Oates 3:364

Deredita, John
Pablo Neruda 7:257
Juan Carlos Onetti 7:278

Deren, Maya
Maya Deren 16:252

Der Hovanessian, Diana
Vicente Aleixandre 36:29
David Kherdian 6:280

Derman, Lisa
Ken Follett 18:156

Dershowitz, Alan M.
Peter Matthiessen 32:293

Desai, Anita
Salman Rushdie 23:365

De Salvo, Louise A.
Robin F. Brancato 35:67

De Santana, Hubert
Brian Moore 19:332

Desilets, E. Michael
Frederick Wiseman 20:471

Desmond, Harold F., Jr.
Melvin Berger 12:38

Des Pres, Terrence
Geoffrey H. Hartman 27:186
Peter Matthiessen 11:360
Czesław Miłosz 22:308

Dessner, Lawrence Jay
Mario Puzo 6:429

De Teresa, Mary
Laura Nyro 17:318

Detro, Gene
Jackson J. Benson 34:412
John Steinbeck 34:412

Detweiler, Robert
John Updike 2:442

Deutsch, Babette
W. H. Auden 2:21
Ben Belitt 22:49
Louise Bogan 4:68
E. E. Cummings 3:116
Richard Eberhart 11:176
T. S. Eliot 2:125
William Empson 8:201
Robert Frost 3:171
Jean Garrigue 8:239
H. D. 3:217
Langston Hughes 35:214
Robinson Jeffers 15:300
Stanley Kunitz 11:319
Marianne Moore 2:290
St.-John Perse 4:398
Ezra Pound 2:339
Kathleen Raine 7:351
John Crowe Ransom 2:361;
24:363
Theodore Roethke 3:432
Carl Sandburg 4:463; 35:345
Edith Sitwell 2:402
Stephen Spender 2:419

Allen Tate **2**:427
Richard Wilbur **9**:568
William Carlos Williams **2**:466
Marya Zaturenska **11**:579

Deutsch, Herbert
Margaret O. Hyde **21**:173

De Van, Fred
Janis Ian **21**:187
Billy Joel **26**:214
Richard Pryor **26**:378

DeVault, Joseph J.
Mark Van Doren **6**:541

Dever, Joe
Edna Ferber **18**:151

Devert, Krystyna
Hermann Hesse **2**:189

Deveson, Richard
Thomas M. Disch **36**:127
Brian Moore **32**:313
Bernice Rubens **31**:352

DeView, Lucille
Peter Maas **29**:307

DeVitis, A. A.
Graham Greene **1**:133

Devlin, Diana
Howard Barker **37**:37
Howard Brenton **31**:68
Edna O'Brien **36**:336

Devlin, John
Ramón Sender **8**:478

DeVoto, Bernard
Van Wyck Brooks **29**:80
Erich Maria Remarque **21**:327

De Vries, Daniel
Stanley Kubrick **16**:387

De Vries, Peter
James Thurber **5**:429

De Vries, Hilary
Tom Stoppard **34**:273

Devrnja, Zora
Charles Olson **9**:412
Charles Simic **9**:478

Dewart, Leslie
William Barrett **27**:18
Jack Williamson **29**:462

Deweese, Beverly
Marion Zimmer Bradley **30**:32

Deweese, Gene
Arthur C. Clarke **35**:127
Lucius Shepard **34**:109

Dewsnap, Terence
Christopher Isherwood **1**:156

Dey, Susnigdha
Octavio Paz **19**:368

DeYoung, Alan J.
Margaret Mead **37**:282

Dial, John E.
José María Gironella **11**:237

Díaz, Janet Winecoff
Fernando Arrabal **18**:17
Miguel Delibes **18**:111
Ana María Matute **11**:363

Dibbell, Carola
Pat Barker **32**:14

Dick, Bernard F.
Michelangelo Antonioni **20**:41
Thomas J. Fleming **37**:122
William Golding **1**:120
John Hersey **2**:188
Iris Murdoch **6**:342; **22**:331
Mary Renault **3**:426
I. A. Richards **14**:454
Stevie Smith **8**:492
Gore Vidal **4**:558

Dick, Kay
Simone de Beauvoir **4**:48

Dickens, Anthony
E. M. Forster **22**:137

Dickens, Byrom
T. S. Stribling **23**:444

Dickens, Monica
Colin Thiele **17**:495

Dickenson, Peter
P. G. Wodehouse **22**:485

Dickey, Chris
Kurt Vonnegut, Jr. **5**:470

Dickey, Christopher
Manlio Argueta **31**:20
Graham Greene **37**:138
Trevanian **29**:432

Dickey, James
Conrad Aiken **1**:3
John Ashbery **2**:16
John Berryman **1**:33
Philip Booth **23**:74
Kenneth Burke **2**:87
Stanley Burnshaw **3**:91
Hayden Carruth **4**:93
E. E. Cummings **1**:68
J. V. Cunningham **3**:120
Robert Duncan **1**:82
Richard Eberhart **3**:133
Ronald G. Everson **27**:133
William Everson **1**:96
Robert Frost **1**:111
Allen Ginsberg **1**:118
Woody Guthrie **35**:193
David Ignatow **4**:247
Robinson Jeffers **2**:214
Galway Kinnell **1**:167
James Kirkup **1**:169
John Logan **5**:252
Louis MacNeice **1**:186
William Meredith **4**:347
James Merrill **2**:272
W. S. Merwin **1**:211
Josephine Miles **1**:215
Marianne Moore **1**:226
Howard Nemerov **2**:305
Mary Oliver **19**:361
Charles Olson **1**:262; **2**:327
Kenneth Patchen **1**:265
Sylvia Plath **2**:337
Herbert Read **4**:439
I. A. Richards **14**:452

Theodore Roethke **1**:290
May Sarton **4**:470
Frederick Seidel **18**:474
Anne Sexton **2**:390
Louis Simpson **4**:497
William Jay Smith **6**:512
William Stafford **4**:519
Allen Tate **6**:527
Derek Walcott **14**:548
Robert Penn Warren **1**:352;
   18:538
Theodore Weiss **3**:515
John Hall Wheelock **14**:571
Reed Whittemore **4**:588
Richard Wilbur **3**:531
William Carlos Williams **1**:370
Yvor Winters **4**:590

Dickey, R. P.
Lawrence Ferlinghetti **6**:183
Robert Lowell **5**:258

Dickey, William
Daniel J. Berrigan **4**:56
John Berryman **13**:75
Hayden Carruth **7**:40
James Dickey **2**:115
William Everson **5**:121
W. S. Merwin **2**:277
George Oppen **7**:281
Richard Wilbur **14**:577

Dickins, Anthony
Vladimir Nabokov **2**:304

Dickinson, Hugh
Eugène Ionesco **6**:250

Dickinson-Brown, R.
Barry Spacks **14**:510
Lewis Turco **11**:551

Dickstein, Lore
Gail Godwin **8**:247
Judith Guest **8**:254
Sue Kaufman **3**:263
Judith Rossner **6**:469
Susan Fromberg Schaeffer
   22:369
Lynne Sharon Schwartz **31**:387
Cynthia Propper Seton **27**:426
Isaac Bashevis Singer **3**:456
Botho Strauss **22**:408

Dickstein, Morris
John Barth **7**:24
Donald Barthelme **6**:29
R. P. Blackmur **2**:61
John Cassavetes **20**:55
Daniel Fuchs **8**:220
John Gardner **3**:184
Günter Grass **11**:252
Galway Kinnell **29**:288
Bernard Malamud **27**:300
Philip Roth **4**:454
Hunter S. Thompson **17**:509
C. K. Williams **33**:442, 445
Tom Wolfe **35**:456
Richard Wright **21**:458
Rudolph Wurlitzer **2**:484

Didion, Joan
Woody Allen **16**:13
John Cheever **8**:137
Elizabeth Hardwick **13**:265
Doris Lessing **2**:240
Norman Mailer **14**:352

V. S. Naipaul **18**:365
J. D. Salinger **12**:511

Dienstag, Eleanor
Sylvia Ashton-Warner **19**:22
Maureen Duffy **37**:113
Lee Kingman **17**:246

Dietemann, Margaret
Arthur Adamov **25**:16

Dietrichson, Jan W.
Daniel Hoffman **23**:239

Diez, Luys A.
Juan Carlos Onetti **7**:280

Digilio, Alice
M. E. Kerr **35**:248
Barbara Pym **37**:379
Cynthia Voight **30**:419
Barbara Wersba **30**:434

Dillard, Annie
Evan S. Connell, Jr. **4**:109

Dillard, R.H.W.
William S. Burroughs **22**:83
W. S. Merwin **8**:389
Wright Morris **18**:351
Vladimir Nabokov **2**:304
Colin Wilson **3**:537

Diller, Edward
Friedrich Dürrenmatt **11**:171

Dillin, Gay Andrews
John Jakes **29**:250

Dillin, John
Jonathan Schell **35**:362

Dillingham, Thomas
Susan Fromberg Schaeffer
   6:488

Dillon, Brooke Selby
Marilyn Sachs **35**:334

Dillon, David
William Goyen **14**:211
John Hawkes **4**:218
Edwin O'Connor **14**:393
Tillie Olsen **13**:433
Wallace Stegner **9**:509

Dillon, George
Gil Orlovitz **22**:332

Dillon, Michael
Thornton Wilder **6**:571

Di Martino, Dave
Pink Floyd **35**:311

Dimeo, Steve
George Roy Hill **26**:197

Dimeo, Steven
Ray Bradbury **3**:85

Dimock, Edward C.
Raja Rao **25**:366

Di Napoli, Thomas
Günter Grass **11**:247

Dinchak, Marla
Laurence Yep **35**:471

Critic Index

Dinnage, Rosemary
Peter Ackroyd **34**:396
A. S. Byatt **19**:77
Isak Dinesen **10**:152
T. S. Eliot **34**:396
E. M. Forster **22**:137
Elizabeth Hardwick **13**:264
Doris Lessing **6**:303
Iris Murdoch **22**:328
Barbara Pym **37**:378
Elizabeth Taylor **29**:409
Fay Weldon **19**:468
Rebecca West **31**:459

Dinoto, Andrea
Walter Farley **17**:118

Di Piero, W. S.
John Ashbery **4**:22
John Hawkes **9**:269
Seamus Heaney **25**:250
Philip Levine **14**:321
Sam Peckinpah **20**:282
R. G. Vliet **22**:442

Dipple, Elizabeth
Iris Murdoch **31**:289

Dirda, Michael
James Dickey **15**:177
Umberto Eco **28**:132
Henry Green **13**:251
Russell C. Hoban **25**:266
John Knowles **10**:303
Vladimir Nabokov **23**:310
D. M. Pinkwater **35**:320
Gilbert Sorrentino **14**:500
John Updike **34**:285
Jack Vance **35**:426
Alice Walker **19**:452

Disch, Thomas M.
William S. Burroughs **22**:84
Arthur C. Clarke **18**:106
Philip José Farmer **19**:168
Piers Paul Read **25**:378
Anne Tyler **18**:529
Gene Wolfe **25**:474
Laurence Yep **35**:474

Ditlea, Steve
Willie Nelson **17**:302

Ditsky, John
Richard Brautigan **12**:69
John Hawkes **2**:186
Erica Jong **8**:313
Joyce Carol Oates **2**:316

Dix, Carol
Martin Amis **4**:20

Dix, Winslow
William X. Kienzle **25**:274

Dixon, Bob
Gunnel Beckman **26**:89
Alan Garner **17**:149
Noel Streatfeild **21**:416

Dixon, John W., Jr.
Elie Wiesel **3**:527

DiZazzo, Raymond
Robert L. Peters **7**:303

Djilas, Milovan
Aleksandr I. Solzhenitsyn **2**:408

Djwa, Sandra
Margaret Laurence **13**:341
E. J. Pratt **19**:381
F. R. Scott **22**:376

Dobbs, Kildare
Hugh Hood **28**:187
Margaret Laurence **3**:278
Alice Munro **6**:341

Dobie, Ann B.
Muriel Spark **2**:416

Dobie, J. Frank
Mari Sandoz **28**:403, 404

Dobrez, L.A.C.
Jean Genet **14**:205

Dobson, Joan L.
Margaret O. Hyde **21**:180
Suzanne Newton **35**:301

Dobyns, Stephen
Julio Cortázar **33**:129, 135
James Tate **25**:427

Doctorow, E. L.
E. L. Doctorow **15**:179
Mary Lee Settle **19**:411

Dodd, Wayne
Madeleine L'Engle **12**:350

Dodsworth, Martin
Robert Bly **2**:65
Donald Davie **8**:163; **31**:110
James Dickey **2**:115
Ian Fleming **30**:133
Marianne Moore **2**:291
Edwin Morgan **31**:273
Peter Porter **33**:318

Doerksen, Daniel W.
Margaret Avison **4**:36

Doerner, William R.
James Herriot **12**:282

Doherty, Andy
Frank Zappa **17**:592

Dohmann, Barbara
Jorge Luis Borges **2**:69
Julio Cortázar **2**:101
Gabriel García Márquez **2**:147
Juan Carlos Onetti **7**:276
João Guimarães Rosa **23**:350
Juan Rulfo **8**:461
Mario Vargas Llosa **3**:493

Dolan, Mary
Frank G. Slaughter **29**:377

Doležel, Lubomír
Milan Kundera **32**:257

Dollard, Peter
Wendell Berry **27**:37
Carl Sandburg **35**:360

Dollard, W.A.S.
Winston Graham **23**:191

Dollen, Charles
William Peter Blatty **2**:64
Paul Gallico **2**:147
Ernest K. Gann **23**:167
N. Scott Momaday **2**:289

Dombroski, Robert S.
Carlo Emilio Gadda **11**:208

Domingues, Larry
Jim Shepard **36**:407

Domini, John
Stratis Haviaras **33**:206
Craig Nova **31**:296

Domowitz, Janet
Alice Adams **13**:3

Dompkowski, Judith A.
Matthew Bruccoli **34**:417
Ross Macdonald **34**:417

Donadio, Stephen
John Ashbery **2**:19
James Baldwin **17**:33
Richard Fariña **9**:195
Sandra Hochman **3**:250

Donaghue, Denis
Donald Barthelme **13**:62

Donahue, Deirdre
Bernard Mac Laverty **31**:255
Gloria Naylor **28**:305

Donahue, Francis
Antonio Buero Vallejo **15**:96
Camilo José Cela **4**:97; **13**:147

Donahue, Walter
Sam Shepard **4**:491

Donahugh, Robert H.
Allan W. Eckert **17**:104
Thomas J. Fleming **37**:127
John Knowles **26**:257
Margaret Mead **37**:280

Donald, David
Bruce Catton **35**:85, 89, 93
Margaret Mead **37**:279

Donald, David Herbert
Alex Haley **12**:246

Donald, Miles
Wilbur Smith **33**:374
Alexander Theroux **25**:431
John Updike **23**:465

Donaldson, Margaret
August Derleth **31**:135

Donaldson, Scott
Ernest Hemingway **13**:276
Philip Roth **1**:293

Donavin, Denise P.
Leon Edel **34**:534
John Ehle **27**:106
Howard Fast **23**:161
Norma Klein **30**:243
Barbara Pym **37**:368

Donegan, Patricia
Ayn Rand **30**:295

Donelson, Kenneth L.
Jay Bennett **35**:45
Robert Cormier **30**:87
James D. Forman **21**:123
Rosa Guy **26**:145
Paul Zindel **26**:472

Donnard, Jean-Hervé
Eugène Ionesco **6**:249

Donnelly, Brian
Derek Mahon **27**:289, 291

Donnelly, Dorothy
Marge Piercy **3**:384
Anne Stevenson **33**:379

Donnelly, John
Thomas Merton **34**:466
Michael Mott **34**:466

Donner, Jorn
Ingmar Bergman **16**:52

Donoghue, Denis
Peter Ackroyd **34**:395
A. R. Ammons **9**:27
John Ashbery **15**:34
W. H. Auden **3**:24
Saul Bellow **2**:51
J. V. Cunningham **31**:101, 103
Elizabeth Bishop **13**:95
R. P. Blackmur **24**:58, 67
Marie-Claire Blais **2**:63
Wayne C. Booth **24**:90
Kenneth Burke **2**:88
Ronald Bush **34**:531
Austin Clarke **9**:167
C. Day Lewis **6**:129
Jacques Derrida **24**:152
Margaret Drabble **22**:127
Richard Eberhart **11**:175
T. S. Eliot **2**:126; **34**:395, 531
Thomas Flanagan **25**:165
John Fowles **10**:188
William H. Gass **11**:225
William Golding **3**:196
Shirley Ann Grau **4**:209
Graham Greene **9**:250; **27**:173
Geoffrey H. Hartman **27**:182,
  186
Seamus Heaney **14**:245; **37**:163
Anthony Hecht **8**:269
Paul Horgan **9**:278
Randall Jarrell **1**:160
Robert Lowell **4**:295
James Merrill **2**:274; **18**:331
W. S. Merwin **2**:277
Marianne Moore **2**:291
Joyce Carol Oates **33**:291
Frank O'Connor **23**:331
Seán O'Faoláin **32**:340, 343
Tom Paulin **37**:355
Robert Pinsky **19**:370
David Plante **23**:341
Ezra Pound **2**:340
Philip Rahv **24**:357
I. A. Richards **24**:400
Philip Roth **6**:476
Frederick Seidel **18**:475
Jaroslav Seifert **34**:262
Christina Stead **2**:422
Mark Strand **18**:515
Allen Tate **6**:527; **9**:521; **11**:526
Charles Tomlinson **2**:437
Lionel Trilling **9**:530; **11**:543;
  24:452
Frank Tuohy **37**:430
Gore Vidal **33**:403
Derek Walcott **2**:460; **25**:451
Anne Waldman **7**:507
Robert Penn Warren **4**:579;
  13:581
René Wellek **28**:450
Rebecca West **7**:525

William Carlos Williams 2:467
Angus Wilson 25:464
Yvor Winters 32:463

Donoghue, Susan
Joni Mitchell 12:435, 436

Donohue, Agnes McNeill
Jessamyn West 17:553

Donohue, John W.
Earl Hamner 12:259

Donovan, Diane C.
Lloyd Alexander 35:28
Sue Ellen Bridgers 26:92
C. J. Cherryh 35:107
Stephen King 37:201

Donovan, Josephine
Sylvia Plath 3:390

Dooley, D. J.
Earle Birney 6:71

Dooley, Dennis M.
Robert Penn Warren 10:517

Dooley, Eugene A.
Evan Hunter 31:228

Dooley, Patricia
William Kotzwinkle 35:255
Barbara Wersba 30:433

Dooley, Roger B.
Thomas J. Fleming 37:121

Dooley, Susan
Joanne Greenberg 30:167

Dooley, Tim
Peter Porter 33:321

Dooley, William Germain
Charles Addams 30:12

Doreski, William
Louise Glück 22:175
Charles Simic 22:383
Richard Tillinghast 29:415

Dorfman, Ariel
Miguel Ángel Asturias 13:39

Dorian, Marguerite
Mircea Eliade 19:147

Dorsey, David
Alex La Guma 19:277

Dorsey, George A.
Margaret Mead 37:268

Dorsey, Margaret A.
Lloyd Alexander 35:25
Gunnel Beckman 26:86
Babbis Friis-Baastad 12:214
Larry Kettelkamp 12:305
Andre Norton 12:458, 459
Scott O'Dell 30:273

Dos Passos, John
E. E. Cummings 12:139

Doubrovsky, J. S.
Eugène Ionesco 6:247

Doubrovsky, Serge
Albert Camus 11:93

Dougherty, Dru
Juan Goytisolo 23:189
Darcy Ribeiro 34:102

Doughtie, Edward
James Dickey 15:176

Douglas, Ann
James T. Farrell 11:196

Douglas, Donald
Carl Van Vechten 33:388

Douglas, Ellen
Josephine Humphreys 34:65
Flannery O'Connor 6:381
May Sarton 4:471

Douglas, George H.
Edmund Wilson 2:477

Douglas, Marjory Stoneman
Noel Streatfeild 21:400

Dowd, Nancy Ellen
Frederick Wiseman 20:468

Dowell, Bob
Flannery O'Connor 21:264

Dowie, James Iverne
Helen Hooven Santmyer 33:357

Dowie, William
Sylvia Plath 17:364

Dowling, Gordon Graham
Yukio Mishima 6:337

Downer, Alan S.
Thornton Wilder 5:495

Downey, Sharon D.
Leon Uris 32:433

Downing, Robert
Orson Welles 20:433

Doxey, William S.
Ken Kesey 3:267
Flannery O'Connor 3:368

Doyle, Charles
James K. Baxter 14:60
See also Doyle, Mike

Doyle, Jacqueline
Sean O'Casey 15:406

Doyle, Mike
Irving Layton 2:236
A. W. Purdy 6:428
Raymond Souster 5:395, 396
See also Doyle, Charles

Doyle, Paul A.
Pearl S. Buck 11:71
Paul Vincent Carroll 10:96
R. V. Cassill 23:104
James T. Farrell 8:205
MacKinlay Kantor 7:195
Seán O'Faoláin 1:259; 7:273
Anne Tyler 28:431
Evelyn Waugh 1:359

Drabble, Margaret
Malcolm Bradbury 32:52
Michael Frayn 3:164
John Irving 13:295
Philip Larkin 8:333; 9:323
Iris Murdoch 4:367
Muriel Spark 8:494
John Updike 15:544

Drabelle, Dennis
Edward Abbey 36:19
David Cudlip 34:38
Frank Tuohy 37:433

Dragonwagon, C.
Stevie Wonder 12:663

Drake, Leah Bodine
Norman MacCaig 36:280

Drake, Robert
Carson McCullers 12:426
Flannery O'Connor 21:264, 273
Reynolds Price 3:405
Eudora Welty 5:478

Draper, Charlotte W.
Andre Norton 12:471

Draper, Gary
Michael Ondaatje 29:343

Draudt, Manfred
Joe Orton 13:436

Draya, Ren
Tennessee Williams 15:579

Dretzsky, George
Marian Engel 36:162

Drew, Fraser
John Masefield 11:356

Drexler, Rosalyn
Anaïs Nin 14:387
Fay Weldon 36:449

Dries, Linda R.
Allan W. Eckert 17:105

Driver, Christopher
Yukio Mishima 4:357
D. M. Thomas 31:433

Driver, Sam N.
Anna Akhmatova 11:6

Driver, Tom F.
Samuel Beckett 29:54
Jean Genet 1:115
Lorraine Hansberry 17:182
Arthur Miller 1:215; 2:279

Druska, John
John Beecher 6:49
John Gregory Dunne 28:125
Mario Puzo 36:360

Dryden, Edgar A.
John Barth 5:52

Duberman, Martin
Ed Bullins 1:47
Laura Z. Hobson 7:163
Albert Innaurato 21:197
David Mamet 15:355

Duberman, Martin B.
John Gregory Dunne 28:120
Nat Hentoff 26:180

Duberstein, Larry
Joel Lieber 6:312

Dubois, Larry
William F. Buckley, Jr. 7:34
Walker Percy 8:445

Du Bois, W. E. Burghardt
Arna Bontemps 18:62

Nella Larsen 37:210
Carl Van Vechten 33:392
Richard Wright 21:434

Du Bois, William
James M. Cain 28:45
Thomas B. Costain 30:93
A. J. Cronin 32:136
Howard Fast 23:158
Laura Z. Hobson 25:269
Conrad Richter 30:308, 323

Dubro, Alec
Neil Diamond 30:111
Kris Kristofferson 26:267
Jim Morrison 17:288
Laura Nyro 17:313

Ducan, Jean
Zibby Oneal 30:280

Ducharme, Edward
Walter M. Miller, Jr. 30:255

Duchêne, Anne
Beryl Bainbridge 22:45
Bruce Chatwin 28:73
Francine du Plessix Gray
22:200
Mark Helprin 22:221
Elizabeth Jane Howard 29:246
Alberto Moravia 18:347
Rosemary Sutcliff 26:441
D. M. Thomas 22:419

Duddy, Thomas A.
Louis Zukofsky 11:581

Dudek, Louis
Daryl Hine 15:281
Irving Layton 15:320
Alden Nowlan 15:399
James Reaney 13:474
Raymond Souster 14:501

Dufault, Peter Kane
Philip Booth 23:73

Duffey, Bernard
W. H. Auden 4:3
H. D. 31:207
Jack Kerouac 1:66
Carl Sandburg 35:358

Duffus, R. L.
Walter D. Edmonds 35:150
Richard Wright 21:435

Duffy, Dennis
Philip Child 19:102
Matt Cohen 19:111

Duffy, Martha
James Baldwin 4:41
Jean Cocteau 1:59
Joan Didion 1:75
Nikki Giovanni 2:164
Gail Godwin 22:180
Lillian Hellman 4:221
D. Keith Mano 10:328
Tom McHale 5:281
Grace Paley 4:393
Walker Percy 2:334
Sylvia Plath 2:336
Judith Rossner 6:470
Bernice Rubens 19:404
Françoise Sagan 36:383

Leon Uris 32:433
Patrick White 3:523

Duffy, Michael
Walter Becker and Donald
Fagen 26:84

Duguid, Lindsay
Ursula K. Le Guin 22:274

Duhamel, P. Albert
Flannery O'Connor 1:253
Paul Scott 9:477

Dukas, Vytas
Vasily Aksenov 22:26, 28

Dukes, Ashley
Emlyn Williams 15:577

Dukore, Bernard F.
Harold Pinter 27:393

Dullea, Gerard J.
Gregory Corso 11:123

Dumas, Bethany K.
E. E. Cummings 12:159

Dunbar, Ernest
Jules Archer 12:21

Duncan, Erika
William Goyen 8:251
Anaïs Nin 8:425

Duncan, Robert
Paul McCartney 35:285
Richard Pryor 26:378
John Wieners 7:536
Frank Zappa 17:591

Dunham, Vera S.
Yevgeny Yevtushenko 26:461

Dunlap, John R.
Martin Cruz Smith 25:414

Dunlea, William
Nevil Shute 30:370
Richard Wright 21:437

Dunlop, John B.
Vladimir Voinovich 10:509

Dunn, Douglas
Dannie Abse 29:20
Giorgio Bassani 9:77
Donald Davie 31:112
John Berryman 4:62
George Mackay Brown 5:78
Noël Coward 29:137
Donald Davie 5:115
Lawrence Durrell 4:147
D. J. Enright 4:156; 8:203
Gavin Ewart 13:209
James Fenton 32:165
W. S. Graham 29:196
Geoffrey Grigson 7:136
John Hawkes 7:141
Seamus Heaney 7:150
Dan Jacobson 14:290
Erica Jong 6:268
Michael Longley 29:292, 294,
296
Norman MacCaig 36:284, 285,
286
Derek Mahon 27:287
Christopher Middleton 13:388
Leslie Norris 14:387

Sylvia Plath 5:339
William Plomer 4:407
Peter Porter 13:452; 33:325
Peter Redgrove 6:446
Kenneth Rexroth 11:473
Jon Silkin 6:499
Anne Stevenson 7:463
Charles Tomlinson 6:534
Andrew Young 5:25

Dunn, Tony
Howard Barker 37:41

Dunne, John Gregory
William F. Buckley, Jr. 37:61
Danny Santiago 33:353

Dunning, Jennifer
Albert Innaurato 21:195

Dunson, Josh
Phil Ochs 17:330, 333

Dupee, F. W.
Kenneth Koch 5:218
Robert Lowell 3:299
Norman Mailer 11:339
Bernard Malamud 3:321
W. S. Merwin 3:338
John Osborne 5:330
J. F. Powers 4:418

DuPlessis, Rachel Blau
Edward Albee 13:6
H. D. 14:229
Muriel Rukeyser 27:412

Dupree, Robert S.
Caroline Gordon 13:245
Allen Tate 6:525

Duprey, Richard A.
Edward Albee 25:32
William Gibson 23:178
Arthur Miller 26:318

Duran, Daniel Flores
Scott O'Dell 30:275

Durán, Manuel
Pablo Neruda 28:312

Durand, Laura G.
Monique Wittig 22:475

Durbin, Karen
Eleanor Clark 5:107

Duree, Barbara Joyce
Lenora Mattingly Weber 12:633

Durgnat, Raymond
Georges Bataille 29:43
Robert Bresson 16:110
Tod Browning 16:122
Luis Buñuel 16:142, 150
John Cassavetes 20:44, 45
Claude Chabrol 16:168
René Clair 20:66
Shirley Clarke 16:216
Rainer Werner Fassbinder
20:119
Federico Fellini 16:273
Jean-Luc Godard 20:129
John Huston 20:168
Kon Ichikawa 20:177
Richard Lester 20:219
Roman Polanski 16:163, 468
Ann Quin 6:442

Jean Renoir 20:291, 304
François Truffaut 20:382
Lina Wertmüller 16:587

Durham, Frank
Julia Peterkin 31:306
Elmer Rice 7:363
T. S. Stribling 23:447

Durham, Philip
Dashiell Hammett 3:218;
19:194

Duroche, L. L.
Martin Heidegger 24:261

Durrant, Digby
Caroline Blackwood 6:80
Penelope Fitzgerald 19:174
Maurice Gee 29:178
Julia O'Faolain 6:383

Durrell, Gerald
Joy Adamson 17:2

Durrell, Lawrence
Odysseus Elytis 15:219
George Seferis 5:385

Dusenbury, Winifred L.
William Saroyan 29:359
Tennessee Williams 30:464

Dust, Harvey
Jules Archer 12:17

Dutton, Robert R.
Saul Bellow 25:86

Duvall, E. S.
Ann Beattie 13:66

Duvall, Elizabeth
Helen Yglesias 22:493

Du Verlie, Claude
Claude Simon 4:497

Dworkin, Ronald
Gay Talese 37:394

Dworkin, Susan
Gretchen Cryer 21:80

Dwyer, David J.
Mary Renault 3:426
Nathalie Sarraute 31:379

Dyck, J. W.
Boris Pasternak 18:381

Dyer, Peter John
René Clair 20:64
Jean Cocteau 16:227
Pier Paolo Pasolini 20:260
Jean Renoir 20:291
Luchino Visconti 16:563
Billy Wilder 20:459

Dyson, A. E.
Jorge Luis Borges 19:50
Ted Hughes 14:269
Sylvia Plath 11:446

Dyson, Claire M.
Kin Platt 26:354

Dyson, Timothy S.
Ronald J. Glasser 37:134

Dyson, William
Ezra Pound 1:276

Dzwonkoski, F. Peter, Jr.
T. S. Eliot 6:163

Eagle, Herbert
Aleksandr I. Solzhenitsyn 9:504
Ludvík Vaculík 7:495

Eagle, Robert
Thomas Hinde 11:274
Alberto Moravia 7:244
Flann O'Brien 4:385

Eagleton, Terry
George Barker 8:45
John Berger 19:39
Donald Davie 8:162
Thom Gunn 6:221
Seamus Heaney 7:150
Hermann Hesse 11:272
Elizabeth Jennings 14:293
William Plomer 8:447
Stevie Smith 8:491
Maura Stanton 9:508
Charles Tomlinson 6:535
John Wain 11:561
Andrew Young 5:525

Eakin, Mary K.
Mary Stolz 12:553

Earl, Pauline J.
Frank B. Gilbreth, Jr. and
Ernestine Gilbreth Carey
17:156

Earle, Adelaide
Mary Stewart 35:391

Early, Len
Bill Bissett 18:59

Earnshaw, Doris Smith
Denise Levertov 28:242
Joyce Carol Oates 33:289

Easterbrook, Gregg
Nicholas M. Guild 33:188

Eastlake, William
A. B. Guthrie, Jr. 23:198

Eastman, Fred
Marc Connelly 7:55

Eastman, Max
William F. Buckley, Jr. 37:55
I. A. Richards 24:374

Easton, Tom
Piers Anthony 35:36
David Brin 34:133
C. J. Cherryh 35:106, 107,
109, 113, 114
Michael Ende 31:144
Frank Herbert 35:206, 207
Stephen King 26:238
Lucius Shepard 34:110
Jack Vance 35:428
Jack Williamson 29:461

Eaton, Anne T.
Sally Benson 17:47
Langston Hughes 35:214
Carl Sandburg 35:347
John R. Tunis 12:593

Eaton, Charles Edward
Robert Frost 9:225

Eaton, Walter Prichard
Padraic Colum **28**:88
Joseph Wood Krutch **24**:285

Eaves, T. C. Duncan
Ezra Pound **34**:507
E. Fuller Torrey **34**:507

Eberhart, Richard
Djuna Barnes **8**:48
William Empson **19**:152
Robert Frost **13**:227
Allen Ginsberg **13**:239
Archibald MacLeish **3**:310
Ezra Pound **7**:324
Kenneth Rexroth **2**:370
Muriel Rukeyser **27**:409

Ebert, Roger
Charles Chaplin **16**:199
John Edgar Wideman **36**:451

Eby, Cecil
Vine Deloria, Jr. **21**:109

Eccleshare, Julia
Diana Wynne Jones **26**:227

Echevarría, Roberto González
Alejo Carpentier **11**:101
Julio Cortázar **10**:114; **13**:158;
34:334
Carlos Fuentes **10**:209
Severo Sarduy **6**:486

Eckley, Grace
Benedict Kiely **23**:259
Edna O'Brien **5**:312

Eckley, Wilton
Harriette Arnow **18**:10

Eckman, Martha
Colin Wilson **14**:583

Economou, George
Yannis Ritsos **31**:328

Edd, Karl
Arthur C. Clarke **35**:129

Eddins, Dwight
John Fowles **10**:183

Eddy, Elizabeth M.
Jonathan Kozol **17**:250

Edel, Leon
Van Wyck Brooks **29**:85
Lawrence Durrell **1**:85
William Faulkner **1**:100
Ernest Hemingway **10**:265
Alain Robbe-Grillet **1**:286
Nathalie Sarraute **1**:303

Edelberg, Cynthia Dubin
Robert Creeley **15**:151

Edelheit, S. J.
Anthony Burgess **13**:126

Edelman, Diane Gersoni
Walter Dean Myers **35**:298

Edelman, Sarah Prewitt
Robert Lowell **15**:344

Edelson, Edward
Carl Sagan **30**:331

Edelstein, Arthur
William Faulkner **1**:102
Janet Frame **6**:190
Jean Stafford **7**:458
Angus Wilson **2**:472

Edelstein, J. M.
Patricia Highsmith **2**:193
Doris Lessing **22**:279

Edelstein, Mark G.
Flannery O'Connor **6**:381

Edenbaum, Robert I.
Dashiell Hammett **3**:219
John Hawkes **2**:185

Eder, Richard
Vasily Aksyonov **37**:14
Frederick Barthelme **36**:50
T. Coraghessan Boyle **36**:60
Raymond Carver **36**:102
Brian Clark **29**:127
Gretchen Cryer **21**:81
Scott Elledge **34**:428
Athol Fugard **14**:191
Albert Innaurato **21**:194
Arthur Kopit **33**:246
Hugh Leonard **19**:283
Iris Murdoch **31**:292
Edna O'Brien **8**:430
Cynthia Ozick **28**:355
Bernard Pomerance **13**:445
Padgett Powell **34**:99
Gerome Ragni and James Rado
17:388
Ntozake Shange **25**:397, 398
Stephen Sondheim **30**:393
Peter Taylor **37**:411
Wendy Wasserstein **32**:439
E. B. White **34**:428
Nancy Willard **37**:465
Lanford Wilson **14**:590

Edinborough, Arnold
Earle Birney **6**:70
Robertson Davies **25**:129
Robert Kroetsch **23**:269
Jay Macpherson **14**:345

Edman, Irwin
Ogden Nash **23**:322
Siegfried Sassoon **36**:387

Edmiston, Susan
Maeve Brennan **5**:72

Edmonds, Ben
Pink Floyd **35**:308
Bob Seger **35**:378

Edmonds, Walter D.
Esther Forbes **12**:204

Edwards, C. Hines, Jr.
James Dickey **4**:121

Edwards, Christopher
Alan Ayckbourn **33**:49

Edwards, Clifford
Andrew Lloyd Webber and Tim
Rice **21**:423

Edwards, Henry
David Bowie **17**:60
Jackson Browne **21**:35
John Lennon **35**:263
Monty Python **21**:224
Lou Reed **21**:304

Bruce Springsteen **17**:479

Edwards, K. Anthony
Henry Gregor Felsen **17**:125

Edwards, Margaret A.
Betty Cavanna **12**:99
Maureen Daly **17**:89
Mary Stolz **12**:546

Edwards, Mary Jane
Paulette Jiles **13**:304
Susan Musgrave **13**:401

Edwards, Michael
René Char **14**:130
Donald Davie **5**:114
Charles Tomlinson **4**:547

Edwards, Paul
Amos Tutuola **14**:540

Edwards, Sharon
Jessamyn West **7**:522

Edwards, Terrance
Ronald Harwood **32**:225

Edwards, Thomas R.
Lisa Alther **7**:14
Kingsley Amis **8**:12
James Baldwin **4**:41
Donald Barthelme **8**:49
Jackson J. Benson **34**:410
Thomas Berger **18**:56
Richard Brautigan **12**:73
Frederick Buechner **2**:83
Charles Bukowski **2**:84
Anthony Burgess **5**:88
Raymond Carver **22**:96
John Cheever **7**:48
Evan S. Connell, Jr. **4**:108
Don DeLillo **27**:76
Joan Didion **32**:148
Stanley Elkin **4**:153
Leslie A. Fiedler **4**:161
Timothy Findley **27**:142
Paula Fox **2**:140
John Gardner **2**:151; **5**:133
Gail Godwin **8**:248
Herbert Gold **4**:193
James Hanley **8**:266
Edward Hoagland **28**:182
Diane Johnson **13**:306
James Jones **10**:293
Yoram Kaniuk **19**:239
Jerzy Kosinski **2**:233
George Lamming **2**:235
Norman Mailer **2**:264
Harry Mathews **6**:616
Peter Matthiessen **7**:211
Mary McCarthy **14**:363
Thomas McGuane **3**:330
Leonard Michaels **6**:324
Brian Moore **7**:237
Alice Munro **19**:347
Craig Nova **31**:298
Joyce Carol Oates **33**:288
Tim O'Brien **19**:358
Ishmael Reed **2**:368
Mordecai Richler **18**:454
Philip Roth **3**:437
André Schwarz-Bart **2**:389
Hubert Selby, Jr. **2**:390
Wilfrid Sheed **4**:488
Gilbert Sorrentino **14**:500

Scott Spencer **30**:407
John Steinbeck **34**:410
John Updike **5**:460; **23**:469
Derek Walcott **4**:576
William Wharton **37**:438
Tom Wolfe **1**:375
Richard Yates **23**:482

Edwards, William D.
Jules Archer **12**:18

Egan, James
Stephen King **37**:201

Eggenschwiler, David
Flannery O'Connor **6**:378
William Styron **5**:419

Egoff, Sheila A.
Julia W. Cunningham **12**:165
Leon Garfield **12**:218
Roderick L. Haig-Brown
21:140
Christie Harris **12**:265
Farley Mowat **26**:338, 339
Rosemary Sutcliff **26**:433, 440
Jill Paton Walsh **35**:433

Egremont, Max
Anna Kavan **13**:317
Seán O'Faoláin **7**:276
Anthony Powell **7**:341; **9**:438
Gillian Tindall **7**:474
Ludvík Vaculík **7**:496

Egudu, Romanus N.
Christopher Okigbo **25**:348,
355

Ehre, Milton
Aleksandr I. Solzhenitsyn **2**:412

Ehrenpreis, Irvin
A. R. Ammons **25**:45
John Ashbery **6**:13
W. H. Auden **9**:58
Ronald Bush **34**:527
Donald Davie **31**:111
T. S. Eliot **13**:200; **34**:527
Ronald Hall **13**:260
Seamus Heaney **37**:162
Anthony Hecht **13**:269
Geoffrey Hill **8**:293
Donald Justice **6**:272
Robert Lowell **1**:180; **8**:353
George Oppen **7**:285
John Updike **5**:455
Robert Penn Warren **18**:537

Ehresmann, Julia M.
Erich von Däniken **30**:427

Eidelman, M.
Anatoli Rybakov **23**:370

Eidus, Janice
Stephen King **37**:206

Einarsson, Stefán
Halldór Laxness **25**:291

Eiseley, Loren
Peter Matthiessen **32**:287
J.R.R. Tolkien **12**:566

Eiseman, Alberta
Betty Cavanna **12**:100
Maureen Daly **17**:89
William Mayne **12**:390
Zoa Sherburne **30**:360, 361
Lenora Mattingly Weber **12**:633

Critic Index

Eisen, Dulcie
  Ronald Tavel 6:529

Eisenberg, J. A.
  Isaac Bashevis Singer 1:310

Eisinger, Chester E.
  Carson McCullers 12:421
  Arthur Miller 6:331

Eisinger, Erica M.
  Marguerite Duras 11:165
  Georges Simenon 18:484

Eisner, Bob
  Smokey Robinson 21:344

Eisner, Lotte H.
  René Clair 20:64
  Fritz Lang 20:210, 213

Eksteins, Modris
  Erich Maria Remarque 21:336

Elderkin, Phil
  Russell Baker 31:28

Eldred, Kate
  David Malouf 28:266

Eldridge, Richard
  Jean Toomer 22:425

Eley, Holly
  Laurie Colwin 23:130
  Virginia Hamilton 26:155, 157

Eliade, Mircea
  Mircea Eliade 19:146

Elias, Robert H.
  James Thurber 5:431

Eliot, T. S.
  Djuna Barnes 29:23
  Marianne Moore 13:392; 19:336
  I. A. Richards 24:371

Elizondo, Salvador
  Octavio Paz 3:376

Elkin, Judith
  Diana Wynne Jones 26:230

Elkin, Sam
  Robert Lipsyte 21:208

Elkin, Stanley
  Frederick Forsyth 2:136

Elledge, Jim
  Stephen Dobyns 37:82
  Robert Hayden 37:159

Elledge, Scott
  Wayne C. Booth 24:89

Elleman, Barbara
  Melvin Berger 12:42
  Robin F. Brancato 35:66
  Barbara Corcoran 17:77
  Paula Danziger 21:86
  Madeleine L'Engle 12:351
  Sonia Levitin 17:265
  Anne McCaffrey 17:282, 284
  Suzanne Newton 35:301
  Katherine Paterson 12:485;
    30:282, 283
  Zilpha Keatley Snyder 17:475

Ellestad, Everett M.
  Pär Lagerkvist 13:333

Elley, Derek
  Mel Brooks 12:79
  Werner Herzog 16:324
  Yasujiro Ozu 16:455
  Pier Paolo Pasolini 20:266, 269
  Ken Russell 16:549
  Carlos Saura 20:315
  François Truffaut 20:404

Ellin, Stanley
  Robert Cormier 12:138; 30:81
  Richard Elman 19:151
  John Gardner 30:157
  Evan Hunter 31:224

Elliott, David
  Roman Polanski 16:470

Elliott, George P.
  Jean Giono 4:187
  Robert Graves 2:176
  Norman Mailer 3:317
  Milton Meltzer 26:305
  Susan Sontag 10:485
  David Wagoner 3:507

Elliott, Janice
  Lynne Reid Banks 23:41
  Patricia Highsmith 2:193
  Michael Moorcock 27:347
  Aleksandr I. Solzhenitsyn 1:321

Elliott, Robert C.
  Ursula K. LeGuin 8:341

Elliott, Susan
  Billy Joel 26:215, 216

Elliott, William I.
  Shusaku Endo 7:95

Ellis, James
  John Knowles 1:169; 26:248

Ellis, Roger
  Michel Tremblay 29:423

Ellis, W. Geiger
  Robert Cormier 30:91

Ellison, Harlan
  Barry N. Malzberg 7:208
  Roman Polanski 16:464

Ellison, Ralph
  Richard Wright 9:583; 21:441

Ellmann, Mary
  John Barth 2:39
  Vladimir Nabokov 1:244
  Joyce Carol Oates 3:364
  Sylvia Plath 17:350
  Richard Price 12:490
  Aleksandr I. Solzhenitsyn 1:321
  J.R.R. Tolkien 12:571
  Michel Tournier 6:538
  Rebecca West 7:526
  Vassily S. Yanovsky 2:485

Ellmann, Richard
  W. H. Auden 9:55
  Giorgio Bassani 9:76
  Samuel Beckett 2:47
  Elizabeth Daryush 19:119
  Seamus Heaney 37:168
  Alfred Kazin 34:558

Elman, Richard
  William Bronk 10:73
  Frederick Busch 10:91
  Allen Drury 37:112
  Daniel Fuchs 22:160
  Thomas McGuane 18:323
  Margaret Mead 37:278
  Richard Price 12:490
  Françoise Sagan 17:426
  Zilpha Keatley Snyder 17:471

Elman, Richard M.
  Arthur A. Cohen 31:91
  Charles Bukowski 9:137
  Hannah Green 3:202
  Jack Spicer 8:497
  Hunter S. Thompson 9:526
  Rudolf Wurlitzer 2:482

Elon, Amos
  Yehuda Amichai 9:22

Elsaesser, Thomas
  Rainer Werner Fassbinder
    20:110

Elsom, John
  Alan Ayckbourn 5:35
  Samuel Beckett 6:43
  Edward Bond 6:85
  Michael Frayn 7:108
  Arthur Miller 15:376
  David Rudkin 14:470
  Sam Shepard 6:496
  Tom Stoppard 5:412
  E. A. Whitehead 5:488

Elstob, Peter
  Len Deighton 4:119

Elston, Nina
  Susan Richards Shreve 23:403

Elton, G. R.
  Antonia Fraser 32:181

Emanuel, James A.
  Langston Hughes 1:147

Emblidge, David
  E. L. Doctorow 11:143

Embree, Ainslie
  Ved Mehta 37:296

Emerson, Donald
  Carson McCullers 12:420

Emerson, Gloria
  Michael Cimino 16:213

Emerson, Ken
  David Bowie 17:61
  David Byrne 26:97
  Ray Davies 21:95, 103
  Van Morrison 21:235
  Smokey Robinson 21:345
  Bruce Springsteen 17:477
  Paul Weller 26:443
  Stevie Wonder 12:657

Emerson, O. B.
  Marion Montgomery 7:232

Emerson, Sally
  Douglas Adams 27:13
  Hermann Hesse 25:261
  Molly Keane 31:233
  William Mayne 12:404
  Piers Paul Read 25:379

Emerson, Stephen
  Gilbert Sorrentino 7:450

Emme, Eugene M.
  Arthur C. Clarke 35:118

Emmons, Winfred S.
  Katherine Anne Porter 1:273

Empson, William
  Wayne C. Booth 24:92
  Cleanth Brooks 24:103

Endres, Robin
  Milton Acorn 15:10

Engel, Bernard F.
  Marianne Moore 1:227

Engel, Eva J.
  Hermann Hesse 17:202

Engel, Howard
  Morley Callaghan 14:102

Engel, Marian
  Penelope Gilliatt 2:160
  Margaret Laurence 3:278
  Françoise Mallet-Joris 11:356
  Joyce Carol Oates 6:372
  Françoise Sagan 6:481
  Michel Tournier 6:537

England, David A.
  Garry Marshall 17:278

Engle, Gary
  Robert Altman 16:22

Engle, Paul
  Charles M. Schulz 12:531

English, Raymond
  Carl Zuckmayer 18:553

Enright, D. J.
  John Ashbery 9:49
  Simone de Beauvoir 14:66
  Heinrich Böll 3:74; 11:52
  Anthony Burgess 4:80; 15:103;
    22:75
  Stanley Burnshaw 3:90
  James Clavell 6:114
  Lawrence Durrell 6:151
  Max Frisch 32:192
  Witold Gombrowicz 4:195
  Günter Grass 2:271; 4:202
  Robert Graves 2:175
  Hermann Hesse 3:243
  Randall Jarrell 9:296
  Yasunari Kawabata 5:206;
    9:316
  Thomas Keneally 14:302;
    27:233
  Carolyn Kizer 15:308
  Milan Kundera 9:321
  Philip Larkin 3:276
  Doris Lessing 3:282
  Norman MacCaig 36:282
  Czesław Miłosz 5:291
  Yukio Mishima 4:353; 27:336
  Vladimir Nabokov 3:352
  V. S. Naipaul 4:371
  Kenzaburō Ōe 36:344
  Ezra Pound 3:395
  Salman Rushdie 31:358
  Stevie Smith 3:460
  C. P. Snow 9:496

Muriel Spark **3**:463
George Steiner **24**:429
John Updike **2**:439

Enslin, Theodore
George Oppen **7**:281

Ensslen, Klaus
Alice Walker **27**:451

Envall, Markku
Paavo Haavikko **34**:179

Eoff, Sherman H.
Jean-Paul Sartre **1**:303
Ramón Sender **8**:477

Ephron, Nora
Erich Segal **3**:447
Garry Trudeau **12**:589

Epps, Garrett
Russell Banks **37**:29
Thomas Berger **11**:47
William Brammer **31**:54
Nicholas Delbanco **13**:174
Molly Keane **31**:233
John Sayles **14**:483
Susan Fromberg Schaeffer
    22:368
Alan Sillitoe **19**:421
Gilbert Sorrentino **22**:394
Elizabeth Spencer **22**:406
John Edgar Wideman **34**:299

Epstein, Helen
Isaac Bashevis Singer **23**:422

Epstein, Joseph
Renata Adler **31**:16
Jonathan Baumbach **23**:55
Rosellen Brown **32**:66
Joan Didion **32**:150
E. M. Forster **4**:165
Gabriel García Márquez **27**:154
Nadine Gordimer **18**:188
Mark Harris **19**:205
Joseph Heller **5**:174
John Irving **23**:253
Alan Lelchuk **5**:241
Bernard Malamud **27**:301
Philip Roth **31**:343
Aleksandr I. Solzhenitsyn **2**:409
Stephen Spender **5**:402
Gay Talese **37**:393
Edmund Wilson **2**:477; **8**:551
Tom Wolfe **35**:449

Epstein, Julia
Anita Brookner **32**:60

Epstein, Lawrence J.
Elie Wiesel **5**:493

Epstein, Leslie
Cynthia Ozick **28**:350
D. M. Thomas **22**:420

Epstein, Seymour
Saul Bellow **13**:72
Dino Buzzati **36**:95
Jerome Charyn **18**:99

Erbes, Bill
C. S. Adler **35**:15

Erickson, Peter
Alice Walker **19**:451

Ericson, Edward, Jr.
Thornton Wilder **10**:533

Ericson, Edward E., Jr.
C. S. Lewis **6**:310
Aleksandr I. Solzhenitsyn
    4:509; **26**:422

Erikson, Kai
Jonathan Schell **35**:366

Erlich, Nancy
Ray Davies **21**:94

Erlich, Richard
Harlan Ellison **13**:203

Erlich, Victor
Joseph Brodsky **6**:96

Ermolaev, Herman
Mikhail Sholokhov **15**:481

Ernst, Margaret
Andre Norton **12**:455

Eron, Carol
John Hawkes **4**:218

Ervine, St. John
Noël Coward **29**:132

Eshleman, Clayton
Aimé Césaire **32**:110
Robert Creeley **36**:120
C. K. Williams **33**:447

Eskin, Stanley G.
Nicholas Delbanco **6**:130

Esmonde, Margaret P.
Ursula K. Le Guin **22**:270
Zilpha Keatley Snyder **17**:474

Esposito, Joseph J.
Larry McMurtry **27**:332

Esslin, Martin
Arthur Adamov **4**:5
Edward Albee **2**:4; **9**:10
John Arden **6**:5
Samuel Beckett **1**:24; **4**:52;
    6:33, 44
Thomas Bernhard **32**:23
Edward Bond **13**:98
Dino Buzzati **36**:85
Friedrich Dürrenmatt **4**:139
Max Frisch **3**:167
Jack Gelber **1**:114
Jean Genet **1**:117
Günter Grass **4**:201
Graham Greene **9**:250
Václav Havel **25**:222
Rolf Hochhuth **4**:231
Eugène Ionesco **1**:154; **4**:252
Arthur Kopit **1**:170
Sławomir Mrozek **3**:344
Robert Pinget **7**:306
Harold Pinter **1**:268; **6**:407,
    414; **27**:392
Peter Shaffer **18**:477
Neil Simon **6**:506
N. F. Simpson **29**:369
Wole Soyinka **14**:505
Peter Weiss **3**:515

Estes, Sally
Robert Cormier **30**:90
Danny Santiago **33**:352
Joan D. Vinge **30**:412

Estes, Sally C.
Sol Gordon **26**:138

Estess, Sybil
Elizabeth Bishop **9**:95
Padgett Powell **34**:100

Estess, Ted L.
Samuel Beckett **11**:41
Elie Wiesel **37**:456

Estrin, Barbara L.
Adrienne Rich **18**:450

Esty, William
James Baldwin **17**:21
Flannery O'Connor **21**:255
Rebecca West **31**:456

Etherton, Michael
Ngugi wa Thiong'o **36**:315

Ettin, Andrew V.
James Merrill **2**:273

Evanier, David
Saul Bellow **25**:85
Eldridge Cleaver **30**:56
Leonard Michaels **25**:319
John Updike **15**:547

Evans, Ann
Judy Blume **12**:46
Rosemary Sutcliff **26**:438

Evans, Don
Ed Bullins **5**:82

Evans, Donald T.
Alice Childress **12**:105

Evans, Eli N.
James Dickey **7**:86

Evans, Ernestine
Jessamyn West **17**:544
Jade Snow Wong **17**:565

Evans, Fallon
J. F. Powers **1**:279

Evans, Gareth Lloyd
Edward Albee **25**:34
Harold Pinter **11**:444

Evans, Gwyneth F.
Christie Harris **12**:267

Evans, Joseph T.
Jacques-Yves Cousteau **30**:104

Evans, M. Stanton
Allen Drury **37**:103, 105

Evans, Oliver
Paul Bowles **1**:41
Babette Deutsch **18**:119
Carson McCullers **12**:425

Evans, Patrick
Frank Sargeson **31**:369

Evans, Robley
J.R.R. Tolkien **3**:478

Evans, T. Jeff
Peter De Vries **28**:106

Evans, Timothy
Isaac Bashevis Singer **11**:499

Evans, William R.
Julian Symons **32**:424
Edmund White III **27**:478

Evarts, Prescott, Jr.
John Fowles **2**:138

Everett, Barbara
Peter Ackroyd **34**:399
Donald Davie **31**:119
T. S. Eliot **34**:399

Everman, Welch D.
Richard Kostelanetz **28**:215

Evers, Larry
Charles R. Larson **31**:240

Everson, Edith A.
E. E. Cummings **15**:157

Evett, Robert
Terrence McNally **7**:219
Manuel Mujica Láinez **31**:278
Lanford Wilson **7**:548

Ewart, Gavin
D. J. Enright **31**:150, 154
Roy Fuller **28**:157
William Sansom **2**:383
Sylvia Townsend Warner
    19:461

Ewen, David
Gerome Ragni and James Rado
    17:385

Ewers, John C.
Jamake Highwater **12**:286

Ewing, Dorothy
Miguel Delibes **18**:110

Exner, R.
Botho Strauss **22**:407

Eyles, Allen
Francis Ford Coppola **16**:231
John Huston **20**:169
Ken Russell **16**:541

Eyre, Frank
H. F. Brinsmead **21**:30
Peter Dickinson **12**:170
Eilís Dillon **17**:98
Leon Garfield **12**:223
Alan Garner **17**:142
William Mayne **12**:396
Philippa Pearce **21**:287
Colin Thiele **17**:494

Eyster, Warren
James Dickey **1**:74

Faas, Ekbert
Gary Snyder **32**:388

Faase, Thomas P.
Andrew M. Greeley **28**:174

Faber, Nancy W.
Frank Bonham **12**:50

Faber, Roderick Mason
Tennessee Williams **19**:474

Fabian, Hans J.
Fritz Hochwälder **36**:239

Fabio, Sarah Webster
Nikki Giovanni **19**:190

Fabre, Michel
James Baldwin **3**:31
Chester Himes **2**:195

Fadiman, Anne
Fran Lebowitz 11:322

Fadiman, Clifton
Taylor Caldwell 28:56, 57
Walter Van Tilburg Clark 28:76
Howard Fast 23:155
William Faulkner 28:139
Arthur Koestler 33:229
Carson McCullers 12:409
Mari Sandoz 28:402
Nevil Shute 30:366
Carl Van Vechten 33:394
Rebecca West 31:455
T. H. White 30:438

Fadiman, Edwin
Laura Z. Hobson 7:163

Faery, Rebecca B.
Richard Wilbur 9:570

Fagan, Carey
John Metcalf 37:304

Fager, Charles E.
Bob Dylan 12:185

Fahey, James
Evan S. Connell, Jr. 4:109

Fahey, Joseph J.
William Barrett 27:21

Fairchild, B. H., Jr.
Steven Spielberg 20:364

Fairweather, Eileen
Pat Barker 32:11

Faith, Rosamond
Rosemary Wells 12:638

Falck, Colin
A. Alvarez 5:16
John Berryman 2:55
William Empson 3:147
Geoffrey Grigson 7:136
Thom Gunn 6:220
Seamus Heaney 7:149
Ted Hughes 9:280
Philip Larkin 3:275, 276
Robert Lowell 2:245; 5:256
George MacBeth 9:340
Paul Muldoon 32:317
Peter Porter 33:319
Anne Sexton 8:483
Charles Tomlinson 2:436

Falcoff, Mark
Joan Didion 32:144

Falk, Doris V.
Lillian Hellman 14:258

Falk, Signi
Tennessee Williams 1:367

Falke, Wayne
Kenzaburō Ōe 10:372
Jun'ichirō Tanizaki 14:525
John Updike 5:453

Falkenberg, Betty
Walter Abish 22:21
Beryl Bainbridge 18:34
Thomas Bernhard 32:21
Milan Kundera 32:264
Primo Levi 37:226
Marge Piercy 18:408

Patrick White 18:549

Fallis, Laurence S.
Ruth Prawer Jhabvala 4:259

Fallowell, Duncan
J. G. Ballard 36:37
Giorgio Bassani 9:77
John Berger 2:54
William Peter Blatty 2:64
Richard Brautigan 12:72
Taylor Caldwell 28:66
Robert Coover 3:114
Mark Helprin 7:152
Ruth Prawer Jhabvala 8:312
Anna Kavan 13:316
Yashar Kemal 29:266
Jerzy Kosinski 3:274
Fran Lebowitz 36:250
Iris Murdoch 4:368
Tim O'Brien 7:272
Seán O'Faoláin 7:274
Mervyn Peake 7:303
David Plante 7:308
Françoise Sagan 9:468
James Salter 7:388
Hubert Selby, Jr. 2:390
Terry Southern 7:454
Muriel Spark 3:465; 8:493
Auberon Waugh 7:514

Fallows, James
William Brammer 31:54
George V. Higgins 18:233

Fandel, John
E. E. Cummings 3:120

Fandray, David F.
David Bowie 17:62

Fanger, Donald
Aleksandr I. Solzhenitsyn 1:319

Fanning, Peter
Alan Garner 17:149
Nat Hentoff 26:185
Paul Zindel 26:478

Fantoni, Barry
S. J. Perelman 15:418
Brian Wilson 12:60

Farber, Jim
Prince 35:323

Farber, Manny
Maya Deren 16:251
John Ford 16:305
Alfred Hitchcock 16:338, 339
John Huston 20:159
Akira Kurosawa 16:394
Paul Schrader 26:386

Farber, Marjorie
Laura Z. Hobson 25:269

Farber, Stephen
Lindsay Anderson 20:15
Francis Ford Coppola 16:231,
232, 235
Michael Cristofer 28:94
George Roy Hill 26:196
Richard Lester 20:225
Sam Peckinpah 20:274
Ken Russell 16:548
Martin Scorsese 20:327
Steven Spielberg 20:358

François Truffaut 20:396
Luchino Visconti 16:569
Orson Welles 20:446
Billy Wilder 20:461, 464, 465

Farmer, Betty Catherine Dobson
Donald Barthelme 13:58

Farmer, Penelope
Alan Garner 17:147
Diana Wynne Jones 26:226,
229
William Mayne 12:401
Philippa Pearce 21:289

Farmiloe, Dorothy
Hugh MacLennan 14:341

Farnsworth, Emily C.
Robert Newton Peck 17:343

Farnsworth, Robert M.
Melvin B. Tolson 36:429

Farrell, Diane
Sol Gordon 26:136
Andre Norton 12:459
Paul Zindel 26:470

Farrell, James T.
James M. Cain 11:84
John Dos Passos 25:139
Ben Hecht 8:269
Frank O'Connor 14:395

Farrell, John P.
Richard Wilbur 3:532

Farrell, Walter C., Jr.
Langston Hughes 35:220, 221

Farrelly, John
Andrew Lytle 22:293

Farrison, W. Edward
Lorraine Hansberry 17:191

Farwell, Harold
John Barth 5:50

Farwell, Ruth
George Mackay Brown 5:77

Farzan, Massud
Ahmad Shamlu 10:469

Fasick, Adele M.
Roderick L. Haig-Brown
21:139

Fassbinder, Rainer Werner
Claude Chabrol 16:181

Fast, Howard
Conrad Richter 30:308

Faulkner, Peter
Angus Wilson 25:464

Faulkner, William
Erich Maria Remarque 21:326

Faulks, Sebastian
Anita Brookner 34:136
Anita Desai 37:71
Yasunari Kawabata 9:316

Fawcett, Anthony
Jackson Browne 21:41

Fawcett, Graham
Anthony Burgess 8:111

Fay, Eliot G.
Jacques Prévert 15:437

Feagles, Anita MacRae
Maia Wojciechowska 26:455

Fearing, Kenneth
George Tabori 19:435

Featherstone, Joseph
Katherine Anne Porter 3:392
Frederick Wiseman 20:468

Featherstone, Simon
Thomas M. Disch 36:127

Feaver, Vicki
Sylvia Townsend Warner
19:460

Feaver, William
Michael Ayrton 7:19
Peter Gent 29:181

Feder, Kenneth L.
Erich von Däniken 30:426

Feder, Lillian
Conrad Aiken 5:8
W. H. Auden 4:33, 34, 35
George Barker 8:43
Samuel Beckett 6:37
T. S. Eliot 6:160
Robert Graves 6:210
Ted Hughes 9:281
Robert Lowell 4:301
Ezra Pound 3:396; 4:414

Federman, Raymond
Samuel Beckett 9:79

Feehan, Paul G.
Woody Guthrie 35:193

Feeney, Joseph J., S.J.
Jessie Redmon Fauset 19:171
Isabelle Holland 21:150

Feidelson, Charles, Jr.
Leon Edel 29:167

Feied, Frederick
John Dos Passos 1:80
Jack Kerouac 1:166

Feifer, George
Aleksandr I. Solzhenitsyn 7:444

Feiffer, Jules
Richard Lester 20:223
Jerome Siegel and Joe Shuster
21:356

Fein, Richard J.
Robert Lowell 3:304

Feinberg, Anat
A. B. Yehoshua 31:469

Feingold, Michael
Dannie Abse 7:2
E. L. Doctorow 15:179
Athol Fugard 9:235
John Guare 8:252,253
Peter Handke 8:263
Beth Henley 23:216, 217
John Hopkins 4:234
Albert Innaurato 21:192, 194
Jim Jacobs and Warren Casey
12:294
Ira Levin 3:294

Miguel Piñero **4**:401
Sam Shepard **17**:444, 445, 447
Elizabeth Swados **12**:557, 561
Tennessee Williams **7**:544

Feinstein, Elaine
Marian Engel **36**:159
Gail Godwin **8**:247
William Golding **2**:169
Nadine Gordimer **3**:202
George MacBeth **5**:265
Olivia Manning **19**:301
Mary McCarthy **3**:329
Grace Paley **6**:339
Christina Stead **5**:403

Feirstein, Frederick
Robert Graves **2**:177

Feld, Michael
Richard Brautigan **12**:63
John Updike **2**:445

Feld, Rose C.
Sally Benson **17**:47
Agatha Christie **12**:114
August Derleth **31**:130
Walter D. Edmonds **35**:152
C. S. Forester **35**:163
Ernest K. Gann **23**:162
Madeleine L'Engle **12**:345
Helen MacInnes **27**:278, 279
Farley Mowat **26**:333
Mary Renault **17**:389
Françoise Sagan **17**:420
Mari Sandoz **28**:400
Mary Stewart **35**:390
Glendon Swarthout **35**:398

Feld, Ross
Paul Blackburn **9**:98
Laurie Colwin **13**:156
William H. Gass **11**:225
Jack Spicer **8**:497
Eudora Welty **14**:566
Tom Wolfe **9**:578

Feldman, Anita
Irwin Shaw **7**:412

Feldman, Hans
Stanley Kubrick **16**:391

Feldman, Irma P.
Helen Yglesia **7**:558

Feldman, Morton
Frank O'Hara **2**:322

Felheim, Marvin
Ben Hecht **8**:272
Lillian Hellman **14**:255
Carson McCullers **1**:208
Eudora Welty **1**:361

Fell, John L.
Rainer Werner Fassbinder **20**:117

Fellows, Jo-Ann
Mazo de la Roche **14**:150

Felsen, Henry Gregor
Henry Gregor Felsen **17**:123

Felstiner, John
Pablo Neruda **1**:247; **2**:309;
5:302

Felton, David
Steve Martin **30**:246
Richard Pryor **26**:379
Lily Tomlin **17**:519

Fender, Stephen
Jacob Epstein **19**:162
Richard Price **12**:491
John Sayles **10**:462

Fenin, George N.
Vittorio De Sica **20**:86
Billy Wilder **20**:457, 458

Fenton, Edward
Mollie Hunter **21**:157
Maia Wojciechowska **26**:454

Fenton, James
W. H. Auden **6**:18
Lynne Reid Banks **23**:41
Giorgio Bassani **9**:76
Douglas Dunn **6**:148
Gavin Ewart **13**:210
Josephine Poole **17**:372
George Steiner **24**:435
Charles Tomlinson **6**:534

Fenves, Peter
Samuel Beckett **29**:59

Ferguson, Alan
Ivo Andrić **8**:20

Ferguson, Charles W.
Thomas B. Costain **30**:98

Ferguson, Frances
Randall Jarrell **13**:301
Robert Lowell **4**:302

Ferguson, Otis C.
Frank Capra **16**:154, 155, 156
Charles Chaplin **16**:190, 192
A. J. Cronin **32**:135
Walter D. Edmonds **35**:146
John Ford **16**:303, 304
Alfred Hitchcock **16**:337
Zora Neale Hurston **30**:211
Rouben Mamoulian **16**:420
Irwin Shaw **23**:395
Orson Welles **20**:432
T. H. White **30**:438

Ferguson, Suzanne
Djuna Barnes **3**:36
Randall Jarrell **2**:209

Fergusson, Francis
René Clair **20**:59

Fernandez, Doreen G.
Bienvenido N. Santos **22**:365

Fernandez, Jaime
Jun'ichirō Tanizaki **8**:511

Fernández-Morera, Dario
Vicente Aleixandre **36**:25

Ferrari, Margaret
Colleen McCullough **27**:317
Marge Piercy **6**:402
Hilma Wolitzer **17**:561

Ferrari, Margaret Burns
Norma Klein **30**:239

Ferrell, Henry C., Jr.
Louis R. Harlan **34**:187

Ferrer, José M.
Garry Marshall **17**:274

Ferrer, Olga Prjevalinskaya
Eugène Ionesco **6**:256

Ferreri, Rosario
Primo Levi **37**:225

Ferres, John H.
Arthur Miller **26**:324

Ferretti, Fred
Norman Lear **12**:326
George Plimpton **36**:357

Ferrier, Carole
Sylvia Plath **17**:369
Diane Wakoski **7**:505

Ferris, Ina
Rudy Wiebe **11**:567

Ferris, Sumner J.
Flannery O'Connor **21**:257

Ferris, William H.
W.E.B. Du Bois **13**:180

Ferrucci, Franco
Italo Calvino **33**:100
Umberto Eco **28**:131

Ferry, David
Theodore Roethke **1**:291

Fetherling, Doug
Hugh Garner **13**:235,236
Patrick Lane **25**:283
A. W. Purdy **14**:435
Mordecai Richler **3**:431
Robin Skelton **13**:506

Fetz, Gerald A.
Martin Walser **27**:463

Feuer, Kathryn B.
Aleksandr I. Solzhenitsyn **7**:445

Feuser, Willfried F.
Chinua Achebe **7**:6

Fialkowski, Barbara
Maxine Kumin **13**:326

Fiamengo, Marya
Susan Musgrave **13**:400

Fickert, Kurt J.
Friedrich Dürrenmatt **4**:139
Hermann Hesse **17**:201

Fiddler, Virginia
Frederick Forsyth **36**:178

Fiedler, Leslie A.
John Barth **3**:38
Saul Bellow **1**:27, 31; **3**:48
Truman Capote **19**:79
Leonard Cohen **3**:109
Bob Dylan **3**:130
Philip José Farmer **19**:164
William Faulkner **1**:101; **3**:149
Allen Ginsberg **2**:162; **3**:193
John Hawkes **3**:221
Ernest Hemingway **1**:143;
3:232, 33
John Hersey **7**:153
Randall Jarrell **1**:160
Arthur Koestler **33**:237
Robert Lowell **2**:246

Norman Mailer **3**:311
Bernard Malamud **9**:341, 351
Henry Miller **2**:282
Alberto Moravia **2**:293
Wright Morris **1**:232
Vladimir Nabokov **1**:239
Ezra Pound **7**:329
John Crowe Ransom **2**:363
Mordecai Richler **5**:375
Henry Roth **6**:470
J. D. Salinger **12**:512
Jerome Siegel and Joe Shuster
21:361
Kurt Vonnegut, Jr. **12**:603
Robert Penn Warren **4**:579
Richard Wilbur **3**:530
Herman Wouk **1**:376

Field, Andrew
Djuna Barnes **29**:32
Vladimir Nabokov **1**:242
Yevgeny Yevtushenko **1**:382

Field, Carol
Paule Marshall **27**:308

Field, Colin
H. F. Brinsmead **21**:26
Eilís Dillon **17**:98
William Mayne **12**:392

Field, Ellen Wilson
George Plimpton **36**:357

Field, George Wallis
Hermann Hesse **1**:147

Field, Joyce
Bernard Malamud **9**:348

Field, Leslie
Bernard Malamud **9**:348

Field, Louise Maunsell
Alvah Bessie **23**:59
Taylor Caldwell **28**:57
Edna Ferber **18**:150
Noel Streatfeild **21**:396

Field, Trevor
Julien Green **11**:261

Fields, Beverly
Anne Sexton **2**:391

Fields, Kenneth
J. V. Cunningham **3**:121
Robert Lowell **4**:299
Mina Loy **28**:247
N. Scott Momaday **2**:290
Marya Zaturenska **6**:585

Fiess, Edward
Edmund Wilson **24**:466

Fifer, Elizabeth
Maxine Hong Kingston **12**:314

Figes, Eva
Edward Bond **23**:72

Filer, Malva E.
Julio Cortázar **10**:117

Finch, John
E. E. Cummings **12**:144

Fincke, Gary
Ben Hecht **8**:271

Critic Index

Fincke, Kate
Isabelle Holland **21**:153

Fine, Dennis
Neil Young **17**:573

Finel-Honigman, Irène
Albert Camus **11**:96

Finger, Louis
John Le Carré **9**:326

Finholt, Richard
James Dickey **10**:142
Ralph Ellison **11**:184

Fink, Rita
Alvah Bessie **23**:61

Finkelstein, Sidney
Louis Aragon **22**:36

Finkle, David
John Fowles **9**:215
Mordecai Richler **18**:459

Finlay, John
Elizabeth Daryush **19**:122

Finlayson, Iain
Peter Rushforth **19**:405

Finley, M. I.
Michael Ayrton **7**:17

Finn, James
James Baldwin **17**:23, 24
Peter Matthiessen **32**:285
François Mauriac **4**:339
P. G. Wodehouse **2**:480

Finn, James D.
Dannie Abse **29**:11

Finne, Elisabeth
Günter Grass **32**:201

Firchow, Peter
Lawrence Durrell **27**:96
Aldous Huxley **8**:305

Firchow, Peter E.
W. H. Auden **11**:17
Aldous Huxley **18**:266

Fireside, Bryna J.
Joan Aiken **35**:20
Ann Schlee **35**:374

Fireside, Harvey
Andrei Sinyavsky **8**:489, 490

Firestone, Bruce M.
Anthony Burgess **10**:89

Firkins, O. W.
Carl Sandburg **35**:338

Firmat, Gustavo Pérez
Dámaso Alonso **14**:24

First, Elsa
Carlos Castaneda **12**:91

Fisch, Harold
Aharon Megged **9**:374
A. B. Yehoshua **31**:469

Fischer, John Irwin
Catharine Savage Brosman
9:135

Fischer, Lucy
René Clair **20**:67

Fischer, Marjorie
Margot Benary-Isbert **12**:30
Joseph Krumgold **12**:317

Fischer, Max
Arthur Koestler **33**:228

Fischer, Michael
Wayne C. Booth **24**:99

Fischler, Alexander
Eugène Ionesco **15**:297

Fisher, Dorothy Canfield
A. B. Guthrie, Jr. **23**:195

Fisher, Elizabeth
Jessamyn West **17**:553

Fisher, Emma
Beryl Bainbridge **18**:32
John Berryman **10**:47
Anaïs Nin **14**:386
Peter Porter **13**:452
R. S. Thomas **13**:544
Yevgeny Yevtushenko **26**:468

Fisher, Margery
Joan Aiken **35**:18, 21
E. M. Almedingen **12**:6
Ruth M. Arthur **12**:25, 26
Honor Arundel **17**:14, 16
Gunnel Beckman **26**:88
Judy Blume **12**:47
Cecil Bødker **21**:11
H. F. Brinsmead **21**:27, 28, 29,
    30, 33
Aidan Chambers **35**:98, 100,
    101
Mavis Thorpe Clark **12**:130,
    131, 132
Robert Cormier **12**:135, 137
Julia W. Cunningham **12**:164,
    165
Maureen Daly **17**:91
Peter Dickinson **12**:169, 174,
    177; **35**:135, 138
Eilís Dillon **17**:95, 96, 97
Walter Farley **17**:118
Esther Forbes **12**:211
Leon Garfield **12**:216, 217,
    218, 223, 227, 231, 233,
    234
Alan Garner **17**:135, 136, 148
S. E. Hinton **30**:206
Mollie Hunter **21**:156, 160, 170
Diana Wynne Jones **26**:224,
    225, 226, 228, 231, 232
Norma Klein **30**:239
William Mayne **12**:389, 405
Emily Cheney Neville **12**:450
Andre Norton **12**:469, 470
Katherine Paterson **12**:485
Philippa Pearce **21**:281, 282,
    287, 288, 290, 291
Richard Peck **21**:298
Josephine Poole **17**:373
Otfried Preussler **17**:375, 376
Zilpha Keatley Snyder **17**:474
Noel Streatfeild **21**:403, 409,
    410, 416
Rosemary Sutcliff **26**:437, 441
Mildred D. Taylor **21**:421

Colin Thiele **17**:493, 494, 495,
    496
J.R.R. Tolkien **12**:586
Rosemary Wells **12**:638
Robert Westall **17**:555, 556,
    559
Laurence Yep **35**:469
Paul Zindel **26**:481

Fisher, Maxine
Paul Zindel **26**:477

Fisher, William J.
William Saroyan **8**:466

Fishman, Charles
A. R. Ammons **25**:47

Fiske, Minnie Maddern
Charles Chaplin **16**:187

Fisketjon, Gary L.
Raymond Carver **22**:97
Thomas McGuane **18**:323

Fison, Peter
C. P. Snow **13**:511

Fitts, Dudley
Peter Davison **28**:99
Langston Hughes **35**:216
Mary Renault **17**:394, 398

Fitzgerald, Edward J.
Howard Fast **23**:156
Mark Harris **19**:200

Fitzgerald, Jennifer
Tom Paulin **37**:356

Fitzgerald, Judith
Margaret Atwood **25**:66
David Donnell **34**:156

Fitzgerald, Penelope
Barbara Pym **19**:388
Stevie Smith **25**:420

Fitzgerald, Robert
Seamus Heaney **7**:151
Robert Lowell **11**:325; **15**:345
Flannery O'Connor **15**:409

Fitzlyon, Kyril
Aleksandr I. Solzhenitsyn **1**:321

Fitzpatrick, Kelly
Nicholas M. Guild **33**:186

Fitzpatrick, Marjorie A.
Marie-Claire Blais **22**:60

Fitzsimmons, Thomas
Elizabeth Hardwick **13**:264

Fiut, Aleksander
Czesław Miłosz **11**:379

Fixler, Michael
Isaac Bashevis Singer **1**:311

Fixx, James F.
Art Buchwald **33**:91

Flagg, Nancy
Jorge Amado **13**:11

Flaherty, Joe
Richard Brautigan **9**:124
James M. Cain **28**:54
Joe McGinniss **32**:300
Edwin Newman **14**:379
George Plimpton **36**:356

Flake, Carol
Paul McCartney **35**:286

Flamm, Dudley
Robert M. Pirsig **4**:404

Flanagan, John T.
John Neihardt **32**:336
Conrad Richter **30**:314, 315
Jessamyn West **17**:551, 552

Flanagan, Kate M.
Sue Ellen Bridgers **26**:91
Walter Dean Myers **35**:296
Marilyn Sachs **35**:335

Flanagan, Margaret
Kent Haruf **34**:57

Flanagan, Thomas
Aharon Appelfeld **23**:36
Benedict Kiely **23**:265

Flanders, Jane
James Dickey **15**:177
Katherine Anne Porter **10**:396;
    27:400

Flanner, Janet
André Malraux **4**:326
Carl Van Vechten **33**:386

Flasch, Joy
Melvin B. Tolson **36**:427

Flatto, Eric
Stanley Kubrick **16**:382

Flaxman, Seymour L.
Hermann Hesse **17**:196

Fleckenstein, Joan S.
Edward Albee **11**:13

Fleischer, Leonard
Woody Allen **16**:6
John A. Williams **5**:496

Fleischer, Leonore
Nora Ephron **17**:110

Fleischmann, Mark
Ray Davies **21**:105

Fleischmann, Wolfgang Bernard
René Wellek **28**:446

Fleishman, Avrom
John Fowles **9**:210

Fleming, Alice
Zilpha Keatley Snyder **17**:471

Fleming, Robert E.
Ronald L. Fair **18**:140
John A. Williams **5**:496

Fleming, Thomas
S. E. Hinton **30**:203

Fleming, Thomas J.
Elizabeth Jane Howard **29**:244
Ira Levin **6**:305
Emily Cheney Neville **12**:450
Michel Tournier **23**:451

Fleshman, Bob
David Madden **15**:350

Fletcher, Angus
Northrop Frye **24**:219

Fletcher, Connie
Ted Berrigan 37:44
Robert Bloch 33:84
Will Harriss 34:192
Elmore Leonard 28:234
J.I.M. Stewart 32:420

Fletcher, John
Arthur Adamov 25:18
Uwe Johnson 5:201
Kamala Markandaya 8:377
Jean-Paul Sartre 7:398

Fletcher, Peggy
Joe Rosenblatt 15:447

Flexner, James Thomas
Esther Forbes 12:209

Flint, F. Cudworth
Ralph Gustafson 36:211

Flint, R. W.
A. R. Ammons 8:15; 9:29
Irving Feldman 7:102
Anthony Hecht 8:267
Randall Jarrell 1:159
James Merrill 34:229
Karl Shapiro 8:486
Charles Tomlinson 13:550

Flippo, Chet
Waylon Jennings 21:201
Kris Kristofferson 26:268
Willie Nelson 17:302, 303, 304, 305
Sam Shepard 17:445

Floan, Howard R.
William Saroyan 1:301

Flood, Charles Bracelen
Thomas J. Fleming 37:123

Flood, Jeanne
Brian Moore 5:294

Flora, Joseph M.
Vardis Fisher 7:103
Günter Grass 6:209
J. E. Wideman 5:490
Nancy Willard 7:539

Flores, Ralph
Frederick Karl 34:552

Flower, Dean
Italo Calvino 33:100
Raymond Carver 22:97
Dan Jacobson 14:291
William Kennedy 34:210
Vladimir Nabokov 15:393
Marge Piercy 14:421
Frederic Raphael 14:438
Hubert Selby, Jr. 8:477
Helen Yglesias 7:559
Al Young 19:479

Flowers, Ann A.
Jay Bennett 35:45
Robin F. Brancato 35:70
Betsy Byars 35:75
Barbara Corcoran 17:78
Peter Dickinson 35:131
Lois Duncan 26:108
Leon Garfield 12:239
Norma Klein 30:240
Norma Fox Mazer 26:291

Katherine Paterson 12:486

Flowers, Betty
Isaac Asimov 26:37
Donald Barthelme 5:56

Flowers, Paul
John Ehle 27:101

Flowers, Sandra Hollin
Ntozake Shange 25:403

Fludas, John
Rita Mae Brown 18:73
Richard Price 12:491

Foell, Earl W.
Thomas B. Costain 30:98
Romain Gary 25:183
Bruce Lancaster 36:245

Fogelman, Phyllis J.
Mildred D. Taylor 21:421

Folejewski, Zbigniew
Maria Dabrowska 15:165, 167
Joseph Wittlin 25:467

Foley, Ann D.
John McPhee 36:295

Foley, Barbara
E. L. Doctorow 18:121

Foley, Michael
Raymond Carver 36:106

Folkart, Burt A.
Richard Brautigan 34:314

Folsom, James K.
Larry McMurtry 27:326

Folsom, L. Edwin
W. S. Merwin 13:384

Fong, Monique
Vittorio De Sica 20:95

Fontenla, Cesar Santos
Carlos Saura 20:320

Fontenot, Chester J.
Alex Haley 8:260
Alice Walker 19:450

Fontenrose, Joseph
John Steinbeck 21:372

Foose, Thomas T.
Jean Renoir 20:287

Foote, Audrey C.
Anthony Burgess 4:81
Zoë Fairbairns 32:163
Nathalie Sarraute 2:386
Christina Stead 5:404
Mary Stewart 7:468

Foote, Bud
Charles R. Larson 31:239

Foote, Jennifer
Richard O'Brien 17:325

Foote, Timothy
W. H. Auden 3:26; 6:24
Anthony Burgess 5:89
Henry Carlisle 33:104
Peter De Vries 2:114
John Gardner 3:187
John le Carré 5:232

V. S. Pritchett 5:352
Aleksandr I. Solzhenitsyn 4:516
Tom Stoppard 4:525
Tom Wolfe 2:481

Forbes, Alastair
Lawrence Durrell 13:189

Forbes, Cheryl
Ralph Bakshi 26:73

Forbes, Jill
René Clair 20:66
Rainer Werner Fassbinder 20:116
Joan Micklin Silver 20:341

Forche, Carolyn
Ai 14:8

Ford, John
Howard Barker 37:32
Snoo Wilson 33:460

Ford, Nick Aaron
Zora Neale Hurston 30:210
Harper Lee 12:341
Willard Motley 18:356
Frank G. Yerby 22:488

Ford, Richard J.
Hermann Hesse 2:189

Ford, Thomas W.
A. B. Guthrie, Jr. 23:202

Foreman, John D.
Evan Hunter 31:222

Forest, James
Eldridge Cleaver 30:65
Peter Matthiessen 32:289

Forman, Jack
Jules Archer 12:18, 20
Frank Bonham 12:51
Bette Greene 30:170
Nat Hentoff 26:184, 185
Norma Fox Mazer 26:290
Scott O'Dell 30:276
Katherine Paterson 12:485, 486
Richard Peck 21:300
Kin Platt 26:352, 354
Barbara Wersba 30:434
Paul Zindel 26:477

Fornacca, Daisy
Dino Buzzati 36:83

Fornatale, Peter
Laura Nyro 17:314
Brian Wilson 12:646

Forrest, Alan
W. H. Auden 3:27
Mario Puzo 2:352

Forrey, Robert
Ken Kesey 11:316
Andrew Sinclair 14:488

Forster, E. M.
Mulk Raj Anand 23:11

Forster, Leonard
Günter Grass 15:262

Forster, Margaret
Iain Banks 34:29

Fortin, René E.
Boris Pasternak 7:296

Foster, David William
Jorge Luis Borges 3:78; 6:89
Camilo José Cela 4:96
Julio Cortázar 10:118
Jorge Ibargüengoitia 37:183
Manuel Mujica Láinez 31:280
Ernesto Sabato 10:445

Foster, Isabel
Robert Francis 15:234

Foster, John Wilson
Seamus Heaney 5:170
Brian Moore 1:225

Foster, Richard
R. P. Blackmur 24:61
Norman Mailer 1:190; 8:365
I. A. Richards 24:393
Allen Tate 24:444

Foster, Richard J.
Arthur Miller 26:315

Foster, Roy
Brian Moore 19:333

Foster, Ruel E.
Jesse Stuart 1:328

Fothergill, C. Z.
N. F. Simpson 29:370

Fotheringham, Hamish
William Mayne 12:388

Foulke, Adrienne
Elizabeth Taylor 29:407

Fowke, Edith
Nevil Shute 30:370

Fowler, Alastair
Michael Moorcock 27:351
Charles M. Schulz 12:532

Fowler, Douglas
Thomas Pynchon 18:438

Fowler, F. M.
Günter Eich 15:203

Fowles, John
G. B. Edwards 25:149

Fowlie, Wallace
Ben Belitt 22:50
Michel Butor 8:119
René Char 9:158
Jean Cocteau 15:133
Jean Genet 5:135
Julien Green 11:258
Henri Michaux 8:392
Anaïs Nin 4:378; 11:398
Jules Romains 7:379

Fox, Charles
Akira Kurosawa 16:396

Fox, Edward
J. G. Ballard 36:48

Fox, Gail
Phyllis Webb 18:542

Fox, Geoff
Bette Greene 30:170
Rosa Guy 26:144
Nat Hentoff 26:187
Scott O'Dell 30:275

Critic Index

Fox, Hank
Janis Ian 21:183

Fox, Hugh
William Carlos Williams 5:509

Fox, Terry Curtis
Rita Mae Brown 18:73
Marguerite Duras 20:103
Max Frisch 18:162
Athol Fugard 14:192
Jean-Luc Godard 20:152
Simon Gray 14:215
John Guare 14:221
Beth Henley 23:214
George V. Higgins 18:235
George Lucas 16:415
Marsha Norman 28:317
Harold Pinter 15:425
Martin Scorsese 20:333

Fox-Genovese, Elizabeth
Susan Cheever 18:102
William Gaddis 8:226
Gail Godwin 22:183

Fraenkel, Heinrich
Leni Riefenstahl 16:521

Fraiberg, Louis
Kenneth Burke 24:130
Joseph Wood Krutch 24:287
Lionel Trilling 24:454
Edmund Wilson 24:476

Fraire, Isabel
Ernesto Cardenal 31:72

Frakes, J. R.
Frederick Forsyth 36:175
J.M.G. Le Clézio 31:246
Robert Ludlum 22:288

Frakes, James R.
Nelson Algren 4:17
Wendell Berry 4:59
E. M. Broner 19:70
R. V. Cassill 23:108
Allen Drury 37:108
Maureen Duffy 37:115
Bruce Jay Friedman 5:127
Joanne Greenberg 30:165
Patricia Highsmith 2:194
Stanley Hoffman 5:185
Julius Horwitz 14:266
Evan Hunter 11:280; 31:224
Diane Johnson 5:198
Peter Maas 29:307
Michael Mewshaw 9:376
Ezekiel Mphahlele 25:332
Muriel Spark 2:418
Richard G. Stern 4:522
Glendon Swarthout 35:403
Richard Tillinghast 29:408

France, Arthur
Lorraine Hansberry 17:185

France, Peter
Anne Hébert 13:267

Francescato, Martha Paley
Julio Cortázar 10:116

Francis, William A. C.
William Price Fox 22:139

Francis, Wynne
Louis Dudek 19:137

Frane, Jeff
Fritz Leiber 25:310

Frank, Armin Paul
Kenneth Burke 2:89

Frank, Joseph
Djuna Barnes 8:47
R. P. Blackmur 24:64
Yves Bonnefoy 15:74
André Malraux 4:327
Aleksandr I. Solzhenitsyn 7:443
Lionel Trilling 24:453

Frank, Margot K.
Vasily Aksyonov 37:12

Frank, Mike
Joseph Heller 11:266

Frank, Pat
Leon Uris 32:431

Frank, Peter
Richard Kostelanetz 28:219

Frank, Sheldon
Edward Abbey 36:13
T. Alan Broughton 19:72
Margaret Laurence 6:289
Steven Millhauser 21:218
Hans Erich Nossack 6:365
Al Young 19:480

Frankel, Bernice
Mary Stolz 12:547

Frankel, Charles
William Barrett 27:17
Arthur Koestler 33:235

Frankel, Haskel
Jonathan Baumbach 23:53
Bruce Jay Friedman 3:165
Joanne Greenberg 30:161
Ronald Harwood 32:223
Muriel Spark 2:417
Glendon Swarthout 35:401
Peter Ustinov 1:346
Charles Webb 7:514
Donald E. Westlake 33:437

Frankenberg, Lloyd
Marianne Moore 19:337
Ogden Nash 23:321

Franklin, Allan
Jorg Luis Borges 9:116

Franklin, H. Bruce
J. G. Ballard 3:32
Robert A. Heinlein 26:175, 179

Franks, Lucinda
Edward Abbey 36:18
Breece D'J Pancake 29:350

Fraser, C. Gerald
Julio Cortázar 34:329
George Oppen 34:358

Fraser, G. S.
Basil Bunting 10:86
Robert Creeley 1:67
C. Day Lewis 6:127
Nigel Dennis 8:172
Lawrence Durrell 4:145; 13:184
Jean Garrigue 2:153
W. S. Graham 29:195
Randall Jarrell 9:296

Robert Lowell 2:249; 11:325
Norman MacCaig 36:279
Hugh MacDiarmid 11:337
W. S. Merwin 1:214
C. P. Snow 4:502
Gary Snyder 1:318
Andrei Voznesensky 15:552
Louis Zukofsky 1:385

Fraser, George
William Empson 33:147

Fraser, John
Louis-Ferdinand Céline 1:56;
4:102
F. R. Leavis 24:298
Yvor Winters 4:592; 8:552

Fraser, Kathleen
Adrienne Rich 3:429

Fraser, Keath
Alden Nowlan 15:398
Sinclair Ross 13:492

Fraser, Robert
Ayi Kwei Armah 33:33

Fraser, Russell
Eugenio Montale 18:341

Fratz, D. Douglas
Frank Herbert 23:222

Fraustino, Lisa
Suzanne Newton 35:302

Frayne, John P.
John Ford 16:320

Frazer, Frances M.
Christie Harris 12:268

Frazer, Mary
Frederick Wiseman 20:477

Frazier, Kermit
John Edgar Wideman 36:452

Fredeman, W. E.
Earle Birney 6:72

Frederick, Linda J.
Ray Davies 21:100

Fredericks, Claude
Brewster Ghiselin 23:169

Fredericks, Pierce
Ernest K. Gann 23:165

Fredrick, E. Coston
Barbara Corcoran 17:75

Free, William J.
Federico Fellini 16:284
Tennessee Williams 15:581

Freed, Donald
Alberto Moravia 27:353

Freedberg, Mike
Smokey Robinson 21:348

Freedberger, Peter
Stan Lee 17:261

Freedman, Morris
Sylvia Ashton-Warner 19:23

Freedman, Ralph
Saul Bellow 1:29
Hermann Hesse 1:146; 17:203

Freedman, Richard
A. Alvarez 13:10
Dino Buzzati 36:89
Taylor Caldwell 28:69
Hortense Calisher 2:96
Dick Francis 2:142
Lois Gould 4:199
Evan Hunter 31:226
Robert Ludlum 22:290
Tim O'Brien 19:356
S. J. Perelman 9:416; 23:337
Wilbur Smith 33:375
George Steiner 24:432
Henri Troyat 23:460
P. G. Wodehouse 5:517

Freedman, Samuel G.
Stephen Sondheim 30:402

Freedman, William
Henry Roth 11:487

Freeman, Anne Hobson
Reynolds Price 13:463

Freeman, David
Steven Bochco and Michael
Kozoll 35:59

Freeman, E.
Albert Camus 32:96

Freeman, Gillian
Robert Nye 13:412

Freeman, Suzanne
M. E. Kerr 35:247
Joyce Maynard 23:290
Norma Fox Mazer 26:296
Susan Richards Shreve 23:404

Freibert, Lucy M.
H. D. 31:206, 210, 213

Frein, George H.
Vine Deloria, Jr. 21:112

Fremantle, Anne
W. H. Auden 1:10
Ernesto Cardenal 31:71
Thomas J. Fleming 37:124
Auberon Waugh 7:513
Vassily S. Yanovsky 18:551

Fremont-Smith, Eliot
Richard Adams 4:6
Martin Amis 4:20
Max Apple 9:33
Louis Auchincloss 4:31
Russell Baker 31:27
Claude Brown 30:33
Arthur C. Clarke 35:124
Laurie Colwin 13:156
E. L. Doctorow 6:132
Lawrence Durrell 6:152
Gael Greene 8:252
Graham Greene 37:140
Barry Hannah 23:211
Joseph Heller 5:173; 11:268
Lillian Hellman 4:221
John Irving 13:294; 23:247
Marjorie Kellogg 2:223
Jascha Kessler 4:269
Arthur Koestler 3:271
Jerzy Kosinski 1:172
John le Carré 9:327
Alan Lelchuk 5:243

Norman Mailer **4**:322
Peter Matthiessen **32**:287
Colleen McCullough **27**:318
Joe McGinniss **32**:304
James A. Michener **5**:289
Chaim Potok **26**:368
Richard Price **6**:426; **12**:490
Mario Puzo **36**:361
Judith Rossner **29**:354
Philip Roth **4**:453, 455
Alix Kates Shulman **10**:476
Gay Talese **37**:396
John Updike **23**:468
Gore Vidal **6**:54
Irving Wallace **7**:510
Patrick White **3**:524

French, Allen
Esther Forbes **12**:206

French, Janet
Sue Ellen Bridgers **26**:92
Otfried Preussler **17**:375

French, Marilyn
Margaret Atwood **15**:39
Christa Wolf **29**:466

French, Ned
William H. Gass **15**:255

French, Philip
Bernardo Bertolucci **16**:101
Jorge Luis Borges **4**:75
Truman Capote **8**:132
Eleanor Clark **19**:107
Graham Greene **3**:212; **6**:220
Richard Lester **20**:219
S. J. Perelman **23**:340

French, Roberts W.
Wendell Berry **27**:32
Philip Booth **23**:75
Joyce Carol Oates **1**:251

French, Warren
William Goldman **1**:123
R. K. Narayan **7**:254
James Purdy **2**:349
J. D. Salinger **1**:297; **12**:514
John Steinbeck **1**:324; **5**:406
Thornton Wilder **1**:366
Richard Wright **21**:447

Frenkel, James
Jack Vance **35**:427

Fretz, Sada
Julia W. Cunningham **12**:165
John Donovan **35**:141
John Neufeld **17**:308

Friar, Kimon
Margaríta Karapánou **13**:314
Yannis Ritsos **6**:463; **31**:324, 327
Vassilis Vassilikos **8**:524

Fricke, David
David Byrne **26**:99
The Clash **30**:51
Mick Jagger and Keith Richard **17**:242
Bob Seger **35**:386
Paul Weller **26**:447
Frank Zappa **17**:592

Friebert, Stuart
Ernst Jandl **34**:196

Fried, Lewis
James T. Farrell **11**:191

Friedberg, Maurice
Aleksandr I. Solzhenitsyn **1**:319; **7**:435

Friedenberg, Edgar Z.
James Baldwin **17**:24
Mark Harris **19**:201
Hermann Hesse **2**:190
Margaret Mead **37**:275
Frederick Wiseman **20**:472

Friedman, Alan
T. Coraghessan Boyle **36**:58
William S. Burroughs **5**:93
John Gardner **7**:112
John Hawkes **27**:198
Erica Jong **18**:279
Yukio Mishima **4**:357
Amos Oz **8**:435
John Rechy **18**:442
Ishmael Reed **2**:367
André Schwarz-Bart **2**:389
John Kennedy Toole **19**:443
Elie Wiesel **3**:528

Friedman, Alan J.
Thomas Pynchon **6**:434

Friedman, Alan Warren
Saul Bellow **8**:69
Lawrence Durrell **1**:87
Bernard Malamud **8**:375

Friedman, Jack
Wendell Berry **4**:59
José Lezama Lima **4**:290

Friedman, John
William Eastlake **8**:200

Friedman, Melvin J.
Bruce Jay Friedman **5**:127
Carolyn G. Heilbrun **25**:252
Eugène Ionesco **6**:256
André Malraux **4**:333
R. K. Narayan **7**:255
Flannery O'Connor **1**:253
Isaac Bashevis Singer **1**:313

Friedman, Norman
E. E. Cummings **1**:69; **12**:149; **15**:153
David Ignatow **7**:174

Friedman, Richard
The Police **26**:365

Friedman, Susan Stanford
H. D. **31**:204, 207

Friedrich, Pia
Pier Paolo Pasolini **37**:349

Friedrichsmeyer, Erhard
Uwe Johnson **15**:302

Frieling, Kenneth
Flannery O'Connor **13**:416

Fries, Maureen
Mary Stewart **35**:394

Friesem, Roberta Ricky
Lenora Mattingly Weber **12**:635

Friesen, Gordon
Phil Ochs **17**:329, 330

Frith, Simon
Elvis Costello **21**:68
Mick Jagger and Keith Richard **17**:240
Bob Marley **17**:272
Smokey Robinson **21**:346
Patti Smith **12**:543
Peter Townshend **17**:538
Paul Weller **26**:445
Neil Young **17**:580

Fritz, Jean
Lloyd Alexander **35**:23, 24, 26, 27
Ruth M. Arthur **12**:24
Judy Blume **30**:23
Betsy Byars **35**:73
Barbara Corcoran **17**:73
Rosa Guy **26**:144
Virginia Hamilton **26**:153, 155
Joseph Krumgold **12**:318
Norma Fox Mazer **26**:293
Milton Meltzer **26**:297
Scott O'Dell **30**:273, 274, 276
Zilpha Keatley Snyder **17**:472
Mary Stolz **12**:553
Mildred D. Taylor **21**:418
Maia Wojciechowska **26**:457
Laurence Yep **35**:470

Frohock, W. M.
James M. Cain **11**:84
Erskine Caldwell **1**:51
James Gould Cozzens **4**:113
John Dos Passos **1**:77
James T. Farrell **1**:97
William Faulkner **1**:99
Ernest Hemingway **1**:141
André Malraux **4**:324; **13**:366
John Steinbeck **1**:323
Robert Penn Warren **1**:351

Frost, Lucy
John Hawkes **3**:223

Fruchtbaum, Harold
Loren Eiseley **7**:90

Frye, Northrop
Charles Chaplin **16**:192
R. S. Crane **27**:71
Louis Dudek **11**:158; **19**:136, 137
Northrop Frye **24**:222
Daryl Hine **15**:280
Dorothy Livesay **15**:339
E. J. Pratt **19**:376, 379
A.J.M. Smith **15**:516
Allen Tate **24**:443

Fryer, Jonathan H.
Christopher Isherwood **9**:292

Frykman, Erik
Norman MacCaig **36**:286

Fuchs, Daniel
Saul Bellow **3**:62

Fuchs, Marcia G.
Jonathan Keates **34**:203

Fuchs, Miriam
Djuna Barnes **29**:30

Fuchs, Vivian
Thomas Keneally **10**:299

Fuchs, Wolfgang
Charles M. Schulz **12**:528

Fuentes, Carlos
Luis Buñuel **16**:137
Julio Cortázar **34**:330

Fugard, Athol
Athol Fugard **14**:189

Fulford, Robert
George Bowering **15**:81
Michael Cimino **16**:214
Mavis Gallant **18**:172
Hugh Hood **28**:187
Kevin Major **26**:285
Brian Moore **3**:340
Mordecai Richler **3**:429
Philip Roth **3**:435
Raymond Souster **14**:504

Fullbrook, Kate
Pat Barker **32**:12

Fuller, Edmund
Paul Bowles **1**:41
Frederick Buechner **4**:80
James Gould Cozzens **1**:65
Jan de Hartog **19**:130
John Ehle **27**:106
Michael Ende **31**:144
James D. Forman **21**:116
Pamela Hansford Johnson **27**:220
James Jones **1**:161
Thomas Keneally **19**:248
Jack Kerouac **1**:165
Bernard Malamud **27**:299
Walter M. Miller, Jr. **30**:253
Alan Paton **4**:395; **25**:360
Mary Renault **17**:392
Carl Sagan **30**:336
Mary Lee Settle **19**:408
Frank G. Slaughter **29**:374
J.R.R. Tolkien **1**:335
Morris L. West **33**:433
Herman Wouk **1**:375

Fuller, Elizabeth Ely
Isak Dinesen **10**:150

Fuller, Henry B.
Rebecca West **31**:451

Fuller, Hoyt W.
Milton Meltzer **26**:299

Fuller, John
Anna Akhmatova **11**:9
Peter Davison **28**:102
Thom Gunn **3**:215
Michael Hamburger **14**:234
Randall Jarrell **2**:208
Diana Wynne Jones **26**:225
Leslie Norris **14**:387
Robert Pinsky **19**:370
William Plomer **4**:406
Ann Quin **6**:441
Kathleen Raine **7**:353
Jon Silkin **6**:499
Andrew Young **5**:523

Fuller, John G.
Colin MacInnes **23**:282

Fuller, John Wesley
Art Buchwald **33**:91

Fuller, Roy
W. H. Auden **3**:25
John Betjeman **34**:306
Aldous Huxley **5**:192
A.J.M. Smith **15**:513
C. P. Snow **19**:427
Stephen Spender **2**:420
Allen Tate **14**:532
Lionel Trilling **9**:530

Fulton, Robin
Pär Lagerkvist **10**:313

Funke, Lewis
John Mortimer **28**:282

Funsten, Kenneth
Robert Creeley **36**:119
Darcy Ribeiro **34**:102
Derek Walcott **25**:456

Furbank, P. N.
Donald Davie **31**:115
Margaret Drabble **22**:120
D. J. Enright **31**:146, 150
E. M. Forster **4**:165, 168
William Golding **17**:176
Elizabeth Jennings **14**:291
Uwe Johnson **10**:284
Norman MacCaig **36**:280
Derek Mahon **27**:287
Gore Vidal **4**:556

Furlong, Vivienne
Honor Arundel **17**:18

Fussell, B. H.
Robert Coover **32**:120
Peter Taylor **4**:543

Fussell, Edwin
Wendell Berry **6**:61
Hayden Carruth **7**:40

Fussell, Paul
Noël Coward **29**:141
Graham Greene **27**:171
Richard F. Hugo **32**:234
Thomas Keneally **8**:318
Siegfried Sassoon **36**:394
Paul Theroux **15**:533
Evelyn Waugh **27**:475, 477

Fussell, Paul, Jr.
Karl Shapiro **4**:486

Fyne, Robert
Aharon Appelfeld **23**:37

Fytton, Francis
Paul Bowles **2**:78

Fyvel, T. R.
Ilya Ehrenburg **18**:133

Gabbard, Krin
Tess Gallagher **18**:170

Gabel, Lars
Marvin Gaye **26**:133

Gabert, Charla
Robert Coover **32**:122

Gabree, John
Mick Jagger and Keith Richard
17:223
John Lennon **35**:261
John Lennon and Paul
McCartney **12**:364

Gadney, Reg
George V. Higgins **7**:158
Patricia Highsmith **2**:194
Ross Macdonald **2**:257
Alistair MacLean **3**:309

Gaev, A.
Vasily Aksenov **22**:25

Gaffney, Elizabeth
Sharon Olds **32**:347
Mary Oliver **34**:248

Gaffney, James
Ayi Kwei Armah **33**:27

Gagné, Sarah
Melvin Berger **12**:42
Larry Kettelkamp **12**:307
Alvin Silverstein and Virginia
B. Silverstein **17**:456

Gaillard, Dawson
Harry Crews **23**:134

Gaillard, Frye
Willie Nelson **17**:304

Gaines, Richard H.
Chester Himes **2**:196

Gaiser, Carolyn
Gregory Corso **1**:63
Nettie Jones **34**:68

Gaither, Frances
Esther Forbes **12**:210

Galassi, Jonathan
John Berryman **6**:63
Frank Bidart **33**:73
Robert Duncan **2**:123
Robert Graves **6**:212
Seamus Heaney **7**:147
Randall Jarrell **9**:297
Czesław Miłosz **22**:309
Eugenio Montale **7**:231
Howard Nemerov **9**:396
George Oppen **13**:434

Galbraith, John Kenneth
Robertson Davies **25**:135
Edwin O'Connor **14**:389
William Safire **10**:446

Gale, David
Suzanne Newton **35**:302

Gale, Zona
August Derleth **31**:129

Gall, Sally M.
Kenneth O. Hanson **13**:263
Eleanor Lerman **9**:329
M. L. Rosenthal **28**:394
Charles Wright **6**:580

Gallagher, Bob
Smokey Robinson **21**:347

Gallagher, D. P.
Adolfo Bioy Casares **8**:94;
13:83
Jorge Luis Borges **6**:88
G. Cabrera Infante **5**:96
Gabriel García Márquez **8**:230
Pablo Neruda **7**:257
Octavio Paz **6**:394
Manuel Puig **10**:420
Mario Vargas Llosa **6**:543

Gallagher, David
G. Cabrera Infante **5**:95
Manuel Mujica Láinez **31**:279
Manuel Puig **3**:407

Gallagher, Donat
Jessica Anderson **37**:19

Gallagher, Jerry
John G. Neihardt **32**:336

Gallagher, Michael
Shusaku Endo **7**:95

Gallagher, Michael Paul
Brian Moore **32**:313

Gallagher, Steve
Stephen King **37**:201

Gallagher, Tess
Laura Jensen **37**:187

Gallant, Mavis
Simone de Beauvior **4**:48
Louis-Ferdinand Céline **7**:46
Günter Grass **4**:205
Vladimir Nabokov **2**:303

Galler, David
Peter Davison **28**:100
Ted Hughes **2**:198
Howard Nemerov **2**:307

Galligan, Edward L.
Georges Simenon **1**:309

Galloway, David
William Melvin Kelley **22**:251

Galloway, David D.
Saul Bellow **3**:51, 55
Stanley Elkin **4**:152
Dan Jacobson **4**:253
J. D. Salinger **3**:445
William Styron **3**:473
John Updike **3**:486

Galt, George
Leon Rooke **34**:251

Gambaccini, Paul
Smokey Robinson **21**:342

Gambaccini, Peter
Billy Joel **26**:217

Gannett, Lewis
Allen Drury **37**:98

Gannon, Edward, S.J.
André Malraux **4**:326

Gannon, Thomas M.
David Bradley, Jr. **23**:82
John Gregory Dunne **28**:127
James A. Michener **29**:313

Gant, Lisbeth
Ed Bullins **5**:82

Ganz, Arthur
Harold Pinter **6**:416

Ganz, Earl
John Hawkes **1**:139
Flannery O'Connor **2**:318

Garbarini, Vic
Paul McCartney **35**:293

Garber, Frederick
Norman Dubie **36**:138
Richard F. Hugo **32**:236
William Stafford **29**:385

Garber, Meg Elliott
Joanne Greenberg **30**:167

Garcia, Irma
Nicholosa Mohr **12**:447

Gard, Roger
Shirley Hazzard **18**:214

Gardiner, Harold C.
Robert Cormier **12**:134

Gardner, Averil
William Empson **19**:156

Gardner, Craig Shaw
Frank Herbert **35**:200
Laurence Yep **35**:473

Gardner, Erle Stanley
Meyer Levin **7**:203

Gardner, Harvey
Jimmy Breslin **4**:76

Gardner, John
Saul Bellow **10**:44
Anthony Burgess **2**:84
Italo Calvino **8**:129; **22**:90
John Cheever **25**:117
E. L. Doctorow **15**:178
John Fowles **9**:215
William H. Gass **1**:114
John Knowles **4**:271
Brian Moore **8**:395
Charles Newman **8**:419
Joyce Carol Oates **19**:354
Walker Percy **8**:442
Philip Roth **2**:379
John Steinbeck **21**:387
William Styron **15**:525
J.R.R. Tolkien **12**:585
Patrick White **9**:567
Thomas Williams **14**:582
Larry Woiwode **6**:578

Gardner, Marilyn
Barbara Corcoran **17**:69
Virginia Hamilton **26**:149
Mary Stolz **12**:554
Maia Wojciechowska **26**:457

Gardner, Peter
Allan W. Eckert **17**:108
John Hersey **9**:277

Gardner, Philip
William Empson **19**:156
D. J. Enright **4**:155; **31**:148
Roy Fisher **25**:160
Philip Larkin **5**:230; **18**:293

Gardner, R. H.
William Inge **19**:228
Arthur Miller **26**:319
Thornton Wilder **35**:444
Tennessee Williams **30**:466

Garebian, Keith
Anne Chislett **34**:146
David Donnell **34**:156
Ralph Gustafson **36**:222
Patrick White **9**:563

Garfield, Brian
Ernest K. Gann **23**:166
Glendon Swarthout **35**:402

Garfield, Evelyn Picon
Julio Cortázar **13**:163

Garfield, Leon
William Mayne **12**:395
Scott O'Dell **30**:276

Garfitt, Roger
George Barker **8**:46
James K. Baxter **14**:60
Martin Booth **13**:103
Joseph Brodsky **6**:96
Robert Creeley **4**:118
Eilís Dillon **17**:99
Douglas Dunn **6**:148
Geoffrey Grigson **7**:136
Donald Hall **13**:259
Anthony Hecht **19**:209
Anna Kavan **5**:206
Reiner Kunze **10**:310
Philip Larkin **8**:332
George MacBeth **5**:263
László Nagy **7**:251
Leslie Norris **14**:388
Julia O'Faolain **6**:383
Vasko Popa **19**:375
Peter Porter **5**:346
Thomas Pynchon **3**:418
Peter Redgrove **6**:445
Bernice Rubens **19**:403
Ward Ruyslinck **14**:471
C. H. Sisson **8**:490
Anne Stevenson **7**:462
Derek Walcott **4**:575

Gargan, Carol
Maya Angelou **35**:30

Garioch, Robert
Elaine Feinstein **36**:168

Garis, Leslie
Doris Lessing **6**:302

Garis, Robert
Herbert Gold **4**:191
Anthony Powell **3**:400

Garland, Phyl
Marvin Gaye **26**:135
Smokey Robinson **21**:348, 349

Garner, Alan
Leon Garfield **12**:219

Garnet, Eldon
B. P. Nichol **18**:367

Garnett, David
T. H. White **30**:436

Garnick, Vivian
Toni Morrison **10**:355

Garrard, J. G.
Aleksandr I. Solzhenitsyn
2:411; **9**:503

Garrett, George
John Cheever **3**:107
Babette Deutsch **18**:119
Gail Godwin **22**:180
Sue Kaufman **8**:317
Wright Morris **3**:342; **18**:351
Leon Rooke **25**:391

Garrett, J. C.
Aldous Huxley **35**:235

Garrett, John
Edmund Crispin **22**:109
Northrop Frye **24**:207

Garrigue, Jean
Romain Gary **25**:183
Mary McCarthy **14**:357
Marianne Moore **1**:228

Garside, E. B.
Farley Mowat **26**:335

Garson, Helen S.
Truman Capote **19**:85
John Hawkes **9**:268; **27**:192

Garvey, Michael
William Trevor **25**:444

Garvin, Larry
Piri Thomas **17**:501

Gascoigne, Bamber
Ann Jellicoe **27**:207

Gasparini, Len
Ronald G. Everson **27**:135
Patrick Lane **25**:284, 286

Gasque, Thomas J.
J.R.R. Tolkien **1**:337

Gass, William H.
Donald Barthelme **3**:43
Jorge Luis Borges **3**:76
Robert Coover **3**:113
Leon Edel **29**:169
Gabriel García Márquez **27**:153
William H. Gass **15**:257
Vladimir Nabokov **3**:351
J. F. Powers **1**:281
Philip Roth **3**:437
Isaac Bashevis Singer **3**:454
Susan Sontag **10**:484

Gassner, John
Edward Albee **3**:6, 7
Robert Anderson **23**:30
Jean Anouilh **3**:11, 12
Samuel Beckett **3**:44, 45
Brendan Behan **8**:63
Eric Bentley **24**:47
William Gibson **23**:177
Lillian Hellman **4**:220
William Inge **8**:307
Eugène Ionesco **4**:250
Joseph Wood Krutch **24**:286
Archibald MacLeish **3**:310
Mary McCarthy **24**:342
Arthur Miller **6**:330; **26**:310
Clifford Odets **28**:331
John Osborne **5**:330
Harold Pinter **3**:386
Thornton Wilder **5**:495
Tennessee Williams **5**:498, 500;
30:462

Gaston, Edwin W., Jr.
Conrad Richter **30**:319

Gaston, Karen C.
Gail Godwin **22**:182

Gaston, Paul M.
John Ehle **27**:103

Gates, David
Samuel Beckett **9**:83

Gates, Henry Louis, Jr.
Sterling A. Brown **23**:100

Gathercole, Patricia M.
Tommaso Landolfi **11**:321

Gathorne-Hardy, J.
Vladimir Nabokov **3**:354

Gatt-Rutter, John
Italo Calvino **11**:89; **22**:89
Pier Paolo Pasolini **37**:346

Gauch, Patricia Lee
Walter Dean Myers **35**:297
Robert Newton Peck **17**:343
Marilyn Sachs **35**:333
Ouida Sebestyen **30**:349

Gaudon, Sheila
Julien Gracq **11**:245

Gaull, Marilyn
E. E. Cumming **12**:156

Gault, John
Stephen King **26**:234

Gaurilović, Zoran
Dobrica Ćosić **14**:132

Gavin, Francis
John Gardner **30**:155

Gavin, Willam
Auberon Waugh **7**:514

Gavin, William F.
Michael Frayn **31**:189

Gavronsky, Serge
Aimé Césaire **32**:113

Gay, Robert M.
Walter D. Edmonds **35**:151

Gayle, Addison, Jr.
Gwendolyn Brooks **1**:46
Ernest J. Gaines **18**:167
Zora Neale Hurston **30**:217
Nella Larson **37**:215
Ezekiel Mphahlele **25**:334

Gaylin, Willard
Lewis Thomas **35**:413

Gealy, Marcia B.
Bernard Malamud **18**:317

Gearing, Nigel
Pier Paolo Pasolini **20**:266

Geary, Joyce
Jade Snow Wong **17**:566

Gebhard, Ann
Barbara Corcoran **17**:75

Geddes, Gary
Raymond Souster **5**:395

Geduld, Harry M.
Woody Allen **16**:8

Geering, R. G.
Shirley Hazzard **18**:216
Christina Stead **2**:42

Geeslin, Campbell
Henry Carlisle **33**:105

Geherin, David
John D. MacDonald **27**:276
Robert B. Parker **27**:364

Geherin, David J.
Joan Didion **8**:173

Gehrz, Robert D.
Franklyn M. Branley **21**:21

Geis, Richard E.
Peter Dickinson **12**:172

Geismar, Maxwell
Nelson Algren **4**:16
John Beecher **6**:48
Saul Bellow **1**:27
Cleanth Brooks **24**:107
Camilo José Cela **13**:145
Eldridge Cleaver **30**:54
James Gould Cozzens **1**:66
John Dos Passos **1**:77
William Faulkner **1**:100
William Gaddis **19**:185
Nadine Gordimer **5**:146
Ernest Hemingway **1**:142
John Hersey **1**:144
Norman Mailer **1**:187
Henry Miller **4**:350
Erich Maria Remarque **21**:332
Henry Roth **6**:471
J. D. Salinger **1**:295
William Styron **1**:329
Leon Uris **7**:490
Herman Wouk **1**:376

Gelb, Arthur
Alice Childress **12**:104

Geldrich-Leffman, Hanna
Siegfried Lenz **27**:256

Geldzahler, Henry
Andy Warhol **20**:414

Gelfant, Blanche H.
Yasunari Kawabata **9**:316
Jack Kerouac **5**:213
Jean Stafford **7**:459
James Welch **14**:558

Gellatly, Peter
C. Day Lewis **6**:128

Gellert, Roger
David Caute **29**:109

Gelpi, Albert J.
Philip Booth **23**:74
H. D. **31**:211
William Everson **14**:164
Adrienne Rich **6**:457

Geltman, Max
Arthur Koestler **8**:325
Ezra Pound **5**:349; **7**:338

Gemmil, Janet P.
Raja Rao **25**:367

Gendzier, Irene L.
David Caute **29**:113

Genêt
Dino Buzzati **36**:85
Françoise Sagan **17**:422, 423

Geng, Veronica
Francis Ford Coppola **16**:246
Paula Danziger **21**:83
Nadine Gordimer **5**:148

Geoghegan, Tom
Peter Maas **29**:304

George, Daniel
Elizabeth Jane Howard **29**:242

George, Diana L.
Lionel Trilling **9**:532

George, Donald W.
Stephen Dobyns **37**:76

George, Michael
J. B. Priestley **5**:350

Georgiou, Constantine
James D. Forman **21**:118
Philippa Pearce **21**:283

Gerald, John Bart
Robert Lowell **3**:302
Robert Stone **5**:11

Gerhardt, Lillian N.
Lloyd Alexander **35**:24
Betty Cavanna **12**:101
S. E. Hinton **30**:203
Mollie Hunter **21**:159

Geringer, Laura
Fran Arrick **30**:18
Toni Cade Bambara **19**:34
Thomas M. Disch **36**:125
Norma Fox Mazer **26**:293
Jill Paton Walsh **35**:432

Gerlach, John
Robert Bresson **16**:118

Gerlach, Larry R.
Thomas J. Fleming **37**:127

German, Howard
Iris Murdoch **15**:383

Gerould, Daniel C.
Vasily Aksenov **22**:26
Tadeusz Rózewicz **9**:463

Gerrard, Charlotte F.
Eugène Ionesco **9**:286

Gerrity, Thomas W.
Jakov Lind **27**:272

Gerrold, David
Gene Roddenberry **17**:403

Gerson, Ben
David Bowie **17**:59
Kris Kristofferson **26**:267
John Lennon and Paul
   McCartney **12**:366, 377

Gerson, Villiers
Isaac Asimov **26**:35
Robert A. Heinlein **26**:161
John Wyndham **19**:474

Gersoni-Edelman, Diane
Paul Zindel **26**:471

Gersoni-Stavn, Diane
See Stavn, Diane Gersoni

Gerstein, Evelyn
Fritz Lang **20**:201

Gersten, Russell
Smokey Robinson **21**:343

Gerstenberger, Donna
Djuna Barnes **29**:26
Iris Murdoch **6**:348

Gertel, Zunilda
José Donoso **4**:128
Juan Carlos Onetti **7**:278

Gervais, Marc
Pier Paolo Pasolini **20**:260

Getz, Thomas H.
Geoffrey Hill **18**:241

Gewen, Barry
Fran Lebowitz **36**:249

Giacoman, Helmy F.
Alejo Carpentier **11**:97

Gianakaris, C. J.
Arthur Miller **15**:376
Peter Shaffer **37**:388

Giannaris, George
Vassilis Vassilikos **8**:524

Giannetti, Louis D.
Federico Fellini **16**:295

Giannone, Richard
Kurt Vonnegut, Jr. **12**:620;
   22:447

Gianturo, Elio
Dino Buzzati **36**:88

Giard, Robert
Claude Chabrol **16**:169, 175

Gibb, Hugh
Thomas McGrath **28**:275

Gibbons, Boyd
James A. Michener **11**:374

Gibbons, Kathryn Gibbs
H. D. **31**:203

Gibbons, Reginald
Robert Hayden **14**:241
Czesław Miłosz **31**:266
Theodore Weiss **14**:553

Gibbs, Beverly J.
Juan Carlos Onetti **10**:374

Gibbs, Robert
Margaret Avison **2**:29
Ronald G. Everson **27**:134

Gibbs, Vernon
Jimmy Cliff **21**:62

Gibbs, Wolcott
Charles Addams **30**:12
Robert Anderson **23**:29
Sally Benson **17**:50
Garson Kanin **22**:229
Emlyn Williams **15**:576
Tennessee Williams **30**:455

Gibian, George
Varlam Shalamov **18**:478
Aleksandr I. Solzhenitsyn **7**:447

Gibson, Arthur
Ingmar Bergman **16**:62

Gibson, Donald B.
James Baldwin **3**:32
Imamu Amiri Baraka **5**:46
Ralph Ellison **3**:143
Langston Hughes **5**:19
Jean Toomer **13**:551

Gibson, Kenneth
Roch Carrier **13**:143

Gibson, Margaret
Judith Wright **11**:578

Gibson, Morgan
Kenneth Rexroth **22**:343

Gibson, Shirley Mann
Marie-Claire Blais **22**:59

Giddings, Paula
Nikki Giovanni **19**:191
Margaret Walker **1**:351

Giddins, Gary
James M. Cain **28**:53
Elias Canetti **25**:114
Philip Roth **31**:341

Gide, André
Hermann Hesse **11**:270
Pär Lagerkvist **7**:199

Gidley, Mick
William Faulkner **3**:156

Gies, Judith
Frederick Busch **18**:86
André Dubus **36**:146
Gail Godwin **31**:198
Francine du Plessix Gray
   22:201
Jayne Anne Phillips **33**:305
Susan Fromberg Schaeffer
   22:368
Lynne Sharon Schwartz **31**:389

Gifford, Henry
Joseph Brodsky **13**:117
Marianne Moore **4**:361

Gifford, Terry
Ted Hughes **37**:175

Gifford, Thomas
Stephen King **26**:240

Gilbert, Elliot L.
Leonard Michaels **25**:315

Gilbert, Harriett
J. G. Ballard **36**:44
André Brink **36**:70
Italo Calvino **33**:98, 100
Julio Cortázar **33**:132
André Dubus **36**:148
Ruth Prawer Jhabvala **29**:261
Ntozake Shange **25**:397
J.I.M. Stewart **32**:421
D. M. Thomas **31**:435

Gilbert, James
Renata Adler **31**:13

Gilbert, Sandra M.
Maya Angelou **12**:13
Norman Dubie **36**:130
Jean Garrigue **8**:239
Sandra Hochman **8**:297
Diane Johnson **5**:200
Kenneth Koch **8**:323

Eleanor Lerman **9**:329
Audre Lorde **18**:308
Sylvia Plath **17**:361
Anne Sexton **4**:484
Kathleen Spivack **6**:521
Diane Wakoski **9**:554

Gilbert, W. Stephen
Howard Barker **37**:33
Caryl Churchill **31**:82, 84
Brian Clark **29**:126
Peter Handke **5**:163
Richard O'Brien **17**:322, 324
J. B. Priestley **5**:350
David Storey **5**:416

Gilbert, Zack
Leon Forrest **4**:164

Gilboy, J. Thomas
David Cudlip **34**:39

Gilder, Joshua
Dee Brown **18**:71
Jerzy Kosinski **15**:316
Alberto Moravia **27**:356

Gilder, Rosamond
Garson Kanin **22**:229
Clifford Odets **28**:330
Tennessee Williams **30**:458

Giles, Dennis
Jean-Luc Godard **20**:151

Giles, James R.
Richard Wright **21**:452

Giles, Mary E.
Juan Goytisolo **10**:243

Gilkes, Michael
Wilson Harris **25**:210, 211, 218

Gill, Brendan
Edward Albee **5**:12; **25**:36
Alan Ayckbourn **5**:36; **8**:34;
   18:29
John Bishop **10**:54
Anne Burr **6**:104
D. L. Coburn **10**:107
Noel Coward **9**:172, 173
James Gould Cozzens **11**:126
Michael Cristofer **28**:96
Christopher Durang **27**:93
Athol Fugard **25**:174, 178
Ernest K. Gann **23**:165
Larry Gelbart **21**:128
William Gibson **23**:180
Charles Gordone **1**:125
John Guare **14**:221
Bill Gunn **5**:152
A. R. Gurney, Jr. **32**:221
Lorraine Hansberry **17**:189
Lillian Hellman **18**:227
Beth Henley **23**:216
John Hopkins **4**:233
Preston Jones **10**:296
Jean Kerr **22**:259
James Kirkwood **9**:319
Pavel Kohout **13**:323
Arthur Kopit **33**:251
Ira Levin **6**:306
David Mamet **9**:360; **34**:220
Terrence McNally **7**:219
Mark Medoff **23**:293
Arthur Miller **6**:334

Peter Nichols **5**:307; **36**:330
Clifford Odets **2**:319
John O'Hara **6**:385
Dorothy Parker **15**:414
Harold Pinter **15**:425
Roman Polanski **16**:464
Gerome Ragni and James Rado
  17:388
Ronald Ribman **7**:358
William Saroyan **8**:468
Murray Schisgal **6**:490
Rod Serling **30**:354, 355
Peter Shaffer **5**:386
Sam Shepard **17**:437
Martin Sherman **19**:416
Neil Simon **6**:505; **11**:495
Isaac Bashevis Singer **15**:509
Stephen Sondheim **30**:399
Elizabeth Spencer **22**:399
John Steinbeck **5**:408
Milan Stitt **29**:390
Tom Stoppard **4**:526; **5**:413;
  8:504; **15**:521; **29**:396
David Storey **2**:424
C. P. Taylor **27**:446
Lily Tomlin **17**:518
Gore Vidal **2**:449
Andy Warhol **20**:419
Thornton Wilder **35**:445
Tennessee Williams **5**:503;
  8:548
Lanford Wilson **7**:547
Robert Wilson **7**:550

Gill, Richard T.
  Frank O'Connor **23**:325

Gillen, Francis
  Donald Barthelme **2**:40

Gillespie, Beryl C.
  Barbara Corcoran **17**:78

Gillespie, Bruce
  Philip K. Dick **30**:121

Gillespie, John
  Scott O'Dell **30**:268
  Kin Platt **26**:350

Gillespie, John T.
  Frank Bonham **12**:51, 55
  Alice Childress **12**:107

Gillespie, Robert
  Eric Ambler **6**:2
  Jorge Luis Borges **6**:91
  John le Carré **9**:326

Gillett, Charlie
  Jimmy Cliff **21**:60

Gillett, John
  Kon Ichikawa **20**:178, 180
  Fritz Lang **20**:209
  Yasujiro Ozu **16**:446
  Satyajit Ray **16**:477
  Josef von Sternberg **20**:374
  Billy Wilder **20**:458

Gilliatt, Penelope
  Woody Allen **16**:2, 7
  Robert Altman **16**:30
  Ralph Bakshi **26**:70
  Samuel Beckett **4**:49
  Claude Chabrol **16**:179
  Shirley Clarke **16**:216

Noel Coward **9**:172
Brian De Palma **20**:76
Rainer Werner Fassbinder
  20:108, 112, 114, 115
Jean-Luc Godard **20**:141
Werner Herzog **16**:326
John Huston **20**:173
Buster Keaton **20**:195
John Landis **26**:272
Richard Lester **20**:230
Monty Python **21**:224
Joe Orton **4**:387
Roman Polanski **16**:472
Satyajit Ray **16**:487
Ken Russell **16**:550
Carlos Saura **20**:317
Melvin Van Peebles **20**:409,
  412
Lina Wertmüller **16**:589, 595
Vassily S. Yanovsky **18**:550

Gillis, William
  Friedrich Dürrenmatt **11**:170

Gilman, Harvey
  Howard Nemerov **6**:362

Gilman, Richard
  Richard Adams **4**:7
  Edward Albee **5**:10
  John Arden **6**:6
  James Baldwin **15**:41; **17**:35,
  44
  Imamu Amiri Baraka **5**:44
  Donald Barthelme **2**:40
  Samuel Beckett **29**:66
  Saul Bellow **6**:49
  Thomas Bernhard **32**:22
  Heinrich Böll **27**:67
  Eldridge Cleaver **30**:55, 68
  J. P. Donleavy **6**:140
  Bruce Jay Friedman **5**:126
  Max Frisch **32**:192
  Carlos Fuentes **22**:163
  William H. Gass **2**:154
  Jack Gelber **1**:114; **6**:196
  Günter Grass **32**:203
  Graham Greene **6**:214
  A. R. Gurney, Jr. **32**:220
  Woody Guthrie **35**:188
  Rolf Hochhuth **11**:274
  Eugène Ionesco **6**:249
  Kenneth Koch **5**:218
  Norman Mailer **2**:260; **8**:367
  Bernard Malamud **18**:320
  William Maxwell **19**:307
  Michael McClure **10**:331
  Arthur Miller **6**:326, 327
  Marsha Norman **28**:320
  Sean O'Casey **5**:319
  Walker Percy **18**:399
  Harold Pinter **6**:405, 406, 410
  Reynolds Price **6**:424
  John Rechy **7**:356
  Philip Roth **3**:438; **22**:358
  Howard Sackler **14**:478
  Irwin Shaw **23**:398
  Robert Shaw **5**:390
  Neil Simon **6**:502
  Susan Sontag **31**:406
  George Steiner **24**:425
  John Updike **2**:440
  Tennessee Williams **5**:499
  Edmund Wilson **24**:478

Richard Wright **21**:440

Gilmore, Mikal
  Bob Marley **17**:269, 270
  Lou Reed **21**:316, 320
  Bruce Springsteen **17**:486
  Stevie Wonder **12**:660

Gilroy, Harry
  Frank B. Gilbreth, Jr. and
    Ernestine Gilbreth Carey
    17:153
  Thor Heyerdahl **26**:189

Gilsdorf, Jeanette
  Robert Creeley **4**:118

Giltrow, Janet
  Marilyn R. Bowering **32**:48

Gimelson, Deborah
  Frederick Barthelme **36**:51

Gindin, James
  Kingsley Amis **2**:4
  Saul Bellow **3**:54
  Truman Capote **3**:100
  Margaret Drabble **10**:165
  E. M. Forster **3**:160
  John Fowles **10**:189
  William Golding **2**:165; **3**:198
  Rosamond Lehmann **5**:238
  Doris Lessing **2**:238; **22**:278
  Iris Murdoch **2**:295; **3**:347
  John Osborne **2**:327
  Philip Roth **3**:436
  Alan Sillitoe **3**:447, 448
  David Storey **2**:423; **4**:528
  John Wain **2**:457
  Angus Wilson **2**:470; **3**:534

Gingell, S.
  William Mitchell **25**:325

Gingher, Robert S.
  John Updike **5**:454

Gingrich, Arnold
  Chester Himes **2**:196

Ginsberg, Allen
  Gregory Corso **11**:123
  Jack Kerouac **2**:228; **14**:306
  Ezra Pound **18**:420

Gioia, Dana
  John Ashbery **25**:56
  Margaret Atwood **25**:69
  Joseph Brodsky **36**:79
  Alfred Corn **33**:118
  Thom Gunn **32**:214
  Maxine Kumin **28**:225
  Frederick Morgan **23**:301
  Katha Pollitt **28**:368
  Craig Raine **32**:354

Giovanni, Nikki
  Virginia Hamilton **26**:149
  Alice Walker **5**:476

Gipson, Carolyn
  W.E.B. Du Bois **2**:120

Girson, Rochelle
  Peter S. Beagle **7**:25

Girvin, Peter
  A. J. Cronin **32**:138

Gish, Robert F.
  A. B. Guthrie, Jr. **23**:200
  Conrad Richter **30**:328

Gitlin, Todd
  James Baldwin **2**:32
  Robert Bly **2**:66
  Steven Bochco and Michael
    Kozoll **35**:54
  Bob Dylan **4**:150
  Paul Goodman **7**:130
  Denise Levertov **2**:243
  Marge Piercy **3**:383

Gitomer, Irene
  Mary Stewart **35**:390

Gitzen, Julian
  Robert Bly **10**:56
  Seamus Heaney **5**:172
  Ted Hughes **4**:237
  Denise Levertov **5**:250
  Peter Redgrove **6**:446
  R. S. Thomas **6**:531
  Charles Tomlinson **2**:437; **4**:548
  Ted Walker **13**:566

Giuliano, William
  Antonio Buero Vallejo **15**:98

Givner, Joan
  Katherine Anne Porter **7**:319;
    10:398; **13**:450; **15**:432
  Eudora Welty **5**:479

Gladstein, Mimi R.
  Ayn Rand **30**:302

Glaessner, Verina
  François Truffaut **20**:404

Glanville, Brian
  George Plimpton **36**:353

Glassco, John
  Jane Rule **27**:418

Glasser, Perry
  Kent Haruf **34**:58

Glasser, William
  J. D. Salinger **8**:464

Glassman, Peter
  Shirley Ann Grau **9**:240
  R. G. Vliet **22**:441

Glastonbury, Marion
  Lynne Reid Banks **23**:43
  John Gregory Dunne **28**:128
  Max Frisch **32**:192
  Russell C. Hoban **25**:264
  Thomas Keneally **27**:233
  Lisa St. Aubin de Teran
    36:420, 423
  Martin Walser **27**:467

Glatstein, Jacob
  Marianne Moore **4**:358

Glauber, Robert H.
  Mary Oliver **19**:361

Glazer, Mitchell
  Paul McCartney **35**:284

Gleason, George
  Jean Craighead George **35**:178
  Sonia Levitin **17**:266
  Robert Newton Peck **17**:342

Gleason, Judith
Aimé Césaire **19**:95
Donald Hall **37**:145

Gleason, Judith Illsley
Chinua Achebe **7**:3

Gleason, Ralph J.
Nelson Algren **10**:7
Lenny Bruce **21**:43
Bob Dylan **6**:156; **12**:181
Martin Mull **17**:299
Paul Simon **17**:459

Gleicher, David
Margaret Atwood **3**:19

Glen, Duncan
Hugh MacDiarmid **4**:311

Glendinning, Victoria
Margaret Atwood **15**:38
Elizabeth Bowen **22**:64
Melvyn Bragg **10**:72
Anthony Burgess **5**:87
Angela Carter **5**:101
Bruce Chatwin **28**:72
Roald Dahl **6**:122
Anita Desai **19**:134
Zöe Fairbairns **32**:162
Elaine Feinstein **36**:169
Penelope Fitzgerald **19**:173
Thomas Flanagan **25**:164
Doris Grumbach **13**:258
James Hanley **13**:262
Chester Himes **7**:159
Russell C. Hoban **7**:160; **25**:264
Ursula Holden **18**:258
Elizabeth Jane Howard **7**:164
Alison Lurie **18**:310
Olivia Manning **19**:303
Joyce Carol Oates **11**:404
Edna O'Brien **13**:416
Barbara Pym **13**:471
Jane Rule **27**:418
Françoise Sagan **9**:468
Alan Sillitoe **6**:500
Stevie Smith **25**:420
J.I.M. Stewart **7**:466
Glendon Swarthout **35**:403
Fay Weldon **11**:565
Eudora Welty **14**:565

Glenn, Jerry
Paul Celan **10**:102, 104; **19**:89

Glenn, Jules
Anthony Shaffer **19**:414

Glick, William
Walter Farley **17**:115

Glicksberg, Charles I.
Arthur Adamov **4**:6
Kenneth Burke **24**:119
Albert Camus **1**:52
Jean Genet **5**:136
Hermann Hesse **3**:244
Aldous Huxley **3**:254
Eugène Ionesco **9**:288; **11**:290
Robinson Jeffers **3**:260
Arthur Koestler **33**:238
Joseph Wood Krutch **24**:281
André Malraux **1**:201
Kenneth Patchen **18**:392
Edmund Wilson **24**:464

Glimm, James York
Thomas Merton **3**:337; **11**:372

Gloag, Julian
Michael Frayn **31**:189

Gloster, Hugh M.
Arna Bontemps **18**:63
Jessie Redmon Fauset **19**:170
Carl Van Vechten **33**:395
Frank G. Yerby **22**:487

Glover, Al
Michael McClure **6**:320

Glover, Elaine
John Fowles **6**:188
Nadine Gordimer **7**:131
Joseph Heller **8**:279
Tim O'Brien **7**:271

Glover, Tony
Chuck Berry **17**:53
Waylon Jennings **21**:202
Patti Smith **12**:534

Glover, Willis B.
J.R.R. Tolkien **1**:340

Glusman, John A.
Stephen Wright **33**:468

Goatley, James L.
Roy A. Gallant **17**:132

Gobeil, Madeleine
Marie-Claire Blais **22**:60

Godard, B.
Audrey Thomas **13**:540

Godard, Barbara
Audrey Thomas **37**:420

Goddard, Donald
Lothar-Günther Buchheim **6**:102

Goddard, Rosalind K.
Milton Meltzer **26**:301

Godden, Rumer
Carson McCullers **12**:418

Godfrey, Dave
Joan Barfoot **18**:35
Hugh MacLennan **14**:343

Godsell, Geoffrey
Allen Drury **37**:100

Godshalk, William L.
Kurt Vonnegut, Jr. **3**:500

Godwin, Gail
Beryl Bainbridge **5**:39
Ann Beattie **13**:64
Julien Green **3**:205
Doris Grumbach **13**:258
Shirley Hazzard **18**:220
Joy Williams **31**:461
Vassily S. Yanovsky **18**:552

Goetz, David R.
William Mastrosimone **36**:291

Goetz, Ronald
Larry Gelbart **21**:128

Goetz-Stankiewicz, Marketa
Václav Havel **25**:225, 229

Going, William T.
T. S. Stribling **23**:448

Goitein, Denise
Nathalie Sarraute **10**:457

Gold, Arthur R.
Arthur A. Cohen **31**:92

Gold, Herbert
Mel Brooks **12**:78
Richard Condon **10**:111
John Dos Passos **4**:136
Doris Grumbach **22**:205
Alistair MacLean **13**:364
James Purdy **28**:376
Aleksandr I. Solzhenitsyn **2**:409
Terry Southern **7**:454
Gore Vidal **6**:550
Donald E. Westlake **33**:440

Gold, Ivan
Pat Barker **32**:13
R. V. Cassill **23**:106
John Ehle **27**:107
Shusaku Endo **14**:162
George V. Higgins **10**:273
Paul Horgan **9**:279
Evan Hunter **31**:225
Jerzy Kosinski **15**:316
Kenzaburō Ōe **36**:348
Frederic Raphael **14**:437
Ishmael Reed **32**:360
Susan Fromberg Schaeffer **22**:369
Robert Stone **23**:424
John Updike **2**:440
John A. Williams **13**:599
Sloan Wilson **32**:447
Helen Yglesias **7**:558

Gold, Pat
Taylor Caldwell **28**:68
Thomas J. Fleming **37**:128

Gold, Peter
José María Arguedas **18**:5

Gold, Renee
Marge Piercy **27**:378

Gold, Richard
Jim Carroll **35**:80

Gold, Sylviane
Peter Nichols **36**:333
Lanford Wilson **36**:465

Goldberg, Isaac
Gregorio López y Fuentes **32**:278

Goldberg, Joe
Neil Diamond **30**:112

Goldberg, Michael
Jim Carroll **35**:80
The Clash **30**:46
Prince **35**:328

Goldberg, Steven
Bob Dylan **6**:154

Goldberg, Vicki
Paul Theroux **11**:530

Goldberger, Judith
Marilyn Sachs **35**:334

Golden, Bernette
Kristin Hunter **35**:226

Golden, Dorothy S.
Josephine Humphreys **34**:66

Golden, Robert E.
Thomas Pynchon **3**:409

Goldensohn, Lorrie
Ben Belitt **22**:54
Norman Dubie **36**:131, 135
Ira Sadoff **9**:466
Maura Stanton **9**:508

Goldfarb, Clare R.
Aleksandr I. Solzhenitsyn **7**:443

Goldhurst, William
John Steinbeck **21**:378

Goldknopf, David
Kurt Vonnegut, Jr. **12**:600

Goldman, Albert
Lenny Bruce **21**:45, 53
Bob Dylan **3**:130; **12**:186
John Lennon and Paul McCartney **12**:367

Goldman, Arnold
Amos Tutuola **29**:435

Goldman, Eric F.
John Steinbeck **21**:370
Dalton Trumbo **19**:445

Goldman, Mark
Bernard Malamud **1**:197

Goldman, Merle
Jules Archer **12**:19

Goldman, Michael
Joyce Carol Oates **3**:361

Goldman, Rowena
Howard Barker **37**:36
Snoo Wilson **33**:465

Goldman, Vivien
Jimmy Cliff **21**:64

Goldman, William
Ross Macdonald **1**:185

Goldmann, Lucien
Witold Gombrowicz **11**:239
Georg Lukács **24**:324

Goldsmith, Arnold L.
Leslie A. Fiedler **24**:203
John Steinbeck **9**:515
Morris L. West **33**:429

Goldsmith, Claire K.
Alvin Silverstein and Virginia B. Silverstein **17**:455

Goldsmith, David H.
Kurt Vonnegut, Jr. **4**:562

Goldstein, Eric
Susan Cheever **18**:102

Goldstein, Laurence
Robert Frost **13**:230
Edwin Honig **33**:212, 213
David Ignatow **4**:248
Adrienne Rich **7**:372
James Wright **3**:541

Goldstein, Malcolm
Thornton Wilder 1:365

Goldstein, Marilyn
Milton Meltzer 26:298

Goldstein, Patrick
Elvis Costello 21:69

Goldstein, Richard
Bob Dylan 3:130; 12:182
John Lennon and Paul
McCartney 12:357
Edmund White III 27:480

Goldstein, Toby
The Clash 30:43
Jonathan Kozol 17:252
Paul McCartney 35:286
Jim Morrison 17:294

Goldstone, Richard H.
Thornton Wilder 6:574

Goldwasser, Noë
Smokey Robinson 21:345

Golffing, Francis
Salvatore Quasimodo 10:429

Gomez, Joseph A.
Ken Russell 16:550

Gömöri, George
Tadeusz Konwicki 28:207
László Nagy 7:251

Goodenough, Ward
Margaret Mead 37:285

Goodfellow, Patricia
A. J. Cronin 32:141

Goodfield, June
Ronald J. Glasser 37:133

Goodfriend, James
Laura Nyro 17:314

Goodheart, Eugene
John Fowles 33:175
F. R. Leavis 24:311
Cynthia Ozick 3:372
Theodore Roethke 1:292
John Seelye 7:405
William Carlos Williams 5:510

Goodman, Charlotte
Joyce Carol Oates 15:400

Goodman, Ellen
Maureen Daly 17:91

Goodman, Henry
Elia Kazan 16:367

Goodman, James
George Seferis 5:385

Goodman, Jan M.
Lois Duncan 26:107

Goodman, Joseph
John Edgar Wideman 36:452

Goodman, Lord
John Mortimer 28:288

Goodman, Paul
James Baldwin 17:23
Ernest Hemingway 1:144

Goodman, Robert L.
David Kherdian 6:280

Goodman, Walter
Thomas Berger 8:83
Josephine Herbst 34:450
Elinor Langer 34:450

Goodrich, Norma L.
Jean Giono 4:187; 11:230

Goodrick, Susan
Robert Crumb 17:86

Goodsell, James Nelson
Jules Archer 12:18
Allan W. Eckert 17:106, 107
Piri Thomas 17:498

Goodstein, Jack
Alain Robbe-Grillet 2:376

Goodwin, June
Laurence Yep 35:468

Goodwin, Michael
Chuck Berry 17:51
John Brunner 10:80
Samuel R. Delany 14:143
Joanna Russ 15:461
Andy Warhol 20:420

Goodwin, Polly
Honor Arundel 17:12
Eilís Dillon 17:94
James D. Forman 21:117
Lee Kingman 17:245
Emily Cheney Neville 12:450
Zoa Sherburne 30:361
Barbara Wersba 30:430

Goodwin, Stephen
Eleanor Clark 19:108
Ella Leffland 19:280
Leonard Michaels 25:317
Walker Percy 2:335
Peter Taylor 1:334
John Kennedy Toole 19:442

Goodwyn, Larry
Larry McMurtry 27:328

Goodyear, Russell H.
Robin F. Brancato 35:69

Gooneratne, Yasmine
Ruth Prawer Jhabvala 29:259

Gordimer, Nadine
Chinua Achebe 3:2
Simone de Beauvoir 14:67
Breyten Breytenbach 37:48
J. M. Coetzee 33:109
V. S. Naipaul 4:372
James Ngugi 3:358
Alan Paton 25:359, 362
Wole Soyinka 36:414

Gordon, Andrew
Ishmael Reed 2:368

Gordon, Caroline
Flannery O'Connor 15:411;
21:255

Gordon, Cecelia
Ruth M. Arthur 12:27

Gordon, David
Margaret Drabble 22:121

Gordon, David J.
Herbert Gold 4:192
William Golding 1:122
Uwe Johnson 5:200
Maxine Kumin 28:221
Brian Moore 1:225
Vladimir Nabokov 1:245
Tom Stoppard 1:328

Gordon, Giles
Caryl Churchill 31:90
Simon Gray 36:210

Gordon, Jan B.
Richard Adams 5:4
John Braine 3:86
Doris Lessing 6:292
Iris Murdoch 3:349

Gordon, Lenore
Sandra Scoppettone 26:402

Gordon, Leonard A.
Ved Mehta 37:292

Gordon, Leonore
Norma Fox Mazer 26:293

Gordon, Lois
Donald Barthelme 23:49
Arthur Miller 26:322

Gordon, Mary
Diane Johnson 13:306
Maxine Hong Kingston 19:249
Mary McCarthy 14:359
Edna O'Brien 13:416; 36:339
Walker Percy 18:401
David Plante 23:346

Gordon, Philip
Ayn Rand 30:300

Gorman, Herbert
Taylor Caldwell 28:57

Gornick, Vivian
Rosellen Brown 32:70
J. M. Coetzee 33:111
Paula Fox 2:140
Nadine Gordimer 18:190
Doris Grumbach 22:205
Lillian Hellman 8:282; 18:227
Jonathan Kozol 17:253
Phillip Lopate 29:298
Alberto Moravia 18:347
Grace Paley 4:391
Marge Piercy 18:407
Anne Tyler 28:432
Gregor von Rezzori 25:384
Helen Yglesias 22:494

Gorra, Michael
Pat Barker 32:13
T. Coraghessan Boyle 36:62
Bernard Mac Laverty 31:257
Jayne Anne Phillips 33:307
Anthony Powell 31:319
Barbara Pym 37:375
Salman Rushdie 31:360
Lynne Sharon Schwartz 31:392

Gose, Elliot
Marie-Claire Blais 13:96
Gwendolyn MacEwan 13:357

Goskowski, Francis
Rosa Guy 26:146
Andrea Lee 36:257

Gosse, Van
The Clash 30:48

Gossett, Louise Y.
William Goyen 14:209
Flannery O'Connor 1:256

Gossman, Ann
Lawrence Durrell 1:87
Iris Murdoch 15:387

Gostnell, David
Alvin Silverstein and Virginia
B. Silverstein 17:456

Gott, Richard
Carlos Castaneda 12:86

Gottesman, Ronald
Frederick Karl 34:553

Gottfried, Martin
Enid Bagnold 25:78
Gretchen Cryer 21:79
Charles Fuller 25:180
William Gibson 23:179
John Guare 14:222; 29:204
A. R. Gurney, Jr. 32:216, 217
Lorraine Hansberry 17:189
Jean Kerr 22:257
Bernard Pomerance 13:445
Howard Sackler 14:479
Ntozake Shange 25:396
Sam Shepard 17:436
Neil Simon 31:395
Stephen Sondheim 30:380, 381,
383, 388, 389
Milan Stitt 29:389
George Tabori 19:438
Michel Tremblay 29:418
Andrew Lloyd Webber and Tim
Rice 21:425, 431
Tennessee Williams 30:469
Lanford Wilson 7:547

Gottlieb, Annie
Maya Angelou 12:11
Henry Bromell 5:74
Anita Brookner 32:59
Marian Engel 36:158
Louis-Ferdinand Céline 4:104
Lois Gould 10:241
Nat Hentoff 26:186
Charles Johnson 7:183
Stephen King 37:203
Joyce Maynard 23:288
Gloria Naylor 28:305
Tillie Olsen 4:386
Sandra Scoppettone 26:401,
404
Lee Smith 25:408

Gottlieb, Elaine
Isaac Bashevis Singer 6:507

Gottlieb, Gerald
Russell Baker 31:26
Jean Craighead George 35:176
John R. Tunis 12:599
Maia Wojciechowska 26:452

Gottschalk, Jane
Ralph Ellison 11:181

Gotz, David M.
Pink Floyd 35:316

Gould, Gerald
Edna Ferber 18:150

Critic Index

Gould, Jack
John Lennon and Paul
McCartney **12**:354

Gould, Jean
Elmer Rice **7**:363

Gould, Lois
Paddy Chayefsky **23**:119

Gould, Stephen Jay
John McPhee **36**:298

Goulianos, Joan Rodman
Lawrence Durrell **8**:193

Govier, Katharine
Marian Engel **36**:163

Gow, Gordon
Lindsay Anderson **20**:18
Michelangelo Antonioni **20**:40
John Cassavetes **20**:45
Claude Chabrol **16**:170
René Clair **20**:66
Vittorio De Sica **20**:88, 91
Bob Fosse **20**:125
George Roy Hill **26**:200, 204
Alfred Hitchcock **16**:353
John Huston **20**:168
Elia Kazan **16**:374
Peter Nichols **36**:328
Nagisa Oshima **20**:246
Sidney Poitier **26**:358
Satyajit Ray **16**:479
Alain Resnais **16**:510
Ken Russell **16**:542, 543
Jerzy Skolimowski **20**:352
Steven Spielberg **20**:359
C. P. Taylor **27**:442
Agnès Varda **16**:555
Peter Weir **20**:428
Orson Welles **20**:439, 452

Gower, Herschel
Peter Taylor **18**:525

Goyen, William
Truman Capote **19**:81
Peter Matthiessen **32**:285
Anaïs Nin **4**:379

Goytisolo, Juan
Carlos Fuentes **10**:204

Grace, Sherrill
Margaret Atwood **25**:64

Grace, William J.
T. H. White **30**:440, 441

Grady, R. F., S.J.
Mary Stewart **35**:393

Grady, Wayne
Matt Cohen **19**:116
Ralph Gustafson **36**:221
Farley Mowat **26**:347
Audrey Thomas **37**:423

Graff, Gerald
Geoffrey H. Hartman **27**:185

Graff, Gerald E.
Donald Barthelme **6**:30
Saul Bellow **6**:54
Stanley Elkin **6**:169
Norman Mailer **8**:372
I. A. Richards **24**:394

Graham, Desmond
Jorge Luis Borges **8**:103
Breyten Breytenbach **23**:84
James Hanley **13**:262
Anthony Hecht **13**:269
Philip Larkin **5**:229
Robert Lowell **11**:329
John Montague **13**:392
Eugenio Montale **9**:388
Edwin Morgan **31**:274
Linda Pastan **27**:370
Peter Porter **13**:453

Graham, John
John Hawkes **3**:221
Ernest Hemingway **3**:236
Gibbons Ruark **3**:441

Graham, Kenneth
Richard Adams **5**:5
Eva Figes **31**:162
Pamela Hansford Johnson
27:221
Yashar Kemal **29**:265
Laurens Van der Post **5**:463

Graham, Maryemma
Frank G. Yerby **22**:491

Graham-Yooll, Andrew
Gabriel García Márquez **15**:253

Grahn, Judy
Alta **19**:19

Granahan, Paul
Piers Anthony **35**:37
C. J. Cherryh **35**:113
Arthur C. Clarke **35**:129
Gene Wolfe **25**:477

**Grande, Brother Luke M.,
F.S.C.**
Marion Montgomery **7**:232

Granetz, Marc
Donald Barthelme **13**:61
John Gardner **18**:183
Sloan Wilson **32**:448

Granfield, Linda
Kevin Major **26**:286

Grange, Joseph
Carlos Castaneda **12**:86

Grant, Annette
Shirley Ann Grau **4**:209
Edward Hoagland **28**:180

Grant, Damian
W. H. Auden **6**:17
Seamus Heaney **5**:172
Sylvia Plath **2**:337
Peter Porter **5**:347

Grant, Joy
Elizabeth Taylor **29**:411

Grant, Judith Skelton
Robertson Davies **13**:173

Grant, Patrick
Robert Graves **11**:257

Grant, Steve
Howard Barker **37**:36, 39
Howard Brenton **31**:64
David Hare **29**:216
C. P. Taylor **27**:441
Snoo Wilson **33**:461

Grau, Shirley Ann
William Goyen **8**:250
Marion Montgomery **7**:233

Graustark, Barbara
Jim Carroll **35**:79

Grave, Elizabeth F.
Franklyn M. Branley **21**:16

Gravel, George E.
Joanne Greenberg **30**:160

Graver, Lawrence
Samuel Beckett **6**:40
Doris Lessing **2**:242
Carson McCullers **1**:209
Iris Murdoch **3**:347
Gilbert Sorrentino **22**:392
Muriel Spark **2**:417
Paul Theroux **8**:513
William Trevor **7**:475

Graves, Elizabeth Minot
Lee Kingman **17**:246
Sonia Levitin **17**:263
Zilpha Keatley Snyder **17**:471

Graves, Peter
Jurek Becker **19**:36
Christa Wolf **14**:595

Graves, Peter J.
Friedrich Dürrenmatt **15**:196

Graves, Robert
Robert Frost **26**:121
Yevgeny Yevtushenko **1**:382

Graves, Tom
Stephen Wright **33**:469

Grawe, Christian
Botho Strauss **22**:407

Gray, Francine du Plessix
Oriana Fallaci **11**:190
Max Frisch **14**:184
Mary Gordon **22**:184
Stratis Haviaras **33**:203

Gray, Hildagarde
C. S. Adler **35**:12
Gunnel Beckman **26**:89
Jay Bennett **35**:45
Robin F. Brancato **35**:67
Lois Duncan **26**:105
Norma Fox Mazer **26**:289
Katherine Paterson **12**:485

Gray, J. Glenn
Martin Heidegger **24**:263

Gray, James
Pearl S. Buck **7**:32
August Derleth **31**:130, 132
Ralph Gustafson **36**:213
Jules Roains **7**:381
Henri Troyat **23**:459

Gray, John
Paul Bowles **2**:79

Gray, Mrs. John G.
Jules Archer **12**:20
Jean Craighead George **35**:178
M. E. Kerr **12**:298

Gray, Larry
John Knowles **26**:262

Gray, Paul
Lisa Alther **7**:12
Roger Angell **26**:30
Samuel Beckett **6**:44
Adolfo Bioy Casares **8**:94
Vance Bourjaily **8**:104
Jimmy Breslin **4**:76
William F. Buckley, Jr. **7**:35
Alex Comfort **7**:54
Evan S. Connell, Jr. **6**:116
Peter De Vries **7**:78
Pete Dexter **34**:45
Thomas M. Disch **7**:86
Scott Elledge **34**:427
Carolyn Forché **25**:170
John Gardner **5**:132
William H. Gass **8**:246
Joanne Greenberg **30**:165
Russell C. Hoban **7**:160
Maureen Howard **5**:189
Elia Kazan **6**:274
William Kennedy **28**:206
Stephen King **26**:242
Maxine Hong Kingston **12**:312
Norman Mailer **28**:259
Bernard Malamud **27**:307
Peter Matthiessen **5**:274
Ted Mooney **25**:329
V. S. Naipaul **7**:253
Seán O'Faoláin **7**:274
Cynthia Ozick **7**:288
Reynolds Price **6**:425
Gregor von Rezzori **25**:385
Marilynne Robinson **25**:386
Robert Stone **5**:409
Julian Symons **32**:428
John Updike **5**:457
Sylvia Townsend Warner
19:459
James Welch **6**:561
Fay Weldon **6**:562
Morris L. West **33**:431
William Wharton **37**:437
E. B. White **34**:427

Gray, Paul Edward
Eleanor Clark **19**:106
John Fowles **1**:109
Iris Murdoch **1**:236
Joyce Carol Oates **1**:251
Eudora Welty **1**:363

Gray, Richard
Erskine Caldwell **14**:96
Donald Davidson **19**:124
William Faulkner **11**:202
Carson McCullers **12**:430
John Crowe Ransom **11**:469
William Styron **11**:520
Tennessee Williams **11**:577

Gray, Ronald
Heinrich Böll **9**:112

Grayden, Robin
Waylon Jennings **21**:204
Kris Kristofferson **26**:270

Greacen, Robert
W. H. Auden **3**:25
Samuel Beckett **4**:50
Margaret Drabble **2**:117
Bernard Kops **4**:274
Doris Lessing **3**:287
Norman MacCaig **36**:287

Harold Robbins **5**:378
Isaac Bashevis Singer **3**:457
Vassilis Vassilikos **4**:551

Grealish, Gerald
Gilbert Sorrentino **14**:498

Grebanier, Bernard
Thornton Wilder **1**:365

Grebstein, Sheldon Norman
Nelson Algren **33**:12
Ernest Hemingway **3**:235
Bernard Malamud **11**:348
John O'Hara **1**:261

Grecco, Stephen
Howard Brenton **31**:69

Greco, Mike
Ralph Bakshi **26**:75

Greeley, Andrew M.
Richard Bach **14**:36
William X. Kienzle **25**:276
Francine du Plessix Gray
22:199

Green, Alan
Peter De Vries **3**:126
Michael Frayn **3**:164

Green, Benny
August Derleth **31**:139
John Fowles **6**:186
Compton Mackenzie **18**:316
Brian Moore **7**:238
V. S. Naipaul **18**:359
John O'Hara **6**:383
S. J. Perelman **15**:417
Charles M. Schulz **12**:533
Noel Streatfeild **21**:417
Julian Symons **32**:427

Green, Calvin
Pier Paolo Pasolini **20**:264
Eric Rohmer **16**:529

Green, Dorothy
Christina Stead **32**:409

Green, Gerald
Thomas Berger **3**:63

Green, Graham
A. J. Cronin **32**:132

Green, Harris
Jim Jacobs and Warren Casey
12:293

Green, James L.
John Hawkes **14**:237

Green, Jim
Ray Davies **21**:103

Green, Kate
Anne Sexton **15**:473

Green, Laurence
Joan Micklin Silver **20**:342

Green, Marc
Robert Altman **16**:43

Green, Martin
Malcolm Bradbury **32**:53
E. L. Doctorow **6**:138
B. S. Johnson **6**:263
Doris Lessing **15**:333
Anthony Powell **31**:315

Philip Roth **15**:449
J. D. Salinger **1**:298

Green, Michelle
Joyce Maynard **23**:289

Green, Paul
Eric Bentley **24**:47

Green, Peter
William Golding **17**:162
R. K. Narayan **28**:301
Gore Vidal **22**:433

Green, Philip
E. E. Cummings **12**:147

Green, Randall
John Hawkes **4**:217
Aleksandr I. Solzhenitsyn **4**:512

Green, Robert J.
Roch Carrier **13**:141
Athol Fugard **9**:233

Green, Robin
Stan Lee **17**:257

Green, Roger Lancelyn
Alan Garner **17**:135

Green, Roland
Piers Anthony **35**:41
Isaac Asimov **26**:58
Marion Zimmer Bradley **30**:29,
32
Roger Zelazny **21**:478

Green, Timothy
W. H. Auden **14**:27

Greenberg, Clement
Arthur Koestler **33**:231

Greenberg, Joanne
Colleen McCullough **27**:321

Greenberg, Judith L.
Patrick Modiano **18**:338

Greenberg, Martin
Reiner Kunze **10**:310

Greenberg, Martin Harry
Robert A. Heinlein **26**:170

Greenblatt, Stephen Jay
Evelyn Waugh **13**:585

Greene, A. C.
Jim Harrison **33**:200

Greene, Daniel
Don L. Lee **2**:237

Greene, Daniel St. Albin
William Kennedy **28**:203

Greene, Douglas G.
Edmund Crispin **22**:111

Greene, George
Paul West **7**:522

Greene, Graham
Sally Benson **17**:47
Frank Capra **16**:154, 155
R. K. Narayan **28**:299

Greene, James
Eugenio Montale **9**:388

Greene, Naomi
Simone de Beauvoir **31**:36

Greene, Robert W.
René Char **14**:124
Francis Ponge **18**:417
Raymond Queneau **10**:430

Greene, Ronald
Kim Stanley Robinson **34**:105

Greenfeld, Josh
Emily Cheney Neville **12**:451
Philip Roth **2**:378
Paul Zindel **6**:586

Greenfield, Jeff
Art Buchwald **33**:94
Jonathan Kozol **17**:255
John Lennon and Paul
McCartney **12**:378
Dan Wakefield **7**:503

Greenfield, Jerome
A. B. Yehoshua **31**:468

Greenfield, Robert
Bernice Rubens **31**:352

Greenland, Colin
J. G. Ballard **36**:44

Greenlaw, M. Jean
John Knowles **26**:265
Suzanne Newton **35**:301
Mary Stewart **35**:397
Laurence Yep **35**:473

Greenman, Myron
Donald Barthelme **6**:29

Greenspan, Miriam
Maxine Hong Kingston **12**:313

Greenspun, Roger
Bernardo Bertolucci **16**:94
Brian De Palma **20**:74
Marguerite Duras **20**:98
Federico Fellini **16**:283
Bob Fosse **20**:122
Alfred Hitchcock **16**:354
Akira Kurosawa **16**:404
Fritz Lang **20**:211
Jean Renoir **20**:303
Carlos Saura **20**:314, 315
Jerzy Skolimowski **20**:349, 353
Melvin Van Peebles **20**:411

Greenstein, Michael
Dorothy Livesay **15**:342

Greenway, John
Woody Guthrie **35**:183, 186
Norman Mailer **2**:262
Joseph Wambaugh **18**:532

Greenwell, Bill
John Cheever **25**:122
Evan Hunter **31**:226
Bette Pesetsky **28**:358
Lynne Sharon Schwartz **31**:389
Christina Stead **32**:413

Greenwell, Scott L.
Mari Sandoz **28**:405

Greenwood, Gillian
Howard Barker **37**:35
Jayne Anne Phillips **33**:308

Greenya, John R.
Ronald L. Fair **18**:139
Budd Schulberg **7**:403

Gregerson, Linda
Mary Oliver **34**:248

Greggs, R.
Robert Westall **17**:559

Gregor, Ian
William Golding **27**:165
Graham Greene **6**:214

Gregor, Ulrich
Leni Riefenstahl **16**:521

Gregory, Charles
Robert Altman **16**:27

Gregory, Helen
Betty Cavanna **12**:103
H. D. **31**:202

Gregory, Hilda
Joyce Carol Oates **1**:251; **2**:315
Mark Strand **6**:522
Nancy Willard **7**:540

Gregory, Horace
Morley Callaghan **14**:99
H. D. **31**:202
Laura Riding **7**:373

Gregory, Kristiana
Kim Stanley Robinson **34**:107

Gregory, Sister M., O.P.
Shelagh Delaney **29**:146

Greider, William
William Safire **10**:447

Greiling, Franziska Lynne
John Knowles **26**:256

Greiner, Donald J.
Djuna Barnes **8**:48
Frederick Busch **10**:91
Robert Frost **26**:127
John Hawkes **1**:138; **4**:213;
7:145; **27**:192
John Updike **23**:472
Kurt Vonnegut, Jr. **3**:499

Grella, George
Ian Fleming **3**:158
Dashiell Hammett **19**:197

Grene, Marjorie
Jacques Derrida **24**:135
Martin Heidegger **24**:270

Grenier, Cynthia
Satyajit Ray **16**:476
Helen Hooven Santmyer **33**:361

Gresham, William Lindsay
Edward Hoagland **28**:179

Gretlund, Jan Nordby
Katherine Anne Porter **27**:402

Grier, Edward F.
Jonathan Williams **13**:600

Grier, Peter
Fran Lebowitz **36**:249
Tom Wolfe **35**:460

Griffin, Bryan
John Irving **13**:27

Critic Index

Griffin, Robert J.
Cid Corman **9**:169

Griffith, Albert J.
Carson McCullers **1**:209
Peter Taylor **1**:334; **4**:542;
18:526
John Updike **5**:455

Griffiths, Eric
William Empson **34**:540

Griffiths, Gareth
Ayi Kwei Armah **33**:25

Grigg, John
Ved Mehta **37**:292

Grigsby, Gordon K.
Kenneth Rexroth **1**:284

Grigsby John L.
Frank Herbert **23**:222

Grigson, Geoffrey
G. B. Edwards **25**:152
Yasunari Kawabata **18**:280
Robert Lowell **3**:302
Kathleen Raine **7**:351
George Steiner **24**:431

Grillo, Jean Bergantini
Steven Bochco and Michael
Kozoll **35**:50

Grimes, Ann
Joyce Maynard **23**:289

Grimwood, Michael
William Faulkner **14**:174

Griswold, Jerry
Ken Kesey **3**:268

Groberg, Nancy
Mark Harris **19**:199

Groden, Michael
William Faulkner **9**:198

Gropper, Esther C.
Hermann Hesse **2**:189; **3**:244

Grosholz, Emily
Donald Davie **31**:124
Richard F. Hugo **18**:264
Mary Oliver **19**:363
Dave Smith **22**:388

Gross, Amy
Lily Tomlin **17**:516

Gross, Barry
Arthur Miller **10**:344

Gross, Beverly
John Barth **14**:49
Jonathan Baumbach **6**:32
Saul Bellow **2**:52
B. H. Friedman **7**:109
Peter Spielberg **6**:514

Gross, Harvey
T. S. Eliot **6**:161
André Malraux **4**:335
Ezra Pound **4**:414

Gross, John
Breyten Breytenbach **37**:50
Anita Brookner **34**:138
Anita Desai **37**:72
William Empson **34**:336, 538
D. J. Enright **31**:155

Ezra Pound **34**:506
V. S. Pritchett **15**:441
George Steiner **24**:426
E. Fuller Torrey **34**:506
A. N. Wilson **33**:457

Gross, Leonard
Michael Cristofer **28**:97

Gross, Michael
David Bowie **17**:62

Gross, Theodore L.
J. D. Salinger **1**:300

Grosskurth, Phyllis
Margaret Atwood **2**:20
Mary McCarthy **24**:349
Gabrielle Roy **14**:463

Grossman, Edward
Simone de Beauvoir **2**:44
Saul Bellow **8**:80
Thomas Berger **3**:63
Heinrich Böll **3**:75
Joseph Heller **5**:181
Doris Lessing **3**:287
Vladimir Nabokov **3**:355
Kurt Vonnegut, Jr. **5**:466

Grossman, Elizabeth
Zöe Fairbairns **32**:163

Grossman, Jan
Václav Havel **25**:219

Grossman, Jill
William Kotzwinkle **35**:259

Grossman, Joel
Philip Roth **9**:459

Grossman, Loyd
Pink Floyd **35**:306
Peter Townshend **17**:536

Grossman, William L.
João Guimarães Rosa **23**:349

Grossvogel, David I.
Agatha Christie **12**:127
Julio Cortázar **10**:112
Jean Genet **14**:196

Groth, Janet
John Cheever **8**:136

Groves, Margaret
Nathalie Sarraute **4**:470

Gruen, John
Charles Addams **30**:15

Grumbach, Doris
Maya Angelou **12**:12
Simone de Beauvoir **4**:49
Kay Boyle **5**:66
Frederick Busch **18**:85
Hortense Calisher **8**:124
R. V. Cassill **23**:109
Arthur A. Cohen **7**:50
Joan Didion **8**:175
E. L. Doctorow **6**:131
Daphne du Maurier **11**:164
Stanley Elkin **4**:154; **14**:158
Marian Engel **36**:162
Leslie A. Fiedler **13**:214
Nadine Gordimer **18**:188
Francine du Plessix Gray
22:201

Stratis Haviaras **33**:204
Susan B. Hill **4**:288
Maureen Howard **5**:188
Ward S. Just **27**:228
Garson Kanin **22**:232
Alison Lurie **4**:307
Cormac McCarthy **4**:342
Mary McCarthy **5**:276
Margaret Mead **37**:282
A. G. Mojtabai **9**:385
Brian Moore **5**:297
Penelope Mortimer **5**:299
Tim O'Brien **19**:357
Julia O'Faolain **6**:383
Aldo Palazzeschi **11**:431
Bette Pesetsky **28**:359
Jayne Anne Phillips **15**:421
Judith Rossner **9**:457
J. R. Salamanca **4**:461
May Sarton **4**:471; **14**:480
Clancy Sigal **7**:425
Henri Troyat **23**:458
Anne Tyler **7**:479
John Updike **15**:546
Nancy Willard **7**:538, 539
Hilma Wolitzer **17**:561, 564
Helen Yglesias **22**:492
Sol Yurick **6**:584

Grunfeld, Frederick V.
John Lennon and Paul
McCartney **12**:361

Grunwald, Beverly
Maureen Daly **17**:90

Grunwald, Henry
Jaroslav Seifert **34**:259

Gubar, Susan
H. D. **14**:225

Gubbins, Bill
Brian Wilson **12**:648

Guerard, Albert, Jr.
C. S. Lewis **27**:259

Guerard, Albert J.
Donald Barthelme **5**:53
Jerome Charyn **5**:103
John Hawkes **2**:183; **3**:222;
15:278; **27**:190
Ayn Rand **30**:293

Guereschi, Edward
Joyce Carol Oates **15**:403
Glendon Swarthout **35**:404

Guernsey, Otis L., Jr.
Sally Benson **17**:49

Guerrard, Philip
Mervyn Peake **7**:301

Guggenheim, Michel
Françoise Sagan **17**:421

Guicharnaud, Jacques
Arthur Adamov **25**:13
Fernando Arrabal **18**:16
Michel de Ghelderode **11**:226
Eugène Ionesco **6**:254
Henri de Montherlant **19**:326
Jean-Paul Sartre **1**:304
Claude Simon **15**:485

Guicharnaud, June
Michel de Ghelderode **11**:226

Guidry, Frederick H.
Thor Heyerdahl **26**:193

Guild, Nicholas
Paul Theroux **11**:530
Richard Yates **23**:480

Guillory, Daniel L.
Josephine Miles **34**:244

Guimond, James
Gilbert Sorrentino **3**:461

Guinn, John
Andrew M. Greeley **28**:178

Guiton, Margaret Otis
Louis Aragon **3**:12
Marcel Aymé **11**:21
Albert Camus **1**:54
Louis-Ferdinand Céline **1**:57
Jean Cocteau **1**:59
Georges Duhamel **8**:186
Jean Giono **4**:183
Julien Green **3**:203
André Malraux **1**:202
François Mauriac **4**:337
Raymond Queneau **2**:359
Jules Romains **7**:381
Jean-Paul Sartre **1**:306

Gullason, Thomas A.
Jackson J. Benson **34**:414
Carson McCullers **4**:344
Flannery O'Connor **1**:259
John Steinbeck **34**:414

Gullette, David
Mark Strand **18**:518

Gullon, Agnes
Pablo Neruda **7**:260

Gunn, Edward
Djuna Barnes **4**:44

Gunn, James
Isaac Asimov **19**:29; **26**:59, 63
Joan D. Vinge **30**:410
Gene Wolfe **25**:474

Gunn, Thom
J. V. Cunningham **31**:98
Donald Davie **31**:109
William Dickey **28**:117
Roy Fuller **28**:148
Barbara Howes **15**:289
David Ignatow **7**:173
Donald Justice **19**:232
W. S. Merwin **13**:383
Christopher Middleton **13**:387
Howard Nemerov **9**:393
Charles Olson **11**:414
Louis Simpson **7**:426, 427

Gunston, David
Leni Riefenstahl **16**:520

Guptara, Prabhu S.
David Dabydeen **34**:150
Anita Desai **37**:68

Guralnick, Peter
Waylon Jennings **21**:205
Willie Nelson **17**:304

Gurewitsch, M. Anatole
William Gaddis **6**:195

Gurian, Jay
Thomas Berger **18**:55

Gurko, Leo
Ernest Hemingway **6**:226
John P. Marguand **10**:331
John Steinbeck **21**:383
Edward Lewis Wallant **5**:477

Gurko, Miriam
Carl Sandburg **35**:357

Gussenhoven, Frances
Joseph Heller **36**:231

Gussow, Adam
Czesław Miłosz **31**:265

Gussow, Mel
Howard Barker **37**:37
Samuel Beckett **29**:65
Ed Bullins **1**:47
Michael Cristofer **28**:95, 97
Christopher Durang **27**:87
Harvey Fierstein **33**:152
Dario Fo **32**:173, 175
Charles Fuller **25**:180
Charles Gordone **1**:125
A. R. Gurney, Jr. **32**:218
Albert Innaurato **21**:190, 191, 193
David Rabe **33**:342
Howard Sackler **14**:480
Ntozake Shange **25**:399
Sam Shepard **17**:438
Milan Stitt **29**:389
Tom Stoppard **29**:395
Elizabeth Swados **12**:558
Wendy Wasserstein **32**:441
Snoo Wilson **33**:465

Gustafson, Ralph
Ronald G. Everson **27**:134

Gustafson, Richard
Reg Saner **9**:469

Gustainis, J. Justin
Thomas J. Fleming **37**:127
Stephen King **12**:311
Steven Millhauser **21**:217
Amos Oz **11**:429

Gutcheon, Beth
Doris Betts **28**:35
Agnes Eckhardt Nixon **21**:245

Gutowski, John A.
Joan Micklin Silver **20**:345

Guttenplan, Don David
Arna Bontemps **18**:65

Gutteridge, Don
Clark Blaise **29**:70
Patrick Lane **25**:289

Guy, David
Virginia Hamilton **26**:158
David Malouf **28**:268

Guzman, Pablo
Prince **35**:323

Guzman, Richard R.
Raja Rao **25**:370

Gwynn, Frederick L.
J. D. Salinger **1**:295

Gysin, Fritz
Jean Toomer **13**:552

Gyurko, Lanin A.
Julio Cortázar **5**:108; **10**:112; **13**:159; **33**:126
Carlos Fuentes **22**:165

Haas, Diane
Judy Blume **12**:46
Barbara Wersba **30**:432

Haas, Joseph
Bob Dylan **12**:180
Jerome Weidman **7**:517

Haavikko, Paavo
Paavo Haavikko **34**:175

Haberl, Franz P.
Max Frisch **9**:218; **14**:184
Botho Strauss **22**:408
Peter Weiss **15**:565

Haberland, Jody
Jane Rule **27**:417

Hack, Richard
Kenneth Patchen **2**:332
Colin Wilson **3**:537

Hackett, C. A.
Henri Michaux **19**:311

Hackett, Francis
Carl Sandburg **35**:338

Hackney, Louise Wallace
John Ford **16**:303

Hadas, Moses
Mary Renault **17**:392
Marguerite Yourcenar **19**:481

Hadas, Pamela White
Marianne Moore **10**:348

Hadas, Rachel
Yannis Ritsos **13**:487; **31**:330
Robert Penn Warren **18**:534

Hadgraft, Cecil
David Malouf **28**:267

Haedens, Kléber
J.M.G. Le Clézio **31**:243

Haenicke, Diether H.
Heinrich Böll **6**:83
Paul Celan **10**:101
Friedrich Dürrenmatt **8**:194
Günter Eich **15**:204
Max Frisch **9**:217
Günter Grass **6**:207
Uwe Johnson **5**:201
Reiner Kunze **10**:310
Anna Seghers **7**:408
Martin Walser **27**:460
Carl Zuckmayer **18**:553

Haffenden, John
John Berryman **10**:45
Robert Lowell **11**:330

Haft, Cynthia
Aleksandr I. Solzhenitsyn **7**:435

Hafter, Ronald
René Wellek **28**:448

Hagan, Candace
Philip Roth **15**:453

Hagan, Patti
Barbara Corcoran **17**:73

Haglin, Donna
Henry Gregor Felsen **17**:123

Hagopian, John V.
James Baldwin **1**:15
William Faulkner **3**:157
J. F. Powers **1**:282

Hague, René
David Jones **7**:189

Hahn, Claire
William Everson **5**:122
Carolyn Forché **25**:170
Jean Garrigue **8**:239
Audre Lorde **18**:309

Hahn, Emily
Martha Gellhorn **14**:196

Haight, Amanda
Anna Akhmatova **25**:26

Hainsworth, J. D.
John Arden **13**:24

Hájek, Igor
Bohumil Hrabal **13**:291

Hajewski, Thomas
Siegfried Lenz **27**:254

Halderman, Marjorie
Larry Kettelkamp **12**:304

Hale, Nancy
Jessamyn West **7**:522; **17**:552, 554

Hale, Thomas A.
Aimé Césaire **19**:97

Hale, William Harlan
Bruce Catton **35**:83

Hales, David
Berry Morgan **6**:340

Haley, Beverly
Ouida Sebestyen **30**:350

Haley, Beverly A.
Paul Zindel **26**:472

Halio, Jay L.
Lawrence Durrell **27**:95
William Gaddis **10**:212
John Gardner **10**:220
Ernest Hemingway **6**:230
John Knowles **26**:246
Mary McCarthy **5**:276
Chaim Potok **26**:373
Reynolds Price **13**:464
Isaac Bashevis Singer **1**:314; **6**:509
C. P. Snow **6**:517
Aleksandr I. Solzhenitsyn **7**:434
Alice Walker **5**:476
Paul West **14**:569

Hall, Donald
Roger Angell **26**:31
Russell Edson **13**:191
Robert Frost **34**:469
Allen Ginsberg **3**:195
Thom Gunn **18**:202
Mark Harris **19**:205
Seamus Heaney **14**:242, 245

Geoffrey Hill **18**:241
Edward Hoagland **28**:185
Richard F. Hugo **18**:263
Roger Kahn **30**:232
Robert Lowell **15**:344
Norman MacCaig **36**:279
Peter Matthiessen **11**:361
Thomas McGrath **28**:278
Rod McKuen **3**:333
Marianne Moore **4**:362
William H. Pritchard **34**:469
Kenneth Rexroth **22**:349
David Wagoner **15**:559
Thomas Williams **14**:583

Hall, Elizabeth
Frank Herbert **12**:275
Stephen King **12**:309

Hall, James
Saul Bellow **3**:50
Elizabeth Bowen **3**:82
William Faulkner **3**:152
Graham Greene **3**:207
Iris Murdoch **2**:296
J. D. Salinger **3**:444
Robert Penn Warren **4**:577

Hall, James B.
Mario Puzo **1**:282

Hall, Joan Joffe
Wendell Berry **4**:59
Marie-Claire Blais **6**:81
Shirley Ann Grau **4**:210
Ursula K. LeGuin **8**:342
Robert Stone **5**:410
John Updike **5**:458
Jessamyn West **17**:550

Hall, John
Gary Snyder **1**:318

Hall, Linda B.
Carlos Fuentes **8**:222
Gabriel García Márquez **10**:214
Maxine Hong Kingston **12**:314

Hall, Mordaunt
Tod Browning **16**:121
Frank Capra **16**:153

Hall, Richard
Breyten Breytenbach **23**:86
Bruce Chatwin **28**:73

Hall, Richard W.
Ezra Pound **5**:348

Hall, Stanley B.
Arthur C. Clarke **35**:120

Hall, Stephen
R. H. W. Dillard **5**:116

Hall, Vernon, Jr.
Paule Marshall **27**:309

Hall, Wade
Jesse Stuart **11**:511

Hallberg, Peter
Halldór Laxness **25**:293

Halle, Louis J.
William Golding **17**:157

Haller, Robert S.
Martin Booth **13**:104
Alan Sillitoe **6**:500

Critic Index

Haller, Scot
Beth Henley **23**:214
John Irving **23**:248

Halliday, Bob
Samuel Beckett **29**:66

Halliday, Mark
Eleanor Lerman **9**:329

Halman, Talat Sait
Yashar Kemal **14**:299, 300, 301; **29**:268

Halpern, Daniel
David Wagoner **5**:475

Halpern, Joseph
Jean-Paul Sartre **24**:416

Halpern, Sue M.
Tom Robbins **32**:368

Halsey, Martha T.
Antonio Buero Vallejo **15**:99

Haltrecht, Monty
Chaim Potok **26**:376

Hamalian, Leo
Jean-Luc Godard **20**:141

Haman, A. C.
Margaret O. Hyde **21**:176

Hamblen, Abigail Ann
Flannery O'Connor **21**:270

Hamburger, Michael
Wendell Berry **27**:36
Paul Celan **19**:93
Günter Grass **32**:197
Martin Heidegger **24**:255
Ernst Jandl **34**:195
Siegfried Lenz **27**:247
Robert Pinsky **19**:370

Hamel, Guy
William Mitchell **25**:328

Hamill, Pete
Seán O'Faoláin **7**:272
Gay Talese **37**:391, 394
Leon Uris **7**:492

Hamill, Sam
Greg Kuzma **7**:197

Hamilton, Alice
Samuel Beckett **10**:31
John Updike **2**:443; **5**:449

Hamilton, Daphne Ann
Melvin Berger **12**:41, 42
Franklyn M. Branley **21**:22
Roy A. Gallant **17**:132

Hamilton, Ian
Kingsley Amis **2**:6
John Landis **26**:273
Robert Lowell **2**:246; **4**:303
Norman MacCaig **36**:282, 284
Louis MacNeice **4**:317
James Merrill **34**:231
Christopher Middleton **13**:387

Hamilton, James Shelley
René Clair **20**:58, 61
John Ford **16**:303
Rouben Mamoulian **16**:420
Jean Renoir **20**:286

Hamilton, Kenneth
Samuel Beckett **10**:31
John Updike **2**:443; **5**:449

Hamilton, Lynne
Judy Blume **30**:23

Hamilton, Mary
Paul Vincent Carroll **10**:98

Hamilton, William
Albert Camus **1**:52
Paul Goodman **7**:128

Hamilton-Paterson, James
Anne McCaffrey **17**:281

Hamley, Dennis
H. F. Brinsmead **21**:32
Diana Wynne Jones **26**:229

Hamlin, William C.
Leonard Michaels **25**:315

Hammond, Graham
Diana Wynne Jones **26**:227

Hammond, John G.
Robert Creeley **8**:151

Hammond, Jonathan
Howard Barker **37**:32
Athol Fugard **9**:229
Snoo Wilson **33**:461

Hammond, Kristin E.
Kin Platt **26**:351

Hammond, Nancy C.
C. S. Adler **35**:14
Robert Cormier **30**:91
M. E. Kerr **35**:250
D. M. Pinkwater **35**:320
Laurence Yep **35**:474

Hamner, Robert D.
V. S. Naipaul **13**:402
Derek Walcott **25**:453

Hampshire, Stuart
Christopher Isherwood **11**:296

Hampson, John
Edmund Crispin **22**:108

Hanckel, Frances
Isabelle Holland **21**:150

Hancock, Geoff
John Metcalf **37**:304

Handa, Carolyn
Conrad Aiken **10**:1

Handlin, Oscar
Bruce Catton **35**:84
Yuri Krotkov **19**:264
Hunter S. Thompson **17**:503

Handy, William J.
John Crowe Ransom **24**:365

Handzo, Stephen
Michelangelo Antonioni **20**:36
Frank Capra **16**:160

Haney, Robert W.
Erich Maria Remarque **21**:333

Hanley, Clifford
Martin Walser **27**:455

Hanley, Karen Stang
C. S. Adler **35**:15
Lloyd Alexander **35**:28

Hanly, Elizabeth
Jorge Ibargüengoitia **37**:185

Hann, Sandra
Aidan Chambers **35**:101

Hanna, Clifford
Jessica Anderson **37**:20

Hanna, Thomas L.
Albert Camus **9**:143

Hannabuss, C. Stuart
Leon Garfield **12**:230, 234
Andre Norton **12**:463
Josephine Poole **17**:372
J.R.R. Tolkien **12**:575

Hannah, Barry
William Eastlake **8**:200

Hanne, Michael
Elio Vittorini **9**:551

Hansen, Arlen J.
Richard Brautigan **3**:90

Hansen, Arthur G.
Richard Bach **14**:35

Hansen, I. V.
Maia Wojciechowska **26**:458

Hansen, Olaf
Peter Handke **10**:259

Hansen, Ron
Stephen King **26**:239

Hanson, Jarice
Steven Bochco and Michael Kozoll **35**:57

Harada, Violet H.
Barbara Corcoran **17**:77

Harbaugh, William H.
Louis R. Harlan **34**:185

Harcourt, Joan
Roch Carrier **13**:141

Harcourt, Peter
Ingmar Bergman **16**:50, 72
Luis Buñuel **16**:141
Federico Fellini **16**:290
Jean-Luc Godard **20**:143
Richard Lester **20**:221
Jean Renoir **20**:292, 305
Alain Resnais **16**:511

Hardee, Ethel R.
Robert Newton Peck **17**:337

Harder, Worth T.
Herbert Read **4**:443

Hardgrave, Robert L., Jr.
Ved Mehta **37**:296

Hardie, Alec M.
Edmund Blunden **2**:65

Hardin, Nancy Shields
Margaret Drabble **3**:129
Doris Lessing **6**:297

Harding, D. W.
Roy Fuller **4**:178
F. R. Leavis **24**:292
I. A. Richards **24**:377

Hardison, O. B., Jr.
Paul Bowles **19**:59
Larry McMurtry **7**:215

Hardré, Jacques
Jean-Paul Sartre **24**:403

Hardwick, Elizabeth
Renata Adler **8**:6
Elizabeth Bishop **32**:40
Lillian Hellman **14**:257
Doris Lessing **3**:285
Flannery O'Connor **15**:408
Marge Piercy **3**:383
Sylvia Plath **17**:355
Alexsandr I. Solzhenitsyn **10**:480
Susan Sontag **31**:416

Hardwick, Mollie
Roald Dahl **18**:108
Penelope Fitzgerald **19**:174

Hardy, Barbara
A. Alvarez **5**:18

Hardy, John Edward
Cleanth Brooks **24**:107
Katherine Anne Porter **15**:428

Hardy, Melody
Arthur C. Clarke **4**:105
Howard Fast **23**:159

Hare, David
Noël Coward **29**:139
Ngaio Marsh **7**:209

Hargrove, Nancy D.
T. S. Eliot **6**:165

Harker, Jonathan
Roman Polanski **16**:462
Satyajit Ray **16**:475

Harker, Ronald
Mary Renault **17**:401

Harkins, William E.
Jaroslav Seifert **34**:256

Harlow, Robert
Jack Hodgins **23**:231

Harmon, Daniel
Waylon Jennings **21**:201

Harmon, Elva
Eilís Dillon **17**:96
William Mayne **12**:392

Harmon, William
Jim Harrison **33**:198
James Wright **28**:468
Louis Zukofsky **18**:560

Haro, Robert P.
Piri Thomas **17**:498

Harold, Brent
William Faulkner **11**:199
Vladimir Nabokov **6**:356

Harper, Howard M., Jr.
John Barth **1**:18
Saul Bellow **1**:33
Jerzy Kosinski **1**:172
Vladimir Nabokov **1**:245
Philip Roth **1**:293

Harper, Michael F.
Robert Alter **34**:515
Joyce Carol Oates **33**:297

Harper, Michael S.
Sterling A. Brown **23**:100
Robert Hayden **9**:269; **14**:241; **37**:152
Ntozake Shange **25**:398

Harper, Ralph
Eric Ambler **4**:18

Harper, Robert D.
Wright Morris **18**:349

Harper, Roy
Jimmy Page and Robert Plant **12**:481

Harrell, Don
James A. Michener **29**:316

Harrigan, Brian
Paul Weller **26**:442

Harrington, Curtis
Josef von Sternberg **20**:371

Harrington, Michael
James Merrill **34**:235
Czesław Miłosz **22**:305
Theodore Roethke **3**:433

Harrington, Stephanie
Norman Lear **12**:327, 334
Agnes Eckhardt Nixon **21**:242

Harris, Bertha
Rita Mae Brown **18**:72
John Hawkes **27**:196
Jane Rule **27**:418

Harris, Bruce
John Lennon **35**:261
John Lennon and Paul McCartney **12**:371
Jimmy Page and Robert Plant **12**:475
Carly Simon **26**:406
Neil Young **17**:569

Harris, Helen
Penelope Gilliatt **13**:239
Ian McEwan **13**:371

Harris, Jane Gary
Boris Pasternak **10**:382

Harris, Janet
June Jordan **11**:312

Harris, John
Robertson Davies **25**:134

Harris, Karen
Robin F. Brancato **35**:66
Barbara Corcoran **17**:78
Robert Cormier **30**:85
Barbara Wersba **30**:431

Harris, Karen H.
Betsy Byars **35**:72
Virginia Hamilton **26**:156
Zoa Sherburne **30**:363
Barbara Wersba **30**:432

Harris, Leo
Peter Dickinson **35**:130
Ngaio Marsh **7**:209
Julian Symons **2**:426

Harris, Lis
Truman Capote **3**:100
Amos Oz **11**:429
Grace Paley **4**:392
Georges Simenon **18**:486

Harris, Marie
Marge Piercy **6**:403

Harris, Mark
Roger Angell **26**:33
E. L. Doctorow **18**:125
George Plimpton **36**:352
Mordecai Richler **18**:455
Isaac Bashevis Singer **23**:422

Harris, Michael
Thomas Berger **5**:60
Andre Dubus **13**:183
John Gardner **5**:133

Harris, Norman
Ishmael Reed **32**:356

Harris, Robert R.
John Gardner **28**:163
Cynthia Ozick **28**:349
Grace Paley **37**:334
William Wharton **18**:542
Richard Yates **23**:483

Harris, Wilson
George Lamming **4**:279
V. S. Naipaul **4**:374

Harrison, Barbara F.
Jean Craighead George **35**:178

Harrison, Barbara Grizzuti
Joan Didion **14**:153
Ruth Prawer Jhabvala **4**:257
Iris Murdoch **6**:343
George Plimpton **36**:355
Adrienne Rich **18**:448
Gay Talese **37**:399

Harrison, Bernard
Muriel Spark **18**:502

Harrison, Ed
Bob Seger **35**:382

Harrison, G. B.
Thomas B. Costain **30**:96

Harrison, George
Nevil Shute **30**:369

Harrison, Jim
Barry Hannah **23**:207
Peter Matthiessen **11**:360; **32**:291
Larry McMurtry **2**:272
Farley Mowat **26**:340

Harrison, Joseph G.
Thomas J. Fleming **37**:120
Arthur Koestler **33**:235
Mary Renault **17**:395

Harrison, Keith
Margot Benary-Isbert **12**:34
John Berryman **3**:69
Marge Piercy **14**:422

Harrison, M. J.
Henri Troyat **23**:461

Harrison, M. John
Thomas M. Disch **36**:123

Harrison, Robert
Julian Symons **32**:425

Harrison, Tony
Lorine Niedecker **10**:360

Harron, Mary
Joan Armatrading **17**:10

Harsent, David
Joe Orton **13**:437

Harss, Luis
Jorge Luis Borges **2**:69
Julio Cortázar **2**:101
Gabriel García Márquez **2**:147
Juan Carlos Onetti **7**:276
João Guimarães Rosa **23**:350
Juan Rulfo **8**:461
Mario Vargas Llosa **3**:493

Hart, Elizabeth
August Derleth **31**:128

Hart, Henry
Carlos Saura **20**:314
Billy Wilder **20**:457, 458, 459

Hart, Jane
Carson McCullers **12**:416

Hart, Jeffrey
E. L. Doctorow **6**:136
Robert Frost **15**:243
Allen Ginsberg **36**:199
Ernest Hemingway **34**:478
John Raeburn **34**:478
Auberon Waugh **7**:514

Hart, John E.
Jack Kerouac **3**:264

Hart, Johnny
Charles M. Schulz **12**:527

Hart, Marc
William X. Kienzle **25**:276

Hart-Davis, Rupert
Agatha Christie **12**:114

Harte, Barbara
Janet Frame **3**:164

Harte, Joe
David Dabydeen **34**:150

Hartfelder, William A., Jr.
Elie Wiesel **37**:457

Harth, Erica
Simone de Beauvoir **14**:68

Hartley, Anthony
Ian Fleming **30**:131

Hartley, George
Philip Larkin **5**:230

Hartley, Lodwick
Katherine Anne Porter **13**:446

Hartley, Lois
Raja Rao **25**:366

Hartman, Charles
Shirley Clarke **16**:218

Hartman, Geoffrey
Kenneth Burke **24**:132
Ross Macdonald **2**:257

Hartman, Geoffrey H.
A. R. Ammons **2**:13
Harold Bloom **24**:76
J. V. Cunningham **31**:101
Jacques Derrida **24**:153
Northrop Frye **24**:216
André Malraux **9**:358
Lionel Trilling **24**:457

Hartos, Marsha
Norma Klein **30**:243

Hartshorne, Thomas L.
Kurt Vonnegut, Jr. **22**:444

Hartt, Julian N.
Mary Renault **3**:426

Hartung, Charles V.
Cleanth Brooks **24**:103

Hartung, Philip T.
John Ford **16**:304
Laurence Olivier **20**:238
Gordon Parks **16**:458
Budd Schulberg **7**:402
Rod Serling **30**:354, 357

Harvey, David D.
Herbert Read **4**:440

Harvey, G. M.
John Betjeman **10**:52

Harvey, James
Jonathan Baumbach **23**:53

Harvey, John
F. R. Leavis **24**:313
V. S. Pritchett **15**:442

Harvey, Lawrence E.
Samuel Beckett **9**:80

Harvey, Robert D.
Howard Nemerov **2**:306

Harvey, Stephen
Anita Brookner **32**:60
David Mamet **34**:222

Haskell, Ann S.
D. M. Pinkwater **35**:317

Haskell, Molly
Woody Allen **16**:6
Marguerite Duras **20**:100
Elaine May **16**:434, 436
François Truffaut **20**:397

Haskins, Jim
Pat Conroy **30**:77

Hasley, Louis
Peter De Vries **1**:72
Joseph Heller **5**:173
S. J. Perelman **3**:381
James Thurber **11**:532
E. B. White **10**:526

Critic Index

Hass, Robert
Joseph Brodsky **36**:78
Stephen Dobyns **37**:79
Robert Lowell **9**:336
James Wright **28**:463

Hass, Victor P.
August Derleth **31**:138
Rosa Guy **26**:141
Evan Hunter **31**:220

Hassall, Anthony J.
Randolph Stow **23**:433

Hassan, Ihab
John Barth **2**:36
Samuel Beckett **1**:23
Saul Bellow **1**:29
Thomas Berger **18**:53
André Breton **2**:81
Frederick Buechner **4**:79
William S. Burroughs **2**:91
Truman Capote **1**:55
J. P. Donleavy **1**:75
Ralph Ellison **1**:94
Jean Genet **2**:159
Allen Ginsberg **2**:164
Herbert Gold **4**:190
Ernest Hemingway **3**:237
Norman Mailer **1**:188, 189;
  4:319
Bernard Malamud **1**:195, 196
Carson McCullers **1**:207, 208
Henry Miller **1**:222
Vladimir Nabokov **1**:239
James Purdy **28**:378
Alain Robbe-Grillet **2**:375
J. D. Salinger **1**:296; **3**:446
Nathalie Sarraute **2**:385
Jean Stafford **7**:455
William Styron **1**:330; **11**:514
Kurt Vonnegut, Jr. **12**:610

Hassett, John J.
José Donoso **4**:129

Hassler, Donald M.
Theodore Sturgeon **22**:412

Hatch, James V.
Alice Childress **12**:106

Hatch, Robert
Ralph Bakshi **26**:67
Anne Burr **6**:104
Francis Ford Coppola **16**:234
Shelagh Delaney **29**:145
Rainer Werner Fassbinder
  20:115, 119
Federico Fellini **16**:300
Ian Fleming **30**:134
Larry Gelbart **21**:130
Werner Herzog **16**:326
Alfred Hitchcock **16**:340
Fletcher Knebel **14**:307
George Lucas **16**:412
Nagisa Oshima **20**:257
Pink Floyd **35**:314
Richard Pryor **26**:382
Carlos Saura **20**:317
François Truffaut **20**:408
Orson Welles **20**:439
Lina Wertmüller **16**:597
Frederick Wiseman **20**:467
Richard Wright **21**:436

Hatch, Ronald
David Donnell **34**:159

Hatcher, Harlan
Julia Peterkin **31**:305

Hatcher, Robert D., Jr.
John McPhee **36**:299

Hatfield, H. C.
George Tabori **19**:435

Hatfield, Henry
Günter Grass **2**:173; **22**:189,
  195

Hattersley, Roy
J. B. Priestley **34**:365

Hattman, John W.
Wendell Berry **27**:32

Hauck, Richard Boyd
Kurt Vonnegut, Jr. **5**:465

Haugaard, Kay
Betty Cavanna **12**:102

Haugh, Robert
John Updike **7**:489

Haugh, Robert F.
Nadine Gordimer **18**:184

Hauptman, Ira
John Buell **10**:81

Hauser, Frank
Ogden Nash **23**:322

Hausermann, H. W.
Herbert Read **4**:438, 439

Havard, Robert G.
Jorge Guillén **11**:262

Haverstick, S. Alexander
John Knowles **4**:271

Havighurst, Walter
Allan W. Eckert **17**:105
Edna Ferber **18**:152
James A. Michener **29**:309
William Mitchell **25**:321
Scott O'Dell **30**:268
Betty Smith **19**:423

Haviland, Virginia
E. M. Almedingen **12**:5
Ruth M. Arthur **12**:25
Margot Benary-Isbert **12**:30
Betty Cavanna **12**:100
Mavis Thorpe Clark **12**:130,
  131
Barbara Corcoran **17**:70
Julia W. Cunningham **12**:165
Eilís Dillon **17**:93
Leon Garfield **12**:218
Jean Craighead George **35**:177
Virginia Hamilton **26**:147
Christie Harris **12**:264
Jamake Highwater **12**:287
Margaret O. Hyde **21**:173
Larry Kettelkamp **12**:304
Joseph Krumgold **12**:317
Jean Lee Latham **12**:323
John Neufeld **17**:307
Andre Norton **12**:456, 466
Scott O'Dell **30**:274
Philippa Pearce **21**:288

Josephine Poole **17**:372
Mary Rodgers **12**:494
Zilpha Keatley Snyder **17**:472
Mary Stolz **12**:546, 550, 555
Colin Thiele **17**:494
Jill Paton Walsh **35**:432
Laurence Yep **35**:469

Hawkes, David
Ch'ien Chung-shu **22**:105

Hawkes, John
Djuna Barnes **29**:25
John Barth **10**:21
John Hawkes **15**:277
Flannery O'Connor **1**:254

Hawkes, Terence
David Lodge **36**:274

Hawkins, Desmond
Pamela Hansford Johnson
  27:214

Hawkins, Robert F.
Vittorio De Sica **20**:85

Hawley, Lucy V.
Walter Dean Myers **35**:299
Marilyn Sachs **35**:335

Haworth, David
Bernice Rubens **19**:402
Morris L. West **6**:563

Hay, John
Eleanor Clark **19**:104
Peter Matthiessen **32**:289
John McPhee **36**:295

Hay, Linda
Marian Engel **36**:160

Hay, Samuel A.
Ed Bullins **5**:83

Hay, Sara Henderson
Brewster Ghiselin **23**:169

Hayakawa, S. Ichiyé
E. E. Cummings **12**:144
T. S. Eliot **24**:162

Haycraft, Howard
Agatha Christie **12**:118
August Derleth **31**:137

Hayden, Brad
Richard Brautigan **12**:72

Hayden, Robert
Robert Hayden **37**:150

Hayes, Alfred
Ernesto Sabato **23**:375

Hayes, Brian P.
Joyce Carol Oates **1**:252

Hayes, E. Nelson
J. R. Salamanca **4**:461

Hayes, Harold
Joy Adamson **17**:6

Hayes, Noreen
J.R.R. Tolkien **1**:336

Hayes, Richard
Robert Anderson **23**:28
Sally Benson **17**:50
Paul Bowles **19**:57
Truman Capote **19**:80
William Gibson **23**:176

Nadine Gordimer **33**:178
Fritz Hochwälder **36**:233
Mary McCarthy **24**:342
Clifford Odets **28**:334

Hayes, Sarah
Rosemary Sutcliff **26**:437

Hayman, David
Samuel Beckett **11**:34
Louis-Ferdinand Céline **7**:42

Hayman, Ronald
Alan Ayckbourn **33**:42
Howard Barker **37**:34
Robert Duncan **7**:88
Roy Fisher **25**:158
Robert Frost **4**:174
Allen Ginsberg **6**:198
David Hare **29**:215
Arthur Miller **6**:331
Charles Olson **5**:327
Anne Sexton **4**:482
Peter Shaffer **14**:485
David Storey **5**:414
Charles Tomlinson **4**:544
Tom Wolfe **15**:586

Haynes, Elizabeth
Andre Norton **12**:459

Haynes, Muriel
Shirley Ann Grau **4**:208
Lillian Hellman **4**:222
Thomas Keneally **5**:210

Hays, H. R.
Robert Bloch **33**:82
Edwin Honig **33**:209

Hays, Peter L.
Henry Miller **9**:379

Hayward, Henry S.
James Clavell **25**:127

Hayward, Max
Andrei Voznesensky **1**:349

Hazard, Lucy Lockwood
John G. Neihardt **32**:331

Hazelton, Lesley
Amos Oz **27**:359

Hazo, Samuel
John Berryman **2**:57
Philip Booth **23**:74
Linda Pastan **27**:369
Yannis Ritsos **31**:326

Hazzard, Shirley
Jean Rhys **2**:371
Patrick White **3**:522

Headings, Philip R.
T. S. Eliot **1**:91

Heald, Tim
Brian Moore **19**:333

Healey, James
Catharine Savage Brosman
  9:135
Michael Casey **2**:100
Leonard Cohen **3**:110

Healey, Robert
Thomas J. Fleming **37**:120

Healey, Robert C.
Chinua Achebe **26**:12
Evan Hunter **31**:219
Gregor von Rezzori **25**:381

Healy, Michael
Wilbur Smith **33**:378

Heaney, Seamus
David Jones **7**:187
Paul Muldoon **32**:319

Hearne, Betsy
Virginia Hamilton **26**:157
Robert Lipsyte **21**:212
D. M. Pinkwater **35**:318
Marilyn Sachs **35**:334
Kin Platt **26**:352

Hearne, John
Wilson Harris **25**:205

Hearron, Thomas
Richard Brautigan **5**:68

Heath, Jeffrey M.
Evelyn Waugh **8**:543

Heath, Melville
Howard Fast **23**:156
Bruce Lancaster **36**:244

Heath, Stephen
Nagisa Oshima **20**:251, 252

Heath, Susan
Martin Amis **9**:25
John Hersey **7**:154
Yasunari Kawabata **5**:208
John Knowles **4**:272
Yukio Mishima **6**:337
Anaïs Nin **4**:379
Richard Price **12**:489
V. S. Pritchett **5**:353
Kurt Vonnegut, Jr. **3**:503

Heath, William
Paul Blackburn **9**:100

Hecht, Anthony
Peter Ackroyd **34**:392
W. H. Auden **2**:22
T. S. Eliot **34**:392
Ted Hughes **2**:198
James Merrill **2**:273
Marianne Moore **2**:291
Howard Nemerov **2**:306
L. E. Sissman **9**:489
Richard Wilbur **9**:570

Heck, Francis S.
Marguerite Duras **11**:166

Heckard, Margaret
William H. Gass **8**:244

Heckman, Don
John Lennon and Paul
McCartney **12**:358

Hector, Mary Louise
Margot Benary-Isbert **12**:32, 33
Mary Stolz **12**:552

Hedden, Worth Tuttle
Zora Neale Hurston **30**:214

Heffernan, Michael
Albert Goldbarth **5**:143
Gibbons Ruark **3**:441
Dave Smith **22**:384

Heffernan, Thomas Farel
Robert Newton Peck **17**:339

Heffernan, Tom
Norma Fox Mazer **26**:290

Hegel, Robert E.
Ch'ien Chung-shu **22**:106

Heidenry, John
Agatha Christie **6**:110
Robert M. Pirsig **4**:405

Heifetz, Henry
Bernardo Bertolucci **16**:84

Heilbrun, Carolyn
Nat Hentoff **26**:182

Heilbrun, Carolyn G.
Christopher Isherwood **14**:279
C. P. Snow **19**:428
Noel Streatfeild **21**:407

Heilbut, Anthony
Stanley Elkin **9**:191

Heilman, Robert B.
Edward Albee **5**:11
Max Frisch **3**:168
Harold Pinter **3**:386
Katherine Anne Porter **15**:426
Tennessee Williams **30**:465

Heimberg, Martha
Shirley Hazzard **18**:220
John Updike **15**:547
Tom Wolfe **15**:586

Heims, Neil
Paul Goodman **4**:198

Heinegg, Peter
Morris L. West **33**:431

Heineman, Alan
Janis Ian **21**:183
Pink Floyd **35**:305
Frank Zappa **17**:586

Heiney, Donald
Jean Anouilh **8**:22
Natalia Ginzburg **11**:227
Alberto Moravia **2**:294
Elio Vittorini **9**:546, 548

Heins, Ethel L.
Lloyd Alexander **35**:26, 27
Ruth M. Arthur **12**:24
Betsy Byars **35**:71, 72
Barbara Corcoran **17**:70
Julia W. Cunningham **12**:166
Peter Dickinson **12**:177
Eilís Dillon **17**:97
Lois Duncan **26**:104
Leon Garfield **12**:231
Rosa Guy **26**:141, 144
Virginia Hamilton **26**:157
Isabelle Holland **21**:148
Lee Kingman **17**:246, 247
Joseph Krumgold **12**:318
Norma Fox Mazer **26**:292
Walter Dean Myers **35**:296
Emily Cheney Neville **12**:451
Scott O'Dell **30**:274
Katherine Paterson **12**:487
Marilyn Sachs **35**:333
Zilpha Keatley Snyder **17**:469,
471

Cynthia Voight **30**:420
Laurence Yep **35**:472

Heins, Paul
Lloyd Alexander **35**:25
Frank Bonham **12**:50
Betsy Byars **35**:73
Christopher Collier and James
L. Collier **30**:73
Robert Cormier **12**:136
Julia W. Cunningham **12**:164,
166
Peter Dickinson **12**:171
John Donovan **35**:139, 141
James D. Forman **21**:116
Alan Garner **17**:142
Rosa Guy **26**:143
Kristin Hunter **35**:226
Mollie Hunter **21**:164
Madeleine L'Engle **12**:347
William Mayne **12**:398, 402
Milton Meltzer **26**:303, 308
Nicholasa Mohr **12**:446
Scott O'Dell **30**:268, 271, 278
Katherine Paterson **30**:284
Philippa Pearce **21**:289
Ouida Sebestyen **30**:346
Zilpha Keatley Snyder **17**:471
Colin Thiele **17**:496
Jill Paton Walsh **35**:429
Barbara Wersba **30**:434
Laurence Yep **35**:468

Heiserman, Arthur
J. D. Salinger **12**:496

Held, George
Jim Harrison **33**:198

Heldman, Irma Pascal
Joan Aiken **35**:18
Robert Ludlum **22**:289

Helfgott, Barbara
Sue Ellen Bridgers **26**:90

Helfgott, Barbara Cutler
Marilyn Sachs **35**:336

Helgesen, Sally
Anita Brookner **34**:142

Heller, Amanda
Max Apple **9**:32
C.D.B. Bryan **29**:103
John Cheever **8**:138
Don DeLillo **8**:171
Joan Didion **8**:175
William Gaddis **6**:194
Mary Gordon **13**:249
Mark Helprin **7**:152
Colleen McCullough **27**:319
Leonard Michaels **6**:325
Luisa Valenzuela **31**:436
Fay Weldon **11**:566
Larry Woiwode **6**:579

Heller, Erich
Martin Heidegger **24**:269

Heller, M. Kay
C. S. Adler **35**:12

Heller, Michael
William Bronk **10**:75
Cid Corman **9**:170
George Oppen **7**:284; **13**:434
Charles Reznikoff **9**:449

Hellmann, John
Mick Jagger and Keith Richard
17:226
Hunter S. Thompson **17**:511
Tom Wolfe **35**:460

Helm.
Rod Serling **30**:354

Helm, Thomas E.
Colleen McCullough **27**:322

Helms, Alan
John Ashbery **2**:18
Robert Bly **10**:61
Richard F. Hugo **18**:261
Galway Kinnell **13**:321
Philip Levine **4**:287
William Meredith **13**:373

Helms, Randel
J.R.R. Tolkien **12**:578

Helwig, David
David Donnell **34**:158

Hemenway, Leone R.
Melvin Berger **12**:39

Hemenway, Robert
Zora Neale Hurston **7**:170;
30:219

Hemesath, James B.
Jim Harrison **33**:199

Hemming, John
Bruce Chatwin **28**:72
Thor Heyerdahl **26**:194

Hemmings, F.W.J.
José Donoso **32**:152
Mary Stewart **7**:467

Hemmings, John
J.M.G. Le Clézio **31**:246

Henault, Marie
Peter Viereck **4**:559

Henderson, Alice Corbin
Padraic Colum **28**:85

Henderson, David w.
David Leavitt **34**:78

Henderson, Katherine Usher
Joan Didion **32**:142

Henderson, Stephen E.
Sterling A. Brown **23**:96, 99

Henderson, Tony
Patricia Highsmith **4**:226

Hendin, Josephine
Gail Godwin **31**:195
Joe McGinniss **32**:305

Hendin, Josephine Gattuso
John Barth **3**:42
Donald Barthelme **6**:28
Richard Brautigan **1**:45
William S. Burroughs **5**:92
Janet Frame **2**:142
John Hawkes **15**:276
John Hersey **2**:188
Marjorie Kellogg **2**:224
Robet Kotlowitz **4**:275
Doris Lessing **3**:286
Michael McClure **6**:316

Critic Index

Joyce Carol Oates 6:371; 9:404
Flannery O'Connor 6:375;
13:421; 21:274
Thomas Pynchon 6:436
Hubert Selby, Jr. 1:307; 4:482
Paul Theroux 5:427
John Updike 9:536
Kurt Vonnegut, Jr. 4:569

Hendley, W. Clark
Philip Roth 31:347

Hendrick, George
Mazo de la Roche 14:148
Jack Kerouac 2:227
Katherine Anne Porter 1:273

Hendricks, Flora
Jessamyn West 17:544

Hendricks, Sharon
Melvin Berger 12:42

Henighan, T. J.
Richard Hughes 1:149

Henkel, Wayne J.
John Knowles 4:272

Henkels, Robert
Robert Pinget 37:362

Henkels, Robert M.
Robert Pinget 37:365

Henkels, Robert M., Jr.
Robert Pinget 13:443, 444;
37:360
Raymond Queneau 10:430

Henkin, Bill
Richard O'Brien 17:325

Henniger, Gerd
Francis Ponge 18:416

Henniker-Heaton, Peter
Arthur C. Clarke 35:119

Henninger, Francis J.
Albert Camus 4:93

Henry, Avril
William Golding 10:237

Henry, Gerrit
Russell Edson 13:190
W. S. Merwin 5:287

Henry, Parrish Dice
Samuel Beckett 29:61

Hentoff, Margaret
Paul Zindel 6:586

Hentoff, Margot
Joan Didion 8:174

Hentoff, Nat
Claude Brown 30:34
Lenny Bruce 21:44, 47, 51
Eldridge Cleaver 30:59
Bob Dylan 12:180
Paul Goodman 4:197
Woody Guthrie 35:185
Alex Haley 12:243
Jonathan Kozol 17:250
Robert Lipsyte 21:207
Colin MacInnes 4:314

Henze, Shelly Temchin
Rita Mae Brown 18:74

Hepburn, Neil
Rayner Heppenstall 10:273
Patricia Highsmith 14:260
Mary Hocking 13:285
Ursula Holden 18:257
Thomas Keneally 5:211; 10:299
David Lodge 36:271
Tim O'Brien 7:272
David Plante 7:308
Frederic Raphael 14:437
William Sansom 6:484
Tom Sharpe 36:401
William Trevor 7:477
John Updike 7:489
Elio Vittorini 14:547
Fay Weldon 9:559

Hepner, Arthur
John R. Tunis 12:594

Herbert, Cynthia
Hilma Wolitzer 17:562

Herbert, Kevin
Mary Renault 17:394

Herbert, Rosemary
Piers Anthony 35:35
C. J. Cherryh 35:106
Jack Vance 35:422
Roger Zelazny 21:479

Herbold, Tony
Dannie Abse 7:2
Michael Hamburger 5:159

Herman, Gary
Peter Townshend 17:528

Herman, Gertrude B.
Maia Wojciechowska 26:458

Hermann, John
J. D. Salinger 12:510

Hern, Nicholas
Peter Handke 15:265

Hernández, Ana María
Julio Cortázar 13:162

Hernlund, Patricia
Richard Brautigan 5:67

Herr, Marian
Otfried Preussler 17:374

Herr, Paul
James Purdy 2:347

Herrera, Philip
Daphne du Maurier 6:147

Herrick, Robert
Julia Peterkin 31:303
T. S. Stribling 23:440

Herrick, William
Manuel Puig 28:373

Herring, Reginald
John Gardner 30:152

Herrnstein, R. J.
Carl Sagan 30:334

Herron, Ima Honaker
William Inge 19:228

Hershinow, Sheldon J.
Bernard Malamud 27:295

Hertz, Peter D.
Hermann Hesse 17:212

Hertzel, Leo J.
J. F. Powers 1:281

Herzberger, David K.
Juan Benet 28:15

Herzog, Arthur
Aldous Huxley 35:239

Heseltine, Harry
Frank Dalby Davison 15:170

Hess, John
Botho Strauss 22:407

Hess, Linda
Shiva Naipaul 32:323

Hesse, Eva
Ezra Pound 7:329

Hesseltine, William B.
MacKinlay Kantor 7:194

Hettinga, Donald R.
Tom Robbins 32:367

Hewes, Henry
Edward Albee 2:2; 13:3
Robert Anderson 23:32
Robert Bolt 14:91
Ed Bullins 5:84
Truman Capote 19:81
William Gibson 23:177
Günter Grass 2:173
Jim Jacobs and Warren Casey
12:293
Garson Kanin 22:230
Jean Kerr 22:257
Terrence McNally 7:216
Alan Paton 25:361
David Rabe 4:425
Gerome Ragni and James Rado
17:379
Anthony Shaffer 19:413
Peter Shaffer 5:388
Stephen Sondheim 30:382
Tom Stoppard 4:524
Melvin Van Peebles 2:447
Gore Vidal 2:450
Joseph A. Walker 19:454
Tennessee Williams 2:465

Hewison, Robert
Jeffrey Archer 28:13
Ursula K. Le Guin 22:275

Hewitt, M. R.
Rosa Guy 26:142

Hewitt, Nicholas
Louis-Ferdinand Céline 15:125

Hewitt, Paulo
Prince 35:324
Paul Weller 26:444, 446, 447

Heyen, William
Robert Bly 5:61
Louise Bogan 4:68
John Cheever 3:106
E. E. Cummings 3:118
James Dickey 2:117
Richmond Lattimore 3:278
Denise Levertov 1:177
Hugh MacDiarmid 2:253

Arthur Miller 6:336
Frederick Morgan 23:296
Theodore Roethke 3:433
M. L. Rosenthal 28:393
Anne Sexton 6:491
W. D. Snodgrass 6:513
William Stafford 4:520
Lewis Turco 11:550
John Updike 3:485
Richard Wilbur 3:533
William Carlos Wiliams 2:468

Heymann, Hans G.
Horst Bienek 7:29

Heywood, Christopher
Peter Abrahams 4:1
Nadine Gordimer 33:182

Hibben, Sheila
Zora Neale Hurston 30:211

Hibberd, Dominic
William Mayne 12:406

Hibbett, Howard
Kōbō Abé 22:12

Hichens, Gordon
Shirley Clarke 16:217

Hickey, Dave
B. H. Friedman 7:108

Hickman, Janet
Mollie Hunter 21:169

Hicks, Granville
Louis Auchincloss 4:28, 30;
9:52, 53; 18:24
James Baldwin 2:31
Amiri Baraka 33:52
Peter S. Beagle 7:25
James M. Cain 28:49
Taylor Caldwell 28:60
Truman Capote 19:80
R. V. Cassill 23:102
James Clavell 25:124
James Gould Cozzens 1:66
José Donoso 32:151
Walter D. Edmonds 35:154
Leslie A. Fiedler 24:189
Herbert Gold 4:189
Shirley Ann Grau 4:207
Mark Harris 19:200
Aldous Huxley 35:233, 235
Dan Jacobson 14:290
Elia Kazan 6:273
Ken Kesey 6:277
John Knowles 26:254
Arthur Koestler 33:230, 238
Richard Kostelanetz 28:212
Jonathan Kozol 17:248
Meyer Levin 7:204
Bernard Malamud 1:200;
11:345
Harry Mathews 6:314
Czesław Miłosz 22:305
Wright Morris 37:310
Flannery O'Connor 1:258
Grace Paley 37:331
Katherine Ann Porter 7:312
Reynolds Price 3:404, 405
Ann Quin 6:442
Ayn Rand 30:294
Mary Renault 17:397
Conrad Richter 30:322

J. D. Salinger **12**:502
Upton Sinclair **15**:499
Robert Stone **23**:424
Randolph Stow **23**:432
John Updike **23**:463
Kurt Vonnegut, Jr. **2**:451;
  12:602
Auberon Waugh **7**:514
Eudora Welty **14**:561
Glenway Wescott **13**:590
Herman Wouk **1**:376
Richard Wright **21**:435, 440

Hicks, Lorne
Patrick Lane **25**:284

Hieatt, Constance B.
John Fowles **15**:231

Hiesberger, Jean Marie
Charles M. Schulz **12**:533

Higgins, Bertram
Fritz Lang **20**:200

Higgins, James
Jonathan Kozol **17**:255

Higgins, R. A.
Peter Gent **29**:182

Higham, Charles
Alfred Hitchcock **16**:342
Andrzej Wajda **16**:578
Orson Welles **20**:443

Highet, Gilbert
Henry Miller **1**:224
Ezra Pound **1**:276

Highsmith, Patricia
Georges Simenon **2**:398

Highwater, Jamake Mamake
Joan Armatrading **17**:7

Hilburn, Robert
Chuck Berry **17**:54
Waylon Jennings **21**:200

Hildick, Wallace
William Mayne **12**:390

Hiley, Jim
Peter Nichols **36**:332

Hill, Art
Roger Angell **26**:32

Hill, Donald L.
Richard Wilbur **3**:530

Hill, Douglas
Margaret Atwood **25**:61
Joan Barfoot **18**:35
John Gardner **28**:161
Michel Tremblay **29**:423

Hill, Eldon C.
Helen Hooven Santmyer **33**:357

Hill, Frances
Penelope Lively **32**:276

Hill, Frank Ernest
Erich Maria Remarque **21**:325
Carl Sandburg **35**:345

Hill, Gladwin
John Gregory Dunne **28**:121

Hill, Helen G.
Norman Mailer **4**:321

Hill, Michael
Prince **35**:327

Hill, Reginald
John Gardner **30**:157
John le Carré **28**:228
Morris L. West **33**:434

Hill, Robert W.
Laurence Lieberman **36**:262

Hill, Susan
Maureen Duffy **37**:115
Penelope Lively **32**:273
Daphne du Maurier **6**:146
Bruce Springsteen **17**:486
Paul Theroux **28**:424

Hill, William B.
Peter De Vries **10**:137
Bruce Lancaster **36**:245

Hill, William B., S.J.
Taylor Caldwell **28**:65
Robert Cormier **12**:133
Paul Gallico **2**:147
Evan Hunter **31**:222
Bernard Malamud **5**:269
Anthony Powell **10**:417
Muriel Spark **2**:418

Hilliard, Stephen S.
Philip Larkin **9**:323

Hillier, Bevis
John Betjeman **34**:312

Hillman, Martin
Len Deighton **22**:118

Hills, Rust
Joy Williams **31**:461

Hillyer, Robert
Siegfried Sassoon **36**:388

Hilton, James
C. S. Forester **35**:169
Jan de Hartog **19**:130
Nevil Shute **30**:368

Hilton, Robert M.
Henry Gregor Felsen **17**:124

Hilty, Hans Rudolf
Odysseus, Elytis **15**:218

Himes, Geoffrey
Seger, Bob **35**:385

Himmelblau, Jack
Miguel Ángel Asturias **8**:25

Hinchcliffe, P. M.
Ethel Davis Wilson **13**:610

Hinchliffe, Arnold P.
John Arden **13**:28
Edward Bond **6**:86
T. S. Eliot **13**:195
Harold Pinter **1**:267

Hinden, Michael
John Barth **3**:41

Hindus, Milton
Louis-Ferdinand Céline **1**:56;
  15:122
Isaac Bashevis Singer **23**:413

Hinerfeld, Susan Slocum
Harriet Doerr **34**:152

Hines, Theodore C.
Isaac Asimov **26**:37

Hingley, Ronald
Anna Akhmatova **25**:30
Aleksandr I. Solzhenitsyn
  1:319; **4**:515; **7**:445
Andrei Voznesensky **1**:349

Hinkemeyer, Joan
John Jakes **29**:249

Hinman, Myra
D. J. Enright **31**:150

Hinton, David B.
Leni Riefenstahl **16**:525

Hinz, Evelyn J.
Doris Lessing **6**:293
Anaïs Nin **1**:248; **4**:377

Hipkiss, Robert A.
Ernest Hemingway **3**:242
Jack Kerouac **29**:269

Hippisley, Anthony
Yuri Olesha **8**:433

Hirsch, Corinne
Isabelle Holland **21**:151

Hirsch, Edward
Robert Hayden **37**:159
Geoffrey Hill **8**:296
Isaac Bashevis Singer **11**:499
Charles Tomlinson **13**:546
James Wright **28**:467
Paul Zweig **34**:379

Hirsch, Foster
Federico Fellini **16**:295
Ernest Hemingway **1**:144
Mary McCarthy **3**:328
Laurence Olivier **20**:242
Tennessee Williams **5**:505;
  19:471

Hirt, Andrew J.
Rod McKuen **3**:332

Hislop, Alan
Richard Elman **19**:150
Jerzy Kosinski **2**:233
Wright Morris **3**:344
Frederic Prokosch **4**:422

Hislop, Ian
Fay Weldon **36**:447

Hiss, Tony
Patti Smith **12**:536

Hitchcock, George
Diane Wakoski **7**:503

Hitchcock, James
Andrew M. Greeley **28**:173

Hitchens, Gordon
Vittorio De Sica **20**:91
Orson Welles **20**:437

Hitrec, Joseph
Ivo Andrić **8**:19

Hjortsberg, William
Angela Carter **5**:101
Rosalyn Drexler **2**:120
Steven Millhauser **21**:215

Hoag, David G.
Melvin Berger **12**:40
Franklyn M. Branley **21**:18, 19,
  20, 22
Roy A. Gallant **17**:132

Hoagland, Edward
Roger Angell **26**:31
Erskine Caldwell **8**:123
Peter Matthiessen **11**:359
Joe McGinniss **32**:302
John McPhee **36**:295, 296
V. S. Naipaul **37**:328
William Saroyan **8**:468; **10**:454
Kurt Vonnegut, Jr. **22**:449

Hoare, Ian
Smokey Robinson **21**:346

Hoban, Russell
Leon Garfield **12**:232
William Mayne **12**:403

Hobbs, Glenda
Harriette Arnow **18**:14, 16

Hobbs, John
Galway Kinnell **13**:318

Hobbs, Mary
Gunnel Beckman **26**:88

Hoberman, J.
Jean-Luc Godard **20**:155
Georg Lukács **24**:338
Nagisa Oshima **20**:256
Pier Paolo Pasolini **20**:270
Satyajit Ray **16**:495
Martin Scorsese **20**:333

Hobsbaum, Philip
F. R. Leavis **24**:308
Sylvia Plath **17**:353

Hobson, Harold
Alan Ayckbourn **33**:47
Howard Brenton **31**:58, 66
Caryl Churchill **31**:82
Michael Frayn **31**:192
Christopher Fry **14**:188
Simon Gray **14**:215; **36**:205
Peter Nichols **36**:327
Edna O'Brien **36**:335

Hobson, Laura Z.
Norman Lear **12**:327
Joyce Carol Oates **33**:286

Hobson, Wilder
Evan Hunter **31**:219

Hochman, Baruch
S. Y. Agnon **4**:12
Isaac Bashevis Singer **1**:312

Hodgart, Matthew
Kingsley Amis **5**:23
Heinrich Böll **27**:60
V. S. Pritchett **5**:353
J.R.R. Tolkien **12**:568

Hodgart, Patricia
Paul Bowles **2**:78

Hodgens, Richard
John W. Campbell **32**:77

Hodges, Elizabeth
Rosemary Sutcliff **26**:426

Hodgkin, Thomas
C.L.R. James **33**:221

Hodgson, Maria
Dirk Bogarde **19**:42

Hoeksema, Thomas
Ishmael Reed **3**:424

Hoellering, Franz
Alfred Hitchcock **16**:338

Hoerchner, Susan
Denise Levertov **5**:247

Hofeldt, Roger L.
Larry Gelbart **21**:129

Hoffa, William Walter
Ezra Pound **2**:343

Hoffman, Barbara
Nora Ephron **17**:112

Hoffman, Charles W.
Max Frisch **32**:188

Hoffman, Daniel
A. R. Ammons **2**:11
W. H. Auden **2**:25
Richard Eberhart **3**:133, 134
Ted Hughes **2**:198
Robert Lowell **2**:247
Carl Sandburg **15**:468
Robin Skelton **13**:507
Anne Stevenson **33**:380
Julian Symons **32**:426

Hoffman, Eva
Marguerite Duras **34**:162
Tadeusz Konwicki **28**:208
Anne Tyler **18**:529

Hoffman, Frederick J.
Conrad Aiken **1**:2
James Baldwin **1**:15
Samuel Beckett **1**:21
Saul Bellow **1**:30
John Dos Passos **1**:79
Jaes T. Farrell **4**:157
William Faulkner **1**:100
John Hawkes **4**:212
Ernest Hemingway **1**:142
Aldous Huxley **11**:281
Flannery O'Connor **15**:410
Katherine Anne Porter **1**:272
Theodore Roethke **3**:434
Philip Roth **4**:451
John Steinbeck **1**:325
William Styron **15**:524
Robert Penn Warren **1**:353

Hoffman, Lyla
James D. Forman **21**:123
Milton Meltzer **26**:304, 306

Hoffman, Michael J.
Henry Miller **1**:224

Hoffman, Nancy Y.
Anaïs Nin **4**:380
Flannery O'Connor **3**:369

Hoffman, Roy
Mary Stewart **35**:376

Hoffman, Stanley
Paul Zindel **26**:475

Hoffman, Stanton
John Rechy **14**:443

Hoffman, Valerie
Thomas J. Fleming **37**:127

Hofmann, Michael
Elizabeth Bishop **32**:43

Hofstadter, Marc
Yves Bonnefoy **15**:73

Hogan, Charles A.
Jonathan Schell **35**:362

Hogan, Lesley
Leon Rooke **25**:392

Hogan, Paula
Margaret O. Hyde **21**:178

Hogan, Randolph
Larry Kettelkamp **12**:305

Hogan, Randy
Donald E. Westlake **33**:439

Hogan, Richard
Kris Kristofferson **26**:269
Paul Weller **26**:445

Hogan, Robert
Paul Vincent Carroll **10**:97
Hugh Leonard **19**:280
Arthur Miller **1**:216
Elmer Rice **7**:361

Hogan, William
Jessamyn West **17**:548

Hoggart, Richard
W. H. Auden **1**:9
Graham Greene **6**:217
Carolyn G. Heilbrun **25**:252

Hokenson, Jan
Louis-Ferdinand Céline **9**:152

Holahan, Susan
Frank O'Hara **5**:324

Holbert, Cornelia
Kenzaburō Ōe **10**:373

Holberton, Paul
Mary Renault **17**:401

Holbrook, Stewart
Woody Guthrie **35**:182

Holden, Anthony
Rayner Heppenstall **10**:272
Daniel Hoffman **13**:286

Holden, David
Piers Paul Read **4**:445

Holden, Jonathan
John Ashbery **15**:30
Stephen Dunn **36**:156
Nancy Willard **7**:540

Holden, Raymond
Carl Sandburg **35**:342

Holden, Stephen
Jackson Browne **21**:35
Neil Diamond **30**:112, 114
Bob Dylan **12**:191
Marvin Gaye **26**:133
Janis Ian **21**:187
Billy Joel **26**:213, 222
Kris Kristofferson **26**:268
John Lennon and Paul
    McCartney **12**:372

Gordon Lightfoot **26**:279, 280
Paul McCartney **35**:284, 288,
    290
Joni Mitchell **12**:438
Van Morrison **21**:234
Martin Mull **17**:298
Laura Nyro **17**:319
The Police **26**:366
Prince **35**:326
Lou Reed **21**:304
Smokey Robinson **21**:349, 351
Buffy Sainte-Marie **17**:431
Carly Simon **26**:408, 409, 412
Paul Simon **17**:463, 464, 467
Patti Smith **12**:535
Elizabeth Swados **12**:561
Lily Tomlin **17**:522
Neil Young **17**:572

Holder, Alan
Robert Lowell **5**:256

Holder, Stephen C.
John Brunner **8**:107

Holditch, W. Kenneth
Tennessee Williams **19**:471

Holland, Bette
Eleanor Clark **5**:106

Holland, Isabelle
Isabelle Holland **21**:148, 154

Holland, Jack
Derek Mahon **27**:292

Holland, Laurence B.
Wright Morris **18**:353

Holland, Mary
Tom Paulin **37**:355

Holland, Norman N.
Federico Fellini **16**:272
Stanley Kubrick **16**:377
Alain Resnais **16**:497

Holland, Philip
Leon Garfield **12**:236

Holland, Robert
Elizabeth Bishop **13**:95
Marilyn Hacker **9**:258
Richard F. Hugo **18**:263
Cynthia Macdonald **13**:356
David Slavitt **14**:491
James Welch **14**:559

Hollander, Deborah
Norma Klein **30**:242

Hollander, John
A. R. Ammons **2**:12
Howard Moss **7**:247
S. J. Perelman **15**:419

Hollindale, Peter
Mollie Hunter **21**:164

Hollinghurst, Alan
William Boyd **28**:37
Brigid Brophy **29**:98
Donald Justice **19**:236
Paul Muldoon **32**:320
Paul Theroux **28**:425
Michel Tournier **23**:455
Gore Vidal **22**:439
Edmund White III **27**:482

Hollington, Michael
Günter Grass **11**:250; **32**:199

Hollingworth, Roy
Ray Davies **21**:92
Neil Diamond **30**:111
Jim Jacobs and Warren Casey
    12:295
John Lennon **35**:263
Andrew Lloyd Webber and Tim
    Rice **21**:428
Pink Floyd **35**:306

Hollis, Christopher
Evelyn Waugh **19**:461

Hollis, James R.
Harold Pinter **11**:439

Hollo, Anselm
Paavo Haavikko **34**:168

Holloway, John
Northrop Frye **24**:211

Hollowell, John
Truman Capote **19**:82

Holman, C. Hugh
John P. Marquand **10**:328
Robert Penn Warren **4**:576

Holmes, Carol
Joseph McElroy **5**:279

Holmes, Charles M.
Aldous Huxley **11**:283

Holmes, Charles S.
James Thurber **5**:439, 441

Holmes, Deborah A.
Marshall McLuhan **37**:256

Holmes, H. H.
Isaac Asimov **26**:36
Roy A. Gallant **17**:126
Robert A. Heinlein **26**:161
Fritz Leiber **25**:301
Andre Norton **12**:456
Jack Williamson **29**:450
John Wyndham **19**:474

Holmes, John
August Derleth **31**:137
M. L. Rosenthal **28**:389

Holmes, John Clellon
Jack Kerouac **2**:227

Holmes, Kay
Emma Lathen **2**:236

Holmstrom, Lakshmi
R. K. Narayan **28**:296

Holroyd, Michael
William Gerhardie **5**:139

Holsaert, Eunice
Madeleine L'Engle **12**:344

Holt, John
Jonathan Kozol **17**:249

Holte, James Craig
Ralph Bakshi **26**:74

Holtz, William
Joseph Wood Krutch **24**:289

Holtze, Sally Holmes
Sue Ellen Bridges **26**:90
Sonia Levitin **17**:266
Mildred D. Taylor **21**:419
Paul Zindel **26**:478

Holzapfel, Tamara
Ernesto Sabato **23**:377

Holzhauer, Jean
Jean Kerr **22**:256

Holzinger, Walter
Pablo Neruda **9**:396

Homan, Richard L.
David Rabe **33**:341

Homann, Frederick A., S.J.
Elie Wiesel **37**:456

Homberger, Eric
Kurt Vonnegut, Jr. **22**:446

Honig, Edwin
Edmund Wilson **24**:475

Hood, Eric
Rosemary Sutcliff **26**:426

Hood, Robert
James D. Forman **21**:118
Jean Craighead George **35**:175
Emily Cheney Neville **12**:449

Hood, Stuart
Josef Škvorecký **15**:510
Aleksandr I. Solzhenitsyn **1**:319

Hook, Sidney
Eric Bentley **24**:44
David Caute **29**:120
Martin Heidegger **24**:257

Hooks, Wayne
Piers Anthony **35**:40

Hooper, William Bradley
Barry Gifford **34**:458
Norma Klein **30**:243
Lawrence Lee **34**:458
Paule Marshall **27**:314
William McPherson **34**:85
Gloria Naylor **28**:304
Barbara Pym **37**:367
William Saroyan **34**:458
Wilbur Smith **33**:378

Hoops, Jonathan
Ingmar Bergman **16**:58
Agnès Varda **16**:558

Hope, Christopher
Nadine Gordimer **5**:147; **18**:187
Paul Muldoon **32**:318
V. S. Naipaul **18**:361
Louis Simpson **9**:486
Derek Walcott **9**:556

Hope, Francis
D. J. Enright **31**:147
John Gardner **30**:151
Norman MacCaig **36**:282
Mary McCarthy **24**:346
Sylvia Plath **17**:345
Frank Tuohy **37**:427

Hope, Mary
Richard Brautigan **12**:74
André Brink **36**:70
Brigid Brophy **11**:68
Bruce Chatwin **28**:72
Eilís Dillon **17**:100
Martha Gellhorn **14**:195
James Hanley **13**:261
Benedict Kiely **23**:265
Tom Sharpe **36**:402
Fay Weldon **11**:566

Hope-Wallace, Philip
Orson Welles **20**:433

Hopkins, Crale D.
Lawrence Ferlinghetti **10**:174

Hopkins, Elaine R.
Michel Tremblay **29**:427

Hopkins, J.G.E.
Maureen Daly **17**:87

Hopkins, Jerry
Jim Morrison **17**:288

Hopkins, Thomas
Jean M. Auel **31**:23

Hopkinson, Shirley L.
E. M. Almedingen **12**:3

Horak, Jan-Christopher
Werner Herzog **16**:330

Horchler, Richard
Arthur A. Cohen **31**:93
John Neufeld **17**:307
James Purdy **28**:378
Frank Tuohy **37**:426

Horgan, John
Tom Paulin **37**:356

Horia, Vintila
Mircea Eliade **19**:144

Horn, Carole
Caroline Blackwood **6**:80

Horn, Richard
Henry Green **13**:253

Hornak, Paul T.
G. Cabrera Infante **25**:104
Colin Wilson **14**:585

Horne, Philip
Ann Schlee **35**:374
Lisa St. Aubin de Teran **36**:420

Horner, Patrick J.
Randall Jarrell **13**:303

Hornyansky, Michael
F. R. Scott **22**:376

Horovitz, Carolyn
Esther Forbes **12**:210
Joseph Krumgold **12**:318
Madeleine L'Engle **12**:347
Rosemary Sutcliff **26**:428

Horowitz, Michael
Jack Kerouac **5**:214

Horowitz, Susan
Ann Beattie **8**:54

Horton, Andrew
James Welch **14**:560

Horton, Andrew S.
Ken Kesey **6**:278
John Updike **7**:487

Horvath, Violet M.
André Malraux **4**:332

Horwich, Richard
John McPhee **36**:296

Horwitz, Carey
Donald Barthelme **23**:47

Horwood, Harold
E. J. Pratt **19**:377

Hosek, Chaviva
Marilyn R. Bowering **32**:47

Hosking, Geoffrey
Aleksandr I. Solzhenitsyn
  18:499
Vladimir Voinovich **10**:507
Alexander Zinoviev **19**:488

Hoskins, Cathleen
Leon Rooke **25**:394

Hough, Graham
Alan Paton **25**:362
John Crowe Ransom **24**:365

Hough, Lynn Harold
Joseph Wood Krutch **24**:281

Hough, Marianne
Zoa Sherburne **30**:362

Hough, Raymond L.
Erich von Däniken **30**:423

House, John
Evan Hunter **31**:229
Tom Robbins **32**:374

Houston, Beverle
Bernardo Bertolucci **16**:92
John Cassavetes **20**:50
Roman Polanski **16**:466

Houston, James
Jean Craighead George **35**:177

Houston, Penelope
Michelangelo Antonioni **20**:23.
  29
Charles Chaplin **16**:197
Paddy Chayefsky **23**:115
John Ford **16**:308
Alfred Hitchcock **16**:341, 342,
  344
Elia Kazan **16**:362
Buster Keaton **20**:189, 193
Richard Lester **20**:223
Laurence Olivier **20**:239
Satyajit Ray **16**:480
Alain Resnais **16**:498
Eric Rohmer **16**:528
Orson Welles **20**:434, 435
Billy Wilder **20**:456

Houston, Robert
Raymond Carver **22**:103
Luis Rafael Sánchez **23**:385
Mary Lee Settle **19**:411

Houston, Stan
Isaac Bashevis Singer **15**:509

Howard, Anthony
Joe McGinniss **32**:300

Howard, Ben
Michael Benedikt **14**:81
Ed Dorn **18**:129
Loren Eiseley **7**:92
Marilyn Hacker **5**:155
Ted Hughes **37**:172
F. T. Prince **22**:339
Anne Sexton **6**:494
John Wain **15**:560

Howard, Elizabeth J.
John Gardner **30**:151

Howard, Esther
Edmund Crispin **22**:109

Howard, Ivor
Larry Gelbart **21**:125

Howard, Jane
C.D.B. Bryan **29**:102
Maxine Kumin **5**:222
Margaret Mead **37**:279

Howard, Joseph Kinsey
A. B. Guthrie, Jr. **23**:196

Howard, Lawrence A.
Robert Newton Peck **17**:340

Howard, Leon
Wright Morris **1**:232

Howard, Lillie P.
Zora Neale Hurston **30**:225

Howard, Maureen
Donald Barthelme **8**:50
Samuel Beckett **11**:43
Jorge Luis Borges **1**:38
Paul Bowles **2**:79
Isak Dinesen **10**:150
Margaret Drabble **2**:117;
  10:163, 165
Eva Figes **31**:170
Mary Gordon **13**:249
Peter Handke **8**:261
Lillian Hellman **8**:281
P. D. James **18**:275
Doris Lessing **6**:301
Toni Morrison **10**:356
Joyce Carol Oates **15**:402
Philip Roth **1**:292
Isaac Bashevis Singer **11**:502
Paul Theroux **15**:533
John Updike **9**:537
Kurt Vonnegut, Jr. **1**:347
Eudora Welty **22**:458
Tennessee Williams **1**:369

Howard, Michael
Len Deighton **22**:116
Evelyn Waugh **27**:474

Howard, Philip
Douglas Adams **27**:12

Howard, Richard
Walter Abish **22**:16
A. R. Ammons **2**:12; **5**:24
John Ashbery **2**:17, 18; **13**:30
W. H. Auden **2**:26; **3**:23
Imamu Amiri Baraka **10**:18
Donald Barthelme **13**:61
Roland Barthes **24**:28
Marvin Bell **8**:67
Frank Bidart **33**:73
Robert Bly **5**:61

Critic Index

Millen Brand **7**:29
Amy Clampitt **32**:116
Alfred Corn **33**:114
Gregory Corso **1**:63
Robert Creeley **15**:150
James Dickey **7**:79
Norman Dubie **36**:129
Irving Feldman **7**:102
Michel Foucault **31**:176
Louise Glück **22**:173
Paul Goodman **7**:128
Daryl Hine **15**:281
Daniel Hoffman **6**:244; **23**:238
John Hollander **5**:185
Richard F. Hugo **32**:235
Uwe Johnson **5**:201
Alfred Kazin **34**:558
Galway Kinnell **5**:215
Kenneth Koch **5**:219
Denise Levertov **5**:245
Philip Levine **5**:251
John Logan **5**:252, 254
William Meredith **4**:348;
   13:372; **22**:301
James Merrill **2**:274
W. S. Merwin **2**:277; **5**:284
Howard Moss **7**:249
Frank O'Hara **5**:323
Sylvia Plath **5**:338
Katha Pollitt **28**:367
Adrienne Rich **3**:428
Raphael Rudnik **7**:384
Gary Snyder **5**:393
William Stafford **7**:460
Mark Strand **18**:515
Jun'ichirō Tanizaki **28**:420
Allen Tate **4**:538
Peter Taylor **18**:523, 524
Mona Van Duyn **3**:491
David Wagoner **5**:473
Robert Penn Warren **6**:557
Theodore Weiss **3**:516
C. K. Williams **33**:441
James Wright **5**:518; **10**:547
Vassily S. Yanovsky **2**:485

Howard, Thomas
Frederick Buechner **2**:82

Howarth, David
Gavin Ewart **13**:209

Howarth, R. G.
Frank Dalby Davison **15**:170

Howarth, William
Jackson J. Benson **34**:406
John Steinbeck **34**:406

Howe, Fanny
Laura Jensen **37**:187
Clarence Major **19**:299

Howe, Irving
James Baldwin **3**:31; **17**:21
Jurek Becker **19**:36
Saul Bellow **3**:49, 60; **8**:79
Raymond Carver **36**:100
Louis-Ferdinand Céline **3**:101
James Gould Cozzens **4**:111
Ralph Ellison **3**:141
William Faulkner **3**:151
Leslie A. Fiedler **24**:190
Paula Fox **2**:139
Robert Frost **3**:170

Daniel Fuchs **8**:221; **22**:155,
  156
Henry Green **13**:252
James Hanley **8**:265
Ernest Hemingway **3**:232
Arthur Koestler **15**:312
György Konrád **4**:273
Jerzy Kosinski **1**:171
Primo Levi **37**:228
Georg Lukács **24**:337
Norman Mailer **3**:311
Bernard Malamud **8**:376
Czesław Miłosz **22**:311
Octavio Paz **3**:377
Sylvia Plath **1**:270; **3**:391
Ezra Pound **2**:344
V. S. Pritchett **13**:467
Philip Rahv **24**:360
Ishmael Reed **13**:477
Philip Roth **2**:380; **3**:440
Delmore Schwartz **10**:466
Varlam Shalamov **18**:479
Ignazio Silone **4**:492, 494
Isaac Bashevis Singer **1**:311;
  23:413
Lionel Trilling **9**:533
Edmund Wilson **3**:538; **24**:489
Richard Wright **3**:545; **9**:585;
  21:437

Howe, Parkman
Jim Harrison **14**:235

Howe, Russell Warren
Alex Haley **12**:247

Howell, Christopher
Harry Martinson **14**:356

Howell, Elmo
Flannery O'Connor **3**:369
Eudora Welty **22**:456

Howell, Margaret C.
C. S. Adler **35**:14

Howes, Victor
Rosellen Brown **32**:66
Peter Davison **28**:100
Howard Fast **23**:159
Robert Francis **15**:236
Joanne Greenberg **30**:163
Kenneth Rexroth **22**:349
Muriel Rukeyser **15**:457
May Swenson **14**:521
James Tate **25**:427

Howlett, Ivan
John Osborne **5**:333

Howley, Edith C.
Isabelle Holland **21**:147
Robert Newton Peck **17**:338

Howley, Veronica
Barbara Corcoran **17**:76

Hoy, David
Jacques Derrida **24**:155
Michel Foucault **34**:342

Hoy, David Couzens
Lucien Goldmann **24**:251

Hoyem, Andrew
Larry Eigner **9**:180

Hoyenga, Betty
Kay Boyle **1**:42

Hoyt, Charles Alva
Bernard Malamud **1**:196
Muriel Spark **2**:414
Edward Lewis Wallant **5**:477

Hubbard, Henry W.
Roy A. Gallant **17**:128

Hubbell, Albert
Farley Mowat **26**:329

Hubbell, Jay B.
John Hall Wheelock **14**:570

Hubert, Renée Riese
André Breton **2**:80
Alain Robbe-Grillet **4**:449
Nathalie Sarraute **4**:470

Hubin, Allen J.
Michael Crichton **6**:119
Edmund Crispin **22**:110
Peter Dickinson **12**:168, 169
John Gardner **30**:152
Harry Kemelman **2**:225
Ruth Rendell **28**:383
Julian Symons **14**:523
Donald E. Westlake **33**:436

Huck, Charlotte S.
Julia W. Cunningham **12**:164
Joseph Krumgold **12**:320

Huck, Janet
Prince **35**:331

Hudacs, Martin J.
William Caunitz **34**:36
Nicholas M. Guild **33**:189

Huddy, Mrs. D.
Eilís Dillon **17**:98

Hudnall, Clayton
Peter Ackroyd **34**:402
T. S. Eliot **34**:402

Hudson, Charles
Wendell Berry **27**:38

Hudson, Christopher
John Montague **13**:390

Hudson, Liam
William H. Gass **15**:256

Hudson, Peggy
Earl Hamner, Jr. **12**:259
Norman Lear **12**:330

Hudson, Theodore R.
Imamu Amiri Baraka **14**:44
Langston Hughes **35**:218

Hudzik, Robert
Laura Jensen **37**:191

Huebner, Theodore
Anna Seghers **7**:408

Huff, Theodore
Charles Chaplin **16**:194

Huffman, James R.
Andrew Lloyd Webber and Tim
  Rice **21**:427

Huggins, Nathan Irvin
Arna Bontemps **18**:65
Carl Van Vechten **33**:399

Hugh-Jones, Stephen
Len Deighton **22**:114

Hughes, Carl Milton
Chester Himes **4**:229
Willard Motley **18**:355
Ann Petry **1**:266
Richard Wright **1**:377
Frank G. Yerby **1**:381

Hughes, Catharine
Edward Albee **2**:3; **9**:6
Robert Anderson **23**:33
Samuel Beckett **2**:47
Daniel J. Berrigan **4**:57
Ed Bullins **5**:82
D. L. Coburn **10**:108
Allen Ginsberg **2**:164
Charles Gordone **4**:199
Rolf Hochhuth **4**:232
Albert Innaurato **21**:192
James Kirkwood **9**:320
Carson McCullers **12**:419
Mark Medoff **6**:323
David Rabe **4**:427
Robert Shaw **5**:391
Sam Shepard **17**:438; **34**:270
Neil Simon **11**:496
Milan Stitt **29**:390
Tom Stoppard **34**:281
Megan Terry **19**:439
Michael Weller **10**:526
Tennessee Williams **2**:466;
  5:502
Lanford Wilson **14**:590

Hughes, Catharine R.
Anthony Shaffer **19**:413
Megan Terry **19**:440
Douglas Turner Ward **19**:457

Hughes, D. J.
Edwin Honig **33**:211

Hughes, Daniel
John Berryman **3**:70

Hughes, David
Gabriel García Márquez **27**:152

Hughes, Dorothy B.
John Gardner **30**:152
Mary Stewart **35**:391
Donald E. Westlake **7**:528

Hughes, Douglas A.
Elizabeth Bowen **15**:77

Hughes, H. Stuart
David Caute **29**:120
Primo Levi **37**:225

Hughes-Hallett, Lucy
Elizabeth Taylor **29**:411

Hughes, James
Louis Auchincloss **9**:53

Hughes, John W.
Dannie Abse **7**:1
Joy Adamson **17**:4
John Ashbery **2**:17
W. H. Auden **2**:26
John Ciardi **10**:106

Hughes, Langston
James Baldwin **17**:21

Hughes, Olga R.
Boris Pasternak **7**:297

Hughes, R. E.
Graham Greene **1**:131

Hughes, Riley
Taylor Caldwell **28**:60, 62
Robert Cormier **12**:133
Ernest K. Gann **23**:164
Evan Hunter **31**:219

Hughes, Robert
Elia Kazan **16**:363

Hughes, Roger
Monty Python **21**:226

Hughes, Serge
Dino Buzzati **36**:85

Hughes, Ted
Joy Adamson **17**:3
Yehuda Amichai **22**:30
Leon Garfield **12**:219
Sylvia Plath **1**:270
Clancy Sigal **7**:423
Isaac Bashevis Singer **15**:503

Hughes-Hallett, Lucy
Thomas Keneally **14**:302
Bernard Slade **11**:508

Hughson, Lois
John Dos Passos **4**:136

Hugo, Richard
Theodore Roethke **8**:458

Hulbert, Ann
Ann Beattie **13**:65
André Brink **36**:72
Rosellen Brown **32**:68
John Cheever **25**:120
Eleanor Clark **19**:107
Joan Didion **14**:152
Harriet Doerr **34**:154
Mavis Gallant **18**:172
Molly Keane **31**:235
Patrick White **18**:548

Hulbert, Debra
Diane Wakoski **4**:572

Hulcoop, John
Phyllis Webb **18**:540

Hull, Elizabeth Anne
Robert Heinlein **14**:254

Hull, Robert A.
Lou Reed **21**:321

Hull, Robot A.
David Byrne **26**:98
Lou Reed **21**:305
Smokey Robinson **21**:350

Hulse, Michael
Roy Fisher **25**:161
Craig Raine **32**:351
Christopher Reid **33**:351

Hume, Kathryn
C. S. Lewis **6**:308

Humes, Walter M.
Robert Cormier **12**:137

Hummer, T. R.
Louis Simpson **32**:382

Humphrey, Robert
William Faulkner **1**:98

Humphreys, Hubert
Jules Archer **12**:19

Humphries, Patrick
The Clash **30**:47
Pink Floyd **35**:313

Humphries, Rolfe
Langston Hughes **35**:214

Hungerford, Alice N.
John Donovan **35**:139
Henry Gregor Felsen **17**:122,
123

Hungerford, Edward B.
Robert Lipsyte **21**:207

Hunt, Albert
John Arden **6**:5

Hunt, David
Lillian Hellman **14**:257

Hunt, George W., S. J.
John Updike **15**:543

Hunt, Peter
Peter Dickinson **12**:176
Leon Garfield **12**:233
William Mayne **12**:406

Hunt, Tim
Jack Kerouac **29**:273

Hunter, Evan
William F. Buckley, Jr. **37**:60
Allen Drury **37**:111
John Gregory Dunne **28**:125
George V. Higgins **18**:234
Peter Maas **29**:306
Irwin Shaw **23**:401
Leon Uris **32**:436

Hunter, Jim
Anne Tyler **11**:552

Hunter, Kristin
Ann Beattie **8**:55
Virginia Hamilton **26**:152
Ouida Sebestyen **30**:345

Hunter, Mollie
Mollie Hunter **21**:161

Hunter, Tim
Stanley Kubrick **16**:382

Hunter, William
Charles Chaplin **16**:189
Fritz Lang **20**:202

Hunting, Constance
Mina Loy **28**:253

Huntington, John
Arthur C. Clarke **18**:105
Ursula K. Le Guin **22**:268

Hurd, Pearl Strachan
Philip Booth **23**:73

Hurren, Kenneth
Samuel Beckett **6**:43
Christopher Fry **2**:144
John Hopkins **4**:234
Peter Nichols **5**:306
Harold Pinter **6**:418
Peter Shaffer **5**:388
Neil Simon **6**:505
Tom Stoppard **4**:527

David Storey **5**:415
James Thurber **11**:534

Hurst, Fannie
Zora Neale Hurston **30**:208

Hurwitz, K. Sue
Piers Anthony **35**:36
C. J. Cherryh **35**:108

Hush, Michele
Brian Wilson **12**:645

Huss, Roy
Michelangelo Antonioni **20**:37

Hussain, Riaz
Philip K. Dick **10**:138

Hutchens, John
Carl Theodor Dreyer **16**:256

Hutchens, John K.
Jessamyn West **17**:546
P. G. Wodehouse **2**:481

Hutchings, W.
Kingsley Amis **13**:12

Hutchins, James N.
Pat Conroy **30**:77

Hutchinson, Joanne
Ivy Compton-Burnett **15**:139

Hutchinson, Tom
Douglas Adams **27**:14

Hutchison, Alexander
Luchino Visconti **16**:571

Hutchison, David
Robert Altman **16**:20

Hutchison, Joanna
Peter Dickinson **12**:172

Hutchison, Paul E.
Kathryn Kramer **34**:74

Hutchison, Percy
A. J. Cronin **32**:129, 130, 131,
132
August Derleth **31**:130
C. S. Forester **35**:160
Zora Neale Hurston **30**:212
Carl Sandburg **35**:346

Huth, Angela
Thomas M. Disch **36**:126
Maurice Gee **29**:178
John Irving **13**:297
Penelope Lively **32**:275
Piers Paul Read **25**:380
Bernice Rubens **31**:351
Lynne Sharon Schwartz **31**:389
Michel Tournier **23**:456
A. N. Wilson **33**:454

Hutman, Norma L.
John Gardner **18**:173

Hutton, Muriel
Noel Streatfeild **21**:410

Hux, Samuel
John Dos Passos **8**:182
M. L. Rosenthal **28**:392

Huxley, Elspeth
Joy Adamson **17**:5

Huxley, Julian
Joy Adamson **17**:4
Aldous Huxley **3**:253

Hydak, Michael G.
Art Buchwald **33**:95

Hyde, Austin T., Jr.
Alvin Silverstein and Virginia
B. Silverstein **17**:456

Hyde, Lewis
Vicente Aleixandre **9**:18
Allen Ginsberg **36**:193

Hyde, Virginia M.
W. H. Auden **3**:23

Hyman, Esther
Nella Larsen **37**:212

Hyman, Nicholas
Ngugi wa Thiong'o **36**:319

Hyman, Sidney
Russell Baker **31**:25
Allen Drury **37**:101

Hyman, Stanley Edgar
W. H. Auden **2**:22
James Baldwin **2**:32
Djuna Barnes **3**:36
John Barth **2**:35
R. P. Blackmur **24**:56
Kenneth Burke **24**:126
Dino Buzzati **36**:89
James M. Cain **28**:45
Truman Capote **3**:99
James Gould Cozzens **11**:124
E. E. Cummings **3**:117
T. S. Eliot **6**:159
William Faulkner **3**:152
Janet Frame **2**:141
Bruce Jay Friedman **3**:165
William Golding **2**:168
Ernest Hemingway **3**:234
Norman Mailer **2**:258
Bernard Malamud **2**:265
Wallace Markfield **8**:378
Henry Miller **2**:283
Marianne Moore **2**:291
Vladimir Nabokov **2**:299
Flannery O'Connor **1**:257
Seán O'Faoláin **7**:273
J. F. Powers **4**:419
James Purdy **2**:348
Thomas Pynchon **2**:353
John Crowe Ransom **2**:363
I. A. Richards **24**:389
Alain Robbe-Grillet **2**:374
J. D. Salinger **3**:444
Isaac Bashevis Singer **3**:452
John Steinbeck **5**:405
Jun'ichiro Tanizaki **8**:510
John Updike **2**:440
Edmund Wilson **24**:472
Yvor Winters **4**:589
Joseph Wittlin **25**:467
Herman Wouk **9**:579

Hyman, Timothy
Federico Fellini **16**:288
Salman Rushdie **31**:354

Hynes, Emerson
August Derleth **31**:137

Hynes, Joseph
    Graham Greene **9**:244
    Evelyn Waugh **3**:511

Hynes, Samuel
    W. H. Auden **1**:11; **3**:24
    C. Day Lewis **10**:130, 131
    T. S. Eliot **10**:172
    E. M. Forster **3**:161
    William Golding **1**:122; **27**:169
    Graham Greene **6**:219; **27**:177
    Louis MacNeice **4**:317; **10**:326
    Jean Rhys **19**:393
    Stephen Spender **5**:401; **10**:488
    J.I.M. Stewart **7**:464
    Vassily S. Yanovsky **18**:550

Ianni, L. A.
    Lawrence Ferlinghetti **2**:133

Iannone, Carol
    Grace Paley **37**:337

Ianzito, Ben
    Margaret O. Hyde **21**:175

Idol, John
    Flannery O'Connor **3**:366

Ignatow, David
    Wendell Berry **27**:35
    Michael S. Harper **22**:209
    Denise Levertov **8**:347
    George Oppen **7**:282
    Gil Orlovitz **22**:333
    Charles Simic **22**:380
    Diane Wakoski **7**:506
    Paul Zweig **34**:378

Inge, M. Thomas
    Donald Davidson **13**:168

Ingoldby, Grace
    Manlio Argueta **31**:21
    Maurice Gee **29**:179

Ingram, Phyllis
    Betty Cavanna **12**:102

Ingrams, Richard
    John Betjeman **34**:311

Innaurato, Albert
    Albert Innaurato **21**:197

Innes, C. D.
    Martin Walser **27**:464

Innes, Michael
    J.I.M. Stewart **32**:419

Innis, Doris
    Jesse Jackson **12**:289

Ionesco, Eugene
    Peter Porter **33**:317

Irby, James E.
    Julio Cortázar **15**:146

Irele, Abiola
    Chinua Achebe **7**:3
    Amos Tutuola **29**:439

Iribarne, Louis
    Czesław Miłosz **22**:307

Irvine, Lorna
    Marian Engel **36**:165

Irving, John
    John Cheever **11**:121
    Toni Morrison **22**:321
    Craig Nova **31**:298
    Jayne Anne Phillips **15**:420

Irwin, Colin
    Billy Joel **26**:214, 220
    Kris Kristofferson **26**:268
    Gordon Lightfoot **26**:281, 282
    Carly Simon **26**:410
    Paul Simon **17**:466

Irwin, John T.
    George P. Elliott **2**:131
    William Faulkner **14**:168
    William Heyen **13**:281
    David Ignatow **7**:177
    Louis MacNeice **1**:187
    Thomas Merton **3**:336
    Stanley Plumly **33**:311
    William Jay Smith **6**:512
    David Wagoner **3**:508
    Theodore Weiss **3**:517

Irwin, Michael
    A. S. Byatt **19**:76
    Isak Dinesen **10**:149
    Andrea Lee **36**:254
    Chaim Potok **26**:373
    V. S. Pritchett **13**:467
    Paul Theroux **11**:528
    John Updike **9**:539

Isaac, Dan
    Rainer Werner Fassbinder
        20:119
    Isaac Bashevis Singer **3**:453
    Elie Wiesel **5**:493

Isaac, Erich
    John le Carré **28**:231
    Chaim Potok **26**:374

Isaac, Rael Jean
    John le Carré **28**:231

Isaacs, Edith J. R.
    Clifford Odets **28**:325, 327

Isaacs, Elizabeth
    Yvor Winters **32**:466

Isaacs, Harold R.
    Lorraine Hansberry **17**:183

Isaacs, Hermine Rich
    Orson Welles **20**:431

Isaacs, James
    Jimmy Cliff **21**:60
    Lou Reed **21**:309

Isaacs, Neil D.
    George Roy Hill **26**:200

Isbell, Harold
    John Logan **5**:253

Isherwood, Christopher
    Katherine Anne Porter **13**:446

Ishiguro, Hidé
    Yukio Mishima **9**:384

Isler, Scott
    David Byrne **26**:95, 98
    Paul McCartney **35**:285
    Jim Morrison **17**:294
    Lou Reed **21**:316, 320

Isola, Carolanne
    Anne McCaffrey **17**:283

Israel, Callie
    Roderick L. Haig-Brown
        21:139

Issacs, Susan
    Jean M. Auel **31**:24

Italia, Paul G.
    James Dickey **10**:139

Itzin, Catherine
    Jack Gelber **6**:197

Ivask, Ivar
    Paavo Haavikko **34**:174

Iverson, Lucille
    Judith Leet **11**:323

Ives, John
    Sonia Levitin **17**:265
    Josephine Poole **17**:372
    Roger Zelazny **21**:465

Iwamoto, Yoshio
    Yasunari Kawabata **18**:281
    Yukio Mishima **9**:381

Iwasaki, Akira
    Akira Kurosawa **16**:397

Iyer, Pico
    Jim Harrison **33**:199
    Barbara Pym **37**:379

Izard, Anne
    Babbis Friis-Baastad **12**:213
    John R. Tunis **12**:597

Jablons, Pam
    Ved Mehta **37**:293

Jack, Peter Monro
    Ogden Nash **23**:318

Jackel, David
    Matt Cohen **19**:112
    James Reaney **13**:476
    Robin Skelton **13**:508
    Raymond Souster **14**:505

Jackson, Al
    Andre Norton **12**:463

Jackson, Angela
    Lucille Clifton **19**:109
    Henry Dumas **6**:145

Jackson, Blyden
    Gwendolyn Brooks **5**:75
    Sterling A. Brown **23**:98
    Robert Hayden **5**:169
    Langston Hughes **5**:191
    Margaret Walker **6**:554

Jackson, Brian
    Philippa Pearce **21**:283

Jackson, David
    James Merrill **34**:241

Jackson, Esther Merle
    Tennessee Williams **7**:540

Jackson, Jane B.
    Richard Peck **21**:300

Jackson, Joseph Henry
    Howard Fast **23**:154
    Roderick L. Haig-Brown
        21:135
    Irving Stone **7**:468

Jackson, Katherine Gauss
    Isabel Colegate **36**:109
    Evan Hunter **31**:222
    Elizabeth Taylor **29**:408

Jackson, Marni
    Nora Ephron **31**:158

Jackson, Miles M.
    Rosa Guy **26**:141

Jackson, Paul R.
    Henry Miller **14**:370, 374

Jackson, Richard
    Stephen Dobyns **37**:78
    Robert Pack **13**:439
    Robert Penn Warren **13**:578
    Charles Wright **13**:614

Jackson, Richard L.
    Ramón Gómez de la Serna
        9:239

Jackson, Robert Louis
    Aleksandr I. Solzhenitsyn **7**:446

Jackson, Seán Wyse
    Dirk Bogarde **19**:43
    D. M. Thomas **22**:418

Jacob, Gilles
    Robert Bresson **16**:110
    François Truffaut **20**:383

Jacob, John
    Thomas McGrath **28**:278
    Jonathan Williams **13**:601

Jacobs, Barry
    Halldór Laxness **25**:292

Jacobs, Diane
    Claude Chabrol **16**:178
    Lina Wertmüller **16**:592

Jacobs, Lewis
    Charles Chaplin **16**:191
    Rouben Mamoulian **16**:422

Jacobs, Nicolas
    David Jones **4**:261

Jacobs, Rita D.
    Saul Bellow **10**:42

Jacobs, Ronald M.
    Samuel R. Delany **8**:168

Jacobs, William Jay
    C. S. Forester **35**:172
    S. E. Hinton **30**:204
    John R. Tunis **12**:598

Jacobsen, Josephine
    Peter Davison **28**:100
    Arthur Gregor **9**:256
    Daniel Hoffman **6**:242
    David Ignatow **4**:249
    Denise Levertov **3**:293
    Howard Moss **14**:375
    James Schevill **7**:401
    Mona Van Duyn **7**:498

Jacobson, Dan
S. Y. Agnon **14**:1
James Baldwin **17**:22
D. J. Enright **4**:155; **31**:147
Ian Fleming **30**:131
Andrei Sinyavsky **8**:490

Jacobson, Irving
Arthur Miller **6**:333; **10**:345

Jacobus, John
Charles M. Schulz **12**:531

Jacobus, Lee A.
Imamu Amiri Baraka **5**:46

Jacoby, Susan
Andrea Lee **36**:253
Gore Vidal **22**:435

Jacoby, Tamar
Athol Fugard **25**:174
Maxine Hong Kingston **19**:250

Jaehne, Karen
Werner Herzog **16**:329

Jaffe, Daniel
A. R. Ammons **2**:12
John Berryman **2**:57
Philip Booth **23**:76
William Melvin Kelley **22**:248
Norman MacCaig **36**:283
Sylvia Plath **17**:346
Gary Snyder **2**:406
Hollis Summers **10**:493
R. G. Vliet **22**:441

Jaffe, Harold
Peter S. Beagle **7**:26
Ernesto Cardenal **31**:79
Kenneth Rexroth **2**:369

Jaffee, Cyrisse
Robin F. Brancato **35**:65
Betty Cavanna **12**:102
Paula Danziger **21**:84
Lois Duncan **26**:106
Stan Lee **17**:261
Hilma Wolitzer **17**:563
Paul Zindel **26**:478

Jahiel, Edwin
Marguerite Duras **6**:150
Antonis Samarakis **5**:381
Vassilis Vassilikos **4**:552

Jahn, Janheing
Camara Laye **4**:282

Jahn, Mike
Chuck Berry **17**:53
Mick Jagger and Keith Richard **17**:229
Jim Morrison **17**:291
Paul Simon **17**:464

Jahner, Elaine
Leslie Marmon Silko **23**:408
Wole Soyinka **36**:412

Jajko, Pamela
Robin F. Brancato **35**:66

Jamal, Zahir
Gail Godwin **22**:181
Olivia Manning **19**:302
Alberto Moravia **11**:384
William Trevor **14**:535
John Wain **15**:561

James, Caryn
Robert Coover **32**:127
Stanley Elkin **27**:124

James, Clive
W. H. Auden **3**:28
John Berryman **25**:89
John Betjeman **6**:66
Ronald Bush **34**:524
T. S. Eliot **34**:524
Lillian Hellman **8**:280
Philip Larkin **5**:225, 229; **33**:262, 266
John le Carré **9**:327
Norman Mailer **3**:317
Aleksandr I. Solzhenitsyn **7**:436
Tom Stoppard **29**:393
Evelyn Waugh **19**:465
Edmund Wilson **24**:481
Yvor Winters **8**:553
Alexander Zinoviev **19**:490

James, D. G.
I. A. Richards **24**:381

James, Jamie
Jim Carroll **35**:78
Toby Olson **28**:345

James, John
David Hare **29**:219

James, Kathryn C.
Christie Harris **12**:263

James, Louis
Louise Bennett **28**:30
Wilson Harris **25**:210
Jean Rhys **14**:447
Derek Walcott **25**:449

James, Stuart
James A. Michener **5**:290

Jameson, Fredric
Larry Niven **8**:426
Jean-Paul Sartre **24**:412, 421

Jameson, Richard T.
Steven Bochco and Michael Kozoll **35**:49

Janeway, Elizabeth
Sylvia Ashton-Warner **19**:22
Pamela Hansford Johnson **7**:184; **27**:217
Jean Kerr **22**:255, 256
Françoise Sagan **17**:417, 420
Elizabeth Spencer **22**:399
John Steinbeck **21**:369
Elizabeth Taylor **29**:408
Jessamyn West **7**:519
Rebecca West **31**:456

Janeway, Michael
Anne Tyler **7**:479
Tom Wicker **7**:533

Janiera, Armando Martins
Kōbō Abé **8**:1
Jun'ichirō Tanizaki **8**:510

Jannone, Claudia
Philip José Farmer **19**:166

Janovicky, Karel
Jaroslav Seifert **34**:259

Janson, Michael
Alta **19**:19

Jarrell, Randall
Conrad Aiken **3**:3
W. H. Auden **2**:21
Ben Belitt **22**:49
John Berryman **13**:75
Elizabeth Bishop **1**:34; **4**:65
R. P. Blackmur **2**:61
Alex Comfort **7**:54
R. S. Crane **27**:70
E. E. Cummings **3**:116
Robert Frost **1**:109; **3**:169
Robert Graves **1**:126; **2**:174
David Ignatow **7**:173
Robinson Jeffers **2**:213
Robert Lowell **1**:178; **2**:246
Josephine Miles **1**:215
Marianne Moore **1**:226; **2**:290; **19**:338
Ezra Pound **2**:340
John Crowe Ransom **2**:361
Theodore Roethke **3**:432
Muriel Rukeyser **6**:478
Carl Sandburg **4**:462
Karl Shapiro **4**:485
Christina Stead **2**:420
Richard Wilbur **3**:530
William Carlos Williams **1**:369; **2**:467
Yvor Winters **32**:454, 459

Jarrett-Kerr, Martin
F. R. Leavis **24**:295

Jaspers, Karl
Czesław Miłosz **22**:304

Jastrow, Robert
Arthur C. Clarke **35**:117

Jaszi, Peter
Stanley Kubrick **16**:382

Jayne, Edward
Roland Barthes **24**:39

Jeanneret, F.
Adolfo Bioy Casares **13**:87

Jeavons, Clyde
Sidney Poitier **26**:359

Jebb, Julian
Bernardo Bertolucci **16**:91
Anita Brookner **34**:137
Alison Lurie **5**:259
François Truffaut **20**:406
Evelyn Waugh **27**:471

Jeffares, A. N.
Molly Keane **31**:234
Seán O'Faoláin **32**:342

Jefferson, Margo
Beryl Bainbridge **5**:39
James Baldwin **17**:43
Rosalyn Drexler **6**:142
Nadine Gordimer **7**:133
Jack Heifner **11**:264
Carolyn G. Heilbrun **25**:254
Elizabeth Jane Howard **7**:164
Gayl Jones **6**:265
Nettie Jones **34**:68
V. S. Naipaul **7**:253
Juan Carlos Onetti **7**:280
Salman Rushdie **31**:354

Jefferson, Margot
Molly Keane **31**:235

Jefferson, M. L.
Ann Schlee **35**:376

Jeffords, Ed
Jim Morrison **17**:289

Jeffrey, David L.
Jack Hodgins **23**:230

Jeffreys, Susan
Erich von Däniken **30**:427
Ann Schlee **35**:374

Jelenski, K. A.
Witold Gombrowicz **7**:123

Jelliffe, R. A.
Robert A. Heinlein **26**:161

Jellinck, Frank
Rex Stout **3**:472

Jemie, Onwuchekwa
Langston Hughes **35**:219

Jenkins, Alan
Lawrence Durrell **27**:95
Derek Walcott **25**:457

Jenkins, Cecil
André Malraux **4**:336

Jenkins, David
A. R. Ammons **5**:28
Patrick Boyle **19**:68

Jenkins, J. S.
Eilís Dillon **17**:97

Jenkins, Peter
Simon Gray **14**:215

Jenkins, Steve
Pink Floyd **35**:314

Jennings, Elizabeth
Robert Frost **3**:171
Seamus Heaney **37**:165

Jerome, Judson
John Ciardi **10**:105
William Dickey **28**:118
Edwin Honig **33**:211
Marge Piercy **27**:376

Jervis, Steven A.
Evelyn Waugh **1**:359

Joad, C.E.M.
Margaret Mead **37**:273

Jochmans, Betty
Agatha Christie **8**:142

Joe, Radcliffe
Gerome Ragni and James Rado **17**:388

Johannesson, Eric O.
Isak Dinesen **29**:153

Johansen, Nancy K.
Betsy Byars **35**:74

John, Roland
Stanley J. Kunitz **6**:287

Johnsen, William F.
Frank Lentricchia **34**:573

Johnson, Abby Ann Arthur
Penelope Gilliatt **10**:229

Johnson, Albert
Lindsay Anderson **20**:14
John Cassavetes **20**:44, 45
Shirley Clarke **16**:217

Johnson, Alexandra
Isaac Bashevis Singer **15**:507
Elie Wiesel **37**:450

Johnson, Ann S.
David Garnett **3**:188

Johnson, Becky
Kristin Hunter **35**:230

Johnson, Carol
Donald Davie **31**:108

Johnson, Carolyn
Hilma Wolitzer **17**:562

Johnson, Colton
Anthony Kerrigan **6**:276

Johnson, Curtis
Guy Davenport, Jr. **6**:125

Johnson, Cynthia
Margaret O. Hyde **21**:177

Johnson, Diane
Beryl Bainbridge **14**:37
Donald Barthelme **13**:59
Saul Bellow **25**:83
C.D.B. Bryan **29**:104
Don DeLillo **8**:172
Joan Didion **8**:176
E. L. Doctorow **37**:80
Nadine Gordimer **5**:147
Edward Hoagland **28**:184
Erica Jong **8**:315
Maxine Hong Kingston **12**:313
Doris Lessing **3**:286; **10**:316
Norman Mailer **14**:354
James Alan McPherson **19**:310
Toni Morrison **10**:355
Joyce Carol Oates **3**:361;
  33:290
Jean Rhys **6**:453
Muriel Spark **3**:465
Alexander Theroux **25**:431
D. M. Thomas **31**:431
Gore Vidal **10**:502
Paul West **7**:524

Johnson, Douglas
Louis-Ferdinand Céline **7**:45
Claude Mauriac **9**:367

Johnson, Ernest A., Jr.
Miguel Delibes **18**:109

Johnson, Gerald W.
Ved Mehta **37**:287

Johnson, Greg
Joyce Carol Oates **15**:401
John Updike **9**:538

Johnson, Halvard
Gary Snyder **1**:318

Johnson, Helen Armstead
Joseph A. Walker **19**:454

Johnson, Ira D.
Glenway Wescott **13**:592

Johnson, James Weldon
Sterling A. Brown **23**:95
Carl Van Vechten **33**:391

Johnson, James William
Katherine Anne Porter **7**:311

Johnson, Joyce
Ayi Kwei Armah **33**:36

Johnson, Kenneth
Richard Wilbur **6**:570

Johnson, Lee R.
Eilís Dillon **17**:99

Johnson, Manly
David Ignatow **14**:277

Johnson, Marigold
Lynne Reid Banks **23**:43
Pamela Hansford Johnson
  27:223
Bernard Malamud **3**:324

Johnson, Nora
Jeffrey Archer **28**:13
Laura Z. Hobson **25**:272
Garson Kanin **22**:233
Norma Klein **30**:240
Darcy O'Brien **11**:405
Françoise Sagan **36**:381

Johnson, Pamela Hansford
Allen Drury **37**:100
Winston Graham **23**:192
Doris Lessing **22**:277
Colin MacInnes **23**:281
Olivia Manning **19**:302
Mary McCarthy **24**:343
Françoise Sagan **17**:419

Johnson, Patricia A.
Langston Hughes **35**:220, 221

Johnson, Patricia J.
J.M.G. Le Clézio **31**:250

Johnson, Paul
Ian Fleming **30**:134
Lillian Hellman **34**:349
Michael Scammell **34**:482
Aleksandr Solzhenitsyn **34**:482

Johnson, Priscilla
Judith Guest **30**:176

Johnson, R. E., Jr.
Agnes Eckhardt Nixon **21**:248

Johnson, Richard
W. H. Auden **2**:26

Johnson, Richard A.
Turner Cassity **6**:107
Anthony Hecht **8**:268
Delmore Schwartz **2**:387

Johnson, Robert K.
Francis Ford Coppola **16**:244
Neil Simon **31**:403

Johnson, Rosemary
John Ashbery **13**:35
May Swenson **14**:520

Johnson, Sidney M.
Hermann Hesse **17**:197

Johnson, Thomas S.
Bob Dylan **12**:194

Johnson, Tom
Archibald Macleish **14**:338
Howard Nemerov **36**:303

Johnson, Wayne L.
Ray Bradbury **15**:85

Johnson, William
Robert Altman **16**:20
Kon Ichikawa **20**:179, 184
Eric Rohmer **16**:532
Martin Scorsese **20**:326
Jerzy Skolimowski **20**:354
Orson Welles **20**:439, 442

Johnson-Masters, Virginia
Gay Talese **37**:401

Johnston, Albert H.
Nora Ephron **17**:110
Patti Smith **12**:541

Johnston, Ann
Kevin Major **26**:287

Johnston, Arnold
William Golding **3**:198

Johnston, Clarie
Nagisa Oshima **20**:250

Johnston, Dillon
Austin Clarke **6**:111
Albert Goldbarth **5**:143
Seamus Heaney **7**:147
Paul Muldoon **32**:315

Johnston, George Sim
Saul Bellow **33**:71
Alfred Kazin **34**:563
Tom Wolfe **35**:466

Johnston, Kenneth G.
William Faulkner **11**:199

Johnston, Neal
Elmore Leonard **28**:236; **34**:215

Johnston, Sheila
Paul McCartney **35**:293

Johnstone, J. K.
E. M. Forster **3**:160

Joly, Jacques
Jean Renoir **20**:294

Jonas, George
Margaret Atwood **3**:19
Gwendolyn MacEwan **13**:357
Raymond Souster **14**:504

Jonas, Gerald
Douglas Adams **27**:12
Poul Anderson **15**:14
Isaac Asimov **9**:49; **19**:27;
  26:59
Arthur C. Clarke **13**:155;
  35:123, 126
Samuel R. Delany **8**:168, 169;
  14:148
Thomas M. Disch **36**:124
Harlan Ellison **13**:203
Robert A. Heinlein **26**:174
Frank Herbert **12**:278, 279;
  23:221; **35**:205, 207
Arthur Koestler **33**:242
Ursula K. LeGuin **8**:343
Stanislaw Lem **15**:330
Barry N. Malzberg **7**:209
Vonda N. McIntyre **18**:326
Larry Niven **8**:426
Andre Norton **12**:470

Frederik Pohl **18**:412
Keith Roberts **14**:464
Joanna Russ **15**:461, 462
Arkadii Strugatskii and Boris
  Strugatskii **27**:438
Kate Wilhelm **7**:538
Jack Williamson **29**:461
Gene Wolfe **25**:473
Roger Zelazny **21**:469

Jones, A. R.
James Baldwin **17**:27
Sylvia Plath **9**:430

Jones, Allan
David Bowie **17**:63, 65
Elvis Costello **21**:66, 68, 69,
  74, 75
Ray Davies **21**:100, 101, 102
Mick Jagger and Keith Richard
  17:235
Laura Nyro **17**:315, 317, 319
Richard O'Brien **17**:324
Pink Floyd **35**:307, 312
Lou Reed **21**:308, 312, 314
Carly Simon **26**:410
Neil Young **17**:576, 577, 580

Jones, Alun R.
Rhys Davies **23**:148
Philip Larkin **13**:335
Eudora Welty **1**:362; **2**:460

Jones, Ann
Joe McGinniss **32**:306

Jones, Bedwyr Lewis
Kate Roberts **15**:445

Jones, Bernard
John Cowper Powys **9**:441

Jones, Brian
Howard Nemerov **2**:306
Peter Porter **33**:318

Jones, C. A.
Edwin Honig **33**:213

Jones, Chris
Athol Fugard **25**:173

Jones, D. A. N.
Howard Barker **37**:31
Marie-Claire Blais **22**:58
Dirk Bogarde **19**:41
William Boyd **28**:37
Ed Bullins **1**:47
John Fowles **6**:184
Julius Horwitz **14**:266
Mervyn Jones **10**:295
Yoram Kaniuk **19**:239
William Kennedy **34**:211
Milan Kundera **19**:267
Colin MacInnes **23**:286
V. S. Naipaul **37**:325
Amos Tutuola **29**:441
John Wain **11**:564
Fay Weldon **11**:565
Vassily S. Yanovsky **18**:551

Jones, D. Allan
John Barth **5**:52

Jones, D. G.
Earle Birney **6**:76; **11**:49
Philip Child **19**:102
Phyllis Gotlieb **18**:192
Anne Hébert **4**:219
Irving Layton **2**:237

Miriam Waddington **28**:437

Jones, Daniel R.
Edward Bond **23**:70

Jones, David R.
Saul Bellow **13**:69

Jones, Du Pre
Sam Peckinpah **20**:272

Jones, E.B.C.
Noel Streatfeild **21**:395

Jones, Edward T.
John Updike **3**:487

Jones, Eldred D.
Wole Soyinka **36**:409

Jones, Ernest
William Maxwell **19**:306
Aldo Palazzeschi **11**:431
Budd Schulberg **7**:403
Elizabeth Spencer **22**:398

Jones, F. Whitney
Ernesto Cardenal **31**:72

Jones, Frank N.
Evan Hunter **31**:221

Jones, Granville H.
Jack Kerouac **2**:226

Jones, Howard Mumford
Alvah Bessie **23**:58
Leon Edel **29**:169
Olivia Manning **19**:299
Philip Rahv **24**:352

Jones, James H.
Louis R. Harlan **34**:183

Jones, John Bush
Simon Gray **36**:203
Harold Pinter **9**:418

Jones, John M.
Kate Roberts **15**:445

Jones, LeRoi
Robert Creeley **15**:149

Jones, Lewis
Seán O'Faoláin **32**:340
Michel Tournier **36**:436
Fay Weldon **36**:445

Jones, Linda T.
Katherine Paterson **30**:284

Jones, Louisa E.
Raymond Queneau **10**:431

Jones, Madison
Andrew Lytle **22**:295

Jones, Margaret E. W.
Ana María Matute **11**:362, 365

Jones, Mervyn
Nadine Gordimer **33**:184
Ved Mehta **37**:291
Peter Nichols **36**:331
Philip Roth **31**:345

Jones, Nettie
Nettie Jones **34**:69

Jones, Patricia
June Jordan **23**:257

Jones, Rhodri
Leon Garfield **12**:227, 235

Jones, Rhonda
Ezekiel Mphahlele **25**:335

Jones, Richard
Graham Greene **14**:218
L. P. Hartley **2**:182
Anthony Powell **7**:346

Jones, Robert F.
James Jones **3**:262

Jones, Roger
Saul Bellow **10**:39
Gary Snyder **32**:394

Jones, Sherman
Louis R. Harlan **34**:188

Jones, Sumie
Jun'ichirō Tanizaki **14**:527

Jong, Erica
Sara Davidson **9**:174
Doris Lessing **3**:287
Marge Piercy **27**:373
Anne Sexton **4**:483; **8**:484
Eleanor Ross Taylor **5**:425

Joost, Nicholas
T. S. Eliot **9**:190
Ernest Hemingway **19**:217
Carl Sandburg **35**:353

Jordan, Alice M.
Henry Gregor Felsen **17**:120
Esther Forbes **12**:207
Lee Kingman **17**:243
Andre Norton **12**:455
John R. Tunis **12**:593

Jordan, Ann
Jean Craighead George **35**:179

Jordan, Clive
Martin Amis **4**:19
Maureen Duffy **37**:114
Elaine Feinstein **36**:168
Masuji Ibuse **22**:226
Dan Jacobson **4**:253
G. Josipovici **6**:271
Milan Kundera **19**:266
Yukio Mishima **4**:356
Thomas Pynchon **6**:432
Gillian Tindall **7**:473
Ludvík Vaculík **7**:494
Kurt Vonnegut, Jr. **4**:567

Jordan, Elaine
Anita Brookner **32**:60

Jordan, Francis X.
Barry Gifford **34**:459
Lawrence Lee **34**:459
Scott O'Dell **30**:276
William Saroyan **34**:459
Gore Vidal **10**:51

Jordan, June
Maya Angelou **12**:13
Millen Brand **7**:30
John Donovan **35**:140
Nikki Giovanni **2**:165
Zora Neale Hurston **7**:171
Gayl Jones **9**:306
Marge Piercy **6**:402
Richard Wright **14**:595

Jose, Nicholas
Noel Hilliard **15**:280

Joseph, Gerhard
John Barth **1**:17

Joseph, Michael
Margery Allingham **19**:12
John Wyndham **19**:475

Josephs, Allen
Manlio Argueta **31**:19
Juan Benet **28**:22
Manuel Puig **28**:374
Luisa Valenzuela **31**:438

Josephy, Alvin M., Jr.
Mari Sandoz **28**:404

Josipovici, Gabriel
Saul Bellow **3**:54; **25**:85
William Golding **27**:168
Vladimir Nabokov **3**:353

Joyce, Joyce Ann
Amiri Baraka **33**:61

Joye, Barbara
Ishmael Reed **13**:476
John A. Williams **13**:598

Joyner, Nancy
Andrew Lytle **22**:297

Judd, Inge
Martin Walser **27**:467

Judell, Brandon
William Kotzwinkle **35**:257

Judson, Horace
Allen Drury **37**:106

Juhasz, Suzanne
Alta **19**:18
Marge Piercy **27**:380

Julian, Janet
Piers Anthony **35**:35, 37

Jumper, Will C.
Robert Lowell **1**:178

Jürma, Mall
Ivar Ivask **14**:287

Jury, Floyd D.
Margaret O. Hyde **21**:180

Justice, Donald
J. V. Cunningham **31**:99

Justus, James H.
John Berryman **4**:60
John Crowe Ransom **4**:431
Karl Shapiro **4**:487
Robert Penn Warren **4**:578, 582

Kabakoff, Jacob
Aharon Megged **9**:375

Kabatchnik, Amnon
William F. Buckley, Jr. **7**:36

Kadish, Doris Y.
Jean Genet **14**:203

Kadison, Chris
Ted Berrigan **37**:45

Kael, Pauline
Woody Allen **16**:4
Robert Altman **16**:23, 28
Michelangelo Antonioni **20**:30, 38
Ingmar Bergman **16**:70
Bernardo Bertolucci **16**:89
Mel Brooks **12**:76
Luis Buñuel **16**:137
John Cassavetes **20**:46, 48
Jimmy Cliff **21**:59
Francis Ford Coppola **16**:233, 240
Brian De Palma **20**:75, 77, 79, 81, 83
Marguerite Duras **20**:102
Federico Fellini **16**:280, 282
Bob Fosse **20**:122
Larry Gelbart **21**:130
Jean-Luc Godard **20**:137, 138, 154
Werner Herzog **16**:325
George Roy Hill **26**:205
John Huston **20**:170, 173
Elia Kazan **16**:364, 373
Stanley Kubrick **16**:378, 393
John Landis **26**:275
Richard Lester **20**:226, 229
George Lucas **16**:409
Norman Mailer **3**:315
Steve Martin **30**:251
Elaine May **16**:432
Sam Peckinpah **20**:281
Sidney Poitier **26**:360
Richard Pryor **26**:381
Satyajit Ray **16**:485, 488
Jean Renoir **20**:296
Erich Rohmer **16**:537
Ken Russell **16**:543
Paul Schrader **26**:389, 394, 399
Martin Scorsese **20**:335
Peter Shaffer **37**:385
Steven Spielberg **20**:357, 360, 366
François Truffaut **20**:383, 384, 385, 392, 404
Agnès Varda **16**:559
Luchino Visconti **16**:570, 575
Peter Weir **20**:429
Lina Wertmüller **16**:591
Frederick Wiseman **20**:469

Kaeppler, Adrienne
Thor Heyerdahl **26**:193

Kaftan, Robert
Morris L. West **33**:432

Kagan, Norman
Stanley Kubrick **16**:385

Kagan, Shel
Frank Zappa **17**:593

Kahn, Lothar
Arthur Koestler **3**:271
Siegfried Lenz **27**:251
Jakov Lind **4**:293
André Schwarz-Bart **4**:479
Isaac Bashevis Singer **23**:416
Peter Weiss **3**:515
Elie Wiesel **3**:527; **37**:452, 455

Kahn, Roger
Robert Lipsyte **21**:211

Critic Index

Kaiser, Marjorie
Joan Aiken 35:21

Kaiser, Walter
George Seferis 11:493

Kakish, William
Peter Hundke 10:260

Kakutani, Michiko
William Boyd 28:41
André Brink 36:69
Ronald Bush 34:524
Peter De Vries 28:111
T. S. Eliot 34:524
Frederick Forsyth 36:177
T. Gertler 34:49
Barbara Guest 34:442
Jim Harrison 33:199
H. D. 34:442
Susan Isaacs 32:255
Jay McInerney 34:82
V. S. Naipaul 37:324
Joyce Carol Oates 33:294
Cynthia Ozick 28:355
Grace Paley 37:333
Jayne Anne Phillips 33:305
Anthony Powell 31:322
John Updike 34:285
Fay Weldon 36:448
Nancy Willard 37:464

Kalb, Marvin L.
Aleksandr I. Solzhenitsyn 26:414

Kalem, T. E.
Edward Albee 2:2; 5:12
Kingsley Amis 3:8
Samuel Beckett 2:47
Ed Bullins 5:84
Anne Burr 6:104
Friedrich Dürrenmatt 4:141
Jules Feiffer 8:216
Robert Graves 2:177
Bill Gunn 5:152
John Hopkins 4:234
Albert Innaurato 21:192
Ira Levin 3:294
Paul McCartney 35:278
Terrence McNally 7:217
Jason Miller 2:284
Peter Nichols 5:307
Sean O'Casey 5:319
Murray Schisgal 6:490
Sam Shepard 34:267
Neil Simon 6:506
Isaac Bashevis Singer 6:511
Aleksandr I. Solzhenitsyn 1:321
Stephen Sondheim 30:381, 384
Tom Stoppard 4:526
David Storey 2:424, 425; 4:530
C. P. Taylor 27:446
Thornton Wilder 6:572
Tennessee Williams 7:545
Robert Wilson 7:550

Kallan, Richard A.
Leon Uris 32:433

Kalstone, David
A. R. Ammons 2:12
John Ashbery 2:17; 13:31
John Berryman 3:69
Elizabeth Bishop 13:95
Alfred Corn 33:114

A. D. Hope 3:250
Philip Levine 5:250
Robert Lowell 11:326
James Merrill 2:273, 275; 13:378
Robert Pinsky 19:371
Adrienne Rich 11:475
James Schuyler 5:383

Kameen, Paul
Daniel J. Berrigan 4:57
Robert Lowell 3:303

Kamin, Ira
Charles Bukowski 9:137

Kaminsky, Stuart M.
Elaine May 16:435

Kamla, Thomas A.
Hermann Hesse 25:259

Kane, B. M.
Christa Wolf 14:594

Kane, Patricia
Chester Himes 7:159

Kanfer, Stefan
Truman Capote 19:85
Jerzy Kosinski 6:285
Terrence McNally 7:218
William McPherson 34:86
Brian Moore 7:237
Paul Simon 17:458
Isaac Bashevis Singer 3:453; 6:510
John Steinbeck 5:408
Dalton Trumbo 19:447
Gore Vidal 22:438

Kanigel, Robert
Margaret Mead 37:283

Kannenstine, Louis F.
Djuna Barnes 29:30

Kanon, Joseph
Robert Altman 16:29
Louis Auchincloss 4:29
Carlos Castaneda 12:88
Daphne du Maurier 6:147
Penelope Gilliatt 2:160
Steven Millhauser 21:216
Jacqueline Susann 3:475
Hunter S. Thompson 17:505
John Updike 2:444

Kantra, Robert A.
Samuel Beckett 3:46

Kao, Donald
Laurence Yep 35:471

Kapai, Leela
Paule Marshall 27:311

Kaplan, Abraham
John Ford 16:306

Kaplan, Fred
Francis Ford Coppola 16:239
Bob Fosse 20:125
Roman Polanski 16:470
François Truffaut 20:381

Kaplan, George
Alfred Hitchcock 16:349

Kaplan, Howard
T. Coraghessan Boyle 36:61

Kaplan, Johanna
Dan Jacobson 4:254
Cynthia Ozick 7:287
Chaim Potok 26:374

Kaplan, Samuel
John Neufeld 17:311

Kaplan, Stephen
Stanley Kubrick 16:382

Kaplan, Sydney Janet
Doris Lessing 6:296

Kaplow, Jeffrey J.
David Caute 29:110

Kapp, Isa
Thomas Berger 18:57
John Cheever 11:120
Joan Didion 32:149
Oriana Fallaci 11:189
Jascha Kessler 4:269
Andrea Lee 36:257
Grace Paley 4:394
Barbara Pym 37:374
Philip Roth 4:459; 22:356
Eudora Welty 22:458

Kappel, Lawrence
Thomas Pynchon 18:439

Karanikas, Alexander
Donald Davidson 19:123

Karatnycky, Adrian
Frederick Forsyth 36:176

Kardokas, Christine
Zilpha Keatley Snyder 17:475

Kareda, Urjo
Marian Engel 36:164
Alice Munro 19:345
Audrey Thomas 37:422

Karimi-Hakkak, Ahmad
Ahmad Shamlu 10:470

Karl, Frederick R.
Samuel Beckett 1:20
Elizabeth Bowen 1:40
John Braine 1:43
Ivy Compton-Burnett 1:60
Lawrence Durrell 1:83
E. M. Forster 1:103
William Golding 1:119
Henry Green 2:178
Graham Greene 1:132
L. P. Hartley 2:181
Joseph Heller 1:140
Aldous Huxley 1:150
Christopher Isherwood 1:155
Pamela Hansford Johnson 1:160
Doris Lessing 1:173, 175
Iris Murdoch 1:233
P. H. Newby 2:310
Anthony Powell 1:277
William Sansom 2:383
C. P. Snow 1:314, 315, 316
Muriel Spark 2:414
Evelyn Waugh 1:357
Angus Wilson 2:471

Karlen, Arno
Edward Dahlberg 7:62

Karlinsky, Simon
Vladimir Nabokov 1:241; 2:305
John Rechy 7:357
Aleksandr I. Solzhenitsyn 2:408
Edmund White III 27:478
Yevgeny Yevtushenko 1:382

Karloff, Boris
Charles Addams 30:11

Karp, David
James Baldwin 17:21
Meyer Levin 7:203

Karriker, Alexandra Heidi
Vasily Aksyonov 37:13

Kasack, Wolfgang
Aleksandr I. Solzhenitsyn 7:434

Kasindorf, Martin
Christopher Hampton 4:212
Norman Lear 12:335

Kasper, Rosemary
M. E. Kerr 35:249

Kass, Judith M.
Robert Altman 16:38, 40

Katope, Christopher G.
Jessamyn West 17:548

Kattan, Naim
Mordecai Richler 5:373

Katz, Bill
Roderick L. Haig-Brown 21:138

Katz, Claire
Flannery O'Connor 6:379, 380

Katz, Donald R.
Thomas McGuane 18:325

Katz, Jonathan
Albert Goldbarth 5:144

Kauf, R.
Fritz Hochwälder 36:239

Kauffmann, Stanley
Kōbō Abé 22:11
Edward Albee 2:3; 5:11, 14; 25:38
Robert Altman 16:29, 44
Lindsay Anderson 20:16
Fernando Arrabal 2:15; 9:41
Alan Ayckbourn 5:37
Ralph Bakshi 26:67, 69, 71
Ingmar Bergman 16:57
John Berryman 3:69
Bernardo Bertolucci 16:90, 94, 100
Mel Brooks 12:80
Ed Bullins 7:36
Luis Buñuel 16:135
Anthony Burgess 2:86
John Cassavetes 20:47, 49
Charles Chaplin 16:203, 206
Michael Cimino 16:213
D. L. Coburn 10:108
Francis Ford Coppola 16:234
Vittorio De Sica 20:95, 96
E. L. Doctorow 6:133
Carl Theodor Dreyer 16:262
Nora Ephron 31:160

Rainer Werner Fassbinder
  20:109, 113
Federico Fellini **16**:279, 281,
  283
Bob Fosse **20**:122, 124, 127
Athol Fugard **5**:130; **9**:230
Larry Gelbart **21**:128
Jean-Luc Godard **20**:139, 140
John Guare **14**:220
Peter Handke **5**:164
Lorraine Hansberry **17**:184
David Hare **29**:211
Beth Henley **23**:217
James Leo Herlihy **6**:234
Werner Herzog **16**:327, 334
George Roy Hill **26**:202, 209
John Huston **20**:175
Buster Keaton **20**:194
James Kirkwood **9**:319
Jerzy Kosinski **1**:171; **2**:233
Stanley Kubrick **16**:382, 383,
  390
J.M.G. Le Clézio **31**:242
Richard Lester **20**:224, 228,
  231
George Lucas **16**:407, 408, 411
Steve Martin **30**:251
Elaine May **16**:435
Albert Maysles and David
  Maysles **16**:439
Arthur Miller **2**:280
Henry Miller **4**:350
Henri de Montherlant **19**:326
Monty Python **21**:225
Peter Nichols **5**:307
Hugh Nissenson **9**:399
Marsha Norman **28**:320
Edna O'Brien **3**:365
Clifford Odets **28**:336
John O'Hara **2**:325
Nagisa Oshima **20**:255
Yasujiro Ozu **16**:448
Pier Paolo Pasolini **20**:260
Miguel Piñero **4**:402
Harold Pinter **3**:386, 387;
  6:417; **15**:421
Roman Polanski **16**:464
Bernard Pomerance **13**:446
Richard Pryor **26**:379, 382
David Rabe **4**:425, 426; **8**:450
Terence Rattigan **7**:356
Satyajit Ray **16**:486
Jean Renoir **20**:300, 302
Gregor von Rezzori **25**:383
Eric Rohmer **16**:531, 537
Ken Russell **16**:543, 547
Françoise Sagan **17**:424
James Salter **7**:387
Carlos Saura **20**:317
Paul Schrader **26**:385, 389
André Schwarz-Bart **2**:388
Martin Scorsese **20**:325, 335
Rod Serling **30**:354
Peter Shaffer **37**:385
Irwin Shaw **7**:412
Sam Shepard **17**:434, 446
Joan Micklin Silver **20**:341
Elizabeth Spencer **22**:401
Steven Spielberg **20**:360, 367
John Steinbeck **5**:408
Tom Stoppard **4**:527; **15**:524
Elizabeth Swados **12**:560
François Truffaut **20**:386, 389

Melvin Van Peebles **20**:410
Gore Vidal **2**:450
Luchino Visconti **16**:567, 570
Kurt Vonnegut, Jr. **2**:452
Andrzej Wajda **16**:584
Joseph A. Walker **19**:455
Orson Welles **20**:453
Lina Wertmüller **16**:587, 591,
  598
Billy Wilder **20**:465
Tennessee Williams **5**:504;
  7:545
Lanford Wilson **14**:593
Robert Wilson **9**:576

Kaufman, Donald L.
  Norman Mailer **2**:263

Kaufman, Joanne
  William Kotzwinkle **35**:258

Kaufman, Marjorie
  Thomas Pynchon **18**:432

Kaufman, Michael T.
  Salman Rushdie **31**:356

Kaufmann, James
  Elmore Leonard **34**:213

Kaufmann, R. J.
  F. R. Leavis **24**:299

Kavanagh, Julie
  Marilynne Robinson **25**:387

Kavanagh, P. J.
  Czesław Miłosz **31**:263
  Siegfried Sassoon **36**:396

Kavanaugh, Patrick
  Frank O'Connor **14**:400

Kaveney, Roz
  Doris Lessing **15**:332
  Frederik Pohl **18**:412

Kay, George
  Eugenio Montale **18**:340

Kaye, Frances W.
  W. P. Kinsella **27**:237

Kaye, Howard
  Yvor Winters **4**:593

Kaye, Lenny
  Jimmy Cliff **21**:59
  Mick Jagger and Keith Richard
    17:224, 239
  Paul McCartney **35**:281
  Jim Morrison **17**:292
  Jimmy Page and Robert Plant
    12:475
  Lou Reed **21**:303, 314
  Smokey Robinson **21**:347
  Paul Simon **17**:446
  Peter Townshend **17**:532
  Stevie Wonder **12**:656

Kaye, Marilyn
  Franklyn M. Branley **21**:23
  Betsy Byars **35**:75, 76
  Aidan Chambers **35**:99
  Christopher Collier and James
    L. Collier **30**:75
  Isabelle Holland **21**:154
  Kristin Hunter **35**:230
  M. E. Kerr **35**:248, 249

Cynthia Voigt **30**:417, 419

Kaysen, Xana
  Jerzy Kosinski **10**:309

Kazin, Alfred
  Renata Adler **8**:7
  James Baldwin **1**:13; **13**:52
  Amiri Baraka **33**:56
  Donald Barthelme **13**:54
  Brendan Behan **1**:25
  Saul Bellow **1**:28; **3**:61
  R. P. Blackmur **24**:55
  Jane Bowles **3**:84
  Paul Bowles **1**:41
  William S. Burroughs **5**:91
  Albert Camus **2**:97
  Elias Canetti **25**:113
  Louis-Ferdinand Céline **9**:158
  John Cheever **3**:108
  James Gould Cozzens **4**:116
  A. J. Cronin **32**:134
  E. E. Cummings **8**:155
  Joan Didion **3**:127
  Lawrence Durrell **1**:83
  Leon Edel **29**:167
  Ralph Ellison **1**:93; **3**:146
  Frederick Exley **6**:170
  William Faulkner **28**:137
  Gabriel García Márquez **2**:149
  William H. Gass **8**:240
  Paul Goodman **4**:195
  Graham Greene **1**:131
  Barbara Guest **34**:445
  H. D. **34**:445
  Joseph Heller **11**:265
  Ernest Hemingway **3**:242
  Edward Hoagland **28**:181
  Maureen Howard **14**:268
  Aldous Huxley **35**:234
  David Ignatow **4**:249
  Jack Kerouac **1**:165
  Alan Lelchuk **5**:241
  Robert Lowell **1**:179
  Georg Lukács **24**:321
  Norman Mailer **1**:187
  Bernard Malamud **1**:194; **3**:326
  Wallace Markfield **8**:379
  John P. Marquand **2**:271
  Mary McCarthy **3**:329
  Carson McCullers **4**:345
  Czesław Miłosz **31**:264
  Vladimir Nabokov **3**:356; **8**:418
  V. S. Naipaul **4**:373; **9**:393
  Joyce Carol Oates **2**:313; **3**:363
  Flannery O'Connor **1**:259;
    3:370
  Julia O'Faolain **19**:359
  John O'Hara **1**:260; **3**:371
  Alan Paton **25**:357
  Walker Percy **2**:334
  Ann Petry **1**:266
  Thomas Pynchon **3**:419
  Kenneth Rexroth **1**:284
  Philip Roth **1**:292
  J. D. Salinger **1**:295, 296;
    3:446, 458
  Karl Shapiro **4**:484
  Isaac Bashevis Singer **1**:310;
    3:457; **9**:487
  C. P. Snow **1**:314
  Aleksandr I. Solzhenitsyn
    2:410; **4**:515
  Susan Sontag **13**:515

John Steinbeck **13**:530
Allen Tate **24**:440
Peter Taylor **4**:543
Paul Theroux **8**:514
John Updike **3**:488; **9**:538;
  23:471
Carl Van Vechten **33**:395
Kurt Vonnegut, Jr. **3**:505
Robert Penn Warren **1**:352;
  4:582
Edmund Wilson **2**:475; **24**:475
Abraham B. Yehoshua **13**:618

Kazin, Pearl
  Brigid Brophy **29**:91

Keane, Patrick
  Galway Kinnell **5**:216

Kearns, Edward
  Richard Wright **1**:379

Kearns, George
  Walter Abish **22**:23
  Elizabeth Bowen **22**:68
  T. Coraghessan Boyle **36**:60
  Alfred Corn **33**:115
  Julio Cortázar **33**:130
  Fumiko Enchi **31**:141
  Athol Fugard **25**:176
  Luis Rafael Sánchez **23**:385
  Danny Santiago **33**:353
  D. M. Thomas **31**:434

Kearns, Kathleen
  T. Coraghessan Boyle **36**:57
  Anita Brookner **32**:61

Kearns, Lionel
  Earle Birney **6**:77

Keates, Jonathan
  Gunnel Beckman **26**:88
  Dirk Bogarde **19**:42
  Jorge Luis Borges **6**:94
  John Fowles **10**:187
  Roy Fuller **28**:157
  Anthony Hecht **19**:208
  John Hersey **7**:155
  Ursula Holden **18**:257
  Tom Sharpe **36**:403
  Peter Straub **28**:409

Keating, H.R.F.
  Jessica Anderson **37**:19
  Robert B. Parker **27**:364

Keating, L. Clark
  Marie-Claire Blais **22**:58

Keating, Peter
  Erica Jong **8**:315

Kee, Robert
  Enid Bagnold **25**:75
  Agatha Christie **12**:115

Keefe, Joan
  Flann O'Brien **10**:362

Keehan, Anne
  Evan Hunter **31**:221

Keeley, Edmund
  Odysseus Elytis **15**:221
  Stratis Haviaras **33**:204
  Yannis Ritsos **31**:328
  George Seferis **11**:492

Critic Index

Keen, Sam
Carlos Castaneda **12**:93

Keenan, Hugh T.
J.R.R. Tolkien **1**:336

Keene, Donald
Yukio Mishima **2**:287; **4**:354
Jun'ichirō Tanizaki **8**:509

Keene, Frances
Françoise Sagan **17**:417

Keeney, Willard
Eudora Welty **1**:361

Keffer, Charles J.
Jeffrey Archer **28**:11
Robin Cook **14**:131
Susan Isaacs **32**:253

Kehoe, William
August Derleth **31**:137

Keils, R. M.
Vladimir Nabokov **11**:391

Keith, Philip
J. E. Wideman **5**:489

Keith, W. J.
Louis Dudek **19**:138
Robert Frost **26**:128
Roderick L. Haig-Brown
21:141
Hugh Hood **28**:194
Rudy Wiebe **14**:573

Keitnor, Wendy
Ralph Gustafson **36**:217, 220

Kelleher, Ed
David Bowie **17**:58
Carly Simon **26**:408

Kelleher, Victor
Muriel Spark **13**:523

Kellen, Konrad
Lina Wertmüller **16**:596

Keller, Jane Carter
Flannery O'Connor **3**:365

Keller, Karl
Aimé Césaire **32**:110, 112
Robert Creeley **36**:119
Robert Frost **34**:472
William H. Pritchard **34**:472

Keller, Marcia
Agatha Christie **12**:117

Kelley, Welbourn
Julia Peterkin **31**:305

Kellman, Steven
Max Frisch **14**:184

Kellman, Steven G.
Milan Kundera **32**:267
Aharon Megged **9**:374
Iris Murdoch **15**:385
Amos Oz **33**:302
Robert Pinget **13**:442

Kellogg, Gene
Graham Greene **3**:208
François Mauriac **4**:339
Flannery O'Connor **3**:365
J. F. Powers **4**:419
Evelyn Waugh **3**:511

Kelly, Aileen
Michael Scammell **34**:483
Aleksandr Solzhenitsyn **34**:483
Henri Troyat **23**:462

Kelly, Ernece B.
Maya Angelou **12**:9

Kelly, Frank
David Madden **15**:350
T. H. White **30**:451

Kelly, James
Rhys Davies **23**:146
Ernest K. Gann **23**:165
Evan Hunter **31**:218
Pamela Hansford Johnson
27:216
Irwin Shaw **7**:411

Kelly, Thomas
Bernard Mac Laverty **31**:254

Kelman, Ken
Carl Theodor Dreyer **16**:259
Leni Riefenstahl **16**:522

Kemball-Cook, Jessica
Andre Norton **12**:465

Kemme, Tom
Shusaku Endo **19**:161
Cay Van Ash **34**:118

Kemp, Barbara
Françoise Sagan **17**:427

Kemp, John C.
Robert Frost **15**:245

Kemp, Peter
Douglas Adams **27**:11
Elizabeth Bishop **32**:39
Frederick Busch **18**:84
I. Compton-Burnett **34**:494
Roald Dahl **18**:108
Lawrence Durrell **13**:189
Buchi Emecheta **14**:160
Thom Gunn **32**:213
John Hawkes **27**:200
Thomas Keneally **27**:231
Doris Lessing **22**:286
David Malouf **28**:269
Iris Murdoch **22**:326
Barbara Pym **19**:387; **37**:377
Bernice Rubens **31**:350
Tom Sharpe **36**:401
Scott Sommer **25**:424
Hilary Spurling **34**:494
D. M. Thomas **22**:417
William Trevor **25**:444
Frank Tuohy **37**:432
Fay Weldon **19**:468

Kemper, Robert Graham
Robert Anderson **23**:31

Kempton, Kenneth Payson
C. S. Forester **35**:161, 162

Kempton, Murray
Gore Vidal **4**:554

Kempton, Sally
John Knowles **26**:258

Kendall, Elaine
Nelson Algren **33**:17
William Kennedy **34**:206
Françoise Sagan **36**:381

Kendall, Paul M.
Thomas B. Costain **30**:99

Kendle, Burton
John Cheever **15**:128

Kendle, Judith
Morley Callaghan **14**:102

Kendrick, Walter
Robert Bloch **33**:84
Leon Edel **34**:536
Stephen King **37**:198
Judith Rossner **29**:355
Susan Sontag **31**:411, 417
Stephen Wright **33**:469

Keneas, Alex
Ira Levin **6**:305

Kenefick, Madeleine
Gayl Jones **6**:265
Cynthia Ozick **7**:290

Kennard, Jean E.
Anthony Burgess **10**:86
William Golding **10**:233
Joseph Heller **8**:275
James Purdy **10**:421
Kurt Vonnegut, Jr. **12**:611

Kennaway, James
Simon Raven **14**:439

Kennebeck, Edwin
Heinrich Böll **27**:55
Walter M. Miller, Jr. **30**:253
James Schuyler **23**:387
Terry Southern **7**:453
Marguerite Yourcenar **19**:482

Kennedy, Andrew K.
John Arden **6**:10
Samuel Beckett **6**:46
T. S. Eliot **6**:166
John Osborne **11**:422
Harold Pinter **6**:419

Kennedy, Dorothy Mintzlaff
Raymond Federman **6**:181
Howard Nemerov **6**:363

Kennedy, Eileen
Penelope Gilliatt **10**:230
Norma Klein **30**:237
Susan Richards Shreve **23**:402
Sloan Wilson **32**:449

Kennedy, Eugene
Thomas Merton **34**:466
Michael Mott **34**:466

Kennedy, Harlan
Michelangelo Antonioni **20**:42
Federico Fellini **16**:300
Werner Herzog **16**:330

Kennedy, John S.
John Steinbeck **1**:323; **13**:532

Kennedy, P. C.
Frank Swinnerton **31**:423

Kennedy, Randall
Philip Caputo **32**:104

Kennedy, Ray
Joseph Wambaugh **3**:509

Kennedy, Raymond
Richard Wright **21**:435

Kennedy, Richard S.
Aldous Huxley **35**:241

Kennedy, Sighle
Arthur Miller **26**:311

Kennedy, Susan
Rita Mae Brown **18**:75
Susan Cheever **18**:101
Anne Redmon **22**:342
J.I.M. Stewart **14**:512

Kennedy, William
Jorge Amado **13**:11
Thomas Bernhard **3**:64
Carlos Castaneda **12**:92
Robertson Davies **2**:113
Don DeLillo **10**:134
Gabriel García Márquez **8**:232
John Gardner **7**:111
Joseph Heller **5**:179
Elia Kazan **6**:273
Jerzy Kosinski **15**:316
William Kotzwinkle **5**:219
Peter Matthiessen **7**:211
Steven Millhauser **21**:219
Mordecai Richler **5**:378
Piri Thomas **17**:500
Mario Vargas Llosa **31**:444

Kennedy, William V.
Thomas J. Fleming **37**:122

Kennedy, X. J.
A. R. Ammons **2**:13
Edward Dahlberg **7**:62
Eleanor Lerman **9**:328
James Merrill **2**:275
Robert Pack **13**:438
David Wagoner **15**:558

Kennelly, Brendan
Seamus Heaney **37**:163
Patrick Kavanagh **22**:236

Kennely, Patricia
Jim Morrison **17**:288, 289

Kenner, Hugh
W. H. Auden **2**:29
Samuel Beckett **11**:43; **29**:53
Ben Belitt **22**:54
Saul Bellow **25**:81
R. P. Blackmur **24**:60
Robert Bly **10**:62
Guy Davenport, Jr. **14**:142
John Dos Passos **8**:182
William Empson **33**:145
Leslie A. Fiedler **24**:196
H. D. **31**:204
Ernest Hemingway **8**:285
Irving Layton **15**:319
J.M.G. Le Clézio **31**:245
Marshall McLuhan **37**:265
James Merrill **34**:234
Marianne Moore **4**:360; **13**:397;
19:340
Vladimir Nabokov **6**:357
George Oppen **7**:283, 285
Sylvia Plath **17**:366
Ezra Pound **2**:345; **4**:412; **7**:325
Mary Renault **11**:472
W. D. Snodgrass **18**:492
Richard G. Stern **4**:522
William Carlos Williams **2**:469;
13:605

James Wright **10**:546
Louis Zukofsky **7**:561, 562

Kennerly, Sarah Law
Jay Bennett **35**:43, 44
Lois Duncan **26**:104
Kin Platt **26**:349, 350

Kenney, Edwin J., Jr.
Elizabeth Bowen **11**:61
Iris Murdoch **6**:345

Kenney, Harry C.
Farley Mowat **26**:335

Kenny, Anthony
Ved Mehta **37**:290

Kenny, Kevin
Norma Klein **30**:243
D. M. Pinkwater **35**:320
Kin Platt **26**:356

Kenny, Mary
Benedict Kiely **23**:265

Kenny, Shirley Strum
Antonia Fraser **32**:183

Kent, Cerrulia
Laura Z. Hobson **7**:164

Kent, George E.
James Baldwin **1**:15
Gwendolyn Brooks **1**:46; **15**:94
Nikki Giovanni **19**:192
Chester Himes **4**:229
Ishmael Reed **13**:477

Kent, Heddie
Franklyn M. Branley **21**:20

Keon, Carol
Pat Jordan **37**:194

Kerans, James
Jean Renoir **20**:289

Kerensky, Oleg
Alan Ayckbourn **33**:40
Howard Brenton **31**:61
Simon Gray **36**:201

Kermode, Frank
W. H. Auden **2**:25; **14**:33
Beryl Bainbridge **8**:37; **22**:46
Roland Barthes **24**:25
Samuel Beckett **2**:46
T. S. Eliot **2**:126, 128
E. M. Forster **10**:178
Northrop Frye **24**:208, 213
William Golding **2**:167, 169;
　17:161, 167; **27**:164
Nadine Gordimer **10**:240
Graham Greene **6**:215
Peter Handke **5**:165
Edwin Honig **33**:210
Christopher Isherwood **11**:296
Stanley Kunitz **14**:312
C. S. Lewis **27**:264
Marshall McLuhan **37**:254
Henry Miller **2**:282
Iris Murdoch **2**:298
Philip Rahv **24**:355
I. A. Richards **14**:453
Philip Roth **3**:440
J. D. Salinger **12**:497
Susan Sontag **31**:413

Muriel Spark **2**:414, 415, 418;
　18:500
Edmund Wilson **24**:478
Marguerite Yourcenar **19**:483

Kern, Anita
Buchi Emecheta **14**:159

Kern, Edith
Samuel Beckett **2**:47; **14**:70

Kern, Gary
Aleksandr I. Solzhenitsyn
　26:420

Kern, Robert
Richard Brautigan **12**:71
Gary Snyder **9**:500

Kernan, Alvin B.
Bernard Malamud **27**:303
Philip Roth **4**:453
Evelyn Waugh **1**:358

Kernan, Margot S.
Claude Chabrol **16**:172

Kerr, Baine
N. Scott Momaday **19**:318

Kerr, Elizabeth M.
William Faulkner **14**:178

Kerr, John Austin, Jr.
José Rodrigues Miguéis **10**:341

Kerr, Peter
Michel Foucault **34**:339

Kerr, Walter
Edward Albee **25**:33
Enid Bagnold **25**:75, 76
Sally Benson **17**:50
Albert Camus **32**:85
Alice Childress **12**:106
Michael Cristofer **28**:95
Gretchen Cryer **21**:79, 80, 82
Shelagh Delaney **29**:144
Harvey Fierstein **33**:154
Charles Fuller **25**:182
William Gibson **23**:173, 174
Charles Gordone **1**:124
Simon Gray **36**:208
David Hare **29**:211, 218
Jan de Hartog **19**:130
Lorraine Hansberry **17**:184, 190
Beth Henley **23**:215, 217
Jim Jacobs and Warren Casey
　12:292
Marsha Norman **28**:318
Clifford Odets **28**:334
Harold Pinter **1**:267
Gerome Ragni and James Rado
　17:386, 387
Martin Sherman **19**:415
Neil Simon **6**:503; **31**:402
Stephen Sondheim **30**:379, 380,
　399
Megan Terry **19**:440
Kurt Vonnegut, Jr. **12**:605
Douglas Turner Ward **19**:458
Andrew Lloyd Webber and Tim
　Rice **21**:426, 432
Michael Weller **10**:526
Tennessee Williams **19**:473
Lanford Wilson **36**:463

Kerrane, Kevin
Robert Coover **7**:59

Kerridge, Roy
Colin MacInnes **23**:286

Kerrigan, Anthony
Jorge Luis Borges **4**:74; **9**:115;
　13:109
Camilo José Cela **13**:145

Kerrigan, John
Paul Muldoon **32**:321

Kerr-Jarrett, Peter
Octavio Paz **6**:397

Kersh, Gerald
José Donoso **32**:152

Kertzer, Jon
Matt Cohen **19**:114
Michael Ondaatje **29**:339

Kessler, Edward
Daniel Hoffman **6**:242
Charles Wright **6**:580

Kessler, Jascha
Vicente Aleixandre **36**:27
Yehuda Amichai **22**:31
A. R. Ammons **5**:28
Imamu Amiri Baraka **2**:34
Samuel Beckett **29**:60
Elizabeth Bishop **32**:36
Sterling A. Brown **23**:101
Charles Bukowski **5**:79
Ernesto Cardenal **31**:78
Robert Creeley **36**:116
James Dickey **7**:79
Loren Eiseley **7**:91
Irving Feldman **7**:101
Lawrence Ferlinghetti **10**:174
Eva Figes **31**:169
Allen Ginsberg **36**:197
Robert Graves **2**:176
Sandra Hochman **8**:297
Edwin Honig **33**:216
Ted Hughes **2**:201
June Jordan **5**:203
Yoram Kaniuk **19**:241
Anthony Kerrigan **4**:269
György Konrád **10**:304
Maxine Kumin **28**:222
Don L. Lee **2**:238
Thomas Merton **3**:335
Czesław Miłosz **31**:267
Pablo Neruda **28**:315
Robert Pack **13**:438
Kenneth Patchen **18**:394
Octavio Paz **10**:388
John Crowe Ransom **11**:467
Muriel Rukeyser **15**:460
Peter Shaffer **37**:383
Karl Shapiro **8**:485; **15**:478
Gary Soto **32**:401
Muriel Spark **8**:492
May Swenson **14**:521
D. M. Thomas **31**:433
John Wain **11**:561, 563
Robert Penn Warren **4**:578
Nancy Willard **37**:464
C. K. Williams **33**:444
Charles Wright **28**:460
James Wright **28**:467
Louis Zukofsky **7**:560

Ketterer, David
Ursula K. Le Guin **22**:267
Theodore Sturgeon **22**:411

Kettle, Arnold
John Berger **2**:55
Ivy Compton-Burnett **3**:111
E. M. Forster **3**:159
Graham Greene **3**:206
Aldous Huxley **3**:252

Key, Jan
Aidan Chambers **35**:100

Keyes, Mary
Phyllis Gotlieb **18**:192

Keyser, Barbara Y.
Muriel Spark **8**:494

Keyser, Lester J.
Federico Fellini **16**:294

Khan, Naseem
Simon Gray **36**:209

Kherdian, David
Philip Whalen **6**:565

Kibera, Leonard
Alex La Guma **19**:275

Kibler, Louis
Alberto Moravia **11**:382; **18**:344

Kibler, Myra L.
Robert Cormier **30**:86

Kidder, Rushworth M.
E. E. Cummings **8**:161; **15**:155,
　158

Kidel, Mark
Bob Dylan **12**:198
The Police **26**:364

Kieffer, Eduardo Gudiño
Jorge Luis Borges **9**:117

Kieley, Benedict
Brendan Behan **11**:44
John Montague **13**:391

Kiely, Robert
Richard Adams **18**:2
Louis Auchincloss **18**:26
Russell Banks **37**:24
Maeve Brennan **5**:73
Frederick Busch **18**:85
Hortense Calisher **2**:96
Susan Cheever **18**:101
Michael Frayn **7**:106
Gabriel García Márquez **2**:148
William H. Gass **2**:155
Bernard Malamud **3**:323
Joyce Carol Oates **19**:356
Anne Redmon **22**:342
Philip Roth **31**:340
Angus Wilson **25**:463

Kieran, Margaret Ford
Walter Farley **17**:117
Mary Stolz **12**:547

Kiernan, Robert F.
John Barth **3**:42
Gore Vidal **33**:405

Kiernan, V. G.
Antonia Fraser **32**:178

Kilgore, Kathryn
Juan Benet **28**:22
Adrienne Rich **36**:367

Killam, G. D.
Chinua Achebe **1**:1; **26**:22
Ngugi wa Thiong'o **36**:317

Killinger, John
Fernando Arrabal **9**:37

Kilpatrick, Thomas L.
T. J. Binyon **34**:33

Kilroy, Thomas
Samuel Beckett **3**:45

Kimball, Arthur G.
Yasunari Kawabata **9**:309
Kenzaburō Ōe **36**:344
Jun'ichirō Tanizaki **14**:526

Kimmel, Eric A.
Emily Cheney Neville **12**:452

Kimzey, Ardis
Leslie Norris **14**:388

Kinder, Marsha
Michelangelo Antonioni **20**:31
Ingmar Bergman **16**:75
Bernardo Bertolucci **16**:92
Luis Buñuel **16**:144
John Cassavetes **20**:50, 52
Richard Lester **20**:223
Roman Polanski **16**:466
Carlos Saura **20**:320
Peter Weir **20**:429

Kindilien, Glenn A.
Saul Bellow **10**:44

King, Bruce
Chinua Achebe **26**:19, 25
Jayanta Mahapatra **33**:278
Nadine Gordimer **10**:240
Ruth Prawer Jhabvala **8**:312
V. S. Naipaul **9**:392
Frank Sargeson **31**:371
Derek Walcott **25**:452

King, Cameron
Derek Walcott **25**:449

King, Charles L.
Ramón Sender **8**:479

King, Cynthia
Christopher Collier and James L. Collier **30**:73
Ouida Sebestyen **30**:346

King, Dolores
Margaret O. Hyde **21**:177

King, Edmund L.
Vicente Aleixandre **36**:25
Jorge Guillén **11**:263

King, Francis
Vasily Aksyonov **37**:14
Louis Auchincloss **18**:26
William Boyd **28**:39
Malcolm Bradbury **32**:57
Bruce Chatwin **28**:74
Isabel Colegate **36**:111, 112
Rhys Davies **23**:148
Margaret Drabble **22**:125
Maureen Duffy **37**:117
Lawrence Durrell **27**:98
Shusaku Endo **14**:161
Herbert Gold **14**:208
Graham Greene **18**:195

Aldous Huxley **5**:193
John Irving **23**:253
Kazuo Ishiguro **27**:203
M. M. Kaye **28**:198
Penelope Lively **32**:274
Bernard Mac Laverty **31**:256
Bobbie Ann Mason **28**:274
Brian Moore **32**:309
Iris Murdoch **11**:388
Shiva Naipaul **32**:327
Barbara Pym **19**:388
Tom Sharpe **36**:401, 403
Muriel Spark **13**:525
Robert Stone **23**:430
Lisa St. Aubin de Teran **36**:423
Fay Weldon **19**:469
Morris L. West **33**:434
A. N. Wilson **33**:452, 456

King, James
F. R. Scott **22**:373

King, Larry L.
Kurt Vonnegut, Jr. **12**:602

King, Nicholas
Rebecca West **31**:458

King, P. R.
Thom Gunn **32**:207
Ted Hughes **37**:171
Philip Larkin **33**:256
Tom Paulin **37**:352

King, Thomas M.
Jean-Paul Sartre **7**:394

Kingsbury, Mary
M. E. Kerr **12**:298

Kingston, Carolyn T.
Margot Benary-Isbert **12**:35
Emily Cheney Neville **12**:453
Scott O'Dell **30**:271

Kingston, Maxine Hong
Bienvenido N. Santos **22**:366

Kington, Miles
Peter Nichols **36**:332

Kinkead, Gwen
Penelope Gilliatt **2**:161

Kinkead-Weekes, Mark
William Golding **27**:165

Kinnamon, Keneth
James Baldwin **13**:52
Richard Wright **21**:451

Kinney, Arthur F.
William Faulkner **28**:141
Dorothy Parker **15**:415

Kinney, Jeanne
Carson McCullers **4**:344; **12**:427

Kinsella, Anna M.
Alberto Moravia **7**:242

Kinsella, Thomas
Austin Clarke **6**:111

Kinsey, Helen E.
Margot Benary-Isbert **12**:33

Kinzie, Mary
Jorge Luis Borges **2**:73
Rosellen Brown **32**:67
Stephen Dobyns **37**:77
Marilyn Hacker **23**:206
Ted Hughes **14**:271
Laura Jensen **37**:191
Howard Nemerov **36**:306
Gary Snyder **32**:395
Charles Wright **28**:459

Kirby, David
A. R. Ammons **25**:44
Stephen Dunn **36**:155

Kirby, Emma
Lenora Mattingly Weber **12**:633

Kirby, Fred
Jim Carroll **35**:77

Kirby, Martin
Walker Percy **8**:440

Kirby-Smith, H. T., Jr.
Elizabeth Bishop **4**:66
Arthur Gregor **9**:254

Kirk, Elizabeth D.
J.R.R. Tolkien **1**:341

Kirk, John M.
Mario Vargas Llosa **15**:549

Kirk, Ron
Michael Moorcock **27**:349

Kirk, Russell
Ray Bradbury **10**:68

Kirke, Ron
D. M. Thomas **22**:418

Kirkham, Michael
Donald Davie **31**:118
Charles Tomlinson **4**:543

Kirkpatrick, Stephen
James Tate **25**:428

Kirsch, Bob
Neil Diamond **30**:112
Paul McCartney **35**:283

Kirsch, Robert
Jascha Kessler **4**:270

Kirton, Mary
Roderick L. Haig-Brown **21**:142

Kirwan, Jack
James A. Michener **29**:316

Kish, A. V.
Mark Helprin **22**:221
Helen Yglesias **22**:493

Kish, Anne V.
Jim Harrison **14**:237

Kisner, Sister Madeleine
T. S. Eliot **15**:216

Kissel, Howard
Harvey Fierstein **33**:156
Neil Simon **31**:398
Stephen Sondheim **30**:392
Tom Stoppard **34**:276
Andrew Lloyd Webber and Tim Rice **21**:433

Kissel, Susan
Robert Coover **15**:145

Kitchen, Paddy
J. M. Coetzee **23**:122
Eva Figes **31**:163, 164
Judith Guest **30**:173
Bessie Head **25**:238
Fay Weldon **36**:447

Kitchin, Laurence
John Arden **13**:24
Arnold Wesker **5**:481

Kitching, Jessie B.
E. M. Almedingen **12**:3

Kitman, Marvin
Larry Gelbart **21**:131
Garry Marshall **17**:277
Arthur Miller **26**:326

Kitses, Jim
Elia Kazan **16**:369

Kittrel, William
Edna Ferber **18**:151

Kizer, Carolyn
Ted Hughes **2**:201

Klaidman, Stephen
Juan Goytisolo **5**:150

Klappert, Peter
Daniel Mark Epstein **7**:97
Kathleen Spivack **6**:520

Klarmann, Adolf D.
Friedrich Dürrenmatt **11**:168

Klaw, Barbara
Evan Hunter **31**:218

Klein, A. M.
A.J.M. Smith **15**:512

Klein, Arnold
William Wharton **37**:440

Klein, Gillian Parker
François Truffaut **20**:398

Klein, Joe
William Brammer **31**:55
Philip Caputo **32**:106
John M. Del Vecchio **29**:150
Ronald J. Glasser **37**:134

Klein, Julia M.
Marilyn French **18**:159
Erica Jong **18**:279
James Purdy **28**:381

Klein, Marcus
Saul Bellow **1**:29
Stanley Elkin **27**:121
Ralph Ellison **1**:94

Klein, T.E.D.
T.E.D. Klein **34**:72

Klein, Theodore
Albert Camus **11**:95

Kleinbard, David
Guillevic **33**:191

Kleinberg, Seymour
Phillip Lopate **29**:301
Isaac Bashevis Singer **3**:458

Klemtner, Susan Strehle
John Fowles **15**:232
William Gaddis **10**:212

Kley, Ronald J.
Margaret O. Hyde **21**:175

Kliman, Bernice W.
Philip Roth **3**:438

Klin, George
Yoram Kaniuk **19**:240

Kline, T. Jefferson
André Malraux **15**:353

Kling, Vincent
Rainer Werner Fassbinder
20:111

Klingel, Gilbert
Jacques-Yves Cousteau **30**:102

Klinkowitz, Jerome
Walter Abish **22**:22
Russell Banks **37**:25
Imamu Amiri Baraka **5**:45
Donald Barthelme **3**:43; **5**:52;
6:29; **13**:60; **23**:46
Jonathan Baumbach **6**:32
Robert Coover **32**:122
Erica Jong **6**:269
Jerzy Kosinski **3**:272
Clarence Major **19**:294, 295
Flann O'Brien **7**:269
Ishmael Reed **32**:361
Tom Robbins **32**:368
Gilbert Sorrentino **3**:462;
22:392
Steven Spielberg **20**:365
Ronald Sukenick **3**:475; **4**:530
Hunter S. Thompson **17**:510
Kurt Vonnegut, Jr. **1**:348;
3:500; **4**:563
Thomas Williams **14**:583

Klockner, Karen M.
Madeleine L'Engle **12**:352
Katherine Paterson **30**:283
Cynthia Voigt **30**:418

Kloman, William
Laura Nyro **17**:312
Gerome Ragni and James Rado
17:380

Klotman, Phyllis R.
Ronald L. Fair **18**:142
Langston Hughes **15**:292
Toni Morrison **22**:314

Klug, M. A.
Saul Bellow **15**:50

Kluger, Richard
Jerome Siegel and Joe Shuster
21:357

Kmetz, Gail Kessler
Muriel Spark **8**:493

Knapp, Bettina Liebowitz
Jean Anouilh **8**:24
Jean Cocteau **8**:145
Georges Duhamel **8**:187
Marguerite Duras **6**:151
Jean Genet **1**:116
Yukio Mishima **27**:343
Anna Kavan **13**:317

Robert Pinget **7**:305
Nathalie Sarraute **8**:469

Knapp, James F.
T. S. Eliot **6**:163
Ken Kesey **11**:317
Delmore Schwartz **2**:387

Knapp, John V.
John Hawkes **7**:145

Knelman, Martin
W. Somerset Maugham **11**:370
William Mitchell **25**:326
Harold Pinter **9**:421
Mordecai Richler **5**:377
Michel Tremblay **29**:419

Knickerbocker, Brad
Allan W. Eckert **17**:108

Knieger, Bernard
S. Y. Agnon **8**:8

Knight, Arthur
Woody Allen **16**:1
Gordon Parks **16**:457

Knight, Damon
Brian Aldiss **14**:10
Isaac Asimov **3**:16
Ray Bradbury **3**:84
John W. Campbell, Jr. **32**:75
Robert A. Heinlein **3**:224
Richard Matheson **37**:245

Knight, G. Wilson
Sean O'Casey **11**:406
John Cowper Powys **7**:347

Knight, Karl F.
John Crowe Ransom **4**:428

Knight, Max
Günter Grass **32**:197

Knight, Susan
Frederick Busch **7**:38
John Gardner **3**:186
József Lengyel **7**:202

Knittel, Robert
Riccardo Bacchelli **19**:31

Knobler, Peter
Jackson Browne **21**:39
Bob Dylan **12**:189
Van Morrison **21**:237
Phil Ochs **17**:333
Bruce Springsteen **17**:476, 484

Knoll, Robert E.
Kay Boyle **19**:64
Wright Morris **18**:351, 355
Ezra Pound **3**:398

Knoll, Robert F.
Ken Russell **16**:542

Knopf, Terry Ann
Agnes Eckhardt Nixon **21**:243,
245

Knopp, Josephine
Elie Wiesel **5**:491

Knorr, Walter L.
E. L. Doctorow **11**:142

Knowles, A. Sidney, Jr.
Marie-Claire Blais **2**:63
Frederic Prokosch **4**:421

Knowles, Dorothy
Eugène Ionesco **11**:290

Knowles, George W.
Marie-Claire Blais **13**:96

Knowles, John
C.D.B. Bryan **29**:100
Pamela Hansford Johnson
27:221
Françoise Sagan **17**:423

Knowlton, James
Walter Abish **22**:21

Knox, Bernard
Primo Levi **37**:230

Knox, George
Kenneth Burke **24**:129

Knox, Wendy
Carolyn Forché **25**:168

Knudsen, Erika
Elisaveta Bagryana **10**:11

Kobel, Peter
Steven Goldsberry **34**:54

Kobler, John
Jerome Siegel and Joe Shuster
21:353

Kobler, Turner S.
Rebecca West **7**:526

Koch, Christopher
Richard Elman **19**:149
Michael Frayn **31**:190

Koch, Kenneth
Frank O'Hara **2**:322
James Schuyler **23**:387

Koch, Stephen
Tish O'Dowd Ezekiel **34**:46
Hermann Hesse **3**:243
Reynolds Price **6**:425
Nathalie Sarraute **8**:472; **31**:385
Christina Stead **5**:404
Gore Vidal **4**:554
Andy Warhol **20**:420

Koch, Vivienne
August Derleth **31**:136
W. S. Graham **29**:192

Kochan, Lionel
Ilya Ehrenburg **34**:436
Anatol Goldberg **34**:436

Kodjak, Andrej
Aleksandr I. Solzhenitsyn
18:495

Koenig, Peter William
William Gaddis **10**:209

Koenig, Rhoda
Roald Dahl **18**:108
Peter De Vries **28**:110
E. L. Doctorow **37**:96
Michael Ende **31**:144
Nora Ephron **31**:158
T. Gertler **34**:50
Mark Helprin **22**:220
Paul Theroux **15**:535
Gore Vidal **33**:411

Koepf, Michael
Raymond Carver **22**:102

Koester, Rudolf
Hermann Hesse **17**:205

Koethe, John
John Ashbery **2**:17; **3**:15
Sandra Hochman **3**:250
James Schuyler **23**:388
Theodore Weiss **3**:517

Kofsky, Frank
Lenny Bruce **21**:56
Mick Jagger and Keith Richard
17:220

Kogan, Rick
Richard Price **12**:489

Koger, Grove
Kristin Hunter **35**:229

Kohler, Dayton
Walter D. Edmonds **35**:148
Carson McCullers **12**:413
Conrad Richter **30**:311
Jesse Stuart **14**:513

Kohn, Hans
E. M. Almedingen **12**:2

Kolb, Muriel
Lois Duncan **26**:102
Alvin Silverstein and Virginia
B. Silverstein **17**:451

Kolker, Robert Phillip
Robert Altman **16**:30
Ken Russell **16**:545
Martin Scorsese **20**:336

Kolodin, Irving
Buffy Sainte-Marie **17**:430

Kolodny, Annette
Thomas Pynchon **3**:412

Kolonosky, Walter F.
Vasily Aksenov **22**:27
Vladimir Voinovich **10**:508

Koltz, Newton
Wright Morris **3**:343
Patrick White **3**:524

Koniczek, Ryszard
Andrzej Wajda **16**:584

Koning, Hans
Jerzy Kosinski **15**:315
Aleksandr I. Solzhenitsyn
18:498

Koningsberger, Hans
John Huston **20**:171

Koon, William
William Price Fox **22**:140

Koper, Peter T.
Ursula K. Le Guin **22**:271

Kopkind, Andrew
Lenny Bruce **21**:57
John Lennon **35**:262
Prince **35**:330

Koprowski, Jan
Joseph Wittlin **25**:471

Korenblum, Toba
Thor Heyerdahl **26**:194

Korg, Jacob
Bernard Malamud **2**:269
Rebecca West **31**:458

Korges, James
Erskine Caldwell **1**:51

Korn, Eric
Philip K. Dick **10**:138
G. B. Edwards **25**:150
Harlan Ellison **13**:203
Rayner Heppenstall **10**:272
John Irving **23**:252
Jack Kerouac **14**:307
Richard O'Brien **17**:323
Judith Rossner **9**:457
Claude Simon **9**:482
Gore Vidal **10**:502
Fay Weldon **11**:566
William Wharton **18**:543
Tom Wolfe **15**:587
Roger Zelazny **21**:470

Kornblatt, Joyce
Joy Williams **31**:464

Kornblum, William
Peter Maas **29**:306

Kornfeld, Matilda
Zilpha Keatley Snyder **17**:473

Kornfeld, Melvin
Jurek Becker **7**:27

Kosek, Steven
Kurt Vonnegut, Jr. **4**:569

Koslow, Jules
Jorge Ibargüengoitia **37**:184

Kostach, Myrna
Rudy Wiebe **6**:566

Kostelanetz, Anne
Nathalie Sarraute **31**:377

Kostelanetz, Richard
R. P. Blackmur **2**:61
Ralph Ellison **3**:141
Ezra Pound **2**:344

Kostis, Nicholas
Julien Green **11**:259

Kostolefsky, Joseph
Frank Capra **16**:156

Kotin, Armine
Jean Arp **5**:33

Kotlowitz, Robert
Gerome Ragni and James Rado
17:382
Howard Sackler **14**:479

Kott, Jan
Andrei Sinyavsky **8**:488

Kotzwinkle, William
Max Apple **33**:20
Jay McInerney **34**:82

Kouidis, Virginia M.
Mina Loy **28**:248

Kountz, Peter
Thomas Merton **11**:372
Frank Zappa **17**:589

Kovács, Katherine Singer
Jorge Luis Borges **19**:49

Kovanda, Karel
Ilya Ehrenburg **34**:434
Anatol Goldberg **34**:434

Kovar, Helen M.
Christie Harris **12**:261

Kozak, Ellen M.
Gene Roddenberry **17**:413

Kozak, Roman
John Lennon **35**:272

Kozarek, Linda
Norma Klein **30**:239

Kozloff, Max
Agnès Varda **16**:557

Kozol, Jonathan
Marjorie Kellogg **2**:223

Kracauer, Siegfried
Fritz Lang **20**:202
Leni Riefenstahl **16**:519
Josef von Sternberg **20**:370

Kraemer, Chuck
Frederick Wiseman **20**:475

Krall, Flo
Jean Craighead George **35**:179

Kramer, Aaron
Stanley J. Kunitz **6**:287

Kramer, Hilton
William Barrett **27**:22
Donald Barthelme **8**:50
Bruce Chatwin **28**:71
E. L. Doctorow **6**:137
Robert Lowell **8**:357
Archibald MacLeish **8**:362
Mary McCarthy **5**:276
Marianne Moore **19**:342
L. E. Sissman **9**:492
Allen Tate **11**:527; **14**:530
Robert Penn Warren **8**:538

Kramer, Jane
André Brink **36**:67
Maxine Hong Kingston **12**:312
V. S. Naipaul **18**:363

Kramer, Lawrence
William Stafford **29**:382

Kramer, Mark
Joe McGinniss **32**:304

Kramer, Nora
Betty Cavanna **12**:99

Kramer, Peter G.
William Goyen **5**:149

Krance, Charles
Louis-Ferdinand Céline **9**:153

Krasny, Michael
Ishmael Reed **32**:361

Krasso, Nicolas
George Steiner **24**:430

Kraus, Elisabeth
John Hawkes **7**:146

Kraus, W. Keith
Kristin Hunter **35**:228

Krause, Walter
James D. Forman **21**:121

Krebs, Albin
Truman Capote **34**:320

Kreidl, John Francis
Alain Resnais **16**:514

Kreitzman, Ruth
Bernardo Bertolucci **16**:86

Krensky, Stephen
Frank Bonham **12**:55
Christopher Collier and James
L. Collier **30**:73
Robert Lipsyte **21**:212

Kresh, Paul
Neil Diamond **30**:111
Isaac Bashevis Singer **23**:417

Kreyling, Michael
Eudora Welty **22**:459

Kreymborg, Alfred
Mina Loy **28**:247

Krickel, Edward
James Gould Cozzens **1**:67
William Saroyan **1**:302

Kridl, Manfred
Maria Dabrowska **15**:165

Kriegel, Harriet
Nora Ephron **17**:112

Kriegel, Leonard
Virginia Spencer Carr **34**:422
John Dos Passos **34**:422
T. S. Eliot **6**:166
James T. Farrell **11**:193
Günter Grass **2**:172
James Jones **10**:293
Iris Murdoch **1**:234
Ezra Pound **7**:333
Harvey Swados **5**:423
Edmund Wilson **2**:475

Krieger, Murray
Northrop Frye **24**:223
I. A. Richards **24**:391

Krim
James Jones **10**:290

Krim, Seymour
William Barrett **27**:23
Leslie A. Fiedler **24**:193
Mark Helprin **32**:232
Ernest Hemingway **19**:219
Jack Kerouac **14**:303

Krispyn, Egbert
Günter Eich **15**:202

Krist, Gary
James Purdy **28**:381

Kroll, Ernest
Peter Viereck **4**:559

Kroll, Jack
Edward Albee **2**:1
Jean Anouilh **3**:12
W. H. Auden **3**:27
Alan Ayckbourn **5**:36
Saul Bellow **6**:55

Mel Brooks **12**:80
Ed Bullins **1**:47
Anne Burr **6**:103, 104
Truman Capote **34**:325
Brian Clark **29**:127
Rosalyn Drexler **2**:119
Frederick Exley **6**:171
Jules Feiffer **8**:216
Harvey Fierstein **33**:157
Jean Genet **2**:158
Amlin Gray **29**:201
Simon Gray **36**:210
John Guare **8**:253; **29**:206
Bill Gunn **5**:152
David Hare **29**:216
Ted Hughes **2**:200
Arthur Kopit **33**:254
Stanley J. Kunitz **6**:286
John Landis **26**:276
Ira Levin **6**:306
David Mamet **9**:360; **34**:221
Steve Martin **30**:251
Terrence McNally **7**:218
Mark Medoff **6**:322
Arthur Miller **2**:280; **6**:334
Jason Miller **2**:284
Rochelle Owens **8**:434
Miguel Piñero **4**:402
Dave Rabe **33**:346
Terence Rattigan **7**:355
Jonathan Reynolds **6**:451
Ronald Ribman **7**:358
Tadeusz Rózewicz **23**:362
Murray Schisgal **6**:490
Sam Shepard **34**:267
Neil Simon **6**:504; **31**:398, 399,
400
Stephen Sondheim **30**:388, 394
Tom Stoppard **5**:414; **29**:402;
34:274, 279
David Storey **2**:424, 426
Elizabeth Swados **12**:559
Lily Tomlin **17**:518
Kurt Vonnegut, Jr. **2**:452
Andrew Lloyd Webber and Tim
Rice **21**:426, 433
Lanford Wilson **7**:548

Kroll, Judith
Sylvia Plath **17**:359

Kroll, Steven
Irvin Faust **8**:215
Elizabeth Jane Howard **29**:245
Thomas McGuane **3**:330
Dan Wakefield **7**:503
Irving Wallace **7**:510

Kronenberger, Louis
Babette Deutsch **18**:118
Edna Ferber **18**:150
Henri de Montherlant **19**:322
Erich Maria Remarque **21**:325
Tennessee Williams **30**:455

Krouse, Agate Nesaule
Agatha Christie **12**:119
Robert B. Parker **27**:364
J.I.M. Stewart **14**:512
Fay Weldon **19**:466

Krulik, Ted
Richard Matheson **37**:248

Krumgold, Joseph
Joseph Krumgold **12**:319

Krupka, Mary Lee
Margot Benary-Isbert **12**:33, 34

Krupnick, Mark L.
Philip Rahv **24**:354

Krutch, Joseph Wood
Brigid Brophy **11**:67
Erskine Caldwell **8**:122
Paul Green **25**:194, 195
Mary McCarthy **24**:341
Clifford Odets **28**:323, 324,
326, 327, 331
Erich Maria Remarque **21**:326
Elmer Rice **7**:360
Irwin Shaw **23**:394
Frank Swinnerton **31**:425
Carl Van Vechten **33**:387
T. H. White **30**:443
Thornton Wilder **35**:436
Emlyn Williams **15**:576, 577
Tennessee Williams **30**:456,
461

Krynski, Magnus Jan
Tadeusz Różewicz **23**:359

Krysl, Marilyn
Marilyn Hacker **23**:204

Krystal, Arthur
T.E.D. Klein **34**:72

Krza, Paul
Edward Abbey **36**:20

Krzyzanowski, Jerzy R.
Tadeusz Konwicki **8**:325

Kubal, David
Raymond Carver **22**:104
G. B. Edwards **25**:152
Barbara Pym **37**:368

Kucewicz, William
Len Deighton **22**:117

Kuczkowski, Richard
Anthony Burgess **13**:125
Don DeLillo **13**:179
Susan Sontag **10**:485

Kuehl, Linda
Doris Lessing **3**:282
Iris Murdoch **3**:345; **15**:381
Marge Piercy **3**:384
Muriel Spark **2**:417
Eudora Welty **5**:479
Thomas Williams **14**:582

Kuehn, Robert E.
Aldous Huxley **11**:284

Kuhn, Doris Young
Julia W. Cunningham **12**:164
Joseph Krumgold **12**:320

Kuhn, Ira
Uwe Johnson **15**:304

Kuhn, Reinhard
J.M.G. Le Clézio **31**:248
Henri Michaux **19**:312, 313

Kuitunen, Maddalena
Dino Buzzati **36**:90

Kulshrestha, Chirantan
Mulk Raj Anand **23**:21

Kuncewicz, Maria
Maria Dąbrowska **15**:166

Kunitz, Isadora
Margaret O. Hyde **21**:174
Alvin Silverstein and Virginia
B. Silverstein **17**:454

Kunitz, Stanley
John Berryman **8**:86
Robert Creeley **8**:152
Carolyn Forché **25**:168
Robert Frost **9**:223
Jean Garrigue **8**:240
H. D. **8**:255; **31**:201
Robert Lowell **9**:334
Marianne Moore **8**:397; **10**:346
John Crowe Ransom **11**:467
Theodore Roethke **8**:458

Kunz, Don
James Welch **14**:559

Kunzle, David
Stan Lee **17**:258

Kupferberg, Herbert
Yoram Kaniuk **19**:238

Kussi, Peter
Milan Kundera **32**:260

Kustow, Michael
Jean-Luc Godard **20**:130
Arnold Wesker **3**:519

Kuzma, Greg
Barry Spacks **14**:510

Kyle, Carol A.
John Barth **9**:65

Labaree, Mary Fleming
Nella Larsen **37**:212

LaBarre, Weston
Carlos Castaneda **12**:88

Laber, Jeri
Ilya Ehrenburg **18**:132
Aleksandr I. Solzhenitsyn
2:411; **4**:514

Labrie, Ross
Thomas Merton **11**:373

Lacey, Henry C.
Amiri Baraka **33**:60

La Charité, Virginia
René Char **9**:167; **11**:113;
14:128
Henri Michaux **19**:314

Lachtman, Howard
Martin Cruz Smith **25**:414

Lacy, Allen
William Barrett **27**:20
Harry Crews **23**:136
Gilbert Sorrentino **14**:501

La Faille, Eugene E.
Piers Anthony **35**:39
Isaac Asimov **26**:58
Kim Stanley Robinson **34**:105
Jack Vance **35**:427

La Farge, Oliver
Howard Fast **23**:153
Robert Lewis Taylor **14**:534

Lafore, Laurence
David Caute **29**:111
Rhys Davies **23**:146
Shirley Hazzard **18**:214
William Maxwell **19**:307
James Alan McPherson **19**:309
R. K. Narayan **28**:295
Paul Theroux **28**:423
Irving Wallace **7**:509
Jessamyn West **17**:550

LaFrance, Marston
Evelyn Waugh **1**:358

LaHood, M. J.
William S. Burroughs **22**:85

LaHood, Marvin J.
Conrad Richter **30**:317, 325

Lahr, John
Edward Bond **13**:103
Noël Coward **29**:139
Dario Fo **32**:172
Arthur Kopit **1**:171
Darcy O'Brien **11**:405
Joe Orton **4**:388; **13**:435, 436
John Osborne **11**:422
Harold Pinter **6**:411
Richard Price **12**:489
Mordecai Richler **18**:454
Sam Shepard **4**:491; **17**:447
Stephen Sondheim **30**:394

Laidlaw, Marc
Stephen King **12**:311

Laing, Alexander
Esther Forbes **12**:208
C. S. Forester **35**:161

Laing, R. D.
Michel Foucault **31**:173

Laitinen, Kai
Paavo Haavikko **18**:205; **34**:173
Hannu Salama **18**:460

Lake, Steve
Ray Davies **21**:96
Gordon Lightfoot **26**:280
Phil Ochs **17**:332
Lou Reed **21**:307
Patti Smith **12**:536

Lalley, Francis A.
Vine Deloria, Jr. **21**:112

Lalley, J. M.
A. B. Guthrie, Jr. **23**:195

Lally, Michael
Charles Bukowski **9**:138
Larry Eigner **9**:182
Kenneth Koch **8**:323
Howard Moss **7**:249
Anne Sexton **6**:493

Lamb, Sister Avila
Piers Anthony **35**:38
David Brin **34**:134

Lambert, Gail Tansill
Fran Arrick **30**:18

Lambert, Gavin
Lindsay Anderson **20**:11
Robert Bresson **16**:102
Luis Buñuel **16**:129
Charles Chaplin **16**:195
Agatha Christie **8**:142

René Clair **20**:63, 64
John Huston **20**:160, 161, 162
Stanley Kubrick **16**:376, 377
Fritz Lang **20**:205
John O'Hara **6**:384
Jean Renoir **20**:288

Lambert, J. W.
Dannie Abse **29**:17
Edward Albee **2**:4
Alan Ayckbourn **5**:35
Howard Barker **37**:32
Peter Barnes **5**:50
Thomas Bernhard **32**:20
Edward Bond **4**:70; **6**:84
Caryl Churchill **31**:83
A. E. Ellis **7**:95
Dario Fo **32**:172
Michael Frayn **7**:108
Athol Fugard **5**:130
Trevor Griffiths **13**:256
David Hare **29**:211
John Osborne **2**:328
J. B. Priestley **34**:363
Sam Shepard **6**:496
Bernard Slade **11**:508
Tom Stoppard **3**:470; **5**:413
David Storey **2**:425; **4**:530
Arnold Wesker **3**:518

Lambert, Marguerite M.
Larry Bograd **35**:64

Lamie, Edward L.
John Brunner **8**:110

Lamming, George
Ishmael Reed **3**:424
Derek Walcott **4**:574

Lamont, Rosette C.
Fernando Arrabal **9**:35
Eugène Ionesco **1**:155; **6**:252,
256; **9**:287
Boris Pasternak **18**:387

Lamott, Kenneth
Maureen Duffy **37**:113
Siegfried Lenz **27**:244

Lamport, Felicia
Laura Z. Hobson **25**:272
S. J. Perelman **5**:337

Lancaster, Bruce
Thomas J. Fleming **37**:118
Halldór Laxness **25**:291

Landau, Deborah
Van Morrison **21**:233

Landau, Elaine
Virginia Hamilton **26**:150

Landau, Jon
Bob Dylan **12**:190
Marvin Gaye **26**:131
George Roy Hill **26**:202
Mick Jagger and Keith Richard
17:221, 224, 233
John Lennon **35**:265, 269, 279
John Lennon and Paul
McCartney **12**:377
Joni Mitchell **12**:438
Van Morrison **21**:231, 232
Jimmy Page and Robert Plant
12:475

Sam Peckinpah **20**:278
Martin Scorsese **20**:324
Bob Seger **35**:379
Paul Simon **17**:461
Bruce Springsteen **17**:478
Andrew Lloyd Webber and Tim
    Rice **21**:429
Stevie Wonder **12**:655, 657

Landess, Thomas
Thomas Merton **1**:211

Landess, Thomas H.
John Berryman **2**:60
Caroline Gordon **6**:205; **13**:247
Andrew Lytle **22**:294
William Meredith **4**:349
Marion Montgomery **7**:234
Julia Peterkin **31**:308, 311
William Jay Smith **6**:512
Allen Tate **4**:540
Mona Van Duyn **3**:491
Eudora Welty **1**:363
James Wright **3**:541

Landis, Joan Hutton
Ben Belitt **22**:52

Landy, Francis
A. Alvarez **13**:9

Lane, Helen R.
Carlos Fuentes **22**:165

Lane, James B.
Harold Robbins **5**:379
Piri Thomas **17**:499

Lane, John Francis
Michelangelo Antonioni **20**:38
Vittorio De Sica **20**:90

Lane, M. Travis
Marilyn Bowering **32**:46
Ralph Gustafson **36**:213, 215,
    221

Lane, Patrick
Andrew Suknaski **19**:433

Lanes, Selma G.
Richard Adams **4**:9
Paula Danziger **21**:84

Lang, Doug
Donald Justice **19**:233
Cynthia MacDonald **19**:291

Lang, Olga
Pa Chin **18**:371

Langbaum, Robert
Samuel Beckett **9**:85
Isak Dinesen **29**:156
E. M. Forster **1**:107
Galway Kinnell **13**:321
M. L. Rosenthal **28**:390

Lange, Victor
Heinrich Böll **27**:62
Martin Heidegger **24**:279

Langer, Elinor
Marge Piercy **18**:408

Langer, Lawrence L.
Simone de Beauvoir **31**:35
Paul Celan **19**:91
Elie Wiesel **37**:450

Langford, Paul
Leon Garfield **12**:233

Langguth, A. J.
Gay Talese **37**:392

Langlois, Jim
William Kotzwinkle **35**:254

Langlois, Walter
Pearl S. Buck **18**:77
André Malraux **9**:355

Langton, Jane
Paula Danziger **21**:85
Virginia Hamilton **26**:151
William Mayne **12**:402
Richard Peck **21**:301
Mary Rodgers **12**:493
Zilpha Keatley Snyder **17**:472,
    473, 474
Cynthia Voigt **30**:420
Jill Paton Walsh **35**:433
Rosemary Wells **12**:637

Lant, Jeffrey
Jonathan Kozol **17**:253

Lantz, Fran
D. M. Pinkwater **35**:318

Lanyi, Ronald Levitt
Trina Robbins **21**:339

Laqueur, Walter
Anatoli Rybakov **23**:370

Lardner, David
Alfred Hitchcock **16**:339

Lardner, John
Irwin Shaw **7**:409

Lardner, Rex
Winston Graham **23**:191
Frank G. Slaughter **29**:377

Lardner, Susan
Toni Cade Bambara **19**:34
John Gregory Dunne **28**:124
Mary Gordon **22**:186
György Konrád **10**:305
Thomas McGuane **18**:324
Joyce Carol Oates **9**:404
Wilfrid Sheed **2**:393

Larkin, Joan
Rita Mae Brown **18**:73
Hortense Calisher **4**:88
June Jordan **23**:256
Audre Lorde **18**:307

Larkin, Philip
Dick Francis **22**:153
Barbara Pym **19**:386

LaRocque, Geraldine E.
Jay Bennett **35**:42
Madeleine L'Engle **12**:348

Larrabee, Eric
Cornelius Ryan **7**:385

Larrieu, Kay
H. D. **34**:443
Barbara Guest **34**:443
Larry Woiwode **10**:542

Larsen, Anne
Lisa Alther **7**:11
William Kotzwinkle **14**:310
Leonard Michaels **6**:325

Larsen, Eric
Charles Newman **8**:419

Larsen, Ernest
Jerome Charyn **18**:100
Gilbert Sorrentino **14**:499

Larson, Charles
Hyemeyohsts Storm **3**:470

Larson, Charles R.
Peter Abrahams **4**:2
Chinua Achebe **5**:1
Rudolfo A. Anaya **23**:25
Ayi Kwei Armah **5**:31; **33**:27,
    29
J. M. Coetzee **23**:122
Leslie A. Fiedler **4**:163; **13**:211
Bessie Head **25**:235, 239
Camara Laye **4**:284
Jayanta Mahapatra **33**:277
Kamala Markandaya **8**:377
Peter Matthiessen **7**:210
V. S. Naipaul **7**:253; **18**:359
R. K. Narayan **7**:255
James Ngugi **7**:263
Raja Rao **25**:369
Simone Schwarz-Bart **7**:404
Leslie Marmon Silko **23**:406
Raymond Sokolov **7**:430
Wole Soyinka **5**:396
Jean Toomer **13**:556
Amos Tutuola **5**:445; **29**:442
Ngugi Wa Thiong'o **13**:583,
    584
James Welch **6**:561

Larson, James
Gunnar Ekelöf **27**:118

Lasagna, Louis
Michael Crichton **2**:108
Margaret O. Hyde **21**:174

LaSalle, Peter
Frederick Barthelme **36**:52
J. M. Coetzee **23**:124
J. F. Powers **8**:448
Cynthia Propper Seton **27**:426
Michel Tournier **36**:435

Lasansky, Terry Andrews
W. P. Kinsella **27**:236

Laschever, Sara
Gordon Vorster **34**:122

Lasdun, James
Anita Brookner **34**:140
J. M. Coetzee **33**:108
Elaine Feinstein **36**:172
Pamela Hansford Johnson
    27:223
Peter Porter **33**:320
Fay Weldon **36**:444

Lask, I. M.
S. Y. Agnon **4**:10

Lask, Thomas
Franklyn M. Branley **21**:15
Richard Brautigan **12**:60
Dino Buzzati **36**:88
Ronald J. Glasser **37**:130
Kenneth O. Hanson **13**:263
Bohumil Hrabal **13**:291
David Ignatow **7**:177

P. D. James **18**:273
William Kotzwinkle **35**:253
J.M.G. Le Clézio **31**:246
Ross Macdonald **1**:185
Clarence Major **19**:294
Frederick Morgan **23**:298
Grace Paley **37**:331
Linda Pastan **27**:368
M. L. Rosenthal **28**:391
John Sayles **14**:484
Georges Simenon **8**:486
Josef Škvorecký **15**:510
W. D. Snodgrass **2**:405
Piri Thomas **17**:502

Laska, P. J.
Imamu Amiri Baraka **10**:21

Laski, Audrey
Bette Greene **30**:169

Laski, Marghanita
Peter Dickinson **35**:131, 132,
    136
Frederick Forsyth **36**:175
John Gardner **30**:154
Patricia Highsmith **14**:260
John le Carré **28**:230
Ruth Rendell **28**:384
J.I.M. Stewart **32**:421
Glendon Swarthout **35**:404
Mario Vargas Llosa **31**:447

Lassell, Michael
Tennessee Williams **11**:573

Lasson, Robert
Mario Puzo **2**:352

Last, B. W.
Ngugi wa Thiong'o **36**:320

Last, Rex
Christa Wolf **29**:467

Latham, Aaron
Jack Kerouac **2**:228

Latham, David
Hugh Hood **28**:191

Lathen, Emma
Agatha Christie **12**:123

Latiak, Dorothy S.
Jules Archer **12**:17

Latimer, Jonathan P.
Francis Ford Coppola **16**:236

Latimer, Margery
Molly Keane **31**:230

Latrell, Craig
Harold Pinter **9**:421

Latshaw, Jessica
Christie Harris **12**:268

Lattimore, Richmond
John Berryman **2**:59
Philip Booth **23**:76
Jorge Luis Borges **2**:73
Edgar Bowers **9**:121
Joseph Brodsky **6**:97
Michael Casey **2**:100
Alan Dugan **6**:144
Daniel Hoffman **6**:243
John Hollander **14**:265
Galway Kinnell **13**:318

Vladimir Nabokov **8**:407
Adrienne Rich **7**:364
I. A. Richards **14**:453
L. E. Sissman **9**:491
Andrei Voznesensky **15**:557

Lattin, Vernon E.
N. Scott Momaday **19**:320

Lauder, Robert E.
Ingmar Bergman **16**:77
John Cassavetes **20**:52, 328
Christopher Durang **27**:91
Jean-Paul Sartre **24**:405

Laughlin, Rosemary M.
John Fowles **2**:138

Laughner, Peter
Lou Reed **21**:310

Laurence, Margaret
Chinua Achebe **7**:3
William Mitchell **25**:322
Wole Soyinka **14**:507
Amos Tutuola **14**:538

Laut, Stephen J., S.J.
R. V. Cassill **23**:105
John Gardner **10**:220

Lavender, Ralph
Alan Garner **17**:150
Diana Wynne Jones **26**:227
Otfried Preussler **17**:375
Robert Westall **17**:557

Lavers, Annette
Sylvia Plath **9**:425

Lavers, Norman
John Hawkes **2**:186

Lavine, Stephen David
Philip Larkin **8**:336

Law, Richard
Joan D. Vinge **30**:416
Robert Penn Warren **13**:570

Lawall, Sarah N.
Yves Bonnefoy **9**:113; **15**:72
Guillevic **33**:193, 194
Francis Ponge **18**:413

Lawhead, Terry
Lois Duncan **26**:108
Milton Meltzer **26**:309

Lawler, Daniel F., S.J.
Eleanor Hibbert **7**:156

Lawler, James R.
René Char **11**:117

Lawless, Ken
J. P. Donleavy **10**:155

Lawrence, D. H.
Edward Dahlberg **7**:61
Ernest Hemingway **10**:263
Carl Van Vechten **33**:393

Lawrence, Isabelle
Lee Kingman **17**:244

Lawrence, Leota S.
C.L.R. James **33**:220

Lawrence, Peter C.
Jean Lee Latham **12**:324

Laws, Frederick
Sally Benson **17**:47

Laws, Page R.
Uwe Johnson **15**:307

Lawson, Lewis A.
William Faulkner **3**:153
Flannery O'Connor **1**:255
Eudora Welty **14**:567

Lawton, A.
Yevgeny Yevtushenko **13**:620

Lazarus, H. P.
Budd Schulberg **7**:401

Lazenby, Francis D.
Milton Meltzer **26**:300

Lazere, Donald
Albert Camus **14**:107

Lea, Sydney
Philip Levine **14**:319
Frederick Morgan **23**:299

Leach, Edmund
Carlos Castaneda **12**:85

Leader, Zachary
Garson Kanin **22**:233

Leaf, David
Brian Wilson **12**:652

Leahy, Jack
David Wagoner **5**:474

Leak, Thomas
Michael Shaara **15**:474

Leal, Luis
Juan Rulfo **8**:462

Leamer, Laurence
Allen Drury **37**:109

Leaming, Barbara
Rainer Werner Fassbinder
20:114

Leapman, Michael
Maurice Gee **29**:179

Lear, Norman
Norman Lear **12**:328

Learmont, Lavinia Marina
Hermann Hesse **2**:191

Leary, Lewis
Lionel Trilling **9**:534

Leary, Timothy
Bob Dylan **12**:193

Leavell, Frank H.
Jesse Stuart **14**:514

Leavis, F. R.
Van Wyck Brooks **29**:84
John Dos Passos **11**:152
T. S. Eliot **24**:171
C. P. Snow **13**:512

Leavitt, David
E. L. Doctorow **37**:95

Leavitt, Harvey
Richard Brautigan **5**:67

Leb, Joan P.
Laura Z. Hobson **25**:272

LeBeau, Bryan F.
Alfred Kazin **34**:559

Lebel, J.-P.
Buster Keaton **20**:190

Leber, Michele M.
Judith Guest **30**:174
Jane Rule **27**:417
Sandra Scoppettone **26**:404

Lebowitz, Alan
Ernest Hemingway **1**:144

Lebowitz, Naomi
Stanley Elkin **4**:152
E. M. Forster **4**:166
J. F. Powers **1**:279

Lechlitner, Ruth
Ben Belitt **22**:48
August Derleth **31**:132

Lecker, Robert
Clark Blaise **29**:74
Ralph Gustafson **36**:219
Jack Hodgins **23**:233
Hugh Hood **15**:286

Lecker, Robert A.
John Metcalf **37**:302

LeClair, Thomas
Isaac Asimov **26**:51
Russell Banks **37**:22
John Barth **7**:23
Saul Bellow **6**:53
Anthony Burgess **1**:48
R. V. Cassill **23**:109
Carlos Castaneda **12**:95
Jerome Charyn **5**:103; **8**:135
Don DeLillo **10**:135; **13**:179
J. P. Donleavy **1**:76; **4**:124;
   6:141; **10**:154
Stanley Elkin **6**:170; **9**:190;
   27:125
John Gardner **8**:236; **18**:179,
   183
John Hawkes **7**:141, 144
Joseph Heller **8**:278
Flannery O'Connor **13**:420
Walker Percy **6**:400; **14**:412
David Plante **7**:307
Thomas Pynchon **6**:435
Tom Robbins **9**:454
Marilynne Robinson **25**:389
Michael Shaara **15**:474
Ronald Sukenick **6**:523
Harvey Swados **5**:420

LeClair, Tom
Max Apple **33**:21
William Wharton **37**:442

LeClercq, Diane
Patricia Highsmith **2**:194
Susan B. Hill **4**:226
William Sansom **6**:483

Ledbetter, J. T.
Galway Kinnell **13**:320
Mark Van Doren **6**:542

Lee, A. Robert
Chester Himes **18**:249

Lee, Alvin
James Reaney **13**:472

Lee, Brian
James Baldwin **17**:35

Lee, Charles
Taylor Caldwell **28**:60, 62
Thomas B. Costain **30**:94, 96
A. J. Cronin **32**:137
Ernest K. Gann **23**:163
Earl Hamner, Jr. **12**:257
Laura Z. Hobson **25**:271
Mary Renault **17**:391
Frank G. Slaughter **29**:375, 376
T. H. White **30**:442

Lee, Dennis
David Donnell **34**:156
Paulette Giles **13**:304
A. W. Purdy **6**:428

Lee, Don L.
Nikki Giovanni **4**:189
Conrad Kent Rivers **1**:285

Lee, Dorothy
Joseph A. Walker **19**:455

Lee, Dorothy H.
Harriette Arnow **18**:13

Lee, Felicia
John Edgar Wideman **34**:300

Lee, Hermione
J. G. Ballard **14**:40
Pat Barker **32**:12
Jurek Becker **19**:36
Elizabeth Bowen **11**:65; **22**:63
Malcolm Bradbury **32**:57
Brigid Brophy **29**:97
Anita Brookner **34**:137
Penelope Fitzgerald **19**:173
Nadine Gordimer **18**:189
Jonathan Keates **34**:201
Thomas Keneally **14**:302
Flannery O'Connor **15**:413
Julia O'Faolain **19**:360
Jayne Anne Phillips **33**:308
Marilynne Robinson **25**:387
Andrew Sinclair **14**:490
J.I.M. Stewart **14**:513
Lisa St. Aubin de Teran **36**:419
Anne Tyler **28**:434

Lee, James W.
John Braine **1**:43

Lee, Judith Yaross
Philip Roth **22**:354

Lee, L. L.
Thomas Berger **18**:54
Walter Van Tilburg Clark **28**:79

Lee, Lance
Thom Gunn **18**:201

Lee, Robert A.
Alistair MacLean **13**:359

Lee, Stan
Stan Lee **17**:261

Leech, Margaret
Esther Forbes **12**:206

Leedom-Ackerman, Joanne
Howard Fast **23**:160

Critic Index

Leeds, Barry H.
Ken Kesey 6:278
Norman Mailer 1:191
D. Keith Mano 2:270

Leeming, Glenda
John Arden 6:9

Leepson, Marc
Sloan Wilson 32:449

Leer, Norman
Bernard Malamud 8:374

Lees, Gene
John Lennon and Paul
McCartney 12:358
Gerome Ragni and James Rado
17:383

Lees-Milne, James
I. Compton-Burnett 34:497
Hilary Spurling 34:497

Leet, Herbert L.
Frank B. Gilbreth and
Ernestine Gilbreth Carey
17:155

Leet, Judith
May Sarton 14:482

Leffland, Ella
Lois Gould 10:242

Legates, Charlotte
Aldous Huxley 11:287

Le Guin, Ursula K.
Italo Calvino 22:89; 33:101
Philip K. Dick 30:125
John Gardner 18:181
Doris Lessing 15:334
Arkadii Strugatskii and Boris
Strugatskii 27:435

Legum, Colin
David Caute 29:123

Lehan, Richard
Walker Percy 2:332
Wilfrid Sheed 2:392
Susan Sontag 1:322

Lehman, David
W. H. Auden 11:20
Ted Berrigan 37:44
Frank Bidart 33:81
Michael S. Harper 22:208
Evan Hunter 31:227
David Ignatow 7:182
William McPherson 34:88
Charles Reznikoff 9:449
Ira Sadoff 9:466

Lehmann, A. G.
Georg Lukács 24:333

Lehmann, John
W. Somerset Maugham 11:370
Edith Sitwell 2:403

Lehmann, Rosamond
Mary Renault 17:390
Conrad Richter 30:308

Lehmann-Haupt, Christopher
Roger Angell 26:28
Aharon Appelfeld 23:35
Louis Auchincloss 18:25
Amiri Baraka 33:60
Thomas Berger 18:56

Peter Brooks 34:520
Rosellen Brown 32:67
Italo Calvino 22:92
Truman Capote 19:85
Henry Carlisle 33:104
Jerome Charyn 18:99
Susan Cheever 18:100
James Clavell 25:126
J. M. Coetzee 33:106
Michael Crichton 2:109
Robert Crumb 17:82
Don DeLillo 27:80
E. L. Doctorow 37:91
Rosalyn Drexler 2:119
Stanley Elkin 14:157
Nora Ephron 31:157
William Price Fox 22:139
Marilyn French 18:159
Robert Frost 34:470
John Gardner 18:180
Gail Godwin 31:197
Francine du Plessix Gray
22:200
Graham Greene 27:172; 37:139
Judith Guest 30:175
Pete Hamill 10:251
Barry Hannah 23:210
George V. Higgins 18:234
P. D. James 18:276
William Kennedy 28:205
John Knowles 26:262
Andrea Lee 36:256
Ella Leffland 19:277, 278
Siegfried Lenz 27:248
Elmore Leonard 34:213
Hugh Leonard 19:282
Bette Bao Lord 23:280
Robert Ludlum 22:291
Peter Maas 29:308
Norman Mailer 28:257
Clarence Major 19:291
Peter Matthiessen 32:292
Ted Mooney 25:330
Joe McGinniss 32:301
Brian Moore 32:308
Wright Morris 37:314
Farley Mowat 26:345
Iris Murdoch 22:329
Charles Newman 2:311
Robert Newton Peck 17:336
Bette Pesetsky 28:357, 359
George Plimpton 36:354, 355,
356
Chaim Potok 26:372
William H. Pritchard 34:470
Richard Price 12:488
Mario Puzo 36:361
Thomas Pynchon 33:338
Piers Paul Read 25:376, 378
Gregor von Rezzori 25:382
Mordecai Richler 18:452
Philip Roth 31:340
Salman Rushdie 31:356
Peter Rushforth 19:406
Jaroslav Seifert 34:260
Irwin Shaw 23:399
Lee Smith 25:407
Martin Cruz Smith 25:412
Paul Theroux 28:428
Lewis Thomas 35:410, 412
Hunter S. Thompson 17:504
Anne Tyler 28:431
Leon Uris 32:432

Gore Vidal 33:403, 409
Kurt Vonnegut, Jr. 22:450
Jill Paton Walsh 35:431
John Edgar Wideman 36:456
Helen Yglesias 22:492
Al Young 19:479

Lehrmann, Charles C.
Romain Gary 25:185

Leib, Mark
Sylvia Plath 3:389

Leiber, Fritz
T.E.D. Klein 34:71
Fritz Leiber 25:304

Leiber, Justin
Fritz Leiber 25:309

Leibold, Cynthia K.
Suzanne Newton 35:303

Leibowitz, Herbert
Elizabeth Bishop 13:91
Robert Bly 2:66
Edward Dahlberg 14:136
Jean Garrigue 2:153
Philip Levine 14:320
Robert Lowell 4:297
Josephine Miles 2:278
Kenneth Rexroth 6:451
Theodore Roethke 3:434
Delmore Schwartz 2:388
Judith Johnson Sherwin 15:479
Isaac Bashevis Singer 3:453
W. D. Snodgrass 2:405
Gary Snyder 5:395
Mona Van Duyn 3:492
Jonathan Williams 13:600
William Carlos Williams 9:574;
22:468
Edmund Wilson 3:540

Leibowitz, Herbert A.
Frank O'Hara 2:321

Leichtling, Jerry
Jackson Browne 21:35

Leigh, David J., S.J.
Ernest Hemingway 6:233
Tadeusz Konwicki 28:211

Leighton, Jean
Simone de Beauvoir 31:33

Leitch, David
Romain Gary 25:187

Leiter, Robert
Janet Frame 6:190
Nadine Gordimer 7:132
Cormac McCarthy 4:342
Jean Rhys 6:453
Clancy Sigal 7:424
Larry Woiwode 10:541

Leiter, Robert A.
William Maxwell 19:308

Leith, Linda
Hubert Aquin 15:17
Marie-Claire Blais 22:59
Matt Cohen 19:112

Leithauser, Brad
Marianne Moore 19:340
Jean Stafford 19:431
Evelyn Waugh 19:465

Lejeune, Anthony
Agatha Christie 12:117
Ian Fleming 30:138
Paul Gallico 2:147
Anthony Powell 7:345
P. G. Wodehouse 2:480

Lejeune, C. A.
René Clair 20:59
Jean Cocteau 16:224
Elia Kazan 16:360

Lekachman, Robert
William F. Buckley, Jr. 18:83
Richard Elman 19:151
Paul E. Erdman 25:156
Ken Follett 18:156
Robert Ludlum 22:290
Martin Cruz Smith 25:413

Lelchuk, Alan
Bernard Malamud 27:298
Isaac Bashevis Singer 11:500

Lellis, George
Rainer Werner Fassbinder
20:107
Martin Scorsese 20:324

Lelyveld, Joseph
Breyten Breytenbach 37:51
Buchi Emecheta 14:160

Lem, Stanislaw
Philip K. Dick 30:117
Arkadii Strugatskii and Boris
Strugatskii 27:436

LeMaster, J. R.
Jesse Stuart 8:507; 11:509

Lemay, Harding
John Knowles 26:246
J. R. Salamanca 4:461

Lembeck, Carolyn S.
Kevin Major 26:286

Lembo, Diana
Scott O'Dell 30:268

Lemmons, Philip
Brian Moore 8:396
William Trevor 7:478

Lemon, Lee T.
Kenneth Burke 2:87, 89
Louis-Ferdinand Céline 3:105
Guy Davenport, Jr. 6:124
Judith Guest 8:254
Jack Kerouac 5:213
Jerzy Kosinski 10:306
Joyce Carol Oates 6:369
John Rechy 1:283
Andrew Sinclair 14:488
C. P. Snow 4:503
Patrick White 5:485
Yvor Winters 4:591

Lenardon, Robert J.
Mary Renault 17:401

Lenburg, Greg
Steve Martin 30:250

Lenburg, Jeff
Steve Martin 30:250

L'Engle, Madeleine
James D. Forman 21:115
Mary Stolz 12:552

Lenhart, Maria
Laurence Yep **35**:470

Lennox, John Watt
Anne Hébert **13**:266

Lensing, George
James Dickey **4**:120
Robert Lowell **1**:183
Louis Simpson **4**:498
Louis Zukofsky **1**:385

Lensing, George S.
William Stafford **29**:380

Lenski, Branko
Miroslav Krleža **8**:329

Lent, Henry B.
John R. Tunis **12**:596

Lentfoehr, Sister Therese
David Kherdian **6**:281

Lentricchia, Frank
Northrop Frye **24**:229

Lenz, Joseph M.
Frank Herbert **35**:199

Leonard, George
Robert Coover **32**:125

Leonard, John
Lisa Alther **7**:12
Max Apple **33**:19
Louis Auchincloss **18**:25
Saul Bellow **6**:56
John Berger **19**:41
E. M. Broner **19**:71
T. Alan Broughton **19**:73
Anthony Burgess **22**:75
Jerome Charyn **18**:98
John Cheever **3**:107; **8**:139;
    25:120
Arthur C. Clarke **35**:120
Arthur A. Cohen **31**:93
Anita Desai **19**:135
Joan Didion **1**:74; **14**:151
Nora Ephron **17**:113
Thomas Flanagan **25**:166
Dick Francis **22**:153
Max Frisch **18**:162
Francine du Plessix Gray
    22:201
Shirley Hazzard **18**:218
Carolyn G. Heilbrun **25**:256
Frank Herbert **23**:219, 221
Maxine Hong Kingston **19**:249
Doris Lessing **3**:285
Jakov Lind **27**:271
Robert Ludlum **22**:289
Alison Lurie **4**:306
Larry McMurtry **2**:271
Margaret Mead **37**:275
V. S. Naipaul **18**:361
Joyce Carol Oates **19**:355
Marge Piercy **27**:372
Thomas Pynchon **3**:414
Wilfrid Sheed **2**:393
Gilbert Sorrentino **14**:499
Gay Talese **37**:398
Alexander Theroux **25**:433
Trevanian **29**:431
Anne Tyler **18**:529
Joseph Wambaugh **18**:532
Donald E. Westlake **33**:439

John Edgar Wideman **36**:451,
    454
Alexander Zinoviev **19**:486

Leonard, Vickie
Marge Piercy **27**:380

Leonard, William J.
Hugh Leonard **19**:283

Leonberger, Janet
Richard Peck **21**:298

Leone, Arthur T.
Jill Paton Walsh **35**:429

Leonhardt, Rudolf Walter
Martin Walser **27**:456

LePellec, Yves
John Updike **15**:540

Le Pelley, Guernsey
William F. Buckley, Jr. **18**:82
G. B. Edwards **25**:150

Leppard, David
Joan Didion **32**:144

Lerman, Leo
Enid Bagnold **25**:74
Gay Talese **37**:390

Lerman, Sue
Agnès Varda **16**:559

Lerner, Laurence
Geoffrey H. Hartman **27**:179
Craig Raine **32**:353
René Wellek **28**:445
A. N. Wilson **33**:455

Lerner, Max
James M. Cain **28**:47
Arthur Koestler **33**:233

Lernoux, Penny
Mario Vargas Llosa **9**:544

LeSage, Laurent
Roland Barthes **24**:25
Marie-Claire Blais **22**:57
Robert Pinget **7**:305
Françoise Sagan **17**:423

Le Shan, Eda J.
Sol Gordon **26**:136

Leslie, Omolara
Chinua Achebe **3**:2
Charles R. Larson **31**:237
Christopher Okigbo **25**:353

Lesser, Rika
Paul Celan **19**:94

Lesser, Wendy
Isabel Colegate **36**:114
David Leavitt **34**:78
Kem Nunn **34**:94

Lessing, Doris
Kurt Vonnegut, Jr. **2**:456

Lester, Julius
Pete Dexter **34**:43
Henry Dumas **6**:146
Lorraine Hansberry **17**:192

Lester, Margot
Dan Jacobson **4**:256
Hugh Nissenson **9**:400

Lester-Massman, Elli
John Edgar Wideman **34**:298

Le Stourgeon, Diana E.
Rosamond Lehmann **5**:235

Letson, Russell
Philip José Farmer **19**:167

Leung, Paul
Margaret O. Hyde **21**:179

Levene, Mark
Arthur Koestler **33**:240

Levensohn, Alan
Brigid Brophy **29**:96
Christina Stead **2**:422

Levenson, Christopher
Patrick Lane **25**:287

Levenson, J. C.
Saul Bellow **1**:29

Levenson, Michael
Herbert Gold **7**:121
Tom McHale **5**:282
John Updike **5**:460

Leventhal, A. J.
Samuel Beckett **11**:32

Lever, Karen M.
John Fowles **15**:234

Leverence, John
Irving Wallace **13**:567

Leverich, Kathleen
Robin F. Brancato **35**:69
Jean Craighead George **35**:179
Cynthia Voigt **30**:417, 418

Levertov, Denise
Imamu Amiri Baraka **14**:42
Russell Edson **13**:190
Guillevic **33**:190
H. D. **14**:223
David Ignatow **7**:173
Gilbert Sorrentino **22**:391
John Wieners **7**:535
Nancy Willard **37**:461

Levett, Karl
Stephen Sondheim **30**:400

Levey, Michael
William Faulkner **1**:102
W. Somerset Maugham **1**:204

Levi, Peter
Peter Ackroyd **34**:388
Donald Davie **31**:115
T. S. Eliot **34**:388
David Jones **4**:261; **13**:307
Shiva Naipaul **32**:327
Peter Porter **33**:324
F. T. Prince **22**:338
Yannis Ritsos **31**:325
Siegfried Sassoon **36**:393
George Seferis **5**:384
Jaroslav Seifert **34**:261
Yevgeny Yevtushenko **1**:381

Leviant, Curt
S. Y. Agnon **4**:12
Jakov Lind **4**:292
Chaim Potok **26**:369
Isaac Bashevis Singer **3**:453
Elie Wiesel **3**:530

Levin, Bernard
Breyten Breytenbach **37**:50
Scott Elledge **34**:432
Howard Fast **23**:157
Michael Scammell **34**:481
Aleksandr I. Solzhenitsyn
    7:436; **34**:481
E. B. White **34**:432

Levin, Betty
Virginia Hamilton **26**:155

Levin, Dan
Yasunari Kawabata **2**:223

Levin, David
James Baldwin **17**:26

Levin, Elena
Yevgeny Yevtushenko **1**:382

Levin, Irene S.
Elizabeth Swados **12**:558

Levin, Martin
Brian Aldiss **5**:14
Jeffrey Archer **28**:13
J. G. Ballard **14**:39
Patrick Boyle **19**:67
Art Buchwald **33**:88
A. S. Byatt **19**:75
James M. Cain **28**:49
Taylor Caldwell **2**:95; **28**:63, 67
Henry Carlisle **33**:103
Austin C. Clarke **8**:143
James Clavell **25**:125
Robert Cormier **12**:134
Margaret Craven **17**:79
Harry Crews **23**:131
Don DeLillo **27**:76
Stephen Dobyns **37**:76
Allen Drury **37**:107
Allan W. Eckert **17**:107
John Ehle **27**:105
Thomas J. Fleming **37**:121, 126
William Price Fox **22**:139
George MacDonald Fraser
    7:106
Paul Gallico **2**:147
Ernest K. Gann **23**:166
Natalia Ginzburg **5**:141
Winston Graham **23**:192
Doris Grumbach **22**:204
A. R. Gurney, Jr. **32**:217
Earl Hamner, Jr. **12**:258
Fletcher Knebel **14**:309
William Kotzwinkle **5**:220;
    35:255
Richard Llewellyn **7**:207
Robert Ludlum **22**:288
Richard Matheson **37**:247
John McGahern **5**:280
Walter M. Miller, Jr. **30**:254
Alice Munro **6**:341
Leslie Norris **14**:388
Craig Nova **7**:267
Marge Piercy **27**:372
J. B. Priestley **2**:347
Ann Quin **6**:441
Frederic Raphael **14**:437
Jean Rhys **2**:371
Judith Rossner **6**:468
Susan Richards Shreve **23**:402
Frank G. Slaughter **29**:377, 378
David Slavitt **14**:491

Critic Index

Lee Smith **25**:406
Wilbur Smith **33**:374, 375
Terry Southern **7**:452
Scott Spencer **30**:404
David Storey **4**:530
Jesse Stuart **8**:507
Hollis Summers **10**:493
Glendon Swarthout **35**:400, 403
Elizabeth Taylor **4**:541
Fredrica Wagman **7**:500
David Harry Walker **14**:552
Morris L. West **33**:430, 431
Donald E. Westlake **33**:437
Thomas Williams **14**:581
Sloan Wilson **32**:447
P. G. Wodehouse **2**:479; **5**:516
Hilma Wolitzer **17**:561
John Wyndham **19**:475
Louis Zukofsky **2**:487

Levin, Meyer
Elmer Rice **7**:358
Henry Roth **6**:472

Levin, Milton
Noel Coward **1**:64

Levine, Bernice
Maia Wojciechowska **26**:454

Levine, George
John Gardner **7**:113
Paul Goodman **2**:171
Juan Carlos Onetti **7**:279
Thomas Pynchon **3**:414

Levine, Joan
Franklyn M. Branley **21**:20

Levine, Joan Goldman
Richard Peck **21**:297

Levine, Judith
André Dubus **36**:148

Levine, June Perry
Vladimir Nabokov **6**:352;
11:396

Levine, Norman
Clark Blaise **29**:71
Frank Sargeson **31**:365

Levine, Paul
Truman Capote **1**:55; **3**:99
J. D. Salinger **12**:498

Levine, Suzanne Jill
Severo Sarduy **6**:486
Mario Vargas Llosa **6**:547

Levinson, Daniel
Walter Abish **22**:17

Levitas, Gloria
Jay Bennett **35**:44
Frank Bonham **12**:54
Lois Duncan **26**:103
Sonia Levitin **17**:263

Levitas, Mitchel
James D. Forman **21**:117

Levitin, Alexis
J.R.R. Tolkien **12**:574

Levitin, Sonia
Sonia Levitin **17**:264

Levitt, Morton P.
Michel Butor **3**:92
Claude Simon **4**:495

Levitt, Paul M.
Brendan Behan **11**:45
Jorge Luis Borges **9**:116
Michel de Ghelderode **11**:226

Levitzky, Sergei
Aleksandr I. Solzhenitsyn **4**:507

Levy, Alan
Art Buchwald **33**:87

Levy, Eric P.
Samuel Beckett **18**:49

Levy, Francis
Thomas Berger **3**:64
Ruth Prawer Jhabvala **4**:257
Megan Terry **19**:441
Frank Tuohy **37**:432

Levy, Frank
Norman Lear **12**:330

Levy, Jacques
Sam Shepard **17**:435

Levy, Paul
Kingsley Amis **13**:14
James Baldwin **15**:41
A. S. Byatt **19**:77
Roald Dahl **6**:122
E. L. Doctorow **11**:141
Doris Lessing **6**:301
William Styron **15**:529

Levy, William Turner
Padraic Colum **28**:90

Lewald, H. Ernest
Ernesto Sabato **10**:446; **23**:376

Lewin, Leonard C.
Art Buchwald **33**:90

Lewis, Alan
David Bowie **17**:59
Marvin Gaye **26**:131
Neil Young **17**:569, 570, 571

Lewis, Allan
Robert Anderson **23**:32
Paddy Chayefsky **23**:114
William Gibson **23**:180
William Inge **19**:227
Clifford Odets **28**:339

Lewis, Anthony R.
Joan D. Vinge **30**:410

Lewis, C. S.
J.R.R. Tolkien **1**:336; **12**:563

Lewis, Caroline
Bob Fosse **20**:124

Lewis, Constance
Ivy Compton-Burnett **15**:141

Lewis, David Levering
Maya Angelou **35**:31

Lewis, Gwyneth
Alfred Corn **33**:120

Lewis, J. Patrick
Howard Nemerov **36**:309

Lewis, Janet
Caroline Gordon **6**:206

Lewis, Lloyd
Carl Sandburg **35**:351

Lewis, Maggie
W. P. Kinsella **27**:239
V. S. Naipaul **37**:329
Anthony Powell **31**:318

Lewis, Marshall
Leni Riefenstahl **16**:520

Lewis, Marvin A.
Rudolfo Anaya **23**:26

Lewis, Naomi
Joan Aiken **35**:18
Betsy Byars **35**:72
Leon Garfield **12**:217
Alan Garner **17**:134
Noel Streatfeild **21**:399, 401
Rosemary Sutcliff **26**:425
Jill Paton Walsh **35**:431, 432,
    434

Lewis, Paula Gilbert
Anne Hébert **29**:239
Gabrielle Roy **10**:440
Michel Tremblay **29**:424

Lewis, Peter
Horst Bienek **11**:48
J. M. Coetzee **23**:124
Autran Dourado **23**:152
Eva Figes **31**:165
Yashar Kemal **29**:267

Lewis, Peter Elfed
Marvin Bell **8**:65
Ruth Prawer Jhabvala **8**:313

Lewis, R.W.B.
R. P. Blackmur **24**:57
Graham Greene **1**:131
André Malraux **4**:328
John Steinbeck **9**:512
Lionel Trilling **24**:449

Lewis, Robert W.
Edward Lewis Wallant **10**:516

Lewis, Robert W., Jr.
Ernest Hemingway **1**:142

Lewis, Robin Jared
E. M. Forster **22**:132

Lewis, Roger
Malcolm Bradbury **32**:56
J.I.M. Stewart **32**:422

Lewis, Sinclair
P. G. Wodehouse **22**:478

Lewis, Stuart
Bruce Jay Friedman **3**:166

Lewis, Theophilus
Gretchen Cryer **21**:78
Langston Hughes **35**:218
Gerome Ragni and James Rado
    17:382
Neil Simon **6**:502, 503
Douglas Turner Ward **19**:457

Lewis, Tom J.
Stanislaw Lem **8**:344

Lewis, Wyndham
William Faulkner **28**:135
Ezra Pound **7**:322

Ley, Charles David
Vicente Aleixandre **9**:10

Ley, Willy
Arthur C. Clarke **35**:118

Leyda, Jay
Akira Kurosawa **16**:395

Lhamon, W. T., Jr.
Anthony Burgess **5**:89
Bob Dylan **6**:158; **12**:192
John Gardner **3**:187
William Kennedy **6**:275
Joseph McElroy **5**:280
Robert M. Pirsig **4**:405
Thomas Pynchon **3**:412; **18**:430
Kurt Vonnegut, Jr. **4**:568

L'heureux, John
John Gardner **34**:550
Bernard Malamud **27**:306

Libby, Anthony
Robert Bly **15**:62
Theodore Roethke **11**:484
William Carlos Williams **2**:470

Libby, Margaret Sherwood
Lloyd Alexander **35**:24
Margot Benary-Isbert **12**:33
Franklyn M. Branley **21**:16
Betty Cavanna **12**:100
Maureen Daly **17**:90
Eilís Dillon **17**:93
James D. Forman **21**:115
Leon Garfield **12**:215
Jean Craighead George **35**:176
Christie Harris **12**:261
Margaret O. Hyde **21**:174
Jean Lee Latham **12**:323
Philippa Pearce **21**:281
Noel Streatfeild **21**:402
Rosemary Sutcliff **26**:426, 427

Libby, Marion Vlastos
Margaret Drabble **5**:117

Libera, Sharon Mayer
Frank Bidart **33**:74

Liberman, M. M.
Katherine Anne Porter **1**:274;
    7:318
Jean Stafford **4**:517

Libhart, Byron R.
Julien Green **11**:260

Librach, Ronald S.
Ingmar Bergman **16**:81

Lichtenberg, Jacqueline
Gene Roddenberry **17**:407

Lichtenstein, Grace
Roger Kahn **30**:231

Lichtheim, George
Lucien Goldmann **24**:234
Georg Lukács **24**:319

Liddell, Robert
Ivy Compton-Burnett **15**:135

Lidoff, Joan
Christina Stead **32**:416

Lieber, Joel
Richard Elman 19:150
Lois Gould 4:199

Lieber, Todd M.
Ralph Ellison 3:144
Robert Frost 9:221
John Steinbeck 5:406

Lieberman, Laurence
Rafael Alberti 7:10
A. R. Ammons 2:11
John Ashbery 9:44
W. H. Auden 2:28
John Berryman 1:33
Edward Brathwaite 11:67
James Dickey 1:73; 2:115
Arthur Gregor 9:252
Michael S. Harper 22:207
Anthony Hecht 8:268
Zbigniew Herbert 9:271
Edwin Honig 33:212
Richard Howard 7:165
Richard F. Hugo 18:259
Galway Kinnell 1:168
Stanley J. Kunitz 6:286
W. S. Merwin 1:212; 3:338
Leonard Michaels 25:314
Frederick Morgan 23:296
Howard Moss 7:248
Howard Nemerov 2:307
Kenneth Patchen 18:394
John Peck 3:378
Kenneth Rexroth 2:371
Muriel Rukeyser 27:409
W. D. Snodgrass 2:405
William Stafford 4:520, 521
Mark Strand 6:521
Melvin B. Tolson 36:426
Ted Walker 13:565
Theodore Weiss 3:517
Reed Whittemore 4:588

Lifton, Robert Jay
Albert Camus 2:99
Masuji Ibuse 22:224
Kurt Vonnegut, Jr. 2:455

Liggett, Priscilla
Larry Bograd 35:63

Light, Carolyn M.
Madeleine L'Engle 12:347

Lillard, Richard G.
Barry Gifford 34:458
Lawrence Lee 34:458
William Saroyan 34:458

Lima, Robert
Jorge Luis Borges 6:88
Ira Levin 6:306
Colin Wilson 3:538

Lindabury, Richard V.
Philip Booth 23:73

Lindberg, Gary
Jack Kerouac 29:277

Lindberg-Seyersted, Brita
Bernard Malamud 9:343

Lindblad, Ishrat
Pamela Hansford Johnson 27:223

Lindborg, Henry J.
Doris Lessing 6:299

Lindegren, Eric
Gunnar Ekelöf 27:109

Lindeman, Jack
Robert Francis 15:235
Edwin Honig 33:210

Lindfors, Bernth
Chinua Achebe 7:4
Ayi Kwei Armah 33:32
Wole Soyinka 36:412
Amos Tutuola 29:439

Lindner, Carl M.
Robert Frost 3:175
James Thurber 5:440

Lindop, Grevel
Dannie Abse 29:20
John Berryman 3:66
Bob Dylan 4:148
Philip Larkin 33:261

Lindquist, Jennie D.
Margot Benary-Isbert 12:32
Walter Farley 17:116
Lee Kingman 17:244
William Mayne 12:387
Zoa Sherburne 30:361
Mary Stolz 12:546, 550
Lenora Mattingly Weber 12:633

Lindsey, Almont
Milton Meltzer 26:299

Lindsey, Byron
Joseph Brodsky 13:116

Lindsey, David A.
Jules Archer 12:22

Lindskoog, Kathryn Ann
C. S. Lewis 27:262

Lindstrom, Naomi
Bob Dylan 12:191

Linehan, Eugene J., S.J.
Taylor Caldwell 2:95
A. J. Cronin 32:140
Allen Drury 37:107
James Herriot 12:283
Irving Wallace 7:509

Lingeman, Richard R.
Richard Bach 14:36
Russell Baker 31:30
James Herriot 12:283
Mary McCarthy 14:362
Charles M. Schulz 12:531
Erich Segal 10:466
William Saroyan 29:360
Garry Trudeau 12:590

Linney, Romulus
Claude Brown 30:34

Lipari, Joseph A.
Robert Hayden 37:159
M. L. Rosenthal 28:398

Lipking, Lawrence
R. S. Crane 27:72

Lippi, Tom
Milan Kundera 32:263

Lippit, Noriko Mizuta
Yukio Mishima 27:345
Jun'ichirō Tanizaki 28:416

Lippmann, Walter
Van Wyck Brooks 29:78

Lipsius, Frank
Herbert Gold 7:121
Bernard Malamud 2:268
Henry Miller 2:283
Thomas Pynchon 6:434

Lipson, Eden Ross
Larry McMurtry 27:333

Lipsyte, Robert
Judy Blume 30:23
Robert Lipsyte 21:213
Walter Dean Myers 35:295
Robert Newton Peck 17:339

Lisca, Peter
John Steinbeck 21:380

Lissner, John
Janis Ian 21:185

Listri, Pier Francesco
Allen Tate 6:525

Litsinger, Kathryn A.
Andre Norton 12:465

Litt, Dorothy E.
John Mortimer 28:286

Littell, Philip
Rebecca West 31:450

Littell, Robert
Howard Fast 23:154
Robert Frost 15:240
Jean Toomer 13:550

Little, Roger
St.-John Perse 4:400; 11:433, 436

Little, Stuart W.
Gay Talese 37:393

Littlejohn, David
James Baldwin 5:40
Imamu Amiri Baraka 5:44
Samuel Beckett 2:45
Jorge Luis Borges 2:68
Cleanth Brooks 24:108
Gwendolyn Brooks 5:75
Lawrence Durrell 4:144
Ralph Ellison 11:179
Jean Genet 2:157
John Hawkes 2:183
Robert Hayden 5:168
Joseph Heller 3:229
Chester Himes 7:159
Langston Hughes 5:190
Robinson Jeffers 2:214
John Oliver Killens 10:300
Henry Miller 2:281, 283
Ann Petry 7:304
Jean Toomer 13:551
J. E. Wideman 5:489
Richard Wright 9:583

Littler, Frank
Isabel Colegate 36:109
Nigel Dennis 8:173
Maureen Duffy 37:114

Litvinoff, Emanuel
Arthur Koestler 33:235

Litwak, Leo E.
Hunter S. Thompson 17:503

Litz, A. Walton
Peter Ackroyd 34:394
T. S. Eliot 34:394

Liv, Gwen
Barbara Corcoran 17:70

Lively, Penelope
Penelope Fitzgerald 19:175
Russell C. Hoban 25:265
Kazuo Ishiguro 27:204
Doris Lessing 22:287
Michael Moorcock 27:352
Barbara Pym 37:369
Ann Schlee 35:374
D. M. Thomas 22:422
Angus Wilson 25:461

Livesay, Dorothy
Milton Acorn 15:8
Louis Dudek 11:159
E. J. Pratt 19:378

Livingstone, Leon
Azorín 11:25

Llorens, David
Nikki Giovanni 19:190

Lloyd, Christopher
Siegfried Sassoon 36:397

Lloyd, Paul M.
Michael Ende 31:144

Lloyd, Peter
Leonardo Sciascia 9:476

Loake, Jonathan
Lisa St. Aubin de Teran 36:422

Lobb, Edward
T. S. Eliot 24:185

Lobdell, Jared C.
August Derleth 31:138

Locke, Alain
Langston Hughes 35:212

Locke, Richard
Donald Barthelme 8:52
Ann Beattie 18:37
Thomas Berger 8:83
Heinrich Böll 3:73
John Cheever 8:139
Joan Didion 8:175
Barry Hannah 23:209
Joseph Heller 11:268
John le Carré 5:233
Vladimir Nabokov 2:303; 8:418
Thomas Pynchon 2:356
John Updike 1:345; 9:540
Mario Vargas Llosa 31:448

Lockerbie, D. Bruce
C. S. Lewis 1:177

Lockhart, Marilyn
Norma Klein 30:242

Locklin, Gerald
Richard Brautigan 12:67

Lockwood, William J.
Ed Dorn 10:159

Critic Index

Loder, Kurt
John Lennon **35**:276
Pink Floyd **35**:309, 314
Prince **35**:329

Lodge, David
Kingsley Amis **2**:10
William S. Burroughs **2**:92
Mary Gordon **13**:250
Graham Greene **1**:134; **3**:206
Ted Hughes **2**:199
Milan Kundera **32**:265
Doris Lessing **15**:332
Norman Mailer **4**:321
Alain Robbe-Grillet **4**:447
Wilfrid Sheed **2**:394
Muriel Spark **13**:525
John Updike **34**:295

Loewinsohn, Ron
Frederick Barthelme **36**:53
Richard Brautigan **12**:59
Padgett Powell **34**:98

Logan, John
E. E. Cummings **3**:117

Logan, William
Gabriel García Márquez **15**:253
Robert Hayden **14**:240
Laura Jensen **37**:190
Michael Ondaatje **14**:410
James Tate **25**:428
Derek Walcott **14**:548

Loggins, Vernon
Julia Peterkin **31**:305

Lohrke, Eugene
Rhys Davies **23**:140

Loke, Margarett
Scott O'Dell **30**:275

Lomas, Herbert
Roy Fuller **4**:179
John Gardner **7**:115
Paul Goodman **4**:196
John Hawkes **7**:143
Robert M. Pirsig **6**:421
Ezra Pound **3**:398

Londré, Felicia Hardison
Mark Medoff **23**:294

Long, John Allan
Anne Tyler **28**:430

Long, Margo Alexander
John Neufeld **17**:311

Long, Robert Emmet
Ernest Hemingway **3**:237
Robert Phillips **28**:362
Edmund Wilson **8**:550

Long, Sidney
Lloyd Alexander **35**:25

Longley, Edna
Douglas Dunn **6**:147
Seamus Heaney **5**:170
Thomas Kinsella **19**:256
Marge Piercy **18**:409

Longley, John Lewis, Jr.
Robert Penn Warren **1**:355

Longstreth, T. Morris
Frank B. Gilbreth and
Ernestine Gilbreth Carey
17:154
Jean Lee Latham **12**:322
Farley Mowat **26**:330

Longsworth, Polly
Madeleine L'Engle **12**:349

Lopez, Daniel
Bernardo Bertolucci **16**:97

Loprete, Nicholas J.
William Saroyan **10**:457

Lorch, Thomas M.
Edward Lewis Wallant **10**:512

Lord, James
Henri Troyat **23**:460

Lorich, Bruce
Samuel Beckett **6**:34

Lorrah, Jean
Marion Zimmer Bradley **30**:29

Losinski, Julie
Christie Harris **12**:263

Lothian, Helen M.
Christie Harris **12**:262

Lotz, Jim
Farley Mowat **26**:334

Loubère, J.A.E.
Claude Simon **15**:490

Louch, A. R.
René Wellek **28**:453

Lounsberry, Barbara
Gay Talese **37**:403

Lourie, Richard
Joseph Brodsky **13**:114

Love, Theresa R.
Zora Neale Hurston **30**:218

Lovecraft, H. P.
August Derleth **31**:126, 127

Loveman, Amy
C. S. Forester **35**:159
William Maxwell **19**:305

Lovering, Joseph P.
Pat Jordon **37**.195

Lovett, R. M.
Carl Van Vechten **33**:387

Low, Alice
Isabelle Holland **21**:147

Lowell, Amy
Robert Frost **13**:222
Carl Sandburg **35**:340

Lowell, Robert
W. H. Auden **1**:9
John Berryman **2**:57
Elizabeth Bishop **32**:28
Randall Jarrell **2**:207; **13**:298
Stanley J. Kunitz **6**:285
Sylvia Plath **17**:347
I. A. Richards **14**:452
Allen Tate **4**:535

Lowenkron, David Henry
Samuel Beckett **6**:40

Lowenthal, Lawrence D.
Arthur Miller **15**:374

Lowie, Robert H.
Margaret Mead **37**:270

Lownsbrough, John
A. G. Mojtabai **29**:319

Lowrie, Rebecca
Maureen Daly **17**:88

Lowrey, Burling
S. J. Perelman **23**:336

Lowry, Beverly
Ellen Gilchrist **34**:166
D. M. Thomas **22**:421

Lowry, Margerie Bonner
Edward Hoagland **28**:180

Lubbers, Klaus
Carson McCullers **12**:423

Lubbock, Richard
Joan D. Vinge **30**:411

Lubow, Arthur
Michael Cimino **16**:211
Fran Lebowitz **36**:247
George Lucas **16**:414

Lucas, Alec
Roderick L. Haig-Brown
21:142
Farley Mowat **26**:341

Lucas, John
Donald Davie **31**:124
Thom Gunn **32**:214
Edwin Morgan **31**:276
Peter Porter **33**:324
Ezra Pound **7**:332
Anne Stevenson **33**:382
William Trevor **25**:442

Luccock, Halford E.
Taylor Caldwell **28**:55

Lucey, Beatus T., O.S.B.
Daphne du Maurier **6**:146

Luchting, Wolfgang A.
José María Arguedas **10**:9
José Donoso **4**:126, 127
Gabriel García Márquez **2**:150
Alain Resnais **16**:499
Luisa Valenzuela **31**:438
Mario Vargas Llosa **10**:496

Lucid, Luellen
Aleksandr I. Solzhenitsyn
10:480

Lucid, Robert F.
Ernest Hemingway **6**:232
Norman Mailer **4**:323

Lucie-Smith, Edward
Sylvia Plath **9**:424

Luckett, Richard
Lenny Bruce **21**:51
Anthony Powell **7**:339
Robert Penn Warren **6**:555
Edmund Wilson **3**:540

Luckey, Eleanore Braun
Honor Arundel **17**:19

Luddy, Thomas E.
Edwin Morgan **31**:273

Ludlow, Colin
David Hare **29**:214
David Mamet **15**:356
Tom Stoppard **15**:520

Ludwig, Jack
Bernard Malamud **2**:269
Mordecai Richler **18**:452

Ludwig, Linda
Doris Lessing **6**:301

Lueders, Edward
Jorge Luis Borges **2**:72
George MacBeth **2**:252
Carl Van Vechten **33**:397

Lugg, Andrew M.
Andy Warhol **20**:417

Lukács, Georg
Aleksandr I. Solzhenitsyn
26:416

Lukacs, John
Russell Baker **31**:31
Aleksandr I. Solzhenitsyn **7**:438

Lukacs, Paul
Anthony Burgess **13**:125

Lukas, Betty
Jeffrey Archer **28**:13

Lukens, Rebecca J.
Mavis Thorpe Clark **12**:132
Madeleine L'Engle **12**:351

Lukowsky, Wes
Roger Kahn **30**:234

Lumley, Frederick
Terence Rattigan **7**:354

Lumport, Felicia
Jessamyn West **7**:520

Lund, Mary
Marian Engel **36**:161

Lundquist, James
J. D. Salinger **12**:518
Kurt Vonnegut, Jr. **12**:615

Lunn, Janet
Kevin Major **26**:286

Lupack, Alan C.
Gwendolyn Brooks **15**:95

Lupoff, Richard
John W. Campbell, Jr. **32**:76
Kurt Vonnegut, Jr. **12**:629

Luria-Sukenick, Lynn
Max Apple **33**:20

Lurie, Alison
Richard Adams **5**:7
Peter Davison **28**:101
Iris Murdoch **3**:348

Lurie, Nancy Oestreich
Vine Deloria, Jr. **21**:108

Luschei, Martin
Walker Percy **3**:378

Lustig, Irma S.
Sean O'Casey **9**:411

Luttwak, Edward
Bernard Malamud **3**:325

Lyall, Gavin
Edmund Crispin **22**:110

Lydenberg, Robin
Jorge Luis Borges **13**:111, 113

Lydon, Michael
Chuck Berry **17**:52

Lydon, Susan
Leslie Epstein **27**:132
John Lennon and Paul
McCartney **12**:362
Toni Morrison **22**:322

Lye, John
A. W. Purdy **14**:433

Lyell, Frank H.
Harper Lee **12**:340

Lyles, Jean Caffey
Richard Bach **14**:35

Lyles, W. H.
Stephen King **12**:310

Lynch, Dennis Daley
William Stafford **7**:462

Lynch, Josephine E.
Noel Streatfeild **21**:399

Lynch, Michael
Richard Howard **7**:168
Michael McClure **10**:332

Lynch, William S.
C. S. Forester **35**:167

Lynd, Helen Merrell
Muriel Rukeyser **27**:409

Lyne, Oliver
Ted Hughes **9**:282

Lynen, John F.
Robert Frost **1**:110

Lynes, Carlos, Jr.
Arthur Adamov **25**:11

Lynes, Russell
Charles Addams **30**:15
Scott Elledge **34**:429
E. B. White **34**:429

Lynn, Kenneth S.
Virginia Spencer Carr **34**:420
John Dos Passos **34**:420
Ernest Hemingway **30**:199
Alfred Kazin **34**:560

Lyon, George W., Jr.
Allen Ginsberg **3**:194

Lyon, James K.
Paul Celan **19**:87

Lyon, Laurence Gill
Jean-Paul Sartre **18**:463

Lyon, Melvin
Edward Dahlberg **1**:72

Lyon, Thomas J.
Gary Snyder **32**:393

Lyons, Bonnie
Margaret Atwood **8**:33
Henry Roth **2**:378; **6**:473
Delmore Schwartz **10**:463

Lyons, Donald
Luchino Visconti **16**:574

Lyons, Eugene
Walker Percy **6**:399
John Updike **3**:486

Lyons, Gene
Peter Ackroyd **34**:392
Jeffrey Archer **28**:11
Peter Benchley **8**:82
Len Deighton **7**:75
Allen Drury **37**:107
T. S. Eliot **34**:392
John Gardner **30**:155
John Hersey **9**:277
John Irving **23**:249
Elia Kazan **6**:274
George MacBeth **9**:340
Helen Hooven Santmyer **33**:358
Peter Straub **28**:410
Hunter S. Thompson **17**:515
John Updike **13**:562; **23**:470
Irving Wallace **7**:510
Robert Penn Warren **8**:540
Richard Yates **7**:555

Lyons, John O.
Vladimir Nabokov **1**:241

Lytle, Andrew
Caroline Gordon **29**:184
Allen Tate **4**:535

Maas, Peter
Frederick Forsyth **36**:177

MacAdam, Alfred J.
José Donoso **32**:155, 160, 161
G. Cabrera Infante **25**:102
Thomas Pynchon **11**:455
João Guimarães Rosa **23**:356

MacAndrew, Andrew R.
Yuri Olesha **8**:430

Macaulay, Jeannette
Camara Laye **4**:285

Macauley, Robie
Toni Cade Bambara **19**:33
R. P. Blackmur **2**:61
Shirley Hazzard **18**:214
James Alan McPherson **19**:310
Jean Rhys **14**:446
M. L. Rosenthal **28**:390
René Wellek **28**:447
Patrick White **9**:566

MacBeth, George
Robert Nye **13**:412

MacBride, James
James M. Cain **28**:48
Helen MacInnes **27**:279
Jessamyn West **17**:544

MacBrudnoy, David
George MacDonald Fraser
7:106

MacCabe, Colin
Jean-Luc Godard **20**:146

MacCaig, Norman
D. J. Enright **31**:146

MacCann, Donnarae
Christopher Collier and James
L. Collier **30**:73

MacCarthy, Desmond
T. S. Eliot **24**:161

Maccoby, Hyam
Ezra Pound **18**:420

MacDiarmid, Hugh
Norman MacCaig **36**:280
Ezra Pound **4**:413

Macdonald, Dwight
Charles Addams **30**:14
Charles Chaplin **16**:199
James Gould Cozzens **4**:111
Federico Fellini **16**:274
Rouben Mamoulian **16**:424
Marshall McLuhan **37**:255
Czesław Miłosz **22**:305
Philip Roth **1**:293
Tom Wolfe **35**:450

MacDonald, John D.
James M. Cain **11**:87

Macdonald, Rae McCarthy
Alice Munro **10**:357

Macdonald, Ross
Nelson Algren **10**:8
Dashiell Hammett **5**:160

MacDonald, Ruth K.
Marilyn Sachs **35**:335

MacDonald, S. Yvonne
Christie Harris **12**:266

MacDonald, Scott
Erskine Caldwell **14**:96

Macdonald, Susan
Pier Paolo Pasolini **20**:262

MacDougall, Ruth Doan
Michael Cunningham **34**:41
Harriet Doerr **34**:152
Sylvia Murphy **34**:92

MacDuffie, Bruce L.
Milton Meltzer **26**:299

MacFadden, Patrick
Albert Maysles and David
Maysles **16**:438, 440
Pier Paolo Pasolini **20**:260

MacFall, Russell
August Derleth **31**:138

Macfarlane, David
Margaret Atwood **25**:65
Clark Blaise **29**:76
Brian Moore **32**:311

MacInnes, Colin
James Baldwin **1**:14; **17**:25
Brendan Behan **15**:44
Shelagh Delaney **29**:143
Alex Haley **12**:244
Gay Talese **37**:393

MacIntyre, Alasdair
Arthur Koestler **1**:170

MacIntyre, Jean
Barbara Corcoran **17**:77

Maciuszko, George J.
Czesław Miłosz **5**:292

Mackay, Barbara
Imamu Amiri Baraka **10**:19
Ed Bullins **7**:37
James Kirkwood **9**:319

MacKay, L. A.
Robert Finch **18**:154

MacKendrick, Louis K.
Hugh Hood **28**:193
Robert Kroetsch **23**:272

MacKenzie, Nancy K.
Babette Deutsch **18**:120

MacKenzie, Robert
Norman Lear **12**:337

MacKethan, Lucinda H.
Lee Smith **25**:409

MacKinnon, Alex
Earle Birney **6**:79

Macklin, F. A.
Leon Uris **32**:432

Macklin, F. Anthony
Robert Altman **16**:34
Stanley Kubrick **16**:381
Gore Vidal **2**:449

MacLaren, I. S.
A.J.M. Smith **15**:517

Maclean, Alasdair
Elizabeth Jennings **14**:292
D. M. Thomas **13**:541

MacLean, Kenneth
William Heyen **18**:229

MacLeish, Archibald
Ezra Pound **3**:399
Carl Sandburg **35**:356

MacLeish, Roderick
Eric Ambler **6**:3
Richard Condon **8**:150
Len Deighton **7**:74
Ken Follett **18**:155
Frederick Forsyth **36**:177
George V. Higgins **4**:224

MacLeod, Anne Scott
Robert Cormier **30**:88

MacManus, Patricia
Shirley Hazzard **18**:214
Grace Paley **37**:330
Françoise Sagan **17**:424

Macmillan, Carrie
Jane Rule **27**:421

Mac Namara, Desmond
Jessamyn West **17**:550

Macnaughton, W. R.
Ernest Hemingway **8**:286

MacPike, Loralee
Thomas J. Fleming **37**:129
Zibby Oneal **30**:279
Cynthia Propper Seton **27**:429
Fay Weldon **19**:470

Critic Index

MacQuown, Vivian J.
Mary Stolz **12**:552

Macrae, Alasdair D. F.
Edwin Morgan **31**:276
D. M. Thomas **31**:430

Macri, F. M.
Anne Hébert **29**:229

MacShane, Frank
Jorge Luis Borges **2**:76
Italo Calvino **22**:93
Edward Dahlberg **1**:71; **14**:138
Barbara Howes **15**:290
Clarence Major **19**:292
W. S. Merwin **1**:212
Alberto Moravia **18**:348
Pablo Neruda **9**:399
Leslie Marmon Silko **23**:407

MacSkimming, Roy
Jack Hodgins **23**:228
Michael Ondaatje **29**:340

MacSween, R. J.
Ivy Compton-Burnett **10**:110
Evelyn Waugh **19**:462

MacTaggart, Garaud
Jimmy Cliff **21**:65

MacWillie, Joan
Noel Streatfeild **21**:396

Madden, David
James M. Cain **3**:96; **11**:86
William Gaddis **1**:113
Wright Morris **1**:230; **3**:343
Sam Shepard **17**:434

Madden, Susan B.
D. M. Pinkwater **35**:319, 320

Maddocks, Fiona
Maya Angelou **35**:33

Maddocks, Melvin
Richard Adams **4**:7
Kingsley Amis **2**:7, 8
John Beecher **6**:48
Jackson J. Benson **34**:408
Heinrich Böll **3**:75
Paul Bowles **2**:78
Truman Capote **34**:324
Padraic Colum **28**:89
J. P. Donleavy **6**:142
Ernest J. Gaines **3**:179
John Gardner **2**:152
Judith Guest **30**:172
Mark Harris **19**:201
Joseph Heller **5**:176
Thomas Keneally **5**:209, 212
Doris Lessing **2**:239; **6**:298, 303
Jakov Lind **27**:271
Bernard Malamud **2**:267
S. J. Perelman **23**:337
Anthony Powell **31**:318
Thomas Pynchon **2**:354
Piers Paul Read **4**:444
Erich Maria Remarque **21**:333
Philip Roth **4**:456
Cornelius Ryan **7**:385
John Steinbeck **34**:408
William Wharton **37**:437
Angus Wilson **3**:536

Maddox, Brenda
Arthur C. Clarke **35**:118

Madison, Charles
James A. Michener **29**:317

Madison, Charles A.
Isaac Bashevis Singer **23**:414

Madsen, Alan
Andre Norton **12**:457

Madsen, Axel
Jerzy Skolimowski **20**:347

Madsen, Børge Gedsø
Kjeld Abell **15**:1

Maes-Jelinek, Hena
Wilson Harris **25**:212

Magalaner, Marvin
E. M. Forster **1**:103
Aldous Huxley **1**:150

Magee, Bryan
Martin Heidegger **24**:271

Magee, William H.
Philip Child **19**:100

Magid, Marion
Shelagh Delaney **29**:145
Tennessee Williams **30**:465

Magid, Nora L.
Mordecai Richler **9**:450; **18**:456
Françoise Sagan **17**:416

Magliola, Robert
Jorge Luis Borges **10**:68

Magnarelli, Sharon
Luisa Valenzuela **31**:439

Magner, James E., Jr.
John Crowe Ransom **4**:431

Magnússon, Sigurður A.
Halldór Laxness **25**:299

Magny, Claude-Edmonde
John Dos Passos **15**:182
William Faulkner **18**:143
André Malraux **15**:351

Maguire, C. E.
Siegfried Sassoon **36**:390

Maguire, Clinton J.
Farley Mowat **26**:337

Maguire, Gregory
Aidan Chambers **35**:101
Joanne Greenberg **30**:168

Maguire, Robert A.
Tadeusz Różewicz **23**:359

Mahlendorf, Ursula
Horst Bienek **7**:28
Christa Wolf **29**:465

Mahon, Derek
Patrick Boyle **19**:68
Austin Clarke **9**:168
Donald Davie **10**:125
Frederick Exley **11**:186
John le Carré **5**:233
József Lengyel **7**:202
Hugh MacDiarmid **19**:289
John Montague **13**:390

Brian Moore **8**:394
Edna O'Brien **8**:429
Tom Paulin **37**:354
Craig Raine **32**:348

Mahon, Vincent
Marilyn French **18**:157

Mahood, M. M.
R. K. Narayan **28**:297

Maida, Patricia D.
Flannery O'Connor **10**:364

Mailer, Norman
Bernardo Bertolucci **16**:92

Maini, Darshan Singhi
Anita Desai **37**:65

Mairowitz, David Zane
Edward Bond **6**:86
Caryl Churchill **31**:83

Mais, S.P.B.
Siegfried Sassoon **36**:385

Maitland, Jeffrey
William H. Gass **11**:224

Maitland, Sara
Thomas M. Disch **36**:127
Edna O'Brien **36**:336
Flann O'Brien **5**:314

Majdiak, Daniel
John Barth **1**:17

Majeski, Jane
Arthur Koestler **8**:324

Majkut, Denise R.
Bob Dylan **4**:148

Major, Clarence
Ralph Ellison **3**:146
Rudolph Wurlitzer **15**:588

Malabre, Alfred L., Jr.
Paul E. Erdman **25**:153

Malamut, Bruce
Jimmy Cliff **21**:63
Steve Martin **30**:246
Pink Floyd **35**:306
Lou Reed **21**:312
Peter Townshend **17**:536

Malanga, Gerard
Jim Carroll **35**:77
Anne Waldman **7**:508

Malcolm, Donald
James Baldwin **17**:22
Allen Drury **37**:101
Mark Harris **19**:200

Malcolm, Janet
Milan Kundera **32**:262
Ved Mehta **37**:295
Maia Wojciechowska **26**:453

Malin, Irving
Kōbō Abé **22**:15
Walter Abish **22**:18
Jonathan Baumbach **23**:52, 55
Saul Bellow **13**:70
Paul Bowles **19**:61
Frederick Busch **7**:39
Hortense Calisher **4**:87
Jerome Charyn **18**:98

Eleanor Clark **5**:105
B. H. Friedman **7**:109
John Hawkes **4**:217
Joseph Heller **5**:182
Ken Kesey **6**:278
Carson McCullers **4**:344
Flannery O'Connor **2**:317
Walker Percy **8**:445
James Purdy **2**:347
Philip Roth **15**:449
Isaac Bashevis Singer **23**:415
Muriel Spark **5**:398; **8**:496
Peter Spielberg **6**:519
Harvey Swados **5**:421
Elie Wiesel **5**:490

Malkin, Lawrence
Harold Pinter **6**:418

Malko, George
Frederick Buechner **4**:80

Malkoff, Karl
Robert Duncan **15**:189
Kenneth Rexroth **1**:284
Theodore Roethke **1**:291
May Swenson **4**:533

Mallalieu, H. B.
John Gardner **7**:116
Pablo Neruda **7**:261
David Pownall **10**:419

Mallerman, Tony
Satyajit Ray **16**:479

Mallet, Gina
Iris Murdoch **1**:237
Tennessee Williams **7**:545

Malley, Terrence
Richard Brautigan **3**:88

Mallon, Thomas
Gore Vidal **33**:404

Malmfelt, A. D.
Brian De Palma **20**:73

Malmström, Gunnel
Pär Lagerkvist **13**:330

Maloff, Saul
Nelson Algren **4**:18; **33**:14
Louis Auchincloss **4**:30
James Baldwin **17**:23
Heinrich Böll **9**:110
Frederick Busch **7**:38
Edward Dahlberg **7**:68
Carlos Fuentes **22**:164
Ernest Hemingway **3**:236
Nat Hentoff **26**:188
Ward S. Just **27**:226
Milan Kundera **9**:321
Norman Mailer **2**:264
Milton Meltzer **26**:303
Vladimir Nabokov **6**:356
Flannery O'Connor **3**:365
Clifford Odets **2**:319
Sylvia Plath **2**:336; **17**:358
Philip Roth **3**:435; **4**:455
Alan Sillitoe **1**:307
Josef Škvorecký **15**:512
Calder Willingham **5**:512
Maia Wojciechowska **26**:450

Malone, Michael
Thomas Berger **18**:57
William F. Buckley, Jr. **37**:61
Ernest K. Gann **23**:168
Barry Hannah **23**:209
Helen Hooven Santmyer **33**:359
Kurt Vonnegut, Jr. **22**:449

Maloney, Douglas J.
Frederick Exley **6**:171

Maloney, Russell
Ogden Nash **23**:320

Maltin, Leonard
Woody Allen **16**:5

Malzberg, Barry N.
Ursula K. LeGuin **13**:349

Mamber, Stephen
Albert Maysles and David
Maysles **16**:441, 442
Frederick Wiseman **20**:470,
473, 476

Maminski, Dolores
Jay Bennett **35**:46

Mandel, Eli
Andrew Suknaki **19**:432

Mandel, Siegfried
Uwe Johnson **5**:200
Mary Renault **17**:393

Mandelbaum, Allen
Giuseppe Ungaretti **7**:481

Mandelbaum, Bernard
Elie Wiesel **11**:570

Mandelbaum, Sara
Adrienne Rich **36**:366

Mander, Gertrud
Peter Weiss **15**:566

Mander, John
Günter Grass **6**:208

Mandić, Oleg
Lucien Goldmann **24**:235

Manfred, Freya
Erica Jong **18**:277

Mangelsdorff, Rich
Michael McClure **6**:318

Mangione, Jerry
Andrea Giovene **7**:116

Manguel, Alberto
André Brink **36**:69
Lawrence Durrell **27**:100
Audrey Thomas **37**:423

Manheimer, Joan
Margaret Drabble **22**:123

Mankiewicz, Don
Jessamyn West **17**:546

Mankiewicz, Don M.
Laura Z. Hobson **25**:271

Manlove, C. N.
J.R.R. Tolkien **12**:580

Mann, Charles W., Jr.
Jonathan Kozol **17**:248

Mann, Elizabeth C.
Mary Stolz **12**:551

Mann, Golo
W. H. Auden **3**:29

Mann, Jeanette W.
Jean Stafford **7**:458

Mann, Jessica
John Gardner **30**:156

Mann, Thomas
Hermann Hesse **11**:270

Mannes, Marya
Françoise Sagan **17**:422

Manning, Olivia
Louis Aragon **22**:36
Beryl Bainbridge **14**:36
Sylvia Townend Warner **7**:511

Manning, Robert J.
Art Buchwald **33**:91

Mano, D. Keith
Richard Adams **4**:9
J. G. Ballard **3**:34
Thomas Berger **5**:60
Daniel J. Berrigan **4**:58
Jorge Luis Borges **2**:71
Philip Caputo **32**:103, 105
John Cheever **3**:108
Evan S. Connell, Jr. **6**:117
Peter DeVries **10**:136
J. P. Donleavy **4**:125
Richard Elman **19**:151
Irvin Faust **8**:214
Gabriel García Márquez **27**:157
William Gerhardie **5**:140
James Hanley **3**:221
Joseph Heller **5**:180
George V. Higgins **4**:224
B. S. Johnson **6**:263, 264
Erica Jong **8**:315
Ward S. Just **27**:229
Yuri Krotkov **19**:264
Siegfried Lenz **27**:250
James A. Michener **11**:376
Vladimir Nabokov **2**:301
Hugh Nissenson **9**:400
Richard O'Brien **17**:325
John O'Hara **2**:325
Philip Roth **4**:458
William Saroyan **10**:456
Alexander Theroux **2**:433
Michel Tournier **36**:434
John Updike **2**:444; **5**:456
Patrick White **3**:525
Elie Wiesel **37**:459
Tennessee Williams **7**:546

Mansbridge, Francis
Rudy Wiebe **14**:573

Mansell, Mark
Isaac Asimov **26**:50
Harlan Ellison **13**:208

Mansfield, Katherine
Enid Bagnold **25**:71

Manso, Susan
Anaïs Nin **8**:424

Mansur, Carole
Fran Lebowitz **36**:250

Manthorne, Jane
Frank Bonham **12**:50, 51
Mavis Thorpe Clark **12**:130
Allan W. Eckert **17**:106
James D. Forman **21**:117
James Herriot **12**:283
Andre Norton **12**:457
Maia Wojciechowska **26**:455

Manuel, Bruce
Wright Morris **37**:314
Jonathan Schell **35**:365

Manuel, Diane Casselberry
Chaim Potok **26**:375
Morris L. West **33**:432

Manvell, Roger
René Clair **20**:63
John Gardner **30**:158
Fritz Lang **20**:204
Jean Cocteau **16**:227
Leni Riefenstahl **16**:521
Wilbur Smith **33**:376
Agnès Varda **16**:554
Andrzej Wajda **16**:577
Orson Welles **20**:433, 447

Mao, Nathan K.
Pa Chin **18**:373

Maples, Houston L.
Joseph Krumgold **12**:318
William Mayne **12**:392
Maia Wojciechowska **26**:451

Marafino, Elizabeth A.
Sonia Levitin **17**:265

Marcello, J. J. Armas
Mario Vargas Llosa **10**:499

Marciniak, Ed
Frank Bonham **12**:50

Marcorelles, Louis
René Clair **20**:65
Elia Kazan **16**:373
Eric Rohmer **16**:528

Marcotte, Edward
Alain Robbe-Grillet **6**:467

Marcus, Adrianne
Anna Kavan **13**:316
Jon Silkin **2**:395
William Stafford **4**:520

Marcus, Greil
Wendell Berry **8**:85
E. L. Doctorow **6**:134
Bob Dylan **12**:197
John Irving **13**:294, 295, 296
John Lennon **35**:269
John Lennon and Paul
McCartney **12**:382
Richard Price **12**:490
John Sayles **10**:460
Patti Smith **12**:535
Raymond Sokolov **7**:431
Robert Wilson **9**:576

Marcus, Mordecai
William Everson **1**:96
Robert Frost **9**:224
Ted Hughes **2**:203
Bernard Malamud **1**:199
Nancy Willard **37**:462

Marcus, Steven
William Golding **2**:165
Dashiell Hammett **10**:252
Bernard Malamud **2**:265
Irving Stone **7**:470
Evelyn Waugh **27**:470

Marcus, Susan F.
Bette Greene **30**:171

Marder, Joan V.
Rosemary Sutcliff **26**:434

Maremaa, Thomas
Robert Crumb **17**:84

Margaronis, Maria
Jonathan Schell **35**:370

Margolies, Edward
John Ehle **27**:103
Chester Himes **18**:244
Richard Wright **21**:443

Margolis, John D.
Joseph Wood Krutch **24**:290

Margolis, Richard J.
Margaret Mead **37**:277

Marguerite, Sister M., R.S.M.
Eleanor Hibbert **7**:155
Erich von Däniken **30**:422

Mariani, John
Aleksandr I. Solzhenitsyn **7**:440

Mariani, Paul
Robert Penn Warren **8**:536
William Carlos Williams **9**:572

Marill-Albérès, René
Jean-Paul Sartre **1**:304

Marine, Gene
Lenny Bruce **21**:49

Marinucci, Ron
Isaac Asimov **19**:29

Marius, Richard
Frederick Buechner **4**:79

Mark, M.
Carly Simon **26**:411
Bruce Springsteen **17**:483

Mark, Rachel
Tom Wolfe **15**:587

Marken, Jack W.
N. Scott Momaday **19**:320

Marker, Frederick J.
Kjeld Abell **15**:3

Markmann, Charles Lam
Julien Green **3**:205
Joyce Carol Oates **2**:313

Markos, Donald
Hannah Green **3**:202

Markos, Donald W.
James Dickey **1**:74

Markow, Alice Bradley
Doris Lessing **6**:297

Marks, Emerson R.
René Wellek **28**:452

Critic Index

Marks, Mitchell
Frederick Busch 7:38

Marling, William
Edward Abbey 36:13, 18

Marnell, Francis X.
Helen Hooven Santmyer 33:361

Marnham, Patrick
Graham Greene 37:137
Paul Theroux 15:535

Marowitz, Charles
John Arden 13:23
Howard Brenton 31:60
Ed Bullins 1:47
Peter Nichols 36:327
John Osborne 5:331
Tom Stoppard 1:327
Tennessee Williams 11:576

Marquard, Jean
André Brink 18:69
Bessie Head 25:237

Marranca, Bonnie
Peter Handke 8:261; 10:256

Mars-Jones, Adam
Anita Brookner 34:139
John Gregory Dunne 28:128
Edna O'Brien 36:341
Cynthia Ozick 28:350

Marsden, Michael T.
Louis L'Amour 25:277, 278

Marsh, Dave
Jackson Browne 21:38
Jimmy Cliff 21:61
Bob Dylan 12:192
Marvin Gaye 26:135
John Lennon 35:264, 270
Steve Martin 30:246
Van Morrison 21:233
Jimmy Page and Robert Plant 12:480
Bob Seger 35:379, 380, 383, 384, 387
Patti Smith 12:539
Bruce Springsteen 17:486
Peter Townshend 17:527, 531, 533, 535, 541
Paul Weller 26:443, 444
Brian Wilson 12:654
Neil Young 17:574

Marsh, Fred T.
A. J. Cronin 32:130
Walter D. Edmonds 35:146
C. S. Forester 35:161, 163, 164
Arthur Koestler 33:228
Andrew Lytle 22:292
Carson McCullers 12:409
Nevil Shute 30:365

Marsh, Irving T.
Roger Kahn 30:230
Jean Lee Latham 12:323

Marsh, Jeffrey
Carl Sagan 30:340

Marsh, Meredith
Raymond Carver 22:101
Ted Mooney 25:330

Marsh, Pamela
Art Buchwald 33:92
Agatha Christie 1:58
Jan de Hartog 19:131
Michael Ende 31:143
Ronald L. Fair 18:140
Michael Frayn 31:190
Romain Gary 25:186
Joseph Krumgold 12:317
John McPhee 36:293
Robert Newton Peck 17:336
Josephine Poole 17:372
Mary Stewart 35:390
Mary Stolz 12:552
Leon Uris 32:432

Marshak, Sondra
Gene Roddenberry 17:407

Marshall, Donald
Geoffrey H. Hartman 27:184
Stanislaw Lem 8:343

Marshall, Donald G.
Jacques Derrida 24:151

Marshall, Elizabeth B.
Manuel Puig 28:372

Marshall, Eliot
Margaret Mead 37:283

Marshall, Margaret
René Clair 20:60
A. B. Guthrie, Jr. 23:196
Josef von Sternberg 20:370

Marshall, Megan
Julian Symons 32:426
Thornton Wilder 15:575

Marshall, Tom
Margaret Atwood 8:29; 25:63
William Heyen 13:282
Gwendolyn MacEwen 13:358
Michael Ondaatje 29:341
P. K. Page 7:292
Leon Rooke 25:393

Mars-Jones, Adam
Judith Rossner 29:356

Marten, Harry
Paul Bowles 19:60
Stanley Kunitz 14:313
Denise Levertov 15:338
Muriel Rukeyser 15:457
Anne Stevenson 33:381

Martin, Allie Beth
Walter Farley 17:118

Martin, B. J.
Noel Streatfeild 21:412

Martin, Brian
Bruce Chatwin 28:72
Alan Sillitoe 19:422
D. M. Thomas 22:418

Martin, Bruce K.
Philip Larkin 13:338
John Steinbeck 21:376

Martin, David
Nevil Shute 30:371

Martin, Dolores M.
G. Cabrera Infante 25:103

Martin, D. R.
David Brin 34:134

Martin, Gerald
Miguel Angel Asturias 13:37

Martin, Graham
Roy Fuller 4:177
Robert Pinget 13:444

Martin, James
Stanley Plumly 33:311
May Sarton 14:480

Martin, Jane
Rhys Davies 23:143
Pamela Hansford Johnson 27:215

Martin, Jay
Robert Lowell 1:181

Martin, John
Russell Baker 31:26

Martin, Judith
Erica Jong 18:278

Martin, Mick
Edward Bond 23:71

Martin, Murray S.
Frank Sargeson 31:373

Martin, Robert A.
Arthur Miller 10:346

Martin, Robert K.
Richard Howard 10:274

Martin, Ruby
Mildred D. Taylor 21:419

Martin, Sandra
Hugh Garner 13:237
Jane Rule 27:419

Martin, Terence
Ken Kesey 11:314

Martin, Wallace
D. J. Enright 8:204

Martin, Wendy
Adrienne Rich 36:374

Martineau, Stephen
Susan Musgrave 13:401
James Reaney 13:475

Martinez, Z. Nelly
José Donoso 8:178

Martins, Wilson
Carlos Drummond de Andrade 18:5
João Guimarães Rosa 23:355

Martinson, Steven D.
Günter Eich 15:205

Martone, John
Robert Creeley 36:122
Richard Kostelanetz 28:218

Martz, Louis L.
Ted Berrigan 37:44
Robert Creeley 1:67
Phyllis Gotlieb 18:192
John Hollander 14:261
X. J. Kennedy 8:320
Philip Levine 33:274

Robert Lowell 1:181
Lisel Mueller 13:400
Joyce Carol Oates 9:403
Robert Pinsky 9:417
Ezra Pound 1:276
Reg Saner 9:469
Jon Silkin 2:396
William Stafford 4:521
Mark Strand 18:515
John Wain 2:458
Al Young 19:477

Martz, William J.
John Berryman 1:34

Marusiak, Joe
Galway Kinnell 29:286

Marvin, K. Shattuck
Thomas B. Costain 30:93

Marwell, Patricia McCue
Jules Archer 12:22

Marx, Paul
Nadine Gordimer 33:185

Marz, Charles
John Dos Passos 25:147

Marzan, Julio
V. S. Naipaul 37:322

Mascaro, Phyllis
Suzanne Newton 35:301

Masing-Delic, Irene
Boris Pasternak 18:389

Masinton, Charles G.
J. P. Donleavy 10:153

Maskell, Duke
E. M. Forster 1:108; 9:203

Maslin, Janet
Elvis Costello 21:72
Ray Davies 21:105
Marguerite Duras 20:103
Rainer Werner Fassbinder 20:114
Alex Haley 12:254
Werner Herzog 16:328
John Landis 26:274, 276
Gordon Lightfoot 26:278
Joni Mitchell 12:440, 443
Laura Nyro 17:318
Mary Rodgers 12:495
Buffy Sainte-Marie 17:431
Carly Simon 26:411
Paul Simon 17:466
Bruce Springsteen 17:480
Lina Wertmüller 16:589
Neil Young 17:573

Mason, Ann L.
Günter Grass 4:204; 11:247

Mason, Clifford
William Melvin Kelley 22:249

Mason, John Hope
David Hare 29:220

Mason, Margaret
Judy Blume 30:22

Mason, Michael
Donald Barthelme 8:53
John Cheever 15:131
Robert Coover 15:143
George V. Higgins 10:273
Colin MacInnes 23:286
Peter Straub 28:409

Massa, Robert
Edna O'Brien 36:341

Massey, Ian
Ray Davies 21:96

Massie, Allan
Anthony Powell 31:321
David Harry Walker 14:552

Massingham, Harold
George Mackay Brown 5:76

Mast, Gerald
Buster Keaton 20:194

Masterman, Len
Roman Polanski 16:468

Masters, Anthony
David Rudkin 14:470
C. P. Taylor 27:444

Match, Richard
Ernest K. Gann 23:163
Winston Graham 23:191
Frank G. Slaughter 29:374, 375
Sloan Wilson 32:444

Mathes, Miriam S.
Lloyd Alexander 35:22
Kin Platt 26:348

Mathes, William
Claude Brown 30:35

Mathews, F. X.
P. H. Newby 13:408, 410

Mathews, Laura
James Hanley 13:261
Richard Price 12:491

Mathews, Richard
Brian Aldiss 14:10
Piers Anthony 35:39
Anthony Burgess 22:72

Mathewson, Joseph
J.R.R. Tolkien 12:566

Mathewson, Rufus W., Jr.
Boris Pasternak 7:299
Mikhail Sholokhov 7:421
Aleksandr I. Solzhenitsyn 7:441

Mathewson, Ruth
Alejo Carpentier 8:134
Joan Didion 8:176
J. P. Donleavy 10:154
Margaret Drabble 8:184
Paula Fox 8:219
James Hanley 13:260
Colleen McCullough 27:320
Leslie Marmon Silko 23:407
Christina Stead 8:500
Robert Penn Warren 8:540

Mathias, Roland
Dannie Abse 29:12

Mathy, Francis
Shiga Naoya 33:363

Matlaw, Myron
Alan Paton 10:387

Matson, Marshall
Margaret Atwood 15:36

Matthews, Anne E.
Margaret O. Hyde 21:177

Matthews, Barbara
Peter Straub 28:411

Matthews, Charles
John Hawkes 2:183

Matthews, Desmond, S.J.
Pat Jordan 37:193

Matthews, Dorothy
J.R.R. Tolkien 12:583

Matthews, Herbert L.
Ved Mehta 37:288

Matthews, J. H.
André Breton 2:80

Matthews, James H.
Frank O'Connor 14:396; 23:329

Matthews, Nancie
Isaac Asimov 26:35
Noel Streatfeild 21:401

Matthews, Pete
Walter Becker and Donald
Fagen 26:83

Matthews, Robin
Robin Skelton 13:507

Matthews, Steve
Robin F. Brancato 35:69

Matthews, T. S.
Edmund Wilson 8:551

Matthews, Virginia H.
Betty Cavanna 12:98

Matthias, John
Elizabeth Daryush 6:123
Michael Hamburger 5:158
Elizabeth Jennings 14:293
David Jones 7:189
Edwin Morgan 31:273
Anne Stevenson 7:463
D. M. Thomas 13:542
R. S. Thomas 6:530

Matyas, Cathy
Ralph Gustafson 36:222

Maugham, W. Somerset
Noël Coward 29:131

Maunder, Gabrielle
Ruth M. Arthur 12:27
Alvin Silverstein and Virginia
B. Silverstein 17:450

Maurer, Robert
A. Alvarez 5:17
Thomas Bernhard 32:16
Robertson Davies 7:73
José Donoso 8:180
Stanley Elkin 27:120
Leslie A. Fiedler 24:198
MacDonald Harris 9:258
Pablo Neruda 9:398
Clancy Sigal 7:425

Maurer, Robert E.
E. E. Cummings 8:155

Mauriac, Claude
Roland Barthes 24:22
Georges Bataille 29:38
Samuel Beckett 2:44
Albert Camus 2:97
Henry Miller 2:281
Alain Robbe-Grillet 2:373
Nathalie Sarraute 2:383
Georges Simenon 2:396

Maurois, André
Aldous Huxley 3:253
Jules Romains 7:381

Maury, Lucien
Pär Lagerkvist 7:198

Maxwell, D. E. S.
Brian Friel 5:128

Maxwell, Emily
Isaac Asimov 26:36
Maia Wojciechowska 26:449

Maxwell, Gavin
Farley Mowat 26:336

Maxwell, William
Scott Elledge 34:431
Eudora Welty 33:424
E. B. White 34:431

May, Charles Paul
Joy Adamson 17:1

May, Clifford D.
Art Buchwald 33:95

May, Derwent
D. J. Enright 31:153
Nadine Gordimer 5:145
Seamus Heaney 37:166
Alfred Hitchcock 16:340
Ted Hughes 14:270
Alison Lurie 4:305
Tadeusz Różewicz 9:463
Louis Simpson 9:485

May, Jill P.
Robert Newton Peck 17:341

May, John R.
Kurt Vonnegut, Jr. 2:455

May, Keith M.
Aldous Huxley 4:242

May, Yolanta
Emma Tennant 13:536

Mayberry, George
Howard Fast 23:155

Mayer, David
Ronald Harwood 32:225, 226
Thornton Wilder 15:574

Mayer, Glenn
Taylor Caldwell 28:67

Mayer, Hans
Friedrich Dürrenmatt 4:140
Witold Gombrowicz 4:193
Günter Grass 4:202
Jean-Paul Sartre 4:473

Mayer, Peter
Vine Deloria, Jr. 21:111

Mayer, Thomas
Maya Deren 16:253

Mayfield, Julian
Eldridge Cleaver 30:57

Mayhew, Alice
Graham Greene 1:134
Claude Mauriac 9:363

Maynard, Robert C.
Alex Haley 8:259
Garry Trudeau 12:588

Maynard, Theodore
Thomas B. Costain 30:95

Mayne, Richard
Saul Bellow 8:70
J.M.G. Le Clézio 31:242
J.I.M. Stewart 7:465

Mayne, William
Eilís Dillon 17:95

Mayo, Clark
Kurt Vonnegut, Jr. 12:617

Mayo, E. L.
Richard F. Hugo 32:235

Mayoux, Jean-Jacques
Samuel Beckett 18:41

Mays, Milton A.
Wayne C. Booth 24:84

Mazrui, Ali A.
Alex Haley 12:249

Mazzaro, Jerome
Elizabeth Bishop 9:88
Donald Davie 31:116
Norman Dubie 36:135
Brewster Ghiselin 23:172
David Ignatow 7:175, 178
Randall Jarrell 6:259
Robert Lowell 4:295, 298
Cynthia Macdonald 19:291
Joyce Carol Oates 3:359
Robert Phillips 28:363
Marge Piercy 27:375
Ezra Pound 4:417
John Crowe Ransom 2:366
W. D. Snodgrass 6:514
R. G. Vliet 22:443
William Carlos Williams 5:508

Mazzocco, Robert
John Ashbery 3:15
Chester Kallman 2:221
Philip Levine 5:251
Mario Luzi 13:354
William Meredith 4:348
James Merrill 34:232
Anne Sexton 6:492
Eleanor Ross Taylor 5:426
Gore Vidal 6:548
Derek Walcott 14:551

McAleer, John
Barbara Pym 37:368

McAleer, John J.
MacKinlay Kantor 7:195
Alain Robbe-Grillet 10:438

McAllister, H. S.
Carlos Castaneda 12:92

Critic Index

McAllister, Mick
Michael McClure **6**:319

McAlpin, Sara, B.V.M.
Eudora Welty **33**:421

McAlpine, Mary
Audrey Thomas **37**:415

McAneny, Marguerite
Richard Kostelanetz **28**:213

McArthur, Colin
Roman Polanski **16**:464
Andrzej Wajda **16**:579

McAuley, Gay
Jean Genet **10**:225
Peter Handke **10**:254

McBride, James
Frank Bonham **12**:49

McBride, Joseph
John Ford **16**:310, 314
Alfred Hitchcock **16**:348
Sidney Poitier **26**:358
Orson Welles **20**:447, 450
Billy Wilder **20**:462, 463, 464

McBroom, Gerry
Joanne Greenberg **30**:166
Barbara Wersba **30**:435

McCabe, Bernard
Jonathan Baumbach **23**:52, 54
Wilfrid Sheed **10**:474

McCaffery, Larry
Donald Barthelme **5**:55
T. Coraghessan Boyle **36**:63
Robert Coover **32**:126
William H. Gass **8**:242

McCaffery, Mark M.
Jim Shepard **36**:406

McCahill, Alice
Elizabeth Taylor **2**:432

McCall, Dorothy
Jean-Paul Sartre **7**:388; **13**:498

McCalla, Nelle
Maureen Daly **17**:89

McCallister, Myrna J.
François Sagan **36**:383

McCandlish, George
Jan de Hartog **19**:132

McCann, Garth
Edward Abbey **36**:14

McCann, John J.
Arthur Adamov **25**:21

McCann, Sean
Brendan Behan **15**:46

McCarten, John
Robert Bolt **14**:88
Alfred Hitchcock **16**:339
Langston Hughes **35**:216
Jean Kerr **22**:256
Douglas Turner Ward **19**:456

McCarthy, Abigail
Cynthia Propper Seton **27**:428
John Updike **15**:546

McCarthy, Colman
P. G. Wodehouse **5**:516

McCarthy, Dermot
Bill Bissett **18**:62

McCarthy, Harold T.
Henry Miller **9**:377
Richard Wright **3**:545

McCarthy, Mary
Alvah Bessie **23**:59
William S. Burroughs **2**:90
Ivy Compton-Burnett **3**:112
Joan Didion **32**:147
Mary McCarthy **14**:361
Vladimir Nabokov **2**:301
Clifford Odets **28**:336
J. D. Salinger **3**:444
Nathalie Sarraute **2**:384
Monique Wittig **22**:472

McCarthy, Paul
John Steinbeck **21**:389

McCartney, Barney C.
Ezekiel Mphahlele **25**:333

McCarty, John Alan
Roman Polanski **16**:467

McCawley, Dwight L.
Theodore Roethke **19**:401

McClain, Harriet
Paula Danziger **21**:86

McClain, John
Larry Gelbart **21**:124
Jean Kerr **22**:255
Stephen Sondheim **30**:376

McClain, Ruth Rambo
Toni Morrison **4**:365

McClanahan, Ed
Richard Brautigan **12**:64

McClatchy, J. D.
A. R. Ammons **5**:31
Alfred Corn **33**:113
Stephen Dobyns **37**:78
Norman Dubie **36**:133
Lawrence Durrell **27**:97
Louise Glück **7**:119; **22**:177
Marilyn Hacker **23**:205
Anthony Hecht **19**:210
Edward Hirsch **31**:216
Richard Howard **7**:167
Ted Hughes **37**:179
Laura Jensen **37**:192
Donald Justice **19**:237
Laurence Lieberman **36**:259
Robert Lowell **8**:355
James Merrill **6**:324
Howard Moss **14**:376
Robert Pinsky **9**:417
Sylvia Plath **5**:346
Ira Sadoff **9**:466
Anne Sexton **15**:471
Charles Simic **22**:383
W. D. Snodgrass **18**:490
Maura Stanton **9**:507
Diane Wakoski **7**:504
Robert Penn Warren **6**:557
Theodore Weiss **8**:546
Philip Whalen **29**:447
Edmund White III **27**:479

Charles Wright **6**:581

McCleary, Dorothy
Eilís Dillon **17**:94

McClellan, Edwin
Yukio Mishima **6**:338

McClellan, Joseph
Mary Stewart **35**:395

McClelland, David
Flann O'Brien **5**:315
Patti Smith **12**:536

McClintock, Michael W.
C. J. Cherryh **35**:109

McCloskey, Mark
Robert Francis **15**:235

McClure, Michael
Sam Shepard **17**:441

McCluskey, John
James Baldwin **17**:39

McCluskey, Sally
John G. Neihardt **32**:335

McComas, J. Frances
Frank Herbert **12**:270

McConnell, Frank
John Barth **7**:25; **14**:57
Saul Bellow **6**:54
Michel Foucault **31**:180
John Gardner **7**:115
Andrew M. Greeley **28**:175
Graham Greene **14**:217; **18**:198
Norman Mailer **14**:353
Tom Robbins **32**:371

McConnell, Ruth M.
William Kotzwinkle **35**:254
Katherine Paterson **30**:288
Laurence Yep **35**:474

McConnell-Mammarella, Joan
Carlo Emilio Gadda **11**:210

McConville, Edward
John Sayles **10**:461

McCord, David
Ogden Nash **23**:321

McCorkle, Elizabeth
Milton Meltzer **26**:305

McCormack, W. J.
Elizabeth Bowen **22**:66

McCormick, E. H.
James K. Baxter **14**:59
Frank Sargeson **31**:364

McCormick, Lynde
Bruce Springsteen **17**:479

McCormick, Ruth
Nagisa Oshima **20**:249, 252

McCourt, James
Noël Coward **29**:141
Eric Rohmer **16**:538

McCown, Robert, S. J.
Flannery O'Connor **21**:255

McCracken, Samuel
Jonathan Schell **35**:368

McCue, Michael
Margaret Craven **17**:80
Anne McCaffrey **17**:283
John Neufeld **17**:310
Laurence Yep **35**:470

McCullers, Carson
Carson McCullers **12**:417

McCullough, Frank
George Garrett **3**:189

McCutcheon, R. S.
Alvin Silverstein and Virginia
B. Silverstein **17**:455

McDaniel, John N.
Philip Roth **31**:334

McDaniel, Richard Bryan
Chinua Achebe **7**:6

McDiarmid, Matthew P.
Hugh MacDiarmid **11**:334

McDonald, Edward R.
Friedrich Dürrenmatt **15**:199

McDonald, Henry
William Price Fox **22**:142
John Gardner **30**:156

McDonald, James L.
John Barth **2**:38
John Knowles **26**:255

McDonald, Marcia
John Crowe Ransom **24**:367

McDonald, Susan S.
Harriet Waugh **6**:560

McDonnell, Christine
Roy A. Gallant **17**:133
Zibby Oneal **30**:280
Noel Streatfeild **21**:417

McDonnell, Jane Taylor
Galway Kinnell **2**:230

McDonnell, John V.
William Barrett **27**:18

McDonnell, Peter J.
Noel Streatfeild **21**:400

McDonnell, Thomas P.
David Lodge **36**:267
Conrad Richter **30**:318

McDonough, Jack
Jackson Browne **21**:36
Jim Carroll **35**:78

McDowell, Danièle
Michel Tournier **23**:452

McDowell, Edwin
Richard Brautigan **34**:315
Glendon Swarthout **35**:402

McDowell, Frederick P. W.
John Braine **1**:43
Lawrnce Durrell **1**:87
E. M. Forster **1**:107; **10**:181
Caroline Gordon **29**:186
Doris Lessing **1**:175
Iris Murdoch **1**:236
Frederic Raphael **2**:366
Muriel Spark **2**:416

McDowell, Myles
Leon Garfield **12**:228
William Mayne **12**:404

McDowell, Robert
Chinua Achebe **26**:14
A. R. Ammons **25**:42
William Least Heat Moon **29**:224
Laura Jensen **37**:190
Thomas Merton **11**:374
Stanley Plumly **33**:315
Louis Simpson **32**:381

McDowell, Robert E.
Thomas Keneally **10**:298

McElroy, Joseph
Samuel Beckett **2**:48
Italo Calvino **5**:99
Vladimir Nabokov **2**:304

McElroy, Wendy
Gabriel García Márquez **10**:217

McEvilly, Wayne
Anaïs Nin **1**:248

McEvoy, Ruth M.
Henry Gregory Felsen **17**:121

McEwan, Ian
David Hare **29**:215
Milan Kundera **32**:264

McEwen, Joe
Smokey Robinson **21**:350

McFadden, George
Wayne C. Booth **24**:91
Robert Lowell **9**:333

McFee, Michael
Laurence Lieberman **36**:263
Dave Smith **22**:389
William Stafford **29**:387

McFee, William
Edna Ferber **18**:151
C. S. Forester **35**:162, 163, 164

McFerran, Douglas
Carlos Castaneda **12**:93

McGann, Jerome
Robert Creeley **2**:106; **8**:151
David Jones **7**:188
X. J. Kennedy **8**:320
Eleanor Lerman **9**:331

McGann, Jerome J.
Michael Benedikt **14**:81
Harold Bloom **24**:70
Turner Cassity **6**:107
Daniel Mark Epstein **7**:97
A. D. Hope **3**:251
Donald Justice **6**:272
Galway Kinnell **13**:320
Muriel Rukeyser **6**:479
Judith Johnson Sherwin **7**:415

McGann, Kevin
Ayn Rand **30**:302

McGee, David
Kris Kristofferson **26**:269
Bruce Springsteen **17**:479

McGeehin, R.
Mary Renault **17**:402

McGerr, Celia
René Clair **20**:69

McGhan, Barry
Andre Norton **12**:459

McGilchrist, Iain
W. H. Auden **9**:57

McGinley, Karen
Sandra Scoppettone **26**:401

McGinley, Phyllis
Margery Allingham **19**:13

McGinnis, Wayne D.
Roman Polanski **16**:471
Kurt Vonnegut, Jr. **8**:529

McGinniss, Joe
Nora Ephron **17**:113
George V. Higgins **4**:222

McGovern, Hugh
Rhys Davies **23**:146
George Tabori **19**:436

McGowan, Sarah M.
Don DeLillo **27**:79

McGrath, Joan
Gwendolyn MacEwen **13**:358

McGregor, Craig
Bob Dylan **4**:148

McGrory, Mary
Taylor Caldwell **28**:59
Helen MacInnes **27**:280
Frank G. Slaughter **29**:373

McGuane, Thomas
Richard Brautigan **1**:44
John Hawkes **2**:185

McGuinness, Arthur E.
Seamus Heaney **14**:242

McGuinness, Frank
Kingsley Amis **1**:6
Andrew Sinclair **2**:400
Frank Tuohy **37**:428

McGuire, Alice Brooks
Betty Cavanna **12**:98
Jean Lee Latham **12**:322

McGuire, Paul, III
Marion Zimmer Bradley **30**:27

McHaffie, Margaret
Christa Wolf **29**:465

McHale, Tom
Diane Johnson **5**:198
D. Keith Mano **2**:270
J. F. Powers **8**:447

McHargue, Georgess
Joan Aiken **35**:17
Lloyd Alexander **35**:27
Barbara Corcoran **17**:71, 74
Peter Dickinson **35**:132
Nicholasa Mohr **12**:447
John Neufeld **17**:308
Scott O'Dell **30**:277
Zilpha Keatley Snyder **17**:473
Barbara Wersba **30**:432, 434
Laurence Yep **35**:469

McHenry, Susan
June Jordan **23**:256

McHugh, Joseph J.
Phillip Lopate **29**:299

McInerney, John
John Knowles **10**:303
Douglas Unger **34**:116

McInerny, Ralph
Anthony Burgess **4**:80

McInnes, Neil
David Caute **29**:116

McIntyre, Jean
Sue Ellen Bridgers **26**:91

McKay, Nellie Y.
Jean Toomer **22**:428

McKay, Ruth Capers
Frank Swinnerton **31**:423

McKegney, Michael
Claude Chabrol **16**:171

McKenna, Andrew J.
Patrick Modiano **18**:338

McKenzie, Alan T.
John Updike **5**:452

McKenzie, Barbara
Mary McCarthy **24**:344

McKeown, Thomas
Donald Davie **31**:110

McKillop, Alan D.
Wayne C. Booth **24**:88

McKinley, Hugh
Anthony Kerrigan **6**:275

McKinley, Robin
Laurence Yep **35**:473

McKinnon, William T.
Louis MacNeice **10**:324

McLachlan, Ian
Timothy Findley **27**:144

McLane, Daisann
Laura Nyro **17**:320
Neil Young **17**:579

McLatchie, Ian B.
W. P. Kinsella **27**:238

McLaughlin, Pat
Charles M. Schulz **12**:533

McLay, C. M.
Margaret Laurence **3**:278
Ethel Davis Wilson **13**:609

McLay, Catherine
William Mitchell **25**:324

McLean, David G.
Lewis Turco **11**:551

McLean, Scott
Frank Herbert **35**:208
Gary Snyder **33**:389

McLellan, Joseph
Richard Adams **18**:1
Richard Bach **14**:36
Russell Baker **31**:29
Donald Barthelme **8**:52
John Berryman **8**:90
Dee Brown **18**:70

Max Frisch **18**:163
Arthur Hailey **5**:156
Robert Heinlein **8**:275
George V. Higgins **10**:274
John le Carré **15**:324
Phillip Lopate **29**:300
J. B. Priestley **34**:362
John Sayles **7**:399
J.R.R. Tolkien **8**:515
Trevanian **29**:431
T. H. White **30**:450

McLennan, Winona
Alvin Silverstein and Virginia B. Silverstein **17**:453

McLeod, A. L.
Thomas Keneally **19**:248
Patrick White **7**:531

McLeod, Alan L.
Thomas Keneally **19**:243

McLuhan, H. M.
F. R. Leavis **24**:294

McLuhan, Herbert Marshall
John Dos Passos **11**:154

McLure, G.
C.L.R. James **33**:218

McMahon, Erik S.
Günter Grass **22**:197

McMahon, Joseph H.
Jean-Paul Sartre **7**:389
Michel Tournier **23**:451, 453

McMahon, Patricia
Alan Garner **17**:151

McMahon-Hill, Gillian
Russell C. Hoban **7**:161

McManus, Jeanne
Rosellen Brown **32**:69

McMichael, Charles T.
Aldous Huxley **35**:243

McMichael, James
May Sarton **4**:471

McMillan, George
Leon Uris **32**:431

McMullen, Roy
Nathalie Sarraute **2**:385

McMurray, George R.
José Donoso **32**:154, 156
Gabriel García Márquez **27**:147

McMurtry, Larry
Vardis Fisher **7**:103
Ernest J. Gaines **11**:217
Ward Just **4**:265
John McPhee **36**:298
Wright Morris **18**:353
Susan Richards Shreve **23**:404

McNally, John
Carson McCullers **12**:429

McNamara, Eugene
Hugh Hood **28**:189

McNamee, Kenneth
T.E.D. Klein **34**:72

McNeil, Helen
Mary Gordon **22**:186
Olivia Manning **19**:304
Jean Rhys **19**:392
Philip Roth **15**:454
Colin Wilson **14**:584

McNeil, Nicholas J., S.J.
Eleanor Hibbert **7**:156

McNeill, William H.
Charles M. Schulz **12**:524

McNelly, Willis E.
Ray Bradbury **10**:70
Robert Heinlein **8**:274
Frank Herbert **12**:277
Kurt Vonnegut, Jr. **2**:452

McNevin, Tom
George V. Higgins **18**:235

McNulty, Faith
Judy Blume **30**:24
Paula Danziger **21**:85
Isabelle Holland **21**:150
Ann Schlee **35**:374

McNulty, John
Sloan Wilson **32**:444

McPheeters, D. W.
Camilo José Cela **4**:98

McPheron, Judith
Jamake Highwater **12**:287

McPherson, Hugo
Morley Callaghan **14**:99
Mordecai Richler **5**:374
Gabrielle Roy **14**:465

McPherson, James
Richard Pryor **26**:377

McPherson, James Alan
Breece D'J Pancake **29**:345

McPherson, Sandra
William Heyen **13**:283
Ted Hughes **37**:176

McPherson, William
Margaret Atwood **8**:30
Paula Fox **8**:218
John Gardner **8**:235
Günter Grass **11**:252
Maxine Hong Kingston **12**:312
Maxine Kumin **5**:222
Ross Macdonald **14**:328
Lewis Thomas **35**:410
John Updike **5**:457; **13**:563

McRobbie, Angela
Pat Barker **32**:14
Anita Brookner **34**:137
Maureen Duffy **37**:116
Zoë Fairbairns **32**:163
Michel Tournier **36**:438
Gore Vidal **33**:408

McRobbie, Kenneth
Seamus Heaney **14**:242

McShane, Joseph M., S.J.
Louis R. Harlan **34**:186

McSweeney, Kerry
Brian Moore **19**:330; **32**:313
V. S. Naipaul **9**:391
Anthony Powell **9**:435
Simon Raven **14**:439

McVay, Douglas
Claude Chabrol **16**:182
Vittorio De Sica **20**:91
Satyajit Ray **16**:475

McWilliams, Dean
Michel Butor **3**:94; **15**:115
Marguerite Duras **3**:129; **20**:100

McWilliams, Donald E.
Frederick Wiseman **20**:471

McWilliams, Nancy R.
John Steinbeck **5**:405

McWilliams, W. C.
Mary Renault **11**:472

McWilliams, Wilson C.
John Steinbeck **5**:405

Meades, Jonathan
Simone de Beauvoir **2**:43
Jorge Luis Borges **1**:39; **3**:77;
  4:74
Louis-Ferdinand Céline **3**:105
Iris Murdoch **2**:297
Vladimir Nabokov **2**:302; **3**:354
Alain Robbe-Grillet **1**:289;
  2:376; **4**:448
Keith Roberts **14**:463
Kurt Vonnegut, Jr. **2**:455

Means, Howard
Roger Kahn **30**:233

Meckier, Jerome
Aldous Huxley **11**:285; **18**:267
Evelyn Waugh **3**:512; **19**:462

Mecklin, John
Jonathan Schell **35**:361

Medawar, Peter B.
Arthur Koestler **6**:281; **8**:324
Lewis Thomas **35**:416

Medjuck, Joe
Monty Python **21**:223

Mednick, Liz
Rita Mae Brown **18**:73
Susan Sontag **13**:518

Medvedev, R. A.
Mikhail Sholokhov **15**:483

Meehan, Thomas
Peter De Vries **28**:112
Bob Dylan **12**:180
Monty Python **21**:227

Meek, Margaret
Peter Dickinson **12**:175
Alan Garner **17**:138, 148, 149,
  150
Mollie Hunter **21**:170
William Mayne **12**:391, 394,
  399, 405
Rosemary Sutcliff **26**:428
Robert Westall **17**:559

Meerloo, Joost A. M.
Aldous Huxley **35**:236

Meeter, Glenn
Kurt Vonnegut, Jr. **4**:566

Megaw, Moira
W. H. Auden **6**:24

Megged, Aharon
S. Y. Agnon **4**:14

Meggers, Betty J.
Margaret Mead **37**:274

Mehrer, Sophia B.
Milton Meltzer **26**:297

Meiners, R. K.
James Dickey **7**:81
Robert Lowell **1**:182
Delmore Schwartz **2**:387
Allen Tate **4**:536; **24**:447

Meinke, Peter
W. H. Auden **6**:20
John Beecher **6**:48
John Dos Passos **4**:136
H. D. **8**:256
Marilyn Hacker **5**:155
Ted Hughes **4**:236
Philip Levine **5**:250
William Meredith **13**:372
Howard Nemerov **2**:307
Muriel Rukeyser **6**:478
Anne Sexton **4**:483
Diane Wakoski **7**:504
Robert Penn Warren **6**:555
Charles Wright **6**:579

Meisel, Perry
Joni Mitchell **12**:440

Meisler, Stanley
Howard Fast **23**:157

Mekas, Jonas
Andy Warhol **20**:415

Melanson, Jim
Richard O'Brien **17**:322

Meldrum, Barbara
Conrad Richter **30**:329

Mellard, James M.
Bernard Malamud **1**:198;
  27:296
François Mauriac **9**:367
Kurt Vonnegut, Jr. **3**:504;
  4:565

Mellen, Joan
Ingmar Bergman **16**:71
Luis Buñuel **16**:135
Jean-Luc Godard **20**:142
Kon Ichikawa **20**:185
Akira Kurosawa **16**:403
Elaine May **16**:434
Nagisa Oshima **20**:253, 255
Eric Rohmer **16**:533
Carlos Saura **20**:314

Mellers, Wilfrid
Bob Dylan **12**:187
John Lennon and Paul
  McCartney **12**:374

Mellor, Anne K.
Nathalie Sarraute **31**:377

Mellor, Isha
Sol Yurick **6**:583

Mellors, John
Martin Amis **4**:20
Louis Auchincloss **6**:15
Beryl Bainbridge **10**:17
Lynne Reid Banks **23**:42
Thomas Berger **5**:60

Caroline Blackwood **9**:101
Dirk Bogarde **19**:43
Elizabeth Bowen **22**:64
Melvyn Bragg **10**:72
Angela Carter **5**:102
Isabel Colegate **36**:111
Peter De Vries **7**:77
Peter Dickinson **35**:135
Shusaku Endo **7**:96; **14**:160
Elaine Feinstein **36**:170, 171
Penelope Fitzgerald **19**:173
John Fowles **6**:188
Athol Fugard **25**:173
Maurice Gee **29**:177
Herbert Gold **14**:208
John Hawkes **7**:141
Bessie Head **25**:237
Mark Helprin **10**:260
Rolf Hochhuth **18**:256
Ursula Holden **18**:258
Jorge Ibargüengoitia **37**:183
Dan Jacobson **4**:253
Ruth Prawer Jhabvala **8**:312
G. Josipovici **6**:270
Jonathan Keates **34**:202
Yashar Kemal **29**:266
Penelope Lively **32**:273, 274,
  276
Bernard Malamud **5**:269
Olivia Manning **19**:303
Ian McEwan **13**:370
Stanley Middleton **7**:219
Yukio Mishima **4**:357
Brian Moore **19**:334
Alberto Moravia **7**:244
Iris Murdoch **4**:369
Craig Nova **31**:296
Julia O'Faolain **6**:382; **19**:360
Seán O'Faoláin **14**:407
V. S. Pritchett **5**:353
Frederic Raphael **14**:438
Piers Paul Read **4**:444; **10**:435;
  25:379, 380
Philip Roth **31**:346
J. R. Salamanca **15**:464
William Sansom **6**:484
Nathalie Sarraute **10**:460
Ann Schlee **35**:373, 375
Penelope Shuttle **7**:422
Alan Sillitoe **6**:499; **19**:420
Wole Soyinka **5**:398
Richard G. Stern **4**:523
David Storey **8**:504
Peter Straub **28**:409
Lisa St. Aubin de Teran **36**:420
Frank Tuohy **37**:431
Ludvík Vaculík **7**:495
John Wain **15**:561
Charles Webb **7**:516
Patrick White **5**:48
A. N. Wilson **33**:451

Mellown, Elgin W.
Jean Rhys **2**:373
John Wain **2**:458

Melly, George
Jean Arp **5**:33

Melnyk, George
Andrew Suknaski **19**:432

Meltzer, R.
John Lennon and Paul
McCartney **12**:382
Jim Morrison **17**:290
Patti Smith **12**:538

Melville, Robert
Herbert Read **4**:438
Susan Sontag **13**:515

Melzer, Annabelle Henkin
Louis Aragon **22**:41

Menand, Louis
Frank Lentricchia **34**:572

Mendelsohn, John
Walter Becker and Donald
Fagen **26**:80
Paul McCartney **35**:280

Mendelsohn, John Ned
David Bowie **17**:57, 58
Ray Davies **21**:91
Jimmy Page and Robert Plant
12:473, 474
Peter Townshend **17**:527
Neil Young **17**:570

Mendelsohn, Michael J.
Clifford Odets **28**:337

Mendelson, David
Eugène Ionesco **6**:255

Mendelson, Edward
John Berryman **4**:61
Thomas Pynchon **3**:415; **6**:439;
33:329

Mengel, Robert M.
Peter Matthiessen **32**:288

Mengeling, Marvin E.
Ray Bradbury **1**:42

Menkiti, Ifeanyi A.
Chinua Achebe **26**:20

Mephisto
Maya Deren **16**:252

Mercer, Peter
John Barth **9**:61

Merchant, Paul
Howard Brenton **31**:63

Merchant, W. Moelwyn
R. S. Thomas **13**:542

Mercier, Jean F.
Ruth M. Arthur **12**:27
Melvin Berger **12**:42
Betty Cavanna **12**:103
Jamake Highwater **12**:288
M. E. Kerr **12**:300
Madeleine L'Engle **12**:352
Katherine Paterson **12**:484, 486
Rosemary Wells **12**:637

Mercier, Vivian
Samuel Beckett **6**:38; **14**:79
Michel Butor **11**:78
Padraic Colum **28**:89
Harry Crews **6**:118
J. P. Donleavy **4**:125
Thomas Flanagan **25**:163
E. M. Forster **2**:135
George V. Higgins **4**:222

Aldous Huxley **5**:193
Iris Murdoch **4**:368
Raymond Queneau **5**:360
Alain Robbe-Grillet **6**:465
Nathalie Sarraute **4**:466
Claude Simon **4**:496

Mercurio, Gregory
Frank Herbert **35**:204

Meredith, William
John Berryman **2**:59; **3**:68;
25:88
Anthony Hecht **8**:268
Robert Lowell **2**:248
Muriel Rukeyser **10**:442

Merguerian, Karen
James D. Forman **21**:122

Merideth, Robert
Norman Mailer **1**:192

Meritt, Carole
Alex Haley **12**:250

Merivale, Patricia
Vladimir Nabokov **1**:242

Merkin, Daphne
Ann Beattie **13**:65
André Brink **18**:68
Michael Brodsky **19**:69
A. S. Byatt **19**:77
Vincent Canby **13**:132
Joan Didion **14**:152
Jacob Epstein **19**:162
Romain Gary **25**:188
Penelope Gilliatt **13**:239
Thomas Keneally **14**:302
Ella Leffland **19**:278
Phillip Lopate **29**:300
A. G. Mojtabai **15**:378
Vladimir Nabokov **23**:311
Breece D'J Pancake **29**:349
Jayne Anne Phillips **15**:421
Chaim Potok **7**:321
V. S. Pritchett **15**:443
Philip Roth **15**:452
Christina Stead **32**:411
John Updike **13**:559; **15**:546
Angus Wilson **25**:463

Mermier, G.
Romain Gary **25**:189, 190

Mermier, Guy
Françoise Sagan **17**:424

Mernit, Susan
June Jordan **23**:255

Merriam, Eve
Jacques Prévert **15**:440

Merrick, Gordon
Truman Capote **19**:82

Merrill, Anthony
Paul Green **25**:196

Merrill, George
Isaac Asimov **26**:37

Merrill, James
Francis Ponge **18**:415

Merrill, Reed B.
William H. Gass **8**:245

Merrill, Robert
Vladimir Nabokov **15**:396
Kurt Vonnegut, Jr. **8**:534

Merrill, Thomas F.
Allen Ginsberg **1**:118
Charles Olson **11**:417; **29**:336

Merry, Bruce
Mario Luzi **13**:352
Elio Vittorini **14**:544

Mersand, Joseph
Elmer Rice **7**:359

Mersmann, James F.
Robert Bly **5**:62
Robert Duncan **4**:142
Allen Ginsberg **4**:182
Denise Levertov **5**:247
Diane Wakoski **7**:507

Merton, John Kenneth
Pamela Hansford Johnson
27:214

Merton, Thomas
Roland Barthes **24**:37
Albert Camus **1**:52
J. F. Powers **1**:281
John Crowe Ransom **24**:362

Mertz, Barbara
Jean M. Auel **31**:23

Meryl, Jay
Norma Klein **30**:242

Meserve, Walter
James Baldwin **17**:36

Mesher, David R.
Bernard Malamud **9**:346;
11:353

Mesic, Michael
James Dickey **4**:121
Chester Kallman **2**:221

Mesic, Penelope
Russell C. Hoban **25**:267

Meškys, Edmund R.
Franklyn M. Branley **21**:18, 19

Mesnet, Marie-Béatrice
Graham Greene **3**:210

Messer, Bill
Peter Dickinson **12**:171

Metcalf, Paul
Charles Olson **9**:413

Metzger, C. R.
Lawrence Ferlinghetti **10**:176

Metzger, Norman
Franklyn M. Branley **21**:24

Mews, Siegfried
Carl Zuckmayer **18**:553, 557

Mewshaw, Michael
Jeffrey Archer **28**:14
Jonathan Baumbach **6**:31
Doris Betts **3**:73
Robertson Davies **7**:74
William Eastlake **8**:200
B. H. Friedman **7**:108
Graham Greene **18**:195

Jack Hodgins **23**:230
Robert F. Jones **7**:192
Stephen King **12**:310
David Slavitt **5**:391
Raymond Sokolov **7**:430
Peter Spielberg **6**:519
Robert Lewis Taylor **14**:534
Paul Theroux **5**:427

Meyer, Ellen Hope
Erica Jong **4**:264
Joyce Carol Oates **2**:315

Meyer, Gerard Previn
Thomas McGrath **28**:276

Meyer, Karl E.
Garry Marshall **17**:278
Frederick Wiseman **20**:475

Meyer, Marianne
Joan Armatrading **17**:10

Meyer, Michael
Harry Martinson **14**:356

Meyer, Thomas
Lorine Niedecker **10**:360
Toby Olson **28**:344

Meyers, Jeffrey
Peter Ackroyd **34**:398
T. S. Eliot **34**:398
E. M. Forster **3**:162; **4**:169
Doris Lessing **2**:241
André Malraux **4**:333
Ezra Pound **34**:507
E. Fuller Torrey **34**:507

Meyers, Richard
Steven Bochco and Michael
Kozoll **35**:50

Meyers, Robert B.
Robert Altman **16**:26

Mezan, Peter
Ken Russell **16**:544

Mezei, Kathy
Anne Hébert **29**:232, 236

Mezey, Robert
Jerome Rothenberg **6**:478
Gary Snyder **9**:498

Micciche, Pauline F.
Roger Zelazny **21**:464

Michaels, Leonard
John Barth **2**:37
Samuel Beckett **11**:43
Thomas Berger **11**:46
Jorge Luis Borges **2**:77
Dashiell Hammett **5**:160
Peter Handke **8**:264
Joseph Heller **11**:269
Erica Jong **8**:314
Bernard Malamud **3**:324
Peter Matthiessen **11**:361
Vladimir Nabokov **8**:417
Robert Stone **23**:427

Michaels, Robert G.
Woody Allen **16**:3

Michalczyk, John J.
Fernando Arrabal **18**:23

Michałek, Bolesław
Andrzej Wajda **16**:581

Michaud, Charles
Evan Hunter 31:229

Michel, Sonya
Joan Micklin Silver 20:342

Michelson, Aaron I.
Robin F. Brancato 35:70
Martha Gellhorn 14:196

Michelson, Bruce
Richard Wilbur 14:579

Michelson, Peter
Leslie A. Fiedler 24:199

Michener, Charles
Albert Maysles and David
  Maysles 16:444
Stephen Sondheim 30:384

Michener, Charles T.
Anthony Powell 3:402; 7:343

Mickelson, Anne Z.
Toni Morrison 22:315

Middlebrook, Diane
Allen Ginsberg 6:199

Middleton, Christopher
Herman Hesse 25:258

Middleton, Victoria
A. G. Mojtabai 29:319

Miesel, Sandra
Poul Anderson 15:11

Mihailovich, Vasa D.
Miroslav Krleža 8:330
Vasko Popa 19:373, 375

Miklitsch, Robert
Robert Hass 18:211

Milano, Paolo
Riccardo Bacchelli 19:32

Milbauer, Jerry
The Police 26:364

Milch, Robert J.
Chaim Potok 2:338

Milder, Robert
Flannery O'Connor 13:417

Mileck, Joseph
Hermann Hesse 17:198

Miles, G. E.
Betty Smith 19:423

Miles, Keith
Günter Grass 15:259

Miles, William
Langston Hughes 1:148

Milford, Nancy
Louise Bogan 4:69

Milivojević, D.
Vasily Aksyonov 37:12

Millar, Daniel
Jean Renoir 20:297

Millar, Gavin
Robert Altman 16:42
Lindsay Anderson 20:13
Ingmar Bergman 16:80
Claude Chabrol 16:172, 184
Michael Cimino 16:210

Millar, Margaret
Daphne du Maurier 6:146

Millar, Neil
John McPhee 36:294
David Harry Walker 14:552

Millar, Sylvia
Erskine Caldwell 14:95
Carlos Saura 20:315

Miller, Adam David
Maya Angelou 35:31
Alex Haley 12:249

Miller, Alice
Rosemary Wells 12:637

Miller, Arthur
Thornton Wilder 35:438

Miller, Baxter
Langston Hughes 10:282

Miller, Charles
Chinua Achebe 26:13
Ayi Kwei Armah 33:23

Miller, Charles L.
Joy Adamson 17:4

Miller, Dan
Robert Bloch 33:84
Marion Zimmer Bradley 30:26
John W. Campbell 32:78
Jack Vance 35:419
Roger Zelazny 21:469

Miller, David M.
Michael Hamburger 5:158
Frank Herbert 35:196

Miller, Faren
Gene Wolfe 25:478

Miller, Gabriel
Alvah Bessie 23:61
Daniel Fuchs 22:157
Alfred Hitchcock 16:353

Miller, Henry
Luis Buñuel 16:127
Blaise Cendrars 18:91
Anaïs Nin 14:379

Miller, James E.
John Berryman 25:98

Miller, James E., Jr.
William Faulkner 6:180
J. D. Salinger 1:298; 12:496

Miller, Jane
Elaine Feinstein 36:167
Ursula Holden 18:257
Julius Horwitz 14:267
Alain Robbe-Grillet 14:462
Simone Schwarz-Bart 7:404

Miller, Jeanne-Marie A.
Imamu Amiri Baraka 2:35
Gwendolyn Brooks 1:46; 4:78
Charles Gordone 4:198

Miller, Jim
Manlio Argueta 31:19
Julio Cortázar 33:136
Ray Davies 21:94
Max Frisch 32:194
Paul McCartney 35:283, 289
Wright Morris 37:313

Van Morrison 21:236
Jimmy Page and Robert Plant
  12:477
Prince 35:331
Smokey Robinson 21:350
Bruce Springsteen 17:482, 485
Brian Wilson 12:644, 648
Neil Young 17:571

Miller, Jim Wayne
Jesse Stuart 11:513

Miller, Jonathan
Lenny Bruce 21:44

Miller, Jordan Y.
Lorraine Hansberry 17:188

Miller, Karl
Kingsley Amis 13:14
Martin Amis 4:21
Beryl Bainbridge 22:44
James Baldwin 17:28
John Berger 19:38
Paula Fox 8:218
Ted Hughes 4:236
Dan Jacobson 4:256
Hugh MacDiarmid 2:254
Flann O'Brien 5:316
Barbara Pym 13:470
Anne Roiphe 9:456
Emma Tennant 13:537
Paul Theroux 11:530
Michel Tournier 6:538

Miller, Marjorie Mithoff
Isaac Asimov 26:39

Miller, Mark Crispin
Steven Bochco and Michael
  Kozoll 35:50
Sam Peckinpah 20:279

Miller, Mary Jane
Harold Pinter 27:385

Miller, Merle
C. S. Forester 35:170
Leon Uris 32:430

Miller, Michael H.
Rosa Guy 26:142

Miller, Neil
Julio Cortázar 2:103

Miller, Nolan
Henry Bromell 5:73
Tillie Olsen 13:433

Miller, Perry
Arthur Koestler 33:234

Miller, R. Baxter
Langston Hughes 15:293

Miller, Sara
Sue Ellen Bridgers 26:91
Anne McCaffrey 17:283

Miller, Stephen
Saul Bellow 25:84
Zbigniew Herbert 9:272

Miller, Tom P.
William Stafford 4:521

Miller, Vincent
T. S. Eliot 9:182
Ezra Pound 13:462

Millgate, Michael
James Gould Cozzens 4:114
John Dos Passos 4:133
William Faulkner 28:139

Millichap, Joseph R.
Carson McCullers 12:428

Milliken, Elizabeth
Tish O'Dowd Ezekiel 34:47

Milliken, Stephen F.
Chester Himes 18:247

Millken, Elizabeth
Pat Jordan 37:196

Mills, James
George V. Higgins 4:222

Mills, John
John Arden 13:26
John Metcalf 37:301
Leon Rooke 25:391
Kurt Vonnegut, Jr. 22:450

Mills, Mary
Mary Stewart 35:397

Mills, Nicolaus
Joan Micklin Silver 20:344

Mills, Ralph J., Jr.
Yves Bonnefoy 9:112
René Char 9:160
Lucille Clifton 19:109
Stephen Dobyns 37:75
Richard Eberhart 3:134, 135
David Ignatow 7:174, 179
Galway Kinnell 29:279
Maxine Kumin 5:222
Denise Levertov 2:243; 3:293
Philip Levine 4:287
Kathleen Raine 7:351
Theodore Roethke 1:291
Anne Stevenson 7:462
Jonathan Williams 13:600

Millstein, Gilbert
Lenny Bruce 21:43
Irvin Faust 8:215
Langston Hughes 35:215
Milton Meltzer 26:304
John R. Tunis 12:598

Milne, Gordon
Allen Drury 37:104

Milne, Tom
Robert Altman 16:42
Ingmar Bergman 16:54, 55
Robert Bresson 16:112, 119
Mel Brooks 12:79
Claude Chabrol 16:175, 178
René Clair 20:68
Francis Ford Coppola 16:232
Vittorio De Sica 20:97
Bob Fosse 20:121
Jean-Luc Godard 20:129, 131
George Roy Hill 26:197, 205
Kon Ichikawa 20:179, 181, 183
Stanley Kubrick 16:379
Akira Kurosawa 16:404
Rouben Mamoulian 16:424
John Osborne 5:330
Yasujiro Ozu 16:447
Gordon Parks 16:459
Sam Peckinpah 20:273

Roman Polanski **16**:463
Satyajit Ray **16**:483, 487, 488, 495
Jean Renoir **20**:292, 293
Martin Scorsese **20**:330, 331
Steven Spielberg **20**:357, 358
Josef von Sternberg **20**:377
Andrzej Wajda **16**:578
Peter Weir **20**:425
Orson Welles **20**:442

Milne, W. Gordon
John Dos Passos **4**:134

Milner, Joseph O.
Sue Ellen Bridgers **26**:93
Ouida Sebestyen **30**:350

Milner, Philip
Toby Olson **28**:342

Milner-Gulland, Robin
Andrei Voznesensky **1**:349
Yevgeny Yevtushenko **1**:381

Milord, James E.
Thomas Merton **34**:462
Michael Mott **34**:462

Milosh, Joseph
John Gardner **10**:220

Miłosz, Czesław
Joseph Brodsky **36**:74
Tadeusz Różewicz **23**:358

Milton, Edith
Beryl Bainbridge **10**:17
Frederick Buechner **9**:136
André Dubus **36**:144
Leslie Epstein **27**:131
Gail Godwin **22**:181
Nadine Gordimer **18**:190
Kazuo Ishiguro **27**:203
Alison Lurie **18**:311
Olivia Manning **19**:303
V. S. Naipaul **18**:361
Barbara Pym **37**:371
Bernice Rubens **31**:351
Jane Rule **27**:420
Alan Sillitoe **10**:477
William Styron **15**:528
D. M. Thomas **22**:420

Milton, John R.
Walter Van Tilburg Clark **28**:82
Vardis Fisher **7**:105
A. B. Guthrie, Jr. **23**:201
N. Scott Momaday **2**:290
James Welch **14**:558

Milton, Joyce
Jules Feiffer **8**:217
Virginia Hamilton **26**:156
Isabelle Holland **21**:151
M. E. Kerr **35**:249
Norma Fox Mazer **26**:291
Scott O'Dell **30**:273
Zibby Oneal **30**:279
Richard Peck **21**:299
Kin Platt **26**:355
Paul Zindel **26**:476

Milun, Richard A.
William Faulkner **6**:177

Milward, John
David Bowie **17**:65
Billy Joel **26**:222
The Police **26**:364
Prince **35**:328

Mindlin, M.
Yehuda Amichai **9**:22

Minemier, Betty
Jacques-Yves Cousteau **30**:106

Miner, Earl
Kōbō Abé **22**:11
Yukio Mishima **27**:337

Miner, Robert G., Jr.
Charles M. Schulz **12**:529

Miner, Valerie
William Wharton **37**:442

Mines, Samuel
Jack Williamson **29**:456

Minogue, Valerie
Michel Butor **11**:82
Alain Robbe-Grillet **10**:437
Nathalie Sarraute **10**:458; **31**:382

Mintz, Alan L.
Andrew M. Greeley **28**:172
Yoram Kaniuk **19**:240
A. B. Yehoshua **31**:471

Minudri, Regina
Charles Addams **30**:16

Miroff, Bruce
Neil Young **17**:569

Mirsky, Jonathan
Jonathan Schell **35**:363

Mirsky, Mark J.
John Hawkes **7**:145
Elie Wiesel **37**:456

Mirsky, Mark Jay
Samuel Beckett **6**:38
Anthony Burgess **4**:83
Günter Grass **4**:205
Flann O'Brien **5**:314
Manuel Puig **3**:407

Mishima, Yukio
Yasunari Kawabata **18**:280

Mitchell, A.C.W.
Kenneth Slessor **14**:497

Mitchell, Chuck
Walter Becker and Donald Fagen **26**:79

Mitchell, Deborah
Roy Fisher **25**:159

Mitchell, Gregg
Paul Simon **17**:460
Bruce Springsteen **17**:476, 478

Mitchell, Henry
S. J. Perelman **23**:338

Mitchell, Judith N.
Rosa Guy **26**:146
Paul Zindel **26**:481

Mitchell, Judy
Bette Green **30**:171

Mitchell, Julian
Ivy Compton-Burnett **10**:110

Mitchell, Juliet
Norman Mailer **1**:192

Mitchell, Lisa
Stevie Smith **25**:421

Mitchell, Loften
Alice Childress **12**:104

Mitchell, Louis D.
Virginia Hamilton **26**:150
Evan Hunter **31**:223

Mitchell, Marilyn L.
John Steinbeck **9**:516

Mitchell, Penelope M.
Roy A. Gallant **17**:128, 130
Christie Harris **12**:263

Mitchell, Roger
Richard F. Hugo **32**:242
Thomas McGrath **28**:279

Mitchell, W.J.T.
Hubert Selby, Jr. **4**:481

Mitchison, Naomi
W. H. Auden **9**:57
Arthur Koestler **33**:227
Mildred D. Taylor **21**:421

Mitgang, Herbert
Giorgio Bassani **9**:75
Jackson J. Benson **34**:406
John Betjeman **34**:305
Virginia Spencer Carr **34**:419
John Dos Passos **34**:419
John Ehle **27**:102
James A. Michener **29**:311
Michael Mott **15**:379
J. B. Priestley **34**:360
Carl Sandburg **15**:468
Leonardo Sciascia **9**:475
John Steinbeck **34**:406
Gay Talese **37**:391

Mittleman, Leslie B.
Kingsley Amis **8**:11

Mitton, Pat
Christie Harris **12**:265

Mitz, Rick
Larry Gelbart **21**:132

Mix, David
Gordon Lightfoot **26**:282

Miyoshi, Masao
Yasunari Kawabata **9**:311
Donald Keene **34**:567
Yukio Mishima **27**:338

Mizejewski, Linda
James Dickey **15**:174

Mizener, Arthur
James Gould Cozzens **4**:115
John Dos Passos **4**:133
Anthony Hecht **8**:266
F. R. Leavis **24**:294
Anthony Powell **10**:408
J. D. Salinger **12**:501
James Thurber **5**:439
Edmund Wilson **2**:475
Sloan Wilson **32**:445

Mo, Timothy
Eva Figes **31**:164
Jennifer Johnston **7**:186
John le Carré **5**:234
Colin MacInnes **4**:35
Wilfrid Sheed **4**:489
Harriet Waugh **6**:559

Moeller, Hans-Bernhard
Peter Weiss **15**:563

Moers, Ellen
Lillian Hellman **2**:187
Adrienne Rich **18**:447

Moffatt, Gregory T., S.J.
Michael Cunningham **34**:41

Moffett, Judith
Thomas M. Disch **36**:127
Daniel Hoffman **13**:287
James Merrill **13**:376; **18**:329

Mohs, Mayo
Andrew M. Greeley **28**:176
Elie Wiesel **37**:451

Moir, Hughes
Christopher Collier and James L. Collier **30**:72

Mojtabai, A. G.
Yasunari Kawabata **5**:208
Yashar Kemal **29**:267
Thomas Keneally **5**:211
Joyce Carol Oates **15**:402
Amos Oz **27**:358
Anne Tyler **18**:530
Richard Yates **8**:555

Mok, Michael
Aleksandr I. Solzhenitsyn **2**:409

Mole, John
Dannie Abse **29**:19
Thom Gunn **32**:214
Ted Hughes **14**:271; **37**:178
Michael Longley **29**:295
Norman MacCaig **36**:288
Derek Mahon **27**:293
Paul Muldoon **32**:321
Tom Paulin **37**:354
Christopher Reid **33**:351
Louis Simpson **7**:428
Anne Stevenson **33**:382
R. S. Thomas **6**:530; **13**:545
Frank Tuohy **37**:430
Theodore Weiss **14**:555

Molesworth, Charles
John Ashbery **15**:26
John Berryman **2**:56; **8**:89
Robert Bly **15**:64
Hayden Carruth **18**:89
Ronald G. Everson **27**:135
Leslie A. Fiedler **24**:200
Louise Glück **22**:175
Marilyn Hacker **23**:205
Robert Hass **18**:210
Ted Hughes **4**:236
Erica Jong **18**:278
Donald Justice **19**:233
Galway Kinnell **3**:269; **29**:282
Richard Kostelanetz **28**:217
Laurence Lieberman **36**:260
Leslie Norris **14**:387
Michael Ondaatje **14**:410

Marge Piercy **14**:421
Robert Pinsky **19**:369
Anne Sexton **8**:483
Charles Simic **22**:381
Gary Snyder **32**:396
Charles Tomlinson **4**:548

Molin, Sven Eric
René Wellek **28**:444

Molina, Ida
Antonio Buero Vallejo **15**:103

Moll, Denise L.
Jay Bennett **35**:46

Molloy, F. C.
John McGahern **9**:370

Molnar, Thomas
Françoise Sagan **17**:419

Moloney, Michael F.
François Mauriac **4**:337

Molyneux, Robert
Erich von Däniken **30**:424, 425

Momaday, N. Scott
Dee Brown **18**:70
Vine Deloria, Jr. **21**:110
Jamake Highwater **12**:288
Leslie Marmon Silko **23**:411

Momberger, Philip
William Faulkner **6**:179

Monaco, James
Woody Allen **16**:15
John Cassavetes **20**:54
Claude Chabrol **16**:182
Francis Ford Coppola **16**:248
Jean-Luc Godard **20**:148
Richard Lester **20**:228
Gordon Parks **16**:460
Alain Resnais **16**:511
Martin Scorsese **20**:333
Andrew Sinclair **14**:489
Steven Spielberg **20**:359, 365
François Truffaut **20**:399
Melvin Van Peebles **20**:412

Monagan, John S.
Anthony Powell **7**:342

Monas, Sidney
Joseph Brodsky **36**:80
Ilya Ehrenburg **18**:134
Aleksandr I. Solzhenitsyn
4:511; **26**:415
Andrei Voznesensky **15**:552

Mondello, Salvatore
Stan Lee **17**:259

Monegal, Emir Rodríguez-
See Rodríguez-Monegal, Emir

Monet, Christina
Mark Medoff **6**:323

Monguió, Luis
Rafael Alberti **7**:8

Monheit, Albert
Roy A. Gallant **17**:126

Monk, Patricia
Robertson Davies **25**:132, 136

Monley, Keith
Frederick Busch **18**:86
Ella Leffland **19**:279

Monogue, Valerie
Harold Pinter **6**:404

Monroe, Harriet
Robert Frost **26**:112
H. D. **31**:201
Marianne Moore **19**:335
John G. Neihardt **32**:329, 330

Monsman, Gerald
J.R.R. Tolkien **1**:339

Monson, Dianne L.
Betsy Byars **35**:73

Montagnes, Anne
Phyllis Gotlieb **18**:192
Brian Moore **5**:297
Audrey Thomas **13**:538

Montague, John
Thomas Kinsella **19**:251
Hugh MacDiarmid **11**:333

Monteiro, George
Bob Dylan **4**:149
Robert Frost **4**:174; **10**:199
Ernest Hemingway **6**:231

Montgomery, Marion
T. S. Eliot **6**:163
Robert Frost **10**:195
Flannery O'Connor **1**:258

Montgomery, Niall
Flann O'Brien **7**:269

Montrose, David
Malcolm Bradbury **32**:57
William Golding **27**:164
Alfred Kazin **34**:562
Bette Pesetsky **28**:358
Siegfried Sassoon **36**:396
Gore Vidal **33**:404
Angus Wilson **34**:580

Moody, Charlotte
Molly Keane **31**:233

Moody, Christopher
Aleksandr I. Solzhenitsyn
26:418

Moody, Jennifer
Lois Duncan **26**:108

Moody, John
Jaroslav Seifert **34**:259

Moody, Michael
Mario Vargas Llosa **9**:544

Moody, Richard
Lillian Hellman **18**:221

Moon, Bucklin
Langston Hughes **35**:214

Moon, Eric
Colin MacInnes **23**:283
Frederic Raphael **14**:436

Moon, Samuel
Anne Hébert **29**:228

Mooney, Bel
Doris Lessing **22**:286

Mooney, Philip
Albert Camus **14**:115

Mooney, Stephen
Josephine Miles **14**:368

Moorcock, Michael
Angus Wilson **3**:535

Moore, Anne Carroll
Margot Benary-Isbert **12**:30

Moore, Brian
Robertson Davies **2**:113

Moore, D. B.
Louis MacNeice **4**:316

Moore, David W.
Isaac Asimov **26**:58

Moore, Emily R.
Mildred D. Taylor **21**:419

Moore, Ernest
Gregorio López y Fuentes
32:278

Moore, Gerald
Chinua Achebe **11**:1
Ezekiel Mphahlele **25**:343

Moore, Harry T.
Arthur Adamov **4**:5
Kay Boyle **5**:65
August Derleth **31**:132, 133, 134
John Dos Passos **4**:132
E. M. Forster **1**:106
Herbert Gold **4**:190
H. D. **31**:203
Rolf Hochhuth **18**:250
Eugène Ionesco **4**:252
James Jones **3**:262
Meyer Levin **7**:204
Henry Miller **4**:350
Alain Robbe-Grillet **2**:374
Nathalie Sarraute **2**:384
Georges Simenon **2**:397
Claude Simon **4**:494
John Steinbeck **5**:405

Moore, Honor
Marilyn Hacker **5**:156
June Jordan **5**:203

Moore, Hugo
Hugh MacDiarmid **4**:311

Moore, Jack B.
Carson McCullers **12**:425
Frank Yerby **7**:556

Moore, John Rees
James Baldwin **2**:31
Samuel Beckett **10**:29
J. P. Donleavy **1**:76; **4**:124
Robert Penn Warren **6**:558

Moore, L. Hugh
Robert Stone **23**:425

Moore, Marianne
E. E. Cummings **12**:141
George Plimpton **36**:351
Ezra Pound **7**:322
Edith Sitwell **9**:493
William Carlos Williams
13:601

Moore, Maxine
Isaac Asimov **9**:49

Moore, Michael
William Wharton **18**:543

Moore, Rayburn S.
Elizabeth Spencer **22**:402

Moore, Richard
George Garrett **3**:192
Maxine Kumin **28**:220

Moore, Stephen C.
John Cheever **7**:49
Robert Lowell **3**:301

Moore, T. Inglis
Kenneth Slessor **14**:495

Moorehead, Caroline
Joyce Maynard **23**:291
David Plante **23**:347
Martin Cruz Smith **25**:414

Moorhead, Wendy
Laurence Yep **35**:469

Moorhouse, Geoffrey
Ved Mehta **37**:294

Moorehouse, Val
Richard Kostelanetz **28**:218

Moorman, Charles
C. S. Lewis **14**:323
J.R.R. Tolkien **1**:337

Moramarco, Fred
John Ashbery **4**:22; **9**:42
Ted Berrigan **37**:44
Robert Creeley **1**:67
Allen Ginsberg **36**:188
David Ignatow **7**:181
Galway Kinnell **2**:229
James Merrill **34**:226
W. S. Merwin **1**:213
Frank O'Hara **13**:424
Ezra Pound **18**:425
James Schevill **7**:401
C. K. Williams **33**:442

Moran, Ronald
Wendell Berry **4**:59
Robert Creeley **4**:117
David Ignatow **4**:248
Marge Piercy **6**:402
Louis Simpson **4**:498
William Stafford **29**:380
James Tate **6**:528

Moran, Terence
Jay McInerney **34**:83

Moravia, Alberto
Truman Capote **13**:132

Mordas, Phyllis G.
Melvin Berger **12**:40

Morel, Jean-Pierre
André Breton **15**:88

Morello-Frosch, Marta
Julio Cortázar **2**:104
Gabriel García Márquez **3**:183

Morgan, Al
Art Buchwald **33**:88, 89
Evan Hunter **31**:220

Morgan, Constance
Helen MacInnes 27:280

Morgan, Edmund S.
Thomas J. Fleming 37:126

Morgan, Edwin
John Berryman 10:47
James Blish 14:83
Malcolm Bradbury 32:51
Anthony Burgess 15:104
Ilya Ehrenburg 18:137
Eva Figes 31:163
Roy Fuller 28:153
W. S. Graham 29:194
Halldór Laxness 25:292
Norman MacCaig 36:281
Hugh MacDiarmid 11:338
Eugenio Montale 9:387
Piers Paul Read 25:376
Frank Sargeson 31:365
Rudolph Wurlitzer 15:587
Yevgeny Yevtushenko 26:468

Morgan, Ellen
Doris Lessing 3:288

Morgan, John
Günter Grass 6:209

Morgan, Robert
Geoffrey Hill 8:294

Morgan, Speer
Wendell Berry 27:33
Dan Jacobson 4:256

Morgan, Ted
Edward Abbey 36:14
Harry Crews 23:136
Norman Mailer 14:354
Farley Mowat 26:346
Alice Munro 19:346

Morgans, Patricia A.
Walter Dean Myers 35:299

Morgenstern, Dan
Andrew Lloyd Webber and Tim
Rice 21:426
Frank Zappa 17:587

Morgenstern, Joseph
Gordon Parks 16:458
Melvin Van Peebles 20:410

Moritz, A. F.
Andrew Suknaski 19:433

Moritz, Albert
Robert Kroetsch 23:276

Morley, Christopher
Enid Bagnold 25:72, 73
Ogden Nash 23:321

Morley, Patricia
John Metcalf 37:299

Morley, Patricia A.
Margaret Atwood 13:41
David Donnell 34:159
Hugh Hood 28:190
Patrick White 7:529

Morley, Sheridan
Terence Rattigan 7:354

Morner, Claudia
Douglas Adams 27:13
Piers Anthony 35:38

Morrell, A. C.
Jean Rhys 19:390

Morris, Alice
Christina Stead 2:422

Morris, C. B.
Rafael Alberti 7:9
Vicente Aleixandre 9:12

Morris, Christopher D.
John Barth 7:23

Morris, George
Paddy Chayefsky 23:117
Brian De Palma 20:82
Eric Rohmer 16:539
Martin Scorsese 20:329
Billy Wilder 20:466

Morris, Gregory
Breece D'J Pancake 29:350

Morris, H. H.
Dashiell Hammett 10:253

Morris, Harry
Louise Bogan 4:68
James Dickey 1:73
Jean Garrigue 2:154
John Hollander 2:197
George MacBeth 2:251
Louis Simpson 4:498
John Steinbeck 21:370

Morris, Ivan
Yasunari Kawabata 2:222

Morris, Jan
Laurens van der Post 5:464

Morris, Jeff
Robert Francis 15:238

Morris, John N.
Ai 14:7
Kenneth O. Hanson 13:263
Donald Justice 6:271
Adrienne Rich 7:370
Mark Strand 6:521
Nancy Willard 7:539
Charles Wright 6:580; 13:612

Morris, Mervyn
Louise Bennett 28:26

Morris, Richard B.
Bruce Lancaster 36:244

Morris, Robert K.
Anthony Burgess 4:81; 5:86
Lawrence Durrell 4:146
John Fowles 6:189
James Hanley 5:167
Doris Lessing 6:290
Olivia Manning 5:271
Anthony Powell 1:278; 3:404;
7:345
V. S. Pritchett 5:354
C. P. Snow 6:515
Thornton Wilder 6:578

Morris, Wesley
John Crowe Ransom 4:433

Morris, Willie
Irwin Shaw 34:369

Morris, Wright
Ernest Hemingway 1:141

Morrison, Blake
Beryl Bainbridge 14:37
William Boyd 28:40
André Brink 18:69
Raymond Carver 36:105
J. M. Coetzee 23:121
Donald Davie 10:124
Jacob Epstein 19:162
Roy Fuller 28:156
Gabriel García Márquez 15:252
Allen Ginsberg 36:198
Patricia Highsmith 14:261
Ted Hughes 37:172
Thomas Keneally 14:301
Philip Larkin 33:267
Eugenio Montale 18:343
Anaïs Nin 14:386
Robert Pinsky 19:370
Frederic Raphael 14:438
Christopher Reid 33:348
Salman Rushdie 31:353
Andrew Sinclair 14:489
Derek Walcott 25:457
Yevgeny Yevtushenko 13:620

Morrison, Harriet
Frank Bonham 12:53

Morrison, Hobe
Stephen Sondheim 30:378, 379

Morrison, J. Allan
Leon Garfield 12:226, 234

Morrison, J. M.
Hugh MacDiarmid 2:254

Morrison, John W.
Jun'ichiro Tanizaki 8:509

Morrison, Lillian
Eilís Dillon 17:93
Mary Stolz 12:549, 551

Morrison, Michael
Andrew M. Greeley 28:169

Morrison, Patt
John Betjeman 34:308

Morrison, Philip
Franklyn M. Branley 21:17
Jacques-Yves Cousteau 30:106
Roy A. Gallant 17:129
Christie Harris 12:262
Thor Heyerdahl 26:191
Larry Kettelkamp 12:304

Morrison, Phylis
Franklyn M. Branley 21:17
Jacques-Yves Cousteau 30:106
Roy A. Gallant 17:129
Christie Harris 12:262
Larry Kettelkamp 12:304

Morrison, Theodore
Robert Frost 1:111

Morrison, Toni
Jean Toomer 22:428

Morrissette, Bruce
Alain Robbe-Grillet 1:27;
14:455

Morrissey, Daniel
John Updike 7:488

Morrow, Lance
John Fowles 6:187
Erica Jong 8:314
Yasunari Kawabata 5:208
James A. Michener 5:290
Yukio Mishima 4:356, 358

Morsberger, Robert E.
Jackson J. Benson 34:415
John Steinbeck 34:415

Morse, David
Smokey Robinson 21:344

Morse, J. Mitchell
Kingsley Amis 2:6
James Baldwin 2:32
Richard Elman 19:150
Bruce Jay Friedman 3:165
Joanne Greenberg 7:134
J.M.G. Le Clézio 31:245
Jakov Lind 2:245
Mary McCarthy 1:207
Vladimir Nabokov 2:299
Peter Weiss 3:514

Morse, John
Gilbert Sorrentino 22:395

Morse, Jonathan
John Dos Passos 11:156

Morse, Samuel French
W. H. Auden 6:18
Margaret Avison 2:29
John Berryman 3:65
Brewster Ghiselin 23:170
Robert Lowell 3:301
Louis Zukofsky 1:385

Morthland, John
The Clash 30:47
Jimmy Cliff 21:63
Waylon Jennings 21:204
Bob Marley 17:269

Mortifoglio, Richard
Marvin Gaye 26:133
Laura Nyro 17:320

Mortimer, John
James Thurber 5:433

Mortimer, Penelope
Elizabeth Bishop 9:89
Nadine Gordimer 7:132
Fay Weldon 6:562
Tom Wolfe 15:586

Mortimer, Peter
C. P. Taylor 27:444

Mortimer, Raymond
Enid Bagnold 25:72
Frank Swinnerton 31:422

Mortimore, Roger
Carlos Saura 20:315

Morton, Brian
I. Compton-Burnett 34:495
Stephen King 37:199
Hilary Spurling 34:495

Morton, Desmond
Thomas Flanagan 25:166

Morton, Donald E.
Vladimir Nabokov 15:390

Morton, Frederic
Richard Elman **19**:149
Romain Gary **25**:184
Erich Maria Remarque **21**:331
Henri Troyat **23**:459
Morris L. West **33**:427
Elie Wiesel **37**:459

Moscoso-Gongora, Peter
José Lezama Lima **10**:319

Moser, Gerald M.
José Rodrigues Miguéis **10**:340

Moses, Carole
Ernest Hemingway **19**:220

Moses, Edwin
Albert Camus **9**:148

Moses, Joseph
E. L. Doctorow **11**:140

Moses, Robbie Odom
Edward Albee **11**:12

Moses, Wilson J.
W.E.B. DuBois **13**:182

Mosher, Harold F., Jr.
Paul Simon **17**:462

Mosher, John
Alfred Hitchcock **16**:338

Moshos, Fran
Ouida Sebestyen **30**:346

Moskowitz, Moshe
Chaim Grade **10**:248

Moskowitz, Sam
John W. Campbell, Jr. **32**:71, 72
Fritz Leiber **25**:301
Theodore Sturgeon **22**:410
Jack Williamson **29**:454
John Wyndham **19**:474

Mosley, Nicholas
J. P. Donleavy **10**:155
D. J. Enright **31**:152
Iris Murdoch **31**:290

Moss, Chuck
Stephen King **37**:207

Moss, Mrs. E. D.
Philippa Pearce **21**:282

Moss, Elaine
Margaret Craven **17**:80
Diana Wynne Jones **26**:231
Madeleine L'Engle **12**:347
Rosemary Sutcliff **26**:438

Moss, Howard
W. H. Auden **6**:20
Elizabeth Bishop **1**:35; **9**:91
Elizabeth Bowen **1**:41; **3**:84
Graham Greene **6**:217
Flann O'Brien **1**:252
Katherine Anne Porter **1**:272
Jean Rhys **6**:454
Nathalie Sarraute **1**:302
Eudora Welty **2**:463

Moss, Leonard
Arthur Miller **1**:217

Moss, Robert
David Caute **29**:118
Frank Tuohy **37**:429

Moss, Robert F.
John Berryman **13**:76
Paddy Chayefsky **23**:119
Lawrence Durrell **6**:153
John O'Hara **6**:384
Richard Wright **14**:596

Moss, Stanley
Stanley J. Kunitz **6**:286

Mossman, Ellott
Boris Pasternak **10**:382

Motion, Andrew
William Boyd **28**:38
Thomas M. Disch **36**:126
Buchi Emecheta **14**:159
D. J. Enright **31**:154
Roy Fisher **25**:157
Max Frisch **32**:191
W. S. Graham **29**:197
John Hollander **14**:265
Thomas Keneally **19**:247
Philip Larkin **33**:263
Michael Longley **29**:294
Derek Mahon **27**:292
Paul Muldoon **32**:319
Seán O'Faoláin **14**:407
Tom Paulin **37**:353
Craig Raine **32**:350
Piers Paul Read **25**:380
James Schuyler **23**:390
D. M. Thomas **22**:418
Yevgeny Yevtushenko **26**:467

Motley, Joel
Leon Forrest **4**:164

Mott, Frank Luther
John G. Neihardt **32**:330

Mott, Michael
A. R. Ammons **8**:15
Geoffrey Grigson **7**:135
Elizabeth Jennings **14**:292
David Jones **7**:186
D. M. Thomas **13**:541
Charles Tomlinson **13**:545

Mottram, Eric
Fielding Dawson **6**:126
Roy Fisher **25**:157
Carolyn Kizer **15**:309
Michael McClure **6**:317
Arthur Miller **1**:218
Gilbert Sorrentino **7**:449
Diane Wakoski **4**:572
Jonathan Williams **13**:601

Moulton, Priscilla L.
E. M. Almedingen **12**:1
Jean Craighead George **35**:176
Christie Harris **12**:262
Lee Kingman **17**:245
Mary Renault **17**:397

Mount, Ferdinand
Harry Crews **23**:133
Peter Handke **10**:257
V. S. Naipaul **37**:327
Bernice Rubens **19**:403

Movius, Geoffrey H.
William Carlos Williams **9**:575

Mowbray, S. M.
Zoë Fairbairns **32**:163
David Plante **23**:345

Moyer, Charles R.
Jonathan Kozol **17**:250

Moyer, Kermit
Robert Altman **16**:34

Moyles, R. G.
Kevin Major **26**:284

Moynahan, Julian
Louis Auchincloss **9**:54
André Brink **36**:66
Frederick Buechner **9**:137
Anthony Burgess **8**:113
R. V. Cassill **23**:109
J. P. Donleavy **4**:126
André Dubus **36**:145
Thomas Flanagan **25**:163
Ernest J. Gaines **11**:218
John Gardner **28**:161
Francine du Plessix Gray **22**:200
John Irving **13**:293
Jack Kerouac **2**:228
Ken Kesey **6**:277
John Knowles **26**:264
John le Carré **15**:326
Tom McHale **3**:331
A. G. Mojtabai **15**:378
Brian Moore **3**:341; **8**:394
Edna O'Brien **36**:340
Seán O'Faoláin **7**:274; **14**:404
Philip Rahv **24**:353
Anne Roiphe **9**:455
Judith Rossner **29**:353
Karl Shapiro **15**:477
Wilfrid Sheed **10**:472
Susan Richards Shreve **23**:404
James Tate **2**:431
Douglas Unger **34**:115
John Wain **15**:562
William Wharton **18**:542

Moynihan, Julian
Alan Sillitoe **19**:421
C. P. Snow **19**:428
James Thurber **11**:532

Mozejko, Edward
Elisaveta Bagryana **10**:13

Muchnic, Helen
Ilya Ehrenburg **18**:137
Mikhail Sholokhov **7**:418, 421
Aleksandr I. Solzhenitsyn **9**:507

Mudrick, Marvin
Donald Barthelme **2**:39
Harold Bloom **24**:82
William S. Burroughs **2**:90
E. M. Forster **2**:135
John Fowles **2**:137
Jerzy Kosinski **2**:231
Doris Lessing **2**:239
Norman Mailer **1**:192
Bernard Malamud **1**:200
Vladimir Nabokov **3**:355
V. S. Naipaul **37**:323
Joyce Carol Oates **2**:314
Nathalie Sarraute **2**:384; **4**:468
David Wagoner **3**:508

Mudrovic, Mike
Claudio Rodríguez **10**:440

Mueller, Lisel
Robert Bly **1**:37
Louise Glück **7**:118; **22**:174
Michael S. Harper **7**:138
Jim Harrison **6**:223
Anthony Hecht **8**:268
W. S. Merwin **1**:212
Sharon Olds **32**:345
Marge Piercy **6**:401
Peter Viereck **4**:559
Alice Walker **6**:553
Reed Whittemore **4**:588

Mugerauer, Robert
Martin Heidegger **24**:266

Muggeridge, John
John Metcalf **37**:301

Muggeridge, Malcolm
Paul Scott **9**:478
P. G. Wodehouse **22**:483

Muir, Edwin
Dannie Abse **29**:12
Djuna Barnes **29**:25
T. S. Eliot **24**:158

Muirhead, L. Russell
C. S. Forester **35**:165

Mukherjee, Bharati
Michael Ondaatje **29**:342

Mukherjee, Meenakshi
Anita Desai **37**:64

Muldoon, Paul
Seamus Heaney **37**:164

Mulhallen, Karen
Robert Kroetsch **23**:273
Audrey Thomas **13**:538

Mulherin, Kathy
Eva Figes **31**:162

Mulkeen, Anne
L. P. Hartley **22**:215

Mullan, Fitzhugh
Lewis Thomas **35**:412

Mullen, Patrick B.
E. E. Cummings **12**:157

Mullen, R. D.
Jack Vance **35**:419
Roger Zelazny **21**:468, 470

Mullen, Richard
Elizabeth Bishop **32**:34

Mullen, Richard D.
James Blish **14**:82

Muller, Al
Laurence Yep **35**:473

Muller, Gilbert H.
William Faulkner **8**:212

Muller, H. J.
R. P. Blackmur **24**:54

Müller-Bergh, Klaus
G. Cabrera Infante **25**:102, 104
José Lezama Lima **4**:288

Mullin, John
T. H. White **30**:449

Mullin, Michael
Orson Welles **20**:451

Mumford, Olive
Larry Kettelkamp **12**:304

Munk, Erika
Martin Duberman **8**:185
Peter Handke **15**:268
David Rudkin **14**:471
Nathalie Sarraute **31**:385
Tom Stoppard **29**:405
Elizabeth Swados **12**:560, 561
Lanford Wilson **14**:591

Murch, A. E.
Edmund Crispin **22**:110

Murch, Anne C.
Arthur Kopit **18**:287

Murchison, John C.
Jorge Luis Borges **2**:71, 75

Murchison, W., Jr.
John Dickson Carr **3**:101

Murchland, Bernard
Albert Camus **2**:97
Jean-Paul Sartre **7**:396

Murdoch, Brian
Heinrich Böll **15**:68
Siegfried Lenz **27**:252

Murdoch, Charles
John Glassco **9**:236

Murdoch, Iris
A. S. Byatt **19**:76
Elias Canetti **25**:106

Murdock, Kenneth B.
Esther Forbes **12**:203

Murillo, L. A.
Jorge Luis Borges **4**:70

Murphy, Brian
Luis Buñuel **16**:134
Eric Rohmer **16**:529

Murphy, Catherine A.
Mary Lavin **18**:306

Murphy, Mrs. J. M.
Honor Arundel **17**:14

Murphy, Reverend James M.
Carlos Fuentes **13**:232

Murphy, Joan
Colin Thiele **17**:495

Murphy, L. J.
Isaac Asimov **26**:59

Murphy, Richard
Thom Gunn **18**:203
Patrick Kavanagh **22**:235
Philip Larkin **5**:231

Murphy, Robert
Allan W. Eckert **17**:104

Murphy, Sylvia
Sylvia Murphy **34**:93

Murr, Judy Smith
John Gardner **10**:219

Murra, John V.
Amos Tutuola **14**:537

Murray, Atholl C.C.
David Jones **7**:188

Murray, Brian
Frederick Barthelme **36**:54
Ezra Pound **34**:510
E. Fuller Torrey **34**:510

Murray, Charles Shaar
Peter Townshend **17**:533

Murray, Donald C.
James Baldwin **13**:53

Murray, Edward
Samuel Beckett **6**:35
William Faulkner **6**:176
Ernest Hemingway **6**:229
Eugène Ionesco **6**:251
Arthur Miller **6**:327, 332
Clifford Odets **28**:337
Alain Robbe-Grillet **6**:466
Tennessee Williams **5**:501

Murray, G. E.
Ai **14**:9
Russell Banks **37**:23
Marvin Bell **31**:49
Alfred Corn **33**:118
Robert Hayden **37**:158
Anthony Hecht **13**:269
Howard Moss **14**:376
Michael Ondaatje **14**:410
Robert Pack **13**:439
Robert Phillips **28**:364
Louis Simpson **32**:377
William Stafford **29**:386
Derek Walcott **14**:550

Murray, Jack
Alain Robbe-Grillet **1**:287

Murray, James G.
A. J. Cronin **32**:139

Murray, John J.
Robert Penn Warren **4**:579

Murray, Michael
Edward Albee **2**:3
Lenny Bruce **21**:52

Murray, Michele
Robert Cormier **12**:134
Paula Fox **2**:140
Doris Grumbach **22**:204
Susan B. Hill **4**:227
William Melvin Kelley **22**:246
Robert Kotlowitz **4**:275
Pär Lagerkvist **7**:200
Mary Lavin **4**:282
William Mayne **12**:399
Grace Paley **4**:392
Frank Tuohy **37**:426

Murray, Peggy
Piers Anthony **35**:38

Murray, Philip
Aldous Huxley **3**:256

Murray, Thomas J.
Mary Lavin **18**:302

Murray, William J.
Melvin Berger **12**:38

Murry, John Middleton
I. A. Richards **24**:372
Siegfried Sassoon **36**:386

Murtaugh, Daniel M.
Marie-Claire Blais **4**:67
Eilís Dillon **17**:100
Wilfrid Sheed **2**:393
John Updike **23**:470

Murtaugh, Kristen
Italo Calvino **22**:94

Mus, David
T. S. Eliot **2**:129

Musher, Andrea
Diane Wakoski **7**:505

Muske, Carol
Jon Anderson **9**:31
Lucille Clifton **19**:110
Adrienne Rich **18**:448; **36**:378
Charles Wright **13**:613

Mutiso, Gideon-Cyrus M.
Alex La Guma **19**:272

Myers, Andrew B.
Alan Garner **17**:137

Myers, Christine
Zoa Sherburne **30**:361

Myers, David
Max Frisch **32**:195

Myers, David A.
Kurt Vonnegut, Jr. **22**:446

Myers, George Jr.
Ted Berrigan **37**:45

Myers, Oliver T.
José Donoso **32**:153

Myers, Robert J.
Lothar-Günther Buchheim
6:100

Myers, Tim
Arthur C. Clarke **18**:107
Nicholas Delbanco **13**:175

Myerson, Jonathan
David Hare **29**:221

Myles, Lynda
George Lucas **16**:416

Myrsiades, Kostas
Stratis Haviaras **33**:202
Yannis Ritsos **6**:463; **13**:487,
488

Mysak, Joe
Russell Baker **31**:31

Nabokov, Peter
Peter Matthiessen **32**:296

Nadeau, Maurice
Louis Aragon **3**:13
Simone de Beauvoir **1**:19
Samuel Beckett **1**:22
Michel Butor **1**:49
Albert Camus **1**:54
Louis-Ferdinand Céline **1**:56
Jean Genet **1**:115
Jean Giono **4**:185
Raymond Queneau **2**:359

Alain Robbe-Grillet **1**:288
Françoise Sagan **3**:444
Nathalie Sarraute **1**:303
Jean-Paul Sartre **1**:305
Claude Simon **4**:495

Nadeau, Robert L.
Djuna Barnes **11**:29
Don DeLillo **27**:80
Tom Robbins **32**:372

Nadel, Norman
Irwin Shaw **23**:398
Neil Simon **31**:394

Naha, Ed
The Police **26**:363
Monty Python **21**:225

Nahal, Chaman
Ernest Hemingway **30**:191

Nahrgang, W. Lee
Fritz Hochwälder **36**:239

Naiden, James N.
Thomas McGrath **28**:277
Lorine Niedecker **10**:360

Naik, M. K.
Mulk Raj Anand **23**:18

Naipaul, Shiva
Miguel Ángel Asturias **8**:27
José Donoso **4**:130

Naipaul, V. S.
Jorge Luis Borges **2**:77
David Caute **29**:108
C.L.R. James **33**:219
R. K. Narayan **28**:293, 298
P. H. Newby **13**:407
Jean Rhys **2**:372
Françoise Sagan **17**:422

Nairn, Tom
Marshall McLuhan **37**:263

Naison, Mark
C.L.R. James **33**:223

Nalley, Richard
Donald Hall **13**:259

Namjoshi, Suniti
Jay Macpherson **14**:347
P. K. Page **18**:377

Nance, William L.
Truman Capote **13**:133

Nance, William L., S.M.
Katherine Anne Porter **7**:314

Napier, Stuart
Frank Herbert **35**:205

Napolin, Leah
E. M. Broner **19**:71

Nardi, Marcia
Babette Deutsch **18**:118

Nardin, Jane
Evelyn Waugh **8**:544

Nardo, A. K.
C. S. Lewis **14**:325

Naremore, James
John Huston **20**:172
Philip Larkin **5**:226

Critic Index

Nassar, Eugene Paul
Ezra Pound **7**:335

Natanson, Maurice
Jean-Paul Sartre **24**:407

Nathan, George Jean
Noel Coward **9**:171
Lillian Hellman **18**:220
Arthur Miller **26**:314
Terence Rattigan **7**:353
Elmer Rice **7**:359
George Tabori **19**:437
Tennessee Williams **30**:460

Nathan, John
Kenzaburō Ōe **36**:346

Nathan, Leonard
Gunnar Ekelöf **27**:118

Natov, Roni
Leon Garfield **12**:239

Naughton, John
A. Alvarez **13**:9
Jeffrey Archer **28**:12
Beryl Bainbridge **18**:33
John Berger **19**:38
Cecil Bødker **21**:13
Arthur A. Cohen **31**:94
Isabel Colegate **36**:111
Autran Dourado **23**:152
Romain Gary **25**:188
Ursula Holden **18**:258
Penelope Lively **32**:274
Bernard Mac Laverty **31**:253
Fay Weldon **36**:443

Navarro, Carlos
Jorge Luis Borges **3**:79

Navasky, Victor S.
Jules Archer **12**:21
Meyer Levin **7**:204

Navone, John J.
Federico Fellini **16**:273

Nazareth, Peter
Charles R. Larson **31**:239
James Ngugi **7**:266

Nebecker, Helen E.
Shirley Jackson **11**:302

Necker, Walter
Joy Adamson **17**:2

Needham, Dorothy
Jacques-Yves Cousteau **30**:106

Needleman, Ruth
Octavio Paz **3**:375

Neeper, Cary
Arthur C. Clarke **35**:125

Neil, Boyd
Michel Tremblay **29**:424

Neil, J. Meredith
Jack Kerouac **14**:306

Neill, Edward
Peter Ackroyd **34**:387
T. S. Eliot **34**:387

Neimark, Paul G.
Agatha Christie **1**:58

Neiswender, Rosemary
E. M. Almedingen **12**:4
Yevgeny Yevtushenko **26**:462

Nekrich, Alexsandr
Alexander Zinoviev **19**:485

Nelsen, Don
Simon Gray **36**:207
Beth Henley **23**:215
Ntozake Shange **25**:397

Nelson, Alix
Nora Ephron **17**:111
Richard Peck **21**:298
Kin Platt **26**:351
Mary Rodgers **12**:494

Nelson, Anne
Jonathan Kozol **17**:254

Nelson, Byron
Howard Barker **37**:40

Nelson, Donald F.
Martin Walser **27**:456

Nelson, Dorothy H.
Esther Forbes **12**:211

Nelson, Elizabeth
Thomas J. Fleming **37**:125

Nelson, Howard
Robert Bly **10**:54
Robert Francis **15**:237

Nelson, Hugh
Harold Pinter **6**:413

Nelson, John A.
Nat Hentoff **26**:186

Nelson, Joyce
Frank Capra **16**:161
Kurt Vonnegut, Jr. **4**:562

Nelson, Paul
David Bowie **17**:64
Jackson Browne **21**:40
Janis Ian **21**:186
Billy Joel **26**:221
John Lennon and Paul
McCartney **12**:378
Willie Nelson **17**:303
Lou Reed **21**:310, 311
Paul Simon **17**:465
Patti Smith **12**:538
Bruce Springsteen **17**:484
Neil Young **17**:576, 581

Nelson, Raymond
Van Wyck Brooks **29**:87
Chester Himes **2**:196

Nelson, Robert C.
Vine Deloria, Jr. **21**:111

Nemerov, Howard
Conrad Aiken **3**:4
Kingsley Amis **2**:5
Djuna Barnes **3**:36
Ben Belitt **22**:50
Kenneth Burke **2**:89
James Dickey **4**:120
Daniel Hoffman **13**:286
Harry Mathews **6**:315
Marianne Moore **4**:359
Howard Moss **7**:247
Kathleen Raine **7**:353

Nesbitt, Bruce
Earle Birney **11**:49

Nesbitt, John D.
Louis L'Amour **25**:279, 281

Nesin, Jeff
Lou Reed **21**:321

Ness, David E.
Lorraine Hansberry **17**:191

Nettelbeck, Colin W.
Louis-Ferdinand Céline **3**:103

Nettleford, Rex
Louise Bennett **28**:28

Neubauer, John
Georg Lukács **24**:335

Neuberger, Richard L.
Allen Drury **37**:99

Neufeld, John
Kristin Hunter **35**:226
Maia Wojciechowska **26**:455

Neufeldt, Leonard
David Wagoner **15**:560

Neumark, Victoria
Carlos Fuentes **13**:232

Nevans, Ronald
Barry Hannah **23**:212
Bette Bao Lord **23**:278

Neves, John
Martin Walser **27**:466

Neville, Robert
Helen MacInnes **27**:281

Nevins, Allan
Walter D. Edmonds **35**:144,
145, 147, 152
Howard Fast **23**:155
Carl Sandburg **35**:349

Nevins, Francis M., Jr.
Ellery Queen **3**:421; **11**:458
Rex Stout **3**:471

Nevius, Blake
Ivy Compton-Burnett **1**:62

New, W. H.
Ethel Davis Wilson **13**:608

New, William H.
Margaret Avison **4**:36
Robertson Davies **7**:73
Simon Gray **9**:241
Hugh Hood **15**:286
William Mitchell **25**:322, 323
Alden Nowlan **15**:399

Newberry, Wilma
Ramón Gómez de la Serna
9:237

Newby, I. A.
Louis R. Harlan **34**:189

Newby, P. H.
Penelope Fitzgerald **19**:174

Newcomb, Horace
Larry Gelbart **21**:127

Newfield, Jack
Bob Dylan **12**:183

Newlin, Margaret
H. D. **14**:225
Sylvia Plath **3**:389

Newlove, Donald
Frederick Barthelme **36**:49
Peter Benchley **4**:53
Joseph Brodsky **4**:78
Howard Fast **23**:159
Günter Grass **22**:195
Thomas Kinsella **4**:271
W. S. Merwin **5**:287
J. D. Salinger **8**:463
Trevanian **29**:431

Newman, Anne R.
Elizabeth Bishop **15**:59

Newman, Barbara
Jamake Highwater **12**:288

Newman, Charles
James Baldwin **13**:48
Donald Barthelme **23**:48
Saul Bellow **6**:59
Sylvia Plath **9**:421
Philip Roth **4**:457

Newman, Christina
Brian Moore **8**:395

Newman, Michael
W. H. Auden **6**:25

Newton, David E.
Isaac Asimov **26**:57
Franklyn M. Branley **21**:22, 23
Roy A. Gallant **17**:130, 133

Newton, Edmund
Wendy Wasserstein **32**:439

Newton, Francis
John Lennon and Paul
McCartney **12**:353

Neyman, Mark
Allan W. Eckert **17**:108

Nichol, B. P.
Earle Birney **6**:76

Nicholas, Brian
Graham Greene **6**:214

Nicholas, Charles A.
N. Scott Momaday **19**:317

Nicholas, Robert L.
Antonio Buero Vallejo **15**:97

Nicholaus, Charles
Van Morrison **21**:236

Nicholls, Peter
Stephen King **37**:206
William Kotzwinkle **35**:258
Gene Wolfe **25**:476

Nichols, Bill
Bernardo Bertolucci **16**:85

Nichols, Kathleen L.
Ernest Hemingway **19**:221

Nichols, Lewis
Irwin Shaw **23**:396

Nichols, Ruth
Diana Wynne Jones **26**:228

Nichols, Stephen G., Jr.
John Hawkes 3:221

Nicholson, C. E.
Theodore Roethke 11:486

Nicholson, Kris
Neil Young 17:575

Nickerson, Edward A.
Robinson Jeffers 15:301

Nickerson, Susan L.
Piers Anthony 35:37, 39
C. J. Cherryh 35:113
Marion Zimmer Bradley 30:32
Anne McCaffrey 17:282, 283, 284
Jack Williamson 29:461

Nicol, Charles
Kingsley Amis 5:22
J. G. Ballard 36:39
Brigid Brophy 6:100
Anthony Burgess 5:90
John Cheever 11:121; 25:116
Peter De Vries 7:77
John Gardner 30:153
Dashiell Hammett 5:162
John Hawkes 4:218; 7:144
John Irving 13:293; 23:252
Milan Kundera 9:320; 19:268
Norman Mailer 4:323
Vladimir Nabokov 1:244
Kurt Vonnegut, Jr. 3:504; 8:534; 12:602

Niemeyer, Gerhart
Aleksandr I. Solzhenitsyn 7:439

Niester, Alan
Frank Zappa 17:590

Nightingale, Benedict
Piers Anthony 35:34
Alan Ayckbourn 5:35; 18:30; 33:41
Howard Barker 37:38
Edward Bond 4:70
Howard Brenton 31:63, 64, 68
David Caute 29:114
Caryl Churchill 31:87, 88
A. E. Ellis 7:93
Dario Fo 32:173, 174
Michael Frayn 7:107; 31:190
Simon Gray 36:205, 206
John Hopkins 4:234
David Mercer 5:284
Slawomir Mrozek 13:399
Peter Nichols 5:305, 306; 36:328, 329
Joe Orton 13:435
John Osborne 5:333
J. B. Priestley 5:350
Gerome Ragni and James Rado 17:382
Anthony Shaffer 19:415
Sam Shepard 34:271
Neil Simon 6:504
Tom Stoppard 5:412; 29:395, 398, 402; 34:272, 277
David Storey 5:415
C. P. Taylor 27:443
Wendy Wasserstein 32:441
E. A. Whitehead 5:488
Snoo Wilson 33:463, 465

Nigro, Kirsten F.
José Donoso 32:153

Nilsen, Alleen Pace
Maya Angelou 12:14
Gunnel Beckman 26:89
Jay Bennett 35:45
Judy Blume 12:44
Robert Cormier 30:85, 87
James D. Forman 21:123
Rosa Guy 26:145
M. E. Kerr 12:300
Norma Klein 30:239
Norma Fox Mazer 26:291
Nicholosa Mohr 12:447
Sandra Scoppettone 26:401
John R. Tunis 12:599

Nimmo, Dorothy
C. S. Adler 35:12
Joan Aiken 35:20
Judy Blume 12:45
S. E. Hinton 30:205
Diana Wynne Jones 26:233
Philippa Pearce 21:290

Nissenson, Hugh
Chaim Potok 2:338; 7:321; 26:368
A. B. Yehoshua 31:468

Nist, John
Carlos Drummond de Andrade 18:3, 4
Laurence Yep 35:474

Nitchie, George W.
Robert Lowell 8:350
George MacBeth 2:251
Marianne Moore 8:397

Niven, Alastair
C.L.R. James 33:223

Nixon, Agnes Eckhardt
Agnes Eckhardt Nixon 21:241, 244

Nixon, Rob
André Brink 36:70

Nkosi, Lewis
André Brink 18:68
Alex La Guma 19:272
Ngugi wa Thiong'o 36:313

Nnolim, Charles E.
Mongo Beti 27:47

Noah, Carolyn
Suzanne Newton 35:301

Noble, David W.
James Baldwin 4:40

Nokes, David
Michael Mewshaw 9:377

Nolan, Mary L.
John Donovan 35:143

Nolan, Paul T.
Marc Connelly 7:55

Nolan, Tom
Neil Diamond 30:112

Noland, W. Richard
Elliott Baker 8:38

Nolen, William A.
Colleen McCullough 27:321

Nomad, Max
Ignazio Silone 4:493

Noonan, Tom
Rainer Werner Fassbinder 20:118

Nordberg, Robert B.
Ward S. Just 27:226
Jonathan Kozol 17:252

Nordell, Roderick
John Ehle 27:105
William Golding 17:172
Mark Harris 19:201
Nat Hentoff 26:185
Peter Matthiessen 32:294
Margaret Mead 37:281
Jerome Siegel and Joe Shuster 21:357

Nordyke, Lewis
Glendon Swarthout 35:399
Robert Lewis Taylor 14:533

Norman, Albert H.
Richard Brautigan 12:58

Norman, Doreen
Otfried Preussler 17:375

Norman, Gurney
Richard Brautigan 12:64

Norman, Marsha
Lillian Hellman 34:352

Norman, Mary Anne
Dee Brown 18:71

Norris, Christopher
William Empson 33:150; 34:543

Norris, Hoke
Frank Tuohy 37:427

Norris, Jerrie
Rosa Guy 26:144

Norris, Ken
George Bowering 15:81

Norris, Leslie
Andrew Young 5:525

Norrish, P. J.
Henri de Montherlant 19:329

Norsworthy, James
Kin Platt 26:353

Norsworthy, James A.
Cecil Bødker 21:14
Jamake Highwater 12:286
Zilpha Keatley Snyder 17:474

North, R. J.
Andre Malraux 13:367

Northey, Margot
Matt Cohen 19:115
Anne Hébert 29:235
Mordecai Richler 18:451

Norton, Dale
Alex Haley 12:248

Norton, Elliot
Lily Tomlin 17:517

Norwood, Gilbert
Agatha Christie 12:113

Norwood, W. D., Jr.
C. S. Lewis 1:177

Nossiter, Bernard D.
Ved Mehta 37:290

Noth, Dominique Paul
Garry Trudeau 12:589

Notken, Debbie
Marion Zimmer Bradley 30:29
C. J. Cherryh 35:107

Notley, Alice
James Schuyler 23:391

Nott, Kathleen
Graham Greene 14:217
Arthur Koestler 33:236

Nouryeh, Christopher
Ben Belitt 22:54

Novak, Barbara
Audrey Thomas 37:418

Novak, Michael
Norman Lear 12:338

Novak, Michael Paul
Robert Hayden 5:169

Novak, William
Grace Paley 6:391
Susan Fromberg Schaeffer 6:488
A. B. Yehoshua 31:470

Novick, Julius
Edward Albee 9:10
John Bishop 10:54
Gretchen Cryer 21:81
Charles Fuller 25:181
Simon Gray 9:242
Albert Innaurato 21:199
Hugh Leonard 19:284
David Mamet 9:360
Sean O'Casey 11:411
David Rabe 4:425
Howard Sackler 14:478
Neil Simon 11:496
Isaac Bashevis Singer 15:509
Tom Stoppard 4:525; 8:504
David Storey 8:505
Tennessee Williams 8:548
Lanford Wilson 14:592

Nowell-Smith, Geoffrey
Michelangelo Antonioni 20:27
Bernardo Bertolucci 16:100
Luis Buñuel 16:131
Richard Lester 20:218
Pier Paolo Pasolini 20:259
Luchino Visconti 16:573

Nowlan, Alden
Ralph Gustafson 36:212
Hugh Hood 15:283

Nuechterlein, James
Bruce Catton 35:95

Nugent, Frank S.
  Tod Browning **16**:121
  John Ford **16**:304
  Jean Renoir **20**:287

Nugent, Robert
  René Char **11**:111

Nwoga, Donatus I.
  Christopher Okigbo **25**:350

Nyabongo, V. S.
  Alice Walker **6**:554

Nyamfukudza, S.
  Ayi Kwei Armah **33**:29

Nye, Robert
  Brigid Brophy **6**:98
  Eva Figes **31**:162
  E. M. Forster **3**:162
  David Garnett **3**:189
  Graham Greene **3**:214
  Hermann Hesse **17**:218
  Mollie Hunter **21**:159
  Bernard Malamud **5**:269
  Michael Moorcock **27**:347
  Anthony Powell **3**:402
  John Cowper Powys **7**:349
  William Sansom **6**:483
  Tom Sharpe **36**:402
  Penelope Shuttle **7**:422

Nye, Russel
  John Lennon and Paul
    McCartney **12**:366

Nygaard, Anita
  Joy Adamson **17**:5

Nyren, D.
  Marie-Claire Blais **13**:97

Nyren, Dorothy
  Frederick Barthelme **36**:49
  Russell Edson **13**:190

Oakley, Helen
  Lenora Mattingly Weber **12**:633

Oates, Joyce Carol
  Harriette Arnow **2**:14
  James Baldwin **5**:42
  Stephen Bochco and Michael
    Kozoll **35**:60
  Paul Bowles **19**:60
  Brigid Brophy **29**:97
  I. Compton-Burnett **34**:499
  Frederick Busch **7**:38
  James M. Cain **3**:95
  Carlos Castaneda **12**:88
  John Cheever **11**:120
  Laurie Colwin **23**:129
  Robert Coover **7**:58
  Alfred Corn **33**:116
  Julio Cortázar **33**:123
  Robert Creeley **8**:152
  Roald Dahl **1**:177
  Robertson Davies **25**:132
  James Dickey **7**:83
  Joan Didion **8**:175
  Margaret Drabble **2**:118; **5**:117
  André Dubus **13**:183; **36**:146
  Marion Engel **36**:159
  James T. Farrell **4**:158
  Eva Figes **31**:169
  Carolyn Forché **25**:170

Janet Frame **2**:141
Tess Gallagher **18**:170
Gail Godwin **5**:142; **22**:179
William Golding **17**:180
William Goyen **8**:250
Joanne Greenberg **30**:162
Jim Harrison **6**:224
Anne Hébert **13**:268; **29**:238
Carolyn G. Heilbrun **25**:252
David Ignatow **14**:276
Maxine Kumin **5**:222
Philip Larkin **8**:337
Mary Lavin **4**:282
Stanislaw Lem **15**:328
Doris Lessing **2**:241
Philip Levine **4**:286, 288
Alison Lurie **18**:310
Norman Mailer **11**:341
Bernard Malamud **3**:323
Leonard Michaels **25**:314
Brian Moore **32**:309
Berry Morgan **6**:339
Alice Munro **6**:342; **19**:346
Iris Murdoch **1**:237; **11**:389;
  31:293
Vladimir Nabokov **2**:304
R. K. Narayan **28**:295
Charles Newman **2**:312; **8**:419
Flannery O'Connor **1**:258
Mary Oliver **19**:362
Breece D'J Pancake **29**:346
Robert Phillips **28**:362
Sylvia Plath **2**:338; **5**:340
Gilbert Rogin **18**:458
Philip Roth **4**:454
J. R. Salamanca **15**:463
Anne Sexton **6**:492
Stevie Smith **25**:422
Hilary Spurling **34**:499
Jean Stafford **19**:430
Elizabeth Taylor **2**:433
Peter Taylor **1**:335
Paul Theroux **8**:512
Lewis Thomas **35**:408
William Trevor **9**:529
John Updike **2**:441; **13**:561
Gore Vidal **33**:410
Kurt Vonnegut, Jr. **12**:603
Fay Weldon **9**:559
Eudora Welty **1**:363
Richard Yates **7**:554

Oberbeck, S. K.
  Kingsley Amis **2**:7
  Amiri Baraka **33**:55
  Frederick Forsyth **5**:125
  John Hawkes **1**:137
  John Hersey **7**:154
  John Irving **13**:293
  Norman Mailer **2**:264
  Joyce Carol Oates **2**:315
  Georges Simenon **2**:398
  Glendon Swarthout **35**:403
  Erich von Däniken **30**:424
  Kurt Vonnegut, Jr. **3**:502
  Stevie Wonder **12**:655

Oberg, Arthur
  Marvin Bell **31**:46
  John Berryman **4**:66; **25**:93
  Galway Kinnell **3**:270
  Greg Kuzma **7**:197
  Philip Levine **2**:244
  John Matthias **9**:362

Josephine Miles **14**:369
Joyce Carol Oates **6**:367
Robert Pack **13**:438
Sylvia Plath **14**:422; **17**:349
Anne Sexton **4**:482
Mona Van Duyn **7**:498
Derek Walcott **9**:556

Oberhelman, Harley D.
  José Donoso **11**:146
  Ernesto Sabato **23**:378

Obolensky, Laura
  Andrea Lee **36**:256

O'Brien, Conor Cruise
  See also **O'Donnell, Donat**
  Jimmy Breslin **4**:76
  Thomas Flanagan **25**:166
  Graham Greene **3**:214
  Seamus Heaney **7**:149

O'Brien, D. V.
  Evan Hunter **31**:228

O'Brien, Darcy
  Patrick Kavanagh **22**:241
  Edna O'Brien **36**:336

O'Brien, Edna
  Françoise Sagan **17**:428

O'Brien, Geoffrey
  Peter Dickinson **35**:138
  Jun'ichirō Tanizaki **28**:419

O'Brien, James H.
  Liam O'Flaherty **5**:321

O'Brien, John
  Robert Coover **32**:125
  Clarence Major **19**:293
  Gilbert Sorrentino **7**:450

O'Brien, Kate
  Elias Canetti **14**:118
  Rhys Davies **23**:142

O'Brien, Tim
  Craig Nova **31**:297

O'Brien, Tom
  Farley Mowat **26**:346
  William Wharton **37**:441

Obstfeld, Raymond
  Elmore Leonard **28**:236

Obuchowski, Chester W.
  Pierre Gascar **11**:220

Obuchowski, Mary Dejong
  Yasunari Kawabata **9**:316

Occhiogrosso, Frank
  Georges Simenon **18**:481

Ochshorn, Susan
  Ann Schlee **35**:372

O'Connell, Kay Webb
  Jean Craighead George **35**:180
  Marilyn Sachs **35**:335

O'Connell, Margaret F.
  Franklyn M. Branley **21**:18

O'Connell, Robert W.
  Margaret O. Hyde **21**:174

O'Connell, Shaun
  Harry Crews **23**:134
  Seamus Heaney **25**:248
  Marjorie Kellogg **2**:224
  Gilbert Sorrentino **7**:447

O'Connor, Flannery
  Flannery O'Connor **21**:254

O'Connor, Garry
  Jean Anouilh **8**:24

O'Connor, Gerald
  J.R.R. Tolkien **12**:576

O'Connor, John J.
  Steven Bochco and Michael
    Kozoll **35**:52
  Larry Gelbart **21**:126
  Earl Hamner, Jr. **12**:258
  Norman Lear **12**:333, 334, 337
  Garry Marshall **17**:275, 276
  Lanford Wilson **7**:547

O'Connor, Mary
  Caroline Gordon **6**:203

O'Connor, William Van
  Kingsley Amis **1**:5
  Donald Davie **5**:113
  D. J. Enright **4**:154
  Leslie A. Fiedler **24**:189
  Elizabeth Jennings **5**:197
  Philip Larkin **3**:275
  Iris Murdoch **1**:234
  Robert Phillips **28**:361
  Ezra Pound **1**:275
  John Wain **2**:458

O'Daniel, Therman B.
  Ralph Ellison **1**:95

Oddo, Sandra Schmidt
  John McPhee **36**:295

Odell, Brian Neal
  Arna Bontemps **18**:64

Oderman, Kevin
  Gary Snyder **32**:393

O'Doherty, Brian
  Flann O'Brien **5**:314

O'Donnell, Donat
  Seán O'Faoláin **14**:402
  George Steiner **24**:424

O'Donnell, Patrick
  John Hawkes **27**:199
  Philip Roth **31**:338

O'Donnell, Thomas D.
  Michel Butor **11**:81
  Claude Simon **15**:495

O'Donovan, Patrick
  Allen Drury **37**:99
  Aldous Huxley **35**:239

O'Faolain, Julia
  Margaret Atwood **25**:69
  Beryl Bainbridge **10**:15; **18**:33
  Mark Helprin **10**:260
  Bernard Mac Laverty **31**:253
  Alice Munro **19**:346
  Edna O'Brien **5**:311
  Seán O'Faoláin **32**:342
  Isaac Bashevis Singer **9**:489

O'Faoláin, Seán
Daphne du Maurier **11**:162
William Faulkner **28**:143
Ernest Hemingway **13**:272

Offerman, Sister Mary Columba
Gunnel Beckman **26**:87

Offit, Sidney
H. F. Brinsmead **21**:28

O'Flaherty, Patrick
Farley Mowat **26**:338

Ogilvie, John T.
Robert Frost **26**:116

Oglesby, Leora
Frank Bonham **12**:50

Ogunyemi, Chikwenye Okonjo
Toni Morrison **10**:354
Amos Tutuola **14**:542

O'Hara, J. D.
Kingsley Amis **8**:11
Donald Barthelme **5**:54
Ann Beattie **8**:54
Samuel Beckett **6**:39; **14**:73;
29:58
Jorge Luis Borges **2**:77
Kay Boyle **5**:66
Richard Brautigan **12**:58
Anthony Burgess **5**:86, 88
Italo Calvino **22**:93
Louis-Ferdinand Céline **4**:103
John Cheever **15**:129
Laurie Colwin **13**:156
Robert Crumb **17**:82
Roald Dahl **6**:121
Edward Dahlberg **7**:71
Don DeLillo **13**:178; **27**:78, 79
William Gaddis **19**:186
Lawrence Durrell **6**:152
William Golding **17**:170
Peter Handke **15**:268
George V. Higgins **4**:223
José Lezama Lima **4**:288
Steven Millhauser **21**:216, 218
Vladimir Nabokov **1**:246
Judith Rossner **6**:469
C. P. Snow **9**:498
Gore Vidal **22**:436
Kurt Vonnegut, Jr. **12**:608
René Wellek **28**:451
Paul West **14**:569

O'Hara, T.
Derek Walcott **4**:575

O'Hara, Tim
Ronald Sukenick **4**:531

O'Hearn, Walter
Farley Mowat **26**:333

Ohmann, Carol B.
Alex Haley **12**:244
J. D. Salinger **12**:516
Muriel Spark **2**:414

Ohmann, Richard M.
Pär Lagerkvist **7**:199
J. D. Salinger **12**:516

Ojaide, Tanure
Wole Soyinka **36**:415

Oka, Takashi
Yukio Mishima **27**:336

Okam, Hilary
Aimé Césaire **19**:98

O'Keeffe, Timothy
Patrick White **3**:521

Okenimkpe, Michael
Ngugi wa Thiong'o **36**:321

Okrent, Daniel
Roger Kahn **30**:234

Okri, Ben
Mongo Beti **27**:53
Anita Desai **19**:134

Okun, Milton
Phil Ochs **17**:330
Buffy Sainte-Marie **17**:430

Olander, Joseph D.
Robert A. Heinlein **26**:170

Olcott, Anthony
Vasily Aksyonov **37**:12
André Brink **36**:71

Olcott, Lynn
Steven Goldsberry **34**:56

Olderman, Raymond M.
John Barth **3**:40
Peter S. Beagle **7**:26
Stanley Elkin **4**:153; **27**:121
John Hawkes **3**:222
Joseph Heller **3**:229
Ken Kesey **3**:266
Thomas Pynchon **3**:411
Kurt Vonnegut, Jr. **3**:505

Oldfield, Michael
Jim Morrison **17**:291
Jimmy Page and Robert Plant
12:477
Bob Seger **35**:379, 380, 381,
385
Carly Simon **26**:408

Oldham, Andrew
Brian Wilson **12**:640

Oldsey, Bernard S.
William Golding **2**:167

Oliphant, Dave
Albert Goldbarth **5**:143

Oliva, Leo E.
Vine Deloria, Jr. **21**:112

Oliver, Edith
Howard Barker **37**:38
Ed Bullins **5**:83; **7**:36
Anne Burr **6**:103
Alice Childress **12**:105
Caryl Churchill **31**:81
Gretchen Cryer **21**:78, 81
Shelagh Delaney **29**:145
Christopher Durang **27**:88, 90
Harvey Fierstein **33**:157
Dario Fo **32**:174
Athol Fugard **14**:191
Charles Fuller **25**:181
Jack Gelber **14**:193
Simon Gray **14**:214, 215
John Guare **8**:253; **14**:220, 221
A. R. Gurney, Jr. **32**:216, 219,
220
Christopher Hampton **4**:211

Beth Henley **23**:214
Albert Innaurato **21**:194
Jim Jacobs and Warren Casey
12:292
Arthur Kopit **18**:286; **33**:253
David Mamet **15**:355, 358
William Mastrosimone **36**:289
Mark Medoff **6**:322
Rochelle Owens **8**:434
Gerome Ragni and James Rado
17:379
Terence Rattigan **7**:355
Jonathan Reynolds **6**:451
Sam Shepard **6**:497; **17**:435,
442
Stephen Sondheim **30**:398
Tom Stoppard **3**:470; **4**:525
Elizabeth Swados **12**:557, 559
George Tabori **19**:437
Megan Terry **19**:440
Kurt Vonnegut, Jr. **12**:605
Derek Walcott **2**:460; **14**:551
Joseph A. Walker **19**:455
Douglas Turner Ward **19**:457,
458
Wendy Wasserstein **32**:440,
441
Richard Wesley **7**:518
Hugh Whitemore **37**:444
Thornton Wilder **35**:445
Lanford Wilson **14**:591

Oliver, Raymond
J. V. Cunningham **31**:105
Arthur Gregor **9**:255
George Steiner **24**:434

Oliver, Roland
Shiva Naipaul **32**:325

Oliver, Roy
Arthur A. Cohen **7**:51

Olivier, Edith
Esther Forbes **12**:203

Olmert, Michael
Philip Roth **4**:452

Olney, James
Chinua Achebe **1**:2
Loren Eiseley **7**:92
Wole Soyinka **36**:414

Olsen, Gary R.
Hermann Hesse **6**:238

Olsen, Miken
Norma Fox Mazer **26**:291

Olshaker, Mark
Rod Serling **30**:358

Olshen, Barry N.
John Fowles **9**:210; **33**:163

Olson, Carol Booth
A. G. Mojtabai **15**:377

Olson, David B.
Robert Penn Warren **10**:518

Olson, Elder
William Empson **33**:142

Olson, Lawrence
Yukio Mishima **2**:288

Olson, Paul A.
Amy Clampitt **32**:115

Olson, Patricia
Morris L. West **33**:434

Olson, Toby
Diane Wakoski **7**:505

O'Malley, Casey
M. E. Kerr **35**:250

O'Malley, Michael
Erich Maria Remarque **21**:334

O'Malley, William J., S.J.
Carl Sagan **30**:338

O'Meally, R. G.
Robert Hayden **37**:159

O'Meally, Robert G.
Sterling A. Brown **23**:98
Robert Hayden **14**:240
Michael Thelwell **22**:416

O'Neal, Susan
Kristin Hunter **35**:225
Robert Lipsyte **21**:208

O'Neill, Kathleen
Michel Butor **11**:80

O'Neill, T.
Pier Paolo Pasolini **37**:343

O'Neill, Tom
Giuseppe Ungaretti **11**:557;
15:537

O'Neill, William L.
Andrew M. Greeley **28**:171

Onley, Gloria
Margaret Atwood **4**:25; **13**:42

Onyeama, Dillibe
Alex Haley **12**:252

Opdahl, Keith
Saul Bellow **3**:51; **15**:55
Jim Harrison **14**:236

Oppenheim, Jane
Len Deighton **22**:114
Susan Isaacs **32**:256

Oppenheim, Shulamith
Leon Garfield **12**:230

Oppenheimer, Dan
Paul Weller **26**:442

Oppenheimer, Joel
Robert Creeley **15**:153
Lawrence Ferlinghetti **27**:136
Anthony Hecht **19**:208
Philip Roth **4**:457
William Saroyan **10**:456;
29:362
L. E. Sissman **18**:489
Andrei Voznesensky **15**:557

Orange, John
David Donnell **34**:156
Hugh Hood **28**:193

Ordóñez, Elizabeth
Ana María Matute **11**:366

O'Reilly, Jane
T. Gertler **34**:51

O'Reilly, Timothy
Frank Herbert **12**:279; **23**:224

Critic Index

Orenstein, Gloria Feman
Fernando Arrabal **18**:20

Orfalea, Greg
William Stafford **29**:383

Orgel, Doris
Emily Cheney Neville **12**:453
Barbara Wersba **30**:431

Oriard, Michael
Don DeLillo **13**:175

Orme, John
Bob Marley **17**:273

Ormerod, Beverley
Édouard Glissant **10**:230

Ormerod, David
V. S. Naipaul **4**:371

Ornstein, Jacob
Camilo José Cela **4**:95

O'Rourke, William
Rosalyn Drexler **2**:120
Craig Nova **7**:267

Orr, Gregory
Josephine Miles **34**:244

Orr, Leonard
Richard Condon **4**:107

Orr, Nancy Young
Barbara Corcoran **17**:69

Ortega, Julio
José María Arguedas **18**:7, 8

Orth, Maureen
Bob Dylan **3**:130
Stevie Wonder **12**:657

Ortiz, Alfonso
Vine Deloria, Jr. **21**:111

Ortiz, Gloria M.
Pablo Neruda **7**:260

Ortiz, Miguel A.
Alice Childress **12**:108
Nicholosa Mohr **12**:448

Ortiz, Simon J.
Leslie Marmon Silko **23**:412

Ortmayer, Roger
Federico Fellini **16**:286

Orton, Gavin
Eyvind Johnson **14**:294

Orwell, George
Alex Comfort **7**:52
Graham Greene **6**:216
Arthur Koestler **33**:227
P. G. Wodehouse **22**:480

Osborn, John Jay, Jr.
George V. Higgins **18**:234

Osborn, Neal J.
Kenneth Burke **2**:87

Osborne, Charles
William Faulkner **1**:102
W. Somerset Maugham **1**:204

Osborne, David
Albert Camus **2**:99

Osborne, John
Noël Coward **29**:140
Joe McGinniss **32**:299

Osborne, Linda B.
Sylvia Ashton-Warner **19**:24
Ella Leffland **19**:278

Osborne, Linda Barrett
Betsy Byars **35**:74
Zibby Oneal **30**:281

Osborne, Trudie
Madeleine L'Engle **12**:345

Osgood, Eugenia V.
Julien Gracq **11**:244

Osler, Ruth
Roderick L. Haig-Brown
21:139

Osnos, Peter
Andrea Lee **36**:252
Martin Cruz Smith **25**:413

Ostriker, Alicia
Ai **4**:16
Cid Corman **9**:170
Alan Dugan **2**:121
Paul Goodman **7**:131
John Hollander **14**:262
Maxine Kumin **28**:224
Sylvia Plath **17**:348
Adrienne Rich **36**:372
Susan Sontag **31**:405
May Swenson **14**:518
Anne Waldman **7**:508

Ostroff, Anthony
Donald Justice **6**:271
Kathleen Spivack **6**:520
Mark Van Doren **6**:542

Ostrom, Alan
William Carlos Williams **1**:370

Ostrovsky, Erika
Louis-Ferdinand Céline **4**:98

O'Toole, Lawrence
Werner Herzog **16**:335
John Landis **26**:274
Paul Schrader **26**:398

Ott, Bill
Maya Angelou **35**:30
T. J. Binyon **34**:32
Pete Dexter **34**:43
Stephen King **26**:240
Sloan Wilson **32**:449

Ottaway, Robert
John Cheever **25**:122

Otten, Anna
Heinrich Böll **2**:66
Michel Butor **8**:120; **15**:120
Robert Pinget **37**:363
Alain Robbe-Grillet **6**:467;
8:453
Nathalie Sarraute **2**:386;
31:380, 382
Claude Simon **4**:497

Ottenberg, Eve
Rosellen Brown **32**:65
Erskine Caldwell **14**:95
Elizabeth Jane Howard **29**:247
William Kotzwinkle **35**:256
Vonda N. McIntyre **18**:327

James Schuyler **23**:389
Alexander Theroux **25**:432

Oughton, John
Marilyn Bowering **32**:48

Overbey, David L.
Luis Buñuel **16**:151
Claude Chabrol **16**:178
Werner Herzog **16**:324, 333
Fritz Lang **20**:212
Richard Lester **20**:227

Överland, Orm
Arthur Miller **15**:371

Oviedo, José Miguel
Mario Vargas Llosa **10**:497,
500

Owen, Carys T.
Louis-Ferdinand Céline **9**:155

Owen, I. M.
Robertson Davies **7**:72
Thomas Flanagan **25**:164
Mavis Gallant **18**:173
Audrey Thomas **37**:417

Owen, Ivon
Robertson Davies **13**:171

Owen, Roger
David Caute **29**:124

Owens, Brad
Mark Harris **19**:205
Lewis Thomas **35**:411
John Kennedy Toole **19**:442

Owens, Iris
Lois Gould **4**:200

Owens, Rochelle
Diane Wakoski **7**:505

Owens, Tony J.
William Faulkner **18**:145

Ower, John
Frank Herbert **12**:273
Mordecai Richler **9**:451
Edith Sitwell **9**:494

Ower, John B.
Edith Sitwell **2**:404

Ownbey, Steve
George V. Higgins **10**:273
Georges Simenon **8**:486

Owomoyela, Oyekan
Chester Himes **7**:159

Oxenhandler, Neal
Jean Cocteau **16**:225
Jean Genet **14**:203
Robert Pinget **37**:361

Oxley, Brian
Geoffrey Hill **18**:240

Ozick, Cynthia
Saul Bellow **10**:43; **33**:67
Frederick Buechner **2**:83
J. M. Coetzee **33**:107
Mark Harris **19**:202
Bernard Malamud **11**:346
Hugh Nissenson **4**:380

Pa Chin
Pa Chin **18**:371

Pace, Eric
Paul E. Erdman **25**:154
Joseph Wambaugh **3**:508

Pace, Mary Kathleen
Suzanne Newton **35**:300

Pacernick, Gary
Millen Brand **7**:30

Pacey, Desmond
Ralph Gustafson **36**:213
F. R. Scott **22**:371
Miriam Waddington **28**:436

Pachter, Henry
Paul Goodman **7**:129

Pachter, Henry M.
Hermann Hesse **6**:236

Pacifici, Sergio J.
Dino Buzzati **36**:87, 90
Elio Vittorini **14**:543

Pack, Robert
James Schevill **7**:400
Mark Strand **18**:514
Nancy Willard **37**:463

Packard, Nancy H.
Grace Paley **6**:393

Packard, Rosalie
Art Buchwald **33**:90

Packard, William
Kenneth Patchen **18**:394

Paddock, Lisa
William Faulkner **18**:147

Page, James A.
James Baldwin **3**:32
Ralph Ellison **3**:145
Richard Wright **3**:546

Page, Malcolm
John Arden **13**:25
Alan Ayckbourn **33**:48

Pagès, Irène M.
Simone de Beauvoir **14**:68

Paige, Nancy E.
Zoa Sherburne **30**:362

Palandri, Angela Jung
Ch'ien Chung-shu **22**:107

Palencia-Roth, Michael
Günter Grass **22**:191

Palevsky, Joan
Isak Dinesen **10**:148

Paley, Bruce
Waylon Jennings **21**:205

Paley, Maggie
Laura Nyro **17**:313

Palley, Julian
Azorín **11**:25

Palmer, Eustace
Chinua Achebe **7**:5
Ayi Kwei Armah **33**:35
Mongo Beti **27**:49
James Ngugi **7**:265
Ngugi wa Thiong'o **36**:315
Amos Tutuola **29**:437

Palmer, James W.
Francis Ford Coppola **16**:242

Palmer, Penelope
Charles Tomlinson **6**:536

Palmer, R. Roderick
Haki R. Madhubuti **6**:313
Sonia Sanchez **5**:382

Palmer, Robert
Ray Davies **21**:92, 93
Smokey Robinson **21**:346, 349
Sam Shepard **17**:445

Palmer, Tony
Bob Dylan **12**:196
Jimmy Page and Robert Plant
12:481

Pancella, John R.
Robert Newton Peck **17**:340

Panek, LeRoy L.
Ian Fleming **30**:147

Paniagua, Lita
Luis Buñuel **16**:134

Panichas, George A.
F. R. Leavis **24**:305

Pannick, David
John Mortimer **28**:287

Pannick, Gerald J.
R. P. Blackmur **24**:68

Panshin, Alexei
C. J. Cherryh **35**:104
Robert A. Heinlein **3**:224
Fritz Leiber **25**:305

Panshin, Cory
C. J. Cherryh **35**:104
Fritz Leiber **25**:305

Panter-Downes, Mollie
Robert Bolt **14**:91
John Le Carré **9**:327

Paolucci, Anne
Federico Fellini **16**:278

Papatzonis, Takis
Giuseppe Ungaretti **11**:557

Parachini, Allan
Waylon Jennings **21**:202
Garry Trudeau **12**:589

Parameswaran, Uma
Derek Walcott **9**:557

Pareles, Jon
Joan Armatrading **17**:9
Walter Becker and Donald
Fagen **26**:84
David Byrne **26**:96, 98
Elvis Costello **21**:70
Ray Davies **21**:104
Bob Dylan **12**:197
Mick Jagger and Keith Richard
17:240
Kris Kristofferson **26**:269
Joni Mitchell **12**:443
Prince **35**:332
William Trevor **25**:446
Frank Zappa **17**:593, 594

Parente, Diane A.
James Dickey **10**:142
Isabelle Holland **21**:149

Parente, Margaret
Scott O'Dell **30**:277

Parente, William J.
Alexsandr I. Solzhenitsyn
10:479

Parham, Sidney F.
Peter Weiss **15**:568

Parini, Jay
Alfred Corn **33**:120
Peter Davison **28**:103
Louise Glück **22**:176
Thom Gunn **32**:210
Daniel Halpern **14**:232
Seamus Heaney **25**:244
Edward Hirsch **31**:215
Brad Leithauser **27**:241
Christopher Middleton **13**:388
Joyce Carol Oates **33**:296
Katha Pollitt **28**:367
Susan Sontag **31**:418
Anne Stevenson **33**:381

Parish, Maggie
Barbara Wersba **30**:433

Parish, Margaret
Barbara Wersba **30**:433

Parisi, John
M. L. Rosenthal **28**:398

Parisi, Joseph
Vicente Aleixandre **36**:32
Robert Frost **34**:473
X. J. Kennedy **8**:320
Josephine Miles **34**:244
William H. Pritchard **34**:473
Susan Fromberg Schaeffer
11:491
Mark Van Doren **6**:543
Robert Penn Warren **18**:536

Park, Clara Claiborne
Brigid Brophy **6**:99
Maxine Kumin **28**:224
James Merrill **13**:377; **18**:330
Stanley Plumly **33**:312
Manuel Puig **28**:371
Luisa Valenzuela **31**:437
Richard Wilbur **9**:568

Park, John G.
Shirley Jackson **11**:302

Park, Sue Simpson
Gwendolyn Brooks **15**:94
Joyce Carol Oates **11**:400

Parke, Andrea
Mary Stolz **12**:548

Parker, A. A.
Edwin Honig **33**:214

Parker, Barbara
Kem Nunn **34**:94

Parker, Dorothy
S. J. Perelman **23**:335
P. G. Wodehouse **22**:478

Parker, Dorothy L.
Pamela Hansford Johnson
27:221

Parker, Geoffrey
Jonathan Keates **34**:202

Parker, John M.
Autran Dourado **23**:151

Parkes, K. S.
Martin Walser **27**:463

Parkes, Stuart
Martin Walser **27**:462

Parkhill-Rathbone, James
C. P. Snow **1**:317; **6**:518

Parkinson, Robert C.
Frank Herbert **12**:271

Parkinson, Thomas
Robert Lowell **1**:179, 180
Gary Snyder **1**:317; **32**:398

Parks, John G.
Lewis Thomas **35**:410

Parr, J. L.
Calder Willingham **5**:510

Parrinder, Patrick
Philip K. Dick **10**:138
B. S. Johnson **9**:302
David Lodge **36**:270
V. S. Naipaul **18**:360
Frederik Pohl **18**:411

Parris, Robert
Françoise Sagan **17**:418

Parrish, Anne
Esther Forbes **12**:202

Parrish, Paul A.
Elizabeth Bowen **11**:59

Parry, Idris
Elias Canetti **25**:108
Hermann Hesse **25**:261

Parsons, Ann
William Carlos Williams **2**:469

Parsons, Gordon
Ruth M. Arthur **12**:27
Leon Garfield **12**:231, 241
Mollie Hunter **21**:156, 158, 167

Parsons, I. M.
Agatha Christie **12**:112

Parsons, Jerry L.
Jack Vance **35**:421, 422, 427

Parsons, Thornton H.
John Crowe Ransom **2**:364

Parton, Margaret
Timothy Findley **27**:140

Partridge, Marianne
Patti Smith **12**:538

Partridge, Ralph
Agatha Christie **12**:113, 114
Edmund Crispin **22**:108, 109

Partridge, Robert
Willie Nelson **17**:304

Pascal, Roy
Georg Lukács **24**:332

Pascal, Sylvia
Stephen King **26**:239

Paschall, Douglas
Theodore Roethke **3**:434

Pasinetti, P. M.
Eleanor Clark **19**:105

Pasolli, Robert
Sam Shepard **17**:434

Pasquariello, Ronald D., F.M.S.
Elie Wiesel **37**:457

Paterson, Gary H.
Kevin Major **26**:285
Norma Fox Mazer **26**:296

Paterson, Katherine
Anita Desai **19**:135
Virginia Hamilton **26**:158
Bette Bao Lord **23**:278
Rosemary Wells **12**:639

Patrouch, Joseph F., Jr.
Isaac Asimov **19**:24
Stephen King **37**:204

Patten, Brian
Isaac Asimov **3**:17
Kurt Vonnegut, Jr. **3**:504

Patten, Frederick
Stephen King **12**:310
Andre Norton **12**:471
Roger Zelazny **21**:468

Patten, Karl
Graham Greene **1**:131

Patterson, Lindsay
Eldridge Cleaver **30**:62

Patterson, Mary Louise
Andrea Lee **36**:253

Patterson, Patricia
Paul Schrader **26**:386

Patterson, Rob
Martin Mull **17**:300

Pattison, Barrie
Brian De Palma **20**:77

Pattow, Donald J.
Dashiell Hammett **19**:198

Paul, Jay S.
William Goyen **14**:211, 212

Paul, Louis
John Steinbeck **21**:365

Paul, Sherman
Paul Goodman **1**:123
Charles Olson **11**:420
Boris Pasternak **7**:295
Edmund Wilson **1**:373

Pauli, David N.
Scott O'Dell **30**:277

Paulin, Tom
Kingsley Amis **13**:15
Robin Cook **14**:131
Robert Coover **15**:145
Thomas Flanagan **25**:167
John Fowles **10**:189
Patricia Highsmith **14**:261
Dan Jacobson **14**:290
Benedict Kiely **23**:264
Jerzy Kosinski **10**:308

Seán O'Faoláin **14**:406
Jim Shepard **36**:405
William Trevor **14**:536
Ian McEwan **13**:370
Barbara Pym **13**:469

Pauls, Ted
Roger Zelazny **21**:464

Pauly, Rebecca M.
Kurt Vonnegut, Jr. **12**:609

Pauly, Thomas H.
John Ford **16**:313

Pautz, Peter D.
Robert Bloch **33**:84

Pavletich, Aida
Joan Armatrading **17**:11
Janis Ian **21**:188
Laura Nyro **17**:321
Buffy Sainte-Marie **17**:431

Pawel, Ernst
Heinrich Böll **2**:67; **9**:109
Hermann Hesse **2**:192
Jakov Lind **2**:245
Martin Walser **27**:467

Paxford, Sandra
Noel Streatfeild **21**:410

Payne, James Robert
Imamu Amiri Baraka **14**:48

Payne, Jocelyn
David Slavitt **14**:491

Payne, Margaret
Mildred D. Taylor **21**:421

Payne, Robert
Winston Graham **23**:193
Yuri Olesha **8**:432
Boris Pasternak **7**:292
Mary Renault **17**:397
Rosemary Sutcliff **26**:432

Paz, Octavio
Elizabeth Bishop **9**:89
André Breton **9**:129
Alexsandr I. Solzhenitsyn
10:478
William Carlos Williams **5**:508

Peabody, Richard, Jr.
Leon Edel **34**:537
Scott Sommer **25**:426

Peacock, Allen
Frederick Busch **18**:86

Peacock, R.
T. S. Eliot **24**:184

Pearce, Howard D.
Paul Green **25**:198, 199

Pearce, Philippa
Alan Garner **17**:136
Philippa Pearce **21**:288

Pearce, Richard
Saul Bellow **8**:72
John Dos Passos **8**:181
John Hawkes **9**:266
Henry Roth **6**:473
William Styron **11**:515

Pearce, Roy Harvey
Robert Frost **26**:120

Pearlman, Sandy
Ray Davies **21**:89
Jim Morrison **17**:287
Lou Reed **21**:302

Pearson, Alan
Joe Rosenblatt **15**:447

Pearson, Carol
Joseph Heller **11**:265

Pearson, Gabriel
John Berryman **2**:55
T. S. Eliot **13**:192
Leslie A. Fiedler **24**:202

Pearson, Haydn S.
Roderick L. Haig-Brown
21:137, 138

Pearson, Ian
W. P. Kinsella **27**:238

Pearson, Norman Holmes
Ezra Pound **2**:340

Pearson, Richard
Jesse Stuart **34**:373

Pease, Howard
Henry Gregor Felsen **17**:121
John R. Tunis **12**:596

Peavy, Charles D.
Larry McMurtry **27**:324
Hubert Selby, Jr. **1**:306
Melvin Van Peebles **20**:410

Pechter, William S.
Lindsay Anderson **20**:16
Ingmar Bergman **16**:48
Frank Capra **16**:158
John Cassavetes **20**:49
Francis Ford Coppola **16**:234,
238
Federico Fellini **16**:282
Elaine May **16**:432
Satyajit Ray **16**:482, 494
Jean Renoir **20**:298
Andrew Lloyd Webber and Tim
Rice **21**:429
Orson Welles **20**:448
Lina Wertmüller **16**:589

Peck, Richard
Robert Cormier **12**:135
Lois Duncan **26**:104
Katherine Paterson **12**:485
Richard Peck **21**:30

Peckham, Morse
Wayne C. Booth **24**:98

Peden, William
James Baldwin **8**:40
Doris Betts **6**:70; **28**:33
Paul Bowles **19**:58
Ed Bullins **7**:37
John Cheever **7**:49
Laurie Colwin **5**:108
James T. Farrell **8**:205
Ernest J. Gaines **11**:217
Mavis Gallant **18**:170
Shirley Ann Grau **9**:240
Chester Himes **7**:159
Langston Hughes **10**:281

Grace Paley **6**:392
Ann Petry **7**:305
William Saroyan **8**:468
Mary Lee Settle **19**:409
Irwin Shaw **7**:411
Isaac Bashevis Singer **6**:509
Jesse Stuart **8**:507
Peter Taylor **18**:523
Tennessee Williams **5**:502
Richard Wright **14**:596

Peel, Mark
John Lennon **35**:275
Paul McCartney **35**:291
Prince **35**:331
Bob Seger **35**:386

Peel, Marie
John Osborne **2**:329
Peter Redgrove **6**:445, 446
Penelope Shuttle **7**:423
Alan Sillitoe **3**:448
David Storey **2**:425
R. S. Thomas **6**:531

Peet, Creighton
Franklyn M. Branley **21**:15
Robert A. Heinlein **26**:160

Pekar, Harvey
Robert Crumb **17**:82
Frank Zappa **17**:585

Pelham, Philip
Dick Francis **22**:151

Pelli, Moshe
S. Y. Agnn **8**:8

Pelorus
Judy Blume **12**:45
Robert Cormier **12**:135
Alan Garner **17**:147

Peltier, Ed
Peter Weir **20**:424

Pemberton, Clive
Leon Garfield **12**:219

Pendergast, Constance
Mavis Gallant **18**:171

Pendleton, Dennis
Douglas Unger **34**:114

Penner, Allen R.
Alan Sillitoe **1**:308

Penner, Dick
Vladimir Nabokov **15**:395

Penner, Jonathan
Margaret Atwood **25**:69
André Dubus **36**:143
Carlos Fuentes **22**:171
Graham Greene **18**:196
Jonathan Keates **34**:203
William Kennedy **28**:204
V. S. Pritchett **15**:443
Philip Roth **15**:450
Susan Richards Shreve **23**:483
Richard Yates **23**:480

Pennington, Jane
Walter Dean Myers **35**:296

Pennington, Lee
Jesse Stuart **11**:508; **34**:373

Penta, Anne Constance
Jane Rule **27**:417

Peppard, Murray B.
Friedrich Dürrenmatt **1**:81

Pepper, Nancy
Anaïs Nin **11**:399

Perazzini, Randolph
Robert Frost **13**:229

Percy, Walker
Walter M. Miller, Jr. **4**:352
Marion Montgomery **7**:232
Jean-Paul Sartre **13**:506
John Kennedy Toole **19**:441
Eudora Welty **1**:362

Percy, William
Joy Adamson **17**:2

Perebinossoff, Phillipe R.
Jean Renoir **20**:308

Perera, Victor
Miguel Ángel Asturias **3**:18

Pérez, Genaro J.
Juan Goytisolo **23**:185

Perez, Gilberto
Beryl Bainbridge **10**:16
Ingmar Bergman **16**:81
Werner Herzog **16**:335
Yuri Krotkov **19**:266
Alan Sillitoe **10**:477
Anne Tyler **11**:553

Pérez Firmat, Gustavo
José Lezama Lima **10**:319

Perkins, David
W. H. Auden **11**:19
Richard Eberhart **11**:179
Howard Nemerov **36**:304
Ezra Pound **3**:397
Carl Sandburg **10**:449

Perkins, Elizabeth
Christina Stead **32**:412

Perkins, Huel D.
Kristin Hunter **35**:227
John A. Williams **13**:599

Perlberg, Mark
Larry Eigner **9**:181
Michael S. Harper **7**:138
George Oppen **7**:285

Perloff, Marjorie
Donald Hall **37**:143

Perloff, Marjorie G.
John Berryman **2**:59
Aimé Césaire **32**:112
Ed Dorn **10**:156
Clayton Eshleman **7**:99
Thom Gunn **3**:216
Seamus Heaney **25**:250
Ted Hughes **2**:204; **4**:235
Richard F. Hugo **6**:244
Erica Jong **6**:270
Galway Kinnell **2**:230
Denise Levertov **2**:243
Philip Levine **33**:273
Robert Lowell **1**:181
Frank O'Hara **2**:322; **5**:325;
13:425

Charles Olson **11**:415
Sylvia Plath **9**:432; **17**:368
Ezra Pound **10**:400
Adrienne Rich **7**:369; **36**:369
Françoise Sagan **6**:482
May Sarton **14**:481
Mark Van Doren **10**:496
Mona Van Duyn **3**:492
Diane Wakoski **7**:504
John Wieners **7**:537
James Wright **3**:542, 544

Perrick, Eve
Ira Levin **3**:294

Perrin, Noel
James Gould Cozzens **11**:132
Walter D. Edmonds **35**:155
Wright Morris **37**:314

Perrine, Laurence
John Ciardi **10**:105

Perry, Charles
Andrew Lloyd Webber and Tim
Rice **21**:431

Perry, Frank
C. S. Adler **35**:13

Perry, Nick
J. G. Ballard **36**:35

Perry, R. C.
Rolf Hochhuth **11**:276

Perry, Ruth
Doris Lessing **15**:330

Pershing, Amy
Pete Dexter **34**:44

Peseroff, Joyce
Sharon Olds **32**:346

Peter, John
Alan Ayckbourn **33**:42
Edward Bond **13**:102
William Golding **17**:158

Peterkiewicz, Jerzy
Witold Gombrowicz **4**:195
Alain Robbe-Grillet **4**:447

Peterkin, Julia
Paul Green **25**:194

Peterman, Michael A.
Farley Mowat **26**:340

Peters, Andrew
Steven Goldsberry **34**:55

Peters, Daniel James
Thomas Pynchon **3**:412

Peters, Jonathan
Chinua Achebe **26**:25

Peters, Julie Stone
Maxine Kumin **28**:223

Peters, Margot
Agatha Christie **12**:119
Robert B. Parker **27**:364
J.I.M. Stewart **14**:512

Peters, Robert
Ted Berrigan **37**:45
Charles Bukowski **5**:80
Clayton Eshleman **7**:99
Michael McClure **6**:317
W. D. Snodgrass **18**:492

Gary Snyder **32**:397
Anne Waldman **7**:508

Peters, Robert L.
Hollis Summers **10**:493

Peters, Ted
Erich von Däniken **30**:424

Petersen, Carol
Max Frisch **18**:160

Petersen, Clarence
Nora Ephron **17**:110
Charles M. Schulz **12**:527
Wilfrid Sheed **2**:392

Petersen, Fred
Ernesto Sabato **23**:376

Petersen, Gwenn Boardman
Yukio Mishima **27**:341
Jun'ichirō Tanizaki **28**:415

Peterson, Levi S.
Edward Abbey **36**:11
A. B. Guthrie, Jr. **23**:200

Peterson, Linda Kauffmann
Betsy Byars **35**:75

Peterson, Mary
Jayne Anne Phillips **15**:419

Peterson, Maurice
Sidney Poitier **26**:360

Peterson, Richard F.
Mary Lavin **18**:303

Peterson, Susan
Steve Martin **30**:246

Peterson, Virgilia
Sylvia Ashton-Warner **19**:22
Jan de Hartog **19**:131
Elizabeth Jane Howard **29**:243
Primo Levi **37**:222
Betty Smith **19**:424
George Tabori **19**:436
Henri Troyat **23**:458
Jessamyn West **17**:548
Monique Wittig **22**:471

Petit, Christopher
Peter Townshend **17**:539

Petric, Vlada
Carl Theodor Dreyer **16**:266

Petrie, Graham
Jean Renoir **20**:302
Eric Rohmer **16**:529
François Truffaut **20**:386

Petrie, Paul
A. Alvarez **5**:16

Petroski, Catherine
Penelope Gilliatt **13**:237

Petrović, Njegoš M.
Dobrica Cosić **14**:132

Petticoffer, Dennis
Richard Brautigan **12**:73

Pettigrew, John
D. J. Enright **31**:146

Pettingell, Phoebe
John Ashbery **25**:54
Ernesto Cardenal **31**:79
Alfred Corn **33**:117
Allen Ginsberg **36**:192
Donald Hall **1**:137
Anthony Hecht **19**:207
Edward Hirsch **31**:214
John Hollander **14**:266
Barbara Howes **15**:289
Brad Leithauser **27**:241
Philip Levine **9**:332; **14**:320
Robert Lowell **8**:353
James Merrill **13**:382
Howard Nemerov **36**:301, 309
Carl Sandburg **35**:358
John Wain **11**:563

Pettit, Arthur G.
Sam Peckinpah **20**:280

Pettit, Michael
Paul Bowles **19**:59

Pettit, Philip
J.R.R. Tolkien **3**:483

Petts, Margo
H. F. Brinsmead **21**:32

Pevear, Richard
A. R. Ammons **3**:10
Wendell Berry **27**:38
Charles Causley **7**:42
Guy Davenport, Jr. **14**:139
Richmond Lattimore **3**:277
Denise Levertov **3**:292
Hugh MacDiarmid **4**:313
James Merrill **3**:334
Pablo Neruda **5**:301
George Oppen **7**:286
Peter Porter **13**:452
Ezra Pound **2**:343
Louis Zukofsky **7**:563

Pew, Thomas W., Jr.
Gary Snyder **32**:394

Peyre, Henri
Marcel Aymé **11**:21
Simone de Beauvoir **1**:19
Albert Camus **1**:53; **14**:106
Louis-Ferdinand Céline **1**:57
René Char **9**:162
Georges Duhamel **8**:186
Romain Gary **25**:184, 186
Jean Giono **4**:185
Julien Green **3**:203
Violette Leduc **22**:261
André Malraux **1**:201
François Mauriac **4**:338
Henri de Montherlant **19**:324
Raymond Queneau **5**:358
Alain Robbe-Grillet **4**:446
Jules Romains **7**:383
Nathalie Sarraute **4**:464
Jean-Paul Sartre **1**:305
Claude Simon **4**:494
Henri Troyat **23**:458, 459, 460

Pfeffercorn, Eli
Abraham B. Yehoshua **13**:616

Pfeiffer, John
Jean M. Auel **31**:22
Franklyn M. Branley **21**:16

Pfeiffer, John R.
John Brunner **8**:105

Pfeil, Fred
John Berger **19**:40
Luis Rafael Sánchez **23**:385

Pfeiler, William K.
Erich Maria Remarque **21**:329

Phelan, Kappo
Tennessee Williams **30**:456

Phelps, Donald
Fielding Dawson **6**:125
Gilbert Sorrentino **7**:451

Phelps, Paul B.
Bienvenido N. Santos **22**:366

Phelps, Robert
Helen MacInnes **27**:280
Walter M. Miller, Jr. **30**:254
Dan Wakefield **7**:502

Phelps, William Lyon
Van Wyck Brooks **29**:79

Philip, Neil
Iain Banks **34**:30
Maureen Duffy **37**:117
Elaine Feinstein **36**:171
Ted Hughes **37**:178
Diana Wynne Jones **26**:230
Rosemary Sutcliff **26**:440, 441
Jill Paton Walsh **35**:434

Phillips, Allen W.
Octavio Paz **3**:376

Phillips, Cassandra
Raymond Carver **22**:98

Phillips, Delbert
Yevgeny Yevtushenko **3**:547

Phillips, Frank Lamont
Maya Angelou **12**:12

Phillips, Gene D.
Ken Russell **16**:551

Phillips, James A.
Vine Deloria, Jr. **21**:109
Pat Jordan **37**:194

Phillips, James E.
Laurence Olivier **20**:237

Phillips, Klaus
Jurek Becker **19**:35

Phillips, Michael Joseph
Richard Kostelanetz **28**:218

Phillips, Norma
Alan Sillitoe **6**:501

Phillips, Robert
A. R. Ammons **25**:45
John Berryman **25**:90
Philip Booth **23**:77
Hortense Calisher **8**:125
Arthur A. Cohen **7**:52
James T. Farrell **4**:158
Allen Ginsberg **6**:199
William Goyen **5**:148, 149;
   14:213
William Heyen **18**:231
Richard Howard **10**:275
Robert Lowell **4**:303

Critic Index

Bernard Malamud 3:325
Carson McCullers 4:345;
  12:432
James Alan McPherson 19:310
Brian Moore 7:239
Joyce Carol Oates 11:404;
  33:288
Jayne Anne Phillips 33:308
Anne Sexton 15:470
Patrick White 4:586
Marya Zaturenska 11:579

Phillips, Robert L., Jr.
Eudora Welty 33:419

Phillips, Steven R.
Ernest Hemingway 3:241

Phillips, William
Susan Sontag 31:409
Edmund Wilson 24:474

Phillipson, John S.
Vine Deloria, Jr. 21:109
Howard Fast 23:161

Phillipson, Michael
Lucien Goldmann 24:250

Philpott, Joan
Josephine Humphreys 34:63

Piacentino, Edward J.
T. S. Stribling 23:449

Piazza, Paul
Christopher Isherwood 14:281
John Knowles 26:263

Picard, Raymond
Roland Barthes 24:23

Piccarella, John
David Byrne 26:96
The Clash 30:45, 49
Pink Floyd 35:315
Smokey Robinson 21:351

Piccione, Anthony
Stanley Plumly 33:310

Piccoli, Raffaello
Riccardo Bacchelli 19:30

Pichaske, David R.
John Lennon and Paul
  McCartney 12:373

Pick, Robert
Ronald Harwood 32:222
Erich Maria Remarque 21:329
Frank Yerby 7:556

Pickar, G. B.
Martin Walser 27:461

Pickar, Gertrud B.
Max Frisch 14:181

Pickar, Gertrud Bauer
Martin Walser 27:458

Pickering, Felix
Benedict Kiely 23:264

Pickering, James S.
Alvin Silverstein and Virginia
  B. Silverstein 17:450

Pickering, Sam, Jr.
Anthony Powell 7:338
P. G. Wodehouse 5:517

Pickering, Samuel
Alan Garner 17:151

Pickering, Samuel F., Jr.
Peter Matthiessen 32:290
Joyce Carol Oates 6:369

Pickford, John
J. B. Priestley 34:366

Pickrel, Paul
Heinrich Böll 27:54
L. P. Hartley 22:211
Aldo Palazzeschi 11:431
Sylvia Townsend Warner 7:511

Picon, Gaëtan
Jean Anouilh 13:21
Michel Butor 8:119
Albert Camus 9:144
Henri Michaux 8:392

Piehl, Kathy
Thomas J. Fleming 37:129
M. E. Kerr 35:250

Piehler, Heide
D. M. Pinkwater 35:320

Pierce, Hazel
Isaac Asimov 26:41

Piercy, Marge
Alta 19:18
Margaret Atwood 3:20
Margaret Laurence 6:289
Judith Rossner 29:353
Joanna Russ 15:461
Alice Walker 9:557

Pifer, Ellen
Vladimir Nabokov 23:312

Pigaga, Thom
John Hollander 2:197

Piggott, Stuart
David Jones 4:261

Pike, B. A.
Margery Allingham 19:13, 14,
  15, 16, 17, 18

Pike, C. R.
Arkadii Strugatskii and Boris
  Strugatskii 27:437

Pilger, John
Michael Cimino 16:211
Joan Didion 32:145

Pinchin, Jane Lagoudis
Lawrence Durrell 13:186
E. M. Forster 13:220

Pinckney, Darryl
James Baldwin 17:44
Russell Banks 37:25
Imamu Amiri Baraka 14:48
Jacob Epstein 19:163
Gayl Jones 9:307
Nettie Jones 34:69
June Jordan 23:257
Paule Marshall 27:315
Jay McInerney 34:84
Toni Morrison 22:322
John Rechy 18:442
Michael Thelwell 22:415
Jean Toomer 22:429
Richard Wright 9:585

Pinckney, Josephine
Zora Neale Hurston 30:208

Pincus, Richard Eliot
Theodore Sturgeon 22:412

Pinkerton, Jan
Peter Taylor 1:333

Pinsker, Sanford
Leslie A. Fiedler 24:204
Joanne Greenberg 30:166
Frederick Karl 34:551
Alfred Kazin 34:561
Bernard Malamud 3:322;
  18:321
Joyce Carol Oates 11:402
Philip Roth 31:337
Isaac Bashevis Singer 3:454
John Updike 7:489

Pinsky, Robert
John Berryman 8:93
Frank Bidart 33:75
Elizabeth Bishop 15:61; 32:33,
  38
J. V. Cunningham 31:104
Seamus Heaney 25:249; 37:167
Ted Hughes 9:282
Philip Larkin 33:268
Philip Levine 9:332
Cynthia MacDonald 13:355
Theodore Roethke 8:461
Raphael Rudnik 7:384
Mark Strand 18:517

Piper, John
John Betjeman 34:307

Pipes, Charles D.
Eva Figes 31:162

Pipkin, Vicki
Neil Diamond 30:113

Pippett, Aileen
Isabel Colegate 36:110
Julia W. Cunningham 12:163
Frank Tuohy 37:428

Pippett, Roger
John Mortimer 28:282

Pirie, Bruce
Timothy Findley 27:142

Pit
Richard O'Brien 17:323

Pitou, Spire
Jean Cayrol 11:110

Pittock, Malcolm
Ivy Compton-Burnett 10:108

Pivovarnick, John
Louis L'Amour 25:282

Plaice, S. N.
Siegfried Lenz 27:255

Planchart, Alejandro Enrique
John Lennon and Paul
  McCartney 12:359

Plant, Richard
Heinrich Böll 27:58
Anne Chislett 34:145
Eleanor Clark 19:105
Gregor von Rezzori 25:381
Henri Troyat 23:457

Plater, William M.
Thomas Pynchon 18:433

Plath, Sara
Ted Berrigan 37:45
Sharon Olds 32:345

Platypus, Bill
C. S. Forester 35:173

Platzner, Robert L.
J. G. Ballard 36:44

Pleasants, Ben
Lisa St. Aubin de Teran 36:421

Pleszczynski, Wladyslaw
James A. Michener 29:317

Plomer, William
C. S. Forester 35:161
Ayn Rand 30:292
Rebecca West 31:453

Plumb, J. H.
Antonia Fraser 32:185

Plumb, Robert K.
Roy A. Gallant 17:126

Plumly, Stanley
Alfred Corn 33:116
Carolyn Forché 25:169
Marilyn Hacker 23:205
Lisel Mueller 13:399
Charles Simic 22:381
James Tate 25:428
C. K. Williams 33:445

Plummer, William
Jerome Charyn 18:99
John M. Del Vecchio 29:149
Stanley Elkin 14:157
Jerzy Kosinski 10:306

Poague, Leland A.
Frank Capra 16:162
Bob Dylan 6:156

Pochoda, Elizabeth
Djuna Barnes 11:30
Milan Kundera 19:268
Tim O'Brien 19:357

Pochoda, Elizabeth Turner
Anna Kavan 13:316
Tadeusz Konwicki 8:327
Alan Lelchuk 5:245
Joyce Carol Oates 6:373

Podhoretz, John
David Lodge 36:276

Podhoretz, Norman
James Baldwin 1:13, 14
Saul Bellow 1:28
Albert Camus 1:52
J. P. Donleavy 1:75
George P. Elliott 2:130
William Faulkner 1:98
William Golding 17:160
Paul Goodman 1:123
Joseph Heller 1:139
Thomas Hinde 6:239
Jack Kerouac 1:165
Milan Kundera 32:268
Norman Mailer 1:188
Bernard Malamud 1:194
Mary McCarthy 1:205

John O'Hara **1**:260
Philip Roth **1**:292
Nathalie Sarraute **1**:302
John Updike **1**:343
Edmund Wilson **1**:372, 373

Poger, Sidney
T. S. Eliot **15**:212

Poggi, Gianfranco
Luchino Visconti **16**:563

Poggioli, Renato
Eugenio Montale **7**:221

Pogrebin, Letty Cottin
Laurie Colwin **23**:130
Norma Klein **30**:235
Richard Peck **21**:295

Poirier, Richard
John Barth **3**:40
Saul Bellow **8**:74
Jorge Luis Borges **3**:77
T. S. Eliot **3**:140
Robert Frost **4**:176; **9**:226
Geoffrey H. Hartman **27**:180
Lillian Hellman **4**:221
John Hollander **14**:264
Jonathan Kozol **17**:251
John Lennon and Paul
    McCartney **12**:368
Norman Mailer **2**:263, 265;
    3:314; **4**:322; **14**:349; **28**:262
Vladimir Nabokov **6**:354
Thomas Pynchon **2**:355; **3**:409;
    18:429
Robert Stone **23**:429
William Styron **3**:474
Gore Vidal **4**:553
Rudolph Wurlitzer **2**:482; **4**:597

Polacheck, Janet G.
Jules Archer **12**:18
James D. Forman **21**:120
Milton Meltzer **26**:300

Poland, Nancy
Margaret Drabble **5**:118

Polar, Antonio Cornejo
José María Arguedas **18**:7

Polishook, Irwin
Allan W. Eckert **17**:107

Politzer, Heinz
Jerome Siegel and Joe Shuster
    21:355

Polk, James
Leslie Marmon Silko **23**:411

Pollack, Pamela D.
Gunnel Beckman **26**:88
Robert Cormier **30**:81
Rosa Guy **26**:143
Norma Fox Mazer **26**:291
Richard Peck **21**:299
Maia Wojciechowska **26**:455

Pollak, Richard
Jan de Hartog **19**:132

Pollitt, Katha
Alice Adams **13**:1, 2
Margaret Atwood **8**:30
Pat Barker **32**:15
Saul Bellow **25**:82
Anita Desai **19**:133

Norman Dubie **36**:134
Leslie Epstein **27**:128
Carolyn Forché **25**:171
Gail Godwin **22**:180
Barbara Guest **34**:444
H. D. **34**:444
Carolyn G. Heilbrun **25**:257
Sandra Hochman **8**:298
Maureen Howard **14**:268
Susan Isaacs **32**:254
Dan Jacobson **14**:291
Yashar Kemal **14**:300
William X. Kienzle **25**:275
Norma Klein **30**:239
Ella Leffland **19**:279
David Malouf **28**:266
Cynthia Ozick **28**:352
Marge Piercy **27**:377
James Purdy **10**:425
Françoise Sagan **17**:428
Lynne Sharon Schwartz **31**:388
Susan Richards Shreve **23**:402
Lee Smith **25**:409
Scott Spencer **30**:405
Anne Tyler **7**:479
Alice Walker **27**:448
William Wharton **18**:542

Pollock, Bruce
Jim Carroll **35**:81
Mick Jagger and Keith Richard
    17:235
Paul Simon **17**:465

Pollock, Zailig
A. M. Klein **19**:262

Polner, Murray
Ronald J. Glasser **37**:131
Roger Kahn **30**:232

Polt, Harriet
Ralph Bakshi **26**:69
Bernard Malamud **18**:322

Polt, Harriet R.
René Clair **20**:66

Pond, Steve
Paul Weller **26**:447

Ponnuthurai, Charles Sarvan
Chinua Achebe **5**:3

Pontac, Perry
Miguel Piñero **4**:401

Pool, Gail
Barbara Pym **37**:377
Anne Sexton **10**:468

Poole, Michael
John Fowles **33**:172

Poore, C. G.
Ogden Nash **23**:317, 318

Poore, Charles
Charles Addams **30**:13
Jessica Anderson **37**:18
Gregorio López y Fuentes
    32:278
Erich Maria Remarque **21**:330
Wilfrid Sheed **2**:392
Jessamyn West **17**:549

Popkin, Henry
Albert Camus **9**:145; **32**:84
Arthur Miller **26**:319

Pops, Martin L.
Charles Olson **29**:327

Porsild, A. E.
Farley Mowat **26**:332

Portch, Stephen R.
Flannery O'Connor **15**:412

Porter, Carolyn
Lina Wertmüller **16**:593

Porter, Katherine Anne
Kay Boyle **19**:61
Ezra Pound **7**:325
Eudora Welty **33**:414

Porter, M. Gilbert
Saul Bellow **2**:54; **8**:72

Porter, Michael
Horst Bienek **11**:48

Porter, Peter
W. H. Auden **14**:31
Amy Clampitt **32**:118
Gavin Ewart **13**:208
James Fenton **32**:166
Roy Fisher **25**:161
Seamus Heaney **14**:244
Ted Hughes **14**:273
Norman MacCaig **36**:285
Derek Mahon **27**:291
Sylvia Plath **17**:352
Craig Raine **32**:350
Christopher Reid **33**:350
Jaroslav Seifert **34**:256
Stevie Smith **3**:460
Judith Wright **11**:578

Porter, Raymond J.
Brendan Behan **8**:64

Porter, Robert
Milan Kundera **4**:276

Porter, Thomas E.
John Ehle **27**:103

Porterfield, Christopher
Kingsley Amis **2**:8
Robert Frost **34**:473
Christopher Fry **2**:143
Ted Hughes **2**:199
William H. Pritchard **34**:473
Donald E. Westlake **7**:528
William Wharton **37**:442

Posnock, Ross
Frank Lentricchia **34**:574

Poss, Stanley
John Hollander **8**:301
Philip Larkin **13**:337
Cynthia Macdonald **13**:355
P. H. Newby **2**:310
Adrienne Rich **7**:370
Theodore Roethke **8**:460
Nancy Willard **7**:539

Postell, Frances
Christie Harris **12**:263

Poster, Mark
Michel Foucault **31**:181

Postlewait, Thomas
Samuel Beckett **18**:46

Potamkin, Harry Allan
Carl Theodor Dreyer **16**:255
Langston Hughes **35**:212

Potok, Chaim
Paul West **7**:523

Potoker, Edward Martin
Michael Mott **15**:379
Judith Rossner **9**:456
Ronald Sukenick **6**:524

Potter, David M.
Bruce Catton **35**:88, 90

Potter, Lois
Antonia Fraser **32**:186

Potter, Vilma Ruskin
Robert Hayden **37**:157

Potts, Charles
Thomas McGrath **28**:277

Potts, Paul
George Barker **8**:43

Potts, Stephen W.
Stanislaw Lem **15**:330

Pouillon, Jean
William Faulkner **8**:208

Pound, Ezra
Robert Frost **15**:239
Mina Loy **28**:245
Marianne Moore **19**:335
William Carlos Williams
    13:602

Povey, John
Chinua Achebe **26**:20

Povey, John F.
Chinua Achebe **1**:1; **7**:6
Cyprian Ekwensi **4**:151
Ngugi wa Thiong'o **36**:318
Wole Soyinka **14**:506

Powdermaker, Hortense
Margaret Mead **37**:272

Powell, Anthony
Evelyn Waugh **3**:513

Powell, Bertie J.
Lorraine Hansberry **17**:193

Powell, Dilys
Elia Kazan **16**:361

Powell, Grosvenor E.
J. V. Cunningham **31**:99
Yvor Winters **32**:465

Powell, Meghan
Stan Lee **17**:262

Powell, Michael
Martin Scorsese **20**:340

Powell, Neil
Donald Davie **31**:117
Thom Gunn **3**:216

Power, K. C.
Michael McClure **6**:321

Power, Victor
Hugh Leonard **19**:281

Powers, Kim
Harvey Fierstein **33**:154

Critic Index

Powers, Thomas
Donald Hall **37**:148
Richard Kostelanetz **28**:213
Tom Wolfe **15**:583

Prado, Holly
Mary Oliver **34**:247
Adrienne Rich **36**:374

Prasad, Madhusudan
Anita Desai **37**:68
Jayanta Mahapatra **33**:281

Pratt, Annis
Doris Lessing **3**:288; **6**:292

Pratt, Fletcher
C. S. Forester **35**:167

Pratt, John Clark
John Steinbeck **1**:326

Pratt, Linda Ray
Sylvia Plath **3**:390

Pratt, Sarah
V. S. Pritchett **13**:468

Pratt, William
John Berryman **10**:45
Joseph Brodsky **6**:97
Daniel Halpern **14**:232
Ezra Pound **18**:427
Andrei Voznesensky **15**:554

Prawer, Siegbert S.
Ernst Jandl **34**:195

Prendergast, Christopher
Roland Barthes **24**:36

Prendowska, Krystyna
Jerzy Kosinski **15**:313

Prescott, Anne Lake
Rosellen Brown **32**:65

Prescott, Orville
Michael Ayrton **7**:17
James Clavell **25**:125
Earl Hamner, Jr. **12**:257
James A. Michener **29**:310
Erich Maria Remarque **21**:330
Conrad Richter **30**:310, 314
Betty Smith **19**:422
J.I.M. Stewart **7**:466
Robert Penn Warren **8**:543

Prescott, Peter S.
Alice Adams **6**:1
Richard Adams **4**:7
Renata Adler **31**:14
Eric Ambler **6**:3
Kingsley Amis **3**:8
Martin Amis **4**:20
Donald Barthelme **5**:54
William Peter Blatty **2**:64
Vance Bourjaily **8**:104
Kay Boyle **5**:65
Robin F. Brancato **35**:67
Richard Brautigan **5**:71
Lothar-Günther Buchheim
6:101
Anthony Burgess **5**:85
William Caunitz **34**:36
Agatha Christie **12**:120
Robert Coover **32**:120
Michael Crichton **6**:119
Robertson Davies **7**:73

Len Deighton **7**:75
Don DeLillo **8**:171
Peter De Vries **7**:78
John Dos Passos **4**:137
Lawrence Durrell **6**:151
Leslie A. Fiedler **4**:161
John Fowles **6**:186
Michael Frayn **3**:165
Ronald J. Glasser **37**:131, 132
Nadine Gordimer **5**:146
Graham Greene **3**:213
Judith Guest **30**:175
Lillian Hellman **4**:221
Mark Helprin **32**:231
George V. Higgins **4**:223
Edward Hoagland **28**:182
Russell C. Hoban **7**:161
Geoffrey Household **11**:277
Dan Jacobson **4**:254
Diane Johnson **5**:198
Robert F. Jones **7**:193
Roger Kahn **30**:232
Thomas Keneally **8**:318
William Kennedy **6**:275;
   28:205, 206
John Knowles **26**:265
Jerzy Kosinski **6**:285
Charles R. Larson **31**:239
John Le Carré **5**:232, 234
Elmore Leonard **34**:214
Doris Lessing **2**:241
Peter Matthiessen **5**:274
Cormac McCarthy **4**:341
John McGahern **5**:280
A. G. Mojtabai **9**:385
Brian Moore **7**:236; **32**:308
Toni Morrison **4**:365
Penelope Mortimer **5**:299
Joyce Carol Oates **6**:374
Flann O'Brien **5**:314
Robert B. Parker **27**:367
Padgett Powell **34**:98
Reynolds Price **6**:425
Thomas Pynchon **33**:338
Philip Roth **2**:378; **4**:455; **6**:475
Jonathan Schell **35**:363
Cynthia Propper Seton **27**:425
Isaac Bashevis Singer **3**:458
Aleksandr I. Solzhenitsyn **4**:516
Muriel Spark **5**:399
Robert Stone **5**:409
Harvey Swados **5**:422
Paul Theroux **5**:428
Michel Tournier **6**:537
William Trevor **7**:478
Frank Tuohy **37**:433
John Updike **5**:455, 458
Gore Vidal **4**:554
Alice Walker **27**:449
Jessamyn West **7**:521
William Wharton **37**:439
Patrick White **3**:524
P. G. Wodehouse **5**:515
Larry Woiwode **6**:579
Richard Yates **7**:555

Presley, Delma Eugene
John Fowles **3**:163
Carson McCullers **4**:346

Press, John
John Betjeman **6**:67
Philip Larkin **8**:339
Norman MacCaig **36**:280
Louis MacNeice **4**:316

Preston, Don
Agnes Eckhardt Nixon **21**:252

Prestwich, J. O.
Rosemary Sutcliff **26**:426

Preuss, Paul
David Brin **34**:135

Price, Derek de Solla
John Brunner **10**:80
Ursula K. LeGuin **8**:343

Price, James
Martin Amis **9**:26
Beryl Bainbridge **8**:37
Caroline Blackwood **9**:101
Frank Capra **16**:157
Margaret Drabble **8**:184

Price, John D.
St.-John Perse **11**:434

Price, L. Brian
Jean Genet **14**:203

Price, Martin
Robert Bolt **14**:87
Mavis Gallant **18**:171
Marjorie Kellogg **2**:224
David Lodge **36**:269, 271
Iris Murdoch **1**:236; **3**:349
Joyce Carol Oates **1**:251
Nathalie Sarraute **4**:469
C. P. Snow **1**:317
David Storey **4**:530
Angus Wilson **5**:514

Price, R.G.G.
Kingsley Amis **2**:7
Paul Bowles **2**:78
Dino Buzzati **36**:88
Isabel Colegate **36**:110
L. P. Hartley **2**:182
Ruth Prawer Jhabvala **29**:253
Robert Kroetsch **23**:270
Josephine Poole **17**:371
Bernice Rubens **31**:350
Elizabeth Taylor **2**:432

Price, Reynolds
Cleanth Brooks **24**:107
Lucille Clifton **19**:110
William Faulkner **1**:102; **3**:151
Francine du Plessix Gray
   22:202
Graham Greene **3**:212
Mark Helprin **22**:220
Toni Morrison **10**:355
Walker Percy **8**:442
Elizabeth Spencer **22**:405
James Welch **6**:560
Eudora Welty **2**:463

Priebe, Richard
Wole Soyinka **3**:463

Priest, Christopher
Joan D. Vinge **30**:411

Priestley, J. B.
T. S. Eliot **3**:135
William Faulkner **3**:150
Ernest Hemingway **3**:232
F. R. Leavis **24**:296
Ezra Pound **3**:394

Priestley, Michael
John Irving **23**:244

Preston, Don
Agnes Eckhardt Nixon **21**:252

Prigozy, Ruth
Larry McMurtry **3**:333

Primeau, Ronald
John Brunner **8**:109

Prince, Peter
Martin Amis **4**:19
Charles Bukowski **5**:80
Anthony Burgess **4**:84
John Fowles **6**:184
Ronald Harwood **32**:224
Thomas Hinde **11**:273
Yashar Kemal **14**:299
Thomas Keneally **5**:210
Larry McMurtry **27**:333
Patrick Modiano **18**:338
Alice Munro **6**:341
David Pownall **10**:419
Piers Paul Read **4**:444; **25**:377
Philip Roth **3**:439

Pring-Mill, Robert
Ernesto Cardenal **31**:76
Pablo Neruda **28**:310

Pringle, David
J. G. Ballard **14**:40; **36**:35

Pringle, John Douglas
Hugh MacDiarmid **4**:312

Pritchard, R. E.
L. P. Hartley **22**:219

Pritchard, William H.
Dannie Abse **7**:1; **29**:19
Margaret Atwood **3**:19
Wendell Berry **8**:85
John Berryman **3**:72; **8**:90
Henry Bromell **5**:74
Anthony Burgess **1**:48; **4**:84
Jerome Charyn **18**:99
Donald Davie **8**:162, 163;
   31:125
Stephen Dunn **36**:154
John Fowles **9**:214; **10**:189
Allen Ginsberg **3**:195
Robert Graves **2**:177
Marilyn Hacker **9**:257
Seamus Heaney **14**:242
John Hollander **5**:187
Ted Hughes **9**:281
Richard F. Hugo **6**:244; **18**:260
William Kennedy **34**:208
Alan Lelchuk **5**:245
Denise Levertov **2**:242; **15**:338
Philip Levine **2**:244
Robert Lowell **1**:184
Louis MacNeice **4**:316
William McPherson **34**:86
Wright Morris **18**:354
Iris Murdoch **8**:406; **31**:295
Vladimir Nabokov **3**:353
Howard Nemerov **6**:363
Anthony Powell **7**:339
Padgett Powell **34**:99
Thomas Pynchon **3**:418
Piers Paul Read **25**:379
Kenneth Rexroth **2**:369
Adrienne Rich **3**:427; **6**:459
Susan Fromberg Schaeffer
   6:489
Cynthia Propper Seton **27**:428
Anne Sexton **15**:473
L. E. Sissman **18**:488

Aleksandr I. Solzhenitsyn **4**:510
Kathleen Spivack **6**:520
Richard G. Stern **4**:523
Robert Stone **5**:410
May Swenson **4**:532
James Tate **25**:429
Elizabeth Taylor **2**:433
Paul Theroux **11**:531
John Updike **3**:487
Richard Wilbur **6**:571
James Wright **3**:544
Rudolph Wurlitzer **4**:597
Richard Yates **7**:556

Pritchett, V. S.
Kingsley Amis **13**:15
Simone de Beauvoir **4**:48;
  14:67
Samuel Beckett **4**:50
Saul Bellow **25**:80
Heinrich Böll **27**:64
Bruce Chatwin **28**:74
Rhys Davies **23**:141
Leon Edel **29**:174
Max Frisch **14**:183
Ernest K. Gann **23**:166
William Golding **2**:168; **17**:160,
  166
Juan Goytisolo **5**:151; **10**:245
Aldous Huxley **35**:240
Ruth Prawer Jhabvala **29**:261
Patrick Kavanagh **22**:234
Molly Keane **31**:235
Arthur Koestler **15**:309
Mary Lavin **18**:301
John le Carré **15**:326
Compton Mackenzie **18**:313
Norman Mailer **2**:262
Carson McCullers **12**:415
William Maxwell **19**:305
John Mortimer **28**:289
Vladimir Nabokov **6**:356
Flann O'Brien **10**:364
Flannery O'Connor **21**:267
Frank O'Connor **14**:395
John Cowper Powys **15**:435
Gregor von Rezzori **25**:382
Michael Scammell **34**:492
Aleksandr I. Solzhenitsyn
  1:320; **34**:492
Paul Theroux **8**:513
James Thurber **5**:433
William Trevor **14**:536
Henri Troyat **23**:461
John Updike **23**:471
Gore Vidal **8**:529
Evelyn Waugh **27**:475

Procopiow, Norma
Marilyn Hacker **5**:155
Eleanor Lerman **9**:329
Anne Sexton **4**:483

Proffer, Carl R.
Michael Scammell **34**:487
Aleksandr I. Solzhenitsyn
  9:506; **34**:487

Profumo, David
Graham Greene **37**:139

Pronko, Leonard Cabell
Arthur Adamov **25**:12
Jean Anouilh **13**:16
Jean Genet **14**:201
Eugène Ionesco **1**:154

Proteus
Agatha Christie **12**:112
Edna Ferber **18**:151

Prothro, Laurie
May Sarton **14**:482

Prouse, Derek
Elia Kazan **16**:364
Laurence Olivier **20**:237

Prucha, Francis Paul
Vine Deloria, Jr. **21**:113

Pruette, Lorne
Ayn Rand **30**:292

Pryce-Jones, Alan
Michael Ayrton **7**:16
John Betjeman **6**:69
Italo Calvino **5**:98
John le Carré **28**:230
Vladimir Nabokov **1**:246

Pryce-Jones, David
Siegfried Lenz **27**:250

Pryor, Thomas M.
Sally Benson **17**:49

Pryse, Marjorie
Helen Yglesias **7**:558; **22**:493

Przekop, Benjamin Paul John
Richard Matheson **37**:247

Puckett, Harry
T. S. Eliot **10**:167

Puckette, Charles McD.
Julia Peterkin **31**:302
T. S. Stribling **23**:439

Puetz, Manfred
John Barth **9**:72
Thomas Pynchon **6**:434

Pugh, Anthony R.
Alain Robbe-Grillet **4**:450

Pulleine, Tim
Woody Allen **16**:9
Claude Chabrol **16**:184
Carlos Saura **20**:319
Peter Weir **20**:428

Punnett, Spencer
Edwin Newman **14**:378

Purcell, H. D.
George MacDonald Fraser
  7:106

Purcell, J. M.
Carolyn G. Heilbrun **25**:255

Purcell, Patricia
Anne Hébert **29**:227

Purdy, A. W.
Earle Birney **6**:73

Purdy, Al
Bill Bissett **18**:59

Purdy, Strother
Luis Buñuel **16**:133

Purdy, Theodore, Jr.
William Maxwell **19**:304

Purtill, Richard
J.R.R. Tolkien **12**:577

Puterbaugh, Parke
Paul McCartney **35**:291

Putney, Michael
Hunter S. Thompson **17**:504

Puzo, Mario
James Baldwin **17**:34

Pybus, Rodney
Paul Muldoon **32**:320
Christina Stead **32**:409

Pye, Ian
John Lennon **35**:270, 272

Pye, Michael
George Lucas **16**:416

Pym, Christopher
Mary Stewart **35**:389
Julian Symons **14**:522

Pym, John
René Clair **20**:69
John Landis **26**:277

Pyros, J.
Michael McClure **6**:320

Quacinella, Lucy
Lina Wertmüller **16**:596

Quammen, David
Michael Ende **31**:143
Bobbie Ann Mason **28**:272
Bette Pesetsky **28**:357
Leon Rooke **25**:392
Danny Santiago **33**:352
Joy Williams **31**:464

Quance, Robert A.
Miguel Delibes **18**:115

Quant, Leonard
Robert Altman **16**:35

Quart, Barbara Koenig
T. Gertler **34**:52
Norma Klein **30**:243
Cynthia Ozick **28**:354
Bette Pesetsky **28**:359

Quennell, Peter
Robert Graves **6**:210

Quigly, Isabel
Danny Abse **29**:12
Robert Bresson **16**:104
Frank Capra **16**:157
Claude Chabrol **16**:168
Natalia Ginzburg **11**:230
Jean-Luc Godard **20**:130
Pamela Hansford Johnson **1**:160
Noel Streatfeild **21**:411
Elio Vittorini **14**:547
Paul Zindel **26**:474

Quilligan, Maureen
Marion Zimmer Bradley **30**:31

Quinn, Sister Bernetta, O.S.F.
Alan Dugan **2**:121
David Jones **4**:259
Ezra Pound **4**:416; **7**:326
William Stafford **7**:460
Allen Tate **4**:539
Derek Walcott **2**:460
  See also Bernetta (Quinn),
  Sister Mary, O.S.F.

Quinn, James P.
Edward Albee **5**:11

Quinn, Joseph L.
Brigid Brophy **29**:92

Quinn, Mary Ellen
Tish O'Dowd Ezekiel **34**:46

Quinn, Michael
William Golding **17**:164

Quinn, Vincent
H. D. **14**:224

Quinton, Anthony
William Barrett **27**:21

Quirino, Leonard
Tennessee Williams **30**:470

R
David Jones **4**:259
Arthur Koestler **6**:281
Aleksandr I. Solzhenitsyn **4**:506

Raab, Lawrence
Norman Dubie **36**:131

Raban, Jonathan
A. Alvarez **5**:18
Kingsley Amis **8**:11
Beryl Bainbridge **5**:40
John Barth **1**:17
Saul Bellow **1**:32
E. L. Doctorow **11**:141
Stanley Elkin **6**:169
James Fenton **32**:167
Eva Figes **31**:162
Nadine Gordimer **5**:145
Erica Jong **4**:265
David Lodge **36**:270
Mary McCarthy **1**:207
Ian McEwan **13**:369
John McGahern **9**:369
Stanley Middleton **7**:220
Brian Moore **1**:225
Iris Murdoch **4**:369
Vladimir Nabokov **6**:359
Jean Rhys **6**:456
Frank Sargeson **31**:366
Tom Sharpe **36**:400
Richard G. Stern **4**:523
Paul Theroux **28**:425
Hunter S. Thompson **17**:505
William Trevor **7**:476
Angus Wilson **25**:458

Rabassa, Gregory
Ernesto Cardenal **31**:72
Alejo Carpentier **11**:99
Julio Cortázar **15**:147
Gabriel García Márquez **3**:180;
  27:148
João Guimarães Rosa **23**:353
Gilbert Sorrentino **22**:392
Mario Vargas Llosa **15**:551

Rabinovitz, Rubin
Kingsley Amis **5**:20
Samuel Beckett **6**:40, 41
Norman Mailer **5**:267
Iris Murdoch **1**:235; **2**:297
C. P. Snow **4**:500
Angus Wilson **5**:512

Critic Index

Rabinowitz, Dorothy
Beryl Bainbridge **8**:36
Elliott Baker **8**:40
Giorgio Bassani **9**:77
Maeve Brennan **5**:72
Anthony Burgess **5**:88
Hortense Calisher **4**:87; **8**:124
John Cheever **3**:107
Laurie Colwin **23**:128
Lois Gould **4**:201
Peter Handke **5**:165
Mark Helprin **7**:152
Dan Jacobson **4**:254
Ruth Prawer Jhabvala **4**:256,
    257; **8**:311
Robert Kotlowitz **4**:275
Mary Lavin **4**:281
Doris Lessing **2**:241
Meyer Levin **7**:205
Larry McMurtry **11**:371
Brian Moore **7**:237
Wright Morris **3**:344
Edna O'Brien **5**:312
John O'Hara **6**:384
Grace Paley **4**:392
S. J. Perelman **5**:337
Philip Roth **3**:437
Anne Sexton **10**:468
John Updike **2**:445
Gore Vidal **4**:553
Dan Wakefield **7**:503
Joseph Wambaugh **3**:509
Harriet Waugh **6**:560
Arnold Wesker **5**:482

Rabinowitz, Morris
James D. Forman **21**:121

Rabkin, David
Alex La Guma **19**:273

Rabkin, Eric S.
Donald Barthelme **13**:58
Robert A. Heinlein **26**:166
Frederik Pohl **18**:410

Rabkin, Gerald
Paul Green **25**:198
Derek Walcott **9**:556

Rachewiltz, Boris de
Ezra Pound **7**:331

Rachleff, Owen S.
Woody Allen **16**:9

Rachlis, Kit
Jackson Browne **21**:41
Elvis Costello **21**:70, 72
Bob Seger **35**:381
Neil Young **17**:582

Rackham, Jeff
John Fowles **2**:138

Radcliff-Umstead, Douglas
Alberto Moravia **11**:381

Rader, Dotson
Hubert Selby, Jr. **4**:481
Yevgeny Yevtushenko **3**:547

Radford, C. B.
Simone de Beauvoir **4**:45, 46

Radhuber, S. G.
Stanley Plumly **33**:310

Radin, Victoria
Sara Davidson **9**:175

Radke, Judith J.
Pierre Gascar **11**:221

Radley, Philippe
Andrei Voznesensky **15**:554

Radner, Rebecca
Gail Godwin **31**:198
Lenora Mattingly Weber **12**:635

Radowsky, Colby
Laurence Yep **35**:472

Radtke, Karen K.
C. S. Adler **35**:15

Radu, Kenneth
Christie Harris **12**:264

Rae, Bruce
John R. Tunis **12**:593

Rae, Simon
Donald Davie **31**:119

Raeburn, John
Frank Capra **16**:163

Rafalko, Robert
Eric Ambler **9**:22

Rafalko, Robert J.
Philip K. Dick **10**:138

Raff, Emanuel
Henry Gregor Felsen **17**:124

Raffel, Burton
Czesław Miłosz **31**:259
J.R.R. Tolkien **1**:337
Louis Zukofsky **11**:580

Raftery, Gerald
Ayn Rand **30**:300

Ragusa, Olga
Italo Calvino **22**:91
Alberto Moravia **2**:292
Pier Paolo Pasolini **37**:341

Rahv, Betty T.
Albert Camus **9**:148
Alain Robbe-Grillet **8**:451
Nathalie Sarraute **8**:469
Jean-Paul Sartre **7**:395

Rahv, Philip
Louis Aragon **22**:34
Saul Bellow **2**:50
Richard Brautigan **12**:57
Leon Edel **29**:171
T. S. Eliot **2**:126
Leslie A. Fiedler **24**:195
Ernest Hemingway **3**:231
Arthur Koestler **33**:232
F. R. Leavis **24**:304
Arthur Miller **2**:278
Delmore Schwartz **10**:462
Aleksandr I. Solzhenitsyn
    2:411; **26**:422

Raidy, William A.
Sam Shepard **17**:449

Raine, Craig
James Fenton **32**:165
Geoffrey Hill **18**:237
Ted Hughes **14**:272
Harold Pinter **6**:419
Anne Stevenson **33**:380

Ted Walker **13**:566

Raine, Kathleen
Brewster Ghiselin **23**:170
David Jones **2**:216; **7**:191
St.-John Perse **4**:399
Herbert Read **4**:440

Rainer, Dachine
Rebecca West **7**:525

Raines, Charles A.
Woody Guthrie **35**:185

Raizada, Harish
R. K. Narayan **28**:294

Rama Rau, Santha
Khushwant Singh **11**:504

Rambali, Paul
Elvis Costello **21**:67

Rampersad, Arnold
Claude Brown **30**:40
Alex Haley **12**:247

Ramras-Rauch, Gila
S. Y. Agnon **4**:14
Yehuda Amichai **22**:32
Yoram Kaniuk **19**:241

Ramsey, Jarold
Leslie Marmon Silko **23**:411

Ramsey, Nancy
Margaret Atwood **25**:70

Ramsey, Paul
Robert Bly **5**:62
Edgar Bowers **9**:121
Hayden Carruth **10**:100
Norman Dubie **36**:130
Larry Eigner **9**:181
John Hollander **14**:265
Eleanor Lerman **9**:328
W. S. Merwin **5**:286
N. Scott Momaday **19**:318
Michael Mott **15**:380
Howard Nemerov **9**:394
Linda Pastan **27**:369
Richard Wilbur **14**:577

Ramsey, R. H.
Robert Kroetsch **23**:271

Ramsey, Roger
Friedrich Dürrenmatt **4**:140
Pär Lagerkvist **10**:311

Ramsey, S. A.
Randolph Stow **23**:438

Ranbom, Sheppard J.
Philip Roth **15**:453

Rand, Richard A.
John Hollander **5**:187

Randall, Dudley
Robert Hayden **5**:168
Audre Lorde **18**:307
Margaret Walker **6**:554

Randall, Francis B.
Ch'ien Chung-shu **22**:105
Yevgeny Yevtushenko **26**:468

Randall, Julia
Howard Nemerov **2**:308
Gabrielle Roy **10**:441

Randall, Margaret
Judith Johnson Sherwin **15**:479

Randall-Tsuruta, Dorothy
Joyce Carol Thomas **35**:406

Ranger, Terence
David Caute **29**:122

Ranjbaran, Esmaeel
Ahmad Shamlu **10**:469

Rank, Hugh
Walter M. Miller, Jr. **30**:257
Edwin O'Connor **14**:390

Ranly, Ernest W.
Kurt Vonnegut, Jr. **2**:453

Ransom, John Crowe
Kenneth Burke **24**:122
Donald Davidson **13**:167
T. S. Eliot **24**:165
William Empson **33**:138
Randall Jarrell **1**:159
Marianne Moore **19**:337
I. A. Richards **24**:382, 385
Allen Tate **4**:535
Yvor Winters **32**:454

Ransom, W. M.
Galway Kinnell **3**:268

Rao, K. B.
Salman Rushdie **23**:367

Rao, K. S. Narayana
R. K. Narayan **28**:299

Raper, Tod
Rod Serling **30**:354

Raphael, Frederic
James Baldwin **17**:41
Michael Frayn **7**:107
Jakov Lind **4**:293

Raphael, Isabel
David Caute **29**:124

Rapisarda, Martin
David Lodge **36**:276

Rascoe, Judith
Laurie Colwin **5**:107
John Gregory Dunne **28**:123
Dick Francis **22**:150

Rasi, Humberto M.
Jorge Luis Borges **2**:74

Raskin, A. H.
Milton Meltzer **26**:298

Rasmussen, Douglas B.
Ayn Rand **30**:304

Raspa, Anthony
Anne Hébert **29**:231

Rasso, Pamela S.
William Heyen **13**:284

Rasula, Jed
Robert White **36**:120

Ratcliff, Michael
Michael Frayn **31**:193
Thomas Keneally **14**:303

Rathbone, Richard
Breyten Breytenbach **23**:86

Rathburn, Norma
Margot Benary-Isbert **12**:32

Ratiner, Steven
Marvin Bell **31**:51

Ratner, Marc L.
John Hawkes **14**:237
William Styron **5**:418

Ratner, Rochelle
Yehuda Amichai **22**:33
Rosellen Brown **32**:66
Clayton Eshleman **7**:100
Carolyn Forché **25**:171
Phillip Lopate **29**:302
Sharon Olds **32**:345
Susan Fromberg Schaeffer
22:370
Patti Smith **12**:541

Rave, Eugene S.
Barbara Corcoran **17**:78

Raven, Simon
Alvah Bessie **23**:60
David Caute **29**:108
Isabel Colegate **36**:109
Ian Fleming **30**:133
Dan Jacobson **14**:289
John Knowles **26**:245
Anthony Powell **31**:313

Ravenscroft, Arthur
Chinua Achebe **11**:1
Bessie Head **25**:233
Wole Soyinka **36**:417

Rawley, James
James Baldwin **15**:43
Donald Barthelme **13**:63

Rawlins, Jack P.
John W. Campbell **32**:81

Rawson, Judy
Dino Buzzati **36**:95

Ray, David
E. E. Cummings **12**:151

Ray, Robert
James Baldwin **2**:34
J.I.M. Stewart **7**:466

Ray, Sheila G.
E. M. Almedingen **12**:7

Rayme, Anne C.
Larry Kettelkamp **12**:307

Raymond, John
Noël Coward **29**:133
Daphne du Maurier **11**:163
Pamela Hansford Johnson
27:216
Françoise Sagan **17**:417
Georges Simenon **3**:449

Raynor, Henry
Laurence Olivier **20**:236

Raynor, Vivien
Evan S. Connell, Jr. **6**:115
Iris Murdoch **3**:348
Edna O'Brien **3**:364

Rayns, Tony
Shirley Clarke **16**:219
Elvis Costello **21**:71
Maya Deren **16**:253
Rainer Werner Fassbinder
20:107, 108
Werner Herzog **16**:321, 322
Richard O'Brien **17**:323
Nagisa Oshima **20**:251

Raysor, Thomas M.
M. H. Abrams **24**:11

Rea, Dorothy
Auberon Waugh **7**:514

Read, Esther H.
Melvin Berger **12**:40

Read, Forrest, Jr.
Ezra Pound **7**:327

Read, Herbert
Georg Lukács **24**:317
Allen Tate **4**:535

Read, Malcolm
Siegfried Lenz **27**:252

Read, S. E.
Robertson Davies **13**:172

Reagan, Dale
Robert Kroetsch **23**:273

Real, Jere
Noël Coward **29**:135
Peter Shaffer **5**:388

Reaney, James
Jay Macpherson **14**:345

Reardon, Betty S.
James D. Forman **21**:122
Jessamyn West **17**:554

Rebay, Luciano
Alberto Moravia **7**:239

Rebovich, David Paul
Carl Sagan **30**:342

Rechnitz, Robert M.
Carson McCullers **1**:209

Rechy, John
Peter Matthiessen **32**:289
William McPherson **34**:87

Reck, Rima Drell
Albert Camus **32**:86
Louis-Ferdinand Céline **7**:44
Françoise Mallet-Joris **11**:355

Reck, Tom S.
James M. Cain **28**:50

Redding, Saunders
John Ehle **27**:105
Shirley Ann Grau **4**:208
Ezekiel Mphahlele **25**:333
Richard Wright **1**:377

Redfern, W. D.
Jean Giono **4**:186

Redman, Ben Ray
Vera Brittain **23**:91
Thomas B. Costain **30**:93
C. S. Forester **35**:160, 163
Erich Maria Remarque **21**:328
Nevil Shute **30**:364

Dalton Trumbo **19**:444
Frank Tuohy **37**:425
Marguerite Yourcenar **19**:482

Redman, Eric
André Brink **18**:69

Redmon, Anne
Judy Blume **12**:45

Redmond, Eugene B.
Clarence Major **19**:293

Reed, Bill
Frank Zappa **17**:586

Reed, Diana
J. G. Ballard **6**:28
John Wyndham **19**:476

Reed, Henry
Rhys Davies **23**:142
Mary Renault **17**:391

Reed, Ishmael
Claude Brown **30**:38
Chester Himes **2**:195
John Edgar Wideman **36**:457

Reed, J. D.
Jim Harrison **33**:196
Richard F. Hugo **32**:235
Mark Stevens **34**:112

Reed, John
Arthur Hailey **5**:156
Ngugi Wa Thiong'o **13**:583

Reed, John R.
William Dickey **3**:127
D. J. Enright **4**:155
William Heyen **18**:233
Daniel Hoffman **6**:243
John Hollander **8**:302
Richard Howard **7**:169; **10**:276
Judith Leet **11**:323
James Merrill **8**:388
Charles Reznikoff **9**:450
David Wagoner **3**:508
Philip Whalen **6**:566

Reed, Peter J.
Kurt Vonnegut, Jr. **3**:495;
12:626

Reed, Rex
Laura Nyro **17**:313
Gordon Parks **16**:460
Stephen Sondheim **30**:385
Tennessee Williams **2**:464

Reedy, Gerard
C. S. Lewis **6**:308
Walker Percy **18**:402

Reedy, Gerard C.
Richard Price **12**:490

Rees, David
Judy Blume **30**:21
Rhys Davies **23**:147
C. S. Forester **35**:171
Rosa Guy **26**:145
Piers Paul Read **25**:375
Paul Zindel **26**:478

Rees, David L.
Philippa Pearce **21**:285
Otfried Preussler **17**:375
Colin Thiele **17**:494

Rees, Goronwy
Rhys Davies **23**:146
Richard Hughes **11**:278
Erich Maria Remarque **21**:328

Rees, Samuel
David Jones **13**:309

Reeve, Benjamin
Grace Paley **4**:393

Reeve, F. D.
Joseph Brodsky **6**:98
Aleksandr I. Solzhenitsyn **1**:319
Alexander Zinoviev **19**:489

Regan, Robert Alton
John Updike **5**:454

Regier, W. G.
W. H. Auden **3**:22
Michael Benedikt **4**:54
Kenneth O. Hanson **13**:263
Howard Moss **14**:375
Howard Nemerov **9**:395
Pablo Neruda **5**:305
Francis Ponge **6**:423

Rehder, Jesse
Randolph Stow **23**:432

Rehmus, E. E.
Gordon Vorster **34**:123

Reibetanz, John
Philip Larkin **8**:334

Reichek, Morton A.
Chaim Grade **10**:249

Reid, Alastair
Jorge Luis Borges **2**:73
Hayden Carruth **18**:89
Bruce Chatwin **28**:71
Pablo Neruda **5**:302
John Updike **13**:561

Reid, Alfred S.
Karl Shapiro **15**:476

Reid, B. L.
V. S. Pritchett **13**:465

Reid, Beryl
Barbara Corcoran **17**:74
Lee Kingman **17**:246
Sonia Levitin **17**:264

Reid, Christopher
Ted Hughes **14**:272
Michael Ondaatje **29**:343

Reid, David
Leonard Michaels **25**:318

Reid, Ian
Frank Sargeson **31**:365, 366

Reigo, Ants
A. W. Purdy **14**:434

Reilly, Alayne P.
Yevgeny Yevtushenko **26**:463

Reilly, John H.
Arthur Adamov **25**:19

Reilly, John M.
Chester Himes **18**:245
B. Traven **11**:538

Critic Index

Reilly, Peter
Joan Armatrading **17**:10
Jimmy Cliff **21**:61
Ray Davies **21**:101
Neil Diamond **30**:113
Janis Ian **21**:184, 185, 186, 187, 188
Billy Joel **26**:213, 214, 215, 216, 217, 221
Kris Kristofferson **26**:269
Paul McCartney **35**:288
Joni Mitchell **12**:436
Monty Python **21**:227
Lou Reed **21**:312
Smokey Robinson **21**:345, 346
Carly Simon **26**:410, 411, 412, 413
Paul Simon **17**:460
Stephen Sondheim **30**:389, 399
Frank Zappa **17**:592

Reilly, Robert J.
C. S. Lewis **3**:298
J.R.R. Tolkien **1**:337; **3**:477

Reingold, Stephen C.
Carl Sagan **30**:335

Reinhardt, Max
Charles Chaplin **16**:187

Reisz, Karel
Vittorio De Sica **20**:86
Elia Kazan **16**:361

Reitberger, Reinhold
Chares M. Schulz **12**:528

Reiter, Seymour
Sean O'Casey **5**:319

Reitman, David
Frank Zappa **17**:588

Reitt, Barbara B.
John Steinbeck **21**:392

Remini, Robert V.
Gore Vidal **8**:526

Remnick, David
Truman Capote **34**:322

Renault, Mary
William Golding **17**:161

Rendle, Adrian
Aidan Chambers **35**:97
Sam Shepard **17**:433
Tom Stoppard **3**:470

Renek, Morris
Erskine Caldwell **8**:123

Renner, Charlotte
John Barth **27**:29

Rennert, Maggie
Mary Stewart **35**:390

Rennie, Neil
Peter Porter **33**:319
Robin Skelton **13**:507

Renoir, Jean
Charles Chaplin **16**:194

Renshaw, Robert
J.R.R. Tolkien **1**:336

Resnik, Henry S.
Amiri Baraka **33**:54
Jonathan Baumbach **23**:54
Nora Ephron **17**:110
Richard Fariña **9**:195
John Irving **13**:292
William Melvin Kelley **22**:248
Wilfrid Sheed **2**:392
J.R.R. Tolkien **12**:566

Restak, Richard
Carl Sagan **30**:333

Restivo, Angelo
Rudolfo A. Anaya **23**:26

Reuss, Richard A.
Woody Guthrie **35**:189

Rexine, John E.
Vassilis Vassilikos **4**:552

Rexroth, Kenneth
Philip Booth **23**:74
Robert Creeley **4**:116
Robert Duncan **1**:82; **2**:123
T. S. Eliot **2**:127
William Everson **1**:96; **14**:162
Leslie A. Fiedler **24**:197
Carolyn Forché **25**:169
Allen Ginsberg **2**:164; **3**:193, 194
William Golding **3**:196
Paul Goodman **2**:169
Robinson Jeffers **2**:211
Pär Lagerkvist **13**:334
Denise Levertov **1**:175; **2**:243; **3**:292
Thomas McGrath **28**:276
W. S. Merwin **2**:278; **3**:338
Henry Miller **1**:219
Marianne Moore **2**:292
Kenneth Patchen **2**:332
Laura Riding **3**:432
Muriel Rukeyser **6**:478; **27**:407, 414
Carl Sandburg **1**:300; **4**:463
Isaac Bashevis Singer **3**:452
Edith Sitwell **2**:403
Gary Snyder **2**:407
Jean Toomer **4**:548
Philip Whalen **6**:565
William Carlos Williams **1**:371; **2**:469
Yvor Winters **4**:594

Reynal, Eugene
Margery Allingham **19**:11

Reynolds, Gary K.
Anne McCaffrey **17**:284

Reynolds, Horace
August Derleth **31**:134
Woody Guthrie **35**:182
Olivia Manning **19**:299

Reynolds, Quentin
Erich Maria Remarque **21**:330

Reynolds, R. C.
Larry McMurtry **7**:215

Reynolds, Siân
Simone de Beauvoir **31**:38

Reynolds, Stanley
Iain Banks **34**:29
José Donoso **32**:161
Frederick Exley **11**:186
Wilson Harris **25**:209
Anna Kavan **5**:205
Yashar Kemal **29**:265
William Kennedy **28**:204
Violette Leduc **22**:262
John Mortimer **28**:287
Chaim Potok **26**:369
Tom Sharpe **36**:399, 402
Paul Theroux **28**:428
Robert Penn Warren **4**:582
A. N. Wilson **33**:454
Tom Wolfe **35**:465

Rezos, Ray
Kris Kristofferson **26**:266

Rheuban, Joyce
Josef von Sternberg **20**:375

Rhoads, Kenneth W.
William Saroyan **10**:455

Rhode, Eric
James Baldwin **17**:40
Robert Bresson **16**:105, 113
Vittorio De Sica **20**:89
Satyajit Ray **16**:477, 479
François Truffaut **20**:381

Rhodes, H. Winston
Frank Sargeson **31**:361, 366, 367

Rhodes, Joseph, Jr.
W.E.B. Du Bois **2**:120

Rhodes, Richard
Chester Himes **2**:194
MacKinlay Kantor **7**:196
Paule Marshall **27**:310
Michael Shaara **15**:474
Wilfrid Sheed **2**:394

Riasanovsky, Nicholas N.
Henri Troyat **23**:462

Ribalow, Harold U.
Lloyd Alexander **35**:22
Meyer Levin **7**:205
Henry Roth **6**:471
Arnold Wesker **3**:518

Ribalow, Menachem
S. Y. Agnon **4**:10

Ribe, Neil
C. S. Lewis **27**:266

Rice, Edward
Thomas Merton **3**:337

Rice, Elmer
Howard Fast **23**:155

Rice, Jennings
Walter D. Edmonds **35**:153

Rice, Julian C.
Ingmar Bergman **16**:76
LeRoi Jones **1**:163
Martin Scorsese **20**:327

Rice, Susan
Gordon Parks **16**:457

Rich, Adrienne
Elizabeth Bishop **32**:38
Hayden Carruth **18**:87
Jean Garrigue **8**:239
Paul Goodman **2**:170
Robert Lowell **3**:304
Robin Morgan **2**:294
Adrienne Rich **36**:370
Eleanor Ross Taylor **5**:425

Rich, Alan
Alan Ayckbourn **8**:34
Enid Bagnold **25**:79
Jules Feiffer **8**:216
Jack Gelber **14**:194
Simon Gray **9**:241
John Guare **8**:253
Albert Innaurato **21**:191, 193
Preston Jones **10**:297
Stephen Sondheim **30**:396
Tom Stoppard **8**:501, 503
Elizabeth Swados **12**:558
Tennessee Williams **7**:545
Lanford Wilson **7**:549

Rich, Frank
Caryl Churchill **31**:85, 87, 89
Christopher Durang **27**:90
Harvey Fierstein **33**:156
Dario Fo **32**:175
Michael Frayn **31**:192
Athol Fugard **25**:177
Charles Fuller **25**:181
Amlin Gray **29**:200
Simon Gray **36**:208
John Guare **29**:205, 208
David Hare **29**:217
Ronald Harwood **32**:227
Albert Innaurato **21**:198
Jean Kerr **22**:258
Arthur Kopit **33**:252
Hugh Leonard **19**:284
David Mamet **34**:220
Garry Marshall **17**:276, 278
William Mastrosimone **36**:289
Peter Nichols **36**:330
Marsha Norman **28**:319
David Rabe **33**:345
Ntozake Shange **25**:400
Sam Shepard **34**:267
Neil Simon **31**:400, 401
Stephen Sondheim **30**:400, 402
Tom Stoppard **34**:274, 275
C. P. Taylor **27**:445
Fay Weldon **36**:444
Hugh Whitemore **37**:447
Lanford Wilson **36**:459, 461, 464

Rich, Nancy B.
Carson McCullers **10**:336

Richards, I. A.
William Empson **33**:149
E. M. Forster **13**:215

Richards, Jeffrey
Frank Capra **16**:160

Richards, Lewis A.
William Faulkner **3**:153

Richards, Marily
Vine Deloria, Jr. **21**:114**

Richardson, D. E.
Wendell Berry 27:35
Catharine Savage Brosman
9:135
Donald Davie 31:112

Richardson, H. Edward
Jesse Stuart 34:374

Richardson, Jack
John Barth 3:39
Saul Bellow 8:71
Brian Clark 29:128
Eldridge Cleaver 30:62
T. S. Eliot 9:182
Trevor Griffiths 13:257
Jack Kerouac 2:227
Arthur Miller 2:280
Vladimir Nabokov 2:300
Peter Shaffer 5:389
Tom Stoppard 4:527
Megan Terry 19:438
Thornton Wilder 35:445

Richardson, Joanna
François Sagan 36:382

Richardson, Maurice
Vasily Aksenov 22:25
Brigid Brophy 29:92
Bruce Chatwin 28:70
Isabel Colegate 36:108
John Knowles 26:246
David Lodge 36:266
Randolph Stow 23:432
Glendon Swarthout 35:400
J.R.R. Tolkien 12:565
Frank Tuohy 37:426
T. H. White 30:444

Richardson, Tony
Luis Buñuel 16:128
John Huston 20:163
Akira Kurosawa 16:395
Jean Renoir 20:288
Josef von Sternberg 20:373
Orson Welles 20:433

Richart, Bette
Phyllis McGinley 14:364

Richie, Donald
Kon Ichikawa 20:177
Donald Keene 34:569
Akira Kurosawa 16:396, 398
Yukio Mishima 2:288; 4:357
Nagisa Oshima 20:246
Yasujiro Ozu 16:450

Richie, Fimie
Luisa Valenzuela 31:437

Richie, Mary
Penelope Mortimer 5:300

Richler, Mordecai
Daniel Fuchs 22:156
Joseph Heller 36:228
Ken Kesey 3:267
Bernard Malamud 2:267
Mordecai Richler 18:458
Jerome Siegel and Joe Shuster
21:361
Isaac Bashevis Singer 15:508
Alexander Theroux 2:433
Paul Theroux 28:425

Richman, Michele H.
Georges Bataille 29:49

Richman, Robert
John Ashbery 25:57
John Gardner 18:180

Richman, Sidney
Bernard Malamud 1:198

Richmond, Al
Alvah Bessie 23:60

Richmond, Jane
E. L. Doctorow 6:131
Thomas McGuane 3:329

Richmond, Velma Bourgeois
Muriel Spark 3:464

Richter, David H.
Jerzy Kosinski 6:283

Richter, Frederick
Kenzaburō Ōe 10:373

Rickey, Carrie
Sidney Poitier 26:361

Ricks, Christopher
Peter Ackroyd 34:390
Giorgio Bassani 9:75
Samuel Beckett 2:48
Harold Bloom 24:80
Ronald Bush 34:526
Charles Causley 7:41
Robert Creeley 2:108
Donald Davie 31:109, 121
Leon Edel 29:173
T. S. Eliot 34:390, 526
William Empson 34:541
William Golding 17:169
Nadine Gordimer 7:131
Marilyn Hacker 5:155
Geoffrey H. Hartman 27:178
Anthony Hecht 19:207
Geoffrey Hill 8:293
Richard Howard 7:167
Galway Kinnell 5:217
David Lodge 36:266
Robert Lowell 1:181; 9:335
Louis MacNeice 1:186
Marshall McLuhan 37:258
Reynolds Price 6:423
Christina Stead 8:499
Peter Taylor 18:524
John Updike 1:346
Robert Penn Warren 6:556
Patrick White 4:586

Ricou, L. R.
Miriam Waddington 28:438

Ricou, Laurence
Jack Hodgins 23:230
Robert Kroetsch 23:270

Ricou, Laurie
Andrew Suknaski 19:434

Riddel, Joseph N.
C. Day Lewis 10:125
Jacques Derrida 24:146
T. S. Eliot 13:195
Geoffrey H. Hartman 27:179

Rideout, Walter B.
John Dos Passos 4:131
Howard Fast 23:157
Randall Jarrell 2:207
Norman Mailer 4:318
Henry Roth 2:377
Upton Sinclair 11:497

Ridge, Lola
Frank Swinnerton 31:421

Ridington, Edith Farr
Taylor Caldwell 28:65

Ridley, Clifford A.
Neil Simon 31:395
Julian Symons 2:426

Ridolfino, Carole
Jean Craighead George 35:177

Riefenstahl, Leni
Leni Riefenstahl 16:521

Rieff, David
Anthony Burgess 13:124
Ilya Ehrenburg 18:138

Riegel, Richard
Jim Carroll 35:79
The Clash 30:43

Riegelhaupt, Joyce F.
Darcy Ribeiro 34:104

Riemer, Jack
Ernesto Cardenal 31:70
Chaim Potok 14:430
Elie Wiesel 11:570; 37:451,
457

Riera, Emilio G.
Luis Buñuel 16:130

Ries, Frank W. D.
Jean Cocteau 15:134

Ries, Lawrence R.
William Golding 10:239
Ted Hughes 9:283
John Osborne 11:424
Anthony Powell 9:439
Alan Sillitoe 10:476
John Wain 11:561

Riesman, David
Margaret Mead 37:273

Riesman, Paul
Carlos Castaneda 12:87

Riggan, William
John Updike 34:291

Righter, William
André Malraux 4:329

Righton, Barbara
Peter Straub 28:411

Riley, Brooks
Lina Wertmüller 16:593

Riley, Clayton
Charles Gordone 1:124
Melvin Van Peebles 20:412

Riley, Craig
John Gardner 34:550

Riley, Jocelyn
Cynthia Propper Seton 27:428

Riley, Peter
Jack Spicer 18:512

Rimanelli, Giose
Alberto Moravia 18:343

Rimer, J. Thomas
Shusaku Endo 19:160
Masuji Ibuse 22:227
Yasunari Kawabata 18:283

Rimland, Ingrid
Denise Levertov 28:243

Rimmon-Kenan, Shlomith
Jorge Luis Borges 19:54

Rinear, David L.
Arthur Kopit 18:289

Ringel, Fred J.
Vera Brittain 23:88

Ringel, Harry
Alfred Hitchcock 16:352

Ringer, Agnes C.
John Knowles 26:263

Ringrose, Christopher Xerxes
Ralph Gustafson 36:214

Rinsler, Norma
Louis Aragon 22:40

Rinzler, Alan
Bob Dylan 12:198

Rinzler, Carol Eisen
Judith Rossner 6:469
Fay Weldon 36:449

Ripley, John
Michel Tremblay 29:419

Ripley, Josephine
Frank B. Gilbreth, Jr. and
Ernestine Gilbreth Carey
17:155

Risdon, Ann
T. S. Eliot 9:190

Risk, Mirna
Primo Levi 37:223

Ritchie, Barbara
Milton Meltzer 26:301

Ritholz, Robert E.A.P.
Martin Mull 17:299

Ritter, Jess
Kurt Vonnegut, Jr. 4:563

Ritter, Karen
Virginia Hamilton 26:152
Lee Kingman 17:247
Norma Fox Mazer 26:294

Ritterman, Pamela
Richard Brautigan 12:57

Ritvo, Harriet
Judith Rossner 29:354

Riva, Raymond T.
Samuel Beckett 1:25

Rivas, Daniel E.
Romain Gary 25:191

Rivera, Francisco
José Donoso 4:129

Rivers, Cheryl
Susan Cheever **18**:102

Rivers, Elias L.
G. Cabrera Infante **25**:102

Rivett, Kenneth
Arthur Koestler **33**:233

Rizza, Peggy
Elizabeth Bishop **4**:66

Rizzardi, Alfredo
Allen Tate **4**:538

Robbe-Grillet, Alain
Samuel Beckett **10**:25

Robbins, Henry
Stanley Elkin **14**:158

Robbins, Ira A.
David Bowie **17**:66
The Clash **30**:51
Elvis Costello **21**:72, 74, 75

Robbins, Jack Alan
Louis Auchincloss **4**:28
Herbert Gold **4**:189
Bernard Malamud **1**:200
Flannery O'Connor **1**:258

Roberts, Cecil
W. Somerset Maugham **11**:370

Roberts, David
R. V. Cassill **4**:94; **23**:106
Carl Sagan **30**:338

Roberts, John
Zora Neale Hurston **30**:224

Roberts, Mark
Wayne C. Booth **24**:86

Roberts, Neil
Ted Hughes **37**:175

Roberts, Paul
William Mitchell **25**:327

Roberts, Philip
Edward Bond **23**:67

Roberts, R. Ellis
Pamela Hansford Johnson **27**:215

Roberts, Sheila
Breyten Breytenbach **23**:86
J. M. Coetzee **23**:123
Athol Fugard **25**:176

Roberts, Thomas J.
Italo Calvino **8**:129

Robertson, Anthony
Hugh Hood **28**:188

Robertson, Deborah G.
Kathryn Kramer **34**:74

Robertson, P.
Otfried Preussler **17**:375

Robertson, R. T.
Mulk Raj Anand **23**:20

Robins, Corinne
Leonard Michaels **25**:319

Robins, Dave
Michael Frayn **31**:191

Robins, Wayne
Joni Mitchell **12**:438
Neil Young **17**:574

Robinson, Beryl
Virginia Hamilton **26**:150
Milton Meltzer **26**:301
Andre Norton **12**:462
Robert Newton Peck **17**:337,
340
Mary Rodgers **12**:494
Ann Schlee **35**:371

Robinson, Christopher
Odysseus Elytis **15**:219

Robinson, David
Robert Altman **16**:19
Luis Buñuel **16**:130
Orson Welles **20**:434

Robinson, Debbie
Roy A. Gallant **17**:130

Robinson, Harlow
Czesław Miłosz **31**:259

Robinson, Henry Morton
T. H. White **30**:443

Robinson, Hubbell
Gordon Parks **16**:459

Robinson, James K.
Robert Francis **15**:239
John Hollander **14**:263
David Ignatow **14**:275
Archibald MacLeish **14**:338
Josephine Miles **14**:370
David Wagoner **15**:559

Robinson, Janice S.
H. D. **31**:212

Robinson, Jill
Alice Adams **6**:2
Anna Kavan **5**:206
Fran Lebowitz **11**:322
Larry McMurtry **11**:371

Robinson, Louie
Norman Lear **12**:332

Robinson, Paul
Gay Talese **37**:394

Robinson, Robert
Saul Bellow **6**:54

Robinson, Spider
Frank Herbert **23**:223
Frederik Pohl **18**:413
Roger Zelazny **21**:479

Robinson, Ted
Ogden Nash **23**:317

Robinson, W. R.
George Garrett **3**:190

Robson, Jeremy
W. H. Auden **4**:33
Leonard Cohen **3**:110

Robson, W. W.
Yvor Winters **32**:464, 465

Rochman, Hazel
Lloyd Alexander **35**:27
Robert Cormier **30**:90
Walter Dean Myers **35**:297,
298
Ouida Sebestyen **30**:350
Joyce Carol Thomas **35**:405

Rockett, W. H.
George Ryga **14**:473

Rockman, Arnold
Marshall McLuhan **37**:264

Rocks, James E.
T. S. Stribling **23**:448

Rockwell, John
Ray Davies **21**:106
Peter Handke **5**:164
Gerome Ragni and James Rado
17:384
Lou Reed **21**:306
Patti Smith **12**:537
Stephen Sondheim **30**:401
Bruce Springsteen **17**:478
Stevie Wonder **12**:661

Rodgers, Audrey T.
T. S. Eliot **6**:162, 166

Rodgers, Bernard F., Jr.
Philip Roth **22**:350

Rodman, Selden
William F. Buckley, Jr. **37**:56
Carlos Fuentes **10**:207
Gabriel García Márquez **27**:157
John Gardner **28**:166
Carl Sandburg **35**:351
Mario Vargas Llosa **31**:447
Derek Walcott **14**:551

Rodrigues, Eusebio L.
Saul Bellow **3**:56; **6**:52

Rodríguez-Monegal, Emir
Adolfo Bioy Casares **13**:84
Jorge Luis Borges **2**:72; **3**:80
Gabriel García Márquez **3**:183
Juan Carlos Onetti **7**:276, 279

Rodriguez-Peralta, Phyllis
José María Arguedas **10**:8

Rodway, Allan
Samuel Beckett **4**:51
Tom Stoppard **8**:502

Roe, Shirley
Roy A. Gallant **17**:131

Roethke, Theodore
Ben Belitt **22**:48

Roffman, Rosaly DeMaios
Donald Keene **34**:569

Rogan, Helen
Maeve Brennan **5**:73
John Gardner **5**:134
Evan Hunter **31**:226
Jennifer Johnston **7**:186
Irving Wallace **7**:510

Rogers, D.
I. A. Richards **14**:455

Rogers, Deborah C.
J.R.R. Tolkien **12**:584

Rogers, Del Marie
Reynolds Price **6**:423

Rogers, Ivor A.
Robert Heinlein **14**:251

Rogers, John Williams
Bruce Lancaster **36**:243

Rogers, Linda
Margaret Atwood **4**:27
Paulette Jiles **13**:304
Susan Musgrave **13**:400
Angus Wilson **5**:515

Rogers, Michael
Peter Benchley **4**:54
Richard Brautigan **12**:70
Bob Dylan **12**:187
John Gardner **3**:188
Richard Price **12**:489
Piers Paul Read **4**:445

Rogers, Norma
Alice Childress **12**:106

Rogers, Pat
Daphne du Maurier **11**:163
A. N. Wilson **33**:457

Rogers, Philip
Chinua Achebe **11**:3

Rogers, Thomas
R. V. Cassill **23**:107
Vladimir Nabokov **6**:358
Tom Stoppard **1**:328

Rogers, Timothy
Alan Garner **17**:135

Rogers, W. G.
Pearl S. Buck **7**:33
James Clavell **25**:125
Allen Drury **37**:102, 105
C. S. Forester **35**:172
Joanne Greenberg **7**:134
Irwin Shaw **23**:398

Rogge, Whitney
Cecil Bødker **21**:13

Roggersdorf, Wilhelm
Erich von Däniken **30**:422

Roginski, Ed
Peter Weir **20**:426

Rogoff, Gordon
David Mamet **9**:361

Rogoff, Leonard
Lee Smith **25**:406

Rogow, Roberta
William Kotzwinkle **35**:257

Rohlehr, Gordon
V. S. Naipaul **4**:372

Rohmann, Gloria P.
Cynthia Voigt **30**:420

Rohmer, Eric
Ingmar Bergman **16**:45
Alfred Hitchcock **16**:357

Rohter, Larry
Carlos Fuentes **8**:223
Yashar Kemal **14**:300

Roiphe, Anne
Earl Hamner, Jr. **12**:259

Rolens, Linda
Margaret Atwood **25**:70

Rollins, Ronald G.
Sean O'Casey **9**:409

Rolo, Charles
Arthur Koestler **33**:234

Rolo, Charles J.
Marcel Aymé **11**:21
Brigid Brophy **29**:91
William Gaddis **19**:185
Romain Gary **25**:185
Martha Gellhorn **14**:195
Aldous Huxley **35**:235
Pär Lagerkvist **7**:198
Françoise Sagan **17**:420
Irwin Shaw **7**:411

Rolph, C. H.
Peter Maas **29**:305

Roman, Diane
Paul Vincent Carroll **10**:98

Romano, John
James Baldwin **17**:42
Donald Barthelme **23**:47
Ann Beattie **8**:56
Thomas Berger **11**:47
Frederick Busch **10**:92
Laurie Colwin **13**:156
John Gardner **18**:182
Graham Greene **18**:196
Barry Hannah **23**:212
Ella Leffland **19**:279
Mary McCarthy **24**:347
Joyce Carol Oates **9**:406
Alan Paton **25**:363
Walker Percy **18**:398
Sylvia Plath **5**:342
John Updike **15**:544
Gore Vidal **10**:501

Rome, Florence
Muriel Spark **3**:465

Romer, Samuel
Alvah Bessie **23**:59

Rompers, Terry
Jim Morrison **17**:294

Ronge, Peter
Eugène Ionesco **6**:249

Rooke, Constance
P. K. Page **18**:380
Katherine Anne Porter **15**:430

Roosevelt, Karyl
Diane Johnson **13**:304
Michael Ondaatje **29**:339

Root, William Pitt
Sonia Sanchez **5**:382
Anne Sexton **4**:483
Peter Wild **14**:580

Rorabacher, Louise E.
Frank Dalby Davison **15**:171

Roraback, Dick
Peter Gent **29**:183

Rorem, Ned
Paul Bowles **2**:79
Tennessee Williams **5**:502

Rorty, Richard
Jacques Derrida **24**:143

Roscoe, Adrian
Ezekiel Mphahlele **25**:341
Ngugi wa Thiong'o **36**:311

Roscoe, Adrian A.
Chinua Achebe **26**:17

Rose, Barbara
Tom Wolfe **35**:455

Rose, Ellen Cronan
Margaret Drabble **22**:125
Doris Lessing **6**:300

Rose, Ernst
Hermann Hesse **1**:145

Rose, Frank
David Byrne **26**:95
Pat Conroy **30**:79
Pink Floyd **35**:309
Lou Reed **21**:312
Peter Townshend **17**:540

Rose, Karel
Norma Fox Mazer **26**:292

Rose, Kate
Richard Brautigan **12**:59

Rose, Lois
J. G. Ballard **3**:33
Arthur C. Clarke **4**:104
Robert A. Heinlein **3**:226
C. S. Lewis **3**:297
Walter M. Miller, Jr. **4**:352

Rose, Marilyn
Julien Green **3**:204

Rose, Marilyn Gaddis
Robert Pinget **13**:441

Rose, Mark
J. G. Ballard **36**:42
Frank Herbert **35**:200

Rose, Phyllis
Margaret Drabble **22**:126
Cynthia Ozick **28**:353
Jean Rhys **19**:394

Rose, Stephen
J. G. Ballard **3**:33
Arthur C. Clarke **4**:104
Robert A. Heinlein **3**:226
C. S. Lewis **3**:297
Walter M. Miller, Jr. **4**:352

Rose, Willie Lee
Alex Haley **8**:260

Rosen, Carol
Sam Shepard **17**:448

Rosen, Charles
M. H. Abrams **24**:12

Rosen, Marjorie
Elaine May **16**:433
Albert Maysles and David
Maysles **16**:444

Rosen, Norma
Paula Fox **8**:218
Judith Guest **30**:174
Françoise Sagan **17**:425

Rosen, R. D.
S. J. Perelman **23**:339
James Tate **6**:528

Rosen, Winifred
Richard Peck **21**:299

Rosenbaum, Jean
Marge Piercy **18**:404; **27**:373

Rosenbaum, Jonathan
Robert Altman **16**:31, 39
Robert Bresson **16**:118
John Cassavetes **20**:50
Carl Theodor Dreyer **16**:268
Rainer Werner Fassbinder
20:108
Yasujiro Ozu **16**:454
Sidney Poitier **26**:360
Roman Polanski **16**:472
Richard Pryor **26**:383
Jean Renoir **20**:304

Rosenbaum, Olga
Bernice Rubens **19**:404

Rosenbaum, Ron
Richard Condon **4**:106

Rosenbaum, S. P.
E. M. Forster **22**:130

Rosenberg, Harold
Stanley Kubrick **16**:390
André Malraux **4**:334
Marshall McLuhan **37**:259
Muriel Rukeyser **27**:403
Anna Seghers **7**:407

Rosenberg, Ross
Philip José Farmer **19**:168

Rosenberger, Coleman
John Ehle **27**:101
Ernest K. Gann **23**:164
Bruce Lancaster **36**:243
Carson McCullers **12**:412
Conrad Richter **30**:316

Rosenblatt, Jon
Sylvia Plath **17**:364

Rosenblatt, Roger
Renata Adler **8**:5
Allen Ginsberg **36**:196
Norman Lear **12**:332
Amos Oz **33**:300
Ishmael Reed **32**:356
Ludvík Vaculík **7**:496
Thornton Wilder **6**:572

Rosenblum, Michael
Vladimir Nabokov **15**:394

Rosenfeld, Alvin H.
Saul Bellow **15**:52
Herbert Gold **7**:122
Primo Levi **37**:224, 227
Jakov Lind **4**:293
Nelly Sachs **14**:476
William Styron **15**:529

Rosenfeld, Isaac
Nadine Gordimer **33**:177

Rosenfeld, Megan
Lillian Hellman **34**:347

Rosenfeld, Paul
Ernest Hemingway **19**:210

Rosenfeld, Sidney
Elias Canetti **14**:124

Rosenfeld, Stella P.
Thomas Bernhard **32**:26

Rosengarten, Herbert
Margaret Atwood **8**:33
William Mitchell **25**:323

Rosenman, John B.
Ray Bradbury **15**:84

Rosenstone, Robert A.
Frank Zappa **17**:585

Rosenthal, David H.
Louis-Ferdinand Céline **7**:45
Austin C. Clarke **8**:143
Nicanor Parra **2**:331

Rosenthal, Lucy
Hortense Calisher **2**:96
Norma Klein **30**:237
Richard Llewellyn **7**:207
Sylvia Plath **2**:336
Cynthia Propper Seton **27**:425
Alix Kates Shulman **2**:395

Rosenthal, M. L.
Yehuda Amichai **9**:25
A. R. Ammons **2**:13
Imamu Amiri Baraka **2**:34;
10:19
John Berryman **2**:56
John Betjeman **2**:60
Kay Boyle **1**:42
John Ciardi **10**:105
Austin Clarke **6**:110
Robert Creeley **2**:105; **36**:122
E. E. Cummings **1**:68
James Dickey **2**:115; **7**:81
Robert Duncan **2**:122
Richard Eberhart **11**:178
T. S. Eliot **2**:125
D. J. Enright **4**:155
Robert Frost **1**:110
Allen Ginsberg **1**:118; **2**:162
Paul Goodman **1**:124; **4**:196
Thom Gunn **18**:203
Michael Hamburger **14**:234
Jim Harrison **6**:223
Daniel Hoffman **23**:237
Ted Hughes **2**:197; **9**:280
Randall Jarrell **13**:299
X. J. Kennedy **8**:320
Galway Kinnell **1**:168
Thomas Kinsella **4**:270; **19**:254
Philip Larkin **3**:275, 277
Denise Levertov **2**:242
Robert Lowell **1**:179; **2**:247
George MacBeth **2**:251
Hugh MacDiarmid **2**:253
W. S. Merwin **1**:211
Marianne Moore **1**:226
Charles Olson **2**:326
Robert L. Peters **7**:304
Sylvia Plath **2**:335
Ezra Pound **1**:274; **7**:332
Kenneth Rexroth **1**:283
Theodore Roethke **3**:432

Critic Index

Delmore Schwartz 2:387
Anne Sexton 2:391
Karl Shapiro 4:484
Charles Tomlinson 2:436
Reed Whittemore 4:588
Richard Wilbur 14:577
C. K. Williams 33:442
William Carlos Williams 1:370

Rosenthal, Michael
David Lodge 36:277

Rosenthal, R.
Paula Fox 2:139

Rosenthal, Raymond
David Caute 29:112
Edward Dahlberg 7:66
Tennessee Williams 8:547

Rosenthal, Stuart
Tod Browning 16:123

Rosenthal, T. G.
Michael Ayrton 7:20
Colin MacInnes 23:283

Rosenzweig, A. L.
Peter Dickinson 12:169

Rosenzweig, Paul
William Faulkner 14:176
John Hawkes 27:194

Roshwald, Miriam
S. Y. Agnon 8:9

Roskolenko, John
John Edgar Wideman 36:450

Ross, Alan
Kingsley Amis 2:7
Alberto Moravia 7:244
Satyajit Ray 16:486

Ross, Alec
David Bowie 17:66, 67

Ross, Anne
Mary Stewart 35:389

Ross, Catherine
Jane Rule 27:422

Ross, Catherine Sheldrick
Hugh MacLennan 14:344

Ross, Charles S.
Tom Wolfe 35:458

Ross, Gary
Margaret Atwood 4:27

Ross, James
Reynolds Price 6:426

Ross, Jerome
Paddy Chayefsky 23:111

Ross, Joan
Alberto Moravia 27:353

Ross, Mary
Vera Brittain 23:91
R. V. Cassill 23:102
A. J. Cronin 32:135
Madeleine L'Engle 12:344
Mary Stewart 35:389
Rebecca West 31:454

Ross, Morton L.
Norman Mailer 1:192

Ross, Nancy Wilson
Sylvia Ashton-Warner 19:20
Ruth Prawer Jhabvala 29:252
Thomas Merton 34:462
Yukio Mishima 27:335
Michael Mott 34:462

Ross, Peter
T. Coraghessan Boyle 36:63

Ross, Robert
Tess Gallagher 18:168, 169

Rosser, Harry L.
Julio Cortázar 33:130

Rossi, Louis R.
Salvatore Quasimodo 10:427

Rossman, Charles
F. R. Leavis 24:309

Rosten, Norman
Lucille Clifton 19:109
James Tate 2:431

Roston, Murray
Aldous Huxley 18:270

Roszak, Theodore
Paul Goodman 2:170

Roth, Philip
Edward Albee 9:1
James Baldwin 17:27
Saul Bellow 6:52
Milan Kundera 32:259
Norman Mailer 5:268
Bernard Malamud 5:269; 8:376
J. D. Salinger 8:464
Fredrica Wagman 7:500

Roth, Susan A.
Barbara Wersba 30:429

Rotha, Paul
Buster Keaton 20:189

Rothberg, Abraham
Graham Greene 3:211
Gary Snyder 9:499
Aleksandr I. Solzhenitsyn
4:507; 7:437

Rothchild, Paul
Jim Morrison 17:285

Rothenberg, Randall
Craig Nova 31:297

Rothenbuecher, Bea
Roman Polanski 16:469

Rother, James
Vladimir Nabokov 11:391
Thomas Pynchon 11:453

Rothery, Agnes
Frans Eemil Sillanpää 19:418

Rothman, Nathan
Nadine Gordimer 33:177

Rothman, Nathan L.
Kay Boyle 19:63
A. J. Cronin 32:136
Evan Hunter 31:217
Jessamyn West 17:543
Frank Yerby 7:556

Rothschild, Elaine
Elaine May 16:431

Rothstein, Edward
Agatha Christie 8:141
Philip Roth 22:359
Scott Spencer 30:406

Rothwell, Kenneth S.
John G. Neihardt 32:333

Rotondaro, Fred
Robert Kroetsch 23:269
Robert Lipsyte 21:211

Rottenberg, Annette T.
Taylor Caldwell 28:63

Rottensteiner, Franz
Philip José Farmer 19:165

Roud, Richard
Michelangelo Antonioni 20:19
Bernardo Bertolucci 16:86
Marguerite Duras 20:101
Jean-Luc Godard 20:132
François Truffaut 20:382, 405
Luchino Visconti 16:566

Roudiez, L. S.
Michel Tournier 36:438

Roudiez, Leon S.
Louis Aragon 22:35
Michel Butor 8:114
Jean Cocteau 15:132
Claude Mauriac 9:363

Roueché, Berton
Trevanian 29:432

Rout, Kathleen
Flannery O'Connor 15:412

Routh, Michael
Graham Greene 9:246

Rovit, Earl
Leslie A. Fiedler 24:205
Ernest Hemingway 30:182

Rovit, Earl H.
Saul Bellow 1:31; 8:71; 13:71
Kay Boyle 19:66
Ralph Ellison 1:93
John Hawkes 2:184
Norman Mailer 8:372
Bernard Malamud 1:195

Rowan, Diana
Heinrich Böll 11:58

Rowan, Louis
Diane Wakoski 7:506

Rowan, Thomas
J. F. Powers 1:281

Rowell, Charles H.
Sterling A. Brown 23:96

Rowland, Richard
Carl Theodor Dreyer 16:257

Rowland, Stanley J., Jr.
Walter M. Miller, Jr. 30:255

Rowley, Brian A.
Erich Maria Remarque 21:334

Rowley, Peter
Paula Fox 2:139
John Knowles 4:272

Rowse, A. L.
Vladimir Nabokov 23:309
Flannery O'Connor 2:318
Barbara Pym 13:469

Roy, Emil
John Arden 15:18
Sean O'Casey 15:403

Roy, Joy K.
James Herriot 12:284

Royal, Robert
Mario Puzo 36:363

Royte, Elizabeth
Michael Cunningham 34:42

Ruark, Gibbons
Andrei Voznesensky 1:349

Ruark, Robert
Lenny Bruce 21:45

Ruben, Elaine
Maureen Howard 5:189

Rubens, Linda Morgan
Vine Deloria, Jr. 21:114

Rubenstein, Joshua
Anatoli Rybakov 23:373

Rubenstein, Roberta
Robert Altman 16:21
Margaret Atwood 8:31
Paddy Chayefsky 23:119
Gail Godwin 22:182
Bessie Head 25:232
Doris Lessing 6:303; 10:316

Rubin, Jay
Donald Keene 34:568

Rubin, Louis, Jr.
William Melvin Kelley 22:246

Rubin, Louis D., Jr.
Donald Davidson 19:126
William Faulkner 1:101
Carson McCullers 10:338
John Crowe Ransom 4:428;
5:365
Carl Sandburg 10:450
Susan Sontag 10:484
William Styron 3:473
Allen Tate 9:523; 14:533
Robert Penn Warren 1:353;
4:577
Eudora Welty 1:361

Rubin, Steven J.
Richard Wright 21:461

Rubins, Josh
Brigid Brophy 11:69
Raymond Carver 36:104
Agatha Christie 6:108
Don DeLillo 27:86
Jacob Epstein 19:162
Helen MacInnes 27:282
Gilbert Sorrentino 22:396
William Trevor 14:537

Rubinstein, E.
Buster Keaton 20:195

Ruby, Kathryn
Linda Pastan 27:369

Ruby, Michael
Charles M. Schulz 12:528

Rucker, Rudy
Tom Robbins 32:373

Ruddick, Sara
Carolyn G. Heilbrun 25:254

Rudin, Ellen
Emily Cheney Neville 12:449
Katherine Paterson 30:283

Rudman, Mark
Robert Lowell 37:238
James Tate 25:429

Rudolf, Anthony
Yehuda Amichai 22:32
Jonathan Schell 35:367

Rueckert, William
Wright Morris 7:245

Ruegg, Maria
Jacques Derrida 24:149

Ruffin, Carolyn F.
Sylvia Ashton-Warner 19:23
Vonda N. McIntyre 18:327
John McPhee 36:294

Rugg, Winifred King
C. S. Forester 35:169

Rugoff, Milton
Irwin Shaw 23:397

Rukeyser, Muriel
Gunnar Ekelöf 27:113
John Crowe Ransom 11:466

Rule, Jane
Rita Mae Brown 18:72

Rule, Philip C.
Thomas J. Fleming 37:124

Rumens, Carol
Maurice Gee 29:178
Colleen McCullough 27:322
Leonard Michaels 25:319
Alice Walker 27:449

Runciman, Lex
Richard F. Hugo 32:251

Ruoff, A. LaVonne
Leslie Marmon Silko 23:408

Rupp, Richard H.
John Updike 1:343

Ruppert, Peter
Max Frisch 18:161

Rushdie, Salman
Italo Calvino 33:97
Gabriel García Márquez 27:150
Günter Grass 22:197
Siegfried Lenz 27:255
Salman Rushdie 31:356
Ernesto Sabato 23:382
Michel Tournier 23:453
Mario Vargas Llosa 31:448

Rushing, Andrea Benton
Audre Lorde 18:309

Ruskamp, Judith S.
Henri Michaux 8:392

Russ, C.A.H.
Siegfried Lenz 27:244

Russ, Joanna
Poul Anderson 15:15
Isaac Asimov 19:28
Ursula K. Le Guin 22:274
Adrienne Rich 18:447
Robert Silverberg 7:425
Kate Wilhelm 7:537
Gene Wolfe 25:472

Russ, Lavinia
Ruth M. Arthur 12:25
Judy Blume 12:44
M. E. Kerr 12:298

Russell, Barry
Howard Brenton 31:58

Russell, Brandon
Joyce Carol Oates 33:296

Russell, Charles
John Barth 7:22
Richard Brautigan 9:123
Jerzy Kosinski 6:284
Vladimir Nabokov 6:353
Ronald Sukenick 6:523

Russell, Delbert W.
Anne Hébert 29:240

Russell, Gillian Harding
David Donnell 34:158

Russell, J.
Honor Arundel 17:18

Russell, John
André Malraux 9:357
Anthony Powell 3:402

Russell, Julia G.
Honor Arundel 17:15
Virginia Hamilton 26:148

Russell, Mariann
Melvin B. Tolson 36:430

Rustin, Bayard
Eldridge Cleaver 30:67

Ruth, John
Jay Bennett 35:45

Rutherford, Anna
Janet Frame 22:145

Ryan, Alan
David Caute 29:118
Walter D. Edmonds 35:157
Brian Moore 32:311

Ryan, Allan A., Jr.
Frederick Forsyth 36:175
Nicholas M. Guild 33:187
Robert Ludlum 22:289

Ryan, Frank L.
Daniel J. Berrigan 4:56
C. S. Forester 35:173
Anne Hébert 4:220
Françoise Sagan 17:426

Ryan, Judith
Christa Wolf 29:467

Ryan, Marjorie
Diane Johnson 5:198

Ryan, Richard W.
Isaac Asimov 26:37
Anne McCaffrey 17:281

Ryan, Stephen P.
Leslie A. Fiedler 24:190

Rybus, Rodney
Seamus Heaney 25:250

Ryf, Robert S.
Henry Green 2:179
B. S. Johnson 9:299
Doris Lessing 10:313
Vladimir Nabokov 6:353
Flann O'Brien 7:268

Ryle, John
John Berger 19:40
Penelope Fitzgerald 19:173
Mark Helprin 10:261

Rysten, Felix
Jean Giono 11:232

Rzhevsky, Leonid
Aleksandr I. Solzhenitsyn 26:417

Saal, Hubert
Paul McCartney 35:278
Mary Renault 17:393
Irwin Shaw 7:411

Saal, Rollene W.
Kristin Hunter 35:224
Anne Tyler 28:429

Sabin, Edwin L.
Lenora Mattingly Weber 12:631

Sabiston, Elizabeth
Philip Roth 6:475
Ludvík Vaculík 7:497

Sabor, Peter
Ezekiel Mphahlele 25:345

Sabri, M. Arjamand
Thomas Pynchon 3:417

Sacharoff, Mark
Elias Canetti 3:98

Sachner, Mark J.
Samuel Beckett 14:71

Sachs, Marilyn
Nicholasa Mohr 12:445, 446
Robert Newton Peck 17:338

Sack, John
Ward S. Just 27:225

Sacks, Peter
James Merrill 34:239

Sackville-West, Edward
Ivy Compton-Burnett 15:137

Saddler, Allen
Ann Jellicoe 27:210
C. P. Taylor 27:442

Sadker, David Miller
Bette Greene 30:170
Kristin Hunter 35:229

Sadker, Myra Pollack
Bette Greene 30:170
Kristin Hunter 35:229

Sadler, Frank
Jack Spicer 18:508

Sadoff, Dianne F.
Gail Godwin 8:247

Sadoff, Ira
Tess Gallagher 18:168
Robert Hass 18:210
Philip Levine 14:315

Säez, Richard
James Merrill 6:323

Safir, Margery
Pablo Neruda 28:312

Sagalyn, Raphael
James H. Webb, Jr. 22:453

Sagan, Carl
Paul West 14:568

Sagar, Keith
Ted Hughes 2:203

Sage, Lorna
Brian Aldiss 14:14
John Barth 27:28
Simone de Beauvoir 31:43
Olga Broumas 10:76
David Caute 29:124
Bruce Chatwin 28:74
Isabel Colegate 36:112
Maureen Duffy 37:116
Elaine Feinstein 36:169
John Hawkes 27:201
Patricia Highsmith 14:261
Erica Jong 6:267
Thomas Keneally 27:232
Iris Murdoch 11:384
Vladimir Nabokov 8:412
Edna O'Brien 36:336
Sylvia Plath 11:450
Philip Roth 15:455
Françoise Sagan 17:429; 36:382
Christina Stead 32:413
Fay Weldon 36:447
Angus Wilson 34:580

Sage, Victor
David Storey 8:505

Said, Edward
V. S. Naipaul 37:319

Said, Edward W.
R. P. Blackmur 2:61
Jacques Derrida 24:140
Michel Foucault 34:340
Lucien Goldmann 24:238
Paul Goodman 2:169
V. S. Naipaul 18:364

Saikowski, Charlotte
Primo Levi 37:222

Sail, Lawrence
James Fenton 32:166
Craig Raine 32:349

Sailsbury, M. B.
Franklyn M. Branley 21:16

Sainer, Arthur
Martin Duberman 8:185
Max Frisch 18:163
Jack Gelber 14:194
Simon Gray 9:242
Michael McClure 6:317

Critic Index

Miguel Piñero **4**:401

St. Aubyn, F. C.
Albert Camus **32**:93

St. John, David
Marvin Bell **31**:49, 50
Norman Dubie **36**:141
Philip Levine **33**:272
Stanley Plumly **33**:315
C. K. Williams **33**:448
Charles Wright **28**:458

St. John-Stevas, Norman
C. S. Lewis **6**:308

St. Martin, Hardie
Blas de Otero **11**:424

Sakurai, Emiko
Fumiko Enchi **31**:140
Kenzaburō Ōe **10**:374
Kenneth Rexroth **11**:474
Shiga Naoya **33**:370

Salamon, Julie
Harriet Doerr **34**:154

Salamon, Lynda B.
Sylvia Plath **17**:350

Salamone, Anthony
Howard Fast **23**:160

Sale, Roger
Richard Adams **18**:2
E. M. Almedingen **12**:3
A. Alvarez **13**:10
Kingsley Amis **5**:22
Saul Bellow **6**:61
Thomas Berger **8**:84
Richard Brautigan **12**:70
Frederick Buechner **2**:83; **6**:103
Anthony Burgess **5**:87
Frederick Busch **10**:94
Agatha Christie **8**:141
Richard Condon **8**:150
Robertson Davies **7**:72
E. L. Doctorow **6**:135
Margaret Drabble **2**:118, 119;
    8:183; **22**:122
George P. Elliott **2**:131
Frederick Exley **6**:172
Leslie A. Fiedler **4**:162
B. H. Friedman **7**:109
Paula Fox **2**:141
Herbert Gold **7**:121
Witold Gombrowicz **7**:122
Joanne Greenberg **30**:163
Dashiell Hammett **5**:161
John Hawkes **4**:214
Mark Helprin **10**:261
Maureen Howard **5**:188; **14**:267
Zora Neale Hurston **30**:222
Ken Kesey **6**:278
Richard Kostelanetz **28**:215
John le Carré **5**:234
Alan Lelchuk **5**:240
Doris Lessing **2**:239, 242;
    6:299, 304
Alison Lurie **4**:306
Ross Macdonald **2**:255
David Madden **5**:266
Norman Mailer **2**:261; **4**:319
Peter Matthiessen **7**:212
Iris Murdoch **8**:404
Tim O'Brien **7**:271

Grace Paley **6**:392
J. F. Powers **8**:447
Richard Price **6**:427
Mario Puzo **36**:359
Judith Rossner **6**:470
Philip Roth **2**:381; **6**:476
Andrew Sinclair **2**:400
Isaac Bashevis Singer **9**:487
Robert Stone **5**:410
Paul Theroux **5**:428
J.R.R. Tolkien **1**:338
Lionel Trilling **24**:458
Anne Tyler **11**:553
John Updike **23**:467
Luisa Valenzuela **31**:436
Mario Vargas Llosa **6**:547
Kurt Vonnegut, Jr. **8**:532
David Wagoner **5**:475
James Welch **14**:558
René Wellek **28**:449
William Wharton **37**:437
Monique Wittig **22**:474
Larry Woiwode **10**:541

Salemi, Joseph S.
William Gaddis **19**:187

Sales, Grover
Jean M. Auel **31**:23

Salisbury, David F.
Ernest K. Gann **23**:168

Salisbury, Harrison E.
Aleksandr I. Solzhenitsyn **4**:511

Salisbury, Stephan
Howard Fast **23**:159

Salkey, Andrew
Ngugi Wa Thiong'o **13**:584

Salmans, Sandra
Scott Sommer **25**:425

Salmon, Sheila
Barbara Corcoran **17**:77

Salomon, I. L.
Robert Duncan **4**:142

Salomon, Louis B.
Carson McCullers **12**:408

Salter, D.P.M.
Saul Bellow **2**:53

Salter, Denis
Jack Hodgins **23**:229

Salvadore, Maria
Betsy Byars **35**:76

Salvadori, Massimo
William F. Buckley, Jr. **37**:58

Salvatore, Caroline
Chaim Potok **26**:368

Salvesen, Christopher
Jane Rule **27**:416

Salway, Lance
Robert Cormier **12**:136
Peter Dickinson **12**:168
Alan Garner **17**:147
S. E. Hinton **30**:206
Barbara Wersba **30**:433
Robert Westall **17**:556

Salzman, Eric
David Byrne **26**:99
Andrew Lloyd Webber and Tim
    Rice **21**:431
Frank Zappa **17**:591

Salzman, Jack
John Dos Passos **4**:138
Jack Kerouac **2**:229
Tillie Olsen **4**:386

Samet, Tom
Henry Roth **11**:488

Sammons, Jeffrey L.
Hermann Hesse **11**:271

Sampley, Arthur M.
Robert Frost **1**:112

Sampson, Edward C.
E. B. White **10**:529

Samuels, Charles Thomas
Richard Adams **4**:7
Michelangelo Antonioni **20**:33
Donald Barthelme **3**:43
Robert Bresson **16**:115
Lillian Hellman **2**:187
Alfred Hitchcock **16**:348
Stanley Kubrick **16**:384
Christina Stead **2**:421; **32**:408
John Updike **1**:344; **2**:442
Kurt Vonnegut, Jr. **2**:454

Samuels, Wilfred D.
John Edgar Wideman **36**:455

Samuelson, David N.
Arthur C. Clarke **18**:103
Robert A. Heinlein **26**:164, 167
Walter M. Miller, Jr. **30**:260,
    261

Sanborn, Sara
Anthony Burgess **4**:84
Rosalyn Drexler **6**:143
Alison Lurie **4**:305
Joyce Carol Oates **3**:363

Sandars, N. K.
David Jones **4**:260

Sandeen, Ernest
R. P. Blackmur **2**:62

Sander, Ellen
Mick Jagger and Keith Richard
    17:223
John Lennon and Paul
    McCartney **12**:364
Paul McCartney **35**:278
Joni Mitchell **12**:435
Paul Simon **17**:459
Neil Young **17**:569
Frank Zappa **17**:585

Sanders, Charles
Theodore Roethke **19**:402

Sanders, Charles L.
Norman Lear **12**:330

Sanders, David
John Hersey **1**:144; **7**:153
Frederick Morgan **23**:300
Robert Phillips **28**:365

Sanders, Ed
Allen Ginsberg **4**:181

Sanders, Frederick L.
Conrad Aiken **3**:5

Sanders, Ivan
Dobrica Ćosić **14**:132
György Konrád **4**:273; **10**:304
Milan Kundera **4**:278
József Lengyel **7**:202
Amos Oz **8**:436

Sanders, Peter L.
Robert Graves **2**:176

Sanders, Ronald
Richard Wright **21**:442

Sanderson, Ivan
Farley Mowat **26**:334

Sanderson, Stewart F.
Compton Mackenzie **18**:315

Sandhuber, Holly
Lois Duncan **26**:107

Sandler, Linda
Margaret Atwood **8**:29, 30
Ernest Buckler **13**:123

Sandoe, James
Margery Allingham **19**:13
Robert Bloch **33**:83
August Derleth **31**:138
Roy Fuller **28**:148
Evan Hunter **31**:219, 220
M. M. Kaye **28**:198
Mary Stewart **35**:388

Sandow, Gregory
Michael Moorcock **27**:352

Sandrof, Ivan
Jean Lee Latham **12**:324

Sands, Douglas B.
Franklyn M. Branley **21**:19

Sandwell, B. K.
Mazo de la Roche **14**:148

Sandy, Stephen
Peter Davison **28**:104

Saner, Reg
William Dickey **28**:119

Sanfield, Steve
Michael McClure **6**:320

Sanhuber, Holly
Christopher Collier and James
    L. Collier **30**:74

Santha, Rama Rau
Ruth Prawer Jhabvala **29**:253

Santí, Enrico-Mario
G. Cabrera Infante **25**:100

Sargeant, Winthrop
Vittorio De Sica **20**:87
Robert Lewis Taylor **14**:534

Sargent, David
Robert Wilson **9**:576

Sargo, Tina Mendes
Luchino Visconti **16**:566

Sarland, Charles
William Mayne **12**:402

Sarlin, Bob
Chuck Berry **17**:54
Janis Ian **21**:186
Mick Jagger and Keith Richard **17**:229
Van Morrison **21**:235
Laura Nyro **17**:316
Neil Young **17**:572

Sarotte, Georges-Michel
William Inge **19**:229
John Rechy **18**:442

Saroyan, Aram
Kenneth Koch **8**:323
Phillip Lopate **29**:299
Frank O'Hara **13**:424
Anne Waldman **7**:508

Saroyan, William
Flann O'Brien **10**:362

Sarratt, Janet P.
Milton Meltzer **26**:302

Sarris, Andrew George
Woody Allen **16**:7, 11
Robert Altman **16**:36, 38, 43
Ralph Bakshi **26**:68
Mel Brooks **12**:75
Michael Cimino **16**:209
Francis Ford Coppola **16**:245
Brian De Palma **20**:80
Rainer Werner Fassbinder **20**:115
Federico Fellini **16**:271, 297
John Ford **16**:308
Bob Fosse **20**:127
Jean-Luc Godard **20**:137, 153
Werner Herzog **16**:333
George Roy Hill **26**:203, 206, 208
Alfred Hitchcock **16**:341, 357
Kristin Hunter **35**:224
John Huston **20**:174
Elia Kazan **16**:364, 366
Buster Keaton **20**:196
Stanley Kubrick **16**:380
Akira Kurosawa **16**:406
John Landis **26**:275
Richard Lester **20**:231, 232
Norman Mailer **3**:315
Sam Peckinpah **20**:282
Roman Polanski **16**:473
Jean Renoir **20**:308
Alain Resnais **16**:504, 518
Carlos Saura **20**:318
Paul Schrader **26**:390, 393, 396
Wilfrid Sheed **4**:487
Joan Micklin Silver **20**:344
Jerzy Skolimowski **20**:354
François Truffaut **20**:383, 404, 406, 407
Lina Wertmüller **16**:599
Billy Wilder **20**:461, 466

Sartre, Jean-Paul
Georges Bataille **29**:34
Albert Camus **14**:104
Aimé Césaire **32**:108
John Dos Passos **11**:153
William Faulkner **9**:197
Jean Genet **2**:155

Sato, Hiroko
Nella Larsen **37**:213

Saunders, Charles
May Swenson **14**:522

Saunders, Mike
Ray Davies **21**:92, 93

Saunders, William S.
James Wright **28**:466

Sauvage, Leo
Charles Fuller **25**:182
David Hare **29**:217
Beth Henley **23**:217
David Mamet **34**:222
Tom Stoppard **34**:280
Hugh Whitemore **37**:446

Sauzey, François
Jean-Paul Sartre **18**:473

Savage, D. S.
E. M. Forster **13**:216
Christopher Isherwood **14**:286
Pamela Hansford Johnson **27**:215
Mary Renault **17**:391

Savage, Jon
Lou Reed **21**:316

Savage, Lois E.
Norma Klein **30**:237
Noel Streatfeild **21**:412

Savory, Teo
Guillevic **33**:192

Savvas, Minas
Yannis Ritsos **13**:487

Sawyer, Roland
Thor Heyerdahl **26**:190

Saxon, Wolfgang
Jesse Stuart **34**:372

Sayre, Henry M.
John Ashbery **15**:31

Sayre, Joel
Garson Kanin **22**:231

Sayre, Nora
Enid Bagnold **25**:77
Marguerite Duras **20**:99
Marian Engel **36**:157
Iris Murdoch **1**:236
Richard O'Brien **17**:325
Anne Roiphe **3**:434
Elizabeth Taylor **2**:432
James Thurber **25**:439
Kurt Vonnegut, Jr. **3**:502

Sayre, Robert
Lucien Goldmann **24**:246

Sayre, Robert F.
James Baldwin **1**:15

Scaduto, Anthony
Bob Dylan **4**:148

Scammell, Michael
Ilya Ehrenburg **34**:438
Anatol Goldberg **34**:438

Scammell, William
John Berger **19**:40
Patrick White **18**:547

Scanlan, Margaret
Iris Murdoch **15**:387

Scanlan, Tom
Thornton Wilder **35**:446

Scanlon, Laura Polla
John Donovan **35**:139
Barbara Wersba **30**:430
Maia Wojciechowska **26**:454

Scannell, Vernon
Martin Booth **13**:103
Randall Jarrell **9**:298
George MacBeth **9**:341
Piers Paul Read **25**:375

Scarbrough, George
Babette Deutsch **18**:119
James Schevill **7**:400

Scarf, Maggie
Lillian Hellman **18**:228
Susan Sontag **10**:487

Schaap, Dick
Peter Gent **29**:181
George Plimpton **36**:354
Mario Puzo **2**:351

Schaar, John H.
Jonathan Schell **35**:364

Schacht, Chuck
Mollie Hunter **21**:169
Diana Wynne Jones **26**:229

Schaefer, J. O'Brien
Margaret Drabble **5**:119

Schaeffer, Susan Fromberg
Nancy Willard **37**:465

Schafer, William J.
Mark Harris **19**:202
David Wagoner **3**:507

Schaffer, Michael
Bruce Catton **35**:94

Schaffner, Nicholas
Ray Davies **21**:107
John Lennon and Paul McCartney **12**:385

Schaire, Jeffrey
Pat Barker **32**:13
Umberto Eco **28**:133
Leon Rooke **34**:251

Schakne, Ann
Roderick L. Haig-Brown **21**:136

Schaller, Joseph G., S.J.
Carolyn Hougan **34**:61

Schamschula, Walter
Václav Havel **25**:223

Schanzer, George O.
Manuel Mujica Láinez **31**:281

Schapiro, Leonard
Aleksandr I. Solzhenitsyn **7**:440

Schatt, Stanley
Langston Hughes **10**:279
Isaac Bashevis Singer **3**:459
Kurt Vonnegut, Jr. **1**:348; **4**:560; **12**:614

Schaub, Thomas Hill
Thomas Pynchon **18**:430

Schechner, Mark
Lionel Trilling **11**:540

Schechner, Richard
Edward Albee **11**:10
Eugène Ionesco **6**:253

Scheer, George F.
Thomas J. Fleming **37**:125

Scheerer, Constance
Sylvia Plath **9**:432

Schein, Harry
Carl Theodor Dreyer **16**:258

Schene, Carol
Norma Klein **30**:240

Scherman, David E.
Milton Meltzer **26**:305

Schevill, James
Peter Davison **28**:99
Richard F. Hugo **32**:234
Kenneth Patchen **18**:395

Schickel, Richard
Woody Allen **16**:3
Robert Altman **16**:24
Michelangelo Antonioni **20**:30
Louis Auchincloss **9**:54
Ingmar Bergman **16**:58, 63
John Cassavetes **20**:47
Charles Chaplin **16**:202
Francis Ford Coppola **16**:236
Joan Didion **1**:75
Nora Ephron **31**:159
Jean-Luc Godard **20**:143
John Landis **26**:271
Norman Lear **12**:333
Alan Lelchuk **5**:242
Richard Lester **20**:227
Ross Macdonald **1**:185
Garry Marshall **17**:276
Steve Martin **30**:251
Monty Python **21**:228
Thomas Pynchon **2**:358
Satyajit Ray **16**:481
Alain Resnais **16**:504
Eric Rohmer **16**:530
Carlos Saura **20**:318
Peter Shaffer **5**:387
Glendon Swarthout **35**:402
Luchino Visconti **16**:567
Andy Warhol **20**:420
Frederick Wiseman **20**:470, 475

Schickele, Peter
John Lennon and Paul McCartney **12**:355

Schieder, Rupert
Jack Hodgins **23**:232, 235

Schier, Donald
André Breton **2**:81

Schier, Flint
Michel Foucault **31**:186

Schiff, Jeff
Mary Oliver **19**:362

Schillaci, Peter P.
Luis Buñuel **16**:140

Schiller, Barbara
Brigid Brophy **11**:68
Mary Stewart **35**:389

Critic Index

Schiller, Jerome P.
I. A. Richards 24:395

Schirmer, Gregory A.
Scott Elledge 34:430
Seamus Heaney 25:243
M. L. Rosenthal 28:395
E. B. White 34:430

Schjeldahl, Peter
Paul Blackburn 9:100
André Breton 2:80; 9:129
Russell Edson 13:191
Gerome Ragni and James Rado 17:384
James Schevill 7:400
Diane Wakoski 11:564

Schlant, Ernestine
Christa Wolf 14:593

Schlesinger, Arthur, Jr.
Woody Allen 16:11
David Caute 29:119
Michael Cimino 16:209
Bob Fosse 20:127
Mary McCarthy 24:343
Paul Schrader 26:391

Schlesinger, Arthur M., Jr.
Marshall McLuhan 37:262

Schlotter, Charles
T. Coraghessan Boyle 36:62
William Caunitz 34:36

Schlueter, June
Samuel Beckett 18:43
Peter Handke 15:269
Arthur Miller 10:346
Tom Stoppard 15:522

Schlueter, Paul
Pär Lagerkvist 7:201
Doris Lessing 1:174; 3:283
Mary McCarthy 1:205
Gabrielle Roy 14:469
Robert Lewis Taylor 14:535

Schmering, Chris
Satyajit Ray 16:494

Schmerl, Rudolf B.
Aldous Huxley 3:255

Schmidt, Arthur
Joni Mitchell 12:437
Brian Wilson 12:641, 645
Frank Zappa 17:589

Schmidt, Elizabeth
Margaret Craven 17:80

Schmidt, Michael
Donald Davie 8:165
Philip Larkin 18:300
George MacBeth 2:252
Edwin Morgan 31:275
Peter Porter 33:319
Jon Silkin 2:396
Stevie Smith 25:419
Charles Tomlinson 13:548
Yevgeny Yevtushenko 26:466

Schmidt, Nancy J.
Amos Tutuola 29:442

Schmidt, Pilar
Lenora Mattingly Weber 12:634

Schmidt, Sandra
James D. Forman 21:116

Schmitt, James
Fritz Hochwälder 36:236

Schmitz, Eugenia E.
Isabelle Holland 21:153

Schmitz, Neil
Donald Barthelme 1:19
Richard Brautigan 3:90
Robert Coover 3:113; 7:58
Thomas Pynchon 6:435
Ishmael Reed 5:368; 6:448
Jonathan Schell 35:366
Al Young 19:478

Schneck, Stephen
Richard Brautigan 1:44
LeRoi Jones 1:162

Schneckloth, Tim
Frank Zappa 17:592

Schneidau, Herbert N.
Ezra Pound 4:408

Schneider, Alan
Edward Albee 11:10

Schneider, Duane
Anaïs Nin 1:248; 11:396

Schneider, Duane B.
Gilbert Sorrentino 22:391

Schneider, Elisabeth
T. S. Eliot 3:140

Schneider, Harold W.
Muriel Spark 13:519

Schneider, Isidor
Kenneth Burke 24:118
Margaret Mead 37:270

Schneider, Mary W.
Muriel Spark 18:504

Schneider, Richard J.
William H. Gass 8:240

Schoeck, R. J.
Allen Tate 24:442

Schoenbaum, S.
Leon Rooke 34:253

Schoenbrun, David
Francine du Plessix Gray 22:199
Cornelius Ryan 7:385

Schoenstein, Ralph
Garry Trudeau 12:590

Schoenwald, Richard L.
Ogden Nash 23:322

Schoffman, Stuart
Nora Ephron 31:158
John Gardner 34:549

Scholes, Robert
Jorge Luis Borges 10:63
Robert Coover 32:120
Lawrence Durrell 8:190
Gail Godwin 22:179
John Hawkes 9:262; 15:273
Robert A. Heinlein 26:166
Frank Herbert 12:276

Ursula K. Le Guin 22:266
Iris Murdoch 22:324
Sylvia Plath 17:351
Frederik Pohl 18:410
Ishmael Reed 5:370
Kurt Vonnegut, Jr. 2:451; 4:561

Schonberg, Harold C.
T. H. White 30:450

Schopen, Bernard A.
John Updike 23:464

Schorer, Mark
Truman Capote 3:98
Walter Van Tilburg Clark 28:77
Leon Edel 29:168
Martha Gellhorn 14:195
Lillian Hellman 4:221
Carson McCullers 4:344
Katherine Anne Porter 7:312
John Steinbeck 21:367
René Wellek 28:443

Schott, Webster
Richard Adams 5:6
Louis Auchincloss 4:31
W. H. Auden 2:25
Donald Barthelme 2:41
Saul Bellow 8:69
William Peter Blatty 2:63
Vance Bourjaily 8:103
Vincent Canby 13:131
R. V. Cassill 23:107, 108
James Clavell 6:113; 25:126
J. M. Coetzee 23:126
Robert Coover 7:57
Michael Crichton 2:108
Thomas J. Fleming 37:123
John Gardner 10:223
Andrew M. Greeley 28:175
Shirley Hazzard 18:219
William Kennedy 34:206
John Knowles 26:261
Ira Levin 6:305
David Madden 15:350
Colleen McCullough 27:319
Larry McMurtry 2:272
Ted Mooney 25:329
Toni Morrison 22:320
Sylvia Plath 2:338
Raymond Queneau 10:432
Philip Roth 3:436
Susan Fromberg Schaeffer 11:492
Georges Simenon 2:398
Harvey Swados 5:421
Thomas Tryon 11:548
Elio Vittorini 6:551
Jessamyn West 7:520
Patrick White 18:549
Tennessee Williams 5:506

Schow, H. Wayne
Günter Grass 11:248

Schrader, George Alfred
Norman Mailer 14:348

Schrader, Paul
Robert Bresson 16:115
Brian De Palma 20:72
Carl Theodor Dreyer 16:263
Albert Maysles and David Maysles 16:440
Yasujiro Ozu 16:449

Sam Peckinpah 20:273

Schraepen, Edmond
William Carlos Williams 9:575

Schraibman, Joseph
Juan Goytisolo 23:188, 189

Schramm, Richard
Philip Levine 2:244
Howard Moss 7:248

Schrank, Bernice
Sean O'Casey 11:411

Schraufnagel, Noel
Kristin Hunter 35:226
Frank G. Yerby 22:491

Schreiber, Jan
Elizabeth Daryush 6:122

Schreiber, Le Anne
Jerome Charyn 8:135
David Lodge 36:274
Adrienne Rich 36:367
Marilynne Robinson 25:386

Schreiber, Ron
Marge Piercy 27:379

Schroeder, Andreas
Michael Ondaatje 14:408

Schroth, Raymond A., S.J.
Andrew M. Greeley 28:170, 173
Norman Mailer 2:261; 3:312
Walter M. Miller, Jr. 30:256

Schruers, Fred
Joan Armatrading 17:9
Ray Davies 21:98
Neil Young 17:576

Schulberg, Budd
Laura Z. Hobson 25:270

Schulder, Diane
Marge Piercy 3:385

Schuler, Barbara
Peter Taylor 1:333

Schulman, Grace
Jorge Luis Borges 13:110
Richard Eberhart 13:134
Pablo Neruda 5:302
Amos Oz 33:301
Octavio Paz 6:395
Adrienne Rich 3:427
Mark Van Doren 6:541
Richard Wilbur 9:569

Schulps, Dave
Elvis Costello 21:67
Ray Davies 21:106
Van Morrison 21:238
Peter Townshend 17:537

Schultheis, Anne Marie
Luisa Valenzuela 31:439

Schulz, Charles M.
Charles M. Schulz 12:527

Schulz, Max F.
John Barth 9:68
Norman Mailer 1:190
Bernard Malamud 1:199
Kurt Vonnegut, Jr. 1:347

Schumacher, Dorothy
Margaret O. Hyde **21**:171

Schürer, Ernst
Fritz Hochwälder **36**:235

Schusler, Kris
Robert Lewis Taylor **14**:534

Schuster, Arian
Richard Brautigan **12**:74

Schuster, Edgar H.
Harper Lee **12**:341

Schwaber, Paul
Robert Lowell **1**:184

Schwartz, Alvin
Jerome Siegel and Joe Shuster **21**:362

Schwartz, Barry N.
Eugène Ionesco **15**:296

Schwartz, Delmore
R. P. Blackmur **24**:53
John Dos Passos **15**:180
T. S. Eliot **24**:166
Randall Jarrell **1**:159
Robinson Jeffers **11**:304
Edmund Wilson **24**:468
Yvor Winters **32**:451

Schwartz, Edward
Katherine Anne Porter **7**:309

Schwartz, Harry
Ronald J. Glasser **37**:133

Schwartz, Howard
Yehuda Amichai **22**:31
David Ignatow **7**:178

Schwartz, Joseph
A. G. Mojtabai **29**:320

Schwartz, Julius
Roy A. Gallant **17**:127

Schwartz, Kessel
Vicente Aleixandre **9**:15; **36**:28
Manlio Argueta **31**:19
Juan Benet **28**:21
Adolfo Bioy Casares **8**:94
Antonio Buero Vallejo **15**:96
Gabriel García Márquez **10**:215
Juan Goytisolo **23**:182, 183
Manuel Mujica Láinez **31**:282
Juan Rulfo **8**:462

Schwartz, Lloyd
Elizabeth Bishop **9**:93, 97

Schwartz, Lynne Sharon
Beryl Bainbridge **5**:40
Rosellen Brown **32**:68
Eleanor Clark **19**:107
Natalia Ginzburg **5**:141
Susan Fromberg Schaeffer **11**:491
Alix Kates Shulman **10**:475
Anne Tyler **11**:552
Fay Weldon **9**:560

Schwartz, Nancy Lynn
E. M. Broner **19**:72
Jill Robinson **10**:438

Schwartz, Paul J.
Samuel Beckett **6**:41
Alain Robbe-Grillet **8**:453

Schwartz, Ronald
Miguel Delibes **8**:169
José Donoso **32**:159
José María Gironella **11**:234
Juan Goytisolo **23**:181

Schwartz, Sanford
Milton Meltzer **26**:302
John Updike **34**:288

Schwartz, Sheila
E. M. Broner **19**:72

Schwartz, Tony
Steve Martin **30**:247

Schwartz, Wendy
Marge Piercy **27**:379

Schwartzenburg, Dewey
Carl Sagan **30**:337

Schwarz, Alfred
Jean-Paul Sartre **18**:469

Schwarz, Egon
Hermann Hesse **17**:211

Schwarzbach, F. S.
Thomas Pynchon **9**:443

Schwarzchild, Bettina
James Purdy **2**:349

Schweitzer, Darrell
Jack Vance **35**:428
Roger Zelazny **21**:474, 478

Schwerer, Armand
Diane Wakoski **7**:506

Scigaj, Leonard M.
Frank Herbert **35**:201

Scobbie, Irene
Pär Lagerkvist **10**:312
Leon Rooke **25**:393

Scobie, Stephen
Bill Bissett **18**:59
John Glassco **9**:237
John Newlove **14**:377
B. P. Nichol **18**:366, 368
Michael Ondaatje **14**:408
Leon Rooke **25**:393

Scobie, Stephen A. C.
F. R. Scott **22**:375

Scobie, W. I.
Melvin Van Peebles **2**:448
Derek Walcott **2**:459

Scofield, Martin
T. S. Eliot **9**:186

Scoggin, Margaret C.
Walter Farley **17**:116
Henry Gregor Felsen **17**:120
Mary Stolz **12**:547, 549, 550, 552
John R. Tunis **12**:594

Scoppa, Bud
Walter Becker and Donald Fagen **26**:79
Jackson Browne **21**:34
Mick Jagger and Keith Richard **17**:228
John Lennon and Paul McCartney **12**:366
Jimmy Page and Robert Plant **12**:479

Neil Young **17**:572, 575

Scott, Alexander
Hugh MacDiarmid **4**:310

Scott, Carolyn D.
Graham Greene **1**:130

Scott, Helen G.
Alfred Hitchcock **16**:346

Scott, J. D.
Gil Orlovitz **22**:334
Andrew Sinclair **2**:400

Scott, James B.
Djuna Barnes **29**:26

Scott, John
Ch'ien Chung-shu **22**:106

Scott, Lael
Mary Stolz **12**:554

Scott, Malcolm
Jean Giono **11**:232

Scott, Nathan A., Jr.
Elizabeth Bishop **32**:41
Charles M. Schulz **12**:522
Lionel Trilling **24**:460
Richard Wright **1**:378

Scott, Paul
Ved Mehta **37**:292

Scott, Peter Dale
John Newlove **14**:377
Mordecai Richler **5**:372

Scott, Tom
Hugh MacDiarmid **4**:309
Ezra Pound **4**:413

Scott, Winfield Townley
Edwin Honig **33**:211
David Ignatow **7**:173
James Purdy **28**:377
Louis Simpson **7**:426

Scott-James, R. A.
Edith Sitwell **9**:493

Scouffas, George
J. F. Powers **1**:280

Scruggs, Charles W.
Ishmael Reed **32**:358
Jean Toomer **4**:549

Scruton, Roger
Lucien Goldmann **24**:254
Marge Piercy **27**:381
Harold Pinter **27**:396
Sylvia Plath **5**:340
Tom Stoppard **29**:403

Scrutton, Mary
Vera Brittain **23**:92

Scudder, Vida D.
T. H. White **30**:438

Sculatti, Gene
Brian Wilson **12**:642

Scupham, Peter
W. H. Auden **6**:16
Elizabeth Daryush **19**:121
Robert Graves **6**:211
H. D. **8**:257
Elizabeth Jennings **14**:293

David Jones **4**:262
D. M. Thomas **13**:542

Seabrook, W. B.
Nella Larsen **37**:212

Sealy, Douglas
Benedict Kiely **23**:265
Michael Longley **29**:294

Searle, Leroy
Dannie Abse **7**:2
Erica Jong **4**:264

Searles, Baird
Anna Kavan **5**:205
Andre Norton **12**:459

Searles, George J.
Joseph Heller **8**:279

Seaver, Richard
Louis-Ferdinand Céline **1**:57

Seay, James
James Wright **3**:543

Secher, Andy
Pink Floyd **35**:313

Sedgwick, Ellery
Esther Forbes **12**:208

See, Carolyn
Josephine Herbst **34**:453
Elinor Langer **34**:453
Kem Nunn **34**:95

Seebohm, Caroline
Isaac Asimov **19**:29
Dirk Bogarde **19**:42
Kamala Markandaya **8**:377

Seed, David
Isaac Bashevis Singer **9**:487

Seed, John
Donald Davie **31**:117

Seeger, Pete
Woody Guthrie **35**:188

Seelye, John
Donald Barthelme **2**:41
Richard Lester **20**:218, 219
Norman Mailer **3**:316
Marge Piercy **3**:383
Charles M. Schulz **12**:531
James Thurber **5**:439
David Wagoner **5**:474

Segal, Erich
Robert Lowell **15**:348

Segal, Lore
Joan Didion **1**:75
James D. Forman **21**:116

Segal, Harold
Gregor von Rezzori **25**:384

Segel, Harold B.
Vasily Aksenov **22**:27
Czesław Miłosz **22**:312

Segovia, Tomás
Octavio Paz **3**:376

Seib, Kenneth
Richard Brautigan **1**:44

Seibles, Timothy S.
James Baldwin **15**:43

Seiden, Melvin
Vladimir Nabokov **2**:302

Seidensticker, Edward
Kōbō Abé **22**:12
Yukio Mishima **27**:337

Seidlin, Oskar
Hermann Hesse **17**:216

Seidman, Hugh
Edward Hirsch **31**:214
Denise Levertov **15**:338
Mary Oliver **19**:362
Linda Pastan **27**:371

Seidman, Robert
John Berger **19**:39

Seitz, Michael
Luchino Visconti **16**:574

Seitz, Michael H.
Richard Pryor **26**:383

Selby, Herbert, Jr.
Richard Price **6**:427

Seldes, Gilbert
Charles Chaplin **16**:188

Seligson, Tom
Piri Thomas **17**:500
Hunter S. Thompson **9**:527

Sellick, Robert
Shirley Hazzard **18**:218

Sellin, Eric
Samuel Beckett **2**:47

Seltzer, Alvin J.
William S. Burroughs **22**:80

Selz, Thalia
Jonathan Baumbach **23**:55

Selzer, David
Peter Porter **5**:346

Semkow, Julie
Joan Micklin Silver **20**:341

Semple, Robert B., Jr.
Allen Drury **37**:103

Sena, Vinad
T. S. Eliot **6**:159

Senkewicz, Robert M.
Bruce Catton **35**:95

Senna, Carl
Julio Cortázar **33**:135
Piers Paul Read **25**:376

Sennwald, Andre
Rouben Mamoulian **16**:421

Serchuk, Peter
Richard F. Hugo **32**:243
Laurence Lieberman **36**:261

Sergay, Timothy
Vasily Aksyonov **37**:13

Sergeant, Howard
Dannie Abse **29**:17
Siegfried Sassoon **36**:391

Servodidio, Mirella D'Ambrosio
Azorín **11**:24

Sesonske, Alexander
Jean Renoir **20**:309

Sessions, William A.
Julia Peterkin **31**:312

Seton, Cynthia Propper
Marilyn French **18**:158
Doris Grumbach **22**:206
Barbara Pym **19**:387
Muriel Spark **18**:505

Settle, Mary Lee
Russell Baker **31**:30

Severin, Timothy
Thor Heyerdahl **26**:193

Sewell, Elizabeth
Muriel Rukeyser **15**:458

Seybolt, Cynthia T.
Jules Archer **12**:21, 22

Seydor, Paul
Sam Peckinpah **20**:283

Seyler, Harry E.
Allen Drury **37**:111

Seymour, Miranda
Italo Calvino **33**:99
Eva Figes **31**:168

Seymour-Smith, Martin
David Caute **29**:113
J. M. Coetzee **23**:126
D. J. Enright **31**:150
Roy Fuller **28**:150
Robert Graves **1**:128

Sgammato, Joseph
Alfred Hitchcock **16**:351

Shack, Neville
William McPherson **34**:89

Shadoian, Jack
Donald Barthelme **1**:18

Shaffer, Dallas Y.
Jules Archer **12**:16
Frank Bonham **12**:53

Shaffer, Peter
Peter Shaffer **37**:382

Shah, Diane K.
Richard O'Brien **17**:325

Shahane, Vasant A.
Ruth Prawer Jhabvala **29**:257

Shahane, Vasant Anant
Khushwant Singh **11**:504

Shakespeare, Nicholas
Morris L. West **33**:434

Shands, Annette Oliver
Gwendolyn Brooks **4**:78, 79
Don L. Lee **2**:238

Shanks, Edward
Siegfried Sassoon **36**:387

Shanley, J. P.
Rod Serling **30**:353

Shannon, James P.
J. F. Powers **1**:279

Shannon, William H.
Thomas Merton **34**:461
Michael Mott **34**:461

Shapcott, Thomas
Frank O'Hara **2**:323
W. R. Rodgers **7**:377

Shapiro, Alan
Donald Davie **31**:125

Shapiro, Anna
Russell Banks **37**:26
Susan Isaacs **32**:256
Stephen King **37**:205
J.I.M. Stewart **32**:423

Shapiro, Charles
Meyer Levin **7**:203
David Madden **5**:265
Joyce Carol Oates **3**:363
Anthony Powell **1**:277
Harvey Swados **5**:420
Jerome Weidman **7**:517

Shapiro, David
John Ashbery **25**:49
Elizabeth Bishop **15**:60
Hayden Carruth **10**:100
X. J. Kennedy **8**:320
Josephine Miles **14**:370
Eric Rohmer **16**:539

Shapiro, Jane
Rosalyn Drexler **6**:143

Shapiro, Karl
W. H. Auden **1**:8; **3**:21
T. S. Eliot **3**:136
Rod McKuen **1**:210
Henry Miller **4**:349
Chaim Potok **26**:367
Ezra Pound **3**:394
Melvin B. Tolson **36**:426
William Carlos Williams **5**:506
Tom Wolfe **35**:451

Shapiro, Laura
Elizabeth Swados **12**:560

Shapiro, Lillian L.
Rosa Guy **26**:145
Kristin Hunter **35**:229

Shapiro, Marianne
Elio Vittorini **14**:546

Shapiro, Paula Meinetz
Alice Walker **6**:553

Shapiro, Susin
Joan Armatrading **17**:7
Jimmy Cliff **21**:61
Janis Ian **21**:184
Lou Reed **21**:315
Carly Simon **26**:409

Shapiro, Walter
Thomas J. Fleming **37**:128
M. M. Kaye **28**:202

Sharma, Govind Narain
Ngugi wa Thiong'o **36**:314

Sharma, P. P.
Arthur Miller **15**:370

Sharman, Vincent
Ralph Gustafson **36**:220

Sharp, Christopher
Ntozake Shange **25**:397
Sam Shepard **34**:267

Sharp, Sister Corona
Friedrich Dürrenmatt **15**:201
Eugène Ionesco **15**:297

Sharp, Francis Michael
Thomas Bernhard **32**:25

Sharp, Jonathan
Alvah Bessie **23**:61

Sharpe, David F.
Henry Carlisle **33**:103

Sharpe, Patricia
Margaret Drabble **10**:162

Sharrock, Roger
T. S. Eliot **24**:179

Shattan, Joseph
Saul Bellow **8**:80

Shattuck, Roger
Renata Adler **31**:15
Jean Arp **5**:32
Saul Bellow **6**:57
Alain Robbe-Grillet **2**:376
Octavio Paz **19**:365
Nathalie Sarraute **31**:384
Michel Tournier **36**:436

Shaughnessy, Mary Rose
Edna Ferber **18**:152

Shaw, Arnold
Chuck Berry **17**:53

Shaw, Bob
Michael Moorcock **27**:350

Shaw, Evelyn
Melvin Berger **12**:37

Shaw, Greg
Monty Python **21**:224
Brian Wilson **12**:647

Shaw, Irwin
James Jones **10**:290

Shaw, Peter
Robert Lowell **8**:351
Hugh Nissenson **9**:400
Ezra Pound **18**:422

Shaw, Robert B.
A. R. Ammons **3**:11
W. H. Auden **2**:26
Wendell Berry **8**:85
Rosellen Brown **32**:63
Stanley Burnshaw **3**:91
Alfred Corn **33**:117
Peter Davison **28**:101
Babette Deutsch **18**:120
James Dickey **2**:117
William Dickey **28**:119
Robert Duncan **7**:88
Stephen Dunn **36**:155
Robert Francis **15**:238
Brewster Ghiselin **23**:171
Allen Ginsberg **6**:201
John Glassco **9**:236
W. S. Graham **29**:196

Richard Howard 7:166
Barbara Howes 15:289
David Ignatow 4:248
Stanley Kunitz 14:313
Philip Larkin 8:338
Brad Leithauser 27:242
Robert Lowell 37:236
William Meredith 4:348
Frederick Morgan 23:299
Howard Nemerov 36:302
Adrienne Rich 6:457
M. L. Rosenthal 28:392
Raphael Rudnik 7:384
Charles Simic 6:501; 9:479;
    22:381
Louis Simpson 32:377
Allen Tate 2:430
Mark Van Doren 6:541
Eudora Welty 14:566
James Wright 28:468
Marya Zaturenska 6:585

Shaw, Russell
Pink Floyd 35:309

Shaw, Spencer G.
Lloyd Alexander 35:28

Shaw, Valerie
Fay Weldon 36:448

Shawe-Taylor, Desmond
Pamela Hansford Johnson
    27:212

Shayon, Robert Lewis
Norman Lear 12:329
Gene Roddenberry 17:403
Rod Serling 30:352, 357

Shea, Robert J.
Budd Schulberg 7:403

Shear, Walter
Bernard Malamud 1:197

Shearer, Ann
Christa Wolf 29:465

Shechner, Mark
Arthur A. Cohen 31:94
Allen Ginsberg 36:185
Tadeusz Konwicki 8:328
Philip Rahv 24:356
Mordecai Richler 18:453
Philip Roth 15:451
Isaac Bashevis Singer 15:508

Shedlin, Michael
Woody Allen 16:2

Sheean, Vincent
Alvah Bessie 23:59

Sheed, Wilfrid
Renata Adler 31:12
Edward Albee 1:4
Roger Angell 26:33
James Baldwin 1:16; 8:42
Robert Coover 7:58
Robert Frost 1:110
William Golding 1:121
Joseph Heller 5:182
James Jones 1:162
Norman Mailer 1:193; 4:320
Terrence McNally 7:216
Arthur Miller 1:217
Alberto Moravia 2:292

Iris Murdoch 1:236
P. H. Newby 13:409
John Osborne 1:263
Walker Percy 2:332
S. J. Perelman 23:339
Neil Simon 6:503
William Styron 1:330
James Thurber 25:436
John Updike 1:343
Kurt Vonnegut, Jr. 1:347
Douglas Turner Ward 19:456
Evelyn Waugh 3:512
Arnold Wesker 3:518
Tennessee Williams 1:369
P. G. Wodehouse 22:482
Tom Wolfe 2:481

Sheehan, Donald
John Berryman 1:34
Richard Howard 7:166
Robert Lowell 1:181

Sheehan, Edward R. F.
Edwin O'Connor 14:392

Sheehan, Ethna
E. M. Almedingen 12:1
Lois Duncan 26:101
Christie Harris 12:261
Mollie Hunter 21:156
Philippa Pearce 21:281

Sheils, Merrill
Frank Herbert 35:206

Shelton, Austin J.
Chinua Achebe 7:4

Shelton, Frank W.
Robert Coover 7:60
Harry Crews 23:137
E. L. Doctorow 37:88
Ernest Hemingway 10:269

Shelton, Robert
Joan Armatrading 17:10
Bob Dylan 12:179

Shepard, Paul
Peter Matthiessen 5:273

Shepard, Ray Anthony
Alice Childress 12:107
Nicholasa Mohr 12:446

Shepard, Richard F.
Lois Duncan 26:102
Sam Shepard 17:433
Elie Wiesel 37:458

Shepherd, Allen
Harry Crews 23:133
Reynolds Price 3:405, 406
Robert Penn Warren 1:355

Shepherd, Naomi
S. Y. Agnon 14:1

Shepherd, R.
Raja Rao 25:368

Shepley, John
Alberto Moravia 27:356

Sheppard, R. Z.
Louis Auchincloss 4:30
Russell Baker 31:28
Saul Bellow 6:55
William Peter Blatty 2:64
Lothar-Günther Buchheim
    6:101

Anthony Burgess 5:85
Philip Caputo 32:106
Peter De Vries 2:114
E. L. Doctorow 6:133
Nora Ephron 17:113
Paul E. Erdman 25:154
Thomas J. Fleming 37:121
Barbara Guest 34:443
Alex Haley 8:260
H. D. 34:443
Frank Herbert 12:270
James Leo Herlihy 6:235
Dan Jacobson 4:254
Bernard Malamud 2:266
S. J. Perelman 5:338
Padgett Powell 34:97
Ishmael Reed 5:370
Harvey Swados 5:422
Michel Tournier 6:537
Anne Tyler 28:433
Douglas Unger 34:115
Mario Vargas Llosa 6:545
Gore Vidal 6:548
Paul West 7:523
Hilma Wolitzer 17:561

Sheps, G. David
Mordecai Richler 13:481

Sher, John Lear
Zoa Sherburne 30:362

Sheridan, Alan
Michel Foucault 31:184

Sheridan, Martin
Jerome Siegel and Joe Shuster
    21:354

Sheridan, Nancy
Betsy Byars 35:75

Sheridan, Robert N.
Henry Gregor Felsen 17:124

Sherman, Beatrice
Margery Allingham 19:13
Sally Benson 17:48
Zora Neale Hurston 30:213
Dalton Trumbo 19:445
T. H. White 30:439, 440

Sherman, Bill
Trina Robbins 21:341

Sherman, Paul
Charles Olson 29:329

Sherman, Stuart
Carl Sandburg 35:343

Sherman, Susan
Adrienne Rich 36:371

Sherrard, Philip
Yannis Ritsos 31:327

Sherrard-Smith, Barbara
Zilpha Keatley Snyder 17:472

Sherrell, Richard E.
Arthur Adamov 25:15

Sherrill, Robert
C.D.B. Bryan 29:103
Art Buchwald 33:95
Peter Matthiessen 32:292
Joe McGinniss 32:301
Jonathan Schell 35:363

Gay Talese 37:395

Sherry, Vincent B., Jr.
W. S. Merwin 18:335

Sherwood, Martin
Isaac Asimov 26:39
Roger Zelazny 21:468

Sherwood, R. E.
Buster Keaton 20:188

Sherwood, Robert E.
Carl Sandburg 35:350, 353

Sherwood, Terry G.
Ken Kesey 1:167

Shetley, Vernon
A. R. Ammons 25:45
John Ashbery 25:59
Norman Dubie 36:138
Laura Jensen 37:190
Galway Kinnell 29:286
James Merrill 34:235
James Schuyler 23:392

Shewey, Don
Joan Armatrading 17:11
William Least Heat Moon
    29:224
Janis Ian 21:188
Billy Joel 26:216, 221
John Lennon 35:275
Lou Reed 21:319
Wole Soyinka 36:413
Frank Zappa 17:594

Shideler, Ross
Gunnar Ekelöf 27:117

Shifreen, Lawrence J.
Henry Miller 14:372

Shimuhara, Nobuo
Margaret Mead 37:277

Shinn, Thelma J.
Flannery O'Connor 6:375
Ann Petry 7:304
William Saroyan 10:452

Shipp, Randy
Robert Lewis Taylor 14:535

Shippey, T. A.
Samuel R. Delany 14:147
Robert Nye 13:414
Frederik Pohl 18:410
Mary Lee Settle 19:410
John Steinbeck 13:535
Arkadii Strugatskii and Boris
    Strugatskii 27:432
Roger Zelazny 21:469

Shippey, Tom
Fritz Leiber 25:305

Shippey, Thomas
Lothar-Günther Buchheim
    6:100

Shiras, Mary
William Meredith 22:301

Shirley, John
Jack Vance 35:421

Shivers, Alfred S.
Jessamyn West 7:520

Critic Index

Shlaes, Amity
Christa Wolf **29**:467

Shockley, Ann Allen
Claude Brown **30**:38

Shockley, Martin
John Steinbeck **21**:368

Shoemaker, Alice
William Faulkner **14**:175

Shore, Rima
Yevgeny Yevtushenko **13**:619

Shores, Edward
George Roy Hill **26**:210

Shorris, Earl
Donald Barthelme **2**:42
Arthur A. Cohen **31**:95
John Gardner **3**:184
William H. Gass **2**:155
Thomas Pynchon **3**:414

Shorris, Sylvia
Russell Banks **37**:24

Short, Robert L.
Charles M. Schulz **12**:522, 525

Shorter, Eric
Alan Ayckbourn **5**:36; **18**:29
Agatha Christie **12**:118
Ronald Harwood **32**:224
Hugh Leonard **19**:282
Thornton Wilder **15**:574

Shorter, Kingsley
Siegfried Lenz **27**:249
Frank Tuohy **37**:429

Shoukri, Doris Enright-Clark
Marguerite Duras **3**:129

Showalter, Dennis E.
Robert Heinlein **14**:246

Showalter, Elaine
Mary McCarthy **3**:329

Showers, Paul
Art Buchwald **33**:93
Peter De Vries **2**:114
James Herriot **12**:283
John Seelye **7**:407
Alvin Silverstein and Virginia
B. Silverstein **17**:454

Shrapnel, Norman
Marge Piercy **18**:406

Shreve, Susan Richards
Andrea Lee **36**:255

Shrimpton, Nicholas
Anita Brookner **32**:59
J. M. Coetzee **23**:124
Zoë Fairbairns **32**:162
M. M. Kaye **28**:200
David Lodge **36**:273
Bernice Rubens **19**:405
Tom Sharpe **36**:402
Irwin Shaw **23**:401
C. P. Snow **19**:428
D. M. Thomas **22**:417
Donald E. Westlake **33**:439
A. N. Wilson **33**:453

Shub, Anatole
Vasily Aksyonov **37**:15
Paddy Chayefsky **23**:113

Shuey, Andrea Lee
M. M. Kaye **28**:202

Shulman, Alix Kates
Grace Paley **37**:335

Shuman, R. Baird
William Inge **1**:153
Clifford Odets **2**:318, 320

Shuttleworth, Martin
Christina Stead **2**:421

Shuttleworth, Paul
Leon Uris **7**:492

Shwartz, Susan M.
Marion Zimmer Bradley **30**:30

Siaulys, Tony
Sonia Levitin **17**:266

Sibbald, K. M.
Jorge Guillén **11**:263

Sibley, Francis M.
Chinua Achebe **26**:22

Sibley, William F.
Shiga Naoya **33**:371

Sicherman, Barbara
Taylor Caldwell **28**:67

Sicherman, Carol M.
Saul Bellow **10**:37

Siconolfi, Michael T., S.J.
Audre Lorde **18**:309

Sidnell, M. J.
Ronald G. Everson **27**:133

Siebert, Sara L.
Maureen Daly **17**:89

Siegal, R. A.
Judy Blume **12**:47

Siegel, Ben
Saul Bellow **8**:78
Bernard Malamud **1**:195
Isaac Bashevis Singer **1**:313

Siegel, Eve
Margaret Atwood **25**:68

Siegel, Joel E.
Robert Altman **16**:33
Albert Maysles and David
Maysles **16**:445

Siegel, Mark
Tom Robbins **32**:369

Siegel, Paul N.
Norman Mailer **5**:266

Siegel, Robert
Philip Booth **23**:76
Al Young **19**:480

Siemens, William L.
Julio Cortázar **5**:110

Sievers, W. David
Tennessee Williams **30**:460

Sigal, Clancy
Kingsley Amis **3**:9; **5**:22
Patrick Boyle **19**:67
Melvyn Bragg **10**:72
E. L. Doctorow **18**:127
Penelope Lively **32**:276

Piers Paul Read **25**:376
Alan Sillitoe **3**:448
James Thurber **25**:440

Sigerson, Davitt
Paul McCartney **35**:289
Brian Wilson **12**:653

Siggins, Clara M.
Taylor Caldwell **2**:95
Alan Garner **17**:146
Lillian Hellman **4**:221
Saul Maloff **5**:270

Signoriello, John
Mollie Hunter **21**:157

Šilbajoris, Rimvydas
Boris Pasternak **10**:387

Silber, Irwin
Bob Dylan **12**:181

Silber, Joan
Cynthia Propper Seton **27**:430
Scott Sommer **25**:426

Silbersack, John
Fritz Leiber **25**:308

Silenieks, Juris
Édouard Glissant **10**:231

Silet, Charles L. P.
David Kherdian **9**:317, 318

Silkin, Jon
Geoffrey Hill **5**:183

Silko, Leslie Marmon
Dee Brown **18**:71
Harriet Doerr **34**:153

Sillanpoa, Wallace P.
Pier Paolo Pasolini **37**:347

Silva, Candelaria
Maya Angelou **35**:32

Silver, Adele Z.
E. M. Broner **19**:70

Silver, Charles
Orson Welles **20**:446

Silver, David
Peter Townshend **17**:527

Silver, George A.
John Berger **19**:37

Silver, Linda
Lois Duncan **26**:103

Silver, Linda R.
Zibby Oneal **30**:279
Sandra Scoppettone **26**:402

Silver, Philip
Dámaso Alonso **14**:22

Silverberg, Robert
Jack Vance **35**:419

Silverman, Hugh J.
Jean-Paul Sartre **18**:472

Silverman, Malcolm
Jorge Amado **13**:11
Autran Dourado **23**:149

Silverman, Michael
Nagisa Oshima **20**:253

Silverstein, Norman
James Dickey **7**:81
Buster Keaton **20**:195

Silvert, Conrad
Peter Matthiessen **7**:210

Silverton, Pete
Elvis Costello **21**:73

Silvey, Anita
Gunnel Beckman **26**:86
S. E. Hinton **30**:205
Milton Meltzer **26**:303
Otfried Preussler **17**:377
Mildred D. Taylor **21**:418

Simels, Steve
Jackson Browne **21**:40
The Clash **30**:43
Jimmy Cliff **21**:64
Ray Davies **21**:95, 100
Billy Joel **26**:223
John Lennon **35**:269, 270, 274
Monty Python **21**:230
Martin Mull **17**:300
Jimmy Page and Robert Plant
12:476
Pink Floyd **35**:309
The Police **26**:365
Lou Reed **21**:305, 308
Gene Roddenberry **17**:414
Patti Smith **12**:537
Bruce Springsteen **17**:485
Peter Townshend **17**:535
Brian Wilson **12**:651
Neil Young **17**:579

Simels, Steven
Jim Carroll **35**:80

Simenon, Georges
Georges Simenon **3**:451

Simic, Charles
Vasko Popa **19**:374

Simmons, Dee Dee
Betsy Byars **35**:71

Simmons, Ernest J.
Mikhail Sholokhov **7**:416, 420

Simmons, John S.
Robert Lipsyte **21**:209

Simmons, Ruth J. S.
Aimé Césaire **19**:97

Simmons, Tom
Richard F. Hugo **18**:263

Simon, John
Edward Albee **2**:1; **5**:13; **11**:11;
13:3, 4; **25**:36
Vicente Aleixandre **36**:30
Woody Allen **16**:7, 13
Robert Altman **16**:33, 36
Lindsay Anderson **20**:14
Jean Anouilh **13**:22
Michelangelo Antonioni **20**:40
Alan Ayckbourn **8**:34; **18**:29;
33:50
Ralph Bakshi **26**:70, 72
James Baldwin **17**:40
Howard Barker **37**:38
Peter Barnes **5**:49
Samuel Beckett **3**:47; **29**:66

Ingmar Bergman **16**:77
Thomas Bernhard **32**:26
Bernardo Bertolucci **16**:100
Robert Bolt **14**:88
Mel Brooks **12**:80
Ed Bullins **5**:84; **7**:36
Anne Burr **6**:104
John Cassavetes **20**:51
Claude Chabrol **16**:179
Caryl Churchill **31**:89
Francis Ford Coppola **16**:240
Michael Cristofer **28**:96, 97
Shelagh Delaney **29**:147
Brian De Palma **20**:74, 76
Martin Duberman **8**:185
Christopher Durang **27**:89, 92
Marguerite Duras **20**:98
Rainer Werner Fassbinder
  20:112
Jules Feiffer **2**:133
Federico Fellini **16**:289, 297,
  300
Lawrence Ferlinghetti **2**:134
Harvey Fierstein **33**:153
Dario Fo **32**:176
Bob Fosse **20**:124
Athol Fugard **9**:230; **14**:191;
  25:177
Peter Gent **29**:182
Frank D. Gilroy **2**:161
Jean-Luc Godard **20**:135
Charles Gordone **1**:124
Günter Grass **11**:252
Simon Gray **14**:215; **36**:207
John Guare **14**:222
Bill Gunn **5**:153
A. R. Gurney, Jr. **32**:218, 219,
  220, 221
Christopher Hampton **4**:211
David Hare **29**:218
Joseph Heller **11**:265
Lillian Hellman **8**:281; **18**:226
Beth Henley **23**:216
George Roy Hill **26**:203, 210
Alfred Hitchcock **16**:353
Rolf Hochhuth **11**:275
Bohumil Hrabal **13**:290
William Inge **8**:308
Albert Innaurato **21**:197, 198
Ann Jellicoe **27**:210
Jean Kerr **22**:259
Pavel Kohout **13**:323
Arthur Kopit **1**:171; **18**:291;
  33:247, 251, 253
Stanley Kubrick **16**:390
Richard Lester **20**:230, 231
Denise Levertov **15**:336
Ira Levin **3**:294
Robert Lowell **4**:299; **11**:324
Norman Mailer **2**:259; **3**:316
David Mamet **15**:356, 358;
  34:221
William Mastrosimone **36**:289
Elaine May **16**:436
Albert Maysles and David
  Maysles **16**:444
Marshall McLuhan **37**:253
Terrence McNally **4**:347;
  7:217, 218, 219
Mark Medoff **6**:321, 322;
  23:293
Christopher Middleton **13**:387
Arthur Miller **2**:279, 280; **6**:335

Jason Miller **2**:284, 285
Czesław Miłosz **22**:310
Vladimir Nabokov **23**:314
Peter Nichols **36**:331, 333
Marsha Norman **28**:317, 319
Joyce Carol Oates **11**:400
Joe Orton **4**:387
John Osborne **2**:328; **11**:421
Nagisa Oshima **20**:245, 256
Rochelle Owens **8**:434
Gordon Parks **16**:460
Pier Paolo Pasolini **20**:262
Sam Peckinpah **20**:274
S. J. Perelman **5**:337
Harold Pinter **3**:386, 387;
  11:443; **15**:425
Sylvia Plath **17**:345
Roman Polanski **16**:471
Bernard Pomerance **13**:446
David Rabe **8**:449, 451; **33**:346
Gerome Ragni and James Rado
  17:381, 388
Satyajit Ray **16**:489
Jean Renoir **20**:307
Jonathan Reynolds **6**:452
Yannis Ritsos **31**:329
Eric Rohmer **16**:538
Howard Sackler **14**:478
Carlos Saura **20**:318
Murray Schisgal **6**:490
Peter Shaffer **5**:387, 389;
  37:384
Ntozake Shange **8**:484; **25**:398,
  399
Sam Shepard **6**:497; **17**:435,
  449; **34**:269
Martin Sherman **19**:415
Joan Micklin Silver **20**:343
Neil Simon **6**:506; **11**:495, 496;
  31:402
Isaac Bashevis Singer **15**:509
Bernard Slade **11**:507
Steven Spielberg **20**:361
John Steinbeck **5**:408
George Steiner **24**:427
Tom Stoppard **3**:470; **4**:525,
  526; **5**:412; **8**:504; **29**:396;
  34:278
David Storey **4**:528; **5**:415, 417
Elizabeth Swados **12**:559, 562
Ronald Tavel **6**:529
C. P. Taylor **27**:446
François Truffaut **20**:385, 405
John Updike **34**:286
Melvin Van Peebles **2**:448
Gore Vidal **2**:450; **4**:554;
  10:503
Andrzej Wajda **16**:578
Derek Walcott **2**:460; **14**:550
Wendy Wasserstein **32**:440
Andrew Lloyd Webber and Tim
  Rice **21**:430
Peter Weiss **3**:513
Fay Weldon **36**:445
Michael Weller **10**:526
Lina Wertmüller **16**:590, 598
Morris L. West **33**:428
Hugh Whitemore **37**:444
Billy Wilder **20**:460
Thornton Wilder **10**:535
Tennessee Williams **2**:464;
  5:501; **7**:544; **8**:549; **11**:571

Lanford Wilson **14**:591, 592;
  36:460, 461, 462, 464
Robert Wilson **7**:550, 551

Simon, John K.
  Michel Butor **15**:112

Simon, Kate
  Rhys Davies **23**:145

Simon, Linda
  Saul Bellow **34**:546
  Daniel Fuchs **34**:546

Simonds, C. H.
  Joan Didion **1**:74
  Gay Talese **37**:392

Simonds, Katharine
  Sally Benson **17**:47

Simonsuuri, Kirsti
  Paavo Haavikko **34**:176

Simpson, Allen
  Albert Camus **11**:96

Simpson, Claude M., Jr.
  Woody Guthrie **35**:184

Simpson, Clinton
  Ilya Ehrenburg **18**:130

Simpson, Elaine
  Andre Norton **12**:456

Simpson, Louis
  Robert Bly **2**:65
  J. V. Cunningham **31**:97
  Donald Davie **31**:123
  Allen Ginsberg **13**:241
  Ronald J. Glasser **37**:131
  James Merrill **8**:380
  Kenneth Rexroth **2**:370
  W. D. Snodgrass **2**:405
  C. K. Williams **33**:446

Simpson, Mona
  Carolyn Hougan **34**:60

Simpson, Sarah
  Kristin Hunter **35**:230

Sims, Rudine
  Ouida Sebestyen **30**:347

Simson, Eve
  Norma Klein **30**:242

Sinclair, Dorothy
  Erich Segal **10**:467
  David Slavitt **14**:491

Sinclair, Karen
  Ursula K. LeGuin **13**:350

Siner, Robin
  Margaret O. Hyde **21**:179

Singer, Alexander
  René Clair **20**:63

Singer, Isaac B.
  Otfried Preussler **17**:376

Singer, Marilyn
  Frank Bonham **12**:54

Singer, Marilyn R.
  Jean Craighead George **35**:178
  Norma Klein **30**:236
  Paul Zindel **26**:471

Singh, G.
  Eugenio Montale **7**:223, 226
  Ezra Pound **2**:342, 344; **7**:334

Singh, Rahul
  M. M. Kaye **28**:200

Singleton, Mary Ann
  Doris Lessing **22**:280

Sinha, Krishna Nandan
  Mulk Raj Anand **23**:15

Sinyavsky, Andrei
  Anna Akhmatova **25**:24
  Robert Frost **4**:174
  Yevgeny Yevtushenko **26**:465

Sire, James W.
  C. S. Lewis **1**:177

Sirkin, Elliott
  Tom Stoppard **34**:281
  Wendy Wasserstein **32**:442

Sisco, Ellen
  Jamake Highwater **12**:286

Sisk, John P.
  Mark Harris **19**:200
  J. F. Powers **1**:280
  Philip Rahv **24**:354

Sissman, L. E.
  Kingsley Amis **2**:7; **5**:22
  Martin Amis **4**:21
  Jimmy Breslin **4**:76
  Michael Crichton **6**:119
  J. P. Donleavy **4**:126
  J. G. Farrell **6**:174
  Natalia Ginzburg **5**:141
  Joseph Heller **8**:278
  Dan Jacobson **4**:255
  Joe McGinniss **32**:300
  Thomas McGuane **3**:329
  Tom McHale **3**:332; **5**:282
  Brian Moore **7**:237
  Gilbert Rogin **18**:458
  Anne Roiphe **3**:434
  John Updike **2**:441
  Evelyn Waugh **3**:513
  Fay Weldon **6**:563
  Emlyn Williams **15**:578
  Edmund Wilson **2**:478
  Al Young **19**:477

Sisson, C. H.
  H. D. **8**:257

Sitterly, Bancroft W.
  Roy A. Gallant **17**:127

Sjöberg, Leif
  Gunnar Ekelöf **27**:111, 113,
  115
  Eyvind Johnson **14**:296, 297
  Harry Martinson **14**:355, 356

Skau, Michael
  Lawrence Ferlinghetti **10**:177

Skelton, Robin
  Ralph Gustafson **36**:212, 215
  Patrick Kavanagh **22**:236
  Anthony Kerrigan **6**:276
  Dorothy Livesay **4**:294
  Derek Mahon **27**:286
  John Metcalf **37**:307
  John Newlove **14**:378

Critic Index

Jane Rule 27:417

Skerrett, Joseph T., Jr.
Ralph Ellison 11:182

Skiles, Don
Jonathan Baumbach 23:56

Skirius, A. John
Carlos Fuentes 22:168

Sklar, Robert
Thomas Pynchon 33:327
J.R.R. Tolkien 12:568

Skloot, Floyd
Laura Jensen 37:186
Thomas Kinsella 19:255

Skodnick, Roy
Gilbert Sorrentino 7:448

Skoller, Don
Carl Theodor Dreyer 16:262

Skow, Jack
John Gardner 5:132
Robert Graves 2:176

Skow, John
Richard Adams 5:5
Richard Brautigan 3:86
Arthur A. Cohen 7:52
Richard Condon 4:107; 6:115
Julio Cortázar 5:109
Robertson Davies 2:113
Allen Drury 37:108
Lawrence Durrell 6:152
Barry Hannah 23:208
Charles Johnson 7:183
Robert F. Jones 7:193
Sue Kaufman 3:263
Yasunari Kawabata 5:208
Milan Kundera 4:277
John D. MacDonald 3:307
Iris Murdoch 4:370
Vladimir Nabokov 6:354
Harold Robbins 5:379
Susan Fromberg Schaeffer 6:488
Irving Stone 7:471
Kurt Vonnegut, Jr. 4:568
Morris L. West 6:564
Patrick White 3:525

Skretvedt, Randy
Steve Martin 30:250

Škvorecký, Josef
Pavel Kohout 13:325
Jaroslav Seifert 34:262

Slade, Joseph W.
James T. Farrell 11:192
Thomas Pynchon 33:332

Slansky, Paul
Martin Mull 17:300

Slate, Ron
Stephen Dobyns 37:76
Stephen Dunn 36:153

Slater, Candace
Elizabeth Bishop 13:88
Salvatore Espriu 9:193

Slater, Jack
Stevie Wonder 12:662

Slater, Joseph
Nelly Sachs 14:475

Slaughter, Frank G.
Millen Brand 7:29
Margaret O. Hyde 21:172

Slavitt, David R.
George Garrett 11:220
Maureen Howard 14:267
Ann Quin 6:441

Slethaug, Gordon E.
John Barth 2:38

Slick, Sam L.
Jorge Ibargüengoitia 37:182

Sloan, James Park
Alice Childress 15:131
David Madden 15:350

Sloman, Larry
Lou Reed 21:306

Slomovitz, Philip
Zora Neale Hurston 30:213

Slonim, Marc
Ilya Ehrenburg 18:133
Mikhail Sholokhov 7:415, 418
Aleksandr I. Solzhenitsyn 1:320
Arkadii Strugatskii and Boris Strugatskii 27:432
Henri Troyat 23:458
Yevgeny Yevtushenko 26:460
Marguerite Yourcenar 19:482

Sloss, Henry
Richard Howard 10:276
James Merrill 8:381, 384
Reynolds Price 3:406
Philip Roth 1:293

Slotkin, Richard
Christopher Collier and James L. Collier 30:74

Slung, Michele
Betsy Byars 35:74
Bette Greene 30:171
Jorge Ibargüengoitia 37:184
P. D. James 18:273
Stephen King 26:237; 37:198
Helen MacInnes 27:284
Cynthia Voigt 30:419

Slusser, George Edgar
Arthur C. Clarke 13:151
Samuel R. Delany 14:143
Harlan Ellison 13:204
Robert Heinlein 14:246
Ursula K. LeGuin 13:345

Small, Robert C.
Joanne Greenberg 30:167
Zibby Oneal 30:281

Smalley, Webster
Langston Hughes 35:217

Smedman, Sarah M.
Katherine Paterson 30:288

Smelser, Marshall
Thomas J. Fleming 37:123

Smeltzer, Sister Mary Etheldra
Larry Kettelkamp 12:306

Smith, A.J.M.
Earle Birney 6:74
Stanley Kunitz 14:312
Irving Layton 15:318
P. K. Page 7:291
F. R. Scott 22:373
A.J.M. Smith 15:515

Smith, Anne
Lisa St. Aubin de Teran 36:419

Smith, Annette
Aimé Césaire 32:110

Smith, Barbara
Ishmael Reed 6:447
Alice Walker 6:553

Smith, Bradford
Roderick L. Haig-Brown 21:136
Bruce Lancaster 36:241

Smith, C.E.J.
Mavis Thorpe Clark 12:130
Leon Garfield 12:231

Smith, Chris
Claude Brown 30:41

Smith, Dave
Philip Booth 23:77
Harry Crews 6:118
Stephen Dunn 36:154
Brewster Ghiselin 23:171
Albert Goldbarth 5:144
Daniel Halpern 14:232
William Heyen 18:232
Richard F. Hugo 32:244, 249
Philip Levine 33:270
Laurence Lieberman 36:260
Cynthia Macdonald 19:290
Craig Nova 31:299
Linda Pastan 27:370
Louis Simpson 7:429; 32:375
Barry Spacks 14:511
Robert Penn Warren 13:581
James Wright 28:469

Smith, David E.
E. E. Cummings 8:158

Smith, Dinitia
Alice Walker 27:451

Smith, Ethanne
Franklyn M. Branley 21:21

Smith, Eleanor T.
Jessamyn West 17:547

Smith, F. C.
Henry Gregor Felsen 17:121

Smith, Gene
Ian Fleming 30:138

Smith, Grover
T. S. Eliot 15:206
Archibald MacLeish 8:359

Smith, H. Allen
Jacqueline Susann 3:476

Smith, Harrison
Taylor Caldwell 28:61
Ilya Ehrenburg 18:132
Madeleine L'Engle 12:345
Mary Renault 17:392
Elizabeth Spencer 22:398

Jessamyn West 17:546

Smith, Iain Crichton
Hugh MacDiarmid 11:336

Smith, Irene
Noel Streatfeild 21:398

Smith, Jack
Josef von Sternberg 20:373

Smith, Janet Adam
Richard Adams 4:8
Lloyd Alexander 35:23
Farley Mowat 26:331
J.R.R. Tolkien 2:435

Smith, Jay
Woody Guthrie 35:184

Smith, Jennifer Farley
Margaret Craven 17:79
Allan W. Eckert 17:108

Smith, Joan
Piri Thomas 17:502

Smith, Julian
Nevil Shute 30:373

Smith, Larry
Lawrence Ferlinghetti 27:138

Smith, Leslie
Edward Bond 23:68

Smith, Liz
Truman Capote 8:133

Smith, Martin Cruz
John le Carré 28:228

Smith, Mason
Richard Brautigan 12:60

Smith, Maxwell A.
Jean Giono 4:184
François Mauriac 4:340

Smith, Michael
Rosalyn Drexler 2:119
Anthony Kerrigan 6:275
John Metcalf 37:303
Tom Stoppard 1:327
Robert Wilson 7:549

Smith, Nancy
Larry Bograd 35:64

Smith, Patricia Keeney
Anne Chislett 34:146
Ralph Gustafson 36:221
William Mastrosimone 36:292

Smith, Patti
Lou Reed 21:308

Smith, Phillip E., II
Charles Olson 11:420

Smith, Raymond J.
James Dickey 10:141

Smith, R. J.
Prince 35:330

Smith, Robert
Jimmy Page and Robert Plant 12:481

Smith, Robert P., Jr.
Mongo Beti 27:46, 53

Smith, Robert W.
Varlam Shalamov 18:479

Smith, Roger H.
John D. MacDonald 3:307

Smith, Sherwin D.
Charles M. Schulz 12:530

Smith, Sidonie Ann
Maya Angelou 12:10

Smith, Stan
Sylvia Plath 17:357

Smith, Starr E.
Virginia Spencer Carr 34:419
John Dos Passos 34:419

Smith, Stephen
J.M.G. Le Clézio 31:251
Michel Tournier 23:456

Smith, Stevie
Edna Ferber 18:152

Smith, William James
Frank O'Connor 23:325
Kurt Vonnegut, Jr. 12:601
Sloan Wilson 32:446

Smith, William Jay
Elizabeth Bishop 13:89
Louis MacNeice 4:315
Frederick Seidel 18:474
Sylvia Townsend Warner
19:459

Smothers, Joyce
Norma Klein 30:240, 241

Smucker, Tom
Steven Bochco and Michael
Kozoll 35:53

Smyth, Pat
William Mayne 12:395

Smyth, Paul
Derek Walcott 4:575

Snelling, O. F.
Ian Fleming 30:135

Snider, David
Piers Anthony 35:40

Sniderman, Stephen L.
Joseph Heller 3:230

Snitow, Ann
Nettie Jones 34:67

Snodgrass, W. D.
Theodore Roethke 8:455

Snow, C. P.
Malcolm Bradbury 32:49
Norman Mailer 4:322

Snow, George E.
Allen Drury 37:106
Aleksandr I. Solzhenitsyn 4:507

Snow, Helen F.
Pearl S. Buck 7:33

Snow, Philip
Thor Heyerdahl 26:193

Snowden, J. A.
Sean O'Casey 9:406

Snyder, Emine
Ezekiel Mphahlele 25:334

Snyder, Louis
Stephen Sondheim 30:387

Snyder, Patrick
John Lennon 35:268
Paul McCartney 35:280

Snyder, Stephen
Pier Paolo Pasolini 20:271

Snyder-Scumpy, Patrick
Martin Mull 17:297, 298

Soares, Manuela
Agnes Eckhardt Nixon 21:251

Sobejano, Gonzalo
Dámaso Alonso 14:20

Sobran, M. J., Jr.
Norman Lear 12:338

Socken, Paul G.
Anne Hébert 13:268; 29:239
Gabrielle Roy 14:469

Soderbergh, Peter A.
Upton Sinclair 11:497

Sodowsky, Alice
George Lucas 16:409

Sodowsky, Roland
George Lucas 16:409

Soete, Mary
Bette Pesetsky 28:358

Soile, Sola
Chinua Achebe 11:4

Sokel, Walter Herbert
Heinrich Böll 9:102

Sokolov, Raymond A.
André Brink 18:67
E. L. Doctorow 6:132
Julius Horwitz 14:267
Dan Jacobson 4:254
Gayl Jones 6:265
Thomas Keneally 8:319
József Lengyel 7:202
John Sayles 7:400
Hilma Wolitzer 17:563

Solecki, Sam
Earle Birney 11:50
Robertson Davies 25:133
Doris Lessing 22:286

Solnick, Bruce B.
George Garrett 11:220

Solomon, Barbara Probst
Juan Goytisolo 5:151
J.M.G. Le Clézio 31:247
João Ubaldo Ribeiro 10:436
Mario Vargas Llosa 10:500

Solomon, Linda
David Bowie 17:61

Solomon, Norman
Jonathan Kozol 17:253

Solomon, Philip H.
Louis-Ferdinand Céline 15:123

Solomon, Stanley J.
Francis Ford Coppola 16:244

Solotaroff, Ted
Roger Angell 26:29
William Trevor 25:446

Solotaroff, Theodore
Saul Bellow 1:33
Paul Bowles 1:41
Anthony Burgess 1:48
William S. Burroughs 1:48
Albert Camus 9:146
Philip Caputo 32:102
Alex Comfort 7:54
George P. Elliott 2:130
John Fowles 6:185
Herbert Gold 7:120
Paul Goodman 1:123
Günter Grass 1:125
Stanislaw Lem 8:344
Bernard Malamud 1:196, 200
Henry Miller 1:219
Flannery O'Connor 1:256
Katherine Anne Porter 1:271
V. S. Pritchett 5:352
James Purdy 2:348
Philip Roth 4:451
Jean-Paul Sartre 1:304
Hubert Selby, Jr. 8:474
Susan Sontag 1:322
George Steiner 24:427
Vladimir Voinovich 10:508
Richard Wright 1:377
Richard Yates 7:553

Solt, Marilyn Leathers
Betsy Byars 35:75

Solvick, Stanley D.
Bruce Catton 35:94

Solzhenitsyn, Alexander
Mikhail Sholokhov 15:480

Somer, John
Kurt Vonnegut, Jr. 4:566

Somers, Paul P., Jr.
Ernest Hemingway 8:283

Sommer, Sally R.
Alice Childress 12:108

Sommers, Joseph
Miguel Ángel Asturias 13:39

Sondheim, Stephen
Stephen Sondheim 30:386

Sondrup, Steven P.
Ernst Jandl 34:200

Sonkiss, Lois
Jamake Highwater 12:286

Sonnenfeld, Albert
Heinrich Böll 9:107
Albert Camus 32:87

Sonntag, Jacob
Amos Oz 8:435
Isaac Bashevis Singer 3:456
Arnold Wesker 3:519

Sontag, Susan
James Baldwin 4:40
Roland Barthes 24:26
Ingmar Bergman 16:56
Robert Bresson 16:106
Albert Camus 4:88

Elias Canetti 25:110
Paul Goodman 2:170
Rolf Hochhuth 4:230
Eugène Ionesco 4:251
Alain Resnais 16:501
Nathalie Sarraute 4:465
Jean-Paul Sartre 4:475
Peter Weiss 15:564

Sonthoff, Helen W.
Phyllis Webb 18:540
Ethel Davis Wilson 13:606

Sorban, M. J., Jr.
Woody Allen 16:8

Sorenson, Marian
Allan W. Eckert 17:103
Lee Kingman 17:245

Sorenson, Somner
Carl Sandburg 35:356

Sorrentino, Gilbert
Paul Blackburn 9:99
Richard Brautigan 12:57
Italo Calvino 22:94
Robert Creeley 2:106
Robert Duncan 2:122
William Gaddis 8:227
Charles Olson 2:327
Manuel Puig 28:374
Luis Rafael Sánchez 23:383
John Wieners 7:535, 536
Louis Zukofsky 7:563

Soskin, William
James M. Cain 28:44
Taylor Caldwell 28:59
Esther Forbes 12:204
Carl Sandburg 35:351
T. H. White 30:437

Sotiron, Michael
Hugh Garner 13:237

Soule, Stephen W.
Anthony Burgess 5:90

Soupault, Philippe
René Clair 20:60

Sourian, Peter
Albert Camus 2:98
Eleanor Clark 5:105
Bette Greene 30:169, 170
Jack Kerouac 2:227
Norman Lear 12:336
Eric Rohmer 16:535
William Saroyan 8:468
Vassilis Vassilikos 4:552

Southerland, Ellease
Zora Neale Hurston 7:171

Southern, David
Michael McClure 6:320

Southern, Jane
Helen MacInnes 27:281

Southern, Terry
William Golding 17:165
Peter Matthiessen 32:286
John Rechy 1:283
Kurt Vonnegut, Jr. 12:601

Critic Index

Southron, Jane Spence
Enid Bagnold **25**:73
Thomas B. Costain **30**:92
Pamela Hansford Johnson **27**:213, 214
Molly Keane **31**:232

Southworth, James G.
E. E. Cummings **3**:115
Robert Frost **3**:168
Robinson Jeffers **3**:257
Archibald MacLeish **3**:309
Laura Riding **7**:373

Souza, Eunice de
Ruth Prawer Jhabvala **29**:258

Souza, Raymond D.
G. Cabrera Infante **25**:100
Octavio Paz **10**:392
Ernesto Sabato **10**:444; **23**:381

Sowton, Ian
Patrick Lane **25**:288
F. R. Scott **22**:373

Soyinka, Wole
Mongo Beti **27**:48

Spackman, W. M.
I. Compton-Burnett **34**:499
Hilary Spurling **34**:499

Spacks, Patricia Meyer
Kingsley Amis **5**:24
Nicholas Delbanco **6**:130
Hannah Green **3**:202
Joseph Heller **5**:183
Jennifer Johnston **7**:186
D. Keith Mano **10**:328
Alberto Moravia **2**:294
Iris Murdoch **6**:347
J. R. Salamanca **15**:463
Anne Sexton **8**:483
Andrew Sinclair **2**:402
Muriel Spark **2**:419; **5**:400
Peter Spielberg **6**:520
J.R.R. Tolkien **1**:336
Elio Vittorini **6**:551
Eudora Welty **2**:464
Paul West **7**:524
Patrick White **4**:587
Joy Williams **31**:464

Spain, Francis Lander
Margot Benary-Isbert **12**:31

Spann, Marcella
Ezra Pound **4**:413

Spanos, William V.
Martin Heidegger **24**:277
Yannis Ritsos **6**:460
Jean-Paul Sartre **18**:466

Sparshott, Francis
Northrop Frye **24**:231

Spaulding, Martha
Laurie Colwin **13**:156
Kamala Markandaya **8**:377
J.R.R. Tolkien **8**:516

Spears, Monroe K.
W. H. Auden **2**:22
John Berryman **2**:57
Cleanth Brooks **24**:114
James Dickey **2**:116
T. S. Eliot **2**:127

Robert Graves **11**:254
Daniel Hoffman **23**:242
Ted Hughes **2**:199
David Jones **2**:217
Madison Jones **4**:263
Maxine Kumin **28**:222
Ursula K. Le Guin **22**:269
Robert Lowell **2**:248
Ezra Pound **2**:342
John Crowe Ransom **2**:366
Karl Shapiro **4**:487
Allen Tate **2**:430; **24**:441
John Kennedy Toole **19**:443
Robert Penn Warren **1**:355; **4**:579; **18**:539
René Wellek **28**:445

Spector, Ivar
Mikhail Sholokhov **7**:420

Spector, Robert D.
Robert Alter **34**:516
William Bronk **10**:73
Len Deighton **22**:114
Stephen Dobyns **37**:74
Robert Duncan **7**:87
D. J. Enright **4**:156
Louise Glück **22**:173
Edwin Honig **33**:209
David Ignatow **7**:174
Carolyn Kizer **15**:308
Halldór Laxness **25**:293
Kenneth Rexroth **2**:371

Speer, Diane Parkin
Robert Heinlein **8**:275

Spence, Jon
Katherine Anne Porter **7**:320

Spence, Jonathan
Kazuo Ishiguro **27**:204

Spencer, Benjamin T.
Edward Dahlberg **7**:70

Spencer, Brent
Donald Hall **37**:145

Spencer, Elizabeth
Elizabeth Spencer **22**:403

Spencer, Jack
André Schwarz-Bart **2**:388

Spencer, Marjorie
Prince **35**:327

Spencer, Sharon
Djuna Barnes **3**:38
Jorge Luis Borges **3**:77
Julio Cortázar **3**:114
Carlos Fuentes **3**:175
Anaïs Nin **4**:376; **14**:381
Alain Robbe-Grillet **4**:448

Spendal, R. J.
James Wright **10**:546

Spender, Stephen
A. R. Ammons **2**:12
W. H. Auden **3**:25, 27
James Baldwin **17**:25
T. S. Eliot **24**:163
James Fenton **32**:169
Günter Grass **22**:196
Robert Graves **2**:177
Thom Gunn **3**:216

Ted Hughes **2**:200
Aldous Huxley **3**:253; **5**:192; **8**:304
David Jones **13**:312
Arthur Koestler **15**:311
F. R. Leavis **24**:293
Philip Levine **4**:287
James Merrill **3**:335
W. S. Merwin **3**:340
Eugenio Montale **7**:225
Elsa Morante **8**:403
Alberto Moravia **27**:356
Sylvia Plath **9**:429
William Plomer **4**:406
Peter Porter **33**:323
Nelly Sachs **14**:475
James Schuyler **5**:383; **23**:389
Gore Vidal **2**:450; **8**:527
Christa Wolf **29**:464
James Wright **3**:541

Sperone, Al J.
Joseph Heller **36**:230

Spice, Nicholas
Michel Tournier **36**:438

Spicer, Edward H.
Carlos Castaneda **12**:85

Spiegel, Alan
Stanley Kubrick **16**:392
Jean-Paul Sartre **7**:398

Spiegelman, Willard
John Betjeman **10**:53
Richard Howard **7**:169
James Merrill **8**:384
Adrienne Rich **7**:370

Spieler, F. Joseph
Robert Wilson **9**:577

Spilka, Mark
Ernest Hemingway **10**:263
Doris Lessing **6**:300
Erich Segal **3**:446
John Steinbeck **21**:385

Spina, James
Jimmy Page and Robert Plant **12**:482

Spinrad, Norman
Jack Vance **35**:417

Spitz, David
William Golding **17**:172

Spitz, Robert Stephen
Pete Hamill **10**:251

Spitzer, Jane Stewart
Leon Uris **32**:437

Spitzer, Nicholas R.
Waylon Jennings **21**:202

Spitzer, Susan
Margaret Drabble **22**:122

Spivack, Kathleen
Robert Lowell **2**:248

Spivey, Herman E.
William Faulkner **6**:176

Spivey, Ted R.
Conrad Aiken **5**:9
Romain Gary **25**:189
Flannery O'Connor **1**:255

Spiwack, David
Jackson Browne **21**:36

Spraggins, Mary Beth Pringle
Monique Wittig **22**:476

Sprague, Rosemary
Marianne Moore **4**:362

Sprague, Susan
Mavis Thorpe Clark **12**:132
Barbara Corcoran **17**:77

Springer, Cole
Frank Zappa **17**:593

Sproul, Kathleen
Nevil Shute **30**:368

Spurling, Hilary
James Fenton **32**:167
Anthony Powell **10**:417

Spurling, John
Peter Barnes **5**:50
Samuel Beckett **6**:42
Peter Benchley **4**:54
Malcolm Bradbury **32**:51
Howard Brenton **31**:58
Graham Greene **37**:135, 138
Anna Kavan **13**:315
Francis King **8**:322
David Mercer **5**:284
Joe McGinniss **32**:301
Yukio Mishima **9**:384
Peter Nichols **5**:308
David Plante **7**:307
Anne Redmon **22**:341
Peter Shaffer **5**:388
Elie Wiesel **5**:491

Squillace, Jacques
Eldridge Cleaver **30**:69

Squires, Radcliffe
Brewster Ghiselin **23**:169
Caroline Gordon **6**:204
Randall Jarrell **6**:260
Robinson Jeffers **11**:305
Mario Luzi **13**:353
Frederic Prokosh **4**:420
Allen Tate **2**:429; **4**:540; **11**:524
Robert Penn Warren **18**:537

Sragow, Michael
Brian De Palma **20**:83
George Roy Hill **26**:209
Stephen King **26**:243
Steve Martin **30**:251

Srivastava, Narsingh
W. H. Auden **14**:26

Stabb, Martin S.
Jorge Luis Borges **19**:44
José Donoso **11**:149

Stableford, Brian M.
Douglas Adams **27**:15
James Blish **14**:84
Ann Swinfen **34**:577

Stade, George
Kingsley Amis **8**:10
E. E. Cummings **3**:119
Guy Davenport, Jr. **14**:142
Don DeLillo **27**:78
E. L. Doctorow **6**:132; **18**:126
John Gregory Dunne **28**:126

Leslie Epstein **27**:131
Max Frisch **18**:163
John Gardner **3**:186
Robert Graves **1**:129
William Kennedy **34**:207
Jerzy Kosinski **3**:272
Alan Lelchuk **5**:243
Elmore Leonard **28**:235
Doris Lessing **15**:331
Joseph McElroy **5**:279
Henry Miller **14**:371
Steven Millhauser **21**:219
Iris Murdoch **22**:328
Jean Rhys **6**:452
Wilfrid Sheed **4**:488
Muriel Spark **2**:416
John Updike **5**:458
Gore Vidal **33**:409
Kurt Vonnegut, Jr. **3**:501

Stadnychenko, Tamara
Ayn Rand **30**:304

Stafford, I. Elizabeth
Lee Kingman **17**:244

Stafford, Jean
Harry Crews **23**:132
M. E. Kerr **12**:296, 298
James A. Michener **5**:289
Jessamyn West **17**:552
Paul West **7**:523

Stafford, William E.
Millen Brand **7**:29
William Dickey **28**:117
Richard Eberhart **19**:142
Loren Eiseley **7**:93
Barbara Howes **15**:289
David Kherdian **6**:280
Kenneth Rexroth **2**:370
M. L. Rosenthal **28**:393
Louis Simpson **7**:427
May Swenson **14**:518
Theodore Weiss **8**:546

Staley, Thomas F.
Margaret Drabble **22**:127

Stallings, Sylvia
Doris Betts **28**:33

Stallknecht, Newton P.
Amos Tutuola **5**:445

Stallman, Robert W.
Ernest Hemingway **13**:271;
19:212

Stambolian, George
Sam Shepard **4**:490

Stamelman, Richard
Yves Bonnefoy **15**:75
Francis Ponge **18**:415

Stamford, Anne Marie
Taylor Caldwell **28**:68
Leslie Epstein **27**:127
Isabelle Holland **21**:149

Stamm, Michael E.
Robert Bloch **33**:85
Stephen King **37**:204, 205

Stamm, Rudolf
Harold Pinter **27**:388

Stamp, Gavin
John Betjeman **34**:310

Stampfer, Judah
Saul Bellow **6**:60
Philip Roth **6**:476

Standard, Elinore
Virginia Hamilton **26**:147

Staneck, Lou Willet
John Neufeld **17**:310

Stanford, Alfred
Thor Heyerdahl **26**:189

Stanford, Ann
May Swenson **4**:533

Stanford, Derek
A. Alvarez **13**:9
Earle Birney **4**:64
Robert Creeley **2**:106
C. Day Lewis **1**:72
Lawrence Durrell **4**:147
Geoffrey Hill **18**:238
Aldous Huxley **5**:192
Elizabeth Jennings **5**:197
Patrick Kavanagh **22**:244
Norman MacCaig **36**:284
Hugh MacDiarmid **4**:313
Louis MacNeice **1**:187
Robert Nye **13**:413
William Plomer **4**:406
Craig Raine **32**:349
Carl Sandburg **15**:470
Stephen Spender **1**:322; **2**:419
Yevgeny Yevtushenko **3**:547

Stanford, Don
Yvor Winters **32**:462

Stanford, Donald E.
Elizabeth Daryush **19**:122
Caroline Gordon **6**:202
Marianne Moore **4**:364
Katherine Anne Porter **27**:402
Ezra Pound **10**:407
Allen Tate **2**:430
Yvor Winters **4**:591

Stange, Maren
Susan Sontag **10**:486

Stanhope, Henry
Wilbur Smith **33**:377

Stankiewicz, Marketa Goetz
Pavel Kohout **13**:323
Sławomir Mrożek **3**:345

Stanleigh, Bertram
Frank Zappa **17**:584

Stanlis, Peter L.
Robert Frost **3**:174

Stannard, Martin
Evelyn Waugh **13**:588

Stansky, Peter
Antonia Fraser **32**:184

Stanton, Michael N.
E. M. Forster **22**:135

Staples, Hugh B.
Randall Jarrell **6**:261
Robert Lowell **2**:246

Stark, Freya
Paul Bowles **19**:58

Stark, John O.
John Barth **7**:22
Jorge Luis Borges **8**:94
E. L. Doctorow **6**:131
William Gaddis **8**:228
Vladimir Nabokov **8**:407

Stark, Myra
Adrienne Rich **11**:477

Starobinski, Jean
Michel Foucault **31**:178

Starr, Carol
John Neufeld **17**:310

Starr, Kevin
Jackson J. Benson **34**:407
James M. Cain **28**:52
E. L. Doctorow **6**:136
John Dos Passos **8**:181
John Steinbeck **34**:407

Starr, Roger
Anthony Powell **3**:403

Stasio, Marilyn
Anne Burr **6**:105
John Hopkins **4**:234
Terrence McNally **4**:346, 347
Jason Miller **2**:284
David Rabe **4**:426
Murray Schisgal **6**:491
Melvin Van Peebles **2**:448

States, Bert O.
R. S. Crane **27**:74
Harold Pinter **6**:412

Stathis, James J.
William Gaddis **19**:186

Stauffer, Donald A.
Rebecca West **31**:455

Stauffer, Helen Winter
Mari Sandoz **28**:406

Stavin, Robert H.
Alvin Silverstein and Virginia
B. Silverstein **17**:450

Stavn, Diane G.
Nat Hentoff **26**:183

Stavn, Diane Gersoni
Frank Bonham **12**:51
Barbara Corcoran **17**:72
Mollie Hunter **21**:157
M. E. Kerr **12**:297
Joseph Krumgold **12**:320
Emily Cheney Neville **12**:451
Barbara Wersba **30**:431

Stavrou, C. N.
Edward Albee **5**:12
Tennessee Williams **30**:463

Steck, Henry J.
Jules Archer **12**:20

Steck, John A.
Al Young **19**:480

Steegmuller, Francis
Patrick Modiano **18**:338

Steel, Ronald
Pavel Kohout **13**:323

Steele, Timothy
W. S. Merwin **18**:336

Steene, Birgitta
Ingmar Bergman **16**:54, 59, 64

Stefanile, Felix
William Bronk **10**:73
Lewis Turco **11**:552

Stegner, Page
J.M.G. Le Clézio **31**:244
Peter Matthiessen **32**:294
Vladimir Nabokov **1**:239

Stegner, Wallace
Jackson J. Benson **34**:405
Walter Van Tilburg Clark **28**:81
N. Scott Momaday **19**:318
John Steinbeck **34**:405

Stein, Benjamin
Joan Didion **8**:177
John Gregory Dunne **28**:123

Stein, Charles
Jerome Rothenberg **6**:477

Stein, Elliott
Andrzej Wajda **16**:584

Stein, Howard F.
Alex Haley **12**:251

Stein, Robert A.
J. V. Cunningham **3**:122

Stein, Robert J.
Margaret O. Hyde **21**:176, 179

Stein, Ruth M.
Jamake Highwater **12**:287
Norma Fox Mazer **26**:293
Anne McCaffrey **17**:283, 284
Robert Newton Peck **17**:342

Steinbeck, Nancy
Kin Platt **26**:356

Steinberg, Karen
Martin Cruz Smith **25**:414

Steinberg, Karen Matlaw
Yuri Krotkov **19**:265
Anatoli Rybakov **23**:372

Steinberg, M. W.
John Arden **15**:23
Robertson Davies **7**:72
A. M. Klein **19**:258, 261
Arthur Miller **1**:215

Steiner, Carlo
Giuseppe Ungaretti **7**:483

Steiner, George
Jorge Luis Borges **2**:70
Malcolm Bradbury **32**:52
Anthony Burgess **22**:78
C. Day Lewis **6**:126
Lawrence Durrell **4**:144
Elaine Feinstein **36**:173
Michel Foucault **31**:174
Paul Goodman **7**:127
Graham Greene **6**:220
Martin Heidegger **24**:275
Aldous Huxley **5**:194
Thomas Keneally **8**:318; **10**:298
F. R. Leavis **24**:303
Georg Lukács **24**:318

Robert M. Pirsig 4:403
Sylvia Plath 11:445
Jean-Paul Sartre 7:397
Aleksandr I. Solzhenitsyn 4:516
John Updike 5:459
Patrick White 4:583
Sloan Wilson 32:447

Stekert, Ellen J.
    Woody Guthrie 35:187

Stendahl, Brita
    Gunnar Ekelöf 27:116

Stengel, Richard
    Brian Moore 19:333

Stenson, Leah Deland
    Sol Gordon 26:137

Stepanchev, Stephen
    John Ashbery 2:16
    Imamu Amiri Baraka 2:34
    Ted Berrigan 37:43
    Elizabeth Bishop 4:65
    Robert Bly 2:65
    James M. Cain 28:47
    Robert Creeley 2:105
    James Dickey 2:115
    Alan Dugan 2:121
    Robert Duncan 2:122
    Jean Garrigue 2:153
    Allen Ginsberg 2:162
    Randall Jarrell 2:208
    Robert Lowell 2:247
    W. S. Merwin 2:276
    Lilika Nakos 29:321
    Charles Olson 2:325
    Kenneth Rexroth 2:369
    Karl Shapiro 4:485
    Irwin Shaw 23:397
    Louis Simpson 4:498
    William Stafford 4:519
    May Swenson 4:532
    Richard Wilbur 6:568

Stephen, Sidney J.
    A. M. Klein 19:260

Stephens, Donald
    Dorothy Livesay 4:294
    Sinclair Ross 13:490
    Rudy Wiebe 6:567

Stephens, George D.
    Thornton Wilder 35:442

Stephens, Martha
    Richard Wright 1:379

Stephens, Robert O.
    Ernest Hemingway 3:239

Stephenson, Edward R.
    John Hawkes 15:277

Stephenson, William
    James Dickey 4:122

Stepto, R. B.
    Maya Angelou 35:30

Stepto, Robert B.
    Michael S. Harper 7:139
    Richard Wright 21:455

Sterba, James P.
    Jacques-Yves Cousteau 30:109

Sterling, Dorothy
    Virginia Hamilton 26:148

Stern, Daniel
    James Baldwin 17:33
    Paul Bowles 2:79
    Margaret Drabble 22:120
    Joanne Greenberg 7:134
    Marjorie Kellogg 2:223
    Jakov Lind 4:292
    Bernard Malamud 3:324
    Chaim Potok 2:339
    Ann Quin 6:441
    Piri Thomas 17:497
    Paul West 7:523
    Elie Wiesel 3:529

Stern, David
    Robert Kotlowitz 4:275
    Amos Oz 5:334

Stern, Frederick C.
    Thomas McGrath 28:278

Stern, Gerald
    Gil Orlovitz 22:335

Stern, J. P.
    Günter Grass 22:192
    Eric Rohmer 16:537

Stern, James
    William Golding 17:158
    Nadine Gordimer 33:177, 179

Stern, Margaret
    Helen MacInnes 27:278

Sterne, Richard C.
    Octavio Paz 10:391

Sterne, Richard Clark
    Jerome Weidman 7:517

Sternhell, Carol
    Simone de Beauvoir 31:43
    Kathryn Kramer 34:75
    Lynne Sharon Schwartz 31:390
    Fay Weldon 36:446

Sternlicht, Stanford
    C. S. Forester 35:173

Sterritt, David
    William Kotzwinkle 35:256

Stetler, Charles
    Richard Brautigan 12:67
    James Purdy 4:423

Steuding, Bob
    Gary Snyder 32:387

Stevens, George
    T. S. Stribling 23:443

Stevens, Georgiana G.
    Vera Brittain 23:90

Stevens, Mark
    David Byrne 26:94

Stevens, Peter
    A. R. Ammons 8:14
    Margaret Atwood 4:24
    Patrick Lane 25:283
    Dorothy Livesay 15:339
    A. W. Purdy 3:408

Stevens, Shane
    Eldridge Cleaver 30:56, 65
    Ronald L. Fair 18:139
    Ronald Harwood 32:223
    William Kennedy 28:203
    John Rechy 7:356
    Paul Theroux 28:423

Stevens, Wallace
    Marianne Moore 10:347

Stevenson, Anne
    Elizabeth Bishop 1:35
    Peter Davison 28:103
    W. S. Graham 29:196
    Michael Hamburger 14:235
    Seamus Heaney 25:242
    Barbara Howes 15:290
    Elizabeth Jennings 14:292, 293
    Primo Levi 37:223
    Paul Muldoon 32:318
    Tom Paulin 37:352
    Marge Piercy 27:376
    David Plante 23:343
    Peter Porter 13:453
    F. T. Prince 22:338
    Christopher Reid 33:349
    Muriel Rukeyser 15:457
    May Swenson 14:521
    R. S. Thomas 13:544
    Charles Tomlinson 13:548

Stevenson, David L.
    James Jones 3:260
    Jack Kerouac 2:226
    William Styron 1:329

Stevenson, Drew
    C. S. Adler 35:12, 14
    Jay Bennett 35:45
    Lois Duncan 26:105
    Kin Platt 26:355
    Laurence Yep 35:472

Stevenson, Patrick
    W. R. Rodgers 7:377

Stevenson, Warren
    Hugh MacLennan 14:343

Stevick, Philip
    Max Apple 33:20
    John Barth 14:57
    Donald Barthelme 8:53
    Wayne C. Booth 24:93
    William S. Burroughs 5:93
    William H. Gass 8:247
    Jerzy Kosinski 6:283
    Jan Stafford 4:518
    Kurt Vonnegut, Jr. 5:465

Stewart, Alastair
    Kon Ichikawa 20:176

Stewart, Alfred D.
    Jack Williamson 29:457

Stewart, Corbet
    Paul Celan 10:102

Stewart, David H.
    George Steiner 24:437

Stewart Douglas
    Robert D. FitzGerald 19:175

Stewart, Garrett
    Buster Keaton 20:197
    Steven Spielberg 20:361

Stewart, Harry E.
    Jean Genet 10:225; 14:201

Stewart, Ian
    Françoise Sagan 17:428

Stewart, J.I.M.
    I. Compton-Burnett 34:498
    Compton Mackenzie 18:316
    Hilary Spurling 34:498
    Angus Wilson 34:581

Stewart, John L.
    John Crowe Ransom 2:362;
    24:367

Stewart, Mary
    Mary Stewart 35:391

Stewart, Robert Sussman
    Heinrich Böll 2:67

Stewart, Ruth Weeden
    William Mayne 12:387

Stille, Alexander
    T. Coraghessan Boyle 36:57
    Michael Ende 31:143
    Pier Paolo Pasolini 37:348

Stiller, Nikki
    Louis Simpson 9:486

Stillman, Clara Gruening
    C.L.R. James 33:218

Stillwell, Robert
    Edwin Honig 33:213

Stilwell, Robert L.
    A. R. Ammons 3:10
    Sylvia Plath 1:269
    Jon Silkin 2:395
    James Wright 3:540

Stimpfle, Nedra
    Kristin Hunter 35:228

Stimpson, Catharine R.
    Thom Gunn 18:199
    Tillie Olsen 13:432
    Marge Piercy 6:403
    J.R.R. Tolkien 1:338
    Edmund White III 27:481

Stineback, David C.
    Allen Tate 9:525

Stinnett, Caskie
    S. J. Perelman 15:419

Stinson, John J.
    Anthony Burgess 4:82

Stitt, Peter
    A. R. Ammons 25:41
    John Ashbery 13:34
    Marvin Bell 31:50
    Wendell Berry 27:35
    John Berryman 10:46
    Frank Bidart 33:77
    Amy Clampitt 32:117
    Stephen Dobyns 37:79, 80
    Norman Dubie 36:134, 135,
    139
    Stephen Dunn 36:152, 155
    Daniel Halpern 14:232
    William Heyen 13:282; 18:232
    Edward Hirsch 31:215
    Richard F. Hugo 32:243

David Ignatow **14**:277
Galway Kinnell **29**:284
Philip Levine **33**:271, 274
Laurence Lieberman **36**:261
James Merrill **18**:330
Linda Pastan **27**:370
Stanley Plumly **33**:312, 314
Katha Pollitt **28**:367
Louis Simpson **7**:429; **32**:376, 378
Dave Smith **22**:387
William Stafford **29**:387
Mark Strand **18**:521
Robert Penn Warren **10**:519
Charles Wright **13**:614; **28**:458
James Wright **10**:542

Stock, Irvin
Saul Bellow **2**:50
Mary McCarthy **1**:206

Stock, Robert
Theodore Weiss **14**:555

Stocking, George W., Jr.
Margaret Mead **37**:280

Stocking, Marion Kingston
Galway Kinnell **1**:168
Gary Snyder **1**:318

Stoelting, Winifred L.
Ernest J. Gaines **18**:165

Stokes, Eric
Kamala Markandaya **8**:378

Stokes, Geoffrey
John Cheever **25**:120
Len Deighton **22**:117
Stanley Elkin **14**:158
Mark Helprin **32**:233
Edward Hoagland **28**:186
John le Carré **15**:325
James Merrill **34**:226
Paul Muldoon **32**:321
Phil Ochs **17**:335
Frank O'Connor **23**:332
Robert Stone **23**:428
Richard Yates **23**:482

Stokes, Thomas L.
Bruce Catton **35**:82

Stoler, Peter
Douglas Adams **27**:15
Carl Sagan **30**:333

Stoltzfus, Ben F.
Ernest Hemingway **13**:279
Alain Robbe-Grillet **1**:285; **14**:456

Stolz, Herbert J.
Larry Kettelkamp **12**:307

Stone, Chuck
Garry Trudeau **12**:590

Stone, Elizabeth
John Fowles **9**:213
John Gardner **8**:234
Cynthia Macdonald **13**:355; **19**:290
Judith Rossner **29**:352
Joan Micklin Silver **20**:344
Lily Tomlin **17**:520

Stone, Laurie
Margaret Atwood **15**:38
Rosellen Brown **32**:65
Raymond Carver **36**:101
Max Frisch **9**:217
Elizabeth Hardwick **13**:266
Shirley Hazzard **18**:219
Mary McCarthy **24**:348
Anaïs Nin **8**:423
Anne Roiphe **9**:455
Judith Rossner **29**:356
Dalton Trumbo **19**:447
Tom Wolfe **15**:584

Stone, Norman
Michael Scammell **34**:489
Aleksandr Solzhenitsyn **34**:489

Stone, Robert
William Kotzwinkle **14**:309
Peter Matthiessen **5**:274

Stone, Rochelle K.
Tadeusz Różewicz **23**:362

Stone, Wilfred
E. M. Forster **15**:229

Stone, William B.
Alice Munro **19**:347

Stoneback, H. R.
William Faulkner **8**:213

Stonehill, Brian
André Dubus **36**:147
Vladimir Nabokov **23**:310

Stones, Rosemary
Virginia Hamilton **26**:152
Philippa Pearce **21**:291

Stonier, G. W.
Charles Chaplin **16**:187

Storch, R. F.
Harold Pinter **6**:409

Storey, Mark
Stevie Smith **25**:418

Storey, Robert
David Mamet **15**:357

Storr, Catherine
Eilís Dillon **17**:98
Leon Garfield **12**:221

Story, Jack Trevor
C. P. Snow **6**:517

Stothard, Peter
Lawrence Durrell **13**:188

Stott, Jon C.
Kevin Major **26**:288
Scott O'Dell **30**:271

Stouck, David
Marie-Claire Blais **2**:63
Hugh MacLennan **2**:257

Stourton, James
Monty Python **21**:228

Stout, Janis P.
Larry McMurtry **27**:329

Stout, Rex
Laura Z. Hobson **25**:270

Stover, Leon E.
Frank Herbert **12**:276

Stowers, Bonnie
Hortense Calisher **4**:88
Saul Maloff **5**:271

Strachan, Don
Thomas M. Disch **36**:127
Nettie Jones **34**:69
John Edgar Wideman **34**:298

Strachan, W. J.
Sylvia Townsend Warner **19**:460

Stracley, Julia
Rhys Davies **23**:142

Strakhovsky, Leonid I.
Anna Akhmatova **25**:23

Strandberg, Victor H.
Cynthia Ozick **28**:353
John Updike **13**:557
Robert Penn Warren **13**:573

Stratford, Philip
Graham Greene **6**:212

Straub, Peter
Michael Ayrton **7**:19
Beryl Bainbridge **8**:36
James Baldwin **4**:43
J. G. Ballard **3**:35
Donald Barthelme **3**:44
John Gregory Dunne **28**:123
Brian Glanville **6**:202
Hermann Hesse **6**:237
Julius Horwitz **14**:266
Jack Kerouac **3**:266
Francis King **8**:321
Margaret Laurence **6**:290
Olivia Manning **5**:273
Thomas McGuane **7**:213
Michael Mewshaw **9**:376
James A. Michener **5**:291
Anaïs Nin **8**:419
Joyce Carol Oates **9**:402
Flann O'Brien **4**:385
Simon Raven **14**:442
Simone Schwarz-Bart **7**:404
Isaac Bashevis Singer **6**:509
Richard G. Stern **4**:523
John Updike **5**:457
Morris L. West **6**:563

Strauch, Carl F.
J. D. Salinger **12**:505

Strauss, Harold
James M. Cain **28**:44
Taylor Caldwell **28**:56
Rhys Davies **23**:141
Arthur Koestler **33**:228
Ayn Rand **30**:291
Dalton Trumbo **19**:44

Strauss, Theodore
Rouben Mamoulian **16**:424

Strauss, Victor
Brigid Brophy **29**:95

Strawson, Galen
Michel Tournier **23**:454

Strawson, P. F.
George Steiner **24**:436

Strebel, Elizabeth Grottle
Jean Renoir **20**:309

Street, Douglas O.
Lawrence Ferlinghetti **6**:183

Strehle, Susan
John Gardner **10**:218

Strell, Lois A.
Piers Anthony **35**:38
Norma Klein **30**:243

Stresau, Hermann
Thornton Wilder **15**:571

Strick, Philip
Ingmar Bergman **16**:80
Philip K. Dick **30**:126
Werner Herzog **16**:330
Kon Ichikawa **20**:182
Nagisa Oshima **20**:246
Pier Paolo Pasolini **20**:264
Jerzy Skolimowski **20**:348
Andrzej Wajda **16**:580
Peter Weir **20**:424

Strickland, Geoffrey
Michel Tournier **36**:433

Strickland, Margaret
Norma Klein **30**:239

Stringer, William H.
Russell Baker **31**:25

Strong, Jonathan
David Plante **23**:342

Strong, Kenneth
Shiga Naoya **33**:369

Strong, L.A.G.
John Masefield **11**:356

Strong, Ray
Antonia Fraser **32**:179

Stroud, Janet G.
Judith Guest **30**:173

Stroupe, John H.
Jean Anouilh **13**:22

Strouse, Jean
Russell Banks **37**:28
Rosellen Brown **32**:64
Bob Dylan **12**:185
Joyce Maynard **23**:290

Strout, Cushing
William Styron **5**:420

Strozier, Robert M.
Peter De Vries **7**:78
S. J. Perelman **5**:337
P. G. Wodehouse **5**:517

Struthers, J. R. (Tim)
Jack Hodgins **23**:235
Hugh Hood **28**:191

Struve, Gleb
Ilya Ehrenburg **18**:131
Vladimir Nabokov **1**:241

Struve, Nikita
Aleksandr I. Solzhenitsyn **7**:433

Stuart, Alexander
Ralph Bakshi **26**:72
Richard O'Brien **17**:323
Pier Paolo Pasolini **20**:266

Critic Index

Stuart, Dabney
Ted Hughes **2**:201
Edwin Morgan **31**:273

Stubblefield, Charles
Sylvia Plath **1**:270

Stubbs, G. T.
Rosemary Sutcliff **26**:433

Stubbs, Harry C.
Isaac Asimov **26**:51
Melvin Berger **12**:38
Franklyn M. Branley **21**:20, 21,
23
Roy A. Gallant **17**:129, 131,
132
Alvin Silverstein and Virginia
B. Silverstein **17**:451, 454

Stubbs, Helen
William Mayne **12**:399

Stubbs, Jean
Julio Cortázar **2**:102
Daphne du Maurier **6**:147
George Garrett **3**:193
Elizabeth Hardwick **13**:265
Eleanor Hibbert **7**:155
Anaïs Nin **8**:421

Stubbs, John C.
John Hawkes **1**:138

Stubbs, Patricia
Muriel Spark **3**:466

Stubing, John L.
Len Deighton **22**:119
Evan Hunter **31**:228

Stuckey, Sterling
Sterling A. Brown **23**:98

Stuckey, W. J.
Pearl S. Buck **18**:76
Caroline Gordon **29**:186

Stuewe, Paul
Joan Barfoot **18**:35
Ernest K. Gann **23**:167
John Gardner **30**:157
Jim Harrison **33**:197
Stephen King **26**:237
Ted Mooney **25**:330
Manuel Mujica Láinez **31**:284
Ernesto Sabato **23**:382
Françoise Sagan **36**:383

Stull, William L.
William S. Burroughs **15**:111

Stumpf, Thomas
Hayden Carruth **7**:41
Daniel Mark Epstein **7**:97
Ishmael Reed **5**:368
Muriel Rukeyser **6**:479

Stupple, A. James
Ray Bradbury **10**:69

Sturgeon, Ray
Joni Mitchell **12**:443

Sturgeon, Theodore
Poul Anderson **15**:10
Isaac Asimov **3**:16
Marion Zimmer Bradley **30**:26
John W. Campbell, Jr. **32**:76
Michael Crichton **2**:108

Harlan Ellison **13**:202
Robert A. Heinlein **26**:178
Frank Herbert **12**:276; **35**:204
Barry N. Malzberg **7**:208

Sturm, T. L.
Robert D. FitzGerald **19**:180

Sturrock, John
Jorge Amado **13**:12
Roland Barthes **24**:33
Jorge Luis Borges **13**:105
Peter De Vries **3**:125
Gabriel García Márquez **8**:233;
10:217
J.M.G. Le Clézio **31**:248
Robert Pinget **37**:358
Alain Robbe-Grillet **8**:454
Nathalie Sarraute **31**:381
Claude Simon **15**:486
Michel Tournier **23**:453
Monique Wittig **22**:476

Styron, William
Philip Caputo **32**:103
Peter Matthiessen **32**:290
Terry Southern **7**:453

Subiotto, Arrigo
Max Frisch **32**:190

Subramani
W. Somerset Maugham **15**:368

Sucharitkul, Somtow
Michael Ende **31**:142
Gene Wolfe **25**:476

Suczek, Barbara
John Lennon and Paul
McCartney **12**:369

Suderman, Elmer F.
John Updike **2**:443; **3**:488

Sugg, Alfred R.
Richard Lester **20**:222

Sugrue, Thomas
Riccardo Bacchelli **19**:31
Rhys Davies **23**:145
Ogden Nash **23**:318, 319
Mary Renault **17**:390
T. H. White **30**:442

Suhl, Benjamin
Jean-Paul Sartre **24**:410

Sukenick, Lynn
Maya Angelou **12**:12
Doris Lessing **3**:288
Anaïs Nin **8**:421
Robert L. Peters **7**:303

Sukenick, Ronald
Carlos Castaneda **12**:89
Rudolph Wurlitzer **2**:483

Suleiman, Jo-Ann D.
Thor Heyerdahl **26**:194
Erich von Däniken **30**:428

Sullivan, Anita T.
Ray Bradbury **3**:85

Sullivan, Dan
Edward Albee **25**:40
Charles Fuller **25**:179
Sam Shepard **34**:265

Sullivan, Eugene V., Jr.
Aidan Chambers **35**:99

Sullivan, Jack
Richard Condon **8**:150
Robin Cook **14**:131
Guy Davenport, Jr. **14**:142
André Dubus **36**:144
Paul Horgan **9**:279
Susan Isaacs **32**:253
Stephen King **12**:309
John Knowles **26**:263
Wright Morris **18**:354
J. B. Priestley **9**:442
Susan Richards Shreve **23**:404
Peter Straub **28**:410
Julian Symons **14**:524
Joan D. Vinge **30**:411

Sullivan, Kevin
Thomas Kinsella **19**:251
Flann O'Brien **5**:316
Sean O'Casey **5**:320
Frank O'Connor **23**:326
Gil Orlovitz **22**:333

Sullivan, Mary
B. S. Johnson **6**:262
William Sansom **6**:483
Fay Weldon **6**:562

Sullivan, Nancy
May Swenson **4**:534

Sullivan, Patrick
Frederick Wiseman **20**:473

Sullivan, Peggy
Gunnel Beckman **26**:87
Barbara Corcoran **17**:72
Lois Duncan **26**:101, 102
Lee Kingman **17**:244
Richard Peck **21**:295

Sullivan, Richard
A. J. Cronin **32**:139
Harper Lee **12**:340
Colin MacInnes **23**:282
William Maxwell **19**:306
William Mitchell **25**:321
Piers Paul Read **25**:376
Betty Smith **19**:423
Mary Stolz **12**:547

Sullivan, Rosemary
Marie-Claire Blais **6**:81
Patrick Lane **25**:286
P. K. Page **18**:378
Theodore Roethke **19**:398

Sullivan, Ruth
Ken Kesey **6**:278

Sullivan, Tom R.
William Golding **8**:249
Michel Tournier **6**:538

Sullivan, Victoria
Saul Bellow **8**:76

Sullivan, Walter
Donald Barthelme **1**:19
Saul Bellow **8**:81
Elizabeth Bowen **11**:64
Eleanor Clark **19**:106
Harry Crews **23**:131
Guy Davenport, Jr. **6**:124
Margaret Drabble **8**:184

Andre Dubus **13**:182
George Garnett **11**:219
William Golding **2**:166, 168
Graham Greene **6**:219
Richard Hughes **11**:278
Bernard Malamud **1**:200
William Maxwell **19**:309
Joyce Carol Oates **6**:368; **9**:405
Flannery O'Connor **2**:317;
21:268
John O'Hara **6**:385
Reynolds Price **13**:464
V. S. Pritchett **13**:465
Jean Rhys **6**:456
Alan Sillitoe **6**:501
William Trevor **14**:535
Anne Tyler **11**:553

Sullivan, Wilson
Irving Stone **7**:470

Sullivan, Zohreh Tawakuli
Iris Murdoch **6**:346; **11**:386

Sullivan-Daly, Tess
Michael Mott **15**:380

Sultan, Stanley
Ezra Pound **7**:331

Sultana, Donald
A. N. Wilson **33**:453

Sultanik, Aaron
E. L. Doctorow **18**:120
Lina Wertmüller **16**:595

Suplee, Curt
Thomas Berger **11**:46

Surette, Leon
George Bowering **15**:84
Ezra Pound **34**:511
E. Fuller Torrey **34**:511

Sussex, Elizabeth
Lindsay Anderson **20**:15
Satyajit Ray **16**:482
Agnès Varda **16**:555
Lina Wertmüller **16**:586
Billy Wilder **20**:460

Sussman, Vic
Fran Lebowitz **36**:248

Sutcliffe, Thomas
Robert Stone **23**:430
Peter Straub **28**:411

Suter, Anthony
Basil Bunting **10**:83, 84

Suther, Judith D.
Eugène Ionesco **11**:292

Sutherland, Bruce
Conrad Richter **30**:308

Sutherland, Donald
Rafael Alberti **7**:10
Octavio Paz **10**:389
St.-John Perse **4**:399
Francis Ponge **6**:422

Sutherland, Fraser
Elizabeth Spencer **22**:405

Sutherland, J. A.
Philip José Farmer **19**:168

Sutherland, John
Vasily Aksyonov **37**:16
Len Deighton **22**:118
Robert Finch **18**:153
Günter Grass **32**:204
Jorge Ibargüengoitia **37**:184
Ruth Prawer Jhabvala **29**:262
P. K. Page **18**:376
Anatoli Rybakov **23**:374
A. N. Wilson **33**:454

Sutherland, Kathryn
Eva Figes **31**:168

Sutherland, Ronald
Roch Carrier **13**:140
Hugh MacLennan **14**:342

Sutherland, Sam
The Clash **30**:46
Elvis Costello **21**:67
Bob Seger **35**:385

Sutherland, Steve
Prince **35**:326

Sutherland, Stuart
A. Alvarez **13**:8
Peter De Vries **10**:137; **28**:107

Sutherland, Zena
Charles Addams **30**:16
C. S. Adler **35**:11, 13, 14
Joan Aiken **35**:16
Fran Arrick **30**:17
E. M. Almedingen **12**:3, 4, 7
Honor Arundel **17**:13
Gunnel Beckman **26**:87
Jay Bennett **35**:44
Melvin Berger **12**:39, 40, 41
Judy Blume **12**:44
Larry Bograd **35**:62, 63
Frank Bonham **12**:49, 50, 51, 52, 53, 54, 55
H. F. Brinsmead **21**:26
Betsy Byars **35**:73, 74
Betty Cavanna **12**:102
Aidan Chambers **35**:100
Alice Childress **12**:107
Mavis Thorpe Clark **12**:132
Christopher Collier and James L. Collier **30**:71, 72, 73
Barbara Corcoran **17**:74, 76, 78
Robert Cormier **30**:87, 90
Paula Danziger **21**:84, 85
Lois Duncan **26**:101, 103, 106, 108
Babbis Friis-Baastad **12**:214
Roy A. Gallant **17**:132
Sol Gordon **26**:137
Rosa Guy **26**:142, 144, 145
Virginia Hamilton **26**:149
Nat Hentoff **26**:184
Isabelle Holland **21**:148, 149, 153, 154
Langston Hughes **35**:219
Mollie Hunter **21**:157
Margaret O. Hyde **21**:178, 179, 180
Jesse Jackson **12**:290, 291
Diana Wynne Jones **26**:226
M. E. Kerr **12**:298; **35**:248
Larry Kettelkamp **12**:305, 306, 307
Lee Kingman **17**:247
Joseph Krumgold **12**:318, 321
Madeleine L'Engle **12**:350
Sonia Levitin **17**:264, 265
Robert Lipsyte **21**:212
Anne McCaffrey **17**:282, 284
Milton Meltzer **26**:298, 302, 307
Nicholosa Mohr **12**:447
Walter Dean Myers **35**:295, 298
John Neufeld **17**:308, 310
Emily Cheney Neville **12**:450, 451, 452
Suzanne Newton **35**:301
Scott O'Dell **30**:276
Zibby Oneal **30**:280
Katherine Paterson **12**:484, 486; **30**:283, 288
Richard Peck **21**:296, 298, 299, 300
Robert Newton Peck **17**:338, 339, 340, 342
Kin Platt **26**:350, 351, 352, 353, 354, 356
D. M. Pinkwater **35**:318
Josephine Poole **17**:373
Marilyn Sachs **35**:335
Ann Schlee **35**:372
Ouida Sebestyen **30**:347
Alvin Silverstein and Virginia B. Silverstein **17**:451, 454, 455
Zilpha Keatley Snyder **17**:470, 473, 475
Mary Stolz **12**:551, 553, 554, 555
Noel Streatfeild **21**:403, 408, 409, 412, 415
Rosemary Sutcliff **26**:436
Mildred D. Taylor **21**:419
Colin Thiele **17**:495, 496
Joyce Carol Thomas **35**:407
John R. Tunis **12**:599
Cynthia Voigt **30**:417, 418
Lenora Mattingly Weber **12**:634
Rosemary Wells **12**:639
Barbara Wersba **30**:432
Jessamyn West **17**:552
Hilma Wolitzer **17**:563
Laurence Yep **35**:471, 472, 473
Paul Zindel **26**:470, 472, 474

Sutton, Graham
W. Somerset Maugham **11**:367

Sutton, Horace
S. J. Perelman **23**:335

Sutton, Martyn
Joan Armatrading **17**:10

Sutton, Roger
Robert Cormier **30**:89
Laurence Yep **35**:473

Sutton, Roger D.
Robin F. Brancato **35**:69

Sutton, Walter
Allen Ginsberg **4**:181
Robert Lowell **4**:303
Thomas Merton **3**:336
Marianne Moore **4**:364
Ezra Pound **3**:395

Suvin, Darko
Eric Bentley **24**:49
Arkadii Strugatskii and Boris Strugatskii **27**:432

Svensson, Frances
Vine Deloria, Jr. **21**:114

Swados, Harvey
Walter Van Tilburg Clark **28**:78
Howard Fast **23**:156
David Ignatow **4**:249

Swanbrow, Diane J.
John Knowles **26**:263

Swann, Brian
Theodore Roethke **19**:396

Sward, Robert
Philip Whalen **29**:445

Swartley, Ariel
Joan Armatrading **17**:8
Walter Becker and Donald Fagen **26**:85
Joni Mitchell **12**:442
Bruce Springsteen **17**:490

Swartney, Joyce
Charles M. Schulz **12**:533

Swayze, Walter E.
Robertson Davies **25**:131

Sweeney, Francis
Thomas J. Fleming **37**:125

Sweeney, Patricia Runk
M. E. Kerr **12**:301

Sweet, Louise
Frederick Wiseman **20**:477

Sweeting, Adam
The Clash **30**:50
Paul Weller **26**:447

Swenson, John
Ray Davies **21**:99
Paul McCartney **35**:292
Willie Nelson **17**:303
Peter Townshend **17**:533, 540
Frank Zappa **17**:591

Swenson, May
Ben Belitt **22**:49
Robin Morgan **2**:294
Muriel Rukeyser **27**:408
Anne Sexton **2**:392
W. D. Snodgrass **2**:406

Swift, John N.
John Cheever **15**:129

Swift, Jonathan
Gerome Ragni and James Rado **17**:385

Swift, Pat
George Barker **8**:44

Swigg, Richard
E. M. Forster **9**:209
Philip Larkin **9**:324

Swigger, Ronald T.
Raymond Queneau **2**:359

Swindell, Larry
Scott Spencer **30**:407

Swinden, Patrick
D. J. Enright **31**:155
C. P. Snow **4**:503

Swing, Raymond
John R. Tunis **12**:596

Swingewood, Alan
Lucien Goldmann **24**:244

Swink, Helen
William Faulkner **3**:154

Swiss, Thomas
Donald Justice **19**:234
Laurence Lieberman **36**:264

Swope, Donald B.
Peter Gent **29**:180

Sykes, Christopher
Aldous Huxley **4**:244; **8**:303; **35**:236

Sykes, Gerald
Jessie Redmon Fauset **19**:169
William Gibson **23**:173
Pamela Hansford Johnson **27**:219, 220
Nevil Shute **30**:369

Sykes, S. W.
Claude Simon **9**:483

Sylvester, R. D.
Joseph Brodsky **13**:114

Sylvester, William
Daniel Hoffman **23**:239

Symons, Julian
Eric Ambler **4**:18
W. H. Auden **2**:28
Beryl Bainbridge **18**:34
John Berryman **2**:59
Edward Brathwaite **11**:66
John Dickson Carr **3**:101
John Cheever **8**:140
Agatha Christie **6**:107; **8**:140; **12**:121, 126
John Creasey **11**:134
C. Day Lewis **6**:129
Len Deighton **4**:119
Thomas M. Disch **36**:126
Friedrich Dürrenmatt **4**:141
James Fenton **32**:164, 169
Ian Fleming **3**:159
Dick Francis **22**:154
Roy Fuller **4**:178
Graham Greene **27**:175
Dashiell Hammett **3**:219
Lillian Hellman **4**:222
Patricia Highsmith **2**:193; **4**:225
Chester Himes **4**:229
Evan Hunter **11**:279; **31**:224
P. D. James **18**:276
Eliabeth Jennings **14**:292
Pamela Hansford Johnson **27**:222
John le Carré **3**:282
John D. MacDonald **3**:307
Ross Macdonald **3**:307
Mary McCarthy **3**:326
Henry Miller **2**:281
Edwin Morgan **31**:272
Ellery Queen **3**:421
Simon Raven **14**:442

Critic Index

Kenneth Rexroth **11**:473
Laura Riding **3**:431
Tadeusz Różewicz **23**:358
Georges Simenon **3**:451; **8**:487;
  18:485
Louis Simpson **4**:498
Maj Sjöwall **7**:501
C. P. Snow **4**:500
Mickey Spillane **3**:469
J.I.M. Stewart **14**:511
Rex Stout **3**:471
William Styron **15**:528
Per Wahlöö **7**:501
Robert Penn Warren **4**:577
Patrick White **3**:523
Angus Wilson **3**:536
Yevgeny Yevtushenko **26**:462

Syrkin, Marie
Henry Roth **6**:472

Szanto, George H.
Alain Robbe-Grillet **1**:288

Szirtes, George
Peter Porter **33**:322

Szogyi, Alex
Lillian Hellman **2**:187
Isaac Bashevis Singer **11**:501

Szporluk, Mary Ann
Vladimir Voinovich **10**:504

Szuhay, Joseph A.
Sandra Scoppettone **26**:405

Tabachnick, Stephen E.
Conrad Aiken **5**:9

Taëni, Rainer
Rolf Hochhuth **18**:252

Tagliabue, John
Muriel Rukeyser **27**:414

Tait, Michael
James Reaney **13**:472

Takiff, Jonathan
Lily Tomlin **17**:521

Talbot, Daniel
Richard Matheson **37**:244

Talbot, Emile J.
Marie-Claire Blais **22**:60
Roch Carrier **13**:144
J.M.G. Le Clézio **31**:250, 251

Talbott, Strobe
Aleksandr I. Solzhenitsyn **4**:516

Talese, Gay
Mario Puzo **36**:362

Taliaferro, Frances
Frederick Barthelme **36**:51
Anita Brookner **32**:61
Frederick Busch **18**:85
Laurie Colwin **13**:157
Andre Dubus **13**:184
Stanley Elkin **27**:125
Nadine Gordimer **5**:147
Maureen Howard **14**:268
Milan Kundera **32**:262
Tom McHale **5**:283
Brian Moore **32**:312
Barbara Pym **37**:376
Françoise Sagan **36**:380

Mark Stevens **34**:111

Tallant, Robert
Doris Betts **28**:32
Elizabeth Spencer **22**:399

Tallenay, J. L.
Charles Chaplin **16**:195

Tallman, Warren
Earle Birney **11**:50
Ernest Buckler **13**:118
Robert Creeley **11**:135
Robert Duncan **15**:187
Jack Kerouac **14**:304
John Rechy **14**:445
Mordecai Richler **3**:430
Sinclair Ross **13**:490

Tambling, Jeremy
Brian Aldiss **14**:15
J.I.M. Stewart **14**:513

Tamkin, Linda
Anaïs Nin **14**:387

Tannen, Deborah
Lilika Nakos **29**:321, 323

Tanner, Alain
Luchino Visconti **16**:561

Tanner, Stephen L.
Ernest Hemingway **8**:288

Tanner, Tony
Walter Abish **22**:19
John Barth **1**:17; **2**:37; **14**:55
Donald Barthelme **2**:40
Richard Brautigan **12**:66
William S. Burroughs **2**:92
William Gaddis **3**:177
John Gardner **2**:152
John Hawkes **2**:185; **7**:143
Ernest Hemingway **10**:266
Norman Mailer **1**:189
Bernard Malamud **2**:267
James Purdy **2**:351; **4**:422
Thomas Pynchon **6**:430, 432;
  33:335
Philip Roth **22**:357
Susan Sontag **1**:322
John Updike **2**:445
Kurt Vonnegut, Jr. **12**:606

Taplin, Oliver
Edward Bond **23**:67

Tapply, Robert S.
Roy A. Gallant **17**:128

Tapscott, Stephen
Friedrich Dürrenmatt **11**:173
Hugh MacDiarmid **19**:288
Stevie Smith **25**:417

Tarantino, Michael
Marguerite Duras **20**:100, 101
Elaine May **16**:437

Targan, Barry
Scott Sommer **25**:425

Tarkka, Pekka
Hannu Salama **18**:461

Tarn, Nathaniel
William H. Gass **1**:114

Tarratt, Margaret
Nagisa Oshima **20**:246
Gordon Parks **16**:459
Luchino Visconti **16**:568
Frederick Wiseman **20**:474

Tarshis, Jerome
J. G. Ballard **3**:34

Tartt, Alison
H. D. **31**:212

Tate, Allen
Edward Dahlberg **14**:134
Donald Davidson **13**:167
John Crowe Ransom **2**:363;
  5:364
I. A. Richards **24**:387
T. S. Stribling **23**:443
Melvin B. Tolson **36**:425
Eudora Welty **1**:362

Tate, Claudia
Nella Larsen **37**:216

Tate, George S.
Halldór Laxness **25**:299

Tate, Greg
Amiri Baraka **33**:62

Tate, J. O.
Flannery O'Connor **13**:421
Thomas Pynchon **33**:340
Alexander Theroux **25**:434

Tate, Robert S., Jr.
Albert Camus **1**:54

Tatham, Campbell
John Barth **1**:18
Raymond Federman **6**:181
Thomas Pynchon **2**:354

Tatum, Charles M.
José Donoso **11**:146

Taubman, Howard
Enid Bagnold **25**:77
James Baldwin **17**:27, 31
Larry Gelbart **21**:125
William Gibson **23**:179
Garson Kanin **22**:230
Arthur Kopit **18**:286
Gerome Ragni and James Rado
  17:379
Stephen Sondheim **30**:379

Taubman, Robert
John Barth **27**:29
Patrick Boyle **19**:67
Anita Brookner **32**:59
William S. Burroughs **22**:85
D. J. Enright **31**:146
John Fowles **33**:173
Michael Frayn **31**:189
Iris Murdoch **31**:291
Cynthia Ozick **7**:287
Sylvia Plath **17**:345
Lisa St. Aubin de Teran **36**:420
D. M. Thomas **22**:419
John Updike **23**:477

Taus, Roger
William Everson **14**:167

Tavris, Carol
Kate Wilhelm **7**:538

Tax, Jeremiah
Nancy Willard **37**:466

Tax, Meredith
Julian Symons **32**:429

Tax, Sol
Margaret Mead **37**:274

Taxel, Joseph
Christopher Collier and James
  L. Collier **30**:73, 74

Taylor, Angus
Philip K. Dick **30**:122

Taylor, Clyde
Imamu Amiri Baraka **5**:47

Taylor, D. W.
Eilís Dillon **17**:99

Taylor, David
John Rechy **18**:443

Taylor, Eleanor Ross
Elizabeth Bishop **15**:59
Sylvia Plath **17**:347

Taylor, F. H. Griffin
George Garrett **3**:192; **11**:219
Robert Lowell **1**:181
Theodore Weiss **3**:516

Taylor, Gordon O.
Mary McCarthy **14**:358
Tennessee Williams **30**:458

Taylor, Harry H.
William Golding **17**:170

Taylor, Henry
Ben Belitt **22**:50
Marvin Bell **8**:64
Irving Feldman **7**:103
X. J. Kennedy **8**:319
William Meredith **13**:373
Howard Nemerov **6**:363
Flannery O'Connor **1**:258
Richard Tillinghast **29**:415
John Hall Wheelock **14**:570
James Wright **5**:521

Taylor, Jane
Galway Kinnell **1**:168

Taylor, John Russell
Lindsay Anderson **20**:17
Robert Anderson **23**:32
Michelangelo Antonioni **20**:28
John Arden **6**:4
Alan Ayckbourn **5**:34; **33**:43,
  44
Howard Barker **37**:36
Brendan Behan **11**:44
Ingmar Bergman **16**:50
Edward Bond **4**:69
Howard Brenton **31**:57
Robert Bresson **16**:108
Mel Brooks **12**:78
Luis Buñuel **16**:132
David Caute **29**:115
Claude Chabrol **16**:180
Caryl Churchill **31**:87
Brian Clark **29**:128, 129
Shelagh Delaney **29**:146
Vittorio De Sica **20**:90
Marguerite Duras **20**:99

Federico Fellini **16**:274, 281, 288
Simon Gray **36**:200, 207
David Hare **29**:220
Alfred Hitchcock **16**:344
John Huston **20**:170, 171
Ann Jellicoe **27**:207
Stanley Kubrick **16**:388
Fritz Lang **20**:208
Hugh Leonard **19**:282
David Mercer **5**:283
John Mortimer **28**:283
Peter Nichols **5**:305
Joe Orton **4**:388
Pier Paolo Pasolini **20**:266
Harold Pinter **11**:436
Terence Rattigan **7**:354
Satyajit Ray **16**:490
Alain Resnais **16**:502
Peter Shaffer **14**:484, 485; **18**:477
Ntozake Shange **25**:399
Robert Shaw **5**:390
N. F. Simpson **29**:367
Tom Stoppard **4**:524
David Storey **4**:528
C. P. Taylor **27**:440, 442
Andy Warhol **20**:423
E. A. Whitehead **5**:488
Billy Wilder **20**:461
Snoo Wilson **33**:463

Taylor, Joseph H.
Milton Meltzer **26**:298

Taylor, Katharine
Sylvia Ashton-Warner **19**:21

Taylor, Lewis Jerome, Jr.
Walker Percy **6**:399

Taylor, Mark
W. H. Auden **3**:27
John Berryman **3**:72
Tom McHale **5**:282
Walker Percy **3**:378
Earl Rovit **7**:383
Edmund Wilson **8**:550
Richard Yates **8**:555

Taylor, Michael
Marian Engel **36**:160
Timothy Findley **27**:141
Brian Moore **32**:310
Leon Rooke **25**:391
Gillian Tindall **7**:474

Taylor, Mildred D.
Mildred D. Taylor **21**:419

Taylor, Millicent
Thomas B. Costain **30**:99, 100

Taylor, Nora E.
Isabelle Holland **21**:149, 151
Mary Stewart **35**:393
Noel Streatfeild **21**:404

Taylor, Rebecca
C. J. Cherryh **35**:106

Taylor, Rebecca Sue
C. J. Cherryh **35**:106

Taylor, Rhoda E.
Margaret O. Hyde **21**:178

Taylor, Stephen
John Huston **20**:169

Taylor, William L.
J.R.R. Tolkien **12**:569

Tchen, John
Milton Meltzer **26**:307

Teachout, Terry
William F. Buckley, Jr. **37**:60
Ayn Rand **30**:303

Teale, Edwin Way
Edward Abbey **36**:12

Tearson, Michael
Jim Carroll **35**:80
Janis Ian **21**:187

Tebbel, John
Charles M. Schulz **12**:527

Téchiné, André
Carl Theodor Dreyer **16**:268

Teich, Nathaniel
Pier Paolo Pasolini **20**:267

Temple, Joanne
John Berryman **3**:72

Temple, Ruth Z.
C. S. Lewis **14**:321
Nathalie Sarraute **1**:303; **2**:386

Templeton, Joan
Sean O'Casey **11**:406

Tenenbaum, Louis
Italo Calvino **5**:97

Tennant, Catherine
Joyce Maynard **23**:289

Tennant, Emma
J. G. Ballard **6**:28
Italo Calvino **5**:100
Elaine Feinstein **36**:170
Thomas Hinde **6**:242
Penelope Mortimer **5**:298

Teo, Elizabeth A.
Jade Snow Wong **17**:567

Terbille, Charles I.
Saul Bellow **6**:52
Joyce Carol Oates **6**:371

Teresa, Vincent
Mario Puzo **2**:352

Terras, Rita
Christa Wolf **29**:463

Terrell, Carroll F.
Ezra Pound **34**:503
E. Fuller Torrey **34**:503

Terrien, Samuel
Fernando Arrabal **2**:15

Terrill, Mary
Carl Van Vechten **33**:385

Terris, Susan
Robin F. Brancato **35**:65
Rosemary Wells **12**:639

Terris, Virginia R.
Muriel Rukeyser **27**:410

Terry, Arthur
Vicente Aleixandre **9**:17
Salvador Espriu **9**:192
Octavio Paz **10**:393

Terry, C. V.
Frank B. Gilbreth, Jr. and Ernestine Gilbreth Carey **17**:154
A. J. Cronin **32**:136

Terry, Sara
Helen MacInnes **27**:283

Terzian, Philip
Anthony Powell **31**:316

Tessitore, John
Francis Ford Coppola **16**:247

Testa, Bart
Gordon Lightfoot **26**:281
Frank Zappa **17**:591

Testa, Daniel
Rudolfo A. Anaya **23**:22

Tetlow, Joseph A.
William X. Kienzle **25**:274

Teunissen, John T.
Doris Lessing **6**:293

Thackery, Joseph C.
Czesław Miłosz **31**:261

Thale, Jerome
C. P. Snow **19**:425

Thane, Elswyth
Thomas J. Fleming **37**:120

Thatcher, A.
Paul Zindel **26**:481

Thayer, C. G.
Antonia Fraser **32**:183

Theall, Donald F.
Arthur C. Clarke **35**:123

Thelwell, Mike
James Baldwin **17**:36

Therese, Sister M.
Marianne Moore **1**:229

Theroux, Paul
Breyten Breytenbach **23**:85
Frederick Buechner **2**:83
Anthony Burgess **5**:89
Henry Carlisle **33**:103
John Cheever **7**:48
Peter De Vries **3**:126; **7**:76
Maureen Duffy **37**:116
Lawrence Durrell **6**:151
George MacDonald Fraser **7**:106
Nadine Gordimer **5**:147
Shirley Ann Grau **4**:209
Graham Greene **3**:213
Ernest Hemingway **6**:229
Susan B. Hill **4**:226
Erica Jong **4**:264
Yashar Kemal **14**:299
John Knowles **4**:272
Milan Kundera **4**:276
David Lodge **36**:275
Mary McCarthy **5**:277
Joe McGinniss **32**:303
Yukio Mishima **4**:356
Brian Moore **3**:341; **7**:236
V. S. Naipaul **4**:373, 374; **7**:252
Christopher Okigbo **25**:349

Cynthia Ozick **7**:288
S. J. Perelman **9**:415
Jean Rhys **2**:372
Georges Simenon **18**:487
Gilbert Sorrentino **22**:391
David Storey **4**:529
Peter Taylor **4**:542
John Updike **13**:563
Gore Vidal **22**:437
Kurt Vonnegut, Jr. **5**:470

Theroux, Phyllis
Jean Kerr **22**:258

Thesen, Sharon Fawcett
Gilbert Sorrentino **14**:498

Thiébaux, Marcelle
Stratis Haviaras **33**:206

Thiher, Allen
Fernando Arrabal **9**:33
Luis Buñuel **16**:149
Louis-Ferdinand Céline **4**:101
Henri de Montherlant **19**:328
François Truffaut **20**:402

Thody, Philip
Roland Barthes **24**:30
Albert Camus **4**:91; **14**:116
Jean-Paul Sartre **4**:476; **24**:407

Thomas, Audrey
Marian Engel **36**:159
Anne Hébert **29**:240

Thomas, Brian
P. G. Wodehouse **22**:485

Thomas, Carolyn
David Jones **7**:191

Thomas, Clara
Margaret Laurence **3**:281; **13**:342

Thomas, D. M.
Anna Akhmatova **25**:29
Martin Booth **13**:103
Eva Figes **31**:167
Francine du Plessix Gray **22**:202
Yuri Krotkov **19**:265
John Matthias **9**:362
Elie Wiesel **37**:453, 458

Thomas, David
James Baldwin **5**:43

Thomas, David P.
Christopher Isherwood **1**:157

Thomas, Della
Charles Addams **30**:15

Thomas, Dylan
Amos Tutuola **29**:434

Thomas, Harry
Laurence Lieberman **36**:261

Thomas, John
Bernardo Bertolucci **16**:84
Tod Browning **16**:122
Jean-Luc Godard **20**:134

Thomas, John Alfred
Josef von Sternberg **20**:369

Thomas, Keith
Antonia Fraser **32**:180

Thomas, M. Wynn
Katherine Anne Porter **10**:394

Thomas, Michael M.
Paul E. Erdman **25**:155

Thomas, Noel L.
Martin Walser **27**:464

Thomas, Paul
Rainer Werner Fassbinder
20:109
Lina Wertmüller **16**:593

Thomas, Peter
John Betjeman **6**:65
Robert Kroetsch **5**:220; **23**:275

Thomas, Ross
Matthew Bruccoli **34**:417
Herbert Gold **14**:209
Ross Macdonald **34**:417
Mario Puzo **36**:362

Thomas, S. L.
John R. Tunis **12**:592

Thompson, Betty
Nadine Gordimer **33**:181

Thompson, Craig
Vera Brittain **23**:91

Thompson, Dody Weston
Pearl S. Buck **18**:78

Thompson, E. P.
Donald Davie **31**:114

Thompson, Eric
Matt Cohen **19**:112
T. S. Eliot **2**:125; **24**:172

Thompson, Howard
Robert Altman **16**:19
Gretchen Cryer **21**:79
Brian De Palma **20**:73
Garry Marshall **17**:274
Martin Scorsese **20**:324
Jerzy Skolimowski **20**:347
Andy Warhol **20**:417

Thompson, Jean C.
Barbara Wersba **30**:430

Thompson, John
James Baldwin **17**:34
John Berryman **3**:71
Bruce Chatwin **28**:73
Irving Feldman **7**:102
Daniel Fuchs **22**:156
Natalia Ginzburg **5**:141
Nadine Gordimer **18**:191
Joseph Heller **5**:176
Robert Lowell **9**:338
Peter Matthiessen **32**:287
Amos Oz **5**:335
John Updike **13**:560
Richard Yates **23**:480

Thompson, Kent
John Gardner **28**:162
Hugh Hood **15**:284; **28**:188

Thompson, Lawrence
Robert Frost **13**:224

Thompson, Leslie M.
Stephen Spender **10**:487

Thompson, Mildred
June Jordan **23**:255

Thompson, Raymond H.
C. J. Cherryh **35**:114

Thompson, R. J.
John Hawkes **4**:214
Mary Lavin **4**:282

Thompson, Robert B.
Robert Frost **13**:230

Thompson, Susan
S. E. Hinton **30**:206

Thompson, Toby
Bruce Jay Friedman **5**:126

Thompson, Tyler
Vine Deloria, Jr. **21**:109

Thomsen, Christian Braad
Rainer Werner Fassbinder
20:105

Thomson, David
Paddy Chayefsky **23**:118
Fritz Lang **20**:213
Peter Shaffer **37**:387

Thomson, George H.
J.R.R. Tolkien **1**:335

Thomson, Jean C.
H. F. Brinsmead **21**:28
Barbara Corcoran **17**:72
Eilís Dillon **17**:97
James D. Forman **21**:117
Leon Garfield **12**:216
Madeleine L'Engle **12**:347
John Neufeld **17**:307, 308
Philippa Pearce **21**:282

Thomson, Peter
Harold Pinter **15**:422

Thomson, R.D.B.
Andrei Voznesensky **15**:554

Thorburn, David
Renata Adler **8**:7
Ann Beattie **8**:57
Judith Guest **8**:254
Norman Mailer **3**:315
Thomas Pynchon **3**:416

Thornber, Robin
Alan Ayckbourn **33**:42

Thorp, Katherine
Isaac Asimov **26**:57

Thorp, Willard
W. D. Snodgrass **2**:404

Thorpe, Michael
J. G. Ballard **36**:42
André Brink **36**:68
Doris Lessing **3**:291
Shiva Naipaul **32**:324

Thurley, Geoffrey
Galway Kinnell **29**:280
Charles Simic **22**:379
Philip Whalen **29**:445

Thurman, Judith
Joyce Carol Oates **6**:374
Jean Rhys **6**:456
Laura Riding **7**:374
Susan Fromberg Schaeffer
22:368
Agnès Varda **16**:560

Thurston, Frederick
Walter D. Edmonds **35**:146

Thurston, Robert
Fritz Leiber **25**:304

Thwaite, Ann
E. M. Almedingen **12**:5

Thwaite, Anthony
Kōbō Abé **22**:14
Joan Aiken **35**:20
W. H. Auden **6**:24
Charles Causley **7**:41
Anita Desai **37**:72
Douglas Dunn **6**:148
Shusaku Endo **19**:160
D. J. Enright **31**:145
Michael Frayn **31**:189
Geoffrey Grigson **7**:136
Seamus Heaney **7**:147; **25**:249
David Jones **7**:187
Yashar Kemal **14**:301
Thomas Keneally **19**:242
Philip Larkin **13**:335
David Lodge **36**:277
Derek Mahon **27**:287
Sylvia Murphy **34**:91
R. K. Narayan **7**:256
Darcy O'Brien **11**:405
Sylvia Plath **14**:426
Peter Porter **33**:318
Ann Schlee **35**:373
Tom Sharpe **36**:399, 400
C. P. Snow **4**:503
Snoo Wilson **33**:466

Tibbetts, John
Frank Capra **16**:165
Josef von Sternberg **20**:377

Tick, Edward
Mario Vargas Llosa **31**:446

Tickell, Paul
Frank Zappa **17**:595

Tiedman, Richard
Jack Vance **35**:424

Tiessen, Hildegard E.
Rudy Wiebe **14**:572

Tiffin, Chris
Thomas Keneally **19**:243

Tiger, Virginia
William Golding **27**:166

Tilden, David
M. M. Kaye **28**:198

Tilden, Freeman
Edward Abbey **36**:12

Tillinghast, Richard
Sterling A. Brown **23**:101
Amy Clampitt **32**:117
Robert Creeley **36**:119
Jim Harrison **33**:197
Galway Kinnell **29**:289

James Merrill **2**:274
Frederick Morgan **23**:300
Katha Pollitt **28**:368
Adrienne Rich **3**:427
Louis Simpson **32**:381
Charles Wright **28**:460

Tillman, Nathaniel
Melvin B. Tolson **36**:424

Tilton, John W.
Anthony Burgess **15**:104
Kurt Vonnegut, Jr. **12**:614

Timmerman, John H.
C. S. Lewis **14**:324

Timms, David
Philip Larkin **5**:223

Timpe, Eugene F.
Hermann Hesse **17**:210

Tindal, Gillian
Louis-Ferdinand Céline **7**:45
Leon Garfield **12**:227

Tindall, William York
Samuel Beckett **1**:22

Tinkle, Lon
A. J. Cronin **32**:137
Jean Lee Latham **12**:324
Hollis Summers **10**:493

Tintner, Adeline R.
Philip Roth **22**:355
François Truffaut **20**:406

Tipmore, David
Joyce Maynard **23**:288

Tisdale, Bob
John Hawkes **4**:215

Tiven, Jon
Paul McCartney **35**:287, 288,
292
Monty Python **21**:226
The Police **26**:363, 364

Tiven, Sally
Paul McCartney **35**:288, 292

Toback, James
Kenzaburō Ōe **36**:343

Tobias, Richard
Thomas Kinsella **19**:256

Tobias, Richard C.
James Thurber **5**:435

Tobin, Patricia
William Faulkner **3**:155

Tobin, Richard L.
Lothar-Günther Buchheim
6:101

Todd, Richard
Renata Adler **8**:4
Louis Auchincloss **9**:54
Donald Barthelme **8**:49
Saul Bellow **6**:55, 61
Thomas Berger **3**:64
Eleanor Bergstein **4**:55
Vance Bourjaily **8**:104
E. L. Doctorow **6**:138
Andre Dubus **13**:183
Bruce Jay Friedman **5**:126

John Hawkes **4**:216
Sue Kaufman **8**:317
William Kotzwinkle **5**:220
Cormac McCarthy **4**:343
Robert Newton Peck **17**:337
Walker Percy **8**:443
Marge Piercy **6**:402
Robert M. Pirsig **6**:420
Judith Rossner **6**:470
John Updike **7**:489
Kurt Vonnegut, Jr. **3**:501
Richard Yates **7**:555

Todisco, Paula
James D. Forman **21**:122
Norma Klein **30**:241
Mary Stewart **35**:396

Toeplitz, Krzysztof-Teodor
Jerzy Skolimowski **20**:348
Andrzej Wajda **16**:579

Toerien, Barend J.
Breyten Breytenbach **23**:83, 84
J. M. Coetzee **23**:122

Toledano, Ralph de
Hugh Whitemore **37**:445

Toliver, Harold E.
Robert Frost **4**:175

Tolkien, J.R.R.
C. S. Lewis **27**:259

Tolomeo, Diane
Flannery O'Connor **21**:276

Tolson, Jay
T. Coraghessan Boyle **36**:59
Jakov Lind **27**:272

Tomalin, Claire
Beryl Bainbridge **10**:15
Charles Newman **2**:311
Paul Theroux **5**:427

Tonks, Rosemary
Adrienne Rich **3**:428

Took, Barry
Monty Python **21**:228

Toolan, David S.
Tom Wicker **7**:535

Toomajian, Janice
Isaac Asimov **26**:59

Torchiana, Donald T.
W. D. Snodgrass **2**:404

Tosches, Nick
Mick Jagger and Keith Richard
17:240
Waylon Jennings **21**:204, 205
Jim Morrison **17**:293
Lou Reed **21**:304
Andrew Lloyd Webber and Tim
Rice **21**:423

Totton, Nick
Beryl Bainbridge **8**:37
J. G. Ballard **14**:39
Heinrich Böll **9**:111
Patrick Boyle **19**:68
Malcolm Bradbury **32**:53
André Brink **18**:67
Gail Godwin **8**:249
James Hanley **8**:265

Mary Hocking **13**:285
Francis King **8**:322
Alistair MacLean **13**:364
Michael Moorcock **27**:349
Iris Murdoch **8**:405
Vladimir Nabokov **8**:417
David Pownall **10**:419
Frederic Raphael **14**:437
Piers Paul Read **10**:434
Elizabeth Taylor **29**:410

Tovey, Roberta
William Kotzwinkle **14**:311
Tadeusz Różewicz **23**:361

Towers, Robert
Renata Adler **8**:4
Russell Banks **37**:30
Donald Barthelme **13**:59
Ann Beattie **18**:38
William Boyd **28**:41
Michael Brodsky **19**:69
Anthony Burgess **22**:76
Italo Calvino **33**:101
Raymond Carver **22**:101
John Cheever **8**:138; **11**:122
Don DeLillo **27**:84
E. L. Doctorow **18**:127; **37**:94
Stanley Elkin **9**:191
John Gardner **8**:233
Graham Greene **18**:197
Lillian Hellman **18**:228
Mark Helprin **22**:222; **32**:229
John Irving **23**:251
Ruth Prawer Jhabvala **29**:263
Diane Johnson **13**:305
William Kennedy **34**:209
Doris Lessing **15**:335
Bernard Malamud **18**:319
Bobbie Ann Mason **28**:273
Ian McEwan **13**:371
Larry McMurtry **7**:214
Leonard Michaels **25**:317
R. K. Narayan **28**:302
Flannery O'Connor **13**:422
Grace Paley **37**:339
Breece D'J Pancake **29**:348
Walker Percy **8**:444; **18**:401
Anthony Powell **9**:435
Padgett Powell **34**:100
V. S. Pritchett **15**:444
Ishmael Reed **32**:360
Philip Roth **9**:461; **15**:451
Salman Rushdie **23**:366
James Salter **7**:387
Wilfrid Sheed **10**:473
Scott Sommer **25**:425
Mark Stevens **34**:112
Peter Taylor **37**:412
Paul Theroux **8**:512; **28**:427
Douglas Unger **34**:116
John Updike **13**:559
Kurt Vonnegut, Jr. **8**:533
Alice Walker **27**:451
Rebecca West **9**:562
William Wharton **18**:543;
37:440

Townley, Rod
Agnes Eckhardt Nixon **21**:247

Towns, Saundra
Gwendolyn Brooks **15**:93

Townsend, John Rowe
Joan Aiken **35**:19
Honor Arundel **17**:18
H. F. Brinsmead **21**:31
Peter Dickinson **12**:172
John Donovan **35**:141
Esther Forbes **12**:211
Leon Garfield **12**:222, 224
Alan Garner **17**:143
Virginia Hamilton **26**:153
S. E. Hinton **30**:204
Jesse Jackson **12**:291
Madeleine L'Engle **12**:350
William Mayne **12**:397
Andre Norton **12**:460
Scott O'Dell **30**:269
Philippa Pearce **21**:289
Rosemary Sutcliff **26**:435
Jill Paton Walsh **35**:430
Barbara Wersba **30**:430
Paul Zindel **26**:471

Townsend, R. C.
William Golding **17**:168

Townshend, Peter
Peter Townshend **17**:534

Toynbee, Philip
D. J. Enright **31**:153
Arthur Koestler **1**:170; **33**:230
Mary Renault **17**:399
Mordecai Richler **5**:375

Trachtenberg, Alan
Henry Miller **4**:351
Tom Wolfe **9**:578

Tracy, Honor
Janet Frame **22**:144
Nadine Gordimer **33**:180
Graham Greene **3**:206

Tracy, Phil
Kingsley Amis **3**:9

Tracy, Robert
Benedict Kiely **23**:267

Trakin, Roy
Lou Reed **21**:321

Traschen, Isadore
William Faulkner **9**:201
Robert Frost **26**:122

Traub, James
Evelyn Waugh **27**:476

Traubitz, Nancy Baker
Tennessee Williams **15**:578

Traum, Happy
Van Morrison **21**:231

Trease, Geoffrey
H. F. Brinsmead **21**:26
Leon Garfield **12**:216, 217
William Mayne **12**:390

Treece, Henry
Herbert Read **4**:437

Treglown, Jeremy
Brian Aldiss **14**:14
Howard Barker **37**:33
Samuel Beckett **29**:57
Brigid Brophy **11**:68
Anthony Burgess **22**:75

Len Deighton **22**:116
Parel Kohout **13**:325
Olivia Manning **19**:302
Joyce Carol Oates **11**:403
Barbara Pym **13**:470
Tom Robbins **9**:454
J.I.M. Stewart **14**:512
A. N. Wilson **33**:450
Snoo Wilson **33**:462

Trenner, Richard
E. L. Doctorow **37**:89

Trensky, Paul I.
Václav Havel **25**:220

Trevor, William
Elizabeth Bowen **22**:64
Margaret Drabble **22**:122
Michael Frayn **31**:189
Frank O'Connor **23**:331
Frank Sargeson **31**:364

Trewin, J. C.
Robert Bolt **14**:89
Agatha Christie **12**:125

Trickett, Rachel
Olivia Manning **19**:302
James Purdy **2**:349
Andrew Sinclair **2**:401
Wallace Stegner **9**:508
Angus Wilson **2**:473

Trilling, Diana
Margery Allingham **19**:12
Ilya Ehrenburg **18**:131
Esther Forbes **12**:209
Martha Gellhorn **14**:194
Aldous Huxley **8**:304
Frank O'Connor **14**:395
Jean Rhys **19**:392
Irwin Shaw **7**:410
Betty Smith **19**:422

Trilling, Lionel
E. M. Forster **1**:104
Robert Graves **2**:174

Trilling, Roger
Bob Marley **17**:270

Trimbur, John
Lawrence Ferlinghetti **27**:137

Trimpi, Helen P.
Edgar Bowers **9**:121, 122

Tripp, John
Dannie Abse **29**:18

Trodd, Kenith
Andrew Sinclair **2**:400

Troeger, Thomas H.
Czesław Miłosz **31**:266

Trombetta, Jim
Lou Reed **21**:314

Trotsky, Leon
André Malraux **13**:364

Trotter, David
Leon Edel **29**:175

Trotter, Stewart
Jean Genet **5**:137
Graham Greene **6**:220

Trowbridge, Clinton
John Updike 2:442

Troy, William
Carl Theodor Dreyer 16:256
Fritz Lang 20:202
Josef von Sternberg 20:370

True, Michael D.
Daniel J. Berrigan 4:58
Robert Francis 15:236
Paul Goodman 2:169
Flannery O'Connor 13:422;
21:271
Karl Shapiro 15:477

Trueblood, Valerie
Margaret Atwood 13:43
Tess Gallagher 18:168
Gilbert Sorrentino 14:499
Derek Walcott 14:548

Trueheart, Charles
John Barth 27:25
Craig Nova 31:299

Truesdale, David A.
Marion Zimmer Bradley 30:28
C. J. Cherryh 35:105

Truffaut, François
Ingmar Bergman 16:70
Luis Buñuel 16:136
Frank Capra 16:161
Charles Chaplin 16:198
John Ford 16:314
Alfred Hitchcock 16:341, 346
Elia Kazan 16:366
Fritz Lang 20:208
Agnès Varda 16:553
Billy Wilder 20:457

Trumbull, Robert
Thor Heyerdahl 26:193

Truscott, Lucian K.
Bob Dylan 3:131

Trussler, Simon
John Arden 15:19

Tsuruta, Kinya
Shusaku Endo 7:96

Tsvetaeva, Marina
Boris Pasternak 18:386

Tube, Henry
Vasily Aksenov 22:26
Masuji Ibuse 22:226

Tuch, Ronald
Charles Chaplin 16:204

Tucker, Carll
Imamu Amiri Baraka 10:19
Ed Bullins 7:37
Jules Feiffer 8:216
Richard Howard 7:169
Albert Innaurato 21:191
Robert Lowell 9:338
Archibald MacLeish 8:363

Tucker, Chris
Kurt Vonnegut, Jr. 22:451

Tucker, James
Anthony Powell 7:338; 10:409

Tucker, Ken
T. Coraghessan Boyle 36:59
Allen Ginsberg 36:195
Stephen King 37:205
Elmore Leonard 28:234

Tucker, Kenneth
Joan Armatrading 17:9
Walter Becker and Donald
Fagen 26:83
David Byrne 26:96
Waylon Jennings 21:203
Steve Martin 30:249
Prince 35:324
Carly Simon 26:410, 413
Patti Smith 12:543
Neil Young 17:576, 580

Tucker, Martin
Chinua Achebe 3:1
Ayi Kwei Armah 33:25
Malcolm Bradbury 32:50
André Brink 18:67
Brigid Brophy 29:93
Claude Brown 30:35
Cyprian Ekwensi 4:152
Nadine Gordimer 3:201
Jan de Hartog 19:131, 132
Ernest Hemingway 3:234
Jerzy Kosinski 1:172
Bernard Malamud 3:322
Ezekiel Mphahlele 25:346
James Ngugi 3:357
Cynthia Ozick 7:287
Alan Paton 4:395
William Plomer 4:406
James Purdy 28:377
Raja Rao 25:365
Ishmael Reed 13:477
Wole Soyinka 3:462; 36:408
Amos Tutuola 5:443
Laurens van der Post 5:463

Tucker, Nicholas
Honor Arundel 17:16
Judy Blume 12:45
Virginia Hamilton 26:151
Barbara Wersba 30:434

Tulip, James
David Malouf 28:269

Tunis, John R.
Maia Wojciechowska 26:449,
454

Tunney, Gene
Budd Schulberg 7:402

Tunstall, Caroline
William Brammer 31:53
Taylor Caldwell 28:61

Tuohy, Frank
Nora Ephron 31:159
Nadine Gordimer 18:188
Ruth Prawer Jhabvala 29:262
Patrick Kavanagh 22:244
Jakov Lind 27:270
Seán O'Faoláin 14:405
Randolph Stow 23:437

Turan, Kenneth
Gene Roddenberry 17:414
Elie Wiesel 11:570

Turco, Lewis
Edward Brathwaite 11:67
Robert Hayden 9:270
Donald Justice 19:232

Turin, Michele
Alix Kates Shulman 10:476

Turkington, Kate
Chinua Achebe 26:16

Turnbull, Colin M.
Christie Harris 12:262

Turnbull, Martin
François Mauriac 4:340

Turnell, Martin
Graham Greene 1:134

Turner, Alice K.
Jamake Highwater 12:285
Colleen McCullough 27:318

Turner, Darwin T.
Zora Neale Hurston 30:214
Ishmael Reed 13:477
Alice Walker 9:558
Richard Wright 21:450
Frank G. Yerby 22:488, 489,
490

Turner, E. S.
Jeffrey Archer 28:11
Art Buchwald 33:93
Mircea Eliade 19:148
Daphne du Maurier 11:164
Monty Python 21:223

Turner, George
Philip K. Dick 30:115

Turner, Gil
Bob Dylan 12:179

Turner, R. H.
Claude Chabrol 16:167

Turner, Steve
Peter Townshend 17:537

Turoff, Robert David
Milton Meltzer 26:306

Tuska, Jon
Louis L'Amour 25:279

Tuttle, Lisa
Douglas Adams 27:11

Tuttleton, James W.
Louis Auchincloss 4:29

Tvardovsky, Alexander
Aleksandr I. Solzhenitsyn
26:415

Twichell, Ethel R.
C. S. Adler 35:15
Norma Fox Mazer 26:295
Milton Meltzer 26:308
Walter Dean Myers 35:297
Katherine Paterson 30:288
Marilyn Sachs 35:334

Tyler, Anne
Richard Adams 18:2
Renata Adler 31:14
Toni Cade Bambara 19:33
Anita Brookner 34:141
John Cheever 11:121

Anita Desai 19:134
Joan Didion 14:151; 32:146
E. L. Doctorow 37:94
Lawrence Durrell 27:99
Jacob Epstein 19:162
Marilyn French 10:191
Mavis Gallant 18:172
Penelope Gilliatt 13:238
Gail Godwin 31:196
Nadine Gordimer 33:181
Caroline Gordon 29:188
Lois Gould 10:241
John Irving 23:244
Sue Kaufman 8:317
Molly Keane 31:234
Thomas Keneally 10:299
Maxine Hong Kingston 19:250
Paule Marshall 27:315
Bobbie Ann Mason 28:271
Joyce Maynard 23:289
Ian McEwan 13:370
Leonard Michaels 25:318
Suzanne Newton 35:302
Grace Paley 37:335
Katherine Paterson 30:283
Jayne Anne Phillips 33:306
Barbara Pym 37:374
Bernice Rubens 19:404
Mary Lee Settle 19:410
Alix Kates Shulman 10:475
Susan Sontag 13:516
Scott Spencer 30:405
Elizabeth Taylor 29:412
Paul Theroux 11:529
D. M. Thomas 31:432
William Trevor 7:478
Angus Wilson 25:462

Tyler, Karen B.[eyard-]
Norma Klein 30:239

Tyler, Parker
Charles Chaplin 16:196
Laurence Olivier 20:235
Agnès Varda 16:554
Andy Warhol 20:416
Orson Welles 20:438

Tyler, Ralph
Richard Adams 5:5
Agatha Christie 6:109
S. J. Perelman 9:416
Jean Rhys 6:455

Tyler, Tony
John Lennon and Paul
McCartney 12:379

Tymn, Marshall B.
Roger Zelazny 21:473

Tyms, James D.
Langston Hughes 5:191

Tynan, Kenneth
Enid Bagnold 25:76
Lenny Bruce 21:47
William Gibson 23:175, 177
Roman Polanski 16:463
N. F. Simpson 29:364, 366
Stephen Sondheim 30:377
Tom Stoppard 15:518
Tennessee Williams 30:462

Tyrmand, Leopold
Witold Gombrowicz 7:124

Tyrrell, Connie
Franklyn M. Branley **21**:23

Tyrrell, William Blake
Gene Roddenberry **17**:407

Tyson, Christy
Piers Anthony **35**:39

Tytell, John
William S. Burroughs **22**:86
Allen Ginsberg **36**:180
Jack Kerouac **3**:264; **29**:272

Ueda, Makoto
Shiga Naoya **33**:366
Jun'ichirō Tanizaki **28**:413

Ugarte, Michael
Juan Goytisolo **23**:187

Uglow, Jennifer
Caroline Gordon **29**:188
Russell C. Hoban **25**:264
Marge Piercy **18**:408

Uhelski, Jaan
Jimmy Page and Robert Plant
12:478

Uibopuu, Valev
Ivar Ivask **14**:287

Ulam, Adam
Agatha Christie **12**:120
Michael Scammell **34**:490
Aleksandr Solzhenitsyn **34**:490

Ulanov, Ann Belford
Margaret Mead **37**:280

Ulfers, Friedrich
Paul Celan **19**:92

Ullman, Montague
Melvin Berger **12**:42
Larry Kettelkamp **12**:308

Ulrich, Mabel S.
A. J. Cronin **32**:133

Underdown, David
Antonia Fraser **32**:183

Underwood, Tim
Jack Vance **35**:422

Unger, Arthur
Alex Haley **12**:253

Unger, Leonard
T. S. Eliot **1**:90

Unsworth, Robert
Larry Bograd **35**:63
Mavis Thorpe Clark **12**:131
James D. Forman **21**:122
Rosa Guy **26**:144
Sonia Levitin **17**:265

Unterecker, John
Lawrence Durrell **1**:84
Ezra Pound **4**:415
Kenneth Rexroth **2**:370

Untermeyer, Louis
Robert Francis **15**:235
Robert Frost **13**:223; **15**:239
Ogden Nash **23**:319
Muriel Rukeyser **27**:403
Carl Sandburg **35**:339, 341

Updike, John
Walter Abish **22**:16
Peter Ackroyd **34**:402
Vasily Aksyonov **37**:16
Michael Ayrton **7**:20
Roland Barthes **24**:29
Ann Beattie **8**:55
Samuel Beckett **6**:45
Saul Bellow **6**:56
Heinrich Böll **27**:68
Jorge Luis Borges **8**:100
William S. Burroughs **22**:83
Italo Calvino **5**:101; **8**:130
Albert Camus **9**:149
Bruce Chatwin **28**:75
John Cheever **7**:50; **25**:121
Julio Cortázar **5**:109
Don DeLillo **10**:135
Margaret Drabble **8**:183
André Dubus **36**:149
T. S. Eliot **34**:402
Shusaku Endo **19**:160, 161
Daniel Fuchs **8**:221
Witold Gombrowicz **7**:124
Günter Grass **2**:172; **4**:206;
32:204
Barry Hannah **23**:207
William Least Heat Moon
29:223
Ernest Hemingway **8**:285
Ruth Prawer Jhabvala **8**:312;
29:263
Gayl Jones **6**:266; **9**:307
Erica Jong **4**:263
Tadeusz Konwicki **28**:210
Jerzy Kosinski **6**:282
Milan Kundera **19**:269
Alex La Guma **19**:275
Ursula K. Le Guin **22**:275
Stanislaw Lem **15**:329
Alberto Moravia **7**:243
Wright Morris **7**:245
Iris Murdoch **6**:344; **22**:330;
31:294
Vladimir Nabokov **2**:301;
3:351; **6**:355; **8**:414, 415,
416, 417; **11**:395
V. S. Naipaul **13**:407
R. K. Narayan **7**:256; **28**:296,
303
Flann O'Brien **7**:269, 270
Tim O'Brien **19**:358
John O'Hara **11**:414
Robert Pinget **7**:306; **37**:359,
364
Harold Pinter **15**:423
Raymond Queneau **5**:359, 362
Jean Rhys **19**:395
Alain Robbe-Grillet **8**:452
Carl Sagan **30**:335
Françoise Sagan **6**:481
J. D. Salinger **12**:513
Simone Schwarz-Bart **7**:405
L. E. Sissman **18**:487
Wole Soyinka **14**:509
Muriel Spark **5**:400
Christina Stead **8**:499, 500
James Thurber **5**:433
William Trevor **25**:444
Anne Tyler **7**:479; **18**:530;
28:434
Sylvia Townsend Warner
7:512; **19**:460

Edmund Wilson **8**:551

Uphaus, Robert W.
Kurt Vonnegut, Jr. **5**:469

Urang, Gunnar
C. S. Lewis **3**:298
J.R.R. Tolkien **2**:434

Urbanski, Marie Mitchell Oleson
Joyce Carol Oates **11**:402

Urbas, Jeannette
Gabrielle Roy **14**:468

Uroff, Margaret D.
Sylvia Plath **3**:391; **17**:354

Uroff, Margaret Dickie
Caroline Gordon **29**:188

Ury, Claude
Jules Archer **12**:17

Usborne, Richard
MacDonald Harris **9**:261

Uscatescu, George
Mircea Eliade **19**:145

Useem, Michael
Jonathan Schell **35**:368

Usmiani, Renate
Friedrich Dürrenmatt **8**:194
Michel Tremblay **29**:425

Uyl, Douglas Den
Ayn Rand **30**:304

Uys, Stanley
Breyten Breytenbach **23**:85

Vaidyanathan, T. G.
Ernest Hemingway **30**:195

Vaizey, John
Kingsley Amis **5**:22

Valdés, Richard A.
Manuel Mujica Láinez **31**:283

Valdéz, Jorge H.
G. Cabrera Infante **25**:105
Julio Cortázar **13**:165

Valentine, Dean
Albert Innaurato **21**:195
Arthur Kopit **33**:247

Valgemae, Mardi
Sławomir Mrozek **13**:398
Jean-Claude Van Itallie **3**:493

Vallee, Lillian
Czesław Miłosz **22**:305

Valley, John A.
Alberto Moravia **7**:243

Vallis, Val
Judith Wright **11**:578

Van Brunt, H. L.
Jim Harrison **6**:224

Van Buren, Alice
Janet Frame **2**:142

Vance, Joel
Chuck Berry **17**:56
David Bowie **17**:63
Jimmy Cliff **21**:63
Marvin Gaye **26**:132
Bob Marley **17**:268

Monty Python **21**:225
Lou Reed **21**:313
Bob Seger **35**:382
Paul Simon **17**:467

Van Cleave, Kit
Julia Peterkin **31**:310

Vande Kieft, Ruth M.
Flannery O'Connor **1**:258
Eudora Welty **1**:360

Vandenbroucke, Russell
Athol Fugard **9**:230

Van den Haag, Ernest
William F. Buckley, Jr. **7**:34

Van den Heuvel, Cor
James Wright **10**:545

Vanderbilt, Kermit
Norman Mailer **3**:319
William Styron **3**:474

Vanderwerken, David L.
Richard Brautigan **5**:69

Van Doren, Carl
Esther Forbes **12**:205, 208
Carl Van Vechten **33**:385

Van Doren, Dorothy
A. J. Cronin **32**:129

Van Doren, Mark
Djuna Barnes **29**:24
René Clair **20**:62
E. E. Cummings **12**:139
Robert Frost **13**:223; **15**:241
Robinson Jeffers **11**:304
John Cowper Powys **7**:346

Van Duyn, Mona
Margaret Atwood **2**:19
Adrienne Rich **3**:427
Anne Sexton **2**:391

Van Dyne, Susan R.
Adrienne Rich **18**:445

Van Gelder, Lawrence
Charles Fuller **25**:179
John Landis **26**:271
Nagisa Oshima **20**:250

Van Gelder, Lindsay
Joan D. Vinge **30**:410

Van Gelder, Robert
August Derleth **31**:133

Vanjak, Gloria
Jim Morrison **17**:290

Van Matre, Lynn
Lily Tomlin **17**:517

Vanocur, Sander
Fletcher Knebel **14**:307

Van Rjndt, Philippe
Morris L. West **33**:433

Vansittart, Peter
José Donoso **32**:152
Lawrence Durrell **13**:189
D. J. Enright **31**:147
Winston Graham **23**:193
Piers Paul Read **10**:436
Elizabeth Taylor **29**:410

Critic Index

Jill Paton Walsh **35**:430

Van Slyke, Berenice
John G. Neihardt **32**:330

Van Spanckeren, Kathryn
John Gardner **28**:166

Van Vechten, Carl
Carl Van Vechten **33**:396

Van Wert, William F.
Kōbō Abé **22**:14
Marguerite Duras **20**:103
Alain Resnais **16**:516

Van Wyngarden, Bruce
Andrea Lee **36**:258

Vardi, Dov
Aharon Appelfeld **23**:35
Abraham B. Yehoshua **13**:617

Vargas Llosa, Mario
José María Arguedas **18**:9
Gabriel García Márquez **3**:181

Vargo, Edward P.
John Updike **7**:486

Vas, Robert
Lindsay Anderson **20**:12
Robert Bresson **16**:105

Vas Dias, Robert
Toby Olson **28**:342

Vásquez Amaral, José
Julio Cortázar **13**:157

Vassal, Jacques
Janis Ian **21**:183
Phil Ochs **17**:331
Buffy Sainte-Marie **17**:431

Vassallo, Carol
Virginia Hamilton **26**:151

Vaughan, Alden T.
Maia Wojciechowska **26**:451

Vaughan, Dai
Carl Theodor Dreyer **16**:265

Vaughan, Stephen
Thomas Keneally **14**:302
Ann Schlee **35**:372

Veidemanis, Gladys
William Golding **17**:169

Veit, Henri C.
Stephen Dobyns **37**:75

Velie, Alan R.
James Welch **14**:561

Venable, Gene
Fletcher Knebel **14**:309
James H. Webb, Jr. **22**:453

Venclova, Tomas
Aleksandr I. Solzhenitsyn
18:497

Vendler, Helen
A. R. Ammons **2**:14; **25**:46
John Ashbery **25**:51
Margaret Atwood **8**:29
John Berryman **3**:68; **10**:46
Frank Bidart **33**:77, 79
Elizabeth Bishop **9**:90

Harold Bloom **24**:81
Olga Broumas **10**:77
Hayden Carruth **7**:41
Amy Clampitt **32**:114
Lucille Clifton **19**:109
E. E. Cummings **3**:119
D. J. Enright **8**:203
Robert Frost **34**:471
Allen Ginsberg **2**:163; **3**:195
Louise Glück **7**:118; **22**:174,
177
Seamus Heaney **7**:152
John Hollander **5**:187
Ted Hughes **37**:180
Richard F. Hugo **6**:245
Randall Jarrell **9**:295
Erica Jong **4**:263
Maxine Kumin **13**:326
Brad Leithauser **27**:242
Philip Levine **33**:272
Audre Lorde **18**:308
Robert Lowell **37**:232
Haki R. Madhubuti **6**:313
Mary McCarthy **3**:328
James Merrill **2**:275; **18**:328
W. S. Merwin **18**:332
Josephine Miles **14**:369
Czesław Miłosz **31**:267
Marianne Moore **19**:341
Howard Moss **7**:250
Howard Nemerov **36**:301
Joyce Carol Oates **3**:361
Frank O'Hara **5**:323
Octavio Paz **4**:397
Sylvia Plath **17**:353
William H. Pritchard **34**:471
Adrienne Rich **7**:367; **18**:444;
36:368, 377
I. A. Richards **14**:454
Irwin Shaw **7**:414
David Slavitt **14**:490
Dave Smith **22**:384, 387
Allen Tate **2**:429
Charles Tomlinson **6**:535
Diane Wakoski **7**:504
Derek Walcott **25**:455
Robert Penn Warren **10**:525;
18:533
Charles Wright **6**:581; **28**:456

Ventimiglia, Peter James
Albert Innaurato **21**:196

Venturi, Lauro
Jean Renoir **20**:288

Venuti, Lawrence
Dino Buzzati **36**:92
Rod Serling **30**:358

Verani, Hugo J.
Juan Carlos Onetti **7**:277

Vernon, Grenville
Clifford Odets **28**:324, 328

Vernon, John
Michael Benedikt **4**:54
William S. Burroughs **15**:108
James Dickey **7**:82
Norman Dubie **36**:133
Richard F. Hugo **18**:264
David Ignatow **4**:247
James Merrill **3**:334
W. S. Merwin **1**:213

Thomas Pynchon **11**:452
C. K. Williams **33**:443

Verschoyle, Derek
Rayner Heppenstall **10**:271

Vesselo, Arthur
Laurence Olivier **20**:235

Vickery, John B.
John Updike **5**:451

Vickery, Olga W.
John Hawkes **4**:213

Vickery, R. C.
Jules Archer **12**:23

Vidal, Gore
Louis Auchincloss **4**:31
John Barth **14**:51
Italo Calvino **5**:98
John Dos Passos **4**:132
William H. Gass **11**:224
E. Howard Hunt **3**:251
Doris Lessing **15**:333
Norman Mailer **2**:265
Carson McCullers **12**:418
Henry Miller **2**:282
Yukio Mishima **2**:287
Vladimir Nabokov **23**:304
Anaïs Nin **4**:376
John O'Hara **2**:323
Thomas Pynchon **11**:452
Ayn Rand **30**:295
Alain Robbe-Grillet **2**:375
Aleksandr I. Solzhenitsyn **4**:510
Susan Sontag **2**:414
Tennessee Williams **7**:546

Vidal-Hall, Judith
Leon Garfield **12**:230

Viereck, Peter
Robert Frost **26**:114

Vigderman, Patricia
Andrea Lee **36**:257
Bobbi Ann Mason **28**:273
Breece D'J Pancake **29**:348

Viguers, Ruth Hill
Lloyd Alexander **35**:23, 24
E. M. Almedingen **12**:2
Ruth M. Arthur **12**:24
Margot Benary-Isbert **12**:33
Betty Cavanna **12**:100
Eilís Dillon **17**:95
Lois Duncan **26**:100, 101
Leon Garfield **12**:218
Jean Craighead George **35**:175,
176
Christie Harris **12**:261, 262
Isabelle Holland **21**:147
Lee Kingman **17**:244, 245
Joseph Krumgold **12**:320
Madeleine L'Engle **12**:345, 346
William Mayne **12**:393
Emily Cheney Neville **12**:450,
451
Scott O'Dell **30**:268
Philippa Pearce **21**:283
Josephine Poole **17**:370
Zoa Sherburne **30**:361
Zilpha Keatley Snyder **17**:469,
470
Mary Stolz **12**:553

Noel Streatfeild **21**:404, 408
Lenora Mattingly Weber **12**:632

Vilhjalmsson, Thor
Gabriel García Márquez **2**:150

Viljanen, Lauri
Frans Eemil Sillanpää **19**:417

Villani, Sergio
Romain Gary **25**:190

Vince, Thomas L.
Rosa Guy **26**:140

Vincent, Celeste H.
Franklyn M. Branley **21**:18

Vincent, Emily
Isabelle Holland **21**:153

Vine, Richard
Stanley Kunitz **11**:319

Vinge, Joan D.
Jack Vance **35**:427

Vining, Mark
Smokey Robinson **21**:344

Vinson, Joe
Isabelle Holland **21**:151

Vintcent, Brian
Marie-Claire Blais **4**:67
Roch Carrier **13**:143
Anne Hébert **4**:220

Vinton, Iris
Robert A. Heinlein **26**:160

Viorst, Judith
Lois Gould **10**:243

Vivas, Eliseo
F. R. Leavis **24**:297
I. A. Richards **24**:379
George Steiner **24**:432
Allen Tate **24**:443
René Wellek **28**:442

Vogel, Christine B.
Barbara Pym **37**:376
Frank G. Slaughter **29**:378

Vogel, Dan
William Faulkner **6**:177, 178
Arthur Miller **6**:333
John Steinbeck **21**:369
Robert Penn Warren **6**:556
Tennessee Williams **5**:504

Volpe, Edmond L.
James Jones **1**:162

Vonalt, Larry P.
John Berryman **3**:66; **4**:60
Marianne Moore **1**:230

Von Däniken, Erich
Erich von Däniken **30**:421

Von Dare, Greg
Cay Van Ash **34**:119

Von Hallberg, Robert
Charles Olson **6**:386
W. D. Snodgrass **18**:495
William Carlos Williams
22:464

Von Hoffman, Nicholas
Aldous Huxley **35**:245

Vonnegut, Kurt, Jr.
Robert Altman **16**:32
Heinrich Böll **27**:61
Joseph Heller **5**:175
Hermann Hesse **17**:219
Stanislaw Lem **15**:328
Hunter S. Thompson **17**:506
Tom Wolfe **35**:449

Von Obenauer, Heidi
Noel Streatfeild **21**:412

Von Tersch, Gary
Buffy Sainte-Marie **17**:431

Voorhees, Richard J.
P. G. Wodehouse **1**:374

Vopat, Carole Gottlieb
Jack Kerouac **3**:265

Voss, Arthur
James T. Farrell **11**:191
John O'Hara **11**:413
Dorothy Parker **15**:414
Jean Stafford **19**:430

Wachtel, Eleanor
Audrey Thomas **37**:419

Wachtel, Nili
Isaac Bashevis Singer **15**:504
A. B. Yehoshua **31**:472

Waddington, C. H.
Lewis Thomas **35**:409

Waddington, Miriam
Joan Barfoot **18**:35
Hugh Garner **13**:234
Ralph Gustafson **36**:212
A. M. Klein **19**:258

Wade, Barbara
Leon Rooke **25**:394

Wade, David
J.R.R. Tolkien **2**:434

Wade, Mason
August Derleth **31**:131

Wade, Michael
Peter Abrahams **4**:2

Wade, Rosalind
Iain Banks **34**:30
Lynne Reid Banks **23**:42
Isabel Colegate **36**:110
Elaine Feinstein **36**:170
L. P. Hartley **22**:215
Ronald Harwood **32**:226

Waelti-Walters, Jennifer R.
Michel Butor **15**:113
J.M.G. Le Clézio **31**:248

Wagenaar, Dick
Yasunari Kawabata **18**:281

Wagenknecht, Edward
Frank G. Slaughter **29**:376

Waggoner, Diana
William Mayne **12**:406

Waggoner, Hyatt H.
E. E. Cummings **3**:117
Robert Duncan **2**:122
T. S. Eliot **2**:127
Robert Frost **3**:173
H. D. **3**:217
Robinson Jeffers **2**:214
Robert Lowell **3**:300
Archibald MacLeish **3**:310
Marianne Moore **2**:292
Ezra Pound **2**:341
John Crowe Ransom **2**:363
Theodore Roethke **3**:432
Carl Sandburg **4**:463
Karl Shapiro **4**:485
Lewis Turco **11**:549
Richard Wilbur **3**:532
William Carlos Williams **2**:468

Wagner, Dave
Robert L. Peters **7**:303

Wagner, Dick
Yukio Mishima **9**:381

Wagner, Geoffrey
R. P. Blackmur **2**:61
Jerome Siegel and Joe Shuster **21**:354
Josef von Sternberg **20**:372

Wagner, Jean
Jean Toomer **22**:423

Wagner, Linda W.
Margaret Atwood **25**:66
John Dos Passos **25**:142
Louise Glück **22**:176
Ernest Hemingway **30**:198
Adrienne Rich **36**:366
William Stafford **29**:379

Wagner, Linda Welshimer
William Faulkner **1**:103
Robert Hass **18**:208
Ernest Hemingway **6**:231; **19**:215
Denise Levertov **1**:176; **5**:247
Philip Levine **9**:332
Phyllis McGinley **14**:365
W. S. Merwin **13**:383
Joyce Carol Oates **19**:349
Diane Wakoski **9**:554, 555

Waidson, H. M.
Heinrich Böll **11**:55; **27**:56

Wain, John
Sylvia Ashton-Warner **19**:20
William Barrett **27**:19
R. P. Blackmur **24**:62
William S. Burroughs **5**:91
Eleanor Clark **19**:105
Edward Dahlberg **7**:66
William Empson **33**:141
C. Day Lewis **6**:127
Günter Grass **2**:173; **4**:202
Michael Hamburger **5**:158
Ben Hecht **8**:270
Ernest Hemingway **3**:233
Aldous Huxley **5**:192
C. S. Lewis **27**:261
Archibald MacLeish **14**:336
Ved Mehta **37**:290
Edwin Morgan **31**:277
Flann O'Brien **4**:383

Sylvia Plath **17**:345
I. A. Richards **24**:390
C. P. Snow **4**:500
Edmund Wilson **24**:476

Wainwright, Andy
Earle Birney **6**:77
Marian Engel **36**:158

Wainwright, Jeffrey
W. S. Graham **29**:198
Ezra Pound **7**:332

Wakefield, Dan
Edward Hoagland **28**:181
Garson Kanin **22**:232
Norma Klein **30**:240
Agnes Eckhardt Nixon **21**:250
J. D. Salinger **12**:500
Harvey Swados **5**:422
John R. Tunis **12**:597
Leon Uris **7**:490

Wakoski, Diane
Clayton Eshleman **7**:98
David Ignatow **4**:248
John Logan **5**:255
Robert Lowell **4**:304
Anaïs Nin **4**:377
Jerome Rothenberg **6**:477
Charles Simic **22**:379

Walcott, Derek
C.L.R. James **33**:222

Walcott, James
Leonard Michaels **25**:318

Walcott, Ronald
Hal Bennett **5**:57, 59
Charles Gordone **4**:199

Walcutt, Charles Child
James Gould Cozzens **4**:114
John O'Hara **1**:262

Waldeland, Lynne
John Cheever **25**:118

Waldemar, Carla
Anaïs Nin **11**:399

Waldmeir, Joseph
Jackson J. Benson **34**:414
John Steinbeck **34**:414
John Updike **5**:450

Waldron, Edward E.
Langston Hughes **15**:291

Waldron, Randall H.
Norman Mailer **3**:314

Waldrop, Rosemary
Hans Erich Nossack **6**:365

Walkarput, W.
Vladimir Nabokov **11**:392

Walker, Alice
Ai **4**:16
Alice Childress **15**:132
Buchi Emecheta **14**:159
Rosa Guy **26**:141
Virginia Hamilton **26**:148
Zora Neale Hurston **30**:223
Flannery O'Connor **6**:381
Derek Walcott **4**:576

Walker, Carolyn
Joyce Carol Oates **3**:360

Walker, Cheryl
Richard Brautigan **12**:68
Stephen Dunn **36**:152
Adrienne Rich **3**:428
Robert Penn Warren **6**:558

Walker, David
Anne Hébert **13**:268; **29**:231

Walker, Evelyn
Scott O'Dell **30**:278

Walker, Greta
Babbis Friis-Baastad **12**:214

Walker, Jim
Clarence Major **19**:292

Walker, John
Manuel Mujica Láinez **31**:284

Walker, Keith
John Rechy **14**:445

Walker, Martin
Robert Ludlum **22**:291

Walker, Michael
Claude Chabrol **16**:173
Jerzy Skolimowski **20**:350

Walker, Robert G.
Ernest Hemingway **8**:287

Walker, Stanley
Mari Sandoz **28**:402

Walker, Ted
Andrew Young **5**:523

Wall, Cheryl A.
Zora Neale Hurston **30**:225

Wall, Chris
Allen Drury **37**:112
Kent Haruf **34**:59

Wall, James M.
Andrew Lloyd Webber and Tim Rice **21**:429

Wall, John
Prince **35**:323

Wall, Richard
Behan, Brendan **15**:46

Wall, Stephen
Isabel Colegate **36**:109, 110
P. H. Newby **13**:408

Wallace, Herbert W.
Alvin Silverstein and Virginia B. Silverstein **17**:455

Wallace, Irving
Irving Wallace **13**:568

Wallace, Margaret
Dee Brown **18**:70
Roderick L. Haig-Brown **21**:135
Zora Neale Hurston **30**:209
Molly Keane **31**:232
Bruce Lancaster **36**:242
Mari Sandoz **28**:401
Frank G. Slaughter **29**:372, 373

Wallace, Michele
Ntozake Shange **8**:485

Critic Index

Wallace, Ronald
Stephen Dunn **36**:152
John Hawkes **15**:274
Vladimir Nabokov **23**:304

Wallace, Willard M.
Thomas J. Fleming **37**:118
Robert Newton Peck **17**:340

Wallace-Crabbe, Chris
Kenneth Slessor **14**:492

Wallenstein, Barry
James T. Farrell **11**:195
Donald Hall **37**:147
Ted Hughes **2**:200

Waller, Claudia Joan
José Lezama Lima **10**:317

Waller, G. F.
Joyce Carol Oates **19**:350
Paul Theroux **8**:514

Waller, Gary F.
T. Alan Broughton **19**:74
William Maxwell **19**:309

Walley, David G.
Peter Townshend **17**:526
Frank Zappa **17**:585, 588

Wallis, Bruce
Katherine Anne Porter **15**:430

Wallis, C. G.
Jean Cocteau **16**:220

Wallrich, William J.
Franklyn M. Branley **21**:16

Walls, Richard C.
Bob Seger **35**:385

Walpole, Hugh
A. J. Cronin **32**:128

Walrond, Eric
Carl Van Vechten **33**:392

Walsh, Chad
Robert Bly **2**:66
Stanley Burnshaw **13**:129
Robert Graves **6**:212
Ted Hughes **2**:197
Aldous Huxley **35**:238
Fletcher Knebel **14**:308
Philip Larkin **5**:228
C. S. Lewis **27**:265
David Lodge **36**:267
Cynthia Macdonald **13**:355
Archibald MacLeish **3**:311
Frederick Morgan **23**:298
Howard Nemerov **2**:306
Conrad Richter **30**:317
Frank G. Slaughter **29**:376
Jerome Weidman **7**:517

Walsh, Jill Paton
H. F. Brinsmead **21**:30
Mollie Hunter **21**:160
Diana Wynne Jones **26**:225
Norma Fox Mazer **26**:289
Rosemary Sutcliff **26**:437

Walsh, John
Malcolm Bradbury **32**:55
Jorge Ibargüengoitia **37**:183
Bernard Mac Laverty **31**:255

Walsh, Moira
Gordon Parks **16**:458

Walsh, Nina M.
Alvin Silverstein and Virginia
B. Silverstein **17**:452

Walsh, Patricia L.
John M. Del Vecchio **29**:151

Walsh, Thomas F.
Katherine Anne Porter **13**:449

Walsh, William
Earle Birney **6**:78
D. J. Enright **31**:151
Robert Finch **18**:155
A. M. Klein **19**:261
F. R. Leavis **24**:301
R. K. Narayan **7**:254; **28**:290
Thomas Tryon **11**:548
Patrick White **3**:521; **4**:583,
584; **7**:532; **9**:567; **18**:546

Walsten, David M.
Yukio Mishima **2**:286

Walt, James
Jean Cayrol **11**:110
Ward Just **4**:266
Violette Leduc **22**:262
John O'Hara **6**:385
J. R. Salamanca **4**:462

Walter, James F.
John Barth **10**:22

Walter, Sydney Schubert
Sam Shepard **17**:435

Walters, Jennifer R.
Michel Butor **3**:93

Walters, Margaret
Brigid Brophy **6**:99

Walton, Alan Hull
Colin Wilson **3**:537; **14**:585

Walton, Eda Lou
Nella Larsen **37**:211
Conrad Richter **30**:306, 307

Walton, Edith H.
Enid Bagnold **25**:73
Sally Benson **17**:46, 48
Maureen Daly **17**:87
August Derleth **31**:128, 129,
131, 135
Esther Forbes **12**:204
Pamela Hansford Johnson
27:213
Mary Renault **17**:390
Rebecca West **31**:454

Walton, Richard J.
Jules Archer **12**:20

Walton, Todd
Scott Sommer **25**:426

Walzer, Judith B.
Marge Piercy **18**:407

Walzer, Michael
J. D. Salinger **12**:503

Wanamaker, John
Joy Adamson **17**:6

Wand, David Hsin-Fu
Marianne Moore **13**:396

Ward, A. C.
W. H. Auden **1**:8
Samuel Beckett **1**:21
Edmund Blunden **2**:65
Ivy Compton-Burnett **1**:62
Noel Coward **1**:64
T. S. Eliot **1**:90
E. M. Forster **1**:104
Christopher Fry **2**:143
Robert Graves **1**:128
Graham Greene **1**:132
Aldous Huxley **1**:150
W. Somerset Maugham **1**:204
Iris Murdoch **1**:234
J. B. Priestley **2**:346
Edith Sitwell **2**:403
C. P. Snow **1**:316
Evelyn Waugh **1**:358
Arnold Wesker **3**:518
P. G. Wodehouse **1**:374

Ward, Allen
John Ehle **27**:102

Ward, Andrew
Bob Dylan **12**:197

Ward, Christopher
Walter D. Edmonds **35**:146

Ward, David E.
Ezra Pound **1**:275

Ward, Ed
Jimmy Cliff **21**:60
Bob Marley **17**:268
Paul Weller **26**:444

Ward, Elizabeth
Pat Barker **32**:12

Ward, J. A.
S. J. Perelman **9**:414

Ward, Jeff
Lou Reed **21**:307

Ward, Leo
Harper Lee **12**:341

Ward, Margaret Joan
Morley Callahan **3**:97

Ward, P.
N. Scott Momaday **19**:318

Ward, Robert
Bruce Springsteen **17**:479
Lily Tomlin **17**:523

Wardle, Irving
Alan Ayckbourn **33**:42
David Caute **29**:113
Caryl Churchill **31**:82, 85
Michael Frayn **31**:191
David Hare **29**:212
Ann Jellicoe **27**:209, 210
Hugh Leonard **19**:282
Richard O'Brien **17**:324
Hugh Whitemore **37**:445
Snoo Wilson **33**:460

Wards, Jeff
Pink Floyd **35**:307

Ware, Cade
Leon Uris **32**:432

Warkentin, Germaine
A. W. Purdy **3**:408
F. R. Scott **22**:377

Warme, Lars G.
Eyvind Johnson **14**:297

Warner, Alan
Patrick Kavanagh **22**:238
Ken Russell **16**:543

Warner, Edwin
Jorge Luis Borges **2**:71

Warner, John M.
John Hawkes **3**:223

Warner, Jon M.
George MacBeth **5**:263

Warner, Rex
E. M. Forster **1**:105

Warner, Sylvia Townsend
T. H. White **30**:451

Warnke, Frank J.
Heinrich Böll **27**:61
William Golding **17**:166
Richard Yates **7**:553

Warnock, Mary
Brigid Brophy **6**:98
Lawrence Durrell **27**:94
Iris Murdoch **8**:404

Warren, Austin
T. S. Eliot **24**:177
E. M. Forster **15**:223

Warren, Robert Penn
James Dickey **10**:140
William Faulkner **28**:141
Robert Frost **26**:114
Caroline Gordon **29**:187
Alex Haley **12**:243
Ernest Hemingway **30**:179
Andrew Lytle **22**:296
Katherine Anne Porter **13**:447;
27:401
T. S. Stribling **23**:440
Eudora Welty **1**:362; **14**:562

Warrick, Patricia S.
Isaac Asimov **26**:53
Philip K. Dick **30**:126
Frank Herbert **23**:219

Warrick, Ruth
Agnes Eckhardt Nixon **21**:252

Warsh, Lewis
Richard Brautigan **3**:86
B. P. Nichol **18**:366

Warshow, Paul
Buster Keaton **20**:197

Warshow, Robert
Arthur Miller **1**:215; **26**:312

Washburn, Martin
Richard Adams **4**:7
Anthony Burgess **4**:84
Nicholas Delbanco **6**:129
John Gardner **3**:187
Lois Gould **4**:200
Juan Goytisolo **5**:150
Günter Grass **4**:206
Dan Jacobson **4**:255

György Konrád **4**:273
Denise Levertov **3**:293
Alison Lurie **4**:306
Lewis Thomas **35**:409

Washburn, Wilcomb E.
Peter Matthiessen **32**:295

Washington, Mary Helen
Arna Bontemps **18**:66
David Bradley, Jr. **23**:80
Nella Larsen **37**:218
Alice Walker **6**:554; **19**:452

Washington, Peter
Roy Fuller **28**:154
Seamus Heaney **7**:149
Peter Porter **13**:451
Stevie Smith **8**:491
R. S. Thomas **13**:544

Wasilewski, W. H.
Theodore Roethke **11**:486

Wasserman, Debbi
Murray Schisgal **6**:490
Sam Shepard **4**:489
Tom Stoppard **4**:525
Richard Wesley **7**:519

Wasserman, Jerry
Leon Rooke **25**:393

Wasserstrom, William
Van Wyck Brooks **29**:86

Waterhouse, Keith
Lynne Reid Banks **23**:40
Harper Lee **12**:341
Doris Lessing **22**:277
Colin MacInnes **23**:282

Waterhouse, Michael
William Golding **27**:161

Waterman, Andrew
Daniel Hoffman **13**:286
John Matthias **9**:361

Waterman, Arthur
Conrad Aiken **3**:5

Waters, Chris
Tim O'Brien **7**:271

Waters, Harry F.
Steven Bochco and Michael
Kozoll **35**:48
Larry Gelbart **21**:131
Norman Lear **12**:335, 338
Garry Marshall **17**:276
Agnes Eckhardt Nixon **21**:242

Waters, Kate
Sandra Scoppettone **26**:404

Waters, Michael
Robert Hass **18**:209

Waterston, Elizabeth
Irving Layton **2**:236

Watkins, Alan
A. N. Wilson **33**:455

Watkins, Floyd C.
Robert Frost **9**:219
Ernest Hemingway **3**:239

Watkins, Mel
James Baldwin **2**:33
David Bradley, Jr. **23**:79
Frederick Forsyth **36**:176
Ernest J. Gaines **11**:218
John Gardner **30**:158
John Jakes **29**:250
Robert Lipsyte **21**:213
Simone Schwarz-Bart **7**:404
Michael Thelwell **22**:416
Alice Walker **5**:476; **27**:450
John Edgar Wideman **36**:454
Al Young **19**:479

Watkins, Tony
Alan Garner **17**:141, 150

Watson, Edward A.
James Baldwin **17**:31

Watson, Elizabeth Porges
C. S. Adler **35**:12

Watson, George
T. S. Eliot **24**:181

Watson, Ian
Marion Zimmer Bradley **30**:28
Elias Canetti **14**:119

Watson, J. P.
J.R.R. Tolkien **2**:434

Watson, Robert
Richard Tillinghast **29**:415

Watson, Wilbur
Henri Troyat **23**:458

Watt, Donald
Isaac Asimov **26**:45

Watt, Donald J.
Aldous Huxley **18**:266

Watt, Douglas
Lenny Bruce **21**:48
Gretchen Cryer **21**:80
David Mamet **34**:218
David Rabe **33**:344
Sam Shepard **34**:265
Neil Simon **31**:398, 399
Stephen Sondheim **30**:380, 383, 387
Andrew Lloyd Webber and Tim
Rice **21**:424

Watt, F. W.
A. M. Klein **19**:260
Raymond Souster **14**:504

Watt, Ian
John Fowles **2**:137

Watt, Roderick H.
Uwe Johnson **15**:305

Watts, Emily Stipes
H. D. **31**:205

Watts, Harold H.
Robert Frost **15**:241
Aldous Huxley **1**:151
Gabriel Marcel **15**:359
Ezra Pound **7**:323

Watts, Michael
Walter Becker and Donald
Fagen **26**:81, 83
David Bowie **17**:60
Jackson Browne **21**:35
Ray Davies **21**:98
Mick Jagger and Keith Richard
17:230, 242
Waylon Jennings **21**:201, 202
John Lennon **35**:266
Jim Morrison **17**:290
Van Morrison **21**:237
Martin Mull **17**:299
Lou Reed **21**:306
Carly Simon **26**:409
Paul Simon **17**:460
Bruce Springsteen **17**:478
Neil Young **17**:571, 575

Watts, Richard
Jean Kerr **22**:257
Lanford Wilson **7**:548

Watts, Richard, Jr.
Robert Anderson **23**:30, 31
Enid Bagnold **25**:76
Paddy Chayefsky **23**:114
Neil Simon **31**:393, 394
Stephen Sondheim **30**:378, 379
Tennessee Williams **30**:455

Waugh, Auberon
Kōbō Abé **22**:13
Michael Ayrton **7**:18
John Betjeman **34**:309
Frederick Forsyth **36**:174
Romain Gary **25**:187
James Leo Herlihy **6**:235
Elizabeth Jane Howard **7**:164
Ruth Prawer Jhabvala **29**:256
Shiva Naipaul **32**:323
Tom Robbins **9**:453
Tom Sharpe **36**:398
Gillian Tindall **7**:474
William Trevor **7**:476
P. G. Wodehouse **5**:516

Waugh, Coulton
Jerome Siegel and Joe Shuster
21:354

Waugh, Evelyn
Graham Greene **14**:216
Aldous Huxley **11**:281
Christopher Isherwood **14**:278

Waugh, Harriet
Jessica Anderson **37**:20
Peter Dickinson **35**:136
Antonia Fraser **32**:186
David Lodge **36**:277
Ruth Rendell **28**:386, 387, 388
Ann Schlee **35**:376
Emma Tennant **13**:536
Fay Weldon **36**:446

Wax, Rosalie H.
Margaret Mead **37**:281

Way, Brian
Edward Albee **9**:2

Wayman, Tom
Miriam Waddington **28**:437

Weales, Gerald
Edward Albee **9**:4
Beryl Bainbridge **4**:39
Eric Bentley **24**:48
Elizabeth Bowen **6**:95
Ivy Compton-Burnett **1**:63
J. P. Donleavy **4**:123
Christopher Durang **27**:92, 93
Charles Fuller **25**:181
Amlin Gray **29**:201
A. R. Gurney, Jr. **32**:218
Lorraine Hansberry **17**:183, 187
John Hawkes **1**:139; **4**:213
John Huston **20**:168
William Inge **19**:226
Robert Lowell **4**:299
Norman Mailer **3**:319; **4**:319
Bernard Malamud **1**:201
William Mastrosimone **36**:290
Mark Medoff **6**:322; **23**:294
Arthur Miller **1**:218
Marsha Norman **28**:318
Clifford Odets **28**:335, 340
Harold Pinter **9**:420
James Purdy **2**:348; **4**:422
David Rabe **4**:427
Gerome Ragni and James Rado
17:380
Ronald Ribman **7**:357
Peter Shaffer **5**:390
Sam Shepard **4**:489; **17**:436
Wole Soyinka **3**:463; **36**:417
Milan Stitt **29**:390
Tom Stoppard **1**:327; **8**:502
David Storey **2**:424
James Thurber **5**:430
Douglas Turner Ward **19**:456
Robert Penn Warren **1**:356
Thornton Wilder **10**:536; **35**:442
Tennessee Williams **1**:368;
2:466; **19**:470
Lanford Wilson **36**:460, 462
Sloan Wilson **32**:445

Weatherby, Harold L.
Andrew Lytle **22**:298

Weatherby, Lonnie
Jorge Ibargüengoitia **37**:183

Weatherhead, A. Kingsley
Robert Duncan **1**:82; **7**:88
Marianne Moore **4**:360
Charles Olson **1**:263
Stephen Spender **1**:323
William Carlos Williams **1**:371

Weathers, Winston
Par Lägerkvist **7**:200

Weaver, John D.
Lenny Bruce **21**:47

Weaver, Mike
William Carlos Williams
13:603

Weaver, Robert
John Metcalf **37**:298

Webb, Bernice Larson
Ian Fleming **30**:143

Webb, Julian
Philip Roth **31**:346

Webb, Phyllis
D. G. Jones **10**:285

Critic Index

Weber, Brom
Thomas Berger **5**:60
Edward Dahlberg **7**:69
Bernard Kops **4**:274
C. P. Snow **4**:503
John Updike **2**:442

Weber, Bruce
Raymond Carver **36**:105

Weber, Robert C.
Robert Duncan **15**:189

Weber, Ronald
Saul Bellow **1**:32
John Knowles **26**:249
Tom Wolfe **35**:453, 466

Webster, Grant
Allen Tate **2**:427

Webster, Harvey Curtis
James Baldwin **17**:20
Dino Buzzati **36**:85
L. P. Hartley **22**:212
Maxine Kumin **13**:329
Bernice Rubens **19**:404
C. P. Snow **13**:514

Webster, Ivan
James Baldwin **4**:43
Gayl Jones **6**:266

Wedgwood, C. V.
Antonia Fraser **32**:180, 181

Weeks, Brigitte
Joan Aiken **35**:18
Judy Blume **12**:46
Betsy Byars **35**:72
Marilyn French **10**:191
Gail Godwin **31**:195
M. M. Kaye **28**:199
M. E. Kerr **12**:301
Iris Murdoch **8**:405
Scott Spencer **30**:406

Weeks, Edward
Margaret Atwood **4**:25
Jorge Luis Borges **1**:39
Brigid Brophy **29**:96
Lothar-Günther Buchheim **6**:102
Pearl S. Buck **7**:33
Bruce Catton **35**:92
Len Deighton **22**:115
Daphne du Maurier **6**:147; **11**:163
Loren Eiseley **7**:91
Howard Fast **23**:155
Edna Ferber **18**:152
Esther Forbes **12**:208
Frank B. Gilbreth, Jr. and Ernestine Gilbreth Carey **17**:153
Nadine Gordimer **33**:179
James Herriot **12**:283
Garson Kanin **22**:231
Yasunari Kawabata **5**:208
Madeleine L'Engle **12**:344
Peter Matthiessen **5**:273, 275; **32**:285
Iris Murdoch **6**:344
Vladimir Nabokov **6**:357
May Sarton **14**:480
André Schwarz-Bart **4**:480
Michael Shaara **15**:474

Irwin Shaw **7**:413
Mikhail Sholokhov **7**:418
Joseph Wambaugh **3**:509
Jessamyn West **7**:519; **17**:545
Herman Wouk **1**:377

Weeks, Ramona
Lucille Clifton **19**:108

Weeks, Robert P.
Ernest Hemingway **19**:214

Weesner, Theodore
Robert Cormier **12**:134

Wegner, Robert E.
E. E. Cummings **12**:153

Weibel, Kay
Mickey Spillane **13**:525

Weigel, Jack W.
Erich von Däniken **30**:422

Weigel, John A.
Lawrence Durrell **1**:86

Weightman, J. G.
David Caute **29**:110
N. F. Simpson **29**:365

Weightman, John
Alan Ayckbourn **5**:37
Simone de Beauvoir **4**:49
Albert Camus **2**:98
Louis-Ferdinand Céline **4**:100
Marguerite Duras **6**:149; **34**:162
A. E. Ellis **7**:94
Romain Gary **25**:191
Jean Genet **5**:136, 139
Jean-Luc Godard **20**:140
Anne Hébert **29**:239
J.M.G. Le Clézio **31**:244
André Malraux **9**:359
Peter Nichols **5**:308
Francis Ponge **6**:422
Gerome Ragni and James Rado **17**:382
Alain Robbe-Grillet **2**:377
Nathalie Sarraute **4**:468, 469
Jean-Paul Sartre **9**:473
Tom Stoppard **5**:412
David Storey **5**:416
Michel Tournier **23**:454; **36**:440
Gore Vidal **4**:555
Monique Wittig **22**:473

Weil, Dorothy
Arna Bontemps **18**:63

Weil, Henry
Philip Roth **22**:358

Weiland, Steven
Wendell Berry **27**:36

Weiler, A. H.
Jean Cocteau **16**:223
Werner Herzog **16**:321
Elia Kazan **16**:362
Alain Resnais **16**:496
Jack Williamson **29**:449
Maia Wojciechowska **26**:453

Weinberg, Helen
Saul Bellow **2**:53
Ralph Ellison **11**:180
Herbert Gold **4**:192
Norman Mailer **2**:261
Philip Roth **4**:452

Weinberg, Herman G.
Josef von Sternberg **20**:374

Weinberger, David
M. M. Kaye **28**:200
Farley Mowat **26**:345
Lewis Thomas **35**:411

Weinberger, Deborah
Adolfo Bioy Casares **13**:86

Weinberger, Eliot
Robert Bly **15**:63

Weinberger, G. J.
E. E. Cummings **8**:160

Weinfield, Henry
Gilbert Sorrentino **7**:448, 449

Weingarten, Sherwood L.
Monty Python **21**:224

Weingartner, Charles
Carl Sagan **30**:336

Weinkauf, Mary S.
Piers Anthony **35**:39, 41
Fritz Leiber **25**:307

Weinstein, Shirley
Maia Wojciechowska **26**:458

Weintraub, Stanley
William Golding **2**:167
C. P. Snow **9**:497, 498

Weir, Alison
Bernard Mac Laverty **31**:254

Weir, Dana
Dave Smith **22**:386

Weir, Emily, C.H.S.
Mary Stewart **35**:394

Weir, Sister Emily
Mary Stewart **35**:393

Weisberg, Robert
Stanley Burnshaw **3**:92
Randall Jarrell **2**:211
Richmond Lattimore **3**:277

Weiskopf, F. C.
Joseph Wittlin **25**:467

Weisman, Kathryn
Margaret O. Hyde **21**:179
Larry Kettelkamp **12**:308

Weismiller, Edward
J. V. Cunningham **31**:96

Weiss, Jonathan M.
Gabrielle Roy **14**:470

Weiss, Nancy Quint
H. F. Brinsmead **21**:26

Weiss, Paulette
Jim Morrison **17**:294

Weiss, Penelope
Edwin Honig **33**:211

Weiss, Peter
Peter Weiss **15**:563

Weiss, Theodore
Dannie Abse **29**:22
Cleanth Brooks **24**:111
Donald Davie **5**:115
Ezra Pound **10**:405
M. L. Rosenthal **28**:396

Weiss, Victoria L.
Marguerite Duras **6**:150

Weissenberger, Klaus
Paul Celan **19**:93

Weixlmann, Joe
John Barth **14**:54
Ronald L. Fair **18**:142

Weixlmann, Sher
John Barth **14**:54

Welburn, Ron
Imamu Amiri Baraka **2**:35
Don L. Lee **2**:237
Clarence Major **19**:291
Dudley Randall **1**:283

Welch, Chris
David Bowie **17**:64
Jimmy Page and Robert Plant **12**:476, 478
Peter Townshend **17**:524, 538

Welch, Elizabeth H.
Jules Archer **12**:19

Welch, Robert D.
Ernesto Cardenal **31**:71

Welcome, John
Dick Francis **22**:152, 153
P. D. James **18**:272

Welding, Pete
Chuck Berry **17**:52
Jimmy Cliff **21**:62
Gordon Lightfoot **26**:278

Weldon, Fay
Françoise Sagan **36**:382

Wellek, René
R. P. Blackmur **2**:62
Cleanth Brooks **24**:111
Van Wyck Brooks **29**:82
Kenneth Burke **2**:89
F. R. Leavis **24**:302
I. A. Richards **24**:395

Weller, Richard H.
Margaret O. Hyde **21**:175

Weller, Sheila
Ann Beattie **8**:55
Gael Greene **8**:252
Diane Wakoski **7**:507

Wells, H. G.
Frank Swinnerton **31**:420

Wells, John
Bob Dylan **12**:200

Wellwarth, George
Arthur Adamov **4**:5
Edward Albee **2**:1
John Arden **6**:8
Samuel Beckett **2**:46
Brendan Behan **8**:63
Friedrich Dürrenmatt **4**:138
Max Frisch **3**:166
Jean Genet **2**:157
Michel de Ghelderode **6**:197
Fritz Hochwälder **36**:233
Eugène Ionesco **4**:251
Arthur Kopit **18**:287
Bernard Kops **4**:274
John Mortimer **28**:283

John Osborne **2**:327
Harold Pinter **3**:385
N. F. Simpson **29**:368
Arnold Wesker **3**:518

Welsh, Mary
Noel Streatfeild **21**:401

Welty, Eudora
Margery Allingham **19**:12
Elizabeth Bowen **6**:94; **22**:65
Annie Dillard **9**:175
E. M. Forster **3**:161
Ross Macdonald **2**:255
S. J. Perelman **23**:334, 337
Katherine Anne Porter **27**:398
V. S. Pritchett **13**:467
Jessamyn West **17**:544
Patrick White **5**:485

Welz, Becky
Betty Cavanna **12**:101

Wendell, Carolyn
C. J. Cherryh **35**:114
Vonda N. McIntyre **18**:326

Werner, Alfred
Hermann Hesse **17**:195
Primo Levi **37**:220

Werner, C.
Amiri Baraka **33**:62

Werner, Craig
Tom Stoppard **15**:520

Wernick, Robert
Wright Morris **3**:343

Wersba, Barbara
Julia W. Cunningham **12**:164,
    165, 166
Leon Garfield **12**:222
Norma Fox Mazer **26**:290
Scott O'Dell **30**:274
Philippa Pearce **21**:283
Noel Streatfeild **21**:409
Jill Paton Walsh **35**:430

Wertham, Fredric
Jerome Siegel and Joe Shuster
    21:355

Wertime, Richard A.
Guy Davenport, Jr. **14**:139
Hubert Selby, Jr. **8**:475

Weschler, Lawrence
Mel Brooks **12**:82

Wescott, Glenway
Katherine Anne Porter **7**:313

Wesker, Arnold
James Fenton **32**:167
William Styron **15**:531

Wesling, Donald
Ed Dorn **10**:157

Wesolek, George
E. E. Cummings **12**:152

West, Anthony
Jorge Amado **13**:11
Yehuda Amichai **9**:22
Jessica Anderson **37**:18
Enid Bagnold **25**:74
James Baldwin **17**:20

Heinrich Böll **27**:55
Paul Bowles **19**:58
Bruce Catton **35**:87
Carlos Fuentes **22**:164
Yukio Mishima **27**:336
Edwin O'Connor **14**:389
Leonardo Sciascia **9**:474
Elizabeth Spencer **22**:398
Sylvia Townsend Warner **7**:512

West, David S.
Ralph Gustafson **36**:219
Robert Kroetsch **23**:275

West, Martha Ullman
David Leavitt **34**:79
Lee Smith **25**:409

West, Paul
Walter Abish **22**:20
Miguel Ángel Asturias **3**:18
Michael Ayrton **7**:18
Samuel Beckett **2**:48
Earle Birney **6**:72
Heinrich Böll **3**:74
Michel Butor **8**:113
Alejo Carpentier **11**:99
Camilo José Cela **13**:146
Louis-Ferdinand Céline **1**:57
Jean Cocteau **15**:132
Evan S. Connell, Jr. **4**:108
Julio Cortázar **2**:103
Guy Davenport, Jr. **6**:123
Len Deighton **22**:115
José Donoso **4**:127
Richard Elman **19**:151
Howard Fast **23**:158
Gabriel García Márquez **10**:215
John Gardner **2**:150
William H. Gass **11**:224
William Golding **1**:122
Peter Handke **5**:166
MacDonald Harris **9**:261
Wilson Harris **25**:202
Uwe Johnson **5**:202
Robert Kroetsch **23**:270
Primo Levi **37**:227
Jakov Lind **2**:245
David Lodge **36**:269
Charles Newman **2**:311
Robert Nye **13**:413
Sylvia Plath **1**:271
André Schwarz-Bart **2**:389
Gilbert Sorrentino **22**:394
Allen Tate **11**:526
Robert Penn Warren **1**:353

West, Ray B.
Katherine Ann Porter **1**:272

West, Rebecca
Carl Sandburg **35**:343
Frank Swinnerton **31**:422

West, Richard
Michael Cimino **16**:211

Westall, Robert
Robert Westall **17**:557

Westbrook, Max
Saul Bellow **1**:30
William Faulkner **1**:101
Ernest Hemingway **1**:143
J. D. Salinger **1**:299
John Steinbeck **1**:326

Robert Penn Warren **1**:355

Westbrook, Perry D.
Mary Ellen Chase **2**:100
R. K. Narayan **28**:293

Westbrook, Wayne W.
Louis Auchincloss **4**:30

Westburg, Faith
Adolfo Bioy Casares **4**:64
Jerzy Kosinski **3**:274

Westerbeck, Colin L., Jr.
Robert Altman **16**:42
Lindsay Anderson **20**:17
Ralph Bakshi **26**:76
Mel Brooks **12**:76, 77
Charles Chaplin **16**:204
Vittorio De Sica **20**:96
Bob Fosse **20**:123
Werner Herzog **16**:327, 336
Sidney Poitier **26**:357, 359
Richard Pryor **26**:383
Paul Schrader **26**:397
Steven Spielberg **20**:359
Lina Wertmüller **16**:587

Westervelt, Linda A.
John Barth **14**:52

Westfall, Jeff
Theodore Roethke **19**:401

Westhuis, Mary G.
Robert Newton Peck **17**:342

Westlake, Donald E.
Gael Greene **8**:252
Elmore Leonard **34**:214

Weston, Jeremy
Roger Zelazny **21**:470

Weston, John
Nat Hentoff **26**:183
Paul Zindel **6**:586

Weston, John C.
Hugh MacDiarmid **11**:335

Weston, Robert V.
Andrew Lytle **22**:299

Weston, Susan B.
Galway Kinnell **29**:281

Wetzsteon, Ross
Charles Gordone **1**:124
Stratis Haviaras **33**:204
Edward Hoagland **28**:184
Albert Innaurato **21**:192
May Sarton **4**:472
Irwin Shaw **23**:399
Lily Tomlin **17**:518

Wevers, Lydia
Frank Sargeson **31**:369

Wexler, Eric
Ronald Bush **34**:524
Ilya Ehrenburg **34**:434
T. S. Eliot **34**:524
John Gardner **34**:548
Anatol Goldberg **34**:434
Frederick Karl **34**:551

Weyant, Jill
William Melvin Kelley **22**:250

Wheatcroft, Geoffrey
David Caute **29**:123

Whedon, Julia
Judy Blume **12**:46
Lois Duncan **26**:104
Penelope Gilliatt **2**:160

Wheeler, Charles
Jeffrey Archer **28**:12
Paul E. Erdman **25**:155
William Safire **10**:447

Wheelock, Carter
Jorge Luis Borges **2**:76; **3**:81;
    4:72; **6**:90; **13**:104
Julio Cortázar **5**:109

Wheelock, John Hall
Allen Tate **4**:536

Whelan, Gloria
Margaret Laurence **13**:342

Whelton, Clark
Joan Micklin Silver **20**:343

Whichard, Nancy Winegardner
Patrick White **4**:583

Whicher, George F.
Ogden Nash **23**:319

Whicher, Stephen E.
E. E. Cummings **3**:116

Whipple, T. K.
Erskine Caldwell **14**:93
Robert Frost **26**:110

Whissen, Thomas R.
Isak Dinesen **10**:144, 149

Whitaker, Jennifer Seymour
Alberto Moravia **7**:243

Whitaker, John T.
Arthur Koestler **33**:229

Whitaker, Muriel
Kevin Major **26**:288

Whitaker, Thomas R.
Conrad Aiken **3**:3

White, Charles, S. J.
Mircea Eliade **19**:147

White, David A.
Martin Heidegger **24**:274

White, E. B.
James Thurber **5**:432

White, Edmund
John Ashbery **6**:11; **15**:33
James Baldwin **17**:41
Amy Clampitt **32**:116
Edward Dahlberg **7**:65
Thomas M. Disch **7**:87
E. L. Doctorow **37**:96
Lawrence Durrell **6**:153
Jean Genet **5**:138
Russell C. Hoban **7**:161
Eugène Ionesco **11**:290
Yasunari Kawabata **5**:207
Marjorie Kellogg **2**:224
Fran Lebowitz **11**:322
José Lezama Lima **4**:290
Harry Mathews **6**:315
William Maxwell **19**:308

James Merrill **18**:328
Yukio Mishima **4**:355
Howard Moss **7**:248
Vladimir Nabokov **2**:304
Ishmael Reed **32**:355
James Schuyler **5**:383
Muriel Spark **18**:505
Jun'ichirō Tanizaki **28**:420
Gore Vidal **8**:527
Paul West **14**:569
Tennessee Williams **5**:503

White, Edward M.
Stratis Haviaras **33**:206

White, Gavin
Farley Mowat **26**:336

White, Gertrude M.
W. D. Snodgrass **10**:477;
18:494

White, Jean M.
Stephen Dobyns **37**:78, 82
Dick Francis **2**:143
Carolyn G. Heilbrun **25**:256
Evan Hunter **31**:223, 224, 226
P. D. James **18**:272
Ross Macdonald **3**:308
George Simenon **2**:398
Maj Sjöwall **7**:502
Per Wahlöö **7**:502
Donald E. Westlake **7**:529;
33:440

White, John
Michael Ayrton **7**:18
Louis R. Harlan **34**:191

White, John J.
MacDonald Harris **9**:259

White, John P.
David Lodge **36**:270

White, Jon Manchip
Gore Vidal **22**:437

White, Olive B.
T. H. White **30**:441

White, Patricia O.
Samuel Beckett **1**:25

White, Ray Lewis
Gore Vidal **2**:448

White, Robert J.
Pier Paolo Pasolini **20**:269

White, Sarah
Anne Stevenson **33**:382

White, Ted
Jerome Siegel and Joe Shuster
21:358

White, Timothy
Jackson Browne **21**:37
Billy Joel **26**:222
Bob Marley **17**:268, 269, 271,
272
Bob Seger **35**:384

White, Victor
Thornton Wilder **10**:536

White, William Allen
Mari Sandoz **28**:400

White, William Luther
C. S. Lewis **3**:295

Whitebait, William
Jean Cocteau **16**:226

Whitehall, Richard
George Roy Hill **26**:196
John Huston **20**:168
Jean Renoir **20**:291

Whitehead, James
Jim Harrison **6**:224
Stanley J. Kunitz **6**:287
Adrienne Rich **3**:427
Gibbons Ruark **3**:441

Whitehead, John
Louis MacNeice **1**:186

Whitehead, Peter
Pier Paolo Pasolini **20**:263

Whitehead, Phillip
Vera Brittain **23**:93

Whitehead, Ralph, Jr.
Hunter S. Thompson **17**:514

Whitehead, Ted
Woody Allen **16**:9
Michael Cimino **16**:210
Peter Townshend **17**:539

Whitehead, Winifred
Eilís Dillon **17**:100

Whiteman, Bruce
Marilyn R. Bowering **32**:48
David Donnell **34**:158

Whitlock, Pamela
Eilís Dillon **17**:93

Whitman, Alden
Henry Carlisle **33**:104
Antonia Fraser **32**:184
Norman Mailer **14**:353

Whitman, Digby B.
John Donovan **35**:140

Whitman, Ruth
Adrienne Rich **6**:459
Anne Sexton **6**:494

Whitney, Phyllis A.
Mary Stolz **12**:551

Whittemore, Bernice
Ilya Ehrenburg **18**:130

Whittemore, Reed
Allen Ginsberg **2**:163
James Kirkwood **9**:320
Larry McMurtry **27**:329
Ogden Nash **23**:323
Charles Olson **2**:326
Tom Robbins **9**:453

Whittington-Egan, Richard
Truman Capote **8**:133
Rayner Heppenstall **10**:272

Whitton, Kenneth S.
Friedrich Dürrenmatt **15**:198

Whitty, John
Tennessee Williams **11**:575

Wickenden, Dan
Brigid Brophy **11**:68; **29**:91
Roy Fuller **28**:149
Jessamyn West **17**:545

Wickenden, Dorothy
Raymond Carver **36**:103
Isabel Colegate **36**:113
André Dubus **36**:146
Ella Leffland **19**:280
Gloria Naylor **28**:305
Susan Fromberg Schaeffer
22:369

Wickes, George
Henry Miller **1**:221
Anaïs Nin **1**:247

Wideman, John
Toni Cade Bambara **19**:34
Breyten Breytenbach **37**:48
Richard Wright **14**:596

Widmer, Kingsley
John Dos Passos **4**:133
Leslie A. Fiedler **4**:160
Allen Ginsberg **13**:239
Herbert Gold **4**:191
Jack Kerouac **14**:305
Henry Miller **1**:220

Wiegand, William
J. D. Salinger **1**:295
Jerome Weidman **7**:516

Wiegner, Kathleen
Michael Benedikt **14**:82
Judith Leet **11**:323
Diane Wakoski **9**:555

Wier, Allen
Laurie Colwin **23**:129

Wiersma, Stanley M.
Christopher Fry **2**:144; **10**:202

Wiesel, Elie
Richard Elman **19**:148
Chaim Grade **10**:246
Anatoli Rybakov **23**:372

Wieseltier, Leon
Yehuda Amichai **9**:24
Harold Bloom **24**:79
Nadine Gordimer **33**:183
Czesław Miłosz **31**:265
Gregor von Rezzori **25**:383
Salman Rushdie **31**:357
Isaac Bashevis Singer **11**:502
Elie Wiesel **3**:529
A. B. Yehoshua **31**:475

Wiggins, William H., Jr.
John Oliver Killens **10**:300

Wightman, G.B.H.
W. S. Graham **29**:197

Wilbur, Richard
Elizabeth Bishop **32**:33
Barbara Howes **15**:288

Wilce, Gillian
Beryl Bainbridge **18**:32
Isabel Colegate **36**:111
Pamela Hansford Johnson
27:222
Gay Talese **37**:402

Wilcher, Robert
Samuel Beckett **11**:35

Wilcox, Barbara
Joyce Maynard **23**:290

Wilcox, Thomas W.
Anthony Powell **7**:341

Wild, John
William Barrett **27**:16

Wilde, Alan
Donald Barthelme **13**:55
Christopher Isherwood **1**:156;
9:290

Wilder, Cherry
Marion Zimmer Bradley **30**:28

Wilder, Thornton
Thornton Wilder **35**:441

Wilder, Virginia
M. E. Kerr **12**:301

Wildgen, Kathryn E.
François Mauriac **9**:368

Wilding, Michael
L. P. Hartley **2**:182
Jack Kerouac **5**:215
Christina Stead **2**:422, 423;
32:406

Wildman, John Hazard
Mary Lavin **4**:281
Joyce Carol Oates **6**:367
Reynolds Price **6**:423
Muriel Spark **13**:520

Wilentz, Amy
Frederick Busch **18**:85

Wiley, Bell I.
Bruce Catton **35**:86

Wiley, Marion E.
Elias Canetti **25**:108

Wilford, John Noble
James A. Michener **29**:315

Wilgus, Neal
Piers Anthony **35**:41

Wilhelm, James J.
Ezra Pound **4**:418

Wilkes, G. A.
Robert D. FitzGerald **19**:178

Wilkes, Paul
Shusaku Endo **14**:162

Wilkie, Brian
C.D.B. Bryan **29**:101

Wilkie, Roy
J. G. Ballard **36**:33

Wilkinson, Burke
Allen Drury **37**:110
C. S. Forester **35**:171
Ernest K. Gann **23**:164

Wilkinson, Doris Y.
Chester Himes **7**:159

Wilkinson, Marguerite
Siegfried Sassoon **36**:385

Wilkinson, Theon
M. M. Kaye **28**:199

Will, Frederic
Martin Heidegger **24**:258

Willard, Mark
Jack Vance **35**:423

Willard, Nancy
Pierre Gascar **11**:222
Pablo Neruda **1**:246; **28**:307
J.R.R. Tolkien **8**:515

Willbanks, Ray
Randolph Stow **23**:434

Willett, Holly
Nat Hentoff **26**:186

Willett, Ralph
Clifford Odets **2**:319

Willey, Basil
I. A. Richards **24**:399

Williams, A. R.
Diana Wynne Jones **26**:232

Williams, Anne
Richard Wilbur **14**:578

Williams, David
Kon Ichikawa **20**:183
Peter Porter **33**:320
Christina Stead **2**:423
John Wyndham **19**:476

Williams, Forrest
Federico Fellini **16**:279

Williams, Gary Jay
Brian Clark **29**:126
Jean Kerr **22**:258

Williams, Gladys
Leon Garfield **12**:226

Williams, H. Moore
Ruth Prawer Jhabvala **29**:253

Williams, Hugo
Horst Bienek **7**:29
Richard Brautigan **12**:60
William S. Burroughs **5**:92
Czesław Miłosz **31**:264
Paul Muldoon **32**:315
James Schuyler **23**:392
Derek Walcott **25**:448
Morris L. West **33**:430
Philip Whalen **29**:447

Williams, John
Henry Miller **1**:223

Williams, Jonathan
Richard Brautigan **3**:87
Rod McKuen **3**:333
Anne Sexton **4**:482

Williams, Linda L.
Bernardo Bertolucci **16**:99

Williams, Liz
Sandra Scoppettone **26**:404

Williams, Lloyd
James Ngugi **7**:262

Williams, Martin
Lenny Bruce **21**:44

Williams, Miller
Donald Davidson **2**:111
John Crowe Ransom **4**:434
Hollis Summers **10**:493
Andrei Voznesensky **1**:349

Williams, Nick B.
T.E.D. Klein **34**:70

Williams, Nigel
Ronald Harwood **32**:226

Williams, Oscar
Muriel Rukeyser **27**:407

Williams, Paul
Ray Davies **21**:88, 90
Mick Jagger and Keith Richard **17**:231
Jim Morrison **17**:285
Bruce Springsteen **17**:482
Brian Wilson **12**:641
Neil Young **17**:568, 577

Williams, R. V.
James Clavell **25**:128

Williams, Raymond L.
Manuel Puig **28**:372
Aleksandr I. Solzhenitsyn **2**:407

Williams, Regina
Rosa Guy **26**:143

Williams, Richard
Joan Armatrading **17**:7
Chuck Berry **17**:52
Allen Ginsberg **6**:201
Van Morrison **21**:232
Laura Nyro **17**:313
Lou Reed **21**:303, 304
Smokey Robinson **21**:343, 344, 348
Carly Simon **26**:407
Paul Simon **17**:461
Bruce Springsteen **17**:477
Andrew Lloyd Webber and Tim Rice **21**:422
Richard Wilbur **6**:568
Brian Wilson **12**:644, 646, 650
Neil Young **17**:569

Williams, Robert V.
Ogden Nash **23**:324

Williams, Sherley Anne
James Baldwin **3**:32
Imamu Amiri Baraka **3**:35; **10**:20
Ralph Ellison **3**:144
Zora Neale Hurston **30**:222
Haki R. Madhubuti **6**:313

Williams, Sherwood
William Wharton **37**:440

Williams, Stanley T.
Mari Sandoz **28**:400

Williams, Tennessee
Paul Bowles **19**:56
William Inge **8**:307
Carson McCullers **12**:412

Williams, T. Harry
Bruce Catton **35**:89, 91, 92

Williams, William Carlos
David Ignatow **14**:274

Marianne Moore **10**:348
Kenneth Patchen **18**:391
Carl Sandburg **15**:466

Williams, Wirt
William Brammer **31**:54

Williamson, Alan
Jon Anderson **9**:31
Frank Bidart **33**:74
Robert Bly **5**:65; **15**:68
Alfred Corn **33**:116, 119
Robert Creeley **15**:153
Louise Glück **22**:176
Ted Hughes **37**:177
Galway Kinnell **5**:216
Robert Lowell **4**:304
Robert Phillips **28**:364
Charles Simic **22**:380
Louis Simpson **32**:380
L. E. Sissman **18**:489
Gary Snyder **5**:394
Barry Spacks **14**:510
Allen Tate **14**:528
Richard Tillinghast **29**:414, 416
C. K. Williams **33**:442
James Wright **3**:541; **5**:519, 521; **28**:472

Williamson, Chilton, Jr.
Norman Lear **12**:331

Williamson, Jack
Robert A. Heinlein **26**:170

Williamson, Michael
Leon Rooke **34**:251

Williamson, Norma B.
Joanne Greenberg **30**:167
Lisa St. Aubin de Teran **36**:421

Williamson, Susan
Walter Dean Myers **35**:299

Willis, David K.
Art Buchwald **33**:93

Willis, Don
Fritz Lang **20**:215
Josef von Sternberg **20**:378

Willis, Donald C.
Luis Buñuel **16**:151
Frank Capra **16**:161
Yasojiro Ozu **16**:455

Willis, Ellen
David Bowie **17**:59
Bob Dylan **3**:131; **12**:183, 186
Lou Reed **21**:317
Paul Simon **17**:459
Stevie Wonder **12**:658

Willis, J. H., Jr.
William Empson **3**:147

Willison, Marilyn
Norma Klein **30**:240

Wills, Garry
James Baldwin **17**:25
Andrew M. Greeley **28**:174
Thomas Keneally **5**:210
James A. Michener **11**:375
Vladimir Nabokov **3**:356
Hunter S. Thompson **17**:514

Willson, Robert F., Jr.
Stephen Dunn **36**:151

Wilmer, Clive
Thom Gunn **32**:209
Czesław Miłosz **22**:310

Wilmington, Michael
John Ford **16**:310, 314
Billy Wilder **20**:462, 463

Wilms, Denise Murko
Lloyd Alexander **35**:27
Jules Archer **12**:23
Cecil Bødker **21**:13
Frank Bonham **12**:55
Betty Cavanna **12**:103
Barbara Corcoran **17**:78
Roy A. Gallant **17**:133
Margaret O. Hyde **21**:180
Larry Kettelkamp **12**:306
Norma Klein **30**:243
Sonia Levitin **17**:266
Walter Dean Myers **35**:296
Marilyn Sachs **35**:334
Ouida Sebestyen **30**:349
Noel Streatfeild **21**:415
Piri Thomas **17**:502
Cynthia Voigt **30**:418

Wilner, Eleanor
Adrienne Rich **7**:369

Wilson, A. N.
Peter Dickinson **35**:135
Thomas Keneally **27**:234
Barbara Pym **19**:388
J.I.M. Stewart **32**:420

Wilson, Angus
Kingsley Amis **3**:9
L. P. Hartley **2**:181
Christopher Isherwood **11**:294
John Cowper Powys **15**:433

Wilson, Arthur
Carl Sandburg **35**:341

Wilson, Barbara Ker
Noel Streatfeild **21**:404

Wilson, Bryan
Kenneth Rexroth **11**:473

Wilson, Carter
Rudolfo A. Anaya **23**:24

Wilson, Clifford
Farley Mowat **26**:330

Wilson, Colin
Jorge Luis Borges **3**:78
Christopher Isherwood **11**:297

Wilson, David
Dirk Bogarde **19**:43
Garson Kanin **22**:232
Yashar Kemal **29**:266
Nagisa Oshima **20**:248
Salman Rushdie **23**:364
Ken Russell **16**:547
François Truffaut **20**:389
Joseph Wambaugh **18**:533

Wilson, Dawn
Conrad Richter **30**:323

Wilson, Douglas
Ernest Hemingway **3**:241

Wilson, Edmund
W. H. Auden **2**:21; **4**:33
Marie-Claire Blais **2**:62; **4**:66

Kay Boyle **19**:62
Van Wyck Brooks **29**:81
James M. Cain **28**:48
Morley Callaghan **3**:97
Agatha Christie **12**:114
Walter Van Tilburg Clark **28**:77
John Dos Passos **4**:130
T. S. Eliot **24**:160
Anne Hébert **4**:219
Ernest Hemingway **30**:178
Joseph Wood Krutch **24**:286
Hugh MacLennan **2**:257
André Malraux **13**:365
William Maxwell **19**:305
Carson McCullers **12**:410
Katherine Anne Porter **7**:309
Aleksandr I. Solzhenitsyn **2**:407
John Steinbeck **13**:529
J.R.R. Tolkien **2**:433
Carl Van Vechten **33**:386
Evelyn Waugh **13**:584; **27**:469
Angus Wilson **2**:470

Wilson, Edwin
Harvey Fierstein **33**:154, 157
Mark Medoff **23**:293
Stephen Sondheim **30**:393, 399
Milan Stitt **29**:390
Tom Stoppard **34**:275

Wilson, Evie
Margaret Craven **17**:80
Anne McCaffrey **17**:283
John Neufeld **17**:310
Laurence Yep **35**:470

Wilson, Frank
Françoise Sagan **17**:427
Susan Sontag **13**:519

Wilson, George
Fritz Lang **20**:213

Wilson, J. C.
Wright Morris **7**:246

Wilson, Jane
Andrew Sinclair **2**:401

Wilson, Jason
Octavio Paz **19**:365

Wilson, Jay
Andy Warhol **20**:416

Wilson, John
Robert Creeley **36**:117

Wilson, Keith
David Kherdian **6**:280

Wilson, Kevin
Bette Greene **30**:170

Wilson, Michiko N.
Kenzaburō Ōe **36**:349

Wilson, Milton
Milton Acorn **15**:8
Earl Birney **6**:74, 75
Ralph Gustafson **36**:212
A.J.M. Smith **15**:514

Wilson, Raymond J.
Isaac Asimov **19**:26

Wilson, Reuel K.
Tadeusz Konwicki **8**:328
Stanislaw Lem **15**:326

Wilson, Robert
Robert Cormier **30**:87
Mark Harris **19**:206
Breece D'J Pancake **29**:347
Richard Yates **23**:483

Wilson, Robley, Jr.
Marvin Bell **31**:46
Daniel J. Berrigan **4**:56
T. Coraghessan Boyle **36**:58
Richard Howard **7**:165
Philip Levine **4**:285

Wilson, Sandy
A. R. Gurney, Jr. **32**:217

Wilson, William E.
Jessamyn West **17**:545

Wilson-Beach, Fay
Ouida Sebestyen **30**:348

Wilton, Shirley
Joan Aiken **35**:18
Isabelle Holland **21**:151

Wimble, Barton
Allan W. Eckert **17**:108

Wimsatt, Margaret
Margaret Atwood **3**:19
Rosellen Brown **32**:63
Robertson Davies **13**:173
Graham Greene **3**:208
Danny Santiago **33**:353
Eudora Welty **33**:425

Wimsatt, W. K.
Northrop Frye **24**:214

Wimsatt, W. K., Jr.
René Wellek **28**:441

Wincelberg, Shimon
Max Apple **33**:21
Elie Wiesel **37**:454

Winch, Terence
Max Apple **33**:19
Russell Banks **37**:23
Jonathan Baumbach **23**:56
Ann Beattie **13**:64
Benedict Kiely **23**:267
W. S. Merwin **8**:388, 390
Flann O'Brien **10**:363
William Trevor **25**:443

Winchell, Mark Royden
Robert Penn Warren **13**:579

Winder, David
James A. Michener **29**:312

Windsor, Philip
Josef Skvorecký **15**:511
Aleksandr I. Solzhenitsyn **7**:441

Winegarten, Renee
Ruth Prawer Jhabvala **4**:258
Bernard Malamud **3**:324; **8**:375
André Malraux **1**:203
Grace Paley **6**:392

Winehouse, Bernard
Conrad Aiken **10**:2

Winfrey, Carey
James H. Webb, Jr. **22**:454

Wing, George Gordon
Octavio Paz **3**:376

Winks, Robin
Donald E. Westlake **33**:437

Winks, Robin W.
William F. Buckley, Jr. **18**:82
Len Deighton **7**:75
Peter Dickinson **35**:137
Howard Fast **23**:160
John Gardner **30**:157
Evan Hunter **31**:227
P. D. James **18**:273
Elmore Leonard **28**:234
Robert B. Parker **27**:363, 364
David Harry Walker **14**:552

Winner, Langdon
Paul McCartney **35**:278

Winner, Viola Hopkins
R. P. Blackmur **24**:66

Winnington, Richard
Vittorio De Sica **20**:85
Alfred Hitchcock **16**:340

Winsten, Archer
Julia Peterkin **31**:304

Winston, Joan
Gene Roddenberry **17**:407

Winston, Richard
Thomas B. Costain **30**:97
Mary Renault **17**:393, 399
T. H. White **30**:446

Winter, Douglas E.
Stephen King **37**:200, 203

Winter, Thomas
Anthony Burgess **4**:81

Winterich, John T.
Frank B. Gilbreth, Jr. and
Ernestine Gilbreth Carey
17:152, 154
Nevil Shute **30**:369

Winters, Yvor
J. V. Cunningham **31**:97, 101
Elizabeth Daryush **19**:119
Robert Frost **10**:192
Mina Loy **28**:246
John Crowe Ransom **24**:364

Wintle, Justin
Jonathan Keates **34**:201
Padgett Powell **34**:101

Wintz, Cary D.
Langston Hughes **10**:279

Wirth-Nesher, Hana
Amos Oz **11**:427

Wise, William
Richard Matheson **37**:245

Wisse, Ruth R.
Saul Bellow **8**:68
Leslie Epstein **27**:128
Chaim Grade **10**:246
Joanne Greenberg **30**:167
Amos Oz **33**:303
Cynthia Ozick **7**:289
Chaim Potok **26**:375

Wistrich, Robert
A. E. Ellis **7**:93

Witcover, Jules
Hunter S. Thompson **17**:507

Witemeyer, Hugh
Guy Davenport, Jr. **14**:141

Witherington, Paul
John Knowles **26**:252
Bernard Malamud **11**:352

Witt, Harold
Conrad Aiken **1**:4

Witte, Stephen
George Lucas **16**:409

Wittels, Anne F.
Michael Cunningham **34**:40

Wittke, Paul
Stephen Sondheim **30**:397

Wixson, Douglas Charles, Jr.
Thornton Wilder **10**:531

Wohlers, H. C.
Melvin Berger **12**:40

Wohlgelernter, Maurice
Frank O'Connor **23**:327

Wohlsen, Theodore O., Jr.
Fritz Hochwälder **36**:239

Woiwode, L.
John Cheever **3**:107

Woiwode, Larry
Wendell Berry **27**:37

Wojahn, David
Norman Dubie **36**:140
Stanley Plumly **33**:316
C. K. Williams **33**:447

Wojciechowska, Maia
Maia Wojciechowska **26**:451

Wojnaroski, Janet B.
Margaret O. Hyde **21**:180

Wolcott, James
John Barth **27**:26
Steven Bochco and Michael
Kozoll **35**:52
William F. Buckley, Jr. **7**:35
Peter De Vries **28**:110
E. L. Doctorow **37**:93
Mary Gordon **22**:185
Alex Haley **12**:253
Peter Handke **10**:255
John Hawkes **27**:197
Norman Lear **12**:333, 337, 338
Fran Lebowitz **36**:248
John le Carré **28**:229
Norman Mailer **14**:351
Laura Nyro **17**:319
Jimmy Page and Robert Plant
12:480
Mordecai Richler **18**:456
Wilfrid Sheed **10**:472
Lily Tomlin **17**:516
Anne Tyler **18**:530
John Updike **34**:284
Gore Vidal **8**:528
Frederick Wiseman **20**:476
Tom Wolfe **35**:464

Wolf, Barbara
Yukio Mishima **2**:288; **6**:338

Wolf, L. N.
C. S. Forester **35**:172

Wolf, Manfred
Brigid Brophy **11**:68

Wolf, William
Ralph Bakshi **26**:73
Gordon Parks **1**:265

Wolfe, Don M.
Shirley Hazzard **18**:213

Wolfe, G. K.
Joanne Greenberg **30**:163
Kurt Vonnegut, Jr. **3**:495

Wolfe, George H.
William Faulkner **9**:203

Wolfe, H. Leslie
Laurence Lieberman **4**:291

Wolfe, Kary K.
Joanne Greenberg **30**:163

Wolfe, Morris
Matt Cohen **19**:111
John Metcalf **37**:307

Wolfe, Peter
Richard Adams **5**:6
A. Alvarez **5**:20
Maeve Brennan **5**:72
Laurie Colwin **5**:108
John Fowles **33**:159
Dashiell Hammett **19**:199
John Knowles **26**:258
Jakov Lind **1**:177
Ross Macdonald **14**:329
Walker Percy **2**:333
Mary Renault **3**:425
Georges Simenon **18**:487
Charles Webb **7**:515
Patrick White **3**:522

Wolfe, Tom
James M. Cain **28**:49
John Lennon and Paul
McCartney **12**:355, 363
S. J. Perelman **23**:338

Wolff, Ellen
Kris Kristofferson **26**:268

Wolff, Geoffrey
John Barth **14**:56
Frederick Buechner **2**:83
Raymond Carver **22**:96
Arthur A. Cohen **7**:52
Julio Cortázar **3**:115
J. P. Donleavy **6**:140
George P. Elliott **2**:131
John Fowles **33**:173
Paula Fox **8**:217
John Gardner **2**:152
Barry Hannah **23**:212
Edward Hoagland **28**:180, 182
James Jones **3**:261
Jerzy Kosinski **1**:171; **3**:272;
6:282
J.M.G. Le Clézio **31**:246
D. Keith Mano **2**:270
Peter Matthiessen **5**:273
Wright Morris **7**:247
Donald Newlove **6**:363
Ezra Pound **2**:342
Thomas Pynchon **2**:356

Isaac Bashevis Singer **3**:456

Wolfley, Lawrence C.
Thomas Pynchon **9**:444

Wolitzer, Hilma
Jessica Anderson **37**:21
Joanne Greenberg **30**:166
Richard Yates **8**:556

Wolkenfeld, J. S.
Isaac Bashevis Singer **1**:311

Wolkoff, Lewis H.
Anne McCaffrey **17**:281
Roger Zelazny **21**:470, 471

Woll, Josephine
Varlam Shalamov **18**:480

Wollen, Peter
John Ford **16**:310

Wollheim, Donald A.
Isaac Asimov **1**:8
Ray Bradbury **1**:42
Arthur C. Clarke **1**:59
Harlan Ellison **1**:93
Philip Jose Farmer **1**:97
Edmond Hamilton **1**:137
Robert A. Heinlein **1**:139
Andre Norton **12**:466
Clifford D. Simak **1**:309
A. E. Van Vogt **1**:347
Kurt Vonnegut, Jr. **1**:348

Womack, John, Jr.
Peter Matthiessen **32**:290

Wong, Jade Snow
Jade Snow Wong **17**:566

Wong, Sharon
John Ehle **27**:105

Wood, Adolf
Louis Auchincloss **18**:25

Wood, Anne
Leon Garfield **12**:232

Wood, Charles
Kurt Vonnegut, Jr. **4**:565

Wood, Clement
Carl Sandburg **35**:342

Wood, Gayle
Margaret Atwood **15**:37

Wood, Karen
Kurt Vonnegut, Jr. **4**:565

Wood, Michael
Miguel Ángel Asturias **3**:18
J. G. Ballard **14**:39
John Barth **2**:37; **27**:27
Donald Barthelme **2**:41
Georges Bataille **29**:48
Samuel Beckett **29**:58
John Betjeman **6**:66
Adolfo Bioy Casares **4**:63
Elizabeth Bishop **9**:95
Harold Bloom **24**:74
Jorge Luis Borges **2**:72
Anthony Burgess **8**:112
Italo Calvino **8**:131; **22**:95
Elias Canetti **25**:109
Alejo Carpentier **11**:101
Evan S. Connell, Jr. **6**:116

Francis Ford Coppola **16**:246
Julio Cortázar **2**:105
Jacques Derrida **24**:138
Lawrence Durrell **6**:153
T. S. Eliot **10**:169
Stanley Elkin **4**:154
William Empson **8**:201
Ken Follett **18**:156
Carlos Fuentes **8**:225; **22**:171
Gabriel García Márquez **15**:254
John Gardner **5**:131; **8**:235
Juan Goytisolo **5**:150
Judith Guest **8**:253
Barry Hannah **23**:209
John Hawkes **4**:219
Seamus Heaney **7**:147
John Hollander **14**:263
Erica Jong **4**:264
William Melvin Kelley **22**:249
John le Carré **15**:324
Violette Leduc **22**:263
Stanislaw Lem **8**:345
John Lennon and Paul
McCartney **12**:365
José Lezama Lima **4**:289
Ross Macdonald **14**:328
Norman Mailer **3**:316
Thomas McGuane **3**:330
A. G. Mojtabai **9**:385
Brian Moore **8**:395
Alberto Moravia **27**:355
Berry Morgan **6**:340
Vladimir Nabokov **2**:303
Pablo Neruda **5**:303
Hans Erich Nossack **6**:365
Craig Nova **31**:296
Robert Nye **13**:413
Joyce Carol Oates **2**:316
Grace Paley **4**:392
Octavio Paz **4**:396
Peter Porter **13**:451
Ezra Pound **2**:345
Anthony Powell **3**:403
Manuel Puig **3**:407; **28**:371
Thomas Pynchon **2**:357; **33**:339
Raymond Queneau **10**:432
Jean Rhys **14**:446
Philip Roth **4**:456
Luis Rafael Sánchez **23**:386
Severo Sarduy **6**:487
Isaac Bashevis Singer **3**:459
Susan Sontag **13**:517
Muriel Spark **5**:399; **8**:495
Robert Stone **23**:426
J.R.R. Tolkien **12**:570
Charles Tomlinson **6**:534
John Updike **2**:445
Mario Vargas Llosa **6**:546;
31:443
Gore Vidal **8**:525
Kurt Vonnegut, Jr. **3**:503
Eudora Welty **2**:463
Angus Wilson **3**:535
Rudolph Wurlitzer **2**:483
Roger Zelazny **21**:468

Wood, Peter
Peter De Vries **2**:114
Alberto Moravia **2**:293

Wood, Robin
Robert Altman **16**:31
Michelangelo Antonioni **20**:34

Ingmar Bergman **16**:60
Frank Capra **16**:164
Claude Chabrol **16**:173
Carl Theodor Dreyer **16**:264
John Ford **16**:311
Alfred Hitchcock **16**:354
Rouben Mamoulian **16**:428
Pier Paolo Pasolini **20**:268
Satyajit Ray **16**:483

Wood, Scott
Rudolfo A. Anaya **23**:22

Wood, Susan
Alice Adams **13**:2
Margaret Atwood **15**:36
T. Alan Broughton **19**:74
Art Buchwald **33**:94
Norman Dubie **36**:133
Penelope Gilliatt **10**:230
Robert Hass **18**:210
Howard Nemerov **36**:302
Joyce Carol Oates **33**:287
David Plante **23**:343
John Wain **11**:564

Wood, William C.
Wallace Markfield **8**:380

Woodbery, W. Potter
John Crowe Ransom **11**:467

Woodburn, James A.
Carl Sandburg **35**:344

Woodburn, John
Nevil Shute **30**:367

Woodcock, George
Margaret Atwood **25**:65
Earle Birney **6**:71, 75; **11**:51
Camilo José Cela **13**:145
Louis-Ferdinand Céline **9**:158
Matt Cohen **19**:113
Robert Finch **18**:154
Roy Fuller **28**:151, 154
Hugh Garner **13**:236
Jean Genet **5**:138
Jack Hodgins **23**:229, 232
W. P. Kinsella **27**:235
Patrick Lane **25**:284
Irving Layton **15**:321
Denise Levertov **5**:246
Hugh MacDiarmid **2**:255
Hugh MacLennan **14**:339
Brian Moore **1**:225; **3**:341
R. K. Narayan **28**:300
Alden Nowlan **15**:399
Joyce Carol Oates **33**:289
A. W. Purdy **14**:431
Herbert Read **4**:441
Kenneth Rexroth **2**:70, 371
Mordecai Richler **5**:375
Gabrielle Roy **14**:469
A.J.M. Smith **15**:515
Andrew Suknaski **19**:432
Audrey Thomas **37**:416
Rudy Wiebe **11**:569

Woodfield, James
Christopher Fry **10**:200; **14**:187

Woodhouse, J. R.
Italo Calvino **22**:87

Woodruff, Stuart C.
Shirley Jackson **11**:301

Critic Index

Woods, Crawford
Ross Macdonald 3:308
Isaac Bashevis Singer 3:457
Hunter S. Thompson 9:526

Woods, George A.
Charles Addams 30:15
Jay Bennett 35:42
Margaret O. Hyde 21:172

Woods, Katherine
A. J. Cronin 32:135
August Derleth 31:134
Nevil Shute 30:366
Henri Troyat 23:457

Woods, Richard, O.P.
Gay Talese 37:401

Woods, William C.
Lisa Alther 7:13
Leon Uris 7:492

Woods, William Crawford
Jim Harrison 6:225

Woodward, C. Vann
Louis R. Harlan 34:184
William Styron 3:473
Eudora Welty 33:424

Woodward, Helen Beal
Vera Brittain 23:93
Frank B. Gilbreth, Jr. and
Ernestine Gilbreth Carey
17:155
Jean Kerr 22:255
Ayn Rand 30:294

Woodward, Kathleen
William Carlos Williams
22:464

Wooldridge, C. Nordhielm
Fran Arrick 30:17, 19
Robin F. Brancato 35:67
Norma Klein 30:241
Norma Fox Mazer 26:295

Woolf, Jenny
Joan Aiken 35:21

Woolf, Virginia
E. M. Forster 15:222
Ernest Hemingway 19:211

Woollcott, Alexander
Dorothy Parker 15:414

Wooster, Martin Morse
C. J. Cherryh 35:106

Wooten, Anna
Louise Glück 7:119

Worden, Blair
Antonia Fraser 32:182, 187

Wordsworth, Christopher
Thor Heyerdahl 26:192
Ann Schlee 35:371
Jill Paton Walsh 35:434

Worsley, T. C.
Ann Jellicoe 27:206
Stephen Spender 10:488
Martin Walser 27:455

Worth, Katharine J.
Edward Bond 13:99

Worthen, John
Edward Bond 23:63

Worton, Michael J.
René Char 11:115

Wray, Wendell
Joyce Carol Thomas 35:406

Wrenn, John H.
John Dos Passos 1:77

Wright, Barbara
Romain Gary 25:188
Michel Tournier 23:452

Wright, Basil
Luis Buñuel 16:129
Charles Chaplin 16:192

Wright, Cuthbert
Compton MacKenzie 18:313

Wright, David
C. Day Lewis 6:126
Seamus Heaney 25:249
Hugh MacDiarmid 19:289

Wright, Elsa Gress
Carl Theodor Dreyer 16:262

Wright, George T.
W. H. Auden 1:10
T. S. Eliot 3:137

Wright, Gordon
David Caute 29:109

Wright, Hilary
Rosemary Sutcliff 26:439

Wright, James
Richard F. Hugo 6:244
Pablo Neruda 28:306, 308
Gary Snyder 32:386

Wright, John M.
David Malouf 28:268

Wright, John S.
Robert Hayden 37:154

Wright, Judith
Robert D. FitzGerald 19:176
Kenneth Slessor 14:493

Wright, Lawrence
Richard Brautigan 34:316

Wright, Madeleine
Nathalie Sarraute 31:379

Wright, Richard
Arna Bontemps 18:63
Zora Neale Hurston 30:211
Carson McCullers 12:408

Wulf, Deirdre
Zoa Sherburne 30:362

Wunderlich, Lawrence
Fernando Arrabal 2:16

Wyatt, David M.
Ernest Hemingway 8:288;
19:223
Robert Penn Warren 8:541

Wyatt, E.V.R.
Jade Snow Wong 17:566

Wyld, Lionel D.
Walter D. Edmonds 35:153,
155

Wylder, Delbert E.
William Eastlake 8:198

Wylie, Andrew
Giuseppe Ungaretti 11:556

Wylie, John Cook
Earl Hamner, Jr. 12:257

Wylie, Philip
Sally Benson 17:49

Wyllie, John Cook
John Ehle 27:103
Earl Hamner, Jr. 12:257

Wymard, Eleanor B.
Annie Dillard 9:177
John Irving 23:246

Wyndham, Francis
Caroline Blackwood 6:79
Elizabeth Bowen 15:78
Agatha Christie 12:120
Aldous Huxley 18:265
Ruth Rendell 28:387

Yablonsky, Victoria
Robin F. Brancato 35:70

Yacowar, Maurice
Woody Allen 16:16
Alfred Hitchcock 16:351

Yagoda, Ben
Margaret Drabble 10:164
Henry Green 13:254
Tom Wolfe 15:585

Yakir, Dan
Peter Weir 20:428

Yamanouchi, Hisaaki
Kōbō Abé 22:13
Yasunari Kawabata 18:285
Yukio Mishima 27:339
Kenzaburō Ōe 36:348
Shiga Naoya 33:370

Yamashita, Sumi
Agatha Christie 12:117

Yannella, Philip R.
Pablo Neruda 5:301
Louis Zukofsky 18:557

Yardley, Jonathan
Chinua Achebe 3:2
Kingsley Amis 2:8
Roger Angell 26:30, 32
Russell Banks 37:26
Frederick Barthelme 36:52
Hal Bennett 5:59
Wendell Berry 4:59; 6:62
Doris Betts 3:73; 28:34, 35
C.D.B. Bryan 29:101, 106
Frederick Buechner 6:102
Harry Crews 6:117, 118
Don DeLillo 27:83
Peter De Vries 7:77; 28:111
James Dickey 2:116
E. L. Doctorow 37:91
Harriet Doerr 34:151
John Gregory Dunne 28:122
John Ehle 27:106
Frederick Exley 6:171
William Faulkner 3:158
Leslie A. Fiedler 13:213
Ellen Gilchrist 34:165

Brian Glanville 6:202
Gail Godwin 31:194, 197
Judith Guest 30:174
James Hanley 5:167, 168
Barry Hannah 23:208
Jim Harrison 6:224
William Least Heat Moon
29:222
John Hersey 9:277
George V. Higgins 7:157
Josephine Humphreys 34:64
Susan Isaacs 32:255
Diane Johnson 5:199
Madison Jones 4:263
Pat Jordan 37:193
Ward Just 4:266; 27:228, 229
Thomas Keneally 8:319; 10:299
John Knowles 4:271; 10:303
Elmore Leonard 28:235
Robert Lipsyte 21:210
John D. MacDonald 27:275
Bernard Malamud 2:267
Saul Maloff 5:271
Cormac McCarthy 4:342
James A. Michener 11:375
A. G. Mojtabai 5:293; 29:319
Wright Morris 37:316
Toni Morrison 4:365
Joyce Carol Oates 33:297
Katherine Paterson 30:287
Robert Newton Peck 17:337
Walker Percy 3:381
Jayne Anne Phillips 33:306
David Plante 23:342, 345
Piers Paul Read 4:444
J. R. Salamanca 4:462
John Seelye 7:406
Irwin Shaw 34:370
Wilfrid Sheed 2:394; 4:488
Robert Stone 23:428
Peter Taylor 37:410
Lewis Thomas 35:415
James Thurber 25:438
Thomas Tryon 3:483
Gore Vidal 33:408
Jerome Weidman 7:518
Eudora Welty 2:462
Tom Wicker 7:533
John Edgar Wideman 36:456
Calder Willingham 5:511, 512

Ya Salaam, Kalumu
Nikki Giovanni 4:189

Yates, Diane C.
Marion Zimmer Bradley 30:29

Yates, Donald A.
Jorge Amado 13:11
John Dickson Carr 3:100
Autran Dourado 23:149
Carlos Fuentes 13:232
João Guimarães Rosa 23:352

Yates, Irene
Julia Peterkin 31:305

Yates, Jessica
Ann Swinfen 34:576

Yates, John
Francis Ford Coppola 16:241

Yates, Nona
David Leavitt 34:79

Yates, Norris W.
Günter Grass **4**:203
James Thurber **5**:433

Yates, Richard
Aidan Chambers **35**:98

Yatron, Michael
Carl Sandburg **35**:355

Yenser, Stephen
Ai **14**:9
A. R. Ammons **25**:43
Stephen Dunn **36**:154
Galway Kinnell **29**:285
Philip Levine **14**:315
Robert Lowell **3**:305
James Merrill **3**:335
Robert Pinsky **19**:372
Adrienne Rich **11**:479
James Schuyler **23**:390
W. D. Snodgrass **18**:493
Robert Penn Warren **8**:537, 540

Yerburgh, Mark R.
Amiri Baraka **33**:61

Yerburgh, Rhoda
Nancy Willard **37**:464

Yglesias, Helen
Cynthia Propper Seton **27**:427
Ludvík Vaculík **7**:494

Yglesias, Jose
Christina Stead **2**:421
Mario Vargas Llosa **6**:547
William Wharton **37**:443

Yglesias, Luis E.
Pablo Neruda **7**:262; **9**:398
Kenneth Rexroth **22**:348

Yoder, Edwin M.
MacKinlay Kantor **7**:195

Yoder, Jon A.
Upton Sinclair **15**:501

Yohalem, John
Clark Blaise **29**:72
Richard Brautigan **5**:70
James McCourt **5**:277
Charles Webb **7**:516
Edmund White III **27**:479

Yoke, Carl B.
Joan D. Vinge **30**:412
Roger Zelazny **21**:474

Yolen, Jane
Jamake Highwater **12**:287
Mollie Hunter **21**:158
Zilpha Keatley Snyder **17**:470

York, David Winston
Chaim Potok **26**:374

Yoshida, Sanroku
Kenzaburō Ōe **36**:350

Young, Alan
Donald Justice **19**:236
Christopher Middleton **13**:389
Edwin Morgan **31**:276
James Schuyler **23**:388

Young, Alan R.
Ernest Buckler **13**:118, 119

Young, B. A.
Eva Figes **31**:161

Young, Charles M.
Mel Brooks **12**:83
Patti Smith **12**:543

Young, Colin
Kon Ichikawa **20**:177

Young, David
John Ashbery **25**:54
Robert Francis **15**:236
Craig Raine **32**:350

Young, Desmond
Jacques-Yves Cousteau **30**:103

Young, Dora Jean
Katherine Paterson **12**:484

Young, Dudley
Carlos Castaneda **12**:84

Young, Israel G.
Bob Dylan **12**:180

Young, J. R.
Waylon Jennings **21**:201

Young, James O.
Jessie Redmon Fauset **19**:170

Young, Jon
Joan Armatrading **17**:10
Chuck Berry **17**:55
Carly Simon **26**:411

Young, Kenneth
Compton Mackenzie **18**:314

Young, Marguerite
John Gardner **30**:154
Carson McCullers **12**:411
Mark Van Doren **10**:495

Young, Peter
Andrei Voznesensky **1**:348

Young, Philip
Ernest Hemingway **13**:273;
30:193, 194

Young, Scott
Farley Mowat **26**:331

Young, Stanley
August Derleth **31**:131
Conrad Richter **30**:307

Young, Stark
Eric Bentley **24**:45
Paul Green **25**:196
Clifford Odets **28**:323, 327,
328
Irwin Shaw **23**:395
Emlyn Williams **15**:576

Young, Thomas Daniel
Donald Davidson **13**:168
Andrew Lytle **22**:298
John Crowe Ransom **4**:433,
436
Peter Taylor **37**:409

Young, Tracy
Lily Tomlin **17**:520

Young, Vernon
Woody Allen **16**:10
Yehuda Amichai **22**:31

W. H. Auden **2**:28
Ingmar Bergman **16**:66
Wendell Berry **27**:35
George Mackay Brown **5**:77
Charles Chaplin **16**:197
Walter Van Tilburg Clark **28**:78
J. V. Cunningham **3**:121
Peter Davison **28**:102
Vittorio De Sica **20**:86, 90
William Dickey **3**:126
Isak Dinesen **29**:164
Gunnar Ekelöf **27**:116
Odysseus Elytis **15**:220
Lawrence Ferlinghetti **6**:183
Brewster Ghiselin **23**:171
William Heyen **18**:231
John Hollander **2**:197
Richard F. Hugo **6**:245; **32**:239
John Huston **20**:172
Donald Justice **19**:232
Galway Kinnell **13**:320
Akira Kurosawa **16**:397
Laurence Lieberman **4**:291
Michael Longley **29**:296
Robert Lowell **5**:258
Cynthia Macdonald **19**:291
Jayanta Mahapatra **33**:276
Peter Matthiessen **32**:291
William Meredith **22**:303
W. S. Merwin **13**:384
Josephine Miles **14**:369
Michael Mott **15**:380
Pablo Neruda **1**:247
Robert Pack **13**:439
Nicanor Parr **2**:331
Roman Polanski **16**:469
Yannis Ritsos **6**:464; **31**:329
Carlos Saura **20**:319
Martin Scorsese **20**:329
Frederick Seidel **18**:475
Jon Silkin **2**:396
Charles Simic **22**:382
David Slavitt **14**:490
Susan Sontag **31**:408
Maura Stanton **9**:508
James Tate **2**:432
Diane Wakoski **2**:459; **4**:573
Ted Walker **13**:566
Peter Weir **20**:429

Youngblood, Gene
Stanley Kubrick **16**:391

Younge, Shelia F.
Joan Armatrading **17**:8

Youree, Beverly B.
Melvin Berger **12**:41

Yourgrau, Barry
William Price Fox **22**:141
Mordecai Richler **18**:452
Peter Rushforth **19**:406

Yucht, Alice H.
Richard Peck **21**:296

Yuill, W. E.
Heinrich Böll **11**:52

Yurchenco, Henrietta
Woody Guthrie **35**:184, 189

Yurieff, Zoya
Joseph Wittlin **25**:468

Zabel, Morton Dauwen
Glenway Wescott **13**:591

Zabriskie, George
Marshall McLuhan **37**:256

Zacharias, Lee
Truman Capote **13**:139

Zahn, Grace M.
Zoa Sherburne **30**:361

Zahorski, Kenneth J.
Roger Zelazny **21**:473

Zaiss, David
Roy Fisher **25**:158

Zak, Michele Wender
Doris Lessing **6**:294

Zaller, Robert
Bernardo Bertolucci **16**:94
Anaïs Nin **4**:377

Zamora, Carlos
Gary Soto **32**:403

Zamora, Lois Parkinson
Julio Cortázar **33**:124, 134

Zarookian, Cherie
Barbara Corcoran **17**:71

Zatlin, Linda G.
Isaac Bashevis Singer **1**:312

Zaturenska, Marya
Laura Riding **7**:373

Zavatsky, Bill
Ed Dorn **10**:157

Zebrowski, George
Arkadii Strugatskii and Boris
Strugatskii **27**:436

Zebrun, Gary
Robert Hayden **37**:153

Zehender, Ted
Tod Browning **16**:123

Zehr, David E.
Ernest Hemingway **8**:286

Zeidner, Lisa
André Dubus **36**:148

Zeik, Michael
Thomas Merton **3**:337

Zelazny, Roger
Philip K. Dick **30**:120

Zelenko, Barbara
Nora Ephron **17**:111

Zeller, Bernhard
Hermann Hesse **2**:190

Zeman, Marvin
Jean Renoir **20**:300

Zern, Ed
Roderick L. Haig-Brown
21:136

Zetterberg, Bettijane
Hilma Wolitzer **17**:562

Zeugner, John F.
Gabriel Marcel **15**:364
Walker Percy **18**:396

Critic Index

Zibart, Eve
Penelope Gilliatt **13**:238

Ziegfeld, Richard E.
Kurt Vonnegut, Jr. **22**:447

Ziff, Larzer
Leslie A. Fiedler **24**:205
Edmund Wilson **24**:488

Zilkha, Michael
Mark Medoff **6**:323

Zimbardo, Rose A.
Edward Albee **13**:3

Zimmerman, Eugenia N.
Jean-Paul Sartre **9**:472

Zimmerman, Paul
R. K. Narayan **7**:256

Zimmerman, Paul D.
John Gregory Dunne **28**:121
E. M. Forster **2**:135
Lois Gould **4**:199
Stanley Kubrick **16**:383
Robert Lipsyte **21**:211
Leni Riefenstahl **16**:524
Melvin Van Peebles **20**:412

Zimmerman, Ulf
Rolf Hochhuth **18**:255
Martin Walser **27**:463, 464,
466

Ziner, Feenie
Frank Bonham **12**:53
Rosemary Sutcliff **26**:437

Zinnes, Harriet
Robert Bly **1**:37
Robert Duncan **1**:83
Anaïs Nin **4**:379; **8**:425
Ezra Pound **3**:399
May Swenson **4**:533, 534
Mona Van Duyn **7**:499

Zinsser, William
Stephen Sondheim **30**:377
James Thurber **25**:439

Ziolkowski, Theodore
Heinrich Böll **2**:67; **6**:83
Günter Grass **22**:195
Hermann Hesse **1**:145, 146;
3:248; **17**:209; **25**:260
Hans Erich Nossack **6**:364

Zipes, Jack D.
Christa Wolf **14**:593

Zivanovic, Judith
Jean-Paul Sartre **9**:470

Zivkovic, Peter D.
W. H. Auden **3**:23

Zivley, Sherry Lutz
Sylvia Plath **9**:431

Zoglin, Richard
Hugh Whitemore **37**:445

Zolf, Larry
Mordecai Richler **5**:376

Zonderman, Jon
Robert Coover **32**:124

Zorach, Cecile Cazort
Heinrich Böll **15**:70

Zoss, Betty
Jesse Jackson **12**:290

Zucker, David
Delmore Schwartz **10**:464

Zuckerman, Albert J.
Vassilis Vassilikos **4**:551

Zuckerman, Lord
Jonathan Schell **35**:369

Zuger, David
Adrienne Rich **7**:372

Zukofsky, Louis
Charles Chaplin **16**:190

Zunser, Jesse
Akira Kurosawa **16**:394

Zvirin, Stephanie
Fran Arrick **30**:19
Jay Bennett **35**:45
Larry Bograd **35**:62, 63, 64
Erich von Däniken **30**:427
Lois Duncan **26**:108
Sol Gordon **26**:138
Nat Hentoff **26**:187
Norma Klein **30**:242
Norma Fox Mazer **26**:295
Walter Dean Myers **35**:298
Katherine Paterson **30**:288
D. M. Pinkwater **35**:319

Zweig, Paul
Richard Adams **5**:6
A. R. Ammons **5**:29
John Ashbery **2**:18
Julio Cortázar **33**:125
James Dickey **15**:178
William Dickey **3**:126
Clayton Eshleman **7**:100
Allen Ginsberg **13**:240
Günter Grass **11**:254
John Hollander **5**:186
David Ignatow **7**:181
Thomas Keneally **27**:232
Kenneth Koch **8**:322
Violette Leduc **22**:263
Philip Levine **4**:286
Jakov Lind **27**:272
Peter Matthiessen **11**:358;
32:296
Leonard Michaels **6**:325
Czesław Miłosz **5**:292; **22**:312
Vladimir Nabokov **3**:354
Pablo Neruda **5**:303
Joyce Carol Oates **15**:402
Frank O'Hara **13**:424
George Oppen **7**:284
Charles Simic **6**:502
William Stafford **7**:461
Diane Wakoski **4**:571
James Wright **3**:542